HBO®'s

Guide to

MOVIES

on

VIDEO-CASSETTE

and

CABLE TV

1991

Harper Perennial

A Division of HarperCollinsPublishers

HOME BOX OFFICE

Senior Editor
Daniel Eagan

Editor
Olga Humphrey

Contributing Editors
Robert Potter

Steve Szilagyi

Ted Winterer

Research Assistants
Katherine Parks

Mary Ellen Donohue

HBO'S GUIDE TO MOVIES ON VIDEOCASSETTE AND CABLE TV 1991. Copyright © 1990 by Home Box Office. All rights reserved. Printed in the United States of America. No part of this book may be used or reproduced in any manner whatsoever without written permission except in the case of brief quotations embodied in critical articles and reviews. For information address Harper-Collins, Publishers, Inc., 10 East 53rd Street, New York, NY 10022.

FIRST EDITION

Designed by Karen Savary

Library of Congress Catalog Card Number 89-19861

ISSN 1050-8996
ISBN 0-06-273074-6

90 91 92 93 94 CC/FC 10 9 8 7 6 5 4 3 2 1

Welcome to the second edition of *HBO's Guide to Movies on Videocassette and Cable TV*, which has been completely revised to make it an even more useful tool for your video shopping. First of all, we have added fifty percent more films, ranging from early silent classics to the latest blockbusters. You'll be able to learn about over 7,000 popular and significant films currently available on tape, in categories from romance to Western, thriller to biography, documentary to musical. And to help you locate your favorites, the entries now include listings of video distributors, allowing you or your video retailer to order hard-to-find tapes directly.

HBO's information about these films comes as a result of its seventeen years as American's premiere pay-TV service. In writing this book, our aim was to provide an unbiased, comprehensive guide to movies, one that would combine the best aspects of film reference guides with the unique information we've gathered for our viewers, including accurate synopses, impartial ratings based on the opinions of HBO viewers, full credits, cautions about potentially offensive material, running times, important awards, and much more.

All films are arranged alphabetically for quick reference. Our method was to list each title in strict alphabetical order, ignoring both initial articles "the," "an" and "a," and punctuation within a title. Numbers are treated as if they were spelled out. The only exceptions are films within a series, which are listed chronologically (e.g., *Rocky II* follows *Rocky*). For films that underwent title changes, we've listed them under their most frequently used names while mentioning alternate titles in the synopsis.

The information included for each film is also arranged for the easiest possible use. The categories are largely self-evident, but some warrant additional clarification.

Subscribers, Not Critics, Rate the Films

Star Recommendations are one of the most important features of the book. After films were screened on the HBO services, researchers polled randomly selected viewers to record their impressions. The findings were entered into a computer program that ranked films according to viewer "satisfaction." The entries in this book received from zero to five stars, as described below:

★ ★ ★ ★ ★ —Excellent
★ ★ ★ ★ —Very Good
★ ★ ★ —Good
★ ★ —Fair
★ —Poor
☆ —Not recommended.

It's worth repeating that these ratings are derived *from our viewers' preferences,* not individual opinions of the HBO staff. Thus, you can be assured that the stars accurately reflect a widespread portion of the mainstream audience and not one critic's particular—and perhaps biased—opinion. For those films that have not yet played on the HBO services, we relied on a panel of evaluators who are expert at estimating viewer tastes. It should be noted that some critically praised films are targeted towards smaller, more demanding audiences than mainstream films. Accordingly, they are not as popular with our viewers, but the synopsis will generally reflect how successfully the film accomplishes its goals. Similarly, older, black-and-white films, foreign films, and documentaries tend to receive lower ratings than expected because they are being compared to the current Hollywood product. However, by using our star rating system, you'll be able to discover a number of underappreciated gems that have been either overlooked or dismissed by critics—the movies our subscribers really enjoy.

Cautions Help Families Plan Their Viewing

Cautions are a second unique feature of our book. Every movie shown on HBO has been carefully screened by our staff of professional evaluators to note the presence of material that could prove offensive to some viewers. Evaluators note, in order of importance to our viewers, whether the movie contains any of the following situations:

Rape	Explicit Language
Nudity	Graphic Violence
Brief Nudity	Violence
Strong Sexual Content	Mild Violence
Adult Situations	Adult Humor

These ten categories are largely self-explanatory. "Adult Situations" refers to material of a violent or sexual nature that parents may not want younger viewers to see. While some older (pre-1960) films contain scenes or themes best appreciated by mature viewers, in general, Hollywood studios treated them in a discreet manner that does not offend contemporary audiences.

As a further guideline, we also include *MPAA Ratings.* These are assigned by the Motion Picture Association of America to alert viewers that material contained within a movie may be deemed inappropriate for young viewers. Where applicable, we have used the following classifications in our entries:

G	"General Audiences. All ages admitted."
PG	"Parental Guidance Suggested. Some material may not be suitable for children."
PG-13	"Parents Strongly Cautioned. Some material may be inappropriate for children under 13."
R	"Restricted. Under 17 requires accompanying parent or adult guardian." (Please note: Age may vary in different jurisdictions.)
NC-17	"No children under 17 admitted." (This rating will ultimately replace the X rating.)
X	"No one under 17 admitted." (Again, age may vary.)

Unless distributors resubmitted titles for new ratings, most theatrical films made before 1968 and all made-for-TV films receive an "NR," or No Rating. Exceptions apply here as well. Most Walt Disney Studio movies, for example, have been recently resubmitted to achieve a "G" rating. In some instances, distributors have added material to home cassette releases that invalidate the MPAA ratings; e.g., cassette versions of *Angel Heart* and *Warrior Queen* contain additional erotic material and no longer qualify as "R" films. Some films are available in both rated and unrated versions. Instances like these have been noted in the synopses.

Distributor Listing Helps You Locate Films

A new feature of this edition is our distributor listing. At the end of each entry we've included the name of the video company that handles the title. Many older films are free to be distributed without any restrictions imposed by copyright laws. For these titles we've listed the distributor as "Various." Should you have difficulty in finding these films, we suggest contacting companies that specialize in older titles. Some of these are Video Yesteryear, Sinister Cinema, Foothill, Corinth, Connoisseur, and Goodtimes. Some titles are out of print, or placed on moratorium. These can still generally be found for rental, particularly from companies like Evergreen or Facets Video, which specialize in hard-to-find titles. Finally, at press time distributors for some films, particularly the newest releases, were not yet cleared. We've included these films because in all likelihood they will be available on tape in the near future.

Genre classifications are included for every film. We provided these categories as a loose umbrella to help guide you in your choice of films. Our genres include: Action-Adventure, Animation, Biography, Comedy, Crime, Dance, Documentary, Drama, Espionage, Family (i.e., recommended for family viewing, not necessarily about the family), Fantasy,

Horror, MFTV (Made for TV), Martial Arts, Music, Musical, Mystery-Suspense, Romance, Sci-Fi, Sex, Sports, War, and Western.

In some instances, a film proves hard to classify because it crosses over two categories, such as a drama that includes a lot of comedy; in these cases, the film will be listed under both genres.

Release Dates can vary widely, particularly for a film that received little or no theatrical exposure. We've generally included the year the film received theatrical release in America; in lieu of that, we've chosen the date the film was copyrighted.

Country of Origin refers not only to where a movie was filmed, but also to where it was produced. For example, although the 1950 version of *Treasure Island* was filmed in Great Britain with English actors, it is considered an American film because it was produced by Walt Disney Studio. Similarly, *Paris, Texas,* although filmed in the United States, is classified as French/German because its production companies were based in those countries.

Running Times proved particularly difficult to verify, especially in those cases where studios added or deleted footage for videocassette release. The running times in this book conform as nearly as possible to the times on videocassette, and should prove reliable in those instances where various versions of a particular film exist.

Synopses provided for each film emphasize plot over critical opinion. Even among our staff of writers, opinions vary greatly over each film. For this reason, we tried to be objective and, as much as possible, restrict our writing to story lines and character descriptions.

Closed captioned versions of numerous films exist for the convenience of the hearing-impaired. If a title has been closed-captioned, the symbol (CC) follows the synopsis.

Subtitled foreign films are preferred to dubbed versions by many viewers. The symbol [S] shows that a film is available on tape with subtitles.

Colorized versions of black-and-white films are becoming increasingly available on video. We use the symbol [C] whenever a black-and-white film has been colorized.

We'd like to acknowledge the many people at HBO who contributed to this project. Michael Fuchs, Chairman of HBO, was enthusiastic and supportive throughout our work. Quentin Schaffer, James F. Noonan, and Sarah Fitzsimmons provided invaluable help. Film evaluators Roger Blunck, Ty Burr, Jim Byerley, and Camilla Carpenter aided with the original research. We are indebted to the assistance received from computer experts Rose Han, Larry Jacobson, and Erica Trantham. We would also like to note help from Marian Anderson and Jonathan Glickman. Finally, Carol Cohen, Susan Randol, and John Day at HarperCollins were crucial in assuring the publication of this book.

Summing up, our purpose in creating *HBO's Guide to Movies on Videocassette and Cable TV* was to help you make the most informed decisions possible about what you watch.

Happy viewing!

AARON LOVES ANGELA 1975
★ ★ R Drama 1:38
☑ Strong sexual content, explicit language
Dir: Gordon Parks, Jr. *Cast:* Irene Cara, Kevin Hooks, Moses Gunn, Robert Hooks, Walt Frazier, Jose Feliciano
▶ Black Harlem teen Kevin Hooks and Puerto Rican counterpart Cara fall in love. Hooks must deal with the lure of the underworld (in the person of his real-life father Robert Hooks, playing a drug dealer) when $250,000 in drug money falls into his hands accidentally. New York City locations lend sweet but thin romance credibility.
Dist.: RCA/Columbia

ABBOTT AND COSTELLO IN HOLLYWOOD 1945
★ NR Comedy 1:24 B&W
Dir: S. Sylvan Simon *Cast:* Bud Abbott, Lou Costello, Frances Rafferty, Robert Stanton, Jean Porter, Mike Mazurki
▶ Bud and Lou play Tinseltown barbers who inadvertently become agents when they try to launch Stanton's acting career. Costello's bout with insomnia and the roller-coaster climax are highlights of this modestly amusing romp. Tour of MGM Studios includes glimpses of Lucille Ball and Butch Jenkins at work.
Dist.: MGM/UA

ABBOTT AND COSTELLO MEET CAPTAIN KIDD 1952
★ NR Comedy 1:10
Dir: Charles Lamont *Cast:* Bud Abbott, Lou Costello, Charles Laughton, Hillary Brooke, Bill Shirley, Fran Warren
▶ Asked to deliver a letter by Warren, Bud and Lou somehow find themselves in possession of a treasure map, which leads to their being kidnapped by the notorious Captain Kidd (Laughton). Mediocre Abbott and Costello vehicle features usually serious Laughton sending up himself.
Dist.: United

ABBOTT AND COSTELLO MEET DR. JEKYLL AND MR. HYDE 1953
★ NR Comedy 1:17 B&W
Dir: Charles Lamont *Cast:* Bud Abbott, Lou Costello, Boris Karloff, Craig Stevens, Helen Westcott
▶ In London, Abbott and Costello get into a jam but are bailed from jail by mad scientist Dr. Jekyll (Karloff), who then hires the duo. He develops a formula that transforms not only himself but Costello into murderous Mr. Hydes. Mixed bag of scares and laughter; the boys did this sort of thing better in *Abbott and Costello Meet Frankenstein.*
Dist.: MCA

ABBOTT AND COSTELLO MEET FRANKENSTEIN 1948
★ ★ ★ NR Comedy 1:23 B&W
Dir: Charles Barton *Cast:* Bud Abbott, Lou Costello, Lon Chaney, Jr., Bela Lugosi, Glenn Strange, Jane Randolph

▶ One of Bud and Lou's most popular films is a surprisingly effective mix of laughs and chills. Plot has the boys getting involved with Dracula (Lugosi), Frankenstein (Strange), the Wolfman (Chaney, Jr.), and a scheme to transplant Costello's brain inside the monster's body.
Dist.: MCA

ABE LINCOLN IN ILLINOIS 1940
★ ★ ★ NR Biography 1:50 B&W
Dir: John Cromwell *Cast:* Raymond Massey, Gene Lockhart, Ruth Gordon, Mary Howard, Dorothy Tree, Harvey Stephens
▶ Earnest, believable biography of Lincoln shows a broader picture of his life—including tragic first love Ann Rutledge (Howard), law practice, debates with Stephen Douglas (Lockhart), and Presidential election—than its competitor, *Young Abe Lincoln.* Massey won an Oscar nomination for his historically accurate portrayal of Lincoln. Adapted by Robert Sherwood from his Pulitzer prize–winning play.
Dist.: Turner

ABILENE TOWN 1946
★ ★ NR Western 1:29 B&W
Dir: Edwin L. Marin *Cast:* Randolph Scott, Ann Dvorak, Edgar Buchanan, Rhonda Fleming, Lloyd Bridges
▶ Marshall Scott has his hands full trying to clean up lawless cowtown while battling members of the Younger gang. Other conflicts include struggle with alcoholic sheriff Buchanan and choosing between kindhearted Fleming and dance-hall gal Dvorak. Polished Western with a good performance from Scott.
Dist.: Cable Ⓒ

ABOMINABLE DR. PHIBES, THE 1971 British
★ ★ PG Horror 1:33
☑ Violence
Dir: Robert Fuest *Cast:* Vincent Price, Joseph Cotten, Hugh Griffith, Terry-Thomas, Virginia North
▶ Price, an evil doctor with a mutilated face and a voice to match, plots revenge against the surgeons who killed his wife on the operating table. Trusty assistant North helps him; doctor Cotten is among those with reason to fear his vendetta. More silly than scary vehicle for the inimitable Price. Sequel: *Dr. Phibes Rises Again.*
Dist.: Vestron

ABOUT LAST NIGHT 1986
★ ★ ★ ★ R Drama 1:53
☑ Nudity, adult situations, explicit language
Dir: Edward Zwick *Cast:* Rob Lowe, Demi Moore, James Belushi, Elizabeth Perkins, George DiCenzo
▶ Glossy romance set in Chicago examines the stormy relationship between Lowe and Moore as they experiment with living together. Sanitized version of playwright David Mamet's *Sexual Perversity in Chicago* scores

points with the supporting work by Belushi and Perkins.
Dist.: RCA/Columbia

ABOVE THE LAW 1988
★ ★ ★ ★ R Action-Adventure 1:44
☑ Explicit language, violence
Dir: Andrew Davis *Cast:* Steven Seagal, Pam Grier, Sharon Stone, Daniel Faraldo, Henry Silva, Ronnie Barron
► Ex-CIA agent Seagal is suspended from Chicago police after he tries to shut down government-sponsored drug ring. When his family is attacked, he introduces his own version of the law to the Windy City villains. Crude but effective thriller marred by muddy politics. Film debut for former bodyguard Seagal (who also produced and co-wrote the story). (CC)
Dist.: Warner

ABRAHAM LINCOLN 1930
★ NR Biography 1:37 B&W
Dir: D. W. Griffith *Cast:* Walter Huston, Una Merkel, Kay Hammond, E. Alyn Warren, Hobart Bosworth
► Factual but slow-moving biography of the great President, ably played by Huston, from his early days as a rural lawyer to the Ford's Theater assassination. Primitive sound, episodic script (by Stephen Vincent Benet), and old-fashioned directing by silent film master Griffith make this difficult to watch.
Dist.: Video Yesteryear

ABSENCE OF MALICE 1981
★ ★ ★ ★ ★ PG Drama 1:56
☑ Adult situations, explicit language, mild violence
Dir: Sydney Pollack *Cast:* Paul Newman, Sally Field, Melinda Dillon, Luther Adler, Bob Balaban
► Ex-newspaperman Kurt Luedtke wrote the screenplay for this engrossing drama of overzealous journalism and its human toll. Newman is a legitimate businessman unjustly implicated in a labor boss murder by journalist Field. He manages to clear his name, get his revenge, and engage in a romance with the conscience-stricken Field. Oscar-nominated performances by Newman, Field, and Dillon.
Dist.: RCA/Columbia

ABSENT MINDED PROFESSOR, THE 1961
★ ★ ★ ★ NR Comedy 1:37 B&W
Dir: Robert Stevenson *Cast:* Fred MacMurray, Nancy Olson, Keenan Wynn, Tommy Kirk, Leon Ames, Ed Wynn
► Delightful screwball comedy with MacMurray as a professor who invents "flubber," an antigravity potion that gives magical flying powers to ordinary rubber. Keenan Wynn plays an industrial spy determined to steal the formula; his father Ed has a cameo as the fire chief. Above-par Disney film was followed by *Son of Flubber*.
Dist.: Buena Vista C

ABSOLUTE BEGINNERS 1986 British
★ PG-13 Musical 1:48
☑ Adult situations, explicit language, violence
Dir: Julien Temple *Cast:* Eddie O'Connell, Patsy Kensit, Ray Davies, David Bowie, Sade Adu
► A young photographer pursues a beautiful model amid London's swinging sixties fashion scene. Expensive adaptation of a cult novel by Colin MacInnes features elaborate musical productions, amusing cameos by rock stars Bowie, Davies, and Sade, and hyperkinetic direction by rock video master Temple.
Dist.: HBO

ABSOLUTION 1981 British
☆ R Drama 1:45
☑ Explicit language, violence
Dir: Anthony Page *Cast:* Richard Burton, Dominic Guard, Dai Bradley, Billy Connolly, Andrew Keir
► At an English Catholic school, priest Burton is put in a quandary when favorite student Guard uses the sanctity of the confessional to admit to murder. Is Guard telling the truth or merely trying to torment his mentor? Cerebral puzzler raises interesting theological questions, but static pacing and unclear character motivations overwhelm Burton's riveting performance.
Dist.: TWE

ABYSS, THE 1989
★ ★ ★ ★ PG-13 Sci-Fi 2:20
☑ Explicit language, violence
Dir: James Cameron *Cast:* Ed Harris, Mary Elizabeth Mastrantonio, Michael Biehn, Todd Graff, Leo Burmester, John Bedford Lloyd
► When a nuclear submarine crashes on the ocean floor, engineer Mastrantonio and her estranged husband Harris investigate. Something not quite human is out there in the water; crazed Navy officer Biehn seeks a literally explosive solution to the mystery. Dazzles the eye if not the mind; startling underwater photography and tense action scenes try to overcome derivative, cluttered plotting. (CC)
Dist.: CBS/Fox

ACCIDENT 1966 British
★ NR Drama 1:45
Dir: Joseph Losey *Cast:* Dirk Bogarde, Stanley Baker, Jacqueline Sassard, Delphine Seyrig, Alexander Knox, Michael York
► Oxford undergraduate's death in a car crash brings into focus competition between teachers Bogarde and Baker, both obsessed with victim's girlfriend Sassard. Intricate flashback structure and cryptic dialogue by playwright Harold Pinter form an intriguing intellectual puzzle about the English class system.
Dist.: HBO

ACCIDENTAL TOURIST, THE 1988
★ ★ ★ PG Drama 2:02
☑ Adult situations

Dir: Lawrence Kasdan *Cast:* William Hurt, Kathleen Turner, Geena Davis, Amy Wright, Bill Pullman, Ed Begley, Jr.

▶ Travel writer Hurt becomes increasingly set in his eccentric ways after his son dies and wife Turner leaves. It takes a relationship with kooky dog trainer Davis to bring him out of his shell. Wonderful adaptation of the Anne Tyler best-seller is alternately funny (Wright shines in scenes of Hurt's bizarre family; don't overlook Hurt's dog) and tender (Hurt telling Davis about his son, Hurt teaching Davis's son to fix sink). Marvelously restrained Hurt registers maximum emotion with the subtlest facial gestures, while delightful, Oscar-winning Davis wins his heart and yours. Nominations for Best Picture, Screenplay Adaptation, and Original Score.
Dist.: Warner

ACCUSED, THE 1988
★★★★★ R Drama 1:55
☑ Rape, nudity, strong sexual content, explicit language, violence
Dir: Jonathan Kaplan *Cast:* Kelly McGillis, Jodie Foster, Bernie Coulson, Leo Rossi, Ann Hearn, Carmen Argenziano
▶ Provocative drama examines the legal difficulties in prosecuting men who gang-raped waitress Foster in a seedy bar. Attorney McGillis reluctantly settles for lesser charge of reckless endangerment; egged on by Foster, she then prosecutes the onlookers who cheered on the rapists. Apart from powerful climax and Foster's bravura, Oscar-winning performance, a routine examination of a potentially devastating subject.
Dist.: Paramount

ACE OF ACES 1933
★ NR War 1:16 B&W
Dir: J. Walter Ruben *Cast:* Richard Dix, Elizabeth Allan, Ralph Bellamy, Theodore Newton, Bill Cagney, Clarence Stroud
▶ Allan accuses fiancé Dix of cowardice when he fails to enlist at the start of World War I. Stung, the principled youth signs up for the Air Corps, where his attitude hardens and he becomes one of the most ruthless killers in the air. Compelling human story and exciting aerial combat.
Dist.: Turner

ACQUA E SAPONE 1985 Italian
☆ PG Comedy 1:25
☑ Adult situations, explicit language, adult humor
Dir: Carlo Verdone *Cast:* Carlo Verdone, Natasha Hovey, Florinda Bolkan, Fabrizio Bracconeri
▶ Portly janitor Verdone works at an all-girls high school and teaches foreign students on the side. When young model Hovey is enrolled at the school, her mother Bolkan hires a priest to tutor the teenager. What Hovey gets instead is Verdone in disguise. An unlikely romance follows as the respectful Verdone tries

to resist his charge's charms. Minor comedy looks good, but suffers from its lack of believability and director/writer/star Verdone's fascination with himself. Ⓢ
Dist.: RCA/Columbia

ACROSS 110TH STREET 1972
★★★★ R Action-Adventure 1:42
☑ Graphic violence
Dir: Barry Shear *Cast:* Anthony Quinn, Yaphet Kotto, Anthony Franciosa, Paul Benjamin
▶ Hard-hitting, slam-bang crime melodrama features Quinn and Kotto as cops caught in the middle of a gang war when three blacks steal $30,000 from a Mafia numbers bank. A suspenseful but quite brutal film that should please action fans (although it didn't please the Legion of Decency, which condemned it).
Dist.: Key

ACROSS THE GREAT DIVIDE 1976
★★★★ G Family 1:40
Dir: Stewart Raffill *Cast:* Robert Logan, Heather Rattray, Mark Hall, George "Buck" Flower
▶ In 1876, orphans Rattray and Hall, left alone in the Rockies after their grandfather's death, bravely continue journeying to Oregon to claim the family land. Lovable con man Logan overcomes their initial distrust and helps them. Touching and exciting family tare. Best scene: driving the grizzly away from an Indian village.
Dist.: Media

ACTION FOR SLANDER 1938 British
★ NR Drama 1:23 B&W
Dir: Tim Whelan *Cast:* Clive Brook, Ann Todd, Margaretta Scott, Arthur Margetson, Ronald Squire, Googie Withers
▶ Self-possessed cavalry officer Brook is accused of cheating at cards, an unforgivable crime in his social set. Shut out by his closest friends, he takes his accuser to court, where a fascinating battle of legal wits ensues. Bringing the wordy script to vivid life is no problem for first-rate British cast.
Dist.: Video Yesteryear

ACTION IN ARABIA 1944
★ NR Espionage 1:12 B&W
Dir: Leonide Moguy *Cast:* George Sanders, Virginia Bruce, Gene Lockhart, Robert Armstrong, Michael Ansara, H. B. Warner
▶ In 1941, Syria is swarming with spies and foreign agents, all gambiting to enlist Arab tribespeople on one side or another of the European conflict. Newspaperman Sanders encounters Bruce as he noses around Damascus for a story; he falls in love, but she may be a Nazi spy. Crisp dialogue makes up for low budget production.
Dist.: Turner

ACTION JACKSON 1988
★★★ R Action-Adventure 1:36

☑ Nudity, explicit language, graphic violence
Dir: Craig Baxley *Cast:* Carl Weathers, Vanity, Craig T. Nelson, Sharon Stone, Sonny Landham
▶ Weathers (Apollo Creed in the *Rocky* movies) is Jackson, a Harvard Law School grad and Detroit supercop trying to win back his stripes after a run-in with corrupt union official/karate expert Nelson. Routine formula picture enlivened by terrific stunts, nonstop (and violent) action, and the presence of sultry rock star Vanity. **(CC)**
Dist.: Warner

ACT OF VENGEANCE 1986
★ ★ ★ ★ NR Biography/MFTV 1:36
☑ Adult situations, explicit language, violence
Dir: John Mackenzie *Cast:* Charles Bronson, Ellen Burstyn, Wilford Brimley, Ellen Barkin
▶ Bronson excels in a change-of-pace role as United Mine Workers official Joseph "Jock" Yablonski, who was eventually murdered for his reformist plans. A compelling true-life drama with a solid cast that includes Burstyn as Yablonski's wife and Brimley as Tony Boyle, the corrupt official convicted of the murder.
Dist.: HBO

ACTORS AND SIN 1952
★ NR Drama 1:22 B&W
Dir: Ben Hecht, Lee Garmes *Cast:* Edward G. Robinson, Eddie Albert, Marsha Hunt, Alan Reed, Dan O'Herlihy, Tracey Roberts
▶ Two-part film: in "Actor's Blood," stage star Robinson tries to cover up the suicide of actress-daughter Hunt by making it look like murder. In the second part, "Woman of Sin," agent Albert sells Hollywood a script written by a nine-year-old girl. Both stories are excellent, with the second being one of the better satires of filmdom.
Dist.: SVS

ADAM 1983
★ ★ ★ ★ NR Drama/MFTV 1:40
Dir: Michael Tuchner *Cast:* Daniel J. Travanti, JoBeth Williams, Martha Scott, Richard Masur, Paul Regina
▶ Superior telemovie about John Walsh (Travanti) and wife Williams's living hell after their child Adam mysteriously disappears. Unhappy true story (Adam was never found) led to missing children's legislation. Wrenching drama with superb performances. In reallife, Walsh went on to host Fox-TV's *Most Wanted.* **(CC)**
Dist.: USA

ADAM HAD FOUR SONS 1941
★ ★ ★ ★ NR Drama 1:48 B&W
Dir: Gregory Ratoff *Cast:* Ingrid Bergman, Warner Baxter, Susan Hayward, Fay Wray, Johnny Downs, Richard Denning
▶ In 1907, European Bergman arrives in America to serve as governess to Baxter's four sons.

Through the years, Bergman and Baxter fall in love and she must defend the family from Hayward, a schemer bent on marrying one son and sleeping with another. An old-style Hollywood soap opera, performed to the hilt by a wonderful Bergman (in her second American film) and a sexy Hayward.
Dist.: RCA/Columbia

ADAM'S RIB 1949
★ ★ ★ ★ NR Comedy 1:41 B&W
Dir: George Cukor *Cast:* Katharine Hepburn, Spencer Tracy, Judy Holliday, Tom Ewell, Jean Hagen
▶ Sixth teaming of Hepburn and Tracy is a classic battle-of-the-sexes comedy. She's a lawyer defending Holliday in a shooting case; he's her husband as well as the opposing attorney. The stars have never been more delightful, and they're supported by an expert cast. Brilliant script by Ruth Gordon and Garson Kanin and smooth direction by Cukor made this one of the most popular of the duo's comedies.
Dist.: MGM/UA

ADIOS AMIGO 1975
☆ PG Western 1:27
☑ Explicit language
Dir: Fred Williamson *Cast:* Fred Williamson, Richard Pryor, James Brown, Mike Henry
▶ In the old West, Williamson is run off his land by a corrupt sheriff but then is rescued by con man Pryor. Later, Williamson returns the favor and frees Pryor when the latter is imprisoned. Good idea, uninspired execution. Pryor's natural wit rises above the thin story and Williamson's lumbering direction but he can't carry the movie on his own.
Dist.: Vidmark

ADVENTURE OF SHERLOCK HOLMES' SMARTER BROTHER, THE 1975
★ ★ ★ PG Comedy 1:31
☑ Adult situations
Dir: Gene Wilder *Cast:* Gene Wilder, Madeline Kahn, Marty Feldman, Dom DeLuise, Leo McKern, Thorley Walters
▶ Sherlock Holmes satire stars Wilder (who also wrote and directed) as Sigerson Holmes, obsessively jealous of his more famous brother but brilliant in his own right, tackling the evil Professor Moriarty (McKern). Feldman provides Watsonesque support as Sigerson's associate. In the broad tradition of Mel Brooks but somewhat sweeter in tone. Comic highlight: a musical number, "The Kangaroo Hop."
Dist.: Magnetic

ADVENTURES IN BABYSITTING 1987
★ ★ ★ ★ PG-13 Comedy 1:39
☑ Explicit language, mild violence
Dir: Chris Columbus *Cast:* Elisabeth Shue, Maia Brewton, Anthony Rapp, Keith Coogan, Calvin Levels, Vincent Philip D'Onofrio, Penelope Ann Miller
▶ A broad comedy of errors in which suburban babysitter Shue and her two young

charges are chased through inner city Chicago by car thieves, street gangs, mobsters, and even blues singers. Debut film from Spielberg protégé Columbus has a naive point of view but is fast-paced entertainment. (CC)
Dist.: Buena Vista

ADVENTURES OF BARON MUNCHAUSEN, THE 1989 British
★ ★ ★ PG Fantasy 2:06 C
☑ Brief nudity, violence
Dir: Terry Gilliam *Cast:* John Neville, Eric Idle, Sarah Polley, Oliver Reed, Uma Thurman, Robin Williams, Charles McKeown, Jonathan Pryce, Jack Purvis, Sting, Valentina Cortese
▶ While trying to save a town from Turkish invaders, eighteenth-century adventurer/teller-of-tall-tales Baron Munchausen (Neville) has several amazing adventures, including a flight in a balloon made of knickers, a cannonball ride, and a dazzling encounter with the disembodied head of the King of the Moon (Williams). Comic spectacle's astonishing visuals hold up surprisingly well on video. (CC)
Dist.: RCA/Columbia

ADVENTURES OF BUCKAROO BANZAI: ACROSS THE 8TH DIMENSION, THE 1984
★ ★ PG Sci-Fi 1:42
☑ Adult situations, explicit language, mild violence
Dir: W. D. Richter *Cast:* John Lithgow, Peter Weller, Ellen Barkin, Christopher Lloyd, Jeff Goldblum
▶ Wild sci-fi farce with neurosurgeon/rock star/race-car driver Banzai (Weller) out to save the Earth from mad scientists, aliens, and World War III. He's aided by the Hong Kong Cavaliers, electroids from Planet 10, and Penny Priddy (Barkin), his dead wife's twin sister. Dense plotting, breathless pacing, and an over-the-top performance from Lithgow have made this a cult item, but the film's tongue-in-cheek style and deliberately obscure story line are not for all tastes.
Dist.: Vestron

ADVENTURES OF BULLWHIP GRIFFIN, THE 1967
★ ★ ★ ★ NR Action-Adventure 1:50
Dir: James Neilson *Cast:* Roddy McDowall, Suzanne Pleshette, Karl Malden, Harry Guardino, Brian Russell, Mike Mazurki
▶ Young Russell, accompanied by proper family butler McDowall, leaves Boston to make his fortune in the San Francisco Gold Rush. Delightful Disney adventure highlighted by a slapstick fistfight between McDowall and Mountain Ox (Mazurki). Barbershop quartet numbers and title cards in the silent film style are amusing touches.
Dist.: Buena Vista

ADVENTURES OF DON JUAN 1949
★ ★ ★ NR Action-Adventure 1:50
Dir: Vincent Sherman *Cast:* Errol Flynn,

Vivoca Lindfors, Robert Douglas, Alan Hale, Romney Brent, Robert Warwick
▶ As a seventeenth-century roué, Flynn forsakes romance to save his queen Lindfors from the machinations of evil duke Douglas. Lavish, action-filled swashbuckler poked fun at Flynn's reputation as a great lover and won a Costume Design Oscar.
Dist.: MGM/UA

ADVENTURES OF HERCULES 1985 Italian
★ PG Action-Adventure 1:30
☑ Violence
Dir: Lewis Coates (Luigi Cozzi) *Cast:* Lou Ferrigno, Milly Carlucci, Sonia Viviani, William Berger, Carlotta Green
▶ Hercules has to recover Zeus's seven thunderbolts by murdering a Fire Monster, the Spider Queen of the Amazons, and assorted other villains. Ferrigno is the muscle-bound hero in this sequel to 1983's *Hercules.* Both films were shot at the same time with Italian unknowns, and feature bad dubbing, cheesy special effects, and ridiculous dialogue. Even kids may be disappointed. Also known as *Hercules II.* (CC)
Dist.: MGM/UA

ADVENTURES OF HUCKLEBERRY FINN, THE 1960
★ ★ ★ NR Family 1:47
Dir: Michael Curtiz *Cast:* Tony Randall, Eddie Hodges, Archie Moore, Patty McCormick, Neville Brand, Buster Keaton
▶ Huckleberry Finn (Hodges) and escaped slave Jim (Moore) travel down the Mississippi via raft into all sorts of adventures, such as encountering con man Randall. Entertaining adaptation of the Mark Twain classic; former boxing champ Moore is the standout in a fine cast.
Dist.: CBS/Fox

ADVENTURES OF HUCKLEBERRY FINN, THE 1985
★ ★ ★ ★ NR Family 2:04
Dir: Peter H. Hunt *Cast:* Patrick Day, Samm-Art Williams, Jim Dale, Frederic Forrest, Lillian Gish, Barnard Hughes
▶ Mark Twain's classic adventure receives a flavorful treatment in this first-rate adaptation. Day is disarming as the shrewd rascal Huck; Williams brings depth and dignity to his role as escaped slave Jim. Peppered with wonderful supporting actors, including Richard Kiley, Geraldine Page, and Butterfly McQueen.
Dist.: MCA

ADVENTURES OF ICHABOD AND MR. TOAD, THE 1949
★ ★ G Animation 1:08
Dir: Jack Kinney, Clyde Geronimi, James Algar *Cast:* Voices of Bing Crosby, Basil Rathbone, Eric Blore, Pat O'Malley, John Floyardt
▶ Two-part Disney cartoon from the studio's golden era. First sequence, based on characters from Kenneth Grahame's *The Wind in the*

Willows and narrated by Rathbone, concerns a stolen car inadvertently purchased by Mr. Toad. Second part is a funny and frightening adaptation of Washington Irving's "The Legend of Sleepy Hollow," narrated and sung in inimitable style by Crosby. Superb animation and music. Split into two cassettes for home video.
Dist.: Buena Vista

ADVENTURES OF MARK TWAIN, THE 1944
★ ★ ★ NR Biography 2:10 B&W
Dir: Irving Rapper   *Cast:* Fredric March, Alexis Smith, Donald Crisp, Alan Hale, C. Aubrey Smith, John Carradine
▶ Respectful biography of the great humorist, capably played by March, follows his picaresque career as a steamboat navigator on the Mississippi, editor in the Wild West, and world-famous lecturer. Not always factual, but shows the inspiration for many of Twain's best stories. Carradine stands out in a large cast as fellow writer Bret Harte.
Dist.: Paramount

ADVENTURES OF MILO AND OTIS, THE 1989 Japanese
★ ★ ★ ★ G Family 1:16
Dir: Masanori Hata   *Cast:* Milo the Cat, Otis the Dog, narrated by Dudley Moore
▶ A buddy movie with fur. Rambunctious kitten Milo becomes fast friends with pug pup Otis. When Milo inadvertently takes a trip downstream in a wooden box, Otis follows his scent. The two team up and set off on adventures with bears, deer, pigs, foxes and raccoons. Japanese production was highly praised for its stunning nature photography and the anthropomorphic reactions of the stars. One of the highest grossing films ever in that country.
Dist.: RCA/Columbia

ADVENTURES OF ROBIN HOOD, THE 1938
★ ★ ★ ★ NR Action-Adventure 1:42
Dir: Michael Curtiz, William Keighley   *Cast:* Errol Flynn, Olivia de Havilland, Basil Rathbone, Claude Rains, Patric Knowles
▶ Perhaps the most famous of all swashbuckling movies, this classic adventure is first-rate on all levels. Flynn is perfect as the charming bandit who steals from the rich and gives to the poor. He's assisted by superb performances by Eugene Pallette, Alan Hale, and other famous character actors, with Rathbone especially memorable as the evil Sir Guy. Sumptuous production values, Oscar-winning score by Erich Korngold, and sparkling Technicolor are big bonuses. An enduring favorite for all ages.
Dist.: MGM/UA

ADVENTURES OF SHERLOCK HOLMES, THE 1939
★ ★ ★ ★ NR Mystery-Suspense 1:22 B&W
Dir: Alfred Werker   *Cast:* Basil Rathbone, Nigel Bruce, Ida Lupino, Alan Marshal, Terry Kilburn, George Zucco

▶ Sequel to *The Hound of the Baskervilles*, which introduced the inspired casting of Rathbone as Holmes and Bruce as his bumbling sidekick Dr. Watson. Professor Moriarty (Zucco), the detective's perennial nemesis, plans to steal the crown jewels while throwing Rathbone off the trail with a series of murders in foggy Victorian England. Gripping, atmospheric fun for all ages; followed by long-running series setting Holmes in modern era, starting with *Sherlock Holmes and the Voice of Terror.* (CC)
Dist.: CBS/Fox

ADVENTURES OF THE WILDERNESS FAMILY, THE 1976
★ ★ ★ ★ ★ G Family 1:39
Dir: Stewart Raffill   *Cast:* Robert Logan, Susan Damante Shaw, Heather Rattray, George 'Buck' Flower
▶ A construction worker moves his family from Los Angeles to a log cabin in Utah so his daughter can recover her health. Adjusting to life in the mountains, they learn to cope with bears, wolves, and other wild animals. The first of many popular family-oriented features in this series benefits from breathtaking photography and a wholesome point-of-view.
Dist.: Media

ADVENTURES OF TOM SAWYER, THE 1938
★ ★ ★ NR Action-Adventure 1:17
Dir: Norman Taurog   *Cast:* Tommy Kelly, Jackie Moran, Ann Gillis, May Robson, Walter Brennan, Victor Jory
▶ Charming adaptation of the Mark Twain classic about the irrepressible Tom Sawyer (Kelly) and his friend Huck Finn (Moran). The novel's best scenes—Tom conning two boys into whitewashing Aunt Polly's (Robson) fence, attending his own funeral, etc.—are reproduced with loving care. Jory is a memorably evil Injun Joe in the film's best sequence, a frightening chase through a mammoth cave. (CC)
Dist.: CBS/Fox

ADVISE AND CONSENT 1962
★ ★ ★ ★ NR Drama 2:19 B&W
Dir: Otto Preminger   *Cast:* Henry Fonda, Charles Laughton, Gene Tierney, Walter Pidgeon, Peter Lawford, Franchot Tone
▶ Ailing President Tone nominates a liberal for Secretary of State. As the Senate debates his choices, politicians resort to blackmail to sway the final vote. Sprawling adaptation of Allen Drury's Pulitzer prize–winning novel is dominated by strong performances by Fonda as the liberal candidate and Laughton as an unscrupulous Southern senator. Tame by today's standards, although still smooth entertainment in the Preminger style.
Dist.: Video Treasures

AFFAIR IN TRINIDAD 1952
★ ★ ★ NR Mystery-Suspense B&W
Dir: Vincent Sherman   *Cast:* Rita Hayworth,

Glenn Ford, Alexander Scourby, Torin Thatcher, Valerie Bettis
▶ Hayworth's comeback vehicle (she took four years off during her marriage to Prince Aly Khan) features Rita as a sultry singer in a Trinidad club whose husband is murdered. Ford, the dead man's brother, suspects Hayworth but eventually falls for her. Entertaining; the leads revive their chemistry from *Gilda* and Hayworth will raise your temperature in numbers choreographed by Bettis.
Dist.: RCA/Columbia

AFFAIRS OF ANNABEL, THE 1938
★ NR Comedy 1:08 B&W
Dir: Ben Stoloff *Cast:* Lucille Ball, Jack Oakie, Ruth Donnelly, Fritz Feld, Bradley Page, Thurston Hall
▶ Hollywood press agent Oakie will do anything to get attention for actress client Ball; his wild schemes land her in the slammer, among other scrapes. Sprightly Tinseltown satire features frisky performances by Oakie and Ball. Stars repeated their roles in sequel *Annabel Takes a Tour.*
Dist.: Turner

AFFAIR TO REMEMBER, AN 1957
★★★★ NR Romance 1:54
Dir: Leo McCarey *Cast:* Cary Grant, Deborah Kerr, Cathleen Nesbitt, Neva Patterson, Richard Denning
▶ Shipboard lovers Grant and Kerr, each engaged to another, postpone their affair, planning to meet after an interval to make sure their feelings are real. Director McCarey's remake of his 1939 classic *Love Affair* continues the original's emphasis on star power and deep emotion. Received four Oscar nominations, including the title song and musical score.
Dist.: CBS/Fox

AFRICAN DREAM, AN 1988 British
★★ PG Drama 1:33
☑ Brief nudity, adult situations
Dir: John Smallcombe *Cast:* Kitty Aldridge, John Kani, Dominic Jephcott, John Carson
▶ In 1906, sensitive Englishwoman Aldridge leaves home to live with rancher husband Jephcott in Africa. Aldridge is appalled by the treatment of natives and forms a relationship with black educator Kani that shocks the whites. Muted pacing and storytelling; the sort of thing "Masterpiece Theatre" does better.
Dist.: HBO

AFRICAN QUEEN, THE 1951
★★★★★ NR Action-Adventure 1:43
Dir: John Huston *Cast:* Katharine Hepburn, Humphrey Bogart, Robert Morley, Peter Bull, Theodore Bikel
▶ In World War I Africa, spinsterish missionary Hepburn and hard-drinking boatman Bogart journey through German-occupied waters in the ramshackle craft *The African Queen.* Bickering and fighting, the unlikely duo fall in love and demolish the Germans' big guns in John Huston's classic adventure tale from the C. S. Forester novel. Marvelous chemistry between the two stars. Bogart's Oscar performance.
Dist.: CBS/Fox

AFRICA SCREAMS 1949
★★ NR Comedy 1:19 B&W
Dir: Charles Barton *Cast:* Bud Abbott, Lou Costello, Hillary Brooke, Max Baer, Buddy Baer, Clyde Beatty, Frank Buck, Shemp Howard, Joe Besser
▶ Department store clerk Bud tries to impress Brooke by pretending Lou is a big-game hunter; as a result, the boys end up in an African jungle searching for lost diamonds and fighting gorillas. Typical slapstick shenanigans boosted by the brothers Baer (real-life heavyweight prizefighters) and famous animal handlers Beatty and Buck.
Dist.: Various ©

AFRICA—TEXAS STYLE! 1967
★ NR Family 1:46
Dir: Andrew Marton *Cast:* Hugh O'Brian, John Mills, Nigel Green, Tom Nardini, Adrienne Corri, Ronald Howard
▶ Roundup time on the old veldt as Mills brings Lone Star cowpunchers O'Brian and Nardini to the Dark Continent to corral endangered wildlife. In addition to baddie Green, Texas boys must cope with recalcitrant beasts, some of whom are more dangerous than your average longhorn. Great family adventure was the basis for TV series "Cowboy in Africa."
Dist.: Republic

AFTER HOURS 1985
★ R Comedy 1:37
☑ Nudity, adult situations, explicit language, violence
Dir: Martin Scorsese *Cast:* Griffin Dunne, Rosanna Arquette, Teri Garr, John Heard, Linda Fiorentino
▶ Dunne plays an uptight word-processing trainer whose date with Arquette turns into a comic nightmare. After losing his bearings in arty downtown New York, his problems escalate when Arquette commits suicide and vigilantes mistake him for a burglar. Offbeat, sophisticated urban comedy has a strong cast, assured direction, and an unpredictable plot. (CC)
Dist.: Warner

AFTER THE FALL OF NEW YORK 1985
Italian/French
★ R Action-Adventure 1:35
☑ Explicit language, violence
Dir: Martin Dolman (Sergio Martino) *Cast:* Michael Sopkiw, Anna Kanakis, Valentine Monnier, Roman Geer, Vincent Scalondro
▶ Twenty years after a devastating nuclear war, a rough-hewn hero named Parsifal leads his gang of misfits into New York to rescue the world's last fertile woman from a hulk known as Big Ape. Lots of mindless action, bad dub-

bing, cheap sets and special effects, and a plot borrowed from *Escape from New York*.
Dist.: Vestron

AFTER THE FOX 1966 U.S./British/Italian
★ ★ NR Comedy 1:42
Dir: Vittorio De Sica   ***Cast:*** Peter Sellers, Victor Mature, Britt Ekland, Martin Balsam
▶ Neil Simon co-wrote the screenplay for this nutty farce about Italian con man Sellers who impersonates a famous film director to pull off a heist. Virtuoso comic performance by Sellers, who indulges his penchant for outlandish disguises. Even the theme song (written by Burt Bacharach and performed by Sellers and the Hollies) is funny.
Dist.: CBS/Fox

AFTER THE REHEARSAL 1984 Swedish
☆ R Drama 1:13
☑ Brief nudity, adult situations, explicit language
Dir: Ingmar Bergman   ***Cast:*** Erland Josephson, Ingrid Thulin, Lena Olin
▶ On an empty stage, theatrical director Josephson has discussions with two actresses, young Olin and older alcoholic Thulin. Past histories, memories, and feelings are bared. Extremely claustrophobic drama has the effect of a long psychoanalytical session. Does not rank with Bergman's best.   Ⓢ
Dist.: RCA/Columbia

AFTER THE THIN MAN 1936
★ ★ ★ NR Mystery-Suspense 1:50 B&W
Dir: W. S. Van Dyke II   ***Cast:*** William Powell, Myrna Loy, Elissa Landi, Joseph Calleia, James Stewart
▶ The second entry in the *Thin Man* series, with Powell and Loy as those wisecracking married detectives, Nick and Nora Charles. In San Francisco, the Charleses (as always, accompanied by their faithful dog Asta) get involved in the case of the missing husband of Nora's cousin. Snappy dialogue, mystery, and comedy mix once more in the typical fashion of the series.
Dist.: MGM/UA

AGAINST A CROOKED SKY 1975
★ ★ G Western 1:29
Dir: Earl Bellamy   ***Cast:*** Richard Boone, Stewart Petersen, Geoffrey Land, Jewel Blanch, Henry Wilcoxon
▶ When his sister Blanch is abducted by Indians, Petersen sets forth with elderly Boone on a mission to find her. Western aimed squarely at the family audience; Boone is fine but the plotting relies on familiar clichés.
Dist.: Vestron

AGAINST ALL FLAGS 1952
★ ★ ★ NR Action-Adventure 1:23
Dir: George Sherman   ***Cast:*** Errol Flynn, Maureen O'Hara, Anthony Quinn, Mildred Natwick, Alice Kelley, Robert Warwick
▶ English officer Flynn poses as pirate to get the goods on buccaneer Quinn and his swashbuckling cutthroats. Flynn rescues captured princess Kelley, wins the heart of female pirate O'Hara, and eventually battles Quinn to the death. Pirate yarn delivered with verve and excitement.
Dist.: KVC

AGAINST ALL ODDS 1984
★ ★ ★ R Mystery-Suspense 2:01
☑ Nudity, adult situations, explicit language, violence
Dir: Taylor Hackford   ***Cast:*** Rachel Ward, Jeff Bridges, James Woods, Richard Widmark, Alex Karras, Swoosie Kurtz
▶ Ex-football player Bridges is hired by sleazy nightclub owner Woods to locate his runaway girlfriend Ward in this sexy, steamy remake of the 1947 *Out of the Past*. Bridges and Ward become lovers and an intricate web of corruption, jealousy, and murder ensues. Stylishly directed by Hackford, this thriller makes up for some confused plotting with plenty of action and sex. Haunting title song by Phil Collins. (CC)
Dist.: RCA/Columbia

AGATHA 1979
★ ★ ★ PG Drama 1:38
☑ Adult situations, explicit language
Dir: Michael Apted   ***Cast:*** Dustin Hoffman, Vanessa Redgrave, Timothy Dalton, Helen Morse, Celia Gregory
▶ Fictional explanation of events during Agatha Christie's famous two-week disappearance in 1926 has the acclaimed mystery writer hatching a real-life murder plot of her own. Redgrave stars as Agatha, the creator of Hercule Poirot and Jane Marple and wife of the philandering Dalton whom she finds at a seaside resort with his secretary. Hoffman plays an earnest journalist who uncovers the real story and falls in love.
Dist.: Warner

AGENCY 1981 Canadian
★ ★ R Mystery-Suspense 1:33
☑ Adult situations, explicit language, violence
Dir: George Kaczender   ***Cast:*** Robert Mitchum, Lee Majors, Valerie Perrine, Saul Rubinek
▶ New York ad agency creative director Majors uncovers a plot to affect the presidential election via subliminal advertising. The trail leads to Mitchum but Majors eventually makes the world safe for democracy in this routine thriller that fails to adequately exploit the talents of a good cast.
Dist.: Vestron

AGNES OF GOD 1985
★ ★ ★ ★ PG-13 Drama 1:39
☑ Adult situations, explicit language
Dir: Norman Jewison   ***Cast:*** Anne Bancroft, Jane Fonda, Meg Tilly, Anne Pitoniak, Winston Rekert
▶ Did Sister Agnes (Tilly) murder her baby or is there a more mystical explanation for this

scandal behind convent walls? It's up to court-appointed shrink Fonda to find out in this talky but engrossing adaptation of John Pielmeier's Broadway hit. Worth seeing for Fonda's sparring with Mother Superior Anne Bancroft (Oscar-nominated, as was Tilly). (CC)
Dist.: RCA/Columbia

AGONY AND THE ECSTASY, THE 1965
★★★ NR Biography 2:20
Dir: Carol Reed *Cast:* Charlton Heston, Rex Harrison, Diane Cilento, Harry Andrews, Alberto Lupo, Adolfo Celi
► Earnest but overlong account of the painting of the ceiling frescoes in the Vatican's Sistine Chapel describes Michelangelo's (Heston) inspiration in terms of a bitter feud with his patron, Pope Julius II (Harrison). Production details are impressive, but plodding pacing and historical inaccuracies are drawbacks. Based on Irving Stone's best-seller.
Dist.: CBS/Fox

AGUIRRE: THE WRATH OF GOD 1972
German
☆ NR Drama 1:34
☑ Explicit language, violence
Dir: Werner Herzog *Cast:* Klaus Kinski, Ruy Guerra, Del Negro, Helena Rojo, Cecilia Rivera, Peter Berling
► Spanish conquistadors led by Kinski penetrate a dense Peruvian jungle in search of a lost city of gold, but find insanity and death instead as they are attacked by wily natives. Compelling account of obsession, shot on location in extraordinary settings, features a magnetic performance by Kinski. Arresting images add to film's impact. [S]
Dist.: Continental

AIR FORCE 1943
★★★★ NR War 2:04 B&W
Dir: Howard Hawks *Cast:* John Garfield, Gig Young, Arthur Kennedy, Charles Drake, Harry Carey, John Ridgely
► Exciting tribute to the crew of the *Mary Ann*, a B-17 Flying Fortress in action over Pearl Harbor, Manila, and the Coral Sea during World War II. Sober, realistic screenplay by Dudley Nichols adds depth to authentic dogfight sequences. Despite anti-Japanese racism, film holds up quite well. Oscar-nominated for writing and photography. **(CC)**
Dist.: CBS/Fox

AIRPLANE! 1980
★★★★ PG Comedy 1:28
☑ Brief nudity, adult situations, violence, adult humor
Dir: Jim Abrahams, Jerry Zucker, David Zucker *Cast:* Robert Hays, Lloyd Bridges, Julie Hagerty, Robert Stack, Peter Graves
► In this wild parody of the *Airport* disaster series, Hays stars as a washed-up, lovelorn pilot flying a planeful of mixed nuts suffering from food poisoning. Directors Abrahams, Zucker, and Zucker imbue the film with an everything-but-the-kitchen-sink sense of humor that propelled it into a runaway hit. A diverse supporting cast features basketball star Kareem Abdul Jabbar and Graves as the copilot/gladiator movie enthusiast.
Dist.: Paramount

AIRPLANE II: THE SEQUEL 1982
★★ PG Comedy 1:24
☑ Brief nudity, adult situations, adult humor
Dir: Ken Finkelman *Cast:* Robert Hays, Julie Hagerty, Lloyd Bridges, William Shatner, Raymond Burr
► In this genial follow-up to the hugely successful *Airplane!*, pilot Hays escapes from an insane asylum to save the space shuttle from destruction. Wide-eyed Hagerty, Hays's former love, is also back from the first film and "Captain Kirk" Shatner has been added to the cast of zanies. Although not as inventive as the first movie, the broad visual humor still brings a few laughs.
Dist.: Paramount

AIRPORT 1970
★★★★★ G Action-Adventure 2:15
Dir: George Seaton *Cast:* Burt Lancaster, Dean Martin, George Kennedy, Helen Hayes, Jean Seberg
► In this granddaddy of the disaster genre, a mad bomber blows up half an airliner in midflight which must then land at a totally snowbound airport. Adapted from Arthur Hailey's best-seller, the movie's all-star cast features Lancaster as the airport manager, Martin as the pilot, Van Heflin as the bomber, and Hayes in an Oscar-winning performance as the little old lady who stows away. Taut, suspenseful, and easily the best of the genre.
Dist.: MCA

AIRPORT 1975 1975
★★★ PG Action-Adventure 1:46
☑ Adult situations
Dir: Jack Smight *Cast:* Charlton Heston, Karen Black, George Kennedy, Efrem Zimbalist, Jr., Susan Clark
► "The stewardess is flying the plane!" a passenger shouts as Black attempts to land a wounded airliner, assisted by Heston's radioed instructions, after a midair collision wipes out the flight crew. Serves up all the genre's key elements—contrived but suspenseful situations, corny dialogue, and an all-star cast (featuring Helen Reddy as a singing nun, Linda Blair as a kidney transplant patient, and Gloria Swanson). An entertaining concoction.
Dist.: MCA

AIRPORT '77 1977
★★★★★ PG Action-Adventure 1:53
☑ Adult situations
Dir: Jerry Jameson *Cast:* Jack Lemmon, Lee Grant, Brenda Vaccaro, Darren McGavin, Christopher Lee, James Stewart
► Millionaire Stewart invites a planeful of people to the opening of his museum, only to

have the plane hijacked by art thieves who proceed to crash it into the Bermuda Triangle. Third in the popular *Airport* series.
Dist.: MCA

ALAMO, THE 1960
★★★ NR Western 2:41
Dir: John Wayne ***Cast:*** John Wayne, Richard Widmark, Laurence Harvey, Patrick Wayne, Linda Cristal, Frankie Avalon
▶ Inspiring re-creation of the famous 1836 siege in Texas, brought to the screen with care and imagination by Wayne, directing for the only time in his career. The Duke gives a tough, sharp performance as Davy Crockett, and he's ably matched by Widmark as a flinty Jim Bowie and Richard Boone as Sam Houston. Superb score by Dimitri Tiomkin.
Dist.: MGM/UA

ALAMO BAY 1985
★★ R Drama 1:39
☑ Brief nudity, adult situations, violence
Dir: Louis Malle ***Cast:*** Amy Madigan, Ed Harris, Ho Nguyen, Donald Moffat, Truyen V. Tran
▶ Harris and Madigan (husband and wife in real life) find themselves on opposite sides of a conflict between Texas fishermen and the Vietnamese refugees who become their competition. Madigan shines as the feisty Glory, who alienates boyfriend Harris when she sides with Vietnamese Nguyen. Harris responds by joining the KKK, leading to an explosive climax in Malle's sensitive fact-based drama. (CC)
Dist.: RCA/Columbia

AL CAPONE 1959
★★ NR Biography/Crime 1:45 B&W
Dir: Richard Wilson ***Cast:*** Rod Steiger, Fay Spain, James Gregory, Martin Balsam, Nehemiah Persoff, Murvyn Vye
▶ Energetic, semidocumentary approach to the infamous Chicago gangster presents an unvarnished look at his career, from his rise as a hit man for Johnny Torrio (Persoff) to his ultimate arrest for income tax evasion. Steiger gives a larger-than-life portrait of Capone; good supporting work by Vye as Bugs Moran and Gregory as an uncompromising cop.
Dist.: Key

ALCHEMIST, THE 1985
☆ R Horror 1:24
☑ Explicit language, violence
Dir: James Armante ***Cast:*** Robert Ginty, Lucinda Dooling, John Sanderford, Viola Kate Stimpson, Robert Glaudini
▶ An 1871 alchemist's curse transforms glassmaker Aaron McCallum (Ginty) into an immortal murderous beast. Then the action cuts to 1955 as the reincarnation of Aaron's wife fights for his soul. Low-budget horror tale for hard-core genre fans.
Dist.: Vestron

ALEXA 1988
☆ R Drama 1:20
☑ Nudity, strong sexual content, explicit language
Dir: Sean Delgado ***Cast:*** Christine Moore, Kirk Bailey, Ruth Corrine Collins
▶ Playwright Bailey, writing play on prostitutes, meets high class call girl Moore. She can't stand Bailey at first but eventually falls for him as her ex-pimp lurks menacingly in the background. Strange movie has attractive cast and cinematography but incoherent story with inconsistent characterizations.
Dist.: Academy

ALEXANDER NEVSKY 1938 Russian
☆ NR War 1:48 B&W
Dir: Sergei Eisenstein ***Cast:*** Nikolai Cherkassov, Nikolai Okhlopkov, Alexander Abrikossov, Dmitri Orlov
▶ Germans invade thirteenth-century Russia, ravaging the countryside until Prince Nevsky (Cherkassov) assembles an army to fight them. Action-packed epic justly famed for its virtuoso editing, in particular during a massive battle on a frozen lake. Music by Sergei Prokofiev. [S]
Dist.: Video Yesteryear

ALEXANDER THE GREAT 1956
★★ NR Biography 2:21
Dir: Robert Rossen ***Cast:*** Richard Burton, Fredric March, Claire Bloom, Danielle Darrieux, Harry Andrews, Stanley Baker
▶ Burton is magnetic as the Greek leader who conquered all of the known world in the fourth century B.C.; March provides powerful counterpoint as his insatiable father Philip. Stirring battle scenes and Burton's tender love affair with Barsine (Bloom) almost salvage film's interminable philosophical debates.
Dist.: MGM/UA

ALFIE 1966 British
★★★ PG Drama 1:53
☑ Adult situations
Dir: Lewis Gilbert ***Cast:*** Michael Caine, Shelley Winters, Julia Foster, Millicent Martin, Shirley Anne Field, Vivien Merchant
▶ Hard-hitting story of a hedonistic Cockney womanizer catapulted Caine to international stardom and his first Oscar nomination. As Alfie, a self-proclaimed "bird-watcher," Caine flits through a series of relationships from Winters, a brassy, well-heeled extrovert in love with another man, to Merchant, a dutiful married woman pregnant by Alfie. For all its humor, startlingly no-nonsense. Nominated for five Academy Awards.
Dist.: Paramount

ALGIERS 1938
★★ NR Drama 1:35 B&W
Dir: John Cromwell ***Cast:*** Charles Boyer, Hedy Lamarr, Sigrid Gurie, Joseph Calleia, Alan Hale, Gene Lockhart
▶ Boyer gave perhaps his most famous performance as Pepe Le Moko, the suave jewel

thief who hides from the law in the Casbah section of Algiers. His sanctuary is jeopardized when he falls in love with Lamarr. Marvelously romantic remake of the French *Pepe Le Moko* with Jean Gabin in title role; Tony Martin assayed the part in 1948's *Casbah*.
Dist.: Video Yesteryear

ALICE 1988 Czech
☆ **NR Animation/Adult 1:24**
Dir: Jan Svankmajer *Cast:* Kristyna Kohoutova
► In this surreal adaptation of *Alice in Wonderland*, Alice (Kohoutova) follows her suddenly alive stuffed rabbit through a desk drawer and encounters strange creatures like the March Hare and the Mad Hatter. Czech animation master Svankmajer uses pixillation, combining live action and puppets to create a disturbing world that will give adults the creeps and frighten unwary children. Dubbed.
Dist.: Warner

ALICE ADAMS 1935
★★★★ **NR Drama 1:40 B&W**
Dir: George Stevens *Cast:* Katharine Hepburn, Fred MacMurray, Fred Stone, Evelyn Venable, Frank Alberston, Hedda Hopper
► Hepburn, a small town girl from the wrong side of the tracks, desperately tries to snag eligible upper-class bachelor MacMurray in spite of her family's gauche background. Sensitive, low-key adaptation of the Booth Tarkington best-seller has a beautifully bittersweet mood, with Hepburn astonishing as the aggressive but still appealing heroine. Both she and the picture won Oscar nominations.
Dist.: Turner

ALICE DOESN'T LIVE HERE ANYMORE 1975
★★★★ **PG Drama 1:52**
☑ Adult situations, explicit language
Dir: Martin Scorsese *Cast:* Ellen Burstyn, Kris Kristofferson, Jodie Foster, Alfred Lutter, Harry Dean Stanton
► Burstyn is absolutely superb in her Oscar-winning turn as Alice Hyatt, a woman left on her own with an eleven-year-old son when her husband is killed in a crash. As Alice rebuilds her life, she finds new work as a singer and waitress, a new man in Kristofferson, and most importantly, new strength in herself. Inspired the popular TV series "Alice."
Dist.: Warner

ALICE IN THE CITIES 1974 German
☆ **NR Drama 1:50 B&W**
☑ Adult situations
Dir: Wim Wenders *Cast:* Rudiger Vogler, Yella Rottlander, Elisabeth Kreuzer, Edda Kochl, Didi Petrikat, Ernest Bohm
► Journalist Vogler has been given custody of Rottlander, a little girl from America. Together they criss-cross the German countryside searching for her grandmother. Slow meditation on the differences between city and

country can be effective, but requires patience. Ⓢ
Dist.: Pacific Arts

ALICE IN WONDERLAND 1950 British/French
★ **NR Animation 1:23**
Dir: Dallas Bower *Cast:* Carol Marsh, Pamela Brown, Stephen Murray, Felix Aylmer
► Mediocre version of the Lewis Carroll classic. Combines live action and puppets (Murray plays Carroll and then provides the voice of one of the Wonderland characters, while Marsh plays Alice) but lacks the inventiveness of the other versions.
Dist.: Monterey

ALICE IN WONDERLAND 1951
★★★★ **G Animation 1:15**
Dir: Clyde Geronimi, Hamilton Luske, Wilfred Jaxon *Cast:* Voices of Kathryn Beaumont, Ed Wynn, Sterling Holloway, Richard Haydn, Jerry Colonna
► Delightful Disney version of Lewis Carroll's novels boasts superb animation, tuneful score, and excellent characterizations, particularly Holloway's amusing Cheshire Cat. Script sacrifices some of Carroll's intellectual humor, concentrating instead on the humor and suspense of young Alice's amazing adventures. Oliver Wallace's orchestrations received an Oscar nomination.
Dist.: Buena Vista

ALICE'S ADVENTURES IN WONDERLAND 1972 British
★ **G Family 1:36**
Dir: William Sterling *Cast:* Fiona Fullerton, Peter Sellers, Dudley Moore, Michael Crawford, Ralph Richardson, Spike Milligan
► Delightful adaptation of the famous book stars Fullerton as Alice, who falls down the White Rabbit's (Crawford) hole, enters Wonderland, and encounters an all-star British cast that includes Sellers as the March Hare, Moore as the Doormouse, and Richardson as the Caterpillar. English stars give this added adult appeal.
Dist.: Vestron

ALICE'S RESTAURANT 1969
★★ **PG Musical 1:50**
☑ Adult situations, explicit language
Dir: Arthur Penn *Cast:* Arlo Guthrie, Pat Quinn, James Broderick, Michael McClanathan
► Folk singer Guthrie plays himself in this adaptation of his famous talking blues "Alice's Restaurant," the story of an arrest for garbage dumping that left Guthrie happily unfit for military service in the Vietnam era. Anyone nostalgic for the days of draft physicals, hippies, and flower children will be in heaven here. The film's natural, easygoing tone is embodied by the star's performance.
Dist.: MGM/UA

ALICE SWEET ALICE 1977
★★ **R Mystery-Suspense 1:48**

☑ Adult situations, violence
Dir: Alfred Sole ***Cast:*** Brooke Shields, Linda Miller, Paula Sheppard, Tom Signorelli, Louis Horton, Lillian Roth
▶ When angelic Shields is brutally murdered during her Holy Communion services, the police believe her malevolent sister Alice (Sheppard) is responsible. Underrated chiller is surprisingly effective and good for a few jolts. Shields, however, dies early in the film. Also known as *Holy Terror* and *Communion.*
Dist.: Goodtimes

ALIEN 1979
★★★ R Sci-Fi 1:57
☑ Explicit language, graphic violence
Dir: Ridley Scott ***Cast:*** Tom Skerritt, Sigourney Weaver, John Hurt, Ian Holm, Harry Dean Stanton, Yaphet Kotto, Veronica Cartwright
▶ A spaceship crew battles a most unpleasant stowaway—an alien creature determined to destroy all life on ship—in Scott's literally gut-wrenching sci-fi thriller. Terrific visual effects combine with Scott's virtuoso style to create nonstop suspense. Weaver is plenty tough as the one person on board who can outwit the alien. Spawned a sequel and many imitators.
Dist.: CBS/Fox

ALIEN FROM L.A. 1988
★ PG Sci-Fi 1:27
☑ Violence
Dir: Albert Pyun ***Cast:*** Kathy Ireland, Thom Mathews, Don Michael Paul, Linda Kerridge, Richard Haines, William R. Moses
▶ Inhibited, squeaky-voiced Valley Girl Ireland travels to Africa to rescue her explorer father Haines, a prisoner in the underground empire of Atlantis. With the help of prospector Moses and alien hunk Mathews, she defeats the villains and blossoms into a beauty. Silly adventure moves quickly but offers few surprises. Cover girl Ireland's swimsuit scenes are unfortunately brief.
Dist.: Media

ALIEN NATION 1988
★★★★ R Sci-Fi 1:34
☑ Explicit language, graphic violence
Dir: Graham Baker ***Cast:*** James Caan, Mandy Patinkin, Terence Stamp, Kevyn Major Howard, Leslie Bevis, Peter Jason
▶ Dome-topped aliens emigrate to tomorrow's Los Angeles, where they fit into society with surprising ease. Patinkin, the first alien promoted to police officer, is paired with Caan, who hates the "newcomers," in a case involving murder and drug smuggling. Dynamite premise and oustanding opening unfortunately give way to routine buddy-cop plotting. Led to TV series.
Dist.: CBS/Fox

ALIEN PREDATOR 1987
★★ R Sci-Fi 1:30
☑ Adult situations, explicit language, graphic violence
Dir: Deran Sarafian ***Cast:*** Dennis Christopher, Martin Hewitt, Lynn-Holly Johnson, Luis Prendes, J. O. Bosso, Yousaf Bokhari
▶ Extraterrestrial microbes attached to downed NASA satellite infect inhabitants of Spanish village, endangering American tourist Christopher and his two pals. Scientist Prendes orders authorities to destroy village before plague spreads as Christopher plots escape plan. Inept adventure, filmed in 1984, features disappointing special effects.
Dist.: TWE

ALIENS 1986
★★★★★ R Sci-Fi 2:17
☑ Explicit language, graphic violence
Dir: James Cameron ***Cast:*** Sigourney Weaver, Carrie Henn, Michael Biehn, Paul Reiser, Lance Henriksen, Bill Paxton, Jenette Goldstein
▶ Astronaut Weaver awakes from fifty-seven years in suspended animation and returns to the original planet from the first *Alien.* With a Marine unit led by Biehn, Weaver takes on a whole army of alien monsters. Director Cameron keeps the action and violence whizzing by in this edge-of-your-seat sci-fi thriller that may even surpass its predecessor. **(CC)**
Dist.: CBS/Fox

ALI: FEAR EATS THE SOUL 1974 German
☆ NR Drama 1:34
☑ Adult situations
Dir: Rainer Werner Fassbinder ***Cast:*** Brigitte Mira, El Hedi Ben Salem, Barbara Valentin, Irm Hermann, Peter Gauhe, Karl Scheydt
▶ Lonely widow Mira meets Arab Ben Salem in a bar, and the two begin a relationship that upsets the ethnic sensibilities of her family. Though they marry, pressures from within and without threaten their happiness. An especially sensitive and clear-eyed portrayal of the complex issue of European racial prejudice. [S]
Dist.: New Yorker

ALL ABOUT EVE 1950
★★★★ NR Drama 2:18 B&W
Dir: Joseph L. Mankiewicz ***Cast:*** Bette Davis, Anne Baxter, George Sanders, Marilyn Monroe, Celeste Holm, Gary Merrill, Thelma Ritter, Hugh Marlowe, Gregory Ratoff
▶ Writer/director Joseph L. Mankiewicz's masterpiece gave Bette Davis the role of a lifetime as Margo Channing, an aging Broadway star suddenly upstaged by young, sweet-faced, ruthlessly ambitious Eve Harrington (Baxter). Witty one-liners fly as the caustic, cantankerous Margo takes on the predatory Eve and the rest of a superb cast. Nominated for fourteen Oscars, winner of six (including Best Picture); a must-see Hollywood classic.
Dist.: CBS/Fox

ALLAN QUATERMAIN AND THE LOST CITY OF GOLD 1987
★ ★ **PG Action-Adventure 1:43**
☑ Explicit language, violence
Dir: Gary Nelson *Cast:* Richard Chamberlain, Sharon Stone, James Earl Jones, Henry Silva, Robert Donner
▶ Chamberlain returns as the dashing adventurer Allan Quatermain in this sequel to *King Solomon's Mines.* Quatermain and his girlfriend Stone battle nasty slave trader Silva while they search for the title lost city. A campy effort with tacky production values that nevertheless offers plenty of action.
Dist.: Media

ALL DOGS GO TO HEAVEN 1989
★ ★ ★ ★ **G Animation 1:24**
Dir: Don Bluth *Cast:* Voices of Burt Reynolds, Dom DeLuise, Judith Barsi, Loni Anderson, Charles Nelson Reilly, Vic Tayback
▶ In 1939 New Orleans, cunning German Shepherd Charlie (voice of Reynolds) reaches heaven after gambling czar/pit bull (Tayback) orders him killed. Charlie comes back to earth for revenge and befriends an orphan girl (Barsi) who can talk to animals. Bouncy full-length cartoon miles above usual kids' fare; should please parents as well. Best tune: the alligator's number. **(CC)**
Dist.: MGM/UA

ALLEGHENY UPRISING 1939
★ ★ **NR Action-Adventure 1:21 B&W**
Dir: William A. Seiter *Cast:* John Wayne, Claire Trevor, George Sanders, Brian Donlevy, Moroni Olsen, Chill Wills
▶ Pre-Revolutionary America provides the setting for Wayne's frontier heroics against Donlevy, an evil gunrunner supplying liquor to the Indians, and Sanders, a British captain determined to control the colony by force. Feisty girlfriend Trevor, a crack shot, helps the Duke during a rigged trial. Modest action vehicle reteamed Wayne and Trevor after their success in *Stagecoach.*
Dist.: Turner C

ALLEGRO NON TROPPO 1977 Italian
★ **PG Animation/Adult 1:25 C/B&W**
☑ Nudity
Dir: Bruno Bozzetto
▶ Classical melodies are illustrated in six sequences, including a bee's eye view of humans, a variation on the story of the snake in the Garden of Eden, and spilled soda giving birth to a whole world. Superb classical music score (includes Stravinsky and Ravel) given imaginative animation. However, humor (especially in the linking live action sequences) is self-conscious and forced.
Dist.: RCA/Columbia

ALLIGATOR 1980
★ ★ **R Horror 1:31**
☑ Explicit language, violence
Dir: Lewis Teague *Cast:* Robert Forster, Robin Riker, Henry Silva, Dean Jagger

▶ An alligator flushed down the toilet twelve years earlier runs amok through Chicago's sewers before surfacing to terrorize innocent bystanders. Police detective Forster can't convince his superiors that anything's wrong, and goes after the gator himself with the help of reptile expert Riker. Modest but enjoyable picture benefits from a tongue-in-cheek screenplay by John Sayles.
Dist.: Vestron

ALL MY SONS 1948
★ ★ ★ **NR Drama 1:34 B&W**
Dir: Irving Reis *Cast:* Edward G. Robinson, Burt Lancaster, Mady Christians, Louisa Horton, Howard Duff, Arlene Francis
▶ Lancaster and Horton, the fiancée of his brother killed in World War II, fall in love. The relationship leads to revelations about Lancaster's dad Robinson, a munitions manufacturer who sold defective parts during the war. Sterling adaptation of Arthur Miller's play features shattering performances by Robinson and Lancaster.
Dist.: MCA

ALLNIGHTER, THE 1987
★ **PG-13 Drama 1:35**
☑ Adult situations, explicit language
Dir: Tamar Simon Hoffs *Cast:* Susanna Hoffs, Dedee Pfeiffer, Joan Cusack, Michael Ontkean, Pam Grier
▶ The misadventures of three roommates on the night before graduation from a party college. Music, dancing, surfing, romance, and prerequisite heartbreak add up to another formula beach movie. Nonstop soundtrack (Mike + the Mechanics, Timbuk 3, etc.) and performance of Hoffs (lead singer of the Bangles rock group) should please fans. Hoffs's mother directed, produced, and co-wrote film.
Dist.: MCA

ALL NIGHT LONG 1981
★ **R Comedy 1:28**
☑ Adult situations, explicit language
Dir: Jean-Claude Tramont *Cast:* Gene Hackman, Barbra Streisand, Dennis Quaid, Diane Ladd
▶ After losing his job, executive Hackman is hired as manager of an all-night drug store. He discovers son Quaid's affair with his fourth cousin Streisand and is soon involved with Streisand himself. Hackman's mid-life crisis is the focus here but Streisand fans might enjoy seeing her in this offbeat mix of comedy and romance.
Dist.: MCA

ALL OF ME 1984
★ ★ ★ ★ **PG Comedy 1:32**
☑ Adult situations, explicit language, adult humor
Dir: Carl Reiner *Cast:* Steve Martin, Lily Tomlin, Victoria Tennant, Jason Bernard, Madolyn Smith
▶ A guru's goof-up leaves half of Martin's

body possessed by eccentric rich woman Tomlin in this hilarious body switch comedy from director Reiner. The simplest bodily function takes on new meaning as these mismatched psyches battle it out. Martin's truly original physical clowning steals the show in this poignant and funny movie.
Dist.: HBO

ALL OVER TOWN 1937
★ **NR Comedy 1:02 B&W**
Dir: James W. Horne   *Cast:* Ole Olsen, Chic Johnson, Mary Howard, Harry Stockwell, Franklin Pangborn, Gertrude Astor
▶ Vaudeville duo Olsen and Johnson are determined to put on a show to save an old theatrical boarding house, but their theater is cursed with a streak of bad luck that may bring their high hopes crashing to the stage. Cheap, old-fashioned comedy is not funny, but offers an interesting glimpse at ancient laugh routines and old comics.
Dist.: SVS

ALL QUIET ON THE WESTERN FRONT 1930
★★★★ **NR War 1:43 B&W**
Dir: Lewis Milestone   *Cast:* Lew Ayres, Louis Wolheim, John Wray, Beryl Mercer, Ben Alexander
▶ In 1914, young student Ayres enlists in the German army. He and his classmates are sent to the front, where they confront the horrors of war. Although dated in some technical aspects, this enduring classic was one of the first and most effective antiwar movies. Filled with emotionally harrowing vignettes and shocking scenes of fighting, it won Oscars for Best Picture and Direction. Adapted from the novel by Erich Maria Remarque.
Dist.: MCA

ALL SCREWED UP 1976 Italian
★ **PG Comedy 1:48**
☑ Adult situations, explicit language
Dir: Lina Wertmuller   *Cast:* Luigi Diberti, Lina Polito, Nini Bignamini, Sara Rapisarda
▶ Tragi-comedy traces the romantic and political complications that ensue when two country bumpkins face a painfully funny adjustment to big city Milan. Their slaughterhouse jobs are rudely cut short by a strike. Final image is memorable but overall film is not as accessible as Wertmuller's *Swept Away*.
Dist.: CBS/Fox

ALL'S FAIR 1988
★ **PG-13 Comedy 1:29**
☑ Explicit language
Dir: Rocky Lang   *Cast:* George Segal, Sally Kellerman, Robert Carradine, Jennifer Edwards, Jane Kaczmarek, Lou Ferrigno
▶ Colonel Segal runs candy company in military manner: his employees must play in weekend war games. Promotion-seeking Edwards and Segal's estranged wife Kellerman decide to join the weekend fun, hiring ninja Ferrigno to train their team for ensuing battle of the sexes. Consistently juvenile, below-the-

belt humor. Edwards and Kaczmarek are appealing but Segal overacts.
Dist.: Media

ALL THAT JAZZ 1979
★★ **R Drama/Musical 2:03**
☑ Nudity, adult situations, explicit language
Dir: Bob Fosse   *Cast:* Roy Scheider, Jessica Lange, Ann Reinking, Leland Palmer, Ben Vereen, John Lithgow
▶ Nine Oscar nominations went to Fosse's dazzling autobiographical musical about choreographer Scheider who juggles ex-wife, mistress, and daughter while simultaneously working on a Broadway musical and a film. A heart attack and a visit from the Angel of Death ensue in this flashy musical for adults, highlighted by Scheider's terrific performance and some wonderful music and dancing. The squeamish should be warned about the graphic open heart surgery scene. **(CC)**
Dist.: CBS/Fox

ALL THE KING'S MEN 1949
★★★★ **NR Biography 1:49 B&W**
Dir: Robert Rossen   *Cast:* Broderick Crawford, John Ireland, Mercedes McCambridge, John Derek, Joanne Dru
▶ Crawford dominates this hard-hitting drama adapted from Robert Penn Warren's Pulitzer prize–winning novel about an ambitious Southern politician. Based on the life of Louisiana's Huey Long, the film shows how a poor farmer uses graft and corruption to become a near-dictator. Superior writing and action highlight a controversial story whose themes are still relevant today. Received seven Oscar nominations, winning Best Picture, Actor (Crawford), and Supporting Actress (McCambridge).
Dist.: RCA/Columbia

. . .ALL THE MARBLES 1981
★★★ **R Drama 1:53**
☑ Nudity, adult situations, explicit language, mild violence
Dir: Robert Aldrich   *Cast:* Peter Falk, Vicki Frederick, Laurene Landon, Burt Young, Tracy Reed
▶ Mild comedy about a small-time manager who pins his hopes for big money on two comely female wrestlers. They make the rounds through small-town Middle America hoping for a shot at a title match in Reno. Considering its subject matter, a surprisingly tame and warm-hearted film that relies heavily on Falk's charm for its humor.
Dist.: MGM/UA

ALL THE PRESIDENT'S MEN 1976
★★★★★ **PG Drama 2:18**
☑ Adult situations, explicit language
Dir: Alan J. Pakula   *Cast:* Robert Redford, Dustin Hoffman, Jason Robards, Jack Warden, Martin Balsam
▶ Landmark film about the investigation by reporters Bob Woodward (Redford) and Carl Bernstein (Hoffman) into the Watergate con-

spiracy won four Oscars, including Supporting Actor for Robards as editor Ben Bradlee. A concise script by William Goldman and uniformly strong action helped explain complex issues to a wide audience in gripping, believable terms. Highly influential documentary approach was imitated in a number of subsequent films. Eight Oscar nominations overall for what has become a modern classic.
Dist.: Warner

ALL THE RIGHT MOVES 1983
★ ★ ★ ★ R Drama 1:26
☑ Nudity, adult situations, explicit language, mild violence, adult humor
Dir: Michael Chapman   *Cast:* Tom Cruise, Craig T. Nelson, Lea Thompson, Charles Cioffi
▶ Popular sports drama was one of Cruise's early hits. He plays an ambitious teen who needs to win a college football scholarship to escape his depressed mining town. When he clashes with coach Nelson after losing an important game, his future looks bleak—until fetching Thompson steps in to help. But the two discover that they still face difficult choices. **(CC)**
Dist.: CBS/Fox

ALL THE RIVERS RUN 1983 Australian
★ ★ ★ ★ ★ NR Romance/MFTV 8:00
Dir: George Miller, Pino Amenta   *Cast:* Sigrid Thornton, John Waters, Charles Tingwell, William Upjohn, Diane Craig
▶ Orphan Philadephia Gordon (Thornton) struggles to assert her independence in nineteenth-century Melbourne's male-dominated society. After a stint as an artist, she falls for the dashing Brenton Edwards (Waters), an adventurer trying to establish a boating company. Gordon goes on to become Australia's first female riverboat pilot in this diverting miniseries adapted from Nancy Cato's novel.
Dist.: HBO

ALL THIS AND HEAVEN TOO 1940
★ ★ ★ NR Romance 2:23 B&W
Dir: Anatole Litvak   *Cast:* Bette Davis, Charles Boyer, Jeffrey Lynn, Barbara O'Neil, Virginia Weidler, June Lockhart
▶ In nineteenth-century France, nanny Davis tends to nobleman Boyer's kids and wins his heart. Although Boyer loves Davis chastely, jealous wife O'Neil suspects an affair. When O'Neil is murdered, Davis is wrongly accused. A multi-Kleenex movie with a shattering ending and fine performances.
Dist.: MGM/UA

ALMOST ANGELS 1962
★ ★ ★ NR Drama 1:25
Dir: Steven Previn   *Cast:* Peter Weck, Vincent Winter, Sean Scully, Hans Holt, Fritz Echardt, Bruni Lobel
▶ Appealing Disney drama about the Vienna Boys Choir takes a tour-guide approach to the world-famous group. Training and rehearsal sessions in beautiful settings provide

most of the action; negligible subplot about two friends who love practical jokes barely detracts from outstanding versions of music by Brahms, Strauss, etc.
Dist.: Buena Vista

ALMOST PERFECT AFFAIR, AN 1979
★ ★ PG Romance 1:32
☑ Brief nudity, adult situations, explicit language
Dir: Michael Ritchie   *Cast:* Keith Carradine, Monica Vitti, Raf Vallone, Christian De Sica
▶ Carradine plays an aspiring director trying to sell his first feature at the Cannes Film Festival. He loses his film to a censor, and turns to producer's wife Vitti for help. Although wildy incompatible, they fall in love. Luscious settings and some fleeting industry satire have more impact than the rather tame love interest.
Dist.: Paramount

ALMOST YOU 1985
★ R Comedy 1:37
☑ Adult situations, explicit language
Dir: Adam Brooks   *Cast:* Brooke Adams, Griffin Dunne, Karen Young, Marty Watt, Christine Estabrook
▶ Dunne is a bored husand who falls in love with Young, the nurse he hired to look after his injured wife Adams. Will he return to his senses? Dunne helped finance this personal project shot in Manhattan. Billed as a "traumatic comedy," its style and tone may be too narrow for most viewers. **(CC)**
Dist.: CBS/Fox

ALOHA, BOBBY AND ROSE 1975
★ ★ ★ PG Drama 1:29
☑ Adult situations, explicit language, violence
Dir: Floyd Mutrux   *Cast:* Paul LeMat, Dianne Hull, Tim McIntire, Leigh French, Robert Carradine
▶ Modest crime melodrama with a familiar theme: LeMat is a Los Angeles auto mechanic mistakenly involved in a robbery. With the cops hot on his trail, he takes off for Mexico with pretty car wash worker Hull. Good actors are hampered by predictable plotting.
Dist.: Media

ALOHA SUMMER 1988
★ ★ ★ PG Drama 1:37
☑ Brief nudity, adult situations, explicit language
Dir: Tommy Lee Wallace   *Cast:* Chris Makepeace, Don Michael Paul, Tia Carrere, Yuji Okumoto, Lorie Griffin
▶ Coming-of-age story set on Hawaii in 1959 follows budding surfer Makepeace as he makes friends, falls in love, and becomes a man. Beautiful scenery, some pointed racial subplots, and top-notch oldies soundtrack add depth to a routine tale.
Dist.: Warner

ALONE IN THE DARK 1982
☆ **R Horror 1:32**
☑ Brief nudity, explicit language, graphic violence
Dir: Jack Sholder ***Cast:*** Jack Palance, Donald Pleasence, Martin Landau, Dwight Schultz, Erland Van Lidth de Jeude
▸ When the electricity fails at Haven, a mental institution operated by Pleasance, four insane killers escape to terrorize the home of new therapist Shultz and his family. Poor slasher fare. Some well-known TV and movie faces are involved in the ugly violence.
Dist.: RCA/Columbia

ALONG CAME JONES 1945
★★ **NR Western/Comedy 1:30 B&W**
Dir: Stuart Heisler ***Cast:*** Gary Cooper, Loretta Young, William Demarest, Dan Duryea, Frank Sully
▸ Entertaining satire of Westerns with Cooper spoofing his typical tight-lipped hero roles by playing Jones, an easygoing, gun-shy drifter mistaken for notorious outlaw Duryea. At first Jones enjoys his newfound celebrity, but he has second thoughts when Duryea challenges him to a showdown. Cooper, who also produced the film, has rarely been as charming.
Dist.: CBS/Fox

ALONG THE GREAT DIVIDE 1951
★★ **NR Western 1:28 B&W**
Dir: Raoul Walsh ***Cast:*** Kirk Douglas, Virginia Mayo, John Agar, Walter Brennan, Ray Teal, Hugh Sanders
▸ Principled marshal Douglas (in his first Western) refuses to budge when a lynch mob condemns Brennan to death. Despite a dangerous desert sandstorm, the lawman and his prisoner set out for a fair trial in the next town. Brennan's daughter Mayo provides the love interest in this well-mounted adventure.
Dist.: Warner

ALPHABET CITY 1984
★★ **R Drama 1:25**
☑ Nudity, adult situations, explicit language, graphic violence
Dir: Amos Poe ***Cast:*** Vincent Spano, Michael Winslow, Kate Vernon, Jami Gertz
▸ Spano, who collects payments for a heroin ring, is ordered to burn down the tenement where his mother and sister live. If he doesn't, he has only one night to escape from Alphabet City, New York's East Village slums. Overwrought direction by underground favorite Poe can't elevate this above B-movie status.
Dist.: CBS/Fox

ALPHAVILLE 1965 French
☆ **NR Sci-Fi 1:40 B&W**
Dir: Jean-Luc Godard ***Cast:*** Eddie Constantine, Anna Karina, Akim Tamiroff, Howard Vernon
▸ Constantine plays futuristic detective Lemmy Caution, who arrives in computer-ruled Alphaville (which looks just like Paris) to find a scientist and hooks up with the man's daughter Karina. Starkly and strikingly photographed by Raoul Coutard with self-mocking in-jokes that will appeal to French New Wave fans only.
Dist.: Various

ALPINE FIRE 1989 Swiss
☆ **R Drama 1:57**
☑ Brief nudity, adult situations
Dir: Fredi M. Murer ***Cast:*** Thomas Nock, Johanna Lier, Dorothea Moritz, Rolf Illig, Tilli Breidenbach, Joerg Odermatt
▸ Eking out a difficult life on the slopes of the Alps, a farm family battles isolation, while brother and sister Nock and Lier become unnaturally close. Remote tale of Alpine incest paints itself into a narrative corner and takes the easy way out with a surreal ending. Background scenery steals the show. [S]
Dist.: Vestron

ALSINO AND THE CONDOR 1982 Nicaraguan
★ **NR Drama 1:29**
☑ Brief nudity, adult situations, explicit language, graphic violence
Dir: Miguel Litten ***Cast:*** Dean Stockwell, Alan Esquivel, Carmen Bunster, Alejandro Parodi
▸ In war-torn Nicaragua, young peasant Esquivel dreams of flying like a bird and is befriended by misguided American military advisor Stockwell. Esquivel's fantasy proves literally crippling as the horrors of war build. Finely textured work reflects fervor of the Nicaraguan revolution but overblown musical score by the Cuban National Symphony clashes with the visual style. Oscar nomination for Best Foreign Language Film.
Dist.: Pacific Arts

ALTERED STATES 1980
★★ **R Sci-Fi 1:42**
☑ Nudity, adult situations, explicit language, graphic violence
Dir: Ken Russell ***Cast:*** William Hurt, Blair Brown, Bob Balaban, Charles Haid, Thaao Penghilis
▸ Hurt gives a terrific performance as obsessed scientist Eddie Jessup, whose experiments on himself to achieve genetic memory bring about some alarming physical transformations. Russell's bravura direction is visually powerful and the hallucination sequences are dazzling and original. A verbose but provocative movie from a script by Paddy Chayefsky (who used the pseudonym "Sidney Aaron" after feuding with Russell).
Dist.: Warner

ALVAREZ KELLY 1966
★★★ **NR Western 1:56 B&W**
Dir: Edward Dmytryk ***Cast:*** William Holden, Richard Widmark, Janice Rule, Patrick O'-Neal, Victoria Shaw
▸ Offbeat Civil War saga tests Holden's neutral politics when he's kidnapped by Confed-

erate colonel Widmark to steal cattle from the North. Holden doesn't realize that as soon as they reach safety, Widmark will kill him for sleeping with Rule.
Dist.: RCA/Columbia

ALWAYS 1985
★ **R Comedy 1:46**
☑ Nudity, adult situations, explicit language
Dir: Henry Jaglom *Cast:* Henry Jaglom, Patrice Townsend, Melissa Leo, Jonathan Kaufer, Joanna Frank, Alan Rachins
▶ An about-to-be-divorced couple hosts two other couples for a Fourth of July weekend. They discuss love and romance and occasionally fall into each other's beds. Low-budget talkfest short on technical polish but long on funny dialogue and warm yet realistic characterizations. Jaglom and Townsend were married and divorced in real life. **(CC)**
Dist.: Vestron

ALWAYS 1989
★★★ **PG Fantasy 2:01**
☑ Adult situations, explicit language
Dir: Steven Spielberg *Cast:* Richard Dreyfuss, Holly Hunter, John Goodman, Brad Johnson, Audrey Hepburn, Keith David
▶ Daredevil firefighter pilot Dreyfuss dies in a crash but is then sent back to earth by angel Hepburn. "I like this job," says Dreyfuss when he finds he can influence things invisibly but doesn't like his ultimate mission: to help pilot Johnson win Hunter, his former girlfriend. Heartfelt remake of *A Guy Named Joe* is impressive although large-scale production threatens to overwhelm romance. Tender moment: Dreyfuss gives tomboyish Hunter "girl clothes." **(CC)**
Dist.: MCA

AMADEUS 1984
★★★★ **PG Drama 2:38**
☑ Brief nudity, adult situations, explicit language, violence
Dir: Milos Forman *Cast:* Tom Hulce, F. Murray Abraham, Elizabeth Berridge, Simon Callow, Jeffrey Jones
▶ Peter Shaffer's play comes to the screen under Forman's meticulous guidance. Abraham won an Oscar as Salieri, the successful but mediocre composer spurred by jealousy to declare psychological war on the prodigy Mozart (Hulce). Superb production, performances, and period detail. Forman's greatest triumph may be in making classical music accessible to the mass audience. Oscars for Best Picture and Director.
Dist.: HBO

AMARCORD 1974 Italian
★ **R Comedy/Drama 2:07**
☑ Brief nudity, adult situations, explicit language
Dir: Federico Fellini *Cast:* Magali Noel, Bruno Zanin, Pupella Maggio, Armando Brancia
▶ The great Fellini's autobiographical ac-

count of life in an Italian town, circa 1930, focusing on Zanin as the director's childhood alter ego. Emphasis is less on plot than on creating a mosaic of atmosphere, childhood discoveries, and rites of passage. Oscar for Best Foreign Film.
Dist.: Warner

AMATEUR, THE 1982
★★★ **R Mystery-Suspense 1:51**
☑ Brief nudity, explicit language, violence
Dir: Charles Jarrott *Cast:* John Savage, Marthe Keller, Christopher Plummer, Arthur Hill, Ed Lauter
▶ CIA codecracker Savage is out for revenge after his girlfriend is killed by a terrorist group in Germany. When his bosses are reluctant to approve the mission, he resorts to blackmail and then finds himself facing both the CIA (who have decided to terminate him) and the terrorists. Interesting premise.
Dist.: CBS/Fox

AMAZING ADVENTURE 1936 British
★ **NR Comedy 1:02 B&W**
Dir: Alfred Zeisler *Cast:* Cary Grant, Mary Brian, Peter Gawthorne, Henry Kendall, Leon M. Lion, John Turnbull
▶ Stung by doctor Gawthorne's criticism of his lifestyle, wealthy London idler Grant bets fifty thousand pounds he can spend one year earning a living. Working as a stove salesman and chauffeur, he wins working girl Brian but then faces choice of losing her or the wager. Technically crude (especially in an inept fight scene) but amiable vehicle for Grant.
Dist.: Various

AMAZING DOBERMANS, THE 1976
★★★ **PG Family 1:34**
☑ Adult situations, explicit language
Dir: Byron Chudnow *Cast:* Fred Astaire, James Franciscus, Barbara Eden, Jack Carter, Billy Barty
▶ Five Doberman dogs, trained by ex-con man Astaire, help Justice Department agent Franciscus thwart a racketeer in this third installment of the Doberman series. Astaire is charming, the dogs are appealing, and the film provides nonviolent family entertainment.
Dist.: Media

AMAZING GRACE AND CHUCK 1987
★★★★ **PG Drama 1:55**
☑ Explicit language
Dir: Mike Newell *Cast:* Jamie Lee Curtis, Alex English, Gregory Peck, William L. Petersen, Joshua Welch Zuehlke
▶ Little League pitcher Zuehlke decides to give up baseball until nuclear weapons are abolished. Basketball star Amazing Grace Smith (Denver Nuggets all-star English) joins him and a worldwide peace movement grows that eventually involves U.S. President Peck.
Dist.: HBO

AMAZING MR. BLUNDEN, THE 1972 British
★ ★ ★ **G Family 1:39**
☑ Adult situations
Dir: Lionel Jeffries   *Cast:* Laurence Naismith, Diana Dors, Garry Miller, Rosalyn Landor, Marc Granger, Lynne Frederick
▶ In this time-travel family fantasy, two children living in 1918 England meet friendly ghost Mr. Blunden (Naismith), who is seeking to right wrongs he did one-hundred years previous. The children return in time with him to help save two youngsters threatened by evil governess Dors. Not up to the level of Jeffries's other family film, the delightful *Railway Children*, but kids may not care that the plot is a tad too complicated.
Dist.: Media

AMAZING TRANSPARENT MAN, THE 1960
☆ **NR Sci-Fi 0:59 B&W**
Dir: Edgar G. Ulmer   *Cast:* Douglas Kennedy, Marguerite Chapman, James Griffith, Ivan Triesault
▶ Criminal Kennedy is rendered invisible by mad doctor Triesault, who plans to use the con for his own nefarious purposes. But Kennedy would rather knock off the local bank. Low-budget B-movie from cult director Ulmer is distinctly unamazing.
Dist.: Sinister

AMAZONS 1987 Argentinian
☆ **NR Fantasy 1:16**
☑ Nudity, adult situations, violence
Dir: Alex Sessa   *Cast:* Windsor Taylor Randolph, Penelope Reed, Joseph Whipp, Danitza Kingsley
▶ Tribal leader Whipp uses his magic powers to dominate Shinar, a rival village that is ruled by women. The Queen of Shinar seeks to reverse this state of affairs by sending Randolph and Reed to retrieve an enchanted sword. Tawdry production, bad dubbing, dumb dialogue, ridiculous sets and costumes, and gratuitous nudity add up to exploitation at its funniest.
Dist.: Concorde

AMAZON WOMEN ON THE MOON 1987
★ **R Comedy 1:24**
☑ Nudity, adult situations, explicit language, adult humor
Dir: John Landis, Joe Dante, Peter Horton, Carl Gottlieb, Robert Weiss   *Cast:* Rosanna Arquette, Ralph Bellamy, Steve Guttenberg, Carrie Fisher, Robert Loggia, Sybil Danning
▶ Compilation film uses a couch potato sucked into his cable system as an anchor for twenty parody sketches such as "Blacks Without Soul," "Son of the Invisible Man," "Reckless Youth," and the title piece, a satire on inept 1950s sci-fi. Irreverent, often vulgar humor and slapdash production values similar to Landis's earlier *Kentucky Fried Movie*.
Dist.: MCA

AMBASSADOR, THE 1985
★ ★ ★ **R Mystery-Suspense 1:30**

☑ Adult situations, explicit language
Dir: J. Lee Thompson   *Cast:* Ellen Burstyn, Robert Mitchum, Rock Hudson, Fabio Testi, Donald Pleasence
▶ Strong cast featured in a rather weak tale of political intrigue in the Middle East. Mitchum plays the ambassador who is being blackmailed with footage of his wife Burstyn's affair with PLO bigwig Testi. Nice performances but technically shoddy with a far-fetched story. Plot was inspired by Elmore Leonard's novel *52 Pick-Up*, later made into a better movie starring Roy Scheider.
Dist.: MGM/UA

AMBASSADOR'S DAUGHTER, THE 1956
★ ★ **NR Comedy 1:42**
Dir: Norman Krasna   *Cast:* Olivia de Havilland, John Forsythe, Myrna Loy, Adolphe Menjou, Tommy Noonan, Edward Arnold
▶ Senator Menjou objects to partying American soldiers stationed in Paris while ambassador's daughter de Havilland has a different view: she falls for G.I. Forsythe, who doesn't know her real identity. Breezy little trifle given life by top-notch performances (especially by the ladies).
Dist.: Showcase

AMBUSHERS, THE 1967
★ ★ **NR Espionage/Action-Adventure 2:00**
Dir: Henry Levin   *Cast:* Dean Martin, Senta Berger, Janice Rule, James Gregory, Albert Salmi, Kurt Kasznar
▶ Third in series featuring Martin as Donald Hamilton's superspy Matt Helm. Space program intrigue provides background as Martin battles villainous Salmi; thin plot works mainly as a vehicle for Martin's boozy joking.
Dist.: RCA/Columbia

AMERICANA 1981
☆ **PG Drama 1:31**
☑ Adult situations, explicit language, violence
Dir: David Carradine   *Cast:* David Carradine, Barbara Hershey, Michael Greene, Arnold Herzstein, Greg Walker, Dan Haggerty
▶ Vietnam vet Carradine drifts into small Kansas town, where he decides to repair an abandoned merry-go-round. Townspeople react in various ways: some offer tools and help, others vandalize the project. Earnest, offbeat, but minor drama suffers from heavy symbolism.
Dist.: Vestron

AMERICAN ANTHEM 1986
★ ★ ★ **PG-13 Drama/Sports 1:42**
☑ Explicit language, violence
Dir: Albert Magnoli   *Cast:* Mitch Gaylord, Janet Jones, Michelle Phillips, Andrew White, John Aprea
▶ Olympic Gold Medal winner Gaylord makes his screen debut in this story of a gymnast with problems both on and off the mat. Jones (Mrs. Wayne Gretzky) co-stars as the fe-

male gymnast who wins his heart. Slick production works best for the gymnastic sequences and for spotlighting the physiques of the leads. Gaylord does okay for a nonactor.
Dist.: Warner

AMERICAN CHRISTMAS CAROL, AN 1979
★★★★ NR Family/MFTV 1:40
Dir: Eric Till ***Cast:*** Henry Winkler, David Wayne, Chris Wiggins, R. H. Thomson, Ken Pogue
▸ Mean-spirited businessman Winkler is visited by ghosts who lead him on a journey back through his life, which changes him forever. Adaptation of Dickens's "A Christmas Carol," set in Depression-era America, provides holiday entertainment. Winkler tries hard in his Scrooge-like role.
Dist.: Vestron

AMERICAN DREAMER 1984
★★★★ PG Action-Adventure 1:45
☑ Explicit language, mild violence
Dir: Rick Rosenthal ***Cast:*** JoBeth Williams, Tom Conti, Giancarlo Giannini, Coral Browne, James Staley
▸ Housewife Williams wins a writing contest and a trip to Paris, where a bump on the head causes her to think she's daring fictional heroine Rebecca Ryan. Embroiled in an espionage plot, she steals the heart of Conti, although he believes she's quite mad. Williams is very appealing and the French locations are lovely in this glossy entertaining fluff. **(CC)**
Dist.: CBS/Fox

AMERICAN FLYERS 1985
★★★★ PG-13 Drama 1:52
☑ Brief nudity, adult situations, explicit language
Dir: John Badham ***Cast:*** David Marshall Grant, Kevin Costner, Rae Dawn Chong, Alexandra Paul, Janice Rule
▸ Formula bike racing movie—entertaining if you overlook the contrivances. Brothers Grant and Costner enter the big race, the twist being that one of them is dying. Upbeat screenplay by Steve Tesich (who won an Oscar for his previous bike movie *Breaking Away*) combines with terrific racing footage and beautiful Colorado Rockies scenery to create a movie that will leave you feeling good, if not totally convinced. **(CC)**
Dist.: Warner

AMERICAN FRIEND, THE 1977
German/French
★★ NR Mystery-Suspense 2:07
☑ Adult situations, explicit language, violence
Dir: Wim Wenders ***Cast:*** Bruno Ganz, Dennis Hopper, Samuel Fuller, Nicholas Ray, Liza Kreuzer
▸ Ganz plays a picture framer with an incurable blood disease who's blackmailed by Hopper into murdering a gangster. The two are drawn into a peculiar relationship when Hopper assists Ganz in further killings. Cult film noir based on *Ripley's Game* by Patricia Highsmith has excellent acting and photography, but its abstract plotting may disappoint action fans. [S]
Dist.: Pacific Arts

AMERICAN GIGOLO 1980
★★★ R Mystery-Suspense 1:57
☑ Nudity, strong sexual content, adult situations, explicit language
Dir: Paul Schrader ***Cast:*** Richard Gere, Lauren Hutton, Hector Elizondo, Nina Van Pallandt, Bill Duke
▸ Handsome gigolo Gere is framed for murder. Will Hutton, the politician's wife who loves him, provide his alibi? Unusual thriller that combines dazzling visuals and steamy love scenes with a basic sincerity and seriousness. Good music score by Giorgio Moroder includes the hit song "Call Me." Gere is fine in a role that requires him to literally show his all.
Dist.: Paramount

AMERICAN GOTHIC 1988
★ R Horror 1:30
☑ Explicit language, violence
Dir: John Hough ***Cast:*** Rod Steiger, Yvonne De Carlo, Michael J. Pollard, Fiona Hutchinson, Sarah Torgov, William Hootkins
▸ Mentally unstable Torgov seeks peace with husband and friends on island off Seattle, only to encounter bizarre older couple, Steiger and De Carlo, with middle-aged children Pollard, Hutchinson, and Hootkins still bedecked in kids' clothes. At first Torgov and her group are welcomed with apple pie and Bible readings, but soon mayhem erupts. Alternately campy and horrifying, unsurprising slasher movie won't satisfy fans of either genre.
Dist.: Vidmark

AMERICAN GRAFFITI 1973
★★★★ PG Drama 1:55
☑ Explicit language
Dir: George Lucas ***Cast:*** Richard Dreyfuss, Ron Howard, Cindy Williams, Mackenzie Phillips, Candy Clark, Paul LeMat, Wolfman Jack, Bo Hopkins, Charles Martin Smith, Kathy Quinlan
▸ Nostalgic and moving story of one memorable night for a group of graduating high school seniors in a small northern California town, circa 1962, a time when kids cruised in their cars to the strains of "Runaway" and other hits. Wonderfully directed by a pre-*Star Wars* Lucas. Look for future stars like Harrison Ford and Suzanne Somers in small parts.
Dist.: MCA

AMERICAN HOT WAX 1978
★★★★ PG Biography/Music 1:31
☑ Explicit language
Dir: Floyd Mutrux ***Cast:*** Tim McIntire, Laraine Newman, Jay Leno, Chuck Berry, Fran Drescher, Jerry Lee Lewis, Screamin' Jay Hawkins
▸ Story of the life and times of disc jockey

Alan Freed (McIntire), the man who hosted radio's first rock 'n' roll show, culminates in a near riot at Brooklyn's Paramount Theater when the cops try to close a rock concert. This enjoyable salute to the oldies but goodies era features Berry, Lewis, and Hawkins performing their own hits. Leno provides comic relief as Freed's driver.

AMERICAN IN PARIS, AN 1951
★ ★ ★ ★ NR Musical 1:53
Dir: Vincente Minnelli *Cast:* Gene Kelly, Leslie Caron, Oscar Levant, Nina Foch, Georges Guetary
▶ In Paris, ex-GI-turned-starving-artist Kelly falls for dancer Caron who's engaged to Guetary. Love, a grand Gershwin score, and MGM musical know-how triumph in this romantic, spectacular production that won seven Oscars (including Best Picture, plus a special award to Kelly). Highlights range from the intimate (Caron and Kelly dancing "Our Love Is Here to Stay" by the Seine; "I Got Rhythm") to the opulent ("I'll Build a Stairway to Paradise" and the famed ballet sequence). Kelly discovered Paris ballet dancer Caron and immediately cast her in her debut film role.
Dist.: MGM/UA

AMERICANIZATION OF EMILY, THE 1964
★ ★ ★ ★ NR Comedy 1:55 B&W
Dir: Arthur Hiller *Cast:* James Garner, Julie Andrews, Melvyn Douglas, James Coburn, Joyce Grenfell
▶ Daring comedy by Paddy Chayefsky takes a bleak look at wartime heroism. Garner plays a Navy officer who preaches pacifism; Andrews is a motor-pool driver who thinks he's a coward. Their relationship is severely tested when Garner is ordered to be the first casualty on Omaha Beach. A witty, racy story with surprisingly serious undertones.
Dist.: MGM/UA ©

AMERICAN JUSTICE 1986
★ ★ R Action-Adventure 1:35
☑ Explicit language, graphic violence
Dir: Gary Grillo *Cast:* Jack Lucarelli, Gerald McRaney, Jameson Parker, Jeannie Wilson, Wilford Brimley
▶ Vacationing ex-cop Lucarelli witnesses a murder and teams with pal Parker to investigate. They uncover an illegal alien trafficking ring run by corrupt cop McRaney. Sturdy action achieves fair amount of tension with "Simon and Simon" co-stars McRaney and Parker on opposite sides of the law. Also known as *Jackals.*
Dist.: Vestron

AMERICAN NINJA 1985
★ ★ ★ R Martial Arts 1:35
☑ Explicit language, graphic violence
Dir: Sam Firstenberg *Cast:* Michael Dudikoff, John LaMotta, Guich Koock, Steve James, Don Stewart
▶ Fourth entry in this martial arts series follows a predictable formula: Dudikoff has amnesia and doesn't know that he's a Ninja master, but he discovers his powers when he sets out to rescue his kidnapped girlfriend from an evil Ninja army. Dudikoff was a last-minute fill-in for Chuck Norris.
Dist.: MGM/UA

AMERICAN NINJA 2: THE CONFRONTATION 1987
★ ★ ★ R Martial Arts 1:30
☑ Explicit language, graphic violence
Dir: Sam Firstenberg *Cast:* Michael Dudikoff, Steve James, Larry Poindexter, Gary Conway, Jeff Weston, Michelle Botes
▶ Army rangers Dudikoff and James are sent to Caribbean island to investigate disappearance of Marines guarding U.S. Embassy. They discover plot by druglord Conway to clone an army of ninja killers in a genetic experiment. Superior sequel to *American Ninja,* filled with action and humor, is stolen by James's energetic performance.
Dist.: Media

AMERICAN NINJA 3: BLOOD HUNT 1989
★ R Martial Arts 1:30
☑ Brief nudity, violence
Dir: Cedric Sundstrom *Cast:* David Bradley, Steve James, Marjoe Gortner, Michele Chan, Yehuda Efroni, Calvin Jung
▶ Evil genetic engineer Gortner wants to test his new super virus on Bradley, a top martial arts expert participating in a tournament on a tropic isle. Believing that Gortner is holding a Japanese master prisoner, Bradley and his friends battle a black-hooded martial arts army to break into Gortner's laboratory. Poorly staged fights and cheap production values make this the weakest of the series.
Dist.: Warner

AMERICANO, THE 1955
★ NR Western 1:25
Dir: William Castle *Cast:* Glenn Ford, Cesar Romero, Frank Lovejoy, Ursula Thiess, Abbe Lane
▶ Ford travels to South America with three prize bulls in tow. There he crosses evil landowner Lovejoy, and teams with popular bandit Romero to defeat him. Despite lively elements, subequatorial Western never gets exciting.
Dist.: Republic

AMERICAN ROULETTE 1988 Australian/British
☆ R Action-Adventure 1:42
☑ Nudity, adult situations, explicit language, violence
Dir: Maurice Hatton *Cast:* Andy Garcia, Kitty Aldridge, Robert Stephens, Al Matthews, Andrew Michelson
▶ Garcia, a poet and president of a South American country, is being pursued by assassins in London. Getting no help from the CIA, he tangles with some goofy Russians, and may not even be able to trust love interest Aldridge. The tone wavers uncertainly be-

tween comedy and danger in this mixed-up, poorly told tale.
Dist.: Vidmark

AMERICAN TAIL, AN 1986
★ ★ ★ ★ G Animation/Musical 1:25
Dir: Don Bluth *Cast:* Voices of Dom DeLuise, Madeline Kahn, Christopher Plummer
▶ Old-fashioned cartoon describes the Russian immigrant experience from the point-of-view of Fievel, a young mouse separated from his family in a harsh turn-of-the-century New York. Typically lavish Steven Spielberg production: richly detailed animation, lush soundtrack (including Oscar-nominated "Somewhere Out There"), and lovable characters. Grim plot may frighten younger viewers. (CC)
Dist.: MCA

AMERICAN WEREWOLF IN LONDON, AN 1981
★ ★ ★ R Horror 1:37
☑ Nudity, explicit language, graphic violence
Dir: John Landis *Cast:* David Naughton, Jenny Agutter, John Woodvine, Griffin Dunne
▶ American students Naughton and Dunne are attacked by a werewolf while backpacking on the English moors. Dunne is killed (although he has an annoying habit of returning from the dead) and Naughton turns into a werewolf. The transformation scenes are truly horrifying, thanks to excellent special effects by Rick Baker. Director Landis mixes comedy and horror effectively.
Dist.: MCA

AMERICATHON 1979
☆ PG Comedy 1:25
☑ Adult situations, explicit language
Dir: Neil Israel *Cast:* Peter Riegert, Harvey Korman, Fred Willard, Zane Buzby, Nancy Morgan, John Ritter, Elvis Costello, Chief Dan George, Tommy Lasorda, Jay Leno, Meat Loaf
▶ When the country goes bankrupt in 1998, President Ritter orders media advisor Riegert to stage a telethon hosted by transvestite sitcom star Korman. Resulting vignettes, filled with brief cameos and walk-ons, are strained and mirthless, although Buzby isn't bad as a Vietnamese punk rocker. Soundtrack includes tunes by Costello, Alan Parsons, and the Beach Boys.
Dist.: Warner

AMIN—THE RISE AND FALL 1981 Kenyan
☆ R Biography/Drama 1:41
☑ Nudity, graphic violence
Dir: Sharad Patel *Cast:* Joseph Olita, Geoffrey Keen, Denis Hills, Leonard Trolley, Diane Mercier
▶ The bloody reign of Idi Amin (Olite), dictator of Uganda, who killed close to half a million of his subjects, and ordered the racist expulsion of close to a hundred thousand more. Gory string of atrocities offered without drama or sense of tragedy.
Dist.: HBO

AMITYVILLE HORROR, THE 1979
★ ★ ★ ★ R Horror 1:58
☑ Adult situations, explicit language, violence
Dir: Stuart Rosenberg *Cast:* James Brolin, Margot Kidder, Rod Steiger, Don Stroud, Murray Hamilton
▶ The Lutzes (Brolin and Kidder) move into an old Long Island mansion that's possessed by the Devil. Priests are unable to protect them from ensuing malevolent events. Popular horror film based on Jay Anson's best-seller about a real Long Island family contained enough scary tricks to spawn two further films.
Dist.: Warner

AMITYVILLE II: THE POSSESSION 1982
★ ★ ★ R Horror 1:44
☑ Rape, nudity, strong sexual content, explicit language, graphic violence
Dir: Damiano Damiani *Cast:* Burt Young, Rutanya Alda, James Olson, Jack Magner, Diane Franklin
▶ Prequel to *The Amityville Horror* sends child-abuser Young and his family of five into Long Island's most famous haunted house, where the Devil causes rape, incest, and murder before possessing a priest. Unsavory characters and gruesome special effects should appeal to hard-core horror fans.
Dist.: Embassy

AMITYVILLE 3-D 1983
★ ★ PG Horror 1:33
☑ Adult situations, explicit language, violence
Dir: Richard Fleischer *Cast:* Tony Roberts, Tess Harper, Robert Joy, Candy Clark, John Beal
▶ Cocky reporter Roberts, skeptical about the famous Amityville house of horrors, buys the place over the objections of colleague Clark and estranged wife Harper and soon finds himself besieged by paranormal phenomena (like man-eating flies who munch the real-estate broker). Originally released in 3-D, this third Amityville flick has some decent effects but suffers from lame scripting and production.
Dist.: Vestron

AMSTERDAM KILL, THE 1978 Hong Kong
★ ★ ★ R Action-Adventure 1:38
☑ Explicit language, violence
Dir: Robert Clouse *Cast:* Robert Mitchum, Bradford Dillman, Richard Egan, Leslie Nielsen, Keye Luke
▶ A narcotics agent who's addicted to heroin is hired by a drug czar to expose rival gangs to the police, but the plan backfires when someone starts tipping off the pushers. Hong

Kong production has good scenery and a solid performance from Mitchum.
Dist.: RCA/Columbia

AMSTERDAMNED 1988 Dutch
★ R Action-Adventure 1:53
☑ Adult situations, explicit language, violence
Dir: Dick Maas *Cast:* Huub Stapel, Monique van de Ven, Hidde Maas, Serge-Henri Valcke, Lou Landre, Tatum Dagelet
▶ When corpses turn up in the canals of Amsterdam, Dutch cop Stapel goes to a diving club in search of the aqua-lunged killer. As the murders continue and authorities fret over the tourist trade, Stapel teams up with tour guide van de Ven to throw a net over the culprit. Glossy presentation has well-staged murders and a crowd-pleasing chase down picturesque canals. [S]
Dist.: Vestron

AMY 1981
★★★★ G Drama 1:40
Dir: Vincent McEveety *Cast:* Jenny Agutter, Barry Newman, Kathleen Nolan, Chris Robinson, Margaret O'Brien, Nanette Fabray
▶ Warm-hearted turn-of-the-century drama about Agutter, a spirited wife who leaves her rich husband to work at a school for handicapped children. With the help of school doctor Newman, she teaches the kids to play football. Excellent Disney film should please parents as well as children.
Dist.: Buena Vista

ANASTASIA 1956
★★★★ NR Drama 1:45
Dir: Anatole Litvak *Cast:* Ingrid Bergman, Yul Brynner, Helen Hayes, Akim Tamiroff, Martita Hunt, Felix Aylmer
▶ Exiled Russian Brynner discovers a suicidal Bergman in Paris and grooms her to pose as Anastasia, the last Czar's daughter who was rumored to have escaped a firing squad that killed the rest of the family, to claim his fortune. Her greatest test comes when she must convince Hayes, Anastasia's grandmother, of her identity. Absorbing drama is perfectly cast; Bergman won a much-deserved Oscar in her first film after a long absence from Hollywood.
Dist.: CBS/Fox

ANATOMY OF A MURDER 1959
★★★★ NR Drama 2:40 B&W
Dir: Otto Preminger *Cast:* James Stewart, Ben Gazzara, Lee Remick, Arthur O'Connell, Eve Arden, George C. Scott
▶ Defense attorney Stewart defends Army lieutenant Gazzara, who killed his wife Remick's rapist. Stewart is then challenged by clever prosecutor Scott. Unforgettable adult drama from director Otto Preminger contains riveting courtroom theatrics. Top-notch performances all around.
Dist.: RCA/Columbia

ANCHORS AWEIGH 1945
★★★★ NR Musical 2:23
Dir: George Sidney *Cast:* Gene Kelly, Frank Sinatra, Kathryn Grayson, Jose Iturbi, Dean Stockwell
▶ Sinatra and Kelly are sailors on a Hollywood spree, finding love and romance in Tinseltown. MGM musical is not the studio's finest hour, but features some outstanding musical numbers, especially Kelly's famous dance with the animated mouse Jerry (of *Tom and Jerry* fame) and Sinatra singing first-rate Sammy Cahn/Jule Styne tunes. [CC]
Dist.: MGM/UA

ANDERSON TAPES, THE 1971
★★★ PG Mystery-Suspense 1:38
☑ Adult situations, explicit language, violence
Dir: Sidney Lumet *Cast:* Sean Connery, Dyan Cannon, Martin Balsam, Ralph Meeker, Alan King, Christopher Walken
▶ New York-based thriller with a cynical kick. Convict Connery emerges from prison and masterminds a heist, unaware that law enforcement officials are watching and taping his every move. Unusually strong cast for the genre features Connery's dependable presence, Cannon as his sexy girlfriend, Balsam as a homosexual, King as a mobster, and a young Walken as "The Kid."
Dist.: RCA/Columbia

. . .AND GOD CREATED WOMAN 1957 French
☆ PG Drama 1:33
☑ Adult situations
Dir: Roger Vadim *Cast:* Brigitte Bardot, Curt Jurgens, Jean-Louis Trintignant, Christian Marquand
▶ Bardot's breakthrough film ran into censorship problems when it was released, but is pretty tame by today's standards. She plays a voluptuous orphan who seduces two of four sons in a straitlaced family. Saint-Tropez locations give Bardot plenty of opportunities to display her body. Vadim used the title twenty years later for a completely different film.
Dist.: Vestron

AND GOD CREATED WOMAN 1988
★★ R Drama 1:40
☑ Nudity, adult situations, explicit language
Dir: Roger Vadim *Cast:* Rebecca De Mornay, Vincent Spano, Frank Langella, Donovan Leitch, Judith Chapman
▶ De Mornay's a convict who proposes to carpenter Spano for parole purposes, but she's really in love with politician Langella. Can she clear up her love life in time to form a rock 'n' roll band? Painless remake of Vadim's notorious 1957 film has some very hot sex scenes, particularly in the opening.
Dist.: Vestron

. . .AND JUSTICE FOR ALL 1979
★★★★★ R Drama 2:00
☑ Nudity, adult situations, explicit language

Dir: Norman Jewison *Cast:* Al Pacino, Jack Warden, John Forsythe, Lee Strasberg, Jeffrey Tambor, Christine Lahti
▶ Comedy and drama are mixed to good advantage by director Jewison in this irreverent and often outrageous look at our legal system. Pacino gives a passionate performance as the lawyer fighting to free a wrongly imprisoned client. His refusal to help corrupt judge Forsythe leads to an inspiring climactic courtroom speech.
Dist.: RCA/Columbia

AND NOTHING BUT THE TRUTH 1982 British
★ NR Drama 1:42
☑ Adult situations, explicit language
Dir: Karl Francis *Cast:* Glenda Jackson, Jon Finch, Kenneth Colley, James Donnelly, Emrys James
▶ When a Welsh family faces eviction from their land, filmmaker Jackson teams up with journalist Finch to investigate. Their trail leads to powerful corporate forces. Surprisingly dry and inaccessible; Jackson and Finch fail to transcend the cryptic plotting. Also known as *Giro City*.
Dist.: Monterey

AND NOW FOR SOMETHING COMPLETELY DIFFERENT 1972 British
★★ PG Comedy 1:29
☑ Adult humor, explicit language
Dir: Ian McNaughton *Cast:* Graham Chapman, John Cleese, Eric Idle, Terry Gilliam, Terry Jones, Michael Palin
▶ Hilarious collection of comic sketches from England's "Monty Python's Flying Circus." Gilliam's brilliant animated sequences connect the skits, which include the classic "Lumberjack Song," the "Upper Class Twit of the Year" contest, and Cleese's turn as a Hungarian tourist with a most inappropriate phrase book. A wild assortment of the troupe's surreal off-the-wall humor.
Dist.: RCA/Columbia

AND NOW MY LOVE 1975 French
★★ PG Romance 2:01
☑ Adult situations, explicit language, violence
Dir: Claude Lelouch *Cast:* Marthe Keller, Andre Dusollier, Charles Denner, Carla Gravina, Gilbert Becaud
▶ Love story about two people who don't actually meet until the climax traces the backgrounds that make their union inevitable: Keller is the daughter of wealthy concentration camp survivors and Dusollier is a convict who becomes a filmmaker. Glossy and sophisticated, although lyrical story is sometimes overwhelmed by the complicated structure. Dubbed.
Dist.: Nelson

ANDREWS' RAIDERS 1956
★★★★ NR Family 1:25
Dir: Francis D. Lyon *Cast:* Fess Parker, Jeffrey Hunter, Jeff York, Kenneth Tobey

▶ During the Civil War, Northern spy Parker leads his team of raiders on a mission to steal a rebel train. Hunter plays the Southern conductor who attempts to thwart the Yankees. A thrilling, wonderful adventure, based on the same true incident that inspired Buster Keaton's *The General*. Also known as *The Great Locomotive Chase*; originally shown in two parts on television's "Wonderful World of Disney."
Dist.: Buena Vista

ANDROCLES AND THE LION 1952
★★ NR Comedy 1:38
Dir: Chester Erskine *Cast:* Jean Simmons, Alan Young, Victor Mature, Robert Newton, Maurice Evans, Elsa Lanchester
▶ Bland adaptation of George Bernard Shaw's satirical play retains enough of his sparkling dialogue to remain intriguing. Young plays a tailor who removes a thorn from a lion's paw, an act of kindness repaid in a Roman arena. Troubled romance between Simmons and Mature adds plot complications. Young was producer Howard Hughes's replacement for Harpo Marx, originally signed to the Androcles role.
Dist.: Nelson

ANDROID 1984
★ PG Sci-Fi 1:20
☑ Brief nudity, adult situations, explicit language, violence
Dir: Aaron Kipstadt *Cast:* Klaus Kinski, Don Opper, Brie Howard, Norbert Weisser, Crofton Hardester, Kendra Kirschner
▶ Naive, obsolete android Opper lives on a space station with mad scientist Kinski. Faced with termination, he goes on a rampage with three escaped convicts. Ultra-low-budget film (shot on sets left over from *Battle Beyond the Stars*) has a charming sense of humor and some touching passages to compensate for weak plot.
Dist.: Media

ANDROMEDA STRAIN, THE 1971
★★★ G Sci-Fi 2:07
Dir: Robert Wise *Cast:* Arthur Hill, David Wayne, James Olson, Kate Reid, Paula Kelly
▶ Mutant strain of bacteria comes to Earth via crashed satellite, threatening all life. At an underground complex, a team of scientists searches for a solution. Race-against-time thriller builds maximum tension and suspense. No-nonsense cast of veteran character actors exemplifies Wise's craftsmanlike, low-key approach to Michael Crichton's best-seller.
Dist.: MCA

AND SOON THE DARKNESS 1970 British
★★ PG Mystery-Suspense 1:38
☑ Adult situations, violence
Dir: Robert Fuest *Cast:* Pamela Franklin, Michele Dotrice, Sandor Eles, John Nettleton, Clare Kelly
▶ English nurses Franklin and Dotrice bicycle through the French countryside, but their va-

cation is disrupted when a sex killer stalks them. Dotrice disappears and the locals are of little help. Moody and ominous thriller is worth a look.
Dist.: HBO

AND THEN THERE WERE NONE 1945
★ ★ ★ ★ NR Mystery-Suspense 1:38 B&W
Dir: René Clair   *Cast:* Barry Fitzgerald, Walter Huston, Louis Hayward, Roland Young, June Duprez, C. Aubrey Smith, Judith Anderson, Mischa Auer, Richard Haydn
▶ Ten guests, each hiding past crimes, are summoned to remote English island for a party. As an unknown killer murders them one by one, they realize they've been trapped in a grotesque plot. Superior whodunit based on Agatha Christie's classic *Ten Little Indians* features tricky script, gripping direction, and uniformly strong performances. Remade in 1966 and 1975.
Dist.: MGM/UA

AND THEN YOU DIE 1987 Canadian
★ R Crime 1:55
☑ Adult situations, explicit language, graphic violence
Dir: Francis Mankiewicz   *Cast:* Kenneth Welsh, R. H. Thomson, Wayne Robson, Pierre Chagnom
▶ Welsh, supporting his nice suburban lifestyle and family as a middleman in Montreal drug trade, finds himself targeted by mob godfathers and maverick cop Thomson. Solid little low budgeter has reprehensible but surprisingly interesting characters, wry humor, and no frills plotting. Not a pretty movie but consistently watchable.
Dist.: Vidmark

AND THE SHIP SAILS ON 1984 Italian
★ PG Drama 2:10
☑ Adult situations, explicit language
Dir: Federico Fellini   *Cast:* Freddie Jones, Barbara Jefford, Victor Poletti, Peter Cellier, Elisa Mainardi, Norma West
▶ Journalist Jones serves as host on an ocean liner setting sail from Naples, Italy, to scatter the ashes of a recently deceased opera singer. On board are a bevy of operatic oddballs, an Austro-Hungarian archduke and his entourage, and a lovesick rhinoceros. Class tensions arise when the ship picks up Serbian refugees. Visually striking, stately drama about colorful characters is mainly for Fellini fans.   Ⓢ
Dist.: RCA/Columbia

ANDY HARDY GETS SPRING FEVER 1939
★ NR Comedy 1:25 B&W
Dir: W. S. Van Dyke II   *Cast:* Mickey Rooney, Lewis Stone, Cecilia Parker, Fay Holden, Ann Rutherford, Helen Gilbert
▶ Spring fever hits America's favorite perky teen Andy Hardy (Rooney) in the person of drama teacher Gilbert. It turns out that she already has a beau but Rooney has his dad

Judge Hardy (Stone) and girlfriend Rutherford to console him. Typical entry in the series.
Dist.: MGM/UA

ANDY HARDY MEETS DEBUTANTE 1940
★ NR Comedy 1:26
Dir: George B. Seitz   *Cast:* Mickey Rooney, Lewis Stone, Judy Garland, Diana Lewis, Fay Holden
▶ When Judge Hardy (Stone) goes to New York on business, young Andy (Rooney) accompanies him and sets his sights on debutante Lewis. Rooney's attempts to infiltrate high society are comic mishaps but Garland helps him. Judy and Mickey don't put on a show this time but are nevertheless charming together.
Dist.: MGM/UA

ANDY HARDY'S DOUBLE LIFE 1942
★ NR Comedy 1:31 B&W
Dir: George B. Seitz   *Cast:* Mickey Rooney, Lewis Stone, Fay Holden, Esther Williams, Robert Blake, Ann Rutherford
▶ Meeting the payments on his old jalopy is Andy's (Rooney) biggest worry until he proposes marriage to two girls—and both accept. Then he discovers his troubles are only beginning. Nice episode in the series introduces a young (and dry) Williams.
Dist.: MGM/UA

ANDY HARDY'S PRIVATE SECRETARY 1941
★ NR Comedy 1:41
Dir: George B. Seitz   *Cast:* Mickey Rooney, Lewis Stone, Fay Holden, Ian Hunter, Ann Rutherford, Gene Reynolds
▶ Andy (Rooney) goes into an anxious frenzy when he discovers that his whole high school class may graduate without him after he fails to pass a final exam. Will school officials give him another chance? Average entry in series.
Dist.: MGM/UA

ANDY WARHOL'S BAD 1971 Italian
☆ R Comedy 1:45
☑ Nudity, adult situations, explicit language, violence
Dir: Jed Johnson   *Cast:* Carroll Baker, Perry King, Susan Tyrrell, Stefania Cassini, Cyrinda Foxe, Mary Boylan
▶ Queens housewife Baker, owner of an electrolysis business, supplements her income running Murder, Inc., dispatching her workers to do away with her clients' unwanted pets and relatives. Poor taste of audacious black comedy will offend many. Last and most expensive of Warhol's Factory films is primarily for devotees.
Dist.: Embassy

ANDY WARHOL'S DRACULA 1974 Italian/French
☆ R Horror/Comedy 1:46
☑ Nudity, adult situations, explicit language, graphic violence
Dir: Paul Morrissey   *Cast:* Joe Dallesandro,

Udo Kier, Arno Juerging, Vittorio De Sica, Roman Polanski, Maxime McKendry
▶ Sex, camp humor, and lots of blood mark this reworking of the Dracula legend, as vampire Kier meets his match in lusty gardener Dallesandro. For the adventurous only. Originally X-rated; also known as *Blood of Dracula*.
Dist.: Video Gems

ANDY WARHOL'S FRANKENSTEIN 1974
Italian/German/French
☆ **R Horror/Comedy 1:34**
☑ Nudity, adult situations, explicit language, graphic violence
Dir: Paul Morrissey *Cast:* Joe Dallesandro, Monique Van Vooren, Udo Kier, Srdjan Zelenovic, Dalila Di Lazzaro
▶ Crazed scientist Kier creates strikingly attractive humanoids out of disinterred body parts. Outrageous version of Mary Shelley's classic horror yarn has plenty of gore and some of the more gruesome sex scenes in movie history. Originally X-rated; also released as *The Frankenstein Experiment* and *Flesh for Frankenstein*.
Dist.: Video Gems

ANGEL 1984
★ ★ ★ **R Drama 1:32**
☑ Nudity, strong sexual content, adult situations, explicit language, violence
Dir: Robert Vincent O'Neil *Cast:* Cliff Gorman, Dick Shawn, Donna Wilkes, Rory Calhoun, Susan Tyrrell
▶ Wilkes plays Angel, a teenager who pays her private high school tuition by turning tricks at night. When a psycho starts murdering her friends, she offers herself as a decoy. Low-grade exploitation became a surprise success due to its memorable ad campaign ("Honor student by day, Hollywood hooker by night"), but film doesn't really deliver on its more lurid themes. Sequel: *Avenging Angel*.
Dist.: HBO

ANGELA 1977 Canadian
★ **NR Drama 1:40**
☑ Adult situations, explicit language, violence
Dir: Boris Sagal *Cast:* Sophia Loren, Steve Railsback, John Vernon, John Huston, Yvon Dufour, Michelle Rossignol
▶ Loren's gangster lover Vernon kidnaps her baby; she retaliates by turning him in to the cops. Twenty years later, Loren falls in love with handsome delivery boy Railsback, who is actually her long lost baby grown to manhood. Murky, ineptly plotted tale of incest and revenge.
Dist.: Nelson

ANGEL AND THE BADMAN 1947
★ ★ ★ ★ ★ **NR Western 1:40 B&W**
Dir: James Edward Grant *Cast:* John Wayne, Gail Russell, Harry Carey, Bruce Cabot, Irene Rich, Lee Dixon
▶ Wayne is Quirt Evans, a wounded outlaw nursed back to health by a pacifist Quaker

family. He falls in love with daughter Russell, who begs him not to seek out his enemy Cabot. Predictable but sincere story expertly handled by veteran Western actors. Thanks to its intelligent, satisfying script, Wayne's first stint as producer stands up better than some of his more action-oriented films.
Dist.: Republic Ⓒ

ANGEL HEART 1987
★ ★ **R Mystery-Suspense 1:53**
☑ Nudity, adult situations, explicit language, violence
Dir: Alan Parker *Cast:* Mickey Rourke, Robert De Niro, Charlotte Rampling, Lisa Bonet, Stocker Fontelieu
▶ In 1955 New York City, Harry Angel (Rourke) is hired by the mysterious Louis Cyphre (De Niro) to look for a missing singer. The trail leads him to New Orleans, voodoo cults, and murder. Parker's controversial movie is atmospheric and visually fascinating but the plot is tangled and confused. Originally rated X, the unrated video version has six extra seconds of steamy sex.
Dist.: IVE

ANGEL OF H.E.A.T. 1982
★ **R Sex 1:33**
☑ Nudity, strong sexual content, explicit language
Dir: Myrl A. Schrlebman *Cast:* Marilyn Chambers, Stephen Johnson
▶ Angel Harmony (Chambers), the top secret agent of a vigilante organization, poses as a mud wrestler so she can spy on a kingpin. Bad acting and cheap production values but plenty of nudity and general sleaziness from wholesome-looking porno queen Chambers.
Dist.: Vestron

ANGELO, MY LOVE 1983
☆ **R Drama 1:54**
☑ Adult situations, explicit language, violence
Dir: Robert Duvall *Cast:* Angelo Evans, Michael Evans, Ruthie Evans, Steve "Patalay" Tsigonoff
▶ Intriguing film uses real-life gypsies in a slight story about a stolen ring worth $10,000. Director Duvall's long friendship with the pint-sized Angelo was the main inspiration behind the project, and his performance is remarkable. So are the glimpses into gypsy life, but the dialogue (often improvised and subtitled) and plot are confusing at times.
Dist.: RCA/Columbia

ANGEL ON MY SHOULDER 1946
★ ★ ★ **NR Fantasy/Comedy 1:41 B&W**
Dir: Archie Mayo *Cast:* Paul Muni, Anne Baxter, Claude Rains, Onslow Stevens, George Cleveland
▶ In order to get revenge on his killer, dead gangster Muni makes pact with devil Rains to come back to earth as a judge. Muni becomes involved with his alter ego's girlfriend Baxter and, much to Rains's chagrin, be-

comes a do-gooder in his new persona. Heavenly fun with winning performances by Muni and Rains.
Dist.: Prism

ANGELS OVER BROADWAY 1940
★ ★ NR Drama 1:20 B&W
Dir: Ben Hecht, Lee Garmes *Cast:* Douglas Fairbanks, Jr., Rita Hayworth, Thomas Mitchell, John Qualen, George Watts
▶ Alcoholic writer Mitchell rescues meek embezzler Qualen from suicide, then suggests entering high stakes poker game to pay back Qualen's stolen loot. Con man Fairbanks and moll Hayworth are only too happy to take advantage of them. Eccentric, sardonic drama set in Manhattan's sleazy underworld builds to unpredictable climax. Co-director Hecht's biting script received an Oscar nomination.
Dist.: RCA/Columbia

ANGELS WITH DIRTY FACES 1938
★ ★ ★ NR Drama 1:37 B&W
Dir: Michael Curtiz *Cast:* James Cagney, Pat O'Brien, Humphrey Bogart, Ann Sheridan, George Bancroft, Dead End Kids
▶ Friends grow up together on the wrong side of the tracks but their paths diverge: Cagney becomes a gangster, O'Brien a priest. Dead End Kids idolize Cagney, setting up the famous climax where O'Brien convinces Cagney to dissuade boys from life of crime. Powerful classic from Warner Brothers' socially conscious period still packs a wallop.
Dist.: MGM/UA

ANGEL III: THE FINAL CHAPTER 1988
★ ★ R Action-Adventure 1:39
☑ Nudity, adult situations, explicit language, violence
Dir: Tom DeSimone *Cast:* Maud Adams, Mitzi Kapture, Mark Blankfield, Kin Shriner, Emile Beaucard, Richard Roundtree
▶ Sequel to *Avenging Angel* finds student hooker grown up as New York photographer Kapture. Reunion with her mother in Los Angeles reveals existence of stepsister held slave in Adams's bordello. Kapture dons prostitute disguise to battle Adams in this tired but still lurid melodrama.
Dist.: New World

ANGEL TOWN 1990
★ ★ R Martial Arts 1:45
☑ Nudity, adult situations, explicit language, violence
Dir: Eric Larson *Cast:* Oliver Gruner, Theresa Saldana, Frank Aragon, Tony Valentino, Peter Kwong, Mike Moroff
▶ Thanks to a housing shortage, French exchange student (and martial arts expert) Gruner must stay in a Los Angeles barrio while getting his degree in engineering. Gang members make life miserable for Gruner's host family until they push the Frenchman too far—then it's time for the ultimate rumble. Tough and rousing.
Dist.: Imperial

ANGRY RED PLANET, THE 1959
☆ NR Sci-Fi 1:23
Dir: Ib Melchior *Cast:* Gerald Mohr, Nora Hayden, Les Tremayne, Jack Kruschen, Paul Hahn
▶ Expedition to Mars faces variety of horrors including giant carnivorous plant, humongous amoeba, and a rodent/crab monster. Upon returning to Earth, scientist Hayden must invent a serum to save the life of the only other survivor. Rather dated special effects, with Martian scenes given special tint through process called Cinemagic.
Dist.: HBO

ANGUISH 1988
★ ★ R Horror 1:29
☑ Explicit language, graphic violence
Dir: Bigas Luna *Cast:* Michael Lerner, Zelda Rubinstein, Talia Paul, Clara Pastor
▶ A genuinely weird little horror movie that cleverly mixes fantasy and reality. Lerner is an orderly who loses his job due to diabetes-induced blindness. Rubinstein is the domineering mother who encourages Lerner to take grisly revenge against his enemies by plucking their eyes out. Gory and sometimes confusing but generally effective. **(CC)**
Dist.: Key

ANIMAL BEHAVIOR 1989
★ ★ PG Comedy 1:25
☑ Explicit language
Dir: H. Anne Riley *Cast:* Karen Allen, Armand Assante, Holly Hunter, Josh Mostel, Richard Libertini
▶ Music teacher Assante falls for scientist Allen, but she's preoccupied with training her pet chimp to communicate with humans. Allen finally starts to thaw, only to misinterpret Assante's casual relationship with single mother Hunter. Botched comedy is inoffensive but bland. **(CC)**
Dist.: HBO

ANIMAL CRACKERS 1930
★ ★ ★ ★ G Comedy 1:38
Dir: Victor Heerman *Cast:* Groucho Marx, Harpo Marx, Chico Marx, Zeppo Marx, Margaret Dumont, Lillian Roth, Louis Sorin, Hal Thompson
▶ Second and least-known Marx Brothers film (legal problems kept it out of circulation for years), based on their Broadway hit by Morrie Ryskind and George S. Kaufman, has some dull passages when the brothers aren't on the screen but also boasts some of their best work. Ignore the uninspired musical comedy plot (about a painting stolen from a Long Island mansion) and concentrate on the wonderful high points: Groucho singing "Hurray for Captain Spaulding," Chico and Harpo playing a vicious game of bridge, etc.
Dist.: MCA

ANIMAL FARM 1955 British
★ ★ NR Animation 1:15
Dir: John Halas, Joy Batchelor *Cast:* Voice

of Maurice Denham, narrated by Gordon Heath
► Political allegory set in a barnyard: pigs lead a revolution and take control of a farm. They base their government on democratic principles until a pig named Napoleon assumes dictatorial powers. Marvelous adaptation of the George Orwell classic is faithful to the source; superbly animated by the British husband-and-wife team of Halas and Batchelor.
Dist.: Video Yesteryear

ANIMAL HOUSE 1978
★★★★ R Comedy 1:48
☑ Nudity, adult situations, explicit language
Dir: John Landis *Cast:* John Belushi, Tim Matheson, Peter Riegert, Karen Allen, Tom Hulce, Stephen Furst, Donald Sutherland, Kevin Bacon, John Vernon, Verna Bloom, Cesare Danova, Bruce McGill
► Much imitated, but seldom surpassed, campus comedy about Delta House, the wild, party-loving fraternity that's the bane of Dean Wormer's (Vernon) existence. The craziest of the Deltas is Belushi's Bluto, a party animal so indestructible that he can smash beer cans on his head without flinching. Film's sense of humor is often tasteless and gross but, just as often, laugh-out-loud funny.
Dist.: MCA

ANIMALS ARE BEAUTIFUL PEOPLE 1975
★★★★★ G Documentary 1:32
Dir: Jamie Uys *Cast:* Narrated by Paddy O'Byrne
► A decade before he made *The Gods Must Be Crazy*, South African director Uys filmed this documentary about African wildlife. Four years in the making, it covers all creatures great and small, from elephants to insects, and the footage is often astonishing.
Dist.: Warner

ANIMALYMPICS 1979
★★★★ NR Animation 1:18
Dir: Steven Lisberger *Cast:* Voices of Gilda Radner, Billy Crystal, Harry Shearer, Michael Fremer
► Winter and Summer Olympics are combined in this animated animal competition hosted by an ostrich resembling Barbara Walters (Radner doing "Baba WaWa"). Commentators also include a turkey and a turtle (Crystal as Howard Cosell and Henry Kissinger). Glossy, inventive, quality animation; a real treat.
Dist.: IVE

ANNA 1987
★★ PG-13 Drama 1:35
☑ Nudity, adult situations, explicit language
Dir: Yurek Bogayevicz *Cast:* Sally Kirkland, Paulina Porizkova, Robert Fields, Gibby Brand, John Robert Tillotson, Joe Aufiery
► Expatriate Czech movie star Kirkland, a struggling actress in New York, welcomes stunning Czech refugee Porizkova into her home. Their friendship deteriorates when Porizkova naively swipes Kirkland's writer/boyfriend Fields and achieves overnight stardom. Low-budget drama, with roots in *All About Eve*, features charming screen debut for model Porizkova and brilliant, Oscar-nominated performance from Kirkland. (CC)
Dist.: Vestron

ANNABEL TAKES A TOUR 1938
★ NR Comedy 1:07 B&W
Dir: Lew Landers *Cast:* Lucille Ball, Jack Oakie, Ruth Donnelly, Bradley Page
► Sequel to *The Affairs of Annabel* features Ball and Oakie reprising their roles as an actress and her press-hungry agent. This time out, Ball goes on tour to plug her latest picture and falls for a married songwriter. Show biz antics were more pleasing first time around.
Dist.: Turner

ANNA CHRISTIE 1930
★★ NR Drama 1:26 B&W
Dir: Clarence Brown *Cast:* Greta Garbo, Marie Dressler, Charles Bickford, Lee Phelps, George F. Marion
► Somewhat creaky early talkie, adapted from a play by one of America's greatest playwrights, Eugene O'Neill, as a vehicle for one of Hollywood's greatest legends, Garbo. Holds interest for her performance as the ex-hooker who finds true love with seaman Bickford and as the movie in which Garbo made a successful transition to the sound era. Advertised at the time with the slogan "Garbo Talks."
Dist.: MGM/UA

ANNA KARENINA 1935
★★★ NR Drama 1:35 B&W
Dir: Clarence Brown *Cast:* Greta Garbo, Fredric March, Freddie Bartholomew, Maureen O'Sullivan, May Robson, Basil Rathbone
► Anna Karenina (Garbo), unhappily married to politician Rathbone in nineteenth-century Russia, falls in love with handsome Count Vronsky (March) but the affair ends in tragedy. The *Anna Christie* team (MGM, director Brown, star Garbo) reunited for this high-quality literary adaptation of Leo Tolstoy's classic. Garbo is superb, as always.
Dist.: MGM/UA

ANNAPOLIS STORY, AN 1955
★ NR War 1:21
Dir: Don Siegel *Cast:* John Derek, Diana Lynn, Kevin McCarthy, Pat Conway, L. Q. Jones, Barbara Brown
► Brothers Derek and McCarthy mix rigorous training for the U.S. Navy officer corps with romantic overtures to Lynn. The brothers quarrel over Lynn; but soon their lives are overshadowed by a more devastating conflict: the Korean War. Corny, by-the-numbers road from service academy to battle.
Dist.: CBS/Fox

ANNA TO THE INFINITE POWER 1983
★ ★ NR Sci-Fi 1:45
Dir: Robert Weimer   *Cast:* Dina Merrill, Martha Byrne, Jack Gilford, Mark Patton, Donna Mitchell
▶ Bright young Byrne, haunted by disaster-filled nightmares, learns she has ESP when her mother Merrill reveals she's the result of a cloning study. Byrne then searches for her telepathic comrades, scattered after the conclusion of the experiment. Tame sci-fi drama will appeal mainly to younger viewers.
Dist.: RCA/Columbia

ANNE OF AVONLEA 1987 Canadian
★ ★ ★ ★ NR Drama/MFTV 3:15
Dir: Kevin Sullivan   *Cast:* Megan Follows, Colleen Dewhurst, Frank Converse, Schuyler Grant, Jonathan Crombie, Patricia Hamilton
▶ Magnificent Canadian TV miniseries with Follows as Anne Shirley, the heroine of Lucy Maude Montgomery's *Anne of Green Gables* and its follow-up books, having grown into young adulthood, teaching at Avonlea, and having her first bittersweet experiences with grownup love. Also known as *Anne of Green Gables: The Sequel.*
Dist.: Buena Vista

ANNE OF GREEN GABLES 1934
★ ★ NR Drama 1:20
Dir: George Nicholls   *Cast:* Anne Shirley, Tom Brown, O. P. Heggie, Helen Westley, Sara Haden, Murray Kinnell
▶ Moving account of bachelor farmer Heggie and his sister Westley who adopt charming pig-tailed orphan Shirley. She wins the hearts of everyone she meets, especially handsome Gilbert Blythe (Brown). Canadian locations help this heartfelt adaptation of Lucy Maud Montgomery's classic novel. Shirley, previously Dawn O'Day, took her screen name from this character. Remade as a Canadian mini-series in 1985.
Dist.: Turner

ANNE OF GREEN GABLES 1985 Canadian
★ ★ ★ NR Drama/MFTV 3:19
Dir: Kevin Sullivan   *Cast:* Megan Follows, Colleen Dewhurst, Patricia Hamilton, Marilyn Lightstone, Charmion King, Richard Farnsworth
▶ Inspired adaptation of L. M. Montgomery's classic novels follows adventures of young orphan Follows in Canadian wilderness community. Sweet, simple story line is touching and uplifting. Double cassette combines two episodes of mini-series, *A New Home* and *A Bend in the Road.* Sequel, *Anne of Avonlea,* appeared in 1987.
Dist.: Buena Vista

ANNE OF THE THOUSAND DAYS 1969 British
★ ★ ★ ★ PG Drama 2:25
☑ Adult situations
Dir: Charles Jarrott   *Cast:* Richard Burton,

Genevieve Bujold, Irene Papas, Anthony Quayle, Michael Hordern, John Colicos
▶ In sixteenth-century England, King Henry VIII (Burton) chooses Anne Boleyn (Bujold) over current wife Katherine (Papas) and marries her, but the union proves ill-fated when Bujold fails to deliver a son. Beautifully mounted and fascinating; superior performances from Burton and Bujold (both Oscar-nominated). Best Picture nominee; won for Costume Design. From Maxwell Anderson's play.
Dist.: MCA

ANNIE 1982
★ ★ ★ ★ ★ PG Musical 2:08
☑ Explicit language
Dir: John Huston   *Cast:* Albert Finney, Carol Burnett, Aileen Quinn, Bernadette Peters, Tim Curry, Geoffrey Holder
▶ Quinn is America's favorite orphan Annie, singing and dancing her way into the heart of billionaire Daddy Warbucks (Finney). Burnett has a comic field day as Miss Hannigan, the drunken orphanage supervisor plotting to reclaim Annie and get her hands on Warbucks's loot. Lavish version of the Broadway musical is overproduced (to the rumored tune of $50 million or so) but still makes fine family fare. Finney is warm and winning and sings surprisingly well. Score includes the hit song "Tomorrow." (CC)
Dist.: RCA/Columbia

ANNIE HALL 1977
★ ★ ★ PG Comedy 1:34
☑ Adult humor
Dir: Woody Allen   *Cast:* Woody Allen, Diane Keaton, Tony Roberts, Carol Kane, Paul Simon, Shelley Duvall
▶ Oscars for Best Picture, Director, and Actress (Keaton) went to Allen's wise and wonderful look at modern relationships. Woody plays neurotic Jewish comic Alvy Singer, recalling his long love affair with Keaton's equally neurotic but WASPy Annie. The crazy humor of Woody's early films is tempered with a new sophistication and maturity. Poignant, funny, and memorable.
Dist.: MGM/UA

ANNIE OAKLEY 1935
★ ★ ★ NR Western 1:30 B&W
Dir: George Stevens   *Cast:* Barbara Stanwyck, Preston Foster, Melvyn Douglas, Moroni Olsen, Andy Clyde, Chief Thundercloud
▶ Stanwyck is charming in her first Western as the rambunctious shooting star of Buffalo Bill's Wild West Show. Entertaining film provides a fairly honest account of her rise from an uncultured Ozarks background to fame and glamour. Foster and Douglas play rivals for her affections, with Chief Thundercloud providing comic relief as Sitting Bull, Annie's mentor.
Dist.: Turner

ANNIHILATORS, THE 1985
★ ★ ★ R Action-Adventure 1:25

☑ Nudity, explicit language, graphic violence
Dir: Charles E. Sellier *Cast:* Christopher Stone, Andy Wood, Lawrence Hilton-Jacobs, Gerrit Graham, Dennis Redfield
▶ In Atlanta, Vietnam vets band together to wipe out three evil gangs. They break up a drug ring, rescue a hijacked school bus, and gain the grudging respect of cops and the homeless. Violent, unpleasant exploitation fare has cheap production values and often unintelligible dialogue.
Dist.: New World

ANN VICKERS 1933
★ NR Drama 1:12 B&W
Dir: John Cromwell *Cast:* Irene Dunne, Walter Huston, Bruce Cabot, Edna May Oliver, Conrad Nagel, Sam Hardy
▶ Dunne is an early feminist, social worker, and eventually warden of a women's prison who bears the stigma of single-motherhood after being abandoned by cad Cabot. Not your usual women's prison movie, but an affecting old-fashioned tearjerker, with Huston and Oliver providing a few laughs amid the suds. Based on the novel by Sinclair Lewis.
Dist.: Turner

A NOS AMOURS 1984 French
☆ R Drama 1:42
☑ Nudity, strong sexual content, adult situations, explicit language
Dir: Maurice Pialat *Cast:* Sandrine Bonnaire, Dominique Besnehard, Maurice Pialat, Evelyne Ker, Cyr Boitard
▶ Young Frenchwoman Bonnaire's approach to sex is one of amoral promiscuity: she loses her virginity to an American drifter and has one-night stands despite steady boyfriend Boitard. Her troubled home life partially explains her behavior in this critically praised but disturbing coming-of-age story. Director Pialat plays the father who walks out on her mother Ker. [S]
Dist.: RCA/Columbia

ANOTHER CHANCE 1988
★★ R Comedy 1:40
☑ Brief nudity
Dir: Jesse Vint *Cast:* Bruce Greenwood, Vanessa Angel, Frank Annese, Jeff East, Anne Ramsey
▶ Daytime soap opera star Greenwood falls for British model Angel but his womanizing puts a damper on the romance until he sees the error of his ways. Pleasant production is attractively cast but suffers from unexplained surreal characters and confusing fantasy ending.
Dist.: Republic

ANOTHER COUNTRY 1984 British
★ PG Drama 1:31
☑ Adult situations, explicit language
Dir: Marek Kanievska *Cast:* Rupert Everett, Colin Firth, Michael Jenn, Robert Addie, Rupert Wainwright, Cary Elwes
▶ Intelligent, small-scaled drama of a 1930s homosexual love affair at a British school. Guy Bennett (Everett) rebels against the system by indulging in Marxist politics (under the influence of best pal Firth) and having an affair with Elwes. Bennett is expelled when his affair is discovered. Based on the life of Guy Burgess, the Englishman who spied for, and eventually defected to, the Soviet Union.
Dist.: Embassy

ANOTHER 48 HRS. 1990
★★★★ R Action-Adventure 1:35
☑ Nudity, adult situations, explicit language, violence
Dir: Walter Hill *Cast:* Eddie Murphy, Nick Nolte, Brion James, Kevin Tighe, Ed O'Ross, Tisha Campbell
▶ Freed from prison, wisemouth Murphy rejoins rumpled cop Nolte to battle a drug lord called the "Iceman," who's targeted them for cold slabs. Almost a note-for-note replay of the original, violent, shoot-'em-up comedy delivers a few laughs in the kind of set pieces where Murphy can't miss, but these moments are few and far between. Script focuses too much on uninteresting baddies.
Dist.: Paramount

ANOTHER MAN, ANOTHER CHANCE 1977 U.S./French
★★ PG Drama 2:08
☑ Rape, explicit language
Dir: Claude Lelouch *Cast:* James Caan, Genevieve Bujold, Francis Huster, Jennifer Warren, Susan Tyrrell
▶ A romantic drama, set in the 1870s American West, featuring Lelouch's customary lyricism. Two widowed people, French immigrant Bujold and American veterinarian Caan, get a second chance at happiness with one another. Appealing characters and excellent photography but overlong and languidly paced.
Dist.: Wood Knapp

ANOTHER THIN MAN 1939
★★ NR Mystery-Suspense 1:45 B&W
Dir: W. S. Van Dyke II *Cast:* William Powell, Myrna Loy, Virginia Grey, Otto Kruger, C. Aubrey Smith, Ruth Hussey
▶ Third entry in the popular *Thin Man* series takes Nick and Nora to Long Island to protect millionaire Smith from murder. Not as distinguished as some of its companion films, but Powell and Loy are as charming and sophisticated as ever, their dog Asta performs his old tricks, and their son Nicky, Jr., makes his first appearance. **(CC)**
Dist.: MGM/UA

ANOTHER TIME, ANOTHER PLACE 1958
★★★ NR Drama 1:38 B&W
Dir: Lewis Allen *Cast:* Lana Turner, Barry Sullivan, Sean Connery, Glynis Johns
▶ American reporter Turner has affair with English counterpart Connery, a married man, during World War II. Turner goes to pieces after

tragedy strikes the relationship but then later recovers to meet Connery's wife. Standard soap opera notable for young Connery's presence.
Dist.: Embassy

ANOTHER WOMAN 1988
★ PG Drama 1:24
☑ Explicit language
Dir: Woody Allen ***Cast:*** Gena Rowlands, Mia Farrow, Ian Holm, Blythe Danner, Gene Hackman, Betty Buckley, Martha Plimpton, John Houseman, Sandy Dennis
▶ Philosophy professor Rowlands, having just turned fifty, examines her life; she discovers she's relied on control to avoid emotion, in the process hurting many around her. Well-made character study with top-flight cast explores the human condition through inner turmoil of gifted New Yorkers. Stark drama marks another of Allen's attempts to deal with more serious subject matter.
Dist.: Orion

A NOUS LA LIBERTE 1931 French
★ NR Comedy 1:27 B&W
Dir: René Clair ***Cast:*** Raymond Cordy, Henri Marchand, Rolla France, Paul Olivier, Jacques Shelly, Andre Michaud
▶ Lively comedy about ne'er-do-well convict pals Cordy and Marchand. Cordy escapes from jail to start a phonograph factory; Marchand joins him later, only to criticize his friend's obsession with quotas and assembly lines. Bouncy, irreverent satire was a major influence on Chaplin's *Modern Times.* [S]
Dist.: Various

ANTARCTICA 1984 Japanese
★★★ G Action-Adventure 1:50
Dir: Koreyoshi Kurahara ***Cast:*** Ken Takakura, Tsunehiko Watase
▶ Real-life Japanese drama about accidentally abandoned sled dogs fighting for survival through a brutal Antarctic winter. The most successful Japanese film ever released in that country includes breathtaking South Pole footage. Sense of genuine disaster may be too intense for younger viewers. **(CC)** [S]
Dist.: CBS/Fox

ANTHONY ADVERSE 1936
★★★ NR Drama 2:21 B&W
Dir: Mervyn LeRoy ***Cast:*** Fredric March, Olivia de Havilland, Edmund Gwenn, Claude Rains, Anita Louise, Gale Sondergaard
▶ Massive, sprawling soap opera from Hervey Allen's best-seller follows the adventures in nineteenth-century Europe and America of the ambitious but illegitimate Adverse (March). His tragic love affair with opera star de Havilland and rivalry with evil business partners Rains and Sondergaard provide the core of the story. Sondergaard, composer Erich Korngold, and cinematographer Tony Gaudio all won Oscars.
Dist.: MGM/UA

ANTONY AND CLEOPATRA 1973 British
★ NR Drama 2:40
Dir: Charlton Heston ***Cast:*** Charlton Heston, Hildegard Neil, Eric Porter, John Castle, Fernando Rey, Juan Luis Galiardo
▶ Faithful adaptation of the Shakespeare play with Heston as Antony, lover of Egyptian queen Cleopatra (Neil) and political rival of Octavius Caesar (Castle). Stagey, low-budget result has some fine moments by Heston and impressive work by Porter as Heston's treacherous aide.
Dist.: Nelson

ANY WEDNESDAY 1966
★★★ NR Comedy 1:49
Dir: Robert Ellis Miller ***Cast:*** Jane Fonda, Jason Robards, Dean Jones, Rosemary Murphy, Ann Prentiss
▶ Wednesday is the day Robards cheats on his wife Murphy with luscious but dim-witted Fonda. The status quo is threatened when salesman Jones learns of the arrangement. Jovial farce from the Muriel Resnik play features fine comic performances from the four leads.
Dist.: Warner

ANY WHICH WAY YOU CAN 1980
★★★★ PG Comedy 1:56
☑ Adult situations, explicit language, violence, adult humor
Dir: Buddy Van Horn ***Cast:*** Clint Eastwood, Sondra Locke, Geoffrey Lewis, William Smith, Harry Guardino, Ruth Gordon
▶ Critics scratched their heads when *Every Which Way But Loose* made more money than any previous Eastwood effort, but even they enjoyed this lighthearted sequel. Original's winning formula remains, with a welcome touch of sensitivity added to the characters. Eastwood repeats his role as a brawling mechanic, this time forced by the mob to face King of the Streetfighters Smith in a no-holds-barred battle in Jackson Hole, Wyoming. Clyde the orangutan is also back, stealing the film with his raunchy gags. Music includes songs by Fats Domino and Glen Campbell.
Dist.: Warner

ANZIO 1968
★★★★ PG War 2:00
☑ Violence
Dir: Edward Dmytryk ***Cast:*** Robert Mitchum, Peter Falk, Arthur Kennedy, Robert Ryan
▶ The Allies invade Italy in the bloody battle of Anzio in World War II; war reporter Mitchum covers the story. Interesting subject with notable cast, but lackluster script is unlikely to please genre fans.
Dist.: RCA/Columbia

APACHE 1954
★★ NR Western 1:31

Dir: Robert Aldrich **Cast:** Burt Lancaster, Jean Peters, John McIntire, Charles Buchinski, John Dehner, Paul Guilfoyle
▶ After Geronimo's surrender, Massai (Lancaster), the last unconquered Apache chief, conducts a guerrilla war against the Army. McIntire plays a cavalry guide sympathetic to Massai's plight; Peters, the chief's beautiful companion. Film's unusual perspective is supportive of Indian rights. Charles Bronson (using his real name Buchinski) has a minor role as a soldier.
Dist.: Playhouse

APARTMENT, THE 1960
★ ★ ★ ★ NR Comedy 2:05 B&W
Dir: Billy Wilder **Cast:** Jack Lemmon, Shirley MacLaine, Fred MacMurray, Ray Walston, Jack Kruschen
▶ Ambitious corporate employee Lemmon tries to work his way up by lending his apartment key to philandering boss MacMurray for assignations with girlfriend MacLaine. Lemmon then falls in love with her himself. Billy Wilder masterfully mixes comedy and drama. Superb acting, especially Lemmon in his archetypal role of the schnook who develops a conscience. Multi-Oscar winner, including Best Picture.
Dist.: MGM/UA

APARTMENT ZERO 1989 British
★ NR Mystery-Suspense 2:04
☑ Adult situations, explicit language, violence
Dir: Martin Donovan **Cast:** Colin Firth, Hart Bochner, Dora Bryan, Liz Smith, Fabrizio Bentivoglio
▶ Repressed film buff Firth runs a revival house in Buenos Aires. Mysterious James Dean-like hunk Bochner answers his ad for a roommate, and Firth's latent homosexuality starts raging. When he becomes suspicious that Bochner may be involved with the recent military government's death squads, the fun has only just begun in this eerie and disturbing psychological thriller. Stylishly directed by Donovan, it missteps only when it crosses the line into camp.
Dist.: Academy

APE, THE 1940
★ NR Horror 1:02 B&W
Dir: William Nigh **Cast:** Boris Karloff, Maris Wrixon, Henry Hall, Gertrude Hoffman
▶ The good news: scientist Karloff has come up with a cure for the condition that crippled and killed his daughter. The bad news: the main ingredient is human spinal fluid, so he dresses as an ape and murders people to make the serum. As ridiculous as it sounds.
Dist.: Various

APE MAN, THE 1943
★ NR Horror 1:04 B&W
Dir: William Beaudine **Cast:** Bela Lugosi, Wallace Ford, Louise Currie, Minerva Urecal
▶ Scientist Lugosi develops a formula that turns him into an ape. Nosy newshounds Currie and Ford get wind of the story and find themselves menaced by the monster. Cheap horror flick with few real scares.
Dist.: Various

APOCALYPSE NOW 1979
★ ★ ★ R Action-Adventure 2:33
☑ Adult situations, violence
Dir: Francis Coppola **Cast:** Martin Sheen, Marlon Brando, Robert Duvall, Frederic Forrest, Sam Bottoms
▶ Coppola's visionary Vietnam film was inspired by Joseph Conrad's novel *Heart of Darkness*. Sheen is the U.S. soldier assigned to "terminate with extreme prejudice" Brando's renegade Colonel Kurtz. His voyage upriver to Kurtz's jungle empire brings home the horrors of war. Excellent performances (especially by Duvall as the gung-ho officer who loves "the smell of napalm in the morning") and stunning visuals. Oscar-winning cinematography by Vittorio Storaro.
Dist.: Paramount

APOLOGY 1986
★ ★ ★ ★ NR Mystery-Suspense/MFTV 1:38
☑ Brief nudity, adult situations, explicit language, violence
Dir: Robert Bierman **Cast:** Lesley Ann Warren, Peter Weller, John Glover, Jimmie Ray Weeks, George Loros, Harvey Fierstein
▶ Conceptual artist Warren solicits anonymous confessions from phone callers in New York City, only to become the target of a serial killer. Weller is the cop who tries to help her in this slick and stylish mystery from the pen of Mark Medoff.
Dist.: HBO

APPALOOSA, THE 1966
★ ★ ★ NR Western 1:38
Dir: Sidney J. Furie **Cast:** Marlon Brando, Anjanette Comer, John Saxon, Emilio Fernandez, Alex Montoya, Rafael Campos
▶ Buffalo hunter Brando's prized Appaloosa horse is stolen by Mexican bandit Saxon. Brando is wounded by Saxon's gang when he tries to recover the horse. He recuperates with the aid of Saxon's ex-lover Comer; they fall in love as Saxon chases them. Off-beat Western features one of Brando's lesser performances.
Dist.: KVC

APPLE DUMPLING GANG, THE 1975
★ ★ ★ ★ G Comedy 1:40
Dir: Norman Tokar **Cast:** Bill Bixby, Susan Clark, Don Knotts, Tim Conway, David Wayne
▶ Lively, wholesome family Western from Walt Disney Studios. Bixby is a gambler who finds himself saddled with three children in this jolly tale of bank robbers and gold mines in the Old West. Most of the comedy is provided by Conway and Knotts as a team of incompetent desperadoes.
Dist.: Buena Vista

APPLE DUMPLING GANG RIDES AGAIN, THE
1979
★ ★ ★ ★ G Comedy 1:29
Dir: Vincent McEveety *Cast:* Tim Conway, Don Knotts, Tim Matheson, Kenneth Mars, Elyssa Davalos
▶ Good old-fashioned Disney fun in this sequel to *The Apple Dumpling Gang*. Former bad guys Conway and Knotts vow to reform, but despite their good intentions, the local sheriff mistakes them for banditos. The bumbling duo redeem themselves by foiling an attempted train robbery.
Dist.: Buena Vista

APPOINTMENT WITH DEATH 1988
★ ★ ★ PG Mystery-Suspense 1:42
☑ Violence
Dir: Michael Winner *Cast:* Peter Ustinov, Lauren Bacall, John Gielgud, Carrie Fisher, Piper Laurie, Hayley Mills, Jenny Seagrove, David Soul
▶ Ustinov returns as Agatha Christie's famous detective Hercule Poirot, whose travels take him to the Holy Land circa 1937. His vacation is interrupted by the murder of wealthy grand dame Laurie. The usual cast of all-star suspects is on hand. Slow and talky at times but spectacular scenery and a sassy Bacall make this painless entertainment. (CC)
Dist.: Warner

APPOINTMENT WITH FEAR 1985
★ R Horror 1:38
☑ Adult situations, explicit language, violence
Dir: Razmi Thomas *Cast:* Michele Little, Michael Wyle, Kerry Remsen, Douglas Rowe, Garrick Dowhen, Deborah Sue Vorhees
▶ The spirit of the Egyptian god Attis inhabits the body of L.A. looney Dowhen and begins a murderous modern-day search for his spiritual son. Quest ends with a group of teens who've got custody of the baby and are staying at a house out in the desert. One by one, they are killed. Despite farfetched premise, oddball suspense/horror pic displays a certain directorial flair.
Dist.: IVE

APPRENTICESHIP OF DUDDY KRAVITZ, THE
1974 Canadian
★ ★ ★ PG Comedy 2:01
☑ Brief nudity, adult situations, explicit language
Dir: Ted Kotcheff *Cast:* Richard Dreyfuss, Randy Quaid, Jack Warden, Denholm Elliott
▶ Wicked comedy about a success-driven schemer in 1940s Montreal gave Dreyfuss his first leading role. He hustles everything from heroin to pinball machines in scenes that are often biting as well as manic. Although uneven, the highlights (including an outrageous barmitzvah home movie directed by Elliott) are hilarious. Mordecai Richler was Oscar-nominated for adapting his novel.
Dist.: Paramount

APPRENTICE TO MURDER 1988
★ ★ PG-13 Drama 1:34
☑ Brief nudity, adult situations, violence
Dir: Ralph L. Thomas *Cast:* Donald Sutherland, Chad Lowe, Mia Sara, Knut Husebo, Rutanya Alda
▶ Young millworker Lowe falls under the spell of faith healer Sutherland, who may have ties to the Devil. Testing his protégé's loyalty, the "Pow Pow" doctor sets out to murder an evil hermit. Atmospheric horror film shot in Norway was based on a purportedly true incident in Pennsylvania, 1927. (CC)
Dist.: New World

APRIL FOOLS, THE 1969
★ ★ ★ ★ PG Comedy 1:35
☑ Adult situations
Dir: Stuart Rosenberg *Cast:* Jack Lemmon, Catherine Deneuve, Peter Lawford, Sally Kellerman
▶ Surburbanite Lemmon, trapped in a bad marriage to Kellerman, falls in love with Deneuve, the wife of his boss Lawford. These kinds of Hollywood movie romances usually end on a bittersweet note, but here Lemmon and Deneuve actually run away together to Paris. Solid cast makes it work. Dionne Warwick sings the hit Bacharach/David title song.
Dist.: CBS/Fox

APRIL FOOL'S DAY 1986
★ ★ R Horror 1:30
☑ Adult situations, explicit language, violence
Dir: Fred Walton *Cast:* Griffin O'Neal, Deborah Foreman, Tom Wilson, Amy Steel, Jay Baker
▶ Spoiled teen Muffy (Foreman) throws a party for her friends on a remote island. Is her insane twin Buffy behind the subsequent murders? Gimmick film from the *Friday the 13th* gang has an attractive cast and good production values, but resorts to familiar slasher stunts. Trick ending will disappoint most viewers. (CC)
Dist.: Paramount

ARABESQUE 1966
★ ★ ★ NR Mystery-Suspense 1:06
Dir: Stanley Donen *Cast:* Gregory Peck, Sophia Loren, Alan Badel, Kieron Moore, Carl Duering, George Coulouris
▶ Glossy, diverting espionage caper with Peck as an Oxford professor and code expert asked to spy on Middle Eastern oil tycoon Badel. When his cover is blown, Peck kidnaps Badel's mistress Loren and embarks on a wild flight to safety. Donen's follow-up to *Charade* is equally romantic and elegant, with Loren particularly fetching in Dior costumes.
Dist.: MCA

ARCH OF TRIUMPH 1948
★ ★ ★ NR Drama 2:00 B&W
Dir: Lewis Milestone *Cast:* Ingrid Bergman, Charles Boyer, Charles Laughton, Louis Calhern, Ruth Warrick

▶ In World War II Paris, doctor Boyer befriends troubled singer Bergman and they fall in love. But Boyer is deported; when he returns, Bergman has a new lover, and Boyer becomes embroiled in plot for revenge against Nazi Laughton. Highly emotional drama with good performances by Boyer and Bergman. Based on the novel by Erich Maria Remarque. *Dist.:* Republic

ARIA 1988 British
☆ **R Musical 1:38**
☑ Nudity, adult situations, violence
Dir: Derek Jarman, Nicolas Roeg, Robert Altman, Bill Bryden, Bruce Beresford, Julien Temple, Jean-Luc Godard, Charles Sturridge, Franc Roddam, Ken Russell *Cast:* Theresa Russell, Nicola Swain, Buck Henry, Anita Morris, Genevieve Page, John Hurt, Beverly D'Angelo, Julie Hagerty, Bridget Fonda
▶ Ten of the world's top directors reinterpret famous operatic arias in rock-video-style vignettes. Some striking sequences (like Roddam's young suicide variation on *Tristan und Isolde*, featuring Fonda), but overall this mixed bag is inaccessible.
Dist.: Academy

ARIZONA HEAT 1988
★ ★ **R Action-Adventure 1:30**
☑ Nudity, explicit language, violence
Dir: John G. Thomas *Cast:* Michael Parks, Denise Crosby, Hugh Farmington, Ron Briskman, Dennis O'Sullivan, Renata Lee
▶ Higher-ups concerned about cop Parks's violent methods team him with femme flatfoot Crosby in the hope that she can cool him down. But while on the trail of a cop killer, lesbian Crosby proves she's no pussycat. Some offbeat touches give this a little more originality than the usual cop film.
Dist.: Republic

ARMED AND DANGEROUS 1986
★ ★ ★ **PG-13 Comedy 1:28**
☑ Brief nudity, adult situations, explicit language, mild violence
Dir: Mark L. Lester *Cast:* John Candy, Eugene Levy, Robert Loggia, Meg Ryan, Kenneth McMillan, Steve Railsback
▶ Cop Candy, who loses his job after a frameup, and inept lawyer Levy become partners at the Guard Dog School. Together they break up a crime ring by crashing Mafia parties. Broad comedy coasts on stars' talents. Candy's impersonation of Divine is priceless. (CC)
Dist.: RCA/Columbia

ARMED RESPONSE 1986
★ ★ **R Action-Adventure 1:26**
☑ Nudity, explicit language, graphic violence
Dir: Fred Olen Ray *Cast:* David Carradine, Lee Van Cleef, Mako, Lois Hamilton, Ross Hagen, Dick Miller
▶ Carradine, a Vietnam vet plagued by

flashbacks, is out to avenge the death of his brother, killed by Japanese gangsters over a stolen jade statue. When his family is kidnapped, he's joined by his ex-cop father Van Cleef in a brutal manhunt. Lots of action and veteran B-characters perk up familiar plot.
Dist.: RCA/Columbia

ARMORED CAR ROBBERY 1950
★ **NR Action-Adventure 1:08 B&W**
Dir: Richard Fleischer *Cast:* Charles McGraw, Adele Jergens, William Talman, Steve Brodie, Don Haggerty, Gene Evans
▶ Talman and his gang pull off a lucrative armored car holdup, killing the buddy of cop McGraw in a shoot-out. Driven to avenge his friend's death, McGraw relentlessly tracks down the killers. Good, tightly directed thriller.
Dist.: Turner

ARMORED COMMAND 1961
★ **NR War 1:45 B&W**
Dir: Byron Haskin *Cast:* Howard Keel, Tina Louise, Warner Anderson, Earl Holliman, Carleton Young, Burt Reynolds
▶ During the Battle of the Bulge, beautiful Louise, a German spy within U.S. ranks, gets involved with American soldiers Holliman and Reynolds. As she attempts to send out key information to her employers, the love triangle becomes increasingly explosive. Effective performance by Reynolds, sexy one from Louise, highlight offbeat war drama.
Dist.: CBS/Fox

ARNOLD 1973
★ ★ **PG Comedy 1:40**
☑ Explicit language, violence
Dir: Georg Fenady *Cast:* Stella Stevens, Roddy McDowall, Farley Granger, Elsa Lanchester, Victor Buono, Shani Wallis
▶ Stevens marries a corpse in order to inherit his estate and then gets worried when the wedding guests are bumped off one by one. Silly comedy from Bing Crosby Productions features imaginative murders and a cast of veteran actors.
Dist.: Vestron

AROUND THE WORLD 1943
★ **NR Musical 1:30 B&W**
Dir: Allan Dwan *Cast:* Kay Kyser, Ish Kabibble, Joan Davis, Mischa Auer, Harry Babbitt, Chester Conklin
▶ Kyser, Kabibble, and the Kollege of Musical Knowledge set off on a tuneful tour of four continents (actually just back lots and soundstage sets). Corny comedy bits are interspersed with entertaining musical numbers, which include "A Moke from Shamokin," "Doodle-Ee-Doo," and "He's Got a Secret Weapon." Connoisseurs of trick canines will enjoy Little Fred's Football Dogs.
Dist.: Turner

AROUND THE WORLD IN 80 DAYS 1956
★ ★ ★ ★ **G Action-Adventure 2:55**
Dir: Michael Anderson *Cast:* David Niven,

Shirley MacLaine, Cantínflas, John Gielgud, Marlene Dietrich, Robert Newton
▶ Large-scale adaptation of the famous Jules Verne story about the efforts of Phileas Fogg (Niven) and his valet Passepartout (Cantínflas) to circle the globe. Producer Michael Todd spared no expense for this blockbuster, which won five Oscars: Best Picture, Screenplay (S. J. Perelman, John Farrow, James Poe), Cinematography, Editing, and Score (Victor Young). Forty-four stars ranging from Frank Sinatra to Jose Greco have cameo parts. Wide-screen process will suffer somewhat on TV.
Dist.: Warner

AROUND THE WORLD UNDER THE SEA 1966
★ **NR Action-Adventure 1:57**
Dir: Andrew Marton   *Cast:* Lloyd Bridges, Shirley Eaton, Brian Kelly, David McCallum, Keenan Wynn, Gary Merrill
▶ Six scientists, all expert divers, set out in an experimental submarine on a dangerous mission to monitor underwater volcanoes. Eaton, the only female on board, causes some tension, but expedition leader Bridges keeps his men firmly in line. Dated science fiction from the makers of TV's "Sea Hunt."
Dist.: MGM/UA

AROUSERS, THE 1973
★ **R Mystery-Suspense 1:27**
☑ Nudity, adult situations, explicit language, violence
Dir: Curtis Hanson   *Cast:* Tab Hunter, Sherry Latimer, Nadyne Turney, Isabel Jewell
▶ Phys ed teacher Hunter kills a young girl to disguise his impotence. Further killings result when the girl's roommate searches for her friend. Low-budget thriller from Roger Corman has become a cult favorite for its case-study approach.
Dist.: Nelson

ARRANGEMENT, THE 1969
★★ **R Drama 2:06**
☑ Adult situations, explicit language, violence
Dir: Elia Kazan   *Cast:* Kirk Douglas, Faye Dunaway, Deborah Kerr, Richard Boone, Hume Cronyn
▶ Suffering a mid-life crisis, successful Madison Avenue ad executive Douglas has a serious car crash. He reexamines his life while convalescing, then goes on a rampage that leaves his wife Kerr and mistress Dunaway in tears. Kazan wrote, produced, and directed this feverish soap opera based on his own novel.
Dist.: Warner

ARROWHEAD 1953
★★ **NR Western 1:45**
Dir: Charles Marquis Warren   *Cast:* Charlton Heston, Jack Palance, Katy Jurado, Brian Keith, Milburn Stone
▶ Apache-raised Army scout Heston is skepti-cal when the Apaches agree to stop fighting and go to a reservation. He's proven right when Palance leads an Apache revolt. Heston and the Army must counterattack. Fast-paced, colorful Western culminates in one-on-one fight between Heston and Palance.
Dist.: Paramount

ARROWSMITH 1931
★★★ **NR Drama 1:39 B&W**
Dir: John Ford   *Cast:* Ronald Colman, Helen Hayes, Beulah Bondi, Myrna Loy, Richard Bennett
▶ In the West Indies, doctor Colman strives to find a cure for bubonic plague, only to lose his own wife Hayes to the disease. Eventually, Colman must decide between preserving his findings or actually stopping a native epidemic. Adaptation of the Sinclair Lewis novel still packs a strong punch; one of Colman's finest hours. A Best Picture nominee.
Dist.: Nelson

ARSENIC AND OLD LACE 1944
★★★ **NR Comedy 1:58 B&W**
Dir: Frank Capra   *Cast:* Cary Grant, Priscilla Lane, Raymond Massey, Peter Lorre, Josephine Hull, Jean Adair
▶ Fast-paced, often hilarious black farce about two sweet old ladies, Hull and Adair, who murder unsuspecting bachelors with homemade elderberry wine. Nephew Grant frantically tries to protect them from the police and two homicidal psychopaths who have unexpectedly dropped in. Adaptation of the hit Joseph Kesselring play was a pet project for Capra, who produced and shot the film in four weeks before entering the Army in 1941.
Dist.: MGM/UA

ARTHUR 1981
★★★★★ **PG Comedy 1:37**
☑ Adult situations, explicit language
Dir: Steve Gordon   *Cast:* Dudley Moore, Liza Minnelli, John Gielgud, Geraldine Fitzgerald, Jill Eikenberry
▶ Winning screwball comedy about drunken heir Moore who falls for Queens waitress Minnelli instead of the debutante Eikenberry he's supposed to marry. Moore (nominated for Best Actor) fits his part perfectly. Gielgud won an Oscar for his role as a caustic valet, as did "Arthur's Theme" for Best Song. Debut director Gordon was also nominated for his screenplay, but tragically died before completing another film. Followed by *Arthur 2 On the Rocks*.
Dist.: Warner

ARTHUR 2 ON THE ROCKS 1988
★★★ **PG Comedy 1:52**
☑ Explicit language
Dir: Bud Yorkin   *Cast:* Dudley Moore, Liza Minnelli, Stephen Elliott, Cynthia Sikes, John Gielgud, Geraldine Fitzgerald
▶ In sequel to immensely popular *Arthur*, lovable billionaire drunk Moore and new bride

Minnelli fall upon hard times as vengeful Elliott, his daughter Sikes spurned by Moore in the original film, conspires to render the newlyweds penniless and homeless. Elliott demands Moore divorce Minnelli and marry Sikes or spend his life on the other side of the tracks. More of Moore's engaging mugging and clowning, but spin-off isn't up to source and employs Gielgud all too briefly. **(CC)**
Dist.: Warner

ARTHUR'S HALLOWED GROUND 1986 British
☆ **NR Drama 1:24**
☑ Explicit language
Dir: Freddie Young *Cast:* Jimmy Jewel, Jean Boht, David Swift, Michael Elphick, Vas Blackwood
▶ Cricket groundskeeper Jewel reluctantly takes on young assistant Blackwood, eventually warms up to him, and battles the Cricket Committee who disagree with his traditional standards. Talky, low-key production is impeccably performed but slowly paced. Impenetrable accents and dialogue are another drawback. Directorial debut for cinematographer Young was made for British television.
Dist.: MGM/UA

ASHANTI 1979 Swiss
★ ★ ★ **R Action-Adventure 1:57**
☑ Nudity, explicit language, violence
Dir: Richard Fleischer *Cast:* Michael Caine, Peter Ustinov, Beverly Johnson, Omar Sharif, Rex Harrison, William Holden
▶ Johnson, the black wife of missionary Caine, is kidnapped by African slave trader Ustinov. Authorities are powerless to help, so Caine hires mercenaries to rescue her. The trail leads from the desert to the yacht of a Middle Eastern prince. Cast (mostly limited to cameos) is the best aspect of this formula adventure.
Dist.: TWE

ASPHALT JUNGLE, THE 1950
★ ★ ★ **NR Crime/Drama 1:52 B&W**
Dir: John Huston *Cast:* Sterling Hayden, Sam Jaffe, Louis Calhern, Jean Hagen, James Whitmore, Marilyn Monroe
▶ Taut, realistic account of a criminal gang planning a perfect robbery with their mastermind Jaffe. Superb performances (including Monroe's best early role), exciting action, and a provocative view of the underworld. Highly influential film received four Oscar nominations and was the unacknowledged inspiration for countless caper movies. Based on a novel by W. R. Burnett.
Dist.: MGM/UA Ⓒ

ASPHYX, THE 1972 British
★ ★ **PG Horror 1:39**
☑ Adult situations, explicit language, violence
Dir: Peter Newbrook *Cast:* Robert Stephens, Robert Powell, Jane Lapotaire, Alex Scott, Ralph Arliss, Fiona Walker
▶ Good production values boost this atmospheric story about Stephens, a nineteenth-century scientist searching for the essence of life. His work unleashes a powerful monster who exacts a stiff price in exchange for giving Stephens immortality. Emphasis is on mood rather than shocks.
Dist.: Magnum

ASSASSINATION 1987
★ ★ ★ **PG-13 Action-Adventure 1:28**
☑ Adult situations, explicit language, violence
Dir: Peter Hunt *Cast:* Charles Bronson, Jill Ireland, Stephen Elliott, Jan Gan Boyd, Eric Stern
▶ Bronson plays a Secret Service agent guarding feisty First Lady Ireland (codenamed "One Mama") from a band of assassins. Cross-country chases stick to tried-and-true action sequences. The relationship between real-life couple Bronson and Ireland is curiously flat. **(CC)**
Dist.: Media

ASSASSINATION OF TROTSKY, THE 1972 French/Italian/British
☆ **R Drama 1:43**
☑ Adult situations, violence
Dir: Joseph Losey *Cast:* Richard Burton, Alain Delon, Romy Schneider, Valentina Cortese, Enrico Maria Salerno
▶ Burton is Trotsky, an aging revolutionary who once led the Russian Red Army; Delon is the man who stalks him. The story switches back and forth between the killer and his intended victim. Always seeming to portend more than it delivers, presentation offers little beyond a probably accurate record of Trotsky's last day. A strangely miscast Burton does his best.
Dist.: Corinth

ASSAULT, THE 1986 Dutch
☆ **PG Drama 2:29**
☑ Violence
Dir: Fons Rademakers *Cast:* Derek de Lint, Marc van Uchelen, Monique van de Ven, John Kraaykamp, Huub van der Lubbe
▶ During World War II, a young Dutch boy watches the Nazis execute his family. Forty years later he still struggles to understand why the incident occurred. Earnest but slow-paced story based on a respected novel by Harry Mulisch won Oscar for Best Foreign Film. Ⓢ]
Dist.: MGM/UA

ASSAULT OF THE KILLER BIMBOS 1988
★ ★ **R Comedy 1:21**
☑ Nudity, adult situations, explicit language, mild violence
Dir: Anita Rosenberg *Cast:* Christina Whitaker, Elizabeth Kaiton, Tammara Souza, Patti Astor, Nick Cassavetes, Griffin O'Neal
▶ Tongue-in-cheek comedy about two go-go dancers and a waitress framed for murder. The girls pick up three "bimboys" and head for Mexico, where they run into the real criminals. Very low-budget (and low-brow) satire merits

some praise for its sympathetic treatment of the heroines.
Dist.: Urban Classics

ASSAULT ON PRECINCT 13 1976
★ ★ ★ R Action-Adventure **1:31**
☑ Explicit language, graphic violence
Dir: John Carpenter   *Cast:* Austin Stoker, Darwin Joston, Laurie Zimmer, Nancy Loomis, Kim Richards
▶ A lone cop, several innocent bystanders, and some death-row prisoners are trapped inside an about-to-be-abandoned police station when a revenge-seeking gang lays siege to it. Explosive, hard-hitting urban crime drama is tremendously suspenseful, thanks to realistic performances by its unknown cast and slam-bang direction from Carpenter. Story was inspired by Howard Hawks's classic western *Rio Bravo.*
Dist.: Media

ASSISI UNDERGROUND, THE 1985
★ ★ ★ ★ PG Drama **1:54**
☑ Violence
Dir: Alexander Ramati   *Cast:* Ben Cross, James Mason, Maximilian Schell, Irene Papas, Karl-Heinz Hackl
▶ In war-torn Assisi, young priest Cross is ordered to hide sixteen Jews from the Germans. Using convents and monasteries, he sets up a forgery ring to outfox the Nazis. Based on a true story, earnest but plodding film features one of Mason's last roles as a bishop determined to help the Jews. A three-hour miniseries version also exists.
Dist.: MGM/UA

AS SUMMERS DIE 1986
★ ★ ★ NR Drama/MFTV **1:27**
Dir: Jean-Claude Tramont   *Cast:* Scott Glenn, Jamie Lee Curtis, Bette Davis, Ron O'Neal, Beah Richards
▶ Glenn, a struggling small-town Southern lawyer in the late 1950s, finds himself defending a poor black woman against the seizure of her oil-rich land by the town's reigning white family. Curtis, as a rebellious Southern belle who wins Glenn's heart, and screen legend Davis co-star as the only family members sympathetic to Glenn's cause. Quality melodrama of little guy who takes on the establishment is enhanced by first-rate cast and splendid Southern atmosphere.
Dist.: HBO

ASYLUM 1972 British
★ ★ PG Horror **1:32**
☑ Adult situations, violence
Dir: Roy Ward Baker   *Cast:* Barbara Parkins, Britt Ekland, Richard Todd, Peter Cushing, Herbert Lom, Charlotte Rampling
▶ Quartet of fright stories by Robert Bloch begins with Todd packing dismembered spouse into freezer; continues with Cushing's efforts to bring his dead son back to life; offers Ekland and Rampling as two halves of a split personality; and concludes with Lom building murderous little mechanical dolls. Cast of familiar faces really delivers the goods. Also known, in a shorter version, as *House of Crazies.*
Dist.: Prism

AS YOU LIKE IT 1936 British
★ NR Comedy **1:36** B&W
Dir: Paul Czinner   *Cast:* Elisabeth Bergner, Laurence Olivier, Sophie Stewart, Henry Ainley
▶ Way before *Tootsie, Yentl,* and other gender reversal stories there was William Shakespeare's comedy of wooing and romance. Rosalind (Bergner), a noblewoman exiled to the forests of Arden, falls for nobleman Orlando (a young Olivier) and disguises herself as a boy to teach him a few lessons in love. Adaptation co-written by J. M. Barrie.
Dist.: Prism

AT CLOSE RANGE 1986
★ ★ ★ R Drama **1:55**
☑ Brief nudity, adult situations, explicit language, violence
Dir: James Foley   *Cast:* Sean Penn, Christopher Walken, Mary Stuart Masterson, Christopher Penn, Millie Perkins, Candy Clark
▶ Moody, frightening thriller with a strong performance from Walken as a father who returns to his family after many years and lures sons (Sean and Christopher Penn) into crime. When the police close in on Walken, he decides that his sons have to die. Vivid evocation of gritty Pennsylvania underclass and often shocking violence. Based on a true story. Madonna sings her hit "Live to Tell." **(CC)**
Dist.: Vestron

AT GUNPOINT 1955
★ ★ NR Western **1:21**
Dir: Alfred Werker   *Cast:* Fred MacMurray, Dorothy Malone, Walter Brennan, Tommy Rettig, John Qualen
▶ MacMurray, owner of a general store and family man to wife Malone and son Rettig, is an unlikely hero when he manages to thwart a gang of cutthroats. Everyone in town, except doc Brennan, turns against him when the gang seeks revenge. Little-known but above-average Western.
Dist.: Republic

ATLANTIC CITY 1981
★ ★ R Drama **1:44**
☑ Nudity, adult situations, explicit language
Dir: Louis Malle   *Cast:* Burt Lancaster, Susan Sarandon, Kate Reid, Michel Piccoli, Hollis McLaren, Robert Joy
▶ Old-time gangster Lancaster and aspiring croupier Sarandon team up to outsmart the Mafia over a dope deal in this offbeat film for sophisticated audiences. The plot is full of melodramatic conventions but they are given a new look and feel by director Malle. The script by playwright John Guare has a genuine understanding of dreamers, and the city, in all its seedy grandeur, provides a meaningful backdrop to the action. Nominated for five

Oscars, including Best Picture. Singer Robert Goulet appears as himself.
Dist.: Paramount

ATOMIC CAFE, THE 1982
★ ★ **NR Documentary 1:32 C/B&W**
Dir: Rafferty Kevin, Loader Jayne, Rafferty Pierce
▶ Nostalgia with an ironic apocalyptic twist. The filmmakers juxtapose archival footage to demonstrate the government's manipulation of American public opinion about The Bomb. Documentary and newsreel footage of real figures—Nixon, Krushchev, Truman, the Rosenbergs—evokes the Cold War. Most disturbing are the "happy talk" propaganda films, such as Bert the Turtle's "Duck and Cover" cartoon warning to children. Repetitive but powerful.
Dist.: HBO

ATOMIC KID, THE 1954
☆ **NR Comedy 1:26 B&W**
Dir: Leslie Martinson *Cast:* Mickey Rooney, Robert Strauss, Elaine Davis, Bill Goodwin, Whit Bissell, Joey Forman
▶ Prospector Rooney is investigating a dummy house on nuclear test site when an A-Bomb goes off. Spared thanks to the properties of a peanut butter sandwich he is eating, the now-radioactive Rooney has all sorts of fanciful powers, such as the ability to trigger wins in slot machines, which attract the attention of spies. Made before radioactivity was considered a subject of profound gloom, light-hearted comedy was scripted by Blake Edwards.
Dist.: Republic

ATOR, THE FIGHTING EAGLE 1983 Italian
☆ **PG Action-Adventure 1:40**
☑ Adult situations, explicit language, violence
Dir: David Hills *Cast:* Miles O'Keeffe, Sabrina Siani, Ritza Brown, Edmund Purdom, Laura Gemser
▶ Low-budget imitation of *Conan the Barbarian* features muscular O'Keeffe in pursuit of his bride Brown, abducted by spider-worshipping sect. Amazonian robber/warrior Siani aids him in his endeavor. Mainly for hard-core sword-and-sorcery fans. Best line: "The Earth trembled like a virgin drawn to the nuptial bed." Followed by sequel *The Blade Master*.
Dist.: HBO

AT SWORD'S POINT 1952
★ ★ **NR Action-Adventure 1:21**
Dir: Lewis Allen *Cast:* Cornel Wilde, Maureen O'Hara, Dan O'Herlihy, Gladys Cooper, Robert Douglas, Alan Hale, Jr.
▶ Evil nobleman Douglas plots against the throne of French queen Cooper. Things look dire until D'Artagnan (Wilde) leads the sons of the four musketeers to the rescue. Lively swashbuckler for fans of derring-do and swordplay. Also known, fittingly, as *Sons of the Musketeers*.
Dist.: Turner

ATTACK FORCE Z 1981 Australian/Taiwanese
★ ★ ★ **NR War 1:24**
☑ Explicit language, violence
Dir: Tim Burstall *Cast:* John Phillip Law, Sam Neill, Mel Gibson, Chris Haywood
▶ During World War II, five Australian commandos are dropped behind enemy lines to bring back an important defector. Surrounded by Japanese soldiers, they must decide between killing the defector or exposing their resistance network. Credible suspense and good acting despite bleak, downbeat tone.
Dist.: Virgin

ATTACK OF THE 50-FOOT WOMAN 1958
★ ★ **NR Sci-Fi 1:06 B&W**
Dir: Nathan Hertz *Cast:* Allison Hayes, William Hudson, Yvette Vickers, Roy Gordon, George Douglas, Ken Terrell
▶ Housewife Hayes, obsessed with her husband Hudson's affairs, is lured into a flying saucer and transformed overnight into a gigantic killer. One of the true lowpoints in cinema, with spectacularly bad acting and dismal special effects. Kitsch fans consider this a classic.
Dist.: CBS/Fox

ATTACK OF THE KILLER TOMATOES 1978
★ **PG Comedy 1:28**
☑ Explicit language
Dir: John De Bello *Cast:* David Miller, George Wilson, Sharon Taylor, Jack Riley, Rock Peace, John De Bello
▶ Title and credits are the best things about this cheapie sci-fi parody. Nonsensical plot (beautiful investigative reporter uncovers rampage of homicidal plants) is simply an excuse for corny jokes and double entendres. Film has a reputation as one of the world's worst, but camp fans can find much funnier examples.
Dist.: Media

AT THE CIRCUS 1939
★ ★ **NR Comedy 1:27 B&W**
Dir: Edward Buzzell *Cast:* Groucho Marx, Harpo Marx, Chico Marx, Kenny Baker, Eve Arden, Margret Dumont, Nat Pendleton
▶ Chico sends for lawyer J. Cheever Loophole (Groucho) to help struggling circus owner Baker save his show. Funniest moments in an uneven vehicle: Groucho singing "Lydia, the Tattooed Lady," his drinking a zillion cups of coffee to buy time for his friends, and the big circus finale.
Dist.: MGM/UA

AT THE EARTH'S CORE 1976 British
★ ★ ★ **PG Action-Adventure 1:30**
☑ Violence
Dir: Kevin Connor *Cast:* Doug McClure, Peter Cushing, Caroline Munro, Cy Grant
▶ Scientist Cushing and cohort McClure find themselves journeying to the center of the world in a pointy earth-boring machine. There they encounter silly-looking monsters in this

lackluster adaptation of an Edgar Rice Burroughs novel; McClure, Connor, and producer Milton Subotsky did much better with Burroughs's *The Land That Time Forgot.*
Dist.: Warner

AT WAR WITH THE ARMY 1950
★ **NR Comedy 1:32 B&W**
Dir: Hal Walker   *Cast:* Dean Martin, Jerry Lewis, Mike Kellin, Polly Bergen, Jean Ruth, Angela Greene
▶ Middling service comedy is of interest as the first Martin/Lewis vehicle. Jerry has a notable encounter with a soda pop machine; Dean parodies Bing Crosby in one of his musical numbers. More restrained than their later efforts.
Dist.: Various

AUDREY ROSE 1977
★ ★ ★ ★ **PG Horror 1:53**
Dir: Robert Wise   *Cast:* Marsha Mason, Anthony Hopkins, John Beck, Susan Swift
▶ Ten years after the car crash death of his daughter Audrey Rose, Hopkins becomes convinced she's been reincarnated as the daughter of Mason and Beck. The emphasis is on domestic relations over horror. Some very scary moments, but the ending is a letdown. Frank De Felitta adapted this supernatural tale from his best-seller.
Dist.: MGM/UA

AUNTIE MAME 1958
★ ★ ★ ★ **NR Comedy 2:26**
Dir: Morton Da Costa   *Cast:* Rosalind Russell, Forrest Tucker, Roger Smith, Peggy Cass, Patric Knowles
▶ In the 1920s, an orphaned boy is adopted by extravagant aunt Russell whose motto is: "Life's a banquet and most poor suckers are starving!" Featuring Russell's colorful star turn and a standout performance by Cass as the very pregnant, unwed Agnes Gooch. Adapted from the best-selling book by Patrick Dennis and later reincarnated as the musical *Mame*, this popular comedy, nominated for six Oscars, was the top-grossing film of 1959.
Dist.: Warner

AU REVOIR LES ENFANTS 1988 French
★ ★ ★ **PG Drama 1:43**
☑ Explicit language
Dir: Louis Malle   *Cast:* Gaspard Manesse, Raphael Fejto, Francine Racette, Stanislas Carre de Malberg, Phillipe Morier-Genoud, François Berleand
▶ At a French boarding school during World War II, Manesse, a Catholic, and Fejto, a Jew trying to avoid capture under a phony name, develop a close relationship that is cut short by the Nazis. Beautifully acted drama, although slowly paced, works up emotional steam. Oscar-nominated for Best Foreign Film. Also known under its English title *Goodbye, Children.* [S]
Dist.: Orion

AURORA ENCOUNTER, THE 1986
★ ★ **PG Sci-Fi 1:30**
☑ Adult situations, explicit language, mild violence
Dir: Jim McCullough   *Cast:* Jack Elam, Peter Brown, Carol Bagdasarian, Spanky McFarland, Dottie West
▶ In 1897, an alien lands his spaceship outside the small town of Aurora, Texas. Only schoolchildren can see the visitor at first, and can't convince their parents that he needs help. Cheap special effects and mediocre acting dampen what is otherwise warm family entertainment.
Dist.: New World

AUTHOR! AUTHOR! 1982
★ ★ ★ ★ **PG Comedy 1:50**
☑ Adult situations, explicit language
Dir: Arthur Hiller   *Cast:* Al Pacino, Tuesday Weld, Dyan Cannon, Alan King, Bob Dishy, Bob (Elliott) & Ray (Goulding)
▶ In a rare comedic role, Pacino portrays a neurotic New York playwright saddled with an impending opening night, adulterous wife Weld, anxiety-ridden friends, and a disintegrating family of five adorable kids, only one of which is his. Diverting domestic comedy delivers a prerequiste happy ending. Written by playwright Israel Horovitz.
Dist.: CBS/Fox

AUTOBIOGRAPHY OF MISS JANE PITTMAN, THE 1974
★ ★ ★ ★ ★ **NR Biography/MFTV 1:50**
Dir: John Korty   *Cast:* Cicely Tyson, Thalmus Rasulala, Richard Dysart, Michael Murphy, Katherine Helmond, Barbara Chaney
▶ Tyson plays a former slave who ages from 19 to 110 to live through the Civil War and become part of the 1960s civil rights movement. Her bravura performance raises this made-for-television movie far above standard fare. Tyson won one of nine Emmys, as did director Korty, screenwriter Tracy Keenan Wynn, and Rick Baker and Stan Wilson for their extraordinary and totally convincing aging makeup work. Adapted from Ernest J. Gaines's epic novel.
Dist.: Prism

AUTUMN LEAVES 1956
★ ★ **NR Drama 1:48 B&W**
Dir: Robert Aldrich   *Cast:* Joan Crawford, Cliff Robertson, Vera Miles, Lorne Greene, Ruth Donnelly, Shepperd Strudwick
▶ Crawford gives an assured performance as a lonely spinster who marries younger Robertson after a whirlwind romance. What starts as an undemanding soap opera turns into a tense psychodrama as Crawford discovers Robertson is already married and mentally deranged as well. Interesting direction and capable supporting cast enhance unpredictable plot.
Dist.: RCA/Columbia

AUTUMN SONATA 1978 Swedish
★ **PG Drama 1:37**
☑ Adult situations
Dir: Ingmar Bergman ***Cast:*** Liv Ullmann, Ingrid Bergman, Lena Nyman, Halvar Bjork, Gunnar Bjornstrand
► After a seven-year separation, concert pianist Bergman visits daughter Ullmann, a parson's wife, to find that a second daughter, wasting away from an undisclosed disease, has been brought out of a state hospital for seemingly charitable reasons. Emotionally charged, this explosive mother-daughter confrontation was the first collaboration between Bergman and the noted Swedish director. [S]
Dist.: Magnetic

AVALANCHE 1978
★★ **PG Action-Adventure 1:31**
☑ Explicit language, mild violence
Dir: Corey Allen ***Cast:*** Rock Hudson, Mia Farrow, Robert Forester, Jeanette Nolan
► Ski lodge operator Hudson defies environmentalists and nature by cutting down a slew of trees uphill from his resort. The result: an avalanche that succeeds in burying the entire lodge, including Hudson's ex-wife Farrow and mother Nolan. Swift pacing, archival footage of an actual massive avalanche, and some exciting trapped-beneath-the-snow sequences raise this formula movie slightly above the average.
Dist.: Nelson

AVENGING ANGEL 1985
★★ **R Action-Adventure 1:33**
☑ Nudity, adult situations, explicit language, violence
Dir: Robert Vincent O'Neil ***Cast:*** Betsy Russell, Rory Calhoun, Susan Tyrrell, Ossie Davis, Robert F. Lyons
► America's favorite "straight A student by day/hustler by night" is back in this sequel to the 1983 *Angel*. Teen tramp Molly/Angel (Russell) has cleaned up her act, gone to college, and is now ready for law school, but her plans change when cop guardian Lyons is killed. Russell then hits the streets to find the murderer. Dumb script and lackadaisical direction but plenty of sleazy atmosphere and tons of revealing outfits for Russell. (CC)
Dist.: New World

AVENGING FORCE 1986
★★★ **R Action-Adventure 1:43**
☑ Adult situations, explicit language, violence
Dir: Sam Firstenberg ***Cast:*** Michael Dudikoff, Steve James, James Booth, John P. Ryan, Bill Wallace, Karl Johnson
► Retired CIA agent/martial arts expert Dudikoff seeks peace on Louisiana homestead. But when liberal black buddy James, a Senate candidate, becomes the target of lunatic-fringe, right-wing terrorist outfit run by psychotic professor Ryan, Dudikoff reprises his one-man army routine. Fine fare for genre fans, with Ryan noteworthy as villain. Dudikoff and James also teamed for *American Ninja* and *American Ninja II*. (CC)
Dist.: Media

AVIATOR, THE 1985
★★★ **PG Action-Adventure 1:36**
☑ Explicit language, violence
Dir: George Miller ***Cast:*** Christopher Reeve, Rosanna Arquette, Tyne Daly, Jack Warden, Sam Wanamaker
► In 1928, mail pilot Reeve and his rich bratty passenger Arquette crash in an isolated mountain region. Antagonists at first, the two grow closer as they fight to survive wolves and other dangers. Adapted from Ernest K. Gann's best-seller, and with plenty of pretty scenery, decent period details, and solid acting, yet the end result lacks spark between the leads.
Dist.: MGM/UA

AWAKENING, THE 1980
★★ **R Horror 1:40**
☑ Adult situations, graphic violence
Dir: Mike Newell ***Cast:*** Charlton Heston, Susannah York, Jill Townsend, Stephanie Zimbalist, Patrick Drury
► Archaeologist Heston discovers the long-lost tomb of an ancient Egyptian princess, whose spirit subsequently possesses Heston's daughter Zimbalist. Unusual story line unravels effectively as moody direction by Newell provides some genuine chills.
Dist.: Warner

AWAY ALL BOATS 1956
★★★ **NR War 1:54**
Dir: Joseph Pevney ***Cast:*** Jeff Chandler, George Nader, Julie Adams, Lex Barker, Keith Andes, Richard Boone
► During World War II, South Seas Navy captain Chandler drives his young recruits mercilessly, losing their respect until lieutenant Nader reveals the compassion behind Chandler's tough exterior. Despite good battle scenes, standard genre fare is mostly cliché.
Dist.: MCA

AWFUL TRUTH, THE 1937
★★★★★ **NR Comedy 1:31 B&W**
Dir: Leo McCarey ***Cast:*** Cary Grant, Irene Dunne, Ralph Bellamy, Cecil Cunningham, Skippy the Terrier
► The awful truth is that recently divorced Grant and Dunne can't stay away from each other. They bicker, fight over custody of the dog (Skippy, the canine who played Asta in *The Thin Man* series), and break up each other's respective new romances. Lively, quintessentially crazy screwball comedy. Witty performances from leads with Bellamy providing his classic hapless foil. Five Oscar nominations, winning for Best Director.
Dist.: RCA/Columbia

BABAR: THE MOVIE 1989
★★★★ **G Animation 1:10**

Dir: John Lawrence Collins   *Cast:* Voices of Gordon Pinsent, Gavin Magrath, Elizabeth Hanna, Sarah Polley, Chris Wiggins, Stephen Ouimette
▶ The story of how Babar, the gentle king of Elephantland, once saved the village of his young friend Celeste. When evil rhinocerouses enslave the village pachyderms, Babar uses his native intelligence and innate decency to thwart his ponderous enemies. Based on the childrens' books created by Jean de Brunhoff, simple animation and unoriginal story will bore parents, but not their young children.
Dist.: IVE

BABE RUTH STORY, THE 1948
★ ★ NR Biography/Sports 1:47 B&W
Dir: Roy Del Ruth   *Cast:* William Bendix, Claire Trevor, Charles Bickford, Sam Levene, William Frawley
▶ Story of the baseball Hall of Famer follows the Babe (Bendix) through his trouble-filled Baltimore childhood, stint in an orphanage, early career as a Red Sox pitcher, and super-stardom as the New York Yankees slugger. Yankee fans might enjoy Bendix's portrayal of the Sultan of Swat as a big, sweet lug, al-though overall result lacks spark.   (CC)
Dist.: CBS/Fox

BABES IN ARMS 1939
★ ★ ★ NR Musical 1:37 B&W
Dir: Busby Berkeley   *Cast:* Judy Garland, Mickey Rooney, Charles Winninger, Guy Kib-bee, June Preisser, Grace Hayes
▶ First musical teaming of Garland and Rooney follows the archetypal "let's put on a show" formula. Rooney (who won an Oscar nomination) writes and directs a hit for his schoolmates, but spoiled teen star Preisser threatens to steal the lead from Garland. Loosely based on a Rodgers and Hart play, and featuring "You Are My Lucky Star," "Where or When," and "The Lady Is a Tramp."
Dist.: MGM/UA

BABES IN TOYLAND 1934
★ ★ ★ ★ ★ NR Family/Fantasy 1:13 B&W
Dir: Gus Meins, Charles Rogers   *Cast:* Stan Laurel, Oliver Hardy, Charlotte Henry, Henry Kleinbach, Felix Knight, Florence Roberts
▶ When evil Kleinbach forces the sweetheart of Little Bo Peep (Henry) into exile and tries to take over Toyland, toymaker's bumbling as-sistants Laurel and Hardy send an army of six-foot wooden soldiers to thwart him. Delightful holiday classic; Laurel and Hardy are wonder-ful as always, and the climactic march of the soldiers will thrill small children. Based on Vic-tor Herbert's operetta; also known as *March of the Wooden Soldiers.*

BABES IN TOYLAND 1961
★ ★ ★ ★ G Family/Fantasy 1961
Dir: Jack Donohue   *Cast:* Ray Bolger, Tommy Sands, Annette Funicello, Ed Wynn, Tommy Kirk, Kevin Corcoran
▶ Pallid, lifeless version of the Victor Herbert operetta about Tom the Piper's Son (Sands), Mary Quite Contrary (Funicello), and their tra-vails with the villainous Barnaby (Bolger) in a land populated by Mother Goose characters. Bland, stylized sets and dull dance sequences make this seem like a TV show with a nursery rhyme theme. A rare fantasy/musical flop for Disney, remade from a 1934 film.
Dist.: Buena Vista

BABES ON BROADWAY 1941
★ ★ NR Musical 1:58 B&W
Dir: Busby Berkeley   *Cast:* Mickey Rooney, Judy Garland, Fay Bainter, Virginia Weidler, Ray McDonald, Richard Quine
▶ Follow-up to *Babes in Arms* repeats suc-cessful high-energy formula as Rooney and Garland try to break into New York's theater world. Lavish production features "F.D.R. Jones" and the Oscar-nominated "How About You?" as well as Rooney's hilarious im-personation of Carmen Miranda. Look for Donna Reed and Margaret O'Brien in small roles; Alexander Woollcott has a brief cameo.
Dist.: MGM/UA

BABETTE'S FEAST 1988 Danish
★ ★ ★ G Drama 1:42
Dir: Gabriel Axel   *Cast:* Stephane Audran, Birgitte Federspiel, Bodil Kjer, Vibeke Hast-rup, Hanne Stensgard, Jarl Kulle
▶ In nineteenth-century Denmark, spinster sis-ters Federspiel and Kjer, leaders of a spartan Protestant sect, take in French refugee Au-dran as their unpaid housekeeper. After many years, Audran wins the lottery and uses her previously hidden culinary skills to teach the sisters and their flock about earthly passions and pleasures. Adaptation of an Isak Dinesen story won Best Foreign Film Oscar. Audan is warm and witty, but stately drama is for dis-criminating tastes.   Ⓢ
Dist.: Orion

BABY BOOM 1987
★ ★ ★ ★ PG Comedy 1:43
☑ Adult situations, explicit language
Dir: Charles Shyer   *Cast:* Diane Keaton, Sam Shepard, Harold Ramis, Mary Kay Place, James Spader
▶ Keaton is steely New York City manage-ment consultant J. C. Wiatt, who finds her fast-track yuppie lifestyle turned upside down when she inherits a baby from a recently de-ceased, long-lost cousin. Eventually, she chucks corporate life for a rural Vermont exis-tence and finds happiness in the arms of small-town veterinarian Shepard. Broad sit-com fun with an adorable kid played by twins Kristina and Michelle Kennedy and a smash-ing star performance by Keaton.   (CC)
Dist.: CBS/Fox

BABY DOLL 1956
★ ★ R Drama 1:54 B&W
☑ Adult situations, explicit language
Dir: Elia Kazan   *Cast:* Carroll Baker, Karl

Malden, Eli Wallach, Mildred Dunnock, Lonny Chapman
▶ Tennesee Williams wrote the screenplay for this odd Southern drama, which caused a furor when it was condemned by the Catholic Legion of Decency for its then shocking child-bride theme. Baker is young Baby Doll, who sleeps in a crib and won't let husband Malden touch her. Wallach is the local cotton-gin king who pursues Baker. Now more dated than outrageous but the performances and Southern atmosphere hold up.
Dist.: Warner

BABY, IT'S YOU 1983
★ ★ R Romance 1:45
☑ Brief nudity, adult situations, explicit language, violence
Dir: John Sayles *Cast:* Rosanna Arquette, Vincent Spano, Joanna Merlin, Jack Davidson
▶ Period high school romance features Arquette as perky, popular Jill, pursued by the "Sheik" (Spano), a greaser from the wrong side of the tracks with a surprisingly tender side. Class differences doom their poignant relationship. Affecting, if predictable; Arquette is sexy and smart and Spano is appealing. Rich in period detail with plenty of 1960s hits on the soundtrack.
Dist.: Paramount

BABY LOVE 1969 British
☆ R Drama 1:32
☑ Nudity, adult situations, explicit language
Dir: Alastair Reid *Cast:* Ann Lynn, Keith Barron, Linda Hayden, Derek Lamden, Diana Dors, Patience Collier
▶ When Dors kills herself, her illegitimate teen daughter Hayden vows revenge against the respectable doctor whom she believes to be her father. While under the doctor's care, she arouses his son to the point of madness, provokes the lesbian leanings of his wife, then sets out to seduce the doctor herself. Trashy stuff.
Dist.: MGM/UA

BABY. . .SECRET OF THE LOST LEGEND 1985
★ ★ ★ PG Action-Adventure 1:35
☑ Brief nudity, adult situations, violence
Dir: B.W.L. Norton *Cast:* William Katt, Sean Young, Patrick McGoohan, Julian Fellowes, Kyalo Mativo
▶ Zoologist Young and her sportswriter husband Katt discover family of brontosauruses in modern-day Africa, and then must save them from ruthless scientist McGoohan. Nice premise routinely scripted. The dinosaurs are cute and their scenes will be irresistible to anyone with a weakness for babies or pets. Family entertainment, although parents should note a slight excess of gunplay.
Dist.: Buena Vista

BABY, TAKE A BOW 1934
★ ★ NR Musical/Family 1:16 B&W

Dir: Harry Lachman *Cast:* Shirley Temple, James Dunn, Claire Trevor, Alan Dinehart, Ray Walker
▶ Thugs try to implicate ex-con Dunn in a necklace robbery; daughter Temple uses her charm to save the day. Creaky antique is notable primarily as Shirley's first starring role. (CC)
Dist.: CBS/Fox

BABY, THE RAIN MUST FALL 1965
★ ★ ★ NR Drama 1:39 B&W
Dir: Robert Mulligan *Cast:* Steve McQueen, Lee Remick, Don Murray, Paul Fix, Josephine Hutchinson
▶ Downbeat drama featuring worthy star performances. McQueen, a guitar-playing ex-con, starts a new life after prison with wife Remick and their four-year-old daughter, but he can't overcome his violent ways. Horton Foote adapted his own play *The Traveling Lady.* Title song was a 1965 hit.
Dist.: RCA/Columbia

BACHELOR AND THE BOBBYSOXER, THE 1947
★ ★ ★ NR Comedy 1:34 B&W
Dir: Irving Reis *Cast:* Cary Grant, Myrna Loy, Shirley Temple, Rudy Vallee, Johnny Sands
▶ After being arrested in a nightclub slugfest, dashing artist Grant comes before judge Loy. When Loy's teenage sister Temple falls for Grant, she sentences him to escort the girl until she gets over the crush. Airy, amusing comedy sustained by Cary's trademark charm and Loy's tart wit. Hugely popular in its time, won 1947 Oscar for Best Original Screenplay by Sidney Sheldon.
Dist.: Turner ©

BACHELOR MOTHER 1939
★ ★ ★ ★ ★ NR Comedy 1:22 B&W
Dir: Garson Kanin *Cast:* Ginger Rogers, David Niven, Charles Coburn, Frank Albertson, Ernest Truex
▶ Salesgirl Rogers's life is turned upside down when she takes in an abandoned baby. Taking an interest in mother and child, department-store heir Niven falls in love. Sweet, charming, swiftly paced romantic comedy still seems fresh today, thanks to great work from Rogers, Niven, Coburn, and an absolutely adorable baby who steals every scene.
Dist.: Turner

BACHELOR PARTY 1984
★ ★ ★ ★ R Comedy 1:51
☑ Nudity, adult situations, explicit language, mild violence, adult humor
Dir: Neil Israel *Cast:* Tom Hanks, Tawny Kitaen, Adrian Zmed, Barry Diamond, Bronson Pinchot
▶ Bawdy comedy about a bachelor party that gets amusingly out of hand. Carefree bachelor Hanks is about to marry Kitaen while her uppity father Grizzard and ex-boyfriend plot to break up the engagement. Plenty of

low-rent humor (including a mule snorting cocaine). Although silly at times, Hanks's brash humor carries the day. **(CC)**
Dist.: CBS/Fox

BACKFIRE 1988
★ ★ ★ **R Mystery-Suspense 1:31**
Dir: Gilbert Cates *Cast:* Karen Allen, Keith Carradine, Jeff Fahey, Dinah Manoff, Dean Paul Martin
▶ Intrigue and double-crossing among Vietnam vet Fahey haunted by war-related nightmares, his scheming wife Allen, her ex-boyfriend Martin, and her new lover Carradine. Loses momentum about midway through, but overall a professional production with a nice nasty edge.
Dist.: Vidmark

BACK FROM ETERNITY 1956
★ ★ **NR Action-Adventure 1:37 B&W**
Dir: John Farrow *Cast:* Robert Ryan, Anita Ekberg, Rod Steiger, Phyllis Kirk, Gene Barry, Beulah Bondi
▶ Plane crash leaves pilot Ryan, prostitute Ekberg, condemned convict Steiger, and others stranded in South America. Two big problems: the natives are headhunters and the plane can't take all of the passengers back to civilization. Remake of Farrow's 1939 *Five Came Back.*
Dist.: United

BACKLASH 1986 Australian
☆ **NR Drama 1:31**
☑ Rape, brief nudity, adult situations, explicit language
Dir: Bill Bennett *Cast:* David Argue, Gia Carides, Lydia Miller, Brian Syron, Anne Smith, Don Smith
▶ When aborigine Miller is raped by her slobbering, crude employer Smith, she is charged with murdering and emasculating him. But did she do it? What follows is a quirky Aussie road movie as Miller is transported across the outback by police officers Argue and Carides. Film's strong suits are its small, amusing moments as Miller and her captors get to know each other. Miller is so natural an actress that it's hard to believe this is her acting debut.
Dist.: Virgin

BACK ROADS 1981
★ ★ ★ **R Comedy 1:34**
☑ Explicit language, violence
Dir: Martin Ritt *Cast:* Sally Field, Tommy Lee Jones, David Keith, Miriam Colon, Michael V. Gazzo
▶ Hooker Field and out-of-work boxer Jones go on the lam when they get into trouble with the law. Foes at first, they eventually fall in love on the road. Escapist comedy is short on plot but the film achieves a pleasant lightweight tone. The leads do what they can with clichéd characters.
Dist.: CBS/Fox

BACK STREET 1961
★ ★ ★ **NR Drama 1:47**
Dir: David Miller *Cast:* Susan Hayward, John Gavin, Vera Miles, Charles Drake, Virginia Grey, Reginald Gardiner
▶ Older but glamorous Hayward falls in love with prominent businessman Gavin, whose alcoholic wife Miles won't give him a divorce. Third sound version of Fannie Hurst's best-selling novel is a glossy but superficial soap opera with an emphasis on haute couture.
Dist.: MCA

BACK TO BACK 1990
★ ★ **R Drama 1:30**
☑ Nudity, explicit language, violence
Dir: John Kincade *Cast:* Bill Paxton, Apollonia, Ben Johnson, Susan Anspach, Luke Askew, Todd Field
▶ Paxton returns to his hometown to clear his father, who has been implicated in an armored car robbery. With the loot from the robbery still missing, Apollonia joins the search, and together they learn some terrible secrets from desert old-timer Johnson. Slack melodrama doesn't pack much of a wallop.
Dist.: MGM/UA

BACK TO BATAAN 1945
★ ★ ★ ★ **NR War 1:35 B&W**
Dir: Edward Dmytryk *Cast:* John Wayne, Anthony Quinn, Beulah Bondi, Fely Franquelli, Richard Loo, Philip Ahn
▶ Action-packed World War II drama about the fall of the Philippines to the Japanese. Wayne is a heroic colonel called back from devastating front-line fighting to help defend Bataan; he arrives too late and witnesses the horrific Death March. Quinn, a Filipino rebel, escapes with the help of guerrillas and rejoins Wayne as the Allied powers finally defeat the enemy. Marred somewhat by flag-waving speeches, but overall a riveting war picture.
Dist.: Turner

BACK TO SCHOOL 1986
★ ★ ★ ★ **PG-13 Comedy 1:36**
☑ Brief nudity, explicit language, adult humor
Dir: Alan Metter *Cast:* Rodney Dangerfield, Sally Kellerman, Ned Beatty, Burt Young, Keith Gordon, Robert Downey, Jr., Sam Kinison
▶ Dangerfield is lovably uncouth Thornton Melon, who made his fortune with a chain of "Tall and Fat" clothing stores. He enrolls in college to help his unhappy son Gordon in this very funny and surprisingly charming comedy. Slob Rodney earns respect and a diploma; his usual one-liners are combined with some real sweetness. Able support from Beatty as "Dean" Martin, Downey as Gordon's eccentric roommate, Kinison as a professor who can't forget Nam, and Kellerman as a literature professor who falls for Rodney. **(CC)**
Dist.: HBO

BACK TO THE BEACH 1987
★ **PG Musical/Comedy 1:32**
☑ Adult situations
Dir: Lyndall Hobbs *Cast:* Annette Funicello, Frankie Avalon, Connie Stevens, Lori Loughlin, Tommy Hinkley, Demian Slade
► Two decades after their string of beach movies captivated teens in the early sixties, the "Big Kahuna" Avalon and his wife Funicello have settled into boring domesticity in Ohio. On vacation to visit daughter Loughlin and her beach-bum boyfriend Hinkley in Southern Cal, Avalon and Funicello reprise many of their youthful high jinks, including his attraction to bad-girl bar owner Stevens. Cameos by Bob Denver, Don Adams, Jerry Mathers, Tony Dow, Pee-wee Herman and David Bowie. **(CC)**
Dist.: Paramount

BACK TO THE FUTURE 1985
★ ★ ★ ★ ★ **PG Sci-Fi/Comedy 1:56**
☑ Adult situations, explicit language, mild violence
Dir: Robert Zemeckis *Cast:* Michael J. Fox, Lea Thompson, Christopher Lloyd, Crispin Glover, Tom Wilson
► Enormously popular time travel fantasy from producer Spielberg and Zemeckis. Typical 1980s teenager Fox is catapulted back to the 1950s by nutty inventor Lloyd's time machine. There Fox meets the teenage versions of his future parents, Thompson and Glover, and must play Cupid to save his own life. One complication—Thompson prefers Fox to the wimpy Glover. An intricate, intelligent plot comes to a quite satisfying conclusion. Terrific performances (especially Glover) in a joyous movie that deftly combines comedy, fantasy, sci-fi, and Freud. Followed by two sequels.
(CC)
Dist.: MCA

BACK TO THE FUTURE II 1989
★ ★ ★ ★ **PG Sci-Fi/Comedy 1:45**
☑ Explicit language, violence
Dir: Robert Zemeckis *Cast:* Michael J. Fox, Christopher Lloyd, Lea Thompson, Elizabeth Shue, Thomas F. Wilson, Charles Fleischer
► Sequel to the appealing megablockbuster finds loopy time-travel expert Doc Brown (Lloyd) transporting Marty McFly (Fox) and girlfriend Shue to 2015 so couple can keep their future offspring from trouble. When arch enemy Biff Tannen—now elderly but just as vitriolic—steals the time machine, Marty and Doc pursue him back to both 1955 and an alternate, bleak present that has been changed by Biff's actions. Even more lavish and special-effects jammed than number one, but lacking the charm that made the original so special. Comic highlights include Fox playing his own daughter complete with bouncy blond do. Follow-up: *Back to the Future Part III.* **(CC)**
Dist.: MCA

BACK TO THE FUTURE PART III 1990
★ ★ ★ ★ **PG Sci-Fi/Comedy 1:58**
☑ Explicit language, mild violence
Dir: Robert Zemeckis *Cast:* Michael J. Fox, Christopher Lloyd, Mary Steenburgen, Thomas F. Wilson, Lea Thompson, Elisabeth Shue, Richard Dysart
► Fox time travels to 1885 to save Lloyd from bandit Mad Dog Tannen (Wilson), his potential murderer. However, Lloyd is tempted to stay behind when he falls in love with schoolmarm Steenburgen. Although it lacks the originality of the first and the second's dense plotting, third entry emerges as the most relaxed of the series, a pleasingly old-fashioned, good-humored Western. Choicest bits: the sweet Steenburgen/Lloyd romance, Wilson's villainy, and the "Clint Eastwood" gags.
Dist.: MCA

BAD AND THE BEAUTIFUL, THE 1952
★ ★ **NR Drama 1:58 B&W**
Dir: Vincente Minnelli *Cast:* Lana Turner, Kirk Douglas, Dick Powell, Gloria Grahame, Walter Pidgeon
► Five Oscars, including Best Supporting Actress (Grahame), went to this well-acted, well-written exposé of the movie business and its treacheries. Douglas is terrific as Jonathan Shields, a ruthless movie producer on the skids who attempts to use the people he stepped on to make a comeback. Turner is also fine as an alcoholic actress. **(CC)**
Dist.: MGM/UA ⓒ

BAD BLOOD 1982 New Zealand
★ ★ **NR Drama 1:45**
☑ Adult situations, explicit language, violence
Dir: Mike Newell *Cast:* Jack Thompson, Carol Burns, Donna Akerstein, Dennis Lill
► In World War II New Zealand, authorities worried about a German invasion decide to confiscate all weapons. Dairy farmer Thompson refuses to give up his guns and becomes the object of a manhunt after killing four policemen. Accomplished, brooding drama is based on a true story.
Dist.: HBO

BAD BOYS 1983
★ ★ ★ **R Drama 2:03**
☑ Rape, adult situations, explicit language, violence
Dir: Rick Rosenthal *Cast:* Sean Penn, Ally Sheedy, Reni Santoni, Esai Morales
► Grim but riveting prison film. Penn is outstanding as Mick O'Brien, a tough Chicago street kid sent to a juvenile correctional facility after a shootout. On the inside, he is confronted by Morales, the rival gang leader who blames Mick for his brother's death. Realistic and powerful.
Dist.: HBO

BAD COMPANY 1972
★ ★ **PG Western 1:33**

☑ Adult situations, explicit language, violence
Dir: Robert Benton *Cast:* Jeff Bridges, Barry Brown, John Savage, Jim Davis, David Huddleston, Jerry Houser
▶ During the Civil War, teenage draft dodgers Bridges and Brown form an outlaw gang of runaways. Director Benton's unjustly neglected antiwar Western combines raunchy humor, gritty action, and appealing performances from a wonderful cast of young actors.
Dist.: Paramount

BAD DAY AT BLACK ROCK 1955
★ ★ ★ ★ NR Drama 1:21
Dir: John Sturges *Cast:* Spencer Tracy, Robert Ryan, Anne Francis, Dean Jagger, Walter Brennan, Lee Marvin
▶ In this tense contemporary Western, Tracy plays a one-armed stranger who stops at Black Rock looking for a Japanese farmer. Despite threats from hostile townspeople, he uncovers a terrible conspiracy. Powerful, disturbing moral drama is still relevant today, thanks to a tough script, fine ensemble acting, and innovative use of CinemaScope. Received Oscar nominations for Best Actor (Tracy), Screenplay and Direction.
Dist.: MGM

BAD DREAMS 1988
★ ★ R Horror 1:24
☑ Adult situations, explicit language, graphic violence
Dir: Andrew Fleming *Cast:* Jennifer Rubin, Bruce Abbott, Richard Lynch, Dean Cameron, Harris Yulin
▶ Rubin, the sole survivor of a mass suicide pact led by cult leader Lynch, awakes from a thirteen-year coma and joins a group run by Abbott. Participants in the therapy session start getting killed. Is Lynch back from the dead to wreck the living? Nicely executed debut flick from young NYU grad Fleming and producer Gale Ann Hurd, although derivative plot is reminiscent of the *Nightmare on Elm St.* movies. (CC)
Dist.: CBS/Fox

BADGE 373 1973
★ ★ R Drama 1:56
☑ Adult situations, explicit language, violence
Dir: Howard W. Koch *Cast:* Robert Duvall, Verna Bloom, Henry Darrow, Eddie Egan
▶ Duvall is a super-tough, maverick cop who, after being unfairly suspended from the force, tracks down the killer of his partner and girlfriend. The real-life French Connection cop, Egan, makes a cameo appearance as Duvall's hardboiled superior caught in the hot spot between friendship and the law. Sturdy, well-acted genre effort.
Dist.: Paramount

BAD INFLUENCE 1990
★ ★ ★ ★ R Mystery-Suspense 1:39
☑ Nudity, adult situations, explicit language

Dir: Curtis Hanson *Cast:* Rob Lowe, James Spader, Lisa Zane, Christian Clemenson, Kathleen Wilhoite, Tony Maggio
▶ Weak-willed market analyst Spader loses a well-earned promotion to a co-worker. He meets mysterious drifter Lowe, who teaches him to take what he wants from life. Spader's dark side emerges as they haunt L.A.'s glitzy, drug-infused underworld. But when murder enters the picture, he realizes things have gone too far. Slick, fascinating psychological murder mystery features well-cast Spader and Lowe, who uses his cool good looks to advantage. First film for Lowe after his sex-video controversy including such a scene as a main plot twist. (CC)
Dist.: RCA/Columbia

BADLANDS 1974
★ ★ ★ PG Drama 1:35
☑ Violence
Dir: Terrence Malick *Cast:* Martin Sheen, Sissy Spacek, Warren Oates, Ramon Bieri, Alan Vint
▶ Based on the true story of Charles Starkweather's murderous binge that left ten people dead, this beautifully photographed and hauntingly scored film contains memorable performances by Sheen and Spacek as two young adults on an all-American joyride/killing spree across the Midwest. When first released, many were shocked by this portrait of two cool, detached criminals mostly bored by their crimes. Today, most critics consider the film a modern classic.
Dist.: Warner

BAD MANNERS 1984
★ ★ R Comedy 1:22
☑ Brief nudity, adult situations, explicit language, violence, adult humor
Dir: Robert Houston *Cast:* Karen Black, Martin Mull, Murphy Dunne, Anne De Salvo
▶ Mildly offensive comedy about life in a Catholic orphanage. De Salvo is Sister Serena, who runs the place with prisonlike discipline, while Mull and Black play a ditsy affluent couple who get more than they bargained for when they adopt a rebellious foundling.
Dist.: HBO

BADMAN'S TERRITORY 1946
★ ★ NR Western 1:37 B&W
Dir: Tim Whelan *Cast:* Randolph Scott, Ann Richards, Gabby Hayes, Ray Collins, James Warren, Morgan Conway
▶ While searching for his brother, sheriff Scott rides into a part of Oklahoma that's used as a hideout for the likes of the James brothers, the Daltons, Belle Starr, and other legendary baddies. Even with so many blue ribbon outlaws on hand, the real villain turns out to be U.S. marshal Conway, who incites trouble to further his political career. Superior Western is well-acted and tightly scripted.
Dist.: Turner

BAD MEDICINE 1985
★ ★ **PG-13 Comedy 1:36**
☑ Adult situations, explicit language, adult humor
Dir: Harvey Miller   *Cast:* Steve Guttenberg, Alan Arkin, Julie Hagerty, Bill Macy
▶ Bad grades force med student Guttenberg south of the border for his degree, where he enrolls in a run-down institution headed by Arkin (whose Spanish accent out-Fernandos Billy Crystal). After a caustic and funny first half, the film loses the courage of its cynicism and turns into a mushy drama of students helping out an impoverished village.   (CC)
Dist.: CBS/Fox

BAD NEWS BEARS, THE 1976
★ ★ ★ ★ ★ **PG Comedy/Family 1:42**
☑ Explicit language
Dir: Michael Ritchie   *Cast:* Walter Matthau, Tatum O'Neal, Vic Morrow, Joyce Van Patten, Jackie Earle Haley
▶ Matthau, an alcoholic pool-cleaner and ex-minor leaguer, is recruited to coach an inept Little League team. With the help of girl pitcher O'Neal, he turns the Bears into winners. Consistently funny baseball comedy with likable characters will appeal to anybody who's ever worn a baseball glove. Nifty direction by Ritchie. Parents should note that the kids' language is a bit spicy.
Dist.: Paramount

BAD NEWS BEARS GO TO JAPAN, THE 1978
★ ★ **PG Comedy/Family 1:32**
☑ Explicit language
Dir: John Berry   *Cast:* Tony Curtis, Jackie Earle Haley, Matthew D. Anton, Erin Blunt, George Gonzales
▶ Seedy huckster Curtis cons the Little Leaguer Bears into a Japanese tour, but by the end the foulmouthed tykes persuade him to go straight. Broad comedy, baseball action, plus some exotic Japanese locations add up to lighweight, easygoing family fare. Amusing cameo by ABC sports commentator Dick Button.
Dist.: Paramount

BAD NEWS BEARS IN BREAKING TRAINING, THE 1977
★ ★ ★ **PG Comedy/Family 1:39**
☑ Explicit language
Dir: Michael Pressman   *Cast:* William Devane, Clifton James, Jackie Earle Haley, Jimmy Baio, Chris Barnes
▶ Little Leaguers from the popular *Bad News Bears* are back in this first of two sequels. This time out, team leader Haley must recruit his estranged dad Devane to be the coach before the kids can play in the Houston Astrodome. Very good-natured and amusing.
Dist.: Paramount

BAD SEED, THE 1956
★ ★ **NR Drama 2:09 B&W**
Dir: Mervyn LeRoy   *Cast:* Nancy Kelly, Patty McCormack, Henry Jones, Eileen Heckart, Evelyn Varden, Jesse White
▶ Child McCormack murders classmate for penmanship medal, then commits other killings. Only horrified mom Kelly suspects the truth. An unnerving experience. Oscar-nominated McCormack delivers perhaps the most chilling child performance ever; Kelly and Heckart were also nominated. Based on the Maxwell Anderson play.
Dist.: Warner

BAD TASTE 1988 New Zealand
★ **NR Sci-Fi 1:30**
☑ Nudity, explicit language, graphic violence
Dir: Peter Jackson   *Cast:* Peter Jackson, Pete O'Herne, Mike Minett, Terry Potter, Craig Smith, Doug Wren
▶ Humans harvested from a small town in New Zealand are the stuff of fast meals for aliens led by Lord Crumb (Wren). Producer/director/star Jackson leads a team of government alien-busters. Between the battles and the people-eating, badly directed cult hit has guts and gore to the absolute max. For strong stomachs.
Dist.: Magnum

BAGDAD CAFE 1988 West German
★ **PG Comedy 1:31**
☑ Nudity, explicit language
Dir: Percy Adlon   *Cast:* Marianne Sägebrecht, Jack Palance, CCH Pounder, Christine Kaufmann, Monica Calhoun, George Aguilar
▶ Stranded by her husband in the Mojave Desert, German tourist Sägebrecht seeks refuge in a seedy cafe/motel. Her presence brings new life to angry owner Pounder and clientele of irregulars like mute tattoo artist Kaufmann and retired Hollywood set painter Palance. Offbeat comedy recommended to those looking for something different.   (CC)
Dist.: Virgin

BAIL JUMPER 1990
☆ **NR Comedy 1:36**
☑ Explicit language
Dir: Christian Faber   *Cast:* Eszter Balint, B. J. Spalding, Tony Askin, Bo Brinkman, Aleandra Auder, Joie Lee
▶ Spunky Balint and gloomy boyfriend Spalding are so much in love they actually give off a type of kinetic enegy. Getting heat for their various illegal activities, the Missouri pair drives to Staten Island, inadvertently setting off twisters, earthquakes, and other natural disasters on the way. Funny and refreshing cult item may be too slow and methodical for some.
Dist.: Angelika

BAJA OKLAHOMA 1988
★ ★ ★ **NR Drama/MFTV 1:45**
☑ Nudity, adult situations
Dir: Bobby Roth   *Cast:* Lesley Ann Warren,

Peter Coyote, Swoosie Kurtz, William Forsythe, Willie Nelson
▶ Bored barmaid Warren longs to escape her
job, her rocky marriage and runaway daughter. Her prayers are answered by the reappearance of ex-boyfriend Coyote, who arranges for her to sing with Willie Nelson. Based
on Dan Jenkins's best-selling novel, this amiable country-western fairy tale features an original soundtrack with eight new songs by Nelson, Emmylou Harris and others.
Dist.: Warner

BAKER'S WIFE, THE 1938 French
☆ **NR Comedy 2:04 B&W**
Dir: Marcel Pagnol *Cast:* Raimu, Ginette
Leclerc, Charles Moulin, Robert Vattier, Robert Brassac
▶ It's crisis time in a small French village when
the wife of local baker Raimu runs off with a
shepherd and the heartsick breadman
refuses to make another loaf until she returns.
Panicked townspeople set out to find the errant spouse, return her to her husband, and
get his hot loaves back on their tables. Warm,
hilarious, and perfectly lighthearted. Ⓢ
Dist.: Corinth

BALBOA 1982
★ **NR Drama 1:31**
Ⓥ Nudity, adult situations, explicit language
Dir: James Polakof *Cast:* Tony Curtis, Carol
Lynley, Steve Kanaly, Lance Armstrong, Joy
Brent, Cassandra Peterson
▶ Entrepreneur Curtis wants to bring legalized
gambling to an island off California, but he's
opposed by a consortium of civic types and
business enemies, including councilman Kanaly, ex-wife Peterson (TV horror host Elvira),
and lawyer Armstrong. To outwit his enemies,
Curtis has former madam Brent appointed to
the building commission, and engages in
threats, blackmail, and other skullduggery. Direct-to-video soap opera is listless and talky.
Dist.: Vestron

BALLAD OF A GUNFIGHTER 1964
★ **NR Western 1:24 B&W**
Dir: Bill Ward *Cast:* Marty Robbins, Joyce
Reed, Bob Barron, Nestor Paiva, Michael
Davis, Laurette Luez
▶ Real-life country star Robbins plays himself
in this low-budget Western loosely based on
"El Paso," his hit song about a cowpoke who
falls for a Mexican girl, only to fall afoul of her
bandit boyfriend. Robbins fans won't want to
miss the singer's first screen appearance, but
there's little here for others.
Dist.: Prism

BALLAD OF CABLE HOGUE, THE 1970
★ ★ ★ ★ **R Western/Comedy 2:01**
Ⓥ Brief nudity, adult situations, explicit lan-
    guage, violence
Dir: Sam Peckinpah *Cast:* Jason Robards,
Stella Stevens, David Warner, Strother Mar-
tin, Slim Pickens
▶ Charming desert-rat Robards, left to die by

his villainous partners, discovers water and
prospers as rest-stop proprietor on stage
route. Stevens, the cow-town harlot, romances and then abandons Robards for a
rich man in Frisco. Warner plays an amiable
wandering preacher. Although highly praised
by critics, Peckinpah fans expecting another
The Wild Bunch may be disappointed in this
character-rich but change-of-pace oater.
Dist.: Warner

BALLAD OF GREGORIO CORTEZ, THE 1983
★ ★ **PG Western 1:39**
Ⓥ Explicit language, graphic violence
Dir: Robert M. Young *Cast:* Edward James
Olmos, James Gammon, Tom Bower, Bruce
McGill, Alan Vint
▶ Mexican cowhand Olmos is unjustly ac-
cused of horse theft and pursued by 600 Texas
Rangers in the biggest manhunt in the state's
history. Artfully re-creating Texas bordertowns
and their inhabitants, this action-packed
Western was developed by Robert Redford's
Sundance Institute and praised for its fresh
and original vision, climactic courtroom
scene, and naturalistic style. Based on a true
1901 incident
Dist.: Nelson

BALLAD OF NARAYAMA, THE 1983
Japanese
☆ **NR Drama 2:10**
Ⓥ Nudity, adult situations, violence
Dir: Shohei Imamura *Cast:* Ken Ogata,
Sumiko Sakamoto, Takejo Aki, Tonpei Hidari,
Shoichi Ozawa
▶ The family of elderly Sakamoto can't bear
to lose her, even though the custom in their
famine-plagued village is for old people to
abandon themselves on the cruel slopes of
Mount Narayama. Sakamoto deliberately
weakens herself, even bashes out her own
teeth, so she can have what she considers the
privilege of perishing as her ancestors did. Despite wonderfully crisp photography, film is
difficult to watch. Ⓢ
Dist.: Janus

BALL OF FIRE 1941
★ ★ ★ ★ **NR Comedy 1:52 B&W**
Dir: Howard Hawks *Cast:* Gary Cooper,
Barbara Stanwyck, Dana Andrews, Oscar
Homolka, Henry Travers, Dan Duryea
▶ Stanwyck is Sugarpuss O'Shea, a nightclub
singer on the lam, who holes up with eight
professors working on a dictionary of Ameri-
can slang, led by gangly Cooper. Coop and
Babs fall in love in this engaging comedy.
Stanwyck has never been sexier, especially in
the classic scene where she teaches Cooper
the meaning of "yum yum."
Dist.: Nelson

BALTIMORE BULLET, THE 1980
★ ★ ★ ★ **PG Drama/Sports 1:43**
Ⓥ Brief nudity, adult situations, explicit lan-
    guage
Dir: Robert Ellis Miller *Cast:* James Coburn,

Omar Sharif, Bruce Boxleitner, Ronee Blakley, Jack O'Halloran
▶ Slick, fast-talking pool hustler Coburn and young partner Boxleitner must raise big money to play a high-stakes rematch with their nemesis Sharif. Simple story and average production values, but good location shooting provides grit and reality. Some remarkable billiards action includes guest appearances by well-known pool sharks.
Dist.: Nelson

BAMBI 1942
★ ★ ★ ★ ★ **G Animation 1:09**
Dir: David Hand *Cast:* Voices of Bobby Stewart, Peter Behn, Stan Alexander
▶ Great Disney animated feature helped ensure the studio's status as producer of classic family entertainment. Fawn Bambi, the new prince of the forest, cavorts with Thumper the Rabbit and Flower the Skunk. When Bambi's mother is shot by hunters, Bambi is guided by his father. Bambi learns his lessons well, and when a forest fire threatens, he and lady love Phylline escape. Exquisitely drawn and detailed, particularly the fire scene which may be the art form at its finest. As with many of the Disney animated films, very young children may be deeply affected by some of the more frightening scenes.
Dist.: Buena Vista

BANANAS 1971
★ ★ **PG Comedy 1:22**
☑ Adult situations, adult humor
Dir: Woody Allen *Cast:* Woody Allen, Louise Lasser, Carlos Montalban, Howard Cosell
▶ Allen is Fielding Mellish, a sex-starved gadget-tester who falls hopelessly in love with Lasser (the then real-life Mrs. Allen), a young political activist. He follows her to the banana republic of San Marcos where he inadvertently manages to unseat the country's dictator and become president. Howard Cosell makes an appearance to host both San Marcos's Assassination of the Week and, later, the on-camera consummation of Allen's marriage. Pure vintage Allen.
Dist.: CBS/Fox

BAND OF OUTSIDERS 1964 French
☆ **NR Drama 1:35 B&W**
Dir: Jean-Luc Godard *Cast:* Anna Karina, Claude Brasseur, Sami Frey, Louisa Colpeyn, Daniele Girard
▶ Three young friends hatch fantasy crimes in a Parisian cafe. With no regard for the consequences, they decide to go through with an actual burglary. Although the subject matter is bleak, whimsical tone and interesting asides (including an impromptu song-and-dance routine) make this one of Godard's most accessible films. French title: *Bande à Part.*
Ⓢ
Dist.: Various

BAND OF THE HAND 1986
★ ★ ★ ★ **R Action-Adventure 1:49**

☑ Adult situations, explicit language, violence
Dir: Paul Michael Glaser *Cast:* Stephen Lang, Michael Carmine, Lauren Holly, John Cameron Mitchell, Danielle Quinn
▶ Crusading Vietnam vet Lang takes five juvenile delinquents into the Florida swamps and trains them to be crimefighters. Once reformed, the fearsome fivesome return to the city to take on a drug lord. Slick, well-made action flick.
Dist.: RCA/Columbia

BANDOLERO! 1968
★ ★ ★ **PG Western 1:47**
☑ Mild violence
Dir: Andrew V. McLaglen *Cast:* James Stewart, Dean Martin, Raquel Welch, George Kennedy, Andrew Prine
▶ Outlaw brothers Stewart and Martin kidnap beautiful widow Welch while fleeing the forces of the law led by sheriff Kennedy. Tough Western adds nothing new to the genre but is generally above average. Stewart stands out among the cast. **(CC)**
Dist.: CBS/Fox

BAND WAGON, THE 1953
★ ★ ★ ★ **NR Musical 1:51**
Dir: Vincente Minnelli *Cast:* Fred Astaire, Cyd Charisse, Oscar Levant, Nanette Fabray, Jack Buchanan
▶ Down-on-his-luck Hollywood star Astaire makes a stab at a Broadway comeback in this classic MGM musical. Wonderful score by Howard Dietz and Arthur Schwartz includes the romantic dance duet "Dancing in the Dark," "A Shine on Your Shoes," "That's Entertainment." Astaire, Fabray, and Buchanan have a great time as little brats in the famous "Triplets" number.
Dist.: MGM/UA

BANG THE DRUM SLOWLY 1973
★ ★ ★ ★ **PG Drama/Sports 1:38**
☑ Brief nudity, adult situations, explicit language
Dir: John Hancock *Cast:* Robert De Niro, Michael Moriarty, Vincent Gardenia, Heather MacRae, Ann Wedgeworth, Danny Aiello
▶ Touching drama of the friendship between baseball players Moriarty and De Niro, who is dying of Hodgkin's Disease. Moriarty is the good-looking "golden boy" pitcher who stands by dim-witted loser De Niro even when his teammates (unaware of De Niro's condition) rag him about the relationship. Sensitively directed by Hancock and adapted by Mark Harris from his novel.
Dist.: Paramount

BANK DICK, THE 1940
★ ★ ★ **NR Comedy 1:19 B&W**
Dir: Edward Cline *Cast:* W. C. Fields, Cora Witherspoon, Una Merkel, Franklin Pangborn, Shemp Howard
▶ Quintessential vehicle for the bulbous-

nosed Fields playing the aptly named Egbert Souse, who prefers drinking at his favorite bar (where the bartender is Howard of the Three Stooges) to hard work. Souse parlays accidental heroism into gigs as a bank guard and film director. Written by Fields under the pseudonym Mahatma Kane Jeeves.
Dist.: MCA

BANKER, THE 1989
★ ★ R Crime 1:35
☑ Nudity, adult situations, explicit language, violence
Dir: William Webb *Cast:* Robert Forster, Duncan Regehr, Shanna Reed, Jeff Conaway, Leif Garrett, Richard Roundtree
▶ Upscale banker Regehr is a serial killer specializing in prostitutes. Cop Forster investigates as his ex-girlfriend Reed, a TV newswoman, covers the story and becomes Regher's next target. Kinky tale promises more than it delivers; weak performance by Conaway as a pimp named "Cowboy."
Dist.: Virgin

BANK SHOT 1974
★ ★ PG Comedy/Crime 1:23
☑ Adult situations, explicit language
Dir: Gower Champion *Cast:* George C. Scott, Joanna Cassidy, Sorrell Booke, Bob Balaban, G. Wood, Clifton James
▶ Crook Scott and his gang set sights on unique bank heist: they plot to steal the entire building by towing it away. Cute caper from a novel by Donald Westlake; Scott and Cassidy are pleasant company.
Dist.: Wood Knapp

BARABBAS 1962
★ ★ ★ ★ NR Drama 2:15
Dir: Richard Fleischer *Cast:* Anthony Quinn, Silvana Mangano, Arthur Kennedy, Katy Jurado, Harry Andrews, Vittorio Gassman, Jack Palance, Ernest Borgnine
▶ Biblical epic about the condemned murderer who was freed in place of Christ is long but consistently engrossing. Quinn gives a determined performance as Barabbas, a nonbeliever who spends years as a slave and gladiator struggling to understand the meaning of Christ's life. Adaptation of a novel by Nobel laureate Par Lagerkvist is filled with spectacle and action.
Dist.: RCA/Columbia

BARBARELLA 1968 French/Italian
★ PG Sci-Fi 1:38
☑ Brief nudity, adult situations, explicit language
Dir: Roger Vadim *Cast:* Jane Fonda, Milo O'Shea, John Phillip Law, David Hemmings
▶ Sexy comic strip adaptation directed by Fonda's then husband Roger Vadim was controversial in its initial release but seems relatively tame now. Fonda is the sci-fi heroine of the future who takes on an evil villainess in a world where sex has been reduced to a handshake and a pill. Fonda, in her pre-political

period, performs a free-floating striptease and wears various scanty costumes. Campy fun.
Dist.: Paramount

BARBARIAN AND THE GEISHA, THE 1958
★ ★ NR Biography 1:45
Dir: John Huston *Cast:* John Wayne, Eiko Ando, Sam Jaffe, So Yamamura, Norman Thomson, James Robbins
▶ Appointed ambassador to Japan in the mid-nineteenth century, Townsend Harris (Wayne) finds his peaceful goals blocked by suspicious natives until a servant (Ando) sent to spy on him falls in love. Wayne is miscast in this slow-moving, heavily fictionalized biography. **(CC)**
Dist.: CBS/Fox

BARBARIAN QUEEN 1985 Argentinian
☆ R Action-Adventure 1:11
☑ Rape, nudity, adult situations, explicit language, violence
Dir: Hector Olivera *Cast:* Lana Clarkson, Katt Shea, Dawn Dunlap, Susana Traverso
▶ Barbarian queen Clarkson's wedding day is interrupted by tribe that enslaves her intended and rapes and kills villagers; Clarkson and her army of busty friends vow vengeance. Comic book story with atrocious acting, so-so production values, and cheesy costumes. Sample dialogue: "Nothing like a virgin to brighten a man's morning."
Dist.: Vestron

BARBARIANS, THE 1987
★ R Action-Adventure 1:27
☑ Nudity, adult situations, explicit language, graphic violence
Dir: Ruggero Deodato *Cast:* Peter Paul, David Paul, Richard Lynch, Eva La Rue, Virginia Bryant, Sheeba Alahani
▶ The Paul brothers play twins condemned as children to slave labor by evil overlord Lynch and now grown into superstrong, untamed young men. Aided by cute, wise-cracking young La Rue, they seek revenge against Lynch while rescuing beautiful queen Bryant. Body-building fans will enjoy the Pauls' bulging muscles, but others will be left cold by adventure set in "some other time and place."
Dist.: Media

BARBAROSA 1982
★ ★ ★ PG Western 1:30
☑ Explicit language, violence
Dir: Fred Schepisi *Cast:* Willie Nelson, Gary Busey, Gilbert Roland, Isela Vega
▶ Critically praised Western shows how legendary outlaw Nelson teaches protégé Busey to survive in the wilderness. Pursued by bounty hunters and killers, they take refuge in a small Mexican village. Stunning photography and Nelson's commanding presence triumph over a sometimes rambling plot. Screen veteran Roland contributes a memorable cameo.
Dist.: J2 Communications

BARBARY COAST 1935
★★ NR Drama 1:37 B&W
Dir: Howard Hawks *Cast:* Miriam Hopkins,
Edward G. Robinson, Joel McCrea, Walter
Brennan, Brian Donlevy, Harry Carey
▶ Fast-paced, rollicking adventure set in 1849
San Francisco with Hopkins as a genteel East-
erner pursued by gangster Robinson and hon-
est gold prospector McCrea. Screenplay by
Ben Hecht and Charles MacArthur spices up
the romantic triangle with bawdy jokes and
innuendoes; action and sets are superb.
Dist.: Nelson

BAREFOOT CONTESSA, THE 1954
★★★ NR Drama 2:08
Dir: Joseph L. Mankiewicz *Cast:* Humphrey
Bogart, Ava Gardner, Edmond O'Brien,
Marius Goring, Rossano Brazzi, Valentina
Cortese
▶ Dancer Gardner is plucked from obscurity
to stardom by director Bogart. However, success has its bitter side: she gets involved with
wealthy tycoon Goring and then marries nobleman Brazzi, whose impotence sets up an
unhappy conclusion. Overdone but quite entertaining; O'Brien does an Oscar-winning,
scene-stealing turn as the press agent.
Dist.: CBS/Fox

BAREFOOT EXECUTIVE, THE 1971
★★★★ G Family 1:36
Dir: Robert Butler *Cast:* Kurt Russell, Joe
Flynn, Harry Morgan, Wally Cox, Heather
North, John Ritter
▶ A television network struggles in the ratings
until Russell finds a chimpanzee with the
unique ability to pick hit shows. The network
can suddenly do no wrong and Russell rises to
the top until the real reason for his animal
cunning comes out. Frisky fun; kids will love the
ape and adults will enjoy the satire.
Dist.: Buena Vista

BAREFOOT IN THE PARK 1967
★★★★ G Comedy 1:45
Dir: Gene Saks *Cast:* Robert Redford, Jane
Fonda, Charles Boyer, Mildred Natwick,
Herb Edelman
▶ Newlywed lawyer Redford and free-spirited
wife Fonda move into a run-down Greenwich
Village apartment. They fight over his stuffi-
ness, as symbolized by his refusal to go "bare-
foot in the park," while Fonda's mom Natwick
is wooed by old charmer Boyer. Youthful, ro-
mantic fun from Neil Simon.
Dist.: Paramount

BARFLY 1987
★★ R Drama 1:39
☑ Nudity, adult situations, explicit lan-
guage, violence
Dir: Barbet Schroeder *Cast:* Mickey Rourke,
Faye Dunaway, Alice Krige, Jack Nance, J.
C. Quinn, Frank Stallone
▶ Convincing but downbeat depiction of life
on the scuzzy side of Los Angeles. Rourke is
Henry, an alcoholic writer who prefers drinking

to the typewriter, Dunaway the fellow alcoholic who shares his bottle and bed. Meandering story line but fine performances from
the two leads. Rourke seems born to play this
part while Dunaway, eschewing her usual
glamour, is surprisingly effective. Based on the
life of the film's screenwriter, poet Charles
Bukowski. **(CC)**
Dist.: Warner

BARKLEYS OF BROADWAY, THE 1949
★★★ NR Musical 1:49
Dir: Charles Walters *Cast:* Fred Astaire, Gin-
ger Rogers, Oscar Levant, Billie Burke, Gale
Robbins
▶ Last Astaire-Rogers film, their only one in
color, is a modest story about a famous musi-
cal team that breaks up when Rogers pursues
a serious acting career. An elegant "They
Can't Take That Away from Me" and Astaire's
witty special effects solo "Shoes With Wings
On" are the highlights.
Dist.: MGM/UA

BARON BLOOD 1972 Italian
☆ PG Horror 1:30
☑ Adult situations, violence
Dir: Mario Bava *Cast:* Joseph Cotten, Elke
Sommer, Massimo Girotti, Rada Rassimov,
Antonio Canafora
▶ Italian horror master Bava brings style and
wit to predictable tale about heir to spooky
castle who is persuaded by Sommer to turn it
into a hotel. He accidentally brings his evil
ancestor Cotten back to life. Resulting mur-
ders are shown in a series of tense sequences.
Dist.: HBO

BARRACUDA 1978
★★ PG Horror 1:30
☑ Explicit language, violence
Dir: Harry Kerwin *Cast:* Wayne-David Craw-
ford, Jason Evers, Bert Freed, Roberta Leigh-
ton
▶ Marine biology students are arrested after
breaking into a chemical plant to take sam-
ples of water they believe has been polluted.
When fishermen start disappearing, the police
turn to the students for help with the case.
Typical drive-in fare with a cast of unknowns.
Dist.: VidAmerica

BARRY LYNDON 1975 British
★★★ PG Drama 3:04
☑ Violence
Dir: Stanley Kubrick *Cast:* Ryan O'Neal,
Marisa Berenson, Patrick Magee, Hardy
Kruger, Steven Berkoff
▶ Master filmmaker Kubrick sumptuously re-
creates the eighteenth century in this adap-
tation of William Makepeace Thackeray's
novel of the rise and eventual ruin of naive but
ambitious Irishman O'Neal in English society.
Natural lighting and painterly visuals enhance
this physically beautiful film. The pace is some-
what slow but the story is engrossing. Oscars

for Costume Design, Cinematography, Musical Score, and Art Direction.
Dist.: Warner

BARTLEBY 1972 British
★ **NR Drama 1:18**
☑ Adult situations
Dir: Anthony Friedmann   *Cast:* Paul Scofield, John McEnery, Thorley Walters, Colin Jeavons
▶ Clerk McEnery isolates himself from society, refusing Scofield's commands without explanation. Scofield fires McEnery but his own dormant humanity is awakened and he becomes drawn to McEnery's plight. Herman Melville's classic tale of nineteenth-century Wall Street has been transposed to modern London but this adaptation is otherwise faithful; superb performances by Scofield and McEnery.
Dist.: Corinth

BASIC TRAINING 1985
★ **R Comedy 1:25**
☑ Nudity, strong sexual content, explicit language
Dir: Andrew Sugarman   *Cast:* Ann Dusenberry, Rhonda Shear, Marty Brill, Angela Aames, Walter Gotell
▶ Glossy professional-looking sex comedy containing all the genre conventions—gratuitous sex, bathroom jokes, and adolescent tone. Dusenberry comes to Washington, D.C., to start a career in government, only to find her bosses more interested in her body than in her work. Subsequently, and to no one's surprise, she uses her female wiles to ascend the Washington ladder.
Dist.: Vestron

BASKET CASE 1982
☆ **R Horror 1:23**
☑ Nudity, adult situations, explicit language, graphic violence
Dir: Frank Henenlotter   *Cast:* Kevin Van Hentenryck, Terri Susan Smith, Beverly Bonner, Lloyd Pace
▶ Low-budget splatter film about young Van Hentenryck, who carries his detached Siamese twin around in a wicker basket. They travel to New York to kill the doctors responsible for separating them. Lowbrow humor, genuinely weird characters, and copious bloodletting made this a cult favorite at midnight screenings. A much more graphic X-rated version is also available.
Dist.: Media

BASKET CASE 2 1990
★★ **R Horror 1:29**
☑ Adult situations, explicit language, graphic violence
Dir: Frank Henenlotter   *Cast:* Kevin Von Hentenryck, Annie Ross, Kathryn Meisle, Heather Rattray, Jason Evers
▶ Van Hentenryk and his partially formed Siamese twin brother join a therapy group for freaks run by Ross out of her house on Staten Island. Assemblage of mutants may be the most grotesque since the bar scene in *Star Wars*, and a million times more sickening. Face-eating, basket-bound "hero" actually finds a mate in this stomach-turning sequel. Horror fans will get the joke, but all others stay away.
Dist.: SGE

BATAAN 1943
★★★ **NR War 1:54 B&W**
Dir: Tay Garnett   *Cast:* Robert Taylor, George Murphy, Thomas Mitchell, Lloyd Nolan, Lee Bowman, Robert Walker
▶ Grim, realistic World War II drama focusing on heroic defense of the Philippines by vastly outnumbered American and native troops. Sturdy cast (including Walker in his film debut as a naive recruit) retains their high spirits despite steadily advancing Japanese. Taylor is particularly convincing in his last film before entering Navy as fighter pilot.
Dist.: MGM/UA

BATMAN 1966
★ **NR Action-Adventure 1:45**
Dir: Leslie H. Martinson   *Cast:* Adam West, Burt Ward, Burgess Meredith, Cesar Romero, Lee Meriwether, Frank Gorshin
▶ The ABC-TV series was so popular that it spawned a feature film at the height of its success. West and Ward as the Caped Crusader and Robin the Boy Wonder are besieged by archenemies Joker (Romero), Penguin (Meredith), Catwoman (Meriwether), and Riddler (Gorshin). Tongue-in-cheek comic-book fun. Followed twenty-three years later by a big-budget version. **(CC)**
Dist.: CBS/Fox

BATMAN 1989
★★★★ **PG-13 Action-Adventure 2:06**
☑ Explicit language, violence
Dir: Tim Burton   *Cast:* Jack Nicholson, Michael Keaton, Kim Basinger, Robert Wuhl, Pat Hingle, Billy Dee Williams, Michael Gough, Jack Palance, Jerry Hall
▶ Millionaire Bruce Wayne (Keaton), orphaned as a child by criminal's bullets, assumes Caped Crusader identity to terrorize Gotham City bad guys. Nicholson, disfigured after Batman drops him in acid vat, emerges as the malevolent Joker to start a crime wave and compete with Batman for reporter Basinger's affections. Gigantic blockbuster strives for both slam-bang action and psychological complexity; magnificently flamboyant Nicholson is complimented by a sober, reflective Keaton. Arrestingly dark Oscar-winning art direction by Anton Furst. Music by Danny Elfman and Prince. **(CC)**
Dist.: Warner

BAT PEOPLE, THE 1974
☆ **PG Horror 1:35**
☑ Explicit language, violence
Dir: Jerry Jameson   *Cast:* Stewart Moss, Ma-

rianne McAndrew, Michael Pataki, Paul Carr, Arthur Space

► On their honeymoon at a ski resort, physician Moss and his wife McAndrew take a side trip to some caverns where he's bitten by a bat. Hallucinations and nightmares about bats ensue, so Moss is hospitalized, but modern medicine can't cure his ailment, and in fact his woes have just begun. Low-budget creature feature mainly for die-hards. Also known as *Angel of Fear*.

Dist.: HBO

BATTERIES NOT INCLUDED 1987
★★★★ PG Sci-Fi 1:46
☑ Explicit language, violence
Dir: Matthew Robbins ***Cast:*** Hume Cronyn, Jessica Tandy, Frank McRae, Elizabeth Peña, Michael Carmine

► Real estate developers harass elderly couple Cronyn and Tandy and other inhabitants of a New York tenement until midget alien spaceships miraculously appear to aid the beleaguered tenants. Special effects hardware tends to outshine the human characters, but basically a heartwarming, wholesome fantasy from producer Steven Spielberg.

Dist.: MCA

BATTLE BEYOND THE STARS 1980
★★ PG Sci-Fi 1:43
☑ Adult situations, adult humor
Dir: Jimmy T. Murakami ***Cast:*** Richard Thomas, Robert Vaughn, George Peppard, John Saxon, Sam Jaffe, Sybil Danning

► When the planet Akir faces destruction at the hands of evil villains, Thomas rounds up interplanetary mercenaries to aid his people. Modest but amusing low-budget sci-fi designed by Roger Corman to capitalize on the *Star Wars* phenomenon (he reused the sets in numerous other films). John Sayles based his screenplay on *The Seven Samurai*.

Dist.: Vestron

BATTLE CRY 1955
★★★ NR War 2:28
Dir: Raoul Walsh ***Cast:*** Van Heflin, Aldo Ray, Mona Freeman, Nancy Olson, James Whitmore, Raymond Massey, Tab Hunter, Dorothy Malone, Anne Francis, Fess Parker

► Elaborate but unfocused adaptation of a Leon Uris best-seller follows the romances of a group of Marines training for battle in the Pacific during World War II. Heflin convincingly portrays the hardened major in charge of the recruits; Ray and Olson conduct a steamy affair. Score by Max Steiner received an Oscar nomination.

Dist.: Warner

BATTLE FOR THE PLANET OF THE APES 1973
★★★ G Sci-Fi 1:26
Dir: J. Lee Thompson ***Cast:*** Roddy McDowall, Claude Akins, John Huston, Natalie Trundy, Lew Ayres, Paul Williams

► Can apes and humans live in peace or are they doomed to fight out the cycle of war enacted in the first four films? Forward-thinking chimpanzee McDowall opts for peace but militaristic gorilla Akins opposes him. Last installment in the series ends on an upbeat note. (CC)

Dist.: Playhouse

BATTLE OF ALGIERS, THE 1966 Italian/Algerian
★ PG Drama 2:05 B&W
☑ Graphic violence
Dir: Gillo Pontecorvo ***Cast:*** Jean Martin, Yacef Saadi, Brahim Haggiag, Tommaso Neri, Fawzia El Kader

► Acclaimed docudrama about Algeria's struggle for independence from France uses graphic, hard-hitting camerawork to show the revolution in human terms. Film's heavy anti-French bias and pseudodocumentary tone raised considerable controversy on release, but it's still an undeniably powerful indictment. [S]

Dist.: Axon

BATTLE OF BRITAIN 1969 British
★★★ G War 2:12
Dir: Guy Hamilton ***Cast:*** Harry Andrews, Michael Caine, Trevor Howard, Curt Jurgens, Kenneth More, Laurence Olivier, Christopher Plummer, Michael Redgrave, Ralph Richardson, Robert Shaw, Susannah York

► Big budget drama about the defense of England against the Nazi Luftwaffe soars during brilliant dogfight sequences; earthbound scenes sink into clichés. Olivier gives a crafty performance as Air Chief Marshal Hugh Dowding, but most roles are as small as cameos. William Walton contributed to the score.

Dist.: MGM/UA

BATTLE OF THE BULGE 1965
★★ NR War 2:35
Dir: Ken Annakin ***Cast:*** Henry Fonda, Robert Shaw, Robert Ryan, Dana Andrews, George Montgomery, Pier Angeli, Telly Savalas, Ty Hardin, Charles Bronson

► Disappointing account of crucial World War II battle sacrifices realism for Hollywood heroics. Shaw is convincing as the German colonel who masterminds the surprise Nazi tank attack in the Ardennes, but Fonda and Ryan are saddled with thankless roles as American officers ill-prepared to meet the onslaught. Expensive, large-scale drama is filled with historical blunders.

Dist.: Warner

BATTLE OF THE SEXES, THE 1960 British
★ NR Comedy 1:30 B&W
Dir: Charles Crichton ***Cast:*** Peter Sellers, Robert Morley, Constance Cummings, Ernest Thesiger, Jameson Clark

► At an Edinburgh textile company, Scottish accountant Sellers reacts with horror when American efficiency expert Cummings changes corporate policies. When he fails to

seduce Cummings, he attempts to murder her. Neat comic turn by Sellers highlights a funny black comedy. Cummings is a worthy foil. Based on a James Thurber short story.
Dist.: Various

BATTLE OF THE WORLDS 1961 Italian
☆ **NR Sci-Fi 1:24 B&W**
Dir: Anthony Dawson (Antonio Margheriti)
Cast: Claude Rains, Bill Carter, Umberto Orsini, Maya Brent
▶ Earth is faced with destruction from a planet heading its way; Rains is the elderly scientist who discovers the secrets of the alien world, including the computer that controls it. Italian import is surprisingly thoughtful, with the wonderful Rains giving a deeply felt performance even under low-budget circumstances.
Dist.: Sinister

BATTLESHIP POTEMKIN 1925 Russian
★ **NR Drama 1:05 B&W**
Dir: Sergei Eisenstein *Cast:* Alexander Antonov, Vladmir Barsky, Grigory Alexandrov, Mikhail Gomorov, Levchenko, Repnikova
▶ Silent film depicts the ill-fated 1905 uprising against the Russian czar by focusing on the mutiny aboard a warship in the Odessa harbor. Writer/director Eisenstein's innovative use of editing and composition to build emotion and drama made this one of the most influential films in history. Famous "Odessa Steps" sequence has been affectionately imitated in such films as Woody Allen's *Bananas* and Brian De Palma's *The Untouchables*. A must for students of the medium.
Dist.: Various

BATTLESTAR GALACTICA 1979
★ ★ ★ **PG Sci-Fi 2:05**
☑ Adult situations
Dir: Richard A. Colla *Cast:* Richard Hatch, Dirk Benedict, Lorne Greene, Ray Milland, Jane Seymour
▶ Greene commands a fleet of spaceships fleeing the Cylons, insect-shaped villains out to eradicate mankind. On the planet Carillon, Greene orders son Hatch and other fighter pilots to battle the aliens. Story and special effects by John Dykstra owe a lot to *Star Wars*. Stitched together from the first and fifth episodes of the failed TV series.
Dist.: Goodtimes

BAT 21 1988
★ ★ ★ ★ **R War 1:45**
☑ Explicit language, graphic violence
Dir: Peter Markle *Cast:* Gene Hackman, Danny Glover, Jerry Reed, David Marshall Grant, Clayton Rohner, Erich Anderson
▶ Hackman, Air Force colonel and intelligence expert, is shot down behind enemy lines during the Vietnam War. Spotter pilot Glover uses radio contact to help maneuver him back through region too dangerous for a rescue mission. Hackman gets a close-up look at the war he'd previously observed only from

30,000 feet. Officer and "grunt" form bond in suspenseful, well-acted war drama based on a true story. **(CC)**
Dist.: Media

BAWDY ADVENTURES OF TOM JONES, THE 1975 British
★ ★ ★ **R Comedy 1:28**
☑ Nudity, strong sexual content
Dir: Cliff Owen *Cast:* Nicky Henson, Trevor Howard, Joan Collins, Terry-Thomas, Arthur Lowe
▶ Henry Fielding's famous bastard, Tom Jones, is back for the first time since the 1963 Albert Finney version. In this good-natured romp, Tom wants to marry the squire's daughter even though he's not in her social class. Good production values and period settings. The story, with many ironic and sexy twists, is true to the spirit of the original. Contains some musical numbers and extensive nudity.
Dist.: MCA

BAY BOY, THE 1985
★ ★ **R Drama 1:44**
☑ Nudity, adult situations, adult humor
Dir: Daniel Petrie *Cast:* Liv Ullmann, Kiefer Sutherland, Peter Donat, Mathieu Carriere, Alan Scarfe
▶ Sensitive coming of age drama set in 1937 Nova Scotia. Sutherland plays a teenager coping with a sickly brother, mother Ullmann, who still grieves over the death of a daughter, and the pangs of first love. As if life weren't complex enough, he also witnesses a murder. Plot clumsily mixes teen sex comedy with more serious elements, but nice period details and breathtaking locations.
Dist.: Orion

BEACHBALLS 1988
☆ **R Comedy 1:18**
☑ Nudity, adult situations, explicit language
Dir: Joe Ritter *Cast:* Phillip Paley, Heidi Helmer, Amanda Goodwin, Steven Rash
▶ Teen lust and assorted beach games in Southern California. With their parents out of town, an aspiring musician pursues a gorgeous blond while his sister goes after a handsome lifeguard. Obvious humor but an attractive cast and plenty of beach lingo ("radical," "bitchin'," "dudes," etc.).
Dist.: Media ⚊

BEACH BLANKET BINGO 1965
★ ★ **NR Comedy 1:38**
Dir: William Asher *Cast:* Frankie Avalon, Annette Funicello, Paul Lynde, Harvey Lembeck, Don Rickles, Buster Keaton, Linda Evans
▶ The *Beach Party* gang mix it up with skydivers, pop stars, motorcycle gangs, and mermaids in this brainless but fun comedy. First-rate nostalgia piece is considered the best in the series. Evans is delightful as Sugar Kane, a singer who allows herself to be kidnapped to

help her career. Strong comic support from Lynde, Rickles, and Keaton.
Dist.: HBO

BEACHCOMBER, THE 1938 British
★ **NR Comedy/Drama 1:27 B&W**
Dir: Erich Pommer *Cast:* Charles Laughton, Elsa Lanchester, Tyrone Guthrie, Robert Newton, Dolly Mollinger
▶ Offbeat adaptation of a W. Somerset Maugham novel, with Laughton giving a flavorful performance as a drunken layabout on a South Seas island. Colonial governor Newton is unable to reform him, but missionary Lanchester uses romance as an inducement to better his position. Curious film bears some resemblance to *The African Queen* in its mixture of comedy and adventure.
Dist.: Video Yesteryear

BEACHES 1988
★ ★ ★ ★ **PG-13 Comedy/Drama 2:00**
☑ Adult situations, explicit language
Dir: Garry Marshall *Cast:* Bette Midler, Barbara Hershey, John Heard, Spalding Gray, Lainie Kazan, James Read
▶ Two very different women meet as kids on an Atlantic City beach and form a lifelong friendship. New Yorker Midler is poor, outspoken, Jewish, and homely; Hershey is rich, reserved, WASPy, and beautiful. Film traces their lives as roommates in New York, romantic rift over stage director Heard, Midler's success as an entertainer and Hershey's sacrifice of her legal career to marriage. Two drift apart as they grow older, but tragedy brings them together again.
Dist.: Buena Vista

BEACH GIRLS 1982
★ ★ **R Comedy 1:31**
☑ Nudity, strong sexual content, explicit language
Dir: Pat Townsend *Cast:* Debra Blee, Val Kline, Jeana Tomasina, James Daughton
▶ Beach blanket comedy features acres of teen flesh as two bikini bunnies vacation at a beach house belonging to a friend's absent uncle. Not much plot but low budget high jinks include seductions, a Peeping Tom's series of accidents, drug smuggling, and a climactic mud wrestling scene.
Dist.: Paramount

BEACH HOUSE 1982
☆ **PG Comedy 1:15**
☑ Explicit language, violence, adult humor
Dir: John Gallagher *Cast:* Ileana Seidel, John Cosola, Kathy McNeil, Richard Duggan, Spence Waugh
▶ Garden State version of *Animal House*: Brooklyn teens take a house in Ocean City for a week and come into conflict (that is, food fights and tequila-drinking contests) with neighboring preppies and Philadelphia punks. Mindless and aimless with plenty of bi-

kini ogling. Typical dialogue: "Hey, gimme a beer, chick."
Dist.: HBO

BEACH PARTY 1963
★ ★ **NR Musical 1:41**
Dir: William Asher *Cast:* Frankie Avalon, Annette Funicello, Bob Cummings, Dorothy Malone, Harvey Lembeck, Jody McCrea
▶ First of a string of successful teen musicals has dated poorly, but still offers fun escapist entertainment. Anthropologist Cummings picks Malibu as the site of his investigations into teenage sex habits, provoking jealous arguments among the kids. Notable for Lembeck's broad parody of a biker, a role he would repeat in *Bikini Beach*, and romantic pairing of Frankie and Annette. Sequel: *Muscle Beach Party*.
Dist.: Warner

BEAR, THE 1984
★ ★ ★ **PG Biography/Sports 1:52**
☑ Explicit language
Dir: Richard Sarafian *Cast:* Gary Busey, Cynthia Leake, Harry Dean Stanton, D'Urville Martin, Jon-Erik Hexum
▶ Inspirational football drama features Busey as the legendary college football coach Paul "Bear" Bryant, who got his nickname wrestling a live bear in his Arkansas hometown. At the University of Alabama, Bear coaches Joe Namath, recruits the school's first black player, survives charges of game fixing, and wins a slew of big games. Busey is outstanding in his return to the biography genre where he previously earned an Oscar nomination playing Buddy Holly.
Dist.: Embassy

BEAR, THE 1989 French
★ ★ ★ ★ ★ **PG Family 1:33**
☑ Mild violence
Dir: Jean-Jacques Annaud *Cast:* Bart the Bear, Douce the Bear, Jack Wallace, Tcheky Karyo, André Lacombe
▶ In 1885 British Columbia, Kodiak bear cub Douce is left to survive on his own after losing his mother to a rock slide. He encounters the gruff, unfriendly, fully grown Bart, recently shot in the shoulder by hunters Wallace and Karyo. Sourpuss Bart reluctantly lets the youngster tag along. Their adventures are told from the bears' point of view and include the two fending off human and animal predators, Bart's stab at romance, and little Douce's sixties-style tripping after ingesting some hallucinogenic mushrooms. International blockbuster features the lush Italian and Austrian Dolomites subbing for the Pacific Northwest. One of the great wilderness adventures of recent years; the kids will love it. **(CC)**
Dist.: RCA/Columbia

BEAR ISLAND 1980 British/Canadian
★ ★ ★ **PG Action-Adventure 1:58**
☑ Explicit language, mild violence
Dir: Don Sharp *Cast:* Donald Sutherland,

Vanessa Redgrave, Richard Widmark, Christopher Lee, Barbara Parkins
▶ Members of a UN science expedition in Norway stumble across abandoned Nazi U-boats filled with gold. As the scientists are killed off one by one, it's up to Sutherland to stop the murders. Large-scale Arctic adventure based on Alistair MacLean's best-seller may please fans of his work, but apart from one snowmobile chase there's very little action.
Dist.: New World

BEAST, THE 1988
★ ★ ★ ★ **R War 1:49**
☑ Explicit language, graphic violence
Dir: Kevin Reynolds **Cast:** George Dzundza, Jason Patric, Steven Bauer, Don Harvey, Stephen Baldwin
▶ During the war in Afghanistan, crazed Soviet Dzundza brutally commands the tank known as "the Beast." Rebellious Russian Patric teams up with Afghan resistance leader Bauer to topple the tank. Muscular action and impressive technology laced with message of brotherhood. High violence level not for the weak of stomach.
Dist.: RCA/Columbia

BEASTMASTER, THE 1982
★ ★ ★ ★ **PG Fantasy 1:58**
☑ Brief nudity, violence
Dir: Don Coscarelli **Cast:** Marc Singer, Tanya Roberts, Rip Torn, John Amos
▶ In a magical feudal world, young warrior Singer uses his telepathy with animals to battle Torn, an evil magician who's enslaved the beautiful virgin Roberts. Derivative sword-and-sorcery epic has enough special effects battles and animal tricks to please younger viewers, although the violence is often excessive.
Dist.: MGM/UA

BEAST MUST DIE, THE 1974 British
★ ★ **PG Horror 1:33**
☑ Violence
Dir: Paul Annett **Cast:** Calvin Lockhart, Peter Cushing, Charles Gray, Anton Diffring, Marlene Clark
▶ Lockhart is a black millionaire who resides in England and lives for the thrill of the hunt; Cushing is among the house guests whom Lockhart suspects may be his dream quarry—a werewolf. Inventive combination of genres and familiar plots. Film stops for a "Werewolf Break" in which viewers have a chance to guess the murderer's identity. Also known as *Black Werewolf.*
Dist.: Prism

BEAST WITHIN, THE 1982
★ ★ **R Horror 1:38**
☑ Rape, nudity, explicit language, graphic violence
Dir: Philippe Mora **Cast:** Ronny Cox, Bibi Besch, Paul Clemens, Don Gordon, R. G. Armstrong
▶ In Mississippi, honeymooning Besch is raped by a mysterious swamp creature. Sev-

enteen years later, her teenage son Clemens, the product of that rape, falls seriously ill. With dad Cox, they return to Mississippi to gather clues about the son's condition. Apparently possessed by the spirit of his dead father, the son turns into a beast and goes on a murderous rampage.
Dist.: MGM/UA

BEAT, THE 1987
★ **R Drama 1:38**
☑ Explicit language, violence
Dir: Paul Mones **Cast:** John Savage, David Jacobson, William McNamara, Kara Glover, Stuart Alexander, David McCarthy
▶ In a crime-ridden New York neighborhood, English teacher Savage tries to encourage street kids to write poetry; they don't respond until the arrival of rebellious Jacobson, whom the teens rally behind but the authorities oppose. Well-intentioned movie with a credible performance by Savage. Sometimes a little too self-consciously poetic but has many thoughtful, inspiring moments.
Dist.: Vestron

BEATLEMANIA 1981
★ **PG Musical 1:36**
☑ Brief nudity
Dir: Joseph Manduke **Cast:** Mitch Weissman, David Leon, Tom Tooley, Ralph Castelli
▶ Adaptation of popular Broadway play features four look-alikes performing thirty Beatles hits. Divided into eight chronological segments consisting mostly of concert footage, although some newsreels and cartoons are included. The songs are great, but film can't hide the fact that these are impersonations, not the real thing.
Dist.: USA

BEAT STREET 1984
★ ★ ★ **PG Musical 1:46**
☑ Explicit language, mild violence
Dir: Stan Lathan **Cast:** Rae Dawn Chong, Guy Davis, Jon Chardiet, Leon Grant
▶ Upbeat teen musical follows old formula of young kids trying to break into show business, this time through break dancing, rapping, and graffiti. Energetic performers, realistic view of racial issues, and authentic South Bronx feel should satisfy hip-hop fans. The real achievement here is the soundtrack (co-produced by Harry Belafonte and re-mix whiz Arthur Baker) featuring Grandmaster Melle Mel, Afrika Bambaataa, Rock Steady, etc.
Dist.: Vestron

BEAT THE DEVIL 1954
★ ★ **NR Comedy 1:29 B&W**
Dir: John Huston **Cast:** Humphrey Bogart, Gina Lollobrigida, Jennifer Jones, Robert Morley, Peter Lorre, Edward Underdown
▶ Low-key satire of caper movies has an extremely unlikely plot: Bogart leads four crooks to Africa on a uranium scam, but the arrival of blond femme fatale Jones and an unex-

pected shipwreck force a change in plans. Nonsensical script (by Huston and Truman Capote) is played straight-faced by the extraordinary cast. A failure on release, film is now a cult favorite.
Dist.: RCA/Columbia

BEAU GESTE 1939
★ ★ ★ NR Action-Adventure 1:54 B&W
Dir: William Wellman ***Cast:*** Gary Cooper, Ray Milland, Robert Preston, Brian Donlevy, Susan Hayward, J. Carrol Naish
► When their brother Beau (Cooper) joins the Foreign Legion after admitting to a jewel theft, Milland and Preston follow to redeem the family name. They are drawn into rebellion against malicious sergeant Donlevy while battling native attacks. Smashing Sahara adventure won Donlevy an Oscar nomination for his genuinely frightening performance. Donald O'Connor plays Beau as a child. Re-made in 1966.
Dist.: MCA

BEAU PERE 1981 French
★ NR Drama 2:00
☑ Nudity, adult situations, explicit language
Dir: Bertrand Blier ***Cast:*** Patrick Dewaere, Ariel Besse, Maurice Ronet, Nicole Garcia, Nathalie Baye
► Musician Dewaere lives with a woman and her teenage daughter Besse. When the woman is killed in a car accident, the girl insists on staying with the musician. She falls for him and he eventually succumbs to her persistent advances. Despite the somewhat controversial subject matter, the film is sensitively handled and at times humorous.
Dist.: Media

BEAUTIFUL BLONDE FROM BASHFUL BEND, THE 1949
★ NR Comedy 1:17
Dir: Preston Sturges ***Cast:*** Betty Grable, Cesar Romero, Rudy Vallee, Olga San Juan, Sterling Holloway, Porter Hall
► Sharpshooting saloon singer Grable aims at unfaithful boyfriend Romero but hits judge Hall in the posterior instead. Grable then goes on the lam and poses as a schoolteacher. She finds romance with Vallee but her past (and Romero) catch up with her. Later Sturges vehicle starts with director's trademark energy and humor but degenerates into a flat slapstick gun battle. **(CC)**
Dist.: Key

BEAUTY AND THE BEAST 1946 French
★ ★ NR Fantasy 1:30 B&W
Dir: Jean Cocteau ***Cast:*** Jean Marais, Josette Day, Marcel André, Mila Parely, Nane Germon, Michel Auclair
► Exquisitely filmed version of the classic fairy tale is one of the landmarks of surrealism. Director Cocteau concentrated on bizarre props and symbolism in telling the story of merchant's daughter Day, who sacrifices herself to a hideous but kind-hearted beast (Marais) to save her father. Evocative but slowly paced, with outstanding photography by Henri Alekan. [S]
Dist.: Nelson

BECKY SHARP 1935
★ NR Drama 1:23
Dir: Rouben Mamoulian ***Cast:*** Miriam Hopkins, Frances Dee, Cedric Hardwicke, Billie Burke, Alison Skipworth, Nigel Bruce
► Loose adaptation of William Makepeace Thackeray's *Vanity Fair* follows adventures of ambitious Becky (Hopkins) as she claws her way up from poverty to the top of nineteenth-century British society. Slow, talky, and only intermittently entertaining; notable primarily as the first feature shot in three-strip Technicolor, which looks fabulous in a recently restored version.
Dist.: KVC

BEDAZZLED 1968 British
★ ★ NR Comedy 1:47
Dir: Stanley Donen ***Cast:*** Peter Cook, Dudley Moore, Eleanor Bron, Raquel Welch, Alba, Robert Russell
► Suicidal short-order cook Moore signs pact with the Devil (Cook) to win the heart of sexy waitress Bron. But the plan goes disastrously awry as the Devil introduces Moore to the seven deadly sins instead. Uneven comic updating of *Faust* has priceless, irreverent, bawdy moments, notably Welch as a steamy Lillian Lust. Written by Cook and Moore (Moore also wrote the music).
Dist.: CBS/Fox

BEDFORD INCIDENT, THE 1965
★ ★ ★ NR Drama 1:42 B&W
Dir: James B. Harris ***Cast:*** Richard Widmark, Sidney Poitier, James MacArthur, Martin Balsam, Wally Cox
► Tough American destroyer commander Widmark stalks Russian sub off the coast of Greenland. His crew begins to crack under the strain, leading to a shocking conclusion. Tense nuclear-age drama is well plotted and well acted by Widmark and Poitier as a journalist on board.
Dist.: RCA/Columbia

BEDKNOBS AND BROOMSTICKS 1971
★ ★ ★ ★ G Family 1:57
Dir: Robert Stevenson ***Cast:*** Angela Lansbury, David Tomlinson, Roddy McDowall, Sam Jaffe, Roy Snart
► A solid Disney classic, based on the story by Mary Norton and set in London during the Blitzkrieg. As the nanny of three orphans Lansbury is hell-bent on helping Churchill stave off the Nazis. With the aid of the Correspondence College of Witchcraft, she takes the children to the cartoon land of Naboombu in search of the ultimate magic spell. A treat for kids and adults.
Dist.: Buena Vista

BEDROOM EYES 1986
★ ★ R Mystery-Suspense 1:35
☑ Nudity, adult situations, violence
Dir: William Fruet *Cast:* Kenneth Gilman, Dayle Haddon, Barbara Law
▶ Peeping Tom stockbroker Gilman spies on lovely Law and gets more show than he bargained for when he witnesses a murder. The cops suspect Gilman and he turns to shrink Haddon for help. Modest thriller plot has interesting premise that never quite gels but enough titillation to intrigue the voyeuristic viewer. Sequel: *Bedroom Eyes II.*
Dist.: Key

BEDROOM EYES II 1989
★ ★ R Mystery-Suspense 1:25
☑ Nudity, adult situations, explicit language, violence
Dir: Chuck Vincent *Cast:* Wings Hauser, Kathy Shower, Linda Blair, Jane Hamilton, Joe Giardina, Kevin Thomsen
▶ Stockbroker Hauser's Peeping Tom days from the original *Bedroom Eyes* are over, but his problems are not. He is married to Shower, having an affair with Blair, and the murderess he helped convict in the first film is back on the streets and out for his blood. Nasty thriller, outlandishly plotted, delivers in the nudity and violence (but not the acting) departments.
Dist.: Vidmark

BEDROOM WINDOW, THE 1987
★ ★ ★ ★ R Mystery-Suspense 1:52
☑ Nudity, adult situations, explicit language, violence
Dir: Curtis Hanson *Cast:* Steve Guttenberg, Elizabeth McGovern, Isabelle Huppert, Paul Shenar, Frederick Coffin
▶ Likable Baltimore executive Guttenberg is having an affair with Huppert, his boss's wife. During a tryst in his apartment, she sees a woman being assaulted outside the bedroom window. To protect her, Guttenberg tells the police he saw the attack and, in true Hitchcock fashion, soon becomes the chief suspect in a rash of killings and must prove his innocence while running from the law. Competent execution of standard thriller fare raised above average by good cast and twisty plot. (CC)
Dist.: Vestron

BEDTIME FOR BONZO 1951
★ ★ NR Comedy 1:23 B&W
Dir: Frederick De Cordova *Cast:* Ronald Reagan, Diana Lynn, Walter Slezak, Jesse White, Lucille Barkley
▶ Trying to prove environment rather than heredity is the main factor in how kids turn out, professor Reagan takes a chimp into his home. Jokes about the future careers of those involved aside (we all know that De Cordova became "The Tonight Show" producer, right?), this is actually a pleasant little diversion.
Dist.: MCA

BEDTIME STORY 1964
★ ★ NR Comedy 1:39
Dir: Ralph Levy *Cast:* Marlon Brando, David Niven, Shirley Jones, Dody Goodman, Aram Stephan, Marie Windsor
▶ Niven is a suave Riviera con man who faces new competition from brash American Brando. It's a battle of brains and wits as the pair vie for Jones's affections and money. Remade in 1988 as *Dirty Rotten Scoundrels.* Fans of that movie will want to see just how faithful the remake is: it replicates the original's plot twists nearly note for note, although the final irony is different.
Dist.: MCA

BEER 1985
★ R Comedy 1:22
☑ Adult situations, explicit language, adult humor
Dir: Patrick Kelly *Cast:* Loretta Swit, Kenneth Mars, Rip Torn, Dick Shawn, William Russ, David Alan Grier
▶ Swit is B. D., advertising executive on the Norbecker beer account, desperately in need of a new campaign. After witnessing three guys thwart a robbery, she signs them as beer spokesmen. Naturally, sales skyrocket with the sexist "whip out your Norbecker" slogan. This Madison Avenue satire, full of shtick and sight gags, has some vaudevillian star turns from Mars, Shawn and Torn but overall is mostly foam. (CC)
Dist.: HBO

BEER DRINKER'S GUIDE TO FITNESS AND FILM MAKING, THE 1988
★ ★ PG Documentary/Comedy 1:24
☑ Explicit language, adult humor
Dir: Fred G. Sullivan *Cast:* Fred G. Sullivan, Polly Sullivan, Tate Sullivan, Katie Sullivan, Kirk Sullivan, Jan Jalenek
▶ In New York's Adirondack Mountains, filmmaker Sullivan struggles to balance the call of his dreams with the need for diaper money. Interviews with friends and neighbors, flashbacks to Sullivan's childhood and career struggles, and phone calls from bill collectors reveal the perils of being a rural filmmaker raising a family. Heartwarming, free-form home movie avoids self-indulgence. Young Tate Sullivan has the best line: "My daddy says if you don't come see this movie, we'll all starve."
Dist.: Trylon

BEES, THE 1978
★ ★ PG Horror 1:23
☑ Violence
Dir: Alfredo Zacharias *Cast:* John Saxon, Angel Tompkins, John Carradine, Claudio Brook, Alicia Encinias
▶ Deadly killer bees, furious at the ecological damage caused by pollution, band together to attack humanity. Hero Saxon joins scientists Carradine and Brook to stop them. Uninspired

low-budget variation on *The Swarm* lacks sting.
Dist.: Warner

BEETLEJUICE 1988
★ ★ ★ PG Fantasy/Comedy 1:30
☑ Adult situations, explicit language, violence
Dir: Tim Burton   *Cast:* Michael Keaton, Alec Baldwin, Geena Davis, Jeffrey Jones, Catherine O'Hara, Winona Ryder, Sylvia Sidney, Robert Goulet, Dick Cavett
► A delightfully deranged and endlessly inventive grand-scale funhouse from director Burton. Keaton is Beetlejuice, a renegade freelance ghost hired by recently deceased newlyweds Davis and Baldwin to evict a real-life family from their home. Jam-packed with ghoulish sight gags and special effects. Younger audiences will appreciate Keaton's hilariously obnoxious performance. Oscar winner for Best Makeup. (CC)
Dist.: Warner

BEFORE DAWN 1945
★ NR Mystery-Suspense 1:00 B&W
Dir: Irving Pichel   *Cast:* Stuart Erwin, Dorothy Wilson, Warner Oland, Dudley Digges, Gertrude W. Hoffman, Oscar Apfel
► Fake psychics plan to project attractive young Wilson onto another plane, but Erwin unravels their plot with the help of Oland and some real psychic powers. Nice little mystery zips right along. Home video version is double-billed with *The Brighton Strangler.*
Dist.: Turner

BEFORE I HANG 1940
★ NR Horror 1:12 B&W
Dir: Nick Grinde   *Cast:* Boris Karloff, Evelyn Keyes, Bruce Bennett, Edward Van Sloan, Ben Taggart
► Scientist Karloff stops at nothing—even murder—to perfect his anti-aging serum. When blood from a dead convict is mixed into the formula, resulting potion has a terrifying effect on Karloff. Stark set design and capable supporting cast heighten Karloff's brooding performance.
Dist.: RCA/Columbia

BEGINNER'S LUCK 1986
★ R Comedy 1:25
☑ Nudity, adult situations, explicit language
Dir: Frank Mouris   *Cast:* Sam Rush, Riley Steiner, Charles Humet, Kate Talbot, Mickey Coburn
► Modest, shaggy dog romantic comedy with a rather skimpy plot. An about-to-be married couple bring their lonely neighbor into their home for a ménage à trois, although there's no sex involved. The leads are pleasant enough but everyone tries a bit too hard to be cute.
Dist.: New World

BEGUILED, THE 1971
★ ★ R Drama 1:49

☑ Brief nudity, adult situations, explicit language, violence
Dir: Don Siegel   *Cast:* Clint Eastwood, Geraldine Page, Elizabeth Hartman, Jo Ann Harris, Darleen Carr, Mae Mercer
► Oddly compelling psychological thriller with Eastwood in an uncharacteristic role as a wounded Union soldier held prisoner in a Confederate girls' boarding school. Sexual tensions lead to gruesome complications as the students and teachers vie for his affections. Interesting but slow-paced, and often gory.
Dist.: MCA

BEHIND THE RISING SUN 1943
★ NR War 1:29 B&W
Dir: Edward Dmytryk   *Cast:* Margo, Tom Neal, J. Carrol Naish, Robert Ryan, Gloria Holden, Don Douglas
► In late 1930s Japan, publisher Naish forces Americanized son Neal to join the army for the Japanese invasion of China. Naish's patriotism backfires, and Japanese army is on its worst behavior overseas. Lead Japanese roles are played by Caucasians. Anti-Japanese story reveals wartime American mindset.
Dist.: Turner

BEHOLD A PALE HORSE 1964
★ ★ NR Drama 1:58 B&W
Dir: Fred Zinnemann   *Cast:* Gregory Peck, Anthony Quinn, Omar Sharif, Mildred Dunnock, Raymond Pellegrin, Paolo Stoppa
► Spanish insurgent Peck, refusing to admit defeat after the 1937 Civil War, conducts guerrilla raids from French outpost. Nemesis Quinn, a police captain, arranges a trap for Peck involving his ailing mother Dunnock. Subtle but talky battle of wits based on Emeric Pressburger's novel *Killing a Mouse on Sunday.*
Dist.: RCA/Columbia

BEING, THE 1983
★ R Horror 1:22
☑ Explicit language, violence
Dir: Jackie Kong   *Cast:* Martin Landau, Jose Ferrer, Dorothy Malone, Ruth Buzzi, Kinky Friedman
► The population of Pottsville, Idaho ("spud capital of the universe"), drops alarmingly when a nuclear waste mutant starts sliming people to death, but mayor Ferrer and toxic dump owner Landau won't admit the monster exists. Zero-budget horror spoof has some nice comic touches and good political points, but don't expect much action.
Dist.: HBO

BEING THERE 1979
★ ★ ★ PG Comedy 2:07
☑ Adult situations, explicit language, adult humor
Dir: Hal Ashby   *Cast:* Peter Sellers, Shirley MacLaine, Melvyn Douglas, Jack Warden, Richard Dysart
► Sellers gives a brilliant performance as Chance, a gardener whose only knowledge of the world comes from TV. People mistake

his naiveté for wisdom, and soon he's advising the President. Literate, incisive screenplay by Jerzy Kosinski actually improves on his novel. Ashby brings a delightfully serene tone to this sophisticated black comedy. Douglas won a supporting actor Oscar for his role as an ailing millionaire.
Dist.: Warner

BELA LUGOSI MEETS A BROOKLYN GORILLA 1952
☆ NR Horror/Comedy 1:05 B&W
Dir: William Beaudine *Cast:* Bela Lugosi, Duke Mitchell, Sammy Petrillo, Charlita, Muriel Landers, Ramona the Chimp
▶ Mitchell and Petrillo, B-movie clones of Dean Martin and Jerry Lewis, are stranded on a jungle island populated by beautiful natives and mad scientist Lugosi. When Lugosi catches Mitchell with the chief's daughter, he changes him into a gorilla. Slapdash nonsense ranks among the world's worst, and funniest, movies. Also known as *The Boys From Brooklyn.*
Dist.: Video Yesteryear

BELIEVERS, THE 1987
★ ★ ★ R Horror 1:40
☑ Nudity, adult situations, explicit language, violence
Dir: John Schlesinger *Cast:* Martin Sheen, Helen Shaver, Harley Cross, Robert Loggia, Richard Masur, Elizabeth Wilson
▶ New York psychiatrist Sheen treats a cop suffering from nightmares about a secret voodoo cult. When the cop commits suicide, Sheen realizes his son may be the cult's next victim. Manipulative but effective horror film has some truly frightening and grotesque sequences.
Dist.: HBO

BELIZAIRE THE CAJUN 1985
★ ★ PG Drama 1:35
☑ Explicit language, violence
Dir: Glen Pitre *Cast:* Armand Assante, Gail Youngs, Michael Schoeffling, Stephen McHattie, Will Patton
▶ Moody period drama about Assante, an 1850s Cajun faith healer who becomes the victim of racial prejudice. After falling in love with a white man's wife, he is falsely accused of murder. Sincere but uneven screenplay by Pitre, a Cajun himself, was developed at Robert Redford's Sundance Institute. Robert Duvall has a brief cameo. (CC)
Dist.: CBS/Fox

BELL, BOOK AND CANDLE 1959
★ ★ ★ NR Comedy 1:43
Dir: Richard Quine *Cast:* James Stewart, Kim Novak, Jack Lemmon, Ernie Kovacs, Hermione Gingold, Elsa Lanchester
▶ Novak, a beautiful modern-day witch, casts spell on staid publisher Stewart on the eve of his wedding. Her warlock brother Lemmon and parapsychology expert Kovacs bring Stewart to rival witch Gingold to break the

spell. Expert cast breezes through this pleasant adaptation of the John Van Druten play.
Dist.: RCA/Columbia

BELLBOY, THE 1960
★ ★ ★ NR Comedy 1:12 B&W
Dir: Jerry Lewis *Cast:* Jerry Lewis, Alex Gerry, Bob Clayton, Sonnie Sands, Bill Richmond
▶ Miami Beach's Fontainebleau Hotel provides the backdrop for series of nonstop sight gags and slapstick jokes linked together by Stanley (Lewis), an inept bellboy who never speaks. Lewis's directing debut is also one of his better solo vehicles. Includes cameos by Maxie Rosenbloom, Milton Berle, and Joe E. Ross.
Dist.: IVE

BELLE OF NEW YORK, THE 1952
★ ★ NR Musical 1:22
Dir: Charles Walters *Cast:* Fred Astaire, Vera-Ellen, Marjorie Main, Keenan Wynn, Alice Pearce, Gale Robbins
▶ In Gay Nineties New York, dashing playboy Astaire pursues chaste social worker Vera-Ellen, but she won't accept him until he gets a respectable job. Lesser Astaire vehicle based on an old vaudeville play features "I Wanna Be a Dancin' Man" and "Let a Little Love Come In."
Dist.: MGM/UA

BELLES OF ST. TRINIAN'S, THE 1955 British
★ ★ NR Comedy 1:26 B&W
Dir: Frank Launder *Cast:* Alastair Sim, Joyce Grenfell, George Cole, Vivienne Martin, Eric Pohlmann, Lorna Henderson
▶ Fast-paced, frequently hilarious farce about a seedy British girls' school, notorious for its bootleg gin, that becomes a hiding place for a kidnapped thoroughbred. Based on Ronald Searle's cartoons, and highlighted by Sim in a dual role as a dotty headmistress and her malevolent brother. Hermione Baddeley and Beryl Reid are marvelous as incompetent faculty members. *Blue Murder at St. Trinian's* was the first of three sequels.
Dist.: HBO

BELL JAR, THE 1979
★ ★ R Drama 1:53
☑ Nudity, adult situations, explicit language
Dir: Larry Peerce *Cast:* Marilyn Hassett, Julie Harris, Anne Jackson, Barbara Barrie, Robert Klein
▶ In the 1950s, an ambitious, gifted college woman travels to New York to become a poet. Unable to cope with the real world, she undergoes shock therapy at a mental institution. Sensitive adaptation of Sylvia Plath's autobiographical novel has superior performances from the talented supporting cast. Extremely depressing despite attempts to lighten the novel's tone.
Dist.: Vestron

BELLMAN AND TRUE 1988 British
★ ★ R Drama 1:58
☑ Adult situations, explicit language, violence
Dir: Richard Loncraine *Cast:* Bernard Hill, Kieran O'Brien, Richard Hope, Frances Tomelty, Derek Newark
► Computer expert Hill and his son are kidnapped by gangsters planning a difficult bank robbery. Hill breaks the bank's alarm system, but can't free his son unless he takes on the crooks. Complex caper film concentrates on realistic personalities involved in compelling conflicts. Still has more than enough gripping moments. Produced by George Harrison.
Dist.: Cannon

BELLS ARE RINGING 1960
★ ★ ★ ★ NR Musical 2:06
Dir: Vincente Minnelli *Cast:* Judy Holliday, Dean Martin, Fred Clark, Eddie Foy, Jr., Jean Stapleton, Frank Gorshin
► A shy telephone answering service operator, Holliday forms warm friendships with her clients and helps them with their problems, especially struggling playwright Martin, with whom she falls in love. Last screen appearance for Holliday, who delightfully re-creates her Tony-winning Broadway triumph in this first-class MGM musical. Songs include "Just in Time."
Dist.: MGM/UA

BELLS OF ST. MARY'S, THE 1945
★ ★ ★ ★ NR Drama 2:06 B&W
Dir: Leo McCarey *Cast:* Bing Crosby, Ingrid Bergman, Henry Travers, Ruth Donnelly, Joan Carroll, Martha Sleeper
► Moving sequel to *Going My Way* sends unorthodox Father Chuck O'Malley (Crosby) to help impoverished parish run by Bergman, a beautiful Sister Superior. She objects to his relaxed ways until recognizing his influence on her schoolchildren. Wistfully sentimental tearjerker received eight Oscar nominations, winning for Best Sound. Highlighted by Crosby's "Aren't You Glad You're You" and Bergman's attempt to teach a youth how to box.
Dist.: Republic

BELOVED ENEMY 1936
★ NR Drama 1:26 B&W
Dir: H. C. Potter *Cast:* Merle Oberon, Brian Aherne, Karen Morley, Jerome Cowan, David Niven
► Polished melodrama set during the 1921 Irish rebellion. Oberon, fiancée of a British officer stationed in Ireland, forms a relationship with rebel leader Aherne that blossoms into love, but political complications threaten tragedy. Glossy and passionate, but less than realistic.
Dist.: Cable

BELOW THE BELT 1979
★ R Drama/Sports 1:31
☑ Adult situations, explicit language, violence

Dir: Robert Fowler *Cast:* Regina Baff, Mildred Burke, John C. Becher, Annie McGreevey, Jane O'Brien
► After witnessing waitress Baff knock out a lecherous customer, a promoter recruits her into the world of women's wrestling. Using the name "Rosa Carlo, the Mexican Spitfire," Baff works her way up to a title match. Despite the seedy settings, a surprisingly affectionate and realistic look at wrestling. Film suffers from shoestring budget.
Dist.: Paragon

BEN 1972
★ ★ PG Horror 1:35
☑ Violence
Dir: Phil Karlson *Cast:* Lee Harcourt Montgomery, Joseph Campanella, Arthur O'Connell, Rosemary Murphy, Meredith Baxter
► Sequel to the horror hit *Willard*. The terror begins when Ben, supersmart leader of the first flick's evil rat pack, befriends troubled Montgomery. Creepy stuff; rodent fearers beware! Hit title tune sung by a young Michael Jackson, first love song about a rat ever to top the charts.
Dist.: Prism

BEND OF THE RIVER 1952
★ ★ ★ NR Western 1:31
Dir: Anthony Mann *Cast:* James Stewart, Arthur Kennedy, Julie Adams, Rock Hudson, Lori Nelson, Jay C. Flippen
► Tough Missouri border raider Stewart guides a group of settlers to a remote Oregon river valley. When their supplies fail to arrive, he rides to Portland to retrieve them from the unscrupulous trader who's hoarding them for gold miners. Sturdy, unsentimental Western has excellent action sequences and another of Stewart's intriguing, fully-rounded characterizations.
Dist.: MCA

BENEATH THE PLANET OF THE APES 1970
★ ★ ★ G Sci-Fi 1:35
Dir: Ted Post *Cast:* James Franciscus, Kim Hunter, Charlton Heston, Maurice Evans, Linda Harrison
► First of four sequels to *Planet of the Apes*. Astronaut Franciscus arrives on the ape-ruled orb to search for the missing Heston and finds himself caught in a war between the primates and an underground mutant race. Not as imaginative as its predecessor but still features striking visual design and ape makeup. Best moments revolve around discovery of buried New York subway system. **(CC)**
Dist.: Playhouse

BENEATH THE 12 MILE REEF 1953
★ NR Action-Adventure 1:42
Dir: Robert Webb *Cast:* Robert Wagner, Terry Moore, Gilbert Roland, J. Carrol Naish, Richard Boone, Peter Graves
► Sponge divers off the Florida Keys squabble over territorial rights near title reef; Wagner, scion of Roland's Greek clan, compounds the

problem by falling for conservative Boone's daughter Moore. Standard underwater fare features octopus battle and attack of the bends; CinemaScope framing will suffer on TV.
Dist.: Cable

BEN HUR 1926
★★ NR Drama 2:28 B&W
Dir: Fred Niblo ***Cast:*** Ramon Novarro, Francis X. Bushman, May McAvoy, Betty Bronson, Claire McDowell, Frank Currier
► Silent version of the Lew Wallace best-seller, with Novarro as the ancient Roman Jew whose eventful life takes him from oar of a naval galley to the foot of Calvary. After nasty centurian Bushman double-crosses him into slavery, he saves the life of naval commander Currier, and becomes an important personage. A spectacular epic, filmed partially in Italy, with literally thousands of extras and an incredibly realistic sea battle. Heart-pounding chariot race holds up especially well.
Dist.: MGM/UA

BEN HUR 1959
★★★★★ NR Action-Adventure 3:32
Dir: William Wyler ***Cast:*** Charlton Heston, Jack Hawkins, Stephen Boyd, Haya Harareet, Cathy O'Donnell, Martha Scott
► During the rule of Caesar, wealthy Jew Heston refuses to turn in rebels, including Jesus of Nazareth, to Roman commander Boyd. Heston is sentenced to be a galley slave while his mother Scott and sister O'Donnell are imprisoned. When Heston saves the life of Roman admiral Hawkins, he's granted his freedom and the chance to seek revenge in rousing chariot race against Boyd. Classic sword-and-sandals spectacle won a record eleven Academy Awards, including Best Picture, Director, and Actor (Heston). **(CC)**
Dist.: MGM/UA

BENIKER GANG, THE 1985
★★★★ G Family 1:27
Dir: Ken Kwapis ***Cast:*** Andrew McCarthy, Jennifer Dundas, Danny Pintauro
► McCarthy stars as Arthur Beniker, a parentless eighteen-year-old who supports four younger orphans by writing an advice column. When their unorthodox family is threatened with adoption, the fivesome run away. Heartwarming sleeper with a cast of fresh young faces.
Dist.: Warner

BENJI 1975
★★★★★ G Family 1:25
Dir: Joe Camp ***Cast:*** Benji, Peter Breck, Cynthia Smith, Christopher Connelly, Patsy Garrett, Mark Slade
► Man's best four-legged friend, Benji, outwits two-legged kidnappers in this delightful family flick. The lovable mutt saves two kids and is adopted by their grateful family. Director Camp heightens our identification with the furry hero by telling the story from Benji's point of view, including a slow-motion love scene with a Pekingese! Country star Charlie Rich sings the Oscar-nominated theme song, "I Feel Love."
Dist.: Vestron

BENJI THE HUNTED 1987
★★★★★ G Family 1:33
Dir: Joe Camp ***Cast:*** Benji, Red Stegall, Joe Camp, Steve Zanolini, Karen Thorndike
► The most popular canine hero since Lassie is back in a warmhearted family film. Kids will have no trouble following the plot: Benji adopts four orphaned cougar cubs whose mother has been killed by a hunter and protects them from bears, wolves, foxes, and eagles. The cuddly cubs prove as adept at stealing scenes as Benji.
Dist.: Buena Vista

BENNY GOODMAN STORY, THE 1955
★★ G Biography/Musical 1:56
Dir: Valentine Davies ***Cast:*** Steve Allen, Donna Reed, Berta Gersten, Herbert Anderson, Robert F. Simon, Sammy Davis, Sr.
► Allen is surprisingly good in his acting debut as the famed clarinetist, and the first-rate music makes up for routine story about his rise from poverty to fame. Goodman dubbed in his own playing, working with the cream of jazz musicians: Harry James, Teddy Wilson, Gene Krupa, Lionel Hampton, etc. That's Sammy Davis's father as Fletcher Henderson.
Dist.: MCA

BERLIN ALEXANDERPLATZ 1983 German
☆ NR Drama/MFTV 15:51
☑ Adult situations, explicit language, violence
Dir: Rainer Werner Fassbinder ***Cast:*** Gunter Lamprecht, Hanna Schygulla, Barbara Sukowa, Gottfried John, Brigitte Mara
► German director Fassbinder's masterpiece, originally made for German television. Lamprecht stars as Franz Biberkopf, a dough-faced ex-con attempting an ultimately doomed effort to start a new life in post World War I Berlin. Serious, powerful themes are handled in a much more accessible style than usual for this noted director. Based on the novel by Alfred Doblin. [S]
Dist.: MGM/UA

BERLIN BLUES 1989 Spanish
☆ PG-13 Drama 1:42
☑ Adult situations, explicit language
Dir: Ricardo Franco ***Cast:*** Julia Migenes, Keith Baxter, Jose Coronado, Javier Gurruchaga, Gerardo Vera
► American Migenes is a Sally Bowles–type pop singer in Cold War Berlin who falls for an East German pianist, then winds up in bed with Baxter, his lonely, middle-aged conductor. The Berlin Wall is not all that stands between this trio, as they work through their differences of age, temperament, and nationality. Older man/showgirl romance

rominiscont of *Tho Bluo Angol* is clunky and tedious. With Euro-pop songs by Lalo Schifrin.
Dist.: Cannon

BERSERK 1967 British
★ ★ NR Horror 1:36
Dir: Jim O'Connolly　*Cast:* Joan Crawford, Ty Hardin, Diana Dors, Michael Gough, Judy Geeson
▶ Tawdry melodrama about circus owner Crawford exploiting an accidental death for publicity purposes. When new high-wire dare-devil Hardin dies, she's suspected of murder. Further killings occur when Geeson, her deranged daughter, arrives. Crawford's next-to-last film.
Dist.: RCA/Columbia

BERT RIGBY, YOU'RE A FOOL 1989
★ R Musical 1:35
☑ Brief nudity, adult situations, explicit language
Dir: Carl Reiner　*Cast:* Robert Lindsay, Anne Bancroft, Corbin Bernsen, Cathryn Bradshaw, Robbie Coltrane, Bruno Kirby
▶ English coal miner Lindsay leaves home after winning a talent contest. He tries for Hollywood stardom but finds a rocky road to the top. Thin plot tries hard to be homage to old musicals but lacks spark and inspiration. Multi-talented stage star Lindsay is a treat, whether doing "Singin' In the Rain" or an Impromptu beer commercial, but deserves a better vehicle. Bancroft contributes a hammy cameo as a producer's wife with a strange lisp and a yen for Lindsay. **(CC)**
Dist.: Warner

BEST BOY 1979
★ ★ NR Documentary 1:44
Dir: Ira Wohl　*Cast:* Phillip Wohl
▶ Uplifting Oscar-winning documentary about "Philly" Wohl, a 52-year-old retarded man living with his parents. Concerned with the fate of Philly's future once his parents die, his cousin Ira helps him become more independent. Philly's enthusiasm for his expanding horizons is contagious; viewers will really get to know him and his family. Deliberately paced but quite moving. Brief appearance by Zero Mostel.
Dist.: Thorn/EMI

BEST DEFENSE 1984
★ ★ R Comedy 1:34
☑ Brief nudity, adult situations, explicit language, adult humor
Dir: Willard Huyck　*Cast:* Dudley Moore, Eddie Murphy, Kate Capshaw, Helen Shaver, George Dzundza, David Rasche
▶ Loud, brassy military comedy actually has two plots. In one, Moore, an inept scientist, uses stolen KGB plans for a "dip-gyro" weapon to further his career. In the second, "Strategic Guest Star" Murphy is stuck in a Middle Eastern war with a dip-gyro that doesn't work. Film's big problem is that the two

stars nover appoar togothor. Writton by Huyck and his wife Gloria Katz. **(CC)**
Dist.: Paramount

BEST FOOT FORWARD 1943
★ ★ ★ NR Musical 1:35
Dir: Edward Buzzell　*Cast:* Lucille Ball, William Gaxton, Virginia Weidler, Tommy Dix, Nancy Walker, Gloria De Haven
▶ Publicity-seeking movie star Ball, playing herself, allows a small-town military academy to name her their prom queen. Chaos results in this amusing, high-spirited romp (with Walker supplying most of the laughs). Includes "Buckle Down Winsocki" and a first-rate "Two O'Clock Jump" by Harry James and his Orchestra.
Dist.: MGM/UA

BEST FRIENDS 1982
★ ★ ★ PG Comedy 1:56
☑ Brief nudity, adult situations, explicit language
Dir: Norman Jewison　*Cast:* Burt Reynolds, Goldie Hawn, Jessica Tandy, Barnard Hughes, Audra Lindley, Ron Silver
▶ Burt and Goldie are live-together L.A. screenwriters who decide to get married. A cross-country honeymoon to meet their respective parents puts strains on their relationship until they realize it's possible to remain best friends. Sophisticated romantic comedy with the stars in top form and a funny supporting turn by Silver as an obnoxious Hollywood producer. Well-observed script by Valerie Curtin and Barry Levinson, who were married at the time and obviously knew the territory.
Dist.: Warner

BEST LITTLE WHOREHOUSE IN TEXAS, THE 1982
★ ★ ★ ★ R Musical 1:54
☑ Nudity, adult situations, explicit language
Dir: Colin Higgins　*Cast:* Burt Reynolds, Dolly Parton, Dom DeLuise, Charles Durning, Jim Nabors, Lois Nettleton
▶ Gaudy, expensive adaptation of the hit Broadway play about the efforts of TV envangelist DeLuise to close down the most popular "chicken ranch" in Texas. Parton is in rare form as the madam of the bordello, and adds two of her own songs to the soundtrack. Although game, Reynolds proves once again that he's not a singer. Durning steals the film with the show's best tune, "Sidestep."
Dist.: MCA

BEST MAN, THE 1964
★ ★ ★ NR Drama 1:42 B&W
Dir: Franklin J. Schaffner　*Cast:* Henry Fonda, Cliff Robertson, Lee Tracy, Edie Adams, Margaret Leighton, Ann Sothern
▶ Backstage machinations at a political convention as Adlai Stevensonesque liberal Fonda and his more ruthless foe Robertson vie for the favor of the dying President, played by Oscar-nominated Tracy. Dirt from both candidates' past comes into play. Incisive look at

the nominating process is more topical than ever. From Gore Vidal's Broadway play.
Dist.: MGM/UA

BEST OF THE BEST 1989
★ ★ ★ PG-13 Martial Arts 1:35
☑ Adult situations, explicit language, violence
Dir: Bob Radler   *Cast:* Eric Roberts, Phillip Rhee, James Earl Jones, Sally Kirkland, Christopher Penn, Louise Fletcher
▶ Roberts, Rhee, and Penn are among five American karate black belts crusty coach Jones must whip into shape to battle the heavily favored Korean team. Victory chances are jeopardized when Roberts breaks training to visit his injured son and Rhee is haunted by his brother's death in the ring. Good actors add humor to a screenplay that is ordinary between the bruising bouts. Kirkland is an unlikely trainer who urges the guys to "inhale joy, courage."
Dist.: SVS

BEST OF TIMES, THE 1986
★ ★ ★ PG-13 Comedy 1:44
☑ Adult situations, explicit language
Dir: Roger Spottiswoode   *Cast:* Robin Williams, Kurt Russell, Pamela Reed, Holly Palance, Donovan Scott
▶ For thirteen years, Williams has been haunted by the memory of the dropped pass that would've won the big high school football game. Finally, he stages a rematch. Underrated small-town comedy from screenwriter Ron Shelton nicely mixes irony and a sense of rueful mid-life regret. Williams is manic and funny, Russell is perfect as his best pal and former star quarterback, and Palance and Reed almost steal the movie as their long-suffering wives. **(CC)**
Dist.: Nelson

BEST REVENGE 1984
★ R Action-Adventure 1:27
☑ Adult situations, explicit language, violence
Dir: John Trent   *Cast:* John Heard, Levon Helm, Alberta Watson, John Rhys-Davies
▶ Heard, a drug smuggler blackmailed into a deal in Morocco, asks for help from best friend Helm. Arrested in a double-cross, they must fight both the police and mobsters to return to Spain. Typical modern-day film noir has a strong performance from former Band drummer Helm.
Dist.: Warner

BEST SELLER 1987
★ ★ ★ ★ R Drama 1:50
☑ Brief nudity, explicit language, violence
Dir: John Flynn   *Cast:* James Woods, Brian Dennehy, Victoria Tennant, Paul Shenar, Allison Balson
▶ Suffering from writer's block, top crime novelist Dennehy agrees to co-author a book on professional hit man Woods's career. But Woods's boss Shenar will stop at nothing to

see that the book is never completed. Larry Cohen's screenplay works best when examining the intriguing relationship between the two leads.
Dist.: Vestron

BEST YEARS OF OUR LIVES, THE 1946
★ ★ ★ ★ NR Drama 2:54 B&W
Dir: William Wyler   *Cast:* Fredric March, Myrna Loy, Dana Andrews, Teresa Wright, Virginia Mayo, Hoagy Carmichael, Harold Russell, Gladys George
▶ Classic study of three World War II veterans readjusting their lives is still riveting today. Heartbreaking and funny by turns, with memorable supporting work by Loy and Wright. Andrews is excellent as a bitter Air Force captain; March won Best Actor as a sergeant who isn't happy working for a bank; but real-life amputee Russell (who won both Supporting Actor and a Special Oscar for inspiring other veterans) is the surprise here. Film won eight Oscars overall, including Best Picture, Direction, Screenplay (Robert E. Sherwood), Editing, and Score.
Dist.: Embassy

BETRAYAL 1983 British
★ R Drama 1:35
☑ Adult situations, explicit language
Dir: David Jones   *Cast:* Ben Kingsley, Jeremy Irons, Patricia Hodge
▶ Playwright Harold Pinter's unconventional look at a long-term extramarital affair receives penetrating screen treatment by three distinguished actors. The story of Hodge's affair with husband Kingsley's best friend Irons unfolds in reverse chronological order. Wonderful trio of performances and witty dialogue, but the arty technique gives this somewhat limited appeal.
Dist.: CBS/Fox

BETRAYAL FROM THE EAST 1945
★ NR War 1:22 B&W
Dir: William Berke   *Cast:* Lee Tracy, Nancy Kelly, Richard Loo, Abner Biberman, Regis Toomey, Philip Ahn
▶ The Japanese want to get their hands on the Panama Canal during World War II. Thinking that former American soldier Tracy can be bought, they try to get him to steal plans for the Big Ditch's defenses. But Tracy, with the help of lovely double-agent Kelly, is just stringing them along. Gung-ho wartime artifact is typical of its type.
Dist.: Turner

BETRAYED 1988
★ ★ ★ ★ R Drama 2:03
☑ Adult situations, explicit language, violence
Dir: Costa-Gavras   *Cast:* Tom Berenger, Debra Winger, John Heard, Betsy Blair, John Mahoney, Richard Libertini
▶ When left-wing talk show host Libertini is murdered by right-wing extremists, FBI honcho Heard dispatches agent Winger on under-

cover mission into the Iowa heartland. Winger falls in love with chief suspect, warm single father/farmer Berenger. As romance deepens, he reveals his secret world of paranoia and hatred, setting up a conflict for Winger between love and morality. Topical thriller with shock power and strong leads.
Dist.: MGM/UA

BETSY, THE 1978
★★★★ R Drama 2:05
☑ Nudity, explicit language
Dir: Daniel Petrie *Cast:* Laurence Olivier, Robert Duvall, Katharine Ross, Tommy Lee Jones, Jane Alexander, Lesley-Anne Down
▶ Amusing adaptation of Harold Robbins's best-seller describes three generations of auto tycoons in terms of incest, homosexuality, and more conventional couplings in Grosse Pointe, Michigan. Labyrinthine plot moves a bit slowly, but not every soap opera boasts Lord Olivier.
Dist.: CBS/Fox

BETSY'S WEDDING 1990
★★★★ R Comedy 1:37
☑ Nudity, adult situations, explicit language
Dir: Alan Alda *Cast:* Alan Alda, Joey Bishop, Madeline Kahn, Anthony LaPaglia, Catherine O'Hara, Joe Pesci, Molly Ringwald, Ally Sheedy, Burt Young, Julie Bovasso
▶ From the moment Ringwald announces her engagement, virtually everything that can possibly go wrong with her large family wedding does, causing no end of headaches for dad Alda and mom Kahn. Meanwhile LaPaglia, the son of a Mafia chieftan, is falling for the bride's sister Sheedy—a cop in need of a little affection. Except for strong work from LaPaglia/Sheedy pair, wonderful cast is stranded in a mass of ennervated clichés. (CC)
Dist.: Buena Vista

BETTER LATE THAN NEVER 1982
★★★ PG Comedy 1:31
☑ Adult situations, explicit language
Dir: Bryan Forbes *Cast:* David Niven, Maggie Smith, Art Carney, Kimberly Partridge, Catherine Hicks
▶ Niven and Carney, two elderly gentlemen who shared a girlfriend years ago in Paris, vie for the affection (and the fortune) of young Partridge, who could be either's granddaughter. Cute diversion with gorgeous Riviera scenery and a wonderful performance by Smith as the child's nanny.
Dist.: CBS/Fox

BETTER OFF DEAD 1985
★★★ PG Comedy 1:37
☑ Explicit language, adult humor
Dir: Savage Steve Holland *Cast:* John Cusack, David Ogden Stiers, Kim Darby, Diane Franklin, Amanda Wyss
▶ Hapless high school student Cusack loses the girl of his dreams to a jock and figures he'd be better off dead. However, he eventually finds happiness with a pretty French exchange student and beats the jock in a ski race. Some overly broad and gross moments but Holland, in his directing debut, provides some truly original and outrageous bits. (CC)
Dist.: CBS/Fox

BETTY BLUE 1986 French
☆ NR Drama 2:00
☑ Nudity, strong sexual content, adult situations, explicit language, violence
Dir: Jean-Jacques Beineix *Cast:* Beatrice Dalle, Jean-Hugues Anglade, Consuelo de Havilland, Gerard Darmon, Clementine Celarie
▶ Flashy, erotic psychodrama about affair between a schizophrenic free spirit Dalle (in an impressive debut) and aspiring writer Anglade. Episodic plot eventually concentrates on Dalle's descent into madness. Director Beineix pumps up the far-fetched story with exotic colors and graphic sex scenes. Has a cult following, and was selected for Best Foreign Film consideration. (CC) [S]
Dist.: CBS/Fox

BETWEEN FRIENDS 1983
★★★★ NR Drama/MFTV 1:40
☑ Adult situations, explicit language
Dir: Lou Antonio *Cast:* Elizabeth Taylor, Carol Burnett, Henry Ramer, Barbara Bush, Stephen Young
▶ Female friendship sustains two recent divorcées through the difficulties of middle-aged single life. Taylor plays a sharp-tongued woman who keeps company with an aging tycoon because she can't imagine life without a man. Burnett is a real estate agent who pursues a series of casual affairs while trying to maintain a relationship with her daughter. Fine performances by two superstars, together for the first time.
Dist.: Vestron

BETWEEN THE LINES 1977
★ R Comedy 1:41
☑ Brief nudity, explicit language
Dir: Joan Micklin Silver *Cast:* John Heard, Lindsay Crouse, Jeff Goldblum, Jill Eikenberry, Gwen Welles, Stephen Collins
▶ The staff of a countercultural Boston newspaper undergoes a collective identity crisis after a conglomerate takeover. Crouse and Goldblum are standouts among the attractive young cast of 1960s survivors facing a new lifestyle. A gentle, humanistic comedy from director Silver.
Dist.: Vestron

BEVERLY HILLS BODYSNATCHERS 1988
☆ NR Comedy 1:45
☑ Brief nudity, adult situations, explicit language
Dir: Jon Mostow *Cast:* Vic Tayback, Frank Gorshin, Rodney Eastman, Warren Selko, Art Metrano
▶ Doctor Gorshin and mortician Tayback finance experiments in reviving the dead with

money borrowed from mafioso Metrano. When Metrano wants his money back, teens Eastman and Selko help Gorshin and Tayback with some high-speed hearse driving. Silly, predictable plot with forced attempts at humor; low budget is apparent.
Dist.: SGE

BEVERLY HILLS COP 1984
★ ★ ★ ★ ★ R Action-Adventure 1:45
☑ Explicit language, violence
Dir: Martin Brest   *Cast:* Eddie Murphy, Judge Reinhold, Lisa Eilbacher, John Ashton, Steven Berkoff, James Russo, Bronson Pinchot
▶ Street-smart Detroit cop Axel Foley (Murphy) travels to Los Angeles to find his friend's killer. Ignoring the L.A. police, Foley pushes his way into upper crust society to uncover a stolen art ring. Expert blend of comedy and action with Murphy in top form was a huge commercial success. Pinchot's career took off after his cameo as an art salesman. Followed by a sequel. **(CC)**
Dist.: Paramount

BEVERLY HILLS COP II 1987
★ ★ ★ ★ R Comedy 1:42
☑ Brief nudity, explicit language, violence, adult humor
Dir: Tony Scott   *Cast:* Eddie Murphy, Judge Reinhold, Jurgen Prochnow, Ronny Cox, John Ashton, Brigitte Nielsen
▶ In this sequel to the 1984 megahit, Detroit cop Axel Foley (Murphy) returns to L.A. to investigate the shooting of pal Cox and comes up against hit woman Nielsen and her gang. Eddie's fans won't be disappointed as he once again gives the verbal shaft to snobs and authority figures at every comic turn. Gilbert Gottfried contributes a hysterical bit as a flaky financial advisor. In all, *Cop II* manages to duplicate the original's formula on a more lavish scale.
Dist.: Paramount

BEVERLY HILLS VAMP 1988
★ R Comedy 1:28
☑ Nudity, adult situations, explicit language, violence
Dir: Fred Olen Ray   *Cast:* Eddie Deezen, Pat McCormick, Tim Conway, Jr., Jay Richardson, Robert Quarry, Britt Ekland
▶ Aspiring filmmaker Deezen and his pals visit madam Ekland's Beverly Hills bordello, only to discover these ladies of the night are vampires. When his friends fall victim to the bloodsucking beauties, Deezen must find a way to save them. Cute concept but generally mirthless. Enlivened by gorgeous women and Deezen's loud clowning.
Dist.: Vidmark

BEWARE, MY LOVELY 1952
★ ★ NR Drama 1:17 B&W
Dir: Harry Homer   *Cast:* Ida Lupino, Robert Ryan, Taylor Holmes, Barbara Whiting, James Williams
▶ Ryan drifts into a small town and survives doing odd jobs. He insinuates himself into widow Lupino's household and slowly takes control of her life. She realizes too late he's a psychopath. Flabby, predictable tale enlivened somewhat by good acting.
Dist.: Republic

BEYOND A REASONABLE DOUBT 1956
★ ★ NR Mystery-Suspense 1:20 B&W
Dir: Fritz Lang   *Cast:* Dana Andrews, Joan Fontaine, Sidney Blackmer, Philip Bourneuf, Shepperd Strudwick, Arthur Franz
▶ To make a case against capital punishment, publisher Blackmer has Andrews pretend he's guilty of murder. When Andrews is sentenced to death, Blackmer heads for the D.A.'s office with information proving his innocence—but then fate intervenes, jeopardizing Andrews. Provocative plot has some genuine surprises, hit home by Lang's typically moody direction and a strong cast.
Dist.: VidAmerica

BEYOND THE DOOR 1975 U.S./Italian
★ R Horror 1:40
☑ Graphic violence
Dir: Oliver Hellman (Ovidio Assonitis)   *Cast:* Juliet Mills, Richard Johnson, David Collin, Jr., Elizabeth Turner, Gabriele Lavia, Nino Segurini
▶ Record producer's wife Mills has an affair with demonic Johnson and becomes pregnant. Unfortunately, her fetus is a Satanic spawn, resulting in the possessed mother's own devilish condition. Script is beyond shame in ripping off *The Exorcist*, though there are some effectively grisly moments.
Dist.: Media

BEYOND THE DOOR II 1979 Italian
☆ R Horror 1:30
☑ Graphic violence
Dir: Mario Bava   *Cast:* John Steiner, Daria Nicolodi, David Colin, Jr., Ivan Rassimov
▶ Nicolodi, along with second husband Steiner and son Colin, moves back into the house she shared with her first husband. When strange things occur, Nicolodi could be hallucinating them—or her late spouse may be possessing Colin to haunt her. Director Bava creates a foreboding mood, but the plot is a tired rehash of old genre elements.
Dist.: Media

BEYOND THE FOREST 1949
★ ★ ★ NR Drama 1:36 B&W
Dir: King Vidor   *Cast:* Bette Davis, Joseph Cotten, Ruth Roman, David Brian, Minor Watson, Dona Drake
▶ "What a dump!" snarls Davis, unhappy wife of doctor Cotten, as she surveys her small-town surroundings. Davis becomes involved with wealthy Chicagoan Brian, but pregnancy and blackmailer Watson complicate her plan to leave Cotten. Extremely trashy, but Davis is as watchable as always.
Dist.: MGM/UA

BEYOND THE LIMIT 1983
★★ **R Drama 1:43**
☑ Nudity, explicit language, violence
Dir: John Mackenzie ***Cast:*** Richard Gere, Michael Caine, Bob Hoskins, Elpidia Carrillo
▸ Unsatisfying if well-mounted adaptation of Graham Greene's best-seller *The Honorary Consul*. Gere, a doctor, gets inadvertently involved when dissidents kidnap British Consul Caine, whose wife is also Gere's lover. Plenty of atmosphere, colorful locations, and good acting, especially from Hoskins as a police chief, but overall less than passionate.
Dist.: Paramount

BEYOND THE POSEIDON ADVENTURE 1979
★★ **PG Action-Adventure 2:02**
☑ Explicit language, mild violence
Dir: Irwin Allen ***Cast:*** Michael Caine, Sally Field, Telly Savalas, Peter Boyle, Jack Warden
▸ Sequel to the immensely popular *The Poseidon Adventure* involves two groups of scavengers. Caine leads the good ones and Savalas is in charge of the bad; they attempt to salvage the ship and some of the survivors we didn't meet the first time around. Large-scale action-adventure resembles its illustrious predecessor so closely, it almost qualifies as a remake.
Dist.: Warner

BEYOND THERAPY 1987
☆ **R Comedy 1:33**
☑ Brief nudity, adult situations, explicit language, adult humor
Dir: Robert Altman ***Cast:*** Glenda Jackson, Tom Conti, Jeff Goldblum, Christopher Guest, Julie Hagerty
▸ Sexual farce about neurotic Hagerty and bisexual Goldblum who meet through a personal ad, their respective incompetent shrinks Conti and Jackson, and Goldblum's jealous male lover Guest. Off-the-padded-wall performances and humor from director Robert Altman and screenwriter Christopher Durang fall flat in this disappointing adaptation of Durang's Broadway play. **(CC)**
Dist.: New World

BEYOND THE STARS 1989
★★ **PG Drama 1:28**
☑ Explicit language
Dir: David Saperstein ***Cast:*** Martin Sheen, Christian Slater, Robert Foxworth, Sharon Stone, Olivia d'Abo, F. Murray Abraham
▸ Aspiring astronaut Slater's ambition is resented by dad Foxworth, an engineer who was fired by NASA, but ex-astronaut Sheen develops a warm relationship with Slater that encourages him to reach for the moon. Honest performances against a beautiful Oregon background, although soap opera plot is weighed down by preachy platitudes. Originally known as *Personal Choice*.
Dist.: IVE

BEYOND THE VALLEY OF THE DOLLS 1970
★ **X Drama 1:49**
☑ Nudity, adult situations, explicit language, violence
Dir: Russ Meyer ***Cast:*** Dolly Read, Cynthia Myers, Marcia McBroom, John LaZar, Michael Blodgett, Edy Williams
▸ Campy "insider's" look at fast track lives of Hollywood's filthy rich focuses on efforts by pop singers Read, Myers, and McBroom to break into show biz. Their experiences involve requisite corrupt actors, homosexual jet-setters, and climactic killing spree. Co-written by film critic Roger Ebert.
Dist.: CBS/Fox

BEYOND THE WALLS 1985 Israeli
☆ **R Drama 1:43**
☑ Explicit language, violence
Dir: Uri Barbash ***Cast:*** Arnon Zadok, Muhamad Bakri, Assi Dayan, Rami Danon
▸ Arabs and Jews, prisoners in an Israeli jail, put aside their disparate backgrounds and go on strike against the brutality of the prison officials. Well-intentioned yet overly grim drama has worthy message of brotherhood but is not easy to watch. Nominated for Best Foreign Film Oscar. Also available in dubbed version. [S]
Dist.: Warner

BIBLE, THE 1966
★★★ **NR Drama 2:54**
Dir: John Huston ***Cast:*** George C. Scott, Peter O'Toole, Ava Gardner, Richard Harris, Franco Nero, Michael Parks, Stephen Boyd, Ulla Bergryd
▸ Colorful, sometimes beautiful, cinematic rendering of the first twenty-two chapters of Genesis, covering the creation of the world, Adam and Eve (Parks, Bergryd), Cain and Abel (Harris, Nero), Noah's Ark, the Tower of Babel, Sodom and Gomorrah, and the plight of Abraham and Sarah (Scott, Gardner). Director Huston plays Noah and also narrates the voice of God.
Dist.: CBS/Fox

BICYCLE THIEF, THE 1949 Italian
★★★ **NR Drama 1:30 B&W**
Dir: Vittorio De Sica ***Cast:*** Lamberto Maggiorani, Enzo Staiola, Lianella Carell, Elena Altieri
▸ In war-torn Italy, thief steals the bike a poor man needs for work. The man and his son search for the culprit. Postwar classic is still penetrating and real forty years after initial release. Tightly woven story, acting, and starkly shaded photography couldn't be better. [S]
Dist.: Various

BIG 1988
★★★★★ **PG Comedy 1:42**
☑ Adult situations, explicit language
Dir: Penny Marshall ***Cast:*** Tom Hanks, Elizabeth Perkins, Robert Loggia, John Heard,

Jared Rushton, David Moscow, Jon Lovitz, Mercedes Ruehl
▶ After being rejected by a fifteen-year-old beauty, thirteen-year-old Moscow asks a mysterious carnival machine to make him big. The next morning he awakens to find his wish come true: he's now adult Hanks! Chased out of his home as an intruder, he moves to New York City with help of shrewd teen pal Rushton. Hanks's childlike perspective and enthusiasm win him a job with toy bigwig Loggia and romance with colleague Perkins. Runaway hit carried by Hanks's sweetly touching little big man, a role that won him his first Oscar nomination.
Dist.: CBS/Fox

BIG BAD JOHN 1990
★ ★ PG-13 Action-Adventure 1:31
☑ Adult situations, explicit language, violence
Dir: Burt Kennedy *Cast:* Jimmy Dean, Jack Elam, Ned Beatty, Doug English, Bo Hopkins, Romy Windsor
▶ Hulking English causes trouble for retired Louisiana sheriff Dean when he kidnaps a girl who may be Dean's illegitimate daughter. With deputy Elam, Dean goes out after him and other baddies with a four-barrel shotgun, until English redeems himself with the mine heroics immortalized in the song upon which the film is loosely based. Violent redneck stuff with expected revenge scenerio is average for the genre. Includes the Charlie Daniels Band's new version of title tune, plus songs by Merle Haggard and Ricky Van Shelton.
Dist.: Magnum

BIG BAD MAMA 1974
★ ★ R Action-Adventure 1:24
☑ Nudity, adult situations, explicit language
Dir: Steve Carver *Cast:* Angie Dickinson, William Shatner, Tom Skerritt, Susan Sennett, Robbie Lee
▶ Dickinson, a widow in depression-era Texas, resorts to bootlegging and bank robbing to keep her family together. Highly diverting *Bonnie and Clyde* clone delivers plenty of action (often bloody), comedy, and steamy sex. Angie's nude scenes made this low-budget Roger Corman production such a cult favorite that a sequel was shot fourteen years later.
Dist.: Warner

BIG BAD MAMA II 1987
★ R Action-Adventure 1:24
☑ Nudity, adult situations, explicit language, violence
Dir: Jim Wynorski *Cast:* Angie Dickinson, Robert Culp, Danielle Brisebois, Julie McCullough, Bruce Glover
▶ Widowed after a shootout over her foreclosed farm, Dickinson hits the road with buxom daughters Brisebois and McCullough for a bank-robbing spree in Depression Texas. Lusty tongue-in-cheek sequel provides plenty

of shootouts and skin; ageless Angie still looks great.
Dist.: MGM/UA

BIG BIRD CAGE, THE 1972
★ R Action-Adventure 1:33
☑ Nudity, adult situations, violence
Dir: Jack Hill *Cast:* Pam Grier, Candice Roman, Anitra Ford, Carol Speed
▶ After being mistakenly implicated in a nightclub robbery, attractive seductress Grier is imprisoned in a brutal work camp. Sprung by revolutionaries, she then competes for the affections of the rebel leader. Philippines-set action vehicle for black star Grier.
Dist.: Warner

BIG BLUE, THE 1988 French
★ ★ PG Action-Adventure 1:58
☑ Adult situations, explicit language
Dir: Luc Besson *Cast:* Jean-Marc Barr, Jean Reno, Rosanna Arquette, Paul Shenar, Sergio Castellito, Jean Bouise
▶ Frenchman Barr and Sicilian Reno, longtime friends, compete against each other in the sport of free-diving, setting new records for depths reached without oxygen tanks. American insurance agent Arquette falls for Barr, but he's more interested in trying to talk to dolphins. Meanwhile Barr and Reno free-dive deeper, pushing the limits of the human body. Gorgeous underwater photography wasted on waterlogged yarn.
Dist.: RCA/Columbia

BIG BRAWL, THE 1980
★ ★ R Martial Arts 1:35
☑ Adult situations, explicit language, graphic violence
Dir: Robert Clouse *Cast:* Jackie Chan, Jose Ferrer, Kristine DeBell, Mako, Ron Max
▶ American debut of Asian superstar Chan starts out as a parody of 1930s gangster films and ends up in a wild free-for-all at the famous Texas Battle Creek Brawl. Producers hoped this good-hearted comedy would position Chan (whose martial arts skills are dazzling) as a successor to Bruce Lee, but he didn't catch on with audiences.
Dist.: Warner

BIG BUS, THE 1976
★ PG Comedy 1:28
☑ Explicit language
Dir: James Frawley *Cast:* Joseph Bologna, Stockard Channing, Ruth Gordon, John Beck, Ned Beatty
▶ Uneven spoof of disaster movies takes place on the first nuclear-powered bus making premier nonstop trip from New York to Denver. Some funny moments (but also some dull stretches) in a genre parody entertaining on a TV sitcom level.
Dist.: Paramount

BIG BUSINESS 1988
★ ★ ★ ★ ★ PG Comedy 1:31
☑ Adult situations, explicit language

Dir: Jim Abrahams *Cast:* Bette Midler, Lily Tomlin, Fred Ward, Edward Herrmann, Michele Placido, Michael Gross
► Two pairs of identical twins are mixed up at birth, sending each set of parents home with mismatched baby girls. Years later Midler is a ruthless New York corporate executive planning to strip-mine small town of Jupiter Hollow with the help of her meek sister Tomlin. Coincidentally, Jupiter Hollow sends the other two sisters to New York to protest: strong-willed, do-gooder Tomlin and yodeling hick Midler. Confusion of identities and biting one-liners yield many laughs in this breezy farce.
Dist.: Buena Vista

BIG CARNIVAL, THE 1951
★ ★ ★ NR Drama 1:51 B&W
Dir: Billy Wilder *Cast:* Kirk Douglas, Jan Sterling, Robert Arthur, Porter Hall
► Powerful drama from director Wilder. When New Mexico man is trapped in a mine shaft cave-in, reporter Douglas exploits the story for all it's worth, endangering the victim further in order to sell papers. Unflattering, bitter portrait of the power of the press with a first-rate Douglas. Also known as *Ace in the Hole.*
Dist.: Turner

BIG CHILL, THE 1983
★ ★ ★ ★ R Drama 1:43
☑ Brief nudity, adult situations, explicit language
Dir: Lawrence Kasdan *Cast:* William Hurt, JoBeth Williams, Glenn Close, Jeff Goldblum, Mary Kay Place, Kevin Kline, Meg Tilly, Tom Berenger
► When a young man commits suicide, his college friends gather for a weekend of self-scrutiny and renewal of old ties in this sharp, literate drama that struck a chord with those who came of age in the 1960s. Outstanding ensemble acting by a dream cast features Hurt as a burned-out Vietnam vet and Place as a lawyer looking for someone to father her baby before her biological clock stops ticking. Hit soundtrack contains lots of sixties classics. (CC)
Dist.: RCA/Columbia

BIG CLOCK, THE 1948
★ ★ ★ NR Mystery-Suspense 1:35 B&W
Dir: John Farrow *Cast:* Ray Milland, Charles Laughton, Maureen O'Sullivan, George Macready, Rita Johnson, Elsa Lanchester
► Suspenseful drama about Milland, a crime magazine editor falsely implicated in a murder and forced by tyrannical publisher Laughton to conduct a search for the killer. Adaptation of Kenneth Fearing's novel features a marvelously twisty plot and first-rate performance by Laughton's real-life wife Lanchester as an abstract artist. Loosely remade in 1987 as *No Way Out.*
Dist.: MCA

BIG COMBO, THE 1955
★ ★ NR Drama 1:29 B&W

Dir: Joseph H. Lewis *Cast:* Cornel Wilde, Richard Conte, Brian Donlevy, Jean Wallace, Robert Middleton, Lee Van Cleef
► Determined cop Wilde attacks mobster Conte's gang despite sadistic beatings by his thugs; Conte's spurned wife provides info that helps topple his crime empire. Fast-paced, influential film noir won critical acclaim for its realism and uncompromising violence.
Dist.: Prism

BIG COUNTRY, THE 1958
★ ★ ★ ★ NR Western 2:45
Dir: William Wyler *Cast:* Gregory Peck, Jean Simmons, Charlton Heston, Carroll Baker, Burl Ives, Charles Bickford
► Ex-seaman Peck, engaged to rancher Bickford's daughter Baker, pursues teacher Simmons instead and gets involved in Bickford/Ives feud over water supply. Heston, Bickford's foreman, provokes more trouble when Simmons is kidnapped. Larger-than-life and rousing Western won Best Supporting Actor Oscar for Ives.
Dist.: MGM/UA

BIG DEAL ON MADONNA STREET 1956
Italian
★ NR Comedy 1:31 B&W
Dir: Mario Monicelli *Cast:* Marcello Mastroianni, Vittorio Gassman, Renato Salvatori, Claudia Cardinale, Rossana Rory, Toto
► Clumsy crook Gassman plots heist of Madonna Street store and enlists equally unskilled helpers, including Mastroianni, for the gig. The robbery predictably and amusingly goes awry. Caper classic evokes virtually nonstop laughter and is vastly superior to its 1984 American remake, *Crackers.* Ⓢ
Dist.: Various

BIG DOLL HOUSE, THE 1971
★ R Action-Adventure 1:33
☑ Nudity, adult situations, explicit language, violence
Dir: Jack Hill *Cast:* Judy Brown, Roberta Collins, Pam Grier, Brooke Mills, Pat Woodell, Sid Haig
► Brown, Grier, and other inmates are the victims of sadistic wardens and guards in a brutal women's prison. Their escape attempt leads to an extremely violent climax. Highly influential exploitation film started a cycle of sexy, tongue-in-cheek prison films. Followed by *The Big Bird Cage.*
Dist.: Embassy

BIG EASY, THE 1987
★ ★ ★ ★ R Mystery-Suspense 1:41
☑ Nudity, adult situations, explicit language, violence
Dir: Jim McBride *Cast:* Dennis Quaid, Ellen Barkin, Ned Beatty, John Goodman, Ebbe Roe Smith, Charles Ludlam
► Brash cop Quaid teaches uptight Assistant D.A. Barkin to mix pleasure with business in this snappy, sassy thriller of New Orleans police corruption. Professional antagonists at first,

they investigate underworld killings; as the bodies pile up, the solution hits closer to home than Quaid anticipated. Lots of Cajun atmosphere, excellent camerawork and music, and spicy sexual electricity between Barkin and Quaid.
Dist.: HBO

BIG FIX, THE 1978
★ ★ ★ PG Mystery-Suspense 1:48
☑ Adult situations, explicit language, violence
Dir: Jeremy Paul Kagan   *Cast:* Richard Dreyfuss, Susan Anspach, Bonnie Bedelia, John Lithgow, F. Murray Abraham
▶ Berkeley-based private eye Moses Wine (Dreyfuss) is hired by ex-sweetheart Anspach to find the culprit who's smearing the political candidate she works for. Is missing ex-sixties radical Abraham involved? Comedy/mystery has an intricate plot, plenty of sixties nostalgia, and works best as a vehicle for Dreyfuss's wisecracking heroics. Adapted by Roger L. Simon from his novel.
Dist.: MCA

BIGGLES 1986 British
★ ★ PG Fantasy 1:48
☑ Explicit language, violence
Dir: John Hough   *Cast:* Neil Dickson, Alex Hyde-White, Fiona Hutchison, Peter Cushing, Michael Siberry
▶ Whenever lightning strikes, modern Manhattan PR man Hyde-White finds himself time traveling to World War I, where he ends up helping British daredevil pilot Dickson battle the Germans. Fanciful fantasy stronger on action scenes than human interaction. The clever ideas would have worked better if played for comedy.   **(CC)**
Dist.: New World

BIG HEAT, THE 1953
★ ★ NR Mystery-Suspense 1:29 B&W
Dir: Fritz Lang   *Cast:* Glenn Ford, Gloria Grahame, Jocelyn Brando, Lee Marvin, Carolyn Jones
▶ Classic thriller from director Lang, almost unparalelled for sheer intensity. Ford is an honest cop who obsessively takes on a crime ring after the bad guys kill his wife. Gangster's moll Grahame pays a heavy price for helping Ford—the menacing Marvin throws scalding coffee in her face in just one of several memorably violent scenes.
Dist.: RCA/Columbia

BIG JAKE 1971
★ ★ ★ ★ ★ PG Western 1:50
☑ Explicit language, violence
Dir: George Sherman   *Cast:* John Wayne, Richard Boone, Maureen O'Hara, Patrick Wayne, Chris Mitchum, Bobby Vinton
▶ As Big Jake, Wayne takes a million dollars to villain Boone to ransom his kidnapped grandson (played by his real-life son John Ethan). Jake tries a double-cross that puts the entire scheme in jeopardy. Some awkward comic touches, but good Mexican scenery, plenty of violence, and a cast of familiar faces (Wayne's fifth film with O'Hara).   **(CC)**
Dist.: CBS/Fox

BIG MAN ON CAMPUS 1989
★ ★ ★ PG-13 Comedy 1:45
☑ Adult situations, explicit language, mild violence
Dir: Jeremy Paul Kagan   *Cast:* Allan Katz, Corey Parker, Cindy Williams, Melora Hardin, Tom Skerritt, Jessica Harper
▶ Hunchback Katz lives in a college bell tower and is discovered when he helps his unrequited love Hardin and her beau Parker in a fight with another student. Professor Skerritt then assigns Parker to live with Katz and teach him how to behave. Surprisingly entertaining modern day takeoff on *The Hunchback of Notre Dame.* Katz wrote the screenplay.
Dist.: Vestron

BIG MO 1973
★ ★ ★ ★ G Drama 1:53
Dir: Daniel Mann   *Cast:* Bernie Casey, Bo Svenson, Janet MacLachlan, Stephanie Edwards, Pauline Myers
▶ Cincinnati Royals basketball star Maurice Stokes (Casey) suffers a paralyzing stroke. His teammate Jack Twyman (Svenson) devotes his life to raising money for Mo's rehabilitation. Sentimental treatment of a true story works on a soap-opera level. Released in theaters as *Maurie.*
Dist.: Vestron

BIG MOUTH, THE 1967
★ ★ ★ NR Comedy 1:47
Dir: Jerry Lewis   *Cast:* Jerry Lewis, Harold J. Stone, Susan Bay, Buddy Lester, Del Moore
▶ Fisherman Lewis hooks the big one; no, not a marlin but a treasure-seeking diver. Bad guys also want the hidden trove and Lewis is in trouble when he gets the map. Zany antics in patented Lewis style.
Dist.: RCA/Columbia

BIG PARADE, THE 1925
★ NR War 2:21 B&W
Dir: King Vidor   *Cast:* John Gilbert, Renee Adoree, Hobart Bosworth, Claire McDowell, Claire Adams, Karl Dane
▶ Wealthy youngster Gilbert goes to the front in World War I, where he meets and falls in love with Adoree, and loses a leg. Considered by many one of the best war (or antiwar) movies ever made, silent classic is highlighted by haunting march of U.S. soldiers through enemy fire into Belleau Wood and contrast between large events and small moments of human warmth.
Dist.: MGM/UA

BIG PICTURE, THE 1988
★ ★ ★ PG-13 Comedy 1:39
☑ Adult situations, explicit language
Dir: Christopher Guest   *Cast:* Kevin Bacon,

Emily Longstreth, J. T. Walsh, Jennifer Jason Leigh, Martin Short, Michael McKean, Tracy Brooks Swope
▶ Student filmmaker Bacon wins award and plenty of attention in Hollywood from agent Short, studio boss Swope, and others, but finds the road to Tinseltown success rather rocky. Actor Guest's directorial debut is never less than genial and often clever; however, inside jabs at movieland may puzzle the uninitiated. Amusing performance by Short.
Dist.: RCA/Columbia

BIG RED 1962
★ ★ ★ ★ NR Family 1:29
Dir: Norman Tokar *Cast:* Walter Pidgeon, Gilles Payant, Emile Genest, Janette Bertrand, George Bouvier, Doris Lussier
▶ Winsome Disney drama set in Canada shows how wealthy businessman and amateur dog breeder Pidgeon's outlook on life is changed by young Payant's attachment to a champion Irish setter. Moving plot and beautiful locations make this perfect viewing for youngsters. Based on a novel by Jim Kjelgaard.
Dist.: Buena Vista

BIG RED ONE, THE 1980
★ ★ ★ ★ PG War 1:53
☑ Explicit language, violence
Dir: Samuel Fuller *Cast:* Lee Marvin, Mark Hamill, Robert Carradine, Bobby DiCicco, Stephane Audran
▶ Autobiographical adventure based on director Fuller's war experiences in the First Infantry Division (the "Big Red One") focuses on veteran sergeant Marvin and his young, untried special infantry squad. Old-fashioned war film is crammed with thrilling action and vivid, firsthand account of fighting. Cult director Fuller spent thirty-five years trying to get this movie made.
Dist.: Warner

BIG SCORE, THE 1983
★ ★ R Action-Adventure 1:25
☑ Nudity, adult situations, explicit language, violence
Dir: Fred Williamson *Cast:* Fred Williamson, Nancy Wilson, Richard Roundtree, John Saxon
▶ Williamson stars as a Dirty Harryish narc who runs afoul of cops and crooks when he's suspected of confiscating a fortune in a large-scale drug bust. Plenty of blood, mayhem, and well-staged action to entertain genre fans yet generally a cut above the usual blaxploitation fare. Singer Wilson provides the love interest.
Dist.: Vestron

BIG SHOTS 1987
★ ★ ★ PG-13 Action-Adventure 1:30
☑ Explicit language, violence
Dir: Robert Mandel *Cast:* Ricky Busker, Darius McCrary, Robert Joy, Robert Prosky, Jerzy Skolimowski

▶ Distraught after the death of his father, eleven-year-old white kid Busker wanders into a ghetto. He's mugged, then befriended by smooth-talking black kid McCrary. The two unlikely pals embark on a wild Chicago-to-Louisiana journey when they come into possession of a hoodlum's car. Freewheeling adventure with an appealing central duo and an upbeat finale, nicely directed by Mandel. (CC)
Dist.: Warner

BIG SKY, THE 1952
★ ★ NR Western 2:20 B&W
Dir: Howard Hawks *Cast:* Kirk Douglas, Dewey Martin, Elizabeth Threatt, Arthur Hunnicutt, Buddy Baer, Steven Geray
▶ In 1830, unruly fur trapper Douglas and grizzled frontiersman Hunnicutt join Geray's expedition up the Missouri River into Blackfoot country. As they haul their boats by hand against the swift current, Crow Indians mount an attack. Long but action-packed Western, based on an A. B. Guthrie novel, is filled with colorful incidents. Hunnicutt won an Oscar nomination for his scene-stealing performance.
Dist.: Turner

BIG SLEEP, THE 1946
★ ★ ★ ★ NR Mystery-Suspense 1:54 B&W
Dir: Howard Hawks *Cast:* Humphrey Bogart, Lauren Bacall, John Ridgely, Martha Vickers, Dorothy Malone, Elisha Cook, Jr.
▶ Outstanding adaptation of Raymond Chandler's novel is one of the most stylish and satisfying mysteries of the 1940s. Bogart is the definitive Philip Marlowe, a laconic private eye drawn into a web of blackmail and murder when he tries to protect Vickers, a millionaire's spoiled daughter. The plot thickens when Marlowe falls for her older sister Bacall. Vivid atmosphere, sparkling dialogue, and great suspense, although the plot is so convoluted that the writers (William Faulkner, Jules Furthman, and Leigh Brackett) turned to Chandler to figure out one of the murders.
Dist.: MGM/UA

BIG SLEEP, THE 1978 British
★ ★ ★ R Mystery-Suspense 1:40
☑ Nudity, explicit language, violence
Dir: Michael Winner *Cast:* Robert Mitchum, Sarah Miles, Candy Clark, Oliver Reed, Joan Collins, Richard Boone
▶ Remake of 1946 film has Mitchum reprising his *Farewell, My Lovely* role as detective Philip Marlowe. Faithful adaptation of the Raymond Chandler novel, updated and set in London, with strong production values and a stellar cast. James Stewart has a cameo as General Sternwood, an ailing millionaire who sets Marlowe off on a complex case involving blackmail and murder.
Dist.: CBS/Fox

BIG STEAL, THE 1949
★ ★ NR Mystery-Suspense 1:11 B&W

Dir: Don Siegel *Cast:* Robert Mitchum, Jane Greer, William Bendix, Patric Knowles
▶ Mitchum and Greer, so memorably teamed in the classic 1947 film noir *Out of the Past*, give the genre another shot in this short but potent thriller from director Siegel. Plot involves stolen army loot; Knowles has it, Greer and Mitchum pursue him south of the border to get it back.
Dist.: Turner

BIG STORE, THE 1941
★ ★ NR Comedy 1:23 B&W
Dir: Charles Riesner *Cast:* Groucho Marx, Harpo Marx, Chico Marx, Tony Martin, Virginia Grey, Margaret Dumont, Douglass Dumbrille
▶ The brothers Marx will always provide a few laughs even in a vehicle that's far from their strongest. Plot involves store detective Wolf J. Flywheel (Groucho) helping department store owner Martin foil the store's villainous manager. The musical interludes (especially Martin singing "Tenement Symphony") are overlong, but there are some funny moments.
Dist.: MGM/UA

BIG STREET, THE 1942
★ ★ ★ ★ NR Drama 1:29 B&W
Dir: Irving Reis *Cast:* Lucille Ball, Henry Fonda, Agnes Moorehead, Sam Levene, Barton MacLane, Eugene Pallette
▶ Lowly busboy Little Pinks (Fonda) worships selfish nightclub singer Ball and devotes his life to her, even after she is crippled. Perhaps Lucy's best dramatic performance and Fonda matches her as the naive busboy. Based on a story by Damon Runyon with some of the same characters as *Guys and Dolls*.
Dist.: Turner

BIG TOP PEE-WEE 1988
★ ★ PG Comedy 1:22
☑ Adult situations
Dir: Randal Kleiser *Cast:* Pee-wee Herman, Kris Kristofferson, Valeria Golino, Penelope Ann Miller, Susan Tyrrell, Albert Henderson
▶ After a storm, farmer Herman emerges from his cellar to discover Kristofferson's circus pitched on his property. Herman falls for trapeze artist Golino, much to the dismay of girlfriend Miller. He decides to join the troupe but must first create an act. Meanwhile the townsfolk want the circus to hit the road. Not up to *Pee-wee's Big Adventure*. (CC)
Dist.: Paramount

BIG TOWN, THE 1987
★ ★ ★ R Drama 1:50
☑ Nudity, adult situations, explicit language
Dir: Ben Bolt *Cast:* Matt Dillon, Diane Lane, Tommy Lee Jones, Bruce Dern, Lee Grant, Tom Skerritt
▶ Dillon, a small-town boy with a talent for craps, heads for Chicago to make his fortune. Although attracted to a single mother, he's seduced by stripper Lane who's married to the dangerous Jones. Stylish but under-

developed drama set in 1957 is highlighted by Jones's swaggering villain and Lane's steamy fan dance.
Dist.: Vestron

BIG TRAIL, THE 1930
★ ★ NR Western 1:50 B&W
Dir: Raoul Walsh *Cast:* John Wayne, Marguerite Churchill, El Brendel, Tully Marshall, Tyrone Power, Sr., David Rollins
▶ Wayne graduated from bit parts to his first starring role in this impressively mounted early sound Western. Story follows pioneers as they cross the Oregon Trail, fighting Indians, staging a buffalo hunt, and fording dangerous rivers. Shot in Grandeur, an early wide-screen process, film's vivid action sequences will lose impact on TV. Dialogue scenes are stilted and unconvincing by today's standards. (CC)
Dist.: CBS/Fox

BIG TREES, THE 1952
★ NR Drama 1:29
Dir: Felix Feist *Cast:* Kirk Douglas, Eve Miller, Patrice Wymore, Edgar Buchanan, John Archer, Alan Hale Jr.
▶ In 1900, Quaker colonists consider California redwoods sacred, alienating those who would use the big trees for lumber. Wheeler-dealer Douglas wants to get his saw on the timber, but he then falls in love with Quaker widow Miller. Lumbering lumber tale acted and directed with a heavy hand (choir music accompanies shots of the forest). Remake of 1938's *Valley of the Giants*.
Dist.: Various

BIG TROUBLE 1986
★ ★ R Comedy 1:33
☑ Explicit language, mild violence, adult humor
Dir: John Cassavetes *Cast:* Alan Arkin, Peter Falk, Beverly D'Angelo, Charles Durning, Paul Dooley, Robert Stack
▶ Curious comedy about insurance salesman Arkin duped into murdering D'Angelo's husband Falk for his $5 million insurance policy. A double-cross leads to trouble with kidnappers and terrorists. This attempt to recapture the lunacy of the leads' *In-Laws* was plagued with production problems (Andrew Bergman dropped out as director and took his name off the screenplay). Barely released to theaters, although there are some funny moments.
Dist.: RCA/Columbia

BIG TROUBLE IN LITTLE CHINA 1986
★ ★ ★ PG-13 Action-Adventure 1:40
☑ Explicit language, violence
Dir: John Carpenter *Cast:* Kurt Russell, Kim Cattrall, Dennis Dun, James Hong, Kate Burton, Suzee Pai
▶ Bizarre action-comedy-kung fu-science-fiction film about macho truck driver Russell and Chinese waiter Dun battling the 2,000-year-old Godfather of Chinatown. Heavy-handed at times, but the stunts and special effects are delightful. Russell does a credible

tongue-in-cheek John Wayne impersonation. (CC)
Dist.: CBS/Fox

BIG WEDNESDAY 1978
★ ★ PG Drama 2:05
☑ Explicit language, adult humor
Dir: John Milius *Cast:* Jan-Michael Vincent, Gary Busey, William Katt, Lee Purcell, Patti D'Arbanville
▶ Male-bonding film about three young men, friends since high school, drawn together by a common love of surfing. Their friendship survives two decades; one gets married and two go off to Vietnam. Spectacular surfing footage, including a twenty-minute "big swell" (when waves can reach 15 feet).
Dist.: Warner

BIKINI BEACH 1964
★ ★ NR Comedy 1:40
Dir: William Asher *Cast:* Frankie Avalon, Annette Funicello, Martha Hyer, Don Rickles, Harvey Lembeck, Keenan Wynn
▶ Surf bums and bunnies face disaster when millionaire Wynn threatens to buy their beach; on top of that, Frankie might lose Annette to British rock star Potato Bug (Avalon, playing dual roles). Mindless escapism features a performance by "Little" Stevie Wonder. Third entry in the *Beach Party* series, followed by *Pajama Party.*
Dist.: Embassy

BILL 1981
★ ★ ★ ★ ★ NR Biography/MFTV 1:37
Dir: Anthony Page *Cast:* Mickey Rooney, Dennis Quaid, Largo Woodruff, Harry Goz, Anna Maria Horsford
▶ True story of mentally retarded Bill Sackler (Rooney), who slowly adjusts to life in the outside world after forty-six years in an institution. Young filmmaker Quaid helps him. Beautiful made-for-TV film about true meaning of friendship. Unforgettable Emmy-winning performance by Rooney and excellent support from Quaid. Followed by sequel "Bill on His Own."
Dist.: USA

BILL & TED'S EXCELLENT ADVENTURE 1989
★ ★ ★ PG Comedy 1:30
☑ Explicit language
Dir: Stephen Herek *Cast:* Keanu Reeves, Alex Winter, Bernie Casey, George Carlin, Terry Camilleri, Jane Wiedlin
▶ California high school students Reeves and Winter are failing history class. Futuristic hipster Carlin appears with his magical telephone booth to transport the hapless dudes through the past so historical figures, like Napoleon and Julius Caesar, can help them pass. Scattered laughs in freewheeling plot. Funniest line: the boys' description of Joan of Arc.
Dist.: Nelson

BILL COSBY—"HIMSELF" 1983
★ ★ ★ ★ ★ PG Documentary/Comedy 1:44
☑ Explicit language, adult humor
Dir: Bill Cosby *Cast:* Bill Cosby
▶ No-frills concert footage of Cosby doing what he does best: complaining about his family, dentists, old age, etc. Patched together from four 1981 performances in Hamilton, Ontario, and featuring some of Cosby's home movies. Sure to please his many fans. (CC)
Dist.: CBS/Fox

BILLION DOLLAR HOBO, THE 1978
★ ★ ★ ★ G Comedy/Family 1:36
Dir: Stuart E. McGowan *Cast:* Tim Conway, Will Geer, Eric Weston, Sydney Lassick, John Myhers
▶ Conway, a hopeless klutz, will inherit a fortune if he can make the long trip to Seattle as a hobo. He sets off with his amazing (and funny) wonder dog Bo, only to run afoul of bad guys who have kidnapped a rare Chinese dog. Amiable family-oriented comedy is uninspired but consistently entertaining.
Dist.: CBS/Fox

BILL OF DIVORCEMENT, A 1932
★ NR Drama 1:09 B&W
Dir: George Cukor *Cast:* John Barrymore, Katharine Hepburn, Billie Burke, David Manners, Henry Stephenson, Paul Cavanagh
▶ Shell-shocked war veteran Barrymore escapes from an asylum, meets daughter Hepburn for the first time, and learns that wife Burke is preparing to remarry. Hepburn believes that mental illness is in her blood, and, fearing to reproduce, calls off her romance with Manners. Young Hepburn is electric in her screen debut. Funny, touching story was remade in 1940.
Dist.: CBS/Fox

BILL ON HIS OWN 1983
★ ★ ★ ★ NR Biography/MFTV 1:40
Dir: Anthony Page *Cast:* Mickey Rooney, Helen Hunt, Teresa Wright, Dennis Quaid, Largo Woodruff, Paul Leiber
▶ Sequel to immensely popular TV movie *Bill* about mentally retarded adult coping with life in the outside world after forty-six years in an institution. Rooney reprises his Emmy-winning turn as Bill Sackter, overcoming another hurdle as friend Quaid and his wife Woodruff move away, learning to read with the help of Wright, and struggling when a fire destroys his small business. Rooney's heartwarming performances as the childlike but determined Sackter revitalized his career.
Dist.: USA

BILLY BUDD 1962
★ ★ NR Drama 2:03 B&W
Dir: Peter Ustinov *Cast:* Robert Ryan, Peter Ustinov, Melvyn Douglas, Terence Stamp, John Neville
▶ Saintly, innocent young sailor Billy Budd

(Stamp) is opposed by iron-handed officer Ryan and weak-willed captain Ustinov is caught in between. Stamp accidentally kills Ryan and Ustinov reluctantly presides at his court-martial. Literary adaptation of Herman Melville's novella really works, thanks to terrific cast and director/star/co-screenwriter Ustinov's craftsmanship. **(CC)**
Dist.: CBS/Fox

BILLY GALVIN 1987
★ ★ ★ **PG Drama 1:35**
☑ Explicit language
Dir: John Gray *Cast:* Karl Malden, Lenny Von Dohlen, Joyce Van Patten, Toni Kalem, Keith Szarabajka
▶ Earnest but predictable melodrama about the conflict between construction worker Malden, who wants his children to have a better life, and his son Billy (Von Dohlen), who wants nothing more than to follow in his father's footsteps. Sincere performances and gritty blue-collar Boston settings add to the film's realism.
Dist.: Vestron

BILLY JACK 1971
★ ★ ★ ★ **PG Action-Adventure 1:54**
☑ Rape, nudity, adult situations, violence
Dir: T. C. Frank (Tom Laughlin) *Cast:* Tom Laughlin, Delores Taylor, Clark Howat, Julie Webb, Kenneth Tobey
▶ Half-Indian ex–Green Beret Billy Jack lives on a reservation that's unpopular with the bigoted townsfolk. When the son of the local kingpin rapes the schoolmarm and kills an Indian boy, Billy Jack murders the boy's killer, takes a bullet in the gut, and then gives himself up so that he can go on to star in the first of two extremely popular sequels, *The Trial of Billy Jack* and *Billy Jack in Washington.* Surprise 1970s megahit was written, directed, and produced (under pseudonym T. C. Frank) by and stars Laughlin and wife, Delores Taylor.
Dist.: Warner

BILLY LIAR 1963 British
★ **NR Comedy 1:36 B&W**
Dir: John Schlesinger *Cast:* Tom Courtenay, Julie Christie, Mona Washbourne, Finlay Currie, Wilfred Pickles
▶ Courtenay excels as the title character, a young man who deals with mundane day-to-day reality by daydreaming, telling lies, and romancing women, including Christie. Memorable characterization will appeal to anyone whose mind ever wandered between nine and five. Schlesinger beautifully directs the Keith Waterhouse/Willis Hall adaptation of their play.
Dist.: HBO

BILLY ROSE'S JUMBO 1962
★ ★ **NR Musical 2:05**
Dir: Charles Walters *Cast:* Doris Day, Stephen Boyd, Jimmy Durante, Martha Raye, Dean Jagger, Billy Barty
▶ Durante and his daughter Day struggle to

keep their Wonder Circus afloat, unaware that rival Jagger has sent his son Boyd, supposedly a roustabout, to sabotage their efforts. Passable romance enlivened by beautiful Rodgers and Hart score ("This Can't Be Love," "The Most Beautiful Girl in the World"), Busby Berkeley choreography, and energetic clowning by Durante and Raye. Adapted by Sidney Sheldon from a Ben Hecht/Charles MacArthur play.
Dist.: MGM/UA

BILLY THE KID 1989
★ ★ **NR Western/MFTV 1:36**
Dir: William A. Graham *Cast:* Val Kilmer, Duncan Regehr, Julie Carmen, René Auberjonois, Wilford Brimley
▶ In 1879 New Mexico, young William Bonney (Kilmer) breaks the law to avenge the death of a kindly ranch owner. As Bonney's renegade reputation grows, governor Brimley pressures sheriff Pat Garrett (Regehr) to hunt him down. A few revisionist touches by screenwriter Gore Vidal, but on the whole a straightforward Western. Fine performance by Kilmer and a cameo by the author. Also known as *Gore Vidal's Billy the Kid.*
Dist.: Turner

BILLY THE KID VS. DRACULA 1966
☆ **NR Western/Horror 1:11**
Dir: William Beaudine *Cast:* Chuck Courtney, John Carradine, Melinda Plowman, Walter Janovitz, Harry Carey, Jr.
▶ Notorious outlaw Courtney has reformed and plans to marry ranch owner Plowman, but wedding is delayed by the arrival of her "uncle" Carradine, a mysterious European with designs on Plowman's neck. Bottom-of-the-barrel production is satisfying if viewed as camp.
Dist.: Video Yesteryear

BILOXI BLUES 1988
★ ★ ★ **PG-13 Comedy 1:44**
☑ Adult situations, explicit language
Dir: Mike Nichols *Cast:* Matthew Broderick, Christopher Walken, Corey Parker, Matt Mulhern, Markus Flanagan, Penelope Ann Miller
▶ In 1945, Brooklyn Jewish youth Broderick has three goals in life: win the Pulitzer prize, lose his virginity, and fall in love with his dream girl. During Army basic training in Biloxi, Mississippi, he achieves two of the three, despite harassment of foul-tempered drill sergeant Walken and antics of his bunkmates. Fine coming-of-age tale with plenty of laughs. Based on the Broadway smash; Broderick character is writer Neil Simon's alter ego. Preceded by *Brighton Beach Memoirs.*
Dist.: MCA

BINGO LONG TRAVELING ALL-STARS AND MOTOR KINGS, THE 1976
★ ★ ★ ★ **PG Drama 1:50**
☑ Explicit language

Dir: John Badham *Cast:* Billy Dee Williams, James Earl Jones, Richard Pryor, Ted Ross
▶ Badham made his film debut with this high-spirited tale of a barnstorming Negro League baseball team in the days when blacks were barred from the majors. Beautifully shot with an evocative period feel. Nice work from Williams as the team leader, Jones as burly catcher, and Pryor as a light-skinned black hoping to pass for Hispanic.
Dist.: MCA

BIRCH INTERVAL 1976
★ ★ **PG Drama 1:45**
☑ Adult situations
Dir: Delbert Mann *Cast:* Eddie Albert, Rip Torn, Ann Wedgeworth, Susan McClung, Anne Revere
▶ In 1947, delicate eleven-year-old McClung is sent to Amish Pennsylvania to live with grandfather Albert. She learns about love and understanding from retarded uncle Torn, only to watch him victimized by local bigots. Sensitive coming-of-age story from Joanna Crawford's novel has beautiful photography and outstanding performances from Albert and Torn.
Dist.: Media

BIRD 1988
★ ★ ★ **R Biography/Music 2:43**
☑ Adult situations, explicit language
Dir: Clint Eastwood *Cast:* Forest Whitaker, Diane Venora, Michael Zelniker, Samuel E. Wright, Keith David, Michael McGuire
▶ Whitaker plays Charlie Parker, legendary saxophone player who changed the nature of jazz during the bebop era. Not always appreciated during his time, Parker struggled with booze and drugs despite the help of faithful wife Venora. Exultant and sorrowful tale of musical mastery and personal disintegration directed by jazz fan Eastwood will please music lovers; its dark look and frequent flashbacks/forwards may leave others restless. Received Oscar for Best Sound.
Dist.: Warner

BIRDMAN OF ALCATRAZ 1962
★ ★ ★ **NR Biography 2:23 B&W**
Dir: John Frankenheimer *Cast:* Burt Lancaster, Karl Malden, Thelma Ritter, Neville Brand, Edmond O'Brien, Hugh Marlowe
▶ True story of prison lifer Robert Stroud (Lancaster), who became an outstanding ornithologist after nursing back to health a sick bird that flew into his cell. Stroud got along better with birds than humans, leading to conflict with tough warden Malden. Wonderful Oscar-nominated performance by Lancaster highlights this long but engrossing film.
Dist.: CBS/Fox

BIRD OF PARADISE 1932
★ ★ **NR Drama 1:20 B&W**
Dir: King Vidor *Cast:* Joel McCrea, Dolores Del Rio, John Halliday, Skeets Gallegher, Lon Chaney, Jr.

▶ Virile playboy McCrea wrecks his yacht on a South Seas island paradise, where he falls for local dark-skinned beauty Del Rio. Marriage plans are upset when the island's volcano god begins to rumble and Del Rio is chosen to sacrifice herself to the fiery crater. Long on lush scenery and hints of eroticism, short on story. First sound film to have background music in every scene; native dance choreographed by Busby Berkeley.
Dist.: Video Yesteryear

BIRD ON A WIRE 1990
★ ★ ★ **PG-13 Action-Adventure/Comedy 1:53**
☑ Brief nudity, adult situations, explicit language, violence
Dir: John Badham *Cast:* Mel Gibson, Goldie Hawn, David Carradine, Bill Duke, Stephen Tobolowsky, Joan Severance
▶ Lawyer Hawn pulls into a gas station and recognizes Gibson, her supposedly long-dead boyfriend who is actually a relocated FBI witness. When the thugs he fingered come gunning for him, the ex-lovers go on the lam. Combined star power energizes a rickety vehicle with surprisingly punchless direction from Badham. Gibson has fun with broad bits, like impersonating a homosexual; Hawn relies on her tried-and-true persona.
Dist.: MCA

BIRDS, THE 1963
★ ★ ★ ★ **PG-13 Mystery-Suspense 2:00**
☑ Violence
Dir: Alfred Hitchcock *Cast:* Rod Taylor, Tippi Hedren, Jessica Tandy, Suzanne Pleshette, Veronica Cartwright
▶ In a small Northern California town, wealthy young Hedren and lawyer Taylor are among those menaced when birds suddenly and mysteriously start attacking people. Hitchcock's technical mastery has never been more apparent than in this classic thriller of nature against man. Eerie visuals plus Bernard Herrmann's synthesized soundtrack (using no actual music) create a constant sense of unease.
Dist.: MCA

BIRD WITH THE CRYSTAL PLUMAGE, THE 1969 Italian
★ **PG Mystery-Suspense 1:38**
☑ Violence
Dir: Dario Argento *Cast:* Tony Musante, Suzy Kendall, Eva Renzi, Enrico Maria Salerno
▶ In Rome, American writer Musante witnesses a woman being murdered in an art gallery. A serial killer is on the loose; the police keep an eye on Musante, who does a little sleuthing himself. Stylish direction by Argento has given this cunning thriller a cult following. Also known as *Phantom of Terror.*
Dist.: United

BIRDY 1984
★ ★ **R Drama 2:00**

☑ Nudity, explicit language, violence
Dir: Alan Parker   **Cast:** Nicolas Cage, Matthew Modine, John Harkins, Sandy Baron, Karen Young
▶ Offbeat character drama directed with care and sensitivity by Parker. Cage and bird-obsessed Modine, childhood pals from Philly, are sent to Vietnam. When the war drives Modine completely off the deep end and into an institution, Cage tries to reach out to him. Terrific performances, especially by Modine, and amazing footage re-creating his fantasies of flight. Not for all tastes but nonetheless powerful and thought provoking. Adapted from William Wharton's acclaimed novel.   **(CC)**
Dist.: RCA/Columbia

BIRTH OF A NATION, THE 1915
★ **NR Drama 2:39 B&W**
Dir: D. W. Griffith   **Cast:** Lillian Gish, Mae Marsh, Henry B. Walthall, Miriam Cooper, Robert Harron, Walter Long
▶ The Ku Klux Klan are the heroes of this silent classic about two families, one from the North and one from the South, during and after the Civil War. Defeated Southerners must bear the insolent rule of newly enfranchised blacks led by would-be rapist Long. Rebel veteran Walthall raises a company of sheeted night riders to frighten the former slaves back to their places. Would have been consigned to obscurity for its racial attitudes except for its historical importance in establishing the full range of the medium's narrative vocabulary—and for the fact that it is a masterpiece, vividly recreating the look of the era it portrays.
Dist.: Cable

BISHOP'S WIFE, THE 1947
★★★★★ **NR Fantasy 1:49 B&W**
Dir: Henry Koster   **Cast:** Cary Grant, Loretta Young, David Niven, Monty Woolley, James Gleason, Elsa Lanchester
▶ As an Angel, Grant comes to Earth to help harried bishop Niven, who neglects wife Young and daughter due to career demands. Classic Christmas story is truly timeless and so filled with charm and sweetness that few will be able to resist. Young is delicate and lovely, Grant his dependably dashing self, Niven convincingly cast against type. A Best Picture Oscar nominee.
Dist.: Nelson   Ⓒ

BITCH, THE 1979 British
★ **R Drama 1:30**
☑ Nudity, strong sexual content, adult situations
Dir: Gerry O'Hara   **Cast:** Joan Collins, Kenneth Haigh, Michael Coby, Ian Hendry, Carolyn Seymour
▶ Follow-up to *The Stud* has disco owner Collins involved in diamond smuggling and fixing horse races to save her failing club. Based on a story by Joan's sister, Jackie, the plot is simply an excuse for frequent sex in beds, pools,

showers, sauna, etc. Exploitation fare should please Collins fans.
Dist.: HBO

BITE THE BULLET 1975
★★★★ **PG Western 2:11**
☑ Explicit language, mild violence
Dir: Richard Brooks   **Cast:** Gene Hackman, Candice Bergen, James Coburn, Ben Johnson, Jan-Michael Vincent, Dabney Coleman
▶ Large-scale Western about wildly different characters involved in a grueling 700-mile endurance race across mountains, deserts, woodlands, and mesas. Old-fashioned entertainment (based on an actual 1908 race sponsored by the *Denver Post*) helped by beautiful photography and strong performances.
Dist.: RCA/Columbia

BITTER SWEET 1940
★ **NR Musical 1:32**
Dir: W. S. Van Dyke II   **Cast:** Jeanette MacDonald, Nelson Eddy, George Sanders, Ian Hunter, Felix Bressart, Lynne Carver
▶ Beautiful Noel Coward score highlights this well-mounted adaptation of his 1929 operetta. Singer MacDonald and composer Eddy elope to turn-of-the-century Vienna, but their happiness is threatened by Sanders, a cad with no respect for marriage. Songs include "Today" and "I'll See You Again."
Dist.: MGM/UA

BITTERSWEET LOVE 1976
★★ **PG Drama 1:30**
☑ Adult situations
Dir: David Miller   **Cast:** Lana Turner, Robert Lansing, Celeste Holm, Robert Alda, Meredith Baxter Birney, Scott Hylands
▶ Birney and Hylands are about to have a baby when they discover they're brother and sister. Should they continue their marriage? "Problem" drama with an intriguing cast (Turner's role as the mother was her first after a long absence from the screen) treats its delicate theme in a romantic, glossy style.
Dist.: Nelson

BLACK AND WHITE IN COLOR 1976 French
★ **PG Comedy 1:40**
☑ Explicit language, violence
Dir: Jean-Jacques Annaud   **Cast:** Jean Carmet, Jacques Dufilho, Catherine Rouvel, Jacques Spiesser
▶ French and German settlers in Africa, having lived without conflict for years, fight one another when World War I breaks out in Europe. Biting antiwar satire from director Annaud beat out *Cousine, Cousine* and *Seven Beauties* for Best Foreign Film Oscar.   Ⓢ
Dist.: Warner

BLACK ARROW, THE 1948
★ **NR Action-Adventure 1:16 B&W**
Dir: Gordon Douglas   **Cast:** Louis Hayward, Janet Blair, George Macready, Edgar Buchanan, Lowell Gilmore, Rhys Williams

▶ In the fifteenth century, Hayward returns from the War of the Roses to learn his father has been murdered. While seeking the killers, he befriends Blair, ward of his wealthy uncle Macready, and later must rescue her from a deadly conspiracy. Loose adaptation of the Robert Louis Stevenson adventure concentrates on novel's second half; excellent climax as Hayward and Macready face off man to man.
Dist.: RCA/Columbia

BLACKBEARD'S GHOST 1968
★ ★ ★ G Fantasy/Comedy 1:47
Dir: Robert Stevenson *Cast:* Peter Ustinov, Dean Jones, Suzanne Pleshette, Elsa Lanchester, Joby Baker, Richard Deacon
▶ Lighthearted Disney fare stars Ustinov as the ghost of legendary pirate Blackbeard, summoned back to life by Jones when gangsters target his home for conversion to a casino. Merry mixture of delightful Ustinov and top-notch special effects.
Dist.: Buena Vista

BLACKBEARD, THE PIRATE 1952
★ NR Action-Adventure 1:39
Dir: Raoul Walsh *Cast:* Robert Newton, Linda Darnell, William Bendix, Keith Andes, Torin Thatcher, Irene Ryan
▶ Newton stars as the notorious pirate Blackbeard, terrorizing the high seas until his adopted daughter Darnell and handsome hero Andes join against him. Highlighted by Newton's patented, entertainingly outlandish villainy and Walsh's typical two-fisted direction.
Dist.: Turner

BLACK BEAUTY 1971 British
★ ★ ★ ★ G Family 1:14
Dir: James Hill *Cast:* Mark Lester, Walter Slezak, Peter Lee Lawrence, Ursula Glas
▶ Young Lester loses his beloved horse Black Beauty when his father is forced to sell his farm. Black Beauty undergoes many adventures in the hands of different owners while Lester tries to get him back. Scrupulous adaptation of Anna Sewell's classic is perfect viewing for children. Also filmed in 1946.
Dist.: Paramount

BLACK BELT JONES 1974
☆ R Martial Arts 1:25
☑ Violence
Dir: Robert Clouse *Cast:* Jim Kelly, Gloria Hendry, Scatman Crothers, Alan Weeks, Eric Laneuville
▶ Bodies go flying as karate king Black Belt Jones (Kelly) takes on bad guys who covet the dojo belonging to the Scatman and his sultry daughter Hendry. American blaxploitation-meets-kung-fu flick reunites real-life martial arts champ Kelly and his *Enter the Dragon* director Clouse.
Dist.: Warner

BLACK BIRD, THE 1975
★ ★ ★ PG Comedy 2:02
☑ Explicit language, mild violence
Dir: David Giler *Cast:* George Segal, Stephane Audran, Lionel Stander, Lee Patrick, Elisha Cook, Jr.
▶ Comedy that is both a parody of and a sequel to the 1941 Bogart classic *The Maltese Falcon*. Story takes place in San Francisco thirty years later, as the priceless statue appears once again and Sam Spade, Jr. (Segal) finds himself involved in the resulting intrigue. Patrick as the secretary Effie and Cook as gunman Wilmer reprise their roles from the original.
Dist.: Goodtimes

BLACKBOARD JUNGLE, THE 1955
★ ★ ★ ★ NR Drama 1:41 B&W
Dir: Richard Brooks *Cast:* Glenn Ford, Anne Francis, Vic Morrow, Louis Calhern, Sidney Poitier, Paul Mazursky
▶ Earnest English teacher Ford takes job at tough New York City vocational school and deals with problems of juvenile delinquents—rape, physical beatings, and blackmail. Eventually he wins the respect of the students. Tough, realistic melodrama presenting a frightening picture of inner-city education caused quite a sensation in its day. A bit dated but still holds up. Song "Rock Around the Clock" represents first Hollywood use of rock music.
Dist.: MGM/UA

BLACK CAESAR 1973
★ R Action-Adventure 1:36
☑ Nudity, language, violence
Dir: Larry Cohen *Cast:* Fred Williamson, Art Lund, Gloria Hendry, Julius W. Harris
▶ After being wounded as a boy by bigoted policeman Lund, Williamson becomes a Harlem crime czar as an adult. The battle against Lund continues, thanks to Williamson's possessing proof of the cop's corruption. Lively and fast-paced. Followed by *Hell Up in Harlem*.
Dist.: Orion

BLACK CAT, THE 1934
★ ★ NR Horror 1:05 B&W
Dir: Edgar G. Ulmer *Cast:* Boris Karloff, Bela Lugosi, David Manners, Jacqueline Wells, Lucille Lund, Henry Armetta
▶ Bizarre horror film pits Lugosi, a doctor determined to avenge his country's honor, against evil architect/devil worshipper Karloff, who he feels betrayed Austria during World War I. Eye-opening sets and intentionally outlandish touches (including hints of necrophilia, sadism, and fish worship) highlight this first of many Karloff-Lugosi teamings. Title was used for completely different films in 1941 and 1984.
Dist.: MCA

BLACK CAULDRON, THE 1985
★ ★ ★ ★ PG Animation 1:21
☑ Mild violence

Dir: Ted Berman, Richard Rich   *Cast:* Voices of Grant Bardsley, Susan Sheridan, Freddie Jones, Nigel Hawthorne, John Byner
▶ Taran, a young lad who hopes to become a warrior, battles the evil Horned King for possession of a magic cauldron that could determine the fate of the world. Aided by Princess Eilonwy and the bumbling Gurgi, Taran breaks into the king's sinister castle. Captivating Disney sword-and-sorcery fantasy features superb animation and a narration by John Huston.
Dist.: Buena Vista

BLACK DRAGONS 1942
★ NR Horror 1:01
Dir: William Nigh   *Cast:* Bela Lugosi, Clayton Moore, Joan Barclay, George Pembroke
▶ Evil Nazi doctor Lugosi operates on Japanese operatives. He transforms them into Caucasians so they can infiltrate America, but soon has to go there himself when his charges turn against him. The best thing you can say about this movie is that it's dated.
Dist.: Video Yesteryear

BLACK EAGLE 1988
★★ R Action-Adventure 1:34
☑ Explicit language, violence
Dir: Eric Karson   *Cast:* Sho Kosugi, Jean-Claude Van Damme, Doran Clark, Bruce French, Kane Kosugi, Shane Kosugi
▶ When a plane containing a top secret guidance system crashes in Malta, American agent Kosugi is dispatched to retrieve it before the Russians do. CIA woman Clark brings along Kosugi's kids (played by his actual children) as cover. Kung fu action includes big battle between Kosugi and Soviet operative Van Damme.
Dist.: Imperial

BLACKENSTEIN 1974
☆ R Horror 1:33
☑ Nudity, explicit language, graphic violence
Dir: William A. Levy   *Cast:* John Hart, Ivory Stone, Andrea King, Joe DiSue, Roosevelt Jackson, James Cougar
▶ A devious assistant interferes with an experimental operation, turning patient DiSue into a giant, gut-gobbling monster—with an Afro. Race-reversal exploitation picture is worse than most.
Dist.: Media

BLACK FURY 1935
★★★ NR Drama 1:32 B&W
Dir: Michael Curtiz   *Cast:* Paul Muni, Karen Morley, William Gargan, Barton MacLane, John Qualen, J. Carrol Naish
▶ Muni delivers a sterling performance as a furious, nearly illiterate coal miner whose attempt to form a new union is undermined by corrupt bosses. Hospitalized by company goons, he resorts to violence against strikebreakers. Assured direction enhances this

message drama based on a real incident in 1929 Pennsylvania.
Dist.: Key

BLACK HOLE, THE 1979
★★ PG Sci-Fi 1:37
☑ Mild violence
Dir: Gary Nelson   *Cast:* Maximilian Schell, Anthony Perkins, Robert Forster, Joseph Bottoms, Yvette Mimieux, Ernest Borgnine
▶ A space expedition led by Forster is trapped by Schell, a mad scientist intent on dragging them into a dangerous black hole. Disney's first PG film has magnificent special effects and two standout nonhuman characters: Vincent, a free-floating minicomputer, and Max, a sinister robot.
Dist.: Buena Vista

BLACK LIKE ME 1964
★★ NR Drama 1:47 B&W
Dir: Carl Lerner   *Cast:* James Whitmore, Roscoe Lee Browne, Sorrell Booke, Will Geer, Dan Priest
▶ Well-meaning exploration of racial problems. Trying to understand what it's like to be black, white writer Whitmore darkens his skin with chemicals and sets out in the world. A true story, from the best-selling book by John Howard Griffin.
Dist.: Various

BLACK MAGIC 1949
★★ NR Drama 1:45 B&W
Dir: Gregory Ratoff   *Cast:* Orson Welles, Nancy Guild, Akim Tamiroff, Raymond Burr, Frank Latimore, Valentina Cortese
▶ In the eighteenth century, villainous Welles uses hypnotism on the rich and powerful in an attempt to control the destiny of Europe. Based on Alexandre Dumas's account of real-life charlatan Cagliostro, historical drama is undermined by Welles's heavy-handed aping of the broad acting styles of the era.
Dist.: IVE

BLACKMAIL 1929 British
★★ NR Mystery-Suspense 1:26 B&W
Dir: Alfred Hitchcock   *Cast:* Anny Ondra, Sara Allgood, Charles Paton, John Longden, Donald Calthrop, Cyril Ritchard
▶ Ondra murders artist Ritchard when he tries to rape her; her boyfriend Longden, a Scotland Yard detective, is assigned to the case. He must protect her from arrest as well as deal with a blackmailer with damaging evidence. First British sound feature has rough passages as well as innovative touches; tense premise and chase through British Museum should satisfy fans of Hitchcock (who has an amusing cameo in a subway car).
Dist.: Various

BLACK MAMA, WHITE MAMA 1973 U.S./Filipino
☆ R Action-Adventure 1:27
☑ Nudity, adult situations, explicit language, graphic violence

Dir: Eddie Romero *Cast:* Pam Grier, Margaret Markow, Sid Haig, Lynn Borden, Zaldy Zshomack, Laurie Burton

► Gimmick exploitation film chains black prostitute Grier to white revolutionary Markow in a sordid Filipino prison ruled by lesbian guards. Mamas manage to escape and join guerrilla group in an attack on the jail. Crude low-budget drama filmed in the Philippines.

Dist.: HBO

BLACK MARBLE, THE 1980

★★ PG Drama 1:53

☑ Adult situations, explicit language, violence

Dir: Harold Becker *Cast:* Robert Foxworth, Paula Prentiss, Harry Dean Stanton, Barbara Babcock, James Woods

► Second collaboration between Becker and Joseph Wambaugh (*The Onion Field*) is an accurate, insightful look at depressed cop Foxworth slowly killing himself with alcohol. Saddled with Prentiss, a sexy new partner who thinks he's obsolete, Foxworth takes on an unimportant dognapping case to prove his moral values are still valid. Stanton excels in another offbeat villain role.

Dist.: Nelson

BLACK MOON RISING 1986

★★★ R Action-Adventure 1:40

☑ Brief nudity, adult situations, explicit language, violence

Dir: Harley Cokliss *Cast:* Tommy Lee Jones, Linda Hamilton, Robert Vaughn, Richard Jaeckel, Lee Ving, Bubba Smith

► Thieves led by industrialist Vaughn steal the Black Moon, a high-tech race car that has secret government evidence hidden inside. Free-lance thief Jones joins up with another free-lancer (Hamilton) to steal the car back from Vaughn's heavily guarded headquarters. Fast and eventful, with a full-throttle finale. (CC)

Dist.: New World

BLACK NARCISSUS 1946 British

★★★ NR Drama 1:41

Dir: Michael Powell, Emeric Pressburger

Cast: Deborah Kerr, Sabu, David Farrar, Flora Robson, Jean Simmons, Kathleen Byron

► Kerr and Byron lead a group of Anglican nuns seeking to maintain a school and hospital in the remote Himalayas. Farrar is the British agent who proves a thorn in their sides; Sabu is the Indian general using the Black Narcissus perfume to woo nubile local Simmons. Conflicts break out among the nuns, a result of mounting pressures and their growing isolation from the world. Wonderfully photographed, unusual but winning drama won Oscars for Cinematography and Set Decoration.

Dist.: Various

BLACK ORPHEUS 1959 French

★★ NR Drama 1:38

Dir: Marcel Camus *Cast:* Breno Mello, Marpessa Dawn, Lourdes de Oliveira, Lea Garcia, Adhemar da Silva, Alexandro Constantino

► Rio de Janeiro carnival is the exotic visual backdrop for a modernized version of the Orpheus and Eurydice legend set to a samba score. Dawn and Mello fall in love but she is killed by her angry ex-boyfriend. Mello attempts to resurrect Dawn. Won Best Foreign Film Oscar. Dubbed. [S]

Dist.: Various

BLACKOUT 1978

★★ R Action-Adventure 1:30

☑ Explicit language, violence

Dir: Eddy Matalon *Cast:* Jim Mitchum, Belinda Montgomery, Robert Carradine, June Allyson, Ray Milland, Jean-Pierre Aumont

► Cop Mitchum pursues four psychopaths, led by Carradine, who take advantage of a blackout to menace residents in an apartment building. Thriller inspired by the massive Manhattan blackout of July 13, 1977 (although film was shot in Canada), combines action and an interesting cast of Hollywood vets as the beleaguered tenants.

Dist.: Nelson

BLACKOUT 1985

★★ NR Mystery-Suspense/MFTV 1:39

☑ Adult situations, explicit language, violence

Dir: Douglas Hickox *Cast:* Richard Widmark, Keith Carradine, Kathleen Quinlan, Michael Beck

► Cop Widmark spends years tracking a psychopath who murdered his wife and children, narrowing his search to Carradine, an amnesiac who's started a new family with nurse Quinlan. Twisty thriller has a surprise ending.

Dist.: Media

BLACKOUT 1989

★ NR Mystery-Suspense 1:30

☑ Explicit language, violence

Dir: Doug Adams *Cast:* Carol Lynley, Gail O'Grady, Michael Keys Hall, Joseph Gian, Deena Freeman, Joanna Miles

► O'Grady returns home after running away four years previous. She suspects that her father has been murdered and buried on the property, or is being held prisoner somewhere in the house. Or maybe her hostile mother Lynley is hiding something? Alas, the answers to these questions evoke more chuckles than chills.

Dist.: Magnum

BLACK PANTHER 1977 British

☆ NR Mystery-Suspense 1:42

☑ Adult situations, explicit language, violence

Dir: Ian Merrick *Cast:* Donald Sumpter, Debbie Farrington, Marjorie Yates, Sylvia O'-Donnell, Andrew Brut, Alison Key

► Wearing a black hood, killer Sumpter earns feline sobriquet while robbing, killing, and

eluding the British police for three years in the early seventies. Based on a true criminal case that made a big splash in the British tabloids, unenlightening docudrama has little to offer American viewers.
Dist.: Vestron

BLACK PIRATE, THE 1926
★ **NR Action-Adventure 1:25 B&W**
Dir: Albert Parker *Cast:* Douglas Fairbanks, Sr., Billie Dove, Anders Randolf, Donald Crisp, Tempe Piggott, Sam De Grasse
▶ The sword of nobleman-turned-pirate Fairbanks is kept busy as he captures treasure-laden ships, rescues the beautiful Dove, and avenges his father's death while working his way back to his rightful station in life. Fairbanks bursts with vitality as he bounds across the painstakingly researched sets. The swashbuckling clichés of future generations are here freshly minted.
Dist.: Video Yesteryear

BLACK RAIN 1989
★★★★ **R Action-Adventure 1:25**
☑ Adult situations, explicit language, violence
Dir: Ridley Scott *Cast:* Michael Douglas, Andy Garcia, Kate Capshaw, Ken Takakura, Yusaku Matsuda
▶ Macho New York City cop Douglas and affable partner Garcia are assigned to escort ruthless Japanese mobster Matsuda back to Osaka. They deliver him to his cronies instead. Mad as hell, Douglas teams up with Japanese flatfoot Takakura to bring the gangster to justice. Infused with director Scott's trademark smoky visuals and fascination with neon; unfortunately, it's formula all the way, and Douglas's virile swagger is strained. Capshaw, as a glamorous nightclub hostess, has little to do except fill in the exposition. For hardcore action fans, there are battles on motorcycle, lethal samurai swordplay, and bloody beatings galore. **(CC)**
Dist.: Paramount

BLACK RAIN 1989 Japanese
☆ **NR Drama 2:03 B&W**
☑ Nudity, explicit language, violence
Dir: Shohei Imamura *Cast:* Yoshiko Tanaka, Kazuo Kitamura, Etsuko Ichihara, Shoichi Ozawa, Norihei Miki
▶ Tanaka is on a boat approaching Hiroshima on the day the atom bomb is dropped. As she walks through the devastated city with her aunt and uncle, all three are doused in radioactive rain. When they return to their village, Tanaka is ostracized for having been exposed to radiation. As her friends and relations die of the poison from the sky, she forms a close relationship with a shell-shocked war veteran. Profoundly sad and moving. Japanese title: *Kuroi Ame.* [S]
Dist.: Angelika

BLACK ROOM, THE 1935
★★ **NR Horror 1:10 B&W**
Dir: Roy William Neill *Cast:* Boris Karloff, Marian Marsh, Robert Allen, Thurston Hall, Katherine De Mille
▶ In the nineteenth-century, evil baron Karloff presides cruelly over a Czech village. His good twin, also played by Karloff, takes over and gladdens the hearts of the townspeople. The bad twin plots against his brother. Well done; Karloff shines in his dual role.
Dist.: RCA/Columbia

BLACK SABBATH 1964 Italian
★★ **NR Horror 1:39**
Dir: Mario Bava *Cast:* Boris Karloff, Susy Anderson, Mark Damon, Jacqueline Pierreux, Milli Monti, Michele Mercier
▶ Intriguing three-part horror anthology narrated by Karloff. In the first episode, based on Chekov's "The Drop of Water," nurse Pierreux makes a bad mistake when she robs a medium's corpse; "The Telephone" is an eerie exercise in suspense as prostitute Mercier is haunted by jailed killer; "The Wurdalak," based on a Tolstoy short story, stars Karloff as a vampire who preys on his own family. Karloff's turn is the standout here, although all three episodes receive stylish direction.
Dist.: HBO

BLACK SIX, THE 1974
☆ **R Action-Adventure 1:30**
☑ Adult situations, explicit language, violence
Dir: Matt Cimber *Cast:* Gene Washington, Carl Eller, Lem Barney, Mercury Morris, Willie Lanier, Joe Greene, Rosalind Miles, Ben Davidson, Maury Wills
▶ Black exploitation movie with a twist to please sports fans: pro football greats Washington, Eller, Barney, Morris, Lanier, and Greene star as Vietnam vet bikers. When Washington's brother is murdered by white motorcyclists, the six confront the killers. Appealing, if amateurish, acting by the athletes.
Dist.: Unicorn

BLACK STALLION, THE 1979
★★★★★ **G Family 1:56**
Dir: Carroll Ballard *Cast:* Kelly Reno, Mickey Rooney, Teri Garr, Clarence Muse, Hoyt Axton
▶ Walter Farley's adventure about young Reno shipwrecked on a desert island with an Arabian thoroughbred receives a lavish production in this beautiful family film. Story follows Reno's reunion with mother Garr and horse-racing adventures with trainer Rooney. Outstanding photography by Caleb Deschanel. Film received a special Oscar for sound editing, and was followed four years later by *The Black Stallion Returns.*
Dist.: MGM/UA

BLACK STALLION RETURNS, THE 1983
★★★★ **PG Family 1:43**
☑ Explicit language, mild violence
Dir: Robert Dalva *Cast:* Kelly Reno, Mickey

Rooney, Vincent Spano, Allen Goorwitz, Teri Garr, Jodi Thelen
► Teenager Reno searches the Sahara for the Black, his beloved horse, kidnapped by an evil Arab. Lacks the magical feel of the original movie but may be more accessible to younger tots. Provides plenty of action, adventure, production values, and Middle Eastern atmosphere. Rousing big race climax will entertain the whole family.
Dist.: MGM/UA

BLACK SUNDAY 1961 Italian
★ ★ NR Horror 1:23 B&W
Dir: Mario Bava *Cast:* Barbara Steele, John Richardson, Ivo Garrani, Andrea Cecchi, Arturo Dominici, Enrico Olivieri
► Steele, a witch brought back to life two hundred years after her original execution, wreaks revenge on the Moldavian descendents of the brother who betrayed her. Director Bava's swooping camera and acute sense of the grisly have won this chilling horror drama cult status over the years.
Dist.: Sinister

BLACK SUNDAY 1977
★ ★ ★ R Mystery-Suspense 2:23
☑ Explicit language, violence
Dir: John Frankenheimer *Cast:* Robert Shaw, Bruce Dern, Marthe Keller, Fritz Weaver, Steven Keats
► Terrorist leader Keller teams up with brainwashed, shellshocked Vietnam vet Dern to explode the Goodyear Blimp over the crowded Super Bowl. Shaw saves the day as a heroic Israeli agent. Somewhat overlong but suspenseful, topical thriller from director Frankenheimer. The climax generates real terror and excitement. Adapted from the Thomas Harris best-seller.
Dist.: Paramount

BLACK VEIL FOR LISA, A 1969
German/Italian
☆ NR Mystery-Suspense 1:27
☑ Adult situations, violence
Dir: Massimo Dallamano *Cast:* John Mills, Luciana Paluzzi, Robert Hoffman, Renata Kasche, Tulio Altamura, Carlo Hintermann
► Narcotics cop Mills learns that wife Paluzzi is cheating on him. After surveilling his unfaithful spouse instead of the bad guys, he ultimately hires a hitman—who proceeds to fall in love with his target. Strained plot and familiar characters.
Dist.: Republic

BLACK WIDOW 1987
★ ★ ★ ★ R Mystery-Suspense 1:42
☑ Nudity, adult situations, explicit language, violence
Dir: Bob Rafelson *Cast:* Debra Winger, Theresa Russell, Nicol Williamson, Sami Frey, Dennis Hopper, Terry O'Quinn
► Winger, a Justice Department investigator, wonders if Russell, a frequent widow, may be murdering her wealthy husbands. Winger be-

comes so obsessed with the case that she forms a friendship with Russell in order to spy on her. The leads are convincing, as well as beautiful, in this absorbing thriller. Eye-catching locations range from the Pacific Northwest to Hawaii. **(CC)**
Dist.: CBS/Fox

BLACK WINDMILL, THE 1974
★ ★ ★ PG Espionage 1:46
☑ Violence
Dir: Don Siegel *Cast:* Michael Caine, Joseph O'Conor, Donald Pleasence, John Vernon, Janet Suzman, Delphine Seyrig
► British spy Caine learns that his agency has kidnapped his son; with the help of his estranged wife Suzman, he races against time to rescue the boy. Strong opening leads to disappointing climax in this middling spy thriller. Pleasence overacts as the creepy chief villain.
Dist.: MCA

BLACULA 1972
☆ PG Horror 1:32
☑ Violence
Dir: William Crain *Cast:* William Marshall, Denise Nicholas, Vonetta McGee, Thalmus Rasulala, Ketty Lester, Elisha Cook, Jr.
► Marshall, an African prince turned into a vampire by Dracula in 1815, searches for new victims in modern day Los Angeles. Stylish, violent, and often amusing picture billed as the first black horror film. Features a surprisingly dignified performance from Marshall. Followed by *Scream, Blacula, Scream.*
Dist.: HBO

BLADE MASTER, THE 1984 Italian
★ PG Action-Adventure 1:32
☑ Adult situations, explicit language, violence
Dir: David Hills *Cast:* Miles O'Keeffe, Lisa Foster, Charles Borromel, David Cain Haughton, Chen Wong
► Sequel to *Ator, the Fighting Eagle.* In prehistoric times, muscular warrior O'Keeffe leads a small band of men to the "Castle of Knowledge" to prevent the ultimate weapon, known as the Geometric Nucleus, from being used to destroy the world. Live action comic book was originally titled *Ator, the Invincible.*
Dist.: Media

BLADE RUNNER 1982
★ ★ R Sci-Fi 2:01
☑ Brief nudity, explicit language, violence
Dir: Ridley Scott *Cast:* Harrison Ford, Rutger Hauer, Sean Young, Daryl Hannah, Edward James Olmos, Joanna Cassidy
► Ford plays a twenty-first-century cop forced out of retirement to track down a rebellious gang of Replicants, androids indistinguishable from humans. During a deadly cat-and-mouse chase through Los Angeles, Ford falls in love with a woman who may be one of the killers. Postmodern film noir highlighted by dazzling production design. Based on *Do*

Androids Dream of Electric Sheep? by Philip K. Dick. Videocassette version contains five minutes of additional footage.
Dist.: Nelson

BLAME IT ON RIO 1984
★ ★ ★ R Comedy 1:40
☑ Nudity, adult situations, explicit language, adult humor
Dir: Stanley Donen *Cast:* Michael Caine, Joseph Bologna, Michelle Johnson, Demi Moore, Valerie Harper
▶ Remake of French farce *One Wild Moment* has Caine and Bologna as best friends who take their teenaged daughters, Moore and Johnson, on a Rio vacation. To his dismay, Caine finds himself seduced by Johnson. Suggestive material handled adroitly by the leads. Beautiful Rio de Janeiro locations.
Dist.: Vestron

BLAME IT ON THE NIGHT 1984
★ ★ ★ PG-13 Drama 1:25
☑ Adult situations, explicit language
Dir: Gene Taft *Cast:* Nick Mancuso, Byron Thames, Leslie Ackerman, Dick Bakalyan, Merry Clayton
▶ After his wife dies, rock 'n' roll star Mancuso gets custody of son Thames, a military academy student who doesn't take easily to the music world. Some moving moments as father and son iron out their differences. Based on an idea by Mick Jagger. Plenty of music from Merry Clayton, Billy Preston, and Ollie E. Brown appearing as themselves.
Dist.: CBS/Fox

BLAST OFF 1967
★ ★ NR Sci-Fi/Comedy 1:35
Dir: Don Sharp *Cast:* Burl Ives, Troy Donahue, Gert Frobe, Terry-Thomas, Hermione Gingold, Jimmy Clitheroe
▶ In Victorian England, American promoter P. T. Barnum (Ives) announces his plan to send Tom Thumb (Clitheroe) on a one-way rocket trip to the moon. Foreign spies seek to steal the spaceship's design, while rocketeer Donahue suggests that his craft is superior and can make the round trip. Film's uninspired high jinks, loosely based on a Jules Verne story, are adequate for kids. Also titled *Those Fantastic Flying Fools.*
Dist.: HBO

BLAZE 1989
★ ★ ★ ★ R Biography/Drama 2:00
☑ Nudity, adult situations, explicit language
Dir: Ron Shelton *Cast:* Paul Newman, Lolita Davidovitch, Jerry Hardin, Gailard Sartain, Jeffrey DeMunn, Robert Wuhl
▶ Bawdy, irreverent look at the scandalous affair in the late 1950s between Louisiana Governor Earl Long and exotic dancer Blaze Starr (Davidovitch). Newman is superb as the feisty Governor, weathering charges of corruption and turning a stay in a mental institution to his advantage by campaigning with the slogan "I'm not crazy." Wry screenplay by

Shelton captures atmosphere and politics of the Deep South perfectly. Based on Starr's memoirs (she can be glimpsed in a dressing room scene). Received an Oscar nomination for Haskell Wexler's photography. **(CC)**
Dist.: Buena Vista

BLAZING SADDLES 1974
★ ★ ★ ★ R Comedy 1:33
☑ Explicit language, violence, adult humor
Dir: Mel Brooks *Cast:* Mel Brooks, Gene Wilder, Cleavon Little, Harvey Korman, Madeline Kahn, Alex Karras
▶ Mel Brooks's wild send-up of the Wild West. Little stars as Bart, the black sheriff challenged by the corrupt villain Hedley Lamarr (Korman). Hugely popular and unabashedly vulgar comedy with many memorable moments including Kahn's uproarious Marlene Dietrich parody, Brooks as a Yiddish-speaking Indian chief, and the notorious eating-beans-around-the-campfire scene.
Dist.: Warner

BLESS THE BEASTS AND CHILDREN 1971
★ ★ PG Drama 1:49
☑ Explicit language, violence
Dir: Stanley Kramer *Cast:* Billy Mumy, Barry Robins, Miles Chapin, Darel Glaser, Jesse White, Ken Swofford
▶ Six private school outcasts, including Mumy and Chapin, are upset when they witness the killing of buffalo. They decide to free a herd slated for slaughter. Sincere adaptation of the Glendon Swarthout novel. Oscar-nominated title song performed by the Carpenters.
Dist.: RCA/Columbia

BLIND ALLEY 1984
★ ★ R Mystery-Suspense 1:31
☑ Nudity, adult situations, explicit language, violence
Dir: Larry Cohen *Cast:* Anne Carlisle, Brad Rijn, John Woehrle, Matthew Stockley, Stephen Lack
▶ After toddler Stockley witnesses a Mafia slaying, hit man Rijn befriends the kid's mom (Carlisle) to learn if Stockley can identify him. Nice use of Greenwich Village locations in this moderately interesting, if not always believable, thriller from the prolific B-movie king Cohen. Also known as *Perfect Strangers.*
Dist.: Nelson

BLIND DATE 1984
★ ★ R Mystery-Suspense 1:39
☑ Nudity, adult situations, explicit language, violence
Dir: Nico Mastorakis *Cast:* Joseph Bottoms, Kirstie Alley, Keir Dullea, James Daughton
▶ Slick formula thriller with some fresh twists. American account executive Bottoms, living in Athens, is blinded in a fall while chasing a serial murder suspect. Medical researcher Dullea outfits Bottoms with experimental artificial vision, which enables him to find the killer. Meandering story line but stylishly shot.
Dist.: Vestron

BLIND DATE 1987
★★★ PG-13 Comedy 1:35
☑ Explicit language
Dir: Blake Edwards *Cast:* Bruce Willis, Kim Basinger, John Larroquette, Joyce Van Patten, Mark Blum
▶ "Just don't get her drunk," is the warning to yuppie Willis about beautiful blind date Basinger. Willis ignores the advice and Basinger proceeds to go "ca-razy," leading him on the wildest night of his life. Charming performances by the likable leads amidst plenty of slapstick gags from director Edwards in this lightweight romantic comedy.
Dist.: RCA/Columbia

BLIND FEAR 1989
★★ R Mystery-Suspense 1:30
☑ Explicit language, violence
Dir: Tom Berry *Cast:* Shelley Hack, Jan Rubes, Jack Langedyk, Kim Coates
▶ Blind inn manager Hack is spending night alone in isolated Maine hotel when vicious trio of thugs invades the premises. Hack takes advantage of the dark to battle the intruders. Fine work from Hack although her co-stars ham it up. Shabby production values but a nifty twist ending.
Dist.: Academy

BLIND FURY 1989
★★★ R Action-Adventure 1:26
☑ Explicit language, violence
Dir: Phillip Noyce *Cast:* Rutger Hauer, Terry O'Quinn, Lisa Bonet, Randall (Tex) Cobb, Meg Foster, Brandon Call
▶ Blinded in Vietnam, jungle fighter Hauer learns samurai techniques from Asian experts. Back in the States, he sets out to save O'-Quinn, a war buddy who's being tormented by crooked gamblers. Hauer and O'Quinn's young son Call head cross country to Vegas for a violent confrontation. Hauer swings a mean sword in this strong action pic based on a popular Japanese movie character.
Dist.: RCA/Columbia

BLIND HUSBANDS 1919
☆ NR Drama 1:38 B&W
Dir: Erich von Stroheim *Cast:* Erich von Stroheim, Gibson Gowland, Sam De Grasse, Francelia Billington, Faye Holderness, Jack Perrin
▶ Among the picturesque Alps, handsome officer von Stroheim romances the bored wife of a stuffy doctor. Hot stuff for its time, silent melodrama satirizing sexual mores has little appeal outside of the historical. Von Stroheim's first as a director.
Dist.: Video Yesteryear

BLIND RAGE 1983 Filipino
★★★ R Action-Adventure 1:20
☑ Explicit language, violence
Dir: Efren C. Pinion *Cast:* D'Urville Martin, Leo Fong, Fred Williamson, Tony Ferrer
▶ International cast in a Filipino thriller. Five blind men pull off a $15 million bank heist but

are killed in the getaway. Williamson is the mercenary hired by the CIA to track down the surviving mastermind. Cheap-looking production and bad dubbing but some action and fiery explosions for genre addicts.
Dist.: MGM/UA

BLINDSIDE 1988
★★ R Mystery-Suspense 1:42
☑ Nudity, adult situations, explicit language, violence
Dir: Paul Lynch *Cast:* Harvey Keitel, Lori Hallier, Lolita David, Michael Rudder
▶ Creepy hotel owner Keitel is immersed in deception and double-crosses when a drug kingpin strongarms him into keeping tabs on one of the guests. A cross between Coppola's *The Conversation* and Hitchcock's *Psycho*, the story can be confusing at times but improves as it goes along. Stylish direction from Lynch.
Dist.: Nelson

BLOB, THE 1958
★★ NR Sci-Fi 1:22
Dir: Irvin S. Yeaworth, Jr. *Cast:* Steve McQueen, Aneta Corseaut, Earl Rowe, Olin Howlin
▶ The original sticky-creature-from-outer-space flick lacks the budget and slick effects of the 1988 remake but it does have a young McQueen as the hero and a certain primitively campy charm all its own. Hilarious theme song (with lyrics like "Beware the blob, it leaps, and creeps, and leaps") by Burt Bacharach and Hal David.
Dist.: Video Gems

BLOB, THE 1988
★★ R Sci-Fi 1:30
☑ Explicit language, violence
Dir: Chuck Russell *Cast:* Kevin Dillon, Shawnee Smith, Joe Seneca, Donovan Leitch, Candy Clark
▶ A meteor brings a pink gelatinous mass to menace a small town in this upscale remake of the 1958 Steve McQueen low-budget classic. Only local bad boy Dillon and feisty cheerleader Smith have the moxie to defeat the sticky monster-mass. Good special effects and old fashioned suspense. Genre fans should lap this up like Jell-O.
Dist.: RCA/Columbia

BLONDE VENUS 1932
★★ NR Drama 1:37 B&W
Dir: Josef von Sternberg *Cast:* Marlene Dietrich, Cary Grant, Herbert Marshall, Sidney Toler, Dickie Moore
▶ When her scientist husband Marshall falls ill, performer Dietrich struggles to support her family and gets involved with Grant. Bizarrely stylized Dietrich/von Sternberg collaboration with a wild plot line: Dietrich degenerates into prostitution and even dons an ape suit for her "Hot Voodoo" song before a final reconciliation with her hubby.
Dist.: MCA

BLOOD ALLEY 1955
★ ★ ★ NR Action-Adventure 1:55
Dir: William Wellman   *Cast:* John Wayne,
Lauren Bacall, Paul Fix, Mike Mazurki, Anita
Ekberg, Joy Kim
▶ Daughter of a doctor murdered by Communists, Bacall persuades Merchant Marine
captain Wayne to ferry a group of Chinese
refugees through the dangerous Straits of Formosa to freedom in Hong Kong. With the Chinese seeking them by land and sea, Wayne
uses a combination of wit and daring to get
them through. Old-fashioned fifties flag-waver
with Wayne in his brawling, two-fisted prime.
Dist.: Warner

BLOOD AND LACE 1971
☆ PG Horror 1:27
Ⓥ Violence
Dir: Philip Gilbert   *Cast:* Gloria Grahame,
Melody Patterson, Vic Tayback, Milton
Selzer, Dennis Christopher
▶ After the brutal slaying of her prostitute
mother, teenager Patterson is sent to strict
Grahame's orphanage. The place gives Pat-
terson the creeps and for good reason: Gra-
hame has runaways murdered and put in the
basement freezer. Dated drive-in flick has hol-
low production values but good performance
by Grahame.
Dist.: HBO

BLOOD AND SAND 1922
★ NR Drama 1:32 B&W
Dir: Fred Niblo   *Cast:* Rudolph Valentino,
Lila Lee, Nita Naldi, George Field, Walter
Long, Leo White
▶ Valentino rises from poverty to become a
top Spanish matador. Although he marries
longtime girlfriend Lee, he has an affair with
wealthy Naldi that leads to his professional
downfall. The plotting veers into cornball
melodramatics, but Valentino still manages to
ooze charisma in an impressive production.
Silent was remade in 1941.
Dist.: Video Yesteryear

BLOOD AND SAND 1941
★ ★ ★ NR Drama 2:03
Dir: Rouben Mamoulian   *Cast:* Tyrone
Power, Linda Darnell, Rita Hayworth, Alla
Nazimova, Anthony Quinn
▶ Bullfighter Power is the toast of the town
until he hooks up with beautiful bad girl Hay-
worth, who lures him away from his wife Dar-
nell and guides him down the road to ruin.
Remake of the Rudolph Valentino silent is a
classic in its own right, thanks to lush direction
from Mamoulian, plush early Technicolor, and
Power's charisma.
Dist.: CBS/Fox

BLOOD BATH AT THE HOUSE OF DEATH
1985 British
☆ NR Horror/Comedy 1:30
Ⓥ Rape, brief nudity, explicit language, violence

Dir: Ray Cameron   *Cast:* Kenny Everett,
Pamela Stephenson, Vincent Price
▶ The body count piles up in this British genre
send-up. Eighteen people are found dead at
Headstone Manor and no explanation for the
killings is uncovered. Everett leads a group of
high-strung parapsychologists who attempt
to disprove the place's "haunted house" reputation. Funniest moment is a lampoon of
John Hurt's death scene in *Alien*.
Dist.: Media

BLOOD BEACH 1981
★ ★ R Horror 1:32
Ⓥ Nudity, adult situations, explicit lan-
guage, graphic violence
Dir: Jeffrey Bloom   *Cast:* John Saxon, Burt
Young, David Huffman, Marianna Hill, Otis
Young, Stefan Gierasch
▶ Various mutilations and deaths are occur-
ring beneath the sands of a Santa Monica
beach, but no remains can be found. Led by
Saxon, police try to locate the mysterious
creature responsible for the mayhem while
keeping skeptical sun worshippers away from
the sea. Average horror has few surprises.
Dist.: Media

BLOODBROTHERS 1978
★ ★ ★ R Drama 1:56
Ⓥ Adult situations, explicit language
Dir: Robert Mulligan   *Cast:* Richard Gere,
Paul Sorvino, Tony Lo Bianco, Lelia Goldoni,
Kenneth McMillan, Marilu Henner
▶ Young Stony DeCoco (Gere) prefers work-
ing in a children's hospital to the construction
work employing his macho dad (Lo Bianco)
and uncle (Sorvino). Domestic strife escalates
as the relatives fight over Stony's future. Old-
fashioned drama of Brooklyn Italian family
was unjustly ignored in its theatrical run. Many
moving moments and strong performances.
Based on the novel by Richard Price.
Dist.: Warner

BLOOD DINER 1987
☆ R Horror/Comedy 1:30
Ⓥ Nudity, explicit language, violence
Dir: Jackie Kong   *Cast:* Rick Burks, Carl
Crew, Roger Dauer, LaNette La France, Lisa
Guggenheim
▶ Brothers Burks and Crew, taking orders from
the brain of their evil late uncle, kill women so
that a goddess can inhabit their assembled
body parts. The boys add the leftover victim
portions to the food in their restaurant and
business picks up. Tacky gross-out comedy is
totally tasteless.
Dist.: Vestron

BLOOD FEUD 1980 Italian
☆ R Drama 1:39
Ⓥ Adult situations, explicit language, vio-
lence
Dir: Lina Wertmuller   *Cast:* Sophia Loren,
Marcello Mastroianni, Giancarlo Giannini,
Tuli Ferro
▶ Widow Loren vows revenge after her hus-

band is killed by the Sicilian Mafia in tho 1920s. She's helped by socialist lawyer Mastroianni and hit man Giannini, both of whom fall in love with her. Powerhouse performances by the three leads in this gritty antifascist drama from Wertmuller, one of the most important Italian directors of the 1970s.
Dist.: CBS/Fox

BLOODFIST 1989
★ R Martial Arts 1:25
☑ Adult situations, explicit language, graphic violence
Dir: Terence H. Winkless *Cast:* Don Wilson, Rob Kaman, Billy Blanks, Kris Aguilar, Joe Maril Avellana, Michael Shaner
► After his half-brother is murdered, California kung-fuer Wilson comes to Manila for revenge. He enters a martial arts competition to face off against his brother's killer, but his quest takes an unexpected turn. Ferocious fight choreography has cast giving its athletic all, but don't expect much in the acting or technical departments.
Dist.: MGM/UA

BLOODHOUNDS OF BROADWAY 1989
★★ PG Comedy 1:30
☑ Adult situations, violence
Dir: Howard Brookner *Cast:* Matt Dillon, Jennifer Grey, Julie Hagerty, Rutger Hauer, Madonna, Esai Morales, Anita Morris, Ethan Phillips, Randy Quaid, Josef Sommer, Dinah Manoff, Fisher Stevens
► Adaptation of Damon Runyon stories set on New Year's Eve, 1928: wounded gambling czar Hauer seeks refuge with series of mistresses; Quaid woos showgirl Madonna (who duets with Grey on "I Surrender, Dear") and tries to welsh on agreement to donate his big feet to science; Dillon has rocky romance with Grey while tracked by bloodhounds as murder suspect; and Phillips pretends to be tough guy to impress Hagerty. Fragmented narrative has tangy dialogue, pungent period settings, and colorful cast. In letterbox format. (CC)
Dist.: RCA/Columbia

BLOODLINE 1979
★★★ R Mystery-Suspense 1:57
☑ Nudity, adult situations, explicit language
Dir: Terence Young *Cast:* Audrey Hepburn, Ben Gazzara, James Mason, Michelle Phillips, Omar Sharif
► After the death of her father, Hepburn struggles for control of his pharmaceutical empire. Plenty of jet-set flash and glamour, intrafamily viciousness, colorful locations (Sardinia, Paris, Rome, New York), intrigue and mystery in this glossy adaptation of Sidney Sheldon's best-seller.
Dist.: Paramount

BLOOD LINK 1986
★ R Mystery-Suspense 1:30
☑ Nudity, adult situations, explicit language, violence
Dir: Alberto DeMartino *Cast:* Michael Mori-

arty, Penelope Milford, Geraldine Fitzgerald, Cameron Mitchell, Sarah Langenfeld
► Dr. Craig Mannings (Moriarty), separated at birth from his Siamese twin Keith (also Moriarty), discovers that his brother has become a lady killer (literally). Good twin tries to thwart bad twin in this farfetched but decently made thriller. Uneven performance by Moriarty in his dual role, but a few genuinely tense moments.
Dist.: Nelson

BLOOD MONEY 1988
★★★ NR Drama/MFTV 1:50
☑ Adult situations, explicit language, violence
Dir: Jerry Schatzberg *Cast:* Andy Garcia, Ellen Barkin, Morgan Freeman, Michael Lombard, John C. McGinley
► Florida-based smuggler Garcia joins hooker Barkin to track down his lawyer brother's murderers. Trail leads to seedy Miami attorney Freeman and Central American arms trafficking. Attractive leads generate heat, but plot runs out of steam. Also known as *Clinton and Nadine* .
Dist.: J2 Communications

BLOOD OF DRACULA'S CASTLE 1967
☆ PG Horror 1:24
☑ Violence
Dir: Al Adamson *Cast:* John Carradine, Alex D'Arcy, Paula Raymond, Ray Young
► Mr. and Mrs. Dracula (D'Arcy and Raymond) like to feast on American women; Carradine and Young are the cohorts assigned to keep the happy couple well supplied with lovely ladies. Low-budget horror is slowly paced and ridiculously plotted.
Dist.: Interglobal

BLOOD OF FU MANCHU 1968 British
★ NR Action-Adventure 1:31 B&W
Dir: Jess Franco *Cast:* Christopher Lee, Richard Greene, George Gotz, Shirley Eaton
► Sinister villain Fu Manchu (Lee) concocts a deadly poison, injects it into ten gorgeous women, and then sends them out into the world to literally kiss his foes to death. Also known as *Against All Odds.* Fourth in the series, followed by *Castle of Fu Manchu.*
Dist.: Republic Ⓒ

BLOOD OF GHASTLY HORROR 1972
☆ PG Horror 1:27
☑ Violence
Dir: Al Adamson *Cast:* John Carradine, Kent Taylor, Tommy Kirk, Regina Carrol
► Mad doc Carradine implants a device in the brain of a Vietnam vet that turns him into a robot-controlled killer. Grade Z horror pic is packed with severed heads, comely victims, and senseless action. Originally made in 1965, new scenes were added in 1971 and 1979, each version becoming increasingly incoherent. Also known as *Psycho a Go-Go!, Fiend With the Electronic Brain, Fiend With the*

Atomic Brain, and *Man With the Synthetic Brain.*
Dist.: VidAmerica

BLOOD OF HEROES, THE 1990
★ ★ R Action-Adventure 1:31
☑ Adult situations, explicit language, graphic violence
Dir: David Peoples ***Cast:*** Rutger Hauer, Joan Chen, Vincent Phillip D'Onofrio, Anna Katarina, Delroy Lindo, Gandhi MacIntyre
► In a grim future, Hauer leads nomadic "Jugger" team. In this violent sport, players must place a dog skull on a pointed stick while their opponents attack them. New "qwik" Chen joins the squad, which eventually plays in a big match, giving disgraced former star Hauer a chance for redemption. Tough yet solemn vision has fine, but derivative, futuristic texture. (CC)
Dist.: HBO

BLOOD OF OTHERS, THE 1984
★ ★ NR Drama/MFTV 2:56
☑ Adult situations, explicit language, mild violence
Dir: Claude Chabrol ***Cast:*** Jodie Foster, Michael Ontkean, Sam Neill, Stephane Audran, Lambert Wilson, Jean-Pierre Aumont
► Romantic saga of star-crossed lovers Ontkean, an antifascist activist from a wealthy background, and Foster, a seamstress and part-time model from a poor upbringing. Vividly played out against the social and policial upheaval of the years proceeding World War II through the German occupation of France. Adapted from the novel by Simone de Beauvoir.
Dist.: Prism

BLOOD OF THE VAMPIRE 1958 British
★ NR Horror
Dir: Henry Cass ***Cast:*** Donald Wolfit, Vincent Ball, Barbara Shelley, Victor Maddern, William Devlin, Bernard Bresslaw
► Maddern accidentally revives vampire Wolfit before he is sentenced to a prison for the criminally insane. There an evil warden conducts illegal, and gruesome, medical experiments. Botched horror outing should have been played for laughs; comes off as dull instead.
Dist.: MPI

BLOOD ON THE MOON 1948
★ ★ NR Western 1:28 B&W
Dir: Robert Wise ***Cast:*** Robert Mitchum, Barbara Bel Geddes, Robert Preston, Walter Brennan, Phyllis Thaxter, Frank Faylen
► Gunfighter Mitchum takes advantage of feud between beautiful rancher Bel Geddes and rival Brennan, helping outlaw Preston in the process. Romance leads to a change of heart and deadly showdown. Brooding, atmospheric Western with unusually rich characterizations.
Dist.: Turner

BLOOD ON THE SUN 1945
★ ★ NR Action-Adventure 1:38 B&W
Dir: Frank Lloyd ***Cast:*** James Cagney, Sylvia Sidney, Wallace Ford, Rosemary De-Camp, Robert Armstrong, Wallace Ford
► Cagney, editor of an English-language newspaper in Tokyo, uncovers evidence of a Japanese plan to conquer the world. Authorities are determined to kill him before he can leave the country with the story. Action-packed adventure with a dynamic Cagney.
Dist.: Video Yesteryear ©

BLOOD RED 1989
☆ R Drama 1:31
☑ Brief nudity, adult situations, violence
Dir: Peter Masterson ***Cast:*** Eric Roberts, Dennis Hopper, Giancarlo Giannini, Burt Young, Carlin Glynn, Lara Harris, Susan Anspach, Julia Roberts
► In turn-of-the-century northern California, young Italian Roberts isn't enthralled with the family wine business headed by dad Giannini. However, when railroad tycoon Hopper attempts to seize their land, Roberts fights back. Handsome period production gets increasingly involving after a slow start, although you'll wish director Masterson had reined in some of the hammier performers.
Dist.: Nelson

BLOOD RELATIONS 1988
★ NR Mystery-Suspense 1:29
☑ Nudity, adult situations, explicit language, violence
Dir: Graeme Campbell ***Cast:*** Jan Rubes, Lydie Dernier, Kevin Hicks, Ray Walston
► Surgeon Rubes, grieving for his late wife, wants to bring her back by using experimental surgery on the brain of Dernier, his son's girlfriend. Meanwhile, Hicks and Dernier plot to kill Rubes. Nasty little movie is well-crafted, with ghoulish twists to the story. Unfortunately, unsavory characters and slack pace limit involvement.
Dist.: Orion

BLOOD SIMPLE 1985
★ ★ R Mystery-Suspense 1:36
☑ Adult situations, explicit language, graphic violence
Dir: Joel Coen ***Cast:*** John Getz, Frances McDormand, Dan Hedaya, Samm-Art Williams, M. Emmet Walsh
► In rural Texas, bar-owner Hedaya hires detective Walsh to kill unfaithful wife McDormand and lover Getz. The plot that follows has to be seen to be believed—as murdered bodies don't quite stay dead and nothing is what it seems—in this visually stylish, ingenious thriller from writer/director Joel Coen and his producer/co-writer brother Ethan.
Dist.: MCA

BLOODSPORT 1987
★ ★ ★ R Martial Arts 1:37
☑ Explicit language, violence
Dir: Newt Arnold ***Cast:*** Jean-Claude Van

Damme, Donald Gibb, Leah Ayres, Roy Chiao, Bolo Yeung, Norman Burton

▶ Slipping out of Defense Intelligence Agency training camp, martial arts expert Van Damme journeys to Hong Kong to compete in the Kumite, a secret full-contact kickboxing tournament. While romancing journalist Ayres and befriending wild-eyed competitor Gibb, Van Damme establishes himself as the likely contender to dethrone reigning champ Yeung. Based on the true story of the first Westerner to win the Kumite. (CC)

Dist.: Warner

BLOODSTONE 1989

★★ PG-13 Comedy 1:31

☑ Brief nudity, adult situations, explicit language, violence

Dir: Dwight Little ***Cast:*** Brett Stimely, Rajni Kanth, Anna Nicholas, Charlie Brill, Jack Kehler, Christopher Neame

▶ Stimely and Nicholas come into possession of a cursed stone while honeymooning in India. When the jewel winds up in the trunk of innocent taxi-driver Kanth, all three become the targets of Neame, a power-hungry Dutchman desperate to get his hands on the stone. Heavy-handed chase comedy, with a funny turn by Brill as a Clouseau-like Indian detective.

Dist.: Forum

BLOOD WEDDING 1981 Spanish

★ NR Dance 1:12

☑ Adult situations

Dir: Carlos Saura ***Cast:*** Antonio Gades, Christina Hoyos, Juan Antonio Jimenez, Pilar Cardenas, Carmen Villena

▶ On his wedding night, Gades is forced into a revenge scheme that proves fatal. Ballet version of Federico Garcia Lorca's classic play, filmed at a full dress rehearsal and interspersed with interviews. Expert flamenco-derived choreography by Gades makes this a favorite among dance buffs. [S]

Dist.: Media

BLOODY MAMA 1970

★★ R Action-Adventure 1:30

☑ Adult situations, violence

Dir: Roger Corman ***Cast:*** Shelley Winters, Don Stroud, Pat Hingle, Robert De Niro, Bruce Dern, Robert Walden

▶ Ma Barker (Winters) teaches sons Walden, De Niro, and Stroud the tricks of the family trade: bank robbery. They prove to be good learners, much to the dismay of the law. B-movie action from the prolific Corman features a pre-stardom performance by De Niro.

Dist.: Vestron

BLOWING WILD 1953

★★ NR Action-Adventure 1:30 B&W

Dir: Hugo Fregonese ***Cast:*** Gary Cooper, Barbara Stanwyck, Ruth Roman, Anthony Quinn, Ward Bond, Juan Garcia

▶ Oil wildcatter Cooper needs a job, but hesitates at working for Quinn because of bad memories over an affair with Quinn's wife Stanwyck. In addition to the triangle, bandits are threatening to dynamite Quinn's rigs. Overblown misfire despite a strong turn by Stanwyck as a ruthless vixen.

Dist.: Republic

BLOW OUT 1981

★★★ R Mystery-Suspense 1:48

☑ Adult situations, explicit language, violence

Dir: Brian De Palma ***Cast:*** John Travolta, Nancy Allen, John Lithgow, Dennis Franz, Peter Boyden

▶ Travolta, a sound-effects expert for a fly-by-night film company, records evidence that a politician may have been murdered, but the only person who believes him is prostitute Allen, who's also a target of the conspiracy. Shooting in his Philadelphia hometown, De Palma and a superb crew push suspense to the limit. Buffs will spot many in-jokes and references to other films.

Dist.: Warner

BLOW-UP 1966 British/Italian

★★ NR Mystery-Suspense 1:51

☑ Nudity, adult situations, explicit language

Dir: Michelangelo Antonioni ***Cast:*** David Hemmings, Vanessa Redgrave, Sarah Miles, Jill Kennington, Verushka

▶ Alienated London photographer Hemmings photographs couple in park, then enlarges pics when he suspects he's stumbled onto a murder. Elegant murder mystery (whose plot influenced *The Conversation* and *Blow Out*, among others) may seem too oblique and arty to some but is still Antonioni's most accessible film. Technically superb, although director's wide-screen compositions may suffer on video.

Dist.: MGM/UA

BLUE ANGEL, THE 1930 German

★★ NR Drama 1:43 B&W

Dir: Josef von Sternberg ***Cast:*** Emil Jannings, Marlene Dietrich, Kurt Gerron, Rosa Valette, Hans Albers, Eduard von Winterstein

▶ Conservative teacher Jannings falls hopelessly in love with tawdry but irresistible cabaret singer Dietrich, sacrificing his career for her casual favors. Morbid, painfully incisive study of human degradation has lost none of its power over the years. Dietrich's Lola-Lola became an international icon as she sang "Falling in Love Again." Based on the novel by Heinrich Mann. [S]

Dist.: KVC

BLUEBEARD 1944

★★ NR Mystery-Suspense 1:13 B&W

Dir: Edgar G. Ulmer ***Cast:*** John Carradine, Jean Parker, Nils Asther, Ludwig Stossel, Teala Loring, Iris Adrian

▶ Carradine excels in a rare starring role as a nineteenth-century Parisian fond of murdering his wives. Parker, his latest girlfriend, notices

something odd about her intended while policeman Asther searches the city for the killer. Taut, low-budget thriller has a strong cult following.
Dist.: Video Yesteryear

BLUEBEARD 1972 French/Italian/German
★ R Drama 2:04
☑ Nudity, adult situations
Dir: Edward Dmytryk *Cast:* Richard Burton, Raquel Welch, Virna Lisi, Joey Heatherton, Nathalie Delon, Karin Schubert
▶ On her honeymoon, American bride Heatherton learns that aristocratic husband Burton has murdered his seven previous brides. Through flashbacks, he explains how their frozen corpses ended up in his basement. Offbeat drama has an impressive cast in unusual roles (Welch plays a nun; Burton, a Nazi).
Dist.: Nelson

BLUEBERRY HILL 1988
★ ★ R Drama 1:29
☑ Brief nudity, adult situations, explicit language
Dir: Strathford Hamilton *Cast:* Margaret Avery, Carrie Snodgress, Matt Lattanzi, Jennifer Rubin
▶ Coming-of-age story features Lattanzi as an aspiring mechanic and Rubin as his girlfriend, a young woman suffering a troubled relationship with her widowed mother Snodgress. Avery is a piano teacher who befriends Rubin in this slowly paced but competently handled melodrama with a good soundtrack of fifties tunes.
Dist.: CBS/Fox

BLUE BIRD, THE 1940
★ NR Fantasy 1:23
Dir: Walter Lang *Cast:* Shirley Temple, Spring Byington, Nigel Bruce, Gale Sondergaard, Eddie Collins, Sterling Holloway
▶ Temple and Collins go on a magical journey to find the bluebird of happiness, encountering Father Time and Mr. Luxury among other eccentric characters. Leaden version of the Maurice Maeterlinck play at least has beautiful production values and a memorable bit by Sondergaard. Remade in 1976.
Dist.: CBS/Fox

BLUE BIRD, THE 1976 U.S./Russian
★ ★ G Fantasy 1:37
Dir: George Cukor *Cast:* Elizabeth Taylor, Cicely Tyson, Jane Fonda, Ava Gardner, Todd Lookinland, Patsy Kensit
▶ Children Lookinland and Kensit search for the mythical bluebird of happiness, encountering Taylor (in four roles), Fonda (as Night), Tyson (Cat), and Gardner (Luxury) along the way. Expensive third film version of the Maurice Maeterlinck children's story is notable as the first U.S./Russian co-production.
Dist.: Playhouse

BLUE CITY 1986
★ R Mystery-Suspense 1:23

☑ Nudity, adult situations, explicit language, violence
Dir: Michelle Manning *Cast:* Judd Nelson, Ally Sheedy, Paul Winfield, Scott Wilson, David Caruso
▶ Brat Pack homage to 1940s film noir mysteries may appeal to teens. Rebellious Nelson returns to his sleazy hometown to discover his dad has been murdered and no one is anxious to nail the culprit. He investigates with help from kid sister Sheedy, who goes undercover as a go-go dancer. Based on a novel by Ross MacDonald.
Dist.: Paramount

BLUE COLLAR 1978
★ ★ ★ R Drama 1:53
☑ Explicit language
Dir: Paul Schrader *Cast:* Richard Pryor, Harvey Keitel, Yaphet Kotto, Ed Begley, Jr., Harry Bellaver
▶ Hard-hitting, realistic thriller about three assembly-line auto workers whose friendship falls apart when they find evidence that their union is corrupt. Schrader's directing debut (he also wrote the screenplay with his brother Leonard) is a graphic, unsettling film with unexpected comic touches. Convincing acting from all three leads.
Dist.: MCA

BLUE COUNTRY 1978 French
☆ PG Comedy 1:44
☑ Adult situations
Dir: Jean-Charles Tacchella *Cast:* Brigette Fossey, Jacques Serres, Ginette Garcin, Armand Meffre
▶ Parisian Fossey moves to the country and has affair with truck driver Serres. The lovers consider cohabitation and marriage. Likable leads cavort against the gorgeous pastel backgrounds of southern France. However, nearly plotless film meanders without achieving the humor and insight of same director's *Cousin, Cousine.* Ⓢ
Dist.: RCA/Columbia

BLUE HAWAII 1961
★ ★ ★ ★ NR Musical 1:41
Dir: Norman Taurog *Cast:* Elvis Presley, Joan Blackman, Nancy Walters, Angela Lansbury, Roland Winters, Iris Adrian
▶ Presley, heir to a pineapple fortune, shocks parents Winters and Lansbury when he turns his back on wealth to work in a tourist bureau. Above-average Presley vehicle has beautiful locations, plenty of romance, and a fine acting job by Lansbury. Elvis sings one of his biggest hits, "Can't Help Falling in Love."
Dist.: CBS/Fox

BLUE HEAVEN 1984
☆ NR Drama 1:40
☑ Explicit language
Dir: Kathleen Dowdey *Cast:* Leslie Denniston, James Eckhouse, Bruce Evers, Lisa Sloan
▶ Successful broadcaster Eckhouse and wife

Denniston start a new life in Atlanta. Eckhouse's drinking problem resurfaces and he grows abusive toward Denniston. She is hospitalized but battles to save her marriage. Flat drama has noble aims but suffers from heavyhanded screenplay and merely average acting.
Dist.: Vestron

BLUE IGUANA, THE 1988
★★ R Comedy 1:30
☑ Adult situations, explicit language, violence
Dir: John Lafia *Cast:* Dylan McDermott, Jessica Harper, James Russo, Pamela Gidley, Dean Stockwell, Tovah Feldshuh
▶ Down-and-out bounty hunter McDermott is hired by the IRS to retrieve contraband loot. South of the border, he finds himself in the middle of a war between mobster Russo and greedy bank owner Harper. Pungent film noir spoof lays on the murky plot details and loco characterizations with an unashamedly heavy hand. **(CC)**
Dist.: Paramount

BLUE LAGOON, THE 1980
★★★ R Drama 1:45
☑ Nudity, adult situations
Dir: Randal Kleiser *Cast:* Brooke Shields, Christopher Atkins, Leo McKern, William Daniels, Elva Josephson, Glenn Kohan
▶ Victorian-era teenagers Shields and Atkins are shipwrecked on a deserted Pacific island. Survival in this tropical paradise proves easy for a number of years; then, as developing adolescents, they struggle with their new sexual attraction to one another. Gorgeous photography by Nestor Almendros.
Dist.: RCA/Columbia

BLUE MAX, THE 1966
★★★ NR War 2:35
☑ Brief nudity, adult situations, violence
Dir: John Guillermin *Cast:* George Peppard, James Mason, Ursula Andress, Jeremy Kemp, Carl Schell, Anton Diffring
▶ In World War I, upstart German infantry soldier Peppard transfers to the air force and ruthlessly manipulates his fellow pilots to win the Blue Max, Germany's highest medal. Thrilling dogfight sequences and Peppard's steamy love scenes with Andress as Mason's unfaithful wife perk up the uneven plotting.
Dist.: CBS/Fox

BLUE MONKEY 1987
★★ R Horror 1:38
☑ Adult situations, explicit language, violence
Dir: William Fruet *Cast:* Steve Railsback, Susan Anspach, Gwynyth Walsh, John Vernon, Joe Flaherty
▶ Deadpan, low-budget horror flick should entertain genre fans. Plot is sort of an earthbound, hospital version of *Alien*, as a monstrous creature (more like a bug than a monkey) menaces doctors and patients. Nothing

new but a decent cast and spooky atmosphere enliven a familiar script.
Dist.: RCA/Columbia

BLUE MURDER AT ST. TRINIAN'S 1958 British
★ NR Comedy 1:26 B&W
Dir: Frank Launder *Cast:* Joyce Grenfell, Terry-Thomas, George Cole, Alistair Sim, Lionel Jeffries
▶ Sequel to *The Belles of St. Trinian's* finds authorities taking control of the girls' school; to escape disciplinary measures, pupils win a trip to Europe and get mixed up in a jewel robbery. Broad slapstick is hit or miss, although Terry-Thomas is delightful as a crooked tour manager.
Dist.: Various

BLUES BROTHERS, THE 1980
★★★★ R Comedy 2:13
☑ Explicit language
Dir: John Landis *Cast:* John Belushi, Dan Aykroyd, James Brown, Cab Calloway, Ray Charles, Carrie Fisher
▶ Jake Blues (Belushi) gets out of prison and teams with brother Elwood (Aykroyd) for "a mission from God"—to reassemble their old band and raise money for the orphanage where they grew up. Blockbuster combo of music (great numbers by Calloway, Charles, and Aretha Franklin), comedy in the "Saturday Night Live" style, and mayhem (plenty of car chases and crashes).
Dist.: MCA

BLUE SKIES AGAIN 1983
★★★ PG Comedy 1:36
☑ Adult situations, explicit language
Dir: Richard Michaels *Cast:* Harry Hamlin, Robyn Barto, Mimi Rogers, Kenneth McMillan, Dana Elcar
▶ Charming, fun performance by Barto as a woman struggling to become the first female minor league baseball player. This easy-to-root-for underdog must overcome harassment from the other players, prejudice, and the resistance of team owner Hamlin before she gets her chance to win the big game in the movie's final inning.
Dist.: Warner

BLUE STEEL 1990
★★★ R Mystery-Suspense 1:42
☑ Adult situations, explicit language, graphic violence
Dir: Kathryn Bigelow *Cast:* Jamie Lee Curtis, Ron Silver, Clancy Brown, Elizabeth Peña, Philip Bosco, Louise Fletcher
▶ After being suspended from the force for shooting a robbery suspect, rookie cop Curtis is romanced by Wall Street commodities broker Silver. She doesn't realize that he is actually a serial killer, slaying victims using bullets with her name on them. Pounding, gutwrenching thriller never bothers to explain Silver's psychosis but is propelled forward by

Bigelow's stunning visuals and Curtis's subtle performance. **(CC)**
Dist.: MGM/UA

BLUE SUNSHINE 1978
★ ★ ★ R Horror 1:37
☑ Explicit language, violence
Dir: Jeff Lieberman   *Cast:* Zalman King, Deborah Winters, Robert Walden, Alice Ghostley, Ray Young
▶ Students who took "Blue Sunshine," a certain brand of acid, at Stanford ten years ago begin to experience shocking and violent aftereffects—they become crazed killers. Some plot holes but this eerie, fairly plausible suspense drama delivers an ample number of thrills and chills.
Dist.: Vestron

BLUE THUNDER 1983
★ ★ ★ ★ R Action-Adventure 1:50
☑ Nudity, adult situations, explicit language, violence
Dir: John Badham   *Cast:* Roy Scheider, Candy Clark, Malcolm McDowell, Warren Oates, Daniel Stern
▶ High-flying, breathlessly paced action-adventure from director Badham. Scheider, a Vietnam vet flying choppers for the L.A.P.D., uncovers an evil government conspiracy involving a high-tech "Blue Thunder" helicopter. He steals the craft, thus setting the stage for an exciting, climactic battle with archenemy McDowell. Plot implausibilities easily outweighed by action, drive, and suspense. **(CC)**
Dist.: RCA/Columbia

BLUE VELVET 1986
★ ★ R Mystery-Suspense 2:00
☑ Rape, nudity, adult situations, explicit language, graphic violence
Dir: David Lynch   *Cast:* Isabella Rossellini, Kyle MacLachlan, Laura Dern, Hope Lange, Dennis Hopper, Dean Stockwell
▶ Young college student MacLachlan returns to his Norman Rockwellish hometown and discovers a web of corruption involving Rossellini, a chanteuse being tortured by psychopath Hopper. Weird stuff is undeniably gripping, thanks to surreal, brilliantly nightmarish direction from Lynch. Hopper is mesmerizing. The graphic sex and violence makes this experience not for everyone, but it is hard to forget. **(CC)**
Dist.: Warner

BLUME IN LOVE 1973
★ ★ R Comedy 1:57
☑ Adult situations, explicit language
Dir: Paul Mazursky   *Cast:* George Segal, Susan Anspach, Kris Kristofferson, Marsha Mason, Shelley Winters
▶ Philandering divorce attorney Blume (Segal) is literally caught with his pants down by wife Anspach, so she divorces him and takes up with hippie Kristofferson. However,

Blume still loves his wife and pursues her obsessively. Compassionate and satirical.
Dist.: Warner

BOARDING SCHOOL 1977 German
★ R Sex/Comedy 1:38
☑ Nudity, strong sexual content, adult situations, explicit language
Dir: Andre Farwagi   *Cast:* Nastassia Kinski, Gerry Sundquist, Stephane D'Amato, Gabrielle Blum, Marion Kracht, Nigel Greaves
▶ At a Swiss boarding school for girls in 1956, precocious students, more interested in learning facts of life than calculus, enlist aid of experienced Kinski in effort to lose virginity. They offer to sell their services to the boy's school across the lake, but the play-for-pay setup goes comically awry. Undraped Kinksi in early stages of her career.
Dist.: Vestron

BOATNIKS, THE 1970
★ ★ ★ G Comedy/Family 1:40
Dir: Norman Tokar   *Cast:* Robert Morse, Stefanie Powers, Phil Silvers, Norman Fell, Mickey Shaughnessy, Wally Cox
▶ Inept jewel thieves Silvers, Fell, and Shaughnessy lose their loot in a harbor overseen by naive Coast Guard ensign Morse. Their outlandish schemes to recover the gems provide plenty of brisk slapstick in this strong Disney comedy.
Dist.: Buena Vista

BOB AND CAROL AND TED AND ALICE 1969
★ ★ R Comedy 1:44
☑ Adult situations, explicit language
Dir: Paul Mazursky   *Cast:* Natalie Wood, Robert Culp, Dyan Cannon, Elliott Gould, Horst Ebersberg
▶ Hip couple Culp and Wood and their square counterparts Gould and Cannon flirt with the notion of wife-swapping in this landmark comedy, which was somewhat of a sexual breakthrough in 1960s Hollywood. May seem a bit dated today, but Mazursky's satiric wit and the fine performances still hold up nicely.
Dist.: RCA/Columbia

BOBBIE JO AND THE OUTLAW 1976
★ ★ R Action-Adventure 1:29
☑ Nudity, adult situations, explicit language, violence
Dir: Mark L. Lester   *Cast:* Marjoe Gortner, Lynda Carter, Jesse Vint, Merrie Lynn Ross, Belinda Belaski
▶ Outlaw Gortner gets his kicks stealing cars and winning shooting contests. He falls for waitress Carter and they shoot their way across New Mexico. Bloody bank robbery leads to heavy pursuit by the law, climaxing in a violent shootout. Sexy action-adventure with a country-western flavor.
Dist.: Vestron

BOBBY DEERFIELD 1977
★ ★ PG Drama 2:04
☑ Brief nudity, explicit language
Dir: Sydney Pollack *Cast:* Al Pacino, Martha Keller, Anny Duperey, Walter McGinn, Romolo Valli
▶ Grand Prix racer Bobby Deerfield (Pacino) survives his dangerous sport by cutting himself off from human emotion, but changes when he falls in love with Keller, a free-spirited but terminally ill woman. Old-fashioned love story based on a novel by Erich Maria Remarque.
Dist.: Warner

BOB LE FLAMBEUR 1957 French
★ PG Drama 1:42 B&W
☑ Adult situations
Dir: Jean-Pierre Melville *Cast:* Isabel Corey, Roger Duchesne, Andre Garet, Daniel Cauchy, Guy Decomble
▶ Funny, jaunty film amazingly fresh after 30 years. Bob Le Flambeur (Duchesne), a former bank robber now living in Paris in semiretirement, spends his time gambling and losing. To recoup his fortune, Bob plans one last heist at the casino at Deauville. Ⓢ
Dist.: RCA/Columbia

BOBO, THE 1967 British
★ ★ NR Comedy 1:43
Dir: Robert Parrish *Cast:* Peter Sellers, Britt Ekland, Rossano Brazzi, Adolfo Celi, Hattie Jacques
▶ Spanish matador Sellers dreams of becoming a singer. He can get a gig at Celi's club by winning Ekland's heart, but it turns out to be mission impossible for the bungling bullfighter. Sellers evokes a few chuckles, but overall not one of his stronger vehicles.
Dist.: Warner

BODY AND SOUL 1947
★ ★ ★ NR Drama/Sports 1:44 B&W
Dir: Robert Rossen *Cast:* John Garfield, Lilli Palmer, Hazel Brooks, Anne Revere, William Conrad, Canada Lee
▶ Dynamic boxing drama with Garfield in one of his best roles as a champion fighter corrupted by gangsters. Ordered to throw his next bout, he returns to his mother Revere and girlfriend Palmer for advice. Oscar-winning editing brings extraordinary tension to boxing scenes.
Dist.: Republic

BODY AND SOUL 1981
★ ★ ★ R Drama/Sports 1:49
☑ Nudity, adult situations, explicit language, violence
Dir: George Bowers *Cast:* Leon Isaac Kennedy, Jayne Kennedy, Muhammad Ali, Peter Lawford, Perry Lang, Michael V. Gazzo
▶ Aspiring medical student and amateur fighter Leon Kennedy, determined to win the welterweight title, learns his little sister suffers from sickle cell anemia. While falling in love with sportswriter Jayne Kennedy, the fighter

contends with mob hood Lawford and trains under watchful eye of Gazzo, with brief assist from Ali as himself. Passable remake of 1947 version from then husband-wife Kennedy team.
Dist.: Republic

BODY DOUBLE 1984
★ ★ ★ R Mystery-Suspense 1:50
☑ Nudity, strong sexual content, adult situations, explicit language, graphic violence
Dir: Brian De Palma *Cast:* Craig Wasson, Melanie Griffith, Gregg Henry, Deborah Shelton, Guy Boyd
▶ L.A. actor Wasson is set up as a murder witness. Obsessively investigating the crime himself, he hooks up with porno queen Griffith, who may provide the key to the killing. Typical De Palma mixture of Hitchcockian plotting, voyeurism, violence, stylish camerawork, and suspense. Definitely not for the squeamish. (CC)
Dist.: RCA/Columbia

BODY HEAT 1981
★ ★ ★ R Mystery-Suspense 1:53
☑ Nudity, adult situations, explicit language, violence
Dir: Lawrence Kasdan *Cast:* William Hurt, Kathleen Turner, Richard Crenna, Ted Danson, Mickey Rourke, J. A. Preston
▶ Luckless lawyer Hurt gets involved with sultry Turner, who's rich, beautiful—and married to Crenna. The lovers plot Crenna's murder with hapless Hurt unaware that Turner's hiding several double crosses up her sexy sleeve. Torrid, steamy thriller successfully updates 1940s-style film noir to the 1980s. Terrific hard-boiled dialogue, stylish visuals from writer/director Kasdan, sizzling chemistry between Hurt and Turner, and noteworthy supporting turns from Danson, Crenna, Preston, and Rourke (in his first major film role).
Dist.: Warner

BODY ROCK 1984
★ ★ PG-13 Musical 1:34
☑ Brief nudity, adult situations, explicit language
Dir: Marcelo Epstein *Cast:* Lorenzo Lamas, Michelle Nicastro, Ray Sharkey, Vicki Frederick, Joseph Whipp
▶ Pushy Brooklyn kid Lamas attempts to make it in the world of breakdancing. On his way to the top, will he forget his old friends from the neighborhood? Lots of music, dancing, and an unrelenting beat in this glitzy look at the New York counterculture scene. Energetic soundtrack assembled by music industry vet Phil Ramone.
Dist.: HBO

BODY SLAM 1987
★ ★ PG Comedy 1:29
☑ Explicit language
Dir: Hal Needham *Cast:* Dirk Benedict,

Tanya Roberts, Roddy Piper, Captain Lou Albano, Barry Gordon
▶ The fortunes of down-on-his-luck promoter Benedict improve when he takes on a new client, former pro wrestler Piper, and combines rock 'n' wrestling in arena shows. But then former manager Albano and his goons mess up the works. Mixture of rock music, comedy, and wrestling has some sexist and racist humor but might amuse those looking for an easy laugh.
Dist.: Nelson

BODY SNATCHER, THE 1945
★ ★ NR Horror 1:17 B&W
Dir: Robert Wise   *Cast:* Boris Karloff, Bela Lugosi, Henry Daniell, Edith Atwater, Russell Wade, Rita Corday
▶ Daniell, a Scottish doctor requiring cadavers for his experiments, turns to Karloff, a menacing cabbie with a disconcerting supply of fresh bodies. Thoughtful Val Lewton version of a Robert Louis Stevenson story features evocatively gloomy atmosphere and restrained performances. Karloff and Lugosi have one scene together, a powerful confrontation.
Dist.: RKO

BOHEMIAN GIRL, THE 1936
★ ★ NR Comedy 1:14 B&W
Dir: James Horne, Charles Rogers   *Cast:* Stan Laurel, Oliver Hardy, Mae Busch, Darla Hood, Jacqueline Wells, Thelma Todd
▶ Gypsies Laurel and Hardy become surrogate parents to a lost little girl who turns out to be the daughter of nobility. Eventually, the now-grown woman is reunited with her family. Above-average vehicle for the comic duo. Funniest scene: Laurel and the wine.
Dist.: Fox Hills

BOLERO 1984
★ R Drama 1:44
☑ Nudity, adult situations, explicit language
Dir: John Derek   *Cast:* Bo Derek, Andrea Occhipinti, George Kennedy, Ana Obregon, Olivia d'Abo
▶ After graduation, sheltered schoolgirl Derek sets out to lose her virginity with an Arab sheik, then falls in love with a bullfighter. Suggestive plot (played mostly for laughs) gives Bo plenty of opportunities to display her assets. Written, shot, edited, and directed by husband John.
Dist.: IVE

BOMBARDIER 1943
★ ★ NR War 1:39 B&W
Dir: Richard Wallace   *Cast:* Pat O'Brien, Randolph Scott, Anne Shirley, Eddie Albert, Walter Reed, Robert Ryan
▶ Team player O'Brien and wild individualist Scott are best friends in Air Corps training school. When the Japanese bomb Pearl Harbor, each contributes to the air war in the way most expressive of his personality. Rousing World War II antique.
Dist.: Turner

BOMBS AWAY 1985
☆ NR Comedy 1:28
☑ Explicit language, adult humor
Dir: Bruce Wilson   *Cast:* Michael Huddleston, Pat McCormick, Michael Santo, Ben Tone, Lori Larsen
▶ Labored, unfunny farce about cab driver Huddleston who mistakenly winds up transporting an atom bomb in his taxi. There's a limit to how many jokes about nuclear weapons one movie can have. McCormick is the only one to walk away with some dignity intact.
Dist.: Nelson

BONJOUR TRISTESSE 1958
★ ★ NR Drama 1:33
Dir: Otto Preminger   *Cast:* Jean Seberg, Deborah Kerr, David Niven, Mylene Demongeot, Geoffrey Horne, Juliette Greco
▶ Through flashbacks, Seberg tells of her last summer on the Riviera with father Niven, a rake whose endless pursuit of women leads to tragedy when he tries to seduce shy Kerr. Superficial soap opera based on Françoise Sagan's novel features beautiful scenery and touching performance by Kerr.
Dist.: RCA/Columbia

BONNIE AND CLYDE 1967
★ ★ ★ ★ NR Crime/Drama 1:51
☑ Adult situations, explicit language, graphic violence, adult humor
Dir: Arthur Penn   *Cast:* Warren Beatty, Faye Dunaway, Michael J. Pollard, Gene Hackman, Estelle Parsons
▶ Legendary Depression-era bank robbers Bonnie Parker (Dunaway) and Clyde Barrow (Beatty) were transformed into glamorous antiheroes by director Penn and producer/star Beatty in one of the great films of the 1960s. Story traces the larcenous couple from their first meeting (Clyde tries to steal Bonnie's mom's car) through their life on the lam to their tragic deaths, deftly mixing violence, comedy, and moments of great tenderness. Oscar nominations went to all five leading players and Best Picture, but only Parsons and the cinematography won.
Dist.: Warner

BONNIE SCOTLAND 1935
★ ★ NR Comedy 1:20 B&W
Dir: James W. Horne   *Cast:* Stan Laurel, Oliver Hardy, Anne Grey, David Torrence, June Lang, James Finlayson
▶ Penniless, Laurel and Hardy take a cattle boat to Scotland in a quest for an uncle's inheritance. Bequeathed only bagpipes and a snuff box, they head for India to join the British Lancers. Slow-moving comedy is one of the duo's lesser efforts.
Dist.: MGM/UA

BON VOYAGE! 1962
★ ★ ★ NR Comedy 2:11
Dir: James Neilson   *Cast:* Fred MacMurray,

Jane Wyman, Michael Callan. Deborah Walley, Tommy Kirk, Kevin Corcoran
▶ All-American dad MacMurray and wife Wyman take the family on a French vacation. Romance blooms between daughter Walley and countess's son Callan while MacMurray must deal with a roué's interest in Wyman. Overlong and only intermittently entertaining.
Dist.: Buena Vista

BON VOYAGE, CHARLIE BROWN (AND DON'T COME BACK!) 1980
★ ★ ★ ★ G Animation 1:15
Dir: Bill Melendez *Cast:* Voices of Daniel Anderson, Debbie Muller, Scott Beach, Casey Carlson
▶ Charles Schulz's "Peanuts" gang is back as Charlie Brown and company spend two weeks as exchange students in France, where they run afoul of a local baron until Linus and his blanket save the day. Simple animation, characteristic of this series, is charming and colorful.
Dist.: Paramount

BOOGEYMAN, THE 1980
★ ★ R Horror 1:30
☑ Nudity, explicit language, graphic violence
Dir: Ulli Lommel *Cast:* Suzanna Love, Ron James, John Carradine, Nicholas Love, Raymond Boyden, Felicite Morgan
▶ Twenty years previous, Love's little brother killed their mother's lover. Now, Love returns to the family home and smashes a mirror when she sees the dead man's ghost. This turns to be very bad luck indeed as a series of grisy murders ensues. Feeble story overloaded with excessive gore.
Dist.: Magnum

BOOGEYMAN II 1983
☆ NR Horror 1:19
☑ Nudity, explicit language, violence
Dir: Ulli Lommel *Cast:* Suzanna Love, Shannah Hall, Ulli Lommel, Shoto von Douglas, Bob Rosenfarb, Rhonda Aldrich
▶ After the events of the original, Love moves to Los Angeles and tells her sad story to filmmaker Lommel. Unfortunately, she's brought a piece of that possessed mirror with her, resulting in butler von Douglas doing in Hollywood party guests. Sequel is more ambitious than its predecessor, but still not very effective.
Dist.: VCII

BOOK OF NUMBERS 1973
★ R Action-Adventure 1:20
☑ Brief nudity, explicit language, violence
Dir: Raymond St. Jacques *Cast:* Raymond St. Jacques, Phillip Michael Thomas, Freda Payne, Hope Clarke, D'Urville Martin
▶ St. Jacques and Thomas play black Northerners who set up a numbers racket in a small Louisiana town despite opposition from the mob and the Ku Klux Klan. Better-than-average exploitation fare has a good feel for its

Depression-era settings and some gospel tunes from pop star Payne.
Dist.: Media

BOOST, THE 1988
★ ★ R Drama 1:35
☑ Brief nudity, adult situations, explicit language, mild violence
Dir: Harold Becker *Cast:* James Woods, Sean Young, John Kapelos, Steven Hill, Kelle Kerr
▶ Ambitious real estate salesman Woods and wife Young become cocaine addicts after business reversals. As life goes increasingly downhill, Woods abuses Young but can't kick the habit. Dated morality tale suffers from unrelentingly depressing tone but provides emotional tour de force for the always fascinating Woods.
Dist.: HBO

BORDER, THE 1982
★ ★ ★ R Drama 1:47
☑ Nudity, adult situations, explicit language, violence
Dir: Tony Richardson *Cast:* Jack Nicholson, Valerie Perrine, Harvey Keitel, Warren Oates, Elpidia Carrillo
▶ Nicholson, a U.S. border patrolman, battles corruption within the ranks when he helps Mexican Carrillo recover her baby from an adoption ring. Gritty, topical, emotionally charged drama with strong supporting performances and haunting music by Ry Cooder. Nicholson's towering work as the conscience-stricken Charlie is the real focal point.
Dist.: MCA

BORDERLINE 1980
★ ★ ★ ★ PG Action-Adventure 1:43
☑ Explicit language, violence
Dir: Jerrold Freedman *Cast:* Charles Bronson, Bruno Kirby, Ed Harris, Wilford Brimley, Michael Lerner
▶ Bronson is solid as a Border Patrol cop searching for his partner's killers. The Feds think drug smugglers are responsible, but Bronson goes after the leader of an illegal alien ring instead. Strong subject matter and supporting performances (notably Harris in his debut role) make this one of Bronson's better vehicles. (CC)
Dist.: CBS/Fox

BORDER RADIO 1987
☆ R Drama 1:24 B&W
☑ Brief nudity, adult situations, explicit language
Dir: Allison Anders, Dean Lent, Kurt Voss
Cast: Chris D., John Doe, Luana Anders, Chris Shearer, Dave Alvin, Iris Berry
▶ Student-style work about small-time rockers D., Doe, and Alvin, who take it on the lam after they rob a welshing club owner. Characters simply wander around inconsequentially in this empty, "artistic" feature. Great sound-

track songs by real-life rockabilly star Alvin.
(CC)
Dist.: Pacific Arts

B.O.R.N. 1988
★ **R Drama 1:31**
☑ Nudity, explicit language, violence
Dir: Ross Hagen   *Cast:* Ross Hagen, P. J.
Soles, Hoke Howell, Russ Tamblyn
▶ When his foster daughters are abducted by
Soles's black market human organ ring,
Hagen finds the cops no help. He tracks down
the kidnappers, who proceed to kill his wife
and son. Hagen's double duty is double trou-
ble, as his flat performance and direction fail
to make a workable concept compelling. Pro-
duction values reflect the low budget.
Dist.: Prism

BORN AGAIN 1978
★ ★ **PG Biography 1:50**
☑ Explicit language
Dir: Irving Rapper   *Cast:* Dean Jones, Anne
Francis, Jay Robinson, Dana Andrews, Raymond St. Jacques, George Brent
▶ Nixon advisor Charles Colson (Jones) is implicated in Watergate scandal and sentenced to prison. Before sentencing, he experiences a spiritual awakening and establishes
prayer groups while still in jail. Jones gives a
subdued, affecting performance as Colson
but the sanctimonious story is distorted in the
character's favor. Unintentional laughs come
from weak actors playing Nixon, Kissinger, and
other famous figures.
Dist.: Nelson

BORN AMERICAN 1986 U.S./Finnish
★ ★ **R Action-Adventure 1:36**
☑ Nudity, explicit language, graphic vio-
lence
Dir: Renny Harlin   *Cast:* Mike Norris, Steve
Durham, David Coburn, Thalmus Rasulala,
Albert Salmi
▶ While exploring Lapland, three young
Americans cross the Russian border on a
whim. Caught by Russian soldiers and tortured
in a gulag, their only hope is to escape across
the hostile Arctic. Norris (Chuck's son) displays
some karate tricks during a training se-
quence. Ultrapatriotic fantasy was filmed in
(and banned from) Finland.
Dist.: Magnum

BORN FREE 1966 British
★ ★ ★ ★ ★ **NR Drama/Family 1:35**
Dir: James Hill   *Cast:* Virginia McKenna, Bill
Travers, Geoffrey Keen, Peter Lukoye
▶ Game warden George Adamson and his
wife Joy (McKenna) raise Elsa, a lion cub, in
captivity. When Elsa matures, they teach her
how to survive in the wilderness. Based on a
true story and shot on location in Kenya, this
heartwarming adaptation of Joy Adamson's
best-selling book will please everyone in the
family. Title song and soundtrack both won
Oscars. Sequel: *Living Free.*
Dist.: RCA/Columbia

BORN IN EAST L.A. 1987
★ ★ **R Comedy 1:24**
☑ Adult situations, explicit language, mild
violence
Dir: Cheech Marin   *Cast:* Cheech Marin,
Paul Rodriguez, David Stern, Kamala Lopez,
Jan-Michael Vincent
▶ Marin, an auto mechanic from East Los Angeles, is accidentally nabbed in a roundup of
illegal aliens. Stuck in Mexico with no money
or papers, he has to rely on shady nightclub
owner Stern to get home. Based on his rock
video parody of Bruce Springsteen's "Born in
the USA," Marin's post-"Cheech and Chong"
debut is a surprisingly good-natured comedy
about a touchy subject.   (CC)
Dist.: MCA

BORN LOSERS 1967
★ ★ ★ **PG Action-Adventure 1:52**
☑ Adult situations, violence
Dir: T. C. Frank (Tom Laughlin)   *Cast:* Tom
Laughlin, Elizabeth James, Jeremy Slate,
William Wellman, Jr.
▶ Vicious bikers terrorize a small town and
threaten to gang-rape beautiful hippie
James. But brave half-breed Laughlin fights
fire with fire to rescue her. Violent motorcycle
film is notable chiefly for the introduction of
Laughlin's "Billy Jack" character, the hero of
three subsequent films. Jane Russell has a
cameo as James's mother.
Dist.: Vestron

BORN ON THE FOURTH OF JULY 1989
★ ★ ★ ★ ★ **R Biography 2:25**
☑ Nudity, adult situations, explicit language, violence
Dir: Oliver Stone   *Cast:* Tom Cruise, Kyra
Sedgwick, Raymond J. Barry, Caroline Kava,
Jerry Levine, Frank Whaley, Willem Dafoe
▶ True story of Vietnam veteran Ron Kovic's
harrowing experiences as he goes from naive,
patriotic Long Island teenager to embittered
paraplegic who is shunned as his country tries
to forget its most unpopular war. Takes up
where Stone's *Platoon* leaves off, and is perhaps more disturbing and heartwrenching
because of the personalness of its story. As
Kovic, Cruise rises to the occasion with his
most powerful and poignant performance
yet. Epic in sweep, richly photographed, and
masterfully written and acted. Look for Tom
Berenger and Abbie Hoffman in cameos.
Nominated for eight Oscars, including Best
Picture, Actor, and Screenplay, it won for Director and Editing.   (CC)
Dist.: MCA

BORN TO DANCE 1936
★ ★ **NR Musical 1:45 B&W**
Dir: Roy Del Ruth   *Cast:* Eleanor Powell,
James Stewart, Virginia Bruce, Sid Silvers,
Una Merkel, Buddy Ebsen
▶ During shore leave, sailor Stewart woos
wholesome hoofer Powell while New York pa-
pers link him with spoiled actress Bruce. Goofy

gobs Silvers and Ebsen have their own on-shore romantic problems. Powell is at her freshest and most vigorous, especially in a flashy finale danced beneath the cannons of a Navy gun turret. A raft of Cole Porter standards like "Easy to Love" and "I've Got You Under My Skin" makes the score close to perfect.
Dist.: MGM/UA

BORN TO KILL 1974
★ ★ R Drama 1:24
☑ Adult situations, explicit language, violence
Dir: Monte Hellman   *Cast:* Warren Oates, Richard B. Shull, Harry Dean Stanton, Troy Donahue, Millie Perkins, Laurie Bird
▶ Offbeat but engrossing story of Oates, a maniacal breeder of fighting cocks who takes a vow of silence until he wins a championship. Voice-overs explaining the action grow tedious, although supporting characters are quirkily amusing and photography by Nestor Almendros is excellent. Filmed in Georgia under the titles *Wild Drifters* and *Gamblin' Man*, and also available as *Cockfighter*.
Dist.: Nelson

BORN TO RACE 1988
★ ★ R Drama/Sports 1:38
☑ Brief nudity, explicit language, mild violence
Dir: James Fargo   *Cast:* Joseph Bottoms, Antonio Sabato, George Kennedy, Marla Heasley, Marc Singer
▶ In North Carolina's Charlotte Speedway, greedy sponsor Kennedy enlists top driver Singer to kidnap sexy Italian engineer Heasley who has important state-of-the-art jalopy blueprints. Good guy driver Bottoms loses his heart to Heasley and comes to her rescue. Sexual chemistry between the leads and authentic locations enliven this racetrack yarn.
Dist.: CBS/Fox

BORN YESTERDAY 1950
★ ★ ★ ★ ★ NR Comedy 1:42 B&W
Dir: George Cukor   *Cast:* Judy Holliday, William Holden, Broderick Crawford, Howard St. John, Frank Otto
▶ Junk dealer millionaire Crawford, upset with crass girlfriend Holliday's lack of social graces, hires newspaperman Holden to coach her. The plan backfires as the not-so-dumb Billie outwits Crawford and falls in love with Holden. Classic screen comedy with Judy's hilarious yet vulnerable characterization winning a well-deserved Oscar. Garson Kanin's Broadway hit also received Best Picture nomination.
Dist.: RCA/Columbia

BOSS'S SON, THE 1978
★ ★ NR Drama 1:41
☑ Explicit language
Dir: Bobby Roth   *Cast:* Asher Brauner, Rudy Solari, Rita Moreno, James Darren, Richie Havens, Henry G. Sanders
▶ Brauner finishes college and joins dad

Solari's carpet business, where he befriends black driver Sanders. He investigates a rash of carpet thefts; the solution to the mystery creates a dilemma. Screenplay creates a highly credible conflict between father and son but low-budget drama is hurt by Brauner's uncharismatic performance.
Dist.: Vestron

BOSS'S WIFE, THE 1986
★ R Comedy 1:23
☑ Nudity, adult situations, explicit language, adult humor
Dir: Ziggy Steinberg   *Cast:* Daniel Stern, Arielle Dombasle, Christopher Plummer, Fisher Stevens, Melanie Mayron, Martin Mull
▶ Stern, a mild-mannered stockbroker, fears for his career and his marriage when, on a company weekend, boss Plummer's gorgeous wife Dombasle pursues him. Extremely broad sex farce with plenty of sight gags. **(CC)**
Dist.: CBS/Fox

BOSTONIANS, THE 1984
★ NR Drama 2:00
☑ Adult situations
Dir: James Ivory   *Cast:* Christopher Reeve, Vanessa Redgrave, Madeleine Potter, Jessica Tandy, Nancy Marchand
▶ In nineteenth-century Boston, young suffragette orator Potter becomes the object of a battle of wills between Redgrave, a spinster tutoring her in feminism, and Reeve, a handsome antifeminist Southern lawyer attempting to woo her away. Slow-moving but first-rate work from Reeve and Redgrave. Picture postcard re-creation of the Henry James novel from the team that later created *A Room With a View*.
Dist.: Vestron

BOSTON STRANGLER, THE 1968
★ ★ R Crime 2:00
☑ Violence
Dir: Richard Fleischer   *Cast:* Tony Curtis, Henry Fonda, George Kennedy, Mike Kellin, Hurd Hatfield, Murray Hamilton
▶ Deliberate, unsensational account of real-life killer Albert DeSalvo (Curtis), seemingly ordinary family man who was actually serial killer of women. Criminologist Fonda investigates and eventually brings Curtis to justice. Superb performances from Curtis and Fonda. **(CC)**
Dist.: CBS/Fox

BOTANY BAY 1953
★ ★ NR Action-Adventure 1:34
Dir: John Farrow   *Cast:* Alan Ladd, James Mason, Patricia Medina, Cedric Hardwicke, Murray Matheson, Dorothy Patten
▶ Eighteenth-century American medical student Ladd, unjustly accused of a crime, is assigned to Australia-bound prison ship captained by Mason. Mason makes Ladd's life miserable, especially after Medina chooses the American over him. Overheated and

melodramatic but not without a certain panache.
Dist.: KVC

BOUDU SAVED FROM DROWNING 1932
French
☆ **NR Comedy 1:27 B&W**
Dir: Jean Renoir ***Cast:*** Michel Simon, Charles Grandval, Marcella Hainia, Severine Lerczynska, Jean Daste
▶ Middle-class businessman Grandval rescues tramp Simon from suicide and brings him home to start a new life. Ungrateful and unrepentant, Simon proceeds to seduce Grandval's wife and maid in this cheerful black comedy. Critically acclaimed for its lyrical photography and unpretentious tone. Loosely remade in 1986 as *Down and Out in Beverly Hills.* [S]
Dist.: Various

BOULEVARD NIGHTS 1979
★★ **R Action-Adventure 1:42**
☑ Adult situations, explicit language, violence
Dir: Michael Pressman ***Cast:*** Richard Yniguez, Danny De La Paz, Marta Du Bois, Betty Carvalho, Carmen Zapata
▶ Affecting melodrama about Yniguez and De La Paz, brothers trapped by poverty and gang warfare in the barrios of East Los Angeles. Yniguez dreams of taking his wife out of the slums, but honor forces him to avenge his mother's murder. Authentic locations and details distinguish this from other gang films.
Dist.: Warner

BOUND FOR GLORY 1977
★★★★ **PG Biography 2:27**
☑ Adult situations
Dir: Hal Ashby ***Cast:*** David Carradine, Ronny Cox, Melinda Dillon, Gail Strickland, Randy Quaid
▶ The autobiography of folk singer Woody Guthrie is transformed into a moving, heartfelt account of Dustbowl America during the Depression. Vignettes of Okies, miners, migrant farmers, and unionizers reveal the inspiration behind Guthrie's songs. Superb photography by Haskell Wexler won an Oscar, as did Leonard Rosenman's scoring of Guthrie's music. Carradine is quite convincing in the lead role.
Dist.: MGM/UA

BOUNTY, THE 1984
★★★★ **PG Drama 2:12**
☑ Nudity, adult situations, explicit language, violence
Dir: Roger Donaldson ***Cast:*** Mel Gibson, Anthony Hopkins, Laurence Olivier, Edward Fox, Daniel Day-Lewis, Bernard Hill
▶ Third Hollywood version of *Mutiny on the Bounty* offers revisionist portraits of the infamous Captain Bligh (Hopkins) and his enemy, Fletcher Christian (Gibson, in a charged, erotic performance). Bligh's bravery as he crosses the ocean in a small boat contrasts well with Christian's adventures on exotic Tahiti, whose breathtaking scenery provides a memorable backdrop to the large-scale action scenes. Robert Bolt's screenplay concentrates on revealing personal details glossed over in the earlier films.
Dist.: Vestron

BOWERY AT MIDNIGHT 1942
★ **NR Mystery-Suspense 1:03 B&W**
Dir: Wallace Fox ***Cast:*** Bela Lugosi, John Archer, Wanda McKay, Tom Neal, Vincent Barnett
▶ Lugosi's skid row storefront mission is actually a cover for his growing criminal empire. But a junkie doctor is resurrecting Lugosi's murdered enemies for revenge. Low-rent nonsense short on shocks or logic.
Dist.: Various

BOXCAR BERTHA 1972
★★ **R Drama 1:28**
☑ Nudity, strong sexual content, adult situations, explicit language, violence
Dir: Martin Scorsese ***Cast:*** Barbara Hershey, David Carradine, Barry Primus, Bernie Casey, John Carradine
▶ Competent low-budget variation on *Bonnie and Clyde* with Hershey turning to crime after the death of her father. Forming a gang with union organizer Carradine, she crosses Depression-era Arkansas robbing banks and kidnapping evil millionaires. Scorsese's studio debut is a fairly typical Roger Corman quickie production.
Dist.: Vestron

BOY AND HIS DOG, A 1975
★★ **R Sci-Fi 1:27**
☑ Strong sexual content, explicit language, violence
Dir: L. Q. Jones ***Cast:*** Don Johnson, Jason Robards, Suzanne Benton, Charles McGraw, Alvy Moore
▶ A pre-"Miami Vice" Johnson stars as Vic, a young man attempting to survive in post-atomic-war America (circa 2024) with the help of his faithful companion, a telepathic talking dog named Blood (voice of Tim McIntire). Blackly comic adaptation of Harlan Ellison's award-winning novella has developed a cult following over the years. Outrageous twist ending, in which Johnson must choose between the dog or Benton, might offend feminists.
Dist.: Media

BOY, DID I GET A WRONG NUMBER! 1966
★★ **NR Comedy 1:39**
Dir: George Marshall ***Cast:*** Bob Hope, Elke Sommer, Phyllis Diller, Cesare Danova, Marjorie Lord
▶ Hollywood starlet Sommer flees to Oregon to escape demands of director Danova. Hope agrees to put her up, then must keep her presence hidden from his wife Lord. Lowbrow Hope vehicle with an emphasis on smirking humor.
Dist.: Playhouse

BOY FRIEND, THE 1971 British
★★★ G Musical 1:50 B&W
Dir: Ken Russell *Cast:* Twiggy, Christopher Gable, Max Adrian, Tommy Tune, Glenda Jackson
▶ Affectionate send-up of Busby Berkeley musicals uses a time-honored plot (aspiring actress gets her big break when the star is injured) as a framework for lavish, glittering production numbers. Former model Twiggy gives a steady performance, and she's backed by top-notch hoofers. Fourteen songs in all (although the British version includes two extra tunes).
Dist.: MGM/UA

BOYFRIENDS AND GIRLFRIENDS 1987 French
★ PG Comedy 1:42
☑ Brief nudity, adult situations, explicit language
Dir: Eric Rohmer *Cast:* Emmannuelle Chaulet, Sophie Renoir, Eric Viellard, François-Eric Gendron, Anne-Laure Meury
▶ Best girlfriends find themselves up to their necks in romantic entanglements in this comic look at love from Rohmer. Shy Chaulet has a crush on cad Gendron, while her shallow pal Renoir is looking to dump nice-guy boyfriend Viellard. Rohmer's special touch with newcomers is evident as ensemble cast of unknowns plays off each other delightfully. Like the rest of his films, for fans only. [S]
Dist.: Orion

BOY IN BLUE, THE 1986
★★★ R Sports/Drama 1:38
☑ Nudity, adult situations, explicit language
Dir: Charles Jarrott *Cast:* Nicolas Cage, David Naughton, Christopher Plummer, Cynthia Dale, Melody Anderson
▶ Canadian variation on the *Rocky* theme based on the life of nineteenth-century rower Ned Hanlan (Cage). Story traces Ned's rise from the working class to the top of his sport, his conflict with villainous sponsor Plummer who tries to get him to throw the big race, and his romance with the sponsor's daughter Dale. Straightforward formula plot delivers the underdog's climactic victory. (CC)
Dist.: CBS/Fox

BOY NAMED CHARLIE BROWN, A 1970
★★★★ G Animation 1:25
Dir: Bill Melendez *Cast:* Voices of Peter Robbins, Pamelyn Ferdin, B. Melendez, Glenn Gilger
▶ First animated feature film about the Peanuts gang brings the precocious bunch to life. The usually hapless Charlie Brown finally finds something he can do well as he wins the school spelling bee and goes on to the national contest. Pleasant, good-humored family entertainment. Music by Rod McKuen. (CC)
Dist.: CBS/Fox

BOYS FROM BRAZIL, THE 1978
★★★★ R Mystery-Suspense 2:03
☑ Brief nudity, explicit language, violence
Dir: Franklin J. Schaffner *Cast:* Gregory Peck, Laurence Olivier, James Mason, Lilli Palmer, Uta Hagen
▶ Intriguing suspense thriller highlighted by the legendary leads. Peck, getting a rare chance to play a villain, has an evil field day as Dr. Josef Mengele, the mad Nazi doctor plotting a Fourth Reich via ninety-four clones of Adolf Hitler (the "boys" of the title). Olivier is Nazi hunter Lieberman, who tries to stop him. From the best-selling novel by Ira Levin.
Dist.: CBS/Fox

BOYS IN COMPANY C, THE 1978
★★★★ R War 2:06
☑ Adult situations, explicit language, violence
Dir: Sidney J. Furie *Cast:* Stan Shaw, Andrew Stevens, James Canning, Michael Lembeck, Craig Wasson
▶ Five young Marine recruits become friends in boot camp before being sent to Vietnam, where they confront the real horrors of war. Sturdy war drama overcomes formula plotting with gritty, authentic action, salty humor (especially in the opening boot-camp sequence), and fine acting, particularly by Shaw.
Dist.: RCA/Columbia

BOYS IN THE BAND, THE 1970
★ R Drama 2:00
☑ Adult situations, explicit language
Dir: William Friedkin *Cast:* Frederick Combs, Leonard Frey, Cliff Gorman, Reuben Greene, Robert La Tourneaux, Laurence Luckinbill
▶ Playwright Mart Crowley adapted his own off-Broadway hit in this landmark (for Hollywood) sympathetic treatment of gays. A group of gays gathers for a birthday party that quickly degenerates into a hornet's nest of confrontations and revelations. Nicely directed by Friedkin and well acted by all.
Dist.: CBS/Fox

BOYS NEXT DOOR, THE 1985
★ R Drama 1:31
☑ Brief nudity, adult situations, explicit language, violence
Dir: Penelope Spheeris *Cast:* Maxwell Caulfield, Charlie Sheen, Christopher McDonald, Hank Garrett, Patti D'Arbanville
▶ Unpopular high school students Caulfield and Sheen, victims of rough upbringings and facing a bleak future as factory workers, vent their rage in a violent spree. Director Spheeris presents a gruesome vision of people who appear innocent but are capable of horrendous crimes. Not pleasant but well made.
Dist.: New World

BOYS TOWN 1938
★★★★ NR Drama 1:36 B&W
Dir: Norman Taurog *Cast:* Spencer Tracy,

Mickey Rooney, Henry Hull, Leslie Fenton, Addison Richards

▶ "There's no such thing as a bad boy," theorizes Father Flanagan (Tracy), real-life figure who opens Nebraska home for juvenile delinquents. He proves the axiom by reforming bad-boy Rooney and others. Old-fashioned sentiment is still enormously appealing. Oscars for Best Actor (Tracy) and Original Story.
Dist.: MGM/UA

BOY WHO COULD FLY, THE 1986
★ ★ ★ ★ PG Fantasy 1:54
☑ Explicit language
Dir: Nick Castle   *Cast:* Jay Underwood, Lucy Deakins, Bonnie Bedelia, Fred Savage, Colleen Dewhurst
▶ Recently widowed Bedelia and her children Deakins and Savage move into a new neighborhood and endure all sorts of personal problems. Deakins befriends Underwood, the autistic boy next door, whose belief that he can fly leads to the uplifting climax. Sweet, mild-mannered drama tugs honestly at the heartstrings and is perfect small-screen family viewing.   (CC)
Dist.: Warner

BOY WITH GREEN HAIR, THE 1948
★ ★ NR Drama 1:22
Dir: Joseph Losey   *Cast:* Dean Stockwell, Robert Ryan, Pat O'Brien, Barbara Hale, Richard Lyon, Walter Catlett
▶ Stockwell awakes one morning to find he has mysteriously become a boy with green hair. The condition leads to ostracism and harassment from his classmates and neighbors. Child actor Stockwell is affecting in this haunting allegory about prejudice. Most disturbing image: the shaved head.
Dist.: King of Video

BRADDOCK: MISSING IN ACTION III 1988
★ ★ ★ ★ R Action-Adventure 1:41
☑ Explicit language, graphic violence
Dir: Aaron Norris   *Cast:* Chuck Norris, Roland Harrah III, Aki Aleong, Miki Kim, Yehuda Efroni
▶ U.S. Army Colonel James Braddock (Norris) returns to Vietnam to liberate his wife and son and a group of Amerasian foundlings. Martial artist supreme, Norris uses every part of his anatomy to destroy the Red villains, but he also gets to show a more sensitive side, even shedding a tear when he embraces his newfound son. Action-packed.
Dist.: Media

BRADY'S ESCAPE 1984
★ ★ ★ NR Action-Adventure 1:36
☑ Violence
Dir: Pal Gabor   *Cast:* John Savage, Kelly Reno, Ildiko Bansagi, Laszlo Mensaros, Dzsoko Bacs
▶ During World War II, Hungarian cowboys, known as Csikos, help downed U.S. aviator Savage escape the Nazis. Reno plays a local kid who befriends Savage and dreams of re-

turning with him to "Vyoming." Low-key, modest action-adventure tale is somber but likable.
Dist.: VidAmerica

BRAIN, THE 1988 Canadian
★ R Horror 1:30
☑ Nudity, explicit language, violence
Dir: Edward Hunt·   *Cast:* Tom Breznahan, Cyndy Preston, David Gale, George Buza, Brett Pearson
▶ Teen Breznahan, a disciplinary problem at school, is ordered to see shrink/TV personality Gale. He discovers Gale has been turning townspeople violent with his giant experimental brain and tries to stop him. Way-out plot provides wild chases, fierce battles, narrow escapes, and a few scattered chuckles.
Dist.: IVE

BRAIN DAMAGE 1988
☆ R Horror/Comedy 1:34
☑ Adult situations, explicit language, graphic violence
Dir: Frank Henenlotter   *Cast:* Rick Herbst, Jennifer Lowry, Gordon MacDonald, Theo Barnes
▶ Ugly little parasite moves from host to host and takes possession of young New Yorker Herbst. The monster feasts on human brains; Herbst must find the strength to battle the thing. Offbeat, twisted humor and plotting are not for every taste; the gore is excessive. (CC)
Dist.: Paramount

BRAIN FROM PLANET AROUS, THE 1958
★ NR Sci-Fi 1:10 B&W
Dir: Nathan Juran   *Cast:* John Agar, Joyce Meadows, Robert Fuller, Henry Travis
▶ Enormous alien brain comes to Earth and takes possession of scientist Agar. Can the evil gray matter's plan to conquer the world be stopped? Not to worry. A benevolent brain also arrives and takes possession of Agar's dog. They battle it out in this so-bad-it's-good B-movie.
Dist.: Rhino

BRAINSTORM 1983
★ ★ PG Sci-Fi 1:46
☑ Brief nudity, adult situations, explicit language, violence
Dir: Douglas Trumbull   *Cast:* Christopher Walken, Natalie Wood, Louise Fletcher, Cliff Robertson, Joe Dorsey
▶ Scientist Walken and wife Wood try to prevent the government from misusing his incredible discovery: a system that transfers perceptual experience from one mind to another. Provocative sci-fi has some murky plotting (Wood's death left some scenes unshot and caused a dispute between the studio and Trumbull) compensated by fine performances (especially Fletcher), thrilling special effects, and exciting subjective camerawork.
Dist.: MGM/UA

BRAIN THAT WOULDN'T DIE, THE 1959
★ NR Sci-Fi 1:21 B&W
Dir: Joseph Green *Cast:* Herb Evers, Virginia Leith, Adele Lamont, Paul Maurice
▶ Campy sci-fi horror B-movie has a plot so wild, it must be seen to be believed. Scientist Evers has problems: he's got a monster in the basement and, when girlfriend Leith is decapitated in a car crash, he keeps the head alive in a solution on his lab table. The bodiless lass spends the rest of the movie begging to be put out of her misery.
Dist.: Warner

BRAINWAVES 1982
★ ★ PG Mystery-Suspense 1:21
☑ Brief nudity, adult situations, explicit language, violence
Dir: Uli Lommel *Cast:* Keir Dullea, Suzanna Love, Tony Curtis, Vera Miles
▶ Young Love falls into a coma after a car accident. Her recovery turns into a nightmare after mad doctor Curtis tampers with her brain. Dullea, her concerned husband, tries to uncover the reason for her psychosis. A good cast and stylish camerawork enliven this pulpy story.
Dist.: Nelson

BRANDED 1950
★ ★ NR Western 1:35
Dir: Rudolph Maté *Cast:* Alan Ladd. Mona Freeman, Charles Bickford, Joseph Calleia, Milburn Stone, Robert Keith
▶ In cahoots with crook Keith. Ladd impersonates the long-lost son of wealthy rancher Bickford in a scheme to get the old man's cash. But Ladd is disarmed by the warmth of Bickford and his family—especially daughter Freeman. Unable to continue the deception, he confesses, and sets out to find the real son. By-the-numbers Western.
Dist.: Paramount

BRANNIGAN 1975 British
★ ★ ★ PG Action-Adventure 1:51
☑ Adult situations, explicit language, violence
Dir: Douglas Hickox *Cast:* John Wayne, Richard Attenborough, Judy Geeson, Mel Ferrer, Del Henney, Lesley-Anne Down
▶ Wayne, a tough Chicago cop, tracks criminal to England, where strict Scotland Yard detective Attenborough proves as much an obstacle as the crook's sneaky lawyer Ferrer. Predictable Wayne vehicle, typical of his later efforts, features strong car chases and fistfights.
Dist.: MGM/UA

BRASS TARGET 1978
★ ★ ★ PG Mystery-Suspense 1:51
☑ Explicit language, violence
Dir: John Hough *Cast:* Sophia Loren, John Cassavetes, George Kennedy, Robert Vaughn, Patrick McGoohan, Max Von Sydow
▶ Intriguing plot based on historical specula-

tion that General George Patton (Kennedy) was murdered to cover up a gold heist conspiracy involving U.S. army officers in post-World War II Germany. Cassavetes is the OSS man who investigates, Von Sydow the assassin working for the bad guys, and Loren is the woman involved with both men.
Dist.: MGM/UA

BRAVADOS, THE 1958
★ ★ ★ NR Western 1:38
Dir: Henry King *Cast:* Gregory Peck, Joan Collins, Stephen Boyd, Albert Salmi, Henry Silva, Kathleen Gallant
▶ Peck, a rancher whose wife has been raped and murdered, pursues four criminals to Mexican frontier town where they face hanging. When they escape, he exacts vengeance on them one by one. Stark, thoughtful Western features a brooding performance by Peck as a vigilante who becomes as evil as his prey.
Dist.: CBS/Fox

BRAVE ONE, THE 1956
★ ★ NR Family 1:40
Dir: Irving Rapper *Cast:* Michel Ray, Rodolfo Hoyos, Elsa Cardenas, Carlos Navarro, Joi Lansing, Fermin Rivera
▶ Mexican farm boy Ray raises a baby bull from calfhood, but then loses his pet when it's slated for the bullring. Ray struggles to save the bull from death. Tender tale is beautifully mounted. Oscar-winning story written by blacklisted Dalton Trumbo under the pseudonym Robert Rich. Bullfighter Rivera plays himself.
Dist.: United

BRAZIL 1985 British
★ R Sci-Fi 2:11
☑ Adult situations, explicit language, violence
Dir: Terry Gilliam *Cast:* Jonathan Pryce, Robert De Niro, Michael Palin, Kim Greist, Katherine Helmond, Ian Richardson
▶ Controversial black comedy about naive bureaucrat Pryce trapped in an Orwellian nightmare by a computer mixup is a wildly inventive but bleak vision of the future as seen by Monty Python member Gilliam. Stunning art direction was nominated for an Oscar, as was the sophisticated screenplay (by Gilliam, Tom Stoppard, and Charles McKeown). Uniformly good cast includes Bob Hoskins in an amusing cameo as a sanitation engineer. (CC)
Dist.: MCA

BREAD AND CHOCOLATE 1978 Italian
★ NR Comedy 1:51
☑ Adult situations, explicit language
Dir: Franco Brusati *Cast:* Nino Manfredi, Anna Karina, Johnny Dorell, Paolo Turco
▶ Italian immigrant Manfredi goes to work in Switzerland to support his family back home. Struggling to survive in a country that considers him inferior in every respect, his compassion for others and sense of humor ultimately

sees him through. Manfredi gives an almost Chaplinesque performance.

BREAKER! BREAKER! 1977
★ ★ PG Action-Adventure 1:26
☑ Violence
Dir: Don Hulette   *Cast:* Chuck Norris, George Murdock, Terry O'Connor, Don Gentry, Michael Augenstein
▶ Kung fu combines with citizens' band radio in this Norris vehicle. He plays a karate-chopping trucker rescuing younger brother Augenstein, the prisoner of some evil small-town types. Norris provides the action/mayhem mix we've come to expect.
Dist.: Embassy

BREAKER MORANT 1980 Australian
★ ★ ★ PG Drama 1:47
☑ Explicit language, violence
Dir: Bruce Beresford   *Cast:* Edward Woodward, Jack Thompson, Bryan Brown, John Waters, Lewis Fitz-Gerald
▶ During the Boer War in South Africa circa 1901, Australian soldiers Woodward, Brown, and Fitz-Gerald are made scapegoats for war crimes by their guilt-ridden British allies. Inexperienced attorney Thompson stoutly defends them in the controversial court-martial. Beautifully crafted, absolutely gripping factbased Australian antiwar drama. Terrific ensemble acting completely involves viewers in their tragic fate. Well worth a look.
Dist.: IVE

BREAKFAST AT TIFFANY'S 1961
★ ★ ★ ★ NR Romance 1:55
Dir: Blake Edwards   *Cast:* Audrey Hepburn, George Peppard, Patricia Neal, Buddy Ebsen, Mickey Rooney, Martin Balsam
▶ Sparkling adaptation of Truman Capote's novella stars Hepburn in a lovely performance as the free-spirited but vulnerable Holly Golightly. Struggling New York writer Peppard, the kept man of wealthy woman Neal, falls for Holly. Director Edwards weaves together an adult film of contrasting yet cohesive moods, from haunting loneliness to broad comedy. Oscar for Best Song, "Moon River."
Dist.: Paramount

BREAKFAST CLUB, THE 1985
★ ★ ★ ★ R Drama 1:37
☑ Explicit language, adult humor
Dir: John Hughes   *Cast:* Molly Ringwald, Ally Sheedy, Emilio Estevez, Anthony Michael Hall, Judd Nelson
▶ Five high school students face eight hours of detention on a Saturday. Nerd Hall, delinquent Nelson, jock Estevez, prom queen Ringwald, and kooky introvert Sheedy use the time to discuss their innermost secrets and really get to know one another. An ambitious and very funny comedy-drama from director Hughes. The excellent young cast keeps all the talk interesting.   **(CC)**
Dist.: MCA

BREAKHEART PASS 1976
★ ★ ★ PG Western 1:32
☑ Adult situations, explicit language, violence
Dir: Tom Gries   *Cast:* Charles Bronson, Ben Johnson, Richard Crenna, Jill Ireland, Charles Durning, Ed Lauter
▶ Crackling Western adventure with Bronson a secret agent on the trail of a gang of killers. Set primarily aboard a luxury steam train, and featuring a full complement of extraordinary stunts: runaway cars, rooftop fistfights, Indian ambushes, etc. Supporting villains include rodeo star Casey Tibbs, boxer Archie Moore, and pro quarterback Joe Kapp.   **(CC)**
Dist.: MGM/UA

BREAKIN' 1984
★ ★ ★ PG Musical 1:27
☑ Adult situations, explicit language, mild violence
Dir: Joel Silberg   *Cast:* Lucinda Dickey, Adolfo "Shabba-Doo" Quinones, Michael "Boogaloo Shrimp" Chambers, Ben Lokey, Christopher McDonald
▶ First feature film devoted entirely to the breakdancing craze. Dickey is a serious dance student turned on to breakin' by her new friends Quinones and Chambers. The dancing establishment refuses to acknowledge the style but the kids prove them wrong by winning parts in a Broadway musical. Plenty of music, dance, energy, and movement.
Dist.: MGM/UA

BREAKIN' 2: ELECTRIC BOOGALOO 1984
★ ★ ★ PG Musical 1:34
☑ Explicit language
Dir: Sam Firstenberg   *Cast:* Adolfo "Shabba-Doo" Quinones, Lucinda Dickey, Michael "Boogaloo Shrimp" Chambers, Susie Bono, Harry Caesar
▶ Breakdancing trio from the original *Breakin'* returns, this time to save a local community center from the greedy hands of evil developers. In the best Judy Garland/Mickey Rooney tradition, they decide to put on a show. Simple, rather predictable plot provides the anchor for lots of music and plenty of acrobatic dancing.
Dist.: MGM/UA

BREAKING ALL THE RULES 1985
★ ★ R Comedy 1:31
☑ Nudity, adult situations, explicit language
Dir: James Orr   *Cast:* Carl Marotte, Thor Bishopria, Carolyn Dunn, Rachel Hayward
▶ Comedy and romantic entanglements highlight lightweight teen fare for the youth audience. Teenagers Marotte, a security guard, and Bishopria spend a day at the amusement park. They woo two pretty girls and become the target of inept hoods who have hidden a valuable diamond in a stuffed toy won by Marotte in a park game.
Dist.: New World

BREAKING AWAY 1979
★ ★ ★ ★ PG Comedy 1:40
☑ Explicit language
Dir: Peter Yates *Cast:* Dennis Christopher, Dennis Quaid, Barbara Barrie, Paul Dooley, Jackie Earle Haley, Robyn Douglass
► Simply wonderful coming-of-age comedy set in Indiana. Christopher is a young man so obsessed with being an Italian bike racing champ that he pedals the day away and speaks with an Italian accent, upsetting salt-of-the-earth dad Dooley and delighting coed Douglass who mistakes him for the real article. The local college boys look down on Christopher and his townie friends; their conflict is resolved in a thrilling bike-race climax. Tender, funny, insightful Oscar-winning script from Steve Tesich. A Best Picture nominee.
Dist.: CBS/Fox

BREAKING GLASS 1980 British
☆ PG Musical 1:44
☑ Adult situations, explicit language
Dir: Brian Gibson *Cast:* Hazel O'Connor, Phil Daniels, Jon Finch, Jonathan Pryce, Peter-Hugo Daly
► Angry punker O'Connor falls prey to music industry pressures, drugs, and her own egotism in this slice-of-life look at British new wave music. Strong performances can't compensate for obvious story line.
Dist.: Paramount

BREAKING IN 1989
★ ★ ★ R Comedy 1:31
☑ Adult situations, explicit language
Dir: Bill Forsyth *Cast:* Burt Reynolds, Casey Siemaszko, Sheila Kelley, Lorraine Toussant, Albert Salmi, Harry Carey
► Veteran burglar Reynolds and novice Siemaszko meet when each breaks into the same house. Reynolds takes the younger man under his wing, teaching him the tricks of the trade, but Siemaszko's free spending arouses police suspicion. Lighthearted look at larceny lacks narrative drive but has appealingly restrained Reynolds and Forsyth's graceful visual touches. Funniest moments: Kelley's poem and the dog in the supermarket. Screenplay by John Sayles. **(CC)**
Dist.: HBO

BREAK OF HEARTS 1935
★ NR Drama 1:20 B&W
Dir: Phillip Moeller *Cast:* Katharine Hepburn, Charles Boyer, John Beal, Jean Hersholt, Sam Hardy, Inez Courtney
► Struggling composer Hepburn falls for world-famous conductor Boyer, but leaves him when she learns of his many affairs. Boyer sinks into alcoholism until Hepburn returns to redeem him. Weepy melodrama is dull and often improbable, despite stars' accomplished performances.
Dist.: Turner

BREAKOUT 1975
★ ★ PG Action-Adventure 1:36

☑ Explicit language, violence
Dir: Tom Gries *Cast:* Charles Bronson, Jill Ireland, Robert Duvall, Randy Quaid, John Huston
► Texas bush pilot Bronson is hired by Ireland to liberate her husband Duvall, who has been unjustly imprisoned in a Mexican jail. Huston plays Duvall's evil grandfather, who is behind the frame-up. Hard-hitting, realistic escape melodrama for fans of Bronson and action.
Dist.: RCA/Columbia

BREAKTHROUGH 1979 German
★ ★ ★ PG War 1:51
☑ Adult situations, explicit language, violence
Dir: Andrew V. McLaglen *Cast:* Richard Burton, Robert Mitchum, Rod Steiger, Helmut Griem, Curt Jurgens, Michael Parks
► Despondent German officer Burton becomes entangled in a plot to assassinate Hitler, maintaining his command long enough to ensure the American seizure of a town pivotal to the Allied victory. Not the usual one-sided pro-American drama but a humane look at individuals on both sides with plenty of action. Sequel to *Cross of Iron.*
Dist.: Worldvision

BREATHLESS 1961 French
★ ★ NR Drama 1:30 B&W
Dir: Jean-Luc Godard *Cast:* Jean-Paul Belmondo, Jean Seberg, Daniel Boulanger, Jean-Pierre Melville, Liliane Robin, Henri-Jacques Huet
► Small-time hood Belmondo, on the run from the law, hooks up with bohemian American Seberg in Paris. Highly influential cult film, a textbook on jump cuts, offbeat camera angles, and improvised acting, legitimized French "New Wave" directors for an international audience. Story by François Truffaut. Filmed again in 1983 with Richard Gere. French title: *A Bout de Souffle.* Ⓢ
Dist.: Various

BREATHLESS 1983
★ ★ R Drama 1:40
☑ Nudity, adult situations, explicit language, violence
Dir: Jim McBride *Cast:* Richard Gere, Valerie Kaprisky, Art Metrano, John P. Ryan, William Tepper
► Updated remake of the 1959 French classic switches the setting to Los Angeles, but retains the basic plot. Gere plays a small-time hood on the run from the cops; Kaprisky is a French college student who can't fight her attraction to him. As the cops close in, she realizes she may have to betray him. Highly stylized, with a bold color scheme and pounding rock soundtrack.
Dist.: Vestron

BREED APART, A 1986
★ ★ ★ ★ R Action-Adventure 1:41
☑ Nudity, adult situations, explicit language, violence

Dir: Philippe Mora   *Cast:* Rutger Hauer, Powers Boothe, Kathleen Turner, Donald Pleasence, John Dennis Johnston
▶ Vet-turned-conservationist Hauer battles famous mountain climber Boothe over a nest of rare bald eagle eggs. Turner plays a local merchant who has to choose between them. Beautiful mountain scenery (shot on location in North Carolina) provides an attractive background to this offbeat adventure.
Dist.: HBO

BREWSTER MCCLOUD 1970
☆ **R Comedy 1:44**
☑ Nudity, adult situations, explicit language
Dir: Robert Altman   *Cast:* Bud Cort, Sally Kellerman, Michael Murphy, William Windom, Shelley Duvall, Stacy Keach
▶ Odd young Cort lives in the Houston Astrodome while developing a pair of wings to support his fantasy of flight. Eventually he's linked to a series of murders in which the victims are covered with bird droppings. Altman's surreal, satiric fantasy has garnered a cult following and is reportedly among the director's favorites.
Dist.: MGM/UA

BREWSTER'S MILLIONS 1985
★ ★ ★ ★ **PG Comedy 1:41**
☑ Violence
Dir: Walter Hill   *Cast:* Richard Pryor, John Candy, Lonette McKee, Stephen Collins, Jerry Orbach, Hume Cronyn
▶ Frantic, large-scale updating of the venerable play has Pryor as a minor league pitcher who must spend $30 million in a month to inherit a vast fortune. Lawyers try to cheat him out of the money, but they haven't counted on his pals: beautiful accountant McKee and chubby teammate Candy (an excellent foil for Pryor). Although first staged in 1907, the premise is still delightful.   **(CC)**
Dist.: MCA

BRIAN'S SONG 1970
★ ★ ★ ★ ★ **G Biography/MFTV 1:13**
Dir: Buzz Kulik   *Cast:* James Caan, Billy Dee Williams, Jack Warden, Judy Pace, Shelley Fabares
▶ Heartbreaking true-life story of the friendship between Chicago Bears football stars Brian Piccolo (Caan) and Gale Sayers (Williams) was one of the most popular of all made-for-TV movies. Dealing honestly with Piccolo's fatal cancer, the story is a rich, rewarding experience full of life and hope. Based on Sayers's *I Am Third.* Winner of many awards, with a sensitive screenplay by William Blinn and beautiful Michel Legrand score. **(CC)**
Dist.: RCA/Columbia

BRIDE, THE 1985
★ **PG-13 Horror 1:58**
☑ Nudity, violence
Dir: Franc Roddam   *Cast:* Sting, Jennifer Beals, Geraldine Page, Clancy Brown, David Rappaport, Phil Daniels
▶ Dr. Frankenstein (Sting) creates wife (Beals) for his monster Victor (Brown), but ends up falling in love with the creature himself. Victor escapes and joins a circus with dwarf Rappaport, but after a tragic murder he returns to claim his bride. Remake of 1935 film presents a more faithful interpretation of Mary Shelley's characters. Rock star Sting turns in a magnetic performance, but Brown and Rappaport have the best moments.   **(CC)**
Dist.: RCA/Columbia

BRIDE OF FRANKENSTEIN, THE 1935
★ ★ ★ **NR Horror 1:15 B&W**
Dir: James Whale   *Cast:* Boris Karloff, Elsa Lanchester, Colin Clive, Ernest Thesiger, Valerie Hobson, Dwight Frye
▶ Sequel to the 1931 *Frankenstein* focuses on mad doctor Clive's disastrous attempt to create a bride (Lanchester) for unhappy monster (Karloff). In this horror classic, director Whale mixes macabre black comedy with poignancy, especially in the famous scene where the blind hermit befriends the monster. Thesiger, as Clive's eerie rival, is nearly as scary as the great Karloff.
Dist.: MCA

BRIDE OF THE MONSTER 1955
☆ **NR Horror 1:09 B&W**
Dir: Edward D. Wood   *Cast:* Bela Lugosi, Tor Johnson, Tony McCoy, Loretta King
▶ Mad doctor Lugosi tries to create a race of super-powered atomic beings in his swamp laboratory; henchman Johnson pitches in by kidnapping subjects for the experiments. Detective McCoy investigates when his fiancée King becomes Lugosi's prisoner. Incompetent movie is screamingly funny. Lowlights include fight with a rubber octopus and unexplained atomic explosion.
Dist.: Video Yesteryear

BRIDE WALKS OUT, THE 1936
★ **NR Comedy 1:21 B&W**
Dir: Leigh Jason   *Cast:* Barbara Stanwyck, Gene Raymond, Robert Young, Ned Sparks, Helen Broderick, Willie Best
▶ Stanwyck and Raymond break up because of her spendthrift ways. When playboy Young offers her unlimited money, she considers forgetting Raymond forever. Stanwyck outshines the rest of the cast in this middling comedy.
Dist.: Turner

BRIDGE OF SAN LUIS REY, THE 1944
★ **NR Drama 1:29 B&W**
Dir: Rowland V. Lee   *Cast:* Lynn Bari, Akim Tamiroff, Francis Lederer, Alla Nazimova, Louis Calhern, Blanche Yurka
▶ Faithful adaptation of Thornton Wilder's novel examines the reactions of superstitious eighteenth-century Peruvians to the collapse of a mountain bridge that kills five villagers. Slowly paced drama about an intriguing subject is notable for its accomplished cast and

unusual production design. Score by Dimitri Tiomkin received an Oscar nomination.
Dist.: New World

BRIDGE ON THE RIVER KWAI, THE 1957 British
★ ★ ★ ★ ★ NR War/Drama 2:44
Dir: David Lean *Cast:* Alec Guinness, William Holden, Jack Hawkins, Sessue Hayakawa, Geoffrey Horne
► Superlative World War II adventure about Allied POWs forced to build a strategic bridge for the Japanese in the jungles of Thailand. Guinness won the Best Actor Oscar as the proud colonel determined to complete the bridge despite Allied saboteurs. Beautifully realized production also won Oscars for Best Picture, Direction, Cinematography, Score, Editing, and Screenplay (Carl Foreman and Michael Wilson were both blacklisted at the time, so the award was given to Pierre Boulle, author of the original novel).
Dist.: RCA/Columbia

BRIDGES AT TOKO-RI, THE 1955
★ ★ ★ ★ NR War 1:43
Dir: Mark Robson *Cast:* William Holden, Fredric March, Grace Kelly, Mickey Rooney, Robert Strauss, Earl Holliman
► Holden, a veteran of World War II, is forced back into action as an aircraft carrier pilot during the Korean War. His mission: destroy five bridges spanning a strategic pass. Rooney and Holliman offer strong support as members of a helicopter rescue team. Vivid adaptation of James Michener's best-seller won an Oscar for Special Effects. Exceptional aerial footage.
Dist.: Paramount

BRIDGE TOO FAR, A 1977 British
★ ★ ★ ★ ★ PG War 3:03
☑ Explicit language, mild violence
Dir: Richard Attenborough *Cast:* Dirk Bogarde, James Caan, Michael Caine, Sean Connery, Edward Fox, Gene Hackman, Anthony Hopkins, Hardy Kruger, Laurence Olivier, Ryan O'Neal, Robert Redford, Maximilian Schell, Liv Ullmann, Arthur Hill
► Multimillion-dollar version of Cornelius Ryan's best-seller. Gripping tale of Operation Market Garden, the Allied Force's attempt to cross the Rhine into Germany—resulting in history's largest airborne assault. Star studded and action packed, with terrific battle scenes, strong dramatic sequences and excellent photography of Dutch locations. Despite three-hour length and disconsolate mood, an epic of great proportions.
Dist.: MGM/UA

BRIEF ENCOUNTER 1945 British
★ ★ ★ NR Romance 1:26 B&W
Dir: David Lean *Cast:* Celia Johnson, Trevor Howard, Stanley Holloway, Joyce Carey, Cyril Raymond
► Chance train station meeting between married doctor Howard and housewife Johnson leads to an ultimately doomed romance.

Adaptation of Noel Coward play is a beautiful and poignant classic, thanks to the superb leads and director Lean, whose intimate touch here will be a revelation to those only familiar with his later spectacles. Celebrated score features Rachmaninoff's "Second Piano Concerto."
Dist.: Paramount

BRIGADOON 1954
★ ★ ★ ★ G Musical 1:48
Dir: Vincente Minnelli *Cast:* Gene Kelly, Cyd Charisse, Van Johnson, Elaine Stewart, Barry Jones
► Americans Kelly and Johnson happen upon a mythical Scottish kingdom that comes to life only once every 100 years. Kelly falls in love with Charisse and must choose between her world and his. Screen adaptation of one of the best-loved Lerner and Loewe musicals features songs like "The Heather on the Hill" and "It's Almost Like Being in Love."
Dist.: MGM/UA

BRIGHT EYES 1934
★ ★ NR Comedy/Family 1:34 B&W
Dir: David Butler *Cast:* Shirley Temple, James Dunn, Jane Withers, Jane Darwell, Judith Allen, Charles Sellon
► Little orphan Temple becomes the object of a three-way custody battle among Allen, wealthy Sellon, and pilot Dunn. One of Temple's best vehicles (and not just because she gets to sing "On the Good Ship Lollipop"). Her relationship with Dunn is surprisingly affecting.
Dist.: Playhouse

BRIGHT LIGHTS, BIG CITY 1988
★ ★ R Drama 1:34
☑ Adult situations, explicit language
Dir: James Bridges *Cast:* Michael J. Fox, Kiefer Sutherland, Dianne Wiest, Phoebe Cates, Swoosie Kurtz, Frances Sternhagen, Tracy Pollan
► Yuppie magazine fact-checker Fox is at the end of his rope: mother Wiest has recently died of cancer, bitchy wife Cates has left him, and he's snorting cocaine to oblivion. Smirking Sutherland is Ted Allagash, his partner in disco and drug excess. Pollan (real-life Mrs. Michael J. Fox) appears as Ted's cousin. Fine camera-work, soundtrack, and supporting actors still add up to bright lights, big deal. From the best-selling book about Manhattan life in the too-fast lane. **(CC)**
Dist.: MGM/UA

BRIGHTON BEACH MEMOIRS 1986
★ ★ ★ PG-13 Comedy 1:50
☑ Adult situations, explicit language
Dir: Gene Saks *Cast:* Blythe Danner, Bob Dishy, Stacey Glick, Judith Ivey, Jonathan Silverman
► Semiautobiographical comedy based on Neil Simon's hit Broadway play. Eugene (Silverman) is a 1930s teen growing up in Brooklyn in a house so small that no one is afforded any privacy. While grappling with raging hor-

mones, Eugene comes to the realization that he'll never pitch for the Yankees. Warmly nostalgic period piece. **(CC)**
Dist.: MCA

BRIGHTON STRANGLER, THE 1945
★ **NR Mystery-Suspense 1:07 B&W**
Dir: Max Nosseck   *Cast:* John Loder, June Duprez, Michael St. Angel, Miles Mander, Rose Hobart, Gilbert Emery
▶ Actor Loder is appearing in a London stage play as a demented killer. After receiving a blow on the head, he embarks on a string of murders, believing himself to be the character he plays onstage. Nicely done thriller.
Dist.: Turner

BRIMSTONE AND TREACLE 1982 British
★ **R Drama 1:25**
☑ Nudity, adult situations, explicit language, violence
Dir: Richard Loncraine   *Cast:* Denholm Elliott, Joan Plowright, Sting, Suzanna Hamilton
▶ Offbeat psychological thriller featuring rock 'n' roll singer Sting in his first starring role. He invades the drab lives of married couple Elliot and Plowright, who are devoted to their catatonic daughter. The mother welcomes his attention; the father fears he has an evil purpose in mind, which of course he does. Sting provides the musical score, along with The Police and The Go-Gos. Screenplay by Dennis Potter, based on his British teleplay.
Dist.: MGM/UA

BRINGING UP BABY 1938
★ ★ ★ ★ **NR Comedy 1:42 B&W**
Dir: Howard Hawks   *Cast:* Katharine Hepburn, Cary Grant, Charles Ruggles, Barry Fitzgerald, May Robson, Walter Catlett
▶ Hysterically funny screwball comedy virtually defines the genre. Shy, bespectacled paleontologist Grant needs just one bone to complete his prized dinosaur skeleton—the same bone snatched by dizzy heiress Hepburn's dog (Asta of the Thin Man movies). A whirlwind plot follows as hurricane Hepburn wins the reluctant Grant's heart. Breathless direction by Hawks and two terrific comic performances by the stars.
Dist.: Turner   C

BRING ME THE HEAD OF ALFREDO GARCIA 1974
★ ★ **R Action-Adventure 1:52**
☑ Brief nudity, adult situations, explicit language, graphic violence
Dir: Sam Peckinpah   *Cast:* Warren Oates, Isela Vega, Gig Young, Robert Webber, Helmut Dantine, Kris Kristofferson
▶ Mexican millionaire hires seedy bar owner Oates to kill Garcia, the man who seduced his daughter. Discovering that Garcia is already dead, Oates chops off his head to receive his fee, and then fights off hitmen, bikers, and other thugs who also want the money. Jarring,

bloody adventure has plenty of Peckinpah's trademark violence.
Dist.: MGM/UA

BRING ON THE NIGHT 1985 British
★ ★ ★ **PG-13 Documentary/Music 1:37**
☑ Adult situations, explicit language
Dir: Michael Apted   *Cast:* Sting, Omar Hakim, Darryl Jones, Kenny Kirkland, Branford Marsalis
▶ Rockumentary traces the founding of a new jazz-oriented band by Sting, former lead singer of the Police, from rehearsals in the lush French countryside to a premiere Paris concert. Devotees of the star will thrill to behind-the-scenes footage. Concert includes such Sting favorites as "Roxanne," "If You Love Somebody Set Them Free," and "Message in a Bottle." **(CC)**
Dist.: Warner

BRINK'S JOB, THE 1978
★ ★ ★ ★ **PG Comedy 1:58**
☑ Explicit language, mild violence
Dir: William Friedkin   *Cast:* Peter Falk, Peter Boyle, Allen Goorwitz, Warren Oates, Gena Rowlands, Paul Sorvino
▶ Suspense and laughs as ringleader Falk and a gang of petty crooks attempt the crime of the century by robbing $2.7 million from Boston's Brink's vault. Eventually costing the government ten times that amount, they're caught less than a week before the statute of limitations runs out. Vivid re-creation of the famous 1950 heist, blessed with a light touch and sturdy cast.
Dist.: MCA

BRITANNIA HOSPITAL 1983 British
☆ **R Comedy 1:56**
☑ Nudity, explicit language
Dir: Lindsay Anderson   *Cast:* Leonard Rossiter, Graham Crowden, Malcolm McDowell, Joan Plowright, Jill Bennett, Mark Hamill, Alan Bates
▶ Chaos reigns at London's venerable Britannia Hospital as the administration copes with riots, strikes, and mass disorder prior to a visit from the Royal Family. Humor is very British, and combined with black comedy elements may not be everyone's cup of tea. McDowell reprises his *O Lucky Man!* role.
Dist.: HBO

BROADCAST NEWS 1987
★ ★ ★ ★ **R Comedy/Drama 2:13**
☑ Brief nudity, adult situations, explicit language
Dir: James L. Brooks   *Cast:* William Hurt, Albert Brooks, Holly Hunter, Robert Prosky, Lois Chiles, Jack Nicholson, Joan Cusack
▶ Brooks's clever, poignant look at three TV newspeople struggling with the problems of love and work in the eighties. Highly principled producer Hunter is attracted to charismatic anchorman Hurt, even though he represents everything she despises professionally. Her best friend Brooks, a brainy journalist

who lacks the slickness to make it on TV, is hopelessly in love with her. Terrific dialogue, wonderful performances for fully rounded, very human characterizations. Oscar nominations for Picture, Director, and the three leads. (CC)
Dist.: CBS/Fox

BROADWAY DANNY ROSE 1984
★ ★ PG Comedy 1:24 B&W
☑ Adult situations, explicit language, mild violence, adult humor
Dir: Woody Allen *Cast:* Woody Allen, Mia Farrow, Nick Apollo Forte, Sandy Baron, Corbett Monica, Jackie Gayle
▶ Danny Rose (Allen), a Broadway agent with a good heart and a bad eye for talent (clients include a blind xylophone player), finds himself on the lam from Mafia hitmen along with gangster's widow Tina (Farrow), the girlfriend of Rose's one hot client, Italian crooner Forte. Farrow eschews her usual delicate persona and does wonders as the gum-chewing, bleached-blond Tina. Sharp dialogue and excellent black-and-white photography in this enchanting comic fable.
Dist.: Vestron

BROADWAY MELODY, THE 1929
★ NR Musical 1:21 B&W
Dir: Harry Beaumont *Cast:* Anita Page, Bessie Love, Charles King, Jed Prouty, Kenneth Thompson, James Gleason
▶ First "all-talking, all-singing, all-dancing" musical is a technically primitive story of Page and Love, sisters looking for a break on Broadway. Both fall in love with singer/dancer King. Although it received three Oscar nominations, winning for Best Picture, it seems awfully crude and awkward today. Title tune and "You Were Meant for Me" are both repeated three times; liveliest song is the charming "Boy Friend." Technicolor version of "The Wedding of the Painted Doll" has apparently been lost, and is now shown in black and white.
Dist.: MGM/UA

BROADWAY MELODY OF 1938 1937
★ ★ ★ NR Musical 1:50 B&W
Dir: Roy Del Ruth *Cast:* Robert Taylor, Eleanor Powell, George Murphy, Binnie Barnes, Buddy Ebsen, Sophie Tucker
▶ Broadway producer Taylor can't finance his next show unless Powell's horse wins at Saratoga. Plot is little more than a thin frame for nine songs, including "Everybody Sing" and "Follow in My Footsteps." Powell's tap solos are superb; Tucker reprises her vaudeville routines; but the real highlight is a young Judy Garland on the verge of stardom singing "Dear Mr. Gable." (CC)
Dist.: MGM/UA

BROADWAY MELODY OF 1940 1940
★ ★ ★ NR Musical 1:42 B&W
Dir: Norman Taurog *Cast:* Fred Astaire, Eleanor Powell, George Murphy, Frank Morgan, Ian Hunter

▶ Astaire and Murphy's dancing team splits up when Murphy lands a solo spot in a show. While Fred woos Powell, Murphy becomes an insufferable star—until he realizes he still needs Fred's help. The stars breeze through this light, glossy MGM comedy. Fourth and final entry in the *Melody* series has a wonderful Cole Porter score ("I Concentrate on You") and a knock-out duet to "Begin the Beguine."
Dist.: MGM/UA

BROKEN ARROW 1950
★ ★ ★ NR Western 1:32
Dir: Delmer Daves *Cast:* James Stewart, Jeff Chandler, Debra Paget, Will Geer, Jay Silverheels
▶ In Civil War Arizona, ex–Union soldier Stewart marries Apache Paget, befriends the warrior Cochise (Chandler), and teams with him to settle battles between whites and Indians. Terrific adventure delivers action, romance, scenery, fine performances, and even a rare (for Hollywood) pro-Indian message. (CC)
Dist.: CBS/Fox

BROKEN BLOSSOMS 1919
★ NR Drama 1:35 B&W
Dir: D. W. Griffith *Cast:* Lillian Gish, Richard Barthelmess, Donald Crisp, Arthur Howard, Edward Piel, George Beranger
▶ Gish is worshipped from afar by Barthelmess, a peaceful Chinese who has been reduced to running a curio shop in London. When Gish is brutally beaten by her boxer father Crisp, Barthelmess takes her in, igniting the father's violent wrath. Silent classic treats plight of culturally displaced Chinese with sensitivity.
Dist.: HBO

BROKEN LANCE 1954
★ ★ ★ NR Western 1:36
Dir: Edward Dmytryk *Cast:* Spencer Tracy, Robert Wagner, Jean Peters, Richard Widmark, Katy Jurado, Hugh O'Brian
▶ Ruthless cattle baron Tracy suffers a stroke struggling to keep his empire intact. Faithful son Wagner is forced into a deadly feud with his scheming brothers (including Widmark in a typically nasty role). Solid, intelligent Western, with Oscar-nominated Jurado particularly impressive as Tracy's wife. Philip Yordan won an Oscar for Original Story (loosely based on *King Lear*).
Dist.: CBS/Fox

BRONCO BILLY 1980
★ ★ ★ PG Comedy 1:56
☑ Adult situations, explicit language
Dir: Clint Eastwood *Cast:* Clint Eastwood, Sondra Locke, Geoffrey Lewis, Scatman Crothers, Bill McKinney
▶ Engaging low-key comedy about the love-hate relationship between Eastwood, owner of a flea-bitten Wild West show, and Locke, a spoiled heiress. Warm, gentle story was a real change-of-pace for Eastwood, who acts and directs with winning simplicity. He even sings

with Merle Haggard (who also performs "Misery and Gin").
Dist.: Warner

BROOD, THE 1979 Canadian
★ ★ R Horror 1:31
☑ Explicit language, graphic violence
Dir: David Cronenberg *Cast:* Oliver Reed, Samantha Eggar, Art Hindle, Cindy Hines, Nuala FitzGerald
▶ Disturbing, extremely gruesome shocker about mad scientist Reed, whose genetic experiments go disastrously awry, spreading a lethal plague on an unsuspecting city. Mentally disturbed mother Eggar's children may hold the key to understanding the virus—if a bizarre mutant doesn't kill them first. Fans of cult director Cronenberg champion the script's allegorical touches.
Dist.: Embassy

BROTHER, CAN YOU SPARE A DIME? 1975
★ ★ ★ PG Documentary 1:45 B&W
☑ Adult situations, violence
Dir: Philippe Mora
▶ In his portrait of the 1930s Depression era, director Mora uses fascinating, previously unseen footage. Compilation documentary intercuts newsreel film of real-life figures with clips from Hollywood classics. Inventive editing, effective use of music.
Dist.: VCI

BROTHER FROM ANOTHER PLANET, THE 1984
★ NR Sci-Fi/Comedy 1:49
☑ Adult situations, explicit language, violence, adult humor
Dir: John Sayles *Cast:* Joe Morton, Darryl Edwards, Steve James, Leonard Jackson, Bill Cobbs
▶ Morton, a mute black alien, escapes from slavery on another planet and arrives in Harlem via Ellis Island. Wise, winsome comedy-allegory from writer/director Sayles gently mixes satire with social comment. Wonderful work from Morton as he adjusts to a strange new world. Sayles appears as an alien bounty hunter tracking Morton. **(CC)**
Dist.: Key

BROTHERHOOD, THE 1968
★ ★ ★ NR Drama 1:38
Dir: Martin Ritt *Cast:* Kirk Douglas, Alex Cord, Irene Papas, Luther Adler, Susan Strasberg, Eduardo Ciannelli
▶ Douglas produced and stars as a mafioso who gets involved in power struggle with younger brother Cord. After Douglas kills Cord's father-in-law Adler, Cord accepts the task of murdering Douglas. Well-done mob tale features fine work from the leads.
Dist.: Paramount

BROTHERHOOD OF SATAN, THE 1971
★ PG Horror 1:32
☑ Violence
Dir: Bernard McEveety *Cast:* Strother Mar-

tin, L. Q. Jones, Charles Bateman, Ahna Capri, Charles Robinson
▶ Producer Jones plays the sheriff of an isolated small town who can't explain why twenty-six citizens have been butchered in four days. Survivors spread the rumor that witches are responsible. Low-budget thriller effectively exploits mob hysteria.
Dist.: RCA/Columbia

BROTHER JOHN 1971
★ ★ PG Comedy/Drama 1:34
☑ Adult situations, violence
Dir: James Goldstone *Cast:* Sidney Poitier, Will Geer, Bradford Dillman, Paul Winfield, Beverly Todd
▶ Poitier, a mysterious drifter, returns to small Southern town when his mother becomes fatally ill. Sheriff Dillman fears Poitier will stir up local blacks, as there are hints that he may be the messiah. Dated, inadequately constructed screenplay begins with interesting clues but never brings tale to climax. Geer outshines Poitier, who gives a surprisingly lackluster performance.
Dist.: RCA/Columbia

BROTHERS KARAMAZOV, THE 1958
★ ★ ★ ★ NR Drama 2:30
Dir: Richard Brooks *Cast:* Maria Schell, Yul Brynner, Lee J. Cobb, William Shatner, Claire Bloom, Richard Basehart, Albert Salmi
▶ Sin, salvation, greed, and depravity are examined in this sophisticated story of a lecherous father, his four sons (one illegitimate), their loves and tragedies. Good-looking all-star cast; based on Dostoyevsky's classic Russian novel.
Dist.: MGM/UA

BROTHER SUN, SISTER MOON 1973
Italian/British
★ ★ ★ PG Drama 2:01
☑ Adult situations
Dir: Franco Zeffirelli *Cast:* Graham Faulkner, Judi Bowker, Alec Guinness, Leigh Lawson, Kenneth Cranham
▶ Lyrical version of the life of St. Francis of Assisi with Faulkner as the young soldier who renounces wealth to found a religious order. Beautiful images overwhelm the plot, which assumes a mystical, wide-eyed approach to Francis's achievements. Guinness has a small role as the Pope who supports Francis. Folksinger Donovan wrote the soundtrack.
Dist.: Paramount

BRUBAKER 1980
★ ★ ★ ★ ★ R Drama 2:12
☑ Brief nudity, explicit language, violence
Dir: Stuart Rosenberg *Cast:* Robert Redford, Yaphet Kotto, Jane Alexander, Murray Hamilton, David Keith, Morgan Freeman
▶ Reform-minded warden Redford disguises himself as a prisoner to investigate a notoriously harsh prison. He uncovers evidence that prisoners are being systematically murdered, then has to confront corrupt prison officials

who want to cover up the conspiracy. Earnest drama was based on a true story. Screenplay by W. D. Richter was nominated for an Oscar. *Dist.:* CBS/Fox

BRUTE MAN, THE 1947
☆ **NR Horror 1:00 B&W**
Dir: Jean Yarbrough *Cast:* Rondo Hatton, Jane Adams, Tom Neal, Donald MacBride
▶ Acid-scarred Hatton hunts down those who caused his deformed condition and befriends blind pianist Adams. Cheaply made scare picture contains element of exploitation: Hatton's disfigured face was actually the result of the disease acromegaly.
Dist.: SVS

BUCCANEER, THE 1959
★ ★ **NR Action-Adventure 2:01**
Dir: Anthony Quinn *Cast:* Yul Brynner, Charlton Heston, Claire Bloom, Charles Boyer, Inger Stevens, Lorne Greene
▶ During the Battle of New Orleans, pirate Jean Lafitte (Brynner) allies himself with American general Andrew Jackson (Heston) to defeat the British and end the War of 1812. Producer Cecil B. DeMille's remake of his own 1938 film is better cast than the original but somehow not a better film.
Dist.: KVC

BUCK AND THE PREACHER 1972
★ ★ **PG Western 1:42**
☑ Explicit language
Dir: Sidney Poitier *Cast:* Sidney Poitier, Harry Belafonte, Ruby Dee, Cameron Mitchell, Denny Miller, Nita Talbot
▶ Two blacks, bunco artist/preacher Belafonte and good guy Poitier, team up to outwit evil whites, including Mitchell, a greedy bounty hunter trying to catch runaway slaves in the old West. Thin story enlivened by the charm and charisma of Poitier and Belafonte. Poitier's directorial debut.
Dist.: RCA/Columbia

BUCKET OF BLOOD, A 1959
★ ★ **NR Horror/Comedy 1:06 B&W**
Dir: Roger Corman *Cast:* Dick Miller, Barboura Morris, Anthony Carbone, Julian Burton, Ed Nelson, John Brinkley
▶ Engaging horror spoof set in an amusingly dated world of beatnik coffeehouses. Miller, a nerdy busboy who longs to impress Morris, stumbles onto a path to success when he turns his dead cat into a sculpture. Low-budget sleeper was written by Charles B. Griffith (*Little Shop of Horrors*).
Dist.: Sinister

BUCK PRIVATES 1941
★ ★ **NR Comedy 1:24 B&W**
Dir: Arthur Lubin *Cast:* Bud Abbott, Lou Costello, The Andrews Sisters, Lee Bowman, Nat Pendleton
▶ Early Bud and Lou vehicle is one of their best efforts. Army comedy high jinks as the boys go to boot camp during the early days of World

War II. Also on hand: the Andrews Sisters (who sing "Boogie Woogie Bugle Boy from Company B" and several others) and Stooge Shemp Howard in a bit part. Spawned a 1947 sequel.
Dist.: MCA

BUCK ROGERS IN THE 25TH CENTURY 1979
★ ★ ★ **PG Sci-Fi 1:28**
☑ Explicit language, violence
Dir: Daniel Haller *Cast:* Gil Gerard, Pamela Hensley, Erin Gray, Henry Silva, Tim O'Connor, Joseph Wiseman
▶ Present-day astronaut Buck Rogers (Gerard) awakes in the twenty-fifth century after being frozen in space and finds a brave new world. He makes a quick adjustment to his new surroundings and saves Earth from an evil villain. Relaxed and diverting despite threadbare special effects. Pilot for Gerard's TV series got a theatrical release but definitely looks better on the small screen.
Dist.: MCA

BUDDY BUDDY 1981
★ ★ ★ **R Comedy 1:36**
☑ Brief nudity, explicit language, mild violence
Dir: Billy Wilder *Cast:* Jack Lemmon, Walter Matthau, Paula Prentiss, Klaus Kinski, Dana Elcar, Miloš Chapin
▶ Mob hitman Matthau rents a hotel room to rub out a government witness but a suicidal Lemmon, in despair over wife Prentiss's affair with sex doctor Kinski, occupies the room next door and keeps foiling Matthau. Fourth teaming of these two stars has an off-the-wall plot taken from the French film *A Pain in the A—*. The last film to date by director Wilder.
Dist.: MGM/UA

BUDDY HOLLY STORY, THE 1978
★ ★ ★ ★ **PG Biography/Music 1:39**
☑ Explicit language
Dir: Steve Rash *Cast:* Gary Busey, Don Stroud, Charles Martin Smith, Maria Richwine, Conrad Janis, Amy Johnston
▶ Honest, enjoyable biography of rock 'n' roll star Buddy Holly. Bravura performance by Busey, Oscar-nominated for his uncanny impersonation of the Lubbock, Texas, musician who achieved early fame before his tragic death. Use of live music (which won the Oscar for Song Adaptation) and accurate period detail brought the late 1950s back to life. Broad sampling of Holly's music: "That'll Be the Day," "Maybe Baby," "Peggy Sue," "Oh Boy," "Every Day," etc.
Dist.: RCA/Columbia

BUDDY SYSTEM, THE 1984
★ ★ ★ ★ **PG Comedy 1:50**
☑ Adult situations, explicit language
Dir: Glenn Jordan *Cast:* Richard Dreyfuss, Susan Sarandon, Nancy Allen, Jean Stapleton, Wil Wheaton
▶ Security guard and aspiring writer Dreyfuss

befriends single mother Sarandon. Her young son wants a father, but Dreyfuss is too busy coping with dizzy girlfriend Allen to realize what he's missing. Likable stars bring warmth to this pleasant romantic trifle. **(CC)**
Dist.: CBS/Fox

BUFFALO BILL 1944
★ ★ ★ **NR Western/Biography 1:30**
Dir: William Wellman **Cast:** Joel McCrea, Maureen O'Hara, Linda Darnell, Thomas Mitchell, Edgar Buchanan, Anthony Quinn
▶ Large-scale biography of Buffalo Bill Cody, the frontier scout whose feats of bravery won him the Congressional Medal of Honor. Starts with a daring rescue of a stagecoach under Indian attack and proceeds through fights with Yellow Hand (Quinn) and establishment of the famous Wild West Show. Heavily romanticized and prone to sentimentality. McCrea is stalwart in the lead role; Mitchell plays dime pulp author Ned Buntline. **(CC)**
Dist.: CBS/Fox

BUFFALO BILL AND THE INDIANS, OR SITTING BULL'S HISTORY LESSON 1976
☆ **PG Western 2:00**
☑ Adult situations, explicit language
Dir: Robert Altman **Cast:** Paul Newman, Joel Grey, Kevin McCarthy, Harvey Keitel, Geraldine Chaplin, Will Sampson
▶ Altman's follow-up to *Nashville* is a sprawling, revisionist look at how Buffalo Bill (Newman) exploited the press to become the nation's first Wild West star. Offbeat, convoluted screenplay (by Altman and Alan Rudolph, based on Arthur Kopit's play *Indians*) gives a weird, hallucinatory cast to the proceedings. Burt Lancaster has a sharp cameo as Ned Buntline, the writer who actually invented most of Bill's adventures.
Dist.: Playhouse

BUG 1975
★ **PG Horror 1:40**
☑ Violence
Dir: Jeannot Szwarc **Cast:** Bradford Dillman, Joanna Miles, Richard Gilliland, Jamie Smith Jackson, Alan Fudge
▶ An earthquake in California unleashes a plague of prehistoric beetles who set their victims on fire. Attempts by scientists to eradicate the insects end in failure. Often nasty film with obvious special effects. B-movie master William Castle's last production (he also had a hand in the screenplay).
Dist.: Paramount

BUGLES IN THE AFTERNOON 1952
★ ★ **NR Western 1:25**
Dir: Roy Rowland **Cast:** Ray Milland, Helena Carter, Hugh Marlowe, Forrest Tucker, Barton MacLane, George Reeves
▶ Fast-paced but routine Western finds Milland under the command of his old enemy Marlowe at Fort Lincoln. Marlowe sends Milland on suicide missions to keep him away

from Carter, but their conflict isn't resolved until the Battle of Little Big Horn.
Dist.: Republic

BUGS BUNNY/ROAD RUNNER MOVIE, THE 1979
★ ★ ★ ★ ★ **G Animation 1:23**
Dir: Chuck Jones **Cast:** Voice of Mel Blanc
▶ Animated anthology marks the return of the world's most popular rabbit (sorry, Peter). Released in honor of Bugs Bunny's fourtieth anniversary. Bugs narrates, joined by zany cohorts Daffy Duck, Yosemite Sam, and Road Runner. Funny opening parodies *Star Wars* and *Superman.*
Dist.: Warner

BUGS BUNNY SUPERSTAR 1975
★ ★ ★ **NR Animation 1:30**
Dir: Larry Jackson **Cast:** Orson Welles, Bob Clampett, Tex Avery, Fritz Freleng
▶ Ten classic cartoons from the 1940s (including Porky Pig, Elmer Fudd, Daffy Duck, Sylvester and Tweetie, in addition to Bugs) are interspersed with period newsreel footage and interviews with Warner Brothers animators. A total delight from start to finish. Our favorite cartoon: Bugs losing the Oscar to James Cagney in *What's Cookin' Doc.*
Dist.: MGM/UA

BUGS BUNNY'S 3RD MOVIE: 1001 RABBIT TALES 1982
★ ★ ★ ★ ★ **G Animation 1:14**
Dir: David Detiege, Art Davis, Bill Perez
Cast: Voice of Mel Blanc
▶ Bugs and Daffy are competing book salesmen for "Rambling House Publications" in Friz Freleng's blend of classic cartoons and new footage of the famous rabbit and his pals. Vocals provided by Mel Blanc, Man of 1000 Voices.
Dist.: Warner

BUGSY MALONE 1976 British
★ ★ ★ **G Comedy 1:33**
Dir: Alan Parker **Cast:** Scott Baio, Jodie Foster, Florrie Dugger, John Cassisi, Martin Lev
▶ Unusual musical spoof of gangster films: the tough-guy clichés are left intact, but they're performed by an all-kid cast whose guns shoot whipped cream instead of bullets. Plot about a feud between rival mobs relies heavily on slapstick chases. Delightful, sometimes coy story should please adults as well as children. Paul Williams did the score.
Dist.: Paramount

BULLDOG DRUMMOND 1929
★ **NR Mystery-Suspense 1:29 B&W**
Dir: F. Richard Jones **Cast:** Ronald Colman, Joan Bennett, Lilyan Tashman, Montagu Love, Lawrence Grant, Claud Allister
▶ Debonair Colman is perfectly cast as H. C. McNeile's popular detective Bulldog Drummond, an aristocrat who seeks excitement by advertising for unusual assignments. Bennett

asks him to free her father from a crooked mental asylum before his estate is stolen. Primitive sound detracts from witty, elegant script. First talkie role for Colman, who received Oscar nominations that year for both this and *Condemned*. Also nominated for sets by William Cameron Menzies. Sequel: *Bulldog Drummond Strikes Back*.
Dist.: Nelson

BULLDOG DRUMMOND'S BRIDE 1939
★ NR Mystery-Suspense 0:55 B&W
Dir: James Hogan *Cast:* John Howard, Heather Angel, H. B. Warner, Reginald Denny, E. E. Clive, Eduardo Cianelli
▶ The great English detective Bulldog Drummond (Howard) finally ties the knot and embarks on a French honeymoon. There's no rest for the weary newlywed as a local bank robbery forces the sleuth into action. Nifty supporting cast, but the plot and direction are average.
Dist.: Sinister

BULL DURHAM 1988
★★★★ R Comedy/Sports 1:55
☑ Nudity, adult situations, explicit language
Dir: Ron Shelton *Cast:* Kevin Costner, Susan Sarandon, Tim Robbins, Trey Wilson, Robert Wuhl, Jenny Robertson
▶ Every year Southern belle/baseball groupie Sarandon dedicates herself to a new player on the minor league Durham Bulls. This season's candidates are bonus baby Robbins, a pitcher with a million-dollar arm and two-cent brain, and veteran Costner, a shrewd catcher with the job of prepping Robbins for the major leagues. Romantic triangle yields comical squeeze play. Saucy, witty, and authentic screenplay from writer/director Shelton, former bush leaguer, hits homer.
Dist.: Orion

BULLETPROOF 1988
★★★ R Action-Adventure 1:34
☑ Rape, brief nudity, adult situations, explicit language, violence
Dir: Steve Carver *Cast:* Gary Busey, Darlanne Fluegel, Henry Silva, Rene Enriquez, L. Q. Jones
▶ As the credits announce, "Gary Busey *is* Bulletproof," a renegade cop sent to Central America to recover Thunderblast, a top-secret tank that's fallen into the hands of the Communists. The bad guys have also kidnapped Fluegel, Bulletproof's lover, so he's fighting mad.
Dist.: RCA/Columbia

BULLFIGHTER AND THE LADY 1951
★ NR Drama 1:27 B&W
Dir: Budd Boetticher *Cast:* Robert Stack, Gilbert Roland, Katy Jurado, Joy Page, Virginia Grey, John Hubbard
▶ American Stack gets bullfighting lessons from Mexican pro Roland but causes his mentor's death in the ring. Stack gets a chance at redemption in this authentic drama from director Boetticher, a bullfighting buff best known for his Randolph Scott Westerns, and producer John Wayne (best known for his own Westerns).
Dist.: Republic

BULLFIGHTERS, THE 1945
★★ NR Comedy 1:01 B&W
Dir: Malcolm St. Clair *Cast:* Stan Laurel, Oliver Hardy, Margo Woode, Richard Lane, Carol Andrews
▶ Inept private dicks Laurel and Hardy travel south of the border on a case, and Stan's resemblance to a star toreador causes comic complications. Made toward the end of the duo's illustrious career and not top-notch stuff, but some amusing bits.
Dist.: CBS/Fox

BULLIES 1986
★★ R Drama
☑ Rape, adult situations, explicit language, graphic violence
Dir: Paul Lynch *Cast:* Stephen Hunter, Janet Laine-Green, Jonathan Crombie, Dehl Berti, Olivia d'Abo
▶ Teenager Crombie arrives in new town with stepdad Hunter and mom Laine-Greene. After mom is raped and dad injured by local rednecks, Crombie takes the law into his own hands. Lynch's stylish direction and Crombie's performance enliven this teen vigilante flick; unfortunately, excessive violence and uneven pacing will turn off some.
Dist.: MCA

BULLITT 1968
★★★★ PG Action-Adventure 1:53
☑ Mild violence
Dir: Peter Yates *Cast:* Steve McQueen, Robert Vaughn, Jacqueline Bisset, Robert Duvall, Simon Oakland
▶ Suspenseful, influential cop thriller with McQueen creating an indelible image as tough guy Bullitt, pursuing the killers of a government witness. Great action scenes, including an incredibly exciting car chase through the streets of San Francisco and a slam-bang airport finale.
Dist.: Warner

BULLSHOT 1985 British
★★ PG Comedy 1:26
☑ Adult situations, explicit language
Dir: Dick Clement *Cast:* Alan Shearman, Diz White, Ron House, Frances Tomelty, Ron Pember, Mel Smith
▶ Shearman (who, with White and House, adapted his British stage hit) stars as Bullshot Crummond, a parody of English hero Bulldog Drummond, who comes to aid of dizzy White when a German count kidnaps her scientist father. Preposterous plot full of slapstick silliness. Endearing cast, especially White, but British wit is a matter of taste.
Dist.: HBO

BULLWHIP 1958
★ ★ **NR Western 1:20**
Dir: Harmon Jones   *Cast:* Guy Madison,
Rhonda Fleming, James Griffith, Don
Beddoe, Peter Adams, Dan Sheridan
▶ Convicted of a crime he didn't com-
mit, Madison is given the option of death or wedlock. After thinking it over briefly, Madison marries, only to discover spouse Fleming is a shrew
who enforces domestic discipline with a bullwhip. Set amid colorful autumn foliage, but
generally lacks grit. Remade with Jack Nicholson as *Goin' South*.
Dist.: Republic

BUNDLE OF JOY 1956
★ ★ ★ **NR Musical 1:38**
Dir: Norman Taurog   *Cast:* Debbie Rey-
nolds, Eddie Fisher, Adolphe Menjou,
Tommy Noonan, Una Merkel, Nita Talbot
▶ Musical remake of *Bachelor Mother* fea-
tures Reynolds in the Ginger Rogers role of the
salesgirl who takes in an abandoned baby.
Fisher, as the son of the department store
owner Menjou, plays David Niven's old part as
her love interest. Pleasant but instantly forget-
table. Bland score includes "I Never Felt This
Way Before."
Dist.: United

BUNNY O'HARE 1972
☆ **PG Comedy 1:32**
☑ Explicit language
Dir: Gerd Oswald   *Cast:* Bette Davis, Ernest
Borgnine, Jack Cassidy, Joan Delaney, John
Astin
▶ Senior citizen Davis, evicted by a cruel
banker, teams up with plumbing supply salesman Borgnine to get revenge. Disguised as
hippies, they embark on a successful crime
wave. Soon other robbers are imitating their
disguises. Bizarre comedy will leave most
viewers speechless. Davis sued the producers
to prevent the film's release.
Dist.: HBO

'BURBS, THE 1989
★ ★ ★ **PG Comedy 1:42**
☑ Explicit language, mild violence
Dir: Joe Dante   *Cast:* Tom Hanks, Bruce
Dern, Carrie Fisher, Rick Ducommun, Corey
Feldman, Henry Gibson, Brother Theodore
▶ Suburbanites Hanks, Dern, and Ducommun
are nonplussed by their new neighbors, the
sinister Klopeks, and use guerrilla tactics to
learn the secret behind their nocturnal activi-
ties. Large-scale comedy concentrates on
slapstick and satirical jabs at suburbia, but
failed to win over audiences.
Dist.: MCA

BURDEN OF DREAMS 1982
☆ **NR Documentary 1:35**
☑ Brief nudity, explicit language
Dir: Les Blank   *Cast:* Werner Herzog, Klaus
Kinski, Claudia Cardinale, Jason Robards,
Jr., Mick Jagger
▶ Engrossing look at the filming of *Fitzcar-*

raldo, a jungle epic plagued by a border war,
disease, and death. Director Herzog had to
start from scratch halfway through when Robards and Jagger dropped out of the cast;
film eventually took five years to complete.
Blank caught fascinating behind-the-scenes
moments, including Kinski's reactions on
board a steamship as it unexpectedly
crashed through rapids. As a study of obsession, this ranks right up there with Herzog's film.
☑
Dist.: Flower Films

BURGLAR 1987
★ ★ ★ ★ **R Action-Adventure 1:40**
☑ Brief nudity, adult situations, explicit language, mild violence
Dir: Hugh Wilson   *Cast:* Whoopi Goldberg,
Bob Goldthwait, Lesley Ann Warren, G. W.
Bailey, James Hardy
▶ Ex-con Goldberg, blackmailed into committing one last burglary by retired cop Bailey,
must prove her innocence when blamed for a
murder. Comedy/thriller from director Wilson
features plenty of shtick from Goldberg, and
from Goldthwait as her wacked-out best
friend. **(CC)**
Dist.: Warner

BURKE AND WILLS 1985 Australian
★ ★ ★ **PG-13 Biography 2:20**
☑ Adult situations, explicit language
Dir: Graeme Clifford   *Cast:* Jack Thompson,
Nigel Havers, Greta Scacchi, Matthew
Farger, Chris Haywood
▶ True story of the 1860 expedition by Irish-
man Burke (Thompson) and English scientist
Wills (Havers) to cross the uncharted Aus-
tralian continent. Among the obstacles in a
three-thousand-mile journey: aborigines, de-
serts, sandstorms, and rats. Large-scale pro-
duction unfortunately loses impact on the
small screen.
Dist.: Nelson

BURMESE HARP, THE 1956 Japanese
★ **NR War/Drama 1:56 B&W**
Dir: Kon Ichikawa   *Cast:* Rentaro Mikuni,
Shoji Yasui, Tatsuya Mihashi, Tanie Kitabaya-
shi, Yunosuke Ito
▶ During World War II, Japanese soldier Yasui
is deeply shaken when a garrison of his countrymen is destroyed by the enemy. Donning a
monk's robes, he begins walking back to his
unit, passing battlefield after battlefield,
where he buries or burns the countless bodies
he finds there. When his unit prepares to leave
for home, he resolves to stay and inter the
thousands of dead still unburied. Unique and
moving antiwar drama is also known as *The
Harp of Burma*.   ☑
Dist.: Various

BURN! 1970 Italian/French
★ ★ **PG Drama 1:52**
☑ Nudity, violence
Dir: Gillo Pontecorvo   *Cast:* Marlon Brando,

Ernesto Marquez, Renato Salvatori, Norman Hill, Tom Lyons

▶ British agent Brando incites Black revolution on a Portugese-controlled Caribbean island, then betrays the revolt's leader when the rebellion succeeds. Overly complex, convoluted political story is emotionally distant if topical and provocative. Brando is fine playing a difficult and unattractive character based on William Walker.

Dist.: Key

BURNDOWN 1989
☆ **NR Action-Adventure 1:27**
☑ Adult situations, explicit language, violence

Dir: James Allen *Cast:* Cathy Moriarty, Peter Firth, Michael McCabe, Hal Orlandini
▶ Reporter Moriarty falls for police chief Firth while investigating murders whose radioactive clues suggest some association with a nearby nuclear plant. Further investigation reveals the cover-up of a nuclear accident and a crew of mutants manning the plant. Likable leads, but villains are cartoons and the plot is silly and unbelievable.

Dist.: Virgin

BURNING, THE 1981
★ ★ **R Horror 1:30**
☑ Adult situations, graphic violence

Dir: Tony Maylam *Cast:* Brian Mathews, Leah Ayres, Brian Backer, Larry Joshua, Jason Alexander, Fisher Stevens
▶ Drunken camp handyman is badly disfigured when kids set him afire in practical joke. Five years later, the handyman returns to menace the campers with garden shears. Formula story is professionally filmed but overly familiar; delivers requisite number of chills, but characters fail to generate much empathy.

Dist.: HBO

BURNING BED, THE 1984
★ ★ ★ ★ **NR Drama/MFTV 1:36**
☑ Violence

Dir: Robert Greenwald *Cast:* Farrah Fawcett, Paul LeMat, Richard Masur, Grace Zabriskie, Penelope Milford
▶ Fawcett, abused by husband LeMat, eventually fights back, killing him by setting their bed on fire while he's still in it. LeMat's brutality becomes an issue in Fawcett's trial. Shattering true story sustained by Emmy-nominated Fawcett's breakthrough performance; she proves her merits as a serious actress. **(CC)**

Dist.: CBS/Fox

BURNING SECRET 1988 U.S/British/German
★ ★ **PG-13 Drama 1:47**
☑ Adult situations

Dir: Andrew Birkin *Cast:* Faye Dunaway, Klaus Maria Brandauer, David Eberts, Ian Richardson, John Nettleton, Martin Obernigg
▶ In 1920s Austria, Dunaway takes her asthmatic son (Eberts) to an Alpine sanatorium. There they meet war-scarred baron Brandauer, who fulfills Eberts's need for male guidance until he turns his attentions to Dunaway, causing Eberts to flee in a jealous rage. Old World romantic drama at times is too stately and refined for its own good.

Dist.: Vestron

BURNT OFFERINGS 1976
★ ★ ★ **PG Horror 1:55**
☑ Violence

Dir: Dan Curtis *Cast:* Karen Black, Oliver Reed, Burgess Meredith, Eileen Heckart, Bette Davis
▶ A clean-cut family rents an ancient mansion from two invalids. The house's evil spirit gradually possesses the family, leading to terror and violence. Moody atmosphere and a fascinating setting (Oakland's Dunsmuir House) account for film's small cult following.

Dist.: MGM/UA

BUSHIDO BLADE, THE 1980 British
★ ★ ★ **R Martial Arts 1:34**
☑ Brief nudity, adult situations, explicit language, graphic violence

Dir: Tom Kotani *Cast:* Richard Boone, Frank Converse, James Earl Jones, Toshiro Mifune, Mako, Sonny Chiba
▶ Period kung-fu drama set in 1854 describes the efforts of American soldiers to recover a sacred sword needed for a treaty-signing ceremony with Japan. Boone (in his last role) plays Commodore Perry; Mifune repeats his role from the *Shogun* mini-series. Jones and Chiba are limited to cameos. Shot on location in Japan. Also known as *The Bloody Bushido Blade.*

Dist.: HBO

BUSINESS AS USUAL 1988 British
★ ★ **PG Drama 1:28**
☑ Explicit language

Dir: Lezli-An Barrett *Cast:* Glenda Jackson, John Thaw, Cathy Tyson, Mark McGann, Eamon Boland, James Hazeldine
▶ British boutique manager Jackson gets sacked for confronting boss Boland about sexual harassment of employee Tyson. Encouraged by her son McGann and father Keegan, both union activists, Jackson files suit against the boutique's owners, despite the objections of househusband Thaw. Based on a true incident.

Dist.: Warner

BUS STOP 1956
★ ★ ★ ★ **NR Romance/Comedy 1:31**
Dir: Joshua Logan *Cast:* Marilyn Monroe, Don Murray, Arthur O'Connell, Betty Field, Eileen Heckart, Hope Lange
▶ In Phoenix, voluptuous cafe singer Monroe is pursued by high-spirited rodeo cowboy Murray. She resists but he is persistent; eventually, true love finds its way. Monroe is both sexy and innocent; Oscar-nominated Murray is marvelous. Based on the William Inge Broadway hit.

Dist.: CBS/Fox

BUSTED UP 1986
☆ **R Action-Adventure 1:32**
☑ Explicit language, violence
Dir: Conrad E. Palmisano   *Cast:* Paul
Coufos, Irene Cara, Stan Shaw, Tony Rosato
▶ Boxer Coufos is in trouble: thugs are threat-
ening to take over his gym, his singer girlfriend
Cara wants to leave him, and he's going blind
in one eye. He stages a winner-takes-all brawl
in a last-ditch effort to pull his life together.
Lots of fights, and Cara gets to sing four songs.
(CC)
Dist.: MCA

BUSTER 1988 British
★ ★ **R Biography 1:33**
☑ Adult situations, explicit language, mild
   violence
Dir: David Green   *Cast:* Phil Collins, Julie
Walters, Larry Lamb, Stephanie Lawrence,
Ellen Beaven, Michael Atwell
▶ True story of bank robber Ronnie "Buster"
Edwards (Collins) who supported wife Walters
and daughter Beaven with small-time crime
until he hit the jackpot by participating in a
$35 million train robbery. Refreshing emphasis
on Buster's personal life with Collins, in his film
debut, evoking maximum sympathy for the
family man/criminal. Soundtrack includes
Collins singing "Groovy Kind of Love" and the
Oscar-nominated "Two Hearts." **(CC)**
Dist.: HBO

BUSTER AND BILLIE 1974
★ ★ **R Romance 1:30**
☑ Rape, adult situations, explicit language,
   violence
Dir: Daniel Petrie   *Cast:* Jan-Michael Vincent, Joan Goodfellow, Pamela Sue Martin,
Clifton James, Robert Englund
▶ "The guys all know about Billie," high school
heartthrob Vincent is told by buddies in reference to good-time girl Goodfellow. Vincent
discovers Goodfellow's more sensitive side,
falls in love, but faces violent opposition from
local toughs. Uninspired love story set in post–
World War II Georgia.
Dist.: RCA/Columbia

BUSTIN' LOOSE 1981
★ ★ ★ ★ **R Comedy 1:34**
☑ Adult situations, explicit language, vio-
   lence
Dir: Oz Scott   *Cast:* Richard Pryor, Cicely
Tyson, Alphonso Alexander, Robert Christian,
George Coe
▶ Rather than return to jail, parolee Pryor
agrees to drive a busload of reform-school
kids across country to a Washington farm.
Along the way he battles breakdowns, bigots,
and antagonistic teacher Tyson who gradu-
ally falls in love with him. Despite the rough
language, a warm, positive comedy. Pryor's
encounter with the KKK is hilarious.
Dist.: MCA

BUTCH AND SUNDANCE: THE EARLY DAYS
1979
★ ★ ★ **PG Western 1:50**
☑ Explicit language, mild violence
Dir: Richard Lester   *Cast:* William Katt, Tom
Berenger, Jill Eikenberry, Jeff Corey, Arthur
Hill
▶ Prequel to *Butch Cassidy and the Sun-
dance Kid* traces the first meeting and subse-
quent adventures of the legendary partners in
crime. Although overshadowed by its hugely
popular predecessor, this is an easy-to-take
Western on its own terms, as director Lester
inventively mixes comedy and action. Katt
and Berenger are a likable duo, resembling
Redford and Newman physically without
mimicking their earlier performances.
Dist.: CBS/Fox

BUTCH CASSIDY AND THE SUNDANCE KID
1969
★ ★ ★ ★ ★ **PG Western 1:52**
☑ Adult situations, explicit language, violence
Dir: George Roy Hill   *Cast:* Robert Redford,
Paul Newman, Katharine Ross, Strother Martin, Henry Jones
▶ Immensely entertaining Western classic
starring Newman and Redford as the infamous, affable outlaws on the run. Ross is the
proper, pristine schoolmarm infatuated with
both of them. Stunt-packed and slickly pack-
aged, this box-office smash won four Oscars,
including Best Screenplay (William Goldman)
and song ("Raindrops Keep Fallin' on My
Head" by Burt Bacharach and Hal David).
Dist.: CBS/Fox

BUTLEY 1974 British
★ **R Drama 2:07**
☑ Adult situations, explicit language
Dir: Harold Pinter   *Cast:* Alan Bates, Jessica
Tandy, Richard O'Callaghan, Susan Engel,
Michael Byrne, Georgina Hale
▶ London University professor Bates's bitter wit
is his way of dealing with a joyless personal life
and career. Tired of his ways, wife Engel finds
someone else, as does Bates's male lover O'-
Callaghan. Blazing performance by Bates in
Simon Gray's adaptation of his play. However,
audiences will have trouble sympathizing with
selfish protagonist who can't even remember
the name of his only child.
Dist.: CBS/Fox

BUTTERFIELD 8 1960
★ ★ ★ **NR Drama 1:49**
Dir: Daniel Mann   *Cast:* Elizabeth Taylor,
Laurence Harvey, Eddie Fisher, Dina Merrill,
Betty Field
▶ Model/prostitute Taylor falls for married Har-
vey and can't come to grips with her illusions
when he refuses to leave his wife. Daring (for
its day) look at sex and love worth seeing for
Taylor's Oscar-winning performance. Based
on a John O'Hara novel.
Dist.: MGM/UA

BUTTERFLIES ARE FREE 1972
★ ★ ★ ★ **PG Comedy/Drama 1:49**
☑ Adult situations, explicit language
Dir: Milton Katselas *Cast:* Goldie Hawn, Edward Albert, Eileen Heckart, Mike Warren
► Hawn falls for blind Albert in the film version of a favorite Broadway play. He breaks free of an overprotective mother (Oscar-winner Heckart) and Goldie matures because of their feisty and funny relationship. Nominated for three Academy awards.
Dist.: RCA/Columbia

BUTTERFLY 1982
☆ **R Drama 1:47**
☑ Nudity, strong sexual content, explicit language, mild violence
Dir: Matt Cimber *Cast:* Stacy Keach, Pia Zadora, Orson Welles, Lois Nettleton, Edward Albert, Ed McMahon
► Sexy nymphet Zadora is reunited with long-lost father Keach, now the guard of an abandoned silver mine. Their passionate affair brings them before Welles, a nasty judge determined to stamp out incest. Low-budget adaptation of a James M. Cain novel is considered a classic by Zadora's fans.
Dist.: Vestron

BUY AND CELL 1988
★ **NR Comedy 1:31**
☑ Nudity, adult situations, explicit language, mild violence
Dir: Robert Boris *Cast:* Robert Carradine, Malcolm McDowell, Imogene Coca, Ben Vereen, Randall "Tex" Cobb
► Framed yuppie stockbroker Carradine makes prison pay in this wacky but implausible comedy. Not ready for life in prison, Carradine, with the help of a motley group of murderers and career criminals, resorts to insider trading to improve conditions. Genuinely funny at times, but the zany sight gags tend to fall flat.
Dist.: New World

BUYING TIME 1989 Canadian
★ ★ **R Action-Adventure 1:37**
☑ Nudity, adult situations, explicit language, violence
Dir: Mitchell Gabourie *Cast:* Jeff Schultz, Page Fletcher, Laura Cruickshank, Dean Stockwell, Leslie Toth, Martin Louis
► Young car washers Schultz and Toth get in trouble with the police, who agree to drop charges if they will go undercover to nab a psychotic killer. Heroin connections and horse doping are subsequently uncovered by the heroes. Overly convoluted plot strains credulity despite decent action and performances (especially Stockwell as a detective).
Dist.: CBS/Fox

BY DAWN'S EARLY LIGHT 1990
★ ★ ★ ★ **NR Action-Adventure/MFTV 1:43**
☑ Brief nudity, adult situations, explicit language, violence
Dir: Jack Sholder *Cast:* Powers Boothe, Rebecca De Mornay, James Earl Jones, Martin Landau, Darren McGavin, Rip Torn, Jeffrey DeMunn, Peter MacNicol, Nicolas Coster
► When a dissident group explodes a nuclear device within the Soviet Union, the American and Russian defense systems set nuclear war in motion. The destruction of the world is imminent, until co-pilots Boothe and De Mornay, plus others along the chain of command, decide to disobey orders. Riveting thriller with nailbiting direction by Sholder. Bruce Gilbert's screenplay is a meticulous blend of technical precision and the human element.
Dist.: HBO

BY DESIGN 1982 Canadian
☆ **R Drama 1:30**
☑ Nudity, adult situations, explicit language
Dir: Claude Jutra *Cast:* Patty Duke Astin, Sara Botsford, Saul Rubinek, Sonia Zimmer
► Lesbians Astin and Botsford are happy and successful fashion designers but want to have a baby. When an adoption agency rejects them because of their lifestyle, they search for a man. Slim plot, but Astin rises above it.
Dist.: HBO

BYE BYE BABY 1989 Italian
☆ **R Drama 1:23**
☑ Nudity, adult situations, explicit language
Dir: Enrico Oldoini *Cast:* Carol Alt, Luca Barbareschi, Brigitte Nielsen, Jason Connery
► Alt breaks up with husband Barbareschi and gets together with Connery; Barbareschi has affair with Nielsen. Nevertheless, Alt and Barbareschi resume their relationship, even during a Club Med vacation with their new loves. Alt and Nielsen look great, as do the Italian backgrounds, but self-absorbed characters and slack screenplay limit interest.
Dist.: Prism

BYE BYE BIRDIE 1963
★ ★ ★ **NR Musical 1:52**
Dir: George Sidney *Cast:* Janet Leigh, Dick Van Dyke, Ann-Margret, Bobby Rydell, Maureen Stapleton, Jesse Pearson
► Conrad Birdie, a hip-swinging rock 'n' roll sensation, is subject to immediate Army call, but not before he appears on Ed Sullivan's show to kiss a local fan, Ann-Margret. Her hometown of Sweet Apple, Ohio, is thrown into a frenzy, particularly her easily agitated dad Lynde. From the hit Broadway musical; Oscar-nominated for Best Sound, Musical Scoring. Songs include "Put on a Happy Face" and "Just One Kiss".
Dist.: RCA/Columbia

BYE BYE BRAZIL 1980 Brazilian
☆ **R Drama 1:50**
☑ Nudity, adult situations, explicit language
Dir: Carlos Diegues *Cast:* Jose Wilker, Betty Faria, Fabio Junior, Zaira Zambelli
► Deliriously languorous trip down the backroads of Brazil with a ragtag carnival determined to delight villagers despite encroachment of TV into jungle. Troupe includes bad

magicians, exotic dancers, and a pair of innocent young lovers along for the ride. A sweetly sensuous, sometimes melancholy paeon to the Brazilian pleasure principle. [S]
Dist.: Warner

CABARET 1972
★★★ PG Musical 2:03
☑ Adult situations, violence
Dir: Bob Fosse ***Cast:*** Liza Minnelli, Joel Grey, Michael York, Helmut Griem, Fritz Weber, Marisa Berenson
► Eight-Oscar winner, set in early 1930s Germany when Nazism was on the rise, and based on the hit Broadway musical. Minnelli, in her Best Actress–winning role, is an aspiring cabaret singer/dancer who falls in love with both York and Griem. Her dreams of stardom are dashed by the shadow of Hitler. Grey is eerily, joyfully decadent in his Best Supporting Actor performance. Stunning music by Kander and Ebb and smashing choreography make this one of the most memorable movie musicals of all time, winning Best Screenplay, Scoring, Director, and more. Songs include "The Money Song" and "Tomorrow Belongs to Me." (CC)
Dist.: CBS/Fox

CABINET OF DR. CALIGARI, THE 1919 German
★ NR Horror 1:28 B&W
Dir: Robert Wiene ***Cast:*** Werner Krauss, Conrad Veidt, Lil Dagover
► Caligari (Krauss) displays Veidt, a somnambulist in a catatonic state, to leering crowds at a circus sideshow. By night Veidt roams over the roofs of the city, searching for a woman he can enslave as his mate. Pioneering horror film influenced decades of movies for its German Expressionist set design and adroit use of light and shadow. Dated in most aspects, but still eerie and unsettling.
Dist.: Various

CABIN IN THE SKY 1943
★★ NR Musical 1:38 B&W
Dir: Vincente Minnelli ***Cast:*** Ethel Waters, Eddie "Rochester" Anderson, Lena Horne, Louis Armstrong, Rex Ingram, Kenneth Spencer
► Delightful all-black musical turns Anderson's indecision between the charms of wife Waters and those of seductive Horne into an allegorical battle between agents from heaven and hell. Excellent score features "Happiness Is Just a Thing Called Joe" and "Taking a Chance on Love." Among the many guest stars are Duke Ellington, Butterfly McQueen, John "Bubbles" Sublett and Ford "Buck" Washington.
Dist.: MGM/UA

CABOBLANCO 1980
★★ R Drama 1:32
☑ Nudity, adult situations, mild violence
Dir: J. Lee Thompson ***Cast:*** Charles Bronson, Jason Robards, Dominique Sanda, Fernando Rey, Camilla Sparv
► Sleepy story of macho hotel owner Bronson, beautiful widow Sanda, and millions in sunken Nazi gold set in postwar coastal Peru. Robards appears as a fugitive war criminal. Lush visual appeal is the film's real plus.
Dist.: Media

CACTUS 1986 Australian
☆ NR Drama 1:35
☑ Nudity, adult situations
Dir: Paul Cox ***Cast:*** Isabelle Huppert, Robert Menzies, Norman Kaye, Monica Maughan, Banduk Marika
► After losing most of her sight in a car accident, Huppert must choose between having a disfiguring operation or giving up what is left of her vision. An affair with a young blind man who collects cactus helps her "see" her way to life-affirming decision. Tear-wringing tale is lyrically photographed, wonderfully acted.
Dist.: Warner

CACTUS FLOWER 1969
★★★★ PG Comedy 1:44
☑ Adult situations
Dir: Gene Saks ***Cast:*** Walter Matthau, Ingrid Bergman, Goldie Hawn, Jack Weston, Rick Lenz
► Frothy adaptation of the Broadway smash. Bergman stars as a dowdy assistant to bachelor/dentist Matthau, who asks her to cover as his "wife" so he won't have to marry girlfriend, Hawn. When she agrees, Matthau falls for her and gets caught in a love triangle. Hawn snagged an Oscar for her role as the spurned girlfriend saved by next-door-neighbor Lenz.
Dist.: RCA/Columbia

CADDY, THE 1953
★★ NR Comedy 1:35 B&W
Dir: Norman Taurog ***Cast:*** Dean Martin, Jerry Lewis, Donna Reed, Barbara Bates, Frank Calleia, Fred Clark
► Martin is a golfer trying to break into the professional circuit; Lewis is his zany caddy-manager. Predictable blend of slapstick and light romance, with cameos from famous pros (Ben Hogan, Sam Snead, Julius Boros, etc.) and an improbable Martin-Lewis duet to "That's Amore."
Dist.: Paramount

CADDYSHACK 1980
★★★★ R Comedy 1:38
☑ Brief nudity, explicit language, adult humor
Dir: Harold Ramis ***Cast:*** Chevy Chase, Rodney Dangerfield, Ted Knight, Michael O'Keefe, Bill Murray
► Megahit comedy about caddy O'Keefe's efforts to win a college scholarship. *Animal House* approach to country clubs works best when pros Murray (as a demented greenskeeper pursuing a gopher), Dangerfield (an unforgettably obnoxious real estate developer), and Chase (in a daffy WASP impersona-

tion) deliver their material. Followed by *Caddyshack II.*
Dist.: Warner

CADDYSHACK II 1988
★ ★ **PG Comedy 1:36**
☑ Brief nudity, explicit language, adult humor
Dir: Allan Arkush *Cast:* Jackie Mason, Robert Stack, Dyan Cannon, Dina Merrill, Jessica Lundy, Brian McNamara
▶ Sequel to immensely popular *Caddyshack* pits loud shirt Mason against stuffed shirt Stack. Since his daughter Lundy longs for preppy country club member McNamara, wealthy-but-ethnic Mason applies to join, antagonizing president Stack and snobby wife Merrill. Winner-take-all golf match climax, with sexy divorcée Cannon rooting for Mason. Despite cameo appearances by Chevy Chase and Dan Aykroyd, spin-off isn't on par with original.
Dist.: Warner

CADILLAC MAN 1990
★ ★ ★ **R Comedy 1:35**
☑ Brief nudity, adult situations, explicit language, mild violence
Dir: Roger Donaldson *Cast:* Robin Williams, Tim Robbins, Pamela Reed, Fran Drescher, Zack Norman, Lori Petty, Annabella Sciorra, Paul Guilfoyle, Lauren Tom, Elaine Stritch
▶ Womanizing car salesman Williams, trying to sell twelve autos in one day to keep his job, is interrupted by the arrival of rifle-bearing cuckold Robbins. When the husband takes hostages, the salesman uses his wits and mouth to keep everyone alive. Oddly winning if inconsistent mixture of comedy and tension, Williams's characterization surprises by emphasizing vulnerability over slickness, just as the movie demonstrates unexpected poignant moments. Two supporting standouts: Williams's married lover Drescher and Chinese waitress Tom. **(CC)**
Dist.: Orion

CAESAR AND CLEOPATRA 1946 British
★ ★ **NR Drama 2:18**
Dir: Gabriel Pascal *Cast:* Vivien Leigh, Claude Rains, Stewart Granger, Flora Robson, Francis L. Sullivan
▶ George Bernard Shaw co-wrote the screenplay for this adaptation of his modern classic play. Playwright's typically intelligent and witty dialogue tells of the relationship between an elderly Caesar (Rains) and a bewitching young Cleopatra (Leigh). Elaborate sets, costumes, and production values.
Dist.: Various

CAGE 1989
★ ★ **R Action-Adventure 1:41**
☑ Explicit language, graphic violence
Dir: Lang Elliot *Cast:* Lou Ferrigno, Reb Brown, Michael Dante, James Shigeta
▶ A pair of old Vietnam buddies unwittingly fall in with gamblers involved in "cage fighting," a sport where two men locked in a cage battle until one is dead or unconscious. Ferrigno and Brown empower a merely functional action story through battles both in and around the cubed circle.
Dist.: Magnum

CAGED FURY 1983
☆ **R Action-Adventure 1:31**
☑ Nudity, adult situations, explicit language, graphic violence
Dir: Cirio Santiago *Cast:* Bernie Williams, Taffy O'Connell, Jennifer Lane, Cirio Santiago
▶ Ten captive white women are being brainwashed by demented Commies somewhere in Asia. Before they can be turned into human time bombs, the girls attempt a daring escape. Rank racial stereotypes, clumsy action, and predictable plot may make even hardcore women-in-prison fans long for a shower.
Dist.: Vidmark

CAGED HEAT 1974
★ **R Action-Adventure 1:24**
☑ Nudity, explicit language, violence
Dir: Jonathan Demme *Cast:* Juanita Brown, Roberta Collins, Erica Gavin, Ella Reid, Rainbeaux Smith, Barbara Steele
▶ An innocent Gavin is unjustly sentenced to a hellish prison run by crippled, sexually repressed warden Steele. Gavin breaks out with two friends, but returns to free the other inmates from the clutches of a maniacal doctor. Oddball humor tempers Demme's directing debut.
Dist.: Nelson

CAGED WOMEN 1982 Italian/French
★ **R Action-Adventure 1:36**
☑ Rape, nudity, explicit language, graphic violence
Dir: Vincent Dawn *Cast:* Laura Gemser, Gabrielle Tinti, Jack Stany
▶ Globe-trotting Emanuelle (Gemser) gets herself thrown into a women's prison so she can report on its brutality for Amnesty International. Once behind bars, heroine becomes a victim of the femme slammer's rampant lesbianism and sadism, including a lengthy scene where she is set upon by vicious attack rats. Exploitative film poses as advocacy for prisoners' rights. Filmed under title *Emanuelle Reports From a Woman's Prison* in conjunction with *Women's Prison Massacre.*
Dist.: Vestron

CAHILL—U.S. MARSHALL 1973
★ ★ ★ **PG Western 1:43**
☑ Violence
Dir: Andrew V. McLaglen *Cast:* John Wayne, George Kennedy, Gary Grimes, Neville Brand, Marie Windsor, Clay O'Brien
▶ Cahill (Wayne) spends so much time chasing badmen that he neglects young sons Grimes and O'Brien. Pa faces a real dilemma when the boys—blackmailed by vicious crook

Kennedy—start robbing banks. Action is quite violent at times.
Dist.: Warner

CAINE MUTINY, THE 1954
★ ★ ★ ★ ★ NR Drama 2:05
Dir: Edward Dmytryk *Cast:* Humphrey Bogart, Van Johnson, Jose Ferrer, Fred Mac-Murray, Robert Francis, E. G. Marshall, May Wynn, Lee Marvin, Tom Tully, Claude Akins
► First-rate adaptation of Herman Wouk's Pulitzer prize–winning novel and Broadway hit, with Bogart in one of his most memorable roles as Queeg, the neurotic captain of a Pacific minesweeper. Johnson plays a lieutenant who questions Queeg's command during a typhoon; Ferrer, the attorney who defends him in a court-martial. Classic study of military loyalty won seven Oscar nominations, including Best Picture and Actor. **(CC)**
Dist.: RCA/Columbia

CAL 1984 Irish
★ R Drama 1:42
☑ Nudity, adult situations, explicit language, graphic violence
Dir: Pat O'Connor *Cast:* Helen Mirren, John Lynch, Donal McCann, John Kavanagh, Ray McAnally
► Moving drama set in Northern Ireland describes the rocky love affair between IRA member Lynch and Mirren, the widow of an assassinated policeman. Told with style and insight, film provides a compelling portrait of Belfast but may be too downbeat for many. Moody score by Mark Knopfler.
Dist.: Warner

CALAMITY JANE 1953
★ ★ ★ ★ NR Musical 1:41
Dir: David Butler *Cast:* Doris Day, Howard Keel, Allyn Ann McLerie, Phil Carey, Gale Robbins, Dick Wesson
► Rambunctious tomboy Day charms Western legend Wild Bill Hickok (Keel) with her sharpshooting and singing. Mild comedy patterned after *Annie Get Your Gun* introduced the Oscar-winning "Secret Love," one of Day's biggest hits.
Dist.: Warner

CALIFORNIA DREAMING 1976
★ ★ R Comedy 1:32
☑ Brief nudity, adult situations, explicit language
Dir: John Hancock *Cast:* Glynnis O'Connor, Seymour Cassel, Dorothy Tristan, Dennis Christopher, Tanya Roberts, Jimmy Van Patten
► Christopher, a nerd from Chicago, moves to California, where he falls for beautiful virginal O'Connor. Will he succumb to the empty morals of surfers and bikini girls, or impress O'Connor with higher goals? Unpretentious beach comedy with a heavy emphasis on sex and a bouncy soundtrack.
Dist.: Vestron

CALIFORNIA SUITE 1978
★ ★ ★ ★ PG Comedy 1:42
☑ Adult situations, explicit language
Dir: Herbert Ross *Cast:* Michael Caine, Maggie Smith, Jane Fonda, Alan Alda, Bill Cosby, Richard Pryor, Elaine May, Walter Matthau
► Writer Neil Simon intercuts four stories set in the Beverly Hills Hotel: divorced Fonda and Alda fight over their teenaged daughter; sexually mismatched English couple Smith and Caine arrive for the Oscar ceremonies; husband Matthau tries to hide a hooker from wife, May; and pals Cosby and Pryor vacation with their wives and find their friendship tested by a series of mishaps. Slick and clever, superb work by Caine and Smith (Oscar, Best Supporting Actress).
Dist.: RCA/Columbia

CALIGULA 1980
☆ X Drama/Sex 2:36
☑ Rape, nudity, strong sexual content, explicit language, graphic violence
Dir: Tinto Brass *Cast:* Malcolm McDowell, Teresa Ann Savoy, Helen Mirren, Peter O'-Toole, John Gielgud
► Big-budget erotica produced by *Penthouse* magazine gained some notoriety for its six minutes of hard-core footage, but for the most part it's a slow, extravagant look at the orgies of two Roman emperors: syphilitic Tiberius (O'Toole) and epileptic Caligula (McDowell). Screenwriter Gore Vidal had his name removed from the credits.
Dist.: Vestron

CALL ME 1988
★ ★ R Mystery-Suspense 1:37
☑ Strong sexual content, adult situations, explicit language, violence
Dir: Sollace Mitchell *Cast:* Patricia Charbonneau, Patti D'Arbanville, Stephen McHattie, Boyd Gaines, Steve Buscemi, Sam Freed
► Lured by an obscene phone call she mistakenly believes is from her beau Freed, hip writer Charbonneau goes to a bar where she's hit on by McHattie. She witnesses the drug-related murder of a transvestite and is terrorized by increasingly threatening calls she assumes come from McHattie, unaware that she's the target of a killer. Sleek, erotic look at trendy downtown New York lacks substance.
Dist.: Vestron

CALL OF THE WILD 1972
German/Spanish/Italian/French
★ ★ PG Action-Adventure 1:20
☑ Violence
Dir: Ken Annakin *Cast:* Charlton Heston, Raimund Harmsdorf, Michele Mercier, George Eastman, Sancho Garcia, Rik Battaglia
► Partners Heston and Harmsdorf attempt to find gold in Alaska but mostly encounter various kinds of trouble. However, loyal dog Buck

rescuos thom from peril. Aduplullon of the Jack London classic is handsomely produced but inadequately scripted, directed, and acted (save for Heston).
Dist.: Vestron

CAME A HOT FRIDAY 1985 New Zealand
☆ **PG Comedy 1:40**
☑ Explicit language, mild violence
Dir: Ian Mune   *Cast:* Peter Bland, Philip Gordon, Billy T. James, Michael Lawrence, Marshall Napier
▶ It's 1949, and a pair of goofy con men chased out of the big city have taken up residence in a small town, where they operate a crudely effective off-track betting scam. The town's resident crooks turn out to be poor losers; when the conmen's takings are unfairly confiscated, the pair plots an explosive sting to get it back. Bright, refreshing fun.
Dist.: Nelson

CAMELOT 1967
★ ★ ★ ★ **G Musical 2:58**
Dir: Joshua Logan   *Cast:* Richard Harris, Vanessa Redgrave, Franco Nero, David Hemmings, Lionel Jeffries
▶ In the mystical kingdom of Camelot, King Arthur (Harris) invites Lancelot (Nero) to join his Knights of the Round Table. Guenevere (Redgrave), Arthur's queen, starts a tragic romance with Lancelot. Large scale adaptation of the Lerner-Loewe hit musical has beautiful production values and an exciting, Oscar-winning score including "If Ever I Would Leave You." Also won Oscars for Set Direction and Costumes.
Dist.: Warner

CAMERON'S CLOSET 1988
★ ★ ★ R **Horror 1:26**
☑ Adult situations, explicit language, violence
Dir: Armand Mastroianni   *Cast:* Cotter Smith, Mel Harris, Scott Curtis, Chuck McCann, Leigh McCloskey, Tab Hunter
▶ Doctor Hunter experiments on his telekinetic son, unleashing a demon who checks into the boy's bedroom closet. When the monster goes on a slaughter spree, a police sergeant linked to the boy by psychic dreams tries desperately to unravel the closet's dark secret. Not particularly original, but good effects, talented actors, and frightening theme will kill sleep for many.
Dist.: SVS

CAMILA 1985 Argentinian
★ **NR Drama 1:45**
☑ Nudity, adult situations, violence
Dir: Maria Louisa Bemberg   *Cast:* Susu Pecoraro, Imanol Arias, Hector Alterio, Elena Tasisto
▶ A young aristocratic woman and a handsome priest fall in love in the strictly Catholic Argentina of 1847. Condemned by the authorities for their forbidden liaison, they flee to a small town, where they are tracked down and put before a firing squad. Oscar nominee from its home country, true story of doomed lovers is emotionally uninvolving, poorly directed. ☐S☐
Dist.: Nelson

CAMILLE 1936
★ ★ ★ ★ **NR Drama 1:48 B&W**
Dir: George Cukor   *Cast:* Greta Garbo, Robert Taylor, Lionel Barrymore, Henry Daniell, Elizabeth Allan
▶ Cukor's meticulous adaptation of Alexandre Dumas's novel and play is justly remembered as a vehicle for Garbo's delicately nuanced performance as the ill-fated Paris courtesan who sacrifices herself for Taylor, the man she loves. The tragic ending has been breaking hearts and bringing tears for over fifty years.
Dist.: MGM/UA

CAMILLE CLAUDEL 1989 French
★ **R Biography 2:29**
☑ Nudity, adult situations, explicit language
Dir: Bruno Nuytten   *Cast:* Isabelle Adjani, Gerard Depardieu, Laurent Grevill, Alain Cuny
▶ In 1880s France, stunning sculptress Camille Claudel (Adjani) is taken on as an apprentice and lover by the famed Rodin (Depardieu). Headstrong, she tries vainly to succeed in a man's milieu, but succumbs to insanity. Overwrought melodrama was Adjani's pet project for many years; at times Claudel's descent into madness is a little too reminiscent of *The Story of Adele H.* Stunning production design and cinematography, with a perfectly cast, bearlike Depardieu making the most of his scenes. Adjani was awarded an Oscar nomination as Best Actress. ☐S☐
Dist.: Orion

CAMORRA: THE NAPLES CONNECTION 1986 Italian
☆ **R Drama 1:45**
☑ Rape, nudity, explicit language
Dir: Lina Wertmuller   *Cast:* Angela Molina, Harvey Keitel, Daniel Ezralow, Francisco Rabal, Paolo Bonacelli, Isa Danieli
▶ Mystery in the Neapolitan underworld of drug dealers, prostitutes, and female impersonators as mafiosi are murdered by a hypodermic poke to the genitals. Appearances point to a gang war, but the real culprits are a group of mothers fed up with drug dealers' exploitation of children. Keitel plays a visiting American hood. Lurid film drives its anti-drug message home with broad, obvious strokes.
Dist.: MGM/UA

CAMPUS MAN 1987
★ ★ **PG Comedy 1:34**
☑ Brief nudity, adult situations, explicit language
Dir: Ron Casden   *Cast:* John Dye, Steve Lyon, Kathleen Wilhoite, Kim Delaney, Miles O'Keeffe, Morgan Fairchild
▶ Unable to pay his tuition, Arizona State Uni-

versity student Dye convinces diving champ roommate Lyon to pose for beefcake calendar. The calendar is a sensation, but Dye soon runs afoul of loan shark O'Keeffe and campus newspaper editor Wilhoite. Amusing adolescent comedy based on a true incident has an amiable tone and good songs by Robert Cray, Corey Hart, E-I-E-I-O, and others.
Dist.: Paramount

CAN-CAN 1960
★ ★ ★ ★ NR Musical 2:11
Dir: Walter Lang *Cast:* Frank Sinatra, Shirley MacLaine, Maurice Chevalier, Louis Jourdan, Juliet Prowse, Marcel Dalio
▶ Nightclub owner MacLaine is sued when she tries to introduce the naughty can-can dance to 1890s Paris. Attorney Sinatra reluctantly agrees to defend her, upsetting his girlfriend. Glossy comedy benefits from an outstanding Cole Porter score ("I Love Paris," "Let's Do It," "Just One of Those Things," etc.). (CC)
Dist.: CBS/Fox

CANCEL MY RESERVATION 1972
★ ★ G Comedy 1:39
Dir: Paul Bogart *Cast:* Bob Hope, Eva Marie Saint, Ralph Bellamy, Forrest Tucker, Anne Archer, Keenan Wynn
▶ New York talk show host Hope's Arizona vacation is complicated by the appearance of a corpse in his hotel room. He must solve the case while hiding the murder from wife Saint. Stiff, unfunny adaptation of a Louis L'Amour novel has pointless walk-ons by Bing Crosby, John Wayne, and Flip Wilson.
Dist.: RCA/Columbia

CANDIDATE, THE 1972
★ ★ ★ PG Drama 1:50
☑ Explicit language
Dir: Michael Ritchie *Cast:* Robert Redford, Peter Boyle, Don Porter, Allen Garfield, Melvyn Douglas
▶ Idealistic attorney Redford agrees to enter a Senate campaign if he can run on his own terms. But he quickly learns he can't win without giving in to powerful interests. Sharp, convincing look at the political scene with uniformly strong performances, particularly by Boyle as the campaign manager and Douglas as Redford's father; incisive, Oscar-winning screenplay by Jeremy Larner.
Dist.: Warner

CANDLESHOE 1977
★ ★ ★ ★ G Family 1:41
Dir: Norman Tokar *Cast:* David Niven, Helen Hayes, Jodie Foster, Leo McKern, Veronica Quilligan
▶ Con man McKern tries to pass off Foster as the long-lost heiress to Hayes's English estate. Butler Niven uses amusing disguises to hide the fact that Hayes is actually penniless. Clever Disney film has a fun plot filled with

twists and double-crosses. Wholesome entertainment for children and adults alike.
Dist.: Buena Vista

CANDY MOUNTAIN 1987
Canadian/French/Swiss
★ R Drama 1:31
☑ Brief nudity, adult situations, explicit language
Dir: Robert Frank, Rudy Wurlitzer *Cast:* Kevin J. O'Connor, Harris Yulin, Tom Waits, Leon Redbone, David Johansen, Joe Strummer
▶ Rock star Johansen finances con man O'Connor as he goes in search of vanished master guitar maker Yulin. Trail leads through U.S. and Canada, as O'Connor encounters unusual characters and gets arrested for running into a parked boat. Offbeat road picture has "hip" cast and co-directors, but manages to turn rather dull.
Dist.: Republic

CANNERY ROW 1982
★ ★ ★ ★ PG Drama 2:00
☑ Brief nudity, adult situations, explicit language
Dir: David S. Ward *Cast:* Nick Nolte, Debra Winger, Audra Lindley, Frank McRae, M. Emmet Walsh
▶ Flavorful, highly romanticized period drama about the picaresque denizens of Monterey in the 1940s. Nolte plays a marine biologist and former baseball star who falls in love with pretty, wisecracking prostitute Winger. Based on two John Steinbeck stories, with a narration by John Huston.
Dist.: MGM/UA

CANNONBALL 1976
★ ★ PG Action-Adventure 1:33
☑ Explicit language
Dir: Paul Bartel *Cast:* David Carradine, Bill McKinney, Veronica Hamel, Gerrit Graham
▶ Not to be confused with the Burt Reynolds flicks, this free-wheeling action-comedy stars Carradine as Cannonball Buckman, a racer intent on winning the "most dangerous race in America" and the $100,000 prize. Features cameos by Martin Scorsese, Sylvester Stallone, Joe Dante, and producer Roger Corman. Lovers of car chases will be in 4-wheel heaven.
Dist.: Warner

CANNONBALL RUN, THE 1981
★ ★ ★ ★ PG Action-Adventure/Comedy 1:36
☑ Nudity, explicit language, adult humor
Dir: Hal Needham *Cast:* Burt Reynolds, Roger Moore, Farrah Fawcett, Dom DeLuise, Dean Martin
▶ Reynolds and guest star buddies DeLuise, Martin, and Moore enter a cross-country race in which there are no rules, no speed limits, no strategies—except avoid the police and get to California first. Though predictable, this action-packed good ol' boy picture was a major

hit, inspiring a sequel. Great for those in the mood for a smash-'em-up.
Dist.: Vestron

CANNONBALL RUN II 1984
★ ★ ★ **PG Action-Adventure/Comedy 1:48**
☑ Nudity, explicit language, adult humor
Dir: Hal Needham *Cast:* Burt Reynolds, Dom DeLuise, Marilu Henner, Frank Sinatra, Dean Martin, Sammy Davis, Jr., Jamie Farr
► Reynolds and DeLuise compete in a cross-country race for a million dollar prize offered by Arab sheik Farr. The contestants include two showgirls masquerading as nuns, two bums masquerading as cops, an orangutan masquerading as a chauffeur, and two long-legged bimbos masquerading as themselves. Lots of mayhem and mangled cars before the winner crosses the finish line.   (CC)
Dist.: Warner

CAN SHE BAKE A CHERRY PIE? 1983
★ ★ **R Comedy 1:30**
☑ Brief nudity, adult situations, explicit language, adult humor
Dir: Henry Jaglom *Cast:* Karen Black, Michael Emil, Michael Margotta, Frances Fisher, Paul Williams
► Abandoned by her husband, Black cautiously starts an affair with divorced hypochondriac Emil. Loose, largely improvised comedy may seem aimless at first, but the film's quirky humor and accomplished performances have their own charm. Shot on New York's Upper West Side.
Dist.: Monterey

CAN'T BUY ME LOVE 1987
★ ★ ★ **PG-13 Comedy 1:34**
☑ Adult situations, explicit language
Dir: Steve Rash *Cast:* Patrick Dempsey, Amanda Peterson, Courtney Gains, Seth Green, Devin De Vasquez
► Nerdy Dempsey wants to be accepted by the popular crowd in high school so he hires beautiful Peterson to be his girlfriend. What starts out as a bogus courtship turns into the real thing in this pert teen comedy that actually has something to say about the price of popularity. (CC)
Dist.: Buena Vista

CAN'T STOP THE MUSIC 1980
★ ★ **PG Musical 1:57**
☑ Brief nudity, adult situations, explicit language
Dir: Nancy Walker *Cast:* Valerie Perrine, Bruce Jenner, The Village People, Steve Guttenberg, Paul Sand
► Aspiring songwriter Guttenberg and ex-model Perrine gather some "Village" types and form the disco group Village People, in this lavish, colorful musical with a pounding dance beat. Olympic decathalon champ Jenner makes his film debut as the square lawyer who falls for Perrine but is nonplussed by her choice of friends. Harmless and gen-

lally campy fluff. Songs include the hit "YMCA."
Dist.: HBO

CAPE FEAR 1962
★ ★ ★ **NR Drama 1:46 B&W**
Dir: J. Lee Thompson *Cast:* Gregory Peck, Robert Mitchum, Polly Bergen, Lori Martin, Martin Balsam, Telly Savalas
► Rapist Mitchum finds Peck, the lawyer responsible for his jail sentence, in a small North Carolina town. He starts a campaign of terror against Peck's family which the police are powerless to stop. Uncomfortably tense drama improves on John D. MacDonald's novel thanks to Mitchum's riveting portrayal of a shrewd psychopath.
Dist.: MCA

CAPRICORN ONE 1978
★ ★ ★ ★ **PG Sci-Fi 2:07**
☑ Explicit language, mild violence
Dir: Peter Hyams *Cast:* Elliott Gould, James Brolin, Karen Black, Telly Savalas, Sam Waterston, O. J. Simpson
► NASA executive Holbrook fakes a Mars mission in a TV studio rather than risk a failure that would jeopardize funding. Nosy reporter Gould investigates the conspiracy and astronauts Brolin, Simpson, and Waterston find themselves running for their lives when the scheme goes awry. Slick, fast paced thriller has terrific chase scenes and an intricate, interesting "it could happen" plot.
Dist.: CBS/Fox

CAPTAIN APACHE 1971
★ **PG Western 1:34**
☑ Adult situations, explicit language, violence
Dir: Alexander Singer *Cast:* Lee Van Cleef, Carroll Baker, Stuart Whitman, Percy Herbert, Charlie Bravo, Elisa Montes
► Indian-born cavalry officer Van Cleef investigates the murder of an Indian commissioner and courts peril to uncover a plot by crooked brothel-owner Whitman to assassinate President Grant. Luridly lit, psychedelic Western is full of gratuitous winks at the viewer. Van Cleef sings the theme song over an irritating opening credits sequence.
Dist.: Prism

CAPTAIN BLOOD 1935
★ ★ ★ ★ **NR Action-Adventure 1:39 B&W**
Dir: Michael Curtiz *Cast:* Errol Flynn, Olivia de Havilland, Lionel Atwill, Basil Rathbone, Guy Kibbee, Ross Alexander
► Seventeenth century English doctor Flynn is sold into Caribbean slavery when a rebellion is crushed. He revolts against his captors, turns pirate, fights colonial governor Atwill, and, in one of cinema's great swordfights, battles fellow pirate Rathbone for de Havilland. Grand classic fueled by Flynn's high spirits. Adapted from a Rafael Sabatini novel.
Dist.: Key ⓒ

CAPTAIN JANUARY 1936
★ ★ ★ NR Musical/Family 1:16 B&W
Dir: David Butler *Cast:* Shirley Temple, Guy Kibbee, Slim Summerville, June Lang, Buddy Ebsen, Jane Darwell
▶ After her parents drown, Temple comes under the care of Kibbee, a kindhearted lighthouse keeper. Their home is threatened when truant officers order her to attend a boarding school. Sturdy Temple vehicle highlighted by her duet with Ebsen to "At the Codfish Ball."
Dist.: CBS/Fox

CAPTAIN KIDD 1945
★ NR Action-Adventure 1:29 B&W
Dir: Rowland W. Lee *Cast:* Charles Laughton, Randolph Scott, Barbara Britton, Reginald Owen, John Carradine, Gilbert Roland, John Qualen, Sheldon Leonard
▶ Infamous pirate Kidd (Laughton) poses as a legitimate captain, winning a commission from the king to guide a treasure past Madagascar. His plans to steal the loot depend on seaman Scott, who may be a spy for the king. Lackluster swashbuckler has a great cast but disappointing production values. Laughton repeated his role in *Abbott and Costello Meet Captain Kidd.*
Dist.: Various

CAPTAIN KRONOS: VAMPIRE HUNTER
1974 British
★ ★ R Horror 1:31
☑ Nudity, adult situations, graphic violence
Dir: Brian Clemens *Cast:* Horst Janson, John Carson, Shane Briant, Caroline Munro, John Cater, Lois Daine
▶ When the undead stalk the English countryside, leaving their female victims prematurely aged, Janson, a sort of monster mercenary, and his hunchbacked assistant Carson are summoned to fight them. Unique premise and stylish direction account for film's cult reputation. The drawbacks: bland acting (save for sexy Munro as the love interest rescued from a stockade) and intrusive music.
Dist.: Paramount

CAPTAIN NEWMAN, M.D. 1963
★ ★ ★ ★ NR Comedy/Drama 2:06
Dir: David Miller *Cast:* Gregory Peck, Tony Curtis, Bobby Darin, Eddie Albert, Angie Dickinson, Jane Withers, Larry Storch, Robert Duvall, Dick Sargent, Ted Bessell
▶ Offbeat combination of drama and comedy set in a mental institution at the close of World War II, focusing on psychiatrist Peck's work with Darin, a war hero suffering from fears of cowardice, and Albert, a colonel guilty over the losses in his command. Curtis supplies the laughs as a slick corporal. Received Oscar nominations for Darin's affecting performance and screenplay adapted from Leo Rosten's novel.
Dist.: MCA

CAPTAIN SCARLETT 1953
★ NR Action-Adventure 1:15

Dir: Thomas Carr *Cast:* Richard Greene, Leonora Amar, Nedrick Young, Manolo Fabregas
▶ Predictable heroics as captain Greene battles injustice and tyranny with the help of princess Amar and brigand Young. Full quota of sword fights, sea battles, and dastardly villains in this low-grade swashbuckler.
Dist.: Republic

CAPTAINS COURAGEOUS 1937
★ ★ ★ ★ NR Drama/Family 1:56 B&W
Dir: Victor Fleming *Cast:* Freddie Bartholomew, Spencer Tracy, Melvyn Douglas, Lionel Barrymore, Mickey Rooney, John Carradine
▶ Child star Bartholomew plays a spoiled heir who falls off an ocean liner and is rescued by Tracy, a gruff Portuguese fisherman. His pleas to be sent home are ignored until the fishermen finish their three-month voyage. Although ungrateful at first, with Tracy's help he learns the value of love and trust. Beautiful adaptation of Rudyard Kipling's novel is outstanding on all levels, with a deeply affecting performance by Tracy that won him a richly deserved Oscar.
Dist.: MGM/UA ⓒ

CAPTAIN'S PARADISE, THE 1953 British
★ ★ NR Comedy 1:29 B&W
Dir: Anthony Kimmins *Cast:* Alec Guinness, Yvonne De Carlo, Celia Johnson, Charles Goldner, Bill Fraser, Sebastian Cabot
▶ Ship captain Guinness's idea of paradise is bigamy; homey Gibraltar bride Johnson and gorgeous North African wife De Carlo are unaware of each other's existence. Although the wives get the last laugh in the end, before that the audience is kept in stitches by the hilarious antics.
Dist.: HBO

CAPTIVE 1986 British
★ ★ R Drama 1:43
☑ Nudity, adult situations, explicit language
Dir: Paul Mayersberg *Cast:* Irina Brook, Oliver Reed, Hiro Arai, Xavier Deluc, Corinne Dacla
▶ Gang kidnaps pretty heiress Brook who lives in a castle with rich father Reed. Drugged, locked up and brainwashed, she reflects on her less-than-loving relationship with daddy and grows closer to her captors. Thinly disguised version of Patty Hearst's life is stylish-looking but lacks depth.
Dist.: Virgin

CAPTIVE HEARTS 1987
★ ★ ★ PG Drama/Romance 1:41
☑ Adult situations, explicit language, violence
Dir: Paul Almond *Cast:* Noriyuki "Pat" Morita, Michael Sarrazin, Chris Makepeace, Mari Sato, Seth Sakai
▶ Tough-talking U.S. airman Sarrazin and baby-faced cohort Makepeace are shot down over Japan during World War II and parachute into an isolated town. Village elder

Morita intervenes to save the Americans from execution and puts them to work. Makepeace soon falls in love with Sato, Morita's widowed daughter-in-law, and the star-crossed lovers must contend with the harsh realities of war.
Dist.: CBS/Fox

CARBON COPY 1981
★ ★ ★ ★ **PG Comedy 1:31**
☑ Adult situations, adult humor
Dir: Michael Schultz   *Cast:* George Segal, Susan Saint James, Denzel Washington, Jack Warden, Dick Martin
▶ White corporate executive Segal, married to Saint James, the daughter of his boss Warden, discovers he has black son Washington by a previous lover. His career and marriage are jeopardized as wife and employer prove less than understanding. Simple, broadly drawn farce pleasantly mixes social comment and comedy. Some clever moments (the son turns out to be the one black kid inept at basketball) and appealing performances by Segal and Washington.
Dist.: Nelson

CARE BEARS ADVENTURE IN WONDERLAND, THE 1987
★ ★ ★ ★ ★ **G Animation 1:15**
Dir: Raymond Jafelice   *Cast:* Voice of Colin Fox
▶ Third in the series is variation on Lewis Carroll's *Alice in Wonderland* as furry heroes accompany Alice through the looking glass to stop evil wizard who has kidnapped princess. Wizard scoffs at bears as "puffballs" but they save the day. Should enthrall tykes between ages three and seven. Sprightly John Sebastian score includes "Welcome Back to Wonderland."
Dist.: MCA

CARE BEARS MOVIE, THE 1985
★ ★ ★ ★ ★ **G Animation 1:15**
Dir: Arna Selznick   *Cast:* Voices of Mickey Rooney, Georgia Engel, Harry Dean Stanton
▶ Cuddly Care Bears to the rescue when a misguided magician's assistant comes under the control of an evil spirit plotting to remove all feelings from the world. Small children are fond of these furry do-gooders and parents will appreciate their message of friendship, caring, and feeling. Catchy title tune by Carole King and a bouncy John Sebastian score merrily move things along. **(CC)**
Dist.: Vestron

CARE BEARS MOVIE II: A NEW GENERATION 1986
★ ★ ★ ★ ★ **G Animation 1:17**
Dir: Dale Schott   *Cast:* Voices of Kay Hadley, Chris Wiggins, Cree Summer Francks, Alyson Court, Michael Fantini
▶ Prequel to the original *Care Bears Movie* traces how the compassionate bears became the guardians of love in the world. The animals help a little girl named Christy, who

trades her soul to the evil Dark Heart in return for summer camp success. All ends happily in this vehicle for small children. **(CC)**
Dist.: RCA/Columbia

CAREFREE 1938
★ ★ ★ **NR Musical 1:20 B&W**
Dir: Mark Sandrich   *Cast:* Fred Astaire, Ginger Rogers, Ralph Bellamy, Jack Carson, Franklin Pangborn, Hattie McDaniel
▶ Lesser Astaire/Rogers vehicle is a lighthearted send-up of psychology. Singing star Rogers won't accept marriage proposal from stuffy lawyer Bellamy, so he hires psychiatrist Astaire to hypnotize her into submission. Duo's eighth teaming has more comedy than music, but the dances and Irving Berlin score (including "Change Partners" and "I Used to Be Color Blind") are still unbeatable.
Dist.: Turner

CAREFUL, HE MIGHT HEAR YOU 1984
Australian
★ ★ ★ ★ **PG Drama 1:53**
☑ Adult situations, explicit language
Dir: Carl Schultz   *Cast:* Nicholas Gledhill, Wendy Hughes, Robyn Nevin, John Hargreaves, Peter Whitford
▶ In 1930s Sydney, two aunts—working class housewife Nevin and sophisticated but neurotic and rich Hughes—fight for custody over Gledhill, their deceased sister's son. Australian *Kramer Vs. Kramer* is slowly paced but well acted. Gledhill is a remarkably subtle child actor and Hughes won an Australian Film Institute Award (one of eight the film received, including Best Picture). **(CC)**
Dist.: CBS/Fox

CARIBE 1988 Canadian
★ **R Action-Adventure 1:29**
☑ Explicit language, violence
Dir: Michael Kennedy   *Cast:* John Savage, Kara Glover, Stephen McHattie, Sam Malkin, Maury Chaykin, Zack Nesis
▶ When her partner in a Central American ammo-selling scheme is killed by a greedy mercenary, Glover hooks up with laid-back Savage who's been eyeballing the deal for the law. As they fight for their lives in the jungle, the pair is aided by a mystical hippie still living out the sixties in a ruined pyramid. Action is sluggish and mixed up, but Belizian scenery has tropical punch.
Dist.: Vestron

CARLTON-BROWNE OF THE F.O. 1958
British
★ **NR Comedy 1:31 B&W**
Dir: Jeffrey Dell, Roy Boulting   *Cast:* Terry-Thomas, Peter Sellers, Luciana Paluzzi, Thorley Walters, Ian Bannen
▶ Extremely British farce about the obscure island of Gallardia, caught in a political tug-of-war over valuable mineral deposits. Thomas stars as Carlton Browne, dim-witted "Chief of Miscellaneous Territories," who gums up Britain's plan to recapture the former col-

ony. With Sellers as the isle's corrupt Prime Minister. Also known as *Man in a Cocked Hat.*
Dist.: HBO

CARMEN 1983 Spanish
☆ **R Drama/Dance 1:39**
☑ Adult situations, nudity, violence
Dir: Carlos Saura ***Cast:*** Antonio Gades, Laura Del Sol, Paco de Lucia, Christina Hoyos, Sebastian Moreno
▶ A choreographer rehearses a flamenco version of Bizet's opera and falls in love with his leading lady, an obsession that turns into tragedy because of the dancer's drug-dealer husband. The drama of love and jealousy verges on the banal but the dancing, enhanced by some fine camerawork, is dramatic and thrilling. [S]
Dist.: Media

CARMEN 1984 French/Italian
★★★★ **PG Music 2:32**
☑ Adult situations, violence
Dir: Francesco Rosi ***Cast:*** Julia Migenes-Johnson, Placido Domingo, Ruggero Raimondi, Faith Esham, Jean-Philippe Lafont
▶ Oft-filmed story about an aristocratic Spanish soldier who loses his heart to a faithless gypsy receives a full operatic treatment here. Distinguished tenor Domingo tops an accomplished cast in a faithful version of Bizet's original score. Beautiful Spanish settings and exotic local color. Also known as *Bizet's Carmen.* [S]
Dist.: RCA/Columbia

CARMEN JONES 1954
★★ **NR Musical 1:45**
Dir: Otto Preminger ***Cast:*** Dorothy Dandridge, Harry Belafonte, Olga James, Pearl Bailey, Diahann Carroll, Roy Glenn
▶ Ambitious updating of Bizet's famous opera, with new lyrics by Oscar Hammerstein II. Set in a World War II parachute factory, story describes tragic affair of beautiful flirt Dandridge (who received an Oscar nomination) and hot-headed soldier Belafonte. Dandridge's singing dubbed by Marilyn Horne.
Dist.: Magnetic

CARNAL KNOWLEDGE 1971
★★ **R Drama 1:38**
☑ Nudity, adult situations, explicit language
Dir: Mike Nichols ***Cast:*** Jack Nicholson, Candice Bergen, Art Garfunkel, Ann-Margret, Rita Moreno, Carol Kane
▶ Caustic drama traces the sexual attitudes of friends Nicholson and Garfunkel from college through middle age. The women in their lives include Smith college student Bergen, voluptuous model Ann-Margret (in an Oscar-nominated performance), prostitute Moreno, and young hippie Kane. Provocative script by cartoonist Jules Feiffer was expertly directed by Nichols.
Dist.: Nelson

CARNIVAL BOAT 1932
★ **NR Drama 1:01 B&W**
Dir: Albert Rogell ***Cast:*** Bill Boyd, Ginger Rogers, Fred Kohler, Hobart Bosworth, Marie Prevost, Edgar Kennedy
▶ Showgirl Rogers comes to timberland on a floating pleasure barge and turns the head of Boyd, a tough logger. Boyd's father, who owns a lumber business, tries to discourage the liaison. Falling trees have been photographed better since, and there's not much else in this slow drama. Rogers's teaming with Astaire was still a year away.
Dist.: Turner

CARNIVAL OF SOULS 1962
★ **NR Horror 1:31 B&W**
Dir: Herk Harvey ***Cast:*** Candace Hilligoss, Sidney Berger, Frances Feist, Herk Harvey, Stan Levitt, Art Ellison
▶ Hilligoss emerges mysteriously uninjured from a horrifying car crash to find herself on a new, strangely menacing plane of reality. Playing organ in a small-town church, she is haunted by zombie-like figures she alone can see, and is drawn to a deserted pavilion full of wildly dancing ghouls. This eerily effective evocation of spiritual disjunction was former industrial filmmaker Harvey's sole feature; filmed for zilch, it became an unexpected cult classic years after its original release.
Dist.: VidAmerica

CARNIVAL ROCK 1957
☆ **NR Drama 1:15 B&W**
Dir: Roger Corman ***Cast:*** Susan Cabot, Dick Miller, Brian Hutton, David Houston, David J. Stewart
▶ Old-time burlesque comic Stewart runs a nightspot on a carnival pier and falls hard for resident singer Cabot. She in turn goes for gambler Hutton, who makes it worse for the broken-hearted former clown by winning his nightclub in a card game. Rock 'n' roll acts including The Platters, Bob Luman, and the Blockbusters are occasionally wheeled on and off. Perfectly adequate rock-era *Pagliacci.*
Dist.: Rhino

CARNIVAL STORY 1954
☆ **NR Drama 1:35**
Dir: Kurt Neumann ***Cast:*** Anne Baxter, Steve Cochran, Lyle Bettger, George Nader, Jay C. Flippen
▶ German tramp Baxter joins a visiting American carnival and winds up in the arms of Cochran, a certified rat. Even after Baxter marries high diver Bettger and joins him in his successful act, she continues to see Cochran, leading to tragedy and death on the midway. Gloomy and unpleasant melodrama has a few nice moments atop an impossibly high diving tower, where the performers pause to enjoy their splendid isolation before leaping into the distant tank.
Dist.: Goodtimes

CARNY 1980
★ ★ R Drama 1:47
☑ Nudity, adult situations, explicit language
Dir: Robert Kaylor *Cast:* Jodie Foster, Gary
Busey, Robbie Robertson, Meg Foster,
Kenneth McMillan, Elisha Cook, Jr.
▶ Eccentric but appealing drama about Foster, a young runaway who comes between
friends Busey and rock star Robertson (in his
first dramatic role) when she joins a seedy carnival. Effective use of sideshow atmosphere
adds depth to the predictable plot. Foster is
excellent in her first "adult" role.
Dist.: Warner

CAROUSEL 1956
★ ★ ★ ★ NR Musical 2:09
Dir: Henry King *Cast:* Cordon MacRae,
Shirley Jones, Cameron Mitchell, Barbara
Ruick, Claramae Turner, Gene Lockhart
▶ Carnival barker MacRae is killed when
committing a robbery to support wife Jones
and unborn child. In heaven, he gets another
chance to return to earth and redeem himself. Sentimental musical fantasy has rather
stagebound production but leads' lovely
voices do justice to a familiar, much-loved
Rodgers and Hammerstein score which includes "If I Loved You," "June Is Busting Out All
Over," and "You'll Never Walk Alone."
Dist.: CBS/Fox

CARPETBAGGERS, THE 1964
★ ★ ★ PG Drama 2:30
Dir: Edward Dmytryk *Cast:* George Peppard, Alan Ladd, Carroll Baker, Bob Cummings, Martha Hyer, Elizabeth Ashley
▶ In the early 1930s, playboy Peppard inherits
millions, buys a movie studio, turns father's
widow Baker into a star, then dumps her for
prostitute Hyer. His friend Nevada Smith (Ladd,
in his last film) is the only one who can bring
him to his senses. Adaptation of Harold Robbins's best-seller loosely based on the life of
Howard Hughes. Steve McQueen played
Ladd's character in a prequel, *Nevada Smith*.
Dist.: Paramount

CARRIE 1976
★ ★ ★ ★ ★ R Horror 1:37
☑ Nudity, adult situations, explicit language, graphic violence
Dir: Brian De Palma *Cast:* Sissy Spacek,
Piper Laurie, William Katt, John Travolta,
Nancy Allen, Amy Irving
▶ Stephen King's novel about a repressed
high school girl with telekinetic powers became an absorbing, frightening hit thanks to
director De Palma's clever tricks. Carrie (Spacek) is tormented at home by religious zealot
mother Laurie and at school by cruel students,
including Allen and Travolta in his film debut.
She unleashes her powers after a particularly
mean practical joke on prom night. Widely
imitated film won Oscar nominations for both
Spacek and Laurie.
Dist.: MGM/UA

CARRIER, THE 1987
☆ R Horror 1:39
☑ Adult situations, explicit language, violence
Dir: Nathan J. White *Cast:* Gregory Fortescue, Steve Dixon, N. Paul Silverman, Paul Urbanski, Patrick Butler, Stevie Lee
▶ In a small town cut off from the rest of the
world by a flood, Fortescue is the unaffected
carrier of a deadly disease that kills its victims
in a sizzling meltdown. The town is split by fear
of the disease, with Fortescue the target of its
anger. Very weak, unprofessional attempt at
low budget *Night of the Living Dead*-style horror.
Dist.: Magnum

CARRY ON DOCTOR 1968 British
★ NR Comedy 1:35
☑ Adult situations, explicit language, adult
humor
Dir: Gerald Thomas *Cast:* Frankie Howerd,
Sidney James, Kenneth Williams, Charles
Hawtrey, Jim Dale, Barbara Windsor
▶ Middling entry in the comedy series relies
on standard formula, although the jokes are
raunchier. This time snake oil quack Howerd
causes an uproar in a hospital staffed by libidinous nurses and Williams, the infamous "Dr.
Tinkle."
Dist.: Paramount

CARRY ON NURSE 1958 British
★ ★ NR Comedy 1:26 B&W
Dir: Gerald Thomas *Cast:* Kenneth Connor,
Kenneth Williams, Charles Hawtrey, Terence
Longdon, Bill Owen, Wilfrid Hyde-White, Hattie Jacques, Shirley Eaton
▶ Second in the popular British comedy series
drags out hoary but nonstop jokes as male
patients in a stodgy hospital plan a revolt
against their doctors and nurses. Humor is
broad but amiable. One of the most popular
entries in the long-lived series.
Dist.: Various

CARS THAT ATE PARIS, THE 1974 Australian
☆ PG Comedy 1:31
☑ Adult situations, explicit language, violence
Dir: Peter Weir *Cast:* Terry Camilleri, John
Meillon, Melissa Jaffa, Kevin Miles, Max Gillies, Bruce Spence
▶ Citizens of Paris, Australia, lure unsuspecting
motorists into traffic accidents; unscrupulous
doctor performs medical experiments on the
victims while looters and mechanics reap a
fortune from the wrecks. Extremely black comedy with a minor cult reputation suffers from
hit-or-miss gags.
Dist.: RCA/Columbia

CAR TROUBLE 1985 British
★ R Comedy 1:33
☑ Adult situations, explicit language, mild
violence
Dir: David Green *Cast:* Julie Walters, Ian

Charleson, Stratford Johns, Vincenzo Ricotta, Hazel O'Connor
► Husband Charleson appears to love his new Jaguar more than he loves wife Walters. So when she accidentally crashes the car while in the arms of another man, Charleson goes into a rage that sets off a zany of cycle of vengeance, including burning down their house and setting up a plane collision. Bickering couple grates, and their actions seem more insane than funny.
Dist.: Virgin

CAR WASH 1976
★ ★ ★ PG Comedy 1:37
☐ Explicit language, adult humor
Dir: Michael Schultz   *Cast:* Richard Pryor, Franklyn Ajaye, Sully Boyar, George Carlin, Irwin Corey, Melanie Mayron
► Fast, rowdy look at the workers and customers at an inner-city L.A. car wash is basically a series of skits tied together by a pounding rock score. Pryor steals the film as Daddy Rich, a wealthy evangelist who shows up in a gold limo to do a song with the Pointer Sisters, but everyone in the large cast gets some bright lines.
Dist.: MCA

CASABLANCA 1943
★ ★ ★ ★ ★ NR Drama 1:42 B&W
Dir: Michael Curtiz   *Cast:* Humphrey Bogart, Ingrid Bergman, Paul Henreid, Claude Rains, Conrad Veidt, Peter Lorre, Sydney Greenstreet, Dooley Wilson
► "Of all the gin joints in all the world, she walks into mine," says cafe owner Rick (Bogart) when old love Bergman arrives in World War II Casablanca with freedom fighter husband Henreid. Will Rick stay neutral or overcome his bitterness and help Bergman and Henreid in the cause? Cynical French captain Rains and Nazi leader Veidt want to know. Immortal Hollywood classic, full of memorable moments, romance, intrigue, and perhaps the most quoted dialogue of any film. When they say they don't make 'em like they used to, this is what they mean. Oscar for Best Picture. (CC)
Dist.: MGM/UA

CASANOVA'S BIG NIGHT 1954
★ ★ ★ NR Comedy 1:26
Dir: Norman Z. McLeod   *Cast:* Bob Hope, Joan Fontaine, Audrey Dalton, Basil Rathbone, Hugh Marlowe, Vincent Price, John Carradine, Lon Chaney, Jr., Raymond Burr
► Hope's uncanny resemblance to the notorious lover prompts duchess to hire him to test motives of son's fiancée Fontaine. Memorable villains Rathbone, Carradine, Chaney, and Burr mistake Hope for the real thing, leading to frequent slapstick chases in this amiable period comedy. Price has an amusing cameo as the "real" Casanova.
Dist.: Paramount

CASE OF THE LUCKY LEGS, THE 1935
★ NR Mystery-Suspense 1:16 B&W
Dir: Archie L. Mayo   *Cast:* Warren William, Genevieve Tobin, Patricia Ellis, Lyle Talbot, Allen Jenkins, Barton MacLane
► A Perry Mason mystery featuring William as Erle Stanley Gardner's sleuthing lawyer and Tobin as wisecracking secretary Della Street. Murder comes into the picture on the good-looking gams of Ellis, a small town girl who becomes a suspect in the slaying of a contest promotor. A few chuckles, and Mason fans will enjoy.
Dist.: Sinister

CASEY'S SHADOW 1978
★ ★ ★ ★ PG Family 1:56
☐ Adult situations, explicit language
Dir: Martin Ritt   *Cast:* Walter Matthau, Alexis Smith, Robert Webber, Murray Hamilton, Andrew S. Rubin
► Cajun horse trainer Matthau and his three sons groom their quarterhorse, Casey's Shadow, for an important race at New Mexico's Ruidoso Downs—even though the owner plans to sell the horse. A well-made, old-fashioned family film, emotionally honest as well as touching. Matthau, playing a good-natured slob, is wonderful, and he receives excellent support from Smith as a wealthy horse breeder.
Dist.: RCA/Columbia

CASINO ROYALE 1967 British
★ ★ NR Comedy 2:11
Dir: John Huston, Ken Hughes, Robert Parrish, Joseph McGrath, Val Guest   *Cast:* Peter Sellers, Ursula Andress, David Niven, Orson Welles, Woody Allen, William Holden, John Huston, George Raft, Jean-Paul Belmondo, Jacqueline Bisset
► Overblown spoof of the 007 series, with a huge all-star cast. The aging Sir James Bond (Niven) is recruited to crush the evil organization SMERSH, but lots of other Bond impersonators have been recruited as well (including Allen as nephew Jimmy Bond) to confuse the enemy.
Dist.: RCA/Columbia

CAST A GIANT SHADOW 1966
★ ★ NR Biography 2:18
Dir: Melville Shavelson   *Cast:* Kirk Douglas, Senta Berger, Angie Dickinson, Yul Brynner, John Wayne, Frank Sinatra
► True story of Colonel Mickey Marcus (Douglas), an American Jew who guided the Israeli Army to victories over Arab enemies in the 1949 war. Along the way, Douglas, although married to Dickinson, finds time for romance with freedom fighter Berger. All-star cast adds punch to fascinating tale.   (CC)
Dist.: KEY

CASTAWAY 1987 British
★ R Drama 1:57
☑ Nudity, adult situations, explicit language
Dir: Nicolas Roeg   *Cast:* Oliver Reed,

Amanda Donohoe, Georgina Hale, Frances Barber, Tony Richards
► The Seychelles Islands provide an exotic tropical backdrop to an intriguing psychological drama based on a true story. Reed signs a book contract to spend a year on a desert island, and selects Donohoe through a personal ad to share the experience. Cut off from civilization, the two prey on each other's weaknesses.
Dist.: Warner

CASTAWAY COWBOY, THE 1974
★ ★ ★ G Comedy 1:31
Dir: Vincent McEveety *Cast:* James Garner, Vera Miles, Robert Culp, Eric Shea, Elizabeth Smith, Manu Tupou
► Texas sailor Garner, shipwrecked on Hawaii in 1850, protects widow Miles from villain Culp, who wants her potato ranch. Likable stars boost the familiar Western-style plot in this enjoyable Disney comedy.
Dist.: Buena Vista

CASTLE OF EVIL 1966
☆ NR Horror 1:21
Dir: Francis D. Lyon *Cast:* Scott Brady, Virginia Mayo, William Thourlby, Lisa Gaye, Hugh Marlowe
► Disfigured in an assault, a crazed scientist arranges for vengeance after his death through look-alike robot Thourlby. But the scientist's attacker reprograms the robot, and it begins attacking those gathered in a spooky castle to hear the scientist's will. Cheap and predictable enough to provide a few camp chuckles.
Dist.: Republic

CASUAL SEX? 1988
★ ★ R Comedy 1:30
☑ Nudity, strong sexual content, explicit language
Dir: Genevieve Robert *Cast:* Lea Thompson, Victoria Jackson, Stephen Shellen, Jerry Levine, Andrew Dice Clay, Mary Gross
► Thompson and Jackson, two of Los Angeles' most eligible beauties, are intimidated by the AIDS crisis and their single status. Looking for Mr. Rights, they venture to a health resort. Thompson fends off crude Clay while batting eyes at a musician; Jackson may have found her man in chiropractor Levine. Amusing look at modern dating woes.
Dist.: MCA

CASUALTIES OF WAR 1989
★ ★ ★ ★ R War 2:00
☑ Rape, nudity, explicit language, graphic violence
Dir: Brian De Palma *Cast:* Michael J. Fox, Sean Penn, Thuy Thu Le, Don Harvey, John C. Reilly, John Leguizamo
► When Vietnam War platoon leader Penn kidnaps and leads rape of native Le, horrified raw recruit Fox faces crisis of conscience. He tries to help Le escape and later brings the matter to the authorities. Gripping throughout

although brutality is not always easy to watch; excellent performances by Fox and Penn, relentless direction by De Palma. David Rabe screenplay based on Daniel Lang article about an actual incident. (CC)
Dist.: RCA/Columbia

CAT AND MOUSE 1978 French
★ PG Mystery-Suspense 1:47
☑ Adult situations
Dir: Claude Lelouch *Cast:* Michele Morgan, Serge Reggiani, Phillipe Leotard, Jean-Pierre Aumont
► Wealthy art collector Aumont is murdered. Police inspector Reggiani suspects the widow Morgan but then begins to fall in love with her. Complex mystery plot combines romance, comedy (especially in scenes with the inspector's dog Sam), and wryly amusing performances.
Dist.: RCA/Columbia

CAT AND THE CANARY, THE 1927
★ NR Mystery-Suspense 2:06 B&W
Dir: Paul Leni *Cast:* Laura La Plante, Creighton Hale, Tully Marshall, Flora Finch, Gertrude Astor, Forrest Stanley
► Relatives of a deceased millionaire are called to a spooky mansion for the reading of his will. La Plante, who might inherit the fortune, is menaced by what appears to be a ghost. Moody atmosphere and wry humor make this a treat for silent film buffs; inspired scores of haunted house movies. Remade in 1939 and 1978.
Dist.: Video Yesteryear

CAT AND THE CANARY, THE 1978 British
★ ★ PG Mystery-Suspense 1:31
☑ Explicit language
Dir: Radley Metzger *Cast:* Honor Blackman, Michael Callan, Edward Fox, Wendy Hiller, Olivia Hussey, Carol Lynley, Peter McEnery, Wilfrid Hyde-White
► Fourth remake of John Willard's 1921 stage play about an assortment of would-be heirs and heiresses gathered in a spooky manse for the reading of a will. Twist has deceased eccentric Hyde-White reading the will himself on film, allowing him to wittily berate greedy relatives who proceed to battle over his fortune. Strong cast delivers conundrum with chuckles and chills.
Dist.: RCA/Columbia

CATASTROPHE 1977
★ ★ ★ ★ PG Documentary 1:31 C/B&W
☑ Graphic violence
Dir: Larry Savadore *Cast:* Narrated by William Conrad
► Extraordinary compilation of natural and man-made disasters from around the world features horrifying newsreel footage of a skyscraper fire in Sao Paulo, the destructive fury of Hurricane Camille, car crashes at the Indy 500, a killer tornado in Ohio, etc. A number of black-and-white sections contain famous

older tragedies (the Hindenburg disaster, the wreck of the *Andrea Doria*, etc.).
Dist.: Nelson

CAT BALLOU 1965
★ ★ ★ ★ NR Western/Comedy 1:36
Dir: Elliot Silverstein *Cast:* Jane Fonda, Lee Marvin, Michael Callan, Dwayne Hickman, Nat "King" Cole, Stubby Kaye
▶ Young Wild West schoolteacher Fonda is forced into a life of crime by a crooked land baron. Threatened by hired killers, she teams up with cattle rustler Callan, con man Hickman, and notorious gunslinger Marvin. Popular spoof of Westerns won Marvin an Oscar for his dual role as the drunken has-been Kid Shelleen and his deadly twin, Silvernose. Wandering minstrels Kaye and Cole provide an amusing commentary on the action as they sing the Oscar-nominated title song.
Dist.: RCA/Columbia

CATCH THE HEAT 1987
☆ R Action-Adventure 1:37
☑ Nudity, adult situations, explicit language, violence
Dir: Joel Silberg *Cast:* David Dukes, Tiana Alexandra, Rod Steiger, Brian Thompson, Jorge Martinez, John Hancock
▶ Glamorous Jewish–Asian drug agent Alexandra poses as an exotic dancer to infiltrate smuggling ring headed by Steiger. Smugglers' scam is to surgically implant heroin instead of silicone in the strippers' bosoms. Alexandra has appealing martial arts expertise, but vulgar, amateurish film throws her. Also known as *Feel the Heat.* (CC)
Dist.: Media

CATCH-22 1970
★ ★ R War/Comedy 1:59
Dir: Mike Nichols *Cast:* Alan Arkin, Richard Benjamin, Art Garfunkel, Martin Balsam, Jack Gilford, Bob Newhart, Anthony Perkins, Paula Prentiss, Jon Voight, Orson Welles, Buck Henry, Charles Grodin, Bob Balaban
▶ An all-star cast brings to life Joseph Heller's classic antiwar novel. As Captain Yossarian, Arkin represents every war-weary soldier. He tries to plead insanity to escape flight duty but, according to catch-22, if he says he's crazy, he can't be crazy.
Dist.: Paramount

CAT FROM OUTER SPACE, THE 1978
★ ★ ★ ★ G Family 1:43
Dir: Norman Tokar *Cast:* Ken Berry, Sandy Duncan, Harry Morgan, Roddy McDowall, McLean Stevenson
▶ Jake, an extraterrestrial feline, crash-lands on Earth and enlists goofy physicist Berry to repair his spaceship. It's a race against time because the Pentagon wants Jake's magic crystal collar. Likable stars, crazy shenanigans, and the typical Disney gloss make this perfect viewing for children.
Dist.: Buena Vista

CATHERINE THE GREAT 1934 British
☆ NR Biography 1:34 B&W
Dir: Paul Czinner *Cast:* Elisabeth Bergner, Douglas Fairbanks, Jr., Flora Robson, Irene Vanbrugh, Gerald du Maurier, Griffith Jones
▶ Tour-de-force performance by Bergner dominates this story of the rise of Catherine from shy German princess to Empress of Russia. Meeting Grand Duke Peter (Fairbanks) by accident, she is swept up in court intrigue as his mother Elizabeth (Robson) plots their marriage. Large-scale spectacle is offset by slow pacing. Marlene Dietrich tackled the same role in *The Scarlet Empress*.
Dist.: Video Yesteryear

CAT ON A HOT TIN ROOF 1958
★ ★ ★ NR Drama 1:48
Dir: Richard Brooks *Cast:* Elizabeth Taylor, Paul Newman, Burl Ives, Jack Carson, Judith Anderson
▶ Dying Big Daddy (Ives) wants an heir. Daughter-in-law Maggie (Taylor) would love to provide one (and get her hands on the family fortune) but hubby Brick (Newman) has psychological problems that preclude this goal. Playwright Tennessee Williams's homosexual subtext was muted here but much of the steamy power of the original play comes through, thanks to some terrific acting. Six Oscar nominations including Best Picture, Actor (Newman) and Actress (Taylor).
Dist.: MGM/UA

CAT PEOPLE 1942
★ ★ NR Horror 1:13 B&W
Dir: Jacques Tourneur *Cast:* Simone Simon, Kent Smith, Tom Conway, Jane Randolph, Jack Holt
▶ Smith falls for Simon. Problem: she may have nasty habit of turning into a killer beast. Producer Val Lewton is the real genius behind this minor classic of the horror genre. Lewton's pictures avoided the gore of today's movies and achieved their scares with provocative ideas and stylized visuals (in contrast especially to the bloody 1982 remake).
Dist.: Turner

CAT PEOPLE 1982
★ ★ R Horror 1:58
☑ Nudity, strong sexual content, adult situations, explicit language
Dir: Paul Schrader *Cast:* Nastassia Kinski, Malcolm McDowell, John Heard, Annette O'Toole, Ruby Dee
▶ When McDowell visits his sister Kinski in New Orleans, he reveals their family's mysterious heritage. Can Kinski consummate her love for zookeeper Heard without turning into a killer feline? Unusual fantasy, not for every taste, creates plenty of spooky atmosphere. Remake is much more graphic (both in sex and in violence) than the 1942 original. Hit theme song by David Bowie.
Dist.: MCA

CAT'S EYE 1985
★ ★ ★ ★ PG-13 Horror 1:30
☑ Explicit language, violence
Dir: Lewis Teague *Cast:* Drew Barrymore, James Woods, Robert Hays, Alan King, Kenneth McMillan, Candy Clark
▶ Three tales of terror from genre master Stephen King: chain smoker Woods suffers through clinic head King's shocking cure, tennis pro Hays accepts gambler McMillan's bet that he can't walk around building ledge and live, and stray cat protects little Barrymore against deadly troll (a remarkable creation from *E.T.* designer Carlo Rambaldi). Strong stuff with touches of tongue-in-cheek humor.
Dist.: Key

CATTLE QUEEN OF MONTANA 1954
★ ★ NR Western 1:28
Dir: Allan Dwan *Cast:* Barbara Stanwyck, Ronald Reagan, Gene Evans, Lance Fuller, Anthony Caruso, Jack Elam
▶ Despite her father's murder, beautiful rancher Stanwyck vows to build an empire equal to villain Evans's spread. Reagan plays a federal agent who exposes Evans's ties to murdering Indians. Stanwyck, who did her own stunts, impressed the local Blackfeet so much that they made her their blood sister. Shot in Montana's Glacier National Park.
Dist.: Buena Vista

CAT WOMEN OF THE MOON 1954
☆ NR Sci-Fi 1:04 B&W
Dir: Arthur Hilton *Cast:* Sonny Tufts, Marie Windsor, Victor Jory, Susan Morrow, Carol Brewster
▶ Astronauts Tufts and Jory lead a trip to the moon, where they battle giant spiders and discover the cat women, whose talents include telepathy and looking great in leotards but not acting. For connoisseurs of camp. Originally shot in 3-D, also known as *Rocket to the Moon.* Remake: *Missile to the Moon.*
Dist.: Nostalgia

CAUGHT 1949
★ ★ ★ NR Drama 1:28 B&W
Dir: Max Ophuls *Cast:* James Mason, Barbara Bel Geddes, Robert Ryan, Curt Bois, Frank Ferguson, Natalie Schafer
▶ Impoverished charm school grad Bel Geddes marries wealthy Ryan but finds money can't buy happiness as he ignores and mistreats her. She leaves Ryan and gets job with idealistic slum doctor Mason. They fall in love but Ryan comes back to threaten their relationship. Soapy plot is quite engrossing; passionate performances and director's striking camera angles (commenting visually on the situations) maximize impact.
Dist.: Republic

CAULDRON OF BLOOD 1967 Spanish/U.S.
☆ PG Horror 1:35
☑ Adult situations, violence
Dir: Edward Mann (Santos Alcocer) *Cast:* Boris Karloff, Viveca Lindfors, Jean-Pierre Au-

mont, Jacqui Speed, Rosenda Monteros, Ruven Rojo
▶ Lindfors attempts to murder husband Karloff, but only succeeds in blinding him. She then goes on a murder spree, bathing her victims in acid and giving their bones to Karloff for use in his sculptures. Turgid, boring shocker is also known as *Blind Man's Bluff.*
Dist.: Republic

CAVEMAN 1981
★ ★ PG Comedy 1:31
☑ Adult humor
Dir: Carl Gottlieb *Cast:* Ringo Starr, Barbara Bach, Dennis Quaid, Shelley Long, Jack Gilford, John Matuszak
▶ Kicked out of his tribe after making eyes at the chief's woman, caveman Starr bands together with other outcasts. With his new friends he discovers fire, music, the wheel, and the love of sincere cavegirl Long. Broad prehistoric spoof has plenty of slapstick, with dialogue mostly of grunts and funny special-effects dinosaurs. Film led to wedding bells for Ringo and Bach.
Dist.: CBS/Fox

C.C. AND COMPANY 1970
★ PG Action-Adventure 1:34
☑ Explicit language, violence
Dir: Seymour Robbie *Cast:* Joe Namath, Ann-Margret, William Smith, Jennifer Billingsley, Don Chastain
▶ Dramatic debut for former quarterback Namath is an inept, unintentionally funny biker drama about vicious goons led by Smith who attempt to gang-rape beautiful hitchhiker Ann-Margret. Namath not only rescues Ann-Margret, earning her love, but also wins control of Smith's gang.
Dist.: Embassy

CEASE FIRE 1985
★ ★ ★ ★ R Drama 1:37
☑ Explicit language, violence
Dir: David Nutter *Cast:* Don Johnson, Lisa Blount, Robert F. Lyons, Richard Chaves, Rick Richards
▶ Vietnam vet Johnson's war flashbacks threaten to destroy his marriage until fellow vet Lyons introduces him to Veterans Center group therapy sessions. Wife Blount helps him on the long road to recovery. Sensitive treatment of a timely subject is slow-paced but emotionally rewarding.
Dist.: HBO

CELLAR DWELLER 1988
★ NR Horror 1:17
☑ Nudity, adult situations, explicit language, violence
Dir: John Buechler *Cast:* Debrah Mulrowney, Brian Robbins, Vince Edwards, Cheryl-Ann Wilson, Jeffrey Combs, Yvonne De Carlo
▶ Aspiring cartoonist Mulrowney joins De Carlo's art institute to work on "Cellar Dweller" comic strip. When she visits studio basement,

she unwittingly releases same monster who appears in her strip. Predictable horror formula receives uninspired treatment.
Dist.: New World

CERTAIN FURY 1985
★ ★ R Action-Adventure 1:27
☑ Rape, nudity, adult situations, explicit language, violence
Dir: Steven Gyllenhaal *Cast:* Tatum O'Neal, Irene Cara, Nicholas Campbell, Moses Gunn, Peter Fonda
► Street-smart tough O'Neal and rich kid Cara are mistakenly implicated in a courtroom shootout. Although enemies, they are forced on the lam together. After encounters with drug dealer Campbell and pimp Fonda, the girls become friends. Sordid exploitation fare handled with flair by the leads.
Dist.: New World

CHAINED HEAT 1983
★ ★ R Action-Adventure 1:35
☑ Rape, nudity, adult situations, explicit language, violence
Dir: Paul Nichols *Cast:* Linda Blair, John Vernon, Sybil Danning, Tamara Dobson, Stella Stevens, Henry Silva
► Convicted of manslaughter, naive Blair ends up in a hellish prison run by warden Vernon (with a hot tub in his office) and his partner Stevens, who also heads a drug and prostitution ring. Blair gets caught in the middle of a feud between black and white inmates, then leads a riot against her corrupt guards. Follow-up to *The Concrete Jungle* has a heavy emphasis on rape and nudity.
Dist.: Vestron

CHAIN REACTION 1980 Australian
★ NR Action-Adventure 1:27
☑ Nudity, explicit language, mild violence
Dir: Ian Barry *Cast:* Steve Bisley, Arna-Maria Winchester, Ross Thompson, Ralph Cotterill, Patrick Ward
► After an accident at a nuclear waste depository, a badly injured worker races against his impending death to warn the world of the intrusion of plutonium 239 into the food chain. A car crash shatters his memory, and the young farm couple who rescues him must fit together the pieces of the deadly puzzle. Anti-nuke polemic is excitingly staged and believable.
Dist.: Nelson

CHALK GARDEN, THE 1964 British
★ ★ NR Drama 1:46
Dir: Ronald Neame *Cast:* Deborah Kerr, Hayley Mills, John Mills, Edith Evans, Felix Aylmer
► When her mother remarries, Laurel (Hayley Mills) is sent to her grandmother Evans's house. Feeling rejected, she becomes a disruptive force until Kerr, a governess with a shady past, teaches her the value of love. Delicate adaptation of an Enid Bagnold play also features

Hayley's father John as the grandmother's butler.
Dist.: MCA

CHALLENGE, THE 1982
★ ★ ★ R Action-Adventure 1:46
☑ Nudity, adult situations, explicit language, graphic violence
Dir: John Frankenheimer *Cast:* Scott Glenn, Toshiro Mifune, Donna Kei Benz, Atsuo Nakamura, Calvin Young
► When American boxer Glenn is hired to transport an antique sword back to Japan, he unknowingly steps into a vicious feud between traditional warrior Mifune and his industrialist brother Nakamura. Intriguing look at ancient rituals in modern-day Japan was co-written by John Sayles. An intense training sequence and violent climax are not for the squeamish.
Dist.: CBS/Fox

CHALLENGE TO BE FREE 1975
★ ★ ★ G Action-Adventure 1:27
Dir: Tay Garnett *Cast:* Mike Mazurki, Jimmy Kane, Vic Christy, Fritz Ford, Tay Garnett
► Burly loner Mazurki frees an injured wolf from a trap set by a no-good Frenchman out to sell animals to profiteers. The authorities come for him and by accident he kills one of them. A manhunt ensues and Mazurki heads for the mountains to avoid the posse. Solid family fare with lots of animal footage and beautiful Alaskan scenery.
Dist.: Media

CHAMBER OF HORRORS 1940 British
★ NR Horror 1:24 B&W
Dir: Norman Lee *Cast:* Leslie Banks, Lilli Palmer, Romilly Lunge, Gina Malo, David Horne
► In an effort to claim a large estate, mad scientist Banks eliminates legal inheritors in his basement torture chamber. Unless the police can stop him, young Palmer will be his next victim. Modest British shocker is best for fetching Palmer's work. Based on *The Door With Seven Locks* by Edgar Wallace.
Dist.: Sinister

CHAMP, THE 1979
★ ★ ★ ★ ★ PG Drama 2:01
☑ Explicit language
Dir: Franco Zeffirelli *Cast:* Jon Voight, Faye Dunaway, Ricky Schroder, Jack Warden, Arthur Hill
► Alcoholic former boxing champion Voight, desperate to keep young son Schroder from glamorous ex-wife Dunaway, decides to make a comeback despite doctor's advice. Touching Voight/Schroder relationship, lushly filmed, in sentimental remake of the 1931 King Vidor classic. Goes unashamedly for the tear ducts. Pro boxer Randall "Tex" Cobb is Voight's foe in the final fight.
Dist.: MGM/UA

CHAMPION 1949
★ ★ ★ NR Drama/Sports 1:39 B&W
Dir: Mark Robson   *Cast:* Kirk Douglas, Marilyn Maxwell, Arthur Kennedy, Paul Stewart, Ruth Roman, John Day
▶ Uncompromising portrait of boxer Douglas's rise to fame and corruption by gangsters ranks among the best sports dramas. Highlighted by brisk direction and uniformly strong acting, particularly Roman's spurned wife and Maxwell's ruthless mistress. Oscar-winning editing boosts fighting sequences; Kennedy received a nomination as Douglas's crippled brother, as did Carl Foreman for adapting Ring Lardner's story.
Dist.: Republic

CHAMPIONS 1984 British
★ ★ ★ ★ PG Biography/Sports 1:54
☑ Adult situations, explicit language
Dir: John Irvin   *Cast:* John Hurt, Edward Woodward, Ben Johnson, Jan Francis, Ann Bell
▶ True sports drama of two incredible comebacks. England's top steeplechase jockey Bob Champion (Hurt) is stricken with cancer at age 31 while his horse Aldaniti is crippled in a race. Both man and beast triumph over their afflictions and win the 1981 Grand National Steeplechase. Inspirational tale suffers from slow pacing but Hurt is excellent. (CC)
Dist.: Nelson

CHANCES ARE 1988
★ ★ ★ ★ PG Comedy 1:48
☑ Adult situations, explicit language
Dir: Emile Ardolino   *Cast:* Cybill Shepherd, Robert Downey, Jr., Ryan O'Neal, Mary Stuart Masterson, Christopher McDonald
▶ When her husband is killed in a car accident, Shepherd mourns for twenty-three years while ignoring O'Neal's advances. Her daughter Masterson falls for Downey, who discovers to his dismay that he's the reincarnation of Shepherd's husband. Romantic comedy earns some genuine chuckles with its elaborate mistaken identity complications.
Dist.: RCA/Columbia

CHANEL SOLITAIRE 1981 U.S./French
★ ★ R Biography 2:04
☑ Adult situations, explicit language
Dir: George Kaczender   *Cast:* Marie-France Pisier, Timothy Dalton, Rutger Hauer, Karen Black, Brigitte Fossey
▶ Glossy rags-to-riches biography of fashion designer Coco Chanel (Pisier), an orphan who rises from seamstress to the leader of Parisian haute couture. Along the way, she falls in love with handsome Brit Dalton but tragedy strikes when he dies in a car accident. Languidly paced but nice-looking soap opera with lovely costumes.
Dist.: Media

CHANGELING, THE 1980 Canadian
★ ★ ★ R Horror 1:47
☑ Adult situations, explicit language, violence
Dir: Peter Medak   *Cast:* George C. Scott, Trish Van Devere, Melvyn Douglas, John Colicos, Jean Marsh
▶ Music professor Scott loses his family in a tragic accident and rents an old house to recuperate. The place turns out to be haunted because title-holder Douglas, a Senator from a prestigious family, had committed an evil act some time back. Real estate agent Van Devere helps Scott crack the secrets of the house. Chilling tale with an intense performance from Scott.
Dist.: Vestron

CHANGE OF HABIT 1969
★ ★ G Drama 1:33
Dir: William Graham   *Cast:* Elvis Presley, Mary Tyler Moore, Barbara McNair, Jane Elliot, Leora Dana
▶ Teaming of Presley and Moore is not either's finest moment. Moore plays a nun who helps doctor Presley run a clinic in a bad New York neighborhood. Fans of the two stars may enjoy seeing them so oddly cast but be warned, Presley barely gets to sing here.
Dist.: MCA

CHANGE OF SEASONS, A 1980
★ ★ ★ R Comedy 1:42
☑ Nudity, adult situations, explicit language
Dir: Richard Lang   *Cast:* Shirley MacLaine, Bo Derek, Anthony Hopkins, Michael Brandon, Mary Beth Hurt
▶ Middle-aged college professor Hopkins is having an affair with Derek, one of his students. Wife MacLaine finds out and responds in kind with young carpenter Brandon. Agreeable romantic comedy with old pros MacLaine and Hopkins providing the acting expertise and Derek giving her all to the hot tub scene.
Dist.: CBS/Fox

CHAN IS MISSING 1982
★ NR Drama 1:20 B&W
☑ Adult situations, explicit language, violence
Dir: Wayne Wang   *Cast:* Wood Moy, Marc Hayashi, Laureen Chew, Judy Nihei, Peter Wang
▶ Critically acclaimed independent film from Chinese-American filmmaker Wang is quality delivered on a home-movie budget ($20,000). Mystery plot, concerning the search of two Chinese cabbies, older man Moy and his young nephew Hayashi, for a missing immigrant in San Francisco's Chinatown, explores the Chinese lifestyle in America.
Dist.: New Yorker

CHAPTER TWO 1979
★ ★ ★ ★ PG Comedy/Drama 2:04
☑ Adult situations, explicit language
Dir: Robert Moore   *Cast:* Marsha Mason, James Caan, Valerie Harper, Joseph Bologna

▶ Playwright Neil Simon adapted his autobiographical Broadway hit, taken from his own painful experiences after the death of his first wife. Caan plays a writer/widower racked with guilt when he falls in love with divorcée Mason. Oscar-nominated turn by Mason, who shines in a role based on her life (she was the second Mrs. Neil Simon). Her "I'm nuts about me" speech provides the film's emotional climax and has become a favored monologue of acting students. **(CC)**
Dist.: RCA/Columbia

CHARADE 1963
★ ★ ★ ★ **NR Mystery-Suspense 1:53**
Dir: Stanley Donen *Cast:* Cary Grant, Audrey Hepburn, Walter Matthau, James Coburn, George Kennedy
▶ In Paris, Hepburn finds herself caught up in intrigue when her husband is murdered. Can she trust the handsome but mysterious Grant who comes to her aid? Stylish and sparkling, with sleek direction by Donen, great Henry Mancini score, and plenty of romantic chemistry from the leads.
Dist.: MCA

CHARGE OF THE LIGHT BRIGADE, THE
1936
★ ★ ★ **NR Action-Adventure 1:56 B&W**
Dir: Michael Curtiz *Cast:* Errol Flynn, Olivia de Havilland, Patric Knowles, Donald Crisp, Henry Stephenson, Nigel Bruce
▶ In 1850s India, British major Flynn saves the life of an evil khan. When the khan orders the massacre of a British outpost, Flynn seeks revenge by leading his troops in a heroic but costly assault on the khan's men. Sweeping, action-packed adventure, loosely based on the Tennyson poem, is justly famed for its thundering climax. Max Steiner's rousing score was nominated for an Oscar. **(CC)**
Dist.: CBS/Fox ©

CHARIOTS OF FIRE 1981 British
★ ★ ★ ★ **PG Drama/Sports 2:03**
☑ Adult situations, explicit language
Dir: Hugh Hudson *Cast:* Ben Cross, Ian Charleson, Ian Holm, John Gielgud, Alice Krige, Cheryl Campbell, Lindsay Anderson, Patrick Magee, Nigel Davenport, Dennis Christopher, Brad Davis
▶ The true story of two British runners in the 1924 Olympics who were of disparate backgrounds but united in their desire to win—Harold Abrahams (Cross), a Jew driven by anti-Semitism, and Eric Liddell (Charleson), a Christian missionary who felt God's presence when he ran. Genuinely stirring, superbly filmed drama exquisitely re-creates the period. Oscars for Best Picture, Original Screenplay, Costume Design, and for Vangelis's stunning musical score.
Dist.: Warner

CHARLEY AND THE ANGEL 1973
★ ★ ★ **G Comedy 1:33**
Dir: Vincent McEveety *Cast:* Fred MacMur-

ray, Cloris Leachman, Harry Morgan, Kurt Russell, Kathleen Cody, Vincent Van Patten
▶ Pleasant Disney fantasy about Depression-era shopkeeper MacMurray, who neglects his family until angel Morgan warns him that his time on earth has expired. MacMurray's new devotion to home alarms his family, especially a son who's mixed up with the mob.
Dist.: Buena Vista

CHARLEY VARRICK 1973
★ ★ ★ **PG Action-Adventure 1:51**
☑ Adult situations, explicit language, violence
Dir: Don Siegel *Cast:* Walter Matthau, Joe Don Baker, Felicia Farr, Andy Robinson, John Vernon, Sheree North
▶ Small-time con Matthau and his partner Robinson mistakenly steal $750,000 from the Mafia; Matthau must find a way to return the money before sadistic hitman Baker finds him. Ingenious, hard-edged caper film has crisp pacing, brutal action sequences, and a wily performance from Matthau. Good example of director Siegel's flair with action pictures.
Dist.: MCA

CHARLIE CHAN AND THE CURSE OF THE DRAGON QUEEN 1981
★ ★ **PG Comedy 1:32**
☑ Adult situations, explicit language
Dir: Clive Donner *Cast:* Peter Ustinov, Lee Grant, Angie Dickinson, Richard Hatch, Brian Keith
▶ Veteran crime solver Charlie Chan (Ustinov) is called out of retirement to help the San Francisco police solve a mysterious series of murders. Accompanied by bumbling grandson Hatch, Chan encounters his old nemesis, the Dragon Queen (Dickinson). Comic mystery has nutty characters, broad performances, and nonstop slapstick.
Dist.: Media

CHARLIE CHAN AT THE OPERA 1936
★ ★ **NR Mystery-Suspense 1:06 B&W**
Dir: H. Bruce Humberstone *Cast:* Warner Oland, Boris Karloff, Keye Luke, Charlotte Henry, Thomas Beck, Margaret Irving
▶ Famous detective Charlie Chan (Oland) solves a puzzling mystery involving murder, amnesia, and imperious opera singer Karloff. Strong cast, good production values, and a musical interlude by Oscar Levant make this enjoyable for everyone; fans consider it one of the best in the series. **(CC)**
Dist.: Key

CHARLIE CHAN AT THE WAX MUSEUM
1940
★ **NR Mystery-Suspense 1:03 B&W**
Dir: Lynn Shores *Cast:* Sidney Toler, Sen Yung, C. Henry Gordon, Marc Lawrence, Joan Valerie
▶ Later Chan entry with Toler assaying the Earl Derr Biggers detective. With Number Two Son Yung, he hunts a killer hiding in a wax museum's chamber of horrors. More jokes than

chills in this middling example of the long-running series. **(CC)**
Dist.: Key

CHARLIE, THE LONESOME COUGAR 1968
★ ★ ★ ★ NR Family 1:15
Dir: Winston Hibler *Cast:* Ron Brown, Brian Russell, Linda Wallace, Jim Wilson
▶ A lumberjack in the Pacific Northwest adopts Charlie, an orphaned cougar cub who stirs up so much trouble around the logging camp that he's caged. The lumberjack realizes Charlie belongs in the wild, and takes him on a long journey into the wilderness. Another fine Disney animal adventure with good photography and a remarkable performance by Charlie. Narrated by Rex Allen.
Dist.: Buena Vista

CHARLOTTE'S WEB 1973
★ ★ ★ ★ ★ G Animation 1:34
Dir: Charles A. Nichols, Iwao Takamoto
Cast: Voices of Debbie Reynolds, Paul Lynde, Henry Gibson, Charles Nelson Reilly
▶ Wilbur is a runt pig slated for the slaughterhouse until his spider friend Charlotte weaves words into her web to convince a superstitious farmer that Wilbur is a miraculous hog. Charming animated musical from E. B. White's beloved children's classic. Bouncy score by Robert B. Sherman and Richard M. Sherman.
Dist.: Paramount

CHARLY 1968
★ ★ ★ ★ PG Drama 1:43
☑ Nudity, adult situations, explicit language
Dir: Ralph Nelson *Cast:* Cliff Robertson, Claire Bloom, Lilia Skala, Leon Janney, Dick Van Patten
▶ Retarded Robertson is turned into a genius by a scientific experiment. He knows a brief period of happiness with teacher Bloom before the process begins to reverse. Some story contrivances and overly busy camerawork but Robertson is moving and poignant in his Oscar-winning role. Based on *Flowers for Algernon* by Daniel Keyes.
Dist.: CBS/Fox

CHARRO! 1969
★ G Western 1:38
Dir: Charles Marquis Warren *Cast:* Elvis Presley, Ina Balin, Victor French, Lynn Kellogg, Barbara Werle, Paul Brinegar
▶ Ex-bandit Presley is kidnapped by a gang of his former criminal cohorts. Their plan is to use him as the scapegoat for the theft of a valuable gold and silver cannon. The King's singing voice is heard only over the credits in this dismally scripted howler.
Dist.: Warner

CHASE, THE 1966
★ ★ NR Drama 2:15
Dir: Arthur Penn *Cast:* Marlon Brando, Jane Fonda, Robert Redford, E. G. Marshall, Angie Dickinson, Janice Rule, Miriam Hopkins, Martha Hyer, Robert Duvall
▶ Overblown melodrama examines the reactions of small-town citizens to the jailbreak of Redford, a local boy imprisoned on false charges. As he tries to join girlfriend Fonda, corrupt banker Marshall encourages a drunken posse to kill him. Upright sheriff Brando is the only man on Redford's side. Lillian Hellman's adaptation of a Horton Foote novel was disowned by director Penn.
Dist.: RCA/Columbia

CHATTAHOOCHIE 1990
★ ★ R Drama 1:37
☑ Adult situations, explicit language, violence
Dir: Mick Jackson *Cast:* Gary Oldman, Dennis Hopper, Frances McDormand, Pamela Reed, M. Emmet Walsh, Ned Beatty
▶ Korean war vet Oldman, unable to adjust to peacetime Florida, botches a suicide attempt. He is institutionalized in the Chattahoochie State Mental Hospital, where conditions are so brutal he is inspired to study law to fight for reforms. Realistic portrayal of hellish milieu is difficult to take, but film's ultimate effect is inspiring. Excellent performances led by Oldman and Reed as his sister. Based on a true story. **(CC)**
Dist.: HBO

CHATTANOOGA CHOO CHOO 1984
★ ★ ★ PG Comedy 1:42
☑ Adult situations, explicit language
Dir: Bruce Bilson *Cast:* George Kennedy, Barbara Eden, Joe Namath, Tony Azito, Melissa Sue Anderson, Clu Gulager
▶ Football team owner Kennedy can inherit one million tax free dollars from his father-in-law if he restores the old man's favorite train and makes a 24-hour Chattanooga-to-New York run. Cheerleaders, players, coach Namath, and Kennedy's chief rival Gulager are along for the ride in this cornball comedy in the tradition of *Harper Valley PTA*.
Dist.: HBO

CHEAP DETECTIVE, THE 1978
★ ★ ★ PG Comedy 1:32
☑ Explicit language
Dir: Robert Moore *Cast:* Peter Falk, Ann-Margret, Madeline Kahn, Marsha Mason, Eileen Brennan, Louise Fletcher, James Coco, Fernando Lamas
▶ Neil Simon's follow-up to *Murder By Death*. Falk reprises his Bogart-like character in a parody plot that involves a *Maltese Falcon*–like search for a dozen diamond eggs and a *Casablanca*-like love triangle. High-spirited fun will please film buffs and Simon fans alike. Fletcher and Lamas (in the Ingrid Bergman and Paul Henried parts) are standouts in an all-star comic cast.
Dist.: RCA/Columbia

CHEAPER TO KEEP HER 1980
★ ★ ★ R Comedy 1:31
☑ Strong sexual content, explicit language
Dir: Ken Annakin *Cast:* Mac Davis, Tovah

Feldshuh, Rose Marie, Jack Gilford, Priscilla Lopez, Ian McShane
▶ Sex comedy about recently divorced detective Davis who is hired by tough attorney Feldshuh to track down men who've lapsed in their alimony payments. Davis's on-the-job adventures include wooing Feldshuh's secretary Lopez and investigating her ex-husband McShane before he ends up with the lady lawyer. Basically a raunchy sitcom. ✏
Dist.: Media

CHECK AND DOUBLE CHECK 1930
☆ **NR Comedy 1:17 B&W**
Dir: Melville Brown *Cast:* Freeman Gosden, Charles Correll, Sue Carol, Charles Morton, Irene Rich, Duke Ellington and His Orchestra
▶ In their only feature film, blackface performers Gosden and Correll portray famous radio and TV characters Amos 'n' Andy, who get mixed up in comic complications when they drive Ellington and his band to a party. Early sound comedy is stilted and uncomfortably racist, although the music is good.
Dist.: Video Yesteryear

CHECKING OUT 1989
★ ★ **R Comedy 1:33**
☑ Nudity, adult situations, explicit language
Dir: David Leland *Cast:* Jeff Daniels, Melanie Mayron, Michael Tucker, Kathleen York, Allan Havey, Ann Magnuson
▶ When his friend Havey suddenly drops dead, airline executive Daniels has a major attack of hypochondria, driving wife Mayron nuts with his conviction he's next to die. It may be a self-fulfilling prophecy as his life starts resembling Havey's. Frenetic comedy fails to squeeze much humor from its one joke.
Dist.: Virgin

CHECK IS IN THE MAIL, THE 1986
★ ★ **R Comedy 1:23**
☑ Brief nudity, adult situations, explicit language
Dir: Joan Darling *Cast:* Brian Dennehy, Anne Archer, Hallie Todd, Chris Hebert, Michael Bowen
▶ Pharmacist Dennehy, having trouble making ends meet for wife Archer and their three kids, declares war on the system. He rips up his credit cards, cancels his automobile insurance, and converts his family to *Whole Earth Catalog*-style living, even to the point of raising chickens to provide eggs. Sitcom-type humor.
Dist.: Media

CHEECH & CHONG'S NEXT MOVIE 1980
★ ★ ★ **R Comedy 1:35**
☑ Nudity, explicit language, adult humor
Dir: Thomas Chong *Cast:* Cheech Marin, Thomas Chong, Evelyn Guerrero, Betty Kennedy, Sy Dramer
▶ Usual dose of silly routines and irreverent "dope humor" for the Chino-Latino duo's many fans. They roll a lot of illegal herb and

wind up at a massage parlor. Predictable but fun.
Dist.: MCA

CHEECH & CHONG'S NICE DREAMS 1981
★ ★ **R Comedy 1:27**
☑ Nudity, explicit language, adult humor
Dir: Thomas Chong *Cast:* Cheech Marin, Thomas Chong, Evelyn Guerrero, Stacy Keach, Timothy Leary
▶ Their third film has "Los Guys" amassing a stash of dinero by dealing drugs out of an ice cream truck. Keach keeps a watchful eye over them as their narcotics agent/boss hooked on the weed. Leary appears as himself, dispensing little pills at an insane asylum. Fans should have a snorting good time.
Dist.: RCA/Columbia

CHEECH & CHONG'S THE CORSICAN BROTHERS 1984
★ **PG Comedy 1:30**
☑ Explicit language, violence, adult humor
Dir: Thomas Chong *Cast:* Cheech Marin, Thomas Chong, Roy Dotrice, Shelby Fiddis, Rikki Marin
▶ Cheech and Chong are a couple of American musicians paid *not* to play on the streets of Paris in this takeoff of the Dumas tale about twins separated at birth but spiritually linked. Not one reference to marijuana, but plenty of other jokes about women, bodily functions, and minorities.
Dist.: Vestron

CHEERS FOR MISS BISHOP 1941
★ ★ **NR Drama 1:35 B&W**
Dir: Tay Garnett *Cast:* Martha Scott, William Gargan, Sterling Holloway, Edmund Gwenn, Sidney Blackmer, Mary Anderson
▶ Well-turned tale of fifty years in life of nineteenth-century midwestern schoolteacher Scott. Two frustrated romances leave her unmarried, so she devotes herself with a passion to educating young minds. Female equivalent to *Goodbye, Mr. Chips*.
Dist.: KVC

CHEETAH 1989
★ ★ ★ ★ **G Family 1:23**
Dir: Jeff Blyth *Cast:* Keith Coogan, Lucy Deakins, Collin Mothupi, Timothy Landfield, Breon Gorman
▶ American teens Coogan and Deakins residing in Kenya adopt baby cheetah Duma and raise her, but realize they must eventually teach her to live in the wild. When Duma is kidnapped to be entered in the racing circuit, they set off to rescue her. Flat Disney fare lacks adventure and a charming enough animal star to appeal to adults. The very young will forgive its shortcomings.
Dist.: Buena Vista

CHERRY 2000 1987
★ ★ **PG-13 Fantasy 1:38**
☑ Brief nudity, adult situations, explicit language, violence

Dir: Steve DeJarnatt *Cast:* Melanie Griffith, David Andrews, Ben Johnson, Tim Thomerson, Pamela Gidley
▶ Futuristic fable of young Andrews who must cross a deadly wasteland to replace his sexy robot wife's malfunctioned chassis. Griffith is great as a daredevil heroine who refuses to wear a crash helmet because it messes up her hair. Mock-sexist and slyly funny fantasy comic strip is a hoot. (CC)
Dist.: Orion

CHEYENNE AUTUMN 1964
★★★ NR Western 2:34
Dir: John Ford *Cast:* Richard Widmark, Carroll Baker, James Stewart, Edward G. Robinson, Karl Malden, Ricardo Montalban, Dolores Del Rio, Sal Mineo, Gilbert Roland
▶ The Cheyenne Indians make a journey to protest their treatment by the white man, only to be pursued by the U.S. cavalry (led by Widmark). Sincere revisionism from, of all people, John Ford. Indians, often the bad guys in his classic Wayne westerns, are here treated with the utmost sympathy and respect.
Dist.: Warner

CHEYENNE SOCIAL CLUB, THE 1970
★★★★ PG Western/Comedy 1:43
☑ Adult situations, explicit language
Dir: Gene Kelly *Cast:* James Stewart, Henry Fonda, Shirley Jones, Sue Ane Langdon, Elaine Devry, Robert Middleton
▶ Cowpoke Stewart and buddy Fonda leave the trail to inspect Stewart's inheritance, the title social club. They are nonplussed when the club turns out to be a brothel. Straitlaced Stewart tries to sell the house while Fonda takes advantage of the situation. Two pros bring some life to tired script.
Dist.: Warner

CHICKEN CHRONICLES, THE 1977
★★★ PG Comedy 1:34
☑ Brief nudity, adult situations, explicit language
Dir: Francis Simon *Cast:* Phil Silvers, Ed Lauter, Steve Guttenberg, Lisa Reeves, Meredith Baer
▶ In a Beverly Hills high school, circa the late 1960s, senior Guttenberg faces problems with the principal, his job at a take-out chicken joint, absentee parents, Vietnam, drugs, and especially sex. Pleasant coming-of-age story is attractively cast and mounted. Silvers overacts amusingly. Guttenberg's film debut.
Dist.: Nelson

CHILD IS WAITING, A 1963
★★★ NR Drama 1:44 B&W
Dir: John Cassavetes *Cast:* Burt Lancaster, Judy Garland, Gena Rowlands, Steven Hill, Bruce Ritchey, Gloria McGehee
▶ Lancaster runs an institution for the mentally retarded, trying to be evenhanded in emotionally charged situations. Teacher Garland must cope with her inclination to favor one particular student. Using actual handicapped children as extras, director Cassavetes unevenly mixes documentry-style footage with plot and improvisation. Results are occasionally powerful.
Dist.: MGM/UA

CHILDREN, THE 1980
★ R Horror 1:31
☑ Adult situations, explicit language, violence
Dir: Max Kalmanowicz *Cast:* Martin Shakar, Gil Rogers, Gale Garnett, Jesse Abrams
▶ Little darlings become deadly brats after their schoolbus is contaminated by radiation. The kids go on the rampage, menacing their parents, the townspeople, and anyone else who gets in their way. Genre fans may like the display of severed limbs.
Dist.: Vestron

CHILDREN OF A LESSER GOD 1986
★★★★ R Drama 1:56
☑ Nudity, adult situations, explicit language
Dir: Randa Haines *Cast:* William Hurt, Marlee Matlin, Piper Laurie, Philip Bosco, Allison Gompf
▶ Tender, beautifully crafted drama of the romance between Hurt, a teacher at a school for the deaf, and Matlin, a rebellious deaf student who refuses to learn how to speak. Completely convincing and moving without being excessively sentimental. Wonderfully acted by the Oscar-nominated Hurt. Matlin, deaf in real life, deservedly won the Oscar for her complex, poignant, and charismatic performance. Also nominated for Best Picture. From Mark Medoff's Tony-winning play. (CC)
Dist.: Paramount

CHILDREN OF PARADISE 1945 French
★★ NR Drama 3:08 B&W
Dir: Marcel Carne *Cast:* Arletty, Jean-Louis Barrault, Pierre Brasseur, Marcel Harrand, Pierre Renoir, Maria Casares
▶ In nineteenth-century Paris, mime Barrault and his comedian friend Brasseur both fall for Arletty, the theater's leading actress, but she chooses wealth over love by becoming a count's mistress. Monumental drama of doomed romance has exquisite acting, shimmering photography, and heartbreaking script by Jacques Prévert. Shot under extraordinary circumstances during the Nazi occupation, and often acclaimed as the greatest French film ever made. [S]
Dist.: Various

CHILDREN OF THE CORN 1984
★★ R Horror 1:33
☑ Explicit language, graphic violence
Dir: Fritz Kiersch *Cast:* Peter Horton, Linda Hamilton, R. G. Armstrong, John Franklin, Courtney Gains, Robby Kiger
▶ Cross-country travelers Horton and Hamilton find themselves menaced in Nebraska town where child Franklin leads killer-kid cult bent on slaughtering adults. Hamilton is kidnapped and Horton must resuce her. Taut,

bloodthirsty shocker is based on the short story by Stephen King.
Dist.: Nelson

CHILD'S PLAY 1988
★ ★ ★ R Horror 1:28
☑ Explicit language, violence
Dir: Tom Holland   *Cast:* Catherine Hicks, Chris Sarandon, Brad Dourif, Alex Vincent, Dinah Manoff, Tommy Swerdlow
▶ Widowed working mom Hicks gives six-year-old son Vincent a "Good Guy" doll for his birthday, unaware that the doll possesses the soul of deceased murderer Dourif. When Vincent's new pal "Chucky" runs amok, no one except the kid believes the demon doll is responsible until it's too late. Sarandon plays the homicide detective who finds himself in pursuit of a toy in this well-crafted spine-tingler.
Dist.: MGM/UA

CHILLY SCENES OF WINTER 1979
★ ★ PG Drama 1:37
☑ Adult situations, explicit language
Dir: Joan Micklin Silver   *Cast:* John Heard, Mary Beth Hurt, Peter Riegert, Kenneth McMillan, Gloria Grahame
▶ Heard, a Salt Lake City civil servant, falls in love with Hurt, just separated from her husband. His passion is so overwhelming that she flees to her family—but Heard still won't give up. Quirky, low-key comedy/drama has a brilliant cameo by Grahame (as Heard's suicidal mother). Adapted from the novel by Ann Beattie, and originally released as *Head Over Heels*.
Dist.: MGM/UA

CHIMES AT MIDNIGHT 1967 Spanish/Swiss
☆ NR Drama 1:55 B&W
Dir: Orson Welles   *Cast:* Orson Welles, Keith Baxter, John Gielgud, Margaret Rutherford, Jeanne Moreau, Norman Rodway
▶ Period drama combines several Shakespeare plays (primarily the two parts of *Henry IV*) to tell story of Prince Hal (Baxter), who outgrows carousing with tubby drinking buddy Falstaff (Welles) to assume mantle of leadership on and off the battlefield. Welles gives a poignant performance and his highly stylized battle scenes are a visual treat. However, dubbing detracts from impact. Also known as *Falstaff*.
Dist.: HBO

CHINA GATE 1957
★ ★ ★ NR Action-Adventure 1:36 B&W
Dir: Samuel Fuller   *Cast:* Gene Barry, Angie Dickinson, Nat King Cole, Lee Van Cleef, Marcel Dalio
▶ In Vietnam, adventurer Barry, his estranged wife Dickinson, and fellow American Cole join a group of Frenchmen in a mission against the Chinese Communists. Hollywood's first look at Vietnam conflict features slambang action (if not complex political analysis) from writer/director Fuller. Cole sings the title tune.
Dist.: Republic

CHINA GIRL 1987
★ ★ R Drama 1:28
☑ Adult situations, explicit language, violence
Dir: Abel Ferrara   *Cast:* James Russo, Sari Chang, Richard Panebianco, David Caruso, Russell Wong
▶ Love affair between young pizza shop worker Panebianco and Chang, a beautiful Chinese teenager, leads to war between Italian and Chinese gangs. The tragedy is played out on the nightclub dance floors and alleyways of New York's Little Italy and Chinatown. Russo is convincing as the hero's older brother, and director Ferrara brings a gritty realism to this modern-day *Romeo and Juliet*. Soundtrack includes Run-D.M.C. and David Johansen.
Dist.: Vestron

CHINA SEAS 1935
★ ★ ★ NR Drama 1:30 B&W
Dir: Tay Garnett   *Cast:* Clark Gable, Jean Harlow, Wallace Beery, Lewis Stone, Rosalind Russell, Robert Benchley
▶ Contrived but highly enjoyable adventure aboard a liner between Shanghai and Singapore, with Gable as a valiant captain battling pirates led by Beery and choosing between English aristocrat Russell and spunky dancehall girl Harlow. Slick, action-filled story may not make much sense, but the stars are wonderful.
Dist.: MGM/UA

CHINA SKY 1945
★ NR War 1:18 B&W
Dir: Ray Enright   *Cast:* Randolph Scott, Ruth Warrick, Ellen Drew, Anthony Quinn, Carol Thurston, Richard Loo
▶ Scott attempts to extend his dramatic range as an American doctor in the Pacific during World War II. He deals with Japanese attacks and becomes close to colleague Warrick while wife Drew casts a jealous shadow. Soapy adaptation of the Pearl Buck novel fails to deliver required impact or emotion.
Dist.: Turner

CHINA SYNDROME, THE 1979
★ ★ ★ ★ ★ PG Drama 2:02
☑ Explicit language
Dir: James Bridges   *Cast:* Jane Fonda, Jack Lemmon, Michael Douglas, Scott Brady, James Hampton, Wilford Brimley
▶ Thrilling account of neophyte TV reporter Fonda, who digs up evidence that a nuclear power plant may have structural flaws. When the plant owners start a cover-up, she has to convince conscientious engineer Lemmon to break ranks and speak out about the danger. Realistic, hard-hitting drama scores points against TV news as well as nuclear power. Lemmon and Fonda both won Oscar nominations, as did the screenplay. **(CC)**
Dist.: RCA/Columbia

CHINATOWN 1974
★★★★ **R Drama 2:11**
[✓] Adult situations, explicit language, violence
Dir: Roman Polanski *Cast:* Jack Nicholson, Faye Dunaway, John Huston, Perry Lopez, John Hillerman, Diane Ladd, Burt Young
► Haunting, beautifully realized mystery set in 1930s Los Angeles. Nicholson is superb as J. J. Gittes, a private eye drawn into a case much larger than he can handle. He finds himself protecting Dunaway, an enigmatic widow who may be responsible for a murder. In an excellent cast, Huston stands out as a genial millionaire who hires Gittes to find his granddaughter. Director Polanski has a memorable cameo as a vicious thug. Influential film received eleven Oscar nominations, winning for Robert Towne's screenplay. Nicholson directed sequel *The Two Jakes* sixteen years later.
Dist.: Paramount

CHINATOWN CONNECTION, THE 1989
★ **NR Martial Arts 1:36**
[✓] Explicit language, violence
Dir: Jean-Paul Ouellette *Cast:* Bruce Ly, Lee Majors II, Pat McCormick, Fitz Houston, Art Camacho, William Ghent
► Maverick L.A. cop Majors is assigned by superior McCormick to team with Ly. Majors joins Ly's elite group known as the "kung fu" police squad and they investigate poisoned coke ring. The trail leads to kingpin Ghent. Macho martial arts action has Ly emulating moves of late Bruce Lee. Majors II is son of Lee Majors.
Dist.: Southgate

CHINESE CONNECTION, THE 1973 Chinese
★★ **R Martial Arts 1:47**
[✓] Explicit language, violence
Dir: Lo Wei *Cast:* Bruce Lee, Miao Ker Hsio, James Tien, Robert Baker
► When his martial arts teacher is murdered, Lee searches through turn-of-the-century Shanghai for the killers. At the same time he faces challenge from Japanese fighters who claim they're superior to Chinese martial arts experts. Apart from obvious dubbing, an excellent showcase for the charismatic Lee.
Dist.: CBS/Fox

CHINO 1973 Italian
★★ **PG Western 1:38**
[✓] Adult situatins, explicit language, violence
Dir: John Sturges *Cast:* Charles Bronson, Jill Ireland, Vincent Van Patten, Marcel Bozzuffi, Melissa Chimenti, Fausto Tozzi
► Downbeat Western about poor New Mexican horse breeder Bronson, who falls in love with Ireland, the sister of wealthy rancher Bozzuffi. Van Patten is a teenage runaway befriended by Bronson. Uncharacteristic role for Bronson, who rejects revenge for peace. His scenes with wife Ireland are subtly erotic.
Dist.: Warner

CHIPMUNK ADVENTURE, A 1987
★★★ **G Animation 1:16**
Dir: Janice Karman *Cast:* Voices of Dody Goodman, Ross Bagdasarian, Jr., Susan Tyrrell
► While their master is away on a business trip, Chipmunks Alvin, Simon, and Theodore are unwittingly duped into being diamond smugglers as they compete against the Chipettes in an around-the-world balloon race. Children will find this highly entertaining despite the simplistic animation. Charming Chipmunks sing "Wooly Bully" and "Quanido Le Guesto." (CC)
Dist.: Warner

CHISUM 1970
★★★★ **G Western 1:51**
Dir: Andrew V. McLaglen *Cast:* John Wayne, Forrest Tucker, Christopher George, Ben Johnson, Glenn Corbett, Geoffrey Deuel
► Quality Western, loosely based on the 1878 Lincoln County land wars, with Wayne playing real-life cattle baron John Chisum. The Duke locks horns with Tucker, a wealthy crook stealing land from farmers. Wayne gets steady support from Johnson as his foreman, but the younger stars (Corbett as Pat Garrett, Deuel as Billy the Kid, George as bounty hunter Dan Nodeen) take up most of the story. Country-and-western star Merle Haggard sings two ballads.
Dist.: Warner

CHITTY CHITTY BANG BANG 1968
★★★★ **G Musical/Family 2:36**
Dir: Ken Hughes *Cast:* Dick Van Dyke, Sally Ann Howes, Lionel Jeffries, Gert Frobe, Benny Hill
► Lavish children's musical based on the novel by Ian Fleming. Van Dyke is a tinkerer and widowed father of two who invents a magical flying car coveted by evil king Frobe. Songs by Richard M. Sherman and Robert B. Sherman include the title tune, "Truly Scrumptious," and "Hushabye Mountain."
Dist.: MGM

CHLOE IN THE AFTERNOON 1972 French
☆ **R Comedy 1:37**
[✓] Brief nudity, adult situations, explicit language
Dir: Eric Rohmer *Cast:* Bernard Verley, Zouzou, Francoise Verley, Daniel Ceccaldi
► Happily married Verley gets involved with bohemian Zouzou. The films of Rohmer are not for everyone, certainly, but patient viewers will be rewarded with insight into human nature and relationships. Deceptively simple camerawork, well-crafted dialogue, and small-scale story add up to the cinematic equivalent of a fine miniature. [S]
Dist.: Media

CHOCOLAT 1989 French
☆ **PG-13 Drama 1:45**

☑ Brief nudity, adult situations, explicit language
Dir: Claire Denis *Cast:* Isaach de Bankolé, Giulia Boschi, François Cluzet, Cécile Ducasse, Mireille Perrier
▶ Traveling in Cameroon, where she was raised, France (Perrier) remembers her childhood. Her beautiful, lonely mother Boschi fights to contain her passion for the family's dignified, but aloof, black servant de Bankolé, who proves little France's (Ducasse) only friend. Beautifully realized and photographed. Subtle details carry lots of emotional power, but may not be for all audiences. [S]
Dist.: Orion

CHOCOLATE SOLDIER, THE 1941
★ NR Musical 1:42 B&W
Dir: Roy Del Ruth *Cast:* Nelson Eddy, Rise Stevens, Nigel Bruce, Florence Bates, Dorothy Gilmore, Nydia Westman
▶ Viennese operetta star Eddy tests wife Stevens's fidelity by disguising himself as a Russian and wooing her. She sees through the ruse and torments him in this pleasant remake of Molnar's *The Guardsman.* A few tunes from Oscar Strauss's original operetta remain; other songs include "While My Lady Sleeps" and "Song of the Flea."
Dist.: MGM/UA

CHOCOLATE WAR, THE 1989
★★ R Drama 1:40
☑ Adult situations, explicit language, violence
Dir: Keith Gordon *Cast:* John Glover, Ilan Mitchell-Smith, Wally Ward, Doug Hutchinson, Adam Baldwin, Brent Fraser
▶ At a rigid Catholic boys' high school, freshman Mitchell-Smith is tyrannized by dictatorial teachers and bullied by a secret club of students led by Ward. Ambitious teacher Glover, hoping for promotion to headmaster, seeks to double the quota of chocolates sold by each boy during the annual fund-raiser; Ward and his clique compel Mitchell-Smith to refuse Glover's demands. Well-crafted but bleak adaptation of Robert Cormier novel. Writing/directing debut for actor Gordon.
Dist.: Virgin

CHOICE OF ARMS 1983 French
★★ NR Action-Adventure 1:57
☑ Explicit language, graphic violence
Dir: Alain Corneau *Cast:* Yves Montand, Gerard Depardieu, Catherine Deneuve, Michel Galabru
▶ Tense crime thriller about retired gangster Montand, whose rural life is upset by young psychopath Depardieu. Unable to turn to the police, Montand must reenter the underworld and kill Depardieu to protect wife Deneuve. Rich characterizations, with Depardieu especially striking as a mad-dog killer. [S]
Dist.: Media

CHOIRBOYS, THE 1977
★★★★ R Action-Adventure 1:59
☑ Brief nudity, adult situations, explicit language
Dir: Robert Aldrich *Cast:* Charles Durning, Louis Gossett, Jr., Perry King, Clyde Kasatsu, Stephen Macht, Tim McIntire, Randy Quaid, Don Stroud, James Woods, Blair Brown, Vic Tayback, Burt Young
▶ Raunchy comedy/drama about L.A. cops who relieve tension by holding wild "choir practice" sex-and-booze parties in MacArthur Park. Story follows ten different choirboys on and off duty. Young (as a grubby vice squad sergeant) stands out in an enormous cast. Based on Joseph Waumbaugh's best-seller.
Dist.: MCA

CHOKE CANYON 1986
★★★ PG Action-Adventure 1:34
☑ Explicit language, violence
Dir: Chuck Bail *Cast:* Stephen Collins, Janet Julian, Lance Henriksen, Bo Svenson, Victoria Racimo
▶ Physicist Collins, developing a new form of clean energy in Choke Canyon, learns that an evil conglomerate is dumping nuclear waste on the site of his experiments. When he threatens to expose the crime, ruthless hitman Svenson is hired to silence him. Fast-paced genre picture features an exciting dogfight between a plane and a futuristic helicopter.
Dist.: Media

C.H.O.M.P.S. 1979
★★★★ G Comedy 1:29
Dir: Don Chaffey *Cast:* Wesley Eure, Valerie Bertinelli, Conrad Bain, Chuck McCann, Red Buttons, Jim Backus
▶ Eure plays a young inventor whose latest project, C.H.O.M.P.S. (the Canine Home Protection System, a Benji-like mechanical guard dog), is the target of bumbling crooks McCann and Buttons. The robot dog saves the day and smoothes the way for a romance between Eure and Bertinelli, his boss's daughter. Younger viewers should love the adorable dog star.
Dist.: Warner

CHOOSE ME 1984
★ R Drama 1:46
☑ Adult situations, explicit language
Dir: Alan Rudolph *Cast:* Genevieve Bujold, Keith Carradine, Lesley Ann Warren, Patrick Bauchau, Rae Dawn Chong, John Larroquette
▶ Offbeat mixture of comedy and drama takes a romantic, stylized look at the love affairs of three unusual loners: radio talk show sex therapist Bujold, womanizing mental patient Carradine, and vulnerable bar owner Warren. Top-notch ensemble acting, wonderful Teddy Pendergrass score, and unpredictable plotting and directing make this a treat for sophisticated viewers.
Dist.: Media

CHOPPING MALL 1986
☆ R Horror 1:16
☑ Nudity, adult situations, explicit lan-
guage, graphic violence
Dir: Jim Wynorski *Cast:* Kelli Maroney, Tony
O'Dell, John Terlesky, Russell Todd, Paul Bar-
tel, Mary Woronov
▶ Eight teenagers are trapped overnight in a
Los Angeles shopping mall guarded by de-
mented, murderous robots. Can they fight
their way out? Campy slasher film played for
laughs is filled with in-jokes and references to
other films (Bartel and Woronov repeat their
Eating Raoul roles).
Dist.: Vestron

CHORUS LINE, A 1985
★ ★ ★ PG-13 Musical 1:53
☑ Explicit language
Dir: Richard Attenborough *Cast:* Michael
Douglas, Terrence Mann, Alyson Reed, Vicki
Frederick, Nicole Fosse, Matt West, Audrey
Landers, Janet Jones
▶ Big-budget adaptation of Broadway's
longest-running musical examines aspiring
dancers auditioning for demanding choreographer Douglas. Through songs and solilo-
quies the anonymous "gypsies" reveal their
secret hopes and fears. The Pulitzer prize–winning play is essentially transferred intact, although composers Marvin Hamlisch and Edward Kleban added Oscar-nominated
"Surprise, Surprise" to the score. Inherently theatrical experience was a major box office disappointment on film. **(CC)**
Dist.: Nelson

CHORUS OF DISAPPROVAL, A 1989 British
★ PG Comedy 1:39
☑ Adult situations
Dir: Michael Winner *Cast:* Jeremy Irons, Anthony Hopkins, Prunella Scales, Patsy Kensit,
Lionel Jeffries, Jenny Seagrove
▶ Timid Irons, transferred to small town by his
company, joins local amateur opera troupe
and finds himself having affairs with Scales,
the wife of director Hopkins, and Seagrove. A
fine cast manages to find some humor in unsympathetic characters. Adaptation of an
Alan Ayckbourn play gets heavy-handed direction from Winner.
Dist.: Southgate

CHOSEN, THE 1978 Italian/British
★ ★ ★ ★ R Horror 1:45
☑ Brief nudity, graphic violence
Dir: Alberto De Martino *Cast:* Kirk Douglas,
Simon Ward, Agostina Belli, Anthony
Quayle, Virginia McKenna, Alexander Knox
▶ While financing a chain of nuclear fission
reactors, industrialist Douglas discovers that
son Ward has designed structural flaws into
the plants—turning them into atom bombs.
When Douglas tries to stop the project, he
learns he's dealing with the Antichrist. Violent,

derivative horror story was based on the Book
of Revelations. Also known as *Holocaust 2000*.
Dist.: Vestron

CHOSEN, THE 1982
★ ★ ★ PG Drama 1:48
☑ Adult situations, mild violence
Dir: Jeremy Paul Kagan *Cast:* Maximilian
Schell, Rod Steiger, Robby Benson, Barry
Miller, Hildy Brooks, Ron Rifkin
▶ Warm, moving adaptation of Chaim
Potok's novel has a simple story line: 1940s
Jewish-American boys—Hasidic Benson and
liberal Miller—become friends in Brooklyn.
Miller is amazed at Benson's strict Hasidic life;
Benson's father Steiger, a rabbi, worries that
his son may be corrupted by nonsectarians.
Religious themes are handled with sincerity
and taste, and insights into friendship and fa-
ther-son relationships have universal appeal.
Dist.: CBS/Fox

CHRISTIAN THE LION 1976 British
★ ★ ★ G Family 1:29
Dir: Bill Travers *Cast:* Bill Travers, Virginia
McKenna, George Adamson, Terence
Adamson
▶ Spouses Travers and McKenna of *Born Free*
fame reunite with wildlife expert George
Adamson (whom Travers portrayed in the
enormously popular film) in this docudrama
about the arduous journey of Christian the
lion. Like Elsa the lioness, Christian was born in
civilization and has to be reacclimated to the
wild. Stars play themselves, in addition to taking turns narrating. Not up the inspiration's
standards, but solid family entertainment
nonetheless.
Dist.: United

CHRISTINE 1983
★ ★ R Horror 1:50
☑ Adult situations, explicit language, violence
Dir: John Carpenter *Cast:* Keith Gordon,
John Stockwell, Alexandra Paul, Robert
Prosky, Harry Dean Stanton
▶ Gordon, a social outcast at school, devotes
all his time to renovating a 1958 Plymouth Fury
named Christine. Best friend Stockwell tries to
warn him that something's wrong with the car,
but the evil spirit possessing the Fury is more
dangerous than they anticipated. Slick adaptation of the Stephen King best-seller has a
good soundtrack showcasing Christine's favorite 1950s rock 'n' roll hits. **(CC)**
Dist.: RCA/Columbia

CHRISTMAS CAROL, A 1938
★ ★ ★ NR Drama/Family 1:09 B&W
Dir: Edwin L. Marin *Cast:* Reginald Owen,
Gene Lockhart, Kathleen Lockhart, Terry Kil-
burn, Leo G. Carroll, Lionel Braham, Ann
Rutherford, Lynne Carver, Barry MacKay
▶ Fine adaptation of the Charles Dickens
classic is a bit more subdued than the 1951
version. Owen gives a measured performance
as the miser whose life is transformed by en-

counters with three ghosts. Strong supporting cast and superb production values add to the enjoyment.
Dist.: MGM/UA Ⓒ

CHRISTMAS CAROL, A 1951 British
★ ★ ★ ★ **NR Drama/Family 1:26 B&W**
Dir: Brian Desmond Hurst   *Cast:* Alastair Sim, Kathleen Harrison, Jack Warner, Michael Hordern, Mervyn Johns, Hermione Baddeley
► Marvelous version of the Charles Dickens tale features Sim in one of his best roles as the tightfisted Scrooge. Encounters with three ghosts on Christmas Eve lead him to confront his own mortality. Strong supporting cast and good use of period detail add to the film's charm. Perennial Christmas favorite lives up to its reputation as a classic. **(CC)**
Dist.: VCI

CHRISTMAS IN CONNECTICUT 1945
★ ★ ★ **NR Comedy 1:41 B&W**
Dir: Peter Godfrey   *Cast:* Barbara Stanwyck, Dennis Morgan, Sydney Greenstreet, Reginald Gardiner, S. Z. Sakall
► Stanwyck, a magazine housekeeping expert, is coerced by editor Greenstreet into bringing war hero Morgan home to her family for the holidays. Unfortunately, Stanwyck doesn't have a home, or a family, and she doesn't know the first thing about housekeeping—but she learns plenty before Greenstreet arrives for dinner. Bright farce has plenty of slapstick to top off its warm holiday mood.
Dist.: MGM

CHRISTMAS IN JULY 1940
★ ★ ★ **NR Comedy 1:07 B&W**
Dir: Preston Sturges   *Cast:* Dick Powell, Ellen Drew, William Demarest, Franklin Pangborn, Raymond Walburn, Ernest Truex, Alan Bridge
► Powell, a struggling but ambitious clerk, enters a coffee slogan contest with a slogan that even fiancée Drew doesn't understand ("If you can't sleep at night, it isn't the coffee, it's the bunk"). When co-workers fool him into thinking he's won, he goes on a spending spree. Merry take on the American Dream from writer/director Sturges.
Dist.: MCA

CHRISTMAS STORY, A 1983
★ ★ ★ ★ **PG Comedy 1:33**
☑ Explicit language
Dir: Bob Clark   *Cast:* Melinda Dillon, Peter Billingsley, Darren McGavin, Ian Petrella, Scott Schwartz
► Imaginative, nostalgic look at Christmas in the 1940s has the feel of a future classic. Adaptation of Jean Shepherd's humorous recollections of the Midwest is primarily about a young boy's obsession for a Red Ryder BB gun, but the film's real successes are its sharply observed vignettes about small-town family life. Nightmarish visit to a department store Santa Claus is one of many highlights.
Dist.: MGM/UA

CHRISTMAS THAT ALMOST WASN'T, THE 1966
★ ★ ★ ★ **G Musical/Family 1:34**
Dir: Rossano Brazzi   *Cast:* Rossano Brazzi, Paul Tripp, Sonny Fox, Mischa Auer, Lydia Brazzi
► Mean millionaire Brazzi buys the North Pole and threatens to evict Santa and Mrs. Claus unless they come up with back rent by Christmas Eve. Children learn of Santa's plight and help him save Christmas. Classic holiday tale delightfully combines animation, live action, and musical numbers including "Why Can't Every Day Be Christmas?"
Dist.: HBO

CHRISTMAS TO REMEMBER, A 1978
★ ★ ★ ★ **NR Family/MFTV 2:00**
Dir: George Englund   *Cast:* Jason Robards, Jr., Eva Marie Saint, Joanne Woodward, George Parry, Bryan Englund, Louise Hockmeyer
► TV movie depicts elderly farm couple Robards and Saint, who take in their city-bred grandson Parry for the holidays during the Depression. Robards, still grieving over the death of only son in World War I, reluctantly warms to Parry. Woodward makes cameo appearance as Parry's mom. Splendid cast assures adaptation of Glendon Swarthout's *The Melodeon* never gets mired in sentimentality.
Dist.: Vestron

CHRISTMAS TREE, THE 1969
★ ★ **G Drama 1:50**
Dir: Terence Young   *Cast:* William Holden, Virna Lisi, Andre Bourvil, Brook Fuller
► Holden and son Fuller are vacationing in Corsica when the boy is exposed to nuclear radiation and contracts terminal cancer. Holden tries to give his son all he wants: he even steals wolves from the zoo to serve as pets. Improbable blend of holiday entertainment and anti-nuclear message.
Dist.: United

CHRISTOPHER STRONG 1933
★ **NR Drama 1:18 B&W**
Dir: Dorothy Arzner   *Cast:* Katharine Hepburn, Colin Clive, Billie Burke, Helen Chandler, Ralph Forbes, Jack LaRue
► In her second movie, Hepburn plays a headstrong pilot preoccupied with breaking records rather than hearts—until she meets Clive, a married politician. Although Hepburn's role has intriguing feminist overtones, film as a whole is dated and uninvolving.
Dist.: Turner

CHRIST STOPPED AT EBOLI 1979 Italian
☆ **NR Drama 2:00**
☑ Adult situations
Dir: Francesco Rosi   *Cast:* Gian Maria Volonté, Irene Papas, Paolo Bonicelli, Alain Cuny, Lea Massari
► Liberal doctor Volonté incurs the wrath of fascists in 1935 Italy and is exiled to a remote village which has yet to experience modern

civilization. Simplicity of villagers' lives is beautifully rendered in this adaptation of Carlo Levi's memoirs. Also known as *Eboli*.
Dist.: RCA/Columbia

CHROME AND HOT LEATHER 1971
☆ **PG Action-Adventure 1:32**
☑ Explicit language, violence
Dir: Lee Frost *Cast:* William Smith, Tony Young, Michael Haynes, Peter Brown, Marvin Gaye
▶ When his wife is killed by bikers, Vietnam veteran Smith gathers his fellow sergeants for revenge. The vets have to master motorcycles before they can tackle the thugs. Some welcome humor is this otherwise standard genre piece.
Dist.: Magnum

CHU CHU AND THE PHILLY FLASH 1981
★ **PG Comedy 1:40**
☑ Explicit language
Dir: David Lowell Rich *Cast:* Alan Arkin, Carol Burnett, Jack Warden, Danny Aiello, Danny Glover, Ruth Buzzi
▶ Former baseball player Arkin and dance instructor Burnett pounce on a briefcase filled with stolen government papers. Although enemies, they work together on a complicated scheme to ransom the goods. Shrill slapstick comedy was written by Arkin's wife, Barbara Dana.
Dist.: CBS/Fox

C.H.U.D. 1984
★ ★ **R Horror 1:28**
☑ Adult situations, explicit language, graphic violence
Dir: Douglas Creek *Cast:* John Heard, Kim Greist, Daniel Stern, Christopher Curry, George Martin
▶ A government plot to dump nuclear waste under Manhattan turns unsuspecting bag people into C.H.U.D.'s: Cannibalistic Humanoid Underground Dwellers. Since the cops won't help, it's up to bored television photographer Heard, his favorite model Greist, and hippie Stern to defeat the monsters. Low-budget exploitation fare has some humor and ecological points to accompany the requisite gore.
Dist.: Media

C.H.U.D. II 1988
★ ★ **R Horror/Comedy 1:25**
☑ Explicit language, violence
Dir: David Irving *Cast:* Brian Robbins, Bill Calvert, Tricia Leigh Fisher, Gerrit Graham, Robert Vaughn, Bianca Jagger
▶ Graham is the last zombie left from government C.H.U.D. program headed by Vaughn. High school teens Calvert and Robbins, having lost their cadaver for a biology project, steal Graham's corpse and accidentally bring him back to life. Graham goes on a killing spree, turning victims into fellow zombies, and soon his small town is crawling with the creatures. Horror sequel to C.H.U.D. plays mostly for

laughs, but has more than enough gore for genre buffs.
Dist.: Vestron

CHUMP AT OXFORD, A 1940
★ ★ **NR Comedy 1:03 B&W**
Dir: Alfred Goulding *Cast:* Stan Laurel, Oliver Hardy, Wilfred Lucas, Forrester Harvey, James Finlayson, Anita Garvin
▶ Last of the top-notch Laurel and Hardy films plays like a series of shorts, with convoluted events landing the boys at Oxford University, where they are the objects of some sinister practical jokes by fellow undergrads. Laurel masterfully plays a role reversal in which a blow on the head makes him think he's an English aristocrat. Peter Cushing is supposedly among the crowd of black-robed student extras.
Dist.: Nostalgia

CIMARRON 1931
★ ★ **NR Western 2:10 B&W**
Dir: Wesley Ruggles *Cast:* Richard Dix, Irene Dunne, Estelle Taylor, Nance O'Neil, William Collier, Jr., Roscoe Ates
▶ Epic Western follows Dix, Dunne, and their family over a forty-year period from the settling of Oklahoma in 1889 to Dunne's election to Congress in 1929. Well-mounted version of Edna Ferber's novel is slow-moving at times, and Dix seems hammy today. Still worth a look for its massive staging of the Oklahoma Land Rush. Oscars for Best Picture, Screenplay Adaptation (Howard Estabrook), and Interior Decoration.
Dist.: MGM/UA

CINCINNATI KID, THE 1965
★ ★ ★ **NR Drama 1:45**
Dir: Norman Jewison *Cast:* Steve McQueen, Edward G. Robinson, Ann-Margret, Karl Malden, Tuesday Weld, Joan Blondell
▶ McQueen, a New Orleans gambler known as the "Cincinnati Kid," takes on long-time champion Robinson, known as "The Man," in a high stakes game of stud poker. Engrossing story builds slowly (with time out for romantic interludes with Weld and Ann-Margret) but segues into a tense finish. McQueen is fine in one of his best roles but acting honors are stolen by Blondell as the dealer, "Ladyfingers."
Dist.: MGM/UA

CINDERELLA 1950
★ ★ ★ ★ ★ **G Animation 1:14**
Dir: Wilfred Jackson, Hamilton Luske, Clyde Geronimi *Cast:* Voices of Ilene Woods, William Phipps, Eleanor Audley, Verna Felton, James MacDonald
▶ Smooth, sentimental version of Perrault's fairy tale adds large cast of animals—comical mice Jacques and Gus-Gus, sinister cat, energetic bluebirds—to classic story of abused stepdaughter who captures dashing prince's heart. Typically strong Disney animation enhanced by tuneful score, including Oscar-

nominated "Bibbidy-Bobbidi-Boo." Highlighted by inspired rendition of Cinderella's transformation into princess. (CC)
Dist.: Buena Vista

CINDERELLA LIBERTY 1973
★★ R Drama/Romance 1:57
☑ Adult situations, explicit language
Dir: Mark Rydell ***Cast:*** James Caan, Marsha Mason, Kirk Calloway, Eli Wallach, Burt Young, Dabney Coleman
▶ While on a pass, sailor Caan meets prostitute Mason, the mother of mulatto son Calloway. Caan falls for her and becomes close to her child but complications, such as Mason's pregnancy, arise in the relationship. Warm and winning; Mason's Oscar-nominated performance is solidly supported by Caan.
Dist.: CBS/Fox

CINDERFELLA 1960
★★ NR Comedy 1:28
Dir: Frank Tashlin ***Cast:*** Jerry Lewis, Ed Wynn, Judith Anderson, Anna Maria Alberghetti, Henry Silva, Count Basie
▶ Sex-changed "Cinderella" with Lewis as the hapless "Fella" who, mistreated by wicked stepmother Anderson, is aided by Fairy Godfather Wynn so he can find true love with charming princess Alberghetti. Pathos and pratfalls, Jerry-style. Songs include "Let Me Be a People."
Dist.: IVE

CINEMA PARADISO 1989 Italian
★★★★ NR Drama 2:03
☑ Adult situations, explicit language
Dir: Giuseppe Tornatore ***Cast:*** Philippe Noiret, Jacques Perrin, Salvatore Cascio, Marco Leonardi
▶ Nostalgia piece starts in post-World War II Italy as young Cascio develops lifelong love of movies and friendship with projectionist Noiret. The child takes over Noiret's job after an accident and film follows character through his first love affair and adulthood. Slowly paced but warm and affectionate salute to cinema. Oscar for Best Foreign Film. [S]
Dist.: HBO

CIRCLE OF IRON 1979
★★ R Martial Arts 1:42
☑ Adult situations, explicit language, graphic violence
Dir: Richard Moore ***Cast:*** David Carradine, Jeff Cooper, Roddy McDowall, Eli Wallach, Christopher Lee
▶ Atypical kung-fu adventure set in a bizarre fantasy land mixes Zen philosophy with well-staged martial arts mayhem. A blind teacher guides young pupil Cooper through battles with monkey people, demons, and bandits to enlightenment at the hands of Zetan the Great (Lee). Carradine, replacing Bruce Lee after his untimely death, plays four roles. Lee wrote the story with James Coburn and Stirling Silliphant.
Dist.: Embassy

CIRCLE OF POWER 1984
★ R Drama 1:37
☑ Nudity, adult situations, explicit language, violence
Dir: Bobby Roth ***Cast:*** Yvette Mimieux, Christopher Allport, Cindy Pickett, John Considine, Scott Marlowe, Walter Olkewicz
▶ Businessmen and their wives attend an Executive Development Training session, expecting director Mimieux to help them cope with a variety of problems. Instead, she instigates a series of ghastly rituals to degrade and humiliate her clients. Offbeat psychodrama is often uncomfortable to watch. Also known as *Mystique* and *Naked Weekend*.
Dist.: Media

CIRCLE OF TWO 1980 Canadian
★★★ PG Drama 1:39
☑ Nudity
Dir: Jules Dassin ***Cast:*** Richard Burton, Tatum O'Neal, Nuala FitzGerald, Patricia Collins, Kate Reid
▶ Tedious account of the platonic affair between Burton, a creatively blocked artist, and O'Neal, a teenager who inspires him to paint again. A touchy subject is handled with delicacy, and Burton gives one of his better later performances. Ryan O'Neal (Tatum's father) appears as an extra in the porno theater where the friends meet.
Dist.: Vestron

CIRCUS, THE 1928
★★ NR Comedy 1:12 B&W
Dir: Charlie Chaplin ***Cast:*** Charlie Chaplin, Merna Kennedy, Allan Garcia, Betty Morrissey, Harry Crocker
▶ Chaplin stumbles into the ring of a small circus and unwittingly becomes its star clown. As he amuses the crowd by simply being himself, he falls in love with beautiful bareback rider Kennedy, who is already in love with tightrope walker Crocker. Chaplin won a special Oscar for directing, producing, and starring in what many consider his funniest full-length feature.
Dist.: Playhouse

CIRCUS OF HORRORS 1960 British
★★ NR Horror 1:28
☑ Violence
Dir: Sidney Hayers ***Cast:*** Anton Diffring, Erika Remberg, Yvonne Monlaur, Donald Pleasence, Kenneth Griffith
▶ Grisly horror film about plastic surgeon Diffring, who uses a small circus to pursue illegal experiments. His altered patients are forced to perform in dangerous circus acts; if they complain, they meet with gruesome "accidents." Alternately ghastly and comic, with heavy overtones of sex and sadism.
Dist.: HBO

CIRCUS WORLD 1964
★★★ NR Drama 2:15
Dir: Henry Hathaway ***Cast:*** John Wayne,

Claudia Cardinale, Rita Hayworth, Lloyd Nolan, Richard Conte, Kay Walsh
► Wayne, owner of a nineteenth-century circus and Wild West show, plans a tour of Europe to search for the mother of foster daughter Cardinale. Shipwreck threatens show's survival, but Wayne's horse stunts and Cardinale's budding trapeze talents save the day. She's also reunited with her mother, Hayworth. Large-scale, eye-pleasing drama features exciting acts by Austria's Franz Althoff Circus.
Dist.: Vestron

CITADEL, THE 1938 British
★ ★ NR Drama **1:52** B&W
Dir: King Vidor *Cast:* Robert Donat, Rosalind Russell, Ralph Richardson, Rex Harrison, Emlyn Williams, Penelope Dudley Ward
► Faithful adaptation of A. J. Cronin's bestselling novel describes the choice idealistic doctor Donat must make between caring for impoverished Welsh village or taking lucrative London practice. Russell offers stirring support as his devoted wife. Earnest but slowly paced picture received four Oscar nominations.
Dist.: MGM/UA

CITIZEN KANE 1941
★ ★ ★ ★ NR Drama **1:59** B&W
Dir: Orson Welles *Cast:* Orson Welles, Joseph Cotten, Ruth Warrick, Agnes Moorehead, Everett Sloane, Dorothy Comingore, Ray Collins, George Coulouris, Paul Stewart
► Welles's film masterpiece about the scandalous public and private life of newspaper publisher Charles Foster Kane (Welles), who dies murmuring "Rosebud" and sets off a nationwide search for the meaning of the word. Sure and penetrating performances by the entire cast, magnificent production values that set a new standard in cinematic craftsmanship, and a stunning musical score by Bernard Herrmann. Nominated for nine Oscars, winning for the screenplay by Welles and Herman Mankiewicz. Indisputably one of the great American classics.
Dist.: Turner

CITY HEAT 1984
★ ★ ★ PG Action-Adventure **1:37**
☑ Adult situations, explicit language, violence
Dir: Richard Benjamin *Cast:* Clint Eastwood, Burt Reynolds, Jane Alexander, Madeline Kahn, Irene Cara, Rip Torn
► Tongue-in-cheek 1930s mystery with private eye Reynolds pursuing two mob gangs who killed his lowlife colleague; Eastwood, spoofing his Dirty Harry role, doubts his former partner's motives. Good showcase for the leads, appearing together for the first time. Eastwood, tight-lipped as ever, is especially funny. (CC)
Dist.: Warner

CITY LIGHTS 1931
★ ★ ★ ★ G Comedy **1:26** B&W
Dir: Charlie Chaplin *Cast:* Charlie Chaplin, Virginia Cherrill, Florence Lee, Harry Myers, Hank Mann
► Chaplin's masterpiece is funny and poignant all at once. The Little Tramp falls in love with a blind flower seller and is befriended by an alcoholic millionaire who likes him when he's drunk but doesn't recognize him while sober. The Tramp's efforts to finance his love's eye operation bring about a delicately understated but incredibly moving finale. Silent, with a musical score by Chaplin.
Dist.: CBS/Fox

CITY LIMITS 1985
★ ★ PG-13 Sci-Fi **1:25**
☑ Brief nudity, adult situations, violence
Dir: Aaron Lipstadt *Cast:* Darrell Larson, John Stockwell, Kim Cattrall, Rae Dawn Chong, John Diehl, Don Opper
► In a postapocalyptic wasteland, teenager Stockwell is caught in a gang war between vicious punks and deadly bikers. Chong and Cattrall play the beautiful women who lead the hero to safety. Robby Benson and James Earl Jones have bit parts.
Dist.: Vestron

CITY OF SHADOWS 1987
★ NR Action-Adventure **1:39**
☑ Rape, adult situations, explicit language, graphic violence
Dir: David Mitchell *Cast:* Paul Coufos, Paul Harding, Tony Rosato, John P. Ryan, Damian Lee
► Cops Coufos and Rosato battle child kidnapping ringleader Lee, whom Coufos can't bring himself to kill for a shocking reason that dates back to his childhood. Sleazy ambiance and excessive bloodshedding set to music by Tangerine Dream; Coufos has a striking presence but the rest of the cast overacts.
Dist.: New World

CITY OF WOMEN 1981 Italian
☆ NR Fantasy/Comedy **2:18**
☑ Nudity, adult situations, explicit language
Dir: Federico Fellini *Cast:* Marcello Mastroianni, Ettore Manni, Anna Prucnal, Bernice Stegers
► Lothario Mastroianni falls asleep on a train and awakens to find stacked Stegers in his compartment. Desperate for a tryst, he follows her to a fantastical city populated solely by feminists out to get him. Delightfully surreal sex comedy is Fellini in top form. Mastroianni is endearingly confused as the chauvinist on the run. Ⓢ
Dist.: New Yorker

CITY ON FIRE 1979 Canadian
★ ★ ★ R Action-Adventure **1:44**
☑ Explicit language, violence
Dir: Alvin Rakoff *Cast:* Barry Newman, Henry Fonda, Ava Gardner, Shelley Winters, Susan Clark
► After a lunatic sets off an explosion in a

chemical refinery, fire engulfs the nearby drought-ridden town, trapping an all-star cast in a hospital. Fonda is the fire chief coping bravely with the disaster; Gardner, an alcoholic TV reporter covering the story; and Newman, a hospital director responsible for the safety of his patients.
Dist.: Nelson

CITY'S EDGE, THE 1983 Australian
☆ **NR Drama 1:30**
☑ Explicit language
Dir: Ken Quinnell   *Cast:* Tommy Lewis, Katrina Foster, Mark Lee, Ralph Cotterill, Hugo Weaving
▶ Weaving moves into a rundown Sydney boarding house owned by aborigine Lewis. He meets drug addict Lee and has an affair with Lee's sister Foster, who is also involved with Lewis. Good acting but lacks plot. Nothing really happens in the first half and the dialogue is stiff.
Dist.: MGM/UA

CITY THAT NEVER SLEEPS 1953
★ **NR Drama 1:30 B&W**
Dir: John H. Auer   *Cast:* Gig Young, Mala Powers, William Talman, Edward Arnold, Chill Wills, Marie Windsor
▶ Chicago cop Young, about to leave his wife for saloon singer Powers, is hired by corrupt lawyer Arnold to escort Talman out of state. When Talman kills Young's father, the detective is jolted back to reality and attempts to nab the killer. Street tough atmosphere enhances cluttered plotting.
Dist.: Republic

CLAIRE'S KNEE 1971 French
☆ **PG Comedy 1:43**
☑ Adult situations
Dir: Eric Rohmer   *Cast:* Jean-Claude Brialy, Aurora Cornu, Beatrice Romand, Laurence De Monaghan
▶ While on vacation, Brialy becomes obsessed with a much younger teenage De Monaghan; specifically he yearns to touch her knee. Dry, civilized adult entertainment in the director's patented mode, emphasizing talk and character development. Fifth in Rohmer's "Six Moral Tales" collection.
Dist.: Media

CLAIRVOYANT, THE 1934 British
★ **NR Drama 1:20 B&W**
Dir: Maurice Elvey   *Cast:* Claude Rains, Fay Wray, Jane Baxter, Mary Clare, Ben Field
▶ In another commanding performance, Rains plays a phony mind reader whose life is transformed when his predictions suddenly come true. When his warnings about a mining disaster are ignored, he is put on trial for causing the accident. Inventive courtroom scene enlivens this intriguing story.
Dist.: Video Yesteryear

CLAMBAKE 1967
★★ **NR Musical 1:39**

Dir: Arthur H. Nadel   *Cast:* Elvis Presley, Shelley Fabares, Will Hutchins, Bill Bixby, Gary Merrill, Angelique Pettyjohn
▶ Texas oil heir Presley trades places with a poor Miami ski instructor to see if he can win women without money. He falls for Fabares, his first student, and steals her away from playboy boyfriend Bixby by entering a big boat race. Lower-grade Presley vehicle includes the title song, "Hey, Hey, Hey," "Who Needs Money," and three other tunes.
Dist.: MGM/UA

CLAN OF THE CAVE BEAR, THE 1986
★★ **R Action-Adventure 1:38**
☑ Rape, brief nudity, violence
Dir: Michael Chapman   *Cast:* Daryl Hannah, Pamela Reed, James Remar, Thomas G. Waites, John Doolittle
▶ Respectful adaptation of Jean M. Auel's best-seller about the transition 35,000 years ago from the Neanderthal age to the Cro-Magnon era. Hannah is Ayla, a beautiful blond woman resented by the swarthy members of her adopted tribe. Mastering weapons reserved for males, she earns respect and becomes a medicine woman. **(CC)**
Dist.: CBS/Fox

CLARA'S HEART 1988
★★★★ **PG-13 Comedy/Drama 1:43**
☑ Adult situations, explicit language
Dir: Robert Mulligan   *Cast:* Whoopi Goldberg, Michael Ontkean, Kathleen Quinlan, Neal Patrick Harris, Spalding Gray, Beverly Todd
▶ Troubled suburban couple Ontkean and Quinlan hire Jamaican housekeeper Goldberg. Obnoxious son Harris resents Goldberg's presence and gives her grief, but unflappable maid has a witty rejoinder for every smart-aleck remark. When parents separate, Harris surrenders to Goldberg's innate warmth. Unapologetically sentimental drama carried by heartfelt performance from Goldberg.
Dist.: Warner

CLASH BY NIGHT 1952
★★★ **NR Drama 1:45 B&W**
Dir: Fritz Lang   *Cast:* Barbara Stanwyck, Paul Douglas, Robert Ryan, Marilyn Monroe, Keith Andes
▶ A disillusioned Stanwyck comes home to Monterey and accepts a marriage of convenience to big-hearted fisherman Douglas. Still unhappy, she starts an affair with cynical projectionist Ryan that leads to tragedy. Somber, downbeat version of a Clifford Odets play notable for its strong acting, expert direction, and vivid atmosphere. Monroe performs capably as a young woman who wants to follow in Stanwyck's footsteps.
Dist.: VCI

CLASH OF THE TITANS 1981 British
★★★★ **PG Fantasy 1:58**
☑ Brief nudity, violence
Dir: Desmond Davis   *Cast:* Laurence Olivier,

Harry Hamlin, Claire Bloom, Judi Bowker, Maggie Smith, Burgess Meredith
► Perseus (Hamlin) battles fearsome obstacles to save the kidnapped Andromeda (Bowker). Although mortal, he receives guidance and protection from the gods (including Olivier as Zeus and Bloom as Hera). Special effects by Ray Harryhausen are often outstanding in this loose adaptation of Greek mythology. Children will be entranced by Pegasus, a flying horse, and the snake-haired Medusa.
Dist.: MGM/UA

CLASS 1983
★ ★ ★ R Comedy/Drama 1:38
☑ Nudity, adult situations, explicit language
Dir: Lewis John Carlino   *Cast:* Rob Lowe, Jacqueline Bisset, Andrew McCarthy, Stuart Margolin, Cliff Robertson, John Cusack
► During a wild weekend in Chicago, naive boarding school student McCarthy has a fling with older woman Bisset, who he later learns is roommate Lowe's mother. Bisset's portrayal of a troubled character brings serious overtones to this preppie comedy.
Dist.: Vestron

CLASS OF '44 1973
★ ★ ★ PG Drama 1:35
☑ Adult situations, explicit language
Dir: Paul Bogart   *Cast:* Gary Grimes, Jerry Houser, Oliver Conant, William Atherton, Sam Bottoms, Deborah Winters
► Sequel to *Summer of '42* focuses on Hermie (Grimes, repeating his earlier role) after he graduates from his Brooklyn high school. Friend Conant enlists in the Marines, but Hermie and Oscy (Houser) enter college instead, where Hermie has a troubling affair with young Winters. Effective period details add to film's nostalgic tone.
Dist.: Warner

CLASS OF MISS MACMICHAEL, THE 1979
British
★ R Comedy 1:33
☑ Strong sexual content, explicit language
Dir: Silvio Narizzano   *Cast:* Glenda Jackson, Oliver Reed, Michael Murphy, Rosalind Cash, Phil Daniels
► At a British school for problem students, dedicated teacher Jackson clashes with incompetent principal Reed over how to handle the rowdy kids. Abrasive humor may offend some. Performances are a mixed bag: high grades for Jackson's brassy performance and Cash's quieter but equally effective one, lower marks for Reed's overacting.   (CC)
Dist.: Media

CLASS OF 1984 1982
★ ★ ★ R Action-Adventure 1:36
☑ Nudity, explicit language, graphic violence
Dir: Mark L. Lester   *Cast:* Perry King, Timothy Van Patten, Merrie Lynn Ross, Roddy McDowall

► Graphic, hard-hitting exposé of shocking conditions in an inner-city high school where rebellious teenagers conduct a guerrilla war against beleaguered teachers King and McDowall. When the punks, led by Van Patten, kidnap and rape King's wife Ross, he goes on the warpath. The violence is often excessive.
Dist.: Vestron

CLASS OF NUKE 'EM HIGH 1986
★ R Horror 1:21
☑ Nudity, adult situations, explicit language, graphic violence
Dir: Richard W. Haines, Samuel Weil   *Cast:* Janelle Brady, Gilbert Brenton, Robert Prichard, R. L. Ryan, James Nugent Vernon
► Leak from a nuclear power plant seeps into the water supply at Tromaville, "The Toxic Waste Capital of the World." The first victims are the high school's Honor Society, clean-cut preppies who are turned overnight into violent mutants. Follow-up to *Toxic Avenger* has the same amusingly disgusting special effects and slapstick humor.
Dist.: Media

CLAY PIGEON, THE 1949
★ NR Action-Adventure 1:03 B&W
Dir: Richard Fleischer   *Cast:* Bill Williams, Barbara Hale, Richard Quine, Richard Loo, Frank Fenton, Martha Hyer
► Seaman Williams gets a rude awakening from a long coma: he has been accused of complicity in a friend's death in a Japanese prison camp. Widow Hale helps Williams prove his innocence. Top-notch B-movie, well-directed by Fleischer. Home video version double billed with 1942's *Call Out the Marines.*
Dist.: Turner

CLEAN AND SOBER 1988
★ ★ ★ ★ ★ R Drama 2:04
☑ Adult situations, explicit language
Dir: Glenn Gordon Caron   *Cast:* Michael Keaton, Kathy Baker, Morgan Freeman, M. Emmet Walsh, Tate Donovan, Brian Benben
► Yuppie cocaine and alcohol addict Keaton has some serious problems: he's embezzled funds from his company and given drugs to a woman who subsequently died. Hiding out in a detox clinic, he spars with counselor Freeman and fellow patient Baker. Once he's out of the hospital, Keaton finds new take on life doesn't necessarily yield easy answers. Convincing, thought-provoking drama generates power from solid supporting cast and impressive first foray into drama by Keaton.
Dist.: Warner

CLEO/LEO 1989
★ ★ R Comedy 1:34
☑ Nudity, strong sexual content, adult situations, explicit language
Dir: Chuck Vincent   *Cast:* Jane Hamilton, Scott Baker, Ginger Lynn Allen, Alan Naggar
► Obnoxious sexist Leo (Baker) is forced into a

river and shot by an angry woman. Leo emerges from the river as a woman, Cleo (Hamilton), and gets new perspective on life in his female incarnation. Body switch formula with a sexual twist, crude humor, and decent performance from Hamilton (known to porno film fans as Veronica Hart).
Dist.: New World

CLEOPATRA 1934
★ ★ **NR Drama 1:35 B&W**
Dir: Cecil B. DeMille *Cast:* Claudette Colbert, Warren William, Henry Wilcoxon, Gertrude Michael, Joseph Schildkraut, C. Aubrey Smith
▶ Typically spectacular and inaccurate interpretation of the life and death of history's most famous queen from director DeMille. Colbert makes a luscious Cleopatra, but William as Caesar and Wilcoxon as Antony are stiff and genteel as her noble Roman suitors. Thrills come from the gigantic crowds of extras, Cleopatra's breathtaking barge, and extravagant replication of Egyptian architectural splendors.
Dist.: Goodtimes

CLEOPATRA 1963
★ ★ ★ **G Drama 4:03**
Dir: Joseph L. Mankiewicz *Cast:* Elizabeth Taylor, Richard Burton, Rex Harrison, Roddy McDowall, Martin Landau, Pamela Brown, Hume Cronyn, Carroll O'Connor
▶ Egyptian queen Cleopatra's (Taylor) affair with Julius Caesar (Harrison) is cut short by his assassination; she then takes up with Roman senator Mark Antony (Burton) for ill-fated romance/political alliance. Lavish epic won notoriety for huge budget and Taylor/Burton affair; Oscar-nominated Harrison outshines his more publicized co-stars. Best Picture nominee nabbed Oscars for Cinematography, Costume Design, Special Effects, Art Direction/Set Decoration.
Dist.: CBS/Fox

CLEOPATRA JONES 1973
★ ★ **PG Action-Adventure 1:29**
☑ Violence
Dir: Jack Starrett *Cast:* Tamara Dobson, Shelley Winters, Bernie Casey, Brenda Sykes, Antonio Fargas
▶ The 6'2" Dobson is Cleopatra Jones, a black CIA narcotics agent who takes on Winters, a lesbian underworld antagonist running an international dope ring. A James Bond-type adventure with a story line straight out of comic books. Fans can check out sequel *Cleopatra Jones and the Casino of Gold.*
Dist.: Warner

CLEOPATRA JONES AND THE CASINO OF GOLD 1975
★ ★ **R Action-Adventure 1:36**
☑ Nudity, explicit language, violence
Dir: Chuck Bail *Cast:* Tamara Dobson, Stella Stevens, Tanny, Norman Fell, Albert Popwell

▶ Sassy black superagent Cleopatra Jones (Dobson) returns to battle larger-than-life drug queen villainess Stevens in this action-packed adventure sequel. Filmed on location in Hong Kong. Good support from Fell and oriental martial arts beauty Tanny.
Dist.: Warner

CLIMB, THE 1987 Canadian
★ ★ **PG Action-Adventure 1:30**
☑ Explicit language
Dir: Don Shebib *Cast:* Bruce Greenwood, James Hurdle, Kenneth Walsh, Ken Pogue
▶ A German expedition climbing a Himalayan peak is beset by problems, including conflict between Greenwood and Hurdle, injuries, an avalanche, and storms. Astonishing scenery steals the show from colorless characterizations and punchless narration. Based on a true story.
Dist.: Virgin

CLINIC, THE 1982 Australian
★ **NR Comedy 1:32**
☑ Nudity, strong sexual content, explicit language, adult humor
Dir: David Stevens *Cast:* Chris Haywood, Simon Burke, Gerda Nicolson
▶ During a typically busy day in a VD clinic, a young medical student is exposed to patients with a variety of sexual ailments, as well as a prostitute, a gay doctor, and a bomb scare. Raunchy shenanigans deftly mixed with more serious issues although has slow spots. Greg Millin based his screenplay on his stint working in an actual clinic.
Dist.: VidAmerica

CLOAK AND DAGGER 1946
★ ★ **NR Action-Adventure 1:46 B&W**
Dir: Fritz Lang *Cast:* Gary Cooper, Lilli Palmer, Robert Alda, Vladimir Sokoloff, J. Edward Bromberg
▶ Towards the end of World War II, physicist Cooper is recruited by the government to find Sokoloff, an atomic scientist held captive by the Nazis in Italy. Partisan Palmer falls for Cooper while helping him spirit Sokoloff out of the country. Engrossing but farfetched intrigue moves quickly.
Dist.: Republic

CLOAK & DAGGER 1984
★ ★ ★ ★ **PG Action-Adventure 1:41**
☑ Explicit language, violence
Dir: Richard Franklin *Cast:* Henry Thomas, Dabney Coleman, Michael Murphy, Christina Nigra, John McIntire
▶ Thomas is an overly imaginative Cloak & Dagger computer game whiz-kid who becomes entangled in a real-life spy caper involving government secrets and enemy agents. Coleman doubles as Thomas's dad and make-believe superhero pal. Appealing adventure with a child hero that's not for kids only. **(CC)**
Dist.: MCA

CLOCKMAKER, THE 1973 French
☆ **NR Drama 1:45**
☑ Adult situations, violence
Dir: Bertrand Tavernier ***Cast:*** Philippe Noiret, Sylvain Rougerie, Jean Rochefort, Jacques Denis, William Sabatier
► Watchmaker Noiret is alarmed when son Rougerie is arrested for killing a factory foreman. While the defiant son's only explanation is that the foreman was "a pig," Noiret becomes unwound and faces the need to reset his life. Thoughtful, effective drama based on a novel by Georges Simenon. [S]
Dist.: Corinth

CLOCKWISE 1986 British
★★ **PG Comedy 1:32**
☑ Adult humor
Dir: Christopher Morhan ***Cast:*** John Cleese, Alison Steadman, Sharon Maiden, Penelope Wilton, Stephen Moore
► Monty Python's Cleese is the most pompous, punctilious headmaster in England. Through a series of silly mishaps, he's late for the most important speech of his life. For those who appreciate British humor.
Dist.: HBO

CLOCKWORK ORANGE, A 1971
★★ **R Drama 2:17**
☑ Nudity, adult situations, explicit language, graphic violence
Dir: Stanley Kubrick ***Cast:*** Malcolm McDowell, Patrick Magee, Adrienne Corri, Aubrey Morris, James Marcus
► Sadistic young McDowell of the near future is "rehabilitated" by a special conditioning treatment. "Cured" of his savage excesses and love for Beethoven, he's a misfit in a still violent society. Brilliantly directed by Kubrick, this strikingly violent film (though tame by today's standards) was nominated for four Academy Awards and is considered a classic by many critics.
Dist.: Warner

CLOSE ENCOUNTERS OF THE THIRD KIND 1977
★★★★ **PG Sci-Fi 2:15**
☑ Adult situations, explicit language
Dir: Steven Spielberg ***Cast:*** Richard Dreyfuss, François Truffaut, Teri Garr, Melinda Dillon, Cary Guffey, Bob Balaban
► Dreyfuss, a power company worker, encounters UFOs and searches for the truth behind his vision. Also on the aliens' trail: scientist Truffaut, leader of an international research team, and Dillon, who's searching for her missing son. Spielberg's stunning, joyous portrait of a quite benign alien invasion culminates in a joining of man and spaceman at Wyoming's Devil's Tower. Technical wizardry combines music, visuals, and great special effects. Reissued in 1980 with new footage as *Close Encouters of the Third Kind: The Special Edition.* **(CC)**
Dist.: RCA/Columbia

CLOSELY WATCHED TRAINS 1966 Czech
★ **NR Comedy 1:29 B&W**
Dir: Jiri Menzel ***Cast:*** Vaclav Neckar, Jitka Bendova, Josef Somr, Vladimir Valenta, Jiri Menzel
► In World War II German-occupied Czechoslovakia, railroad employee Neckar attempts to lose his virginity, then turns his attention to a more serious matter: blowing up a Nazi train. Alternately amusing and moving mix of moods. Oscar winner for Best Foreign Film. [S]
Dist.: RCA/Columbia

CLOUD DANCER 1979
★★ **PG Drama 1:48**
☑ Explicit language, violence
Dir: Barry Brown ***Cast:*** David Carradine, Jennifer O'Neill, Joseph Bottoms, Colleen Camp, Albert Salmi, Nina Van Pallandt
► Old-fashioned adventure about stunt pilot Carradine whose daring exploits in a flying circus upset his friends. O'Neill is a photographer who causes Carradine to rethink his priorities when she reveals he's a father; Bottoms, a fellow pilot who falls victim to drugs. Good aerial sequences overcome a mechanical plot.
Dist.: Prism

CLOUDS OVER EUROPE 1939 British
★★★ **NR Action-Adventure 1:22 B&W**
Dir: Tim Whelan ***Cast:*** Laurence Olivier, Valerie Hobson, Ralph Richardson, George Curzon, George Merritt
► English newspaper reporter Hobson alerts brother Richardson, a Scotland Yard detective, about a secret German ray that can disable British planes. With Olivier's help, he pursues the ship carrying the weapon. Droll sense of humor and outstanding stars spark this early anti-Nazi effort.
Dist.: Nelson

CLOWN, THE 1953
★ **NR Drama 1:32 B&W**
Dir: Robert Z. Leonard ***Cast:*** Red Skelton, Tim Considine, Jane Greer, Loring Smith, Philip Ober, Walter Reed
► Maudlin show-biz remake of *The Champ* features Skelton in a rare dramatic role as a down-on-his-luck vaudeville star who battles alcoholism with the help of his devoted son Considine. Through perseverance and grit, he wins the lead in a new TV show. Charles Bronson and Roger Moore have bit parts.
Dist.: MGM/UA

CLOWN HOUSE 1988
★ **R Horror 1:21**
☑ Explicit language, violence
Dir: Victor Salva ***Cast:*** Nathan Forrest Winters, Brian McHugh, Sam Rockwell, Tree, Byron Weible, David C. Reinecker
► Despite young Winters's terror of clowns, his bullying older brother Rockwell forces him to attend a performance of the Jolly Brothers Circus. Unfortunately, escaped mental patients have invaded the show disguised as clowns

and pursue the boys back to their deserted Victorian house. Low-budget horror downplays gore while emphasizing suspense.
Dist.: RCA/Columbia

CLOWN MURDERS, THE 1975 Canadian
☆ **NR Drama 1:36**
☑ Adult situations, explicit language, violence
Dir: Martyn Burke *Cast:* Steven Young, Susan Keller, Lawrence Dane, John Candy
▶ A wheeler-dealer is about to purchase a farm on Halloween. His pals dress up as clowns and abduct his wife to prevent the deal. This practical joke turns deadly as the clowns argue among themselves and someone starts shooting. Builds some moderate tension but characters won't hold your interest.
Dist.: TWE

CLOWNS, THE 1971 Italian
☆ **G Documentary 1:30**
Dir: Federico Fellini
▶ Director Fellini recalls his childhood fascination with clowns, interviews retired and current ones, and stages a circus. Visually evocative production shows Fellini's touch throughout and is much more accessible to mainstream audiences than the director's fiction films. Nice musical score by Nino Rota.
Dist.: Media

CLUB, THE 1980 Australian
★ **Drama 1:39**
☑ Brief nudity, adult situations, explicit language
Dir: Bruce Beresford *Cast:* Jack Thompson, Graham Kennedy, Frank Wilson, Harold Hopkins
▶ Pro rugby coach Thompson faces opposition from the front office, bickering among his players, and lackluster performance by the team's newly signed star. Beresford elicits fine ensemble acting but the script is talky and the subject unlikely to excite American audiences.
Dist.: Academy

CLUB PARADISE 1986
★ ★ **PG-13 Comedy 1:44**
☑ Explicit language
Dir: Harold Ramis *Cast:* Robin Williams, Rick Moranis, Peter O'Toole, Adolph Caesar, Twiggy, Andrea Martin
▶ Williams is a burned-out fireman trying to turn a ramshackle Caribbean resort into a tropical paradise. Subplots include nerds trying to pick up women, guests lost in the jungle, and a local revolution. Williams sparkles, despite heat stroke material. Reggae star Jimmy Cliff's bouncy tunes give the film a lift. (CC)
Dist.: Warner

CLUE 1985
★ ★ **PG Mystery-Suspense/Comedy 1:27**
☑ Explicit language, violence

Dir: Jonathan Lynn *Cast:* Eileen Brennan, Tim Curry, Madeline Kahn, Christopher Lloyd, Michael McKean
▶ Plastic game pieces come to life and you guess who killed whom and with what. Host Mr. Boddy and Yvette, his bosomy French maid, greet guests Mrs. White, Mrs. Peacock, Mr. Green, Miss Scarlet and Colonel Mustard before the lights go out and Boddy is killed. Or is he? Theaters offered one of three endings; all appear on videotape. Especially good performances from Kahn and McKean. (CC)
Dist.: Paramount

COACH 1978
★ ★ ★ **PG Drama 1:40**
☑ Brief nudity, explicit language
Dir: Bud Townsend *Cast:* Cathy Lee Crosby, Michael Biehn, Keenan Wynn, Steve Nevil
▶ Crosby is hired as coach of boys' high school basketball team over opposition from Wynn. She promises to quit if the team loses once; although the guys don't take her seriously at first, she turns them into winners. Player Biehn falls in love with her. Diverting vehicle for Crosby, who is as cool and fresh as a mint candy.
Dist.: Media

COAL MINER'S DAUGHTER 1980
★ ★ ★ ★ ★ **PG Biography/Music 2:05**
☑ Adult situations, explicit language, mild violence
Dir: Michael Apted *Cast:* Sissy Spacek, Tommy Lee Jones, Beverly D'Angelo, Levon Helm, Phyllis Boyens, Ernest Tubb
▶ Heartwarming story of country-western legend Loretta Lynn. Perceptive script and sympathetic direction results in compelling portraits of the people in her life: dirt-poor father Helm, husband Mooney (Jones), and best friend Patsy Cline (D'Angelo). Location shooting captures the Appalachian essence of Tennessee and Kentucky. Spacek, who sang the songs herself, won an Oscar for her uncanny imitation of the singer. The film also received five other nominations (including Best Picture and Screenplay).
Dist.: MCA

COAST TO COAST 1980
★ ★ ★ **PG Comedy 1:34**
☑ Adult situations, explicit language
Dir: Joseph Sargent *Cast:* Dyan Cannon, Robert Blake, Quinn Redeker, Michael Lerner, Maxine Stuart
▶ Semi-loony but very rich Cannon escapes from a New York hospital and hitches a ride to California with debt-ridden truck driver Blake. The unlikely pair fall in love while fleeing an assortment of villains. Smash finale includes a ten-wheeler driven into a Beverly Hills living room.
Dist.: Paramount

COBRA 1986
★ ★ ★ R Action-Adventure 1:27
☑ Explicit language, graphic violence
Dir: George Pan Cosmatos *Cast:* Sylvester Stallone, Brigitte Nielsen, Reni Santoni, Andrew Robinson, Art La Fleur
▶ Unconventional L.A. cop Marion "Cobra" Cobretti (Stallone) takes on a neo-fascist gang of killers in this efficient, action-packed thriller reuniting Sly with his *Rambo: First Blood Part II* director. Stallone's then-wife Nielsen portrays the murder witness who's on the gang's hit list. Macho heaven for Stallone fans as their man successfully invades *Dirty Harry* territory. **(CC)**
Dist.: Warner

COCA-COLA KID, THE 1985 Australian
★ R Comedy 1:34
☑ Nudity, explicit language
Dir: Dusan Makavejev *Cast:* Eric Roberts, Greta Scacchi, Bill Kerr, Chris Haywood, Max Gillies
▶ Roberts is an American hotshot Coca-Cola executive who tries to discover why Australia's Anderson Valley is the one spot in the whole country where Coke isn't sold. May not be for mainstream audiences but will reward the patient viewer with its original moments. Arresting visuals and a buoyant performance by Scacchi as a troubled secretary. **(CC)**
Dist.: Vestron

COCAINE WARS 1986
★ ★ R Action-Adventure 1:22
☑ Nudity, adult situations, explicit language, violence
Dir: Hector Olivera *Cast:* John Schneider, Kathryn Witt, Federico Luppi, Royal Dano, Rodolfo Ranni
▶ DEA agent Schneider gathers evidence on South American drug kingpin Luppi, but his cover is blown by his old girlfriend, reporter Witt. When Luppi kidnaps Witt, Schneider arms himself for a one-man assault on his headquarters. Diverting exploitation fare for action fans.
Dist.: Media

COCKTAIL 1988
★ ★ ★ ★ R Drama 1:40
☑ Adult situations, explicit language
Dir: Roger Donaldson *Cast:* Tom Cruise, Bryan Brown, Elisabeth Shue, Lisa Banes, Laurence Luckinbill, Kelly Lynch
▶ Cocky young Cruise rises to the top of New York bartending trade under corrupt tutelage of Brown. In Jamaica, Cruise has romance with wealthy Shue. Will her love redeem him? Shallow but brassy and energetic. Cruise, Shue, and Jamaica look terrific; Brown plays his role to the hilt, spouting the wisdom he calls "Coughlin's Law." Most outlandish scene: Cruise reciting poetry in bar. Hard-rocking soundtrack includes Bobby McFerrin's "Don't Worry, Be Happy," Beach Boys' "Kokomo," and

John Cougar Mellencamp's version of Buddy Holly's "Rave On."
Dist.: Buena Vista

COCOANUTS, THE 1929
★ ★ NR Comedy 1:36 B&W
Dir: Robert Florey, Joseph Santley *Cast:* Groucho Marx, Harpo Marx, Chico Marx, Zeppo Marx, Mary Eaton, Margaret Dumont, Kay Francis, Oscar Shaw
▶ First Marx Brothers film is a straight transfer of their Broadway hit by George S. Kaufman and Irving Berlin. Primitive sound and camerawork make it extremely difficult to watch, but fans will want to see some of the brothers' best routines: a hilarious rigged auction, the "viaduct" skit, and all of Groucho's scenes with Dumont. Berlin score includes "Monkey-Doodle-Doo" and "When My Dreams Come True."
Dist.: MCA

COCOON 1985
★ ★ ★ ★ ★ PG-13 Fantasy 1:57
☑ Brief nudity, adult situations, explicit language
Dir: Ron Howard *Cast:* Don Ameche, Wilford Brimley, Steve Guttenberg, Hume Cronyn, Brian Dennehy, Jessica Tandy, Jack Gilford, Maureen Stapleton, Gwen Verdon, Tahnee Welch, Linda Harrison, Clint Howard
▶ Old codgers Ameche, Brimley and Cronyn are suddenly rejuvenated when they find a swimming pool filled with mysterious cocoons: a fountain of youth provided by benevolent aliens led by Dennehy. Magical, upbeat comedy/fantasy with a touching script and wonderful ensemble acting. Ameche, whose breakdancing scene brings down the house, won the Oscar for Best Supporting Actor. Spawned sequel. **(CC)**
Dist.: CBS/Fox

COCOON: THE RETURN 1988
★ ★ ★ ★ ★ PG Fantasy 1:56
☑ Explicit language
Dir: Daniel Petrie *Cast:* Don Ameche, Wilford Brimley, Hume Cronyn, Jack Gilford, Steve Guttenberg, Maureen Stapleton
▶ Undersea earthquake endangers alien cocoons, so Ameche, Brimley, and Cronyn return to Earth to help recover them. They cheer up old buddy Gilford and rescue a space dweller from marine biologists. Slick sequel benefits greatly from the charm of its geriatric cast members (led by Ameche re-creating his Oscar-winning role), but lacks the magic of the original.
Dist.: CBS/Fox

CODE NAME: EMERALD 1985
★ ★ ★ ★ PG Action-Adventure 1:35
Dir: Jonathan Sanger *Cast:* Ed Harris, Max Von Sydow, Eric Stoltz, Helmut Berger, Horst Buchholz
▶ Tense espionage thriller features Harris as a World War II double agent fighting to keep the Nazis from discovering the time and place of

D-Day. Good-looking spy drama with believable performances; a nail-biter. **(CC)**
Dist.: CBS/Fox

CODE NAME: TRIXIE 1973
★ R Horror 1:43
☑ Graphic violence
Dir: George Romero *Cast:* Lane Carroll, W. G. McMillan, Harold Wayne Jones, Lloyd Hollar, Lynn Lowry
► An Army plane carrying a germ weapon crashes near a small town, unleashing a virus that causes its victims to run murderously wild. While scientists desperately search for a cure, the Army quarantines the town, trapping those who have not yet been infected. Filmed in director Romero's home state of Pennsylvania, downbeat horror pic has a powerful sense of immediacy. Also known as *The Crazies*.
Dist.: Vista

CODENAME: WILDGEESE 1986
German/Italian
★ ★ ★ R Action-Adventure 1:42
☑ Explicit language, violence
Dir: Anthony M. Dawson (Antonio) Margheriti) *Cast:* Ernest Borgnine, Lewis Collins, Lee Van Cleef, Mimsy Farmer, Klaus Kinski
► A team of mercenaries led by Collins is hired to destroy a Communist-run drug ring in the jungles of Thailand. The mission is accomplished, with the help of intrepid chopper pilot Van Cleef, in quite violent fashion. Plenty of explosions, dismembered limbs, and general brutality in a film longer on action than plot logic.
Dist.: New World

CODE OF SILENCE 1985
★ ★ ★ ★ R Action-Adventure 1:40
☑ Explicit language, graphic violence
Dir: Andrew Davis *Cast:* Chuck Norris, Henry Silva, Bert Remsen, Mike Genovese, Nathan Davis
► Chicago cop Norris defies the "code of silence" by testifying against a policeman who wrongly shot a teenager. The decision does not make him popular with his peers and thus he must stand alone against two warring drug gangs. First-rate Norris vehicle combines the anticipated action with more depth in its plotting and characterization. Chuck's best performance to date.
Dist.: HBO

COFFY 1973
☆ R Action-Adventure 1:31
☑ Nudity, adult situations, explicit language, violence
Dir: Jack Hill *Cast:* Pam Grier, Booker Bradshaw, Robert DoQui, William Elliott, Allan Arbus
► High-grade exploitation fare gave Grier one of her best roles as a tough nurse whose sister is turned into a junkie by greasy dealers. Grier uses her wit, beautiful body, and shotgun

to eliminate the villians. Fast-paced, sexy, and extremely violent.
Dist.: Orion

COHEN & TATE 1989
★ R Mystery-Suspense 1:26
☑ Explicit language, graphic violence
Dir: Eric Red *Cast:* Roy Scheider, Adam Baldwin, Harley Cross, Cooper Huckabee, Suzanne Savoy, Marco Perella
► Two contract killers, old pro Scheider and sadistic hothead Baldwin, kidnap nine-year-old murder witness Cross and drive him to Houston mob bosses. To escape, kid exploits hitmen's warring personalities. Ugly but oddly gripping thriller in which Red's bravura style and situation's intrinsic suspense overcome illogical plot. Baldwin's psychopathic portrait is one of the most loathsome movie characters in recent memory. **(CC)**
Dist.: Nelson

COLD FEET 1984
☆ PG Comedy 1:36
☑ Adult situations, explicit language
Dir: Bruce van Dusen *Cast:* Griffin Dunne, Blanche Baker, Marrissa Chibas, Mark Cronogue, Kurt Knudson
► Dunne, a TV writer/director who just broke up with wife Baker, becomes friendly with research scientist Chibas who just broke up with boyfriend Cronogue. After bad dates with other people and some wrangling with their respective ex's, Dunne and Chibas find their relationship turning into a romance in this New York-based comedy. Music by Todd Rundgren. **(CC)**
Dist.: CBS/Fox

COLD FEET 1989
★ R Comedy 1:34
☑ Nudity, adult situations, explicit language, violence
Dir: Robert Dornhelm *Cast:* Keith Carradine, Sally Kirkland, Tom Waits, Rip Torn, Bill Pullman, Jeff Bridges
► Carradine, his girlfriend Kirkland, and his psychotic partner Waits smuggle stolen gems inside a stallion. When Carradine steals the horse and gives them the slip, heading for brother Pullman's ranch, Kirkland and Waits pursue. Offbeat and uneven; Kirkland's trashy wardrobe and screenwriters Thomas McGuane and Jim Harrison's off-center dialogue provide some amusement to a bizarre plot. **(CC)**
Dist.: IVE

COLD FRONT, THE 1989
★ ★ NR Crime 1:36
☑ Adult situations, explicit language, violence
Dir: Paul Bnarbic *Cast:* Martin Sheen, Michael Ontkean, Beverly D'Angelo, Jan Rubes
► In Vancouver, Drug Enforcement Agency representative Sheen and Canadian lawman Ontkean team up to investigate the murder of

a Korean consulate worker. The trail leads to a terrorist. D'Angelo, who sings over the end credits, plays Sheen's ex-wife and renewed love interest. Convoluted film has terrific cinematography.
Dist.: HBO

COLDITZ STORY, THE 1955 British
★ ★ ★ **NR Drama 1:37 B&W**
Dir: Guy Hamilton *Cast:* John Mills, Eric Portman, Christopher Rhodes, Lionel Jeffries, Bryan Forbes, Theodore Bikel
► Tense World War II drama about POWs determined to break out of the Colditz Castle, an "escape-proof" Nazi prison. When attempts by Polish and French inmates fail, Pat Reid (Mills) concocts a daring plan that requires bravery and split-second timing. Authentic and exciting film was based on a true story.
Dist.: HBO

COLD RIVER 1982
★ ★ ★ **PG Action-Adventure 1:32**
☑ Adult situations, explicit language, mild violence
Dir: Fred G. Sullivan *Cast:* Suzanne Weber, Pat Petersen, Brad Sullivan, Richard Jaeckel, Robert Earl Jones
► Children Weber and Petersen are stranded in the Adirondacks when father Jaeckel has a fatal heart attack. The pair brave the winter elements under the protection of old trapper Jones but they must deal with an escaped con by themselves. Meatier, somewhat more mature fare than others in the wilderness genre. Independent filmmaker Sullivan's experiences with making this movie are humorously detailed in his *Beerdrinker's Guide to Fitness and Film Making.*
Dist.: CBS/Fox

COLD ROOM, THE 1983
★ ★ **NR Mystery-Suspense/MFTV 1:35**
☑ Rape, adult situations, explicit language, violence
Dir: James Dearden *Cast:* George Segal, Amanda Pays, Renee Soutendijk, Warren Clarke, Anthony Higgins
► Engrossing psychological thriller about father Segal and daughter Pays who visit East Berlin and find themselves supernaturally drawn into a forty-year-old intrigue. Atmosphere enhanced by location shooting, including Checkpoint Charlie, the former crossing point between West and East Berlin. Written and directed by Dearden from the novel by Jeffrey Caine.
Dist.: Media

COLD SASSY TREE 1989
★ ★ ★ ★ **NR Drama/MFTV 1:37**
Dir: Joan Tewkesbury *Cast:* Faye Dunaway, Richard Widmark, Neil Patrick Harris, Francis Fisher, Lee Garlington, John Jackson
► Northerner Dunaway travels to a small Southern town, where she marries Widmark, a wealthy widower. The marriage is one of con-venience for Dunaway, who wants a home and place to settle down; but for Widmark, the relationship is important enough for him to endure the scorn of the town. As Dunaway opens up to him, a terrible secret comes to light. Good adaptation of the novel by Olive Ann Burns, with nice period re-creations.
Dist.: Turner

COLD STEEL 1987
★ ★ **R Action-Adventure 1:30**
☑ Nudity, adult situations, explicit language, violence
Dir: Dorothy Ann Puzo *Cast:* Brad Davis, Sharon Stone, Jonathan Banks, Adam Ant, Jay Acovone
► Davis, a tough cop who doesn't play by the rules, investigates his father's brutal murder. The trail leads to old friend Banks and vicious British punk Ant. Competently filmed if predictable cop film with its fair share of car chases, violence, and shootouts.
Dist.: RCA/Columbia

COLD SWEAT 1974 Italian/French
★ **PG Action-Adventure 1:34**
☑ Violence
Dir: Terence Young *Cast:* Charles Bronson, Liv Ullmann, James Mason, Jill Ireland, Jean Topart, Yannick Delulle
► Bronson, a former drug dealer, retires to France with wife Ullmann and daughter Delulle, but his past comes back to haunt him when Southern smuggler Mason sets up one more drug run. After his family is kidnapped, Bronson goes on a rampage, taking hostage Mason's mistress Ireland. Adapted from Richard Matheson's *Ride the Nightmare.*
Dist.: Video Gems

COLLECTOR, THE 1965
★ ★ ★ **NR Mystery-Suspense 1:59**
Dir: William Wyler *Cast:* Terence Stamp, Samantha Eggar, Mona Washbourne, Maurice Dallimore
► Young, neurotic Stamp collects butterflies and decides to take on another hobby: "collecting" a fiancée for himself. He kidnaps beautiful student Eggar and tries to force her into falling in love with him. Powerful suspense drama, both disturbing and highly entertaining. Compelling performances by Stamp and Eggar in what is essentially a two-character movie; claustrophobic tension created by director Wyler. From the John Fowles best-seller.
Dist.: RCA/Columbia

COLLEGE 1927
★ ★ **NR Comedy 1:38 B&W**
Dir: James W. Horne *Cast:* Buster Keaton, Ann Cornwall, Harold Goodwin, Snitz Edwards, Florence Turner
► Keaton is so devoted to studying that he delivers a speech denouncing sports at his high school graduation. When he falls for coed Cornwall, who has eyes for the college jock, he embarks on a crash program to become an athlete. Although not as tightly

plotted as Keaton's best, this delightful silent comedy finds him at the height of his powers. Highlights: a disastrous baseball tryout and marvelous acrobatics in a soda fountain.
Dist.: Video Yesteryear

COLLISION COURSE 1987
★ ★ ★ **PG Action-Adventure 1:45**
☑ Explicit language, violence
Dir: Lewis Teague   *Cast:* Jay Leno, Noriyuki "Pat" Morita, Chris Sarandon, Tom Noonan, Ernie Hudson
► Japanese cop Morita teams up with Detroit policeman Leno to investigate car industry–related murders. Formula mismatched partners tale enlivened by action, stunts, violence, and a wild car chase finale through the streets of Detroit. Humor is a little heavy on the racial slurs but Morita adds a touch of class and comedian/talk show host Leno does a nice job in his first major movie role.
Dist.: HBO

COLONEL REDL 1985
German/Hungarian/Austrian
☆ R Drama 2:29
☑ Nudity, adult situations, explicit language
Dir: Istvan Szabo   *Cast:* Klaus Maria Brandauer, Armin Mueller-Stahl, Hans Christian Blech, Gudrun Landgrebe, Jan Miklas
► Before World War I, lower-middle-class cadet Brandauer rises to colonel in the German Army Secret Service despite his homosexuality. Ordered to find a fall guy for an upcoming trial, Brandauer falls in love with a young Italian and finds himself being scapegoated. Overlong epic with mannered performance by Brandaeur as the real-life Redl.
§
Dist.: Orion

COLOR ME DEAD 1969
★ R Mystery-Suspense 1:31
☑ Nudity, violence
Dir: Eddie Davis   *Cast:* Tom Tryon, Carolyn Jones, Rick Jason, Patricia Connolly
► Remake of *D.O.A.* features Tryon as the man who is given a fatal poison and must find a cure and the killer before he bites the dust. Although Tryon tries hard, color this not as suspenseful as the 1949 version or as colorful as the 1988 version.
Dist.: Republic

COLOR OF MONEY, THE 1986
★ ★ ★ ★ R Drama 1:57
☑ Nudity, adult situations, explicit language, mild violence
Dir: Martin Scorsese   *Cast:* Paul Newman, Tom Cruise, Mary Elizabeth Mastrantonio, Helen Shaver, John Turturro, Forest Whitaker
► In this follow-up to 1961's *The Hustler,* Newman won his long-awaited Oscar as "Fast Eddie" Felson, instructing rebellious but talented protégé Cruise in the ways of pool. Teacher and pupil separate but meet again for a climactic game. Bravura direction by Scorsese, flavorful dialogue from screenwriter

Richard Price, terrific performances from Newman, Cruise, and Mastrantonio (as Cruise's hard-boiled girlfriend).
Dist.: Buena Vista

COLOR PURPLE, THE 1985
★ ★ ★ ★ ★ PG-13 Drama 2:32
☑ Adult situations, explicit language, violence
Dir: Steven Spielberg   *Cast:* Danny Glover, Whoopi Goldberg, Margaret Avery, Willard E. Pugh, Oprah Winfrey, Adolph Caesar
► Spielberg abandoned the world of aliens and adventurers for this controversial but visually beautiful adaptation of Alice Walker's best-seller which traces the struggle and eventual triumph of Celie (Goldberg), a poor black woman under the brutal thumb of husband Glover in 1909–47 rural South. Some criticized Spielberg's approach as sugarcoated but the performances are excellent (especially TV talk show hostess Winfrey in her first dramatic role) and the story is overflowing with powerful emotions. Nominated for eleven Oscars, including Best Picture. **(CC)**
Dist.: Warner

COLORS 1988
★ ★ ★ R Action-Adventure 2:00
☑ Nudity, adult situations, explicit language, graphic violence
Dir: Dennis Hopper   *Cast:* Sean Penn, Robert Duvall, Maria Conchita Alonso, Randy Brooks, Brand Bush, Don Cheadle
► Hotheaded rookie cop Penn and streetwise veteran Duvall are partnered to patrol tough Los Angeles neighborhood plagued by warfare between rival gangs, the Bloods and the Crips. Penn romances barrio girl Alonso, but his aggressive approach to street punks alienates and infuriates her, Duvall, and the gangs. Realistic, hard-hitting look at cop/gang battle for control of the streets is not for the squeamish. **(CC)**
Dist.: Orion

COLOSSUS: THE FORBIN PROJECT 1969
★ ★ ★ PG Sci-Fi 1:40
☑ Adult situations
Dir: Joseph Sargent   *Cast:* Eric Braeden, Susan Clark, Gordon Pinsent, William Schallert, Georg Stanford Brown, Marion Ross
► Colussus, a powerful computer that controls the American defense system, hooks up with its Russian counterpart Guardian to dominate the world. Scientist Braeden, who created the computer, now finds he can't outwit it. Unusual, intelligent sci-fi hampered by flat pacing. James Bridges wrote the provocative screenplay. Also known as *The Forbin Project.*
Dist.: MCA

COMA 1978
★ ★ ★ PG Mystery-Suspense 1:52
☑ Adult situations, explicit language, violence
Dir: Michael Crichton   *Cast:* Genevieve Bu-

Jold, Michael Douglas, Elizabeth Ashley, Richard Widmark, Rip Torn, Tom Selleck
▶ When a close friend goes into a permanent coma during an otherwise routine operation, intrepid doctor Bujold begins investigating similar incidents. She uncovers a sinister medical conspiracy, even though boyfriend Douglas is doubtful. Taut, quickly paced hospital thriller from the best-selling novel by Robin Cook. Bujold gives an intelligent, immensely sympathetic performance as the beleaguered heroine.
Dist.: MGM/UA

COMANCHEROS, THE 1961
★ ★ ★ ★ NR Western 1:47
Dir: Michael Curtiz *Cast:* John Wayne, Stuart Whitman, Ina Balin, Lee Marvin, Patrick Wayne
▶ Texas Rangers Wayne and Whitman battle the Comancheros, an outlaw band supplying guns and liquor to the dreaded Commanche Indians. Solid Western, neither Wayne's best nor worst, with the Duke well suited to his tough, sarcastic role. Whitman, gunslinger Marvin, Wayne's son Pat, and a rousing Elmer Bernstein score add extra zing. **(CC)**
Dist.: CBS/Fox

COME AND GET IT 1936
★ ★ ★ NR Drama 1:39 B&W
Dir: Howard Hawks, William Wyler *Cast:* Edward Arnold, Joel McCrea, Frances Farmer, Walter Brennan, Andrea Leeds, Frank Shields
▶ Sprawling epic of the Pacific Northwest and larger-than-life timberman Arnold, who sacrifices love for wealth. Farmer, playing both the woman Arnold rejects and her daughter whom he tries to wed, considered this her best film. Based on Edna Ferber novel. Contains some fascinating lumbering sequences. Brennan, as Arnold's pal, won the first of three Supporting Oscars.
Dist.: Embassy

COME BACK TO THE 5 & DIME, JIMMY DEAN, JIMMY DEAN 1982
★ PG Drama 1:49
☑ Adult situations, explicit language, adult humor
Dir: Robert Altman *Cast:* Cher, Karen Black, Sandy Dennis, Sudie Bond, Kathy Bates
▶ Six women in the James Dean fan club reunite in a run-down Texas five and dime near where the actor shot *Giant.* Revelations start pouring out in Ed Graczyk's heavy-handed adaptation of his own play, which is transformed into affecting drama by the fine performances of the three leads and Altman's artful direction.
Dist.: Virgin

COMEDY OF TERRORS, THE 1964
★ ★ NR Horror/Comedy 1:28
Dir: Jacques Tourneur *Cast:* Vincent Price,

Peter Lorre, Boris Karloff, Basil Rathbone, Joe E. Brown, Joyce Jameson
▶ In turn-of-the-century New England, business is slow for undertakers Price and Karloff, so Price and gnomish aide Lorre turn to murder to bring in new customers. Mean-spirited landlord Rathbone is the victim who won't stay dead. Broad spoof succeeds due to all-star cast of horror heavies.
Dist.: HBO

COMES A HORSEMAN 1978
★ ★ ★ ★ PG Western/Drama 1:58
☑ Explicit language, mild violence
Dir: Alan J. Pakula *Cast:* Jane Fonda, James Caan, Jason Robards, George Grizzard, Richard Farnsworth, Mark Harmon
▶ In the 1940s, independent ranchers—tomboyish spinster Fonda and World War II vet Caan—join forces to battle Robards, a land baron intent on amassing an empire. Austere, slowly paced Western filmed in Colorado's majestic Wet Mountain Valley convincingly updates a traditional theme. Farnsworth won a Supporting Actor nomination for his role as Fonda's aging hired hand.
Dist.: CBS/Fox

COMFORT AND JOY 1984 Scottish
★ PG Comedy 1:45
☑ Adult situations, violence
Dir: Bill Forsyth *Cast:* Bill Paterson, Eleanor David, C. P. Grogan, Alex Norton, Patrick Malahide, Rikki Fulton
▶ A mild-mannered Scottish radio disc jockey (Paterson), saddened when his girlfriend leaves him, throws himself into a mission to reconcile two Mafia families warring over local ice cream racket. Good-natured, subtle bit of Scottish artillery from Forsyth, who invests the slim story with his trademark whimsy and dry humor. Best appreciated by sophisticated viewers.
Dist.: MCA

COMIC, THE 1969
★ ★ PG Comedy 1:35
☑ Explicit language
Dir: Carl Reiner *Cast:* Dick Van Dyke, Michele Lee, Mickey Rooney, Cornel Wilde, Nina Wayne, Steve Allen
▶ Silent film star Van Dyke destroys his career through egotism and alcoholism, then rejects friends who try to help him. Sincere but heavy-handed study of a doomed figure (a composite of several screen clowns) is ultimately mawkish and unrevealing.
Dist.: RCA/Columbia

COMIC BOOK CONFIDENTIAL 1988
★ ★ ★ NR Documentary 1:30 C/B&W
☑ Explicit language
Dir: Ron Mann *Cast:* William M. Gaines, Stan Lee, Jack Kirby, Harvey Kurtzman, Robert Crumb, Gilbert Shelton, Bill Griffith, Art Spiegelman, Lynda Barry, Harvey Pekar, Sue Coe
▶ History of the comic book from the thirties to

the eighties is hip, sassy, and entertaining. High points are interviews with living legends like Gaines, Kurtzman, and Crumb, some of whom narrate panels of their work. Comics fans will be in hog heaven; but even those who know the form only through Sunday papers will enjoy this laugh-, image-, and music-packed look at a truly amazing art form.

COMING HOME 1978
★★★★★ R Drama 2:07
☑ Nudity, adult situations, explicit language
Dir: Hal Ashby ***Cast:*** Jane Fonda, Jon Voight, Bruce Dern, Penelope Milford, Robert Ginty, Robert Carradine
▶ Fonda, the proper, repressed wife of Vietnam Marine captain Dern, does volunteer work at a local veteran's hospital, where she falls in love with paraplegic vet Voight. The husband, freaked out by the war, returns to find his wife radically changed and independent. One of Hollywood's first attempts to explore Vietnam veterans, but the political slant takes a back seat to the touching and emotionally charged love story. Outstanding Oscar-winning performances by Voight and Fonda. Score of classic sixties music adds to the period feel.
Dist.: MGM/UA

COMING TO AMERICA 1988
★★★★ R Comedy 1:55
☑ Nudity, adult situations, explicit language, adult humor
Dir: John Landis ***Cast:*** Eddie Murphy, James Earl Jones, Arsenio Hall, John Amos, Madge Sinclair, Shari Headley
▶ Pressured into an arranged marriage by his father Jones, pampered African prince Murphy travels to America with sidekick Hall in search of true love. Murphy meets beautiful Headley in Queens, New York, and to be near her gets a job in the burger joint owned by her dad, Amos. Romantic prospects look bright until Jones interferes. Despite critical condemnation, fans flocked to Murphy vehicle; part of the fun comes from identifying Murphy and Hall in multiple disguises.
Dist.: Paramount

COMMANDO 1985
★★★★ R Action-Adventure 1:30
☑ Brief nudity, explicit language, graphic violence
Dir: Mark L. Lester ***Cast:*** Arnold Schwarzenegger, Rae Dawn Chong, Dan Hedaya, Vernon Wells, James Olson, Alyssa Milano
▶ Retired commando Schwarzenegger returns to action when daughter Milano is kidnapped. Not much in the way of plot, but plenty of energetic, powerhouse action scenes. Chong, as a stewardess along for Arnie's violent ride, is appealing and the big man evinces a nice sense of humor. "I like you, Sully, you're a funny guy," he tells one thug. "That's why I'll kill you last." (CC)
Dist.: CBS/Fox

COMMANDOS STRIKE AT DAWN, THE 1942
★★★ NR War 1:39 B&W
Dir: John Farrow ***Cast:*** Paul Muni, Anna Lee, Lillian Gish, Cedric Hardwicke, Alexander Knox
▶ Nazis invade a small Norwegian fishing community and take Muni's daughter captive. He escapes to England, where admiral Hardwicke convinces him to lead a raid on a Nazi airfield. Interesting Irwin Shaw screenplay concentrates on the personal impact of the war.
Dist.: RCA/Columbia

COMMISSAR 1988 Russian
☆ NR Drama 1:50 B&W
☑ Adult situations
Dir: Aleksandr Askoldov ***Cast:*** Nonna Mordukova, Rolan Bykov, Raisa Nedaskovskaya, Vasily Shukshin
▶ During the 1922 Russian Civil War, hefty, fearless commissar Mordukova finds herself pregnant. Sent to live with a large Jewish family until the birth of the baby, she learns important lessons about justice and tolerance. Visually striking, with richly textured story. Made in 1967, production so infuriated the authorities for dealing with Soviet anti-Semitism that it was banned for twenty-one years; director Askoldov was never allowed to make another movie. [S]
Dist.: IFE

COMMUNION 1989
★★★ R Sci-Fi 1:47
☑ Nudity, adult situations, explicit language, mild violence
Dir: Phillippe Mora ***Cast:*** Christopher Walken, Lindsay Crouse, Joel Carlson, Frances Sternhagen, Andreas Katsulas, Basil Hoffman
▶ Why is writer Walken suffering fear and depression? What is filling his mind with unsettling images? After a hypnotic session, Walken finds out he has been visited by space aliens. Film based on best-seller by Whitley Streiber is full of superior performances, but has same flaw as book: we're expected to swallow it as true.
Dist.: Virgin

COMPANY OF WOLVES, THE 1985 British
★ R Horror 1:35
☑ Adult situations, violence
Dir: Neil Jordan ***Cast:*** Angela Lansbury, David Warner, Stephen Rea, Tusse Silberg, Sarah Patterson
▶ Young Patterson, visiting grandmother Lansbury, has a series of peculiar dreams about wolves. Eccentric, unpredictable, and extremely adult approach to "Little Red Riding Hood" overflowing with Freudian symbols. Alternately comic and horrifying, with an amusing cameo by Terence Stamp as the Devil. (CC)
Dist.: Vestron

COMPETITION, THE 1980
★★★★ PG Drama 2:09

☑ Adult situations, explicit language
Dir: Joel Oliansky *Cast:* Richard Dreyfuss, Amy Irving, Lee Remick, Sam Wanamaker, Joseph Cali
▶ Talented pianists Dreyfuss and Irving compete for first prize in a contest despite their growing love for one another. Well-acted with effective Dreyfuss in a complex, not always sympathetic role. Irving is fine but Remick, as her bitchy mentor, almost steals the movie.
Dist.: RCA/Columbia

COMPLEAT BEATLES, THE 1984
★ ★ ★ ★ NR Documentary/Music 2:00
☑ Adult situations
Dir: Patrick Montgomery *Cast:* Paul McCartney, John Lennon, Ringo Starr, George Harrison, Brian Epstein, George Martin
▶ Exhaustive documentary on the Beatles uses interviews, newsreel footage, and concert excerpts to describe every facet of their career. Although their personal lives aren't ignored, the film concentrates squarely on the music, from their start as the Quarrymen to their breakup after "Let It Be." Narration (by Malcolm McDowell) will inform and entertain even the most knowledgeable fans.
Dist.: MGM/UA

COMPROMISING POSITIONS 1985
★ ★ R Mystery-Suspense 1:38
☑ Brief nudity, adult situations, explicit language, mild violence
Dir: Frank Perry *Cast:* Susan Sarandon, Raul Julia, Edward Herrmann, Judith Ivey, Mary Beth Hurt, Joe Mantegna
▶ A quiet Long Island community goes into shock when philandering gum surgeon Mantegna (in a funny cameo) is murdered. Local homemaker Sarandon turns sleuth to investigate the case, much to the chagrin of stuffy hubby Herrmann. Murder suburban style is handled with humor, nifty dialogue, and a little romance (between Sarandon and cop Julia). Susan Isaacs adapted from her bestseller. **(CC)**
Dist.: Paramount

COMPUTER WORE TENNIS SHOES, THE 1970
★ ★ ★ ★ G Comedy 1:30
Dir: Robert Butler *Cast:* Kurt Russell, Cesar Romero, Joe Flynn, William Schallert, Alan Hewitt
▶ Above-average Disney comedy about not-too-bright college student Russell, transformed into a genius after he's accidentally zapped with a supercomputer's data bank. Unfortunately, gangster Romero's records are transferred into Russell as well, leading to a series of well-executed chases. Russell repeated his successful role in sequels: *Now Your See Him, Now You Don't* and *The Strongest Man in the World.*
Dist.: Buena Vista

CONAN THE BARBARIAN 1982
★ ★ R Action-Adventure 1:55
☑ Nudity, adult situations, graphic violence
Dir: John Milius *Cast:* Arnold Schwarzenegger, Sandahl Bergman, James Earl Jones, Max Von Sydow, Ben Davidson
▶ Robert E. Howard's pulp hero Conan comes to the screen in the muscular, hulking presence of Schwarzenegger. Violent saga traces the rise of Conan from enslaved orphaned boy to revenge-seeking barbarian who goes after his parents' killer, the evil Thulsa Doom (Jones). Macho tale is full of blood, gore, rippling biceps, and beautiful women.
Dist.: MCA

CONAN THE DESTROYER 1984
★ ★ ★ PG Action-Adventure 1:43
☑ Violence
Dir: Richard Fleischer *Cast:* Arnold Schwarzenegger, Grace Jones, Wilt Chamberlain, Mako, Sarah Douglas, Olivia d'Abo
▶ Schwarzenegger's sequel to *Conan the Barbarian.* Conan is recruited by scheming queen Douglas to accompany virginal princess d'Abo to a castle containing a magical gem. Along the way, Schwarzenegger hooks up with hoops legend Chamberlain and disco queen Jones. An improvement over the first movie. **(CC)**
Dist.: MCA

CONCERT FOR BANGLADESH, THE 1972
★ ★ ★ ★ ★ G Documentary/Music 1:39
Dir: Saul Swimmer *Cast:* George Harrison, Bob Dylan, Eric Clapton, Ringo Starr, Leon Russell, Ravi Shankar
▶ Decent recording of former Beatle Harrison's 1971 benefit for the starving masses of Bangladesh. Extended opening Ravi Shankar set is tough to watch for non-sitar buffs but film picks up considerably when Harrison, Dylan, Clapton, and Starr rock out. Songs include "My Sweet Lord" and "Mr. Tambourine Man."
Dist.: HBO

CONCORDE—AIRPORT '79, THE 1979
★ ★ ★ PG Action-Adventure 2:03
☑ Adult situations, violence
Dir: David Lowell Rich *Cast:* Alain Delon, Susan Blakely, Robert Wagner, Sylvia Kristel, George Kennedy, Eddie Albert, Charo, John Davidson, Andrea Marcovicci, Cicely Tyson, Jimmie Walker, Sybil Danning
▶ Fourth episode in the *Airport* series throws an all-star cast into extreme jeopardy aboard a Concorde flight to the Moscow Olympics. Evil tycoon Wagner sabotages the plane over the Alps, forcing the resourceful crew and passengers to fight for their lives.
Dist.: MCA

CONCRETE JUNGLE, THE 1982
★ ★ ★ R Action-Adventure 1:39
☑ Rape, nudity, adult situations, explicit language
Dir: Tom DeSimone *Cast:* Jill St. John, Tracy Bregman, Barbara Luna, June Barrett

► Framed in a drug bust, young WASP Bregman winds up in a women's prison ruled by corrupt warden St. John. She becomes the pawn of lesbian heroin dealer Luna who dominates the other inmates. Exploitation fare includes all the expected elements: beatings in the showers, cat fights in the cafeteria, etc.
Dist.: RCA/Columbia

CONDORMAN 1981
★ PG Comedy 1:30
☑ Explicit language
Dir: Charles Jarrott ***Cast:*** Michael Crawford, Oliver Reed, Barbara Carrera, James Hampton, Dana Elcar, Jean-Pierre Kalfon
► Superhero spoof stars Crawford as comic strip artist who gets involved in CIA/KGB intrigue and assumes the identity of a winged hero. Carrera provides the romantic interest as the Russian operative who wins Crawford's heart. Lighthearted Disney fare.
Dist.: Buena Vista

CONFESSIONAL, THE 1975 British
☆ R Mystery-Suspense 1:48
☑ Adult situations, explicit language
Dir: Peter Walker ***Cast:*** Anthony Sharp, Susan Penhaligan, Stephanie Beacham, Norman Eshley, Sheila Keith
► No one believes a young woman who claims a well-respected priest has been secretly tape-recording her sexual confessions. Priest eventually goes mad and embarks on a murder spree that includes his own mother. Talky, slow-paced, and uncompelling. Originally titled *House of Mortal Sin.*
Dist.: Prism

CONFIDENTIALLY YOURS 1983 French
★ PG Mystery-Suspense 1:46 B&W
☑ Adult situations, explicit language, violence
Dir: François Truffaut ***Cast:*** Fanny Ardant, Jean-Louis Trintignant, Philippe Laudenbach, Caroline Sihol, Philippe Morier-Genoud, Xavier Saint Macary
► When real estate agent Trintignant is suspected of murdering his wife's lover, his devoted secretary Ardant tries to prove him innocent. Truffaut's last film is a stylishly made homage to old movies, crisply photographed by Nestor Alemendros and marvelously acted by Ardant. However, unlikable Trintignant and out-of-left-field resolution detract. [S]
Dist.: Key

CONFORMIST, THE 1970
Italian/French/German
☆ R Drama 1:55
☑ Nudity, adult situations, explicit language
Dir: Bernardo Bertolucci ***Cast:*** Jean-Louis Trintignant, Stefania Sandrelli, Dominique Sanda, Pierre Clementi
► Psychological portrait of weak-willed Trintignant, who joins the Italian Fascist party in 1938 to further his radio career. His beliefs are tested when he's ordered to kill his college professor. Powerful, intellectually astute film has stunning photography and a beautiful score by Georges Delerue. [S]
Dist.: Paramount

CONNECTICUT YANKEE IN KING ARTHUR'S COURT, A 1949
★★★ NR Fantasy 1:46
Dir: Tay Garnett ***Cast:*** Bing Crosby, William Bendix, Cedric Hardwicke, Rhonda Fleming, Virginia Field
► Crosby, a nineteenth-century Yankee blacksmith, is magically transported back in time to Camelot, where he astounds King Arthur (Hardwicke) with his "magic" compass and kitchen matches. Dubbed "Sir Boss," he pursues a romance with Fleming. Premise is all that remains of Mark Twain's grimly humorous novel, but Crosby's easygoing performance and tunes like "Busy Doing Nothing" are delightful. Pointlessly remade in 1979 as *The Unidentified Flying Oddball.*
Dist.: MCA

CONQUEROR, THE 1956
★★★ G Action-Adventure 1:51
Dir: Dick Powell ***Cast:*** John Wayne, Susan Hayward, Pedro Armendariz, Agnes Moorehead, Thomas Gomez, Lee Van Cleef
► Mongol leader Wayne kidnaps Tartar bride-to-be Hayward, the daughter of his father's killer, and then falls in love with her. Exotic action adventure has a silly story and miscast leads (although Wayne is fun to watch), but plenty of action and spectacle in the "cast of thousands" battle scenes. Excellent music score by Victor Young.
Dist.: MCA

CONQUEROR WORM, THE 1968 British
★★ NR Horror
☑ Brief nudity, adult situations, violence
Dir: Michael Reeves ***Cast:*** Vincent Price, Ian Ogilvy, Rupert Davies, Hilary Dwyer, Robert Russell, Patrick Wymark
► Price and cohort Russell are granted license to search the English countryside for witches. Price abducts Dwyer after murdering her uncle, then attempts to torture and execute her boyfriend Ogilvy. Competent shocker with a strong turn by Price as the "Witchfinder General" (which was the film's British title).
Dist.: HBO

CONQUEST 1984 Italian/Spanish/Mexican
☆ R Fantasy 1:38
☑ Rape, nudity, adult situations, explicit language, graphic violence
Dir: Lucio Fulci ***Cast:*** Jorge Rivero, Andrea Occhipinti, Sabrina Siani, Conrado San Martin, Violetta Cela, Maria Scola
► Two wandering warriors on a primitive world battle fur-bearing man-beasts sent to kill them by evil demigod Siani. Ponderously mystical tale has laughable monsters, blurry visuals, and not a trace of script logic.
Dist.: Media

CONQUEST OF SPACE 1955
★ ★ NR Sci-Fi 1:20
Dir: Byron Haskin   *Cast:* Eric Fleming, Walter Brooke, Ross Martin, Phil Foster, William Hopper, Mickey Shaughnessy
▶ Astronauts fly to Mars but one crew member thinks that such a mission goes against God and he tries sabotage. However, God proves to be on the side of progress in the end. Special effects overshadow bland plotting and performances. Produced by George Pal.
Dist.: JCI

CONQUEST OF THE PLANET OF THE APES 1972
★ ★ ★ PG Sci-Fi 1:27
☑ Explicit language, violence
Dir: J. Lee Thompson   *Cast:* Roddy McDowall, Don Murray, Ricardo Montalban, Natalie Trundy, Hari Rhodes
▶ After dogs and cats are killed by a virus in the near future, apes are trained to do menial labor and other unpleasant tasks. They live under the iron hand of stern human governor Murray until intelligent talking ape McDowall leads a revolt. Fourth in the Apes series is a surprisingly taut and suspenseful effort. (CC)
Dist.: CBS/Fox

CONRACK 1974
★ ★ ★ ★ ★ PG Drama 1:46
☑ Explicit language
Dir: Martin Ritt   *Cast:* Jon Voight, Hume Cronyn, Paul Winfield, Madge Sinclair, Tina Andrews
▶ Moving story of young white schoolteacher Voight helping a group of culturally deprived black youngsters on a remote island off the South Carolina coast. Voight gives an extremely appealing and tender performance and the kids are wonderful. Based on the book *The Water Is Wide* by Pat Conroy. (CC)
Dist.: CBS/Fox

CONSOLATION MARRIAGE 1931
★ NR Drama 1:22 B&W
Dir: Paul Sloane   *Cast:* Irene Dunne, Pat O'Brien, John Halliday, Matt Moore, Leslie Vail, Myrna Loy
▶ Reporter O'Brien meets Dunne in a bar and learns she's just broken up with boyfriend Vail. Although broken-hearted over losing Loy, O'Brien marries Dunne. Their union is threatened when Loy returns unexpectedly. Great cast adds some spark to predictable melodrama.
Dist.: Turner

CONSPIRACY: THE TRIAL OF THE CHICAGO 8 1987
★ ★ ★ NR Drama/MFTV 1:58
☑ Explicit language
Dir: Jeremy Kagan   *Cast:* Peter Boyle, Robert Carradine, Elliott Gould, Robert Loggia, Michael Lembeck, David Opatoshu
▶ Made-for-cable dramatization of the trial of the "Chicago 8," the antiwar activists accused of inciting the riots that disrupted the 1968 Democratic national convention. Newsreel footage, interviews with the real defendants as they are today, and dialogue based on the court transcripts combine to re-create the circuslike atmosphere of the trial.
Dist.: HBO

CONSUMING PASSIONS 1988 U.S./British
★ R Comedy 1:40
☑ Adult situations, explicit language
Dir: Giles Foster   *Cast:* Vanessa Redgrave, Jonathan Pryce, Tyler Butterworth, Freddie Jones, Sammi Davis, Prunella Scales
▶ Three workmen meet a sticky end when chocolate factory management trainee Butterworth accidentally pushes them into a vat. Amazingly, the public responds to this "new ingredient" and the company searches for fresh meat to add to the candies. Offbeat black comedy bon bon from Britain for those with unusual tastes. Based on a play by Monty Python graduates Michael Palin and Terry Jones.
Dist.: Virgin

CONTEMPT 1963 French/Italian
★ ★ NR Drama 1:43
☑ Nudity, adult situations, explicit language
Dir: Jean-Luc Godard   *Cast:* Brigitte Bardot, Jack Palance, Michel Piccoli, Fritz Lang, Giorgia Moll, Jean-Luc Godard
▶ Idealistic playwright Piccoli is lured into writing a screenplay of *The Odyssey* to please extravagant wife Bardot; she derides him for selling out and starts an affair with producer Palance. Challenging but perceptive look at the process of writing for the screen was director Godard's subtle dig at his own producer, Joseph E. Levine. S
Dist.: Nelson

CONTINENTAL DIVIDE 1981
★ ★ ★ ★ PG Romance 1:43
☑ Brief nudity, adult situations, explicit language
Dir: Michael Apted   *Cast:* John Belushi, Blair Brown, Allen Goorwitz, Carlin Glynn, Tony Ganios
▶ Crack Chicago reporter Belushi is assigned to a story about reclusive ornithologist Brown who is doing research in the Rockies. They fall in love but must work out a solution to their separate careers in this modern variation on the Tracy/Hepburn formula. Agreeable, pleasant romantic comedy with a charming Brown and a nice, surprisingly low-key Belushi.
Dist.: MCA

CONTROL 1987
★ ★ ★ NR Drama/MFTV 1:22
Dir: Giuliano Montaldo   *Cast:* Burt Lancaster, Kate Nelligan, Ben Gazzara, Kate Reid, Erland Josephson, Ingrid Thulin
▶ Fifteen volunteers from around the world agree to test a state-of-the-art nuclear bomb shelter for twenty days. Malfunction in the ventilating system increases tensions, but the

participants quickly learn of an even greater threat. Timely message drama with an all-star cast, including Gazzara as a reporter, Nelligan as a peace activist, and Lancaster as supervisor of the experiment.
Dist.: HBO

CONVERSATION, THE 1974
★ ★ **PG Drama 1:53**
☑ Adult situations, explicit language
Dir: Francis Ford Coppola *Cast:* Gene Hackman, John Cazale, Allen Garfield, Frederic Forrest, Cindy Williams, Teri Garr, Robert Duvall, Harrison Ford
▶ Expert wire-tapper Hackman is hired to spy on Forrest and Williams. Reviewing his tapes, Hackman realizes someone is planning a murder, but professional pride prevents him from telling his employers (Duvall and Ford). On all levels a stunning, deeply disturbing film. Nominated for Best Picture, Screenplay (Coppola), and Sound (Walter Murch).
Dist.: Paramount

CONVERSATION PIECE 1977 Italian
☆ **R Drama 1:52**
☑ Nudity, adult situations, explicit language, violence
Dir: Luchino Visconti *Cast:* Burt Lancaster, Silvana Mangano, Helmut Berger, Claudia Marsani, Stefano Patrizi, Claudia Cardinale
▶ Aging American professor Lancaster lives in a Roman house filled with paintings called "conversation pieces." When decadent Mangano, lover Berger, and daughter Marsani move into the upstairs apartment, sexual intrigue and death intrude upon Lancaster's well-ordered life. Static, talky drama of corruption was filmed in English.
Dist.: HBO

CONVOY 1978
★ ★ ★ ★ **PG Action-Adventure 1:51**
☑ Explicit language
Dir: Sam Peckinpah *Cast:* Kris Kristofferson, Ali MacGraw, Ernest Borgnine, Burt Young, Madge Sinclair
▶ Good-natured trucker movie based on the hit song by C. W. McCall describes the feud between Rubber Duck (Kristofferson) and Borgnine, a hotheaded speed-trap cop. Borgnine sets up a roadblock to arrest the Duck, who turns to his CB buddies for help. MacGraw is a photojournalist along for the ride. Above-average truck stunts and scenery add to the excitement.
Dist.: HBO

COOGAN'S BLUFF 1968
★ ★ ★ **R Action-Adventure 1:34**
☑ Nudity, adult situations, explicit language, violence
Dir: Don Siegel *Cast:* Clint Eastwood, Lee J. Cobb, Susan Clark, Tisha Sterling, Don Stroud, Betty Field
▶ Arizona deputy Eastwood is fish out of water when he comes to New York City to fetch criminal Stroud, who is being held by NYPD.

Stroud escapes, but he's no match for Clint's Wild West techniques. Initial Eastwood/Siegel (*Dirty Harry*) teaming is satisfying, if not as exciting as later efforts. Inspiration for TV series "McCloud" makes effective use of New York locale.
Dist.: MCA

COOKIE 1989
★ ★ ★ **R Comedy 1:33**
☑ Explicit language, violence
Dir: Susan Seidelman *Cast:* Peter Falk, Emily Lloyd, Michael V. Gazzo, Dianne Wiest, Brenda Vaccaro, Jerry Lewis
▶ Punkette mafia princess Cookie (Lloyd) is at odds with mob boss dad, Dapper Dino (Falk), who's just finished a thirteen-year stretch in prison and can't figure out his wise-talking daughter. Generation gap closes as Cookie proves she can drive a getaway stretch limo like a pro, and helps her dad outwit crooked associates and a politically ambitious D.A. Fun, breezy; Mafia lite. **(CC)**
Dist.: Warner

COOK, THE THIEF, HIS WIFE & HER LOVER, THE 1990 British
☆ **NC-17 Drama 2:00**
☑ Nudity, adult situations, explicit language, violence
Dir: Peter Greenaway *Cast:* Michael Gambon, Helen Mirren, Alan Howard, Richard Bohringer
▶ Brutish thug Gambon abuses wife Mirren while dining nightly at his opulent new restaurant, savoring feasts prepared by submissive cook Bohringer. When Mirren begins an affair with Howard, the spouses dish up their own unique blends of revenge on each other. Startling, uncompromising film has been given differing interpretations by many. Sumptuously designed and acted, but will put off most due to its excessiveness and violence. Also available in an R-rated version.
Dist.: Vidmark

COOLANGATTA GOLD, THE 1988 Australian
★ **PG-13 Drama 1:56**
☑ Brief nudity, adult situations, explicit language
Dir: Igor Auzins *Cast:* Joss McWilliam, Nick Tate, Robyn Nevin, Josephine Smulders, Grant Kenny, Colin Friels
▶ Dad Tate prefers older son Friels over younger McWilliam and trains him for upcoming "Iron Man" competition. When Friels is accidentally injured, Tate blames McWilliam, who responds by entering the contest against his brother. Exciting race sequences although family squabbles grow tiresome. Bill Conti score adds to *Rocky*-esque flavor.
Dist.: IVE

COOL HAND LUKE 1967
★ ★ ★ ★ **PG Drama 2:06**
☑ Adult situations, explicit language
Dir: Stuart Rosenberg *Cast:* Paul Newman, George Kennedy, Strother Martin, J. D. Can-

non, Jo Van Fleet, Clifton James, Lou Antonio, Wayne Rogers, Anthony Zerbe, Ralph Waite, Harry Dean Stanton, Dennis Hopper, Joe Don Baker
▶ Enormously popular prison story features a sterling performance by Newman as a petty thief who refuses to submit to authority on a Southern chain gang. Although brutal at times, film's many vignettes are surprisingly funny and upbeat. As the warden, Strother delivers the memorable line, "What we have here is a failure to communicate." Newman and screenwriters Donn Pearce and Frank R. Pierson were nominated for Oscars; Kennedy, as a harsh gang foreman, won Best Supporting Actor.
Dist.: Warner

COP 1988
★ ★ ★ **R Mystery-Suspense 1:45**
☑ Nudity, adult situations, explicit language, graphic violence
Dir: James B. Harris   *Cast:* James Woods, Lesley Ann Warren, Charles Durning, Charles Haid, Randi Brooks
▶ Maverick cop Woods tackles the police department and his inner demons while obsessively investigating a series of grisly slayings. Chilling, gritty murder mystery with a twisty plot, sleazy but smart dialogue, and an edgy, compelling performance by the unique Woods as a cop so tough he's almost unhinged. Fine support from Durning as Woods's born-again superior.
Dist.: Paramount

COPACABANA 1947
★ ★ **NR Musical/Comedy 1:30 B&W**
Dir: Alfred E. Green   *Cast:* Groucho Marx, Carmen Miranda, Steve Cochran, Gloria Jean, Ralph Sanford
▶ Groucho plays a two-bit agent with one client, Miranda. She auditions twice (once wearing a wig) for nightclub manager Cochran, and wins two jobs at the Copa. Predictable complications ensue in this frantic but generally stale comedy. "Tico, Tico" is the best song.
Dist.: Republic

CORNBREAD, EARL AND ME 1975
★ ★ **PG Drama 1:34**
☑ Adult situations, explicit language
Dir: Joseph Manduke   *Cast:* Moses Gunn, Rosalind Cash, Madge Sinclair, Keith Wilkes, Tierre Turner, Larry Fishburne
▶ High school basketball star Cornbread (pro hoops star Wilkes), idolized by ghetto youths Turner and Fishburne, is mistaken for a rapist by two cops and then fatally shot. The cops try to intimidate potential witnesses when Cornbread's family fights to clear his name. Well-intentioned, modest black family drama.
Dist.: HBO

CORNERED 1945
★ ★ **NR Mystery-Suspense 1:43 B&W**
Dir: Edward Dmytryk   *Cast:* Dick Powell,

Walter Slezak, Micheline Cheirel, Nina Vale, Morris Carnovsky, Edgar Barrier
▶ Canadian veteran Powell searches post–World War II Buenos Aires for the Nazis who murdered his French wife. Underworld figures insist the Germans are already dead, but Powell obsessively pursues clues that place him in jeopardy. Tough, crackling film noir with gritty plotting and compelling performances.
Dist.: Turner

CORN IS GREEN, THE 1945
★ ★ ★ **NR Drama 1:54 B&W**
Dir: Irving Rapper   *Cast:* Bette Davis, John Dall, Nigel Bruce, Joan Lorring, Rhys Williams
▶ In Wales circa 1895, middle-aged schoolteacher Davis goes to work in a backward mining town and takes a brilliant but untutored young Dall under her wing. The relationship that develops between student and pupil changes both in deeply moving ways. Excellent work from both Davis and Dall. Based on the play by Emlyn Williams.
Dist.: MGM/UA

CORPSE VANISHES, THE 1942
★ **NR Horror 1:04 B&W**
Dir: Wallace Fox   *Cast:* Bela Lugosi, Luana Walters, Tristram Coffin, Elizabeth Russell, Kenneth Harlan, Vince Barnett
▶ Mad scientist Lugosi uses glandular secretions to keep his elderly wife Russell alive. His technique: kidnap virginal brides from their weddings. Middling Lugosi vehicle suffers from low budget and uninspired plotting.
Dist.: Sinister

CORRUPT 1984
★ **R Drama 1:39**
☑ Adult situations, explicit language, graphic violence
Dir: Roberto Faenza   *Cast:* Harvey Keitel, John Lydon, Sylvia Sidney, Nicole Garcia, Leonard Mann
▶ Exploration of strange sadomasochistic relationship between Keitel, a corrupt New York City policeman, and confessed cop-killer Lydon (a.k.a. Johnny Rotten). Story starts with a bang but goes downhill. Street grit with psychological pretensions plays like a weird hybrid of *Mean Streets* and *The Night Porter.*
Dist.: HBO

CORRUPT ONES, THE 1967
French/Italian/German
★ **NR Action-Adventure 1:32**
Dir: James Hill   *Cast:* Robert Stack, Elke Sommer, Nancy Kwan, Christian Marquand, Werner Peters
▶ After escaping Chinese Communists, photographer Stack is given a medallion by the black marketeer who rescued him. When his benefactor is killed, he is besieged by gangsters seeking the object, which holds the key to a treasure. Solid but unremarkable international thriller. Also known as *Hell to Macao* and *The Peking Medallion.*
Dist.: Nelson

CORSICAN BROTHERS, THE 1941
★ ★ ★ ★ NR Action-Adventure 1:51 B&W
Dir: Gregory Ratoff *Cast:* Douglas Fairbanks, Jr., Ruth Warrick, Akim Tamiroff, H. B. Warner, J. Carrol Naish
▶ Separated twin brothers avenge the deaths of their parents (caused by a family feud on Corsica), while vying for the hand of the same woman. Light, tongue-in-cheek version of the Dumas classic, full of sword fights, battles, and heroic deeds, features Fairbanks at his swashbuckling best.
Dist.: IVE

CORVETTE SUMMER 1978
★ ★ PG Action-Adventure 1:36
☑ Brief nudity, explicit language
Dir: Matthew Robbins *Cast:* Mark Hamill, Annie Potts, Eugene Roche, Kim Milford, Richard McKenzie
▶ High school student Hamill obsessively searches for stolen Corvette. The trail leads to Las Vegas, where hooker Potts helps him. Attractive, amiable youth adventure/comedy with nicely staged action and genuine chemistry between the appealing Hamill and Potts, whose wacky comic style is original and refreshing.
Dist.: MGM/UA

COTTON CLUB, THE 1984
★ ★ R Drama 2:01
☑ Adult situations, explicit language, violence
Dir: Francis Coppola *Cast:* Richard Gere, Gregory Hines, Diane Lane, Lonette McKee, Bob Hoskins
▶ Against the background of Harlem's legendary Cotton Club, struggling musician Gere has a dangerous affair with gangster's moll Lane. His best pal, tap dancer Hines, gets involved with McKee, a black singer trying to pass for white. Flashy gangster epic is long on atmosphere, dancing, music, and technique but somewhat short on plot and likable characters. (CC)
Dist.: Nelson

COUCH TRIP, THE 1988
★ ★ R Comedy 1:38
☑ Adult situations, explicit language
Dir: Michael Ritchie *Cast:* Dan Aykroyd, Charles Grodin, Donna Dixon, Walter Matthau, Richard Romanus, Mary Gross
▶ Swindler Aykroyd, confined to a mental institution, escapes and then successfully poses as a Beverly Hills radio sex therapist. Psychiatry and L.A. lifestyle are satirized in this vehicle for Aykroyd's motor-mouthed comic style. Grodin steals scenes as the unhinged shrink replaced by Aykroyd. (CC)
Dist.: Orion

COUNTDOWN 1968
★ ★ ★ NR Sci-Fi 1:41
Dir: Robert Altman *Cast:* James Caan, Joanna Moore, Robert Duvall, Barbara Baxley, Michael Murphy, Ted Knight

▶ NASA officials forsake safety precautions in a race against the Russians to the moon. At the same time, dedicated astronaut Duvall is replaced by civilian scientist Caan, a move which seriously affects their private lives. Once-provocative film has dated badly (particularly its technology); still an honest effort to portray the space program realistically.
Dist.: Warner

COUNT DRACULA 1971
Spanish/Italian/German
★ PG Horror 1:36
☑ Adult situations, violence
Dir: Jess Franco *Cast:* Christopher Lee, Herbert Lom, Klaus Kinski, Soledad Miranda, Maria Rohm
▶ Slow-paced, faithful adaptation of Bram Stoker's horror classic, with Lee playing the vampire as a respectable older man who gains a youthful appearance after his bloody meals. Lom is surprisingly dignified as the Count's nemesis Van Helsing. Kinski steals the show as the bug-chewing Renfield.
Dist.: Republic

COUNT OF MONTE CRISTO, THE 1934
★ ★ ★ NR Action-Adventure 1:56 B&W
Dir: Rowland V. Lee *Cast:* Robert Donat, Elissa Landi, Louis Calhern, Sidney Blackmer, Raymond Walburn
▶ Superb adaptation of Alexander Dumas's classic tale of Edmond Dantes, a man unjustly imprisoned twenty years for treason—and his revenge. Rousing combination of adventure, romance, and intrigue receives a first-rate production; Donat is convincing in a difficult role.
Dist.: Media C

COUNTRY 1984
★ ★ ★ ★ PG Drama 1:48
☑ Explicit language, violence
Dir: Richard Pearce *Cast:* Jessica Lange, Sam Shepard, Wilford Brimley, Matt Clark, Therese Graham, Levi L. Knebel
▶ An Iowa farm family faces foreclosure unless they can repay a Federal loan. When a tornado destroys their equipment, husband Shepard loses faith and turns to alcohol. Determined to keep the farm, wife Lange organizes a support group with her neighbors. Down-to-earth slice of Americana provides a compelling look at modern-day problems. Lange won a Best Actress nomination.
Dist.: Buena Vista

COUNTRY GIRL, THE 1954
★ ★ ★ NR Drama 1:44 B&W
Dir: George Seaton *Cast:* Bing Crosby, Grace Kelly, William Holden, Anthony Ross, Gene Reynolds, Jacqueline Fontaine
▶ Alcoholic actor Crosby returns to stage in director Holden's play. As he struggles to stay sober, Crosby's wife Kelly gets into disputes with Holden about the situation; later, more loving feelings grow between these two. Towering trio of performances highlight adapta-

tion of Clifford Odets play; Kelly and the screenplay won Oscars.
Dist.: Paramount

COUNT YORGA, VAMPIRE 1970
★★ PG Horror 1:31
☑ Adult situations, explicit language, violence
Dir: Bob Kelljan ***Cast:*** Robert Quarry, Roger Perry, Donna Anders, Michael Murphy, Michael Macready
▶ Sunny Southern California is the new home base for Count Yorga (Quarry), a peculiar medium who lures unsuspecting young couples to seances. When Anders wakes up one morning missing several pints of blood, husband Murphy sets out to kill the Count. Amusing, effective updating of the Dracula story is played more for laughs than chills.
Dist.: HBO

COUP DE GRACE 1976 French/German
☆ NR Drama 1:36 B&W
☑ Adult situations, violence
Dir: Volker Schlondorff ***Cast:*** Margarethe von Trotta, Matthias Habich, Rudiger Kirschstein, Valeska Gert, Mathieu Carriere, Marc Eyraud
▶ Von Trotta, brother Habich, and Prussian officer Kirschstein are together on a Latvian estate during the Allied campaign against the Bolsheviks in 1919. Red sympathizer Von Trotta loves Red-hater Kirschstein, but he has eyes for her brother. As shells explode around them, Von Trotta and Kirschstein play out their political roles to their tragic conclusion. Vivid, dreamlike imagery, but action is vague and distant. Based on a novel by Marguerite Yourcenar. [S]
Dist.: RCA/Columbia

COUP DE TETE 1980 French
★ R Comedy 1:28
☑ Nudity, explicit language
Dir: Jean-Jacques Annaud ***Cast:*** Patrick Dewaere, France Dougnac, Jean Bouise, Michel Aumont, Paul Le Person
▶ Dewaere, a soccer player, is dropped from his small-town team when he injures the team's star. Then he's wrongly jailed on a rape charge but gains his freedom and his vengeance when the team needs him again. Lightweight comedy from France features adept performance by Dewaere.
Dist.: RCA/Columbia

COUP DE TORCHON 1981 French
★ NR Comedy/Drama 2:08
☑ Nudity, explicit language, violence
Dir: Bertrand Tavernier ***Cast:*** Philippe Noiret, Isabelle Huppert, Stephane Audran, Jean-Pierre Marielle, Eddy Mitchell
▶ In West Africa circa 1938, French police official Noiret, fed up with being harassed by community members, decides to kill his tormentors. Exotic background provides a nice contrast to theme of absurdities of civilization but the black comic tone is hard to handle. Definitely original. French director Tavernier adapted from American pulp novelist Jim Thompson's *Pop. 1280*.
Dist.: Nelson

COUPE DE VILLE 1990
★★★ PG-13 Comedy/Drama 1:39
☑ Adult situations, explicit language
Dir: Joe Roth ***Cast:*** Patrick Dempsey, Arye Gross, Daniel Stern, Annabeth Gish, Rita Taggart, Joseph Bologna, Alan Arkin, James Gammon
▶ In 1963, brothers Stern, Dempsey, and Gross are ordered by dad Arkin to drive a 1954 Cadillac Coupe de Ville from Detroit to Miami as a gift for their mom Taggart. The boys' disparate personalities make for lots of fussing and fighting until brotherly love eventually emerges. Coming-of-age journey covers familiar dramatic territory, yet cast makes it a pleasant trip. **(CC)**
Dist.: MCA

COURAGE MOUNTAIN 1990
★★ PG Family 1:38
☑ Mild violence
Dir: Christopher Leitch ***Cast:*** Juliette Caton, Charlie Sheen, Jan Rubes, Leslie Caron, Yorgo Voyagis
▶ During World War I, now-adolescent Heidi (Caton) leaves grandfather Rubes in Switzerland and goes off to Italian boarding school. When the Italian army takes over the school and the girls are forced to work in a soap factory, Caton organizes an escape as her soldier boyfriend Sheen heads to the rescue. Youngsters should enjoy this simple retelling of the familiar story with stunning Alpine scenery.
Dist.: RCA/Columbia

COURAGEOUS MR. PENN 1941 British
★ NR Biography 1:19 B&W
Dir: Lance Comfort ***Cast:*** Clifford Evans, Deborah Kerr, Dennis Arundell, Aubrey Mallalieu, D. J. Williams
▶ Biography of seventeenth-century British nobleman William Penn (Evans), who renounced aristocracy to join the Quaker religious group. Persecuted by authorities, Penn leads a shipload of Quakers to the colonies, where he founds Pennsylvania. Kerr is the best aspect of this slow-moving and inaccurate story. British title: *Penn of Pennsylvania*.
Dist.: Video Yesteryear

COURIER, THE 1988 British
☆ R Drama 1:27
☑ Adult situations, explicit language, violence
Dir: Joe Lee, Frank Deasy ***Cast:*** Padraig O'Loingsigh, Cait O'Riordan, Gabriel Byrne, Ian Bannen, Patrick Bergin, Andrew Connolly
▶ Bike messenger O'Loingsigh discovers that dealer Byrne has been using him to transport drugs. When Byrne's actions lead to death of O'Longsigh's best friend, he tries to get revenge. Impenetrable accents and unlikable

characters give audience little stake in the story. O'Riordan's husband Elvis Costello did the music.
Dist.: Vestron

COURT JESTER, THE 1956
★ ★ ★ ★ NR Comedy 1:41
Dir: Norman Panama, Melvin Frank   *Cast:* Danny Kaye, Glynis Johns, Basil Rathbone, Angela Lansbury, Mildred Natwick, Cecil Parker
► Forest outlaw Kaye becomes involved in scheme to restore rightful heir to the throne of England. In order to infiltrate the castle, Kaye impersonates the court jester. One of Kaye's funniest vehicles features good score, excellent supporting cast, and the comic's famous routine, "The pellet with the poison's in the vessel with the pestle."
Dist.: Paramount

COURT-MARTIAL OF BILLY MITCHELL, THE 1955
★ ★ NR Drama 1:50
Dir: Otto Preminger   *Cast:* Gary Cooper, Charles Bickford, Ralph Bellamy, Rod Steiger, Elizabeth Montgomery, Fred Clark
► True story of Gen. Mitchell (Cooper), an Army officer whose insistent demands for a new air force service and criticism of Army brass led to his trial by Washington, D.C., authorities. Aided by congressman Bellamy, Mitchell makes a favorable courtroom impression until prosecutor Steiger attacks his personal life. Earnest, somber production given a jolt by Steiger's theatrics. Screenplay by Milton Sperling and Emmet Lavery received an Oscar nomination.
Dist.: Republic

COUSIN, COUSINE 1976 French
★ ★ R Romance/Comedy 1:35
☑ Nudity, adult situations
Dir: Jean-Charles Tacchella   *Cast:* Marie-Christine Barrault, Victor Lanoux, Marie-France Pisier, Guy Marchand
► Barrault and Lanoux, whose unfaithful spouses Marchand and Pisier have a brief affair with one another, become friends and then lovers. Exhilarating French comedy deals delightfully with middle-class values. Film's European attitude toward sex and relationships is still accessible to American audiences. Oscar-nominated for Best Foreign Film, Original Screenplay, and Actress (Barrault). American remake in 1989: *Cousins.* Ⓢ
Dist.: CBS/Fox

COUSINS 1989
★ ★ ★ ★ PG-13 Romance/Comedy 1:51
☑ Brief nudity, adult situations, explicit language
Dir: Joel Schumacher   *Cast:* Ted Danson, Isabella Rossellini, Sean Young, William L. Petersen, Lloyd Bridges, Norma Aleandro
► Danson and Rossellini play cousins by marriage who, after discovering affair between their respective spouses Young and Petersen,

become friends and eventually lovers. Sunny remake of the 1975 French *Cousin, Cousine* is vibrantly shot, brightly cast (especially the winningly vulnerable Rossellini), and laced with humor and good cheer.
Dist.: Paramount

COVERED WAGON, THE 1923
☆ NR Western 1:43 B&W
Dir: James Cruze   *Cast:* Lois Wilson, J. Warren Kerrigan, Ernest Torrence, Charles Ogle, Ethel Wales, Alan Hale
► Early Western re-creates the overland trek of America's pioneers on actual locations with a cast of over 3,000, including 1,000 Indians. Based on the recollections of those who were actually there, with stunning views of the beleaguered prairie schooners and their captains, silent offering is the cinema's first large-scale Western. Still watchable despite corny plot.
Dist.: Paramount

COVER GIRL 1944
★ ★ ★ NR Musical 1:47
Dir: Charles Vidor   *Cast:* Rita Hayworth, Gene Kelly, Lee Bowman, Phil Silvers, Jinx Falkenburg, Otto Kruger, Eve Arden, Ed Brophy
► Dancer Hayworth forsakes Brooklyn nightclub owner Kelly for Broadway when she is chosen as a magazine model, but comes to her senses before the close of this lavish, exuberant musical. Silvers, Kelly's pal, and Arden, editor Kruger's assistant, provide the laughs; Kelly performs two admirable dances; and Hayworth looks stunning. Oscar-winning score includes "Long Ago and Far Away" and "Put Me to the Test" by Jerome Kern and Ira Gershwin.
Dist.: RCA/Columbia

COVERGIRL 1984 Canadian
★ R Drama 1:33
☑ Nudity, strong sexual content, explicit language
Dir: Jean-Claude Lord   *Cast:* Jeff Conaway, Irena Ferris, Cathie Shiriff, Roberta Leighton, Deborah Wakeman, Kenneth Welsh
► Beautiful young Ferris and fashion mogul Conaway meet in a traffic accident and fall in love. He turns her into a top model and, when threatened by a corporate takeover, she teams with other models to save the day. Sleek behind-the-scenes look at modeling has attractive actors and fair amount of nudity and debauchery.
Dist.: HBO

COWBOYS, THE 1972
★ ★ ★ ★ PG Western 2:08
☑ Adult situations, explicit language, violence
Dir: Mark Rvdell   *Cast:* John Wayne, Roscoe Lee Browne, Bruce Dern, Colleen Dewhurst, Slim Pickens, Lonny Chapman
► When his ranch hands abandon cattle drive for gold rush, Wayne turns to eleven

youngsters to help guide his steers four hundred miles across the wilderness. Maniacal killer Dern dogs their steps, leading to a violent confrontation. Slow-paced Western's disturbing themes made this a rare box-office failure for Wayne, but he turns in an exemplary performance as a two-fisted teacher who turns his young charges into men.
Dist.: Warner

CRACKERS 1984
★ **PG Comedy 1:32**
☑ Adult situations, explicit language, adult humor
Dir: Louis Malle   *Cast:* Donald Sutherland, Sean Penn, Jack Warden, Wallace Shawn, Larry Riley
▶ Ringleader Sutherland and his inept gang of amateur thieves bungle a pawnshop heist in San Francisco's seedy Mission District in this droll comic caper. A good cast does its best with some broad comic stereotypes. Remake of the 1960 Italian *Big Deal on Madonna Street.*
Dist.: MCA

CRACK HOUSE 1989
☆ **R Action-Adventure 1:30**
☑ Nudity, adult situations, explicit language, graphic violence
Dir: Michael Fischa   *Cast:* Jim Brown, Anthony Geary, Richard Roundtree, Cheryl Kay, Angel Tompkins
▶ Evil drug kingpin Brown seduces budding art student Kay into a life of drugs and squalor. Her boyfriend, a gang member who once tried to go straight for her, joins with cop Roundtree to infiltrate Brown's crack house and get her out. Super-lurid cheapie is overexploitative and underproduced.
Dist.: Warner

CRACKING UP 1985
★ ★ **PG Comedy 1:26**
☑ Explicit language, adult humor
Dir: Jerry Lewis   *Cast:* Jerry Lewis, Sammy Davis, Jr., Milton Berle, Herb Edelman, Foster Brooks
▶ Lewis is a nerd who tries to ice-skate at a roller rink and fails even at suicide. After a series of zany vignettes, psychiatrist Edelman dubs him a hopeless case. Not vintage Lewis; even die-hard fans might be disappointed.
Dist.: Warner

CRACK IN THE MIRROR 1987
★ **NR Drama 1:30**
☑ Nudity, adult situations, explicit language, violence
Dir: Robby Benson   *Cast:* Robby Benson, Tawney Kitaen, Danny Aiello, Sally Kirkland, Kevin Gray, Judy Tenuta
▶ Debt-plagued yuppie Benson agrees to caretake crack-dealer Gray's apartment and business while Gray is hiding out from Mafia boss Aiello. Soon, Benson and wife Kitaen are hooked on crack themselves, and when Gray returns, things turn deadly. The first U.S. feature

to be shot on high-definition videotape and transferred to 35mm film, cheap exploitation could have used a better script.
Dist.: Academy

CRAIG'S WIFE 1936
★ ★ **NR Drama 1:14 B&W**
Dir: Dorothy Arzner   *Cast:* Rosalind Russell, John Boles, Billie Burke, Dorothy Wilson, Jane Darwell
▶ In her first starring role, Russell plays a self-absorbed woman who loves her house and possessions more than her husband. Surprisingly good melodrama was based on a Pulitzer prize–winning play and directed by one of the few women directors of the 1930s.
Dist.: RCA/Columbia

CRASHOUT 1955
★ **NR Action-Adventure 1:22**
Dir: Lewis R. Foster   *Cast:* William Bendix, Arthur Kennedy, Luther Adler, William Talman, Gene Evans, Marshall Thompson
▶ Bendix and Kennedy are among six prisoners who break out of jail and attempt to recover some hidden loot. Making their task difficult is a police manhunt and conflict between themselves. Good B-movie has zippy pacing and decent performances.
Dist.: Republic

CRATER LAKE MONSTER, THE 1977
☆ **PG Horror 1:25**
☑ Violence
Dir: William R. Stromberg   *Cast:* Richard Cardella, Glenn Roberts, Mark Siegel, Bob Hyman, Kacey Cobb, Michael Hoover
▶ When a meteor hits the bottom of Crater Lake, it revives a napping dinosaur. A scientist wants to study the creature, but the monster goes on a violent rampage. Above-average special effects, but below-par direction and performances on top of a bland script.
Dist.: United

CRAWLING EYE, THE 1958 British
★ **NR Sci-Fi 1:25**
Dir: Quentin Lawrence   *Cast:* Forrest Tucker, Janet Munro, Warren Mitchell, Laurence Payne
▶ In the Swiss Alps, scientist Tucker and psychic Munro confront one of the most grotesque-looking monsters in movie history, consisting of a giant single eye and tentacles, which hides in a cloud and feasts on unwary tourists. Surprisingly moody and well-made.
Dist.: Media

CRAWLING HAND, THE 1963
☆ **NR Horror 1:29 B&W**
Dir: Herbert L. Strock   *Cast:* Peter Breck, Kent Taylor, Rod Lauren, Arline Judge, Richard Arlen, Alan Hale, Jr.
▶ The disembodied hand of an astronaut infected by space fungus goes on a murderous rampage, casting suspicion on an unwitting teen and baffling cop Hale. Nothing special,

except for the presence of the Rivington's "Papa Oom Mow Mow" on the soundtrack.
Dist.: Amvest

CRAWLSPACE 1986
☆ R Horror 1:20
☑ Nudity, adult situations, explicit language, graphic violence
Dir: David Schmoeller *Cast:* Klaus Kinski, Tahne Caine, Talia Balsam, Carol Francis, David Abbott
▶ Creepy Kinski plays the son of a Nazi war criminal who runs a boarding house for pretty women only. New tenant Balsam gets suspicious and fears the walls hide more than rats. Well made B-grade movie is for horror fans only.
Dist.: Lightning

CRAZY MAMA 1975
★ ★ PG Action-Adventure 1:21
☑ Adult situations, explicit language
Dir: Jonathan Demme *Cast:* Cloris Leachman, Stuart Whitman, Ann Sothern, Jim Backus, Linda Purl
▶ Leachman plays a crazy widow wanted for bigamy, robbery, kidnapping, assaulting an officer and numerous traffic violations. She resorts to crime to win back the family farm lost during the Depression. Early effort by director Demme provides lots of laughs and adventure.
Dist.: Embassy

CRAZY MOON 1986 Canadian
★ ★ ★ PG-13 Drama 1:29
☑ Adult situations, explicit language
Dir: Allan Eastman *Cast:* Kiefer Sutherland, Vanessa Vaughan, Peter Spence, Ken Pogue, Eve Napier
▶ Sutherland is a poor little rich boy withdrawn from life, passing time listening to 1930s music, dressing a female mannequin, and photographing dog droppings. He comes out of his eccentric shell when he falls for Anne (real-life deaf actress Vaughan), a deaf girl who teaches him to swim. Drama chronicles their relationship with effective doses of humor and sensitivity. (CC)
Dist.: Nelson

CRAZY PEOPLE 1990
★ ★ ★ R Comedy 1:30
☑ Adult situations, explicit language
Dir: Tony Bill *Cast:* Dudley Moore, Daryl Hannah, Paul Reiser, Mercedes Ruehl, J. T. Walsh, Bill Smitrovich
▶ Suffering a nervous breakdown, ad man Moore writes a series of brutally frank slogans. He is institutionalized and falls for fellow patient Hannah, but suddenly his truth-in-advertising campaign is the rage of the industry. Terrific premise gets only middling execution, but some of the satiric jabs are a scream. Our favorites: the airline slogan ("Most of our passengers get there alive") and the Greek tourist campaign. (CC)
Dist.: Paramount

CREATION OF THE HUMANOIDS 1962
☆ NR Sci-Fi 1:15
Dir: Wesley E. Barry *Cast:* Don McGowan, Frances McCann, Erica Elliot, Don Dolittle
▶ In a futuristic postapocalyptic society, robots do much of the work but still face prejudice from humans who disparage them as "clickers." McGowan leads anti-robot group but then discovers a shocking fact about his own origin. Low-budget sci-fi may be stiffly acted but has a thoughtful screenplay with imaginative ideas.
Dist.: Raedon

CREATOR 1985
★ ★ ★ R Comedy 1:47
☑ Nudity, adult situations, explicit language
Dir: Ivan Passer *Cast:* Peter O'Toole, Mariel Hemingway, Vincent Spano, David Ogden Stiers, Virginia Madsen
▶ Student Spano works for unorthodox scientist O'Toole, who's trying to clone his long-dead wife from an egg donated by friendly nymphomaniac Hemingway. A crisis occurs when Spano's girlfriend Madsen falls into a coma. Plot wanders in many directions and the movie mixes many different moods, but the actors are charming and elicit a surprising amount of genuine emotion.
Dist.: HBO

CREATURE 1985
★ R Sci-Fi 1:35
☑ Nudity, adult situations, violence
Dir: Gordon Hessler *Cast:* Klaus Kinski, Stan Ivar, Robert Jaffe, Annette McCarthy, John Stinson
▶ On one of Saturn's cobwebby moons, snaggle-toothed, saliva-dripping monsters are on the loose to eat a team of American researchers. Low-budget thriller is tasty fare for sci-fi lovers and horror fans. With Kinski in one of his mad-scientist-lecher roles. (CC)
Dist.: Media

CREATURE FROM BLACK LAKE 1976
★ PG Horror 1:37
☑ Violence
Dir: Joy Houck, Jr. *Cast:* Jack Elam, Dennis Fimple, Dub Taylor, John David Carson, Bill Thurman
▶ College students Carson and Fimple enter the Louisiana swamps and have encounters with a big hairy creature. Could it be Bigfoot? Supporting cast includes Elam as a drunk and Thurman as the local sherriff. Not bad as Bigfoot movies go but of course that isn't saying much.
Dist.: MCA

CREATURE FROM THE BLACK LAGOON 1954
★ ★ NR Horror 1:18 B&W
Dir: Jack Arnold *Cast:* Richard Carlson, Julie Adams, Richard Denning, Antonio Moreno, Whit Bissell
▶ Scientists on Amazon expedition battle

monstrous creature from murky depths. The monster targets a beautiful woman in one of the most popular horror movies of the 1950s. From the director of *Incredible Shrinking Man* and *It Came From Outer Space*. Beautifully shot and quite chilling. Originally in 3-D.
Dist.: Goodtimes

CREATURE FROM THE HAUNTED SEA 1961
☆ NR Horror 1:12 B&W
Dir: Roger Corman *Cast:* Anthony Carbone, Betsy Jones-Moreland, Edward Wain, Robert Beam
▶ On a war-torn Caribbean island, Carbone transports a group of counterrevolutionaries to safety on his boat. He murders them and takes their money, pinning the killings on a fictional sea monster. The joke's on Carbone when an actual creature shows up to menace him and his gang.
Dist.: Video Yesteryear

CREATURES THE WORLD FORGOT 1971
British
☆ PG Fantasy 1:34
☑ Adult situations, violence
Dir: Don Chaffey *Cast:* Julie Ege, Tony Bonner, Robert John, Sue Wilson, Rosalie Crutchley
▶ After their chief's death, twin cavemen vie for tribal leadership and the hand of gorgeous cavewoman Ege. Other problems faced by the tribe: a dangerous antelope hunt and a volcanic eruption. Not much plot or dialogue. Audiences may have trouble following this despite showcase of former Miss Norway Ege's charms.
Dist.: RCA/Columbia

CREEPER, THE 1948
★ NR Horror 1:03 B&W
Dir: Jean Yarbrough *Cast:* Eduardo Cianelli, Onslow Stevens, June Vincent, Ralph Morgan, Janis Wilson, John Baragrey
▶ Scientists Stevens and Morgan discover a West Indian formula that turns men into cats. Morgan thinks this isn't such a hot idea, but makes the fatal mistake of disagreeing with Stevens, who has been transformed into a murderous meow-er. Straightforward chiller is no catastrophe, but neither is it very scary.
Dist.: IVE

CREEPING FLESH, THE 1972 British
★ PG Horror 1:33
☑ Violence
Dir: Freddie Francis *Cast:* Christopher Lee, Peter Cushing, Lorna Heilbron, George Benson, Kenneth J. Warren
▶ Scientist Cushing experiments on ancient skeleton that grows flesh when touched with water, injecting his daughter Heilbron with resulting serum. His brother Lee, head of an insane asylum, plots to steal skeleton and discover secret of evil. Good cast strengthens intriguing monster plot.
Dist.: RCA/Columbia

CREEPING TERROR, THE 1964
☆ NR Horror 1:15 B&W
Dir: Art J. Nelson *Cast:* Vic Savage, Shannon O'Neill, William Thourlby, Louise Lawson
▶ Alien monster munches on lots of innocent people, including soldiers and teenagers at a prom. Sheriff Savage and scientist Thourlby team up to stop the creature. Generally considered by grade-Z movie fans to be one of the worst horror movies ever made, this amateurish, inanely scripted effort may be good for a few laughs.
Dist.: United

CREEPSHOW 1982
★ ★ R Horror 1:57
☑ Explicit language, graphic violence
Dir: George A. Romero *Cast:* Hal Holbrook, Adrienne Barbeau, Fritz Weaver, Leslie Nielsen, Carrie Nye, Ed Harris, Ted Danson, Viveca Lindfors, Stephen King
▶ Five horror vignettes written by Stephen King based on the infamous E. C. *Creepshow* comic books. Great for genre junkies with short attention spans, stories range from a return of the undead to angry roaches on the rampage. With King's son Joe as the boy reading the comics. Led to a sequel.
Dist.: Warner

CREEPSHOW 2 1987
★ ★ R Horror 1.29
☑ Adult situations, explicit language, graphic violence explicit language, graphic violence
Dir: Michael Gornick *Cast:* Lois Chiles, George Kennedy, Dorothy Lamour, David Holbrook, Tom Savini
▶ *Creepshow* sequel serves up three stories for another horror anthology connected by animation. From a wooden Indian that comes to life to an oil slick that devours teens, the tales are quick and to the gruesome point, but will leave horror fans wanting more. Low-budget technical aspects translate well to the small screen. (CC)
Dist.: New World

CRIES AND WHISPERS 1972 Swedish
★ ★ R Drama 1:34
☑ Nudity, adult situations
Dir: Ingmar Bergman *Cast:* Liv Ullmann, Ingrid Thulin, Harriet Andersson, Erland Josephson, Kari Sylwan, George Arlin
▶ Sisters Thulin and Ullmann, visiting dying sister Andersson, are haunted by their own unhappy pasts; servant Sylwan has a more positive outlook to share with Andersson. Powerful and magnificently crafted. Oscar nominations for Best Picture, Director, Screenplay, Costume Design; won for Cinematography. Ⓢ
Dist.: Warner

CRIME AND PASSION 1976
★ R Comedy 1:32
☑ Adult situations, explicit language, violence
Dir: Ivan Passer *Cast:* Omar Sharif, Karen

Black, Joseph Bottoms, Bernhard Wicki, Heinz Ehrenfreund, Elma Karlowa
► When his stock gambles fail, financial advisor Sharif finds himself pursued by assassins hired by angry industrialist Wicki. Sharif persuades his girlfriend Black to marry Wicki, but the killers refuse to back off. Sharif's dignified performance and beautiful Alpine locations are the only assets of this mediocre comedy.
Dist.: Vestron

CRIMES AND MISDEMEANORS 1989
★ ★ ★ PG-13 Comedy/Drama 1:44
☑ Adult situations, explicit language
Dir: Woody Allen *Cast:* Woody Allen, Alan Alda, Mia Farrow, Anjelica Huston, Martin Landau, Sam Waterston, Jerry Orbach, Claire Bloom, Joanna Gleason, Daryl Hannah
► When mistress Huston threatens to make trouble, respected ophthalmologist Landau considers murder to protect his marriage. Lighter half of plot concerns idealistic documentarian Allen falling for Farrow but finding competition from glib TV producer Alda. Complex look at contemporary morality is sometimes overly ambitious but remains provocative throughout. Landau was Oscarnominated as was Allen for direction and script, but Alda is the scene stealer here. Funniest bits: Allen's movie about Alda and latter's definition of comedy. (CC)
Dist.: Orion

CRIMES OF PASSION 1984
★ ★ R Drama 1:42
☑ Nudity, strong sexual content, adult situations, explicit language, violence
Dir: Ken Russell *Cast:* Kathleen Turner, Anthony Perkins, John Laughlin, Annie Potts, Bruce Davison
► Unhappy suburban husband Laughlin gets involved with Turner, who lives a double life: designer by day, streetwalker by night. Meanwhile, someone's stalking Turner; perhaps bizarre street preacher Perkins? Russell's often outrageous movie goes over the top with blatantly wild dialogue and plot twists in a disturbing look at adult sexuality in America. Explicit sex and nudity; available in an unrated video version. (CC)
Dist.: New World

CRIMES OF THE HEART 1986
★ ★ ★ PG-13 Comedy/Drama 1:45
☑ Adult situations, adult humor
Dir: Bruce Beresford *Cast:* Diane Keaton, Jessica Lange, Sissy Spacek, Sam Shepard, Tess Harper, Hurd Hatfield
► Entertaining adaptation of Beth Henley's Pulitzer prize–winning play focuses on three sisters who have a reunion in their small Southern hometown. Keaton is upset over her thirtieth birthday; Spacek just shot her husband because of his "stinking looks"; and Lange has given up her singing career for a job with a dog food company. Alternately zany and

heartwarming, with accomplished direction providing an excellent showcase for the leads. Spacek, Harper and Henley were all nominated for Oscars. (CC)
Dist.: Warner

CRIMEWAVE 1986
★ PG-13 Comedy 1:22
☑ Explicit language, violence
Dir: Sam Raimi *Cast:* Louise Lasser, Paul L. Smith, Brion James, Bruce Campbell, Reed Birney
► Rodent exterminators run riot in this farce spoofing gangster films of the thirties. Through a series of mishaps, small businessman Birney finds himself awaiting execution for murders he didn't commit. Off-the-wall comedy written by Joel and Ethan Coen. (CC)
Dist.: Nelson

CRIME ZONE 1988
★ ★ ★ R Sci-Fi 1:33
☑ Nudity, adult situations, explicit language, violence
Dir: Luis Llosa *Cast:* David Carradine, Peter Nelson, Sherilyn Fenn, Michael Shaner
► "Subgrade" lovers Nelson and Fenn want to escape their repressive futuristic society so they agree to steal a computer disc for Carradine in exchange for his help. Carradine double-crosses them and the lovers go on the lam. Familiar story gets surprising production values out of its low budget. Roger Corman executive produced.
Dist.: MGM/UA

CRIMINAL CODE, THE 1931
★ ★ NR Drama 1:35 B&W
Dir: Howard Hawks *Cast:* Walter Huston, Phillips Holmes, Constance Cummings, Mary Doran, Boris Karloff, John Sheehan
► District attorney Huston convicts Holmes, who killed a man in self-defense, then is appointed warden at the prison where Holmes is jailed. Holmes starts an affair with Huston's daughter Cummings, but faces solitary confinement for refusing to squeal on another inmate. Dated prison melodrama has unexpectedly good touches, in particular Karloff's role as a deadly prisoner.
Dist.: RCA/Columbia

CRIMINAL COURT 1946
★ ★ NR Mystery-Suspense 1:03 B&W
Dir: Robert Wise *Cast:* Tom Conway, Martha O'Driscoll, June Clayworth, Robert Armstrong, Addison Richards, Pat Gleason
► Attorney Conway defends O'Driscoll, who is accused of killing blackmailer Armstrong. Conway knows she didn't do it: in fact, he is the killer, and must prove this in court to help his client. Clever if unlikely plot, nicely directed by Wise. Home video version double billed with 1939's *The Saint Strikes Back.*
Dist.: Turner

CRIMINAL LAW 1989
★ ★ ★ R Mystery-Suspense 1:57

☑ Nudity, adult situations, explicit language, violence
Dir: Martin Campbell *Cast:* Gary Oldman, Kevin Bacon, Tess Harper, Karen Young, Joe Don Baker
▶ Oldman, a young Boston defense attorney, wins an acquittal for wealthy young client Bacon, who turns out to be a psychotic killer. When Bacon goes on a murderous rampage, the lawyer risks his career and life to trap him. Straightforward thriller gets boggeddown in ethical issues but does provide food for thought. Reverse casting works beautifully: Bacon makes a great psycho while English actor Oldman is fine in his first American role.
Dist.: HBO

CRIMSON CULT, THE 1970 British
★ **PG Horror 1:27**
☑ Violence
Dir: Vernon Sewell *Cast:* Boris Karloff, Christopher Lee, Mark Eden, Barbara Steele, Virginia Wetherell, Michael Gough
▶ Searching for his missing brother, Eden enters sinister Lee's mansion, where the lovely Wetherell persuades him to stay for a while. Soon Eden is haunted by Steele, a witch burned at the stake years before, and must enlist the aid of supernatural expert Karloff. Noteworthy mainly for eighty-year-old horror veteran Karloff in one of his last roles.
Dist.: HBO

CRIMSON PIRATE, THE 1952
★ ★ ★ **NR Action-Adventure 1:44**
Dir: Robert Siodmak *Cast:* Burt Lancaster, Nick Cravat, Eva Bartok, Torin Thatcher, James Hayter, Christopher Lee
▶ Pirate Lancaster intends to exploit battle between Caribbean rebels and Spanish rulers for his own profitable purposes, but when he meets gorgeous freedom fighter Bartok, it's viva la revolution! Enormously exuberant entertainment sparked by Lancaster's high spirits and Hayter's turn as an inventor.
Dist.: Warner

CRISIS AT CENTRAL HIGH 1981
★ ★ ★ ★ **NR Drama/MFTV 2:05**
Dir: Lamont Johnson *Cast:* Joanne Woodward, Charles Durning, William Russ, Henderson Forsythe, Calvin Levels, Regina Taylor
▶ Docudrama focuses on the 1957 school integration crisis in which bigoted locals opposed the Supreme Court order that nine black students be admitted to previously all-white Central High in Little Rock, Arkansas. Superlative telemovie with a powerhouse, Emmy-nominated performance by Woodward as Elizabeth Huckaby, the prim but principled teacher who stood up for the students. Based on Huckaby's journal.
Dist.: Vestron

CRISS CROSS 1949
★ ★ **NR Crime 1:27 B&W**
Dir: Robert Siodmak *Cast:* Burt Lancaster,

Yvonne De Carlo, Dan Duryea, Stephen McNally, Richard Long, Tony Curtis
▶ Lancaster plays an armored car driver who gets involved with gorgeous De Carlo. De Carlo's criminal husband Duryea ropes Lancaster into a robbery plan; Lancaster plots to run away with De Carlo but a series of double crosses ensues. Hard-hitting crime drama.
Dist.: MCA

CRITICAL CONDITION 1987
★ ★ **R Comedy 1:40**
☑ Adult situations, explicit language
Dir: Michael Apted *Cast:* Richard Pryor, Rachel Ticotin, Ruben Blades, Joe Dallesandro, Sylvia Miles
▶ During a hospital blackout, fast-talking con man Pryor impersonates a doctor and copes with the ordeal, heightened by a crazed killer, a fire, and other assorted crises. Not Pryor's best vehicle but he gets his share of laughs out of the hospital high jinks. (CC)
Dist.: Paramount

CRITTERS 1986
★ ★ ★ **PG-13 Horror 1:26**
☑ Explicit language, graphic violence
Dir: Stephen Herek *Cast:* Dee Wallace Stone, M. Emmet Walsh, Billy Green Bush, Scott Grimes, Nadine Van Der Velde, Don Oppor
▶ Krites—vicious alien furballs—escape from space prison and land in Kansas, where they terrorize an isolated farm family. While Mom Stone fights off the monsters, son Grimes races into town for help. He finds two alien bounty hunters who mount an attack on the Krites. Low-budget mixture of comedy and science fiction has some particularly nasty violence. Followed by *Critters 2.*
Dist.: RCA/Columbia

CRITTERS 2: THE MAIN COURSE 1988
★ ★ **PG-13 Horror 1:26**
☑ Nudity, explicit language, violence
Dir: Mick Garris *Cast:* Scott Grimes, Liane Curtis, Don Opper, Barry Corbin
▶ Grimes returns to quiet little Grovers Bend to visit grandma and soon encounters ravenous outer space critters. Sheriff Corbin provides little help but alien bounty hunters save the day. Never takes itself too seriously and moves along nicely; cute touches take edge off the violence and Corbin is very funny. However, monsters are rather cheap-looking. (CC)
Dist.: RCA/Columbia

CROCODILE 1979 Thai
☆ **R Horror 1:35**
☑ Adult situations, explicit language, graphic violence
Dir: Herman Cohen *Cast:* Nat Puvanai, Tany Tim, Angela Wells, Kirk Warren
▶ Combination of atomic test gone awry and malignant Nature spawns gigantic crocodile that attacks residents of Thai beach resort. Scientists and hunters are unable to cope with

fearsome creature. Low-budget exploitation is bloody and predictable.
Dist.: HBO

CROCODILE DUNDEE 1986 Australian
★ ★ ★ ★ ★ PG-13 Action-Adventure 1:34
☑ Adult situations, explicit language
Dir: Peter Faiman *Cast:* Paul Hogan, Linda Kozlowski, Mark Blum, David Gulpilil, Michael Lombard
▶ Down Under darling Paul "Throw another shrimp on the barbie" Hogan stars in this half-adventure, half-romance as Mick "Crocodile" Dundee, who saves sexy American reporter Kozlowski from an Outback crocodile attack. She, in turn, invites him to her jungle, Manhattan, where they fall in love and he faces new perils: room service, assorted muggers, transvestites, and Kozlowski's boyfriend Blum. Hogan, making his film debut, also co-wrote the screenplay to this surprise, worldwide blockbuster hit. Followed by sequel. (CC)
Dist.: Paramount

CROCODILE DUNDEE II 1988 U.S./Australian
★ ★ ★ ★ PG Action-Adventure 1:50
☑ Explicit language, violence
Dir: John Cornell *Cast:* Paul Hogan, Linda Kozlowski, John Meillon, Ernie Dingo, Hechter Ubarry
▶ G'day, amigo—Mick "Crocodile" Dundee (Hogan) is back and living in New York City with movie #1 flame Sue (Kozlowski). When her ex-husband is murdered after taking photos of Colombian cocaine dealers, the thugs chase Sue and Mick to Australia. On his own turf, no one can compete with the affable Aussie knife-thrower/alligator wrestler.
Dist.: Paramount

CROMWELL 1970 British
★ ★ G Biography 2:21
Dir: Ken Hughes *Cast:* Richard Harris, Alec Guinness, Robert Morley, Dorothy Tutin, Frank Finlay, Timothy Dalton
▶ Dull account of the seventeenth-century duel between Cromwell (Harris), a Puritan bent on reforming the English court, and Charles I (Guinness), an ineffectual ruler devoted to his Catholic queen (Tutin). Lackluster history lesson won an Oscar for Costume Design.
Dist.: RCA/Columbia

CROOKS AND CORONETS 1970 British
★ PG Comedy 1:46
☑ Adult situations
Dir: Jim O'Connolly *Cast:* Telly Savalas, Edith Evans, Warren Oates, Cesar Romero, Harry H. Corbett, Nicky Henson
▶ Backed by Romero and helped by British thief Corbett, American crooks Savalas and Oates plan to rob dotty old Evans's British estate. The Yanks become her houseguests but like their hostess so much they can't bring themselves to pull off the heist. Minor crime

comedy has spry Evans stealing the show. Also known as *Sophie's Place.*
Dist.: Warner

CROSS COUNTRY 1983
★ ★ R Drama 1:32
☑ Nudity, strong sexual content, adult situations, explicit language, graphic violence
Dir: Paul Lynch *Cast:* Richard Beymer, Nina Axelrod, Michael Ironside, Brent Carver, Michael Kane
▶ Call girl is brutally murdered and police suspect Beymer, a TV advertising exec who was involved with her. Detective Ironside pursues him across Canada. Gritty and unsavory, but the twisty plot effectively exploits elements of suspense and action.
Dist.: Nelson

CROSS CREEK 1983
★ ★ ★ ★ PG Biography 2:00
☑ Explicit language, violence
Dir: Martin Ritt *Cast:* Mary Steenburgen, Rip Torn, Malcolm McDowell, Alfre Woodard, Dana Hill, Peter Coyote
▶ In 1928, after her marriage crumbles, author Marjorie Kinnan Rawlings (Steenburgen) relocates from New York to the swamps of Florida, where the locals inspire her to write the children's classic *The Yearling.* Sweet, old-fashioned movie is slowly paced but excellently crafted and filled with real emotion. Steenburgen gives a warm and sensitive performance with fine work from Woodward and Torn, both nominated for Best Supporting Oscars.
Dist.: HBO

CROSSED SWORDS 1978
★ ★ ★ PG Action-Adventure 1:53
☑ Mild violence
Dir: Richard Fleischer *Cast:* Oliver Reed, Raquel Welch, Mark Lester, Ernest Borgnine, George C. Scott, Rex Harrison, Charleton Heston, David Hemmings, Sybil Danning
▶ Opulent version of Mark Twain's *The Prince and the Pauper,* with Lester in dual role as heir to the throne who switches places with earthy ragamuffin on a lark that backfires. Reed is his swashbuckling rescuer; con man Scott and aristocrat Harrison strike strongest dramatic sparks. Screenplay by George MacDonald Fraser. Also known as *The Prince and the Pauper.*
Dist.: Media

CROSSFIRE 1947
★ ★ NR Crime 1:26 B&W
Dir: Edward Dmytryk *Cast:* Robert Young, Robert Mitchum, Robert Ryan, Gloria Grahame, Sam Levene, Paul Kelly
▶ Bigoted soldier Ryan murders Jewish Levene. Cop Young and Army man Mitchum team up to investigate and bring the killer to justice. Groundbreaking look at anti-Semitism creates much tension while hitting home a

powerful message; outstanding performances by Mitchum, Young, and Ryan.
Dist.: Nelson

CROSS FIRE 1989
☆ **R Action-Adventure 1:44**
☑ Nudity, adult situations, explicit language, violence
Dir: Anthony Maharaj   *Cast:* Richard Norton, Michael Meyer, Daniel Dietrich, Eric Hahn, Wren T. Brown, Paul Holmes
▶ Norton, a Vietnam vet from Australia, hits skid row after the war. Authorities force him into a dangerous mission to recover Holmes, his former commander who's now held prisoner in the jungle. As Norton closes in on the villains, he discovers he has leprosy. Low-rent adventure filled with tired clichés.
Dist.: Nelson

CROSSING DELANCEY 1988
★ ★ ★ **PG Romance 1:37**
☑ Adult situations
Dir: Joan Micklin Silver   *Cast:* Amy Irving, Peter Riegert, Jeroen Krabbe, Reizl Bozyk, Sylvia Miles, George Martin
▶ Irving is a thirty-four-year-old New Yorker with a rent-controlled apartment and a fine job managing a book store; but she's very single, much to the dismay of her grandmother Bozyk. Matchmaker Miles introduces Irving to pickle merchant Riegert, but she prefers the more upscale company of womanizing writer Krabbe. Modern fairy tale romance uses rich neighborhood atmosphere, understated Riegert, and charming Irving for fine result.
Dist.: Warner

CROSS MY HEART 1987
★ **R Comedy 1:31**
☑ Nudity, adult situations, explicit language
Dir: Armyan Bernstein   *Cast:* Martin Short, Annette O'Toole, Paul Reiser, Joanna Kerns, Jessica Puscas
▶ Short and O'Toole nervously embark on their third date. Sex and even commitment could be in the offing but the secrets they've kept from each other (she chain-smokes and has a young daughter; he's lost his job but pretends he's been promoted) could sabotage the romance. Thin plot filled with sitcom story twists but likable leads and some insight into 1980s dating mores.
Dist.: MCA

CROSS OF IRON 1977 British/West German
★ ★ ★ ★ **R Action-Adventure 2:00**
☑ Violence
Dir: Sam Peckinpah   *Cast:* James Coburn, Maximilian Schell, James Mason, David Warner, Senta Berger
▶ Solid World War II adventure told from the German point of view. Opportunistic captain Schell, out to win a medal, comes into conflict with Coburn, a battle-scarred sergeant trying to protect his young troops from the advancing Russians. Harrowing battle sequences

highlight this realistic look at the war. Followed by a sequel, *Breakthrough*.
Dist.: Media

CROSSOVER 1980 Canadian
★ ★ **R Drama 1:37**
☑ Nudity, adult situations, explicit language
Dir: John Guillermin   *Cast:* James Coburn, Kate Nelligan, Fionnula Flanagan, Les Carlson, Candy Kane
▶ Coburn is Patman, an Irish orderly who works the night shift in a hospital psychiatric ward. He befriends the insane, gradually loses his mind and becomes a patient himself. Intense film-noir portrait of a man's deterioration. Filmed in Vancouver. Also known as *Mr. Patman*.
Dist.: Vestron

CROSSOVER DREAMS 1985
★ **NR Drama 1:25**
☑ Adult situations, explicit language
Dir: Leon Ichaso   *Cast:* Ruben Blades, Shawn Elliot, Tom Signorelli, Elizabeth Peña, Frank Robles
▶ Spanish Harlem barrio crooner Rudy (real-life salsa star Blades) longs to "cross over" to the Anglo charts and make it as a mainstream pop singer. With Robles as sleazeball manager/furniture salesman who pitches lines like "Plastic is forever," Low-budget but heartfelt.
Dist.: HBO

CROSSROADS 1986
★ ★ ★ ★ **R Drama 1:39**
☑ Adult situations, explicit language
Dir: Walter Hill   *Cast:* Ralph Macchio, Joe Seneca, Jami Gertz, Joe Morton, Robert Judd
▶ Juilliard classical guitar student Macchio and Willie Brown (Seneca), an aging Mississippi blues musician, travel to the heart of the Delta. Once there, they recapture the crossroads of Willie's memory and release him from a contract made with the devil years ago. Leisurely paced character study with a strong blues soundtrack by Ry Cooder and first-rate performance by Seneca. **(CC)**
Dist.: RCA/Columbia

CROWD, THE 1928
★ ★ **NR Drama 1:30 B&W**
Dir: King Vidor   *Cast:* Eleanor Boardman, James Murray, Bert Roach, Estelle Clark, Daniel G. Tomlinson, Lucy Beaumont
▶ Eager young Murray arrives in New York, determined to make his mark in the world. He marries Boardman and starts a family but finds his dreams elusive. Then, in one of the most heartrending scenes in all silent cinema, a tragedy occurs on his own street. Towering classic, unflinching in its realism yet ultimately moving.
Dist.: MGM/UA

CRUCIBLE OF HORROR 1971 British
☆ **PG Horror 1:31**

☑ Violence
Dir: Viktors Ritelis   *Cast:* Michael Gough, Sharon Gurney, Yvonne Mitchell, David Butler, Nicholas Jones
▶ Gough mistreats wife Mitchell and daughter Gurney, so they poison him and contrive to make it appear a suicide. Just as they are congratulating themselves on a job well done, villain returns from the dead. Slow and familiar. Also known as *Velvet House.*
Dist.: Warner

CRUEL SEA, THE 1953 British
★ ★ ★ ★ NR War 2:04 B&W
Dir: Charles Frend   *Cast:* Jack Hawkins, Donald Sinden, Denholm Elliott, John Stratton, Stanley Baker
▶ Realistic World War II drama examines the crew of a typical corvette during its hazardous convoy runs across the Atlantic. Hawkins is outstanding as a dedicated skipper torn between protecting his men and battling the Nazis. Often brutal plot is handled in a convincing documentary fashion. Screenwriter Eric Ambler won an Oscar nomination for his adaptation of Nicholas Monssarrat's bestseller.
Dist.: HBO

CRUISING 1980
★ ★ R Drama 1:46
☑ Strong sexual content, adult situations, explicit language, graphic violence
Dir: William Friedkin   *Cast:* Al Pacino, Paul Sorvino, Karen Allen, Richard Cox, Don Scardino
▶ Innocent New York cop Pacino goes undercover to ferret out a dangerous killer menacing the lower strata of the gay world. More an exploration of the sadomasochistic lifestyle than murder mystery, this controversial film was criticized for its one-sided, sensationalistic depiction of homosexuals.
Dist.: CBS/Fox

CRUSOE 1989
★ ★ ★ PG-13 Drama 1:31
☑ Violence
Dir: Caleb Deschanel   *Cast:* Aidan Quinn, Ade Sapara, Elvis Payne, Richard Sharp, Scamp the Dog
▶ Revisionist version of Daniel Dafoe's *Robinson Crusoe* stars Quinn as a nineteenth-century slave trader who, shipwrecked on an island, gains a new attitude toward humanity due to relationship with native warrior Sapara. Immaculate production is treat for the eyes and the emotions. Quinn pulls off what is essentially a one-man show but watch out for canine scene-stealer Scamp. **(CC)**
Dist.: Virgin

CRY-BABY 1990
★ ★ PG-13 Musical/Comedy 1:30
☑ Adult situations, explicit language
Dir: John Waters   *Cast:* Johnny Depp, Amy Locane, Susan Tyrrell, Traci Lords, Polly Bergen, Ricki Lake, Patricia Hearst, Dave Nelson, Iggy Pop, Mink Stole, Joe Dallesandro, Troy Donohue
▶ Campy parody of fifties and sixties teen musicals features Depp as the cool, swaggering Cry-Baby who leads the rebellious Drapes gang and sings evil rock 'n' roll. Locane is a squeaky-clean blond in the Squares who longs to cut loose and shimmy with him. Spirited spoof is given Waters's typically demented treatment. Not up to *Hairspray*, but lots of fun nonetheless. Look for Willem Dafoe and Joey Heatherton among the cast of eccentrics. **(CC)**
Dist.: Paramount

CRY DANGER 1951
★ ★ NR Mystery-Suspense 1:20 B&W
Dir: Robert Parrish   *Cast:* Dick Powell, Rhonda Fleming, Richard Erdman, William Conrad, Regis Toomey, Jean Porter
▶ After serving a five-year prison term for a crime he didn't commit, Powell is pardoned. Teaming with crippled Erdman, he sets out to clear his name. The trail involves his ex-girlfriend Fleming, gangster Conrad, and a missing $100,000. Nicely plotted film noir has convincing atmosphere and intriguing characterizations.
Dist.: Republic

CRY FOR ME BILLY 1971
★ ★ ★ R Western 1:33
☑ Rape, nudity
Dir: William A. Graham   *Cast:* Cliff Potts, Xochitl, Harry Dean Stanton, Don Wilbanks
▶ Potts makes mistake of sticking up for the Indians after they are mistreated and then massacred by the local cavalry. Cowpoke compounds crime by falling in love with Indian girl Xochitl, who commits suicide after being violated by troopers. Depressing film also pops up under names *Face the Wind*, *Count Your Bullets*, *Apache Massacre*, *The Long Tomorrow.*
Dist.: Media

CRY FREEDOM 1987 British
★ ★ ★ ★ PG Biography/Drama 2:37
☑ Explicit language, violence
Dir: Richard Attenborough   *Cast:* Kevin Kline, Denzel Washington, Penelope Wilton, Kevin McNally, John Thaw, Timothy West
▶ Black activist Steven Biko (Washington) fights against South African apartheid and raises the consciousness of white liberal editor Donald Woods (Kline). When Biko is martyred in prison, Woods attempts to escape the country to tell the world his story. Forthright, deeply felt, and engrossing true account features rich camerawork, strong production values, and excellent performances. Washington was Oscar-nominated.
Dist.: MCA

CRY IN THE DARK, A 1988
★ ★ ★ ★ PG-13 Drama 2:01
☑ Explicit language
Dir: Fred Schepisi   *Cast:* Meryl Streep, Sam

Neill, Bruce Myles, Charles Tingwell, Nick Tate, Neil Fitzpatrick
► True story of Lindy Chamberlain (Streep), an Australian woman who found herself charged with murder after a wild dog stole her baby. Public opinion and a media circus prejudiced the case against Lindy. Husband Michael (Neill) stood by her side even after the stress threatened their marriage. Interesting indictment of judicial system. Trial sequence a bit long, but Streep, with perfect Australian accent, creates a fully rounded, hard-edged protagonist.
Dist.: Warner

CRY OF BATTLE 1963
★ NR War 1:39 B&W
Dir: Irving Lerner *Cast:* Van Heflin, Rita Moreno, James MacArthur, Leopoldo Salcedo, Sidney Clute, Marilou Munoz
► MacArthur, a young man from a wealthy background, arrives in the Philippines soon after Pearl Harbor. His inexperience is soon a thing of the past, as he joins the fight against the Japanese and competes with Heflin for Moreno. Although leads try valiantly, story is ordinary.
Dist.: Prism

CRY OF THE BANSHEE 1970 British
☆ PG Horror 1:27
☑ Brief nudity, adult situations, violence
Dir: Gordon Hessler *Cast:* Vincent Price, Elisabeth Bergner, Essy Persson, Hugh Griffith, Patrick Mower, Hilary Dwyer
► In the sixteenth century, witch Bergner puts a curse on Price when he slays her children. Evil spirit Mower then terrorizes Price and his family. Average B grade witch-burning fare, with lines like "Take care of your tongue, woman!" and "You're much too pretty to be a witch."
Dist.: HBO

CRYSTAL HEART 1987
★★★ R Drama 1:43
☑ Nudity, adult situations, explicit language
Dir: Gil Bettman *Cast:* Tawny Kitaen, Lee Curreri, May Heatherly, Lloyd Bochner, Simon Andreu
► Born without immune defenses and confined to a glass laboratory in his parents' L.A. mansion, Curreri falls in love with free-spirited rock star Kitaen. When she goes on tour, he forsakes his hermetically sealed environment for a final fling. Good-looking leads and heartfelt script.
Dist.: New World

CRYSTALSTONE 1988 British/Spanish
★ PG Family 1:43
☑ Explicit language, mild violence
Dir: Antonio Pelaez *Cast:* Kamlesh Gupta, Laura Jane Goodwin, Frank Grimes, Edward Kelsey, Sydney Bromley, Terence Bayler
► Two orphaned Spanish children battle a hook-handed heavy and follow clues in an ancient diary to search for fabulous crystal-

stone, a sacred Aztec diamond. Their adventure takes them to a mysterious island along with a strange sea captain who just may be their long lost El Papa. Nice ingredients go flat on screen.
Dist.: Forum

CRY UNCLE! 1971
☆ R Comedy 1:27
☑ Nudity, explicit language, adult humor
Dir: John G. Avildsen *Cast:* Allen Garfield, Madeleine le Roux, Devin Goldenberg, David Kirk
► When an eccentric millionaire is accused of murdering his mistress, he hires private detective Garfield to clear his name. Ordinary detective plot used as vehicle for graphic humor and plenty of skin. Although pudgy Garfield is amusing, shots of him in the nude are no fun. Overall crudeness will offend many.
Dist.: Prism

CRY VENGEANCE 1954
★ NR Drama 1:23 B&W
Dir: Mark Stevens *Cast:* Mark Stevens, Martha Hyer, Skip Homeier, Joan Vohs, Douglas Kennedy
► After serving time in prison on a frame-up, Stevens searches for the man who killed his family. Trail leads to Alaska and businessman Kennedy, but Stevens is trapped in what looks like another double cross when hitman Homeier arrives. Trim story told with conviction.
Dist.: Republic

CUBA 1979
★★ R Drama 2:02
☑ Nudity, explicit language, violence
Dir: Richard Lester *Cast:* Sean Connery, Brooke Adams, Jack Weston, Hector Elizondo, Denholm Elliott, Lonette McKee
► Working for the British government, mercenary Connery rekindles his affair with tobacco plantation owner Adams, who's now married to a spineless playboy. He must convince her to leave Cuba before Castro comes to power. Strong supporting cast and good period detail provide an intriguing look at Havana in 1958.
Dist.: Key

CUJO 1983
★★★ R Horror 1:29
☑ Adult situations, explicit language, graphic violence
Dir: Lewis Teague *Cast:* Dee Wallace, Danny Pintauro, Daniel Hugh-Kelly, Christopher Stone, Ed Lauter
► Horror master Stephen King deviates from his usual supernatural bent to tell the terrifying story of mother Wallace and son Pintauro, trapped in their stalled car for days by a mammoth St. Bernard. Stalwart genre fans will love this simply crafted chiller.
Dist.: Warner

CULPEPPER CATTLE COMPANY, THE 1972
★★★ PG Western 1:32

☑ Violence
Dir: Dick Richards *Cast:* Gary Grimes, Billy
"Green" Bush, Luke Askew, Bo Hopkins,
Geoffrey Lewis
▶ Sixteen-year-old Grimes joins a Texas cattle
drive and is exposed to the harsh, unforgiving
Wild West of the post–Civil War era. Meticu-
lously authentic production will please West-
ern fans, but violent plot is very downbeat.
Dist.: CBS/Fox

CURFEW 1989
☆ R Drama 1:24
☑ Adult situations, explicit language, violence
Dir: Gary Winick *Cast:* Kyle Richards, Wendell Wellman, John Putch, Jean Brooks,
Frank Miller
▶ Richards is the daughter of a district attorney targeted for vengeance by Wellman and
Putch, rapist/killers who've just escaped from
jail. Though Richards once chafed at having
to meet a strict curfew, she learns the real
meaning of harsh treatment when her family
is kidnapped and tormented by the two villains. Little suspense or plot interest in this direct-to-video release.
Dist.: New World

CURLY TOP 1935
★ ★ ★ NR Musical/Family 1:15 B&W
Dir: Irving Cummings *Cast:* Shirley Temple,
John Boles, Rochelle Hudson, Jane Darwell,
Esther Dale, Arthur Treacher
▶ Orphan Temple wins the heart of millionaire
Boles, then encourages his romance with her
older sister Hudson. Above-average Temple
vehicle features the songs "When I Grow Up,"
"The Simple Things in Life," and "Animal
Crackers in My Soup." Treacher provides
comic relief as Boles's butler. **(CC)**
Dist.: CBS/Fox

CURSE, THE 1987
★ R Horror 1:30
☑ Adult situations, explicit language, vio-
lence
Dir: David Keith *Cast:* Wil Wheaton,
Claude Akins, Malcolm Danare, Cooper
Huckabee, John Schneider, Amy Wheaton
▶ Meteorite lands on Tennessee farm and
contaminates the water supply. Youths Wil
and Amy Wheaton (real-life siblings) watch in
horror as toxin turns stepfather Akins and oth-
ers into disfigured psychotics; state official
Schneider comes to the rescue. Directorial
debut for actor Keith is loosely based on the
H. P. Lovecraft yarn "The Color Out of Space."
(CC)
Dist.: Media

CURSE OF FRANKENSTEIN, THE 1957 British
★ ★ NR Horror 1:23
Dir: Terence Fisher *Cast:* Peter Cushing,
Christopher Lee, Hazel Court, Robert Ur-
quhart, Valerie Gaunt
▶ Efficient version of Mary Shelley's classic tells
in flashbacks the story of Baron Victor Franken-

stein's (Cushing) experiments in creating
human life. Lee takes a realistic approach in
portraying the creature. Popular Hammer Studios picture revitalized the horror genre and
led to six further entries in the series. Sequel:
Revenge of Frankenstein.
Dist.: Warner

CURSE OF THE CAT PEOPLE, THE 1944
★ ★ NR Horror 1:10 B&W
Dir: Gunther von Fritsch, Robert Wise *Cast:*
Simone Simon, Kent Smith, Jane Randolph,
Ann Carter, Elizabeth Russell, Julia Dean
▶ Wise made his directorial debut in this fol-
low-up to producer Val Lewton's 1942 *Cat
People.* Simon, the panther-possessed hero-
ine of the first movie, returns as imaginary
playmate of her husband's (Smith) little
daughter, Carter. Focus is not on terror but on
psychological portrait of the child and family.
Dist.: Turner

CURSE OF THE DEMON 1958 British
★ ★ ★ NR Horror 1:22 B&W
Dir: Jacques Tourneur *Cast:* Dana An-
drews, Peggy Cummins, Niall MacGinnis,
Maurice Denham
▶ Psychologist Andrews investigates a murder
and refuses to believe supernatural explana-
tions until it's almost too late, as satanic cultist
MacGinnis conjures creature to kill him.
Moody and chilling; atmospheric direction by
Tourneur creates a sense of constant men-
ace.
Dist.: RCA/Columbia

CURSE OF THE LIVING CORPSE 1964
★ NR Horror 1:24 B&W
Dir: Del Tenney *Cast:* Helen Warren, Roy
Scheider, Margot Hartman, Robert Milli,
Hugh Franklin, Candace Hillgloss
▶ A wealthy man, fearing an illness which
makes him appear dead, warns his family
there'll be hell to pay if he's buried alive. Natu-
rally, they don't listen and he comes back to
kill them. Scheider made his film debut in this
occasionally scary, but mostly routine, effort.
Dist.: Prism

CURSE OF THE PINK PANTHER 1983
★ ★ PG Comedy 1:50
☑ Brief nudity, explicit language, mild vio-
lence, adult humor
Dir: Blake Edwards *Cast:* Ted Wass, David
Niven, Robert Wagner, Capucine, Joanna
Lumley, Herbert Lom
▶ Inspector Clouseau is missing in this post–
Peter Sellers reprise of the Panther series. Wass
plays Clifton Sleigh, a bumbling New York cop
legendary for his ineptitude, hired to find Clou-
seau and the missing "Panther Diamond."
Niven plays a charming jewel thief. Glossy
and adequately cast, but pale in comparison
to past Panther plots.
Dist.: MGM/UA

CURSE OF THE WEREWOLF, THE 1961 British
★ ★ NR Horror 1:31

Dir: Terence Fisher *Cast:* Clifford Evans, Oliver Reed, Yvonne Romain, Anthony Dawson, Josephine Llewellyn, Richard Wordsworth
▶ After a long, interesting prologue establishing the title monster's pedigree, Reed emerges as a young man unfortunately tainted with wolf's blood. Though sent to a monastery, he breaks out to be with the woman he loves. Reed is a natural as the tragic lupine hero in this well-done Hammer Studios picture.
Dist.: MCA

CURTAINS 1983 Canadian
★ ★ R Horror 1:29
☑ Rape, nudity, adult situations, explicit language, graphic violence
Dir: Jonathan Stryker (Richard Ciupka)
Cast: John Vernon, Samantha Eggar, Linda Thorson, Anne Ditchburn
▶ Actress Eggar commits herself to a mental institution to research a "mad woman" movie role. Shocked to discover director Vernon is interviewing other actresses for her part, she escapes and shows up at his mansion where five other contenders, all dying for the role, assemble for auditions. Muddled exploitation was plagued by production problems.
Dist.: Vestron

CUTTER'S WAY 1981
★ ★ R Mystery-Suspense 1:49
☑ Nudity, adult situations, explicit language, violence
Dir: Ivan Passer *Cast:* Jeff Bridges, John Heard, Lisa Eichhorn, Ann Dusenberry, Stephen Elliot
▶ Santa Barbara hustler Bridges witnesses a murderer dumping a body. His best pal, embittered and crippled Vietnam vet Heard, becomes obsessed with proving a powerful businessman is the killer. Dark, moody, underrated thriller's convincingly sordid milieu and ambiguous ending are not for everyone, but the three leads are terrific, especially Heard's snarling, larger-than-life portrayal. Originally released as *Cutter and Bone.*
Dist.: MGM/UA

CYBORG 1989
★ ★ R Sci-Fi 1:26
☑ Nudity, adult situations, explicit language, graphic violence
Dir: Albert Pyun *Cast:* Jean-Claude Van Damme, Deborah Richter, Vincent Klyn, Alex Daniels, Dayle Haddon`
▶ A Cyborg, half-human and half-robot, has the key to a potion that will cure the world of a deadly plague, but she's been kidnapped by Klyn and a gang of post-punk goons. Splendidly muscular Van Damme sets out to save her, and does so after stylized knife fights, gun battles, and brutal hand-to-hand combat. At one point, Van Damme is crucified. Audience may feel the same.
Dist.: Warner

CYCLONE 1987
★ ★ R Action-Adventure 1:26
☑ Brief nudity, explicit language, violence
Dir: Fred Olen Ray *Cast:* Heather Thomas, Jeffrey Combs, Ashley Ferrare, Dan Robinson
▶ Motorcycle enthusiasts Thomas and Combs go dancing at a rock club when Combs is murdered with an icepick. Thomas discovers her dead boyfriend's secret project, a transformer for a hydrogen-powered motorcycle wanted by both the CIA and KGB, which she must return to friendly hands.
Dist.: RCA/Columbia

CYRANO DE BERGERAC 1950
★ ★ ★ NR Drama 1:52 B&W
Dir: Michael Gordon *Cast:* Jose Ferrer, Mala Powers, William Prince, Morris Carnovsky, Ralph Clanton
▶ Adaptation of Edmond Rostand's classic romantic tragedy. Soldier/poet Cyrano (Ferrer) loves the fair Roxanne (Powers) but is too ashamed of his repulsive nose to woo her. He puts his great wit at the service of handsome Christian (Prince), who also loves Roxanne but is too tongue-tied to tell her. Brilliant Oscar-winning performance by Ferrer. Story later adapted by Steve Martin into the comedy *Roxanne.*
Dist.: Republic

DA 1988
★ ★ ★ PG Drama 1:42
☑ Explicit language
Dir: Matt Clark *Cast:* Martin Sheen, Barnard Hughes, William Hickey, Karl Hayden, Doreen Hepburn
▶ Sheen returns to Ireland for the funeral of adoptive father Hughes and has a confrontation with his Da's ghost. Reminiscences of times past include a painful incident when Da tried to drown the family dog and his interference with Sheen's attempt at losing his virginity. Talky and seemingly stagebound at times but touching nonetheless. Hughes re-creates his stage role from Hugh Leonard's Tony Award–winning play. **(CC)**
Dist.: Virgin

DAD 1989
★ ★ ★ ★ PG Drama 1:57
☑ Adult situations, explicit language
Dir: Gary David Goldberg *Cast:* Jack Lemmon, Ted Danson, Olympia Dukakis, Kathy Baker, Kevin Spacey, Ethan Hawke
▶ Danson is an emotionally remote banker forced to touch base with his family after mother Dukakis has a heart attack, leaving dad Lemmon helpless. Mom recovers, but Dad is diagnosed with cancer, and Danson leaves his job to nurse him. After yet another shocking health revelation, the whole family learns to love and trust their feelings. Film is rich with comedy, pathos, and Lemmon at his most brilliant. **(CC)**
Dist.: MCA

DADDY LONG LEGS 1955
★ ★ ★ NR Musical 2:06
Dir: Jean Negulesco *Cast:* Fred Astaire, Leslie Caron, Terry Moore, Thelma Ritter, Fred Clark, Charlotte Austin
▶ Effective but slow-moving May-December romance about playboy Astaire who supports beautiful French orphan Caron. They fall in love to a tuneful Johnny Mercer score (including the Oscar-nominated "Something's Got to Give"). Highlighted by Astaire's drum specialty number.
Dist.: Vestron

DADDY'S BOYS 1988
☆ R Mystery-Suspense 1:25
☑ Nudity, adult situations, explicit language, violence
Dir: Joe Minion *Cast:* Daryl Haney, Laura Burkett, Raymond J. Barry, Dan Shor, Christian Clemenson
▶ Depression-era dad Barry and three sons go on a robbing/kidnapping spree after losing farm. Son Haney splits from kin to take up with local drab Burkett whom he gets pregnant. Family is reunited for bloody shoot-out with greedy landowner. Roger Corman cheapie was said to have been scripted and shot in three weeks to take advantage of standing sets from another film.
Dist.: RCA/Columbia

DADDY'S GONE A-HUNTING 1969
★ PG Mystery-Suspense 1:48
☑ Adult situations, explicit language, violence
Dir: Mark Robson *Cast:* Carol White, Scott Hylands, Paul Burke, Mala Powers, Barry Cahill
▶ Happily married White's new baby is kidnapped by an old boyfriend still furious over long-ago abortion. Crazy ex kills family cat, tries to feed baby poison formula, and finally threatens to hurl infant from roof of hotel. Modestly effective suspense from Lorenzo Semple, Jr., scripter of *Pretty Poison*.
Dist.: Warner

DAFFY DUCK'S MOVIE: FANTASTIC ISLAND 1983
★ ★ ★ ★ G Animation 1:18
Dir: Friz Freleng *Cast:* Voices of Mel Blanc, Les Tremayne
▶ Classic Looney Tuners Porky Pig, Tweety Pie and Sylvester, Pepe Le Pew and more team up in this spoof of TV's "Fantasy Island." Daffy Duck is the Ricardo Montalban-type host and Speedy Gonzales is hilarious in a brief Herve Villechaize parody.
Dist.: Warner

DAFFY DUCK'S QUACKBUSTERS 1988
★ ★ ★ ★ G Animation 1:20
Dir: Greg Ford, Terry Lennon *Cast:* Voices of Mel Blanc, Mel Tormé
▶ Eleven vintage Warner Brothers cartoons are linked with new material in a plot involving a ghost-hunting service operated by Daffy

Duck. Featured are Chuck Jones's "The Abominable Snow Rabbit," Friz Freleng's "Hyde and Go Tweet," and Robert McKimson's "Prize Pest." New shorts include 1987's "The Duxorcist" and "Night of the Living Duck," the latter featuring Tormé's warbling. The old stuff is best, but new material is superior to same in previous four W.B. compilations. **(CC)**
Dist.: Warner

DAISY MILLER 1974
★ G Drama 1:31
Dir: Peter Bogdanovich *Cast:* Cybill Shepherd, Barry Brown, Cloris Leachman, Mildred Natwick, Eileen Brennan
▶ Spoiled American Shepherd tours Europe with mother Leachman and bratty little brother, shocking nineteenth-century polite society with her flirting and directness before tragedy strikes. Beautifully detailed period piece with lavish costumes and sumptuous settings. From the Henry James novel.
Dist.: Paramount

DAKOTA 1945
★ ★ NR Western 1:22 B&W
Dir: Joseph Kane *Cast:* John Wayne, Vera Ralston, Walter Brennan, Ward Bond, Mike Mazurki, Ona Munson
▶ Wayne elopes with Ralston, whose father is a railroad tycoon, and heads for the Dakota Territory. On a steamship to Fargo, he is robbed by crooks working for Bond, who plans to use inside information about a new train route to cheat Fargo farmers. Wayne sides with the farmers in the subsequent land war. Large-scale Western never builds up steam.
Dist.: Republic

DAKOTA 1989
★ ★ ★ PG Drama 1:36
☑ Explicit language, violence
Dir: Fred Holmes *Cast:* Lou Diamond Phillips, Eli Cummins, DeeDee Norton, Jordan Burton, Steven Ruge
▶ Phillips is a troubled youth who gets into a fight at a drive-in and winds up working off the damages at a ranch. With his mechanical abilities, Phillips makes himself useful to the rancher, falls in love with foreman's daughter Norton, and "finds himself" in the great outdoors. Simple and heart-tugging. **(CC)**
Dist.: HBO

DAKOTA INCIDENT 1956
★ ★ NR Western 1:22
Dir: Lewis R. Foster *Cast:* Linda Darnell, Dale Robertson, John Lund, Ward Bond, Regis Toomey, Skip Homeier
▶ Robertson robs a bank and flees with fallen woman Darnell. Lund, a bank clerk implicated in the crime, is run out of town on a stagecoach with politician Bond and singer Toomey. All must rely on each other when Indians attack. High body count in an otherwise routine Western.
Dist.: Republic

DALEKS—INVASION EARTH 2150 A.D.
1966 British
★ **NR Sci-Fi 1:24**
Dir: Gordon Flemyng *Cast:* Peter Cushing,
Bernard Cribbins, Ray Brooks, Jill Curzon,
Andrew Keir, Roberta Tovey
▶ Cushing stars as Dr. Who, a brilliant scientist
accidentally propelled into a future where
Daleks, evil creatures from outer space, have
taken over London. Cushing, with a little help
from his friends, manages to overcome the
invaders. Second feature inspired by the BBC
television series; first was 1965's *Dr. Who and
the Daleks.*
Dist.: HBO

DAM BUSTERS, THE 1954 British
★ ★ ★ **NR War 1:59 B&W**
Dir: Michael Anderson *Cast:* Richard Todd,
Michael Redgrave, Ursula Jeans, Basil Sydney, Derek Farr, Patrick Barr
▶ During World War II, scientist Redgrave invents a new bomb to destroy Nazis' strategic
and previously impregnable dams; wing commander Todd trains his pilots for the almost
impossible mission. Based on actual incidents,
this first-rate war drama maintains tension by
sticking to the facts. Thrilling climax received
an Oscar nomination for special effects.
Dist.: HBO

DAMES 1934
★ ★ **NR Musical 1:30 B&W**
Dir: Ray Enright *Cast:* Joan Blondell, Dick
Powell, Ruby Keeler, ZaSu Pitts, Hugh Herbert, Guy Kibbee
▶ Bumbling millionaire Herbert wants to
spend a fortune to close "scandalous" Broadway musicals; instead, his partner Kibbee is
blackmailed by chorus girl Blondell into investing in Powell's latest show. Silly plot takes back
seat to eye-opening Busby Berkeley versions
of "I Only Have Eyes for You," "Try to See It My
Way," and other tunes.
Dist.: MGM/UA

DAMIEN—OMEN II 1978
★ ★ ★ **R Horror 1:47**
☑ Explicit language, graphic violence
Dir: Don Taylor *Cast:* William Holden, Lee
Grant, Lew Ayres, Sylvia Sidney, Robert Foxworth, Jonathan Scott-Taylor
▶ Damien (Scott-Taylor), Satan's spawn from
the 1976 original, has grown into a spoiled,
obnoxious teenager. Reading the Book of
Revelations at military school, the little Antichrist learns his true identity—and kills his second set of relatives. Holden plays the business
tycoon father who thinks Damien is an angel.
For more carnage, see *The Final Conflict,* the
third title in this popular supernatural horror
trilogy.
Dist.: CBS/Fox

DAMNATION ALLEY 1977
★ ★ **PG Sci-Fi 1:27**
☑ Violence
Dir: Jack Smight *Cast:* Jan-Michael Vin-

cent, George Peppard, Dominique Sanda,
Paul Winfield, Jackie Earle Haley
▶ After a nuclear holocaust, a small band of
survivors cross America to the last outpost of
humanity in upstate New York. Along the dangerous route, they encounter tornadoes, giant
cockroaches, and murderous hillbillies.
Comic-book screenplay enlivened by good
special effects and well-paced action.
Dist.: CBS/Fox

DAMNED, THE 1969 Italian/German
★ **R Drama 2:41**
☑ Nudity, adult situations, violence
Dir: Luchino Visconti *Cast:* Dirk Bogarde, Ingrid Thulin, Helmut Griem, Helmut Berger,
Charlotte Rampling
▶ Challenging study of a rich, amoral family
of German industrialists that divides and disintegrates under Nazi influence. Incest, adultery, homosexuality, and mass murder
abound as family members struggle among
themselves for dominance and power. Academy Award nominations for Best Story and
Screenplay.
Dist.: Warner

DAMNED RIVER 1989
★ **R Action-Adventure 1:33**
☑ Rape, brief nudity, adult situations, explicit language, violence
Dir: Michael Schroeder *Cast:* Stephen
Shellen, Lisa Aliff, John Terlesky, Mark Pop-
pel, Bradford Bancroft
▶ College friends travel to Zimbabwe for
whitewater rafting down the Zambezi River.
Unfortunately, their guide Shellen turns out to
be a psychopath who proceeds to menace
them. After a fast start, story turns increasingly
rancid; Shellen's brutal behavior is never really
explained. Spectacular scenery. **(CC)**
Dist.: CBS/Fox

DAMN THE DEFIANT! 1962 British
★ ★ ★ **NR War 1:41**
Dir: Lewis Gilbert *Cast:* Alec Guinness, Dirk
Bogarde, Maurice Denham, Nigel Stock,
Anthony Quayle, Peter Gill
▶ Aboard an eighteenth-century British warship, captain Guinness finds himself caught
between his evil lieutenant Bogarde and a
crew ready to mutiny against Bogarde's iron
fist. Fighting among themselves, the British
must also battle the French. Handsome production featuring first-rate Guinness and Bogarde.
Dist.: RCA/Columbia

DAMN YANKEES 1958
★ ★ ★ **NR Musical 1:50**
Dir: George Abbott, Stanley Donen *Cast:*
Tab Hunter, Gwen Verdon, Ray Walston,
Shannon Bolin, Nathaniel Frey
▶ Middle-aged Hunter makes deal with the
Devil (Walston) to live out his dream of being
a youthful baseball star. Entertaining version
of the Broadway musical hit with Verdon
nicely re-creating her stage role as Lola, the

devil's sexy helper. Bob Fosse (who choreographed) appears briefly. Oscar-nominated Adler/Ross score includes "Whatever Lola Wants," "Two Lost Souls," "You Gotta Have Heart."
Dist.: Warner

DAMSEL IN DISTRESS, A 1937
★ ★ ★ NR Musical 1:40 B&W
Dir: George Stevens *Cast:* Fred Astaire, George Burns, Gracie Allen, Joan Fontaine, Reginald Gardiner, Ray Noble
► American dancing star Astaire romances English aristocrat Fontaine, helped by his pals Burns and Allen. Breezy musical based on a P. G. Wodehouse novel and play has a wonderful Gershwin score, including "A Foggy Day in London Town," "Nice Work If You Can Get It," and "I Can't Be Bothered Now." Choreographer Hermes Pan won an Oscar for his work on the delightful "Fun House" sequence.
Dist.: Turner

DANCE, CHARLIE, DANCE 1937
☆ NR Musical 1:05 B&W
Dir: Frank McDonald *Cast:* Stuart Erwin, Jean Muir, Glenda Farrell, Allen Jenkins, Addison Richards, Charles Foy
► Two dishonest promoters trick wealthy bumpkin Erwin into pouring his money into a flop Broadway show. But the tables turn when the canny rustic retools the show and makes it a hit. An amusing farce, based on the play *The Butter and Egg Man* by George S. Kaufman.
Dist.: Turner

DANCE, GIRL, DANCE 1940
★ ★ NR Drama 1:29 B&W
Dir: Dorothy Arzner *Cast:* Maureen O'Hara, Louis Hayward, Lucille Ball, Virginia Field, Ralph Bellamy, Maria Ouspenskaya
► Unable to find work, ballerina O'Hara auditions at a burlesque hall, where she falls prey to unscrupulous males despite guidance from veteran dancer Ball. A cult item for its early feminist stance, but overall a dull and unsatisfying melodrama.
Dist.: Turner

DANCE OF THE DAMNED 1989
☆ R Horror 1:23
☑ Nudity, strong sexual content, violence
Dir: Katt Shea Rubin *Cast:* Starr Andreeff, Cyril O'Reilly, Deborah Ann Nassar, Maria Ford, Athena Worthy, Tom Ruben
► Suicidal nightclub stripper Andreeff agrees to spend night with vampire O'Reilly after court bars her from visiting her son. Vampire is sexy, brooding, long-haired and immortal; get-together goes beyond the usual "wham, bam, fang you ma'am." Far from worst modern variation on this theme.
Dist.: Virgin

DANCE OF THE DWARFS 1983
★ ★ PG Action-Adventure 1:33
☑ Brief nudity, explicit language, violence

Dir: Gus Trikonis *Cast:* Peter Fonda, Deborah Raffin, John Amos, Carlos Palomino
► Anthropologist Raffin hires alcoholic he-man Fonda to copter her into jungle to find mysterious tribe of primitive dwarfs. Helicopter crashes, and the two must fend for themselves in jungle inhabited by, among others, witch doctor Amos. As pair continues quest, death and boredom pursue in a thousand forms, including monsters who look like Creature from Black Lagoon. Also called *Jungle Heat*.
Dist.: TWE

DANCERS 1987
★ ★ ★ PG Drama/Dance 1:39
☑ Adult situations, explicit language
Dir: Herbert Ross *Cast:* Mikhail Baryshnikov, Allesandra Ferri, Leslie Browne, Thomas Rall, Lynn Seymour, Julie Kent
► While supervising production of *Giselle* in Italy, world's best dancer and notorious womanizer Baryshnikov romances young ballerina Kent, despite warnings from his jaded former lovers Ferri and Browne. Soon the backstage romance mirrors the tragic tale of the ballet being rehearsed. Baryshnikov, Browne, and director Ross reprise their successful teaming from *The Turning Point.* **(CC)**
Dist.: Warner

DANCE WITH A STRANGER 1985 British
★ ★ R Drama 1:42
☑ Adult situations, explicit language, violence
Dir: Mike Newell *Cast:* Miranda Richardson, Rupert Everett, Ian Holm, Matthew Carroll, Tom Chadbon
► Powerful if downbeat true story of Ruth Ellis (Richardson), the nightclub hostess who killed wealthy beau Everett and then, in 1955, became the last woman executed in England. Low-key, realistic drama refuses to pander to our emotions, but the amazing Richardson makes Ruth a woman to remember. **(CC)**
Dist.: Vestron

DANCING IN THE DARK 1986 Canadian
★ NR Drama 1:37
☑ Brief nudity, adult situations, explicit language
Dir: Leon Marr *Cast:* Martha Henry, Neil Munro, Rosemary Dunsmore, Richard Monette
► Shattering psychological drama about fortyish housewife Henry whose entire life revolves around the meticulous care she gives to her home and husband Munro. With no opinions or interests of her own, she is ultimately able to make a personal breakthrough only after a shocking tragedy. Henry is splendid thanks in part to amazing direction from Marr, who also wrote the screenplay. Slow pacing makes it only for discriminating audiences.
Dist.: New World

DANCING LADY 1933
★ ★ NR Musical 1:34 B&W

Dir: Robert Z. Leonard *Cast:* Joan Crawford, Clark Gable, Franchot Tone, Fred Astaire, Nelson Eddy, May Robson
▶ Crawford is a poor but spunky dancer; Tone, a wealthy playboy sponsoring her in a Broadway play; and Gable, the director who resents Tone's interference. Glossy romance includes "Everything I Have Is Yours" and "Hold Your Man," but it's notable chiefly for Astaire's film debut in a short duet with Crawford. The Three Stooges and Robert Benchley supply comic relief.
Dist.: MGM/UA

DANDY IN ASPIC, A 1968 British
☆ **R Espionage 1:47**
☑ Adult situations, violence
Dir: Anthony Mann *Cast:* Laurence Harvey, Tom Courtenay, Mia Farrow, Lionel Stander, Harry Andrews, Peter Cook
▶ British civil servant Harvey is actually a Russian agent, leaking information leading to assassinations of British operatives. When English agent Courtenay gets on his trail, Harvey is in trouble because the Russians think he's too valuable to return home. Intricate plot should satisfy genre fans. After Mann died during production, Harvey took over director's chair.
Dist.: RCA/Columbia

DANGEROUS 1935
★ ★ **NR Drama 1:18 B&W**
Dir: Alfred E. Green *Cast:* Bette Davis, Franchot Tone, Margaret Lindsay, Alison Skipworth, John Eldredge, Dick Foran
▶ Davis, an alcoholic actress, has sunk to the bottom when millionaire Tone decides to rehabilitate her. Their romance is threatened by Davis's wastrel husband Eldredge and Tone's fiancée Lindsay. Turgid soap opera is notable for Davis's larger-than-life, Oscar-winning performance.
Dist.: MGM/UA

DANGEROUS CURVES 1988
★ **PG Comedy 1:33**
☑ Explicit language
Dir: David Lewis *Cast:* Tate Donovan, Danielle von Zerneck, Grant Heslov, Valeri Breiman, Karen Lee Scott, Leslie Nielsen, Elizabeth Ashley, Robert Stack, Robert Klein
▶ Youths Donovan and Heslov take what looks like an easy job: deliver a new Porsche to Stack's daughter. Stop in San Diego turns into disaster when the car is stolen and offered as first prize in a beauty pageant. Painless high jinks with attractive youngsters; older stars are merely along for the ride.
Dist.: Vestron

DANGEROUS LIAISONS 1988
★ ★ ★ **R Drama 2:00**
☑ Nudity, strong sexual content, adult situations, explicit language, violence
Dir: Stephen Frears *Cast:* Glenn Close, John Malkovich, Michelle Pfeiffer, Swoosie Kurtz, Keanu Reeves, Uma Thurman, Mildred Natwick, Peter Capaldi

▶ Adaptation by Christopher Hampton of his London and Broadway hit, *Les Liaisons Dangereuses*, pits eighteenth-century French nobles and former lovers Close and Malkovich in a battle of sexual intrigue. Malkovich seeks to seduce virginal convent girl Thurman to further Close's revenge against Thurman's fiancé; he soon finds a greater challenge in devout and self-righteous Pfeiffer. Meanwhile, Close educates the teenage Reeves in the ways of love. Hampton's screenplay and the sumptuous costumes won Oscars.
Dist.: Warner

DANGEROUS LOVE 1988
★ **R Mystery-Suspense 1:36**
☑ Nudity, explicit language, violence
Dir: Marty Ollstein *Cast:* Lawrence Monoson, Brenda Bakke, Peter Marc, Elliott Gould, Anthony Geary, Teri Austin
▶ A psychopath murders the girls at the Dream Date Video Club, taping his dark deeds. Cop Gould suspects hapless Monoson; his partner Bakke goes undercover to find the real killer. Unconvincing screenplay unevenly acted: Monoson is fine, but Bakke is incredibly miscast as a policewoman. Slick direction by Ollstein falters in the action scenes.
Dist.: Media

DANGEROUSLY CLOSE 1986
★ ★ **R Drama 1:35**
☑ Brief nudity, adult situations, explicit language, violence
Dir: Albert Pyun *Cast:* John Stockwell, J. Eddie Peck, Carey Lowell, Bradford Bancroft
▶ Fast times at Vista Verde High. An activist pack of good-looking, ultra-privileged do-gooders keeps class delinquents in check, sometimes overstepping disciplinary boundaries. The "wrong element" is suddenly dropping dead. Stockwell plays ringleader Randy; Lowell, his naive girlfriend Julie. Slick MTV-type editing will please teens and vigilantes. (CC)
Dist.: Media

DANGEROUS MISSION 1954
☆ **NR Mystery-Suspense 1:15**
Dir: Louis King *Cast:* Victor Mature, Piper Laurie, William Bendix, Vincent Price, Betta St. John, Steve Darrell
▶ Laurie, bystander at a gangland rubout, flees New York with both the cops and the mob on her tail. At Montana's Glacier National Park she is befriended by Mature and Price, but can't tell which one of them is trying to kill her. Lackluster thriller is filled with plot holes. Originally shot in 3-D.
Dist.: Fox Hills

DANGEROUS MOONLIGHT 1941 British
★ **NR War 1:37 B&W**
Dir: Brian Desmond Hurst *Cast:* Anton Walbrook, Sally Gray, Derrick de Marney, Cecil Parker, Percy Parsons, Kenneth Kent
▶ Polish pianist Walbrook lets his fingers do the flying, joining the British Royal Air Force

during World War II. The Battle of Britain causes him to suffer amnesia, but wife Gray finds a way to bring his memory back. War film successfully combines romance, aerial sequences, and classical music. Also known as *Suicide Squadron.*
Dist.: Turner

DANGEROUS MOVES 1984 Swiss
★ ★ ★ NR Drama 1:40
☑ Explicit language
Dir: Richard Dembo *Cast:* Michel Piccoli, Leslie Caron, Liv Ullmann, Alexandre Arbatt, Bernhard Wicki, Wojtek Pszoniak
▶ Aging Russian grandmaster Piccoli takes on upstart defector Arbatt in a championship chess match. Tense psychological battle heats up as Piccoli contends with a failing heart and Arbatt's brash conduct while the younger man struggles with a faltering marriage to Ullmann and his increasing paranoia. Winner of Oscar for Best Foreign Film. Ⓢ
Dist.: Warner

DANGEROUS ORPHANS 1986 New Zealand
★ R Action-Adventure 1:30
☑ Adult situations, explicit language, violence
Dir: John Laing *Cast:* Peter Stevens, Jennifer Ward-Lealand, Michael Hurst, Ross Girven, Peter Bland
▶ Pals from youth, three orphans kill a drug courier, then go to Geneva and withdraw money from the gang's bank account. Stevens, one of the orphans, is carrying on with Ward-Lealand, the ex-wife of one of the gang's leaders, making him target number one when the gang decides to take revenge. Not much plot sense, but a slick veneer goes a long way in this empty thriller.
Dist.: Academy

DANGEROUS WHEN WET 1953
★ ★ ★ NR Musical 1:35
Dir: Charles Walters *Cast:* Esther Williams, Fernando Lamas, Jack Carson, Charlotte Greenwood, William Demarest
▶ Sneaky entrepreneur Carson sponsors young Arkansas girl Williams in her attempt to swim the English Channel. Along the way she's wooed by champagne salesman Lamas. Lush production values and an animated sequence with Tom and Jerry highlight this MGM musical. Lamas and Williams later became husband and wife.
Dist.: MGM/UA

DANGER ZONE, THE 1987
☆ R Action-Adventure 1:28
☑ Nudity, adult situations, explicit language
Dir: Henry Vernon *Cast:* Robert Canada, Jason Williams, Mike Wiles, Axel Roberts
▶ All-girl rock group is traveling to Las Vegas for talent show when their station wagon breaks down. They take refuge in a ghost town that happens to be the headquarters of grubby biker gang involved in drug smuggling. Band repels rattlesnake with hair spray,

endures other indignities until old prospector and cop come to rescue. Too slimy to be entertaining.
Dist.: Nelson

DANGER ZONE II: REAPER'S REVENGE 1989
☆ R Horror 1:35
☑ Rape, nudity, adult situations, explicit language, violence
Dir: Geoffrey G. Bowers *Cast:* Jason Williams, Robert Random, Jane Higginson, Alisha Das
▶ Williams, the undercover cop who nailed bikers in *Danger Zone*, is targeted for payback when Random, their leader, is sprung on niggling legal technicality. After kidnapping Williams's girl, Random heads for desert, with Williams and other wronged types on his tail. Dull brawl evens score in story where sadism substitutes for action.
Dist.: Forum

DANIEL 1983
★ ★ R Drama 2:09
☑ Adult situations, explicit language, violence
Dir: Sidney Lumet *Cast:* Timothy Hutton, Mandy Patinkin, Lindsay Crouse, Edward Asner, Amanda Plummer, Ellen Barkin
▶ Fictionalized account of the famous Rosenberg espionage trial from the point of view of the doomed couple's children. Story cuts back and forth in time as Daniel (Hutton), the angry son of socialists Patinkin and Crouse executed for giving away atomic secrets, investigates his past. Strongest scene: Patinkin using a cereal box to explain capitalism to his young son. Ambitious drama with political overtones adapted from E. L. Doctorow's novel *The Book of Daniel.*
Dist.: Paramount

DANIEL BOONE 1936
★ NR Western 1:15 B&W
Dir: David Howard *Cast:* George O'Brien, Heather Angel, John Carradine, Ralph Forbes, Clarence Muse
▶ Minor tale of the famous frontiersman leading settlers from North Carolina to the wilds of eighteenth-century Kentucky. Their new home is threatened when fur trader Carradine incites hostile Indian tribes against them. O'Brien is suitably heroic in the title role.
Dist.: Cable

DANNY BOY 1982 Irish
☆ R Drama 1:30
☑ Brief nudity, adult situations, explicit language, graphic violence
Dir: Neil Jordan *Cast:* Stephen Rea, Alan Devlin, Veronica Quilligan, Peter Caffrey, Honor Heffernan, Ray McAnally
▶ Musician Rea trades his saxophone for an Uzi to track down the masked killers of his band's manager and an innocent girl. All-Irish production has a peculiar, morally confused attitude toward revenge, expecting audi-

ence to continue to like formerly gentle Rea even after he becomes a savage killer. Also known as *Angel.*
Dist.: RCA/Columbia

DANTON 1983 French/Polish
★★ PG Drama 2:16
☑ Brief nudity, violence
Dir: Andrzej Wajda ***Cast:*** Gerard Depardieu, Wojtek Pszoniak, Anne Alvaro, Roland Blanche, Patrice Chereau
▸ Depardieu is magnetic as Danton, an idealistic radical seeking an end to the Reign of Terror in 1793. He is opposed by Robespierre (Pszoniak), a strict lawyer who uses the Revolution for personal goals. Working with French and Polish actors, director Wajda took an intellectual approach to the French Revolution, pointing out its parallels with contemporary Poland. [S]
Dist.: RCA/Columbia

DARBY O'GILL AND THE LITTLE PEOPLE 1959
★★★★ NR Fantasy/Family 1:59
Dir: Robert Stevenson ***Cast:*** Albert Sharpe, Sean Connery, Janet Munro, Jimmy O'Dea, Kieron Moore
▸ Evil spells abound when an about-to-retire Irish caretaker Darby O'Gill (Sharpe) falls down a well and runs afoul of local leprechaun king O'Dea. Darby manages to outwit the wee folk and orchestrate the marriage of daughter Munro to his handsome young successor Connery. Magical bit of blarney with some uncomfortably frightening moments from Walt Disney Studios.
Dist.: Buena Vista

DARING DOBERMANS, THE 1973
★★★ G Drama/Family 1:30
Dir: Byron Chudnow ***Cast:*** Charles Knox Robinson, Tim Considine, David Moses, Claudio Martinez, Joan Caulfield
▸ Fun sequel to *The Doberman Gang.* The larcenous dogs are taken over by a new gang of crooks for a daring heist too dangerous for humans to perform, but an Indian lad throws a monkey wrench into their plans. Best for children and dog lovers. **(CC)**
Dist.: CBS/Fox

DARK, THE 1978
★★ R Sci-Fi 1:32
☑ Explicit language, violence
Dir: John Cardos ***Cast:*** William Devane, Cathy Lee Crosby, Richard Jaekel, Keenan Wynn, Jacquelyn Hyde, Casey Kasem
▸ Devane's a pulp writer, Crosby's a TV newscaster, Jaekel's a cop, and they're all trying to find out what mysterious force is killing, mutilating, and decapitating Los Angelenos. Culprit is gradually revealed as blue-jeans-wearing alien, who kills with laser-beam eyes. Just another monster movie.
Dist.: Media

DARK AGE 1988 U.S./Australian
★★ R Action-Adventure 1:30
☑ Nudity, violence
Dir: Arch Nicholson ***Cast:*** John Jaratt, Nikki Coghill, Max Phipps, Burnam Burnam
▸ A twenty-five-foot aquatic creature with huge teeth is devouring swimmers, causing bad publicity for a commerce-hungry town. A three-man team goes out to kill it. Sounds like *Jaws*, but it's a crocodile. Aussie variation on bite theme has little suspense but good local flavor, thanks to aboriginal story angle and Queensland setting.
Dist.: Nelson

DARK COMMAND 1940
★★ NR Western 1:34 B&W
Dir: Raoul Walsh ***Cast:*** John Wayne, Claire Trevor, Walter Pidgeon, Roy Rogers, George "Gabby" Hayes, Porter Hall, Marjorie Main, Raymond Walburn
▸ Texan Wayne becomes sheriff of a Kansas town divided over the slave question before the Civil War. Schoolteacher Pidgeon forms a band of Confederate guerrilla raiders that terrorizes the townpeople. Both also spar over Trevor. Potent Western has action, spectacle, and memorable stunts by Yakima Canutt.
Dist.: Republic

DARK CORNER, THE 1946
★★★ NR Mystery-Suspense 1:39 B&W
Dir: Henry Hathaway ***Cast:*** Mark Stevens, Lucille Ball, Clifton Webb, William Bendix, Kurt Kreuger
▸ Tough, exciting mystery about private eye Stevens framed for murder. Chased by both the crooks and the cops, he turns to secretary Ball (in a rare dramatic role) for help. Highly enjoyable example of film noir is notable for its terse dialogue, twisty plot, and moody atmosphere. Bendix is especially effective as a sadistic killer.
Dist.: CBS/Fox

DARK CRYSTAL, THE 1982 British
★★★★ PG Fantasy 1:30
☑ Mild violence
Dir: Jim Henson, Frank Oz ***Cast:*** Voices of Stephen Garlick, Lisa Maxwell, Billie Whitelaw, Perry Edwards
▸ Good versus evil in a fantasy setting where vulturish Skeksis have rid the universe of all but two Gelflings (tiny humanoids). The brave duo, aided by some ancient mystics, attempts to save the world from destruction by finding a missing shard from the Dark Crystal that supplies the evil beings with their power. Solemn, reverential kids' fantasy with amazing puppetry by Muppet master Henson.
Dist.: HBO

DARK EYES 1987 Italian/Russian
★ NR Comedy/Drama 1:58
☑ Nudity, adult situations
Dir: Nikita Mikhalkov ***Cast:*** Marcello Mastroianni, Silvana Mangano, Marthe Keller, Elena Sofonova, Pina Cei

► Wealthy idler Mastroianni visits a ritzy spa and is rejuvenated by a romance with beautiful young (but unhappily married) Russian Sofonova. Sumptuous turn-of-the-century decor often upstages the plot (based on several Chekhov short stories). Poignant, Oscar-nominated performance by Mastroianni as the born-again romantic.
Dist.: CBS/Fox

DARK FORCES 1983 Australian
★ PG Drama 1:36
☑ Adult situations, brief nudity, explicit language, violence
Dir: Simon Wincer ***Cast:*** Robert Powell, David Hemmings, Broderick Crawford, Carmen Duncan
► Senator Hemmings's son is dying of leukemia. He enlists the aid of healer Powell, who cures the boy but puts the entire family, including Hemmings's wife Duncan, under his spell. Intriguing themes are sometimes given a too-simplistic treatment. Wincer's fluid direction, however, keeps this one from sinking. Also known as *Harlequin*.
Dist.: Media

DARK HABITS 1984 Spanish
☆ NR Comedy 1:35
☑ Adult situations, explicit language, nudity
Dir: Pedro Almodóvar ***Cast:*** Cristina S. Pascual, Julieta Serrano, Marisa Paredes, Carmen Maura
► Trashy nightclub singer Pascual is on the lam after her boyfriend dies of a drug overdose. She seeks refuge at the Convent of the Humble Redeemers, an order filled with heroin-shooting, bongo-playing, murdering nuns. Warped comedy takes potshots at an already much-lampooned subject, but director Almodóvar adds a few unique and hilarious touches of his own. [S]
Dist.: CineVista

DARK MIRROR, THE 1946
★★ NR Drama 1:25 B&W
Dir: Robert Siodmak ***Cast:*** Olivia de Havilland, Lew Ayres, Thomas Mitchell, Richard Long, Charles Evans
► Acting field day for de Havilland playing a good sister and her evil twin. Both become murder suspects; shrink Ayres is the man who investigates the case and wins the two women's hearts. Quite involving; technical effects are pretty good. Oscar nomination for Original Story.
Dist.: Republic

DARK OF THE NIGHT 1985 New Zealand
★ NR Horror 1:28
☑ Adult situations, explicit language, violence
Dir: Gaylene Preston ***Cast:*** Heather Bolton, David Letch, Margaret Umbers, Suzanne Lee, Gary Stalker, Perry Piercy
► Bolton buys a used Jaguar as a symbol of her independence but gradually learns the car is haunted by Piercy, victim of a murderous hitchhiker. Bolton also finds herself pursued by three menacing men in this slowly paced horror fantasy. Originally released as *Mr. Wrong*.
Dist.: Lightning

DARK PASSAGE 1947
★★★ NR Mystery-Suspense 1:46 B&W
Dir: Delmer Daves ***Cast:*** Humphrey Bogart, Lauren Bacall, Bruce Bennett, Agnes Moorehead, Tom D'Andrea
► Unjustly accused Bogart escapes prison, changes his identity via plastic surgery, and goes after the real killer. First-rate Warner Brothers thriller with interesting use of subjective camera, San Francisco locations, and Bogart/Bacall chemistry (their third teaming).
Dist.: Key

DARK PAST, THE 1948
★★★ NR Drama 1:14 B&W
Dir: Rudolph Maté ***Cast:*** William Holden, Lee J. Cobb, Nina Foch, Adele Jergens, Stephen Dunne
► Holden, a vicious young killer, is as afraid of his own dreams as he is of the law until shrewd psychiatrist Cobb helps him understand why he kills. With Foch as the gorgeous moll. Notable as one of Hollywood's first attempts to illustrate Freudian ideas. Remake of *Blind Alley*.
Dist.: RCA/Columbia

DARK PLACES 1974 British
★★ PG Horror 1:15
☑ Explicit language, violence
Dir: Don Sharp ***Cast:*** Christopher Lee, Joan Collins, Herbert Lom, Robert Hardy, Jane Birkin
► Mental hospital administrator Hardy inherits an estate from a dying man and searches for the money supposedly stashed there. The place is haunted, causing the administrator to go beserk and embark on a murderous rampage. Straightforward suspenser has good production values. Collins skillfully plays a scheming bitch.
Dist.: Nelson

DARK STAR 1974
★ G Sci-Fi 1:30
☑ Explicit language
Dir: John Carpenter ***Cast:*** Brian Narelle, Andreijah Pahich, Cal Kuniholm, Dan O'-Bannon, Joe Sanders
► Four astronauts, trapped in outer space with little chance for reentry, battle an alien and continue their mission to destroy unstable planets. Early low-budget effort of director Carpenter with campy acting but inventive touches and offbeat humor.
Dist.: VCI

DARK TOWER 1989
☆ R Horror 1:31
☑ Adult situations, explicit language, violence
Dir: Ken Barnett ***Cast:*** Michael Moriarty,

Jenny Agutter, Carol Lynley, Theodore Bikel, Anne Lockhart, Kevin McCarthy
▶ Moriarity is a security chief at a Barcelona skyscraper being plagued by mysterious deaths, including a falling window washer and an evisceration by elevator. Parapsychologist Bikel traces building's jinx to ghost of architect's murdered husband. With help of exorcist McCarthy, Bikel battles demons and tower is purged. Artily slow film has foolish, one-note plot.
Dist.: Forum

DARK VICTORY 1939
★ ★ ★ ★ **NR Drama 1:46 B&W**
Dir: Edmund Goulding *Cast:* Bette Davis, George Brent, Geraldine Fitzgerald, Humphrey Bogart, Ronald Reagan
▶ Not-a-dry-eye-in-the-house department. Socialite Davis learns she's contracted a fatal disease and tries to make the rest of her days meaningful. Classy Warners tearjerker with bravura performance by the great Bette (Oscar-nominated, as was the movie), ably supported by Brent as the doctor who loves her and Bogart as her stable master. **(CC)**
Dist.: MGM/UA Ⓒ

DARLING 1965 British
★ ★ ★ **NR Drama 2:02 B&W**
Dir: John Schlesinger *Cast:* Julie Christie, Dirk Bogarde, Laurence Harvey, Roland Curram, José Luis de Villalonga, Alex Scott
▶ Psychological study of amoral model Christie, who casually uses and discards men. Slick, cynical look at the Swinging Sixties has dated poorly, although its treatment of abortion and orgies was once controversial. Bogarde registers strongly as a TV newsman who abandons his family for Christie. Nominated for five Oscars, winning for Best Actress (Christie), Screenplay (by Frederic Raphael), and Costume Design.
Dist.: Nelson

D.A.R.Y.L. 1985
★ ★ ★ ★ **PG Sci-Fi 1:39**
☑ Explicit language, mild violence
Dir: Simon Wincer *Cast:* Mary Beth Hurt, Michael McKean, Kathryn Walker, Colleen Camp, Barrett Oliver
▶ Suburbanites Hurt and McKean adopt amnesiac ten-year-old Daryl (Oliver), who turns out to be a robot on the lam from a government project (his name stands for Data Analysing Robot Youth Lifeform). The boy develops human feelings but the government baddies try to reclaim him anyway. Sweet-natured family adventure with an upbeat ending. **(CC)**
Dist.: Paramount

DAS BOOT 1982 German
★ ★ ★ ★ **R War 2:30**
☑ Explicit language, violence
Dir: Wolfgang Petersen *Cast:* Jurgen Prochnow, Herbert Gronemeyer, Klaus Wenne-

man, Hubertus Bengsch, Martin Semmelrogge
▶ During World War II, world-weary U-boat commander Prochnow navigates his desperate crew through numerous close encounters with the British and masterminds the raising of the damaged ship when it sinks to the ocean floor. Technically superb German antiwar drama combines claustrophobic feel within the ship with exciting battle sequences outside. Nominated for six Oscars. Dubbed version features original cast members doing their own voices. ⒮
Dist.: RCA/Columbia

DATE WITH AN ANGEL 1987
★ ★ ★ **PG Fantasy 1:45**
☑ Explicit language
Dir: Tom McLoughlin *Cast:* Michael Knight, Emmanuelle Beart, Phoebe Cates, David Dukes, Phil Brock
▶ Young Knight, unsure about his engagement to wealthy Cates, falls in love with an angel (the beautiful French actress Beart) who crash-lands in his swimming pool. Comedy/fantasy/romance in the *Splash* vein lacks the directoral magic to really fly but has an appealing cast and generally charming lightweight tone.
Dist.: HBO

DATE WITH JUDY, A 1948
★ **NR Musical 1:43**
Dir: Richard Thorpe *Cast:* Wallace Beery, Jane Powell, Elizabeth Taylor, Carmen Miranda, Xavier Cugat, Robert Stack
▶ Powell suspects her father Beery may be having an affair with Miranda, but he's just taking dancing lessons to surprise his wife in this frothy slice of small-town Americana. Powell also competes with a radiant Taylor for Stack's affections. Miranda does "Cuanto La Gusta"; other tunes include "It's a Most Unusual Day" and "Temptation." **(CC)**
Dist.: MGM/UA

DAUGHTER OF DR. JEKYLL 1957
☆ **NR Horror 1:11 B&W**
Dir: Edgar G. Ulmer *Cast:* John Agar, Gloria Talbot, Arthur Shields, John Dierkes, Martha Wentworth
▶ Talbot is told that she is the offspring of the infamous killer, and comes under suspicion when a rash of murders occurs. Actual culprit appears to be a werewolf in this low-budget, uninspired, and unamusing twist on the Robert Louis Stevenson classic.
Dist.: Key

DAVID AND BATHSHEBA 1951
★ ★ ★ ★ **NR Drama 1:56**
Dir: Henry King *Cast:* Gregory Peck, Susan Hayward, Raymond Massey, Kieron Moore, James Robertson Justice, Jayne Meadows
▶ Biblical story of King David (Peck), who falls in love with married Bathsheba (Hayward) and sends her husband Moore off to battle. However, hardship falls upon his kingdom,

suggesting that powers above are none too pleased. Intelligent epic was nominated for three Oscars (Screenplay, Music, Cinematography). **(CC)**
Dist.: CBS/Fox

DAVID AND LISA 1962
★ ★ NR Drama 1:29 B&W
☑ Adult situations
Dir: Frank Perry *Cast:* Keir Dullea, Janet Margolin, Howard da Silva, Neva Patterson, Clifton James
▶ Disturbed adolescent Dullea, placed in a mental home, begins to blossom because of his relationship with young schizophrenic Margolin. Independently made tale of love conquering madness is a minor classic. Sincere, well-intentioned direction by Perry overcomes the modest budget. Nicely acted by Dullea and Margolin.
Dist.: RCA/Columbia

DAVID COPPERFIELD 1935
★ ★ ★ ★ NR Drama 2:13 B&W
Dir: George Cukor *Cast:* Freddie Bartholomew, Frank Lawton, W. C. Fields, Madge Evans, Maureen O'Sullivan, Edna May Oliver, Roland Young, Basil Rathbone
▶ Orphaned as a child, young Copperfield (Bartholomew) faces a bleak future in his stepfather's sweatshop, but through pluck and the help of friends he achieves success. Masterful adaptation of Charles Dickens's beloved classic captures the author's spirit and humor without sacrificing pacing. Superb direction and a perfect cast: Fields (Mr. Micawber), Young (Uriah Heep), and Rathbone (the villainous Murdstone) are particularly impressive. **(CC)**
Dist.: MGM/UA

DAVY CROCKETT AND THE RIVER PIRATES 1956
★ ★ G Action-Adventure 1:21
Dir: Norman Foster *Cast:* Fess Parker, Buddy Ebsen, Jeff York, Kenneth Tobey, Clem Bevans, Irvin Ashkenazy
▶ Frontiersman Crockett (Parker) meets fellow legend Mike Fink (York) in a series of adventures up and down the Mississippi River. Despite being pieced together out of two separate Disney TV shows, this superior production is solid entertainment, with Ebsen particularly strong as Crockett's sidekick George Russel, and a thoroughly competent group of familiar faces as Fink's crew of rowdy rivermen.
Dist.: Buena Vista

DAWN! 1979 Australian
★ ★ NR Biography 1:51
☑ Explicit language
Dir: Ken Hannam *Cast:* Bronwyn Mackay-Payne, Tom Richards, John Diedrich, Bunney Brooke
▶ Story of Dawn Fraser (Mackay-Payne), a chunky Australian teenager who became a three-time Olympic gold medal-winner. A strong individual, Fraser is always getting in

hot water with athletic authorities. Biopic is straightforward and honest, but also predictable and a bit dull.
Dist.: VidAmerica

DAWN OF THE DEAD 1979
★ NR Horror 2:05
☑ Explicit language, graphic violence
Dir: George A. Romero *Cast:* David Emge, Ken Foree, Scott Reiniger, Gaylen Ross, David Crawford
▶ Two military men, a TV reporter, and a lovely blond are trapped in a shopping center filled with menacing zombies in director Romero's follow-up to his 1968 cult classic *Night of the Living Dead.* Very bloody and gory; violence level will offend many. However, horror fans will be in heaven with the extremely effective, if revolting, special effects. Original R rating was revoked when producers inserted additional graphic violence.
Dist.: HBO

DAWN OF THE MUMMY 1981
★ NR Horror 1:33
☑ Graphic violence
Dir: Armand Weston *Cast:* Brenda King, George Peck, Barry Sateels
▶ A mummy is awakened from nearly five thousand years of sleep when four gorgeous models and their photographers invade his tomb. The hapless women are then pursued by the bandaged monster. Silly screenplay is enlivened by occasionally scary moments.
Dist.: HBO

DAWN PATROL, THE 1938
★ ★ ★ NR War 1:43 B&W
Dir: Edmund Goulding *Cast:* Errol Flynn, David Niven, Basil Rathbone, Donald Crisp, Melville Cooper, Barry Fitzgerald
▶ British Royal Flying Corps pilots rely on boyish bravado to counter the deadly toll of daily missions behind enemy lines. Flynn is outstanding as an ace wracked with guilt when he's promoted to squadron leader. Sentimental World War I drama is famous for its thrilling dogfight sequences. Original made in 1930 by Howard Hawks.
Dist.: Key

DAY AFTER, THE 1983
★ ★ ★ ★ NR Drama/MFTV 2:00
Dir: Nicholas Meyer *Cast:* Jason Robards, JoBeth Williams, John Lithgow, John Cullum, Steven Guttenberg, Amy Madigan
▶ Controversial made-for-television movie details the beginning and aftermath of a nuclear war. Shattering scenes of radiation's effects on a midwestern American community are directed with a heavy hand. Much more effective is the earlier scene in which missiles zooming out of their silos suddenly disrupt the quiet of an ordinary day.
Dist.: Embassy

DAY AT THE RACES, A 1937
★ ★ ★ NR Comedy 1:51 B&W

Dir: Sam Wood *Cast:* Groucho Marx, Harpo Marx, Chico Marx, Allan Jones, Maureen O'-Sullivan, Margaret Dumont, Douglass Dumbrille
► Delicious Marx Brothers shenanigans in a racetrack and a sanitarium as horse doctor Dr. Hackenbush (Groucho) treats wealthy hypochondriac Dumont for "double blood pressure." Hilarious scenes include Harpo and Chico saving Groucho from a scheming vixen by wallpapering her out of Dumont's sight and Chico's famous "Tootsie fruitsie" racetrack tip to Groucho. Does have a dated scene of black stereotypes who mistake Harpo for an angel.
Dist.: MGM/UA

DAYDREAMER, THE 1966
★ ★ ★ **NR Family 1:41**
Dir: Jules Bass *Cast:* Paul O'Keefe, Jack Gilford, Ray Bolger, Margaret Hamilton, voices of Hayley Mills, Tallulah Bankhead, Victor Borge, Patty Duke, Boris Karloff, Robert Goulet
► Opens with scenes of Hans Christian Anderson (O'Keefe) and his father Gilford, then uses puppets to perform his fables. Included are the tale of the boy who saw through "The Emperor's New Clothes" and "The Little Mermaid" (voice of Mills) who wanted to become human. Disney's version of the latter story remains superior, but otherwise this is fine for kids.
Dist.: Nelson

DAY FOR NIGHT 1973 French
★ **PG Comedy/Drama 1:56**
☑ Adult situations, explicit language
Dir: François Truffaut *Cast:* Jacqueline Bisset, Jean-Pierre Aumont, François Truffaut, Valentina Cortese, Alexandra Stewart
► Delightful inside look at moviemaking with director Truffaut playing shrink, social director, and confidant to his cast and crew as the behind-the-scenes love stories become more complicated than the movie being filmed. Oscar for Best Foreign Film, and Oscar nomination for Best Supporting Actress Cortese, who is so good that Ingrid Bergman apologized when she beat her for the award.
Dist.: Warner

DAY IN THE DEATH OF JOE EGG, A 1972 British
☆ **R Comedy/Drama 1:46**
☑ Nudity, adult situations, explicit language
Dir: Peter Medak *Cast:* Alan Bates, Janet Suzman, Peter Bowles, Sheila Gish, Joan Hickson
► Bates and Suzman, parents of a retarded spastic they call "Joe Egg," cope with their inner pain by telling sick jokes and playing out fantasies. Although Bates and Suzman give accomplished performances, this bleak, talky adaptation of the Peter Nichols play is extremely depressing.
Dist.: RCA/Columbia

DAY OF THE ANIMALS 1977
★ ★ **PG Horror 1:37**
☑ Violence
Dir: William Girdler *Cast:* Christopher George, Leslie Nielsen, Michael Ansara, Lynda Day George, Richard Jaeckel
► Animals run amok due to the destruction of earth's ozone layer in this thriller from the makers of *Grizzly*. Forest guide George tries to protect city slickers from killer beasts, including bears, cougars, wolves, hawks, vultures, and snakes. Tense thriller enhanced by Lalo Schifrin score.
Dist.: Media

DAY OF THE DEAD 1985
★ ★ **R Horror 1:42**
☑ Explicit language, graphic violence
Dir: George A. Romero *Cast:* Lori Cardille, Terry Alexander, Joseph Pilato, Jarlath Conroy, Antone DiLeo, Jr.
► The last few humans alive hole up in an underground compound in Florida in the third part of Romero's zombie trilogy. Production values and budget are higher than earlier entries but the familiar formula remains the same: plenty of blood and guts, well-done gore effects, and marauding zombies. Will gross out some, scare the rest.
Dist.: Media

DAY OF THE DOLPHIN, THE 1973
★ ★ ★ ★ **PG Action-Adventure 1:44**
Dir: Mike Nichols *Cast:* George C. Scott, Trish Van Devere, Paul Sorvino, Fritz Weaver, Edward Herrmann
► Scientist Scott teaches two dolphins to talk but evil conspirators try to use the mammals in an assassination scheme. Criticized as simplistic upon initial release but holds up as sweet and enchanting adventure fare, ideal for younger moviegoers. Lyrical direction from Nichols, charming dolphins, and a heartbreaking ending.
Dist.: Nelson

DAY OF THE JACKAL, THE 1973
British/French
★ ★ ★ ★ **PG Action-Adventure 2:20**
Dir: Fred Zinnemann *Cast:* Edward Fox, Alan Badel, Tony Britton, Cyril Cusack, Michael Lonsdale, Derek Jacobi
► In 1962, a terrorist organization hires the Jackal (Fox), the world's best professional hitman, to assassinate French President Charles de Gaulle. French policeman Lonsdale learns of the plot, but the Jackal uses baffling disguises to stay one step ahead of the cops. Methodical semidocumentary approach to Frederick Forsyth's best-seller is short on characterizations but builds incredible tension.
Dist.: MCA

DAY OF THE LOCUST, THE 1975
★ ★ **R Drama 2:24**
☑ Nudity, adult situations, explicit language, violence
Dir: John Schlesinger *Cast:* Donald Suther-

land, Karen Black, William Atherton, Burgess Meredith, Geraldine Page

▶ Ambitious look at the dark underside of 1930s Hollywood, as personified by lonely accountant Sutherland, young studio artist Atherton, and loose woman Black with whom they are involved. Meredith shines as Black's alcoholic father. Schlesinger's hellish vision culminates in a nightmarish riot at a movieland premiere. From Nathanael West's classic novel.
Dist.: Paramount

DAY OF THE TRIFFIDS, THE 1963 British
★ ★ NR Sci-Fi 1:35
Dir: Steve Sekely *Cast:* Howard Keel, Nicole Maurey, Janette Scott, Kieron Moore, Mervyn Johns

▶ A brilliant meteor shower blinds nearly everyone on Earth, sparing eye-patient Keel. Trains, planes, and boats crash, groping crowds panic in the burning cities, and plantlike aliens suddenly appear, making a disgusting sucking sound as they stalk human prey. Some nice effects and poignant situations with the suddenly sightless, but the title monsters, looking like a cross between Big Bird and a clematis, fail to give fright.
Dist.: Goodtimes

DAY OF WRATH 1943 Danish
☆ NR Drama 1:40 B&W
Dir: Carl Theodor Dreyer *Cast:* Thorkild Roose, Lisbeth Movin, Sigrid Neiiendam, Preben Lerdoff Rye, Anna Svierkier

▶ Stark, unnerving account of an illicit affair between Movin, bride of elderly pastor Roose, and his son Rye, set against the hysteria surrounding witch trials in seventeenth-century Denmark. Critically praised story's ornate visuals and troubling moral issues will reward patient viewers, but slow pacing and solemn tone are drawbacks. Also known as *Vredens Dag* and *Dies Irae*. Ⓢ
Dist.: Various

DAYS OF GLORY 1944
★ NR War 1:26 B&W
Dir: Jacques Tourneur *Cast:* Gregory Peck, Alan Reed, Maria Palmer, Lowell Gilmore, Tamara Toumanova, Hugo Haas

▶ Soviet resistance fighter Peck falls for ballerina Toumanova while facing Nazi peril in World War II Russia. Attempting to turn the tide of the Nazi invasion, the Russians counterattack, and the two lovers brave fatal danger for their country. In his film debut, Peck considerably outshines the other unknowns in this slow piece of wartime filler.
Dist.: Turner

DAYS OF HEAVEN 1978
★ ★ PG Drama 1:35
☑ Brief nudity, explicit language, mild violence
Dir: Terrence Malick *Cast:* Richard Gere, Brooke Adams, Sam Shepard, Linda Manz, Robert Wilke

▶ Factory worker Gere leaves Chicago for the Texas Panhandle with girlfriend Adams and sister Manz. They find work with Shepard, a wealthy farmer who starts a tragic affair with Adams. Technically breathtaking period drama has some of the most beautiful images ever captured on film. Nestor Almendros (assisted by Haskell Wexler) won an Oscar for his photography. Shepard's acting debut.
Dist.: Paramount

DAYS OF THRILLS AND LAUGHTER 1961
★ ★ ★ NR Documentary 1:33 B&W
Dir: Robert Youngson *Cast:* Charlie Chaplin, Stan Laurel, Oliver Hardy, Carole Lombard, Douglas Fairbanks, Fatty Arbuckle, Ben Turpin, Charlie Chase, Harry Langdon, Harry Houdini

▶ Compilation of silent screen comedy's greatest moments boasts exemplary narration, good music, and unusual clips. Novelties include Laurel and Hardy before they were a team, Turpin matching wits with Cameo the Wonder Dog, and Houdini himself rescuing a damsel at the brink of Niagara Falls. Viewers will long for more of same.
Dist.: MPI

DAYS OF THUNDER 1990
★ ★ ★ ★ PG-13 Drama 1:45
☑ Adult situations, explicit language
Dir: Tony Scott *Cast:* Tom Cruise, Robert Duvall, Nicole Kidman, Randy Quaid, Michael Rooker, Cary Elwes

▶ Under the wing of veteran manager Duvall, car crazy Cruise enters the stock car circuit, shooting for the Daytona 500, and searching for an identity. Severely injured in a crash, he recovers under the romantic care of doctor Kidman, and must overcome an obstacle he's never known before: fear. Thunderous soundtrack, heart-stopping races, and thrilling, driver's-eye camera work compensate for formulaic plot. Duvall delivers another expert performance. Screenplay by Robert Towne from a story written with Cruise.
Dist.: Paramount

DAYS OF WINE AND ROSES 1962
★ ★ ★ ★ NR Drama 1:57 B&W
Dir: Blake Edwards *Cast:* Jack Lemmon, Lee Remick, Charles Bickford, Jack Klugman, Alan Hewitt, Jack Albertson

▶ Newlyweds Lemmon and Remick fall into alcoholism as he brings job pressures home with him. Alcoholics Anonymous provides a cure for Lemmon but Remick finds beating the bottle not so easy. Superb Oscar-nominated performances by Lemmon and Remick highlight this adaptation of J. P. Miller's television play. Henry Mancini/Johnny Mercer title tune won Oscar.
Dist.: Warner

DAY THE EARTH CAUGHT FIRE, THE 1962 British
★ ★ ★ NR Sci-Fi 1:39 B&W
Dir: Val Guest *Cast:* Edward Judd, Janet

Munro, Leo McKern, Michael Goodliffe, Bernard Braden

▶ Cynical reporter Judd covers what is literally the hottest story of all time: when the Americans and Russians conduct nuclear tests on the same day, the Earth is thrown off its orbit and starts moving dangerously closer to the sun. Realistic treatment emphasizes character over special effects, resulting in blistering tension.
Dist.: HBO

DAY THE EARTH STOOD STILL, THE 1951
★ ★ ★ ★ NR Sci-Fi 1:28 B&W
Dir: Robert Wise *Cast:* Michael Rennie, Patricia Neal, Hugh Marlowe, Bobby Gray, Sam Jaffe

▶ Benevolent alien Rennie, accompanied by a huge robot, lands his flying saucer in Washington, D.C., to bring a message of peace to violence-prone humans. Widow Neal aids him but humanity is suspicious. Powerful, still topical fifties sci-fi classic generates plenty of suspense and food for thought. Rennie is a fine alien and there's a haunting Bernard Herrmann score.
Dist.: CBS/Fox

DAY TIME ENDED, THE 1980
☆ PG Sci-Fi 1:19
☑ Adult situations
Dir: John (Bud) Cardos *Cast:* Jim Davis, Christopher Mitchum, Dorothy Malone, Marcy Lafferty, Scott Kolden, Natasha Ryan

▶ Family living out in desert is visited first by a tiny humanoid alien, followed by a sinister little spaceship. Next thing they know, dinosaurs are battling it out in their backyard and the sky is full of colorful UFOs. Kids might not mind silly script that barely connects some passable special effects. Original title: *Time Warp.*
Dist.: Media

DAYTON'S DEVILS 1968
☆ NR Drama 1:47
Dir: Jack Shea *Cast:* Rory Calhoun, Leslie Nielsen, Lainie Kazan, Hans Gudegast, Barry Sadler

▶ Nielsen assembles a team of professional criminals to steal a million-dollar payroll from a nearby Air Force base. Training, preparation, and disguises make up the bulk of this familiar yarn. Kazan gets to sing "Sunny."
Dist.: Republic

DAY WILL DAWN, THE 1942 British
★ NR War 1:40 B&W
Dir: Harold French *Cast:* Hugh Williams, Griffiths Jones, Deborah Kerr, Ralph Richardson, Griffith Manes, Francis L. Sullivan

▶ Foreign correspondent Williams learns that Nazis are constructing a submarine base in a Norwegian village. With the help of native girlfriend Kerr, he plots sabotage. Well-made, rousing adventure with an excellent supporting cast. Also known as *The Avengers.*
Dist.: Video Yesteryear

D.C. CAB 1983
★ ★ ★ R Comedy 1:39
☑ Nudity, adult situations, explicit language, mild violence
Dir: Joel Schumacher *Cast:* Adam Baldwin, Charlie Barnett, Irene Cara, Max Gail, Mr. T, Gary Busey

▶ Low-key Southerner Baldwin joins Washington's worst taxi company, where his rowdy new colleagues are soon involved in a kidnapping. Good-natured nonsense is consistently funky, fast-paced, and funny. As enormous redneck twins, David and Peter Barbarian stand out in the talented cast. Giorgio Moroder adds a hot soundtrack. (CC)
Dist.: MCA

D-DAY, THE SIXTH OF JUNE 1956
★ ★ ★ NR War 1:46
Dir: Henry Koster *Cast:* Robert Taylor, Richard Todd, Dana Wynter, Edmond O'Brien, John Williams, Jerry Paris

▶ While waiting on a landing boat for the invasion of Normandy to begin, Taylor thinks back to his love affair with Wynter, wife of wounded British officer Todd. Taylor also has problems with O'Brien, an egotistical colonel willing to risk lives to enhance his reputation. Good action sequences boost melodramatic plot.
Dist.: Key

DEAD, THE 1987
★ ★ PG Drama 1:23
Dir: John Huston *Cast:* Anjelica Huston, Donal McCann, Rachel Dowling, Cathleen Delany, Helena Carroll, Dan O'Herlihy

▶ During a Dublin Christmas party in 1904, husband McCann realizes he knows very little about wife Huston. Low-key, scrupulous adaptation of the James Joyce story features superb ensemble acting from an all-Irish cast and marvelous attention to period detail. The stunning climax is a fitting coda to John Huston's illustrious career. Oscar nominations for Best Adapted Screenplay (by son Tony Huston) and for Costume Design. (CC)
Dist.: Vestron

DEAD AIM 1989
★ ★ R Action-Adventure 1:31
☑ Nudity, adult situations, explicit language, violence
Dir: William VanDerKloot *Cast:* Ed Marinaro, Darrell Larson, Cassandra Gava, Isaac Hayes, Corbin Bernsen, John Hancock

▶ Atlanta vice cop Marinaro is investigating the murders of topless dancers when he falls for stripper Gava. The FBI moves in when they discover that the case involves Bulgarian drug dealers, but Marinaro goes deeper and uncovers business involving diplomats and a sex party. Marinaro is a charmless tough guy. Also known as *Mace.*
Dist.: Vestron

DEAD AND BURIED 1981
★ ★ R Horror 1:34
☑ Explicit language, graphic violence
Dir: Gary A. Sherman *Cast:* James Farentino, Melody Anderson, Jack Albertson, Dennis Redfield, Nancy Locke Hauser
▶ Mad mortician/plastic surgeon Albertson gives new meaning to "life after death" as residents of Potter's Bluff mysteriously become zombies. Grim and grisly crimes start occuring all over town. First-rate makeup with a gallery of decomposing faces.
Dist.: Vestron

DEAD BANG 1989
★ ★ ★ R Action-Adventure 1:49
☑ Brief nudity, adult situations, explicit language, violence
Dir: John Frankenheimer *Cast:* Don Johnson, Penelope Ann Miller, William Forsythe, Bob Balaban, Tate Donovan, Frank Military
▶ When his wife kicks him out, L.A. cop Johnson has plenty of time to chase Military, a suspect in the killing of a police officer. Military and his buddies are white supremacists, motorcycling to a major hate conclave in Colorado and killing minorities along the way. Johnson follows them to their survival bunker for an extended shoot-out. Gritty, no-frills pulp.
Dist.: Warner

DEAD CALM 1989 Australian
★ ★ ★ R Mystery-Suspense 1:35
☑ Brief nudity, adult situations, explicit language, violence
Dir: Phillip Noyce *Cast:* Nicole Kidman, Sam Neill, Billy Zane
▶ Slick, stylish thriller creates loads of claustrophobic tension using the simplest ingredients. After their child dies, Naval officer Neill and his wife Kidman take to their boat to recover. When psychotic American Zane invites himself aboard, it's high terror on the high seas. Edge-of-your-seat excitement is handsomely produced and tautly directed.
Dist.: Warner

DEAD EASY 1982 Australian
☆ NR Action-Adventure 1:32
☑ Brief nudity, explicit language, violence
Dir: Bert Deling *Cast:* Scott Burgess, Rosemary Paul, Tim McKenzie, Max Phipps, Joe Martin, Jack O'Leary
▶ Burgess, a hustler who runs a seamy Sydney nightclub, finds himself caught between rival gangs who kill with machetes and piano wire. After his club is blown up, Burgess, his hooker girlfriend, and a young cop fighting a bad rap flee the villains in a supercharged, two-ton truck. Jazzy-looking film captures underworld milieu, but lacks sympathetic characters.
Dist.: Media

DEAD END 1937
★ ★ ★ NR Drama 1:33 B&W
Dir: William Wyler *Cast:* Sylvia Sidney, Joel McCrea, Humphrey Bogart, Claire Trevor, Marjorie Main, Ward Bond
▶ Sidney Kingsley's powerful play about the slums of New York received a first-rate interpretation from director Wyler, screenwriter Lillian Hellman, and an exceptional cast. Episodic plot weaves a broad spectrum of characters—criminal on the run Bogart, struggling architect McCrea, working girl Sidney watching her brother turn to crime—into a raw, uncompromising examination of poverty. Film introduced the Dead End Kids (Billy Halop, Leo Gorcey, Huntz Hall, etc.), who went on to star in *Angels With Dirty Faces* and the Bowery Boys series.
Dist.: Nelson

DEAD END CITY 1989
★ R Action-Adventure 1:25
☑ Adult situations, explicit language, violence
Dir: Peter Yuval *Cast:* Dennis Cole, Greg Cummins, Christine Lunde, Robert Zdar, Durrell Nelson
▶ Youth gangs become a tool of a twisted government urban renewal project designed to raze the city. Tough loner Cummins decides to stay and fight for his turf and family factory, teaming up with friends and snooty newsperson Lunde to battle a nasty gang called the Ratts. Okay for the action.
Dist.: Action International

DEAD-END DRIVE-IN 1986 Australian
☆ R Action-Adventure 1:27
☑ Nudity, adult situations, explicit language, violence
Dir: Brian Trenchard-Smith *Cast:* Ned Manning, Natalie McCurry, Peter Whitford, Wilbur Wilde, Brett Climo
▶ In near-future New South Wales, fascist government locks up unruly kids and their revved-up jalopies in a drive-in prison. Cocky Manning plots to escape, which he accomplishes by literally driving through the roof in a wild finale. Imaginative, funny, action-packed Aussie fare has appeal similar to the *Mad Max* trilogy. **(CC)**
Dist.: New World

DEAD HEAT 1988
★ ★ R Action-Adventure/Comedy 1:27
☑ Explicit language, graphic violence
Dir: Mark Goldblatt *Cast:* Treat Williams, Joe Piscopo, Lindsay Frost, Darren McGavin, Vincent Price, Clare Kirkconnell
▶ Los Angeles cops Williams and Piscopo following a trail of jewel heists learn thieves are zombies reanimated by coroner McGavin. Duo try to crack the undead ring, but Williams gets killed in the action. Can he be brought back to life as a zombie crime-stopper? Played for laughs that never come. **(CC)**
Dist.: New World

DEAD HEAT ON A MERRY-GO-ROUND 1966
★ ★ NR Crime 1:44
Dir: Bernard Girard *Cast:* James Coburn,

Camilla Sparv, Aldo Ray, Nina Wayne, Robert Webber, Rose Marie
▶ Ex-convict Coburn plots airport bank robbery timed to coincide with the arrival of the Russian premier. As part of the scheme, he woos women, steals jewelry and art, and marries Sparv to provide himself a new identity. Swiftly paced, irreverent caper has charming Coburn and somewhat dated sixties look. Harrison Ford makes his film debut in a bit part as a bellboy.
Dist.: RCA/Columbia

DEADLINE 1987 German
★ R Drama 1:39
☑ Explicit language, violence
Dir: Nathaniel Gutman *Cast:* Christopher Walken, Marita Marschall, Hywel Bennett, Arnon Zadok, Amos Lavie, Ette Ankri
▶ Walken is a world-weary TV journalist dispatched to war-torn Lebanon in 1983. An exclusive interview with a PLO bigshot turns out to be a fraud and soon Walken has angered the warring factions. Political drama convinces with footage shot in Jaffa, Israel, but story is often tiring and passionless.
Dist.: Virgin

DEADLINE AT DAWN 1946
★ ★ NR Mystery-Suspense 1:23 B&W
Dir: Harold Clurman *Cast:* Susan Hayward, Paul Lukas, Bill Williams, Joseph Calleia, Osa Massen, Lola Lane
▶ In New York City, dim-witted sailor Williams enlists dance hall girl Hayward's help when he is implicated in a murder. They uncover plenty of suspects, but can they catch the killer before sunrise? Complicated film noir with brooding atmosphere and pungent dialogue. Screenplay by Clifford Odets from a novel by Cornell Woolrich. Theater director Clurman's first and last film.
Dist.: Turner

DEADLY BLESSING 1981
★ ★ R Horror 1:42
☑ Nudity, adult situations, explicit language, graphic violence
Dir: Wes Craven *Cast:* Maren Jensen, Susan Buckner, Sharon Stone, Lisa Hartman, Lois Nettleton, Ernest Borgnine
▶ Effective low-budget chiller about sexy widow Jensen terrorized by the Hittites, a repressive Texas religious sect. Leader Borgnine banishes the widow and her friends, leading to gruesome, lethal confrontations. Unusual feminist subtext and a quirky sense of morality set this a notch above other films in the genre.
Dist.: Embassy

DEADLY BREED 1989
★ ★ NR Action-Adventure 1:23
☑ Rape, adult situations, explicit language, violence
Dir: Charles T. Kanganis *Cast:* William Smith, Addison Randall, Blake Bahner, Joe Vance, Michelle Berger
▶ Police captain Smith is the mastermind behind a gang of right-wing skinheads on a killing spree. Bahner, an innocent parole officer being framed for the murders, links up with a lady cop to solve the case after his wife is raped and killed by Smith's bald-pated henchmen. A sturdy thriller with good performances.
Dist.: Raedon

DEADLY COMPANIONS, THE 1961
★ ★ ★ NR Western 1:30
☑ Violence
Dir: Sam Peckinpah *Cast:* Maureen O'-Hara, Brian Keith, Steve Cochran, Chill Wills, Strother Martin, Will Wright
▶ Civil War vet Keith enlists former enemy Wills and cohort Cochran to rob a bank, planning to murder them later. Instead, he accidentally kills O'Hara's son. To make amends, Keith forces the gang to accompany O'Hara through Apache land to bury the boy. Debut film for director Peckinpah is an efficient Western with intriguing character conflicts.
Dist.: New World

DEADLY DREAMS 1988
★ R Horror 1:19
☑ Nudity, strong sexual content, adult situations, explicit language, violence
Dir: Kristine Peterson *Cast:* Mitchell Anderson, Juliette Cummins, Xander Berkley, Thom Babbes, Beach Dickerson
▶ Anderson's recurring nightmares are the result of a long-buried horror involving murder of his parents on Christmas Eve ten years previous. His older brother and girlfriend spin a deadly plot, from which he emerges to exact cold revenge. Dreary and low-budgeted, but somewhat interesting.
Dist.: Virgin

DEADLY EMBRACE 1989
★ NR Mystery-Suspense 1:23
☑ Adult situations, explicit language, violence
Dir: Ellen Cabot *Cast:* Jan-Michael Vincent, Ty Randolph, Linnea Quigley, Ken Abraham, Jack Carter
▶ When rich businessman Vincent leaves gorgeous wife Randolph alone with hunk houseboy Abraham, nature takes its course. Sudden appearance of Abraham's cute girlfriend Quigley complicates idyll; blackmail and double crossing make it dangerous. Plot fails to grab in this cheapo film noir.
Dist.: Prism

DEADLY EYES 1983
★ R Horror 1:27
☑ Nudity, explicit language, graphic violence
Dir: Robert Clouse *Cast:* Sam Groom, Sara Botsford, Scatman Crothers, Lisa Langlois, Cec Linder
▶ Old fashioned "monster on the loose" story about a colony of giant rats plaguing a big-city subway system. High school teacher Groom and health inspector Botsford fall in

love while tackling the overgrown rodents. Highlights include nighttime attacks on a movie theater and bowling alley. *Dist.:* Warner

DEADLY FORCE 1983
★ ★ ★ R Action-Adventure 1:35
☑ Nudity, adult situations, explicit language, graphic violence
Dir: Paul Aaron *Cast:* Wings Hauser, Joyce Ingalls, Paul Shenar, Al Ruscio, Arlen Dean Snyder
▶ Racing against the L.A. police, tough ex-cop-turned-bounty-hunter Hauser tracks down a homicidal psychopath. The cops close the case after a murder, but Hauser, joining forces with ex-wife Ingalls, won't let up until his revenge is complete.
Dist.: Nelson

DEADLY FRIEND 1986
★ ★ R Horror 1:32
☑ Explicit language, graphic violence
Dir: Wes Craven *Cast:* Matthew Laborteaux, Kristy Swanson, Michael Sharrett, Anne Twomey, Anne Ramsey, Richard Marcus
▶ Offbeat horror film about young inventor Laborteaux whose robot "BB" protects his friends from bullies. When girl next door Swanson is murdered by her father, Laborteaux implants BB's memory chip into her brain, bringing her back to life as a vengeful automaton. Surprisingly lighthearted, with Ramsey turning in a funny performance as the neighborhood busybody. (CC)
Dist.: Warner

DEADLY HERO 1972
★ ★ R Mystery-Suspense 1:42
☑ Explicit language, violence
Dir: Ivan Nagy *Cast:* Don Murray, Diahn Williams, James Earl Jones, Lilia Skala, George S. Irving, Treat Williams
▶ With heroes like policeman Murray, musician Diahn Williams doesn't need enemies. First he uses excessive force to save her from attacker Jones, then he stalks her when she complains about it. Gritty New York thriller is well-acted but unevenly written and directed.
Dist.: Nelson

DEADLY ILLUSION 1987
★ ★ R Mystery-Suspense 1:30
☑ Adult situations, explicit language, violence
Dir: Larry Cohen, William Tannen *Cast:* Billy Dee Williams, Morgan Fairchild, Vanity, John Beck, Joe Cortese
▶ Hired by a businessman to kill his wife, unlicensed private dick Williams tries to warn her instead and is framed for murder. Entertaining B movie with likable Williams, clever dialogue, and engaging tongue-in-cheek tone. Nice use of New York City locations, including a fight scene staged in the Rockefeller Center Christmas tree.
Dist.: RCA/Columbia

DEADLY INTENT 1988
★ ★ R Mystery-Suspense 1:27
☑ Adult situations, explicit language, violence
Dir: Nigel Dick *Cast:* Lisa Eilbacher, Steve Railsback, Maud Adams, Fred Williamson, David Dukes, Lance Henrickson
▶ Villainous double-crosser Henrickson is killed after he brings the fabulous Window Stone of Naboth back from South America. When the gem disappears, Henrickson's former boss Adams and numerous other unsavory types look for it in all the wrong places. The bodies pile up, but uneventful mystery never comes to life.
Dist.: Prism

DEADLY INTRUDER, THE 1985
★ NR Horror 1:24
☑ Nudity, adult situations, explicit language, violence
Dir: John McCauley *Cast:* Chris Holder, Molly Cheek, Tony Crupi, Danny Bonaduce, Stuart Whitman, Laura Melton
▶ Psychotic killer escapes from institution and terrorizes rural town, baffling policeman Whitman. Meanwhile, drifter Crupi kidnaps young Cheek, who suspects Crupi may be the missing lunatic. Mediocre horror film suffers from lackluster acting and tired plot.
Dist.: HBO

DEADLY PASSION 1985 South African
☆ R Mystery-Suspense 1:38
☑ Nudity, adult situations, explicit language, violence
Dir: Larry Larson *Cast:* Brent Huff, Ingrid Boulting, Harrison Coburn, Lynn Maree
▶ It's love at first sight for Huff and recently widowed Boulting. New romance, however, could lose Boulting her share of late husband's will. Defying corrupt business manager, Huff tries to get Boulting her rightful dough, unwittingly setting himself up for double cross. Low-budget *Body Heat* occasionally verges on soft porn.
Dist.: Vestron

DEADLY REACTOR 1989
★ NR Sci-Fi 1:22
☑ Rape, adult situations, explicit language, violence
Dir: David Heavener *Cast:* Stuart Whitman, David Heavener, Darwyn Swalve, Allyson Davis
▶ Postapocalyptic spaghetti Western has gunslinger Heavener going after an endormorphic gang leader named Hog who raped his sister and killed his family. Heavener is called "the Reactor" because he waits for adversary to make first move, then reacts. Modestly successful; apes Eastwood/Leone Westerns right down to the music.
Dist.: Action International

DEADLY STRANGERS 1974 British
★ ★ NR Mystery-Suspense 1:33

Brief nudity, adult situations, explicit language, violence
Dir: Sidney Hayers *Cast:* Hayley Mills, Simon Ward, Sterling Hayden, Ken Hutchison, Peter Jeffrey
▶ Violent patient escapes from mental institution in the British countryside. Later, Mills, haunted by unhappy love affair, gets a lift from Ward. Is he the killer? Decent performances by Mills and Ward, although those who remember Mills from her child star days may be shocked to see her topless here. Mild tension with surprise ending.
Dist.: Paragon

DEADLY WEAPON 1989
☆ **PG-13 Sci-Fi 1:30**
Adult situations, explicit language, violence
Dir: Michael Miner *Cast:* Rodney Eastman, Kim Walker, Gary Frank, Michael Horse
▶ Eastman is a fifteen-year-old boy who finds an anti-matter pistol accidently lost by the Army in a train wreck. With the powerful weapon in hand, the boy blasts his mean dad and kidnaps the town's authority figures in a pink Cadillac. Joyride ends when the vengeance-besotted kid must be neutralized by the Army. High concept dissolves into mishmash.
Dist.: TWE

DEAD MAN OUT 1989
★ ★ ★ **NR Drama/MFTV 1:30**
Adult situations, explicit language, violence
Dir: Richard Pearce *Cast:* Danny Glover, Ruben Blades, Tom Atkins
▶ In a state whose law demands that a condemned prisoner must be legally sane before he can be executed, psychiatrist Glover is given the assignment of restoring mental health to doomed killer Blades. Locked together into small rooms, Glover and Blades face off in powerfully tense confrontations. Grimly authentic prison setting; Blades gives an outstanding performance.
Dist.: HBO

DEAD MAN WALKING 1987
★ **R Action-Adventure 1:30**
Nudity, adult situations, explicit language, graphic violence
Dir: Gregory Brown *Cast:* Wings Hauser, Brion James, Jeffrey Combs, Pamela Ludwig
▶ A futuristic plague has wiped out much of the earth, big corporations rule the world, and the population is divided into sectors housing the dying, the soon-to-be dying, and the healthy. When a corporate executive is murdered and daughter Ludwig is kidnapped, amoral bounty hunter Hauser is hired to cross the disease lines and bring her back. Repellent characters, ugly doings, and pinched-looking production will turn off all but fans of ultra-violence.
Dist.: Republic

DEAD MEN DON'T WEAR PLAID 1982
★ ★ **PG Comedy 1:29 B&W**
Explicit language, adult humor
Dir: Carl Reiner *Cast:* Steve Martin, Rachel Ward, Carl Reiner, Reni Santoni, George Gaynes
▶ Private-eye parody with Martin as a 1940s detective hired by beautiful Ward to solve the murder of her noted cheesemaker/scientist father. Consistently amusing deadpan comedy based on a clever gimmick: clips of old movies are seamlessly woven into the narrative so that Martin gets to interact with Barbara Stanwyck, Humphrey Bogart, Ingrid Bergman, Fred MacMurray, and other stars of that era. Superlative editing, lighting, sets, and black-and-white cinematography make the device work perfectly.
Dist.: MCA

DEAD OF NIGHT 1945 British
★ ★ ★ **NR Horror 1:44 B&W**
Dir: Cavalcanti, Charles Crichton, Basil Dearden, Robert Hamer *Cast:* Mervyn Johns, Roland Culver, Googie Withers, Michael Redgrave, Basil Radford, Naunton Wayne, Judy Kelly, Miles Malleson, Sally Ann Howes, Ralph Michael, Frederick Valk
▶ Landmark omnibus horror film uses architect Johns's nightmare as a linking device for five separate ghost stories: "The Hearse Driver," "The Christmas Story," "The Haunted Mirror," "The Golfing Story," and "The Ventriloquist's Dummy." Eerie, macabre film suffers from varying quality, but the frightening final sequence—in which ventriloquist Redgrave's dummy slowly drives him insane—was so successful it was expanded into the feature-length *Magic.*
Dist.: HBO

DEAD OF WINTER 1987
★ ★ ★ **R Mystery-Suspense 1:40**
Violence
Dir: Arthur Penn *Cast:* Mary Steenburgen, Roddy McDowall, Jan Rubes, William Ruff, Mark Malone
▶ Struggling actress Steenburgen is lured to an isolated, snowbound house with the promise of a part and soon finds herself an unwilling accomplice to scheme of blackmailers Rubes and McDowall. Old-fashioned suspense thriller with an intricate, surprising plot. Creepy atmosphere, several real scares, and nifty work from Steenburgen in three roles. **(CC)**
Dist.: CBS/Fox

DEAD PIT 1989
☆ **R Horror 1:32**
Nudity, adult situations, explicit language, violence
Dir: Brett Leonard *Cast:* Jeremy Slate, Danny Gochnauer, Cheryl Lawson, Steffen Gregory Foster
▶ Lovely young amnesiac Lawson, admitted to mental hospital, somehow reactivates an evil brain sealed into a chamber twenty years

before by doctor Gochnauer. Mad doc stalks wards and unleashes lobotomized ghouls who terrorize patients. Poor example of the genre.
Dist.: Imperial

DEAD POETS SOCIETY 1989
★ ★ ★ ★ ★ PG Drama 1:24
☑ Adult situations, explicit language, brief nudity
Dir: Peter Weir *Cast:* Robin Williams, Robert Dean Leonard, Ethan Hawke, Josh Charles, Gale Hansen, Norman Lloyd, Kurtwood Smith
▶ In 1959 Vermont, Williams is an unorthodox English teacher at a stuffy prep school. Inspired by his passion for life, Leonard and his friends resurrect the "Dead Poets Society," which Williams started when he was a student at the school. Leonard then disobeys stern father Smith, leading to crisis for all. Surprise hit is bolstered by Williams's touching and humorous perfomance, which sustains film even when he's not on screen. Weir's direction is often heavy-handed, but film's messages remain universal. Nominated for four Oscars, including Best Picture and Actor, it won for Tom Schulman's screenplay. **(CC)**
Dist.: Buena Vista

DEAD POOL, THE 1988
★ ★ ★ ★ R Action-Adventure 1:31
☑ Explicit language, violence
Dir: Buddy Van Horn *Cast:* Clint Eastwood, Patricia Clarkson, Evan C. Kim, Liam Neeson, David Hunt, Michael Currie
▶ After jailing a Mafia kingpin, San Francisco cop Harry Callahan (Eastwood) finds himself the center of unwanted publicity, in particular a betting pool predicting celebrities' deaths. Fifth entry in the *Dirty Harry* series maintains formula's high body count while emphasizing humor. Manic car chase highlights sturdy Eastwood vehicle.
Dist.: Warner

DEAD RECKONING 1947
★ ★ ★ ★ NR Mystery-Suspense 1:40 B&W
Dir: John Cromwell *Cast:* Humphrey Bogart, Lizabeth Scott, Morris Carnovsky, William Prince, Wallace Ford
▶ Steamy whodunit features Bogart as a man determined to solve his army buddy's mysterious disappearance and death—until he learns his friend was a convicted murderer. Sultry Scott plays Bogey's love interest. Underrated film holds up extremely well.
Dist.: RCA/Columbia

DEAD RINGERS 1988 Canadian
★ ★ R Drama 1:55
☑ Nudity, adult situations, explicit language, violence
Dir: David Cronenberg *Cast:* Jeremy Irons, Genevieve Bujold, Heidi Von Palleske, Barbara Gordon, Shirley Douglas, Stephen Lack
▶ Irons is eerily convincing in a dual role as identical twin gynecologists who sink into

drug addiction and insanity after deceiving actress Bujold in romance. Director Cronenberg fashioned a true incident into a macabre, perversely fascinating fantasy that is unnerving without being overly graphic. Howard Shore's rich score adds to film's compelling style. **(CC)**
Dist.: Media

DEADTIME STORIES 1987
★ R Horror 1:23
☑ Explicit language, violence
Dir: Jeffrey Delman *Cast:* Michael Mesmer, Brian DePersia, Scott Valentine, Phyllis Craig, Anne Redfern
▶ Once upon a time. . .little DePersia asked for a bedtime story from his Uncle Mike (Mesmer) and got Lizzie Borden and the Three Bears, variations on the Brothers Grimm and more. Cute idea, but not scary enough to give anyone bad dreams.
Dist.: Cinema Group

DEAD ZONE, THE 1983
★ ★ ★ ★ R Mystery-Suspense 1:43
☑ Brief nudity, explicit language, violence
Dir: David Cronenberg *Cast:* Christopher Walken, Brooke Adams, Tom Skerritt, Herbert Lom, Martin Sheen
▶ Schoolteacher Walken awakens from a five-year coma with the eerie power to predict the future. Besieged by pleas for help from people who want to know their fate, he retreats into anonymity—until he realizes that a politician may lead the country into war. Restrained adaptation of the Stephen King novel has a few gory moments, but is primarily an absorbing psychological thriller. **(CC)**
Dist.: Paramount

DEALERS 1989 British
★ ★ R Drama/Romance 1:35
☑ Adult situations, explicit language
Dir: Colin Bucksey *Cast:* Paul McGann, Rebecca De Mornay, Derrick O'Conner, John Castle, Paul Guilfoyle
▶ In the fast-paced world of British high finance McGann is a hot-shot money trader for Whitney Paine. Cool American De Mornay is hired because of her conservative touch. In no time these handsome yuppies are taking risks on the floor and in bed. Glossy Brit answer to *Wall Street* lacks the latter's penetrating incisiveness, but is equally adept at showing us the lifestyles of the rich and reckless. McGann and De Mornay smolder, but the film ultimately fizzles.
Dist.: Academy

DEAL OF THE CENTURY 1983
★ ★ PG Comedy 1:38
☑ Adult situations, explicit language, violence, adult humor
Dir: William Friedkin *Cast:* Chevy Chase, Sigourney Weaver, Gregory Hines, Vince Edwards, Wallace Shawn
▶ Struggling arms dealer Chase gets mixed up with Latin American fascists and beautiful

widow Weaver while selling faulty aircraft to unsuspecting Third Worlders. However, the "deal of the century" is sabotaged by Chase's born-again partner Hines, who begins to question his career choice. Irreverent arms-race satire.
Dist.: Warner

DEAR AMERICA: LETTERS HOME FROM VIETNAM 1987
★ ★ ★ ★ PG-13 Documentary/MFTV 1:27 C/B&W
☑ Explicit language, violence
Dir: Bill Couturie
▶ Award-winning documentary examines the Vietnam War from viewpoint of soldiers' first-hand accounts of the fighting. Accompanied by masterful use of NBC stock footage, out-takes, and Super-8 home movies, the soldiers' letters are moving, illuminating, and often un-bearably painful. Actors contributing to the voice-overs include Tom Berenger, Robert De Niro, Sean Penn, Randy Quaid, Martin Sheen, and Kathleen Turner. Produced by HBO, film received such high praise that it was subse-quently released in theaters.
Dist.: HBO

DEAR BRIGITTE 1965
★ ★ NR Comedy 1:40
Dir: Henry Koster *Cast:* James Stewart, Fa-bian, Glynis Johns, Billy Mumy, John Wil-liams, Brigitte Bardot
▶ Popular family-oriented comedy about young math whiz Mumy, who won't help fa-ther Stewart handicap horse races until Dad introduces him to Bardot. Since Stewart needs the money to finance a humanities founda-tion, he flies to Paris with Mumy to see the great star. Whimsical piece of contemporary Americana also features Ed Wynn as a ferry-boat captain. **(CC)**
Dist.: CBS/Fox

DEAR, DEAD DELILAH 1972
☆ R Horror 1:37
☑ Explicit language, graphic violence
Dir: John Farris *Cast:* Agnes Moorehead, Will Geer, Michael Ansara, Patricia Carmi-chael, Dennis Patrick, Anne Meacham
▶ Southerner Moorehead has money and a mansion, but she's also dying and confined to a wheelchair. Seeking to get their greedy hands on her bucks, her relatives come a call-ing. Axe murders ensue. Grotesque effort con-veys a certain nasty intensity, but most audi-ences will simply be offended.
Dist.: Nelson

DEAR WIFE 1950
★ NR Comedy 1:27 B&W
Dir: Richard Haydn *Cast:* William Holden, Joan Caulfield, Billy De Wolfe, Mona Free-man, Edward Arnold, Harry Von Zell
▶ Family comedy features Holden and Caul-field as a young married couple who must live with her parents. Complications ensue when Holden is drafted to run against Arnold, his politician father-in-law, for the state senate. Holden, Caulfield, and De Wolf sparkle in this innocent charmer. Sequel to *Dear Ruth.*
Dist.: KVC

DEATH BEFORE DISHONOR 1987
★ ★ ★ R Action-Adventure 1:35
☑ Explicit language, violence
Dir: Terry Leonard *Cast:* Fred Dryer, Brian Keith, Joanna Pacula, Paul Winfield, Kasey Walker
▶ It's hardheaded Marine gunnery Sgt. Dryer to the rescue when Arab terrorists kidnap Col-onel Keith and the U.S. government refuses to negotiate. The impregnable terrorist hideout is no match for the fists and grenades of Dryer in this *Rambo*esque yarn that encourages you to cheer the Marines and hiss the Arabs. **(CC)**
Dist.: New World

DEATH DRIVER 1978
★ ★ NR Action-Adventure 1:33
☑ Adult situations, violence
Dir: Jimmy Huston *Cast:* Earl Owensby, Mike Allen, Patty Shaw, Mary Ann Hearn
▶ Once the World Motor Rodeo Champion, Owensby leaves his unfaithful wife and seeks to regain his title ten years later. After much womanizing and car crashing with buddy Allen, Owensby must attempt the stunt in which he was critically injured a decade ear-lier. Low-budget drive-in offering tells story of real-life stunt driver Rex Randolph.
Dist.: HBO

DEATH DRUG 1978
☆ PG-13 Drama 1:13
☑ Adult situations, explicit language
Dir: Oscar Williams *Cast:* Phillip Michael Thomas, Vernee Watson, Rosalind Cash, Frankie Crocker
▶ Struggling musician Thomas records a disco album that goes platinum but then becomes addicted to PCP. He suffers hallucinations about vermin and white women, beats his wife Watson, and jeopardizes his budding re-cording career. Antidrug message hit clumsily home by tawdry production with an over-wrought Thomas. Home video version includes Thomas's video clip, "Just the Way I Planned It."
Dist.: Academy

DEATH HUNT 1981
★ ★ ★ ★ R Action-Adventure 1:37
☑ Explicit language, graphic violence
Dir: Peter Hunt *Cast:* Charles Bronson, Lee Marvin, Andrew Stevens, Angie Dickinson, Carl Weathers, Ed Lauter
▶ Bronson plays real-life fugitive Albert John-son, wrongly accused of murder in 1930s Yukon. Mountie Marvin reluctantly leaves lady love Dickinson to track the "Mad Trapper" in the biggest manhunt in Canadian history. Knockout combination of male stars.
Dist.: CBS/Fox

DEATH IN VENICE 1971 Italian/French
★ **PG Drama 2:10**
☑ Adult situations
Dir: Luchino Visconti   *Cast:* Dirk Bogarde,
Marisa Berenson, Bjorn Andresen, Silvana
Mangano, Mark Burns, Romolo Valli
▶ On the verge of a nervous breakdown in
Venice, aging German composer Bogarde
finds his dormant emotions reawakened by
pretty young boy Andresen. Bogarde follows
his obsession around the decaying city with-
out making contact, even as his health rap-
idly deteriorates. Adaptation of the Thomas
Mann novella is beautifully shot and makes
powerful use of Mahler's Third and Fifth symphonies, but result is not for all tastes.
Dist.: Warner

DEATH KISS, THE 1933
★ **NR Mystery-Suspense 1:14 B&W**
Dir: Edwin L. Marin   *Cast:* Bela Lugosi,
David Manners, Adrienne Ames, John Wray,
Vince Barnett, Edward Van Sloan
▶ Three leads from *Dracula*—Lugosi, Manners,
Van Sloan—are reunited in a low-budget
whodunit about a murder on a movie set. Skip
the mystery, which is a muddled mixture of
tension and farce, and concentrate on the
behind-the-scenes look at movie making at
the dawn of the sound era. Filmed in the for-
mer Tiffany Studios.
Dist.: Cable

DEATHMASK 1983
★ **NR Mystery-Suspense 1:43**
☑ Brief nudity, explicit language, violence
Dir: Richard Friedman   *Cast:* Farley
Granger, Lee Bryant, John McCurry, Ruth
Warrick, Arch Johnson, Danny Aiello
▶ A guilty conscience about the death of his
daughter triggers cop Granger's ten-year obsession with a child-murder case. Unable to
identify the victim, Granger carries a plaster
death mask of the child everywhere he goes,
consults a psychic, and finally untangles the
web of medical deceit behind the killing. Cast
is effective in morbid, downbeat story.
Dist.: Prism

**DEATH OF A CENTERFOLD: THE DOROTHY
STRATTEN STORY** 1981
★ ★ ★ **NR Biography/MFTV 1:40**
Dir: Gabrielle Beaumont   *Cast:* Jamie Lee
Curtis, Bruce Weitz, Robert Reed, Mitchell
Ryan, Tracy Reed
▶ TV docudrama about Dorothy Stratten
(Curtis), the actress and *Playboy* centerfold,
focuses on her relationship with Paul Snider
(Weitz), the husband/manager who eventu-
ally killed her and then committed suicide in
a jealous rage. Good performance by Curtis.
Same story was covered (more graphically
and perhaps more pretentiously) in Bob
Fosse's *Star 80*.
Dist.: MGM/UA

DEATH OF AN ANGEL 1986
★ **PG Drama 1:32**

☑ Explicit language, violence
Dir: Petru Popescu   *Cast:* Bonnie Bedelia,
Nick Mancuso, Pamela Ludwig, Alex Colon,
Abel Franco
▶ Ludwig, the crippled daughter of widowed
Episcopal priest Bedelia, runs away to seek
cure from faith healer Mancuso. Bedelia fol-
lows and gets involved in Mancuso's quest to
find a miraculous cross. Well-intentioned but
plodding and obscure.
Dist.: New Star Entertainment

DEATH OF A SALESMAN 1951
★ **NR Drama 1:55 B&W**
Dir: Laslo Benedek   *Cast:* Fredric March,
Mildred Dunnock, Kevin McCarthy, Cameron Mitchell, Howard Smith
▶ Screen version of Arthur Miller play about
Willy Loman (March), the salesman whose
tragic pursuit of the American Dream poisoned his relationship with his sons. Innovative
cinematic techniques by director Benedek
and solid acting by March, but the 1985 Dustin Hoffman version has more dramatic intensity.
Dist.: Karl/Lorimar

DEATH OF A SALESMAN 1985
★ ★ ★ **NR Drama/MFTV 2:14**
Dir: Volker Schlondorff   *Cast:* Dustin Hoff-
man, Kate Reid, John Malkovich, Stephen
Lang, Charles Durning
▶ Hoffman won both Emmy and Golden
Globe awards for his titanic performance as
Willy Loman, the sixty-year-old salesman who
dreams of being "well liked." Skillful rendition
of Arthur Miller's Pulitzer prize–winning play
from the Broadway revival cast. Biff, the good
kid crushed by his overbearing father, is bril-
liantly played by Malkovich.   **(CC)**
Dist.: Warner

DEATH OF A SCOUNDREL 1956
★ **NR Drama 1:59 B&W**
Dir: Charles Martin   *Cast:* George Sanders,
Yvonne De Carlo, Zsa Zsa Gabor, Victor
Jory, Nancy Gates, Coleen Gray
▶ Secretary De Carlo relates the tale of Sand-
ers, a vile man without a single redeeming
quality whose corpse turns up in a posh Park
Avenue apartment. Sanders begins his career
by informing on his brother, and goes on to do
wrong to everybody who loves him or does
business with him. Sanders attacks his villain-
ous role with relish in this interesting drama.
Dist.: VCI

DEATH OF A SOLDIER 1986 Australian
★ ★ **R Drama 1:36**
☑ Nudity, explicit language, violence
Dir: Philippe Mora   *Cast:* James Coburn,
Reb Brown, Maurie Fields, Max Fairchild, Bill
Hunter
▶ True story of American soldier Edward J.
Leonski (Brown), who was court-martialed and
hanged for strangling women in World War II
Australia. Military lawyer Coburn tries to win a
stay of execution for the unbalanced soldier.

Interesting story, credible work from Coburn and Brown, but the last third of film gets static, talky, and preachy. **(CC)**
Dist.: CBS/Fox

DEATH ON THE NILE 1978 British
★ ★ ★ ★ **PG Mystery-Suspense 2:20**
⊡ Violence
Dir: John Guillermin *Cast:* Peter Ustinov, David Niven, Mia Farrow, Bette Davis, Maggie Smith, Angela Lansbury, George Kennedy, Jack Warden, Lois Chiles, Olivia Hussey, Simon MacCorkindale, Jane Birkin
▶ Belgian detective Hercule Poiret (Ustinov) settles in for a cruise down the Nile, which is rudely disrupted by several murders. Follow-up to *Murder on the Orient Express* is leisurely paced but scenic fun with terrific cast of suspects. As Poiret, Ustinov brings a genial grace to the role.
Dist.: HBO

DEATH RACE 2000 1975
★ **R Action-Adventure 1:20**
⊡ Explicit language, graphic violence, adult humor
Dir: Paul Bartel *Cast:* David Carradine, Sylvester Stallone, Simone Griffeth, Louisa Moritz, Mary Woronov
▶ In the year 2000, hit-and run driving is no longer a felony—it's the national sport. Five male/female teams compete in a futuristic road race where running down a woman is worth 10 points, an elderly person, 100. Carradine is Frankenstein, the half-man, half-machine leader of one team; Griffeth, a political rebel, is assigned to eliminate him; and megastar Stallone is a competitor. Film has cult following.
Dist.: Warner

DEATHROW GAMESHOW 1987
☆ **R Comedy 1:18**
⊡ Nudity, adult situations, explicit language, violence
Dir: Mark Pirro *Cast:* John McCafferty, Robin Blythe, Beano, Mark Lasky, Debra Lamb
▶ TV gameshow "Live or Die" has an unusual premise: prisoners can win prizes or reprieves, but if they lose they are executed on the air. Host McCafferty finds himself targeted by the mob after a mafioso is one of the losers. Idea is stronger than the, pardon the expression, execution.
Dist.: Media

DEATH SHIP 1980 Canadian
★ **R Horror 1:27**
⊡ Nudity, explicit language, graphic violence
Dir: Alvin Rakoff *Cast:* George Kennedy, Nick Mancuso, Richard Crenna, Sally Ann Howes, Kate Reid
▶ Eight survivors of a sunken cruise ship board a haunted cargo boat navigated by Nazi ghosts. Possessed by the former Nazi captain, Kennedy goes insane; Crenna's believable

performance as a frightened man determined to save his family keeps the film afloat.
Dist.: Nelson

DEATH SPA 1988
★ **R Horror 1:30**
⊡ Nudity, adult situations, explicit language, graphic violence
Dir: Michael Fische *Cast:* William Bulmiller, Brenda Bakke, Merritt Buttrick, Rosalind Cash, Ken Foree
▶ A series of strange killings occurs at a high tech health spa, including one customer ripped apart by a Nautilus machine. The culprit: the ghost of owner Bulmiller's late ex-wife, who has possessed her twin brother Buttrick. Cunning concept undercut by too-sober tone; film lacks the tongue-in-cheek wit of its ad slogan ("You'll sweat blood").
Dist.: MPI

DEATHSPORT 1978
★ **R Sci-Fi 1:23**
⊡ Nudity, violence
Dir: Henry Suso, Allan Arkush *Cast:* David Carradine, Claudia Jennings, Richard Lynch, William Smithers
▶ The year is 3000 and good guys like Carradine still battle bad guys in this sci-fi gladiator picture. Saber-wielding Ranger Guides ride horses and fight evil cannibal mutants who drive motorcycles known as "Death Machines." Crash scenes light up the screen every few minutes. Sequel of sorts to *Death Race 2000*.
Dist.: Warner

DEATHSTALKER 1983
★ **R Action-Adventure 1:20**
⊡ Rape, nudity, adult situations, explicit language, graphic violence
Dir: John Watson *Cast:* Richard Hill, Barbi Benton, Richard Brooker, Lana Clarkson, Bernard Erhard
▶ Low-budget sword-and-sorcery semispoof in which a king loses his empire and daughter Benton (the former Playmate) to cruel magician Erhard, who rules with the aid of mutant guards. Muscleman Deathstalker (Hill) possesses the "sword of justice" and flexes his pecs to fight ill will. A little sex, lots of t&a and an endless barrage of bloodletting hold the works together.
Dist.: Vestron

DEATHSTALKER II 1987
★ **R Action-Adventure 1:17**
⊡ Nudity, explicit language, violence
Dir: Jim Wynorski *Cast:* John Terlesky, Monique Gabrielle, John La Zar
▶ Prince Terlesky rescues princess Gabrielle and battles evil wizard who has made a double of Gabrielle to take her throne away. Zombies and amazons are on the perilous path to victory for the hunky hero. Insipid sword and sorcery emphasizes rippling biceps and bare breasts.
Dist.: Vestron

DEATH TAKES A HOLIDAY 1934
★★★ NR Fantasy 1:18 B&W
Dir: Mitchell Leisen ***Cast:*** Fredric March, Evelyn Venable, Guy Standing, Katherine Alexander, Gail Patrick, Helen Westley
► March delivers another distinguished performance as Death, who disguises himself as an Italian prince to learn why humans fear him. While visiting with nobleman Standing, Death finds himself drawn to the beautiful but ethereal Venable. Slowly paced and predictable romance has an oddly compelling tone and touching sentiments.
Dist.: MCA

DEATHTRAP 1982
★★★ PG Mystery-Suspense 1:56
☑ Adult situations, explicit language, violence
Dir: Sidney Lumet ***Cast:*** Michael Caine, Christopher Reeve, Dyan Cannon, Irene Worth, Henry Jones
► Caine plays a famous but fading Broadway playwright whose faltering career prompts him to plot several "murders" in the hope of stealing the younger Reeve's superior play. Well acted, funny mindteaser with enough twists and turns to bait any mystery fan. Based on Ira Levin's Broadway play.
Dist.: Warner

DEATH VALLEY 1982
★★ R Mystery-Suspense 1:28
☑ Nudity, graphic violence
Dir: Dick Richards ***Cast:*** Paul LeMat, Catherine Hicks, Stephen McHattie, Wilford Brimley, Peter Billingsley
► Billingsley vacations in Death Valley with mom Hicks and her new boyfriend LeMat. He accidentally learns the identity of killer McHattie who in turn pursues Billingsley across the desert. A bit more exciting than a mouthful of sand—but not by much.
Dist.: MCA

DEATH WISH 1974
★★★★ R Action-Adventure 1:29
☑ Rape, adult situations, explicit language, Violence
Dir: Michael Winner ***Cast:*** Charles Bronson, Hope Lange, Vincent Gardenia, Steven Keats, William Redfield, Stuart Margolin, Stephen Elliott, Olympia Dukakis, Christopher Guest, Jeff Goldblum
► After muggers murder his wife and cripple his daughter, mild-mannered businessman Bronson takes the law into his own hands. Stalking would-be attackers on the streets of New York, he metes out his own brand of justice. Highly graphic film was a commercial success and spawned many sequels and numerous imitators, even though its premise of vigilante law disturbed many critics.
Dist.: Paramount

DEATH WISH II 1982
★★★★ R Action-Adventure 1:28
☑ Rape, nudity, explicit language, graphic violence
Dir: Michael Winner ***Cast:*** Charles Bronson, Jill Ireland, Vincent Gardenia, J. D. Cannon, Anthony Franciosa, Robin Sherwood
► Vigilante architect Bronson finds Los Angeles no more peaceful than New York: a gang of thugs steals his wallet, attacks his maid, and kidnaps and rapes his daughter. After his daughter dies trying to escape, Bronson hunts the culprits. Hard-hitting and convincing; predictable plot repeats original formula but Bronson evokes audience empathy.
Dist.: Warner

DEATH WISH 3 1985
★★★ R Action-Adventure 1:30
☑ Rape, nudity, adult situations, explicit language, graphic violence
Dir: Michael Winner ***Cast:*** Charles Bronson, Deborah Raffin, Ed Lauter, Martin Balsam, Gavan O'Herlihy
► Further adventures of vigilante Paul Kersey (Bronson). Here he avenges an army pal's death brought on by a punky street gang. Excessive violence: Bronson blows away scores of people, single-handedly, without changing facial expression.
Dist.: MGM/UA

DEATH WISH 4: THE CRACKDOWN 1987
★★★★ R Action-Adventure 1:32
☑ Rape, explicit language, graphic violence
Dir: J. Lee Thompson ***Cast:*** Charles Bronson, Kay Lenz, George Dickerson, Soon-Teck Oh, Perry Lopez
► Citizen's arrest, Bronson style. When girlfriend Lenz's teen daughter overdoses on cocaine, architect/vigilante Paul Kersey (Bronson) wipes out the top hoods in L.A.'s drug trade, maintaining his right to remain violent. Ultimate shootout in skating rink parking lot. (CC)
Dist.: Media

DECAMERON, THE 1970
French/Italian/German
☆ X Drama 1:56
☑ Nudity, strong sexual content
Dir: Pier Paolo Pasolini ***Cast:*** Franco Citti, Ninetto Davoli, Angela Luce, Patrizia Capparelli, Jovan Jovanovic, Silvana Mangano
► Director Pasolini appears as frescoist Giotto to introduce eight tales from the work of fourteenth-century storyteller Boccaccio. Though the original stories are earthy, Pasolini uses contemporary license to make them sexually explicit. Other films in the director's pornographic medieval trilogy are *Canterbury Tales* and *Arabian Nights.* [S]
Dist.: Water Bearer

DECAMERON NIGHTS 1953 British
★ NR Drama 1:28
Dir: Hugo Fregonese ***Cast:*** Joan Fontaine, Louis Jourdan, Binnie Barnes, Joan Collins, Godfrey Tearle

▶ In the fourteenth century, author Boccaccio (Jourdan) woos Fontaine with three of his stories, "Paganino the Pirate," "Wager for Virtue," and "The Doctor's Daughter." Jourdan and Fontaine also star in each of the tales, all concerning love and fidelity. Ornate but lifeless costume drama sanitizes original stories almost beyond recognition.
Dist.: Various

DECEIVERS, THE 1988
★ ★ ★ PG-13 Action-Adventure 1:52
☑ Violence
Dir: Nicholas Meyer *Cast:* Pierce Brosnan, Saeed Jaffrey, Shashi Kapoor, Helena Michell, Keith Michell
▶ In nineteenth-century India, English officer Brosnan disguises himself as an Indian to infiltrate killer cult and becomes caught up in their murderous ways. Handsomely mounted period piece with a provocative premise falls short due to confused, ambiguous screenplay and slack pacing. Brosnan gamely struggles with his difficult role but the lively Kapoor outshines him.
Dist.: Warner

DECEPTION 1946
★ ★ NR Drama 1:52 B&W
Dir: Irving Rapper *Cast:* Bette Davis, Claude Rains, Paul Henreid, John Abbott, Benson Fong
▶ Teacher Davis loves musician Henreid but her conductor ex-beau Rains disrupts her chance at happiness. Soap operaish Warner Brothers drama is loads of fun, mainly because Rains has a great time playing the wicked interloper.
Dist.: MGM/UA

DECLINE OF THE AMERICAN EMPIRE, THE 1986 Canadian
☆ R Comedy/Drama 1:41
☑ Nudity, adult situations, explicit language
Dir: Denys Arcand *Cast:* Dominque Michel, Dorothee Berryman, Louise Portal, Genevieve Rioux, Pierre Curzi, Remy Girard
▶ Super-literate comedy of modern manners where sophisticated friends gather for dinner and discuss their sexual histories. Smug Girard is a womanizer, Curzi is divorced, Michel has written a book about the decay of society and Jacques, a homosexual, talks of the thrill of indiscriminate sex. Incisive observations and caustic wit; not for all tastes. [S]
Dist.: MCA

DECLINE OF WESTERN CIVILIZATION, THE 1981
☆ NR Documentary/Music 1:40
☑ Explicit language, violence
Dir: Penelope Spheeris *Cast:* Circle Jerks, Alice Bag Band, Fear, Germs, X, Black Flag
▶ Startling documentary about the late 1970s Los Angeles punk rock scene is a definitive portrait of a disturbing subculture. Concert footage of raw, violent music is interspersed with chilling interviews of the musicians and

their fans. Some of the bands achieved legendary status, but sadly many of the performers are now dead. Followed in 1988 by a sequel on heavy metal music.
Dist.: Media

DECLINE OF WESTERN CIVILIZATION PART II: THE METAL YEARS, THE 1988
★ R Documentary/Music 1:30
☑ Explicit language, violence
Dir: Penelope Spheeris *Cast:* Joe Perry, Steven Tyler, Alice Cooper, Gene Simmons, Paul Stanley, Lemmy
▶ Sequel to documentary on punk rockers follows similar formula while focusing on heavy metal music. Interviews with members of Aerosmith, Kiss, Motorhead, Poison, Megadeath, Faster Pussycat, and other groups alternate with brief concert footage to provide an eye-opening look at performers and groupies. Highlighted by chilling talk with Chris Holmes of W.A.S.P., filmed drinking vodka in his swimming pool.
Dist.: RCA/Columbia

DECOY FOR TERROR 1970 Canadian
☆ NR Horror 1:30
☑ Violence
Dir: Erick Santamaria *Cast:* William Kirwin, Jean Christopher, Neil Sedaka, Andree Champagne
▶ Mad painter Kirwin stalks and murders his models in this lurid low-budget thriller. Sedaka shows up at an early poolside scene, sings, and mercifully leaves before the killing starts. Too crude to be scary but will entertain those who enjoy laughing at bad movies.
Dist.: New World

DEEP, THE 1977
★ ★ ★ PG Action-Adventure 2:03
☑ Brief nudity, violence
Dir: Peter Yates *Cast:* Robert Shaw, Jacqueline Bisset, Nick Nolte, Louis Gossett, Jr., Eli Wallach
▶ While skin diving off Bermuda, young Americans Nolte and Bisset discover a World War II ship with a fortune in morphine aboard. Drug dealer and voodoo expert Gossett has designs on the treasure, but crusty recluse Shaw comes to the Americans' aid. Amazing underwater photography and Bisset's eye-catching outfits provide most of the excitement in this adaptation of Peter Benchley's best-seller.
Dist.: RCA/Columbia

DEEP IN MY HEART 1954
★ ★ ★ ★ NR Biography/Musical 2:12
Dir: Stanley Donen *Cast:* Jose Ferrer, Merle Oberon, Helen Traubel, Doe Avedon, Walter Pidgeon, Paul Henreid, Rosemary Clooney, Jane Powell, Vic Damone, Ann Miller, Cyd Charisse, Howard Keel, Tony Martin
▶ Star-studded biography of composer Sigmund Romberg (ably played by Ferrer) and his rise to fame with the help of writer Dorothy Donnelly (Oberon) and showman Florenz Ziegfeld (Henreid). Hits such as "The Desert

Song," "Lover Come Back to Me," and "Softly, As in a Morning Sunrise" are performed by a long list of guest stars. Gene Kelly appears in his only film performance with brother Fred.
Dist.: MGM/UA

DEEP IN THE HEART 1984 British
★ ★ R Action-Adventure 1:39
☑ Rape, nudity, adult situations, explicit language, graphic violence
Dir: Tony Garnett   *Cast:* Karen Young, Clayton Day, Suzie Humphreys, Helena Humann, Ben Jones
► Pretty Dallas schoolteacher Young is raped on a date with gun-collecting attorney Day. When the cops refuse to do anything about the crime, she becomes a sharpshooter to get revenge. Antihandgun and feminist themes add some spark to this low-budget action picture. Also known as *Handgun.*
Dist.: HBO

DEEP RED 1975 Italian
☆ R Horror 1:38
☑ Graphic violence
Dir: Dario Argento   *Cast:* David Hemmings, Daria Nicolodi, Gabriele Lavia, Clara Calamai, Macha Meril
► In Rome, Englishman Hemmings sees a psychiatrist fall victim to a serial killer. He investigates and is stalked by the murderer. Directed by Argento in his trademark fashion in which bravura visuals overwhelm a muddled plot. Also known as *Hatchet Murders.*
Dist.: HBO

DEEP SPACE 1988
☆ R Sci-Fi 1:30
☑ Explicit language, violence
Dir: Fred Olen Ray   *Cast:* Charles Napier, Ann Turkel, Bo Svenson, Ron Glass, Julie Newmar, James Booth
► Cocoon-like thing, apparently from another planet, hatches into a killer monster that terrorizes Los Angeles. Detective Napier and partner Glass try to stop the creature, which is actually the creation of government scientist Booth. Cheap special effects, few plot surprises.
Dist.: TWE

DEEPSTAR SIX 1988
★ ★ ★ R Horror 1:40
☑ Explicit language, violence
Dir: Sean S. Cunningham   *Cast:* Greg Evigan, Nancy Everhard, Taurean Blacque, Miguel Ferrer, Cindy Pickett
► Captain Blacque, right-hand man Evigan, and Evigan's pregnant lover Everhard are members of an undersea research crew menaced by a monster crustacean. Generates some scares as attractive stars run for their collective lives, but special effects and formula screenplay are merely okay.
Dist.: IVE

DEER HUNTER, THE 1978
★ ★ ★ ★ R Drama 3:03
☑ Adult situations, explicit language, graphic violence
Dir: Michael Cimino   *Cast:* Robert De Niro, John Cazale, John Savage, Christopher Walken, Meryl Streep, George Dzundza, Chuck Aspegren
► Ambitious epic about the effect of the Vietnam War on the blue-collar inhabitants of a Pennsylvania steel town. Filled with magnificent performances—including De Niro as an embittered POW, Streep as an abandoned wife, Cazale (in his last role) as a neurotic alcoholic, and Savage as a maimed vet—and beautiful production values. A milestone for its sympathetic treatment of veterans, film was awarded nine Oscar nominations, winning for Picture, Director, Supporting Actor (Walken), Sound, and Editing.
Dist.: MCA

DEF-CON 4 1985
★ ★ R Sci-Fi 1:28'
☑ Explicit language, graphic violence
Dir: Paul Donovan   *Cast:* Lenore Zahn, Maury Chaykin, Kate Lynch, Kevin King, John Walsch, Tim Choate
► Three astronauts return to Earth after World War III and find Nova Scotia overrun by sadistic thugs. When their partner is killed, Choate and his lover Zahn begin the arduous journey to safety in Central America. Grim post-apocalyptic fable suffers from a low budget and cast of unknowns.
Dist.: New World

DEFENCE OF THE REALM 1986 British
★ ★ PG Mystery-Suspense 1:36
☑ Brief nudity, mild violence
Dir: David Drury   *Cast:* Gabriel Byrne, Greta Scacchi, Denholm Elliott, Ian Bannen, Bill Paterson
► Jumbled thriller about investigative reporter Byrne, whose articles destroy politician Bannen's career. When colleague Elliott is murdered, Byrne learns he's been set up by the government. Aided by secretary Scacchi, Byrne sets out to expose the villains. Film combines intriguing themes—terrorism, nuclear politics, press responsibilities—in a confusing manner. (CC)
Dist.: Nelson

DEFENSE PLAY 1988
★ ★ PG Action-Adventure 1:33
☑ Explicit language, mild violence
Dir: Monte Markham   *Cast:* David Oliver, Susan Ursitti, Monte Markham, Eric Gilliom, William Frankfather
► Air Force Colonel Markham's son Oliver uncovers Soviet sabotage of prototype mini-helicopters and eventually takes on the spy in battle of remote control choppers. Unlikely plot with echoes of *WarGames* gets swift direction from Markham. Solid supporting cast although Oliver is bland in the lead.
Dist.: TWE

DEFIANCE 1980
★ ★ ★ ★ PG Action-Adventure 1:42
☑ Adult situations, explicit language, graphic violence
Dir: John Flynn *Cast:* Jan-Michael Vincent, Theresa Saldana, Fernando Lopez, Danny Aiello, Art Carney
▶ Between voyages, merchant seaman Vincent finds his New York neighborhood besieged by vicious young punks. When kindly shopkeeper Carney is beaten, Vincent rallies his old friends to defeat the gang. Gritty vigilante drama is restrained and realistic.
Dist.: Vestron

DEFIANT ONES, THE 1958
★ ★ ★ ★ NR Action-Adventure 1:37 B&W
Dir: Stanley Kramer *Cast:* Tony Curtis, Sidney Poitier, Theodore Bikel, Charles McGraw, Lon Chaney, Jr., Cara Williams
▶ Black convict Poitier and prejudiced white Curtis escape chain gang while still handcuffed together. The pair overcome initial differences to insure mutual survival. Tremendous excitement with something to say; Poitier and Curtis are excellent. Oscars for Best Cinematography and Screenplay; nominated for Picture, Actor (Curtis, Poitier), Supporting Actor (Bikel), Supporting Actress (Williams), Director.
Dist.: MGM/UA

DEJA VU 1985
★ ★ R Drama 1:34
☑ Adult situations, mild violence
Dir: Anthony Richmond *Cast:* Jaclyn Smith, Shelley Winters, Claire Bloom, Nigel Terry
▶ Screenwriter Terry notices the uncanny resemblance between his fiancée and famous 1930s dancer (Smith in a dual role) who died in a suspicious fire. Bizarre coincidences lead him to believe that the dancer has possessed his fiancée. Smith's then-husband shot and directed this handsome fantasy.
Dist.: Warner

DELICATE BALANCE, A 1973
★ PG Drama 2:12
☑ Explicit language
Dir: Tony Richardson *Cast:* Katharine Hepburn, Paul Scofield, Lee Remick, Kate Reid, Joseph Cotton, Betsy Blair
▶ Film version of the Pulitzer prize–winning Edward Albee play has Hepburn and Scofield as a wealthy New England couple whose home is invaded by neurotic family members and disturbed best friends. Direction is discreet to the point of nonexistence in this static, talky American Film Theater production.
Dist.: CBS/Fox

DELIGHTFULLY DANGEROUS 1945
★ NR Musical 1:32 B&W
Dir: Arthur Lubin *Cast:* Jane Powell, Ralph Bellamy, Constance Moore, Arthur Treacher, Louise Beavers, Morton Gould and His Orchestra
▶ Country teenager Powell is shocked to

learn her New York sister Moore is working as a stripper, and pressures producer Bellamy into hiring her for his legitimate Broadway show. Antiseptic musical features title tune and "Once Upon a Song."
Dist.: Video Dimensions

DELIVERANCE 1972
★ ★ ★ ★ R Action-Adventure 1:49
☑ Rape, explicit language, violence
Dir: John Boorman *Cast:* Jon Voight, Burt Reynolds, Ned Beatty, Ronny Cox, Bill McKinney, Herbert "Cowboy" Coward
▶ Brutal, riveting adventure about backwoods novices Voight, Beatty, and Cox who join macho guide Reynolds on a white-water rafting trip in Georgia. Classic man-against-the-elements premise is taken one step further by the introduction of terrifying hillbillies intent on rape and murder. Stark photography and haunting bluegrass score (including the pop hit "Dueling Banjos") helped make this an enormous success. Nominated for Best Picture and Director. Based on the novel by James Dickey (who has a cameo as the sheriff).
Dist.: Warner

DELTA FORCE, THE 1986
★ ★ ★ ★ R Action-Adventure 2:09
☑ Explicit language, violence
Dir: Menahem Golan *Cast:* Lee Marvin, Chuck Norris, Martin Balsam, Shelley Winters, Joey Bishop, George Kennedy
▶ When Palestinian terrorists hijack a TWA flight in Athens and take a group of hostages to Beirut, Marvin and his crack commando unit Delta Force are summoned to help. Lone wolf Norris rejoins his old comrades for Israel-based rescue mission. Actioner revises facts of 1985 hijacking to give Yanks revenge on terrorists, but genre fans won't quibble with such details as Norris and company bust up the bad guys with great gusto. **(CC)**
Dist.: Media

DEMENTED 1980
★ R Horror 1:32
☑ Rape, Nudity, explicit language, graphic violence
Dir: Arthur Jeffreys *Cast:* Sallee Elyse, Bruce Gilchrist, Bryan Charles, Chip Matthews, Deborah Alter, Kathryn Clayton
▶ After being gang raped by four masked men, Elyse is sent to an asylum, but time does not heal her emotional wounds. After her release, seduction and sharp objects become her chosen weapons of revenge against her attackers. Grotesque shocker has a few flashes of humor.
Dist.: Media

DEMENTIA 13 1963
☆ NR Horror 1:21 B&W
Dir: Francis Ford Coppola *Cast:* William Campbell, Luana Anders, Bart Patton, Mary Mitchell, Patrick Magee, Eithne Dunne
▶ When her husband dies of a heart attack,

Anders drowns his corpse so she won't be cut off from his family fortune. Relative Campbell shows up for a memorial service for his late sister, who died in the same lake. Anders schemes more, but killings continue even after she is victimized. Coppola's baroque direction highlights this horror flick.
Dist.: Cable

DEMETRIUS AND THE GLADIATORS 1954
★ ★ NR Drama 1:41
Dir: Delmer Daves *Cast:* Victor Mature, Susan Hayward, Michael Rennie, Debra Paget, Anne Bancroft, Jay Robinson, Ernest Borgnine, William Marshall, Richard Egan
▶ Sequel to *The Robe* finds the Christian slave Demetrius (Mature) forced to fight in the Roman gladiator ring. Paget's apparent death and his subsequent seduction by Hayward make Mature question his faith until St. Peter (Rennie) shows him the way back. Not as inspirational as its predecessor but nevertheless exciting. **(CC)**
Dist.: CBS/Fox

DEMI-PARADISE, THE 1943 British
☆ NR Comedy 1:55 B&W
Dir: Anthony Asquith *Cast:* Laurence Olivier, Margaret Rutherford, Penelope Dudley Ward, Leslie Henson, Felix Aylmer
▶ On his first visit to England in 1939, Russian scientist Olivier is put off by the seeming coldness of the English people. When he returns three years later, World War II is on, and the English welcome him as the citizen of an allied country. Olivier's portrayal of the Russian is a technical tour de force in this warm, funny parable of a stranger in a strange land. Also known as *Adventure for Two.*
Dist.: Video Yesteryear

DEMON, THE 1981
★ ★ NR Horror 1:33
☑ Nudity, adult situations, explicit language, graphic violence
Dir: Percival Rubens *Cast:* Jennifer Holmes, Cameron Mitchell, Craig Gardner, Zoli Markey, Mark Tannous
▶ Vicious alien monster attacks women with a steel claw, saving their body parts in plastic bags. Authorities are baffled by the mounting murders. Unremarkable horror exploitation filmed in South Africa.
Dist.: VidAmerica

DEMON OF PARADISE 1987
☆ R Horror 1:23
☑ Nudity, adult situations, explicit language, violence
Dir: Cirio H. Santiago *Cast:* Kathryn Witt, William Steis, Laura Banks, Fred Bailey
▶ A huge, scaly lizard is reported causing mayhem in Banks's Hawaiian resort. Banks and PR man Bailey exploit the situation for publicity while herpetologist Witt plots to stop the beast. Picture postcard Hawaiian settings

are the backdrop for laughable man-in-a-rubber suit creature.
Dist.: Warner

DEMONOID, MESSENGER OF DEATH 1981
☆ R Horror 1:18
☑ Adult situations, explicit language, violence
Dir: Alfred Zacharias *Cast:* Samantha Eggar, Stuart Whitman, Roy Cameron Jenson, Narciso Busquets, Erika Carlson, Lew Saunders
▶ While in Mexico, Eggar and husband Jenson discover a silver box containing the Devil's left hand. When the hand escapes it triggers an outbreak of self-inflicted amputations. Poor production and wretched performances. Also known as *Demonoid* and *Macabra.*
Dist.: Media

DEMON SEED 1977
★ ★ R Sci-Fi 1:34
☑ Nudity, adult situations, violence
Dir: Donald Cammell *Cast:* Julie Christie, Fritz Weaver, Gerrit Graham, Berry Kroeger
▶ Weaver invents Proteus IV, an organic supercomputer with the ability to reproduce. Proteus traps Weaver's wife Christie in a computer-controlled apartment, then proceeds to impregnate her. Bizarre science-fiction story has interesting special effects and stylish direction. Robert Vaughn supplies the computer's voice.
Dist.: MGM/UA

DEMONS OF THE MIND 1972 British
★ R Horror 1:25
☑ Adult situations, explicit language, violence
Dir: Peter Sykes *Cast:* Paul Jones, Patrick Magee, Yvonne Mitchell, Robert Hardy, Gillian Hills, Michael Hordern
▶ Nineteenth-century doctor Magee confronts baron Jones, who believes his children are possessed by demons and has been locking them up in his castle. Uninspired psychological drama with a dollop of horror.
Dist.: HBO

DEMONWARP 1988
☆ NR Horror 1:31
☑ Nudity, adult situations, explicit language, violence
Dir: Emmett Alston *Cast:* George Kennedy, David Michael O'Neill, Pamela Gilbert, Billy Jacoby, Colleen McDermott, Hank Stratton
▶ Teenager O'Neill and his friends go camping in the woods, only to be attacked by a Bigfoot-like monster. Kennedy, whose daughter was kidnapped by the creature, joins the young folk to hunt it down. Attractive cast sheds clothes frequently, providing a distraction from lackluster plotting and an unscary monster.
Dist.: Vidmark

DERSU UZALA 1975 Japanese/Russian
★ ★ G Drama 2:17

Dir: Akira Kurosawa *Cast:* Maxim Munzuk, Yuri Solomine
▶ In 1902, Mongolian guide Dersu Uzala (Munzuk) teaches Russian surveyor Solomine how to survive the Siberian wilderness. Their friendship deepens over the years as Dersu reveals the wonders and dangers of nature to the surveyor. Deliberate pacing and exotic locations enhance this simple, poignant film. Based on a true story, and winner of the Best Foreign Film Oscar. S
Dist.: Nelson

DESERT BLOOM 1986
★ ★ **PG Drama 1:46**
☑ Adult situations, explicit language, mild violence
Dir: Eugene Corr *Cast:* Jon Voight, JoBeth Williams, Ellen Barkin, Allen Garfield, Annabeth Gish
▶ Modest, touching coming-of-age story set in 1950 Las Vegas focuses on awkward teenager Gish and her eccentric family. Aunt Sara (Barkin) moves in while awaiting her divorce, sparking a confrontation between father Voight, a troubled veteran who runs a gas station, and mother Williams. Good sense of period detail (including a funny account of A-bomb tests) and sensitive performances.
Dist.: RCA/Columbia

DESERT FOX, THE 1951
★ ★ ★ **NR War 1:28 B&W**
Dir: Henry Hathaway *Cast:* James Mason, Cedric Hardwicke, Jessica Tandy, Luther Adler, Everett Sloane, Richard Boone
▶ True story of the brilliant World War II German commander Erwin Rommel (Mason) traces his North African campaign against the British. Later, Rommel turns against Hitler and participates in an ill-fated plot against the Führer's life. Sympathetic account dominated by Mason's characterization; he played Rommel again two years later in *The Desert Rats.*
Dist.: CBS/Fox

DESERT HEARTS 1986
★ ★ **R Drama 1:27**
☑ Nudity, adult situations, explicit language
Dir: Donna Deitch *Cast:* Helen Shaver, Patricia Charbonneau, Audra Lindley, Andra Akers, Dean Butler
▶ In the 1950s, repressed professor Shaver visits Nevada dude ranch to obtain divorce and is pursued by younger Charbonneau. They fall in love; Shaver deals with society pressure and her own misgivings. Passionate lesbian love story with intelligent direction by Deitch and strong, committed performances by the leads. Steamy love scene is pretty explicit.
Dist.: Vestron

DESIGN FOR LIVING 1933
★ ★ ★ **NR Comedy 1:30 B&W**
Dir: Ernst Lubitsch *Cast:* Fredric March, Gary Cooper, Miriam Hopkins, Edward Everett Horton, Franklin Pangborn, Isabel Jewell
▶ Elegant but risqué comedy of manners about commercial artist Hopkins who sets up a ménage à trois in Paris with playwright March and painter Cooper. Although rivals, March and Cooper join together to break up Hopkins's marriage of convenience to stuffy millionaire Horton. Surprisingly adult farce about sexual politics was adapted by Ben Hecht from a Noel Coward play.
Dist.: MCA

DESIRE 1936
★ ★ **NR Comedy 1:36 B&W**
Dir: Frank Borzage *Cast:* Marlene Dietrich, Gary Cooper, John Halliday, William Frawley, Akim Tamiroff
▶ Dietrich has one of her most alluring roles as a Parisian jewel thief who drags American engineer Cooper into her scheme to cross the Spanish border. Polished, extremely witty romantic comedy made Dietrich a mainstream star in America. She also gets to sing "Awake in a Dream."
Dist.: MCA

DESIREE 1954
★ ★ **NR Drama 1:50**
Dir: Henry Koster *Cast:* Marlon Brando, Jean Simmons, Merle Oberon, Michael Rennie, Cameron Mitchell, Cathleen Nesbitt
▶ Young and penniless Napoleon Bonaparte (Brando) wants to marry beautiful Desiree (Simmons) but her dad bars the match. Bonaparte rises to power and marries Josephine (Oberon); Desiree weds nobleman Rennie but still carries a torch for her lost love. An oddly cast Brando still shines. (CC)
Dist.: CBS/Fox

DESIRE UNDER THE ELMS 1958
★ **NR Drama 1:51 B&W**
Dir: Delbert Mann *Cast:* Sophia Loren, Anthony Perkins, Burl Ives, Frank Overton, Pernell Roberts
▶ Story of seduction and murder set against the stark backdrop of 1840 New England. Elderly farmer Ives weds young Italian immigrant Loren; she seduces Ives's son Perkins in order to produce an heir. The affair ends in tragedy. Strong chemistry between Loren and Perkins in this adaptation of the Eugene O'Neill play. Oscar-nominated cinematography and top Elmer Bernstein score.
Dist.: KVC

DESK SET 1957
★ ★ ★ ★ **NR Comedy 1:43**
Dir: Walter Lang *Cast:* Spencer Tracy, Katharine Hepburn, Gig Young, Joan Blondell, Dina Merrill
▶ Sparks fly when the unbeatable team of Tracy and Hepburn mixes business with pleasure at a broadcast network. Hepburn is especially delightful as an intellectual researcher capable of throwing fear and trepidation into the coils of efficiency expert Tracy's computer in this comedy-romance about the onslaught of office automation.
Dist.: CBS/Fox

DESPAIR 1979 German
☆ **NR Drama 1:59**
☑ Brief nudity, adult situations, explicit language
Dir: Rainer Werner Fassbinder **Cast:** Dirk Bogarde, Andrea Ferreol, Volker Spengler, Klaus Lowitsch, Bernhard Wicki, Alexander Allerson
▶ In 1930s Berlin, Bogarde, the neurotic owner of a chocolate factory, tries to switch identities with drifter Lowitsch to collect on an insurance policy. Surreal psychodrama with bleak comic overtones was adapted by playwright Tom Stoppard from Vladimir Nabokov's novel.
Dist.: Warner

DESPERADOS, THE 1969
★ ★ **PG Western 1:30**
☑ Adult situations, explicit language, violence
Dir: Henry Levin **Cast:** Vince Edwards, Jack Palance, George Maharis, Neville Brand, Sylvia Sims
▶ Even after the Civil War, Palance leads family band of Confederate guerrillas in plundering and murdering. Palance's son Edwards breaks with the group and starts a new life in Texas. Six years later, Palance and company show up, forcing a deadly confrontation between Edwards and his family. Bloody and action-packed.
Dist.: RCA/Columbia

DESPERATE HOURS, THE 1955
★ ★ ★ **NR Mystery-Suspense 1:52 B&W**
Dir: William Wyler **Cast:** Humphrey Bogart, Fredric March, Arthur Kennedy, Martha Scott, Gig Young, Dewey Martin
▶ Escaped prisoner Bogart and two accomplices break into March's suburban home and hold his family hostage. March cooperates with his captors but then manages to outwit them. Nail-biting adaptation of the Joseph Hayes play and novel; well acted by all with razor-sharp direction by Wyler.
Dist.: Paramount

DESPERATELY SEEKING SUSAN 1985
★ ★ **PG-13 Comedy 1:43**
☑ Brief nudity, adult situations, explicit language
Dir: Susan Seidelman **Cast:** Rosanna Arquette, Madonna, Aidan Quinn, Robert Joy, Mark Blum ·
▶ Bump on the noggin gives bored New Jersey hausfrau Arquette amnesia and makes her think she's wild young Madonna. Arquette finds herself in the middle of caper plot and falls for film projectionist Quinn. Sly, hip direction by Seidelman creates a funky New York City fantasyland that accounts for this comedy's shaggy, offbeat charm. The ladies, solidly supported by Quinn, are fine.
Dist.: HBO

DESTINATION MOON 1950
★ ★ **NR Sci-Fi 1:31**
Dir: Irving Pichel **Cast:** Warner Anderson,

John Archer, Tom Powers, Dick Wesson, Erin O'Brien-Moore, Ted Warde
▶ Four astronauts make the hazardous journey to the moon, then learn they don't have enough fuel to return to Earth. Although dated, this landmark science fiction film, based on Robert Heinlein's *Rocketship Galileo*, was one of the first to take a realistic approach to space travel. Producer George Pal won an Oscar for Special Effects.
Dist.: Media

DESTINATION TOKYO 1944
★ ★ ★ **NR War 2:15 B&W**
Dir: Delmer Daves **Cast:** Cary Grant, John Garfield, Alan Hale, John Ridgely, Dane Clark, Faye Emerson
▶ Rousing World War II drama follows the crew of the *Copperfin* submarine on a perilous mission to Tokyo Bay. Wonderful cast features a rugged Grant as the commander and Garfield in one of his best performances as a skirt-chasing sailor. Deliberately claustrophobic set design makes the many highlights (including an improvised appendectomy and a nerve-wracking depth charge sequence) feel even more authentic.
Dist.: MGM/UA ☐

DESTROYER, THE 1988
★ **R Horror 1:34**
☑ Nudity, adult situations, explicit language, graphic violence
Dir: Robert Kirk **Cast:** Deborah Foreman, Clayton Rohner, Lyle Alzado, Anthony Perkins, Tobias Andersen, Lannie Garrett
▶ While working on screenwriter boyfriend Rohner's prison picture, stuntperson Foreman has nightmares about electrocuted convict Alzado. Her dreams come horribly true, as a still-alive Alzado menaces her and the crew, including director Perkins. Gory tale features lifeless performances.
Dist.: Virgin

DESTRUCTORS, THE 1974 British
★ ★ ★ **PG Drama 1:29**
☑ Adult situations, violence
Dir: Robert Parrish **Cast:** Michael Caine, Anthony Quinn, James Mason, Maureen Kerwin, Marcel Bozzuffi, Catherine Rouvel
▶ Narcotics agent Quinn hires hitman Caine to eliminate well-protected druglord Mason. Caine worms his way into Mason's drug ring, but his cover is blown when Quinn suddenly changes plans. Interesting cast and French locations add spark to this crime thriller. Also known as *The Marseilles Contract*.
Dist.: Vestron

DESTRY RIDES AGAIN 1939
★ ★ ★ ★ **NR Western/Comedy 1:34 B&W**
Dir: George Marshall **Cast:** Marlene Dietrich, James Stewart, Mischa Auer, Charles Winninger, Brian Donlevy, Una Merkel
▶ Classic Western comedy from the Max Brand novel about soft-spoken, milk-drinking sheriff Stewart who cleans up a corrupt frontier

town without resorting to violence. Dietrich's Frenchy, a saloon singer with a heart of gold, was a turning point in her career. She sings "See What the Boys in the Back Room Will Have," and gets into one of the wildest catfights in filmdom with Merkel. Top-notch supporting work from veteran character actors Auer, Winninger, Allen Jenkins, and Samuel S. Hinds.
Dist.: MCA

DETECTIVE, THE 1954 British
★★ NR Mystery-Suspense 1:31 B&W
Dir: Robert Hamer *Cast:* Alec Guinness, Joan Greenwood, Peter Finch, Cecil Parker, Bernard Lee, Sidney James
▶ Smooth, entertaining mystery based on G. K. Chesterton's Father Brown (Guinness), a mild-mannered priest with an unexpected talent for detecting. Flambeau (Finch), a notorious jewel thief, steals a rare crucifix; Brown is determined to retrieve the cross as well as reform Flambeau. Diverting fun with superior performances. Also known as *Father Brown*.
Dist.: RCA/Columbia

DETECTIVE, THE 1968
★★ NR Mystery-Suspense 1:54
Dir: Gordon Douglas *Cast:* Frank Sinatra, Lee Remick, Ralph Meeker, Jack Klugman, William Windom, Jacqueline Bisset
▶ Sinatra, a hard-bitten New York cop investigating the murder of a homosexual, uncovers evidence of widespread police corruption. Twisty, fast-paced mystery based on the Roderick Thorp novel features a creditable performance by Sinatra. Look for Robert Duvall and Sugar Ray Robinson in small roles.
Dist.: CBS/Fox

DETECTIVE SCHOOL DROPOUTS 1986
★★ PG Comedy 1:30
☑ Adult situations, explicit language
Dir: Filippo Ottoni *Cast:* David Landsberg, Lorin Dreyfuss, Christian De Sica, Valeria Golino, Rick Battaglia, Francesco Cinieri
▶ Pint-sized Landsberg, obsessed with detective stories, becomes student to Dreyfuss, an incompetent private eye who's only interested in Landsberg's money. Pursuing a murder/kidnapping case, the duo find themselves stranded in Italy with no passports or money. Undemanding comedy written by Landsberg and Dreyfuss (Richard's brother) has an unexpectedly innocent tone.
Dist.: MGM/UA

DETOUR 1945
★★ NR Drama 1:07 B&W
Dir: Edgar G. Ulmer *Cast:* Tom Neal, Ann Savage, Claudia Drake, Edmund MacDonald, Tim Ryan
▶ Nihilistic film noir about Neal, a hitchhiker inexorably drawn into a maze of blackmail and murder, has become a cult favorite over the years. Savage is memorable as a heartless vixen who pawns Neal off as the long-lost heir to a fortune in a scheme to defraud a

widow. Shot in six days on a shoestring budget.
Dist.: KVC

DETROIT 9000 1973
★★ R Action-Adventure 1:46
☑ Brief nudity, adult situations, explicit language, violence
Dir: Arthur Marks *Cast:* Alex Rocco, Hari Rhodes, Vonetta McGee, Ella Edwards, Scatman Crothers
▶ When masked gunmen rob the mostly black guests at a posh political fund-raiser, white cop Rocco and black cop Rhodes are paired on the case. The two can barely stand each other but turn color-blind when the going gets rough. Dated blaxploitation buddy pic suffers from passage of time.
Dist.: HBO

DEVIL AND DANIEL WEBSTER, THE 1941
★★★★ NR Fantasy 1:49 B&W
Dir: William Dieterle *Cast:* Edward Arnold, Walter Huston, James Craig, Simone Simon, Anne Shirley, Gene Lockhart
▶ Nineteenth-century New England farmer Craig unwittingly sells his soul to Mr. Scratch (Huston); it's up to lawyer Daniel Webster (Arnold) to rescue him. Wonderful Americana, faithfully adapted from Stephen Vincent Benét's short story, is a delightful showcase for Huston and Arnold. Bernard Herrmann's score won an Oscar.
Dist.: Nelson

DEVIL AND MAX DEVLIN, THE 1981
★★★★ PG Comedy 1:36
☑ Explicit language
Dir: Steven Hilliard Stern *Cast:* Elliott Gould, Bill Cosby, Susan Anspach, Adam Rich, Julie Budd, David Knell
▶ Mean landlord Gould killed by a bus winds up in Hell, where Devil Cosby offers him freedom in return for three "unsullied" souls. Although he hates children, Gould sets out to befriend, and betray, three innocent kids. Some mild and inoffensive profanity; otherwise, a typically light Disney comedy.
Dist.: Buena Vista

DEVIL AND MISS JONES, THE 1941
★★★ NR Comedy 1:32 B&W
Dir: Sam Wood *Cast:* Jean Arthur, Robert Cummings, Charles Coburn, Edmund Gwenn, Spring Byington, William Demarest
▶ Stuffy multimillionaire Coburn, alarmed at unionizing efforts in one of his department stores, disguises himself as a sales clerk to check conditions first-hand. Arthur, salesperson in shoe department, takes Coburn under her wing. Marvelous comedy raises points still relevant today. Coburn and screenwriter Norman Krasna received Oscar nominations.
Dist.: Republic

DEVIL AT 4 O'CLOCK, THE 1961
★★ NR Action-Adventure 2:06
Dir: Mervyn LeRoy *Cast:* Spencer Tracy,

Frank Sinatra, Kerwin Mathews, Jean-Pierre Aumont, Gregoire Aslan, Barbara Luna
▸ Sinatra is one of three prisoners rebuilding a leper colony chapel on a South Seas island. When a volcano explodes, Tracy, an embittered, alcoholic priest, enlists the prisoners' help in guiding the colony children through the jungle to safety. Large-scale adventure dampened somewhat by downbeat tone.
Dist.: RCA/Columbia

DEVIL BAT, THE 1941
★ NR Horror 1:08 B&W
Dir: Jean Yarbrough ***Cast:*** Bela Lugosi, Dave O'Brien, Suzanne Kaaren, Arthur Q. Brian
▸ Lugosi stars as a town physician who is in reality an evil scientist. He performs experiments on bats in his laboratory, turning them into bloodsuckers that kill anyone wearing a certain scent. Also known as *Killer Bats;* remade as *The Flying Serpent.* Standard low-budget nonsense.
Dist.: Video Yesteryear

DEVIL BAT'S DAUGHTER 1946
★ NR Horror 1:06 B&W
Dir: Frank Wisbar ***Cast:*** Rosemary La Planche, Michael Hale, John James, Molly Lamont, Nolan Leary, Monica Mars
▸ Sequel to 1941's *The Devil Bat* finds La Planche consulting with shrink Hale regarding nightmares about her late father. Maybe she's crazy—or maybe dad is a vampire as real killings commence. Then again, it's possible the shrink can't be trusted. Better than the original, which is faint praise.
Dist.: SVS

DEVIL DOLL, THE 1936
★★ NR Horror 1:19 B&W
Dir: Tod Browning ***Cast:*** Lionel Barrymore, Maureen O'Sullivan, Frank Lawton, Robert Greig, Lucy Beaumont
▸ Truly bizarre horror film about escaped convict Barrymore who avenges himself on the people who framed him by shrinking them down to doll-size. Great sets and special effects add to the film's grotesque humor. Barrymore, posing as the owner of a doll store, plays most of the second half in drag. Noted director Erich von Stroheim contributed to the screenplay.
Dist.: MGM/UA

DEVIL IN THE FLESH 1987 Italian/French
☆ X Drama 1:50
☑ Nudity, strong sexual content, adult situations, explicit language
Dir: Marco Bellocchio ***Cast:*** Maruschka Detmers, Federico Pitzalis, Anita Laurenzi, Riccardo De Torrebruna, Alberto Di Stasio, Anna Orso
▸ In this loose updating of Raymond Radiguet's classic novel (filmed before in 1946), Detmers portrays an unstable woman engaged to an imprisoned terrorist. Before he is freed, she takes teenager Pitzalis as her lover. First mainstream film to include an explicit, unsimulated sex act. [S]
Dist.: Orion

DEVILS, THE 1971 British
★ R Drama 1:48
☑ Nudity, adult situations, graphic violence
Dir: Ken Russell ***Cast:*** Vanessa Redgrave, Oliver Reed, Dudley Sutton, Max Adrian, Gemma Jones
▸ Reed plays an unpopular priest accused of witchcraft by a band of hysterical nuns in this controversial adaptation of Aldous Huxley's *The Devils of Loudun* and the John Whiting play. Set in seventeenth-century France, with powerful images and impressive art direction. Close-ups of leprosy and exorcistic torture may offend some viewers.
Dist.: Warner

DEVIL'S PLAYGROUND, THE 1976 Australian
★ NR Drama 1:47
☑ Nudity, explicit language
Dir: Fred Schepisi ***Cast:*** Arthur Dignam, Nick Tate, Simon Burke, Charles McCallum, John Frawley, Jonathon Hardy
▸ Thoughtful examination of the repressive atmosphere at an Australian Catholic seminary in the early 1950s, contrasting the students' growing physicality with their teachers' morbid fear of sex. Subdued but assured direction from Schepisi, who also wrote the script.
Dist.: IFE

DEVIL'S RAIN, THE 1975
★★ PG Horror 1:25
☑ Violence
Dir: Robert Fuest ***Cast:*** Ernest Borgnine, Ida Lupino, William Shatner, Tom Skerritt, Eddie Albert, John Travolta
▸ Borgnine leads a cult of devil worshippers devoted to destroying the descendents of Shatner's family for having done them a bad turn three hundred years earlier. High points include Borgnine turning into a ram-horned demon, and final set piece in which title precipitation melts cultists (including a briefly viewed Travolta) into streaming rivulets. Borgnine's unique features are well-exploited to highlight his evil role in this superior schlock.
Dist.: United

DEVIL THUMBS A RIDE, THE 1947
★ NR Mystery-Suspense 1:03 B&W
Dir: Felix Feist ***Cast:*** Lawrence Tierney, Ted North, Nan Leslie, Betty Lawford, Andrew Tombes, Harry Shannon
▸ Never drink, drive, and pick up hitchhikers—a lesson North should have obeyed before he picked up thumb tripper Tierney, who turns out to be a mad killer. The police pursue the murderer. Tense if contrived B-movie's plot concept has become a familiar genre staple. Home video version double billed with 1945's *Having Wonderful Crime.*
Dist.: Turner

DEVONSVILLE TERROR, THE 1983
★ R Horror 1:22
☑ Nudity, explicit language, violence
Dir: Ulli Lommel *Cast:* Suzanna Love, Robert Walker, Donald Pleasence, Paul Wilson, Mary Walden, Deanna Haas
▶ In 1683, three young women are burned as witches in a New England town. Three hundred years later, teacher Love, environmentalist Walden, and controversial radio host Haas arrive and the townsfolk begin to believe they are the reincarnated witches. Small town setting serves as nice contrast to terror but plotting and special effects are below par.
Dist.: Nelson

D.I., THE 1957
★★ NR Crime 1:46 B&W
Dir: Jack Webb *Cast:* Jack Webb, Don Dubbins, Monica Lewis, Jackie Loughery, Lin McCarthy
▶ No-nonsense Parris Island drill instructor Webb turns boot camp into living hell for his greenhorn recruits, in particular weak-willed mama's boy Dubbins, who's trying to uphold a family tradition of strong soldiers. Webb (who also produced and directed) dominates the story.
Dist.: Warner

DIABOLIQUE 1955 French
★★ NR Mystery-Suspense 1:47 B&W
Dir: Henri-Georges Clouzot *Cast:* Simone Signoret, Vera Clouzot, Paul Meurisse, Charles Vanel, Jean Brochard
▶ At a boarding school, a brutal man's unhappy mistress (Signoret) and his equally troubled wife (Clouzot) plot off the murder—or do they? The wife keeps thinking she's seen the dead man in this shocking, suspenseful chiller that influenced many subsequent movies. Ⓢ
Dist.: Various

DIAL M FOR MURDER 1954
★★★ PG Mystery-Suspense 1:45
Dir: Alfred Hitchcock *Cast:* Ray Milland, Grace Kelly, Robert Cummings, John Williams, Anthony Dawson
▶ Husband Milland plots to get rid of wife Kelly, who is having an affair with Cummings, by blackmailing killer Dawson into attacking her. Plan goes awry when she kills her assailant. Hitchcock thriller (from Frederick Knott's stage play) generates a good deal of tension (especially in Kelly's life-and-death struggle with Dawson over a pair of scissors). Originally shot in 3-D.
Dist.: Warner

DIAMOND HEAD 1962
★★★ NR Drama 1:47
Dir: Guy Green *Cast:* Charlton Heston, Yvette Mimieux, George Chakiris, James Darren, France Nuyen
▶ Heston stars as the domineering family head of a pineapple empire who opposes his

sister's love for a full-blooded Hawaiian, even though he himself keeps a native mistress. Based on the popular novel of bigotry and family squabbles by Peter Gilman. Colorful Hawaiian backdrop.
Dist.: RCA/Columbia

DIAMONDS ARE FOREVER 1971 British
★★★★ PG Espionage/Action-Adventure 1:59
☑ Adult situations, violence
Dir: Guy Hamilton *Cast:* Sean Connery, Jill St. John, Charles Gray, Lana Wood, Jimmy Dean
▶ Las Vegas is the backdrop as super spy James Bond (Connery) battles the villainous Blofeld (Gray), who organizes diamond smuggling operation to equip his deadly space satellite. Connery returned to the role after temporarily quitting (George Lazenby starred in 1969's *On Her Majesty's Secret Service*) and his class and panache make him the ultimate Bond. Not the best in the series but still tons of fun gadgets, action, and pretty girls (St. John and Natalie's sister Lana Wood as the aptly named "Plenty O'Toole").
Dist.: MGM/UA

DIARY OF A CHAMBERMAID 1964 French
☆ NR Drama 1:19 B&W
Dir: Louis Buñuel *Cast:* Jeanne Moreau, Michel Piccoli, Georges Geret, Françoise Lugagne, Daniel Ivernel, Jean Ozenne
▶ In 1939, the bourgeoisie of fascist France are seen through the eyes of Moreau, a spunky chambermaid who turns from town to province to acquire a wealthy mate. With director Buñuel at the helm, the bourgeoisie are characterized as bizarre maniacs. Pointed, often amusing satire was also tackled by Jean Renoir in 1946. Ⓢ
Dist.: Media

DIARY OF A COUNTRY PRIEST 1950 French
☆ NR Drama 2:00 B&W
Dir: Robert Bresson *Cast:* Claude Laydu, Nicole Ladmiral, Jean Riveyre, Nicole Maurey, Andre Guibert, Martine Lemaire
▶ Simple cleric Laydu struggles to bring out the spiritual side of the small town to which he has been assigned. He succeeds in helping countess Arkell, who had withdrawn from man and God. Nonactor Laydu brings a dour grace to his role in this slow examination of faith in the day-to-day world. Ⓢ
Dist.: Various

DIARY OF A LOST GIRL 1929 German
☆ NR Drama 1:44 B&W
Dir: G. W. Pabst *Cast:* Louise Brooks, Fritz Rasp, Josef Ravensky, Sybille Schmitz, Valeska Gert
▶ Rape victim Brooks gives birth to a child, sinks into prostitution, loses a wealthy husband, and goes further down the road to degradation in this powerful silent tale of sin in Weimar Germany. Brooks is the epitome of screen beauty, and Pabst maintains a morbid control

over the seamy underside of life. Pair also teamed for 1928's *Pandora's Box.*
Dist.: Video Dimensions

DIARY OF A MAD HOUSEWIFE 1970
★ R Drama 1:34
☑ Nudity, adult situations, explicit language
Dir: Frank Perry ***Cast:*** Carrie Snodgress, Richard Benjamin, Frank Langella, Lorraine Cullen, Peter Boyle
▶ Stuck in an unhappy marriage to lawyer Benjamin, Manhattan housewife Snodgress turns to selfish writer Langella for sex and solace. Feminist social satire still packs a punch, thanks to compelling performance from Snodgress (Oscar nominated) and nicely nasty support from Langella.
Dist.: MCA

DIARY OF ANNE FRANK, THE 1959
★ ★ ★ ★ NR Biography 2:50 B&W
Dir: George Stevens ***Cast:*** Millie Perkins, Joseph Schildkraut, Shelley Winters, Richard Beymer, Lou Jacobi
▶ Perkins gives a remarkably moving performance as the Jewish girl hiding with her family in an Amsterdam attic for two years before being discovered by the Nazis. Actors are well cast; Winters won Supporting Actress Oscar for her role as Mrs. Van Daan. Based on the award-winning play inspired by Anne's diary, the film captures the horror of the Holocaust but also the hope and courage of the people under its. threat. Winner of three Academy Awards and remade as a TV movie.
Dist.: CBS/Fox

DICK TRACY 1990
★ ★ ★ PG Action-Adventure 1:50
☑ Violence, adult situations
Dir: Warren Beatty ***Cast:*** Warren Beatty, Charlie Korsmo, Glenne Headly, Al Pacino, Madonna, Dustin Hoffman, William Forsythe, Charles Durning, Mandy Patinkin, Paul Sorvino, Dick Van Dyke, James Caan, Lawrence Steven Meyers, William Forsythe
▶ Comic strip cop Tracy (Beatty) battles crime boss Big Boy Caprice (Pacino), rescues young Korsmo from a life on the street, fends off singer Breathless Mahoney (Madonna), all the while contemplating matrimony with Tess Trueheart (Headly). Utilizing the limited palette of Chester Gould's comic strip, production designer Richard Sylbert and cinematographer Vittorio Storaro created a beautifully detailed fantasy universe for the script's two-dimensional characters. Villains like Flattop (Forsythe) and Little Face (Meyers) are remarkably realized, though given little to do. Best acting is from Pacino, who sweats blood to bring life to his scenes. Songs by Stephen Sondheim; score by Danny Elfman.
Dist.: Buena Vista

DICK TRACY, DETECTIVE 1945
★ NR Mystery-Suspense 1:02 B&W
Dir: William Berke ***Cast:*** Morgan Conway,

Anne Jeffreys, Mike Mazurki, Jane Greer, Lyle Latell
▶ First feature film (after four serials) based on Chester Gould's square-jawed comic strip detective. Tracy (Conway) is on the trail of Split-face, a knife-scarred escaped convict who is systematically murdering the members of the jury who convicted him. Hero's girl Tess Trueheart (Jeffreys) is taken hostage by the Split-face mob. Low-budget effort has no relation to Warren Beatty's 1990 feature. Led to many sequels.
Dist.: Various

DICK TRACY MEETS GRUESOME 1947
★ NR Mystery-Suspense 1:05 B&W
Dir: John Rawlins ***Cast:*** Boris Karloff, Ralph Byrd, Anne Gwynne, Edward Ashley, June Clayworth
▶ Karloff has a field day as Gruesome, a notorious criminal whose immobilizing gas enables him to rob and kill with impunity. More humor than mystery in this above-average entry in the series based on the famous comic book hero.
Dist.: Various

DIE, DIE MY DARLING 1965 British
★ ★ NR Horror 1:37
Dir: Silvio Narrizano ***Cast:*** Tallulah Bankhead, Stefanie Powers, Peter Vaughn, Donald Sutherland, Yootha Joyce
▶ Religious zealot Bankhead kidnaps dead son's fiancée Powers and locks her in a basement to purify her soul. Creepy shocker in the *Whatever Happened to Baby Jane?* vein is notable primarily for a campy performance by Bankhead (in her last role). Sutherland has an amusing bit as an illiterate handyman.
Dist.: RCA/Columbia

DIE HARD 1988
★ ★ ★ ★ ★ R Action-Adventure 2:11
☑ Adult situations, explicit language, violence
Dir: John McTiernan ***Cast:*** Bruce Willis, Alan Rickman, Bonnie Bedelia, Alexander Godunov, Reginald VelJohnson, Paul Gleason
▶ Terrorists "hijack" Century City skyscraper, holding employees at a Christmas party hostage while they crack the computer code to a fortune in bonds. Only hitch: New York cop Willis, who upsets each step of oily villain Rickman's perfectly timed plan. Powerhouse thriller features amazing stunts, relentless pacing, and agreeable tongue-in-cheek humor. Beefed-up Willis is impressive in one of the year's top hits.
Dist.: CBS/Fox

DIE HARD 2 1990
★ ★ ★ ★ ★ R Action-Adventure 2:04
☑ Brief nudity, explicit language, violence
Dir: Renny Harlin ***Cast:*** Bruce Willis, Bonnie Bedelia, William Atherton, Reginald VelJohnson, Franco Nero, William Sadler, John Amos, Dennis Franz, Art Evans, Fred Dalton Thompson, Tom Bower, Sheila McCarthy

► Cop Willis is at Washington airport when terrorists take it over to nab extradited dictator Nero. He must battle the bad guys, whose machinations threaten several planes in flight, including wife Bedelia's, while handicapped by airport officials' stupidity. Smash sequel may lack original's freshness but cleverly escalates the danger with several sub-plots. Action highlight: Willis trapped in plane. Comic highlight: the "Fax" pun.
Dist.: CBS/Fox

DIE LAUGHING 1980
★★ PG Comedy 1:47
☑ Adult situations, explicit language, violence
Dir: Jeff Werner ***Cast:*** Robby Benson, Charles Durning, Linda Grovenor, Elsa Lanchester, Bud Cort
► Singing cabdriver Benson stumbles into a spy conspiracy when a passenger is murdered in his taxi. He dodges killers while protecting a chimp who holds a secret formula that could destroy the world. A must for Robby's fans: he produced and wrote, and sings five of his songs.
Dist.: Warner

DIE, MONSTER, DIE! 1965
★ NR Horror 1:18
Dir: Daniel Haller ***Cast:*** Boris Karloff, Nick Adams, Freda Jackson, Suzan Farmer, Terence de Marney, Patrick Magee
► American scientist Adams visits his fiancée Farmer's parents in England. Invalid mother Jackson begs Adams to take Farmer away, but he wants to solve the puzzle behind father Karloff's mutant houseplants first. Middling horror picture based on an H. P. Lovecraft story with Karloff suitably menacing as the wheelchair-bound villain.
Dist.: HBO

DIFFERENT STORY, A 1978
★★★★ PG Drama 1:48
☑ Adult situations, explicit language
Dir: Paul Aaron ***Cast:*** Perry King, Meg Foster, Valerie Curtin, Peter Donat
► Gay King and lesbian Foster form a close relationship that turns into love and marriage. Foster and King bring depth and conviction to this uneven but sensitive love story.
Dist.: Nelson

DILLINGER 1945
★★★ NR Crime 1:10 B&W
Dir: Max Nosseck ***Cast:*** Edmund Lowe, Anne Jeffreys, Lawrence Tierney, Eduardo Ciannelli, Marc Lawrence, Elisha Cook, Jr.
► Inaccurate but highly entertaining look at the notorious gangster, ably performed by Tierney in what may be his best role. Dillinger is depicted as a psychopath who will kill anyone who gets in the way of his plans for a criminal empire. Shot on a shoestring budget, fast, hard-edged B-movie received an Oscar nomination for Philip Yordan's screenplay. Bears little resemblance to the 1973 picture.
Dist.: CBS/Fox

DILLINGER 1973
★★ R Biography/Crime 1:36
☑ Adult situations, explicit language, graphic violence
Dir: John Milius ***Cast:*** Warren Oates, Ben Johnson, Michelle Phillips, Cloris Leachman, Harry Dean Stanton, Geoffrey Lewis
► Oates is suitably hard-bitten as Dillinger, Public Enemy Number One until his confrontation with G-man Melvin Purvis (Johnson) outside Chicago's Biograph Theatre in 1934. Violent film plays loose with the facts, but contains absolutely mesmerizing gun battles. Richard Dreyfuss has a small role as Baby Face Nelson.
Dist.: Vestron

DIMPLES 1936
★★ NR Musical/Family 1:18 B&W
Dir: William A. Seiter ***Cast:*** Shirley Temple, Frank Morgan, Helen Westley, Robert Kent, Stepin Fetchit
► Above-average Temple vehicle set in nineteenth-century New York. A sidewalk dancer adopted by society matron Westley, Shirley prefers to stay with lovable grandfather Morgan, a harmless pickpocket. Songs (choreographed by Bill Robinson) include "Hey, What Did the Bluebird Say?" and "Oh Mister Man Up in the Moon." (CC)
Dist.: CBS/Fox

DIM SUM: A LITTLE BIT OF HEART 1985
★ PG Comedy 1:28
☑ Adult situations
Dir: Wayne Wang ***Cast:*** Laureen Chew, Kim Chew, Victor Wong, Ida F. O. Chung, Cora Miao
► Portraying a Chinese-American family living in San Francisco, real-life mother (Laureen Chew) and daughter (Kim Chew) explore the complexities of human relationships. Series of sweet-humored vignettes concentrate on the widowed mother's desire to see her last daughter married complicated by her fear of living alone. As a free-spirited uncle, Wong bears witness that the way of Confucius may no longer be appropriate for contemporary Chinese. [S]
Dist.: Pacific Arts

DINER 1982
★★ R Comedy/Drama 1:50
☑ Adult situations, explicit language
Dir: Barry Levinson ***Cast:*** Steve Guttenberg, Daniel Stern, Mickey Rourke, Kevin Bacon, Ellen Barkin, Paul Reiser, Timothy Daly, Michael Tucker
► Nostalgic look at buddies in 1959 Baltimore who rely on friendship to cope with life after high school. Married Stern, engaged Guttenberg, trying-to-be-engaged Daly, and playing-the-field Rourke all hang out at the local diner to swap stories about music and sex.

Warmly written and engaging, this small film was an unexpected hit, especially for director Levinson, who returned to his hometown locale for *Tin Man*.
Dist.: MGM/UA

DINGAKA 1965 South African
★ **NR Drama 1:38**
Dir: Jamie Uys *Cast:* Stanley Baker, Juliet Prowse, Ken Gampu, Siegfried Mynhardt, Bob Courtney, Gordon Hood
► Gampu is caught in a deadly cycle of revenge when his daughter is murdered as a result of superstitions and rituals in a tribal village; sympathetic lawyer Baker and his wife Prowse attempt to aid the native. Earnest drama suffers from preachy tone and clichéd characters.
Dist.: Nelson

DINNER AT EIGHT 1933
★★★ **NR Comedy 1:53 B&W**
Dir: George Cukor *Cast:* Marie Dressler, John Barrymore, Wallace Beery, Jean Harlow, Lionel Barrymore, Billie Burke, Lee Tracy, Edmund Lowe, Madge Evans, Jean Hersholt, Karen Morley, May Robson
► Dizzy socialite Burke plans an exclusive dinner for visiting royalty, but her guests have varying reactions to the invitation. All-star cast shines in this sophisticated version of the long-running Broadway hit by George S. Kaufman and Edna Ferber. Harlow and Beery get the best laughs as a brawling couple; Barrymore is at his most romantic as a doomed matinee idol.
Dist.: MGM/UA

DINNER AT THE RITZ 1937 British
★★ **NR Mystery-Suspense 1:17 B&W**
Dir: Harold D. Schuster *Cast:* Annabella, Paul Lukas, David Niven, Romney Brent, Francis L. Sullivan
► When her French banker father is murdered in England, Annabella has no one to turn to for help except Niven, a mysterious government official who may have ulterior motives. Glossy but not especially compelling mystery with good early work from Niven.
Dist.: Video Yesteryear

DINO 1957
★★ **NR Drama 1:36 B&W**
Dir: Thomas Carr *Cast:* Sal Mineo, Brian Keith, Susan Kohner, Frank Faylen, Joe De Santis, Penny Santon
► Just released from a reformatory, juvenile delinquent Mineo faces a difficult choice: return to a life of crime, or accept pleas by girlfriend Kohner and social worker Keith to reform. Earnest performances give this small-scale drama some merit. Reworking of a Reginald Rose TV play.
Dist.: Republic

DIPLOMANIACS 1933
☆ **NR Comedy 1:03 B&W**
Dir: William A. Seiter *Cast:* Bert Wheeler, Robert Woolsey, Marjorie White, Louis Calhern, Edgar Kennedy, Hugh Herbert
► Joseph L. Mankiewicz–penned comedy about Wheeler and Woolsey, barbers to the Adoop Indian tribe, being sent to Geneva to make peace among battling delegates at an international conference. Some first-rate comedy here, and much that is truly odd. The satire is a little dated though.
Dist.: Turner

DIRT BIKE KID, THE 1986
★★★ **PG Comedy 1:30**
☑ Explicit language
Dir: Hoite Caston *Cast:* Peter Billingsley, Stuart Pankin, Anne Bloom, Patrick Collins, Danny Breen
► Billingsley plays a pint-size Evel Knievel in this family comedy. As little Jack, he helps save the local hot-dog stand from being mowed down for a new bank site with his magic motorcycle that really takes off—right into the sky. Impressive stuntwork and comic timing. **(CC)**
Dist.: Nelson

DIRTY DANCING 1987
★★★★★ **PG-13 Romance/Dance 1:41**
☑ Adult situations, explicit language
Dir: Emile Ardolino *Cast:* Patrick Swayze, Jennifer Grey, Jerry Orbach, Jack Weston, Cynthia Rhodes
► Gigantic box-office hit set in the summer of '63. While vacationing at a Catskills resort with her parents, seventeen-year-old Grey falls for Swayze, a sexy dance instructor from the wrong side of the dining hall. Packed with exciting dance sequences, glossy production values, and a nostalgic music score. "I've Had the Time of My Life" won the 1987 Oscar for Best Song.
Dist.: Vestron

DIRTY DOZEN, THE 1967
★★★★ **NR War 2:30**
☑ Adult situations, mild violence
Dir: Robert Aldrich *Cast:* Lee Marvin, Ernest Borgnine, Charles Bronson, Jim Brown, John Cassavetes, Richard Jaeckel, George Kennedy, Trini Lopez, Robert Ryan, Telly Savalas, Donald Sutherland, Clint Walker
► Tough, unorthodox major Marvin trains twelve hardened convicts for a suicide commando mission behind German lines during World War II. Highly entertaining war adventure expertly combines action, humor, and tension. Cassavetes won a Supporting Oscar nomination for his role as a foulmouthed psychotic. **(CC)**
Dist.: MGM/UA

DIRTY HARRY 1971
★★★★★ **R Action-Adventure 1:42**
☑ Violence
Dir: Don Siegel *Cast:* Clint Eastwood, Reni Santoni, Harry Guardino, Andy Robinson, John Vernon, John Larch
► Psychotic killer Robinson demands $200,000

ransom for his young hostage. The San Francisco police agree to the deal—except for detective Harry Callahan (Eastwood), who ignores the rules to track down the murderer. First and best of the *Dirty Harry* series is a swift, cunning thriller filled with memorable dialogue and taut action. Followed by *Magnum Force*.
Dist.: Warner

DIRTY LAUNDRY 1987
★ PG-13 Comedy 1:20
☑ Explicit language, adult humor
Dir: William Webb ***Cast:*** Leigh McCloskey, Jeanne O'Brien, Frankie Valli, Sonny Bono, Carl Lewis, Greg Louganis
► Soundman McCloskey walks out of local laundromat with what he thinks is his laundry but is actually a bag containing a million bucks in mafia drug money. McCloskey meets attractive reporter O'Brien and they find themselves in the midst of a wild chase. Undemanding sit-com-style humor.
Dist.: SVS

DIRTY MARY, CRAZY LARRY 1974
★★ PG Action-Adventure 1:33
☑ Explicit language, violence
Dir: John Hough ***Cast:*** Peter Fonda, Susan George, Adam Roarke, Vic Morrow, Fred Daniels, Roddy McDowall
► Daredevil racer Fonda and pal Roarke extort $150,000 from supermarket manager McDowall. With the police in hot pursuit, they take off across California in their new top-of-the-line stock car. George plays a groupie they pick up along the way. Nonstop chase has above-average stunts and car wrecks.
Dist.: CBS/Fox

DIRTY ROTTEN SCOUNDRELS 1988
★★★★ PG Comedy 1:42
☑ Explicit language, adult humor
Dir: Frank Oz ***Cast:*** Steve Martin, Michael Caine, Glenne Headly, Barbara Harris, Anton Rodgers, Ian McDiarmid, Dana Ivey
► Suave con man Caine has cushy Riviera scam going until crass American Martin invades his territory. Martin blackmails Caine into reluctant partnership, then becomes his rival in a bet to see who can win the heart and wallet of heiress Headly. Remake of the 1964 *Bedtime Story* hilariously combines broad comic antics with sharp plot twists. Top-notch Martin/Caine teamwork is abetted nicely by Headly. Funniest scene: Martin's impersonation of Caine's lunatic brother.
Dist.: Orion

DIRTY TRICKS 1981 Canadian
★★ PG Comedy 1:31
☑ Adult situations, explicit language, violence
Dir: Alvin Rakoff ***Cast:*** Elliott Gould, Kate Jackson, Arthur Hill, Rich Little, Nicholas Campbell, Angus MacInnes
► When his student is murdered after uncovering a startling George Washington letter, Harvard professor Gould is the target of two different sets of hitmen. Jackson is an investigative reporter who falls for Gould while covering the case. Light-hearted comedy dampened by overly realistic violence.
Dist.: Nelson

DISCREET CHARM OF THE BOURGEOISIE, THE 1972 French
★★ PG Comedy 1:40
☑ Adult situations
Dir: Luis Buñuel ***Cast:*** Fernando Rey, Delphine Seyrig, Stephane Audran, Bulle Ogier, Jean-Pierre Cassel, Julian Bertheau
► Deliberately confusing but still exhilarating film is actually an elaborate practical joke: six wealthy friends are continually interrupted as they sit down to dinner. Subtle blend of illusion and reality creates the feel of an incomprehensible dream, but adventurous viewers will be rewarded by brilliant acting and often hilarious writing by Buñuel and Jean-Claude Carriere. Oscar-nominated for the screenplay, and winner of the Best Foreign Film Oscar. Also available in a dubbed version. [S]
Dist.: Media

DISORDERLIES 1987
★★★ PG Comedy 1:26
☑ Brief nudity, explicit language
Dir: Michael Schultz ***Cast:*** Ralph Bellamy, Damon Wimbley, Darren Robinson, Mark Morales, Tony Plana, Anthony Geary
► Debt-ridden Geary plots the death of wealthy uncle Bellamy by hiring the Fat Boys rap group (Wimbley, Robinson and Morales) as his nurses. But the rappers turn the tables on Geary and his Mafia hitmen and restore Bellamy's spirits in broad slapstick reminiscent of the Three Stooges. Highlight is the film's only rap number, "Baby You're a Rich Man." (CC)
Dist.: Warner

DISORDERLY ORDERLY, THE 1964
★★ NR Comedy 1:30
Dir: Frank Tashlin ***Cast:*** Jerry Lewis, Glenda Farrell, Susan Oliver, Everett Sloane, Karen Sharpe, Jack E. Leonard
► Lewis saves for medical school by working as a hospital orderly. Unfortunately, he's afflicted with "identification empathy," causing him to suffer the same pains as his patients. Typically broad Lewis slapstick highlighted by a climactic ambulance chase. Sharpe as a nurse and Oliver as a suicidal patient are rivals for Jerry's affections.
Dist.: Paramount

DISORGANIZED CRIME 1989
★★★★ R Comedy 1:38
☑ Explicit language, mild violence
Dir: Jim Kouf ***Cast:*** Corbin Bernsen, Lou Diamond Phillips, Ruben Blades, Fred Gwynne, Ed O'Neill, Hoyt Axton, Daniel Roebuck, William Russ
► New Jersey crook Bernsen assembles gang of robbers to pull off Montana bank heist.

However, the clumsy crooks have to do it without the mastermind when Bernsen is forced to flee from cops O'Neill and Roebuck. Modestly engaging caper never takes itself too seriously. Ingratiating cast has an infectious good time; Gwynne is the standout.
Dist.: Buena Vista

DISTANT DRUMS 1951
★ **NR Action-Adventure 1:41**
Dir: Raoul Walsh   *Cast:* Gary Cooper, Mari Aldon, Richard Webb, Arthur Hunnicutt, Ray Teal, Robert Barrat
▶ Cooper leads an Army expedition against gunrunners in 1840 Florida. Surrounded by hostile Seminoles, he and his men are pushed deep into the Everglades, where they are picked off by unseen assailants. Interesting reworking of director Walsh's *Objective, Burma!* has good action to compensate for dull passages.
Dist.: Republic

DISTANT HARMONY 1988
★★★ **G Documentary/Music 1:25**
Dir: DeWitt Sage   *Cast:* Luciano Pavarotti, Kallen Esperian, Madelyn Renee
▶ Documentary covers 1986 tour of China by renowned tenor Pavarotti and the Genoa Opera. The star performs arias from *La Boheme,* gives a master class to Chinese singers, and becomes the first Westerner to sing in Beijing's Great Hall of the People. Opera fans will especially enjoy Pavarotti's closing "Come Back to Sorrento." Scenery vibrantly recorded by cinematographer Miroslav Ondricek.
Dist.: Pacific Arts

DISTANT THUNDER 1988
★★★ **R Drama 1:54**
☑ Adult situations, explicit language, violence
Dir: Rick Rosenthal   *Cast:* John Lithgow, Ralph Macchio, Kerrie Keane, Jamey Sheridan, Reb Brown, Denis Arndt
▶ High schooler Macchio journeys to Pacific Northwest for reunion with father Lithgow, a shell-shocked Vietnam vet he hasn't seen in a decade. Unable to cope with society, Lithgow retreats to the wilderness with other displaced vets. There he finally confronts the memories of his war experiences. Earnest but low-keyed drama is glum and often maudlin.
Dist.: Paramount

DISTANT VOICES, STILL LIVES 1989 British
☆ **PG-13 Drama 1:25**
☑ Adult situations, explicit language, violence
Dir: Terence Davies   *Cast:* Freda Dowie, Pete Postlethwaite, Angela Walsh, Dean Williams, Lorraine Ashbourne
▶ Highly stylized collection of disparate scenes from the life of a desperately unhappy working-class British family. Story centers on father Postlethwaite's erratic behavior: abusive one minute, loving the next. The family drowns its sorrows by often breaking into song.

Hampered by the lack of a narrative thread, film's obvious artiness indeed makes this one "distant."
Dist.: IVE

DIVA 1982 French
★★ **R Mystery-Suspense 1:58**
Dir: Jean-Jacques Beineix   *Cast:* Wilhelminia Wiggins Fernandez, Frederic Andrei, Richard Bohringer, Thuy An Luu, Jacques Fabbri
▶ Messenger Andrei tapes reclusive opera star idol Fernandez and gets involved in a complex maze of intrigue. Thriller plot is an excuse to display the dazzling talents of director Beineix, who creates a New Wave Paris full of hip visual references and throws in some jazzy action and chases to boot. Ⓢ
Dist.: MGM/UA

DIVINE NYMPH, THE 1979 Italian
★★ **NR Drama 1:30**
☑ Brief nudity, adult situations
Dir: Giuseppe Patrone Griffi   *Cast:* Laura Antonelli, Terence Stamp, Marcello Mastroianni, Michelle Placido
▶ Vixenish beauty Antonelli plays rich noblemen Stamp and Mastroianni against one another amid orgiastic decadence of the twenties. Fiery triangle fizzles as lovers fall to fascism and suicide, and Antonelli goes into hiding. Ornate sets and period detail steal the show from pointless plot. Brief nude scene will disappoint Antonelli fans. Ⓢ
Dist.: MPI

DIVORCE OF LADY X, THE 1938 British
★★ **NR Comedy 1:32**
Dir: Tim Whelan   *Cast:* Merle Oberon, Laurence Olivier, Binnie Barnes, Ralph Richardson
▶ Frothy drawing-room farce about London divorce attorney Olivier forced to share his hotel room during a storm with pretty debutante Oberon, who Olivier assumes is his client Richardson's wife. Slight plot is buoyed by the charming stars and elegant early use of Technicolor.
Dist.: Nelson

D.O.A. 1949
★★★ **NR Mystery-Suspense 1:23 B&W**
Dir: Rudolph Maté   *Cast:* Edmond O'Brien, Pamela Britton, Luther Adler, Neville Brand, Henry Hart
▶ Strong film noir has a fascinating premise: accountant O'Brien, vacationing in San Francisco, learns he's been given a lethal poison. He searches desperately for his murderer before the poison takes effect. Terse dialogue and accomplished direction have made this a cult favorite. Remade in 1988 and in 1969 as *Color Me Dead.*
Dist.: KVC Ⓒ

D.O.A. 1988
★★★ **R Mystery-Suspense 1:40**
☑ Explicit language, violence

Dir. Rocky Morton, Annabel Jankel *Cast:*
Dennis Quaid, Meg Ryan, Charlotte Rampling, Daniel Stern, Jay Patterson, Jane
Kaczmarek
▶ Berkeley professor Quaid, poisoned by a
slow-acting but fatal serum, has twenty-four
hours to find his killers. With Ryan's help, he
confronts an antagonistic group of suspects,
including academic rival Patterson, jealous
best friend Stern, and villainous benefactor
Rampling. Updated remake of the 1949 film
noir classic maintains the original's intriguing
premise, but sacrifices plotting for baroque visuals and flashy camera tricks.   **(CC)**
Dist.: Buena Vista

DOBERMAN GANG, THE 1972
★ ★ ★ **G Drama/Family 1:27**
Dir: Byron Chudnow *Cast:* Byron Mabe, Hal
Reed, Julie Parrish, Simmy Bow, Jojo D'A-
more, John Tull
▶ Con man Mabe doesn't trust his bumbling
cronies to pull off a difficult bank heist, so he
kidnaps six Dobermans and dog trainer Reed
to perform the robbery without human error.
Ingenious and charming low-budget film led
to a sequel, *The Daring Dobermans.* **(CC)**
Dist.: CBS/Fox

DOCKS OF NEW YORK, THE 1928
★ **NR Drama 1:16 B&W**
Dir: Josef von Sternberg *Cast:* George
Bancroft, Betty Compson, Olga Baclanova,
Mitchell Lewis, Clyde Cook
▶ Haunting, richly detailed story of Bancroft, a
two-fisted stoker in a ship boiler room, and
Compson, a fallen woman he rescues from
suicide. Superb direction adds to the poi-
gnancy of their relationship. Silent master-
piece is among the most beautifully photo-
graphed films of the era. Cassette version
features an organ score by Gaylord Carter.
Dist.: Paramount

DOC SAVAGE: THE MAN OF BRONZE 1975
★ ★ **G Action-Adventure 1:40**
Dir: Michael Anderson *Cast:* Ron Ely, Darrell Zwerling, Paul Gleason, Paul Wexler, Michael Miller, Pamela Hensley
▶ Pulp superhero Doc Savage (Ely) and five
associates travel to 1930s Latin America to
investigate the murder of Ely's father and battle the villainous Wexler. Adaptation of the
Kenneth Robeson novels is generally friendly
and appealing. John Phillip Sousa score is
corny, and special effects from producer
George Pal surprisingly tame, but strapping
Ely is perfectly cast.
Dist.: Warner

DOCTOR AND THE DEVILS, THE 1985
★ **R Horror 1:33**
☑ Nudity, explicit language, violence
Dir: Freddie Francis *Cast:* Timothy Dalton,
Jonathan Pryce, Twiggy, Julian Sands, Ste-
phen Rea, Beryl Reid
▶ Nineteenth-century British laws limit doctor
Dalton's access to a steady source of cadav-

ers for his students; vagabonds Pryce and Rea
come up with a gruesome grave-robbing
scheme to supply his needs. Old-fashioned
horror film adapted from a 1940s Dylan
Thomas screenplay was based on a famous
1830s body-snatching case. Filmed in England. **(CC)**
Dist.: Key

DOCTOR AT LARGE 1957 British
★ **NR Comedy 1:38**
Dir: Ralph Thomas *Cast:* Dirk Bogarde,
Muriel Pavlow, Donald Sinden, James Ro-
berston Justice, Shirley Eaton
▶ Third entry in the "Doctor" series finds Dr.
Simon Sparrow (Bogarde) still searching for a
lucrative practice and still preoccupied with
beautiful women. Looking through want ads
prompts a trip to the Riviera. Plenty of laughs
in this lightweight but amiable comedy.
Based on the novels by Richard Gordon.
Dist.: VidAmerica

DOCTOR AT SEA 1955 British
★ **NR Comedy 1:34**
Dir: Ralph Thomas *Cast:* Dirk Bogarde, Brigitte Bardot, Brenda de Banzie, James Robertson Justice, Maurice Denham
▶ Doctor Bogarde avoids a forced marriage
by signing on as a freighter's medic. The crew
takes an instant dislike to him but eventually
he wins their respect and the love of pretty
French lass Bardot. Simple but pleasant comedy with fine Bogarde in a rare comedic role
and a charming young Bardot. Sequel to the
1954 *Doctor in the House.*
Dist.: VidAmerica

DOCTOR DEATH, SEEKER OF SOULS 1973
☆ **R Horror 1:27**
☑ Explicit language, graphic violence
Dir: Eddie Saeta *Cast:* John Considine,
Barry Coe, Cheryl Miller, Stewart Moss, Leon
Askin, Moe Howard
▶ Scientist Considine has lived for one thousand years but needs new bodies to keep his
soul going. Askin is the disfigured assistant who
helps the good doctor; Miller is the secretary
who is the unwilling subject of Considine's latest experiment. Howard's last performance is
one of the few highlights of an otherwise forgettable flick.
Dist.: Prism

DOCTOR DETROIT 1983
★ ★ **R Comedy 1:30**
☑ Nudity, adult situations, explicit language, violence, adult humor
Dir: Michael Pressman *Cast:* Dan Aykroyd,
Howard Hesseman, Donna Dixon, T. K.
Carter, Fran Drescher, Kate Murtagh
▶ Academia collides with street life when
nerdy professor Aykroyd is roped into impersonating a Chicago pimp. Prof's fright-
wigged, claw-handed "Doctor Detroit" persona helps him gallantly save beleaguered
hookers-with-hearts-of-gold from dreaded
mobster known as "Mom" (Murtagh). Durable

premise, frantic execution given life by Dan's clowning and the attractive ladies. James Brown performs at the climactic Hooker's Ball. Aykroyd met future wife Dixon on the set.
Dist.: MCA

DOCTOR DOLITTLE 1967
★ ★ ★ ★ NR Musical/Family 2:24
Dir: Richard Fleischer   *Cast:* Rex Harrison, Samantha Eggar, Anthony Newley, Richard Attenborough, Peter Bull, Geoffrey Holder
▶ Musical adaptation of Hugh Lofting's children's classic. Eccentric doctor Harrison, who prefers beasts to people, goes on journey with fiancée Eggar and discovers strange creatures. Pacing lags in this mammoth production, but some decent moments from Rex and the Leslie Bricusse score (Oscar-winning Best Song, "Talk to the Animals"). **(CC)**
Dist.: CBS/Fox

DOCTOR IN DISTRESS 1963 British
★ NR Comedy 1:42
Dir: Ralph Thomas   *Cast:* Dirk Bogarde, James Robertson Justice, Samantha Eggar, Barbara Murray, Mylene Demongeot, Donald Houston
▶ Two intertwining medical love stories: crusty surgeon Justice is hit by Cupid's arrow when he meets physiotherapist Murray while model/actress Eggar has a similar effect on younger doctor Bogarde. Lighthearted lark is running on empty, although series continued without Bogarde and with decreasing inspiration.
Dist.: VidAmerica

DOCTOR IN THE HOUSE 1954 British
★ ★ NR Comedy 1:32
Dir: Ralph Thomas   *Cast:* Dirk Bogarde, Muriel Pavlow, Kenneth More, Donald Sinden, Kay Kendall, James Robertson Justice
▶ First in a long series of medical comedies focuses on intern Bogarde's efforts to seduce women and latch onto a wealthy practice. Unfortunately, he's guided by three students who have already failed their first year at school. Well-cast story is consistently bright and funny.
Dist.: Paramount

DOCTORS' WIVES 1971
★ ★ R Drama 1:42
Ⓥ Explicit language, strong sexual content
Dir: George Schaefer   *Cast:* Dyan Cannon, Richard Crenna, Gene Hackman, Carroll O'Connor, Ralph Bellamy, Rachel Roberts
▶ Trashy Cannon decides to seduce four other doctor husbands but is shot by her own jealous mate; incident provokes the other doctors' wives to grapple with their failing marriages. Bad-taste soap opera evokes tongue-in-cheek humor; Roberts's description of a lesbian encounter is the film's low-comedy high point.
Dist.: RCA/Columbia

DOCTOR TAKES A WIFE, THE 1940
★ ★ ★ ★ NR Comedy 1:28 B&W
Dir: Alexander Hall   *Cast:* Loretta Young, Ray Milland, Reginald Gardiner, Gail Patrick, Edmund Gwenn
▶ Lively little romantic comedy about two marriage-haters forced to live together for publicity purposes. Young and Milland star as the bachelorette/authoress and medical college instructor who lock horns in a sprightly battle of the sexes.
Dist.: RCA/Columbia

DOCTOR X 1932
★ ★ NR Horror 1:20
Dir: Michael Curtiz   *Cast:* Lionel Atwill, Lee Tracy, Fay Wray, Preston Foster, Arthur Edmund Carewe
▶ Newspaper reporter Tracy tracks New York's "Moon Murderer" to scientist Atwill's Long Island mansion. Tracy romances Atwill's daughter Wray, unaware that experiments with deadly "synthetic flesh" are proceeding in her father's lab. Although long considered a cult treasure, this fails to lives up to expectations. Three noteworthy aspects: inventive Anton Grot sets, Max Factor makeup, and two-strip Technicolor hues restored to their original glory on cassette.
Dist.: MGM/UA

DOCTOR ZHIVAGO 1965
★ ★ ★ ★ ★ PG Drama 3:17
Dir: David Lean   *Cast:* Omar Sharif, Julie Christie, Tom Courtenay, Rod Steiger, Geraldine Chaplin, Alec Guinness, Ralph Richardson, Rita Tushingham
▶ Sweeping epic of the Russian Revolution seen through the eyes of sensitive doctor Sharif and his beautiful lover, Christie. Enormously popular romance, based on the novel by Nobel Laureate Boris Pasternak, is filled with thrilling spectacle. Winner of five Oscars, including Screenplay (Robert Bolt) and score (Maurice Jarre). **(CC)**
Dist.: MGM/UA

DODES'KA-DEN 1970 Japanese
☆ NR Drama 2:20
Ⓥ Explicit language
Dir: Akira Kurosawa   *Cast:* Yoshitaka Zushi, Kin Sugai, Toshiyuki Tonomura, Tomoko Yamazaki
▶ The lives of various dwellers of a squalid Tokyo slum examined with sympathy and insight by the master Japanese director. Virtually plotless story line follows a man who dreams of building a palace while his son begs for food, a homeless retarded boy, a daughter who supports her father by making artificial flowers, etc. Slowly paced and extremely sentimental. Ⓢ
Dist.: Nelson

DODGE CITY 1939
★ ★ ★ NR Western 1:45
Dir: Michael Curtiz   *Cast:* Errol Flynn, Olivia

de Havilland, Ann Sheridan, Bruce Cabot,
Frank McHugh, Alan Hale
▶ Rousing, large-scale adventure with Flynn
(in his first Western) donning a sheriff's star to
clean up a corrupt frontier town. The dashing
star shows off his prowess by stopping a stam-
pede, a burning runaway train, and an enormous barroom brawl (a classic of its kind). Provided the story line for Mel Brooks's Western
satire *Blazing Saddles.*
Dist.: Playhouse

DODSWORTH 1936
★ ★ ★ NR Drama 1:41 B&W
Dir: William Wyler *Cast:* Walter Huston, Ruth
Chatterton, Paul Lukas, Mary Astor, David
Niven, Maria Ouspenskaya
▶ Intelligent, moving drama about retired
auto tycoon Huston, social-climbing wife
Chatterton, and the changes they undergo
during a European vacation. Niven plays a
gigolo who seduces Chatterton; Astor, a
divorcée who comforts Huston. Sincere adap-
tation of a Sinclair Lewis novel is notable for its
sympathetic, adult treatment of marriage.
Nominated for seven Academy Awards, in-
cluding Best Picture, Actor, Director, and
Screenplay.
Dist.: Nelson

DOG DAY 1983 French
☆ NR Mystery-Suspense 1:45
☑ Rape, nudity, adult situations, explicit
language, graphic violence
Dir: Yves Boisset *Cast:* Lee Marvin, Miou-
Miou, Bernadette Lafont, Victor Lanoux, Tina
Louise
▶ Marvin pulls off an armored car robbery and
buries the loot on a French farm. Farm wife
Miou-Miou hides Marvin, but her loutish hus-
band finds him. Before long, they are all killing
and raping each other. Possibly meant as a
black comedy, horridly violent ordeal has no
sympathetic characters and very little in the
way of suspense.
Dist.: Vestron

DOG DAY AFTERNOON 1975
★ ★ ★ ★ R Drama 2:04
☑ Adult situations, explicit language, vio-
lence
Dir: Sidney Lumet *Cast:* Al Pacino, John
Cazale, James Broderick, Charles Durning,
Chris Sarandon
▶ Pacino stars in a true story of a New York
City man who holds up a bank to finance a
sex change operation for his lover Sarandon.
Plan goes awry and Pacino is forced to nego-
tiate with the cops. Pacino's no-holds-barred
performance is tops. Gritty suspense, master-
fully directed by Lumet. Oscar-nominated for
Best Picture, Director, Actor (Pacino), and Sup-
porting Actor (Sarandon). Oscar for Best Origi-
nal Screenplay.
Dist.: Warner

DOG OF FLANDERS, A 1959
★ ★ ★ ★ NR Family 1:36

Dir: James B. Clark *Cast:* David Ladd, Donald Crisp, Theodore Bikel, Max Croiset,
Monique Ahrens, Siohban Taylor
▶ Turn-of-the-century Belgium provides picturesque backdrop for heartwarming story of
orphaned Ladd's efforts to save sickly dog.
Crippled grandfather Crisp, a milkman, sacrifices his meager food to help the canine. Third
film version of Ouida's beloved children's
novel retains original's bittersweet charm.
Ideal for younger viewers.
Dist.: Paramount

DOGS IN SPACE 1987 Australian
☆ R Drama 1:48
☑ Explicit language, violence
Dir: Richard Lowenstein *Cast:* Michael Hutchence, Saskia Post, Nique Needles,
Deanna Bond, Chris Haywood
▶ Title canines are a grungy punk rock band
who live communally with other youngsters in
a garbage-strewn house. Hutchence is a
junkie who sticks needles in arms of girlfriend
Post, while other middle-class dropouts get
sick in bathroom and the music blasts nonstop. Nonnarrative film revels in squalor and
pointlessness of characters' lives.
Dist.: CBS/Fox

DOGS OF WAR, THE 1980 British
★ ★ ★ R Action-Adventure 2:02
☑ Explicit language, violence
Dir: John Irvin *Cast:* Christopher Walken,
Tom Berenger, Colin Blakely, Hugh Millais,
Paul Freeman, JoBeth Williams
▶ Perceptive adaptation of Frederick For-
syth's best-seller about mercenaries concen-
trates on callous American Walken, captured
and tortured in the tiny African republic of
Zangaro. He escapes and returns home to or-
ganize a coup against Zangaro's tyrant. Jar-
ring battle scenes frame an unusually de-
tailed look at Third World politics.
Dist.: MGM/UA

DOG TAGS 1989
☆ R War 1:33
☑ Nudity, explicit language, violence
Dir: Romano Scavolini *Cast:* Clive Wood,
Mike Monty, Baird Stafford, Robert Hau-
frecht, Chris Hilton
▶ Commando Wood saves some G.I.s from a
Communist prison, then leads the ragtag
band on a secret mission to find a downed
helicopter. When the chopper turns out to be
filled with gold dog tags, the survivors of the
jungle trek get greedy. Cynical, pretentious
exploitation picture has little to offer action
fans.

DOIN' TIME 1985
★ R Comedy 1:17
☑ Nudity, adult situations, explicit lan-
guage, mild violence
Dir: George Mendeluk *Cast:* Jeff Altman,
Dey Young, Richard Mulligan, John Vernon,
Jimmie Walker, Judy Landers, Mike Mazurki,
Muhammad Ali

▶ Innocent Altman is incarcerated in an "animal house" penitentiary where the prisoners enjoy parties, music, and women. Dim new warden Mulligan fails to restore law and order; Altman fights guard in televised bout that may get him sprung. Not as funny as it thinks it is.
Dist.: Warner

DOIN' TIME ON PLANET EARTH 1988
☆ PG Comedy 1:25
☑ Adult situations, explicit language
Dir: Charles Matthau   *Cast:* Nicholas Strouse, Hugh Gillin, Gloria Henry, Hugh O'-Brian, Adam West, Andrea Thompson
▶ Arizona lad Strouse learns from his computer that he's an alien, but can't return home until he unlocks code secreted in his DNA. To open his DNA package, he must seduce singer Thompson. Offbeat black comedy suffers from low budget and hit-or-miss gags. Directing debut for Matthau (son of Walter Matthau) features cameos by Maureen Stapleton and Roddy McDowall.
Dist.: Warner

$ (DOLLARS) 1971
★ ★ ★ R Action-Adventure 2:01
☑ Nudity, adult situations, explicit language
Dir: Richard Brooks   *Cast:* Warren Beatty, Goldie Hawn, Gert Frobe, Robert Webber, Scott Brady, Arthur Brauss
▶ Breezy heist film set in Germany features a charming Beatty as a security expert who loots three safe deposit boxes with the help of Hamburg hooker Hawn. The victims—dope dealer Brauss, mob courier Webber, and crooked Army sergeant Brady—pursue Beatty and Hawn in a clever climactic chase.
Dist.: RCA/Columbia

DOLLMAKER, THE 1984
★ ★ ★ NR Drama/MFTV 2:30
Dir: Daniel Petrie   *Cast:* Jane Fonda, Levon Helm, Amanda Plummer, Susan Kingsley, Geraldine Page, Christine Ebersol
▶ Illiterate whittling folk artist Fonda finds hard times when she and her children leave the Kentucky hills to follow husband Helm to Detroit during World War II. She struggles to adjust to her new way of life while attempting to pursue her craft. Fonda won an Emmy for her strong, simple performance in this above-par TV offering. **(CC)**
Dist.: CBS/Fox

DOLLS 1987
★ ★ R Horror 1:18
☑ Explicit language, violence
Dir: Stuart Gordon   *Cast:* Ian Patrick Williams, Carolyn Purdy-Gordon, Carrie Lorraine, Stephen Lee, Guy Rolfe, Bunty Bailey
▶ London family caught in a storm takes refuge in a gloomy mansion filled with handmade dolls. Young Lorraine notices something odd about the toys, but cruel stepmother Purdy-Gordon and weak-willed father Williams ignore her warnings. Satisfying effort has

ingenious special effects, nice comic sensibility, and relatively toned-down gore.
Dist.: Vestron

DOLL'S HOUSE, A 1973 British
★ G Drama 1:35
Dir: Patrick Garland   *Cast:* Claire Bloom, Anthony Hopkins, Ralph Richardson, Denholm Elliott, Anna Massey, Edith Evans
▶ Ibsen's proto-feminist drama is lifted almost intact from a 1971 Broadway stage presentation, with Bloom as the wife who makes a stand for independence from stuffy banker husband Hopkins. The crisis is reached when Hopkins's ill health requires an expensive trip to the country, and Bloom takes out a dubious loan to pay for it. Bloom and Hopkins excellently portray their characters' respective growth and disintegration, but tasteful rendering lacks pizzazz.
Dist.: MPI

DOMINICK AND EUGENE 1988
★ ★ ★ ★ PG-13 Drama 1:51
☑ Adult situations, explicit language
Dir: Robert M. Young   *Cast:* Tom Hulce, Ray Liotta, Jamie Lee Curtis, Todd Graff, Mimi Cecchini, Robert Levine
▶ Hulce, mildly retarded twin of medical student Liotta, works as a Pittsburgh garbageman to pay his brother's tuition. Their carefully balanced relationship is threatened when Liotta considers transferring to school in California. Emotionally charged soap opera boasts terrific acting in difficult roles. Curtis is appealing as Liotta's girlfriend.
Dist.: Orion

DOMINIQUE 1978 British
★ PG Mystery-Suspense 1:40
☑ Adult situations, mild violence
Dir: Michael Anderson   *Cast:* Cliff Robertson, Jean Simmons, Jenny Agutter, Simon Ward, Ron Moody, Judy Geeson
▶ Robertson drives his unstable wife Simmons to suicide. After her funeral, he finds himself cracking up as he is haunted by mysterious images and sounds. Classy, old-fashioned ghost story starts off very slowly but steadily builds atmosphere and tension. Retitled *Dominique Is Dead.*
Dist.: Prism

DOMINO 1988 Italian
☆ R Drama 1:35
☑ Nudity, strong sexual content, explicit language
Dir: Ivana Massetti   *Cast:* Brigitte Nielsen, Thomas Arana, Daniela Azzone, Lucien Bruchon, Pascal Druant, Cyrus Ellis
▶ Filmmaker Nielsen, depressed over her inability to fall in love, discusses the problem with her pet turtle, various men, and a prostitute. She has an affair with a married sound engineer, but is really more turned on by a mysterious man who spies on her. Unintentional laugh riot features artsy photography, soft core plotting, pretentious dialogue, and

Nielsen in various states of undress. Soundtrack makes liberal misuse of Billie Holiday.
Dist.: IVE

DOMINO PRINCIPLE, THE 1977
★★★ R Mystery-Suspense 1:35
☑ Violence
Dir: Stanley Kramer ***Cast:*** Gene Hackman, Candice Bergen, Edward Albert, Mickey Rooney, Richard Widmark
► Prisoner Hackman is busted out of jail by mysterious organization that wants him to commit a political assassination. He demurs and they come after him and wife Bergen. Director Kramer tries to create a mood of mid-seventies post-Watergate mistrust and paranoia; fine cast.
Dist.: CBS/Fox

DONA FLOR AND HER TWO HUSBANDS
1978 Brazilian
★ R Fantasy/Comedy 1:46
☑ Nudity, adult situations, explicit language
Dir: Bruno Barreto ***Cast:*** Sonia Braga, Jose Wilker, Mauro Mendonca, Dinorah Brillanti
► Widow Braga marries a straightlaced and sexually dull pharmacist. Her deceased husband, an irresponsible but exciting womanizer and gambler, returns in the form of a nude ghost, leading to an unusual ménage à trois. Exotic comedy with likable Braga, colorful Bahia backgrounds and tuneful Brazilian music. Extremely racy; remade and toned down in America as Sally Field's *Kiss Me Goodbye*. [S]
Dist.: Warner

DON IS DEAD, THE 1973
★ R Drama 1:54
☑ Brief nudity, adult situations, explicit language, violence
Dir: Richard Fleischer ***Cast:*** Anthony Quinn, Frederic Forrest, Robert Forster, Al Lettieri, Angel Tompkins, Vic Tayback
► When the old Don dies, the Cosa Nostra is in danger of falling apart. Quinn is elected as the new Don, but Forrest and Lettieri refuse to obey him. They send former Playmate Tompkins to keep Quinn occupied while they declare war on his men. Bloody, violent attempt to cash in on *The Godfather* follows a routine gangster formula.
Dist.: MCA

DONKEY SKIN 1971 French
☆ NR Fantasy 1:30
☑ Adult situations
Dir: Jacques Demy ***Cast:*** Catherine Deneuve, Jean Marais, Jacques Perrin, Delphine Seyrig, Fernand Ledoux, Micheline Presle
► Dying queen Deneuve makes king Marais promise never to marry anyone less beautiful than she. The royal daughter (also Deneuve) is thus the only woman pretty enough to wed him. To avoid incest, fairy godmother Seyrig disguises her as a servant in a donkey skin. Grandly produced, if somewhat precious, adult fairy tale. Pretty score by Michel Legrand. [S]
Dist.: Nelson

DONOVAN'S BRAIN 1953
★★ NR Sci-Fi 1:21 B&W
Dir: Felix Feist ***Cast:*** Lew Ayres, Gene Evans, Nancy Davis, Steve Brodie, Lisa K. Howard
► Scientist Ayres keeps dead man's brain alive and pulsating, then becomes possessed by its evil spirit. Wife Davis (the future Mrs. Reagan) frets in the background. Pretty good B-movie chiller with a cult following. The type of movie Steve Martin spoofed in *The Man With Two Brains*.
Dist.: MGM/UA

DONOVAN'S REEF 1963
★★★★ NR Comedy 1:39
Dir: John Ford ***Cast:*** John Wayne, Lee Marvin, Elizabeth Allen, Jack Warden, Cesar Romero, Dorothy Lamour, Victor McLaglen
► Rambunctious comedy set in the South Pacific about burly bar owner Wayne, his old Navy buddy Marvin, and veteran Warden who's taken a Polynesian wife. Plot deals with the boys hiding Warden's new family from prim Boston visitor Allen. Sentimental in stretches, but the island locations make a beautiful backdrop to Wayne's slapstick fistfights with Marvin.
Dist.: Paramount

DON'S PARTY 1982 Australian
★★ NR Comedy 1:30
☑ Nudity, strong sexual content, explicit language, adult humor
Dir: Bruce Beresford ***Cast:*** John Hargreaves, Pat Bishop, Jeannie Drynan, Graeme Blundell, Veronica Lang, Graham Kennedy
► In 1969 Australia, a teacher throws an election night party for his friends and their mates. A mood of "quiet desperation" builds as couples pair off. This sexual vaudeville, intercut with political ironies, was an early effort from director Beresford.
Dist.: VidAmerica

DON'T CRY, IT'S ONLY THUNDER 1982
★★★★ PG Drama 1:48
☑ Adult situations, explicit language, violence
Dir: Peter Werner ***Cast:*** Dennis Christopher, Susan Saint James, Roger Aaron Brown, Lisa Lu, James Whitmore, Jr., Thu Thuy
► U.S. Army medic Christopher, working in a Saigon hospital, is recruited by nuns to steal black market supplies for their orphanage. Moved by the orphans' plight, he recruits pretty young doctor Saint James to help him. Inspirational story, based on a true incident, is handled with compassion and humor.
Dist.: RCA/Columbia

DON'T DRINK THE WATER 1969
★★ G Comedy 1:40

Dir: Howard Morris   *Cast:* Jackie Gleason, Estelle Parsons, Ted Bessell, Michael Constantine, Joan Delaney, Richard Libertini
▶ American tourists Gleason, Parsons, and Delaney inadvertently wind up in a Communist country. They are accused of being spies and become the focus of an international incident. Flat farce adapted from the Woody Allen play has a few chuckles but end results will leave both Allen and Gleason fans feeling shortchanged.
Dist.: Nelson

DONT LOOK BACK 1967
★ **NR Documentary 1:35 B&W**
Dir: D. A. Pennebaker   *Cast:* Bob Dylan, Joan Baez, Donovan (Leitch), Bobby Neuwirth, Alan Ginsberg, Albert Grossman
▶ Little concert footage, but lots of backstage and hotel room talk as filmmaker Pennebaker follows elusive and oracular sixties music star Bob Dylan on 1965 tour in Great Britian. Most intimate portrait of Dylan ever filmed shows the soon-to-be-superstar baiting the press, writing songs, and exchanging riffs with Donavan. Still fresh and surprising, film set tone for scores of docus to come. Songs include "Don't Think Twice, It's All Right," "The Times They Are a Changin'," "It's All Over Now, Baby Blue," and "Subterranean Homesick Blues," a sequence since excerpted as a rock video.
Dist.: Paramount

DON'T LOOK NOW 1973 British/Italian
★★ **R Drama 1:50**
☑ Nudity, adult situations, explicit language
Dir: Nicolas Roeg   *Cast:* Julie Christie, Donald Sutherland, Hilary Mason, Clelia Matania, Massimo Serato, Renato Scarpa
▶ After the death of their daughter, art historian Sutherland and wife Christie are approached by blind seer Mason, who claims she can contact the deceased girl. Haunting, richly detailed occult thriller from a Daphne du Maurier story makes marvelous use of gloomy Venice settings. Confusing plot doesn't detract from violent climax or charged love scenes between Sutherland and Christie.
Dist.: Paramount

DON'T OPEN UNTIL CHRISTMAS 1984 British
☆ **R Horror 1:26**
☑ Nudity, explicit language, violence
Dir: Edmund Purdom   *Cast:* Edmund Purdom, Alan Lake, Belinda Mayne, Gerry Sundquist, Mark Jones, Caroline Munro
▶ A knife-wielding maniac is carving up all the Santas in London, and it's up to harried Scotland Yard inspector Purdom to catch him. Decoy cops in Santa suits are no avail, and killer proceeds to dispatch witnesses as well. Story's holiday doings are gruesome and unpleasant.
Dist.: Vestron

DON'T RAISE THE BRIDGE, LOWER THE RIVER 1968
★★ **G Comedy 1:39**
Dir: Jerry Paris   *Cast:* Jerry Lewis, Terry-Thomas, Jacqueline Pearce, Bernard Cribbins, Patricia Routledge
▶ Wide-eyed American expatriate Lewis finds his marriage to Pearce in trouble as a result of his bizarre money-making plans. Con man Terry-Thomas lures him into scheme to steal top secret oil drill. Slapstick overwhelms plot in typical Lewis vehicle. Director Paris cameos as a baseball umpire.
Dist.: RCA/Columbia

DOOMED TO DIE 1940
★ **NR Mystery-Suspense 1:09**
Dir: William Nigh   *Cast:* Boris Karloff, Marjorie Reynolds, Grant Withers, Melvin Lang, Guy Usher, Catherine Craig
▶ When a rich shipping mogul is murdered in the company of his daughter's boyfriend, the beau becomes the number-one suspect. However, brilliant Chinese sleuth Mr. Wong (Karloff) sets out to prove they've got the wrong man. A Chinatown tong war and big boat fire are elements in this ingenious fifth entry in the series.
Dist.: Video Yesteryear

DOOR TO DOOR 1984
★★ **PG Comedy 1:34**
☑ Explicit language
Dir: Patrick Bailey   *Cast:* Ron Leibman, Arliss Howard, Jane Kaczmarek, Alan Austin, Mimi Honze
▶ Leibman shines as a glib, larcenous salesman who entices Howard into a scam to sell vacuums. Since Leibman doesn't work for the vacuum company, they're soon pursued by angry, tenacious detective Austin. Thin comedy coasts on the strength of its stars.
Dist.: Media

DORIAN GRAY 1970 British/Italian
☆ **R Horror 1:32**
☑ Nudity, adult situations, explicit language, violence
Dir: Massimo Dallamano   *Cast:* Helmut Berger, Richard Todd, Herbert Lom, Marie Liljedahl, Margaret Lee, Maria Rohm
▶ In London, Dorian Gray (Berger) lives a life of lust, sin, and depravity of which his friend Lom heartily approves. However, Gray's portrait, painted by Todd, deteriorates even as his appearance doesn't. Adaptation of the Oscar Wilde classic is loose in every sense of the word. Pure exploitation, poorly acted, written, and directed.
Dist.: Republic

DO THE RIGHT THING 1989
★★ **R Drama 2:00**
☑ Nudity, explicit language, violence
Dir: Spike Lee   *Cast:* Danny Aiello, Ossie Davis, Ruby Dee, Richard Edson, Giancarlo Esposito, Spike Lee, Bill Nunn, John Turturro, Robin Harris, Rosie Perez, John Savage

► Bed-Stuy, Brooklyn, pizza parlor proprietor Aiello is proud of his relationship with neighborhood blacks like his employee Lee. However, during a sizzling summer day, racial tensions build to the point of violence. Explosive exploration probes racism's root causes through complex characterizations and streetsmart dialogue, although not everyone will agree with its conclusion. Standouts in the large cast include Davis as "Da Mayor" and Harris as sidewalk commentator Sweet Dick Willie. Oscar nominations for Aiello and Lee's screenplay. **(CC)**
Dist.: MCA

DOUBLE DEAL 1984 Australian
★ ★ NR Mystery-Suspense 1:30
☑ Adult situations, mild violence
Dir: Brian Kavanagh *Cast:* Louis Jourdan, Angela Punch-McGregor, Warwick Comber, Peter Cummins
► Punch-McGregor, a young fashion model bored with marriage to older Jourdan, fakes her own kidnapping and runs off with prowler Comber on a mini-crime spree. Prowler, model, and wronged husband all double-cross each other. Plot twists and turns toward a surprise ending involving a priceless opal. Decent little mystery.
Dist.: Virgin

DOUBLE DYNAMITE 1951
★ NR Comedy 1:21 B&W
Dir: Irving Cummings *Cast:* Frank Sinatra, Jane Russell, Groucho Marx, Don McGuire, Harry Hayden
► Bank teller Sinatra loves co-worker Russell, but can't afford romance until a gangster showers him with money from a horse race long shot. When a shortage in the bank's accounts appears, Sinatra is suspected of being an embezzler. Even Groucho can't rescue this lackluster comedy.
Dist.: Turner

DOUBLE EXPOSURE 1982
★ R Mystery-Suspense 1:35
☑ Nudity, adult situations, explicit language, violence
Dir: William Hillman *Cast:* James Stacy, Michael Callan, Joanna Pettet, Cleavon Little, Seymour Cassel, William Hillman
► Photographer Stacy has an attitude problem toward women: he likes to kill them. When models and prostitutes drop right and left, Stacy's shrink gets suspicious, but needs more info before going to cops. Meanwhile, Stacy begins affair with sweet blond who doesn't suspect his real nature. Gruesome violence.
Dist.: Vestron

DOUBLE EXPOSURE 1987
★ R Comedy 1:43
☑ Nudity, adult situations, explicit language, violence
Dir: Nico Mastorakis *Cast:* Mark Hennessy, Scott King, Hope Marie Carlton, John Vernon

► A pair of California beach bums photographing attractive derrieres accidentally snap a murder in progress. Trail begins with gorgeous blond with a tattoo on her rear end. Certain anatomical part is butt of much humor. Fundamentally sophomoric idea lacks plot interest. Also known as *Terminal Exposure*.
Dist.: Vestron

DOUBLE INDEMNITY 1944
★ ★ ★ ★ NR Mystery-Suspense 1:47 B&W
Dir: Billy Wilder *Cast:* Fred MacMurray, Barbara Stanwyck, Edward G. Robinson, Porter Hall, Jean Evans, Tom Powers
► Nifty crime melodrama from the James M. Cain novel. Treacherous housewife Stanwyck plots the murder of her husband with the help of cynical insurance agent MacMurray. Insurance investigator Robinson pieces together the scheme. Blistering dialogue and a devious plot by Wilder and Raymond Chandler made this one of the most memorable films of the forties. Robinson is outstanding. Received seven Oscar nominations.
Dist.: MCA

DOUBLE LIFE, A 1947
★ ★ ★ NR Drama 1:43 B&W
Dir: George Cukor *Cast:* Ronald Colman, Signe Hasso, Edmond O'Brien, Shelley Winters, Ray Collins, Phillip Loeb
► Absorbing drama won Colman an Oscar for his work as a brilliant stage actor who can't separate his roles from reality. Rehearsals for *Othello* lead to tragic complications as unreasonable jealousy consumes his life. Winters's turn as a waitress attracted to Colman made her a star. Miklos Rozsa's brooding score also won an Oscar; intelligent script by Ruth Gordon and Garson Kanin received a nomination. Look for John Derek as a stenographer and Paddy Chayefsky as a photographer.
Dist.: Republic

DOUBLE McGUFFIN, THE 1979
★ ★ ★ PG Family 1:41
☑ Explicit language
Dir: Joe Camp *Cast:* Elke Sommer, George Kennedy, Ernest Borgnine, Ed "Too Tall" Jones, Lyle Alzado, Dion Pride
► A group of youngsters stumble on a plot to assassinate Sommer, a Middle Eastern leader. Clues lead them to a corpse and a cache of arms, but evidence keeps disappearing and cops are dubious. Kids take it upon themselves to trap baddies. High-quality family picture from makers of *Benji* has Orson Welles in uncredited voiceover.
Dist.: Vestron

DOUBLE TROUBLE 1967
★ ★ ★ NR Musical 1:30
Dir: Norman Taurog *Cast:* Elvis Presley, Annette Day, John Williams, Yvonne Romain, The Wiere Brothers, Chips Rafferty
► During a European tour Elvis helps young heiress Day elude murderous uncle Williams,

who's after her inheritance. Bumbling smugglers also chase the duo in this lightweight blend of comedy, action, and music. Killer version of "Long Legged Girl" lights up the film. *Dist.:* MGM/UA

DOWN AND OUT IN BEVERLY HILLS 1986
★ ★ ★ ★ R Comedy 1:37
▢ Brief nudity, adult situations, explicit language
Dir: Paul Mazursky *Cast:* Nick Nolte, Bette Midler, Richard Dreyfuss, Little Richard, Tracy Nelson, Elizabeth Peña
▶ Homeless bum Nolte attempts suicide in swimming pool but is rescued and taken in by wealthy coat-hanger manufacturer Dreyfuss and his vulgar, frustrated wife Midler. Mazursky's jubilant remake of Jean Renoir's French classic *Boudu Saved From Drowning* expertly mixes sexual farce (Nolte seducing various members of Dreyfuss's household) and lyricism (Nick reciting Shakespeare's "What a piece of work is man" speech to Dreyfuss). Wonderful performances from all, including star turn from Mike the dog. *Dist.:* Buena Vista

DOWN ARGENTINE WAY 1940
★ ★ NR Musical 1:32
Dir: Irving Cummings *Cast:* Don Ameche, Betty Grable, Carmen Miranda, Charlotte Greenwood, J. Carrol Naish, The Nicholas Brothers
▶ Horse fancier Grable finds romance in Argentina with horse breeder Ameche, unaware that their families have been feuding for years. Bright, bouncy musical lacks substance but is consistently entertaining. Received three Oscar nominations, including title tune and photography. Miranda's Hollywood debut is eye-catching; the Nicholas Brothers have a sensational specialty number. *Dist.:* CBS/Fox

DOWN BY LAW 1986
★ R Drama 1:46 B&W
▢ Nudity, adult situations, explicit language
Dir: Jim Jarmusch *Cast:* Tom Waits, John Lurie, Roberto Benigni, Nicoletta Braschi, Ellen Barkin
▶ Minimalist comedy about three losers—down-and-out DJ Waits, slimy pimp Lurie, and Italian tourist Benigni—and their unlikely escape from a Louisiana jail. Slight plot is static and uninvolving until the arrival of Benigni, who steals the film with his cheerfully mangled English. Waits and Lurie collaborated on the soundtrack. (CC)
Dist.: CBS/Fox

DOWNHILL RACER 1969
★ ★ ★ PG Drama/Sports 1:42
▢ Adult situations, explicit language
Dir: Michael Ritchie *Cast:* Robert Redford, Gene Hackman, Camilla Sparv, Karl Michael Vogler, Jim McMullan, Christian Dormer
▶ When a top racer gets hurt, U.S. ski team

coach Hackman offers tryouts for a new on spot roster. Complaining loner Redford irritates many but makes squad. Tour of European race circuit, rivalry with McMullan, the country's best skier, and affair with Sparv, assistant to wealthy ski manufacturer Vogler, precede climax at Olympics. Racing footage, with avid downhiller Redford doing much of his own stunt work, will delight skiers, but others may be put off by cynical look at heroism and unusually cold Redford.
Dist.: Paramount

DOWNTOWN 1990
★ ★ ★ R Action-Adventure 1:36
▢ Brief nudity, explicit language, violence
Dir: Richard Benjamin *Cast:* Anthony Edwards, Forest Whitaker, Penelope Ann Miller, Joe Pantoliano, David Clennon, Art Evans
▶ Edwards, a rookie cop in the cushy Main Line suburbs, is reassigned to inner-city Philadelphia after angering wealthy businessman Clennon. Although despised by his mostly black colleagues, Edwards teams up with Whitaker to break up a drug ring. Two leads display great chemistry, but can't overcome clichéd plot. Comic overtones don't mix well with heavy bloodletting. (CC)
Dist.: CBS/Fox

DOWN TWISTED 1987
★ R Action-Adventure 1:29
▢ Explicit language, violence
Dir: Albert Pyun *Cast:* Carey Lowell, Charles Rocket, Linda Kerridge, Nicholas Guest
▶ Rich L.A. art collector steals religious artifact from banana republic, setting off a wild round of deadly double-crossing among scoundrels on two continents. Rocket, a wisecracking gunrunner, and Lowell are kidnapped and taken to South America, but escape to track the artifact to an airport locker. Fast-moving action; low-voltage cast.
Dist.: Media

DRACULA 1931
★ ★ ★ NR Horror 1:15 B&W
Dir: Tod Browning *Cast:* Bela Lugosi, Helen Chandler, David Manners, Dwight Frye, Edward Van Sloan, Herbert Bunston
▶ Countless sequels, remakes, and ripoffs have not diminished the stature of this classic adaptation of the Bram Stoker novel. Lugosi is unforgettable as the Transylvanian count who moves to London, puts Chandler under his vampire spell, but meets his match in professor Van Sloan. Very, very scary.
Dist.: MCA

DRACULA 1979
★ ★ ★ R Horror 1:49
▢ Adult situations, violence
Dir: John Badham *Cast:* Frank Langella, Laurence Olivier, Donald Pleasence, Kate Nelligan, Trevor Eve, Tony Haygarth
▶ Moody, atmospheric version of the famous Bram Stoker story, with Langella emphasizing

the erotic nature of the notorious vampire. He moves to England and falls for Nelligan, daughter of local doctor Pleasence, while fighting off Olivier, the father of another victim. Adapted from the hit Broadway play.
Dist.: MCA

DRACULA AND SON 1979 French
★ **PG Horror/Comedy 1:18**
☑ Brief nudity, adult situations, explicit language, violence
Dir: Eduard Molinaro *Cast:* Christopher Lee, Bernard Menez, Marie-Helene Brielle, Catherine Breillat, Jack Boudet
▶ Count Dracula (Lee) and son Menez are forced to move from Romania to London. Dracula gets a job playing himself in a movie, Menez works in a slaughterhouse, and the two compete to win a woman who looks like the Count's late wife. Clumsy spoof with tired performance from Lee. Sample dialogue: "May the cross be with you."
Dist.: RCA/Columbia

DRACULA'S DOG 1978
★ ★ **R Horror 1:30**
☑ Explicit language, graphic violence
Dir: Albert Band *Cast:* Michael Pataki, Reggie Nadler, Jose Ferrer, Jan Shutan, Libbie Chase, John Levin
▶ After Dracula's tomb is exhumed, the Count's dog Zoltan comes back to life. Accompanied by vampire Nadler, the mutt goes to America in search of Pataki, a relative of his master. Transylvanian inspector Ferrer follows. Fangless flick is also known as *Zoltan, Hound of Dracula.*
Dist.: United

DRACULA'S WIDOW 1987
★ **R Horror 1:26**
☑ Nudity, adult situations, explicit language, violence
Dir: Christopher Coppola *Cast:* Sylvia Kristel, Josef Sommer, Lenny Von Dohlen, Marc Coppola, Stefan Schnabel, Rachel Jones
▶ Von Dohlen, owner of Hollywood Wax Museum, opens a crate from Transylvania and releases Kristel, famed vampire's lovely spouse. She embarks on a killing spree that baffles Los Angeles cop Sommer. Anemic horror semispoof fails to add much to vampire myths.
Dist.: HBO

DRACULA VS. FRANKENSTEIN 1971
☆ **PG Horror 1:30**
☑ Violence
Dir: Al Adamson *Cast:* J. Carrol Naish, Lon Chaney, Jr., Zandor Vorkov, Russ Tamblyn, Jim Davis, Anthony Eisley
▶ Dr. Frankenstein (Naish) and assistant Chaney operate from under an amusement park, where they are still in the business of collecting body parts. When the doc's creation meets Dracula (Vorkov), the result is what many believe is among the worst horror movies ever made. Self-parodying turkey fea-

tures a guest appearance by Forrest J. Acker-man, publisher of "Famous Monsters of Filmland" magazine.
Dist.: VidAmerica

DRAGNET 1954
★ ★ **NR Crime 1:29**
Dir: Jack Webb *Cast:* Jack Webb, Ben Alexander, Richard Boone, Ann Robinson, Stacy Harris, Virginia Gregg
▶ Sergeant Joe Friday (Webb) and his partner Alexander tackle murder by the Red Spot Gang, building their case from four bullet shells and a footprint. Feature spinoff from the popular TV series predictably focuses on police tactics, not characterizations. Remade as a comedy in 1987; Webb also directed a TV movie under the same title in 1969. **(CC)**
Dist.: MCA

DRAGNET 1987
★ ★ ★ **PG-13 Comedy 1:46**
☑ Brief nudity, explicit language, adult humor
Dir: Tom Mankiewicz *Cast:* Dan Aykroyd, Tom Hanks, Christopher Plummer, Harry Morgan, Alexandra Paul, Elizabeth Ashley, Dabney Coleman
▶ Affectionate takeoff of Jack Webb's TV series updated to present-day Los Angeles. As Sgt. Joe Friday's nephew, Aykroyd gives a dead-on parody of Webb's tight-lipped delivery. With his new partner Hanks (who has the best lines), Aykroyd tackles a puzzling case involving lisping pornographer Coleman, corrupt televangelist Plummer, and "the virgin Connie Swail" (Paul). Jokes trail off after a bright start.
Dist.: MCA

DRAGONFLY SQUADRON 1954
★ ★ **NR War 1:23 B&W**
Dir: Lesley Selander *Cast:* John Hodiak, Barbara Britton, Bruce Bennett, Chuck Connors, Gerald Mohr, Jess Barker
▶ Right before the Korean War, tough American Air Force major Hodiak trains a Korean unit that subsequently proves its mettle in battle. The officer also has a rocky love life, as his girlfriend Britton is married to doctor Bennett. Good fight scenes, so-so dramatic ones.
Dist.: SVS

DRAGON SEED 1944
★ ★ **NR Drama 2:25 B&W**
Dir: Jack Conway, Harold S. Bucquet *Cast:* Katharine Hepburn, Walter Huston, Aline MacMahon, Akim Tamiroff, Turhan Bey, Hurd Hatfield
▶ Sincere effort to examine the impact of Japanese invaders on rural Chinese during World War II. Hepburn must convince husband Bey to resist the invasion; father-in-law Huston disagrees with her until the Japanese reach his farm. Adaptation of Pearl S. Buck's novel suffers from slow pacing and miscasting of Caucasians as Orientals.
Dist.: MGM/UA

DRAGONSLAYER 1981
★ ★ ★ PG Fantasy 1:48
☑ Brief nudity, violence
Dir: Matthew Robbins *Cast:* Peter Mac-
Nicol, Caitlin Clarke, Ralph Richardson,
John Hallam, Peter Eyre, Albert Salmi
► Sixth-century British sorcerer Richardson
and young apprentice MacNicol are re-
cruited to rid kingdom of a dragon. When king
Eyre tests Richardson in battle with villainous
Hallam, the old wizard dies. Although his edu-
cation in magic is incomplete, MacNicol
takes on the dragon and soon finds he's over-
matched. First-rate fantasy with realistic
dragon and authentic Dark Ages setting.
Dist.: Paramount

DRAW! 1984
★ ★ ★ ★ NR Western/MFTV 1:38
☑ Nudity, adult situations, explicit language, violence
Dir: Steven Hilliard Stern *Cast:* Kirk Douglas,
James Coburn, Alexandra Bastedo, Graham
Jarvis, Derek McGrath, Len Birman
► Reformed outlaw Douglas, downplaying his
gunslinging reputation to live last years in
peace, must unwillingly kill the sheriff in Bell
City and take actress Bastedo hostage to
save his skin from angry mob. While romance
blooms between the captor and his prisoner,
the townspeople hire lawman Coburn, Douglas's longtime nemesis, to bring the gunfighter
to justice. Western with a surprise ending benefits from location shoot in Canada and presence of screen veterans Douglas and Coburn.
Dist.: Media

DR. BLACK, MR. HYDE 1976
☆ R Horror 1:40
☑ Nudity, explicit language
Dir: William Grain *Cast:* Bernie Casey,
Rosalind Cash, Marie O'Henry, Ji-Tu Cum-
buka, Milt Kogan, Stu Gilliam
► Black doctor working on cure for cirrhosis of
the liver turns ghastly white and begins killing
prostitutes after injecting himself with experimental serum. Chase finale sees monster
climbing Watts Towers. Preposterous black exploitation version of the Robert Louis Stevenson classic. Also known as *The Watts Monster*
and *Dr. Black and Mr. White.*
Dist.: United

DR. CYCLOPS 1940
★ ★ ★ NR Horror 1:15
Dir: Ernest B. Shoedsack *Cast:* Albert Dekker, Janice Logan, Thomas Coley, Charles
Halton, Victor Kilian
► Mad scientist Dekker snares unwary jungle
travelers and shrinks them to doll-size; ordinary
objects pose unexpected threats as they try
to escape. Low-budget exploitation redeemed somewhat by clever special effects
(which received an Oscar nomination, one of
the few given to horror films of that era).
Dist.: MCA

DREAM A LITTLE DREAM 1989
★ ★ ★ PG-13 Comedy/Fantasy 1:39
☑ Adult situations, explicit language
Dir: Marc Rocco *Cast:* Corey Feldman,
Corey Haim, Jason Robards, Piper Laurie,
Harry Dean Stanton, Meredith Salenger
► Feldman is teenager failing at school who
finds romance with Salenger when bicycle
crash imbues them with the personalities of
elderly neighbors Robards and Laurie; Robards's spirit also helps Feldman on his SAT
exams. Nonstop soundtrack, mixing heavy
metal with Frank Sinatra, plus Rocco's flashy
visual style add zing to confusing body switch
antics. **(CC)**
Dist.: Vestron

DREAM CHASERS, THE 1984
★ ★ ★ PG Family 1:37
☑ Explicit language
Dir: Arthur Dubs, David Jackson *Cast:* Harold Gould, Justin Dana, Carolyn Carradine,
Jeffrey Tambor
► Paperboy Dana has cancer and a father
with little time for him. Antiques dealer Gould's
family wants him to close up shop and go to
an old age home. These two friends run away
to Wyoming together. Credible performances
by Gould and Dana enliven this calculated
crowd-pleaser; touches the heart despite
barely adequate direction. **(CC)**
Dist.: Playhouse

DREAMCHILD 1985 British
★ PG Drama 1:30
☑ Adult situations
Dir: Gavin Millar *Cast:* Coral Browne, Ian
Holm, Peter Gallagher, Caris Corfman,
Nicola Cowper, Amelia Shankley
► Elderly Browne, who as a child provided
Lewis Carroll (Holm) with the inspiration for
Alice in Wonderland, recalls her relationship
with the author while on a visit to 1932 New
York City. Meanwhile, young assistant Cowper
is wooed by brash reporter Gallagher. Com-
plex screenplay by Dennis Potter weaves a
delicate, magical spell as it movingly explores
art and memory. An unusual, underap-
preciated treat.
Dist.: Warner

DREAMER 1979
★ ★ PG Drama/Sports 1:33
☑ Explicit language
Dir: Noel Nosseck *Cast:* Tim Matheson,
Susan Blakely, Jack Warden, Richard B.
Schull, Barbara Stuart
► Hollywood's stab at applying familiar sports
formula to bowling. Underdog bowler Mathe-
son tries to beat the odds and win the big
match while having problems with girlfriend
Blakely. Contains an unforgettable scene in
which Matheson's coach Warden literally
bowls himself into a fatal heart attack. And
we thought boxing was dangerous!
Dist.: CBS/Fox

DREAM LOVER 1986
★★ R Drama 1:11
☑ Adult situations, explicit language, violence
Dir: Alan J. Pakula *Cast:* Kristy McNichol, Ben Masters, Paul Shenar, Justin Deas, Gayle Hunnicutt, Matthew Penn
► Young flutist McNichol suffers recurring nightmares after being attacked by an intruder. She turns to scientist Masters from the Yale Sleep Laboratory for help. Together they uncover a disturbing secret about her past. Intriguing subject suffers from repetitive plotting and unsettling dream sequences.
Dist.: MGM/UA

DREAM OF KINGS, A 1969
★★★★ R Drama 1:49
☑ Adult situations, explicit language, violence
Dir: Daniel Mann *Cast:* Anthony Quinn, Irene Papas, Inger Stevens, Sam Levene, Radames Pera, Val Avery
► Stubborn, proud Greek-American Quinn ekes out a living by gambling and dispensing advice to the troubled souls of his poor Chicago neighborhood. Son Pera is gravely ill and Quinn tries to raise the money to take him to Greece where he hopes the boy will recover. Solid performances and real emotion in this small, but rewarding, film.
Dist.: Warner

DREAM OF PASSION, A 1978 Greek
☆ R Drama 1:50
☑ Adult situations, explicit language
Dir: Jules Dassin *Cast:* Melina Mercouri, Ellen Burstyn, Andreas Voutsinas, Despo Diamantidou, Dimitris Papamichael
► In Greece, Euripides's ancient drama *Medea* is being rehearsed by actress Mercouri. In a publicity stunt, she is introduced to incarcerated American Burstyn, who, á la Medea, is accused of murdering her children to spite an unfaithful husband. The woman begin to form a strange and unsettling bond. Leads are dynamic, but twist on the classic tragedy proves dramatically unfinished.
Dist.: Nelson

DREAMSCAPE 1984
★★★ PG-13 Sci-Fi 1:39
☑ Nudity, adult situations, explicit language, violence
Dir: Joseph Ruben *Cast:* Dennis Quaid, Max Von Sydow, Christopher Plummer, Eddie Albert, Kate Capshaw
► Engaging sci-fi with tantalizing premise: psychic Quaid with ability to enter other people's dreams is asked to help troubled President Albert and manages to stave off telepathic assassination attempt masterminded by right-winger Plummer. Director Ruben pulls out all the stops in the inventive dream scenes.
Dist.: HBO

DREAM TEAM, THE 1989
★★★★ PG-13 Comedy 1:53
☑ Explicit language, violence
Dir: Howard Zieff *Cast:* Michael Keaton, Christopher Lloyd, Peter Boyle, Stephen Furst, Lorraine Bracco, Dennis Boutsikaris
► Psychiatrist Boutsikaris takes mental patients Keaton, Lloyd, Boyle, and Furst to Yankee Stadium outing but witnesses a killing and is knocked out before they get there. Stranded in New York City, these half-wits somehow pull themselves together to outwit the killers. High-spirited, consistently amusing merriment with Boyle a special treat as the ad man who thinks he's the Savior. Funniest scenes: Boyle in church and Keaton in the restaurant. **(CC)**
Dist.: MCA

DRESSED TO KILL 1946
★ NR Mystery-Suspense 1:12 B&W
Dir: Roy William Neill *Cast:* Basil Rathbone, Nigel Bruce, Patricia Morison, Edmond Breon, Frederick Worlock, Carl Harbord
► Rathbone as Sherlock Holmes tracks down three music boxes containing Bank of England engraving plates stolen by villain Morison. Twelfth and final picture starring Rathbone as the great sleuth shows the series's age. Fearful of losing his own identity to the role that made him famous, Rathbone left the series to pursue a career on the stage.
Dist.: Various C

DRESSED TO KILL 1980
★★★ R Mystery-Suspense 1:45
☑ Nudity, explicit language, graphic violence
Dir: Brian De Palma *Cast:* Michael Caine, Angie Dickinson, Nancy Allen, Keith Gordon, Dennis Franz
► A psychopath stalks two women—lonely suburban housewife Dickinson and feisty hooker Allen—through the streets of New York. Caine plays a psychiatrist who may hold the clue to the killer's identity. Film's frequent shocks are made all the more frightening by De Palma's stylized direction. Buffs will enjoy the many references to Hitchcock films. (CC)
Dist.: Republic

DRESSER, THE 1983 British
★★★ PG Drama 1:58
☑ Adult situations, explicit language
Dir: Peter Yates *Cast:* Albert Finney, Tom Courtenay, Edward Fox, Zena Walker, Eileen Atkins, Michael Gough
► Sterling adaptation of London and New York stage hit is an affectionate look at touring British acting troupe's efforts to do Shakespeare during the German blitz. Actor/manager Sir (Finney) is egomaniacal, spoiled, and losing his faculties. It's dresser Courtenay who has the herculian task of primping, prodding, and pleading with the spiritually fatigued, war-weary Sir to ensure that the show does go

oh. Finney (Oscar-nominated) and Courtenay are magnificent, alternately riotous and tragic. **(CC)**
Dist.: RCA/Columbia

DRESSMAKER, THE 1988 British
☆ **NR Drama 1:32**
☑ Adult situations, nudity
Dir: Jim O'Brien *Cast:* Joan Plowright, Billie Whitelaw, Jane Horrocks, Tim Ransom, Peter Postlethwaite
▶ In 1944 Liverpool, teen Horrocks lives with her two aunts: repressed spinster Plowright and live-wire widow Whitlaw. When Horrocks starts dating illiterate, oversexed Yank Ransom, the complicated relationship between the four leads to tragedy. Tour-de-force acting turns by Plowright and Whitelaw. On the surface, slow-paced and precise, but at its heart, a psychological shocker with a very creepy conclusion.
Dist.: Capitol

DR. HACKENSTEIN 1988
☆ **R Horror/Comedy 1:28**
☑ Explicit language, violence
Dir: Richard Clark *Cast:* David Muir, Stacey Travis, Catherine Davis Cox, Anne Ramsey, Phyllis Diller
▶ After their car crashes, a trio of pretty girls must spend the night at the home of Dr. Hackenstein, a mad scientist who just happens to be looking for some female body parts for a human pastiche. Diller, aunt of one of the girls, is worried and goes to the sheriff. Witless, charmless.
Dist.: Virgin

DRIFTER, THE 1988
★ ★ **R Drama 1:28**
☑ Nudity, adult situations, explicit language, violence
Dir: Larry Brand *Cast:* Kim Delaney, Timothy Bottoms, Miles O'Keeffe, Al Shannon
▶ While on a business trip, Los Angeles fashion designer Delaney picks up hunky hitchhiker O'Keeffe after he fixes her flat tire. They have a one-night stand before Delaney returns to L.A. and boyfriend Bottoms. O'Keeffe then relentlessly pursues her. Trashy but fast-paced and effective. Delaney is sexy and sympathetic.
Dist.: MGM/UA

DRIVER, THE 1978
★ ★ ★ **PG Action-Adventure 1:31**
☑ Explicit language, violence
Dir: Walter Hill *Cast:* Ryan O'Neal, Bruce Dern, Isabelle Adjani, Ronee Blakley, Matt Clark
▶ Stripped-down, existential chase film with O'Neal playing a crack getaway driver pursued by obsessive cop Dern. Adjani and Blakley have thankless roles as love interests. Pretentious at times (the characters don't even have names), but the car stunts and fights are first rate. **(CC)**
Dist.: CBS/Fox

DRIVER'S SEAT, THE 1974 Italian
★ **R Drama 1:41**
☑ Adult situations, explicit language, violence
Dir: Giuseppe Patroni Griffi *Cast:* Elizabeth Taylor, Ian Bannen, Guido Mannari, Mona Washbourne, Maxence Mailfort, Andy Warhol
▶ Flashy, confusing approach to Muriel Spark's intricate novella follows neurotic English spinster Taylor as she arranges a date with a man she knows will kill her. Filled with abstract touches and cinematic tricks, and perhaps too vague even for Taylor's fans.
Dist.: Embassy

DRIVING FORCE 1990 Australian
☆ **R Action-Adventure 1:30 ***
☑ Nudity, explicit language, violence
Dir: A. J. Prowse *Cast:* Sam J. Jones, Catherine Bach, Don Swayze, Stephanie Mason, Billy Blanks
▶ Rivalry among tow truck drivers begins when single dad Jones discovers that Swayze and other truckers are sparking collisions and mistreating customers to win business. When Jones tries to interfere, situation explodes into incidents of mounting violence. Silly resolution in this direct-to-video offering will strain the credulity of action fans.
Dist.: Academy

DRIVING ME CRAZY 1990
★ **NR Documentary 1:25**
☑ Explicit language
Dir: Nick Broomfield *Cast:* André Heller, Mercedes Ellington, Howard Porter, Andrew Braunsberg
▶ Nutty, revealing documentary salvaged from Broomfield's disastrous efforts to film the making of an all-black stage musical in Germany. After being hired by the show's backers, Broomfield is immediately beset by budget cuts and bad advice, while at the same time getting on everyone's nerves with his own clumsy doings. A compelling and hilarous peek into the way show business projects come together and fall apart.
Dist.: Virgin

DRIVING MISS DAISY 1989
★ ★ ★ ★ ★ **PG Drama 1:39**
☑ Explicit language
Dir: Bruce Beresford *Cast:* Morgan Freeman, Jessica Tandy, Dan Aykroyd, Patti LuPone, Esther Rolle
▶ In 1948 Atlanta, Aykroyd hires black Freeman as chauffeur for his crusty Jewish mother Tandy. She doesn't warm to Freeman immediately but their gradual closeness through twenty-five years is beautifully rendered in this delicately understated yet very moving adaptation by Alfred Uhry of his Pulitzer prize-winning play. Immaculate direction by Beresford, superb performances by Freeman and

Tandy. Won Oscars for Picture, Actress (Tandy), and Screenplay Adaptation. **(CC)**
Dist · Warner

DR. JEKYLL AND MR. HYDE 1920
★ ★ **NR Horror 1:03 B&W**
Dir: John S. Robertson *Cast:* John Barrymore, Martha Mansfield, Brandon Hurst, Nita Naldi, Charles Lane, Louis Wolheim
▶ Obsessed with the problem of human evil, doctor Barrymore invents a potion that isolates his bestial nature, effectively splitting himself into two personalities, one good and one not so good. Barrymore is remarkably intense in this early adaptation of the Robert Louis Stevenson novel.
Dist.: Video Yesteryear

DR. JEKYLL AND MR. HYDE 1932
★ ★ ★ **NR Horror 1:30 B&W**
Dir: Rouben Mamoulian *Cast:* Fredric March, Miriam Hopkins, Rose Hobart, Holmes Herbert, Edgar Norton
▶ London doctor March's experiments in chemistry turn him into monstrous Mr. Hyde, who befriends lady of the night Hopkins and sinks into depravity and murder. Superior adaptation of the Robert Louis Stevenson classic with stylish direction. March's Oscar-winning turn is the only Best Actor award given to the lead in a horror film.

DR. JEKYLL AND MR. HYDE 1941
★ ★ ★ **NR Horror 1:54 B&W**
Dir: Victor Fleming *Cast:* Spencer Tracy, Ingrid Bergman, Lana Turner, Donald Crisp, Ian Hunter, Barton MacLane
▶ Tracy stars as Dr. Jekyll, the scientist whose experiments change him into the beastly Mr. Hyde. The transformations threaten his relationship with fiancée Turner as he gets involved with prostitute Bergman and becomes a murderer. Adaptation of the Robert Louis Stevenson work is nicely directed and well acted, especially by Bergman, but fails to erase the memory of Fredric March's Oscar-winning performance in the 1932 version.
Dist.: MGM/UA

DR. JEKYLL & SISTER HYDE 1972 British
★ **PG Horror 1:34**
☑ Violence
Dir: Roy Ward Baker *Cast:* Ralph Bates, Martine Beswick, Gerald Sim, Lewis Flander, Susan Broderick, Neil Wilson
▶ Heartthrob physician Bates accidentally creates a formula that causes instant sex change operations. After turning a male insect into a female insect, he samples it on himself and changes into psychotic femme Beswick. Eventually, he/she gets into trouble by tangling the genders of his/her lovers. Never develops beyond the obvious.
Dist.: HBO

DR. NO 1962 British
★ ★ ★ ★ **PG Espionage/Action-Adventure 1:51**
☑ Adult situations, violence
Dir: Terence Young *Cast:* Sean Connery, Ursula Andress, Joseph Wiseman, Jack Lord, Bernard Lee
▶ First James Bond film set a winning formula for the subsequent series. Agent 007 is sent to Jamaica to investigate the murder of a fellow spy. With the help of CIA contact Lord and beautiful Andress, he uncovers a scheme by the nefarious Dr. No (Wiseman) to divert missiles from Cape Canaveral. More plot and less humor than the other Bond pictures, but the sets and stunts are amazing. As for Connery, nobody does it better. **(CC)**
Dist.: MGM/UA

DROWNING POOL, THE 1975
★ ★ ★ **PG Mystery-Suspense 1:48**
☑ Adult situations, violence
Dir: Stuart Rosenberg *Cast:* Paul Newman, Joanne Woodward, Anthony Franciosa, Murray Hamilton, Gail Strickland, Melanie Griffith
▶ Newman's second stab at detective Lew Harper, here employed by former lover Woodward to discover who's blackmailing her. Harper soon finds himself entangled with an oil tycoon, oversexed teen Griffith, a hooker, and assorted menacing types. Colorful New Orleans settings, Newman's charm, and slick plotting make for intelligent and diverting escapism. From the Ross MacDonald novel.
Dist.: Warner

DR. PHIBES RISES AGAIN 1972 British
★ ★ **PG Horror 1:34**
☑ Violence
Dir: Robert Fuest *Cast:* Vincent Price, Robert Quarry, Hugh Griffith, Valli Kemp, Peter Cushing, Terry-Thomas
▶ Mad doctor Price, seeking to revive his late wife, goes to Egypt in search of resurrection formula. There he battles wealthy Quarry for possession of the superpowered stuff. Sequel to *The Abominable Dr. Phibes* features Price's patented campy humor.
Dist.: Vestron

DR. STRANGELOVE OR: HOW I LEARNED TO STOP WORRYING AND LOVE THE BOMB 1964 British
★ ★ ★ ★ **PG Comedy 1:35 B&W**
☑ Adult situations, adult humor
Dir: Stanley Kubrick *Cast:* Peter Sellers, George C. Scott, Sterling Hayden, Keenan Wynn, Slim Pickens, James Earl Jones
▶ General Jack D. Ripper (Hayden) launches an unauthorized nuclear attack on Russia; amid escalating tensions, President Sellers and his advisors fruitlessly try to halt the bombers. Peerless Cold War black comedy won Oscar nominations for Best Picture; biting script by Kubrick, Terry Southern, and Peter George; direction; and Sellers's tour-de-force performance in a triple role (he also plays a

British Group Captain and the lunatic Strangelove).
Dist.: RCA/Columbia

DR. SYN 1937 British
★ NR Action-Adventure 1:20 B&W
Dir: Roy William Neill *Cast:* George Arliss, Margaret Lockwood, John Loder, Roy Emerton, Graham Moffatt, Frederick Burtwell
► Arliss's last screen appearance casts him as an ex-pirate who is thought dead but is actually the town vicar. The new identity provides perfect cover for his smuggling activities. Crisply told tale was remade twice in 1962 as Disney's *Dr. Syn, Alias the Scarecrow* and *Night Creatures* with Peter Cushing. Disney version is best of the three.
Dist.: Video Yesteryear

DR. SYN, ALIAS THE SCARECROW 1962
★ ★ NR Family 1:38
Dir: James Neilson *Cast:* Patrick McGoohan, George Cole, Tony Britton, Kay Walsh, Patrick Wymark, Geoffrey Keen
► Respectable country parson McGoohan is secretly the Scarecrow, an ex-pirate who harasses the tyrannical King's customs men, smuggles liquor, and divides the money among his overtaxed parishioners. Old-fashioned, high-grade production provides swashbuckling diversion for both kids and their parents. Also known as *The Scarecrow of Romney Marsh*.
Dist.: Buena Vista

DR. TERROR'S HOUSE OF HORRORS 1965 British
★ ★ NR Horror 1:38
Dir: Freddie Francis *Cast:* Peter Cushing, Christopher Lee, Roy Castle, Donald Sutherland, Neil McCallum, Alan Freeman, Max Adrian, Edward Underdown, Ursula Howells, Peter Madden
► Engrossing horror anthology set aboard a train. Five travelers befriend Cushing, who uses tarot cards to predict their deaths. An architect has a run-in with a werewolf; a musician angers the gods by stealing secret voodoo music; doctor Sutherland becomes convinced his wife is a vampire; critic Lee is tormented by an artist's dismembered hand; and a vine threatens all humanity. Literate and credible.
Dist.: Republic

DRUGSTORE COWBOY 1989
★ ★ ★ R Drama 1:40
☑ Brief nudity, adult situations, explicit language, violence
Dir: Gus Van Sant *Cast:* Matt Dillon, Kelly Lynch, James LeGros, Heather Graham, James Remar, William S. Burroughs
► In 1971 Portland, junkie Dillon leads fellow addicts Lynch, Graham, and LeGros in drugstore robberies to support their habit. When one of the foursome dies, he realizes it may be time to go straight. Potentially bleak subject matter is given surprisingly graceful direction

by Van Sant, mixing realistic detail with moments of mournful humor. Relaxed, intelligent performance by Dillon. Pacing slows considerably in second half. Based on an unpublished novel by James Fogle.
Dist.: IVE

DRUM 1976
★ ★ ★ R Drama 1:40
☑ Brief nudity, strong sexual content, graphic violence
Dir: Steve Carver *Cast:* Warren Oates, Ken Norton, Isela Vega, Yaphet Kotto, Pam Grier, Fiona Lewis, Rainbeaux Smith
► Sequel to *Mandingo* reprises the original's look at life on a squalid nineteenth-century Southern plantation. Sold into slavery, former heavyweight boxer Norton rebels against owner Oates's cruelty. Smith, Oates's daughter, further incites the slaves with her scanty attire.
Dist.: Vestron

DRUM BEAT 1954
★ NR Western 1:51
Dir: Delmer Daves *Cast:* Alan Ladd, Audrey Dalton, Marisa Pavan, Robert Keith, Charles Bronson, Elisha Cook, Jr.
► Former Indian fighter Ladd is appointed by the President to make peace with California's Modocs, with whom he has been friendly for years. Renegade redman Bronson imperils Ladd's mission, killing his childhood sweetheart and forcing a showdown. Ladd carries well-written, fact-based tale, with a strong contribution from Bronson.
Dist.: VCI

DRUMS 1938 British
★ ★ NR Action-Adventure 1:36
Dir: Zoltan Korda *Cast:* Sabu, Raymond Massey, Valerie Hobson, Roger Livesey, Desmond Tester, David Tree
► High-spirited adventure set in colonial India with Sabu playing a prince forced into hiding by Massey, his evil uncle. He takes refuge in a British garrison, where kindly captain Livesey adopts him as the troop's mascot. Sabu proves his courage when Massey mounts an ambush on the British.
Dist.: Embassy

DRUMS ALONG THE MOHAWK 1939
★ ★ ★ ★ ★ NR Drama 1:43
☑ Adult situations, mild violence
Dir: John Ford *Cast:* Claudette Colbert, Henry Fonda, Edna May Oliver, John Carradine, Jessie Ralph, Ward Bond
► Sturdy frontier saga set in Revolutionary New York: cultured newlywed Colbert must adjust to the wilderness when husband Fonda goes off to fight marauding Indians. Superb slice of Americana is filled with battles, romance, humor, and tragedy. Oliver received an Oscar nomination as a feisty frontier matriarch. **(CC)**
Dist.: CBS/Fox

DR. WHO AND THE DALEKS 1965 British
★ NR Sci-Fi 1:23
Dir: Gordon Flemyng *Cast:* Peter Cushing,
Roy Castle, Jennie Linden, Roberta Tovey,
Barrie Ingham, Michael Coles
▶ Feature based on the popular British sci-fi TV
show stars Cushing as Dr. Who, who is acci-
dentally transported to another planet along
with his granddaughters and Castle. The fear-
less foursome battle evil aliens called Daleks.
Series fans should enjoy this, but it won't con-
vert the uninitiated. Followed by *Daleks—In-
vasion Earth 2150 A.D.*.
Dist.: HBO

DRYING UP THE STREETS 1976
☆ NR Drama 1:30
☑ Nudity, adult situations, explicit language
Dir: Robin Spry *Cast:* Don Francis, Len
Cariou, Sarah Torgov
▶ A heroin-addicted father meets all the
usual seedy characters as he goes looking for
his daughter who's become involved with the
world of pornography. Similar in plot to, but
not as good as, the George C. Scott vehicle
Hardcore, grainy-looking low-budgeter is a
big down.
Dist.: Vestron

DRY WHITE SEASON, A 1989
★ ★ ★ R Drama 1:46
☑ Explicit language, violence
Dir: Euzhan Palcy *Cast:* Donald Sutherland,
Marlon Brando, Zakes Mokae, Susan Saran-
don, Jurgen Prochnow, Winston Ntsohna
▶ Sutherland is white prep school teacher in
South Africa who gradually becomes involved
in investigation of police atrocities when his
black gardener Ntsohna and son are victim-
ized by sadistic security chief Prochnow.
Brando is eccentrically brilliant as a liberal
lawyer, but in real-life disassociated himself
from the film, which makes anti-apartheid
points with exploitation film tactics. Brando
was nominated for Best Supporting Actor
Oscar. **(CC)**
Dist.: CBS/Fox

DU BARRY WAS A LADY 1943
★ ★ NR Musical 1:41
Dir: Roy Del Ruth *Cast:* Red Skelton, Lucille
Ball, Gene Kelly, Virginia O'Brien, Zero Mostel, Tommy Dorsey and His Orchestra
▶ Sanitized version of a bawdy Cole Porter
play with Skelton and Kelly both pursuing Ball,
a gorgeous showgirl. Skelton wins the Irish
Sweepstakes, accidentally drinks a mickey,
and dreams he's back in the court of Louis XIV.
Includes a few great Porter tunes: "Katie Went
to Haiti," "Friendship," "Did You Evah?". Dorsey
and his Orchestra (in period costumes and
wigs!) do "I'm Getting Sentimental Over You."
Dist.: MGM/UA

DUCHESS AND THE DIRTWATER FOX, THE
1976
★ ★ ★ PG Comedy 1:44
☑ Adult situations, violence, adult humor

Dir: Melvin Frank *Cast:* George Segal, Goldie Hawn, Conrad Janis, Thayer David, Jennifer Lee, Roy Jenson
▶ Flat comedy set in the Wild West pairs gambler Segal and saloon singer Hawn in offbeat
adventures trying to keep proceeds of a bank
robbery from outlaws, Mormon settlers, and a
Jewish wedding party. Song-and-dance
numbers prove as irritating as Segal's mugging.
Dist.: CBS/Fox

DUCK SOUP 1933
★ ★ ★ NR Comedy 1:10 B&W
Dir: Leo McCarey *Cast:* Groucho Marx,
Harpo Marx, Chico Marx, Zeppo Marx, Louis
Calhern, Margaret Dumont, Raquel Torres,
Edgar Kennedy
▶ In the mythical kingdom of Freedonia, petty
tyrant Rufus T. Firefly (Groucho) declares war
on neighboring Sylvania; Chico and Harpo
are inept spies out to steal his war plans. Pur-
ists rate this unique blend of slapstick and sav-
age political satire the Brothers' best work.
Among the many highlights are a dazzling
mirror sequence and Harpo's encounter with
lemonade vendor Kennedy. Zeppo's last film.
Dist.: MCA

DUCK, YOU SUCKER! 1972 Italian
★ ★ ★ PG Western 2:19
☑ Adult situations, explicit language, vio-
lence
Dir: Sergio Leone *Cast:* Rod Steiger, James
Coburn, Romolo Valli, Maria Monti, Rick
Battaglia, Franco Graziosi
▶ Lavish, action-filled epic about the Mexican
revolution, with Coburn outstanding as an Irish
terrorist who teams up with bandit Steiger—a
disarmingly unwilling hero—to rob a bank.
Stunning set pieces include an unforgettable
train collision. Another strong work by Leone,
but as with most of his films there are a number
of versions available. Alternate title *A Fistful of
Dynamite* is twenty minutes shorter.
Dist.: MGM/UA

DUDES 1988
★ R Action-Adventure 1:30
☑ Explicit language, violence
Dir: Penelope Spheeris *Cast:* Jon Cryer,
Daniel Roebuck, Catherine Mary Stewart,
Flea, Lee Ving, Calvin Bartlett
▶ Aimless punk rockers Cryer, Roebuck, and
Flea set off on cross-country trek. Camping out
in the desert, they are attacked by tattooed
tough Ving and his gang of sadistic rednecks,
who steal their money and slay Flea. When
police offer no help, Cryer and Roebuck,
aided by sharp-shooting Stewart, seek their
own revenge. Hodgepodge of comedy,
drama, and fantasy sabotages standard action premise.
Dist.: IVE

DUEL 1971
★ ★ ★ ★ PG Drama/MFTV 1:30
☑ Explicit language

Dir: Steven Spielberg   *Cast:* Dennis Weaver, Eddie Firestone, Gene Dynarksi, Tim Herbert, Charles Seel, Alexander Lockwood
▶ Driving through the desert, salesman Weaver is menaced by the unseen driver of a ten-ton diesel truck. Streamlined plot by Richard Matheson, relentless pacing, and impressive technical credits helped establish director Spielberg's reputation. Originally made for TV, then released theatrically with peripheral scenes about Weaver's family added. Jack A. Marta's slick photography received an Emmy nomination.
Dist.: MCA

DUEL AT DIABLO 1966
★ ★ ★ NR Western 1:43
☒ Adult situations, violence
Dir: Ralph Nelson   *Cast:* James Garner, Sidney Poitier, Bibi Andersson, Dennis Weaver, Bill Travers, William Redfield
▶ Trailsman Garner guides a shipment of ammunition through hostile Indian country while defusing racial tensions caused by black horsemaster Poitier and the half-breed son of Andersson, raped by the Apaches. Garner's rival, greenhorn Army lieutenant Travers, provokes further trouble when he breaks down during an Indian ambush. Old-fashioned Western is often excessively violent.
Dist.: Wood Knapp

DUEL IN THE SUN 1946
★ ★ ★ NR Western 2:10
Dir: King Vidor   *Cast:* Jennifer Jones, Joseph Cotten, Gregory Peck, Lionel Barrymore, Lillian Gish, Walter Huston
▶ Overwrought, controversial Western has an improbable plot, but triumphs through sheer spectacle. Thousands of extras and an extravagant production frame the tragic story of half-breed Jones torn between amoral cowpoke Peck and his refined brother Cotten. Barrymore is commanding as their invalid father; Gish (Barrymore's wife) and Jones were Oscar-nominated. Narrated by Orson Welles.
Dist.: CBS/Fox

DUELLISTS, THE 1978 British
★ ★ PG Drama 1:41
☒ Violence
Dir: Ridley Scott   *Cast:* Keith Carradine, Harvey Keitel, Albert Finney, Edward Fox, Cristina Raines
▶ Sober, beautifully filmed account of a feud between two French officers during the Napoleonic Wars. Keitel pursues Carradine for sixteen years before they resolve their argument. Adaptation of a Joseph Conrad story is most notable for its remarkable photography and attention to period detail. Scott's directing debut.
Dist.: Paramount

DUET FOR ONE 1986
★ ★ R Drama 1:47
☒ Brief nudity, adult situations, explicit language

Dir: Andrei Konchalovsky   *Cast:* Julie Andrews, Alan Bates, Max Von Sydow, Rupert Everett, Margaret Courtenay
▶ Old-fashioned three-hanky weeper stars Andrews as a world-famous violinist stricken with multiple sclerosis. Forced to retire at the peak of her career and dumped by husband Bates for a secretary, she is left to contemplate suicide as her body degenerates. Andrews's perky disposition adds some light to this terminally grim fare.
Dist.: MGM/UA

DUMBO 1941
★ ★ ★ ★ ★ G Animation 1:04
Dir: Ben Sharpsteen   *Cast:* Voices of Edward Brophy, Sterling Holloway, Verna Felton, Herman Bing, Cliff Edwards
▶ Infant circus elephant Dumbo is ridiculed for oversized ears until he discovers his deformity allows him to fly and becomes the star of the show. Flawless Disney classic will delight all ages; youngsters will especially identify with shy, nonspeaking Dumbo and the ugly duckling story line. Musical score won an Oscar; songs include "Look Out for Mr. Stork," Oscar-nominated "Baby of Mine," and unforgettable "Pink Elephants on Parade." **(CC)**
Dist.: Buena Vista

DUNE 1984
★ ★ ★ PG-13 Sci-Fi 2:20
☒ Explicit language, violence
Dir: David Lynch   *Cast:* Kyle MacLachlan, Francesca Annis, Jose Ferrer, Brad Dourif, Linda Hunt, Freddie Jones, Richard Jordan, Virginia Madsen
▶ Great-looking but ultimately disappointing sci-fi epic from Frank Herbert's elaborate cult classic, once thought to be unfilmable. The time is A.D. 10,991. Young messiah MacLachlan travels to the planet Dune, an arid wasteland containing a valuable narcotic spice guarded by giant sandworms. He leads its lowly inhabitants to victory over an evil emperor and his minions. Rock-star Sting plays a minor role as a smiling dispenser of pain. **(CC)**
Dist.: MCA

DUNERA BOYS, THE 1985 Australian
★ ★ R Drama 2:30
☒ Explicit language
Dir: Ben Lewin   *Cast:* Joseph Spano, Bob Hoskins, Joseph Furst, John Meillon, Warren Mitchell, Mary-Anne Fahey
▶ At the outset of World War II, British authorities round up immigrants suspected of being Nazi spies and deport them to Australian prison camps. Plan is bizzare error as most deportees are Jews, and haphazard roundup accidentally nets Cockneys like Hoskins. Cut down from Australian TV miniseries, funny, fast-moving film shows how deportees cope despite cruel treatment. Based on a true incident.
Dist.: Prism

DUNGEONMASTER, THE 1985
★ **PG-13 Sci-Fi 1:14**
☑ Violence
Dir: Rose Marie Turko, John Buechler, Charles Band, David Allen, Steve Ford, Peter Manoogian, Ted Nicolaou *Cast:* Jeffrey Byron, Leslie Wing, Richard Moll, Danny Dick
► Sword and sorcery goes yuppie when computer whiz Byron travels back in time to rescue aerobics instructor sweetheart Wing from mad magician Moll. With the help of his "pet" computer Cal, Byron zaps every bad dude in sight with just a flick of his wrist. Special effects are purely primitive. Also known as *Ragewar.*
Dist.: Vestron

DUNWICH HORROR, THE 1970
★ ★ **PG Horror 1:30**
☑ Adult situations, violence
Dir: Daniel Haller *Cast:* Sandra Dee, Dean Stockwell, Ed Begley, Sam Jaffe, Donna Baccala, Lloyd Bochner
► In New England, college student Dee becomes intended victim of Satanic family cult through her involvement with Stockwell. Professor Begley attempts to rescue her from the evil worshippers. Moody, atmospheric terror, nicely adapted from an H. P. Lovecraft story, gets eerie direction from Haller.
Dist.: Nelson

DUST 1986 Belgian/French
☆ **NR Drama 1:27**
☑ Rape, adult situations
Dir: Marion Hansel *Cast:* Jane Birkin, Trevor Howard, John Matshikiza, Nadine Uwampa, Lourdes Christina Savo
► Birkin is effective as a lonely spinster devoted to care of elderly father Howard on isolated South African sheep ranch. Sexual tension is unleashed when young black couple moves in as caretakers, and severly repressed Birkin goes slowly mad. Examination of power and shifting social roles is based on novel *In the Heart of the Country* by J. M. Coetzee.
Dist.: Monarch

DUSTY 1982 Australian
★ ★ ★ ★ **NR Drama 1:28**
Dir: John Richardson *Cast:* Bill Kerr, Noel Trevarthen, Carol Burns, Nick Holland, John Stanton
► An Australian rancher raises a dingo pup into a prize-winning sheep dog. When the call of the wild lures "Dusty" back to the bush, other ranchers blame the dog for an increase in slaughtered sheep. A touching, nicely produced family film, both interesting and educational.
Dist.: Media

DUTCH TREAT 1987
★ **R Comedy 1:24**
☑ Adult situations, explicit language
Dir: Boaz Davidson *Cast:* David Landsberg, Lorin Dreyfuss, The Dolly Dots, Terry Camilleri, Linda Lutz
► Landsberg and Dreyfuss are thrown into a

Dutch jail after their cruise ship knife-throwing act goes awry. In Holland, they meet all-girl singing group The Dolly Dots, and pretend to be big record execs. Complications resolve when Dutch warblers really do get recording contract. Lightweight entertainment has a certain dumb charm.
Dist.: MGM/UA

DYNAMITE CHICKEN 1972
★ **R Documentary 1:16**
☑ Nudity, Adult situations, explicit language
Dir: Ernie Pintoff *Cast:* Richard Pryor, John Lennon, Yoko Ono, The Ace Trucking Company, Joan Baez, Ron Carey
► Social protest documentary combines comedy skits and news footage dealing with racial, sexual, and political issues. Frantic, now-dated assemblage of clips includes a nun stripping, shots of L.B.J. and Nixon, and a discussion of a man who threw excrement on draft board files. Pryor's routines do not show him at his best.
Dist.: Monterey

EACH DAWN I DIE 1939
★ ★ ★ **NR Action-Adventure 1:32 B&W**
Dir: William Keighley *Cast:* James Cagney, George Raft, Jane Bryan, George Bancroft, Maxie Rosenbloom, Victor Jory
► Framed by corrupt politicians, reporter Cagney is sent to jail, where he becomes friends with gangster Raft. Cagney is blamed when Raft escapes, so Raft returns to the pen to rescue him. Smashing prison drama is preposterous at times, but Cagney ("I'll get out if I have to kill every screw in the hole") is dynamic, and Raft matches him with a superior tough-guy performance.
Dist.: MGM/UA

EAGLE, THE 1925
★ **NR Action-Adventure 1:14 B&W**
Dir: Clarence Brown *Cast:* Rudolph Valentino, Vilma Banky, Louise Dresser, Albert Conti, James Marcus
► Silent feature stars Valentino as a Russian soldier who seeks revenge against Marcus for stealing his father's land by becoming the masked hero, the "Black Eagle." Romance with Marcus's daughter Banky complicates the mission. Old-style adventure features the star at his most dashing and romantic.
Dist.: Video Yesteryear

EAGLE HAS LANDED, THE 1977
★ ★ ★ ★ **PG Mystery-Suspense 2:03**
☑ Mild violence
Dir: John Sturges *Cast:* Michael Caine, Donald Sutherland, Robert Duvall, Jenny Agutter, Donald Pleasence
► During World War II, German operatives led by Caine and IRA man Sutherland infiltrate a small English town in a plot to kill Winston Churchill. Well-crafted, satisfying action-adventure from the Jack Higgins best-seller presented from the point of view of sympathetic

Germans. Nifty surprise ending, solid work from Caine, Sutherland, and Duvall.
Dist.: CBS/Fox

EAGLE'S WING 1979 British
★ PG Western 1:38
☑ Explicit language, violence
Dir: Anthony Harvey *Cast:* Martin Sheen, Sam Waterston, Caroline Langrishe, Harvey Keitel, Stephane Audran, John Castle
▸ City-born Sheen and Indian Waterston compete to capture a magnificent white stallion, learning about each other and the limits of their own dreams and ambitions in the process. Artsy Western is good-looking, but plot is obscure, and there is little here for action fans.
Dist.: Media

EARLY FROST, AN 1985
★★★★ NR Drama/MFTV 1:37
Dir: John Erman *Cast:* Gena Rowlands, Ben Gazzara, Sylvia Sidney, Aidan Quinn, D. W. Moffett, John Glover
▸ Rowlands and Gazzara are shocked to discover their son Quinn is not only gay but is dying of AIDS. Made-for-television drama, one of the first to deal with the controversial subject, soars way above average because of a power-packed cast and an Emmy-winning script by Rom Cowen and Daniel Lipman, based on a Sherman Yellen story.
Dist.: RCA/Columbia

EARRINGS OF MADAME DE. . ., THE 1954 French
★ NR Drama 1:45 B&W
Dir: Max Ophuls *Cast:* Charles Boyer, Danielle Darrieux, Vittorio De Sica, Mireille Perrey, Jean Debucourt, Serge Lecointe
▸ In nineteenth-century France, general Boyer gives wife Darrieux a pair of earrings, which she sells, and which come back to her again, first through her husband's mistress, and then through her own affair with young baron De Sica. Very handsome production saves this very slight story, which relies a bit too much on coincidence for believability. Also known as *Diamond Earrings.* [S]
Dist.: Foothill

EARTH GIRLS ARE EASY 1989
★★★ PG Comedy 1:40
☑ Adult situations, explicit language
Dir: Julien Temple *Cast:* Geena Davis, Jeff Goldblum, Jim Carrey, Damon Wayans, Julie Brown, Charles Rocket, Michael McKean
▸ Valley gal Davis has just broken up with boyfriend Rocket when aliens Goldblum, Carrey, and Wayans land in her swimming pool. After beautician pal Brown gives the furry trio a body wax, the girls expose them to L.A. nightlife and Davis finds love with Goldblum. Thin but genial screenplay colorfully directed by Temple. Brown co-wrote the screenplay and sings her clever composition, "'Cause I'm a Blonde." **(CC)**
Dist.: Vestron

EARTHLING, THE 1980 Australian
★★★★ PG Drama 1:37
☑ Adult situations, violence
Dir: Peter Collinson *Cast:* William Holden, Ricky Schroder, Jack Thompson, Olivia Hamnett, Alwyn Kurts
▸ City kid Schroder is orphaned while camping in the Australian wilderness. Chased by packs of wild animals, he seems doomed until he meets grizzled traveler Holden, who teaches him the rudiments of survival. Features stunning nature footage.
Dist.: Vestron

EARTHQUAKE 1974
★★★★ PG Action-Adventure 2:09
☑ Explicit language, violence
Dir: Mark Robson *Cast:* Charlton Heston, Ava Gardner, Lorne Greene, George Kennedy, Victoria Principal, Walter Matthau, Genevieve Bujold, Richard Roundtree, Lloyd Nolan
▸ California crumbles in this early disaster movie, startling audiences with ear-splitting "Sensurround," which created shock waves inside the theatre. Kennedy is a policeman who takes charge of the rescue operation while buildings quiver and collapse, streets buckle, and crammed elevators plummet. Packed with action and suspense.
Dist.: MCA

EARTH VS. THE FLYING SAUCERS 1956
★★ NR Sci-Fi 1:23 B&W
Dir: Fred F. Sears *Cast:* Hugh Marlowe, Joan Taylor, Donald Curtis, Morris Ankrum, Tom Browne Henry
▸ Friendly flying saucers land on Earth and are greeted by gunfire, so the angry aliens respond with full-scale warfare. Marlowe stars as a scientist who discovers the space-creatures' weakness. Outstanding early special effects by Ray Harryhausen include the destruction of the Lincoln emorial and other Washington monuments.
Dist.: RCA/Columbia

EASTER PARADE 1948
★★★★★ NR Musical 1:43
Dir: Charles Walters *Cast:* Fred Astaire, Judy Garland, Ann Miller, Peter Lawford, Jules Munshin
▸ After partner Miller leaves him, dancer Astaire plucks Garland from the chorus to be his new sidekick. Garland and Astaire end up making beautiful professional and personal music together. A joy from start to finish; top-notch period (early-twentieth-century New York) re-creation with the stars at their peak. Many wonderful Irving Berlin songs include the title tune, Astaire and Garland clowning as "A Couple of Swells," and the beautiful and unjustly overlooked "It Only Happens When I Dance With You." Oscar for Musical Scoring.
Dist.: MGM/UA

EAST OF EDEN 1955
★★★★★ NR Drama 1:55

Dir: Elia Kazan *Cast:* James Dean, Julie Harris, Raymond Massey, Burl Ives, Richard Davalos, Jo Van Fleet
▶ In World War I Salinas Valley, Dean, rebellious son of stern father Massey, seeks truth about estranged mother Van Fleet (Supporting Actress Oscar winner) and finds love with Harris, his brother's girlfriend. Stirring, passionate direction by Kazan; lovely, winsome performance by Harris; intense but vulnerable work by Dean; and haunting Leonard Rosenman score make this adaptation of the John Steinbeck novel a memorable and emotional piece of Americana.
Dist.: Warner

EASY COME, EASY GO 1967
★ ★ NR Musical 1:35
Dir: John Rich *Cast:* Elvis Presley, Dodie Marshall, Pat Priest, Pat Harrington, Skip Ward, Frank McHugh, Elsa Lanchester
▶ Romantic comedy with a nautical theme: Navy frogman Presley, go-go dancer Marshall, and old wharf rat McHugh team up to salvage treasure from a sunken Spanish galleon. Lanchester offers a kooky character bit for comic relief; Elvis sings "Yoga Is as Yoga Does" and "You Gotta Stop."
Dist.: Paramount

EASY LIVING 1949
★ ★ NR Drama 1:17 B&W
Dir: Jacques Tourneur *Cast:* Victor Mature, Lucille Ball, Lizabeth Scott, Sonny Tufts, Lloyd Nolan, Jack Paar
▶ Mature, the aging halfback star of the New York Chiefs, faces endless nagging from wife Scott as retirement nears. Medical problems and loss of coaching job to rival Tufts bring him to edge of despair, but team secretary Ball offers unexpected support. Earnest sports soap opera features credible performances.
Dist.: Turner

EASY MONEY 1983
★ ★ ★ R Comedy 1:39
☑ Nudity, adult situations, explicit language, adult humor
Dir: James Signorelli *Cast:* Rodney Dangerfield, Joe Pesci, Geraldine Fitzgerald, Candice Azzara, Taylor Negron, Jennifer Jason Leigh
▶ Fun-loving Dangerfield stands to inherit $10 million if he can abstain from his favorite vices—boozing, gambling, and cavorting—for a year. With Pesci as his plumber pal and Leigh as his blond daughter married to a Puerto Rican gang member. Co-writer Dangerfield may get no respect, but fans adore his one-liners. **(CC)**
Dist.: Vestron

EASY RIDER 1969
★ ★ ★ R Drama 1:35
☑ Explicit language, violence
Dir: Dennis Hopper *Cast:* Peter Fonda, Dennis Hopper, Jack Nicholson, Luana Anders, Robert Walker, Jr., Karen Black

▶ The sixties classic that encouraged an American generation to tune in, turn on, and drop out. Fonda and Hopper motorcycle from Southern California to New Orleans encountering drugs, hippies, hookers, and death. Nicholson won his first Academy Award nomination for his performance as an alcoholic lawyer. Debut directorial effort by Hopper.
Dist.: RCA/Columbia

EASY WHEELS 1989
★ ★ R Comedy 1:34
☑ Brief nudity, adult situations, explicit language, violence
Dir: David O'Malley *Cast:* Paul LeMat, Eileen Davidson, Mayove Bransfield, Jon Menick, Barry Livingston, George Plimpton
▶ Crazed feminist bikers kidnap infants in effort to establish gal-o-centric world order. Led by Davidson, biker babes come up against LeMat and his all-male cycle tribe. When Davidson takes a shine to big lug LeMat, she arranges an orgy for both groups that turns into a duel-to-the-death rumble on wheels. Consciousness-lowering spoof of Grade C biker films goes overboard in pursuit of laughs and gets some.
Dist.: Fries

EAT A BOWL OF TEA 1989
★ PG-13 Drama 1:44
☑ Adult situations, explicit language, violence
Dir: Wayne Wang *Cast:* Russell Wong, Victor Wong, Cora Miao, Lau Siu Ming, Law Lan
▶ Young Chinese-American couple are happily married, but are pressured by older community members to have children. As a result, performance-anxious husband Russell Wong becomes impotent, and wife Miao has affair with gambler, causing breach in marriage, family shame, and disrupted lives. Film is low-key, but colorful and gently amusing. Cast is spunky, attractive.
Dist.: RCA/Columbia

EATING RAOUL 1982
★ R Comedy 1:23
☑ Nudity, adult situations, violence, adult humor
Dir: Paul Bartel *Cast:* Paul Bartel, Mary Woronov, Buck Henry, Robert Beltran
▶ Cult film about Paul and Mary Bland (Bartel and Woronov), a mild-mannered modern couple who resort to murder to finance their dream of owning a gourmet restaurant. With Beltran as Raoul, a local thief who meets an unhappy fate when he tries to horn in on their plans. Offbeat black comedy for those with exotic tastes.
Dist.: CBS/Fox

EAT MY DUST 1976
★ ★ PG Action-Adventure 1:30
☑ Explicit language, violence
Dir: Charles B. Griffith *Cast:* Ron Howard,

Christopher Norris, Warren Kemmerling, Dave Madden, Paul Bartel
► Sheriff Kemmerling organizes a posse after son Howard steals a stock car from pro racer Big Bubba Jones (Madden). But no one can stop Howard and his girl Norris. Fast-paced but relentless Roger Corman production is essentially one long car chase.
Dist.: Nelson

EAT THE PEACH 1986 Irish
★ **NR Comedy 1:35**
☑ Explicit language
Dir: Peter Ormrod *Cast:* Stephen Brennan, Eamon Morrissey, Catherine Byrne, Niall Toibin, Joe Lynch, Tony Doyle
► Unemployed Brennan and Morrissey are inspired by an Elvis movie to build cylindrical motorcycle stunt track in Brennan's backyard. Financing scheme with smuggled booze, pair actually build crazy structure and prepare for fame and fortune on opening day. Whimsical, appealing film has great Irish folk rock score, gorgeous scenery, and solid acting. **(CC)**
Dist.: CBS/Fox

EAT THE RICH 1988 British
☆ **R Comedy 1:32**
☑ Explicit language, violence
Dir: Peter Richardson *Cast:* Ronald Allen, Robbie Coltrane, Sandra Dorne, Jimmy Fagg, Lemmy, Lanah Pellay
► Pellay, an androgynous black waiter fired from posh London restaurant, gets revenge by forming revolutionary gang, taking over the place, killing wealthy folk, and then putting them on the menu. Irreverent, Monty Pythonesque comedy is bizarre and darkly comic.
Dist.: RCA/Columbia

ECHOES 1981
★ **R Drama 1:31**
☑ Nudity, adult situations, explicit language
Dir: Arthur Allan Seidelman *Cast:* Richard Alfieri, Nathalie Nell, Mercedes McCambridge, Ruth Roman, Gale Sondergaard
► Psychological examination of young painter Alfieri tormented by a past incarnation. Nell is a French dancer/love interest trying to understand his violent dreams. Very arty and theatrical; at times too farfetched and dreamlike.
Dist.: VidAmerica

ECHOES OF PARADISE 1987 Australian
★ **R Drama 1:32**
☑ Nudity, adult situations, explicit language
Dir: Philip Noyce *Cast:* Wendy Hughes, John Lone, Steven Jacobs, Peta Toppano, Rod Mullinar, Gillian Jones
► Unhappily·married Hughes goes to Thailand and finds fulfillment in the arms of Balinese dancer Lone. But he hides a secret past, and when Hughes's husband comes looking for her, she must choose between continuing her life abroad, or returning to her family in Sydney. Lone lends offbeat presence to other-

wise slow-moving film. Released in Australia as *Shadows of the Peacock.*
Dist.: Academy

ECHO PARK 1986 U.S./Austrian
★ **R Comedy/Drama 1:32**
☑ Brief nudity, adult situations, explicit language
Dir: Robert Dornhelm *Cast:* Tom Hulce, Susan Dey, Christopher Walker, Michael Bowen, Shirley Jo Finney
► Aspiring poet/pizza delivery man Hulce, mother/stripper/aspiring actress Dey and Austrian weightlifter Bowen share an old duplex apartment house in Echo Park, a low-rent, hilly address in East L.A., and wait for their big breaks. Offbeat, sweet, and occasionally very funny.
Dist.: Paramount

ECSTASY 1933 Czech
★ **NR Drama 1:08 B&W**
☑ Brief nudity, adult situations
Dir: Gustav Machaty *Cast:* Hedy Kiesler (Lamarr), Aribert Mog, Jaromir Rogoz, Leopold Kramer, Andre Nox
► Young Keisler (who later became Hedy Lamarr) has an affair with an engineer after her new husband is unable to perform. While she is swimming in a lake, her horse walks off with her clothes, resulting in a nude scene that won the film enduring notoriety. Although mild by today's standards, this was banned around the world and condemned by both the Pope and Hitler. A dull movie with a fascinating history.
Dist.: Video Yesteryear

EDDIE AND THE CRUISERS 1983
★ ★ ★ ★ **PG Drama 1:35 C**
☑ Adult situations, explicit language, mild violence
Dir: Martin Davidson *Cast:* Tom Berenger, Michael Paré, Ellen Barkin, Helen Schneider, Joe Pantoliano
► Variation on the rock nostalgia formula in which TV reporter Barkin investigates early sixties band, Eddie (Paré) and the Cruisers. The group dissolved after Eddie's mysterious car crash but his body was never found and tapes of their last album disappeared. Music startlingly Springsteen-esque. With Berenger as the first ex-band member to be interviewed.
Dist.: Nelson

EDDIE AND THE CRUISERS II: EDDIE LIVES 1989
★ ★ ★ **PG Drama 1:40**
☑ Adult situations, explicit language
Dir: Jean-Claude Lord *Cast:* Michael Paré, Marina Orsini, Bernie Coulson, Matthew Laurance, Anthony Sherwood
► Sequel to *Eddie and the Cruisers* sees New Jersey rock legend Eddie (Paré) living incognito as Montreal construction worker after faking own death. When "posthumously" released tapes of his band go platinum, Eddie decides to get back in business under differ-

ent name. Springsteen-style tunes supplied by
real life rockers John Cafferty and the Beaver
Brown Band. **(CC)**
Dist.: IVE

EDDIE MACON'S RUN 1983
★ ★ ★ **PG Action-Adventure 1:31**
☑ Rape, brief nudity, adult situations, explicit language, violence
Dir: Jeff Kanew   *Cast:* Kirk Douglas, John
Schneider, Lee Purcell, Leah Ayres, Lisa
Dunsheath
▶ In his first film, Schneider, wrongly convicted
on trumped-up charges, escapes from jail
and heads for Mexico. Douglas is the vengeful
cop who pursues him in a grueling chase; Purcell, the heiress who helps him cross Texas.
Based on James McLendon's novel.
Dist.: MCA

EDDIE MURPHY RAW 1987
★ ★ **R Documentary/Comedy 1:31**
☑ Explicit language, adult humor
Dir: Robert Townsend   *Cast:* Eddie Murphy
▶ No-frills film of Murphy's one-man show at
New York's Felt Forum is a must for his fans. His
targets include Mr. T, Bill Cosby, Michael Jackson, and sex—all handled in hilarious but
coarse language that may offend unsuspecting viewers. **(CC)**
Dist.: Paramount

EDGE OF DARKNESS 1943
★ ★ ★ **NR War 2:00 B&W**
Dir: Lewis Milestone   *Cast:* Errol Flynn, Ann
Sheridan, Walter Huston, Helmut Dantine,
Ruth Gordon, Judith Anderson
▶ During World War II, Nazis invade a Norwegian town but find more trouble than they
could have imagined; fisherman Flynn, his girlfriend Sheridan, widow Anderson, and doctor
Huston are among the leaders of an underground resistance movement that battles the
Germans through both nonviolent and violent
means. Tense and well-crafted. **(CC)**
Dist.: CBS/Fox

EDGE OF SANITY 1989 British
★ **R Horror 1:30**
☑ Nudity, adult situations, explicit language
Dir: Gerard Kikoine   *Cast:* Anthony Perkins,
Glynis Barber, Sarah Maur-Thorp, David
Lodge, Ben Cole, Lisa Davis
▶ Dr. Jekyll (Perkins) has not been working
late at the hospital, as he told his wife. In fact,
he's been sniffing his experimental cocaine
potions and turning into Jack the Ripper, a
persona that allows him to compensate for
childhood trauma by fileting prostitutes. Film
flops as kinky update of old tale, being neither
sexy nor frightening. Perkins's strained performance proves he's possibly played one
psycho too many. **(CC)**
Dist.: Virgin

EDUCATING RITA 1983 British
★ ★ ★ ★ **PG Comedy 1:50**
☑ Adult situations, explicit language

Dir: Lewis Gilbert   *Cast:* Michael Caine,
Julie Walters, Michael Williams, Maureen
Lipman, Jeananne Crowley, Malcolm Douglas
▶ Alcoholic literature professor Caine finds a
prize pupil in eager-to-learn lower-class hairdresser Walters. He admires her streetsmart wit
and wonders if in educating Rita, he's changing her for the worse. Nevertheless both
teacher and student end up learning from
one another. Consistently funny and truly
touching with wonderful Oscar-nominated
performances by Caine and Walters; Willy
Russell screenplay, based on his play, was
also nominated. **(CC)**
Dist.: RCA/Columbia

EDUCATION OF SONNY CARSON, THE
1974
★ ★ **R Drama 1:44**
☑ Explicit language, violence
Dir: Michael Campus   *Cast:* Rony Clayton,
Don Gordon, Joyce Walker, Paul Benjamin,
Thomas Hicks
▶ Honest, hard-edged look at black ghetto
life follows Carson's (Clayton) descent into
crime after joining a gang. Powerful assault on
racism and inescapable poverty, with a sincere, positive outlook that overcomes the
film's budget limitations.
Dist.: Fox Hills

EGG AND I, THE 1947
★ ★ ★ **NR Comedy 1:48 B&W**
Dir: Chester Erskine   *Cast:* Claudette Colbert, Fred MacMurray, Marjorie Main, Percy
Kilbride, Louise Allbritton
▶ MacMurray and Colbert are delightful as
the city-bred MacDonalds, who buy a
chicken farm and cope with rural life. Main
and Kilbride team for their roles as Ma and Pa
Kettle, the hick couple next door who have so
many children they don't know what to do.
Based on the best-selling novel by Betty MacDonald; led to a series of Ma and Pa Kettle
movies.
Dist.: KVC

EGYPTIAN, THE 1954
★ ★ ★ **NR Drama 2:20**
Dir: Michael Curtiz   *Cast:* Edmund Purdom,
Jean Simmons, Victor Mature, Gene Tierney,
Michael Wilding, Peter Ustinov, Bella Darvi
▶ Sprawling, soap opera treatment of ancient Egypt. Wilding plays an epileptic Pharaoh whose physician Purdom has affairs with
Simmons and Darvi. Mature, a valiant soldier,
must choose between the Pharoah's religion
or traditional creeds. Expensive costume epic
delivers spectacle with elephantine pacing.
Dist.: CBS/Fox

EIGER SANCTION, THE 1975
★ ★ ★ ★ **R Espionage/Action-Adventure
2:08**
☑ Adult situations, explicit language, violence
Dir: Clint Eastwood   *Cast:* Clint Eastwood,

George Kennedy, Vonetta McGee, Jack Cassidy, Thayer David
▶ Ex-spy Eastwood is lured out of retirement to assassinate a hit man. After the mission, black stewardess McGee tricks him into killing another spy, one of three men climbing the dangerous Eiger mountain. Espionage themes are upstaged by thrilling, brutal climbing sequences in Monument Valley and the Alps. Based on a best-seller by Trevanian.
Dist.: MCA

8½ 1963 Italian
☆ **NR Drama 2:18 B&W**
Dir: Federico Fellini ***Cast:*** Marcello Mastroianni, Claudia Cardinale, Anouk Aimee, Sandra Milo, Barbara Steele
▶ Classic autobiographical "film within a film" from Italian master moviemaker Fellini. A visual diary about a film director's difficulties making the very film we are seeing, it offers the viewer the chance to glimpse Fellini's memories, fantasies, and problems. Won an Academy Award for Best Foreign Film in 1963. A masterpiece for sophisticated tastes. [S]
Dist.: Vestron

18 AGAIN! 1988
★★★★ **PG Comedy 1:40**
☑ Brief nudity, adult situations, explicit language
Dir: Paul Flaherty ***Cast:*** George Burns, Charlie Schlatter, Tony Roberts, Anita Morris, Red Buttons
▶ Entry in the popular body switch genre has eighty-one-year-old tycoon Burns wishing he were eighteen again like his grandson Schlatter. He gets his wish: after a car crash, his mind possesses Schlatter's body. Personable Schlatter has Burns's trademarks (leer, pause, cigar) down pat, and Burns is even better in this affectionate comedy. **(CC)**
Dist.: New World

EIGHT MEN OUT 1988
★★ **PG Drama/Sports 2:00**
☑ Explicit language
Dir: John Sayles ***Cast:*** John Cusack, Clifton James, D. B. Sweeney, Christopher Lloyd, Charlie Sheen, David Strathairn, Michael Lerner, John Mahoney, Don Harvey, Michael Rooker, Perry Lang, Bill Irwin
▶ Tragic true story of the 1919 "Black Sox" scandal, the fixing of the World Series by the Chicago White Sox and a group of gamblers. Sayles's handsome period piece about our national pastime basically sides with the players who were motivated by the stinginess of team owner Charles Comiskey (James). Sober drama with many standouts in the large cast: Cusack as Buck Weaver, the player who may have been the scandal's biggest victim, Strathairn as the aging pitcher Eddie Cicotte, Sayles and author Studs Terkel as the sportwriters who blew open the scandal.
Dist.: Orion

8 MILLION WAYS TO DIE 1986
★★★ **R Drama 1:55**
☑ Nudity, explicit language, violence
Dir: Hal Ashby ***Cast:*** Jeff Bridges, Rosanna Arquette, Alexandra Paul, Randy Brooks, Andy Garcia
▶ Hard-boiled melodrama about vendetta of alcoholic ex-cop Bridges against Garcia, head of a drug and prostitution ring. Arquette is a high-priced call girl who plays the two off each other. Adaptation of Lawrence Block's cult thriller inexplicably drops New York setting, but makes good use of tawdry Los Angeles locations. Oliver Stone worked on the screenplay. **(CC)**
Dist.: CBS/Fox

84 CHARING CROSS ROAD 1987
★★★ **PG Drama 1:39**
☑ Explicit language
Dir: David Jones ***Cast:*** Anne Bancroft, Anthony Hopkins, Judi Dench, Maurice Denham, Jean De Baer
▶ Struggling New York writer Helene Hanff (Bancroft) orders rare books from London book dealer Frank Doel (Hopkins) and a warm relationship, spanning many years, develops by mail. True story (adapted from Hanff's memoir) of lovers who never meet is literate, civilized entertainment. All talk, little action, but the talk's good and two pros shine.
Dist.: RCA/Columbia

84 CHARLIE MOPIC 1989
★★★ **R War 1:35**
☑ Explicit language, violence
Dir: Patrick Duncan ***Cast:*** Jonathan Emerson, Nicholas Cascone, Jason Tomlins, Cristoper Burgard, Glenn Morshower, Richard Brooks
▶ Vietnam movie presents its characters and events through the point of view of a cameraman filming an American platoon. Story covers conflict between inexperienced officer Emerson and tough sergeant Brooks, an enemy ambush, and several casualties of war. Unusual technique gives familiar characterizations a unique perspective. Realistic dialogue and atmosphere from Vietnam vet Duncan.
Dist.: RCA/Columbia

EL BRUTO 1952 Mexican
☆ **NR Drama 1:23 B&W**
Dir: Luis Buñel ***Cast:*** Pedro Armendariz, Katy Jurado, Andres Soler, Rosita Arenas, Roberto Meyer, Jose Munoz
▶ Insensitive landlord Soler hires muscular hulk Armendariz to strong-arm a group of tenants who are resisting eviction. The not-very-bright Armendariz accidentally kills one of the tenant organizers, and falls in love with Arenas, the victim's daughter. Moving, if unsubtle. [S]
Dist.: Media

EL CID 1961
★★★★★ **NR Action-Adventure 3:04**

Dir: Anthony Mann *Cast:* Charlton Heston, Sophia Loren, Raf Vallone, Genevieve Page, Hurd Hatfield
▶ Story of the great eleventh-century Spanish warrior El Cid (Heston), who battled Moorish invaders. Mammoth costume spectacle has grand sweep and pageantry. Stiff dialogue but spectacular battle scenes, larger-than-life performances by Heston and Loren (as the great love of El Cid's life), surging musical score by Miklos Rozsa.
Dist.: Vestron

EL CONDOR 1970
★ **R Western 1:42**
☑ Nudity, explicit language, violence
Dir: John Guillermin *Cast:* Jim Brown, Lee Van Cleef, Patrick O'Neal, Marianna Hill, Iron Eyes Cody
▶ Outlaws Brown and Van Cleef team up to steal a treasure of gold hidden in a remote Mexican fortress. Mexican general O'Neal tries to thwart them. Undistinguished story and wooden acting but plenty of action, gunfire, and sex in this scenic made-in-Spain Western.
Dist.: Warner

EL DORADO 1967
★ ★ ★ ★ ★ **NR Western 2:06**
Dir: Howard Hawks *Cast:* John Wayne, Robert Mitchum, James Caan, Arthur Hunnicutt, Edward Asner, Christopher George
▶ Rousing Howard Hawks Western with plenty of action. Gunslinger Wayne and drifter Caan help sober up drunken sheriff Mitchum; the trio find themselves in the midst of a blood feud between ranchers. The stars are in top two-fisted form and George provides nifty support as a badman with a code of honor.
Dist.: Paramount

ELECTRA GLIDE IN BLUE 1973
★ **PG Drama 1:53**
☑ Explicit language, violence
Dir: James William Guercio *Cast:* Robert Blake, Billy Green Bush, Mitchell Ryan, Jeannine Riley, Elisha Cook, Jr.
▶ Diminutive Arizona motorcycle cop Blake dreams of being a detective and gets his chance when he discovers an apparent suicide in a desert shack. Overly arty direction by Guercio goes too heavy on the close-ups, but Blake is solid and there's a fine motorcycle chase.
Dist.: MGM/UA

ELECTRIC DREAMS 1984
★ ★ ★ **PG Romance 1:36**
☑ Adult situations, explicit language, mild violence, adult humor
Dir: Steve Barron *Cast:* Lenny Von Dohlen, Virginia Madsen, Maxwell Caulfield, Bud Cort, Don Fellows
▶ Supersmart computer (voice of Cort) helps bumbling architect Von Dohlen woo gorgeous neighbor Madsen. Machine develops human feelings for the girl and turns against its owner. Leads are appealing but script doesn't develop interesting premise. Rock video director Barron directs this love story in high-tech fashion. Liberal use of pop music includes Culture Club's overlooked gem, "Love Is Love."
Dist.: MGM/UA

ELECTRIC HORSEMAN, THE 1979
★ ★ ★ ★ ★ **PG Drama 2:00**
☑ Adult situations, explicit language
Dir: Sydney Pollack *Cast:* Robert Redford, Jane Fonda, Valerie Perrine, Willie Nelson, John Saxon, Wilford Brimley
▶ Pleasant modern-day Western about alcoholic ex-rodeo champ Redford who sobers up long enough to hijack a prize horse exploited by an evil Las Vegas conglomerate. Skeptical TV reporter Fonda publicizes his ride across Utah to find a wilderness home for the horse. Disarmed by Redford's sincerity, she gradually falls in love. Film debut for country-western star Willie Nelson, who plays Redford's rodeo pal and sings his hit "Mama Don't Let Your Babies Grow Up to Be Cowboys."
Dist.: MCA

ELENI 1985
★ ★ ★ **PG Biography/Drama 1:57**
☑ Violence
Dir: Peter Yates *Cast:* Kate Nelligan, John Malkovich, Linda Hunt, Oliver Cotton, Ronald Pickup
▶ True story of *New York Times* reporter Nicholas Gage's (Malkovich) present-day search for the Communist guerrillas who murdered his mother Eleni (Nelligan) during the 1948 Greek Civil War. Film cuts between Gage's investigations and flashbacks explaining the reasons for Eleni's execution. Nelligan is impressive in a demanding role. **(CC)**
Dist.: Nelson

ELEPHANT BOY 1937 British
★ ★ **NR Drama/Family 1:21 B&W**
Dir: Robert Flaherty, Zoltan Korda *Cast:* Sabu, Walter Hudd, Allan Jeayes, W. W. Holloway, Bruce Gordon, D. J. Williams
▶ Dated but intriguing adventure about young animal trainer Sabu whose favorite elephant is sold to a mean dealer. Sabu steals the elephant and escapes into the jungle, where he discovers a herd of wild pachyderms. Film's semidocumentary approach provides a fascinating view of India in the 1930s; heartwarming subject matter should please children. Film debut for Sabu, a former stableboy who later starred in *The Thief of Bagdad*.
Dist.: Nelson

ELEPHANT MAN, THE 1980
★ ★ ★ ★ **PG Drama 2:03 B&W**
☑ Adult situations
Dir: David Lynch *Cast:* Anthony Hopkins, John Hurt, Anne Bancroft, John Gielgud, Wendy Hiller, Freddie Jones
▶ Moving true story probes the real life of John Merrick (Hurt), the horribly deformed "Ele-

phant Man" rescued from life as a sideshow attraction by compassionate doctor Hopkins in Victorian England. Unsensational account deliberately and gracefully directed by Lynch. Exquisite black-and-white photography, top performances by a restrained Hopkins and a poignant Hurt (under tons of extraordinary makeup). Eight Oscar nominations (Hurt, Lynch, and Best Picture). Not based on the Broadway play.
Dist.: Paramount

11 HARROWHOUSE 1974 British
★★ PG Comedy/Crime 1:38
☑ Explicit language, violence
Dir: Aram Avakian ***Cast:*** Charles Grodin, Candice Bergen, James Mason, Trevor Howard, John Gielgud
► Fast-paced, amusing heist film stars Grodin as a diamond merchant who enlists the help of girlfriend Bergen to rob the vault of a gem cartel headed by Gielgud. Howard plays a seedy millionaire who initiates the scheme. Adapted by Grodin from Gerald A. Browne's best-selling novel. **(CC)**
Dist.: CBS/Fox

ELIMINATORS 1986
★★ PG Action-Adventure 1:36
☑ Explicit language, violence
Dir: Peter Manoogian ***Cast:*** Patrick Reynolds, Denise Crosby, Andrew Prine, Conan Lee, Roy Dotrice
► Injured flyer Reynolds, turned into "mandroid" (half-man, half robot) by mad doctor Dotrice, teams with jungle guide Prine, pretty scientist Crosby, and ninja Lee to seek his revenge. Comic book sci-fi adventure, loaded with gadgets, cute robots, and special effects, doesn't take itself too seriously. **(CC)**
Dist.: CBS/Fox

ELLIE 1983
☆ R Comedy 1:40
☑ Nudity, adult situations, explicit language
Dir: Peter Wittman ***Cast:*** Shelley Winters, Pat Paulsen, Edward Albert, Sheila Kennedy, Patrick Toyat, Robert Keith
► Winters is widowed mom to three hillbilly hammerheads. Claiming that her live-in lover is her brother, she marries a crippled man and kills him by rolling him into a lake. Cripple's gorgeous daughter Kennedy starts offing the sons in revenge. Dirty Dogpatch doin's should entertain those on same mental level as the characters.
Dist.: Vestron

ELMER GANTRY 1960
★★★★ NR Drama 2:26
Dir: Richard Brooks ***Cast:*** Burt Lancaster, Jean Simmons, Arthur Kennedy, Shirley Jones, Dean Jagger, Edward Andrews
► Adaptation of the Sinclair Lewis novel stars Lancaster as the titular salesman-turned-evangelist. In the 1920s Midwest, he sees barnstorming preacher Simmons in action and cons her into letting him join her troupe. Gripping exposé of commercialized religion has even more impact today. Oscars went to writer/director Brooks, Lancaster, and Jones as Gantry's jilted girlfriend who turns to prostitution; also nominated for Best Picture and Scoring by André Previn. Cameo by singer Patti Page.
Dist.: CBS/Fox

EL NORTE 1984
★★★ R Drama 2:19
☑ Adult situations, explicit language, violence
Dir: Gregory Nava ***Cast:*** Zaide Silva Gutierrez, David Villalpando, Ernesto Gomez Cruz, Alicia Del Lago, Lupe Ontiveros, Trinidad Silva
► When their father is killed and mother kidnapped by the army, a Guatemalan brother and sister decide to escape to America. After an arduous border crossing, they find life in the promised land not what was promised. Visually accomplished direction by Nava evokes the plight of the immigrant with emotion and intelligence. Oscar-nominated for Best Original Screenplay. [S]
Dist.: CBS/Fox

EL SUPER 1979
☆ NR Drama 1:30
☑ Adult situations
Dir: Leon Ichaso, Orlando Jimenez-Leal
Cast: Raymundo Hidalgo-Gato, Zully Montero, Reynaldo Medina, Efrain Lopez-Neri, Ana Margarita Martinez-Casado, Elizabeth Peña
► Building super Hidalgo-Gato still pines for his native Cuba after ten years in New York. Cold weather, a broken boiler, and daughter Peña's pregnancy make him consider moving to a warmer climate. Quality low-budget drama, essentially high spirited despite the characters' poverty. Not much plot but well acted. [S]
Dist.: New Yorker

ELUSIVE CORPORAL, THE 1962 French
☆ NR War/Drama 1:49 B&W
Dir: Jean Renoir ***Cast:*** Jean-Pierre Cassel, Claude Brasseur, Claude Rich, Jean Carmet, O. E. Hasse, Mario David
► Cassel gives a fine performance as a French corporal captured by the Germans who makes several escape attempts, sometimes accompanied by cohorts Brasseur and Rich, before finally finding freedom. Overlooked later Renoir effort, ranking just a bit below his best. Often cited as a companion piece to *Grand Illusion*, but much lighter in spirit.
Dist.: Video Yesteryear

ELVES 1989
☆ NR Horror 1:36
☑ Nudity, adult situations, explicit language, graphic violence
Dir: Jeff Mandel ***Cast:*** Dan Haggerty, Julie

Austin, Deanna Lund, Borah Silver, Mansell Rivers-Bland, Christopher Graham
▶ Teen Austin is stalked by evil elves, products of a Nazi genetic engineering experiment who must mate with a virgin to produce the Fourth Reich. Haggerty, an alcoholic department store Santa, tries to save her. Tongue-in-cheek humor fails to alleviate nutty plotting and grotesque violence. Best dialogue exchange: "Is everything all right?" "No, Willy, Gramps is a Nazi."
Dist.: AIP

ELVIRA MADIGAN 1967 Swedish
★ **PG Romance 1:35**
☑ Brief nudity, adult situations
Dir: Bo Widerberg   *Cast:* Pia Degermark, Thommy Berggren, Lennart Malmen, Nina Widerberg, Cleo Jensen
▶ Poetic, expressionistic love story from Sweden about an affair in 1900 between an army officer and a circus tightrope walker that ends in suicide. Visually striking art film is slowly paced and has little in the way of conventional plot development, characterization, or dialogue. Beautiful Mozart score.
Dist.: Thorn/EMI

ELVIRA, MISTRESS OF THE DARK 1988
★ ★ **PG-13 Comedy 1:36**
☑ Adult situations, explicit language, violence, adult humor
Dir: James Signorelli   *Cast:* Cassandra Peterson, Edie McClurg, Daniel Greene, W. Morgan Sheppard, Susan Kellermann, Pat Crawford Brown
▶ Friendly witch inherits New England home, incurring wrath of puritanical parents with her eye-opening wardrobe and uninhibited approach to sex. Teens naturally love her, and rally to her support when she's sentenced to burn at the stake. Crude but good-natured comedy capitalizing on Peterson's TV horror movie hostess role offers an encyclopedia of breast jokes.
Dist.: New World

ELVIS 1979
★ ★ ★ ★ **NR Biography/MFTV 2:29**
Dir: John Carpenter   *Cast:* Kurt Russell, Shelley Winters, Season Hubley, Pat Hingle, Bing Russell
▶ Story of Elvis Presley's rise from truck driver to superstar and his drug-infused fall. Russell is nothing short of extraordinary in an electrifying, magnetic portrayal that sets the standard for Elvis impersonations. Excellent support from Winters as his mother. Made for television but doesn't look it—Carpenter's direction provides a big-screen feel. Russell and Hubley fell in love while doing the movie and married, but were later divorced.
Dist.: Vestron

ELVIS & ME 1988
★ ★ ★ **NR Biography/MFTV 3:20**
Dir: Larry Peerce   *Cast:* Dale Midkiff, Susan

Walters, Billy Green Bush, Jon Cypher, Linda Miller, Anne Haney
▶ The future Mrs. Presley (Walters) is fourteen-year-old Army brat Priscilla Beaulieu when she first takes up with the King (Midkiff), and goes on to ride the roller coaster of ups and downs that was his later career. The real-life Priscilla Presley served as a consultant in this authorized adaptation of her own memoir. Rather bland retelling of a familiar story.   **(CC)**
Dist.: New World

ELVIS ON TOUR 1972
★ ★ **G Documentary/Music 1:33**
Dir: Pierre Adidge, Robert Abel   *Cast:* Elvis Presley, Glen D. Hardin, James Burton
▶ Concert documentary has the unfortunate distinction of being Presley's last film. Onstage performances include "Love Me Tender," a high-velocity "Burning Love," and many other tunes. Brief backstage scenes are interspersed with archival footage from the King's early days.
Dist.: MGM/UA

ELVIS: THAT'S THE WAY IT IS 1970
★ ★ ★ ★ **G Documentary/Music 1:37**
Dir: Denis Sanders   *Cast:* Elvis Presley
▶ Documentary of Elvis preparing for and performing his act at Las Vegas's International Hotel. Interspersed are many brief interviews with aids, fans, hotel personnel. The Elvis of 1970 was still in pretty good shape and he puts on a rousing and thoroughly professional show. Songs include "All Shook Up," "Blue Suede Shoes," "Bridge Over Troubled Water."
Dist.: MGM/UA

EMBRYO 1976
★ ★ ★ **PG Sci-Fi 1:43**
☑ Nudity, violence
Dir: Ralph Nelson   *Cast:* Rock Hudson, Barbara Carrera, Diane Ladd, Roddy McDowall, Anne Schedeen, John Elerick
▶ Scientist Hudson administers growth hormone to fetus of dying pregnant woman. Result is beautiful, full-grown Carrera, gifted with brilliant mind but lacking normal life experience. Hudson promptly falls for her, but since he's tampered with nature Carrera turns out to be more than he'd anticipated. A few notches above average sci-fi fare.
Dist.: IVE

EMERALD FOREST, THE 1985
★ ★ ★ ★ **R Action-Adventure 1:53**
☑ Nudity, violence
Dir: John Boorman   *Cast:* Powers Boothe, Meg Foster, Charley Boorman, Estee Chandler, Tetchie Agbayani
▶ American construction engineer Boothe spends ten years searching for his son Boorman, kidnapped by a remote tribe in the Amazon jungle. Decidedly different adventure from director Boorman supposedly based on fact. Exotic locations, dazzling camerawork,

and convincing native cast transport the audience into another world. (CC)
Dist.: Nelson

EMIL AND THE DETECTIVES 1964
★★★ NR Mystery-Suspense 1:39
Dir: Peter Tewksbury *Cast:* Walter Slezak, Brian Russell, Roger Mobley, Heinz Schubert, Peter Erlich
► In West Berlin, a group of precocious kids band together to thwart the plans of a trio of comically sinister thieves. Polished entertainment in the wholesome Disney tradition. Based on a children's novel by Erich Kastner.
Dist.: Buena Vista

EMILY 1976 British
☆ R Sex 1:26
☑ Nudity, strong sexual content
Dir: Christopher Neame *Cast:* Koo Stark, Sarah Brackett, Victor Spinetti, Jane Hayden, Ina Skriver, Richard Oldfield
► In 1928, seventeen-year-old Stark returns to England after a year at boarding school. While not realizing her mother Brackett supports their luxurious life-style through sex parties, Stark explores her own sexuality with American Oldfield. Glossy vehicle for Stark, one-time girlfriend of England's Prince Andrew. Music by Rod McKuen.
Dist.: MGM/UA

EMMANUELLE 1974 French
★★ X Sex 1:32
☑ Rape, nudity, strong sexual content, explicit language
Dir: Just Jaeckin *Cast:* Sylvia Kristel, Alain Cuny, Marika Green, Daniel Sarky
► In Bangkok, Kristel, the young wife of French diplomat Sarky, gets involved with experienced older man Cuny, who introduces her to kinky pleasures. One of the breakthrough erotic films still generates enough heat to light up your TV. [S]
Dist.: RCA/Columbia

EMPEROR JONES, THE 1933
☆ NR Drama 1:12 B&W
Dir: Dudley Murphy *Cast:* Paul Robeson, Dudley Digges, Frank Wilson, Fredi Washington, Ruby Elzy
► Dated adaptation of the Eugene O'Neill play is of interest today as one of Robeson's best vehicles. He plays a brooding, egotistical railroad porter who flees to Haiti after murdering a friend. Trader Digges (the only white member of the cast) hires Jones to keep his native workers in line. Jones becomes a tyrant, and declares himself emperor of the island. Unusual studio sets enhance the story's gloomy atmosphere.
Dist.: Nelson

EMPIRE OF THE ANTS 1977
★ PG Sci-Fi 1:29
☑ Violence
Dir: Bert I. Gordon *Cast:* Joan Collins, Robert Lansing, John David Carson, Albert Salmi, Jacqueline Scott
► "This is no picnic!" Good-natured thrills and chills about a colony of gigantic ants who've grown by eating radioactive waste. The insects attack pre-*Dynasty* Collins, head of a group of crooked real estate investors, and her colleagues. They make their way to a village only to discover the sugar refinery is controlled by the ants. Based on an H. G. Wells story; sometimes silly, but mostly fun.
Dist.: Nelson

EMPIRE OF THE SUN 1987
★★★★ PG Drama 2:25
☑ Adult situations, explicit language, violence
Dir: Steven Spielberg *Cast:* Christian Bale, John Malkovich, Miranda Richardson, Joe Pantoliano, Rupert Frazer, Nigel Havers, Leslie Phillips, Masato Ibu, Emily Richard, Ben Stiller, Paul McGann
► Spielberg's poetic, hallucinatory account of eleven-year-old Bale's harrowing adventures in Japanese-occupied China during World War II. Separated from his upper-class British parents, bruised and ignored, Bale is "adopted" by shady Yank seaman Malkovich and his pal Pantoliano. Together, they survive the grueling conditions of a refugee camp and, from afar, Bale witnesses the nuking of Nagasaki. Screenplay by Tom Stoppard, adapted from J. G. Ballard's fictionalized account of his childhood in Shanghai. (CC)
Dist.: Warner

EMPIRE STRIKES BACK, THE 1980
★★★★★ PG Sci-Fi/Action-Adventure 2:04
☑ Adult situations, violence
Dir: Irvin Kershner *Cast:* Mark Hamill, Harrison Ford, Carrie Fisher, Billy Dee Williams, Alec Guinness, Frank Oz
► Second episode of the *Star Wars* trilogy delivers the expected action and amazing special effects while rounding out the characters. Han Solo (Ford) and Princess Leia (Fisher) battle an organic asteroid; Luke Skywalker (Hamill) furthers his training with the irascible Yoda (Oz); and Darth Vader reveals a startling secret about his past. New characters include Williams as Lando Calrissian, an untrustworthy trader. Winner of an Oscar for Sound and a special award for Special Effects. Sequel: *Return of the Jedi.* (CC)
Dist.: CBS/Fox

EMPTY BEACH, THE 1985 Australian
★★ NR Mystery-Suspense 1:33
☑ Nudity, explicit language, violence
Dir: Chris Thomson *Cast:* Bryan Brown, Anne Maria Monticelli, Belinda Giblin, Rat Barett, John Wood, Nick Tate
► Pretty blond Giblin asks private eye Brown to investigate the apparent suicide of her husband ten years earlier. Brown discovers that the late hubby was mixed up with shady char-

acters, some of whom are willing to kill to keep Brown's nose out of their business. Witness cinematographer John Seale glorifies sunny Sydney locales; rest of film is decent, if standard, detective fare.
Dist.: Vestron

EMPTY CANVAS, THE 1964 French/Italian
★ **NR Drama 1:58**
Dir: Damiano Damiani   *Cast:* Bette Davis, Horst Buchholz, Catherine Spaak, Isa Miranda, Lea Padovani, Daniela Rocca
▶ Painter Buchholz adores beautiful Spaak, who does not return his feelings despite the promise of his family wealth. Davis, Buchholz's understanding mother, gives him solace when the relationship falters. Awful adaptation of an Alberto Morovia novel. Not even Davis can save it.
Dist.: Nelson

ENCHANTED COTTAGE, THE 1945
★ ★ ★ **NR Fantasy 1:31 B&W**
Dir: John Cromwell   *Cast:* Dorothy McGuire, Robert Young, Herbert Marshall, Mildred Natwick, Spring Byington, Richard Gaines
▶ Suicidal veteran Young, horribly disfigured in World War I, finds romance with plain girl McGuire. They move into a honeymoon cottage in New England, where the power of love reveals the true beauty behind their physical shortcomings. Delicate adaptation of an Arthur Pinero play offers endearingly understated performances and tone.
Dist.: Turner

ENCHANTED FOREST, THE 1945
★ **NR Family 1:18**
Dir: Lew Landers   *Cast:* Harry Davenport, Edmund Lowe, Brenda Joyce, Billy Severn, John Litel, Clancy Cooper
▶ Hermit Davenport can talk to animals and trees, thoroughly enjoying his enchanted forest home. He saves lost little boy Severn and passes on his knowledge, although encroaching civilization threatens his lifestyle. Underrated sleeper, great for kids. Perfectly cast Davenport is a delight.
Dist.: Prism

ENCHANTED ISLAND 1958
☆ **NR Action-Adventure 1:34**
Dir: Allan Dwan   *Cast:* Dana Andrews, Jane Powell, Don Dubbins, Arthur Shields, Ted de Corsia, Friedrich Ledebur
▶ Tired of life aboard their nineteenth-century whaler, seamen Andrews and Dubbins jump ship and live among the cannibals of an island in the tropical Marquessas. Powell is the lovely cannibal girl Fayaway, the possibly mythical creation of Herman Melville in this clumsy adaptation of his autobiographical first novel *Typee.*
Dist.: VCI

ENCORE 1951 British
★ ★ **NR Drama 1:29 B&W**
Dir: Harold French, Pat Jackson, Anthony

Pelissier   *Cast:* Nigel Patrick, Roland Culver, Kay Walsh, Noel Purcell, Glynis Johns, Terence Morgan
▶ Pleasant omnibus of three W. Somerset Maugham short stories: "The Ant and the Grasshopper" (brothers feud over money); "Winter Cruise" (Walsh makes life miserable for passengers on a luxury liner); "Gigolo and Gigolette" (Johns wants her husband to quit high diving). Smoothly diverting.
Dist.: Axon

END, THE 1978
★ ★ ★ **R Comedy 1:40**
☑ Adult situations, explicit language
Dir: Burt Reynolds   *Cast:* Burt Reynolds, Sally Field, Dom DeLuise, Strother Martin, David Steinberg
▶ Ambitious black comedy about real-estate huckster Reynolds, who believes he has a fatal blood disease and decides to kill himself. DeLuise is hilarious as a schizophrenic who assists Reynolds in his suicide attempts. Reynolds's second stab at directing is uneven but often wildly funny, and filled with hilarious cameos: Joanne Woodward, Norman Fell, Myrna Loy, Kristy McNichol, Robby Benson, Carl Reiner, etc.
Dist.: CBS/Fox

ENDANGERED SPECIES 1982
★ ★ ★ **R Drama 1:37**
☑ Brief nudity, adult situations, explicit language, graphic violence
Dir: Alan Rudolph   *Cast:* Robert Urich, JoBeth Williams, Paul Dooley, Hoyt Axton, Peter Coyote
▶ Ex-cop Urich moves to Colorado for peace and quiet, then stumbles across a series of bizarre cattle mutilations that threatens his daughter's safety. Williams plays a spunky sheriff who helps him on the case. Odd blend of romantic thriller and science fiction was based on fact.
Dist.: MGM/UA

ENDGAME 1983 Italian
★ **NR Sci-Fi 1:39**
☑ Rape, nudity, violence
Dir: Steven Benson   *Cast:* Al Cliver, Laura Gemser, George Eastman, Jack Davis
▶ World War III is over, and for kicks the inhabitants of fascist-ruled New York turn to Endgame, a brutal televised death sport. Cliver, a hero of the game, assembles a martial arts army to lead a group of persecuted misfits out of the city. Film has altogether too much crotch stomping and too few thrills.
Dist.: Media

ENDLESS LOVE 1981
★ ★ **R Romance 1:55**
☑ Nudity, adult situations, explicit language
Dir: Franco Zeffirelli   *Cast:* Brooke Shields, Martin Hewitt, Shirley Knight, Don Murray, Richard Kiley, Beatrice Straight
▶ Teenage Hewitt takes revenge on girlfriend Shields's family when her parents break up

their precocious romance. Lush, romantic adaptation of Scott Spencer's novel was a popular examination of lost love. Knight is compelling as Shields's bright but insecure mother. Oscar-nominated title song by Lionel Ritchie.
Dist.: Vestron

ENDLESS NIGHT 1971 British
★ ★ NR Mystery-Suspense **1:39**
☑ Adult situations, violence
Dir: Sidney Gilliat *Cast:* Hayley Mills, Hywel Bennett, Shirley Knight, George Sanders, Richard Kiley, Britt Ekland
▶ Mills, the "sixth richest girl in the world," upsets her family when she falls in love with chauffeur Bennett. But it's a visit from Mills's mysterious old friend Ekland that spells true peril. Confusing flashbacks make it hard to follow this adaptation of an Agatha Christie mystery. Also known as *Agatha Christie's Endless Night*.
Dist.: HBO

ENDLESS SUMMER, THE 1966
★ ★ NR Documentary/Sports **1:35**
Dir: Bruce Brown *Cast:* Mike Hynson, Robert August
▶ California surfers August and Hynson travel around the world sampling the breakers to find the perfect wave. Legendary documentary will be a revelation to non-enthusiasts of the sport, stunningly conveying the dangerous beauty of the ocean, and the near-mystical dedication of those who challenge it.
Dist.: Pacific Arts

END OF THE LINE 1987
★ ★ ★ PG Drama **1:45**
☑ Explicit language
Dir: Jay Russell *Cast:* Wilford Brimley, Levon Helm, Mary Steenburgen, Barbara Barrie, Bob Balaban, Holly Hunter
▶ Hard times hit the small town of Clifford, Arkansas, when the Southland conglomerate closes its railyard. Best friends Brimley and Helm hijack an old engine and ride to the company's headquarters in Chicago to force management to reopen the yard. Upbeat, folksy comedy was a labor of love for Steenburgen, who also produced. Kevin Bacon has a small role as Brimley's raffish ex-son-in-law. (CC)
Dist.: Warner

END OF THE ROAD 1970
★ X Drama **1:50**
☑ Nudity, adult situations, explicit language, violence
Dir: Aram Avakian *Cast:* Stacy Keach, Harris Yulin, Dorothy Tristan, James Earl Jones, Grayson Hall, James Coco
▶ Peculiar, haunting adaptation of John Barth's novel centers on teacher Keach, recently released from mental institution, and his affair with faculty wife Tristan, but story veers into meditations on abortion, drug use, the NASA moon program, and quack Jones's shock treatments for depression. Screenplay

by director Avakian, Dennis McGuire, and Terry Southern. (CC)
Dist.: CBS/Fox

ENEMIES, A LOVE STORY 1989
★ ★ ★ ★ R Drama **1:58**
☑ Nudity, adult situations, explicit language
Dir: Paul Mazursky *Cast:* Ron Silver, Anjelica Huston, Lena Olin, Margaret Sophie Stein, Alan King
▶ In 1949 New York, Holocaust survivor Silver has a big problem. He's married to three women: happily servile Stein, who saved him from the Nazis; fiery Olin, who keeps him on an emotional and sexual rollercoaster; and first wife Huston, whom he thinks was killed in the war. Alternately humorous, tragic, life-affirming; one of Mazursky's best. Period details bring post-War New York's ethnic neighborhoods vividly to life. Based on the novel by Isaac Bashevis Singer. Huston and Olin were Oscar-nominated. (CC)
Dist.: Media

ENEMY BELOW, THE 1957
★ ★ ★ NR War **1:38**
Dir: Dick Powell *Cast:* Robert Mitchum, Curt Jurgens, Theodore Bikel, Russell Collins, Kurt Kreuger, Al (David) Hedison
▶ Tense account of cat-and-mouse battle between Mitchum's destroyer escort and Jurgens's Nazi U-boat in the North Atlantic during World War II is a compelling study of bravery in unforgiving circumstances. Streamlined direction, realistic performances, and accurate portrayal of military tactics contribute to nail-biting suspense. Based on a novel by D. A. Rayner; Walter Rossi's special effects received an Oscar.
Dist.: CBS/Fox

ENEMY FROM SPACE 1957 British
★ NR Sci-Fi **1:24** B&W
Dir: Val Guest *Cast:* Brian Donlevy, Michael Ripper, Sidney James, Bryan Forbes, John Longdon, Vera Day
▶ When strange meteors fall to Earth, a factory springs up at the site. Alien life forms take over the lives of earthlings to conquer the planet one person at a time. The lone scientist who learns the secret is, of course, not believed. Good British version of always-interesting *Invasion of the Body Snatchers* theme. Also known as *Quatermass II*; followed by *Five Million Years to Earth* in 1968.
Dist.: Corinth

ENEMY MINE 1985
★ ★ ★ ★ PG-13 Sci-Fi **1:48**
☑ Explicit language violence
Dir: Wolfgang Petersen *Cast:* Dennis Quaid, Louis Gossett, Jr., Brion James, Richard Marcus, Carolyn McCormick
▶ In the twenty-first century, astronaut Quaid and reptilian Drac (Gossett) are marooned on the forbidding planet Fryine IV. Although enemies, they learn they must work together to survive. Gossett, almost unrecognizable under

his scaly makeup, is surprisingly sympathetic. (CC)
Dist.: CBS/Fox

ENEMY TERRITORY 1987
★ ★ R Action-Adventure 1:29
☑ Explicit language, graphic violence
Dir: Peter Manoogian *Cast:* Gary Frank, Ray Parker, Jr., Jan-Michael Vincent, Frances Foster, Tony Todd, Deon Richmond
► Engrossing but violent exploitation film about meek white insurance agent Frank trapped overnight in a ghetto high-rise controlled by Todd and his Vampires gang. Frank teams up with crippled Vietnam vet Vincent and a Good Samaritan telephone repairman (pop singer Parker in his acting debut) to fight his way out of the building. High body count will please action fans. (CC)
Dist.: CBS/Fox

ENFORCER, THE 1951
★ ★ NR Drama 1:27 B&W
Dir: Bretaigne Windust *Cast:* Humphrey Bogart, Zero Mostel, Ted de Corsia, Everett Sloane, Roy Roberts, Lawrence Tolan
► Crusading district attorney Bogart's case against mob kingpin Sloane is jeopardized when his chief witness dies. To prosecute "Murder Inc.", Bogart must secure another witness's safety before the mob finds her. Hard-hitting, graphic exposé has a memorable gallery of villains.
Dist.: Republic

ENFORCER, THE 1976
★ ★ ★ ★ ★ R Action-Adventure 1:36
☑ Brief nudity, explicit language, graphic violence
Dir: James Fargo *Cast:* Clint Eastwood, Harry Guardino, Tyne Daly, Bradford Dillman, John Mitchum
► Third Dirty Harry film pits him against Revolutionary Strike Force terrorists who have kidnapped San Francisco's mayor. What's worse, he's been given feisty feminist Daly as his new partner. Eastwood, in fine form, trades in his .44 for a bazooka at the climax. Followed by *Sudden Impact.*
Dist.: Warner

ENIGMA 1983 British/French
★ ★ ★ ★ PG Drama 1:41
☑ Brief nudity, adult situations, explicit language, mild violence
Dir: Jeannot Szwarc *Cast:* Martin Sheen, Sam Neill, Brigitte Fossey, Derek Jacobi, Michael Lonsdale, Frank Finlay
► East German defector Sheen is ordered back to East Berlin to stop the KGB assassination of five dissidents. Desperate for information, he forces old girlfriend Fossey to start an affair with Neill, the Russian mastermind behind the plot. Solid cast emphasizes the personal aspects of espionage.
Dist.: Embassy

ENORMOUS CHANGES AT THE LAST MINUTE 1983
★ NR Drama 1:50
☑ Adult situations, explicit language
Dir: Mirra Bank, Ellen Hovde, Muffie Meyer
Cast: Ellen Barkin, Kevin Bacon, Maria Tucci, Lynn Milgrim
► Three separate stories adapted from a collection by Grace Paley. First has newly divorced Barkin going on welfare and making hard choices about love and money. In second, Milgrim discovers a shocking secret about her parents' past. And third sees social worker Tucci in affair with cab driver Bacon. Film makes close human relationships seem sad and impossible. John Sayles scripted.
Dist.: Vidmark

ENSIGN PULVER 1964
★ ★ NR Comedy 1:44
Dir: Joshua Logan *Cast:* Robert Walker, Jr., Burl Ives, Walter Matthau, Tommy Sands, Millie Perkins
► Follow-up to the classic *Mister Roberts* details the further adventures of free-spirited Ensign Pulver (Walker assumes the role Jack Lemmon played in the original). Genial service comedy but not in the same league as the earlier film. Large cast includes bit parts by young Jack Nicholson and Larry Hagman.
Dist.: Warner

ENTER LAUGHING 1967
★ ★ NR Comedy 1:52
Dir: Carl Reiner *Cast:* José Ferrer, Shelley Winters, Reni Santoni, Elaine May, Jack Gilford, Janet Margolin, David Opatoshu, Michael J. Pollard, Don Rickles
► Against the objections of parents Winters and Opatoshu, young Santoni attempts a stage career in a theater owned by hammy former star Ferrer. His initial efforts are predictably disastrous in this amusing adaptation of Reiner's semiautobiographical Broadway hit.
Dist.: RCA/Columbia

ENTERTAINER, THE 1960 British
★ ★ ★ NR Drama 1:36 B&W
Dir: Tony Richardson *Cast:* Laurence Olivier, Brenda de Banzie, Joan Plowright, Roger Livesey, Alan Bates, Albert Finney
► One of the high points of Olivier's career is his Oscar-nominated performance as Archie Rice, a music hall has-been who refuses to admit his lack of talent. John Osborne's relentlessly bleak play describes Rice's brutal treatment of his family, brought to vivid life by a wonderful supporting cast. Film debut for Plowright, who later married Olivier. Remade as a TV movie with Jack Lemmon in 1975.
Dist.: Film Forum

ENTERTAINING MR. SLOANE 1970 British
☆ NR Comedy 1:34
☑ Nudity, adult situations
Dir: Douglas Hickox *Cast:* Beryl Reid, Harry Andrews, Peter McEnery, Alan Webb
► Sexy young Mr. Sloane (McEnery) meets

spinster Reid and her middle-aged homosexual brother Andrews. Using his wiles, Sloane ingratiates himself, and soon the siblings are fighting for his affection. Outstanding acting from Reid, Andrews, and McEnery can't make up for this talky and generally unsuccessful adaptation of the Joe Orton play.
Dist.: HBO

ENTER THE DRAGON 1973
★★★★ R Martial Arts 1:39
☑ Violence
Dir: Robert Clouse ***Cast:*** Bruce Lee, John Saxon, Jim Kelly, Ahna Capri, Shih Kien, Yang Tse
► Lee's last role before his death is one of the best of all kung-fu pictures. On a mission to avenge his sister's death, he teams up with ex–Army buddies Saxon and Kelly to infiltrate druglord Kien's island fortress. Strong production values and a nice comic sensibility add depth to the formulaic plot. An excellent showcase for Lee's grace and skill (he also choreographed the fights).
Dist.: Warner

ENTER THE NINJA 1981
★★ R Martial Arts 1:39
☑ Adult situations, explicit language, graphic violence
Dir: Menahem Golan ***Cast:*** Franco Nero, Susan George, Sho Kosugi, Alex Courtney, Will Hare, Christopher George
► Martial arts expert Nero enlists the aid of his friend Courtney to defend his Filipino plantation from Christopher George, a greedy real estate developer. Susan George, Nero's sexy wife, proves just as adept as the men in fighting off the villains. Characters and plot take a back seat to the action scenes.
Dist.: MGM/UA

ENTITY, THE 1983
★★★ R Horror 2:05
☑ Nudity, explicit language, violence
Dir: Sidney J. Furie ***Cast:*** Barbara Hershey, Ron Silver, David Labisoa, George Coe, Margaret Blye, Jacqueline Brooks
► Single mom Hershey thinks she is being raped by huge, invisible demon. Closed-minded shrink Silver tries to convince her that it's all in her mind. Relief comes in the form of parapsychologists, who put Hershey into lab environment and freeze the libidinous spirit when it comes to get her. Standard possession stuff is supposedly based on true incident.
Dist.: CBS/Fox

ENTRE NOUS 1983 French
★ PG Drama 1:50
☑ Brief nudity, adult situations, explicit language, violence
Dir: Diane Kurys ***Cast:*** Miou-Miou, Isabelle Huppert, Guy Marchand, Jean-Pierre Bacri
► Huppert and Miou-Miou, both survivors of World War II, form a close, fifteen-year friendship that sustains them through the breakup of their respective marriages. Compassionate yet tough-minded drama from French director Kurys with fully rounded, three-dimensional characterizations. Not so much a "woman's film" as a human one which concedes the male point of view without condescension or dogma. [S]
Dist.: MGM/UA

EQUALIZER 2000 1987 Filipino
☆ R Action-Adventure 1:19
☑ Adult situations, explicit language, violence
Dir: Cirio H. Santiago ***Cast:*** Richard Norton, Corinne Wahl, William Steis, Robert Patrick, Frederick Bailey
► In yet another postapocalyptic scenario where guns and gas are the big motivators, the multi-shot title weapon being especially coveted. Norton, a pumped-up loner, finds himself teamed with real-life porn/model Wahl against the bad guys who are hoarding fuel. Silly film joins crowd on long skirts of *Mad Max* series.
Dist.: MGM/UA

EQUUS 1977
★★ R Drama 2:18
☑ Nudity, adult situations, explicit language, violence
Dir: Sidney Lumet ***Cast:*** Richard Burton, Peter Firth, Colin Blakely, Joan Plowright, Eileen Atkins, Jenny Agutter
► Disillusioned shrink Burton probes the mind of teenager Firth, who blinded six horses. Burton begins to envy the troubled youth's passion. Thought-provoking, passionate drama about insanity vs. repression from the play by Peter Shaffer. Overly literal direction by Lumet (especially in the horse-blinding scene); dynamic Oscar-nominated work by Burton.
Dist.: MGM/UA

ERASERHEAD 1978
☆ NR Horror 1:30 B&W
☑ Adult humor
Dir: David Lynch ***Cast:*** John Nance, Charlotte Stewart, Allen Joseph, Jeanne Bates, Judith Anna Roberts
► Grotesquely fascinating cult film. In a squalid tenement apartment, a horribly mutated baby is born to a repressed couple. Exploration of the relationship between monster and man marked Lynch's auspicious but unsettling feature debut.
Dist.: RCA/Columbia

ERENDIRA 1983 French/German/Mexican
☆ NR Drama 1:43
☑ Rape, nudity, explicit language, violence
Dir: Ruy Guerra ***Cast:*** Irene Papas, Claudia Ohana, Michael Lonsdale, Oliver Rufus
► Grande dame Pappas forces beautiful granddaughter Ohana into prostitution after girl accidentally burns down house. She obeys, but later plots with young boy to kill grandma and escape. Screenplay by Nobel Prize-winner Gabriel Garcia Marquez is based on one of his own stories. Director's effort to

find visual equivalent of Marquez's "magic realism" results in film that departs from all realism, magic or otherwise. Papas gives her all in a project best chalked up as a nice try. [S]
Dist.: Media

ERIK 1990
★ NR Action-Adventure 1:30
☑ Explicit language, violence
Dir: Michael Kennedy ***Cast:*** Stephen McHattie, Deborah Van Valkenburgh, Aharon Ipale, Ismael Carlo, Michael Champion, Dennis A. Pratt
► Mercenary McHattie, a Vietnam veteran, is hired by a Central American dictator. However, he finds his loyalty changing due to his romance with Van Valkenburgh, a journalist sympathetic to the rebels. Turgid action pic is dully directed. McHattie lacks charisma in the title role.
Dist.: SVS

ERIK THE VIKING 1989 British
★★ PG-13 Fantasy/Comedy 1:44
☑ Adult situations, explicit language, violence
Dir: Terry Jones ***Cast:*** Tim Robbins, Mickey Rooney, Eartha Kitt, Terry Jones, John Cleese, Imogen Stubbs
► Sensitive viking Erik (Robbins) is tired of pillaging, raping, and murdering. He visits eccentric soothsayer Kitt, who tells him to travel to the end of the earth to find the Horn Resounding, which will bring the violent age to an end. He sets off with motley crew on adventures taking them to peaceful and goofy land of Hy-Brasil and the very nasty Pit of Hell. Outlandish fantasy is filled with deadpan humor of the Monty Python sort. Lots of potential, but unfortunately misses more than it hits.
Dist.: Orion

ERNEST GOES TO CAMP 1987
★★ PG Comedy 1:33
☑ Mild violence
Dir: John Cherry ***Cast:*** Jim Varney, Victoria Racimo, John Vernon, Iron Eyes Cody, Lyle Alzado
► Film debut for Varney's popular TV commercial character has Ernest babysitting six tough inner-city kids at Camp Kikakee. Meanwhile, an evil building contractor tries to trick Indian chief Cody into giving up the camp's lease. Critics hated this film, but audiences were delighted by its goofy sense of humor and outlandish slapstick stunts. **(CC)**
Dist.: Buena Vista

ERNEST GOES TO JAIL 1990
★★ PG Comedy 1:21
☑ Mild violence
Dir: John Cherry ***Cast:*** Jim Varney, Gailard Sartain, Bill Byrge, Barbara Bush, Barry Scott, Randall "Tex" Cobb
► Third in the series features Ernest P. Worrell (Varney) as a juror who resembles a death row inmate (also Varney). When the jury tours the prison, a switch is made, leaving the hapless Ernest in jail and slated for execution. Varney's broad clowning seems to please kids, although adults might appreciate Bush and canine actor Barkley better. **(CC)**
Dist.: Buena Vista

ERNEST SAVES CHRISTMAS 1988
★★ PG Comedy 1:29
☑ Explicit language
Dir: John Cherry ***Cast:*** Jim Varney, Douglas Seale, Oliver Clark, Noelle Parker, Gailard Sartain, Billie Bird
► Seale plays Santa Claus, eager to retire and looking for a replacement, but his first choice, Florida kiddie show host Clark, turns down the offer. Worse yet, customs men seize Santa's reindeer and a teen hoodlum swipes his bag of gifts. To the rescue comes oddball cab driver Varney. Fans of Varney's mugging, rubber-faced Ernest P. Worrell, made famous in TV commercials and *Ernest Goes to Camp*, won't be disappointed, but others may miss the point.
Dist.: Buena Vista

ERRAND BOY, THE 1962
★★ NR Comedy 1:32 B&W
Dir: Jerry Lewis ***Cast:*** Jerry Lewis, Brian Donlevy, Howard McNear, Fritz Feld, Sig Ruman, Doodles Weaver
► Wacky Lewis gets Hollywood movie studio job and Tinseltown will never be the same. "Bonanza" stars Lorne Greene, Michael Landon, Dan Blocker, and Pernell Roberts, along with Stooge Joe Besser, have cameos.
Dist.: IVE

ESCAPADE 1955 British
★ NR Comedy 1:28 B&W
Dir: Philip Leacock ***Cast:*** John Mills, Yvonne Mitchell, Alastair Sim, Jeremy Spenser, Peter Asher, Andrew Ray
► Temperamental pacifist Mills does not practice what he preaches at home, leading to possible breakup with wife Mitchell and strained relationships with his three sons. The boys proceed to gain both his and the world's attention with a dramatic maneuver. Unique, ahead-of-its time movie. Child and adult performers enhance a magnificent message.
Dist.: Video Yesteryear

ESCAPADE IN JAPAN 1957
★ NR Family 1:33
Dir: Arthur Lubin ***Cast:*** Cameron Mitchell, Teresa Wright, Jon Provost, Roger Nakagawa, Phillip Ober, Clint Eastwood
► American lad Provost is saved by Japanese fishermen when his plane goes down in the ocean. Taken to their village, he runs away to look for his parents with fisherman's son Nakagawa. Eastwood has a tiny role in this lightweight family offering, notable mainly for picturesque glimpses of Japan.
Dist.: VCI

ESCAPE ARTIST, THE 1982
★ ★ ★ **PG Drama 1:36**
☑ Explicit language
Dir: Caleb Deschanel   *Cast:* Griffin O'Neal, Raul Julia, Teri Garr, Joan Hackett, Gabriel Dell, Desi Arnaz, Jackie Coogan, Huntz Hall
▶ Whimsical, family-oriented story about famous magician's gifted son O'Neal (in his film debut) who uses his skills to expose mayor Arnaz's corrupt administration. Plenty of amusing magic tricks for children; adults will appreciate the unusual set design and nostalgic cameos by Coogan and former Bowery Boys Dell and Hall. From the makers of *The Black Stallion.*
Dist.: Vestron

ESCAPE FROM ALCATRAZ 1979
★ ★ ★ ★ **PG Mystery-Suspense 1:52**
☑ Adult situations, explicit language, violence
Dir: Don Siegel   *Cast:* Clint Eastwood, Patrick McGoohan, Roberts Blossom, Jack Thibeau, Fred Ward, Paul Benjamin
▶ Taut, authentic account of the only successful escape from the notorious Alcatraz Island prison. Eastwood is Frank Morris, a hardened con who masterminds the breakout with his pals Thibeau and Ward. McGoohan plays a remarkably chilling warden. Expert direction and a streamlined, unsentimental script add to the suspense.
Dist.: Paramount

ESCAPE FROM NEW YORK 1981
★ ★ ★ **R Sci-Fi 1:39**
☑ Brief nudity, adult situations, explicit language, graphic violence
Dir: John Carpenter   *Cast:* Kurt Russell, Lee Van Cleef, Ernest Borgnine, Donald Pleasence, Isaac Hayes, Adrienne Barbeau
▶ Manhattan in 1997 is a walled-in maximum security prison for murderers, terrorists, and perverts. Hayes, the Duke of New York, kidnaps President Pleasence; war-hero-turned-convict Snake Plissken (Russell) has twenty-four hours to free him. Brutal, lightning-paced stunts, inventive special effects and Russell's marvelously macho hero will delight action fans. Borgnine is amusing as the Big Apple's last cabbie.
Dist.: Nelson

ESCAPE FROM SAFEHAVEN 1989
☆ **R Action-Adventure 1:25**
☑ Nudity, explicit language, graphic violence
Dir: Brian Thomas Jones   *Cast:* Rick Gianasi, John Wittenbauer, Roy MacArthur, William Beckwith, Sammi Gavitch
▶ The South Bronx needs little set dressing to serve as the backdrop for this post-apocalypse cheapie. Gianasi is a stranger who helps a beaten-down family battle British-accented persecutors. With costumes pulled from someone's punk closet, amateurish effort lacks action or sense.
Dist.: SVS

ESCAPE FROM THE PLANET OF THE APES 1971
★ ★ ★ **G Sci-Fi 1:38**
Dir: Don Taylor   *Cast:* Roddy McDowall, Kim Hunter, Bradford Dillman, Natalie Trundy, Eric Braeden, Sal Mineo
▶ Third episode in the simian series is set in the human world of 1971. Apes Cornelius (McDowall), Zira (Hunter), and Milo (Mineo) flee their exploding world to Earth in the spaceship Charlton Heston left behind in the first film. Fearing that pregnant Zira's child will cause the overthrow of the human race, U.S. government officials hunt the "dangerous" chimps. Two more sequels followed.   **(CC)**
Dist.: CBS/Fox

ESCAPE TO ATHENA 1979 British
★ ★ ★ **PG Action-Adventure 1:42**
☑ Explicit language, violence
Dir: George Pan Cosmatos   *Cast:* Roger Moore, Telly Savalas, David Niven, Claudia Cardinale, Richard Roundtree, Sonny Bono
▶ Odd World War II comedy-adventure about an unlikely group of Allied POWs who team up with art-loving Nazi warden Moore and Greek Resistance leader Savalas to both destroy a German missile base and loot ancient art treasures. Elliott Gould and Stefanie Powers play USO entertainers who join the plot when their plane is shot down.
Dist.: CBS/Fox

ESCAPE TO BURMA 1955
★ ★ **NR Action-Adventure 1:16**
Dir: Allan Dwan   *Cast:* Barbara Stanwyck, Robert Ryan, David Farrar, Murvyn Vye, Robert Warwick, Reginald Denny
▶ Unjustly charged of murder, Ryan flees to Stanwyck's jungle plantation. Arrival of policeman Farrar disrupts their passionate affair. Subsequent chase through backlot jungle features encounters with leopards and elephants. Second-rate adventure lacks credibility.
Dist.: Buena Vista

ESCAPE TO WITCH MOUNTAIN 1975
★ ★ ★ ★ ★ **G Fantasy 1:37**
Dir: John Hough   *Cast:* Eddie Albert, Ray Milland, Donald Pleasence, Kim Richards, Ike Eisenmann, Denver Pyle
▶ Monterey provides the setting for an amiable Disney fantasy about Richards and Eisenmann, orphans with peculiar powers who are coerced by Milland and Pleasence into predicting the stock market. Albert is a gruff old bachelor who helps the kids escape. Smooth entertainment features some unusual sci-fi twists.
Dist.: Buena Vista

ESCAPE 2000 1981 Australian
☆ **R Action-Adventure 1:32**

☑ Nudity, explicit language, graphic violence
Dir: Brian Trenchard-Smith **Cast:** Steve Railsback, Olivia Hussey, Michael Craig, Carmen Duncan
► In the not-too-distant future, Railsback and Hussy are jailed as "deviates." Craig offers pair their freedom if they survive after serving as prey for hunting party arranged to amuse visiting VIPs. Leads pull through to inspire prison revolt; end-title card reminds: "Revolution begins with misfits." Horridly gruesome presentation has no action, no suspense, just sadistic killing. Originally titled *Turkey Shoot.*
Dist.: Nelson

ETERNALLY YOURS 1939
★ NR Drama 1:31 B&W
Dir: Tay Garnett **Cast:** Loretta Young, David Niven, Hugh Herbert, Billie Burke, C. Aubrey Smith, Raymond Walburn, ZaSu Pitts, Broderick Crawford, Eve Arden
► Magician Niven woos Young away from her fiancé Crawford, but after they are married she tires of his daredevil tricks. Niven pursues his wayward wife to the 1939 New York World's Fair in this glossy if insubstantial entertainment. Exceptional supporting cast.
Dist.: Video Yesteryear ☐

E.T. THE EXTRA-TERRESTRIAL 1982
★ ★ ★ ★ ★ PG Family/Fantasy 2:00
☑ Explicit language, mild violence
Dir: Steven Spielberg **Cast:** Dee Wallace, Henry Thomas, Drew Barrymore, Peter Coyote, Robert MacNaughton
► Extraterrestrial stranded on Earth is befriended by young Thomas. Soon the kid's brother MacNaughton, sister Barrymore, and mom Wallace share the secret, but government authorities lurk close behind. The #1 box-office champ of all time, Spielberg's fantasy weaves a magical spell, combining realistic suburban detail with flights of fancy. Moving Thomas/E.T. relationship puts the film's many imitators to shame. Uplifting, sweet, original, and E.T. is totally convincing. A Best Picture nominee.
Dist.: MCA

EUREKA 1984 British
★ R Drama 2:09
☑ Nudity, explicit language, violence
Dir: Nicolas Roeg **Cast:** Gene Hackman, Theresa Russell, Rutger Hauer, Jane Lapotaire, Ed Lauter, Mickey Rourke
► Gold prospector Hackman strikes it rich in Canada, but is too paranoid about enemies to enjoy his success. Retiring to a tropical island, he watches wife Lapotaire sink into alcoholism and daughter Russell be seduced by gigolo Hauer. Gloomy melodrama about obsession has a typically creditable performance from Hackman.
Dist.: MGM/UA

EUROPEANS, THE 1979 British
★ NR Drama 1:30

☑ Adult situations
Dir: James Ivory **Cast:** Lee Remick, Robin Ellis, Lisa Eichhorn, Tim Woodward, Wesley Addy, Tim Choate
► Baroness Remick and artist Woodward are siblings from Europe who suddenly descend on American cousins and cause gentle havoc. New England girl Eichhorn ignores clergyman beau for colorful Woodward. Remick dangles two Americans, one young and one old, on her romantic string. Encounter between old and new worlds changes each character. Almost every frame of this subtle and splendidly acted Merchant/Ivory production takes place in a blaze of autumnal foliage. Based on the novel by Henry James.
Dist.: Vestron

EVEL KNIEVEL 1971
★ PG Biography 1:30
☑ Mild violence
Dir: Marvin J. Chomsky **Cast:** George Hamilton, Sue Lyon, Rod Cameron, Bert Freed, Dub Taylor
► Campy biography of Evel Knievel (Hamilton), king of stuntmen, whose daredevil motorcycle jumps earned him fortune and fame. Story traces his youth in Butte, Montana, to the jump over the fountain at Caesar's Palace that almost killed him. Knievel played himself in *Viva Knievel.*
Dist.: MPI

EVERGREEN 1934 British
★ NR Musical 1:31 B&W
Dir: Victor Saville **Cast:** Jessie Matthews, Sonnie Hale, Betty Balfour, Barry Mackay, Ivor MacLaren, Hartley Power
► Matthews, one of England's most popular musical figures, plays a dual role: a singing star blackmailed into giving up her daughter, and the full-grown daughter who attempts to pass as her mother on the stage. Rodgers and Hart score, including "Dancing on the Ceiling" and "Dear, Dear," helped make this the most successful of early British musicals.
Dist.: Various

EVERLASTING SECRET FAMILY, THE 1989 Australian
☆ NR Drama 1:34
☑ Nudity, strong sexual content, adult situations, explicit language
Dir: Michael Thornhill **Cast:** Arthur Dignam, Mark Lee, Dennis Miller, Heather Mitchell, Paul Goddard, John Meillon
► Strange, embarrassing story based on the premise that Australia is ruled by secret homosexual cabal that recruits likely schoolboys as new members. Story is based on youthful Lee's attempts to raise status in shadowy organization as the lover of powerful senator Dignam, and later the senator's son. Idea is novel, but execution is painfully pretentious and lacks any sense of humor.
Dist.: August Entertainment

EVERYBODY'S ALL-AMERICAN 1988
★★★★ R Drama 2:07
☑ Brief nudity, adult situations, explicit language, violence
Dir: Taylor Hackford ***Cast:*** Dennis Quaid, Jessica Lange, Timothy Hutton, John Goodman, Raymond Baker, Carl Lumbly
▸ Football star Quaid, Louisiana's "Grey Ghost," and beauty queen Lange seem destined for a perfect marriage, but their relationship sours once Quaid's sports career is over. Ambitious soap opera covering a twenty-five-year span is smoothly entertaining rather than incisive. Goodman, a bigoted tackle addicted to gambling, and Lumbly, a black athlete defeated by discrimination, are impressive.
Dist.: Warner

EVERYBODY WINS 1990
★★ R Drama 1:37
☑ Brief nudity, adult situations, explicit language
Dir: Karel Reisz ***Cast:*** Debra Winger, Nick Nolte, Will Patton, Jack Warden, Kathleen Whilhoite, Judith Ivey
▸ Egged on by Winger, a mysterious woman who seems to be schizophrenic, New England private eye Nolte reopens a case in which the wrong man may have been convicted of murder. Suspects include Patton, leader of a biker gang, but Nolte's biggest problem is indifference from corrupt authorities. Film's biggest problem is an indecipherable screenplay by Arthur Miller; listless direction and complete absence of tension and plausibility don't help. (CC)
Dist.: Orion

EVERY GIRL SHOULD BE MARRIED 1948
★★ NR Comedy 1:25 B&W
Dir: Don Hartman ***Cast:*** Cary Grant, Franchot Tone, Diana Lynn, Betsy Drake, Alan Mowbray
▸ Department store clerk Drake spots doctor/eligible bachelor Grant and does everything in her power to snare him, including using boss Tone as a fake beau. Lightweight romantic comedy was Drake's film debut; Grant married her a year later.
Dist.: Turner [C]

EVERY MAN FOR HIMSELF AND GOD AGAINST ALL 1975 German
☆ NR Drama 1:50
☑ Explicit language
Dir: Werner Herzog ***Cast:*** Bruno S., Walter Ladengast, Brigitte Mira, Hans Musaus, Willy Semmelrogge
▸ In early nineteenth-century Nuremberg, young Kaspar Hauser (Bruno S.) is thrust into civilization after being raised in almost complete isolation. At first incapable of speech, he is gradually trained to accept society. Based on a true incident, this provocative, moving film cemented director/screenwriter Herzog's world-wide reputation. Bruno S., a former street singer, gives a mesmerizing performance. Also known as *The Mystery of Kaspar Hauser.* [S]
Dist.: Paramount

EVERYTHING YOU ALWAYS WANTED TO KNOW ABOUT SEX BUT WERE AFRAID TO ASK 1972
★★ R Comedy 1:27
☑ Strong sexual content, adult humor
Dir: Woody Allen ***Cast:*** Woody Allen, Gene Wilder, Burt Reynolds, Tony Randall, Lynn Redgrave, Lou Jacobi, John Carradine, Louise Lasser, Anthony Quayle
▸ Wildly funny if uneven takeoff on Dr. David Reuben's best-seller includes episodes about Wilder's love for a sheep; mad doctor Carradine's bizarre creation: a giant breast that terrorizes countryside ("These things usually travel in pairs," someone notes); game show entitled "What's My Perversion?"; and look inside the human body during sex, featuring Reynolds and Randall in a master control room and Allen as a hapless sperm.
Dist.: Key

EVERY TIME WE SAY GOODBYE 1986 Israeli
★★ PG-13 Romance 1:35
☑ Brief nudity, adult situations, explicit language
Dir: Moshe Mizrahi ***Cast:*** Tom Hanks, Cristina Marsillach, Benedict Taylor, Anat Atzmon
▸ In World War II Jerusalem, American pilot Hanks falls in love with Sephardic Jew Marsillach. Her large and very traditional family sets up roadblocks to the romance. Will true love prevail? Israeli backdrops are the only lively things about this run-of-the-mill, lukewarm romance. Marsillach is gorgeous, but Hanks seems uncomfortably out of place.
Dist.: Vestron

EVERY WHICH WAY BUT LOOSE 1978
★★★★ PG Comedy 1:55
☑ Brief nudity, explicit language, violence
Dir: James Fargo ***Cast:*** Clint Eastwood, Sondra Locke, Geoffrey Lewis, Beverly D'Angelo, Ruth Gordon
▸ Eastwood, playing a boozy truck driver and barroom brawler, chases beautiful singer Locke from California to Denver. Along the way he fights off slimy bikers and redneck cops. Extremely broad comedy was a gigantic pop hit, inspiring the sequel *Any Which Way You Can.* Filled with wacky fights, great country-western songs (by Mel Tillis, Charlie Rich, and others), and scene-stealing comic relief from Clyde, Eastwood's ribald pet orangutan.
Dist.: Warner

EVIL, THE 1978
★★★★ R Horror 1:28
☑ Explicit language, graphic violence
Dir: Gus Trikonis ***Cast:*** Richard Crenna, Joanna Pettet, Victor Buono, Andrew Prine, Cassie Yates
▸ Doctor Crenna rents huge gothic mansion

in the country for his drug rehabilitation summer program. The building is haunted by the Evil One (Buono), who imprisons the group inside. Scary excursion into the realm of the supernatural that won favorable critical attention.
Dist.: Embassy

EVIL DEAD, THE 1983
★ NR Horror 1:25
☑ Adult situations, graphic violence
Dir: Sam Raimi *Cast:* Bruce Campbell, Ellen Sandweiss, Betsy Baker, Hal Delrich, Sarah York
▶ Energetic blend of fun and fear. Clean-cut kids camp out in a deserted cabin with resurrected evil spirits. Grisly, campy special effects include contorted faces, dismembered limbs, and geysers of spurting blood. Sequel appeared four years later.
Dist.: HBO

EVIL DEAD II 1987
★ X Horror 1:25
☑ Explicit language, graphic violence
Dir: Sam Raimi *Cast:* Bruce Campbell, Sarah Berry, Dan Hicks, Cassie Wesley, Rick Francis
▶ Campbell and girlfriend Berry go to mountain cabin where they find recording which literally raises the dead; Campbell must fight the demons when they turn Berry into one of them. Skillful camerawork and inventive humorous touches bring horrific life to genre clichés; however, silly-looking monster and excessive violence wear out viewer patience.
Dist.: Vestron

EVIL OF FRANKENSTEIN, THE 1964 British
★ NR Horror 1:24
Dir: Freddie Francis *Cast:* Peter Cushing, Peter Woodthorpe, Kiwi Kingston, Sandor Eles, Duncan Lamont
▶ Sequel to *Revenge of Frankenstein* stars Cushing as Doctor Frankenstein, who melts the ice to thaw his frozen monster (Kingston). Woodthorpe, brought in to help the good doctor, attempts to use the creature for his own evil purposes. Lackluster entry in the Hammer series.
Dist.: MCA

EVILSPEAK 1982
★ R Horror 1:29
☑ Nudity, explicit language, graphic violence
Dir: Eric Weston *Cast:* Clint Howard, R. G. Armstrong, Joseph Cortese, Claude Earl Jones, Haywood Nelson
▶ Tubby nerd Howard is tormented by fellow students at ritzy military academy until he hacks around on computer and punches up Satan. Evil pigs attack school secretary in shower, and by end of film, hell-empowered Howard is flying through school with bloody sword, reaping the heads of hateful kids. Su-

pernatural revenger is not quite bad enough to be funny.
Dist.: CBS/Fox

EVIL THAT MEN DO, THE 1984
★★★ R Action-Adventure 1:30
☑ Nudity, adult situations, explicit language, graphic violence
Dir: J. Lee Thompson *Cast:* Charles Bronson, Theresa Saldana, Jose Ferrer, Joseph Maher, Raymond St. Jacques, John Glover
▶ Slickly made, vengeance-glorifying actioner stars Bronson as a former political assassin. He's recruited out of retirement to rub out Maher, an evil sadist working for a fascist Central American government. Filmed in Mexico. (CC)
Dist.: RCA/Columbia

EVIL UNDER THE SUN 1982 British
★★★★ PG Mystery-Suspense 1:56
☑ Explicit language, violence
Dir: Guy Hamilton *Cast:* Peter Ustinov, Maggie Smith, Diana Rigg, James Mason, Roddy McDowall, Sylvia Miles, Jane Birkin, Colin Blakely, Nicholas Clay
▶ Agatha Christie's super-sleuth Hercule Poirot (Ustinov) sets out to salvage his reputation and solve the murder of famous, bitchy actress Rigg found strangled at a sunny Adriatic resort. Smith, McDowall, and Mason are among the many guests with potential motives. Soundtrack is an anthology of Cole Porter hits.
Dist.: HBO

EXCALIBUR 1981 British
★★★★ PG Action-Adventure 2:20
☑ Nudity, adult situations, violence
Dir: John Boorman *Cast:* Nigel Terry, Helen Mirren, Nicholas Clay, Cherie Lunghi, Nicol Williamson, Robert Addie
▶ Beautiful but long-winded historical epic traces the rise of King Arthur (Terry), the fall of Camelot, the destruction of the evil Mordred (Addie), the quest for the Holy Grail, and the sword-in-the-stone legend. Williamson is superb as Merlin, a virile wizard/trickster. Filmed in breathtaking Irish locales. Adapted from the Malory classic *Le Morte d'Arthur*.
Dist.: Warner

EXECUTIONER, THE 1970 British
★★ PG Action-Adventure 1:47
☑ Adult situations
Dir: Sam Wanamaker *Cast:* George Peppard, Joan Collins, Keith Michell, Judy Geeson, Oscar Homolka
▶ British intelligence agent Peppard tracks down fellow agent Michell suspected of double dealing with the Soviets, but is sidetracked by an old flame. Talky spy-drama that's heavier on drama than action.
Dist.: RCA/Columbia

EXECUTIONER'S SONG, THE 1982
★★★★ NR Biography/MFTV 3:20
☑ Nudity, adult situations, violence

Dir: Lawrence Schiller *Cast:* Tommy Lee Jones, Rosanna Arquette, Christine Lahti, Eli Wallach, Steven Keats, Jordan Clarke
► Norman Mailer adapted his own best-seller about Gary Gilmore (Jones), the parolee who turned to robbery and murder when he was unable to make it in the outside world and then begged the state to execute him so he could die with dignity. Searing portrait of a man who could find no peace in this life; bravura Emmy-winning performance by Jones complemented by Arquette's sizzling turn as his girlfriend Nicole Baker.
Dist.: USA

EXECUTIVE ACTION 1973
★ ★ PG Drama 1:31
⊙ Adult situations, violence
Dir: David Miller *Cast:* Burt Lancaster, Robert Ryan, Will Geer, Gilbert Green, Ed Lauter, Deanna Darrin
► Political melodrama explains the assassination of John F. Kennedy in terms of a military conspiracy instigated by high-placed officials Lancaster and Ryan. Farfetched in the extreme, with an exploitative use of Dallas newsreel footage. Ryan's last film.
Dist.: Warner

EXECUTIVE SUITE 1954
★ ★ ★ ★ NR Drama 1:44 B&W
Dir: Robert Wise *Cast:* William Holden, June Allyson, Barbara Stanwyck, Fredric March, Walter Pidgeon, Louis Calhern, Shelley Winters, Paul Douglas, Nina Foch, Dean Jagger
► The head of a large furniture concern has suddenly died. Who will replace him? Film's contenders include a rogues' gallery of corporate types; from March's amoral toady to Pidgeon's rat-race-weary senior VP. The women are all wives, secretaries, or mistresses; but Stanwyck is also a stockholder, and eventually casts deciding vote. Diverting entertainment based on the book by Cameron Hawley. (CC)
Dist.: MGM/UA

EX-MRS. BRADFORD, THE 1936
★ ★ NR Mystery-Suspense 1:20 B&W
Dir: Stephen Roberts *Cast:* William Powell, Jean Arthur, James Gleason, Eric Blore, Robert Armstrong, Lila Lee
► Doctor Powell must solve a murder in which all clues point to him as the killer. He turns to ex-wife Arthur, a mystery writer, for help. Wonderful chemistry between the leads makes this a treat for fans of the *Thin Man* style of sophistication.
Dist.: Media

EXODUS 1960
★ ★ ★ NR Drama 3:33
Dir: Otto Preminger *Cast:* Paul Newman, Eva Marie Saint, Lee J. Cobb, Sal Mineo, Ralph Richardson, Peter Lawford, Hugh Griffith, Felix Aylmer, John Derek, Jill Haworth
► Preminger's large-scale epic about the founding of the state of Israel details the ef-

forts of Jewish underground rebel Newman leading the battles against the British and the Arabs. Overlong but exciting, with a sweeping, Oscar-winning Ernest Gold score. Based on Leon Uris's best-seller.
Dist.: CBS/Fox

EXORCIST, THE 1973
★ ★ ★ ★ R Horror 1:58
⊙ Adult situations, explicit language graphic violence
Dir: William Friedkin *Cast:* Ellen Burstyn, Linda Blair, Max Von Sydow, Jason Miller, Lee J. Cobb
► Well-wrought horror classic of extraordinarily powerful impact adapted from William Peter Blatty's best-selling novel about a demonically possessed child. When Blair, daughter of movie star Burstyn, is transformed into a repellent monster, young priest Miller tries and fails to rid her body of the spirit. He calls in Father Merrin (Von Sydow) for an elaborate exorcism. Nominated for ten Oscars including Best Picture, Actress, and Director; won for Sound and Blatty's screenplay. One of the top-grossing films of all time.
Dist.: Warner

EXORCIST II: THE HERETIC 1977
★ ★ R Horror 1:43
⊙ Explicit language, violence
Dir: John Boorman *Cast:* Linda Blair, Richard Burton, Louise Fletcher, Kitty Winn, James Earl Jones, Max Von Sydow
► Chilling sequel to the 1974 megahit resumes Regan's (Blair) story four years later. Subjected to terrifying nightmares, she's treated by psychoanalyst Fletcher and, under hypnosis, discovers she's still possessed by the demon Pazuzu. Father Lamont (Burton) searches throughout Africa for Kakumo (Jones), who'd been exorcised of Pazuzu years ago by Father Merrin (Sydow). Professional cast, good production values and special effects.
Dist.: Warner

EXPENDABLES, THE 1988
★ R Action-Adventure 1:29
⊙ Nudity, explicit language, violence
Dir: Cirio H. Santiago *Cast:* Anthony Finetti, Peter Nelson, Loren Haynes, Kevin Duffis
► Finetti is a Vietnam war captain assigned a platoon of misfits—including a religious nut, a bitter black, and sneering racist—and given impossible missions. Guys keep screwing up and getting in trouble with senior officers. Lots of good shooting and explosions, but rest is just half-baked *Dirty Dozen*.
Dist.: Media

EXPERIENCE PREFERRED. . .BUT NOT ESSENTIAL 1983 British
★ PG Drama 1:14
⊙ Nudity, adult situations
Dir: Peter John Duffell *Cast:* Elizabeth Edmonds, Sue Wallace, Geraldine Griffith, Karen Meagher, Ron Bain

▶ Edmonds is an innocent college student working at a Welsh seaside summer resort in 1962. With the help of Scottish chef Bain, she is initiated into certain rites of passage. Charmingly told, honest, and surprising, but also "small" and very British.
Dist.: MGM/UA

EXPERIMENT IN TERROR 1962
★ ★ ★ ★ NR Mystery-Suspense 2:03 B&W
Dir: Blake Edwards   *Cast:* Glenn Ford, Lee Remick, Stefanie Powers, Roy Poole, Ned Glass, Ross Martin
▶ Bank teller Remick must pay an extortionist $100,000 to rescue her kidnapped younger sister Powers. Ford heads an FBI manhunt closing in on the villain, at terrible cost to informants. Brisk, forceful thriller makes good use of San Francisco locations and eerie Henry Mancini score.
Dist.: RCA/Columbia

EXPERIMENT PERILOUS 1944
★ NR Drama 1:31 B&W
Dir: Jacques Tourneur   *Cast:* Hedy Lamarr, George Brent, Paul Lukas, Albert Dekker, Carl Esmond
▶ Lamarr is trapped in a marriage to wealthy Lukas, who may be trying to drive her insane. When psychiatrist Brent falls for her, Lukas ups the ante by staging deadly "accidents." Familiar story given a big lift by adroit direction and compelling performances.
Dist.: Fox Hills   C

EXPERTS, THE 1989
★ PG-13 Comedy 1:34
☑ Adult situations, mild violence
Dir: Dave Thomas   *Cast:* John Travolta, Arye Gross, Kelly Preston, Deborah Foreman, James Keach, Charles Martin Smith, Jan Rubes, Brian Doyle Murray
▶ Manhattan nightclub bouncer Travolta and buddy Gross are hired by Smith to liven up a dull cornbelt town that seems lost in the 1950s. Introduction of Walkmans and VCRs turns townsfolk into culture-mad consumers, but Travolta and Gross soon discover they're helping to train future KGB agents. Lackluster comedy isn't disgraceful, just boring; Travolta is even disarming at times. Filmed in 1987. (CC)
Dist.: Paramount

EXPLORERS 1985
★ ★ ★ PG Sci-Fi 1:50
☑ Explicit language, mild violence
Dir: Joe Dante   *Cast:* Ethan Hawke, River Phoenix, Jason Presson, Amanda Peterson, Dick Miller
▶ Junior high misfits—dreamer Hawke, computer goon Phoenix, and rebel Presson—create a blue soap bubble that can rocket to outer space. Enchanting story with well-executed high-flying effects.   (CC)
Dist.: Paramount

EXPOSED 1983
★ ★ R Mystery-Suspense 1:39
☑ Nudity, adult situations, explicit language, violence
Dir: James Toback   *Cast:* Nastassja Kinski, Rudolf Nureyev, Ian McShane, Harvey Keitel, Bibi Andersson
▶ Kinski, a young Midwestern beauty, seeks her fortune in New York, where she is discovered by fashion photographer McShane. Her luck changes when eccentric violinist Nureyev enlists her to thwart vicious South American terrorist Keitel, who has a weakness for pretty women. Bizarre political thriller is often confusing.
Dist.: MGM/UA

EXQUISITE CORPSES 1988
☆ NR Drama 1:33
☑ Adult situations, explicit language, violence
Dir: Temistocles Lopez   *Cast:* Zoë Tamerlaine Lund, Gary Knox, Daniel Chapman, Ruth Collins, Robert Lund
▶ It's one thing after another for out-of-town trumpeter Knox, who comes to New York, gets mugged and thrown out on street, but eventually winds up with hot cabaret act thanks to coaching from gay club owner Robert Lund. Trouble starts when he gets involved with the sultry wife of a millionaire. Hip but amateurish film noir features wooden acting, uneven score by real-life musician Knox.
Dist.: Monarch

EXTERMINATING ANGEL, THE 1962 Mexican
☆ NR Drama 1:35 B&W
Dir: Luis Buñuel   *Cast:* Silvia Pinal, Enrique Rambal, Jacqueline Andere, Jose Baviera, Augusto Benedico, Luis Beristein
▶ While enjoying an elegant dinner, a group of wealthy people discover that they can't leave the room. Piece by piece, their civilized facades crumble in funny, pointed, and surreal ways. Incisive metaphor for stifling nature of social life is outrageous in the masterly Buñuel way.   S
Dist.: New York Film Annex

EXTERMINATOR, THE 1980
★ ★ ★ R Action-Adventure 1:41
☑ Explicit language, graphic violence
Dir: James Glickenhaus   *Cast:* Christopher George, Samantha Eggar, Robert Ginty, Steve James
▶ Low-budget melodrama about former soldier-turned-vigilante Ginty who seeks revenge on the punks who attacked and paralyzed his friend. He kills them and is pursued, in turn, by police. Excessively violent production was successful enough to spawn a sequel.
Dist.: Nelson

EXTERMINATOR 2 1984
★ ★ ★ R Action-Adventure 1:28
☑ Nudity, adult situations, explicit language, graphic violence

Dir: Mark Buntzman   *Cast:* Robert Ginty, Deborah Geffner, Frankie Faison, Mario Van Peebles, Bruce Smolanoff

▶ In this sequel, urban crime avenger Ginty fights New York punks with his own special weapon, an armed city sanitation truck. Every bit as violent and action-packed as the original. With Geffner as his dancer girlfriend who gets her legs broken, inciting Ginty to revenge.
Dist.: MGM/UA

EXTREME PREJUDICE 1987
★ ★ ★ R Action-Adventure 1:45
☑ Brief nudity, adult situations, explicit language, graphic violence
Dir: Walter Hill   *Cast:* Nick Nolte, Powers Boothe, Rip Torn, Maria Conchita Alonso, Michael Ironside

▶ Texas Ranger Nolte and his partner Torn battle white-suited drug peddler Boothe and Ironside's high-tech bank robbers in an effort to keep their border town safe. When Boothe kidnaps Alonso, a singer in a honky tonk, Nolte infiltrates his Mexican hideout to rescue her—unaware that Ironside is planning a massacre there. Highly stylized mayhem convincingly updates Western themes in contemporary settings.
Dist.: IVE

EXTREMITIES 1986
★ ★ ★ ★ R Drama 1:30
☑ Rape, nudity, explicit language, violence
Dir: Robert M. Young   *Cast:* Farrah Fawcett, James Russo, Alfre Woodard, Diana Scarwid, Sandy Martin

▶ Unpleasant but gripping story of Fawcett who turns the tables on rapist Russo. Brutal, tense and talky. Fawcett's striking performance as victim-vanquisher furthered her critical reputation. Based on William Mastrosimone's Off-Broadway hit, with Fawcett and Russo reprising their stage roles. **(CC)**
Dist.: Paramount

EYE FOR AN EYE, AN 1981
★ ★ ★ R Martial Arts 1:44
☑ Nudity, adult situations, explicit language, violence
Dir: Steve Carver   *Cast:* Chuck Norris, Christopher Lee, Richard Roundtree, Mako, Matt Clark

▶ Actioner pits kung-fu goodness against heroin madness. Norris stars as an ex-cop called in to solve the murder of a TV newswoman. He discovers she was investigating a large heroin-smuggling ring and proceeds to dish out physical punishment to a small army of stuntmen. Lots of bone-shattering encounters and narrow escapes to please kick-fight fans.
Dist.: Nelson

EYE OF THE EAGLE 1986
★ R Action-Adventure 1:22
☑ Explicit language, violence
Dir: Cirio H. Santiago   *Cast:* Brett Clark, Robert Patrick, Ed Crick, William Steis, Cec Verell

▶ U.S. servicemen supposedly listed MIA or POW in Vietnam conflict are not really dead or in prison, but have formed renegade platoon to carry out nasty missions on own initiative. Verell is a reporter who's tracking down the story, and Clark is the tough-guy sergeant she's assigned to. Lots of machine gunning and explosions, but some Americans will find the slur against MIAs and POWs offensive.
Dist.: MGM/UA

EYE OF THE NEEDLE 1981
★ ★ ★ ★ R Mystery-Suspense 1:52
☑ Nudity, adult situations, violence
Dir: Richard Marquand   *Cast:* Donald Sutherland, Kate Nelligan, Ian Bannen, Christopher Cazenove, Philip Martin Brown

▶ While attempting to complete a crucial mission during World War II, ruthless German spy Sutherland is shipwrecked on a deserted Scottish island and befriended by lonely woman Nelligan. Despite the presence of Cazenove, her crippled, embittered husband, they have an affair. Based on Ken Follett's best-selling suspense novel.
Dist.: MGM/UA

EYE OF THE TIGER 1987
★ ★ ★ ★ R Action-Adventure 1:32
☑ Explicit language, violence
Dir: Richard Sarafian   *Cast:* Gary Busey, Yaphet Kotto, Seymour Cassel, William Smith, Denise Galik

▶ Vigilante film pits lean and mean Busey against an army of desert bikers who've killed his wife and traumatized his daughter. Using tricks he learned in Vietnam and prison (he was framed for a murder he didn't commit), Busey begins his one-man cleanup operation. When his daughter is kidnapped from the hospital, Busey really gets mad. Good-looking vengeance exploitation film combines *Walking Tall* and *Death Wish*.
Dist.: IVE

EYES OF A STRANGER 1981
★ ★ ★ R Mystery-Suspense 1:25
☑ Nudity, adult situations, explicit language, violence
Dir: Ken Wiederhorn   *Cast:* Lauren Tewes, Jennifer Jason Leigh, John DiSanti, Peter DePre, Gwen Lewis

▶ TV star Tewes makes her feature-film debut as a Miami newscaster who discovers the identity of a killer/rapist. Coincidentally, he lives in her apartment building and, when he corners Tewes's deaf-dumb-blind sister, the film culminates in a vividly bloody and gruesome finale. Strictly a stalk-and-slaughter affair offering the molestation and murder of women as entertainment; with shopworn clichés, including a woman-in-the-shower scene.
Dist.: Warner

EYES OF LAURA MARS, THE 1978
★ ★ ★ ★ R Mystery-Suspense 1:43
🚫 Nudity, explicit language, graphic violence
Dir: Irvin Kershner *Cast:* Faye Dunaway, Tommy Lee Jones, Raul Julia, René Auberjonois, Brad Dourif
▶ Classy and haunting whodunit with Dunaway as a chic fashion photographer obsessed and possessed by deadly premonitions about a series of murders involving her friends and associates. Though she can see the killings she is powerless to prevent them. Jones is the policeman assigned to the case. Screenplay by John Carpenter and David Zelag Goodman provides a twisty, kinky, and genuinely scary conclusion to this stylish thriller. Title song "Prisoner" sung by Barbra Streisand. (CC)
Dist.: RCA/Columbia

EYEWITNESS 1981
★ ★ ★ R Mystery-Suspense 1:42
☑ Adult situations, explicit language, violence
Dir: Peter Yates *Cast:* William Hurt, Sigourney Weaver, Christopher Plummer, Kenneth McMillan, Pamela Reed, James Woods, Morgan Freeman
▶ When a man is murdered in his building, janitor Hurt pretends to know something about the crime in order to entice the interest of beautiful TV news reporter Weaver. Quirky, interesting thriller with less emphasis on conventional suspense (though there's plenty) than on the unusual love story and complex characterizations. Terrific dialogue (especially Hurt's deadpan come-ons) from writer Steve Tesich, skillful use of New York City locations, and great performances.
Dist.: CBS/Fox

FABULOUS BAKER BOYS, THE 1989
★ ★ ★ ★ ★ R Drama 1:50
☑ Brief nudity, adult situations, explicit language
Dir: Steve Kloves *Cast:* Jeff Bridges, Michelle Pfeiffer, Beau Bridges, Jennifer Tilly, Ellie Raab
▶ The Baker boys are piano playing brothers who have a tired lounge act, performing such ditties as "Feelings" and "People." When hardened ex-prostitute Pfeiffer joins the act as a singer, they start sizzling on stage, but the personal relationships among all three become more tangled offstage. Solid character piece features inspired casting of the Bridges brothers and a memorable performance from Oscar-nominated Pfeiffer, who smolders during the "Making Whoopee" number. (CC)
Dist.: IVE

FABULOUS DORSEYS, THE 1947
★ ★ NR Biography/Musical 1:28 B&W
Dir: Alfred E. Green *Cast:* Tommy Dorsey, Jimmy Dorsey, Janet Blair, Paul Whiteman, William Lundigan, Sara Allgood

▶ Sanitized biography of the feuding big band leaders and their musical growth from a grim Pennsylvania steel town to the top of the charts. Songs include "Marie," "The Object of My Affection," "Green Eyes," and a wild version of "Art's Blues" by Art Tatum and Charlie Barnet.
Dist.: Various

FACE IN THE CROWD, A 1957
★ ★ NR Drama 2:06 B&W
Dir: Elia Kazan *Cast:* Andy Griffith, Patricia Neal, Anthony Franciosa, Walter Matthau, Lee Remick
▶ Fascinating, still topical look at a media-created monster. Homespun hobo Lonesome Rhodes (Griffith), promoted into TV stardom by reporter Neal, rises in politics but is corrupted by power. Griffith, totally convincing in his first movie, is ably supported by Neal, Matthau, and a breathtakingly beautiful Remick as the teenage baton twirler who is Lonesome's undoing. Incisive script and direction from the *On the Waterfront* team.
Dist.: Warner

FADE TO BLACK 1980
★ R Horror 1:42
☑ Brief nudity, adult situations, explicit language, violence
Dir: Vernon Zimmerman *Cast:* Dennis Christopher, Linda Kerridge, Tim Thomerson, Morgan Paull, Marya Small
▶ Young film buff Christopher exacts revenge on his various tormentors by staging their murders in the styles of his favorite movies. Mixture of suspense and comedy doesn't always gel but contains good shocks, lots of cinematic references, and decent performances from Christopher and Australian Marilyn Monroe look alike, Kerridge.
Dist.: Media

FAHRENHEIT 451 1967 British
★ NR Sci-Fi 1:52
Dir: François Truffaut *Cast:* Julie Christie, Oskar Werner, Cyril Cusack, Anton Diffring, Jeremy Spenser
▶ Books are outlawed and burned in a futuristic totalitarian state. Fireman Werner turns against the government when young rebel Christie introduces him to the joys of reading. Truffaut's visually stylized adaptation of the Ray Bradbury novel is literate and intelligent.
Dist.: MCA

FAIL-SAFE 1964
★ ★ ★ ★ NR Drama 1:52 B&W
Dir: Sidney Lumet *Cast:* Henry Fonda, Walter Matthau, Fritz Weaver, Dan O'Herlihy, Sorrell Booke, Larry Hagman
▶ Supposedly error-proof codes are scrambled, sending bombers armed with nuclear weapons to destroy Moscow. As President, Fonda pleads with the Russians not to retaliate while his military advisors try to stop the planes. Uniformly strong performances add to the nail-biting tension in this intelligent adap-

tation of the Eugene Burdick/Harvey Wheeler best-seller.
Dist.: RCA/Columbia

FAKE OUT 1982
★★ NR Drama 1:36
☑ Rape, nudity, adult situations, explicit language, violence
Dir: Matt Cimber **Cast:** Pia Zadora, Telly Savalas, Desi Arnaz, Jr., Larry Storch
▶ Las Vegas entertainer/mobster's girl Zadora is thrown into prison after refusing to testify against her boyfriend. Even though she leads the inmates in Jane Fonda exercise classes, they gang-rape her anyway. She agrees to talk, falls in love with her police bodyguard, and dodges several gun barrages. After she and her bodyguard turn the tables on crooked detective Savalas, they win $50,000 at the roulette wheel. Cheap and trashy entertainment with plenty of unintentional laughs.
Dist.: HBO

FALCON AND THE SNOWMAN, THE 1985
★★★★ R Biography/Drama 2:11
☑ Nudity, adult situations, explicit language, violence
Dir: John Schlesinger **Cast:** Timothy Hutton, Sean Penn, David Suchet, Lori Singer, Pat Hingle, Dorian Harewood
▶ True story of Christopher Boyce (Hutton) and Daulton Lee (Penn), suburban California kids who sold secrets to the Russians. Downbeat but absorbing docudrama made with craftsmanlike precision by director Schlesinger. Penn is stunning in a performance that's flamboyant without ever seeming overdone; Hutton is equally effective as the quieter Boyce. **(CC)**
Dist.: Vestron

FALCON'S ADVENTURE, THE 1946
★ NR Mystery-Suspense 1:01 B&W
Dir: William Berke **Cast:** Tom Conway, Madge Meredith, Edward S. Brophy, Robert Warwick, Myrna Dell, Steve Brodie
▶ The Falcon (Conway) helps Meredith escape from crooks seeking a valuable formula. He then becomes a murder suspect. So-so thirteenth in the series proved to be unlucky, marking Conway's last appearance in the role. Home video version double billed with 1950's *Armored Car Robbery.*
Dist.: Turner

FALCON'S BROTHER, THE 1942
★★ NR Mystery-Suspense 1:03 B&W
Dir: Stanley Logan **Cast:** George Sanders, Tom Conway, Jane Randolph, Don Barclay, Cliff Clark, Ed Gargan
▶ Writer Michael Arlen's dashing troubleshooter Sanders, aided by his brother Conway, investigates a ring of Nazi spies in South America. When Sanders is murdered, Conway assumes his role as the Falcon and solves the case. Fair example of the B-movie series has one unusual aspect: Sanders, tired of his role,

was killed off and replaced by his real-life brother Conway.
Dist.: Media

FALCON TAKES OVER, THE 1942
★★ NR Mystery-Suspense 1:03 B&W
Dir: Irving Reis **Cast:** George Sanders, Lynn Bari, James Gleason, Allen Jenkins, Helen Gilbert, Ward Bond
▶ Third in a series of modest B-films based on Michael Arlen's roguish detective is a loose adaptation of Raymond Chandler's *Farewell, My Lovely* (remade with Dick Powell in 1944's *Murder, My Sweet* and again with Robert Mitchum in 1975 under the original title). Bond plays Moose Malloy, a hulking ex-con who hires the Falcon (Sanders) to find his old girlfriend. Bari is a reporter who helps crack the case.
Dist.: Turner

FALLEN IDOL, THE 1948 British
★★★ NR Drama 1:34 B&W
Dir: Carol Reed **Cast:** Ralph Richardson, Michele Morgan, Bobby Henrey, Sonia Dresdel, Denis O'Dea, Jack Hawkins
▶ Ambassador's young son Henrey idolizes Richardson, a butler trapped in an unhappy marriage to Dresdel. When she dies in a suspicious accident, the boy tries to protect Richardson from the police. Engrossing, superbly crafted film successfully captures a child's point of view without stinting on tension. Won Oscar nominations for director Reed and screenwriter Graham Greene, who next collaborated on *The Third Man.*
Dist.: Prism

FALLEN SPARROW, THE 1943
★★ NR Mystery-Suspense 1:34 B&W
Dir: Richard Wallace **Cast:** John Garfield, Maureen O'Hara, Walter Slezak, Patricia Morison, Martha O'Driscoll, Bruce Edwards
▶ Garfield, a veteran of the Spanish Civil War, is hounded in New York City by Nazis, in particular crippled Gestapo agent Slezak. His goal: find a German battle flag Garfield is concealing. Taut adaptation of the Dorothy Hughes novel establishes terrific atmosphere despite plot holes.
Dist.: Fox Hills

FALLING IN LOVE 1984
★★★★ PG-13 Romance 1:46
☑ Adult situations, explicit language
Dir: Ulu Grosbard **Cast:** Robert De Niro, Meryl Streep, Harvey Keitel, Jane Kaczmarek, David Clennon, Dianne Wiest
▶ Westchester commuters De Niro and Streep, each happily married, fall in love. Michael Cristofer's script realistically captures the way two ordinary (and often inarticulate) people might stumble into romance. Old-fashioned love story with crisp cinematography, nice use of New York City locations, pleasant Dave Grusin score, and sweet,

scaled-down performances from two acting heavyweights. (CC)
Dist.: Paramount

FALLING IN LOVE AGAIN 1980
★★ PG Drama 1:39
☑ Adult situations, explicit language
Dir: Steven Paul *Cast:* Elliott Gould, Susannah York, Stuart Paul, Kaye Ballard, Michelle Pfeiffer
► Wistful and modestly entertaining story of husband Gould and wife York reminiscing about youthful times. While vacationing in New York, they rediscover their lost love. Debut directorial effort from then twenty-one-year-old Paul.
Dist.: Embassy

FALL OF THE HOUSE OF USHER 1960
★★★ NR Horror 1:19
Dir: Roger Corman *Cast:* Vincent Price, Mark Damon, Myrna Fahey, Harry Ellerbee, Bill Borzage, George Paul
► Price, proprietor of a haunted house, tries to break up sister Fahey's engagement to Damon. He tells his potential brother-in-law of the family curse that is passed down through generations; the terror starts when Damon doesn't listen. First of Corman's Edgar Allan Poe adaptations is elegantly crafted and very scary. One of the series' best is also known as *House of Usher.*
Dist.: Warner

FALL OF THE ROMAN EMPIRE, THE 1964
★★ NR Drama 2:26
Dir: Anthony Mann *Cast:* Sophia Loren, Stephen Boyd, James Mason, Alec Guinness, Christopher Plummer, Omar Sharif, Anthony Quayle, John Ireland
► Power corrupts Emperor Commodus (Plummer), bringing about the decline and fall of Rome despite the efforts of noble reformer Mason and rival Boyd in this big, colorful epic that shows its massive budget. Strong cast, sumptuous sets, wall-to-wall armies and action make up for excess length and flawed story.
Dist.: Vestron

FAME 1980
★★★ R Drama/Musical 2:13
☑ Nudity, adult situations, explicit language
Dir: Alan Parker *Cast:* Irene Cara, Lee Curreri, Paul McCrane, Barry Miller, Gene Anthony Ray, Maureen Teefy, Laura Dean, Eddie Barth, Anne Meara, Debbie Allen, Albert Hague
► Feverish musical drama follows students of New York's High School for the Performing Arts from opening auditions to graduation. Some contrived, melodramatic plotting (especially in Cara's dealings with a sleazeball photographer) but plenty of music, dancing, humor (watch for one student's O. J. Simpson impression), stunning cinematography, and youthful high spirits. Won Best Song and Score Oscars. Ray and fellow cast members Allen and Hague re-created their roles for the TV series.
Dist.: MGM/UA

FAMILY, THE 1973 Italian
★★ R Action-Adventure 1:34
☑ Explicit language, violence
Dir: Sergio Sollima *Cast:* Charles Bronson, Jill Ireland, Telly Savalas, Umberto Orsini, George Savalas
► Hired killer Bronson is romanced by Ireland, a police agent trying to solve some murders. Bronson must ambush her as the cops pick up his trail. Straightforward story provides enough action and violence to satisfy hard-core fans; sturdy performances by Bronson and Savalas but tacky-looking production values.
Dist.: Vestron

FAMILY, THE 1987 Italian
★ PG Drama 2:07
☑ Explicit language
Dir: Ettore Scola *Cast:* Vittorio Gassman, Fanny Ardant, Stefania Sandrelli, Andrea Occhipinti, Jo Ciampa
► Eighty years in the life of an Italian clan observed through the loves, feuds, marriage, and grandparenthood of its patriarch, portrayed by three different actors, lastly Gassman. Film dares to tell crowded story without leaving the family's apartment, with relatives coming and going, businesses rising and falling, and wars beginning and ending. Warm, mellow and full of richly observed details. Long but rewarding film succeeds as imitation of life. [S]
Dist.: Vestron

FAMILY BUSINESS 1989
★★★ R Drama
☑ Explicit language, violence
Dir: Sidney Lumet *Cast:* Dustin Hoffman, Sean Connery, Matthew Broderick, Rosana de Soto, Janet Carroll, Victoria Jackson
► Straight-living Hoffman disapproves of a million-dollar caper being planned by his son Broderick, an MIT scholar, and elderly father Connery, scalliwag of long standing. Unable to dissuade them, Hoffman goes along to look out for the boy, who unfortunately gets caught. This is a dilemma for dad and granddad, who could free boy by turning selves in. Can't decide if it's crime caper or family drama, but cast, especially Connery, is the main attraction. Adapted by Vincent Patrick from his novel. (CC)
Dist.: RCA/Columbia

FAMILY GAME, THE 1984 Japanese
☆ NR Comedy 1:47
☑ Explicit language
Dir: Yoshimitsu Morita *Cast:* Yusaku Matsuda, Juzo Itami, Saori Yuki, Junichi Tsujita, Ichirota Miyagawa
► Little Miyagawa is doing poorly at school, so his well-off parents hire tutor Matsuda, whose unorthodox methods soon have house in uproar. Very original lampoon of Japanese middle class puts visually striking direction in

service of often slapstick comedy. Film was voted best of year in home country, and Westerners will enjoy its insights into soul of new Japan. [S]
Dist.: SVS

FAMILY JEWELS, THE 1965
★★ NR Comedy 1:40
Dir: Jerry Lewis ***Cast:*** Jerry Lewis, Sebastian Cabot, Donna Butterworth, Gene Baylor, Milton Frome, Herbie Faye
▶ A field day for Lewis fans: he wrote, produced, directed, and played seven roles in this sentimental comedy. Young Butterworth inherits a fortune, then must decide which of seven uncles (that's right, they're all Jerry) will be her guardian. Nonfans beware.
Dist.: Paramount

FAMILY LIFE 1972 British
☆ NR Drama 1:45
☑ Adult situations, explicit language, violence
Dir: Ken Loach ***Cast:*** Sandy Ratcliff, Bill Dean, Grace Cave, Malcolm Tierney, Hilary Martyn
▶ Teenager Ratcliff's disapproving parents force her to undergo an abortion. When Ratcliff rebells, leaving home with her boyfriend Tierney, her parents have her committed. Grim, depressing story is well-acted but strident and dated. Also known as *Wednesday's Child.*
Dist.: RCA/Columbia

FAMILY PLOT 1976
★★★★ PG Mystery-Suspense 2:00
☑ Explicit language, violence
Dir: Alfred Hitchcock ***Cast:*** Karen Black, Bruce Dern, Barbara Harris, William Devane, Ed Lauter, Cathleen Nesbitt
▶ Possibly bogus psychic Harris and companion Dern are hired to find long-lost heir Devane, who happens to be an extortionist in midst of a kidnapping scheme. Lighthearted mystery/comedy, Hitchcock's last effort, finds the director in sprightly form. Some nifty chases and filmmaking with a very appealing performance by Harris.
Dist.: MCA

FAN, THE 1981
★★ R Mystery-Suspense 1:35
☑ Adult situations, explicit language, graphic violence
Dir: Edward Bianchi ***Cast:*** Lauren Bacall, James Garner, Maureen Stapleton, Michael Biehn
▶ Bacall, a well-known movie star rehearsing her first Broadway musical, is stalked by psychotic fan Biehn. One-note performance by Biehn, but Bacall anchors the film with her solid, sympathetic performance. Straightforward thriller with dark mood, plot holes, and graphic violence.
Dist.: Paramount

FANCY PANTS 1950
★★★★ NR Comedy 1:33
Dir: George Marshall ***Cast:*** Bob Hope, Lucille Ball, Bruce Cabot, Jack Kirkwood, Lea Penman, Hugh French
▶ Hope does a funny impersonation of an Englishman with a very stiff upper lip who accompanies rough-hewn oil businesswoman Ball to her home on the New Mexico frontier. Riotous cricket match and encounter with Rough Rider Teddy Roosevelt highlight this genial remake of 1935's *Ruggles of Red Gap.*
Dist.: Paramount

FANDANGO 1985
★★ PG Comedy 1:31
☑ Brief nudity, explicit language
Dir: Kevin Reynolds ***Cast:*** Kevin Costner, Sam Robards, Judd Nelson, Chuck Bush, Brian Cesak
▶ Five University of Texas college buddies have a final fling before assuming official adulthood. Nelson stars as the group scold and Costner as the ringleader. Sweet, stylish, and romantic. Originally a student short called *Proof,* film attracted Steven Spielberg's attention and was expanded into a feature.
Dist.: Warner

FANNY 1932 French
★ NR Drama 2:05 B&W
Dir: Marcel Pagnol ***Cast:*** Raimu, Orane Demazis, Pierre Fresnay, Fernand Charpin, Alida Rouffe, Robert Vattier
▶ Fresnay goes off to sea, leaving his father Raimu to look after his girlfriend Demazis. Pregnant with Fresnay's child, she marries widower Charpin to avoid a scandal, but the sailor's return could complicate their future. Second of Pagnol's trilogy, including *Marius* and *Cesar,* is the most emotional and satisfying. [S]
Dist.: Corinth

FANNY 1961
★★★★ NR Drama 2:13
Dir: Joshua Logan ***Cast:*** Leslie Caron, Maurice Chevalier, Charles Boyer, Horst Buchholz, Baccaloni, Lionel Jeffries
▶ Ambitious Buchholz abandons pregnant girlfriend Caron for the sea; she sadly enters a marriage of convenience with the adoring but older Chevalier. American adaptation of Marcel Pagnol's Marseilles Trilogy (which also included *Marius* and *Cesar*) was originally a Broadway musical scored by Harold Rome; film inexplicably omits songs, but earthy, sentimental plot is still moving. Received five Oscar nominations, including one for Jack Cardiff's beautiful photography.
Dist.: Warner

FANNY AND ALEXANDER 1983 Swedish
★★ R Drama 3:11
☑ Brief nudity, adult situations, explicit language
Dir: Ingmar Bergman ***Cast:*** Pernilla Allwin,

Bertil Guve, Ewa Froling, Jan Malmsjo, Harriet Andersson, Erland Josephson
► Siblings Fanny and Alexander are raised in a warmhearted theatrical family, then must adjust when their father dies and mother remarries a stern pastor. Rich, almost Dickensian sense of character, sensitive evocation of childhood viewpoint, exquisite cinematography, and lavish period details. Very demanding but rewarding for discerning viewers. Four Oscars, including Best Foreign Film and Cinematography. Dubbed.
Dist.: Nelson

FANNY HILL 1983 British
☆ R Comedy 1:32
☑ Nudity, adult situations, explicit language
Dir: Gerry O'Hara   *Cast:* Lisa Raines, Wilfrid Hyde-White, Oliver Reed, Shelley Winters, Paddy O'Neil
► In eighteenth-century England, poor girl Raines arrives in the city and works her way up the social ladder while learning to appreciate the more sordid metropolitan pleasures. Reed and Hyde-White appear to be having fun; for that matter, so does everybody else in this soft porn costume outing. Don't look for deep characterizations.
Dist.: MGM/UA

FANTASIES 1981
☆ R Drama 1:21
☑ Nudity, adult situations
Dir: John Derek   *Cast:* Bo Derek, Peter Hooten, Anna Alexiadis, Pheacton Gheorghitais, Constantine Beladames
► Derek and Hooten fall in love when they return to the Greek island where they were born. Unfortunately, they're brother and sister. Incest problem is resolved when a local official remembers that they aren't really brother and sister after all. Shot in 1973 when starlet was only sixteen, soft-porn Bo peep show led to her marriage to director Derek. Also known as *Once Upon a Love.*
Dist.: CBS/Fox

FANTASIST, THE 1986 Irish
★ ★ R Mystery-Suspense 1:38
☑ Nudity, strong sexual content, adult situations, explicit language, graphic violence
Dir: Robin Hardy   *Cast:* Moira Harris, Christopher Cazenove, Timothy Bottoms, John Kavanagh, Mick Lally, James Bartley
► After leaving her uncle's farm for a Dublin teaching job, Harris is attracted to married American writer Bottoms, whose wife is subsequently murdered. Inspector Cazenove investigates and suddenly Harris gets obscene phone calls. Is she the next victim? A mixed bag: intriguing premise, pretty Irish scenery, fine performances by Harris and Cazenove, but hurt by psychological pretensions, red herrings, and Bottoms's overacting.
Dist.: Republic

FANTASTIC PLANET 1973 Czech/French
⚛ PG Animation/Adult 1:12
☑ Nudity, adult situations
Dir: Rene Laloux   *Cast:* Voices of: Barry Bostwick, Marvin Miller, Olan Soule, Cynthia Alder, Nora Heflin, Hal Smith
► The giant, glowing-eyed inhabitants of the planet Yagam are unthinkingly cruel to the tiny Oms, who are actually descended from humans. One of the Oms is taken in by the giants, and uses his position to help his people revolt. Unusual animation style with shaded figures and artsy backgrounds won many prizes, but subdued action and lack of humor may limit appeal.
Dist.: United

FANTASTIC VOYAGE 1966
★ ★ ★ ★ NR Sci-Fi 1:40
Dir: Richard Fleischer   *Cast:* Stephen Boyd, Raquel Welch, Edmond O'Brien, Donald Pleasence, Arthur O'Connell
► Scientists and their craft are minaturized and injected inside defector's body in order to save his life, but there's a spy on board who must be handled. Eye dazzling special effects and production design, plus Raquel in a tight-fitting suit.
Dist.: CBS/Fox

FAR COUNTRY, THE 1955
★ ★ ★ NR Western 1:37
Dir: Anthony Mann   *Cast:* James Stewart, Ruth Roman, Corinne Calvet, Walter Brennan, John McIntire, Jay C. Flippen
► Stewart and Brennan bring a herd of cattle from Wyoming to Alaska to exploit the gold boom but lose the steers to evil sheriff McIntire. Stewart refuses to take revenge until two close friends are murdered. First-rate Western written by Borden Chase features a stinging performance by Stewart and incisive direction by Mann.
Dist.: KVC

FAR EAST 1983
★ ★ NR Drama 1:38
☑ Adult situations, explicit language, violence
Dir: John Duigan   *Cast:* Bryan Brown, Helen Morse, John Bell, Raina McKeon, Sinan Leong
► Somewhere in the Far East, bar owner Brown renews affair with old flame Morse, now married to journalist Bell. When Bell disappears while battling corrupt officials, Morse turns to Brown for help. Sizzling chemistry between Morse and Brown and excellent direction from Duigan enliven a well-rendered but old-fashioned plot.
Dist.: Virgin

FAREWELL, MY LOVELY 1975 British
★ ★ ★ ★ R Mystery-Suspense 1:31
☑ Brief nudity, adult situations, explicit language, violence
Dir: Dick Richards   *Cast:* Robert Mitchum,

Charlotte Rampling, John Ireland, Sylvia Miles, Jack O'Halloran, Sylvester Stallone
▶ In 1940s L.A., private eye Philip Marlowe (Mitchum) is hired by overgrown ex-con O'-Halloran to track down ex-lover Rampling. Solidly plotted, true-blue adaptation of the Raymond Chandler novel (filmed previously as *Murder, My Sweet* and *The Falcon Takes Over*) expertly evokes neon-drenched film noir atmosphere. Terrific cast (Miles was Oscar-nominated) led by Mitchum, who is simply perfect as the weary Marlowe.
Dist.: Nelson

FAREWELL TO ARMS, A 1932
★ ★ NR Romance 1:30 B&W
Dir: Frank Borzage   *Cast:* Helen Hayes, Gary Cooper, Adolphe Menjou, Mary Philips, Jack LaRue, Blanche Federici
▶ First film version of Ernest Hemingway's classic World War I novel stars Cooper as an American ambulance driver who falls in love with English nurse Hayes. War, illness, and major Menjou's machinations are obstacles to the romance. Borzage's intelligent yet emotional direction brings out strong Hayes/Cooper romantic chemistry. Best Picture nominee won Oscars for Cinematography and Sound Recording.
Dist.: Various

FAREWELL TO ARMS, A 1957
★ ★ ★ NR Romance 2:28
Dir: Charles Vidor   *Cast:* Rock Hudson, Jennifer Jones, Vittorio De Sica, Oscar Homolka, Mercedes McCambridge
▶ During World War I, American ambulance driver Hudson falls in love with English nurse Jones but the romance ends tragically. Well-made romantic tearjerker. Fine supporting turn by Oscar-nominated De Sica as Hudson's friend. Adaptation of the Ernest Hemingway novel (filmed previously in 1932 with Gary Cooper and Helen Hayes) was final film for producer David O. Selznick.
Dist.: Prism

FAREWELL TO THE KING 1988
★ ★ ★ PG-13 Drama 1:57
☑ Adult situations, violence
Dir: John Milius   *Cast:* Nick Nolte, Nigel Havers, James Fox, Marily Tokuda, Frank McRae, Aki Aleong
▶ Nolte, a World War II deserter, becomes leader of an Iban tribe in remote Borneo. British captain Havers parachutes in to warn them of impending Japanese attack, but Nolte is determined to keep his jungle kingdom a sanctuary from civilization. Beautiful locations and rousing action sequences help compensate for superficial plot.
Dist.: Orion

FAR FROM HOME 1989
★ ★ R Mystery-Suspense 1:30
☑ Nudity, adult situations, explicit language, violence
Dir: Meiert Avis   *Cast:* Drew Barrymore, Matt

Frewer, Richard Masur, Susan Tyrrell, Jennifer Tilly, Andras Jones
▶ Frewer and teen daughter Barrymore move into sleazy Nevada trailer park run by Tyrrell. Frewer is upset when Barrymore runs around with local boys. Meanwhile, a killer stalks the park, frying Tyrrell by throwing an electric fan in her bathtub. Tense if not particularly pleasant; Barrymore leads a fine cast but you'll guess the killer's identity early on.
Dist.: Vestron

FAR FROM THE MADDING CROWD 1967
British
★ ★ ★ ★ PG Drama 2:49
☑ Adult situations, violence
Dir: John Schlesinger   *Cast:* Julie Christie, Peter Finch, Terence Stamp, Alan Bates, Prunella Ransome
▶ Willful Bathseba Everdene (Christie) inherits a farm and in the process of running it destroys three men who love her: herdsman and former suitor Bates, gentleman farmer Finch, and dashing cavalryman Stamp. Lush, extravagant adaptation of Thomas Hardy's novel set in the moors of the fictional Wessex. Filled with sexual passion, cataclysmic encounters, and murderous rages in the best tradition of romantic tragedy. Christie is luminous and sensual in her first reteaming with *Darling* director Schlesinger.
Dist.: MGM/UA

FARMER'S DAUGHTER, THE 1947
★ ★ ★ NR Comedy 1:37 B&W
Dir: H. C. Potter   *Cast:* Loretta Young, Joseph Cotten, Ethel Barrymore, Charles Bickford, Rose Hobart, Rhys Williams
▶ Swedish farm girl Young moves to the big city and secures work as a maid for congressman Cotten and his kingmaker mom Barrymore. Young proves a model servant until her outspoken candor wins her nomination for a congressional seat from Cotten's rival party. Lively romantic comedy pokes fun at backroom politics and uptight city slickers. Young won an Oscar for her delightful performance.
Dist.: CBS/Fox

FARMER TAKES A WIFE, THE 1953
★ ★ NR Musical 1:21
Dir: Henry Levin   *Cast:* Betty Grable, Dale Robertson, Thelma Ritter, John Carroll, Eddie Foy, Jr., Charlotte Austin
▶ Remake of the 1935 drama about life along the Erie Canal during the mid-nineteenth century trades the original's charm for a brassy but undistinguished Harold Arlen/Dorothy Fields score. In this version Grable is the keelboat cook who falls for Robertson despite her misgivings about his love of farming. Songs include "We're Doing It for the Natives of Jamaica." **(CC)**
Dist.: CBS/Fox

FAR NORTH 1988
★ ★ PG-13 Comedy 1:30
☑ Adult situations, explicit language

Dir: Sam Shepard *Cast:* Jessica Lange, Charles Durning, Tess Harper, Donald Moffat, Ann Wedgeworth, Patricia Arquette
▶ Durning, patriarch of an all-female rural Minnesota family, demands the death of his horse Mel when he's thrown in a riding accident. The assignment falls to daughter Lange, who must also cope with her bitter sister Harper, flighty mother Wedgeworth, and promiscuous niece Arquette. Shepard's directing debut is intermittently amusing but also shrill and aimless.
Dist.: Nelson

FAR PAVILIONS, THE 1984
★ ★ ★ ★ **NR Romance/MFTV 1:50**
☑ Adult situations, mild violence
Dir: Peter John Duffell *Cast:* Ben Cross, Amy Irving, Omar Sharif, John Gielgud, Christopher Lee
▶ Cross, an India-born Englishman, has dual allegiances as an officer to the Corps of Guides and as the lover of Anjuli (Irving), a beautiful Indian princess. Epic tale of treachery and romantic intrigue set during the British raj. Originally made for cable and released in reedited version for home video. Based on the best-selling book.
Dist.: HBO

FASTEST GUITAR ALIVE, THE 1967
★ **NR Musical/Western 1:27**
Dir: Michael Moore *Cast:* Roy Orbison, Sammy Jackson, Maggie Pierce, Joan Freeman, Lyle Bettger
▶ Pop star Orbison's film debut is a flat, unconvincing Western played mostly for laughs. He's a Confederate who becomes an unwilling outlaw at the end of the Civil War. Along with buddy Jackson and some dance hall girls, he fights off renegades with a combination guitar/rifle. Songs, including title tune and "Whirlwind," are nothing special.
Dist.: MGM/UA

FAST FOOD 1989
★ ★ **PG-13 Comedy 1:32**
☑ Adult situations, explicit language
Dir: Michael A. Simpson *Cast:* Clark Brandon, Randal Patrick, Tracy Griffith, Jim Varney, Traci Lords, Michael J. Pollard, Kevin McCarthy, Pamela Springsteen
▶ After eight years of college, Brandon and Patrick finally graduate and open up a fast food joint. Burger business booms when duo add aphrodisiac as an ingredient. Rival mogul Wrangler Bob (Varney) plots against them. Moderately amusing teen comedy should appeal to its intended audience (although women may be offended by some sexist humor). Above-average cast with Griffith the standout.
Dist.: Fries

FAST FORWARD 1985
★ ★ ★ **PG Drama/Dance 1:51**
☑ Explicit language, mild violence
Dir: Sidney Poitier *Cast:* John Scott Clough,

Don Franklin, Tamara Mark, Gretchen Palmer, Tracy Silver
▶ Eight young dancers from Ohio compete in a New York City dance contest but have to struggle to make ends meet. Hey, let's put on a show! Eight stars are born overnight. Clough plays fast-talking Matt, the leader of the bright young cast. Lively choreography by Rick Atwell enriched by New York City street breakdancers. **(CC)**
Dist.: RCA/Columbia

FAST TALKING 1986 Australian
★ ★ **NR Drama 1:35**
☑ Adult situations, explicit language
Dir: Ken Cameron *Cast:* Rod Zuanic, Toni Allaylis, Chris Truswell, Gail Sweeny, Steve Bisley
▶ Troubled teen Zuanic sells drugs at school and has problems with teachers and principal. Home life is not much better: brother is a junkie and dad beats Zuanic and kills his dog. Is it any wonder mom walked out on them? Downbeat character study creates little empathy for the protagonist.
Dist.: Nelson

FAST TIMES AT RIDGEMONT HIGH 1982
★ ★ ★ **R Drama 1:30**
☑ Nudity, adult situations, explicit language
Dir: Amy Heckerling *Cast:* Sean Penn, Jennifer Jason Leigh, Judge Reinhold, Phoebe Cates, Robert Romanus, Brian Backer, Ray Walston, Forest Whitaker, James Russo, Pamela Springsteen, Martin Brest
▶ Lively, often raunchy, look at Southern California high school students transcends its youth comedy origins, thanks to Heckerling's amazingly subtle and compassionate direction. Leigh supplies the movie's soul as girl experiencing loss of innocence and Cates the spice as the woman of Reinhold's dreams. Penn provides the laughs as surfer boy Jeff Spicoli, dueling with history teacher Mr. Hand (Walston).
Dist.: MCA

FAST-WALKING 1981
★ ★ **R Drama 1:56**
☑ Nudity, explicit language, violence
Dir: James B. Harris *Cast:* James Woods, Tim McIntire, Kay Lenz, Robert Hooks
▶ "Fast-Walking" Miniver (Woods) is a smirking, laid-back prison guard/part-time pimp who helps inmates smuggle drugs and sneak into a nearby brothel. When famous black activist Hooks is convicted, Fast-Walking concocts a get-rich-quick scam to arrange the militant's escape. Bleak and cynical but well-made prison drama.
Dist.: CBS/Fox

FATAL ATTRACTION 1987
★ ★ ★ ★ ★ **R Drama 2:00**
☑ Nudity, adult situations, explicit language, violence
Dir: Adrian Lyne *Cast:* Michael Douglas,

Glenn Close, Anne Archer, Ellen Hamilton Latzen, Stuart Pankin

► Cautionary tale about the dangers of extramarital affairs stars Douglas as a happily married lawyer forced to deal with the repercussions of a one-night stand with sexy but neurotic book editor Close. Box-office smash garnered national attention for its antiadultery themes and thrill-packed suspense. Extremely well cast; Oscar-nominated for Best Picture, Director, Actor, Actress, Supporting Actress.
Dist.: Vestron

FATAL BEAUTY 1987
★ ★ ★ R Action-Adventure 1:44
☑ Nudity, adult situations, explicit language, graphic violence
Dir: Tom Holland *Cast:* Whoopi Goldberg, Sam Elliott, Ruben Blades, Harris Yulin, John P. Ryan

► Surefire crowd pleaser. Whoopi ("Don't call me bitch!") Goldberg plays a tough-but-tender narcotics detective hot on the trail of a drug dealer pushing a particularly potent and deadly cocaine called "fatal beauty." As the bodies pile up, Whoopi gets involved with the drug king's chief bodyguard Elliott. Shoot-outs and chase scenes directed with technical competence; excessive killings and relentless violence deliver power-packed antidrug message. **(CC)**
Dist.: MGM/UA

FAT CITY 1972
★ ★ PG Drama 1:31
☑ Adult situations, explicit language
Dir: John Huston *Cast:* Stacy Keach, Jeff Bridges, Susan Tyrrell, Candy Clark, Nicholas Colasanto

► Keach, a boozing, battered pug, attempts boxing comeback while younger naive Bridges enters fight game. Huston's adaptation of Leonard Gardner's novel is not for the upbeat *Rocky* crowd. A gritty, painfully real look at losers on the sleazier side of the tracks. Short on plot, long on atmosphere.
Dist.: RCA/Columbia

FATHER GOOSE 1964
★ ★ ★ NR Comedy 1:55
Dir: Ralph Nelson *Cast:* Cary Grant, Leslie Caron, Trevor Howard, Jack Good, Pip Sparke, Nicole Felsette

► Good-natured World War II comedy with Grant in a change-of-pace role as an alcoholic beachcomber coerced by Howard into monitoring Japanese planes on a South Seas island. Grant's troubles multiply when prim French schoolteacher Caron and her young students are stranded on the island. Light romantic adventure won a Best Screenplay Oscar for Frank Tarloff and Peter Stone.
Dist.: Republic

FATHER OF THE BRIDE 1950
★ ★ ★ ★ NR Comedy 1:33 B&W
Dir: Vincente Minnelli *Cast:* Spencer Tracy,

Elizabeth Taylor, Joan Bennett, Don Taylor, Billie Burke

► A honey of a picture about American family life circa 1950. Tracy is tops as the tightly squeezed, self-important father of the bride—alternately torn by jealousy, devotion, pride, and righteous wrath. Champagne cast includes Bennett as the adoring mother, breathtakingly beautiful Liz as the bride-to-be, and Taylor as the overshadowed groom. Adapted from Edward Streeter's novel and nominated for Best Picture, Actor and Screenplay. Led to equally delightful sequel, *Father's Little Dividend.* **(CC)**
Dist.: MGM/UA

FATHER'S LITTLE DIVIDEND 1951
★ ★ ★ ★ NR Comedy 1:21 B&W
Dir: Vincente Minnelli *Cast:* Spencer Tracy, Elizabeth Taylor, Joan Bennett, Don Taylor, Billie Burke

► Charming sequel to *Father of the Bride* reassembles the same popular cast of characters. Tracy has just settled into life as a father-in-law when daughter Taylor announces her pregnancy. Disapproving at first, Tracy eventually succumbs to baby-talk, even though the child starts bawling whenever grandpa comes close.
Dist.: Prism

FAT MAN AND LITTLE BOY 1989
★ ★ ★ ★ PG-13 Drama 2:06
☑ Adult situations, explicit language
Dir: Roland Joffe *Cast:* Paul Newman, Dwight Schultz, John Cusack, Bonnie Bedelia, Laura Dern, Natasha Richardson

► True story of the Manhattan Project, America's effort to create an atomic bomb before the Nazis during World War II, focuses on top scientist Robert Oppenheimer (Schultz) and Leslie Groves (Newman), an iron-willed general who used manipulation, flattery, and force to keep Oppenheimer and project in line. Subplot involves physicist Cusack's exposure to radiation. Imposing history lesson is impressively cast and mounted. **(CC)**
Dist.: Paramount

FATSO 1980
★ ★ PG Comedy 1:30
☑ Brief nudity, explicit language
Dir: Anne Bancroft *Cast:* Dom DeLuise, Anne Bancroft, Ron Carey, Candice Azzara, Michael Lombard

► Sentimental love story about overweight DeLuise who can't stop eating, even when he chains and bolts his refrigerator door. His nagging sister Bancroft screeches when poor Dom eats the icing from a birthday cake. Dom seems hopeless until he meets angelic salesgirl Azzara, and finds the best diet is love. DeLuise gives one of his best screen performances. Bancroft's debut as writer/director. **(CC)**
Dist.: CBS/Fox

FEAR 1988
★ R Mystery-Suspense 1:36
☑ Adult situations, explicit language, violence
Dir: Robert Ferretti *Cast:* Cliff De Young, Kay Lenz, Robert Factor, Scott Schwartz, Geri Betzler, Frank Stallone
► De Young and Lenz and their kids head to a remote mountain cabin to patch up family problems. Their domestic strife seems insignificant when they are taken hostage by four homicidal escaped convicts. Low-budget suspenser offers nothing new to genre.
Dist.: Virgin

FEAR, ANXIETY, AND DEPRESSION 1989
☆ R Comedy 1:34
☐ Adult situations, explicit language
Dir: Todd Solondz *Cast:* Todd Solondz, Jill Wisoff, Alexandra Gersten, Max Cantor, Jane Hamper, Stanley Tucci
► Aspiring playwright Solondz struggles with life, love, and his work. He abandons overweight girlfriend Wisoff for performance artist Hamper and hangs out with pretentious painter Cantor. New York University graduate Solondz's debut has a couple of laughs, but is mostly self-indulgent and derivative. Not helped by director's own whiny performance.
Dist.: Virgin

FEAR CITY 1985
★ ★ ★ R Action-Adventure 1:36
☑ Nudity, explicit language, graphic violence
Dir: Abel Ferrara *Cast:* Jack Scalia, Tom Berenger, Melanie Griffith, Billy Dee Williams, Rossano Brazzi, Rae Dawn Chong
► Excellent cast elevates this familiar story of psycho-killer who wipes out topless dancers in New York's "fleshpot" district. Ex-boxer Berenger tackles the case; Griffith is a stripper who almost gets slashed.
Dist.: HBO

FEAR IN THE NIGHT 1972 British
★ PG Mystery-Suspense 1:22
☐ Adult situations, explicit language, violence
Dir: Jimmy Sangster *Cast:* Joan Collins, Peter Cushing, Judy Geeson, Ralph Bates, James Cossins
► Lurid account of Collins, wife of crippled boys' school headmaster Cushing, conspiring with teacher Bates to drive his wife Geeson insane. Her ultimate plan is to have Geeson murder Cushing. Monotonous drama suffers most from Collins's shrill acting.
Dist.: HBO

FEARLESS VAMPIRE KILLERS, OR PARDON ME, BUT YOUR TEETH ARE IN MY NECK, THE 1967 British
★ NR Comedy 1:47
☑ Adult situations, mild violence
Dir: Roman Polanski *Cast:* Jack MacGowran, Roman Polanski, Alfie Bass, Jessie Robins, Sharon Tate, Ferdy Mayne

► Gruff Professor MacGowran and bumbling assistant Polanski infiltrate a mountain castle to save innkeeper's daughter Tate from vampires celebrating their annual ball. Uneven but often devastating horror satire has a strong cult reputation. Also known as *Dance of the Vampires.* Various reedited versions are available.
Dist.: MGM/UA

FEAR NO EVIL 1981
★ R Horror 1:39
☑ Nudity, explicit language, graphic violence
Dir: Frank LaLoggia *Cast:* Stefan Arngrim, Elizabeth Hoffman, Kathleen McAllen, Daniel Edin
► Baby who spurts blood during baptism grows up to be demonically possessed, telekinetically endowed teen Arngrim. He kills his rival for Hoffman's affections but she turns out to be angelically possessed, sent from above to thwart him. Creepy atmosphere evokes a few chills but inexperienced actors and crude technical quality reflect low budget.
Dist.: Nelson

FEAR STRIKES OUT 1957
★ ★ ★ NR Biography/Sports 1:40 B&W
Dir: Robert Mulligan *Cast:* Anthony Perkins, Karl Malden, Norma Moore, Adam Williams, Peter J. Votrian, Perry Wilson
► True story of baseball player Jimmy Pearsall (Perkins) whose promising career was nearly ruined by mental illness. His uneasy relationship with father Malden plays major role in his condition. Interesting look at price of sports stardom; Perkins is credible and sympathetic.
Dist.: Paramount

FEDS 1988
★ ★ ★ PG-13 Comedy 1:31
☑ Adult situations, explicit language, violence
Dir: Dan Goldberg *Cast:* Rebecca De Mornay, Mary Gross, Ken Marshall, Fred Dalton Thompson, Larry Cedar, James Luisi
► Broad comedy about FBI recruits Gross, a bookworm unaccustomed to physical activity, and De Mornay, an ex-Marine stymied by lack of legal expertise, who become partners during slapstick training program. Amiable jokes include picking up sailors, mastering firearms, and winning simulated terrorist exercise.
Dist.: Warner

FELLINI SATYRICON 1969 Italian
☆ R Drama 2:09
☑ Nudity, explicit language
Dir: Federico Fellini *Cast:* Martin Potter, Hiram Keller, Max Born, Capucine, Salvo Randone
► Two best friends, in love with the same boy, pursue the object of their affections through the Roman Empire. Along the way, they encounter orgies, feasts, festivals, and murders.

Outrageous cinematic journey with vivid colors and shocking visuals. Director Fellini creates an entire world of illusion. Based on a first century A.D. novel by Petronius. Certainly not for all tastes.
Dist.: MGM/UA

FERRIS BUELLER'S DAY OFF 1986
★ ★ ★ ★ PG-13 Comedy 1:43
☑ Explicit language
Dir: John Hughes *Cast:* Matthew Broderick, Alan Ruck, Mia Sara, Jennifer Grey, Jeffrey Jones
▶ Teenpic maestro Hughes's story about free-spirited, suburban whiz kid Broderick who fakes out his parents and takes the day off from school with his girlfriend Sara and reclusive best friend Ruck. Smart-alecky Ferris engages in a battle of wits with frustrated school principal Jones, treats his friends to an expensive lunch, a baseball game, and leads a parade through the streets of Chicago. Will Ferris get home before his mom? A treat for anyone who ever played hooky—or wanted to. (CC)
Dist.: Paramount

FEUD, THE 1990
★ R Comedy 1:37
☑ Adult situations, explicit language, violence
Dir: Bill D'Elia *Cast:* René Auberjonois, Scott Allegrucci, Gale Mayron, Joe Grifasi, David Strathairn, Ron McLarty
▶ Family man McLarty gets into a petty argument with hardware-store owner Grifasi. When Grifasi's store burns down, and McLarty's car blows up, they are convinced each other is responsible, and the battle is joined. Misunderstandings spiral out of control as family members go after one another. Wacky comedy updates Thomas Berger's novel from the thirties to the fifties, probably to accommodate the cool rockabilly soundtrack; odd, but lots of laughs.
Dist.: Vidmark

FEVER 1987 Australian
★ ★ NR Mystery-Suspense 1:30
☑ Nudity, adult situations, explicit language, violence
Dir: Craig Lahiff *Cast:* Bill Hunter, Gary Sweet, Mary Regan, Jim Holt
▶ In a quiet Australian town, cop Hunter brings cash from botched drug deal home to show wife Regan, and finds her in bed with lover Sweet. There is a struggle and Sweet is apparently killed. Hunter and Regan plot getaway but more surprises are coming in this derivative but twisty and involving import.
Dist.: Academy

FEVER PITCH 1985
★ ★ ★ R Drama 1:35
☑ Brief nudity, adult situations, explicit language, mild violence
Dir: Richard Brooks *Cast:* Ryan O'Neal, Catherine Hicks, Rafael Campos, Bridgette Andersen, Chad Everett
▶ Los Angeles sportswriter O'Neal investigates the world of gambling and becomes addicted himself. Everett stars as his loan shark, and Andersen as his daughter who takes him to Gamblers Anonymous. Downbeat and intense. (CC)
Dist.: CBS/Fox

FFOLKES 1980
★ ★ ★ PG Mystery-Suspense 1:40
☑ Adult situations, explicit language, graphic violence
Dir: Andrew V. McLaglen *Cast:* Roger Moore, Anthony Perkins, James Mason, Michael Parks, David Hedison
▶ Mr. ffolkes (Moore), frogman–connoisseur–misogynist–cat lover, is called in by the British Admiral to foil the takeover of two oil rigs in the North Sea. Thoroughly plausible and pithy suspense.
Dist.: MCA

FIDDLER ON THE ROOF 1971
★ ★ ★ ★ ★ G Musical 2:59
Dir: Norman Jewison *Cast:* Chaim Topol, Norma Crane, Leonard Frey, Molly Picon, Paul Mann
▶ Big-budget movie version of one of Broadway's longest-running musicals about Tevye, a Jewish milkman in Czarist Russia, his tart-tongued wife Golde, and his five nubile but dowry-less daughters. As persecution of the Jews intensifies, Tevye and his family are forced to leave their home. Bock/Harnick score includes "If I Were A Rich Man." Adapted from Shalom Aleichem stories and nominated for five Oscars (including Best Picture, Actor, Director); won for Oswald Morris's cinematography.
Dist.: MGM/UA

FIELD OF DREAMS 1989
★ ★ ★ ★ ★ PG Fantasy 1:46
☑ Explicit language
Dir: Phil·Alden Robinson *Cast:* Kevin Costner, Amy Madigan, James Earl Jones, Burt Lancaster, Ray Liotta, Timothy Busfield
▶ "If you build it, he will come," says a mysterious voice to Iowa farmer Costner. When he plows over his cornfield and turns it into a baseball diamond, the ghost of Shoeless Joe Jackson (Liotta) appears. Costner then receives another mystical instruction: to bring reclusive novelist Jones to his field of dreams. A magical, lyrical fantasy, sublimely shot and acted, culminating in a moving climax and an unforgettable final image. Best Picture nominee was also nominated for James Horner's lovely score and Robinson's screenplay adaptation of W. P. Kinsella's novel *Shoeless Joe.* (CC)
Dist.: MCA

FIELD OF HONOR 1986 Dutch
☆ R Action-Adventure 1:35
☑ Explicit language, adult situations, violence
Dir: Hans Scheepsmaker *Cast:* Everett

McGill, Ron Brandsteder, Jun-Kyung Lee, Frank Schaafsma, Hey Young Lee
▶ McGill is a basically honorable squad sergeant turned into brutal maniac by battle, especially when his sexually dallying unit is slaughtered by Chinese attack. Korean war told from the point of view of Dutch soldiers turns out to be not much different from innumerable clichéd World War II films. Only difference is more talk.
Dist.: MGM/UA

FIELD OF HONOR 1987 French
☆ **PG Drama 1:27**
☑ Adult situations, graphic violence
Dir: Jeanne-Pierre Denis *Cast:* Cris Campion, Pascale Rocard, Eric Wapler, Frederic Mayer, Marcelles Dessalles
▶ After selling his low draft number to a rich kid, Campion finds himself in thick of the nineteenth-century Franco-Prussian War, knee deep in battle, blood, and gaily uniformed bodies. In a deserted farmhouse, he links up with lost little German boy and they try to get back to France. War never looked so pretty as in this interesting and beautifully photographed film, where battle is resignedly accepted as part of natural flow of things.
Ⓢ
Dist.: Orion

FIENDISH PLOT OF DR. FU MANCHU, THE
1980 British
★ ★ **PG Comedy 1:40**
☑ Explicit language, adult humor
Dir: Piers Haggard *Cast:* Peter Sellers, Sid Caesar, Helen Mirren, David Tomlinson, Simon Williams, Steve Franken
▶ In his last film, Sellers plays a dual role as both the devilish Dr. Fu Manchu, now 168 years old and hunting for the elixir of youth, and Fu's adversary Nayland Smith, the retired Scotland Yard inspector tracking him down. Lightweight, daffy comedy in the *Pink Panther* vein.
Dist.: Warner

FIEND WITHOUT A FACE 1958 British
★ **NR Sci-Fi 1:14 B&W**
Dir: Arthur Crabtree *Cast:* Marshall Thompson, Terence Kilburn, Michael Balfour, Kim Parker, Kyanston Reeves, Gil Winfield
▶ A scientist's experiment in making energy from thoughts goes awry, creating instead brain monsters who zip around the Canadian countryside murdering people. Thompson, a major at a nearby base, battles the killer craniums. Terrifying chiller, tautly directed.
Dist.: Republic

FIFTH AVENUE GIRL 1939
★ **NR Comedy 1:23 B&W**
Dir: Gregory La Cava *Cast:* Ginger Rogers, Walter Connolly, Verree Teasdale, James Ellison, Tim Holt, Franklin Pangborn
▶ Millionaire Connolly, feeling neglected by his family, hires impoverished Rogers to pose as his mistress. Rogers's fresh outlook on life

causes Connolly's family to rethink their money-grubbing ways in this well-meant but extremely lightweight concoction.
Dist.: Turner

FIFTH FLOOR, THE 1980
★ ★ **R Drama 1:30**
☑ Nudity, adult situations, explicit language
Dir: Howard Avedis *Cast:* Bo Hopkins, Dianne Hull, Sharon Farrell, Mel Ferrer
▶ Young disco dancer Hull is wrongly committed to a mental institution where there's more violence, sadism, and rape than therapy. Hopkins is effectively creepy as the guard who takes advantage of Hull. Spartan production was allegedly based on an actual account.
Dist.: Media

FIFTH MUSKETEER, THE 1979 Austrian
★ ★ ★ **PG Action-Adventure 1:43**
☑ Adult situations, mild violence
Dir: Ken Annakin *Cast:* Beau Bridges, Sylvia Kristel, Ursula Andress, Cornel Wilde, Lloyd Bridges, Jose Ferrer, Rex Harrison, Olivia de Havilland, Alan Hale, Jr., Ian McShane
▶ Louis XIV secures his throne by imprisoning his twin brother Philippe (Beau Bridges in a dual role), but with the help of the elderly Four Musketeers (Wilde, Ferrer, Bridges, and Alan Hale, Jr.) Philippe escapes and mounts an attack on the king. Lavish but slowly paced swashbuckler, based on Alexander Dumas's *The Man in the Iron Mask*, features steady support from veteran actors McShane, de Havilland, and Harrison as the king's minister Colbert.
Dist.: RCA/Columbia

55 DAYS AT PEKING 1963
★ ★ ★ **NR Action-Adventure 2:30**
Dir: Nicholas Ray *Cast:* Charlton Heston, Ava Gardner, David Niven, Flora Robson, John Ireland, Harry Andrews, Paul Lukas
▶ Boxer Rebellion of 1900 traps diplomatic staffs from eleven countries inside a walled compound; supplies run low during protracted siege as prisoners await rescue by their armies. Large-scale action sequences, impressive sets, and Dimitri Tiomkin score outweigh frequently confusing plot in this sprawling epic. Robson gives the best performance as the Empress Dowager.
Dist.: Vestron

52 PICK-UP 1986
★ ★ ★ **R Mystery-Suspense 1:54**
☑ Nudity, adult situations, explicit language, graphic violence
Dir: John Frankenheimer *Cast:* Roy Scheider, Ann-Margret, Vanity, John Glover, Robert Trebor, Lonny Chapman, Clarence Williams III
▶ Successful businessman Scheider, blackmailed by creepy pornographers Glover, Trebor, and Williams, devises a cunning but dangerous revenge scheme. Hard-edged adaptation of Elmore Leonard's novel revels in its lurid, sleazy atmosphere. Glover is excep-

tionally sinister as he sedates Scheider's wife Ann-Margret with heroin. (CC)
Dist.: Media

FIGHTER ATTACK 1953
★★ NR War 1:21
Dir: Lesley Selander ***Cast:*** Sterling Hayden, J. Carrol Naish, Joy Page, Kenneth Tobey, Anthony Caruso, Frank DeKova
► Hayden is an American flier in 1944 Italy who takes one last mission, to destroy a German supply dump, before returning home. Despite being shot down, he hooks up with Italian Resistance fighters Naish and Page to achieve his objective. Sturdy, above-average war drama.
Dist.: Republic

FIGHT FOR US 1989 Filipino/French
☆ R Drama 1:34
☑ Rape, violence
Dir: Lino Brocka ***Cast:*** Phillip Salvador, Dina Bonnevie, Gina Alajar, Bembol Roco, Ginnie Sobrino, Abbo de la Cruz
► Ex-revolutionary Salvador, released from a Philippine prison when the Aquino regime takes over, investigates a priest's death in a mountain village. He is reunited with ex-lover Alajar and must deal with the corruption and violence that still plague the country. Cloudy politics don't lessen impact of central human story. [S]
Dist.: Cannon

FIGHTING BACK 1982
★★★★ R Action-Adventure 1:38
☑ Brief nudity, explicit language, graphic violence
Dir: Lewis Teague ***Cast:*** Tom Skerritt, Patti LuPone, Michael Sarrazin, Yaphet Kotto, David Rasche, Donna Devarona
► Outraged at the crime in his South Philadelphia neighborhood, deli owner Skerritt organizes a security patrol to rid the area of crooks. But his crusade turns ugly when the patrol takes on vigilante overtones. Crude but effective thriller in the *Death Wish* mold is graced with an unusually capable cast.
Dist.: Paramount

FIGHTING FATHER DUNNE 1948
★ NR Drama 1:33 B&W
Dir: Ted Tetzlaff ***Cast:*** Pat O'Brien, Darryl Hickman, Charles Kemper, Una O'Connor, Arthur Shields
► St. Louis priest O'Brien starts a home for problem boys, dishing out discipline and love in equal doses to help his charges overcome lives of crime. His hardest case is Hickman, who committed a murder for private reasons and refuses to repent. Sincere but plodding.
Dist.: Turner

FIGHTING KENTUCKIAN, THE 1949
★★★ NR Western 1:40
Dir: George Waggner ***Cast:*** John Wayne, Vera Ralston, Philip Dorn, Oliver Hardy, Marie Windsor, John Howard
► Heading home after the Battle of New Orleans, Wayne falls in love with Ralston, the daughter of an evil French aristocrat. Wayne calls on his fellow Kentucky rifleman to defeat the aristocrat's attempt to steal farmland. In one of his few roles without Stan Laurel, Hardy is endearing as a stout-hearted sidekick. Briskly entertaining film was also produced by Wayne.
Dist.: Republic

FIGHTING PRINCE OF DONEGAL, THE 1966
★★★ NR Action-Adventure 1:52
Dir: Michael O'Herlihy ***Cast:*** Peter McEnery, Susan Hampshire, Tom Adams, Gordon Jackson, Andrew Keir, Maurice Roeves
► Stirring period drama about the efforts of prince McEnery to rally rival clans against British oppressors in eleventh-century Ireland. When his mother and fiancée are kidnapped by Jackson's troops, McEnery mounts an assault on his castle. Excellent Disney adaptation of Robert T. Reilly's *Red Hugh, Prince of Donegal.*
Dist.: Buena Vista

FIGHTING SEEBEES, THE 1944
★★★ NR War 1:40 B&W
Dir: Edward Ludwig ***Cast:*** John Wayne, Susan Hayward, Dennis O'Keefe, William Frawley, Duncan Renaldo, Leonid Kinsky
► On a Pacific Island, Wayne turns his construction crew into a military unit to fight the Japanese. His propensity for disobeying orders angers Navy commander O'Keefe, but ultimately proves heroic. Hayward plays a reporter who adores Wayne despite O'Keefe's attentions. Brawny, two-fisted, very entertaining. Quintessential Wayne performance.
Dist.: Republic

FINAL ASSIGNMENT 1982
★★★ PG Drama 1:37
☑ Adult situations, explicit language
Dir: Paul Almond ***Cast:*** Genevieve Bujold, Michael York, Burgess Meredith, Colleen Dewhurst, Alexandra Stewart, Richard Gabourie
► Intrepid TV reporter Bujold, on assignment in Moscow, has an affair with Russian press officer York while unearthing deadly steroid experiments on children. With the KGB hot on her trail, she agrees to smuggle out of Russia a child who needs a brain operation. Jewish fur trader Meredith helps her in the scheme.
Dist.: Vestron

FINAL CHAPTER: WALKING TALL 1977
★★★★ R Action-Adventure 1:52
☑ Adult situations, explicit language, violence
Dir: Jack Starrett ***Cast:*** Bo Svenson, Margaret Blye, Forrest Tucker, Lurene Tuttle, Morgan Woodward, Leif Garrett
► Third and last feature about real-life Tennessee sheriff Buford Pusser (Svenson) rehashes the formula started in *Walking Tall*:

Pusser and his baseball bat make mincemeat out of villains who try to corrupt his small town. Followed by a short-lived TV series.
Dist.: Vestron

FINAL COMEDOWN, THE 1972
☆ **R Action-Adventure 1:24**
☑ Explicit language, graphic violence
Dir: Oscar Williams   *Cast:* Billy Dee Williams, Raymond St. Jacques, D'Urville Martin, R. G. Armstrong, Celia Kaye, Pamela Jones
▶ Young black Williams, infuriated when unjustly passed over for a job in favor of a white, fights the system violently along with fellow revolutionaries St. Jacques and Martin. The cops provide the opposition. Film is posed half-way between straight action and a serious critique of racism. Also known as Blast.
Dist.: Nelson

FINAL CONFLICT, THE 1981
★ ★ ★ **R Horror 1:48**
☑ Nudity, strong sexual content, explicit language, graphic violence
Dir: Graham Baker   *Cast:* Sam Neill, Rossano Brazzi, Don Gordon, Lisa Harrow, Mason Adams
▶ Third episode in the *Omen* trilogy follows a middle-aged Damien Thorn (Neill) as he plots control of the world from his post as U.S. Ambassador to Britain. Monks led by Brazzi gather seven magical daggers—the only weapons that can kill the Antichrist. Gut-wrenching gore includes murder by incineration and steam iron.
Dist.: CBS/Fox

FINAL COUNTDOWN, THE 1980
★ ★ ★ ★ **PG Sci-Fi 1:43**
☑ Adult situations, explicit language, mild violence
Dir: Don Taylor   *Cast:* Kirk Douglas, Martin Sheen, Katharine Ross, James Farentino, Ron O'Neal, Charles Durning
▶ On December 7, 1979, the nuclear aircraft carrier *Nimitz* slips through a time warp into 1941. Captain Douglas must decide whether to interfere with Japan's attack on Pearl Harbor and thereby change the course of history. Intriguing premise undermined by talky plot. Shot with the Navy's cooperation, the film provides a fascinating look at the *Nimitz*.
Dist.: Vestron

FINAL EXAM 1981
★ **R Horror 1:30**
☑ Brief nudity, adult situations, graphic violence
Dir: Jimmy Huston   *Cast:* Cecile Bagdadi, Joel S. Rice, Ralph Brown, Deanna Robbins, Sherry Willis-Birch
▶ A junior college is stalked by a crazed murderer who likes to hang out at the gym and massacre unwary students. Routine effort is long on clichés and short on characterization; plot will remind genre fans of *Prom Night*.
Dist.: Nelson

FINAL JUSTICE 1985
★ ★ ★ **R Action-Adventure 1:30**
☑ Nudity, explicit language, graphic violence
Dir: Greydon Clark   *Cast:* Joe Don Baker, Rossano Brazzi, Bill McKinney, Venantino Venantini, Greydon Clark, Helena Abella
▶ Texas sheriff Baker captures Italian criminal Venantini and is assigned to take him to Europe. When Venantini escapes in Malta, Baker pursues in gun-blazing cowboy fashion. Abella plays the Maltese policewoman who becomes Baker's partner. Baker's broadly energetic performance highlights simplistic but chase-filled plot.
Dist.: Vestron

FINAL MISSION 1984
★ ★ ★ **NR Action-Adventure 1:41**
☑ Nudity, adult situations, explicit language, graphic violence
Dir: Cerio Santiago   *Cast:* Richard Young, John Dresden, Kaz Garaz, Christine Tudor
▶ Los Angeles SWAT-team cop's family is killed by a drug kingpin, his sworn enemy since their days as Green Berets in Laos. The cop tracks the dealer to Northern California, where they have a bloody confrontation. Low-budget exploitation delivers extremely violent action.
Dist.: HBO

FINAL OPTION, THE 1983 British
★ ★ ★ **R Drama 2:05**
☑ Adult situations, explicit language, violence
Dir: Ian Sharp   *Cast:* Lewis Collins, Judy Davis, Richard Widmark, Edward Woodward, Robert Webber, Tony Doyle
▶ Crackerjack secret agent Collins infiltrates an antinuclear terrorist group headed by sociopath Davis. Collins's bravery is tested when the terrorists seize the American Embassy, demanding the destruction of a nuclear submarine base. Misleading billing for Widmark, who has exactly one scene as the Secretary of State. Originally titled *Who Dares Wins*.
Dist.: MGM/UA

FINAL TERROR, THE 1983
★ ★ **R Horror 1:24**
☑ Nudity, explicit language, graphic violence
Dir: Andrew Davis   *Cast:* John Friedrich, Adrian Zmed, Daryl Hannah, Rachel Ward, Mark Metcalf, Ernest Harden, Jr.
▶ Mysterious evil force in the California forest kills two motorcycle riders, then, one by one, picks off a group of teenage campers. They rush back to their bus, only to discover that the evil force still lurks among them. Well-made but routine horror film notable only for the presence of future stars Ward, Hannah, and Zmed.
Dist.: Vestron

FINDERS KEEPERS 1984
★ ★ **R Comedy 1:35**

☑ Adult situations, explicit language, mild violence
Dir: Richard Lester *Cast:* Michael O'Keefe, Beverly D'Angelo, Louis Gossett, Jr., David Wayne, Ed Lauter, Brian Dennehy
▶ Frantic nonstop slapstick about various crooks and con artists after $5 million hidden in a veteran's coffin. Failed roller derby manager O'Keefe dons a soldier's uniform to guard the coffin on its train journey to Nebraska; D'Angelo plays his sexy accomplice and Gossett, his foster father. Wayne stands out as the world's oldest conductor. **(CC)**
Dist.: CBS/Fox

FINE MADNESS, A 1966
★ ★ NR Comedy 1:43
Dir: Irvin Kershner *Cast:* Sean Connery, Joanne Woodward, Jean Seberg, Patrick O'Neal, Colleen Dewhurst
▶ One of Sean Connery's best and most overlooked non-Bond performances, showing off his comedic side. He plays rebellious poet Samson Shillitoe, continually running afoul of the women in his life and various forms of authority in this black satire.
Dist.: Warner

FINE MESS, A 1986
★ ★ ★ PG Comedy 1:30
☑ Adult situations, explicit language
Dir: Blake Edwards *Cast:* Ted Danson, Howie Mandel, Maria Conchita Alonso, Richard Mulligan, Paul Sorvino, Jennifer Edwards
▶ Actor Danson learns that gangsters have doped a horse so he and waiter pal Mandel bet on it. The chase is on when the bad guys discover the duo's involvement. Slapstick shenanigans are overly broad and done at breakneck speed. Edwards's daughter Jennifer is likable as Howie's girlfriend. **(CC)**
Dist.: RCA/Columbia

FINGERS 1978
☆ R Drama 1:30
☑ Strong sexual content, explicit language, violence
Dir: James Toback *Cast:* Harvey Keitel, Jim Brown, Tisa Farrow, Tanya Roberts, Michael V. Gazzo, Marian Seldes, Danny Aiello
▶ Keitel leads double life thanks to mismatched parents: he works as collector for mobster dad Gazzo while practicing to follow in pianist mom Seldes's footsteps. He goes deeper into the underworld when he falls for black gangster Brown's girlfriend Farrow. Lots of raw verve and energy but difficult to identify with unsympathetic hero.
Dist.: Media

FINIAN'S RAINBOW 1968
★ ★ ★ ★ G Musical/Comedy 2:21
Dir: Francis Ford Coppola *Cast:* Fred Astaire, Petula Clark, Tommy Steele, Keenan Wynn, Al Freeman, Jr.
▶ Screen legend Astaire's last major musical. Irish rascal Finian McLonergan buries a pot of leprechaun gold in Rainbow Valley. Daughter Clark gets three wishes and turns Wynn, racist white Southern senator, black. Nimble dancing and tuneful score includes "How Are Things in Glocca Morra?" Carefully adapted from Harburg and Saidy's Broadway play. Early directorial effort from Coppola.
Dist.: Warner

FINNEGAN BEGIN AGAIN 1985
★ ★ ★ ★ NR Drama/MFTV 1:54
☑ Adult situations, explicit language
Dir: Joan Micklin Silver *Cast:* Robert Preston, Mary Tyler Moore, Sylvia Sidney, Sam Waterston, David Huddleston
▶ Feel-good love story of the touching and funny relationship between Moore and Preston. He plays a top-notch reporter reduced to writing a lonely hearts column; Moore's a widowed teacher having an affair with married funeral director Waterson. A platonic, mutually supportive friendship develops into a romance between the mismatched pair. Directed with style and grace by Silver.
Dist.: HBO

FIRE AND ICE 1983
★ ★ PG Animation/Adult 1:15
☑ Mild violence
Dir: Ralph Bakshi *Cast:* Voices of Randy Norton, Cynthia Leake, Steve Sandor, Sean Hannon, Leo Gordon
▶ Sword and sorcery shenanigans from animator Bakshi and co-producer Frank Frazetta, an influential comic book artist. In a vaguely prehistoric jungle occupied by reptilian creatures, a fire princess is kidnapped by an evil ice king and then rescued by a brave warrior. Predictable story but innovative production techniques stretch the confines of animation.
Dist.: RCA/Columbia

FIRE AND ICE 1987
★ PG Drama/Sports 1:20
☑ Adult situations
Dir: Willy Bogner *Cast:* John Eaves, Suzy Chaffee, Tom Sims, Steve Link, John Denver
▶ Ski bum Eaves, Canadian freestyle champ, hitchhikes to Aspen in pursuit of ski bunny Chaffee. His frequent fantasies trigger production numbers involving acrobatic skiing, ski surfing, hang gliding, wind surfing, and other feats of derring-do. Not much of a plot, but lots of eye-popping athletic feats and scenic international locales. **(CC)**
Dist.: Nelson

FIRE AND SWORD 1982 German/Irish
☆ R Drama 1:30
☑ Nudity, adult situations, violence
Dir: Veith Von Furstenberg *Cast:* Christoph Waltz, Leigh Lawson, Peter Firth
▶ Wounded English knight Tristan, washed ashore on Irish coast, is tended by princess Isolde. They fall in love but unfortunately she is already engaged to his uncle, the king. More trouble occurs for the couple when she is ac-

cused of witchcraft. Gorgeously mounted period piece fails to engage the emotions due to limp performances and pacing.
Dist.: Vestron

FIRE BIRDS 1990
★★★ PG-13 Action-Adventure 1:25
☑ Explicit language, violence
Dir: David Green ***Cast:*** Nicolas Cage, Tommy Lee Jones, Sean Young, Bryan Kestner, Dale Dye, Bert Rhine
► Tough Army instructor Jones trains Cage and Young to fly new Apache attack choppers to avenge American deaths at the hands of evil South American drug pilot Rhine. It's *Top Gun* with rotors and an obvious script. But the final aerial combat sequence (designed by *Top Gun* air choreographer Richard T. Stevens) is a pip, with the choppers swinging gracefully through the sky like deadly mobiles. (CC)
Dist.: Buena Vista

FIRE DOWN BELOW 1957
★★ NR Action-Adventure 1:56
Dir: Robert Parrish ***Cast:*** Rita Hayworth, Robert Mitchum, Jack Lemmon, Herbert Lom, Anthony Newley, Bernard Lee
► When gorgeous Hayworth, a woman with a past, becomes a passenger on boat of smugglers Mitchum and Lemmon, a shipboard triangle is the result. Friends Lemmon and Mitchum become foes, but it is Mitchum to the rescue when Lemmon's life is endangered by a collision. Clichéd story but nice performances and Caribbean scenery.
Dist.: RCA/Columbia

FIREFOX 1982
★★★★ PG Action-Adventure 2:16
☑ Explicit language, violence
Dir: Clint Eastwood ***Cast:*** Clint Eastwood, Freddie Jones, David Huffman, Warren Clarke, Ronald Lacey, Kenneth Colley
► Guilt-driven Vietnam veteran Eastwood is the only American who can fly Russia's newest secret weapon, the "mind-controlled" Firefox jet. Will his war flashbacks endanger his efforts to infiltrate the Firefox compound? Special effects climax adds some spark to the typical Eastwood heroics.
Dist.: Warner

FIRE IN THE NIGHT 1990
☆ NR Action-Adventure 1:29
☑ Explicit language
Dir: John Steven Soet ***Cast:*** John Martin, Graciela Casillas, Patrick St. Esprit, Muni Zano, Burt Ward, E. J. Peaker
► Casillas, pursued and nearly raped by obnoxious St. Esprit, challenges her tormentor to a martial arts bout, even though his father can put her family out of business. Cement contractor Zano trains her. Feeble-minded and amateurish. Bodybuilder Casillas is miscast.
Dist.: New World

FIREMAN'S BALL, THE 1968 Czech
★ NR Comedy 1:13
☑ Adult situations, explicit language
Dir: Milos Forman ***Cast:*** Vaclav Stocker, Josef Svet, Ian Vistrcil, Josef Kolb
► Elderly fire brigade commander, dying of cancer, is feted by former associates. However, the fireman's ball turns into a series of comic mishaps. Sophisticated audiences should enjoy this Best Foreign Film nominee, an early effort of director Forman with some hilarious moments. [S]
Dist.: RCA/Columbia

FIRE OVER ENGLAND 1937 British
★★★ NR Drama 1:29 B&W
Dir: William K. Howard ***Cast:*** Laurence Olivier, Flora Robson, Leslie Banks, Raymond Massey, Vivien Leigh, Robert Newton
► Fast-paced, relatively accurate historical epic about dashing British spy Olivier, who steals plans for the Spanish Armada invasion from the court of King Philip (Massey). Robson would repeat her interpretation of Queen Elizabeth in *The Sea Hawk*. Olivier's scenes with Leigh, who plays a lady-in-waiting, led to their real-life affair.
Dist.: KVC

FIREPOWER 1979
★★★★ R Action-Adventure 1:44
☑ Explicit language, violence
Dir: Michael Winner ***Cast:*** Sophia Loren, James Coburn, O. J. Simpson, Eli Wallach, Anthony Franciosa, Vincent Gardenia
► Widowed by a suspicious chemical plant fire, Loren vows revenge on the arsonist. She's aided by government agents, bounty hunters, and mobsters. Bang-bang film treats us to multiple explosions: a Caribean hideaway, a yacht, a helicopter, five jeeps, and a boat dock.
Dist.: CBS/Fox

FIRES ON THE PLAIN 1959 Japanese
☆ NR War/Drama 1:45 B&W
Dir: Kon Ichikawa ***Cast:*** Eiji Funakoshi, Mantaro Ushio, Yoshihiro Hamaguchi, Osamu Takizawa
► In the chaos of the Japanese defeat in the Philippines during World War II, tubercular Funakoshi and other desperate soldiers kill, scrape, and scavenge for food and shelter. With escape cut off by deadly American tank fire, the crazed and destitute men turn to cannibalism. Horrifying antiwar film spares no details in its vision of humanity reduced to its basest instincts. [S]
Dist.: Various

FIRESTARTER 1984
★★★★ R Horror 1:54
☑ Explicit language, violence
Dir: Mark L. Lester ***Cast:*** Drew Barrymore, David Keith, George C. Scott, Martin Sheen, Art Carney
► In this Stephen King adaptation, gifted Barrymore can telepathically ignite fires without

matches. Blessing becomes a curse when she and dad Keith are pursued by sinister government assassin Scott. Incendiary horror fun will kindle genre-fans' enthusiasm with brisk pace and first-rate cast. **(CC)**
Dist.: MCA

FIREWALKER 1986
★ ★ ★ **PG Action-Adventure 1:50**
☑ Violence
Dir: J. Lee Thompson   *Cast:* Chuck Norris, Louis Gossett, Jr., Melody Anderson, Will Sampson, Sonny Landham
▶ Norris and Gossett, American soldiers of fortune, search for lost Aztec treasure in Mexico. Billed as Norris's "first comedy role" but with enough bone-cracking and carnage to please fans of the kung-fu star. **(CC)**
Dist.: Media

FIRE WITH FIRE 1986
★ ★ ★ **PG-13 Drama/Romance 1:44**
☑ Adult situations, explicit language, violence
Dir: Duncan Gibbins   *Cast:* Virginia Madsen, Craig Sheffer, Kate Reid, Jeffrey Jay Reid, Jon Polito, Jean Smart
▶ Convent school student Madsen meets Sheffer, an inmate at nearby work camp for delinquents, and it's love at first sight. Authorities punish Sheffer when the lovers meet clandestinely, so they run off together to a remote cabin; but disapproving nuns and police are hot on their trail. Opposite-side-of-the-tracks romance will appeal mainly to fans of the genre.
Dist.: Paramount

FIRST BLOOD 1982
★ ★ ★ ★ **R Action-Adventure 1:33**
☑ Nudity, explicit language, graphic violence
Dir: Ted Kotcheff   *Cast:* Sylvester Stallone, Richard Crenna, Brian Dennehy, David Caruso, Jack Starrett
▶ Tormented ex-Green Beret John Rambo (Stallone), honed like a machine in survival and attack skills, eludes a vicious gang of backwoods cops in this first of the riveting Rambo series. Crenna appears as his old commanding officer who calls him back to his Green Beret family. Gigantic box-office smash.
Dist.: HBO

FIRSTBORN 1984
★ ★ ★ ★ **PG Drama 1:43**
☑ Adult situations, explicit language, violence
Dir: Michael Apted   *Cast:* Teri Garr, Peter Weller, Christopher Collet, Corey Haim, Sarah Jessica Parker, Robert Downey, Jr.
▶ Single mother Garr and sons Collet and Haim are getting along just fine until she begins a romance with drug dealer Weller. He proves a villainous interloper and sets the family at odds. Eventually, elder son Collet stands up to Weller. Fine premise and convincing job by cast sabotaged by uninspired and violent ending. **(CC)**
Dist.: Paramount

FIRST DEADLY SIN, THE 1980
★ ★ ★ **R Action-Adventure 1:52**
☑ Adult situations, explicit language, violence
Dir: Brian G. Hutton   *Cast:* Frank Sinatra, Faye Dunaway, David Dukes, Brenda Vaccaro, Martin Gabel
▶ Sinatra is a battle-weary detective tracking a perverted killer who stalks the streets of New York. Dunaway appears in a thankless role as the cop's dying wife, lying in a hospital bed. Stuffy, somber film based on the best-selling novel by Lawrence Sanders.
Dist.: Warner

FIRST FAMILY 1980
★ **R Comedy 1:40**
☑ Explicit language, adult humor
Dir: Buck Henry   *Cast:* Bob Newhart, Gilda Radner, Madeline Kahn, Richard Benjamin, Bob Dishy
▶ Henry wrote and directed this White House spoof. Newhart is a dim-witted President with drunk wife Kahn and nymphomaniac daughter Radner. The Prez trades white middle-class Americans to an African nation in return for a tank of dung with magical veggie-growing properties. Lively, tacky comedy worthy of a few laughs.
Dist.: Warner

FIRST LEGION, THE 1951
★ ★ **NR Drama 1:26 B&W**
Dir: Douglas Sirk   *Cast:* Charles Boyer, Barbara Rush, William Demarest, Lyle Bettger
▶ Boyer is a wise priest who has his doubts about a comatose fellow cleric's miraculous cure. Attending physician Bettger confesses that the incident has a sound medical explanation; Boyer wonders if he must now disillusion crippled Rush, who's hoping for a similar cure. Strong performance by Boyer as a man who passes through skepticism to a deeper faith.
Dist.: Vestron

FIRST LOVE 1977
★ ★ ★ **R Romance 1:28**
☑ Nudity, adult situations, explicit language
Dir: Joan Darling   *Cast:* William Katt, Susan Dey, John Heard, Beverly D'Angelo, Robert Loggia
▶ College students Katt and Dey fall in love for the first time and deal with fidelity, responsibility and passion. Refreshingly frank yet old-fashioned love story with a very attractive cast.
Dist.: Paramount

FIRST MAN INTO SPACE 1959 British
★ **NR Sci-Fi 1:18 B&W**
Dir: Robert Day   *Cast:* Marshall Thompson, Marla Landi, Bill Edwards, Robert Ayres, Bill Nagy, Carl Jaffe

▶ Daring astronaut flies through a meteor cloud and returns to Earth with an alien hidden inside his body. Since the alien needs human blood to survive, the astronaut turns into a vampirelike killer. His brother must defeat the menace. Stark thriller's effectiveness limited by cheap production values.
Dist.: Rhino

FIRST MEN IN THE MOON 1964 British
★ ★ ★ NR Sci-Fi 1:43
Dir: Nathan Juran *Cast:* Edward Judd, Lionel Jeffries, Martha Hyer, Erik Chitty, Betty McDowall, Miles Malleson
▶ Tongue-in-cheek adaptation of H.G. Wells's novel follows the crew of an 1899 expedition to the moon, where they are attacked by Ray Harryhausen's devilish special-effects monsters. Broad but entertaining story should please younger viewers. Peter Finch has a bit part as a process server.
Dist.: RCA/Columbia

FIRST MONDAY IN OCTOBER 1981
★ ★ ★ R Comedy/Drama 1:39
☑ Brief nudity, explicit language
Dir: Ronald Neame *Cast:* Jill Clayburgh, Walter Matthau, Barnard Hughes, James Stephens, Jan Sterling
▶ Matthau is a crusty old Supreme Court justice shocked to learn the very female Clayburgh is filling the newly vacated Court seat. Though they disagree on nearly every critical issue, lovable sourpuss Matthau and high-spirited Clayburgh make an appealing pair.
Dist.: Paramount

FIRST NAME: CARMEN 1984 French/Swiss
☆ NR Drama 1:25
☑ Nudity, explicit language, violence
Dir: Jean-Luc Godard *Cast:* Maruschka Detmers, Jacques Bonaffe, Myriel Roussel, Cristophe Odent, Jean-Luc Godard
▶ When Detmers's terrorist gang robs a bank, guard Bonaffe tries to stop them but then becomes her lover. An affair with echoes of Bizet's *Carmen* ensues. The director plays Detmers's "Uncle Jean," a mental patient/filmmaker. Story is merely an excuse for a Godardian mixture of brooding sexuality and non sequitur observations. [S]
Dist.: Connoisseur

FIRST POWER, THE 1990
★ ★ ★ R Horror 1:38
☑ Explicit language, graphic violence
Dir: Robert Resnikoff *Cast:* Lou Diamond Phillips, Tracy Griffith, Jeff Kober, Mykel T. Williamson, Elizabeth Arlen, Dennis Lipscomb
▶ Cop Phillips pursues serial killer Kober, who has been given the power of resurrection by Satan. With the killer's spirit flitting from body to body, Phillips needs the help of psychic Griffith and nun Arlen to exorcise him. Shallow and formulaic; Griffith never gets a bead on her part. (CC)
Dist.: Nelson

FIRST TIME, THE 1981
★ R Comedy 1:36
☑ Adult situations, explicit language, adult humor
Dir: Charlie Loventhal *Cast:* Tim Choate, Krista Errickson, Marshall Effron, Wendy Fulton, Raymond Patterson, Wallace Shawn, Cathryn Damon
▶ Blossom College film student Choate schemes to lose his virginity with the advice of black roommate Patterson and school psychologist Effron. His chances drop drastically when mother Damon unexpectedly enrolls. Clever adolescent comedy with an amusing turn by Shawn as an eccentric professor. Directing debut for twenty-two-year old Loventhal, a Brian De Palma protégé.
Dist.: HBO

FIRST TURN-ON, THE 1984
☆ R Comedy 1:25
☑ Nudity, adult situations, explicit language, violence, adult humor
Dir: Michael Herz, Samuel Weil *Cast:* Georgia Harrell, Michael Sanville, Googy Gress, John Flood, Heidi Miller, Gilda Gumbo
▶ Trapped in a cave by a flatulence-caused landslide, a group of campers exchange stories about how each lost his or her virginity. A fat camper tells of the thanks he got from a blond he saved from a gang rape while the nature counselor recalls a game of "doctor." Packed with crude sex and bodily function gags.
Dist.: Vestron

FIRST YANK INTO TOKYO 1945
★ NR War 1:23 B&W
Dir: Gordon Douglas *Cast:* Tom Neal, Barbara Hale, Marc Cramer, Richard Loo, Keye Luke, Leonard Strong
▶ American pilot Neal is surgically altered to appear Oriental so he can sneak into World War II Japan and contact captured scientist Cramer. Complicating the mission: the presence of Neal's former sweetheart Hale and the suspicions of his old college buddy Loo, a Japanese officer. Great premise, okay execution.
Dist.: Turner

FISH CALLED WANDA, A 1988
★ ★ ★ R Comedy 1:47
☑ Nudity, adult situations, explicit language, violence
Dir: Charles Crichton *Cast:* John Cleese, Jamie Lee Curtis, Kevin Kline, Michael Palin, Maria Aitken, Tom Georgeson
▶ In London, Brits Georgeson and Palin and Yanks Curtis and Kline steal diamonds and quickly start double-crossing each other. Georgeson winds up in jail, but he's hidden the loot, so Curtis comes on to his lawyer Cleese to learn the hiding spot. Meanwhile, meek Palin fails miserably in mission to kill little old lady, the crime's only witness. Side-split-

ting farce marries Monty Python irreverence and American caper comedy. Sleeper hit, written by Cleese and Crichton, given sure-handed treatment by the seventy-seven-year-old director. Oscar nominations for Crichton (Best Director and Screenplay) and Cleese (Screenplay); Kline won for Supporting Actor.
Dist.: CBS/Fox

FISH HAWK 1980 Canadian
★ ★ ★ ★ G Family 1:34
Dir: Donald Shebib *Cast:* Will Sampson, Charlie Fields, Geoffrey Bowes, Mary Pirie, Don Francks
► Turn-of-the-century tale of Fish Hawk (Sampson), an elderly alcoholic Indian who befriends Ozark farm boy Fields, but dreams of returning to his people. Nicely mounted, high quality family fare with enthralling wildlife footage.
Dist.: Media

FISH THAT SAVED PITTSBURGH, THE 1979
★ ★ PG Comedy 1:43
Ⓥ Explicit language
Dir: Gilbert Moses *Cast:* Julius Erving, Jonathan Winters, Meadowlark Lemon, Kareem Abdul-Jabbar, Stockard Channing, Flip Wilson
► Channing is an astrologer who assembles a team of Pisces-only basketball players that turns the Pittsburgh franchise into a winner. Real-life NBA super-star Erving, as the team's best player, demonstrates his spectacular slam dunk. Lots of basketball, fast action and laughs.
Dist.: Warner

F.I.S.T. 1978
★ ★ ★ ★ PG Drama 2:23
Ⓥ Explicit language, violence
Dir: Norman Jewison *Cast:* Sylvester Stallone, Rod Steiger, Peter Boyle, Melinda Dillon, David Huffman, Tony Lo Bianco
► Episodic tale traces Stallone's Hoffa-like rise from Hungarian immigrant to president of a trucking union in the late 1930s. Along the way, he accepts mob favors that eventually lead to a senate hearing investigation. First-rate acting delivers professional and convincing portraits, especially Steiger as the prosecuting senator, Boyle as a double-dealing union boss and Lo Bianco as an oily Mafia connection. Excellent set decoration and use of color; photography by Laslo Kovacs.
Dist.: MGM/UA

FIST FIGHTER 1989
★ ★ R Action-Adventure 1:37
Ⓥ Brief nudity, adult situations, explicit language, graphic violence
Dir: Frank Zuniga *Cast:* George Rivero, Edward Albert, Mike Connors, Brenda Bakke, Matthias Hues
► Fighter Rivero arrives in South American town for revenge against Hues, who killed his friend. Crippled hustler Albert trains him for the

big match but Hues's scheming manager Connors gets Rivero thrown in jail. Bonecrushing bouts overshadow stingy production and banal (sometimes dubbed) dialogue. Rivero was known as Jorge Rivero when he starred with John Wayne in *Rio Lobo.*
Dist.: IVE

FISTFUL OF DOLLARS, A 1967 Italian
★ ★ ★ NR Western 1:36
Ⓥ Violence
Dir: Sergio Leone *Cast:* Clint Eastwood, Marianna Koch, John Wells, Pepe Calvo, Wolfgang Lukschy, Sieghardt Rupp
► Eastwood, a mysterious mercenary, cleans up a corrupt Mexican village by manipulating rival families against each other. First "spaghetti Western," based loosely on Kurosawa's *Yojimbo,* has dazzling direction and a haunting Ennio Morricone score. Eastwood's shrewd performance as The Man With No Name made him an international star. Highly influential and entertaining picture was followed by *For a Few Dollars More.* **(CC)**
Dist.: MGM/UA

FISTS OF FURY 1973 Chinese
★ ★ R Martial Arts 1:43
Ⓥ Explicit language, violence
Dir: Lo Wei *Cast:* Bruce Lee, Maria Yi, Han Ying Chieh, Tony Liu, Malalene, Paul Tien
► Out to avenge his teacher's murder, Lee uncovers a Japanese drug smuggling ring. Extremely violent kung fu film suffers from poor dubbing and wooden acting, although Lee's acrobatic stunts are as amazing as ever.
Dist.: CBS/Fox

FITZCARRALDO 1982 German
★ ★ PG Action-Adventure 2:37
Ⓥ Brief nudity, adult situations, violence
Dir: Werner Herzog *Cast:* Klaus Kinski, Claudia Cardinale, Jose Lewgoy, Miguel Angel Fuentes, Paul Hittscher, Huerequeque Bohorquez
► In turn-of-the-century South America, obsessed dreamer Kinski sets out to build an opera house in the middle of the jungle—even though he has to drag a full-sized steamboat over a forbidding mountain to reach his site. Massive epic is paradoxically a highly personal achievement for Herzog, who surmounted extraordinary production difficulties to complete the film (which were documented in *Burden of Dreams*). Ⓢ
Dist.: Warner

FIVE CAME BACK 1939
★ ★ NR Action-Adventure 1:15 B&W
Dir: John Farrow *Cast:* Chester Morris, Lucille Ball, Wendy Barrie, John Carradine, Allen Jenkins, Joseph Calleia
► Ball is among a dozen passengers in an Amazon plane crash. As the pilots try to fix the plane, cannibals lurk nearby. Only five survivors will be able to make the journey back.

Compelling screenplay co-written by Nathanael West. Remade as *Back From Eternity.*
Dist.: Turner

FIVE CARD STUD 1968
★★ **PG Western 1:43**
☑ Violence
Dir: Henry Hathaway   *Cast:* Dean Martin, Robert Mitchum, Inger Stevens, Roddy McDowall, Katherine Justice, Yaphet Kotto
► Despite Martin's objections, five poker players lynch a cheating gambler. As the five are murdered one by one, Martin teams up with stern preacher Mitchum to unmask the killer. Routine Western loses steam when the villain is identified halfway through the picture.
Dist.: Paramount

FIVE CORNERS 1988
★ **R Drama 1:32**
☑ Explicit language, violence
Dir: Tony Bill   *Cast:* Jodie Foster, Tim Robbins, Todd Graff, John Turturro, Daniel Jenkins, Elizabeth Berridge
► Slice of 1960s Bronx life has pet store worker Foster turning to peace-loving activist Robbins for help when rapist Turturro gets out of jail and comes calling. Quirky John Patrick Shanley screenplay has touches of originality but uneasily mixes comedy with violence; Foster and company manage to overcome the uneven tone. Marvelous sixties soundtrack.
Dist.: Cannon

FIVE DAYS ONE SUMMER 1982
★★ **PG Drama 1:48**
☑ Adult situations, mild violence
Dir: Fred Zinnemann   *Cast:* Sean Connery, Betsy Brantley, Lambert Wilson, Jennifer Hilary, Anna Massey
► Connery and Brantley, a doctor and his niece masquerading as husband and wife, take a holiday in 1930s Switzerland, hoping to consummate a long-postponed affair. She has eyes for their handsome young mountaineer guide Wilson, so the two men vie for her love. Tasteful production in a beautiful Alpine setting.
Dist.: Warner

FIVE EASY PIECES 1970
★★★ **R Drama 1:36**
☑ Nudity, adult situations, explicit language
Dir: Bob Rafelson   *Cast:* Jack Nicholson, Karen Black, Lois Smith, Susan Anspach, Billy Green Bush, Fannie Flagg
► Bobby Dupea (Nicholson) forsakes his musical talent and oppressive middle-class family for oil rig work, one-night stands, and poker games. Moody study of alienation has Oscar-nominated Nicholson as one of his quintessential antiheroes. Several powerful scenes include Jack's one-way conversation with his crippled dad and the famous bit where he orders a "chicken salad sandwich on whole wheat toast" from an uncooperative waitress. Best Picture nominee.
Dist.: RCA/Columbia

FIVE GOLDEN DRAGONS 1967 British
★ **NR Action-Adventure 1:32**
Dir: Jeremy Summers   *Cast:* Robert Cummings, Margaret Lee, Klaus Kinski, Dan Duryea, Christopher Lee, George Raft
► Swinging American Cummings goes to Hong Kong on vacation and ends up seeing the sordid side of town as he finds himself battling a sinister crime syndicate led by Lee. Cummings, never particularly convincing as an action hero, is a little long in the tooth for his role in this chintzy adventure.
Dist.: Republic

FIVE MILES TO MIDNIGHT 1963
U.S./Italian/French
★ **NR Mystery-Suspense 1:50 B&W**
Dir: Anatole Litvak   *Cast:* Sophia Loren, Anthony Perkins, Gig Young, Jean-Pierre Aumont, Yolande Turner, Tommy Norden
► In Paris, Loren marries Perkins, a younger American whose jealousy breaks up the marriage. He apparently dies in a plane crash, but shows up very much alive and needing his wife's help in an insurance fraud scheme. Despite a twisty plot premise, not nearly as exciting as it should be.
Dist.: SVS

FIVE WEEKS IN A BALLOON 1962
★★ **NR Action-Adventure 1:41**
Dir: Irwin Allen   *Cast:* Red Buttons, Fabian, Barbara Eden, Cedric Hardwicke, Peter Lorre
► English explorer Hardwicke, reporter Buttons, and slave trader Lorre are among the crew of a nineteenth-century balloon expedition in uncharted Africa. Diverse cast in a lighthearted adaptation of the Jules Verne adventure from disaster-movie king Allen.
Dist.: CBS/Fox

FLAME AND THE ARROW, THE 1950
★★★★ **NR Action-Adventure 1:28**
Dir: Jacques Tourneur   *Cast:* Burt Lancaster, Virginia Mayo, Robert Douglas, Aline MacMahon, Frank Allenby, Nick Cravat
► High-spirited swashbuckler gave Lancaster one of his zestiest roles as Dardo, a Robin Hood type who matches wits with cruel tyrant Allenby in the Italian Alps. After a daring escape from the gallows, Lancaster disguises himself as an acrobat to rescue the beautiful Mayo from Allenby's castle. Lancaster did most of his own stunts in this well-mounted production, which won Oscar nominations for Ernest Haller's cinematography and Max Steiner's score.
Dist.: Warner

FLAME OF BARBARY COAST 1945
★★ **NR Drama 1:31 B&W**
Dir: Joseph Kane   *Cast:* John Wayne, Ann Dvorak, Joseph Schildkraut, William Frawley, Virginia Grey
► San Francisco singer Dvorak stakes visiting Montana rancher Wayne at cards, and loses everything to a cheat. After honing his card

skills out of town, Wayne returns, recovers Dvorak's money, and opens his own gambling house. When they're together, the two lovers feel the earth move—unfortunately, it's the San Francisco earthquake, destroying Wayne's business. Low budget effort fails to catch fire. **Dist.:** Republic

FLAME OF THE ISLANDS 1955
★ NR Drama 1:30
Dir: Edward Ludwig   *Cast:* Yvonne De Carlo, Howard Duff, Zachary Scott, Kurt Kaznar, Barbara O'Neil, James Arness
► Singer De Carlo opens a Bahamas casino with Scott and Kaznar, and is reunited with ex-boyfriend Duff. Unfortunately, he has ties to the Mob, which covets De Carlo's operation. Between bullets and battles, De Carlo gets to sing "Bahama Mama" and "Take It or Leave It" in this flavorsome Carribean stew.
Dist.: Republic

FLAMINGO KID, THE 1984
★ ★ ★ PG-13 Comedy 1:40
☑ Adult situations, explicit language
Dir: Garry Marshall   *Cast:* Matt Dillon, Richard Crenna, Janet Jones, Jessica Walter, Hector Elizondo, Fisher Stevens
► Charming, extremely likable coming-of-age movie about Dillon, a 1963 Brooklyn teenager who gets a summer job as a cabana boy at El Flamingo, a fancy Long Island beach club. A good kid but no genius, Dillon idolizes the club's materialistic cardsharp Crenna and his gorgeous niece Jones (in real life, Mrs. Wayne Gretsky). By Labor Day, though, Jeffrey returns to the values taught by father Elizondo, a poor but honest plumber. Soundtrack is loaded with period rock 'n' roll hits. **(CC)**
Dist.: Vestron

FLAMING STAR 1960
★ ★ ★ NR Western 1:41
Dir: Don Siegel   *Cast:* Elvis Presley, Barbara Eden, Steve Forrest, Dolores Del Rio, John McIntire, Rudolph Acosta
► Presley gives a strong performance as a half-breed Indian torn between siding with Kiowa mother Del Rio and white father McIntire when the Kiowas declare war. Rescuing brother Forrest during a foolish attack on the Indians' village, Presley incurs the wrath of his tribe. Despite two opening songs (including "Old Shep"), a solid Western decrying racial prejudice rather than a musical.
Dist.: CBS/Fox

FLANAGAN 1985
☆ R Drama 1:40
☑ Brief nudity, adult situations, explicit language
Dir: Scott Goldstein   *Cast:* Philip Bosco, Geraldine Page, William Hickey, Linda Thorson, Olympia Dukakis
► Bosco, a fifty-three-year-old New York City cab driver, dreams of becoming a Shakespearean actor but is plagued with personal and professional difficulties including es-

tranged wife Dukakis, mistress Thorson, and rejection by producers. Talky and static drama has good urban texture and wonderful Bosco. Also known as *Walls of Glass*.
Dist.: Media

FLASHBACK 1990
★ ★ ★ R Comedy 1:48
☑ Explicit language, violence
Dir: Franco Amurri   *Cast:* Dennis Hopper, Kiefer Sutherland, Carol Kane, Cliff De Young, Paul Dooley, Richard Masur, Michael McKean, Kathleen York
► Straitlaced FBI agent Sutherland is assigned to escort unrepentant sixties radical Hopper from San Francisco to Spokane. During the journey, the hippie at first outwits but then loosens up the yuppie. Clever premise undone by Amurri's lazy direction and David Loughery's blundering screenplay. However, Hopper lends project both gravity and humor. **(CC)**
Dist.: Paramount

FLASHDANCE 1983
★ ★ ★ ★ R Drama/Dance 1:36
☑ Nudity, explicit language
Dir: Adrian Lyne   *Cast:* Jennifer Beals, Michael Nouri, Lilia Skala, Cynthia Rhodes, Belinda Bauer, Phil Burns
► Megahit of 1983, a Cinderella-in-Pittsburgh fantasy about beautiful welder Beals who lives to dance. By day she handles acetylene torches, by night she gyrates to a pulsating Giorgio Moroder soundtrack. Lyne directs new-wave dancing and sweaty female workouts with vim and vigor. Sizzling Irene Cara sings Oscar-winning "What a Feeling." Also nominated for the song "Maniac," Editing and Cinematography. **(CC)**
Dist.: Paramount

FLASH GORDON 1980
★ ★ ★ PG Sci-Fi 1:51
☑ Explicit language, violence
Dir: Mike Hodges   *Cast:* Max Von Sydow, Timothy Dalton, Sam J. Jones, Melody Anderson, Chaim Topol, Ornella Muti
► Lavish high-camp revival pits comic-strip hero Flash (Jones) and pretty, putty-brained Dale Arlen (Anderson) against against the merciless Emperor Ming (Von Sydow) in a battle to save the planet. Sexy innuendos abound on the planet Mongo, where inhabitants sport gold-lamé outfits.
Dist.: MCA

FLASH OF GREEN, A 1984
★ NR Drama 2:11
☑ Brief nudity, adult situations, explicit language, violence
Dir: Victor Nunez   *Cast:* Ed Harris, Blair Brown, Richard Jordan, George Coe, Joan Goodfellow, Jean De Baer
► Moody, complex melodrama about Florida Keys newspaper reporter Harris who betrays a local conservation group despite his love for its leader Brown. Producer Jordan is magnetic

as a corrupt politician. Director-writer-cameraman Nunez captures the unique feel of the Keys, but his adaptation of John D. MacDonald's novel suffers from extreme length and offbeat pacing.
Dist.: Media

FLASHPOINT 1984
★ ★ ★ R Mystery-Suspense **1:34**
☑ Explicit language, violence
Dir: William Tannen   *Cast:* Kris Kristofferson, Treat Williams, Rip Torn, Kevin Conway, Mark Slade, Tess Harper
▶ Texas border patrolmen Kristofferson and Williams find a skeleton and a cache of 1963 money inside an abandoned jeep. Kristofferson wants to retire with the loot in Mexico, but Williams connects the money to a deadly conspiracy. Competent adventure has an accomplished performance from Torn as a sheriff.
Dist.: HBO

FLAT TOP 1952
★ ★ NR War **1:25**
Dir: Lesley Selander   *Cast:* Sterling Hayden, Richard Carlson, Bill Phipps, Keith Larsen, William Schallert, John Bromfield
▶ During World War II, fighter pilot Hayden commands an air craft carrier in the Pacific. He has conflicts with both his superiors and his own men, but gets a chance to prove his mettle during a Japanese attack. Fast-paced war drama won an Oscar nomination for film editing.
Dist.: Republic

FLESH + BLOOD 1985
★ ★ R Action-Adventure **2:05**
☑ Nudity, adult situations, explicit language, violence
Dir: Paul Verhoeven   *Cast:* Rutger Hauer, Jennifer Jason Leigh, Tom Burlinson, Jack Thompson, Susan Tyrrell
▶ In 1501 Europe, soldier of fortune Hauer, betrayed by a lord, kidnaps his daughter Leigh. They fall in love but her fiancé Burlinson arrives to rescue her. Gorgeously photographed epic re-creates the Dark Ages with gusto and carnage, although characters are unsympathetic. Overripe dialogue is excessively vulgar; hot tub seduction scene is quite steamy.
Dist.: Vestron

FLESH AND THE DEVIL 1927
★ ★ NR Drama **1:49** B&W
Dir: Clarence Brown   *Cast:* Greta Garbo, John Gilbert, Lars Hanson, Barbara Kent, William Orlamond, George Fawcett
▶ Garbo exerts a fatal fascination upon the Austrian officer corps, provoking her husband's death in a duel, and coming between best friends Gilbert and Hanson. Rich, velvety silent, with the incomparable Garbo and Gilbert striking sparks in their love scenes.
Dist.: MGM/UA

FLESHBURN 1984
★ R Action-Adventure **1:31**
☑ Adult situations, explicit language, violence
Dir: George Gage   *Cast:* Steve Kanaly, Karen Carlson, Macon McCalman, Robert Chimento, Sonny Landham, Duke Stroud
▶ Indian Vietnam vet Landham escapes from insane asylum, kidnaps the psychiatrists who committed him there, and abandons them in the desert. The shrinks struggle to survive as Landham practices black magic against them. Survival tale with aspirations to larger meaning. Also known as *Fear in a Handful of Dust*.
Dist.: Media

FLETCH 1985
★ ★ ★ PG Comedy **1:38**
☑ Adult situations, explicit language
Dir: Michael Ritchie   *Cast:* Chevy Chase, Dana Wheeler-Nicholson, Joe Don Baker, Tim Matheson, Richard Libertini, M. Emmet Walsh
▶ Rich Matheson claims to be dying and hires investigative reporter Chase to murder him so wife Wheeler-Nicholson can collect the insurance. Chase investigates and uncovers a drug smuggling ring. Relaxed, diverting comedy/mystery with Chevy's most pleasing film work to date. His offhand delivery of screenwriter Andrew Bergman's non sequiturs ("Can I borrow your towel?" he asks a half-naked Wheeler-Nicholson, "my car just hit a water buffalo") is endearing. (CC)
Dist.: MCA

FLETCH LIVES 1989
★ ★ ★ PG Comedy **1:35**
☑ Adult situations, explicit language
Dir: Michael Ritchie   *Cast:* Chevy Chase, Hal Holbrook, Julianne Phillips, R. Lee Ermey, Cleavon Little, Randall "Tex" Cobb
▶ Los Angeles reporter/master-of-disguise Chase goes to Louisiana to claim mansion he has inherited and gets involved in murder and intrigue. Someone is trying to scare Chase's property and evangelist Ermey is among the suspects. Follow-up to *Fletch* lacks its comic consistency but thin plot provides good vehicle for Chase's patented wit. Funniest scenes: Chevy's impersonation of a faith healer and interruption of a KKK gathering. (CC)
Dist.: MCA

FLICKS 1982
☆ R Comedy **1:18**
☑ Nudity, adult situations, explicit language, adult humor
Dir: Peter Winograd   *Cast:* Pamela Sue Martin, Joan Hackett, Martin Mull, Betty Kennedy, Richard Belzer, Barry Pearl
▶ Inconsistent collection of film parodies includes mock movie trailers and newsreel, as well as animated segment about cartoon characters' retirement home. Other episodes: *House of the Living Corpse*, about a couple

who move into mutant-plagued neighborhood, and a detective parody with an insect hero. Not very funny, save for a few Mull bits.
Dist.: Media

FLIGHT OF THE EAGLE, THE 1983 Swedish
★ NR Drama 2:21
☑ Violence
Dir: Jan Troell ***Cast:*** Max Von Sydow, Goran Stangertz, Sverre Anker, Eva von Hanno
▶ True story of the ill-fated 1897 expedition that attempted to reach the North Pole in a hydrogen-filled balloon in order to claim the land for Sweden. The three explorers were never seen alive again but, in 1930, their remains—including a detailed diary—were discovered by the crew of a Norwegian ship. Artful but slow drama was Sweden's entry as Best Foreign Film.
Dist.: Active Home Video

FLIGHT OF THE NAVIGATOR, THE 1986
★★★★ PG Sci-Fi 1:28
☑ Explicit language
Dir: Randal Kleiser ***Cast:*** Joey Cramer, Cliff De Young, Veronica Cartwright, Matt Adler, Sarah Jessica Parker, Howard Hesseman
▶ Disney time-tripper about twelve-year-old Cramer who falls into a ravine in 1978, wakes up a moment later, and discovers it's 1986! Panic-stricken, he runs home but finds his parents have moved. NASA scientists discover the kid's been riding on a flying saucer. A lively and touching adventure, grand fun for the whole family.
Dist.: Buena Vista

FLIGHT OF THE PHOENIX 1965
★★★★ NR Action-Adventure 2:27
Dir: Robert Aldrich ***Cast:*** James Stewart, Richard Attenborough, Peter Finch, Hardy Kruger, Ernest Borgnine, Ian Bannen, Dan Duryea, George Kennedy
▶ Grueling adventure about a small band of survivors stranded in the Arabian desert after their plane crashes. Exciting tribute to endurance is realistic and unpredictable, with Stewart delivering another thoughtful performance as the pilot. Fine support from Attenborough as an alcoholic navigator and Kruger as a German designer. (CC)
Dist.: CBS/Fox

FLIGHT TO MARS 1951
★ NR Sci-Fi 1:12
Dir: Lesley Selander ***Cast:*** Marguerite Chapman, Cameron Mitchell, Arthur Franz, Virginia Huston, Morris Ankrum, John Litel
▶ A spaceship from Earth crashes on Mars, uncovering an underground civilization. Martian princess Chapman helps the Earthlings, who include Mitchell and Franz, return to their home planet. Slightly above-average grade B sci-fi has some good story ideas but cheesy sets and costumes.
Dist.: Fries

FLIM FLAM MAN, THE 1967
★★★ NR Comedy 1:55
Dir: Irvin Kershner ***Cast:*** George C. Scott, Sue Lyon, Michael Sarrazin, Harry Morgan, Jack Albertson, Slim Pickens
▶ In the South, old-time bunco artist Scott hooks up with AWOL soldier Sarrazin and teaches him the tricks of the trade. Sarrazin tries to turn Scott straight but learns there's no reforming a dishonest man. Engaging; Scott and Sarrazin make an entertaining team. (CC)
Dist.: CBS/Fox

FLIPPER 1963
★★★★ G Family 1:30
Dir: James B. Clark ***Cast:*** Chuck Connors, Luke Halpin, Connie Scott, Jane Rose, Joe Higgins, Mitzi the Dolphin
▶ Florida youngster Halpin nurses a wounded dolphin back to health. Connors, his fisherman father, returns Flipper to the wild, breaking Halpin's heart. Will Flipper remember his old friend? Wholesome family film, basis for the hit TV series, will enthrall kids.
Dist.: MGM/UA

FLOATING WEEDS 1959 Japanese
☆ NR Drama 1:59
Dir: Yasujiro Ozu ***Cast:*** Ganjiro Nakamura, Machiko Kyo, Haruko Sugimura, Ayako Wakao, Koji Mitsui, Hiroshi Kawaguchi
▶ After a twelve-year separation, theater performer Nakamura reunites with former mistress Sugimura and son Kawaguchi. Bitter current mistress Kyo tries to get back at Nakamura by having one of the actresses in their starving troupe seduce the son. Critically hailed for its precision and dramatic power, remake of director's own 1936 silent film may be too remote for some. Also known as *Drifting Weeds*. [S]
Dist.: Connoisseur

FLORIDA STRAITS 1986
★★★ PG-13 Action-Adventure/MFTV 1:37
☑ Explicit language, violence
Dir: Mike Hodges ***Cast:*** Raul Julia, Fred Ward, Daniel Jenkins, Jaime Sanchez, Victor Argto
▶ Old style soldier-of-fortune adventure about Cuban refugee Julia who hires a Florida charter boat owned jointly by Ward and Jenkins to track down the gold he buried 20 years ago, before going to Castro's prison. Their exciting seafaring journey is interrupted by patrol boats and a renegade army. Excellent casting, superior technical credits, and an exciting wind-up. (CC)
Dist.: Orion

FLOWER DRUM SONG 1961
★★★ NR Musical 2:13
Dir: Henry Koster ***Cast:*** Nancy Kwan, James Shigeta, Miyoshi Umeki, Juanita Hall, Jack Soo
▶ Hong Kong immigrant Umeki is brought to San Francisco to wed nightclub owner Soo in

an arranged marriage, but instead falls in love with handsome stranger Shigeta. Soo's top singer Kwan is also intent on marriage in this pleasant adaptation of a Broadway hit. Rodgers and Hammerstein score includes "I Enjoy Being a Girl" and "Don't Marry Me." *Dist.:* MCA

FLOWERS IN THE ATTIC 1987
★ ★ ★ PG-13 Mystery-Suspense 1:31
☑ Explicit language, violence
Dir: Jeffrey Bloom *Cast:* Louise Fletcher, Victoria Tennant, Kristy Swanson, Jeb Stuart Adams, Ben Granger
▶ Nasty gothic-style melodrama, adapted from V. C. Andrews's huge best-seller. Disinherited from the family fortune for marrying her uncle, truly weird, gold-digging mom Tennant hides her four kids in the attic until her daddy dies (and she can inherit his dough). Grandma Fletcher sadistically tortures kids; mom poisons them. Stiff and dreary acting; mindless story will only appeal to those who loved the book.
Dist.: New World

FLY, THE 1958
★ ★ NR Sci-Fi/Horror 1:30
Dir: Kurt Neumann *Cast:* Al (David) Hedison, Patricia Owens, Vincent Price, Herbert Marshall
▶ Housefly gets caught in machine with scientist Hedison during his matter transference experiment. Result: one man with a fly's head and one fly with a man's head. Cult favorite with the unforgettable scene of Price and Marshall encountering the fly who pleads: "Help me!" Pretty good sci-fi, not as dramatic or nearly as grisly as David Cronenberg's 1986 remake.
Dist.: CBS/Fox

FLY, THE 1986
★ ★ ★ R Sci-Fi/Horror 1:36
☑ Brief nudity, adult situations, explicit language, graphic violence
Dir: David Cronenberg *Cast:* Jeff Goldblum, Geena Davis, John Getz, Joy Boushel, Les Carlson
▶ Bookish scientist Goldblum genetically fuses himself with a fly. His journalist girlfriend Davis stands by her man—even when he starts climbing walls and has skin that resembles burnt cheese. High-tech eighties gore, plus a hearty dose of black humor, updates this remake of the fifties camp classic; decidedly not for the squeamish. Sequel: 1989's *The Fly II.* Goldblum and Davis married later. (CC)
Dist.: CBS/Fox

FLY II, THE 1989
★ ★ ★ R Sci-Fi/Horror 1:45
☑ Adult situations, violence, explicit language
Dir: Chris Walas *Cast:* Eric Stoltz, Daphne Zuniga, Lee Richardson, John Getz, Frank Turner, Ann Marie Lee

▶ Stoltz, brilliant son of the Jeff Goldblum character in the 1986 *The Fly*, follows in his father's footsteps by conducting matter transference experiments. Girlfriend Zuniga remains loyal even as Stoltz's chromosomes go haywire, transforming him into a giant fly. Competent sequel overcomes slow start for a rousing finale; plenty of gore and gooey special effects. Director Walas won an Oscar for makeup in the first film.
Dist.: CBS/Fox

FLYING DEUCES 1939
★ ★ ★ NR Comedy 1:05
Dir: Edward Sutherland *Cast:* Stan Laurel, Oliver Hardy, Jean Parker, Reginald Gardiner, Charles Middleton, James Finlayson
▶ When Hardy's romance with Parisian waitress Parker falls through, he and Laurel are stopped from drowning their sorrows in the Seine by an officer of the Foreign Legion who encourages them to enlist. Disenchanted under arms, the boys learn that getting out of the Legion is a good deal more difficult than getting in. Not one of Laurel and Hardy's great pictures, but fairly rollicking; the pair delivers a gentle song-and-dance interlude to "Shine on Harvest Moon."
Dist.: Republic

FLYING DOWN TO RIO 1933
★ ★ ★ NR Musical 1:29 B&W
Dir: Thornton Freeland *Cast:* Dolores Del Rio, Gene Raymond, Raoul Roulien, Ginger Rogers, Fred Astaire, Blanche Frederici
▶ Dated musical romance, focusing on pilot/bandleader Raymond's rivalry with singer Roulien over the beautiful Del Rio, is an amusing Depression relic with an incredible climax: dozens of chorus girls perform the title song while strapped to the wings of airborne biplanes. Notable primarily as the first pairing of Astaire and Rogers. Although fourth- and fifth-billed, their version of "The Carioca" helped establish them as America's premier dancing team.
Dist.: Turner

FLYING LEATHERNECKS 1951
★ ★ ★ NR War 1:42 B&W
Dir: Nicholas Ray *Cast:* John Wayne, Robert Ryan, Don Taylor, William Harrigan, Janis Carter, Jay C. Flippen
▶ World War II drama examines the conflict between Wayne, a harsh, demanding major of an air squadron in Guadalcanal, and Ryan, a captain who thinks the young pilots need more compassionate treatment. Good use of newsreel dogfights boosts familiar plot. Flippen is a delight as a resourceful sergeant. Produced by Howard Hughes.
Dist.: Turner Ⓒ

FLYING TIGERS 1942
★ ★ ★ NR War 1:42
Dir: David Miller *Cast:* John Wayne, John Carroll, Anna Lee, Paul Kelly, Gordon Jones, Mae Clarke

▶ Tribute to American fighter pilots stationed in China during World War II has squadron leader Wayne (in his first war picture) coping with his unruly fliers as well as the Japanese. Carroll has an interesting role as a recklessly mercenary pilot (the Tigers received $500 for each downed enemy plane).
Dist.: Republic

FOG, THE 1980
★ ★ R Horror 1:26
☑ Violence
Dir: John Carpenter *Cast:* Adrienne Barbeau, Hal Holbrook, Janet Leigh, Jamie Lee Curtis, John Houseman
▶ Dense fog hides a colony of vengeful, shipwrecked ghosts in the California town of Antonion Bay. In her first film, Barbeau stars as a deejay who broadcasts from the isolated lighthouse. Eerie and elegant tale of the macabre.
Dist.: Embassy

FOLLOW ME, BOYS 1966
★ ★ ★ ★ G Family 2:11
Dir: Norman Tokar *Cast:* Fred MacMurray, Vera Miles, Lillian Gish, Charles Ruggles, Kurt Russell
▶ Small-town scoutmaster (a perfectly cast MacMurray) and wife Miles, unable to have kids of their own, become surrogate parents to kids in their troop. Later, they actually adopt troubled young Russell. Sentimental if sometimes melodramatic Disney film still conveys genuine emotion.
Dist.: Buena Vista

FOLLOW THAT DREAM 1962
★ ★ ★ NR Musical 1:50
Dir: Gordon Douglas *Cast:* Elvis Presley, Arthur O'Connell, Anne Helm, Joanna Moore, Jack Kruschen, Simon Oakland
▶ Elvis and pop O'Connell claim squatters' rights to government land in Florida, then defeat thugs to establish a home for four orphans. Mild Presley entry features "What a Wonderful Life," "On Top of Old Smoky," and "Home Is Where the Heart Is." Action scenes allow the King to show off his judo moves.
Dist.: MGM/UA

FOLLOW THE FLEET 1936
★ ★ ★ ★ NR Musical 1:50 B&W
Dir: Mark Sandrich *Cast:* Fred Astaire, Ginger Rogers, Randolph Scott, Harriet Hilliard, Astrid Allwyn, Harry Beresford
▶ In a turnabout to their usual glamorous roles, Astaire plays a wisecracking sailor and Rogers, a dancehall hostess. Earthy setting and plot are secondary to the splendid dances and Irving Berlin score: "I'm Putting All My Eggs in One Basket," "Let Yourself Go," "Let's Face the Music and Dance," etc. Thin but charming comedy relief provided by Scott and Hilliard (Harriet of TV's "Ozzie and Harriet"). Look quickly for Lucille Ball and Betty Grable in bit parts.
Dist.: Turner

FOOD OF THE GODS 1976
★ ★ PG Horror 1:29
☑ Violence
Dir: Bert I. Gordon *Cast:* Marjoe Gortner, Pamela Franklin, Ida Lupino, Ralph Meeker, Jon Cypher
▶ Campy low-budgeter based on H. G. Wells's foreboding sci-fi novel about ecology gone beserk. Feeding on a mysterious food substance, giant rats, wasps, and man-eating worms proliferate and roam the earth. Special effects are on par with the dialogue ("I know a rat when I see one, mister.").
Dist.: Vestron

FOOD OF THE GODS II 1989
☆ R Horror 1:31
☑ Explicit language, violence
Dir: Damian Lee *Cast:* Paul Coufos, Lisa Schrage, Colin Fox, Frank Moore, Real Andrews, Jackie Burroughs
▶ Against a backdrop of animal rights protests, university scientist Coufos experiments with a special growth hormone that is accidentally ingested by some rats. Once grown to enormous size, the rodents begin devouring coeds. Sequel to 1976 giant animal movie is as stupid as it sounds.
Dist.: IVE

FOOL FOR LOVE 1985
★ R Drama 1:45
☑ Explicit language, violence
Dir: Robert Altman *Cast:* Sam Shepard, Kim Basinger, Harry Dean Stanton, Randy Quaid, Martha Crawford
▶ Sagebrush soap opera long on talk, short on action. Obscure screenplay by Shepard (adapted from his Off-Broadway play) tells the tale of the on-again, off-again, possibly incestuous romance between has-been, love-crazed rodeo cowboy Shepard and a strung-out Basinger. Ghosts from the past also visit the seedy motel on the edge of the Mojave Desert where the story takes place. Saving graces: intense, steely-eyed performance by Shepard and a sultry, Monroe-like Basinger.
Dist.: MGM/UA

FOOLIN' AROUND 1980
★ ★ ★ PG Comedy 1:40
☑ Adult situations, explicit language
Dir: Richard T. Heffron *Cast:* Gary Busey, Annette O'Toole, Eddie Albert, Tony Randall, Cloris Leachman, John Calvin
▶ Sweet Oklahoma bumpkin Busey goes to college, meets rich girl O'Toole, and falls in love. She's forced to choose between him and Calvin, the straitlaced do-gooder approved by mother Leachman. Modest mix of slapstick and romance makes for a cute and entertaining film.
Dist.: Nelson

FOOLISH WIVES 1922
☆ NR Drama 1:47 B&W
Dir: Erich von Stroheim *Cast:* Erich von Stro-

Dietrich, John Lund, Millard Mitchell, Bill Murphy
► Arthur, head of a congressional investigation into Berlin's postwar black market, locks horns with Lund, a cynical American officer. She forces Lund to offer his mistress, nightclub chanteuse Dietrich, as bait to catch a missing Nazi. Caustic, dark-toned comedy restored Dietrich's popularity after a long box-office decline. She sings "Black Market" and "Ruins of Berlin."
Dist.: MCA

FOREIGN BODY 1986 British
★ ★ PG-13 Comedy 1:51
☑ Nudity, adult situations, explicit language
Dir: Ronald Neame *Cast:* Victor Banerjee, Warren Mitchell, Geraldine McEwan, Denis Quilley, Amanda Donohoe, Trevor Howard
► Wide-eyed Banerjee borrows, bribes, and bluffs his way from Calcutta to London, where he finds romantic and financial success while posing as a doctor. Old-fashioned comedy has amiable cast and smart pacing to compensate for inconsequential plot.
Dist.: HBO

FOREIGN CORRESPONDENT 1940
★ ★ ★ ★ NR Mystery-Suspense 2:00 B&W
Dir: Alfred Hitchcock *Cast:* Joel McCrea, Laraine Day, Herbert Marshall, George Sanders, Albert Basserman, Robert Benchley
► Smashing wartime thriller, one of the best espionage films ever, drops naive reporter McCrea into a maelstrom of Nazi intrigue and double-crosses as he tracks a missing diplomat through Europe. Top-notch Hitchcock work delivers many of his famous set pieces (an assassination in the rain, a shocking plane crash, etc.) with devious, breathless pacing. Oscar nominations for Picture, Screenplay, and Cinematography.
Dist.: Warner

FOREVER, LULU 1987
★ R Comedy 1:26
☑ Nudity, explicit language, violence
Dir: Amos Kollek *Cast:* Hanna Schygulla, Deborah Harry, Alec Baldwin, Annie Golden, Paul Gleason
► Cheap imitation of *Desperately Seeking Susan* starring accomplished Polish-born actress Schygulla in her first English-language role. She plays a down-on-her-luck East Village writer/temp for a toilet seat company who encounters a series of "only in New York" events. Harry appears to mutter ten words and add some cachet. Schygulla embarrassingly muddles through this mess.
Dist.: RCA/Columbia

FOR KEEPS? 1988
★ ★ ★ ★ PG-13 Comedy 1:38
☑ Adult situations, explicit language
Dir: John G. Avildsen *Cast:* Molly Ringwald, Randall Batinkoff, Miriam Flynn, Kenneth Mars, Conchata Ferrell
► They're very young, very much in love, and

she's very pregnant. Ringwald is an adolescent forced to deal with adult problems; newcomer Batinkoff the confused but well-meaning father. Sweet, lighthearted comedy includes documentary footage of a live birth. Fine supporting cast.
Dist.: RCA/Columbia

FOR LOVE OF IVY 1968
★ ★ G Comedy 1:41
Dir: Daniel Mann *Cast:* Sidney Poitier, Abbey Lincoln, Beau Bridges, Nan Martin, Carroll O'Connor, Hugh Hurd
► Worried that maid Lincoln might quit, a white Long Island family arranges a romance with Poitier, a trucking executive and part-time gambler. Undemanding comedy based on a story by Poitier includes songs by Shirley Horn and B. B. King.
Dist.: CBS/Fox

FOR ME AND MY GAL 1942
★ ★ ★ NR Musical 1:44 B&W
Dir: Busby Berkeley *Cast:* Judy Garland, George Murphy, Gene Kelly, Marta Eggerth, Ben Blue, Keenan Wynn
► Garland quits her vaudeville team to work with Kelly (making his film debut), but rival singer Eggerth and the onslaught of World War I sabotage their chances for success. Ragged musical sparkles during the frequent numbers, especially a disarming version of the title song and "Oh You Beautiful Doll." (CC)
Dist.: MGM/UA

FORMULA, THE 1980
★ ★ ★ R Drama 1:57
☑ Adult situations, explicit language, violence
Dir: John G. Avildsen *Cast:* George C. Scott, Marlon Brando, Marthe Keller, John Gielgud, Beatrice Straight
► High quality suspense about L.A. detective Scott investigating a murder case that involves giant, powerful oil cartels and a Nazi formula for synthetic fuel. Brando is haggard but still fascinating in his small part as an oil executive. Complex, novelistic story written by best-selling author Steve Shagan.
Dist.: MGM/UA

FOR PETE'S SAKE 1974
★ ★ ★ PG Comedy 1:30
☑ Explicit language, adult humor
Dir: Peter Yates *Cast:* Barbra Streisand, Michael Sarrazin, Estelle Parsons, William Redfield, Molly Picon
► Old-time boisterous farce with Streisand as Henrietta, a Brooklyn housewife who'll do anything for her taxi-driving husband, Sarrazin. After borrowing $3,000 to pay for hubby's college education, Babs is forced by greedy loan sharks to take up prostitution, drug dealing, and cattle rustling. Action and chase scenes are aptly handled but this faux-screwball

comedy is probably best suited to Streisand aficionados.
Dist.: RCA/Columbia

FOR QUEEN AND COUNTRY 1989 British
★ **R Drama 1:48**
☐ Explicit language, violence
Dir: Martin Stellman   *Cast:* Denzel Washington, Dorian Healy, Amanda Redman, George Baker, Bruce Payne
▶ After duty in Northern Ireland, soldier Washington returns to his London neighborhood, which is dominated by criminals, drugs, and brutal police. He has interracial relationship with Redman and tries to stay straight, but frustrations with society point him toward crime. Extremely grim portrait of Thatcher-era England with complex performances.

FORT APACHE 1948
★ ★ ★ ★ **NR Western 2:08 B&W**
Dir: John Ford   *Cast:* Henry Fonda, John Wayne, Shirley Temple, Ward Bond, John Agar, Victor McLaglen
▶ Ambitious but inexperienced colonel Fonda, overriding the objections of veteran captain Wayne, endangers the soldiers at his new post by inciting nearby Apaches to war. Somber, richly detailed Western, shot in Monument Valley, has a commanding performance by Fonda in a rare villainous role. The first of director Ford's "cavalry trilogy," followed by *She Wore a Yellow Ribbon* and *Rio Grande.*
Dist.: Turner   Ⓒ

FORT APACHE, THE BRONX 1981
★ ★ ★ ★ **R Drama 2:03**
☐ Nudity, adult situations, explicit language, violence
Dir: Daniel Petrie   *Cast:* Paul Newman, Edward Asner, Ken Wahl, Rachel Ticotin, Pam Grier, Danny Aiello
▶ Tough-talking street melodrama takes disturbing look at New York's South Bronx at its down-and-dirty worst. In and around Fort Apache, the embattered precinct house, cops Newman and Wahl battle nonstop crime. After witnessing two cops commit a heinous crime, a disillusioned Newman must wrestle with his conscience. Good performances, especially from Ticotin as Newman's girlfriend, and energetically directed action add up to an exciting urban nightmare story.
Dist.: Vestron

FOR THE LOVE OF BENJI 1977
★ ★ ★ ★ **G Comedy/Family 1:24**
Dir: Joe Camp   *Cast:* Benji, Patsy Garrett, Ed Nelson, Cynthia Smith
▶ The world's most expressive, cuddly canine is back for his second comedy-adventure. Government bad-guy Nelson chases Benji, who is accidentally carrying secret information on his paw, through the crowded streets of a lovely-to-look-at Athens. Cleverly shot through Benji's point of view. Lovable, suspenseful story for all ages.
Dist.: Vestron

FORTRESS 1985 Australian
★ ★ ★ **NR Drama/MFTV 1:28**
☐ Brief nudity, adult situations, explicit language, violence
Dir: Arch Nicholson   *Cast:* Rachel Ward, Sean Garlick, Marc Gray, Rebecca Rigg, Bradley Meehan
▶ Australian schoolteacher Ward and her young students are kidnapped by two mask-wearing thugs and carted off at gunpoint to an underground cavern. Hair-raising fight-for-survival story with a thrill-packed finish. Adapted from the novel by Gabrielle Lord.
Dist.: HBO

FORTUNE COOKIE, THE 1966
★ ★ ★ **NR Comedy 2:05 B&W**
Dir: Billy Wilder   *Cast:* Jack Lemmon, Walter Matthau, Ron Rich, Cliff Osmond, Judi West
▶ Sports cameraman Lemmon is accidentally injured by football player Rich while filming a game. Lemmon's shyster lawyer cousin, the aptly named Whiplash Willie (Matthau, in a wonderful Oscar-winning performance), tries to exploit the situation for all it's worth but Lemmon suffers pangs of guilt. Sharp demonstration of Wilder's wit and Lemmon/Matthau's comic chemistry.
Dist.: Magnetic

FORTY CARATS 1973
★ ★ **PG Romance/Comedy 1:50**
☐ Adult situations
Dir: Milton Katselas   *Cast:* Liv Ullmann, Edward Albert, Gene Kelly, Binnie Barnes, Deborah Raffin, Nancy Walker
▶ New York realtor Ullmann falls in love with Albert, a great guy half her age, but is afraid of what her friends will think. Ullmann's good-natured ex-husband Kelly urges her to follow her heart. Sweet love story with Liv learning life begins at forty.
Dist.: RCA/Columbia

48 HRS. 1982
★ ★ ★ ★ **R Action-Adventure 1:36**
☐ Nudity, adult situations, explicit language, violence
Dir: Walter Hill   *Cast:* Nick Nolte, Eddie Murphy, Annette O'Toole, Frank McRae, James Remar, David Patrick Kelly
▶ Boozy but tough police detective Nolte springs glib con man Murphy (in a smashing film debut) from jail to track down two psychopath cop killers. Cunning blend of rugged action and gritty comedy was a huge hit, inspiring a rash of "buddy-cop" films. This is one of the few that delivers the goods. Murphy's bit in a redneck bar has become a classic.
Dist.: Paramount

FORTY-NINTH PARALLEL, THE 1941 British
★ ★ ★ **NR War 1:47 B&W**
Dir: Michael Powell   *Cast:* Anton Walbrook, Eric Portman, Leslie Howard, Laurence Olivier, Glynis Johns, Niall MacGinnis
▶ Early in World War II, six Nazis led by Portman are stranded in Canada after their submarine

sinks. They trek across Canada in an effort to reach then-neutral U.S., have violent encounters with writer Howard and radio operator Olivier, and come to reside in a nonviolent religious community. One of the best films to come out of the war won Oscar for Best Story. Also known as *The Invaders*.
Dist.: VidAmerica

FORTY-SECOND STREET 1933
★★★ NR Musical 1:38 B&W
Dir: Lloyd Bacon ***Cast:*** Warner Baxter, Bebe Daniels, George Brent, Una Merkel, Ruby Keeler, Dick Powell, Guy Kibbee, Ginger Rogers
► Desperate director Baxter banks everything on temperamental leading lady Daniels, but turns to newcomer Keeler when Daniels breaks her ankle. Seminal musical is filled with classic lines ("You're going out a youngster, but you've *got* to come back a star!") and extravagant Busby Berkeley routines. Songs include "You're Getting to Be a Habit With Me," "Forty-Second Street," and "Shuffle off to Buffalo."
Dist.: MGM/UA

FOR YOUR EYES ONLY 1981 British
★★★★ PG Espionage/Action-Adventure 2:08
☑ Brief nudity, adult situations, explicit language, violence
Dir: John Glen ***Cast:*** Roger Moore, Carole Bouquet, Chaim Topol, Lynn-Holly Johnson, Julian Glover
► In his fifth Bond film, Moore is trapped in a runaway helicopter, stalked in the snow, flung to the sharks, hurled off a cliff—all in the name of national security. Bouquet joins him as a Greek beauty out to avenge her father's death and help save the world. Has more substance than the traditional Bond fare.
Dist.: MGM/UA

FOUL PLAY 1978
★★★★ PG Comedy 1:51
☑ Explicit language, mild violence
Dir: Colin Higgins ***Cast:*** Goldie Hawn, Chevy Chase, Burgess Meredith, Rachel Roberts, Dudley Moore, Billy Barty
► Slick, amusing murder/mystery finds Hawn accidentally involved in a plot to murder the Pope. Chase, as a nutty police detective, stumbles his way into her heart. Fine supporting cast features Barty as a Bible salesman and Moore in his first big American role, which launched his movie career here. Charming, endearing, and very funny.
Dist.: Paramount

FOUNTAINHEAD, THE 1949
★★★ NR Drama 1:54 B&W
Dir: King Vidor ***Cast:*** Gary Cooper, Patricia Neal, Raymond Massey, Kent Smith, Robert Douglas
► Architect Cooper asserts his right to artistic integrity by blowing up an apartment house when the builders distort his original designs. You don't have to agree with author Ayn Rand's philosophy to enjoy this compelling adaptation of her best-seller. Blistering sexual chemistry between Cooper and Neal and dynamic visuals from director Vidor.
Dist.: Key

FOUR ADVENTURES OF REINETTE AND MIRABELLE 1989 French
☆ NR Comedy 1:35
☑ Adult situations
Dir: Eric Rohmer ***Cast:*** Joëlle Miquel, Jessica Forde, Phillipe Laudenbach, Yasmine Haury, Marie Rivière, Béatrice Romand
► Parisian Forde and ruralist Miquel become friends during summer vacation. In the country, they attempt to discover mystical morning light known as the "blue hour." In Paris, they learn lessons in morality, including encounters with a shoplifter and a surly waiter plus bet between the women that gabby Miquel can't keep silent for a day. Deliberately episodic and slight with some enchanting moments. [S]
Dist.: New Yorker

4D MAN 1959
★ NR Sci-Fi 1:25
Dir: Irwin S. Yeaworth, Jr. ***Cast:*** Robert Lansing, Lee Meriwether, James Congdon, Guy Raymond, Robert Strauss, Patty Duke
► Scientist Lansing discovers method of altering his molecular structure so he can travel through solid objects. Unfortunately, his new talent leads to a life of crime. Girlfriend Meriwether is concerned about her beau's transformation in this nifty little genre gem. Also known as *Master of Terror*.
Dist.: New World

FOUR FACES WEST 1948
★ NR Western 1:29 B&W
Dir: Alfred E. Green ***Cast:*** Joel McCrea, Frances Dee, Charles Bickford, William Conrad, Joseph Calleia
► McCrea robs a bank to save his family ranch but fully intends to pay the money back when he can. Bickford plays lawman Pat Garrett, who tracks McCrea down, only to discover the fugitive's basic integrity and honesty. Western emphasizes honest emotion, first-rate performances.
Dist.: Republic

FOUR FEATHERS, THE 1939 British
★★★★ NR Action-Adventure 1:55
Dir: Zoltan Korda ***Cast:*** Ralph Richardson, John Clements, June Duprez, C. Aubrey Smith, Jack Allen
► In 1898, young officer Clements resigns commission and is given feathers as a symbol of cowardice by his disapproving comrades and fiancée. When his regiment fights in the Sudan, Clements disguises himself as a native and proves his bravery, returning the feathers to their sources one by one. Riproaring, rousing adventure with fine cast and beautiful

color photography. Genuine classic is by far the best of four versions of the story.
Dist.: Embassy

FOUR FRIENDS 1981
★ ★ R Drama 1:54
☑ Nudity, adult situations, explicit language, violence
Dir: Arthur Penn   *Cast:* Craig Wasson, Jodi Thelen, Jim Metzler, Michael Huddleston, Reed Birney, James Leo Herlihy
▶ Collaboration of Penn and screenwriter Steve Tesich traces young immigrant Wasson, his pals, and Thelen, the free-spirited girl they all love in the 1960s. Uneven but heartfelt film conveys sense of turbulent lives in a turbulent decade. Some terrific moments but also loses some of its tension after a shocking plot twist at the hero's wedding.
Dist.: Warner

FOUR HORSEMEN OF THE APOCALYPSE, THE 1962
★ ★ ★ NR Drama 2:31
Dir: Vincente Minnelli   *Cast:* Glenn Ford, Ingrid Thulin, Lee J. Cobb, Charles Boyer, Paul Henreid, Paul Lukas, Yvette Mimieux
▶ Large-scale but unrealistic remake of the 1921 Valentino silent film about a family fighting on opposing sides in war (updated to World War II). The Four Horsemen are Conquest, War, Pestilence and Death—a biblical allusion to the end of the earth. Entertaining, old-fashioned melodrama.
Dist.: MGM/UA

400 BLOWS, THE 1959 French
★ ★ ★ NR Drama 1:44 B&W
Dir: François Truffaut   *Cast:* Jean-Pierre Leaud, Albert Remy, Patrick Auffray, Claire Maurier
▶ Troubled teenager Antoine Doinel (Leaud) turns to petty crime as parents and social institutions fail him. Technically adventurous and insightful, Truffaut's autobiographical directoral debut is one of the most memorable films of the French New Wave. Adventures of Doinel continued in four subsequent movies. Ⓢ
Dist.: CBS/Fox

FOUR IN A JEEP 1951 Swiss
★ NR Drama 1:23 B&W
Dir: Leopold Lindtberg   *Cast:* Viveca Lindfors, Ralph Meeker, Joseph Yadin, Michael Medwin, Dinan, Paulette Dubost
▶ American Meeker, Englishman Medwin, Russian Yadin, and Frenchman Dinan are military policemen whose beat is post–World War II Vienna. Lindfors, the wife of a mutual friend who may be a spy, becomes the focus for conflict among the foursome. Ambitious but turgid drama.
Dist.: SVS

FOUR JACKS AND A JILL 1942
★ NR Musical 1:08 B&W
Dir: Jack Hively   *Cast:* Ray Bolger, Desi Arnaz, Anne Shirley, June Havoc, Eddie Foy, Jr., Jack Briggs
▶ Singer Havoc's gangster boyfriend makes her quit the business, leaving band members Briggs, Bolger, and Foy in a jam. To keep their nightclub job, they hire down-and-out Shirley, pretending she's a foreign vocal star. Remake of 1929's *Street Girl* and 1937's *That Girl From Paris* has energy, but not much else. Songs include "I'm in Good Shape for the Shape I'm In" and "You Go Your Way and I'll Go Crazy."
Dist.: Turner

FOUR MUSKETEERS, THE 1975
★ ★ ★ ★ PG Action-Adventure 1:48
☑ Adult situations, violence
Dir: Richard Lester   *Cast:* Michael York, Raquel Welch, Oliver Reed, Richard Chamberlain, Faye Dunaway, Frank Finlay, Christopher Lee, Charlton Heston
▶ York, Reed, Chamberlain, and Finlay battle the evil Milady (Dunaway) in this sequel to Richard Lester's *The Three Musketeers.* Begins with the same high spirits, comedy, and adventure of its predecessor but darkens as it goes on. Larger-than-life tale is engrossing and surprisingly emotion-packed, especially if you've already seen the first film (shot simultaneously, the two were released as separate movies).
Dist.: USA

FOUR SEASONS, THE 1981
★ ★ ★ ★ PG Comedy/Drama 1:47
☑ Brief nudity, adult situations, explicit language
Dir: Alan Alda   *Cast:* Alan Alda, Carol Burnett, Sandy Dennis, Len Cariou, Rita Moreno, Jack Weston
▶ Conversational comedy/drama written, directed, and starring the affable Alda concerns three middle-class, middle-aged couples who vacation together four times over the course of a year. They cook, crack jokes, quip, and engage in heart-to-heart talks. Then Dennis and Cariou divorce, causing midlife crises all around. Harmless and endearing with a few amusing moments. Lovely locations in New England and the Virgin Islands; poignant Vivaldi score. Alda was Oscar-nominated for both directing and acting.
Dist.: MCA

4TH MAN, THE 1979 Dutch
☆ NR Drama 1:44
☑ Nudity, adult situations, explicit language
Dir: Paul Verhoeven   *Cast:* Jeroen Krabbe, Renee Soutendijk, Thom Hoffman, Dolf de Vries, Geert De Jong, Hans Veerman
▶ Bisexual writer Krabbe seduces bewitching beautician Soutendijk because he's interested in her fiancé, then learns that her three previous husbands died in "accidents." Will he be the fourth? An art house favorite for its strong eroticism and alluring production de-

sign, but frequent symbolic interludes are heavy going. $\boxed{S}$
Dist.: Cinematheque

FOURTH PROTOCOL, THE 1987 British
★ ★ ★ ★ R Drama 1:59
☑ Nudity, adult situations, explicit language, violence
Dir: John Mackenzie *Cast:* Michael Caine, Pierce Brosnan, Joanna Cassidy, Ned Beatty, Julian Glover, Michael Gough
► Unorthodox British agent Caine uncovers a KGB plot to discredit NATO by destroying a strategic airbase with a miniature nuclear bomb. Racing against time, he tracks down Brosnan, the Russian spy assembling the bomb. Efficient version of Frederick Forsyth's best-seller sacrifices characterizations for non-stop plotting.
Dist.: Warner

FOURTH WAR, THE 1990
★ ★ ★ R Action-Adventure 1:49
☑ Explicit language, violence
Dir: John Frankenheimer *Cast:* Roy Scheider, Jurgen Prochnow, Tim Reid, Lara Harris, Harry Dean Stanton
► American colonel Scheider, an unconverted cold warrior in the age of detente, is assigned to a base on the German/Czech border across from similarly belligerent Russian Prochnow. When the Soviet guns down a defector, Scheider seizes the opportunity to start his own private war. Engrossing thriller. Frankenheimer's direction puts a worthwhile spin on a shallow screenplay. **(CC)**
Dist.: HBO

FOX AND HIS FRIENDS 1975 German
☆ NR Drama 2:03
☑ Adult situations
Dir: Rainer Werner Fassbinder *Cast:* Rainer Werner Fassbinder, Peter Chatel, Karlheinz Bohm, Adrian Hoven, Ulla Jacobsson, Christiane Maybach
► Homosexual carnival barker Fassbinder wins the lottery and enters a higher social set through new lover Chatel. But Chatel and his family cynically exploit the low-class lug, with unhappy results. Insightful dissection of class attitudes, but some may find it pretentious. $\boxed{S}$
Dist.: Corinth

FOXES 1980
★ ★ R Drama 1:46
☑ Adult situations, explicit language, violence
Dir: Adrian Lyne *Cast:* Jodie Foster, Scott Baio, Sally Kellerman, Randy Quaid, Lois Smith, Cherie Currie, Marilyn Kagan, Kandice Stroh
► Earthy coming-of-age melodrama follows troubled Los Angeles teenagers Foster, Currie, Kagan, and Stroh as they cope with broken homes, drugs, and sex. Foster is outstanding in this realistic approach to modern problems,

and Quaid contributes a strong bit as Kagan's boyfriend. **(CC)**
Dist.: CBS/Fox

FOXTRAP 1986 U.S./Italian
★ ★ R Action-Adventure 1:28
☑ Nudity, adult situations, explicit language, violence
Dir: Fred Williamson *Cast:* Fred Williamson, Chris Connelly, Arlene Golonka, Donna Owen, Beatrice Palme, Cleo Sebastian
► Los Angeles bodyguard Williamson is hired by millionaire Connelly to find his missing niece Owen. The often violent trail takes Williamson to France and Rome before he finds her, and then it's back to California for more plot twists and shoot-outs. Scenic if sloppily plotted vehicle for supercool Fred.
Dist.: Vestron

FOXTROT 1976 Mexican/Swiss
★ ★ R Drama 1:30
☑ Adult situations, explicit language
Dir: Arturo Ripstein *Cast:* Peter O'Toole, Charlotte Rampling, Max Von Sydow, Jorge Luke, Helen Rojo, Claudio Brook
► Wealthy O'Toole and Rampling go to an island to escape World War II. As their supplies run out, the balance of power changes between them and their servants Von Sydow and Luke. Glamorous production with a ravishing Rampling, but funereal pace and bleak climax prove alienating. Also known as *The Other Side of Paradise.*
Dist.: Nelson

FOXY BROWN 1974
☆ R Action-Adventure 1:34
☑ Rape, nudity, adult situations, explicit language, graphic violence
Dir: Jack Hill *Cast:* Pam Grier, Antonio Fargas, Peter Brown, Terry Carty, Kathryn Loder, Harry Holcombe
► Tough nurse Grier takes revenge on the drug dealers responsible for the murder of her cop boyfriend. First target is her junkie brother Fargas. Extremely violent exploitation features particularly repulsive punishments for druglords Brown and Loder.
Dist.: Orion

FRAMED 1975
★ ★ R Action-Adventure 1:46
☑ Nudity, adult situations, explicit language, violence
Dir: Phil Karlson *Cast:* Joe Don Baker, Conny Van Dyke, Gabriel Dell, John Marley, Brock Peters
► Professional gambler Baker, framed for murder by corrupt cops, spends four years in jail plotting his revenge. Predictable story competently handled. From the makers of *Walking Tall.*
Dist.: Paramount

FRANCES 1982
★ ★ ★ ★ R Biography 2:20

☑ Rape, nudity, adult situations, explicit language, violence
Dir: Graeme Clifford *Cast:* Jessica Lange, Kim Stanley, Sam Shepard, Bart Burns, Jeffrey DeMunn, Jordan Charney
▶ Disturbing biography of volatile beauty Frances Farmer (Lange), tracing her tragic decline from promising 1930s movie career to incarceration in mental institutions. Relentlessly downbeat story despite impressive performances from Lange, Shepard (playing a steady friend), and Stanley (returning to the screen after a lengthly absence as Farmer's domineering mother). Lange and Stanley won Oscar nominations.
Dist.: HBO

FRANKENHOOKER 1990
★ R Horror 1:30
☑ Nudity, explicit language, graphic violence
Dir: Frank Henenlotter *Cast:* James Lorinz, Patty Mullen, Charlotte Helmkamp, Shirley Stoler, Louise Lasser, Joseph Gonzalez
▶ Utility worker Lorinz keeps girlfriend Mullen's head alive in his garage after her body is chewed up by a runaway lawnmower. Hoping to reconstruct her, he acquires body parts from hapless hookers whom he feeds a special kind of crack that makes them explode. Gruesome and twisted scenes of horror and dismemberment multiply to blackly humorous excess in this stomach-turning offering from the director of *Basket Case.*
Dist.: SGE

FRANKENSTEIN 1931
★★★ NR Horror 1:11 B&W
Dir: James Whale *Cast:* Boris Karloff, Colin Clive, Mae Clarke, John Boles, Edward Van Sloan, Dwight Frye
▶ Mad Dr. Frankenstein (Clive) creates monster Karloff out of parts of corpses but finds he cannot control his creation. Frightened townspeople storm Karloff with torches but the indestructible creature lives on in countless sequels. Adaptation of Mary Shelley's novel is a screen classic, thanks to Karloff's tremendously sympathetic monster, Clive's intensity, and Whale's shadowy, atmospheric direction.
Dist.: MCA

FRANKENSTEIN MEETS THE WOLF MAN 1943
★★★ NR Horror 1:13 B&W
Dir: Roy William Neill *Cast:* Lon Chaney, Jr., Ilona Massey, Bela Lugosi, Patric Knowles, Maria Ouspenskaya, Lionel Atwill
▶ Team-up of two favorite monsters: the Wolfman (Chaney) and Frankenstein (Lugosi). Plot involves the Wolfman looking for Dr. Frankenstein to cure his condition. Alas, all he finds is the monster, who prefers fighting to problemsolving.
Dist.: MCA

FRANKENSTEIN'S DAUGHTER 1959
☆ NR Horror 1:25 B&W

Dir: Richard Cunha *Cast:* John Ashley, Sandra Knight, Donald Murphy, Sally Todd, Harold Lloyd, Jr.
▶ Suburban neighbors never suspect that the real name of Dr. Frank (Murphy) is actually Frankenstein, and that he's created a crude, bandaged monster in his basement. With a special potion he goes on to revive a dead teenage girl, and she's not pretty. Unimaginative makeup and plot.
Dist.: Media

FRANKIE AND JOHNNY 1966
★★ NR Musical 1:27
Dir: Frederick De Cordova *Cast:* Elvis Presley, Donna Douglas, Harry Morgan, Sue Ane Langdon, Nancy Kovack
▶ Mildly entertaining musical based on the famous title song. Presley is Johnny, a riverboat gambler down on his luck; Douglas plays Frankie, his jealous lover. Shapely Kovack provides the spark that sets the song's plot into motion. Other numbers include "When the Saints Go Marching In," "Petunia," and "What Every Woman Lives For."
Dist.: MGM/UA

FRANTIC 1958 French
★ NR Mystery-Suspense 1:31 B&W
Dir: Louis Malle *Cast:* Jeanne Moreau, Maurice Ronet, Georges Poujouly, Yori Bertin, Jean Wall
▶ Lovers Moreau and Ronet plot the murder of Wall—her husband and his boss—but are tripped up by a few unanticipated twists in this generally absorbing thriller. Feature debut for director Malle. Based on the novel *Elevator to the Gallows* by Noel Calef. Ⓢ
Dist.: Video Yesteryear

FRANTIC 1988
★★★★ R Mystery-Suspense 2:00
☑ Brief nudity, adult situations, explicit language, violence
Dir: Roman Polanski *Cast:* Harrison Ford, Betty Buckley, Emmanuelle Seigner, John Mahoney, Jimmie Ray Weeks, Gerard Klein
▶ Ford, an American doctor, searches the streets of Paris for missing wife Buckley despite the indifference of the police and embassy officials. Sexy young Seigner holds the key to the kidnapping. Polished execution from Polanski, chic French locations, and Ford's refreshingly human heroism (he even gets jet lag) overcome mechanical plotting. (CC)
Dist.: Warner

FRATERNITY VACATION 1985
★★ R Comedy 1:34
☑ Nudity, adult situations, explicit language, violence
Dir: James Frawley *Cast:* Stephen Geoffreys, Sheree J. Wilson, Cameron Dye, Leigh McCloskey, Tim Robbins
▶ Amiable sex farce about spring break in Palm Springs. Two rival fraternities bet on who can win beautiful but aloof Wilson. Geoffreys is

especially adept as a perpetually amorous nerd. Bouncy tunes by Bananarama. (CC)
Dist.: New World

FREAKS 1932
☆ **NR Horror 1:05 B&W**
Dir: Tod Browning ***Cast:*** Wallace Ford, Olga Baclanova, Leila Hyams, Roscoe Ates, Harry Earles
► A community of circus freaks takes terrible revenge upon a beautiful trapeze performer who marries one of their troupe and then tries to poison him for his money. Strangely disturbing horror flick with a cast of physically deformed people alienated audiences of its day but retains its bizarre power.
Dist.: MGM/UA

FREAKY FRIDAY 1976
★★★★ **G Comedy 1:35**
Dir: Gary Nelson ***Cast:*** Barbara Harris, Jodie Foster, John Astin, Patsy Kelly, Dick Van Patten, Ruth Buzzi
► Suburban teen Foster magically gets her wish to switch places with her mom Harris. Spending time in new incarnations proves neither kids nor adults have it easy. Breezy and lightweight in the Disney way. Insightful adaptation of her own book by Mary Rodgers; ingratiating performances by Foster and Harris.
Dist.: Buena Vista

FREEBIE AND THE BEAN 1974
★★★★ **R Action-Adventure/Comedy 1:53**
☑ Explicit language, violence
Dir: Richard Rush ***Cast:*** Alan Arkin, James Caan, Loretta Swit, Valerie Harper, Jack Kruschen, Alex Rocco
► Cops Arkin and Caan battle gangsters by chasing, shooting, and slugging their way through the streets of San Francisco. Rambunctious and energetic; Caan and Arkin make an engaging pair. Funniest scene: the cops drive through a bedroom window.
Dist.: Warner

FREEWAY 1988
★★ **R Drama 1:31**
☑ Nudity, adult situations, explicit language, violence
Dir: Francis Della ***Cast:*** Darlanne Fluegel, James Russo, Billy Drago, Richard Belzer, Michael Callan, Joey Palese
► Sniper loose on Los Angeles freeways kills Fluegel's husband. Policeman Callan has no leads, although the killer strikes up relationship with radio psychologist Belzer. Russo, a neurotic ex-cop, convinces revenge-obsessed Fluegel to offer herself as decoy to the sniper. Wooden acting is a major drawback to this lurid treatment of a provocative subject.
Dist.: New World

FRENCH CONNECTION, THE 1971
★★★★★ **R Crime 1:44**
☑ Adult situations, explicit language, violence
Dir: William Friedkin ***Cast:*** Gene Hackman, Fernando Rey, Roy Scheider, Tony Lo Bianco
► New York City cop Popeye Doyle (Hackman) obsessively tries to bust international drug ring. Cat and mouse chase follows between Hackman and the elusive French mastermind Rey. A stunning thriller, unsurpassed for sheer visceral excitement. Director Friedkin combines street-smart grit with gut-wrenching suspense, especially in the incredible chase where Hackman pursues a runaway subway train. Oscars for Best Picture, Director, Screenplay, Editing, and Actor (Hackman, who is brilliant).
Dist.: CBS/Fox

FRENCH CONNECTION II, THE 1975
★★★ **R Crime 1:59**
☑ Adult situations, explicit language, violence
Dir: John Frankenheimer ***Cast:*** Gene Hackman, Fernando Rey, Bernard Fresson, Jean-Pierre Castaldi, Charles Milot
► Tough New York cop Popeye Doyle (Hackman) trails slippery drug king Rey to Marseilles. Doyle, a fish out of water, grates on nerves of French cop Fresson, but finally nabs his man. Pretty good sequel. Not as exciting as the original but outstanding work from Hackman (especially in a harrowing sequence where he goes cold turkey after bad guys inject him with drugs), effective locations and chases. (CC)
Dist.: CBS/Fox

FRENCH DETECTIVE, THE 1979 French
★ **NR Mystery-Suspense 1:30**
☑ Explicit language
Dir: Pierre Granier-Deferre ***Cast:*** Lino Ventura, Patrick Dewaere, Victor Lanoux
► When a policeman is killed by thugs working for politician Lanoux, cop Ventura finds himself suddenly taken off the investigation. Despite these machinations, Ventura and partner Dewaere track the killers anyway. First-rate performances and confident direction, although ambiguous finale leaves too many questions unanswered. [S]
Dist.: RCA/Columbia

FRENCH LESSON 1986 British
☆ **PG Romance 1:30**
☑ Adult situations, explicit language
Dir: Brian Gilbert ***Cast:*** Jane Snowden, Alexandre Sterling, Diana Blackburn, Oystein Wilk, Jacqueline Doyen, Raoul Delfosse
► British student Snowden goes to France in 1961. After passing up opportunities with Norwegian student Wilk and an engaged man, she falls for Frenchman Sterling. Scenic but slow-paced Harlequin-style romance in English and subtitled French. Produced by David Puttnam. (CC) [S]
Dist.: Warner

FRENCH LIEUTENANT'S WOMAN, THE 1981
★★ **R Drama 1:59**

☑ Brief nudity, adult situations, explicit language
Dir: Karel Reisz *Cast:* Meryl Streep, Jeremy Irons, Leo McKern, Hilton McRae, Emily Morgan
▶ Dark-hued romance featuring a fine performance by Streep as a jilted 1860s Victorian governess who draws the attention of officer Irons. Screenwriter Harold Pinter reworks the John Fowles novel by creating a movie-within-a-movie; the leads are also twentieth-century actors falling in love while shooting the film. Well-crafted and sumptuously photographed. Garnered five Oscar nominations, including Best Actress and Screenplay.
Dist.: MGM/UA

FRENCH LINE, THE 1954
★ NR Musical 1:42
Dir: Lloyd Bacon *Cast:* Jane Russell, Gilbert Roland, Arthur Hunnicut, Mary McCarty, Paula Corday, Craig Stevens
▶ Wealthy Texan Russell, tired of being wooed for her money, hires a woman to impersonate her while she takes an ocean voyage. The ruse leads to misunderstandings in shipboard romance with Frenchman Roland. Howard Hughes produced this showcase for Russell's physical attributes. Songs include "With a Kiss" and "Wait Till You See Paris." Originally filmed in 3-D.
Dist.: Turner

FRENCH POSTCARDS 1979
★ PG Comedy 1:31
☑ Brief nudity, adult situations, explicit language
Dir: Willard Huyck *Cast:* Miles Chapin, Blanche Baker, David Marshall Grant, Debra Winger, Marie-France Pisier, Valerie Quennessen
▶ American college students Chapin, Grant, and Baker arrive in Paris for a year's study and find romance and adventure. Lightweight fluff with a minimal story, given charm and atmosphere by the Paris locations and the attractive young cast. Mandy Patinkin has a brief but funny bit as an overzealous Iranian lover.
Dist.: Paramount

FRENCH QUARTER 1977
★ R Fantasy 1:41
☑ Nudity, adult situations, explicit language
Dir: Dennis Kane *Cast:* Bruce Davison, Virginia Mayo, Lindsay Bloom, Alisha Fontaine, Lance LeGault, Vernel Bagneris
▶ Bayou blond Fontaine becomes a topless dancer in the French Quarter of New Orleans. She passes out at a voodoo practitioner's place and awakes as a nineteenth-century prostitute. The two time periods and story lines are intercut in this weird item that veers uneasily between ambitious artiness and softcore sexiness.
Dist.: Monarch

FRENCH WAY, THE 1940 French
☆ NR Musical 1:13 B&W

Dir: Jacques De Baroncelli *Cast:* Josephine Baker, Micheline Presle, Georges Marchal, Almos, Jean Tissier, Lucien Baroux
▶ Nightclub entertainer Baker takes charge when her landlord's son cannot get together with the girl of his choice thanks to a *Romeo and Juliet*-style family feud. Fans of Baker will not want to miss their heroine as she does her trademark shimmy and warbles "No Nina" and "To Live Together Under One Roof."
☒
Dist.: Video Dimensions

FRENCH WOMAN, THE 1978 French
★★ R Romance 1:50
☑ Nudity, strong sexual content, adult situations, explicit language
Dir: Just Jaeckin *Cast:* Françoise Fabian, Dayle Haddon, Murray Head, Maurice Ronet, Klaus Kinski, Robert Webber
▶ Heads of state and government officials are among the clients of high-class madam Fabian. When a photographer uses his relationship with the prostitutes to take compromising photos of powerful customers, the CIA suspects that Fabian is involved. Steamy but shallow; beautiful bodies, dull story. Dubbed. Also known as *Madame Claude*.
Dist.: Vestron

FRENZY 1972 British
★★ R Mystery-Suspense 1:56
☑ Rape, nudity, adult situations, violence
Dir: Alfred Hitchcock *Cast:* Jon Finch, Barry Foster, Barbara Leigh-Hunt, Anna Massey, Alec McCowen, Vivien Merchant
▶ The "necktie murderer" is raping and killing women in London. The cops suspect sullen Finch but they may have the wrong man. Hitchcock's second-to-last movie is one of his best later efforts. Favorite moments: the body hidden in the lorry, the camera pulling back from a murder scene, and the dryly humorous dinnertime discussions between cop McCowen and wife Merchant.
Dist.: MCA

FRESH HORSES 1988
★★ PG-13 Drama 1:45
☑ Adult situations, explicit language
Dir: David Anspaugh *Cast:* Molly Ringwald, Andrew McCarthy, Patti D'Arbanville, Ben Stiller, Leon Russom, Molly Hagan
▶ McCarthy, an industrious college student engaged to a wealthy Cincinnati girl, becomes obsessed with Ringwald, a teenage dropout from a mysterious Kentucky farm. McCarthy falls in love despite evidence that Ringwald is a pathological liar and married prostitute. Somber, ambitious romance based on Larry Ketron's play suffers from slow pacing.
Dist.: RCA/Columbia

FRIDAY FOSTER 1975
☆ R Action-Adventure 1:30
☑ Nudity, explicit language, violence
Dir: Arthur Marks *Cast:* Pam Grier, Yaphet

Kotto, Godfrey Cambridge, Thalmus Rasulala, Eartha Kitt, Jim Backus
► Photographer Grier investigates the assassinations of black politicians, and discovers that gangster Backus could be behind scheme. Based on the comic strip of the same name, this otherwise mediocre black exploitation does have Grier bringing her usual style and grace to a much-maligned genre.
Dist.: Orion

FRIDAY THE 13TH 1980
★ ★ R Horror 1:35
☑ Nudity, adult situations, explicit language, graphic violence
Dir: Sean S. Cunningham *Cast:* Harry Crosby, Betsy Palmer, Adrienne King, Laurie Bartram, Mark Nelson
► Psychotic Mommy (Palmer) hacks up young counselors at Camp Crystal Lake to avenge the death of her son, who drowned twenty years ago while his counselors were making love. Box office surprise smash spawned innumerable sequels and a TV series.
Dist.: Paramount

FRIDAY THE 13TH, PART 2 1981
★ ★ R Horror 1:27
☑ Nudity, explicit language, graphic violence
Dir: Steve Miner *Cast:* Adrienne King, Amy Steel, John Furey, Betsy Palmer, Kirsten Baker
► Steel, the only survivor of the first *Friday the 13th*, tries to pull her life together but mysteriously disappears. Camp Crystal Lake is rejuvenated after five years and stories of the drowned child Jason are told around the campfires. And someone is still stalking the nubile teens.
Dist.: Paramount

FRIDAY THE 13TH, PART 3 1982
★ ★ R Horror 1:35
☑ Brief nudity, adult situations, explicit language, graphic violence
Dir: Steve Miner *Cast:* Dana Kimmell, Richard Brooker, Paul Kratka, Tracy Savage, Jeffrey Rogers
► Shot in 3-D, this third in the popular brand-name series is strictly formula: vanload of brainless teens + Camp Crystal Lake = bloody massacre. Relentless slashing and gashing grow wearisome.
Dist.: Paramount

FRIDAY THE 13TH—THE FINAL CHAPTER 1984
★ ★ R Horror 1:30
☑ Nudity, adult situations, explicit language, graphic violence
Dir: Joseph Zito *Cast:* Crispin Glover, Kimberly Beck, Barbara Howard, Erich Anderson, Corey Feldman, Alan Hayes
► Is Jason dead? The folks at the morgue think so until the killer's corpse rises up to kill the coroner. Maniac then goes to Crystal Lake to prey on new teens in town. Artful Harry Man-

fredini score, effective sound effects, and inventive killing methods will make you scream; ludicrous ending will not. **(CC)**
Dist.: Paramount

FRIDAY THE 13TH PART V: A NEW BEGINNING 1985
★ ★ R Horror 1:32
☑ Nudity, adult situations, explicit language, graphic violence
Dir: Danny Steinmann *Cast:* John Shepherd, Melanie Kinnaman, Shavar Ross, Richard Young, Marco St. John
► Shepherd, after disposing of goalie-masked killer Jason in previous sequel, checks into camp for disturbed youngsters. History repeats itself in bloody fashion as machete murders maul staff and guests. Fifth installment hits familiar menacing notes: high corpse count, scary background music, and convincingly distressed cast. **(CC)**
Dist.: Paramount

FRIDAY THE 13TH PART 6: JASON LIVES 1986
★ ★ R Horror 1:27
☑ Adult situations, explicit language, graphic violence
Dir: Tom McLoughlin *Cast:* Thom Mathews, Jennifer Cooke, David Kagen, Kerry Noonan, Renee Jones
► Jason's grave is dug up and a metal fence post is driven through his heart. Lightning strikes—and the wearer of the hockey mask is resurrected to slaughter with reckless abandon. Noninventive and routine; only so many ways to slice and dice.
Dist.: Paramount

FRIDAY THE 13TH PART VII—THE NEW BLOOD 1988
★ ★ R Horror 1:30
☑ Nudity, adult situations, explicit language, graphic violence
Dir: John Buechler *Cast:* Lar Park Lincoln, Kevin Blair, Susan Blu, Terry Kiser, Kane Hodder, Heidi Kozak
► Telekinetic teen Lincoln, attempting to psychically revive her late father, instead accidentally resurrects goalie-masked killer Jason. It's bloody business as usual as Jason uses spikes, chain-saws, and his own brute strength to slay promiscuous teenagers. Up to the series's gory standard. **(CC)**
Dist.: Paramount

FRIDAY THE 13TH PART VIII: JASON TAKES MANHATTAN 1989
★ ★ R Horror 1:40
☑ Nudity, adult situations, explicit language, graphic violence
Dir: Rob Hedden *Cast:* Jensen Daggett, Scott Reeves, Peter Mark Richman, Barbara Bingham, Kane Hodder, V. C. Dupree
► Goalie-masked killer Jason (Hodder) attacks high schoolers aboard New York-bound cruise ship. Daggett, who had a childhood encounter with Jason, escapes to Manhattan

with her boyfriend Reeves and uncle Richman. Guess who follows? Hedden's energetic direction pumps new blood into old formula although title is somewhat misleading (they don't reach NYC until near the end).
Dist.: Paramount

FRIEDA 1947 British
★ NR Drama 1:38 B&W
Dir: Basil Dearden *Cast:* David Farrar, Glynis Johns, Mai Zetterling, Flora Robson, Albert Lieven, Barbara Everest
► After World War II, English pilot Farrar marries German Zetterling, who aided his escape from the Nazis. But when he brings her home, his family (save for sympathetic sister-in-law Johns) and local townspeople refuse to accept his bride. Landmark study of prejudice is still fresh and timely today, thanks to excellent cast and direction.
Dist.: Video Yesteryear

FRIENDLY FIRE 1979
★ ★ ★ ★ NR Drama/MFTV 2:25
Dir: David Greene *Cast:* Carol Burnett, Ned Beatty, Sam Waterston, Dennis Erdman, Timothy Hutton
► Typical suburban mom Burnette defies officialdom to learn the truth behind the military blunder that led to the death of her son by American ordnance in Vietnam. Beatty is excellent as her husband in this somewhat extended, but sincere, drama of home front agony. **(CC)**
Dist.: CBS/Fox

FRIENDLY PERSUASION 1956
★ ★ ★ ★ NR Drama 2:18
Dir: William Wyler *Cast:* Gary Cooper, Dorothy McGuire, Anthony Perkins, Marjorie Main, Richard Eyer
► Acclaimed drama of Civil War violence and its effects on the lives of a peace-loving Quaker family in Indiana, based on the novel by Jessamyn West. Parents Cooper and McGuire must cope with son Perkins's desire to go off to battle. Warm and charming film notched six Academy Award nominations, including Best Picture, Director, Supporting Actor (Perkins), and the title song. **(CC)**
Dist.: CBS/Fox

FRIENDS, LOVERS & LUNATICS 1989 Canadian
★ R Comedy 1:28
☑ Adult situations, explicit language
Dir: Stephen Withrow *Cast:* Daniel Stern, Sheila McCarthy, Damir Andrei, Elias Koteas, Page Fletcher, Deborah Foreman
► Eccentric artist Stern pines so hard for exgirlfriend McCarthy that he follows her and boyfriend Andrei on their countryside vacation. Promising comic start goes for naught as plot takes disastrous turn when lunatic thugs Koteas and Fletcher take the lovers hostage. Stern is fun but script shifts focus away from him.
Dist.: Fries

FRIGHT NIGHT 1985
★ ★ ★ R Horror 1:46
☑ Nudity, explicit language, violence
Dir: Tom Holland *Cast:* Chris Sarandon, William Ragsdale, Amanda Bearse, Roddy McDowall, Stephen Geoffreys
► Teenage Ragsdale learns that neighbor Sarandon is a vampire. When girlfriend Bearse falls under fiend's evil spell, TV horror host McDowall agrees to help Ragsdale. Some plot holes but generally ingenious blend of horror and humor. Handsome Sarandon is a creepily effective bloodsucker; nice work from McDowall and Geoffreys as the hero's nerdy buddy. **(CC)**
Dist.: RCA/Columbia

FRIGHT NIGHT II 1988
★ ★ ★ R Horror 1:41
☑ Nudity, explicit language, violence
Dir: Tommy Lee Wallace *Cast:* Roddy McDowall, William Ragsdale, Traci Lin, Julie Carmen, Russell Clark, Merritt Butrick
► Ragsdale, after visiting shrink, is about to accept events of *Fright Night* as figments of his imagination until sexy vampire Carmen and three bloodsucking pals move into friend McDowall's building. Ragsdale and McDowall reteam to fight the newcomers. Sequel will entertain fans of the original but lacks its predecessor's verve.
Dist.: IVE

FRINGE DWELLERS, THE 1987 Australian
★ PG Drama 1:38
☑ Brief nudity, adult situations, explicit language
Dir: Bruce Beresford *Cast:* Kristina Nehm, Justine Saunders, Bob Maza, Kylie Belling, Denis Walker, Ernie Dingo
► Rebellious aborigine Nehm resents both her impoverished family's lack of education and the dominating white culture. She convinces the family to move to an all-white neighborhood, but assimiliation and upward mobility prove elusive. American audiences may relate with surprising ease to the aborigines' Westernized life-style, but Nehm's climactic choice undercuts sympathy for the character. Skillfully directed by Beresford, finely acted by a cast of unknowns.
Dist.: SVS

FRISCO KID, THE 1979
★ ★ ★ ★ PG Western/Comedy 1:59
☑ Explicit language, violence, adult humor
Dir: Robert Aldrich *Cast:* Gene Wilder, Harrison Ford, Ramon Bieri, Val Bisoglio, Leo Fuchs
► Western spoof stars Wilder as a naive Polish rabbi who crosses America to head a San Francisco congregation during the Gold Rush. Ford is hilarious as a kindhearted bank robber who takes Wild-West Wilder under his wing.
Dist.: Warner

FRITZ THE CAT 1972
★ X Animation/Adult 1:18

☑ Nudity, strong sexual content, adult situations, explicit language, violence
Dir: Ralph Bakshi *Cast:*
▶ Countercultural cat accidentally burns down his NYU dorm, then forsakes college life for sex, drugs, battles with the police, and a cross-country jaunt with other creatures. Freewheeling and outrageously controversial cartoon is for adults only. Based on the comic strip by R. Crumb.
Dist.: Warner

FROGS 1972
★ PG Horror 1:31
☑ Mild violence
Dir: George McCowan *Cast:* Ray Milland, Sam Elliott, Joan Van Ark, Adam Roarke, Judy Pace
▶ Southern despot Milland despoils surrounding bayou, enraging the reptiles and amphibians living there. They patriotically wait until the Fourth of July to attack the wheelchair-bound Milland and his family. Funny on a camp level. **(CC)**
Dist.: Warner

FROM BEYOND 1986
★ R Horror 1:25
☑ Nudity, adult situations, explicit language, graphic violence
Dir: Stuart Gordon *Cast:* Jeffrey Combs, Barbara Crampton, Ken Foree, Ted Sorel, Carolyn Purdy-Gordon
▶ Fantastic horror entry from the warped minds that created *Re-Animator.* Dr. Pretorious (Sorel) invents a machine that allows him to see the bizarre inhabitants of the beyond, but they can also see him. Mind-boggling special effects turn the professor's assistant Combs into a bald-headed brain eater. **(CC)**
Dist.: Vestron

FROM BEYOND THE GRAVE 1973 British
★ ★ PG Horror 1:38
☑ Adult situations, violence
Dir: Kevin Connor *Cast:* Peter Cushing, Donald Pleasence, Margaret Bannen, Ian Bannen, David Warner, Lesley-Anne Down, Margaret Leighton
▶ Cushing, the sinister owner of an antiques shop, is the macabre host for four occult tales in this well-mounted horror anthology. Uneven quality, with "The Elemental" (in which Leighton plays an unconventional psychic) the standout.
Dist.: Warner

FROM HELL TO VICTORY 1979
French/Italian/Spanish
★ ★ ★ PG War 1:40
☑ Adult situations, explicit language, violence
Dir: Hank Milestone *Cast:* George Peppard, Anny Duperey, George Hamilton, Horst Buchholz, Sam Wanamaker, Jean-Pierre Cassel
▶ In August, 1939, six friends promise to meet

each year in Paris on the same day, but go their separate ways when World War II breaks out. Peppard leads a commando team in blowing up a Nazi installation, Buchholz fights for the Germans, Duperey is captured by the Gestapo, and Wanamaker suffers cancer. Satisfying combination of wartime danger and romance. Duperey shines although Hamilton is miscast as a Frenchman.
Dist.: Media

FROM HERE TO ETERNITY 1954
★ ★ ★ ★ NR War/Drama 1:53 B&W
Dir: Fred Zinnemann *Cast:* Burt Lancaster, Montgomery Clift, Deborah Kerr, Frank Sinatra, Donna Reed, Philip Ober, Ernest Borgnine, Jack Warden
▶ Classic story about Army life in Hawaii before Pearl Harbor boasts blockbuster cast and gripping script. Clift is a rebellious bugler; Lancaster, a career soldier having an affair with officer's wife Kerr, which climaxes In their famous beach love scene. Nominated for thirteen Oscars and won eight, including Best Picture, Director, Supporting Actor (Sinatra) and Supporting Actress (Reed). Based on the James Jones best-seller.
Dist.: RCA/Columbia

FROM HOLLYWOOD TO DEADWOOD 1988
★ ★ R Mystery-Suspense/Comedy 1:42
☑ Adult situations, explicit language, violence
Dir: Rex Pickett *Cast:* Scott Paulin, Jim Haynie, Barbara Schock, Jurgen Doeres, Chris Mulkey, Mike Genovese
▶ Odd couple of private eyes, uptight Paulin and slob Haynie, are hired by a film studio to find actress Schock, who has disappeared during a production. As the trail takes them to Santa Fe and Deadwood, South Dakota, Paulin becomes obsessed with their quarry. Terrific start blows apart due to excessive inside movie references. However, Haynie is hilarious.
Dist.: Media

FROM MAO TO MOZART: ISAAC STERN IN CHINA 1980
★ ★ ★ G Documentary/Music 1:24
Dir: Murray Lerner *Cast:* Isaac Stern, David Golub, Tan Shuzhen
▶ World-renowned violinist Stern visits China and displays his virtuosity and passionate love for music in lectures and concerts. Noteworthy for revelations by Shuhzen of the Shanghai Conservatory of Music about his imprisonment during Chairman Mao's Cultural Revolution. Spirited account of East meeting West won Oscar for Best Documentary.
Dist.: Warner

FROM RUSSIA, WITH LOVE 1963 British
★ ★ ★ NR Espionage/Action-Adventure 1:58
Dir: Terence Young *Cast:* Sean Connery, Daniela Bianchi, Lotte Lenya, Pedro Armendariz, Robert Shaw
▶ Action in Istanbul and the Orient Express as

Agent 007 (Connery) gets involved with beautiful Russian spy Bianchi as part of sinister Soviet plot. Very exciting James Bond thriller, one of the best in the series, is more realistic than later, more comic-book efforts and features two of 007's most memorable villains in the stoic Shaw and the creepy Lenya, of the stiletto-toed shoes.
Dist.: MGM/UA

FROM THE HIP 1987
★ ★ ★ **PG Comedy 1:52**
☑ Adult situations, explicit language
Dir: Bob Clark   *Cast:* Judd Nelson, Elizabeth Perkins, John Hurt, Darren McGavin, Nancy Marchand
▶ Outrageous tactics help advance ambitious young defense attorney Nelson but he must wrestle with his conscience when he suspects new client Hurt is guilty of murder. Some laughs, if you can suspend your disbelief, but smug hero Judd is unappealing. Glib screenplay by David E. Kelley.   **(CC)**
Dist.: Warner

FROM THE TERRACE 1960
★ ★ ★ ★ **NR Drama 2:28**
Dir: Mark Robson   *Cast:* Paul Newman, Joanne Woodward, Myrna Loy, Ina Balin, Leon Ames
▶ Young Newman marries pampered socialite Woodward and succeeds in the rat race as his marriage deteriorates. He then falls in love with the more down-to-earth Balin. High-class soap opera version of John O'Hara's popular novel of the idle rich, power, romance, and success. Newman and Woodward make it work as an entertaining romantic drama in the lush Hollywood tradition.
Dist.: CBS/Fox

FRONT, THE 1976
★ ★ ★ **PG Drama 1:31**
☑ Adult situations, explicit language
Dir: Martin Ritt   *Cast:* Woody Allen, Zero Mostel, Herschel Bernardi, Michael Murphy, Andrea Marcovicci
▶ During the McCarthy era, cashier Allen serves as a "front," submitting scripts under his own name so that blacklisted writers can continue to work. Allen rises to the top of the TV biz but develops a conscience when a congressional committee wants him to fink on his pals. Politically oversimplified but still effective comedy/drama. Mostel stands out as an actor driven to suicide by the witchhunt. Many involved in the film were blacklisted (including Mostel, Ritt, Bernardi, and screenwriter Walter Bernstein).
Dist.: RCA/Columbia

FRONT PAGE, THE 1931
★ ★ **NR Comedy 1:41 B&W**
Dir: Lewis Milestone   *Cast:* Adolphe Menjou, Pat O'Brien, Mary Brian, Edward Everett Horton, Walter Catlett
▶ First film version of the Ben Hecht/Charles MacArthur play. O'Brien is the reporter and

Menjou his rascal editor covering the escape of an about-to-be-executed man in Chicago. Despite its age and three subsequent remakes (*His Girl Friday*, the Lemmon-Matthau *Front Page*, *Switching Channels*), the comedy still remains fresh and fast-paced.
Dist.: KVC

FUGITIVE, THE 1947
★ ★ ★ **NR Drama 1:44 B&W**
Dir: John Ford   *Cast:* Henry Fonda, Dolores Del Rio, Pedro Armendariz, Ward Bond, Leo Carrillo, J. Carrol Naish
▶ Fonda gives a memorable performance as a doubt-wracked priest trapped in a Mexico where Catholicism has been outlawed. Although the peasants are desperate for religious guidance, Fonda faces death each time he reveals his identity. Stark photography by Gabriel Figueroa is one of the best aspects of this loose adaptation of Graham Greene's *The Power and the Glory*.
Dist.: Turner

FUGITIVE KIND, THE 1960
★ ★ **NR Drama 2:15 B&W**
Dir: Sidney Lumet   *Cast:* Marlon Brando, Anna Magnani, Joanne Woodward, Maureen Stapleton, R. G. Armstrong, Victor Jory
▶ Itinerant musician Brando arrives in small Southern burg, gets involved with unhappily married woman Magnani. Town tramp Woodward also becomes interested in Brando. Based on Tennessee Williams's play *Orpheus Descending*; some strong moments from the three stars but not on par with the playwright's best work.
Dist.: Key

FULLER BRUSH MAN, THE 1948
★ ★ ★ **NR Comedy 1:33 B&W**
Dir: S. Sylvan Simon   *Cast:* Red Skelton, Janet Blair, Hillary Brooke, Don McGuire, Adele Jergens
▶ Bumbling door-to-door salesman Skelton stumbles across a murder mystery which he tries to solve with girlfriend Blair. Broad slapstick climax in a factory revives some old silent-film gags. Skelton briefly reprised his role in 1950's semisequel *The Fuller Brush Girl* starring Lucille Ball.
Dist.: RCA/Columbia

FULL METAL JACKET 1987
★ ★ ★ ★ **R War 1:56**
☑ Adult situations, explicit language, graphic violence
Dir: Stanley Kubrick   *Cast:* Matthew Modine, Arliss Howard, Vincent D'Onofrio, Dorian Harewood, Lee Ermey, Adam Baldwin
▶ Blistering anti-Vietnam indictment from director Kubrick traces group of Marine recruits, led by ironic Private Joker (Modine), from boot camp to battlefield. The basic training sequence, a mini-movie in itself, contains amazingly foulmouthed dialogue, great work from real-life drill sarge Ermey, and a shattering cli-

max. The Vietnam scenes provide a gripping and visually powerful portrait of war. (CC)
Dist.: Warner

FULL MOON HIGH 1981
★★ PG Horror/Comedy 1:34
☑ Brief nudity, adult situations, explicit language, adult humor
Dir: Larry Cohen ***Cast:*** Adam Arkin, Roz Kelly, Elizabeth Hartman, Ed McMahon, Joanne Nail, Kenneth Mars
► Arkin, football star of Full Moon High, travels to Romania with his right-wing CIA agent dad McMahon and gets bitten by a werewolf. Upon his return, Arkin finds himself hungry for dog food, unable to play football, and ostracized by the community. Twenty years later, the ageless Arkin returns to his school, determined to make the football squad. Zany spoof has its moments.
Dist.: HBO

FULL MOON IN BLUE WATER 1988
★★ R Drama 1:34
☑ Explicit language
Dir: Peter Masterson ***Cast:*** Gene Hackman, Teri Garr, Burgess Meredith, Elias Koteas
► Southern-fried story stars Hackman as Floyd, the owner of the Blue Water Bar and Grill, unable to shake the blues after his wife's disappearance in a boating accident several years before. He indulges in fantasies of her return while Garr, a Texas schoolbus driver, struts around in high heels and miniskirt hoping to attract his attention. Amiable and leisurely with down-home humor and fine performances from the ever reliable Hackman and the sweetly wacky Garr. (CC)
Dist.: Media

FULL MOON IN PARIS 1984 French
☆ R Comedy 1:42
☑ Nudity
Dir: Eric Rohmer ***Cast:*** Pascale Ogier, Fabrice Luchini, Tcheky Karyo, Christian Vadim, Virginia Thevenet
► Young Ogier is torn between boyfriends Karyo, Luchini, and Vadim and two places (Paris and surrounding suburb) while searching for elusive happiness. When she finally decides what she wants, it is no longer available to her. A shade below top Rohmer but still insightful and witty in his fashion. Ogier died shortly after release. [S]
Dist.: Media

FUNERAL, THE 1987 Japanese
☆ NR Comedy
☑ Brief nudity, adult situations, explicit language
Dir: Juzo Itami ***Cast:*** Tsutomu Yamazaki, Nobuko Miyamoto, Kin Sugai, Shuji Otaki
► Darkly comic look at how the Japanese deal with death. Married couple Yamazaki and Miyamoto must put their lives on hold as they attend the elaborate three-day ritual after her father has died. Wry, shrewd observations. Miyamoto is the director's wife. [S]
Dist.: Republic

FUNERAL HOME 1982 Canadian
★ R Horror 1:33
☑ Adult situations, explicit language, violence
Dir: William Fruet ***Cast:*** Lesleh Donaldson, Kay Hawtrey, Barry Morse, Dean Garbett, Stephen Miller
► Donaldson, a teenager living with her grandmother Hawtrey, hears strange voices from the basement. Her curiosity turns to terror when she learns grandmom's house used to be a funeral parlor. Is her dead grandfather trying to contact her? Modest shocker strongly resembles *Psycho*.
Dist.: Paragon

FUNERAL IN BERLIN 1966 British
★★★ NR Espionage 1:42
Dir: Guy Hamilton ***Cast:*** Michael Caine, Eva Renzi, Paul Hubschmid, Oscar Homolka, Guy Doleman
► Sequel to *The Ipcress File* finds secret agent Harry Palmer (Caine) in Berlin trying to arrange the defection of a Soviet officer through a bogus funeral. Slick production and Caine's delicious wry humor make follow-up a worthy successor.
Dist.: Paramount

FUNHOUSE, THE 1981
★ R Horror 1:35
☑ Nudity, explicit language, graphic violence
Dir: Tobe Hooper ***Cast:*** Elizabeth Berridge, Miles Chapin, Cooper Huckabee, Largo Woodruff, Sylvia Miles, Kevin Conway
► Four teens hole up in carnival funhouse for the night. Witnessing barker Conway's monster son kill fortune-teller Miles, they become the murderer's next targets. Atmospheric and not without tension; game cast tries hard but the violence and downbeat tone wear thin.
Dist.: MCA

FUN IN ACAPULCO 1963
★★★ NR Musical 1:37
Dir: Richard Thorpe ***Cast:*** Elvis Presley, Ursula Andress, Elsa Cardenas, Paul Lukas, Larry Domasin, Alejandro Rey
► Presley plays a trapeze artist with vertigo who settles down to an easier job as lifeguard at a resort hotel. He must conquer his fear of heights to win lovely Andress. Scenery outrates the songs, which include "The Bullfighter Was a Lady," "There's No Room to Rhumba in a Sports Car," and "You Can't Say No in Acapulco."
Dist.: CBS/Fox

FUNLAND 1987
☆ PG-13 Comedy 1:26
☑ Adult situations, explicit language, violence
Dir: Michael Simpson ***Cast:*** William Win-

dom, David L. Lander, Bruce Mahler, Robert Sacchi, Lane Davies, Clark Brandon
▶ Lander, a clown who is spokesman for the Funland amusement park, is fired when the mob takes it over. Former owner Windom, murdered by the Mafia, comes back from the dead and teams up with Lander for revenge. Miserable mishmash of various genres with overstated acting.
Dist.: Vestron

FUNNY 1988
★ ★ ★ NR Documentary/Comedy 1:21
☑ Brief nudity, explicit language, adult humor
Dir: Bran Ferren   *Cast:* Dick Cavett, Bob Balaban, Melissa Gilbert, Alan King, Susan Ruttan, Peter Boyle
▶ There's not a special effect in sight in Oscar-winning technical whiz Ferren's directorial debut, a cunning compilation of many people, including celebrities, telling their favorite jokes. Basically a novelty item, but it doesn't wear thin. Some hysterical moments, with the ordinary folk sometimes outshining the actors.

FUNNY FACE 1957
★ ★ ★ ★ NR Musical 1:43
Dir: Stanley Donen   *Cast:* Audrey Hepburn, Fred Astaire, Kay Thompson, Michel Auclair, Robert Flemyng, Suzy Parker
▶ Elegant May-December romance, with Astaire playing a fashion photographer (based on Richard Avedon) who turns young bookstore clerk Hepburn into an internationally famous model. Slight plot buoyed by beautiful Paris locations, Oscar-nominated costumes by Edith Head and Hubert de Givenchy, and a wonderful George and Ira Gershwin score: "He Loves and She Loves," "How Long Has This Been Going On," "Clap Yo' Hands."
Dist.: Paramount

FUNNY FARM 1988
★ ★ ★ PG Comedy 1:41
☑ Explicit language
Dir: George Roy Hill   *Cast:* Chevy Chase, Madolyn Smith, Kevin O'Morrison, Joseph Maher, Jack Gilpin
▶ Sports reporter Chase moves to bucolic New England town to write a novel. But his neighbors are anything but friendly, his dream house causes slapstick complications, and his marriage to Smith falls apart when she writes a successful children's book. Mildly amusing comedy suits Chase's easygoing charm.
Dist.: Warner

FUNNY GIRL 1968
★ ★ ★ ★ ★ G Biography/Musical 2:27
Dir: William Wyler   *Cast:* Barbra Streisand, Omar Sharif, Kay Medford, Anne Francis, Walter Pidgeon
▶ Charismatic musical biography of Ziegfeld Follies comedienne Fanny Brice portrays the familiar backstage story of star's rise from obscurity to fame and her doomed love for no-good Sharif. Major box-office hit with Streisand

singing "People," "Don't Rain on My Parade," "My Man," and more. Schmaltzy, tuneful and funny. Nominated for eight Oscars, including Best Picture. Streisand's Best Actress Oscar was shared with Katharine Hepburn for *The Lion in Winter.*
Dist.: RCA/Columbia

FUNNY LADY 1975
★ ★ ★ ★ ★ PG Biography/Musical 2:21
☑ Adult situations, explicit language
Dir: Herbert Ross   *Cast:* Barbra Streisand, James Caan, Omar Sharif, Roddy McDowall, Ben Vereen, Heidi O'Rourke
▶ Successful Ziegfeld star Fanny Brice (Streisand), divorced from Nicky Arnstein (Sharif), meets and marries showman Billy Rose (Caan). They drift apart and, by the time she realizes she loves him, he's fallen for Olympic swimming star Eleanor Holm (O'Rourke). "I'm her Nick," Caan tells Streisand. Sequel to megahit *Funny Girl* features showstopping hits "How Lucky Can You Get" (Oscar nominated) and oldies "Me and My Shadow" and "Paper Moon." Also nominated for Cinematography, Sound, Scoring, and Costume Design.
Dist.: RCA/Columbia

FUNNY MONEY 1983 British
★ ★ NR Comedy 1:32
☑ Nudity, explicit language
Dir: James Kenelm Clarke   *Cast:* Gregg Henry, Elizabeth Daily, Gareth Hunt, Annie Ross, Derren Nesbitt
▶ Two Yankee con artists, lounge pianist Henry and hooker Daily, team up at a London hotel to collect as many credit cards as possible from the guests. Corny and predictable, with a smattering of sexy jokes.
Dist.: Vestron

FUNNY THING HAPPENED ON THE WAY ON THE WAY TO THE FORUM, A 1966
★ ★ ★ ★ NR Comedy 1:39
Dir: Richard Lester   *Cast:* Zero Mostel, Phil Silvers, Jack Gilford, Buster Keaton, Michael Crawford
▶ Mostel, a scheming slave in ancient Rome, tries everything to win his freedom, dragging protesting accomplice Gilford along on outrageous schemes involving pimp Silvers and naive lover Crawford. Frantic adaptation of the Broadway hit has some wonderful slapstick, particularly by Keaton in his last feature. Stephen Sondheim score (including "Comedy Tonight" and "Lovely") won an Oscar.
Dist.: CBS/Fox

FUN WITH DICK AND JANE 1977
★ ★ ★ ★ PG Comedy 1:35
☑ Explicit language, adult humor
Dir: Ted Kotcheff   *Cast:* George Segal, Jane Fonda, Ed McMahon, Dick Gautier, Allan Miller
▶ Suburban couple Segal and Fonda live the American dream until Segal loses his job as an aerospace engineer. When bills pile up, they

turn to crime. Wry, polished comedy with a political point.
Dist.: RCA/Columbia

FURTHER ADVENTURES OF TENNESSEE BUCK, THE 1988
★ ★ R Action-Adventure 1:30
⊡ Rape, nudity, adult situations, explicit language, violence
Dir: David Keith *Cast:* David Keith, Kathy Shower, Brant Von Hoffman, Sydney Lassick, Sillaiyoor Selvarajan, Tiziana Stella
▶ Hunter Keith is hired to take yuppie Van Hoffman and wife Shower on a jungle safari. Shower and Keith have clashing personalties but he eventually becomes her rescuer and lover when cannibals capture her. Derivative but diverting escapism with exotic Borneo locations and action aplenty.
Dist.: Media

FURY, THE 1978
★ ★ ★ R Mystery-Suspense 1:58
⊡ Explicit language, violence
Dir: Brian De Palma *Cast:* Kirk Douglas, Andrew Stevens, John Cassavetes, Carrie Snodgress, Amy Irving
▶ Stevens, a young man with ESP, is kidnapped by bad-guy secret-agent Cassavetes. Father Douglas desperately attempts to get him back safely. Irving plays a girl with psychokinetic powers enlisted to help. Bloody and violent, with a literally explosive ending.
Dist.: CBS/Fox

FUTURE HUNTERS 1989 Filipino
★ R Action-Adventure/Fantasy 1:40
⊡ Nudity, explicit language, violence
Dir: Cirio H. Santiago *Cast:* Robert Patrick, Linda Carol, Ed Crick, Richard Norton, Bob Schott, Ursula Marquez
▶ Norton, hero from 2025, arrives in 1986 to help Patrick and Carol battle biker gang. He gives them a magic spearhead that will enable them to thwart Nazi doctor Crick and possibly change the future. The chase goes from Los Angeles to Hong Kong to Manila in this badly done and badly dubbed action fantasy. Some kung fu action for martial arts fans.
Dist.: Vestron

FUTURE-KILL 1985
★ R Sci-Fi 1:25
⊡ Nudity, explicit language, graphic violence
Dir: Ronald Moore *Cast:* Edwin Neal, Marilyn Burns, Doug Davis
▶ Social consciousness and blood-and-guts are combined in this unusual low-budgeter featuring the stars of *The Texas Chain Saw Massacre*. Neal plays Splatter, a punked-out No-Nukes activist who wears armor over his radiation wounds and kills with his hooklike hand. In Barbarella garb, tough-chick Burns supplies ammo to fraternity boys to get rid of Splatter and his goons.
Dist.: Vestron

FUTUREWORLD 1976
★ ★ ★ PG Sci-Fi 1:47
⊡ Adult situations, explicit language, mild violence
Dir: Richard T. Heffron *Cast:* Peter Fonda, Blythe Danner, Arthur Hill, Jim Antonio, John P. Ryan, Stuart Margolin
▶ Sequel to *Westworld* concerns scientist Ryan's conspiracy to replace world leaders with robot replicas. Investigative reporters Fonda and Danner find their lives in jeopardy when they stumble across the plan while touring Ryan's amusement complex. NASA's Houston Space Center provides a realistic backdrop to this entertaining fantasy. Yul Brynner repeats his *Westworld* role in a brief cameo.
Dist.: Warner

FUZZ 1972
★ ★ PG Action-Adventure 1:32
⊡ Adult situations, mild violence
Dir: Richard A. Colla *Cast:* Burt Reynolds, Jack Weston, Tom Skerritt, Raquel Welch, Yul Brynner, Charles Martin Smith
▶ Black comedy about off-the-wall cops in a tough Boston precinct is episodic but fast-paced. Welch, an alluring undercover cop, and Smith, a baby-faced punk, stand out in the large cast. Humor is often vulgar, but Reynolds in a nun's habit is a sight to see. Adapted by Evan Hunter from a novel written under his Ed McBain pseudonym.
Dist.: CBS/Fox

F/X 1986
★ ★ ★ R Action-Adventure 1:48
⊡ Adult situations, explicit language, violence
Dir: Robert Mandel *Cast:* Bryan Brown, Brian Dennehy, Diane Venora, Cliff Young, Mason Adams, Jerry Orbach
▶ Justice Department official Adams hires movie special effects wizard Brown to fake the assassination of mobster Orbach. Double-crossed, Brown becomes the target of a police manhunt. Props and tricks help him survive the taut chase that makes up most of the film. Twisty plot and accurate use of New York locations enliven this smooth entertainment. (CC)
Dist.: HBO

GABRIELA 1984 Brazilian
★ ★ R Comedy 1:42
⊡ Nudity, strong sexual content, adult situations, explicit language, mild violence
Dir: Bruno Barreto *Cast:* Marcello Mastroianni, Sonia Braga, Antonio Cantafora, Paulo Goulart, Nelson Xavier
▶ Mastroianni plays a libidinous Bahian tavernkeeper who procures lusty peasant girl Braga to be his cook, lover and eventually, his bride. Sexy Braga is the film's biggest draw. Based on Jorge Amado's novel, also made into a top Brazilian soap opera. Ⓢ
Dist.: MGM/UA

GABY—A TRUE STORY 1987
★ ★ ★ ★ ★ R Biography/Drama 1:54
☑ Nudity, adult situations, explicit language
Dir: Luis Mandoki *Cast:* Rachel Levin,
Norma Aleandro, Liv Ullmann, Lawrence
Monoson, Robert Loggia
► Tasteful and compassionate story of Gaby
Brimmer (Levin), born with such severe cerebral palsy that all but her left foot was completely paralyzed. Her fully functioning mind,
however, enabled her to become a famous
writer. The leads are played so realistically
that critics thought both actors were disabled
in real life. Aleandro won an Oscar nomination for her role as the woman who devotes
her life to Gaby. An inspiring, beautiful movie.
Dist.: RCA/Columbia

GALACTIC GIGOLO 1987
☆ R Comedy 1:20
☑ Nudity, adult situations, explicit language
Dir: Gorman Bechard *Cast:* Carmine
Capobianco, Debi Thibeault, Ruth Collins,
Angela Nicholas, Frank Stewart
► Alien Capobianco, wearing silver-lamé
bell-bottomed outfit, arrives in hick town in
search of sex with earth women. He discovers
earth girls are indeed easy but must contend
with gangsters. Feeble collection of low-brow
jokes with amateurish acting and cheesy pro-
duction values.
Dist.: Urban Classics

GALAXINA 1980
☆ R Sci-Fi/Comedy 1:36
☑ Brief nudity, explicit language, adult
humor
Dir: William Sachs *Cast:* Stephen Macht,
Dorothy Stratten, Avery Schreiber, James
David Hinton
► Silly sci-fi satire falls flat with cheap production and a vulgar, humorless script. In her last
film, Stratten (former *Playboy* Playmate whose
murder was the subject of *Star 80* and *Death
of a Centerfold: The Dorothy Stratten Story*),
gives a wooden performance as a beautiful
robot pursued by men.
Dist.: MCA

GALAXY EXPRESS 1980 Japanese
★ ★ G Animation 1:30
Dir: Taro Sin *Cast:* Voices of B. J. Ward,
Corey Burton
► In the future, a young boy takes a trip on a
celestial train, the Galaxy Express, to get a
new mechanical body. Bandits kidnap the
lad's companion. Overdone music score plus
animation on the level of Saturday morning
TV. Should entertain the younger kids but
there is little for adults here.
Dist.: Nelson

GALAXY OF TERROR 1981
★ R Sci-Fi 1:21
☑ Nudity, explicit language, graphic vio-
lence
Dir: B. D. Clark *Cast:* Edward Albert, Erin

Moran, Ray Walston, Bernard Behrens, Zalman King
► A space-ship rescue mission lands on the
planet Morganthus to investigate the strange
deaths of a sister ship's crew. The team, led by
Moran, is eliminated one by one when their
innermost fears materialize (e.g., one worm-
hating female is molested and "slimed" by a
giant squishy nightcrawler). Borrows generously from *Aliens.*
Dist.: Nelson

GALLIPOLI 1981 Australian
★ ★ ★ PG War 1:51
☑ Brief nudity, explicit language, violence
Dir: Peter Weir *Cast:* Mel Gibson, Mark Lee,
Bill Kerr, Robert Grubb, David Argue
► Naive young Australians Gibson and Lee
join the army to fight in World War I and are
sent to Gallipoli, the site of a devastating bat-
tle. Harrowing war drama boasts excellent
performances and stunning production val-
ues.
Dist.: Paramount

GAL YOUNG 'UN 1979
★ NR Drama 1:45
☑ Adult situations
Dir: Victor Nunez *Cast:* Dana Preu, David
Peck, J. Smith, Gene Densmore, Jenny
Stringfellow, Tim McCormick
► During Prohibition, widow Preu retires to her
world of home and work, only to have her
still-vulnerable emotions played upon by
Peck, a young dandy who wants to set up a
still on her property. From a story by Marjorie
Kinnan Rawlings, winning low-budget effort
has powerful characterizations, good string
band score.
Dist.: Academy

GAMBIT 1966
★ ★ ★ NR Action-Adventure 1:49
Dir: Ronald Neame *Cast:* Shirley MacLaine,
Michael Caine, Herbert Lom, Roger C. Carmel, John Abbott
► In Hong Kong, criminal Caine enlists Eurasian MacLaine in his scheme to outwit
wealthy Arab Lom for possession of a valuable
statue. Ingeniously plotted and stylishly performed by Caine and MacLaine. Underrated
on initial release; has become a cult favorite
over the years.
Dist.: MCA

GAMBLER, THE 1974
★ ★ R Drama 1:51
☑ Adult situations, explicit language
Dir: Karel Reisz *Cast:* James Caan, Paul
Sorvino, Lauren Hutton, Morris Carnovsky,
Burt Young, Jacqueline Brookes
► College professor Axel Freed (Caan) is a
compulsive gambler who runs up a $44,000
debt to the Mafia. Intense character study is
nicely directed by Reisz and finely acted by
Caan, Sorvino, Carnovsky, and especially
Brookes as Caan's concerned mother.
Dist.: Paramount

GAME OF DEATH 1979
★ R Martial Arts 1:41
☑ Explicit language, violence
Dir: Robert Clouse ***Cast:*** Bruce Lee, Gig Young, Dean Jagger, Colleen Camp, Hugh O'Brian, Kareem Abdul-Jabbar, Chuck Norris
▶ Kung-fu film star Lee, shot in the face by an evil crime syndicate, must undergo reconstructive plastic surgery. With a new identity, he gets even by eliminating the mob with his bare hands (and feet). Martial arts idol Lee died midway during production and a double was substituted. Best sequence is a fight between the real Lee and basketball star Abdul-Jabbar.
Dist.: CBS/Fox

GAMERA 1966 Japanese
★ NR Sci-Fi 1:28 B&W
Dir: Noriaki Yuasi ***Cast:*** Brian Donlevy, Albert Dekker, John Baragrey, Diane Findlay, Dick O'Neill, Eiji Funakoshi
▶ An atomic detonation has the unfortunate side effect of awakening giant flying turtle Gamera from his ages-long Arctic sleep. The beastie proceeds to menace cities. American military officer Donlevy and Secretary of Defense Dekker team up with Japanese scientists to stop Gamera. At best, turtle is number two among Japanese monsters, but he does spit fire harder. Also known as *Gamera the Invincible*.
Dist.: Sinister

GAMMA PEOPLE, THE 1956 British
☆ NR Sci-Fi 1:18 B&W
Dir: John Gilling ***Cast:*** Paul Douglas, Eva Bartok, Leslie Phillips, Walter Rilla, Philip Leaver, Martin Miller
▶ Reporter Douglas and photographer Phillips are heading to the Salzburg Music Festival when their train is derailed in the nation of Gudavia. Aided by Bartok, they uncover dictator/scientist Rilla's gamma ray experiments on children. Entertaining, if odd, sci-fi with weak special effects.
Dist.: RCA/Columbia

GANDHI 1982 British/Indian
★★★★★ PG Biography 3:11
☑ Violence
Dir: Richard Attenborough ***Cast:*** Ben Kingsley, John Gielgud, Martin Sheen, Candice Bergen, Trevor Howard, Edward Fox, John Mills, Ian Charleson, Athol Fugard, Saeed Jaffrey
▶ Epic chronicle of Mahatma Gandhi's life, from his early days as an attorney fighting prejudice in South Africa to his success as India's spiritual and political leader. Kingsley creates an uncannily accurate portrait of the nonviolent leader, killed by an assassin in 1948. Lavish, grand-scaled production won eight Oscars, including Best Picture, Actor, Director, Cinematography, and Costumes.
Dist.: RCA/Columbia

GARBAGE PAIL KIDS MOVIE, THE 1987
★★ PG Comedy 1:40
☑ Mild violence
Dir: Rod Amateau ***Cast:*** Anthony Newley, Mackenzie Astin, Katie Barberi, Ron MacLachlan, Kevin Thompson, Phil Fondacaro
▶ Young Astin knocks over garbage can in antique store owner Newley's shop. Out come seven maladjusted midgets with talent for various disgusting antisocial behaviors. Friendship ensues although Newley fears Garbage Pail Kids will be locked up in State Home for the Ugly. Raucous and rude; parents will not want their children emulating these characters. Based on the popular bubblegum cards.
Dist.: KVC

GARBO TALKS 1984
★★ PG-13 Comedy/Drama 1:44
☑ Adult situations, explicit language, adult humor
Dir: Sidney Lumet ***Cast:*** Anne Bancroft, Ron Silver, Catherine Hicks, Carrie Fisher, Howard da Silva, Steven Hill, Dorothy Loudon, Harvey Fierstein
▶ Loving son Silver attempts to grant dying mother Bancroft's final wish: to meet ultrareclusive Greta Garbo. Offbeat charmer with flaky humor and a sentimental heart. **(CC)**
Dist.: CBS/Fox

GARDEN OF ALLAH, THE 1936
★★ NR Romance 1:18
Dir: Richard Boleslawski ***Cast:*** Marlene Dietrich, Charles Boyer, Basil Rathbone, C. Aubrey Smith, Tilly Losch, John Carradine
▶ After the death of her father, long-suffering Dietrich flees to the Algerian desert, where she falls under the spell of Boyer, a moody ex-monk hiding a dark secret about his past. Murky, stilted romance won an Oscar for its ravishing Technicolor.
Dist.: CBS/Fox

GARDEN OF THE FINZI-CONTINIS, THE 1971 Italian
★★ R Drama 1:34
☑ Brief nudity, adult situations
Dir: Vittorio De Sica ***Cast:*** Dominique Sanda, Lino Capolicchio, Helmut Berger, Fabio Testi, Romolo Valli
▶ In Italy, a wealthy Jewish family pays little heed to the winds of World War II, realizing too late the danger that threatens them. Testi, the lover of daughter Sanda, is killed in battle as the government orders the imprisonment of the Jews. Engrossing, cautionary tale won Best Foreign Film Oscar. [S]
Dist.: Warner

GARDENS OF STONE 1987
★★★★ R Drama 1:52
☑ Adult situations, explicit language
Dir: Francis Coppola ***Cast:*** James Caan, Anjelica Huston, James Earl Jones, D. B. Sweeney, Dean Stockwell, Mary Stuart Masterson

▶ Sober examination of the Vietnam War years told from the perspective of soldiers assigned to Arlington National Cemetery. Caan is a grizzled sergeant who wants a transfer to an infantry training post; Huston plays his journalist girlfriend. Blustery sergeant Jones and recruit's fiancée Masterson stand out in this accomplished but curiously detached drama. (CC)
Dist.: CBS/Fox

GAS 1981 Canadian
★ R Comedy 1:34
☑ Adult situations, explicit language, adult humor
Dir: Les Rose ***Cast:*** Donald Sutherland, Susan Anspach, Howie Mandel, Sterling Hayden, Helen Shaver, Peter Aykroyd
▶ Midwestern city goes through gasoline shortage when tycoon Hayden hoards supply to drive up prices. Reporter Anspach investigates, and wild disc jockey Sutherland circles overhead in helicopter to keep townsfolk informed as gas lines form. Crazy, nonstop slapstick humor features many outrageous stunts.
Dist.: Paramount

GASLIGHT 1944
★★★ NR Mystery-Suspense 1:54 B&W
Dir: George Cukor ***Cast:*** Ingrid Bergman, Charles Boyer, Joseph Cotten, Dame May Whitty, Angela Lansbury
▶ In Victorian London, wealthy young Bergman marries seemingly wonderful Boyer who proceeds to make her think she's going insane. The evil plan works all too well until detective Cotten enters the case. Gripping and atmospheric. Three great performances: Bergman (Oscar-winning), Boyer (Oscar-nominated), and Lansbury (also nominated in her debut as the maid). Best Picture nominee was remade from a 1939 British film.
Dist.: MGM/UA

GAS-S-S-S! 1970
★ PG Comedy 1:19
☑ Explicit language, violence
Dir: Roger Corman ***Cast:*** Bud Cort, Cindy Williams, Robert Corff, Ben Vereen, Talia Shire, Marshall McLuhan
▶ Nerve gas kills everyone over thirty, leaving isolated bands of murderous teens ruling the country. Corman's version of the apocalypse is an overwrought, fragmented black comedy that doesn't quite conquer its low-budget limitations. Some worthwhile moments from the young cast, many on the verge of stardom. Music by Country Joe and the Fish.
Dist.: Vestron

GATE, THE 1987 Canadian
★★ PG-13 Horror 1:32
☑ Explicit language, violence
Dir: Tibor Takacs ***Cast:*** Stephen Dorff, Christa Denton, Louis Tripp, Kelly Rowan, Jennifer Irvin
▶ Young Dorff and his friend Tripp explore a suburban backyard hole, unwittingly freeing the Demon Lord and his horde of ghastly trolls into contemporary suburbia. Dreary first half-hour gives way to a fun plot, clever special effects, and strong climax.
Dist.: Vestron

GATE OF HELL 1954 Japanese
★★ NR Drama 1:30
Dir: Teinosuke Kinugasa ***Cast:*** Machiko Kyo, Kazuo Hasegawa, Isao Yamagata, Koreya Senda
▶ In twelth-century Japan, an emperor grants a warrior any wish he desires. He chooses another man's wife but she sacrifices herself rather than live without the man she loves. Vividly staged war scenes are combined with passionate romantic tragedy in a foreign classic with broad appeal. Won Oscars for Best Foreign Film and Costume Design, plus New York Film Critics Award and Best Film at Cannes Film Festival. [S]
Dist.: Nelson

GATES OF HEAVEN 1978
☆ NR Documentary 1:25
☑ Adult situations
Dir: Errol Morris
▶ Look at a California pet cemetery consists mainly of interviews with proprietor Floyd McClure and his clients. McClure and his partners provided full-service funerals but eventually went out of business. Highly acclaimed documentary may strike a chord in animal devotees but is probably too bizarre for mainstream audiences.
Dist.: RCA/Columbia

GATHERING, THE 1977
★★★★★ NR Drama/MFTV 1:34
Dir: Randal Kleiser ***Cast:*** Edward Asner, Maureen Stapleton, Bruce Davison, Veronica Hamel, Gregory Harrison, Lawrence Pressman
▶ Asner, a lonely, dying father, reaches out to alienated wife Stapleton and children for one last Christmas celebration. Exquisite Emmy-winning tearjerker pulls out all the stops on its way to a sentimental climax. Sequel, *The Gathering, Part II*, appeared in 1979.
Dist.: Worldvision

GATOR 1976
★★★★ PG Action-Adventure 1:56
☑ Adult situations, violence
Dir: Burt Reynolds ***Cast:*** Burt Reynolds, Jack Weston, Lauren Hutton, Jerry Reed, Alice Ghostley, Mike Douglas
▶ Moonshiner Reynolds (reprising his *White Lightning* character) is coerced by pushy New York Fed Weston into ratting on his friend, local crime czar Reed. After a romantic liaison with TV reporter Hutton, Reynolds takes on corrupt governor Douglas instead. Directing debut for Reynolds.
Dist.: MGM/UA

GATOR BAIT 1973
★ R Action-Adventure 1:31

☑ Strong sexual content, explicit language, violence
Dir: Ferd Sebastian, Beverly Sebastian
Cast: Claudia Jennings, Sam Gilman, Doug Dirkson, Clyde Ventura, Ben Sebastian, Tracy Sebastian
► In the Louisiana swamp, Cajun Jennings is caught poaching gators and then blamed for the accidental death of Ben Sebastian, whose powerful clan pursue her for revenge. Trashy exploitation fare with skimpy screenplay. Jennings's accent is laughable.
Dist.: Paramount

GATOR BAIT II—CAJUN JUSTICE 1989
☆ **R Action-Adventure 1:35**
☑ Rape, nudity, adult situations, explicit language, violence
Dir: Ferd Sebastian, Beverly Sebastian
Cast: Jan MacKenzie, Tray Loren, Paul Muzzcat, Brad Kepnick, Jerry Armstrong, Ben Sebastian
► Loren, brother of Claudia Jennings's character in *Gator Bait*, marries city girl MacKenzie. Bad guys kidnap and rape MacKenzie while leaving Loren for dead. MacKenzie escapes from her tormentors and uses a shotgun and poison snakes in quest for vengeance. Low-grade item with surprisingly few action scenes. **(CC)**
Dist.: Paramount

GAUNTLET, THE 1977
★★★★ **R Action-Adventure 1:49**
☑ Nudity, explicit language, violence
Dir: Clint Eastwood ***Cast:*** Clint Eastwood, Sondra Locke, Pat Hingle, William Prince, Bill McKinney
► Disillusioned Phoenix cop Eastwood escorts hard-bitten hooker Locke from Las Vegas to testify in a mob trial. Gradually, they realize corrupt politicians want them both dead. Escalating violence provides plenty of thrills and humor, especially during an eye-opening fight between a motorcycle and helicopter. Eastwood brings welcome depth to his character.
Dist.: Warner

GAY DIVORCEE, THE 1934
★★★ **NR Musical 1:47 B&W**
Dir: Mark Sandrich ***Cast:*** Fred Astaire, Ginger Rogers, Alice Brady, Edward Everett Horton, Erik Rhodes, Eric Blore
► First starring vehicle for Astaire and Rogers is a dated but enjoyable farce: Rogers, a wife planning a divorce, mistakes Astaire for her court corespondent Rhodes. Achingly romantic dances include "A Needle in a Haystack," "Night and Day," and the Oscar-winning "The Continental." Low point in the strained comic relief is Horton's duet with a young Betty Grable to "Let's K-nock K-nees."
Dist.: Turner

GAY LADY, THE 1949 British
★ **NR Comedy 1:35**
Dir: Brian Desmond Hurst ***Cast:*** Jean Kent, James Donald, Hugh Sinclair, Bill Owen, Andrew Crawford, Lana Morris
► Kent, an actress in the Gay Nineties, rises to the top of the theater world, breaking up with balloonist beau Crawford in the process. She weds lord Donald but begins to long for the old days. Romp highlighted by handsome period production values.
Dist.: Unicorn

GENE KRUPA STORY, THE 1959
★★ **NR Biography/Music 1:41 B&W**
Dir: Don Weis ***Cast:*** Sal Mineo, Susan Kohner, James Darren, Susan Oliver, Yvonne Craig
► Mineo stars in this antiseptic biography of the great jazz drummer, portraying his fall from grace due to drug addiction. He's obviously miscast, but the songs are first-rate: "Memories of You" (sung by Anita O'Day), "Indiana" (with Red Nichols), "Cherokee," "Drum Crazy," etc.
Dist.: RCA/Columbia

GENERAL, THE 1927
★★★★ **NR Comedy 1:18 B&W**
Dir: Buster Keaton ***Cast:*** Buster Keaton, Marion Mack, Glen Cavender, Jim Farley, Frederick Vroom, Joe Keaton
► Union soldiers hijack train containing Mack, Confederate engineer Keaton's girlfriend; he singlehandedly pursues them into a Northern compound in one of film's greatest chase sequences. Keaton's silent masterpiece not only contains some of his best sight gags, but also provides a meticulous reconstruction of the Civil War era. Based on a real incident. Remade by Disney in 1956 as *The Great Locomotive Chase*.
Dist.: Various

GENERAL DELLA ROVERE 1959 Italian
☆ **NR Drama 2:12 B&W**
Dir: Roberto Rossellini ***Cast:*** Vittorio De Sica, Hannes Messemer, Sandra Milo, Giovanna Ralli, Anne Vernon, Mary Greco
► During World War II, the Nazis force petty con man De Sica to pose as a Resistance general so he can get information from Italian prisoners. However, De Sica begins to identify with his role, resisting his mission to the point of martyrdom. Extraordinary performance by De Sica and a supremely moving climax highlight this very special film. Oscar nomination for screenplay. [S]
Dist.: Various

GENERAL DIED AT DAWN, THE 1936
★★ **NR Action-Adventure 1:37**
Dir: Lewis Milestone ***Cast:*** Gary Cooper, Madeleine Carroll, Akim Tamiroff, Dudley Digges, Porter Hall, William Frawley
► In China, American adventurer Cooper smuggles gold for opponents of evil warlord Tamiroff. Carroll, the daughter of Tamiroff's ally Hall, is sent to trap Cooper but falls in love with him instead. Riproaring adventure makes good use of Cooper's star power. Marvelous

direction. Cameo appearances by Milestone and film's screenwriter Clifford Odets, in addition to author John O'Hara.
Dist.: MCA

GENERATION 1969
★ ★ **PG Comedy 1:44**
☑ Adult situations, explicit language
Dir: George Schaefer *Cast:* David Janssen, Kim Darby, Peter Duel, Carl Reiner, James Coco, Sam Waterston
▶ Father Janssen is upset when daughter Darby and her husband Duel desire to deliver their baby in their Greenwich Village apartment. Despite a strong cast, this generation gap comedy probably seemed quaint even on initial release. William Goodhart adapted his Broadway play.
Dist.: Nelson

GENEVIEVE 1953 British
★ ★ **NR Comedy 1:26**
Dir: Henry Cornelius *Cast:* John Gregson, Dinah Sheridan, Kay Kendall, Kenneth More, Geoffrey Keen
▶ Gregson and More and their vintage autos compete in a London-to-Brighton road race. Their hapless mates, Sheridan and Kendall, view the battle as juvenile madness. One of the most entertaining and lighthearted romps ever to come out of England. Kendall is delightful.
Dist.: White Knight

GENTLE GIANT 1967
★ ★ ★ **NR Family 1:33**
Dir: James Neilson *Cast:* Dennis Weaver, Vera Miles, Clint Howard, Ralph Meeker, Huntz Hall, Charles Martin
▶ Seven-year-old Florida boy Howard befriends a lumbering but harmless bear. Despite Howard's pleas, father Weaver, a wildlife officer, returns the bear to the Everglades. But the bear proves to be a hero when he saves Weaver's life. Pleasant family-oriented story led to the TV series "Gentle Ben."
Dist.: Republic

GENTLEMAN JIM 1942
★ ★ ★ **NR Biography/Sports 1:44 B&W**
Dir: Raoul Walsh *Cast:* Errol Flynn, Alexis Smith, Jack Carson, Alan Hale, John Loder, Ward Bond
▶ Story of nineteenth-century heavyweight boxing champion "Gentleman" Jim Corbett (Flynn), whose dandyish ways outside the ring belied his skill inside it. Few directors handled male bonding as well as Walsh, especially in demonstrating Corbett's relationship with defeated rival Bond, which goes from baiting to mutual respect in touching fashion. **(CC)**
Dist.: CBS/Fox

GENTLEMEN PREFER BLONDES 1953
★ ★ ★ ★ **NR Musical 1:31**
Dir: Howard Hawks *Cast:* Jane Russell, Marilyn Monroe, Charles Coburn, Elliott Reid, Tom Noonan, George Winslow

▶ Flashy musical about the antics of Anita Loos's famous golddigger Lorelei (Monroe), en route to Paris with best friend Russell to marry a millionaire. Russell falls for private eye Reid, who's searching for incriminating evidence against Monroe. She has an innocent flirtation with elderly jeweler Coburn. Songs include Monroe's classic "Diamonds Are a Girl's Best Friend" and "Two Little Girls From Little Rock." Followed by *Gentlemen Marry Brunettes.*
Dist.: CBS/Fox

GEORGY GIRL 1966 British
★ ★ **NR Comedy 1:39 B&W**
Dir: Silvio Narizzano *Cast:* Lynn Redgrave, Alan Bates, James Mason, Charlotte Rampling, Rachel Kempson, Bill Owen
▶ Homely Redgrave wins the heart of parents' employer Mason while falling for her promiscuous roommate Rampling's lover Bates. When Rampling has an unwanted baby, Redgrave treats the child as her own. Funny and affecting. Bates, Mason, and Rampling are excellent; Redgrave's Oscar-nominated performance is unforgettable. Hit Tom Springfield/Jim Dale theme sung by The Seekers.
Dist.: RCA/Columbia

GETAWAY, THE 1972
★ ★ ★ ★ **PG Action-Adventure 2:02**
☑ Adult situations, explicit language, violence
Dir: Sam Peckinpah *Cast:* Steve McQueen, Ali MacGraw, Ben Johnson, Sally Struthers, Al Lettieri, Slim Pickens
▶ Double-crossed after a bank robbery, excon McQueen and girlfriend MacGraw must kill their accomplices and Johnson, the crooked cop who framed them, before escaping to Mexico. Violent, fast-paced version of cult favorite Jim Thompson's novel with topnotch action sequences.
Dist.: Warner

GET CRAZY 1983
★ **R Comedy 1:32**
☑ Nudity, adult situations, explicit language, adult humor
Dir: Allan Arkush *Cast:* Malcolm McDowell, Allen Goorwitz, Daniel Stern, Gail Edwards, Miles Chapin, Ed Begley, Jr., Lou Reed
▶ Hip, good-natured rock satire takes place during a New Year's Eve concert at the Saturn Theater as rock promoter Goorwitz puts together a superstar show to save the lease on his building. Filled with amusing cameos (Bobby Sherman, Fabian, Mary Woronov, etc.) and dead-on parodies of Mick Jagger (McDowell) and Bob Dylan (Reed).
Dist.: Nelson

GET OUT YOUR HANDKERCHIEFS 1978 French
★ ★ **R Comedy 1:49**
☑ Nudity, strong sexual content, adult situations, explicit language
Dir: Bertrand Blier *Cast:* Gerard Depardieu, Carole Laure, Patrick Dewaere, Riton

► Depardieu stars in this unconventional story of a man who will do anything to satisfy his sexually frustrated wife Laure, including introducing her to precocious thirteen-year-old Mozart prodigy, Riton. Eyebrow-raising, controversial black comedy won an Oscar for Best Foreign film. Strictly adult fare.
Dist.: Warner

GETTING EVEN 1986
★ ★ ★ R Mystery-Suspense **1:30**
☑ Nudity, explicit language, violence
Dir: Dwight H. Little   *Cast:* Audrey Landers, Edward Albert, Joe Don Baker, Blue Deckert, Dan Shackelford
► Big Texas corporations battle over secret nerve gas stolen from the Russians. Ridiculous plot involves recovering the poison gas (hidden on top of a Dallas skyscraper) before the city goes up with a bang. Farfetched, clumsy thriller with modest suspense.
Dist.: Vestron

GETTING IT ON 1983
★ ★ R Comedy **1:33**
☑ Nudity, adult situations, explicit language, adult humor
Dir: William Olsen   *Cast:* Martin Yost, Heather Kennedy, Jeff Edmond, Kathy Brickmeier, Mark Alan Ferri, Charles King Bibby
► Teenagers Yost and Edmond videotape female classmates' bedroom escapades and then charge friends a fee for viewing. The camera comes in handy to blackmail principal Bibby, who decides to expel Edmond. Unsexy sex comedy longer on titillation than actual glimpses of bare skin.
Dist.: Vestron

GETTING IT RIGHT 1989 British
★ ★ ★ ★ R Comedy **1:42**
☑ Brief nudity, adult situations, explicit language
Dir: Randal Kleiser   *Cast:* Jesse Birdsall, Helena Bonham Carter, Peter Cook, John Gielgud, Jane Horrocks, Lynn Redgrave
► Birdsall is a thirty-one-year-old virgin who still lives at home in London with his mum and dad. When a pal invites him to a trendy party, he hits it off with miserable socialite Redgrave and is pursued by unhinged blue-blood Carter. At work, he develops a sudden liking for assistant Horrocks, and finds himself juggling three very different women. Whimsical, low-key, coming-of-age comedy was inspired by classic British satires of the sixties, like *Georgy Girl*; not in that league, but enjoyable nonetheless.
Dist.: Forum

GETTING OF WISDOM, THE 1977 Australian
★ ★ NR Drama **1:41**
☑ Explicit language
Dir: Bruce Beresford   *Cast:* Susannah Fowle, Barry Humphries, John Waters, Sheila Helpmann, Hilary Ryan
► Fowle is a rough-hewn country girl sent off to a Victorian girls' school where the other stu-

dents make fun of her. Even the teachers are nonplussed by her unpolished honesty. But the strong-willed Fowle eventually wins them over with her free spirit and musical talents. Beautifully shot turn-of-the-century re-creations hampered by heavy Australian accents and slow pacing.
Dist.: CBS/Fox

GETTING STRAIGHT 1970
☆ R Comedy **2:06**
☑ Nudity, adult situations, explicit language, violence
Dir: Richard Rush   *Cast:* Elliott Gould, Candice Bergen, Robert F. Lyons, Jeff Corey, Max Julien, Cecil Kellaway
► Vietnam veteran Gould returns to his old college to teach and secure a graduate degree. He has an affair with student Bergen (among others), fights with the faculty and administrators, and finds himself caught up in campus unrest. Spirited performances by Gould and Bergen, interesting direction by Rush highlight dated portrayal of sixties turmoil. Look for Harrison Ford in a brief part as a party host.
Dist.: RCA/Columbia

GHOST AND MRS. MUIR, THE 1947
★ ★ ★ ★ ★ NR Fantasy/Romance **1:44** B&W
Dir: Joseph L. Mankiewicz   *Cast:* Rex Harrison, Gene Tierney, George Sanders, Vanessa Brown, Edna Best, Natalie Wood
► Widow Tierney and her daughter Wood move into a seaside cottage haunted by Harrison, the ghost of a nineteenth-century sea captain. Harrison falls in love with Tierney and rescues her from financial woes, but the material world soon interferes with the spiritual romance. Lavishly produced fantasy with two great stars is one of filmdom's most romantic stories and should not be confused with the TV series.
Dist.: CBS/Fox

GHOSTBUSTERS 1984
★ ★ ★ ★ ★ PG Comedy **1:45**
☑ Explicit language, violence
Dir: Ivan Reitman   *Cast:* Bill Murray, Dan Aykroyd, Sigourney Weaver, Harold Ramis, Rick Moranis, Annie Potts, Ernie Hudson
► Columbia University parapsychologists Murray, Aykroyd, and Ramis lose their grant and go into business as free-lance exorcists. Their first major gig: dealing with Weaver's haunted refrigerator ("Usually you don't see such behavior in a major appliance," deadpans Murray). Her building turns out to be a receiving tower for ghosts and spirits, and the intrepid boys battle a giant Staypuff Marshmallow man, among others. Hilarious mixture of ectoplasmic monsters, action, and comedy. Murray is a scream. The highest grossing comedy of all time. **(CC)**
Dist.: RCA/Columbia

GHOSTBUSTERS II 1989
★ ★ ★ ★ ★ PG Comedy 1:42
☑ Adult situations, explicit language
Dir: Ivan Reitman *Cast:* Bill Murray, Dan Aykroyd, Sigourney Weaver, Harold Ramis, Ernie Hudson, Annie Potts, Rick Moranis, Peter MacNicol
▶ Million-dollar lawsuits from the damage they caused in the original have forced the Ghostbusters out of business: Murray now hosts a hilariously bogus cable psychic show, Hudson and Aykroyd entertain "yuppie larvae" at kid parties. However, when seventeenth-century bad guy and underground river of slime threaten New York, who ya gonna call to save the city? Smile-inducing sequel adds new twists to familiar fun, such as MacNicol's bizarrely accented art restorer and an animate Statue of Liberty. (CC)
Dist.: RCA/Columbia

GHOST DAD 1990
★ ★ ★ PG Family 1:30
☑ Adult situations
Dir: Sidney Poitier *Cast:* Bill Cosby, Kimberly Russell, Denise Nicholas, Ian Bannen, Christine Ebersole, Barry Corbin
▶ Widowed father Cosby is killed in an auto accident and realizes he is a ghost when a speeding bus passes right through him. Back at home, his children have trouble coping with their pop's new powers—like invisibility. Slow moving family comedy may please Cosby's young TV fans, but not much of a knee-slapper for adults.
Dist.: MCA

GHOST FEVER 1987
★ PG Comedy 1:26
☑ Adult situations, explicit language
Dir: Alan Smithee *Cast:* Sherman Hemsley, Luis Avalos, Jennifer Rhodes, Deborah Benson, Pepper Martin
▶ Low-budget comedy with breakdancing ghosts. Hemsley and Avalos are bumbling black detectives in the Deep South. Sent to evict two old ladies from a creepy mansion, they are met by a bigoted antebellum ghost.
Dist.: Nelson

GHOST GOES WEST, THE 1936 British
★ ★ ★ NR Comedy 1:25 B&W
Dir: René Clair *Cast:* Robert Donat, Jean Parker, Eugene Pallette, Elsa Lanchester, Ralph Bunker
▶ Eighteenth-century Scotsman Murdoch (Donat) dies a coward and is forced to haunt his castle. When American Pallette buys the castle and moves it to Florida, the ghost and his modern-day descendant Donald (also Donat) go along: Murdoch to redeem his honor, Donald to win Pallette's daughter Parker. Whimsical comedy by Robert Sherwood has an appealingly light tone.
Dist.: Nelson

GHOSTS ON THE LOOSE 1943
★ NR Comedy 1:04 B&W

Dir: William Beudine *Cast:* Leo Gorcey, Huntz Hall, Bobby Jordan, Sammy Morrison, Bela Lugosi, Ava Gardner
▶ Gardner, the engaged sister of East Side Kid Hall, is to inhabit Nazi spy Lugosi's hideout. Bela pretends the house is haunted to frighten everyone away from the place. Minor fun fest for those wanting a glimpse of gorgeous young Gardner, or of Lugosi clowning. The East Side Kids were later renamed "The Bowery Boys." Also known as *The East Side Kids Meet Bela Lugosi.*
Dist.: Video Yesteryear

GHOST STORY 1981
★ ★ ★ R Horror 1:51
☑ Nudity, explicit language, mild violence
Dir: John Irvin *Cast:* Fred Astaire, Melvyn Douglas, Douglas Fairbanks, Jr., John Houseman, Craig Wasson, Patricia Neal, Alice Krige
▶ Elderly New Englanders Astaire, Houseman, Fairbanks, and Douglas assuage their guilt over a dark secret in the past by telling each other ghost stories. The appearance of Fairbanks's son Wasson and mysterious beauty Krige expose the friends to new horrors. Disappointing adaptation of Peter Straub's bestseller is notable for strong performances by Astaire and Douglas (in his last film).
Dist.: MCA

GHOST TOWN 1988
★ ★ R Horror 1:25
☑ Adult situations, explicit language, violence
Dir: Richard Governor *Cast:* Franc Luz, Catherine Hickland, Jimmie F. Skaggs, Penelope Windust, Bruce Glover, Blake Conway
▶ An old Western town has risen from the dust of time, and its ghostly inhabitants are terrorized by zombie desperado Skaggs. Modern day sheriff Luz is called upon to destroy badguy spirits after Skaggs kidnaps woman who reminds him of dead flame. Intriguing premise sets this apart from other low-budget horror films, and ghosts, gore, and gunplay will please fans of the genre.
Dist.: New World

GHOUL, THE 1933 British
★ NR Horror 1:13 B&W
Dir: T. Hayes Hunter *Cast:* Boris Karloff, Cedric Hardwicke, Ernest Thesiger, Dorothy Hyson, Anthony Bushell, Ralph Richardson
▶ Dying Egyptologist Karloff swears he will return from the dead if his valuable jewel is stolen. Lawyer Hardwicke and phony cleric Richardson are among those coveting the gem. When it turns up missing, Karloff keeps his creepy promise. Above-average fright flick with a great cast.
Dist.: Sinister

GHOUL, THE 1975 British
★ ★ NR Horror 1:28
☑ Violence

Dir: Freddie Francis   *Cast:* Peter Cushing, John Hurt, Alexandra Bastedo, Gwen Watford, Don Henderson
▶ During the 1920s, two couples race their cars after a party and are separated in the fog. Despite a stranger's warning, one woman goes to a mansion where a menacing monster lurks. Restrained flick has spooky haunted house atmosphere but lacks plot punch (especially at the inane climax) to satisfy jaded genre fans.
Dist.: Media

GHOULIES 1985
★ ★ **PG-13 Horror 1:21**
☑ Explicit language, violence
Dir: Luca Bercovici   *Cast:* Peter Liapis, Lisa Pelikan, Michael Des Barres, Jack Nance, Peter Risch
▶ When Liapis and girlfriend Pelikan move into an old house, he becomes obsessed with the occult. Suddenly, nasty little minions of the Devil (John Buechler's cutesy hand puppets) appear to wreak bloody havoc. Corny *Gremlins* imitator.
Dist.: Vestron

GHOULIES II 1987
★ **PG-13 Horror 1:35**
☑ Explicit language, violence
Dir: Albert Band   *Cast:* Damon Martin, Royal Dano, Phil Fondacaro, J. Downing, Kerry Remsen
▶ In this follow-up to the campy original, the pint-size puppet beasties terrorize a carnival sideshow. Fondacaro is a sideshow star who suggests using magic to exterminate the vicious pests. With silly-looking monsters and a minimum of violence, this "horror" film plays mainly for laughs.
Dist.: Vestron

GIANT 1956
★ ★ ★ ★ **G Drama 3:18**
Dir: George Stevens   *Cast:* Elizabeth Taylor, Rock Hudson, James Dean, Carroll Baker, Mercedes McCambridge, Jane Withers, Chill Wills, Dennis Hopper, Sal Mineo
▶ Ten Oscar nominations (and a win for director Stevens) went to this rousing multigenerational saga from the Edna Ferber best-seller. Texan Hudson brings home Eastern bride Taylor, who must contend with jealousy of his unmarried sister McCambridge, the attentions of wild young ranch hand Dean, and a racial dispute. As the years pass, Dean grows wealthy but disillusioned in the oil biz, while Hudson and Taylor raise three kids on the Riata, the largest cattle ranch in Texas. Blockbuster combines romance, comedy, and drama. Dean's final film.   **(CC)**
Dist.: Warner

G.I. BLUES 1960
★ ★ ★ **NR Musical 1:44**
Dir: Norman Taurog   *Cast:* Elvis Presley, James Douglas, Robert Ivers, Juliet Prowse, Leticia Roman, The Jordanaires
▶ Presley's first film after military service capitalized on his well-publicized assignment in Germany. Leader of a combo with two other soldiers, he bets that he can spend the night with cabaret singer Prowse. Strong assortment of songs, including "Wooden Heart," "Blue Suede Shoes," and "Shopping Around."
Dist.: CBS/Fox

GIDGET 1959
★ ★ ★ **NR Comedy 1:35**
Dir: Paul Wendkos   *Cast:* Sandra Dee, James Darren, Cliff Robertson, Arthur O'Connell, Mary Laroche, Tom Laughlin
▶ Frothy comedy introduced famed teenybopper Gidget (Dee), an insecure "girl midget" convinced she'll never win a boyfriend until surfers Darren and Robertson vie for her affections. Dee is ideal as the heroine (based on Frederick Kohner's novel about his daughter). Led to a string of less successful features and two TV series. Sequel: *Gidget Goes Hawaiian.*
Dist.: RCA/Columbia

GIDGET GOES HAWAIIAN 1961
★ ★ **NR Comedy 1:42**
Dir: Paul Wendkos   *Cast:* James Darren, Michael Callan, Deborah Walley, Carl Reiner, Peggy Cass, Eddie Foy, Jr.
▶ Walley replaces Sandra Dee, the original Gidget, in this painless sequel to the 1959 film. The lovable teen takes a Hawaiian vacation with her parents, trying to forget Stateside boyfriend Darren by flirting with handsome surfers. She's in for a big surprise when Darren shows up unexpectedly. Led to a feature sequel (*Gidget Goes to Rome*) as well as TV movies and series.
Dist.: RCA/Columbia

GIDGET GOES TO ROME 1963
★ ★ **NR Comedy 1:44**
Dir: Paul Wendkos   *Cast:* Cindy Carol, James Darren, Jessie Royce Landis, Cesare Danova, Jeff Donnell
▶ Gidget (Carol) and her longtime steady "Moondoggie" (Darren) vacation in Rome. After several lovers' quarrels, Darren serenades himself back into Gidget's heart. Last of the film series is cute, scenic, simple, and predictable.
Dist.: RCA/Columbia

GIFT, THE 1983 French
★ **R Comedy 1:50**
☑ Nudity, adult situations, explicit language
Dir: Michel Lang   *Cast:* Pierre Mondy, Claudia Cardinale, Clio Goldsmith, Jacques Francois, Cecile Magnet
▶ Instead of a gold watch, friends of retiring bank employee Mondy give him an unusual "gift": high-priced call girl Goldsmith. Routine bedroom farce based on the popular Italian stage comedy *Even Bankers Have Souls* is cheerful and silly but markedly uneven.
Dist.: HBO

GIG, THE 1985
★ NR Comedy/Drama 1:28
☑ Adult situations
Dir: Frank D. Gilroy ***Cast:*** Wayne Rogers, Cleavon Little, Andrew Duncan, Jerry Matz, Daniel Nalbach
► Small-scale, big-hearted comedy about a group of middle-aged men who get their dream opportunity: a two-week Catskills gig for their amateur Dixieland band. Little plays the only professional musician in the group. Jazzy mix of mid-life crisis and Borscht Belt music.
Dist.: Warner

GIGI 1958
★★★★ G Musical 1:55
Dir: Vincente Minnelli ***Cast:*** Maurice Chevalier, Leslie Caron, Louis Jourdan, Hermione Gingold, Eva Gabor
► Caron is superb as Gigi, a turn-of-the-century Parisian tomboy who refuses to grow up, resisting her family's efforts to train her as a courtesan. She has no interest in love until she meets Jourdan. Memorable Lerner and Loewe score includes "Thank Heaven for Little Girls," sung by Chevalier, who received an honorary Oscar for career achievement. Winner of nine Academy Awards, including Best Picture, Director, and Screenplay by Alan Jay Lerner (based on the spicy Colette novel).
Dist.: MGM/UA

GILDA 1946
★★★★ NR Drama 1:50 B&W
Dir: Charles Vidor ***Cast:*** Rita Hayworth, Glenn Ford, George Macready, Joseph Calleia, Steven Geray
► Casino owner Macready rescues Ford from a mugger, then hires him as bodyguard to gorgeous wife Hayworth, unaware that Ford and Hayworth were once lovers. Confusing but stylish film noir gave Hayworth one of her best roles. Her striptease to "Put the Blame on Mame" has become Hollywood legend.
Dist.: RCA/Columbia

GILDA LIVE 1980
★★ R Documentary/Comedy 1:30
☑ Explicit language
Dir: Mike Nichols ***Cast:*** Gilda Radner, Don Novello, Paul Schaffer
► Filmed version of Radner's one-woman Broadway show, with material culled mostly from NBC's "Saturday Night Live." Familiar characters include crude commentator Rosanne Rosannadanna, nerd Lisa Loopner, punk-singer Candy Slice and others. With Novello as Vatican gossip columnist Father Guido Sarducci. Aficionados of "SNL" will love Gilda, but may also yearn for the other Not Ready for Prime Time Players.
Dist.: Warner

GIMME AN 'F' 1984
☆ R Comedy 1:43
☑ Nudity, adult situations, explicit language
Dir: Paul Justman ***Cast:*** Stephen Shellen, Mark Keyloun, John Karlen, Jennifer C. Cooke
► When Camp Beaver View sponsors a cheerleading competition, nobody expects the clumsy Moline Ducks to put on a good show, least of all camp honcho Karlen. But with help of hunk instructor Shellin, girls are whipped into shape to perform a sexy production number. Don't look for a lot of nudity in this superlightweight teen fluff.
Dist.: Key

GIMME SHELTER 1970
★★ PG Documentary/Music 1:31
☑ Explicit language, violence
Dir: David Maysles, Albert Maysles, Charlotte Zwerin ***Cast:*** The Rolling Stones, Jefferson Airplane, Ike and Tina Turner, Marvin Belli, Sonny Barger, The Flying Burrito Brothers
► Brilliant but extremely disturbing documentary on the 1969 Rolling Stones tour of America, focusing on the notorious Altamont concert. While the Stones perform some of their best songs ("Sympathy for the Devil," "Brown Sugar," etc.), film's most compelling moments are Mick Jagger's reactions to footage of a murder in the audience by the Hell's Angels, ironically hired as security.
Dist.: RCA/Columbia

GINGER ALE AFTERNOON 1989
☆ R Drama
☑ Adult situations, explicit language
Dir: Rafal Zielinski ***Cast:*** Dana Andersen, John M. Jackson, Yeardly Smith
► Three-character drama set in a trashy trailer court. Andersen and Jackson are a married couple who are expecting a child and fight constantly. Jackson, who already resents nascent son, is having an affair with equally unpleasant neighbor Smith. Uninteresting, unlikeable characters just won't shut up. Screenplay by Gina Wendkos from her play.
Dist.: Academy

GINGER AND FRED 1986 Italian
★ PG-13 Drama 2:06
☑ Adult situations, explicit language
Dir: Federico Fellini ***Cast:*** Giulietta Masina, Marcello Mastroianni, Franco Fabrizi, Frederick Von Ledenburg, Martin Blau
► One-time forties dance stars Mastroianni and Masina, now ravaged by time, are reunited for television special. Lovely lead performances, visual inventiveness, satiric jabs at TV, and straightforward storytelling. Fairly accessible for a Fellini film but with some dull stretches; lacks the magic of his best efforts. [S]
Dist.: MGM/UA

GIRL, A GUY, AND A GOB, A 1941
★ NR Comedy 1:31 B&W
Dir: Richard Wallace ***Cast:*** George Murphy, Lucille Ball, Edmond O'Brien, Henry

Travers, Franklin Pangborn, George Cleveland
▶ Ball is the girl, Murphy's the gob, and O'Brien's the guy in this Harold Lloyd–produced comedy triangle. Strong supporting characters like pet shop owner Pangborn, combined with always-professional leads, make this a pleasant watch.
Dist.: Turner

GIRL CAN'T HELP IT, THE 1956
★ **NR Comedy 1:37**
Dir: Frank Tashlin *Cast:* Tom Ewell, Jayne Mansfield, Edmond O'Brien, Julie London, Henry Jones, John Emery
▶ Theatrical agent Ewell, brokenhearted over ex-girlfriend London, has six weeks to turn mobster's moll Mansfield into a star. Thin, silly plot emphasizing Mansfield's anatomy redeemed by seventeen rock gems: "Blue Monday" (Fats Domino), "Be Bop a Lula" (Gene Vincent), "Ready Teddy" (Little Richard), etc.
Dist.: CBS/Fox

GIRL CRAZY 1943
★ ★ ★ **NR Musical 1:39 B&W**
Dir: Norman Taurog *Cast:* Mickey Rooney, Judy Garland, Gil Stratton, Robert E. Strickland, June Allyson, Nancy Walker
▶ First-rate Rooney-Garland comedy, their eighth teaming, finds ladies' man Rooney stuck in an all-boys' school in the desert. He falls for dean's daughter Garland, and promotes a rodeo to save the school from closing. Wonderful Gershwin score includes "Fascinating Rhythm," "Embraceable You," "But Not For Me," and Busby Berkeley's stupendous production of "I Got Rhythm."
Dist.: MGM/UA

GIRLFRIENDS 1978
★ **PG Comedy/Drama 1:28**
☑ Brief nudity, adult situations, explicit language
Dir: Claudia Weill *Cast:* Melanie Mayron, Anita Skinner, Eli Wallach, Christopher Guest, Bob Balaban
▶ Affectionate film about dumpy but likable Jewish girl Mayron and her Midwestern roommate Skinner, fresh out of college and living in Manhattan. Though made on a shoestring budget, an attention-getting first feature by documentary maker Weill.
Dist.: Warner

GIRL FROM PETROVKA, THE 1974
★ ★ **PG Comedy 1:43**
☑ Adult situations, explicit language
Dir: Robert Ellis Miller *Cast:* Goldie Hawn, Hal Holbrook, Anthony Hopkins, Gregoire Aslan, Anton Dolin
▶ Young Russian Hawn falls in love with American journalist Holbrook but faces government disapproval of the relationship. Pre-glasnost tale is flatly directed and scripted; the leads are effective but don't generate enough chemistry to overcome the flaws.
Dist.: MCA

GIRL HAPPY 1965
★ ★ ★ ★ **NR Musical 1:36**
Dir: Boris Sagal *Cast:* Elvis Presley, Shelley Fabares, Harold J. Stone, Gary Crosby, Joby Baker, Nita Talbot
▶ Chicago mobster Stone sends singer Presley to Fort Lauderdale over spring break to keep an eye on his beautiful daughter Fabares. Inevitable romance blossoms between lesser Presley numbers: "Wolf Call," "Fort Lauderdale Chamber of Commerce," "Do the Clam," etc.
Dist.: MGM/UA

GIRL HUNTERS, THE 1963 British
★ ★ **NR Mystery-Suspense 1:43 B&W**
Dir: Roy Rowland *Cast:* Mickey Spillane, Shirley Eaton, Lloyd Nolan, Hy Gardner, Scott Peters
▶ Author Spillane plays tough guy private eye Mike Hammer and co-wrote this adaptation of his novel. Plot involves Hammer's investigation of a political assassination, which also yields clues to the murder of the detective's secretary. Sleazy, violent, energetic. Spillane gives a monotonous, inexpressive performance.
Dist.: Sinister

GIRL IN A SWING, THE 1988 British/U.S.
☆ **R Mystery-Suspense 1:52**
☑ Nudity, adult situations, explicit language
Dir: Gordon Hessler *Cast:* Meg Tilly, Rupert Frazer, Nicholas Le Provost, Elspet Gray, Lorna Heilbron
▶ Title lass is a porcelain figurine acquired by ceramics dealer Frazer, a shy fellow who's taken up with Tilly, a mysterious Danish woman. Tilly seems to have no past, and is consumed by guilt and uncertainty. After they are married, Tilly's horrid secret comes to consume her in strangely supernatural form. Moody and creepy, but doesn't make much sense. Based on a novel by Richard Adams. (CC)
Dist.: HBO

GIRL IN EVERY PORT, A 1952
★ ★ **NR Comedy 1:26 B&W**
Dir: Chester Erskine *Cast:* Groucho Marx, Marie Wilson, William Bendix, Don DeFore, Gene Lockhart
▶ Lowbrow antics about troublemaking sailors Marx and Bendix trying to switch a slowpoke horse with its speedy twin. Wilson plays a pretty cabdriver who's onto the scheme. Generally mirthless comedy represents a low point in Groucho's career.
Dist.: Republic

GIRL IN THE PICTURE, THE 1986 Scottish
★ ★ **PG-13 Romance/Comedy 1:30**
☑ Adult situations
Dir: Cary Parker *Cast:* John Gordon-Sinclair, Irina Brook, David McKay, Gregor Fisher, Caroline Guthrie
▶ Harmless comedy from American-born writer/director Parker about the break-up and

reconciliation of live-in lovers, Gordon-Sinclair and Brook. Charming cast and low-key humor with lovely shots of Glasgow and a guitar-tinged musical score.
Dist.: Vestron

GIRL MOST LIKELY, THE 1957
★ ★ ★ NR Musical 1:38
Dir: Mitchell Leisen *Cast:* Jane Powell, Cliff Robertson, Keith Andes, Kaye Ballard, Tommy Noonan, Una Merkel
▶ Jaunty musical remake of *Tom, Dick and Harry* features Powell in the Ginger Rogers role of the girl who can't decide which of three boyfriends (Andes, Robertson, or Noonan) to marry. Wealthy Andes has the bucks but you should put your money on handsome Robertson. Hugh Martin/Ralph Blane songs include "I Don't Know What I Want" and "All the Colors of the Rainbow."
Dist.: United

GIRL OF THE GOLDEN WEST, THE 1938
★ NR Musical 2:00 B&W
Dir: Robert Z. Leonard *Cast:* Jeanette MacDonald, Nelson Eddy, Walter Pidgeon, Leo Carrillo, Buddy Ebsen, Leonard Penn
▶ Rough-and-ready saloon owner Mac-Donald falls in love with highwayman Eddy. Jealous sheriff Pidgeon is about to apprehend Eddy when MacDonald steps in and stakes marriage to the sheriff against Eddy's freedom in a single draw of the cards. Weak songs can't help the script past the slow spots. Comic-relief Ebsen does a wonderful, shambling dance about halfway through that will keep some from tuning out.
Dist.: MGM/UA

GIRL ON A MOTORCYCLE, THE 1968
British/French
☆ R Drama 1:31
⊡ Nudity, adult situations
Dir: Jack Cardiff *Cast:* Marianne Faithfull, Alain Delon, Roger Mutton, Marius Goring, Catherine Jourdan
▶ Sixties period piece, with real-life rock star Faithfull as a loose woman who leaves her husband to speed from lover to lover on a motorcycle. Also known as *Naked Under Leather*, exploitation offering features abundant nudity and sixties light show effects. From a novel by Andre Pieyre de Mandiargue.
Dist.: Monterey

GIRLS! GIRLS! GIRLS! 1962
★ ★ ★ ★ NR Musical 1:46
Dir: Norman Taurog *Cast:* Elvis Presley, Stella Stevens, Laurel Goodwin, Jeremy Slate, Benson Fong
▶ Poor tuna fisherman Presley doubles as a nightclub singer to pay the mortgage on his father's boat. He's pursued by singer Stevens (who sings "The Nearness of You") and the wealthy Goodwin. Typical Presley effort has pretty Hawaiian locations and a marvelous version of "Return to Sender."
Dist.: CBS/Fox

GIRLS JUST WANT TO HAVE FUN 1985
★ ★ ★ PG Musical 1:27
⊡ Explicit language
Dir: Alan Metter *Cast:* Sarah Jessica Parker, Helen Hunt, Lee Montgomery, Sharron Shayne, Jonathan Silverman
▶ Bubble-headed high school antics of a group of Chicago kids out to win a dance contest and land a spot on their favorite TV show. Relentlessly silly, predictable characters: rich bitch, army brat, Catholic-school girl, preppie, uptight dad, and misty-eyed mom. Inspired by Cyndi Lauper's hit song, although neither Cyndi nor her voice are anywhere in evidence. **(CC)**
Dist.: New World

GIRLS' NITE OUT 1983
☆ R Horror 1:32
⊡ Nudity, adult situations, explicit language, graphic violence
Dir: Robert Deubel *Cast:* Julie Montgomery, James Carroll, Suzanne Barnes, Rutanya Alda, Hal Holbrook
▶ Campus killer has special grudge against cheerleaders. Fortunately for him, the only contestants in a college scavenger hunt are young women who have no qualms about journeying out on lonely streets, alone, at midnight. Numerous grotesque attacks in a strictly low-rent horror flick. Also known as *The Scaremaker*.
Dist.: HBO

GIVE 'EM HELL, HARRY! 1975
★ ★ ★ PG Drama 1:42
⊡ Explicit language
Dir: Steve Binder *Cast:* James Whitmore
▶ Former President Harry Truman (Whitmore) recalls his tumultuous political career and offers opinions on subsequent Presidents (with especially unkind words for Nixon). Whitmore won well-earned Oscar nomination for his portrayal of the irreverent, salty-tongued Truman in this film version of his one-man show.
Dist.: Worldvision

GIVE MY REGARDS TO BROAD STREET
1984 British
★ ★ PG Musical 1:49
⊡ Adult humor
Dir: Peter Webb *Cast:* Paul McCartney, Tracey Ullman, Bryan Brown, Ringo Starr, Linda McCartney, Ralph Richardson
▶ A silly love song from an ex-Beatle. Paul plays a superstar rocker whose master tapes have mysteriously disappeared—along with one of his employees. If Paul doesn't find the tapes by midnight, his company will be taken over by a ruthless villain who wears sunglasses indoors. McCartney fans should ignore the plot and concentrate on the songs: "Ballroom Dancing," "Yesterday," "Good Day Sunshine," and many others. **(CC)**
Dist.: CBS/Fox

GIZMO! 1979
★ ★ ★ G Documentary 1:16

Dir: Howard Smith
▶ Zany chronicle of eccentric American inventions: antisnore devices, dimple-making machines, wet diaper alarms, and bathing caps for beards, culled from footage dating back to the 1930s. Director Smith, who won an Academy Award for his documentary *Marjoe*, displays a fine sense of the golly-gee-whiz ridiculous.
Dist.: Warner

GLACIER FOX, THE 1978 Japanese
★ ★ ★ ★ G Documentary 1:30
Dir: Koreyski Kurahara
▶ Extremely well-made Japanese nature film dramatizes the life cycle of a fox couple and offspring. The baby foxes are adorable, but film does not shrink from realities of nature. Some children may be upset when the mother fox dies in a leg-hold trap (a simulation in which no animal was actually harmed). Eye-pleasing photography contrasts chilly glacial winter with short, lush spring.
Dist.: IVE

GLASS KEY, THE 1942
★ ★ NR Mystery-Suspense 1:25 B&W
Dir: Stuart Heisler *Cast:* Brian Donlevy, Veronica Lake, Alan Ladd, Bonita Granville, Richard Denning, William Bendix
▶ Corrupt political boss Donlevy backs a reform candidate for governor, despite pleas from right-hand-man Ladd to consider the impact on local gangs. When Donlevy is implicated in a murder, it's up to Ladd to clear his name. Blistering adaptation of Dashiell Hammett's novel has unexpected depth, vivid characters, and Bendix's memorably sadistic attack on Ladd. Plot bears a strong resemblance to 1990's *Miller's Crossing*.
Dist.: MCA

GLASS MENAGERIE, THE 1987
★ ★ ★ ★ PG Drama 2:10
☑ Adult situations
Dir: Paul Newman *Cast:* Joanne Woodward, Karen Allen, John Malkovich, James Naughton
▶ Reverential rendition of Tennessee Williams's American stage classic about an aging Southern belle and her children: Tom, a frustrated poet, and crippled Laura, who finds solace in her cherished glass animals. Polished performances, lavish photography, and sensitive direction from Woodward's husband Newman, but production suffers from static, stagey atmosphere.
Dist.: MCA

GLEAMING THE CUBE 1988
★ ★ PG-13 Drama 1:45
☑ Adult situations, explicit language, violence
Dir: Graeme Clifford *Cast:* Christian Slater, Steven Bauer, Min Luong, Art Chudabala, Le Tuan
▶ When cops claim that his adopted Vietnamese stepbrother Chudabula committed

suicide, skateboarding teen Slater sets out to prove he was murdered. While searching through Los Angeles' Little Saigon, he uncovers evidence of an evil conspiracy. Highlighted by amazing skateboarding stunts by real-life experts Mike McGill, Gator Rogowski, and others.
Dist.: Vestron

GLEN AND RANDA 1970
★ R Sci-Fi 1:34
☑ Nudity
Dir: Jim McBride *Cast:* Steven Curry, Shelley Plimpton, Woodrow Chamblis, Garry Goodrow
▶ Guided only by an old "Wonder Woman" comic book, postapocalyptic orphan Curry goes in quest of what he believes is a city called Metropolis. Along the way, he meets Plimpton, and the two try to make sense of the rusting wreckage of civilization. Sober and thoughtful film is a bit too slow and episodic to compete with later entries in Hollywood's postannihilation derby.
Dist.: United

GLENN MILLER STORY, THE 1954
★ ★ ★ G Biography/Musical 1:56
Dir: Anthony Mann *Cast:* James Stewart, June Allyson, Charles Drake, George Tobias, Henry Morgan, Marion Ross
▶ Story of bandleader Glenn Miller from his rise to the top to his tragic death during World War II. Sweet Stewart/Allyson romance, lively big-band music, and good period settings spark this highly enjoyable biography. Songs include: "Pennsylvania 6-5000," "In the Mood," "Chattanooga Choo-Choo." Sound on video version is digitally reprogrammed for stereo.
Dist.: MCA

GLEN OR GLENDA 1953
☆ PG Drama 1:10 B&W
☑ Adult situations
Dir: Edward D. Wood, Jr. *Cast:* Bela Lugosi, Lyle Talbot, Daniel Davis, Dolores Fuller, Tommy Haynes, Timothy Farrell
▶ Straightfaced account of Davis's attempt to tell fiancée Fuller about his transvestism is acknowledged to be one of the world's worst movies. Delirious combination of "scientific" commentary, baffling stock footage, and Lugosi delivering curses from someone's basement make this an unintentional comic delight. Directing debut for Wood, who also stars under the pseudonym Daniel Davis. Among the many variant titles are *I Led Two Lives, He or She,* and *The Transvestite.*
Dist.: Video Yesteryear

GLITCH! 1988
☆ R Comedy 1:30
☑ Nudity, adult situations, explicit language
Dir: Nico Mastorakis *Cast:* Will Egan, Steve Donmyer, Julia Nickson, Dick Gautier
▶ Egan and Donmyer are a pair of lunkheads who hit the jackpot when they masquerade

as movie moguls and audition hundreds of bikini-clad hopefuls for a movie. Egan falls for actress indignant about sexism; Donmyer falls down and squeals a lot. When thugs come looking for the real moguls, the phony pair try to escape in ladies' duds. Fails to amuse even by the very low standards it sets for itself.
Dist.: Academy

GLITTER DOME, THE 1984
★ ★ NR Crime/MFTV 1:34
⊡ Nudity, adult situations, explicit language, violence
Dir: Stuart Margolin *Cast:* James Garner, Margot Kidder, John Lithgow, Colleen Dewhurst, Christianne Laughlin, John Marley
► Funny and shocking Hollywood panorama, adapted from Joseph Wambaugh's best-selling novel. Burned-out detectives Garner and Lithgow spearhead an investigation into the murder of a Tinseltown movie mogul, leading them through a maze of performers, bookies, dope dealers and users, prostitutes, rollerskaters, porn producers, and has-beens. With Kidder as a tough-talking movie star who falls for Garner.
Dist.: HBO

GLORIA 1980
★ ★ ★ PG Action-Adventure 2:01
⊡ Adult situations, explicit language, violence
Dir: John Cassavetes *Cast:* Gena Rowlands, Buck Henry, John Adames, Julie Carmen, Lupe Guarnica
► Rowlands was Oscar-nominated for her hard-boiled portrayal of a former gangster's moll with a heart of gold who rescues Adames, the son of her slain neighbor Henry, a Mafia money-counter. When Adames refuses to relinquish his dad's accounting book, Gloria turns gunslinger to keep them both from being killed. Bristling with near-misses, New York City chase scenes, sudden encounters, and shoot-outs; written and directed by Rowlands's husband, Cassavetes.
Dist.: RCA/Columbia

GLORY 1989
★ ★ ★ ★ ★ R War/Drama 2:02
⊡ Adult situations, graphic violence, explicit language
Dir: Edward Zwick *Cast:* Matthew Broderick, Denzel Washington, Cary Elwes, Morgan Freeman, Jhimi Kennedy, Andre Braugher
► Moving tribute to the Civil War's 54th Regiment, the nation's first all-black fighting unit. Led by young eastern liberal Broderick, the 54th found that their biggest hurdles were getting shoes and uniforms, receiving the same pay as white soldiers, and just being allowed to go into battle so they could prove their mettle. Authentically detailed and magnificently photographed, with some of the greatest battle scenes of any recent war film. Although sometimes maudlin, and with a

weak lead performance by Broderick, film is nevertheless an emotionally stirring and potent history lesson. Nominated for five Oscars, it won three, including Washington as Best Supporting Actor. (CC)
Dist.: RCA/Columbia

GLORY BOYS, THE 1984 British
☆ NR Action-Adventure 1:50
⊡ Adult situations, violence
Dir: Michael Ferguson *Cast:* Rod Steiger, Anthony Perkins, Joanna Lumley, Alfred Burke, Gary Brown, Aaron Harris
► In London, Arab terrorist Brown teams up with IRA assassin Harris in a plot to kill visiting Israeli physicist Steiger. Alcoholic security agent Perkins is assigned to protect the scientist from "The Glory Boys." Workmanlike plot, blandly written and directed.
Dist.: Prism

GLORY! GLORY! 1989
★ ★ ★ ★ NR Comedy/MFTV 3:30
⊡ Brief nudity, adult situations, explicit language
Dir: Lindsay Anderson *Cast:* Richard Thomas, Ellen Greene, James Whitmore, Barry Morse, Winston Reckert
► Mild-mannered evangelist Thomas takes over his father's TV ministry and tries to liven things up by hiring foul-mouthed rock singer Greene as musical entertainment. When Greene becomes a national sensation, a TV newsmagazine begins investigating the ministry's finances. Funny satire bites without taking the usual cheap shots at TV ministers. Greene is pure energy, but Whitmore steals the show as a worldly veteran of the gospel trail.
Dist.: Orion

GLOVE, THE 1980
★ R Action-Adventure 1:28
⊡ Explicit language, violence
Dir: Ross Hagen *Cast:* John Saxon, Rosey Grier, Jack Carter, Aldo Ray, Keenan Wynn, Joan Blondell
► Competent B-movie stars Saxon as an ex-ballplayer/bounty hunter who wants out of the business of tracking bad guys. First he must defeat vengeful escaped prisoner Grier and his notoriously dangerous steel glove that can maim, kill, and destroy just about anything. Action fans will devour the bruiser, he-man showdown.
Dist.: Media

GNOME-MOBILE, THE 1967
★ ★ ★ G Comedy 1:30
Dir: Robert Stevenson *Cast:* Walter Brennan, Tom Lowell, Matthew Garber, Ed Wynn, Karen Dotrice
► Marvelous Disney fantasy based on an Upton Sinclair novel features Brennan in a dual role as a curmudgeonly timber tycoon and a 943-year-old gnome who lives on the tycoon's land. Amusing plot climaxes in a wonderful car chase that frees the tycoon

from a mental institution and the gnome from a freak show. Wynn's last film.
Dist.: Buena Vista

GODDESS, THE 1958
★ ★ NR Drama 1:45 B&W
Dir: John Cromwell *Cast:* Kim Stanley, Lloyd Bridges, Patty Duke, Steven Hill, Betty Lou Holland, Joyce Van Patten
▶ First screenplay by Paddy Chayefsky (*Network*) portrays twenty years in the life of a voluptuous movie star not unlike Marilyn Monroe. Landmark performance by Stanley covers Depression-era adolescence in the squalor of a Southern slum town, two unhappy marriages (one to ex-boxing champ Bridges), rise to international stardom, and demise due to alcoholism and drug dependency.
Dist.: RCA/Columbia

GODFATHER, THE 1972
★ ★ ★ ★ ★ R Drama 2:55
☑ Adult situations, explicit language, violence
Dir: Francis Ford Coppola *Cast:* Marlon Brando, Al Pacino, James Caan, Robert Duvall, Richard Castellano, John Cazale, Diane Keaton, Talia Shire, Sterling Hayden, John Marley, Richard Conte, Abe Vigoda
▶ Story of the Corleones, fictionalized leaders of the Mafia empire, from the turn of the century to the 1950s. Emotion-packed epic with family theme focuses on changing relationship between Don Vito (Brando) and his sons: hot-tempered Sonny (Caan), weak Fredo (Cazale), and sensitive Michael (Pacino), who is drawn into the family biz despite his desire to live apart. A movie you can't refuse. Powerhouse cast led by the stunning Brando; wonderfully crafted filmmaking from Coppola. Oscars for Best Picture, Actor (Brando), Screenplay Adaptation.
Dist.: Paramount

GODFATHER, PART II, THE 1974
★ ★ ★ ★ R Drama 3:23
☑ Brief nudity, adult situations, explicit language, graphic violence
Dir: Francis Ford Coppola *Cast:* Al Pacino, Robert Duvall, Robert De Niro, Diane Keaton, Talia Shire, John Cazale, Lee Strasberg, Michael V. Gazzo, G. D. Spradlin, Joe Spinell, Harry Dean Stanton, Danny Aiello
▶ Follow-up to *The Godfather* projects the Mafia saga into the future and reveals its past. Michael Corleone (Pacino) extends the family empire into Nevada but pays an emotionally steep price by destroying his marriage. Young Don Vito Corleone (De Niro) flees turn-of-the-century Sicily and enters organized crime in Little Italy's immigrant ghetto. Double story line adds richness and texture to the saga and may even surpass the magnificent original. Won six Oscars: Best Picture, Director, Supporting Actor (De Niro), Screenplay Adaptation, Art Direction, and Score.
Dist.: Paramount

GODFATHER SAGA, THE 1977
★ ★ ★ ★ ★ NR Drama 7:30
☑ Adult situations, explicit language, violence
Dir: Francis Ford Coppola *Cast:* Marlon Brando, Al Pacino, Robert De Niro, Robert Duvall, James Caan, Diane Keaton, Talia Shire, John Cazale
▶ Television reediting combines *The Godfather* and *The Godfather, Part II* so story unfolds in chronological order. Includes scenes that didn't make the final cuts of the theatrical films. A genuine masterpiece, no matter how you slice it. **(CC)**
Dist.: Paramount

GOD'S LITTLE ACRE 1958
★ ★ PG Drama 1:50 B&W
☑ Adult situations
Dir: Anthony Mann *Cast:* Robert Ryan, Tina Louise, Aldo Ray, Buddy Hackett, Jack Lord, Vic Morrow
▶ Rural Georgia farmer Ryan and his sons Lord and Morrow obsessively search for gold on their land; son-in-law Ray goes into the mill business while Lord's wife Louise cheats on him. Adaptation of the Erskine Caldwell novel features convincing atmosphere and strong performances.
Dist.: Prism

GODS MUST BE CRAZY, THE 1984 South African
★ ★ ★ PG Comedy 1:49
☑ Brief nudity, explicit language, violence
Dir: Jamie Uys *Cast:* Marius Weyers, Sandra Prinsloo, Louw Verwey, Sam Boga, Nic De Jager, N!xau
▶ Sleeper hit is an oddball comedy adventure that begins when a pilot flying over the Kalahari desert tosses an empty Coke bottle into the midst of a tribe of bushmen who accept it as a gift from the gods. Slapstick fun also involves a clumsy microbiologist who studies animal manure, a beautiful journalist fleeing the city, bumbling Communist guerrillas, a vainglorious safari operator, and a fine supporting cast of giraffes, elephants and hippos. Uys does an ace job writing, directing, and producing with charm and perfect pitch. **(CC)**
Dist.: CBS/Fox

GODS MUST BE CRAZY II, THE 1990 South African
★ ★ ★ ★ PG Comedy 1:37
☑ Explicit language
Dir: Jamie Uys *Cast:* N!xau, Lena Ferugia, Hans Strydom, Eiros, Nadies, Erick Bowen
▶ In the Kalahari, bushman N!xau searches for his children after they hop on an ivory poacher's truck. He also rescues anthropologist Strydom, who has become separated from New Yorker Ferugia after a plane crash. Slapstick sequel is pleasant and good-humored, although not as inventive as its hugely

successful predecessor. The kids and animals are adorable. (CC)
Dist.: RCA/Columbia

GOD TOLD ME TO 1977
★ ★ R Horror 1:35
▣ Nudity, adult situations, explicit language
Dir: Larry Cohen *Cast:* Tony Lo Bianco, Sandy Dennis, Sylvia Sidney, Deborah Raffin
▶ New York City detective Lo Bianco investigates a string of murders with one common thread: the killers all claim God told them to do it. He uncovers a secret society and a cosmic war between the forces of good and evil. Combination of religion and violence may upset some but director Cohen delivers a surprisingly gripping and creepy film.
Dist.: Nelson

GODZILLA, KING OF THE MONSTERS 1956
Japanese
★ ★ NR Sci-Fi 1:20
Dir: Inoshiro Honda, Terry Morse *Cast:* Raymond Burr, Takashi Shimura, Momoko Kochi, Akira Takarada
▶ Nuclear test has unwanted side effect: gigantic creature Godzilla revives from hibernation. He attacks Tokyo, proving immune to weapons until a scientist figures out how to thwart him. Spawned many sequels but clearly the best of the series; creates a genuinely ominous mood. Dubbed.
Dist.: Vestron

GODZILLA 1985 1985 Japanese
★ PG Sci-Fi 1:31
▣ Explicit language, violence
Dir: Kohju Hashimoto *Cast:* Raymond Burr, Keiju Kobayashi, Ken Tanaka, Yasuko Sawaguchi, Shin Takuma
▶ Cheapo sequel to the 1956 exploitation hit. Basically the same plot: fire-snorting Godzilla awakes from ocean deep to come ashore and trample Tokyo. Burr, who played a reporter in the original, returns as a Godzilla expert. It's sayonara sucker when the not-so-jolly green giant is lured into a volcano. Cheesylooking and badly dubbed but fun for the small screen.
Dist.: New World

GODZILLA VS. MOTHRA 1964 Japanese
★ ★ NR Sci-Fi 1:30
Dir: Inoshiro Honda *Cast:* Akira Takarada, Yuriko Hoshi, Hiroshi Koizumi, Emi Ito, Yumi Ito
▶ Giant fir-breathing monster Godzilla attacks humanity once again; little twin mutant sisters Ito and Ito convince humongous moth Mothra to battle Godzilla. Plenty of destruction and special effects fireworks. Also known as *Godzilla vs. the Thing*. Dubbed.
Dist.: Paramount

GODZILLA VS. THE SMOG MONSTER 1972
Japanese
☆ G Sci-Fi 1:25
Dir: Yoshimitsu Banno *Cast:* Akira Yamau-

chi, Hiroyuki Kawase, Toshie Kimura, Toshio Shibaki
▶ Long before today's Hollywood stars dreamed of celebrating Earth Day, Japan's King of Monsters showed his environmental consciousness by fighting a giant creature made out of pollution who menaces his country. Scientist Yamauchi helps Godzilla save the planet. Dubbed.
Dist.: Orion

GOING APE! 1981
★ ★ ★ PG Comedy 1:27
▣ Adult situations, explicit language
Dir: Jeremy Joe Kronsberg *Cast:* Tony Danza, Jessica Walter, Stacey Nelkin, Danny DeVito, Art Metrano
▶ If Danza can take care of his late father's beer-swilling orangutans for five years, he'll inherit five million bucks. Hitmen go after one of the apes, but Danza, girlfriend Walter, and their hairy charges triumph. DeVito plays his usual demented character, giving the scenestealing primates their only competition. Pretty bad; not even up to the Bonzo films.
Dist.: Paramount

GOING BANANAS 1988
★ ★ PG Comedy 1:33
▣ Explicit language
Dir: Boaz Davidson *Cast:* Dom DeLuise, Jimmie C. Walker, David Mendenhall, Warren Berlinger, Herbert Lom
▶ On an African safari, young Mendenhall befriends a talking chimp who's been chosen for the circus by corrupt policeman Lom. Highstrung custodian DeLuise and native guide Walker pose as clowns to free the ape. Harmless nonsense filled with good-natured slapstick will amuse younger viewers. (CC)
Dist.: Media

GOING HOLLYWOOD: THE WAR YEARS 1989
★ ★ ★ ★ ★ NR Documentary 1:16 C/B&W
▣ Adult situations, mild violence
Dir: Julian Schlossberg *Cast:* Van Johnson, Douglas Fairbanks, Jr., Joan Leslie, Roddy McDowall, Tony Randall, Sylvia Sidney
▶ Van Johnson is the personable host of this examination of Hollywood's part in perking up the nation during World War II. Clips from period films (like *Thirty Seconds Over Tokyo* and *Sahara*) are interspersed with comments from stars from the time; pin-up girls and homefront activities are also covered. Entertaining and enlightening.
Dist.: Warner

GOING IN STYLE 1979
★ ★ ★ ★ ★ PG Comedy 1:38
▣ Explicit language
Dir: Martin Brest *Cast:* George Burns, Art Carney, Lee Strasberg, Charles Hallahan, Pamela Payton-Wright
▶ Inspired casting: Burns, Carney and Strasberg as retired 70-year-olds who share an apartment in Queens, a park bench and an

uneventful, atrophied life. Then Burns convinces the others to rob a Manhattan bank. Tender, contemplative study of gallantry and last stands from writer/director Brest.
Dist.: Warner

GOING MY WAY 1944
★★★★ NR Drama 2:06 B&W
Dir: Leo McCarey ***Cast:*** Bing Crosby, Barry Fitzgerald, Rise Stevens, Frank McHugh, Gene Lockhart, William Frawley
► Moving account of the relationship between Fitzgerald, crusty pastor of a run-down church, and Crosby, the cocky young priest who revives the parish's fortunes. Though often skirting the maudlin, direction by Oscar-winning McCarey (who copped another Oscar for Best Original Story) is too emotional and polished to resist. Grand entertainment also won Oscars for Crosby, Fitzgerald, Best Picture, Screenplay, and "Swinging on a Star." Crosby's rendition of "Too-ra-loo-ra-loo-ral" is one of the highlights of his career. Sequel: *The Bells of St. Mary's.*
Dist.: MCA

GOING PLACES 1974 French
★★★ R Comedy 1:24
☑ Rape, nudity, strong sexual content, adult situations, explicit language
Dir: Bertrand Blier ***Cast:*** Gerard Depardieu, Patrick Dewaere, Miou-Miou, Jeanne Moreau, Brigitte Fossey
► Outlaws Depardieu and Dewaere roam around France, stealing and pillaging. They pursue several women, including beautician Miou-Miou, convict Moreau, and mom Fossey. Controversial sex comedy from French director Blier pleased some critics but outraged many others. [S]
Dist.: RCA/Columbia

GOING UNDERCOVER 1988
★ PG-13 Comedy 1:22
☑ Adult situations, explicit language, violence
Dir: James Kenelm Clarke ***Cast:*** Chris Lemmon, Jean Simmons, Lea Thompson, Mills Waterson
► The wife of a meteorology professor pulls the name of private eye Lemmon from a phone book and has him follow spoiled stepdaughter Thompson around Europe. Brat leads Lemmon on a merry chase that becomes earnest when she is kidnapped and Lemmon must save her. Humor is forced throughout, and some may find casual drug jokes offensive. Also known as *Yellow Pages.*
Dist.: Vidmark

GOIN' SOUTH 1978
★★★ PG Comedy 1:48
☑ Adult situations, adult humor
Dir: Jack Nicholson ***Cast:*** Jack Nicholson, Mary Steenburgen, Christopher Lloyd, John Belushi, Veronica Cartwright, Danny DeVito
► Shaggy horse-thief Nicholson is saved from the gallows by beautiful widow Steenburgen, who invokes a frontier law allowing her to marry him. Nicholson attacks his role with relish in this offbeat, amusing Western comedy. Film debuts for Steenburgen and Belushi, who has a small role as a Mexican bandit.
Dist.: Paramount

GO, JOHNNY, GO! 1958
★★ NR Musical 1:15 B&W
Dir: Paul Landres ***Cast:*** Jimmy Clanton, Alan Freed, Sandy Stewart, Jo-Ann Campbell, Chuck Berry, Eddie Cochran, Jackie Wilson, Ritchie Valens
► Deejay Freed turns orphan Clanton into a national rock 'n' roll sensation. Like many other rock movies of the fifties, this has its share of camp laughs and insincere performances. But there's nothing camp about the work by Berry ("Little Queenie," "Johnny B. Goode"), Cochran ("Teenage Heaven"), and especially Wilson ("You'd Better Know It")—who fairly leaps off the screen. Sole screen appearance of Valens ("La Bamba"), who died in a plane crash before the film was released.
Dist.: Video Treasures

GOLD DIGGERS OF 1933 1933
★★★ G Musical 1:36 B&W
Dir: Mervyn LeRoy ***Cast:*** Warren William, Joan Blondell, Aline MacMahon, Ruby Keeler, Dick Powell, Ginger Rogers, Guy Kibbee
► Blockbuster musical combines laughs, romance, and outrageous Busby Berkeley numbers into a very satisfying entertainment. Songwriter Powell foots the bill for a new show, scandalizing his blueblood brother William; chorines Blondell, MacMahon, and Keeler team up to save the day. Surprisingly racy; highlighted by Rogers's pig Latin version of "We're in the Money."
Dist.: MGM/UA

GOLD DIGGERS OF 1935 1935
★★ NR Musical 1:35 B&W
Dir: Busby Berkeley ***Cast:*** Dick Powell, Adolphe Menjou, Gloria Stuart, Alice Brady, Glenda Farell, Winifred Shaw
► Medical student Powell is the desk clerk at quick-tempered Menjou's New England resort. When the staff decides to stage a show for charity, it turns out to be among the most eye-poppingly great set of musical numbers ever put on celluloid. Director Berkeley gives this film what may be his greatest achievement: the Oscar-winning "Lullaby of Broadway" sequence, as well as numerous other fine production numbers.
Dist.: MGM/UA

GOLDEN BOY 1939
★★ NR Drama/Sports 1:41 B&W
Dir: Rouben Mamoulian ***Cast:*** Barbara Stanwyck, Adolphe Menjou, William Holden, Lee J. Cobb, Joseph Calleia, Sam Levene
► Archetypal boxing drama made Holden a star as a violinist who turns to fighting to help his immigrant father Cobb. Stanwyck is re-

strained and believable as the woman who corrupts Holden's dreams. Fight scenes are expertly staged, but film version softens the ending of Clifford Odets's hit play.
Dist.: RCA/Columbia

GOLDEN CHILD, THE 1986
★ ★ ★ **PG-13 Action-Adventure 1:34**
☑ Explicit language, violence
Dir: Michael Ritchie *Cast:* Eddie Murphy, Charlotte Lewis, Charles Dance, Victor Wong, J. L. Reate
▶ Murphy is hired to locate Reate, a Tibetan child with magical powers kidnapped by equally endowed bad guy Dance. Elaborate special effects in an often illogical plot combine *Beverly Hills Cop* "fish out of water" formula with Indiana Jones–style adventure. Wisecracking Eddie, with help from villainous Dance and voluptuous Lewis, is the main attraction. **(CC)**
Dist.: Paramount

GOLDENGIRL 1979
★ ★ ★ ★ **PG Drama 1:45**
☑ Adult situations, explicit language
Dir: Joseph Sargent *Cast:* Susan Anton, James Coburn, Leslie Caron, Robert Culp, Harry Guardino, Curt Jurgens
▶ Neo-Nazi doctor Jurgens experiments on adopted daughter Anton to create a Super Sprinter programmed to win three gold medals at the Moscow Olympics. Coburn is the girl's shrewd sports agent and Caron, her live-in behavioral psychologist. Plot is predictable but fans of tall, leggy blonds may not notice.
Dist.: Nelson

GOLDEN NEEDLES 1974
★ ★ **PG Action-Adventure 1:28**
☑ Violence
Dir: Robert Clouse *Cast:* Joe Don Baker, Elizabeth Ashley, Jim Kelly, Burgess Meredith, Ann Sothern
▶ Yanks Baker and Ashley, evil millionaire Meredith, and Hong Kong gangster vie for possession of a gold figurine with magic healing powers. Director Clouse gets maximum mileage from camp *Maltese Falcon* clone through zippy pacing and constant barrage of brawls and chases. Baker and Ashley are no Bogart and Astor but they get by on tongue-in-cheek vigor.
Dist.: HBO

GOLDEN RENDEZVOUS 1977
★ ★ ★ **NR Mystery-Suspense 1:42**
☑ Violence
Dir: Ashley Lazarus *Cast:* Richard Harris, Ann Turkel, David Janssen, Burgess Meredith, John Vernon
▶ Caribbean-bound casino/cargo ship is seized by terrorists who plant a nuclear device on board. Their aim: to extort bullion from nearby U.S. Treasury ship. Their foe: gallant First Officer Harris. Lively action flick marred by awkward scripting and gorgeous Turkel's stiff performance. Adapted from Alistair MacLean's novel.
Dist.: Vestron

GOLDEN SEAL, THE 1983
★ ★ ★ ★ **PG Action-Adventure 1:35**
☑ Explicit language, mild violence
Dir: Frank Zuniga *Cast:* Steve Railsback, Michael Beck, Penelope Milford, Torquil Campbell, Seth Sakai
▶ According to legend, a golden seal will appear someday to teach man to live in harmony with nature. Youngster Campbell happens upon the mystical animal while it's giving birth. Friendship blooms and the kid must protect his animal pal from greedy adults. The seal and the spectacular Aleutian Island settings steal the story from the adult cast members.
Dist.: Embassy

GOLDEN VOYAGE OF SINBAD, THE 1974 British
★ ★ ★ **G Fantasy 1:45**
Dir: Gordon Hessler *Cast:* John Phillip Law, Caroline Munro, Tom Baker, Douglas Wilmer, Gregoire Aslan, John Garfield, Jr.
▶ Sinbad (Law) rescues beautiful Munro and battles monsters and villainous Baker (of "Dr. Who" fame) while seeking treasure. Entertaining adventure for children features special effects whiz Ray Harryhausen's clever creatures and beasties. **(CC)**
Dist.: RCA/Columbia

GOLDFINGER 1964 British
★ ★ ★ ★ ★ **PG Espionage/Action-Adventure 1:52**
Dir: Guy Hamilton *Cast:* Sean Connery, Gert Frobe, Honor Blackman, Shirley Eaton, Harold Sakata
▶ It's secret agent James Bond (Connery) to the rescue when archvillain Goldfinger (Frobe) tries to rob Fort Knox. Along the way, 007 tumbles with Goldfinger's sexy pilot Pussy Galore (Blackman) and tackles his menacing Korean bodyguard, the derby-throwing Oddjob (Sakata). Quintessential Bond is pedal-to-the-metal entertainment; great gadgets (including Bond's Aston Martin with the ejector seat,) fine Connery, and flip dialogue: "Do you expect me to talk, Goldfinger?" "No, Mr. Bond, I expect you to die!" **(CC)**
Dist.: MGM/UA

GOLD RUSH, THE 1925
★ ★ ★ ★ **NR Comedy 1:12 B&W**
Dir: Charlie Chaplin *Cast:* Charlie Chaplin, Georgia Hale, Mack Swain, Tom Murray
▶ The Little Tramp (Chaplin) prospects during the Klondike Gold Rush. He struggles with starvation (especially in the famous Thanksgiving Day shoe dinner), tangles with a menacing prospector, and has a bittersweet relationship with dance hall girl Hale. Chaplin classic is moving, full of memorable visuals, and funny; deservedly one of his best-loved works.
Dist.: Various

GOLDWYN FOLLIES, THE 1938
★ NR Musical 2:00
Dir: George Marshall **Cast:** Adolphe Menjou, Andrea Leeds, Kenny Baker, The Ritz Brothers, Zorina, Edgar Bergen
▶ Producer Menjou hires simple country girl Leeds to advise him on how to add "humanity" to his films. Premise unleashes tepid romance, unfunny sketch comedy, and a solemnly "artistic" George Balanchine dance sequence. Relentlessly middlebrow color extravaganza is worth seeing for Baker's unsurpassable rendering of Gershwin's "Love Walked In."
Dist.: Nelson

GONE IN 60 SECONDS 1974
★ PG Action-Adventure 1:43
☑ Explicit language, mild violence
Dir: H. B. Halicki **Cast:** H. B. Halicki, Marion Busia, Jerry Augirda, James McIntire
▶ Family car-theft ring has only five days to deliver forty-eight stolen cars to dock for South American clients. Auto-snatchers drive fast and furious, eluding fleet of cop cars in long, long chase sequence. Film will be hit with those who are amused by movement alone, no characters, no drama.
Dist.: Media

GONE WITH THE WIND 1939
★ ★ ★ ★ ★ G Drama 3:42
Dir: Victor Fleming **Cast:** Clark Gable, Vivien Leigh, Olivia de Havilland, Leslie Howard, Hattie McDaniel, Butterfly McQueen, Thomas Mitchell, Barbara O'Neil, Victor Jory, Laura Hope Crews, Ann Rutherford, Evelyn Keyes
▶ Hollywood moviemaking at its zenith. Margaret Mitchell's Civil War saga was perfectly realized under the guidance of producer David O. Selznick and four different directors. Now part of history: the search for Scarlett, the burning of Atlanta scene, the green dress made from Miss Ellen's portieres, Rhett's tears, Prissy "birthing" Miss Mellie's baby, and Mammy's red petticoat. Perhaps the greatest love story ever told, even though Rhett didn't give a damn. Oscars for Leigh, McDaniel (the first black ever to win), Best Picture, Director, Screenplay, Cinematography, Interior Decoration, and Editing. Restored for its fiftieth anniversary. **(CC)**
Dist.: MGM/UA

GOODBYE, COLUMBUS 1969
★ ★ ★ PG Comedy 1:45
☑ Brief nudity, adult situations, explicit language
Dir: Larry Peerce **Cast:** Richard Benjamin, Ali MacGraw, Jack Klugman, Nan Martin, Michael Meyers
▶ Poor librarian Benjamin falls for pampered Jewish-American Princess MacGraw. Her dad Klugman prods him to be more ambitious. The lovers' relationship eventually hits a snag when she goes off to college. Satiric look at life

in well-heeled suburbia from Philip Roth's acclaimed novel.
Dist.: Paramount

GOODBYE EMMANUELLE 1978 French
★ R Sex 1:38
☑ Strong sexual content, nudity, adult situations, explicit language
Dir: François Leterrier **Cast:** Sylvia Kristel, Umberto Orsini, Alexandra Stewart, Jean-Pierre Bouvier
▶ Beautiful Emmanuelle (Kristel) lives on the Seychelles Islands with her hubby. He openly fools around but proves less than tolerant when she has a fling with a handsome Frenchman. Lovely scenery, nice color, shapely bodies, but too much talk between the too-few sex scenes.
Dist.: HBO

GOODBYE GIRL, THE 1977
★ ★ ★ ★ ★ PG Comedy 1:51
☑ Explicit language
Dir: Herbert Ross **Cast:** Richard Dreyfuss, Marsha Mason, Quinn Cummings, Barbara Rhodes, Nicol Williamson
▶ Jilted by her live-in lover, hard-luck ex-dancer Mason and precocious ten-year-old daughter Cummings must adjust to weird new roommate Dreyfuss. After hating each other on sight, the leads trade insults, wisecracks, misunderstandings and outrage—and then fall in love. Crackling original screenplay by Neil Simon (written for then-wife Mason) helped Dreyfuss win an Oscar as Elliot Garfield, an actor forced to play Richard III in full drag. One of the top-grossing films of 1978; six Oscar nominations.
Dist.: MGM/UA

GOODBYE, MR. CHIPS 1939
★ ★ ★ ★ NR Drama 1:54 B&W
Dir: Sam Wood **Cast:** Robert Donat, Greer Garson, Paul von Henreid, Terry Kilburn, John Mills
▶ Shy, rigid schoolmaster Donat marries beautiful free spirit Garson, whom he meets on vacation. She brings out his gentler side and he becomes a much beloved teacher. Donat's tremendous performance beat out Clark Gable's Rhett Butler for the Oscar. Classic tearjerker is heartwarming and heartwrenching, particularly when Donat insists on teaching his class despite a personal tragedy. **(CC)**
Dist.: MGM/UA

GOODBYE, MY LADY 1956
★ ★ ★ NR Family 1:34
Dir: William Wellman **Cast:** Walter Brennan, Phil Harris, Brandon de Wilde, Sidney Poitier, William Hopper, Louise Beavers
▶ Mississippi orphan de Wilde, who lives with uncle Brennan, adopts stray pup Lady. A warm boy/dog relationship forms but the lad is faced with a dilemma when the real owners seek their lost pet. Timeless family classic, win-

ningly performed and directed. Based on the novel by James Street.
Dist.: Warner

GOODBYE, NEW YORK 1985 U.S./Israeli
★ **R Comedy 1:31**
☑ Adult situations, explicit language
Dir: Amos Kollek *Cast:* Julie Hagerty, Amos Kollek, David Topaz, Aviva Ger, Shmuel Shiloh
▶ Fed up with her job and her unfaithful husband, pampered New Yorker Hagerty impulsively flies to Paris but overdoses on Valium and ends up in Israel minus luggage and money. She's befriended by soldier Kollek while adjusting to life in the Holy Land. Humor alternates between sophisticated cultureclash jabs and cornball slapstick. Technically crude but charming.
Dist.: Vestron

GOODBYE, NORMA JEAN 1976
★ **R Drama 1:35**
☑ Rape, nudity, explicit language
Dir: Larry Buchanan *Cast:* Misty Rowe, Terence Locke, Patch Mackenzie, Preston Hanson
▶ Norma Jean Baker (Rowe), a.k.a. Marilyn Monroe, rises from orphan to Hollywood stardom. Along the way, she is raped twice, molested several times, attempts suicide, experiences terrifying visions, and has affairs with men and women. More fiction than fact in this low-budget sexploitation flick.
Dist.: HBO

GOODBYE PEOPLE, THE 1984
★★ **PG Drama 1:44**
☑ Explicit language
Dir: Herb Gardner *Cast:* Judd Hirsch, Martin Balsam, Pamela Reed, Ron Silver, Gene Saks, Michael Tucker
▶ Forty-something Hirsch, unhappy with his life and job, goes to Coney Island to observe the sunrise and gets caught up in elderly Balsam's dream of reviving his hot dog stand. Gardner adapted his Broadway play too faithfully; the self-conscious script is extremely talky, though a good cast tries hard to please. (CC)
Dist.: Nelson

GOODBYE PORK PIE 1981 New Zealand
★ **R Comedy 1:45**
☑ Explicit language
Dir: Geoff Murphy *Cast:* Tony Barry, Shirley Gruar, Kelly Johnson, Claire Oberman
▶ Road comedy about juvenile delinquent Johnson who steals a rental car and picks up ditzy Oberman and abandoned lover Barry. Together they become fugitives, pursuing a cross-country career in petty larceny that—as in so many films since *Bonnie and Clyde*—captures the heart of the nation. "Small" film from small country is engaging and unpretentious.
Dist.: Nelson

GOOD EARTH, THE 1937
★★★★ **NR Drama 2:18 B&W**
Dir: Sidney Franklin *Cast:* Paul Muni, Luise Rainer, Walter Connolly, Tilly Losch, Charley Grapewin, Jessie Ralph
▶ Vivid drama about Chinese peasant Muni fighting backbreaking poverty with wife Rainer. Their farm ruined by drought, Rainer is later swept up in a massive revolution. Newfound wealth corrupts Muni, who faces further tragedy from a plague of locusts. Meticulous adaptation of Pearl S. Buck's prize-winning novel highlighted by superb special effects and Karl Freund's Oscar-winning photography. Rainer received her second consecutive Oscar (after *The Great Ziegfeld*). Last film overseen by noted producer Irving G. Thalberg.
Dist.: MGM/UA

GOOD FATHER, THE 1987 British
★ **R Drama 1:30**
☑ Brief nudity, adult situations, explicit language
Dir: Mike Newell *Cast:* Anthony Hopkins, Jim Broadbent, Harriet Walter, Fanny Viner, Simon Callow, Joanne Whalley
▶ Bitter divorcé Hopkins befriends teacher Broadbent, whose marriage is also on the rocks. When his buddy's wife Viner plans to take the couple's son and move to Australia with her lesbian lover, Hopkins makes it a personal crusade to fight her. Uncompromising and well acted, but fuzzy camerawork, poor sound recording, and generally sour tone. (CC)
Dist.: CBS/Fox

GOOD GUYS WEAR BLACK 1979
★★★ **PG Martial Arts 1:36**
☑ Violence, explicit language
Dir: Ted Post *Cast:* Chuck Norris, Anne Archer, James Franciscus, Lloyd Haynes, Dana Andrews
▶ Fast and furious kung fu stunts highlight this hard-hitting, efficient action-adventure. Corrupt politician Franciscus betrays special U.S. unit led by Norris to the Vietcong. Norris and some others survive but Franciscus takes another shot at them in the States. Plausible story is given realistic treatment.
Dist.: Vestron

GOOD MORNING, BABYLON 1987 Italian
★ **PG-13 Drama 1:58**
☑ Nudity, adult situations
Dir: Paolo Taviani, Vittorio Taviani *Cast:* Vincent Spano, Joaquim de Almeida, Greta Scacchi, Desiree Becker, Omero Antonutti, Charles Dance
▶ Brothers Spano and de Almeida, down-on-their-luck Italian craftsmen, set out for America. They reach Hollywood and are hired by the great film director D. W. Griffith (Dance) to help build the sets for his epic *Intolerance*, but tragedy mars their stab at the American

Dream. Picturesque production but not very convincing plotting.
Dist.: Vestron

GOOD MORNING, VIETNAM 1987
★ ★ ★ ★ R Comedy/Drama 2:00
☑ Adult situations, explicit language
Dir: Barry Levinson *Cast:* Robin Williams, Forest Whitaker, Tung Thanh Tran, Chintara Sukapatana, Bruno Kirby, Robert Wuhl
▶ Fictionalized version of real-life disc jockey Adrian Cronauer's (Williams) Vietnam years during which he delighted U.S. troops and outraged his stuffy superiors with his hysterical brand of iconoclastic patter. Hugely popular comedy/drama. A couple of less-than-stellar dramatic subplots include Williams's romance with a Vietnamese girl and his friendship with her brother, but the film comes joyously alive whenever Williams is in the booth. Williams received an Oscar nomination. **(CC)**
Dist.: Buena Vista

GOOD MOTHER, THE 1988
★ ★ ★ R Drama 1:44
☑ Nudity, adult situations, explicit language
Dir: Leonard Nimoy *Cast:* Diane Keaton, Liam Neeson, Teresa Wright, Ralph Bellamy, Jason Robards, Jr., James Naughton
▶ Divorced mother Keaton's only passion in life is her beloved daughter; then sculptor Neeson unleashes her pent-up sexuality. Keaton seems to be having it all, until ex-husband Naughton asserts that her sex life has been a bad influence on their daughter and sues for custody. Emotionally charged drama with controversial moral. Based on Sue Miller's best-selling novel.
Dist.: Buena Vista

GOOD NEIGHBOR SAM 1964
★ ★ ★ NR Comedy 2:10
Dir: David Swift *Cast:* Jack Lemmon, Romy Schneider, Edward G. Robinson, Dorothy Provine, Mike Connors, Anne Seymour
▶ Ad exec Lemmon wins account from ultra-wholesome dairy magnate Robinson, then agrees to impersonate neighbor Schneider's husband so she can collect an inheritance. The plan backfires when Robinson decides to promote the couple in his ads. Winning comedy with a good performance by Lemmon as an innocent trapped in escalating disasters.
Dist.: RCA/Columbia

GOOD NEWS 1947
★ ★ ★ NR Musical 1:33
Dir: Charles Walters *Cast:* June Allyson, Peter Lawford, Patricia Marshall, Joan McCracken, Ray McDonald, Mel Torme
▶ Giddy, lavish, 1920s musical: Lawford is a football star tutored by librarian Allyson so he can play in the big game; Marshall is Allyson's glamorous rival. Fun score highlighted by "Varsity Drag" and the Oscar-nominated "Pass the Peace Pipe."
Dist.: MGM/UA

GOOD SAM 1948
★ ★ NR Comedy 1:56 B&W
Dir: Leo McCarey *Cast:* Gary Cooper, Ann Sheridan, Ray Collins, Edmund Lowe, Joan Lorring, Clinton Sundberg
▶ Department store manager Cooper can't resist helping other people, a virtue that almost ruins his life when he tries to prevent a clerk from committing suicide. Disappointing satirical comedy never catches fire, although Sheridan is droll as Cooper's wife.
Dist.: Republic

GOOD, THE BAD, AND THE UGLY, THE
1967 Italian/Spanish
★ ★ ★ NR Western 2:41
☑ Adult situations, violence
Dir: Sergio Leone *Cast:* Clint Eastwood, Eli Wallach, Lee Van Cleef, Aldo Giuffre, Chelo Alonso, Mario Brega
▶ Stunning climax to Leone's "Dollars" trilogy finds bounty hunter Eastwood, crook Wallach, and Army sergeant Van Cleef all scrambling for a fortune in gold hidden in a coffin. The Civil War, shown in sweeping detail, has an increasingly violent impact on their uneasy alliance. Sequel to *For a Few Dollars More* is among the best of all spaghetti Westerns. Highly influential score by Ennio Morricone.
Dist.: MGM/UA

GOOD TO GO 1986
☆ R Drama 1:27
☑ Rape, explicit language, violence
Dir: Blaine Novak *Cast:* Art Garfunkel, Robert DoQui, Harris Yulin, Reginald Daughtry, Hattie Winston
▶ Garfunkel is a reporter with a drinking problem who gets involved in the rape of an off-duty nurse by a young gang. Fingers are pointing at a disco specializing in go-go music, and the club owner is furious. Garfunkel character is remote, and relentless music track will torture all but fans of Redds & the Boys, Trouble Funk, Chuck Brown & the Soul Searchers, and other featured go-go groups. Also known as *Short Fuse.*
Dist.: Vidmark

GOOD WIFE, THE 1987 Australian
★ R Drama 1:37
☑ Brief nudity, adult situations, explicit language
Dir: Ken Cameron *Cast:* Rachel Ward, Bryan Brown, Sam Neill, Steven Vidler, Jennifer Claire
▶ In 1939 New South Wales, Ward, unhappily married to crude lumberjack Brown (Ward's real-life husband), has a brief affair with brother-in-law Vidler and then develops an unrequited passion for bartender Neill. Beautifully shot period piece engages the eyes but not the mind; the plot gets increasingly contrived in the second half.
Dist.: Paramount

GOONIES, THE 1985
★ ★ ★ ★ PG Fantasy 1:54

☑ Explicit language, violence
Dir: Richard Donner   *Cast:* Sean Astin, Josh Brolin, Corey Feldman, Martha Plimpton, Ke Huy Quan, John Matuszak, Anne Ramsey, Joe Pantoliano
▶ Spielberg-produced fantasy about a group of overimaginative pre-teens in an Oregon coastal town who find a pirate map and search for the buried treasure. They must grab the loot before mean Mama Fratelli (Ramsey) and her brood close in. Brisk caper gives kid cast opportunity to exude warmth and personality while providing roller-coaster thrills. (CC)
Dist.: Warner

GORDON'S WAR 1973
★ R Action-Adventure 1:30
☑ Explicit language, graphic violence
Dir: Ossie Davis   *Cast:* Paul Winfield, Carl Lee, David Downing, Tony King, Gilbert Lewis, Grace Jones
▶ Vietnam veteran Winfield returns home to Harlem and discovers that his wife has died from a drug overdose. He goes to war once more, gathering army buddies Lee, Downing, and King for an all-out assault on pushers and pimps. Black vigilante flick a cut above usual exploitation fare of the period, thanks to Davis's hard-driving direction and Winfield's sturdy presence.
Dist.: CBS/Fox

GORGO 1961 British
★★ NR Horror 1:18
Dir: Eugene Lourie   *Cast:* Bill Travers, William Sylvester, Vincent Winter, Bruce Seton, Joseph O'Conor, Howard Lang
▶ A sixty-five-foot monster is captured off the coast of England and put on display in a carnival-like setting in London. A little boy who shares a strange link with the beast watches as its mother (who is three times as large) comes to its rescue, destroying London in the process. Superior in concept and special effects to *Godzilla* and other films of this genre. Models of well-known London buildings are particularly well done.
Dist.: United

GORGON, THE 1964 British
★ NR Horror 1:23
Dir: Terence Fisher   *Cast:* Peter Cushing, Christopher Lee, Richard Pasco, Barbara Shelly, Michael Goodliffe
▶ People are being murdered and turned to stone in a small German village. Brain surgeon Cushing and professor Lee discover that the town is haunted by the spirit of Medusa's sister, who has possessed Cushing's assistant and given her a killing glance. Villainess has nice serpentine coiffure, and suspense builds amid dank and solemn atmosphere.
Dist.: RCA/Columbia

GORILLA, THE 1939
★ NR Comedy 1:06 B&W

Dir: Alan Dwan   *Cast:* Jimmy Ritz, Harry Ritz, Al Ritz, Anita Louise, Patsy Kelly, Bela Lugosi
▶ The Ritz Brothers are slapstick detectives hired to stake out a spooky mansion where a murderer in a gorilla suit is supposedly at large. Complicating matters is a real gorilla, recently escaped from a traveling circus. The Ritz Brothers try hard but aren't very funny in this third remake of the Ralph Spence play.
Dist.: Video Dimensions

GORILLAS IN THE MIST 1988
★★★★★ PG-13 Biography 2:05
☑ Adult situations, explicit language, violence
Dir: Michael Apted   *Cast:* Sigourney Weaver, Bryan Brown, John Omirah Miluwi, Julie Harris, Iain Cuthbertson
▶ Fascinating true story of anthropologist Dian Fossey (Weaver), who studied the mountain gorillas of Africa and helped save them from extinction. She has an affair with photographer Brown, but her real love is the animals; she protects them from poachers to the point of obsession. Heartfelt production dominated by Weaver's mesmerizing performance; her relationship with the amazing apes has many stirring moments. Wonderful support by Miluwi, exotic African locations. Film received five Oscar nominations, including Weaver as Best Actress.
Dist.: MCA

GORKY PARK 1983
★★★★ R Mystery-Suspense 2:08
☑ Nudity, adult situations, explicit language, graphic violence
Dir: Michael Apted   *Cast:* William Hurt, Lee Marvin, Brian Dennehy, Joanna Pacula, Ian Bannen
▶ When three mutilated bodies are found in Moscow's Gorky Park, Russian inspector Hurt investigates a diverse group of suspects: American fur trader Marvin, New York cop Dennehy, and beautiful dissident Pacula with whom Hurt falls in love. Convoluted but atmospheric mystery with an unusual premise adapted from Martin Cruz Smith's best-seller. Solid work from Hurt.
Dist.: Vestron

GORP 1980
★★ R Comedy 1:30
☑ Brief nudity, adult situations, explicit language
Dir: Joseph Ruben   *Cast:* Michael Lembeck, Dennis Quaid, Phillip Casnoff, Fran Drescher, David Huddleston, Rosanna Arquette
▶ Summer-camp waiters Lembeck and Casnoff have a penchant for pranks: showing porno films on Parents' Day, spiking food with speed, sneaking into the girls' dorm dressed as werewolves, upsetting camp owner Huddleston no end. Wild, vulgar little movie plays like a cross between *Animal House* and *Meatballs.*
Dist.: HBO

GOSPEL 1982
★ ★ ★ ★ **G Documentary/Music 1:29**
Dir: David Leivick, Frederick A. Ritzenberg
Cast: James Cleveland, Walter Hawkins, Mighty Clouds of Joy, Shirley Caesar
▶ A series of gospel acts performed on stage before a *very* live, often frenzied audience, some of whom had to be carried out. High-energy concert works up quite a sweat. All music, no commentary. Performers are terrific; expect plenty of shouting.
Dist.: Monterey

GOSPEL ACCORDING TO ST. MATTHEW, THE 1966 Italian/French
☆ **NR Drama 2:15**
Dir: Pier Paolo Pasolini *Cast:* Enrique Irazoqui, Margherita Caruso, Susanna Pasolini, Marcello Morante
▶ Stark corrective to overblown biblical epics, Pasolini's austere reading of single evangelist stresses simple humanity of divine subject. Settings are stark, and nonprofessional cast, which includes Pasolini's mother, appears to be chosen for faces and figures which suggest Renaissance paintings. No leap of faith is necessary to enjoy this aesthetically powerful film.
Dist.: Various

GOSPEL ACCORDING TO VIC 1986 Scottish
★ ★ ★ **PG-13 Comedy/Drama 1:27**
☑ Adult situations, explicit language
Dir: Charles Gormley *Cast:* Tom Conti, Helen Mirren, David Hayman, Brian Pettifer, Jennifer Black
▶ In Glasgow, Conti, a teacher of remedial students, achieves notoriety when he finds he can work miracles. Slightly off-kilter story told with sincerity and blessed with Conti's quirky and captivating antihero. Talky script and wry humor may be too low-key for some viewers. Also known as *Heavenly Pursuits.* **(CC)**
Dist.: CBS/Fox

GOTCHA! 1985
★ ★ ★ ★ **PG-13 Comedy 1:41**
☑ Brief nudity, adult situations, explicit language, violence
Dir: Jeff Kanew *Cast:* Anthony Edwards, Linda Fiorentino, Nick Corri, Klaus Lowitsch, Alex Rocco
▶ UCLA student Edwards excels at mock assassination game called "Gotcha," then finds himself in real-life danger when he gets involved with sexy Fiorentino in Europe. Personable hero, attractive leading lady, and impressive location scenery (Paris, East Berlin). Lots of easy laughs. **(CC)**
Dist.: MCA

GO TELL THE SPARTANS 1978
★ ★ ★ ★ **R War 1:53**
☑ Adult situations, violence, explicit language
Dir: Ted Post *Cast:* Burt Lancaster, Craig Wasson, Jonathan Goldsmith, Marc Singer, Joe Unger
▶ Lancaster, the commanding officer of an outpost near Dienbienphu, where the French were slaughtered in 1954, tries to impart his instincts and experiences to green troops who know little of jungle fighting. A true sleeper, this unsung Vietnam-era drama predates some of the better known efforts in the genre. Lancaster and Wasson are sympathetic and believable.
Dist.: Vestron

GOTHIC 1987 British
☆ **R Drama 1:28**
☑ Nudity, adult situations, explicit language, violence
Dir: Ken Russell *Cast:* Gabriel Byrne, Julian Sands, Natasha Richardson, Myriam Cyr, Timothy Spall
▶ On a stormy night in 1816, the poets Shelley (Sands) and Byron (Byrne), Mary Shelley (Richardson), Byron's girlfriend Cyr, and Dr. Polidori (Spall) tell ghost stories and confront each other. Mary Shelley is inspired to write *Frankenstein.* Florid nonsense goes over the top and stays there. Russell provides lots of flash but unappealing characters grate on the nerves.
Dist.: Vestron

GO WEST 1940
★ ★ **NR Comedy 1:21 B&W**
Dir: Edward Buzzell *Cast:* Groucho Marx, Harpo Marx, Chico Marx, John Carroll, Diana Lewis, Walter Woolf King
▶ Groucho, Chico, and Harpo head for the wild, wild West and battle a villain over a priceless land deed. Not top-notch Marx but some funny stuff: Groucho getting bilked by his brothers, hilarious train-chase finale.
Dist.: MGM/UA

GRACE QUIGLEY 1985
★ ★ **PG Comedy 1:27**
☑ Explicit language, violence
Dir: Anthony Harvey *Cast:* Katharine Hepburn, Nick Nolte, Elizabeth Wilson, Chip Zien, William Duell
▶ Elderly Hepburn witnesses hitman Nolte commit murder and blackmails him into bumping off unhappy old folks who want to end their lives but can't bring themselves to commit suicide. A warm if unlikely relationship develops between Nolte and Hepburn. Two pros add class to this uneasy, sometimes bizarre mixture of killing and comedy.
Dist.: MGM/UA

GRADUATE, THE 1967
★ ★ ★ ★ ★ **PG Comedy 1:45**
☑ Adult situations, explicit language
Dir: Mike Nichols *Cast:* Dustin Hoffman, Anne Bancroft, Katharine Ross, William Daniels, Murray Hamilton
▶ Directionless college grad Hoffman (in his first starring role) has affair with much older Mrs. Robinson (Bancroft), wife of his dad's friend, and then falls for her daughter Ross. One of the most influential films of the sixties is a witty comedy of manners and a sharp portrait of a generation. Jazzily directed by Ni-

chols, beautifully acted by all. Clever Buck Henry/Calder Willingham script is filled with memorable dialogue: "Plastics" and "Mrs. Robinson, you're trying to seduce me. . .aren't you?" Score by Simon and Garfunkel includes "Mrs. Robinson," "Sounds of Silence." Oscar for Best Director, nominated for Best Picture, Actor, Actress. (CC)
Dist.: Nelson

GRADUATION DAY 1981
★ R Horror 1:36
☑ Adult situations, explicit language, violence
Dir: Herb Freed ***Cast:*** Christopher George, Patch Mackenzie, E. J. Peaker, E. Danny Murphy, Michael Pataki
► As graduation day approaches, someone is killing off members of a high school track team. The suspects: a creepy principal, gung-ho track coach, female Navy ensign whose sister was the first victim, and a punk rocker. Low-budget entry in the kill-a-teen genre. Some suspense for hard-core blood and gore freaks but the story is strictly routine.
Dist.: RCA/Columbia

GRAND HIGHWAY, THE 1987 French
★ R Drama 1:44
☑ Brief nudity, explicit language
Dir: Jean-Loup Hubert ***Cast:*** Anemone, Richard Bohringer, Vanessa Guedj, Christine Pascal, Antoine Hubert
► Hubert, a sensitive nine-year-old boy, is left with people in the country while his mother goes off to have a baby. Through friendship with neighbor Guedj, and involvement in the tumultuous lives of his guardians Bohringer and Anemone, he becomes aware of the physical and emotional facts of life. Tender, episodic look at a boy's summer of discovery was a big hit in its home country. [S]
Dist.: Image

GRAND HOTEL 1932
★★★ NR Drama 1:55 B&W
Dir: Edmund Goulding ***Cast:*** Greta Garbo, John Barrymore, Joan Crawford, Wallace Beery, Lionel Barrymore, Jean Hersholt, Lewis Stone
► All-star spectacular weaves together lives of several guests at a Berlin hotel. Aging dancer Garbo "wants to be alone" until thief John Barrymore breaks into her room to steal her jewels; dying Lionel Barrymore gets involved with secretary Crawford and her brutal boss Beery. Oscar for Best Picture. (CC)
Dist.: MGM/UA

GRAND ILLUSION 1937 French
★ NR Drama 1:50 B&W
Dir: Jean Renoir ***Cast:*** Jean Gabin, Pierre Fresnay, Erich von Stroheim, Marcel Dalio, Dita Parlo
► In a World War I prison camp, titled French POW Fresnay is befriended by his German captor and fellow aristocrat von Stroheim. Fresnay helps inmates Dalio and Gabin escape, forcing von Stroheim to kill him. Deservedly legendary antiwar classic, masterfully directed by the great Renoir. [S]
Dist.: KVC

GRANDMOTHER'S HOUSE 1989
★★ R Horror 1:29
☑ Explicit language, violence
Dir: Peter Rader ***Cast:*** Eric Foster, Kim Valentine, Brinke Stevens, Ida Lee, Len Lesser
► To grandmother's house go Foster and Valentine after their father dies. A body is found on the property and Foster witnesses some other odd doings. Could grandparents Lee and Lesser be killers? Occasional unusual touches lift this slightly above genre standard. Kid actors outshine the adults.
Dist.: Academy

GRAND PRIX 1966
★★★★ NR Drama/Sports 2:49
☑ Adult situations, mild violence
Dir: John Frankenheimer ***Cast:*** James Garner, Eva Marie Saint, Yves Montand, Toshiro Mifune, Brian Bedford, Jessica Walter
► American Garner, Brit Bedford, and Corsican Montand are among the drivers whose pursuit of a racing championship is complicated by on-track accidents and off-track romances. Mildly entertaining script enhanced by good cast and visually spectacular racing footage. Three Oscars: Sound, Film Editing, Sound Effects. (CC)
Dist.: MGM/UA

GRAND THEFT AUTO 1977
★★★ PG Action-Adventure 1:24
☑ Explicit language, violence
Dir: Ron Howard ***Cast:*** Ron Howard, Nancy Morgan, Marion Ross, Pete Isackson, Barry Powers, Rance Howard
► Young Howard and fiancée Morgan elope to Las Vegas in a Rolls Royce after her millionaire dad Cahill refuses to approve their marriage. Good-natured action comedy turns into one gigantic car chase when they're pursued by Pop and others. Directorial debut for Howard, co-written by and co-starring his dad Rance.
Dist.: Warner

GRANDVIEW, U.S.A. 1984
★★ R Drama 1:37
☑ Nudity, adult situations, explicit language, mild violence, adult humor
Dir: Randal Kleiser ***Cast:*** Jamie Lee Curtis, Patrick Swayze, C. Thomas Howell, Troy Donahue, Jennifer Jason Leigh
► Teenager Howell becomes involved with older Curtis, who owns the local demolition derby, leading to conflict with his dad who wants to build country club on Curtis's property. Small-town slice-of-life comedy suffers from mechanical plotting and condescending humor; redeemed in part by the performances, particularly the always winsome Curtis. (CC)
Dist.: CBS/Fox

GRAPES OF WRATH, THE 1940
★ ★ ★ ★ ★ NR Drama 2:09 B&W
Dir: John Ford *Cast:* Henry Fonda, Jane
Darwell, John Carradine, Dorris Bowden,
Charley Grapewin, John Qualen
▶ In the 1930s, the Oklahoma Dust Bowl
forces farm families like the Joads to migrate
to California, where the dispossessed clan
become virtual slaves at a labor camp. Tom
Joad (Fonda) refuses to be beaten by adver-
sity and demands fair treatment for the work-
ers. Grueling, heartbreaking masterpiece tells
an epic story of determination and struggle.
Fonda's "I'll be there" speech is one of the
most moving moments in all cinema. Director
Ford and Darwell (as Ma Joad) won Oscars.
From John Steinbeck's Pulitzer prize-winning
novel. (CC)
Dist.: CBS/Fox

GRASSHOPPER, THE 1970
★ R Drama 1:35
☑ Nudity, explicit language
Dir: Jerry Paris *Cast:* Jacqueline Bisset, Jim
Brown, Joseph Cotten, Corbett Monica,
Ramon Bieri
▶ Bissett is a young Canadian girl whose life
goes steadily downhill between the ages of
nineteen and twenty-two. She quits her bank
job, becomes a Las Vegas showgirl, marries
athlete Brown, is widowed, turns to drugs, becomes kept woman, and ultimately descends
into prostitution and utter despair. In the end,
she gets "last word" by skywriting obscenity
across sky. Brown is surprisingly good in otherwise overwrought drama.
Dist.: Warner

GRASS IS GREENER, THE 1960
★ ★ NR Comedy 1:45
Dir: Stanley Donen *Cast:* Cary Grant, Deb-
orah Kerr, Robert Mitchum, Jean Simmons,
Moray Watson
▶ Strained, talky adaptation of a minor British
play about an English couple (Grant and Kerr)
whose marriage is threatened by visiting
Texas oilman Mitchum. Grant, in a polished
performance, summons old girlfriend Simmons
to stir Kerr's jealousy. Noel Coward songs
("Mad Dogs and Englishmen," "The Stately
Homes of England") provide most of the
humor.
Dist.: Republic

GRAVEYARD SHIFT 1987
★ ★ ★ R Horror 1:28
☑ Nudity, adult situations, explicit language, violence
Dir: Gerard Ciccoritti *Cast:* Silvio Oliviero,
Helen Papas, Cliff Stoker, Dorin Ferber
▶ Papas is a busy TV producer who discovers
she has only a few months to live. Though married, she decides to have fling with taxi driver
Oliviero. Hunk hackie Oliviero likes the night
shift for a reason: he's a vampire; Papas discovers his secret when she catches him with
his fangs in a blond. Pretty good minor effort

has lots of nudity and effective late-night atmosphere.
Dist.: Virgin

GRAY LADY DOWN 1978
★ ★ ★ ★ PG Mystery-Suspense 1:51
☑ Explicit language, mild violence
Dir: David Greene *Cast:* Charlton Heston,
Stacy Keach, David Carradine, Ned Beatty
▶ A nuclear sub commanded by Heston is
sunk after being rammed by a freighter. The
Navy attempts to rescue the stricken ship but
an earth tremor covers the escape hatch. Fi-
nally, an experimental diving vessel comes to
the rescue. Undersea thriller is a tense, nail-
biting affair with a solid cast.
Dist.: MCA

GREASE 1978
★ ★ ★ ★ PG Musical 1:50
☑ Explicit language
Dir: Randal Kleiser *Cast:* John Travolta,
Olivia Newton-John, Stockard Channing,
Jeff Conaway, Didi Conn, Eve Arden
▶ The summertime romance of wholesome
Sandy (Newton-John) and greaser Danny
(Travolta) is disrupted by the advent of school
but love eventually triumphs. Broadway sen-
sation about the 1950s makes for a tuneful,
lively movie musical. Sprightly numbers ex-
pertly choreographed by Patricia Birch, pizazz
from Travolta, charm and torch songs from
Newton-John, and fine supporting work from
Channing.
Dist.: Paramount

GREASE 2 1982
★ ★ PG Musical 1:54
☑ Explicit language
Dir: Patricia Birch *Cast:* Maxwell Caulfield,
Michelle Pfeiffer, Lorna Luft, Eve Arden, Con-
nie Stevens, Tab Hunter
▶ Britisher Caulfield arrives at raucous Rydell
High and falls for Stephanie (Pfeiffer), a mem-
ber of the Pink Ladies gang. She thinks he's a
nerd so he disguises himself as a biker to
sweep her off her feet. Young, attractive cast,
ample dancing, and toe-tapping tunes in this
insubstantial but fast-paced sequel.
Dist.: Paramount

GREASED LIGHTNING 1977
★ ★ ★ PG Biography/Sports 1:36
☑ Explicit language
Dir: Michael Schultz *Cast:* Richard Pryor,
Beau Bridges, Pam Grier, Cleavon Little, Vincent Gardenia, Richie Havens
▶ True story of Wendell Scott (Pryor), a black
stock-car racer who overcame bigotry and
poverty to become a national champion. An
effective change-of-pace dramatic performance by Pryor. Slowly paced at first but well-
staged racing sequences rev movie up to
speed.
Dist.: Warner

GREAT ADVENTURE, THE 1975
★ ★ PG Action-Adventure 1:27

☑ Mild violence
Dir: Paul Elliotts (Gianfranco Baldanello)
Cast: Joan Collins, Jack Palance, Fred Romer, Elizabeth Virgil
▶ Young Romer and his dog survive dangerous Alaskan Rockies to arrive in corrupt Gold Rush town where he intends to take over his dead father's newspaper. Sultry dance hall hostess Collins helps him battle crooked Palance for its control. Tepid, lackluster adventure based on the Jack London tale.
Dist.: Media

GREAT BALLS OF FIRE! 1989
★ ★ ★ ★ **PG-13 Biography 1:48**
◯ Adult situations, explicit language, violence
Dir: Jim McBride *Cast:* Dennis Quaid, Winona Ryder, Alec Baldwin, John Doe, Lisa Blount, Trey Wilson
▶ Highly entertaining biography of rock 'n' roll star Jerry Lee Lewis (Quaid) traces his meteoric rise to stardom, marriage to thirteen-year-old cousin Myra (Ryder), and the resulting scandal. Far from penetrating, but both the film and Quaid get by on energy, high spirits, and exuberance. Baldwin is a standout as Lewis's cousin Rev. Jimmy Swaggart and Ryder is winning. Songs (dubbed by Lewis) include "Breathless," "Whole Lotta Shakin'," and the title tune (also performed by the Killer in a clip that precedes the film in its home video incarnation). **(CC)**
Dist.: Orion

GREAT BANK HOAX, THE 1977
★ ★ ★ **PG Comedy 1:29**
◯ Adult situations, explicit language
Dir: Joseph Jacoby *Cast:* Richard Basehart, Ned Beatty, Charlene Dallas, Burgess Meredith, Michael Murphy, Paul Sand, Arthur Godfrey
▶ Bank officers Basehart, Beatty, and Meredith fake a robbery so they can cover up an embezzlement and collect the insurance. The plan begins to unravel when culprit Sand wants to return the money. Easygoing caper ambles along pleasantly if not speedily. Also known as *Shenanigans* and *The Great Georgia Bank Hoax.*
Dist.: Warner

GREAT CARUSO, THE 1951
★ ★ ★ ★ **G Biography/Music 1:49**
Dir: Richard Thorpe *Cast:* Mario Lanza, Ann Blyth, Dorothy Kirsten, Jarmila Novotna
▶ Life and times of legendary opera star Enrico Caruso (Lanza) details his Italian childhood, his American success and happy marriage to beautiful socialite Blyth, and his tragic early death. Lanza was born to play this role and music lovers will feast on the many operatic classics in this gorgeous MGM production.
Dist.: MGM/UA

GREAT DICTATOR, THE 1940
★ ★ ★ **G Comedy 2:05 B&W**
Dir: Charles Chaplin *Cast:* Charles Chaplin, Paulette Goddard, Jack Oakie, Henry Daniell, Billy Gilbert
▶ Chaplin plays a dual role: a Hitler-like dictator and his lookalike, a poor Jewish barber. An identity switch eventually thwarts the fascist. Superb spoof of totalitarianism with many memorable moments, including Chaplin's playing with a globe/balloon and the battles between Charlie and Oakie (uproariously funny as a Mussolini-like leader).
Dist.: CBS/Fox

GREAT ESCAPE, THE 1963
★ ★ ★ ★ **NR War 2:48**
Dir: John Sturges *Cast:* Steve McQueen, James Garner, Richard Attenborough, Charles Bronson, James Coburn, David McCallum
▶ Allied prisoners plan a daring mass escape from a German POW camp by digging three underground tunnels. Thrilling adventure offers all-star macho cast, humor, clever plotting, action, and the unforgettable jaunty music theme. McQueen was never cooler than as the "Cooler King," so nicknamed because of the time he spent in solitary. Script by James Clavell from a true story. **(CC)**
Dist.: MGM/UA

GREATEST, THE 1977
★ ★ **PG Biography/Sports 1:41**
◯ Explicit language
Dir: Tom Gries *Cast:* Muhammad Ali, Ernest Borgnine, Lloyd Haynes, John Marley, Robert Duvall, James Earl Jones
▶ A relaxed and confident Ali plays himself in this biography of his rise to the heavyweight championship, battles with bigotry, conversion to Islam, marriages, being stripped of the title for his refusal to fight in Vietnam, and triumphant resurgence against George Foreman. Actual fight footage enhances this predictable but entertaining movie.
Dist.: RCA

GREATEST SHOW ON EARTH, THE 1952
★ ★ ★ ★ **NR Drama 2:33**
Dir: Cecil B. DeMille *Cast:* Betty Hutton, Charlton Heston, Cornel Wilde, Dorothy Lamour, Gloria Grahame, James Stewart
▶ Best Picture Oscar went to this epic look at life under the big top. Trapeze artist Hutton falls for daring new star Wilde while still harboring a yen for boss Heston. Showgirl Grahame also loves Wilde while clown Stewart (who remains in makeup throughout) hides a mysterious past. Despite these passions (and a train wreck disaster), the show must go on.
Dist.: Paramount

GREATEST STORY EVER TOLD, THE 1965
★ ★ ★ ★ ★ **G Drama 2:21**
Dir: George Stevens *Cast:* Max Von Sydow, Charlton Heston, Roddy McDowall, Robert Loggia, Jose Ferrer, Dorothy McGuire
▶ Von Sydow is Christ in this most grandiose of biblical epics tracing His life from birth to crucifixion and resurrection. Top-quality holi-

day fare has one of the most star-studded casts ever assembled; John Wayne, Sidney Poitier, Claude Rains, Angela Lansbury, and Telly Savalas are among the cameos. (CC)
Dist.: Paramount

GREAT EXPECTATIONS 1947 British
★★★★ NR Drama 1:58 B&W
Dir: David Lean *Cast:* John Mills, Valerie Hobson, Bernard Miles, Finlay Currie, Jean Simmons, Alec Guinness, Martita Hunt
▶ Pip, a young orphan devoted to the wealthy Estella, receives a mysterious bequest that enables him to improve his social standing. From the thrilling opening in a gloomy cemetery to the fiery climax, this masterpiece is generally regarded as the best of all the Charles Dickens adaptations. Mills, the older Pip, and Guinness, Pip's raffish London friend, are superb, but the most remarkable performance is Hunt's haunting Miss Havisham. Won Oscars for set design and Guy Green's cinematography. (CC)
Dist.: Learning Corp. of America

GREAT FLAMARION, THE 1945
★ NR Drama 1:18 B&W
Dir: Anthony Mann *Cast:* Erich von Stroheim, Mary Beth Hughes, Dan Duryea, Stephen Barclay, Lester Allen
▶ Femme fatale Hughes lures circus sharpshooter von Stroheim into a plot to dispose of her husband Duryea. Despite predictable plotting, moody low-budget B-movie is unexpectedly appealing, thanks to Mann's concise direction and von Stroheim's powerful acting.
Dist.: Sinister

GREAT GABBO, THE 1929
★ NR Drama 1:38 B&W
Dir: James Cruze *Cast:* Erich von Stroheim, Betty Compson, Don Douglas, Marjorie King, Helen Kane
▶ Bizarre study of von Stroheim, a jealous, psychotic ventriloquist who ruins his stage act with Compson before losing his identity to his dummy. Early talkie has campy touches (notably "The Web of Love," a stage number involving a giant spider), but overall is too dull and outlandish to be entertaining. Primitive sound and camerawork are big drawbacks.
Dist.: Cable

GREAT GATSBY, THE 1974
★★★ PG Drama 2:23
☑ Adult situations, explicit language
Dir: Jack Clayton *Cast:* Robert Redford, Mia Farrow, Sam Waterston, Bruce Dern, Karen Black, Lois Chiles
▶ In the Roaring Twenties, mysterious self-made millionaire Jay Gatsby (Redford) throws mammoth parties at his Long Island estate. He hopes to get close to Daisy Buchanan (Farrow), the woman he loved and lost years back, now married to boorish blueblood Dern. Overly literal adaptation of F. Scott Fitz-

gerald's magnificent novel fails to do justice to book's serious themes and suffers from miscast leads. Enjoyable, though, for the lavish period re-creation and for Waterston's sharp performance as narrator Nick.
Dist.: Paramount

GREAT GUNS 1941
★★ NR Comedy 1:14 B&W
Dir: Monty Banks *Cast:* Stan Laurel, Oliver Hardy, Sheila Ryan, Dick Nelson, Edmund MacDonald, Charles Trowbridge
▶ When their wealthy young master Nelson is drafted, servants Laurel and Hardy enlist in the army so they can keep their eye on him. Sergeant MacDonald finds the duo to be incompentent soldiers but the guys prove their worth in maneuvers. Mild vehicle for the comedy team.
Dist.: CBS/Fox

GREAT GUY 1936
★ NR Drama 1:06 B&W
Dir: John G. Blystone *Cast:* James Cagney, Mae Clarke, James Burke, Edward Brophy, Henry Kolker
▶ Bureau of Weights and Measures official Cagney looks into corruption in the food industry, discovering that gangsters are cheating the public with crooked schemes. His investigation leads him to a mayor and a millionaire. Lively vehicle for a typically energetic Cagney.
Dist.: Video Yesteryear

GREAT IMPOSTOR, THE 1961
★★ NR Biography 1:52 B&W
Dir: Robert Mulligan *Cast:* Tony Curtis, Edmond O'Brien, Karl Malden, Arthur O'Connell, Gary Merrill, Raymond Massey
▶ Doctor, Marine, prison warden, academic, and monk are some of the roles assayed in the colorful life of impostor Ferdinand Demara (Curtis). Fanciful true story is generally enjoyable, thanks to Curtis's panache and a good supporting cast.
Dist.: MCA

GREAT LOVER, THE 1949
★★★ NR Comedy 1:20 B&W
Dir: Alexander Hall *Cast:* Bob Hope, Rhonda Fleming, Roland Young, Roland Culver, Jim Backus, George Reeves
▶ Scoutmaster Hope takes troop on European cruise. He falls in love with penniless duchess Fleming and must save the day when a murderer appears on board. Lighthearted suspense comedy in a sophisticated milieu with an irresistible Hope compensating for some weak songs and a tentative Fleming.
Dist.: RCA/Columbia

GREAT MCGINTY, THE 1940
★★★ NR Comedy 1:21 B&W
Dir: Preston Sturges *Cast:* Brian Donlevy, Muriel Angelus, Akim Tamiroff, Allyn Joslyn, William Demarest
▶ In a corrupt election, bum Donlevy im-

presses party boss Tamiroff by voting thirty-seven times for the same politician. He rises to governor, is stricken by conscience and has a falling-out with Boss Tamiroff. Marvelous satire from writer/director Sturges with unforgettable characterizations (Tamiroff as the politician so corrupt he controls both machine and reform parties) and scenes (Donlevy reading children's story to his stepkids). Oscar for Best Screenplay.
Dist.: MCA

GREAT MOUSE DETECTIVE, THE 1986
★ ★ ★ ★ ★ G Animation 1:12
Dir: Barry Mattinson *Cast:* Voices of Vincent Price, Barrie Ingham, Val Bettin, Susanne Pollatschek, Candy Candido, Alan Young
▶ Sherlock Holmes and Dr. Watson return as animated characters, Basil of Baker Street and faithful companion Dr. Dawson. In foggy London town, the dynamic duo foil the evil scheme of rat Professor Rattigan (voice of Price). Pleasing story moves at fast clip with delightful visuals. A family entertainment winner.
Dist.: Buena Vista

GREAT MUPPET CAPER, THE 1981
★ ★ ★ ★ G Comedy/Family 1:38
Dir: Jim Henson *Cast:* The Muppets, Charles Grodin, Diana Rigg, John Cleese, Peter Falk, Robert Morley
▶ Fired from their jobs as reporters for a big-city paper, Kermit and company investigate a jewel theft in London. Good-natured charm and innocence, inspired routines (Kermit dances like Fred Astaire, Miss Piggy swims in an Esther Williams number), and London locations deliver delightful fun. Rigg and Grodin bring panache to their Muppet interactions.
Dist.: Playhouse

GREAT NORTHFIELD, MINNESOTA RAID, THE 1972
★ ★ ★ PG Western 1:31
☑ Adult situations, explicit language, violence
Dir: Philip Kaufman *Cast:* Cliff Robertson, Robert Duvall, Luke Askew, R. G. Armstrong, Dana Elcar, Donald Moffat
▶ Famed badman Cole Younger (Robertson) considers hanging up his gun, but his friend Jesse James (Duvall) will have none of the straight life. The pair and their gang then team up for a Minnesota bank robbery. Intelligent direction by Kaufman and good performances from Robertson and Duvall.
Dist.: MCA

GREAT OUTDOORS, THE 1988
★ ★ ★ ★ PG Comedy 1:30
☑ Explicit language
Dir: Howard Deutsch *Cast:* Dan Aykroyd, John Candy, Stephanie Faracy, Annette Bening, Chris Young, Ian Giatti
▶ Auto parts salesman Candy takes his Chicago family to bucolic lakeside retreat, but his

serenity is destroyed by arrival of obnoxious brother-in-law Aykroyd and his snobby family. Broad comedy from John Hughes relies heavily on stars' charm and silly sight gags.
Dist.: MCA

GREAT RACE, THE 1965
★ ★ ★ NR Comedy 2:33
Dir: Blake Edwards *Cast:* Tony Curtis, Natalie Wood, Jack Lemmon, Peter Falk, Keenan Wynn, Larry Storch
▶ Grand-scaled comedy about a 1908 transcontinental road race. *Some Like It Hot* costars Curtis and Lemmon are reunited on opposite sides: Curtis is the handsome hero who wins suffragette Wood, Lemmon has a scenery-chewing field day as the mustache-twirling villain. Highlight: one of the most lavish pie-throwing fights ever filmed.
Dist.: Warner

GREAT SANTINI, THE 1980
★ ★ ★ ★ PG Drama 1:55
☑ Explicit language
Dir: Lewis John Carlino *Cast:* Robert Duvall, Blythe Danner, Michael O'Keefe, Stan Shaw, Lisa Jane Persky
▶ Duvall is superb as Bull Meechum, a tough marine pilot without any real battles to fight, who runs his household like a boot camp. O'Keefe was Oscar nominated for his portrayal of Duvall's emotionally torn adolescent son. A luminous Danner plays a sensitive and loving Southern belle mother. Originally released as *The Ace*; based on Pat Conroy's novel.
Dist.: Warner

GREAT SCOUT AND CATHOUSE THURSDAY, THE 1976
★ ★ ★ PG Comedy 1:36
☑ Adult situations
Dir: Don Taylor *Cast:* Lee Marvin, Oliver Reed, Robert Culp, Elizabeth Ashley, Strother Martin, Kay Lenz
▶ Trapper Marvin and Harvard-educated Indian Reed team up to retrieve fortune in gold stolen by Culp, who has used the money to buy into what passes for high society in the Wild West. Lenz is attractive as a prostitute romanced by Marvin, but lumbering Western spoof lacks inspiration.
Dist.: Vestron

GREAT SMOKEY ROADBLOCK, THE 1976
★ ★ PG Comedy 1:24
☑ Explicit language
Dir: John Leone *Cast:* Henry Fonda, Eileen Brennan, John Byner, Dub Taylor, Susan Sarandon, Melanie Mayron
▶ Diagnosed as terminally ill, truck-driving old-timer Fonda steals back his repossessed vehicle and sets off across the country on one last run. Loading up with madam Brennan and her crew of prostitutes in Wyoming, he becomes a folk hero as he outraces and outfoxes the highway patrol. Fonda at his charm-

ing and irascible best. Shown on network TV as *The Last of the Cowboys.*
Dist.: Media

GREAT TEXAS DYNAMITE CHASE, THE 1976
★★★ R Action-Adventure 1:28
☑ Nudity, violence
Dir: Gus Trikonis ***Cast:*** Claudia Jennings, Jocelyn Jones, Johnny Crawford, Chris Pennock
▶ Bonnie and Clyde with a twist of women's lib: two pretty Texas girls, escaped con (*Playboy* centerfold) Jennings and obnoxious ex-bank teller Jones, join forces to rob banks, outsmart the cops and enrapture various men. Workable and offbeat, with bits of real humor.
Dist.: Warner

GREAT TRAIN ROBBERY, THE 1979 British
★★★★ PG Drama 1:51
☑ Explicit language
Dir: Michael Crichton ***Cast:*** Sean Connery, Donald Sutherland, Lesley-Anne Down, Alan Webb, Malcolm Terris
▶ In 1855, arch-criminal Connery enlists mistress Down and master lockpicker Sutherland in a daring scheme to hijack gold bullion from a train. Sly caper film, based on a real incident, features an excellent cast and gorgeous production values. Connery, who did his own stunts, is especially impressive. Director Crichton wrote the screenplay from his best-selling novel.
Dist.: MGM/UA

GREAT WALDO PEPPER, THE 1975
★★★ PG Drama 1:47
☑ Adult situations, explicit language
Dir: George Roy Hill ***Cast:*** Robert Redford, Bo Svenson, Bo Brundin, Margot Kidder, Susan Sarandon, Phil Bruns
▶ After World War I, pilot Redford barnstorms through the countryside before getting his long-delayed chance to battle German ace Brundin when both are hired as movie stuntmen. Eye-boggling aerial footage was obviously a labor of love for director Hill, a licensed pilot, but the script meanders. Redford exudes charisma in the title role.
Dist.: MCA

GREAT WALL, A 1986 U.S./Chinese
★★★ PG Comedy 1:40
☑ Explicit language
Dir: Peter Wang ***Cast:*** Peter Wang, Sharon Iwai, Kelvin Han Yee, Li Qinqin, Hu Xiaoguang, Shen Guanglan
▶ Chinese-American computer executive Wang takes his family to Peking to visit his sister; resulting clash of values is shown with amusing insight in this lighthearted comedy. First U.S./Chinese co-production is short on plot, but scenery and characters are fascinating. [S]
Dist.: Pacific Arts

GREAT ZIEGFELD, THE 1936
★★★ NR Biography/Musical 2:56 B&W
Dir: Robert Z. Leonard ***Cast:*** William Powell, Luise Rainer, Myrna Loy, Frank Morgan, Reginald Owen, Nat Pendleton
▶ Long, detailed account of showman Flo Ziegfeld (Powell), his turbulent affair with Anna Held (Rainer), his up-and-down career, and his happy but tragically brief marriage to Billie Burke (Loy). Filled with cameos from Fanny Brice, Ray Bolger, etc., and memorable songs like "A Pretty Girl Is Like a Melody," "Rhapsody in Blue," "Look for the Silver Lining" and many more. Won three Oscars, including Best Picture and Actress (Rainer).
Dist.: MGM/UA

GREED 1924
★ NR Drama 2:20 B&W
Dir: Erich von Stroheim ***Cast:*** Gibson Gowland, ZaSu Pitts, Jean Hersholt, Chester Conklin, Dale Fuller, Sylvia Ashton
▶ Driven by avaricious wife Pitts, dentist Gowland becomes a California gold prospector. The desire for wealth overcomes all other satisfactions in their lives, driving Gowland dramatically insane. Silent adaptation of Frank Norris's novel *McTeague* is still powerful stuff, though history of heavy editing (original was eight hours long) makes it more effective in parts rather than as a flowing narrative.
Dist.: MGM/UA

GREEKS HAD A WORD FOR THEM, THE 1932
☆ NR Comedy 1:19 B&W
Dir: Lowell Sherman ***Cast:*** Joan Blondell, Ina Claire, Madge Evans, David Manners, Lowell Sherman
▶ In a New York of Broadway lights, top hats, and nightclubs, Blondell, Claire, and Evans set their hats to marry rich men. Fate throws a couple of millionaires their way, but the girls learn that all is not fair in love and golddigging. Merry progenitor of films like *How to Marry a Millionaire*, as well as the musical Gold Diggers series, snappy comedy is also known as *Three Broadway Girls.*
Dist.: Cable

GREEK TYCOON, THE 1978
★★★ R Drama 1:46
☑ Adult situations, explicit language
Dir: J. Lee Thompson ***Cast:*** Anthony Quinn, Jacqueline Bisset, Raf Vallone, Edward Albert, Camilla Sparv, Charles Durning
▶ Greek shipping magnate Theo Tomasis (Quinn) marries Liz Cassidy (Bisset), the stylish widow of an assassinated President. Despite unimaginable wealth, they grapple with the same emotional problems as couples everywhere. Lush scenery provides a dramatic backdrop to this provocative romance loosely based on the life of billionaire Aristotle Onassis.
Dist.: MCA

GREEN BERETS, THE 1968
★★★ G War 2:21
Dir: John Wayne, Ray Kellogg ***Cast:*** John Wayne, David Janssen, Jim Hutton, Aldo Ray, Raymond St. Jacques, Bruce Cabot
▶ Wayne's tribute to the Special Forces soldiers based in Vietnam is an old-fashioned war adventure filled with large-scale action scenes. Wayne commands a regiment defending a strategic hill from swarming Vietcong, then leads his men on a mission to kidnap an enemy general. Janssen is a cynical reporter gradually won over to the Berets' methods. Received scathing reviews on release for its right-wing tone. Based on Robin Moore's novel.
Dist.: Warner

GREEN DOLPHIN STREET 1947
★★ NR Drama 2:21 B&W
Dir: Victor Saville ***Cast:*** Lana Turner, Van Heflin, Donna Reed, Richard Hart, Frank Morgan, Edmund Gwenn
▶ Broad, sweeping tale of a tangled love, played across two continents and three oceans during the nineteenth century. Hart marries Reed, joins the Navy, and winds up in New Zealand, where he mistakenly sends for her sister Turner to join him. Hart and Turner fall in love and establish a lumber business. Good costume romance, with a plot that turns on the slip of a pen.
Dist.: MGM/UA

GREEN ICE 1981 British
★★★ PG Action-Adventure 1:55
☑ Adult situations, explicit language, violence
Dir: Ernest Day ***Cast:*** Ryan O'Neal, Anne Archer, Omar Sharif, Domingo Ambriz, John Larroquette
▶ On-the-skids electronics engineer O'Neal teams up with sophisticated Archer to rob a fortune in emeralds from Colombian tycoon Sharif. Black-market thugs and left-wing guerrillas add to the tension. Highlighted by a daring raid by hot air balloon. **(CC)**
Dist.: CBS/Fox

GREEN PASTURES 1936
★ NR Drama 1:30 B&W
Dir: William Keighley, Marc Connelly ***Cast:*** Rex Ingram, Oscar Polk, Eddie "Rochester" Anderson, Frank Wilson, George Reed, Abraham Gleaves
▶ While listening to a Sunday School lesson, a little boy imagines scenes from the Bible enacted by an all-black cast led by Ingram as "de Lawd." Film is well-meaning, but modern viewers will find patronizing racial stereotypes depressing. The Hall Johnson Choir drones syrupy spirituals throughout.
Dist.: Key

GREEN ROOM, THE 1979 French
☆ PG Drama 1:34
☑ Adult situations
Dir: François Truffaut ***Cast:*** François Truffaut, Nathalie Baye, Jean-Pierre Moulin, Jean Daste, Jane Lobre
▶ Widowed World War I veteran Truffaut builds altar to his late wife whose memory he worships; not even friendship with similarly mournful Baye can alter his single-minded obsession. Immaculately crafted, occasionally moving adaptation of writings of Henry James finds director/star Truffaut in an unusually somber mood. [S]
Dist.: Warner

GREGORY'S GIRL 1982 Scottish
★★ PG Comedy 1:29
☑ Adult situations, explicit language
Dir: Bill Forsyth ***Cast:*** Gordon John Sinclair, Dee Hepburn, Chic Murray, Clare Grogan, Jake D'Arcy
▶ Gawky high school student Sinclair falls for Hepburn, his soccer team's female goalie, but eventually finds true love with one of her friends, Grogan. Filmmaker Forsyth transforms a seemingly mundane story of an adolescent crush into something magical, romantic, and slyly humorous. Thick Scottish brogues may prove too wearying for the impatient.
Dist.: Nelson

GREMLINS 1984
★★★★ PG Fantasy 1:46
☑ Adult situations, explicit language, violence
Dir: Joe Dante ***Cast:*** Zach Galligan, Phoebe Cates, Hoyt Axton, Frances Lee McCain, Polly Holliday, Keye Luke
▶ Failed inventor Axton gives son Galligan a cuddly "mogwai" for Christmas, but Galligan ignores warnings against feeding the pet after midnight and getting it wet. The result: hordes of vicious gremlins prone to deadly practical jokes invade a small town. Steven Spielberg production has fascinating special effects and a mordant sense of humor. Sequel in 1990. **(CC)**
Dist.: Warner

GREMLINS II: THE NEW BATCH 1990
★★★ PG-13 Horror/Comedy 1:45
☑ Explicit language, violence
Dir: Joe Dante ***Cast:*** Zach Galligan, Phoebe Cates, John Glover, Robert Prosky, Robert Picardo, Christopher Lee, Haviland Morris, Hulk Hogan, John Astin, Rick Ducommun, Henry Gibson, Leonard Maltin, Dick Butkus, Bubba Smith, Dick Miller, Jackie Joseph, voices of Tony Randall, Howie Mandell, Jeff Bergman
▶ Cuddly creature Gizmo is captured by genetic scientist Lee, whose lab is located in a glitzy Manhattan office tower owned by Glover, a Donald Trump–like real estate mogul. After being exposed to water, Gizmo spawns hundreds of scaley, drooling gremlins, whose violent antics go quickly out of control. Returning from the first outing are sweethearts Cates and Galligan, who may be all that stands in the way of a totally gremlinized

Gotham. Very funny sequel gets laughs from pop culture references, rib-tickling cameos, and the title creatures' hilariously ill-mannered behavior.
Dist.: Warner

GREY FOX, THE 1983 Canadian
★ ★ ★ ★ **PG Western 1:31**
☑ Adult situations, explicit language, mild violence
Dir: Philip Borsos *Cast:* Robert Farnsworth, Jackie Burroughs, Wayne Robson, Ken Pogue, Timothy Webber, Gary Reineke
▶ After decades in jail, "Gentleman Bandit" Farnsworth must adjust to a new world of steam trains and motion pictures. Burroughs plays an early feminist who befriends the robber. Warm, elegiac Western, set in turn-of-the-century Canada, is a good showcase for ex-stuntman Farnsworth's thoughtful, expressive performance.
Dist.: Media

GREYFRIARS BOBBY 1961 British
★ ★ ★ **NR Family 1:31**
Dir: Don Chaffey *Cast:* Donald Crisp, Laurence Naismith, Alex MacKenzie, Kay Walsh, Duncan MacRae, Gordon Jackson
▶ In nineteenth-century Scotland, Skye terrier Bobby loves his recently deceased master so much that he visits his grave every night. Both Naismith and cemetery caretaker Crisp develop a fondness for the pooch, who becomes a cause célèbre when a constable insists he get a collar. Touching Disney tale has one of the most adorable dogs in movie history, plus fine period atmosphere.
Dist.: Buena Vista

GREYSTOKE: THE LEGEND OF TARZAN, LORD OF THE APES 1984
★ ★ ★ **PG Drama 2:10**
☑ Brief nudity, violence
Dir: Hugh Hudson *Cast:* Christopher Lambert, Ian Holm, Andie MacDowell, Ralph Richardson, Nigel Davenport, James Fox, Cheryl Campbell, Ian Charleson
▶ Sophisticated, lavish retelling of the Edgar Rice Burroughs classic stars Lambert as the Sixth Earl of Greystoke, born in the jungle to shipwrecked parents and raised by apes. "Civilized" by Belgian explorer Holm, Tarzan is brought to England to claim his inheritance. Incredible ape makeup by Rick Baker is one of the highlights. Film debut for MacDowell (whose southern voice was dubbed over by Glenn Close). Richardson's final film. **(CC)**
Dist.: Warner

GRIEVOUS BODILY HARM 1988 Australian
★ ★ ★ **R Mystery-Suspense 1:36**
☑ Nudity, adult situations, explicit language, violence
Dir: Mark Joffe *Cast:* Colin Friels, John Waters, Bruno Lawrence, Joy Bell, Chris Stalker
▶ Violent schoolteacher Waters realizes his supposedly late wife may still be alive, kills a possible witness, and goes on a rampage.

Corrupt cop Lawrence investigates and unscrupulous reporter Friels covers the story as the bodies and plot twists pile up in this absorbing mystery. Nicely cast and directed if not terribly original.
Dist.: Fries

GRISSOM GANG, THE 1971
★ ★ **R Action-Adventure 2:07**
☑ Adult situations, explicit language, violence
Dir: Robert Aldrich *Cast:* Kim Darby, Scott Wilson, Tony Musante, Robert Lansing, Irene Dailey, Connie Stevens
▶ In the 1930s, gangster mom Dailey and her clan nab rich girl Darby and demand ransom; Dailey's son Wilson and Darby fall in love. Slambang action in an off-beat story; characterizations and performances are bizarre but compelling (especially the over-the-top Wilson).
Dist.: CBS/Fox

GRIZZLY 1976
★ ★ ★ **PG Action-Adventure 1:32**
☑ Explicit language, graphic violence
Dir: William Girdler *Cast:* Christopher George, Andrew Prine, Richard Jaeckel, Joan McCall, Joe Dorsey
▶ Enraged grizzly goes on the rampage in a Georgia forest; heroic ranger George and dedicated naturalist Jaeckel pursue the beast, hampered by meddling reporter McCall. Violent action takes precedence over characterizations in this low-budget mayhem modeled after *Jaws*.
Dist.: Media

GROOVE TUBE, THE 1974
★ ★ **R Comedy 1:13**
☑ Nudity, adult situations, explicit language, adult humor
Dir: Ken Shapiro *Cast:* Ken Shapiro, Chevy Chase, Richard Belzer, Buzzy Linhart
▶ In ten sketches masquerading as the program "The Groove Tube," writer/director/producer Shapiro takes a jaundiced look at TV commercials, Hollywood glitz, children's shows (where a clown reads from *Fanny Hill*) and more. Cult curio is wildly irreverent, with loads of scatological humor. Pre–"Saturday Night Live" Chevy Chase appears as a newscaster.
Dist.: Media

GROSS ANATOMY 1989
★ ★ ★ ★ **PG-13 Comedy 1:47**
☑ Adult situations, explicit language
Dir: Thom Eberhardt *Cast:* Matthew Modine, Daphne Zuniga, Christine Lahti, Zakes Mokae, Todd Field, John Scott Clough
▶ Cocky student Modine plans to glide through medical school on the strength of his retentive memory, alienating tough doctor Lahti who wants him to do better. Modine romances lab parter Zuniga and deals with second semester crises involving roommate Field and Lahti. Ultimately upbeat sleeper missed

theatrically but personable cast and entertaining story should give it new life on video. (CC)
Dist.: Buena Vista

GROTESQUE 1988
★ **R Horror 1:30**
◻ Explicit language, violence
Dir: Joe Tornatore *Cast:* Linda Blair, Tab Hunter, Donna Wilkes, Guy Stockwell, Nels Van Patten, Brad Wilson
▶ Blair and friend Wilkes go to the mountains for a family reunion and are menaced by a punker gang. After a retarded relative escapes from his basement cage and kills two of the punks, Blair's plastic surgeon uncle Hunter uses the tools of his trade to finish the job. Laughable story with little suspense although Hunter tries hard.
Dist.: Media

GROUNDSTAR CONSPIRACY, THE 1972
★★ **PG Mystery-Suspense 1:35**
◻ Violence
Dir: Lamont Johnson *Cast:* George Peppard, Michael Sarrazin, Christine Belford, Cliff Potts, James Olson, James McEachin
▶ Bomb goes off at government space project, killing several researchers. Is scientist/survivor Sarrazin involved? Inquiring agent Peppard wants to know. Overlooked and underrated suspenser features taut direction, first-rate performances, and intricate plotting.
Dist.: MCA

GROUND ZERO 1988 Australian
★★★ **PG-13 Mystery-Suspense 1:40**
◻ Explicit language, violence
Dir: Michael Pattinson, Bruce Myles *Cast:* Colin Friels, Jack Thompson, Donald Pleasence, Natalie Bate
▶ Cameraman Friels connects his father's death thirty years ago to nuclear bomb tests and battles government thugs intent on preserving a cover-up. Paranoid thriller gets off to a slow start but builds logically to create a fair amount of tension; Friels is sympathetic.
Dist.: IVE

GROUP, THE 1966
★★★ **NR Drama 2:30**
Dir: Sidney Lumet *Cast:* Candice Bergen, Joan Hackett, Elizabeth Hartman, Shirley Knight, Joanna Pettet, Jessica Walter, Mary-Robin Redd, Kathleen Widdoes, James Broderick, Larry Hagman, Richard Mulligan, Hal Holbrook
▶ Eight women friends graduate from Vassar in the 1930s and find the real world fraught with difficulties. Walter becomes a successful but lonely author, Bergen turns to lesbianism, Knight gets involved with a married man, and Pettet suffers through a bad marriage with tragic consequences. Juicy all-star soap opera from the Mary McCarthy best-seller.
Dist.: Key

GRUNT! THE WRESTLING MOVIE 1985
☆ **R Comedy 1:30**
◻ Explicit language, violence
Dir: Allan Holzman *Cast:* Jeff Dial, Robert Glaudini, Marilyn Dodds Farr, Greg Magic Schwartz, Bill Grant, Steve Cepello
▶ Filmmaker Dial investigates possibility that wrestler Schwartz, an apparent suicide after accidentally decapitating an opponent six years previous, may have returned to the ring as "The Mask." Vulgar comedy with unfunny cursing and choppy editing. Wrestling fans may enjoy the climactic ten-man bout.
Dist.: Warner

GUADALCANAL DIARY 1943
★★★★ **NR War 1:33 B&W**
Dir: Lewis Seiler *Cast:* Preston Foster, Lloyd Nolan, William Bendix, Richard Conte, Anthony Quinn
▶ One of Hollywood's best World War II actioners about Marines battling the Japanese to capture a strategic Pacific base. Features the usual disparate cast of characters brought together to fight like brothers, with Bendix stealing the show as a Brooklyn taxi driver. Based on the book by Richard Tregaskis.
Dist.: CBS/Fox

GUARDIAN, THE 1984
★★★ **NR Crime/MFTV 1:41**
◻ Rape, adult situations, explicit language, graphic violence
Dir: David Greene *Cast:* Louis Gossett, Jr., Martin Sheen, Arthur Hill, Tandy Cronyn
▶ No-nonsense ex–military man Gossett is hired as a security guard for a crime-plagued Manhattan apartment building. He is pitted against ultra-liberal tenant Sheen, who's concerned that Gossett is taking the law into his own hands. Engrossing crime drama.
Dist.: Vestron

GUARDIAN, THE 1990
★★★ **R Horror 1:35**
◻ Nudity, adult situations, explicit language, violence
Dir: William Friedkin *Cast:* Jenny Seagrove, Dwier Brown, Carey Lowell, Brad Hall, Miguel Ferrer, Natalia Nogulich
▶ Brown and Lowell hire beautiful Seagrove to look after their infant son. In her private life, Seagrove combines tree-worship with human sacrifice, and her hidden agenda as a nanny includes giving up the baby's life to a fearsome neighborhood plant. Some scares in spite of silly plot. Based on Dan Greenberg's novel *The Nanny.*
Dist.: MCA

GUESS WHO'S COMING TO DINNER 1967
★★★★★ **NR Drama 1:48**
Dir: Stanley Kramer *Cast:* Spencer Tracy, Katharine Hepburn, Sidney Poitier, Katharine Houghton, Cecil Kellaway
▶ College senior Houghton announces to upper-middle-class parents Tracy and Hep-

burn her intention to marry brilliant research physician Poitier, who happens to be black. Graceful, entertaining story about the social turmoil experienced by both her family and his. Perhaps best known as the final film pairing of Hepburn and Tracy (he died a few weeks after the movie was shot). Garnered Oscars for Hepburn and the screenplay; nomination for Tracy. (CC)
Dist.: RCA/Columbia

GUIDE FOR THE MARRIED MAN, A 1967
★ ★ ★ **NR Comedy 1:29**
Dir: Gene Kelly *Cast:* Walter Matthau, Robert Morse, Inger Stevens, Lucille Ball, Jack Benny, Art Carney
▶ Although married to beautiful Stevens, Matthau is led down the path of infidelity by his womanizing pal Morse before seeing the error of his ways. Ball, Benny, and Carney are among the cameo guest stars in sequences illustrating Morse's advice. Broad, obvious, but very amusing; Morse and Matthau make a great pair.
Dist.: CBS/Fox

GULAG 1985
★ ★ ★ ★ ★ **NR Drama/MFTV 2:10**
⊡ Nudity, explicit language, violence
Dir: Roger Young *Cast:* David Keith, Malcolm McDowell, David Suchet, Warren Clarke, Nancy Paul
▶ American sportscaster Keith is railroaded by the KGB into a Russian labor camp. Struggling with the bitter cold and the cruelty of the guards, he plots a daring breakout with fellow prisoner McDowell. Top-notch escape drama.
Dist.: Prism

GULLIVER'S TRAVELS 1939
★ ★ **NR Animation 1:14**
Dir: Dave Fleischer *Cast:* Voices of Lanny Ross, Jessica Dragonette
▶ Shipwrecked Gulliver washes ashore in Lilliput and helps the tiny residents defeat the enemy Blefuscians while nurturing romance between the son and daughter of the rival kings. Attempt by the Fleischer brothers to create a Disney-style feature is fully animated, with well-painted backgrounds and an amusing lead character in the person of Gabby, the garrulous night watchman. But caricatured Lilliputians and realistic Gulliver don't seem to inhabit the same universe. Still worth seeing by children and adults. Songs include "All's Well" and the Oscar-nominated "Faithful Forever."
Dist.: Goodtimes

GULLIVER'S TRAVELS 1977 British/Belgian
★ **G Family 1:20**
Dir: Peter Hunt *Cast:* Richard Harris, Catherine Schell, Norman Shelley, Meredith Edwards, voices of Julian Glover, Murray Melvin
▶ Mix of live action and animation features Harris as a man who is shipwrecked on an island of very small people. Kids old enough to

have seen *Who Framed Roger Rabbit* won't think much of the animation, and the songs by Michel Legrand are as bland as can be. Based on Jonathan Swift's classic book.
Dist.: United

GUMBALL RALLY, THE 1976
★ ★ ★ **PG Action-Adventure 1:47**
⊡ Adult situations
Dir: Chuck Bail *Cast:* Michael Sarrazin, Tim McIntire, Raul Julia, Gary Busey, Norman Burton, John Durren, Susan Flannery
▶ Oddball motorists stage a cross-country auto race. Violating every traffic law from New York to Los Angeles, they escape the vengeful cop out to stop them. Harmless and fast-moving, with some good gags and tons of car crashes.
Dist.: Warner

GUMSHOE 1972 British
★ **PG Comedy 1:28**
⊡ Adult situations, violence
Dir: Stephen Frears *Cast:* Albert Finney, Billie Whitelaw, Janice Rule, Frank Finlay, Fulton MacKay, Carolyn Seymour
▶ Ordinary Brit Finney decides to try his hand at the private eye business. He soon finds himself up to his neck in intrigue and danger with gunrunner Rule and members of his own family. English parody of American genre films will appeal to sophisticated tastes. Musical score by theatrical composer Andrew Lloyd Webber.
Dist.: RCA/Columbia

GUMSHOE KID, THE 1989
★ ★ **R Mystery-Suspense 1:30**
⊡ Nudity, adult situations, explicit language
Dir: Joseph Manduke *Cast:* Jay Underwood, Tracy Scoggins, Vince Edwards, Pamela Springsteen
▶ Harvard-bound Underwood has to get a job after his father dies, and takes over half of inherited detective agency run by Edwards. His first job goes haywire when Scoggins, whom he is supposed to be following, is spirited away by thugs. Police are unhelpful, and Underwood and Scoggins soon find themselves enmeshed in KGB/CIA mess. Film has a little action, a few laughs, some cute asides. Time passes.
Dist.: Academy

GUNFIGHT, A 1971
★ ★ ★ **PG Western 1:33**
⊡ Adult situations, explicit language
Dir: Lamont Johnson *Cast:* Kirk Douglas, Johnny Cash, Jane Alexander, Karen Black, Raf Vallone, Eric Douglas
▶ Former gunfighter Douglas now lives quietly with wife Alexander and works as celebrity bouncer at a local bar. Into town rides over-the-hill gunslinger Cash, prompting speculation about a shoot-out between the two legends. Cash and Douglas decide to make a buck on the local tongue-wagging and charge admission to their showdown. Unusual,

atmospheric Western was financed by oil-rich Jicarilla Apaches of New Mexico.
Dist.: Thorn/EMI

GUNFIGHT AT THE O.K. CORRAL 1957
★ ★ ★ ★ NR Western 2:02
Dir: John Sturges *Cast:* Burt Lancaster, Kirk Douglas, Rhonda Fleming, Jo Van Fleet, John Ireland, Lyle Bettger, Earl Holliman, Dennis Hopper, Lee Van Cleef, Jack Elam
▶ Gripping, authentic account of the friendship between lawman Wyatt Earp (Lancaster) and gunslinger Doc Holliday (Douglas) and the events leading up to their famous shootout with the Clanton gang. Memorable acting, richly detailed script, and taut direction aided film's popular success and helped reestablish the importance of the Western genre. Director Sturges returned to the subject in 1967's *Hour of the Gun.*
Dist.: Paramount

GUNFIGHTER, THE 1950
★ ★ ★ ★ NR Western 1:24 B&W
Dir: Henry King *Cast:* Gregory Peck, Helen Westcott, Millard Mitchell, Jean Parker, Karl Malden, Skip Homeier
▶ Peck gives a bravura performance as Johnny Ringo, an aging gunslinger haunted by his past as he waits in a grimy frontier town for a glimpse of estranged wife Westcott and son. Somber, thoughtful Western is first-rate on all levels, particularly the assured, steady direction and Homeier's memorable turn as a novice gunman trying to goad Peck into a confrontation.
Dist.: CBS/Fox

GUN FURY 1953
★ ★ NR Western 1:23
Dir: Raoul Walsh *Cast:* Rock Hudson, Donna Reed, Phil Carey, Roberta Haynes, Lee Marvin, Neville Brand
▶ Compact Western set in Arizona, with Hudson and Reed playing newlyweds terrorized by Carey, a genuinely disturbing villain. When Reed is kidnapped, Hudson must sink to Carey's level to rescue her. Originally released in 3-D.
Dist.: RCA/Columbia

GUNGA DIN 1939
★ ★ ★ ★ NR Action-Adventure 1:57 B&W
Dir: George Stevens *Cast:* Cary Grant, Victor McLaglen, Douglas Fairbanks, Jr., Sam Jaffe, Eduardo Ciannelli, Joan Fontaine
▶ An outstandingly heroic trio of British sergeants (Grant, McLaglen, and Fairbanks) grapple with a murderous Thugee cult in colonial India, helped by native water boy Jaffe, who dreams of becoming a soldier. Rousing blend of action, humor, and romance, loosely based on the Rudyard Kipling poem, is one of Hollywood's greatest adventures.
Dist.: Turner Ⓒ

GUNG HO! 1943
★ ★ NR War 1:28 B&W

Dir: Ray Enright *Cast:* Randolph Scott, Grace McDonald, Peter Coe, Noah Beery, Jr., J. Carrol Naish, Robert Mitchum
▶ Scott molds a motley group of World War II Marines into a crack team of jungle warriors. Objective: the Japanese-held island of Makin. Crazed Japanese defenders have their hands full with tough lieutenant Naish and mean grunts Mitchum and Coe. Based on the exploits of an actual battalion.
Dist.: Republic Ⓒ

GUNG HO 1986
★ ★ ★ ★ PG-13 Comedy 2:00
☑ Adult situations, explicit language
Dir: Ron Howard *Cast:* Michael Keaton, George Wendt, Gedde Watanabe, Mimi Rogers, John Turturro, Soh Yamamura
▶ Car plant foreman Keaton convinces Japanese company to take over his hometown's abandoned auto factory, then is caught in the middle when the new bosses' strict ways clash with American methods. Terrific premise cheerfully directed, niftily acted by cocky Keaton and uptight Watanabe. Script could have used some more fine tuning, but overall, quite pleasing. (CC)
Dist.: Paramount

GUNS OF NAVARONE, THE 1961
★ ★ ★ ★ ★ NR War 2:39
Dir: J. Lee Thompson *Cast:* Gregory Peck, David Niven, Anthony Quinn, Anthony Quayle, Stanley Baker
▶ On the Greek island of Kheros, a worn-out World War II garrison faces Axis annihilation unless a group of Allied commandos led by Peck can dismantle the two radar-controlled German cannons guarding their evacuation route. High-powered Hollywood triumph-over-impossible-odds story based on Alistair MacLean's best-seller. Nominated for seven Academy Awards, deservedly winning Best Special Effects. Lesser 1978 sequel: *Force 10 From Navarone.*
Dist.: RCA/Columbia

GUNS OF THE MAGNIFICENT SEVEN 1969
★ ★ ★ G Western 1:46
Dir: Paul Wendkos *Cast:* George Kennedy, Monte Markham, James Whitmore, Reni Santoni, Joe Don Baker, Fernando Rey, Bernie Casey, Tony Davis, Scott Thomas
▶ Second follow-up to *The Magnificent Seven* features Kennedy (in the Yul Brynner gunslinger role) getting his outlaw gang back together when he is hired to free rebel leader Rey from a Mexican prison. All the tried-and-true elements have been assembled: a cast of solid pros, Elmer Bernstein score, and tons of guns.
Dist.: MGM/UA

GUS 1976
★ ★ ★ G Comedy 1:36
Dir: Gary McEveety *Cast:* Edward Asner, Don Knotts, Gary Grimes, Tim Conway, Liberty Williams

▶ More family fun from the folks at Disney. Asner and Knotts, the owner and coach, respectively, of a struggling football team, find fortunes reversed by an unlikely new player: a field-goal-kicking mule. Former pros Johnny Unitas and Dick Butkus appear, but realism is not film's strong suit.
Dist.: Buena Vista

GUY NAMED JOE, A 1944
★★★★ **NR Fantasy 2:00 B&W**
Dir: Victor Fleming *Cast:* Spencer Tracy, Irene Dunne, Van Johnson, Ward Bond, James Gleason, Lionel Barrymore, Esther Williams, Barry Nelson, Blake Edwards
▶ Killed in battle, pilot Tracy finds himself assigned as a guardian angel to novice flier Johnson. To Tracy's consternation, Johnson pursues his old girlfriend Dunne, herself a flying ace. Large-scale fantasy was a popular World War II hit, although blend of whimsy, sentimentality, and ghosts seems forced today. Steven Speilberg remade this in 1989 as *Always*.
Dist.: MGM/UA

GUYS AND DOLLS 1955
★★★★ **NR Musical 2:29**
Dir: Joseph L. Mankiewicz *Cast:* Marlon Brando, Jean Simmons, Frank Sinatra, Vivian Blaine, Stubby Kaye
▶ In Damon Runyon's New York, Nathan Detroit (Sinatra) tries to finance his floating crap game by betting gambler Sky Masterson (Brando) that he can't win the heart of Salvation Army officer Simmons. All-star cast delivers the goods in this professional and entertaining adaptation of Frank Loesser's Broadway smash. Hummable songs include "Luck Be a Lady," "If I Were a Bell." **(CC)**
Dist.: CBS/Fox

GYMKATA 1985
★ **R Martial Arts 1:30**
☑ Graphic violence
Dir: Robert Clouse *Cast:* Kurt Thomas, Tetchie Agbayani, Richard Norton, Edward Bell, John Barrett
▶ Gymnastics gold medalist Thomas is sent to compete in a remote Himalayan country's life-and-death endurance contest that grants the winner one wish. Loud bone-crunching outshines acting and dialogue. Based on Dan Tyler Moore's novel, *The Terrible Game*.
Dist.: MGM/UA

GYPSY 1963
★★★ **NR Biography/Musical 2:23**
Dir: Mervyn LeRoy *Cast:* Rosalind Russell, Natalie Wood, Karl Malden, Paul Wallace, Betty Bruce, Ann Jillian
▶ Stage mother Russell pushes daughters Jillian and Wood into theatrical careers, which proceed on a downward course until Wood finds a niche as stripper Gypsy Rose Lee. Although she overacts, Russell is effective. Brassy musical adaptation of the Jule Styne/Steven Sondheim Broadway hit. Songs include "Ev-

erything's Coming Up Roses" and "Let Me Entertain You."
Dist.: Warner

HADLEY'S REBELLION 1984
★★★ **PG Drama 1:36**
☑ Explicit language, mild violence
Dir: Fred Walton *Cast:* Griffin O'Neal, William Devane, Charles Durning, Adam Baldwin
▶ O'Neal, a youngster from Georgia, attends California boarding school and tries to prove himself to the other kids with his wrestling prowess. Sensitively crafted coming-of-age drama with decent performances. **(CC)**
Dist.: CBS/Fox

HAIL! HAIL! ROCK 'N' ROLL 1987
★★ **PG Documentary/Music 2:00**
☑ Explicit language
Dir: Taylor Hackford *Cast:* Chuck Berry, Keith Richards, Eric Clapton, Robert Cray, ·Etta James, Julian Lennon, Linda Ronstadt, Bruce Springsteen, Little Richard
▶ Marvelous tribute to rock pioneer Chuck Berry on his sixtieth birthday. Interviews from top musicians combine with fascinating concert footage that climaxes in an all-star bash in his St. Louis hometown. Astute direction and editing reveal Berry as a complex, contradictory figure. Richards, Springsteen, Little Richard, and many others contribute valuable insights. Also known as *Chuck Berry Hail! Hail! Rock 'n' Roll*.
Dist.: MCA

HAIL MARY 1985 French/Swiss
☆ **NR Drama 1:47**
☑ Nudity, strong sexual content, adult situations, explicit language
Dir: Jean-Luc Godard *Cast:* Myriem Roussel, Thierry Rode, Philippe Lacoste, Juliette Binoche, Manon Anderson
▶ In this modern retelling of the Nativity, Virgin Mary works at a gas station, Joseph is her moody cabdriver boyfriend, and the angel Gabriel is a seedy stranger. Story provides the peg for Godard's voice-over reveries about womanhood, spirituality, and sex. Controversial drama was condemned by the Catholic Church.
Dist.: Vestron

HAIL THE CONQUERING HERO 1944
★★★★★ **NR Comedy 1:41 B&W**
Dir: Preston Sturges *Cast:* Eddie Bracken, Ella Raines, Bill Edwards, Raymond Walburn, William Demarest, Freddie Steele, Jimmy Conlin, Alan Bridge, Franklin Pangborn
▶ Demarest and his fellow Marines, veterans of Guadalcanal, donate their medals to embarrassed 4-F reject Bracken so he can return home a hero. Despite Bracken's protests, his gullible neighbors nominate him for mayor. Devastating satire on wartime patriotism is a sheer delight from start to finish. Familiar Sturges character actors handle the sparkling

dialogue with aplomb. Nominated for Best Screenplay.
Dist.: MCA

HAIR 1979
★★ PG Musical 2:01
☑ Nudity, explicit language
Dir: Milos Forman *Cast:* John Savage, Treat Williams, Beverly D'Angelo, Annie Golden, Dorsey Wright, Don Dacus, Charlotte Rae
▸ Oklahoma farm boy Savage, in New York City for his induction, gets sidetracked by a tribe of hippies obsessed with turning him on to drugs, sex, and peace. Forman's glowing tribute to the euphoria of flower children, adapted from the 1968 Broadway love-rock musical, features be-ins, draft dodgers, hippie rags, and lots of hair. Far-out performances, exuberant Twyla Tharp cheoreography, and seminal sixties soundtrack: "Aquarius," "Easy to be Hard," White Boys/Black Boys," more.
Dist.: MGM/UA

HAIRSPRAY 1988
★★ PG Comedy 1:34
☑ Explicit language
Dir: John Waters *Cast:* Divine, Ricki Lake, Debbie Harry, Sonny Bono, Jerry Stiller, Pia Zadora, Ric Ocasek
▸ With the support of parents Divine and Stiller, perky chubette Lake auditions for a popular teen dance show in 1960s Baltimore. She wows the kids with her Mashed Potato but garners the wrath of rival Amber and Amber's parents Harry and Bono. Bubble-headed series of teenage crises and crushes also touches on the civil rights movement, but plot is secondary to the campy acting and lacquered bouffants. Cult director Waters at his most goofball benign. Film was his most popular success, crossing over to mainstream audiences. (CC)
Dist.: RCA/Columbia

HALF LIFE 1986
★★★ NR Documentary 1:26
☑ Adult situations
Dir: Dennis O'Rourke
▸ Highly charged documentary makes case that U.S. weapons testers deliberately exposed South Sea islanders to H-bomb radiation in 1950s. Lovely photography of gorgeous islands poisoned by radiation; tragic interviews with victims, some of whom unwittingly played in fallout as if it were snow.
Dist.: Kino

HALF MOON STREET 1986
★★ R Drama 1:30
☑ Nudity, strong sexual content, explicit language, violence
Dir: Bob Swaim *Cast:* Michael Caine, Sigourney Weaver, Patrick Kavanagh, Faith Kent, Ram John Holder
▸ Unconventional Weaver is a serious scholar by day, high-class hooker by night. Caine, a diplomat and client, involves her in the world of international intrigue. Film boasts remarkable technical credits (costumes, production, etc.), a too-violent climax and lots of Sigourney-in-the-buff shots. Based on Paul Theroux's novella. (CC)
Dist.: Nelson

HALF OF HEAVEN 1988 Spanish
☆ NR Comedy/Drama 2:07
☑ Adult situations, explicit language
Dir: Manuel Gutienez Aragon *Cast:* Angela Molina, Margarita Lozano, Antonio V. Valero, Nacho Martinez, Santiago Ramos, Francisco Merino
▸ Offbeat, fantastical tale in which Molina goes from being a poor wet nurse to mistress of the ritziest restaurant in Madrid. Along the way, she learns everything from how to market animal innards to the art of giving a banquet. Unfolding at a gentle pace, story is full of earthy, engaging characterizations. [S]
Dist.: Pacific Arts

HALLOWEEN 1978
★★★ R Horror 1:31
☑ Brief nudity, adult situations, explicit language, violence
Dir: John Carpenter *Cast:* Donald Pleasence, Jamie Lee Curtis, P. J. Soles, Nancy Loomis, Charles Cyphers
▸ A young boy is institutionalized after killing his sister. Fifteen years later, on Halloween, he escapes to menace baby-sitter Curtis and her high school pals. Evocative direction by Carpenter (who also wrote the chilling music score) uses inventive camerawork and deceptively peaceful settings to create a fantastic fright flick. Curtis is quite good as the terrorized heroine. Followed by three sequels.
Dist.: Media

HALLOWEEN II 1981
★★ R Horror 1:32
☑ Nudity, explicit language, graphic violence
Dir: Rick Rosenthal *Cast:* Jamie Lee Curtis, Donald Pleasence, Charles Cyphers, Pamela Susan Shoop, Lance Guest
▸ Just when you thought it was safe to go trick-or-treating. . . Sequel begins where the first left off: Curtis is in the hospital recovering from her ordeal when the crazed killer, not really dead as believed, tracks her down. Not nearly as subtle or confident as the first flick but delivers blood, gore, and a few solid jolts.
Dist.: MCA

HALLOWEEN III: SEASON OF THE WITCH 1982
★★ R Horror 1:38
☑ Adult situations, explicit language, graphic violence
Dir: Tommy Lee Wallace *Cast:* Tom Atkins, Stacey Nelkin, Dan O'Herlihy, Ralph Strait
▸ After one of his patients is killed, doctor Atkins and the murdered man's daughter Nelkin investigate. They uncover a scheme by mad toy manufacturer O'Herlihy to kill children via deadly Halloween masks. Slickly mounted

horror film is well executed but series fans be warned: story is unrelated to first two *Halloween* flicks.
Dist.: MCA

HALLOWEEN IV: THE RETURN OF MICHAEL MYERS 1988
★ ★ ★ R Horror 1:28
⊙ Brief nudity, explicit language, graphic violence
Dir: Dwight H. Little   *Cast:* Donald Pleasence, Ellie Cornell, Danielle Harris, George P. Wilbur, Michael Pataki
► En route to a new mental home, homicidal slasher Michael Myers (Wilbur) escapes and heads for his hometown to ravage his sole surviving relative, little niece Harris (who's the daughter of the Jamie Lee Curtis character from the first movie in the series). Wilbur is pursued by gimpy-legged doctor Pleasence. Special effects include an exploding gas station, a gruesome electrocution, and lots of corpses. Film's twist ending sets the stage for a whole new series of sequels.
Dist.: CBS/Fox

HALLOWEEN 5: THE REVENGE OF MICHAEL MYERS 1989
★ ★ R Horror 1:36
⊙ Explicit language, graphic violence
Dir: Dominique Othenin-Girard   *Cast:* Danielle Harris, Donald Pleasence, Donald L. Shanks, Wendy Kaplan, Ellie Cornell
► It's that time of year again, and Michael Myers (Shanks) is back to do his bit for population control. Having been buried alive in the previous installment, Myers tunnels out and starts looking once again for his little niece Jamie (Harris). Nutty psychiatrist Pleasence uses Jamie to catch him and put him in jail. Michael, however, won't stay jailed for long. Viewers know it all already.   **(CC)**
Dist.: CBS/Fox

HALLS OF MONTEZUMA 1950
★ ★ ★ ★ NR War 1:53
Dir: Lewis Milestone   *Cast:* Richard Widmark, Jack Palance, Karl Malden, Robert Wagner, Richard Hylton, Richard Boone, Skip Homeier, Jack Webb
► During World War II, lieutenant Widmark leads American Marines, including Palance and Wagner, on a dangerous mission to locate a Japanese rocket site in the South Pacific. The men are forced to take prisoners to achieve their objective. Riveting war drama, superbly acted and directed.
Dist.: CBS/Fox

HAMBONE AND HILLIE 1984
★ ★ ★ ★ PG Family 1:30
⊙ Violence
Dir: Roy Watts   *Cast:* Lillian Gish, O. J. Simpson, Timothy Bottoms, Candy Clark, Jack Carter
► Elderly Gish, returning to L.A. after visiting grandson Bottoms in New York City, loses mutt Hambone at the airport. The resilient pet makes a cross-country journey and is eventually reunited with owner. Simple story provides vehicle for the cutest cinematic canine since Benji.
Dist.: HBO

HAMBURGER HILL 1987
★ ★ ★ ★ R War 1:34
⊙ Nudity, adult situations, explicit language, graphic violence
Dir: John Irvin   *Cast:* Michael Patrick Boatman, Tegan West, Dylan McDermott, Courtney Vance, Tommy Swerdlow, Steven Weber
► In 1969, fresh American recruits are launched into a hellish battle against the North Vietnamese for possession of a hill. Forthright staging by Irvin and raw script by Vietnam vet James Carabatsos give an authentic grunt's-eye-view of war's carnage and confusion. Very graphic violence makes for disturbing end; difficult to view but hard to ignore.
Dist.: Vestron

HAMBURGER. . .THE MOTION PICTURE 1986
★ R Comedy 1:30
☑ Nudity, adult situations, explicit language
Dir: Mike Marvin   *Cast:* Leigh McCloskey, Dick Butkus, Randi Brooks, Chuck McCann, Jack Blessing, Debra Blee
► After being expelled from four colleges, young McCloskey must clean up his act or be disinherited. He enrolls in a twelve-week course at Burgerbuster University for a degree in the fast-food biz. A few laughs and some nubile topless coeds; cinematic equivalent of a Big Mac.   **(CC)**
Dist.: Media

HAMLET 1948 British
★ ★ NR Drama 2:33 B&W
Dir: Laurence Olivier   *Cast:* Laurence Olivier, Eileen Herlie, Basil Sydney, Jean Simmons, Norman Wooland, Stanley Holloway, Anthony Quayle
► Overwhelming performance by Olivier as the mad prince of Denmark distinguishes this noteworthy drama. Although play is abridged somewhat, cast and directing rank this among the best of Shakespeare adaptations. Simmons is suitably ethereal as Ophelia; John Gielgud supplies the voice of Hamlet's father's ghost. Best Picture winner also received Oscars for Olivier and the stark set design.
Dist.: Paramount

HAMLET 1969 British
★ G Drama 1:58
Dir: Tony Richardson   *Cast:* Nicol Williamson, Gordon Jackson, Anthony Hopkins, Judy Parfitt, Mark Dignam, Marianne Faithfull
► Respectable adaptation of Shakespeare's tragedy pits Williamson's intense interpretation of Hamlet against Hopkins's larger-than-life performance as Claudius. Peculiar casting

of pop star Faithfull as Ophelia is surprisingly successful. Look for Anjelica Huston as one of the court ladies.
Dist.: RCA/Columbia

HAMMETT 1982
★ **PG Mystery-Suspense 1:37**
☺ Brief nudity, adult situations, explicit language, violence
Dir: Wim Wenders *Cast:* Frederic Forrest, Peter Boyle, Marilu Henner, Roy Kinnear, Elisha Cook, Jr., Lydia Lei
▶ In 1928, Pinkerton detective Boyle asks aspiring mystery writer Dashiell Hammett (Forrest) for help on a baffling case involving missing Chinese woman Lei. Francis Ford Coppola produced this atmospheric but confusing thriller. Evocative sets, outstanding photography, and amusing in-jokes almost salvage the often tedious plot.
Dist.: Warner

HAND, THE 1981
★ **R Horror 1:44**
☺ Nudity, adult situations, explicit language, graphic violence
Dir: Oliver Stone *Cast:* Michael Caine, Andrea Marcovicci, Annie McEnroe, Bruce McGill, Viveca Lindfors
▶ Intellectually challenging thriller about cartoonist Caine whose drawing hand is severed in a car accident. Psychologically as well as physically damaged, he destroys his marriage and sinks into murderous fantasies. Caine gives an astute performance in this sometimes gory shocker.
Dist.: Warner

HANDFUL OF DUST, A 1988 British
★ **PG Drama 1:58**
☺ Brief nudity, adult situations, explicit language
Dir: Charles Sturridge *Cast:* James Wilby, Kristin Scott Thomas, Rupert Graves, Anjelica Huston, Judi Dench, Alec Guinness
▶ In 1930s England, stuffy Wilby is devoted to country estate, while bored wife Thomas takes social-climbing lover Graves in the city. Affair plus family tragedy prove fatal to the marriage. "Masterpiece Theatre"-style filmmaking meticulously re-creates the period, but heartless characters make for unsatisfying experience. Based on the Evelyn Waugh novel.
Dist.: RCA/Columbia

HANDLE WITH CARE 1977
★ ★ **PG Comedy 1:38**
☺ Adult situations, explicit language
Dir: Jonathan Demme *Cast:* Paul LeMat, Candy Clark, Ann Wedgeworth, Bruce McGill, Hobert S. Blossom, Charles Napier
▶ Inventive comedy, released at the height of the CB craze, examines the wacky inhabitants of a Southwestern town—all fascinated with citizen-band radios—in a series of winsome vignettes. Napier, as a bigamist trucker,

shines in this smoothly entertaining story. Originally titled *Citizens Band*.
Dist.: Paramount

HANDMAID'S TALE, THE 1990
★ ★ **R Drama 1:49**
☺ Nudity, strong sexual content, adult situations, explicit language, violence
Dir: Volker Schlondorff *Cast:* Natasha Richardson, Faye Dunaway, Aidan Quinn, Elizabeth McGovern, Victoria Tennant, Robert Duvall
▶ In a bleak near-future where the few fertile women are enslaved for their reproductive capacity, Richardson is forced to live with government commander Duvall and wife Dunaway but may find real love and escape with chauffeur Quinn. Ambitious adaptation of Margaret Atwood's novel has several disturbing scenes but Jennifer Bartlett's striking production design may be too pretty for the subject. McGovern is outstanding as Richardson's lesbian friend. Screenplay by Harold Pinter. **(CC)**
Dist.: HBO

HANDS OF ORLAC, THE 1960 British/French
★ **NR Horror 1:35 B&W**
Dir: Edmond T. Gréville *Cast:* Mel Ferrer, Christopher Lee, Dany Carrel, Felix Alymer, Donald Pleasence, Donald Wolfit
▶ Concert pianist Ferrer loses his hands in a plane crash. Surgeon Wolfit gives him new mitts that used to belong to a killer.'Now the musician thinks himself capable of killing. Lee is the menacing magician who blackmails Ferrer. Remake of 1935's *Mad Love* starring Peter Lorre is not bad, but not as good as the original.
Dist.: Sinister

HANDS OF STEEL 1986 Italian
★ **R Action-Adventure 1:34**
☺ Explicit language, violence
Dir: Martin Dolman (Sergio Martino) *Cast:* Daniel Greene, Janet Agren, John Saxon, George Eastman, Amy Werba
▶ Mysterious Italian assassin Greene bungles an assignment and flees to the Arizona desert, where he befriends beautiful Agren. Greene defends her from brutal arm wrestlers who later ambush him in a trap. When Agren rescues him, he reveals that he's a high-tech mandroid. Low-budget exploitation suffers from poor dubbing and special effects.
Dist.: Vestron

HANDS OF THE RIPPER 1971 British
★ **R Horror 1:22**
☺ Adult situations, explicit language, violence
Dir: Peter Sadsy *Cast:* Eric Porter, Angharad Rees, Jane Merrow, Keith Bell, Derek Godfrey, Dora Bryan
▶ As a child, Jack the Ripper's daughter Rees witnessed her dad killing her mother. Traumatized by the experience, she fears her own capacity for violence and consults psychia-

trist Porter. A possibly fatal attraction ensues. Shocker done with intelligence and style is worth a look.
Dist.: VidAmerica

HANGAR 18 1980
★ ★ ★ PG Sci-Fi 1:37
☑ Adult situations, explicit language, violence
Dir: James L. Conway *Cast:* Darren McGavin, Robert Vaughn, Gary Collins, James Hampton, Philip Abbott, Joseph Campanella
▶ UFO collides with an earth satellite and crashes in Arizona. White House official Vaughn whisks spaceship off to top-secret location and plants cover story that NASA's astronauts wrecked satellite. To clear names, astros try to blow lid off government cover-up. For the gullible only.
Dist.: Worldvision

HANG 'EM HIGH 1968
★ ★ ★ R Western 1:54
☑ Adult situations, explicit language, violence
Dir: Ted Post *Cast:* Clint Eastwood, Inger Stevens, Ed Begley, Bruce Dern, Dennis Hopper, Ben Johnson
▶ Innocent rancher Eastwood swears revenge on the men who tried to lynch him. Derivative Hollywood version of Eastwood's highly successful spaghetti Westerns is violent, technically polished, and filled with strong supporting work, including Western veteran Bob Steele as a dungeon prisoner.
Dist.: MGM/UA

HANGMAN'S KNOT 1952
★ ★ NR Western 1:21
Dir: Roy Huggins *Cast:* Randolph Scott, Donna Reed, Claude Jarman, Jr., Richard Denning, Lee Marvin, Jeanette Nolan
▶ Rebel leader Scott and his men attack a Union gold train during the Civil War, learning afterwards that the war is over and they are now considered common criminals. A gang of bad guys posing as lawmen trap them in an isolated stagecoach station, and Scott must fight them off, while trying to convince his men to return the gold. Tight, tough, and well-directed Western keeps things tense and has a sense of humor.
Dist.: Goodtimes

HANKY PANKY 1982
★ ★ ★ PG Comedy 1:43
☑ Explicit language, violence
Dir: Sidney Poitier *Cast:* Gene Wilder, Gilda Radner, Kathleen Quinlan, Richard Widmark, Robert Prosky, Josef Sommer
▶ Neurotic Chicago architect Wilder is chased by cops, spies, and villains because of a tape containing secret weapons data. Attempt to recapture the success of *Stir Crazy* is a limp mistaken-identity thriller notable for the

first screen teaming of Wilder and Radner, his wife-to-be. (CC)
Dist.: RCA/Columbia

HANNAH AND HER SISTERS 1986
★ ★ PG-13 Comedy 1:47
☑ Adult situations, explicit language
Dir: Woody Allen *Cast:* Woody Allen, Mia Farrow, Michael Caine, Barbara Hershey, Dianne Wiest, Max Von Sydow, Maureen O'-Sullivan, Lloyd Nolan, Carrie Fisher, Daniel Stern, Tony Roberts, Sam Waterston, Julie Kavner, John Turturro, Joanna Gleason, Bobby Short
▶ In the tradition of *Annie Hall*, Allen's fourteenth film as writer/director is warmhearted, wise, and funny. Quirky contemporary drama concerns very different sisters Farrow, Wiest, and Hershey and their relationships with men, women friends, showbiz parents O'Sullivan and Nolan, and each other. Sterling cast. Three cheers and three Oscars (Caine, Wiest, and Screenplay).
Dist.: HBO

HANNA K 1983 French
★ R Drama 1:50
☑ Adult situations, explicit language, mild violence
Dir: Costa-Gavras *Cast:* Jill Clayburgh, Jean Yanne, Gabriel Byrne, Mohammed Bakri
▶ Quirky Hanna Kaufman (Clayburgh) practices law in Jerusalem. While defending Moslem Bakri for illegally crossing the border, she finds herself caught between her growing personal involvement with him, her pregnancy by Israeli Byrne, and her estranged husband Yanne. Controversial because of its ambiguous Palestinian stand.
Dist.: MCA

HANNA'S WAR 1988
★ ★ PG-13 Biography 2:30
☑ Adult situations
Dir: Menahem Golan *Cast:* Ellen Burstyn, Maruschka Detmers, Anthony Andrews, Donald Pleasence, David Warner, Vincenzo Ricotta
▶ True story of Jewish martyr Hanna Senesh (Detmers), who fled anti-Semitism in her native Hungary for Palestine in the 1930s, but then returned as a British operative to help her people. Sincere but overlong and oversimplified; spirited Detmers well supported by Burstyn as her mother.
Dist.: Media

HANOI HILTON, THE 1987
★ ★ ★ R War 2:10
☑ Explicit language, violence
Dir: Lionel Chetwynd *Cast:* Michael Moriarty, Jeffrey Jones, Paul LeMat, Gloria Carlin, David Soul, Aki Aleong
▶ In a Vietnamese camp, American prisoners of war suffer torture under major Aleong's iron hand. Moriarty leads the men who resist Aleong; LeMat is among those who are not

quite so principled. Grueling drama is solidly acted but heavy-handed, with a right-wing viewpoint unique among recent Vietnam films. Carlin plays a Jane Fonda figure who visits the camp and is resented by the Americans. (CC)
Dist.: Warner

HANOVER STREET 1979
★★★★ PG Romance 1:49
☑ Brief nudity, adult situations, explicit language
Dir: Peter Hyams *Cast:* Harrison Ford, Lesley-Anne Down, Christopher Plummer, Alec McCowen, Richard Masur
▸ Ford, an American bomber pilot, and Down, a married Englishwoman, meet in London during the Blitzkrieg and fall in love. Coincidentally, Down's husband Plummer, a British intelligence officer, and Ford are brought together on a crucial mission behind enemy lines, not knowing they love the same woman. Old-fashioned, nostalgic romance.
Dist.: RCA/Columbia

HANS BRINKER AND THE SILVER SKATES 1979
★★★ NR Family 1:43
Dir: Robert Scheerer *Cast:* Eleanor Parker, Richard Basehart, Cyril Ritchard, John Gregson, Robin Askwith
▸ The beloved story of poor Dutch boy Gregson's determination to help his invalid father and win a pair of silver skates. Expert acting from Parker; Basehart and Ritchard add class. Wholesome family classic shot on location in Amsterdam.
Dist.: Warner

HANS CHRISTIAN ANDERSEN 1952
★★★★★ NR Biography/Musical 1:52
Dir: Charles Vidor *Cast:* Danny Kaye, Farley Granger, (Renee) Jeanmaire, John Brown, Roland Petit
▸ Kaye shines in this musical biography of Hans Christian Andersen, a storytelling cobbler forced to leave his Danish village because children play hooky to listen to his wonderful stories. He journeys to Copenhagen, where he falls in love with beautiful ballerina Jeanmaire, who inspires one of his most famous stories, "The Little Mermaid." Well-crafted production. Music by Frank Loesser and Franz Liszt adds imagination and vibrancy.
Dist.: Nelson

HANUSSEN 1988 Hungarian
★ R Drama 2:20
☑ Brief nudity, adult situations, explicit language
Dir: Istvan Szabo *Cast:* Klaus Maria Brandauer, Erland Josephson, Ildiko Bansagi, Walter Schmidinger, Karoly Eperjes, Grazina Szapolowska
▸ Based on a real-life character, Brandauer is a charismatic psychic who becomes darling of early Nazi movement, only to fall afoul of goose-steppers when he foresees too much. Brandauer is onscreen almost constantly in this obvious, declamatory film. Nominated for Best Foreign Film Oscar, it's a comedown from director's previous efforts. [S]
Dist.: RCA/Columbia

HAPPIEST MILLIONAIRE, THE 1967
★★★★ NR Musical/Family 2:24
Dir: Norman Tokar *Cast:* Fred MacMurray, Lesley Ann Warren, Tommy Steele, Greer Garson, John Davidson
▸ Philadelphia blue-blood MacMurray's chaotic household includes patient wife Garson, teenage daughter Warren, two sons, Irish butler Steele, and twelve pet alligators. MacMurray is training for World War I Marines while Warren gets engaged to a New York gentleman (Davidson). Patriotic Disney production with lavish sets and beautiful costumes. Most hummable tune: "Fortuosity."
Dist.: Buena Vista

HAPPY BIRTHDAY TO ME 1981
★★ R Horror 1:51
☑ Brief nudity, adult situations, explicit language, graphic violence, adult humor
Dir: J. Lee Thompson *Cast:* Glenn Ford, Melissa Sue Anderson, Tracy Bregman, Jack Blum, Matt Craven
▸ Anderson, a preppie at Crawford Academy, is welcomed into "The Top Ten," an elite social clique. A jealous maniac takes revenge, reducing them to "The Top Nine" . . .and so on. Cutlery is the murder weapon of choice in this unappetizing teen slaughter film.
Dist.: RCA/Columbia

HAPPY HOOKER, THE 1975
★ R Sex/Comedy 1:37
☑ Brief nudity, strong sexual content, explicit language
Dir: Nicholas Sgarro *Cast:* Lynn Redgrave, Jean-Pierre Aumont, Tom Poston, Nicholas Powell, Conrad Janis, Anita Morris
▸ Dutch girl Redgrave arrives in New York to marry, has change of heart, becomes high-class prostitute, and eventually starts her own establishment. Silly comedy plays tamely now. Based on real-life hooker Xaviera Hollander's best-selling memoir.
Dist.: Warner

HAPPY NEW YEAR 1973 French
☆ PG Comedy 1:54
☑ Explicit language, violence
Dir: Claude Lelouch *Cast:* Lino Ventura, Françoise Fabian, Charles Gerard, Andre Falcon
▸ It starts off as a happy new year for crook Ventura when he is released from prison. Plotting a new heist, he gets involved with store owner Fabian and is pursued by the cops. Caper benefits from director Lelouch's sure touch. American remake appeared in 1987. Also available in a dubbed version. [S]
Dist.: Nelson

HAPPY NEW YEAR 1987
★★ PG Comedy 1:26
[✓] Explicit language
Dir: John G. Avildsen ***Cast:*** Peter Falk, Charles Durning, Wendy Hughes, Tom Courtenay, Joan Copeland
► Ex-con Falk plots jewel heist with buddy Durning while romancing antiques dealer Hughes in West Palm Beach. Agreeable American remake of Claude Lelouch's French film with Falk donning some neat disguises. Gently humorous and diverting though moves slowly and fails to deliver big laughs.
Dist.: RCA/Columbia

HARDBODIES 1984
★★ R Comedy 1:27
[✓] Nudity, adult situations, explicit language
Dir: Mark Griffiths ***Cast:*** Grant Cramer, Gary Wood, Teal Roberts, Michael Rapport, Sorrells Pickard
► Middle-aged clods Wood, Rapport, and Pickard rent a house on Venice beach and hire local blond surfer-stud Cramer to teach them how to score. The lessons pay off, and soon the place is wall-to-wall bimbettes. Witless and obvious, but successfully delivers a good-looking young cast that lives up to the title. (CC)
Dist.: RCA/Columbia

HARDBODIES 2 1986
★ R Comedy 1:28
[✓] Nudity, adult situations, explicit language
Dir: Mark Griffiths ***Cast:*** Brad Zutaut, Fabiana Udenio, James Karen, Sam Temeles, Alba Francesca, Roberta Collins
► Zutaut, Temeles, and Wilmot arrive in Greece to work on a low-budget picture. The leading lady has not yet been cast; auditions are held on a cruise ship/floating university right out of an adolescent boy's fantasy, with mandatory topless attendants.
Dist.: RCA/Columbia

HARD CHOICES 1986
★★ NR Drama 1:31
[✓] Nudity, explicit language, violence
Dir: Rick King ***Cast:*** Margaret Klenck, Gary McCleery, John Seitz, John Sayles, John Snyder, Spalding Gray
► Tennessee teen McCleery is jailed as accomplice in robbery/cop shooting. Social worker Klenck, unable to provide help, springs him and they become lovers on the lam. Commendable low-budget effort with naturalistic settings and performances. Slightly slow-paced but soap opera star Klenck is outstanding. Based on a true story.
Dist.: Warner

HARDCORE 1979
★★★ R Drama 1:48
[✓] Nudity, adult situations, explicit language
Dir: Paul Schrader ***Cast:*** George C. Scott, Peter Boyle, Season Hubley, Dick Sargent, Leonard Gaines
► Scott, an upright, God-fearing Midwesterner, sees his runaway daughter in a porn movie and searches for her through L.A.'s sleazy netherworld of prostitution and pornography. Hubley plays a hooker with a gold-plated heart who helps him. Strong, hard-hitting drama pulls no punches.
Dist.: RCA/Columbia

HARD COUNTRY 1981
★★★ NR Drama 1:42
[✓] Adult situations, explicit language
Dir: David Greene ***Cast:*** Jan-Michael Vincent, Kim Basinger, Michael Parks, Gailard Sartain, Daryl Hannah, Tanya Tucker
► Poor man's *Urban Cowboy* about unhappy factory worker Vincent and his frustrated girlfriend Basinger living in a dreary west Texas town. They dream of California, where he can escape his brother, who's got an eye for Basinger, and she can become a stewardess. In her film debut, country-western singer Tucker plays a local-girl-made-good and Hannah appears as Basinger's kid sister. Original R rating was revoked when producers inserted additional graphic violence.
Dist.: J2 Communications

HARD DAY'S NIGHT, A 1964 British
★★★★ G Musical/Comedy 1:27 B&W
Dir: Richard Lester ***Cast:*** John Lennon, Paul McCartney, George Harrison, Ringo Starr, Wilfred Brambell, Victor Spinetti
► The Beatles head for a TV gig in London while Paul's grandfather Brambell gets into trouble. "At least he's a clean old man," the boys muse. Exuberant direction by Lester employs all sorts of playful cinematic techniques to convey the youth, humor, and enthusiasm of the Fab Four. One of the most entertaining musicals ever; enjoyable even to non-Beatles fans.
Dist.: MPI

HARDER THEY COME, THE 1973 Jamaican
★★ R Drama/Musical 1:38
[✓] Nudity, adult situations, explicit language, violence
Dir: Perry Henzell ***Cast:*** Jimmy Cliff, Carl Bradshaw, Janet Bartley, Ras Daniel Hartman
► Jamaican singer Cliff turns to crime when a corrupt producer wrecks his dream for a recording contract. Cliff becomes a legendary outlaw as his songs rise on the charts. Cult classic manages to be raw and uncompromising yet upbeat and exciting at the same time. Exhilarating reggae score by the charismatic Cliff includes title tune, "You Can Get It if You Really Want," "Many Rivers to Cross," "Sitting in Limbo." (In English, but subtitles get you through the thick accents.) [S]
Dist.: HBO

HARDER THEY FALL, THE 1956
★★★★ NR Drama 1:49 B&W
Dir: Mark Robson ***Cast:*** Humphrey Bogart, Rod Steiger, Jan Sterling, Mike Lane, Max Baer, Jersey Joe Walcott

▶ Promoter Steiger exploits glass-jawed boxer Lane, fixing his fights all the way to a title shot. Ex-sportswriter Bogart is hired to publicize the pug but ends up exposing fight game corruption. Bogart, in his last screen role, does a fine job in this brutally effective inside look at boxing.
Dist.: RCA/Columbia

HARDLY WORKING 1981
★ ★ ★ PG Comedy 1:29
☑ Explicit language, adult humor
Dir: Jerry Lewis *Cast:* Jerry Lewis, Susan Oliver, Roger C. Carmel, Deanna Lund, Billy Barty
▶ Predictable Lewis vehicle about an out-of-work clown bungling a series of jobs. Lewis appears in every frame to fall down, spill drinks, or mug in front of the camera. He even tries to score with an ugly woman who turns out to be Jerry in drag. For Lewis fans only.
Dist.: CBS/Fox

HARD ROCK ZOMBIES 1985
☆ R Comedy 1:34
☑ Nudity, adult situations, explicit language
Dir: Krishna Shah *Cast:* E. J. Curcio, Sam Mann, Geno Andrews, Mick McMains, Jennifer Coe, Lisa Toothman
▶ Heavy metal rockers murdered by Hitler cult are turned into zombies by singer Curcio, a specialist in Satanic lyrics. Teens flock to the living dead musicians, prompting local authorities to ban rock music. Low-budget comedy scores some good points about heavy metal, although horror elements are silly. Shot in conjunction with horror spoof *American Drive-In,* in which it appears as film-within-film.
Dist.: Vestron

HARD TIMES 1974
★ ★ ★ ★ ★ PG Drama 1:33
☑ Adult situations, explicit language, violence
Dir: Walter Hill *Cast:* Charles Bronson, James Coburn, Jill Ireland, Strother Martin, Maggie Blye, Michael McGuire
▶ Nineteen-thirties New Orleans provides colorful backdrop for episodic tale of burly streetfighter Bronson and his rise to wealth through a series of no-holds-barred bouts staged by manager Coburn. Vivid atmosphere and brutal fights compensate for sketchy plot. Bronson, fifty-four at the time, is in amazing shape. Promising directorial debut for Hill.
Dist.: RCA/Columbia

HARD TO HOLD 1984
★ ★ PG Romance 1:33
☑ Brief nudity, strong sexual content, explicit language
Dir: Larry Peerce *Cast:* Rick Springfield, Patti Hansen, Janet Eilber, Albert Salmi, Gregory Itzen
▶ Springfield plays a famous rock musician in love with frosty psychologist Eilber, who's far too serious for his frivolous world. Fashion model Hansen is his songwriting collaborator/

sometime girlfriend. Made-for-teens movie has all the vim and spontaneity of a broken record, but Springfield fans may not notice. (CC)
Dist.: MCA

HARD TO KILL 1990
★ ★ ★ ★ R Action-Adventure 1:37
☑ Brief nudity, adult situations, explicit language, graphic violence
Dir: Bruce Malmuth *Cast:* Steven Seagal, Kelly Le Brock, Bill Sadler, Frederick Coffin
▶ Los Angeles cop Seagal is shot after videotaping dirty deal between politician and mobster. He emerges from the resulting seven year coma to find the incriminating evidence and get back at the villains. Helping him is sympathetic nurse Le Brock (the real-life Mrs. Seagal). Star's mild on-screen manner is dropped for blistering displays of martial arts mastery and gunplay that proved big at the box office. (CC)
Dist.: Warner

HARD TRAVELING 1985
★ ★ NR Drama 1:47
☑ Adult situations, explicit language
Dir: Dan Bessie *Cast:* Ellen Geer, J. E. Freeman, Barry Corbin, James Gammon, Jim Haynie
▶ Earnest, low-key story set during the post-Depression years. Uneducated drifter Freeman meets struggling mother Geer, who finds some good in him. Trying to make ends meet, he commits a crime that tests her love for him. Some fine moments, but film lacks the dramatic richness of more successful slices of Americana like *Tender Mercies.* Based on the novel *Bread and a Stone* by Alvah Bessie, one of the Hollywood Ten and the director's father.
Dist.: New World

HARD WAY, THE 1980 British
★ NR Mystery-Suspense 1:28
☑ Adult situations, violence
Dir: Michael Dryhurst *Cast:* Patrick McGoohan, Lee Van Cleef, Donal McCann, Edna O'Brien
▶ Burned-out hitman McGoohan wants to quit his profession, but boss Van Cleef won't let him. To make matters worse, McGoohan's sympathetic wife O'Brien is threatened by the crime syndicate. Very understated; more of a character study than an action-packed thriller. Filmed in Ireland.
Dist.: TWE

HAREM 1985 French
★ NR Drama 1:53
☑ Nudity, explicit language
Dir: Arthur Joffe *Cast:* Nastassja Kinski, Ben Kingsley, Dennis Goldson, Zohra Segal, Michel Robin
▶ Love-struck Arab sheik Kingsley kidnaps New York career girl Kinski and deposits her in his desert harem, where the ladies watch porno movies on the VCR. Yet, despite appearances, the sensitive sheik has been sav-

ing himself for the woman he loves. Color, cinematography and Kinski are visual treats but muddled, confusing story can be exasperating.
Dist.: Vestron

HARLAN COUNTY, U.S.A. 1976
★ ★ PG Documentary 1:43
☑ Explicit language
Dir: Barbara Kopple
▶ Emotional story of a thirteen-month coal strike in eastern Kentucky shows hardships of miners' lives and desperation of their fight against the owners. Unforgettable images include miners' wives throwing themselves into road to stop strikebreakers' cars. Academy Award-winning documentary is one-sided, didactic, but rich with solidarity and human warmth.
Dist.: RCA/Columbia

HARLEM NIGHTS 1989
★ ★ ★ R Comedy 1:55
☑ Adult situations, explicit language, violence
Dir: Eddie Murphy *Cast:* Eddie Murphy, Richard Pryor, Redd Foxx, Danny Aiello, Jasmine Guy, Della Reese, Michael Lerner, Arsenio Hall, Stan Shaw
▶ Murphy's debut as writer/director is at best disappointing. Playing thirties-era nightclub owners, Murphy and Pryor concoct a complex scheme to rip off Aiello-led gangsters. Plot staggers through a score of clichés on the way to a credulity-straining conclusion. Murphy's personal charm shines through, however, and veteran Reese sparkles in the role of a madam. **(CC)**
Dist.: Paramount

HARLOW 1965
★ ★ ★ ★ NR Biography 2:05
Dir: Gordon Douglas *Cast:* Carroll Baker, Peter Lawford, Red Buttons, Mike Connors, Angela Lansbury
▶ "Blond bombshell" Jean Harlow (Baker) rises to Hollywood stardom in the 1930s. Marriage to studio executive Lawford ends in his suicide and leads to drink, promiscuity, and her own tragic demise. Superior of the two 1965 film bios of Harlow (the other starred Carol Lynley) plays fast and loose with fact but is nonetheless entertaining.
Dist.: Paramount

HAROLD AND MAUDE 1971
★ ★ ★ PG Comedy 1:32
☑ Adult situations, explicit language, mild violence
Dir: Hal Ashby *Cast:* Ruth Gordon, Bud Cort, Cyril Cusack, Vivian Pickles, Ellen Geer
▶ Macabre black comedy starring Cort and Gordon as a taboo odd couple. Twenty-year-old Harold is rich and suicidal; Maude is old, poor, and full of life. They meet at a funeral and fall in love. Director Ashby captures a goofy sentimentality—happily bizarre and, occasionally, madly funny. Movie has de-

voted cult following. Written by Colin Higgins.
Dist.: Paramount

HARPER 1966
★ ★ ★ ★ NR Mystery-Suspense 2:01
Dir: Jack Smight *Cast:* Paul Newman, Lauren Bacall, Julie Harris, Arthur Hill, Janet Leigh, Pamela Tiffin
▶ Newman's first detective role finds him pursuing kidnappers of Bacall's millionaire husband; his investigation uncovers a deadly smuggling ring involving drug-addicted nightclub singer Harris. Expert cast is fun to watch. Screenwriter William Goldman adapted Ross MacDonald's *The Moving Target.*
Dist.: Warner

HARPER VALLEY P.T.A. 1978
★ ★ ★ PG Comedy 1:42
☑ Adult situations, explicit language
Dir: Richard Bennett *Cast:* Barbara Eden, Nanette Fabray, Ronny Cox, Susan Swift, Louis Nye, Pat Paulsen
▶ Jeannie C. Riley's hit song is transformed into a broad attack on small-town hypocrisy, with sexy mother Eden turning tables on the snobbish leaders of her local P.T.A. Fabray is delightful as Eden's friend. Popular comedy led to a TV series.
Dist.: Vestron

HARRY AND SON 1984
★ ★ ★ ★ PG Drama 1:57
☑ Brief nudity, adult situations, explicit language, adult humor
Dir: Paul Newman *Cast:* Paul Newman, Robby Benson, Joanne Woodward, Ellen Barkin, Wilford Brimley
▶ Heartfelt family drama describes the clash between aging blue-collar widower Newman and his free-spirited son Benson, an aspiring writer. A labor of love for Newman, who worked on the script and produced as well as directed.
Dist.: Vestron

HARRY AND THE HENDERSONS 1987
★ ★ ★ ★ PG Comedy 1:51
☑ Adult situations, mild violence
Dir: William Dear *Cast:* John Lithgow, Melinda Dillon, Don Ameche, Joshua Rudoy, Margaret Langrick, Kevin Peter Hall
▶ The Hendersons, a typical suburban Seattle family, run over the legendary Bigfoot on a camping trip. Dad Lithgow brings Bigfoot (played by Hall) home, where the lovable monster wreaks widespread chaos. Family-oriented comedy from Steven Spielberg features an amusing performance from Ameche as a skeptical Bigfoot expert. **(CC)**
Dist.: MCA

HARRY AND TONTO 1974
★ ★ ★ ★ R Comedy/Drama 1:15
☑ Adult situations, explicit language
Dir: Paul Mazursky *Cast:* Art Carney, Ellen Burstyn, Chief Dan George, Geraldine Fitz-

gerald, Larry Hagman, Melanie Mayron, Josh Mostel

▶ Touching, bittersweet tale about an independent, seventy-two-year-old New York City widower/retired teacher, Harry (Carney), rejuvenated by a cross-country trip with his pet cat, Tonto. Oscar-winner Carney maintains a gentle dignity and resilience throughout various encounters with his obnoxious offspring, hitchhiker Mayron, grandson Mostel, an aging radical, a former sweetheart, a homicidal Indian chief, and a happy hooker. (CC)

Dist.: CBS/Fox

HARRY AND WALTER GO TO NEW YORK 1976

★★★ PG Comedy 2:00

☑ Adult situations, explicit language

Dir: Mark Rydell ***Cast:*** James Caan, Elliott Gould, Michael Caine, Diane Keaton, Charles Durning

▶ Turn-of-the-century farce about fleabag vaudevillians Gould and Caan trying to safecrack their way into Caine's exclusive uppercrust criminal set. Zany antics, song and dance, a couple of sight gags, and a few stretches of ho-hum. A disappointment from director Rydell and all-star cast.

Dist.: RCA/Columbia

HARRY'S WAR 1981

★★★ PG Comedy 1:38

☑ Explicit language

Dir: Keith Merrill ***Cast:*** Edward Herrmann, Geraldine Page, Elisha Cook, Jr., Salome Jens, David Ogden Stiers

▶ There is one big, unambiguous heavy in this movie, and its initials are IRS. Herrmann is a decent postman driven to declare war on the revenue arm when dotty old junk dealer Page drops dead while defending herself against a whopping tax bill. Armed to the teeth, Herrmann barricades himself in a junkshop until he gets his day in court via national TV. Not bad, but best if seen around April fifteenth.

Dist.: Thomson

HARRY TRACY, DESPERADO 1982 Canadian

★★★ PG Western 1:40

☑ Brief nudity, adult situations, explicit language, violence

Dir: William A. Graham ***Cast:*** Bruce Dern, Helen Shaver, Michael C. Gwynne, Gordon Lightfoot

▶ The old West is fading away, but not prison-escapee Dern, the last surviving member of the Wild Bunch. Pursued by marshall Lightfoot and in the company of sweetheart Shaver, Dern is determined not to be taken alive. Humorous, elegiac Western was nominated for seven Canadian Oscars, including Best Picture. Also known as *Harry Tracy*.

Dist.: Vestron

HARUM SCARUM 1965

★★★ NR Musical 1:25

Dir: Gene Nelson ***Cast:*** Elvis Presley, Mary Ann Mobley, Fran Jeffries, Michael Ansara, Jay Novello, Billy Barty

▶ Movie star Presley is kidnapped by band of assassins while on Middle East tour. He finds himself in the midst of a murder plot, rescues maidens in distress, and wins the heart of beautiful princess Mobley. Tune-filled Presley adventure as the King brings his big beat to Baghdad.

Dist.: MGM/UA

HARVEST 1937 French

★ NR Drama 1:45 B&W

Dir: Marcel Pagnol ***Cast:*** Gabriel Gabrio, Orane Demazis, Fernandel, Edouard Delmont, Henri Poupon

▶ Gabrio, the last inhabitant of an old village, plants, tends, and harvests its crops. Companion Demazis has been raped by a gang of foresters, and Gabrio acquires her from husband Fernandel through an act of primitive barter. Divided into segements representing the seasons, simple tale of peasant life is rewarding, but slow. Unornamented story is not for all tastes. [S]

Dist.: Various

HARVEY 1950

★★ NR Comedy 1:44 B&W

Dir: Henry Koster ***Cast:*** James Stewart, Josephine Hull, Peggy Dow, Charles Drake, Cecil Kellaway, Jesse White

▶ Elwood P. Dowd (Stewart) is the nicest man you'd ever want to meet but there's a problem: his best pal is a six-foot-tall invisible rabbit. Sister Hull considers having him committed in this popular screen comedy featuring one of Stewart's drollest performances. Hull won Oscar for Best Supporting Actress. Videotape version contains an introduction by Stewart.

Dist.: MCA

HARVEY GIRLS, THE 1946

★★★ NR Musical 1:41

Dir: George Sidney ***Cast:*** Judy Garland, John Hodiak, Ray Bolger, Angela Lansbury, Preston Foster, Cyd Charisse

▶ High-spirited, beautifully photographed musical based on the real-life Fred Harvey chain of railroad restaurants and their Eastern waitresses who helped civilize frontier towns in the Old West. Garland, playing a mail-order bride, is at the peak of her talent, singing the Oscar-winning "On the Atchison, Topeka and the Santa Fe."

Dist.: MGM/UA

HASTY HEART, THE 1949 British

★★★ NR Drama 1:39 B&W

Dir: Vincent Sherman ***Cast:*** Ronald Reagan, Richard Todd, Patricia Neal, Anthony Nicholls, Howard Crawford, Ralph Michael

▶ During World War II, wounded Scotsman Todd alienates a ward in a military hospital; doctors are afraid to tell him that he has a terminal disease. Reagan and fellow patients try to bring him out of his shell, succeeding only to have him withdraw again when he

learns that he will soon die. Wonderfully moving drama based on a stage play by John Patrick has what may be Reagan's best performance.
Dist.: Warner

HATARI! 1962
★ ★ ★ ★ ★ **NR Action-Adventure 2:37**
Dir: Howard Hawks   *Cast:* John Wayne, Elsa Martinelli, Red Buttons, Hardy Kruger, Gerard Blain
▶ American Wayne leads team that traps wild animals in East Africa for zoos around the world. Wayne clashes with photographer Martinelli, who does a story on the operation. Simple plot is dominated by terrific footage of animals, especially two baby elephants, and stunning African settings. Overlong but will appeal to kids. Score by Henry Mancini is a highlight.
Dist.: Paramount

HAUNTED HONEYMOON 1986
★ ★ **PG Comedy 1:23**
☑ Explicit language, violence
Dir: Gene Wilder   *Cast:* Gene Wilder, Gilda Radner, Dom DeLuise, Jonathan Pryce, Paul Smith
▶ Thirties radio stars Wilder and Radner intend to wed but first Wilder must overcome his fears during a weekend at his spooky ancestral home. Strange things happen: a werewolf goes on the prowl and someone is after Aunt Kate's (DeLuise) fortune. Despite all the promising elements, this one's real short on laughs. Radner's given little to work with, and DeLuise in drag is still no relief from the tedium.
Dist.: HBO

HAUNTED PALACE, THE 1963
★ ★ **NR Horror 1:23**
Dir: Roger Corman   *Cast:* Vincent Price, Debra Paget, Lon Chaney, Jr., Frank Maxwell, Leo Gordon
▶ Price, a descendant of devil worshipers, moves into New England family home with bride Paget and becomes possessed by his dead relative. Corman adaptation of an H. P. Lovecraft story is full of fog, thunder, eerie music, and other haunted-house effects.
Dist.: HBO

HAUNTED SUMMER 1988
★ **R Drama 1:55**
☑ Nudity, adult situations, explicit language
Dir: Ivan Passer   *Cast:* Philip Anglim, Laura Dern, Alice Krige, Eric Stoltz, Alex Winter
▶ In 1816, a summer of sexual and literary passions ensues when poets Byron (Anglim) and Shelly (Stoltz) holiday with half-sisters Dern and Krige (as the future Mary Shelly, whose *Frankenstein* was inspired by these events). Adding to the intrigue: bisexual Byron's lover Dr. Polidori (Winter). Fascinating subject matter (also covered in Ken Russell's *Gothic*) should have been better; energetic Anglim and company can't do much with the ornate dialogue. Scenic but surprisingly placid direction from the usually more passionate Passer.
Dist.: Media

HAUNTING, THE 1963
★ ★ ★ **G Horror 1:52 B&W**
Dir: Robert Wise   *Cast:* Julie Harris, Claire Bloom, Richard Johnson, Russ Tamblyn, Lois Maxwell
▶ For research, anthropologist Johnson takes a group of people to an allegedly haunted house, where supernatural forces plague them. Promising idea never coalesces despite good performances and amusingly gothic direction by Wise, who opts for suggestiveness over blood and gore.
Dist.: MGM/UA

HAUNTING OF JULIA, THE 1981
British/Canadian
★ **R Horror 1:36**
☑ Adult situations, explicit language, violence
Dir: Richard Loncraine   *Cast:* Mia Farrow, Keir Dullea, Tom Conti, Jill Bennett, Robin Gammell
▶ Distraught over the death of her daughter, Farrow moves into mansion determined to forge a new life with husband Dullea. Unfortunately, evil spirit possessing the house has malevolent designs on the couple. Some effective shocks marred by predictable plotting.
Dist.: Magnum

HAUNTS 1977
★ ★ **PG Horror 1:38**
☑ Adult situations, violence
Dir: Herb Freed   *Cast:* May Britt, Cameron Mitchell, Aldo Ray, William Gray Espy, Susan Nohr
▶ Sheriff Ray is baffled when a scissors-wielding fiend begins terrorizing his small-town bailiwick. Eyebrows raise in the direction of a sexually repressed farm girl who believes she was raped by a goat. Atmospheric film demands patience for slight rewards.
Dist.: Media

HAVING WONDERFUL CRIME 1945
★ ★ **NR Mystery-Suspense 1:10 B&W**
Dir: Edward Sutherland   *Cast:* Pat O'Brien, George Murphy, Carole Landis, Lenore Aubert, George Zucco
▶ Newlyweds Murphy and Landis pull private eye O'Brien into an intricate mystery involving missing magician Zucco. The trio discover a body, only to lose it again and again in this tongue-in-cheek mystery. Loses inspiration well before the climax.
Dist.: Turner

HAVING WONDERFUL TIME 1938
★ ★ **NR Comedy 1:10 B&W**
Dir: Alfred Santell   *Cast:* Ginger Rogers, Douglas Fairbanks, Jr., Peggy Conklin, Lucille Ball, Lee Bowman, Eve Arden, Red Skelton, Jack Carson, Ann Miller
▶ Glossy romantic comedy set in New York's

Catskills resort area pairs city worker Rogers with debonair Fairbanks. She resists at first but eventually succumbs to his charms. Good support from Arden, Carson, and Skelton (in his film debut).
Dist.: Turner

HAWAII 1966
★ ★ ★ **NR Drama 3:12**
Dir: George Roy Hill *Cast:* Julie Andrews, Max Von Sydow, Richard Harris, Gene Hackman, Jocelyne La Garde, Manu Tupou, Carroll O'Connor, George Rose, Bette Midler, John Cullum
▶ Von Sydow, a straitlaced missionary, attempts to convert Hawaiian natives in the 1820s; wife Andrews is torn between defending his methods and her love for sea captain Harris. Overlong, sprawling drama covers the first half of James Michener's *Hawaii.* Received six Oscar nominations, including La Garde's role as the native queen. *The Hawaiians* covers the second half of the book.
Dist.: MGM/UA

HAWKS 1989 British
★ ★ ★ **R Drama 1:50**
☑ Nudity, adult situations, explicit language
Dir: Robert Ellis Miller *Cast:* Timothy Dalton, Anthony Edwards, Janet McTeer, Jill Bennett, Sheila Hancock, Connie Booth
▶ Terminally ill patients Dalton and Edwards escape British hospital and head for final fling at Amsterdam bordello. They pick up pregnant McTeer along the way; romance develops between Dalton and McTeer with Edwards playing matchmaker. Gallant mixture of sentiment and wry humor; McTeer is the standout.
Dist.: Paramount

HAWK THE SLAYER 1980 British
★ ★ **NR Action-Adventure 1:35**
☑ Adult situations, violence
Dir: Terry Marcel *Cast:* Jack Palance, John Terry, Bernard Bresslaw, Ray Charleson, Peter O'Farrell
▶ Sword and sorcery tale with a plot lifted right from the comic books. Hawk (Terry) vows to avenge the death of his father and takes on the forces of darkness headed by Voltan (Palance). Plenty of swordplay and solid action keep things moving at a brisk pace. Teens may enjoy but violence is unsuitable for younger kids.
Dist.: IVE

HAWMPS! 1976
★ ★ ★ **G Family 1:53**
Dir: Joe Camp *Cast:* James Hampton, Christopher Connelly, Slim Pickens, Denver Pyle, Gene Conforti, Jack Elam
▶ Horse soldiers in Old West are befuddled when U.S. Government gets bright idea to augment equine force with camels. Based on actual historical incident, cornball genre spoof has requisite saloon fight, shoot-out, stock cavalry characters. Cast walks more

than a mile for camels, but slight premise is stretched mighty thin.
Dist.: Vestron

HEAD 1968
★ ★ ★ **G Comedy 1:26**
Dir: Bob Rafelson *Cast:* David Jones, Michael Nesmith, Mickey Dolenz, Peter Tork, Teri Garr, Frank Zappa
▶ The Monkees, TV's answer to the Beatles, hired Rafelson and Jack Nicholson (who appears in one scene) to assemble this plotless time capsule of the psychedelic era. Resulting pastiche of film clips, newsreel footage, cheerful tunes, and bizarre cameos (Annette Funicello, Sonny Liston, Victor Mature, etc.) has enough far-out laughs to appeal to cultists.
Dist.: RCA/Columbia

HEAD OFFICE 1986
★ ★ **PG-13 Comedy 1:31**
☑ Brief nudity, adult situations, explicit language, adult humor
Dir: Ken Finkelman *Cast:* Judge Reinhold, Eddie Albert, Jane Seymour, Danny DeVito, Rick Moranis, Wallace Shawn, Lori-Nan Engler, Don Novello, Michael O'Donoghue
▶ Business school grad Reinhold enters corporation and encounters diverse group: ruthless boss Albert, tax cheat DeVito, female exec Seymour sleeping her way to top, and burnouts Shawn and Moranis. Reinhold romances the boss's rebellious daughter Engler and teams with her to stop company corruption. Snappy satire with amusing cast of goofballs, although fun wears thin in second half.
Dist.: HBO

HEARSE, THE 1980
★ ★ **PG Horror 1:39**
☑ Adult situations, explicit language
Dir: George Bowers *Cast:* Trish Van Devere, Joseph Cotten, David Gautreaux, Donald Hotton, Perry Lang
▶ After the death of her aunt, an unstable Van Devere returns to her family home. She is menaced by a mysterious man driving a large black hearse. Is she going crazy or is there really something evil going on? Formula shocker with sympathetic work from Trish as the beleaguered heroine.
Dist.: Media

HEART 1987
☆ **R Drama 1:31**
☑ Explicit language, violence
Dir: James Lemmo *Cast:* Brad Davis, Frances Fisher, Steve Buscemi, Robinson Frank Adu, Jesse Doran, Bill Costello
▶ Washed-up boxer Davis is chosen to fight up-and-coming contender Costello. Girlfriend Fisher thinks Davis is a fool to accept the challenge and his greedy manager Buscemi takes a bribe to fix the fight. However, Davis proves he has the heart of a winner. If you've seen *Rocky,* you know the ending but perform-

ances by Davis and Buscemi transcend genre clichés.
Dist.: New World

HEARTACHES 1981 Canadian
★ ★ ★ R Drama 1:32
☑ Adult situations, explicit language
Dir: Donald Shebib *Cast:* Margot Kidder, Annie Potts, Robert Carradine, Winston Rekert
▶ Pregnant Potts runs away from husband Carradine rather than fess up that another man fathered her child. In Toronto, she hooks up with brassy blond Kidder who has romantic problems of her own. Harmless lightweight fluff with an appealing Potts.
Dist.: Vestron

HEART BEAT 1980
★ R Drama 1:48
☑ Nudity, adult situations, explicit language
Dir: John Byrum *Cast:* Nick Nolte, Sissy Spacek, John Heard, Ray Sharkey, Ann Dusenberry
▶ An intriguing subject: Beat Generation founder Jack Kerouac's (Heard) unconventional relationship with his pal Neal Cassady (Nolte) and the woman they both love, Cassady's wife Carolyn (Spacek). First-rate production and cinematography, but script fails to penetrate the surface. Superlative Sissy outshines her two male co-stars.
Dist.: Warner

HEARTBEEPS 1981
★ PG Fantasy 1:17
☑ Explicit language
Dir: Allan Arkush *Cast:* Andy Kaufman, Bernadette Peters, Randy Quaid, Melanie Mayron, Kenneth McMillan, Christopher Guest
▶ At a futuristic factory, robots Kaufman and Peters, trained as helpers to humans, decide they prefer each other to the company of people. They create a child out of spare parts and set out to see the world. Sweet but insubstantial flight of fancy stymies talented players in robot makeup and doesn't develop inventive premise.
Dist.: MCA

HEARTBREAKERS 1984
★ ★ R Drama 1:38
☑ Nudity, adult situations, explicit language
Dir: Bobby Roth *Cast:* Peter Coyote, Nick Mancuso, Carole Laure, Kathryn Harrold, James Laurenson, Carol Wayne
▶ Up-and-coming artist Coyote and jealous best pal Mancuso look for meaning in their lives as they approach middle age. Their attraction to the same woman, Laure, causes a rift between them. Generally insightful look at male-female relationships with sharp performances (notably Wayne).
Dist.: Vestron

HEARTBREAK HOTEL 1988
★ ★ ★ ★ PG-13 Comedy 1:30
☑ Adult situations, explicit language
Dir: Chris Columbus *Cast:* David Keith, Tuesday Weld, Charlie Schlatter, Angela Goethals, Jacque Lynn Colton, Chris Mulkey
▶ In 1972 Ohio, teen Schlatter's mom Weld drinks too much. Who wouldn't? Her husband has left her, her boyfriend Mulkey beats her, and she gets in a car accident. Schlatter decides to cheer up mom by kidnapping her idol Elvis Presley (Keith). Outrageous concept gets talky execution, but Schlatter is sympathetic and Keith does a fabulous Elvis impersonation. Most heartwarming scene: Elvis teaching Schlatter's sister not to be afraid of the dark.
Dist.: Buena Vista

HEARTBREAK KID, THE 1972
★ ★ PG Comedy 1:44
☑ Adult situations, explicit language
Dir: Elaine May *Cast:* Charles Grodin, Cybill Shepherd, Eddie Albert, Jeannie Berlin, Audra Lindley
▶ While honeymooning with his clinging bride Berlin, newlywed Grodin falls for WASP dream girl Shepherd. He wins her over the objections of her stern Midwestern pop Albert but finds victory bittersweet. Grodin's ironic demeanor is engaging, but it's the Oscar-nominated Berlin (May's daughter) who is the real surprise. A comedy of intelligence and nuance as screenwriter Neil Simon (adapting Bruce Jay Friedman's story) eschews his usual one-liners. Expert direction by May.
Dist.: Media

HEARTBREAK RIDGE 1986
★ ★ ★ ★ R War 2:10
☑ Brief nudity, explicit language, violence
Dir: Clint Eastwood *Cast:* Clint Eastwood, Marsha Mason, Everett McGill, Moses Gunn, Eileen Heckart, Bo Svenson, Mario Van Peebles
▶ Unorthodox, foulmouthed gunnery sergeant Eastwood turns a squadron of misfits into gung-ho fighting machines ready to tackle the Communists in Grenada. Handled with flair by Eastwood, who shows a welcome sensitive side in scenes with his ex-wife Mason. Van Peebles is a standout among the recruits. (CC)
Dist.: Warner

HEARTBURN 1986
★ ★ ★ R Comedy 1:48
☑ Adult situations, explicit language, adult humor
Dir: Mike Nichols *Cast:* Meryl Streep, Jack Nicholson, Maureen Stapleton, Jeff Daniels, Stockard Channing, Richard Masur, Catherine O'Hara, Steven Hill, Milos Forman, Karen Akers, Mercedes Ruehl
▶ New York writer Streep marries Washington columnist Nicholson but then finds he's fooling around. Witty dialogue, classy production, but ultimately unsatisfying story development and conclusion. A dark-haired Streep shows another side of her amazing range, finding

humor and heartbreak as the wronged wife. Nicholson has less to do but does have film's comic highlight, serenading pregnant Streep with a medley of songs about babies. From Nora Ephron's roman à clef about her breakup with Watergate reporter Carl Bernstein. **(CC)**
Dist.: Paramount

HEART CONDITION 1990
★ ★ ★ **R Comedy 1:36**
☑ Adult situations, explicit language, violence
Dir: James D. Parriot *Cast:* Bob Hoskins, Denzel Washington, Chloe Webb, Roger E. Mosley, Ja'net DuBois, Alan Rachins
▶ Bigoted Los Angeles vice cop Hoskins receives heart transplant from dead black lawyer Washington. Demoted to desk jockey, Hoskins is stunned when Washington's ghost appears to help him solve his murder. Messy if lively mixture of genres doesn't quite gel but scores with occasional humor and Hoskins/ Washington teamwork.
Dist.: RCA/Columbia

HEART IS A LONELY HUNTER, THE 1968
★ ★ ★ ★ **G Drama 2:04**
Dir: Robert Ellis Miller *Cast:* Alan Arkin, Sondra Locke, Laurinda Barrett, Stacy Keach, Chuck McCann, Cicely Tyson
▶ Touching adaptation of a Carson McCullers novel about the efforts of small-town deaf-mute Arkin to help the people around him. Earnest, episodic, extremely downbeat story won Oscar nominations for Arkin and for Locke as a spoiled teenager. Film debuts for Locke and Keach. **(CC)**
Dist.: Warner

HEARTLAND 1981
★ ★ ★ **PG Drama 1:36**
☑ Adult situations, mild violence
Dir: Richard Pearce *Cast:* Rip Torn, Conchata Ferrell, Barry Primus, Lilia Skala, Megan Folson, Amy Wright
▶ In 1910 Wyoming, widow Ferrell with young daughter Folson is hired as housekeeper by dour rancher Torn. They marry and see each other through the hardships and isolation of pioneer life. Slow and thoughtful with fine performances and gorgeous photography of the Wyoming countryside.
Dist.: HBO

HEART LIKE A WHEEL 1983
★ ★ ★ **PG Biography/Sports 1:53**
☑ Adult situations, explicit language, violence
Dir: Jonathan Kaplan *Cast:* Bonnie Bedelia, Beau Bridges, Leo Rossi, Hoyt Axton, Bill McKinney, Dean Paul Martin
▶ True story about drag racer Shirley Muldowney (Bedelia), a housewife who battled the odds to win the national championship an unprecedented three times. Honest, engrossing biography has a sensational performance

from Bedelia. Bridges plays her rival/lover Connie Kalitta. **(CC)**
Dist.: CBS/Fox

HEART OF DIXIE 1989
★ ★ ★ **PG Drama 1:36**
☑ Adult situations, explicit language
Dir: Martin Davidson *Cast:* Ally Sheedy, Virginia Madsen, Phoebe Cates, Treat Williams, Don Michael Paul, Kyle Secor
▶ Nice-looking cast and cool '57 Ford in tale of Southern college girls chasing dreams on cusp of sixties. Liberal news photog Williams is on hand to help sorority girl Sheedy get on right side of integration issue. Madsen shines as an ambitious beauty queen. Based on novel *Heartbreak Hotel* by Anne Rivers Siddons.
Dist.: Orion

HEART OF MIDNIGHT 1988
★ **R Mystery-Suspense 1:33**
☑ Nudity, explicit language, violence
Dir: Matthew Chapman *Cast:* Jennifer Jason Leigh, Peter Coyote, Gale Mayron, Sam Schacht, Brenda Vaccaro, Frank Stallone
▶ Leigh inherits a creepy sex club from an uncle, an AIDS victim. When strange and violent things start happening, Leigh turns to police officer Coyote. But is Coyote a real cop? Is Leigh crazy and just imagining it all? Viewers can't tell, and soon cease to care.
Dist.: Virgin

HEARTS AND ARMOUR 1982 Italian
☆ **NR Action-Adventure 1:41**
☑ Rape, adult situations, violence
Dir: Giacomo Battiato *Cast:* Tanya Roberts, Barbara De Rossi, Zeudi Araya, Rick Edwards, Leigh McCloskey
▶ Christian knight Orlando battles the Moors while his lover Angelica fights off would-be rapists in an action-filled sword-and-sorcery epic based on *Orlando Furioso*. Pillage and sword-play dominate this often confusing Italian production.
Dist.: Warner

HEARTS AND MINDS 1974
☆ **R Documentary 1:52**
☑ Nudity, adult situations, explicit language, violence
Dir: Peter Davis
▶ Groundbreaking documentary on the Vietnam War combines newsreel footage (some of it quite horrifying) with interviews covering a wide assortment of individuals, from General Westmoreland to a paraplegic vet. Offended some right-wingers when it won an Oscar, but overall a reasoned approach to a troubling period in history.
Dist.: Paramount

HEARTS OF FIRE 1988
★ **R Drama 1:35**
☑ Adult situations, explicit language
Dir: Richard Marquand *Cast:* Bob Dylan,

Fiona, Rupert Everett, Julian Glover, Suzanne Bertish, Richie Havens

► Aspiring rock star Fiona falls for aging superstar Dylan. The romance hits hard times when her success eclipses his and she gets involved with younger rocker Everett. Well-staged concert footage and music-world atmosphere. Problem: Dylan can sing but can't act, Everett can act but can't sing, and the slushy love triangle plot is weak. (CC)

Dist.: Warner

HEARTS OF THE WEST 1975
★★ PG Comedy 1:42
☑ Adult situations, explicit language
Dir: Howard Zieff ***Cast:*** Jeff Bridges, Andy Griffith, Donald Pleasence, Blythe Danner, Alan Arkin

► In the 1930s, Bridges, a naive Iowan, heads west to write cowboy stories and ends up a star in B-movie Westerns. Along the way, he finds romance with script girl Danner and clashes with veteran stunt man Griffith and egotistical director Arkin. Amiable comedy highlighted by sweetness of Bridges and Danner.

Dist.: MGM/UA

HEAT 1972
☆ R Drama 1:40
☑ Nudity, adult situations, explicit language
Dir: Paul Morrissey ***Cast:*** Sylvia Miles, Joe Dallesandro, Andrea Feldman, Pat Ast, Ray Vestal

► Omnisexual hunk Dallesandro moves in with never-was star and sometime game-show contestant Miles as she struggles with her neurotic daughter. When Dallesandro decides the relationship is over, Miles goes after him with a pistol. Like many of director Morrissey's films produced by Andy Warhol, this noisy echo of *Sunset Boulevard* has its own obnoxious integrity, and actually nails the truth about some self-obsessed lives. Also known as *Andy Warhol's Heat*.

Dist.: Paramount

HEAT 1987
★★★ R Action-Adventure 1:42
☑ Adult situations, explicit language, violence
Dir: Dick Richards ***Cast:*** Burt Reynolds, Peter MacNicol, Karen Young, Neill Barry, Howard Hesseman, Diana Scarwid

► In Las Vegas, adventurer/compulsive gambler Reynolds helps friend Young avenge a beating at the hands of gangster Barry and thus runs afoul of the mob. A nice turn by MacNicol as a wimpy rich guy Reynolds teaches how to fight. Glittery backgrounds, action, sex, violence, and Burt's trademark macho posing.

Dist.: Paramount

HEAT AND DUST 1983 British
★ R Drama 2:10
☑ Nudity, adult situations, mild violence
Dir: James Ivory ***Cast:*** Julie Christie, Greta Scacchi, Christopher Cazenove, Shashi Kapoor, Susan Fleetwood

► In India, modern Englishwoman Christie investigates the life of her great-aunt Scacchi, who caused scandal in the 1920s by running off with Indian prince Kapoor. As past intercuts with present, Christie also falls for a native man. Visually extravagant, superbly acted drama, epic in scope, may be too leisurely paced for most.

Dist.: MCA

HEATED VENGEANCE 1985
★★ R Action-Adventure 1:30
☑ Nudity, explicit language, violence
Dir: Edward Murphy ***Cast:*** Richard Hatch, Jolina Mitchell-Collins, Michael J. Pollard, Robert Walker, Jr., Dennis Patrick

► In Bangkok, Vietnam vet Hatch looks up old girlfriend Mitchell-Collins. Reunion is rudely disrupted when he's kidnapped by the head of a heroin ring, an ex-comrade Hatch court-martialed during the war. Survival training enables Hatch to escape his tormentors. Okay low budget actioner.

Dist.: Media

HEATHERS 1989
★★ R Comedy 1:42
☑ Explicit language, violence
Dir: Michael Lehman ***Cast:*** Winona Ryder, Christian Slater, Shannen Doherty, Kim Walker, Lisanne Falk, Penelope Milford

► Ryder is the fourth wheel in a powerful high school clique composed of three other girls all named Heather (Doherty, Falk, Walker). Tired of their cruel putdowns, Ryder joins seductive newcomer Slater to rebel against the Heathers' tyranny. She has a change of heart when Slater's plans include murder. Biting script, inventive visuals, and attractive young cast carry this black comedy, but teen suicide subject matter and dark humor may disturb some.

Dist.: New World

HEAT OF DESIRE 1984 French
★ R Comedy 1:29
☑ Nudity, adult situations, explicit language, mild violence
Dir: Luc Beraud ***Cast:*** Patrick Dewaere, Clio Goldsmith, Jeanne Moreau, Guy Marchand, Pierre Dux

► Against the background of political upheavals, professor Dewaere leaves his wife for sexy Goldsmith. His obsession grows even as she manipulates him. Half-baked plotting but Clio radiates heat, desire, spontaneity, and grace as she glides unclothed from moonlit balcony to bedroom. [S]

Dist.: RCA/Columbia

HEATWAVE 1983 Australian
★★ R Drama 1:33
☑ Nudity, adult situations, explicit language, violence
Dir: Phillip Noyce ***Cast:*** Judy Davis, Richard Moir, Chris Haywood, Bill Hunter

▶ Davis, the leader of squatters protesting housing development, has affair with project's architect Moir. He turns against the corrupt developers. Intelligent and sincere, with Davis giving her usual accomplished performance, but overly preachy and excessively talky.
Dist.: HBO

HEAVEN 1987
★ **PG-13 Documentary 1:20**
☑ Adult situations, explicit language
Dir: Diane Keaton
▶ An unseen Keaton interviews diverse group—kids, hippies, Salvation Army officers, Hawaiians, oldsters, boxing promoter Don King—on their views of God and heaven. Interspersed are clips from Hollywood movies on these subjects. Keaton's candid camera captures some bizarrely funny responses but this quirky documentary is likely to bore some.
Dist.: Pacific Arts

HEAVEN CAN WAIT 1943
★ ★ ★ ★ **NR Fantasy/Comedy 1:52**
Dir: Ernst Lubitsch *Cast:* Gene Tierney, Don Ameche, Charles Coburn, Marjorie Main, Laird Cregar, Eugene Pallette
▶ Elegant, lighthearted fantasy about sophisticated rake Ameche trying to convince the Devil he deserves damnation for his busy love life. Flashbacks set in the Gay Nineties show Ameche's genuine love for the beautiful Tierney. Effortless comedy is a prime example of the suave "Lubitsch touch."
Dist.: CBS/Fox

HEAVEN CAN WAIT 1978
★ ★ ★ ★ ★ **PG Fantasy/Comedy 1:40**
☑ Adult situations, explicit language
Dir: Warren Beatty, Buck Henry *Cast:* Warren Beatty, Julie Christie, James Mason, Jack Warden, Dyan Cannon, Charles Grodin, Buck Henry, Vincent Gardenia
▶ "Does the phrase 'not being a good sport' have any meaning to you?" asks inept angel Henry when pro football player Beatty protests celestial foul-up that killed him too early. Henry's superior Mason gives Beatty the new body of a millionaire threatened by murderous wife Cannon and her lover Grodin. Beatty plays in the Super Bowl and falls for environmentalist Christie. Absolutely wonderful romantic comedy/fantasy won nine Oscar nominations including Best Picture and Actor (Beatty). Remake of 1941's *Here Comes Mr. Jordan.*
Dist.: Paramount

HEAVEN HELP US 1985
★ ★ ★ **R Comedy 1:44**
☑ Brief nudity, explicit language, adult humor
Dir: Michael Dinner *Cast:* Donald Sutherland, John Heard, Andrew McCarthy, Kevin Dillon, Mary Stuart Masterson, Malcolm Danare
▶ In 1965 Brooklyn, Catholic schoolboys—new kid McCarthy, tough guy Dillon, and

brainy but fat Danare—form an unlikely friendship and rebel against a stern Brother's rule. Solid performances by all, and the McCarthy/Masterson romance is quite fetching. Overlooked but worth watching.
Dist.: HBO

HEAVENLY BODIES 1985 Canadian
★ ★ **R Musical 1:29**
☑ Brief nudity, adult situations, explicit language, violence
Dir: Lawrence Dane *Cast:* Cynthia Dale, Richard Rebiere, Laura Henry, Walter George Alton, Stuart Stone
▶ Young Dale opens her own aerobics studio, falls in love with football player Rebiere, and gets job with TV station. Life should be great, but then rival aerobicist schemes against her. Climax has the two women facing off in a dance contest. *Flashdance* clone offers enough jumping around and hot bods to last a lifetime.
Dist.: CBS/Fox

HEAVENLY KID, THE 1985
★ ★ ★ **PG-13 Fantasy/Comedy 1:27**
☑ Adult situations, explicit language, mild violence
Dir: Cary Medoway *Cast:* Lewis Smith, Jason Gedrick, Jane Kaczmarek, Richard Mulligan, Mark Metcalf
▶ Mild-mannered comedy/fantasy with a familiar plot. In the early 1960s, James Dean–like hipster Smith dies in a drag race. Up in heaven, he's given the assignment to return to Earth and help present-day klutzy teen Gedrick, who turns out to be his illegitimate son.
Dist.: HBO

HEAVENS ABOVE! 1963 British
★ **NR Comedy 1:58 B&W**
Dir: Roy Boulting *Cast:* Peter Sellers, Cecil Parker, Isabel Jeans, Eric Sykes, Bernard Miles
▶ Sellers, a guileless small-town parson, inadvertently causes nationwide uproar when he convinces the rich to share with poor. Eventually, he is shipped off to outer space to stop him from causing further trouble. Religious satire, considered daring in 1963, lacks impact now. Heavy British dialects, at times difficult to understand, may hinder enjoyment. Strictly for Sellers fans.
Dist.: HBO

HEAVEN'S GATE 1980
★ ★ **R Western 3:40**
☑ Rape, nudity, adult situations, explicit language, violence
Dir: Michael Cimino *Cast:* Kris Kristofferson, Christopher Walken, John Hurt, Sam Waterston, Isabelle Huppert, Jeff Bridges, Brad Dourif, Joseph Cotten, Mickey Rourke
▶ In 1890s Wyoming, sheriff Kristofferson sides with immigrants as wealthy cattlemen make land grab, setting off the Johnson County War. He also vies with foe Walken for the affections of French madam Huppert. Cimino's mega-

budget Western is famous for sinking the United Artists studio. Murkily plotted and overlong, but the mammoth production has some moments of epic grandeur: a dance in Harvard, a community roller skate in Wyoming. An edited-down version failed to bring any cohesion to the story.
Dist.: MGM/UA

HEAVY PETTING 1989
★ ★ ★ R Documentary 1:20 C/B&W
☑ Nudity, strong sexual content, explicit language
Dir: Obie Benz *Cast:* Josh Mostel, Spalding Gray, Abbie Hoffman, Allen Ginsberg, William Burroughs, Laurie Anderson, David Byrne, Sandra Bernhardt, Ann Magnuson
▶ Hilarious footage from fifties and sixties sex education films frustratingly interrupted by sexual reminiscences of dull performance artists and underground icons. Sample memory has poet Ginsberg getting slugged for telling girl she has big breasts.
Dist.: Academy

HEAVY TRAFFIC 1973
★ R Animation/Adult 1:16
☑ Strong sexual content, explicit language, violence
Dir: Ralph Bakshi *Cast:* Voices of Joseph Kaufman, Beverly Hope Atkinson, Frank De Kova, Terri Haven, Mary Dean Lauria, Jamie Farr
▶ Young aspiring cartoonist living with his parents fails in attempt to lose virginity when he accidentally bumps local tramp off the roof. Later, he falls for a black woman as his life intersects with mobsters and other neighborhood types. Gritty New York atmosphere captured by Bakshi's deft, daring animation. Bittersweet tale for adults.
Dist.: Warner

HEDDA 1975 British
★ ★ PG Drama 1:43
Dir: Trevor Nunn *Cast:* Glenda Jackson, Timothy West, Jennie Linden, Patrick Stewart, Peter Eyre
▶ Two-time Oscar winner Jackson received another Best Actress nomination for her stunning portrayal of Ibsen's Hedda Gabler, the intelligent, well-bred but quite lethal wife of the scholarly Eyre. She's well-matched by supporting cast: West as moralizing judge, Stewart as possible former lover, and Linden as the woman who idolizes Stewart and rouses Jackson's willful destructiveness.
Dist.: Media

HEIDI 1937
★ ★ ★ ★ ★ NR Family 1:27 B&W
Dir: Allan Dwan *Cast:* Shirley Temple, Jean Hersholt, Arthur Treacher, Helen Westley, Pauline Moore, Thomas Beck
▶ Temple is perfectly cast as a German orphan sent to live with grandfather Hersholt in the Alps; she wins his heart but is sold by her evil aunt to a wealthy family. Fans clamored

for Temple to appear in Johanna Spyri's enduring classic, which proved one of her most popular films. **(CC)**
Dist.: CBS/Fox

HEIDI 1968
★ ★ ★ ★ G Family 1:44
Dir: Delbert Mann *Cast:* Maximilian Schell, Jennifer Edwards, Jean Simmons, Michael Redgrave, Walter Slezak
▶ Living in the Swiss Alps with her kindly grandfather, the orphan Heidi is taken to the city to be a playmate for her crippled cousin. Respected group of actors, including Blake Edwards's daughter, Jennifer, as Heidi, adds class to this well-loved story. Script by Earl Hammer, Jr.
Dist.: Vestron

HEIRESS, THE 1949
★ ★ ★ ★ NR Drama 1:55 B&W
Dir: William Wyler *Cast:* Olivia de Havilland, Montgomery Clift, Ralph Richardson, Miriam Hopkins, Vanessa Brown
▶ First-rate adaptation of the 1881 Henry James novel and Broadway play. De Havilland won her second Oscar for an awesome performance as the plain-looking daughter of tyrannical Richardson. She falls tragically in love with fortune-hunter Clift, who abandons Olivia when her father threatens to disown her and then returns seven years after Richardson's death. A true Hollywood classic. Also won Oscars for Score, Art Direction, Costumes.
Dist.: MCA

HEIST, THE 1988
★ ★ ★ NR Mystery-Suspense/MFTV 1:37
Dir: Stuart Orme *Cast:* Pierce Brosnan, Tom Skerritt, Wendy Hughes, Robert Prosky, Noble Willingham, Tom Atkins
▶ Fresh out of jail, Brosnan wants to get back at the man who framed him: race-track security chief Skerritt. Skerritt gets suspicious when he sees Brosnan hanging around the track, but he is not prepared for the complicated sting Brosnan is quietly and cleverly arranging. Amusing race-track characters enliven this well-scripted suspense yarn.
Dist.: HBO

HE KNOWS YOU'RE ALONE 1980
★ ★ R Horror 1:30
☑ Nudity, explicit language, violence
Dir: Armand Mastroianni *Cast:* Don Scardino, Caitlin O'Heaney, Elizabeth Kemp, Tom Rolfing, Tom Hanks, Patsy Pease
▶ Killer Rolfing, jilted by his beloved, stalks brides-to-be. O'Heaney, his next intended victim, escapes with the help of old boyfriend Scardino. Effective thriller manages to avoid genre's gory tactics. Predictable plotting but acceptable scare ratio.
Dist.: MGM/UA

HELLBENDERS 1967 U.S./Italian/Spanish
☆ NR Western 1:32
Dir: Sergio Corbucci *Cast:* Joseph Cotten,

Norma Bengell, Julian Mateos, Angel Aranda, Maria Martin

▶ During the Civil War, Southerner Cotten and his three sons steal a huge fortune from the Union, then become the object of a desert manhunt. Cheaply produced Western doesn't stint on action, but offers little in the way of characterization, intelligent storytelling, or good performances.
Dist.: Nelson

HELLBOUND: HELLRAISER II 1988 British
★ ★ **R Horror 1:38**
☑ Nudity, explicit language, graphic violence
Dir: Tony Randel   *Cast:* Clare Higgins, Ashley Laurence, Kenneth Cranham, Imogen Boorman

▶ Laurence is treated by shrink Cranham after witnessing her returned-from-dead uncle murdering her father in *Hellraiser*. Laurence then teams with fellow patient Boorman to rescue dad from hell. Flashy sequel boasts impressive special effects and imaginative monsters from the mind of writer Clive Barker. However, repulsive violence and indecipherable plotting grow wearisome.
Dist.: New World

HELLCATS OF THE NAVY 1957
★ ★ **NR War 1:21 B&W**
Dir: Nathan Juran   *Cast:* Ronald Reagan, Nancy Davis, Arthur Franz, Robert Arthur, William Leslie

▶ In World War II, submarine commander Reagan is criticized by first officer Franz for leaving behind diver during an operation. Reagan eventually proves his heroism and works things out with long-suffering nurse/girlfriend Davis. Okay war drama was the only film pairing of America's future first couple.
Dist.: RCA/Columbia

HELL COMES TO FROGTOWN 1988
★ ★ ★ **R Horror 1:26**
☑ Nudity, adult situations, explicit language, violence
Dir: R. J. Kizer   *Cast:* Roddy Piper, Sandahl Bergman, Nicholas Worth, Cec Ferrell, Rory Calhoun

▶ In a postnuclear world where most of the men are sterile, Piper, one of the last virile men, and government agent Bergman battle mutants who have kidnapped fertile women. Loony plot played for chuckles. Appealing leads and fantastic mutant makeup add up to futuristic fun.
Dist.: New World

HELLFIGHTERS 1969
★ ★ ★ **G Action-Adventure 2:01**
Dir: Andrew V. McLaglen   *Cast:* John Wayne, Katharine Ross, Jim Hutton, Vera Miles, Jay C. Flippen, Bruce Cabot

▶ Wayne circles the globe snuffing out dangerous oil-well fires, but has a tougher time dealing with ex-wife Miles—especially when his right-hand man Hutton proposes to their

daughter Ross. Middling Wayne vehicle (based on real-life hero Red Adair) has excellent special effects.
Dist.: MCA

HELLFIRE 1949
★ **NR Western 1:30**
Dir: R. G. Springsteen   *Cast:* William Elliot, Marie Windsor, Forrest Tucker, Jim Davis, H. B. Warner, Paul Fix

▶ A minister is fatally wounded saving gambler Elliot's life. Honoring his savior's last wish, Elliot attempts to complete construction of a church by collecting the reward money on fugitive Windsor. Unusual plot gets uncertain direction and performances.
Dist.: Republic

HELL HIGH 1989
☆ **R Horror 1:19 0**
☑ Nudity, adult situations, explicit language, graphic violence
Dir: Douglas Grossman   *Cast:* Christopher Stryker, Maureen Mooney, Christopher Cousins, Millie Prezioso, Jason Brill

▶ Gratuitously cruel and ugly teen slaughter film about students who torment mentally unstable teacher until she leaps out a window. Teens think she's dead, but teach comes back to erase them one by one. Nothing here, even for gore fans. Also known as *Real Trouble* and *Raging Fury*.
Dist.: Prism

HELLHOLE 1985
★ **R Mystery-Suspense 1:35**
☑ Nudity, explicit language, violence
Dir: Pierre de Moro   *Cast:* Judy Landers, Ray Sharkey, Mary Woronov, Marjoe Gortner, Edy Williams, Terry Moore

▶ Amnesiac Landers, sent to "hellhole" sanatorium after witnessing mother's death, encounters mom's killer Sharkey and lesbian mad scientist Woronov. Lurid piece of exploitation delivers the sleazy goods: nudity, violence, dreadful dialogue, preposterous story, bad acting (save for delightful Woronov). (CC)
Dist.: RCA/Columbia

HELL IN THE PACIFIC 1968
★ ★ ★ **G War 1:43**
Dir: John Boorman   *Cast:* Lee Marvin, Toshiro Mifune

▶ During World War II, American pilot Marvin finds himself stranded on Pacific island with Japanese officer Mifune. At first the two engage in a battle of wits, but learn they must team up to survive. Two-character battle is well-acted and generally exciting.
Dist.: CBS/Fox

HELL IS FOR HEROES 1962
★ ★ ★ **NR War 1:30 B&W**
Dir: Don Siegel   *Cast:* Steve McQueen, Bobby Darin, Fess Parker, Harry Guardino, James Coburn, Bob Newhart

▶ During World War II, rebellious young private

McQueen pulls off a battlefield triumph that results in his court martial for disobeying orders. Tense combat scenes, with hard-bitten warriors Parker, Coburn, and Guardino taking all the enemy can give, and Darin and Newhart (in his first film role) providing something like comic relief. Good war movie.
Dist.: Paramount

HELL NIGHT 1981
★ ★ R Horror **1:42**
☑ Adult situations, explicit language, graphic violence
Dir: Tom DeSimone *Cast:* Linda Blair, Vincent Van Patten, Kevin Brophy, Peter Barton
▶ College frat pledges must spend a night in a haunted house for initiation. Students are bumped off one by one by the thing that lurks below the house in an underground labyrinth. Standard genre fare: a few goose bumps, okay production values, effective special effects, some charm from chubby Linda.
Dist.: Media

HELLO AGAIN 1987
★ ★ ★ PG Comedy **1:36**
Dir: Frank Perry *Cast:* Shelley Long, Corbin Bernsen, Judith Ivey, Sela Ward, Gabriel Byrne
▶ Klutzy Long chokes to death on a South Korean chicken ball, then returns from the dead to find hubby Bernsen and best friend Ward in bed together. Screwball dialogue plays off variations on: "I wouldn't be caught dead in that dress." Funny turn by Ivey as Long's psychic sister. Director Perry and writer Susan Isaacs also collaborated on *Compromising Positions.*
Dist.: Buena Vista

HELLO, DOLLY 1969
★ ★ ★ ★ G Musical **2:26**
Dir: Gene Kelly *Cast:* Barbra Streisand, Walter Matthau, Louis Armstrong, Michael Crawford, Tommy Tune, E. J. Peaker
▶ In turn-of-the-century New York, matchmaker Streisand gets involved in romantic intrigues with wealthy Matthau's employees and family, all the while hoping to snag Matthau for herself. Bouncy Jerry Herman score, extravagant period re-creation, and Armstrong/Streisand title tune duet highlight adaptation of the Broadway musical hit, in turn based on Thornton Wilder's play *The Matchmaker.* (CC)
Dist.: CBS/Fox

HELLO MARY LOU: PROM NIGHT II 1987 Canadian
★ ★ R Horror **1:36**
☑ Nudity, adult situations, explicit language, violence
Dir: Bruce Pittman *Cast:* Lisa Schrage, Michael Ironside, Wendy Lyon, Justin Louis, Richard Monette
▶ Thirty years after slutty Hamilton High prom queen Mary Lou was set afire by a jealous beau, a nice girl is possessed by her ghost to wreak some violent havoc. Carrie's prom was high tea at the Plaza compared to the carnage in these corridors. Stylish staging gets new-minted thrills out of recycled plot; sequel to *Prom Night.* (CC)
Dist.: Virgin

HELL ON FRISCO BAY 1955
★ ★ NR Mystery-Suspense **1:28**
Dir: Frank Tuttle *Cast:* Alan Ladd, Edward G. Robinson, Joanne Dru, William Demarest, Fay Wray, Jayne Mansfield
▶ After serving five years for a murder he didn't commit, newly freed ex-cop Ladd is out for vengeance. Forgoing the sympathy of wife Dru, he scours the underworld until Wray, a gangster's girlfriend, leads him to Robinson, the crime kingpin who set him up. Old-fashioned crime story lags until Robinson makes his snarling entrance.
Dist.: United

HELLRAISER 1987 British
★ ★ R Horror **1:33**
☑ Explicit language, graphic violence
Dir: Clive Barker *Cast:* Andrew Robinson, Clare Higgins, Ashley Laurence, Sean Chapman, Oliver Smith, Robert Hines
▶ Magical box causes all sorts of problems for two brothers, turning one into a monster who enlists the other's wife into helping him satisfy his blood thirst. Excessive gore will surely turn off some, but those who can watch may enjoy writer/director Barker's original touches. Followed by *Hellbound: Hellraiser II.* (CC)
Dist.: New World

HELL'S ANGELS ON WHEELS 1967
★ NR Action-Adventure **1:35**
Dir: Richard Rush *Cast:* Adam Roarke, Jack Nicholson, Sabrina Scharf, Jana Taylor, John Garwood, Sonny Barger
▶ Bored gas station attendant Nicholson joins Hell's Angels to steal away leader Roarke's girlfriend. Typical low-budget biker nonsense redeemed somewhat by Nicholson's broad performance and the presence of real-life Angels leader Barger.
Dist.: Inter Global

HELLSTROM CHRONICLE, THE 1971
★ ★ ★ ★ G Documentary **1:30**
Dir: Walon Green *Cast:* Lawrence Pressman
▶ Fact-based theories of fictional doctor Pressman, who opines that insects will inherit the earth. Vibrant photography captures the beauty of nature with up-close insect footage. Fascinating and educational. Academy Award winner, Best Documentary.
Dist.: RCA/Columbia

HELL TO ETERNITY 1960
★ ★ ★ NR War **2:12** B&W
Dir: Phil Karlson *Cast:* Jeffrey Hunter, David Janssen, Vic Damone, Patricia Owens, Sessue Hayakawa
▶ Hunter plays real-life World War II Silver Star

winner Guy Gabaldon, a Hispanic American raised by Japanese Americans who uses his knowledge of the language to persuade Japanese soldiers to surrender during the battle of Saipan. Good battle action in this strong drama about a brave and compassionate war hero.
Dist.: Key

HELL UP IN HARLEM 1973
★ R Action-Adventure 1:36
☐ Brief nudity, adult situations, explicit language, graphic violence
Dir: Larry Cohen *Cast:* Fred Williamson, Julius W. Harris, Gloria Hendry, Margaret Avery, D'Urville Martin, Tony King
▶ Sequel to *Black Caesar* features Williamson reprising his crime kingpin role. In this installment, he battles a corrupt district attorney while keeping an eye on his own ambitious assistant King. Avery plays Williamson's girlfriend. Violent brew is only for fans of the original.
Dist.: Orion

HELP! 1965 British
★ ★ ★ ★ G Musical/Comedy 1:30
Dir: Richard Lester *Cast:* John Lennon, Paul McCartney, George Harrison, Ringo Starr, Leo McKern, Eleanor Bron
▶ Religious zealots McKern and Bron need a sacred ring to complete a human sacrifice; Starr, who received the ring from a fan, becomes their target. Second Beatles film sacrifices irreverent wit of *A Hard Day's Night* for slapstick, James Bond parodies, and beautiful locations in Austria and the Bahamas. Still a consistent delight, especially the superb score ("You've Got to Hide Your Love Away," "Ticket to Ride," "You're Gonna Lose That Girl," etc.).
Dist.: MPI

HELTER SKELTER 1976
★ ★ ★ NR Drama/MFTV 3:14
Dir: Tom Gries *Cast:* George DiCenzo, Steve Railsback, Nancy Wolfe, Marilyn Burns, Christina Hart
▶ Made-for-television adaptation of the bestseller details the investigation of the Sharon Tate murders and the subsequent trial of Charles Manson (Railsback) and his murderous "family." Well done, with a haunting performance by Railsback and a very convincing supporting cast. (CC)
Dist.: CBS/Fox

HENNESSY 1975 British
★ ★ ★ PG Drama 1:43
☐ Violence
Dir: Don Sharp *Cast:* Rod Steiger, Lee Remick, Richard Johnson, Trevor Howard, Peter Egan, Ian Hogg
▶ When his wife and child are murdered in a Belfast gunfight, Steiger plots to blow up the British Parliament during an appearance by the Royal Family. Both Scotland Yard and the

IRA are determined to thwart the scheme. Farfetched plot undermines standard heroics.
Dist.: HBO

HENRY V 1944
★ ★ ★ ★ NR Drama 2:17
Dir: Laurence Olivier *Cast:* Laurence Olivier, Robert Newton, Leslie Banks, Renee Asherson, Esmond Knight, Leo Genn
▶ Brilliant adaptation of Shakespeare's play, with swashbuckling Olivier as the young Prince of Wales who leads his men to victory against the French. A sweeping, visually stunning production justly famed for its elaborate framing device (opening as a typical seventeenth-century Globe Theatre production, then expanding into dazzling location footage). Olivier received a special Oscar for "outstanding achievement as actor, producer, and director."
Dist.: Paramount

HENRY V 1989 British
★ ★ PG Drama 2:18
☐ Violence
Dir: Kenneth Branagh *Cast:* Kenneth Branagh, Derek Jacobi, Paul Scofield, Emma Thompson, Robbie Coltrane, Ian Holm, Brian Blessed, Alec McCowen, Richard Briers, Christian Bale, Judi Dench
▶ Adaptation of the Shakespeare play follows maturation of King Henry (Branagh) as he leads the English against French in Battle of Agincourt and woos Princess Katherine (Thompson, also Mrs. Branagh). Sly, energetic performance by Branagh successfully follows in Olivier's footsteps. Fluid and accessible; could serve as a fine introduction to the Bard for younger viewers. Oscar nominations for Branagh's acting and direction; won for costume design. (CC)
Dist.: CBS/Fox

HENRY: PORTRAIT OF A SERIAL KILLER
1990
★ ★ NR Drama 1:23
☐ Rape, nudity, graphic violence
Dir: John McNaughton *Cast:* Michael Rooker, Tracy Arnold, Tom Towles
▶ Towles and Rooker kill innocent victims for kicks, videotaping their slaughter of one family so they can watch it over and over. Rooker kills Towles when he finds him raping his own sister. Gruesome murder and mutilation spree is presented without drama or attempt at psychological insight. Originally rated X.
Dist.: MPI

HER ALIBI 1988
★ ★ ★ ★ PG Comedy 1:31
☐ Adult situations, explicit language, mild violence
Dir: Bruce Beresford *Cast:* Tom Selleck, Paulina Porizkova, William Daniels, James Farentino, Tess Harper, Patrick Wayne
▶ Mystery writer Selleck provides a alibi for murder suspect Porizkova and decides to use her real-life case as the source for his next

book. The two hole up in his country house, where he falls in love with her. There's only one complication: he begins to suspect she really is a killer who has targeted him as her next victim. Strained attempt at a romantic comedy is never convincing.
Dist.: Warner

HERBIE GOES BANANAS 1980
★★★ G Comedy 1:40
Dir: Vincent McEveety *Cast:* Charlie Martin Smith, Cloris Leachman, John Vernon, Steven W. Burns, Elyssa Davalos, Harvey Korman
▶ Smith and Burns take their VW to Brazil for a race but Herbie gets sidetracked into other adventures, battling villainous Vernon and playing matador in a bullfight. Fourth and final entry in the series finds the beloved bug running out of comic gas. Usual Disney touches will please youngsters.
Dist.: Buena Vista

HERBIE GOES TO MONTE CARLO 1977
★★★ G Comedy 1:45
Dir: Vincent McEveety *Cast:* Dean Jones, Don Knotts, Julie Sommars, Jacques Marin, Roy Kinnear, Eric Braeden
▶ Jones enters Herbie the Love Bug in a Paris-to-Monte Carlo race. Complicating victory chances are car's infatuation with another auto and Marin's museum heist scheme. Third in the Disney series should please those who enjoyed the first two, although fun is beginning to wear thin.
Dist.: Buena Vista

HERBIE RIDES AGAIN 1974
★★★★★ G Comedy 1:28
Dir: Robert Stevenson *Cast:* Helen Hayes, Ken Berry, Stefanie Powers, John McIntire, Keenan Wynn, Huntz Hall
▶ Bright Disney sequel to *The Love Bug* continues the adventures of the Volkswagen with magical powers. This time Herbie teams up with Hayes to thwart real estate developer Wynn's plot to build the world's tallest building.
Dist.: Buena Vista

HERCULES 1959 Italian
★★★ G Action-Adventure 1:43
Dir: Pietro Francisci *Cast:* Steve Reeves, Sylva Koscina, Gianna Maria Canale, Ivo Garrani, Fabrizio Mioni
▶ Hercules (the well-developed Reeves) searches for the missing Jason and the Argonauts, wins beautiful princess Koscina, and fights ape men, amazons, animals, and monsters. Lousy dubbing, but this comic-book muscleman adventure is undeniably fun. Sequel *Hercules Unchained* released in 1960.
Dist.: VidAmerica

HERCULES 1983 Italian
★ PG Action-Adventure 1:38
☑ Explicit language, violence
Dir: Lewis Coates (Luigi Cozzi) *Cast:* Lou

Ferrigno, Mirella D'Angelo, Sybil Danning, Ingrid Anderson, William Berger, Brad Harris
▶ Ferrigno battles evil gods and deadly monsters to rescue his beloved Cassiopeia (Anderson) from fiery doom in a volcano. Plodding, witless version of the Hercules legend relies too much on shoddy special effects. Followed by *Adventures of Hercules*. **(CC)**
Dist.: MGM/UA

HERCULES UNCHAINED 1960 Italian
★★ G Action-Adventure 1:41
Dir: Pietro Francisi *Cast:* Steve Reeves, Sylva Koscina, Primo Carnera, Sylvia Lopez, Carlo D'Angelo, Gabrielle Antonini
▶ Sequel to the 1959 *Hercules* again features beefcake king Reeves in the title role. Returning to his birthplace with bride Koscina and Ulysses (Antonini), the mighty one suffers amnesia and is sidetracked to an island where he becomes consort to queen Lopez. Colorful, action-packed, poorly dubbed and acted. In other words, campy entertainment.
Dist.: Nelson

HERE COMES MR. JORDAN 1941
★★★★ NR Fantasy/Comedy 1:33 B&W
Dir: Alexander Hall *Cast:* Robert Montgomery, Evelyn Keyes, Claude Rains, Rita Johnson, Edward Everett Horton, James Gleason
▶ Heavenly mixup kills boxer Montgomery before his time; angels Rains and Horton find him a replacement body—a millionaire about to be murdered by scheming wife Johnson. Charming, sophisticated fantasy is one of Hollywood's enduring classics. Received Oscar nominations for Best Picture, Director, Actor (Montgomery), and Supporting Actor (Gleason as a skeptical fight manager); Harry Segall won for Best Story; and Sidney Buchman and Seton I. Miller won for Best Screenplay. Remade by Warren Beatty in 1978 as *Heaven Can Wait*.
Dist.: RCA

HERE COME THE TIGERS 1978
★★★ PG Comedy 1:30
☑ Explicit language
Dir: Sean S. Cunningham *Cast:* Richard Lincoln, James Zvanut, Samantha Grey, Manny Lieberman, William Caldwell, Fred Lincoln
▶ Rookie cop Lincoln takes on thankless task of coaching racially mixed Little League team composed of foul-mouthed, inept no-accounts. Team seems destined to be the league doormat until arrival of new talent, including a Japanese power-hitting karate champ, a rehabilitated Hispanic delinquent, and a deaf pitcher. Dime store knockoff of *The Bad News Bears*.
Dist.: HBO

HERO AIN'T NOTHIN' BUT A SANDWICH, A 1978
★★★ PG Drama 1:47
☑ Adult situations, explicit language
Dir: Ralph Nelson *Cast:* Cicely Tyson, Paul

Winfield, Larry B. Scott, Helen Martin, Glynn Turman, David Groh
► Troubled Los Angeles ghetto youth Scott turns to drugs as mother Tyson and foster father Winfield struggle to set him on a constructive course. Sincere, realistic drama suffers somewhat from preachy tone and distracting subplot between high school teachers Turman and Groh. Well-meaning drama based on a book by Alice Childress.
Dist.: Nelson

HERO AND THE TERROR 1988
★ ★ ★ R Action-Adventure 1:36
☑ Adult situations, explicit language, violence
Dir: William Tannen *Cast:* Chuck Norris, Brynn Thayer, Steve James, Jack O'Halloran, Jeffrey Kramer, Ron O'Neal
► Broadening his macho image, Norris plays an L.A. cop who feels guilty about undeserved credit in nabbing serial killer O'Halloran. He's understandably dismayed when the "Terror" killer escapes from jail and resumes his butchery. Accomplished thriller shortchanges kung fu scenes, but has a strong climax in the Wiltern Theater.
Dist.: Media

HERO AT LARGE 1980
★ ★ ★ PG Comedy 1:38
☑ Explicit language
Dir: Martin Davidson *Cast:* John Ritter, Anne Archer, Bert Convy, Kevin McCarthy, Harry Bellaver, Anita Dangler
► Aspiring actor Ritter makes public appearances as the heroic Captain Avenger; when he foils a holdup, the city thinks a real hero now protects them. The mayor's agents Convy and McCarthy exploit the actor for an upcoming election. Ritter excels in a "Three's Company"-type nice-guy role.
Dist.: MGM/UA

HEROES 1977
★ ★ ★ PG Comedy 1:53
☑ Explicit language
Dir: Jeremy Paul Kagan *Cast:* Henry Winkler, Sally Field, Harrison Ford, Val Avery, Olivia Cole, Hector Elias
► Vietnam vet Winkler escapes from a mental institution and travels cross-country to start a worm farm. Field plays a fiancée on the run who aids him. Uneven blend of whimsy and melodrama gave Winkler his first starring role in films. Ford is excellent in an early role.
Dist.: MCA

HEROES DIE YOUNG 1960
★ NR War 1:16
Dir: Gerald S. Shepard *Cast:* Krika Peters, Scott Borland, Robert Getz, James Strother, Malcolm Smith, Donald Joslyn
► Rumanian Peters aids Strother's Allied commando team on a mission to set up the bombing of Nazi-held oil fields. Romance develops between her and soldier Borland, but

the movie's title proves tragically true for some of the men. Fast-paced and fact-based.
Dist.: CBS/Fox

HE'S MY GIRL 1987
★ ★ PG-13 Comedy 1:44
☑ Brief nudity, adult situations, explicit language
Dir: Gabrielle Beaumont *Cast:* T. K. Carter, David Hallyday, Misha McK, Jennifer Tilly, Warwick Sims, David Clennon
► Missouri rocker Hallyday wins a trip to Los Angeles; his manager Carter resorts to dressing in drag to accompany him. Clennon, a sleazy L.A. hustler, sets his sights on Hallyday's beautiful "date." Cute sex farce gets a tremendous lift from Carter's lively performance.
Dist.: IVE

HESTER STREET 1975
★ PG Drama 1:32 B&W
☑ Adult situations
Dir: Joan Micklin Silver *Cast:* Steven Keats, Carol Kane, Mel Howard, Dorrie Kavanaugh, Doris Roberts, Stephen Strimpell
► In 1896 New York, Jewish immigrant Keats adjusts to American ways; his Old World wife Kane alienates him by sticking to tradition. Keats forsakes Kane for another woman but eventually gets his comeuppance. Wonderfully expressive performance by Kane was Oscar nominated; slow pace and muted dramatic impact may limit appeal.
Dist.: Vestron

HE WALKED BY NIGHT 1948
★ ★ NR Mystery-Suspense 1:19 B&W
Dir: Alfred Werker *Cast:* Richard Basehart, Scott Brady, Roy Roberts, Whit Bissell, Jack Webb, Jimmy Cardwell
► Thief Basehart consistently outwits the cops by using a police radio to keep tabs on them. Detectives Brady and Roberts corner him. The manhunt intensifies when Basehart escapes by killing an officer. Taut direction by Werker and an uncredited Anthony Mann heighten the suspense.
Dist.: Sinister

HEY BABU RIBA 1987 Yugoslavian
☆ R Drama 1:49
☑ Nudity, adult situations, explicit language
Dir: Jovan Acin *Cast:* Gala Videnovic, Relja Bacic, Nebojsa Bakocevic, Marko Todorovic, Dragan Bjelogrlic
► Four men get together to reminisce about Videnovic, the love of their lives who became pregnant when they were all teenagers and left the country. Unanswered question of paternity gives pretext for touching, funny flashbacks to boys' lives in fifties Yugoslavia. Viewers share characters' nostalgic ache in this wonderfully funny, heart-wrenching film.
Ⓢ
Dist.: Orion

HEY GOOD LOOKIN' 1982
★ R Animation/Adult 1:16

☑ Nudity, adult situations, explicit language, adult humor
Dir: Ralph Bakshi ***Cast:*** Voices of Richard Romanus, David Proval, Jesse Welles, Tina Bowman, Danny Wells
▸ Ambitious animated drama uses the adventures of gang leader Romanus and his friend Proval as a metaphor for life in Brownsville during the early 1950s. Occasionally interesting visuals and a realistic atmosphere can't compensate for routine gang war plot.
Dist.: Warner

HEY THERE, IT'S YOGI BEAR 1964
★★★★ NR Animation 1:29
Dir: William Hanna, Joseph Barbera ***Cast:*** Voices of Daws Butler, Don Messick, Julie Bennett, Mel Blanc, Hal Smith, J. Pat O'Malley
▸ The bear from Jellystone Park makes it to the big screen, along with sidekick BooBoo, sometime antagonist Ranger Smith, girl bear Cindy, and pals Grifter and Cornpone, to best corrupt circus operator Snively. Hanna-Barbera animation gets boring quickly, although characters' voices are less obnoxious than those in some of the pair's offerings. Songs include title tune and "Ven-E, Ven-O, Ven-A."
Dist.: KVC

HIDDEN, THE 1987
★★★ R Sci-Fi 1:37
☑ Explicit language, violence
Dir: Jack Sholder ***Cast:*** Michael Nouri, Kyle MacLachlan, Ed O'Ross, Clu Gulager, Claudia Christian, Clarence Christian
▸ Ingenious thriller with sci-fi overtones: oddball FBI agent MacLachlan joins Los Angeles homicide cop Nouri on a manhunt for a psycho killer who's apparently already dead. But then why does a meek accountant go on a wild crime spree? And why does MacLachlan chew Alka-Seltzer tablets? Enjoyable low-budget sleeper starts with a dynamite car chase and rarely lets up.
Dist.: Media

HIDDEN FORTRESS, THE 1958 Japanese
★ NR Action-Adventure 2:06 B&W
Dir: Akira Kurosawa ***Cast:*** Toshiro Mifune, Misa Uehara, Minoru Chiaki, Kamatari Fujiwara, Susumu Fujita, Takashi Shimura
▸ Two bumbling mercenaries join forces with fugitive general Mifune in guiding a fortune in gold and haughty deposed princess Uehara across enemy territory. Influential "samurai Western" will delight Kurosawa fans; others may find its stately pacing and uneven acting hard to take. Characters and rousing action sequences were the original inspiration for *Star Wars*. Japanese version contains additional footage. [S]
Dist.: Media

HIDE IN PLAIN SIGHT 1980
★★★ PG Drama 1:32
☑ Explicit language, mild violence
Dir: James Caan ***Cast:*** James Caan, Jill Eikenberry, Robert Viharo, Joe Grifasi, Barbara Rae
▸ Caan plays a Buffalo, New York, factory worker who becomes the innocent victim of the federal witness protection program. His ex-wife marries a two-bit crook who testifies against the mob and, overnight, disappears with Caan's family. The government refuses to reveal the whereabouts of Caan's children, now living under an assumed identity with their mother and stepfather. Based on a true story; Caan's directorial debut.
Dist.: MGM/UA

HIDEOUS SUN DEMON, THE 1959
☆ NR Horror 1:14
Dir: Robert Clarke ***Cast:*** Robert Clarke, Patricia Manning, Nan Peterson, Patrick Whyte, Fred La Porta, Bill Hampton
▸ Reversing the traditional monster/moonlight connection, Clarke is a radioactive atomic scientist who turns into a lizard-like humanoid when exposed to sunlight. Since he also eats people, the scaly monster is hunted by the authorities, who close in on him atop a giant gas tank. This low-budget fifties horror item is among those particularly relished by bad-movie fans.
Dist.: Nostalgia

HIDER IN THE HOUSE 1989
★★ R Mystery-Suspense 1:49
☑ Adult situations, explicit language, violence
Dir: Matthew Patrick ***Cast:*** Gary Busey, Mimi Rogers, Michael McKean, Kurt Christopher Kinder, Candy Huston, Elizabeth Ruscio
▸ After his release from a mental institution, Busey moves to the attic of Rogers's family house. While killing anyone who gets near his hiding place, he becomes infatuated with her. Well-crafted, small-scale thriller is better suited for video than the big screen. Good performance by Busey.
Dist.: Vestron

HIDING OUT 1987
★★★★ PG-13 Comedy 1:39
☑ Explicit language, violence
Dir: Bob Giraldi ***Cast:*** Jon Cryer, Keith Coogan, Annabeth Gish, Gretchen Cryer, Oliver Cotton
▸ Cryer, a twenty-seven-year-old Boston commodities trader, testifies against mobsters and then poses as a high school student in Delaware to avoid getting killed. Within a week, he becomes the most popular kid in school, runs for student council president and dates class beauty Gish; then the Feds and the bad guys catch up with him. Affable teen comedy from Giraldi, king of the music video, also feature's Cryer's real-life mom, Gretchen, as Aunt Lucy.
Dist.: HBO

HIDING PLACE, THE 1975
★★★ PG Drama 2:25
☑ Mild violence

Dir: James F. Collier *Cast:* Julie Harris, Eileen Heckart, Arthur O'Connell, Jeanette Clift, Robert Rietty, Pamela Sholto
▶ Following the moral dictates of their religion, Christians Harris, O'Connor, and Clift resist Nazi laws and provide a safe haven for Jews trying to escape occupied Holland. Eventually, their faith must stand the test of the concentration camps. Based on the life of evangelist Corrie Ten Boom and financed by the Billy Graham organization, presentation has brooding atmosphere and an excellent performance by Harris.
Dist.: Republic

HIGH AND LOW 1962 Japanese
☆ **NR Mystery-Suspense 2:22 B&W**
Dir: Akira Kurosawa *Cast:* Toshiro Mifune, Tatsuya Mihashi, Yutaka Sada, Tatsuya Nakadai, Kyoko Kagawa
▶ Wealthy industrialist Mifune receives word that kidnappers have abducted his chauffeur's son, believing that the boy was his. Despite their mistake, the kidnappers still demand ransom, and Mifune must choose between ruining himself financially and saving the boy's life. Setting most of the first part of the film in Mifune's hilltop mansion, director Kurosawa slowly increases tension, finally releasing it in a frenzy of action and revelation down in the city slums. A knockout entertainment in the Hollywood film noir tradition. Based on a novel by Ed McBain. [S]
Dist.: Pacific Arts

HIGH ANXIETY 1977
★★★ **PG Comedy 1:30**
☑ Explicit language
Dir: Mel Brooks *Cast:* Mel Brooks, Madeline Kahn, Cloris Leachman, Harvey Korman, Ron Carey
▶ Psychiatrist Brooks, head of the Psycho-Neurotic Institute for the Very, Very Nervous, hides the fact he suffers from high anxiety—sort of like vertigo but worse. He must deal with his neurosis, a sadistic Nurse Diesel (Leachman), several flipped-out patients, and a hint of murderous skullduggery in the padded cells. Witty homage to Hitchcock features Brooks's usual brand of lunacy and low-brow humor.
Dist.: CBS/Fox

HIGH-BALLIN' 1978
★★★ **PG Action-Adventure 1:38**
☑ Brief nudity, explicit language
Dir: Peter Carter *Cast:* Peter Fonda, Jerry Reed, Helen Shaver, Chris Wiggins, David Ferry
▶ Independent trucker Reed, pressured to sign on with Wiggins's crooked transport company, teams up with buddy Fonda and fellow driver Shaver to fight Wiggins's thugs. Good stunts and serious themes help this competent genre piece.
Dist.: Vestron

HIGH COUNTRY, THE 1981 Canadian
★★★★ **PG Drama 1:38**
☑ Nudity, explicit language
Dir: Harvey Hart *Cast:* Timothy Bottoms, Linda Purl, George Sims, Jim Lawrence, Bill Berry
▶ Escaped con Bottoms hooks up with learning-disabled runaway Purl. They hide out in the mountains and fall in love. Thin story, shallow characterizations, but beautiful scenery and genuine romantic chemistry between the appealing leads.
Dist.: Vestron

HIGHER AND HIGHER 1943
★ **NR Musical 1:30 B&W**
Dir: Tim Whelan *Cast:* Michele Morgan, Jack Haley, Frank Sinatra, Leon Errol, Victor Borge, Mel Tormé
▶ Having lost his fortune, Errol schemes to marry off his maid Morgan to Sinatra, a wealthy neighbor. Sudden appearance of shifty con man Borge disrupts the plan. Fast-paced but bland musical is notable mostly for Sinatra's first big film role. Songs include "I Couldn't Sleep a Wink Last Night" and "A Lovely Way to Spend an Evening."
Dist.: Turner

HIGHER EDUCATION 1987
★ **R Comedy 1:35**
☑ Brief nudity, adult situations
Dir: John Sheppard *Cast:* Kevin Hicks, Isabelle Mejias, Lori Hallier, Stephen Black, Maury Chaykin
▶ Small-town boy Hicks goes to big city college, has mob-connected roommate, commences affair with older art teacher Mejias. Hicks's heart really belongs to a girl his own age, but when his art teacher gets pregnant, he offers to marry her. Nothing new here for anyone who's seen *The Graduate*, but cast, especially Mejias, has a certain charm.
Dist.: Palisades

HIGHEST HONOR, THE 1984 Australian/Japanese
★★★ **R War 1:39**
☑ Explicit language, violence
Dir: Peter Maxwell, Seiji Maruyama *Cast:* John Howard, Atsuo Nakamura, Stuart Wilson, Michael Aitkens
▶ Disguised as Malaysians, members of Australia's Z Force infiltrate Singapore on a daring mission to destroy enemy ships during World War II. Captured by the Japanese, Captain Page (Howard) develops an unusual relationship with interpreter Nakamura. Well-meaning; based on a true story. [S]
Dist.: Nelson

HIGH FREQUENCY 1988 Italian
☆ **PG Family 1:45**
☑ Mild violence
Dir: Faliero Rosati *Cast:* Vincent Spano, Oliver Benny, Anne Canovas, Isabelle Pasco
▶ High atop Mount Blanc, Spano is a satellite relay attendant who has established a ham

radio friendship with eleven-year-old Benny in far off Maine. When Spano sees a murder on one of the channels he's monitoring, he and Benny work together to piece together the clues and solve the crime. Mystery has little intensity; not much here for adults.
Dist.: Virgin

HIGH HOPES 1989 British
★ **NR Comedy 1:52**
☑ Adult situations, explicit language, adult humor
Dir: Mike Leigh *Cast:* Philip Davis, Ruth Sheen, Edna Dore, Philip Jackson, Heather Tobias, Lesley Manville
▶ Tender, funny satire follows working class liberals Davis and Sheen as they try to make sense of life in Thatcher England, where his aged mother Dore is treated like garbage by her yuppie neighbors and sister Tobias is out of control as she acquires possessions. Rich and rewarding for those willing to take the trip.
Dist.: Academy

HIGHLANDER 1986
★ ★ ★ **R Action-Adventure 1:51**
☑ Nudity, adult situations, explicit language, graphic violence
Dir: Russell Mulcahy *Cast:* Christopher Lambert, Sean Connery, Roxanne Hart, Clancy Brown, Beatie Edney
▶ Two parallel stories, set in medieval Scotland and modern-day New York, where immortal heroes Lambert and Brown battle for several centuries to win the ultimate prize of Total Knowledge. Enough head-chopping for even the most jaded fan. Flashy directing, costumes, settings; score combines rock group Queen with traditional Scottish folk music. Sequel in 1990. **(CC)**
Dist.: HBO

HIGH NOON 1952
★ ★ ★ ★ **NR Western 1:25 B&W**
Dir: Fred Zinnemann *Cast:* Gary Cooper, Grace Kelly, Lloyd Bridges, Thomas Mitchell, Katy Jurado, Lon Chaney, Jr.
▶ On his wedding day, about-to-retire sheriff Cooper learns that an outlaw gang is gunning for him at high noon. He must stand alone as no one in town will help him; even his Quaker wife Kelly doesn't want him to get involved. Unforgettable Western generates maximum suspense by unfolding in close to real time. Oscars to the great Coop and Dimitri Tiomkin's score and theme song.
Dist.: Republic

HIGH PLAINS DRIFTER 1973
★ ★ ★ ★ **R Western 1:45**
☑ Rape, adult situations, explicit language, graphic violence
Dir: Clint Eastwood *Cast:* Clint Eastwood, Verna Bloom, Marianna Hill, Mitchell Ryan, Jack Ging, Billy Curtis
▶ Inhabitants of a corrupt mining town hire mysterious gunman Eastwood to protect them from three vengeful ex-cons. Eastwood

proceeds to destroy the town and everyone in it. Provocative, harshly violent Western has extraordinary locations and a subtle sense of humor.
Dist.: MCA

HIGHPOINT 1984 Canadian
★ ★ **PG Action-Adventure 1:28**
☑ Explicit language, violence
Dir: Peter Carter *Cast:* Richard Harris, Christopher Plummer, Beverly D'Angelo, Kate Reid, Peter Donat, Robin Gammell
▶ Industrialist Plummer double-crosses the Mafia and CIA, in the process framing unemployed accountant Harris for a ten-million-dollar theft. Jumbled thriller with comic overtones boils down to a series of routine chases.
Dist.: Embassy

HIGH RISK 1981
★ ★ ★ **R Action-Adventure 1:32**
☑ Explicit language, violence
Dir: Stewart Raffill *Cast:* James Brolin, Lindsay Wagner, Anthony Quinn, Cleavon Little, Bruce Davison, James Coburn
▶ Filmmaker Brolin and three friends rob Colombian druglord Coburn but fall prey to Quinn's banditos before they can flee the country. Offbeat caper film with plenty of humor and an unusual cast. Ernest Borgnine has an amusing cameo as an arms dealer.
Dist.: Nelson

HIGH ROAD TO CHINA 1983
★ ★ ★ ★ **PG Action-Adventure 1:45**
☑ Explicit language, violence
Dir: Brian G. Hutton *Cast:* Tom Selleck, Bess Armstrong, Jack Weston, Robert Morley, Wilford Brimley
▶ In 120s Asia, heiress Armstrong hires hard-drinking pilot Selleck to locate her missing dad Brimley before his business partner Morley can have him declared legally dead and take over their empire. Nice aerial photography, plenty of action, and a pleasing Selleck in this entertaining high flyer.
Dist.: Warner

HIGH SCHOOL CAESAR 1960
★ **NR Drama 1:15 B&W**
Dir: O'Dale Ireland *Cast:* John Ashley, Gary Vinson, Lowell Brown, Steve Stevens, Judy Nugent, Daria Massey
▶ Ignored by his wealthy parents, Ashley takes out his frustrations at school, setting up his own gang of teenage hooligans. Fortunately, there are some clean-cut kids who won't stand for such nonsense, and they battle the bad guys. Silly story is not without a certain vitality. Home video version hosted by Mamie Van Doren.
Dist.: Rhino

HIGH SCHOOL CONFIDENTIAL 1958
★ **NR Drama 1:25 B&W**
Dir: Jack Arnold *Cast:* Russ Tamblyn, Jan Sterling, John (Drew) Barrymore, Mamie Van

Doren, Diane Jergens, Charles Chaplin, Jr., Jackie Coogan

▶ Narcotics agent Tamblyn goes undercover in a California high school to break up a heroin ring. Unintentionally hilarious exposé with bizarre casting is a revealing time capsule of the late 1950s. Former child star Coogan plays the drug kingpin. Look for Michael Landon as one of the students. Jerry Lee Lewis opens with a killer version of the title song.
Dist.: Republic

HIGH SEASON 1988 British
★ ★ R Comedy 1:44
⊡ Nudity, adult situations, explicit language
Dir: Clare Peploe   *Cast:* Jacqueline Bisset, James Fox, Irene Papas, Paris Tselios, Sebastian Shaw, Kenneth Branagh
▶ Estranged couple (photographer Bisset and sculptor Fox) live in separate houses on the beautiful Greek island of Rhodes with their teenage daughter. Even though they all become involved with several expatriates, tourists, artists, and spies, plot never gels. Directorial debut for Peploe, real-life wife of Bernardo Bertolucci.
Dist.: Nelson

HIGH SIERRA 1941
★ ★ ★ NR Crime 1:40 B&W
Dir: Raoul Walsh   *Cast:* Humphrey Bogart, Ida Lupino, Arthur Kennedy, Joan Leslie, Henry Travers
▶ Aging gangster Mad Dog Earle (Bogart) befriends a crippled Leslie and reluctantly participates in one last caper. The plan goes awry, setting the stage for a tragic mountainside conclusion. Poignant performance by Bogart, brisk direction by Walsh in this Warner Brothers classic.
Dist.: CBS/Fox

HIGH SOCIETY 1956
★ ★ ★ NR Musical 1:47
Dir: Charles Walters   *Cast:* Grace Kelly, Bing Crosby, Frank Sinatra, Celeste Holm, John Lund, Louis Armstrong
▶ Top-drawer musical remake of *The Philadelphia Story* stars Kelly as a frosty Newport society beauty dithering over three men: her priggish fiancé Lund; her ex-husband Crosby, a wealthy jazz devotee; and brash reporter Sinatra, on hand to cover her wedding for a gossip magazine. Cole Porter hits include "Did You Evah?", "You're Sensational," and the Oscar-nominated "True Love." Bing and Satchmo sing "Now You Have Jazz."
Dist.: MGM/UA

HIGH SPIRITS 1988 U.S./British
★ ★ PG-13 Fantasy/Comedy 1:36
⊡ Adult situations, explicit language
Dir: Neil Jordan   *Cast:* Daryl Hannah, Peter O'Toole, Steve Guttenberg, Beverly D'Angelo, Jennifer Tilly, Liam Neeson
▶ Faced with losing ancestral castle, Irish hotel owner O'Toole hires locals to impersonate ghosts to lure tourist trade. Not all of the

spirits turn out to be fake: guest Guttenberg forsakes shrewish wife D'Angelo for spectacular specter Hannah. Perky concept benefits from vivacious cast and beguiling local color. Special effects, however, are merely passable. (CC)
Dist.: Media

HIGH STAKES 1989
☆ R Drama 1:37
⊡ Nudity, adult situations, explicit language, violence
Dir: Amos Kolek   *Cast:* Sally Kirkland, Robert LuPone, Richard Lynch, Kathy Bates, Sarah Geller
▶ Kirkland is a stripper with a heart of gold who takes in stockbroker LuPone after he's been left mugged and beaten on the street. LuPone is disillusioned after a friend's suicide, but he and Kirkland hit it off. Things go bad when Kirkland's pimp appears, demanding cash. Film is turgid underutilization of 1987 Oscar nominee Kirkland's talents.
Dist.: Vidmark

HIGH TIDE 1987 Australian
★ ★ ★ PG-13 Drama 1:41
⊡ Adult situations, explicit language
Dir: Gillian Armstrong   *Cast:* Judy Davis, Jan Adele, Claudia Karvan, Colin Friels, John Clayton
▶ Davis shines as a backup singer left to fend for herself in a remote trailer park. She forms a friendship with teenaged Adele, gradually revealing that she is the mother who abandoned Adele years before. Moving drama reunited Davis with Armstrong, her director in *My Brilliant Career.*
Dist.: Nelson

HIGH VELOCITY 1976
★ PG Action-Adventure 1:45
⊡ Explicit language, violence
Dir: Remi Kramer   *Cast:* Ben Gazzara, Paul Winfield, Britt Ekland, Keenan Wynn, Alejandro Rey, Victoria Racimo
▶ Wynn is an executive who lives in a miserable tropical country with wife Ekland. While attending a polo match, he is kidnapped by guerrillas, and the powerful multinational for which he works hires Vietnam vets Gazzara and Winfield to get him back. Hard-hitting, gritty, and realistic actioner has conviction, but little in the way of characterization.
Dist.: Media

HILLBILLYS IN A HAUNTED HOUSE 1967
☆ NR Musical 1:28
Dir: Jean Yarbrough   *Cast:* Ferlin Husky, Joi Lansing, Linda Ho, John Carradine, Lon Chaney, Jr., Basil Rathbone, Merle Haggard, Molly Bee, Sonny James
▶ On their way to a Nashville music jamboree, Husky and Lansing are forced to spend the night in a spooky old mansion during a storm. House happens to be headquarters for atomic spy Ho and henchpersons Rathbone, Chaney, and Carradine. Last film for Rath-

bone has dumb humor, good music, with short singing appearances by Haggard, James, and other Nashville greats. Sequel of sorts to *Las Vegas Hillbillys*.
Dist.: United

HILLS HAVE EYES, THE 1977
★ R Horror 1:29
☑ Nudity, explicit language, graphic violence
Dir: Wes Craven *Cast:* Susan Lanier, Robert Houston, Virginia Vincent, Russ Grieve, Dee Wallace
▶ A typical American family goes camping and is harassed by man-eating mutants. Gory cult film loaded with nasty plot twists. Sequel also directed by horror master Craven.
Dist.: Vestron

HILLS HAVE EYES PART II, THE 1985
★ R Horror 1:27
☑ Nudity, explicit language, graphic violence
Dir: Wes Craven *Cast:* Michael Berryman, John Laughlin, Tamara Stafford, Kevin Blair, John Bloom, Janus Blyth
▶ A group of motocross enthusiasts, late for the big race, take a short-cut across the desert and are chased by a family of cannibal mutants. Chock-full of footage from the first film, including the first doggie flashback in movie history.
Dist.: HBO

HINDENBURG, THE 1975
★★★★ PG Mystery-Suspense 2:05
☑ Violence
Dir: Robert Wise *Cast:* George C. Scott, Anne Bancroft, Roy Thinnes, Gig Young, Burgess Meredith, Charles Durning, William Atherton, Richard Dysart
▶ Star-studded spectacle combines actual newsreel footage with loony dialogue to dramatize the 1937 explosion of the German zeppelin in Lakehurst, New Jersey. Special effects provide ample thrills. Disaster movie fans may not mind such lackluster scripting as Scott, the good German, saying: "I have an uneasy sense of disaster."
Dist.: MCA

HIPS, HIPS, HOORAY 1934
☆ NR Comedy 1:08 B&W
Dir: Mark Sandrich *Cast:* Bert Wheeler, Robert Woolsey, Dorothy Lee, Thelma Todd, George Meeker
▶ Comedy team Wheeler and Woolsey are selling a new flavored lipstick when they fall for beauty parlor owner Todd and makeup demonstrator Lee. Trying to save Lee's business, they get mixed up with stolen stocks and bonds, and wind up on a cross-country race that leads to some pretty silly sight gags with automobiles. Mostly an excuse for girls and gams, tired comedy has good songs by screenwriters Harry Ruby and Bert Kalmar, in-

cluding a "Keep Romance Alive" sung by Ruth Etting.
Dist.: Blackhawk

HIS GIRL FRIDAY 1940
★★★ NR Comedy 1:32 B&W
Dir: Howard Hawks *Cast:* Cary Grant, Rosalind Russell, Ralph Bellamy, Gene Lockhart, Helen Mack, Porter Hall, Ernest Truex, Roscoe Karns, John Qualen, Billy Gilbert, Alma Kruger
▶ On the eve of a politically vital execution, scheming editor Grant tries everything to keep star reporter and ex-wife Russell from marrying insurance agent Bellamy. Outstanding remake of *The Front Page* rates among Hollywood's best comedies. Razor-sharp dialogue, breathless pacing, savagely cynical plot, and a brilliant cast add up to first-rate entertainment. Remade into the lackluster *Switching Channels*.
Dist.: Various

HISTORY IS MADE AT NIGHT 1937
★★★ NR Drama 1:37 B&W
Dir: Frank Borzage *Cast:* Charles Boyer, Jean Arthur, Colin Clive, Leo Carrillo, George Meeker, Lucien Prival
▶ Fascinating melodrama about insanely jealous husband's efforts to ruin wife Arthur's life by framing her lover (Boyer) for murder. Wildly improbable, but compelling direction and intensely romantic tone give story rare depth and resonance. Highlighted by a stunning climax aboard a luxury liner threatened by icebergs.
Dist.: Vestron

HISTORY OF THE WORLD—PART I 1981
★★★ R Comedy 1:32
☑ Explicit language, nudity
Dir: Mel Brooks *Cast:* Mel Brooks, Dom DeLuise, Madeline Kahn, Harvey Korman, Cloris Leachman, Hugh Hefner, Sid Caesar, Gregory Hines, Orson Welles, Bea Arthur, Jackie Mason, Henny Youngman
▶ String of burlesque blackouts and slapstick vignettes takes potshots at mankind. Brooks looks at cave dwellers, unholy Christian hosts, the Romans, high-stepping torturers of the Spanish Inquisition, and the French Revolution. No-holds-barred comedy epic for the legion of Mel's fans, featuring many cameo appearances.
Dist.: CBS/Fox

HIT, THE 1985 British
★ R Mystery-Suspense 1:39
☑ Adult situations, explicit language, violence
Dir: Stephen Frears *Cast:* John Hurt, Terence Stamp, Tim Roth, Laura Del Sol, Fernando Rey
▶ Gang boss hires hitmen Hurt and Roth to kidnap squealer Stamp. Stamp doesn't put up a struggle; he actually seems to enjoy the bumpy journey as the others transport him to his doom. Beautiful Spanish countryside and

strong performances by Stamp and Roth. However, this offbeat film works overtime not to be taken seriously; unfortunately it succeeds.
Dist.: Nelson

HIT AND RUN 1982
★ **PG Mystery-Suspense 1:30**
☑ Explicit language, violence
Dir: Chuck Braverman *Cast:* Paul Perri, Claudia Cron, Will Lee, Bart Braverman
▶ N. Y. cabbie Perri is trying to forget the eye-patched driver who years ago killed his wife in a hit and run accident. One night, Perri is lured into a mansion where he finds eye-patch dead, and he is framed for the murder. With the assistance of an army of N. Y. cabbies, he tries to clear his name. Low-budget film has no-name cast, but does good job with limited materials. Realistic locations.
Dist.: HBO

HITCHER, THE 1986
★ ★ ★ ★ **R Mystery-Suspense 1:37**
☑ Explicit language, graphic violence
Dir: Robert Harmon *Cast:* Rutger Hauer, C. Thomas Howell, Jennifer Jason Leigh, Jeffrey DeMunn, Henry Darrow
▶ In Texas, young Howell picks up hitchhiker Hauer who turns out to be murderous lunatic. Hauer stalks Howell and Leigh, the waitress he befriends. Harrowing thriller creates edge-of-your-seat suspense. Classy cinematography by John Seale. **(CC)**
Dist.: HBO

HITCH-HIKER, THE 1952
★ ★ **NR Mystery-Suspense 1:11 B&W**
Dir: Ida Lupino *Cast:* Edmond O'Brien, Frank Lovejoy, William Talman, Jose Torvay, Sam Hayes, Wendell Niles
▶ On their way to a Mexican fishing trip, O'-Brien and Lovejoy pick up hitchhiker Talman. Bad move: he turns out to be a psychotic killer seeking to use them to get out of the country. The vacationers find that escaping Lovejoy is a perilous proposition. Relentless direction by Lupino makes this a gripping minor classic.
Dist.: Sinister

HITLER 1962
★ ★ **NR Biography 1:43 B&W**
Dir: Stuart Heisler *Cast:* Richard Basehart, Cordula Trantow, Maria Emo, Martin Kosleck, John Banner, Carl Esmond
▶ Biography of the Nazi dictator (Basehart) deals with his relationship with Eva Braun (Emo), traces the last few days of his reign, and culminates in his suicide. Shrill screenplay emphasizes the Führer's personal life; inadequate performances don't help.
Dist.: CBS/Fox

HITLER: THE LAST TEN DAYS 1973
British/Italian
★ **PG Drama 1:45**
☑ Adult situations, explicit language
Dir: Ennio De Concini *Cast:* Alec Guinness, Doris Kunstmann, Simon Ward, Adolfo Celi, Diane Cilento, Eric Porter
▶ Claustrophobic account of the last ten days of Hitler's (Guinness) life set exclusively in the bunker where he hid with Eva Braun (Kunstmann) and a handful of staff members. Brilliant Riefenstahl footage from *Triumph of the Will* leaves the rest of the film looking cheap and unimaginative. Talky and painfully uneventful.
Dist.: Paramount

HIT LIST 1989
★ ★ **R Action-Adventure 1:27**
☑ Explicit language, violence
Dir: William Lustig *Cast:* Jan-Michael Vincent, Lance Henriksen, Rip Torn, Leo Rossi, Jere Burns, Ken Lerner
▶ Hitman hired to kill grand jury witnesses accidentally kidnaps Vincent's son, beats up his wife, and kills his friend. This gets Vincent mad, and rest of plot is excuse for shoot-outs and car chases down familiar L.A. locations. Hard-boiled action picture is just average for its genre.
Dist.: RCA/Columbia

HIT THE DECK 1955
★ ★ **NR Musical 1:52**
Dir: Roy Rowland *Cast:* Jane Powell, Tony Martin, Debbie Reynolds, Ann Miller, Vic Damone, Russ Tamblyn, Walter Pidgeon, Gene Raymond
▶ Sailors Martin, Damone, and Tamblyn get shore leave in San Francisco and find romance with Powell, Reynolds, and Miller. Tamblyn takes time out to visit his admiral father Pidgeon. Perky cast heats up an otherwise unremarkable musical. Songs include "Sometimes I'm Happy" and "More Than You Know."
Dist.: MGM/UA

HIT THE ICE 1943
★ **NR Comedy 1:29 B&W**
Dir: Charles Lamont *Cast:* Bud Abbott, Lou Costello, Ginny Simms, Patric Knowles, Elyse Knox, Sheldon Leonard
▶ Cameramen Abbott and Costello, innocent bystanders implicated in a bank heist, go to Sun Valley to avoid arrest. Also at the resort is Leonard, the real robber. Our heroes pose as waiters to recover the stolen loot. Snappy vehicle is one of the duo's funniest. Simms sings four songs, including "Slap Polka."
Dist.: MCA

H-MAN, THE 1958 Japanese
☆ **NR Sci-Fi 1:19**
Dir: Inoshiro Honda *Cast:* Kenji Sahara, Yumi Shirakawa, Akihiko Hirata, Eitaro Ozawa, Koreya Senda, Mitsuru Sato
▶ As if Tokyo residents didn't have enough trouble from Godzilla, a radioactive substance starts turning them into slime balls which subsequently reproduce and mess up the sewers. Scientist Hirata is among those

looking for an answer. Plot may sound inane, but this actually isn't that bad.
Dist.: RCA/Columbia

HOBSON'S CHOICE 1954 British
★ ★ ★ NR Comedy 1:47 B&W
Dir: David Lean *Cast:* Charles Laughton, John Mills, Brenda de Banzie, Prunella Scales, Daphne Anderson, Richard Wattis
▶ Hard-drinking bootmaker Laughton makes life miserable for his three single daughters. De Banzie, the eldest, rebels by marrying Mills, dad's assistant, and turning him into Laughton's business rival. A comedy with heart, laughs, and fine performances from Laughton, Mills, and de Banzie.
Dist.: HBO

HOG WILD 1980 Canadian
★ PG Comedy 1:37
☑ Adult situations, explicit language
Dir: Les Rose *Cast:* Michael Biehn, Patti D'Arbanville, Tony Rosato, Angelo Rizacos, Martin Doyle, Matt Craven
▶ Rosato's motorcycle gang rumbles into a small town and makes life miserable for the clean-cut teenagers. High schooler Biehn gets involved with Rosato's girlfriend D'Arbanville, battles the gang, and faces off against its leader in a climactic motorcycle race. Youth comedy is often tasteless, occasionally mildly amusing.
Dist.: Nelson

HOLCROFT COVENANT, THE 1985 British
★ ★ ★ R Mystery-Suspense 1:52
☑ Nudity, adult situations, explicit language, violence
Dir: John Frankenheimer *Cast:* Michael Caine, Anthony Andrews, Victoria Tennant, Lilli Palmer, Michael Lonsdale
▶ Caine stars as the son of a Nazi financial wizard who has been instructed to use his inheritance to make amends for Hitler's crimes. A series of creepy events leads his mother Palmer to believe the money is being used to build a new Nazi empire. Unconvincing, muddled thriller with modest suspense. Based on the Robert Ludlum novel.
Dist.: Warner

HOLD THAT GHOST 1941
★ ★ NR Comedy 1:26 B&W
Dir: Arthur Lubin *Cast:* Bud Abbott, Lou Costello, Richard Carlson, Evelyn Ankers, Joan Davis, The Andrews Sisters, Ted Lewis
▶ Delightful Abbott and Costello foolishness with an unusually strong supporting cast. Haunted high jinks are the order of the day when the boys come into possession of a dead gangster's house. Davis shines in a wacky duet with Bud; the Andrews Sisters and vaudeville great Lewis offer four songs.
Dist.: MCA

HOLE IN THE HEAD, A 1959
★ ★ ★ NR Drama 2:00
Dir: Frank Capra *Cast:* Frank Sinatra, Eddie

Hodges, Edward G. Robinson, Carolyn Jones, Thelma Ritter, Keenan Wynn
▶ Sinatra dreams of turning his Miami Beach hotel property into a Disneyland-like amusement park, while the bank threatens to foreclose his mortgage. Robinson, his hard-nosed businessman brother, might help, but only if Sinatra gives up Hodges, his neglected but loving son. Charmless characters and unbelievable story; song "High Hopes" won Academy Award.
Dist.: MGM/UA

HOLIDAY 1938
★ ★ ★ ★ NR Comedy 1:31 B&W
Dir: George Cukor *Cast:* Cary Grant, Katharine Hepburn, Doris Nolan, Lew Ayres, Edward Everett Horton
▶ Successful young Grant would like to retire at thirty and enjoy the world; wealthy fiancée Nolan disapproves, as do her stuffy parents. Grant finds a more sympathetic ear—and true love—in Nolan's free-thinking sister Hepburn. Glorious adaptation of Philip Barry's play boasts amazing ensemble acting.
Dist.: RCA/Columbia

HOLIDAY AFFAIR 1949
★ ★ NR Romance 1:27 B&W
Dir: Don Hartman *Cast:* Robert Mitchum, Janet Leigh, Wendell Corey, Gordon Gebert, Esther Dale, Henry O'Neill
▶ Widow Leigh is set on marrying solid but dull Corey, hoping to provide security for herself and little son Gebert. Into their lives walks free spirit Mitchum, a store clerk whom the boy adores and Leigh tries to resist, although her heart begins to tell her otherwise. Christmas-set heartwarmer deserves to be better known, with Mitchum and Leigh giving perhaps their most likable performances.
Dist.: Turner

HOLIDAY INN 1942
★ ★ ★ ★ ★ NR Musical 1:41 B&W
Dir: Mark Sandrich *Cast:* Bing Crosby, Fred Astaire, Marjorie Reynolds, Virginia Dale, Walter Abel, Louise Beavers
▶ Crosby retires from show biz to New England but finds farm chores harder than singing. Solution: turn the farm into an inn open only on holidays. Extremely slight plot about romantic triangle with Astaire and Reynolds barely gets in the way of first-rate Irving Berlin songs, including Oscar-winning perennial "White Christmas," "Happy Holidays," and "Easter Parade." Fred's routine with firecrackers is one of his best specialty numbers.
Dist.: MCA

HOLLYWOOD BOULEVARD 1976
★ R Comedy 1:22
☑ Nudity, adult situations, explicit language
Dir: Joe Dante, Allan Arkush *Cast:* Candice Rialson, Mary Woronov, Rita George, Jeffrey Kramer, Dick Miller, Paul Bartel
▶ Innocent blond Rialson arrives in Hollywood and gets gig at Miracle Pictures, a studio

churning out one B-movie a week. She becomes a target when reigning star Woronov tries to eliminate the competition. Some uproarious satire and inside moviemaking jokes from producer/mogul Roger Corman. Low budget shows, but generally fun stuff in this early Dante effort.
Dist.: Warner

HOLLYWOOD GHOST STORIES 1986
★ ★ NR Documentary 1:15
☑ Violence
Dir: James Forsher *Cast:* John Carradine, Elke Sommer, Susan Strasberg, William Peter Blatty
▶ Documentary is the cinematic equivalent of a Halloween grab bag. A little of everything: from *Exorcist* scribe Blatty introducing highlights from Hollywood's haunted house films to actresses Sommer and Strasberg discussing their experiences with the spirit world. Also includes a look at cinematic spook comedies and investigations into the deaths and afterlives of Rudolph Valentino and George Reeves.
Dist.: Warner

HOLLYWOOD HIGH 1977
★ R Comedy 1:21
☑ Nudity, adult situations, explicit language
Dir: Patrick Wright *Cast:* Marcy Albrecht, Sherry Hardin, Rae Sperling, Susanne, Marla Winters
▶ Four beach bunnies attend Hollywood High but are more preoccupied with surfing, giggling, and making out. Winters, an aging movie sexpot, lets the girls hang out at her place, as long as she can ogle their young male friends.
Dist.: Vestron

HOLLYWOOD HIGH II 1981
★ R Comedy 1:20
☑ Brief nudity, adult situations, explicit language
Dir: Caruth C. Byrd *Cast:* April May, Donna Lynn, Camille Warner, Brad Cowgill, Drew Davis
▶ Teen clan at Hollywood High are now seniors but their penchant for bad marks, sex, drugs, and rotten manners may put graduation out of reach. Once again, they prefer romping on the beach to hitting the books. Along the way, they pull pranks on a cop. Inane dialogue, rude teenagers, bad acting.
Dist.: Vestron

HOLLYWOOD HOT TUBS 1984
★ R Comedy 1:43
☑ Nudity, adult situations, explicit language, mild violence
Dir: Chuck Vincent *Cast:* Paul Gunning, Donna McDaniel, Michael Andrew, Katt Shea, Jewel Shepard
▶ Arrested for desecrating the famed "Hollywood" sign, spoiled California teen Gunning avoids the slammer by working as a hot-tub repairman. Big event: a wild party whose

guests include a wacked-out horror movie star, overaged Hell's Angels, a woman with whips, a chimpanzee, and a marimba band. Mindless, hedonistic fluff.
Dist.: Vestron

HOLLYWOOD OR BUST 1956
★ ★ ★ NR Comedy 1:35
Dir: Frank Tashlin *Cast:* Dean Martin, Jerry Lewis, Anita Ekberg, Pat Crowley, Maxie Rosenbloom, Willard Waterman
▶ Lewis is dying to meet Ekberg, his favorite star; Martin forges the winning lottery ticket for a car to drive his pal cross-country for a blind date with her. Strained comedy was the duo's last film together. Songs include "The Wild and Woolly West."
Dist.: Paramount

HOLLYWOOD SHUFFLE 1987
★ ★ R Comedy 1:21
☑ Adult situations, explicit language, violence
Dir: Robert Townsend *Cast:* Robert Townsend, Anne-Marie Johnson, Helen Martin, Keenan Ivory Wayans, Paul Mooney
▶ Fresh and unexpected satire from actor/writer/director/producer Townsend. He plays a black middle-class actor who struggles to become a star, but encounters only roles for pimps, muggers, and slaves. NAACP members appear to say, "You'll never play the Rambos till you stop playing the Sambos!" Funny, sweet, and amazingly well made for its low budget.
Dist.: Virgin

HOLLYWOOD VICE SQUAD 1986
★ ★ R Drama 1:40
☑ Nudity, strong sexual content, explicit language, violence
Dir: Penelope Spheeris *Cast:* Trish Van Devere, Ronny Cox, Frank Gorshin, Leon Isaac Kennedy, Carrie Fisher, Ben Frank
▶ Episodic cop drama on the order of TV's "Hill Street Blues" has multiple story lines, numerous chases, and lewd jokes. Fisher is one of pair going after S&M filmmakers; Van Devere is the mother of a prostitute; and Kennedy is cop trying to entrap wiry pimp Gorshin. Mix of black humor and drama might have worked with better editing and direction, but this lacks both.
Dist.: Magnum

HOLY INNOCENTS, THE 1984 Spanish
☆ PG Drama 1:48
☑ Adult situations
Dir: Mario Camus *Cast:* Alfredo Landa, Francisco Rabal, Terele Pavez, Belén Ballesteros, Juan Sanchez, Susana Sanchez
▶ Earthy peasants who live in tune with animals and nature are contrasted with the highhanded aristocrats who rule their lives in this look at near-feudal conditions in Franco's Spain. Poorly structured, slow-moving story

puts its political agenda ahead of need to create empathy for characters. ⓢ
Dist.: Warner

HOMBRE 1967
★ ★ ★ ★ NR Western 1:51
☑ Adult situations, explicit language, mild violence
Dir: Martin Ritt *Cast:* Paul Newman, Fredric March, Richard Boone, Diane Cilento, Cameron Mitchell
▶ Newman, an Apache-raised white man, boards a stagecoach full of prejudiced passengers. When the travelers are attacked by bandits, Newman leads them to safety in the hills and defends them from the marauders. Film successfully crossbreeds 1960s social consciousness with classic genre elements. Newman makes a terrific antihero. From an Elmore Leonard novel.
Dist.: CBS/Fox

HOME AND THE WORLD 1984 Indian
☆ NR Drama 2:10
☑ Adult situations
Dir: Satyajit Ray *Cast:* Soumitra Chatterjee, Victor Banerjee, Swatilekha Chatterjee, Gopa Aich, Jennifer Kapoor
▶ Historical drama of turn-of-the-century India, with Banerjee as a landowner who watches helplessly as wife Swatilekha Chatterjee falls in love with his old college friend Soumitra Chatterjee, now a political radical organizing a boycott against the British. Beautiful, rarified tapestry of Indian life has little in the way of action or plot. ⓢ
Dist.: Nelson

HOMEBODIES 1974
★ ★ PG Horror 1:36
☑ Violence
Dir: Larry Yust *Cast:* Frances Fuller, Ian Wolfe, Ruth McDevitt, Paula Trueman, Douglas Fowley, Linda Marsh
▶ Six oldsters get no help when they are evicted from their homey brownstone, so they take matters into their own hands and start killing people. Shocked victims include social worker Marsh, their landlord, construction workers, and Fowley, the owner of a construction company. Shot in Cincinnati, grisly but well-done film should be on any A list of B pictures. Septuagenarian actors, led by TV commercial vet Trueman, have a ball.
Dist.: Nelson

HOMEBOY 1988
★ NR Drama 1:58
☑ Brief nudity, adult situations, explicit language, violence
Dir: Michael Seresin *Cast:* Mickey Rourke, Christopher Walken, Debra Feuer, Thomas Quinn, Kevin Conway, Antony Alda, Ruben Blades
▶ Boxer Rourke comes to town for bouts but is too punch drunk to compete. He becomes an accomplice to petty crook Walken, but accepts one last fight to help girlfriend Feuer's

struggling amusement park. Meandering, barely coherent movie gets overemphatic direction from Seresin. Holding his face at odd angles, Rourke gives a curiously remote performance. Effectively gritty cinematography by Gale Tattersall, but the dialogue is often unintentionally funny.
Dist.: IVE

HOMECOMING, THE 1971
★ NR Drama/MFTV 1:20
Dir: Fielder Cook *Cast:* Richard Thomas, Patricia Neal, Edgar Bergen, Ellen Corby, Cleavon Little, Andrew Duggan
▶ Heartwarming pilot movie for long-running TV series "The Waltons" recounts the events of Christmas Day, 1933, in the lives of a rural American family. Neal, Cook, and writer Earl Hamner, Jr., were all nominated for Emmys; Hamner's autobiographical source novel was previously filmed as the 1963 Henry Fonda/Maureen O'Hara vehicle *Spencer's Mountain.* Seasonally rebroadcast as "The Homecoming—A Christmas Story." (CC)
Dist.: Playhouse

HOMECOMING, THE 1973
★ PG Drama 1:51
☑ Adult situations, explicit language
Dir: Peter Hall *Cast:* Cyril Cusak, Ian Holm, Michael Jayston, Vivien Merchant, Terence Rigby, Paul Rogers
▶ After a long absence, professor Jayston returns from America to England with wife Merchant. While visiting the home of Jayston's father and three other male relatives, Merchant's deeper sexual nature is tapped, and one of the men proposes setting her up as a prostitute in London. Based on a play by Harold Pinter, highly praised American Film Theater production may leave some bored and baffled.
Dist.: CBS/Fox

HOME FROM THE HILL 1960
★ ★ ★ ★ NR Drama 2:30
☑ Adult situations
Dir: Vincente Minnelli *Cast:* Robert Mitchum, Eleanor Parker, George Peppard, George Hamilton, Everett Sloane, Luana Patten
▶ Convoluted soap opera based on William Humphrey's novel about two generations of a wealthy Deep South family. Patriarch Mitchum must intervene when legitimate son Hamilton and illegitimate son Peppard clash over Patten. Includes many fine moments—in particular a well-orchestrated boar hunt—but length and generally overblown tone are drawbacks.
Dist.: MGM/UA

HOME MOVIES 1979
★ ★ PG Comedy 1:30
☑ Adult situations, explicit language
Dir: Brian De Palma *Cast:* Keith Gordon, Nancy Allen, Kirk Douglas, Gerrit Graham, Vincent Gardenia, Mary Davenport

► While taking a film course with pompous professor Douglas, teenage nerd Gordon decides to film his own hectic family life for class project. At the same time, he's fallen in love with his weird older brother's fiancée Allen, and he's determined to win her away. Flimsy, offhand film was made by De Palma with aid of film students from Sarah Lawrence and good-naturedly financed by some of his big Hollywood pals. It was probably a good learning experience for the kids.
Dist.: Vestron

HOME OF THE BRAVE 1949
★ ★ ★ NR War 1:25 B&W
Dir: Mark Robson   *Cast:* James Edwards, Douglas Dick, Steve Brodie, Jeff Corey, Lloyd Bridges, Frank Lovejoy
► Black soldier Edwards is paralyzed while on a South Seas mission during World War II. Under psychiatrist Corey's guidance, he confronts the racism that caused his injury. Provocative message drama was one of the first Hollywood films to deal with discrimination. Intelligent screenplay by Carl Foreman based on a Broadway play by Arthur Laurents.
Dist.: Republic

HOMER AND EDDIE 1989
★ ★ R Drama 1:40
Ⓥ Adult situations, explicit language, violence
Dir: Andrei Konchalovsky   *Cast:* James Belushi, Whoopi Goldberg, Karen Black, Ernestine McClendon, Nancy Parsons, Anne Ramsey
► Belushi is a mental defective after a baseball beaning. Goldberg has a brain tumor that makes her rob and murder. The two share a car and various adventures on the way to visit Belushi's dying father in Oregon. Stars chew the scenery but fail to convince in this depressing, irritating, sometimes sadistic drama. **(CC)**
Dist.: HBO

HOMEWORK 1982
☆ R Comedy 1:30
Ⓥ Nudity, adult situations, explicit language
Dir: James Beshears   *Cast:* Joan Collins, Michael Morgan, Shell Kepler, Lanny Horn, Carrie Snodgress
► Adolescent tease about good-looking but virginal punk-rock singer Morgan, with Collins as the older woman who makes a man of him. Crude and sloppy; more embarrassing than libido-stirring.
Dist.: MCA

HONEY, I SHRUNK THE KIDS 1989
★ ★ ★ ★ ★ PG Family 1:33
Ⓥ Mild violence
Dir: Joe Johnston   *Cast:* Rick Moranis, Matt Frewer, Marsha Strassman, Kristine Sutherland, Jared Rushton, Thomas Brown
► Hapless inventor Moranis doesn't think his miniaturizer works but it goes off while he is out, shrinking not only his own children but

neighbor Frewer's. The kids are thrown out with the garbage and must make their way through the suddenly giant-size perils of their backyard. Marvelous fun from first inventive moment to last. Our favorite parts: making friends with the ant and the kids' perilous encounter with a bowl of cereal. Accompanied by the Roger Rabbit cartoon, *Tummy Trouble.* **(CC)**
Dist.: Buena Vista

HONEYMOON 1985
☆ R Mystery-Suspense 1:40
Ⓥ Nudity, explicit language, violence
Dir: Patrick Jamain   *Cast:* Nathalie Baye, John Shea, Richard Berry, Marla Lukofsky, Peter Donat, Greg Ellwand
► Baye is a foreigner whose visa has run out, so she goes to an agency that sets her up in a phony marriage with Shea that will allow her to stay in U.S. Marriage of convenience turns into marriage from hell as Shea proves to be a psycho. Downbeat drama lacks suspense.
Dist.: Forum

HONEYMOON KILLERS, THE 1970
★ R Mystery-Suspense 1:50 B&W
Ⓥ Adult situations, mild violence
Dir: Leonard Kastle   *Cast:* Shirley Stoler, Tony Lo Bianco, Doris Roberts, Mary Jane Higby
► Stark, hypnotic, true story of obese nurse Stoler and her charming boyfriend Lo Bianco, electrocuted in 1951 for murdering "lonely hearts club" women after robbing them of their savings. Bizarre drama has a cult following.
Dist.: Vestron

HONEYSUCKLE ROSE 1980
★ ★ ★ PG Drama 1:59
Ⓥ Adult situations, explicit language
Dir: Jerry Schatzberg   *Cast:* Willie Nelson, Dyan Cannon, Amy Irving, Slim Pickens, Charles Levin, Bobbie Nelson
► Nelson's first starring film is a semi-autobiographical account about the conflict between a country-western musician's heavy touring schedule and his home life. Nelson's wife Cannon is understandably upset when he starts an affair with young musician Irving. First-rate music (including Nelson's Oscar-nominated "On the Road Again") outweighs sometimes improbable plot. C&W fans can spot many stars: Johnny Gimble, Hank Cochran, Emmylou Harris, etc. Also known as *On the Road Again.*
Dist.: Warner

HONKY TONK FREEWAY 1981
★ ★ PG Comedy 1:46
Ⓥ Adult situations, explicit language, adult humor
Dir: John Schlesinger   *Cast:* William Devane, Beverly D'Angelo, Beau Bridges, Jessica Tandy, Hume Cronyn, Geraldine Page, George Dzundza, Teri Garr, Howard Hesseman, Paul Jabara

▶ Devane, Mayor of Ticlaw, a small Florida town heavily dependent on tourists, resorts to bribery and kidnapping when the state fails to build the town an exit ramp on the new interstate. Broad slapstick and episodic vignettes result in a chaotic structure that's only intermittently amusing. Large cast strikes some sparks, but can't salvage the film (a notorious failure on release).
Dist.: HBO

HONKYTONK MAN 1982
★ ★ ★ **PG Drama 2:03**
☑ Adult situations, explicit language, mild violence
Dir: Clint Eastwood   *Cast:* Clint Eastwood, Kyle Eastwood, John McIntire, Alexa Kenin, Verna Bloom, Matt Clark
▶ Consumptive country singer Eastwood and nephew Kyle (Eastwood's son) travel the backroads of Depression-era South in hopes of arranging Grand Ole Opry audition. Atypical Eastwood effort is both subtle and charming: excellent production values capture the 1930s; strong cast adds unpredictable touches. Linda Hopkins and Marty Robbins (who died before the film's release) are among the musicians contributing to the soundtrack.
Dist.: Warner

HOODLUM EMPIRE 1952
★ **NR Drama 1:38 B&W**
Dir: Joseph Kane   *Cast:* Brian Donlevy, Claire Trevor, Forrest Tucker, Vera Ralston, Luther Adler, John Russell
▶ A battle against mobster Adler's organization occurs on two fronts: reformed gangster Russell and his army buddies fight the bad guys while senator Donlevy, in a role inspired by Estes Kefauver, investigates them. Fine performances by Donlevy and Adler highlight an ordinary screenplay.
Dist.: Republic

HOOPER 1978
★ ★ ★ ★ **PG Action-Adventure 1:39**
☑ Explicit language
Dir: Hal Needham   *Cast:* Burt Reynolds, Jan-Michael Vincent, Sally Field, Brian Keith, John Marley, Robert Klein
▶ Affectionate tribute to stuntmen concentrates on the rivalry between aging pro Reynolds and newcomer Vincent, who challenges him to an especially dangerous stunt. Large-scale set pieces are predictably impressive (both Reynolds and director Needham started out in stunts); strong ensemble acting adds to the fun. Klein is marvelous as an egomaniacal director.
Dist.: Warner

HOOSIERS 1986
★ ★ ★ ★ **PG Drama 1:55**
☑ Adult situations
Dir: David Anspaugh   *Cast:* Gene Hackman, Barbara Hershey, Dennis Hopper, Sheb Wooley, Fern Persons

▶ Heartwarming slice of Americana stars Hackman as a scandal-haunted, unconventional basketball coach leading a losing high school team to victory, and redeeming himself. Set in small-town Indiana, where basketball is worshipped. With Hopper as the town drunk/ex-basketball star Hackman hires as his assistant coach. Both screenwriter Angelo Pizzo and director Anspaugh are real-life Hoosiers. Oscar nominations went to Hopper for Best Supporting Actor and the film's musical score. **(CC)**
Dist.: Vestron

HOPE AND GLORY 1987 British
★ ★ ★ **PG-13 Drama 1:53**
☑ Adult situations, explicit language
Dir: John Boorman   *Cast:* Sebastian Rice Edwards, Sarah Miles, David Hayman, Derrick O'Connor, Sammi Davis, Ian Bannen
▶ The London Blitz of World War II as seen through the eyes of a ten-year-old boy (Edwards) whose mother Miles tries to hold together the family, including rebellious daughter Davis. Boorman's memoir takes an unusual child's point of view: the war seems like one great happy adventure (when the bombing cancels school, one lad thanks Hitler!). A magical movie, alternately funny and dramatic, with a wonderful feel for the past. A Best Picture nominee. **(CC)**
Dist.: Nelson

HOPPITY GOES TO TOWN 1941
★ ★ **NR Animation 1:17**
Dir: Dave Fleischer   *Cast:* Voices of Kenny Gardner, Gwen Williams, Jack Mercer, Ted Pierce, Mike Meyer, Stan Freed
▶ Juvenile bug Hoppity romances a sexy katydid and battles an evil beetle while beleaguered insect community flees from the hobnailed soles of oncoming humanity. Best of the Fleischer brothers' full-length cartoons is good fun for kids. Songs by Hoagy Carmichael and Frank Loesser. Also known as *Mr. Bug Goes to Town.*
Dist.: Republic

HOPSCOTCH 1980
★ ★ ★ ★ **R Comedy 1:45**
☑ Adult situations, explicit language
Dir: Ronald Neame   *Cast:* Walter Matthau, Glenda Jackson, Ned Beatty, Sam Waterston, Herbert Lom
▶ Polished performances from pros Matthau and Jackson. He's a CIA agent put out to pasture; she's his girlfriend/co-conspirator helping him to expose the bureau's misdeeds and dirty tricks. Light-as-a-feather espionage caper capitalizes on leads' proven chemistry from their first film, *House Calls.*
Dist.: Nelson

HORRIBLE DR. HICHCOCK, THE 1962 Italian
☆ **NR Horror 1:17**
Dir: Robert Hampton (Riccardo Freda)
Cast: Robert Flemyng, Barbara Steele,

Teresa Fitzgerald, Harriet White, Montgomery Glenn

► Dr. Hichcock (Flemyng) truly is horrible, especially to his wives: after killing the first to satisfy his necrophilia, he attempts to bring her back by using second spouse Steele's blood. Lurid fright fest creates an effective, if unpleasantly grisly atmosphere. Sequel: *The Ghost.*

Dist.: Republic

HORROR CHAMBER OF DR. FAUSTUS, THE 1959 French/Italian

★ NR Horror 1:28 B&W

Dir: Georges Franju ***Cast:*** Pierre Brasseur, Alida Valli, Edith Scob, Francois Guerin, Juliette Mayniel, Beatrice Altariba

► Plastic surgeon Brasseur is obsessed with reconstructing the face of daughter Scob, scarred in an auto accident. To this end, he has assistant Valli lure girls to his laboratory, where he neatly removes their faces. Dreamlike chiller is not soon forgotten. Also known as *Eyes Without a Face.* [S]

Dist.: Various

HORROR EXPRESS 1972 British/Spanish

★★ R Horror 1:35

☑ Violence

Dir: Eugenio Martin ***Cast:*** Christopher Lee, Peter Cushing, Telly Savalas, Alberto de Mendoza, Silvia Tortosa, Julio Peña

► English scientist Lee discovers a fossilized creature in 1906 China and transports it home on the Trans-Siberian Express. The monster comes to life, killing passengers by absorbing their brains with its glowing red eyes. Captain Savalas's soldiers board the train, but are no match for the thing. Creepy creature effects undercut by pompous dialogue and blatant use of a model train.

Dist.: Goodtimes

HORROR OF DRACULA 1958 British

★★★ NR Horror 1:22

Dir: Terence Fisher ***Cast:*** Christopher Lee, Peter Cushing, Michael Gough, Melissa Stribling, Carol Marsh, John Van Eyssen

► Adaptation of the Bram Stoker classic introduced Lee's uniquely sinister yet charismatic portrayal of Count Dracula, who moves to London, puts pretty young Marsh under his spell, but finds opposition from Cushing. Measures up well to the 1931 Bela Lugosi version and certainly surpasses its own six sequels.

Dist.: Warner

HORROR OF FRANKENSTEIN, THE 1970 British

★★ R Horror 1:35

☑ Graphic violence

Dir: Jimmy Sangster ***Cast:*** Ralph Bates, Kate O'Mara, Graham James, Veronica Carlson, Dennis Price, David Prowse

► Bates plays Victor Frankenstein, son of the monster-making count, who kills his dad and then takes the family business to new lows of depravity by murdering locals to provide body parts for his own creation, the hulking Prowse.

Dist.: HBO

HORROR OF PARTY BEACH, THE 1964

☆ NR Horror 1:12 B&W

Dir: Del Tenney ***Cast:*** John Scott, Alice Lyon, Allen Laurel, Marilyn Clark, Eulabelle Moore

► Drums of radioactive waste turn victims of a shipwreck into awkward, lurching monsters who rise from the sea and terrorize groups of Connnecticut teenagers at various beach locations. With rock music by the Del Aires, "first horror monster musical" is on nearly everybody's list of the world's worst movies. Monster costumes are particularly bad.

Dist.: Prism

HORROR PLANET 1982 British

☆ R Sci-Fi/Horror 1:26

☑ Rape, nudity, graphic violence

Dir: Norman J. Warren ***Cast:*** Judy Geeson, Robin Clarke, Jennifer Ashley, Stephanie Beachum, Victoria Tennant, Steven Grives

► Astronaut Geeson is raped and impregnanted by an outer space monster. Now endowed with super powers, she attacks her fellow crew members. Later, Geeson gives birth to two little creatures. Violent effort has better acting than usual for the genre, but the ending is a letdown. Also known as *Inseminoid.*

Dist.: Nelson

HORROR SHOW 1989

★ R Horror 1:34

☑ Nudity, adult situations, explicit language, graphic violence

Dir: James Issac ***Cast:*** Lance Henriksen, Brion James, Rita Taggart, Deedee Pfieffer, Aron Eisenberg, Thom Bray

► When hot seat fails to fry mass murderer James, he secretly takes up residence in home of Henriksen, the cop who nabbed him. Meat-cleaver-wielding maniac dismembers Henricksen's daughter's boyfriend, and it is Henriksen who is blamed. Grubbily shot bloodbath is actually second sequel to the pretty good *House*, but fans of that film shouldn't bother with this one.

Dist.: MGM/UA

HORSE FEATHERS 1932

★★★ NR Comedy 1:09 B&W

Dir: Norman Z. McLeod ***Cast:*** Groucho Marx, Harpo Marx, Chico Marx, Zeppo Marx, Thelma Todd, David Landau, Robert Greig, Nat Pendleton

► The brothers dismantle a college: president Groucho advocates tearing down the dorms ("Where will the students sleep?" "Where they always sleep, in the classroom."); his son Zeppo fools around with college widow Todd; speakeasy bouncer Chico and dog-catcher Harpo join the football team and enter a kidnapping plot. Sidesplitting fun from Groucho's

opening credo (expressed in the clever song, "I'm Against It") to the gridiron finale.
Dist.: MCA

HORSE IN THE GRAY FLANNEL SUIT, THE
1968
★ ★ ★ ★ **G Comedy/Family 1:54**
Dir: Norman Tokar   *Cast:* Dean Jones, Diane Baker, Lloyd Bochner, Fred Clark, Ellen Janov
▶ Advertising exec Jones purchases a horse to use in a campaign to boost sagging aspirin sales. His plan fails but all isn't lost: the horse turns out to be a steeplechase champ and wins the big race. Family comedy from Disney.
Dist.: Buena Vista

HORSEMEN, THE 1971
☆ **PG Action-Adventure 1:50**
☑ Brief nudity, violence
Dir: John Frankenheimer   *Cast:* Omar Sharif, Leigh Taylor-Young, Jack Palance, David De, Peter Jeffrey, Mohammed Shamsi
▶ Unusual look at the Afghani sport of buzkashi, a type of superviolent polo played with a calf's head for a ball. Sharif overcomes an amputated leg and an uneasy relationship with father Palance to win the championship. Looks better than it sounds; scenery and action compensate for unfocused story.
Dist.: RCA/Columbia

HORSE'S MOUTH, THE 1958 British
★ **NR Comedy 1:33**
Dir: Ronald Neame   *Cast:* Alec Guinness, Kay Walsh, Renee Houston, Mike Morgan, Michael Gough, Robert Coote
▶ Wild look at the art world through the off-the-wall antics of Guinness, an artist/vagrant who paints on unusual surfaces and moves uninvited into the home of wealthy collector Coote. Guinness's behavior gets crazier as his artworks become more grandiose, his friends move in, and the walls come tumbling down. A hilarious tour de force for Guinness, who adapted the screenplay from Joyce Cary's novel.
Dist.: Janus

HORSE SOLDIERS, THE 1959
★ ★ ★ **NR Western 1:59**
Dir: John Ford   *Cast:* John Wayne, William Holden, Constance Towers, Hoot Gibson, Althea Gibson
▶ Stirring Ford adventure. Wayne is a Union officer leading a march through the Confederacy. Along the way, he tangles with liberal doctor Holden and pretty Southern sympathizer Towers. All the elements of a Ford cavalry picture, including great action and pageantry, yet falls short of his classic trilogy. (CC)
Dist.: CBS/Fox

HORSE WITHOUT A HEAD, THE 1963
★ ★ ★ **NR Action-Adventure/Family 1:29**
Dir: Don Chaffey   *Cast:* Jean-Pierre Aumont,

Herbert Lom, Leo McKern, Pamela Franklin, Vincent Winter
▶ A kindly junk dealer gives a group of poor children a headless toy horse. Soon both the law and criminals are in pursuit of the kids, for the horse contains stolen loot. Fine Disney family fare, shot in Britain, was originally aired in two parts on TV.
Dist.: Buena Vista

HOSPITAL, THE 1972
★ ★ ★ **PG Comedy 1:44**
☑ Adult situations, explicit language
Dir: Arthur Hiller   *Cast:* George C. Scott, Diana Rigg, Barnard Hughes, Nancy Marchand, Lenny Baker, Stockard Channing, Richard Dysart, Stephen Elliott, Roberts Blossom, Robert Walden, Frances Sternhagen
▶ Best Screenplay Oscar went to Paddy Chayefsky for this acerbic black comedy, which does for hospitals what his *Network* did for TV. Impotent doctor Scott has his sexual confidence restored by free spirit Rigg but must deal with a series of crises, including a psychopathic murderer on the loose in the corridors. Greatly enhanced by Scott's sardonic performance. **(CC)**
Dist.: CBS/Fox

HOSTAGE 1987
★ ★ **R Action-Adventure 1:34**
☑ Explicit language, violence
Dir: Hanro Moehr   *Cast:* Wings Hauser, Karen Black, Kevin McCarthy, Nancy Locke, Robert Whitehead, Billy Second
▶ Arab terrorists hijack South African plane; vets Hauser and McCarthy assemble a mission to rescue Locke (Hauser's real-life wife) and her ailing son. Hang-glider assault provides some chills to offset perfunctory script; Black offers good comic support as fading sexpot passenger.
Dist.: RCA/Columbia

HOT DOG. . .THE MOVIE 1984
★ ★ **R Comedy 1:36**
☑ Nudity, adult situations, explicit language, mild violence, adult humor
Dir: Peter Markle   *Cast:* David Naughton, Tracy N. Smith, Patrick Houser, John Patrick Reger, Shannon Tweed
▶ Set in Lake Tahoe, *Hot Dog* (ski lingo for showing off) is mostly spectacular ski stunts and naked women. Plot concerns ski-slope rivalry between the American team led by wholesome farm boy Houser and the Australian team led by ruthless Reger. With Naughton as the American team's oldest member; Playmate Tweed as ski bunny on the make. Includes a major wet T-shirt contest. (CC)
Dist.: CBS/Fox

HOTEL 1967
★ ★ ★ ★ **PG Drama 2:05**
☑ Adult situations, explicit language
Dir: Richard Quine   *Cast:* Rod Taylor, Karl Malden, Catherine Spaak, Melvyn Douglas,

Richard Conte, Merle Oberon, Michael Rennie, Kevin McCarthy
► Adaptation of Arthur Hailey's novel about the glamorous guests and management of New Orleans's venerable St. Gregory Hotel, which is forced either to modernize or to sell. Large and colorful cast includes a superb Douglas as the gentleman owner who loves his hotel but is resistant to change and Malden as an 'amusingly elusive thief. Adapted into a TV series.
Dist.: Warner

HOTEL COLONIAL 1987 U.S./Italian
★ ★ **R Action-Adventure 1:43**
☑ Brief nudity, explicit language, violence
Dir: Cinzia Torrini *Cast:* John Savage, Rachel Ward, Robert Duvall, Massimo Troisi
► Savage searches the Amazon for brother Duvall's murderer. He encounters friendly embassy aide Ward, bad-guy locals, a filthy jail, a colorful cockfight, a comfy hotel—and his brother, very much alive. Meandering, slow-paced, and unusually cast. Excellent location shooting in Mexico.
Dist.: Nelson

HOTEL NEW HAMPSHIRE, THE 1984
★ **R Comedy 1:48**
☑ Rape, adult situations, explicit language, violence, adult humor
Dir: Tony Richardson *Cast:* Jodie Foster, Beau Bridges, Rob Lowe, Nastassja Kinski, Wilford Brimley, Jennifer Dundas, Paul McCrane, Matthew Modine
► Lives and loves of New England hotel owner Bridges and his children, including homosexual McCrane, writer Dundas who won't grow, and Lowe and Foster, both in love with one another. Wild plot includes a shy Kinski who hides in a bear suit, revolutionaries, and family's revenge against Foster's rapist Modine. Visually inventive adaptation of John Irving's best-seller captures the author's bittersweet, whimsical tone. Enjoyable for those tuned in to Irving's wavelength; others may find characters relentlessly eccentric.
Dist.: Vestron

HOTEL RESERVE 1944 British
★ **NR Mystery-Suspense 1:19 B&W**
Dir: Lance Comfort, Max Greene, Victor Hanbury *Cast:* James Mason, Lucie Mannheim, Herbert Lom, Patricia Medina, Anthony Shaw, Clare Hamilton
► On the eve of World War II, visiting marine biologist Mason photographs Riviera sea life, and is arrested when someone substitutes spy photos for the roll of film he drops off at the developers. To clear himself, Mason must uncover the backgrounds of all the people at his hotel. Involving dilemma based on a novel by Eric Ambler, with Mason in top form.
Dist.: Turner

HOTEL TERMINUS: THE LIFE AND TIMES OF KLAUS BARBIE 1988
☆ **NR Documentary 4:27**
☑ Adult situations, explicit language
Dir: Marcel Ophuls
► Oscar-winning documentary proves a scathing examination of the moral climate that allowed Klaus Barbie to become "the butcher of Lyon." The Germans recall the young Barbie as a gentle boy and good scholar, while the French remember his love of torture. Hard-hitting and uncompromising. Follows in the tradition of Ophuls's *The Sorrow and the Pity.*
Dist.: Virgin

HOT LEAD AND COLD FEET 1978
★ ★ ★ **G Western/Comedy 1:59**
Dir: Robert Butler *Cast:* Jim Dale, Darren McGavin, Karen Valentine, Jack Elam, Don Knotts
► Cowtown is turned upside down when a rich, cantankerous codger named Jasper Bloodshy dies, leaving his estate to one of two identical twin sons; sweet-tempered Salvation Army officer and crazed bandit "Wild Billy" fight it out for the inheritance. Dale plays all three parts. With Knotts as the sheriff preparing for a shoot-out. Boisterous, fast-paced Disney fun.
Dist.: Buena Vista

HOT MOVES 1984
★ **R Comedy 1:26**
☑ Nudity, adult situations, explicit language, mild violence, adult humor
Dir: Jim Sotos *Cast:* Michael Zorek, Adam Silbar, Jeff Fishman, Johnny Timko, Jill Schaelen
► Four Southern California teens vow to lose their virginity before summer ends. Fishman tries to score with hookers on Hollywood Boulevard, Zorek hits on a bowling alley waitress, and Silbar plays up to his reluctant girlfriend. Conversely, Timko is pursued by a female impersonator disguised as a housewife.
Dist.: Vestron

HOT POTATO 1976
☆ **PG Martial Arts 1:27**
☑ Explicit language, violence
Dir: Oscar Williams *Cast:* Jim Kelly, George Memmoli, Geffrey Binney, Irene Tsu, Judith Brown, Sam Hiona
► Oriental villain Hiona kidnaps Brown, the daughter of an American senator, to blackmail her father. Karate expert Kelly must rescue the girl before she becomes lunch for the bad guy's tigers. Standard Kelly vehicle, short on plot twists, long on chops and kicks. (CC)
Dist.: Warner

HOT PURSUIT 1987
★ ★ ★ **PG-13 Comedy 1:33**
☑ Adult situations, explicit language, mild violence
Dir: Steven Lisberger *Cast:* John Cusack, Wendy Gazelle, Robert Loggia, Monte Markham, Shelley Fabares, Jerry Stiller
► Due to a failed chemistry exam, likable

preppie Cusack misses a Caribbean cruise with girlfriend Guzelle and her folks Markham and Fabares. When he's granted a reprieve, Cusack embarks on a hellish three-day odyssey to catch up to Gazelle. Appealing comedy, thanks to Cusack's charisma and picturesque locales.
Dist.: Paramount

HOT RESORT 1985
★ **R Comedy 1:31**
☑ Nudity, explicit language, adult humor
Dir: John Robins   *Cast:* Tom Parsekian, Michael Berz, Bronson Pinchot, Daniel Schneider, Linda Kenton, Frank Gorshin
▶ Cut off from the beautiful girls at a St. Kitts resort, three summer employees go on strike until management agrees to let them compete in a boat-race audition for a TV commercial. Leering teen comedy with an emphasis on bikinis and gross-out humor marks an early effort for Pinchot. Kenton was 1985 *Penthouse* Pet of the Year.
Dist.: MGM/UA

HOT STUFF 1979
★ ★ ★ **PG Comedy 1:31**
☑ Adult situations, explicit language
Dir: Dom DeLuise   *Cast:* Dom DeLuise, Suzanne Pleshette, Jerry Reed, Luis Avalos, Ossie Davis
▶ Miami cop Reed is infuriated when burglars are released on technicalities. With partners Reed, sexy Pleshette, and DeLuise, he sets up a fencing front to bust criminals selling stolen goods. Amiable, mildly entertaining fluff.
Dist.: RCA/Columbia

HOT TARGET 1985 New Zealand
★ ★ **R Drama 1:33**
☑ Nudity, strong sexual content, explicit language, violence
Dir: Denis Lewiston   *Cast:* Simone Griffeth, Steve Marachuk, Brian Marshall, Peter McCauley, Elizabeth Hawthorne, Ray Henwood
▶ Bored corporate wife Griffeth meets attractive criminal Marachuk, whose disgusting come-on intrigues her. Griffeth really gets turned on after Marachuk murders her husband. Will the couple get away with the crime? Griffeth is gorgeous and doesn't hesitate to shed her clothes for the camera. Not much else of interest in this trashy melodrama. Also known as *Restless.*
Dist.: Vestron

HOT TO TROT 1988
★ ★ **PG Comedy 1:23**
☑ Adult situations, explicit language
Dir: Michael Dinner   *Cast:* Bob Goldthwait, Dabney Coleman, Virginia Madsen, Cindy Pickett, Jim Metzler
▶ Goldthwait inherits a talking horse (voice of John Candy) and half-share in brokerage. Horse's tips propel Goldthwait to fortune, but scheming stepbrother Coleman plots to discover the success formula. Outrageously stri-

dent performances and flimsy screenplay; tolerable for kids and Goldthwait fans. Danny Elfman score includes nifty Muzak version of "We're in the Money."
Dist.: Warner

HOT TOUCH 1981
★ ★ **NR Drama 1:33**
☑ Nudity, adult situations, explicit language, violence
Dir: Roger Vadim   *Cast:* Wayne Rogers, Samantha Eggar, Marie-France Pisier, Patrick Macnee, Melvyn Douglas
▶ Caper film about cop Rogers, who goes undercover as an artist and is blackmailed into forging a pair of missing masterpieces. With gorgeous girlfriend Pisier, he exposes a crooked art dealer. Unbalanced mixture of romance, comedy, drama, and suspense; lackluster and punchless.
Dist.: TWE

HOT T-SHIRTS 1979
★ **R Comedy 1:26**
☑ Nudity, adult situations, explicit language, adult humor
Dir: Chuck Vincent   *Cast:* Ray Holland, Glenn Marc, Stephanie Landor, Pauline Rose, Corinne Alphen
▶ Small-town bar owner revives his flagging business by instituting a wet T-shirt competition, leading to a heated rivalry between the local girls and snooty college co-eds. Despite suggestive subject matter, leering comedy fails to deliver the goods.
Dist.: Warner

HOUND OF THE BASKERVILLES, THE 1939
★ ★ ★ **NR Mystery-Suspense 1:20 B&W**
Dir: Sidney Lanfield   *Cast:* Basil Rathbone, Nigel Bruce, Wendy Barrie, Lionel Atwill, Richard Greene, John Carradine
▶ It's Sherlock Holmes (Rathbone) and Dr. Watson (Bruce) to the rescue when young nobleman Greene is menaced by a legendary beast. Intelligently mounted adaptation retained Sir Arthur Conan Doyle's Victorian period (later efforts were updated to World War II era) and an explicit reference to Holmes's drug habit in the closing line, "Watson, the needle!" Cerebral Rathbone and bumbling Bruce left an indelible impression in these roles and appeared in further episodes.
Dist.: CBS/Fox

HOUND OF THE BASKERVILLES, THE 1959 British
★ ★ **NR Mystery-Suspense 1:26**
Dir: Terence Fisher   *Cast:* Peter Cushing, Andre Morell, Christopher Lee, Marla Landi
▶ Not bad Hammer Studios remake of the Holmes classic with horror star Cushing as the great detective and Morell as his Watson. They take on the case of Sir Baskerville (Lee) whose estate is haunted by the curse of a murderous dog. **(CC)**
Dist.: CBS/Fox

HOUR OF THE ASSASSIN 1987
★ ★ R Action-Adventure 1:33
☑ Nudity, explicit language, violence
Dir: Luis Llosa   *Cast:* Erik Estrada, Robert Vaughn, Alfredo Alvarez Calderon, Lourdes Berninzon
▶ The enemies of the new president-elect of a banana republic hire ex–Green Beret Estrada to assassinate him at the inauguration. Slowly making his way toward the capital, one-man army Estrada is pursued by Vaughn, a CIA agent. Lots of killings, car chases, and explosions on way to routine denouement. Estrada is totally wooden, and even usually good Vaughn walks through part.
Dist.: MGM/UA

HOUSE 1986
★ ★ ★ R Horror 1:32
☑ Explicit language, graphic violence
Dir: Steve Miner   *Cast:* William Katt, Kay Lenz, George Wendt, Richard Moll, Mary Stavin
▶ After his aunt commits suicide, writer Katt moves into her big old house. She claimed the house was haunted and, when monsters start coming out of closets, he suspects she was right. Familiar story enlivened by inventive touches, emphasizing chuckles over tingles. Not really scary (monsters look fake) but well produced fun should play nicely on the small screen. (CC)
Dist.: New World

HOUSE II: THE SECOND STORY 1987
★ ★ PG-13 Horror 1:28
☑ Explicit language, violence
Dir: Ethan Wiley   *Cast:* Arye Gross, Jonathan Stark, Royal Dano, Bill Maher, Lar Park Lincoln, John Ratzenberger
▶ Sequel in name only. Gross, his girlfriend Lincoln, and hustling best pal Stark move into creepy digs where Gross's parents were done in twenty-five years earlier. The horror begins when Gross resurrects long-dead great-great-grandfather Dano. Arbitrary plotting, a few jolts. (CC)
Dist.: New World

HOUSE ACROSS THE BAY, THE 1940
★ NR Mystery-Suspense 1:26 B&W
Dir: Archie Mayo   *Cast:* George Raft, Joan Bennett, Lloyd Nolan, Gladys George, Walter Pidgeon, June Knight
▶ Torch-singer Bennett marries crooked night-club owner Raft, who goes to jail on a tax rap to avoid angry criminal brethren. Unfortunately, his sentence turns out to be longer than he expected, and when he busts out and finds Bennett romancing Pidgeon, he gets shooting mad. Average suspenser with radiant leads.
Dist.: Monterey

HOUSEBOAT 1958
★ ★ ★ ★ NR Comedy 1:50
Dir: Melville Shavelson   *Cast:* Cary Grant,

Sophia Loren, Martha Hyer, Harry Guardino, Paul Petersen, Murray Hamilton
▶ Widowed Washington lawyer Grant hires music conductor's daughter Loren to look after his three children on Potomac houseboat. Grant and Loren, although pursued by others, fall in love. Lighthearted and lots of fun; Grant and Loren interact beautifully with each other and the children. Sam Cooke sings the Oscar-nominated "Almost in Your Arms"; screenplay was also nominated.
Dist.: Paramount

HOUSE CALLS 1978
★ ★ ★ ★ PG Comedy 1:38
☑ Adult situations, explicit language
Dir: Howard Zieff   *Cast:* Walter Matthau, Glenda Jackson, Art Carney, Richard Benjamin, Candice Azzara, Dick O'Neill
▶ Slapstick hospital antics combine with sophisticated sexual innuendos when recently widowed surgeon/would-be ladykiller Matthau falls for divorcée Jackson while rewiring her broken jaw. He's forced to choose between the hectic single life and Glenda's home and hearth. Middle-age comedy/romance serves as apt vehicle for powerhouse leads, with strong support from Carney as an out-to-lunch doctor going senile.
Dist.: MCA

HOUSEKEEPER, THE 1987 Canadian
★ R Mystery-Suspense 1:37
☑ Brief nudity, adult situations, explicit language, violence
Dir: Ousama Rawi   *Cast:* Rita Tushingham, Ross Petty, Tom Kneebone, Shelley Peterson, Jonathan Crombie, Jessica Steen
▶ Dyslexic Tushingham kills her dad after he makes fun of her impediment. She then takes a job with a doctor's family without telling of her handicap, leading to friction and a violent (and rather repellent) climax. Tushingham is memorable, but this Canadian-made feature fails to build sufficient suspense.
Dist.: Warner

HOUSEKEEPING 1987
★ ★ ★ PG Drama 1:56
☑ Adult situations
Dir: Bill Forsyth   *Cast:* Christine Lahti, Andrea Burchill, Sara Walker, Anne Pitoniak, Barbara Reese
▶ Beautifully observed, quirky drama about sisters Walker and Burchill, orphaned by their mother's suicide and cared for by their long-lost, eccentric Aunt Sylvie (Lahti). Haunting performances (especialy from Lahti and Walker) examine the nature of impossible attachments and vagrant lives. Based on Marilynne Robinson's well-regarded novel. (CC)
Dist.: RCA/Columbia

HOUSE OF FEAR, THE 1945
★ ★ NR Mystery-Suspense 1:08 B&W
Dir: Roy William Neill   *Cast:* Basil Rathbone,

Nigel Bruce, Aubrey Mather, Dennis Hoey, Paul Cavanagh, Holmes Herbert

► After attempting to move Sherlock Holmes and Dr. Watson into World War II era, long-running series returned the duo to Victorian times. In a dreary Scottish mansion, someone is killing off the seven middle-aged members of the "Good Comrades Club." A curse on the manor decrees that no inhabitant shall go to the grave in one piece. Indeed, those slain die in ways that make identification impossible, posing a formidable test for Holmes's renowned powers of deduction.
Dist.: CBS/Fox

HOUSE OF GAMES 1987
★ ★ R Mystery-Suspense 1:41
☑ Adult situations, explicit language, violence
Dir: David Mamet   *Cast:* Lindsay Crouse, Joe Mantegna, Mike Nussbaum, Lilia Skala, J. T. Walsh

► Repressed shrink Crouse attempts to study con man Mantegna and his gang and becomes involved in a series of scams. Twisty, satisfying plot has a few predictable spots but generally keeps the audience off balance. Playwright Mamet's feature debut is a visually sleek thriller. Frosty Crouse (Mrs. Mamet) and frisky Mantegna work beautifully together.
Dist.: HBO

HOUSE OF THE LONG SHADOWS 1983
British
★ ★ ★ PG Horror 1:42
☑ Explicit language, violence
Dir: Peter Walker   *Cast:* Peter Cushing, Vincent Price, Christopher Lee, John Carradine, Desi Arnaz, Jr., Richard Todd

► Spooky spoof about young author Arnaz who tries to write his new novel in a deserted gothic mansion, only to be interrupted by murder. Price, Lee, Cushing, and Carradine are the film's most menacing bogeymen. Based on George M. Cohan's novel *Seven Keys to Baldpate.*
Dist.: MGM/UA

HOUSE OF THE RISING SUN 1986
★ NR Mystery-Suspense 1:26
☑ Brief nudity, adult situations, explicit language, violence
Dir: Greg Gold   *Cast:* Frank Annese, Jamie Barrett, Tawny Moyer

► Newspaper reporter Barrett goes undercover as high-class escort to get the goods on murderer, stylishly dressed pimp Annese. She finds herself attracted to him and becomes his lover, but he gives chase when he learns her true identity. Suspenser plays like a full-length music video.
Dist.: Prism

HOUSE OF WAX 1953
★ ★ ★ PG Horror 1:28
☑ Adult situations, violence
Dir: Andre de Toth   *Cast:* Vincent Price,

Frank Lovejoy, Carolyn Jones, Phyllis Kirk, Paul Picerni, Charles Buchinski

► Wax sculptor Price disappears after fire started by evil partner and then returns with a new wax museum. People begin to wonder: how does he get those figures so realistic? It wouldn't have anything to do with murder, would it? Originally filmed in 3-D but ingenious thriller works just fine without the gimmick. Macabre wax museum atmosphere, deliciously mad Vincent.
Dist.: Warner

HOUSE ON CARROLL STREET, THE 1988
★ ★ PG Mystery-Suspense 1:41
☑ Explicit language, mild violence
Dir: Peter Yates   *Cast:* Kelly McGillis, Jeff Daniels, Mandy Patinkin, Jessica Tandy, Jonathan Hogan

► An old-fashioned thriller set in 1950s New York City. Blacklisted McGillis uncovers mysterious goings-on at the house next door involving Joe McCarthyish senator Patinkin. G-man Daniels helps her through treacherous maze of murder and espionage. New York never looked spiffier in this splendid period re-creation, although the plot relies too heavily on coincidence. (CC)
Dist.: HBO

HOUSE ON HAUNTED HILL 1958
★ ★ NR Horror 1:15 B&W
Dir: William Castle   *Cast:* Vincent Price, Carol Ohmart, Richard Long, Alan Marshal

► Mysterious millionaire Price invites group of people to spend the night at his haunted mansion, offering ten grand each if they stay until dawn. Murder is on the menu for the guests, including Price's unfaithful wife and her lover. William Castle gimmick movie, originally filmed in "Percepto" (including a skeleton flying over the audience), is enjoyable but not to be taken seriously. (CC)
Dist.: CBS/Fox

HOUSE ON SKULL MOUNTAIN, THE 1974
☆ PG Horror 1:25
☑ Violence
Dir: Ron Honthaner   *Cast:* Victor French, Janee Michelle, Jean Durand, Mike Evans, Xernona Clayton, Lloyd Nelson

► The reading of a dying black woman's will brings her relatives together at the spooky house on Skull Mountain. Killings begin and the butler, in this case voodoo-practicing Durand, did it. French is the Caucasian who learns something surprising about his ancestry while battling the butler. Black cast is trite flick's sole novelty.
Dist.: CBS/Fox

HOUSE ON SORORITY ROW, THE 1983
★ ★ R Horror 1:31
☑ Brief nudity, explicit language, violence
Dir: Mark Rosman   *Cast:* Kathryn McNeil, Eileen Davidson, Janis Zido, Robin Meloy

► Sorority girls accidentally kill their bitchy house mother and dump the corpse into the pool. Then someone starts killing the girls. Could the house mother have risen from the dead? Bad acting plus a plot with few surprises in an already oversaturated genre. Many false scares, too few real ones. *Dist.:* Vestron

HOUSE PARTY 1990
★★ **R Comedy 1:40**
☑ Adult situations, explicit language
Dir: Reginald Hudlin *Cast:* Christopher Reid, Robin Harris, Christopher Martin, Tisha Campbell
▶ Exhuberant black teen comedy follows the adventures of Kid (Reid), who gets grounded by dad Harris on the night of a big party. Kid sneaks out and finds himself in uproarious scrapes with a trio of hoods and bigoted cops ("Freeze, Negroes!") before making it to the festivities brimming with rap music and hot dancing. First feature from the Hudlin Brothers (Reginald also scripted; Warrington produced) won the grand prize at the U.S. Film Festival. More than a teen flick: funny, perceptive, energetic, and pure fun. **(CC)**
Dist.: RCA/Columbia

HOUSE THAT DRIPPED BLOOD, THE 1971 British
★ **PG Horror 1:41**
☑ Violence
Dir: Peter John Duffell *Cast:* Denholm Elliott, Peter Cushing, Christopher Lee, Ingrid Pitt, John Bennett, Jon Pertwee
▶ Anthology features four stories set in an English country mansion: writer Elliott is stalked by killer, the house becomes a wax museum and setting for more murders, Lee falls victim to voodoo doll, and actor Pertwee takes vampire role too seriously. Sturdy cast and literate screenplay by Robert Bloch combine scares and laughs.
Dist.: Prism

HOUSE WHERE EVIL DWELLS, THE 1982
★ **R Horror 1:28**
☑ Nudity, adult situations, explicit language, graphic violence
Dir: Kevin Connor *Cast:* Susan George, Edward Albert, Doug McClure, Amy Barrett, Mayo Hattori
▶ Americans Albert and George rent a house outside Kyoto, unaware the place is haunted by ghosts of a samurai, his unfaithful wife, and her lover. All hell breaks loose as the spirits menace the tenants. Offensive characters (you may be rooting for the ghosts), silly special effects (like giant crabs), plenty of sex and violence.
Dist.: MGM/UA

HOWARDS OF VIRGINIA, THE 1940
★★ **NR Drama 1:58 B&W**
Dir: Frank Lloyd *Cast:* Cary Grant, Martha Scott, Cedric Hardwicke, Alan Marshal, Richard Carlson, Paul Kelly
▶ Revolutionary War epic traces surveyor Grant's growing involvement with the rebel cause against a backdrop of familiar events (the Boston Tea Party, Valley Forge, etc.). Although shot in Williamsburg, dull historical pageant feels contrived and inauthentic.
Dist.: RCA/Columbia

HOWARD THE DUCK 1986
★★ **PG Fantasy 1:50**
☑ Adult situations, explicit language
Dir: Willard Huyck *Cast:* Lea Thompson, Jeffrey Jones, Tim Robbins, Ed Gale, Chip Zien
▶ A cigar-chomping alien duck is accidentally transported to Cleveland via a wayward laser. Befriended by aspiring rock star Thompson, the feathered hero defends her against a gang of punks. Mild satire then turns into overproduced orgy of frenetic chase scenes, car crashes, and light shows as Howard saves the world from an evil Duck Warlord (Jones). Critics and audiences alike found George Lucas production a turkey. **(CC)**
Dist.: MCA

HOW GREEN WAS MY VALLEY 1941
★★★★ **NR Drama 1:58 B&W**
Dir: John Ford *Cast:* Walter Pidgeon, Maureen O'Hara, Donald Crisp, Anna Lee, Roddy McDowall, Sara Allgood
▶ Emotionally powerful adaptation of Richard Llewellyn's novel shows changes in a nineteenth-century Welsh coal-mining village, seen through the eyes of a young boy whose parents sacrifice to give him a better life. Inspiring, often heartbreaking film received ten Oscar nominations, winning for Best Picture, Ford's magnificent direction, Crisp's stern but loving father, Arthur Miller's lyrical photography, and impressive set design.
Dist.: CBS/Fox

HOW I GOT INTO COLLEGE 1989
★★★ **PG-13 Comedy 1:27**
☑ Explicit language
Dir: Savage Steve Holland *Cast:* Anthony Edwards, Corey Parker, Lara Flynn Boyle, Finn Carter, Charles Rocket, Brian Doyle-Murray
▶ One of the rare teen films that actually respects its characters, this sleeper outlines travails of Parker, low-scoring high school senior who is desperate to get into same college as girl-of-his-dreams Boyle. Parker impresses admissions board with funny, highly self-referential video. Director Holland's flip funnybone puts an odd spin on the material. Story and cast are quite appealing. **(CC)**
Dist.: CBS/Fox

HOW I WON THE WAR 1967 British
★ **NR Comedy 1:51**
☑ Violence
Dir: Richard Lester *Cast:* Michael Crawford, John Lennon, Roy Kinnear, Lee Montague, Jack MacGowran
▶ In World War II North Africa, eccentric officer Crawford drives his troops crazy with his ridiculous demands. Impressively shot black com-

edy makes sharp contrast between its lunatic characters and the realistic horrors of war but the very British accents and humor may not be readily accessible to Americans. Crawford is remarkable and Lennon (who appears briefly) is fascinating.
Dist.: MGM/UA

HOWLING, THE 1981
★ ★ R Horror 1:30
☑ Nudity, explicit language, graphic violence
Dir: Joe Dante   *Cast:* Dee Wallace, Patrick Macnee, Dennis Dugan, John Carradine, Christopher Stone, Slim Pickens
▶ TV reporter Wallace survives attack from a lunatic and then recuperates with husband Stone at a secluded retreat. Bad idea: the place turns out to be a coven of werewolves who intend to make Wallace their next furry member. Very convincing special effects provide lots of gore. Director Dante and co-writer Sayles (who appears in a cameo) deliver a beautifully conceived and executed movie that transcends its B-movie origins.
Dist.: Embassy

HOWLING II: YOUR SISTER IS A WEREWOLF 1985
★ R Horror 1:24
☑ Nudity, adult situations, explicit language, graphic violence
Dir: Philippe Mora   *Cast:* Christopher Lee, Annie McEnroe, Reb Brown, Sybil Danning, Marsha Hunt
▶ In L.A., Brown investigates the death of his sister, rumored to be a werewolf. Then, accompanied by reporter McEnroe and psychic investigator Lee, It's off to Transylvania to confront werewolf leader Danning. Feeble sequel, inferior to the original. Production values are good; script and performances aren't, although Danning outcleavages Hunt.
Dist.: HBO

HOWLING III: THE MARSUPIALS 1987
Australian
★ PG-13 Horror 1:34
☑ Nudity, explicit language, violence
Dir: Philippe Mora   *Cast:* Barry Otto, Imogen Annesley, Leigh Biolos, Max Fairchild, Dasha Blahova
▶ Marsupial werewolf Annesley escapes from her commune and falls for a crew member in a horror film. Her cohorts track her down. More professional than *Howling II* but not as good as the original. Hammy acting, ridiculous script, intrusive rock score, more laughs than scares. Some fine camerawork and a few audacious ideas.
Dist.: Vista

HOWLING IV...THE ORIGINAL NIGHTMARE 1988
★ ★ R Horror 1:32
☑ Nudity, adult situations, explicit language, violence
Dir: John Hough   *Cast:* Romy Windsor, Michael T. Weiss, Anthony Hamilton, Susanne Severeid
▶ Novelist Windsor and nervous husband Weiss rent a country cottage to get away from it all. There they meet an exotic woman who seduces Weiss, and is later revealed to be a she-wolf. It seems the woods are crawling with werewolves who are tearing people apart. With help of friend Hamilton, Windsor manages to round them up in bell tower for fiery finish. Not much in the way of special effects or believable acting.
Dist.: IVE

HOWLING V: THE REBIRTH 1989
★ ★ R Horror 1:30
☑ Nudity, explicit language, violence
Dir: Neal Sundstrom   *Cast:* Philip Davis, Victoria Catlin, Elizabeth She, William Shockley, Clive Turner
▶ A group of people are stranded in an old Hungarian castle during a blizzard. One of them is a werewolf. It could be debonair count Davis, bimbo She, movie star Stavin or any of the others trekking through the castle's underground labyrinth. Whoever it is, one by one, the guests are having their throats ripped out. Low-budget horror seems to have cast competing over who can give worst performance.
Dist.: IVE

HOW SWEET IT IS! 1968
★ ★ ★ NR Comedy 1:39
Dir: Jerry Paris   *Cast:* James Garner, Debbie Reynolds, Maurice Ronet, Paul Lynde, Marcel Dalio, Terry-Thomas
▶ Reynolds arranges for husband Garner to chaperone their son and his girlfriend to Europe. Meanwhile, she is conned by Terry-Thomas into renting a villa that belongs to Ronet, an amorous Frenchman who then pursues her. Sixties-style sitcom is sustained by stars, although dated elements include Garner wearing peace medallions, plus a psychedelic title sequence.
Dist.: Warner

HOW THE WEST WAS WON 1963
★ ★ ★ ★ ★ G Western 2:25
Dir: John Ford, Henry Hathaway, George Marshall   *Cast:* John Wayne, James Stewart, Debbie Reynolds, Gregory Peck, Carroll Baker, George Peppard, Henry Fonda, Lee J. Cobb, Eli Wallach, Walter Brennan, Robert Preston
▶ Tale traces family of New England farmers as they head West in the 1830s through two subsequent generations of trials and tribulations. This one has it all: comedy, romance, drama, adventure. Wide-screen Western classic loses scope on the TV screen but all-star cast and sweep of the story make it almost like a mammoth (and very engrossing) miniseries. Divided into chapters, each with its own director. A Best Picture nominee.
Dist.: MGM/UA

HOW TO BEAT THE HIGH COST OF LIVING
1980
★ ★ ★ ★ PG Comedy 1:44
⊡ Nudity, adult situations, explicit language
Dir: Robert Scheerer *Cast:* Susan Saint James, Jane Curtin, Jessica Lange, Dabney Coleman, Richard Benjamin, Fred Willard
▶ Caper comedy about Oregon ladies St. James, Curtin, and Lange, who are mad as hell about skyrocketing prices and decide not to take it anymore. They pull off a shopping mall heist. Predictable but happy spoof provides undemanding entertainment.
Dist.: Vestron

HOW TO GET AHEAD IN ADVERTISING
1989 British
★ R Comedy 1:35
⊡ Brief nudity, adult situations, explicit language
Dir: Bruce Robinson *Cast:* Richard E. Grant, Rachel Ward, Richard Wilson, Jacqueline Tong, John Shrapnel, Susan Woolridge
▶ Overachiever Grant is a neurotic advertising genius having trouble with a new account: a pimple cream. When a huge boil with a face grows on his neck and starts talking, Grant goes over the edge. Hilarious satire has moments of true originality, but seems to retread the same jokes. (CC)
Dist.: Virgin

HOW TO MARRY A MILLIONAIRE 1953
★ ★ ★ ★ NR Comedy 1:35
Dir: Jean Negulesco *Cast:* Marilyn Monroe, Betty Grable, Lauren Bacall, William Powell, David Wayne, Rory Calhoun
▶ Trying to land millionaire husbands, models Monroe, Gable, and Bacall pool their funds to rent a posh Manhattan penthouse into which they plan to lure their victims. The golddiggers' plans go awry when two fall for men who appear to be poor. Frothy fun with sprightly dialogue from writer/producer Nunnally Johnson. First comedy to use wide-screen CinemaScope process.
Dist.: CBS/Fox

HOW TO MURDER YOUR WIFE 1965
★ ★ ★ ★ NR Comedy 1:58
Dir: Richard Quine *Cast:* Jack Lemmon, Virna Lisi, Terry-Thomas, Eddie Mayehoff, Claire Trevor, Sidney Blackmer
▶ Cartoonist and avowed bachelor Lemmon awakes from a debauch to find himself wed to Italian spitfire Lisi, who'd popped out of a cake at a party. Researching an incident for his comic strip, Lemmon enacts a murder and the disposal of a dummy body, only to have his actions mistaken for a real crime when his unwanted wife mysteriously disappears. Brisk diversion with nice color and art direction.
Dist.: MGM/UA

HOW TO STEAL A MILLION 1966
★ ★ ★ NR Comedy 2:07
Dir: William Wyler *Cast:* Audrey Hepburn, Peter O'Toole, Eli Wallach, Hugh Griffith, Charles Boyer, Marcel Dalio
▶ Delicious comedy caper set in Paris. Hepburn, daughter of art forger Griffith, must steal one of her father's fakes from a heavily guarded museum before authenticators examine it. She turns to security expert O'Toole, who concocts an elaborate break-in. Smoothly entertaining film features a winning performance by Boyer.
Dist.: CBS/Fox

HOW TO STUFF A WILD BIKINI 1965
★ ★ NR Comedy 1:30
Dir: William Asher *Cast:* Annette Funicello, Dwayne Hickman, Brian Donlevy, Harvey Lembeck, Beverly Adams, Buster Keaton, Frankie Avalon, Mickey Rooney
▶ Witch doctor Keaton's flying bikini makes Adams the hit of the beach; she steals Hickman away from Funicello, who's also pining over Naval Reserve recruit Avalon. Sixth *Beach Party* entry shows its age. Guests include the Kingsmen and Brian Wilson as one of the surf bums. Sequel *Ghost in the Invisible Bikini* sinks even further.
Dist.: Warner

HOW TO SUCCEED IN BUSINESS WITHOUT REALLY TRYING 1967
★ ★ ★ NR Musical 2:01
Dir: David Swift *Cast:* Robert Morse, Michele Lee, Rudy Vallee, Anthony Teague, Maureen Arthur, Kay Reynolds
▶ Window washer J. Pierpont Finch (Morse) charms and worms his way up the corporate ladder, impressing boss Vallee and falling for secretary Lee along the way. Adaptation of the Pulitzer Prize–winning musical satire feels like a photographed play, but it's irresistible nevertheless. Perfect performance by Morse. Grand Frank Loesser score includes "I Believe in You," "Brotherhood of Man," and "Been a Long Day." Funniest scene: Vallee and Morse singing "rip the chipmunks off the field" in "Grand Old Ivy."
Dist.: MGM/UA

HUCKLEBERRY FINN 1939
★ ★ ★ ★ NR Comedy/Drama 1:30 B&W
Dir: Richard Thorpe *Cast:* Mickey Rooney, Walter Connolly, William Frawley, Rex Ingram, Minor Watson, Jo Ann Sayers
▶ Rooney is ideally cast as Mark Twain's young hero, who resists attempts to make him respectable by escaping on a Mississippi River raft with runaway slave Ingram. They meet con men Connolly and Frawley and must later deal with Ingram's capture. Superior adaptation of the classic. Also known as *The Adventures of Huck Finn.*
Dist.: MGM/UA

HUCKLEBERRY FINN 1974
★ ★ ★ ★ G Musical/Family 1:54
Dir: J. Lee Thompson *Cast:* Jeff East, Paul Winfield, Harvey Korman, David Wayne
▶ Charming musical adaptation of Mark

Twain's classic. Among the adventures facing young Huck (East) and freedom-bound slave Jim (Winfield) are hooking up with the rascally "King" (Korman). Score by Robert and Richard Sherman (*Mary Poppins, Chitty Chitty Bang Bang*). **(CC)**
Dist.: Vestron

HUCKLEBERRY FINN 1975
★ ★ ★ ★ **NR Family/MFTV 1:16**
Dir: Robert Totten   *Cast:* Ron Howard, Antonio Fargas, Jack Elam, Merle Haggard, Donny Most, Sarah Selby
▶ Made-for-television adaptation of Mark Twain's classic about young Huck Finn (Howard) and runaway slave Jim (Fargas) journeying down the Mississippi via raft. Simply presented, well produced, but rather uninspired. Howard is convincing, if not endearing, as Huck; Fargas is miscast as Jim. Easy-to-take lesson in tolerance for younger kids.
Dist.: CBS/Fox

HUD 1963
★ ★ ★ **NR Drama 1:52 B&W**
☑ Rape, adult situations, violence
Dir: Martin Ritt   *Cast:* Paul Newman, Patricia Neal, Melvyn Douglas, Brandon de Wilde, John Ashley, Whit Bissell
▶ Ne'er-do-well Newman returns to father Douglas, feuds with him about how to save struggling ranch, tries to rape maid Neal, and loses the respect of nephew de Wilde. Great drama still remarkably fresh thanks to Newman's Oscar-nominated performance. Equally fine are Oscar-winning Neal and Douglas. Based on a Larry McMurtry novel.
Dist.: Paramount

HUMAN COMEDY, THE 1943
★ ★ ★ **NR Drama 1:58 B&W**
Dir: Clarence Brown   *Cast:* Mickey Rooney, Frank Morgan, James Craig, Marsha Hunt, Fay Bainter, Ray Collins, Donna Reed, Van Johnson, Robert Mitchum, "Butch" Jenkins
▶ Warmly sentimental look at how the people of a small California town are affected by World War II. Rooney excels as a telegraph messenger, a job that means delivering tragic news to friends, but child star Jenkins steals the picture as his brother. William Saroyan won an Oscar for his story; film received four other nominations.
Dist.: MGM/UA ©

HUMAN DUPLICATORS, THE 1964
☆ **NR Sci-Fi 1:23**
Dir: Hugo Grimaldi   *Cast:* George Nader, Barbara Nichols, George Macready, Hugh Beaumont, Richard Kiel, Richard Arlen
▶ Alien Kiel prepares for his planet's invasion of Earth by creating android copies of human bigwigs. Professor Macready and government operative Nader try to stop him, only to get duplicated themselves. The alien, meanwhile, falls in love with a blind woman. Later retitled *Jaws of the Alien* to capitalize on Kiel's recur-

ring role in James Bond movies, but inane under any name.
Dist.: IVE

HUMAN FACTOR, THE 1979
★ **R Drama 1:55**
☑ Nudity, adult situations, explicit language
Dir: Otto Preminger   *Cast:* Nicol Williamson, Richard Attenborough, John Gielgud, Robert Morley, Iman, Derek Jacobi
▶ Family man Williamson is unlikely suspect when a double agent is discovered in British Secret Service. Williamson turns out to be the culprit: years before he made a deal with USSR to get black wife Iman out of South Africa. He must leave his family behind when the net tightens around him. Intimate spy drama, adapted by Tom Stoppard from Graham Greene novel, suffers from below average production values. Subtle, understated acting from Williamson, but lovely model Iman is lifeless as his wife.
Dist.: MGM/UA

HUMAN MONSTER, THE 1939 British
★ **NR Horror 1:16 B&W**
Dir: Walter Summers   *Cast:* Bela Lugosi, Hugh Williams, Greta Gynt, Edmond Ryan, Wilfrid Walter, Arthur E. Owen
▶ A London home for the blind provides cover for evil doctor Lugosi's experiments. When Lugosi's victims are found floating in the Thames, enabling him to collect on their insurance policies, Scotland Yard inspector Williams investigates. Superior Lugosi vehicle achieves some truly frightening moments. Based on the novel by Edgar Wallace. Also known as *Dark Eyes of London*.
Dist.: Video Yesteryear

HUMANOIDS FROM THE DEEP 1980
★ **R Horror 1:20**
☑ Rape, nudity, explicit language, graphic violence
Dir: Barbara Peeters   *Cast:* Doug McClure, Ann Turkel, Vic Morrow, Cindy Weintraub, Anthony Penya, Denise Galik
▶ Gruesome monsters attack a fishing community, prompting an investigation by scientist Turkel and fisherman McClure. Lurid but enjoyable low-budget shocker, with a heavy emphasis on gore and nudity, scores some points with its pro-environment stance.
Dist.: Warner

HUMONGOUS 1982 Canadian
★ ★ **R Horror 1:34**
☑ Rape, adult situations, explicit language, graphic violence
Dir: Paul Lynch   *Cast:* Janet Julian, David Wallace, Janit Baldwin, John Wildman
▶ In 1946, a woman survives a rape attack on an island. In the present, a group of teens lost in a fog are shipwrecked on the island where the rape victim still lives in isolation. Someone (or something) starts bumping off the teens. Adequate suspense, distasteful violence.
Dist.: Nelson

HUNCHBACK OF NOTRE DAME, THE 1923
★ ★ NR Drama 2:13 B&W
Dir: Wallace Worsley *Cast:* Lon Chaney, Patsy Ruth Miller, Norman Kerry, Ernest Torrence, Raymond Hatton, Kate Lester
▶ The story of Quasimodo (Chaney), the deformed bell ringer of Paris's Notre Dame Cathedral. The hunchback's poignant, ultimately ill-fated love for gypsy girl Miller plays against the background of the fifteenth-century reign of Louis the XI. Lavish, visually astonishing silent adaptation of the Victor Hugo novel with an amazing physical transformation by Chaney.
Dist.: Video Yesteryear

HUNCHBACK OF NOTRE DAME, THE 1939
★ ★ ★ ★ NR Drama 1:57 B&W
Dir: William Dieterle *Cast:* Charles Laughton, Maureen O'Hara, Thomas Mitchell, Cedric Hardwicke, Edmond O'Brien, Walter Hampden
▶ In Fifteenth-century Paris, hideous hunchback Quasimodo (Laughton) rescues gypsy O'Hara from angry crowd outside Notre Dame Cathedral, but ultimately becomes tragic victim of church officials. Laughton's poignant performance is a magnificent blend of makeup and acting. Based on the often-filmed Victor Hugo novel; Lon Chaney starred in the 1923 silent version, Anthony Quinn in the 1957, and Anthony Hopkins in the telemovie.
Dist.: Various ☒

HUNDRA 1984 Italian
☆ NR Action-Adventure 1:49
☑ Rape, nudity, adult situations, explicit language, graphic violence
Dir: Matt Cimber *Cast:* Laurene Landon, John Ghaffari, Marissa Casel, Romiro Oliveros
▶ Landon, sole survivor of a woman warrior tribe massacred by male marauders, ventures into the city to get impregnated and continue her race. She finds love with a handsome healer but must overcome an evil king. Intentionally silly adventure/parody. Landon plays this like a valley girl with a thorn in her side.
Dist.: Media

HUNGER, THE 1983
★ ★ R Horror 1:36
☑ Nudity, adult situations, explicit language, violence
Dir: Tony Scott *Cast:* Catherine Deneuve, David Bowie, Susan Sarandon, Cliff De Young, Beth Ehlers
▶ In present-day New York City, two-hundred-year-old vampire Bowie is rapidly aging. His immortal mate Deneuve tries to reverse the process by recruiting brilliant scientist Sarandon. Deneuve seduces Sarandon and then tries to lay claim to her soul. Arresting visuals and vivid sex scenes but muddled storytelling and lurid bloodletting.
Dist.: MGM/UA

HUNK 1987
★ PG Comedy 1:42

☑ Explicit language, adult humor
Dir: Lawrence Bassoff *Cast:* John Allen Nelson, Steve Levitt, Deborah Shelton, Rebeccah Bush, James Coco, Robert Morse
▶ Brainy computer wimp Levitt, jilted by girlfriend for aerobics instructor, is lured by sexy witch Shelton into making deal with the devil (Coco). Result: Levitt's turned into handsome hunk Nelson. Slapdash direction, but flimsy froth provides handsome bods and mindless fun.
Dist.: RCA/Columbia

HUNTER, THE 1980
★ ★ ★ ★ PG Action-Adventure 1:37
☑ Adult situations, explicit language, violence
Dir: Buzz Kulik *Cast:* Steve McQueen, Eli Wallach, Kathryn Harrold, Levar Burton, Ben Johnson
▶ Old-fashioned bounty hunter McQueen tries to catch up with a new breed of leaner, meaner criminal. Several excellent chase scenes (in a Nebraska cornfield and a Chicago elevated train), convincingly seedy environment, energetic Burton, and vitality from McQueen (dying when this was made) in his last film.
Dist.: Paramount

HUNTER'S BLOOD 1987
★ ★ R Action-Adventure 1:41
☑ Explicit language, graphic violence
Dir: Robert C. Hughes *Cast:* Sam Bottoms, Kim Delaney, Clu Gulager, Mayf Nutter, Ken Swofford, Joey Travolta
▶ City boy Bottoms and four friends take hunting trip in backwoods Oklahoma. They run afoul of redneck poachers, who stalk the vacationers and kidnap Bottoms's girlfriend Delaney. Well directed, but characters are stereotypes and plot seems recycled from better movies. **(CC)**
Dist.: Nelson

HUNT FOR RED OCTOBER, THE 1990
★ ★ ★ ★ PG Action-Adventure 2:15
☑ Violence
Dir: John McTiernan *Cast:* Sean Connery, Alec Baldwin, Scott Glenn, James Earl Jones, Sam Neill, Richard Jordan
▶ Renegade Russian commander Connery heads his submarine toward the United States. Is he planning to attack or defect? CIA analyst Baldwin thinks the latter and must race time to prove his theory as both the Americans and Russians hunt the *Red October*. Rousing, large-scale adventure gets more exciting as it goes along. Magnificently crafted by director McTiernan and perfectly cast with Connery and Baldwin leading a huge roster of manly types. Based on the Tom Clancy best-seller. **(CC)**
Dist.: Paramount

HUNT THE MAN DOWN 1950
★ NR Crime 1:08 B&W
Dir: George Archainbaud *Cast:* Gig Young,

Lynne Roberts, Willard Parker, Gerald Mohr, Mary Anderson, James Anderson

▶ Lawyer Young agrees to defend James Anderson, an innocent man convicted of murder twelve years ago. When he reopens the investigation, more killings occur. Can Young catch the guilty party? Conventional but well done. Home video version double billed with 1937's *Smashing the Rackets*.
Dist.: Turner

HURRICANE, THE 1937
★ ★ NR Action-Adventure 1:43 B&W
Dir: John Ford *Cast:* Jon Hall, Dorothy Lamour, Mary Astor, Raymond Massey, C. Aubrey Smith

▶ Rousing, first-class adventure and South Seas spectacular from master director Ford. Massey plays an uncompromising governor obsessed with imprisoning native Hall, who eventually saves Massey's wife Astor during the relentless hurricane finale. Spellbinding disaster climax directed by special effects wizard James Basevi. Alfred Newman's score includes the pop hit "Moon of Manikoora."
Dist.: Nelson

HURRICANE 1979
☑ ★ ★ ★ PG Action-Adventure 2:00
Brief Nudity, explicit language
Dir: Jan Troell *Cast:* Timothy Bottoms, Jason Robards, Mia Farrow, Max Von Sydow, Trevor Howard, Dayton Ka'Ne

▶ Dino De Laurentis's $22 million remake of John Ford's 1937 classic of love and torrential rain. There's trouble in Pago Pago when Farrow defies stern father Robards and falls for native Ka'ne, whose dialogue includes such gems as: "I see you are getting very wet." Most of the cast drowns in the waterlogged climax.
Dist.: Paramount

HURRY, CHARLIE, HURRY 1942
★ NR Comedy 1:05 B&W
Dir: Charles E. Roberts *Cast:* Leon Errol, Mildred Coles, Kenneth Howell, Cecil Cunningham, George Watts, Eddie Conrad

▶ Errol is a man named Daniel Boone, but has little resemblance to the famous pioneer: he's a harried husband who lies to nagging wife Cunningham to go on a fishing trip. His scheme backfires when his fib about knowing an important politician is believed all over town. Good-humored but far from hilarious. Home video version double billed with 1942's *Seven Days Ashore*.
Dist.: Turner

HUSH. . .HUSH, SWEET CHARLOTTE 1965
★ ★ ★ ★ NR Horror 2:13
Dir: Robert Aldrich *Cast:* Bette Davis, Olivia de Havilland, Joseph Cotten, Agnes Moorehead, Cecil Kellaway

▶ Not a sequel, more a blood relation to *Whatever Happened to Baby Jane?* featuring the same producer/director Aldrich, star Davis, and gothic gore and bitchery. Old-pro bravura performances include Oscar-nominated Moorehead as Velma, housekeeper to the deteriorating Southern mansion where de Havilland and Cotten plot to turn poor Bette into a blabbering maniac. Also received six other nominations. **(CC)**
Dist.: Key

HUSTLE 1975
★ ★ ★ ★ R Mystery-Suspense 2:00
☑ Nudity, strong sexual content, violence
Dir: Robert Aldrich *Cast:* Burt Reynolds, Catherine Deneuve, Ben Johnson, Paul Winfield, Eileen Brennan, Eddie Albert

▶ Los Angeles detective Reynolds, involved with high-class hooker Deneuve, investigates death of young woman found on beach. The trail leads to Albert, a lawyer with mob connections. Johnson, the dead girl's father, is also involved in the investigation. Cynical stuff with a powerful kick; Reynolds is quite sympathetic.
Dist.: Paramount

HUSTLER, THE 1961
★ ★ ★ ★ NR Drama 2:15 B&W
Dir: Robert Rossen *Cast:* Paul Newman, Jackie Gleason, Piper Laurie, George C. Scott, Myron McCormick, Murray Hamilton

▶ Pool hustler "Fast" Eddie Felson (Newman) takes on Minnesota Fats (Gleason), has a doomed affair with crippled Laurie, and almost loses his soul to gambler Scott. Tense, compelling drama with Newman in one of his most complex and full-bodied performances. Scott, Laurie, and Gleason offer superb support. Razor-sharp cinematography and editing, taut direction by Rossen. Followed twenty-five years later by Scorsese's *The Color of Money*. **(CC)**
Dist.: CBS/Fox

I AM A CAMERA 1955 British
★ ★ NR Drama 1:38 B&W
Dir: Henry Cornelius *Cast:* Julie Harris, Laurence Harvey, Shelley Winters, Ron Randell, Lea Seidl, Anton Diffring

▶ In pre-WWII Berlin, Harris is a fun-loving chanteuse while Winters is a Jewish girl who encounters the first wave of Hitler's anti-Semitism. Harvey portrays poor, struggling writer Christopher Isherwood, whose *Berlin Stories* inspired John van Druten's play from which this intelligent film was adapted. Source material later evolved into the Broadway musical and hit film *Cabaret*.
Dist.: Monterey

I AM A FUGITIVE FROM A CHAIN GANG 1932
★ ★ ★ ★ ★ NR Drama 1:33 B&W
Dir: Mervyn LeRoy *Cast:* Paul Muni, Glenda Farrell, Helen Vinson, Preston Foster, Edward J. McNamara

▶ World War I vet Muni, unwilling accomplice in a petty crime, is caught and sentenced to brutal Southern chain gang. He escapes and establishes a law-abiding life, but the past catches up with him. Gripping Depression-era

drama, relentlessly directed by LeRoy and stunningly acted by Muni. Shattering climax: "How do you live?" asks Muni's friend. "I steal," he says from the shadows. Fact-based drama remade by HBO as *The Man Who Broke a Thousand Chains.* Based on Robert E. Burns's autobiographical story.
Dist.: Key

I AM THE CHEESE 1983
★ ★ **PG Drama 1:35**
☑ Explicit language
Dir: Robert Jiras *Cast:* Robert MacNaughton, Robert Wagner, Hope Lange, Don Murray, Cynthia Nixon
▶ Troubled teen MacNaughton recalls childhood traumas that led to his institutionalization. Past and present are intercut as therapist Wagner tries to help him. Quiet but high-quality, low-budget drama from Robert Cormier's popular novel for young adults. Nonlinear story requires concentration to follow.
Dist.: Vestron

ICE CASTLES 1979
★ ★ ★ ★ **PG Drama 1:49**
☑ Explicit language
Dir: Donald Wrye *Cast:* Robby Benson, Lynn-Holly Johnson, Colleen Dewhurst, Tom Skerritt, Jennifer Warren
▶ Teen ice-skater Johnson forsakes beau Benson and widowed dad Skerritt to rise to the top. When an accident nearly blinds her, she reaffirms her ties to them and beats the odds to skate again. Well-done sentiment evokes laughs and tears. Ice Capades star Johnson makes a winsome debut. Moving Marvin Hamlisch score features Melissa Manchester singing Oscar-nominated "Through the Eyes of Love."
Dist.: RCA/Columbia

ICE HOUSE 1989
☆ **NR Drama 1:26**
☑ Adult situations, explicit language, violence
Dir: Eagle Pennell *Cast:* Melissa Gilbert, Bo Brinkman, Andreas Manolikakis, Buddy Quaid, Katie Wagner
▶ Texans Gilbert and Brinkman came to Hollywood to make it big in show biz but are now drug-addicted failures. She becomes wealthy Manolikakis's lover; he wants to return to Texas with her and confronts her about their past. Gilbert tries to change her wholesome image in real-life husband Brinkman's screenplay but overall result resembles a bad stage play.
Dist.: Monarch

ICEMAN 1984
★ ★ ★ **PG Action-Adventure 1:40**
☑ Explicit language, violence
Dir: Fred Schepisi *Cast:* Timothy Hutton, Lindsay Crouse, John Lone, Josef Sommer, David Strathairn, Danny Glover
▶ Caveman Lone is found preserved in ice. Revived by scientists, he makes a painful adjustment to his new surroundings, although an-thropologist Hutton develops a strong rapport with him (even teaching him to sing Neil Young's "Heart of Gold"). Intriguing adventure with a magnetic performance by Lone and solid work from Hutton, but an overly mystical ending.
Dist.: MCA

ICEMAN COMETH, THE 1973
★ **PG Drama 3:59**
☑ Adult situations
Dir: John Frankenheimer *Cast:* Lee Marvin, Fredric March, Robert Ryan, Jeff Bridges, Martyn Green, Moses Gunn
▶ Ryan, March, Bridges, and other desperate men nurse drinks and illusions as they palaver in a bar called the Hell Hole. Biggest blower of hot air is Marvin, whose bravado cannot hide the guilty secret that makes him the most deluded loser of them all. Cast does well in straightforward rendering of Eugene O'Neill's electrifying stage play.
Dist.: CBS/Fox

ICE PALACE 1960
★ ★ ★ **NR Drama 2:23**
Dir: Vincent Sherman *Cast:* Richard Burton, Robert Ryan, Martha Hyer, Jim Backus, Carolyn Jones, Ray Danton
▶ The drive for Alaskan statehood is the backdrop for the rivalry between Burton and Ryan. Burton ruthlessly pursues money, battles Ryan for Jones's affections, goes against public opinion on the statehood question, then is reconciled with his former enemy through marriage. Based on the Edna Ferber novel.
Dist.: Warner

ICE PIRATES, THE 1984
★ ★ **PG Sci-Fi 1:34**
☑ Adult situations, violence, adult humor
Dir: Stewart Raffill *Cast:* Robert Urich, Mary Crosby, Michael D. Roberts, Anjelica Huston, John Matuszak, Ron Perlman
▶ Pirate leader Urich and his buccaneer band aid princess Crosby in a battle against an evil empire for the most valuable commodity in the universe: water. Tongue-in-cheek attempt to crossbreed swashbuckler genre with sci-fi trappings. Aimless script, bland effects, some fun for the younger set.
Dist.: MGM/UA

ICE STATION ZEBRA 1968
★ ★ ★ ★ **G Action-Adventure 2:30**
Dir: John Sturges *Cast:* Rock Hudson, Ernest Borgnine, Patrick McGoohan, Jim Brown, Tony Bill, Lloyd Nolan
▶ Nuclear submarine races to the North Pole to retrieve a strategic Russian satellite. Hudson, the commander, must also identify a saboteur among suspects including Communist defector Borgnine, British secret agent McGoohan, and Brown, a captain bitter over discrimination. Despite impressive Arctic settings, large-scale adventure based on Alistair

MacLean's best-seller is typical Cold War espionage
Dist.: MGM/UA

I CONFESS 1953
★★★★ NR Mystery-Suspense 1:35 B&W
Dir: Alfred Hitchcock *Cast:* Montgomery Clift, Anne Baxter, Karl Malden, Brian Aherne, Roger Dann
► Priest Clift hears murderer's confession. Religious code prohibits him from revealing the information, so he becomes cop Malden's number-one suspect. Somber but involving thriller from master Hitchcock. Intense performance by Clift, evocative use of Quebec locations.
Dist.: Warner

I COULD GO ON SINGING 1963 British
★★★ NR Musical/Drama 1:39
Dir: Ronald Neame *Cast:* Judy Garland, Dirk Bogarde, Jack Klugman, Aline MacMahon, Gregory Phillips, Pauline Jameson
► In London, American singer Garland is reunited with English doctor Bogarde, the old flame who raised their child without her. Her new relationship with them is not without problems. Soapy, sometimes overwrought, melodrama with music. Garland goes emotionally all out in her last screen appearance. Songs, performed at the London Palladium, include the title tune and "By Myself."
Dist.: MGM/UA

IDIOT'S DELIGHT 1939
★★ NR Comedy 1:45 B&W
Dir: Clarence Brown *Cast:* Norma Shearer, Clark Gable, Edward Arnold, Charles Coburn, Joseph Schildkraut, Burgess Meredith
► Glamorous adaptation of Robert Sherwood's Pulitzer prize–winning play concerns a mixed bag of travelers stranded in an Alpine retreat at the outbreak of World War II. Gable, leader of a cut-rate song-and-dance troupe, rekindles a romance with Shearer, now mistress to munitions industrialist Arnold. Antiwar stance seems naive today, but Gable does a delightful version of "Puttin' on the Ritz."
Dist.: MGM/UA

IDOLMAKER, THE 1980
★★★ PG Drama 1:59
☑ Adult situations, explicit language
Dir: Taylor Hackford *Cast:* Ray Sharkey, Peter Gallagher, Tovah Feldshuh, Paul Land, Maureen McCormick
► In the late 1950s, failed-songwriter-turned-producer Sharkey stops at nothing to make stars out of unknown Philadelphia kids Land and Gallagher. Flashy inside look at the music biz, inspired by the careers of Fabian and Frankie Avalon, with nice period detail, exciting concert footage, and an energetic performance by Sharkey.
Dist.: MGM/UA

I DON'T GIVE A DAMN 1988 Israeli
★ R Drama 1:32
☑ Nudity, adult situations
Dir: Samuel Imberman *Cast:* Ikka Zohar, Anath Waxman, Liora Grossman, Shmuel Vilojni, Shlomo Tarshish, Dudu Ben
► Young Israeli soldier Zohar goes to war a happy, diffident youth with a lovely girlfriend, comes home an embittered paraplegic. Adjustment to home life is hard, and Zohar manages to alienate the ones who love him most. Story of ruined young life is affecting, but film has a naively pretty look in parts, poor editing, and nonexistent pacing. [S]
Dist.: TWE

I DREAM TOO MUCH 1935
★ NR Musical 1:37 B&W
Dir: John Cromwell *Cast:* Lily Pons, Henry Fonda, Eric Blore, Osgood Perkins, Lucien Littlefield, Lucille Ball
► Fonda is miscast as an unsuccessful operatic composer who, after encouraging wife Pons's stab at singing stardom, is upset when she reaches the top before he does. Middling musical's score mixes opera excerpts (from Verdi's *Rigoletto* and others) with Jerome Kern/Dorothy Fields songs.
Dist.: Turner

IF. . . 1969 British
☆ R Drama 1:51 C/B&W
☑ Nudity, explicit language
Dir: Lindsay Anderson *Cast:* Malcolm McDowell, David Wood, Christine Noonan, Richard Warwick, Robert Swann, Peter Jeffrey
► At a British boarding school, student McDowell leads a violent rebellion against the establishment. Exemplary performances with McDowell making an unforgettable debut in this strikingly original film. Sharply satiric, but avant-garde narrative techniques may alienate the casual viewer.
Dist.: Paramount

IF EVER I SEE YOU AGAIN 1978
★★★ PG Romance 1:45
☑ Adult situations, explicit language
Dir: Joe Brooks *Cast:* Joe Brooks, Shelley Hack, Jimmy Breslin, Jerry Keller, George Plimpton
► Composer/widower Brooks looks up old school flame Hack and they renew their affair. He loses her again but then wins her back. Actor/co-writer/director Brooks also wrote the swooning music (a chore he repeated in *You Light Up My Life*).
Dist.: RCA/Columbia

IF I WERE RICH 1933 British
☆ NR Comedy 1:03 B
Dir: Zoltan Korda *Cast:* Robert Donat, Wendy Barrie, Edmund Gwenn, Clifford Heatherley, Morris Harvey
► Wealthy Donat, forced to work for a living when the Depression hits, is ordered to turn off con man Gwenn's electricity. Gwenn tries to involve Donat in one of his schemes while Donat becomes interested in Gwenn's

daughter Barrie. Amiable comedy is also known as *Cash* and *For Love of Money.*
Dist.: Video Yesteryear

IF YOU COULD SEE WHAT I HEAR 1982
★ ★ ★ ★ ★ **PG Biography 1:43**
☒ Adult situations, explicit language
Dir: Eric Till   *Cast:* Marc Singer, R. H. Thomson, Sarah Torgov, Shari Belafonte Harper
▶ True story traces the college years of the blind singer/TV personality Tom Sullivan (Singer) as he deals with the realities of his condition and has several affairs before settling down with Torgov. Focus is on the humorous aspects of Sullivan's situation rather than the usual teary-eyed manipulation. Sunny and uplifting.
Dist.: Vestron

I GO POGO 1980
★ ★ **G Animation 1:22**
Dir: Marc Chinoy   *Cast:* Voices of Vincent Price, Ruth Buzzi, Jonathan Winters, Jimmy Breslin, Arnold Stang, Skip Hinnant
▶ Walt Kelly's beloved comic strip characters are portrayed in a puppet-animated satire of the political process. Story has Pogo, a reluctant candidate for President, endorsed by the opposition since he seems so likely to lose. Likeable tone and nice songs, but this particular style of puppet animation lacks enough movement and detail to remain interesting for the length of a feature.
Dist.: Buena Vista

I HATE ACTORS! 1988 French
☆ **PG Comedy 1:31 C/B&W**
☒ Explicit language, adult situations
Dir: Gerard Krawczyk   *Cast:* Jean Poiret, Patrick Floersheim, Michel Blanc, Bernard Blier, Pauline Lafont, Michel Galabru
▶ There's been a murder on the set of a forties Hollywood costume epic. Who's the killer? Is it harassed studio boss Blier? Has-been star Galabru? Stunning blond Lafont? This gentle send-up of Hollywood film noir rounds up the usual suspects of the genre. Still, as a Gallic take on a classic era in American film, it is mildly amusing. Gerard Depardieu does a quick cameo. ☒
Dist.: IVE

IKIRU 1952 Japanese
★ **NR Drama 2:23 B&W**
Dir: Akira Kurosawa   *Cast:* Takashi Shimura, Nobuo Kaneko, Kyoko Seki, Miki Odagiri, Yunosuke Ito
▶ Minor government clerk Shimura reassesses his life when his doctor tells him he has only a year to live. Deriving no comfort from his grown children, he becomes obsessed with the construction of a playground in a last, desperate grab for purpose. Prepare to be emotionally clobbered by a deeply moving, if depressing, work of art. ☒
Dist.: Media

I'LL CRY TOMORROW 1955
★ ★ ★ ★ **NR Biography 1:57 B&W**
Dir: Daniel Mann   *Cast:* Susan Hayward, Richard Conte, Eddie Albert, Jo Van Fleet, Don Taylor, Ray Danton
▶ Frank biography of Broadway and Hollywood star Lillian Roth (Hayward), whose career was destroyed by alcoholism. Forced onto the stage at an early age by her domineering mother (Van Fleet), Roth turned to drink after the sudden death of her first husband. Disastrous marriages to Taylor and sadist Conte further her decline. Oscar-nominated Hayward gives an intense performance in this uncompromising adaptation of Roth's best-selling autobiography. Oscar for Best Costumes.
Dist.: MGM/UA

ILLEGALLY YOURS 1988
★ ★ **PG Comedy 1:34**
☒ Adult situations, mild violence
Dir: Peter Bogdanovich   *Cast:* Rob Lowe, Colleen Camp, Kenneth Mars, Kim Myers, L. B. Stratten
▶ When Camp, the object of Lowe's childhood crush nineteen years ago, goes on trial for attempted murder, Lowe lies about the relationship to get on the jury. Love develops as Lowe helps Camp prove her innocence. Breezy style recalls thirties screwball comedy; paper-thin plot overloads the shtick. Stratten, Bogdanovich's current wife and sister of the late Dorothy Stratten, has a small role. (CC)
Dist.: CBS/Fox

ILLUSTRATED MAN, THE 1969
★ **PG Sci-Fi 1:43**
☒ Adult situations, violence
Dir: Jack Smight   *Cast:* Rod Steiger, Claire Bloom, Robert Drivas, Jason Evers, Don Dubbins, Tim Weldon
▶ In 1933 California, hobo Drivas encounters Steiger, who is covered with magical tattoos that come to life to illustrate three different stories: Steiger and Bloom—then real-life spouses—as parents of superpowered children, Steiger as astronaut caught in endless downpour, and Steiger and Bloom trapped in nuclear conflict. Based on the book by Ray Bradbury.
Dist.: Warner

I LOVE MY WIFE 1970
★ ★ **R Comedy 1:35**
☒ Nudity, adult situations, explicit language
Dir: Mel Stuart   *Cast:* Elliott Gould, Brenda Vaccaro, Angel Tompkins, Dabney Coleman, Joan Tompkins, Leonard Stone
▶ When wife Vaccaro becomes pregnant, med student Gould seduces nurses and has affair with model Tompkins. Vaccaro learns of his infidelity and rebuffs him; he eventually sees the error of his ways, but will she take him

back? Risqué Robert Kaufman screenplay provides little entertainment.
Dist.: MCA

I LOVE N.Y. 1987
★ ★ **NR Romance/Comedy 1:32**
☑ Brief nudity, adult situations, explicit language
Dir: Alan Smithee (Gianni Bozzachi) *Cast:* Scott Baio, Kelly Van Der Velden, Christopher Plummer, Jennifer O'Neill, Jerry Orbach, Virna Lisi
▶ Brash young photographer Baio gets break when he is assigned to snap big-time actor Plummer and falls for thespian's lovely daughter Van Der Velden. Despite dad's opposition, love blooms between beauty and shutterbug. Sweet if ordinary romantic comedy has appealing cast and nice New York locations.
Dist.: Magnum

I LOVE YOU 1981 Brazilian
★ ★ **R Comedy 1:44**
☑ Nudity, strong sexual content, explicit language, mild violence
Dir: Arnaldo Jabor *Cast:* Sonia Braga, Paulo Cesar Pereio, Vera Fischer, Tarcisio Meira, Maria Lucia Dahl
▶ When his girlfriend leaves him, wealthy bra manufacturer Pereio invites Braga up to his luxurious high-rise apartment. Pretending to be a prostitute, she helps him enact a variety of sexual fantasies, which lead to a what is supposed to be genuine emotional involvement. Braga's near-continuous nudity pushes this poorly made, would-be-arty sex comedy close to porn. ☒
Dist.: MGM/UA

I LOVE YOU, ALICE B. TOKLAS 1968
★ ★ **R Comedy 1:33**
☑ Nudity, adult situations
Dir: Hy Averback *Cast:* Peter Sellers, Jo Van Fleet, Leigh Taylor-Young, David Arkin, Joyce Van Patten
▶ Successful L.A. lawyer Sellers jilts fiancée Van Patten in favor of young hippie Taylor-Young after munching marijuana brownies. He grows his hair long and moves into his car, but finds the hippie world just as constraining as straight life. Freaked-out Sellers has never been more charming. Although obviously dated, script by Paul Mazursky and Larry Tucker remains surprisingly funny.
Dist.: Warner

I LOVE YOU TO DEATH 1990
★ ★ ★ **R Comedy 1:36**
☑ Brief nudity, adult situations, explicit language, mild violence
Dir: Lawrence Kasdan *Cast:* Kevin Kline, Tracey Ullman, Joan Plowright, River Phoenix, William Hurt, Keanu Reeves, James Gammon, Victoria Jackson, Phoebe Cates
▶ Ullman turns a blind eye to husband Kline's infidelities until finally confronted with the truth. She conspires with mother Plowright and admirer Phoenix to murder him. However, the

philanderer proves impossible to kill despite several attempts on his life. Very amusing in fits and starts, although there are flat stetches in between. Best gags involve Kline walking around with a hole in his chest. Funniest performers: Hurt and Reeves as a pair of blissfully stoned hit men. Based on a true story. **(CC)**
Dist.: RCA/Columbia

I, MADMAN 1989
★ **R Horror 1:33**
☑ Violence
Dir: Tibor Takacs *Cast:* Jenny Wright, Clayton Rohner, Randall William Cook, Steven Memel, Stephanie Hodge, Bruce Wagner
▶ Bookstore clerk Wright's imagination runs away from her: a murderous, mutilating monster comes to life from novels she's read. Her cop boyfriend Rohner thinks there must be a more practical explanation for the subsequent killings. He's wrong. Outlandish plot is competently acted and directed.
Dist.: Media

IMAGE, THE 1990
★ ★ ★ ★ **NR Drama/MFTV 1:47**
☑ Brief nudity, adult situations, explicit language
Dir: Peter Werner *Cast:* Albert Finney, John Mahoney, Kathy Baker, Marsha Mason, Swoosie Kurtz
▶ Finney, the on-air star of America's most popular TV newsmagazine, suffers a crisis of conscience when one of his investigative reports results in the suicide of a man mistakenly implicated in wrongdoing. While Finney's marriage to Mason crumbles, he has an affair with long-time associate Baker, and tries to stay on top of a developing armed forces scandal. Authentic behind-the-scenes atmosphere and a marvelous Finney make this worth seeing.
Dist.: HBO

IMAGEMAKER, THE 1986
★ **R Drama 1:29**
☑ Nudity, adult situations, violence
Dir: Hal Weiner *Cast:* Michael Nouri, Jessica Harper, Anne Twomey, Jerry Orbach, Farley Granger
▶ Former Presidential media consultant Nouri attempts to expose corruption while the government tries to stop him. Nouri must also deal with his wife's suicide in this well-acted but only intermittently successful political thriller. Script is vague at critical points, so the movie is not always easy to follow.
Dist.: Vestron

IMAGINE: JOHN LENNON 1988
★ ★ ★ ★ **R Documentary/Biography 1:43**
☑ Brief nudity, adult situations, explicit language
Dir: Andrew Solt *Cast:* John Lennon, Yoko Ono, Paul McCartney, Ringo Starr, George Harrison, Julian Lennon
▶ Interviews, rare live concert footage, and astounding home movies trace Lennon's rise

to Beatle stardom, his eventful relationship with wife Ono, the break-up of the group, involvement in drugs and other controversies, solo career, and death. Like its subject, film is quirky, abrasive, moving, funny, and sometimes brilliant. Superbly remixed music soundtrack.
Dist.: Warner

I'M ALL RIGHT, JACK 1959 British
★ ★ ★ **NR Comedy 1:48**
Dir: John Boulting, Roy Boulting *Cast:* Ian Carmichael, Peter Sellers, Terry-Thomas, Richard Attenborough, Dennis Price, Margaret Rutherford
▶ Naive youth Carmichael enters industry and upsets union leaders by improving plant efficiency. The union calls a strike that spreads and cripples Britain. Astute, biting satire features a remarkable cast of comics in peak form. Sellers's pompous shop steward is one of his best performances.
Dist.: HBO

I MARRIED A MONSTER FROM OUTER SPACE 1958
★ **NR Sci-Fi 1:18 B&W**
Dir: Gene Fowler *Cast:* Tom Tryon, Gloria Talbott, Ken Lynch, John Eldredge, Jean Carson, Maxie Rosenbloom
▶ Newlywed Talbott begins to realize husband Tryon (the future best-selling author) is acting bizarre. You would too, if you were possessed by a horrifying alien! Terse and moody B-movie, far from the exploitation flick the title suggests.
Dist.: Paramount

I MARRIED AN ANGEL 1942
★ **NR Musical 1:24 B&W**
Dir: W. S. Van Dyke II *Cast:* Jeanette MacDonald, Nelson Eddy, Edward Everett Horton, Binnie Barnes, Reginald Owen, Douglass Dumbrille
▶ Banker Eddy meets MacDonald at a ball, then dreams that she's an angel. They marry, but her honesty causes business problems for him. Final MacDonald/Eddy teaming ends famous screen partnership on a sour note. Based loosely on the Rodgers and Hart stage musical. Songs include "Spring Is Here" and "A Twinkle in Your Eye."
Dist.: MGM/UA

I MARRIED A WITCH 1942
★ ★ ★ ★ **NR Fantasy/Comedy 1:16 B&W**
Dir: René Clair *Cast:* Fredric March, Veronica Lake, Robert Benchley, Susan Hayward, Cecil Kellaway, Robert Warwick
▶ Delightful fantasy about father/daughter witches Kellaway and Lake who wait four hundred years for revenge against their persecutors, the Wooley family. Modern-day Wooley (March) is a sluffy gubernatorial candidate; through devilish tricks, Lake breaks up his engagement to Hayward. First-rate comedy

boasts sharp dialogue, funny special effects, and a twisty plot from Thorne Smith.
Dist.: Lightning

I'M DANCING AS FAST AS I CAN 1982
★ ★ ★ **R Drama 1:46**
☑ Adult situations, explicit language, violence
Dir: Jack Hofsiss *Cast:* Jill Clayburgh, Nicol Williamson, Dianne Wiest, Geraldine Page, Joe Pesci, Ellen Greene
▶ True story of TV producer Barbara Gordon (Clayburgh), who finds refuge from her stressful existence in Valium and then battles to overcome her addiction. Well-acted but very grim psychological drama pulls no punches in indicting medical profession and drug companies. Clayburgh, strongly supported by Page and Wiest, is in top form. Based on Gordon's best-selling book.
Dist.: Paramount

I'M GONNA GIT YOU SUCKA 1988
★ ★ ★ **R Comedy 1:27**
☑ Nudity, explicit language, violence
Dir: Keenan Ivory Wayans *Cast:* Keenan Ivory Wayans, Bernie Casey, Antonio Fargas, John Vernon, Isaac Hayes, Jim Brown
▶ After a ten-year Army stint, Wayans returns home to discover his brother has died of an overdose of gold neck chains and left behind a debt to Vernon, the "Mr. Big" of a local crime syndicate. When Vernon gets rough with Wayans's family, he enlists the aid of Casey, Hayes, Brown, and Fargas, all over-the-hill former black heroes/role models. Wild and woolly spoof does to blaxploitation movies what *Airplane!* did to the disaster genre.
Dist.: MGM/UA

IMITATION OF LIFE 1959
★ ★ ★ ★ **NR Drama 2:04**
Dir: Douglas Sirk *Cast:* Lana Turner, John Gavin, Sandra Dee, Dan O'Herlihy, Susan Kohner, Juanita Moore
▶ Actress Turner and black maid Moore are close to each other but not to their daughters; Turner ignores Dee to rise to the top while Kohner rejects Moore to pass for white. Tearjerker benefits from Sirk's sure hand and Turner's strong performance. Remake of 1934 Claudette Colbert vehicle based on the Fannie Hurst novel.
Dist.: MCA

IMMEDIATE FAMILY 1989
★ ★ ★ ★ **PG-13 Drama 1:35**
☑ Adult situations, explicit language
Dir: Jonathan Kaplan *Cast:* Glenn Close, James Woods, Mary Stuart Masterson, Kevin Dillon
▶ Infertile Close and Woods meet pregnant teen Masterson who wants to give up her baby. They develop a poignant bond with Masterson and her boyfriend Dillon as all nervously await the delivery. Nicely produced, with touching performance from Masterson,

but the gloss can't hide the fact that this is glorified TV fodder. **(CC)**
Dist.: RCA/Columbia

IMMORTAL SERGEANT, THE 1943
★ ★ ★ ★ **NR War 1:31 B&W**
Dir: John M. Stahl *Cast:* Henry Fonda, Maureen O'Hara, Thomas Mitchell, Allyn Joslyn, Reginald Gardiner, Melville Cooper
▶ In World War II Libya, mild-mannered corporal Fonda finds himself suddenly thrust into command when the senior officers of his patrol are killed in action. Recalling the spiritual guidance of old sergeant Mitchell, and the love of girl-back-home O'Hara, Fonda draws upon inner reserves of valor to lead his men into battle. Involving war story, directly told. **(CC)**
Dist.: Key

I, MOBSTER 1958
★ ★ **NR Crime 1:22 B&W**
Dir: Roger Corman *Cast:* Steve Cochran, Lita Milan, Robert Strauss, Lili St. Cyr, John Brinkley, Yvette Vickers
▶ As gangster Cochran testifies to a Senate committee, his sordid life and times unfold in flashback. Given his start in the crime biz by Strauss, Cochran rises to the top through drug selling, union busting, and assassination, despite the qualms of girlfriend Milan and his parents. Slam-bang saga snappily directed by Corman.
Dist.: Nelson

IMPACT 1949
★ ★ **NR Mystery-Suspense 1:51 B&W**
Dir: Arthur Lubin *Cast:* Brian Donlevy, Ella Raines, Charles Coburn, Helen Walker, Anna May Wong, Mae Marsh
▶ Walker and her lover plan to murder her husband Donlevy, but instead it is the boyfriend who gets killed. More twists occur: Donlevy is believed dead, Walker is imprisoned, then events cause the cuckold to consider coming out of hiding. Suspenseful sleeper has an excellent cast and a clever plot.
Dist.: Sinister

IMPORTANCE OF BEING EARNEST, THE
1952 British
★ ★ **NR Comedy 1:35**
Dir: Anthony Asquith *Cast:* Michael Redgrave, Michael Denison, Edith Evans, Joan Greenwood, Dorothy Tutin, Margaret Rutherford
▶ Debonair London bachelor Redgrave uses the nom de plume "Ernest" to cover up his escapades while he's courting country beauty Gwendolen (Greenwood). His plans go awry when his friend Denison pretends to be Ernest to woo Redgrave's ward Cecily (Tutin). Spirited adaptation of Oscar Wilde's classic comedy of errors is played to the hilt by an extraordinary cast. Greenwood is especially alluring as the secretly daring Gwendolen.
Dist.: Paramount

IMPOSSIBLE SPY, THE 1987
★ ★ ★ ★ **NR Espionage/MFTV 1:29**
☑ Explicit language, violence
Dir: Jim Goddard *Cast:* John Shea, Eli Wallach, Michal Bat-Adam, Sasson Gabai, Rami Danon, Haim Girafi
▶ True story of the Israeli spy Elie Cohen (Shea), who infiltrates the Syrian government, befriends Arab bigwig Gabai, and rises in the corridors of power. Cohen risks his life to provide Israel with information that later leads to victory in the Six-Day War. Gripping tale portrays the costs of espionage in very human terms.
Dist.: HBO

IMPROPER CHANNELS 1981 Canadian
★ ★ ★ **PG Comedy 1:32**
☑ Adult situations, explicit language, violence
Dir: Eric Till *Cast:* Alan Arkin, Mariette Hartley, Monica Parker, Harry Ditson, Sarah Stevens
▶ Parents Arkin and Hartley fight the bureaucracy to get their daughter back when an overzealous social worker mistakenly institutionalizes her. Winning performances, appealing "little guys vs. the system" theme. Unevenly paced but generally satisfying.
Dist.: Vestron

IMPULSE 1984
★ ★ **R Sci-Fi 1:31**
☑ Nudity, adult situations, explicit language, graphic violence, adult humor
Dir: Graham Baker *Cast:* Tim Matheson, Meg Tilly, Hume Cronyn, John Karlen, Bill Paxton
▶ City girl Tilly and med student beau Matheson return to small town when her mom attempts suicide. They discover people are suddenly and violently acting out their impulses without any moral restraints. A toxic waste leak turns out to be the cause. Interesting concept, disappointing development.
Dist.: Vestron

IMPULSE 1990
★ ★ **R Action-Adventure 1:48**
☑ Nudity, adult situations, explicit language, violence
Dir: Sondra Locke *Cast:* Theresa Russell, Jeff Fahey, George Dzundza, Alan Rosenberg
▶ Vice-cop Russell romances district attorney Fahey, who is searching for a missing witness on an important case. While undercover as a prostitute, Russell is picked up by none other than Fahey's missing witness, and finds herself sought for murder when he turns up dead. Russell is beautiful, though somewhat remote in this functional but complicated thriller.
Dist.: Warner

IN A LONELY PLACE 1950
★ ★ ★ **NR Drama 1:34 B&W**
Dir: Nicholas Ray *Cast:* Humphrey Bogart,

Gloria Grahame, Frank Lovejoy, Martha Stewart, Robert Warwick, Art Smith
► Screenwriter Bogart is the chief suspect in a savage murder until neighbor Grahame supplies an alibi. They fall in love, but Bogey's cynicism and unprovoked outbursts force Grahame to question their affair. Astute adaptation of the Dorothy B. Hughes novel is a superb example of film noir, with Bogart delivering one of his most complex performances. *Dist.:* RCA/Columbia

IN A SHALLOW GRAVE 1988
★ ★ R Drama 1:32
☑ Adult situations, explicit language, violence
Dir: Kenneth Bowser   *Cast:* Michael Biehn, Maureen Mueller, Michael Beach, Patrick Dempsey, Thomas Boyd Mason, Mike Pettinger
► Soldier Biehn is horribly disfigured during the battle of Guadalcanal. He returns home to Virginia and woos old flame Mueller from afar by letters sent through drifter Dempsey. But Mueller falls for Dempsey. A good performance by Biehn highlights a well-intentioned but uneven adaptation of the James Purdy novel. *Dist.:* Warner

IN CELEBRATION 1975 British
★ PG Drama 1:50
☑ Adult situations, explicit language
Dir: Lindsay Anderson   *Cast:* Alan Bates, James Bolam, Brian Cox, Constance Chapman, Gabrielle Day, Bill Owen
► Bates, Bolam, and Cox are three brothers who've gone different ways in life, rising above their working class background. Seeing one another again at a celebration of their parents' fortieth wedding anniversary, they open up about their hopes, realities, and disillusionment. Adaptation of David Storey's play combines drama, comedy, and a wonderful sense of humanity. *Dist.:* CBS/Fox

INCIDENT, THE 1967
★ ★ ★ NR Drama 1:39 B&W
Dir: Larry Peerce   *Cast:* Tony Musante, Martin Sheen, Beau Bridges, Brock Peters, Ruby Dee, Jack Gilford, Thelma Ritter, Donna Mills, Ed McMahon, Gary Merrill
► After committing a mugging, thugs Sheen and Musante invade a New York subway car at two A.M. and terrorize the passengers, including elderly Gilford and Ritter. The riders are reluctant to resist the punks. Only soldier Bridges finally fights back. Edgy urban suspense with a fine cast. *Dist.:* CBS/Fox

IN COLD BLOOD 1968
★ ★ ★ ★ R Crime 2:14 B&W
☑ Adult situations, explicit language, violence
Dir: Richard Brooks   *Cast:* Robert Blake,

Scott Wilson, John Forsythe, Paul Stewart, Gerald S. O'Loughlin
► Intelligent adaptation of Truman Capote's best-seller follows killers Blake and Wilson (both giving the performances of their lives) from the motiveless murder of a Midwest family to their capture and eventual execution. Chilling masterpiece exudes a constant sense of foreboding. Outstanding editing and photography. Four Oscar nominations including Best Director. *Dist.:* RCA/Columbia

IN COUNTRY 1989
★ ★ ★ ★ R Drama 2:00
☑ Adult situations, explicit language, violence
Dir: Norman Jewison   *Cast:* Bruce Willis, Emily Lloyd, Kevin Anderson, Joan Allen, Judith Ivey, Peggy Rea
► Kentucky teenager Lloyd finds letters written by her late Vietnam vet dad and wants to know more about the father who died "in country." Willis plays her uncle, an alcoholic vet who must pull himself out of his stupor to enlighten Emily and deal with his own pain. Heartrending adaptation of Bobbie Ann Mason's best-seller has splendid change-of-pace performance from Willis. Wrenching climax set at Vietnam Veterans Memorial in Washington, D.C. **(CC)** *Dist.:* Warner

INCREDIBLE JOURNEY, THE 1963
★ ★ ★ G Family 1:20
Dir: Fletcher Markle   *Cast:* Emile Genest, John Drainie, Tommy Tweed, Sandra Scott, Syme Jago, Marion Finlayson
► When their owners leave for the summer, three pets—bull terrier Bodger, Siamese cat Lao, and Labrador retriever Luath—are sent to stay with a friend 250 away. The pets embark on an action-filled adventure across the Canadian wilderness to rejoin the family, encountering bears, lynx, and porcupines as well as some eccentric humans. Highly enjoyable Disney picture with beautiful scenery and amazing animal stunts. *Dist.:* Buena Vista

INCREDIBLE MELTING MAN, THE 1978
★ R Horror 1:26
☑ Nudity, explicit language, graphic violence
Dir: William Sachs   *Cast:* Alex Rebar, Burr DeBenning, Myron Healey, Michael Alldredge, Ann Sweeny, Lisle Wilson
► A trip to Saturn leaves astronaut Rebar with a degenerating, radioactive disease that turns him into a melting-skin maniac who must snack on people to survive. Doctor DeBenning tries to track him down. Give this points for originality and creepy music but watch out for nauseating special effects. *Dist.:* Vestron

INCREDIBLE MR. LIMPET, THE 1964
★ ★ ★ NR Family/Fantasy 1:42

Dir: Arthur Lubin *Cast:* Don Knotts, Carole Cook, Jack Weston, Andrew Duggan; voice of Elizabeth MacRae
► Fish-lover Knotts, deemed unfit for World War II Navy service, suddenly gets his wish when he falls into the water and turns into an animated fish. In his new guise, he not only aids the Navy, but finds a fish girlfriend more understanding than his wife Cook. Goofy, friendly fun. (CC)
Dist.: Warner

INCREDIBLE SHRINKING MAN, THE 1957
★ ★ ★ ★ NR Sci-Fi 1:21 B&W
Dir: Jack Arnold *Cast:* Grant Williams, Randy Stuart, April Kent, Paul Langton, William Schallert
► After passing through radioactive cloud, Williams begins to shrink. Science is unable to reverse the process and Williams faces personal humiliation and life-and-death battles with house pets and spiders. Director Arnold skillfully creates a disturbing mood in this strikingly original sci fi classic. From Richard Matheson's novel; inspired Lily Tomlin's 1981 comedy *The Incredible Shrinking Woman*.
Dist.: MCA

INCREDIBLE SHRINKING WOMAN, THE 1981
★ ★ ★ PG Comedy 1:28
☑ Explicit language, adult humor
Dir: Joel Schumacher *Cast:* Lily Tomlin, Charles Grodin, Ned Beatty, Henry Gibson, Elizabeth Wilson, Mark Blankfield
► Amusing reworking of *The Incredible Shrinking Man*. Tomlin, a typical suburban housewife, is bombarded with so many pollutants that she starts to shrink. Uneven as satire, but plenty of laughs. Special-effects master Rick Baker does an impressive turn as a gorilla; Tomlin briefly reprises her Ernestine character.
Dist.: MCA

IN CROWD, THE 1988
★ ★ ★ PG Drama 1:35
☑ Adult situations
Dir: Mark Rosenthal *Cast:* Donovan Leitch, Joe Pantoliano, Jennifer Runyon, Wendy Gazelle
► Wealthy teen Leitch (son of 1960s pop star Donovan) sacrifices girlfriend Gazelle and college goals to appear on a TV dance show, where he disrupts a troubled romance between hoodlum Pantoliano and Runyon, the show's dancing star. Modest teen romance set in 1960s Philadelphia has an outstanding oldies soundtrack and plenty of dance numbers. (CC)
Dist.: Orion

INCUBUS, THE 1982 Canadian
★ ★ R Horror 1:32
☑ Rape, nudity, adult situations, language, graphic violence
Dir: John Hough *Cast:* John Cassavetes, Kerrie Keane, Helen Hughes, Erin Flannery, Duncan McIntosh, John Ireland

► Rapist terrorizes small Wisconsin town, leading surgeon Cassavetes to suspect daughter's boyfriend McIntosh. With the help of beautiful reporter Keane, he sets a trap for the villain. Weak low-budget horror effort relies too much on violence and silly special effects.
Dist.: Vestron

IN DANGEROUS COMPANY 1988
★ ★ R Mystery-Suspense 1:25
☑ Adult situations, explicit language
Dir: Ruben Preuss *Cast:* Cliff De Young, Tracy Scoggins, Chris Mulkey, Henry Darrow, Steven Keats
► Detective De Young protects old flame Scoggins from an angry ex-boyfriend, then allows himself to be pillow-talked by her into scheme to steal rare Degas painting from her current millionaire beau Keats. Stunning Scoggins has a few more surprises up her sexy sleeve but unfortunately lacks chemistry with the bland De Young. Sharply paced and shot.
Dist.: Forum

INDEPENDENCE DAY 1983
★ ★ ★ R Drama 1:50
☑ Brief nudity, adult situations, explicit language, violence
Dir: Robert Mandel *Cast:* Kathleen Quinlan, David Keith, Dianne Wiest, Frances Sternhagen, Cliff De Young
► Spunky small-town waitress Quinlan dreams of big-city photography career. Can she leave behind her lover, mechanic Keith? Both have problems: her mother Sternhagen is dying and his sister Wiest is being abused by husband De Young. Naturalistic atmosphere and forceful performances (notably Wiest's) in this pleasing soap opera drama.
Dist.: Warner

INDESTRUCTIBLE MAN, THE 1956
★ NR Horror 1:10 B&W
Dir: Jack Pollexfan *Cast:* Lon Chaney, Jr., Marian Carr, Robert Shayne, Ross Elliott, Kenneth Terrell, Marvin Ellis
► Convict Chaney is executed but is then revived by scientist Shayne. The criminal goes on a rampage against old colleagues who did him wrong, but his life after death proves ill-fated. Generic plot juiced up by unsubtle, yet intense, performances and direction.
Dist.: Goodtimes

INDIANA JONES AND THE LAST CRUSADE 1989
★ ★ ★ ★ ★ PG-13 Action-Adventure 2:06
☑ Violence
Dir: Steven Spielberg *Cast:* Harrison Ford, Sean Connery, Denholm Elliott, Allison Doody, John Rhys-Davies, River Phoenix
► After rollicking prologue where teenage Indiana Jones (Phoenix) acquires trademark hat and bullwhip, film cuts to 1938 as Ford tries to rescue his prickly professor dad Connery, whose lifelong quest for the Holy Grail has run him afoul of the Nazis. Third in the series has all the required danger and derring-do (espe-

cially the tank battle and chases on land and air), plus nifty Ford/Connery teamwork. Funniest moments: the encounter with Hitler, Connery's revelation of relationship with femme fatale Doody, and the origin of Indiana's nickname. **(CC)**
Dist.: Paramount

INDIANA JONES AND THE TEMPLE OF DOOM 1984
★ ★ ★ ★ **PG Action-Adventure 1:58**
☑ Explicit language, violence
Dir: Steven Spielberg **Cast:** Harrison Ford, Kate Capshaw, Ke Huy Quan, Amrish Puri, Roshan Seth
► Adventurer Indiana Jones (Ford), sidekick Quan, and nightclub singer Capshaw (who opens the movie with a nifty Chinese version of "Anything Goes") flee Shanghai gang and land in India. There Indy helps villagers recover a sacred stone from an evil cult. Breakneck-paced sequel to *Raiders of the Lost Ark* crams in enough amazing derring-do and outrageous stunts for ten movies. Lags a bit in the Temple of Doom sequence (and small kids may be upset when a cultist rips out a human heart from a victim's chest); otherwise, Spielberg never gives you a chance to catch your breath. **(CC)**
Dist.: Paramount

INDIAN PAINT 1964
★ **G Family 1:31**
Dir: Norman Foster **Cast:** Johnny Crawford, Jay Silverheels, Pat Hogan, Robert Crawford, Jr., George J. Lewis, Joan Hollmark
► Indian teenager Crawford rescues a tribal horse from thieves. The horse returns the favor when the teen is menaced by wolves. A sweet man/animal relationship develops in this sturdy if unremarkable fare that should please the children. Nicely photographed by Floyd Crosby.
Dist.: United

INDISCREET 1931
★ **NR Comedy 1:14 B&W**
Dir: Leo McCarey **Cast:** Gloria Swanson, Ben Lyon, Arthur Lake, Barbara Kent, Monroe Owsley
► After dumping her no-good boyfriend, Swanson discovers that her little sister Kent has become involved with him. Attempting to break up the relationship, she nearly loses current beau Lyon. Mixed-up mess veers uncertainly between subplots, but McCarey/Swanson collaboration is consistently watchable. Songs include "Come to Me."
Dist.: Video Yesteryear

INDISCREET 1958
★ ★ ★ **NR Romance 1:40**
Dir: Stanley Donen **Cast:** Cary Grant, Ingrid Bergman, Cecil Parker, Phyllis Calvert, Megs Jenkins, David Kossoff
► Single financier Grant, pretending to be married to keep from getting involved in a serious relationship, woos film star Bergman.

She eventually turns the tables on him. Stylish romance with Cary and Ingrid generating class and charm, as always.
Dist.: Various

INDISCRETION OF AN AMERICAN WIFE 1954 U.S./Italian
★ **NR Romance/Drama 1:03 B&W**
Dir: Vittorio de Sica **Cast:** Jennifer Jones, Montgomery Clift, Richard Beymer, Gino Cervi, Paolo Stoppa
► At the Rome train station, American housewife Jones, heading home after an affair with Italian Clift, has one last meeting with her lover. Clift wants her to remain but she is reluctant. Short, bittersweet love story with stars and director wringing emotion out of an extremely slim plot. Truman Capote was one of four credited screenwriters.
Dist.: CBS/Fox

I NEVER PROMISED YOU A ROSE GARDEN 1977
★ ★ ★ **R Drama 1:29**
☑ Nudity, explicit language
Dir: Anthony Page **Cast:** Bibi Andersson, Kathleen Quinlan, Reni Santoni, Susan Tyrrell, Signe Hasso, Diane Varsi
► Teenager Quinlan is institutionalized by her parents. With the help of understanding therapist Andersson, she comes to grips with her private demons. Harrowing, realistic drama; strong performances by Quinlan and Andersson. Based on the Joanne Greenberg bestseller.
Dist.: Warner

I NEVER SANG FOR MY FATHER 1970
★ ★ ★ **PG Drama 1:30**
☑ Adult situations
Dir: Gilbert Cates **Cast:** Melvyn Douglas, Gene Hackman, Dorothy Stickney, Estelle Parsons, Elizabeth Hubbard, Conrad Bain
► New Yorker Hackman plans to move to California with divorcée Hubbard but mom Stickney's death and cantankerous dad Douglas's opposition complicate the plan. Teaming of Douglas and Hackman as the battling father and son is worth the price of admission; both were Oscar-nominated. Based on the Robert Anderson play.
Dist.: RCA/Columbia

INFERNO 1980 Italian
★ **R Horror 1:23**
☑ Graphic violence
Dir: Dario Argento **Cast:** Irene Miracle, Leigh McCloskey, Eleonora Giorgi, Daria Nicolodi, Alida Valli, Sacha Pitoeff
► Miracle discovers that her Manhattan apartment building is one of three hellish headquarters for demons in the world. When her knowledge proves fatal, her brother McCloskey seeks the answers behind her death. The prolific Argento directs in his typically overheated style. Score by Keith Emerson.
Dist.: CBS/Fox

INFORMER, THE 1935
★★★ **NR Drama 1:31 B&W**
Dir: John Ford ***Cast:*** Victor McLaglen, Heather Angel, Preston Foster, Margot Grahame, Wallace Ford, Una O'Connor
▸ Searing adaptation of Liam O'Flaherty's novel gave McLaglen the role of his life as Gypo Nolan, a hulking Dubliner who betrays his IRA friend to the British for twenty pounds. Stark, uncompromising classic builds to an unbearable climax. Won Oscars for McLaglen, director Ford, screenplay by Dudley Nichols, and Max Steiner's score. Remade in 1968 as *Up Tight*, with the setting changed from 1922 Ireland to black American ghetto.
Dist.: Various

IN HARM'S WAY 1965
★★★★ **NR War 2:45 B&W**
Dir: Otto Preminger ***Cast:*** John Wayne, Kirk Douglas, Patricia Neal, Tom Tryon, Paula Prentiss, Brandon de Wilde, Jill Haworth, Dana Andrews, Stanley Holloway, Burgess Meredith, Franchot Tone, Patrick O'Neal
▸ Large-scale epic focuses on the aftermath of Pearl Harbor. Naval officer Wayne leads an American counterattack on the Japanese; commander Douglas, after disgracing himself by molesting Haworth, proves heroic in battle. Satisfying mixture of action and personal drama, as Wayne romances Neal and reconciles with estranged son de Wilde. **(CC)**
Dist.: Paramount

INHERITORS, THE 1984 Austrian
☆ **NR Drama**
☑ Nudity, explicit language, violence
Dir: Walter Bannert ***Cast:*** Nikolas Vogel, Roger Schauer, Anneliese Stoceckl-Eberhard, Jaromir Borek, Klaus Novak
▸ Teenager Vogel, troubled at both school and home, joins neo-Nazi party that denies the existence of the Holocaust and wants to purify German workforce. As his rift with his family grows so does his violent allegiance to the hate group. Cautionary picture may attract the curious but grim story leaves us without hope or humanity to hang on to. Also available dubbed. [S]
Dist.: Nelson

INHERIT THE WIND 1960
★★★ **NR Drama 2:07 B&W**
Dir: Stanley Kramer ***Cast:*** Spencer Tracy, Fredric March, Gene Kelly, Florence Eldridge, Dick York
▸ In 1925 Tennessee, teacher York is put on trial for advocating evolution. Attorney Tracy (based on Clarence Darrow) defends him against fundamentalist March (based on William Jennings Bryan) while cynical reporter Kelly (based on H. L. Mencken) looks on. Movie version of the Lawrence and Lee Broadway play (inspired by the Scopes "Monkey" Trial) provides glib but entertaining courtroom theatrics and larger-than-life performances by Tracy and March.
Dist.: CBS/Fox

INITIATION, THE 1984
★ **R Horror 1:37**
☑ Nudity, adult situations, explicit language, graphic violence
Dir: Larry Stewart ***Cast:*** Clu Gulager, Vera Miles, James Read, Daphne Zuniga, Marilyn Kagan
▸ Sorority initiation turns into a real-life Hell Night when a knife-wielding asylum escapee terrorizes nubile coeds. Formula slasher film with a surprise ending. Filmed in the Dallas-Fort Worth area.
Dist.: HBO

IN-LAWS, THE 1979
★★★★ **PG Comedy 1:43**
☑ Explicit language, adult humor
Dir: Arthur Hiller ***Cast:*** Peter Falk, Alan Arkin, Richard Libertini, Nancy Dussault, Penny Peyser, Michael Lembeck
▸ Conservative dentist Arkin does a favor for his future in-law, CIA agent Falk, and through a series of esculating disasters winds up facing a firing squad in a South American dictatorship. Madcap farce is often side-splittingly funny, with Libertini a standout for his performance as a crazed tyrant. Charming leads were reteamed to lesser effect in 1985's *Big Trouble*.
Dist.: Warner

IN LIKE FLINT 1967
★★★★ **NR Espionage 1:54**
Dir: Gordon Douglas ***Cast:*** James Coburn, Lee J. Cobb, Jean Hale, Andrew Duggan, Anna Lee, Yvonne Craig
▸ Coburn reprises his role as secret agent Derek Flint, this time battling a Virgin Islands-based organization of beautiful women. The ladies, cosmetics experts who've invented brainwashing hair dryers, now scheme to gain control of a nuclear-armed space station and take over the world. Sequel to *Our Man Flint* runs out of steam due to excessive campiness.
Dist.: CBS/Fox

IN NAME ONLY 1939
★★★ **NR Drama 1:42 B&W**
Dir: John Cromwell ***Cast:*** Carole Lombard, Cary Grant, Kay Francis, Charles Coburn, Helen Vinson, Peggy Ann Garner
▸ Scheming Francis marries wealthy Grant for his family's money. Grant sees through her act but his parents don't; they side with her when Cary finds real love with widow Carole. Emotion-packed tearjerker with a superb cast.
Dist.: Turner

INNERSPACE 1987
★★★★ **PG Fantasy/Comedy 2:00**
☑ Explicit language
Dir: Joe Dante ***Cast:*** Dennis Quaid, Martin Short, Meg Ryan, Kevin McCarthy, Fiona Lewis, Vernon Wells

► Quaid, a guinea pig for a top-secret government miniaturization experiment, is accidentally injected into the body of nerdish grocery clerk Short. As spies pursue Short, Quaid's girlfriend Ryan helps him evade the bad guys. Steven Spielberg production has typically good special effects, inventive premise, and cheerful tone. Short is outstanding; his SCTV pals Joe Flaherty and Andrea Martin have brief cameos. Won a Visual Effects Oscar. (CC)
Dist.: Warner

INNOCENT, THE 1979 Italian
★ R Drama 1:41
☑ Nudity, adult situations
Dir: Luchino Visconti ***Cast:*** Giancarlo Giannini, Laura Antonelli, Jennifer O'Neill, Rina Morelli, Massimo Girotti
► In nineteenth-century Italy, wealthy nobleman Giannini ignores beautiful wife Antonelli to pursue mistress O'Neill, but regrets his actions when he learns Antonelli is having her own affair. Lush, beautifully photographed romance became an art house favorite for its charged eroticism. Visconti's last film. [S]
Dist.: Vestron

INNOCENT MAN, AN 1989
★★★★ R Drama 1:53
☑ Rape, explicit language, violence
Dir: Peter Yates ***Cast:*** Tom Selleck, F. Murray Abraham, Laila Robins, David Rasche, Richard Young, Todd Graff
► Cops Rasche and Young mistakenly raid Selleck's house on a drug bust and cover up error by framing Selleck into a prison term. Con Abraham helps Selleck survive the rigors of jail; Selleck and wife Robins later enlist Abraham to plot revenge against the detectives. Paranoid plot served with canny professionalism; Selleck gives a solid performance.
Dist.: Buena Vista

INN OF THE SIXTH HAPPINESS, THE 1958
★★★★ NR Biography 2:41
Dir: Mark Robson ***Cast:*** Ingrid Bergman, Curt Jurgens, Robert Donat, Ronald Squire
► Biography of Gladys Alward (Bergman), an Englishwoman who opened a mission in China and won the love and respect of the locals. She falls for Eurasian colonel Jurgens and helps war orphans during World War II. Mandarin Donat converts to Christianity out of esteem for her. Bergman shines in this satisfying combination of religion, romance, and adventure. Donat is also superb in his last screen appearance.
Dist.: CBS/Fox

IN OLD CALIFORNIA 1942
★★ NR Western 1:28 B&W
Dir: William McGann ***Cast:*** John Wayne, Binnie Barnes, Albert Dekker, Helen Parrish, Patsy Kelly, Edgar Kennedy
► During the California Gold Rush, Boston pharmacist Wayne journeys West to start a business. Corrupt politician Dekker, already upset that singer girlfriend Barnes is attracted to the Easterner, tries to frame Wayne when he leads a ranchers' rebellion. Fast-paced vehicle for the Duke.
Dist.: Republic

IN PERSON 1935
★ NR Comedy 1:25 B&W
Dir: William Seiter ***Cast:*** Ginger Rogers, George Brent, Alan Mowbray, Grant Mitchell, Samuel S. Hinds, Joan Breslau
► How can film star Rogers escape her legion of howling, demanding, autograph-hunting fans? Why not try rendering her glamorous self unrecognizably plain and passing as someone else? Rogers's first solo starring role is okay, but really only marks time between *Top Hat* and *Follow the Fleet*.
Dist.: Turner

IN PRAISE OF OLDER WOMEN 1979 Canadian
★★ R Drama 1:48
☑ Nudity, strong sexual content, explicit language
Dir: George Kaczender ***Cast:*** Tom Berenger, Karen Black, Susan Strasberg, Alexandra Stewart, Helen Shaver
► Succession of various older women initiate young Berenger into the pleasures of sex, love, and literature. Plenty of heavy breathing but the doltish dialogue and stilted (though explicit) love scenes are ultimately more embarrassing than erotic.
Dist.: Embassy

INQUIRY, THE 1987 Italian
★★ NR Drama 1:50
☑ Violence
Dir: Damiano Damiani ***Cast:*** Keith Carradine, Harvey Keitel, Phyllis Logan, Angelo Infanti, Lina Sastri, John Forgeham
► Roman authorities send officer Carradine to Palestine to investigate rumors that the body of Christ, crucified three years earlier, is missing. Carradine, unsatisfied with explanations by Pontius Pilate (Keitel), questions witnesses who knew Christ personally. Biblical epic's offbeat premise proves unexpectedly absorbing.
Dist.: HBO

IN SEARCH OF A GOLDEN SKY 1984
★★★★ PG Family 1:35
☑ Mild violence
Dir: Jefferson Richard ***Cast:*** Charles Napier, George "Buck" Flower, Cliff Osmond, Anne Szesny, Shane Wallace
► Crusty old coot Flower, a hermit in the Pacific Northwest, is dismayed when two nephews and a niece arrive for an unexpected visit, but grows to appreciate their youthful spirits. Wholesome wilderness story features beautiful photography and scene-stealing fun from a racoon and bear cub. (CC)
Dist.: CBS/Fox

IN SEARCH OF THE CASTAWAYS 1962
★ ★ ★ Ⓖ Fantasy/Family 1:40
Dir: Robert Stevenson *Cast:* Maurice
Chevalier, Hayley Mills, George Sanders,
Wilfrid Hyde-White, Michael Anderson, Jr.,
Inia Te Wiata
▶ Young Mills enlists singing professor Cheva-
lier to find her missing sea captain father. The
search leads from South America to Australia,
with Chevalier's expedition battling giant
condors, earthquakes, volcanoes, and canni-
bals. Enjoyable Disney fantasy based on a
Jules Verne story.
Dist.: Buena Vista

INSIDE MOVES 1980
★ ★ ★ ★ PG Drama 1:53
☑ Adult situations, explicit language
Dir: Richard Donner *Cast:* John Savage,
David Morse, Diana Scarwid, Harold Russell,
Bert Remsen, Tony Burton
▶ Crippled after a suicide attempt, Savage
finds solace with similarly handicapped patrons of a San Francisco bar. He falls in love
with waitress Scarwid and befriends injured
basketball star Morse. Donner, director of such
heralded films as *Superman* and *The Omen*,
did some of his best work with this sleeper
filled with warmth, humor, fine ensemble acting, and sharply observed, sympathetic characters.
Dist.: Warner

INSIDE OUT 1975
★ ★ PG Action-Adventure 1:37
☑ Mild violence, explicit language
Dir: Peter Duffell *Cast:* Telly Savalas, Robert
Culp, James Mason, Aldo Ray, Charles Kor-
vin
▶ Savalas joins with Culp and Mason in a plot
to steal a stash of gold hidden in East Germany. But first they have to free the only occu-
pant of a Berlin maximum security prison so he
can reveal where the loot is. London, Amsterdam, and Berlin locales add international
touch to this well-executed caper. Also known
as *Hitler's Gold* and *The Golden Heist*.
Dist.: Warner

INSIDE OUT 1987
☆ R Drama 1:27
☑ Adult situations, explicit language
Dir: Robert Taicher *Cast:* Elliott Gould,
Howard Hesseman, Jennifer Tilly, Beah Rich-
ards, Nicole Norman, John Bleifer
▶ Gould gives a strong performance as a
New York gambler trapped in his apartment
by agoraphobia. Despite help from best
friend Hesseman and call girl Tilly, his fear of
open spaces leads to tragedy. Intriguing idea
undermined by static presentation.
Dist.: Warner

INSIGNIFICANCE 1985 British
★ R Drama 1:48
☑ Adult situations, explicit language, vio-
lence
Dir: Nicolas Roeg *Cast:* Michael Emil,

Theresa Russell, Tony Curtis, Gary Busey, Will
Sampson
▶ Political, emotional, intellectual, and sexual
machinations in a 1953 New York hotel
among characters similar to Albert Einstein
(Emil), Marilyn Monroe (Russell), Joe DiMaggio
(Busey), and Joe McCarthy (Curtis). Ambitious
concept works as an intellectual exercise but
script is too obscure for general tastes. Affecting performances by Russell and Emil.
Dist.: Warner

INSPECTOR GENERAL, THE 1949
★ ★ ★ ★ NR Comedy 1:42
Dir: Henry Koster *Cast:* Danny Kaye, Walter
Slezak, Barbara Bates, Elsa Lanchester,
Gene Lockhart, Alan Hale
▶ Clumsy Kaye benefits from case of mistaken
identity in czarist Russia: locals think he is a
bigwig and give him red carpet treatment.
Adaptation of the Nikolai Gogol play provides
effective vehicle for Kaye, whose wife, Sylvia
Fine, wrote the lyrics for the musical numbers.
Dist.: Various

INSTANT JUSTICE 1986 British
★ ★ R Action-Adventure 1:41
☑ Brief nudity, explicit language, violence
Dir: Denis Amar *Cast:* Michael Paré, Tawny
Kitaen, Peter Crook, Charles Napier, Linda
Bridges
▶ Tough, two-fisted Marine Paré leaves the
Corps to avenge death of his sister Bridges in
Madrid. Kitaen plays a prostitute who reluc-
tantly agrees to help him. Solid action helps
camouflage flimsy plot.
Dist.: Warner

INTERIORS 1978
★ ★ PG Drama 1:32
☑ Adult situations, explicit language
Dir: Woody Allen *Cast:* Diane Keaton, Ger-
aldine Page, Maureen Stapleton, Mary Beth
Hurt, E. G. Marshall, Sam Waterston, Kristin
Griffith
▶ Allen's first serious work as a writer-director
(he does not appear) is populated by mem-
bers of a desperately unhappy family. Keaton,
a successful poet in analysis, and her sisters
Hurt and Griffith deal with the divorce of their
parents Page and Marshall and his subse-
quent remarriage to Stapleton. Memorable
and affecting, in the style of Ingmar Bergman.
Warning: Woody Allen fans hoping for laughs,
look elsewhere.
Dist.: MGM/UA

INTERMEZZO 1936 Swedish
★ NR Drama 1:28 B&W
Dir: Gustav Molander *Cast:* Gosta Ekman,
Inga Tiblad, Ingrid Bergman, Bullen Ber-
glund, Britt Hagman
▶ Original Swedish version of the weepy love
story set against a musical backdrop. Ekman
is a married concert violinist who falls in love
with young music teacher Bergman, and
abandons his wife—for a time. The Hollywood

version is more accessible, but Bergman is even more beautiful here. [S]
Dist.: Crocus

INTERMEZZO 1939
★ ★ ★ NR Drama/Romance 1:10 B&W
Dir: Gregory Ratoff *Cast:* Leslie Howard, Ingrid Bergman, Edna Best, John Halliday, Cecil Kellaway, Enid Bennett
▶ American remake of Swedish film of same name has Bergman reprising her role as a bright-eyed piano teacher. Married, world-weary violinist Howard falls for Bergman; he abandons wife Best and children for new love, but is haunted by familial responsibilities. In her first English-speaking role, Bergman electrified American audiences in this touching, tender romance. Memorable theme music by Heinz Provost became an enormous pop hit.
Dist.: CBS/Fox

INTERNAL AFFAIRS 1990
★ ★ ★ ★ R Mystery-Suspense 1:55
☑ Brief nudity, adult situations, explicit language, violence
Dir: Mike Figgis *Cast:* Richard Gere, Andy Garcia, Nancy Travis, Laurie Metcalf, Annabella Sciorra, William Baldwin
▶ Gritty police thriller stars Gere as a sleazy, corrupt officer being investigated by Internal Affairs agents Garcia and Metcalf. Gere resorts to psychological mind games (like insinuating that he's slept with Garcia's wife Travis) and even murder to trip up the inquiry. Slick production, tension-filled atmosphere, and a perfectly smarmy Gere make this one a winner. **(CC)**
Dist.: Paramount

INTERNATIONAL HOUSE 1933
★ ★ NR Comedy 1:10 B&W
Dir: Edward Sutherland *Cast:* W. C. Fields, Peggy Hopkins Joyce, George Burns, Gracie Allen, Bela Lugosi, Cab Calloway, Stuart Erwin, Franklin Pangborn, Rudy Vallee, Sterling Holloway
▶ Inventor displays his television device at a Chinese hotel, bringing all sorts of crazy types, like Soviet military man Lugosi, to bid for it. Cockeyed plot is a terrific excuse for Fields to interact with great cast of vaudevillians and clowns. Burns and Allen offer some sparkling routines.
Dist.: MCA

INTERNATIONAL VELVET 1978 British
★ ★ ★ ★ PG Drama/Family 2:07
☑ Adult situations
Dir: Bryan Forbes *Cast:* Tatum O'Neal, Christopher Plummer, Anthony Hopkins, Nanette Newman
▶ Sequel to 1944's horse-racing drama *National Velvet*. English Steeplechase winner Velvet Brown (Newman) is now forty and her American niece O'Neal is destined to follow in auntie's equestrienne footsteps. Plummer plays Newman's writer boyfriend; Hopkins is

first-class as O'Neal's stern, no-nonsense trainer. Polished family entertainment.
Dist.: MGM/UA

INTERNECINE PROJECT, THE 1973 British
★ ★ PG Mystery-Suspense 1:35
☑ Adult situations, violence
Dir: Ken Hughes *Cast:* James Coburn, Lee Grant, Keenan Wynn, Harry Andrews, Ian Hendry, Michael Jayston
▶ Wealthy but evil Coburn decides to do in his enemies in a unique way, creating an elaborate plan in which they will kill one another. Underrated thriller deserves a look, although Hughes's stodgy direction threatens to flatten out a clever and original premise. Produced and co-written by Barry Levinson. **(CC)**
Dist.: CBS/Fox

INTERNS, THE 1962
★ ★ NR Drama 2:02 B&W
Dir: David Swift *Cast:* Michael Callan, Cliff Robertson, James MacArthur, Nick Adams, Suzy Parker, Haya Harareet, Telly Savalas, Stefanie Powers, Buddy Ebsen
▶ Glossy soap opera about a year in the lives of four interns at a big-city hospital. Adams falls for a dying patient; Robertson struggles with his ethics when model Parker requests an abortion; Callan juggles affairs with a nurse and a socialite; MacArthur pursues a nurse who hates doctors. Predictable material notable for many future TV stars. Led to a 1964 sequel, *The New Interns*, as well as a brief TV series.
Dist.: RCA/Columbia

INTERVAL 1978 U.S./Mexican
★ PG Drama 1:24
☑ Adult situations
Dir: Daniel Mann *Cast:* Merle Oberon, Robert Wolders, Claudio Brook, Russ Conway, Charles Bateman, Britt Leach
▶ In Mexico, sixtyish Oberon has an affair with younger Wolders. Haunting her current happiness is a past tragedy. Soppy May/December romance was more convincing off-screen than on—Oberon and Wolders later married. Oberon's last film was written by Gavin Lambert.
Dist.: Nelson

IN THE GOOD OLD SUMMERTIME 1949
★ ★ ★ ★ ★ NR Musical 1:43
Dir: Robert Z. Leonard *Cast:* Judy Garland, Van Johnson, S. Z. Sakall, Spring Byington, Clinton Sundberg, Buster Keaton
▶ Charming musical remake of *The Shop Around the Corner* switches the setting of the 1940 film to turn-of-the-century Chicago. Garland and Johnson, impersonal co-workers in Sakall's music shop, are unaware they're secretly romantic pen pals. Tuneful score includes the title song and "I Don't Care."
Dist.: MGM/UA

IN THE HEAT OF THE NIGHT 1967
★ ★ ★ ★ NR Mystery-Suspense 1:49

Dir: Norman Jewison *Cast:* Sidney Poitier, Rod Steiger, Warren Oates, Lee Grant, William Schallert, Scott Wilson

► "They call me Mister Tibbs!" says Philadelphia detective Poitier, trying to command respect from redneck Mississippi sheriff Steiger. Teaming to solve a murder, the two warily grow to respect one another. Mystery with a message features powerhouse performances from Steiger and Poitier. Oscars for Best Picture, Actor (Steiger), Editing, Sound, and Screenplay. Poitier reprised Tibbs in *They Call Me Mister Tibbs!* and *The Organization.*
Dist.: MGM/UA

IN THE MOOD 1987
★ ★ ★ PG-13 Biography 1:38
☑ Brief nudity, adult situations, explicit language
Dir: Phil Alden Robinson *Cast:* Patrick Dempsey, Beverly D'Angelo, Talia Balsam, Michael Constantine, Betty Jinett

► True story of Sonny Wisecarver (Dempsey), a.k.a. "The Woo Woo Kid," a teenager who caused a sensation in 1944 by running off with married mother Balsam. After that relationship is annulled, he finds romance and more legal trouble with D'Angelo, another older woman. Consistently buoyant romantic comedy with classy period details and likable performances. A neglected treat. (CC)
Dist.: Warner

IN THE REALM OF THE SENSES 1976
Japanese/French
☆ NR Drama 1:55
☑ Nudity, strong sexual content, adult situations, explicit language, violence
Dir: Nagisa Oshima *Cast:* Tatsuya Fuji, Eiko Matsuda, Aio Nakajima, Meika Seri

► In 1930s Japan, geisha Matsuda develops an irrational obsession with married man Fuji that leads to murder. Based on a real incident, this stylish but gloomy drama consists almost entirely of sexual couplings filmed in graphic detail. Gained some notoriety when it was seized as obscene by United States Customs officials. ⬚S⬚
Dist.: Fox/Lorber

IN THE SHADOW OF KILIMANJARO 1986
U.S./British/Kenyan
★ R Horror 1:37
☑ Nudity, adult situations, explicit language, graphic violence
Dir: Raju Patel *Cast:* John Rhys-Davies, Timothy Bottoms, Irene Miracle, Michele Carey

► In drought-plagued Africa, baboons go insane from hunger and thirst and start attacking humans. Game commissioner Bottoms tries to warn the authorities of the danger but gets little cooperation. Meanwhile, locals hole up at the hotel as the mad monkeys close in. Bloodthirsty man-against-nature tale suffers from obviously faked footage.
Dist.: IVE

IN THE SPIRIT 1990
☆ R Comedy 1:33
☑ Explicit language
Dir: Sandra Seacat *Cast:* Elaine May, Marlo Thomas, Jeannie Berlin, Peter Falk, Melanie Griffith, Olympia Dukakis

► After leaving California, May and husband Falk move in with her New York spiritualist friend Thomas. When someone tries to kill them, the women flee and later set a trap for the murderer. Terrific cast plays broad caricatures in a not-so-terrific movie. Sloppy direction and messy plotting add up to few laughs. Berlin co-wrote the screenplay and co-stars as Thomas's prostitute friend.
Dist.: Academy

IN THIS OUR LIFE 1942
★ ★ NR Drama 1:37 B&W
Dir: John Huston *Cast:* Bette Davis, Olivia de Havilland, George Brent, Dennis Morgan, Charles Coburn, Billie Burke

► Selfish Davis dumps Brent to steal her sister de Havilland's husband Morgan. After ruining his life, Davis makes a play for Brent, now involved with de Havilland, and creates other troubles. Wild, windy melodrama plot, not one of Huston's finest hours, does feature a classic bad girl performance by Davis.
Dist.: MGM/UA

INTIMATE CONTACT 1987 British
★ ★ ★ ★ NR Drama/MFTV 2:39
☑ Adult situations, explicit language
Dir: Waris Hussein *Cast:* Claire Bloom, Daniel Massey, Sylvia Sims, Abigail Cruttenden, Mark Kingston, Lizzy McInnerny

► Affluent Englishman Massey contracts AIDS from a prostitute. Wife Bloom supports him through the fatal ordeal, befriends other victims of the disease, faces ostracism from neighbors, and becomes crusader against ignorance and prejudice. Sensitive and realistic portrayal of controversial medical issue; Bloom is outstanding.
Dist.: HBO

INTIMATE POWER 1989
★ NR Action-Adventure 1:40
☑ Nudity, adult situations, violence
Dir: Jack Smight *Cast:* F. Murray Abraham, Maud Adams, Amber O'Shea, James Michael Gregory, Jonathan Vuille

► Free-spirited nineteenth-century French schoolgirl O'Shea is kidnapped by pirates and sold into Sultan Abraham's harem. O'Shea wins Abraham's heart, arouses his wife Adams's deadly jealousy, gives birth to a son, gets involved in palace intrigue, and rises to a position of great power. Plush adaptation of the historical novel *Sultana* by Prince Michael of Greece. Also known as *The Favorite.* (CC)
Dist.: HBO

INTOLERANCE 1916
☆ NR Drama 3:28 B&W
☑ Brief nudity, violence

Dir: D. W. Griffith **Cast:** Lillian Gish, Robert Harron, Mae Marsh, Constance Talmadge, Bessie Love, Alfred Paget
▶ The crucifixion of Christ, the fall of Babylon, the massacre of the Huguenots, and the destruction of a family by moral crusaders are examples of man's inhumanity to man portrayed in this legendary silent spectacle. Made by director Griffith in response to criticism of his previous film *Birth of a Nation*, episodic pageant contains some of the most expensive scenes in the history of the cinema, as well as many small, intimately affecting vignettes.
Dist.: Video Yesteryear

INTO THE FIRE 1987 Canadian
★ **R Drama 1:33**
☑ Nudity, adult situations, explicit language, violence
Dir: Graeme Campbell **Cast:** Susan Anspach, Art Hindle, Olivia d'Abo, Lee Montgomery
▶ Hot doings at the chilly Wolf Lodge. Drunken nympho Anspach is planning to kill her cruel husband/lodge-owner for the insurance money. Newly arrived hunk Montgomery is drawn into the scheme, even though he lusts after waitress d'Abo. Despite the cold, everyone has his or her shirt off at some point, and the murderous plot heats up to point where nearly everyone is dead. Anspach camps it up wildly in this heavy-breathing murder fest. Also known as *The Legend of Wolf Lodge*.
Dist.: Vestron

INTO THE HOMELAND 1987
★ ★ ★ **NR Drama/MFTV 1:55**
☑ Violence
Dir: Lesli Linka Glatter **Cast:** Powers Boothe, C. Thomas Howell, Paul LeMat, Cindy Pickett, David Caruso, Arye Gross
▶ Ex-cop Boothe infiltrates white supremacist group to find his runaway teenage daughter. Boothe abducts her boyfriend Howell, the son of group leader LeMat, and attempts to deprogram him. Riveting drama with unsettling contemporary political overtones. Script by Anna Hamilton Phelan, who also wrote *Mask*.
Dist.: Warner

INTO THE NIGHT 1985
★ ★ ★ ★ **R Mystery-Suspense 1:55**
☑ Nudity, adult situations, explicit language, graphic violence
Dir: John Landis **Cast:** Jeff Goldblum, Michelle Pfeiffer, David Bowie, Richard Farnsworth, Vera Miles, Dan Aykroyd
▶ Insomniac Goldblum finds something to do with his restless nights when he accidentally gets involved with the beautiful Pfeiffer, who is battling Arabs for possession of stolen emeralds. Uneven but stylish mixture of comedy, romance, and intrigue. Occasionally marred by excessive violence, but flick is often fun and exciting. Cameo appearances from many

Hollywood directors including Lawrence Kasdan, David Cronenberg, and Jonathan Demme. **(CC)**
Dist.: MCA

INTRUDER 1988
★ **R Horror 1:30**
☑ Explicit language, graphic violence
Dir: Scott Spiegel **Cast:** Elizabeth Cox, Renée Estevez, Danny Hicks, David Byrnes, Sam Raimi, Eugene Glazer
▶ Cox, a cashier at the Walnut Lake supermarket, is visited by ex-boyfriend Byrnes, an ex-convict who gets into a dispute with her co-workers. Later, a mad killer stalks the store aisles. Could Byrnes be the guilty party? Unpretentious terror flick is a tiny cut above its lurid genre. **(CC)**
Dist.: Paramount

INVADERS FROM MARS 1953
★ ★ **NR Sci-Fi 1:20**
Dir: William Cameron Menzies **Cast:** Jimmy Hunt, Helena Carter, Arthur Franz, Morris Ankrum, Leif Erickson
▶ Young Hunt is the only witness when aliens invade a small town. He tries in vain to convince the authorities of what he's seen. B-movie sci-fi enlivened by striking visuals from director Menzies, best remembered as a significant production designer. Remade in 1986.
Dist.: Media

INVADERS FROM MARS 1986
★ ★ **PG Sci-Fi 1:33**
☑ Explicit language, violence
Dir: Tobe Hooper **Cast:** Karen Black, Hunter Carson, Timothy Bottoms, Laraine Newman, James Karen, Louise Fletcher
▶ Carson witnesses a spaceship land outside his bedroom window but no one in town believes the boy's tale of aliens, perhaps because they're being possessed by the invaders. Hooper creates some crackerjack tension in the movie's first half, sort of a child's-point-of-view paranoid thriller. Second half, with silly-looking monsters and military response to the threat, bogs down. Remake of the 1953 B-movie. **(CC)**
Dist.: Media

INVASION OF THE BEE GIRLS 1974
★ **R Sci-Fi 1:25**
☑ Nudity, explicit language, violence
Dir: Denis Sanders **Cast:** Victoria Vetri, William Smith, Anitra Ford, Cliff Osmond, Wright King
▶ Nude mutant women come on to guys, buzzing sounds begin, and then each man instantly dies. Motif is repeated over and over. Awful music, cheapo production values; for fans of gratuitous nudity only.
Dist.: Nelson

INVASION OF THE BODY SNATCHERS 1956
★ ★ ★ ★ **NR Sci-Fi 1:20 B&W**
Dir: Don Siegel **Cast:** Kevin McCarthy,

Dana Wynter, Carolyn Jones, King Donovan, Larry Gates, Sam Peckinpah
► Small-town doctor McCarthy and girlfriend Wynter try to hold on to their humanity and their lives when friends and neighbors are turned into emotionless "pod people" by alien force. Siegel's low-key, evocative direction creates classic moments of terror: the greenhouse confrontation, McCarthy yelling "You're next!" as passing drivers ignore him. Based on the Jack Finney novel.
Dist.: Republic Ⓒ

INVASION OF THE BODY SNATCHERS 1978
★ ★ ★ PG Sci-Fi 1:56
☑ Brief nudity, explicit language, violence
Dir: Philip Kaufman *Cast:* Donald Sutherland, Brooke Adams, Leonard Nimoy, Jeff Goldblum, Veronica Cartwright, Art Hindle
► Jazzy remake of the 1956 classic effectively takes terror out of 1950s small town and into modern-day San Francisco, where city health official Sutherland and colleague Adams find epidemic of soulless alien automatons in their midst. Celebrity shrink Nimoy also gets involved. Literate screenplay and glittery cinematography create credibly creepy atmosphere.
Dist.: MGM/UA

INVASION OF THE FLESH HUNTERS 1982
Italian/Spanish
☆ NR Horror 1:31
☑ Nudity, adult situations, explicit language, graphic violence
Dir: Anthony M. Dawson (Antonio) Margheriti) *Cast:* John Saxon, Elizabeth Turner, John Morghen, Cindy Hamilton, Tony King
► More gross than engrossing tale of ex-Vietnam G.I.'s infected with a strange virus that turns them into cannibals who devour innocent Atlantans. Veteran actor Saxon plays the commanding officer trying to resist the disease, despite being infected. Blood and gore galore.
Dist.: Vestron

INVASION U.S.A. 1985
★ ★ ★ R Action-Adventure 1:48
☑ Brief nudity, adult situations, explicit language, graphic violence
Dir: Joseph Zito *Cast:* Chuck Norris, Richard Lynch, Melissa Prophet, Alexander Zale, Alex Colon
► Villainous Soviet agent Lynch and cohorts shamelessly seek to destroy the American way of life by blowing up shopping malls at Christmastime and shooting innocent suburbanites at home. One-man National Guard Norris is called in to kill the Russian terrorists and save democracy. Overwrought and extremely violent melodrama.
Dist.: MGM/UA

INVISIBLE GHOST, THE 1941
★ NR Horror 0:58 B&W
Dir: Joseph H. Lewis *Cast:* Bela Lugosi,

Polly Ann Young, John McGuire, Clarence Muse, Terry Walker, Betty Compson
► Wealthy Lugosi makes the mistake of not marrying well: his wife is an insane shrew who hypnotizes him into becoming a murderer. Not particularly scary or memorable, although the star and director Lewis bring some intensity to an otherwise routine plot.
Dist.: Video Yesteryear

INVISIBLE KID, THE 1988
★ ★ PG Fantasy/Comedy 1:36
☑ Nudity, explicit language
Dir: Avery Crouse *Cast:* Karen Black, Jay Underwood, Wally Ward, Chynna Phillips, Brother Theodore
► High school nerd Underwood invents a green slime that renders swallower invisible for half an hour, just enough time to peek in the cheerleaders' locker room with wimpy pal Ward and help win the big basketball game. Black, sporting countless curlers and a huge bathrobe, plays Grover's ditsy mom. Lightweight screwball comedy for kids.
Dist.: Media

INVISIBLE MAN, THE 1933
★ ★ ★ NR Horror 1:11 B&W
Dir: James Whale *Cast:* Claude Rains, Gloria Stuart, William Harrigan, Dwight Frye, Una O'Connor, E. E. Clive
► Scientist Rains invents process to render himself invisible. Unfortunately, his mind is affected and he becomes a raving megalomaniac. Amazing special effects (even by today's standards), wonderfully atmospheric direction by Whale, incredible vocal performance by the unseen Rains ("Power to rule, power to make the world grovel at my feet," he says in that magnificent voice). A classic, from the H. G. Wells novel.
Dist.: MCA

INVISIBLE RAY, THE 1936
★ NR Horror/Sci-Fi 1:22 B&W
Dir: Lambert Hillyer *Cast:* Boris Karloff, Bela Lugosi, Frances Drake, Frank Lawton, Beulah Bondi, Walter Kingsford
► Scientist Karloff discovers a radioactive substance in a meteor which unfortunately transforms him into a crazed killer. Colleague Lugosi tries to produce a cure. Superior pairing of the two horror stars with a plot much more original than their usual efforts.
Dist.: MCA

INVITATION AU VOYAGE 1983 French
☆ R Drama 1:33
☑ Nudity, adult situations
Dir: Peter Del Monte *Cast:* Laurent Malet, Aurore Clément, Mario Adorf, Nina Scott
► Rock star Scott and twin brother Malet have incestuous relationship. When she is accidentally killed, he puts her body in a bass fiddle case and journeys through France, meeting strange people and eventually assuming her identity. Unusual story is meticu-

lously mounted but heavy symbolism and weird characters will alienate most. [S]
Dist.: RCA/Columbia

INVITATION TO A WEDDING 1982 British
★★ PG Comedy 1:38
☑ Adult situations, explicit language
Dir: Joseph Brooks *Cast:* Ralph Richardson, John Gielgud, Susan Brooks, Paul Nicholson
► Implausible, nonsensical tale of young Nicholson who fills in for a busy groom at his wedding rehearsal and is accidentally betrothed to bride-to-be Brooks. Richardson is the befuddled English minister who marries them. In an extremely unlikely role, Gielgud is a born-again Texan evangelist.
Dist.: Vestron

INVITATION TO THE DANCE 1956
★ NR Dance 1:32
Dir: Gene Kelly *Cast:* Gene Kelly, Igor Youskevitch, Claire Sombert, David Kasday, David Paltenghi, Daphne Dale
► Three-part film told entirely in dance and mime. In "Circus," Kelly plays a lovestruck clown trying to win Sombert from trapeze artist Youskevitch; "Ring Around the Rosy" reworks the circular love affairs of *La Ronde*; "Sinbad the Sailor" is a fun version of the genie-in-a-lamp classic set in a magical animated world. Ambitious attempt to popularize dance features music by Jacques Ibert, André Previn, and Roger Edens.
Dist.: MGM/UA

I OUGHT TO BE IN PICTURES 1982
★★★★ PG Comedy 1:47
☑ Brief nudity, adult situations, explicit language
Dir: Herbert Ross *Cast:* Walter Matthau, Ann-Margret, Dinah Manoff, Lance Guest, Lewis Smith
► New Yorker Manoff arrives in Hollywood to look up long-lost father Matthau, a bitter screenwriter who spends more time at the racetrack than at the typewriter. Father and daughter, with dad's sympathetic girlfriend Ann-Margret mediating, eventually resolve their problems. Solid acting in a funny Neil Simon script.
Dist.: CBS/Fox

IPCRESS FILE, THE 1965 British
★★★★ NR Espionage 1:47
Dir: Sidney J. Furie *Cast:* Michael Caine, Nigel Green, Sue Lloyd, Guy Doleman, Gordon Jackson
► British agent Harry Palmer (Caine) investigates kidnappings of top scientists; the trail leads to a traitor in his own organization. Twisty and intelligent; Caine gives a marvelously low-key and subtle performance. First and best of the Harry Palmer series adapted from the Len Deighton novel. Sequels *Funeral in Berlin* and *Billion Dollar Brain* followed.
Dist.: MCA

IPHIGENIA 1977 Greek
☆ NR Drama 2:10
☑ Adult situations
Dir: Michael Cacoyannis *Cast:* Irene Papas, Costa Kazakos, Costa Carras, Tatiana Papamoskou, Cristos Tsangas, Panos Michalopoulos
► King Agamemnon (Kazakos), his army, and a thousand ships lie becalmed in the Mediterranean on their way to Troy to retrieve the kidnapped Helen. Much to the distress of Queen Clytemnestra (Papas), oracles want Agamemnon to sacrifice his twelve-year-old daughter Iphigenia to the gods. Papas is very strong, but adaptation of 404 B.C. play by Euripides is unsatisfying. [S]
Dist.: RCA/Columbia

I REMEMBER MAMA 1948
★★★★★ NR Drama 2:14 B&W
Dir: George Stevens *Cast:* Irene Dunne, Barbara Bel Geddes, Oscar Homolka, Philip Dorn, Edgar Bergen, Ellen Corby, Cedric Hardwicke, Rudy Vallee
► Norwegian family emigrates to San Francisco, where they cheerfully struggle to make ends meet as loving mama Dunne pulls them through ups and downs. Shy aunt Corby and blustering uncle Homolka are among those who inspire eldest daughter Bel Geddes to write about her family. Old-fashioned heartwarmer with humor and genuine emotion. Oscar nominations to Dunne, Corby, Bel Geddes, Homolka. Based on the play by John Van Druten and the book *Mama's Bank Account* by Kathryn Forbes.
Dist.: Turner

IRISHMAN, THE 1978 Australian
★★ NR Drama 1:48
☑ Adult situations
Dir: Donald Crombie *Cast:* Michael Craig, Simon Burke, Robin Nevin, Lou Brown, Andrew Maguire
► In the early twentieth-century Australian outback, teenager Burke works in a mine, has conflict with his hardheaded Irish father Craig, and falls for an aborigine woman. Beautiful Australian vistas, evocative of the American Old West, provide backdrop for sturdy drama of father-son battles. Slow-paced but will reward patient viewers.
Dist.: Vestron

IRMA LA DOUCE 1963
★★ NR Comedy 2:26
Dir: Billy Wilder *Cast:* Shirley MacLaine, Jack Lemmon, Lou Jacobi, Herschel Bernardi, Joan Shawlee, Hope Holiday
► Adaptation of Broadway play concerns overzealous, bumbling Parisian cop Lemmon who raids Jacobi's bistro to rid it of prostitutes and winds up arresting his boss Bernardi. Sacked from the force, Lemmon works as streetwalker MacLaine's procurer but, smitten

by love, grows jealous of her work. Amiable comedy won Oscar for André Previn's score.
Dist.: Key

IRON EAGLE 1986
★ ★ ★ PG-13 Action-Adventure 1:57
☑ Explicit language, violence
Dir: Sidney J. Furie   *Cast:* Louis Gossett, Jr., Jason Gedrick, David Suchet, Tim Thomerson
▶ Macho movie about young Gedrick's attempt to rescue his pilot father Thomerson, shot down in a small Arab country. Aided by combat veteran Gossett, he breaks into the top secret Air Force computer, steals two jets, drops a few bombs, and fights it out with rival MIGs. Turns into battle between teen Rambo and entire Middle East country. Striking aerial photography. **(CC)**
Dist.: CBS/Fox

IRON EAGLE II 1988
★ ★ ★ PG Action-Adventure 1:40
☑ Explicit language, violence
Dir: Sidney J. Furie   *Cast:* Louis Gossett, Jr., Mark Humphrey, Stuart Margolin, Alan Scarfe, Sharon H. Brandon, Maury Chaykin
▶ Sequel to popular aviation adventure finds Gossett, now a general, recruiting multinational team of pilots to destroy Third World nuclear weapons plant. Hotdog flier Humphrey, bitterly anti-Soviet, finds himself falling for beautiful Russian aviatrix Brandon during grueling training sessions. Inventive dogfights provide plenty of excitement.
Dist.: IVE

IRON MAJOR, THE 1943
★ ★ NR Biography/Sports 1:25 B&W
Dir: Ray Enright   *Cast:* Pat O'Brien, Ruth Warrick, Robert Ryan, Leon Ames, Russell Wade, Richard Martin
▶ Football coach Frank Cavanaugh (O'Brien) believes in three things: God, country, and the family—the latter being fortunate, as he raises a brood of ten while coaching at Dartmouth. Rising to the rank of major in World War I, he is wounded and nearly blinded in battle, but returns to support his family and produce winning football teams until the very last. It's the kind of role O'Brien was born to play, with dynamite pep talks and demonstrations of quiet courage in the face of doom. Based on a true story.
Dist.: Turner

IRON TRIANGLE, THE 1989
★ ★ R War 1:31
☑ Adult situations, explicit language, violence
Dir: Eric Weston   *Cast:* Beau Bridges, Haing S. Ngor, Johnny Hallyday, Liem Whatley, James Ishida
▶ During the Vietnam War, American Army captain Bridges is captured by Vietcong guerrilla Whatley and Communist disciple Ishida, who hates Whatley and Bridges with equal vehemence. On the trip north, Whatley

flees with Bridges to spare him from Ishida; the pragmatic American and idealistic North Vietnamese learn to respect each other. Portrayal of war from the Vietcong perspective is more intriguing for its premise than for the result.
Dist.: IVE

IRON WARRIOR 1987 Italian
☆ PG-13 Action-Adventure 1:22
☑ Nudity, violence
Dir: Al Bradley   *Cast:* Miles O'Keeffe, Savina Gersak, Iris Peynado, Elisabeth Kaza, Tim Lane
▶ Evil goddess steals one of two twins raised by good goddess and, eighteen years later, the two do battle. Sample dialogue: "And what if they kill you?" "Then I'll be dead." Senseless plot, lackluster swordplay and mix-and-match mythology with K-Mart special effects. **(CC)**
Dist.: Media

IRONWEED 1987
★ ★ ★ R Drama 2.23
☑ Nudity, explicit language, violence
Dir: Hector Babenco   *Cast:* Jack Nicholson, Meryl Streep, Carroll Baker, Tom Waits, Fred Gwynne, Michael O'Keefe
▶ Prestigious but grim tale of late 1930s homeless people. Bum Nicholson, haunted by the death of his infant son, hangs out with fellow boozer Streep, visits ex-wife Baker, and confronts the wreckage of his life. Relentlessly downbeat despite impressive performances by Oscar-nominated leads. Based on the Pulitzer prize–winning novel by William Kennedy (who also wrote the screenplay).
Dist.: Vestron

IRRECONCILABLE DIFFERENCES 1984
★ ★ ★ ★ PG Comedy 1:53
☑ Adult situations
Dir: Charles Shyer   *Cast:* Drew Barrymore, Ryan O'Neal, Shelley Long, Sharon Stone, Sam Wanamaker
▶ Coy nine-year-old Barrymore hires lawyer Wanamaker and sues to divorce bickering parents Long and O'Neal. Flashbacks recall the couple's relationship. Set in the world of Hollywood writers and directors with many in-jokes. **(CC)**
Dist.: Vestron

ISADORA 1969 British
★ ★ PG Biography/Dance 2:11
☑ Adult situations, explicit language
Dir: Karel Reisz   *Cast:* Vanessa Redgrave, James Fox, Jason Robards, Ivan Tchenko, John Fraser, Bessie Love
▶ True story of the controversial and free-spirited dancer Isadora Duncan (Redgrave) traces her involvements with artist Fox, tycoon Robards, and poet Tchenko, her innovations in modern dance, the deaths of her children, and her own tragic demise. Ambitious but overly precious direction by Reisz frames inter-

esting performance by Redgrave. Also known as *The Loves of Isadora*.
Dist.: MCA

I SEE A DARK STRANGER 1947 British
★ ★ NR Mystery-Suspense 1:52 B&W
Dir: Frank Launder   *Cast:* Deborah Kerr, Trevor Howard, Raymond Huntley, Michael Howard, Norman Shelley
▶ Kerr, a young Irish girl, hates the English and unwittingly becomes a pawn of a Nazi agent until British officer Howard helps her. Perky, spirited performance by beautiful Kerr highlights fine suspense drama with touches of witty comedy. Also known as *The Adventuress*.
Dist.: VidAmerica

I SENT A LETTER TO MY LOVE 1981 French
★ PG Drama 1:42
Ⓥ Adult situations
Dir: Moshe Mizrahi   *Cast:* Simone Signoret, Jean Rochefort, Delphine Seyrig
▶ Middle-aged Signoret cares for invalid brother Rochefort. When he places a personal ad, she inadvertently answers and, unable to reveal the coincidence, continues the correspondence. Good premise, but tepid drama is slowly paced. Some touching moments; Seyrig is delightful as the neighbor who eventually wins Rochefort's heart.   Ⓢ
Dist.: Thorn/EMI

ISHTAR 1987
★ PG-13 Comedy 1:47
Ⓥ Brief nudity, explicit language
Dir: Elaine May   *Cast:* Warren Beatty, Dustin Hoffman, Isabelle Adjani, Charles Grodin, Tess Harper, Jack Weston
▶ Forty-million-dollar rocky road caper about dunderheaded songwriters Beatty and Hoffman booked by agent Weston into a club in strife-torn North Africa. Once there, they become patsies for gorgeous terrorist Adjani and manipulative CIA agent Grodin. Awful songs are constantly repeated, killing all the humor. Stars try hard, but the reverse casting backfires. Far from entertaining box-office bust and artistic embarrassment for writer/director Elaine May.   (CC)
Dist.: RCA/Columbia

ISLAND, THE 1980
★ ★ R Mystery-Suspense 1:54
Ⓥ Nudity, adult situations, explicit language, graphic violence
Dir: Michael Ritchie   *Cast:* Michael Caine, David Warner, Angela Punch-McGregor, Don Henderson, Jeffrey Frank
▶ New York journalist Caine travels to Bermuda Triangle island to investigate reports of bizarre disappearances. He unwisely brings along his twelve-year-old son Frank. They are soon abducted by a incest-ridden gang of toothless pirates led by Warner. Excessive blood and gore, sloppy photography, stilted action scenes, and waterlogged plot from Peter Benchley.
Dist.: MCA

ISLAND AT THE TOP OF WORLD, THE 1974
★ ★ G Fantasy/Family 1:33
Dir: Robert Stevenson   *Cast:* David Hartman, Donald Sinden, Jacques Marin, Mako, David Gwillim, Agneta Eckemyr
▶ In 1907, history professor Hartman joins rich Englishman Sinden on an arduous Arctic expedition to find the Brit's missing son. The intrepid adventurers encounter a lost civilization of Vikings. Old-fashioned Disney adventure gains momentum as it goes along. Fine production values and special effects.
Dist.: Buena Vista

ISLAND OF ADVENTURE 1981 British
★ ★ NR Family 1:25
Dir: Anthony Squire   *Cast:* Norman Bowler, Wilfrid Brambell, Catherine Schell, John-Rhys Davies
▶ Four curious teens on vacation in Cornwall sail out to the deserted Island of Gloom, a locale they've been warned away from. There they discover a mysterious network of tunnels, and are kidnapped by a gang of terrorist counterfeiters. Youthful derring-do, based on the novel by Enid Blyton.
Dist.: Nelson

ISLAND OF DR. MOREAU, THE 1977
★ ★ PG Horror 1:38
Ⓥ Brief nudity
Dir: Don Taylor   *Cast:* Burt Lancaster, Michael York, Barbara Carrera, Nigel Davenport, Richard Basehart
▶ Classic 1896 H. G. Wells story about mad scientist Lancaster working on his wild-beast-into-man serum. Shipwrecked sailor York falls for the doc's beautiful adopted daughter Carrera and discovers his evil experiments. Not as good as the 1933 original *Island of Lost Souls* but does boast fine performances from an admirable cast and appropriately lush jungle background.
Dist.: Vestron

ISLAND OF THE BLUE DOLPHINS 1964
★ NR Family 1:33
Dir: James B. Clark   *Cast:* Celia Kaye, Larry Domasin, Ann Daniel, George Kennedy, Carlos Romero, Hal Jon Norman
▶ In the early 1800s, Kaye, a young Aleutian girl, is marooned on a remote Alaskan island. She befriends the wild dogs living there and survives on perserverance and luck. Offbeat adventure, adapted from Scott O'Dell's popular children's novel, was based on a true incident.
Dist.: MCA

ISLANDS IN THE STREAM 1977
★ ★ ★ ★ PG Drama 1:44
Ⓥ Explicit language
Dir: Franklin J. Schaffner   *Cast:* George C. Scott, David Hemmings, Claire Bloom, Susan Tyrrell, Gilbert Roland
▶ On the eve of World War II, famous sculptor Scott enjoys a solitary existence in the West Indies. Visits by his three sons and one of his

ex-wives cause him to reexamine his life. Adaptation of Ernest Hemingway's unfinished last novel is heartfelt and emotion-packed. Classy, Oscar-nominated cinematography and a great Scott.
Dist.: Paramount

ISLE OF THE DEAD 1945
★ ★ NR Horror 1:12 B&W
Dir: Mark Robson *Cast:* Boris Karloff, Ellen Drew, Marc Cramer, Katherine Emery, Helen Thimig, Jason Robards, Sr.
▶ In 1912, Greek general Karloff uncovers evidence of grave-robbing on a remote Balkan island. He pursues the culprits despite rumors of vampires and an outbreak of the plague. Unusual horror film has a gripping, unsettling tone and an eerie performance by Drew, one of the suspected vampires.
Dist.: Fox Hills

I SPIT ON YOUR GRAVE 1978
☆ R Mystery-Suspense 1:41
☑ Rape, nudity, explicit language, violence
Dir: Meir Zarchi *Cast:* Camille Keaton, Eron Tabor, Richard Pace, Anthony Nichols
▶ Keaton takes summer house in Connecticut and is beaten and raped by four locals. She recovers and takes the law into her own hands, getting vengeance via castration, axe, and other methods. Revenge may be sweet but this very brutal movie isn't. Star is grandniece of Buster Keaton. Also known as *Day of the Women*.
Dist.: VidAmerica

ISTANBUL 1990
☆ PG-13 Mystery-Suspense 1:22
☑ Adult situations, explicit language, violence
Dir: Mats Arehn *Cast:* Timothy Bottoms, Twiggy, Robert Morley, Emma Kihlberg, Lena Endre, Celal Khosrowshahi
▶ *N.Y. Times* correspondent Bottoms goes to Turkey with his young daughter to follow up on a strange videotape he has received from a relation in Istanbul. At a Turkish hotel, mysterious things occur that make him question his sanity. He befriends Englishman Morley and enigmatic Twiggy, while arms-dealing bad guys target his daughter for abduction. Lackluster international thriller short on suspense, with mildly interesting Turkish backdrop.
Dist.: Magnum

IT CAME FROM BENEATH THE SEA 1955
★ ★ NR Sci-Fi 1:20 B&W
Dir: Robert Gordon *Cast:* Faith Domergue, Kenneth Tobey, Ian Keith, Donald Curtis, Dean Maddox, Jr.
▶ San Francisco is the target of an enraged giant octopus. Navy sub commander Tobey tries to thwart the beast, which creates Bay City havoc before being nuked. Sci-fi thriller most notable for Ray Harryhausen's special effects.
Dist.: RCA

IT CAME FROM HOLLYWOOD 1982
★ PG Comedy 1:20 C/B&W
☑ Explicit language, adult humor
Dir: Malcolm Leo, Andrew Solt *Cast:* Dan Aykroyd, John Candy, Cheech Marin, Thomas Chong, Gilda Radner
▶ Casserole of clips from Hollywood's most laughably bad movies, including *Glen or Glenda* and *Attack of the 50-Foot Woman*. Awful, campy fun is perfect for midnight movie fans.
Dist.: Paramount

IT CAME FROM OUTER SPACE 1953
★ ★ NR Sci-Fi 1:20 B&W
Dir: Jack Arnold *Cast:* Richard Carlson, Barbara Rush, Russell Johnson, Kathleen Hughes, Charles Drake
▶ In an Arizona desert town, astronomer Carlson witnesses spaceship landing and then finds townspeople's personalities suddenly changed. Eerie and intelligent chiller, nicely directed by Arnold. Ultimately benign view of aliens was rare for the paranoid fifties. Originally filmed in 3-D and based on a Ray Bradbury story.
Dist.: MCA

IT HAPPENED AT THE WORLD'S FAIR 1963
★ ★ ★ NR Musical 1:45
Dir: Norman Taurog *Cast:* Elvis Presley, Joan O'Brien, Gary Lockwood, Vicky Tiu, H. M. Wynant
▶ Presley plays a daredevil pilot who romances nurse O'Brien at the 1962 Seattle World's Fair. Charming subplot involves young Tiu's efforts to stay out of an orphanage. Ten Elvis tunes, including "One Broken Heart for Sale," "Cotton Candy Land," and "I'm Falling in Love Tonight." Look for young Kurt Russell in this, his first film. He would later play the King in the telemovie *Elvis*.
Dist.: MGM/UA

IT HAPPENED ONE NIGHT 1934
★ ★ ★ ★ NR Comedy 1:45 B&W
Dir: Frank Capra *Cast:* Clark Gable, Claudette Colbert, Walter Connolly, Roscoe Karns, Alan Hale
▶ Pampered heiress Colbert runs away from dad Connolly and travels incognito. Hard-edged reporter Gable pretends he doesn't recognize her to get the big scoop. They hit the road together and antagonism gives way to love. Terrific romantic comedy with many classic scenes: Colbert and Gable arguing over hitchhiking methods, Gable putting up the "Walls of Jericho," group sing-along on a bus. Oscar sweep: Picture, Director, Actor, Actress, Screenplay (first film to accomplish this feat). **(CC)**
Dist.: RCA/Columbia

I, THE JURY 1982
★ ★ ★ R Action-Adventure 1:51
☑ Nudity, strong sexual content, adult situations, explicit language, violence
Dir: Richard T. Heffron *Cast:* Armand As-

sante, Barbara Carrera, Alan King, Laurene Landon, Geoffrey Lewis, Paul Sorvino
▶ Tough private eye Mike Hammer (Assante) investigates the murder of his Vietnam buddy and gets involved with sex therapist Carrera, whose clinic may be connected to the case. The pace is fast, the violence frequent, the atmosphere seedy, and the women numerous and often unclad in this flavorful adaptation of Mickey Spillane's pulp classic.
Dist.: CBS/Fox

IT LIVES AGAIN 1978
★ **R Horror 1:31**
☑ Adult situations, explicit language, graphic violence
Dir: Larry Cohen *Cast:* Frederic Forrest, Kathleen Lloyd, John P. Ryan, John Marley, Eddie Constantine
▶ Lurid sequel to *It's Alive* with Ryan reprising his earlier role as the distressed father of a homicidal infant. He warns parents Forrest and Lloyd that their child may also be a monster while police conduct a manhunt for two other killer babies. Good special effects by Rick Baker and lush Bernard Herrmann score helped make this a cult favorite among horror fans.
Dist.: Warner

IT'S A GIFT 1934
★ ★ ★ **NR Comedy 1:13 B&W**
Dir: Norman Z. McLeod *Cast:* W. C. Fields, Jean Rouverol, Julian Madison, Kathleen Howard, Tom Bupp, Baby LeRoy
▶ Henpecked grocer Harold Bissonette (Fields) pins his dreams on California and drags his protesting family cross-country to a ramshackle orange grove. Unforgettable comedy may be the best, and bitterest, of Fields's work. Contains one classic scene after another: Baby LeRoy's encounter with molasses, Fields's herculean efforts to get to sleep, insufferable salesman T. Roy Barnes looking for Carl LaFong, etc. Highly recommended to his fans.
Dist.: KVC

IT'S ALIVE 1974
★ **PG Horror 1:30**
☑ Adult situations, graphic violence
Dir: Larry Cohen *Cast:* John P. Ryan, Sharon Farrell, Andrew Duggan, Guy Stockwell, James Dixon
▶ Infant mutant bounds out of the womb to bite and claw people to shreds. Escaping the hospital, it crawls around L.A., killing innocents and assaulting milk trucks. Ryan and Farrell play the horrified parents. Led to two sequels.
Dist.: Warner

IT'S ALIVE III: ISLAND OF THE ALIVE 1987
★ **R Horror 1:30**
☑ Adult situations, explicit language, graphic violence
Dir: Larry Cohen *Cast:* Michael Moriarty, Karen Black, Laurene Landon, Gerrit Graham, James Dixon

▶ Third go-round (after *It Lives Again*) for the killer babies, now quarantined on a desert island. Moriarty, father of one of the mutants, accompanies an expedition to the island to save them from extermination. After considerable carnage (much of it tongue-in-cheek), the tots escape and kidnap Black, their mom. Clever exploitation scores some effective satirical points.
Dist.: Warner

IT'S ALWAYS FAIR WEATHER 1955
★ ★ ★ **NR Musical 1:42**
Dir: Stanley Donen, Gene Kelly *Cast:* Gene Kelly, Cyd Charisse, Dan Dailey, Dolores Gray, Michael Kidd
▶ World War II buddies Kelly, Dailey, and Kidd vow to meet in ten years. Their reunion proves bittersweet as youthful hopes and dreams have fallen by the wayside. Wide-screen production may lose something on video but first-rate musical scenes such as the trash-can dance and a roller skating number highlight third Donen/Kelly collaboration (after *On the Town* and *Singing in the Rain*).
Dist.: MGM/UA

IT'S A MAD, MAD, MAD, MAD WORLD 1963
★ ★ ★ **G Comedy 3:12**
Dir: Stanley Kramer *Cast:* Spencer Tracy, Edie Adams, Milton Berle, Sid Caesar, Ethel Merman, Jonathan Winters, Buddy Hackett, Mickey Rooney, Phil Silvers
▶ Three hours of wackiness with huge all-star cast. Story has comedians racing wildly to find a hidden cache of stolen money, under the watchful eye of sober sheriff Tracy. Big and splashy, lots of fun. Cameos by Dick Shawn, Peter Falk, The Three Stooges, Buster Keaton, Jimmy Durante, Jim Backus, Don Knotts, and many more.
Dist.: CBS/Fox

IT'S A WONDERFUL LIFE 1946
★ ★ ★ ★ ★ **NR Drama 2:09 B&W**
Dir: Frank Capra *Cast:* James Stewart, Donna Reed, Lionel Barrymore, Thomas Mitchell, Henry Travers, Gloria Grahame, Beulah Bondi, Frank Faylen, Ward Bond, H. B. Warner
▶ Small-towner George Bailey (Stewart) finds his dreams thwarted by rich and greedy Barrymore. He's driven to the point of suicide until angel Travers shows him what life would be like if he'd never been born. Christmas classic grows more popular every year, and deservedly so: combines whimsical humor, romance, and fantasy with realistic despair. Towering performance by Stewart; Reed is touching as his sweet wife; Travers a delight as the bumbling angel. Wonderful movie with life-affirming ending.
Dist.: Various Ⓒ

IT SHOULD HAPPEN TO YOU 1954
★ ★ ★ **NR Comedy 1:27 B&W**
Dir: George Cukor *Cast:* Judy Holliday,

Jack Lemmon, Peter Lawford, Michael O'-Shea

▶ Kooky New Yorker Holliday wants to feel special and important, so she purchases billboard space to advertise her name in huge letters. Soap company executive Lawford makes a deal with her to get the prime space; in return he buys her several other billboards. Boyfriend Lemmon is nonplussed by her sudden notoriety. Vibrant performance by Holliday in this breezy comedy. Lemmon's film debut.
Dist.: RCA/Columbia

IT'S IN THE BAG 1945
★ ★ NR Comedy 1:27 B&W
Dir: Richard Wallace *Cast:* Fred Allen, Binnie Barnes, Robert Benchley, Don Ameche, Jack Benny, William Bendix
▶ Flea circus operator, family man, and real-life radio personality Allen has his world turned upside-down when he inherits a fortune from a murdered uncle. Unfortunately, the cash is hidden in one of several antique chairs which Allen must recover from characters like penny-pincher Benny and gangster Bendix. More zany than funny. Written by Alfred Hitchcock's wife and sometime-collaborator Alma Reville, plot is similar to a 1943 British film with same title and Mel Brooks's later *The Twelve Chairs.*
Dist.: Republic

IT'S MY TURN 1980
★ ★ ★ R Romance/Comedy 1:31
☑ Adult situations, explicit language
Dir: Claudia Weill *Cast:* Jill Clayburgh, Michael Douglas, Charles Grodin, Teresa Baxter
▶ Smart but spacey mathematician Clayburgh lives in Chicago with aloof architect Grodin, but falls for her stepmother's brash, bearded ex-baseball player son Douglas in New York. A warm, witty look at romance. Title song by Diana Ross.
Dist.: RCA/Columbia

IT TAKES TWO 1988
★ ★ PG-13 Comedy 1:21
☑ Adult situations, explicit language
Dir: David Beaird *Cast:* George Newbern, Leslie Hope, Kimberly Foster, Barry Corbin, Anthony Geary, Bill Bolender
▶ Jittery Texas groom-to-be Newbern buys sports car in Dallas for a last fling before his wedding, but the adventure turns into a comic nightmare that changes his life forever. Amiable plot has engaging offbeat style and appealing performances by Newbern and fiancée Hope.
Dist.: CBS/Fox

IVANHOE 1952
★ ★ ★ NR Action-Adventure 1:46
Dir: Richard Thorpe *Cast:* Robert Taylor, Elizabeth Taylor, Joan Fontaine, George Sanders, Emlyn Williams, Robert Douglas
▶ In twelfth-century England, the noble Saxon knight Ivanhoe (Taylor) defeats a Norman plot against the king while rescuing both his betrothed Fontaine and beautiful Jewess Taylor from the dastardly De Bois-Builbert (Sanders). Faithful, lavish adaptation of Sir Walter Scott's medieval epic offers dazzling sweep and spectacle.
Dist.: MGM/UA

IVAN THE TERRIBLE, PART I 1944 Russian
☆ NR Drama 1:36 B&W
Dir: Sergei Eisenstein *Cast:* Nikolai Cherkassov, Pavel Kadochnikov, Mikhail Zharov, Ludmila Tselikovskaya, Serafima Birman
▶ In the sixteenth century, Ivan (Cherkassov) becomes the first czar of a united Russia, defeating foreign foes while battling court intrigues after the assassination of his wife (Tselikovskaya). Fascinating story, told in epic proportions, unfortunately lacks a sense of humanity. Best enjoyed by students who can appreciate Eisenstein's intricate editing and massive production design. Music by Sergei Prokofiev. Followed by a sequel. Ⓢ
Dist.: Video Yesteryear

IVAN THE TERRIBLE, PART II 1946 Russian
☆ NR Drama 1:22 C/B&W
Dir: Sergei Eisenstein *Cast:* Nikolai Cherkassov, Serafima Birman, Pavel Kadochnikov, Mikhail Zharov, Alexei Buchma
▶ Sixteenth-century Russian czar Ivan (Cherkassov) consolidates his power by conducting a purge of Moscow's aristocracy, in the process foiling a murder plot by his aunt (Birman). Second part of Eisenstein's planned trilogy about Ivan was banned by Stalin, resurfacing only in 1958. Contains a remarkable banquet sequence in color. Brief test shots for the third episode have recently surfaced. Ⓢ
Dist.: Video Yesteryear

I'VE HEARD THE MERMAIDS SINGING 1987 Canadian
★ ★ NR Comedy 1:24
☑ Adult situations, explicit language
Dir: Patricia Rozema *Cast:* Sheila McCarthy, Paule Baillargeon, Ann-Marie McDonald, John Evans
▶ Ditzy McCarthy describes herself as "organizationally impaired," but manages to get a job at an art gallery nonetheless. She begins to worship her sophisticated and talented boss Baillargeon, but eventually realizes that things aren't always what they seem. Amazing debut work from both Rozema and the immediately endearing McCarthy. Charming, wise, and witty.
Dist.: Nelson

I VITELLONI 1953 Italian
★ NR Drama 1:44 B&W
Dir: Federico Fellini *Cast:* Franco Interlenghi, Franco Fabrizi, Alberto Sordi, Leopoldo Trieste, Riccardo Fellini, Leonora Ruffo
▶ In a small Italian town, five young friends hang out together as the shadow of adulthood looms. Interlenghi makes mature deci-

sions about his life; womanizer Fabrizi gets a girl pregnant, which leads to a bad marriage. One of Fellini's most beloved films. Oscar nomination for original screenplay. Ⓢ
Dist.: Various

I WALKED WITH A ZOMBIE 1943
★ ★ **NR Horror 1:09 B&W**
Dir: Jacques Tourneur *Cast:* Frances Dee, Tom Conway, James Ellison, Edith Barrett, Christine Gordon, Teresa Harris
▶ American planter Conway hires nurse Dee to look after his mysteriously catatonic wife Barrett on Haiti. While denying her love for Conway, Dee tries voodoo to "cure" Barrett. Imaginative film uses evocative atmosphere to suggest rather than show horror, emphasizing tension over shocks. A treat for sophisticated viewers (who will also appreciate plot's close resemblance to *Jane Eyre*).
Dist.: Media

I WANNA HOLD YOUR HAND 1978
★ **PG Comedy 1:44**
☑ Explicit language
Dir: Robert Zemeckis *Cast:* Nancy Allen, Bobby DiCicco, Marc McClure, Susan Newman, Theresa Saldana, Eddie Deezen
▶ February 1964: the Beatles are set to appear on the Ed Sullivan show. Several New Jersey teenagers travel to New York City to see their idols. Nostalgic look at Beatlemania captures fan hysteria with energetic crowd shots, inventive comic plot, a fresh young cast, and numerous Fab Four hits on the soundtrack. Overlooked early effort from the director of *Back to the Future* and *Who Framed Roger Rabbit.*
Dist.: Warner

I WANT TO LIVE! 1958
★ ★ ★ **NR Biography 2:00 B&W**
Dir: Robert Wise *Cast:* Susan Hayward, Simon Oakland, Virginia Vincent, Theodore Bikel, Wesley Lau, Philip Coolidge
▶ Relentlessly downbeat story of Barbara Graham (Hayward), a hardened convict and drug addict sentenced to death in 1955 for the murder of a widow. Hayward is mesmerizing in an Oscar-winning performance, but film raised considerable controversy by insisting (without evidence) Graham was innocent. Bleak but compelling story received five other Oscar nominations.
Dist.: MGM/UA

I WAS A TEENAGE ZOMBIE 1987
★ **NR Horror 1:32**
☑ Nudity, adult situations, explicit language, graphic violence
Dir: John Elias Michalakias *Cast:* Michael Rubin, George Seminara, Steve McCoy, Peter Bush, Cassie Madden, Cindy Keiter
▶ Five teens victimized by unscrupulous pusher McCoy kill him and dump his body in polluted river. Toxic wastes revive McCoy as a zombie who murders Rubin. Remaining teens use the river to transform Rubin into a "good

guy" zombie who engages McCoy in battle. Campy exploitation film shot on shoestring budget has become cult favorite at midnight shows. Extraordinary soundtrack includes tunes by the Fleshtones, Smithereens, Del Fuegos, Violent Femmes, Alex Chilton, and Los Lobos.
Dist.: Nelson

I WENT TO THE DANCE 1989
★ **NR Documentary/Music 1:24**
☑ Explicit language
Dir: Les Blank, Chris Strachwitz *Cast:* Clifton Chenier, Queen Ida, Dennis McGee, The Falcons, The Hackberry Ramblers, Rockin' Sidney
▶ Lively, informative documentary mixes Cajun music and history, exploring the origins and development of the people and their art from the eighteenth century through today. Rough-hewn production values and subtitles (used to translate Cajun lyrics) are mild distractions from the marvelous music. Also known as *J'ai Été au Bal.* Ⓢ
Dist.: Flower Films

I WILL, I WILL . . . FOR NOW 1976
★ ★ ★ **R Comedy 1:47**
☑ Explicit language
Dir: Norman Panama *Cast:* Elliott Gould, Diane Keaton, Paul Sorvino, Victoria Principal, Robert Alda, Candy Clark
▶ Divorced couple Gould and Keaton are still attracted to one another. They negotiate a contract to guide their renewed relationship and then go to a sex clinic for further help. Meanwhile, lawyer Sorvino pursues Keaton. Good cast in a bawdy and sometimes bittersweet sex comedy.
Dist.: Media

JABBERWOCKY 1977 British
★ **PG Comedy 1:40**
☑ Brief nudity, graphic violence
Dir: Terry Gilliam *Cast:* Michael Palin, Max Wall, John Le Mesurier, Annette Badland, Terry Jones
▶ Monty Python meets Lewis Carroll in Gilliam's daft adaptation of the famous poem. Befuddled Palin seeks his fortune in the realm of King Bruno the Questionable so that he can marry Griselda Fishfinger (Badland). Sophomoric farce, predictably insane, with plenty of blood splatterings. Warning: when the King says, "Off with his head!" Gilliam obeys.
Dist.: RCA/Columbia

JACK AND THE BEANSTALK 1952
★ **NR Family 1:18 C/B&W**
Dir: Jean Yarbrough *Cast:* Bud Abbott, Lou Costello, Buddy Baer, Dorothy Ford, Shaye Cogan, James Alexander
▶ When the precocious brat he's babysitting reads him "Jack and the Beanstalk," Costello dreams he's the lad who trades the family cow for magic beans. He climbs the beanstalk and battles the giant Baer. Characters from his life reappear in the fairy tale: Abbott

is Mr. Finklepuss, a cheating butcher. Very funny clowning from Costello, although garish production is as hard on the eyes as lame songs, including "I Fear Nothing," are on the ear.
Dist.: Goodtimes

JACKIE ROBINSON STORY, THE 1950
★ ★ NR Biography/Sports 1:17 B&W
Dir: Alfred E. Green *Cast:* Jackie Robinson, Ruby Dee, Minor Watson, Louise Beavers, Richard Lane, Bernie Hamilton
▶ Robinson plays himself in this earnest biopic that traces his days at UCLA, encounters with racial prejudice, courtship and marriage to Dee, and breaking of the baseball color barrier with the Brooklyn Dodgers. Full of corny touches (such as "America the Beautiful" underscoring Robinson's last speech), but still documents a valuable history lesson.
Dist.: Goodtimes

JACK LONDON 1943
☆ NR Biography 1:34 B&W
Dir: Alfred Santell *Cast:* Michael O'Shea, Susan Hayward, Osa Massen, Harry Davenport, Frank Craven, Virginia Mayo
▶ Fanciful biography, with O'Shea as the well-known novelist whose writings about his youthful adventures in the Alaska gold fields won him acclaim. While he travels around the world seeking war and danger, his wife Hayward waits at home. London's coverage of the Russo-Japanese war gives an excuse for heavily played anti-Japanese propaganda that dates this otherwise invigorating adventure. Also known as *The Adventures of Jack London.*
Dist.: KVC

JACKNIFE 1989
★ ★ ★ ★ R Drama 1:42
☑ Adult situations, explicit language, violence
Dir: David Jones *Cast:* Robert De Niro, Ed Harris, Kathy Baker, Tom Isbell, Charles Dutton, Loudon Wainwright III
▶ After a long separation, Vietnam vet De Niro tries to pull his old buddy Harris out of an alcohol-induced depression over the war. Harris resents De Niro's help and courtship of his sister Baker, but De Niro's tactics ultimately force Harris to confront his memories of the war. Powerhouse casting sparks Stephen Metcalfe's adaptation of his Off-Broadway play.
Dist.: HBO

JACK'S BACK 1988
★ ★ R Mystery-Suspense 1:35
☑ Nudity, adult situations, explicit language, violence
Dir: Rowdy Herrington *Cast:* James Spader, Cynthia Gibb, Rod Loomis, Rex Ryon, Robert Picardo
▶ Los Angeles prostitutes are murdered in the style used by Jack the Ripper one hundred years ago. Young medic Spader, cute doctor Gibb, uptight chief doctor Ryon, and intern

Loomis track the serial killer. Some psychological depth attempted in this routine thriller. (CC)
Dist.: Paramount

JACKSON COUNTY JAIL 1976
★ ★ R Action-Adventure 1:23
☑ Rape, strong sexual content, explicit language, violence
Dir: Michael Miller *Cast:* Yvette Mimieux, Tommy Lee Jones, Robert Carradine, Howard Hesseman, Betty Thomas
▶ While driving cross country, producer Mimieux is unjustly imprisoned and then raped by her jailer. She kills her attacker and escapes with convicted murderer Jones. Roger Corman–produced film features zippy pacing, lots of action, exceptional performances by Jones and Mimieux. Warning: rape scene is extremely graphic.
Dist.: Warner

JAGGED EDGE 1985
★ ★ ★ ★ ★ R Mystery-Suspense 1:49
☑ Brief nudity, adult situations, explicit language, violence
Dir: Richard Marquand *Cast:* Jeff Bridges, Glenn Close, Peter Coyote, Robert Loggia, Leigh Taylor-Young
▶ Solid courtroom drama with lawyer Close defending newspaper publisher Bridges on charges of ruthlessly murdering his wife. She finds herself falling for him. Close's unmannered acting is perfectly balanced by Bridges's finely shaded performance, adding crackling tension to the riveting conclusion. Loggia shines in an Oscar-nominated performance as a seedy private investigator with a memorable exit line. **(CC)**
Dist.: RCA

JAGUAR LIVES! 1979
★ PG Action-Adventure 1:30
☑ Violence
Dir: Ernest Pintoff *Cast:* Joe Lewis, Christopher Lee, Donald Pleasence, Barbara Bach, John Huston, Woody Strode
▶ Incoherent action epic has combination Superman and 007 Lewis battling various kung fu armies across a total of sixteen different international locations. They call him: Jaguar. Awful music, bad dubbing, but viewers may enjoy running into familiar faces Lee, Pleasence, Huston, and Bach in perfectly dopey contexts.
Dist.: TWE

JAILHOUSE ROCK 1957
★ ★ ★ NR Musical 1:36 B&W
Dir: Richard Thorpe *Cast:* Elvis Presley, Judy Tyler, Mickey Shaughnessy, Jennifer Holden, Dean Jones, The Jordanaires
▶ Presley kills a man while defending a woman's honor, then learns to sing in prison. With Tyler's help he becomes a rock 'n' roll sensation, but turns on his old friends when fame goes to his head. Stark plot and outstanding songs ("Treat Me Nice," "Baby I Don't

Care," "Don't Leave Me Now," etc.) set this well above other Presley vehicles. Elvis sizzles throughout, particularly during the title tune. *Dist.:* MGM/UA

JAKE SPEED 1986
★ ★ PG Action-Adventure 1:45
☑ Explicit language, violence
Dir: Andrew Lane   *Cast:* Wayne Crawford, Dennis Christopher, Karen Kopins, John Hurt, Leon Ames, Donna Pescow
▶ Fictional paperback hero Jake Speed (Crawford) and sidekick Christopher come to life to help Kopins rescue her kidnapped sister in Africa. Tongue-in-cheek derring-do, reminiscent of *Romancing the Stone*, suffers from erratic pacing and storytelling, and co-writer Crawford's bland performance.   **(CC)** *Dist.:* New World

JAMAICA INN 1939 British
★ NR Mystery-Suspense 1:38 B&W
Dir: Alfred Hitchcock   *Cast:* Charles Laughton, Maureen O'Hara, Leslie Banks, Robert Newton, Emlyn Williams, Wylie Watson
▶ In the early eighteenth century, young O'Hara uncovers a den of thieves and pirates who prey on passing ships. With the help of insurance agent Newton, she pins the blame on local squire Laughton. Competent but slow-moving adaptation of Daphne du Maurier's novel suffers from Laughton's overacting. Atypical Hitchcock effort lacks his usual touches.
Dist.: Various

JAMES JOYCE'S WOMEN 1985
☆ R Drama 1:29
☑ Adult situations, explicit language
Dir: Michael Pierce   *Cast:* Fionnula Flanagan, Chris O'Neil, Timothy O'Grady, Tony Lyons, Paddy Dawson
▶ A journalist visits James Joyce's wife Nora (Flanagan) in Switzerland to interview her about her famed husband. Flashbacks tell the story of their lives, and excerpts from *Ulysses* (with Flanagan as Molly Bloom) and *Finnegan's Wake* are interwoven into the film. Only fans of Joyce will be able to appreciate this esoteric homage to his genius.
Dist.: MCA

JANE AND THE LOST CITY 1987 British
☆ PG Action-Adventure 1:32
☑ Adult situations, explicit language, violence
Dir: Terry Marcel   *Cast:* Sam J. Jones, Maud Adams, Kirsten Hughes, Jasper Carrott, Elsa O'Toole
▶ Lackluster British entry into Indiana Jones territory is based on the long-running World War II comic strip, "Jane," about a nubile heroine who's constantly losing her dress in battle. In this adventure, Churchill orders Jane into the African jungle to search for diamonds to support the war effort. And, yes, Jane disrobes several times while escaping the Nazis.
Dist.: New World

JANE AUSTEN IN MANHATTAN 1980
☆ PG Drama 1:50
☑ Adult situations
Dir: James Ivory   *Cast:* Anne Baxter, Robert Powell, Sean Young, Kurt Johnson, Katrina Hodiak, Tim Choate
▶ Rival Soho theatrical companies vie for a grant to present a newly discovered play by Jane Austen. Powell's company is experimental; Baxter's is classical. Film is not up to level of other Merchant-Ivory offerings. As in *Slaves of New York*, Ivory doesn't quite get contemporary Gotham into believable focus.
Dist.: Nelson

JANE EYRE 1944
★ ★ ★ ★ NR Drama 1:37 B&W
Dir: Robert Stevenson   *Cast:* Joan Fontaine, Orson Welles, Margaret O'Brien, Peggy Ann Garner, John Sutton
▶ In nineteenth-century England, shy governess Fontaine takes a job with mysterious, wealthy Welles. They fall in love but he has a dark secret that could threaten their happiness. Sterling adaptation of the classic Charlotte Brontë novel. Moody camerawork captures haunting atmosphere of the moors. **(CC)**
Dist.: CBS/Fox

JANIS 1975
★ ★ ★ R Documentary/Biography/Music 1:36
☑ Explicit language
Dir: Howard Alk, Seaton Findley   *Cast:* Janis Joplin, Big Brother and the Holding Company
▶ Documentary on rock star Janis Joplin concentrates on concert footage, showing her in performance between 1967 and 1970. Includes her classic songs ("Piece of My Heart," "Ball and Chain," "Me and Bobby McGee"), but glosses over her drug addiction and death. Visit to her tenth high school reunion provides a revealing glimpse into her character.
Dist.: MCA

JANUARY MAN, THE 1989
★ ★ R Mystery-Suspense 1:37
☑ Brief nudity, adult situations, explicit language, mild violence
Dir: Pat O'Connor   *Cast:* Kevin Kline, Mary Elizabeth Mastrantonio, Susan Sarandon, Harvey Keitel, Danny Aiello, Rod Steiger, Alan Rickman
▶ When serial killer claims eleventh victim, unorthodox detective Kline is assigned to the case. Romance blooms between Kline and Mastrantonio, the mayor's daughter, as they bumble their way to a solution. Quirky John Patrick Shanley screenplay disappoints greatly after his wonderful *Moonstruck*; O'Connor's misdirection makes matters worse. A talented cast is left stranded in this critical and box-office bomb.
Dist.: CBS/Fox

JASON AND THE ARGONAUTS 1963
★ ★ ★ G Fantasy 1:44
Dir: Don Chaffey   *Cast:* Todd Armstrong,
Nancy Kovack, Gary Raymond, Laurence
Naismith, Niall MacGinnis, Honor Blackman
▶ Cheated out of his birthright, Jason (Armstrong) assembles a band of heroes to retrieve the golden fleece and claim his throne.
Captivating adventure based on Greek mythology with outstanding Ray Harryhausen
special effects. The giant statue Talos, monstrous harpies, and deadly skeleton warriors
are only a few of the highlights in this immensely entertaining fantasy.
Dist.: RCA/Columbia

JAWS 1975
★ ★ ★ ★ ★ PG Action-Adventure 2:04
☑ Graphic violence, explicit language
Dir: Steven Spielberg   *Cast:* Roy Scheider,
Robert Shaw, Richard Dreyfuss, Lorraine
Gary, Murray Hamilton
▶ Triple-Oscar-winning fish-tale about an Atlantic resort town terrorized by a twenty-five-
foot man-eating great white shark. Chief of
police Scheider, salty old shark-hunter Shaw,
and cocky young oceanographer Dreyfuss
battle the killer creature to the death. Spielberg's first major triumph spawned three sequels and numerous imitators. Based on the
best-selling novel by Peter Benchley and
filmed on Martha's Vineyard. Considered by
many to be the best of its genre. The evocative score by John Williams has become syn-
onymous with terror.
Dist.: MCA

JAWS 2 1978
★ ★ ★ PG Action-Adventure 1:56
☑ Explicit language, violence
Dir: Jeannot Szwarc   *Cast:* Roy Scheider,
Lorraine Gary, Murray Hamilton, Joseph
Mascolo, Jeffrey Kramer
▶ Scheider reprises his role as resort-town
sheriff, convinced another killer shark is stalk-
ing vacationing swimmers. No one believes
him until the fish rears its mechanical head to
gobble teens tartare. Sequel lacks the quality
cast and meticulously calculated suspense
that made the original a box-office splash.
Dist.: MCA

JAWS 3 1983
★ ★ PG Action-Adventure 1:38
☑ Explicit language, graphic violence
Dir: Joe Alves   *Cast:* Dennis Quaid, Bess
Armstrong, Simon MacCorkindale, Louis
Gossett, Jr., John Putch, Lea Thompson
▶ Third entry in the *Jaws* series shifts the set-
ting to Florida's Sea World theme park, where
Quaid (supposedly the son of sheriff Roy
Scheider of the earlier films) and marine biolo-
gist Armstrong capture a great white shark.
Mother shark arrives for a bloody revenge. Shot
in 3-D, film's best effects will be lost on TV.
Dist.: MCA

JAWS THE REVENGE 1987
★ ★ PG-13 Action-Adventure 1:30
☑ Explicit language, graphic violence
Dir: Joseph Sargent   *Cast:* Michael Caine,
Lorraine Gary, Lance Guest, Karen Young,
Mitchell Anderson
▶ Holding a personal grudge against the
Brody clan, the killer shark swims all the way to
the Bahamas to stalk Gary and her only re-
maining son Guest. Caine plays a rakish pilot
romantically pursuing her. By now, the fourth
remake in the *Jaws* series has lost most of its
bite. **(CC)**
Dist.: MCA

JAZZ ON A SUMMER'S DAY 1960
★ NR Documentary/Music 1:25
Dir: Bert Stern   *Cast:* Louis Armstrong, Count
Basie, Mahalia Jackson, Chuck Berry, Duke
Ellington, Thelonious Monk, Gerry Mulligan,
Dinah Washington, Anita O'Day, Chico
Hamilton, Sonny Stitt, Big Maybelle
▶ Influential documentary captures musical
performances and relaxed local ambiance
around the Newport Jazz Festival, held over a
two-day period in 1959. The big names in jazz
are all here—as well as rocker Berry. Set the
pattern for future music documentaries like
Monterey Pop and its imitators.
Dist.: New Yorker

JAZZ SINGER, THE 1927
★ ★ NR Musical 1:28 B&W
Dir: Alan Crosland   *Cast:* Al Jolson, May
McAvoy, Werner Oland, Eugene Besserer,
Bobby Gordon, William Demarest
▶ Pioneering talkie changed the movie industry forever, although large portions of the
film are actually silent. Jolson plays an aspiring
Broadway star whose mainstream ambitions
conflict with those of cantor father Oland, who
wants son to follow in his professional and religious footsteps. Jolson is unforgettable, singing "Mammy," "Toot, Toot, Tootsie Goodbye,"
and others.
Dist.: CBS/Fox

JAZZ SINGER, THE 1980
★ ★ ★ ★ PG Drama/Musical 1:56
☑ Adult situations, explicit language
Dir: Richard Fleischer   *Cast:* Neil Diamond,
Laurence Olivier, Lucie Arnaz, Catlin Adams,
Franklyn Ajaye, Paul Nicholas
▶ Singer Diamond reaches for the pop music
pinnacle, but Jewish cantor dad Olivier wants
him to follow in family footsteps. Diamond has
affair with promoter Arnaz but eventually sees
the emptiness of success. Old-fashioned sentiment laid on with conviction is a guaranteed
audience pleaser. Most heartrending moment: Olivier declaring "I have no son." Diamond's score includes "Love on the Rocks,"
"Hello Again," and "America." Earlier versions
starred Al Jolson (1927) and Danny Thomas
(1953).
Dist.: Paramount

J.D. AND THE SALT FLAT KID 1978
★ ★ ★ PG Family 1:30
☑ Mild violence
Dir: Alex Grasshoff *Cast:* Jesse Turner, Dennis Fimple, Slim Pickens, Hope Summers, Johnny Paycheck
► Country singers Turner and Fimple leave their small Texas hometown to try their luck in Nashville. On the way, they are mistaken for kidnappers and pursued by lamebrained sheriff Pickens. Car chase comedy imbued with crossover country music is simple and wholesome, with a pleasing windup at the Grand Ole Opry.
Dist.: Nelson

JEAN DE FLORETTE 1987 French
★ ★ PG Drama 2:02
☑ Explicit language
Dir: Claude Berri *Cast:* Yves Montand, Gerard Depardieu, Daniel Auteuil, Elisabeth Depardieu, Ernestine Mazurowna
► Hunchback Depardieu moves from the city to the French countryside and tries to make it as a farmer. Greedy neighbors Montand and Auteuil plot against him. Placidly paced but lovingly rendered French drama with excellent performances, beautiful production, and old-fashioned literary feel. Story reaches its conclusion in *Manon of the Spring.* Ⓢ
Dist.: Orion

JEKYLL AND HYDE. . .TOGETHER AGAIN 1982
★ ★ ★ R Comedy 1:27
☑ Nudity, adult situations, explicit language
Dir: Jerry Belson *Cast:* Mark Blankfield, Bess Armstrong, Tim Thomerson, Krista Errickson
► Raunchy parody of Robert Louis Stevenson's *The Strange Case of Dr. Jekyll and Mr. Hyde.* Straitlaced surgeon Blankfield inhales white powder that turns him into a bushy-haired, gold-chain-wearing swinger. Irreverent, tasteless humor, heavy on sex and drug references.
Dist.: Paramount

JEREMIAH JOHNSON 1972
★ ★ ★ ★ ★ PG Western 1:51
☑ Violence
Dir: Sydney Pollack *Cast:* Robert Redford, Will Geer, Stefan Gierasch, Allyn Ann McLerie, Josh Tyner
► Nineteenth-century mountain man Redford survives winter, wilderness, and rival trappers. After Indians kill his family, Redford seeks revenge. Rambles at times but excellent photography and locations, thoughtful direction by Pollack, respectful view of Indians, and convincing performance by Redford combine for an extraordinary adventure.
Dist.: Warner

JERICHO MILE, THE 1979
★ ★ ★ NR Drama/MFTV 1:37
☑ Violence
Dir: Michael Mann *Cast:* Peter Strauss,
Brian Dennehy, Richard Lawson, Roger E. Mosely, Geoffrey Lewis, Miguel Pinero
► Angry convicted killer Strauss, who takes out his frustrations by running each day around the jail yard, is timed at a world-class pace. Against the background of prison tensions, he begins training for Olympic trials. Riveting telemovie combines both inspirational uplift and cynicism. Magnificently directed by Mann at authentic Folsom Prison locations. Superb Strauss garnered one of production's three Emmy Awards.
Dist.: Nelson

JERK, THE 1979
★ ★ ★ R Comedy 1:34
☑ Adult situations, explicit language, adult humor
Dir: Carl Reiner *Cast:* Steve Martin, Bernadette Peters, Bill Macy, Catlin Adams, Mabel King, Richard Ward
► Eager-beaver, happy idiot Martin discovers he's not the natural son of black sharecroppers King and Ward and sets out to find his place in the world. An off-the-wall inventor, he makes and loses a fortune, then marries Peters, the cornet-playing cosmetologist of his dreams. Goofy, innocent, nonstop lunacy reminiscent of Jerry Lewis.
Dist.: MCA

JESSE JAMES 1939
★ ★ ★ NR Western 1:46
Dir: Henry King *Cast:* Tyrone Power, Henry Fonda, Nancy Kelly, Randolph Scott, Brian Donlevy, Jane Darwell
► When their mother Darwell is murdered by villainous railroad agent Donlevy, Jesse James (Power) and his brother Frank (Fonda) are forced into a life of crime. Large-scale adventure is pure hokum as biography, but for action and entertainment it's hard to beat. Outstanding production values and cast, with John Carradine memorably evil as Bob Ford. Fonda starred in the sequel, *The Return of Frank James.*
Dist.: CBS/Fox

JESSE JAMES MEETS FRANKENSTEIN'S DAUGHTER 1966
☆ NR Western/Horror 1:28
Dir: William Beaudine *Cast:* John Lupton, Cal Bolder, Narda Onyx, Steven Geray, Felipe Turich, Rosa Turich
► Unwilling outlaw Jesse James (Lupton) and his pal Bolder hide from a posse with Baron Frankenstein's granddaughter (Onyx). She proceeds to transplant the famous monster's brain into Bolder, turning him into the deadly Igor. Can Jesse escape? Low-budget cross-genre nonsense offers plenty of unintentional laughs.
Dist.: Nelson

JESUS 1979
★ ★ ★ ★ G Drama 1:56
Dir: Peter Sykes, John Kirsh *Cast:* Brian

Deacon, Rivka Noiman, Joseph Shiloah, Niko Nitai, Gadi Rol
► Unusually faithful approach to the life of Jesus Christ in an almost literal adaptation of the Gospel of Luke. Filmed in the Holy Land with an all-Israeli cast (with the exception of Shakespearean actor Deacon, in the lead). Sober and satisfying. Narration by Alexander Scourby.
Dist.: Warner

JESUS CHRIST SUPERSTAR 1973
★★★ G Musical 1:46
Dir: Norman Jewison ***Cast:*** Ted Neeley, Carl Anderson, Yvonne Elliman, Barry Dennen, Bob Bingham, Josh Mostel
► Controversial rock opera version of the final weeks of Jesus's life, including the Last Supper and Crucifixion. Interesting visuals by director Jewison injects contemporary elements by including modern jets and tanks during Judas's production number. Andrew Lloyd Webber/Tim Rice score includes "I Don't Know How to Love Him."
Dist.: MCA

JESUS OF MONTREAL 1989 Canadian
★ R Drama 2:00
☑ Nudity, adult situations, explicit language, violence
Dir: Denys Arcand ***Cast:*** Lothaire Bluteau, Catherine Wilkening, Johanne-Marie Tremblay, Rémy Girard, Robert Lepage, Gilles Pelletier
► In Montreal, actor Bluteau agrees to play Jesus in a staging of the Passion Play. He researches the role and develops a special understanding of it but the play causes a violent controversy. Modernized parable played with intelligence and intensity. Oscar nomination for Best Foreign Film. [S]

JETSONS: THE MOVIE 1990
★★★ G Animation 1:22
Dir: William Hanna, Joseph Barbera ***Cast:*** Voices of: George O'Hanlon, Mel Blanc, Penny Singleton, Tiffany, Patric Zimmerman, Don Messick
► In the distant future, company man George Jetson is promoted by squat boss Mr. Spacely to head a mining operation on a far-off asteroid. While confronting sit-com domestic problems with wife Jane and offspring Judy and Elroy, Jetson must choose between exposing Spacely's environmentally unsound mining practices or keeping his job. Figures have some dimension thanks to computer-assisted shading, but their movements are still simplistic. Feature version of the former TV series is strictly for kids.
Dist.: MCA

JEWEL OF THE NILE, THE 1985
★★★★ PG Action-Adventure 1:46
☑ Brief nudity, explicit language, violence
Dir: Lewis Teague ***Cast:*** Michael Douglas, Kathleen Turner, Danny DeVito, Avner Eisenberg, Spiros Focas
► *Romancing the Stone* alumni Douglas, Turner, and DeVito return six months later to track down yet another valuable "jewel"—this one is lost somewhere in the blistering Sahara desert. Lots of cliff-hanging action, expensive-looking explosions, and good technical credits, but the Douglas/Turner matchup feels a little like a retread. (CC)
Dist.: CBS/Fox

JEZEBEL 1938
★★★ NR Drama 1:44 B&W
Dir: William Wyler ***Cast:*** Bette Davis, Henry Fonda, George Brent, Fay Bainter, Margaret Lindsay, Richard Cromwell
► In pre–Civil War New Orleans, belle Davis causes scandal by wearing a red dress instead of traditional white to the big ball which leads to breakup with beau Fonda. Later, Fonda reenters her life and she gets chance for redemption. Oscar-winning performance by Davis is magnificent. Large-scale production received five other nominations, with Bainter garnering Best Supporting Actress.
Dist.: MGM/UA

JIGSAW MAN, THE 1984 British
★★ PG Espionage 1:31
☑ Explicit language, violence
Dir: Terence Young ***Cast:*** Laurence Olivier, Michael Caine, Susan George, Robert Powell, Eric Sevareid
► Double-crosses run rampant when defector Caine returns to England to recover a microfilmed list of Soviet agents he hid long before. Not to worry: British Secret Service Agent Olivier is on Caine's case. Fourth pairing of the two British superstars makes for an appealing caper. From the best-seller by Dorothea Bennett (Mrs. Terence Young.)
Dist.: HBO

JIMI HENDRIX 1973
★★★★ R Documentary/Biography 1:42
☑ Adult situations, explicit language
Dir: Joe Boyd, John Head, Gary Weis ***Cast:*** Jimi Hendrix, Eric Clapton, Mick Jagger, Pete Townshend, Dick Cavett
► Thoughtful look at the public and private life of guitar genius Jimi Hendrix. Concert footage of the star's flashy stage doings is interspersed with recollections from family and friends like Jagger and Clapton. Opens a window into the confused world in which Hendrix developed his talent.
Dist.: Warner

JIMMY THE KID 1982
★★★★ PG Family 1:26
☑ Explicit language, mild violence
Dir: Gary Nelson ***Cast:*** Gary Coleman, Paul LeMat, Ruth Gordon, Dee Wallace, Don Adams, Cleavon Little
► Tried-and-true caper in which a precocious kid outwits scatterbrained adults. Unhappy, rich, twelve-year-old Coleman learns to have fun and make friends after being kidnapped by bumbling bad guys LeMat, Wallace, and

Gordon. Nonthreatening, above-average family film. Based on the novel by Donald E. Westlake.
Dist.: HBO

JINXED! 1982
★ ★ R Comedy 1:42
☑ Brief nudity, adult situations, explicit language
Dir: Don Siegel *Cast:* Bette Midler, Ken Wahl, Rip Torn, Val Avery
▶ Tacky Vegas singer Midler can't stand her overbearing boyfriend Torn, who then causes blackjack dealer Wahl to run into a streak of bad luck. Midler and Wahl team up to do away with Torn in this uneven stab at black comedy. Plagued by widely publicized production problems.
Dist.: MGM/UA

JOAN OF ARC 1948
★ NR Drama 1:40
Dir: Victor Fleming *Cast:* Ingrid Bergman, Jose Ferrer, J. Carrol Naish, Ward Bond, Francis L. Sullivan
▶ Farm girl Joan of Arc (Bergman) leads French armies against England and is later tried as a heretic and burned at the stake. Opulent spectacle, with stalwart Ingrid breathing life into slack pacing and musty screenplay (based on the Maxwell Anderson play).
Dist.: VidAmerica

JOAN OF PARIS 1942
★ ★ NR Drama B&W
Dir: Robert Stevenson *Cast:* Michele Morgan, Paul Henreid, Thomas Mitchell, Alan Ladd, May Robson, Alexander Granach
▶ During the Nazi occupation, French barmaid Morgan becomes unwittingly involved with a group of downed English flyers trying to get back to Britain, eventually risking her life to bluff the Gestapo. Stirring wartime romance, with Ladd strong in an early supporting role.
Dist.: Turner

JOCK PETERSEN 1975 Australian
☆ R Drama 1:37
☑ Nudity, adult situations, explicit language
Dir: Tim Burstall *Cast:* Jack Thompson, Jacki Weaver, Joey Hohenfels, Amanda Hunt, Wendy Hughes, Arthur Dignam
▶ Married Thompson tosses over his career in electronics to return to college and study the finer things in life. Among these is married tutor Hughes, whose affair with Thompson considerably complicates his academic career. Finely written piece delves into characters, makes them interesting. Also known as *Petersen.*
Dist.: Nelson

JOCKS 1987
★ R Comedy 1:31
☑ Nudity, adult situations, explicit language, adult humor
Dir: Steve Carver *Cast:* Scott Strader, Perry

Lang, Mariska Hargitay, Richard Roundtree, R. G. Armstrong, Christopher Lee
▶ Juvenile pranksters must get their act together and win big tennis tournament or their program will be cancelled. By-the-numbers teen fare won't disappoint genre fans: frantic pacing, idiotic situations, clichéd characters, muscular guys, busty gals, and raunchy shenanigans including strip blackjack game.
Dist.: RCA/Columbia

JOE 1970
★ ★ R Drama 1:47
☑ Nudity, explicit language, violence
Dir: John G. Avildsen *Cast:* Peter Boyle, Dennis Patrick, Susan Sarandon, Audrey Caine, K. Callan, Patrick McDermott
▶ Business exec Patrick accidentally murders his daughter Sarandon's junkie boyfriend and then meets bigoted hard-hat Joe (Boyle), who convinces him, "Plenty of people would consider you a hero." Controversial flower-people-vs.-Archie Bunker drama made big impression when first released. Noted for fine performance by Boyle; early effort from Avildsen, who later directed *Rocky.* Sarandon's film debut.
Dist.: Vestron

JOE COCKER: MAD DOGS AND ENGLISHMEN 1971 British
★ PG Documentary/Music 1:59
☑ Brief nudity, explicit language
Dir: Pierre Adidge *Cast:* Joe Cocker, Leon Russell, Rita Coolidge, Carl Radle, John Price
▶ Rockumentary covers Cocker's 1971 American tour. Concert scenes, including backing from Russell and Coolidge, are electric, but only die-hard Cocker fans will be able to sit through nonmusical sequences of life on the road. Songs include "Delta Lady," "With a Little Help From My Friends," "Feelin' Alright," and "The Letter."
Dist.: RCA/Columbia

JOE KIDD 1972
★ ★ ★ PG Western 1:27
☑ Explicit language, violence
Dir: John Sturges *Cast:* Clint Eastwood, Robert Duvall, John Saxon, Don Stroud, Stella Garcia, James Wainwright
▶ When his ranch in New Mexico is raided, Eastwood joins a posse to catch the Mexican-American guerrillas responsible. But posse leader Duvall proves as dangerous as the fugitives. Despite marvelous locomotive climax, muddled Western is a disappointment. Written by Elmore Leonard.
Dist.: MCA

JOE LOUIS STORY, THE 1953
★ NR Biography/Sports 1:28 B&W
Dir: Robert Gordon *Cast:* Coley Wallace, Paul Stewart, Hilda Simms, James Edwards, John Marley, Anita Ellis
▶ Biography of the great boxing champ (played by heavyweight contender Wallace)

begins with his 1951 defeat by Rocky Marciano and then flashes back to his humble Detroit beginnings, rise from contender to champion, two memorable bouts with German Max Schmeling, and various personal and professional problems. Simplistic portrait of Louis as a beleaguered nice guy who gives up violin lessons to box, but fight footage shows his real talent and ferocity. Ellis winningly sings "I'll Be Around."
Dist.: Goodtimes

JOE VERSUS THE VOLCANO 1990
★★★ **PG Comedy 1:35**
☑ Adult situations, explicit language
Dir: John Patrick Shanley *Cast:* Tom Hanks, Meg Ryan, Lloyd Bridges, Robert Stack, Dan Hedaya, Ossie Davis
► Stricken with a fatal "brain cloud," Hanks quits his job, then is hired by millionaire Bridges to appease South Pacific islanders by jumping into their volcano. The adventure gives him a new lease on life and romance with Bridges's daughter (Ryan, in one of her three roles). *Moonstruck* screenwriter Shanley's directorial debut hits some false notes yet emerges as an upbeat but poignant comic fantasy. Off-center humor neatly played by ace cast. **(CC)**
Dist.: Warner

JOEY 1985
★★★ **PG Drama 1:37**
☑ Adult situations, explicit language, mild violence
Dir: Joseph Ellison *Cast:* Neill Barry, Linda Thorson, Elisa Heinsohn, James Quinn, John Snyder
► Ode to doo-wop music follows the lives of rebellious teen rocker Barry and his once famous 1950s crooner dad Quinn, now an alcoholic who works in a gas station. Music from the Ramones, Stray Cats, The Silhouettes, Jay Hawkins, The Elegants, The Limelights; with songs, "Why Do Fools Fall in Love?," "Boy From New York City," "Get a Job," and more.
Dist.: VidAmerica

JOHN AND JULIE 1955 British
★★ **NR Family 1:22**
Dir: William Fairchild *Cast:* Constance Cummings, Colin Gibson, Lesley Dydley, Noel Middleton, Wilfrid Hyde-White, Peter Sellers
► Two English schoolchildren, determined to see the coronation of Queen Elizabeth II, run away to London (150 miles away) and have a series of adventures en route. Very appealing child actors backed by a swell adult supporting cast make this superior family programming.
Dist.: IVE

JOHNNY ANGEL 1945
★★ **NR Mystery-Suspense 1:19 B&W**
Dir: Edwin L. Marin *Cast:* George Raft, Claire Trevor, Signe Hasso, Lowell Gilmore, Hoagy Carmichael, Marvin Miller

► Well-shot but talky film noir, with Raft playing a hard-bitten sea captain who noses around the New Orleans underworld for the men who killed his father. With the help of glib cabbie Carmichael, Raft uncovers a plot involving $5 million in gold bullion. Strong support from Miller as a mentally unstable villain and Trevor as his untrustworthy wife.
Dist.: Turner

JOHNNY BE GOOD 1988
★★★ **R Comedy 1:26**
☑ Nudity, adult situations, explicit language
Dir: Bud Smith *Cast:* Anthony Michael Hall, Paul Gleason, Robert Downey, Jr., Uma Thurman, Seymour Cassel
► Star high school quarterback Hall is tempted by aggressive college recruiters promising illegal cash, fast cars, and willing cheerleaders. With Downey as his best friend, Thurman as his girl. Cameos by Jim McMahon and Howard Cosell. **(CC)**
Dist.: Orion

JOHNNY BELINDA 1948
★★★★ **NR Drama 1:42 B&W**
Dir: Jean Negulesco *Cast:* Jane Wyman, Lew Ayres, Charles Bickford, Stephen McNally, Agnes Moorehead
► In rural New England, deaf-mute Wyman is befriended by doctor Ayres. She is put on trial when she kills McNally, who raped and impregnated her. Moving drama with an outstanding performance by Wyman that copped Best Actress Oscar.
Dist.: MGM/UA

JOHNNY DANGEROUSLY 1984
★★★ **PG-13 Comedy 1:30**
☑ Explicit language, adult humor
Dir: Amy Heckerling *Cast:* Michael Keaton, Dom DeLuise, Maureen Stapleton, Joe Piscopo, Danny DeVito, Griffin Dunne
► Spoof of gangster movies and the Prohibition era. Keaton plays Johnny Dangerously, a mamma's boy/hoodlum; Dunne, his straight-arrow D.A. brother; Piscopo, a sleazy mobster named Vermin; and Stapleton, Johnny's ailing mother who talks dirty. Dopey slapstick humor, fun for those who appreciate opening song by Weird Al Yankovic. **(CC)**
Dist.: CBS/Fox

JOHNNY GOT HIS GUN 1971
★ **PG War 1:51**
☑ Brief nudity, adult situations, explicit language
Dir: Dalton Trumbo *Cast:* Timothy Bottoms, Jason Robards, Donald Sutherland, Diane Varsi, Kathy Fields
► Frightening and depressing story of young World War I soldier Bottoms who loses most of his body, face, and limbs in a bomb blast; only his mind survives intact. His flashbacks include past experiences with father Robards and girlfriend Fields, and strange visions of Jesus Christ

(Sutherland). Jarring antiwar film was based on Trumbo's novel.
Dist.: Media

JOHNNY GUITAR 1954
★ ★ ★ NR Western 1:50
Dir: Nicholas Ray *Cast:* Joan Crawford, Sterling Hayden, Mercedes McCambridge, Scott Brady, Ward Bond, Ben Cooper, Ernest Borgnine, Royal Dano, John Carradine
▶ Bizarre Western pits Crawford, saloon owner with a shady past, against McCambridge, a two-fisted moral crusader determined to drive her out of Arizona. Hayden is a worn-out gunfighter who observes the duel from the sidelines. Interpreted variously as a Freudian psychodrama, an anti-McCarthy parable, and an auteur classic, film wavers precariously between high camp and enjoyable nonsense.
Dist.: Republic

JOHNNY HANDSOME 1989
★ ★ ★ R Action-Adventure 1:33
☑ Nudity, adult situations, explicit language, violence
Dir: Walter Hill *Cast:* Mickey Rourke, Scott Wilson, Ellen Barkin, Lance Henrikson, Morgan Freeman, Elizabeth McGovern, Forest Whitaker
▶ Rourke is an inarticulate crook with a horribly scarred mug. While he is in prison, plastic surgeon Whitaker gives him a new face, but policeman Freeman wonders: will it make him a new man? Once free, Rourke romances McGovern and executes a robbery that turns into a gunfight. Freeman and Whitaker are the best things about this sordid, hard-driving melodrama. **(CC)**
Dist.: IVE

JOHNNY TIGER 1966
☆ NR Drama 1:40
Dir: Paul Wendkos *Cast:* Robert Taylor, Geraldine Brooks, Chad Everett, Brenda Scott, Marc Lawrence, Ford Rainey
▶ Professor Taylor and his three kids move to the Florida Everglades, where he attempts to teach modern ways to the Seminole Indians. Chief Rainey opposes him, but his grandson Everett, who falls in love with Taylor's daughter Scott, is more sympathetic. Well-intentioned if hardly earth-shattering drama features a good performance by Taylor.
Dist.: Republic

JOHNNY TREMAIN 1957
★ ★ ★ NR Drama 1:20
Dir: Robert Stevenson *Cast:* Hal Stalmaster, Luana Patten, Jeff York, Sebastian Cabot, Richard Beymer, Walter Sande
▶ In 1773 Boston, silversmith's apprentice Stalmaster, victimized by British nobleman Cabot, is persuaded by Paul Revere to join the revolutionary movement. Involving Disney adaptation of Esther Forbes's novel explains the war for independence in human terms; accurate,

exciting production is perfect for the entire family.
Dist.: Buena Vista

JO JO DANCER, YOUR LIFE IS CALLING 1986
★ ★ ★ R Comedy/Drama 1:37
☑ Nudity, adult situations, explicit language
Dir: Richard Pryor *Cast:* Richard Pryor, Debbie Allen, Carmen McRae, Diahnne Abbott, Barbara Williams
▶ This is your life, Richard Pryor. Extremely personal account of funny man's near-fatal accident freebasing cocaine. Half dead, the spirit of Jo Jo Dancer rises from the hospital bed to relive his life and discover the reason for his drug dependency. Odd mixture of maudlin drama, self-absorbed fantasy, and hard reality enlivened by a few uproarious monologues.
Dist.: RCA

JOKE OF DESTINY, A 1984 Italian
☆ PG Comedy 1:45
☑ Adult situations, explicit language
Dir: Lina Wertmuller *Cast:* Ugo Tognazzi, Piera Degli Esposti, Gastone Moschin, Renzo Montagnani, Valeria Golino
▶ Tognazzi, the popular Italian comedian, stars in a more-than-usually confused Wertmuller mix of sex, politics and slapstick. An Italian politician is trapped inside his terrorist-proof limousine when it breaks down in front of rival Tognazzi's house. Tognazzi's wacky wife Esposti and amorous daughter Golino trigger confusion and embarrassment. Slightly better if viewer has some familiarity with Italian politics. Complete title is *A Joke of Destiny, Lying in Wait Around the Corner Like a Bandit.* [S]
Dist.: Warner

JOLSON SINGS AGAIN 1949
★ ★ ★ NR Biography/Musical 1:36
Dir: Henry Levin *Cast:* Larry Parks, Barbara Hale, William Demarest, Bill Goodwin, Ludwig Donath, Tamara Shayne
▶ Sequel to popular musical biography picks up the singer's life after his divorce. Singing for the troops overseas during World War II, Jolson (Parks) falls in love with nurse Hale. After their wedding, work begins on the original picture, setting up unusual scene in which Parks as Jolson meets Parks as Parks. Once again, story is merely an excuse for a tune-a-thon, with "Give My Regards to Broadway," "You Made Me Love You," and "I'm Looking Over a Four-Leaf Clover" among the many numbers.
Dist.: RCA/Columbia

JOLSON STORY, THE 1946
★ ★ ★ NR Biography/Musical 2:08
Dir: Alfred E. Green *Cast:* Larry Parks, Evelyn Keyes, William Demarest, Bill Goodwin, Ludwig Donath, Tamara Shayne
▶ Parks plays singing great Al Jolson, as picture charts his rise through vaudeville to top of pop charts and star role in *The Jazz Singer*, the

first talkie feature. Jolson assisted with the production and dubbed the songs in this sanitized biopic. Resulting sing-along concentrates on the many tunes such as "Swanee," "My Mammy," "April Showers," "You Made Me Love You," and "By the Light of the Silvery Moon."
Dist.: RCA/Columbia

JONATHAN LIVINGSTON SEAGULL 1973
★★ G Drama 1:55
Dir: Hall Bartlett ***Cast:***
▶ Based on Richard Bach's early-seventies best-selling book. Allegorical tale of a seagull who forsakes his flock to fly to new heights and learn the meaning of perfection. Shot from a spectacular bird's-eye view. With effective music by Neil Diamond.
Dist.: Paramount

JOSEPHA 1982 French
★★ R Drama 1:54
☑ Nudity, adult situations, explicit language
Dir: Christopher Frank ***Cast:*** Miou-Miou, Claude Brasseur, Bruno Cremer, Anne Laure Meury, Francois Perrot
▶ Marriage falls apart between struggling actor Brasseur and long-suffering wife Miou-Miou. She leaves him and has affair with the gentle and wealthy Cremer but can't quite get her ex-husband completely out of her life. Sincerely felt, well-acted, but overlong effort is ultimately a bit wearying. Dubbed.
Dist.: RCA/Columbia

JOSEPH ANDREWS 1977 British
★ R Comedy 1:39
☑ Nudity, adult situations, explicit language, adult humor
Dir: Tony Richardson ***Cast:*** Ann-Margret, Peter Firth, Michael Hordern, Beryl Reid, Jim Dale, Natalie Ogle, John Gielgud, Hugh Griffith, Peggy Ashcroft
▶ Eighteenth-century footman Firth becomes the object of Lady Booby's (Ann-Margret) amorous attentions in a farcical plot of escalating mistaken identities. Gorgeously mounted adaptation of Henry Fielding's novel lacks the bawdy humor and rapid pacing of director Richardson's earlier *Tom Jones*, but Reid is outstanding as Mrs. Slipslop.
Dist.: Paramount

JOSHUA 1976
☆ PG Western 1:30
☑ Violence
Dir: Larry Spangler ***Cast:*** Fred Williamson, Isela Vega, Calvin Bartlett, Brenda Venus, Stacy Newton, Kathryn Jackson
▶ Black veteran Williamson returns home after the Civil War to learn his mother has been murdered by a gang. A homesteader whose wife was also victimized joins him for a mission of revenge. Below-par oater with a screenplay by Williamson. Poor production values, predictable story. Also known as *The Black Rider.*
Dist.: Magnum

JOSHUA THEN AND NOW 1985 Canadian
★★★ R Comedy 1:58
☑ Nudity, adult situations, explicit language
Dir: Ted Kotcheff ***Cast:*** James Woods, Alan Arkin, Gabrielle Lazure, Michael Sarrazin, Linda Sorensen
▶ Joshua Shapiro (Woods), a Jewish-Canadian writer, recalls his life and times through flashbacks. Joshua then: ex-gangster dad Arkin tells him about sex and uninhibited mom does a strip-tease at his bar mitzvah. Joshua now: caught in a trumped-up homosexual scandal and abandoned by aristocratic gentile wife Lazure. Based on Mordechai Richler's semiautobiographical novel. **(CC)**
Dist.: CBS/Fox

JOUR DE FETE 1948 French
☆ NR Comedy 1:10 B&W
Dir: Jacques Tati ***Cast:*** Jacques Tati, Guy Decomble, Paul Frankeur, Santa Relli, Maine Vallee, Roger Rafal
▶ Tati plays a rural French postman who sets about modernizing his system of mail delivery after being inspired by a film about the U.S. Postal Service. His efforts trigger mild chaos in a little French village preparing to celebrate Bastille Day. Near-silent directoral debut by comic master Tati is technically rough, but filled with superbly timed sight gags and wry observations of human behavior. [S]
Dist.: Various

JOURNEY BACK TO OZ 1972
★★★★ G Animation 1:30
Dir: Hal Sutherland ***Cast:*** Bill Cosby, voices of Liza Minnelli, Margaret Hamilton, Jack E. Leonard, Paul Lynde, Ethel Merman, Mickey Rooney, Rise Stevens, Danny Thomas, Mel Blanc, Milton Berle
▶ Cosby hosts animated sequel to *The Wizard of Oz* in which Dorothy returns to the enchanted land only to find it in the grip of the Wicked Witch of the West. Crude animation makes remarkable lineup of star voices the main reason for seeing this one. Big kick is Minnelli as Dorothy, her mother's role in the live film, and original witch Hamilton as Aunt Em. Has songs, but not an "Over the Rainbow" in the bunch.
Dist.: MGM/UA

JOURNEY INTO FEAR 1942
★★ NR Mystery-Suspense 1:11 B&W
Dir: Norman Foster ***Cast:*** Orson Welles, Joseph Cotten, Dolores Del Rio, Ruth Warrick, Agnes Moorehead, Everett Sloane
▶ American munitions expert Cotten becomes the target of Nazi assassins in Istanbul; Turkish spy Welles assures him he'll be safe aboard a rusty freighter, but as the ship leaves port, Cotten sees that the killers are also on board. Taut, realistic thriller (scripted by Welles and Cotten from Eric Ambler's best-seller) is filled with brilliant touches. Welles was re-

placed as director by Foster after filming started.
Dist.: Turner

JOURNEY OF NATTY GANN, THE 1985
★ ★ ★ ★ PG Action-Adventure/Family
1:45
☑ Explicit language, mild violence
Dir: Jeremy Paul Kagan *Cast:* Meredith Salenger, John Cusack, Lainie Kazan, Verna Bloom, Scatman Crothers
▶ Feisty fourteen-year-old tomboy Natty Gann (Salenger) embarks on a cross-country journey to find her father, sent to Seattle on a logging job. She rides the rails with teen drifter Cusack, escapes a train wreck, and thwarts a charging bull, accompanied by a friendly wolf. Authentic Depression-era setting helps this spirited Disney adventure appeal to sophisticated youths without sacrificing family values.
Dist.: Buena Vista

JOURNEY TO THE CENTER OF THE EARTH 1959
★ ★ ★ NR Sci-Fi 2:09
Dir: Henry Levin *Cast:* James Mason, Pat Boone, Arlene Dahl, Diane Baker, Peter Ronson
▶ Scientist Mason, his star pupil Boone, widow Dahl, Nordic assistant Ronson and his pet duck Gertrude attempt an underground expedition to the center of the earth. They encounter landslides, volcanic tremors, giant reptiles, a subterranean shipwreck, the lost city of Atlantis, and an evil Count during their arduous trek. Perfect casting, top cinematography and special effects, first-rate Bernard Herrmann score enhance a Jules Verne adaptation that delivers fun, fantasy, and adventure. (CC)
Dist.: CBS/Fox

JOURNEY TO THE CENTER OF TIME 1967
★ ★ NR Sci-Fi 1:22
Dir: David L. Hewitt *Cast:* Scott Brady, Anthony Eisley, Gigi Perreau, Abraham Sofaer, Poupee Gamin, Lyle Waggoner
▶ Scientist Sofaer and his associates develop a time machine that accidentally beams them into an alien-invaded seventieth-century Earth. Traveling backwards is no picnic either, thanks to some nasty dinosaurs. Cheesy and cheap. Director Hewitt handled this theme much more effectively in his screenplay for 1964's *The Time Travelers.*
Dist.: Academy

JOURNEY TO THE FAR SIDE OF THE SUN
1969 British
★ ★ G Sci-Fi 1:39
Dir: Robert Parrish *Cast:* Roy Thinnes, Ian Hendry, Patrick Wymark, Lynn Loring, Loni von Friedl, Herbert Lom
▶ Scientists discover a new planet hidden behind the sun; astronauts Thinnes and Hendry are sent to explore it. A crash landing leaves them trapped in a strange new world. Good

special effects and a devious trick ending highlight this tidy low-budget effort.
Dist.: MCA

JOURNEY TO THE 7TH PLANET 1961
☆ NR Sci-Fi 1:20
Dir: Sidney Pink *Cast:* John Agar, Greta Thyssen, Ann Smyrner, Mimi Heinrich, Carl Ottosen, Ove Sprogoe
▶ At the dawn of the twenty-first century, Agar leads five-man United Nations expedition to Uranus. Planet's bitterly cold landscape hides a terrifying monster who preys on the astronauts' fears with startling illusions. Dated special effects and dubbing of Danish cast members lessen the story's impact.
Dist.: HBO

JOY OF LIVING 1938
★ ★ NR Musical 1:31 B&W
Dir: Tay Garnett *Cast:* Irene Dunne, Douglas Fairbanks, Jr., Alice Brady, Guy Kibbee, Eric Blore, Lucille Ball
▶ Stage star Dunne is taken advantage of by her greedy family. Handsome Bostonian Fairbanks seeks to change this state of affairs while winning Dunne's heart. Slim story provides opportunities for stars to shine. Heavenly Jerome Kern/Dorothy Fields score includes "A Heavenly Party," "Just Let Me Look at You," and "What's Good About Goodnight?"
Dist.: Turner

JOY OF SEX 1984
★ R Comedy 1:33
☑ Nudity, explicit language, adult humor
Dir: Martha Coolidge *Cast:* Michelle Meyrink, Cameron Dye, Christopher Lloyd, Charles Van Eman
▶ The kids at Southern California's Richard M. Nixon High School hold farting contests and try to lose their virginity. Tasteless teen comedy no worse than others in the genre, but that's not saying much. Bears no resemblance to the best-selling book of the same title.
Dist.: Paramount

JOYRIDE 1977
★ ★ ★ R Drama 1:32
☑ Nudity, adult situations, explicit language
Dir: Joseph Ruben *Cast:* Desi Arnaz, Jr., Robert Carradine, Melanie Griffith, Anne Lockhart, Tom Ligon
▶ Disenchanted young Californians Arnaz, Carradine, and Griffith dump their boring jobs and head to Alaska for adventure. When their money runs out, they rob a bank, take Lockhart hostage, and flee from the police. Well-acted, good-looking, low-budget production.
Dist.: Vestron

JOYSTICKS 1983
★ R Comedy 1:28
☑ Nudity, explicit language, adult humor
Dir: Greydon Clark *Cast:* Joe Don Baker, Leif Green, Jim Greenleaf, Scott McGinnis
▶ Offensive low-grade farce features Baker as a parent who disapproves of decadent teen-

age fun at the local video arcade. With Green as the nerd and Greenleaf as an overweight slob who redeems himself through video game expertise. Originally titled *Video Madness*.
Dist.: Vestron

JUAREZ 1939
★★ NR Biography 2:12 B&W
Dir: William Dieterle ***Cast:*** Paul Muni, Bette Davis, Brian Aherne, Claude Rains, John Garfield, Donald Crisp
► True story of Mexican Benito Pablo Juarez (Muni), who led revolution against Emperor Aherne, Empress Davis, and Napoleon III (Rains), the power behind the throne. Epic-scaled and entertaining; Muni and Rains are terrific.
Dist.: Key

JUBAL 1956
★★★ NR Western 1:41
Dir: Delmer Daves ***Cast:*** Glenn Ford, Ernest Borgnine, Rod Steiger, Valerie French, Felicia Farr, Noah Beery, Jr.
► Ford, a Wyoming drifter, signs on with Steiger's ranch, attracting Steiger's wife Farr. Jealous Borgnine claims that Ford and Farr are lovers, leading to a series of tense shoot-outs. Gloomy, adult Western will make more sense to viewers familiar with *Othello*.
Dist.: RCA/Columbia

JUBILEE TRAIL 1954
★ NR Western 1:43
Dir: Joseph Kane ***Cast:*** Vera Ralston, Joan Leslie, Forrest Tucker, John Russell, Ray Middleton, Pat O'Brien
► A wagon train full of disparate characters makes its way from Louisiana to Califonia. Among the migrants are showgirl Ralston, alcoholic physician O'Brien, and Leslie, whose brother Middleton objects to her marriage. Excellent ensemble enlivens plot you've seen before.
Dist.: Republic

JUDGE AND THE ASSASSIN, THE 1975
French
☆ NR Drama 2:10
☑ Adult situations
Dir: Bertrand Tavernier ***Cast:*** Philippe Noiret, Michel Galabru, Isabelle Huppert, Jean-Claude Brialy, Renee Faure, Jean Bretonniere
► Amid political turmoil in nineteenth-century France, judge Noiret gets the unwelcome task of determining the mental state of Galabru, a vicious child-killer who may be feigning insanity. Critically hailed, deceptively simple story is powerful and incisive, though not for all tastes.
[S]
Dist.: Corinth

JUDGEMENT DAY 1989
★ PG-13 Horror 1:33
☑ Explicit language, violence
Dir: Ferde Grofé, Jr. ***Cast:*** Kenneth McLeod, David Anthony Smith, Monte Markham, Cesar Romero, Gloria Hayes, Peter Mark Richman
► While vacationing in Central America, young Americans McLeod and Smith visit a village where Satan rules once a year, thanks to a deal struck by Romero. The locals traditionally evacuate for the day, but the friends are endangered when they get stuck in town. Average horror flick.
Dist.: Magnum

JUDGE PRIEST 1934
★★★ NR Comedy 1:19 B&W
Dir: John Ford ***Cast:*** Will Rogers, Henry B. Walthall, Tom Brown, Anita Louise, Rochelle Hudson, Hattie McDaniel
► Southern man faces assault charges in a trial rather than reveal he's the father of "orphan" Louise. Slim plot is an undemanding framework for enjoyable Rogers vehicle. As a no-nonsense judge, the famous humorist offers wry observations on small-town foibles. Sentimental comedy's beautifully realized atmosphere is marred only by some racist caricatures. Director Ford remade story in 1953 as *The Sun Shines Bright*.
Dist.: Various

JUDGMENT AT NUREMBERG 1961
★★★★ NR Drama 3:09 B&W
Dir: Stanley Kramer ***Cast:*** Spencer Tracy, Burt Lancaster, Richard Widmark, Marlene Dietrich, Judy Garland, Maximilian Schell, Montgomery Clift, William Shatner
► After World War II, American judge Tracy presides over the Nuremberg war crimes trials, resisting pressure for a "not guilty" verdict as testimony from Holocaust survivors Garland and Clift (both Oscar nominated) proves damning. Absorbing and intelligent, if overlong, examination of the issues. Phenomenal cast includes Schell's mesmerizing, Oscar-winning turn as the German defense attorney. A Best Picture nominee.
Dist.: MGM/UA

JUDGMENT IN BERLIN 1988
★★ PG Drama 1:32
☑ Adult situations, mild violence
Dir: Leo Penn ***Cast:*** Martin Sheen, Sean Penn, Sam Wanamaker, Max Gail, Jurgen Heinrich, Heinz Hoenig
► True story of East German couple who hijacked Polish plane to U.S. base in West Berlin. Seeking to avoid an international incident, American authorities summon judge Sheen to decide the hijackers' fate. Penn (whose father directed) shines in the small but key part as a witness.
Dist.: RCA/Columbia

JUGGERNAUT 1974 British
★★★ PG Action-Adventure 1:49
☑ Explicit language, violence
Dir: Richard Lester ***Cast:*** Richard Harris, Omar Sharif, David Hemmings, Anthony Hopkins, Shirley Knight, Ian Holm

▶ Blackmailer plants several bombs aboard a luxury liner; Harris and a band of demolitions experts race against time to defuse them. Tense, realistic thriller is a nerve-wracking battle of wits. Strong cast performs capably. (CC)
Dist.: Key

JULES AND JIM 1962 French
★★ NR Drama 1:50 B&W
Dir: François Truffaut ***Cast:*** Oskar Werner, Jeanne Moreau, Henri Serre, Marie Dubois, Vanna Urbino
▶ Best friends Werner and Serre share a love for Moreau in pre–World War I France. An unusual three-way triangle unfolds with ultimately tragic consequences. Magnificently directed by Truffaut. The charismatic and sexy Moreau is completely convincing as the restless object of two men's obsession. [S]
Dist.: CBS/Fox

JULIA 1977
★★★★ PG Drama 1:57
☑ Adult situations, mild violence
Dir: Fred Zinnemann ***Cast:*** Jane Fonda, Vanessa Redgrave, Maximilian Schell, Jason Robards, Meryl Streep
▶ Vibrant and mesmerizing story adapted from a chapter in Lillian Hellman's popular memoir *Pentimento*. Oscar-winner Redgrave plays Julia, Hellman's wealthy childhood friend, who becomes a political activist in 1930s Europe and involves Lillian (Fonda) in the intrigue. Robards also snagged an Oscar for his role as mystery writer Dashiell Hammett. In her film debut, Streep appears briefly as Hellman's friend.
Dist.: CBS/Fox

JULIA AND JULIA 1988 Italian
★ R Mystery-Suspense 1:37
☑ Nudity, adult situations, explicit language
Dir: Peter Del Monte ***Cast:*** Kathleen Turner, Sting, Gabriel Byrne, Gabriele Ferzetti, Angela Goodwin
▶ Psychological thriller stars Turner as the beautiful, long-widowed Julia, still trying to forget husband Byrne's tragic death. When she comes home one day to find him alive and tending to their supposed son, the intrigue has only just begun. Promising premise gets muddled in its own illogical plot turns. Sting shows up as Turner's ominous lover. Originally shot on video. (CC)
Dist.: CBS/Fox

JULIET OF THE SPIRITS 1965 Italian
★ NR Drama 2:28
Dir: Federico Fellino ***Cast:*** Giulietta Masina, Sandra Milo, Mario Pisu, Valentina Cortese, Lou Gilbert, Sylva Koscina
▶ Oppressed by life with unfaithful husband Pisu, thirtysomething housewife Masina takes refuge in a world of fantasy. Colorful, outrageous extravaganza is fully pleasing, though far outside the ordinary. Masina (director Fellini's wife) proves she is one of the most fascinating women in cinema. [S]
Dist.: Various

JULIUS CAESAR 1953
★★ NR Drama 2:01 B&W
Dir: Joseph L. Mankiewicz ***Cast:*** Marlon Brando, James Mason, Louis Calhern, John Gielgud, Deborah Kerr, Edmond O'Brien, Greer Garson
▶ Notable Hollywood rendering of Shakespeare's tragedy features the always-fascinating Brando stretching his acting muscles as Marc Antony, confidante to doomed Roman emperor Julius Caesar (Calhern). Among the all-star cast, Gielgud is another standout as Cassius. Received five Oscar nominations, including Best Picture and Actor (Brando), winning for Art Direction. Produced by John Houseman, with a screenplay by the director.
Dist.: MGM/UA

JUMPIN' JACK FLASH 1986
★★★★ R Mystery-Suspense/Comedy 1:45
☑ Adult situations, explicit language, mild violence
Dir: Penny Marshall ***Cast:*** Whoopi Goldberg, Stephen Collins, John Wood, Carol Kane, Annie Potts, Jon Lovitz
▶ New York City bank computer programmer Goldberg receives messages on her screen from spy trapped behind the Iron Curtain. When she tries to aid him, she's caught up in chases and intrigue. Upbeat comedy/thriller with bright moments and blue language from Whoopi. The computer terminal relationship between Whoopi and the unseen spy is novel and affecting. Oddball cast of co-workers adds some spice. Feature directorial debut of Marshall. (CC)
Dist.: CBS/Fox

JUNGLE BOOK, THE 1942
★★★ NR Drama/Family 1:55
Dir: Zoltan Korda ***Cast:*** Sabu, Joseph Calleia, John Qualen, Rosemary DeCamp, Ralph Byrd, Frank Puglia
▶ Rudyard Kipling's classic tale of Mowgli (Sabu), the boy raised by wolves and then introduced to the public in India. Mowgli grows disenchanted with civilized but violent society and decides to return to the jungle. Wonderful family fare, remade in 1967 as an animated Disney film.
Dist.: Various

JUNGLE RAIDERS 1986 Italian
★ PG-13 Action-Adventure 1:42
☑ Adult situations, explicit language, violence
Dir: Anthony M. Dawson (Antonio Margheriti) ***Cast:*** Christopher Connelly, Marina Costa, Lee Van Cleef, Alan Collins, Dario Pontonutti
▶ In 1938 Malaya, museum curator Costa hires dashing mercenary Connelly to retrieve

the Ruby of Gloom, a jewel hidden in booby-trapped caves. Routine treatment of predictable action fare hampered by sloppy dubbing and poor special effects.
Dist.: MGM/UA

JUNGLE WARRIORS 1984 German/Mexican
☆ **R Action-Adventure 1:33**
☑ Nudity, explicit language, violence
Dir: Ernst R. von Theumer *Cast:* Nina Van Pallandt, Paul Smith, Marjoe Gortner, John Vernon, Woody Strode, Sybil Danning
▶ A fashion crew's plane is forced to land in the jungle by evil drug traders. Danning, the drug king's sister, tortures the models, who are also molested by horny locals and then caught in the middle of a battle between the druggies, the mob, and the feds. Lame dialogue with performances to match; cheap thrills for the exploitation crowd.
Dist.: Media

JUNIOR BONNER 1972
★★★ **PG Drama 1:40**
☑ Adult situations, explicit language
Dir: Sam Peckinpah *Cast:* Steve McQueen, Robert Preston, Ida Lupino, Ben Johnson, Joe Don Baker, Barbara Leigh
▶ Aging rodeo rider McQueen returns to his small home-town after many years to discover that his parents, Preston and Lupino, are estranged and his brother Baker, now a phony real estate wheeler-dealer, has subdivided the family homestead. During a local rodeo, brief fling with Leigh, and barroom brawl, McQueen shines as the cowboy who learns you can't go home on the range again. Unusual and whimsical effort from director Peckinpah, known for his essays in violence.
Dist.: CBS/Fox

JUPITER'S THIGH 1984 French
★ **PG Comedy 1:36**
☑ Brief nudity, adult situations
Dir: Philippe de Broca *Cast:* Annie Girardot, Philippe Noiret, Francis Perrin, Catherine Alric
▶ Caper comedy has Girardot as a police inspector on her honeymoon in Greece getting involved with the theft of ancient statuary. Sequel to *Dear Inspector* has outrageous escapes and vigorous chases over gorgeous Greek countryside. Girardot is delightful. Also known as *Somebody's Stolen the Thigh of Jupiter.* Ⓢ
Dist.: Nelson

JUST A GIGOLO 1979 German
☆ **R Drama 1:45**
☑ Nudity, adult situations, explicit language
Dir: David Hemmings *Cast:* David Bowie, Marlene Dietrich, Sydne Rome, Kim Novak, David Hemmings, Maria Schell
▶ Dietrich's last film appearance. She sings the title song, and makes more of an impression in her three minutes on screen than anything else in the film. Story has Bowie returning to Germany from World War I to become a

male escort to the likes of Novak in Weimar's moral sink. Soundtrack is best, with terrific twenties tunes from Manhattan Transfer. Cut down from longer, supposedly more coherent European version.
Dist.: Water Bearer

JUST ANOTHER MISSING KID 1981 Canadian
★★★★ **NR Documentary/MFTV 1:27**
☑ Adult situations, explicit language
Dir: John Zaritsky *Cast:* Narrated by Ian Parker
▶ A disturbing true story: Canadian teenager Eric Wilson disappears in the U.S. and his family hires a private eye because authorities are indifferent to "just another missing kid." Wilson was murdered and the killers eventually caught but given lenient sentences. Fascinating indictment of flawed U.S. justice system won Best Documentary Oscar.
Dist.: CBC Enterprises

JUST AROUND THE CORNER 1938
★★ **NR Musical 1:10 B&W**
Dir: Irving Cummings *Cast:* Shirley Temple, Joan Davis, Charles Farrell, Amanda Duff, Bill Robinson, Bert Lahr
▶ The Depression drops Temple's father Farrell from architect to maintenance man. However, the plucky youngster manages to befriend a millionaire and convince him to finance dad. Cheerful Temple vehicle features duets with Robinson and Lahr to songs like "I'll Be Lucky With You," "I Love to Walk in the Rain," and "This Is a Happy Little Ditty." (CC)
Dist.: CBS/Fox

JUST BETWEEN FRIENDS 1986
★★★★ **PG-13 Drama 1:51**
☑ Brief nudity, adult situations, explicit language
Dir: Allan Burns *Cast:* Mary Tyler Moore, Christine Lahti, Ted Danson, Sam Waterston, Jane Geer
▶ Moore is unaware that her new pal Lahti is having an affair with her husband Danson. When tragedy strikes, the friendship is tested by the revelation that Lahti is pregnant with Danson's child. Old-fashioned, agreeable mixture of laughter and tears. Lahti is the standout among four good performances.
Dist.: HBO

JUSTINE 1969
★ **R Drama 1:55**
☑ Nudity, adult situations
Dir: George Cukor *Cast:* Anouk Aimee, Dirk Bogarde, Robert Forster, Anna Karina, John Vernon, Michael York
▶ Aimee, a Jewish woman living in Egypt, attempts to send weapons to Palestine Jews. Also involved in the plan: her husband Vernon, her lover York, York's girlfriend Karina, and her British friend Bogarde. Atmospheric, beauti-

fully shot adaptation of Lawrence Durrell's *The Alexandria Quartet.* (CC)
Dist.: CBS/Fox

JUST ONE OF THE GUYS 1985
★★★★ PG-13 Comedy 1:40
☑ Brief nudity, explicit language, mild violence, adult humor
Dir: Lisa Gottlieb ***Cast:*** Joyce Hyser, Clayton Rohner, Billy Jacoby, Toni Hudson, William Zabka, Leigh McCloskey
▸ Cute high school journalism student Hyser finds she isn't taken seriously so she decides to disguise herself as a boy. In her male incarnation, she befriends nerd Rohner, bolsters his confidence, and then falls for him. Teen *Tootsie* has some funny moments ("Of course you're confused," Hyser's little brother tells her, "you're wearing my underwear.") but suffers from obvious plotting. (CC)
Dist.: RCA/Columbia

JUST TELL ME WHAT YOU WANT 1980
★★ R Comedy 1:53
☑ Brief nudity, adult situations, explicit language
Dir: Sidney Lumet ***Cast:*** Ali MacGraw, Alan King, Peter Weller, Myrna Loy, Dina Merrill, Tony Roberts, Keenan Wynn
▸ TV producer MacGraw tries to break free of her powerful mogul beau King by marrying young writer Weller. But King outmaneuvers her at every turn and wins her back. Cynical romantic comedy with an amusingly bombastic performance by King and able support from Loy, Merrill, Roberts, and Wynn. Screenplay by Jay Presson Allan was based on her novel.
Dist.: Warner

JUST THE WAY YOU ARE 1984
★★★★ PG Drama 1:35
☑ Nudity, adult situations
Dir: Edouard Molinaro ***Cast:*** Kristy McNichol, Michael Ontkean, Robert Carradine, Lance Guest, Timothy Daly, Kaki Hunter
▸ Unhappy disabled musician McNichol takes skiing vacation and has doctor put a cast on her leg to disguise her condition. Life turns into a glorious adventure and she meets Mr. Right (Ontkean)—but how will he react when he learns the truth? Spunky Kristy takes the potential sappiness out of the story and makes a very sympathetic heroine. (CC)
Dist.: MGM/UA

KAGEMUSHA 1980 Japanese
★★ PG Action-Adventure 2:39
☑ Violence
Dir: Akira Kurosawa ***Cast:*** Tatsuya Nakadai, Tsutomu Yamazaki, Kenichi Hagiwara, Kota Yui, Hideji Otaki
▸ In sixteenth-century Japan, small-time crook Nakadai, lookalike for a great warlord, is used by the clan to impersonate the leader after his death. Nakadai slowly grows into his new role. Grand epic from Japan's master director combines magnificent battle scenes and beautiful color photography with moments of psychological insight. Loses some impact on TV. [S]
Dist.: Magnetic

KAMIKAZE '89 1982 German
☆ NR Drama 1:46
☑ Nudity, adult situations, explicit language, violence
Dir: Wolf Gremm ***Cast:*** Rainer Werner Fassbinder, Gunther Kaufmann, Boy Gobert, Arnold Marquis, Richy Mueller, Brigitte Mira
▸ Weird film about a bomb placed in skyscraper is supposed to take place in a then-futuristic Germany of 1989. There is some question as to whether the bomb is real or not; but that is far from the only puzzling aspect of this mystifying anti-utopia, where alchohol is banned and all media are ruled by a single conglomerate. Main reason to watch is for performance by Fassbinder as a police lieutenant, his last as an actor. Based on a book by Per Wahloo. [S]
Dist.: CBS/Fox

KANDYLAND 1987
★ R Drama 1:29
☑ Nudity, adult situations, explicit language, violence
Dir: Robert Schnitzer ***Cast:*** Kim Evenson, Charles Laulette, Sandahl Bergman, Cole Stevens, Bruce Baum
▸ Perky Evenson, bored with her dry-cleaning job, gets the stage bug when she enters a bikini contest. She becomes a stripper under Bergman's tutelege but almost loses the love of Laulette, her hot-tempered boyfriend. Glossy T & A vehicle for former *Playboy* Playmate Evenson.
Dist.: New World

KANGAROO 1987 Australian
☆ R Drama 1:45
☑ Brief nudity, adult situations, explicit language, violence
Dir: Tim Burstall ***Cast:*** Colin Friels, Judy Davis, John Walton, Julie Nihill, Hugh Keays-Byrne
▸ Controversial English writer Friels and his German-born wife Davis move to Australia in the 1920s. Friels falls under the spell of right-wing radical leader Keays-Byrne but later turns against him. Good performances by real-life husband and wife Friels and Davis, but adaptation of a semiautobiographical D. H. Lawrence novel is torturously talky.
Dist.: MCA

KANSAN, THE 1943
★★ NR Western 1:19 B&W
Dir: George Archainbaud ***Cast:*** Richard Dix, Jane Wyatt, Victor Jory, Albert Dekker, Eugene Pallette, Robert Armstrong
▸ Pausing in Kansas on his way west, Dix finds himself town marshal after he thwarts an attack by the James gang. While romancing Wyatt, he goes on to battle Dekker, a corrupt

banker who thinks he's got the town in his pocket. Satisfactory sagebrush saga.
Dist.: KVC

KANSAS 1988
★ ★ ★ R Drama 1:48

☑ Adult situations, explicit language, mild violence

Dir: David Stevens *Cast:* Matt Dillon, Andrew McCarthy, Leslie Hope, Alan Toy, Brent Jennings, Andy Romano

▶ McCarthy meets vagrant Dillon and finds himself passive participant in latter's bank robbery. They separate and McCarthy becomes involved with farmer's daughter Hope; fugitive Dillon's return threatens McCarthy's future. Authentic cornbelt ambiance provides background for young leads to stretch their talents. (CC)
Dist.: Media

KANSAS CITY CONFIDENTIAL 1953
★ ★ NR Mystery-Suspense 1:38 B&W

Dir: Phil Karlson *Cast:* John Payne, Coleen Gray, Preston Foster, Jack Elam, Neville Brand, Lee Van Cleef

▶ Foster masterminds a robbery in which his crooks' identities are protected by masks. Florist Payne, unjustly accused of the crime, tracks the gang to Mexico for revenge. He must pose as a con to break into the gang. Small-scale film noir is sordid, compelling, and at times preposterous. Has many of the qualities—and drawbacks—of 1950s pulp thrillers.
Dist.: Goodtimes

KARATE KID, THE 1984
★ ★ ★ ★ ★ PG Drama 2:07

☑ Explicit language, violence

Dir: John G. Avildsen *Cast:* Ralph Macchio, Noriyuki "Pat" Morita, Elisabeth Shue, Martin Kove, William Zabka

▶ New Jersey teen Macchio moves to Southern California and runs afoul of martial arts bully. Kindly Oriental handyman (Oscar-nominated Morita) comes to the rescue with karate lessons, training Macchio for a karate tournament showdown with his tormentor. The Macchio-Morita relationship is warm and appealing. A winner; you'll cheer for the underdog. (CC)
Dist.: RCA/Columbia

KARATE KID, PART II, THE 1986
★ ★ ★ ★ ★ PG Drama 1:53

☑ Explicit language, violence

Dir: John G. Avildsen *Cast:* Ralph Macchio, Noriyuki "Pat" Morita, Nobu McCarthy, Danny Kamekona, Tamlyn Tomita, Yuji Okumoto

▶ With Macchio in tow, Morita returns to his native Okinawa to visit his dying father, resolve a thirty-year-old feud, and resume a romance with his childhood sweetheart (McCarthy). Macchio finds love of his own with the charming Tomita and also battles a bully.

Sequel repeats likable characters and inspiring, warmhearted plotting. (CC)
Dist.: RCA/Columbia

KARATE KID, PART III, THE 1989
★ ★ ★ ★ PG Action-Adventure 1:51

☑ Explicit language, violence

Dir: John Alvidsen *Cast:* Ralph Macchio, Noriyuki "Pat" Morita, Robyn Lively, Thomas Ian Griffith, Martin Kove, Sean Kanan

▶ Third in this popular series has Macchio disregarding mentor Morita's wishes and going up against nasty Kanan in Karate tournament. Macchio is not to be blamed, as bad guys have punched out lady pal Lively and torn up a precious bonsai tree. With whatever good about the premise exhausted in the earlier films, *Rocky*-director Alvidsen must shamelessly pump for revenge to hold audience interest. (CC)
Dist.: RCA/Columbia

KEEP, THE 1983
★ ★ R Horror 1:38

☑ Rape, nudity, adult situations

Dir: Michael Mann *Cast:* Scott Glenn, Alberta Watson, Jurgen Prochnow, Robert Prosky, Gabriel Byrne, Ian McKellen

▶ Nazi soldiers under the command of sensitive officer Prochnow hole up in imposing Rumanian edifice known as "the keep." Monster hidden within its walls murders soldiers and threatens all humanity. Artful visual style from "Miami Vice" creator Mann fails to compensate for ponderous pacing, stilted script, and lack of real shocks. Pulsating score by Tangerine Dream.
Dist.: Paramount

KEEPING TRACK 1987 Canadian
★ R Mystery-Suspense 1:42

☑ Brief nudity, explicit language, violence

Dir: Robin Spry *Cast:* Margot Kidder, Michael Sarrazin, Ken Pogue, Alan Scarfe

▶ Bank executive Kidder and TV news anchorman Sarrazin witness a shooting and find themselves battling killers, cops, and a government cover-up. Standard suspenser features acceptable performances and scenic Montreal locations, but suffers from creaky, farfetched plotting. (CC)
Dist.: Nelson

KELLY'S HEROES 1970
★ ★ ★ ★ PG War 2:24

☑ Adult situations, explicit language, violence

Dir: Brian G. Hutton *Cast:* Clint Eastwood, Telly Savalas, Don Rickles, Donald Sutherland, Carroll O'Connor, Gavin McLeod

▶ During World War II, Eastwood learns where a fortune in gold is hidden behind enemy lines. As the Allies advance, he assembles a ragtag band of misfits to steal the gold. Sprawling, consistently entertaining adventure has an expert cast and pleasant tongue-in-cheek tone.
Dist.: MGM/UA

KENNEL MURDER CASE, THE 1933
★ ★ NR Mystery-Suspense 1:13 B&W
Dir: William Curtiz   *Cast:* William Powell, Mary Astor, Eugene Pallette, Ralph Morgan, Helen Vinson, Jack LaRue
▶ When murder slips through the gates of a posh Long Island kennel club, Philo Vance (Powell) is unleashed to dog the culprit using his faithful Doberman to help make the collar. Powell's last of four outings as urbane wag Vance is his best. Based on the S. S. Van Dine novel *The Return of Philo Vance.*
Dist.: Cable

KENTUCKIAN, THE 1955
★ ★ ★ NR Western 1:44
Dir: Burt Lancaster   *Cast:* Burt Lancaster, Dianne Foster, Diana Lynn, John McIntire, Una Merkel, Walter Matthau
▶ Rugged frontier adventure finds Lancaster and his son involved in a vicious family feud when they leave Kentucky for Texas. Lancaster's only directing effort gave Matthau his film debut as a whip-wielding villain.
Dist.: Playhouse

KENTUCKY FRIED MOVIE, THE 1977
★ ★ R Comedy 1:24
☑ Nudity, explicit language
Dir: John Landis   *Cast:* Evan C. Kim, Bill Bixby, Henry Gibson, George Lazenby, Master Bong Soo Han, Donald Sutherland
▶ From the director of *Animal House* and the creators of *Airplane!* a generally amusing and frequently off-color collection of skits satirizing 1950s TV shows, disaster movies, kung-fu flicks, sexploitation movies, and commercials. Some terrible jokes but many very funny ones too.
Dist.: Media

KEY, THE 1958 British
★ ★ NR Drama 2:05 B&W
Dir: Carol Reed   *Cast:* William Holden, Sophia Loren, Trevor Howard, Oscar Homolka, Kieron Moore, Bernard Lee
▶ During World War II, naval captains share a flat and lover Loren, giving the apartment key to the next officer as each goes off to fight. Holden becomes the latest beneficiary of the arrangement, but soon genuine feelings develop between him and Loren. Stars' charisma sustains story through rocky passages.
Dist.: RCA/Columbia

KEY EXCHANGE 1985
★ R Romance/Comedy 1:36
☑ Nudity, adult situations, explicit language
Dir: Barnett Kellman   *Cast:* Brooke Adams, Ben Masters, Daniel Stern, Danny Aiello, Tony Roberts
▶ Writer Masters enjoys sexual freedom and resists girlfriend Adams's request for commitment while his best pal Stern separates from his wife. Adaptation of Kevin Wade's off-Broadway play has attractive cast, but insights into singles scene are pretty dated.

Comic highlight: Masters pretending to be a "Sterile Single" on TV talk show.   (CC)
Dist.: CBS/Fox

KEY LARGO 1948
★ ★ ★ NR Drama 1:41 B&W
Dir: John Huston   *Cast:* Humphrey Bogart, Lauren Bacall, Edward G. Robinson, Lionel Barrymore, Claire Trevor, Thomas Gomez, Jay Silverheels
▶ During a hurricane, tyrannical gangster Robinson takes over a Florida hotel. Disillusioned World War II vet Bogart is reluctant to get involved until Bacall gives him the inspiration to fight back. Strongly acted if overly talky drama. Trevor won Best Supporting Actress Oscar.
Dist.: MGM/UA   ⓒ

KHARTOUM 1966 British
★ ★ NR Action-Adventure 2:14
Dir: Basil Dearden   *Cast:* Charlton Heston, Laurence Olivier, Richard Johnson, Ralph Richardson, Johnny Sekka, Michael Hordern
▶ True story of the 1885 siege of Khartoum, in which Sudanese natives, led by holy man "The Mahdi" (Olivier), eventually defeated British troops led by Sir Charles "Chinese" Gordon (Heston) after a long and arduous battle. Intelligent screenplay and superb performances by Heston and Olivier make this epic a cut above the genre norm.
Dist.: MGM/UA

KICKBOXER 1989 British
★ ★ ★ R Martial Arts 1:45
☑ Nudity, explicit language, violence
Dir: Mark DiSalle   *Cast:* Jean-Claude Van Damme, Dennis Alexio, Dennis Chan, Haskell Anderson, Rochelle Ashana, Tong Po
▶ Van Damme beats people to a pulp in kickboxing style known as "Muay Thai," which he learns from inscrutable *Karate Kid*-style tutor Chan. Special target is Po, who crippled Van Damme's brother in a brutal encounter. Lots of violent action with nice Thai backgrounds. (CC)
Dist.: HBO

KID, THE 1921
★ NR Comedy 1:00 B&W
Dir: Charlie Chaplin   *Cast:* Charlie Chaplin, Jackie Coogan, Carl Miller, Edna Purviance
▶ The Little Tramp adopts abandoned Coogan and serves as father and mother to him. Their relationship is threatened when the child's actual mother seeks to reclaim him. Silent classic is heartwarming and always amusingly sentimental; Chaplin and young Coogan made an unbeatable team.
Dist.: CBS/Fox

KIDCO 1984
★ ★ ★ ★ PG Comedy/Family 1:44
☑ Adult situations, explicit language
Dir: Ronald F. Maxwell   *Cast:* Scott Schwartz, Cinnamon Idles, Tristine Skyler, Elizabeth Gorcey, Maggie Blye

▶ Sixth-grader Schwartz and his pals go into business, cornering the local manure market. Adult competition and the IRS are no match for these pint-sized entrepreneurs. Predictable, but as cheerfully produced as a corn flakes commercial; inspired by a true story. (CC)
Dist.: CBS/Fox

KID COLTER 1989
★ ★ ★ ★ PG Family 1:42
☑ Explicit language, mild violence
Dir: David O'Malley   *Cast:* Jim Stafford, Jeremy Shamos, Greg Ward, Hal Terrence, Jim Turner
▶ Twelve-year-old city boy Shamos goes to visit divorced dad in the country. Resistant at first to charm of nature, Shamos gets to know dad and the woods better and realizes that there are secrets of nature he has yet to learn. Before returning to city, he is kidnapped by spies, dumped in the wilderness, and must fend for himself in the hostile terrain. Film has some farfetched moments, but all in all it's superior family entertainment.   (CC)
Dist.: Playhouse

KID FROM BROOKLYN, THE 1946
★ ★ ★ ★ NR Musical/Comedy 1:54
Dir: Norman Z. McLeod   *Cast:* Danny Kaye, Virginia Mayo, Vera-Ellen, Steve Cochran, Eve Arden, Lionel Stander
▶ Mild-mannered milkman Kaye gets into nightclub tussle with middleweight boxing champ Cochran. The press wrongly reports that Kaye knocked out Cochran, thus setting the stage for milkman's pugilistic career. Broadly appealing Kaye vehicle highlighted by "Pavlova," a nifty modern dance parody number. Wisecracking Arden brightens up this remake of the 1936 Harold Lloyd comedy *The Milky Way.*
Dist.: Nelson

KID GALAHAD 1962
★ ★ NR Musical 1:35
Dir: Phil Karlson   *Cast:* Elvis Presley, Gig Young, Lola Albright, Joan Blackman, Charles Bronson, Ned Glass
▶ Boxing promoter Young discovers young fighter Presley at his Catskills camp and turns him into title contender Kid Galahad. Weak remake of a 1937 Edward G. Robinson film includes "King of the Whole Wide World" and "Love Is for Lovers." Bronson is effectively understated as Presley's incorruptible trainer.
Dist.: MGM/UA

KID MILLIONS 1934
★ NR Musical 1:30 C/B&W
Dir: Roy Del Ruth   *Cast:* Eddie Cantor, Ann Sothern, Ethel Merman, George Murphy, Edgar Kennedy, Nicholas Brothers
▶ Lower East Side singer Cantor inherits $77 million and goes on a wild spending spree with his girlfriend Sothern. Dated but tuneful comedy works best during the frequent specialty numbers. Songs include "When My Ship Comes In," "Mandy," and "Ice Cream Fantasy" (look quickly for Goldwyn Girl Lucille Ball in this number).
Dist.: Nelson

KIDNAPPED 1960
★ ★ ★ ★ G Action-Adventure 1:34
Dir: Robert Stevenson   *Cast:* Peter Finch, James MacArthur, Bernard Lee, Niall MacGinnis, Finlay Currie, Peter O'Toole
▶ In eighteenth-century Scotland, young MacArthur is tricked out of a fortune and impressed as a cabin boy on a ship to the New World. He befriends Scottish rebel Finch, who leads him on a series of daring adventures against the English. Third film version of Robert Louis Stevenson's adventure receives typically polished Disney treatment.
Dist.: Buena Vista

KIDNAPPED 1986
★ ★ R Action-Adventure 1:38
☑ Nudity, strong sexual content, explicit language, violence
Dir: Howard Avedis   *Cast:* David Naughton, Barbara Crampton, Lance LeGault, Chick Vennera, Kim Evenson, Jimmie C. Walker
▶ Young Evenson is abducted and forced into pornographic films. Her older sister Crampton joins forces with Santa Barbara police detective Naughton to rescue her. Low-budget exploitation film with a full quota of nudity and sadistic violence.
Dist.: Virgin

KIDNAPPING OF THE PRESIDENT, THE 1980 Canadian
★ ★ ★ R Drama 1:33
☑ Adult situations, explicit language, violence
Dir: George Mendeluk   *Cast:* William Shatner, Hal Holbrook, Van Johnson, Ava Gardner, Miguel Fernandes, Cindy Girling
▶ During a Toronto visit, the President (Holbrook) is taken hostage by South American terrorists; Secret Service agent Shatner must rescue him. The Vice President (Johnson) and wife Gardner want Shatner to fail. Workmanlike thriller with a good performance from Fernandes as the terrorist leader.
Dist.: Continental

KIDS ARE ALRIGHT, THE 1979 British
★ ★ PG Documentary/Music 1:47
☑ Explicit language
Dir: Jeff Stein   *Cast:* Pete Townshend, Roger Daltrey, John Entwistle, Keith Moon, Kenny Jones
▶ Fascinating look at rock supergroup The Who is a chaotic collection of concert footage, rock videos, and interviews with the group and their friends (Ringo Starr, Tom Smothers, etc.). Fourteen first-rate songs, including: "Happy Jack," "Baba O'Riley," "Won't Get Fooled Again." Final sequence, filmed in Dolby Stereo, features deceased drummer Moon's replacement Jones.
Dist.: HBO

KILL AND KILL AGAIN 1981
★ ★ PG Martial Arts 1:40
☐ Violence
Dir: Ivan Hall *Cast:* James Ryan, Anneline Kriel, Ken Gampu, Norman Robinson, Stan Schmidt, Bill Flynn
► Sequel to *Kill or Be Killed* with Ryan repeating his role as a heroic martial arts master. This time he battles a mad billionaire who plans to poison the world's water supply. Ryan is alerted to the case by former Miss World Kriel, whose scientist father has been kidnapped. Fast, lighthearted action should please kung fu fans.
Dist.: Media

KILLER ELITE, THE 1975
★ ★ ★ PG Action-Adventure 2:00
☐ Explicit language, graphic violence
Dir: Sam Peckinpah *Cast:* James Caan, Robert Duvall, Arthur Hill, Gig Young, Mako, Bo Hopkins
► While protecting Asian politician Mako, bodyguard Caan learns that his nemesis Duvall is assembling an assassination team. Extended chases and double-crosses are the best aspects of this political thriller. Caan makes a strong impression as the badly wounded hero.
Dist.: MGM/UA

KILLER FISH 1979 Italian/Brazilian
☆ PG Action-Adventure 1:41
☐ Explicit language, violence
Dir: Anthony M. Dawson (Antonio) Margheriti) *Cast:* Lee Majors, Karen Black, James Franciscus, Margaux Hemingway, Marisa Berenson, Gary Collins
► Laconic tough guy Majors and his neurotic partner Black steal a fortune in gems from a Brazilian industrial complex. They hide the loot in the bottom of a lake, unaware that villain Franciscus has stocked it with hungry piranha. Mindless thriller is perfectly cast. Also known as *Treasure of the Piranha.* (CC)
Dist.: Key

KILLER FORCE 1975
★ ★ R Action-Adventure 1:40
☐ Adult situations, explicit language, violence
Dir: Val Guest *Cast:* Telly Savalas, Peter Fonda, Hugh O'Brian, O. J. Simpson, Maud Adams, Christopher Lee
► Savalas, chief of security at a South African diamond mine, asks local deputy Fonda to investigate a series of thefts, unaware that Fonda is masterminding an assault on the mine's vaults. Competent adventure highlighted by an extended break-in sequence.
Dist.: Vestron

KILLER INSIDE ME, THE 1976
★ ★ R Drama 1:39
☐ Brief nudity, adult situations, explicit language, violence
Dir: Burt Kennedy *Cast:* Stacy Keach, Susan Tyrrell, Tisha Sterling, Keenan Wynn, Charles McGraw, John Dehner
► Battling redneck hoodlums, Montana sheriff Keach succumbs to a violent psychosis brought on by childhood traumas. Disappointing, flashback-ridden adaptation of Jim Thompson's cult novel is worth a look for Keach's thoughtful performance and a superb turn by Tyrrell as a hard-bitten hooker.
Dist.: Warner

KILLER KLOWNS FROM OUTER SPACE 1988
☆ PG-13 Sci-Fi 1:22
☐ Explicit language, violence
Dir: Stephen Chiodo *Cast:* Grant Cramer, Suzanne Snyder, John Allen Nelson, Royal Dano, John Vernon, Michael Siegel
► A small town is terrorized by aliens who look like grotesque circus clowns. Red-nosed "klowns" kill by hitting people with acid pies, spinning them into cotton candy cocoons, etc. Vernon is fine as the town cop, but everything else about this strained satire of fifties sci-fi flicks is tenth-rate.
Dist.: Media

KILLER PARTY 1986
★ R Horror 1:32
☐ Nudity, adult situations, explicit language, violence
Dir: William Fruet *Cast:* Martin Hewitt, Ralph Seymour, Elaine Wilkes, Paul Bartel, Sherry Willis-Burch, Alicia Fleer
► Sorority pledges plan a series of practical jokes for an April Fool's party at a haunted house, but something goes terribly wrong as the guests meet gruesome deaths. Minor horror piece sticks to a familiar formula.
Dist.: CBS/Fox

KILLERS, THE 1964
★ ★ NR Drama 1:35
Dir: Don Siegel *Cast:* Lee Marvin, Angie Dickinson, John Cassavetes, Ronald Reagan, Clu Gulager, Claude Akins
► Marvin and Gulager assassinate Cassavetes and then pursue Reagan, a gangster who sold out Cassavetes in robbery scheme. Fast-paced film is notable for Reagan's atypical bad guy role in his last film. Based on the Ernest Hemingway story and originally made for TV. Previously filmed in 1946 with Burt Lancaster.
Dist.: MCA

KILLERS FROM SPACE 1954
☆ NR Sci-Fi 1:11 B&W
Dir: W. Lee Wilder *Cast:* Peter Graves, James Seay, Steve Pendleton, Barbara Bestar, John Merrick
► A plane crash during a nuclear test apparently kills scientist Graves, but he then reappears with a mysterious scar on his chest. FBI man Pendleton is suspicious, as he should be: Graves has been resurrected and hypnotized by bulging-eyed aliens intent on invading Earth. Stolid filmmaking features cardboard

acting, dumb dialogue. Weak special effects include blown-up footage of real lizards to show alien menagerie of "giant" creatures.
Dist.: Goodtimes

KILLER SHREWS, THE 1959
☆ **NR Horror 1:10 B&W**
Dir: Ray Kellogg *Cast:* James Best, Ingrid Goude, Ken Curtis, Baruch Lumet, Gordon McLendon
▶ Best brings supplies to an isolated island where nutty doc Lumet has concocted a serum that turns miniature mammals into man-eating monsters the size of golden retrievers. Cheerfully dumb creature pic parsimoniously lensed in Texas in tandem with *The Giant Gila Monster*. Lumet is father of Sidney Lumet, the well-known director.
Dist.: Sinister

KILLING, THE 1956
★ ★ ★ ★ **NR Mystery-Suspense 1:25 B&W**
Dir: Stanley Kubrick *Cast:* Sterling Hayden, Coleen Gray, Vince Edwards, Jay C. Flippen, Marie Windsor, Ted de Corsia, Elisha Cook, Jr., Joe Sawyer, Timothy Carey
▶ Ex-convict Hayden and Windsor's henpecked husband Cook are among the conspirators plotting a racetrack heist. A clever plan is concocted, but then things go disastrously wrong. Kubrick's detached yet edgy direction creates a superior thriller. Characterizations, especially the perverse Cook/Windsor relationship, have unusual depth for the genre. Screenplay co-written by Jim Thompson.
Dist.: MGM/UA

KILLING AFFAIR, A 1988
★ ★ **R Drama 1:40**
☑ Nudity, adult situations, explicit language, violence
Dir: David Saperstein *Cast:* Peter Weller, Kathy Baker, John Glover, Bill Smitrovich, Rhetta Hughes
▶ In 1943 West Virginia, a vicious labor boss is found murdered. Widow Baker strikes up an unsettling relationship with Weller, a drifter who might be the killer. Bleak Southern gothic melodrama is often confusing. Inauspicious directing debut for Saperstein, author of *Cocoon*.
Dist.: Prism

KILLING FIELDS, THE 1984 British
★ ★ ★ ★ **R Drama 2:22**
☑ Adult situations, explicit language, graphic violence
Dir: Roland Joffe *Cast:* Sam Waterston, Haing S. Ngor, John Malkovich, Craig T. Nelson, Julian Sands, Athol Fugard
▶ Morally overwhelming masterwork about friendship, survival, and war based on a true story. *New York Times* journalist Sydney Schanberg (Waterston) escapes the fall of Cambodia aided by his native assistant Dith Pran (Ngor), but Pran is left behind to face the horrors of the Khmer Rouge holocaust. Ngor, a

doctor who survived the brutal political upheaval in Cambodia, is astonishing his first time acting. Three Oscars, including Best Supporting Actor (Ngor), Editing and Cinematography. Also nominated for Picture, Director, and Actor (Waterston). **(CC)**
Dist.: Warner

KILLING FLOOR, THE 1984
★ ★ ★ **PG Drama/MFTV 1:57**
☑ Explicit language
Dir: William Duke *Cast:* Damien Leake, Moses Gunn, Alfre Woodard, Clarence Feder, Ernest Rayford
▶ Southern blacks trying to make a life in Chicago during World War I include Leake and wife Woodard. Working at the stockyards, Leake gets involved with the touchy business of union organizing. Unemployment troubles lead to violent riots and a tense standoff outside the slaughterhouse. Sincere, well-acted drama brings period dilemma to vivid life. Originally made for PBS's "American Playhouse."
Dist.: Orion

KILLING HEAT 1984 Swedish
☆ **NR Drama 1:44**
☑ Nudity, adult situations, violence
Dir: Michael Raeburn *Cast:* Karen Black, John Thaw, John Kani, John Moulder-Brown
▶ The African interior has proven to be a rough place for women in many films, but Black marries farmer Thaw, moves there anyway, and starts going mad from the heat, the bugs, and the lack of water. Worse, she alien ates the farm's black laborers, especially the houseboy, setting herself up for a bad end. Situation is hopeless and film is relentlessly depressing. Also known as *The Grass is Singing*; based on a story by Doris Lessing.
Dist.: Key

KILLING OF ANGEL STREET, THE 1981 Australian
★ ★ **NR Drama 1:41**
☑ Adult situations, explicit language, violence
Dir: Donald Crombie *Cast:* Liz Alexander, John Hargreaves, Alexander Archdale, Reg Lyle, Gordon McDougall
▶ A seemingly respectable real estate group uses bludgeoning tactics to get residents out of charming row houses targeted for demolition. Alexander is spurred to action when her father, a leader of the residents' action group, mysteriously dies. She eventually uncovers a conspiracy between business and government. Little entertainment in this paranoid and self-righteous treatment of a supposedly true story.
Dist.: VidAmerica

KILLING OF SISTER GEORGE, THE 1968 British
☆ **R Drama 2:19**
☑ Nudity, strong sexual content, adult situations, explicit language

Dir: Robert Aldrich *Cast:* Beryl Reid, Susannah York, Coral Browne, Ronald Fraser, Patricia Medina, Hugh Paddick

▶ Lesbian actress Reid faces personal and professional problems: she's written out of her BBC soap opera and her lover York gets involved with another woman. Subject matter may offend some; Reid's powerhouse performance dominates. Lengthy seduction scene near film's conclusion originally earned X rating.

Dist.: CBS/Fox

KILLING TIME, THE 1987
★★★ R Mystery-Suspense 1:35
☑ Nudity, adult situations, explicit language, violence
Dir: Rick King *Cast:* Beau Bridges, Kiefer Sutherland, Wayne Rogers, Joe Don Baker, Camelia Kath, Janet Carroll

▶ Small-town California sheriff Bridges and his ex-lover Kath plot the death of her arrogant developer husband Rogers, but their plan is threatened by the arrival of new deputy Sutherland, secretly a serial killer. Twisty modern-day film noir has an unpredictable story line and agreeably unsavory characters.

Dist.: New World

KILL ME AGAIN 1989
★★ R Mystery-Suspense 1:34
☑ Adult situations, explicit language, violence
Dir: John Dahl *Cast:* Val Kilmer, Joanne Whalley-Kilmer, Michael Madsen, Jonathan Gries, Michael Greene, Bibi Besch

▶ Brazen Madsen and his siren girlfriend Whalley-Kilmer relieve some mob accountants of a million in cash. He cramps Whalley-Kilmer's style, so she knocks him unconscious and takes the loot. She then enlists unsuspecting private eye Kilmer to fake her death and get Madsen off her trail. Steamy film noir brims with double crosses and the very watchable Whalley-Kilmer.

Dist.: MGM/UA

KILL OR BE KILLED 1980
★★ PG Martial Arts 1:30
☑ Violence
Dir: Ivan Hall *Cast:* James Ryan, Norman Combes, Charlotte Michelle, Danie DuPlessis

▶ Ex-Nazi karate coach forces his star students to compete against a Japanese team led by his nemesis from World War II. Martial arts master Ryan rebels, leading to an action-filled climax involving his kidnapped girlfriend. Fast-paced exploitation picture, filmed in South Africa, led to sequel *Kill and Kill Again.*

Dist.: Media

KILLPOINT 1984
★ R Action-Adventure 1:32
☑ Rape, nudity, adult situations, explicit language, graphic violence
Dir: Frank Harris *Cast:* Leo Fong, Richard

Roundtree, Cameron Mitchell, Stack Pierce, Hope Holiday, Diana Leigh

▶ Vicious thugs led by Mitchell and Pierce overwhelm a small-town arsenal, then use the weapons to terrorize local citizens. Kung-fu expert Fong and Federal agent Roundtree battle the gang. Standard low-budget thriller is often uncomfortably racist.

Dist.: Vestron

KILL SLADE 1989
☆ PG-13 Action-Adventure 1:22
☑ Explicit language, violence
Dir: D. Bruce McFarlane *Cast:* Patrick Dollaghan, Lisa Brady, Danny Keogh, Anthony Fridjhon, Vusi Dibakwane, Alfred Nokwe

▶ Someone's stealing from a U.N. relief program in Africa, and reporter Brady wants to find out who it is. Bad guys hire ne'er-do-well soldier of fortune Slade to kidnap her. Mismatched pair develops familiar screen-style bickering romance while trekking across veldt. Mediocre *Romancing the Stone* clone has clichéd script, bad actors.

Dist.: Orion

KIM 1951
★★★★ G Action-Adventure 1:53
Dir: Victor Saville *Cast:* Errol Flynn, Dean Stockwell, Paul Lukas, Robert Douglas, Thomas Gomez, Cecil Kellaway

▶ Young Stockwell, orphaned in colonial India, befriends horse-thief Flynn and ascetic Lukas; disguised as a native, he takes part in a secret plot to repel a Russian invasion of the Khyber Pass. Adaptation of Rudyard Kipling's classic adventure captures the novel's exotic atmosphere and sweeping action. Remade as a TV movie in 1984.

Dist.: MGM/UA

KIND HEARTS AND CORONETS 1949 British
★★★ NR Comedy 1:45 B&W
Dir: Robert Hamer *Cast:* Dennis Price, Alec Guinness, Joan Greenwood, Valerie Hobson, Miles Malleson, Audrey Fildes

▶ Conniving cad Price, the unacknowledged offspring of a duke, conspires to kill those who stand between him and the inheritance he believes is rightfully his. In an unparalleled acting feat, Guinness plays the eight family members, including the duke himself, whom Price must slay in order to acquire the title. Memorable and notorious black comedy made Guinness an international star; witty dialogue and wicked send-up of English manners still amuse today.

Dist.: HBO

KIND OF LOVING, A 1962 British
★★ NR Drama 1:52 B&W
Dir: John Schlesinger *Cast:* Alan Bates, June Ritchie, Thora Hird, Bert Palmer, Gwen Nelson, Malcolm Patton

▶ Factory workers Bates and Ritchie, forced to marry when she becomes pregnant, move in with her domineering mother Hird. Marriage goes awry when she miscarries and forsakes

sex and he hits the bottle; two eventually realize they must escape Hird's clutches to save the marriage and achieve a "kind of loving." Simple story sustained by grimy realism, fine performances, and sure-handed direction by Schlesinger.
Dist.: HBO

KINDRED, THE 1987
★ ★ R Horror 1:29
☑ Explicit language, violence
Dir: Jeffrey Obrow *Cast:* David Allen Brooks, Rod Steiger, Amanda Pays, Talia Balsam, Kim Hunter
▶ Geneticist Brooks discovers late scientist's mom Hunter created nasty things in the lab (such as turning Brooks's brother into a tentacled creature). Mad doctor Steiger complicates Brooks's efforts to annihilate mom's experiments. Above-par "don't go in the basement" flick. Fair number of chills as well as unintentional chuckles.
Dist.: Vestron

KING AND I, THE 1956
★ ★ ★ ★ NR Musical 2:13
Dir: Walter Lang *Cast:* Deborah Kerr, Yul Brynner, Rita Moreno, Martin Benson, Terry Saunders
▶ Stern Siamese monarch Brynner is softened by the influence of English governess Kerr as their clashing cultures and personalties eventually give way to un unspoken love. Magnificent performance by Brynner (who won one of film's three Oscars) in this sumptuously produced and moving adaptation of the Broadway musical. Brynner/Kerr "Shall We Dance?" duet highlights a wonderful Rodgers and Hammerstein score. A Best Picture nominee. Story was originally brought to the screen in 1946's *Anna and the King of Siam.*
Dist.: CBS/Fox

KING CREOLE 1958
★ ★ ★ ★ NR Musical 1:56 B&W
Dir: Michael Curtiz *Cast:* Elvis Presley, Carolyn Jones, Dolores Hart, Dean Jagger, Liliane Montevecchi, Walter Matthau, Vic Morrow
▶ Presley plays a New Orleans singer drawn into the underworld by his love for Jones, mistress to nightclub owner Matthau. Morrow makes a good impression as a young gang leader. Unusually dramatic plot for a musical was adapted from Harold Robbins's early best-seller *A Stone for Danny Fisher.* Elvis's last film before entering the Army includes "Hard-Headed Woman" and "Trouble."
Dist.: CBS/Fox

KING DAVID 1985
★ ★ ★ PG-13 Drama 1:54
☑ Rape, brief nudity, violence
Dir: Bruce Beresford *Cast:* Richard Gere, Edward Woodward, Alice Krige, Denis Quilley, Hurd Hatfield
▶ Biblical epic of the story of David (Gere), from his battle with Goliath through his ascension to the throne. He falls for Bathsheba (Krige) and has her husband killed. Although film is respectful and well produced, Gere is miscast and the pacing lags. **(CC)**
Dist.: Paramount

KINGDOM OF THE SPIDERS 1977
★ ★ PG Horror 1:30
☑ Violence
Dir: John Cardos *Cast:* William Shatner, Tiffany Bolling, Woody Strode, Lieux Dressler, Altovise Davis, Marcy Rafferty
▶ An Arizona desert town is attacked by terrifying tarantulas whose food supply has been destroyed by insecticides. Veterinarian Shatner and scientist Bolling team up to battle them. Intelligent screenplay and Cardos's above-average direction transcend the premise of this genre fare.
Dist.: VCI

KING IN NEW YORK, A 1957 British
★ G Comedy 1:44 B&W
Dir: Charles Chaplin *Cast:* Charles Chaplin, Dawn Addams, Oliver Johnston, Maxine Audley, Harry Green, Michael Chaplin
▶ After a revolution in his country, deposed king Chaplin flies to New York, where he is exposed to American phenomena like night life, television, and plastic surgery. When a young boy's parents are accused of being Communists, the monarch comes to their aid. Chaplin makes his political points awkwardly, yet this late effort is still an enjoyable showcase for his great talent.
Dist.: CBS/Fox

KING KONG 1933
★ ★ ★ ★ NR Sci-Fi 1:40 B&W
Dir: Merian C. Cooper, Ernest B. Schoedsack *Cast:* Fay Wray, Bruce Cabot, Robert Armstrong, Frank Reicher, Sam Hardy
▶ Enduring classic stands head and shoulders above any of the remakes and imitators. On a trip to Skull Island, Wray is captured by a fifty-foot gorilla known as Kong. After her rescue, Kong is brought to New York, where he is billed as the Eighth Wonder of the World. He wreaks havoc on the city when he escapes and seeks out true love Wray. Climax atop the Empire State Building is one of filmdom's great moments.
Dist.: Turner ©

KING KONG 1976
★ ★ ★ PG Sci-Fi 2:14
☑ Explicit language, violence
Dir: John Guillermin *Cast:* Jessica Lange, Jeff Bridges, Charles Grodin, John Randolph, René Auberjonois
▶ Producer De Laurentiis's $24 million remake of the 1933 classic boasts touches of feminism, Freud, and ecology in the script; a wealth of special effects including an updated climax where Kong climbs one of the World Trade Center Towers; and Lange in her film debut. Not as charming as the original, but enlivened by bravura performances from

Grodin and the marvelous mechanical beast.
Dist.: Paramount

KING KONG LIVES 1986
★ ★ **PG-13 Sci-Fi 1:45**
☑ Adult situations, explicit language, violence
Dir: John Guillermin *Cast:* Brian Kerwin, Linda Hamilton, John Ashton, Peter Michael Goetz, Peter Elliot, George Yiasomi
▶ Sequel to 1976 film reveals giant ape kept on life-support systems after fall from World Trade Center. Borneo hunter Kerwin brings enormous female Kong to help doctor Hamilton perform needed surgery on the King. Two apes fall in love, escape, but fall prey to bloodthirsty hunters. Despite improved special effects, pointless adventure strains credibility. **(CC)**
Dist.: Warner

KING KONG VS. GODZILLA 1963 Japanese
☆ NR Sci-Fi **1:30**
Dir: Thomas Montgomery, Inoshiro Honda
Cast: Michael Keith, James Yagi, Tadao Takashima, Mie Hama, Kenji Sahara, Harry Holcomb
▶ Roused from an iceberg, Godzilla descends upon Tokyo, only to find his way blocked by Kong, who's been enjoying life as a fishermen's deity. Heavyweights duke it out in front of Mount Fuji, while structures underfoot take a beating. English language scenes edited in later for U.S. audience. One of the better Godzilla films.
Dist.: Goodtimes

KING LEAR 1988 U.S./Swiss
☆ **PG Drama 1:31**
☑ Explicit language
Dir: Jean-Luc Godard *Cast:* Burgess Meredith, Molly Ringwald, Jean-Luc Godard, Peter Sellars, Norman Mailer
▶ Descendant of William Shakespeare (American theater director Sellars) follows retired mobster Meredith and daughter Ringwald as they reenact scenes from *King Lear.* French director Godard (working in English) uses Shakespeare's text as a vehicle for obscure critique of pop culture that may appeal to his following but will leave most in the cold.
Dist.: Media

KING OF COMEDY, THE 1983
★ **PG Comedy/Drama 1:49**
☑ Adult situations, explicit language, mild violence
Dir: Martin Scorsese *Cast:* Robert De Niro, Jerry Lewis, Sandra Bernhard, Diahnne Abbott, Shelley Hack
▶ Show-biz junkie and general nebbish Rupert Pupkin (De Niro) worships urbane TV talkshow host Lewis. Desperate to become a celebrity and win an appearance on late night TV, De Niro and sidekick Bernhard kidnap Lewis and hold him hostage. Top-notch acting from entire cast (especially the restrained Lewis) but some critics found De Niro's charac-

ter too unlikable; others were put off by Scorsese's moralizing tone.
Dist.: RCA/Columbia

KING OF HEARTS 1967 French/British
★ ★ **NR Comedy 1:42**
Dir: Philippe de Broca *Cast:* Alan Bates, Genevieve Bujold, Adolfo Celi, Pierre Brasseur, Jean-Claude Brialy
▶ Funny and touching parable was an enormous underground hit in the late sixties–early seventies. Amiable Scotsman Bates is sent to a small village during World War I to defuse a bomb. He doesn't realize that the townsfolk have fled, replaced by charming lunatics from a local asylum. Now a little dated and simpleminded, but definitely worth a look.
Dist.: MGM/UA

KING OF JAZZ, THE 1930
★ ★ **NR Musical 1:33**
Dir: John Murray Anderson *Cast:* Laura LaPlante, John Boles, Jeanette Loff, The Rhythm Boys, Slim Summerville, Paul Whiteman and His Orchestra
▶ Knockout musical-and-comedy revue built around Whiteman's orchestra, featuring music by Gershwin (and others), comedy skits, and band sessions. A young Bing Crosby appears uncredited as part of his singing group The Rhythm Boys. "Rhapsody in Blue" production finale is outstanding. A visual feast in two-strip Technicolor, film won Oscar for Interior Decoration.
Dist.: MCA

KING OF KINGS 1961
★ ★ ★ ★ ★ **NR Drama 2:44**
Dir: Nicholas Ray *Cast:* Jeffrey Hunter, Robert Ryan, Harry Guardino, Rip Torn, Siobhan McKenna, Hurd Hatfield
▶ Story of Christ (Hunter), told against the backdrop of Jewish resistance to Roman rule, traces his life through birth in the manger, wandering in the desert, the Sermon on the Mount, and the Last Supper. Cast-of-thousands spectacular is satisfying holiday fare.
Dist.: MGM/UA

KING OF THE GYPSIES 1978
★ ★ ★ **R Drama 1:52**
☑ Nudity, adult situations, explicit language
Dir: Frank Pierson *Cast:* Sterling Hayden, Shelley Winters, Susan Sarandon, Judd Hirsch, Eric Roberts, Brooke Shields
▶ Inside look at three generations of gypsies and the succession of power from "king" Hayden to his reluctant grandson Roberts. Colorful *Godfather* clone re-creates a very foreign, nomadic way of life replete with fortune tellers and all-night celebrations. Written by Pierson from the nonfiction best-seller by Peter Maas.
Dist.: Paramount

KING OF THE MOUNTAIN 1981
★ ★ **PG Drama 1:30**
☑ Adult situations, explicit language
Dir: Noel Nosseck *Cast:* Harry Hamlin, Jo-

seph Bottoms, Richard Cox, Dennis Hopper, Dan Haggerty, Seymour Cassel

▶ Three young Angelenos—garage mechanic Hamlin, aspiring songwriter Bottoms, and junior record producer Cox—pursue careers by day and drag race on Mulholland Drive by night. They pal around with over-the-hill hippie Hopper and risk their macho lives, staking claim to title: "king of the mountain."
Dist.: Embassy

KING RAT 1965
★ ★ ★ ★ **NR War 2:13 B&W**
Dir: Bryan Forbes *Cast:* George Segal, Tom Courtenay, James Fox, Patrick O'Neal, Denholm Elliott, John Mills

▶ In Singapore in 1945, POW Segal ensures his survival but incurs the hatred of his fellow prisoners by exploiting the black market in a Japanese prison camp. Officers Elliott and Mills aid him in return for money and food, while Provost Marshal Courtenay opposes him. Powerful, unvarnished drama based on the novel by James Clavell.
Dist.: RCA/Columbia

KINGS AND DESPERATE MEN 1983
Canadian
☆ **PG-13 Drama 1:58**
☑ Adult situations, violence
Dir: Alexis Kanner *Cast:* Patrick McGoohan, Alexis Kanner, Andrea Marcovicci, Margaret Trudeau, Robin Spry, Frank Moore

▶ A gang of terrorists takes obnoxious radio host McGoohan and wife Trudeau hostage to publicize their demand that an unfairly imprisoned cohort be freed. Judge who passed sentence is also held, and terrorists attempt escape after he dies in their custody. McGoohan towers over the other actors in the film, but the story is a lemon, and the whole is made worse by show-offy direction.
Dist.: Magnum

KING SOLOMON'S MINES 1937 British
★ ★ **NR Action-Adventure 1:20 B&W**
Dir: Robert Stevenson *Cast:* Paul Robeson, Cedric Hardwicke, Roland Young, John Loder, Anna Lee

▶ Robeson rules this version of the H. Rider Haggard novel, helping white explorers Hardwicke, Young, and Lee seek the fabled diamond hoard, while they help him recapture the throne of his tribe. Latter is accomplished via old gag where the civilized types awe the natives by predicting an eclipse. A powerful screen presence, Robeson belts out a tune and keeps otherwise sagging effort alive. Remade in 1950, 1977, and 1985.
Dist.: Janus

KING SOLOMON'S MINES 1950
★ ★ ★ ★ **NR Action-Adventure 1:42**
Dir: Compton Bennett *Cast:* Andrew Marton, Deborah Kerr, Stewart Granger, Richard Carlson, Hugo Haas

▶ Exciting adventure spectacle sends Granger's white-hunter and Indiana Jones prototype Quatermain into the jungle on quest for the legendary diamond mines of the biblical King Solomon. Kerr leads the group, which is imperiled by stampedes and savage natives, and imprisoned in a cave, before learning the secret of the mines. Nominated for three Academy Awards including Best Picture; won for photography and editing.
Dist.: MGM/UA

KING SOLOMON'S MINES 1985
★ ★ **PG-13 Action-Adventure 1:40**
☑ Explicit language, violence
Dir: J. Lee Thompson *Cast:* Richard Chamberlain, Sharon Stone, Herbert Lom, John Rhys-Davies, Ken Gampu, Shai K. Ophir

▶ In Africa, adventurer Chamberlain helps Stone search for her missing father, who has been captured by Germans seeking coveted diamond-mine treasure map. Romance develops as the intrepid duo face cannibals, wild animals, and other dangers. Moves along quickly if mindlessly. Exotic scenery helps; cardboard characterizations do not. Sequel: *Allan Quatermain and the Lost City of Gold.*
Dist.: MGM/UA

KING SOLOMON'S TREASURE 1976
Canadian
☆ **NR Action-Adventure 1:30**
☑ Violence
Dir: Alvin Rakoff *Cast:* David McCallum, John Colicos, Patrick Macnee, Britt Ekland, Hugh Rose

▶ A gold medallion is explorer Allan Quatermain's first clue to the whereabouts of a lost Phoenician city. Dinosaurs, a volcano, and natives are among the obstacles to the adventurer's quest. Lackluster adaptation of the H. Rider Haggard classic makes the middling Richard Chamberlain Quatermain movies look better in comparison.
Dist.: VCI

KINJITE—FORBIDDEN SUBJECTS 1989
★ ★ ★ **R Action-Adventure 1:37**
☑ Nudity, explicit language, violence
Dir: J. Lee Thompson *Cast:* Charles Bronson, Perry Lopez, Juan Fernandez, Peggy Lipton, James Pax

▶ When pimp Fernandez kidnaps daughter of Japanese businessman Pax, Los Angeles cop Bronson investigates although he's no fan of Pax (who once made a play for Bronson's daughter). Bronson vehicle has a bit more variety than his recent outings, with an attempt at a three-dimensional character, but contrived story is often distasteful.
Dist.: Warner

KIPPERBANG 1982 British
★ **PG Comedy/Drama 1:25**
☑ Explicit language
Dir: Michael Apted *Cast:* John Albasiny, Abigail Cruttenden, Maurice Dee, Alison Steadman, Garry Cooper, Robert Urquhart

▶ In suburban England, circa 1948, awkward adolescent Albasiny dreams of kissing class-

mate Cruttenden, who likes someone else. However, a romantic part in the school play may grant the lad his wish. Well-observed but juiceless coming-of-age tale clumsily mixes in a subplot about teacher Steadman's possible pregnancy. Cruttenden is quite charming.
Dist.: MGM/UA

KIPPS 1941 British
★ **NR Comedy 1:22 B&W**
Dir: Carol Reed   *Cast:* Michael Redgrave, Diana Wynyard, Arthur Riscoe, Phyllis Calvert, Max Adrian, Helen Haye
▶ In a small turn-of-the-century English village, shopkeeper Redgrave has his life turned upside down by a large inheritance. Despite being pursued by the upper-class Wynyard, he settles down with long-time sweetheart Calvert, who loses patience with his new hoity-toity ways. Based on a novel by H. G. Wells, preachy story fails to involve. Also known as *The Remarkable Mr. Kipps*; inspired the musical *Half a Sixpence.*
Dist.: Cable

KISMET 1955
★★★ **NR Musical 1:53**
Dir: Vincente Minnelli   *Cast:* Howard Keel, Ann Blyth, Dolores Gray, Vic Damone, Monty Woolley, Sebastian Cabot
▶ In ancient Baghdad, rascal con man Keel is forced by wicked Wazir (Cabot) to persuade Caliph (Damone) to wed a princess. Keel outwits the Wazir and helps daughter Blyth win Caliph's heart. Screen version of the popular Broadway musical is an Arabian Nights tale of comedy and romance. Songs include "Stranger in Paradise," "This Is My Beloved," "Baubles, Bangles and Beads."   **(CC)**
Dist.: MGM/UA

KISS, THE 1988
★★ **R Horror 1:40**
☑ Nudity, adult situations, explicit language, graphic violence
Dir: Pen Desham   *Cast:* Joanna Pacula, Meredith Salenger, Mimi Kuzyk, Pamela Collyer, Nicholas Kilbertus, Jan Rubes
▶ Beautiful model Pacula visits family of her niece Salenger. Dad Kilbertus is bewitched by gorgeous Pacula, but Salenger senses the truth: Pacula is really murderous witch who'd like to possess her. Stylishly directed and above-par acting for the genre, but, gross violence and increasingly contrived plotting hurt.
Dist.: RCA/Columbia

KISS DADDY GOODNIGHT 1987
☆ **R Drama 1:27**
☑ Nudity, adult situations, violence
Dir: Peter Ily Huemer   *Cast:* Uma Thurman, Paul Dillon, Paul Richards, Steve Buscemi, Jennifer Lee Mitchell, Annabelle Gurwitch
▶ Rich bozos are fed knockout drops by slumgoddess Thurman, who swipes their valuables and returns to her pad. There her loser boyfriend is trying to put together a punk band. Cold teen Thurman swipes a dagger that's

involved in a murder from one of her johns. Murky, pretentious entry into low-budget, Lower East Side lowlife sub-genre has little to hold viewers' attention.
Dist.: Academy

KISSIN' COUSINS 1964
★★ **NR Musical 1:36**
Dir: Gene Nelson   *Cast:* Elvis Presley, Arthur O'Connell, Glenda Farrell, Jack Albertson, Pam Austin, Yvonne Craig
▶ Dual role for Presley: he's an Air Force officer ordered to buy O'Connell's land for a missile base and a distant cousin in love with a WAC. O'Connell's moonshine operations provide most of the comedy; Elvis sings "It's a Long Lonely Highway," "Barefoot Ballad," "Smokey Mountain Boy," etc.
Dist.: MGM/UA

KISS ME GOODBYE 1982
★★★★ **PG Fantasy/Comedy 1:41**
☑ Adult situations, explicit language, adult humor
Dir: Robert Mulligan   *Cast:* Sally Field, James Caan, Jeff Bridges, Claire Trevor, Paul Dooley
▶ Widow Field is set to wed straitlaced lawyer Bridges but her happiness is complicated by the ghostly appearance of late husband Caan. Cozy Americanized remake of the much spicier Brazilian *Dona Flor and Her Two Husbands.* Obvious at times (Field talks to an "invisible" Caan with everybody else wondering what's going on), but perky Field and dryly humorous Bridges are likable.
Dist.: CBS/Fox

KISS ME, KATE 1953
★★★ **NR Musical 1:50**
Dir: George Sidney   *Cast:* Kathryn Grayson, Howard Keel, Ann Miller, Bobby Van, Keenan Wynn, Bob Fosse
▶ Sometimes stiff adaptation of Cole Porter's Broadway hit (itself based on Shakespeare's *The Taming of the Shrew*) is a sophisticated comedy of errors about lovers, prima donnas, and gangsters staging a musical. Outstanding Oscar-nominated score includes "Wunderbar," "So in Love," "Why Can't You Behave?" and Miller's scorching tapping to "Too Darn Hot."
Dist.: Magnum

KISS OF THE SPIDER WOMAN 1985
U.S./Brazilian
★★★ **R Drama 1:59 C/B&W**
☑ Adult situations, explicit language, violence
Dir: Hector Babenco   *Cast:* William Hurt, Raul Julia, Sonia Braga, Jose Lewgoy
▶ Hurt, an apolitical gay, and Julia, a political prisoner, are cellmates in a South American jail. Hurt entertains the initially reluctant Julia by retelling scenes from old movies, and a close relationship develops between the men. Superb direction by Babenco weaves a magical spell. Magnificent Oscar-winning

performance by Hurt is tender, subtle, and convincing. Julia holds his own in this enthralling drama. A Best Picture nominee. **(CC)**
Dist.: Nelson

KISS TOMORROW GOODBYE 1950
★ ★ NR Crime 1:42 B&W
Dir: Gordon Douglas *Cast:* James Cagney, Barbara Payton, Helena Carter, Ward Bond, Luther Adler, Barton MacLane
▶ After breaking out of prison, Cagney robs, kills, bribes policemen, and mistreats trashy girlfriend Payton. Corrupt cops Bond and MacLane try to get a piece of Cagney's action but he outwits them. Tough and terse, with the star creating another memorable criminal characterization. Based on a novel by Horace McCoy.
Dist.: Republic

KITCHEN TOTO, THE 1988 British
★ ★ PG-13 Drama 1:36
☑ Violence
Dir: Harry Hook *Cast:* Edwin Mahinda, Bob Peck, Phyllis Logan, Kirsten Hughes, Robert Urquhart, Nicholas Chase
▶ In politically troubled 1950s Kenya, young black Mahinda becomes houseboy for British family after his father is killed. Mahinda finds his allegiance divided between his white employers and the black rebels. Beautifully filmed and socially conscious, but melancholy tone and slow pace limit appeal. Mahinda gives a beguilingly natural performance.
Dist.: Warner

KITTY AND THE BAGMAN 1982 Australian
★ ★ R Comedy 1:35
☑ Nudity, adult situations, explicit language, violence
Dir: Donald Crombie *Cast:* Liddy Clarke, John Stanton, Val Lehman, Gerard McGuire, Collette Mann, Reg Evans
▶ Felonious females are the focus of this lavish Australian tribute to American gangster films. Clarke is a small-town innocent who quickly learns big city ways, and is set up in nightclub to compete with queen-of-the-waterfront Lehman. Bagman Stanton is caught between the two women, who each in her own tough, shrewd way, control gambling houses, brothels, and merchants. Colorful sting caper is well-acted and well-mounted.
Dist.: Nelson

KITTY FOYLE 1940
★ ★ ★ NR Drama 1:45 B&W
Dir: Sam Wood *Cast:* Ginger Rogers, Dennis Morgan, James Craig, Eduardo Ciannelli, Gladys Cooper
▶ Ambitious Kitty Foyle (Rogers) works on a Philadelphia magazine for wealthy blueblood Morgan. They start an affair and plan to marry, but his disapproving family force Kitty to flee to New York. Tragedy and then eventual happiness follow in this soap opera, which nabbed

Rogers a Best Actress Oscar. A Best Picture nominee.
Dist.: VidAmerica

KLONDIKE FEVER 1980
★ ★ ★ PG Action-Adventure 1:58
☑ Adult situations, explicit language, violence
Dir: Peter Carter *Cast:* Rod Steiger, Angie Dickinson, Jeff East, Lorne Greene, Barry Morse
▶ During his Alaskan Gold Rush youth, writer Jack London (East) stands up to the brutality and corruption of the gold miners, helps madam Dickinson set up her own saloon, saves a husky dog from being mistreated, and battles town tyrant Steiger. Fast-paced adventure. Also known as *Jack London's Klondike Fever.*
Dist.: Vestron

KLUTE 1971
★ ★ ★ ★ R Mystery-Suspense 1:54
☑ Adult situations, explicit language, mild violence
Dir: Alan J. Pakula *Cast:* Jane Fonda, Donald Sutherland, Charles Cioffi, Roy Scheider, Dorothy Tristan, Rita Gam
▶ Pennsylvania detective Sutherland investigates friend's disappearance in New York City and centers on hooker Fonda, who's being stalked by a psychopath. Consistently provocative adult thriller with a nail-biting finale. Fascinating Oscar-winning performance by Fonda dominates the film, with Sutherland providing understated support.
Dist.: Warner

KNIFE IN THE WATER 1962 Polish
★ NR Drama 1:34
Dir: Roman Polanski *Cast:* Leon Niemczyk, Jolanta Umecka, Zygmunt Malanowicz
▶ A young couple pick up a student hitchhiker and take him sailing. Out on a tranquil lake, things get tense as a rivalry builds between the student and the husband, culminating in mysterious doings. Director Polanaski's first feature is subtle and remote, but powerfully executed. Ⓢ
Dist.: Various

KNIGHTRIDERS 1981
★ R Action-Adventure 2:26
☑ Brief nudity, adult situations, explicit language, violence
Dir: George A. Romero *Cast:* Ed Harris, Gary Lahti, Tom Savini, Amy Ingersoll
▶ A traveling troupe of entertainers combines medieval costumes with motorcycles and lives according to the laws of Camelot. The group's king is challenged by a pretender to the throne. Unusual film is a wry change-of-pace for horror director Romero.
Dist.: Media

KNIGHTS AND EMERALDS 1987 British
★ PG Comedy 1:34

☑ Adult situations, explicit language, violence
Dir: Ian Emes   **Cast:** Christopher Wild, Beverley Hills, Warren Mitchell, Bill Leadbiter, Rachel Davies, Tracie Bennett
▶ Look at the subculture of teen marching bands has Wild drumming for hapless outfit called the Knights while all his friends are in the bodacious black Crusaders. Loyal to the Knights, Wild falls for a girl from their dance troupe, only to have her prefer a skinhead bully. During big band competition finale, Wild risks racial ostracism and defects to black band. Film gives fascinating glimpses into Britian's complex race/class situation.   **(CC)**
Dist.: Warner

KNIGHTS OF THE CITY 1986
★ R Drama/Music 1:29 C/B&W
☑ Adult situations, explicit language, violence
Dir: Dominic Orlando   **Cast:** Leon Isaac Kennedy, John Mengatti, Nicholas Campbell, Janine Turner
▶ When not making music, street gang led by Kennedy battles rivals over turf. Kennedy romances record company executive's daughter Turner and the gang wins a talent contest. However, they must revert to knives to settle their final confrontation. Noisy, crudely shot entry in the breakdance/rap craze represents last gasp of the dying genre.
Dist.: New World

KNIGHTS OF THE ROUND TABLE 1953
★★★ NR Action-Adventure 1:55
Dir: Richard Thorpe   **Cast:** Robert Taylor, Ava Gardner, Mel Ferrer, Anne Crawford, Stanley Baker, Felix Aylmer
▶ In medieval England, Sir Lancelot (Taylor) faithfully serves King Arthur (Ferrer) but his heart roams in the direction of Arthur's wife Queen Guinevere (Gardner). Well-mounted version of a now-familiar triangle.
Dist.: MGM/UA

KNIGHT WITHOUT ARMOUR 1937 British
★★ NR Drama 1:41 B&W
Dir: Jacques Feyder   **Cast:** Marlene Dietrich, Robert Donat, Irene Vanbrugh, Herbert Lomas, Miles Malleson, David Tree
▶ British agent Donat saves countess Dietrich from revolutionaries, but the two still find themselves caught between the Red and White armies in the Russian Revolution. Donat makes a handsome hero for Dietrich's glamorous aristocrat in this lavish, compelling production.
Dist.: Nelson

K-9 1989
★★★★ PG-13 Action-Adventure/Comedy 1:42
☑ Explicit language, violence
Dir: Rod Daniel   **Cast:** James Belushi, Mel Harris, Kevin Tighe, Ed O'Neill, Jerry Lee the Dog
▶ Police officer Belushi is hot on the trail of drug kingpin Tighe. He's assigned a new partner for the case: German shepherd K-9. The duo manages to pick up the scent and show Tighe a trick or two. Lame twist on the buddy genre features an abrasive, unappealing Belushi and tired jokes.   **(CC)**
Dist.: MCA

KNOCK ON ANY DOOR 1949
★★ NR Drama 1:40 B&W
Dir: Nicholas Ray   **Cast:** Humphrey Bogart, John Derek, George Macready, Allene Roberts, Susan Perry
▶ Socially conscious drama stars Bogart as an attorney defending cop-killer Derek on the grounds of his deprived childhood. This liberal philosophy may seem quaint to some but Bogart's climactic courtroom "knock on any door" speech is a rouser.
Dist.: RCA/Columbia

KNUTE ROCKNE—ALL AMERICAN 1940
★★★★ NR Biography/Sports 1:36 B&W
Dir: Lloyd Bacon   **Cast:** Pat O'Brien, Ronald Reagan, Gale Page, Donald Crisp, Albert Basserman
▶ Biography of football coach Knute Rockne (O'Brien), who guided Notre Dame to many gridiron victories, is conventional but still entertaining. Reagan is George Gipp, the dying player who asks O'Brien to "tell the boys to win one for the Gipper." O'Brien does just that in an inspirational speech that is now part of cinema, sports, and political history.
Dist.: MGM/UA Ⓒ

KOTCH 1971
★★★★ PG Comedy 1:53
☑ Adult situations, explicit language
Dir: Jack Lemmon   **Cast:** Walter Matthau, Deborah Winters, Felicia Farr, Ellen Geer, Charles Aidman, Lucy Saroyan
▶ Senior citizen Matthau lives with son Aidman and daughter-in-law Farr. Farr and Matthau fight. She tries to send him to an old age home; he responds by running away and befriending unmarried mother-to-be Winters. Affecting comedy won Oscar nominations for the wonderful Matthau, editing, sound, and the Johnny Mercer/Marvin Hamlisch song, "Life Is What You Make It." Lemmon's only directorial effort to date.
Dist.: CBS/Fox

KOYAANISQATSI 1983
★ NR Documentary 1:27
Dir: Godfrey Reggio
▶ Reggio collaborated with composer Philip Glass and cinematographer Ron Fricks to illuminate the Hopi Indian concept of "life out of balance." Powerful score and stunning photographic techniques show natural wonders and man's technological invasion of them. Assault dazzles the senses, though mainstream audiences may be overwhelmed by the experience.
Dist.: Pacific Arts

KRAMER VS. KRAMER 1979
★ ★ ★ ★ ★ **PG Drama 1:45**
☑ Brief nudity, adult situations, explicit language
Dir: Robert Benton *Cast:* Dustin Hoffman, Meryl Streep, Justin Henry, JoBeth Williams, Jane Alexander, Howard Duff
▶ Enormously moving film about parental love examines the growing relationship between father Hoffman and son Henry after they're abandoned by wife/mother Streep. A fierce child-custody battle ensues when Streep returns to claim her son. Oscars for Best Picture, Actor (Hoffman), Supporting Actress (Streep), and Adapted Screenplay (by Benton from the Avery Corman novel). **(CC)**
Dist.: RCA/Columbia

KRULL 1983
★ ★ ★ **PG Fantasy 1:56**
☑ Adult situations, violence
Dir: Peter Yates *Cast:* Ken Marshall, Lysette Anthony, Freddie Jones, Francesca Annis, David Battley, Liam Neeson
▶ Once upon a time on a far-off planet, prince Marshall was aided by a bandit, a sorcerer, and a cyclops in a quest to rescue his beloved Anthony kidnapped by an evil monster. Elaborate fantasy adventure will entertain kids but adults may find it laughable. Fanciful special effects and set design, but awkwardly directed by the usually dependable Yates. **(CC)**
Dist.: RCA/Columbia

KRUSH GROOVE 1985
★ ★ ★ **R Musical 1:34**
☑ Brief nudity, adult situations, explicit language
Dir: Michael Schultz *Cast:* Blair Underwood, Sheila E. (Escovedo), Run-D.M.C., Kurtis Blow, Fat Boys, LL Cool J
▶ Slight plot about young entrepreneur Underwood and his fledgling record company provides the framework for top-notch songs performed by rap's early stars. Sheila E. makes the strongest impression, but film catches Run-D.M.C., the Fat Boys, and the Beastie Boys (in a brief cameo) on the verge of stardom. Soundtrack album was a huge success. **(CC)**
Dist.: Warner

KUNG FU MASTER 1989 French
☆ **R Drama 1:20**
☑ Adult situations, explicit language
Dir: Agnes Varda *Cast:* Jane Birkin, Mathieu Demy, Charlotte Gainsbourg, Lou Doillon, Eva Simonet, Judy Campbell
▶ Fourteen-year-old Demy is deeply involved in a martial arts video game. He's also involved in a glorious May/December romance with middle-aged Birkin, mother of one of his friends. When Birkin's daughter discovers mother and Demy locked in loving embrace, she is shocked. Affair ends amid universal tut-tutting. Silly, self-indulgent film has anti-AIDS

messages awkwardly interpolated into action. Released on video as *Le Petit Amour.*
☑
Dist.: Prism

KWAIDAN 1964 Japanese
☆ **NR Horror 2:40**
Dir: Masaki Kobayashi *Cast:* Rentaro Mikuni, Keiko Kishi, Katsuo Nakamura, Ganemon Nakamura, Michiyo Aratama, Tatsuya Nakadai
▶ Delicately frightening Japanese treatment of four ghost stories taken from the works of turn-of-the-century American author Lafcadio Hearn. A samurai wakes in bed with a corpse; a woodcutter marries a ghost with breath of ice; a minstrel is summoned to sing for samurai spirits; and a warrior is haunted by a face in a cup of tea. Eerie and beautiful. ☑
Dist.: Various

LA BALANCE 1982 French
☆ **R Action-Adventure 1:42**
☑ Adult situations, explicit language, graphic violence
Dir: Bob Swaim *Cast:* Nathalie Baye, Philippe Leotard, Richard Berry, Maurice Ronet, Christophe Malavoy, Jean-Paul Connart
▶ Berry leads an elite police group whose informer has been killed by crime kingpin Ronet. Leotard, a small-time hood living off prostitute Baye, has his arm twisted into helping Berry get back at Ronet in a sting operation. Visceral, hard-hitting police thriller. **(CC)**
☑
Dist.: CBS/Fox

LA BAMBA 1987
★ ★ ★ **PG-13 Biography/Music 1:49**
☑ Brief nudity, adult situations, explicit language
Dir: Luis Valdez *Cast:* Lou Diamond Phillips, Esai Morales, Rosana De Soto, Elizabeth Peña, Danielle von Zerneck, Joe Pantoliano, Marshall Crenshaw, Brian Setzer
▶ Uplifting musical about migrant laborer Ritchie Valens (Phillips), who bucks the odds against Hispanics by becoming a rock star. Film concentrates on Valens's problems with his criminal brother Morales and romance with Donna (von Zerneck) before his tragic death in a plane crash. Los Lobos did the soundtrack, which includes "Come on Let's Go" and the title tune. **(CC)**
Dist.: RCA/Columbia

LA BETE HUMAINE 1938 French
☆ **NR Drama 1:45 B&W**
Dir: Jean Renoir *Cast:* Jean Gabin, Simone Simon, Fernand Ledoux, Julien Carette, Blanchette Brunoy, Jean Renoir
▶ Railroad employee Ledoux kills wife Simon's lover in a fit of jealousy. Brutal engineer Gabin witnesses the crime, says nothing, and later becomes Simon's lover himself. Soon, Gabin is faced with necessity of killing Ledoux. Gabin

is sensational in this gripping adaptation of the Emile Zola novel. [S]
Dist.: Various

LA BOUM 1981 French
☆ **NR Comedy/Drama 1:40**
☑ Adult situations
Dir: Claude Pinoteau *Cast:* Claude Brasseur, Brigitte Fossey, Sophie Marceau, Denise Grey, Bernard Giraudeau, Dominique Lavanant
► When her family moves to a new neighborhood, thirteen-year-old Marceau tries to cope with the change. Adding to her troubles is marital rift between parents Brasseur and Fossey. Well-observed, but aimless, coming-of-age story with an engaging performance by Marceau. Cast and director reunited for 1982 sequel *La Boum 2*. [S]
Dist.: RCA/Columbia

LABYRINTH 1986
★★★★ **PG Fantasy/Family 1:42**
☑ Explicit language
Dir: Jim Henson *Cast:* David Bowie, Jennifer Connelly, Toby Froud, Shelley Thompson, Christopher Malcolm, Natalie Finland
► When goblins kidnap her baby brother, teenager Connelly enters a magical labyrinth to find him. She's aided by a helpful dwarf and other odd creatures. Henson's puppets should delight the kiddies but, aside from David Bowie as the king of the goblins, there's not much here for adults. (CC)
Dist.: Nelson

LABYRINTH OF PASSION 1982 Spanish
☆ **NR Comedy 1:409**
☑ Nudity, strong sexual content, adult situations, explicit language
Dir: Pedro Almodóvar *Cast:* Cecilia Roth, Imanol Arias, Malta Fernandez-Murk, Helga Line
► Off-the-wall sex farce was director Almodóvar's first foray into film. Lunatic characters include: nymphomaniac Sexilia (Roth); her gynecologist dad who does artificial insemination on budgies; the gay Shah of Tyran's son (Arias) who sleeps with terrorists; and a laundress (Fernandez-Murk) involved in an incestuous relationship. A raucous romp, but obviously not for everyone. [S]
Dist.: CineVista

LA CAGE AUX FOLLES 1979 French/Italian
★★ **R Comedy 1:37**
☑ Adult situations, explicit language
Dir: Edouard Molinaro *Cast:* Ugo Tognazzi, Michel Serrault, Michel Galabru, Claire Maurier
► Gay nightclub owner Tognazzi and his star performer/lover Serrault attempt to impersonate a straight couple to please their son's priggish prospective in-laws. Hilarious boulevard farce with Serrault especially amusing. Most sidesplitting scene: Tognazzi teaching Serrault how to act like a "man." Three Oscar nominations; inspired the Tony-winning Broadway musical. Led to several sequels. [S]
Dist.: MGM/UA

LA CAGE AUX FOLLES II 1981 French/Italian
★ **R Comedy 1:39**
☑ Adult situations, explicit language, violence, adult humor
Dir: Edouard Molinaro *Cast:* Ugo Tognazzi, Michel Serrault, Mark Bodin, Benny Luke, Gianrico Tondinelli, Michel Galabru
► Gay nightclub owner Tognazzi and his transvestite companion Serrault become involved with cops and spies when Serrault unwittingly gets his hands on stolen microfilm. The lovers flee to Italy but find little peace there. Re-creating their original roles, Tognazzi and Serrault still evoke laughs. [S]
Dist.: CBS/Fox

LA CAGE AUX FOLLES 3: THE WEDDING 1985 French
★ **PG-13 Comedy 1:31**
☑ Adult situations, explicit language
Dir: Georges Lautner *Cast:* Ugo Tognazzi, Michel Serrault, Michel Galabru, Benny Luke
► The St. Tropez nightclub of lovers Serrault and Tognazzi has fallen on hard times. One glimmer of hope: Serrault will inherit a fortune if he can marry and produce an heir within eighteen months. Third in the popular comedy series from France. Some fun but the original is still the best. [S]
Dist.: RCA/Columbia

LADIES CLUB, THE 1986
★★ **R Action-Adventure 1:30**
☑ Rape, adult situations, explicit language, graphic violence
Dir: A. K. Allen *Cast:* Karen Austin, Diana Scarwid, Christine Belford, Bruce Davison, Shera Danese, Beverly Todd
► Policewoman Austin and doctor Belford join up with other victimized women to kidnap and castrate career rapists. Their activities embroil the city in controversy, and the women must decide how long they will continue their crusade. Nasty revenge movie exploits rape for full voyeuristic impact.
Dist.: Media

LA DOLCE VITA 1960 Italian
★★ **NR Drama 2:55 B&W**
Dir: Federico Fellini *Cast:* Marcello Mastroianni, Yvonne Furneaux, Anita Ekberg, Anouk Aimee, Magali Noel, Alain Cuny
► Roman gossip columnist Mastroianni has serious literary aspirations but craves money too much to pursue them. Instead, his life is an aimless round of womanizing and trivial glamour events beloved of tabloid readers. Part slice-of-life look at Italy, part satire of money as route to happiness, and part elaborate joke by director Fellini. Trend-setting film will delight buffs, but length, rambling structure, and often banal dialogue will bore those with conventional tastes. [S]
Dist.: Republic

LADY AND THE TRAMP 1955
★ ★ ★ ★ ★ G Animation 1:16
Dir: Hamilton Luske, Clyde Geronimi, Wilfred Jackson *Cast:* Voices of Peggy Lee, Barbara Luddy, Larry Roberts, Stan Freberg, Verna Felton
▶ Lady, a pampered pedigreed spaniel, runs away when forced to play second fiddle to her owners' new baby. She falls in puppy love with a mutt from the other side of the tracks named Tramp after their famous romantic spaghetti dinner scene. Peggy Lee provides the voice for a blowsy Pekinese and Si and Am, two slinky cats who sing "We Are Siamese If You Please." Charming and witty Disney effort has become a popular favorite. **(CC)**
Dist.: Buena Vista

LADY BEWARE 1987
★ ★ R Mystery-Suspense 1:48
☑ Nudity, strong sexual content, explicit language, violence
Dir: Karen Arthur *Cast:* Diane Lane, Michael Woods, Cotter Smith, Peter Nevargic, Tyra Ferrell, Viveca Lindfors
▶ Lane, a sultry Pittsburgh window dresser, turns the tables on a psychopathic Peeping Tom who's been torturing her with devious tricks. Journalist Smith may be a suspect or a friend. Lane has one provocative bath-time nude scene. Mildly exploitive thriller.
Dist.: IVE

LADY CHATTERLEY'S LOVER 1982
French/British
★ ★ R Drama 1:43
☑ Nudity, strong sexual content, adult situations, explicit language, mild violence
Dir: Just Jaeckin *Cast:* Sylvia Kristel, Shane Briant, Nicholas Clay, Ann Mitchell
▶ After husband Briant is wounded in World War I, Lady Chatterley (Kristel) takes handsome caretaker Clay for a lover. Classy production values enhance tasteful sex scenes, but this sappy rendering of D. H. Lawrence's novel suffers from overwrought music, marginal characterizations, and languid pacing.
Dist.: MGM/UA

LADY EVE, THE 1941
★ ★ ★ ★ NR Comedy 1:34 B&W
Dir: Preston Sturges *Cast:* Barbara Stanwyck, Henry Fonda, Charles Coburn, Eugene Pallette, William Demarest, Eric Blore, Melville Cooper
▶ Shipboard romance flounders when wealthy paleontologist Fonda discovers cardsharp Stanwyck originally intended to bilk him. She plots delicious revenge by posing as British royalty. Fonda is charmingly innocent (he thinks it can't be same girl because "they look too much alike"), Stanwyck devastatingly sexy (particularly in the hair-ruffling scene), and the Sturges stock company swell, espe-

cially Demarest as the aide who insists: II's the same dame."
Dist.: MCA

LADY FOR A NIGHT 1941
★ NR Drama 1:27 B&W
Dir: Leigh Jason *Cast:* Joan Blondell, John Wayne, Ray Middleton, Philip Merivale, Blanche Yurka, Edith Barrett
▶ Hoping to be accepted in high society, riverboat gambling queen Blondell marries gentleman Middleton in exchange for covering his debts. Leaving old friends like political boss Wayne behind, she starts a new life, but becomes the number-one suspect when Middleton is mysteriously murdered. Wayne has little to do in this leaden melodrama.
Dist.: Republic

LADY FRANKENSTEIN 1971 Italian
☆ R Horror 1:24
☑ Nudity, adult situations, violence
Dir: Mel Welles *Cast:* Joseph Cotten, Sara Bay, Paul Muller, Peter Whiteman, Herbert Fux, Mickey Hargitay
▶ Baron Frankenstein (Cotten) creates a monster that kills him and ravages the countryside. His daughter Bay's solution: fashion a second creature from the brain of a crippled assistant and the body of a muscular gardener to avenge her father's death. Tawdry shocker has a fair amount of sex and some unintentional humor (especially the alienlike monster and a soundtrack full of gurgles) to keep it interesting.
Dist.: Nelson

LADY FROM LOUISIANA 1941
★ NR Drama 1:22 B&W
Dir: Bernard Vorhaus *Cast:* John Wayne, Ona Munson, Ray Middleton, Henry Stephenson, Helen Westley, Jack Pennick
▶ Lawyer Wayne is fighting vice in turn-of-the-century New Orleans, where the lovely Munson takes over a lottery racket formerly run by her dad. Munson doesn't know how corrupt an enterprise she's inherited, but Wayne does—and he's got the bad guys on trial when a monstrous flood comes crashing through the courthouse. The elements are all here, but story never works up speed.
Dist.: Republic

LADY FROM SHANGHAI, THE 1948
★ NR Mystery-Suspense 1:27 B&W
Dir: Orson Welles *Cast:* Rita Hayworth, Orson Welles, Everett Sloane, Glenn Anders, Ted de Corsia
▶ Sailor Welles is seduced by femme fatale Hayworth (then Mrs. Welles) and is implicated in a murder plot by her crippled husband Sloane. Twisty film noir highlighted by Welles's exciting cinematic techniques (as exemplified by the celebrated hall of mirrors finale).
Dist.: RCA/Columbia

LADYHAWKE 1985
★ ★ ★ ★ PG-13 Fantasy 2:01

[✓] Explicit language, violence
Dir: Richard Donner *Cast:* Matthew Broderick, Rutger Hauer, Michelle Pfeiffer, Leo McKern, John Wood
► Offbeat and original story of thirteenth-century cursed lovers. Young pickpocket Broderick meets mysterious knight Hauer who's always accompanied by a hawk. Every night, the hawk turns into Pfeiffer and the knight becomes a wolf; they are actually lovers trapped in an awful spell cast by jealous bishop Wood. Handsome medieval fantasy with romance, adventure, and strong period flavor. (CC)
Dist.: Warner

LADY IN A CAGE 1964
★ NR Mystery-Suspense 1:33 B&W
Dir: Walter Grauman *Cast:* Olivia de Havilland, Jeff Corey, Ann Sothern, James Caan, Scatman Crothers
► De Havilland plays a wealthy woman trapped in an elevator and menaced by a trio of thugs including a young Caan. Taut thriller builds up claustrophobic tension.
Dist.: Paramount

LADY IN QUESTION, THE 1940
★ NR Comedy/Drama 1:21 B&W
Dir: Charles Vidor *Cast:* Brian Aherne, Rita Hayworth, Glenn Ford, Irene Rich, George Coulouris, Evelyn Keyes
► Parisian bicycle shopkeeper Aherne, serving as a juror, successfully lobbies for murder suspect Hayworth's acquittal. Hiding her identity from his family, he gives her a job, only to have his son Ford fall in love with her. Enjoyable American remake of the French *Heart of Paris* features first teaming of Hayworth and Ford.
Dist.: RCA/Columbia

LADY IN RED, THE 1979
★ ★ ★ R Biography/Crime 1:33
[✓] Nudity, adult situations, explicit language, graphic violence
Dir: Lewis Teague *Cast:* Pamela Sue Martin, Robert Conrad, Louise Fletcher, Robert Hogan, Laurie Heineman
► Gangster saga from gun moll's point of view. Abused by her dad, Polly Franklin (Martin) moves to Chicago, works in a sweatshop, goes to prison, and becomes a prostitute. She falls for John Dillinger (Conrad) and, after he's gunned down, turns to a life of crime. Lurid, frenzied plotting with lots of stabbings, sadistic murders, and sex. Roger Corman production has a screenplay by John Sayles.
Dist.: Vestron

LADY IN WHITE 1988
★ ★ ★ PG-13 Mystery-Suspense 1:52
[✓] Explicit language, violence
Dir: Frank LaLoggia *Cast:* Lukas Haas, Katherine Helmond, Len Cariou, Alex Rocco, Lucy Lee Flippin
► Imaginative nine-year-old Haas is locked in a spooky school closet on Halloween night. He sees the ghost of a murdered girl and is almost strangled by a mysterious killer. Absorbing blend of horror and the supernatural has tricky plotting and a peculiar tone. (CC)
Dist.: Virgin

LADY JANE 1986 British
★ ★ ★ PG-13 Biography 2:22
[✓] Brief nudity, adult situations
Dir: Trevor Nunn *Cast:* Helena Bonham Carter, Cary Elwes, John Wood, Jane Lapotaire, Joan Bennett
► Old-fashioned historical epic based on the life of Lady Jane Grey (Carter), who was crowned Queen of England at the age of sixteen in 1553 and reigned for only nine days. With Elwes as Guilford Dudley, Jane's handsome teenaged husband, and Lapotaire as her rival, the vehemently pro-Catholic Princess Mary (who became legendary queen "Bloody" Mary). (CC)
Dist.: Paramount

LADYKILLERS, THE 1955 British
★ ★ ★ ★ NR Comedy 1:30
Dir: Alexander Mackendrick *Cast:* Alec Guinness, Katie Johnson, Cecil Parker, Herbert Lom, Peter Sellers
► Gang of crooks led by a buck-toothed Guinness moves in with petite, elderly Johnson, who's unaware of their true professions. When she stumbles across their loot, they decide she must die. Black comedy is decidedly morbid but ingenious.
Dist.: HBO

LADY OF BURLESQUE 1943
★ ★ NR Mystery-Suspense 1:31 B&W
Dir: William Wellman *Cast:* Barbara Stanwyck, Michael O'Shea, J. Edward Bromberg, Iris Adrian, Pinky Lee, Gloria Dickson
► Stanwyck bears the perils of police raids and the importunities of comic O'Shea as one of a company of strippers performing in an old opera house gone to seed. When a killer starts strangling her fellow performers with their own G-strings, Stanwyck teams up with O'Shea to solve the mystery. Stanwyck is good form in this entertaining adaptation of Gypsy Rose Lee's mystery novel *The G-String Murders.*
Dist.: Video Yesteryear

LADY ON THE BUS 1978 Brazilian
★ R Comedy 1:26
[✓] Nudity, strong sexual content, adult situations
Dir: Neville d'Almeida *Cast:* Sonia Braga, Nuno Leal Maia, Jorge Doria, Paulo Cesar Pereio, Yara Amaral
► Bewitching Brazilian temptress Braga is a frigid newlywed, unresponsive to her handsome husband Maia. Her solution is to try other lovers, from her husband's best friend (Pereio), to his father, to casual strangers riding the bus. Shot in Rio de Janeiro. [S]
Dist.: Vestron

LADY SCARFACE 1941
★ NR Mystery-Suspense 1:09 B&W
Dir: Frank Woodruff *Cast:* Dennis O'Keefe, Judith Anderson, Frances Neal, Mildred Coles, Eric Blore, Marc Lawrence
► Wisecracking cop O'Keefe and magazine photgrapher Neal are tracking down a gang leader responsible for deadly crimes, little realizing that the man they are after is a woman—Anderson, whose scarred visage has made her antisocial. Anderson is effective, but her efforts are disfigured by a poor script.
Dist.: Turner

LADY SINGS THE BLUES 1972
★★★★ R Biography/Musical 2:22
☑ Brief nudity, adult situations, explicit language, violence
Dir: Sidney J. Furie *Cast:* Diana Ross, Billy Dee Williams, Richard Pryor, James Callahan, Paul Hampton
► In her film debut, Diana Ross plays Billie Holiday, the legendary black jazz singer whose life and brilliant career was destroyed by drug addiction. With Richard Pryor as "Piano Man" and Williams as her lover. Songs include: "Strange Fruit" and "God Bless the Child." Very loosely based on Holiday's book co-written with William Duffy. Nominated for five Oscars (Actress, Screenplay, Art Direction, Score, and Costumes).
Dist.: Paramount

LADY TAKES A CHANCE, A 1943
★★★★ NR Comedy 1:26 B&W
Dir: William A. Seiter *Cast:* Jean Arthur, John Wayne, Charles Winninger, Phil Silvers, Mary Field
► Arthur, a sharp New York City girl traveling out West, misses her bus and finds herself stranded with cowpoke Wayne. He introduces the self-confident Easterner to the rough-and-tumble ways of the region, and she teaches him a trick or two, as they overcome misunderstandings and fall in love. Charming comedy.
Dist.: VidAmerica

LADY VANISHES, THE 1938 British
★★★★ NR Mystery-Suspense 1:37 B&W
Dir: Alfred Hitchcock *Cast:* Margaret Lockwood, Michael Redgrave, Paul Lukas, Dame May Whitty, Naunton Wayne, Basil Radford, Googie Withers
► Returning home from a Balkan vacation, young Lockwood strikes up a friendship with elderly Whitty. When Whitty disappears during a train journey, Lockwood turns to arrogant folklorist Redgrave for help. They uncover a sinister spy conspiracy in this deft mixture of suspense and comedy, one of Hitchcock's most enjoyable movies. Cricket fanciers Wayne and Radford proved so popular as comic relief that they teamed up in many subsequent films.
Dist.: Media

LADY VANISHES, THE 1980
★★★ PG Mystery-Suspense 1:39
☑ Adult situations, explicit language
Dir: Anthony Page *Cast:* Elliott Gould, Cybill Shepherd, Angela Lansbury, Herbert Lom, Arthur Lowe, Ian Carmichael
► Dear old British lady Lansbury disappears off a train in 1939 Germany, and Shepherd is the madcap heiress who's trying to get to the bottom of the mystery. Life magazine photog Gould is on hand to lend amusing assistance, and the plot comes to have international significance in tense, pre-war atmosphere. Real mystery is what, besides color, filmmakers thought bland new version would have that dazzling Hitchcock version didn't.
Dist.: Media

L'AGE D'OR 1930 French
☆ NR Comedy 1:03 B&W
Dir: Louis Buñuel *Cast:* Gaston Modot, Lya Lys, Max Ernst, Pierre Prevert, Caridad de Laberdesque, Lionel Salem
► Surrealist masterpiece co-scripted by director Buñuel and painter Salvador Dali tells of lovers Lys and Modot, whose affection is disrupted by the state, the class system, the church, and other hampering forces. Lots of irreverent jokes and unexpected turns of imagery. [S]
Dist.: Corinth

LAGUNA HEAT 1987
★★★★ NR Mystery-Suspense/MFTV 1:50
☑ Brief nudity, adult situations, explicit language, violence
Dir: Simon Langton *Cast:* Harry Hamlin, Jason Robards, Jr., Rip Torn, Catherine Hicks, Anne Francis
► Wry, witty suspense drama about the sleepy picture-postcard town of Laguna Beach, jolted awake by two brutal murders. In a plot full of razor-sharp twists and turns, former police detective Hamlin investigates the crimes and discovers a long-buried secret that hits painfully close to home. Based on T. Jefferson Parker's best-selling thriller.
Dist.: Warner

LAIR OF THE WHITE WORM, THE 1988 British
★ R Horror 1:34
☑ Nudity, adult situations, explicit language, violence
Dir: Ken Russell *Cast:* Amanda Donohoe, Hugh Grant, Catherine Oxenberg, Sammi Davis, Peter Capaldi, Stratford Johns
► Archaeologist Capaldi unearths ancient skull that proves a crucial element in neighbor Donohoe's search for virgins to feed local giant white worm. Delirious horror extravaganza, loosely based on a Bram Stoker novel, is nifty fun on a camp level. Donohoe is amazingly alluring as an aristocratic vampire priestess.
Dist.: Vestron

LA LECTRICE 1989 French
☆ **R Drama 1:38**
☑ Nudity, adult situations, explicit language
Dir: Michel Deville *Cast:* Miou-Miou, Christian Ruché, Sylvie Laporte, Michel Raskine, Brigitte Catillon, Régis Royer
▶ Lots of literary in-jokes here, as Miou-Miou plays a professional reader, paid to read aloud from works of Duras, de Sade, Marx and others. Her clients are a variety of strange French people, some of whom have fantasies about her, others about whom she has fantasies, all of whom are served above and beyond the call of duty. Very interesting intellectual exercise may be inaccessible to some. [S]
Dist.: Orion

LA MARSELLAISE 1938 French
☆ **NR Drama 2:10 B&W**
Dir: Jean Renoir *Cast:* Pierre Renoir, Lise Delamare, Leon Larive, William Haguet, Louis Jouvet, Aime Clairond
▶ The stirring French patriotic song grows from a rough melody to a rousing anthem in the throats of five hundred determined peasants marching from Marseilles to Paris during the French Revolution of 1789. Re-creation of the epoch-making trek to the Tuilleries celebrated the one-hundred-fiftieth anniversary of the song. Despite some splendid touches, pageant lacks dramatic impact. [S]
Dist.: Various

LAMBADA 1990
☆ **PG Drama/Dance 1:44**
☑ Adult situations, explicit language, mild violence
Dir: Joel Silberg *Cast:* J. Eddie Peck, Melora Hardin, Shabba-Doo, Ricky Paul Goldin, Basil Hoffman, Dennis Burkley
▶ Beverly Hills math teacher Peck has a secret life, teaching dancing and equations to East L.A. kids at night. When student Hardin discovers Peck's nocturnal activities, it takes a climactic math contest to save his job. Manufactured Brazilian dance craze gets another surprisingly sexless Hollywood treatment. Attractive leads, innocuous plot. Highlight: Peck and Hardin dancing "I Like the Rhythm."
Dist.: Cannon

LAND BEFORE TIME, THE 1988
★★★★ **G Animation 1:13**
Dir: Don Bluth *Cast:* Voices of Pat Hingle, Helen Shaver, Gabriel Damon, Candice Houston, Burke Barnes
▶ In a time when dinosaurs rule the earth, changes in climate make the land inhospitable for plant eaters. Baby brontosaurus Littlefoot and his family leave their home in search of the bountiful Great Valley. Separated from his elders and pursued by a flesh-eating tyrannosaurus, Littlefoot must team with child dinosaurs from differing species to find the promised land. Old-fashioned animation from purist Bluth stands out among today's static, cost-cutting cartoons.
Dist.: MCA

LANDLORD BLUES 1987
★ **NR Drama 1:37**
☑ Explicit language
Dir: Jacob Burkhardt, William Gordy *Cast:* Mark Boone, Jr., Raye Dowell, Richard Litt, Nona Hendryx, Gigi Williams, Gerard Little
▶ When scuzzy landlord Litt tries to evict bicycle repairman Boone, he fights back by enlisting his friends in a scam to double-cross Litt with a phony lease. To make him even more despicable, the filmmakers have made the property-owning fiend a drug dealer, too. Set in New York's Lower East Side, low-budget independent has a few laughs and a certain hip charm.
Dist.: Monarch

LAND THAT TIME FORGOT, THE 1975 British
★★★ **PG Action-Adventure 1:31**
☑ Mild violence
Dir: Kevin Connor *Cast:* Doug McClure, John McEnery, Susan Penhaligon, Keith Barron, Anthony Ainley, Godfrey James
▶ American McClure and Englishwoman Penhaligon come aboard the German World War I submarine that sunk their ship. They become allies with captain McEnery when the sub is grounded in a lost world where prehistoric monsters still roam. Imaginative adventure is the first, and clearly the best, of the McClure/Connor Edgar Rice Burroughs adaptations. Followed by *The People That Time Forgot.*
Dist.: Vestron

LA NUIT DE VARENNES 1982 French/Italian
★ **R Drama 2:13**
☑ Nudity, adult situations
Dir: Ettore Scola *Cast:* Marcello Mastroianni, Jean-Louis Barrault, Hanna Schygulla, Harvey Keitel, Jean-Claude Brialy
▶ The French revolution is roaring, the king is making a hasty getaway, and aged voluptuary Cassanova (Mastroianni), libertarian pamphleteer Thomas Paine (Keitel), and other historical characters bump into each other on a night of consequences fateful to the future of France. Mastroianni is perfect as the pouchy libertine, and Schygulla is stunning in this colorful, satisfying historical concoction. [S]
Dist.: RCA/Columbia

LA PASSANTE 1982 French/German
☆ **NR Drama 1:46**
☑ Adult situations, violence
Dir: Jacques Rouffio *Cast:* Romy Schneider, Michel Piccoli, Wendelin Werner, Helmut Griem, Gerard Klein, Dominique Labourier
▶ Though a dedicated pacifist, Piccoli shocks those who know him by killing a former Nazi living under the identity of a South American diplomat. Flashbacks reveal the trauma of Piccoli's childhood with mother Schneider in Nazi Germany. Deftly intercuts between past

and present to build drama. Schneider died two days before the movie's release. [S]
Dist.: Pacific Arts

LA RONDE 1950 French
★★ NR Drama 1:37 B&W
Dir: Max Ophuls *Cast:* Simone Signoret, Anton Walbrook, Serge Reggiani, Simone Simon, Daniel Gelin, Danielle Darrieux, Jean-Louis Barrault, Gerard Philipe
▶ Walbrook serves as the cynical master of ceremonies for an elegant but bleak comedy of manners about the intertwined affairs of various lovers, starting and ending with young prostitute Signoret. Witty, polished adaptation of Arthur Schnitzler's play was nominated for Best Screenplay. [S]
Dist.: Nelson

LASSITER 1984
★★★★ R Action-Adventure 1:40
☑ Nudity, adult situations, explicit language, violence
Dir: Roger Young *Cast:* Tom Selleck, Jane Seymour, Lauren Hutton, Bob Hoskins, Joe Regalbuto, Ed Lauter
▶ Pre-World War II intrigue set in London follows the exploits of suave cat burglar Selleck, forced by the police to steal uncut diamonds from the German embassy. Selleck's mission includes seducing beautiful Nazi courier Hutton. Glamorous adventure sparked by Hoskins's hard-boiled cop.
Dist.: Warner

LAST AMERICAN HERO, THE 1973
★★★ PG Biography/Sports 1:33
☑ Nudity, adult situations, explicit language, mild violence
Dir: Lamont Johnson *Cast:* Jeff Bridges, Valerie Perrine, Geraldine Fitzgerald, Art Lund, Gary Busey, Ned Beatty
▶ When his dad is busted for moonshining, hot-rodder Bridges joins the racing circuit to pay for a lawyer. He rises to pro stardom, remaining his own man despite the demands of promoters and sponsors. Underrated movie with good work from Bridges and exciting demo derby and stock car footage. Based on the life of flamboyant auto racer Junior Jackson. Retitled *Hard Driver.*
Dist.: CBS/Fox

LAST AMERICAN VIRGIN, THE 1982
★★ R Comedy 1:33
☑ Nudity, adult situations, explicit language
Dir: Boaz Davidson *Cast:* Lawrence Monoson, Diane Franklin, Steve Antin, Joe Rubbo, Louisa Moritz, Brian Peck
▶ Three horny teenagers—ladies' man Antin, chubby Rubbo, and shy Monoson—set their sights on beautiful Franklin. Predictable teen comedy scores some points for its fairly realistic look at high school rituals and knockout soundtrack featuring the Cars, the Police, Devo, Blondie, Commodores, and others.
Dist.: MGM/UA

LAST ANGRY MAN, THE 1959
★★★★ NR Drama 1:40 B&W
Dir: Daniel Mann *Cast:* Paul Muni, David Wayne, Betsy Palmer, Luther Adler, Joby Baker, Billy Dee Williams
▶ Muni is magnificent in his Oscar-nominated portrayal of a Brooklyn doctor who refuses the blandishments of fame and fancy medicine to minister to the slum dwellers who have been his lifelong concern. Williams is a young street tough who may have a brain tumor, but who resists Muni's efforts to help him. Themes of television exploitation and medical priorities are still contemporary. Muni's last film was remade as a TV movie in 1974.
Dist.: RCA/Columbia

LAST CHASE, THE 1981 Canadian
★★ PG Sci-Fi 1:41
☑ Brief nudity, adult situations, explicit language, violence
Dir: Martyn Burke *Cast:* Lee Majors, Burgess Meredith, Chris Makepeace, Alexandra Stewart, George Touliatos
▶ After an oil shortage and a plague hit America, an authoritarian government takes over. Driving is banned but ex-auto racer Majors begs to differ: he hits the road with whiz kid Makepeace to join a renegade band of drivers in California. The regime attempts to stop them. Crafty conception motors along speedily if not memorably.
Dist.: Vestron

LAST COMMAND, THE 1928
☆ NR Drama 1:28 B&W
Dir: Josef von Sternberg *Cast:* Emil Jannings, Evelyn Brent, William Powell, Nicholas Soussanin, Michael Visaroff, Jack Raymond
▶ Formerly an officer of the Czar, elderly Jannings is reduced to working as an extra in Hollywood movies. When he is hired to play the part of a Russian officer, memories of the danger and glory of his past life come rushing back. Ironies pile on ironies, but this wise and moving silent drama builds to a conclusion that is as genuinely stirring as it is knowingly self-referential. Jannings won the first Best Actor Oscar in part for his performance here.
Dist.: Paramount

LAST COMMAND, THE 1955
★★★ NR Action-Adventure 1:50
Dir: Frank Lloyd *Cast:* Sterling Hayden, Anna Maria Alberghetti, J. Carrol Naish, Arthur Hunnicutt, Ernest Borgnine, Slim Pickens
▶ Remember the Alamo! Hayden is lusty, brawling Jim Bowie, who goes against former pal General Santa Anna (Naish) and holes up an old monastery with the likes of Davy Crockett (Hunnicutt) to battle to the death against 7,000 Mexican regulars. Though smaller-scaled than other treatments of the subject, this still-rousing version boasts excellent performances by a grand Hayden and a poignant Pickens.
Dist.: Republic

LAST DAYS OF POMPEII, THE 1935
★ ★ NR Action-Adventure 1:36 B&W
Dir: Ernest B. Schoedsack *Cast:* Preston
Foster, Alan Hale, Basil Rathbone, John
Wood, Louis Calhern, Dorothy Wilson
▶ When his family is killed by a nobleman,
blacksmith Foster becomes an amoral gladiator. Sent to Judea, he allies himself with the
weak-willed Pontius Pilate (Rathbone). He repents in time to save Christians from the eruption of Mount Vesuvius. Long-winded historical
epic of interest only for Rathbone's superb
acting and the famous special-effects climax.
Dist.: Turner C

LAST DETAIL, THE 1973
★ ★ R Drama 1:44
☑ Adult situations, explicit language
Dir: Hal Ashby *Cast:* Jack Nicholson, Otis
Young, Randy Quaid, Carol Kane, Michael
Moriarty
▶ Career sailors Nicholson and Young are as-
signed to escort petty thief Quaid from Vir-
ginia to a New Hampshire naval prison. On
the road, the two lifers teach the hapless
Quaid about living, but the brief taste of free-
dom proves bittersweet. Powerhouse movie,
alternately bawdy and moving, with a blister-
ing performance by Jack as "Badass" Bud-
dusky and some of the saltiest dialogue in film
history. Oscar nominations went to Nicholson,
Quaid, and Robert Towne's screenplay.
Dist.: RCA/Columbia

LAST DRAGON, THE 1985
★ ★ ★ PG-13 Action-Adventure 1:48
☑ Explicit language, violence
Dir: Michael Schultz *Cast:* Taimak, Vanity,
Julius J. Carry III, Faith Prince, Leo O'Brien,
Jim Moody
▶ The world's first kung-fu musical has a cluttered plot that makes almost no sense, but its
high-tech, action-packed style has a goofy
charm. Taimak plays a young black who idolizes Bruce Lee; he's drawn into various battles
with gangsters and the Shogun of Harlem
when he falls for nightclub VJ Vanity. Romance between the attractive leads is credible, and humor sparks the inevitable martial
arts showdowns. Also known as *Berry Gordy's
The Last Dragon.*
Dist.: CBS/Fox

LAST EMBRACE 1979
★ ★ ★ R Mystery-Suspense 1:43
☑ Nudity, violence
Dir: Jonathan Demme *Cast:* Roy Scheider,
Janet Margolin, Sam Levene, John Glover,
Christopher Walken, Jacqueline Brookes
▶ Government agent Scheider, having suf-
fered a nervous breakdown after his wife's
death, receives a death threat in Hebrew and
becomes involved in a series of murders.
Some farfetched plotting but inventive direc-
tion by Demme keeps the thrills coming

quickly. Evocative Miklos Rozsa score, exciting
Niagara Falls finale.
Dist.: CBS/Fox

LAST EMPEROR, THE 1987
Italian/British/Chinese
★ ★ ★ ★ PG-13 Biography 2:46
☑ Brief nudity, adult situations, explicit lan-
guage, violence
Dir: Bernardo Bertolucci *Cast:* John Lone,
Joan Chen, Peter O'Toole, Ying Ruocheng,
Dennis Dun, Ryuichi Sakamoto
▶ Epic biography of Pu Yi (Lone), who was
crowned Chinese emperor at age three in
1908 but whose rule was essentially powerless
and anachronistic. Eventually arrested by the
Communists and reeducated, he lived out his
days as a common gardener. Stunning imag-
ery, filmed on location in China's Forbidden
City, highlights this rare epic that is basically
an intimate character study. Gorgeous sets,
costumes, and art direction. Won nine Oscars,
including Best Picture. (CC)
Dist.: Nelson

LAST EXIT TO BROOKLYN 1990 U.S./German
★ R Drama 1:40
☑ Rape, nudity, strong sexual content, Adult
situations, explicit language, violence
Dir: Uli Edel *Cast:* Stephen Lang, Jennifer
Jason Leigh, Burt Young, Peter Dobson, Jerry
Orbach, Ricki Lake, Alexis Arquette, Zette
▶ In 1952 Brooklyn, factory worker Lang's
major role in a bitter strike is compromised by
his obsession with transvestite Zette. Another
grim story line concerns co-worker Dobson's
prostitute wife Leigh, who helps hubby roll soldiers and then sinks further into degeneracy.
Raw, pounding adaptation of the controversial Hubert Selby novel features powerhouse
acting from Lang and Leigh. However, sordid
story hits the same hard notes throughout,
making this hard to endure.
Dist.: RCA/Columbia

LAST FIGHT, THE 1983
★ ★ ★ R Drama/Sports 1:29
☑ Nudity, adult situations, explicit language, violence
Dir: Fred Williamson *Cast:* Willie Colon,
Ruben Blades, Fred Williamson, Joe Spinell,
Darlanne Fluegel, Don King
▶ Singer-turned-boxer Blades signs with
shady promoter Colon but then turns against
him when Colon's thugs kill his girlfriend. Despite a blood clot in his head, Blades gets
revenge and a shot at the title. Low-budget
boxing film leaves no cliché unturned. Captures environment with conviction, but characters are not sympathetic.
Dist.: HBO

LAST FOUR DAYS, THE 1978 Italian
☆ PG Drama 1:38
☑ Explicit language
Dir: Carlo Lizzani *Cast:* Rod Steiger, Henry
Fonda, Franco Nero, Lisa Gastoni
▶ During the last four days of the life of Italian

dictator Benito Mussolini (Steiger), he flees to the mountains, forming a phantom government in the hope of escaping to Switzerland or the United States. Hollow examination of a potentially interesting subject. Good period details but lackluster performances. Music by Ennio Morricone. Dubbed.
Dist.: Vestron

LAST GAME, THE 1983
★★ PG Drama 1:30
[✓] Adult situations
Dir: Martin Beck ***Cast:*** Howard Segal, Ed. L. Grady, Terry Alden, Jerry Rushing, Mike Allen, Toby Wallace
► A high school quarterback almost loses his girl and his big chance on the field to a rival player from a wealthy family. Though his father's heart is failing, the working class hero may be the only hope as the team falters in the big game. Touching story in an interesting milieu.
Dist.: HBO

LAST HOUSE ON THE LEFT, THE 1972
☆ R Horror 1:31
[✓] Rape, nudity, graphic violence
Dir: Wes Craven ***Cast:*** David Hess, Lucy Grantham, Sandra Cassell, Marc Sheffler, Jeramie Rain
► After a rock concert, two young girls are abducted by a demented Manson-like foursome who torture, rape, and murder them. The gang, in turn, meets an even more gruesome death from one of the girls' vengeful parents. Sickening violence, blood, and gore turn off any sympathy toward the parents.
Dist.: Vestron

LAST HURRAH, THE 1958
★★★★ NR Drama 2:01 B&W
Dir: John Ford ***Cast:*** Spencer Tracy, Jeffrey Hunter, Dianne Foster, Pat O'Brien, Basil Rathbone, Donald Crisp, James Gleason, Edward Brophy, John Carradine, Frank McHugh, Jane Darwell
► Long-time Boston mayor Frank Skeffington (Tracy) enters his last campaign against a weak candidate backed by conservative patrician forces. Compelling Tracy vehicle based on Edwin O'Connor's best-seller features outstanding character actors.
Dist.: RCA/Columbia

LAST INNOCENT MAN, THE 1987
★★★★★ NR Mystery-Suspense/MFTV 1:53
[✓] Adult situations, explicit language, violence
Dir: Roger Spottiswoode ***Cast:*** Ed Harris, Roxanne Hart, Clarence Williams III, Darrell Larson, Bruce McGill, David Suchet
► Hot-shot Portland lawyer Harris, disillusioned with defending guilty clients, falls for Hart, estranged wife of murder suspect Larson. Harris accepts Larson's case and is quickly trapped in a baffling web of deceit and treachery. Superior courtroom drama adapted from attorney Phillip Margolin's novel raises engrossing ethical questions. Excellent acting, particularly by Harris.
Dist.: Warner

LAST LAUGH, THE 1924 German
★ NR Drama 1:17 B&W
Dir: F. W. Murnau ***Cast:*** Emil Jannings, Mary Delschaft, Kurt Hiller, Emelie Kurtz, Hans Unterkirchen, Olaf Strom
► At a Berlin hotel, haughty doorman Jannings enjoys preening until he is brought down to earth by his demotion to washroom attendant. Only an ironic reversal can change his sad plight. Murnau's bravura direction and a superb performance by Jannings elevate this silent to classic status. Remarkable camerawork is still effective today.
Dist.: Cable

LAST MARRIED COUPLE IN AMERICA, THE 1980
★★★ R Comedy 1:42
[✓] Nudity, adult situations, explicit language
Dir: Gilbert Cates ***Cast:*** George Segal, Natalie Wood, Richard Benjamin, Arlene Golonka, Valerie Harper
► When all their friends start getting divorces, happily married Segal and Wood wonder if they should, too. With Dom DeLuise as their jolly porno film star/plumber friend who eggs them on. Ribald comedy concludes traditional ways are still the best.
Dist.: MCA

LAST METRO, THE 1981 French
★★ PG Drama 2:13
[✓] Adult situations, mild violence
Dir: François Truffaut ***Cast:*** Catherine Deneuve, Gérard Depardieu, Jean Poiret, Heinz Bennent, Andrea Ferreol
► Elegant yet empty melodrama set in Nazi-occupied Paris features Deneuve as the wife of a theater director. She tries to produce a play while hiding Jewish husband Bennent underneath the stage. Deneuve is the film's best asset. Nominated for Best Foreign Film.
[S]
Dist.: CBS/Fox

LAST MILE, THE 1932
★ NR Drama 1:09 B&W
Dir: Sam Bischoff ***Cast:*** Preston Foster, Howard Phillips, George E. Stone, Noel Madison, Alan Roscoe, Paul Fix
► Foster is outstanding as Killer Mears, a vicious inmate on death row. After swiping a guard's keys and taking a hostage, Mears leads the other prisoners in an ultimately ill-fated revolt. Material still retains its raw power despite the passage of time. Foster's role was played on stage by Spencer Tracy and Clark Gable.
Dist.: Video Yesteryear

LAST OF PHILIP BANTER, THE 1986 Spanish/Swiss
★ R Drama 1:43

☑ Nudity, adult situations, explicit language, violence
Dir: Hervé Hachuel ***Cast:*** Scott Paulin, Irene Miracle, Gregg Henry, Kate Vernon, Tony Curtis
▶ As his marriage to Curtis's daughter Miracle breaks up, Paulin finds a manuscript which tells of events in his life. The line between fact and fantasy blurs as Paulin suspects that pal Henry and gorgeous Vernon, both characters in the manuscript, are plotting against him. Stylishly made but confusing, with too-cold Paulin performance. Henry contributes three songs to the soundtrack.
Dist.: Republic

LAST OF SHEILA, THE 1973
★★ PG Mystery-Suspense 1:59
☑ Adult situations, explicit language
Dir: Herbert Ross ***Cast:*** James Coburn, James Mason, Dyan Cannon, Ian McShane, Joan Hackett, Dyan Cannon, Raquel Welch, Richard Benjamin
▶ Movie producer Coburn invites six urbane Hollywood friends on a Mediterranean cruise aboard his yacht *Sheila*. Playing whodunit parlor games, Coburn searches for the person who caused his wife's death. A slew of red herrings keeps audience guessing. Script by Stephen Sondheim and Anthony Perkins.
Dist.: Warner

LAST OF THE FINEST, THE 1990
★★★ R Action-Adventure 1:46
☑ Adult situations, explicit language, violence
Dir: John Mackenzie ***Cast:*** Brian Dennehy, Joe Pantoliano, Jeff Fahey, Bill Paxton, Michael C. Gwynne, Henry Stolow
▶ Dennehy leads a special police squad that goes outside the law to nail drug thug Gwynne. Things get complicated, however, as Gwynne is also involved in a major arms deal, and Dennehy's hard-working cops get twenty-two million illegal bucks—and a heck of an ethical problem—dropped in their laps. Derivative, but lean, mean, and enjoyable, with nice twist being the inclusion of the cops' wives in the decision-making process.
Dist.: Orion

LAST OF THE MOHICANS, THE 1936
★★ NR Action-Adventure 1:31 B&W
Dir: George B. Seitz ***Cast:*** Randolph Scott, Binnie Barnes, Heather Angel, Hugh Buckler, Bruce Cabot
▶ As the French-Indian War rages across upstate New York, indefatigable frontiersman Hawkeye (Scott), along with two Mohicans, guides a British officer and his family across French lines. They are pursued over rough terrain by a war party of villainous Hurons led by Cabot. Good adaptation of James Fenimore Cooper's novel has vigorous, large-scale battle scenes and fine acting.
Dist.: Media

LAST OF THE RED HOT LOVERS 1972
★ PG Comedy 1:38
☑ Adult situations, explicit language
Dir: Gene Saks ***Cast:*** Alan Arkin, Sally Kellerman, Paula Prentiss, Renée Taylor, Bella Bruck, Sandy Balson
▶ Married restaurateur Arkin, in throes of midlife crisis, dreams of restoring passion to his life. Using his mother's unoccupied apartment, he tries to start affairs with Kellerman, Prentiss, and Taylor. Commercially unsuccessful adaptation of Neil Simon's play.
Dist.: Paramount

LAST PLANE OUT 1983
★★★ PG Action-Adventure 1:37
☑ Explicit language, mild violence
Dir: David Nelson ***Cast:*** Jan-Michael Vincent, Mary Crosby, Julie Carmen, William Windom, David Huffman
▶ American journalist Vincent has an affair with Nicaraguan Carmen during the last days of the Samosa regime. When Samosa is toppled, Vincent is pursued by rebels who suspect him of working for the CIA. Blandly directed, though it picks up steam as it goes along. Based on the true story of film's co-producer, Jack Cox. **(CC)**
Dist.: CBS/Fox

LA STRADA 1956 Italian
★★ NR Drama 1:45 B&W
Dir: Federico Fellini ***Cast:*** Anthony Quinn, Giulietta Masina, Richard Basehart, Aldo Silviani, Marcella Rovere, Livia Venturini
▶ Circus strongman Quinn, realizing his oneman show needs an extra attraction, acquires dim-witted peasant Masina to play trumpet and drums while he performs. He treats his sidekick/mistress poorly during their itinerant life; at a carnival, sympathetic clown/acrobat Basehart seeks to free Masina from servitude. Spare direction from Fellini, simple story, and Chaplinesque Masina yielded Oscar for Best Foreign Film. Released in Europe in 1954. [S]
Dist.: Nelson

LAST REMAKE OF BEAU GESTE, THE 1977
★★ PG Comedy 1:23
☑ Explicit language, adult humor
Dir: Marty Feldman ***Cast:*** Marty Feldman, Ann-Margret, Michael York, Peter Ustinov, James Earl Jones, Trevor Howard
▶ Spoof of the three film versions of P. C. Wren's novel stars bug-eyed Feldman and blond Adonis York as an unlikely pair of identical twins who join the French Foreign Legion. With Ann-Margret as the femme fatale who weds Howard, the Geste twins' father, and nearly kills him in bed. Uneven, bawdy comedy.
Dist.: MCA

LAST RESORT 1986
★ R Comedy 1:19
☑ Nudity, explicit language, adult humor
Dir: Zane Busby ***Cast:*** Charles Grodin,

Robin Pearson Rose, John Ashton, Ellen Blake, Megan Mullally, Jon Lovitz
► Businessman Grodin takes wife and kids for a Caribbean vacation at Club Sand that turns into a series of comic disasters. Talented Chuck deserves much better. Frantic pacing, smutty and predictable humor, and crude slapstick.
Dist.: Vestron

LAST RITES 1988
★ ★ R Drama 1:43
☑ Nudity, adult situations, explicit language, violence
Dir: Donald P. Bellisario *Cast:* Tom Berenger, Daphne Zuniga, Chick Vennera, Anne Twomey, Dane Clark, Paul Dooley
► New York City priest Berenger takes on-the-run Zuniga under his wing after her mafioso lover is gunned down. He finds himself in turmoil as he juggles his allegiances to God, family, and his own Mafia connections, while resisting the tempting Zuniga. Slow pace and ridiculous plot turns detract from handsome production and story's steamy undercurrents. (CC)
Dist.: CBS/Fox

LAST STARFIGHTER, THE 1984
★ ★ ★ PG Sci-Fi 1:40
☑ Explicit language, violence
Dir: Nick Castle *Cast:* Robert Preston, Lance Guest, Barbara Bosson, Dan O'Herlihy, Catherine Mary Stewart
► Videogame whiz Guest, living in a trailer, gets whisked away to another galaxy by alien headhunter Preston. He helps save the universe from evil invaders. O'Herlihy, underneath layers of lizard makeup, plays an intergalactic good guy. Sweet-natured sci-fi tale for kids.
Dist.: MCA

LAST SUMMER 1969
★ ★ ★ R Drama 1:37
☑ Rape, nudity, adult situations, explicit language
Dir: Frank Perry *Cast:* Barbara Hershey, Richard Thomas, Bruce Davidson, Cathy Burns, Ernesto Gonzalez, Peter Turgeon
► Adaptation of an Evan Hunter novel concerns unchaperoned teens on the loose in New York's Fire Island resort. They get drunk, play revealing game of "truth or dare," smoke marijuana, and experiment with sex. Rivalry between sluttish Hershey and shy Burns leads to brutality. Fine, insightful look at teen gamesmanship and cruelty.
Dist.: CBS/Fox

LAST TANGO IN PARIS 1973 French/Italian
☆ X Drama 2:09
☑ Nudity, strong sexual content, explicit language
Dir: Bernardo Bertolucci *Cast:* Marlon Brando, Maria Schneider, Jean-Pierre Leaud, Massimo Girotti, Darling Legitimus, Catherine Allegret
► Highly controversial film about an obsessive

affair between Brando and Schneider, a young stranger he meets in a deserted apartment. Notorious for its frank treatment of sexuality, story is rewarding as a psychological case study. Expert direction and Brando's startling performance were awarded Oscar nominations. Memorable Gato Barbieri score.
S
Dist.: MGM/UA

LAST TEMPTATION OF CHRIST, THE 1988
★ ★ R Drama 2:40
☑ Nudity, adult situations, violence
Dir: Martin Scorsese *Cast:* Willem Dafoe, Harvey Keitel, Barbara Hershey, David Bowie, Andre Gregory, Harry Dean Stanton
► Despite miracles and a growing following, Jesus Christ (Dafoe) struggles with his sense of mission. Condemned to the cross by the Romans, Christ has a vivid fantasy of what his life might be as a normal man. Scorsese directs with a blazing intensity that matches the protagonist's restless searching. Unconventional story created much controversy but actually arrives at a pious (and moving) conclusion. Scorsese was nominated for an Oscar. From the novel by Nikos Kazantzakis.
Dist.: MCA

LAST TIME I SAW PARIS, THE 1954
★ ★ ★ ★ NR Romance 1:56
Dir: Richard Brooks *Cast:* Elizabeth Taylor, Van Johnson, Donna Reed, Walter Pidgeon, Eva Gabor
► Tragic love story of Johnson and Taylor, a young couple in post–World War II Paris who strike it rich with Texas oil stocks. Their once-happy marriage turns sour when they start living frivolously and drinking heavily. With Pidgeon as Taylor's expatriate father. Glossy, slightly altered adaptation of F. Scott Fitzgerald's "Babylon Revisited."
Dist.: Goodtimes

LAST TRAIN FROM GUN HILL 1959
★ ★ ★ NR Western 1:34
Dir: John Sturges *Cast:* Kirk Douglas, Anthony Quinn, Carolyn Jones, Earl Holliman, Ziva Rodann, Brad Dexter
► Sheriff Douglas tracks down Holliman, his wife's killer and the son of his best friend Quinn. Quinn's henchmen are determined to rescue Holliman before Douglas takes him out of town. Sturdy Western is an intriguing study of loyalty.
Dist.: CBS/Fox

LAST TYCOON, THE 1976
★ ★ ★ PG Drama 2:02
☑ Adult situations
Dir: Elia Kazan *Cast:* Robert De Niro, Robert Mitchum, Jeanne Moreau, Tony Curtis, Jack Nicholson, Ingrid Boulting, Donald Pleasence, Peter Strauss, Ray Milland, Dan Andrews, Theresa Russell, John Carradine, Anjelica Huston
► In 1930s Hollywood, brilliant young movie mogul De Niro pursues an elusive Boulting,

who reminds him of his late wife, but he is unable to control her as he does his film productions. Intelligent, meticulously crafted adaptation of F. Scott Fitzgerald's last, unfinished novel features one of De Niro's subtlest and most effective performances.
Dist.: Paramount

LAST WALTZ, THE 1978
★ ★ ★ **PG Documentary/Music 1:56**
ⓤ Explicit language
Dir: Martin Scorsese *Cast:* The Band, Bob Dylan, Neil Young, Van Morrison, Eric Clapton, Emmylou Harris
▶ The 1976 farewell performance of The Band (supplemented by guest stars Ringo Starr, Neil Diamond, Dr. John, Joni Mitchell, and others) is arguably the best rock concert film ever. First-rate direction by Scorsese, intercutting onstage numbers with penetrating backstage interviews. Highlights: guitar duet between Clapton and Robbie Robertson of The Band so intense that Eric breaks a string and a climactic sing-along of "I Shall Be Released." Songs include "The Night They Drove Old Dixie Down," "The Weight," "Up on Cripple Creek," many more.
Dist.: MGM/UA

LAST WARRIOR, THE 1989
★ ★ **R War 1:34**
ⓥ Nudity, adult situations, explicit language, violence
Dir: Martin Wragge *Cast:* Gary Graham, Maria Holvoe, Cary-Hiroyuki Tagawa, John Carson, Steven Ito, Al Karaki
▶ On a secluded island during the last days of World War II, American Marine observer Graham discovers Japanese counterpart Tagawa, assigned to make place safe for wounded battleship. The two men battle to the death with novice nun Holvoe, also stranded there, caught in the middle. Well-crafted survival story.
Dist.: SVS

LAST WAVE, THE 1977 Australian
★ ★ **PG Mystery-Suspense 1:46**
ⓤ Explicit language, violence
Dir: Peter Weir *Cast:* Richard Chamberlain, Olivia Hamnett, David Gulpilil, Frederick Parslow
▶ Unusual Australian thriller about lawyer Chamberlain defending five aborigines accused of murdering their friend. After witnessing a rain of frogs and apocalyptic winds, he suspects ancient tribal rituals and black magic were responsible for the killing. Spine-tingling and spooky.
Dist.: Warner

LAST WINTER, THE 1984 Israeli
★ ★ **R Drama 1:30**
ⓥ Nudity, adult situations, explicit language
Dir: Riki Shelach *Cast:* Yona Elian, Kathleen Quinlan, Stephen Macht, Zipora Peled
▶ Israeli Elian and American Quinlan search for their missing husbands after the 1973 Yom Kippur War. Although they identify the same man as their man, they eventually become friends. Central situation can evoke a good cry although cloying music and awkward dialogue are detriments.
Dist.: RCA/Columbia

LAST WOMAN ON EARTH, THE 1961
☆ **NR Sci-Fi 1:11**
Dir: Roger Corman *Cast:* Antony Carbone, Edward Wain, Betsy Jones-Moreland
▶ A passing phenomenon temporarily robs the earth of its oxygen, killing everybody except skin divers Carbone, Jones-Moreland, and Wain (actually Robert Towne, screenwriter here and, much later, of *Chinatown*). As the planet's last female, Jones-Morland becomes the object of rivalry between the two men. Unconvincing story with unappealing characters.
Dist.: Sinister

LAST WORD, THE 1980
★ ★ ★ **PG Drama 1:42**
ⓤ Explicit language
Dir: Roy Boulting *Cast:* Richard Harris, Karen Black, Martin Landau, Dennis Christopher, Biff McGuire, Penelope Milford
▶ Inventor Harris refuses to leave his apartment when the government decides to tear down his neighborhood. He takes a cop hostage, becomes a hero when the story is nationally televised, and uses some of his inventions to ward off an invading SWAT team. Socially conscious and well-meaning.
Dist.: Nelson

LAST YEAR AT MARIENBAD 1962
French/Italian
☆ **NR Drama 1:33 B&W**
Dir: Alain Resnais *Cast:* Delphine Seyrig, Giorgio Albertazzi, Sacha Pitoeff, Françoise Bertin, Luce Garcia-Ville
▶ While the idle rich play their games at a lavish spa, Albertazzi tries to convince the already attached Seyrig that in a previous meeting she promised to run away with him. The other guests, seen only in profile, mill about, and Albertazzi's fantasies become Seyrig's reality. Slow, arty (a string quartet saws away in silence), and incomprehensible.
ⓢ
Dist.: Various

LAS VEGAS HILLBILLYS 1966
★ **NR Musical 1:30**
Dir: Arthur C. Pierce *Cast:* Ferlin Husky, Jayne Mansfield, Mamie Van Doren, Richard Kiel, Connie Smith, John Harmon
▶ Inheriting a casino is no windfall for country boy Husky, who heads west, meets Mansfield, and arrives in Las Vegas to find his legacy in tumbledown shape. With an assist from barmaid Van Doren, he puts on a big country music show to get the cash to fix the place up. Appearances by Sonny James, Del Reeves, Roy Drusky, Bill Anderson, Wilma Burgess, and the Duke of Paducah make this wackily cast

item an interesting curiosity for country music fans. Sequel of sorts: *Hillbillys in a Haunted House*.
Dist.: United

L'ATALANTE 1934 French
☆ **NR Drama 1:29 B&W**
Dir: Jean Vigo   *Cast:* Jean Dasté, Dita Parlo, Michel Simon, Gilles Margaritis, Louis Lefèvre, Diligent Raya
▶ Barge captain Dasté marries Parlo, but the former country girl is made restive by life on ship. On a visit to Paris, she attracts peddler Margaritis, causing jealous Dasté to take to sea without her in revenge. In the long run, nothing can keep these powerful lovers apart in this earthy and unusual romance. The original French version has recently been restored using the director's shooting script. Ⓢ
Dist.: Foothill

LATE SHOW, THE 1977
★ ★ ★ **PG Mystery-Suspense 1:34**
Ⓥ Explicit language, violence
Dir: Robert Benton   *Cast:* Art Carney, Lily Tomlin, Bill Macy, Howard Duff, Joanna Cassidy
▶ Elderly private eye Carney is hired by wacky Tomlin to find her missing cat. The trail leads them into a complex web of murder and blackmail. Sophisticated contemporary mystery with a sense of humor and a sterling Carney performance.
Dist.: Warner

LATINO 1985
★ **NR War 1:45**
Ⓥ Rape, nudity, explicit language, violence
Dir: Haskell Wexler   *Cast:* Robert Beltran, Annette Cardona, Tony Plana, Julio Medina, Gavin McFadden, Luis Torrentes
▶ Vietnam vet Beltran joins the Contras fighting the Sandinistas in Nicaragua. Romance with Nicaraguan Cardona plus witnessing his own side's torture techniques gives Beltran doubts about the Contra cause. Betrays both Wexler's leftist political slant and his filmmaking skill; dialogue is didactic but location shooting gives realistic feel. In English and Spanish. (CC) Ⓢ
Dist.: CBS/Fox

LA TRAVIATA 1982 Italian
★ ★ ★ ★ **G Music 1:50**
Dir: Franco Zeffirelli   *Cast:* Teresa Stratas, Placido Domingo, Cornell MacNeil, Alan Monk
▶ Courtesan Stratas falls in love with wealthy MacNeil's son Domingo. MacNeil convinces Stratas she'll ruin Domingo's life, and she breaks off the relationship before a deathbed reconciliation. Lavish allstar production of Verdi's timeless opera. Based on Alexandre Dumas's "Marguerite and Armand," the same story that inspired *Camille*. Ⓢ
Dist.: MCA

LA TRUITE 1982 French
☆ **R Drama 1:45**
Ⓥ Nudity, adult situations, explicit language
Dir: Joseph Losey   *Cast:* Isabelle Huppert, Jeanne Moreau, Jean-Pierre Cassel, Daniel Olbrychski, Lisette Malidor, Maggie Smith
▶ Supposedly innocent farm-girl Huppert is lured away from her homosexual husband by four jaded-jet setters who take her to Japan. Along the way, she meets flamboyant widow Smith, and proceeds to manipulate supposed sophisticates to get what she wants: her own trout farm. The sexual attitudes are very pre-AIDS in this extremely stylish but incoherent story. Also known by its English title, *The Trout*.
Ⓢ
Dist.: RCA/Columbia

LAUGHING POLICEMAN, THE 1974
★ ★ **R Drama 1:51**
Ⓥ Adult situations
Dir: Stuart Rosenberg   *Cast:* Walter Matthau, Bruce Dern, Louis Gossett, Jr., Albert Paulsen, Anthony Zerbe, Val Avery
▶ Working on tips from a dangerously untrustworthy informer, cop partners Matthau and Dern track a violent killer through the seamy underside of San Francisco's homosexual community. Brutal thriller is somewhat dated, but plot is realistic and bloody. Based on a novel by Per Wahloo and Maj Sjowall. (CC)
Dist.: CBS/Fox

LAURA 1944
★ ★ ★ ★ **NR Mystery-Suspense 1:27 B&W**
Dir: Otto Preminger   *Cast:* Gene Tierney, Dana Andrews, Clifton Webb, Vincent Price, Judith Anderson, Dorothy Adams
▶ Investigating a murder, detective Andrews falls under the spell of the beautiful victim (Tierney). Witty, stylish mystery a landmark film noir of the 1940s. Highlighted by Webb's delicious role as acerbic columnist Waldo Lydecker, film received five Oscar nominations (winning for Joseph LaShelle's photography). Romantic theme by David Raksin became a classic ballad.
Dist.: Magnetic

LAVENDER HILL MOB, THE 1951 British
★ ★ ★ **NR Comedy 1:22 B&W**
Dir: Charles Crichton   *Cast:* Alec Guinness, Stanley Holloway, Sidney James, Alfie Bass, Marjorie Fielding, John Gregson
▶ Mild-mannered bank worker Guinness enlists aid of sculptor pal Holloway and pro crooks James and Bass to hijack armored car containing gold bullion. Thieves melt the loot into small, souvenir Eiffel Towers for smuggling to Paris; plan goes awry when English schoolgirls purchase some of the miniatures. Hilarious, tongue-in-cheek comedy with a delightful Guinness and madcap antics. Oscar winner for screenplay by T. E. B. Clarke. Look for young Audrey Hepburn in opening sequence..
Dist.: HBO

L'AVVENTURA 1960 Italian
☆ **NR Drama 2:25 B&W**
Dir: Michelangelo Antonioni   *Cast:* Monica Vitti, Gabriele Ferzetti, Lea Massari, Dominique Blanchar, James Addams
▶ Wealthy friends go on an expedition to a rocky isle off the coast of Sicily where Massari disappears. They search for a while, then sail back to town. Time passes, and Massari's lover Ferzetti and best friend Vitti start cuddling up. Once plot premise is established, nothing much happens, which is what this ironically titled, critically praised movie is all about. For adventurous tastes only.   [S]
Dist.: Various

LAWLESS LAND, THE 1988
☆ **R Action-Adventure 1:18**
☑ Nudity, violence
Dir: Jon Hess   *Cast:* Nick Corri, Leon, Xander Berkeley, Amanda Peterson, Patricio Bunster, Walter Kliche
▶ In a grim future, Corri and Peterson fall in love over the objections of her dad Kliche, an important official. The lovers marry but Corri is imprisoned. He escapes and flees with Peterson as bounty hunters pursue them. Blah drive-in fodder. Filmed in Chile; Roger Corman was executive producer.
Dist.: MGM/UA

LAW OF DESIRE 1987 Spanish
☆ **NR Comedy/Drama 1:40**
☑ Nudity, adult situations, explicit language, violence
Dir: Pedro Almodóvar   *Cast:* Eusebio Poncela, Carmen Maura, Antonio Banderas, Miguel Molina
▶ Film director Poncela is in love with Molina, but he has to contend with obsessive fan Banderas who is determined to have him. Other characters include Poncela's transsexual, sex-bomb sister Maura. Outrageous tragicomedy by Spain's hottest director since Buñuel is for select audiences.   [S]
Dist.: CineVista

LAWRENCE OF ARABIA 1962 British
★ ★ ★ ★ ★ **G Biography/Action-Adventure 3:25**
Dir: David Lean   *Cast:* Peter O'Toole, Alec Guinness, Anthony Quinn, Jack Hawkins, Claude Rains, Anthony Quayle, Arthur Kennedy, Omar Sharif, Jose Ferrer
▶ Seven Oscars, including Best Picture and Director, went to this magnificent screen biography of T. E. Lawrence (O'Toole), the enigmatic Britisher who attempted to unite Arab factions to revolt against the Turks during World War I. In the process, he befriends tribal leader Sharif (Oscar-nominated), faces self-doubt over his own love of killing, and survives torture. Oscar-nominated O'Toole is brilliant; Lean's direction conveys epic sweep and grandeur, as does Maurice Jarre's score. Recently restored to Lean's original cut and re-released theatrically.
Dist.: RCA/Columbia

LEADER OF THE BAND 1987
★ ★ ★ **PG Comedy 1:31**
☑ Adult situations, explicit language
Dir: Nessa Hyams   *Cast:* Steve Landesberg, Gailard Sartain, Mercedes Ruehl, James Martinez, Calvert Deforest
▶ Itinerant musician Landesberg takes job conducting unruly high school marching band and whips his charges into championship form. Bland story is nevertheless peppy and heartwarming, thanks in large measure to engaging comic timing from Landesberg.
Dist.: IVE

LEAGUE OF GENTLEMEN, THE 1960 British
★ ★ **NR Comedy 1:53 B&W**
Dir: Basil Dearden   *Cast:* Jack Hawkins, Nigel Patrick, Roger Livesey, Richard Attenborough, Bryan Forbes
▶ A shady group of ex-servicemen are recruited for a complicated bank heist by Hawkins, their former sergeant. They almost pull it off until fate trips them up. Engrossing and witty caper flick performed and directed with great style.
Dist.: IVD

LEAN ON ME 1989
★ ★ ★ ★ ★ **PG-13 Biography 1:48**
☑ Explicit language, violence
Dir: John G. Avildsen   *Cast:* Morgan Freeman, Beverly Todd, Robert Guillaume, Alan North, Lynne Thigpin, Robin Bartlett
▶ True story of black school principal Joe Clark (Freeman), who turned around troubled New Jersey school by literally locking out the hoodlums and ruling the kids with a wooden bat, if not an iron hand. Although criticized for simplistic approach that basically lionizes the controversial Clark, film packs an undeniably uplifting punch. See it for Freeman's magnetic yet subtle performance.   **(CC)**
Dist.: Warner

LEARNING TREE, THE 1969
★ ★ ★ ★ **PG Drama 1:47**
☑ Adult situations
Dir: Gordon Parks   *Cast:* Kyle Johnson, Estelle Evans, Dana Elcar, Mita Waters, Alex Clarke
▶ In a small 1920s Kansas town, young black Johnson gets a taste of racial prejudice when a murder he witnesses is wrongly pinned on a black. *Life* magazine photographer Parks adapted his own autobiographical novel with satisfying results.
Dist.: Warner

LEATHER BOYS, THE 1966 British
★ **NR Drama 1:45 B&W**
☑ Adult situations, explicit language, mild violence, adult humor
Dir: Sidney J. Furie   *Cast:* Rita Tushingham,

Colin Campbell, Dudley Sutton, Gladys Henson

▶ Biker/mechanic Campbell marries his high school sweetheart Tushingham. After a happy if inexpensive honeymoon, the passion goes out of the relationship. Example of so-called "kitchen sink" school of drama. Mirroring the protagonists' disaffection, story moves from humorous hopefulness to darker emotions.
Dist.: Vestron

LEATHERFACE: TEXAS CHAINSAW MASSACRE III 1990
★ R Horror 1:21
☑ Adult situations, explicit language, graphic violence
Dir: Jeff Burr   *Cast:* Kate Hodge, Viggo Mortenson, William Butler, Ken Foree, Joe Unger, R. A. Mihailoff
▶ California-bound couple Hodge and Butler stop for gas in Texas. Big mistake: the creepy attendant shoots at them and they flee, only to be menaced by murderous Leatherface (Mihailoff) and his malevolent clan. Fans of the first two movies will not be disappointed. The rest will find this gory and gross.
Dist.: RCA/Columbia

LE BAL 1982 French/Italian
☆ NR Drama 1:52
☑ Adult situations
Dir: Ettore Scola   *Cast:* Christophe Allwright, Marc Berman, Regis Bouquet, Chantal Capron, Nani Noel, Jean-François Perrier
▶ A Parisian dance hall is the setting for a social history of the twentieth century told entirely through dancing and its accompanying rituals. Sans dialogue, short episodes display the troupe of eleven men and nine women as representative types of each era, flirting, fighting, and losing one another. A real curiosity.
Dist.: Warner

LE BEAU MARRIAGE 1982 French
☆ PG Comedy 1:40
☑ Adult situations, explicit language
Dir: Eric Rohmer   *Cast:* Béatrice Romand, Andre Dussollier, Arielle Dombasle, Feodor Atkine, Sophie Renoir
▶ After breaking up with her married lover, Parisian art student Romand decides it's high time she found a husband. She sets her cap for lawyer Dussollier but he proves to be reluctant quarry. Glum central performance by Romand dampens Rohmer's usual effervescence although Dombasle is charming as her best friend. Ⓢ
Dist.: Media

LE CAVALEUR 1980 French
☆ NR Comedy 1:44
☑ Adult situations
Dir: Philippe de Broca   *Cast:* Jean Rochefort, Nicole Garcia, Catherine Alric, Catherine Leprince, Lila Kedrova, Carole Lixon
▶ Womanizing pianist Rochefort gets a rude shock when he falls for the young daughter of

an old flame. The youngster makes middle-aged Rochefort feel his years, forcing him into a bittersweet reconciliation with time. Some charming moments in this light comedy, whose title might be translated as "The Skirt Chaser." Ⓢ
Dist.: RCA/Columbia

LE DERNIER COMBAT 1984 French
☆ R Sci-Fi 1:30 B&W
☑ Nudity, violence
Dir: Luc Besson   *Cast:* Pierre Jolivet, Jean Bouise, Fritz Wepper, Christiane Kruger, Jean Reno, Maurice Lamy
▶ In a postapocalyptic world where no one can speak, Jolivet builds an airplane that takes him to a mostly devastated Paris. There he encounters a hulking creature of the id (Reno) and doctor Bouise, who's locked himself in a hospital with a female prisoner. No dialogue and black-and-white photography are the gimmicks in this portentously barren exercise.
Dist.: RCA/Columbia

LEFT-HANDED GUN, THE 1958
★★ NR Western 1:42 B&W
Dir: Arthur Penn   *Cast:* Paul Newman, Lita Milan, John Denner, Hurd Hatfield, James Congdon, James Best
▶ Debunking the myth of Billy the Kid, Newman portrays the legendary gunfighter as a stupid, backstabbing killer. Outraged by the murder of his only friend, Newman and saddlemates Best and Congdon go on a killing spree, pursued by his old pal Sheriff Pat Garrett (Denner). Popping in and out of the story is pulp writer Hatfield, who creates the Billy the Kid of folk-lore. Newman stands out in psychological Western.
Dist.: Warner

LEFT HAND OF GOD, THE 1955
★★ NR Action-Adventure 1:27
Dir: Edward Dmytryk   *Cast:* Humphrey Bogart, Gene Tierney, Lee J. Cobb, Agnes Moorehead, E. G. Marshall, Jean Porter
▶ In 1947 China, American soldier-of-fortune Bogart disguises himself as a monk to flee employ of local warlord Cobb. In a small village, Bogart must continue pretense to appease missionaries Moorehead and Marshall; he even brings comfort to the locals with his phony ceremonies and sermons. Plot thickens when Bogart falls for mission nurse Tierney and Cobb arrives to insist Bogart rejoin him. Bogart excels in one of his last roles.
Dist.: CBS/Fox

LEGACY, THE 1979
★★★ R Horror 1:40
☑ Adult situations, explicit language, violence
Dir: Richard Marquand   *Cast:* Katharine Ross, Sam Elliott, John Standing, Ian Hogg, Margaret Tyzack
▶ In England to do interior design work, American couple Elliott and Ross find themselves

unwilling guests in a haunted manor. Competent suspenser. Workmanlike direction by Marquand generates tension even though the story is predictable.
Dist.: MCA

LEGAL EAGLES 1986
★ ★ ★ ★ PG Mystery-Suspense 1:56
☑ Adult situations, explicit language, violence
Dir: Ivan Reitman *Cast:* Robert Redford, Debra Winger, Daryl Hannah, Brian Dennehy, Terence Stamp
▶ Prosecutor Redford and defense lawyer Winger team up when flaky but beautiful performance artist Hannah gets involved in art fraud and murder. Sophisticated comedy/mystery scores with plenty of action, old-fashioned romance, and clever verbal sparring. Husky-voiced Debra and charming Robert make an immensely appealing team. (CC)
Dist.: MCA

LEGEND 1986 British
★ ★ ★ PG Fantasy 1:30
☑ Violence
Dir: Ridley Scott *Cast:* Tom Cruise, Mia Sara, David Bennent, Tim Curry, Alice Playten, Billy Barty
▶ It's Cruise to the rescue when the Lord of Darkness (Curry) kidnaps the unicorn that prevents evil from taking over the world. Lovely production design, vibrant cinematography, and intricate costumes bring fairy tale world to life, but sappy story has the sophistication of a greeting card. (CC)
Dist.: MCA

LEGEND OF BILLIE JEAN, THE 1985
★ ★ ★ PG-13 Drama 1:36
☑ Adult situations, explicit language, violence
Dir: Matthew Robbins *Cast:* Helen Slater, Keith Gordon, Christian Slater, Richard Bradford, Peter Coyote, Martha Gehmen
▶ Texas teenager Billie Jean (Slater) demands reimbursement when bullies trash her brother's motorcycle. Her brother (Christian Slater, no relation to Helen) accidentally shoots bully's dad Bradford. When the siblings go on the lam, Billie Jean becomes a folk hero. Agreeable cast but simplistic story lacks dramatic weight. (CC)
Dist.: CBS/Fox

LEGEND OF BOGGY CREEK, THE 1972
★ G Horror 1:30
Dir: Charles B. Pierce *Cast:* Willie E. Smith, John P. Hixon, John W. Oates, Jeff Crabtree, Buddy Crabtree
▶ Docudrama concerns alleged Bigfoot-like monster running wild near small town of Foulke, Arkansas. Creature attacks several people, roots around garbage cans, and occasionally sticks its arm through a living room window. Tame stuff for horror fans, but G rating offered scares to small kids and made crude

picture a hit. Followed by *Return to Boggy Creek* and *The Barbaric Beast of Boggy Creek Part II.*
Dist.: Vestron

LEGEND OF HELL HOUSE, THE 1973 British
★ ★ ★ PG Horror 1:34
☑ Adult situations, explicit language, violence
Dir: John Hough *Cast:* Pamela Franklin, Roddy McDowall, Clive Revill, Gayle Hunnicutt, Roland Culver, Peter Bowles
▶ Millionaire Culver hires four people to spend a week in an allegedly haunted house to determine truth of the rumors: McDowall, a veteran of the house's eerie effects; Franklin, a spiritualist in touch with the spooks; Revill, a skeptical scientist; and Hunnicutt, Revill's wife. Occasionally harrowing look at occult phenomena.
Dist.: CBS/Fox

LEGEND OF THE LONE RANGER, THE 1981
★ ★ ★ PG Western 1:38
☑ Explicit language, violence
Dir: William A. Fraker *Cast:* Klinton Spilsbury, Michael Horse, Christopher Lloyd, Jason Robards, Richard Farnsworth
▶ The Lone Ranger (Spilsbury) dons mask to track his brother's murderer. Teaming up with his childhood Indian friend Tonto (Horse), he gets his man and rescues President Grant (Robards) in the process. Old-fashioned Western, classily produced and photographed. Action aplenty and rousing score (including the familiar "William Tell Overture") but lackluster leads. Robards and Silver the horse are delightful, however.
Dist.: CBS/Fox

LEGEND OF THE LOST 1957
★ ★ NR Action-Adventure 1:49
Dir: Henry Hathaway *Cast:* John Wayne, Sophia Loren, Rossano Brazzi, Kurt Kaznar, Sonia Moser, Angela Portaluri
▶ Seeking a fabled treasure in the Sahara Desert, Brazzi hires guide Wayne to help him. Lovely Loren joins the expedition over Wayne's initial objections; she later becomes the object of rivalry between the men. Cast, director, and premise suggest old-style entertainment, but picture doesn't gel. Surprisingly lethargic pace and lack of chemistry between the leads.
Dist.: MGM/UA

LEGEND OF THE WEREWOLF 1975 British
★ NR Horror 1:27
☑ Violence
Dir: Freddie Francis *Cast:* Peter Cushing, David Rintoul, Ron Moody, Hugh Griffith, Roy Castle, Lynn Dalby
▶ A young boy is stolen and raised by a wolfpack. He grows up to be Rintoul, arrives in nineteenth-century Paris, and turns into a werewolf. Professor Cushing investigates. Far

from legendary; plotting and special effects pale in comparison to recent genre efforts. **Dist.:** Media

LE JOUR SE LEVE 1939 French
☆ **NR Drama 1:30 B&W**
Dir: Marcel Carne **Cast:** Jean Gabin, Jacqueline Laurent, Jules Berry, Arletty, Mady Berry
▶ Factory worker Gabin kills a man and hides in his apartment. Soon the apartment is surrounded by police, and a barricaded Gabin muses in flashback on his thwarted love for two women, and how the evil machinations of dog trainer Berry—the murder victim—have led him to this end. With its dark interiors, barred shadows, and atmosphere of malaise and confinement, this critically hailed French classic is one of the first examples of the film noir style. Also known as *Daybreak*. [S]
Dist.: Video Yesteryear

LE MILLION 1931 French
☆ **NR Comedy 1:21 B&W**
Dir: Rene Clair **Cast:** Annabella, Rene Lefevre, Vanda Greville, Paul Olivior, Louis Allibert, Constantin Stroesco
▶ Two penniless French artists are at the mercy of their creditors until they purchase a winning lottery ticket—which they leave in a jacket pocket. When the jacket is stolen and later winds up on the back of an opera singer set to leave for the States, a frenzied chase ensues. Splendid, stylized musical comedy remains in a category by itself, with magical sets and creative early use of sound. [S]
Dist.: Video Yesteryear

LEMON DROP KID, THE 1951
★★★ **NR Comedy 1:31 B&W**
Dir: Sidney Lanfield **Cast:** Bob Hope, Marilyn Maxwell, Lloyd Nolan, Jane Darwell, Andrea King, Fred Clark
▶ Fast-paced comedy with Hope in top form as a bookie who gives a bad tip to gangster Nolan. He has a month to pay back Nolan's money, but his schemes backfire hilariously. Sweet version of "Silver Bells" caps off this adaptation of a Damon Runyon story.
Dist.: RCA/Columbia

LEMON SISTERS, THE 1990
★ **PG-13 Comedy/Drama 1:29**
☑ Adult situations, explicit language
Dir: Joyce Chopra **Cast:** Diane Keaton, Carol Kane, Kathryn Grody, Elliott Gould, Aidan Quinn, Ruben Blades, Richard Libertini
▶ In Atlantic City, friends Keaton, Kane, and Grody are part of a singing trio that has seen better times. They try to raise the money to open their own club, but other commitments get in the way. Weakly written screenplay and lack of strong direction leave three fine actresses floundering.
Dist.: HBO

LENNY 1974
★★★ **R Biography 1:51 B&W**
☑ Nudity, adult situations, explicit language
Dir: Bob Fosse **Cast:** Dustin Hoffman, Valerie Perrine, Jan Miner, Stanley Beck, Gary Morton
▶ Rise and fall of controversial comedian and social gadfly Lenny Bruce (Hoffman), as seen by the people who knew him best: self-destructive stripper/wife Perrine, overbearing mother Miner, and ruthless manager Beck. Fosse brilliantly blends elements of documentary, drama, and stand-up comedy. Critically acclaimed biography was nominated for several Oscars including Best Actor, Director, Picture, and Screenplay. **(CC)**
Dist.: MGM/UA

LEONARD PART VI 1987
★ **PG Comedy 1:25**
☑ Adult situations, explicit language
Dir: Paul Weiland **Cast:** Bill Cosby, Tom Courtenay, Joe Don Baker, Moses Gunn, Pat Colbert
▶ Such a super dud that Cosby offered to buy back the film from Columbia Pictures—and with good cause. He plays 007-type agent fighting to save the world from homicidal house cats, brook trout, and lobsters. **(CC)**
Dist.: RCA/Columbia

LEOPARD IN THE SNOW 1978 Canadian
★★ **PG Romance 1:30**
☑ Adult situations
Dir: Gerry O'Hara **Cast:** Keir Dullea, Susan Penhaligon, Kenneth More, Billie Whitelaw
▶ Penhaligon, stranded in a snowstorm, is taken in by leopard-owning stranger Dullea, an ex-race car driver who has isolated himself from the world since the accident which left him limping and his brother dead. The two eventually fall in love. First film production from Harlequin Romance should please die-hard romantics.
Dist.: Nelson

LEOPARD MAN, THE 1943
★★ **NR Mystery-Suspense 1:06 B&W**
Dir: Jacques Tourneur **Cast:** Dennis O'-Keefe, Margo, Jean Brooks, Isabel Jewell, James Bell, Margaret Landry
▶ New Mexican nightclub promoter O'Keefe rents a leopard to increase business, but the cat escapes just before a series of brutal murders terrifies the town. Snug little thriller from producer Val Lewton (*Cat People*) has terrific atmosphere and tension.
Dist.: Fox Hills

LEPKE 1974
★★★ **R Biography/Crime 1:38**
☑ Adult situations, explicit language, violence
Dir: Menahem Golan **Cast:** Tony Curtis, Anjanette Comer, Michael Callan, Warren Berlinger, Milton Berle
▶ Jewish gangster Curtis rises from New York delinquent to narcotics king and leader of

"Murder Inc." but is eventually arrested by the Feds. Reminiscent of (although not as good as) the gangster classics of the 1930s. May appeal to genre fans.
Dist.: Warner

LES COMPERES 1984 French
★★ PG Comedy 1:32
☑ Adult situations, explicit language, violence
Dir: Francis Veber ***Cast:*** Gerard Depardieu, Pierre Richard, Anny Duperey, Bruno Allain, Patrick Blondell, Stephane Bierry
▶ When teen Bierry vanishes en route to the Riviera with his girlfriend, his mom Duperey persuades two of her former lovers that the boy is his son. Macho reporter Depardieu and meek poet Richard then search for the boy and, when they meet and learn of their common goal, each seeks to prove more worthy of Bierry's affection than the other. Fine, fast-paced French farce. [S]
Dist.: Media

LES GIRLS 1957
★★★★ NR Musical 1:54
Dir: George Cukor ***Cast:*** Gene Kelly, Mitzi Gaynor, Kay Kendall, Taina Elg, Jacques Bergerac
▶ An MGM winner. Former dancer Kendall writes sensational book and is sued for libel by another member of her troupe. Conflicting stories come out in courtroom flashbacks. Sumptuous musical with energetic dancing, lavish production numbers, excellent Cole Porter tunes , terrific cast (especially Kendall) and Oscar-winning costumes.
Dist.: MGM/UA

LES MISERABLES 1935
★★★★ NR Drama 1:49 B&W
Dir: Richard Boleslawski ***Cast:*** Fredric March, Charles Laughton, John Beal, Cedric Hardwicke, Rochelle Hudson
▶ In nineteenth-century France, starving peasant Jean Valjean (March) is imprisoned for stealing a loaf of bread. He emerges from jail and becomes respectable citizen but is relentlessly pursued by inspector Laughton. Most highly regarded of the four big screen filmings of Victor Hugo classic which also inspired the recent Broadway musical. Shows its age in spots but still succeeds.
Dist.: CBS/Fox

LESS THAN ZERO 1987
★★ R Drama 1:38
☑ Nudity, adult situations, violence
Dir: Marek Kanievska ***Cast:*** Andrew McCarthy, Jami Gertz, Robert Downey, Jr., James Spader, Tony Bill
▶ College student McCarthy returns to Beverly Hills for Christmas vacation, rekindles romance with coke-snorting model Gertz, and tries to save his self-destructive pal Downey from pusher Spader. Candid peek at the rich and debauched, junior division, based on the best-selling novel by Bret Easton Ellis. Gorgeous graphics, superbly sardonic performance by Downey, but self-absorbed adolescents generate little sympathy. **(CC)**
Dist.: CBS/Fox

LETHAL OBSESSION 1988 German
☆ R Mystery-Suspense 1:36
☑ Nudity, adult situations, explicit language, violence
Dir: Peter Patzak ***Cast:*** Peter Maffay, Tahnee Welch, Elliott Gould, Massimo Ghini, Armin Mueller-Stahl, Michael York
▶ Cop Maffay and partner Ghini investigate a crime czar's triple murder of drug dealers; Maffay is paralyzed in explosion that also kills Welch's dad. He recovers but sticks to his wheelchair to fool the bad guys, who then kidnap Welch. Visually exciting but dramatically inert. Good actors are wasted in uninteresting roles. Dubbed.
Dist.: Vidmark

LETHAL PURSUIT 1988
☆ NR Mystery-Suspense 1:35
☑ Adult situations, violence
Dir: Don Jones ***Cast:*** Mitzi Kapture, Blake Bahner, John Stuart Wildman, Stephanie Johnson, Blake Gibbons, William Kerr
▶ Sexy rock singer Kapture returns to her hometown with guitarist boyfriend Wildman. There she encounters a teenager wounded by a murderous band of car thieves, led by her ex-boyfriend Bahner. Bahner and company attack the lovers. Repellent tale told on a bare-bones budget.
Dist.: Southgate

LETHAL WEAPON 1987
★★★★★ R Action-Adventure 1:49
☑ Brief nudity, explicit language, violence
Dir: Richard Donner ***Cast:*** Mel Gibson, Danny Glover, Gary Busey, Mitchell Ryan, Tom Atkins, Darlene Love
▶ Veteran cop Glover, a staid family man, is paired with Gibson, an undercover narc on the verge of a nervous breakdown. Together they discover that a routine suicide is a cover-up for a drug ring. High-voltage thriller with a driven performance from Gibson, breathless pacing, and stunning action pieces. Huge popular success led to a sequel. **(CC)**
Dist.: Warner

LETHAL WEAPON 2 1989
★★★★★ R Action-Adventure 1:54
☑ Brief nudity, adult situations, explicit language, graphic violence
Dir: Richard Donner ***Cast:*** Mel Gibson, Danny Glover, Joe Pesci, Joss Ackland, Derrick O'Connor, Patsy Kensit
▶ Wild Los Angeles cop Gibson and his more restrained partner Glover uncover drug money laundering scheme by South African envoy Ackland, who uses diplomatic immunity to bend the law. When the bad guys kill cops, the partners don't just get mad but get even. Super sequel has Pesci adding extra dimension to already sparkling Gibson/Glover

buddy chemistry. Thrilling large-scale, nearly nonstop action is tempered with moments of humor and humanity, like Glover's visa application at South African consulate and Gibson's supermarket pickup of Kensit. **(CC)**
Dist.: Warner

LET IT BE 1970 British
★ ★ G Documentary/Music 1:21
Dir: Michael Lindsay-Hogg *Cast:* John Lennon, Paul McCartney, George Harrison, Ringo Starr, Billy Preston, Yoko Ono
▶ Documentary on the Beatles' recording session for their last album drags at times, but provides revealing glimpses of their methods and personalities. The music is, of course, wonderful: "Get Back," "I Dig a Pony," "Two of Us," etc. Climaxes with their last live performance, a rooftop concert. Won an Oscar for Best Score. A must for their fans, as it includes songs not found on the album ("Shake, Rattle, and Roll," "Besame Mucho," "Kansas City," etc.).
Dist.: CBS/Fox

LET IT RIDE 1989
★ ★ ★ PG-13 Comedy 1:26
☑ Explicit language
Dir: Joe Pytka *Cast:* Richard Dreyfuss, David Johansen, Teri Garr, Jennifer Tilly, Allen Garfield, Michelle Phillips
▶ Miami cabbie Dreyfuss promises estranged wife Garr that he'll give up gambling. However, a fifty-dollar bet on a forty-to-one shot at the track starts him on a winning streak that's too hot to ignore. Likably larky vehicle perfectly showcases Dreyfuss's manic comic style. Delightful support by bodacious Tilly.
Dist.: Paramount

LET'S DANCE 1950
★ ★ NR Musical 1:52
Dir: Norman Z. McLeod *Cast:* Betty Hutton, Fred Astaire, Roland Young, Ruth Warrick, Shepperd Strudwick, Melville Cooper
▶ War widow Hutton finds herself married into a stuffy family of Boston Brahmins who don't approve of her working in a nightclub with her young son. To save him from a life of degredation, the in-laws hire lawyers to initiate a custody suit. Astaire dances well as Hutton's former partner, but their pairing lacks chemistry. Dull story doesn't help.
Dist.: Paramount

LET'S DO IT AGAIN 1975
★ ★ ★ ★ PG Comedy 1:53
☑ Explicit language, adult humor
Dir: Sidney Poitier *Cast:* Sidney Poitier, Bill Cosby, Calvin Lockhart, John Amos, Jimmie C. Walker, Ossie Davis
▶ Fun sequel to *Uptown Saturday Night*, with Poitier and Cosby reprising their roles as larcenous brothers of "The Sons and Daughters of Shaka Lodge." This time they use Poitier's hexing powers to hypnotize bony Walker into thinking he's a prizefighter. Followed by *A Piece of the Action*.
Dist.: Warner

LET'S GET HARRY 1986
★ ★ ★ ★ R Action-Adventure 1:47
☑ Explicit language, violence
Dir: Stuart Rosenberg *Cast:* Michael Schoeffling, Tom Wilson, Glen Frey, Gary Busey, Robert Duvall, Mark Harmon
▶ When his brother Harmon is kidnapped by Colombian terrorists, Schoeffling and three Illinois friends set out to rescue him. Shallow but well-made thriller with a full quota of exciting violence. Duvall gives a wonderful performance as the mercenary who aids the heroes.
Dist.: HBO

LET'S GET LOST 1989
★ ★ NR Documentary/Biography 1:59
B&W
☑ Nudity, adult situations, explicit language
Dir: Bruce Weber *Cast:* Chet Baker
▶ Clear-eyed examination of charismatic trumpeter Baker, whose talent and personal charm are contrasted with his abusive rages, irresponsibility in relationships, and thirty-five-year addiction to heroin. Presentation is a bit long considering Baker's ranking as an artist, but director Weber makes the most of Baker's magnificent ruin of a face. (Epilogue informs that soon after filming, Baker died in what may have been suicide—or murder.)
Dist.: BMG

LET'S MAKE LOVE 1960
★ ★ ★ NR Musical/Comedy 1:58
Dir: George Cukor *Cast:* Marilyn Monroe, Yves Montand, Tony Randall, Frankie Vaughan, Wilfrid Hyde-White, David Burns
▶ Wealthy industrialist Montand investigates rehearsals of Off-Broadway play satirizing him and, mistaken for an actor by the director, is asked to play himself in the spoof. Stunned by the beauty of leading lady Monroe, Montand accepts the part and hires guest stars Bing Crosby, Milton Berle, and Gene Kelly to give him a cram course in the tricks of the trade. Not as funny as it could be, but worthy for luminous Monroe and sly Randall as Montand's PR man. Songs include superb version of "My Heart Belongs to Daddy" by Monroe.
Dist.: CBS/Fox

LET'S SCARE JESSICA TO DEATH 1971
★ ★ ★ PG Horror 1:29
☑ Violence
Dir: John Hancock *Cast:* Zohra Lampert, Barton Heyman, Kevin O'Connor, Gretchen Corbett, Alan Manson, Mariclare Costello
▶ Lampert has just been released from a mental institution, but she begins to suspect her newfound sanity when she discovers that her Connecticut town is full of vampires. Is she still mad? Or have husband Heyman and friends cooked up a scheme to make her think so? Pretty good scares.
Dist.: Paramount

LET'S SPEND THE NIGHT TOGETHER 1983
★ ★ PG Documentary/Music 1:30
☑ Explicit language

Dir: Hal Ashby *Cast:* Mick Jagger, Keith Richards, Charlie Watts, Bill Wyman, Ron Wood, Ian Stewart

▶ Well-staged documentary of the Rolling Stones' 1981 American tour features twenty-five of their songs performed in concert. Apart from a few oldies ("Time Is on My Side," "Satisfaction"), songs are from later stages in their career: "Start Me Up," "Miss You," "Waiting on a Friend," etc. Best for their fans.
Dist.: Embassy

LETTER, THE 1940
★★★★ NR Drama 1:35 B&W
Dir: William Wyler *Cast:* Bette Davis, Herbert Marshall, James Stephenson, Gale Sondergaard, Bruce Lester, Elizabeth Earl
▶ While rubber plantation owner Marshall is away from Malaysian home, wife Davis kills her secret lover and pleads self-defense. Then dead man's widow (Sondergaard) produces letter from Davis luring victim to his death. Potentially melodramatic adaptation of a W. Somerset Maugham story elevated by dynamic Davis in unsympathetic role. Her most memorable line: "I still love the man I killed."
Dist.: MGM/UA C

LETTER FROM AN UNKNOWN WOMAN 1948
★★ NR Drama 1:30 B&W
Dir: Max Ophuls *Cast:* Joan Fontaine, Louis Jourdan, Mady Christians, Marcel Journet, Art Smith
▶ Fontaine loves concert pianist Jourdan from afar, eventually meeting and having an affair with him on the eve of his departure on a concert tour. Pregnant with his child, Fontaine marries another man, but is unable to forget Jourdan. Moving drama has plush production values and splendidly nuanced performances.
Dist.: Republic

LETTER TO BREZHNEV 1986 British
★ R Romance 1:34
☑ Nudity, adult situations, explicit language
Dir: Chris Bernard *Cast:* Alexandra Pigg, Alfred Molina, Peter Firth, Margi Clarke, Tracy Lea, Ted Wood
▶ In Liverpool, young Englishwoman Pigg has quick fling with Russian sailor Firth while her friend Clarke romances Firth's pal Molina. After the Russians leave, a lovesick Pigg writes a letter to Soviet premier Brezhnev about the situation and gets a surprising answer. Good performances and buoyant feel, but accents are so thick subtitles would have come in handy. (CC)
Dist.: Warner

LETTER TO THREE WIVES, A 1949
★★★★ NR Drama 1:43 B&W
Dir: Joseph L. Mankiewicz *Cast:* Jeanne Crain, Linda Darnell, Ann Sothern, Kirk Douglas, Paul Douglas, Jeffrey Lynn, Thelma Ritter
▶ During a day trip, three wives learn that one

of their husbands is running off with notorious flirt Addie Ross (voice of Celeste Holm). Crain worries that she doesn't fit into spouse Lynn's social set; Sothern wonders if Kirk Douglas resents her writing income; Darnell is convinced that burly Paul Douglas has lost interest in her. Ingenious and witty, with Mankiewicz winning Oscars for his directing and screenplay.
Dist.: CBS/Fox

LEVIATHAN 1989
★★★ R Sci-Fi/Horror 1:38
☑ Explicit language, violence
Dir: George Pan Cosmatos *Cast:* Peter Weller, Richard Crenna, Amanda Pays, Daniel Stern, Ernie Hudson, Michael Carmine, Lisa Eilbacher, Hector Elizondo, Meg Foster
▶ After retrieving a safe from a sunken Russian ship that was conducting genetic experiments, two crew members of an undersea mining company turn into mutant monsters. Can the remaining members survive the ensuing onslaught? Formula plot in an underwater setting delivers expected number of jolts and shocks. Eerie score by Jerry Goldsmith. (CC)
Dist.: MGM/UA

LIANNA 1983
★ R Drama 1:55
☑ Nudity, strong sexual content, adult situations, explicit language
Dir: John Sayles *Cast:* Linda Griffiths, Jane Hallaren, Jon DeVries, Jo Henderson
▶ Lianna (Griffiths), married to insensitive film professor DeVries, finds she prefers Hallaren to him and leaves husband and children to be with her lover. Humanistic lesbian love story with naturalistic dialogue from the screenwriter/director.
Dist.: Vestron

LIAR'S MOON 1982
★★★★ PG Drama 1:45
☑ Nudity, adult situations
Dir: David Fisher *Cast:* Matt Dillon, Cindy Fisher, Christopher Connelly, Hoyt Axton, Yvonne De Carlo, Broderick Crawford
▶ In 1949 Texas, youngsters Dillon and pregnant Fisher run off to get married, only to discover they may be brother and sister. Fisher considers an abortion before the truth is learned. Intimate melodrama with an appealing Dillon; nicely produced and affecting.
Dist.: Vestron

LIBELED LADY 1936
★★★ NR Comedy 1:38 B&W
Dir: Jack Conway *Cast:* Jean Harlow, William Powell, Myrna Loy, Spencer Tracy, Walter Connolly
▶ Newspaper editor Tracy, facing libel suit from heiress Loy, hires Powell to romance her into an embarrassing position. Plan backfires when Powell really falls in love. Furiously fast and funny romantic comedy with brisk dia-

logue, ingenious plotting, and terrific performances.
Dist.: MGM/UA

LIBERATION OF L.B. JONES, THE 1970
★ ★ R Drama 1:44
☑ Adult situations, explicit language, violence
Dir: William Wyler *Cast:* Lee J. Cobb, Anthony Zerbe, Roscoe Lee Browne, Lola Falana, Lee Majors, Barbara Hershey
▶ Southern attorney Cobb and nephew Majors represent black funeral director Browne; he wants to sue wife Falana for divorce over her affair with white policeman Zerbe. Zerbe wants Falana not to contest the divorce, but she needs alimony to raise his child. Zerbe then turns violent. Too many sub-plots overcomplicate final work of director Wyler's distinguished career.
Dist.: RCA/Columbia

LICENCE TO KILL 1989 British
★ ★ ★ ★ ★ PG-13
Espionage/Action-Adventure 2:15
☑ Adult situations, violence
Dir: John Glen *Cast:* Timothy Dalton, Carey Lowell, Robert Davi, Talisa Soto, Anthony Zerbe, Wayne Newton, David Hedison, Priscilla Barnes
▶ Dalton is back for his second go-round as the inimitable James Bond. When close friends Hedison and Barnes are brutally attacked after their nuptials by pock-marked Latin drug kingpin Davi, Agent 007 has a personal vendetta to settle, even though his license to kill has been revoked. Hyperactive action scenes, state-of-the-art special effects, supersexy Bond girls Lowell and Soto, and the oiliest villain in years put the series back on the fast track. Final sequence involving elaborate attack on trucks carrying cocaine-spiked gasoline is a thrill a second. (CC)
Dist.: MGM/UA

LICENSE TO DRIVE 1988
★ ★ ★ ★ PG-13 Comedy 1:28
☑ Adult situations, explicit language
Dir: Greg Beeman *Cast:* Corey Haim, Corey Feldman, Heather Graham, Carol Kane, Richard Masur, Grant Goodeve
▶ Teenager Haim is obsessed with getting his driver's license. He fails road test but "borrows" stepfather's Cadillac anyway for date with dream girl Graham. A series of comic disasters ensues in this lightweight comedy with lots of wild stunts, car crashes, and colorful supporting characters. (CC)
Dist.: CBS/Fox

LIES 1985
★ ★ R Mystery-Suspense 1:30
☑ Nudity, adult situations, explicit language, violence
Dir: Jim Wheat, Ken Wheat *Cast:* Ann Dusenberry, Gail Strickland, Bruce Davison, Clu Gulager, Terence Knox, Bert Remsen
▶ Actress Dusenberry is hired for a movie role

as a murder witness who supposedly committed suicide in real life. However, in the first of several twists, she learns there is no film, the woman is alive, and is subject of a battle for an inheritance. Dusenberry gives an accomplished performance in an otherwise average thriller. (CC)
Dist.: Key

LIFE AND DEATH OF COLONEL BLIMP, THE
1943 British
★ ★ NR Drama 2:43
Dir: Michael Powell *Cast:* Roger Livesey, Deborah Kerr, Anton Walbrook, Roland Culver, James McKechnie, Albert Lieven
▶ Extraordinary portrait of a stereotypical British soldier examines his career from dashing officer in the Boer War to outmoded reactionary during World War II. Livesey is remarkable in a difficult part; Kerr excels in multiple roles as the women in his life. Heavily cut after harsh criticism from Winston Churchill and recently restored to full length on videocassettes.
Dist.: VidAmerica

LIFE AND TIMES OF JUDGE ROY BEAN, THE
1972
★ ★ ★ PG Western 2:00
☑ Adult humor
Dir: John Huston *Cast:* Paul Newman, Ava Gardner, Jacqueline Bisset, Anthony Perkins, Victoria Principal, John Huston
▶ Revisionist Western spoof about outlaw Bean (Newman), who takes over a Texas frontier town and proceeds to rob and hang assorted travelers. Violent, disjointed, occasionally funny tall tale is filled with cameos: Stacy Keach, Tab Hunter, Roddy McDowall, Ned Beatty, etc. Gardner plays Lily Langtry, Bean's idol.
Dist.: Warner

LIFE BEGINS FOR ANDY HARDY 1941
★ NR Drama 1:40 B&W
Dir: George B. Seitz *Cast:* Mickey Rooney, Lewis Stone, Judy Garland, Fay Holden, Ann Rutherford, Patricia Dane
▶ Andy Hardy (Rooney) is out of high school, and despite father Stone's objections, he's determined to experience real life in New York. Staying in cheap rooms and working as an office boy, Rooney is brushed by big city heartbreak, and hears the voice of sexual experience in divorcée Dane. Good, relatively sober departure from usually buoyant Hardy mold.
Dist.: MGM/UA

LIFEBOAT 1944
★ ★ ★ ★ ★ NR Drama 1:37 B&W
Dir: Alfred Hitchcock *Cast:* Tallulah Bankhead, William Bendix, Walter Slezak, Mary Anderson, John Hodiak, Henry Hull, Hume Cronyn, Canada Lee
▶ During World War II, survivors of a German sub attack are stranded on a lifeboat in the middle of the Atlantic. Despite mixed backgrounds, they team together to defeat a Nazi

threat. Although limited to one set, technological tour de force is a riveting thriller. Bankhead gives her best screen performance; Cronyn and Lee also register strongly. Hitchcock and writer John Steinbeck received Oscar nominations. **(CC)**
Dist.: CBS/Fox

LIFEFORCE 1985
★ ★ **R Sci-Fi 1:41**
Ⓥ Nudity, adult situations, explicit language, violence
Dir: Tobe Hooper *Cast:* Steve Railsback, Peter Firth, Frank Finlay, Mathilda May
▶ Space mission led by Railsback discovers bodies of alien vampires and brings them to London. The creatures come to life and suck the lifeforce out of people. Railsback must finally confront sexy head vampire May. A good start but story gets pretty silly. Special effects and the naked-throughout Ms. May are eye-filling.
Dist.: Vestron

LIFEGUARD 1976
★ ★ ★ **PG Drama 1:33**
Ⓥ Adult situations, explicit language
Dir: Daniel Petrie *Cast:* Sam Elliott, Anne Archer, Kathleen Quinlan, Stephen Young, Parker Stevenson
▶ California lifeguard Elliott, past thirty and feeling insecure, considers getting a more stable job and settling down with his high school sweetheart Archer. A simple story nicely played by Elliott and Archer.
Dist.: Paramount

LIFE OF EMILE ZOLA, THE 1937
★ ★ ★ **NR Biography 1:56 B&W**
Dir: William Dieterle *Cast:* Paul Muni, Gale Sondergaard, Joseph Schildkraut, Gloria Holden, Donald Crisp
▶ Life and times of Zola (Muni), France's most famous crusading journalist and author. Story focuses on Zola helping unjustly accused Jewish soldier Schildkraut in the notorious Dreyfus Affair. Effective biography with a strong Oscar-nominated performance by Muni. Oscar wins for Best Picture and Schildkraut as Best Supporting Actor.
Dist.: MGM/UA

LIFE OF OHARU, THE 1952 Japanese
☆ **NR Drama 2:26 B&W**
Dir: Kenji Mizoguchi *Cast:* Kinuyo Tanaka, Toshiro Mifune, Hisako Yamane, Yuriko Hamada, Ichiro Sugai, Toshiake Konoe
▶ Tanaka begins life as the honored daughter of a samurai, but a poor choice of lovers brings her down in the world, and she tumbles from mistress to prostitute. By the time she is fifty, a life of precipitous ups and downs has taken its toll. Hailed as a masterpiece, slow and highly pictorial tale will please the discriminating. Ⓢ
Dist.: Video Yesteryear

LIFE WITH FATHER 1947
★ ★ ★ ★ **NR Comedy 1:58**
Dir: Michael Curtiz *Cast:* William Powell, Irene Dunne, Elizabeth Taylor, Edmund Gwenn, ZaSu Pitts, Jimmy Lydon
▶ First-rate adaptation of the Broadway hit is a warm, nostalgic look at the foibles of irascible Victorian father Powell and his often unruly family. Essentially a series of reminiscences, beautifully shot film is consistently funny and touching. Based on the book by Clarence Day, Jr.
Dist.: Various

LIFT, THE 1983 Dutch
★ **R Horror 1:35**
Ⓥ Nudity, adult situations, explicit language, violence
Dir: Dick Maas *Cast:* Huub Stapel, Willeke van Ammelrooy, Josine van Dalsum, Hans Veerman, Ab Abspoel
▶ An elevator takes on a murderous life of its own, suffocating passengers, decapitating a night watchman, and throwing a blind man down the shaft. Mechanic Stapel and female reporter van Ammelrooy investigate. Novel notion brings fresh blood to tired genre, although ending is unsatisfying. Ⓢ
Dist.: Media

LIGHT AT THE EDGE OF THE WORLD, THE 1971 Liechtensteinian/Spanish
★ ★ **PG Action-Adventure 1:41**
Ⓥ Rape, violence
Dir: Kevin Billington *Cast:* Kirk Douglas, Yul Brynner, Samantha Eggar, Jean-Claude Drouot, Fernando Rey, Renato Salvatori
▶ Pirates take over an isolated lighthouse on a rugged, uninhabited island. Led by Brynner, they douse the light and loot the ships that then run aground. All the keepers have been killed but Douglas, who hides in a cave. Refusing to join the pirates, Douglas must struggle to defeat them and attract a relief ship. Loosely based on a story by Jules Verne, film sets up pirates' nefariousness in far too brutal a fashion. Two leads lend their considerable charisma to lost cause.
Dist.: Media

LIGHTHORSEMEN, THE 1988 Australian
★ ★ ★ **PG War 1:56**
Ⓥ Brief nudity, explicit language, violence
Dir: Simon Wincer *Cast:* Jon Blake, Peter Phelps, Tony Bonner, Bill Kerr, John Walton, Anthony Andrews
▶ Old-fashioned adventure about the Australian cavalrymen who played a decisive role in the battle of Beersheba during World War I. Episodic plot follows four friends preparing for the battle, in particular Phelps, a young recruit with pacifist leanings. Sincere but plodding, apart from the rousing climax.
Dist.: Warner

LIGHT IN THE FOREST, THE 1958
★ ★ ★ **NR Western/Family 1:33**
Dir: Herschel Daugherty *Cast:* James

MacArthur, Fess Parker, Wendell Corey, Carol Lynley, Joanne Dru, Jessica Tandy
▶ Intriguing Disney adaptation of the Conrad Richter novel tells of MacArthur, a young man raised by Indians who must readjust to life in white society. Army scout Parker helps him make the transition, but MacArthur despises his racist uncle Corey. MacArthur falls in love with Corey's indentured servant Lynley, but romance is threatened when his old tribe wants to use him as ploy in war against whites.
Dist.: Buena Vista

LIGHT OF DAY 1987
★ ★ **PG-13 Drama 1:47**
☑ Explicit language
Dir: Paul Schrader *Cast:* Michael J. Fox, Gena Rowlands, Joan Jett, Michael McKean, Thomas G. Waites, Cherry Jones
▶ Honest but grim account about the efforts of Fox and Jett, a Cleveland brother and sister, to break out of their blue-collar background through rock 'n' roll. Jett's painful relationship with cancer-ridden mother Rowlands exacerbates her problems. Story tends to wander, but rock star Jett is impressive in her film debut. Originally named *Born In the USA* until Bruce Springsteen borrowed the title for his rock anthem; the Boss returned the favor by writing film's theme song.
Dist.: Vestron

LIGHTSHIP, THE 1986
★ ★ **PG-13 Drama 1:30**
☑ Explicit language, violence
Dir: Jerzy Skolimowski *Cast:* Robert Duvall, Klaus Maria Brandauer, Michael Lyndon, Tom Bower, Robert Costanzo, Badja Djola
▶ Ship captain Brandauer and his estranged son Lyndon resolve their differences after they are taken hostage by Duvall's gang of fugitives. Some claustrophobic tension in the psychological duel, but film is hindered by meandering story, excessive talk, and overly mannered performance by Duvall (his accent is so thick you may not understand what he's saying). **(CC)**
Dist.: CBS/Fox

LIGHT YEARS 1988
★ **PG Animation 1:29**
☑ Nudity
Dir: René Laloux *Cast:* Voices of Glenn Close, Jennifer Grey, Christopher Plummer, John Shea, Penn Jillette, David Johansen
▶ Ambitiously plotted animated feature begins on a beautiful planet where invaders are turning the inhabitants to stone. To find out what's going on, Queen Ambisextra (Close) sends agent Sylvan (Shea) out into a universe swarming with genetic mutants, Metal Men, and mind twisting sci-fi paradoxes. Isaac Asimov adapted the screenplay from a French original, but his talents are not up to saving this pretentious, poorly animated snooze-fest.
Dist.: Vidmark

LIKE FATHER LIKE SON 1987
★ ★ ★ **PG-13 Comedy 1:39**
☑ Adult situations, explicit language
Dir: Rod Daniel *Cast:* Dudley Moore, Kirk Cameron, Margaret Colin, Catherine Hicks, Patrick O'Neal, Sean Astin
▶ Thanks to an Indian brain transference serum, prominent heart surgeon Moore and his sixteen-year-old son Cameron accidentally exchange bodies and have to live each other's lives. Adult/teen switcheroo is hardly a new premise, but the leads are charming and Moore generates some genuine laughs as a befuddled adolescent.
Dist.: RCA/Columbia

LI'L ABNER 1940
★ **NR Comedy 1:18 B&W**
Dir: Albert S. Rogell *Cast:* Granville Owen, Martha O'Driscoll, Mona Ray, Buster Keaton, Chester Conklin, Edgar Kennedy
▶ You'd think a comedy based on the comic strip characters created by Al Capp with Keaton as Lonesome Polecat, Kennedy as Cornelius Cornpone, not to mention Conklin (as well as Owen as Li'l Abner, O'Driscoll as Daisy Mae, and Ray as Mammy Yokum) would be pretty funny. But, apart from some inventive Keaton bits, this isn't funny at all. Not up to the 1959 musical remake.
Dist.: Video Yesteryear

LILI 1953
★ ★ ★ ★ **G Musical 1:21**
Dir: Charles Walters *Cast:* Leslie Caron, Mel Ferrer, Jean-Pierre Aumont, Zsa Zsa Gabor, Kurt Kasznar, Amanda Blake
▶ Sixteen-year-old French orphan Caron joins carnival and falls in love with magician Aumont. Heartbroken to learn that Aumont's assistant Gabor is also his wife, Caron is consoled by puppeteer Ferrer, a crippled former dancer whose bitterness she has mistaken for cruelty. Delightful Caron was nominated for an Oscar; music won Academy Award. Turned into the 1961 Broadway hit *Carnival*. Best bit: Caron and Ferrer's puppets sing famous "Hi-Lili, Hi-Lo."
Dist.: MGM/UA

LILIES OF THE FIELD 1963
★ ★ ★ **NR Drama 1:34 B&W**
Dir: Ralph Nelson *Cast:* Sidney Poitier, Lilia Skala, Lisa Mann, Isa Crino
▶ Black handyman Poitier builds church under the watchful supervision of German nuns led by Skala. Moving, humanistic drama with an Oscar-winning performance by Poitier (the first black actor ever to win in this category). Also received nominations for Best Picture and Supporting Actress Skala. **(CC)**
Dist.: CBS/Fox

LILITH 1964
★ ★ **NR Drama 1:54 B&W**
Dir: Robert Rossen *Cast:* Warren Beatty, Jean Seberg, Peter Fonda, Kim Hunter, Jessica Walter, Gene Hackman

▶ Beatty, occupational therapist at an exclusive mental institution, is drawn against his will into an affair with alluring patient Seberg. Respectful adaptation of J. R. Salamanca's novel has thoughtful performances to offset its slow pacing and downbeat tone.
Dist.: RCA/Columbia

LILY IN LOVE 1985 U.S./Hungarian
★ **PG-13 Comedy 1:46**
☑ Adult situations
Dir: Karoly Makk *Cast:* Christopher Plummer, Maggie Smith, Elke Sommer, Adolph Green, Szabo Sandor
▶ Writer Smith doesn't feel her ham actor hubby Plummer is quite right for her script. He disguises himself as an Italian matinee idol to seduce her and win the role. Genteel continental fluff with lovely Hungarian locations. Smith and Plummer transcend the flat dialogue with smooth timing and poise.
Dist.: Vestron

LIMELIGHT 1952
★★★ **NR Comedy/Drama 2:25 B&W**
Dir: Charles Chaplin *Cast:* Charles Chaplin, Claire Bloom, Nigel Bruce, Buster Keaton, Sydney Chaplin
▶ Elderly vaudevillian Chaplin rescues suicidal ballet dancer Bloom and they support each other through career ups and downs. The innocence and goodness of the central relationship is hard to resist in this sweetly sentimental Chaplin talkie. Stiff performance by Chaplin's son Sydney but Buster shines in his too-brief routine with Charlie. Chaplin co-wrote the Oscar-winning score.
Dist.: CBS/Fox

LIMIT UP 1989
★ **PG-13 Comedy/Fantasy 1:28**
☑ Adult situations, explicit language
Dir: Richard Martini *Cast:* Nancy Allen, Dean Stockwell, Brad Hall, Danitra Vance, Ray Charles
▶ Chicago stock exchange runner Allen, thwarted in her ambition to become a trader, sells her soul to Satanic employee Vance. She attempts to short circuit the deal when she learns the terms involve causing a worldwide famine. Amiable comedy attempts to tap into yuppie success fantasies, but the screenplay isn't clever enough to bring it off. **(CC)**
Dist.: Virgin

LINK 1986
★★★ **R Horror 1:43**
☑ Brief nudity, violence
Dir: Richard Franklin *Cast:* Elisabeth Shue, Terence Stamp, Steven Pinner, Richard Garnett, David O'Hara
▶ American student Shue takes housekeeping gig with Stamp, an English doctor studying apes. She becomes the object of a rampaging orangutan's affections. Pace lags until orangutan goes ape in the last part of the movie. Weak screenplay leaves the human

actors stranded although the monkey shines in this brutal thriller.
Dist.: HBO

LIONHEART 1987
★★ **PG Action-Adventure 1:44**
☑ Explicit language, violence
Dir: Franklin J. Schaffner *Cast:* Eric Stoltz, Gabriel Byrne, Nicola Cowper, Dexter Fletcher, Deborah Barrymore, Nicholas Clay
▶ Young knight Stoltz leads group of sideshow escapees and orphans to join the Crusades but must battle Black Knight Byrne who seeks to enslave them. Promising story gets lost in clumsy telling. Stoltz lacks the charisma to carry this large-scale production, although villainous Byrne does well.
Dist.: Warner

LION IN WINTER, THE 1968
★★★★ **PG Drama 2:14**
☑ Adult language
Dir: Anthony Harvey *Cast:* Katharine Hepburn, Peter O'Toole, Anthony Hopkins, Timothy Dalton, Jane Merrow
▶ Hepburn won her third Oscar as Eleanor of Aquitaine, the imprisoned wife of King Henry II (O'Toole). Amid jousting contests and period pageants, the King and Queen squabble over which of their three sons should inherit the throne in twelfth-century England. Elaborate plotting and witty dialogue. Also won Oscars for Screenplay and Musical Score.
Dist.: Nelson

LION OF AFRICA, THE 1987
★★★★ **NR Action-Adventure/MFTV 1:49**
Dir: Kevin Connor *Cast:* Brian Dennehy, Brooke Adams, Joseph Shiloa, Don Warrington
▶ In West Africa, no-nonsense doctor Adams hires feisty trader Dennehy and his battered truck to fetch desperately needed medical shipment. Friction blossoms into romance during their adventurous trek. Old-fashioned entertainment with exotic Kenyan locales.
Dist.: Warner

LION OF THE DESERT 1981 Libyan/British
★★★★ **PG Drama 2:40**
☑ Graphic violence
Dir: Moustapha Akkad *Cast:* Anthony Quinn, Oliver Reed, Raf Vallone, Rod Steiger, John Gielgud
▶ In 1929 Libya, Bedouin Omar Mukhtar (Quinn) guides his people against Italian invaders led by vicious general Reed. True story is impressive in scope with well-staged battle scenes, spectacular desert vistas, and grand Maurice Jarre score. Too long, however.
Dist.: USA

LION, THE WITCH & THE WARDROBE, THE 1979
★★★★ **NR Animation 1:40**
Dir: Bill Melendez *Cast:* Voices of Dick Vosborough, Rachel Warren, Victor Spinetti, Don Parker, Liz Proud, Beth Porter

▶ Four children pass through an antique wardrobe in a old country house and enter a magical land called Narnia where many adventures await them. Superior adaptation of the classic fairy tale from the first of the seven books in *The Chronicles of Narnia* by C. S. Lewis. **(CC)**
Dist.: Vestron

LIPSTICK 1976
★ ★ ★ **R Drama 1:29**
☑ Rape, nudity, violence, explicit language
Dir: Lamont Johnson   *Cast:* Margaux Hemingway, Chris Sarandon, Anne Bancroft, Mariel Hemingway, Perry King
▶ Model Margaux Hemingway is raped by Sarandon. Despite the efforts of prosecutor Bancroft, he gets off. When Sarandon attacks her little sister Mariel, Margaux takes the law into her own hands. Volatile antirape drama with uncomfortably graphic rape scenes.
Dist.: Paramount

LIQUID SKY 1983
☆ **R Sci-Fi 1:52**
☑ Rape, nudity, adult situations, explicit language, violence
Dir: Slava Tsukerman   *Cast:* Anne Carlisle, Paula Sheppard, Susan Doukas, Otto Von Wernherr, Bob Brady, Elaine Grove
▶ Lesbian model Carlisle, reeling from a brutal rape, is attacked by miniature UFO seeking brain secretions formed during intercourse. Eccentric low-budget combination of sci-fi, black comedy, New Wave fashion, and punk sensibilities has mild cult following, but underground humor has already dated badly. Carlisle's androgynous beauty is an asset in her dual role (she's also a male heroin addict).
Dist.: Media

LISA AND THE DEVIL 1975 Italian
☆ **R Horror 1:33**
☑ Adult situations, explicit language, graphic violence
Dir: Mickey Lion (Mario Bava)   *Cast:* Telly Savalas, Elke Sommer, Robert Alda, Silva Koscina, Alessio Orano, Alida Valli
▶ In Italy, tourist Sommer encounters demonic Savalas in a shop. Suddenly, she seems possessed, and neither doctors nor priest Alda are able to exorcise her. Lurid and ludicrous. Bava's baroque visuals can't disguise an incoherent story. And if Savalas is the Devil, why does he suck a lollipop, àla "Kojak"? Also known as *House of Exorcism*.
Dist.: Various

LISBON 1956
★ **NR Action-Adventure 1:30**
Dir: Ray Milland   *Cast:* Ray Milland, Maureen O'Hara, Claude Rains, Frances Lederer, Yvonne Furneaux, Percy Marmont
▶ In Lisbon, O'Hara hires Rains to rescue her husband from a Communist country and then kill him so she can inherit his money. Unaware of the real nature of the mission, boat captain Milland is enlisted to help. Competent adventure, with Rains stealing scenes from actor/director Milland.
Dist.: Republic

LISTEN TO ME 1989
★ ★ ★ **PG-13 Drama 1:47**
☑ Brief nudity, adult situations, explicit language, mild violence
Dir: Douglas Day Stewart   *Cast:* Kirk Cameron, Jami Gertz, Roy Scheider, Amanda Peterson, Tom Quill, George Wyner
▶ Scheider is debating coach at a college where competitive colloquy is the hottest sport. Cameron and Gertz are two of his premiere verbal sparrers, but off the podium they suffer romantic problems. In the finale, the two team up to debate the abortion issue with a couple of Harvard smoothies in a national college contest. No deep thinking on sensitive issues here, but novel teen pic may also please adults. **(CC)**
Dist.: RCA/Columbia

LIST OF ADRIAN MESSENGER, THE 1963
★ ★ **NR Mystery-Suspense 1:38 B&W**
Dir: John Huston   *Cast:* George C. Scott, Dana Wynter, Clive Brook, Gladys Cooper, Herbert Marshall, John Merivale
▶ Scott, a retired British colonel, is given a list of eleven names by Merivale, the title character. When Merivale dies, Scott learns that the eleven have met similar fates; all were World War II POWs whose escape plans were betrayed to the Japanese by a cohort. Scott pursues the murderer, a master of disguise, before he kills again. Numerous red herrings feature uncredited appearances by Tony Curtis, Kirk Douglas, Burt Lancaster, Robert Mitchum, Frank Sinatra, and director Huston, all in heavy disguise. Fine mystery even without the gimmick; shot in Ireland.
Dist.: MCA

LISZTOMANIA 1975 British
☆ **R Biography/Music 1:44**
☑ Nudity, strong sexual content, adult situations, explicit language
Dir: Ken Russell   *Cast:* Roger Daltrey, Sara Kestelman, Paul Nicholas, Fiona Lewis, Veronica Quilligan, Ringo Starr
▶ Daltrey is composer Franz Liszt and Nicholas is his buddy Richard Wagner in this surreal, outrageous, and sexually obsessed biographical fantasy. Director Russell re-creates Liszt as the first rock idol, with the composer's music updated by English rocker Rick Wakeman. Russell is always flamboyant, but here he aims to shock even the most adventurous.
Dist.: Warner

LITTLE BIG HORN 1951
★ **NR Western 1:26 B&W**
Dir: Charles Marquis Warren   *Cast:* Lloyd Bridges, John Ireland, Marie Windsor, Reed Hadley, Jim Davis, Hugh O'Brian
▶ Cavalry captain Bridges gets wind of the impending Indian attack at Little Big Horn. He sets out with his men, including rival Ireland, to

warn General Custer, but the Indians ambush them at every turn. If you're familiar with history, you probably know how this story ends, but tightly constructed movie transcends its built-in historical handicap.
Dist.: Paramount

LITTLE BIG MAN 1970
★ ★ ★ ★ ★ **PG Western 2:13**
☑ Adult situations, violence
Dir: Arthur Penn   *Cast:* Dustin Hoffman, Faye Dunaway, Martin Balsam, Richard Mulligan, Chief Dan George, Jeff Corey
▶ Adaptation of Thomas Berger's novel about Jack Crabb (Hoffman), a 121-year-old-man who reminisces about his days as a young pioneer, adopted Indian, drinking pal of Wild Bill Hickok, medicine show hustler, and survivor of Custer's Last Stand. Monumental, enthralling epic with superior performances and compassionate view of Indians.   **(CC)**
Dist.: CBS/Fox

LITTLE CAESAR 1930
★ ★ ★ **NR Crime 1:17 B&W**
Dir: Mervyn LeRoy   *Cast:* Edward G. Robinson, Douglas Fairbanks, Jr., Glenda Farrell, Stanley Fields, Sidney Blackmer, Ralph Ince
▶ The rise and fall of crime kingpin Robinson. Hard-hitting gangster film with a magnetic performance by the great Eddie G. Includes one of the great curtain lines in cinema history: "Mother of mercy, is this the end of Rico?"
Dist.: Fox Hills

LITTLE COLONEL, THE 1935
★ ★ **NR Family 1:20 B&W/C**
Dir: David Butler   *Cast:* Shirley Temple, Lionel Barrymore, Evelyn Venable, John Lodge, Hattie McDaniel, Bill "Bojangles" Robinson
▶ Superior Temple vehicle, set in the post–Civil War South, has Shirley smoothing over a feud between her grandfather Barrymore, a Confederate colonel, and mother Venable, who made the mistake of marrying Yankee Lodge. Temple does one of her most famous routines, a stairstep tap dance with Robinson. **(CC)**
Dist.: CBS/Fox

LITTLE DARLINGS 1980
★ ★ ★ **R Comedy 1:34**
☑ Adult situations, explicit language, adult humor
Dir: Ronald F. Maxwell   *Cast:* Kristy McNichol, Tatum O'Neal, Matt Dillon, Armand Assante, Maggie Blye
▶ Teen campers McNichol and O'Neal bet on who'll be first to lose her virginity. O'Neal tries to score with counselor Assante while McNichol falls for fellow camper Dillon. Tasteful handling of a tricky theme elicits sympathetic performances from the leads. Amusing and occasionally touching.
Dist.: Paramount

LITTLE DORRIT 1988 British
★ **G Drama 6:00**

Dir: Christine Edzard   *Cast:* Alec Guinness, Derek Jacobi, Cyril Cusack, Joan Greenwood, Sarah Pickering, Roshan Seth
▶ Wonderfully detailed, two-part rendering of Dickens's novel has splendid Oscar-nominated performance by Guinness as Dorrit's father, terrific costumes, and lots of nineteenth-century atmosphere. It's the story of how middle-aged Clenham (Jacobi) helps the family of Little Dorrit (Pickering), and how she in turn is able to help him. Teeming with splendidly portrayed secondary characters, and engrossing subplots, this lengthy film passes quickly and leaves pleasant memories. Part one is titled *Nobody's Fault*; part two is *Little Dorrit's Story*.   **(CC)**
Dist.: Warner

LITTLE DRUMMER GIRL, THE 1984
★ ★ ★ **R Espionage 2:10**
☑ Brief nudity, adult situations, explicit language, violence
Dir: George Roy Hill   *Cast:* Diane Keaton, Klaus Kinski, Yorgo Voyagis, Sami Frey, Michael Cristofer
▶ Crack Israeli intelligence team headed by Kinski recruits American actress Keaton to help catch a Palestinian terrorist. She falls for Israeli agent Voyagis, assigned to teach her the espionage business. Faithful adaptation of John le Carré's best-selling novel is often contrived, but leads give uniformly powerful performances and European and Middle Eastern locations are spectacular.   **(CC)**
Dist.: Warner

LITTLE FOXES, THE 1941
★ ★ ★ ★ **NR Drama 1:56 B&W**
Dir: William Wyler   *Cast:* Bette Davis, Herbert Marshall, Teresa Wright, Richard Carlson, Patricia Collinge, Dan Duryea
▶ In the turn-of-the-century South, a family of greedy carpetbaggers schemes among and against one another to build a factory on a lovely former plantation. Nine Oscar nominations (including Picture, Director, Davis, Collinge, Wright) went to this juicy film version of Lillian Hellman's play. Davis gives one of her best performances as a woman willing to risk everything, even her husband's life, to get what she wants.
Dist.: Nelson

LITTLE GIRL WHO LIVES DOWN THE LANE, THE 1976
★ ★ **PG Mystery-Suspense 1:33**
☑ Violence
Dir: Nicholas Gessner   *Cast:* Jodie Foster, Martin Sheen, Scott Jacoby, Mort Shuman, Alexis Smith
▶ Reclusive thirteen-year-old Foster, who lives in isolated house, is befriended by handicapped teen Jacoby. Foster is endangered when child molester Sheen discovers her. Subtle thriller with an effective performance by Foster.
Dist.: Vestron

LITTLE LORD FAUNTLEROY 1936
★ ★ ★ NR Drama 1:44 B&W
Dir: John Cromwell   *Cast:* Freddie Bartholomew, C. Aubrey Smith, Dolores Costello, Mickey Rooney, Guy Kibbee
▶ Warmhearted adaptation of the classic Frances Hodgson Burnett story about poor Brooklyn boy Bartholomew, who is the heir to a fortune and a title if he can win the heart of grumpy English grandfather Smith. Rooney stands out in a small part as a shoeshine boy. (CC)
Dist.: Various

LITTLE MEN 1940
★ NR Drama 1:24 B&W
Dir: Norman Z. McLeod   *Cast:* Kay Francis, Jack Oakie, George Bancroft, Jimmy Lydon, Ann Gillis, Charles Esmond
▶ Tough-kid Lydon is among the lads who learn the enduring values of life in an orphanage run by Francis, who is Jo—the now-grown-up heroine of Louisa May Alcott's *Little Women*. Not in the same league as 1933's *Little Women*, treacly tale still has its champions.
Dist.: Cable

LITTLE MERMAID, THE 1989
★ ★ ★ ★ ★ G Animation 1:22
Dir: John Musker, Ron Clements   *Cast:* Voices of Jodi Benson, Pat Carroll, Samuel E. Wright, Kenneth Mars, Buddy Hackett, Christopher Daniel Barnes
▶ Defying her sea king father, mermaid Ariel (Benson) trades her beautiful voice to witch Carroll in exchange for legs so she can win prince Barnes. He must "Kiss the Girl" (one of two Oscar-nominated songs in tuneful Oscar-winning Howard Ashman-Alan Menken score) within three days for her to stay human. Adorable adaptation of Hans Christian Anderson tale is a merry and moving experience. Most delightful scene: Sebastian the Crab (Wright) singing Oscar-winning "Under the Sea."   (CC)
Dist.: Buena Vista

LITTLE MINISTER, THE 1934
★ NR Comedy 1:50 B&W
Dir: Richard Wallace   *Cast:* Katharine Hepburn, John Beal, Donald Crisp, Andy Clyde, Beryl Mercer, Billy Watson
▶ Early Hepburn vehicle, with the star as a whimsical elfin gypsy girl who captures the heart of new minister Beal. Romance appears impossible until her true identity is revealed. Soft-focus adaptation of a popular play by *Peter Pan* author James M. Barrie is fey, but enjoyable.
Dist.: Turner

LITTLE MISS BROADWAY 1938
★ ★ NR Musical 1:10 B&W
Dir: Irving Cummings   *Cast:* Shirley Temple, George Murphy, Jimmy Durante, Phyllis Brooks, Edna May Oliver, Edward Ellis
▶ Temple loses her parents and is taken under the wing of Ellis, who manages a show-business hostelry catering to the likes of song-and-patter man Durante. Hard-hearted Oliver owns the place, and when she decides to evict the show people, Temple gets idea of putting on a show to pay everyone's back rent. Moppet star is irresistible, as usual, especially in tandem with Durante and Murphy. Delightful songs include title tune and "Be Optimistic."   (CC)
Dist.: CBS/Fox ⓒ

LITTLE MISS MARKER 1980
★ ★ ★ ★ PG Comedy 1:42
☑ Explicit language
Dir: Walter Bernstein   *Cast:* Walter Matthau, Julie Andrews, Tony Curtis, Bob Newhart, Lee Grant, Sara Stimson
▶ Crabby bookie Sorrowful Jones (Matthau) gets stuck with six-year-old Stimson, left as collateral after her father commits suicide because of his racetrack losses. Sorrowful and the kid are befriended by beautiful widow Andrews. Matthau magic and Andrews charm make this sentimental Damon Runyon story good for family viewing. Remake of the 1934 Shirley Temple vehicle.
Dist.: MCA

LITTLE MONSTERS 1989
★ ★ ★ PG Comedy 1:40
☑ Explicit language, violence
Dir: Richard Alan Greenberg   *Cast:* Howie Mandel, Fred Savage, Daniel Stern, Margaret Whitton, Rick Ducommun, William Murray Weiss
▶ Mandel is a monster who inhabits the fantasy world under youngsters' beds. New kid in the neighborhood Savage discovers and befriends Mandel, but then must battle monsters when they kidnap his little brother. Far-fetched adventure has some delightfully inventive moments in the manner of *Beetlejuice*, but it may be too scary for the younger children who are its natural audience. Mandel's monster shtick will get on everybody's nerves.
Dist.: Vestron

LITTLE MURDERS 1971
☆ R Comedy 1:50
☑ Adult situations, explicit language, violence
Dir: Alan Arkin   *Cast:* Elliott Gould, Marcia Rodd, Vincent Gardenia, Elizabeth Wilson, Jon Korkes, Donald Sutherland
▶ With crime, mugging, and murder everyday events in New York, photographer Gould (his specialty is dog excrement) has let himself sink into a state of near-comatose apathy. It takes the love and commitment of Rodd and her zany family to draw Gould back into the real world—a place where tragedy lurks just outside the window. Disturbing black comedy based on the stage play by cartoonist Jules Feiffer has unfortunately proven prophetic. Director Arkin has a dazzling cameo.
Dist.: Key

LITTLE NIGHT MUSIC, A 1977
★ PG Musical 2:05
☑ Adult situations
Dir: Harold Prince   *Cast:* Elizabeth Taylor, Diana Rigg, Len Cariou, Lesley-Anne Down, Hermione Gingold, Lawrence Guittard
▶ In 1905 Vienna, lawyer Cariou, his virginal wife Down, his old flame Taylor, his teenage son, and Taylor's lover Guittard gather for a summer weekend at Gingold's estate. Couples break up and reunite in new pairs. Stiff staging by theater director Prince but nice work from Rigg and Cariou and wonderfully witty, sophisticated Stephen Sondheim score (including "Send in the Clowns"). Adaptation of the Broadway hit based on Bergman's *Smiles of a Summer Night.* Oscar for Best Song Score.
Dist.: Nelson

LITTLE NIKITA 1988
★★★★ PG Mystery-Suspense 1:38
☑ Explicit language, violence
Dir: Richard Benjamin   *Cast:* Sidney Poitier, River Phoenix, Richard Jenkins, Caroline Kava, Richard Bradford
▶ While tracking KGB official, FBI agent Poitier interviews teenaged Phoenix, whose parents turn out to be Russian agents themselves. A stunned Phoenix is then kidnapped by Poitier's quarry. Farfetched tale has some plot holes but maintains interest throughout. (CC)
Dist.: RCA/Columbia

LITTLE PRINCE, THE 1974 British
★★★ G Musical 1:28
Dir: Stanley Donen   *Cast:* Richard Kiley, Steven Warner, Bob Fosse, Gene Wilder, Joss Ackland, Clive Revill
▶ Pilot Kiley crash-lands in the desert and meets young interplanetary traveler Warner. Warner has encounters with a snake (Fosse) and a fox (Wilder), and learns about life. Tender adaptation of the Antoine de Saint-Exupéry children's classic. Lerner and Loewe score highlighted by Wilder singing "Closer and Closer."
Dist.: Paramount

LITTLE PRINCESS, THE 1939
★★ NR Family 1:33
Dir: Walter Lang   *Cast:* Shirley Temple, Richard Greene, Anita Louise, Cesar Romero, Ian Hunter
▶ Legendary charmer with Temple as a poor little rich girl sent to boarding school after her father is killed in the Boer War. Shirley escapes and discovers her father's still alive but stricken with amnesia. Predictably, the sight of his darling daughter quickly cures him.
Dist.: Various

LITTLE ROMANCE, A 1979
★★★ PG Romance/Comedy 1:50
☑ Explicit language
Dir: George Roy Hill   *Cast:* Laurence Olivier,

Sally Kellerman, Diane Lane, Arthur Hill, Thelonious Bernard
▶ Precocious teens Lane and Bernard, hassled by their parents, run away from Paris to Italy. Dapper, elderly ex-con Olivier helps them in their quest to reach Venice and kiss under the Bridge of Sighs. A sweet movie with pretty locations. The youngsters are winning and natural, and Lord Larry is a sly scene-stealer.
Dist.: Warner

LITTLE SEX, A 1982
★★ R Comedy 1:35
☑ Adult situations, explicit language, adult humor
Dir: Bruce Paltrow   *Cast:* Tim Matheson, Kate Capshaw, Edward Herrmann, John Glover, Wallace Shawn
▶ After Matheson marries Capshaw, older brother Herrmann bets him that he can't stay faithful. Tempted by beautiful women at every turn, the poor newlywed is in danger of losing Capshaw to ex-beau Glover when he strays. Harmless sit-com romantic comedy.
Dist.: MCA

LITTLE SHOP OF HORRORS, THE 1960
★ NR Horror/Comedy 1:10 B&W
Dir: Roger Corman   *Cast:* Jonathan Haze, Jackie Joseph, Dick Miller, Mel Welles, Jack Nicholson
▶ On Skid Row, lowly florist's assistant Haze becomes popular when he creates a new plant. However, Audrey, Jr. (named after the girl of his dreams), snacks on human blood and is soon demanding, "Feed Me!" B-movie cult classic, shot in two days, is raw and quite funny. Young Nicholson is hysterical as a masochistic dental patient. Inspired the off-Broadway musical and 1986 film.
Dist.: Vestron   ☐

LITTLE SHOP OF HORRORS 1986
★★ PG-13 Musical 1:34
☑ Explicit language, violence
Dir: Frank Oz   *Cast:* Rick Moranis, Ellen Greene, Vincent Gardenia, Steve Martin, John Candy, Bill Murray
▶ Funny, fractured musical set in a Skid Row flower shop. Life of nebbish Moranis changes after he buys a mysterious plant during a solar eclipse. But to keep the plant alive, he must feed it fresh blood. Singing and dancing with Moranis are his love interest Audrey (Greene), ruthless boss Gardenia, and demented dentist Martin. Levi Stubbs, the voice of the plant, shines. Original, outrageous, tuneful, and fun; based on Roger Corman's 1960 horror-movie spoof. (CC)
Dist.: Vestron

LITTLEST HORSE THIEVES, THE 1977
★★★ G Comedy/Family 1:44
Dir: Charles Jarrott   *Cast:* Alastair Sim, Peter Barkworth, Maurice Colbourne, Andrew Harrison, Benje Bolgar, Chloe Franks
▶ Franks, daughter of coal mine manager in

turn-of-the-century England, mounts a campaign to protect ponies from abuse in the mines. With her friends Harrison and Bolger, she hides the ponies in a church while the miners vote on their fate. Sim's last film has interesting moral points. Strong Disney effort.
Dist.: Buena Vista

LITTLEST REBEL, THE 1935
★★ NR Musical/Family 1:10 B&W
Dir: David Butler ***Cast:*** Shirley Temple, John Boles, Bill "Bojangles" Robinson, Jack Holt, Karen Morley
▶ Memorable Temple feature set in the South during the Civil War. Temple saves soldier daddy Boles, convicted as a spy, from death sentence by persuading Abe Lincoln to let him go free. Songs include "Those Endearing Young Charms" and "Polly Wolly Doodle" in a famous tap-dancing duet with "Bojangles" Robinson. **(CC)**
Dist.: CBS/Fox

LITTLE THIEF, THE 1989 French
☆ NR Drama 1:49
☑ Adult situations, explicit language
Dir: Claude Miller ***Cast:*** Charlotte Gainsbourg, Didier Bezace, Simon de la Brosse, Raoul Billery, Chantal Banlier
▶ In 1950 France, alienated teen Gainsbourg lives with relatives after being abandoned by her mother. She turns to petty thievery to get attention and eventually falls in love with kindred spirit de la Brosse. François Truffaut planned this as his next film before he died. Miller took up the project and result is an affecting and sensitive homage to the late director. [S]
Dist.: HBO

LITTLE TREASURE 1985
★★ R Action-Adventure 1:38
☑ Brief nudity, explicit language, mild violence
Dir: Alan Sharp ***Cast:*** Margot Kidder, Ted Danson, Burt Lancaster, Joseph Hacker, Malena Doria
▶ Stripper Kidder, told by dying father Lancaster of buried stolen loot in New Mexico ghost town, teams with lapsed seminary student Danson to find the treasure. It's a bumpy road to love and money for this mismatched pair in director Sharp's easy-to-take adventure. **(CC)**
Dist.: RCA/Columbia

LITTLE VERA 1988 Russian
★ NR Drama 2:10
☑ Nudity, adult situations, explicit language, mild violence
Dir: Vassili Pitchul ***Cast:*** Natalia Negoda, Andrei Sokolov, Yuri Nazarov, Ludmila Zaisova, Alexander Niegreva
▶ Teenaged Vera (Negoda) is living in typical cramped Soviet squalor with her parents. When she gets pregnant, boyfriend Sokolov moves in. With no privacy, apartment becomes a pressure cooker, and before long Vera's father stabs Sokolov and she starts losing her mind. Though frank setting and language made it a landmark of early glasnost-era Soviet cinema, film is only routine kitchen sink drama. Outside of Negoda's occasional nudity, there's not much novel here for westerners. [S]
Dist.: Water Bearer

LITTLE WOMEN 1933
★★★★ NR Drama 1:55 B&W
Dir: George Cukor ***Cast:*** Katharine Hepburn, Joan Bennett, Paul Lukas, Edna May Oliver, Jean Parker, Frances Dee, John Lodge, Douglass Montgomery, Spring Byington
▶ Faithful adaptation of Louisa May Alcott's classic about the coming-of-age of four New England sisters during the Civil War is an irresistible tearjerker. Luminous performance by Hepburn as Jo, an aspiring writer who fears the family may fall apart when sister Meg (Dee) marries Brooke (Lodge). Nominated for three Oscars, winning for superb screenplay by Sarah Y. Mason and Victor Heerman.
Dist.: MGM/UA

LITTLE WOMEN 1949
★★ NR Drama 2:01
Dir: Mervyn LeRoy ***Cast:*** June Allyson, Peter Lawford, Margaret O'Brien, Elizabeth Taylor, Janet Leigh, Mary Astor
▶ Allyson is Jo, Taylor is Amy, O'Brien is Beth, and Leigh is Meg in this slick adaptation of the episodic Louisa May Alcott novel about sisters coping and growing up while their father is away at war. Casting makes sense, but film lacks the heart of the 1933 version. **(CC)**
Dist.: MGM/UA

LIVE A LITTLE, LOVE A LITTLE 1968
★★ NR Musical 1:30
Dir: Norman Taurog ***Cast:*** Elvis Presley, Michele Carey, Don Porter, Rudy Valee, Dick Sargent, Sterling Holloway
▶ Film number twenty-eight for the King. This time, he's a photographer who sneakily snaps for a *Playboy*-type magazine while also working for a straitlaced conservative publisher in the same building. Love with model Carey complicates his life even further in this mildly amusing outing. Songs include "Wonderful World" and "A Little Less Conversation."
Dist.: MGM/UA

LIVE AND LET DIE 1973 British
★★★★★ PG Espionage/Action-Adventure 2:01
☑ Adult situations, explicit language, violence
Dir: Guy Hamilton ***Cast:*** Roger Moore, Yaphet Kotto, Jane Seymour, Clifton James, Geoffrey Holder, Bernard Lee, Lois Maxwell
▶ The trail leads from Harlem to New Orleans as secret agent James Bond (Moore) goes after Kotto, a villain who mixes voodoo with drug dealings. Action includes a wild chase through the Louisiana swamps, with good-ol'-

boy sheriff James providing comic relief so effectively they brought him back for *The Man With the Golden Gun*. Moore makes a debonair debut as agent 007, Seymour provides the love interest as Solitaire, and Paul McCartney does the theme song in this typically effective Bond concoction.
Dist.: MGM/UA

LIVES OF A BENGAL LANCER, THE 1935
★ ★ ★ NR Action-Adventure 1:49 B&W
Dir: Henry Hathaway *Cast:* Gary Cooper, Franchot Tone, Richard Cromwell, Guy Standing, C. Aubrey Smith, Monte Blue
▶ Rousing adventure set in colonial India: daredevil Tone and nervous Cromwell, neglected son of troop commander Standing, join Cooper in foiling a native uprising. A delight from start to finish, with a snake-charming sequence and a grueling torture session among the highlights. Unusually accurate classic received six Oscar nominations.
Dist.: MCA

LIVING DAYLIGHTS, THE 1987 British
★ ★ ★ ★ PG Espionage/Action-Adventure 2:11
☑ Violence
Dir: John Glen *Cast:* Timothy Dalton, Maryam d'Abo, Jeroen Krabbe, Joe Don Baker, John Rhys-Davies, Art Malik
▶ The sixteenth installment of the world's most popular secret agent features Dalton as the newest James Bond. Helping with the defection of KGB agent Krabbe, 007 and svelte blond d'Abo toboggan their way over the Iron Curtain. Then the unflappable Bond gets mixed up with ruthless American arms dealer Baker and Afghan freedom fighter Malik. Exotic scenery, breathless chase scenes, and socko production values add up to Bond business as usual. **(CC)**
Dist.: CBS/Fox

LIVING DESERT, THE 1953
★ ★ ★ ★ G Documentary 1:39
Dir: James Algar
▶ Trendsetting documentary uses striking footage to portray the seasonal life cycle of an American desert and its inhabitants. Oscar winner for Best Documentary despite controversy surrounding some staged animal rituals. First in Disney's True-Life Adventure series. Narrated by Winston Hibler.
Dist.: Buena Vista

LIVING FREE 1972 British
★ ★ ★ ★ G Drama/Family 1:31
Dir: Jack Couffer *Cast:* Susan Hampshire, Nigel Davenport, Geoffrey Keen, Edward Judd, Peter Lukoye
▶ Sequel to *Born Free* continues the efforts of real-life conservationist Joy Adamson to protect Elsa's three lion cubs. Less inspired than the original, although the Kenya locations are beautiful.
Dist.: RCA/Columbia

LIVING ON TOKYO TIME 1987
☆ NR Comedy 1:23
☑ Adult situations, explicit language
Dir: Steven Okazaki *Cast:* Minako Ohashi, Ken Nakagawa, Mitzie Abe, Bill Bonham, Brenda Aoki
▶ Ohasi is a nineteen-year-old Japanese dishwasher living in San Francisco. She marries Japanese-American rock guitarist Nakagawa to get her green card. Couple finds they are really from two different cultures as they struggle to get acquainted. Shoe-string budget and inarticulate characters limit this one's appeal.
Dist.: Nelson

LOBSTER MAN FROM MARS 1988
☆ PG Comedy 1:33
☑ Explicit language
Dir: Stanley Sheff *Cast:* Tony Curtis, Deborah Foreman, Patrick Macnee, Billy Barty, Anthony Hickox, Tommy Sledge
▶ Curtis is a movie mogul who needs a terrible pic for tax purposes, and happens to come across just what the accountant ordered in title film within film. There, a seafood-styled monster terrorizes American Southwest, with professor Macnee and hard-boiled detective Sledge among its pursuers. Many individual bits are clever and amusing in this amiable genre spoof, but overall level of inspiration is far below *Airplane!* level.
Dist.: IVE

LOCAL HERO 1983 Scottish
★ ★ PG Comedy 1:51
☑ Adult situations, explicit language
Dir: Bill Forsyth *Cast:* Peter Riegert, Burt Lancaster, Fulton MacKay, Dennis Lawson, Peter Capaldi, Jenny Seagrove
▶ Houston oil company executive Riegert is sent by eccentric boss Lancaster to buy seaside Scottish town where petrol has been discovered. He falls under the spell of the place—and who wouldn't? Everything is slightly and magically off kilter: there's biologist Seagrove who may be a mermaid, innkeeper Lawson who doubles as a lawyer/town spokesman, and the sky's nightly show of northern lights. Forsyth's lyrical comedy is intelligent and subtle, full of unexpected and unexplained juxtapositions. Lancaster is marvelous. Whimsical tale will reward patient viewers.
Dist.: Warner

LOCK UP 1989
★ ★ ★ ★ R Action-Adventure 1:40
☑ Explicit language, graphic violence
Dir: John Flynn *Cast:* Sylvester Stallone, Donald Sutherland, John Amos, Tom Sizemore, Sonny Landham
▶ *Rocky* in prison as Stallone is victimized by a vengeful warden, sadistic guards, and a psychotic prisoner until he is driven to take drastic measures. Film delivers both prison and Stallone genre goods with torture, sa-

dism, solitary confinement, stabbing, loyal buddies, filthy traitors, a muddy football game, and star prevailing over incredible odds. But ugly, grunting violence is unrelenting, and film is not for the faint at heart.
Dist.: IVE

LODGER, THE 1926 British
★ ★ NR Mystery-Suspense 2:13 B&W
Dir: Alfred Hitchcock *Cast:* Ivor Novello, Marie Ault, Arthur Chesney, Malcolm Keen, June
▶ Jack the Ripper–like killer terrifies London, turning every stranger into a suspect. When Novello moves into a boarding house, his mysterious ways draw the attention of detective Keen. Provocative silent film is the first of Hitchcock's thrillers and contains his favorite themes in early forms. A transparent floor is one of his many arresting visual touches.
Dist.: Video Yesteryear

LOGAN'S RUN 1976
★ ★ ★ PG Sci-Fi 2:00
☑ Brief nudity, adult situations
Dir: Michael Anderson *Cast:* Michael York, Jenny Agutter, Richard Jordan, Peter Ustinov, Farrah Fawcett-Majors, Roscoe Lee Browne
▶ In the year 2274, an enclosed society encourages a pleasure-seeking lifestyle but then kills its citizens at age thirty. Cop York rebels against the system and flees with fellow resister Agutter. York's colleague Jordan pursues. Fast-paced sci-fi mixes action, ingenious effects, and provocative ideas.
Dist.: MGM/UA

LOLA MONTES 1955 French
★ NR Drama 1:50
Dir: Max Ophuls *Cast:* Martine Carol, Peter Ustinov, Anton Walbrook, Ivan Desny, Oskar Werner
▶ A New Orleans circus ringmaster (Ustinov) tells the story of his main attraction, the famous courtesan Lola Montes (Carol). Through flashbacks we see her affairs with various European lovers, including the King of Bavaria (Walbrook). Technically breathtaking but emotionally distant period drama is considered a critical masterpiece; Ophuls's last film.
Ⓢ
Dist.: Nelson

LOLITA 1962 British
★ NR Comedy 2:32 B&W
Dir: Stanley Kubrick *Cast:* James Mason, Sue Lyon, Shelley Winters, Peter Sellers, Marianne Stone, Diana Decker
▶ Mason, a middle-aged professor, marries sex-starved widow Winters in order to start an affair with her daughter Lyon, a precocious teen. Peculiar black comedy tones down the controversial novel; still an unnerving look at sexual obsession and hypocrisy. Outstanding acting, particularly Sellers in multiple disguises as a rake who pursues Lolita. Vladimir Nabo-

kov received an Oscar nomination for adapting his novel.
Dist.: MGM/UA

LONELINESS OF THE LONG DISTANCE RUNNER, THE 1962 British
★ ★ ★ ★ NR Drama 1:43 B&W
Dir: Tony Richardson *Cast:* Tom Courtenay, Michael Redgrave, Avis Bunnage, Peter Madden, Alec McCowen, James Fox
▶ Eighteen-year-old Courtenay robs a bakery, is sent to reformatory, and encounters strict governor Redgrave. Redgrave believes in rehabilitation through sports. Courtenay's running ability gains him some freedom and recognition, but competition fails to curb his rebellious instincts. Critically acclaimed but bleak look at alienated youth.
Dist.: Sheik

LONELY ARE THE BRAVE 1962
★ ★ ★ NR Western 1:47 B&W
Dir: David Miller *Cast:* Kirk Douglas, Walter Matthau, Gena Rowlands, Michael Kane, Carroll O'Connor
▶ Nonconformist cowboy Douglas, indifferent to the social order of the modern Southwest, escapes from jail after intentionally getting arrested to help a friend. Sheriff Matthau pursues but grows to respect his quarry. Crisply told and thoughtful; from a Dalton Trumbo screenplay.
Dist.: MCA

LONELY GUY, THE 1984
★ ★ R Comedy 1:30
☑ Adult situations, explicit language
Dir: Arthur Hiller *Cast:* Steve Martin, Charles Grodin, Judith Ivey, Robyn Douglass, Steve Lawrence, Dr. Joyce Brothers
▶ Greeting card writer Martin is exposed to the perils of singlehood when girlfriend Douglass kicks him out. Fellow "lonely guy" Grodin provides solace. Martin eventually finds new love with divorcée Ivey. Mild-mannered but sometimes poignant comedy is at its best when it sticks to the realities of urban life (as when Martin tries to eat alone inconspicuously). Nicely mournful chemistry between Grodin and Martin. Uneven script co-written by Neil Simon from Bruce Jay Friedman's *The Lonely Guy's Book of Life.*
Dist.: MCA

LONELYHEARTS 1958
★ ★ NR Drama 1:42 B&W
Dir: Vincent J. Donehue *Cast:* Montgomery Clift, Robert Ryan, Myrna Loy, Dolores Hart, Maureen Stapleton, Jackie Coogan
▶ Cynical editor Ryan assigns sensitive reporter Clift to write an advice column for the lovelorn. Against his will, Clift is drawn into the personal problems of his readers. Turgid melodrama, based very loosely on Nathanael West's *Miss Lonelyhearts,* is worth a look for its strong cast. Stapleton received an Oscar nomination in her film debut.
Dist.: MGM/UA

LONELY HEARTS 1981 Australian
★ **R Comedy 1:35**
☑ Brief nudity, adult situations, explicit language
Dir: Paul Cox *Cast:* Wendy Hughes, Norman Kaye, Jon Finlayson, Julia Blake, Jonathan Hardy
▶ Kaye is a solitary bachelor in his mid-fifties who meets virginal, insecure Hughes through an introduction agency. Courtship is slow procession of ups and downs for these two, and when the long-awaited sexual encounter happens, Hughes can't handle it and flees. How much viewers like it will depend on their tolerance for painful dissections of "little" lives. Won Australian Film Institute's Best Film award in 1982.
Dist.: Nelson

LONELY LADY, THE 1983
★ **R Drama 1:31**
☑ Rape, nudity, explicit language
Dir: Peter Sasdy *Cast:* Pia Zadora, Lloyd Bochner, Bibi Besch, Joseph Cali, Anthony Holland, Ray Liotta
▶ Aspiring writer Zadora endures rape, abortion, lesbianism, a nervous breakdown, and professional jealousy during her climb to fame in Hollywood. Sloppy adaptation of a Harold Robbins best-seller takes a glamorous view of the seedy side of show biz. Best for Zadora's fans, who will treasure her Oscar acceptance speech.
Dist.: MCA

LONELY MAN, THE 1957
★ ★ **NR Western 1:27 B&W**
Dir: Henry Levin *Cast:* Anthony Perkins, Jack Palance, Elaine Aiken, Neville Brand, Claude Akins, Lee Van Cleef
▶ Gunfighter Palance is trying to make amends to son Perkins, who is bitter about having been abandoned as a child. Attempting to reform and reestablish relationship with old flame Aiken, Palance clashes with gambler Brand and his henchman Van Cleef. Plenty of gunplay, though main focus is on the father/son relationship.
Dist.: KVC

LONELY PASSION OF JUDITH HEARNE, THE 1987 British
★ ★ **R Drama 1:50**
☑ Nudity, adult situations, explicit language
Dir: Jack Clayton *Cast:* Maggie Smith, Bob Hoskins, Wendy Hiller, Alan Devlin, Prunella Scales
▶ In 1950s Dublin, repressed alcoholic piano teacher Smith is wooed by con man Hoskins, her landlady's brother. Well-acted but downbeat British drama. Sad characters are beautifully rendered by a perfect cast.
Dist.: Warner

LONE WOLF MCQUADE 1983
★ ★ ★ ★ **PG Action-Adventure 1:47**
☑ Nudity, adult situations, explicit language, graphic violence
Dir: Steve Carver *Cast:* Chuck Norris, David Carradine, Barbara Carrera, Leon Isaac Kennedy, Robert Beltran
▶ Trashy, obvious, heavy-handed and a great deal of fun. Norris plays the title character, an independent Texas Ranger assigned Mexican partner Beltran to combat his "Lone Wolf" image. They uncover Carradine's gun-smuggling operation with the help of federal agent Kennedy. Tight-knit action flick climaxes with a to-the-death karate fight between martial arts masters Norris and Carradine.
Dist.: Vestron

LONG, DARK NIGHT, THE 1977
★ ★ ★ **R Mystery-Suspense 1:39**
☑ Explicit language, violence
Dir: Robert Clouse *Cast:* Joe Don Baker, Hope Alexander-Willis, Richard B. Shull, R. G. Armstrong, Ned Wertimer, Bibi Besch
▶ Well-made thriller from the director of *Enter the Dragon.* A pack of dogs, abandoned by vacationing tourists, starts attacking people on a resort island. Marine biologist Baker, his girlfriend Alexander-Willis, fisherman Armstrong, and country store owner Shull are among the menaced humans who make a last stand. Originally titled *The Pack.*
Dist.: Warner

LONG DAY'S JOURNEY INTO NIGHT 1962
★ ★ **NR Drama 2:16 B&W**
Dir: Sidney Lumet *Cast:* Katharine Hepburn, Ralph Richardson, Jason Robards, Jr., Dean Stockwell, Jeanne Barr
▶ Recriminations and arguments afflict the Tyrone family—drug-addicted mother Hepburn, stingy actor father Richardson, alcoholic son Robards, and his sickly writer brother Stockwell—in their Connecticut home as Hepburn makes a long day's journey into madness. Masterful adaptation of Eugene O'Neill play features superb performances. Hepburn was Oscar-nominated.
Dist.: Republic

LONGEST DAY, THE 1962
★ ★ ★ **G War 3:00 B&W**
Dir: Ken Annakin, Andrew Marton, Bernhard Wicki *Cast:* John Wayne, Robert Mitchum, Henry Fonda, Robert Ryan, Rod Steiger, Robert Wagner, Richard Burton, Mel Ferrer, Jeffrey Hunter
▶ Extravagant epic with an all-star cast repeats in exhaustive detail the events of D-Day, June 6, 1944, when the Allies launched the crucial invasion of Normandy. Told in three parts: preparations by the high command, activities by Resistance heroes and paratroopers, and the bloody assault on Omaha Beach. Among the many actors are Richard Todd, Jean-Louis Barrault, Red Buttons, Stuart Whitman, and Gert Frobe.
Dist.: CBS/Fox

LONGEST YARD, THE 1974
★ ★ ★ ★ **R Comedy/Sports 1:59**
☑ Explicit language, violence

Dir: Robert Aldrich   *Cast:* Burt Reynolds, Eddie Albert, Ed Lauter, Michael Conrad, James Hampton, Bernadette Peters

▶ Ex-pro-football-star-turned-convict Reynolds organizes other prisoners into a team to take on the brutal guards. Corrupt warden Albert schemes to insure the guards' victory. Brawny football comedy with uproarious, literally bone-crunching humor. Rousing football game finale; one of Burt's best performances.
Dist.: Paramount

LONG GONE 1987
★ ★ ★ ★ NR Comedy/Sports/MFTV 1:52
☑ Brief nudity, adult situations, explicit language
Dir: Martin Davidson   *Cast:* William L. Petersen, Virginia Madsen, Dermot Mulroney, Larry Riley, Henry Gibson, Teller Lasarow

▶ Winning baseball comedy set in the 1950s follows the misadventures of the Tampico Stogies, a third-rate minor league team managed by hard-bitten pitcher Petersen. He recruits talent that turns the club into a contender, but at the risk of losing his job and his girlfriend Madsen. Solid cast and nostalgic settings add to the fun.
Dist.: Warner

LONG GOOD FRIDAY, THE 1982 British
★ ★ ★ R Crime/Drama 1:54
☑ Brief nudity, adult situations, explicit language, violence
Dir: John Mackenzie   *Cast:* Bob Hoskins, Helen Mirren, Eddie Constantine, Dave King

▶ Swift and sharp-edged British gangster film. While cajoling American mobsters to invest in a major real estate deal, crime kingpin Hoskins and his mistress Mirren are threatened by terrorist bomb attacks from unknown sources. Complicated plot and heavy Cockney accents require concentration, but Hoskins's riveting transformation from smooth talker to raging ogre desperate for revenge is well worth the effort.
Dist.: HBO

LONG, HOT SUMMER, THE 1958
★ ★ ★ NR Drama 1:57
Dir: Martin Ritt   *Cast:* Paul Newman, Joanne Woodward, Anthony Franciosa, Orson Welles, Lee Remick, Angela Lansbury

▶ Drifter Newman enters into a sharecropping contract with Welles, richest man in a backwater Mississippi county, while pursuing his spinster daughter Woodward. Seamless adaptation of several William Faulkner stories captures the author's atmospheric view of corruption and redemption in small-town South. First teaming of Newman and Woodward led to their marriage. Remade as a TV movie in 1985.
Dist.: CBS/Fox

LONG JOHN SILVER 1954 Australian
★ NR Action-Adventure 1:49
Dir: Byron Haskin   *Cast:* Robert Newton, Connie Gilchrist, Kit Taylor, Grant Taylor, Syd Chambers, Rod Taylor

▶ "Ar-r-r-r-r-w, Jim!" Newton was born to play Long John Silver, and he proved it in Disney's *Treasure Island* and in this Australian sequel by the same director. Here, Newton and young Jim Hawkins (Taylor) are stranded on a desert island after an aborted mutiny, and must battle a rival gang of pirates to win a king's ransom in gold. Lots of fun, with Gilchrist a match for the star as a marriage-minded innkeeper.
Dist.: Cable

LONG RIDERS, THE 1980
★ ★ ★ R Western 1:39
☑ Adult situations, explicit language, graphic violence
Dir: Walter Hill   *Cast:* David Carradine, Keith Carradine, Robert Carradine, James Keach, Stacy Keach, Dennis Quaid, Randy Quaid, Christopher Guest, Nicholas Guest, Pamela Reed

▶ First-rate Western about the James-Younger gang has an unusual gimmick: the notorious outlaws are played by real-life brothers. The Carradines are the Youngers; the Keaches play Frank and Jesse James; the Quaids are the Miller brothers; and the Guests portray the villainous Ford brothers. Historically accurate, brutally violent, and consistently engrossing. Reed is a memorably sexy Belle Starr. Ry Cooder soundtrack adds to film's authencity.
Dist.: MGM/UA

LONGSHOT, THE 1986
★ ★ PG-13 Comedy 1:29
☑ Explicit language, adult humor
Dir: Paul Bartel   *Cast:* Tim Conway, Jack Weston, Harvey Korman, Ted Wass, Anne Meara, Stella Stevens

▶ Working on a tip from a Mexican stableboy, four friends borrow money from gangsters to bet on a sureshot. But they pick the wrong horse, leading to long chases and slapstick complications. Not to be confused with Conway's family-oriented efforts: humor here is often scatological and racist. A bizarre project for executive producer Mike Nichols.
Dist.: HBO

LONGTIME COMPANION 1990
★ ★ ★ R Drama 1:36
☑ Nudity, adult situations, explicit language
Dir: Norman René   *Cast:* Stephen Caffrey, Patrick Cassidy, Brian Cousins, Bruce Davison, Campbell Scott, Mark Lamos

▶ Wealthy Davison, soap opera writer Lamos, actor Cassidy, lawyer Caffrey, and exercise instructor Scott all have one thing in common: the menace of AIDS. At first, the disease is only a news story casting a slight cloud over a happy Fire Island summer; but as the disease begins taking its toll, each man is forced to confront his own personal tragedy. A sensitive, nonsensational story, written by Craig Lucas.
Dist.: Vidmark

LONG VOYAGE HOME, THE 1940
★ ★ ★ NR Drama 1:44 B&W
Dir: John Ford *Cast:* John Wayne, Thomas Mitchell, Ian Hunter, Barry Fitzgerald, John Qualen, Ward Bond, Mildred Natwick
▶ Moving drama about merchant marines in 1939, drawn from four Eugene O'Neill one-act plays. Wayne gives one of his best performances as a naive Swede protected by more experienced seamen on a dangerous ammunition convoy. Natwick has a memorable role as a waterfront prostitute. Nominated for six Oscars, including Best Picture and Screenplay (Dudley Nichols).
Dist.: Warner

LONG WEEKEND, THE 1977 Australian
☆ NR Horror 1:40
☑ Nudity, explicit language, violence
Dir: Colin Eggleston *Cast:* John Hargreaves, Briony Behets, Mike McEwen, Michael Aitkins, Roy Day, Sue Kiss von Soly
▶ Hargreaves and Behets are an unhappily married couple who take to the hills to air their differences. Nature, however, has other plans for the camping couple, and a mysterious ecological force working through ordinary animals and weapons confuses and destroys them. Unintentionally hilarious film has idiotic plot, illogical character behavior, and numerous continuity lapses.
Dist.: Media

LOOK BACK IN ANGER 1959 British
★ ★ NR Drama 1:39 B&W
Dir: Tony Richardson *Cast:* Richard Burton, Claire Bloom, Mary Ure, Edith Evans, Donald Pleasence, Gary Raymond
▶ In England, impoverished Burton takes out his frustrations on wife Ure and has an affair with her friend Bloom. A passionate performance from young Burton and a fragile and sensuous one from Ure are featured in this high-quality drama based on John Osborne's play.
Dist.: Embassy

LOOKER 1981
★ ★ PG Mystery-Suspense 1:30
☑ Nudity, explicit language, violence
Dir: Michael Crichton *Cast:* Albert Finney, Susan Dey, James Coburn, Leigh Taylor-Young, Dorian Harewood
▶ Successful Los Angeles plastic surgeon Finney is set up as the fall guy for a string of murders involving beautiful models who were also his patients. He teams with Dey, tracks down the real killers, and uncovers an ambitious politician's plot to hypnotize people via TV commercials. Glossy but farfetched thriller.
Dist.: Warner

LOOKING FOR MR. GOODBAR 1977
★ ★ ★ R Drama 2:16
☑ Strong sexual content, explicit language, graphic violence
Dir: Richard Brooks *Cast:* Diane Keaton,

Richard Gere, William Atherton, Tuesday Weld, Richard Kiley, Tom Berenger
▶ Catholic schoolteacher Keaton leads a self-destructive double life. She helps deaf children by day and cruises seedy singles bars to pick up men by night. Keaton gives a tour-de-force performance as an emotionally and physically crippled woman; but the film's marital murder scene and violent sex don't do justice to Judith Rossner's sensitive novel. Gere and Berenger play some of the men in Keaton's life.
Dist.: Paramount

LOOKING GLASS WAR, THE 1970 British
★ ★ PG Espionage 1:46
☑ Adult situations, explicit language
Dir: Frank Pierson *Cast:* Christopher Jones, Pia Degermark, Ralph Richardson, Anthony Hopkins, Paul Rogers, Susan George
▶ Polish refugee Jones is forced by British Intelligence into a suicidal mission behind the Iron Curtain. Despite help from free-spirited hippie Degermark, he is unable to shake his KGB pursuers. Dreary Cold War thriller based on a John le Carré novel has a good performance by Richardson as an untrustworthy British agent.
Dist.: RCA/Columbia

LOOKIN' TO GET OUT 1982
★ R Drama 1:45
☑ Brief nudity, adult situations, explicit language, violence
Dir: Hal Ashby *Cast:* Jon Voight, Ann-Margret, Burt Young, Bert Remsen, Richard Bradford
▶ Voight and Young are New York gamblers in debt to loan sharks. They flee to Las Vegas and, helped by over-the-hill cardsharp Remsen, sneak into a high-stakes blackjack game. With Ann-Margret as Voight's former flame. Haphazard story co-written and co-produced by Voight was a flop at the box office.
Dist.: CBS/Fox

LOOK WHO'S TALKING 1989
★ ★ ★ ★ ★ PG-13 Comedy 1:33
☑ Adult situations, explicit language
Dir: Amy Heckerling *Cast:* John Travolta, Kirstie Alley, George Segal, voice of Bruce Willis, Olympia Dukakis, Abe Vigoda
▶ Accountant Alley, pregnant by married Mr. Wrong (Segal), decides to have the baby. Cab driver Travolta, on the scene when she delivers, may be Mr. Right—at least baby Mikey thinks so and, in the film's justly famous and uproarious gimmick, gives us this and other opinions in the voice of Bruce Willis. Frisky and ferociously funny; Willis's wisecracks complement ingratiating leads.
Dist.: RCA/Columbia

LOONEY, LOONEY, LOONEY BUGS BUNNY MOVIE, THE 1981
★ ★ ★ ★ ★ G Animation 1:20

Dir: Friz Freleng   **Cast:** Voices of Mel Blanc, June Foray, Frank Nelson
▶ Master animator Freleng displays his talents in this festival of Bugs Bunny's greatest hits. In a spoof of the Academy Awards, the gang attends "The Oswald Awards," a chance to view clips of their stellar careers. Highlight is Bugs Bunny's 1958 Oscar-winning cartoon *Knighty Knight Bugs*. Solid family fun.
Dist.: Warner

LOOPHOLE 1980 British
★★★ **NR Drama 1:45**
☑ Adult situations, explicit language, violence
Dir: John Quested   **Cast:** Albert Finney, Martin Sheen, Susannah York, Colin Blakely, Jonathan Pryce, Robert Morely, Alfred Lynch
▶ Mildly entertaining caper film has gang leader Finney recruiting architect Sheen, along with debt-ridden Blakely, Price, and Lynch, to rob London's most secure bank via sewer. Morely is a dewlapped banker, and York is Sheen's shrill wife. A bit of a walkthrough for everyone involved. Based on a novel by Robert Pollock.
Dist.: Media

LOOSE CANNONS 1990
★★ **R Comedy 1:34**
☑ Nudity, adult situations, explicit language, violence
Dir: Bob Clark   **Cast:** Dan Aykroyd, Gene Hackman, Dom DeLuise, Robert Prosky
▶ Kitten-loving cop Hackman is paired with Aykroyd, a certified zany with a personality disorder that causes him to assume different characters at a moment's notice. They're after modern-day Nazis who are trying to blackmail a German politician with scandalous footage. Porn king DeLuise is also after the film. Unfunny waste of the leads. **(CC)**
Dist.: RCA/Columbia

LOOSE CONNECTIONS 1984 British
☆ **PG Comedy/Drama 1:30**
☑ Adult situations, explicit language
Dir: Richard Eyre   **Cast:** Lindsay Duncan, Stephen Rea, Gary Olsen, Jan Niklas
▶ Englishwoman Duncan advertises for company on a drive to a Munich feminist convention. Auto worker Rea, who claims to be gay, is her only reply. On the road, they disagree about everything from politics to music, but love develops. Old-fashioned formula plot imbued with modern consciousness. Fine performances by Duncan and Rea.
Dist.: Pacific Arts

LOOSE SHOES 1980
★ **R Comedy 1:16**
☑ Nudity, explicit language, adult humor
Dir: Ira Miller   **Cast:** Bill Murray, Howard Hesseman, Avery Schreiber, Buddy Hackett, Susan Tyrrell
▶ Wacky series of fake movie trailers which are actually parodies of Woody Allen movies, biker pictures, sci-fi films, and other genre movies. Skits vary wildly, including "Welcome to Bacon County," Jewish "Star Wars," and a Chaplin takeoff, "The Yid and the Kid." Some of the material was criticized for being offensive and racist. Originally titled *Coming Attractions*.
Dist.: CBS/Fox

LOOT 1972 British
★ **PG Comedy 1:41**
☑ Adult situations, explicit language
Dir: Silvio Narizzano   **Cast:** Lee Remick, Richard Attenborough, Milo O'Shea, Hywell Bennett, Roy Holder
▶ Bennett and Holder knock off a bank and hide the loot in the coffin of Holder's just deceased mum. Idiot detective Attenborough arrives to investigate. Alluring Remick plays the murderous nurse trying to convince widower O'Shea to become her eighth husband. Delirious farce adapted from Joe Orton's play leaves his brilliant dialogue intact, but the direction unfortunately detracts.
Dist.: WesternWorld

LORD JIM 1965 British
★★★★ **NR Drama 2:34**
Dir: Richard Brooks   **Cast:** Peter O'Toole, James Mason, Curt Jurgens, Eli Wallach, Jack Hawkins, Paul Lukas
▶ Ambitious but uneven version of Joseph Conrad's novel, with O'Toole giving a fascinating performance as a British officer who spends a lifetime making up for one moment of cowardice. South Seas period adventure filmed in Cambodia and Hong Kong has plenty of spectacle and an outstanding supporting cast, particularly Mason's unscrupulous mercenary.
Dist.: RCA/Columbia

LORD OF THE FLIES 1963 British
★★ **NR Drama 1:30 B&W**
☑ Brief nudity, adult situations, explicit language, violence
Dir: Peter Brook   **Cast:** James Aubrey, Tom Chapin, Hugh Edwards, Roger Elwin, Tom Gaman
▶ A group of English schoolboys is stranded by a plane crash on a lush, tropical island. While waiting to be rescued, they lose their civilized manners and revert to a kind of tribal barbarism. Especially horrid is their torment of Piggy, an asthmatic fat boy. Based on the modern classic by Nobel prize–winner William Golding. Remade with an American cast in 1990.
Dist.: Various

LORD OF THE FLIES 1990
★★★ **R Action-Adventure 1:27**
☑ Adult situations, explicit language, violence
Dir: Harry Hook   **Cast:** Balthazar Getty, Chris Furrh, Danuel Pipoly, Badgett Dale, Edward Taft, Andrew Taft
▶ A group of adolescents are marooned on a tropical island, where Getty organizes them in

a civilized way for survival. As the months go by, rebel Furrh leads them down the road of tribalism, murder, and cruelty. Plodding direction leaves only sumptuous photography to hold the attention in this Americanized remake of the 1964 British film based on William Golding's novel. **(CC)**
Dist.: Nelson

LORD OF THE RINGS, THE 1978
★ ★ ★ ★ PG Animation/Adult 2:13
☑ Mild violence
Dir: Ralph Bakshi   *Cast:* Voices of Christopher Guard, John Hurt, William Squire, Michael Sholes
▶ Fantasy based on a portion of Tolkien's trilogy about a hobbit named Frodo and other creatures in Middle Earth competing for a magic ring. Ambitious adventure, but you need to be familiar with the books to understand what's happening; strictly for Tolkien fans.
Dist.: HBO

LORDS OF DISCIPLINE, THE 1983
★ ★ ★ R Drama 1:42
☑ Brief nudity, explicit language, graphic violence
Dir: Franc Roddam   *Cast:* David Keith, Judge Reinhold, Robert Prosky, G. D. Spradlin, Barbara Babcock, Rick Rossovich, Mark Breland
▶ Well-crafted, hard-hitting drama about 1960s cadet life in a strict Southern military academy. To preserve decorum, senior cadet Keith is asked by his cigar-chomping colonel Prosky to protect the school's first black student, Breland. Keith soon uncovers a sadistic secret society, the Ten, that uses Klan-like tactics to terrorize and humiliate certain undesirable cadets. Absorbing but brutal film about military macho was based on Pat Conroy's dynamic novel.
Dist.: Paramount

LORDS OF FLATBUSH, THE 1974
★ PG Drama 1:25
☑ Adult situations, explicit language, mild violence
Dir: Stephen F. Verona, Martin Davidson
Cast: Perry King, Sylvester Stallone, Henry Winkler, Susan Blakely, Paul Mace
▶ In 1950s Brooklyn, leather jacketed high school students Stallone, Winkler, King, and Mace hang out together and cause havoc. King falls for new student Blakely; Stallone is reluctantly dragged Into marriage by his pregnant girlfriend. Limited budget shows, but those nostalgic for the era (or curious for glimpses at pre-stardom King, Winkler, and a pudgy Sly) might take a look.
Dist.: RCA/Columbia

LORDS OF THE DEEP 1989
★ PG-13 Sci-Fi 1:22
☑ Explicit language, violence
Dir: Mary Ann Fisher   *Cast:* Bradford Dillman, Priscilla Barnes, Melody Ryane, Daryl Haney, Ed Lottimer, Greg Sobeck
▶ In 2020, Dillman's underwater expedition encounters an alien life form. Barnes deduces the aliens are benign but something is wrong: one crew member is turned into a gelatinous mass and others are being murdered. Limp pacing, inadequate special effects, campy dialogue. Good for a few laughs if not much suspense.
Dist.: MGM/UA

LOSIN' IT 1983
★ ★ R Comedy 1:40
☑ Nudity, explicit language, violence
Dir: Curtis Hanson   *Cast:* Tom Cruise, Jackie Earle Haley, Shelley Long, John Stockwell, John P. Navin, Jr.
▶ Teens Cruise, Haley, Stockwell, and Navin go to Tijuana to lose their virginity. Cruise hooks up with Long, in town to seek a divorce, while the others get involved in some wild misadventures of their own. Modest, agreeable youth comedy; above average for the genre.
Dist.: Nelson

LOS OLVIDADOS 1950 Mexican
☆ NR Drama 1:28 B&W
Dir: Luis Buñuel   *Cast:* Alfonso Mejia, Roberto Cobo, Estela Inda, Miguel Inclan, Jesus Navarro, Mario Ramirez
▶ Bleak, unsentimental look at juvenile delinquents in the worst slums of Mexico City. Episodic plot shows Mejia's degradation at the hands of Cobo, a corrupt older boy, but film's strongest aspect is its unsparing portrayal of hopeless poverty. Buñuel's confident direction, including an eerie dream sequence, propelled him to a new level of international acclaim. Also known as *The Young and the Damned.* ⓢ
Dist.: Video Yesteryear

LOST AND FOUND 1979
★ ★ ★ PG Comedy 1:45
☑ Adult situations, explicit language
Dir: Melvin Frank   *Cast:* George Segal, Glenda Jackson, Maureen Stapleton, Hollis McLaren, John Cunningham, Paul Sorvino
▶ Affable widowed professor Segal and persnickety British divorcée Jackson meet by accident—in a car crash—and fall in love. Sophisticated adult comedy tries to capture the spirit of *A Touch of Class* but falls far short. Cameo appearances by Martin Short and John Candy.
Dist.: RCA/Columbia

LOST ANGELS 1989
★ ★ ★ R Drama 1:56
☑ Nudity, adult situations, explicit language
Dir: Hugh Hudson   *Cast:* Donald Sutherland, Adam Horovitz, Amy Locane, Don Bloomfield, Celia Weston, Graham Beckel
▶ Nobody loves middle-class teen Horovitz, who is dumped into a private rnental hospital where Sutherland is the only dedicated doc.

Outside, in Los Angeles world of violent youth gangs, drugs, and materialism, other teens are not doing so good either. Horovitz thinks he loves Locane, but she two-times him. Confused plot mars director Hudson's attempt at a modern *Rebel Without a Cause*; but caucasian rapper Horovitz is superb in his film debut. (CC)
Dist.: Orion

LOST BOYS, THE 1987
★ ★ ★ ★ R Horror 1:37
☑ Explicit language, violence
Dir: Joel Schumacher *Cast:* Jason Patric, Corey Haim, Dianne Wiest, Barnard Hughes, Kiefer Sutherland, Jami Gertz
▶ Divorced Wiest moves with her kids Patric and Haim to a California town that contains a pack of bike-riding teen vampires (led by scary Sutherland). Haim tries to save Patric after the bloodsuckers add him to their group. Slick and flashy fun, mixing comedy and horror in music video style. (CC)
Dist.: Warner

LOST COMMAND, THE 1966
★ ★ NR Action-Adventure 2:07
Dir: Mark Robson *Cast:* Anthony Quinn, Alain Delon, George Segal, Michele Morgan, Maurice Monet, Claudia Cardinale
▶ After his country's defeat in Indochina, French paratrooper Quinn is transferred to Algeria, where he whips a new unit into shape and battles Arab terrorist Segal. Complicating the assignment is fellow officer Delon's affair with Segal's sister Cardinale. Overlong but occasionally exciting.
Dist.: RCA/Columbia

LOST EMPIRE, THE 1983
★ R Sci-Fi/Comedy 1:26
☑ Nudity, strong sexual content, adult situations, explicit language, graphic violence
Dir: Jim Wynorski *Cast:* Melanie Vincz, Angela Aames, Raven de la Croix, Paul Coufos, Angus Scrimm, Bob Tessier
▶ On the Pacific isle of Golgotha, a bevy of beautiful, busty, and half-clothed women warriors investigate a death cult run by the sinister Dr. Sin Do (Scrimm). Tessier, a familiar baddie, wears ridiculous paste-on eyebrows that vary from scene to scene. Raunchy, low-budget adventure spoof borders on soft porn.
Dist.: Vestron

LOST HONOR OF KATHARINA BLUM, THE 1975 German
★ NR Drama 1:46
☑ Adult situations, violence
Dir: Volker Schlondorff *Cast:* Margarethe von Trotta, Angela Winkler, Mario Adorf, Dieter Laser, Heinz Bennent, Jurgen Prochnow
▶ Winkler, a typical waitress, becomes the object of a nightmarish media inquest after she has a brief affair with a suspected terrorist. Food for thought in an age of increasing media power. Remade for American TV in

1984 as "The Lost Honor of Kathryn Beck."
Ⓢ
Dist.: Nelson

LOST HORIZON 1937
★ ★ ★ ★ NR Action-Adventure 2:13 B&W
Dir: Frank Capra *Cast:* Ronald Colman, H. B. Warner, Sam Jaffe, Jane Wyatt, Thomas Mitchell, John Howard, Edward Everett Horton, Margo, Isabel Jewel
▶ A planeload of passengers is forced down in Tibet where they discover Shangri-La, a paradise hidden in a mountain valley. Capra's version of James Hilton's utopian novel creaks a little but, overall, still stands as an unusual, lavish and entertaining film classic. Oscar nominations for Picture, Supporting Actor (Warner) and Score. Remade in 1973 as a musical. Recently restored with footage cut from the original version.
Dist.: RCA/Columbia

LOST IDOL, THE 1989
★ NR Action-Adventure 1:40
☑ Explicit language, violence
Dir: P. Chalong *Cast:* Erik Estrada, James Phillips, Myra Chasen
▶ During Vietnam war, American soldiers discover golden idol in Cambodian temple. Dastardly leader, Phillips, guns them all down so he can come back later to get it. Unknown to him, one soldier, Estrada, has survived. Years later, the two must temporarily team up in a convoluted quest for the shiney statue and Estrada's kidnapped daughter. Some shooting, but not much derring-do in this limp actioner.
Dist.: SGE

LOST IN AMERICA 1985
★ ★ R Comedy 1:31
☑ Adult situations, explicit language
Dir: Albert Brooks *Cast:* Albert Brooks, Julie Hagerty, Maggie Roswell, Garry Marshall, Michael Greene, Tom Tarpey
▶ Advertising exec Brooks and his wife Hagerty decide to drop out, sell everything and hit the road to find America, mimicking their *Easy Rider* idol, Peter Fonda. Roughing it in a $40,-000 Winnebago, they arrive in Vegas, where their life and luck changes after Hagerty goes crazy at the roulette wheel. Brooks's right-on-the-money look at a yuppie mid-life crisis may not appeal to all, but those who appreciate his humor will howl. (CC)
Dist.: Warner

LOST MOMENT, THE 1947
★ NR Drama 1:28 B&W
Dir: Martin Gabel *Cast:* Robert Cummings, Susan Hayward, Agnes Moorehead, Joan Lorring, Eduardo Cianelli, Frank Puglia
▶ Hayward lives in a creepy Venetian manse with elderly aunt Moorehead, who was once romantically linked with a long-missing poet. Publisher Cummings pays a visit to see if he can get his hands on her possibly valuable correspondence. But all is not as it seems, as

Hayward may be slightly off her rocker. Poor editing mars the continuity but not the tension of this interesting adaptation of Henry James's *The Aspern Papers.*
Dist.: Republic

LOST PATROL, THE 1934
★★ NR War 1:14 B&W
Dir: John Ford ***Cast:*** Victor McLaglen, Boris Karloff, Wallace Ford, Reginald Denny, Billy Bevan, Alan Hale
► British cavalry troops stranded at an oasis in the Mesopotamian desert are picked off one by one by Arab snipers. Grim, fast-paced World War I adventure features steady direction, engrossing performances (particularly Karloff's religious fanatic), and surprisingly enjoyable sense of gloom.
Dist.: Fox Hills

LOST WEEKEND, THE 1945
★★★ NR Drama 1:41 B&W
Dir: Billy Wilder ***Cast:*** Ray Milland, Jane Wyman, Phillip Terry, Howard da Silva, Frank Faylen
► Writer Milland hits the bottle instead of the typewriter. With his brother Terry and girlfriend Wyman powerless to stop him, he goes through hell before pulling himself together. Landmark film about alcoholism, vividly directed by Wilder and superbly acted by the Oscar-winning Milland. Also Oscars for Best Picture, Director, Screenplay.
Dist.: MCA

LOUISIANA 1984
★★★ NR Drama/MFTV 2:06
☑ Adult situations, explicit language, violence
Dir: Philippe de Broca ***Cast:*** Margot Kidder, Ian Charleson, Victor Lanoux, Lloyd Bochner, Len Cariou
► In the nineteenth-century South, Kidder survives the loss of her children and two husbands. Despite the destruction of her pre–Civil War life, she manages to hang on to her beloved planatation and Charleson, the man she truly loves. Romantic saga in the tradition of *Gone With the Wind.*
Dist.: Prism

LOUISIANA STORY 1948
★★ NR Drama 1:17 B&W
Dir: Robert Flaherty ***Cast:*** Joseph Boudreaux, Lionel Le Blanc, E. Beinvenu, Frank Hardy, C. T. Guedry
► Life in the Cajun backwaters of Louisiana is disrupted with the arrival of oil company derricks at the previously pristine swamps. Young Boudreaux and his family try not to have their lives distrupted, but a blown well challenges the riggers and threatens the bayou. Sumptuously photographed docudrama has music by Virgil Thompson. Financed by Standard Oil.
Dist.: Video Yesteryear

LOULOU 1980 French
☆ NR Drama 1:50
☑ Nudity, adult situations
Dir: Maurice Pialat ***Cast:*** Isabelle Huppert, Gerard Depardieu, Guy Marchand, Humbert Balsan, Bernard Tronczyk, Christian Boucher
► Huppert leaves respectable husband Marchand for Depardieu, a charismatic, criminally inclined rat she meets in a disco. Marchand offers his errant wife a job at his office, but Depardieu exerts a fatal charm over her. Same old story, engagingly told thanks to excellent leads. [S]
Dist.: New Yorker

LOVE AFFAIR 1939
★★★ NR Romance 1:27 B&W
Dir: Leo McCarey ***Cast:*** Irene Dunne, Charles Boyer, Maria Ouspenskaya, Lee Bowman, Astrid Allwyn, Maurice Moscovich
► Dunne and Boyer fall in love aboard a luxury liner. Since both are engaged to others, they agree not to see each other for six months to determine if their feelings can stand the test of time. When the day comes for them to meet again, an accident changes their affair in a way neither had foreseen. Witty and bright, yet full of deep emotion; right up there with the other greats from Hollywood's golden year of 1939.
Dist.: Burbank

LOVE AMONG THE RUINS 1975
★★★ NR Romance/Comedy/MFTV 1:40
Dir: George Cukor ***Cast:*** Katharine Hepburn, Laurence Olivier, Colin Blakely, Joan Sims, Richard Pearson, Leigh Lawson
► In London, wealthy widow Hepburn is sued by a much younger man for breach of promise. She enlists barrister Olivier to defend her, not realizing he is a former beau from forty years ago who has adored her his entire life. James Costigan's script is an engaging trifle, wondrously adorned by Hepburn and especially Olivier at his most rapturously romantic. Directed with just the right light touch by Cukor. **(CC)**
Dist.: CBS/Fox

LOVE AND ANARCHY 1973 Italian
★ R Drama 1:48
☑ Adult situations, explicit language
Dir: Lina Wertmuller ***Cast:*** Giancarlo Giannini, Mariangela Melato, Lina Polito, Eros Pagni, Pina Cel
► Italy in the fascist-ruled thirties sees Gianinni traveling to Rome to assassinate Mussolini. Holing up in a whorehouse while he awaits his chance, Gianinni falls in love with brothel-inmate Polito and begins to lose his resolve. Full of vitality and great performances, film explores political questions considered interesting in the early seventies, and suggests that bawdyhouses may be last outposts of freedom under totalitarianism. [S]
Dist.: RCA/Columbia

LOVE AND BULLETS 1979 British
★★★★ PG Action-Adventure 1:43

☑ Adult situations, explicit language, violence
Dir: Stuart Rosenberg *Cast:* Charles Bronson, Rod Steiger, Jill Ireland, Bradford Dillman, Strother Martin
▶ Bronson is a tough Arizona cop sent to Switzerland to bring back mobster's moll Ireland. When he falls in love with her, the mobsters fear she'll leak information and have her killed. Bronson takes private revenge. Inoffensive adventure yarn with pleasing Swiss location shots. **(CC)**
Dist.: CBS/Fox

LOVE AND DEATH 1975
★ ★ ★ PG Comedy 1:25
☑ Adult humor
Dir: Woody Allen *Cast:* Woody Allen, Diane Keaton, Frank Adu, Olga Georges-Picot, Harold Gould, Alfred Luther, Zvee Scooler
▶ Woody's hilarious spoof of *War and Peace*. Boris (Allen), a nineteenth-century Slav, is imprisoned for attempting to assassinate Napoleon and has two hours to review his life. He muses about Keaton, his unrequited love, Russian philosophy, art, war, and religion ("I will dwell in the House of the Lord for six months with an option to buy"). Vintage, not-to-be-missed Allen.
Dist.: CBS/Fox

LOVE AT FIRST BITE 1979
★ ★ ★ PG Comedy 1:36
☑ Explicit language
Dir: Stan Dragoti *Cast:* George Hamilton, Susan Saint James, Richard Benjamin, Dick Shawn, Arte Johnson
▶ Evicted from his Transylvania castle, modern-day Count Dracula (Hamilton) jets to New York, gets drunk on a skid-row wino's blood, and meets the girl of his dreams, Saint James, in a disco. Her psychiatrist boyfriend Benjamin frantically tries to warn Saint James but she falls for the sexy Prince of Darkness anyway. Hammy, lightweight, and amusing.
Dist.: Vestron

LOVE AT LARGE 1990
★ ★ R Romance/Comedy 1:37
☑ Explicit language, violence
Dir: Alan Rudolph *Cast:* Tom Berenger, Elizabeth Perkins, Anne Archer, Kate Capshaw, Annette O'Toole, Ted Levine, Ann Magnuson, Kevin J. O'Connor, Neil Young, Ruby Dee
▶ Hired by secretive Archer to follow a man, detective Berenger mistakenly ends up on the trail of bigamist Levine, married to both O'-Toole and Capshaw. Meanwhile, Berenger's girlfriend Magnuson hires Perkins to tail him. Rudolph's usual blend of stylized filmmaking and colorful casting evokes a few smiles, but casual pace and half-baked story ultimately prove tiresome.
Dist.: Orion

LOVE AT STAKE 1988
☆ R Comedy 1:26

☑ Explicit language
Dir: John Moffitt *Cast:* Patrick Cassidy, Kelly Preston, Bud Cort, David Graf, Stuart Pankin, Dave Thomas
▶ In 1692 Salem, Cassidy and Preston fall in love as judge Pankin and mayor Thomas plot to exploit the witch trials for their own financial gain. Preston is then accused of witchcraft. Dreadful premise for a comedy; simpleminded humor includes enema and chastity belt jokes. Formerly known as *Burnin' Love*.
Dist.: Nelson

LOVE BUG, THE 1968
★ ★ ★ ★ ★ G Family 1:50
Dir: Robert Stevenson *Cast:* Dean Jones, Michele Lee, Buddy Hackett, David Tomlinson, Joe Flynn
▶ Herbie, a perky green Volkswagen Bug with human feelings, adopts high-spirited but losing race-car driver Jones and carries him to victory. With Tomlinson as the villain who gets Herbie drunk before the road race. Charming Disney family fantasy led to three sequels: *Herbie Rides Again*, *Herbie Goes to Monte Carlo*, and *Herbie Goes Bananas*. **(CC)**
Dist.: Buena Vista

LOVE CHILD 1982
★ ★ ★ ★ R Drama 1:37
☑ Nudity, adult situations, explicit language
Dir: Larry Peerce *Cast:* Amy Madigan, Beau Bridges, Mackenzie Phillips, Albert Salmi, Joanna Merlin
▶ Young convict Madigan has a secret affair with Bridges, a guard at Florida's Broward Correctional Institute. She then fights for the right to give birth behind bars. Sporting a greased-back ducktail, Phillips plays a tough lesbian inmate who befriends Madigan. Rough around the edges, but the intriguing drama was based on a true story.
Dist.: Warner

LOVE FINDS ANDY HARDY 1938
★ ★ ★ NR Drama 1:30 B&W
Dir: George B. Seitz *Cast:* Mickey Rooney, Judy Garland, Lewis Stone, Cecilia Parker, Lana Turner, Ann Rutherford
▶ Andy Hardy (Rooney) gets in big trouble with girlfriend Rutherford when he is spotted squiring Turner around in his car. Both are forgotten when Garland shows up to sing at a local dance. Garland's introduction to wholesome series adds to its already considerable charm.
Dist.: MGM/UA

LOVE HAPPY 1949
★ ★ NR Comedy 1:31 B&W
Dir: David Miller *Cast:* Harpo Marx, Chico Marx, Groucho Marx, Ilona Massey, Vera-Ellen, Raymond Burr, Eric Blore, Marilyn Monroe
▶ Harpo and Chico put on a Broadway show with the help of some starving performers, while detective Groucho sleuths for missing diamonds that have found their way into a

sardine can. Stories come together when Harpo unwittingly steals the can from a grocery store, and villainess Massey gets involved in the show's production to retrieve it. Some laughs here despite disjointed script. Then-unknown Monroe is onscreen only long enough to earn a brief Groucho leer.
Dist.: Republic

LOVE IN GERMANY, A 1984 French/German
☆ R Drama 1:47
Ⓥ Nudity, adult situations
Dir: Andrzej Wajda   *Cast:* Hanna Schygulla, Piotr Lysak, Marie Christine Barrault, Daniel Olbrychski, Armin Mueller-Stahl
▶ During World War II, German shopkeeper Schygulla has an affair with Lysak, a Polish prisoner of war who is doing forced labor in her town. Although Schygulla does not try to hide the affair, local authorities are pressured to take action against the lovers. Lovely Schygulla and the rest of the cast are excellent, but the atmosphere of Nazi-era corruption is familiar, and broadly drawn characters fail to convince. Ⓢ
Dist.: RCA/Columbia

LOVE IN THE AFTERNOON 1957
★ ★ ★ NR Comedy 2:10 B&W
Dir: Billy Wilder   *Cast:* Gary Cooper, Audrey Hepburn, Maurice Chevalier, Van Doude, John McGiver
▶ Texas millionaire Cooper, intrigued by a chance encounter with beautiful Parisian Hepburn, becomes so preoccupied by their "casual" affair that he hires detective Chevalier to trace true identity. Chevalier's charm and the fabulous locations more than compensate for Cooper's stiff performance in this breezy May-December romance. **(CC)**
Dist.: CBS/Fox

LOVE IS A DOG FROM HELL 1988 Belgian
☆ NR Drama 1:30
Ⓥ Nudity, adult situations, explicit language
Dir: Dominique Deruddere   *Cast:* Josse De Pauw, Geert Hunaerts, Michael Pas, Gene Bervoets, Amid Chakir, Florence Beliard
▶ Adaptation of stories by American writer Charles Bukowski traces luckless young man's misadventures with women over a twenty-year period; acne and drinking prove obstacles to success until he finally finds a perfect woman (who happens to be a corpse). Odd, terribly sad tale is done with honesty and candor but never works up much sympathy for the hapless hero. Ⓢ

LOVE IS A MANY SPLENDORED THING 1955
★ ★ ★ NR Romance 1:42
Dir: Henry King   *Cast:* Jennifer Jones, William Holden, Torin Thatcher, Isobel Elsom, Murray Matheson, Richard Loo
▶ Jones garnered a well-earned Oscar nomination as real-life Han Suyin, a Eurasian doctor who falls in love with married American reporter Holden. Racial prejudice, Holden's wife,

and the Korean War keep the lovers apart in this extremely romantic and moving love story. Best Picture nominee; won for Score, Song, and Costume Design.
Dist.: CBS/Fox

LOVELESS, THE 1983
★ R Drama 1:24
Ⓥ Nudity, adult situations, explicit language, violence
Dir: Kathryn Bigelow, Monty Montgomery   *Cast:* Willem Dafoe, Robert Gordon, Marin Kanter, J. Don Ferguson, Tina L'Hotsky, Lawrence Matarese
▶ In the late 1950s, motorcycle gang led by Dafoe invades small Georgia town, taking over a diner and saloon and menacing local girls. Dafoe's encounter with Kanter forces a deadly confrontation with her father Ferguson. Ambitious homage to *The Wild One* has stunning visuals but pretentious attitude. Good soundtrack includes songs by Gordon, Marshall Crenshaw, and Little Richard.
Dist.: Media

LOVE LETTERS 1984
★ ★ R Romance 1:28
Ⓥ Nudity, strong sexual content
Dir: Amy Jones   *Cast:* Jamie Lee Curtis, James Keach, Amy Madigan, Bud Cort, Matt Clark
▶ Romantic drama about young L.A. disc jockey Curtis, who discovers old love letters that reveal her deceased mother once had an adulterous affair. Curtis then begins a passionate romance of her own with Keach, a married man.
Dist.: Vestron

LOVELINES 1984
★ ★ R Comedy 1:34
Ⓥ Nudity, explicit language, adult humor
Dir: Rod Amateau   *Cast:* Greg Bradford, Mary Beth Evans, Michael Winslow, Don Michael Paul, Tammy Taylor
▶ Low-budget teen sex comedy stars former coverboy Bradford and Evans as students from rival high schools and lead singers of competitive bands. Despite protests from their peers, the two fall in love and play a duet. No-think entertainment with strictly mainstream music. **(CC)**
Dist.: CBS/Fox

LOVELY BUT DEADLY 1982
☆ R Action-Adventure 1:35
Ⓥ Brief nudity, violence
Dir: David Sheldon   *Cast:* Lucinda Dooling, John Randolph, Mel Novak, Mary McDonough, Richard Herd
▶ After her brother fatally overdoses on angel dust, teenage martial arts expert Dooling vows vengeance on her high school's drug pushers, who include the captain of the football team. Hard-chopping heroine is a novel genre twist, but tawdry production values and

obviously fake sound effects undercut her impact.
Dist.: Vestron

LOVE MACHINE, THE 1971
★ R Drama 1:48
☑ Adult situations, explicit language
Dir: Jack Haley, Jr. *Cast:* John Phillip Law, Dyan Cannon, Robert Ryan, Jackie Cooper, David Hemmings
▸ Dated adaptation of Jacqueline Susann's steamy 1960s best-seller about handsome Robin Stone (Law), a ruthless and libidinous TV newscaster who uses people to reach the top of the network pile. The frequent love scenes are fairly tame by 1990s standards. Borders on campy today.
Dist.: RCA/Columbia

LOVE ME OR LEAVE ME 1955
★★★★ NR Biography/Musical 2:02
Dir: Charles Vidor *Cast:* Doris Day, James Cagney, Cameron Mitchell, Robert Keith, Tom Tully, Harry Bellaver
▸ Gangster Martin "the Gimp" Snyder (Cagney) turns dance-hall singer Ruth Etting (Day) into one of the most popular stars of the Roaring Twenties. But Snyder's insane jealousy leads to tragedy when Etting starts an affair with her pianist, Mitchell. Absorbing biography has strong performances from the leads and a standard-filled soundtrack ("Mean to Me," "Ten Cents a Dance," "I'll Never Stop Loving You," etc.). Received six Oscar nominations, winning for the story by Daniel Fuchs. (CC)
Dist.: MGM/UA

LOVE ME TENDER 1956
★★★★ NR Western 1:29 B&W
Dir: Robert D. Webb *Cast:* Elvis Presley, Richard Egan, Debra Paget, Mildred Dunnock, William Campbell, James Drury
▸ The Civil War sets brother against brother. Elvis marries Paget because sibling Egan is presumed dead in battle. Trouble begins when Egan returns in possession of a stolen payroll. Motion picture debut of a young and vibrant Elvis. He sings "Poor Boy," "Old Shep," and the title song, among others.
Dist.: CBS/Fox

LOVE ON THE DOLE 1941 British
★ NR Drama 1:40 B&W
Dir: John Baxter *Cast:* Deborah Kerr, Clifford Evans, Joyce Howard, Frank Cellier, Mary Merrall, George Carney
▸ Mill worker Kerr wants to marry Evans, but his pride won't let him wed while he's on relief. A workers' demonstration in which Evans is involved turns violent, and Kerr considers marrying a man she doesn't love because she thinks it might help her family. There's some humor in this sad story of British working class life in the thirties.
Dist.: Video Yesteryear

LOVE ON THE RUN 1979 French
☆ PG Drama 1:30 C/B&W
☑ Adult situations
Dir: François Truffaut *Cast:* Jean-Pierre Leaud, Marie-France Pisier, Claude Jade, Dani, Dorothee, Rosy Varte
▸ Antoine Doinel (Leaud) wakes with new love Dorothee on the morning of his divorce from old love Jade, runs into even older love Pisier, and reminisces in flashback on his romantic life to date. Final, gently nostalgic installment of director Truffault's Doinel series incorporates generous clips from previous outings, including *The 400 Blows, Love at Twenty, Stolen Kisses*, and *Bed and Board.* [S]
Dist.: RCA/Columbia

LOVERBOY 1989
★★★ PG-13 Comedy 1:38
☑ Adult situations, explicit language
Dir: Joan Miklin Silver *Cast:* Patrick Dempsey, Kate Jackson, Kirstie Alley, Barbara Carrera, Kim Miyori, Nancy Valen
▸ In hot water with girlfriend Valen, delivery boy Dempsey offers stud services to lonely female doctors and businesswomen along with pizza deliveries (code word: "extra anchovies"). Just this close to earning his college tuition, Dempsey is hunted down by jealous husbands and chased back into Valen's arms. Only slightly better than the usual teen sex comedy. (CC)
Dist.: RCA/Columbia

LOVER COME BACK 1962
★★★ NR Romance/Comedy 1:47
Dir: Delbert Mann *Cast:* Rock Hudson, Doris Day, Tony Randall, Edie Adams, Jack Oakie, Ann B. Davis
▸ Sprightly Madison Avenue comedy: Day is an ad executive furious over rival Hudson's sneaky tactics, especially when she learns that the product in his latest campaign doesn't even exist. Leads are charming, and they receive fine support from Randall and Adams.
Dist.: KVC

LOVERS AND LIARS 1981 Italian
★★ R Comedy/Drama 1:36
☑ Nudity, explicit language
Dir: Mario Monicelli *Cast:* Goldie Hawn, Giancarlo Giannini, Aurore Clément, Claudine Auger
▸ Giannini, a Cassanova type, tries to whisk fun-loving American tourist Hawn to Pisa for a tryst, but is foiled by a series of mishaps. Potentially good setup falls flat; Giannini and Hawn, as she declares in the movie, "simply don't get along." Also known as *Travels With Anita.*
Dist.: Nelson

LOVERS AND OTHER STRANGERS 1970
★★ PG Comedy 1:44
☑ Adult situations, adult humor
Dir: Cy Howard *Cast:* Gig Young, Beatrice Arthur, Bonnie Bedelia, Anne Jackson, Harry

Guardino, Michael Brandon, Richard Castellano, Anne Meara, Bob Balaban, Cloris Leachman, Diane Keaton
▶ Honest, frequently hilarious comedy about the surfacing tensions between two families as they prepare for Bedelia's marriage to Brandon. Incisive vignettes and accomplished cast (including Keaton in her film debut) add up to delightful entertainment. Received nominations for Castellano (introducing the phrase "So what's the story?") and screenplay (based on a play by Renée Taylor and Joseph Bologna); "For All We Know" won Best Song Oscar.
Dist.: CBS/Fox

LOVES AND TIMES OF SCARAMOUCHE, THE
1975 Italian
☆ **PG Comedy 1:35**
Ⓥ Adult situations
Dir: Enzo G. Castellari   *Cast:* Michael Sarrazin, Ursula Andress, Aldo Maccione, Giancarlo Prete, Michael Forest, Romano Puppo
▶ Notorious French scamp Scaramouche (Sarrazin) hops from the bed of one Empiregowned lovely to the next, and outwits the plodding romantic strategies of a lunkheaded Napoleon (Maccione). With the exception of Maccione's funny Little Corporal, lusty, peppy costumer bounds by without many laughs.
Dist.: Nelson

LOVESICK 1983
★★ **PG Romance/Comedy 1:36**
Ⓥ Adult situations, explicit language, adult humor
Dir: Marshall Brickman   *Cast:* Dudley Moore, Elizabeth McGovern, Alec Guinness, John Huston, Wallace Shawn
▶ Moore, a psychiatrist with a posh Manhattan office and pretty wife, develops an obsessive crush on his latest patient, McGovern. Disregarding professional ethics and supposedly good sense, they begin a passionate romance. Guinness, as a comic Sigmund Freud, occasionally appears to ask Moore: "Didn't you read my chapter on termination?"
Dist.: Warner

LOVES OF CARMEN, THE 1948
★★★ **NR Drama 1:37 B&W**
Dir: Charles Vidor   *Cast:* Rita Hayworth, Glenn Ford, Victor Jory, Arnold Moss
▶ Amoral temptress Hayworth, married to gypsy Jory, has affair with handsome soldier Ford that brings misfortune to them both. Follow-up to the Hayworth/Ford *Gilda* has the same sizzling sexual chemistry of its predecessor.
Dist.: RCA/Columbia

LOVE SONGS 1986 Canadian/French
☆ **NR Romance 1:47**
Ⓥ Adult situations, explicit language
Dir: Elie Chouraqui   *Cast:* Catherine Deneuve, Christopher Lambert, Nick Mancuso,

Dayle Haddon, Richard Anconina, Charlotte Gainsbourg
▶ When Deneuve's writer husband Mancuso leaves her and their two kids, she begins an affair with aspiring rock singer Lambert. His budding career and her indecision about divorce cause the couple conflict. Flat, unexceptional love story has attractive leads but one-note script. Surprisingly insipid Michel Legrand score.   Ⓢ
Dist.: Vestron

LOVESPELL 1979
☆ **NR Romance 1:31**
Ⓥ Adult situations
Dir: Tom Donovan   *Cast:* Richard Burton, Kate Mulgrew, Nicholas Clay, Cyril Cusak, Geraldine Fitzgerald, Niall Toibin
▶ Also known as *Tristan and Isolt*, new retelling of sixth-century romance has Burton and Mulgrew as the doomed lovers whose story, some say, triggered the age of chivalry. Set in ancient Britain, with lovely locations, authentic costumes, and rousing music by Ireland's Chieftains. Not Burton's best performance, however.
Dist.: Continental

LOVE STORY 1970
★★★★ **PG Drama 1:39**
Dir: Arthur Miller   *Cast:* Ali MacGraw, Ryan O'Neal, Ray Milland, John Marley, Katherine Balfour
▶ Rich Ivy Leaguer O'Neal falls for poor but sassy co-ed MacGraw and, despite objections of his dad Milland, they marry. Their happiness is shattered when she becomes terminally ill. Most often-quoted line: "Love means never having to say you're sorry." Megahit tearjerker was based on Erich Segal's bestseller and won an Oscar for Francis Lai's score. Sequel: *Oliver's Story*.
Dist.: Paramount

LOVE STREAMS 1984
★ **PG-13 Drama 2:02**
Ⓥ Adult situations, explicit language, violence
Dir: John Cassavetes   *Cast:* Gena Rowlands, John Cassavetes, Diahnne Abbott, Seymour Cassel
▶ Intensely emotional drama about alienated writer Cassavetes and his sister Rowlands, helping each other work through their various (and many) neuroses and discovering that life is really worth living. A brilliant roller coaster of human emotion for Cassavetes fans; long, rambling psychodrama for everyone else.
Dist.: MGM/UA

LOVE WITH THE PROPER STRANGER 1963
★★★★★ **NR Drama 1:42 B&W**
Dir: Robert Mulligan   *Cast:* Natalie Wood, Steve McQueen, Edie Adams, Herschel Bernardi, Tom Bosley, Harvey Lembeck
▶ Although engaged to Bosley, Wood has a one-night stand with musician McQueen that

leaves her pregnant. Their search for an abortionist is the unlikely but oddly moving premise of this offbeat drama set in New York. Wood received one of five Oscar nominations; Adams shines as McQueen's stripper girlfriend. **(CC)**
Dist.: Paramount

LOVING 1970
★ ★ R Drama 1:30
☑ Nudity, adult situations, explicit language
Dir: Irvin Kirschner *Cast:* George Segal, Eva Marie Saint, Sterling Hayden, Keenan Wynn, Nancie Phillips, Janis Young
► Commercial artist Segal keeps wife Saint in Connecticut, enjoys mistress Young in Manhattan, and tries to snag a big commission from eccentric tycoon Hayden. Segal nearly holds it all together until he is seduced by neighbor Phillips into some unexpectedly interrupted lovemaking. Occasionally funny drama, with Segal's characterization especially on target.
Dist.: SVS

LOVING COUPLES 1980
★ ★ ★ PG Comedy 1:37
☑ Adult situations, explicit language
Dir: Jack Smight *Cast:* Shirley MacLaine, James Coburn, Susan Sarandon, Stephen Collins, Sally Kellerman
► Saucy sex comedy about MacLaine and Coburn taking up with younger lovers Collins and Sarandon before realizing there's no bed like home. Smooth cast of professionals gives polish to routine screenplay.
Dist.: Vestron

LOVING YOU 1957
★ ★ ★ ★ NR Musical 1:41
Dir: Hal Kanter *Cast:* Elvis Presley, Lizabeth Scott, Wendell Corey, Dolores Hart, James Gleason, The Jordanaires
► Promoter Scott and country-western star Corey turn hillbilly truckdriver Presley into a rock 'n' roll sensation, but Presley has second thoughts about his new career when he loses girlfriend Hart. Elvis, at the height of his powers, does a fine acting job in a story loosely based on his own life. Great soundtrack: "Teddy Bear," "Hot Dog," "Mean Woman Blues," title song, etc.
Dist.: Warner

LOWER DEPTHS, THE 1957 Japanese
☆ NR Drama 2:05 B&W
Dir: Akira Kurosawa *Cast:* Toshiro Mifune, Isuzu Yamada, Ganjiro Nakamura, Kyoko Kagawa, Bokuzen Hidari
► Yamada is the landlady of a low-life hovel housing gamblers, prostitutes, tinkers, and other social cast-offs. Though married, she loves thieving resident Mifune; he, however, is attracted to Yamada's sister Kagawa. They futilely try to make sense of their lives. Director Kurosawa does a good job adapting the Maxim Gorky play to a Japanese milieu.
Dist.: SVS

LT. ROBIN CRUSOE, U.S.N. 1966
★ ★ G Family 1:50
Dir: Byron Paul *Cast:* Dick Van Dyke, Nancy Kwan, Akim Tamiroff, Arthur Malet, Tyler McVey
► Updated *Robinson Crusoe* stars Van Dyke as a navy pilot who fends for himself on a deserted island. His man Friday is native girl Wednesday (Kwan); other companionship is provided by a chimp. Disney comedy provides a good vehicle for Van Dyke, and Kwan is appealing. However, there are tedious stretches.
Dist.: Buena Vista

LUCAS 1986
★ ★ ★ ★ PG-13 Comedy/Drama 1:40
☑ Explicit language
Dir: David Seltzer *Cast:* Corey Haim, Kerri Green, Charlie Sheen, Courtney Thorne-Smith, Winona Ryder
► Brainy but shrimpy high schooler Lucas (Haim) falls for friend Green, although she prefers sensitive jock Sheen. To prove himself, Haim tries out for the football team. For a change, film offers three-dimensional teenage characters in a sweetly affecting story. Intelligent dialogue and winning performances; modest in scope but quite evocative. **(CC)**
Dist.: CBS/Fox

LUCKY JIM 1957 British
★ ★ NR Comedy 1:35
Dir: John Boulting *Cast:* Ian Carmichael, Terry-Thomas, Hugh Griffith, Sharon Acker, Jean Anderson, Maureen Connell
► At a small English college, professor Carmichael's efforts to impress his superiors run aground on a series of comic disasters. Amusing performances by Carmichael and Terry-Thomas highlight this entertaining adaptation of the Kingsley Amis novel.
Dist.: HBO

LUCKY LUCIANO 1974 Italian/French/U.S.
★ ★ R Crime 1:50
☑ Adult situations, explicit language, violence
Dir: Francesco Rosi *Cast:* Gian Maria Volonté, Rod Steiger, Charles Siragusa, Edmond O'Brien, Vincent Gardenia, Silverio Blasi
► Intriguing account of famed gangster's career after deportation to Italy in the 1950s. Real-life narcotics investigator Siragusa adds touch of authenticity in showing the ten-year campaign to end Luciano's criminal empire; Steiger is convincing as an informer.
Dist.: Nelson

LUCKY PARTNERS 1940
★ NR Comedy 1:39 B&W
Dir: Lewis Milestone *Cast:* Ronald Colman, Ginger Rogers, Jack Carson, Spring Byington, Cecilia Loftus, Harry Davenport
► Through strangers, Colman and Rogers split a lottery ticket as a lark—with Rogers promis-

ing to go to Niagara Falls with him if they win. When the ticket pays off, Rogers must make the promised journey, earning the ire of fiancé Carson. No big boffs here, but mildly interesting example of what was once considered a racy bedroom farce. Based on the Sacha Guitry story "Bonne Chance."
Dist.: Turner

LUMIERE 1976 French
☆ **R Drama 1:35**
☑ Brief nudity, explicit language
Dir: Jeanne Moreau ***Cast:*** Jeanne Moreau, Francine Racette, Lucia Bose, Caroline Cartier, Keith Carradine
▸ A film "by women and about women" dramatizing the conflicts and compromises experienced by four actresses in the course of pursuing their profession. Director/star Moreau knows whereof she speaks, and cast, with the exception of a leaden Carradine, performs superbly. [S]
Dist.: Nelson

LURKERS 1988
☆ **R Horror 1:30**
☑ Nudity, adult situations, violence
Dir: Roberta Findlay ***Cast:*** Christine Moore, Gary Warner, Marina Taylor, Carissa Channing, Tom Billett
▸ Despite lurid title, few viewers will lurk long enough to see the end of this poorly made thriller about young cellist Moore haunted by emissaries of Satan. Moore's mother, it seems, was a witch, and her revenant is just one of the otherworldly horrors with whom Moore must contend. Poor directing, acting, and script are among horrors with which viewers must contend. Not even for fans of the genre.
Dist.: Media

LUST FOR LIFE 1956
★★★★ **NR Biography 2:02**
Dir: Vincente Minnelli ***Cast:*** Kirk Douglas, Anthony Quinn, James Donald, Pamela Brown, Everett Sloane
▸ Painter Vincent Van Gogh (Douglas) struggles with poverty, heartbreak, mental illness, and a world that ignores his artistic genius. Compelling drama may be the best movie ever made about an artist; Douglas's intense performance captures Van Gogh's inner workings. Stunning color photography, Oscar-winning supporting performance by Quinn as Van Gogh's friend, the artist Gauguin.
Dist.: MGM/UA

LUST IN THE DUST 1985
★ **R Western/Comedy 1:24**
☑ Nudity, explicit language, violence, adult humor
Dir: Paul Bartel ***Cast:*** Tab Hunter, Divine, Lainie Kazan, Geoffrey Lewis, Cesar Romero
▸ Offbeat camp Western, decidedly tasteless but often fun. Big mama Rosie (drag queen Divine) and singer Margarita (Kazan) vie for gunslinger Hunter's attention. The rivalry ends, however, when by matching derriere tattoos they realize they are long-lost sisters! Saucy and irreverent. (CC)
Dist.: New World

LUSTY MEN, THE 1952
★★★ **NR Drama 1:53 B&W**
Dir: Nicholas Ray ***Cast:*** Susan Hayward, Robert Mitchum, Arthur Kennedy, Arthur Hunnicutt, Frank Faylen, Walter Coy
▸ Washed up rodeo star Mitchum coaches Kennedy to stardom on the ropin' and ridin' circuit. The more successful Kennedy becomes, the more he neglects wife Hayward, allowing Mitchum to make a play for her. Rivalry between the two men is settled in the rodeo ring. No previous interest in rodeo is necessary to appreciate the deeper resonances of this offbeat American classic. One of Mitchum's best roles; inspired by a story in *Life* magazine.
Dist.: United

LUV 1967
☆ **NR Comedy 1:35**
Dir: Clive Donner ***Cast:*** Jack Lemmon, Peter Falk, Elaine May, Nina Wayne, Eddie Mayehoff
▸ Lemmon plays an inept loser who's rescued from a suicide attempt by old school friend Falk; in return, Falk asks Lemmon to help him divorce May. Lemmon marries May, Falk ends up with buxom gym teacher Wayne—but both couples are still unhappy. Plodding adaptation of a Murray Schisgal play fails to reproduce the original's comic tone.
Dist.: RCA/Columbia

M 1931 German
★★★ **NR Drama 1:39 B&W**
Dir: Fritz Lang ***Cast:*** Peter Lorre, Otto Wernicke, Gustav Grundgens, Theo Lingen, Theodore Loos, Georg John
▸ Child murderer Lorre terrifies and outrages Berlin. When the police prove incompetent, the city's criminals conduct their own manhunt. Provocative, critically praised film suffers from dated passages, but its cumulative impact is astonishing and nerve-wracking. Lorre's chilling film debut made him an international star. [S]
Dist.: Various

MAC AND ME 1988
★★★ **PG Fantasy/Family 1:33**
☑ Explicit lanugage
Dir: Stewart Raffill ***Cast:*** Jade Calegory, Christine Ebersole, Jonathan Ward, Katrina Caspary, Lauren Stanley, Vinnie Torrente
▸ Baby alien Mac (Mysterious Alien Creature) is left behind when government scientists attempt to nab his family. Mac hides out in California home and is befriended by handicapped boy Calegory. Resemblance to *E.T.* very apparent but sweet story evokes its own charm.
Dist.: Orion

MACAO 1952
★ ★ NR Mystery-Suspense 1:20 B&W
Dir: Josef von Sternberg   *Cast:* Robert
Mitchum, Jane Russell, William Bendix,
Gloria Grahame, Thomas Gomez, Philip
Ahn, Brad Dexter
▶ On the run from a frame-up, Mitchum winds
up on tropical Macao along with singer Russell and undercover dick Bendix. Mitchum has
a turbulent affair with Russell, while becoming
involved in Bendix's mission to nab crime big
shot Dexter by luring him off the island into
international waters. Some fight scenes were
directed by Nicholas Ray, causing director
von Sternberg to disown the film despite his
obvious influence on its steamy, cluttered
decor. Mitchum and Russell make a hot
combo.
Dist.: Nostalgia

MACARONI 1985 Italian
★ ★ PG Comedy/Drama 1:44
☑ Explicit language
Dir: Ettore Scola   *Cast:* Jack Lemmon, Marcello Mastroianni, Daria Nicolodi, Isa
Danieli, Maria Luisa Saniella, Patrizzia Sacchi
▶ Uptight American businessman Lemmon
arrives in Naples and is reunited with Mastroianni, brother of his World War II flame
Danieli. Mastroianni has kept the romance
alive by writing his sister love letters and signing Lemmon's name. Lemmon loosens up
under Mastroianni's guidance. Pleasing performances by the two stars. In English and
(sporadically) subtitled Italian.
Dist.: Paramount

MACARTHUR 1977
★ ★ ★ ★ PG Biography 2:10
☑ Violence
Dir: Joseph Sargent   *Cast:* Gregory Peck,
Dan O'Herlihy, Ed Flanders, Marj Dusay
▶ The life and times of General Douglas
MacArthur (Peck) from World War II to his dis-
missal during the Korean War. Sacrifices cine-
matic excitement in favor of historical accu-
racy, but the excellent portrayal by Peck and
the fine supporting players (Flanders as Tru-
man, O'Herlihy as FDR) make it worthwhile.
Dist.: MCA

MACBETH 1948
★ NR Drama 1:52 B&W
Dir: Orson Welles   *Cast:* Orson Welles, Dan
O'Herlihy, Edgar Barrier, Roddy McDowall,
Robert Coote, Jeanette Nolan
▶ Aristocrat Welles is needled by wife Nolan
into killing Barrier and others who stand be-
tween him and the Scottish throne. Action is
predicted by a trio of witches. Director/star
Welles's adaptation of Shakespeare's tragedy
is artistically ambitious, but suffers from a shoe-
string budget. Videotape is original, uncut
length.
Dist.: Republic

MACBETH 1971 British
★ ★ R Drama 2:20
☑ Nudity, graphic violence
Dir: Roman Polanski   *Cast:* Jon Finch, Francesca Annis, Martin Shaw, Nicholas Shelby,
John Stride, Stephan Chase
▶ Macbeth (Finch), egged on by scheming
wife Annis and witches' prophecy, attempts
to usurp the crown of Scotland. Bloody version
of Shakespeare's tragedy seems like a cathar-
sis for director Polanksi (he made it after wife's
murder by the Charles Manson family).
Unusual interpretation of the classic has some
terrific swordplay and stunning visuals.
Dist.: RCA/Columbia

MACK, THE 1973
★ R Drama 1:50
☑ Explicit language
Dir: Michael Campus   *Cast:* Max Julien,
Richard Pryor, Roger Mosley, Don Gordon
▶ Black pimp Julien rises to the top of his pro-
fession and comes into conflict with corrupt
white cops and the Mafia. Dated black ex-
ploitation; even Pryor's small part as Julien's
sidekick doesn't enliven stereotyped plot.
Dist.: Nelson

MACKENNA'S GOLD 1969
★ ★ ★ PG Western 2:08
☑ Explicit language, violence
Dir: J. Lee Thompson   *Cast:* Gregory Peck,
Omar Sharif, Telly Savalas, Camilla Sparv,
Keenan Wynn, Julie Newmar, Lee J. Cobb,
Raymond Massey, Burgess Meredith, An-
thony Quayle, Edward G. Robinson, Eli Wal-
lach
▶ Sheriff Peck memorizes and burns Indian
map to a mythical golden canyon; he be-
comes the target of innumerable greedy
prospectors and killers in this long, disappoint-
ing Western. Large cast fails to spark episodic
story.
Dist.: RCA/Columbia

MACKINTOSH MAN, THE 1973
★ ★ ★ PG Espionage 1:38
☑ Violence
Dir: John Huston   *Cast:* Paul Newman,
James Mason, Dominique Sanda, Harry Andrews, Ian Bannen
▶ British intelligence sends Interpol agent
Newman to trap Mason, a parliament member who is actually working for the Communists. Good characters, charismatic cast, atmospheric Maurice Jarre score, and colorful
locations in England, Ireland, and Malta; but
contrived plotting makes for a less than satisfying whole.
Dist.: Warner

MACK THE KNIFE 1990
☆ PG-13 Musical 2:00
☑ Adult situations, explicit language, vio-
   lence
Dir: Menahem Golan   *Cast:* Raul Julia,
Richard Harris, Julie Walters, Julia Migenes,
Roger Daltry, Rachel Robertson

▶ Adaptation of the Kurt Weill/Bertolt Brecht *Threepenny Opera* stars Julia as Mack the Knife, nineteenth-century London's most notorious criminal and womanizer who continues his evil ways even after eloping with underage Polly Peachum (Robertson). Migenes is the prostitute who eventually betrays Julia, Daltry the streetsinger who does the title tune. Golan's misdirection distorts original meaning and encourages talented cast to overact. Compensations are the brilliant score and Julia.
Dist.: RCA/Columbia

MACON COUNTY LINE 1975
★ ★ ★ R Action-Adventure 1:29
☑ Adult situations, explicit language, violence
Dir: Richard Compton   *Cast:* Alan Vint, Cheryl Waters, Max Baer, Jr., Geoffrey Lewis, Joan Blackman, Jesse Vint
▶ Baer, who also wrote and produced, stars as a redneck sheriff whose wife Blackman is brutally murdered. The prime suspects are outsiders Waters, Alan Vint, and Jesse Vint; a deputy finds out too late that Baer is pursuing the wrong people. Taut Southern thriller set in the early 1950s led to a sequel, *Return to Macon County.*
Dist.: Embassy

MADAME BOVARY 1949
★ ★ ★ ★ NR Drama 1:55 B&W
Dir: Vincente Minnelli   *Cast:* Jennifer Jones, James Mason, Van Heflin, Louis Jourdan, Gene Lockhart, Gladys Cooper
▶ Lavish production of Gustave Flaubert's classic, with Mason portraying the writer as he defends himself from censors. Through flashbacks, he reveals the story of Emma Bovary (Jones), a nineteenth-century libertine whose extramarital affairs lead to tragedy. Novel's plot is softened considerably, but passion and spectacle remain intact. "Emma Bovary Waltz" stands among Minnelli's best dances.
Dist.: MGM/UA

MADAME ROSA 1977 French
★ ★ PG Drama 1:45
☑ Adult situations, explicit language
Dir: Moshe Mizrahi   *Cast:* Simone Signoret, Claude Dauphin, Sammy Ben Youb, Gabriel Jabbour
▶ Profoundly moving, Oscar-winning Best Foreign Film about an aging ex-prostitute/Auschwitz survivor and an orphaned 14-year-old Arab boy, Ben Youb. Her dying mission in life is to save him from becoming a "fancy man" of the French quarter. Huffing and puffing her way up tenement stairs, painfully aware her mind is slipping into senility, Signoret is unforgettable and heartbreaking. A very different kind of love story, often funny in spite of its downbeat subject.
Dist.: Vestron

MADAME SOUSATZKA 1988 British
★ ★ PG-13 Drama 2:02

☑ Adult situations, explicit language
Dir: John Schlesinger   *Cast:* Shirley MacLaine, Peggy Ashcroft, Twiggy, Navin Chowdhry, Leigh Lawson, Shabana Azmi
▶ In London, eccentric piano teacher MacLaine takes Indian teenager Chowdhry under her wing, teaching him not only how to play but how to live. Prodigy blossoms under her tutelage, but rift eventually occurs between pupil and mentor. Flamboyant MacLaine performance is hard to resist, as is the very appealing Chowdhry.
Dist.: MCA

MADAME X 1966
★ ★ ★ NR Drama 1:40
Dir: David Lowell Rich   *Cast:* Lana Turner, John Forsythe, Ricardo Montalban, Burgess Meredith, Constance Bennett, Keir Dullea
▶ Version of an oft-filmed Alexandre Bisson play is a smoothly produced soap opera about bored diplomat's wife Turner whose affair with playboy Montalban leads to prostitution, blackmail, and murder. In a tragic twist, she is defended in court by Dullea, the son who never knew her. Turner's dedicated performance overcomes the often maudlin plot.
Dist.: MCA

MAD DOG MORGAN 1976 Australian
★ ★ R Western 1:42
☑ Adult situations, explicit language, violence
Dir: Philippe Mora   *Cast:* Dennis Hopper, Jack Thompson, David Gulpilil, Frank Thring, Michael Pate, Walls Eaton
▶ After failing as a prospector during the mid-1800s, Hopper turns to robbery and winds up in prison. Once released, he teams with aborigine Gulpilil for an infamous crime spree. Well-made, extremely violent Western is based on the legendary outlaw of Australia's gold rush era.
Dist.: HBO

MADE FOR EACH OTHER 1939
★ ★ ★ ★ NR Drama 1:31 B&W
Dir: John Cromwell   *Cast:* Carole Lombard, James Stewart, Lucile Watson, Charles Coburn, Ward Bond
▶ Superior melodrama about young love on an uphill climb. Stewart and Lombard, in fine comedic form, struggle with marriage, parenting, and interfering in-laws. The engaging script by Jo Swerling climaxes in the near death of the couple's first child.   (CC)
Dist.: Key Ⓒ

MADE IN HEAVEN 1987
★ ★ PG Fantasy/Romance 1:41
☑ Brief nudity, adult situations
Dir: Alan Rudolph   *Cast:* Timothy Hutton, Kelly McGillis, Maureen Stapleton, Ann Wedgeworth, Mare Winningham
▶ Fairy-tale romance begins in the 1940s when Hutton dies while saving a drowning child. Up in heaven, he falls for fellow angel McGillis. When she's returned to earth to fulfill

her destiny, he follows. Featherweight concoction sags as the couple tries to find each other on earth. Includes surprising cameo appearances by Neil Young, Ellen Barkin, Tom Petty, and Debra Winger as a man.
Dist.: Warner

MADE IN THE U.S.A. 1987
★ R Drama 1:26
☑ Nudity, adult situations, explicit language
Dir: Ken Friedman *Cast:* Christopher Penn, Lori Singer, Adrian Pasdar, Jackie Murphy, Judy Baldwin, Dean Paul Martin
► Punks Penn and Pasdar pick up Singer and go on a crime spree across America. Downbeat road movie with unpleasant characters and heavy-handed preaching against the evils of toxic waste. Well made but not much fun to sit through.
Dist.: Nelson

MADHOUSE 1974 British
★ PG Horror 1:29
☑ Violence
Dir: Jim Clark *Cast:* Vincent Price, Peter Cushing, Robert Quarry, Adrienne Corri, Natasha Pyne
► Horror actor Price, famous for his role as Doctor Death, spends twelve years in an asylum after finding his fiancée beheaded. He is released but his comeback is sabotaged by a series of murders. Above-average genre plot features noteworthy Price but is pretty tame in the fright department.
Dist.: Virgin

MADHOUSE 1990
★ ★ ★ PG-13 Comedy 1:30
☑ Adult situations, explicit language
Dir: Tom Ropelewski *Cast:* John Larroquette, Kirstie Alley, Alison LaPlaca, John Diehl, Jessica Lundy, Bradley Gregg, Dennis Miller, Robert Ginty
► Larroquette and wife Alley are living happily in the Los Angeles suburbs when his unemployed cousin Diehl and wife Lundy drop in for a visit, starting a procession of unwanted houseguests that doesn't end until the harried couple fights back. Sit-com-style humor, always frisky and occasionally hilarious, should be right at home on the small screen. Funniest performer: LaPlaca as Alley's gold-digging sister. (CC)
Dist.: Orion

MADIGAN 1968
★ ★ ★ NR Action-Adventure 1:41
Dir: Don Siegel *Cast:* Richard Widmark, Henry Fonda, Inger Stevens, Harry Guardino, Susan Clark, James Whitmore
► Cops Widmark and Guardino, in hot water with police commissioner Fonda for letting killer get away, attempt to recapture him. Gritty, intelligent thriller with good performances, authentic New York City locations, and a shattering finale. Widmark re-created his role in the subsequent TV series.
Dist.: MCA

MAD MAX 1980 Australian
★ R Action-Adventure 1:33
☑ Explicit language, graphic violence
Dir: George Miller *Cast:* Mel Gibson, Joanne Samuel, Hugh Keays-Byrne, Steve Bisley, Tim Burns
► In the not-too-distant future, Australian policeman Gibson goes on a rampage of revenge when vicious biker gang attacks his wife and child. Visceral excitement, fast-paced action, and well-executed stunts in this tough and unusual futuristic fantasy. Dubbed voices substitute for the Australian accents. Sequel: *The Road Warrior.*
Dist.: Vestron

MAD MAX BEYOND THUNDERDOME 1985 Australian
★ ★ PG-13 Action-Adventure 1:47
☑ Violence
Dir: George Miller, George Ogilvie *Cast:* Mel Gibson, Tina Turner, Helen Buday, Bruce Spence, Angelo Rossitto, Frank Thring
► "Two men enter, one man leaves," announces feudal society queen Turner as Max (Gibson) prepares for gladiatorial combat in the futuristic arena known as Thunderdome. Gibson also befriends a tribe of wild children in this third entry in the Mad Max series. Less action-oriented than its predecessors, with a higher budget, more elaborate costumes and sets, and Mel adding some humanity to his charismatic hero. Still, plenty of thrills, especially in the rousing Thunderdome sequence. Tina is a high-style villain. (CC)
Dist.: Warner

MAD MISS MANTON, THE 1938
★ ★ NR Mystery-Suspense 1:20 B&W
Dir: Leigh Jason *Cast:* Barbara Stanwyck, Henry Fonda, Sam Levene, Frances Mercer, Stanley Ridges, Vicki Lester
► Madcap heiress Stanwyck discovers a body that somehow disappears before the police arrive on the scene. Police lieutenant Levene has no patience for her amateur sleuthing, but newspaper reporter Fonda likes Stanwyck almost as much as a hot scoop. Screwball comedy/mystery/romance in a neat little package.
Dist.: Turner

MAD MONSTER, THE 1942
★ NR Horror 1:12 B&W
Dir: Sam Newfield *Cast:* Johnny Downs, George Zucco, Anne Nagel, Sarah Padden, Glenn Strange, Mae Busch
► When university scientists expel Zucco from their midst, he takes revenge by turning simple peasant Strange into a wolfman-type monster who not only slaughters a few of the offending scientists, but anyone else he can get his paws on. As bad as they come.
Dist.: Sinister

MAD MONSTER PARTY 1967
★ ★ NR Animation 1:34
Dir: Jules Bass *Cast:* Voices of Boris Karloff,

Phyllis Diller, Gale Garnett, Ethel Ennis, Allen Swift

▶ Baron Frankenstein (Karloff), head of a monsters' organization, is calling it a monstrous career; Dracula, the Invisible Man, and other creatures gather to pick a successor. Meanwhile, the Baron's nerdy nephew falls for his uncle's assistant, the sultry Francesca (Garnett). Clever and charming, perfect for kids weaned on horror films. Romantic subplot is actually very sweet. Garnett sings "Never Was a Love Like Mine (For You)."

Dist.: Nelson

MAGIC 1978
★★★ R Mystery-Suspense 1:38
☑ Brief nudity, explicit language, violence
Dir: Richard Attenborough ***Cast:*** Anthony Hopkins, Ann-Margret, Burgess Meredith, Ed Lauter, E. J. Andre, Jerry Houser

▶ Ventriloquist-magician Hopkins, insecure about the success of his latest dummy Fats, flees a lucrative TV contract for his Catskills hometown. There he rekindles a romance with high school sweetheart Ann-Margret (delivering another fine performance), who's trapped in an unhappy marriage with redneck Lauter. Thriller similar to an episode in *Dead of Night* gives away most of its surprises in the first half-hour. Screenplay by William Goldman from his novel.

Dist.: Nelson

MAGICAL MYSTERY TOUR 1968 British
★ NR Musical 1:00
Dir: The Beatles ***Cast:*** John Lennon, Paul McCartney, Ringo Starr, George Harrison, Viv Stanshall, Victor Spinetti

▶ Beatle drummer Starr and his aunt join a bizarre bus trip whose stops provide the excuse for proto rock videos featuring the Fab Four. Sophomoric, self-indulgent production rates zero as a movie, but the musical segments are imaginative. Songs range from the stimulating "I Am a Walrus" to the soporific "Blue Jay Way." Stanshall (of the Bonzo Dog Doo-Dah Band) contributes his winning croon to a charmingly sleazy strip club sequence.

Dist.: Media

MAGIC CHRISTIAN, THE 1970 British
★ PG Comedy 1:33
☑ Adult situations, explicit language, adult humor
Dir: Joseph McGrath ***Cast:*** Peter Sellers, Ringo Starr, Richard Attenborough, Laurence Harvey, Christopher Lee, Spike Milligan

▶ Millionaire Sellers sets out to prove to adopted son Starr that people will do anything for money. Irreverent, often tasteless satire is structurally a mess, but many of the vignettes are priceless. Filled with cameos: Graham Chapman, John Cleese, Raquel Welch, etc. Typical scene: Yul Brunner in drag singing "Mad About the Boy" to Roman Polanski. Other songs include Badfinger's "Come and Get It."

Dist.: Republic

MAGIC FLUTE, THE 1974 Swedish
★ G Music 2:14
Dir: Ingmar Bergman ***Cast:*** Ulric Cold, Josef Kostlinger, Erik Saeden, Birgit Nordin, Trina Urrila

▶ Superior adaptation of Mozart's opera about a prince who must rescue the kidnapped daughter of the Queen of the Night. Assured direction captures intimate details as well as the sweep of Mozart's score. Only drawbacks: cast sings in Swedish, not German; length may be excessive for non-opera fans. On all other levels a delightful, rewarding experience. [S]

Dist.: Paramount

MAGICIAN, THE 1958 Swedish
☆ NR Drama 1:42 B&W
Dir: Ingmar Bergman ***Cast:*** Max Von Sydow, Ingrid Thulin, Gunnar Bjornstrand, Naima Wifstrand, Bengt Ekerot, Bibi Anderson

▶ Parable of mortality and art set in the nineteenth century, with Von Sydow leading a troupe of illusionists into a dark town whose inhabitants refuse to believe in magic. Nothing is what it appears to be as Von Sydow confounds the villagers, and director Bergman confounds the viewer with camera tricks and special effects. In the end, even death itself may be only a trick. Rich, moody, and atmospheric. [S]

Dist.: Various

MAGICIAN OF LUBLIN, THE 1979
★★ R Drama 1:45
☑ Nudity, adult situations, explicit language
Dir: Menahem Golan ***Cast:*** Alan Arkin, Louise Fletcher, Valerie Perrine, Shelley Winters, Lou Jacobi, Maia Danzinger

▶ Arkin, a nervy, second-rate magician in turn-of-the-century Poland, claims he can fly, but works most of his wonders in the bedroom, seducing a bevy of women, including his wife, peasant Perrine, and, he hopes, aristocratic Fletcher. Arkin goes from magician to prophet, but not many will want to follow along. Film fails to capture the zest of the Isaac Bashevis Singer book upon which it is based. Winters is grossly repellent as the mother of Arkin's stage assistant.

Dist.: Warner

MAGIC OF LASSIE, THE 1978
★★★★★ G Family 1:40
Dir: Don Chaffey ***Cast:*** James Stewart, Mickey Rooney, Pernell Roberts, Stephanie Zimbalist, Michael Sharrett, Alice Faye

▶ Evil millionaire Roberts, unable to buy neighbor Stewart's vineyard, steals Stewart's dog instead. Can Lassie find her way home across the vast Rockies? Children will love the canine star's comeback (her first film since

1952); adults will enjoy the singing by Faye, Stewart, and Pat and Debby Boone.
Dist.: MGM/UA

MAGIC SWORD, THE 1962
★ **NR Fantasy 1:20**
Dir: Bert I. Gordon *Cast:* Basil Rathbone, Estelle Winwood, Gary Lockwood, Anne Helm, Liam Sullivan, Richard Kiel
▶ Villainous magician Rathbone would like to feed princess Helm to his dragon, but legendary slayer St. George (Lockwood) has other ideas. Fantasy world is well-populated with knights of various humors and human oddities like pinhead Kiel, but clearly from an era less obsessed with special effects and slam-bang action than our own.
Dist.: Video Yesteryear

MAGIC TOWN 1947
★★ **NR Comedy 1:43 B&W**
Dir: William Wellman *Cast:* James Stewart, Jane Wyman, Kent Smith, Regis Toomey, Donald Meek, Mary Currier
▶ Public opinion pollster Stewart leads a team into a small town which statistics tell him is America's most perfectly average. When newspaper editor Wyman blows the whistle on him, the town is almost destroyed by resulting media attention. Scripted by Robert Riskin, writer of many of Frank Capra's most popular films, cornball hokum could have used the master's touch.
Dist.: Republic

MAGNIFICENT AMBERSONS, THE 1942
★★★ **NR Drama 1:28 B&W**
Dir: Orson Welles *Cast:* Joseph Cotten, Dolores Costello, Anne Baxter, Tim Holt, Agnes Moorehead, Ray Collins
▶ Fascinating study of the Amberson family, wealthy, turn-of-the-century Midwesterners who fail to adapt to changing times. Technically innovative film is also rich in characterizations: Cotten as a compassionate inventor, Holt an insufferable heir, Oscar-nominated Moorehead his spinster aunt. Director Welles wrote the screenplay from Booth Tarkington's novel. Laserdisk version contains additional information about the uneven ending (which was reshot by the studio).
Dist.: Turner

MAGNIFICENT OBSESSION 1954
★★★★ **NR Drama 1:48**
Dir: Douglas Sirk *Cast:* Jane Wyman, Rock Hudson, Barbara Rush, Otto Kruger, Agnes Moorehead
▶ Playboy Hudson is responsible for blinding Wyman in an accident. He changes his lifestyle, becomes a doctor, and gets a chance to help the woman he injured. They fall in love although she is unaware of her benefactor's true identity. Soap opera love story acted with conviction and emotion by the leads.
Dist.: MCA

MAGNIFICENT SEVEN, THE 1960
★★★★ **NR Western 2:06**
Dir: John Sturges *Cast:* Yul Brynner, Eli Wallach, Steve McQueen, Charles Bronson, Robert Vaughn, James Coburn, Horst Buchholz, Brad Dexter
▶ Americanized version of Japanese classic *The Seven Samurai* depicts Mexican village terrorized by outlaw Wallach and his band of cutthroats. Townsfolk hire tough hombre Brynner and six other mercenaries, including McQueen, Bronson, Vaughn, and Coburn, to fight for them. Rousing and perpetually popular Western carried by fine performances from cast of relative unknowns who later became stars. Elmer Bernstein score so enthralled audiences it became the signature tune of Marlboro cigarettes. Three sequels followed.
Dist.: MGM/UA

MAGNUM FORCE 1973
★★★★★ **R Action-Adventure 2:02**
☑ Nudity, explicit language, violence
Dir: Ted Post *Cast:* Clint Eastwood, Hal Holbrook, Felton Perry, Mitchell Ryan, David Soul, Tim Matheson
▶ Brutal sequel to *Dirty Harry*: rogue cops form an execution squad to rid San Francisco of its crime leaders. Detective Harry Callahan (Eastwood) is the one man who can stop them, because "shooting is all right, as long as the right people get shot." Fast, violent, and more popular than the original, with a thrilling car chase and an unnerving bomb sequence. Followed by *The Enforcer*.
Dist.: Warner

MAHLER 1974 British
★ **PG Biography/Music 1:55**
☑ Adult situations, adult humor
Dir: Ken Russell *Cast:* Robert Powell, Georgina Hale, Richard Morant, Lee Montague, Rosalie Crutchley
▶ Biography of composer Gustav Mahler (Powell) traces his troubled relationship with wife Hale, religious problems, and tortured inner life. Nice photography and classical music, but overwrought imagery and odd mixture of fact and fantasy à la Ken Russell are for very specialized tastes only.
Dist.: HBO

MAHOGANY 1975
★★★★ **PG Drama 1:48 B&W**
☑ Adult situations
Dir: Berry Gordy *Cast:* Diana Ross, Billy Dee Williams, Anthony Perkins, Jean-Pierre Aumont, Nina Foch
▶ Gay photographer Perkins turns Ross, a poor Chicago girl, into the internationally famous model Mahogany. Rich Frenchman Aumont helps develop her wildly successful clothing designs, but Mahogany realizes she can only be happy with struggling politician Williams. Glossy soap opera with an emphasis on fashion. Oscar-nominated theme, "Do You

Know Where You're Going To," became a pop hit for Ross.
Dist.: Paramount

MAIDS, THE 1975 British
☆ PG Drama 1:35
☑ Brief nudity, explicit language
Dir: Christopher Miles   *Cast:* Glenda Jackson, Susannah York, Vivien Merchant, Mark Burns
▶ While their master Merchant's away, Parisian maid sisters Jackson and York engage in role-playing games in which one pretends to be Merchant, and plot against their employer. Jean Genet play is stylishly brought to screen by Miles with wondrous acting by the three principals. However, claustrophobic feel and illusion/reality theme make this heavy going.
Dist.: CBS/Fox

MAID'S NIGHT OUT 1938
★ NR Comedy 1:04 B&W
Dir: Ben Holmes   *Cast:* Joan Fontaine, Allan Lane, Hedda Hopper, George Irving, William Brisbane, Billy Gilbert
▶ Wealthy Fontaine falls in love with milkman Lane, who thinks she is only the maid in her big house. She in turn doesn't know that Lane is really a millionaire temporarily delivering dairy to win a bet. Fontaine's mother Hopper (the real-life gossip columnist) doesn't approve, until the wacky finale. Light, happy fun.
Dist.: Turner

MAID TO ORDER 1987
★ ★ ★ PG Comedy 1:36
☑ Brief nudity, explicit language
Dir: Amy Jones   *Cast:* Ally Sheedy, Beverly D'Angelo, Michael Ontkean, Valerie Perrine, Tom Skerritt, Dick Shawn
▶ Fairy tale reversal for pouty brat packer Sheedy who's transformed from bored Beverly Hills heiress to maid by flaky fairy godmother D'Angelo. Household chores and a romance with the chauffeur humanize Sheedy, educating her about what's really important in life. Riches-to-rags tale spun with simplicity and enthusiasm. Comic turns by Perrine and Shawn as Sheedy's wealthy, snobby employers who hoard tin foil.
Dist.: IVE

MAIN EVENT, THE 1979
★ ★ ★ ★ PG Comedy 1:49
☑ Adult situations, explicit language
Dir: Howard Zieff   *Cast:* Barbra Streisand, Ryan O'Neal, Paul Sand, Patti D'Arbanville, Whitman Mayo
▶ After her business manager flees with all her money, bankrupt perfume company owner Streisand has only one asset left: O'Neal, a boxer she once acquired as a tax write-off. She nags him back into the ring; they fall in love. Attempts to recapture the chemistry the leads displayed in *What's Up Doc?*
Dist.: Warner

MAJOR BARBARA 1941 British
★ ★ NR Comedy 2:16 B&W
Dir: Gabriel Pascal   *Cast:* Wendy Hiller, Rex Harrison, Robert Morley, Robert Newton, Emlyn Williams, Deborah Kerr, Sybil Thorndike
▶ Hiller, a Salvation Army Major, clashes with her surprisingly benevolent munitions mogul father Morley. Her admirer Harrison is caught in between the two. Cynically amusing film version of the George Bernard Shaw play features Kerr in her film debut.
Dist.: Janus

MAJOR DUNDEE 1965
★ NR Western 2:04
Dir: Sam Peckinpah   *Cast:* Charlton Heston, Richard Harris, Jim Hutton, James Coburn, Senta Berger, Warren Oates, Slim Pickens, Ben Johnson
▶ Apaches attack a Southwestern jail; Union Army warden Heston assembles his prisoners—including Confederate captain Harris, who's been sentenced to death—to chase the Indians into Mexico. Good cast and violent action.
Dist.: RCA/Columbia

MAJOR LEAGUE 1989
★ ★ ★ ★ ★ R Comedy 1:47
☑ Adult situations, explicit language
Dir: David S. Ward   *Cast:* Tom Berenger, Charlie Sheen, Corbin Bernsen, Margaret Whitton, James Gammon, Rene Russo, Wesley Snipes, Bob Uecker
▶ Owner Whitton has Cleveland Indians stocked with the worst players that can be found so baseball team will lose big, allowing her to move it to Florida. However, catcher Berenger and manager Gammon have different ideas and rally the ragtag bunch to victory. Uproarious on- and off-field shenanigans with cleverly staged game scenes. There's even a romantic subplot of Berenger pursuing ex-girlfriend Russo. Standouts are Sheen as the punk-haired ex-con flamethrower with control problems and Snipes as fleet-footed Willie Mays Hayes. (CC)
Dist.: Paramount

MAKE ME AN OFFER 1955 British
★ ★ NR Comedy 1:22
Dir: Cyril Frankel   *Cast:* Peter Finch, Adrienne Corri, Rosalie Crutchley, Finlay Currie, Meier Tzelniker, Alfie Bass
▶ While competing with rivals Currie and Tzelniker, antiques dealer Finch tries to raise money to buy a valuable Wedgewood vase that has turned up in the attic of a non-expert. Set in a rarified milieu, auction-house comedy offers some sophisticated laughs.
Dist.: Nelson

MAKE MINE MINK 1960 British
★ NR Comedy 1:40 B&W
Dir: Robert Asher   *Cast:* Terry-Thomas, Athene Seyler, Hattie Jacques, Billie Whitelaw, Elspeth Duxbury, Caroline Leigh

▶ Society doyenne Seyler lights on the idea of using stolen fur coats to raise funds for charity. Sputtering ex-military officer Terry-Thomas is enlisted as part of a gang that embarks on a hilarious career of amateur crime. Wonderful caper comedy.
Dist.: Vestron

MAKING CONTACT 1986
★★★ PG Fantasy 1:19
☑ Explicit language
Dir: Roland Emmerich *Cast:* Joshua Morrell, Eva Kryll, Jan Zierold, Tammy Shields
▶ Nine-year-old Morrell, mourning the death of his father, finds a mysterious dummy with magical but deadly powers. Some impressive special effects but the ending is pretty weird. Too intense for younger kids, okay for the older ones.
Dist.: New World

MAKING LOVE 1982
★★ R Drama 1:51
☑ Adult situations, strong sexual content, explicit language
Dir: Arthur Hiller *Cast:* Michael Ontkean, Kate Jackson, Harry Hamlin, Wendy Hiller, Arthur Hill
▶ Doctor Ontkean, seemingly happily married to TV executive Jackson, discovers that he has a preference for men, particularly Hamlin. His marriage falls apart when Jackson learns the truth. Attractive cast in a compassionate (if sanitized) look at once-taboo subject matter.
Dist.: CBS/Fox

MAKING MR. RIGHT 1987
★★ PG-13 Comedy 1:38
☑ Adult situations, explicit language
Dir: Susan Seidelman *Cast:* John Malkovich, Ann Magnuson, Ben Masters, Glenne Headly, Laurie Metcalf, Polly Bergen
▶ Miami PR exec Magnuson despairs of finding Mr. Right until she is hired to publicize naive android Malkovich, made by grouchy scientist (Malkovich again) in his own image. Magnuson teaches the robot social graces and falls for him. Kooky comedy with inventive visuals and production design, delightful Magnuson, and Malkovich having fun with his dual role. However, pacing and too many of the bits fall flat.
Dist.: HBO

MAKING THE GRADE 1984
★★ R Comedy 1:45
☑ Nudity, adult situations, explicit language
Dir: Dorian Walker *Cast:* Judd Nelson, Jonna Lee, Carey Scott, Dana Olsen, Gordon Jump, Walter Olkewicz
▶ Obnoxious young millionaire Olsen hires street-smart punk Nelson to impersonate him at prep school while he bops across Europe. Nelson turns the snooty academy upside down in this predictable genre effort.
Dist.: MGM/UA

MALAREK 1988 Canadian
★★★ R Drama 1:45
☑ Brief nudity, adult situations, explicit language, violence
Dir: Roger Cardinal *Cast:* Elias Koteas, Kerrie Keane, Al Waxman, Kahil Karn, Michael Sarrazin
▶ Long-haired mailroom boy Koteas convinces newspaper boss Keane to give him a shot as a cub reporter. On the job, the former street kid witnesses a police shooting that leads him to uncover brutality at a juvenile detention center. Gritty urban crime melodrama has a lot going for it, especially Koteas, who plays the rough-edged hero with the talent and intensity of a young De Niro. Based on a true story.
Dist.: SVS

MALCOLM 1986 Australian
★★ PG-13 Comedy 1:30
☑ Adult situations, explicit language, mild violence
Dir: Nadia Tass *Cast:* Colin Friels, John Hargreaves, Lindy Davies, Chris Haywood, Charles Tingwell
▶ Slow-witted Friels is a mechanical genius who loses his job and takes in ex-con Hargreaves and his girlfriend Davies as roommates to improve his finances. The trio form a close relationship and plot a heist together. Some charm and wit but gets off to a slow start.
Dist.: Vestron

MALIBU BIKINI SHOP, THE 1987
★★ R Comedy 1:38
☑ Nudity, adult situations
Dir: David Wechter *Cast:* Michael David Wright, Bruce Greenwood, Barbara Horan, Debra Blee, Jay Robinson
▶ Stuffy yuppie Wright and his ne'er-do-well brother Greenwood inherit bikini store from their aunt. Wright loosens up under the influence of would-be designer Horan and then battles a guru for possession of the place. Inconsequential comedy features miles of tan lines. **(CC)**
Dist.: CBS/Fox

MALIBU EXPRESS 1985
★ R Mystery-Suspense 1:41
☑ Nudity, strong sexual content, violence
Dir: Andy Sidaris *Cast:* Darby Hinton, Sybil Danning, Barbara Edwards, Brett Clark, Kimberly McArthur, Lorraine Michaels
▶ Mysterious Contessa Danning hires slow-talking Texas private eye Hinton to investigate sale of computer secrets to the Russians. Hayseed dialogue, wooden acting, and nonstop nudity featuring four *Playboy* Playmates (including Playmate of the Year Edwards) as well as some beefcake for the ladies.
Dist.: MCA

MALICIOUS 1974 Italian
☆ R Comedy 1:38
☑ Nudity, strong sexual content

Dir: Salvatore Samperi *Cast:* Laura Antonelli, Turi Ferro, Alessandro Momo, Tina Aumont, Angela Luce, Gianluigi Chrizzi
▶ When housekeeper Antonelli joins the household of recent widower Ferro and his three sons, all four males pursue her. Fourteen-year-old Momo blackmails and manipulates her into fulfilling his fantasies. Combination of comedy, social comment, and eroticism benefits greatly from Antonelli's loveliness and Vittorio Storaro's luscious cinematography. Dubbed.
Dist.: Paramount

MALONE 1987
★★★ R Action-Adventure 1:32
☑ Explicit language, violence
Dir: Harley Cokliss *Cast:* Burt Reynolds, Cliff Robertson, Lauren Hutton, Kenneth McMillan, Scott Wilson, Cynthia Gibb
▶ In a remote mountain town, burnt-out CIA assassin Reynolds befriends gas station owner Wilson and his daughter Gibb. He protects them against Robertson, a fascist trying to take over the burg. Standard Reynolds vehicle has pleasant scenery and pert Gibb but is hampered by his overly solemn acting and the slow pacing.
Dist.: Orion

MALOU 1983 German
☆ R Drama 1:35
☑ Nudity, adult situations
Dir: Jeanine Meerapfel *Cast:* Ingrid Caven, Grischa Huber, Helmut Griem, Ivan Desny, Marie Colbin
▶ Huber, wife of architect Griem, examines her mother Caven's past to learn something about her own problems. In flashbacks, Caven marries a Jew, is forced to flee Germany during World War II, and finally becomes an impoverished alcoholic. Handsome production builds little momentum but might reward those with a taste for soap opera. [S]
Dist.: Nelson

MALTA STORY, THE 1954 British
★ NR War 1:38
Dir: Brian Desmond Hurst *Cast:* Alec Guinness, Jack Hawkins, Anthony Steel, Muriel Pavlow
▶ Reconnaissance photographer Guinness is shot down over Malta during World War II. While the island is besieged by Nazis, Guinness gets involved with local girl Pavlow, whose brother is conniving with the enemy. Real-life action footage, including some captured from the Germans, sets the grim tone for this action-packed feature. Ably illuminates a hard-fought episode in the war.
Dist.: Nelson

MALTESE FALCON, THE 1941
★★★★★ NR Mystery-Suspense 1:40
B&W
Dir: John Huston *Cast:* Humphrey Bogart, Mary Astor, Peter Lorre, Sydney Greenstreet, Lee Patrick, Elisha Cook, Jr., Ward Bond, Gladys George, Barton MacLane
▶ Detective Sam Spade is hired by an enigmatic Astor to find a valuable antique, but she doesn't tell him that a gang of swindlers is also after the bird. Irresistible mystery based on Dashiell Hammett's novel set a high standard for private eye films. Bogart excels in his first major role as the hard-boiled Spade; outstanding support from Lorre as an effeminate con man, Greenstreet (in his film debut) as the notorious fat man, and Cook, a jittery gunman. Directing debut for Huston (whose father Walter appears in a cameo). (CC)
Dist.: MGM/UA [C]

MAMA, THERE'S A MAN IN YOUR BED
1990 French
★ NR Comedy 1:48
☑ Nudity, adult situations
Dir: Coline Serreau *Cast:* Daniel Auteuil, Firmine Richard, Pierre Vernier, Maxime Leroux, Gilles Privat
▶ Fluffy fairy tale of interracial romance between businessman Auteuil and Richard, his long-time office cleaning lady. Relationship begins when Richard reveals to Autueil that she has discovered a business conspiracy against him, and intensifies after Auteuil hides from the police in her apartment. Richard makes her character thoroughly believable, but little else bears close scrutiny in this mildly entertaining story. [S]

MAME 1974
★★ PG Musical 2:13
☑ Adult situations, explicit language
Dir: Gene Saks *Cast:* Lucille Ball, Robert Preston, Beatrice Arthur, Jane Connell, Bruce Davison, Joyce Van Patten
▶ Ball, at sixty-two and no great singer, was miscast as the eccentric Auntie Mame in this musical version of the durable Patrick Dennis novel. Arthur is her best friend, Van Patten plays Gooch, and Preston is Mame's Southern love interest. Funniest scene: Ball, pretending to ride in the fox hunt, passes the master of the hounds, then the hounds, then the fox. Score includes "We Need a Little Christmas" and "If He Walked Into My Life."
Dist.: Warner

MAMMA DRACULA 1980 Belgian/French
☆ NR Comedy 1:30
☑ Nudity, explicit language
Dir: Boris Szulzinger *Cast:* Louise Fletcher, Maria Schneider, Marc-Henri Wajnberg, Alexander Wajnberg, Jess Hahn, Jimmy Shuman
▶ Schneider is a police officer investigating Fletcher, a modern day countess who must bathe daily in the blood of virgins to retain her eternal youth. Joke is that these days, virgins are hard to come by. A stiff.
Dist.: TWE

MAN ALONE, A 1955
★★ NR Western 1:36

Dir: Ray Milland   *Cast:* Ray Milland, Mary Murphy, Ward Bond, Raymond Burr, Arthur Space, Lee Van Cleef
► Wrongly accused of six murders, fugitive Milland hides out with sheriff Bond's daughter Murphy, who is quarantined because of her father's illness. They fall in love as a lynch mob hones in on the wanted man. Milland's directoral debut is well-crafted and entertaining although familiar.
Dist.: Republic

MAN AND A WOMAN, A 1966 French
★ ★ ★ **NR Romance 1:43**
Dir: Claude Lelouch   *Cast:* Anouk Aimee, Jean-Louis Trintignant, Pierre Barouh, Valerie Lagrange
► Two widowed people, script girl Aimee and race-car driver Trintignant, embark on a love affair haunted by memories of the tragic past. Lyrical contemporary classic won two Oscars (Best Foreign Film, Screenplay) and is one of the most popular French films ever in America. Outstanding musical score by Frances Lai. Followed by a sequel twenty years later. (CC) [S]
Dist.: Warner

MAN AND A WOMAN: 20 YEARS LATER, A
1986 French
★ **PG Romance 1:52**
[v] Adult situations, mild violence
Dir: Claude Lelouch   *Cast:* Anouk Aimee, Jean-Louis Trintignant, Evelyne Bouix, Marie-Sophie Pochat
► Film producer Aimee, making a movie about her old love Trintignant, realizes she still loves him. She switches to another topic for her movie and uncovers a murderer. Self-indulgent and convoluted, although film buffs may admire Lelouch's intricate editing. Great music from the original is used again. [S]
Dist.: Warner

MAN AND BOY 1971
★ ★ **G Western 1:38**
Dir: E. W. Swackhamer   *Cast:* Bill Cosby, Gloria Foster, George Spell, Leif Erickson, Douglas Turner Ward, Yaphet Kotto
► Homesteader Cosby returns from the Civil War to discover his horses have been stolen. Accompanied by son Spell and burly sidekick Kotto, he sets out on an odyssey across the Southwest to recover them. Earnest family-oriented adventure with Cosby in an unusual noncomic performance.
Dist.: RCA/Columbia

MAN, A WOMAN AND A BANK, A 1979
Canadian
★ ★ ★ **PG Comedy 1:42**
[v] Adult situations, explicit language
Dir: Noel Black   *Cast:* Donald Sutherland, Brooke Adams, Paul Mazursky, Allen Magicovsky, Nick Rice
► Standard caper movie with an off-beat love story. Electronic masterminds Mazursky

and Sutherland break the code of a bank's computer, but while stealing the building's blueprints, they get photographed by Adams. Trying to recover the pictures, Sutherland falls in love with her. Originally titled *A Very Big Withdrawal.*
Dist.: Charter

MAN CALLED ADAM, A 1966
★ **NR Drama 1:42 B&W**
Dir: Leo Penn   *Cast:* Sammy Davis, Jr., Ossie Davis, Cicely Tyson, Louis Armstrong, Frank Sinatra, Jr., Mel Tormé
► Jazz trumpeter Davis is wracked with guilt over the death of his family in a traffic accident. During a tour of the South, he endures racial prejudice and management indifference while falling for civil rights worker Tyson. Except for a brief, upbeat song from the ever-ebullient Tormé, drama is depressing and impenetrable.
Dist.: Nelson

MAN CALLED FLINTSTONE, THE 1966
★ ★ ★ **NR Animation 1:27**
Dir: Joseph Barbera, William Hanna   *Cast:* Voices of Alan Reed, Mel Blanc, Jean Vander Pyl, June Foray
► Full-length feature starring the characters from television's first prime-time animated series. Spy spoof has Fred Flintstone mistaken for a well-known secret agent, causing problems when he, wife Wilma and friends Barney and Betty Rubble travel to Paris. Stilted animation style barely holds viewer interest. Songs include "Pensate Amore," sung by Louis Prima.
Dist.: Hanna Barbera

MAN CALLED HORSE, A 1970
★ ★ ★ ★ ★ **PG Western 1:49**
[v] Graphic violence
Dir: Elliot Silverstein   *Cast:* Richard Harris, Judith Anderson, Jean Gascon, Manu Tupou, Corinna Tsopei
► While hunting in the Dakota Territory in the early 1800s, English aristocrat Harris is captured by Sioux Indians. He endures torturous rituals (shown in horrifying detail) and proves his manhood. Eventually, he becomes the tribe's great white chief and marries Indian princess Tsopei. Features authentic Sioux rituals and language. Sequels: *Return of a Man Called Horse* and *Triumphs of a Man Called Horse.* (CC)
Dist.: CBS/Fox

MAN CALLED PETER, A 1955
★ ★ ★ ★ **NR Biography 1:57**
Dir: Henry Koster   *Cast:* Richard Todd, Jean Peters, Marjorie Rambeau, Jill Esmond, Les Tremayne, Robert Burton
► True story of Scottish clergyman Peter Marshall (Todd), who moves to the United States, wins a following through the wisdom and power of his sermons, and eventually becomes Church of Presidents pastor over the objections of conservative members of his congregation. Peters is Marshall's understand-

ing wife in this intelligent and inspirational biography. Excellent performance by Todd.
Dist.: CBS/Fox

MANCHURIAN AVENGER 1985
☆ **R Western 1:21**
☑ Explicit language, violence
Dir: Ed Warnick   *Cast:* Bobby Kim, Bill Wallace, Michael Stuart, Leila Hee, Jose Payo
▶ Oriental cowboy Kim returns to his Wild West hometown and discovers his father has been killed. He battles a gang of evildoers; although outnumbered, Kim's kung fu feet are faster than their six-shooters. Low-budget effort has plenty of action but amateurish acting.
Dist.: HBO

MANCHURIAN CANDIDATE, THE 1962
★ ★ ★ ★ **NR Mystery-Suspense 2:06 B&W**
Dir: John Frankenheimer   *Cast:* Frank Sinatra, Laurence Harvey, Janet Leigh, Angela Lansbury, James Gregory, Henry Silva
▶ Korean War vet Harvey returns to the U.S. as a hero. No one save his nightmare-plagued pal Sinatra suspects that Harvey is actually a killing machine brainwashed by his Communist captors. Audacious thriller works on many levels: crackerjack suspense, political satire, social comment, and even prophecy. Intricate direction by Frankenheimer and wonderful acting all around; Harvey is quite poignant and Lansbury does an Oscar-nominated turn as his monstrous mom. Not to be missed. Video version includes interviews with Sinatra and Frankenheimer. **(CC)**
Dist.: MGM/UA

MANDELA 1987
★ ★ ★ ★ **NR Biography/MFTV 2:15**
Dir: Philip Saville   *Cast:* Danny Glover, Alfre Woodard, John Indi, John Matshikiza, Nathan Dambusa Mdledle
▶ True story of Nelson Mandela (Glover), black South African lawyer whose stand against apartheid awakened the world's conscience. Film traces his involvement with the African National Congress, treason trial, decision to support armed resistance, imprisonment since the 1960s, and the dedication of his wife Winnie (Woodard). Inspiring drama with outstanding performances by Glover and Woodard.
Dist.: HBO

MANDINGO 1975
★ ★ ★ **R Drama 2:07**
☑ Nudity, adult situations, explicit language, violence
Dir: Richard Fleischer   *Cast:* James Mason, Susan George, Perry King, Richard Ward, Ken Norton, Brenda Sykes
▶ Lurid adaptation of Kyle Onstott's bestseller about a Southern plantation ruled with an iron hand by Mason. Heir King ignores wife George for an affair with slave Sykes, at the same time exploiting her husband (heavy-weight boxer Norton, in his film debut) in brutal match fights. Norton reprised his role in the sequel *Drum*.
Dist.: Paramount

MAN FACING SOUTHEAST 1987 Argentinian
☆ **R Drama 1:48**
☑ Nudity, adult situations
Dir: Eliseo Subiela   *Cast:* Lorenzo Quinteros, Hugo Soto, Inés Vernengo, Rubens W. Correa, David Edery
▶ At a Buenos Aires mental hospital, no one seems to know where brilliant new patient Soto came from. He claims to be from outer space; psychiatrist Quinteros begins to believe him. Although intelligent and provocative, excessively verbose and somber. For the arthouse crowd only.   Ⓢ
Dist.: New World

MAN FOR ALL SEASONS, A 1966
★ ★ ★ ★ ★ **G Drama 2:00**
Dir: Fred Zinnemann   *Cast:* Paul Scofield, Robert Shaw, Wendy Hiller, Susannah York, Leo McKern, Orson Welles
▶ Refusing to endorse the divorce of King Henry VIII (Shaw), Chancellor of England Thomas More (Scofield) pays the price in martyrdom. Asked to conform for the sake of "fellowship," More refuses. Towering, superbly mounted film version of the Robert Bolt play, which he adapted. Scofield's justifiably acclaimed and immensely moving portrait leads a great cast. Oscars for Best Picture, Director, Actor (Scofield), Screenplay, Costumes, and Cinematography. **(CC)**
Dist.: RCA/Columbia

MAN FRIDAY 1975 British
★ ★ ★ **PG Drama 1:55**
☑ Explicit language, brief nudity
Dir: Jack Gold   *Cast:* Peter O'Toole, Richard Roundtree, Peter Cellier, Christopher Cabot, Sam Seabrook, Stanley Clay
▶ Variation on Daniel Defoe's *Robinson Crusoe* emphasizes the racial conflicts between marooned sailor O'Toole and black native Roundtree, a fugitive who washes up on the island. In this version, O'Toole establishes a master-slave relationship which the wily Roundtree manages to reverse. Offbeat and extremely talky.
Dist.: CBS/Fox

MAN FROM COLORADO, THE 1948
★ ★ ★ ★ ★ **NR Western 1:39**
Dir: Henry Levin   *Cast:* Glenn Ford, William Holden, Ellen Drew, Ray Collins, Edgar Buchanan, Jerome Courtland
▶ Mentally scarred by the Civil War, Ford becomes increasingly unstable and bloodthirsty after he is appointed judge of a small Colorado town. Best friend Holden, now the town's marshal, is torn between obeying Ford's commands and checking his sadism. Well-mounted psychological Western from a story by Borden Chase.
Dist.: RCA/Columbia

MAN FROM LARAMIE, THE 1955
★ ★ ★ ★ NR Western 1:44
Dir: Anthony Mann *Cast:* James Stewart, Arthur Kennedy, Donald Crisp, Cathy O'-Donnell, Alex Nicol
▶ Mysterious stranger Stewart seeks the identity of the man who sold rifles to the Apaches and was thus responsible for his brother's death. The trail leads him to powerful rancher Crisp, his evil son Nicol, and his foreman Kennedy. Taut and suspenseful psychological Western with scenes of shocking violence.
Dist.: RCA/Columbia

MAN FROM SNOWY RIVER, THE 1982
Australian
★ ★ ★ ★ PG Action-Adventure 1:44
☑ Explicit language, mild violence
Dir: George Miller *Cast:* Kirk Douglas, Jack Thompson, Tom Burlinson, Sigrid Thornton, Lorraine Bayly, Chris Haywood
▶ After his father's death, young Burlinson gets a job with wealthy rancher Douglas, who objects when his daughter Thornton falls for him. Burlinson proves himself by rescuing a missing prized colt. Sweeping adventure with gorgeous cinematography, incredible landscapes, exciting horse stampedes, and stirring music. Douglas has fun in a dual role as the rancher and his brother.
Dist.: CBS/Fox

MAN FROM THE ALAMO, THE 1953
★ ★ ★ NR Western 1:19
Dir: Budd Boetticher *Cast:* Glenn Ford, Julia Adams, Victor Jory, Hugh O'Brian, Chill Wills, Jeanne Cooper
▶ Chosen by lot to escape from the Alamo and warn its defenders' dependants, Ford leaves the doomed fortress to discover that the families, including his own, have been slaughtered. Though branded a coward, Ford devotes himself to tracking down the killers. Unusual Western, with a fine story and snappy pace.
Dist.: KVC

MANGO TREE, THE 1982 Australia
★ NR Drama 1:33
☑ Adult situations, explicit language
Dir: Kevin Dobson *Cast:* Geraldine Fitzgerald, Christopher Pate, Robert Helpmann, Diane Craig, Gerald Kennedy
▶ In pre-World War I Australia, young Pate reflects on past incidents, including an affair with his French teacher and the death of a loved one, before he leaves his hometown. Sensitive coming-of-age story is unevenly acted: Fitzgerald outshines the uncharismatic Pate.
Dist.: VidAmerica

MANHATTAN 1979
★ ★ R Comedy 1:36 B&W
☑ Adult situations, explicit language, adult humor
Dir: Woody Allen *Cast:* Woody Allen, Diane Keaton, Michael Murphy, Mariel Hemingway, Anne Byrne, Meryl Streep
▶ TV writer Allen has his share of romantic problems: wife Streep left him for another woman, his affair with teenager Hemingway makes him uncomfortable, and his pursuit of flighty Keaton is complicated by her love for his married best pal Murphy. Sophisticated ode to New York City with superb black-and-white photography and Gershwin score. Great moment: Woody, having been told by Keaton about her gorgeously attractive ex-boyfriend, runs into the guy and discovers he's shrimpy Wallace Shawn.
Dist.: MGM/UA

MANHATTAN PROJECT, THE 1986
★ ★ ★ ★ PG-13 Drama 1:58
☑ Explicit language
Dir: Marshall Brickman *Cast:* John Lithgow, Christopher Collet, Jill Eikenberry, Cynthia Nixon, John Mahoney
▶ In Ithaca, amateur high school physicist Collet suspects that new government scientist Lithgow is making nuclear warheads. Collet steals a bottle of plutonium and constructs an atom bomb to show how dangerous Lithgow's facility is. Topical thriller has a professional performance from Lithgow and pleasant comic touches. (CC)
Dist.: HBO

MANHUNT, THE 1986 Italian
★ NR Western 1:30
☑ Explicit language, violence
Dir: Larry Ludman *Cast:* Ernest Borgnine, John Ethan Wayne, Bo Svenson, Henry Silva, Henry Harmstorf
▶ Modern-day Western features son of film legend John Wayne as a would-be horse trainer wrongfully accused of stealing and imprisoned in a sadistic Arizona jail. Borgnine is sufficiently sinister as the wealthy rancher intent on keeping Wayne in the slammer.
Dist.: Media

MANHUNTER 1986
★ ★ ★ ★ R Action-Adventure 1:58
☑ Violence
Dir: Michael Mann *Cast:* William L. Petersen, Kim Greist, Dennis Farina, Brian Cox, Joan Allen, Tom Noonan
▶ Gripping, nerve-wracking thriller about psychopathic killer Noonan who murders entire families. He's pursued by ex–FBI forensic specialist Petersen. Cox is splendidly creepy as a mad psychiatrist in contact with the killer. Based on Thomas Harris's novel *Red Dragon*. (CC)
Dist.: Warner

MANIAC 1934
☆ NR Horror 1:07 B&W
Dir: Dwain Esper *Cast:* Bill Woods, Horace Carpenter, Ted Edwards, Phyllis Diller, Thea Ramsey, Jennie Dark
▶ Mad scientist Carpenter is working on a project to revive the dead when he is killed by

assistant Woods, who takes on his master's identity. Craziness multiplies with duel of syringes between battling beauties, a rapist who thinks he's an ape out of a Poe story, and distasteful acts galore. A camp classic to some, this antique sleazefest will surprise those accustomed to wholesome Hollywood product of this era.
Dist.: Video Yesteryear

MANIAC 1962 British
★ NR Mystery-Suspense 1:26 B&W
Dir: Michael Carreras *Cast:* Kerwin Mathews, Nadia Gray, Donald Houston, Justine Lord, Liliane Brousse, George Pastelle
▶ While traveling in France, American artist Mathews takes a shine to Gray, whose mother Brousse wants him to help plan husband Houston's escape from a mental asylum. But as Mathews discovers, there is more to the plot than meets the eye. Fairly good; topped off with a nice twist.
Dist.: RCA/Columbia

MANIAC 1977
☆ PG Mystery-Suspense 1:27
Ⓥ Explicit language, violence
Dir: Richard Compton *Cast:* Oliver Reed, Deborah Raffin, Stuart Whitman, Jim Mitchum, Paul Koslo
▶ Maniac Koslo, dressed as a war-painted Indian, terrorizes the wealthy Arizona town of Paradise. After murdering several people with a bow and arrow, he demands a $5 million ransom. Stone-faced Reed does his best to track down the killer. Sturdy suspense.
Dist.: Nelson

MANIAC COP 1988
★ ★ ★ R Horror 1:32
Ⓥ Nudity, adult situations, explicit language, graphic violence
Dir: William Lustig *Cast:* Tom Atkins, Bruce Campbell, Laurene Landon, Richard Roundtree, Sheree North
▶ Monstrously strong killer cop—who may or may not be human—stalks the streets of New York. No-nonsense lieutenant Atkins investigates the case; North has an unusual part as the maniac's crippled girlfriend. Gory chiller with strained attempts at black humor.
Dist.: TWE

MAN IN GREY, THE 1943 British
★ NR Drama 1:56 B&W
Dir: Leslie Arliss *Cast:* Margaret Lockwood, James Mason, Phyllis Calvert, Stewart Granger, Helen Haye, Martita Hunt
▶ Calvert, the kindly wife of wealthy Mason, helps impoverished school chum Lockwood by hiring her as a nurse. Vixenish Lockwood proceeds to steal Mason and attempts to push Calvert together with good-looking newcomer Granger. No good deed goes unpunished in this enjoyable Regency soap opera, whose success made Mason a star.
Dist.: Vestron

MAN IN LOVE, A 1987 French/Italian
★ R Romance 1:48
Ⓥ Nudity, adult situations, explicit language
Dir: Diane Kurys *Cast:* Peter Coyote, Greta Scacchi, Peter Riegert, Jamie Lee Curtis, Claudia Cardinale, John Berry
▶ In Rome to make a movie, American leading man Coyote falls in love with leading lady Scacchi. Jeopardizing the affair: her dying mother Cardinale and his wife Curtis. Lush production with steamy love scenes marred by a banal soap opera plot.
Dist.: Nelson

MAN IN THE GLASS BOOTH, THE 1975
★ ★ PG Drama 1:57
Ⓥ Adult situations, explicit language
Dir: Arthur Hiller *Cast:* Maximilian Schell, Lois Nettleton, Luther Adler, Lawrence Pressman, Henry Brown
▶ Schell, a wealthy Jew living in New York, is kidnapped by Israeli agents and put on trial as a Nazi war criminal, an identity he readily embraces. But is he really the notorious Adolf Karl Dorff? Initially engrossing adaptation of Robert Shaw's play receives a fiery, Oscar-nominated performance from Schell but gets increasingly muddled and confused in the second half. Most riveting moment: Schell's "Am I Jewish?" speech.
Dist.: CBS/Fox

MAN IN THE IRON MASK, THE 1939
★ ★ NR Action-Adventure 1:50 B&W
Dir: James Whale *Cast:* Louis Hayward, Joan Bennett, Warren William, Joseph Schildkraut, Alan Hale, Albert Dekker
▶ Fearing an overthrow, cruel King Louis XIV of France encases his good twin brother in an iron mask and throws him in the Bastille. The Three Musketeers rescue Hayward as the monarch attempts to wed an unwilling Bennett. Hayward is outstanding, playing both brothers in this exciting adaptation of the Alexandre Dumas classic.
Dist.: Video Treasures Ⓒ

MAN IN THE WHITE SUIT, THE 1952 British
★ ★ NR Comedy 1:25 B&W
Dir: Alexander Mackendrick *Cast:* Alec Guinness, Joan Greenwood, Cecil Parker, Michael Gough, Ernest Thesiger
▶ Shy chemist Guinness develops a wondrous white fabric that never gets dirty or wears out. Its acceptance by consumers poses a serious threat to both labor and management and they plot to thwart him. Marvelous satire boasts one of Sir Alec's best performances.
Dist.: HBO

MANITOU, THE 1978
★ ★ ★ PG Horror 1:43
Ⓥ Brief nudity, graphic violence
Dir: William Girdler *Cast:* Tony Curtis, Susan Strasberg, Stella Stevens, Michael Ansara, Ann Sothern, Burgess Meredith
▶ Con man Curtis is shocked when a lump on his girlfriend Strasberg's back turns into the

fetus of a 400-year-old evil medicine man. Indian variation on *The Exorcist* has an improbable script that the cast plays tongue-in-cheek. Good special effects brighten last effort from director Girdler, who was killed in a helicopter crash before film's release.
Dist.: Nelson

MANNEQUIN 1987
★ ★ ★ ★ **PG Comedy 1:30**
☑ Explicit language
Dir: Michael Gottlieb   *Cast:* Andrew McCarthy, Kim Cattrall, Estelle Getty, James Spader, Meshach Taylor, Carole Davis
▶ Struggling Philadelphia window dresser McCarthy skyrockets to fame with the help of mannequin Cattrall, actually an Egyptian princess brought to life by a magic spell. Airy fantasy makes good use of Wanamaker's department store setting; Taylor adds some fun as McCarthy's effeminate colleague. Starship's "Nothing's Gonna Stop Us Now" was an Oscar-nominated song. **(CC)**
Dist.: Media

MAN OF FLOWERS, A 1984 Australian
☆ **NR Drama 1:31**
☑ Nudity, adult situations, explicit language
Dir: Paul Cox   *Cast:* Norman Kaye, Alyson Best, Chris Haywood, Sarah Walker, Werner Herzog, Barry Dickens
▶ Repressed middle-aged Kaye befriends art class model Best, who is torn between abusive artist boyfriend Haywood and lesbian lover Walker. Haywood schemes against Kaye but Kaye gets the last laugh. Weird story with characters to match, although Cox's direction makes them surprisingly palatable. Kaye is wonderful but plodding pace may alienate some. Herzog appears in flashbacks as Kaye's mean father.
Dist.: Vestron

MAN OF LA MANCHA 1972
★ ★ ★ **PG Musical 2:09**
☑ Adult situations, explicit language
Dir: Arthur Hiller   *Cast:* Peter O'Toole, Sophia Loren, James Coco, Harry Andrews, John Castle, Brian Blessed
▶ In seventeenth-century Spain, rich nobleman Don Quixote (O'Toole) imagines himself to be a knight and charges at windmills, seeing them as dragons. Everyone thinks he's crazy, but servant Sancho Panza (Coco) sticks by him and even Loren, the hardened prostitute he loves, is moved by his valor. Gallant performance by O'Toole, Loren's beauty, and the unforgettable musical score (including "The Impossible Dream") overcome Hiller's lumbering direction.
Dist.: CBS/Fox

MAN ON FIRE 1987 French/Italian
★ ★ ★ **R Mystery-Suspense 1:33**
☑ Adult situations, explicit language, violence
Dir: Elie Chouraqui   *Cast:* Scott Glenn, Jade Malle, Joe Pesci, Brooke Adams, Jonathan Pryce, Danny Aiello
▶ In Italy, ex-CIA agent Glenn is hired as bodyguard to twelve-year-old Malle; a tender relationship develops. When she is kidnapped by extortionists, he tracks them down to rescue her. Some sweet moments between Glenn and Malle but Chouraqui's flashy, overly busy direction fails to build enough suspense. Based on the novel by A. J. Quinnell.
Dist.: Vestron

MANON OF THE SPRING 1987 French
★ ★ **PG Drama 1:53**
☑ Brief nudity
Dir: Claude Berri   *Cast:* Yves Montand, Daniel Auteuil, Emmanuelle Beart, Hippolyte Girardot, Elisabeth Depardieu
▶ Beautiful shepherd Beart gets revenge on Auteuil and Montand, villains who dammed up her father's spring, leading to his accidental death. Classy continuation of *Jean de Florette*. Perfect acting, tasteful atmosphere and production values, but slow pacing. ⓢ
Dist.: Orion

MAN ON THE EIFFEL TOWER, THE 1949
★ ★ **NR Mystery-Suspense 1:37**
Dir: Burgess Meredith   *Cast:* Charles Laughton, Franchot Tone, Burgess Meredith, Wilfrid Hyde-White, Jean Wallace, Patricia Roc
▶ As Georges Simenon's fictional detective Maigret, Laughton attempts to discover the killer of a wealthy woman in Paris. Despite the apparent guilt of blind knife-grinder Meredith, Laughton persists until he has cornered the real killer. Dark, moody thriller with nice Paris locales. Directing debut for Meredith.
Dist.: Cable

MAN OUTSIDE 1986
★ **PG-13 Drama 1:49**
☑ Explicit language, violence
Dir: Mark Stouffer   *Cast:* Kathleen Quinlan, Robert Logan, Bradford Dillman, Levon Helm
▶ Attorney Logan, a recluse since his wife's death, teams with teacher Quinlan to prove his innocence when he is wrongly accused of killing children. Low-budget independent film has slick production values and sincere acting but suffers from awkward scripting and direction.
Dist.: Virgin

MAN'S FAVORITE SPORT? 1964
★ ★ ★ **NR Comedy 2:00**
Dir: Howard Hawks   *Cast:* Rock Hudson, Paula Prentiss, Maria Perschy, Charlene Holt, John McGiver, Roscoe Karns
▶ Public relations expert Prentiss pushes sporting goods salesman Hudson into entering a fishing contest, even though he's never fished before. Attempt to capture the lunacy of screwball comedies is marked by broad slapstick and an energetic cast.
Dist.: MCA

MAN THEY COULD NOT HANG, THE 1939
★ ★ NR Horror 1:12 B&W
Dir: Nick Grinde *Cast:* Boris Karloff, Lorna Gray, Robert Wilcox, Roger Pryor, Don Beddoe
▶ Genius doctor Karloff conducts experiments in reviving the dead with a heart device but is executed after a student dies during one of the tests. Revived by an assistant with his own invention, Karloff seeks vengeance against those responsible for his death. Taut chiller is one of Karloff's stronger vehicles.
Dist.: RCA/Columbia

MAN WHO BROKE 1,000 CHAINS, THE 1987
★ ★ ★ ★ NR Biography/MFTV 1:53
☑ Explicit language, violence
Dir: Daniel Mann *Cast:* Val Kilmer, Charles Durning, Elisha Cook, Jr., Kyra Sedgwick, Sonia Braga
▶ True story of Robert Ellis Burns (Kilmer), World War I vet sentenced to hard labor in a brutal Georgia work camp after being forced to participate in an armed robbery. Burns escapes and establishes a new life as a respected Chicago magazine publisher. When his real identity emerges, his captors want him to serve out his term. Strong drama inspired previous Hollywood classic *I Am a Fugitive From a Chain Gang.*
Dist.: Warner

MAN WHO CAME TO DINNER, THE 1941
★ ★ NR Comedy 1941 B&W
Dir: William Keighley *Cast:* Monty Woolley, Bette Davis, Ann Sheridan, Jimmy Durante, Billie Burke, Mary Wickes
▶ Bombastic critic Woolley slips on the ice outside a family's home and injures his leg. Afraid of a lawsuit, they do everything they can to make him feel at home; he proceeds to entertain himself by completely invading and rearranging their lives. Woolley delivers his most famous performance in this amusing adaptation of the Broadway play by George S. Kaufman and Moss Hart.
Dist.: MGM/UA

MAN WHO COULD WORK MIRACLES, THE 1937 British
★ NR Fantasy 1:22 B&W
Dir: Lothar Mendes *Cast:* Roland Young, Ralph Richardson, Joan Gardner, Ernest Thesiger, Wallace Lupino, George Zucco
▶ Meek draper's clerk Young is chosen by "the gods" to be the possessor of unlimited powers as an experiment to see if the human race is worth saving. Young proceeds on an unlikely course of actions that ranges from curing freckles to stopping the earth's rotation, but his powers can't get him what he really wants. Based on a short story by H. G. Wells, film has good special effects and some amusing moments amid the social commentary.
Dist.: Nelson

MAN WHO FELL TO EARTH, THE 1976 British
★ R Sci-Fi 2:20
☑ Nudity, strong sexual content, explicit language
Dir: Nicolas Roeg *Cast:* David Bowie, Rip Torn, Candy Clark, Buck Henry, Bernie Casey
▶ Alien Bowie comes to Earth to get water for his drought-stricken planet. He sets up a company and makes a fortune, only to be plotted against by mysterious business interests. Great-looking, thought-provoking sci-fi with intricate direction by Roeg and strong performance by Bowie (his film debut). Occasionally murky plotting loses steam towards the end. Based on the novel by Walter Tevis.
Dist.: RCA/Columbia

MAN WHO HAUNTED HIMSELF, THE 1970 British
★ PG Fantasy 1:34
☑ Adult situations
Dir: Basil Dearden *Cast:* Roger Moore, Hildegard Neil, Alastair Mackenzie, Hugh Mackenzie, Kevork Malikyan
▶ Executive Moore recovers from a traffic accident to discover that a psychologically twisted alter ego has escaped from his mind while he was in limbo. Doppelganger wreaks havoc in Moore's business and personal life. Intriguing story is based on an episode from Alfred Hitchcock's TV show. Director Dearden himself died in a car crash a year after filming.
Dist.: HBO

MAN WHO KNEW TOO MUCH, THE 1934 British
★ ★ NR Mystery-Suspense 1:15 B&W
Dir: Alfred Hitchcock *Cast:* Leslie Banks, Edna Best, Peter Lorre, Hugh Wakefield, Nova Pilbeam, Pierre Fresnay
▶ While vacationing in Switzerland with their daughter Pilbeam, Best and Banks learn from dying Fresnay of Lorre's plot to assassinate a foreign dignitary in London. When Lorre and his associates kidnap Pilbeam to prevent the couple from going to the authorities, Banks and Best must try to rescue their girl and stop the killing on their own. Gripping suspenser boasts Lorre's first English-speaking role. Remade by Hitchcock in 1956.
Dist.: Various

MAN WHO KNEW TOO MUCH, THE 1956
★ ★ ★ ★ NR Mystery-Suspense 2:00
Dir: Alfred Hitchcock *Cast:* James Stewart, Doris Day, Brenda de Banzie, Bernard Miles, Ralph Truman, Christopher Olsen
▶ Vacationing in Morocco, American doctor Stewart and his wife Day, a retired singing star, stumble across a clue to an assassination. But they can't tell the police because their son Olsen has been kidnapped by the killers. Expansive reworking of Hitchcock's 1935 classic is preferred by some critics for Stewart's engaging performance and the famous Albert

Hall climax. Day's version of "Que Sera, Sera" won an Oscar for best song.
Dist.: MCA

MAN WHO LOVED CAT DANCING, THE 1973
★★ PG Western 1:51
☑ Adult situations, explicit language, violence
Dir: Richard Sarafian *Cast:* Burt Reynolds, Sarah Miles, Lee J. Cobb, Jack Warden, George Hamilton, Bo Hopkins
▸ Fugitive outlaw Reynolds and his gang kidnap Hamilton's wife Miles. Hamilton and bounty hunter Cobb pursue as captive and captor fall in love. Unusual and at times turgid; however, Reynolds and Miles demonstrate a good deal of chemistry.
Dist.: MGM/UA

MAN WHO LOVED WOMEN, THE 1977 French .
★★ NR Comedy 1:59
Dir: François Truffaut *Cast:* Charles Denner, Brigitte Fossey, Leslie Caron, Nelly Borgeaud
▸ A large number of women attend Denner's funeral. Through flashbacks, his womanizing adventures are recounted. Low-key Truffaut comedy with gentle comic ironies (like the hero being rejected by an older woman who prefers younger men) and a memorable performance by the underrated Denner. Remade in America by Blake Edwards. [S]
Dist.: RCA/Columbia

MAN WHO LOVED WOMEN, THE 1983
★★ R Comedy 1:50
☑ Nudity, explicit language
Dir: Blake Edwards *Cast:* Burt Reynolds, Julie Andrews, Kim Basinger, Marilu Henner, Cynthia Sikes, Jennifer Edwards
▸ Compulsive womanizer Reynolds just can't say no to beautiful women, including psychiatrist Andrews who tries to probe his psyche. American remake of Truffaut's French film is sober and repetitive but sometimes affecting. Funniest scenes involve Reynolds getting accidentally glued to a dog and delightful Basinger as a Texan who enjoys making love in public places. **(CC)**
Dist.: RCA/Columbia

MAN WHO SHOT LIBERTY VALANCE, THE 1962
★★★★ NR Western 2:02 B&W
Dir: John Ford *Cast:* James Stewart, John Wayne, Vera Miles, Lee Marvin, Edmond O'-Brien, Andy Devine, Woody Strode, Lee Van Cleef, Strother Martin, Ken Murray
▸ Greenhorn lawyer Stewart, trying to bring civilization to the frontier town of Shinbone, runs up against Valance (Marvin), a bullying killer. Stewart turns to rancher Wayne for help. Sprawling, elegiac drama eloquently sums up director Ford's favorite Western themes. Notable supporting work from Strode, Van Cleef, and Martin; Gene Pitney's version of the theme song became a pop hit.
Dist.: Paramount

MAN WHO WASN'T THERE, THE 1983
★★★ R Comedy 1:51
☑ Nudity, adult situations, explicit language, adult humor
Dir: Bruce Malmuth *Cast:* Steve Guttenberg, Jeffrey Tambor, Lisa Langlois, Art Hindle, Morgan Hart, Bill Forsythe
▸ Washington, D.C., government employee Guttenberg is about to marry finacée Hart when he gets his hands on invisibility formula coveted by various villains. Much of the humor comes from the fact that Guttenberg must be naked in order to remain completely unseen. Originally released in 3-D.
Dist.: Paramount

MAN WHO WOULD BE KING, THE 1975
★★★★ PG Action-Adventure 2:09
☑ Violence
Dir: John Huston *Cast:* Sean Connery, Michael Caine, Christopher Plummer, Saeed Jaffrey, Shakira Caine
▸ Rogue British soldiers Connery and Caine leave colonial India and enter the remote kingdom of Kafiristan. Caine wants to plunder the royal treasure and move on but Connery, mistaken for a god and installed as king by the natives, develops deadly delusions of grandeur. Glorious adventure with director Huston weaving a magical narrative spell against an epic background. Exuberant Connery and crafty Caine play off each other beautifully. Plummer gives able support as the writer Rudyard Kipling (on whose story the film is based). Four Oscar nominations (Screenplay, Costumes, Art Direction, Editing). **(CC)**
Dist.: CBS/Fox

MAN WHO WOULD NOT DIE, THE 1975
★ PG Mystery-Suspense 1:23
☑ Adult situations, violence
Dir: Robert Arkless *Cast:* Dorothy Malone, Keenan Wynn, Aldo Ray, Alex Sheafe, Joyce Ingalls, Fred Scollay
▸ After two people die at sea near St. Thomas, investigator Sheafe hooks up with Ingalls, a victim's daughter. But is her father really dead? Gangster Wynn wants to know because a million-dollar scam may be at stake. Interesting premise, adapted from a Charles Williams novel, gets muddled execution.
Dist.: Worldvision

MAN WITH BOGART'S FACE, THE 1980
★★★ PG Comedy 1:51
☑ Brief nudity, adult situations
Dir: Robert Day *Cast:* Robert Sacchi, Franco Nero, Olivia Hussey, Michelle Phillips, Victor Buono, Misty Rowe
▸ Business picks up for detective Sacchi when plastic surgery turns him into a Bogart lookalike. He gets hired by two beautiful women to crack two different cases. Remarkable imper-

sonation of Bogie by Sacchi in a likable parody plot that should please film buffs. The one joke does wear thin by the end.
Dist.: CBS/Fox

MAN WITH ONE RED SHOE, THE 1985
★ ★ ★ PG Comedy 1:32
☑ Adult situations, mild violence
Dir: Stan Dragoti   *Cast:* Tom Hanks, Dabney Coleman, Lori Singer, James Belushi, Charles Durning, Edward Herrmann
▶ Eccentric musician Hanks is a patsy caught between CIA rivals Durning and Coleman. Beautiful spy Singer helps Hanks to escape. More frantic than truly funny but Hanks makes the frenzy easy to take. Lots of physical humor in this American remake of the French *The Tall Blond Man With One Black Shoe.* (CC)
Dist.: CBS/Fox

MAN WITHOUT A STAR 1955
★ ★ ★ NR Western 1:29
Dir: King Vidor   *Cast:* Kirk Douglas, Jeanne Crain, Claire Trevor, William Campbell, Richard Boone, Jay C. Flippen
▶ Drifting cowboy Douglas befriends young farmboy Campbell; both are hired by Crain, a rancher who is plotting a range war. Although unwilling to fight, Douglas must confront sadistic killer Boone. Intelligent Western also features a song from Douglas ("And the Moon Grew Brighter and Brighter").
Dist.: MCA

MAN WITH THE GOLDEN ARM, THE 1955
★ ★ NR Drama 1:59 B&W
Dir: Otto Preminger   *Cast:* Frank Sinatra, Kim Novak, Eleanor Parker, Darren McGavin, Arnold Stang
▶ Heroin addict Sinatra tries to go straight. Nagging wife Parker provides little understanding and pusher McGavin pressures him. Only local vamp Novak can help him. Unrelenting drama tackles difficult subject honestly. One of Sinatra's best performances; classic jazz score by Elmer Bernstein.
Dist.: MGM/UA

MAN WITH THE GOLDEN GUN, THE 1974
British
★ ★ ★ ★ PG Espionage/Action-Adventure 2:05
☑ Violence, explicit language
Dir: Guy Hamilton   *Cast:* Roger Moore, Christopher Lee, Britt Ekland, Maud Adams, Herve Villechaize, Clifton James
▶ James Bond (Moore) takes on Scaramanga (Lee), a golden-gun-wielding assassin plotting to corner the market on solar energy, and his midget sidekick Villechaize. Moore's second 007 outing has gadgets, gimmicks, beautiful women, exotic Southeast Asia locations, and Lee, one of the best villians of the series. James reprises his Southern sheriff from *Live and Let Die.*
Dist.: MGM/UA

MAN WITH TWO BRAINS, THE 1983
★ ★ R Comedy 1:30
☑ Nudity, explicit language, adult humor
Dir: Carl Reiner   *Cast:* Steve Martin, Kathleen Turner, David Warner, Paul Benedict, Richard Brestoff, James Cromwell
▶ Brilliant brain surgeon Dr. Michael Hfuhruhurr (Martin) marries sexy but unfaithful Turner. Frustrated in his marriage, Martin finds true love with a disembodied female brain that is able to communicate (voice provided by Sissy Spacek). Nutty mad-scientist parody is uneven but frequently sidesplitting and occasionally endearing. Funniest moments: a lakeside love scene with his beloved brain, the drunk test, and Merv Griffin's cameo.
Dist.: Warner

MAN, WOMAN AND CHILD 1983
★ ★ ★ ★ PG Drama 1:41
☑ Adult situations, explicit language
Dir: Dick Richards   *Cast:* Martin Sheen, Blythe Danner, Craig T. Nelson, Sebastian Dungan, David Hemmings, Nathalie Nell
▶ Sheen, a happily married family man, and his wife Danner are shocked when he learns he has illegitimate child Dungan from a fling ten years ago in France. High-grade, sentimental soap opera pulls out all the stops and gets the tear ducts going. Based on an Erich Segal novel.
Dist.: Paramount

MARATHON MAN 1976
★ ★ ★ ★ ★ R Mystery-Suspense 2:05
☑ Adult situations, explicit language, violence
Dir: John Schlesinger   *Cast:* Dustin Hoffman, Laurence Olivier, Roy Scheider, William Devane, Marthe Keller, Fritz Weaver
▶ "Is it safe?" demands escaped Nazi war criminal Olivier as he tortures Columbia grad student Hoffman with a dentist drill in a now-classic scene. This is just one of Hoffman's predicaments when Scheider, his intelligence-agent brother, becomes embroiled in Olivier's diamond-smuggling scheme. Tense thriller with bravura direction by Schlesinger providing nonstop excitement. Olivier was nominated for an Oscar.
Dist.: Paramount

MARAT/SADE 1966 British
☆ NR Drama 1:55
Dir: Peter Brook   *Cast:* Patrick Magee, Clifford Rose, Glenda Jackson, Ian Richardson, Brenda Kempner, Ruth Baker
▶ A play about French revolutionary leader Jean-Paul Marat (Richardson) and his assassination by Charlotte Corday (Jackson, in her film debut) is directed by the Marquis de Sade (Magee) with a cast of mental patients. Play-within-the-movie gets out of hand as crazed actors periodically go berserk. Based on the stage offering by Peter Weiss, movie is exhausting, but an experience worth having. Full title is *The Persecution and Assassination of*

Jean-Paul Marat as Performed by the Inmates of the Asylum of Charenton Under the Direction of the Marquis de Sade.
Dist.: Water Bearer

MARCH OR DIE 1977 British
★★ PG Action-Adventure 1:46
☑ Violence
Dir: Dick Richards ***Cast:*** Gene Hackman, Terence Hill, Max Von Sydow, Catherine Deneuve, Ian Holm
► Bitter French Foreign Legionnaire Hackman reluctantly leads his troops (including thief Hill) on a mission to protect Louvre Museum curator Von Sydow's Sahara dig on a site that is holy to Holm's Arab tribe. Ignored at the box office but rates a look on video for the fine cast and gorgeous John Alcott cinematography. Has some of the flavor of 1930s adventure films.
Dist.: CBS/Fox

MARIA CHAPDELAINE 1984 Canadian/French
☆ NR Drama 1:48
☑ Mild violence
Dir: Gilles Carle ***Cast:*** Carole Laure, Nick Mancuso, Claude Rich, Amulette Garneau, Pierre Curzi, Donald Lautrec
► In turn-of-the-century Quebec, eldest daughter Laure and her devout family work hard to survive the frigid frontier. Farmer Curzi and wealthy Lautrec both adore her, but she loves lumberjack Mancuso. Personal tragedies cast a shadow on her happiness. Immaculate production, fetching Laure are the bright lights in this slow-paced, overly melodramatic soap opera. [S]
Dist.: Media

MARIA'S LOVERS 1984
★ R Drama 1:49
☑ Nudity, adult situations, explicit language
Dir: Andrei Konchalovsky ***Cast:*** Nastassja Kinski, John Savage, Robert Mitchum, Keith Carradine, Vincent Spano, Anita Morris
► World War II hero Savage comes home and marries old girlfriend Kinski. He turns out to be impotent and skips town. She becomes pregnant by itinerent musician Carradine. Will Savage take her back? Turgid, offbeat romance rarely works up emotional urgency.
Dist.: MGM/UA

MARIE 1985
★★★★ PG-13 Biography 1:51
☑ Explicit language, violence
Dir: Roger Donaldson ***Cast:*** Sissy Spacek, Jeff Daniels, Keith Szarabajka, Lisa Banes, Morgan Freeman, Fred Thompson
► True story of how Marie Ragghianti (Spacek), an abused mother of three, left her husband, went to college, and rose to become the first female chief of Tennessee's parole board. Uncovering widespread political corruption, she single-handedly took the administration to court. Gutsy little-person-versus-the-establishment theme is given substance by believable cast, compelling Spacek, and virtuoso directing from Donaldson. Adapted from book by Peter Maas. **(CC)**
Dist.: MGM/UA

MARIE ANTOINETTE 1938
★ NR Biography/Drama 2:29 B&W
Dir: W. S. Van Dyke II ***Cast:*** Norma Shearer, Tyrone Power, John Barrymore, Robert Morley, Gladys George, Anita Louise
► Lonely Austrian princess Shearer romances Power, marries King Louis XVI (Morley), and sets new records for extravagant royal spending on the way to a date with the guillotine during the French Revolution. Grand historical spectacular in the old Hollywood style is solid in every department, with Barrymore a standout as Louis XV.
Dist.: MGM/UA

MARINE RAIDERS 1944
★★ NR War 1:30 B&W
Dir: Harold Schuster ***Cast:*** Pat O'Brien, Robert Ryan, Ruth Hussey, Frank McHugh, Barton MacLane, Richard Martin
► Marine major O'Brien and fellow officer Ryan perform heroically during the Battle of Guadalcanal. They have more to fear from each other than the enemy: friction occurs when O'Brien tries to break up Ryan's romance with Hussey. Merely average screenplay is enlivened by boisterous performances from the leads.
Dist.: Turner

MARIUS 1931 French
★ NR Drama 2:05 B&W
Dir: Alexander Korda ***Cast:*** Raimu, Pierre Fresnay, Charpin, Alida Rouffe, Orane Demazis, Paul Dullac
► Sailor Fresnay longs for the sea, leaving his relationship with true-blue Demazis in dry dock. A filmed play, using the same cast then performing it in a long run in Paris. Funny and heartbreaking first part of the Marseilles trilogy by Marcel Pagnol, which includes *Fanny* and *Cesar,* provided the inspiration for the stage musical *Fanny*. [S]
Dist.: Various

MARJOE 1972
★★ PG Documentary 1:28
☑ Adult situations, explicit language
Dir: Howard Smith, Sarah Kernochan ***Cast:*** Marjoe Gortner
► Frank, Oscar-winning documentary takes a look at the career of evangelist Gortner from early childhood to age 28, when he tired of revival circuit's hypocrisy and retired. Portait of religion for profit may offend true believers, but Gortner's candor is disarming. Filmmakers deftly combine new footage and older shots of "world's youngest evangelist."
Dist.: RCA/Columbia

MARJORIE MORNINGSTAR 1958
★★★★ NR Drama 2:03
Dir: Irving Rapper ***Cast:*** Natalie Wood,

Gene Kelly, Claire Trevor, Ed Wynn, Martin Milner, Carolyn Jones
▶ Aspiring actress Wood falls for Kelly, the entertainment director at a mountain resort. To please Wood's disapproving parents, Kelly goes to New York in an unsuccessful bid for stardom in the larger world. Meanwhile, Kelly's former assistant Milner is enjoying triumph as a playwright while falling in love with Wood. Poorly cast film is an interesting failure. Jewish elements were extremely toned down in adapting the script from the Herman Wouk novel.
Dist.: Republic

MARKED WOMAN 1937
★ ★ ★ NR Drama 1:36 B&W
Dir: Lloyd Bacon *Cast:* Bette Davis, Humphrey Bogart, Jane Bryan, Eduardo Ciannelli, Isabel Jewell, Allen Jenkins
▶ Rapid, hard-hitting crime exposé about vicious gangster Ciannelli who mistreats the "hostesses" at his posh gambling den. Crusading DA Bogart begs Davis to testify against Ciannelli, but his thugs threaten her with death. Based on the real-life trial of Lucky Luciano, with Davis giving a fiery performance. (CC)
Dist.: MGM/UA

MARK OF THE DEVIL 1970 British/German
☆ NR Horror 1:30
☑ Graphic violence
Dir: Michael Armstrong *Cast:* Herbert Lom, Udo Kier, Olivera Vuco, Reggie Nalder
▶ In seventeenth-century Australia, Lom presides over the trials of witches, subjecting them to unspeakable tortures for his own pleasure, and presumably that of the viewer. Repellent chiller has lots of blood and screaming, but nary a scare.
Dist.: HBO

MARK OF THE VAMPIRE 1935
★ ★ NR Horror 1:01 B&W
Dir: Tod Browning *Cast:* Lionel Barrymore, Elizabeth Allan, Bela Lugosi, Lionel Atwill, Carol Borland, Jean Hersholt
▶ Strikingly sexy vampiress Borland joins with dad Lugosi to scare the bejabbers out of unsavory types staying in Lugosi's cobwebbed castle. Viewers may feel cheated by the ending, but the rest is well worth seeing for Borland's classic look and the spooky atmosphere—among the best in director Browning's horror films.
Dist.: MGM/UA

MARLENE 1986 German
★ ★ NR Documentary 1:36 C/B&W
Dir: Maximilian Schell *Cast:* Marlene Dietrich
▶ Documentary features film clips from Dietrich's best movies (*Blue Angel, Destry Rides Again, Touch of Evil*), stage appearances, and photos, intercut with an audio interview of Marlene today (she refused to be photographed). The star is still feisty and opin-

ionated, as this unusual documentary proves. Subtitles are used when she lapses into German.
Dist.: Nelson

MARNIE 1964
★ ★ PG Drama 2:10
☑ Adult situations, violence
Dir: Alfred Hitchcock *Cast:* Sean Connery, Tippi Hedren, Diane Baker, Martin Gabel, Louise Latham, Bruce Dern
▶ Wealthy Philadelphia scion Connery becomes obsessed with kleptomaniac secretary Hedren. She resists him but he blackmails her into marriage and tries to discover the roots of her neurosis. The director's startling use of color highlights this intense drama which emphasizes psychological exploration over conventional suspense.
Dist.: MCA

MAROONED 1969
★ ★ ★ G Sci-Fi 2:14
Dir: John Sturges *Cast:* Gregory Peck, Richard Crenna, James Franciscus, David Janssen, Gene Hackman, Lee Grant
▶ American astronauts Crenna, Hackman, and Franciscus are stranded in outer space. Concerned NASA official Peck struggles to rescue them before their oxygen runs out. Tense and quite plausible thriller won Oscar for Best Special Effects.
Dist.: RCA/Columbia

MARRIAGE CIRCLE, THE 1924
★ NR Comedy 1:54 B&W
Dir: Ernst Lubitsch *Cast:* Florence Vidor, Monte Blue, Creighton Hale, Marie Provost, Adolphe Menjou, Esther Ralston
▶ In Vienna, Provost, whose marriage to professor Menjou is rocky, falls for doctor Blue, her best friend Vidor's husband, while Hale chases Vidor. Silent romantic roundelay, elegantly directed by Lubitsch and acted with élan by its ensemble. Director remade this in 1932 as *One Hour With You.*
Dist.: Video Yesteryear

MARRIAGE OF MARIA BRAUN, THE 1978 German
★ ★ R Drama 2:00
☑ Nudity, adult situations, explicit language
Dir: Rainer Werner Fassbinder *Cast:* Hanna Schygulla, Klaus Lowitsch, Ivan Desny, Gottfried John, Gisela Uhlen, Gunter Lamprecht, George Byrd
▶ In the ruins of postwar Berlin, a liberated but vulnerable Schygulla (in a splendid performance) forges financial independence despite a tragic affair with black American soldier Byrd that sends husband Lowitsch to jail. Challenging look at German society will delight sophisticated viewers with its subtle humor. Ⓢ
Dist.: RCA/Columbia

MARRIED TO THE MOB 1988
★ ★ ★ ★ R Comedy 1:43

☑ Adult situations, explicit language, violence
Dir: Jonathan Demme *Cast:* Michelle Pfeiffer, Matthew Modine, Dean Stockwell, Mercedes Ruehl, Alec Baldwin, Joan Cusack
▶ When her hit man husband is rubbed out, Pfeiffer tries to flee the Long Island Mafia by moving into a New York tenement. She's pursued by Mafia don Stockwell and FBI agent Modine in a comedy of errors. Screwball approach to gangsters is colorful, although plot runs out of steam despite fine performances by Pfeiffer and Stockwell. Amusing cast also includes David Johansen and Sister Carol East; score by David Byrne features songs by New Order, Deborah Harry, and Brian Eno. Stockwell received an Oscar nomination as Best Supporting Actor.
Dist.: Orion

MARRIED WOMAN, THE 1965 French
☆ **NR Drama 1:34 B&W**
Dir: Jean-Luc Godard *Cast:* Macha Meril, Philippe Leroy, Bernard Noel, Margaret Le Van, Chris Tophe, Roger Leenhardt
▶ Married Meril merrily carries on with lover Noel while pilot husband Leroy is out of town. Going back and forth between the two men, she has gotten pregnant—but who is the father? Multifaceted Godardian experiment is not for those who like neat endings. [S]
Dist.: Foothill

MARTIANS GO HOME 1990
★ **PG-13 Comedy 1:30**
☑ Brief nudity, adult situations, explicit language
Dir: David Odell *Cast:* Randy Quaid, Margaret Colin, Anita Morris, Barry Sobel, Vic Dunlop, John Philbin
▶ Composer Quaid's welcoming music for a "close encounter" sci-fi movie is accidentally transmitted into space, attracting a host of real aliens of the looney kind. Anarchic Martians led by Sobel dedicate themselves to destroying Earthling sanity with crude practical jokes. Shrill, ham-fisted goofiness.
Dist.: IVE

MARTIN 1978
★★ **R Horror 1:35 C/B&W**
☑ Nudity, adult situations, explicit language, graphic violence
Dir: George Romero *Cast:* John Amplas, Lincoln Maazel, Elayne Nadeau, Sarah Venable, Tom Savini, Frank Middleton
▶ Unusual updating of the vampire myth finds disturbed young Amplas drugging his victims with a hypodermic and cutting into veins with razors to extract his mealtime pleasure. Traditional ways of defeating him are useless, but grandfather Maazel is determined to put a stop to the family curse. Cult classic is chilling and effective, finding baroque horror in the seemingly everyday and ordinary.
Dist.: HBO

MARTIN'S DAY 1985 Canadian
★★★★ **PG Drama 1:39**
☑ Explicit language
Dir: Alan Gibson *Cast:* Richard Harris, Justin Henry, James Coburn, Lindsay Wagner, Karen Black, John Ireland
▶ Escaped convict Harris kidnaps young Henry. As cop Coburn and lady shrink Wagner close in, the kid and the con grow to be friends. Well-handled formula story given substance by an impressive cast. (CC)
Dist.: CBS/Fox

MARTY 1955
★★★ **NR Drama 1:39 B&W**
Dir: Delbert Mann *Cast:* Ernest Borgnine, Betsy Blair, Esther Minciotti, Karen Steele, Jerry Paris, Frank Sutton
▶ Bronx butcher Borgnine spends lonely nights hanging out with his male pals. They object when he finally finds romance with plain Blair. Wonderful and heartwarming with a superb Ernie. Paddy Chayefsky's sensitive script has lines that have achieved classic status ("Whaddaya wanna do tonight, Marty?"). Oscars for Best Picture, Actor (Borgnine), Screenplay (Chayefsky), Director.
Dist.: MGM/UA

MARVIN AND TIGE 1983
★★★★ **PG Drama 1:44**
☑ Adult situations, explicit language
Dir: Eric Weston *Cast:* John Cassavetes, Billy Dee Williams, Gibran Brown, Denise Nicholas-Hill
▶ In Atlanta, orphaned black boy Brown is talked out of committing suicide by white alcoholic Cassavetes. A father-son relationship develops between the two. Extremely predictable slice-of-life realism. Fine performances can't compensate for uninspired plotting, glacial pacing, and an excess of pathos.
Dist.: Nelson

MARY OF SCOTLAND 1936
★★ **NR Drama 2:03 B&W**
Dir: John Ford *Cast:* Katharine Hepburn, Fredric March, Florence Eldridge, Douglas Walton, John Carradine, Moroni Olsen
▶ Fictionalized account of the conflict between Mary (Hepburn), the Catholic Queen of Scotland, and Elizabeth (Eldridge), the Anglican Queen of Britain. March, Mary's third husband, gives the strongest performance in this somber, gloomy historical epic. Adapted from a Maxwell Anderson play.
Dist.: Turner

MARY POPPINS 1964
★★★★★ **G Musical/Family 2:26**
Dir: Robert Stevenson *Cast:* Julie Andrews, Dick Van Dyke, David Tomlinson, Glynis Johns, Ed Wynn
▶ Julie Andrews won an Oscar for her effervescent performance as the world's greatest nanny, Mary Poppins. She and whimsical chimney sweep Uncle Bert (Van Dyke) take the Banks children for tea parties on the ceil-

ing and other fantasy adventures. When her work is finished, Mary opens her umbrella and flies away. Charming Disney adaptation of the P. L. Travers books won five Oscars, including Visual Effects, Editing, Score, and song "Chim Chim Cher-ee." Other songs include "A Spoon Full of Sugar" and "Supercalifragilisticexpialidocious."
Dist.: Buena Vista

MASCULINE-FEMININE 1966 French/Swedish
☆ **NR Drama 1:43 B&W**
Dir: Jean-Luc Godard *Cast:* Jean-Pierre Leaud, Chantal Goya, Marlene Jobert, Michel Debord, Catherine-Isabelle Duport
► The young people of Paris are the focus of this mostly irritating pastiche ostensibly based on stories by Guy de Maupassant, but actually reflecting director Godard's then-growing obsession with cinematic alienation devices. Leaud is a romantic young market researcher who falls for pop singer Goya. Not for the narrative-minded. [S]
Dist.: Video Dimensions

M*A*S*H 1970
★★★★★ **PG War/Comedy 1:56**
☑ Nudity, adult situations, explicit language, violence, adult humor
Dir: Robert Altman *Cast:* Donald Sutherland, Elliott Gould, Sally Kellerman, Robert Duvall, Tom Skerritt, Gary Burghoff, Jo Ann Pflug, René Auberjonois, Fred Williamson, Roger Bowen, John Schuck, Bud Cort
► During the Korean War, Sutherland, Gould, and Skerritt, irreverent, fun-loving doctors at a Mobile Army Surgical Hospital, contend with straitlaced surgeon Duvall and his lover, head nurse Kellerman. Antics include exposing Kellerman in the shower to prove she's a blond, curing a suicidal dentist's impotence, and climactic, unorthodox football game with rival unit. Ring Lardner's hilarious screenplay won an Oscar; nominated for Best Picture, Director, and Supporting Actress (Kellerman). Spawned one of most successful series in TV history, with Burghoff reprising his role as Radar O'Reilly.
Dist.: CBS/Fox

M*A*S*H: GOODBYE, FAREWELL & AMEN 1983
★★★★★ **NR Comedy/MFTV 2:00**
Dir: Alan Alda *Cast:* Alan Alda, Mike Farrell, Harry Morgan, David Ogden Stiers, Loretta Swit, Jamie Farr
► Concluding two-hour episode of the popular network series "M*A*S*H" explores the final days of the Korean War, as Hawkeye (Alda), BJ (Farrell), Colonel Potter (Morgan), Charles (Stiers), Margaret (Swit), Klinger (Farr), and the rest of the 4077th learn of the declaration of peace, watch the camp (including the infamous Swamp) be dismantled, and bid fond farewells to each other. Broadcast debut scored one of the highest Nielsen ratings in TV history.
Dist.: CBS/Fox

MASK 1985
★★★★★ **PG-13 Drama 2:00**
☑ Adult situations, explicit language
Dir: Peter Bogdanovich *Cast:* Cher, Sam Elliott, Eric Stoltz, Estelle Getty, Richard Dysart, Laura Dern
► Stoltz, a grotesquely disfigured teen with a sense of humor ("You never seen anyone from the planet Vulcan before?") lives with hardened motorcycle mom Cher. He wins the heart of rich blind girl Dern before succumbing to his disease. Fictional tearjerker, based on a true story, features uniformly outstanding performances and a touching spirit of hope and courage. (CC)
Dist.: MCA

MASQUE OF THE RED DEATH, THE 1964
★★ **NR Horror 1:26**
Dir: Roger Corman *Cast:* Vincent Price, Hazel Court, Jane Asher, David Weston, Patrick Magee, Skip Martin
► Medieval prince Price uses murder and sadism to control his peasants while a deadly plague sweeps the countryside. Stylish, evocative horror based on two Edgar Allan Poe short stories is among the best of Corman's features. Superb production design and bleak touches of humor add to the fun.
Dist.: Vestron

MASQUE OF THE RED DEATH, THE 1989
★★ **R Horror**
☑ Nudity, adult situations, explicit language, violence
Dir: Larry Brand *Cast:* Patrick Macnee, Adrian Paul, Clare Hoak, Jeff Osterhage, Tracy Reiner
► In olden times, prince Paul ascends the throne under the advice of elder statesman Macnee. Inside the prince's castle, there are orgies and debauchery; outside, a mysterous plague devastates the peasantry. The prince and his minions think they are immune, until a mysterious, red-cloaked stranger appears. Roger Corman produced this cheap remake of his own vastly superior 1964 adaptation of the Edgar Allan Poe story.
Dist.: MGM/UA

MASQUERADE 1988
★★★★ **R Mystery-Suspense 1:47**
☑ Nudity, adult situations, explicit language, violence
Dir: Bob Swaim *Cast:* Rob Lowe, Meg Tilly, Kim Cattrall, Doug Savant, John Glover
► Hamptons heiress Tilly falls for penniless boat skipper Lowe, but are his motives pure or monetary? Among those interested in the answer: Tilly's malevolent stepfather Glover and Savant, the cop who loves her. Stylishly shot and cleverly plotted thriller spins a web of murder and blackmail. Beautiful Hamptons

settings provide an inside look at the life-styles of the rich and famous.
Dist.: CBS/Fox

MASSACRE AT CENTRAL HIGH 1976
★ R Drama 1:28
☑ Nudity, explicit language, violence
Dir: Renee Daalder ***Cast:*** Derrel Maury, Andrew Stevens, Robert Carradine, Kimberly Beck, Roy Underwood, Rainbeaux Smith
► Transfer student Maury, tormented by bullies, wreaks clever revenge only to discover new problems in his high school's rearranged social structure. Peculiar exploitation picture has a cult reputation for offering satire as well as violence and nudity.
Dist.: MCA

MASS APPEAL 1984
★★★★ PG Comedy/Drama 1:39
☑ Adult situations, explicit language
Dir: Glenn Jordan ***Cast:*** Jack Lemmon, Zeljko Ivanek, Charles Durning, Louise Latham
► Extroverted priest Lemmon clashes with young firebrand seminarian Ivanek. However, gradual respect builds between them, putting Lemmon in a dilemma when superior Durning wants to kick Ivanek out of the clergy. Lemmon and Ivanek play off each other with humanity and humor. Based on Bill C. Davis's Broadway hit. (CC)
Dist.: Vestron

MASSIVE RETALIATION 1984
★ NR Drama 1:29
☑ Explicit language, violence
Dir: Thomas A. Cohen ***Cast:*** Tom Bower, Karlene Crockett, Peter Donat, Marilyn Hassett, Susan O'Connell
► Three northern California families are so worried about the threat of nuclear war that they establish a heavily fortified survivalists' retreat. Their worst fears come true when an atom bomb explodes during war games. Intriguing Cold War paranoia premise sabotaged by low-budget execution and lackluster plotting.
Dist.: Vestron

MASTER OF THE WORLD 1961
★★ NR Fantasy 1:44
Dir: William Witney ***Cast:*** Vincent Price, Charles Bronson, Henry Hull, Mary Webster
► In the nineteenth-century, visionary scientist Price is determined to impose peace on the world with his invention, an advanced flying machine. American agent Bronson attempts to thwart Price when his plans get out of hand. Not bad period thriller from a Jules Verne novel.
Dist.: Warner

MASTERS OF THE UNIVERSE 1987
★★★ PG Fantasy 1:46
☑ Explicit language, violence
Dir: Gary Goddard ***Cast:*** Dolph Lundgren, Frank Langella, Meg Foster, Billy Barty, Courteney Cox, Chelsea Field
► On the magical planet Eternia, superhero He-Man (Lundgren) battles evil Skeletor (Langella) to rescue the imprisoned Sorceress of Greyskull Castle. He-Man comes to Earth, where two teens help in his struggle. Juvenile sword-and-sorcery epic based on a line of popular Mattel toys (also the inspiration for an animated TV series). (CC)
Dist.: Warner

MATADOR 1988 Spanish
☆ NR Comedy/Drama 1:50
☑ Rape, nudity, adult situations, violence
Dir: Pedro Almodóvar ***Cast:*** Assumpta Serna, Nacho Martinez, Carmen Maura, Antonio Banderas, Eva Cobo, Juliete Serrano
► Has-been matador Martinez now teaches bullfighting; among his students is wimpy Banderas who idolizes his master. When bizarre murders plague the city, Banderas takes the blame to prove his manhood. Kinky black comedy mixes sex and death into a naughty and lethal brew. Almodóvar's sense of humor is doubtlessly not for everyone. [S]
Dist.: CineVista

MATEWAN 1987
★★★ PG-13 Drama 2:12
☑ Explicit language, violence
Dir: John Sayles ***Cast:*** Chris Cooper, Will Oldham, Mary McDonnell, James Earl Jones, Jace Alexander, Ken Jenkins
► In 1920, rural West Virginia coal miners organize a union against their company's abusive tactics, but their effort is thrown into disarray with the arrival of Italian and black scabs. Somber, straightforward treatment of a real-life incident has strong ensemble acting from the large cast and impressive period details. Director Sayles has a cameo as fire-and-brimstone preacher. (CC)
Dist.: Warner

MATILDA 1978
★ G Comedy 1:45
Dir: Daniel Mann ***Cast:*** Elliott Gould, Robert Mitchum, Harry Guardino, Clive Revill, Karen Carlson, Lionel Stander, Roy Clark, Whammo the Kangaroo
► Promoter Gould is small potatoes until he hooks up with a unique contender for the heavyweight championship: Matilda, a boxing kangaroo. The Mafia tries to kidnap the slugging marsupial while ASPCA official Carlson objects to Matilda's exploitation. Cute, offbeat fare based on a Paul Gallico novel.
Dist.: Vestron

MATTER OF TIME, A 1976 U.S./Italian
★★ PG Drama 1:37
☑ Adult situations, explicit language
Dir: Vincente Minnelli ***Cast:*** Liza Minnelli, Ingrid Bergman, Charles Boyer, Tina Aumont, Gabriele Ferzetti, Fernando Rey
► Director Minnelli's last film is an embarrassing mishmash about maid Liza Minnelli's rise

to fame as a movie star through the inspiration of a dying contessa (Bergman). Set primarily in 1949, although flashback structure is often confusing. Film debut for Bergman's daughter Isabella Rossellini, who plays a nun at her mother's deathbed.
Dist.: Vestron

MAURICE 1987 British
★ R Drama 2:15
☑ Brief nudity, adult situations
Dir: James Ivory ***Cast:*** James Wilby, Rupert Graves, Hugh Grant, Billie Whitelaw, Denholm Elliott, Ben Kingsley
► Long, arty, and genteel drama about passionate Maurice (Wilby) and scholarly Clive (Grant), who meet while studying at Cambridge. Excellent commentary on socially and sexually repressed Edwardian England. With Kingsley as quack hypnotist who advises Maurice to "take excerise and stroll around with a gun" to cure his homosexuality. Based on E. M. Forster's 1914 novel. **(CC)**
Dist.: Warner

MAVERICK QUEEN, THE 1956
★★ NR Western 1:32
Dir: Joseph Kane ***Cast:*** Barbara Stanwyck, Barry Sullivan, Scott Brady, Mary Murphy, Wallace Ford, Howard Petrie
► Butch Cassidy (Petrie), the Sundance Kid (Brady), and the Wild Bunch are up to their old outlaw tricks, this time in cahoots with saloon owner and Southern aristocrat Stanwyck. All goes well until Stanwyck falls for Sullivan, the Pinkerton man who's been sent to break up the gang. Lively oater based on a novel by Zane Grey.
Dist.: Republic

MAX AND HELEN 1990
★★★★ NR Drama/MFTV 1:34
Dir: Philip Saville ***Cast:*** Treat Williams, Martin Landau, Alice Krige, Jodhi May, Jonathan Phillips
► During World War II, Williams, his fiancée Krige, and her sister May are prisoners in a Nazi work camp. He escapes, but his arrest in the Soviet Union prevents him from helping the women. When the lovers meet years later, past events cast a shadow on the reunion. Sensitive, moving, well-acted true story based on the book by Nazi hunter Simon Wiesenthal (played here by Landau).
Dist.: Turner

MAX DUGAN RETURNS 1983
★★★★ PG Comedy 1:38
☑ Adult situations, explicit language
Dir: Herbert Ross ***Cast:*** Marsha Mason, Jason Robards, Donald Sutherland, Matthew Broderick, Dody Goodman, Sal Viscuso
► Whimsical Neil Simon comedy about single mother Mason's struggle to raise son Broderick. Her long-estranged father Robards shows up unexpectedly to shower her with gifts, arousing the suspicion of amorous cop Sutherland. Polished entertainment features brief appearances by Sutherland's son Kiefer and baseball expert Charley Lau.
Dist.: CBS/Fox

MAXIE 1985
★★★ PG Fantasy/Comedy 1:38
☑ Adult situations, explicit language
Dir: Paul Aaron ***Cast:*** Glenn Close, Mandy Patinkin, Ruth Gordon, Barnard Hughes, Googy Gress, Valerie Curtin
► Sexy 1920s flapper returns to inhabit body of clerical secretary Close, confusing both her husband Patinkin and boss Hughes. Close performs admirably in a dual role, but the screenplay, adapted from Jack Finney's novel *Marian's Wall*, is predictable and schmaltzy. Final film for the great Gordon, who plays the landlady.
Dist.: HBO

MAXIMUM OVERDRIVE 1986
★★ R Horror 1:37
☑ Explicit language, violence
Dir: Stephen King ***Cast:*** Emilio Estevez, Pat Hingle, Laura Harrington, Yeardley Smith, John Short, Ellen McElduff
► When Earth passes through the tail of a comet, formerly inanimate machines come to life. Malevolent trucks besiege a small group of survivors—including ex-con Estevez and hitchhiker Harrington—at a North Carolina Dixie Boy restaurant, leading to relentless crashes and carnage. Directing debut by horror master King runs out of gas after an intriguing start. Ear-splitting score by hard-rock group AC/DC.
Dist.: Warner

MAXIMUM SECURITY 1989
☆ R Action-Adventure 1:30
☑ Explicit language, violence
Dir: Mike Snyder ***Cast:*** Irene Cara, Peter Kowanko, Paula Bond, Joseph Culp
► When her husband is sent to an island penal colony, Cara, unaware of his association with terrorists, parachutes into this hell and is captured by a band of women warriors. Absolutely atrocious in all departments—acting, editing, production—except maybe scenery.
Dist.: New World

MAYERLING 1936 French
★ NR Romance 1:36 B&W
Dir: Anatole Litvak ***Cast:*** Charles Boyer, Danielle Darrieux, Suzy Prim, Jean Dax, Gabrielle Dorziat
► Sensitive, moving account of the doomed love affair in the late nineteenth century between Rudolph (Boyer), crown prince of Austria, and Marie Vetsera (Darrieux), his young mistress. Classic romance notable for its discreet, subtle handling of a real-life scandal. Superb performances from the leads made them international stars. [S]
Dist.: Nelson

MAYTIME 1937
★ NR Musical 2:12 B&W
Dir: Robert Z. Leonard *Cast:* Jeanette MacDonald, Nelson Eddy, John Barrymore, Herman Bing, Rafaela Ottiano, Paul Porcasi
► Famous opera star MacDonald meets and falls in love with penniless singer Eddy, although she's already engaged to manager Barrymore. MacDonald goes through with the marriage, but her love for Eddy defies the years to find a kind of consummation on the opera stage. Old fashioned, but still pleasant. In addition to numerous operatic snippets, songs include Sigmund Romberg's "Will You Remember" and a wonderful duet to James A. Bland's "Carry Me Back to Old Virginny."
Dist.: MGM/UA

MCCABE & MRS. MILLER 1971
★ ★ R Western 2:01
☑ Nudity, adult situations, explicit language, violence
Dir: Robert Altman *Cast:* Warren Beatty, Julie Christie, René Auberjonois, Keith Carradine, William Devane, Shelley Duvall, John Schuck, Bert Remsen, Michael Murphy
► In the turn-of-the-century Pacific Northwest, a combination saloon-bordello run by small-time gambler Beatty and ambitious prostitute Christie attracts the attention of sinister big-money interests. Innovative, richly detailed film was critically praised, but its revisionist approach to Western myths may disturb some viewers. Christie's work received an Oscar nomination. Score by Leonard Cohen.
Dist.: Warner

MCGUFFIN, THE 1985 British
★ NR Mystery-Suspense 1:44
☑ Adult situations, explicit language, violence
Dir: Colin Bucksey *Cast:* Charles Dance, Anna Massey, Ann Todd, Phyllis Logan, Mark Rylance, Jerry Stiller
► London film critic Dance witnesses a murder in the window opposite his own. When the police fail to investigate, he pursues the matter and discovers some incriminating photo negatives. Homage to Hitchcock starts stunningly but falls apart in second half due to plot holes and murky motivations.
Dist.: SVS

MCQ 1974
★ ★ ★ ★ PG Action-Adventure 1:46
☑ Explicit language, violence
Dir: John Sturges *Cast:* John Wayne, Eddie Albert, Diana Muldaur, Colleen Dewhurst, Clu Gulager, Al Lettieri
► When a colleague is murdered, Wayne quits the Seattle police force to find his killer. The trail leads to lonely barmaid Dewhurst and evil drug dealer Lettieri, but Wayne also uncovers evidence implicating his former employers. Rare contemporary role for the Duke is a fast-paced thriller in the *Dirty Harry* mold.
Dist.: Warner

MCVICAR 1980 British
★ R Biography/Crime 1:30
☑ Brief nudity, explicit language, violence
Dir: Tom Clegg *Cast:* Roger Daltrey, Adam Faith, Cheryl Campbell, Steven Berkoff, Brian Hall
► Rock singer Daltrey gives an honest, gritty performance as real-life bank robber Tom McVicar, Britain's Public Enemy No. 1 for his sensational escape from a maximum-security prison. After a reunion with common-law wife Campbell, he plots one more robbery. McVicar wrote the screenplay based on his book; soundtrack includes songs by Daltrey's group The Who.
Dist.: Vestron

ME AND HIM 1989 German
★ R Comedy 1:34
☑ Strong sexual content, explicit language
Dir: Doris Dörrie *Cast:* Griffin Dunne, Ellen Greene, Carey Lowell, Craig T. Nelson, Kelly Bishop, voice of Mark Linn-Baker
► New York architect Dunne finds his penis can suddenly talk to him. Bored with his owner's monogamous, workaholic existence, the organ convinces Dunne to forgo wife Greene and pursue other women, chiefly co-worker Lowell (who is also being chased by their boss Nelson). Premise is outrageous enough to attract the curious but the humor grows increasingly offensive. Nastiest line: Linn-Baker's description of Lowell's legs. (CC)
Dist.: RCA/Columbia

MEAN DOG BLUES 1978
★ ★ ★ ★ R Action-Adventure 1:48
☑ Brief nudity, adult situations, explicit language, violence
Dir: Mel Stuart *Cast:* George Kennedy, Gregg Henry, Kay Lenz, Scatman Crothers, Tina Louise, William Windom
► Unjustly convicted of manslaughter, country-western singer Henry is sent to a brutal prison farm run by sadistic warden Kennedy, who owns a vicious Doberman. When guards attempt to rape his pregnant wife Lenz, Henry decides to escape. Modest, hard-hitting prison drama with a sympathetic underdog hero.
Dist.: Vestron

MEAN JOHNNY BARROWS 1976
☆ R Crime 1:31
☑ Explicit language, violence
Dir: Fred Williamson *Cast:* Fred Williamson, Jenny Sherman, Aaron Banks, Roddy McDowall, Stuart Whitman, Elliot Gould
► After leaving the Army, combat hero Williamson is forced to take menial jobs to support himself until he becomes a mafia hit man. War breaks out on the homefront between two feuding mob families. Plenty of action and gunplay, below-average technical val-

ues. Odd casting includes McDowall and Whitman as mafiosos.
Dist.: Unicorn

MEAN SEASON, THE 1985
★ ★ ★ R Drama 1:44
☑ Nudity, explicit language, graphic violence
Dir: Philip Borsos *Cast:* Kurt Russell, Mariel Hemingway, Richard Jordan, Richard Masur, Joe Pantoliano, Andy Garcia
▶ Miami reporter Russell boosts his career with exclusive stories on the "Numbers Killer," serial murderer Jordan, despite girlfriend Hemingway's fear that he's becoming a collaborator in the deaths. Taut, hard-edged thriller takes some frightening twists.
Dist.: HBO

MEAN STREETS 1973
★ R Drama 1:52
☑ Brief nudity, explicit language, graphic violence
Dir: Martin Scorsese *Cast:* Harvey Keitel, Robert De Niro, Amy Robinson, David Proval, Richard Romanus, Cesare Danova
▶ New York hood Keitel sabotages his career in the Mafia by helping debt-ridden, irresponsible friend De Niro. Director Scorsese's first critical success has strong performances and impressive Little Italy atmosphere, but a gloomy, gritty, and episodic story line. David and Robert Carradine have brief cameos. **(CC)**
Dist.: Warner

MEATBALLS 1979 Canadian
★ ★ ★ ★ PG Comedy 1:33
☑ Brief nudity, adult situations, explicit language, adult humor
Dir: Ivan Reitman *Cast:* Bill Murray, Chris Makepeace, Kate Lynch, Russ Banham, Kristine DeBell, Sarah Torgov
▶ Camp counselor Murray leads his sad-sack troopers against a rival camp in a summer olympics, finding time for romance with Lynch and helping quiet kid Makepeace along the way. Some hilarious high jinks are interspersed with touching moments in this lightweight and winning summertime fun. Irreverent Bill is truly irresistible.
Dist.: Vestron

MEATBALLS PART II 1984
★ ★ PG Comedy 1:35
☑ Adult situations, explicit language
Dir: Ken Wiederhorn *Cast:* Archie Hahn, John Mengatti, Tammy Taylor, Kim Richards, Ralph Seymour, Richard Mulligan, John Larroquette
▶ Street punk Mengatti becomes summer camp counselor, takes care of handicapped kid and extraterrestrial, and must fight in a boxing match for ownership of the camp. Follow-up contains no characters from the first film and has nowhere near its freshness and comic style. Mulligan and Larroquette are wasted. **(CC)**
Dist.: RCA/Columbia

MEATBALLS III 1987
★ R Comedy 1:34
☑ Nudity, explicit language, adult humor
Dir: George Mendeluk *Cast:* Sally Kellerman, Al Waxman, Patrick Dempsey, Shannon Tweed
▶ At camp North Star, nerdy teen Dempsey makes the transition to stud under the guidance of his favorite porn queen Kellerman, who has died but been given the opportunity to return to Earth to do a good deed. Lewd and crude, with none of the charm of the original.
Dist.: IVE

MECHANIC, THE 1972
★ ★ ★ PG Action-Adventure 1:40
☑ Adult situations, violence
Dir: Michael Winner *Cast:* Charles Bronson, Jan-Michael Vincent, Keenan Wynn, Jill Ireland, Linda Ridgeway
▶ Bronson gives a steady performance as a "mechanic," an ace assassin under contract to the Mafia. He takes young apprentice Vincent under his wing during a series of hits in Los Angeles and Naples. Good script features an especially tricky ending. Bronson's real-life wife Ireland has a brief role as a prostitute.
Dist.: MGM/UA

MEDIUM COOL 1969
★ R Drama 1:51
☑ Nudity, explicit language, violence
Dir: Haskell Wexler *Cast:* Robert Forster, Verna Bloom, Peter Bonerz, Marianna Hill, Peter Boyle
▶ Cinematographer-turned-director Wexler blends documentary footage and fiction in this tale of TV news cameraman Forster covering the violent events of the 1968 Democratic Convention in Chicago. Sophisticated cult classic explores the question of reality versus television.
Dist.: Paramount

MEDUSA TOUCH, THE 1978 British
★ ★ ★ ★ PG Mystery-Suspense 1:50
☑ Explicit language, violence
Dir: Jack Gold *Cast:* Richard Burton, Derek Jacobi, Lee Remick, Lino Ventura, Marie-Christine Barrault
▶ Burton, a man with superhuman powers, tells psychiatrist Remick he can cause a 747 to crash, ruin a moon landing, even make Westminster Abbey crumble, simply by willing it. When he's mysteriously bludgeoned to death while watching TV, police inspector Ventura is recruited to solve the crime.
Dist.: CBS/Fox

MEET DR. CHRISTIAN 1939
★ NR Drama 1:03 B&W
Dir: Bernard Vorhaus *Cast:* Jean Hersholt, Dorothy Lovett, Robert Baldwin, Enid Bennett, Paul Harvey, Marcia Mae Jones
▶ Dedicated physician Hersholt goes up against mayor Harvey to get hospital built in little town of Rivers End, Minnesota. The doc

has to save the mayor's daughter to bring the politician around. Warm, interesting opener for a series of movies based on a popular radio show starring Hersholt.
Dist.: Video Yesteryear

MEET JOHN DOE 1941
★ ★ ★ NR Drama 2:03 B&W
Dir: Frank Capra *Cast:* Gary Cooper, Barbara Stanwyck, Edward Arnold, Walter Brennan, James Gleason, Spring Byington
▶ Newspaper columnist Stanwyck creates a fictional Good Samaritan who catches the public's fancy; political candidate Arnold orders her to find a real "John Doe" to help his campaign. Washed-up pitcher Cooper agrees to take the role, but rebels when he discovers Arnold's corrupt intentions. Top-notch drama with an intriguing theme, sparkling comic touches, and outstanding performances. Director Capra filmed three different endings before settling for the final version.
Dist.: Various [C]

MEET ME IN ST. LOUIS 1944
★ ★ ★ ★ ★ NR Musical 1:53
Dir: Vincente Minnelli *Cast:* Judy Garland, Margaret O'Brien, Lucille Bremer, Tom Drake, Mary Astor, Leon Ames, Marjorie Main
▶ As St. Louis prepares to host the 1903 World's Fair, papa Ames wants to move his family to New York. But the children prefer the comforts of home, including boy next door Drake, Halloween trick or treating, and a Christmas ball. Heartfelt and moving, with immaculate direction by Minnelli, beautiful camerawork and period settings, and wonderful performances. Score includes "The Trolley Song," "Under the Bamboo Tree," the title tune, and "Have Yourself a Merry Little Christmas" (sung by Judy to Margaret in a heart-tugging scene).
Dist.: MGM/UA

MEGAFORCE 1982
★ ★ PG Action-Adventure 1:39
☑ Explicit language, violence
Dir: Hal Needham *Cast:* Barry Bostwick, Persis Khambatta, Michael Beck, Edward Mulhare, George Furth, Henry Silva
▶ Ace Hunter (Bostwick) and his Megaforce (a multinational army of good guys using advanced weaponry) are recruited by major Khambatta to rescue her beleaguered desert nation from rebel leader Silva. Harmless fantasy packed to the gills with stunts, but Bostwick is miscast, the humor falls flat, and the comic-book plot is lifeless.
Dist.: CBS/Fox

MELANIE 1982 Canadian
★ ★ ★ ★ PG Drama 1:49
☑ Nudity, adult situations, explicit language, mild violence
Dir: Rex Bromfield *Cast:* Glynnis O'Connor,

Burton Cummings, Paul Sorvino, Trudy Young, Don Johnson
▶ Illiterate Arkansas native O'Connor travels to Los Angeles to reclaim son abducted by estranged husband Johnson. There lawyer Sorvino helps her with custody battle and reading lessons but it is rocker Cummings who becomes the new man in her life. Charming sleeper with immensely likable O'Connor characterization.
Dist.: Vestron

MELODY 1971 British
★ G Drama 1:43
Dir: Waris Hussein *Cast:* Jack Wild, Mark Lester, Tracy Hyde, Sheila Steafel, Kate Williams, Roy Kinnear
▶ Adolescent Lester wants to marry Hyde, but his parents obstinately disapprove. Even Lester's special friend Wild thinks it's a bad idea, as the sensitive youngsters try to find a place for themselves in regimented world. A charming young cast makes idiotic situation somewhat sympathetic, and soundtrack full of mellow songs from The Bee Gees and Crosby, Stills, and Nash makes it bearable.
Dist.: Embassy

MELODY CRUISE 1933
★ NR Musical 1:16 B&W
Dir: Mark Sandrich *Cast:* Charlie Ruggles, Phil Harris, Helen Mack, Greta Nissen, Chick Chandler, June Brewster
▶ Millionaire Harris and pal Ruggles are on their way to California on a steamship loaded with beautiful girls. Despite Ruggles's best efforts to keep him single, Harris get stuck on Mack; but before they can tie the knot, Mack jumps ship in a huff, and Harris must chase her down. Racy musical highlighted by wild visuals and solid turns by vaudeville professionals Ruggles and Harris.
Dist.: Turner

MELVIN AND HOWARD 1980
★ ★ R Comedy/Drama 1:35
☑ Nudity, adult situations, explicit language
Dir: Jonathan Demme *Cast:* Paul LeMat, Jason Robards, Jr., Mary Steenburgen, Michael J. Pollard, Jack Kehoe, Dabney Coleman, Pamela Reed, Gloria Grahame
▶ Critically acclaimed, real-life story about Utah gas station attendant Melvin Dummar (LeMat), who once gave eccentric billionaire Howard Hughes (Robards) a ride in his truck. When Hughes dies, Melvin produces a hand-scrawled will listing himself as beneficiary for $156 million. Robards was nominated for a Best Supporting Oscar and Steenburgen won Best Supporting Actress for her role as Melvin's quirky wife.
Dist.: MCA

MEMBER OF THE WEDDING, THE 1953
★ ★ ★ ★ NR Drama 1:29 B&W
Dir: Fred Zinnemann *Cast:* Ethel Waters, Julie Harris, Brandon de Wilde, Arthur Franz, Nancy Gates, William Hansen

▶ Southern twelve-year-old Harris, desperate to become an adult, imposes herself on her brother's wedding plans. Black cook Waters is the only person who understands her turmoil. Splendid coming-of-age drama adapted from Carson McCullers's novel and Broadway hit is a heartbreaking examination of adolescence. Harris, in her film debut, received an Oscar nomination for her remarkable performance (she was twenty-five at the time).
Dist.: RCA/Columbia

MEMORIES OF ME 1988
★★★★ PG-13 Comedy/Drama 1:44
☑ Adult situations, explicit language
Dir: Henry Winkler ***Cast:*** Billy Crystal, Alan King, JoBeth Williams, Janet Carroll, David Ackroyd, Sean Connery
▶ After a heart attack, New York doctor Crystal reexamines his life and heads to Hollywood for reconciliation with estranged dad King, a career movie extra. They find making up is hard to do; Crystal's girlfriend Williams is caught in the middle. Mixture of laughter and tears aims straight at the heart. Connery contributes cameo playing himself. Funniest scene: King's rendition of "Too Pooped to Pop."
Dist.: CBS/Fox

MEMORY OF US, THE 1974
★ PG Drama 1:33
☑ Adult situations
Dir: H. Kaye Dyal ***Cast:*** Ellen Geer, Jon Cypher, Robert Hogan, Barbara Colby, Rose Marie, Will Geer
▶ Unhappy housewife Geer goes to a motel room every day to be alone. When her unfaithful husband confronts her, she lies, claiming she is also having an affair, and later hires someone to pose as her lover. Subject matter touches on familiar marital woes but Geer's self-indulgent characterization leaves script (which she wrote) without an emotional center. Flat plotting and direction.
Dist.: Academy

MEN, THE 1950
★★★★ NR Drama 1:25 B&W
Dir: Fred Zinnemann ***Cast:*** Marlon Brando, Teresa Wright, Everett Sloane, Jack Webb, Richard Erdman
▶ During World War II, lieutenant Brando receives a spinal injury that leaves him a paraplegic. Falling into depression, he spurns support from fiancée Wright and doctor Sloane and avoids rehabilitation therapy. An honest, sensitive account of war victims. Brando's film debut. Carl Foreman's screenplay received an Oscar nomination.
Dist.: Republic

MEN 1986 German
★ NR Comedy 1:39
☑ Nudity, adult situations, explicit language, violence
Dir: Doris Dorrie ***Cast:*** Heiner Lauterbach, Uwe Ochsenknecht, Ulrike Kreiner, Janna Marangosoff
▶ Workaholic executive Lauterbach discovers wife Kreiner is having an affair with scruffy artist Ochsenknecht. Using a false name, Lauterbach moves in with Ochsenknecht and gets revenge by turning him into a yuppie clone of himself. A bauble with bite; savvy screenplay puts some clever twists on male bonding. [S]
Dist.: Vista

MEN DON'T LEAVE 1990
★★★★ PG-13 Drama 1:53
☑ Adult situations, explicit language
Dir: Paul Brickman ***Cast:*** Jessica Lange, Chris O'Donnell, Charlie Korsmo, Arliss Howard, Tom Mason, Joan Cusack
▶ Lange is warm and appealing as a mother trying to hold her family together after the death of her husband. Forced to sell her house, Lange moves to Baltimore, where in addition to employment difficulties she must handle the troubled emotions of teen sons O'Donnell and Korsmo, and face the prospect of starting a new relationship. Refreshing and likable thanks to wonderful cast and energetic direction. **(CC)**
Dist.: Warner

MEN'S CLUB, THE 1986
★ R Drama 1:35
☑ Nudity, adult situations, explicit language
Dir: Peter Medak ***Cast:*** Roy Scheider, David Dukes, Richard Jordan, Harvey Keitel, Craig Wasson, Treat Williams
▶ What do men talk about in group therapy? According to ex-baseball star Scheider, homebody Dukes, salesman Keitel, doctor Williams, nice guy Wasson, and loony psychiatrist Jordan, they discuss women and act out their hostilities. Then they relocate their session to a bordello. Talky and pretentious, with obnoxious characters. Based on Leonard Michaels's controversial novel about male bonding.
Dist.: Paramount

MEPHISTO 1981 Hungarian
★ NR Drama 2:15
☑ Nudity, adult situations, explicit language, violence
Dir: Istvan Szabo ***Cast:*** Klaus Maria Brandauer, Krystyna Janda, Karin Boyd, Rolf Hoppe
▶ Stylish, handsome, and well-acted film set in prewar Nazi Germany. Gifted actor Brandauer wins the admiration of a Nazi benefactor and the opportunity to rise in the theater if he will renounce his past politics and friendships. Heavy going but can be a dynamic and hypnotic experience for sophisticated audiences willing to accept rather complicated plot. Based on a book by Klaus Mann (son of Thomas Mann) that was banned in Germany for almost forty years. Won an Oscar for Best Foreign Film. [S]
Dist.: HBO

MEPHISTO WALTZ, THE 1971
★★ R Horror 1:48
☑ Adult situations, explicit language, violence
Dir: Paul Wendkos ***Cast:*** Alan Alda, Jacqueline Bisset, Barbara Parkins, Curt Jurgens, Bradford Dillman, William Windom
► Journalist Alda interviews dying pianist Jurgens. He turns out to be a satanist who possesses Alda; Alda's wife Bisset senses something amiss and also gets involved with the devil. Overlooked chiller is genuinely atmospheric and spooky; the ending is truly haunting.
Dist.: CBS/Fox

MERCENARY FIGHTERS 1988
★ R Action-Adventure 1:31
☑ Nudity, explicit language, violence
Dir: Riki Shelach ***Cast:*** Peter Fonda, Reb Brown, Ron O'Neal, Jim Mitchum, Robert DoQui, Joanna Weinberg
► American mercenaries led by Fonda are hired to wipe out African rebels threatening massive dam project that will uproot natives from their homeland. Influenced by beautiful nurse Weinberg, Brown shifts allegiance to the rebels, provoking dissension among the Americans. Low-budget exploitation concentrates on fights and explosions rather than plotting.
Dist.: Media

MERRY CHRISTMAS, MR. LAWRENCE 1983 British/Japanese
★★ R Drama 2:03
☑ Brief nudity, adult situations, explicit language, graphic violence
Dir: Nagisa Oshima ***Cast:*** David Bowie, Tom Conti, Ryuichi Sakamoto, Takeshi, Jack Thompson
► Heroic British soldier Bowie is held captive in a Japanese prisoner-of-war camp during World War II. Two alien cultures clash as captain Sakamoto tries to impose his own ideas of discipline and honor on Bowie. Includes graphic depictions of brutal beheadings and disembowelments. Based on a novel by Sir Laurens van der Post. Mostly in English with subtitles for occasional Japanese dialogue. Memorable score composed by Sakamoto, a music superstar in Japan. [S]
Dist.: MCA

MERRY WIDOW, THE 1934
★ NR Musical 1:39 B&W
Dir: Ernst Lubitsch ***Cast:*** Maurice Chevalier, Jeanette MacDonald, Una Merkel, Edward Everett Horton, George Barbier, Herman Bing
► The fanciful kingdom of Marshovia fears that its economy may collapse after wealthy widow MacDonald takes her free-spending ways to Paris. Irresistible roué Chevalier is ordered by king Barbier to travel to City of Lights, turn on the charm, and bring her back home. Merry in every way, with MacDonald at her most sparkling, and a charming Chevalier. Based on the operetta by Franz Lehar, with new lyrics by Lorenz Hart, among others. Songs include "Girls, Girls, Girls" and "The Merry Widow Waltz."
Dist.: MGM/UA

MESMERIZED 1985 Australian/British/New Zealand
★ PG Drama 1:33
☑ Adult situations
Dir: Michael Laughlin ***Cast:*** Jodie Foster, John Lithgow, Michael Murphy, Harry Andrews, Dan Shor
► In 1880 New Zealand, Foster is put on trial for murder. Flashbacks show her past tribulations, including miserable marriage to miser Lithgow, aborted attempt to leave him, blackmail, and a miscarriage. Ludicrous story and lugubrious pacing waste the considerable talents of Foster and Lithgow. Also known as *My Letter to George.*
Dist.: Vestron

MESSENGER OF DEATH 1989
★★★ R Action-Adventure 1:30
☑ Explicit language, violence
Dir: J. Lee Thompson ***Cast:*** Charles Bronson, Trish Van Devere, Laurence Luckinbill, John Ireland, Marilyn Hassett
► Denver reporter Bronson investigates murders of women and children. Small-town newspaper owner Van Devere helps him link the killings to religious sect, powerful society types, and water rights battle. Pretty Colorado scenery is background for patented Bronson heroics, with explosions, chases, shootouts, and killings galore.
Dist.: Media

METALSTORM: THE DESTRUCTION OF JARED-SYN 1983
★ PG Sci-Fi 1:23
☑ Explicit language, violence
Dir: Charles Band ***Cast:*** Jeffrey Byron, Mike Preston, Tim Thomerson, Kelly Preston, R. David Smith
► Can peacekeeping Ranger (Byron) stop evil warlord Jared-Syn (Preston) from taking over the universe? Poor man's *Mad Max* with a muddled plot was filmed in the California desert—and looks it. Clunky and low budget fare, for hard-core fantasy devotees only.
Dist.: MCA

METEOR 1979
★★★ PG Action-Adventure 1:46
☑ Adult situations, explicit language, violence
Dir: Ronald Neame ***Cast:*** Sean Connery, Natalie Wood, Karl Malden, Martin Landau, Brian Keith, Trevor Howard
► Gigantic meteor hurtles toward Earth, causing mudslides, earthquakes, and other disasters as American scientist Connery teams with Soviet counterpart Keith to find a solution. Familiar genre formula has all-star cast, clichéd

characters. Acceptable special effects generate some suspense.
Dist.: Warner

METROPOLIS 1926 German
★ ★ NR Sci-Fi 2:00 B&W
Dir: Fritz Lang *Cast:* Brigitte Helm, Alfred Abel, Gustav Froehlich, Rudolf Klein-Rogge, Fritz Rasp
▶ Influential silent film classic about a futuristic society divided into haves and have-nots. Helm, a beautiful robot controlled by mad scientist Klein-Rogge, leads exploited workers in a tragic uprising. Plot is alternately silly and dull, but extraordinary special effects set precedent for future sci-fi films. Rock producer Giorgio Moroder added a pop soundtrack to a shortened, partially colorized version in 1984.
Dist.: Vestron

MEXICAN SPITFIRE 1939
☆ NR Comedy 1:07 B&W
Dir: Leslie Goodwins *Cast:* Lupe Velez, Leon Errol, Donald Woods, Linda Hayes, Cecil Kellaway, Elizabeth Risdon
▶ When businessman Woods marries dynamic Latin singer Velez, his former girlfriend Hayes tries unsuccessfully to tear them apart. Painless vehicle for Velez, whose acting is charming if not polished. Errol shines in a dual role. Followed by a series of sequels. Home video version double billed with 1936's *Smartest Girl in Town*.
Dist.: Turner

MIAMI BLUES 1990
★ ★ ★ R Action-Adventure 1:37
☑ Brief nudity, adult situations, explicit language, graphic violence
Dir: George Armitage *Cast:* Alec Baldwin, Jennifer Jason Leigh, Fred Ward, Charles Napier, Obba Babatunde, Nora Dunn
▶ Career con Baldwin kills a Hare Krishna panhandler at the Miami airport. While detective Hoke Moseley (Ward) searches for him, he hooks up with naive prostitute Leigh. After a confrontation, Baldwin steals Moseley's false teeth, gun, and badge, and embarks on a wild crime spree in the name of the law. Jittery adaptation of Charles Willeford's pulp thriller has splendid characterizations and vivid settings, but the violence is excessive.
Dist.: Orion

MIAMI CONNECTION 1987
★ ★ R Martial Arts 1:20
☑ Nudity, adult situations, explicit language, graphic violence
Dir: Richard Park *Cast:* Y. K. Kim, Vincent Hirsch, William Ergle, Kathy Collier
▶ Ruthless drug dealer Ergle and a cruel ninja leader try to eliminate Dragonsound, a clean-living rock band that says "no" to drugs. But bandmembers are all martial arts masters, so Ergle and his bad-mannered minions get pulverized when they eventually take them on.

Well-choreographed fight sequences make this worth seeing for action aficionados.
Dist.: Liberty

MICKI & MAUDE 1984
★ ★ ★ ★ PG-13 Comedy 1:58
☑ Adult situations, explicit language
Dir: Blake Edwards *Cast:* Dudley Moore, Amy Irving, Ann Reinking, Richard Mulligan, George Gaynes, Wallace Shawn
▶ TV newsman Moore wants a child and manages to impregnate both his wife Reinking and mistress Irving. Moore compounds the difficulty by marrying Irving, trying to separate his two wives and lives. Outrageous farce has some flat moments but lots of funny stuff, too (as in the climactic double delivery scene). (CC)
Dist.: RCA/Columbia

MIDDLE AGE CRAZY 1980
★ ★ ★ R Comedy/Drama 1:35
☑ Nudity, adult situations, explicit language
Dir: John Trent *Cast:* Bruce Dern, Ann-Margret, Graham Jarvis, Deborah Wakeham, Geoffrey Bowes
▶ Forty proves to be a dangerous age for Dern: he can't keep up with wife Ann-Margret's sexual appetite, his dad dies, and his son impregnates a girlfriend and wants to leave college. Dern buys a Porsche and has an affair with cheerleader Wakeham. Believable if banal story with effectively subdued performances by the leads. Based on the country song by Sonny Throckmorton.
Dist.: CBS/Fox

MIDNIGHT 1934
★ NR Drama 1:20 B&W
Dir: Chester Erskine *Cast:* Sidney Fox, O. P. Heggie, Henry Hull, Margaret Wycherly, Lynn Overman, Humphrey Bogart
▶ Jury foreman Heggie nails a woman in court for murder, when all had supposed she would get off because it was a crime of passion. On the night the woman is to be electrocuted, Heggie steadfastly stands by the conviction—only to have it thrown in his face when his daughter is brought up on charges for killing gangster Bogart. Stagey, New York-lensed low budgeter holds interest with novel dilemma. Released on videotape as *Call It Murder*.
Dist.: Goodtimes

MIDNIGHT 1981
★ R Horror 1:28
☑ Adult situations, explicit language, graphic violence
Dir: John Russo *Cast:* Lawrence Tierney, Melanie Verliin, John Amplas, John Hall, Charles Jackson, Doris Hackney
▶ After a fight with her stepfather Tierney, teenager Verliin runs away from home. She hitches a ride with two strangers, but the trio then get captured by an evil family. Director Russo co-wrote *Night of the Living Dead*, but this pointlessly gory effort is not nearly in that

league. Also known as *Backwoods Massacre.*
Dist.: Vidmark

MIDNIGHT 1989
★ R Horror 1:30
☑ Nudity, adult situations, explicit language, violence
Dir: Norman Thaddeus Vane *Cast:* Lynn Redgrave, Tony Curtis, Steve Parrish, Karen Witter, Frank Gorshin, Wolfman Jack
► Redgrave has always had spotty taste in film roles, but this puerile shocker may be her career low. Here she plays a TV horror movie hostess whose enemies, including ex-lover Parrish, producer Curtis, and agent Gorshin, all die horribly. Lots of gore, but nothing scary. Horror fans stay away.
Dist.: SVS

MIDNIGHT COP 1989 German
★ R Mystery-Suspense 1:36
☑ Nudity, adult situations, explicit language, violence
Dir: Pater Patzak *Cast:* Armin Mueller-Stahl, Michael York, Morgan Fairchild, Frank Stallone, Julia Kent, Monica Bleibtreu
► Mueller-Stahl is a cop on the trail of a killer who rubs his victims' faces with vaseline. D.A. York looks on from the sidelines as drug dealer Stallone is implicated. Mueller-Stahl baits trap for killer with hooker Fairchild. Quirky, tongue-in-cheek serial slaughter story has some original touches.
Dist.: Vidmark

MIDNIGHT COWBOY 1969
★ ★ R Drama 1:53
☑ Nudity, strong sexual content, adult situations, explicit language, violence
Dir: John Schlesinger *Cast:* Dustin Hoffman, Jon Voight, Sylvia Miles, John McGiver, Brenda Vaccaro, Barnard Hughes
► Seamy, downbeat look at New York street life brings young Texan Voight, an aspiring gigolo, to the big city. When his dreams don't match reality, Voight agrees to let tubercular street hustler Hoffman manage him. As winter sets in, the two dream of moving to Florida before Hoffman's health worsens. First X-rated (later revised to R) movie to win Best Picture; director Schlesinger and screenwriter Waldo Salt also won Academy Awards. Hoffman, Voight, and Miles were Oscar-nominated. "Everybody's Talking," sung by Harry Nilsson, was huge hit.
Dist.: MGM/UA

MIDNIGHT CROSSING 1988
★ ★ R Mystery-Suspense 1:44
☑ Nudity
Dir: Roger Holzberg *Cast:* Faye Dunaway, Daniel J. Travanti, John Laughlin, Kim Cattrall, Ned Beatty
► Travanti takes blind wife Dunaway on Laughlin's boat for a Caribbean cruise, supposedly to celebrate their anniversary but actually to recover a fortune in illicit loot. Love affairs, murder, double crosses follow. Thriller

has enough plot twists to keep you guessing, but the acting ranges from good (Dunaway, Laughlin) to overdone (Travanti, Beatty).
Dist.: Vestron

MIDNIGHT EXPRESS 1978
★ ★ ★ ★ R Drama 1:59
☑ Nudity, explicit language, graphic violence
Dir: Alan Parker *Cast:* Brad Davis, Randy Quaid, Irene Miracle, Bo Hopkins, John Hurt, Paul Smith
► True story of Billy Hayes (Davis), a young American convicted of drug smuggling in Turkey and sentenced to an inhumane prison. Hard-hitting, well-acted (especially by Oscar-nominated Hurt as Davis's junkie prison pal), but the brutality and violence are unrelenting. Some charged the portrayal of the Turks bordered on racism. Screenwriter Oliver Stone won an Oscar, as did Giorgio Moroder's musical score.
Dist.: RCA/Columbia

MIDNIGHT LACE 1960
★ ★ ★ NR Mystery-Suspense 1:48
Dir: David Miller *Cast:* Doris Day, Rex Harrison, John Gavin, Myrna Loy, Roddy McDowall, Herbert Marshall
► Transparent thriller about Day, recently married to wealthy tycoon Harrison, tormented by death threats regarded as lies by Scotland Yard. Day's only supporter, construction foreman Gavin, may be hiding a dangerous secret. Stars struggle gamely with implausible plot.
Dist.: MCA

MIDNIGHT MADNESS 1980
★ ★ PG Comedy 1:52
☑ Explicit language, adult humor
Dir: David Wechter, Michael Nankin *Cast:* David Naughton, Debra Clinger, Eddie Deezen, Stephen Furst, Maggie Roswell, Michael J. Fox
► Games-obsessed L.A. grad student organizes nighttime scavenger hunt that pits jocks, sorority girls, nerds, and good guys against one another. Harmless teen farce from Disney Studios lacks the tasteless humor of other genre efforts.
Dist.: Buena Vista

MIDNIGHT RUN 1988
★ ★ ★ ★ R Action-Adventure 2:02
☑ Explicit language, violence
Dir: Martin Brest *Cast:* Robert De Niro, Charles Grodin, Yaphet Kotto, John Ashton, Dennis Farina, Joe Pantoliano
► Bounty hunter De Niro accepts what looks like an easy assignment: transport mild-mannered CPA Grodin from New York to Los Angeles. Unfortunately, FBI agents and the Mob are also after Grodin, leading to a frantic cross-country chase involving biplanes, buses, helicopters, freight trains, and large-scale shootouts. Brisk action sequences are bal-

anced by stars' remarkable chemistry in this high-spirited comic adventure.
Dist.: MCA

MIDSUMMER NIGHT'S DREAM, A 1935
★ ★ NR Comedy 2:12 B&W
Dir: Max Reinhardt, William Dieterle *Cast:* James Cagney, Dick Powell, Olivia de Havilland, Mickey Rooney, Joe E. Brown, Hugh Herbert, Jean Muir, Victor Jory, Billy Barty
▶ Lavish production of Shakespeare's comedy about mischievous sprites who magically disrupt the affairs of eight lovers is a surprisingly respectful version of the Bard. Cagney makes a delightful Bottom, Rooney an energetic Puck; the other roles are uneven, but Jory and Barty register strongly. Only film by famous impresario Reinhardt won Oscars for photography and editing. De Havilland's film debut.
Dist.: Key

MIDSUMMER NIGHT'S SEX COMEDY, A 1982
★ ★ PG Comedy 1:28
☑ Adult situations, adult humor
Dir: Woody Allen *Cast:* Woody Allen, Mia Farrow, Jose Ferrer, Julie Hagerty, Mary Steenburgen, Tony Roberts
▶ Romantic complications ensue when three couples (inventor Allen and his frustrated wife Steenburgen, pompous professor Ferrer and his fiancée Farrow, doctor Roberts and his nurse/mistress Hagerty) spend a weekend at a country house. Sweet-tempered, lyrical farce with radiant cinematography and lovely turn-of-the-century settings. Humor is gentler than in previous Woody efforts.
Dist.: Warner

MIDWAY 1976
★ ★ ★ ★ ★ PG War 2:11
☑ Explicit language, violence
Dir: Jack Smight *Cast:* Charlton Heston, Henry Fonda, James Coburn, Hal Holbrook, Toshiro Mifune, Robert Mitchum
▶ Newsreel and studio footage are edited together in a fact-based account of the World War II Battle of Midway, in which American air and sea power combined to deliver a key blow against Japanese forces. When not fighting the battle, captain Heston helps his son deal with a Japanese-American girlfriend. Originally released in Sensurround.
Dist.: MCA

MIGHTY JOE YOUNG 1949
★ ★ NR Sci-Fi 1:34 B&W
Dir: Ernest B. Schoedsack *Cast:* Terry Moore, Robert Armstrong, Ben Johnson, Frank McHugh
▶ Showman Armstrong returns from Africa with a great ape and lovely young Moore, whose piano rendition of "Beautiful Dreamer" soothes the savage beast. From the creators of *King Kong* and bearing more than a passing resemblance to it; neither ape nor movie

is on the scale of Kong but both are appealing and fun. Oscar for Special Effects.
Dist.: Turner   C

MIGHTY QUINN, THE 1989
★ ★ ★ R Mystery-Suspense 1:38
☑ Adult situations, explicit language, violence
Dir: Carl Schenkel *Cast:* Denzel Washington, Robert Townsend, James Fox, Esther Rolle, Mimi Rogers, M. Emmett Walsh, Sheryl Lee Ralph
▶ Washington, the chief of police of a Bahamian island, investigates a murder on the estate of wealthy Fox. The prime suspect is Washington's joyously irresponsible childhood friend Townsend, whom he must coax out of hiding. Cool, carefree suspenser is as colorful as the lush Caribbean locales. (CC)
Dist.: CBS/Fox

MIKE'S MURDER 1984
★ ★ R Drama 1:49
☑ Brief nudity, adult situations, explicit language, violence
Dir: James Bridges *Cast:* Debra Winger, Mark Keyloun, Paul Winfield, Darrell Larson, Brookers Alderson
▶ Winger walks on L.A.'s wild side, investigating the death of Mike (Keyloun), her tennisbum lover with a sordid double life. Winfield plays a record producer who loved Mike, too. Offbeat and intriguing crime drama set against gritty atmosphere of drugs and murder.
Dist.: Warner

MIKEY AND NICKY 1976
☆ R Drama 1:45
☑ Adult situations, explicit language, violence
Dir: Elaine May *Cast:* Peter Falk, John Cassavetes, Ned Beatty, Joyce Van Patten, Sanford Meisner
▶ Small-time hood Falk sells out pal Cassavetes to the mob. The duo spend a long night together as the hit man closes in. Gritty, realistic look at the underworld features high-energy performances by Falk and Cassavetes, but rather unlikable characters. Marred by slow pacing, patchwork editing, and inferior camerawork.
Dist.: Warner

MILAGRO BEANFIELD WAR, THE 1988
★ ★ ★ ★ R Drama 1:58
☑ Explicit language, violence
Dir: Robert Redford *Cast:* Ruben Blades, Sonia Braga, Daniel Stern, John Heard, Chick Vennera, Christopher Walken
▶ Chicano handyman Vennera "borrows" water to irrigate his dried-up beanfield and sets off a confrontation with powerful interests. Local radical Braga and lawyer Heard side with Vennera, sheriff Blades is caught in the middle, while bad guy Walken is brought in to eliminate Vennera. Little-guy-versus-the-sys-

tem fable plods a bit but is generally whimsical and charming. Good cast with a delightful pig stealing the show. Film won the Oscar for Best Original Score.
Dist.: MCA

MILDRED PIERCE 1945
★★★★ NR Drama 1:53 B&W
Dir: Michael Curtiz ***Cast:*** Joan Crawford, Jack Carson, Zachary Scott, Eve Arden, Ann Blyth, Bruce Bennett
► Outstanding melodrama about impoverished divorcée Crawford (in one of her greatest roles) who struggles to succeed with a restaurant chain only to face disaster at the hands of her heartless lover Scott and spoiled daughter Blyth. Brilliant script (based on James M. Cain's novel) and astute direction helped Crawford win an Oscar for her portrayal of a gutsy heroine; film received five other nominations.
Dist.: CBS/Fox

MILES FROM HOME 1988
★★★ R Drama 1:52
☑ Adult situations, explicit language, violence
Dir: Gary Sinise ***Cast:*** Richard Gere, Kevin Anderson, Penelope Ann Miller, John Malkovich, Judith Ivey, Brian Dennehy
► Brothers Gere and Anderson burn down the family farm rather than let the bank take possession after foreclosure. They go on the lam through the Midwest, becoming folk heroes. Provocative story contains one of Gere's most emotionally charged performances, but the film is hindered by Sinise's overblown direction. Malkovich contributes a sharply cynical cameo as a reporter.
Dist.: Warner

MILKY WAY, THE 1936
★★ NR Comedy 1:28 B&W
Dir: Leo McCarey ***Cast:*** Harold Lloyd, Adolphe Menjou, Verree Teasdale, William Gargan, Lionel Stander, Helen Mack
► Mild-mannered milkman Lloyd inadvertently knocks out the middleweight boxing champion. Promoter Menjou exploits the situation, making the world believe Lloyd's the real thing, but then the poor sap must really get in the ring. Zippy romp is Lloyd's best sound vehicle along with *The Sin of Harold Diddlebock*. Remake: *The Kid From Brooklyn*.
Dist.: Video Yesteryear

MILKY WAY, THE 1970 French
☆ PG Drama 1:42
☑ Adult situations
Dir: Luis Buñuel ***Cast:*** Paul Frankeur, Laurent Terzieff, Alain Cuny, Bernard Verley, Michel Piccoli, Pierre Clementi
► On the road to a Spanish shrine, pilgrims Frankeur and Terzieff have surreal encounters with rogues, clerics, and religious characters, including Christ himself. A free-flowing meditation on the sacred in general, and Catholicism in particular, with Bible types speaking only scripture. Despite his famous irreverence, director Buñuel engages the Church on a deeply emotional level. [S]
Dist.: Media

MILLENIUM 1989
★★ PG Sci-Fi 1:48
☑ Adult situations, explicit language, violence
Dir: Michael Anderson ***Cast:*** Kris Kristofferson, Cheryl Ladd, Daniel J. Travanti, Robert Joy
► Kristofferson investigates mid-air plane crash and encounters Ladd, time traveller from the future who is pulling present-day people off planes to repopulate her barren world. Unique premise gets increasingly silly; dialogue evokes unintentional laughs. Screenplay by John Varley based on his short story "Air Raid."
Dist.: IVE

MILLION DOLLAR DUCK 1971
★★★ G Comedy 1:32
Dir: Vincent McEveety ***Cast:*** Dean Jones, Sandy Duncan, Joe Flynn, Tony Roberts, James Gregory, Lee Harcourt Montgomery
► Struggling scientist Jones brings home radiation-exposed duck from the lab as a pet for son Montgomery. Family financial worries may be over when duck starts laying golden eggs, but nosy neighbor Flynn reports them to the Treasury Department. Lively, consistently funny Disney comedy is entertaining from start to finish.
Dist.: Buena Vista

MILLION DOLLAR MERMAID 1952
★★ NR Biography 1:55
Dir: Mervyn LeRoy ***Cast:*** Esther Williams, Victor Mature, Walter Pidgeon, David Brian, Donna Corcoran, Jesse White
► Life story of turn-of-the-century Australian swimmer Annette Kellerman (Williams), who set records but gained her greatest notoriety introducing the one-piece bathing suit to America. Promoter Mature guides her to stardom and becomes her love interest. Sensational water ballet directed by Busby Berkeley is the highlight of this old-style and very entertaining biography. Oscar nomination for cinematography.
Dist.: MGM/UA

MILLION DOLLAR MYSTERY 1987
★★ PG Comedy 1:30
☑ Explicit language, mild violence
Dir: Richard Fleischer ***Cast:*** Tom Bosley, Rich Hall, Kevin Pollak, Pam Matteson, Eddie Deezen, Wendy Sherman
► Government official Bosley keels over in desert cafe, revealing to assorted onlookers that he has hidden four caches of $1 million. The hunt is on as a busty waitress, her alcoholic brother, nerdy newlyweds, a rock group, a ninja, and a cop search for the dough. Also looking: movie audiences who were offered $1 million by the producers if they could guess

the hiding place. Relentlessly zany chase comedy.
Dist.: HBO

MILPITAS MONSTER, THE 1976
☆ **NR Horror 1:21**
☑ Violence
Dir: Robert L. Burrill   *Cast:* Douglas Hagdohl, Scott A. Henderson, Scott Parker, Daniel Birkhead, Michael Pegg
▶ Milpitas, a northern California town, is menaced by a creature created by toxic waste dumping. Among the victims: local teens at a high school dance. Low budget nonsense, ineptly scripted, directed, and acted. Sound effects by Ben Burtt, who did much better with his Oscar-winning work for *Star Wars.*
Dist.: VCI

MIN AND BILL 1930
★ **NR Drama 1:10 B&W**
Dir: George Hill   *Cast:* Marie Dressler, Wallace Beery, Dorothy Jordan, Marjorie Rambeau, Frank McGlynn
▶ Dressler, the owner of a cheap waterfront hotel, dotes on fisherman Beery while caring for Jordan, whom she adopted as a child. Her fortunes are complicated when school officials take Jordan away from her, and her evil mother shows up to make trouble. Amusing byplay with Beery is best part of this heart-tugging tale. Dressler won Best Actress Oscar for her performance, and she and Beery took the same roles three years later in *Tugboat Annie.*
Dist.: MGM/UA

MINDGAMES 1989
★ **R Mystery-Suspense 1:33**
☑ Adult situations, explicit language, violence
Dir: Bob Yari   *Cast:* Maxwell Caulfield, Edward Albert, Shawn Weatherly, Matt Norero
▶ Albert and wife Weatherly are on camping trip with their son Norero when they pick up hitchhiker Caulfield, a psychotic psychology student who seduces Weatherly in the sand dunes and attempts to murder her husband. After a slow-moving and dully plotted first half, the story manages to hook the audience.
Dist.: CBS/Fox

MIND KILLER 1987
★ **R Horror 1:26**
☑ Nudity, adult situations, explicit language, violence
Dir: Michael Krueger   *Cast:* Joe McDonald, Christopher Wade, Shirley Ross, Kevin Hart
▶ Nerdy librarian McDonald is a flop at picking up chicks until he reads a mind-control manual and brainwashes women into falling in love with him. Working overtime to satisfy his every desire, McDonald's seething brain reaches uncontrollable proportions, explodes out of his skull, and hunts his friends. Attack of

the killer id is low-budget and scary, with ultra-gross special effects.
Dist.: Prism

MINISTRY OF VENGEANCE 1989
☆ **R Action-Adventure 1:38**
☑ Adult situations, explicit language, graphic violence
Dir: Peter Maris   *Cast:* John Schneider, James Tolkan, Ned Beatty, Apollonia, Yaphet Kotto, George Kennedy
▶ When Arab terrorists kill his wife and young daughter, American minister Schneider takes off his clerical robes and trains at survival camp run by Nam buddy Tolkan for mission of revenge. Heavy on torture, killings, and explosions; the climax is disappointing and the acting overdone.
Dist.: Media

MINOR MIRACLE, A 1983
☆ **PG Family 1:41**
☑ Explicit language
Dir: Terrell Tannen   *Cast:* John Huston, Pele, Peter Fox, Severn Darden
▶ Elderly priest Huston tries to raise money for his struggling San Diego orphanage but is opposed by politicians who covet the real estate. When Huston contracts cancer, the orphans contact soccer star Pele, who helps stage big game to save the orphanage. Warmhearted tale should please family audience.
Dist.: Nelson

MINUTE TO PRAY, A SECOND TO DIE, A
1967 Italian
★ ★ **NR Western 1:37**
Dir: Franco Giraldi   *Cast:* Alex Cord, Arthur Kennedy, Robert Ryan, Nicoletta Machiavelli, Mario Brega, Renato Romano
▶ Bad guys of every stripe have descended on the town of Escondido, where they are waiting for governor Ryan to grant them amnesty. Among them is wanted gunman Cord, who must evade bounty hunters to take advantage of the Ryan's largesse. Nice-looking spaghetti Western with an interesting parade of villains.
Dist.: CBS/Fox

MIRACLE MILE 1988
★ ★ **R Sci-Fi 1:35**
☑ Nudity, adult situations, explicit language, violence
Dir: Steve DeJarnatt   *Cast:* Anthony Edwards, Mare Winningham, Mykel T. Williamson, Denise Crosby
▶ Musician Edwards intercepts a chance phone call and learns that World War III is about to start. Can he get his waitress girlfriend Winningham out of L.A. before panic overcomes the streets and the bombs fall? Impudent thriller with house-afire pacing and visually ingenious direction, although quirky plotting and crazy dialogue relegate this to cult status.
Dist.: HBO

MIRACLE OF MORGAN'S CREEK, THE 1944
★ ★ ★ ★ NR Comedy 1:38 B&W
Dir: Preston Sturges   *Cast:* Eddie Bracken,
Betty Hutton, William Demarest, Diana Lynn,
Porter Hall, Alan Bridge
▶ Outrageous World War II comedy about
small-town flirt Trudy Kockenlocker (Hutton)
who thinks she married someone named
"Ratzkiwatzki" after an all-night party with soldiers from a nearby base. Learning she's pregnant, she tricks 4F reject Bracken into marriage. All-out assault on American morals is
one of the raciest and funniest farces ever
filmed, with superb supporting work from a
large cast of comic pros. Director Sturges received an Oscar nomination for his screenplay.
Dist.: Paramount

MIRACLE OF OUR LADY OF FATIMA, THE
1952
★ ★ NR Drama 1:42
Dir: John Brahm   *Cast:* Gilbert Roland, Angela Clarke, Frank Silvera, Jay Novello,
Sherry Jackson, Frances Morris
▶ A trio of young Portuguese shepherds have
a series of visions of the Virgin Mary. Word gets
out, and mobs of pilgrims flock to the little
town, annoying baffled Church officials and
militantly atheist authorities. All are stunned
when the Virgin treats the crowd to a cosmic
miracle. Roland is well-cast as the children's
cheerfully skeptical adult friend in this tasteful
and occasionally humorous account of 1917's
real-life miracle. Also known as *Miracle of
Fatima.*
Dist.: Warner

MIRACLE OF THE BELLS, THE 1948
★ ★ NR Drama 2:00 B&W
Dir: Irving Pichel   *Cast:* Fred MacMurray,
Valli, Frank Sinatra, Lee J. Cobb, Charles
Meredith
▶ Cynical press agent MacMurray falls in love
with chorus girl Valli, and gets her the lead in
a major film. When Valli dies before her break-
through can be released, MacMurray travels
with her body back to her little home town
with a strange request for parish priest Sinatra.
The sentiment gets a bit thick, but Valli is su-
perb and the story is unique.
Dist.: Warner C

MIRACLE OF THE WHITE STALLIONS 1963
★ ★ NR Family 1:58
Dir: Arthur Hiller   *Cast:* Robert Taylor, Lilli
Palmer, Curt Jurgens, Eddie Albert, James
Franciscus, John Larch
▶ During World War II, Vienna riding school
colonel Taylor attempts to evacuate prized
white stallions from the war-torn city before
they are injured, although the Germans (save
for sympathetic Jurgens) want to keep the
horses in town. Winning wartime adventure
highlighted by performances of Austria's famous Lippizan horses.
Dist.: Buena Vista

MIRACLE ON 34TH STREET 1947
★ ★ ★ ★ ★ NR Fantasy/Comedy 1:36
B&W
Dir: George Seaton   *Cast:* Maureen O'Hara,
John Payne, Natalie Wood, Edmund
Gwenn, Thelma Ritter
▶ Enduring holiday classic features Gwenn
going to work as Macy's Santa Claus for exec-
utive O'Hara. While trying to persuade O'-
Hara's daughter, a very young and cynical
Wood, that Santa is real, Gwenn is institution-
alized. O'Hara's fiancé, lawyer Payne, must
convince the court of Gwenn's sanity and the
very existence of Santa Claus. Heartwarming,
much-beloved Christmas favorite works like a
charm. Gwenn, story writer Valentine Davis
and screenwriter Seaton all garnered Oscars.
Dist.: CBS/Fox C

MIRACLES 1986
★ ★ ★ PG Comedy/Drama 1:27
☑ Explicit language, violence
Dir: Jim Kouf   *Cast:* Teri Garr, Tom Conti,
Paul Rodriguez, Christopher Lloyd
▶ Newly divorced Garr and Conti are kid-
napped by thieves Rodriguez and Lloyd and
taken south of the border. There they get into
further misadventures and rediscover their
feelings for one another. Likable stars de-
served a better script.
Dist.: HBO

MIRACLE WORKER, THE 1962
★ ★ ★ ★ NR Biography 1:47 B&W
Dir: Arthur Penn   *Cast:* Anne Bancroft, Patty
Duke, Victor Jory, Inga Swenson, Andrew
Prine
▶ Determined Annie Sullivan (Bancroft) at-
tempts to teach deaf, dumb, and blind child
Helen Keller (Duke) some semblance of lan-
guage. An inspiring true story from the William
Gibson Broadway play. Galvanizing, Oscar-
winning performances by Bancroft and Duke.
Dist.: MGM/UA

MIRACLE WORKER, THE 1979
★ ★ ★ ★ ★ NR Biography/MFTV 1:38
Dir: Paul Aaron   *Cast:* Patty Duke Astin, Me-
lissa Gilbert, Diana Muldaur, Charles Siebert
▶ TV remake of the William Gibson classic has
Astin, who won an Oscar for playing Helen
Keller in the original, portraying the teacher
Annie Sullivan. Co-producer Gilbert plays Kel-
ler. The now-familiar story of blind deaf-mute
Keller learning to communicate through Sul-
livan's guidance remains powerful, thanks to
these two gifted actresses.
Dist.: Warner

MIRAGE 1965
★ ★ ★ NR Mystery-Suspense 1:49 B&W
Dir: Edward Dmytryk   *Cast:* Gregory Peck,
Diane Baker, Walter Matthau, Kevin
McCarthy, Jack Weston, Walter Abel
▶ Scientist Peck runs out of a blacked-out sky-
scraper just after an associate has fallen from
a high window. Some people appear to be
trying to kill him, and he seems to have lost his

memory. Does his situation have anything to do with an anti-radiation formula he has discovered? Muddled but entertaining, with Matthau appealing as a sympathetic cop. Remade in 1968 as *Jigsaw*.
Dist.: KVC

MIRROR CRACK'D, THE 1980 British
★ ★ ★ PG Mystery-Suspense 1:46
☑ Adult situations
Dir: Guy Hamilton *Cast:* Angela Lansbury, Elizabeth Taylor, Rock Hudson, Kim Novak, Tony Curtis, Geraldine Chaplin
▶ Amateur detective extraordinaire Miss Marple (Lansbury) gets on the case when a murder occurs during a reception for a film production company. Among the possible suspects: co-star Taylor, her husband/director Hudson, rival Novak, secretary Chaplin, and Novak's producer husband Curtis. Lighthearted whodunnit is a bit slowly paced but fun, especially when Taylor and Novak try to out-bitch one another.
Dist.: HBO

MISADVENTURES OF MERLIN JONES, THE 1963
★ ★ ★ G Comedy 1:28
Dir: Robert Stevenson *Cast:* Tommy Kirk, Annette Funicello, Leon Ames, Stuart Erwin, Alan Hewitt, Connie Gilchrist
▶ Genius college student Merlin Jones (Kirk) reads judge Ames's mind and concludes he's planning a heist. After this misunderstanding is cleared up, Kirk actually does hypnotize the judge into the theft of a chimp from the science lab. Friendly Disney fun. Followed by *The Monkey's Uncle*.
Dist.: Buena Vista

MISCHIEF 1985
★ ★ ★ R Comedy 1:37
☑ Nudity, adult situations, explicit language
Dir: Mel Damski *Cast:* Doug McKeon, Chris Nash, Kelly Preston, Catherine Mary Stewart, Jami Gertz
▶ Fifties fable in which rebel Nash initiates shy teen McKeon into the mysteries of dating and sex. McKeon has brief fling with high school sex kitten Preston while Nash eventually splits town with new flame Stewart. Hardly virgin territory but competently rendered nostalgia piece. (CC)
Dist.: CBS/Fox

MISFITS, THE 1961
★ ★ NR Drama 2:04 B&W
Dir: John Huston *Cast:* Clark Gable, Marilyn Monroe, Montgomery Clift, Thelma Ritter, Eli Wallach, Estelle Winwood
▶ Moody study of the stormy relationship between aging cowhand Gable and divorcée Monroe in Reno. She opposes his job of roping wild horses for dog food. More absorbing for its participants than its plot. Gable, who did his own stunts, died before film's release; Monroe

never completed another picture. Script by Arthur Miller, Monroe's husband at the time.
Dist.: MGM/UA

MISHIMA 1985
☆ R Drama 2:00 C/B&W
☑ Nudity, adult situations, explicit language, violence
Dir: Paul Schrader *Cast:* Ken Ogata, Masayuki Shionoya, Hiroshi Mikami, Junya Fukuda, Shigeto Tachihara, Junkichi Orimoto
▶ Intricate, visually fascinating biography of noted Japanese author Yukio Mishima (Ogata) combines black-and-white footage of his troubled life with opulent color excerpts from three novels: *Temple of the Golden Pavilion, Kyoko's House,* and *Runaway Horses.* Intellectually demanding and only intermittently successful experiment features a score by Philip Glass. (CC) Ⓢ
Dist.: Warner

MISS FIRECRACKER 1989
★ ★ PG Comedy 1:45
☑ Adult situations, explicit language
Dir: Thomas Schlamme *Cast:* Holly Hunter, Mary Steenburgen, Tim Robbins, Scott Glenn, Ann Wedgeworth, Alfre Woodard
▶ Yazoo City, Mississippi, native Hunter aspires to greatness, but she's insecure. She pins her hopes on winning the town's Miss Firecracker contest so she can finally be somebody. Adapted by Beth Henley from her Off-Broadway play (which also starred Hunter), ensemble piece featuring cast of looney but vulnerable eccentrics proves tedious, not very funny, and a retread of better material. (CC)
Dist.: HBO

MISSING 1982
★ ★ ★ ★ PG Drama 2:02
☑ Brief nudity, explicit language, violence
Dir: Costa-Gavras *Cast:* Jack Lemmon, Sissy Spacek, John Shea, Melanie Mayron, David Clennon, Janice Rule
▶ American Shea disappears during a coup in Latin America. Searching for him, his anguished wife Spacek and father Lemmon uncover possible U.S. government involvement. Intriguing political thriller, inspired by a true story. Beautifully crafted direction by Costa-Gavras. Lemmon is outstanding as the conservative businessman who gradually sees the error of his ways; Spacek is also fine. Oscar for Best Screenplay Adaptation; nominated for Picture, Actor (Lemmon), and Actress (Spacek).
Dist.: MCA

MISSING IN ACTION 1984
★ ★ ★ ★ R Action-Adventure 1:41
☑ Nudity, explicit language, violence
Dir: Joseph Zito *Cast:* Chuck Norris, M. Emmet Walsh, Lenore Kasdorf, James Hong, David Tress
▶ Determined soldier Norris returns to Vietnam to rescue American POWs. Although he's helped by Army buddy and black marketeer

Walsh, Norris wins his battles almost single-handedly. Plenty of firebombs, car chases, hand-to-hand combat, evil Vietnamese officers, and gung-ho action. Equally popular follow-up: *Missing in Action 2—The Beginning.*
Dist.: MGM/UA

MISSING IN ACTION 2—THE BEGINNING
1985
★★★★ R Action-Adventure 1:35
☑ Explicit language, violence
Dir: Lance Hool *Cast:* Chuck Norris, Steven Williams, Bennett Ohta, Soon-Teck Oh, Cosie Costa
▶ Sturdy prequel to *Missing in Action.* American colonel Norris is captured when his helicopter crashes in Vietnam. He's imprisoned and tortured by the sadistic Vietcong. Among other atrocities, the V.C. put Norris's head in a bag with a rat, which really makes Chuck mad. Of course, he outfoxes his torturers and gets a large measure of revenge.
Dist.: MGM/UA

MISSING LINK, THE 1988 French/Belgian
★★★ PG Animation/Adult 1:35
☑ Nudity, adult situations, explicit language
Dir: Picha *Cast:* Voices of Ron Venable, John Graham, Bob Kaliban, Christopher Guest, Clark Warren, Mark Smith
▶ The missing link in human evolution is found and reared by dinosaurs after being abandoned by his prehistoric tribe. When he is old enough to realize the difference between himself and his adoptive parents, he searches for his people. Inventive animation from cartoonist Picha; music by Leo Sayer. In English.
Dist.: MCA

MISSING LINK, THE 1988
★★ PG Drama 1:31
☑ Violence
Dir: David Hughes, Carol Hughes *Cast:* Peter Elliott, narrated by Michael Gambon
▶ In Africa, one million years ago, man-ape Elliott discovers that his wife and child have been killed by the next stage in the evolutionary cycle—Man. Elliott wanders the land where food is now in short supply. Prehistoric saga has the quality of a documentary. Makeup by two-time Oscar winner Rick Baker.
Dist.: MCA

MISSION, THE 1986 British
★★★★ PG Action-Adventure 2:05
☑ Adult situations, explicit language, violence
Dir: Roland Joffe *Cast:* Robert De Niro, Jeremy Irons, Ray McAnally, Aidan Quinn, Cherie Lunghi, Ronald Pickup
▶ The jungles of eighteenth-century Brazil provide a dramatic backdrop to an intriguing power struggle between a Jesuit religious society promoting the interests of the Indian natives and government officials determined to consolidate their power over the colony. De Niro delivers another commanding performance as a soldier whose faith is tested by poli-

tics, but film's themes are sometimes obscured by the elaborate production values. Oscar-winning cinematography by Chris Menges. **(CC)**
Dist.: Warner

MISSIONARY, THE 1982 British
★ R Comedy 1:27
☑ Brief nudity, adult situations, explicit language, adult humor
Dir: Richard Loncraine *Cast:* Michael Palin, Maggie Smith, Trevor Howard, Denholm Elliott, Michael Hordern, Phoebe Nicholls
▶ In 1906, idealistic British missionary Palin returns from Africa and is assigned to a home for fallen women. Palin tends to his charges beyond the call of duty, falling into bed with them and being seduced by the mission's wealthy patron (Smith). Daffy comedy with thin story is longer on small chuckles than big laughs. Sumptuous period settings, delightful Smith and Nicholls.
Dist.: HBO

MISSION KILL 1985
★★ R Action-Adventure 1:37
☑ Adult situations, explicit language, graphic violence
Dir: David Winters *Cast:* Robert Ginty, Cameron Mitchell, Merete Van Kamp, Olivia d'Abo, Henry Darrow, Eduardo Lopez Rojas
▶ Demolitions expert Ginty is trapped in the middle of a Central American revolution when his Marine pal Mitchell is killed by rebels. After witnessing atrocities ordered by dictator Rojas and his underling Darrow, Ginty conducts series of terrorist attacks that turn him into folk hero. Workmanlike low-budget action offers good stunts and competent acting.
Dist.: Media

MISSISSIPPI BURNING 1988
★★★★ R Drama 2:00
☑ Adult situations, explicit language, violence
Dir: Alan Parker *Cast:* Gene Hackman, Willem Dafoe, Frances McDormand, Brad Dourif, Lee Ermey, Gailard Sartain
▶ In 1964, young, by-the-book FBI honcho Dafoe and good ol' boy assistant Hackman investigate the suspicious disappearance of three civil rights workers in backwoods Jessup County. When it seems likely that local citizens killed the three using KKK nighttime terror tactics, Dafoe ups the ante by calling in hundreds of Bureau men. Disastrous results force Dafoe to yield to Hackman's more unorthodox approach. Based on real events, gripping, often disturbing drama takes more than a few liberties with the facts but always entertains. Nominated for seven Oscars, including Best Picture, Actor (Hackman), Supporting Actress (McDormand), and Director; won for Cinematography.
Dist.: Orion

MISS MARY 1986 Argentinian
☆ **R Drama 1:40**
☑ Adult situations, explicit language
Dir: Maria Luisa Bemberg *Cast:* Julie Christie, Nacha Guevara, Tato Pavlovsky, Gerardo Romano, Luisina Brando, Donald McIntyre
► Prim Englishwoman Christie gets governess job with a wealthy but weird Argentine family just before World War II. Christie helps the two daughters through adolescence but a scandal occurs when she sleeps with their brother. Ponderous pace, confusing structure. Mostly in English, a few subtitles. [S]
Dist.: New World

MISSOURI BREAKS, THE 1976
★★★★ **PG Western 2:06**
☑ Violence
Dir: Arthur Penn *Cast:* Marlon Brando, Jack Nicholson, Randy Quaid, Frederic Forrest, Harry Dean Stanton, Kathleen Lloyd
► Nicholson plays a bumbling horse thief pursued by mercenary lawman Brando. Despite an unusual showdown in a bubble bath, the picture rambles, neither a straight Western nor a spoof. A dream cast, talented director, and stylish screenwriter (novelist Tom McGuane) produced a resounding box office dud. Critics were especially hard on Brando for a performance deemed overblown and completely at odds with the rest of the film.
Dist.: Key

MISS SADIE THOMPSON 1953
★★★ **NR Drama 1:31**
Dir: Curtis Bernhardt *Cast:* Rita Hayworth, Jose Ferrer, Aldo Ray, Russell Collins, Charles Buchinski
► Hayworth is a sultry prostitute who turns a tropical island upside down, stealing the heart of innocent soldier Ray and awakening lust in missionary Ferrer. Fourth cinematic version of W. Somerset Maugham's short story "Rain" updates scene to Marine-occupied isle and adds a somewhat happier ending than most. Sexy Hayworth sings "The Heat Is On" in a smokey room full of soldiers. Originally in 3-D.
Dist.: RCA/Columbia

MISTAKEN IDENTITY 1936
☆ **NR Comedy 1:15 B&W**
Dir: Phil Rosen *Cast:* Chick Chandler, Evalyn Knapp, Berton Churchill, Patricia Farr, Richard Carle, Bradley Page
► At a posh hotel where no one is whom they appear to be, Churchill and two other genial con men try to convince each other that they are millionaires. Churchill and daughter Farr pretend to be everything from tobacco tycoons to Russian royalty in this amusing romp filled with funny situations. Also known as *Three of a Kind*.
Dist.: Video Yesteryear

MISTER ROBERTS 1955
★★★★ **NR Comedy 1:56**
Dir: John Ford, Mervyn LeRoy *Cast:* Henry Fonda, James Cagney, Jack Lemmon, William Powell, Betsy Palmer
► During World War II, cargo ship officer Mister Roberts (Fonda) battles authoritarian captain Cagney on behalf of his men (including Lemmon's jaunty Ensign Pulver and Powell's kindly doctor) while yearning for the excitement of real wartime action. Terrific adaptation of the Pulitzer prize–winning novel and play is alternately funny and moving. Perfectly cast Fonda is solid; Oscar-winning Lemmon steals the show. A Best Picture nominee.
Dist.: Warner

MISUNDERSTOOD 1984
★★★★ **PG Drama 1:35**
☑ Adult situations
Dir: Jerry Schatzberg *Cast:* Gene Hackman, Rip Torn, Henry Thomas, Huckleberry Fox, Susan Anspach
► Melodrama about Hackman, a workaholic shipping magnate based in Tunisia who neglects his sons Thomas and Fox. The three come to terms with each other after Mom dies (cameo by Anspach). As usual Hackman rises above sudsy material.
Dist.: MGM/UA

MIXED BLOOD 1985
☆ **NR Drama 1:37**
☑ Adult situations, explicit language, graphic violence
Dir: Paul Morrissey *Cast:* Marila Pera, Richard Ulacia, Geraldine Smith, Rodney Harvey, Angel David, Linda Kerridge
► With her son Ulacia, Brazilian Pera runs a Lower East Side drug gang whose fourteen-year-old members are too young to serve time. Ulacia falls for uptown blond Kerridge, who is kidnapped along with Pera by a rival Spanish gang. Roughly made, uncomfortably unpolished look at the drug world is considered tongue-in-cheek by some.
Dist.: Media

MOBY DICK 1956
★★ **NR Action-Adventure 1:56**
Dir: John Huston *Cast:* Gregory Peck, Richard Basehart, Leo Genn, Orson Welles, Harry Andrews, Bernard Miles, James Robertson Justice
► Despite warnings from ominous preacher Welles, seaman Basehart sets sail aboard a whaling ship leaving New Bedford in 1840. The obsessed Captain Ahab (Peck), scarred and peg legged, then announces to the crew they are on a vengeance mission to kill Moby Dick, the great white whale that disfigured him. Fine adaptation of the Herman Melville classic, with screenplay by director Huston and sci-fi author Ray Bradbury.
Dist.: CBS/Fox

MODEL BEHAVIOR 1985
☆ **NR Comedy 1:26**
☑ Nudity, adult situations
Dir: Bud Gardner *Cast:* Richard Bekins,

Bruce Lyons, Anne Howard, Lisa McMillan, Antonio Fargas

▶ A hustler and an ad agency drone scheme to meet beautiful women by pretending to be a photographer and a Hollywood talent agent. Not bad sex comedy premise but execution lacks wit and imagination. Some nice looking bodies but actual nudity and sex is downplayed.
Dist.: Vestron

MODERN GIRLS 1986
★ ★ PG-13 Comedy 1:22
☑ Adult situations, explicit language, adult humor
Dir: Jerry Kramer *Cast:* Daphne Zuniga, Virginia Madsen, Cynthia Gibb, Clayton Rohner, Chris Nash

▶ During a night out for three fun-loving roommates, Madsen pursues a disc jockey, gets strung out on pills, and must be saved by her pals from manhandling. Gibb briefly hooks up with rocker Rohner, and Zuniga eventually ends up with teacher (also Rohner) previously dumped by Madsen. Fluffy look at the Los Angeles club scene. Sample dialogue: "Cool people have feelings too."
Dist.: Paramount

MODERN PROBLEMS 1981
★ ★ PG Comedy 1:31
☑ Explicit language, adult humor
Dir: Ken Shapiro *Cast:* Chevy Chase, Patti D'Arbanville, Mary Kay Place, Dabney Coleman, Nell Carter

▶ Hapless air traffic controller Chase acquires telekinetic powers, transforming his jealous tirades over girlfriend D'Arbanville and ex-wife Place into special effects showcases. Chase and the underutilized cast often seem on automatic pilot as the script drags, but some comic bits are memorable.
Dist.: CBS/Fox

MODERN ROMANCE 1981
★ R Comedy 1:34
☑ Nudity, adult situations, explicit language
Dir: Albert Brooks *Cast:* Albert Brooks, Kathryn Harrold, Bruno Kirby, Jane Hallaren, James L. Brooks

▶ Breaking up is hard to do for Brooks and on-again/off-again girlfriend Harrold. Mostly one-man show for Brooks's jealous neuroses, but Harrold is a stunner in her limited screen time. Director James L. Brooks (no relation) makes cameo appearance spoofing the filmmaking biz. Cult followers of Brooks and his quirky, angst-driven humor won't be disappointed, but nonbelievers will wonder what all the fuss is about.
Dist.: RCA/Columbia

MODERNS, THE 1988
★ ★ R Drama 2:06
☑ Nudity, adult situations, explicit language, violence
Dir: Alan Rudolph *Cast:* Keith Carradine,

Linda Fiorentino, Genevieve Bujold, Geraldine Chaplin, Wallace Shawn, John Lone

▶ In 1926 Paris, struggling painter Carradine romances ex-wife Fiorentino under the nose of her current husband Lone, a wealthy collector, and gets involved in an art forging scheme. Colorful but not very compelling drama of American expatriates. Pretty music and cinematography, but overlong story with absurd portrayals of famous figures (Hemingway, Gertrude Stein, Alice B. Toklas).
Dist.: Nelson

MODERN TIMES 1936
★ ★ ★ ★ G Comedy 1:27 B&W
Dir: Charlie Chaplin *Cast:* Charlie Chaplin, Paulette Goddard, Henry Bergman, Chester Conklin

▶ Factory worker Chaplin suffers through machine-induced nervous breakdown, a strike, a jail sentence, and other modern problems while finding companionship with an orphan (his fetching then-wife Goddard). Chaplin's last silent film does have music (including "Smile"), sound effects, brief dialogue, and Charlie singing a delightful nonsensical song. A gem, masterfully combining hilarious slapstick, machine-age satire, tenderness, and heartbreak.
Dist.: CBS/Fox

MOGAMBO 1953
★ ★ ★ NR Action-Adventure 1:56
Dir: John Ford *Cast:* Clark Gable, Ava Gardner, Grace Kelly, Donald Sinden, Laurence Naismith

▶ Sparks fly in a triangle between safari guide Gable, married Englishwoman Kelly, and jetsetter Gardner during an upriver trip in Central Africa. Old-fashioned entertainment, Hollywood style. Amusing dialogue, exotic locations, romance, and bubbling star chemistry. Our favorite scene: Ava giving her bubble gum to a chimp. Remake of the 1932 *Red Dust*, which also starred Gable.
Dist.: MGM/UA

MOLLY MAGUIRES, THE 1970
★ ★ ★ PG Drama 2:05
☑ Adult situations, explicit language, violence
Dir: Martin Ritt *Cast:* Sean Connery, Richard Harris, Samantha Eggar, Frank Finlay, Anthony Zerbe, Art Lund

▶ In 1876 Pennsylvania, company spy Harris infiltrates the Mollies, an Irish mineworkers union violently battling inhuman conditions. He befriends leader Connery and romances miner's daughter Eggar but eventually must betray them. Ambitious, fact-based drama has handsome period production, strong performances, and haunting Henry Mancini score.
Dist.: Paramount

MOMMIE DEAREST 1981
★ ★ ★ PG Drama 2:09
☑ Explicit language, violence

Dir: Frank Perry   *Cast:* Faye Dunaway, Diana Scarwid, Steve Forrest, Howard da Silva, Mara Hobel

▶ In a tour-de-force performance, Dunaway transforms herself passionately and completely into Joan Crawford. Based on Christina Crawford's autobiography about growing up the adopted and abused daughter of the movie queen, the film generally lacks insight and depth. Nonetheless, it has become a kind of cult classic for its glossy good looks, memorable performances (da Silva is brilliant as L. B. Mayer) and quotable dialogue ("No wire hangers!").
Dist.: Paramount

MONA LISA 1986 British
★ ★ R Drama 1:40
☑ Nudity, adult situations, explicit language, violence
Dir: Neil Jordan   *Cast:* Bob Hoskins, Cathy Tyson, Michael Caine, Clarke Peters, Kate Hardie, Robbie Coltrane

▶ Cockney ex-con Hoskins is hired by crime czar Caine as a driver for high class call girl Tyson. Hoskins falls for her and risks his life to search for her missing friend. Dominating, magnetic performance by Hoskins makes his unusual relationship with the haunting Tyson quite touching. Stylish direction by Jordan conveys a convincingly sleazy atmosphere, yet the movie is basically sentimental. Hoskins received an Oscar nomination for Best Actor.
Dist.: HBO

MONDO CANE 1963 Italian
★ R Documentary 1:47
☑ Nudity, adult situations, graphic violence
Dir: Gualtiero Jacopetti

▶ Documentary look at gruesome customs and sights throughout the world: puppy cooking in Formosa, hog slaughter in New Guinea, Bikini turtles dying of radiation, etc. Shocking and a box office success in its time but now merely the stuff of nightmares. Oscar nomination for Best Song ("More"). Dubbed.
Dist.: Various

MONDO NEW YORK 1988
☆ NR Documentary 1:22
☑ Nudity, adult situations, explicit language, graphic violence
Dir: Harvey Keith   *Cast:* Rick Aviles, Charlie Barnett, Ann Magnuson, Karen Finlay, Dean Johnson, Phoebe Legere

▶ Look at New York City's East Village performance art scene includes no-holds-barred turns by controversial Finlay, who breaks eggs over her naked body while reciting antiyuppie diatribe, and Johnson, a six-foot-plus bald drag queen who performs a deliberately outrageous rap song. Alternately provocative and offensive; grotesque violence includes people biting the heads off mice and chickens.
Dist.: MPI

MONEY PIT, THE 1986
★ ★ ★ ★ PG Comedy 1:31
☑ Adult situations, explicit language
Dir: Richard Benjamin   *Cast:* Tom Hanks, Shelley Long, Maureen Stapleton, Alexander Godunov, Joe Mantegna, Philip Bosco

▶ Flaky musician Long and her live-in lawyer/lover Hanks attempt to renovate a rundown mansion. Outlandish special effects include collapsing stairways, exploding plumbing, falling doors, and defective wiring. Godunov is Long's arrogant ex-husband.   **(CC)**
Dist.: MCA

MONKEY BUSINESS 1931
★ ★ ★ ★ NR Comedy 1:27 B&W
Dir: Norman Z. McLeod   *Cast:* Groucho Marx, Harpo Marx, Chico Marx, Zeppo Marx, Thelma Todd, Tom Kennedy

▶ In the first of their films to be written directly for the screen, the loopy brothers stow away on a luxury liner. Chaos reigns, aided by a pair of gangsters and Groucho's wooing of Todd. Plenty of laughs; fine work from the brothers and Todd assure fans and newcomers a good time.
Dist.: MCA

MONKEY BUSINESS 1952
★ ★ ★ NR Comedy 1:37 B&W
Dir: Howard Hawks   *Cast:* Cary Grant, Ginger Rogers, Charles Coburn, Marilyn Monroe, Hugh Marlowe, George "Foghorn" Winslow

▶ While scientist Grant experiments to find a youth potion, one of his lab chimps laces water fountain with a successful version of the formula. Grant reverts to college shenanigans with lab secretary Monroe; he and wife Rogers later slide all the way back to preadolescence. Amusing screwball romp delivered by an expert cast.
Dist.: CBS/Fox

MONKEY GRIP 1982 Australian
☆ NR Drama 1:41
☑ Nudity, adult situations, explicit language
Dir: Ken Cameron   *Cast:* Noni Hazlehurst, Colin Friels, Alice Garner, Harold Hopkins, Candy Raymond, Michael Caton

▶ Recently divorced writer Hazlehurst lives with her daughter in a Melbourne commune. She has affair with junkie actor Friels but his heroin addiction makes the relationship a turbulent one. Talented cast tries to breathe life into self-absorbed, self-indulgent characters.
Dist.: Nelson

MONKEYS, GO HOME! 1967
★ ★ ★ NR Family 1:29
Dir: Andrew V. McLaglen   *Cast:* Maurice Chevalier, Dean Jones, Yvette Mimieux, Bernard Woringer, Jules Munshin, Alan Carney

▶ Jones travels to France to claim his inheritance, an olive farm. After priest Chevalier warns him about the odds against making a profit, Jones decides to use chimps as workers. Mimieux helps him and becomes his girlfriend.

Disney film a notch below their usual high standard, but kids should go bananas for the chimps.
Dist.: Buena Vista

MONKEY SHINES: AN EXPERIMENT IN FEAR 1988
★ ★ ★ R Horror 1:55
☑ Nudity, adult situations, explicit language, violence
Dir: George A. Romero *Cast:* Jason Beghe, John Pankow, Kate McNeil, Joyce Van Patten, Christine Forrest, Boo the Monkey
► When law student Beghe is rendered quadraplegic, scientist Pankow provides experimental monkey Boo to assist him with daily chores. Boo takes the task too close to heart, going on a murderous rampage against Beghe's enemies. After low-gear start, Romero masterfully builds to hair-raising shudders; amazing performance by Boo the Monkey. (CC)
Dist.: Orion

MONKEY'S UNCLE, THE 1965
★ ★ ★ NR Family 1:27
Dir: Robert Stevenson *Cast:* Tommy Kirk, Annette Funicello, Leon Ames, Frank Faylen, Arthur O'Connell, Norman Grabowski
► Sequel to *The Misadventures of Merlin Jones* features Kirk as the young genius who teaches a chimp English. After applying his monkey lessons on two human idiots, Kirk turns his attentions to a man-powered flying machine. Perky monkeyshines from Disney. The Beach Boys and Funicello sing the title song.
Dist.: Buena Vista

MON ONCLE 1958 French
☆ NR Comedy 1:50
Dir: Jacques Tati *Cast:* Jacques Tati, Jean-Pierre Zola, Adrienne Servantie, Alain Becourt, Lucien Fregis, Betty Schneider
► Director Tati plays a disheveled, unaffected man, in contrast to his brother-in-law Zola, who resides in a sanitized suburban home cluttered with the latest gadgets. Tati's nephew Becourt prefers his uncle's simple life, but neither can completely escape modernization. In this sight-gag satire of technology addicts, Tati reprises the character he created in *Mr. Hulot's Holiday*. Oscar winner for Best Foreign Film. Dubbed version available.
Ⓢ
Dist.: Nelson

MON ONCLE D'AMERIQUE 1980 French
★ PG Drama 2:05
☑ Adult situations
Dir: Alain Resnais *Cast:* Gerard Depardieu, Nicole Garcia, Roger Pierre, Marie Dubois, Nelly Bourgeaud, Henri Laborit
► Real-life behavioral scientist Laborit provides commentary on executive Depardieu's adjustment to corporate upheaval and married man Pierre's affair with actress Garcia. Talky and dry but still provocative; the fictional situations interweave with Laborit's theories in complex and surprisingly humorous fashion. Recommended only for discerning moviegoers. Ⓢ
Dist.: Nelson

MONSIEUR HIRE 1989 French
★ PG-13 Drama 1:21
☑ Brief nudity, adult situations, explicit language
Dir: Patrice Leconte *Cast:* Michel Blanc, Sandrine Bonnaire, Luc Thuiller, André Wilms
► Lonely Blanc lives across the street from Bonnaire, whom he spies on. When a murder occurs in the neighborhood, Blanc realizes her petty criminal boyfriend Thuiller is responsible. Precise, subtle psychological thriller is beautifully crafted. Terrific performances from Blanc and Bonnaire. Ⓢ
Dist.: Orion

MONSIEUR VERDOUX 1947
★ ★ ★ ★ NR Comedy 2:04 B&W
Dir: Charles Chaplin *Cast:* Charles Chaplin, Martha Raye, Maddy Correll, Isobel Elsom, William Frawley
► Former bank teller Chaplin supports his crippled wife and child by wedding rich ladies and murdering them for their money. Cynical black comedy, a departure for writer/director/star/composer Chaplin. Overlong and belabors its point but original and unusual. Best scenes pair Chaplin with his gabby would-be victim Raye.
Dist.: CBS/Fox

MONSIGNOR 1982
★ ★ ★ R Drama 2:02
☑ Nudity, adult situations, explicit language, violence
Dir: Frank Perry *Cast:* Christopher Reeve, Genevieve Bujold, Fernando Rey, Jason Miller, Joe Cortese, Leonardo Cimino
► Corrupt priest Reeve rises to Vatican treasurer, making deals with the mob and seducing novice Bujold. Earnest mix of religion, crime, and soap opera passion is sometimes unintentionally laugh-provoking, as when Bujold stops short in church on discovering her lover is a priest, causing a traffic jam of nuns bunching up behind her.
Dist.: CBS/Fox

MONSTER CLUB, THE 1980 British
☆ NR Comedy/Horror 1:37
☑ Brief nudity, mild violence
Dir: Roy Ward Baker *Cast:* Vincent Price, Donald Pleasence, John Carradine, Stuart Whitman, Richard Johnson, Britt Ekland
► Three tales united by framing device of vampire Price welcoming newcomer Carradine into monsters' disco club: a monster disguised as an antique dealer woos a woman, vampire Johnson is hunted by Pleasence, and film director Whitman's encounter with a scary location. Price and Carradine are funnier than the main stories.
Dist.: IVE

MONSTER FROM GREEN HELL 1957
☆ **NR Horror 1:11 B&W**
Dir: Kenneth Crane *Cast:* Jim Davis, Robert E. Griffin, Barbara Turner, Joel Fluellen, Vladimir Sokoloff, Eduardo Cianelli
▶ Wasps go up in a space probe and come down in the jungle, where a dose of radiation causes them to grow into huge, nonflying monsters. The beasts nonplus Davis, who is leading an expedition into the jungle to recover the space capsule. Giant insect tale has been done better elsewhere. Devotees of bad movies will enjoy the way the dialogue desperately stalls off special effects until the bitter end.
Dist.: Sinister

MONSTER HIGH 1989
☆ **R Comedy/Sci-Fi 1:30**
☑ Nudity, adult situations, explicit language
Dir: Rudiger Poe *Cast:* Dean Iandoli, Diana Frank, David Marriot, David Bloch
▶ High schooler Iandoli adores coed Frank, who also becomes object of alien Marriot's affections when outer space men land in town. Iandoli attempts to outsmart the invaders and save the world. A couple of clever touches, but low-budget production runs short of real laughs.
Dist.: RCA/Columbia

MONSTER IN THE CLOSET 1986
☆ **PG Horror/Comedy 1:27**
☑ Brief nudity, explicit language, violence
Dir: Bob Dahlin *Cast:* Donald Grant, Denise DuBarry, Claude Akins, Howard Duff, Henry Gibson, Paul Dooley
▶ Comedy of terrors attempts to spoof 1950s horror classics. Grant, a Clark Kent–type reporter, investigates a baffling series of brutal closet murders. Along with biology teacher DuBarry, madly in love with him, and Nobel Prize–winning scientist Gibson, he discovers the culprit is a ravenous, hunchback monster. High point: DuBarry on national TV, pleading, "Destroy all closets!" **(CC)**
Dist.: Warner

MONSTER MAKER, THE 1944
★ **NR Horror 1:02 B&W**
Dir: Sam Newfield *Cast:* J. Carrol Naish, Ralph Morgan, Wanda McKay, Terry Frost, Glenn Strange, Sam Flint
▶ Nutty doctor Naish and muscleman Strange inject concert pianist Morgan with germs, giving him a disfiguring disease. Naish's idea is to cure him, and make a big impression on McKay, the pianist's beautiful daughter. Plan backfires, of course. Wretched script and low-budget lensing fail to redeem creepy premise.
Dist.: Video Yesteryear

MONSTER SQUAD, THE 1987
★ ★ ★ **PG-13 Horror/Comedy 1:22**
☑ Explicit language, violence
Dir: Fred Dekker *Cast:* Andre Gower,
Robby Kiger, Stephen Macht, Duncan Regehr, Tom Noonan, Brent Chalam
▶ It's up to a group of monster-movie-loving schoolchildren to save the day when Frankenstein, Dracula, the Mummy, the Wolfman, and the Creature from the Black Lagoon descend on a small town. Simple story geared for the younger set, who should love it. Appealing kid actors and tongue-in-cheek humor, but not really that scary.
Dist.: Vestron

MONTENEGRO 1981 Swedish/British
★ **R Comedy 1:34**
☑ Nudity, adult situations, explicit language
Dir: Dusan Makavejev *Cast:* Susan Anspach, Erland Josephson, Jamie Marsh, Per Oscarsson, Bora Todorovic, Svetzovar Cvetkovic
▶ Upscale American housewife Anspach, living in Sweden with husband Josephson and children, forsakes her boring marriage for a quick and passionate affair with Yugoslavian hunk Cvetkovic. Offbeat, steamy comedy from avant-garde director Makavejev.
Dist.: HBO

MONTEREY POP 1968
★ ★ ★ **NR Documentary/Music 1:28**
Dir: James Desmond, Barry Feinstein, D. A. Pennebaker, Albert Maysles, Roger Murphy, Richard Leacock, Nick Proferes *Cast:* Jefferson Airplane, Janis Joplin, Jimi Hendrix, The Mamas and Papas, Otis Redding, The Who
▶ Landmark documentary about the 1967 rock 'n' roll festival at Monterey captures some of the sixties' brightest stars at their peaks. Highlights include Joplin's mesmerizing "Ball and Chain," a white-hot performance by Redding, Hendrix's dazzling guitar workout, and a blockbuster rendition of "My Generation" by The Who.
Dist.: SVS

MONTE WALSH 1970
★ ★ ★ ★ **PG Western 1:40**
☑ Adult situations
Dir: William A. Fraker *Cast:* Lee Marvin, Jeanne Moreau, Jack Palance, Mitch Ryan, Jim Davis, John "Bear" Hudkins
▶ Cowpoke chums Marvin and Palance face dwindling options when their ranch is closed by Eastern money interests; Marvin must also confront his lover Moreau's fatal consumption in this somber Western. Noted photographer Fraker's directorial debut eloquently describes passing of an era. **(CC)**
Dist.: CBS/Fox

MONTH IN THE COUNTRY, A 1988 British
★ ★ **PG Drama 1:36**
☑ Adult situations
Dir: Pat O'Connor *Cast:* Colin Firth, Kenneth Branagh, Natasha Richardson, Patrick Malahide
▶ Art restorer Firth, still haunted by memories of service in World War I, accepts the job of

rejuvenating a mysterious church fresco. In the process, he begins to fall in love with parson's wife Richardson. Exceedingly tasteful British drama is well-acted but terribly genteel and slowly paced.
Dist.: Warner

MONTY PYTHON AND THE HOLY GRAIL
1974 British
★ ★ ★ PG Comedy 1:29
☑ Adult situations, explicit language, violence, adult humor
Dir: Terry Gilliam, Terry Jones *Cast:* Graham Chapman, John Cleese, Eric Idle, Michael Palin, Terry Jones, Terry Gilliam
▶ Merry takeoff on medieval era features the Python gang as King Arthur and the knights of the Round Table on a quest for the Holy Grail. Obstacles in their path include renegade knights obsessed with shrubbery and a bridge guard who demands answers to three questions (like "What's your favorite color?"). Many priceless moments: Cleese apologizing after slaughtering party of innocents, cowardly Idle objecting to minstrel's singing of how he "runneth away," and knight continuing duel despite severed limbs.
Dist.: RCA/Columbia

MONTY PYTHON LIVE AT THE HOLLYWOOD BOWL 1982 British
★ ★ ★ R Documentary/Comedy 1:21
☑ Explicit language, adult humor
Dir: Terry Hughes *Cast:* Graham Chapman, John Cleese, Terry Gilliam, Eric Idle, Terry Jones, Michael Palin
▶ Inimitable Pythons perform new skits and re-create old favorites in front of a crowd of adoring Angelenos. Troupe's acid wit and bawdy antics are at their finest here. Those who have acquired the taste will be amused; those who tire of dead parrot jokes should stay away.
Dist.: HBO

MONTY PYTHON'S LIFE OF BRIAN 1979 British
★ ★ R Comedy 1:34
☑ Explicit language, violence, adult humor
Dir: Terry Jones *Cast:* Graham Chapman, John Cleese, Eric Idle, Michael Palin, Terry Jones, Terry Gilliam
▶ The life and times of one Brian of Nazareth (Chapman), a somewhat reluctant messiah born the same day as Jesus. Religious satire has moments of inspired lunacy, such as crucified people singing the cheery "Always Look on the Bright Side of Life." Python fans will love it although others may be offended by irreverant humor.
Dist.: Warner

MONTY PYTHON'S THE MEANING OF LIFE
1983 British
★ ★ R Comedy 1:47
☑ Nudity, adult situations, explicit language, violence, adult humor
Dir: Terry Jones *Cast:* Terry Gilliam, John

Cleese, Eric Idle, Terry Jones, Graham Chapman, Michael Palin
▶ Plotless grab-bag of skits from the ever-irreverent Brits. Here the Pythons cast their satirical eye at big issues: death, the afterlife, contraception, and twenty-five-course meals, with typically rude and raucous results. Fans will no doubt be delighted, although many find the sketches of uneven quality. Warning: do not view this on a full stomach.
Dist.: MCA

MOON IN THE GUTTER, THE 1983 French
☆ R Drama 2:06
☑ Nudity, explicit language, violence
Dir: Jean-Jacques Beineix *Cast:* Nastassia Kinski, Gerard Depardieu, Victoria Abril, Vittorio Mezzogiorno
▶ Hulking dockworker Depardieu seeks the rapist who drove his sister to suicide. Enter sultry rich brat Kinski to distract him from the squalor of his life; exit all semblance of a coherent plot. Lots of pretty images. Ⓢ
Dist.: RCA/Columbia

MOON IS BLUE, THE 1953
★ ★ ★ PG Comedy 1:39 B&W
☑ Adult situations
Dir: Otto Preminger *Cast:* William Holden, David Niven, Maggie McNamara, Tom Tully, Dawn Addams, Gregory Ratoff
▶ New York architect Holden falls for young actress McNamara, who disrupts his home by flirting with Niven, his prospective father-in-law. Mild adaptation of a dated Broadway farce stirred some controversy for its adult themes. Title song and McNamara (in her film debut) received Oscar nominations.
Dist.: Magnetic

MOONLIGHTING 1982 British
★ ★ PG Drama 1:37
☑ Explicit language
Dir: Jerzy Skolimowski *Cast:* Jeremy Irons, Eugene Lipinski, Jiri Stanislav, Eugeniusz Hacziewicz
▶ Four Polish workers are sent to London to remodel a townhouse. Foreman Irons is the only one who speaks English. When he learns of Solidarity upheavals back home, he keeps the news from the others so they will finish the job. Quiet and reflective political meditation; well acted by Irons but placid pace may try patience. For sophisticated tastes. **(CC)** Ⓢ
Dist.: MCA

MOON OVER MIAMI 1941
★ ★ ★ NR Musical 1:31
Dir: Walter Lang *Cast:* Don Ameche, Betty Grable, Robert Cummings, Charlotte Greenwood, Carole Landis, Jack Haley
▶ Waitress Gable pretends to be a rich socialite in hopes of landing a wealthy husband. Millionaire Cummings proposes to her, but Grable finds herself falling for his penniless pal Ameche. Light, colorful entertainment, with plenty of songs including "Miami," "I've Got

You All to Myself," and "Kindergarten Conga."
(CC)
Dist.: Key

MOON OVER PARADOR 1988
★ ★ ★ PG-13 Comedy 1:45
☺ Adult situations, explicit language, violence
Dir: Paul Mazursky *Cast:* Richard Dreyfuss,
Raul Julia, Sonia Braga, Jonathan Winters,
Fernando Rey, Sammy Davis, Jr.
▶ When a Latin American dictator dies,
power-behind-the-throne Julia convinces
New York actor Dreyfuss to impersonate the
dead man. Dreyfuss gets involved with the
dictator's mistress Braga, CIA man Winters,
and land reform plan. Fizzy farce has infectious spirit; scattershot humor frequently hits
home. Dreyfuss struts his stuff amusingly and
Davis contributes a hilarious cameo.
Dist.: MCA

MOON PILOT 1962
★ ★ ★ NR Sci-Fi 1:38
Dir: James Neilson *Cast:* Tom Tryon, Brian
Keith, Edmond O'Brien, Dany Saval, Tommy
Kirk
▶ Playful chimp "volunteers" astronaut Tryon
to be the first man in orbit; beautiful alien
Saval suddenly arrives with a rocket-fuel formula to ensure the mission's success. Pleasant
Disney comedy pokes harmless fun at NASA;
romance between Saval and Tryon (later a
best-selling author) provides plenty of laughs.
Dist.: Buena Vista

MOONRAKER 1979 British
★ ★ ★ ★ PG Espionage/Action-Adventure
2:06
☺ Adult situations, explicit language
Dir: Lewis Gilbert *Cast:* Roger Moore, Lois
Chiles, Michael Lonsdale, Richard Kiel, Corinne Clery
▶ This time around (the 11th in the series)
aeronautics tycoon Lonsdale threatens the
world with nerve gas dispensed from his personal fleet of space shuttles. Bond saves the
planet by overcoming menacing Venetian
gondoliers and a tram car tango in Rio with
Jaws (Kiel). Glossy, action-packed fun with
standard exotic locales, nifty spy hardware,
ribald wit, and an explosive finale in space.
Dist.: MGM/UA

MOONRISE 1948
★ NR Drama 1:30 B&W
Dir: Frank Borzage *Cast:* Dane Clark, Gail
Russell, Ethel Barrymore, Allyn Joslyn, Rex Ingram, Henry Morgan
▶ In a southern town, Clark, the son of an executed murderer, faces persecution from the
locals. When he accidentally kills one of his
tormentors, he finds refuge in the swamp. Russell is Clark's schoolteacher girlfriend. Standard story with good performances and dark
direction from Borzage.
Dist.: Republic

MOONSHINE COUNTY EXPRESS 1977
★ ★ PG Action-Adventure 1:36
☺ Adult situations, explicit language, violence
Dir: Gus Trikonis *Cast:* John Saxon, Susan
Howard, William Conrad, Morgan Woodward, Claudia Jennings, Maureen McCormick
▶ Sexy sisters Howard, Jennings, and McCormick go after evil bootlegger Conrad, who
they think killed their moonshining father.
Bankrolled by a stash of Prohibition liquor, and
with help from Conrad's underling Saxon, the
girls take over their county. Lightweight lowbudget drama with plenty of action.
Dist.: Warner

MOON'S OUR HOME, THE 1936
★ NR Comedy 1:16 B&W
Dir: William A. Seiter *Cast:* Margaret Sullavan, Henry Fonda, Charles Butterworth,
Beulah Bondi, Walter Brennan, Margaret
Hamilton
▶ Movie star/deb Sullavan and adventurewriter Fonda meet and marry, neither knowing
that the other is famous. On their wedding
night, Sullavan uses a scent that drives Fonda
away, and the rest of the film is taken up with
their bickerings and reunions. Not all that
good; the few funny lines may have come
from pens of Dorothy Parker and husband
Alan Campbell, who are credited with "additional dialogue."
Dist.: KVC

MOON-SPINNERS, THE 1964
★ ★ ★ ★ NR Mystery-Suspense 1:58
Dir: James Neilson *Cast:* Hayley Mills, Eli
Wallach, Pola Negri, Peter McEnery, Joan
Greenwood, Irene Papas
▶ While vacationing in Crete, young Mills befriends wounded Englishman McEnery, a suspect trying to clear his name of robbery
charges. Modest Disney thriller, based on a
Mary Stewart novel, has beautiful settings and
good work from Wallach and Negri as the villains.
Dist.: Buena Vista

MOONSTRUCK 1987
★ ★ ★ ★ PG Romance/Comedy 1:43
☺ Adult situations, explicit language
Dir: Norman Jewison *Cast:* Cher, Nicolas
Cage, Vincent Gardenia, Olympia Dukakis,
Danny Aiello, John Mahoney, Julie Bovasso,
Feodor Chaliapin, Anita Gillette
▶ Magical look at love, Italian-American
style. Brooklyn widow Cher, about to settle into
a passionless marriage with Aiello, is pursued
by his wild one-handed brother Cage. Meanwhile, Cher's dad Gardenia showers trinkets
on Gillette while her long-suffering mom Dukakis meets wolfish NYU professor Mahoney. Perfect combination of romantic atmosphere,
warmth, and deadpan dialogue, especially in
the conversations between Cher and caustictongued Dukakis. Oscars for Cher, Dukakis,

and John Patrick Shanley's script. A Best Picture nominee. **(CC)**
Dist.: MGM/UA

MOONTRAP 1989
★ ★ **R Sci-Fi 1:30**
☑ Explicit language, violence
Dir: Robert Dyke *Cast:* Walter Koenig, Bruce Campbell, Leigh Lombardi, Robert Kurcz, John J. Saunders, Reavis Graham
▶ On a mysterious spaceship orbiting the Earth, astronauts Koenig and Campbell discover a spore that can turn itself into a killer robot. The pair then land on the moon, where they encounter ancient civilization survivor Lombardi and a whole robot army. Good performances by the leads plus suspenseful story overcome inexpensive special effects.
Dist.: SGE

MORE THE MERRIER, THE 1943
★ ★ ★ ★ **NR Comedy 1:44 B&W**
Dir: George Stevens *Cast:* Jean Arthur, Joel McCrea, Charles Coburn, Richard Gaines, Bruce Bennett
▶ Popular comedy based on Washington's World War II housing shortage, with Arthur a single woman who rents out a room to genial Coburn. Concerned about her love life, Coburn rents half his space to handsome Air Force mechanic McCrea. Buoyant romantic comedy received six Oscar nominations, with Coburn winning for his crusty Cupid. Remade with Cary Grant as *Walk, Don't Run.*
Dist.: RCA/Columbia

MORGAN: A SUITABLE CASE FOR TREATMENT 1966 British
★ **NR Comedy 1:37 B&W**
Dir: Karel Reisz *Cast:* David Warner, Vanessa Redgrave, Robert Stephens, Irene Handl
▶ Talented but unstable painter Warner is divorced by wife Redgrave. Refusing to accept her affair with wealthy art dealer Stephens, he kidnaps her. Bittersweet comedy is sometimes eccentric, funny, and endearing, but suffers from Reisz's dated visual tricks. Warner is super in a difficult role.
Dist.: HBO

MORGAN STEWART'S COMING HOME 1987
★ ★ ★ **PG-13 Comedy 1:28**
☑ Explicit language
Dir: Alan Smithee *Cast:* Jon Cryer, Lynn Redgrave, Nicholas Pryor, Paul Gleason, Viveka Davis
▶ Confused 17-year-old Cryer is brought home after years of boarding school to bolster dad Pryor's Senate campaign, which is based on family values. Redgrave, his uptight, no-nonsense mom, displays little patience or understanding. Convoluted plot involves corrupt aide Gleason, blackmail, a safe-deposit box, and a wild chase on girlfriend Davis's moped.
Dist.: HBO

MORITURI 1965
★ ★ **NR Drama 2:03 B&W**
Dir: Bernhard Wicki *Cast:* Marlon Brando, Yul Brynner, Janet Margolin, Trevor Howard, Wally Cox, William Redfield
▶ Brynner is the captain of a German cargo ship delivering rubber from Japan to France during World War II. He doesn't know that Nazi SS agent Brando is really a British spy, determined to incite mutiny among American POWs. Brando and Brynner are wonderful antagonists, and worth seeing in this study of divided loyalties. Also known as *The Saboteur, Code Name Morituri.* **(CC)**
Dist.: CBS/Fox

MORNING AFTER, THE 1986
★ ★ ★ ★ **R Mystery-Suspense 1:43**
☑ Brief nudity, adult situations, explicit language, violence
Dir: Sidney Lumet *Cast:* Jane Fonda, Jeff Bridges, Raul Julia, Diane Salinger, Richard Foronjy, Geoffrey Scott
▶ Alcoholic actress Fonda wakes up with the ultimate hangover: a dead body in her bed and no memory of the night before. Bridges is the mysterious redneck who may be her savior or her undoing. A satisfying thriller with Oscar-nominated Fonda and Bridges giving their all to unusually complex characterizations for the genre. Effectively moody direction by Lumet. **(CC)**
Dist.: Warner

MORNING GLORY 1933
★ ★ **NR Drama 1:14 B&W**
Dir: Lowell Sherman *Cast:* Katharine Hepburn, Douglas Fairbanks, Jr., Adolphe Menjou, Mary Duncan, C. Aubrey Smith
▶ Hepburn, a stagestruck New England girl, receives an indifferent welcome in New York until she meets promising playwright Fairbanks. Touching, small-scale, and somewhat dated drama was based on Zoe Akins's Broadway hit. Hepburn won her first Oscar for her glowing performance.
Dist.: Turner

MOROCCO 1930
★ ★ **NR Drama 1:32 B&W**
Dir: Josef von Sternberg *Cast:* Gary Cooper, Marlene Dietrich, Adolphe Menjou, Ulrich Haupt, Juliette Compton, Francis McDonald
▶ Moody drama about exotic nightclub singer Dietrich's infatuation with Foreign Legionnaire Cooper moves slowly, but Lee Garmes's stunning Oscar-nominated photography provides dazzling backdrop for romantic drama. Dietrich, who also received an Oscar nomination in her Hollywood debut, performs one of her most notorious songs, "What Am I Bid for These Apples."
Dist.: KVC

MORONS FROM OUTER SPACE 1985 British
☆ **PG-13 Comedy 1:26**
☑ Explicit language, adult humor

Dir: Mike Hodges *Cast:* Jimmy Nail, Mel Smith, Paul Brown, Joanne Pearce, Griff Rhys Jones, James B. Sikking
▶ Less-than-brilliant alien tourists from the planet Blob land in England, where they are transformed into international singing stars. Broad spoof has an engaging opening and pockets of laughter, but overall it's predictable and lowbrow.
Dist.: Cannon

MORTUARY 1983
★ R Horror 1:31
☑ Nudity, adult situations, explicit language, violence
Dir: Howard Avedis *Cast:* Mary McDonough, David Wallace, Bill Paxton, Lynda Day George, Christopher George
▶ Young McDonough suspects her father's death was no accident and traces the killing to a crazed mortician's son who works in his father's embalming room. Gross low-budget horror.
Dist.: Vestron

MOSCOW DOES NOT BELIEVE IN TEARS 1980 Russian
★★ NR Drama 2:30
☑ Adult situations
Dir: Vladimir Menschow *Cast:* Vera Alentova, Irina Muravyova, Raisa Ryazanova, Alexei Batalov, Alexander Fatiushin
▶ Three country women move to Moscow to seek fortunes and husbands. One marries an alcoholic hockey player, a second is impregnated and deserted by the father but becomes a successful factory boss, and the third has a happy marriage to a simple man. Old-fashioned, rambling soap opera offers insight into Russian life-style. Oscar for Best Foreign Film. [S]
Dist.: RCA/Columbia

MOSCOW ON THE HUDSON 1984
★★★ R Comedy 1:57
☑ Nudity, adult situations, explicit language, mild violence
Dir: Paul Mazursky *Cast:* Robin Williams, Maria Conchita Alonso, Cleavant Derricks, Alejandro Rey, Savely Kramarov, Elya Baskin
▶ Russian musician Williams defects in Bloomingdale's and faces difficult (if often comic) adjustment to life in America. Making the transition easier are new girlfriend Alonso and black pal Derricks. A gentle and compassionate melting pot of laughter and tears. Brave and winning performance from Williams, whose accent is perfect. (CC)
Dist.: RCA/Columbia

MOSQUITO COAST, THE 1986
★★ PG Action-Adventure 1:59
☑ Explicit language, violence
Dir: Peter Weir *Cast:* Harrison Ford, Helen Mirren, River Phoenix, Martha Plimpton, Andre Gregory
▶ Eccentric inventor Ford, disillusioned with life in America, moves his family to a Central American jungle. His attempt to build an ideal community is noble but misguided and ultimately tragic. Original and interesting adventure, beautifully mounted and artfully directed. Although Ford brilliantly extends his acting range, it's difficult to empathize with his eccentric and often unlikable character. Based on Paul Theroux's best-selling novel. (CC)
Dist.: Warner

MOST DANGEROUS GAME, THE 1932
★★ NR Mystery-Suspense 1:03 B&W
Dir: Ernest B. Schoedsack, Irving Pichel
Cast: Joel McCrea, Fay Wray, Leslie Banks, Robert Armstrong, Steve Clemento, Noble Johnson
▶ McCrea, Wray, and Armstrong are shipwrecked on an island ruled by Russian count Banks. Although treated hospitably at first, the three quickly learn that Banks intends to use them as prey in a sadistic hunt. Gripping, genuinely frightening adaptation of Richard Connell's famous story has been the unofficial inspiration for countless chase films.
Dist.: KVC

MOST DANGEROUS MAN ALIVE, THE 1961
★ NR Sci-Fi 1:22 B&W
Dir: Allan Dwan *Cast:* Ron Randell, Debra Paget, Elaine Stewart, Anthony Caruso, Gregg Palmer
▶ After running smack dab into the middle of a cobalt explosion, gangster Randell metamorphoses into an indestructible man of steel. Ex-girlfriend Paget and fellow crooks become targets of his revenge, while true-blue Stewart tries salvage what little good is left in him. Combination of crime melodrama and sci-fi is well-handled and strangely compelling.
Dist.: Vestron

MOTEL HELL 1980
★ R Horror 1:43
☑ Nudity, explicit language, graphic violence
Dir: Kevin Connor *Cast:* Rory Calhoun, Paul Linke, Nancy Parsons, Nina Axelrod, Wolfman Jack, Elaine Joyce
▶ Uneasy blend of horror and black comedy centered around the remote hotel where Farmer Vincent (Calhoun) prepares his famous sausages. Beautiful biker Axelrod discovers Vincent's horrifying secret ingredient, leading to bloody confrontations. Dueling chainsaws sequence provides the most laughs.
Dist.: MGM/UA

MOTHER, JUGS AND SPEED 1976
★★★ PG Comedy 1:35
☑ Explicit language, adult humor
Dir: Peter Yates *Cast:* Bill Cosby, Raquel Welch, Harvey Keitel, Allen Garfield, Larry Hagman, Bruce Davison
▶ Keitel, Welk, and Cosby are big-city ambulance attendents working for Garfield and responding to a variety of emergency situations

both comic and tragic. Attempt at a M*A*S*H-style mix of sex, medics, and wis-cracks is okay, but some of the jokes are taste-less.
Dist.: Key

MOTHER LODE 1983
★★ **PG Action-Adventure 1:43**
☑ Explicit language, violence
Dir: Charlton Heston   *Cast:* Charlton Heston, Nick Mancuso, Kim Basinger, John Marley
► City dwellers Mancuso and Basinger crash-land on a mountain lake while searching for a missing friend. They encounter Scottish prospector Heston whose crazy brother (also Heston) is killing anyone who comes near his claim. Gorgeous Canadian wilderness scenery, colorful if overbearing Heston (whose son Fraser wrote the script), but a rather turgid narrative.
Dist.: Vestron

MOTHRA 1962 Japanese
★★ **NR Sci-Fi 1:41**
Dir: Inoshiro Honda, Lee Kresel   *Cast:* Franky Sakai, Hiroshi Koizumi, Kyoko Kagawa, Emi Ito, Yumi Ito, Jerry Ito
► Six-inch-tall twin princesses are kidnapped from their island home by unscrupulous Kagawa for display in his nightclub. The girls pray to god Mothra for help and soon an enormous caterpillar hatches on their island. Creature makes its way to Tokyo in search of the girls, laying waste to Japan. Dubbed into English by Toho Studios, creators of the Godzilla and Gammera monsters.
Dist.: RCA/Columbia

MOULIN ROUGE 1952
★★★ **NR Biography 2:03**
Dir: John Huston   *Cast:* Jose Ferrer, Zsa Zsa Gabor, Suzanne Flon, Eric Pohlmann, Colette Marchand, Christopher Lee
► With legs stunted in a childhood accident, artist Henri de Toulouse-Lautrec (Ferrer) tries to make the most of life, drawing the denizens of Paris's red light district and falling in love with prostitutes and models. The color is superb, and the opening can-can scenes are exhilarating, but tale soon descends into joyless drama. Nominated for five Oscars, including Best Picture; won for Best Costume Design (Color).
Dist.: MGM/UA

MOUNTAIN, THE 1956
★ **NR Drama 1:45**
Dir: Edward Dmytryk   *Cast:* Spencer Tracy, Robert Wagner, Claire Trevor, William Demarest, Anna Kashfi, E. G. Marshall
► When an airliner crashes into a towering Alp, unprincipled Wagner climbs up to loot the dead bodies. Decent brother Tracy, an experienced mountaineer, follows him, and later defies him to rescue lone survivor Kashfi.

A few thrills, with beautiful color photography of the French Alps. **(CC)**
Dist.: Paramount

MOUNTAIN FAMILY ROBINSON 1979
★★★★ **G Family 1:39**
Dir: John Cotter   *Cast:* Robert Logan, Susan Damante Shaw, William Bryant, Heather Rattray, Ham Larsen, George "Buck" Flower
► Pa Robinson (Logan) and his family build a log cabin on the site of his uncle's mining claim in the Colorado Rockies. A mining agent wants to run them off the land, but friendly prospector Flower helps save the day. Good-natured family adventure from the makers of the *Wilderness Family* series.
Dist.: Media

MOUNTAIN MEN, THE 1980
★★★★ **R Western 1:40**
☑ Rape, adult situations, explicit language, graphic violence
Dir: Richard Lang   *Cast:* Charlton Heston, Brian Keith, Victoria Racimo, Stephen Macht, John Glover, David Ackroyd
► Aided by sidekick Keith, Wyoming fur trapper Heston protects Racimo, the runaway wife of sadistic Indian chief Macht. Throwback to old-fashioned Westerns written by Heston's son Fraser Clarke Heston. An extremely violent adventure.
Dist.: RCA/Columbia

MOUNTAINS OF THE MOON 1990
★★★ **R Biography/Action Adventure 2:15**
☑ Nudity, adult situations, violence
Dir: Bob Rafelson   *Cast:* Patrick Bergin, Iain Glen, Richard E. Grant, Fiona Shaw, Bernard Hill, John Savident
► True story of explorers Richard Burton (Bergin) and John Hanning Speke (Glen) covers their dangerous mid-nineteenth-century expedition to find the source of the Nile and subsequent falling out over credit for the discovery. Magnificent production, stirringly directed by Rafelson, with incredible locations, vivid characters and music. Flaws: script doesn't fully explore central relationship and glosses over question of Speke's homosexuality.
Dist.: IVE

MOUSE THAT ROARED, THE 1959 British
★★★ **NR Comedy 1:23**
Dir: Jack Arnold   *Cast:* Peter Sellers, Jean Seberg, David Kossoff, William Hartnell, Monty Landis
► Grand Fenwick, the smallest nation on Earth, declares war on the U.S. in the hopes of being defeated and reaping the benefits of foreign aid. The country accidentally captures a bomb inventor and becomes a feared power. Nifty political satire with Sellers hilarious in three roles: the wily prime minister, a bumbling field marshal, and the Grand Duchess.
Dist.: RCA/Columbia

MOVERS & SHAKERS 1985
★ **PG Comedy 1:19**
☑ Adult situations
Dir: William Asher *Cast:* Walter Matthau, Charles Grodin, Vincent Gardenia, Tyne Daly, Bill Macy, Gilda Radner
▶ Hollywood studio head Matthau paid $1 million for the film rights to "Sex in Love," a self-help manual; now he has to convince screenwriter Grodin to turn it into a romance. Wry show biz satire written and produced by Grodin has a great cast, including cameos from Steve Martin and Penny Marshall, but takes too broad an approach to easy targets.
Dist.: MGM/UA

MOVIE MOVIE 1978
★ ★ **PG Comedy 1:46 C/B&W**
☑ Explicit language
Dir: Stanley Donen *Cast:* George C. Scott, Trish Van Devere, Red Buttons, Barry Bostwick, Harry Hamlin, Art Carney
▶ Delightful comedy/homage to 1930s flicks is divided into two parts: the black-and-white "Dynamite Hands" about delivery boy Hamlin who turns boxer to pay for his sister's eye operation, and the color musical "Baxter's Beauties of 1933" about dying producer Scott putting together one last Broadway hit. Never less than genial and often quite diverting. A great cast with droll Scott and disarming Bostwick (singing and dancing "Just Shows to Go Ya") the standouts.
Dist.: CBS/Fox

MOVING 1988
★ ★ **R Comedy 1:29**
☑ Explicit language, adult humor
Dir: Alan Metter *Cast:* Richard Pryor, Beverly Todd, Dave Thomas, Dana Carvey, Randy Quaid, Stacey Dash
▶ New Jersey transit engineer Pryor uproots his family for a new job in Idaho. Slapstick complications include Rambo-esque neighbor Quaid, psychopathic driver Carvey, and the world's worst moving team. Small cameos by Rodney Dangerfield and Morris Day add to the fun. **(CC)**
Dist.: Warner

MOVING OUT 1982 Australian
★ ★ **NR Drama 1:31**
☑ Explicit language
Dir: Michael Pattison *Cast:* Vince Colosimo, Maurice Divencentis, Tibor Gyapjas, Sally Cooper, Desiree Smith, Nicole Miranda
▶ Teenager Colosimo, the son of Italian immigrants, is torn between his ethnic background and his desire to be a regular Australian. School, love, and his family's impending move provide other problems for him in this modestly plotted but nicely directed and acted coming-of-age story.
Dist.: VidAmerica

MOVING VIOLATION 1976
★ ★ **PG Action-Adventure 1:32**
☑ Explicit language, violence

Dir: Charles S. Dubin *Cast:* Stephen McHattie, Kay Lenz, Eddie Albert, Lonny Chapman, Will Geer, Dick Miller
▶ Oil man Geer orders sheriff Chapman to murder a deputy. When young lovers McHattie and Lenz witness the crime, Chapman attempts to frame the couple for the killing. Lenz and McHattie try to prove their innocence as car chases ensue. Zippy direction and non-stop action make this a B-plus movie.
Dist.: CBS/Fox

MOVING VIOLATIONS 1985
★ ★ ★ **PG-13 Comedy 1:31**
☑ Adult situations, explicit language, adult humor
Dir: Neil Israel *Cast:* John Murray, Jennifer Tilly, James Keach, Brian Backer, Ned Eisenberg, Clara Peller
▶ Rambunctious comedy about students in a compulsory driver education class consists of a series of broad skits in the style of *Police Academy.* Leading man Murray delivers a studied imitation of his brother Bill; Sally Kellerman and Fred Willard offer amusing cameos. **(CC)**
Dist.: CBS/Fox

MR. ACE 1946
★ **NR Drama 1:24 B&W**
Dir: Edwin L. Marin *Cast:* George Raft, Sylvia Sidney, Stanley Ridges, Sara Haden, Jerome Cowan
▶ Sydney is an ambitious congresswoman who's learned how to be tough in a man's world. But to get what she wants, she has to deal with Raft, a suave mobster who controls the local political machine. Slick but unexceptional gangster story, with female politico the most interesting angle.
Dist.: SVS

MR. & MRS. SMITH 1941
★ ★ ★ **NR Comedy 1:35 B&W**
Dir: Alfred Hitchcock *Cast:* Carole Lombard, Robert Montgomery, Gene Raymond, Jack Carson, Philip Merivale, Lucile Watson
▶ Sprightly screwball farce about Montgomery and Lombard, a quarrelsome but devoted husband and wife who discover that their marriage isn't legal. Comic misunderstandings force Montgomery to move to his men's club while his law partner Raymond pursues Lombard. Unusual project for Hitchcock, who directed as a favor for Lombard.
Dist.: Turner

MR. ARKADIN 1955 English/French
☆ **NR Drama 1:39 B&W**
Dir: Orson Welles *Cast:* Orson Welles, Michael Redgrave, Patricia Medina, Akim Tamiroff, Paola Mori, Robert Arden
▶ Wealthy European financier Welles claims to have amnesia and hires would-be blackmailer Arden to investigate his past. When everyone Arden interviews meets foul play, he suspects that Welles has something to hide, probably from daughter Mori. More than a

few echoes of director Welles's *Citizen Kane* here, including odd camera angles, overlapping dialogue, and dramatic lighting. But title character inspires neither sympathy nor interest, and Arden is too weak to carry what's left of the story. Also known as *Confidential Report*.
Dist.: Video Dimensions

MR. BILLION 1977
★★ PG Action-Adventure 1:33
☑ Explicit language
Dir: Jonathan Kaplan ***Cast:*** Terence Hill, Valerie Perrine, Jackie Gleason, Slim Pickens, Chill Wills, Dick Miller
▶ Italian mechanic Hill inherits a billion dollars, but he must reach San Francisco within twenty days to get the money. Gleason, a lawyer who covets the fortune, throws every possible obstacle in Hill's way. Cross-country chase with comic overtones offers a full range of cliff-hanging situations. **(CC)**
Dist.: CBS/Fox

MR. BLANDINGS BUILDS HIS DREAM HOUSE 1948
★★★★ NR Comedy 1:34 B&W
Dir: H. C. Potter ***Cast:*** Cary Grant, Myrna Loy, Melvyn Douglas, Reginald Denny, Sharyn Moffett, Connie Marshall
▶ Tired of their cramped apartment, Manhattanites Grant and Loy purchase a dream house in Connecticut. Their troubles start when architect Denny informs them he'll have to raze the house and build a new one from scratch. Homeowners will sympathize with this amusing adaptation of Eric Hodgins's best-selling novel. An interesting contrast to the similar plot of 1986's *The Money Pit*.
Dist.: Turner

MR. DEEDS GOES TO TOWN 1936
★★★ NR Comedy 1:58 B&W
Dir: Frank Capra ***Cast:*** Gary Cooper, Jean Arthur, Lionel Stander, George Bancroft, Douglass Dumbrille, Raymond Walburn
▶ Small-town tuba player Longfellow Deeds (Cooper) inherits $20 million dollars. Big-city reporter Arthur exploits him to sell papers but then falls for the big galoot. When Coop wants to give his fortune to the needy, unscrupulous business types attempt to have him declared insane. Funny, sweet, and endearing Capra classic is a joy. Marvelous chemistry between Cooper and Arthur. Film introduced phrase "pixilated" to the American public. Oscar for Best Director, nominations for Picture, Actor (Cooper), Screenplay, Sound.
Dist.: RCA/Columbia

MR. HOBBS TAKES A VACATION 1962
★★★★ NR Comedy 1:57
Dir: Henry Koster ***Cast:*** James Stewart, Maureen O'Hara, Fabian, Lauri Peters, Lili Gentle, John Saxon, Reginald Denny
▶ Witty satire on family togetherness. St. Louis banker Stewart and wife O'Hara rent a ramshackle West Coast beach house, but their vacation is almost ruined by a series of humorous calamities. O'Hara fends off advances from amorous yacht club member Denny, daughter Peters is so upset by her new braces that she won't go on dates, etc. As expected, Stewart handles each disaster with aplomb. **(CC)**
Dist.: CBS/Fox

MR. HULOT'S HOLIDAY 1954 French
★ NR Comedy 1:26 B&W
Dir: Jacques Tati ***Cast:*** Jacques Tati, Nathalie Pascaud, Michelle Rolla, Valentine Camax, Louis Perrault, Andre DuBois
▶ Shy and clumsy bachelor Tati takes a vacation on the Britanny coast, oblivious to the chaos created by his every move. Gags include misadventures in a kayak, disruption of several card games, and finale in a fireworks factory. Employing slapstick humor and his superb skills as a mime, writer/director/star Tati uses very little dialogue and nonstop visual comedy in a style reminiscent of the early silent films. [S]
Dist.: Nelson

MR. KLEIN 1977 French
★ PG Drama 2:02
☑ Adult situations
Dir: Joseph Losey ***Cast:*** Alain Delon, Jeanne Moreau, Michael Lonsdale, Juliet Berto, Suzanne Flon
▶ In Nazi-occupied Paris, wealthy art dealer Delon takes financial advantage of fleeing Jews. But when he is mistaken for a Jew by the authorities, he finds himself in a desperate search for an elusive double who can establish his identity. Sometimes effective story gets lost in script's cultivated ambiguities. [S]
Dist.: RCA/Columbia

MR. LOVE 1986 British
★★ PG-13 Comedy 1:31
☑ Adult situations, explicit language, mild violence
Dir: Roy Battersby ***Cast:*** Barry Jackson, Maurice Denham, Margaret Tyzack, Julia Deakin
▶ Meek gardener Jackson, trapped in a bad marriage and despised by his own daughter, finds romance with several different lonely women, including usher Deakin. Odd film is slowly paced and may try your patience. Jackson is sympathetic and Deakin does a fine Ingrid Bergman impression. **(CC)**
Dist.: Warner

MR. LUCKY 1943
★★★ NR Comedy 1:38 B&W
Dir: H. C. Potter ***Cast:*** Cary Grant, Laraine Day, Charles Bickford, Gladys Cooper, Alan Carney, Paul Stewart
▶ Breezy romantic comedy set in World War II. Crooked gangster Grant prepares a gambling night for a wealthy charity, planning to steal the money for his shipboard casino. He has second thoughts about the scheme when

he meets beautiful charity official Day. Debonair Grant shows off his Cockney rhyming slang in this popular hit that led to a TV series. *Dist.:* Turner

MR. MAJESTYK 1974
★ ★ PG Action-Adventure 1:43
☑ Adult situations, explicit language, violence
Dir: Richard Fleischer   *Cast:* Charles Bronson, Al Lettieri, Linda Cristal, Lee Purcell, Paul Koslo
▶ Watermelon grower Bronson, unjustly jailed for exploiting migrant workers, helps crimelord Lettieri escape from prison in return for his own freedom. Lettieri's men subsequently terrorize Bronson until he sets out for revenge. Unexpected plotting by Elmore Leonard raises this above other Bronson vehicles.
Dist.: MGM/UA

MR. MOM 1983
★ ★ ★ ★ ★ PG Comedy 1:31
☑ Adult situations, explicit language
Dir: Stan Dragoti   *Cast:* Michael Keaton, Teri Garr, Martin Mull, Ann Jillian, Christopher Lloyd
▶ Detroit auto engineer Keaton loses his job and turns househusband, taking care of the kids while wife Garr gets a job in advertising. Garr is pursued by boss Mull and Keaton by neighbor Jillian but they stick together and overcome the problems of role reversal. Hugely popular comedy is uplifting and quite endearing. Keaton is more restrained than usual but very appealing and the children are superb. **(CC)**
Dist.: Vestron

MR. MOTO'S LAST WARNING 1939
★ NR Mystery-Suspense 1:10 B&W
Dir: Norman Foster   *Cast:* Peter Lorre, Ricardo Cortez, George Sanders, Virginia Field, John Carradine, Robert Coote
▶ On the eve of World War II, Sanders and Cortez apparently kill the famous detective Mr. Moto (Lorre). They then go ahead with their plan to sabotage the French fleet at the Suez Canal, only to be thwarted by a very much alive Moto. Superior series effort is cleverly plotted.
Dist.: Video Yesteryear

MR. NICE GUY 1987
★ PG-13 Comedy 1:32
☑ Nudity, adult situations, explicit language
Dir: Henry Wolford   *Cast:* Mike MacDonald, Jan Smithers, Joe Silver, Harvey Atkin, Howard Jerome
▶ Security guard MacDonald is hired by company specializing in killings and assassinations. MacDonald proves good at the gig, wins the heart of lady shrink Smithers, and takes on her mafioso father. Broad burlesque jokes but few real laughs.
Dist.: New World

MR. NORTH 1988
★ ★ PG Comedy 1:32
☑ Adult situations
Dir: Danny Huston   *Cast:* Anthony Edwards, Robert Mitchum, Lauren Bacall, Harry Dean Stanton, Anjelica Huston, Mary Stuart Masterson, Virginia Madsen, Tammy Grimes, David Warner
▶ In 1926 Newport, Edwards, a young tutor with mysterious powers, helps ailing millionaire Mitchum and foils scheming heirs. Sunny fable offers beguiling hero and comforting message although whimsical style is not for all tastes. Adaptation of a Thornton Wilder novel was final film for executive producer/co-writer John Huston; directing mantle was passed to son Danny.
Dist.: Virgin

MR. PEABODY AND THE MERMAID 1948
★ ★ NR Fantasy/Comedy 1:29 B&W
Dir: Irving Pichel   *Cast:* William Powell, Ann Blyth, Irene Hervey, Andrea King, Clinton Sundberg
▶ Pre-*Splash* oddity features Powell as a fifty-year-old married man on the brink of a mid-life crisis. Vacationing in the Caribbean, he goes fishing and, instead of supper, snags mermaid Blyth. The problem: no one else can see her. Funniest scene: Powell tries to convince Blyth to wear a bra. Doesn't really work but, as always, the charming Powell can do no wrong. Script by Nunnally Johnson.
Dist.: Republic

MR. ROBINSON CRUSOE 1932
★ NR Action-Adventure 1:10 B&W
Dir: Edward Sutherland   *Cast:* Douglas Fairbanks, William Farnum, Earle Browne, Maria Alba
▶ Wealthy Fairbanks makes a thousand-dollar bet that he can rough it on a tropical island for one month. His resourcefulness puts the odds in his favor. He also finds romance with a native girl. Entertaining lark, with a high-spirited Fairbanks performance against a lovely South Sea background. Silent, with sound effects and music.
Dist.: Video Yesteryear

MR. SKEFFINGTON 1944
★ ★ ★ NR Drama 2:26 B&W
Dir: Vincent Sherman   *Cast:* Bette Davis, Claude Rains, Walter Abel, Richard Waring, Marjorie Riordan, Charles Drake
▶ When her brother Waring steals money from Rains's bank, socialite Davis agrees to marry the banker if he'll drop charges. After Waring dies in World War I, she leaves Rains for a life of hedonism in Europe. Diphtheria, a dishonest daughter, and World War II help bring about a reconciliation in this tumultuous soap opera. Tour-de-force Davis performance compensates for frequently soggy passages.
Dist.: MGM/UA

MRS. MINIVER 1942
★ ★ ★ NR Drama 2:14 B&W

Dir: William Wyler   *Cast:* Greer Garson, Walter Pidgeon, Dame May Whitty, Teresa Wright, Reginald Owen, Henry Travers

▶ Gentle matriarch Garson heads an ordinary English family whose small domestic dramas are played out against the background of the increasingly deadly Nazi war against Britain. Story advances through solidly constructed episodes, each demonstrating a new facet of the family's essential decency, and by extension, that of the English people. Patriotic tribute to a proud people still packs a wallop. Won Oscars for Best Picture, Actress (Garson), and Director.
Dist.: MGM/UA

MR. SMITH GOES TO WASHINGTON 1939
★ ★ ★ ★ NR Drama 2:10 B&W
Dir: Frank Capra   *Cast:* James Stewart, Jean Arthur, Claude Rains, Thomas Mitchell, Edward Arnold, Guy Kibbee, Eugene Pallette, Beulah Bondi, Harry Carey

▶ Innocent scout leader Stewart is appointed Senator and soon uncovers Washington corruption. Feeling that "lost causes are the only ones worth fighting for" and helped by secretary Arthur, Smith battles his one-time mentor Rains and ruthless boss Arnold over a fraudulent land scam. Stirring and memorable Capra classic; Stewart and Rains (both Oscar nominees) are superb. Climactic filibuster, with Stewart fighting fatigue and loss of voice to keep going, is Capra at his most inspiring. Best Picture nominee.
Dist.: RCA/Columbia

MRS. SOFFEL 1984
★ ★ ★ PG-13 Drama 1:51
☑ Adult situations, violence
Dir: Gillian Armstrong   *Cast:* Diane Keaton, Mel Gibson, Matthew Modine, Edward Herrmann, Trini Alvarado

▶ A true story set in 1901 Pittsburgh: repressed warden's wife Keaton falls in love with prisoner Gibson and helps him escape. They become lovers on the lam, pursued by the law. Keaton and Gibson provide passion but sluggish script and dim lighting dampen their fire. Resourceful but heavy-handed direction from Australian Armstrong. **(CC)**
Dist.: MGM/UA

MRS. WIGGS OF THE CABBAGE PATCH 1934
★ NR Comedy/Drama 1:20 B&W
Dir: Norman Taurog   *Cast:* Pauline Lord, W. C. Fields, ZaSu Pitts, Evelyn Venable, Kent Taylor, Charles Middleton

▶ Old-fashioned tale of plucky Mrs. Wiggs (Lord), who holds together her poor family despite a missing husband, mortgage problems, and personal tragedy. Venable is the rich girl who befriends the family; Pitts is the pal who attempts to win Fields through Wiggs's cooking. Fields fans be warned: although wonder-

ful as always, he's really a supporting player here.
Dist.: Goodtimes

MR. WINKLE GOES TO WAR 1944
★ ★ NR Comedy 1:18 B&W
Dir: Alfred E. Green   *Cast:* Edward G. Robinson, Ruth Warrick, Ted Donaldson, Bob Haymes, Richard Lane, Robert Armstrong

▶ Mild-mannered bank clerk Robinson, seeking to quit his job after fourteen years, is suddenly drafted into the Army during World War II. Making a successful transition from hypochondriac to hero, he thwarts a Japanese attack in the Pacific. Warm, enchanting comedy. Charming change-of-pace performance by Robinson, sweetly aided by young Donaldson as his orphan pal.
Dist.: RCA/Columbia

MR. WONG, DETECTIVE 1938
★ NR Mystery-Suspense 1:09 B&W
Dir: William Nigh   *Cast:* Boris Karloff, Grant Withers, Maxine Jennings, Evelyn Brent, Lucien Prival, William Gould

▶ First in a series of six films starring Karloff as Chinese sleuth Wong finds him trying to solve a string of killings erupting over the possession of a deadly new gas. Complicating things are a gang of spies led by the cunning Brent, who would like to acquire the gas formula. Charlie Chan ripoff has some interesting twists.
Dist.: Various

MR. WONG IN CHINATOWN 1939
★ NR Mystery-Suspense 1:10 B&W
Dir: William Nigh   *Cast:* Boris Karloff, Grant Withers, Marjorie Reynolds, Huntley Gordon, Peter George Lynn, William Royle

▶ A Chinese princess is killed by a poison dart when she seeks help at Wong's (Karloff) apartment. "Now we've seen everything," says cop Withers, but Wong's troubles have just begun, as his investigation uncovers a gunrunning ring. Below-par entry in the series, although Reynolds adds some snap as Withers's girlfriend, a curious reporter.
Dist.: Goodtimes

MUGSY'S GIRLS 1985
☆ R Comedy 1:30
☑ Adult situations, explicit language
Dir: Kevin Brodie   *Cast:* Ruth Gordon, Laura Brannigan, Eddie Deezen, James Marcel, Joanna Dierek, Rebecca Forstadt

▶ Sorority girls need money to pay off their house mortgage so they enter a Las Vegas mud wrestling tournament. Singer Brannigan (making her film debut) and old pro Gordon (as the house mother) deserve better than this crude college comedy.
Dist.: Vestron

MUMMY, THE 1932
★ ★ ★ NR Horror 1:12 B&W
Dir: Karl Freund   *Cast:* Boris Karloff, Zita Johann, David Manners, Edward Van Sloan, Arthur Byron, Bramwell Fletcher

▶ Archaeologists ignore warnings on an Egyptian sarcophagus, unleashing a malicious mummy condemned to eternal life for a taboo love affair. Spunky heroine Johann, who resembles his ancient sweetheart, turns to the supernatural to escape his dusty embrace. Eerie horror film accomplishes more through suggestive atmosphere than explicit violence. Inspired four sequels and a British remake in 1959.
Dist.: MCA

MUMMY, THE 1959 British
★ ★ **NR Horror 1:28**
Dir: Terence Fisher *Cast:* Peter Cushing, Christopher Lee, Yvonne Fumeaux, Eddie Byrne, Felix Aylmer, Raymond Huntley
▶ Lively remake of the 1932 classic shows the dire consequences when arrogant archaeologist Cushing robs an ancient Egyptian grave. Mummy Lee pursues Cushing's expedition back to London, where he kidnaps beautiful reincarnation of his dead lover. Fast-paced and frightening production helped rejuvenate moribund horror genre.
Dist.: Warner

MUNCHIES 1987
★ **PG Comedy 1:22**
☑ Adult situations, explicit language, violence
Dir: Bettina Hirsch *Cast:* Harvey Korman, Charles Stratton, Nadine Van Der Velde, Alix Elias, Charlie Phillips, Paul Bartel
▶ Anthropologist Korman discovers a lovable furry creature, which his son Stratton hopes to market. The scientist's brother steals the animal, which unexpectedly multiplies and transforms into a bevy of vicious killers. Low-budget thriller modeled after *Gremlins* takes some funny digs at consumerism.
Dist.: MGM/UA

MUPPET MOVIE, THE 1979
★ ★ ★ ★ ★ **G Comedy/Family 1:34**
Dir: James Frawley *Cast:* The Muppets, Charles Durning, Richard Pryor, Steve Martin, Bob Hope, Mel Brooks
▶ Kermit heads for Hollywood to break into show biz and is pursued by Doc Hopper (Durning), who wants him as spokesfrog for a chain of fried frogs' legs franchises. "A whole nation of frogs on little tiny crutches," fears Kermit. Great family entertainment: kids will love the antics of Miss Piggy and company, adults will enjoy movie references and big star cameos (the funniest is Martin's surly waiter). Hummable Paul Williams songs include the Oscar-nominated "Rainbow Connection."
Dist.: CBS/Fox

MUPPETS TAKE MANHATTAN, THE 1984
★ ★ ★ ★ ★ **G Comedy/Family 1:34**
Dir: Frank Oz *Cast:* The Muppets, Dabney Coleman, Art Carney, Joan Rivers, Liza Minnelli, Lonny Price
▶ Kermit and friends, a big hit with a college variety show, try to make it on the Great White Way. Shyster lawyer Coleman and a case of frog amnesia are two of the obstacles on the road to Broadway success and a possible Kermit/Miss Piggy wedding. Well-honed fun from Jim Henson's troupe. Our favorite scene: the rats cook breakfast. **(CC)**
Dist.: CBS/Fox

MURDER! 1930 British
★ ★ **NR Mystery-Suspense 1:48 B&W**
Dir: Alfred Hitchcock *Cast:* Herbert Marshall, Norah Baring, Phyllis Konstam, Edward Chapman, Miles Mander, Esme Percy
▶ Patrician Marshall is the lone dissenter on a jury determined to convict young actress Baring of murder. To review the evidence and prove her innocence, Marshall reconstructs the crime as a play, focusing suspicion on transvestite trapezist Percy. Compelling early Hitchcock mystery pioneered many suspense-generating cinematic techniques, including the first voiceover interior monologue.
Dist.: Video Yesteryear

MURDER AT THE VANITIES 1934
★ **NR Musical 1:29 B&W**
Dir: Mitchell Leisen *Cast:* Jack Oakie, Kitty Carlisle, Carl Brisson, Victor McLaglen, Duke Ellington, Gail Patrick
▶ It's opening night at a new show of Earl Carroll's Vanities, and someone backstage is knocking people off. The show goes on with musical numbers like "Marijuana" and Ellington's "Ebony Rhapsody" as detective McLaglen tries to deduce the identity of the killer from among the colorful showfolk. Amusing hybrid of sleuthing and song, but don't look for any brilliant mystery.
Dist.: MCA

MURDER BY DEATH 1976
★ ★ ★ ★ **PG Comedy 1:34**
☑ Adult situations, explicit language
Dir: Robert Moore *Cast:* Peter Falk, Peter Sellers, Alec Guinness, Maggie Smith, Eileen Brennan, James Coco, David Niven, Elsa Lanchester, Nancy Walker
▶ Eccentric millionaire Lionel Twain (Truman Capote) invites the world's super sleuths to dinner and a murder in Neil Simon's funny parody of great fictional film detectives. Guests include Sam Diamond (Falk), Sidney Wang (Sellers), Nick and Nora Charleston (Smith and Niven), Jessica Marbles (Lancaster), and Milo Perrier (Coco). Guinness is the blind butler, Walker the deaf cook. Tour-de-force performances from sterling cast.
Dist.: RCA/Columbia

MURDER BY DECREE 1979 Canadian/British
★ ★ ★ ★ **PG Mystery-Suspense 2:04**
☑ Graphic violence
Dir: Bob Clark *Cast:* Christopher Plummer, James Mason, Donald Sutherland, Genevieve Bujold, David Hemmings, John Gielgud, Susan Clark, David Hemmings, Frank Finlay, Anthony Quayle
▶ Sherlock Holmes (Plummer) investigates

Jack the Ripper's murders of prostitutes in Victorian London and comes across a cover-up involving highly placed people. Satisfying mystery provides sturdy, old-fashioned plotting with a dash of post-Watergate cynicism. Director Clark creates a nice sense of danger lurking in the foggy streets. Amusing chemistry between Plummer's surprisingly outgoing Holmes and Mason's deliciously droll Watson. *Dist.:* Nelson

MURDER BY PHONE 1982 Canadian
★ R Mystery-Suspense 1:19
☑ Nudity, adult situations, explicit language, violence
Dir: Michael Anderson *Cast:* Richard Chamberlain, John Houseman, Sara Botsford, Robin Gammell, Gary Reineke, Barry Morse
► When people who pick up their phones get zapped by high-voltage surges, scientist Chamberlain investigates. Despite the help of artist Botsford, he finds his way blocked by what appears to be an official conspiracy. Inferior Canadian product also known as *Bells*. *Dist.:* Warner

MURDER BY TELEVISION 1935
☆ NR Mystery-Suspense 1:00 B&W
Dir: Clifford Sandforth *Cast:* Bela Lugosi, June Collyer, Huntley Gordon, George Meeker, Claire McDowell, Henry Mowbray
► A professor mysteriously dies while demonstrating a new television device. Lugosi plays twins, one of whom is next victim, leaving the other to uncover the killer. Interesting to note that television was science fiction in 1935, and screenwriters felt free to implicate it in mysterioso happenings. But cheaply made programmer is definitely worth missing. *Dist.:* Video Yesteryear

MURDERERS AMONG US: THE SIMON WIESENTHAL STORY 1989
U.S./British/Hungarian
★ ★ ★ ★ NR Biography/MFTV 2:55
☑ Violence
Dir: Brian Gibson *Cast:* Ben Kingsley, Renee Soutendijk, Craig T. Nelson, Louisa Haigh, Jack Shepherd, Paul Freeman
► Freed from a Nazi concentration camp, demoralized Simon Wiesenthal (Kingsley) finds a reason for living after U.S. Army officer Craig talks him into helping track down war criminals. Battling time and indifference, Wiesenthal plays a vital part in the Nuremberg trials, and sets up his own clearing house for war crimes information. Eventually, he is instrumental in bringing some of Hitler's most evil henchmen to justice. Realistic concentration camp scenes in this earnest and moving true story. *Dist.:* HBO

MURDERERS' ROW 1966
★ NR Espionage/Action-Adventure 1:48
Dir: Henry Levin *Cast:* Dean Martin, Ann-Margret, Karl Malden, Camilla Sparv, Beverly Adams, Jacqueline Fontaine

► Madman Malden threatens Washington with a deadly Helio Beam; dashing secret agent Matt Helm (Martin) defeats him while rescuing the beam's inventor and his mod daughter, Ann-Margret. Poor sequel to *The Silencers* is a strained spy spoof with music ("I'm Not the Marrying Kind," "If You're Thinking What I'm Thinking," etc.). *Dist.:* RCA/Columbia

MURDER, MY SWEET 1944
★ ★ ★ NR Mystery-Suspense 1:35 B&W
Dir: Edward Dmytryk *Cast:* Dick Powell, Claire Trevor, Anne Shirley, Otto Kruger, Mike Mazurki, Miles Mander
► Hulking ex-con Mazurki hires private eye Philip Marlowe (Powell) to find his girlfriend, but the seemingly easy case turns into a nightmare of drugs, theft, and murder. First-rate adaptation of Raymond Chandler's *Farewell, My Lovely* ranks among the best of 1940s mysteries. Crooner Powell revived a flagging career with his first tough-guy role, and received excellent support from Trevor and Shirley as the treacherous women in the mystery. *Dist.:* Various

MURDER ONE 1988 Canadian
★ R Crime 1:35
☑ Rape, nudity, adult situations, explicit language, graphic violence
Dir: Graeme Campbell *Cast:* Henry Thomas, James Wilder, Stephen Shellen, Errol Slue
► A grim true story: Georgia convicts Wilder and Shellen break out of prison, pick up little brother Thomas, and go on a brutal spree of rape and murder. Straightforward, generally well acted, but repellent; the violent last half hour is especially hard to watch. *Dist.:* Nelson

MURDER ON THE ORIENT EXPRESS 1974 British
★ ★ ★ ★ PG Mystery-Suspense
☑ Adult situations, explicit language, violence
Dir: Sidney Lumet *Cast:* Albert Finney, Lauren Bacall, Martin Balsam, Ingrid Bergman, Jacqueline Bisset, Sean Connery, John Gielgud, Wendy Hiller, Anthony Perkins, Vanessa Redgrave, Richard Widmark, Michael York
► During the 1930s, brilliant Belgian detective Hercule Poirot (Finney) is vacationing on the fabled Orient Express when a murder takes place. Poirot contends with an all-star passenger list of suspects aboard the snowbound train. Luxurious entertainment weaves a spell from the astonishing opening montage detailing a Lindbergh-style kidnapping to the stunning solution. Oscar-nominated Finney submerges himself completely into his character; Bergman won a Supporting Actress Oscar as the missionary who talks of "little brown babies." *Dist.:* Paramount

MURMUR OF THE HEART 1971
French/German/Italian
☆ **NR Comedy 1:58**
☑ Nudity, adult situations
Dir: Louis Malle ***Cast:*** Lea Massari, Benoit Ferreux, Daniel Gelin, Marc Winocourt, Michel Lonsdale
► Adolescent Ferreux, initiated into manhood by his older brothers, is still close to his glamorous mother Massari. When he discovers she is having an affair, their relationship undergoes some amusing and unique changes. Wittily observed French coming-of-age tale deals with provocative themes in a very natural way, but what makes it so charming may be off-putting for some. [S]
Dist.: Orion

MURPHY'S LAW 1986
★★★★ **R Action-Adventure 1:37**
☑ Nudity, explicit language, graphic violence
Dir: J. Lee Thompson ***Cast:*** Charles Bronson, Kathleen Wilhoite, Carrie Snodgress, Robert F. Lyons, Richard Romanus, Angel Tompkins
► Tough cop Bronson is framed for murdering his ex-wife by Snodgress, a killer he once sent to jail. Bronson escapes while handcuffed to foulmouthed teen Wilhoite. They grow to be friends while he attempts to nab Snodgress. Violent and distasteful although Bronson fans will like the action. Suitably nasty performance by Snodgress. **(CC)**
Dist.: Media

MURPHY'S ROMANCE 1985
★★★★★ **PG-13 Romance/Comedy 1:48**
☑ Brief nudity, adult situations, explicit language
Dir: Martin Ritt ***Cast:*** Sally Field, James Garner, Brian Kerwin, Corey Haim, Dennis Burkley
► Newly divorced Field and twelve-year-old son Haim move to a small town in Arizona to run a horse ranch. Crusty town druggist Garner helps her establish the ranch. Their budding, May-September romance is threatened by the unexpected appearance of her ne'er-do-well ex-husband Kerwin. Effortlessly good leads in a display of old-fashioned, homespun values. **(CC)**
Dist.: RCA/Columbia

MURPHY'S WAR 1971 British
★★ **PG Action-Adventure 1:46**
☑ Violence
Dir: Peter Yates ***Cast:*** Peter O'Toole, Sian Phillips, Philippe Noiret, Horst Janson, John Hallam
► In World War II South America, Irishman O'Toole survives his ship's sinking by Janson's German U boat. After doctor Phillips tends to him, O'Toole rebuilds a seaplane and teams with his rescuer Noiret for a revenge campaign, even after the war has been declared over. Exciting if standard adventure benefits from Yates's hard-driving direction and O'Toole's panache.
Dist.: Paramount

MURROW 1986
★★★★ **NR Biography/MFTV 1:50**
☑ Explicit language
Dir: Jack Gold ***Cast:*** Daniel J. Travanti, Dabney Coleman, Edward Herrmann, David Suchet, John McMartin, Robert Vaughn
► Sincere and probing biodrama of revered newsman Edward R. Murrow (Travanti). Film charts his rise from broadcaster on CBS Radio in London during the war years to his successful transition to television. Risking right wing ire, he is the first to openly attack Joe McCarthy, turning public opinion against the senator. Travanti turns in an exemplary performance as Murrow.
Dist.: Vestron

MUSCLE BEACH PARTY 1964
★★ **NR Comedy 1:34**
Dir: William Asher ***Cast:*** Frankie Avalon, Annette Funicello, Luciana Paluzzi, John Ashley, Don Rickles, Rock Stevens
► "Surf's up!" Frankie and Annette take on weight-lifting bullies hogging the beach. Great example of 1960s camp has surprising bonuses: songs by Beach Boys' Brian Wilson, "Little" Stevie Wonder's screen debut, Peter Lorre's last performance (in an unbilled cameo), and early role by Rock Stevens (later Peter Lupus of TV's "Mission: Impossible"). Followed by *Bikini Beach*.
Dist.: HBO

MUSIC BOX 1989
★★★★★ **PG-13 Drama 2:04**
☑ Adult situations, explicit language
Dir: Costa-Gavras ***Cast:*** Jessica Lange, Armin Mueller-Stahl, Frederic Forrest, Lukas Haas, Donald Moffat
► In Chicago, lawyer Lange represents her Hungarian-born father Mueller-Stahl against charges that he is a Nazi war criminal who raped, tortured, and murdered without remorse. Riveting courtroom drama inspired by recent headlines is emotion-packed and suspenseful. Wonderful showcase for Lange, who received an Oscar nomination. **(CC)**
Dist.: IVE

MUSIC MAN, THE 1962
★★★★★ **G Musical 2:31**
Dir: Morton Da Costa ***Cast:*** Robert Preston, Shirley Jones, Buddy Hackett, Hermione Gingold, Paul Ford, Ron Howard
► Professor Harold Hill (Preston) convinces the gullible townsfolk of River City, Iowa, that he can teach their children music through his so-called Think Method. His conscience is pricked when he falls for local librarian Jones. Brassy, supremely entertaining Meredith Wilson musical is as American as apple pie. Preston is marvelous as the charismatic con man in a role he created on Broadway. Won Oscar

for Best Song Score (including such well-loved tunes as "Till There Was You" and "Seventy-Six Trombones"). (CC)
Dist.: Warner

MUSIC TEACHER, THE 1989 Belgian
★ **PG Drama 1:40**
☑ Adult situations
Dir: Gerard Corbiau *Cast:* José Van Dam, Anne Roussel, Philippe Volter, Sylvie Fennec, Patrick Bauchau, Marc Schreiber
► In turn-of-the century Europe, acclaimed baritone Van Dam retires from the stage and begins a career as a music teacher. His first students are lovely Roussel and former pick-pocket Volter. The protégés prepare to compete with students of Van Dam's arch rival Bauchau. Slow, too-precious look at psychological games played against the backdrop of opera, but the music is magnificent. [S]
Dist.: Orion

MUSSOLINI: THE DECLINE AND FALL OF IL DUCE 1985
★★★ **NR Biography/MFTV 1:52**
☑ Violence
Dir: Alberto Negrin *Cast:* Susan Sarandon, Anthony Hopkins, Bob Hoskins, Annie Girardot, Barbara De Rossi
► Sweeping portrait focuses on the years 1943–45 in the life of the Italian dictator Mussolini (Hoskins) and the bitter political and family struggle as his son-in-law Hopkins opposes the Germans, who order Il Duce to execute him. Well-crafted epic filmed in Italy.
Dist.: Nelson

MUTANT 1984
★ **R Horror 1:39**
☑ Adult situations, explicit language, violence
Dir: John Cardos *Cast:* Wings Hauser, Lee Montgomery, Jody Medford, Mark Clement, Cary Guffey, Jennifer Warren
► When his brother is killed by zombies, products of nearby toxic waste, Hauser seeks revenge. Some good chills and zombie transformations, but plagued by poor production: the film quality is so murky that it's difficult to figure out what's going on.
Dist.: Vestron

MUTANT ON THE BOUNTY 1989
★ **PG-13 Sci-Fi/Comedy 1:34**
☑ Rape, adult situations, explicit language, violence
Dir: Robert Torrance *Cast:* John Roarke, Deborah Benson, John Furey, Kyle T. Heffner, John Fleck, Victoria Catlin
► Sophmoric, inane sci-fi spoof about friendly mutant Heffner on board spaceship *USS Bounty* aspires to being a galactic *Rocky Horror Picture Show*. Schlock production values, stupid script, and a hero with a gross complexion render this one a stinker.
Dist.: Southgate

MUTANTS IN PARADISE 1989
☆ **NR Comedy 1:30**
☑ Adult humor
Dir: Scott Apostolu *Cast:* Brad Greenquist, Ray "Boom Boom" Mancini, Edith Massey
► Poor horror spoof about balding researcher Greenquist who has to come up with a major scientific discovery to avoid losing his meal ticket. He bamboozles hospital patient Mancini into participating in harmful nuclear tests. Aims for Monty Python hipness but misses the mark totally. Hammy acting adds to the discomfort.
Dist.: TWE

MUTILATOR, THE 1985
☆ **R Horror 1:26**
☑ Nudity, adult situations, explicit language, violence
Dir: Buddy Cooper *Cast:* Matt Mitler, Ruth Martinez, Bill Hitchcock, Frances Raines, Morley Lampley
► Father is driven crazy when his little son accidentally kills mom. Ten years later at a beach house, the son and his teen pals are savagely mutilated one by one. Is dad on the loose? Few surprises in this amateurish entry in the slasher genre.
Dist.: Vestron

MUTINY ON THE BOUNTY 1935
★★★★ **NR Action-Adventure 2:12 B&W**
Dir: Frank Lloyd *Cast:* Clark Gable, Charles Laughton, Franchot Tone, Herbert Mundin, Eddie Quillan, Donald Crisp, Dudley Digges
► Virile, commanding adventure outshines its subsequent remakes. The familiar story of the 1787 mutiny has Gable as mutiny leader Fletcher Christian, Laughton as evil Captain Bligh, and Tone as the midshipman caught between the two. Oscar for Best Picture and Actor nominations to the three leads.
Dist.: MGM/UA [C]

MUTINY ON THE BOUNTY 1962
★★★★★ **NR Action-Adventure 2:59**
Dir: Lewis Milestone *Cast:* Marlon Brando, Trevor Howard, Richard Harris, Hugh Griffith, Richard Haydn, Tarita
► The uprising of Fletcher Christian (Brando) and the crew of the *H.M.S. Bounty* against stern disciplinarian Captain Bligh (Howard) is leisurely painted on a broad canvas, with palmy South Sea locations and a larger-than-life-sized re-creation of the ship. Brando's portrayal of Christian as a pained, lisping dandy has been criticized, but the characterization works brilliantly against Howard's tight-lipped Bligh, and gives a cockeyed slant to what otherwise might have been simply a pale remake of the 1935 hit. Nominated for seven Oscars.
Dist.: MGM/UA

MY AMERICAN COUSIN 1985 Canadian
★ **PG Drama 1:25**
☑ Adult situations, explicit language
Dir: Sandy Wilson *Cast:* Margaret Langrick,

John Wildman, Richard Donat, Jane Mortifee

▶ In rural Canada during the summer of 1959, bored twelve-year-old Langrick, battling with mom Mortifee about boys and rock music, develops a wild crush on her California cousin Wildman, a James Dean–like stud. Wry observations, believable performances, gorgeous scenery, but a little too predictable and low-key.
Dist.: Media

MY BEAUTIFUL LAUNDRETTE 1986 British
★ ★ R Comedy/Drama 1:38
☑ Nudity, adult situations, explicit language
Dir: Stephen Frears   *Cast:* Daniel Day-Lewis, Gordon Warnecke, Saeed Jaffrey, Roshan Seth, Shirley Anne Field, Rita Wolf
▶ In a shabby, racially torn London neighborhood, young Pakistani Warnecke and his Cockney lover Day-Lewis take over a failing laundry and turn it into a sleek neon moneymaker. Warnecke also deals with bigotry and sexual intrigue within his own upwardly mobile family. Alternately jolly and sad art film makes sharp social comment; overloaded plot and thick accents may render it inaccessible to some. **(CC)**
Dist.: Warner

MY BEST FRIEND IS A VAMPIRE 1988
★ ★ ★ PG Comedy 1:29
☑ Explicit language
Dir: Jimmy Huston   *Cast:* Robert Sean Leonard, Evan Mirand, Cheryl Pollak, René Auberjonois, Fannie Flagg, David Warner
▶ Texas grocery boy Leonard, seduced by a mysterious woman, is puzzled by his growing teeth and sudden aversion to garlic until Auberjonois explains that he's become a vampire. Can he still win a date with pretty musician Pollak while avoiding demented vampire killer Warner? Predictable but pleasant comedy with a nice soundtrack. **(CC)**
Dist.: HBO

MY BLOODY VALENTINE 1981 Canadian
★ ★ R Horror 1:31
☑ Adult situations, explicit language, graphic violence
Dir: George Mihalka   *Cast:* Paul Kelman, Lori Hallier, Neil Affleck, Keith Knight, Alf Humphreys
▶ After a twenty-year hiatus, the people of Valentine Bluffs hold a fair in honor of their patron saint. Youngsters explore a nearby cave, ignoring warnings about the murderer buried there during the last fair. Subsequent pickax killings include good jolts for gore fans.
Dist.: Paramount

MY BODYGUARD 1980
★ ★ ★ ★ PG Comedy 1:35
☑ Explicit language, violence
Dir: Tony Bill   *Cast:* Chris Makepeace, Adam Baldwin, Matt Dillon, Joan Cusack, Ruth Gordon, Martin Mull
▶ Makepeace, a transfer student at a Chicago high school, becomes the victim of punks led by Dillon until he hires menacing older classmate Baldwin as his bodyguard. Modest, appealing comedy benefits from an honest script, realistic characters, and fine supporting cast.
Dist.: CBS/Fox

MY BRILLIANT CAREER 1979 Australian
★ ★ ★ G Drama 1:40
Dir: Gillian Armstrong   *Cast:* Judy Davis, Sam Neill, Wendy Hughes, Robert Grubb, Max Cullen, Pat Kennedy
▶ In the nineteenth-century Australian outback, a headstrong girl of limited means rejects the safety of marriage to become a writer. Davis is remarkable in her film debut as the unconventional heroine; Neill, her suitor, is properly romantic. Stunning locations enhance this uplifting drama, based on a semiautobiographical novel by Miles Franklin.
Dist.: Vestron

MY CHAUFFEUR 1986
★ ★ R Comedy 1:37
☑ Nudity, adult situations, explicit language
Dir: David Beaird   *Cast:* Deborah Foreman, Sam J. Jones, Sean McClory, Howard Hesseman, E. G. Marshall, Penn and Teller
▶ Exclusive limo service is forced to hire woman driver Foreman; manager Hesseman gives her horrible assignments to break her spirit. But Foreman's bubbly personality wins over the other drivers, and she also manages to snag boss's son Jones. Disarming throwback to 1930s screwball comedies is effectively light and smooth. Film debut for magician team Penn and Teller.
Dist.: Vestron

MY DARLING CLEMENTINE 1946
★ ★ ★ ★ NR Western 1:37 B&W
Dir: John Ford   *Cast:* Henry Fonda, Linda Darnell, Victor Mature, Walter Brennan, Tim Holt, Cathy Downs, Ward Bond, John Ireland
▶ When his brother is murdered on a cattle drive, Wyatt Earp (Fonda) becomes sheriff of Tombstone to find his killers. Earp forms an uneasy alliance with the tubercular Doc Holliday (Mature) while gathering evidence against the evil Clanton gang. Vivid characters (particularly Brennan as Old Man Clanton), exceptional photography, and a plot crammed with memorable sequences—climaxing in an exciting rendering of the famous gunfight at OK Corral—make this outstanding Western one of the true classics of the genre. **(CC)**
Dist.: CBS/Fox

MY DEAR SECRETARY 1948
★ NR Comedy 1:34 B&W
Dir: Charles Martin   *Cast:* Laraine Day, Kirk Douglas, Keenan Wynn, Helen Walker, Rudy Vallee
▶ Day goes from personal secretary to wife of wild-living novelist Douglas. She's expected to put up with his depravity, but when she grabs

the spotlight with a highly praised novel of her own, his nose gets out of joint. Appealing comedy with a superior supporting cast.
Dist.: KVC

MY DEMON LOVER 1987
★ **PG-13 Comedy 1:26**
☑ Adult situations, explicit language, violence
Dir: Charlie Loventhal *Cast:* Scott Valentine, Michelle Little, Arnold Johnson, Robert Trebor, Alan Fudge, Gina Gallego
▶ Uneven blend of horror and comedy: young Little is a loser in love until she meets Valentine, who has the unfortunate habit of turning into various monsters whenever he's aroused. Little sets out to prove that her new boyfriend isn't a serial killer dubbed the Mangler. Stars outdo iffy special effects.
Dist.: RCA/Columbia

MY DINNER WITH ANDRE 1981
☆ **PG Drama 1:50**
☑ Explicit language
Dir: Louis Malle *Cast:* Wallace Shawn, Andre Gregory, Jean Lenauer, Roy Butler
▶ Playwright Shawn meets his friend Gregory, an experimental theater director, for dinner. Over their meal Gregory regales Shawn with stories about his search for the meaning of life. One-of-a-kind film was a surprise art-house hit despite divided critical reception. Nonstop talk is occasionally engrossing, sometimes obscure and pretentious.
Dist.: Pacific Arts

MY FAIR LADY 1964
★ ★ ★ ★ ★ **G Musical 2:50**
Dir: George Cukor *Cast:* Rex Harrison, Audrey Hepburn, Stanley Holloway, Wilfrid Hyde-White, Gladys Cooper, Jeremy Brett
▶ Upper-crust English professor Henry Higgins (Harrison) attempts to transform Cockney flower girl Eliza Doolittle (Hepburn) into a respectable lady. Simply grand: Harrison is wonderfully imperious, Hepburn is winningly winsome, and the showstopping Lerner and Loewe score includes "The Rain in Spain," "On the Street Where You Live," and "Get Me to the Church on Time" (sung by Oscar-nominated Holloway). Eight Oscars for Best Picture, Director, Actor (Harrison), Cinematography, Costume Design (Cecil Beaton), Music, Art Direction, and Sound. Based on the Broadway musical inspired by George Bernard Shaw's *Pygmalion.* **(CC)**
Dist.: CBS/Fox

MY FAVORITE BRUNETTE 1947
★ ★ ★ **NR Comedy 1:29 B&W**
Dir: Elliott Nugent *Cast:* Bob Hope, Dorothy Lamour, Peter Lorre, Lon Chaney, Jr., Reginald Denny
▶ Glamorous Lamour mistakes baby photographer Hope for a hard-boiled private eye, and involves him in a search for a missing baron. Prime Hope vehicle crammed with quips, sight gags, and funny performances (particularly Lorre's self-parody of a menacing villain).
Dist.: Various ©

MY FAVORITE WIFE 1940
★ ★ ★ ★ **NR Comedy 1:28 B&W**
Dir: Garson Kanin *Cast:* Cary Grant, Irene Dunne, Randolph Scott, Gail Patrick, Ann Shoemaker, Scotty Beckett
▶ Dunne, lost at sea for seven years, returns home to find hubby Grant married to Patrick. Grant calls off his honeymoon, only to learn that Dunne was marooned with handsome bodybuilder Scott. Stars are in peak form in this delightfully effervescent comedy of errors. Received three Oscar nominations, including Best Story.
Dist.: Turner

MY FAVORITE YEAR 1982
★ ★ ★ **PG Comedy 1:29**
☑ Adult situations, explicit language, adult humor
Dir: Richard Benjamin *Cast:* Peter O'Toole, Mark Linn-Baker, Jessica Harper, Joseph Bologna, Lainie Kazan, Bill Macy
▶ "If I were truly plastered, could I do this?" asks flamboyant film star O'Toole as he drunkenly somersaults into rehearsals for a live comedy TV show in 1950s New York. Concerned host Bologna assigns young writer Linn-Baker to keep O'Toole out of trouble. Linn-Baker fails miserably but memorably as the two men form a close relationship. Wonderfully sweet and winning; dominated by O'Toole's glorious Oscar-nominated turn as the aging swashbuckler. Highlights: O'Toole's gallant dance with an elderly admirer and the Central Park ride on horseback.
Dist.: MGM/UA

MY FORBIDDEN PAST 1951
★ **NR Drama 1:21 B&W**
Dir: Robert Stevenson *Cast:* Robert Mitchum, Ava Gardner, Melvyn Douglas, Janis Carter, Gordon Oliver, Basil Ruysdael
▶ In 1890 New Orleans, Gardner inherits a family fortune accrued by an ill-famed grandmother. Although she can buy anything she wants, Gardner can't have college professor Mitchum, who is married to Carter. A murder threatens both Mitchum and Gardner. Stuffy costume melodrama is dull and preposterous.
Dist.: Turner

MY LEFT FOOT 1989 Irish
★ ★ ★ ★ **R Biography 1:43**
☑ Adult situations, explicit language
Dir: Jim Sheridan *Cast:* Daniel Day-Lewis, Brenda Fricker, Ray McAnally, Hugh O'Conor, Fiona Shaw
▶ True story of Irishman Christy Brown (Day-Lewis), who refused to let cerebral palsy keep him from living life to the fullest. Young Christy (O'Conor) is written off as a vegetable until one day he uses his left foot to write. Fiercely protective mom Fricker scrimps to buy him a wheelchair. He grows up to become a painter

and writer, but love still eludes him. Phenomenal achievement from first-time director Sheridan. Oscar-winner Day-Lewis turns in one of the most technically accomplished and heartrending performances of recent years. Other Oscar nominations included Best Picture, Director, and Adapted Screenplay; Fricker won Best Supporting Actress. (CC)
Dist.: HBO

MY LIFE AS A DOG 1987 Swedish
★★ PG-13 Comedy/Drama 1:41
☑ Nudity, adult situations
Dir: Lasse Hallstrom ***Cast:*** Anton Glanzelius, Tomas von Bromssen, Anki Liden, Melinda Kinnaman, Kicki Rundgren
► When his mother falls fatally ill, young Glanzelius is packed off to live with relatives in a rural village populated by a cast of endearing eccentrics. Beneath the adolescent high jinks lurks the boy's ongoing struggles with guilt, loss, and his first love. More than just another coming-of-age tale, this Oscar nominee is graced with compelling warmth, wit, and wisdom and a sweetly artless performance by Glanzelius. Hallstrom was nominated for Best Director. Also available in a dubbed version. [S]
Dist.: Paramount

MY LIFE TO LIVE 1962 French
☆ NR Drama 1:25 B&W
Dir: Jean-Luc Godard ***Cast:*** Anna Karina, Saddy Rebbot, Andre S. Labarthe, Guylaine Schlumberger, Gerard Hoffman, Monique Messine
► Parisian shopgirl Karina leaves her husband and goes from being an aspiring actress to a prostitute. Divided into twelve segments of varying length, avant garde feature is a good place to sample director Godard's experiments when they still carried the crackling air of discovery. French title: *Vivre Sa Vie.* [S]
Dist.: Cable

MY LITTLE CHICKADEE 1940
★★★ NR Comedy 1:23 B&W
Dir: Edward Cline ***Cast:*** W. C. Fields, Mae West, Joseph Calleia, Dick Foran, Margaret Hamilton, Donald Meek
► West loves mysterious masked bandit Calleia, but enters a marriage of convenience with Fields, a card sharp who takes their marriage vows a bit too seriously. Low-key Western spoof never catches fire, but the card games and a memorable wedding night with a goat are prime Fields scenes. The two stars wrote the screenplay.
Dist.: MCA

MY LITTLE GIRL 1987
★★ PG-13 Drama 1:53
☑ Adult situations, explicit language
Dir: Connie Kaiserman ***Cast:*** Mary Stuart Masterson, James Earl Jones, Geraldine Page, Anne Meara, Pamela Payton-Wright, Peter Gallagher
► Rich girl Masterson volunteers at a children's detention center, befriends some of the homeless kids, and aids in an escape when one of the girls is sent to another institution. Independent film done with obvious care and sensitivity lacks dramatic urgency, but has committed performances by Masterson, Jones, and Page.
Dist.: Prism

MY LITTLE PONY, THE MOVIE 1986
★★★★★ G Animation 1:30
Dir: Michael Joens ***Cast:*** Voices of Danny DeVito, Madeline Kahn, Cloris Leachman, Rhea Perlman, Tony Randall
► Wicked witch threatens carefree Ponyland with a living slime called "the Smooze." Will the pastel Ponies see their world turned to shades of gray? Tiny tots will be kept in suspense by this feature-length pitch for Little Pony products. (CC)
Dist.: Vestron

MY MAN ADAM 1985
★★ R Comedy 1:24
☑ Nudity, adult situations, explicit language, violence
Dir: Roger L. Simon ***Cast:*** Raphael Sbarge, Page Hannah, Veronica Cartwright, Dave Thomas
► Restless teen Sbarge daydreams of being a famous journalist. His fantasies and much more come true when Hannah involves him in exposing a car-theft ring. He gets the scoop and the girl. Walter Mitty–like premise is sabotaged by meandering plot. (CC)
Dist.: CBS/Fox

MY MAN GODFREY 1936
★★★★ NR Comedy 1:35 B&W
Dir: Gregory La Cava ***Cast:*** William Powell, Carole Lombard, Alice Brady, Eugene Pallette, Gail Patrick, Mischa Auer, Alan Mowbray, Franklin Pangborn
► Daffy heiress Lombard wins a society treasure hunt with the help of Powell, a down-and-out but curiously civilized hobo. When she hires him as a butler, Powell straightens out her wacky household. Exceptional screwball comedy whose social points make sense today; received six Oscar nominations, including Auer's hilarious supporting role as a gorilla-impersonating gigolo.
Dist.: Various

MY MOM'S A WEREWOLF 1989
★★ PG Comedy 1:24
☑ Adult situations, explicit language, mild violence
Dir: Michael Fisha ***Cast:*** Susan Blakely, John Saxon, Katrina Caspary, John Schuck, Ruth Buzzi, Marilyn McCoo
► Blakely's new boyfriend Saxon takes suspicious nip out of her toe. Soon she is serving bloody roast beef, growing fangs, and sprouting body hair. Her daughter Caspary turns to

gypsy Buzzi for advice. Sitcommish fare scores the occasional chuckle.
Dist.: Prism

MY NAME IS NOBODY 1974
French/German/Italian
★ ★ ★ **PG Western 1:55**
☑ Adult situations, violence
Dir: Tonino Valerii *Cast:* Henry Fonda, Terence Hill, Leo Gordon, Geoffrey Lewis, R. G. Armstrong
▶ At the turn of the century, legendary outlaw Fonda is retiring to Europe, where he hopes to lead the easy life. Young admirer Hill can't bear to see his hero go out of the picture quietly, and contrives to have him battle an army of baddies before taking his bow. Tongue-in-cheek spaghetti Western written by Sergio Leone is a little long, but has a certain charm.
Dist.: KVC

MY NEW PARTNER 1985 French
★ **R Comedy 1:44**
☑ Nudity, explicit language, violence
Dir: Claude Zidi *Cast:* Philippe Noiret, Thierry Lhermitte, Régine, Grace de Capitani
▶ Corrupt Paris cop Noiret finds that idealistic new partner Lhermitte disapproves of his shady ways. However, after getting involved with prostitute de Capitani, the young man teams with the old pro in plan to rob drug dealers. Pretty accessible to American audiences; the actors make amoral characters sympathetic. ⓢ
Dist.: Media

MY NIGHT AT MAUD'S 1969 French
☆ **PG Comedy 1:51 B&W**
☑ Adult situations
Dir: Eric Rohmer *Cast:* Jean-Louis Trintignant, Francoise Fabian, Marie-Christine Barrault, Antoine Velez
▶ Trintignant, a philosophical and very principled Catholic, has just fallen for younger Barrault, but ends up spending a night with alluring divorcée Fabian. Their encounter is mostly provocative but platonic conversation, yet it resonates in his life in highly unexpected ways. One of Rohmer's best was Oscar-nominated for Best Foreign Film and Original Screenplay. ⓢ
Dist.: Media

MY OTHER HUSBAND 1984 French
★ **PG-13 Comedy 1:50**
☑ Adult situations
Dir: Georges Lautner *Cast:* Miou-Miou, Roger Hanin, Eddy Mitchell, Rachid Ferrache, Chalotte de Turckheim, Dominique Lavanant
▶ With amazing aplomb, Miou-Miou juggles two households unbeknownst to each other. During the week, she's with husband Hanin and son Ferrache, while on weekends she lives happily with lover Mitchell and their two kids. Good-natured comedy is filled with laughs and tender moments. Miou-Miou is a delight. ⓢ
Dist.: RCA/Columbia

MYRA BRECKENRIDGE 1970
☆ **R Comedy 1:34**
☑ Rape, nudity, strong sexual content, adult situations, explicit language
Dir: Michael Sarne *Cast:* Mae West, John Huston, Raquel Welch, Rex Reed, Farrah Fawcett, Jim Backus
▶ West, starring in her first film in thirty-seven years at the age of seventy-eight, plays a film critic who undergoes a sex-change operation before launching an attack on America's love affair with virile male movie stars. Embarrassingly bad adaptation of Gore Vidal's controversial novel concentrates exclusively on leering innuendos and double entendres.
Dist.: CBS/Fox

MY SCIENCE PROJECT 1985
★ ★ ★ **PG Sci-Fi/Comedy 1:35**
☑ Explicit language, violence
Dir: Jonathan Betuel *Cast:* John Stockwell, Fisher Stevens, Danielle von Zerneck, Raphael Sbarge, Dennis Hopper, Richard Masur
▶ High school senior Stockwell needs a science project to graduate and comes up with a whopper when he stumbles upon a relic from outer space. Soon he's warping through time and wreaking havoc on his hometown until he decides some things are better left alone. Hopper steals the show as a hippie science teacher.
Dist.: Buena Vista

MY SIDE OF THE MOUNTAIN 1969
★ ★ ★ **G Family 1:40**
Dir: James B. Clark *Cast:* Ted Eccles, Theodore Bikel, Tudi Wiggins, Frank Perry, Peggi Loder
▶ Under the influence of author Henry David Thoreau, young Eccles leaves home to live in the wilderness for a year. With a falcon and racoon for pets, he lives in a hollow tree and meets Bikel, a wandering folk singer who becomes a special friend. Thoughtful and enjoyable family entertainment.
Dist.: Paramount

MY STEPMOTHER IS AN ALIEN 1988
★ ★ ★ **PG-13 Sci-Fi/Comedy 1:50**
☑ Adult situations, explicit language, adult humor
Dir: Richard Benjamin *Cast:* Dan Aykroyd, Kim Basinger, Jon Lovitz, Alyson Hannigan, Joseph Maher
▶ Alien Basinger arrives on Earth to learn how scientist Aykroyd sent her planet off course. Basinger finds both earthly phenomena (like cheeseburgers and Jimmy Durante songs) and Aykroyd fascinating, leading to intergalactic marriage. Aykroyd effectively plays straight man to the effervescent Basinger. Lo-

vitz adds some mirth as Aykroyd's horny brother.
Dist.: RCA/Columbia

MYSTERIANS, THE 1959 Japanese
★ **NR Sci-Fi 1:25**
Dir: Inoshiro Honda *Cast:* Kenji Sahara, Yumi Shirakawa, Momoko Kochi, Akihiko Hirata
▶ Survivors from the destruction of the planet Mysteroid land on Earth, protesting peaceful intentions. Soon the aliens show their hand, rampaging for Earth women with whom they can procreate. The monsters are some of Japan's most imaginatively bizarre in this far-out offering from the creators of Godzilla.
Dist.: United

MYSTERIOUS ISLAND 1961 British
★★★ **NR Fantasy/Action-Adventure 1:41**
Dir: Cy Endfield *Cast:* Michael Craig, Joan Greenwood, Michael Callan, Gary Merrill, Herbert Lom
▶ Union soldiers escape Confederate prison via balloon, crash-land at sea, and are washed up on the shores of a strange island containing giant creatures, pirates, Captain Nemo (Lom), and a live volcano. Exciting escapist fantasy from the pages of Jules Verne. Ray Harryhausen special effects wizardry and Bernard Herrmann score add to the fun. (CC)
Dist.: RCA/Columbia

MYSTERY MANSION 1984
★★ **PG Family 1:35**
☑ Violence
Dir: David E. Jackson *Cast:* Dallas McKennon, Greg Wynne, Randi Brown, Jane Ferguson
▶ Young Brown explores the secrets of a spooky mansion with crusty old caretaker McKennon. Escaped convicts in pursuit of buried treasure terrorize the girl and kidnap her aunt, but McKennon scares them away with fake ghosts. Standard family fare with enough diversion for young and old alike.
Dist.: Media

MYSTERY OF ALEXINA, THE 1986 French
☆ **NR Drama 1:26**
☑ Nudity, adult situations
Dir: René Feret *Cast:* Philippe Vuillemin, Valérie Stroh, Véronique Silver, Bernard Freyd, Marianne Basler
▶ In the 1850s, convent-educated Alexina (Vuillemin) is hired to teach at boarding school and has affair with co-worker Stroh. It is then revealed that Alexina was born a man but mislabelled sexually at birth. Society pressures doom the romance. Extremely arty and odd. [S]
Dist.: Nelson

MYSTERY OF THE WAX MUSEUM 1933
★★ **NR Horror 1:17**
Dir: Michael Curtiz *Cast:* Lionel Atwill, Fay Wray, Glenda Farrell, Allen Vincent, Frank McHugh, Arthur Edmond
▶ Journalist Farrell suspects that wax-museum owner Atwill is replacing some melted figures with the bodies of murder victims. Farrell's roommate Wray falls into Atwill's clutches, and is placed in a fiendish device that will coat her body in hot wax. Well-done horror picture inspired 1953's equally good 3-D *House of Wax.*
Dist.: MGM/UA

MYSTERY TRAIN 1989
★ **R Comedy/Drama 1:53**
☑ Nudity, adult situations, explicit language
Dir: Jim Jarmusch *Cast:* Masatoshi Nagase, Youki Kudoh, Steve Buscemi, Nicoletta Braschi, Elizabeth Bracco, Screamin' Jay Hawkins, Joe Strummer, Rick Aviles, Elizabeth Bracco
▶ In Memphis, where the spirit of the late Elvis Presley is omnipresent, three seemingly unrelated tales overlap in unusual ways. Young Japanese tourists Nagase and Kudoh visit landmarks related to the King; widow Braschi arrives to take her husband's body back to Italy; and Strummer, Aviles, and Buscemi hold up a liquor store. Hip sensibility of director Jarmusch may be indecipherable for many.
Dist.: Orion

MYSTIC PIZZA 1988
★★★ **R Romance 1:42**
☑ Adult situations, explicit language
Dir: Donald Petrie *Cast:* Julia Roberts, Annabeth Gish, Lili Taylor, Vincent D'Onofrio, William R. Moses, Adam Storke
▶ Roberts, Gish, and Taylor, waitresses at Mystic Pizza restaurant in Connecticut, have summer of romantic ups and downs: Taylor faints before fiancée D'Onofrio at the altar, Gish falls for married Moses, and poor girl Roberts gets involved with rich law student Storke. Winning cast transcends familiar material.
Dist.: Virgin

MY TUTOR 1983
★★★ **R Comedy 1:37**
☑ Nudity, strong sexual content, adult situations, explicit language, adult humor
Dir: George Bowers *Cast:* Caren Kaye, Matt Lattanzi, Kevin McCarthy, Bruce Bauer, Arlene Golonka, Crispin Glover
▶ Sexy tutor Kaye is retained by wealthy Southern Cal family to assure that son Lattanzi gets into Yale. Guess what she winds up teaching him? Credible romance and some better-than-average comic bits. Look for Glover in a small turn as a horny high school chum.
Dist.: MCA

NABONGA 1944
★ **NR Action-Adventure 1:15 B&W**
Dir: Sam Newfield *Cast:* Buster Crabbe, Julie London, Fifi D'Orsay, Barton MacLane, Bryant Washburn
▶ London crash-lands in the Congo jungle with a stash of stolen loot. She is discovered by

a gorilla, who befriends her. When Crabbe comes to recover the money, they all band together to take on baddies MacLane and D'Orsay. Also known as *Gorilla*.
Dist.: Sinister

NADINE 1987
★ ★ ★ PG Comedy 1:23
☑ Explicit language, violence
Dir: Robert Benton   *Cast:* Jeff Bridges, Kim Basinger, Rip Torn, Gwen Verdon, Glenne Headly, Jerry Stiller
► In 1954 Austin, manicurist Basinger is trying to recover revealing photos from photographer Stiller when someone murders him over a valuable map. Basinger and her soon-to-be-ex-husband Bridges fall in love all over again as they battle bad guy Torn for possession of the map. Good-natured, if unoriginal, diversion. Handsome Bridges and saucy Basinger make an attractive couple.   **(CC)**
Dist.: CBS/Fox

NAKED AND THE DEAD, THE 1958
★ ★ ★ NR War 2:13
Dir: Raoul Walsh   *Cast:* Aldo Ray, Cliff Robertson, Raymond Massey, William Campbell, Richard Jaeckel, James Best, Joey Bishop, L. Q. Jones
► Hard-hitting World War II adventure about a doomed platoon's efforts to occupy a Pacific island. Officers Robertson and Massey argue over the welfare of their unit; Ray and his men encounter fierce resistance from the Japanese. Adapted from Norman Mailer's novel.
Dist.: VCI

NAKED CAGE, THE 1986
★ R Action-Adventure 1:37
☑ Nudity, adult situations, explicit language, violence
Dir: Paul Nicholas   *Cast:* Shari Shattuck, Angel Tompkins, Lucinda Crosby, Christina Whitaker, Faith Minton, Stacey Shaffer
► Innocent bank clerk Shattuck takes the rap for a robbery masterminded by Whitaker. They are sentenced to a women's prison run by Tompkins, an evil lesbian warden. Crosby, a guard trying to expose Tompkins's corruption, befriends Shattuck and rescues her during a tear gas attack. Low-budget exploitation relies on predictable material.
Dist.: Media

NAKED FACE, THE 1985
★ ★ ★ R Drama 1:45
☑ Brief nudity, adult situations, explicit language, violence
Dir: Bryan Forbes   *Cast:* Roger Moore, Rod Steiger, Elliott Gould, Art Carney, Anne Archer, David Hedison
► Cops Steiger and Gould try to pin a series of murders on Chicago psychiatrist Moore, whose court testimony endangered a colleague. Moore hires eccentric private eye Carney to clear his name. Slick adaptation of Sidney Sheldon's first novel with an above-average cast, especially Moore in a change of pace from his James Bond roles.
Dist.: MGM/UA

NAKED GUN: FROM THE FILES OF POLICE SQUAD, THE 1988
★ ★ ★ ★ PG-13 Comedy 1:30
☑ Adult situations, explicit language, adult humor
Dir: David Zucker   *Cast:* Leslie Nielsen, Priscilla Presley, Ricardo Montalban, George Kennedy, O. J. Simpson, Reggie Jackson, Nancy Marchand
► When partner Simpson is nearly killed, L.A. cop Nielsen investigates and uncovers crooked mogul Montalban's plot to assassinate visiting Queen Elizabeth. Hilarious from beginning to end: Simpson turns getting shot into comic art, Nielsen and Presley send up MTV in a mock video, and the climax features the funniest baseball game in recent memory. Straight-faced Nielsen demonstrates genuine comic flair; amusing cameo from Jackson as outfielder turned brainwashed assassin. Written by Jim and Jerry Zucker, Jim Abrahams, and Pat Proft from their TV series.
Dist.: Paramount

NAKED IN THE SUN 1957
★ NR Action-Adventure 1:28
Dir: R. John Hugh   *Cast:* James Craig, Lita Milan, Barton MacLane, Tony Hunter, Jim Boles
► Osceola (Craig), chief of the Seminole Indians, fights a trader who hunts slaves and sells them to plantation owners. The bloody battle escalates when his wife Milan is kidnapped by the enemy. Interesting subject matter transcends indifferent execution. Based on a true story.
Dist.: Republic

NAKED JUNGLE, THE 1954
★ ★ ★ NR Action-Adventure 1:35
Dir: Byron Haskin   *Cast:* Eleanor Parker, Charlton Heston, William Conrad, Abraham Sofaer
► In South America, mail-order bride Parker finds her plantation-owner husband Heston a cold fish. When an army of soldier ants descends on the place, they band together to fight them and fall in love. Interesting, unusual premise generates maximum suspense. Great special effects, strong chemistry between Parker and Heston. Underrated and worth a look.
Dist.: Paramount

NAKED PREY, THE 1966
★ ★ ★ ★ NR Action-Adventure 1:34
Dir: Cornel Wilde   *Cast:* Cornel Wilde, Gert van de Berg, Ken Gampu, Patrick Mynhardt, Jose Sithole, Richard Mashiya
► In the 1860s, an ivory expedition is ambushed by natives led by Gampu. They give Wilde, the only survivor, a short head start before chasing him through the jungle. Harrowing adventure shot in a documentary style

on fascinating African locations received a Best Screenplay nomination.
Dist.: Paramount

NAKED SPUR, THE 1953
★ ★ ★ ★ NR Western 1:31
Dir: Anthony Mann *Cast:* James Stewart, Janet Leigh, Robert Ryan, Ralph Meeker, Millard Mitchell
▶ Obsessed bounty hunter Stewart and two untrustworthy partners—grizzled prospector Mitchell and dishonorably discharged soldier Meeker—capture bandit Ryan in the Colorado Rockies. As they return to Abilene, Ryan preys on the weaknesses of his captors, using greed and fear to arrange an escape. Unusually sophisticated Western features taut direction, masterful acting, and an incisive, Oscar-nominated screenplay. Highly recommended to fans of the genre.
Dist.: MGM/UA

NAKED VENGEANCE 1985 Filipino
★ ★ ★ ★ R Action-Adventure 1:37
☑ Rape, nudity, adult situations, explicit language, graphic violence
Dir: Cirio H. Santiago *Cast:* Deborah Tranelli, Kaz Garas, Bill McLaughlin, Ed Crick, Nick Nicholson
▶ Widowed after her husband is shot dead by a rapist, Tranelli returns to her hometown and runs afoul of sleazy gang who proceed to rape her and kill her parents. Tranelli recuperates and then gets revenge against the rednecks. Vigilante plot with a dash of feminism.
Dist.: Vestron

NAKED YOUTH 1959
☆ NR Drama 1:09
Dir: John F. Schreyer *Cast:* Carol Ohmart, Robert Hutton, Steve Rowland, Jan Brooks, Robert Arthur, John Goddard
▶ Sensational fifties juvenile delinquent drama about a group of kids who break out of their easygoing detention facility and light out for Mexico. Once there, they encounter every vice thought to titillate moviegoers. For those who like to laugh at cheap, sleazy movies.
Dist.: Rhino

NAM ANGELS 1988 Filipino
★ ★ ★ R War 1:33
☑ Brief nudity, explicit language, graphic violence
Dir: Cirio H. Santiago *Cast:* Brad Johnson, Vernon Wells, Kevin Duffis, Rick Dean, Mark Venturini
▶ In Vietnam, two of lieutenant Johnson's men are captured by renegade white Wells and his tribesmen. With the promise of going after Wells's gold, Johnson recruits four Hell's Angels for the rescue mission. Combination of biker and war genres provides nonstop battles.
Dist.: Media

NAME OF THE ROSE, THE 1986
Italian/German/French
★ ★ ★ R Mystery-Suspense 2:09
☑ Nudity, adult situations, violence
Dir: Jean-Jacques Annaud *Cast:* Sean Connery, F. Murray Abraham, Christian Slater, William Hickey, Ron Perlman, Michael Lonsdale, Elya Baskin
▶ From the Umberto Eco best-seller set in Northern Italy, 1327. Liberal monk Connery and young protégé Slater solve a series of monastery murders. The shadow of the Inquisition (led by evil Abraham) looms large over the investigation. A thinker's medieval mystery plot, eerily atmospheric, marred by dismal pacing. Witty performance by Connery holds it together. Best scenes: Connery's advice to Slater about women and his confession of his own dark secret. **(CC)**
Dist.: Nelson

NAPOLEON 1927 French
★ G Biography 3:55 C/B&W
Dir: Abel Gance *Cast:* Albert Dieudonne, Gina Manes, Vladimir Roudenko, Antonin Artaud, Pierre Batcheff, Abel Gance
▶ Monumental silent epic on the life of Napoleon (Dieudonne), from his childhood through his courtship of Josephine (Manes) and triumphant military campaign in Italy. Lost for years, this version was reconstructed in 1981 by historian Kevin Brownlow and released with a new score by Carmine Coppola. Film's best effects (particularly the stunning, hand-colored, three-screen climax) will not transfer well to TV.
Dist.: MCA

NAPOLEON AND SAMANTHA 1972
★ ★ ★ ★ G Action-Adventure/Family 1:31
Dir: Bernard McEveety *Cast:* Johnnie Whitaker, Jodie Foster, Michael Douglas, Will Geer, Henry Jones, Rex Holman
▶ Oregon kids Whitaker and Foster adopt a circus lion. When Whitaker's grandfather Geer dies, the kids, preferring the company of mountain man Douglas to being put in a state institution, run away with their feline friend. First-rate Disney fare.
Dist.: Buena Vista

NARROW MARGIN, THE 1952
★ ★ ★ NR Mystery-Suspense 1:11 B&W
Dir: Richard Fleischer *Cast:* Charles McGraw, Marie Windsor, Jacqueline White, Gordon Gebert, Queenie Leonard
▶ Detective McGraw accompanies a witness, mobster's widow Windsor, on a cross-country train trip. Although not fond of his responsibility, he must protect her from assassins trying to prevent her from testifying. Superbly suspenseful thriller, not to be missed. Remade in 1990 with Gene Hackman and Anne Archer. Home video version double billed with 1941's *The Saint's Vacation.*
Dist.: Turner

NASHVILLE 1975
★ R Comedy/Drama 2:39
☑ Nudity, adult situations, explicit language, violence
Dir: Robert Altman   *Cast:* Henry Gibson, Karen Black, Ronee Blakley, Keith Carradine, Geraldine Chaplin, Lily Tomlin, Michael Murphy, Barbara Harris, Allen Garfield, Ned Beatty, Barbara Baxley, Shelley Duvall, Keenan Wynn, Scott Glenn, Gwen Welles, Jeff Goldblum, Bert Remsen, Robert DoQui
► Altman's look at country music characters and the dreams that bring them to Nashville. The most memorable: mother of two deaf children (Tomlin) having an affair with womanizing singer Carradine, country music star Blakley suffering nervous breakdown, and no-talent Welles humiliated into becoming a stripper. Some may find the seeming lack of focus disconcerting; however, the film is as richly populated as a Dickens novel. Five Oscar nominations included Best Picture and Supporting Actresses Blakley and Tomlin; won for Best Song (Carradine's "I'm Easy").
Dist.: Paramount

NASHVILLE GIRL 1976
★ ★ R Drama 1:30
☑ Nudity, adult situations, explicit language
Dir: Gus Trikonis   *Cast:* Monica Gayle, Glenn Corbett, Roger Davis, Johnny Rodriguez, Jesse White
► Raped by a neighbor, young Gayle leaves her farm for Nashville, determined to become a country-western star. But success doesn't come easy: she is forced to work in a massage parlor and sleep with phony agents and producers before recording her songs. Sincere but predictable drama with a strong country-western soundtrack. Film debut for pop star Rodriguez, who plays himself. Also known as *New Girl in Town* and *Country Music Daughter.*
Dist.: Nelson

NASTY HABITS 1977
★ PG Comedy 1:32
☑ Adult situations, explicit language
Dir: Michael Lindsay-Hogg   *Cast:* Glenda Jackson, Melina Mercouri, Geraldine Page, Sandy Dennis, Anne Jackson, Anne Meara
► The Watergate scandal in nun's clothing: scheming sister Jackson plots to win election to succeed the dying abbess through burglary and bugging. Great cast, ingenious idea—but the one joke wears thin very quickly and the Nixonian satire is now dated.
Dist.: Media

NATE AND HAYES 1983 U.S./New Zealand
★ ★ ★ PG Action-Adventure 1:40
☑ Explicit language, graphic violence
Dir: Ferdinand Fairfax   *Cast:* Tommy Lee Jones, Michael O'Keefe, Max Phipps, Jenny Seagrove
► In a characterization based on an actual historical figure, good-hearted pirate Bully Hayes (Jones) teams up with missionary O'-

Keefe to rescue Seagrove, O'Keefe's kidnapped fiancée. Convincing period re-creation of 1880s South Seas, lovely New Zealand scenery, plenty of action, but unconvincing performances, feeble humor and screenplay.
Dist.: Paramount

NATIONAL LAMPOON'S CHRISTMAS VACATION 1989
★ ★ ★ PG-13 Comedy 1:37
☑ Explicit language
Dir: Jeremiah S. Chechik   *Cast:* Chevy Chase, Beverly D'Angelo, Randy Quaid, Diane Ladd, Mae Questel, William Hickey
► Once again the best laid plans of family man Chase end in comic calamity as his traditional Christmas celebration is interrupted by invading in-laws, uninvited slob cousin Quaid, a power failure, and other disasters. Third entry in the series may not be up to the first but improves on the second. Quaid steals the show but cat lovers should beware of family pet's encounter with the Christmas lights. (CC)
Dist.: Warner

NATIONAL LAMPOON'S CLASS REUNION 1982
★ R Horror/Comedy 1:25
☑ Nudity, adult situations, explicit language, violence
Dir: Michael Miller   *Cast:* Gerrit Graham, Michael Lerner, Stephen Furst, Zane Buzby, Anne Ramsey, Shelley Smith
► Tenth-year reunion for the class of 1972 at Lizzie Borden High. Gathered for the festivities are a stuffy yacht salesman, the class prig, a fat guy, and other odd types. The antics get out of hand when someone starts bumping off the alumni. Overstated satire, ludicrously scripted and unevenly acted, has a few clever bits. Chuck Berry guest stars but doesn't even sing one whole song.
Dist.: Warner

NATIONAL LAMPOON'S EUROPEAN VACATION 1985
★ ★ ★ PG-13 Comedy 1:30
☑ Nudity, explicit language, adult humor
Dir: Amy Heckerling   *Cast:* Chevy Chase, Beverly D'Angelo, Dana Hill, Jason Lively, Victor Lanoux, Eric Idle
► All-American dad Clark W. Griswold (Chase) from *National Lampoon's Vacation* is back with his family on a European jaunt won on a game show. Perils of London driving, French women, and Italian kidnappings are some of the comic mishaps that befall the merry bunch. Chase is funny and there is some amusing slapstick although not quite up to the original. (CC)
Dist.: Warner

NATIONAL LAMPOON'S VACATION 1983
★ ★ ★ ★ R Comedy 1:38
☑ Nudity, adult situations, explicit language, adult humor
Dir: Harold Ramis   *Cast:* Chevy Chase, Bev-

erly D'Angelo, Imogene Coca, Randy Quaid, Anthony Michael Hall, John Candy, Christie Brinkley

▶ Middle-class dad Clark Griswold (Chase) takes wife D'Angelo and kids on a cross-country trip to "Wally World," a Disneyland-like theme park. Some unlucky but very funny situations follow: visits with redneck relative Quaid, obnoxious aunt Coca, a St. Louis ghetto detour, and an encounter in a swimming pool with stunning Brinkley. Lively, outrageous, frequently rib-tickling; Chase anchors the craziness with surprising humanity.
Dist.: Warner

NATIONAL VELVET 1945
★ ★ ★ ★ ★ G Drama/Family 2:05
Dir: Clarence Brown *Cast:* Mickey Rooney, Elizabeth Taylor, Donald Crisp, Anne Revere, Angela Lansbury, Juanita Quigley, Reginold Owen

▶ Heartwarming family film follows the adventures of young Taylor and ex-jockey Rooney as they train a long-shot for England's Grand National steeplechase. Sterling performances by all involved, with Crisp in grand form as Taylor's crusty father. Revere received a Supporting Oscar as her sensitive mother; climactic race helped win an Oscar for editor Robert Kern. Followed in 1977 by *International Velvet.* (CC)
Dist.: MGM/UA

NATIVE SON 1950 Argentinian
★ NR Drama 1:45 B&W
Dir: Pierre Chenal *Cast:* Richard Wright, Jean Wallace, Gloria Madison, Nicholas Joy, Ruth Roberts, Charles Cane

▶ Wright, adapting his own novel, is Bigger Thomas, a black Chicago driver who kills Wallace, the daughter of his wealthy employers. He is eventually caught and put on trial. Peculiar independent effort is not a bad try, and Wright does well for a nonactor. However, neither this nor the 1986 remake do justice to the book.
Dist.: International Film Forum

NATIVE SON 1986
★ PG Drama 1:52
☑ Explicit language, violence
Dir: Jerrold Freedman *Cast:* Victor Love, Matt Dillon, Elizabeth McGovern, Geraldine Page, Oprah Winfrey, Akosua Busia

▶ In 1930s Chicago, young black Love is hired as chauffeur to wealthy white family. He accidentally kills their daughter, is caught, and put on trial. Well-intentioned but slow-moving adaptation of Richard Wright's classic novel. Despite good cast, subdued filmmaking never catches fire. (CC)
Dist.: Vestron

NATURAL, THE 1984
★ ★ ★ ★ ★ PG Drama/Sports 2:18
☑ Adult situations, explicit language, violence
Dir: Barry Levinson *Cast:* Robert Redford,

Robert Duvall, Glenn Close, Kim Basinger, Barbara Hershey, Wilford Brimley, Richard Farnsworth, Darren McGavin

▶ Redford plays Roy Hobbs, a baseball natural whose promising career is cut short by madwoman Hershey's bullet. Sixteen years later, Hobbs makes a comeback, overcoming his injury, self-doubts, and the allure of femme fatale Basinger to win the pennant and first love Close. Purists disliked this slick and sanitized adaptation of Bernard Malamud's darkly Arthurian fable, but Redford and the all-star cast shimmer in Caleb Deschanel's lustrous cinematography. (CC)
Dist.: RCA/Columbia

NATURAL ENEMIES 1979
☆ R Drama 1:40
☑ Adult situations, explicit language
Dir: Jeff Kanew *Cast:* Hal Holbrook, Louise Fletcher, Viveca Lindfors, Jose Ferrer

▶ Connecticut housewife Fletcher's marriage to Holbrook has become tired and tedious since her nervous breakdown. He considers killing her, himself, and their three children. Literate to a fault; generally intelligent writing gets bogs down in depressing pretensions. Holbrook and Fletcher are credible, however.
Dist.: RCA/Columbia

NAUGHTY MARIETTA 1935
★ NR Musical 1:46 B&W
Dir: W. S. Van Dyke II *Cast:* Jeanette MacDonald, Nelson Eddy, Frank Morgan, Elsa Lanchester, Douglass Dumbrille, Cecilia Parker

▶ French aristocrat MacDonald flees an unwanted betrothal on a ship full of single women going to New Orleans. She falls in love with Eddy after he and his Indian scouts rescue her from pirates. First of eight MacDonald/Eddy screen pairings doesn't utilize MacDonald's dramatic gifts as well as later films, but does feature some of Victor Herbert's most popular songs, including "Ah, Sweet Mystery of Life" and "Italian Street Song." Nominated for Best Picture.
Dist.: MGM/UA

NAUGHTY NINETIES, THE 1945
★ NR Comedy 1:16 B&W
Dir: Jean Yarbrough *Cast:* Bud Abbott, Lou Costello, Alan Curtis, Rita Johnson, Henry Travers, Lois Collier

▶ Showboat captain Travers is in danger of losing his ship to gamblers. Abbott and Costello try to help him in their usual bumbling manner. Lackluster comic vehicle has many tedious stretches, but also one classic highlight: the "Who's On First?" routine.
Dist.: MCA

NAVIGATOR, THE 1924
★ ★ ★ NR Comedy 1:00 B&W
Dir: Donald Crisp, Buster Keaton *Cast:* Buster Keaton, Kathryn McGuire, Frederick Vroom, Noble Johnson, Clarence Burton, Donald Crisp

► Keaton, a millionaire completely inept in the real world, is stranded on a luxury liner adrift in the ocean and deserted except for McGuire, a dizzy heiress who has repeatedly rejected his marriage proposals. Classic silent comedy is filled with unusually inventive and daring sight gags.
Dist.: Various

NAVIGATOR: AN ODYSSEY ACROSS TIME, THE 1989 New Zealand
☆ **PG Fantasy/Action-Adventure 1:32 C/B&W**
☑ Violence
Dir: Vincent Ward *Cast:* Bruce Lyons, Chris Haywood, Hamish McFarlane, Marshall Napier, Noel Appleby, Paul Livingston
► In 1348 Cumbria, the Black Plague has decimated most of the population. Young McFarlane has a recurring nightmare that he feels holds the key to a cure. He, brother Lyons, and others dig a hole and emerge on the other side of the world, which turns out to be 1988 New Zealand. Fantastical, wildly original adventure starts out slowly, but builds to breathtaking finale. Thick accents, gritty black-and-white photography, and bizarre time-travel elements, however, limit its appeal.
Dist.: Trylon

NAZARIN 1961 Mexican
☆ **NR Drama 1:32 B&W**
Dir: Luis Buñuel *Cast:* Francisco Rabal, Rita Macedo, Marga Lopez Tarso, Ofelia Guilmain, Jesus Fernandez
► Village priest Rabal encounters rebuffs and ridicule when he attempts to pattern his life after Christ. Taking to the road with unlikely companions, he tries to help his fellow man, and learns that he must accept humanity as it is before he can do so. Enlightening.
Ⓢ
Dist.: Cable

NEAR DARK 1987
★ **R Horror 1:35**
☑ Explicit language, graphic violence
Dir: Kathryn Bigelow *Cast:* Adrian Pasdar, Jenny Wright, Lance Henriksen, Bill Paxton, Jenette Goldstein, Joshua Miller
► Young cowboy Pasdar is lured into a traveling pack of vampires by strange but pretty Wright. He reluctantly takes part in their deadly games, finding himself more and more drawn into their world. Wonderfully fresh and original variation on vampire theme is technically and visually superb. Some may find the remarkably vivid violence unpleasant.
Dist.: HBO

NECROMANCER 1989
☆ **R Horror 1:28**
☑ Rape, nudity, adult situations, explicit language, violence
Dir: Dusty Nelson *Cast:* Elizabeth Kaitan, Russ Tamblyn, John Tyler, Rhonda Durton, Stan Hurwitz, Lois Masten

► Acting student Kaitan is gang raped by her classmates, who force her to keep silent about the crime. She contacts sorceress Masten, who possesses her and seduces her attackers to gain violent revenge. Horror film serves up a familiar plot with verve but not much originality.
Dist.: Virgin

NECROPOLIS 1987
☆ **R Horror 1:17**
☑ Nudity, adult situations, explicit language, violence
Dir: Bruce Hickey *Cast:* Leeanne Baker, Jacquie Fitz, Michael Conte, William K. Reed, Jett Julian
► Baker, a three-hundred-year-old witch disguised as a black-leather punker, preys on Manhattan's homeless. Local reverend Reed joins puzzled cop Conte in battling her. Dismal low-budget effort with poor acting and shoddy special effects.
Dist.: Vestron

NEIGHBORS 1981
★ **R Comedy 1:35**
☑ Adult situations, explicit language
Dir: John G. Avildsen *Cast:* John Belushi, Dan Aykroyd, Cathy Moriarty, Kathryn Walker, Igors Gavon, Tim Kazurinsky
► There goes the neighborhood as shameless couple Aykroyd and Moriarty move next door to stoical suburbanite Belushi and wife Walker. New arrivals proceed to disrupt Belushi's staid existence. Adaptation of the Thomas Berger novel gets off to a strong start with Belushi doing surprisingly well in his quiet role; humor lags in the second half.
Dist.: RCA/Columbia

NEON MANIACS 1986
★ ★ **R Horror 1:31**
☑ Brief nudity, adult situations, explicit language, violence
Dir: Joseph Mangine *Cast:* Alan Hayes, Leilani Sarelle, Donna Locke, Victor Elliot Brandt
► Monsters ambush teenagers partying under San Francisco's Golden Gate Bridge. Police won't believe Sarelle, the only survivor, so she teams up with boyfriend Hayes and amateur filmmaker Locke to destroy the menace. Average horror entry with an agreeable sense of humor and a full quota of gore.
Dist.: Vestron

NEPTUNE FACTOR, THE 1973 Canadian
★ **G Sci-Fi 1:34**
Dir: Daniel Petrie *Cast:* Ben Gazzara, Yvette Mimieux, Walter Pidgeon, Ernest Borgnine, Chris Wiggins, Donnelly Rhodes
► An undersea earthquake traps a manned sea lab in a trench on the ocean floor. Gazzara commands the sub sent to rescue the beleaguered crew. Giant mutant fish make his mission near impossible. Waterlogged

screenplay strands veteran cast. As silly as it sounds. **(CC)**
Dist.: CBS/Fox

NEPTUNE'S DAUGHTER 1949
★ ★ NR Musical 1:32
Dir: Edward Buzzell *Cast:* Esther Williams, Red Skelton, Ricardo Montalban, Betty Garrett, Keenan Wynn, Xavier Cugat
▶ Bathing suit manufacturer/model Williams is pursued by millionaire polo player Montalban. Meanwhile, her sister Garrett chases masseur Skelton because she thinks he's Montalban in this colorful, delightful musical. Highlights: Williams and Montalban dueting on Frank Loesser's Oscar-winning "Baby It's Cold Outside" and Cugat's conga. **(CC)**
Dist.: MGM/UA

NEST, THE 1987
★ ★ R Horror 1:29
☑ Adult situations, explicit language, graphic violence
Dir: Terence H. Winkless *Cast:* Robert Lansing, Lisa Langlois, Franc Luz, Terri Treas, Stephen Davies, Diana Bellamy
▶ Small town mayor Lansing permits research corporation to conduct genetic experiments. Move backfires when mutant cannibal cockroaches are created; not only do they munch humans but they turn into what they eat (resulting in a cat-roach, among other monstrosities). Sheriff Luz tries to save the day. Farfetched but competent B-movie with yucky special effects.
Dist.: MGM/UA

NESTING, THE 1981
★ ★ R Horror 1:44
☑ Brief nudity, explicit language, graphic violence
Dir: Armand Weston *Cast:* Robin Groves, Christopher Loomis, Michael David Lally, John Carradine, Gloria Grahame
▶ Novelist Groves battles her fear of open spaces by renting an old house. Right after she arrives, weird things begin to happen: landlord Carradine suffers a stroke, bizarre erotic dreams plague her, she discovers the house was formerly a brothel, and a series of deaths occurs. Slightly above average.
Dist.: Warner

NETWORK 1976
★ ★ ★ ★ R Comedy 2:01
☑ Brief nudity, adult situations, explicit language
Dir: Sidney Lumet *Cast:* Faye Dunaway, William Holden, Peter Finch, Robert Duvall, Ned Beatty, Beatrice Straight
▶ "I'm mad as hell and I'm not gonna take it anymore!" With these words, TV news anchorman Finch revives his faltering career and becomes the popular "mad prophet of the airwaves." Although veteran newsman Holden worries that friend Finch is really insane, ruthless executive Dunaway exploits the situation for big ratings. Blistering satire of television

with Oscar-winning performances by Finch (his last role), Dunaway, and Straight (for one great scene as Holden's wronged wife); also won for Original Screenplay (Paddy Chayefsky).
Dist.: MGM/UA

NEVADA SMITH 1966
★ ★ ★ NR Western 2:15
Dir: Henry Hathaway *Cast:* Steve McQueen, Karl Malden, Brian Keith, Arthur Kennedy, Suzanne Pleshette, Pat Hingle, Martin Landau
▶ When his parents are murdered by outlaws, half-breed McQueen enlists the aid of sharpshooter Keith in tracking them down. Sturdy Western features hard-edged action and a strong cast (including Landau's sneaky villain). McQueen's character is based on a role played by Alan Ladd in 1964's *The Carpetbaggers*. Remade for TV in 1975 with Cliff Potts.
Dist.: Paramount

NEVER CRY WOLF 1983
★ ★ ★ ★ PG Action-Adventure 1:45
☑ Nudity, adult situations, explicit language, violence
Dir: Carroll Ballard *Cast:* Charles Martin Smith, Brian Dennehy, Zachary Ittimangnaq, Samson Jorah, Hugh Webster, Martha Ittimangnaq
▶ Biologist Smith is sent into the Canadian Arctic to study wolves. The relationship that develops between him and the animals is moving yet subtle. Breathtaking cinematography and locations, intelligent ecological message, and welcome humor (as when Smith snacks on mice to better understand his charges). Absorbing Arctic adventure based on Farley Mowat's best-seller.
Dist.: Buena Vista

NEVERENDING STORY, THE 1984
German/British
★ ★ ★ ★ PG Fantasy/Family 1:34
☑ Violence
Dir: Wolfgang Petersen *Cast:* Noah Hathaway, Barrett Oliver, Tami Stronach, Moses Gunn, Patricia Hayes, Gerald McRaney
▶ Little boy Oliver reads "special" book that tells of young warrior Hathaway's quest to stop a stormlike entity from destroying a fantasy world. Oliver enters the story to help save the day. Good-natured family adventure, filled with charming monsters, magic, and special effects. Imaginative direction by Petersen. **(CC)**
Dist.: Warner

NEVER GIVE A SUCKER AN EVEN BREAK 1941
★ ★ NR Comedy 1:11 B&W
Dir: Edward Cline *Cast:* W. C. Fields, Gloria Jean, Margaret Dumont, Leon Errol, Franklin Pangborn, Susan Miller
▶ Crazy, wildly surreal bit of nonsense starts with Fields pitching movie idea to producer Pangborn. Story within the story has Fields fall-

ing out of an airplane in pursuit of his beloved bottle and visiting the mountaintop home of wealthy but monstrous Dumont. Free-falling fun was the great comic's last starring role.
Dist.: KVC

NEVER LOVE A STRANGER 1958
☆ NR Drama 1:31 B&W
Dir: Robert Stevens *Cast:* John Drew Barrymore, Lita Milan, Peg Murray, Robert Bray, Steve McQueen
▶ Jewish orphan Barrymore is mistakenly placed in a Catholic orphanage. Authorities try to move him to a different home, but the experience leaves Barrymore embittered, and he plunges into a life of crime. Unconvincing story produced by Harold Robbins and based on his novel.
Dist.: Republic

NEVER ON SUNDAY 1960 Greek
★ ★ ★ NR Comedy 1:31 B&W
Dir: Jules Dassin *Cast:* Melina Mercouri, Jules Dassin, Titos Vandis, Mitsos Liguisos, Despo Diamantidou, George Foundas
▶ Greek prostitute Mercouri plies her trade six days a week but "never on Sunday." Visiting American intellectual Dassin takes Mercouri (his wife in real life) under his wing and tries to teach her a more legit life-style; in the end, it is Dassin who ends up learning from his pupil. Mercouri's marvelous Oscar-nominated turn dominates this frisky tale. Title tune won Best Song Oscar; also nominated for screenplay and direction.
Dist.: MGM/UA

NEVER ON TUESDAY 1989
☆ R Comedy 1:30
☑ Nudity, adult situations, explicit language
Dir: Adam Rifkin *Cast:* Claudia Christian, Andrew Lauer, Pete Berg, Gilbert Gottfried, Charlie Sheen, Judd Nelson
▶ Lauer and Berg, Ohio boys headed West, have an accident and are stranded along the highway with the attractive Christian—who fends off their advances by telling them she's a lesbian. Nelson, Sheen, and Gottfried have brief cameos as passersby who refuse to give the threesome a lift. Experimental technique sinks this unfunny, direct-to-video release. **(CC)**
Dist.: Paramount

NEVER SAY NEVER AGAIN 1983
★ ★ ★ ★ PG Espionage/Action-Adventure 2:14
☑ Brief nudity, adult situations, explicit language, violence
Dir: Irvin Kershner *Cast:* Sean Connery, Klaus Maria Brandauer, Max Von Sydow, Barbara Carrera, Kim Basinger, Bernie Casey
▶ Arch-villain Brandauer hijacks two cruise missiles to hold the world hostage, but doesn't count on the resolute superagent 007. High-spirited James Bond adventure based on *Thunderball*, with Connery making a welcome

return after a thirteen-year absence to the role he originated. Carrera is especially alluring as the evil Fatima Blush.
Dist.: Warner

NEVER SO FEW 1959
★ ★ ★ ★ NR War 2:04
Dir: John Sturges *Cast:* Frank Sinatra, Gina Lollobrigida, Peter Lawford, Steve McQueen, Richard Johnson, Charles Bronson
▶ During World War II, American captain Sinatra leads Burmese unit against the Japanese but causes an international incident when he retaliates against Chinese attack on an American convoy. Romantic subplot concerns his dalliance with Lollobrigida while on leave in Calcutta. Top cast in zingy wartime adventure briskly directed by Sturges.
Dist.: MGM/UA

NEVER STEAL ANYTHING SMALL 1959
★ ★ NR Musical 1:34
Dir: Charles Lederer *Cast:* James Cagney, Shirley Jones, Roger Smith, Cara Williams, Nehemiah Persoff, Royal Dano
▶ Gangster Cagney seeks presidency of a dockhands' union by illicit means while resorting to a frame-up to steal Jones away from her husband Smith. An ambitious misfire, adapted from the play *The Devil's Hornpipe* by Maxwell Anderson and Rouben Mamoulian. Anderson co-wrote the songs, which include "I'm Sorry, I Want a Ferrari" and "It Takes Love to Make a Home."
Dist.: MCA

NEVER TOO YOUNG TO DIE 1986
★ ★ R Action-Adventure 1:37
☑ Nudity, adult situations, explicit language, violence
Dir: Gil Bettman *Cast:* John Stamos, Vanity, Gene Simmons, George Lazenby, Peter Kwong
▶ Hermaphrodite Simmons kills agent Lazenby and plots to pollute Los Angeles water supply. Lazenby's son Stamos and lover Vanity team up to thwart Simmons and get revenge. Teenage James Bond–style thriller is poorly written but may appeal to fans of soap star Stamos and rock star Vanity. **(CC)**
Dist.: Nelson

NEW ADVENTURES OF PIPPI LONGSTOCKING, THE 1988
★ ★ ★ G Family 1:40
Dir: Ken Annakin *Cast:* Tami Erin, Eileen Brennan, Dennis Dugan, Dianne Hull, George DiCenzo, Dick Van Patten
▶ Separated from her sea captain father by a tidal wave, young Pippi washes ashore in small Florida town, where her pranks and practical jokes incur the wrath of mean orphanage mistress Brennan. Kids should enjoy elaborate food fights and special effects. Erin, in her film debut, is the perfect physical type

for the pigtailed heroine of Astrid Lindgren's classic children's novels.
Dist.: RCA/Columbia

NEW CENTURIONS, THE 1972
★ ★ ★ R Crime 1:43
☑ Adult situations, explicit language, graphic violence
Dir: Richard Fleischer *Cast:* George C. Scott, Stacy Keach, Jane Alexander, Scott Wilson, Rosalind Cash, Erik Estrada
▶ Rookie Los Angeles cop Keach is shown the ropes by grizzled old pro Scott. Keach's marriage to Alexander deteriorates under the pressures of police lifestyle; Scott falls apart when he is sent into retirement. Strong performances by Scott and Keach, but fans of the Joseph Wambaugh best-seller may be disappointed by the less-than-faithful screenplay.
Dist.: RCA/Columbia

NEW KIDS, THE 1985
★ ★ ★ R Mystery-Suspense 1:29
☑ Rape, explicit language, graphic violence
Dir: Sean S. Cunningham *Cast:* Shannon Presby, Lori Loughlin, James Spader, Eddie Jones, John Philbin, Eric Stoltz
▶ Orphaned by a car crash, teen siblings Presby and Loughlin move in with Florida relatives and run afoul of vicious local bullies. After the gang tries to rape Loughlin, the brother and sister fight back. Competently filmed but banal junior version of *Death Wish.* **(CC)**
Dist.: RCA/Columbia

NEW LEAF, A 1971
★ ★ G Comedy 1:42
☑ Adult situations
Dir: Elaine May *Cast:* Walter Matthau, Elaine May, Jack Weston, George Rose, William Redfield, James Coco
▶ His trust fund exhausted, aging libertine Matthau woos wealthy but woefully klutzy botanist May, planning to murder her after their wedding. Uneven black comedy is not for all tastes, but director/writer/star May's script contains priceless moments. Excellent support by Rose as an imperturbable valet and Weston as a scheming lawyer.
Dist.: Paramount

NEW LIFE, A 1988
★ ★ ★ PG-13 Comedy/Drama 1:45
☑ Adult situations, explicit language
Dir: Alan Alda *Cast:* Alan Alda, Ann-Margret, Hal Linden, Veronica Hamel, John Shea, Mary Kay Place
▶ Workaholic Wall Streeter Alda is divorced by wife Ann-Margret and gingerly enters the Manhattan singles scene. Both find new relationships with younger lovers: he with heart specialist Hamel and she with sculptor Shea. Alda's willingness to poke fun at himself is endearing. Sometimes reaches for easy laughs but pleasantly evokes real-life pains and joys. **(CC)**
Dist.: Paramount

NEWMAN'S LAW 1974
★ ★ ★ PG Action-Adventure 1:38
☑ Adult situations, explicit language, violence
Dir: Richard T. Heffron *Cast:* George Peppard, Roger Robinson, Eugene Roche, Gordon Pinsent, Abe Vigoda, Louis Zorich
▶ Honest cop Peppard and partner Robinson connect a murder to a drug dealer. When the crime czar subsequently frames Peppard on a drug charge, Peppard attempts to get even. Corruption within the force complicates his task. Gritty, hard-hitting action in a familiar plot.
Dist.: MCA

NEW MOON 1940
★ NR Musical 1:45 B&W
Dir: Robert Z. Leonard *Cast:* Jeanette MacDonald, Nelson Eddy, Mary Boland, George Zucco, H. B. Warner, Grant Mitchell
▶ In the late eighteenth century, French aristocrat Eddy pretends to be a servant to escape the wrath of the king. Sent to America, he is indentured to heiress MacDonald, from whose service he escapes to become a pirate. Hard to keep interested in the slow-moving plot, but worth sticking around for songs like Sigmund Romberg and Oscar Hammerstein's "Stout-Hearted Men" and Handel's "Ombre Ma Fui." Look for Buster Keaton in a very small role as a prisoner called "LuLu."
Dist.: MGM/UA

NEWSFRONT 1978 Australian
★ PG Drama 1:51 C/B&W
☑ Brief nudity, adult situations, explicit language
Dir: Phillip Noyce *Cast:* Bill Hunter, Gerard Kennedy, Wendy Hughes, Angela Punch, Chris Haywood
▶ Original, absorbing drama about the rivalry between Hunter and Kennedy, brothers who work for competing newsreel companies in post–World War II Australia. Fresh approach to the subject uses actual documentary footage to round out the characters' lives. Technically impressive film provides a rewarding, nostalgic look at the period.
Dist.: Nelson

NEW YEAR'S EVIL 1981
☆ R Horror 1:28
☑ Nudity, explicit language, violence
Dir: Emmett Alston *Cast:* Roz Kelly, Kip Niven, Chris Wallace, Grant Cramer, Louisa Moritz, Jed Mills
▶ Los Angeles disc jockey Kelly is hosting a televised New Year's Eve bash when an anonymous caller tells her he will kill someone at midnight in four time zones. The murderer succeeds three times and then heads for Kelly. Script fails to make you care about the victims

despite above-par direction. Less violent than you would expect.
Dist.: Warner

NEW YORK, NEW YORK 1977
★ ★ ★ PG Musical 2:43
☑ Explicit language
Dir: Martin Scorsese *Cast:* Liza Minnelli, Robert De Niro, Lionel Stander, Mary Kay Place, Diahnne Abbott, Dick Miller
▶ Lavish but downbeat musical about the troubled affair between saxophonist De Niro and singer Minnelli during the post–World War II Big Band era. Boasts a strong score by John Kander and Fred Ebb (title song, "There Goes the Ball Game,") and good performances from the leads, but unfocused plot has tedious stretches. Abbott does a great "Honeysuckle Rose." Reissue and cassette versions also include "Happy Endings," a song cut from the original release.
Dist.: MGM/UA

NEW YORK NIGHTS 1984
★ R Sex 1:43
☑ Nudity, strong sexual content, adult situations, explicit language
Dir: Simon Nuchtern *Cast:* Corinne Alphen, George Ayer, Bobbi Burns, Cynthia Lee, Marcia McBroom, Willem Dafoe, William Dysart
▶ Anthology of nine erotic stories, set in modern-day New York and loosely based on *La Ronde*. In "The Porno Star and the Financier," Lee seduces Dysart for a part in a mainstream film; "The Authoress and the Photographer" features a female boxing match; etc. Alphen, 1982 *Penthouse* Pet of the Year, performs an explicit striptease.
Dist.: Vestron

NEW YORK STORIES 1989
★ ★ PG Comedy/Drama 2:10
☑ Adult situations, explicit language
Dir: Woody Allen, Francis Coppola, Martin Scorsese *Cast:* Nick Nolte, Rosanna Arquette, Heather McComb, Talia Shire, Woody Allen, Mae Questel, Mia Farrow, Giancarlo Giannini, Don Novello, Carole Bouquet
▶ Anthology of three stories about Manhattan: in Scorsese's "Life Lessons," artist Nolte suffers through obsessive passion for Arquette; Coppola's "Life Without Zoe" concerns lively young McComb's adventures in and around the Sherry-Netherland hotel; Allen's "Oedipus Wrecks" takes a nagging mother joke to absurd and hilarious lengths.
Dist.: Buena Vista

NEXT OF KIN 1989
★ ★ ★ ★ R Action-Adventure 1:51
☑ Explicit language, violence
Dir: John Irvin *Cast:* Patrick Swayze, Liam Neeson, Adam Baldwin, Helen Hunt, Andreas Katsulas, Bill Paxton
▶ When their brother Paxton is murdered by the mob, Swayze, a Kentucky hillbilly turned

Chicago cop, wants to arrest the killer, but backwoods brother Neeson prefers a bloodier revenge. Eventually, Swayze does resort to mountain-style vigilante vengeance. Terrific premise has you rooting for Swayze, although Neeson steals a few scenes. Ferocious finale makes up for sluggish early going. **(CC)**
Dist.: Warner

NEXT ONE, THE 1981
☆ NR Sci-Fi 1:45
☑ Adult situations, explicit language
Dir: Nico Mastorakis *Cast:* Keir Dullea, Adrienne Barbeau, Jeremy Licht, Peter Hobbs, Phaedon Georgitsis
▶ In Greece with son Licht, widow Barbeau discovers Dullea on beach after his apparent arrival from outer space. They have a romance; he evinces miraculous powers and later claims to be Jesus Christ's brother. Death is not terminal, as one character here points out, but this overly symbolic story comes close. Winning performance by Barbeau overcomes the pretentiousness.
Dist.: Vestron

NEXT YEAR IF ALL GOES WELL 1983 French
☆ R Comedy 1:35
☑ Nudity, explicit language
Dir: Jean-Loup Hubert *Cast:* Isabelle Adjani, Thierry Lhermitte, Marie-Anne Chazel, Michel Dussarat, Bernard Crommbe
▶ Accountant Adjani wants to become pregnant but her live-in lover Lhermitte, a hypochondriac cartoonist, wants no part of fatherhood. She breaks up with him, both see other people, but then they reconcile and she gets her wish. However, their troubles are not over. Modest vehicle for leads' comedic talents.
Ⓢ
Dist.: HBO

NIAGARA 1953
★ ★ ★ NR Mystery-Suspense 1:29
Dir: Henry Hathaway *Cast:* Marilyn Monroe, Joseph Cotten, Jean Peters, Casey Adams, Denis O'Dea, Richard Allan
▶ Disturbing film noir about femme fatale Monroe plotting the murder of her weak-willed husband Cotten, a veteran recovering from a stay in a mental institution. Peters, a bride honeymooning at the same Niagara Falls motel, finds her loyalty and courage tested when the scheme takes an unexpectedly grim twist. Gritty drama catches Monroe on the verge of superstardom.
Dist.: CBS/Fox

NICE GIRLS DON'T EXPLODE 1987
★ PG Comedy 1:32
☑ Brief nudity
Dir: Chuck Martinez *Cast:* Barbara Harris, Wallace Shawn, Michelle Meyrink, William O'Leary, Belinda Wells, James Nardini
▶ Slight, whimsical comedy about young Meyrink, who sets objects on fire when she thinks about romance—a major drawback when she falls in love. Mother Harris, who

shares the curse, concocts goofy methods for dealing with men while Meyrink tries to explain her problem to boyfriend O'Leary.
Dist.: New World

NICHOLAS AND ALEXANDRA 1971 British
★ ★ ★ **PG Drama 3:03**
☑ Adult situations
Dir: Franklin J. Schaffner   *Cast:* Michael Jayston, Janet Suzman, Roderic Noble, Tom Baker, Harry Andrews, Irene Worth
▶ Historically accurate epic about Nicholas (Jayston), the last Russian czar, and the events surrounding the 1917 Bolshevik revolution. Suzman is superb as Alexandra, the czarina mesmerized by mad monk Rasputin (Baker). Filled with interesting cameos (Laurence Olivier, Michael Redgrave, John Wood, etc.). Received six Oscar nominations, winning for art design and costumes.
Dist.: RCA/Columbia

NICHOLAS NICKLEBY 1947 British
★ ★ **NR Drama 1:48 B&W**
Dir: Alberto Cavalcanti   *Cast:* Derek Bond, Cedric Hardwicke, Alfred Drayton, Sally Ann Howes, Stanley Holloway, Bernard Miles, Sybil Thorndike, Cathleen Nesbitt
▶ When his father dies, young Nickleby (Bond) takes teaching position at an orphanage run by a cruel family, then flees with a crippled pupil. He also protects his sister and his beloved from rich, manipulative uncle Hardwicke. Old-fashioned sentiment and morality, painstakingly detailed costumes and sets, fascinating performances (especially Hardwicke) in this adaptation of the Charles Dickens classic.
Dist.: Various

NICKEL MOUNTAIN 1985
★ ★ ★ **NR Drama 1:28**
☑ Brief nudity, adult situations, explicit language, violence
Dir: Drew Denbaum   *Cast:* Michael Cole, Heather Langenkamp, Patrick Cassidy, Brian Kerwin, Grace Zabriskie, Don Beddoe
▶ Rural waitress Langenkamp refuses to have an abortion when boyfriend Cassidy deserts her for college. She forms a relationship with older diner owner Cole that deepens into true love. Polished, low-key tearjerker with a winning performance from Langenkamp. Based on a John Gardner novel.
Dist.: Warner

NIGHT AMBUSH 1957 British
★ ★ **NR War 1:33 B&W**
Dir: Michael Powell, Emeric Pressburger   *Cast:* Dirk Bogarde, Marius Goring, David Oxley, Cyril Cusak
▶ During World War II, British soldiers Bogarde and Oxley kidnap German general Goring from Crete. Arrogant Goring sneers at their attempts to transport him to Cairo, but the laugh is on him as the two thwart his cleverest attempts to escape. Fast-moving adventure

with lots of energy. Also known as *Ill Met by Moonlight.*
Dist.: VidAmerica

NIGHT AND DAY 1946
★ ★ **NR Biography/Musical 2:08**
Dir: Michael Curtiz   *Cast:* Cary Grant, Alexis Smith, Monty Woolley, Ginny Simms, Jane Wyman, Eve Arden
▶ Star-studded biography of Cole Porter (Grant), wealthy Ivy Leaguer who became a legendary composer only to suffer a crippling accident. Smith plays his loyal wife. Well-mounted production ignores controversy surrounding his private life for excellent renditions of his remarkable songs. Grant attempts "You're the Top"; Mary Martin re-creates her Broadway hit "My Heart Belongs to Daddy." Other tunes include "Begin the Beguine," "I've Got You Under My Skin," "Just One of Those Things," "What Is This Thing Called Love."
Dist.: Key

NIGHT AT THE OPERA, A 1935
★ ★ ★ ★ **NR Comedy 1:32 B&W**
Dir: Sam Wood   *Cast:* Groucho Marx, Harpo Marx, Chico Marx, Allan Jones, Kitty Carlisle, Margaret Dumont, Sig Rumann, Walter Woolf King
▶ Riotously funny classic has the brothers helping opera singer Jones outwit a nasty rival while Groucho battles Rumann for wealthy patron Dumont's affections. Highlights: the stateroom scene, Chico and Groucho negotiating the "sanity clause," the boys trying to disguise themselves as aviators for a City Hall ceremony.
Dist.: MGM/UA

NIGHT BEFORE, THE 1988
★ ★ **PG-13 Comedy 1:25**
☑ Adult situations, explicit language, mild violence
Dir: Thom Eberhardt   *Cast:* Keanu Reeves, Lori Loughlin, Theresa Saldana, Trinidad Silva, Suzanne Snyder
▶ School beauty Loughlin attends prom with wimpy Reeves because she lost a bet. Date escalates into disaster as couple ends up on wrong side of the tracks and pimp Silva nabs Loughlin. Engaging youth comedy gets better as it goes along; Reeves and Loughlin are tart and attractive. **(CC)**
Dist.: HBO

NIGHTBREAKER 1989
★ ★ ★ **NR Drama/MFTV 1:39**
Dir: Peter Markle   *Cast:* Martin Sheen, Emilio Estevez, Lea Thompson, Melinda Dillon, Joe Pantoliano, Nicholas Pryor
▶ Fact-based story of the American government using soldiers to test the effects of nuclear detonations in the 1950s. Despite the concern of girlfriend Thompson, psychologist Estevez takes part in the experiment. Thirty years later, the doctor, now played by Es-

tevez's real-life father Sheen, returns to the site. Probing drama with good performances.
Dist.: Turner

NIGHTBREED 1990
★ ★ ★ R Horror 1:41
☑ Explicit language, graphic violence
Dir: Clive Barker *Cast:* Craig Sheffer, Anne Bobby, David Cronenberg, Charles Haid, Hugh Quarshie, Hugh Ross
► When he is accused of murders actually committed by psychiatrist Cronenberg, Sheffer hides out in Midian, an underground city of monsters. The killer shrink pursues him. Typically overwrought Barker concoction has his trademark gore and convoluted plotting. Horror director Cronenberg proves an effective actor. Barker's screenplay is based on his own novel, *Cabal.*
Dist.: Media

NIGHT CALLER FROM OUTER SPACE 1965
British
★ NR Sci-Fi 1:24 B&W
Dir: John Gilling *Cast:* John Saxon, Maurice Denham, Patricia Haines, Alfred Burke, Jack Watson, Stanley Meadows
► Scientist Saxon is part of a team that discovers a mysterious sphere at the site of a UFO landing. Is there a connection between the UFO and the mysterious disappearance of attractive women who've answered a modeling ad in a London newspaper? Solidly done. Also known as *The Night Caller* and *Blood Beast From Outer Space.*
Dist.: SVS

NIGHTCOMERS, THE 1972 British
★ ★ R Drama 1:36
☑ Nudity, violence
Dir: Michael Winner *Cast:* Marlon Brando, Stephanie Beacham, Thora Hird, Harry Andrews, Verna Harvey, Christopher Ellis
► On a turn-of-the-century English estate, children Ellis and Harvey become obsessed with mysterious gardener Brando, who has an affair with their governess Beacham. Powerfully brooding performance by Brando. Inspired by Henry James's novel *The Turn of the Screw.*
Dist.: Nelson

NIGHT CREATURE 1978
☆ PG Action-Adventure 1:23
☑ Adult situations, violence
Dir: Lee Madden *Cast:* Donald Pleasence, Nancy Kwan, Ross Hagen, Lesly Fine, Jennifer Rhodes
► Hunter Pleasence lives among helpful natives like Kwan on a spectacular jungle island in Southeast Asia. Terror stalks in the form of black leopard with a taste for native flesh. Tries to build suspense and sense of menace with irritating cuts and jerky camera movements. Cat is not scary.
Dist.: VCI

NIGHT CROSSING 1982 British
★ ★ ★ ★ PG Action-Adventure/Family
1:46
☑ Mild violence
Dir: Delbert Mann *Cast:* John Hurt, Jane Alexander, Glynnis O'Connor, Beau Bridges, Doug McKeon, Ian Bannen
► Two dissident East German families attempt to escape their country via hot-air balloon. Their first effort fails so they try again while the authorities investigate. Terrific true story from Walt Disney Studios.
Dist.: Buena Vista

NIGHTFALL 1988
★ PG-13 Sci-Fi 1:23
☑ Nudity, violence, strong sexual content
Dir: Paul Mayersberg *Cast:* David Birney, Sarah Douglas, Alexis Kanner, Starr Andreeff
► When a world with three suns and constant daylight is suddenly threatened by darkness, scientist Birney battles religious cultist Kanner for the planet's leadership. Incomprehensible plotting (including scene of Douglas willingly having her eyes poked out) and bombastic dialogue mar this loose adaptation of Isaac Asimov's short story.
Dist.: MGM/UA

NIGHT FLYERS 1987
☆ R Sci-Fi 1:29
☑ Explicit language, violence
Dir: T. C. Blake (Robert Collector) *Cast:* Catherine Mary Stewart, Michael Praed, John Standing, Lisa Blount, Michael Des Barres
► Something is menacing the crew aboard a twenty-first-century spaceship mission to an unexplored planet. Suspects include captain Praed and the craft's computer. Pleasing production values but *Alien* clone lacks the jolts that made its role model special.
Dist.: HBO

NIGHTFORCE 1986
★ ★ R Action-Adventure 1:22
☑ Nudity, adult situations, explicit language, violence
Dir: Lawrence D. Foldes *Cast:* Linda Blair, James Van Patten, Chad McQueen, Cameron Mitchell, Richard Lynch, Dean R. Miller
► Central American revolutionary group kidnaps daughter of U.S. Senator Mitchell so he will reverse his position on their country. Blair leads the kidnapped girl's young pals in a rescue raid. Unbelievable and overly familiar, with dreadful script and direction. Almost succeeds at being unintentionally funny.
Dist.: Vestron

NIGHT GALLERY 1969
★ ★ ★ NR Horror/MFTV 1:35
Dir: Boris Sagal, Steven Spielberg, Barry Shear *Cast:* Roddy McDowall, Ossie Davis, Richard Kiley, Tom Bosley, George Macready, Joan Crawford
► First-rate pilot for Rod Serling's anthology TV series is notable for Spielberg directing Joan

Crawford as a blind woman who regains her sight the night of a New York blackout. Other episodes feature Kiley as a Nazi war criminal in South America and McDowall plotting against uncle Macready. Latter segment, the best of the three, features marvelously subtle interplay between McDowall and Davis.
Dist.: MCA

NIGHT GAME 1989
★ ★ R Mystery-Suspense 1:37
☑ Nudity, adult situations, explicit language, violence
Dir: Peter Masterson *Cast:* Roy Scheider, Karen Young, Richard Bradford, Paul Gleason, Carlin Glynn, Lane Smith
▶ When a psychopath preys on Galveston women, cop Scheider, an ex-baseball player involved with Young, investigates. He is hard up for clues until he ties the murders to the national pastime: the killer is coordinating his activities with Houston Astros games. Novel concept gets less-than-original execution. Solid performance from Scheider, amusingly supported by Bradford as his foul-mouthed superior. Evocative Galveston locations.
Dist.: HBO

NIGHT GAMES 1980
★ R Drama 1:43
☑ Nudity, explicit language
Dir: Roger Vadim *Cast:* Cindy Pickett, Joanna Cassidy, Barry Primus, Paul Jenkins
▶ Memories of being raped leave Californian Pickett frigid, much to husband Primus's chagrin. She retreats into a sexual fantasy world that becomes all too real when a scorned suitor tries to kill her. Titillating pulp has perky Cindy and lots of skin. Sunk by feeble flashbacks and laughable psychology.
Dist.: Embassy

NIGHTHAWKS 1981
★ ★ ★ ★ R Action-Adventure 1:39
☑ Adult situations, explicit language, graphic violence
Dir: Bruce Malmuth *Cast:* Sylvester Stallone, Billy Dee Williams, Lindsay Wagner, Rutger Hauer, Persis Khambatta, Nigel Davenport
▶ New York City cops Stallone and Williams pursue vicious international terrorist Hauer. Fast-paced and exciting action (especially when Hauer hijacks the Roosevelt Island tramway) overcomes story contrivances. Sly gives one of his best non-*Rocky* performances and Hauer is menacing. Wagner is wasted in an undeveloped role as Stallone's ex-wife.
Dist.: MCA

NIGHT IN CASABLANCA, A 1946
★ ★ ★ NR Comedy 1:25 B&W
Dir: Archie Mayo *Cast:* Groucho Marx, Harpo Marx, Chico Marx, Charles Drake, Lois Collier, Lisette Verea
▶ Groucho takes a job at Hotel Casablanca not knowing that his three predecessors have been murdered. Treasure-seeking Nazis are

the key to the killings; Groucho teams with Chico and Harpo to thwart them. Perhaps the best of the brothers' later efforts. Classic bit: Harpo's reaction when criticized for leaning against building.
Dist.: IUD

NIGHT IN HEAVEN, A 1983
★ ★ R Drama 1:23
☑ Nudity, adult situations, explicit language, mild violence
Dir: John G. Avildsen *Cast:* Christopher Atkins, Lesley Ann Warren, Robert Logan, Deborah Rush, Carrie Snodgress
▶ Teacher Warren, unhappily married to aerospace worker Logan, finds solace in the arms of male stripper Atkins, who is also one of her students. Dull drama with uncertain tone and half-baked story. Includes brief scene of frontal male nudity. (CC)
Dist.: CBS/Fox

NIGHT IN THE LIFE OF JIMMY REARDON, A 1988
★ ★ R Comedy 1:32
☑ Brief nudity, adult situations, explicit language
Dir: William Richert *Cast:* River Phoenix, Ann Magnuson, Meredith Salenger, Ione Skye, Louanne, Matthew Perry
▶ Phoenix plays a glib teen Lothario in a "what-a-night-I'm-having" comedy. Amid seductions and chaos, he tries to scam up airfare to escape to Hawaii with his girl Salenger. Featuring director Richert's usual lunacy and literacy, film will disappoint those expecting ordinary coming-of-age fare; recommended for anyone with a taste for the ironic and offbeat. (CC)
Dist.: CBS/Fox

NIGHTMARE AT NOON 1988
★ ★ R Horror 1:36
☑ Explicit language, violence
Dir: Nico Mastorakis *Cast:* George Kennedy, Bo Svenson, Wings Hauser, Brion James
▶ A town's water supply is purposely contaminated as part of an experiment. The locals turn into murderous maniacs: not even mothers and ministers are immune from the effect. Svenson leads the survivors in hunting down the silent albino behind the scheme. Most of the budget seems to have gone for stunts, shoot-outs, and explosions; farfetched but far from boring.
Dist.: Republic

NIGHTMARE CASTLE 1966 Italian
☆ NR Horror 1:30 B&W
Dir: Allan Grunewald *Cast:* Barbara Steele, Paul Mueller, Helga Line, Lawrence Clift, Rik Battaglia
▶ Unbalanced scientist Mueller kills wife Steele and her lover, places their hearts in an urn, and uses their blood to make servant Line young and beautiful. After marrying Steele's sister to inherit her fortune, Miller tangles with

doctor Clift, who begins to suspect that something is up. Slow, moody, and visually arresting. Also known as *Faceless Monsters* and *Lovers From Beyond the Tomb*.
Dist.: Sinister

NIGHTMARE ON ELM STREET, A 1984
★ ★ ★ R Horror 1:31
☑ Adult situations, explicit language, graphic violence
Dir: Wes Craven *Cast:* John Saxon, Ronee Blakley, Robert Englund, Heather Langenkamp, Amanda Wyss, Nick Corri, Johnny Depp
▶ The first appearance of now-infamous Freddy Krueger (Englund), the disfigured, finger-knived bogeyman who preys on promiscuous teens. Years ago vigilantes torched child murderer Freddy; he returns to lethally haunt the dreams of his killers' kids. Some slice-and-dice clichés, but for the most part director Craven manages to find real horror amid ordinary life. Mainly for fans of the genre. (CC)
Dist.: Media

NIGHTMARE ON ELM STREET, PART 2: FREDDY'S REVENGE, A 1985
★ ★ ★ R Horror 1:25
☑ Brief nudity, adult situations, explicit language, graphic violence
Dir: Jack Sholder *Cast:* Mark Patton, Robert Englund, Kim Myers, Robert Rusler, Clu Gulager, Hope Lange
▶ More rude awakenings from Freddy (Englund). New kid in town Patton learns too late to leave on his night light. Freddy takes over Patton's body; teen makes few new friends during spree of mayhem and murder. Patton's girlfriend Myers saves the day with exorcism, but only the naive believe Freddy won't crawl under the covers again soon. Squeamish stay away. (CC)
Dist.: Media

NIGHTMARE ON ELM STREET 3: DREAM WARRIORS, A 1987
★ ★ ★ R Horror 1:36
☑ Brief nudity, adult situations, explicit language, graphic violence
Dir: Chuck Russell *Cast:* Robert Englund, Heather Langenkamp, John Saxon, Patricia Arquette, Craig Wasson
▶ Seven nightmare-plagued Elm Street kids are sent to a psychiatric hospital, where intern Langenkamp (reprising her role from the series original) realizes Freddy is at work once again. Freddy's undying appeal and the clever visual effects compensate for illogical script and some truly bad acting. Cameos by Dick Cavett and Zsa Zsa Gabor. (CC)
Dist.: Media

NIGHTMARE ON ELM STREET 4: THE DREAM MASTER, A 1988
★ ★ ★ R Horror 1:33
☑ Brief nudity, adult situations, explicit language, graphic violence

Dir: Renny Harlin *Cast:* Robert Englund, Lisa Wilcox, Rodney Eastman, Danny Hassel, Andras Jones, Tuesday Knight
▶ When Freddy returns to Elm Street (yes, a few people still live there) and quickly offs his dream dates from prior flicks, it's up to Wilcox, the new kid on the block, to do the screaming. She ultimately employs the services of the Dream Master, the guardian of good dreams. More body counts, quips from the affably demonic Freddy, and expensive special effects.
Dist.: Media

NIGHTMARE ON ELM STREET 5: THE DREAM CHILD, A 1989
★ ★ ★ R Horror 1:30
☑ Adult situations, explicit language, graphic violence
Dir: Stephen Hopkins *Cast:* Robert Englund, Lisa Wilcox, Joe Seely, Whitby Hertford, Danny Hassel, Beatrice Boepple
▶ High school senior Wilcox has dreams about boogeyman Freddy Kruger (Englund), Freddy's lapsed nun mother, and a toddler named Jacob. Coincidentally, Wilcox is pregnant and her child will be named Jacob; Freddy covets the baby's soul. Fifth fright fest has Kruger crooning lullabies, plus added production values and special effects. (CC)
Dist.: Media

NIGHTMARES 1983
★ ★ R Horror 1:40
☑ Explicit language, graphic violence
Dir: Joseph Sargent *Cast:* Emilio Estevez, Richard Masur, Cristina Raines, Veronica Cartwright, Lance Henriksen, Moon Zappa, Timothy James, William Sanderson, Robin Gammell
▶ Anthology pic featuring four horror tales of varying quality: a woman will do anything for a cigarette, youngster enters deadly video game, car menaces priest, and giant rat is misunderstood. Originally shot on a low budget for network TV but released theatrically, so effects are not up to par with rest of genre. For dedicated thrillseekers only.
Dist.: MCA

'NIGHT, MOTHER 1986
★ ★ ★ PG-13 Drama 1:36
☑ Adult situations, explicit language
Dir: Tom Moore *Cast:* Anne Bancroft, Sissy Spacek
▶ Overwhelmed by despair, Spacek calmly and methodically prepares to kill herself. Over the course of an hour and a half, her mother Bancroft tries to convince her life is worth living, no matter how bleak. Not for all tastes. Some might be put off by the soul-baring, but two topflight actresses shine in a faithful adaptation of the Pulitzer prize–winning play by Marsha Norman. (CC)
Dist.: MCA

NIGHT MOVES 1975
★ ★ R Mystery-Suspense 1:39
☑ Nudity, adult situations, violence

Dir: Arthur Penn   *Cast:* Gene Hackman, Jennifer Warren, Susan Clark, Edward Binns, Melanie Griffith, James Woods, Harris Yulin
▶ L.A. detective Hackman, hired to find runaway teen Griffith, tracks her down to the Florida Keys and brings her home. The mystery deepens when someone is murdered in the seemingly cut-and-dried case. Moody, intelligent film noir, as much an allegory about social malaise as it is a mystery. Muddled plotting but solid performance by Hackman, sizzling one from the underrated Warren. One of the most overlooked films of the 1970s.
Dist.: Warner

NIGHT NURSE, THE 1977 British
☆ NR Horror 1:18
☑ Violence
Dir: Igor Auzins   *Cast:* Davina Whitehouse, Kay Taylor, Gary Day
▶ A night nurse is hired to care for a wheelchair-bound former opera star, not knowing that the woman's housekeeper has just killed someone. The housekeeper obviously resents the newcomer; the nurse begins to realize the maid's murderous intentions. Ordinary thriller with choppy editing.
Dist.: Paragon

NIGHT OF THE COMET 1984
★ ★ PG-13 Sci-Fi 1:35
☑ Explicit language, violence
Dir: Thom Eberhardt   *Cast:* Catherine Mary Stewart, Kelli Maroney, Robert Beltran, Mary Woronov, Geoffrey Lewis, Sharon Farrell
▶ Campy day-after saga of Southern Cal sisters Stewart and Maroney who are among the few to weather a comet's impact and lethal fallout. Battling zombies and survivalists, the valley girls search for the remnants of civilization and a couple of cute dudes. At least as silly as it sounds but nonetheless diverting. (CC)
Dist.: CBS/Fox

NIGHT OF THE CREEPS 1986
★ ★ R Horror/Comedy 1:28 C/B&W
☑ Nudity, explicit language, graphic violence
Dir: Fred Dekker   *Cast:* Jason Lively, Steve Marshall, Jill Whitlow, Tom Atkins
▶ In 1959, a young man is killed by an alien slug. In 1986, college students Lively and Marshall steal his corpse from lab for frat initiation, thus unleashing little creatures that turn people into murderous zombies. Dekker's tongue-in-cheek wit enlivens standard scare plot. Best line comes as zombies approach sorority house: "The good news is that your dates are here. . .the bad news is they're dead!"
Dist.: HBO

NIGHT OF THE DEMONS 1987
★ R Horror 1:29
☑ Nudity, explicit language, violence
Dir: Kevin S. Tenney   *Cast:* Lance Fenton, Cathy Podewell, Alvin Alexis, Hal Havins, Mimi Kinkade, Linnea Quigley

▶ Teens attend a Halloween party thrown by weird witchcraft-loving classmates Kinkade and Quigley at the site of a former funeral parlor. They should have stayed in bed as demons emerge to menace them. Mild gore and above-par technique by genre standards. However, unsympathetic characters try your patience.
Dist.: Republic

NIGHT OF THE GENERALS 1967 British
★ ★ NR War/Mystery-Suspense 2:28
Dir: Anatole Litvak   *Cast:* Peter O'Toole, Omar Sharif, Tom Courtenay, Donald Pleasence, Joanna Pettet, Christopher Plummer
▶ When a prostitute is brutally slain in 1942 Warsaw, German intelligence agent Sharif narrows the suspects to three top-ranking Nazi generals, including the ruthless O'Toole. Sharif tries to bring the killer to justice; the mystery widens to include a plot against Hitler and extends twenty years beyond the war. Tension-filled.
Dist.: RCA/Columbia

NIGHT OF THE HUNTER, THE 1955
★ ★ ★ ★ NR Drama 1:33 B&W
Dir: Charles Laughton   *Cast:* Robert Mitchum, Shelley Winters, Lillian Gish, Evelyn Varden, Billy Chapin, Sally Jane Bruce
▶ Mitchum delivers an unforgettable performance as a psychopath posing as a minister who marries convict's widow Winters to search her house for hidden loot. Her children Chapin and Bruce escape with the money, but are pursued downriver by the preacher. Unnerving, dreamlike study of innocence and corruption was Laughton's only film as a director. Screenplay by James Agee.
Dist.: MGM/UA

NIGHT OF THE IGUANA, THE 1964
★ ★ ★ NR Drama 2:05 B&W
Dir: John Huston   *Cast:* Richard Burton, Ava Gardner, Deborah Kerr, Sue Lyon, Skip Ward, Grayson Hall
▶ In Puerto Vallarta, hard-drinking former priest Burton works as tour guide and gets entangled with three women—pretty, young Lyon, spinsterish artist Kerr, and slatternly hotel owner Gardner—one of whom may be able to halt his physical and mental deterioration. Generally engrossing Tennessee Williams adaptation. Burton, Gardner, and Kerr are outstanding; Oscar for Best Costume Design.
Dist.: MGM/UA

NIGHT OF THE JUGGLER 1980
★ ★ ★ R Action-Adventure 1:41
☑ Explicit language, graphic violence
Dir: Robert Butler   *Cast:* James Brolin, Cliff Gorman, Richard Castellano, Abby Bluestone, Dan Hedaya, Julie Carmen
▶ Deranged kidnapper Gorman mistakenly abducts ex-cop Brolin's daughter. Brolin defies the police in an effort to rescue her. Well-executed chases dominate this relentless re-

venge film exploiting realistically seedy New York locations.
Dist.: Media

NIGHT OF THE LIVING DEAD 1968
★ ★ ★ ★ NR Horror 1:36 B&W
☑ Graphic violence
Dir: George A. Romero *Cast:* Duane Jones, Judith O'Dea, Russell Streiner, Karl Hardman, Keith Wayne, Judith Ridley
▶ Pursued by man-eating zombies, seven people in a farmhouse struggle to survive a night of terror. Grainy, low-budget pic was panned by critics for its ghoulish and graphic effects, but today the gore seems tame. Became one of the most successful cult films ever, acknowledged as a genre classic and now frequently aped in commercials and videos. Romero went on to complete trilogy with *Dawn of the Dead* and *Day of the Dead.*
Dist.: Various [C]

NIGHT OF THE SHOOTING STARS, THE
1983 Italian
★ ★ R Drama 1:46
☑ Adult situations, violence
Dir: Paolo Taviani, Vittorio Taviani *Cast:* Omero Antonutti, Margarita Lozano, Claudio Bigagil, Massimo Bonetti, Norma Martel
▶ An Italian woman recalls World War II, when the inhabitants of her village took to the roads in search of approaching American troops. For some, the journey is a lark, for others, it's an uprooting of their whole lives. Best part is harrowing, confused battle in a wheat field between the wanderers and fascist fellow-villagers: the squealing terror of a teenaged fascist bully about to be shot is unforgettable. Magical, lyrical film is unusual and unsettling.
[S]
Dist.: MGM/UA

NIGHT OF THE ZOMBIES 1983
Spanish/Italian
☆ R Horror 1:40
☑ Nudity, explicit language, graphic violence
Dir: Vincent Dawn *Cast:* Frank Garfield, Magrit Newton, Selan Karay, Gaby Renom
▶ In New Guinea, scientists experimenting with overpopulation solution mess up big: their vapor turns people into flesh-eating zombies. Reporter Newton, her cameraman boyfriend, and a commando team battle the bloodthirsty beings. Dreadful in all departments; appalling scenes of cannibalism. Poorly dubbed.
Dist.: Vestron

NIGHT PATROL 1984
★ ★ R Comedy 1:22
☑ Nudity, adult situations, explicit language, adult humor
Dir: Jackie Kong *Cast:* Linda Blair, Pat Paulsen, Jaye P. Morgan, Jack Riley, Billy Barty, Murray Langston
▶ Rookie cop Langston is transferred to the rough night shift—a schedule that interferes

with his career as the Unknown Comic. He runs into further trouble when a thief steals his stand-up costume. Extremely broad slapstick with hit-or-miss gags and a lifeless performance by Blair. (CC)
Dist.: New World

NIGHT PORTER, THE 1974 Italian
★ R Drama 1:58
☑ Rape, nudity, strong sexual content
Dir: Liliana Cavani *Cast:* Dirk Bogarde, Charlotte Rampling, Philippe Leroy, Gabriele Ferzetti, Giuseppe Addobbati
▶ Unsettling examination of the sadomasochistic relationship between concentration camp guard Bogarde and Rampling, one of his victims. Meeting again in 1958, they resume their affair. Controversial film takes a serious, nonexploitative approach to the subject, but graphic sexuality may offend some viewers.
Dist.: Nelson

NIGHT SCHOOL 1981
★ R Horror 1:28
☑ Nudity, adult situations, explicit language, graphic violence
Dir: Ken Hughes *Cast:* Leonard Mann, Rachel Ward, Drew Snyder, Joseph R. Sicari, Nicholas Cairis
▶ Boston cop Mann investigates a series of decapitations which lead to Snyder, a promiscuous anthropology professor at a women's college. Evidence of demonic cults hampers Mann's work. Routine slasher film enlivened by Ward, a sexy student, in her first major film role.
Dist.: CBS/Fox

NIGHT SHIFT 1982
★ ★ ★ R Comedy 1:46
☑ Nudity, adult situations, explicit language, violence
Dir: Ron Howard *Cast:* Michael Keaton, Shelley Long, Henry Winkler, Gina Hecht, Pat Corley, Bobby DiCicco
▶ Much-abused nebbish Winkler seeks peace through night job at a morgue, only to encounter manic colleague Keaton. Soon the odd couple are running an escort service out of the morgue and expanding into legit businesses. Winkler falls in love with Long, the sweetest of the hookers. Sanitized sitcom about prostitution, but many laughs, fine performances, and engaging romance. Keaton's feature debut made him a star.
Dist.: Warner

NIGHTS OF CABIRIA 1957 Italian
★ ★ NR Drama 1:50
Dir: Federico Fellini *Cast:* Giulietta Masina, François Périer, Amadeo Nazzari, Aldo Silvani, Dorian Gray
▶ Kindhearted prostitute Masina has brief affair with movie star Nazzari and then falls for Périer. Her hopes for the straight life with him are cruelly dashed, but her essential optimism remains. Bittersweet drama has knockout performance by Masina (Fellini's wife). Oscar for

Best Foreign Film; inspired the Broadway musical *Sweet Charity*. $\boxed{\text{S}}$
Dist.: Foothill

NIGHT STALKER, THE 1987
★ ★ ★ R Mystery-Suspense 1:31
☑ Nudity, adult situations, explicit language, graphic violence
Dir: Max Kleven *Cast:* Charles Napier, Michelle Reese, Katherine Kelly Lang, Robert Viharo, Joey Gian, Robert Zdar
▶ Hard-drinking, often-suspended cop Napier pursues ritualistic murderer of prostitutes who appears to get stronger each time he kills. Standard rehashing of B-movie premise boasts brisk action, some barbed dialogue, and skid row hero.
Dist.: Vestron

NIGHTSTICK 1987
★ ★ R Action-Adventure 1:32
☑ Violence, explicit language
Dir: Joseph Scanlan *Cast:* Bruce Fairbairn, Kerrie Keane, Robert Vaughn, John Vernon, Leslie Nielsen
▶ Lone-wolf cop Fairbairn tracks three terrorists threatening to blow up Manhattan unless they're paid a $5 million ransom. Cop's bosses Vaughn and Nielsen argue, girlfriend Keane gets kidnapped, and he confronts the bad guys for a climatic shoot-out in a deserted warehouse.
Dist.: RCA/Columbia

NIGHT THE LIGHTS WENT OUT IN GEORGIA, THE 1981
★ ★ ★ PG Drama 1:52
☑ Brief nudity, adult situations, explicit language
Dir: Ronald F. Maxwell *Cast:* Kristy McNichol, Dennis Quaid, Mark Hamill, Don Stroud, Arlen Dean Snyder
▶ Country singer Quaid and his sister McNichol travel to Nashville. After getting into trouble with the law, Quaid is sentenced to a work farm; McNichol falls in love with cop Hamill, who tries to help him. Agreeable drama bears little resemblance to the hit title song. Quaid and McNichol perform on the soundtrack (which also includes country-western stars Glen Campbell and George Jones).
Dist.: TWE

NIGHT THEY RAIDED MINSKY'S, THE 1969
★ ★ ★ PG Comedy 1:40
☑ Adult situations
Dir: William Friedkin *Cast:* Jason Robards, Britt Ekland, Norman Wisdom, Forrest Tucker, Denholm Elliott, Elliott Gould
▶ Vaudeville comic Robards persuades naive Amish girl Ekland to perform a religious dance in order to thwart attempts by censors to close his theater. Flavorful account of the history of striptease humorously re-creates famous burlesque skits. Film debut for Gould; charming cameo by Bert Lahr in his last role. Narrated by Rudy Vallee. **(CC)**
Dist.: CBS/Fox

NIGHT TO REMEMBER, A 1942
★ ★ NR Mystery-Suspense/Comedy 1:32 B&W
Dir: Richard Wallace *Cast:* Loretta Young, Brian Aherne, Jeff Donnell, William Wright, Sidney Toler, Gale Sondergaard
▶ Debonair mystery writer Aherne and perky wife Young move into a Greenwich Village apartment where she hopes he'll leave the genre behind in favor of a good love story. But when a corpse winds up in their backyard, they do some real-life sleuthing of their own. Aherne and Young couldn't be more charming in this obvious but enjoyable *Thin Man* clone.
Dist.: RCA/Columbia

NIGHT TO REMEMBER, A 1958 British
★ ★ ★ ★ NR Drama 2:03 B&W
Dir: Roy Ward Baker *Cast:* Kenneth More, Ronald Allen, Robert Ayres, Honor Blackman, Anthony Bushell, David McCallum, Jill Dixon, Frank Lawton, Laurence Naismith
▶ Authentic, documentary-style reconstruction of the famous 1912 wreck of the "unsinkable" *Titanic*, told from the perspective of second officer More as he oversees rescue operations. Large cast is uniformly impressive; vignettes of passengers are alternately touching and uplifting. Adapted by Eric Ambler from Walter Lord's best-selling novel.
Dist.: Paramount

NIGHT VISITOR, THE 1970 Swedish/U.S.
★ PG Mystery-Suspense 1:46
☑ Violence
Dir: Laslo Benedek *Cast:* Max Von Sydow, Liv Ullmann, Trevor Howard, Per Oscarsson, Rupert Davies, Andrew Keir
▶ Imprisoned for a crime he didn't commit, Von Sydow sneaks out to kill those who framed him, afterwards slipping back into his cell with the perfect alibi. Inspector Howard leads the investigation, not suspecting an inmate in an escape-proof prison. Ullmann and Oscarsson are among Von Sydow's victims in this improbable, leaden thriller.
Dist.: United

NIGHT WATCH 1973 British
★ ★ PG Drama 1:40
☑ Explicit language, violence
Dir: Brian G. Hutton *Cast:* Elizabeth Taylor, Laurence Harvey, Billie Whitelaw, Robert Lang, Tony Britton
▶ When her husband dies in a car accident, Taylor suffers a nervous breakdown. After recovering, she witnesses what may be a murder across the street, but her suave second husband Harvey insists she's hallucinating. Uneven thriller from a Lucille Fletcher play relies too heavily on red herrings.
Dist.: Fox Hills

NIGHTWING 1979
★ ★ PG Horror 1:45
☑ Explicit language, violence
Dir: Arthur Hiller *Cast:* Nick Mancuso, David

Warner, Kathryn Harrold, Stephen Macht, Strother Martin, Ben Piazza

▶ Mancuso, a sheriff on an Arizona Indian reservation, and his girlfriend Harrold, a nurse, join exterminator Warner in battling a plague of vampire bats. Infrequent tense moments are obscured by subplots involving spiritualism, Indian rights, and Macht's scheme to steal mineral deposits. Based on Martin Cruz Smith's novel.
Dist.: RCA/Columbia

NIGHT ZOO 1987 Canadian
☆ **R Drama 1:55**
☑ Adult situations, explicit language, violence
Dir: Jean-Claude Lauzon   *Cast:* Gilles Maheu, Roger Le Bel, Corrado Mastropasqua, Lorne Brass, Germain Houde
▶ Maheu gets out of prison and is reunited with father Le Bel. The ex-con tries to patch up his uneasy relationship with dad while fending off a former partner and a corrupt cop who want the $200,000 drug money he has stashed away. Nasty tale includes shooting of an animal as a plot twist; redeemed somewhat by emotional father/son relationship. Also known as *Un Zoo La Nuit.* ③
Dist.: New World

NIJINSKY 1980
★ ★ **R Biography 2:09**
☑ Adult situations, explicit language
Dir: Herbert Ross   *Cast:* Alan Bates, George de la Pena, Leslie Browne, Alan Badel, Carla Fracci, Colin Blakely
▶ Ballet dancer de la Pena plays the famed Russian dancer Nijinsky in this account of his homosexual relationship with impresario Serge Diaghilev (Bates), marriage to Browne, and descent into madness. Has handsome period settings (circa 1912–13) and Ross's usual solid craftsmanship but end result is emotionally remote. Acting is uneven: Bates is first-rate but de la Pena, while an arresting presence, lacks the acting experience to bring off the complex role. **(CC)**
Dist.: Paramount

NIKKI, WILD DOG OF THE NORTH 1961
★ ★ ★ ★ **NR Family 1:14**
Dir: Jack Couffer   *Cast:* Jean Coutu, Emile Genest, Uriel Luft, Robert Rivard
▶ French Canadian trader Coutu, already owner of malamute puppy Nikki, adopts orphan bear cub Neewa. The two animals don't get along at first but must learn to survive in the wilderness together when they are separated from their master. Gorgeous Canadian scenery provides backdrop for wonderful Disney adventure.
Dist.: Buena Vista

9½ WEEKS 1986
★ ★ **R Drama 1:53**
☑ Nudity, strong sexual content, adult situations, explicit language
Dir: Adrian Lyne   *Cast:* Mickey Rourke, Kim

Basinger, Margaret Whitton, David Margulies, Christine Baranski

▶ Screen adaptation of Elizabeth McNeill's novel about an obsessive, all-consuming love affair between Wall Street wheeler-dealer Rourke and art gallery employee Basinger that lasts as long as the title indicates. Recently divorced, Basinger is shy about sex until Rourke seduces her into some of his kinky fantasies. Plenty of erotic spark between the leads. Unrated, more explicit version available on homevideo.
Dist.: MGM/UA

9 DEATHS OF THE NINJA 1985
★ ★ ★ **R Martial Arts 1:34**
☑ Adult situations, explicit language, graphic violence
Dir: Emmett Alston   *Cast:* Sho Kosugi, Brent Huff, Emmila Leshah, Blackie Dammett, Regina Richardson
▶ Manila tourist bus is hijacked by a lesbian ringleader and her amazon army; passengers are dragged through the desert. Antiterrorist team, headed by Japanese martial arts master Kosugi, is dispatched to rescue the hostages. Lots of kicking and maiming.
Dist.: Media

976-EVIL 1988
★ **R Horror 1:33**
☑ Nudity, adult situations, explicit language, graphic violence
Dir: Robert Englund   *Cast:* Stephen Geoffreys, Sandy Dennis, Patrick O'Bryan, Jim Metzler, Maria Rubell, Lezlie Deane
▶ Geoffreys, a nerd who lives with his religious fanatic mom Dennis, dials a 976 number that grants his wishes. Awful things then start happening to Geoffrey's tormentors but the price is his soul. Directorial debut for Englund (Freddy Kruger in the *Nightmare on Elm Street* movies) makes very little sense and certainly doesn't stint on the gore. Fine performances, way above genre par.
Dist.: RCA/Columbia

1918 1985
★ **NR Drama 1:32**
Dir: Ken Harrison   *Cast:* Matthew Broderick, Hallie Foote, William Converse-Roberts, Michael Higgins, Rochelle Oliver
▶ Atmospheric period piece, adapted by Horton Foote from his stage play and set in a small Texas town during the last weeks of World War I. Broderick wants to enlist in the army while his father Higgins wants to send him off to work. The family is struck down by the Spanish influenza epidemic. Restrained, very talky, and slow-moving. **(CC)**
Dist.: CBS/Fox

1984 1985 British
★ **R Drama 1:51**
☑ Nudity, adult situations, violence
Dir: Michael Radford   *Cast:* John Hurt, Suzanna Hamilton, Richard Burton, Cyril Cusack, Gregor Fisher

▶ Chilling film adaptation of George Orwell's futuristic classic. In a totalitarian society, under Big Brother's constant surveillance, civil servant Hurt works at the Ministry of Truth, shows signs of dissatisfaction, and is arrested for having sex with clandestine rebel Hamilton. He's tortured and "cured" by interrogator Burton. Brilliant production design and superior work from distinguished cast, but the tone is uniformily dark and depressing.
Dist.: IVE

1941 1979
★ ★ ★ **PG Comedy 1:58**
☑ Explicit language, adult humor
Dir: Steven Spielberg *Cast:* Dan Aykroyd, John Belushi, Lorraine Gary, Robert Stack, John Candy, Eddie Deezen, Toshiro Mifune, Christopher Lee, Warren Oates, Murray Hamilton, Tim Matheson, Slim Pickens, Joe Flaherty
▶ After the bombing of Pearl Harbor, a Japanese sub sighted off the coast of California panics the people of Los Angeles. Mammoth comedy about war hysteria suffers from overkill, but the special effects are extraordinary.
Dist.: MCA

1900 1977 Italian/French/German
★ **R Drama 4:05**
☑ Nudity, adult situations, explicit language
Dir: Bernardo Bertolucci *Cast:* Burt Lancaster, Robert De Niro, Gerard Depardieu, Dominique Sanda, Donald Sutherland, Sterling Hayden
▶ Monumental epic chronicles the history, politics, and social changes of a small Italian province from 1900 to the defeat of Mussolini in 1945. Story concerns two boys, best friends, both born on January 1, 1900. One is fatherless peasant Depardieu and the other, De Niro, is heir to a vast estate. Their relationship is shaped by volatile social forces. Visually stunning but excessively long.
Dist.: Paramount

1990: THE BRONX WARRIORS 1983 Italian
☆ **R Action-Adventure 1:24**
☑ Explicit language, violence
Dir: Enzo G. Castellari *Cast:* Vic Morrow, Christopher Connelly, Fred Williamson, Mark Gregory, Stefania Girolami, John Sinclair
▶ In a gang-dominated Bronx, Girolami, the future president of the Manhattan Corp., is rescued from a rapist by motorcyclist Gregory. They fall in love, but he must then contend with murderous Manhattanite Morrow and rival gang leader Williamson. Slick production values fail to alleviate repellent characterizations and dreadful dialogue.
Dist.: Media

1969 1988
★ ★ **R Drama 1:35**
☑ Nudity, adult situations, explicit language
Dir: Ernest Thompson *Cast:* Bruce Dern, Kiefer Sutherland, Robert Downey, Jr., Ma-

riette Hartley, Winona Ryder, Joanna Cassidy
▶ Flower power finds its way to small-town Maryland as college students Sutherland and Downey contend with the Vietnam War and domestic woes. Downey turns on, flunks out, and gets arrested for breaking into his draft board office; Sutherland's pacifism alienates his dad Dern but attracts Downey's sister Ryder. Sutherland and Ryder excel, but psychedelic melodrama from writer/director Thompson can be overly earnest.
Dist.: Media

NINE TO FIVE 1980
★ ★ ★ ★ ★ **PG Comedy 1:49**
☑ Explicit language, adult humor
Dir: Colin Higgins *Cast:* Jane Fonda, Lily Tomlin, Dolly Parton, Dabney Coleman, Sterling Hayden
▶ Slapstick sermon on job equality. Office workers Fonda, Tomlin, and Parton, pushed to the wall by their chauvinist boss Coleman, kidnap him while they wait for proof he's an embezzler. Terrific team acting but Tomlin steals the show. ("I'm no fool. I killed the boss . . .they're going to fire me for that.") Led to a TV series. Parton, in her screen debut, sings hit title song she also wrote.
Dist.: CBS/Fox

90 DAYS 1986 Canadian
★ **NR Comedy 1:40**
☑ Adult situations, explicit language
Dir: Giles Walker *Cast:* Stefan Wodoslowsky, Christine Pak, Sam Grana, Fernanda Tavares, Daisy De Bellefeuille
▶ Charming, low-budget comedy about two men in crisis. Womanizer Wodoslowsky has been dumped by both his wife and mistress; lovelorn Grana has ninety days to decide whether to marry Korean mail-order bride Pak before her visa expires. Deft comic performances. **(CC)**
Dist.: CBS/Fox

99 WOMEN 1969 British/Spanish
☆ **R Drama 1:30**
☑ Rape, nudity, adult situations, violence
Dir: Jess Franco *Cast:* Maria Schell, Mercedes McCambridge, Luciana Paluzzi, Herbert Lom, Maria Rohm
▶ Island women's prison warden McCambridge brutally mistreats her charges until superintendent Schell arrives to improve conditions. The demoted McCambridge plots against the newcomer. Unbelievably lurid flick features frequent nudity and sleazy subplots involving lesbianism and men's prison warden Lom.
Dist.: Republic

92 IN THE SHADE 1975
★ **R Drama 1:33**
☑ Nudity, adult situations, explicit language, violence
Dir: Thomas McGuane *Cast:* Peter Fonda, Warren Oates, Margot Kidder, Burgess

Meredith, Harry Dean Stanton, Sylvia Miles, Elizabeth Ashley
▶ Drifter Fonda returns home to Key West to open a fishing charter business, provoking a dangerous feud with rival captain Oates. Subtle, picturesque cult favorite was adapted by director McGuane from his novel. Interesting cast also includes William Hickey and Louise Latham.
Dist.: CBS/Fox

NINJA III—THE DOMINATION 1984
★ ★ R **Martial Arts 1:35**
☑ Nudity, adult situations, explicit language, violence
Dir: Sam Firstenberg *Cast:* Lucinda Dickey, Sho Kosugi, Jordan Bennett, David Chung, T. J. Castronova
▶ Telephone worker Dickey, possessed by the spirit of an evil ninja, perplexes cop boyfriend Bennett when she goes on a killing spree. Kosugi is the only ninja who can exorcise the demon. Lively sequel to *Revenge of the Ninja* blends martial arts action (expertly choreographed by Kosugi) with touches of the supernatural.
Dist.: MGM/UA

NINJA TURF 1986
★ ★ R **Martial Arts 1:26**
☑ Explicit language, violence
Dir: Richard Park *Cast:* Jun Chong, Phillip Rhee, James Lew, Rosanna King, Bill Wallace, Dorin Mukama
▶ Teenager Chong, a kung fu whiz with a boozing mom, gets involved in gang warfare and drug dealing while battling arch-rival Rhee. The action is sometimes impressive; the acting and production values are not. Chong and Rhee acted, respectively, as executive producer and producer of the film.
Dist.: RCA/Columbia

NINOTCHKA 1939
★ ★ ★ ★ NR **Comedy 1:50 B&W**
Dir: Ernst Lubitsch *Cast:* Greta Garbo, Melvyn Douglas, Ina Claire, Sig Rumann, Felix Bressart, Bela Lugosi
▶ Garbo, in her first comedy, is stunning as a stern Communist sent to Paris to reprimand comrades indulging in the luxuries of capitalism. Debonair gigolo Douglas does his best to seduce the icy Ninotchka. Elegant comedy takes some gentle stabs at social satire, but succeeds best as a delightful romance. Both Garbo and the screenplay by Charles Brackett, Walter Reisch, and Billy Wilder received Oscar nominations.
Dist.: MGM/UA

NINTH CONFIGURATION, THE 1980
★ R **Drama 1:55**
☑ Nudity, explicit language, graphic violence
Dir: William Peter Blatty *Cast:* Stacy Keach, Scott Wilson, Jason Miller, Ed Flanders, Neville Brand, Robert Loggia, Moses Gunn
▶ Keach plays a new psychiatrist at a military

mental institution who may be more insane than his patients. Obscure, jumbled concoction of pompous speeches and sadistic violence was cut into several confusing versions by the studio. Director Blatty also produced and wrote the screenplay from his novel *Twinkle, Twinkle, Killer Kane.*
Dist.: New World

NOBODY'S FOOL 1986
★ ★ PG-13 **Comedy 1:47**
☑ Adult situations, explicit language
Dir: Evelyn Purcell *Cast:* Rosanna Arquette, Eric Roberts, Mare Winningham, Jim Youngs, Louise Fletcher, Gwen Welles
▶ Kooky small-town waitress Arquette, broken-hearted over losing a local boy to a rich girl, falls for Roberts, the lighting director of a visiting theatrical troupe. Oddball romance by Beth Henley is filled with disarming peripheral characters and her trademark touches of black comedy. (CC)
Dist.: Warner

NO DEPOSIT, NO RETURN 1976
★ ★ ★ ★ ★ G **Comedy/Family 1:58**
Dir: Norman Tokar *Cast:* David Niven, Darren McGavin, Don Knotts, Herschel Bernardi, Barbara Feldon, Kim Richards, Brad Savage
▶ Lonely children Richards and Savage persuade bumbling crooks McGavin and Knotts to stage a phony kidnapping so they can visit their mother in Hong Kong. Grandfather Niven, a multimillionaire, turns detective to track down the kids. Disney blend of comedy and action has an unusually good cast of comic veterans.
Dist.: Buena Vista

NO HOLDS BARRED 1989
★ ★ ★ PG-13 **Comedy 1:32**
☑ Adult situations, explicit language, violence, adult humor
Dir: Thomas J. Wright *Cast:* Hulk Hogan, Joan Severance, Kurt Fuller, Tiny Lister, Mark Pellagrino
▶ Unable to break wrestling king Hogan's contract with a rival network, mogul Fuller plots champ's defeat in the ring at the hands of ex-con Lister. Severance is hired to use her wiles on Hogan but falls for him instead. Broadly comedic vehicle for Hogan, a commanding figure if not a great actor. Wrestling fans will not be disappointed. (CC)
Dist.: RCA/Columbia

NOMADS 1986
★ R **Action-Adventure 1:35**
☑ Nudity, adult situations, explicit language, violence
Dir: John McTiernan *Cast:* Pierce Brosnan, Lesley-Anne Down, Adam Ant, Hector Mercado, Anna-Maria Montecelli, Mary Woronov
▶ French anthropologist Brosnan transmits his soul to Los Angeles doctor Down; she discovers he was battling evil spirits in the form of punk rockers led by a mute Ant. Intriguing

body-switching premise undermined by confusing crosscutting; still, some successful shocks.
Dist.: Paramount

NO MAN OF HER OWN 1932
★ NR Drama 1:25 B&W
Dir: Wesley Ruggles *Cast:* Clark Gable, Carole Lombard, Dorothy Mackaill, Grant Mitchell, Elizabeth Patterson, Lillian Harmer
► Gambler Gable flees New York to escape debts. He falls for small-town librarian Lombard, and proposes when she dares him to marry her. But Lombard has a tough task reforming him back in the Big Apple. Sole screen pairing of future husband and wife Gable and Lombard is stiff and predictable.
Dist.: KVC

NO MAN'S LAND 1987
★ ★ ★ R Drama 1:46
☑ Adult situations, explicit language, violence
Dir: Peter Werner *Cast:* Charlie Sheen, D. B. Sweeney, Lara Harris, Randy Quaid, Bill Duke, M. Emmet Walsh
► Rookie cop Sweeney takes undercover job in a "chop shop" specializing in stolen Porsches. Under the influence of seductive car thief Sheen, Sweeney turns to crime. Stylish, fast-paced thriller with above-average car chases raises interesting moral issues. **(CC)**
Dist.: Orion

NO MERCY 1986
★ ★ ★ ★ R Action-Adventure 1:48
☑ Adult situations, explicit language, graphic violence
Dir: Richard Pearce *Cast:* Richard Gere, Kim Basinger, Jeroen Krabbe, George Dzundza, Gary Basaraba, William Atherton
► Undercover Chicago cop Gere, vowing revenge for his partner's murder, tracks the killers to the Louisiana bayous. There he uncovers a conspiracy involving pony-tailed druglord Krabbe and his illiterate moll Basinger. Sexy leads and tense action enliven familiar plot.
Dist.: RCA/Columbia

NONE BUT THE LONELY HEART 1944
★ ★ ★ NR Drama 1:53 B&W
Dir: Clifford Odets *Cast:* Cary Grant, Ethel Barrymore, Barry Fitzgerald, June Duprez, Jane Wyatt, George Coulouris
► Ambitious but grim story of the London slums: Cockney con man Grant drifts into a crime ring run by Coulouris. He repents when he learns his impoverished mother Barrymore is dying of cancer. Grant received an Oscar nomination for his change-of-pace role; Barrymore won Best Supporting Actress.
Dist.: Fox Hills

NON-STOP NEW YORK 1937 British
★ NR Mystery-Suspense 1:12 B&W
Dir: Robert Stevenson *Cast:* Anna Lee, John Loder, Frank Collier, Desmond Tester, William Dewhurst, Francis L. Sullivan

► Witness to a New York mob rubout, English actress Lee returns to London, where she learns that an innocent man has been charged with the crime. With the bad guys trying to get their hands on her, she stows away on board a futuristic airliner in a desperate race to get back to the Big Apple and testify. Okay suspenser, but the real star is the big airplane, actually more of a flying, art deco ocean liner, sumptuously furnished with lounges, staterooms, and even an observation porch. Lots of fun.
Dist.: Sinister

NO NUKES 1980
★ ★ ★ PG Documentary/Music 1:43
☐ Explicit language
Dir: Danny Goldberg, Julian Schlossberg, Anthony Potenza *Cast:* Jackson Browne, David Crosby, The Doobie Brothers, John Hall, Graham Nash, Bonnie Raitt, Gil Scott-Heron, Carly Simon, Bruce Springsteen, Stephen Stills, James Taylor, Jesse Colin Young
► Lively series of concerts at Madison Square Garden were sponsored by MUSE (Musicians for Safe Energy) and feature some of the more politically active greats of rock 'n' roll. Cameras catch an energetic version of "Mockingbird" by James Taylor and Carly Simon; another Crosby, Stills, and Nash reunion; Jackson Browne's spirited "Running on Empty"; and Bruce Springsteen (captured for the first time on film) feverishly hurling himself into inspired versions of "The River," "Thunder Road," and a roof-raising "Quarter to Three."
Dist.: CBS/Fox

NO RETREAT, NO SURRENDER 1986
★ ★ ★ PG Martial Arts 1:24
☑ Explicit language, violence
Dir: Corey Yuen *Cast:* Kurt McKinney, Jean-Claude Van Damme, J. W. Fails, Kathie Sileno, Kim Tai Chong
► Seattle karate student McKinney, tormented by local thugs, turns to the ghost of Bruce Lee (Chong) for help. McKinney vindicates himself by battling psychopathic Russian athlete Van Damme. Amateurish martial arts drama picks up some steam during the frequent fights.
Dist.: New World

NO RETREAT, NO SURRENDER II 1989 Hong Kong
★ ★ R Martial Arts 1:32
☑ Explicit language, violence
Dir: Corey Yuen *Cast:* Loren Avedon, Max Thayer, Cynthia Rothrock, Matthias Hues
► Crude, serviceable martial arts adventure, with Avedon going into the jungle to rescue a woman kidnapped by fiendish Russian muscleman Hues. After dispatching hordes of Southeast Asian martial arts experts with his own brand of Tae Kwan Doe, Avedon and buddy Thayer load a helicopter with ordnance for the final showdown. Good fights,

but even action fans will find the plot hard to swallow.
Dist.: Forum

NORMAN LOVES ROSE 1982 Australian
★ **R Comedy 1:38**
☑ Adult situations, explicit language
Dir: Henri Safran   *Cast:* Carol Kane, Tony Owen, Warren Mitchell, Myra de Groot, David Downer
▶ Thirteen-year-old Norman (Owen) loves Rose (Kane), his older brother's wife. According to ancient Jewish law, he would be required to marry Rose if his brother died. This gives Norman ideas. Cute little comedy with sparkling performances.
Dist.: Vestron

NORMA RAE 1979
★ ★ ★ ★ ★ **PG Drama 1:54**
☑ Adult situations, explicit language, mild violence
Dir: Martin Ritt   *Cast:* Sally Field, Ron Leibman, Beau Bridges, Pat Hingle, Barbara Baxley, Gail Strickland
▶ Small-town Southern worker Norma Rae (Field) helps fast-talking Jewish organizer Leibman unionize the cotton mill where her family has worked for generations. The friendship between Field and Leibman is played against her marriage to Bridges, a goodhearted but confused electrician. Enormously affecting, intelligent film with plenty of heart showcases a spectacular Oscar-winning performance by Field.
Dist.: CBS/Fox

NORSEMAN, THE 1978
★ **PG Action-Adventure 1:30**
☑ Mild violence
Dir: Charles B. Pierce   *Cast:* Lee Majors, Cornel Wilde, Mel Ferrer, Jack Elam, Chris Connelly, Susie Coelho
▶ Coming on like nautical Hell's Angels, Majors and a gang of tenth-century Viking warriors sail to what will someday be called America to rescue king Ferrer from what will someday be called Indians. Plenty of fighting and familiar faces in this hokey non-epic, which features Sonny Bono–ex Coelho as an Indian maid who helps Majors out of a jam.
Dist.: Vestron

NORTH BY NORTHWEST 1959
★ ★ ★ ★ ★ **NR Mystery-Suspense 2:16**
Dir: Alfred Hitchcock   *Cast:* Cary Grant, Eva Marie Saint, James Mason, Jessie Royce Landis, Martin Landau, Leo G. Carroll
▶ Madison Avenue exec Grant finds his world turned upside down when he is mistaken for a CIA agent. Pursued by both cops and enemy spies (led by Mason), he gets involved with mysterious Saint on a cross-country chase. One of Hitchcock's best films is fast-paced, witty, and tremendously exciting. Many classic scenes: the murder at the UN, the crop-

duster sequence, and the cliff-hanging Mount Rushmore climax.
Dist.: MGM/UA

NORTH DALLAS FORTY 1979
★ ★ ★ **R Comedy/Sports 1:58**
☑ Nudity, adult situations, explicit language
Dir: Ted Kotcheff   *Cast:* Nick Nolte, Mac Davis, Charles Durning, Dayle Haddon, Bo Svenson, Steve Forrest
▶ Over-the-hill wide receiver Nolte, needing drugs to overcome his aches and pains, gradually realizes the corruption of the owners and coaches. A winner, both on and off the field: convincing bone-crunching football action, terrific relationship between Nolte and quarterback pal Davis, and some great raucous humor (especially in Davis's bawdy "Wait til I get to the weird part" story). Based on the Peter Gent novel.
Dist.: Paramount

NORTHERN PURSUIT 1943
★ ★ **NR War 1:34 B&W**
Dir: Raoul Walsh   *Cast:* Errol Flynn, Julie Bishop, Helmut Dantine, John Ridgely, Gene Lockhart
▶ During World War II, Flynn, a Canadian mountie of German descent, befriends Nazi spy Dantine in order to infiltrate an enemy cabal. Top-level wartime thriller with some fine action during an avalanche and ski chase.
Dist.: Key

NORTH SHORE 1987
★ ★ ★ **PG Drama 1:36**
☑ Explicit language
Dir: William Phelps   *Cast:* Matt Adler, Nia Peeples, John Philbin, Gregory Harrison, Gerry Lopez
▶ Arizona surfer Adler rejects the security of college to challenge the waves at Hawaii's famous North Shore. While training for a dangerous pipeline contest, Adler meets beautiful native Peeples and receives inspiration from older "soul surfer" Harrison. Undemanding fare with above-average wave footage.
Dist.: MCA

NORTH STAR, THE 1943
★ ★ **NR War 1:45 B&W**
Dir: Lewis Milestone   *Cast:* Anne Baxter, Dana Andrews, Walter Huston, Farley Granger, Erich von Stroheim, Jane Withers
▶ Von Stroheim leads Nazis on an attack of a small Ukranian town, where residents Baxter, Granger, and Withers flee to join a guerrilla band, and doctor Huston stays to witness enemy atrocities. Produced during World War II by some of Hollywood's leading Stalinists (like scriptwriter Lillian Hellman), some of whom were later called upon to explain pro-Soviet angle to the House Un-American Activities Committee. Obvious, sentimental tragedy is hardly worth the trouble it caused. An edited version is entitled *Armored Attack*.
Dist.: Republic   Ⓒ

NORTH TO ALASKA 1960
★ ★ ★ ★ NR Western 2:00
Dir: Henry Hathaway *Cast:* John Wayne,
Stewart Granger, Ernie Kovacs, Fabian,
Capucine, Mickey Shaughnessy
▶ Light-hearted Western romp with gold-min-
ing partners Wayne and Granger battling
over saucy Capucine, a replacement for
Granger's Seattle mail-order bride. Kovacs, an
unctuous con man and Capucine's former
lover, attempts to steal their mine with a rival
claim. Good vehicle for Wayne, who revels in
his comic role. Title tune became a pop hit for
Johnny Horton. **(CC)**
Dist.: CBS/Fox

NORTHWEST PASSAGE 1940
★ ★ ★ ★ NR Action-Adventure 2:05
Dir: King Vidor *Cast:* Spencer Tracy, Robert
Young, Walter Brennan, Ruth Hussey, Nat
Pendleton, Louis Hector
▶ In the mid-eighteenth century, frontiersman
Tracy coerces artist Young and crony Brennan
into joining his border patrol. Their perilous mission: subdue rampaging Indians supported by
the French in upstate New York. Highlights of
this rousing adventure include a gripping sequence in which Tracy's men must drag their
boats over a mountain to mount a surprise
attack. Adapted from the first part of Kenneth
Roberts's best-seller about the exploits of real-
life patriot Robert Rogers.
Dist.: MGM/UA

NOSFERATU 1922 German
★ ★ NR Horror 1:03 B&W
Dir: F. W. Murnau *Cast:* Max Schreck, Alexander Granach, Greta Schroeder, Gustav
von Wangenheim
▶ The very shadows are alive in this silent, expressionistic treatment of Bram Stoker's *Dracula*. Cadaverously thin and hollow-eyed,
Schrek may be the most sinister of all cinema
vampires as he rises stiffly from his coffin to terrorize young Jonathan Harker (Granach) and
his virginal fiancée Schroeder. Disquieting episodes include the discovery of the ghost ship,
loaded to the gunnels with rats and corpses.
Inspired scores of vampire films, including a
1979 remake.
Dist.: Various

NOSFERATU, THE VAMPYRE 1979 German
★ PG Horror 1:47
☑ Violence
Dir: Werner Herzog *Cast:* Klaus Kinski, Isabelle Adjani, Bruno Ganz, Jacques Dufilho,
Roland Topor
▶ Eerie but slow-paced remake of the 1922
silent film presents an intellectual version of
the Dracula legend. Ganz plays a lawyer who
stumbles across the horrid secret behind mysterious count Kinski; Ganz's wife Adjani sacrifices herself to destroy the vampire. Visually
stunning picture benefits from oddly comic
touches and Kinski's magnetic performance.

Shorter, English-language version also available. ⓢ
Dist.: Crown

NO SMALL AFFAIR 1984
★ ★ R Comedy 1:42
☑ Brief nudity, adult situations, explicit language
Dir: Jerry Schatzberg *Cast:* Jon Cryer, Demi
Moore, George Wendt, Peter Frechette, Elizabeth Daily, Ann Wedgeworth
▶ Precocious teen photographer Cryer sets
his sights on an indifferent "older" woman, aspiring rock singer Moore. Predictable adolescent comedy salvaged by Cryer's ingratiating
performance and glossy San Francisco locations. **(CC)**
Dist.: RCA/Columbia

NO SURRENDER 1986 British
☆ R Comedy 1:40
☑ Adult situations, explicit language, violence
Dir: Peter Smith *Cast:* Michael Angelis, Avis
Bunnage, James Ellis, Tom Georgeson, Bernard Hill, Ray McAnally, Joanne Whalley
▶ Biting satire about Northern Ireland's woes
finds Angelis the new manager of a Liverpool
nightspot. On New Year's Eve he must contend with busloads of elderly Orangemen,
Irish Catholic pensioners, the senile residents
of a retirement home, and a terrorist hiding
out in the toilet, among other cantankerous
patrons. Brutally funny film about the desperate times we live in should find small but appreciate audience.
Dist.: Prism

NOT FOR PUBLICATION 1984
★ R Comedy 1:27
☑ Adult situations, explicit language
Dir: Paul Bartel *Cast:* Nancy Allen, David
Naughton, Laurence Luckinbill, Alice Ghostley, Richard Paul, Barry Dennen
▶ Old-fashioned farce set in the 1950s about
the double life of plucky heroine Allen, who's
both a muckraking reporter for an exposé rag
and assistant to reform mayoral candidate
Luckinbill. Romance blossoms between Allen
and Naughton, a photographer she's hired to
check into Luckinbill's background. Fitfully
amusing but rarely inspired.
Dist.: HBO

NOTHING IN COMMON 1986
★ ★ ★ ★ PG Comedy/Drama 1:59
☑ Brief nudity, adult situations, explicit language
Dir: Garry Marshall *Cast:* Tom Hanks,
Jackie Gleason, Eva Marie Saint, Bess Armstrong, Hector Elizondo, Barry Corbin
▶ High-flying advertising whiz kid Hanks is
grounded by the divorce of parents Gleason
and Saint and their sudden dependence on
him. Hanks's transformation from hilarious-but-
unlikable yuppie to responsible, loving son Is,
by turns, funny, touching, and overly sentimental. Fine supporting help from Elizondo as

Hanks's boss and Armstrong as his girlfriend. Gleason's final film.
Dist.: HBO

NOTHING PERSONAL 1980 Canadian/U.S.
★★ PG Comedy 1:37
☑ Brief nudity, adult situations, explicit language
Dir: George Bloomfield *Cast:* Donald Sutherland, Suzanne Somers, Lawrence Dane, Roscoe Lee Brown, Dabney Coleman, Saul Rubinek
▸ Big Business is out to destroy some Alaskan seals, and pot-smoking, sixties-nostalgic professor Sutherland is determined to save them. Somers is sexy attorney who signs on to help him. Enduring blackmail and other runarounds, two manage to fall in love and find a seal-positive legal loophole. Flat, inane comedy flops on all levels.
Dist.: Vestron

NOTHING SACRED 1937
★★★★ NR Comedy 1:15
Dir: William Wellman *Cast:* Carole Lombard, Fredric March, Charles Winninger, Walter Connolly, Sig Rumann, Frank Fay
▸ Ambitious New York reporter March plans a sob story on dying Vermonter Lombard. When her incompetent doctor Winninger reverses his initial diagnosis, March won't back off and persuades Lombard to feign illness and journey to the city in style. She's honored by a grief-stricken populace until her ruddy good health raises eyebrows. Classic screwball comedy provides nonstop laughs at a breakneck pace, with script by Ben Hecht and additional dialogue by Ring Lardner, Jr., and Budd Schulberg.
Dist.: Various

NO TIME FOR SERGEANTS 1958
★★★★ NR Comedy 1:51 B&W
Dir: Mervyn LeRoy *Cast:* Andy Griffith, Nick Adams, Myron McCormick, Murray Hamilton, Howard Smith, Don Knotts
▸ Hillbilly Will Stockdale (Griffith) joins the Air Force, where his down-home ways bring him into conflict with no nonsense sarge McCormick. Fresh, alive, and very funny with marvelous performances by Griffith and McCormick. Griffith's second film was adapted from Ira Levin's Broadway play and Mac Hyman's novel.
Dist.: Warner

NOT OF THIS EARTH 1988
★ R Sci-Fi 1:20
☑ Nudity, explicit language, violence
Dir: Jim Wynorski *Cast:* Traci Lords, Arthur Roberts, Ace Mask, Lenny Juliano, Roger Lodge, Becky LeBeau
▸ Roger Corman-produced remake of his own 1957 sci-fi schlocker drapes a limp plot about blood-sucking aliens around the often-bared body of Lords, formerly a real-life porn star. Jokey, campy film is full of nudity and double-entendres.
Dist.: MGM/UA

NOTORIOUS 1945
★★★★ NR Mystery-Suspense 1:41 B&W
Dir: Alfred Hitchcock *Cast:* Cary Grant, Ingrid Bergman, Claude Rains, Louis Calhern, Leopoldine Konstantin, Reinhold Schunzel
▸ In post-World War II South America, Federal agent Grant blackmails German playgirl Bergman into marrying Nazi Rains. When she uncovers a conspiracy involving uranium, Rains slowly poisons her. Fascinating drama executed with breathless pacing and superlative plotting; on top of the suspense, Grant and Bergman conduct a memorable romance. Rains and screenwriter Ben Hecht both received Oscar nominations. **(CC)**
Dist.: CBS/Fox

NOT QUITE PARADISE 1986 British
★ R Drama 1:46
☑ Brief nudity, adult situations, explicit language, violence
Dir: Lewis Gilbert *Cast:* Joanna Pacula, Sam Robards, Kevin McNally, Todd Graff, Selina Cadell
▸ Foreign workers on an Israeli kibbutz encounter a variety of adventures, ranging from a run-in with Arabs to a budding romance between American medical student Robards and Pacula, a no-nonsense native in charge of the kibbutz. Uneven mixture of drama, comedy, and romance offers a good performance by Cadell as a neurotic Englishwoman. [S]
Dist.: New World

NOW AND FOREVER 1983 Australian
★★★★ R Romance 1:32
☑ Nudity, adult situations, explicit language, violence
Dir: Adrian Carr *Cast:* Cheryl Ladd, Robert Coleby, Carmen Duncan, Christine Amor, Alex Scott
▸ Boutique owner Ladd turns to alcohol and pills when her writer husband Coleby is wrongly convicted of rape. Beautiful Australian countryside, lush visuals. Unfortunately, the soap opera plot has many holes and Cheryl's characterization generates little sympathy. Based on the Danielle Steel novel.
Dist.: MCA

NO WAY OUT 1987
★★★★★ R Mystery-Suspense 1:54
☑ Nudity, adult situations, explicit language, violence
Dir: Roger Donaldson *Cast:* Kevin Costner, Gene Hackman, Sean Young, Will Patton, Howard Duff, George Dzundza, Iman
▸ Gripping thriller about Costner, a Navy career man assigned as a CIA liaison to Secretary of Defense Hackman. While searching for a Russian mole, Costner realizes he is being framed for the murder of Hackman's mistress Young. Taut, convincing plot was loosely

based on Kenneth Fearing's novel *The Big Clock* (filmed under that title in 1948). *Dist.:* HBO

NO WAY TO TREAT A LADY 1968
★ ★ ★ NR Mystery-Suspense 1:48
Dir: Jack Smight   *Cast:* Rod Steiger, Lee Remick, George Segal, Eileen Heckart, Murray Hamilton, Michael Dunn
▶ Deranged serial killer Steiger, a master of disguise, slays New York women while in costume. Police detective Segal romances key witness Remick as he pursues Steiger in a battle of wits. Well-crafted romantic suspenser is both humorous and grisly.
Dist.: Paramount

NOWHERE TO HIDE 1987 Canadian
★ ★ ★ R Mystery-Suspense 1:30
☑ Explicit language, violence
Dir: Mario Azzopardi   *Cast:* Amy Madigan, Daniel Hugh Kelly, Robin MacEachern, Michael Ironside, John Colicos, Charles Shamata
▶ When her husband is murdered while investigating suspicious helicopter crashes, ex-Marine and mother Madigan must recover his evidence before assassins find her. Competent thriller features an above-average performance by Madigan as the indomitable heroine. **(CC)**
Dist.: Warner

NOW, VOYAGER 1942
★ ★ ★ ★ NR Romance 1:57 B&W
Dir: Irving Rapper   *Cast:* Bette Davis, Claude Rains, Paul Henreid, Gladys Cooper, Bonita Granville, Ilka Chase, Janis Wilson
▶ Davis, the ugly duckling in a New England family, is transformed into a swan under guidance of kindly shrink Rains. She finds shipboard romance with married Henreid and helps his troubled daughter. Davis is superb in one of the most romantic movies ever made. Many unforgettable moments: Henreid lighting two cigarettes at once; Davis's famous line, "Don't let's ask for the moon! We have the stars!" Oscar-winning score by Max Steiner.
Dist.: MGM/UA

NOW YOU SEE HIM, NOW YOU DON'T 1972
★ ★ ★ G Family 1:28
Dir: Robert Butler   *Cast:* Kurt Russell, Cesar Romero, Joe Flynn, Jim Backus, William Windom, Michael McGreevey
▶ College student Russell inadvertently creates an invisibility formula. He uses his newfound power to help dean Flynn defeat millionaire Backus in a golf match to raise money for the school. However, crook Romero swipes the potion for a bank heist. Genial, entertaining sequel to *The Computer Wore Tennis Shoes.* Golf stars Billy Casper and Dave Hill have cameos.
Dist.: Buena Vista

NUMBER SEVENTEEN 1932 British
★ ★ NR Mystery-Suspense 1:23 B&W
Dir: Alfred Hitchcock   *Cast:* Leon M. Lion, Anne Grey, John Stuart, Donald Calthrop, Barry Jones, Garry Marsh
▶ Tramp Lion, detective Stuart, and ingenue Grey scramble through a deserted house for a stolen necklace in this early Hitchcock thriller. Tongue-in-cheek adaptation of a dated stage play gives way in the second half to a train chase that works up considerable thrills (despite the use of obvious miniatures).
Dist.: Various

NUNS ON THE RUN 1990 British
★ ★ ★ PG-13 Comedy 1:34
☑ Nudity, adult situations, explicit language
Dir: Jonathan Lynn   *Cast:* Eric Idle, Robbie Coltrane, Camille Coduri, Janet Suzman, Doris Hare, Lila Kaye
▶ Weary crooks Idle and Coltrane run away with the loot from their gang's latest bank heist. Seeking refuge from the law and their irate boss in a convent, they don habits and become Sister Euphemia of the Five Wounds and Sister Inviolata of the Immaculate Conception. Retread comedy doesn't wring any new juice from tired material, but hefty, leacherous Coltrane steals every scene he's in.
Dist.: CBS/Fox

NUN'S STORY, THE 1959
★ ★ ★ NR Drama 2:29
Dir: Fred Zinnemann   *Cast:* Audrey Hepburn, Peter Finch, Edith Evans, Peggy Ashcroft, Dean Jagger, Mildred Dunnock
▶ Young Hepburn becomes a nun. Serving as a nurse in a Belgian mental institution and a Congolese hospital, she begins to question stern church doctrine. World War II proves to be a turning point in her wrestling with her conscience. Outstanding, engrossing drama features one of Oscar-nominated Hepburn's most complex performances. A Best Picture nominee.
Dist.: Warner

NURSE EDITH CAVELL 1939
★ NR War 1:48
Dir: Herbert Wilcox   *Cast:* Anna Neagle, Edna May Oliver, George Sanders, ZaSu Pitts, May Robson, H. B. Warner
▶ Nurse Neagle operates a kind of underground railroad devoted to smuggling refugees, noncombatants, and escaped prisoners out of German-occupied Belgium during World War I. Germans uncover the network, and Neagle goes before a firing squad. Based on a true story, movie opened just as World War II was breaking out, and served to solidify attitudes against the Nazis. Moving and dignified.
Dist.: Video Yesteryear

NUTCRACKER: THE MOTION PICTURE 1986
★ ★ ★ G Dance/Family 1:25
Dir: Carroll Ballard   *Cast:* Hugh Bigney,

Vanessa Sharp, Patricia Barker, Wade Walthall, Russell Burnett
▶ The much loved classical ballet, set to Tchaikovsky's unforgettable score. In twelve-year-old Clara's dream, her Christmas gift, the Nutcracker, and a legion of toy soldiers wage battle with mice while the tree decorations come to life. Charmingly sinister sets and creatures were designed by children's book illustrator Maurice Sendak. Ballet lovers will rejoice. Performed by the Pacific Northwest Ballet and narrated by Julie Harris.
Dist.: Paramount

NUTS 1987
★ ★ ★ ★ R Drama 1:58
☑ Adult situations, explicit language, violence
Dir: Martin Ritt *Cast:* Barbra Streisand, Richard Dreyfuss, Maureen Stapleton, Eli Wallach, Robert Webber, Karl Malden, Leslie Nielson
▶ High-priced prostitute Streisand is indicted for manslaughter after killing a customer. Against the advice of court-appointed attorney Dreyfuss, she refuses to plead insanity, demanding her day in court. Psychological fireworks erupt when her stepfather Malden takes the stand. High-powered, well-cast courtroom drama was adapted from Tom Topor's Broadway play. (CC)
Dist.: Warner

NUTTY PROFESSOR, THE 1963
★ ★ NR Comedy 1:47
Dir: Jerry Lewis *Cast:* Jerry Lewis, Stella Stevens, Kathleen Freeman, Ned Flory, Norman Alden, Howard Morris, Del Moore
▶ Hoping to win the love of beautiful student Stevens, nerdy professor Julius Kelp (Lewis) creates a potion that transforms him into the obnoxious but dashing Buddy Love (also Lewis). The double life gets complicated when the formula wears off at inconvenient times. One of Lewis's best and deservedly most popular films; his usual broad clowning is tempered with heart.
Dist.: Paramount

OBLONG BOX, THE 1969 British
★ PG Horror 1:31
☑ Violence
Dir: Gordon Hessler *Cast:* Vincent Price, Christopher Lee, Alistair Williamson, Hilary Dwyer, Peter Arne, Harry Baird
▶ British aristocrat Price injects his brother Williamson, mutilated on African safari, with witch doctor's drug that gives the appearance of death before entombing him. But grave robbers take the body to scientist Lee, who revives the "corpse." Price must confront Williamson to stop subsequent murders. Slowly paced adaptation of an Edgar Allan Poe story sacrifices chills for too much talk.
Dist.: HBO

OBSESSED 1988 Canadian
☆ PG-13 Drama 1:42

☑ Adult situations, explicit language
Dir: Robin Spry *Cast:* Kerrie Keane, Daniel Pilon, Saul Rubinek, Lynne Griffin, Mireille Deyglum, Colleen Dewhurst
▶ When American businessman Rubinek accidentally runs over a child while driving in Montreal, he panics and returns to America. Victim's mom Keane tries everything she can to get Rubinek back to Canada to stand trial, but law forbids extradition for this particular crime. Film is unforgiving of Rubinek, but dramatizes the human and legal frailties behind the heartbreaking situation.
Dist.: New Star

OBSESSION 1976
★ ★ ★ ★ PG Mystery-Suspense 1:38
☑ Adult situations, explicit language, mild violence
Dir: Brian De Palma *Cast:* Cliff Robertson, Genevieve Bujold, John Lithgow, Sylvia Kumba Williams, Wanda Blackman
▶ In 1959, New Orleans businessman Robertson cooperates with police when his wife Bujold and daughter are kidnapped; as a result, they are killed. Sixteen years later in Rome, the guilt-ridden Robertson meets his late wife's lookalike (also Bujold) and marries her. History repeats itself when she is kidnapped. Lush, emotional Hitchcockian thriller. Sweeping Bernard Herrmann score, sincere performances, and bravura camerawork create a rich mood of danger and romance.
Dist.: RCA/Columbia

O.C. AND STIGGS 1987
☆ R Comedy 1:50
☑ Brief nudity, adult situations, explicit language
Dir: Robert Altman *Cast:* Neill Barry, Daniel Jenkins, Martin Mull, Jane Curtin, Dennis Hopper, Paul Dooley, Jon Cryer, Ray Walston
▶ Boisterous Phoenix teens Barry and Jenkins spend idle summer persecuting insurance mogul Dooley and his kin. Overly ambitious, anarchic satire of Sun Belt life is alternately hilarious and dumb. Director Altman's foray into teen comedy sports good individual gags and splendid supporting cast, but don't expect it to add up to much. (CC)
Dist.: CBS/Fox

OCEAN DRIVE WEEKEND 1985
☆ PG-13 Comedy 1:38
☑ Adult situations, explicit language, nudity
Dir: Bryan Jones *Cast:* Charles Redmond, Robert Peacock, P. J. Grethe, Konya Dee
▶ Southern college students in the sixties head to South Carolina beaches for fun, sun, beer and sex. Two of them have forged a check to finance their holiday. Cheap, trashy, unfunny teen comedy never got a theatrical release.
Dist.: Vestron

OCEAN'S ELEVEN 1960
★ ★ ★ NR Comedy 2:08

Dir: Lewis Milestone *Cast:* Frank Sinatra, Dean Martin, Sammy Davis, Jr., Peter Lawford, Angie Dickinson, Richard Conte, Cesar Romero, Joey Bishop
▶ All-star caper film built around a clever premise: Sinatra and ten buddies, all Airborne veterans, come up with a scheme to rob five Las Vegas casinos on New Year's Eve. Complications set in when local gangster Romero hears of the plot. Cast includes Akim Tamiroff, Henry Silva, Red Skelton, Shirley MacLaine, and George Raft.
Dist.: Warner

OCTAGON, THE 1980
★ ★ ★ R Martial Arts 1:44
☑ Brief nudity, adult situations, explicit language, graphic violence
Dir: Eric Karson *Cast:* Chuck Norris, Lee Van Cleef, Karen Carlson, Art Hindle, Kim Lankford, Tadashi Yamashita
▶ Retired martial arts champ Norris makes comeback when gang of ninja killers slay his date Lankford. Soon Norris is on the trail of kung fu terrorists. Climactic battle at gang's HQ, the Octagon, leads to duel-to-the-death between Norris and villains' leader Yamashita. Better-than-average chop socky with usual Oriental mysticism, sultry girls, and violence a-plenty.
Dist.: Media

OCTAMAN 1971
☆ NR Sci-Fi 1:30
☑ Violence
Dir: Harry Essex *Cast:* Kerwin Mathews, Pier Angeli, Jeff Morrow, Jerry Guardino, Norman Fields, David Essex
▶ Explorers including Mathews and Angeli head to Mexico, where they encounter an unusual monster: a six-armed octopus that lumbers around on two feet. Monster effects are the early work of Rick Baker, who went on to fame in far better films later in the decade. Angeli died of a barbiturate overdose during the filming of this perfectly dreadful creature pic.
Dist.: Prism

OCTOBER 1928 Russian
☆ NR Drama 1:43 B&W
Dir: Sergei Eisenstein *Cast:* Grigori Alexandrov, Nikandrof, N. Popov, Boris Livanov, Eduard Tisse
▶ The Russian Revolution and Bolshevik coup are powerfully, if fancifully, re-created on an epic scale in this Soviet-made silent, commissioned for the tenth anniversary of the 1918 events. Director Eisenstein brings his considerable artistry to bear on historical characters like Lenin (Nikandrof), Kerensky (Popov), and Trotsky. Impressive propaganda is also known as *Ten Days That Shook the World* after the John Reed book on which it is loosely based.
Dist.: Evergreen

OCTOPUSSY 1983 British
★ ★ ★ ★ PG Espionage/Action-Adventure 2:10
☑ Adult situations, explicit language, violence
Dir: John Glen *Cast:* Roger Moore, Maud Adams, Louis Jourdan, Kristina Wayborn, Kabir Bedi, Steven Berkoff
▶ Hawkish Soviet general Berkoff attempts to start a superpower war, assisted by beautiful smuggler Adams and villainous art dealer Jourdan. Many exotic locales include an Indian island populated only by scantily-clad women. Breathtaking stunts, droll and urbane Jourdan, and Moore's best turn as 007. Thirteenth installment in the always popular series.
Dist.: MGM/UA

ODD ANGRY SHOT, THE 1979 Australian
★ NR Comedy 1:30
☑ Nudity, explicit language, violence
Dir: Tom Jeffrey *Cast:* John Hargreaves, Graham Kennedy, Bryan Brown, John Jarratt
▶ Unusual Vietnam war comedy about Aussie volunteer special forces fighting alongside U.S. troops. Aussies go to war as sporting amateurs, but are soon initiated into the bloody business at at hand. Grim, funny, and believable film, with Brown as one of the Down Under fighters.
Dist.: Vestron

ODD COUPLE, THE 1968
★ ★ ★ ★ G Comedy 1:45
Dir: Gene Saks *Cast:* Jack Lemmon, Walter Matthau, John Fiedler, Herb Edelman, Carole Shelley, Monica Evans
▶ When his wife leaves him, finicky Felix Unger (Lemmon) moves in with his sloppy sportswriter pal, Oscar Madison (Matthau). Felix's obsessively neat behavior quickly conflicts with Oscar's messy poker games. Time and the popular Tony Randall/Jack Klugman TV series have not diminished the appealing Lemmon/Matthau teamwork in this hilarious and endearing adaptation of Neil Simon's smash Broadway hit.
Dist.: Paramount

ODD JOB, THE 1977 British
★ NR Comedy 1:26
☑ Nudity, explicit language, mild violence
Dir: Peter Medak *Cast:* Graham Chapman, David Jason, Simon Williams, Diana Quick, Edward Hardwicke
▶ Monty Pythonite Chapman is a suicidal abandoned husband who programs an odd-job man to kill him. When his wife returns, he changes his mind about the suicide business, but the odd-job man hasn't changed his, and Chapman must escape his murderous efforts. Funny film is very British, with old-fashioned comic types hearkening back to the Ealing Studio comedies.
Dist.: Vestron

ODD JOBS 1986
★ **PG-13 Comedy 1:29**
☑ Adult situations, explicit language, mild violence
Dir: Mark Story   *Cast:* Paul Reiser, Robert Townsend, Scott McGinnis, Paul Provenza, Rick Overton, Julianne Phillips
▶ When their schemes to get rich quick with summer jobs fail, Reiser and four college friends form a moving company that draws the wrath of rival Cabrezzi Brothers goons. Capable cast does wonders with the story's breezy high jinks, but inventive writing is undercut by scattershot direction. Notable for appearances by Phillips (then Mrs. Bruce Springsteen), radio personality Don Imus, and "Body by Jake" Steinfeld.
Dist.: HBO

ODD MAN OUT 1947 British
★ ★ ★ **NR Mystery-Suspense 1:55 B&W**
Dir: Carol Reed   *Cast:* James Mason, Kathleen Ryan, Robert Newton, F. J. McCormick, Cyril Cusack, Dan O'Herlihy, Robert Beatty
▶ Irish rebel Mason, critically wounded during a robbery, seeks refuge in the slums of Belfast while a British manhunt closes in on him. An unforgettable masterpiece of tension, written, directed, and performed admirably. Mason is especially remarkable in what may be his best role.
Dist.: Paramount

ODESSA FILE, THE 1974 British
★ ★ ★ **PG Action-Adventure 2:08**
☑ Adult situations, explicit language, violence
Dir: Ronald Neame   *Cast:* Jon Voight, Maximilian Schell, Maria Schell, Mary Tamm, Derek Jacobi, Peter Jeffrey
▶ After reading a concentration camp survivor's diary, German journalist Voight is determined to find Schell, a missing SS agent responsible for mass murders. Israelis train him to infiltrate Odessa, a secret neo-Nazi organization harboring Schell. Brooding adaptation of a Frederick Forsyth best-seller showcases a strong performance by Voight, but plot is often confusing. (CC)
Dist.: RCA/Columbia

ODE TO BILLY JOE 1976
★ ★ ★ **PG Drama 1:46**
☑ Adult situations
Dir: Max Baer   *Cast:* Robby Benson, Glynnis O'Connor, Joan Hotchkis, Sandy McPeak, James Best
▶ Feature-length interpretation of Bobbie Gentry's 1976 hit song concerns young lovers Benson and O'Connor facing problems in rural 1953 South. Benson, hiding a tragic secret, commits suicide; O'Connor comes to maturity when she discovers his past. Accurate period details help this sincere but overwrought melodrama.
Dist.: Warner

ODYSSEY OF THE PACIFIC 1982
Canadian/French
★ ★ **NR Family 1:40**
Dir: Fernando Arrabal   *Cast:* Mickey Rooney, Jonathan Starr, Anik, Guy Hoffman, Ky Huot Uk, Vera Dalton
▶ Crippled raconteur Rooney chatters with a trio of children including Starr, sister Anik, and adopted Cambodian orphan Uk. Aside from claiming to be the Emperor of Peru, Rooney introduces the children to a railroad engine he once operated, giving Uk the idea of driving the vehicle back across the ocean. Okay fantasy for the younger set.
Dist.: MCA

OFF BEAT 1986
★ ★ **PG Comedy 1:33**
☑ Adult situations, explicit language
Dir: Michael Dinner   *Cast:* Judge Reinhold, Meg Tilly, Cleavant Derricks, Joe Mantegna, Jacques d'Amboise, Amy Wright
▶ Pal of librarian Reinhold doesn't want to perform in a police dance benefit; Reinhold takes his place and falls in love with police hostage negotiator Tilly. Ensuing impersonation leads to amusing but predictable complications; supporting actors (Anthony Zerbe, Fred Gwynne, Harvey Keitel, etc.) provide most of the laughs in this middling comedy.
Dist.: Buena Vista

OFFERINGS 1989
☆ **R Horror 1:34**
☑ Adult situations, explicit language, violence
Dir: Christopher Reynolds   *Cast:* Loretta Leigh Bowman, Elizabeth Greene, G. Michael Smith, Jerry Brewer, Richard A. Buswell
▶ A human being is served up on a pizza in this poorly made cannibal movie. Insane boy eats mom, goes to mental hospital, then returns ten years later to get back at kids who once taunted him. Dull regional horror offering lacks any genre thrills. Direct-to-video release.
Dist.: Southgate

OFFICER AND A GENTLEMAN, AN 1982
★ ★ ★ ★ ★ **R Drama/Romance 2:04**
☑ Nudity, adult situations, explicit language, violence
Dir: Taylor Hackford   *Cast:* Richard Gere, Debra Winger, Louis Gossett, Jr., David Keith, Robert Loggia, Lisa Blount, Lisa Eilbacher
▶ Loner pilot-in-training Gere meets his match in hardnosed drill instructor Gossett while romancing local Puget Sound girl, Winger. Gere's best buddy Keith drops out and then blows it with his townie belle; but Gere has the right stuff and learns to become both a warrior and a lover. Hugely popular if somewhat obvious film combines old-style steamy romance and boot camp rite-of-passage. Gossett won an Oscar for his fine sup-

porting portrayal of a tough but humane mentor.
Dist.: Paramount

OFFICIAL STORY, THE 1985 Argentinian
★★ **NR Drama 1:53**
[✓] Adult situations
Dir: Luis Puenzo *Cast:* Norma Aleandro, Hector Alterio, Chela Ruiz, Chunchuna Villafane, Hugo Arana
▶ Argentinian Aleandro finds her comfortable, upper-class life disrupted when she suspects her adopted daughter is the offspring of a political prisoner killed by the military dictatorship. Her right-wing husband Alterio seeks to allay her concerns, but her investigation reveals he is a partner in the corrupt government. Winner of an Oscar for Best Foreign Film, picture shrewdly reveals its politics through a moving human story. [S]
Dist.: Pacific Arts

OFF LIMITS 1953
★★ **NR Comedy 1:29 B&W**
Dir: George Marshall *Cast:* Bob Hope, Mickey Rooney, Marilyn Maxwell, Eddie Mayehoff, Stanley Clements, Marvin Miller
▶ Boxing promoter Hope calls it quits when he's drafted, despite pleas from young recruit Rooney to help him train. Hope changes his mind when he learns Rooney's aunt (Maxwell) is a gorgeous nightclub singer. Fast-paced comedy filled with Army gags features an amusing cameo by Jack Dempsey.
Dist.: KVC

OFF LIMITS 1988
★★★ **R Mystery-Suspense 1:42**
[✓] Nudity, explicit language, violence
Dir: Christopher Crowe *Cast:* Willem Dafoe, Gregory Hines, Fred Ward, Amanda Pays, Kay Tong Lim, Scott Glenn
▶ Saigon 1968 provides an unusual setting for a nasty murder mystery: undercover Army detectives Dafoe and Hines search the grimy underworld for a high-ranking superior who's murdering prostitutes. Pays is a nun whose missionary work helps the cops. Conventional thriller graced by unusually good leads and taut atmosphere. (CC)
Dist.: CBS/Fox

OFF THE WALL 1982
★★ **R Comedy 1:25**
[✓] Adult situations, explicit language
Dir: Rick Friedberg *Cast:* Paul Sorvino, Rosanna Arquette, Patrick Cassidy, Billy Hufsey, Ralph Wilcox, Mickey Gilley, Brianne Leary
▶ Nutty little prison story has Cassidy and Hufsey thrown into tough Southern lockup after they cover for governor's daughter Arquette, who's caused a traffic accident. Once behind bars, Cassidy falls for warden Sorvino's daughter Leary, and Hufsey gets roped into a nationally televised tag-team wrestling match. Nothing sophisticated here, but script shows an original sense of humor.
Dist.: Vestron

OF HUMAN BONDAGE 1934
★★★ **NR Drama 1:23 B&W**
Dir: John Cromwell *Cast:* Leslie Howard, Bette Davis, Frances Dee, Reginald Owen, Reginald Denny, Kay Johnson
▶ Howard, a sensitive, clubfooted medical student, falls under the spell of cockney waitress Davis, a heartless tramp who destroys his life. Powerful adaptation of W. Somerset Maugham's novel still packs an emotional punch. Davis approaches her breakthrough role with relish. Remade in 1946 and 1964.
Dist.: Various [C]

OF HUMAN BONDAGE 1964
★★★★ **NR Drama 1:39 B&W**
Dir: Ken Hughes *Cast:* Kim Novak, Laurence Harvey, Robert Morley, Siobhan McKenna, Roger Livesey
▶ Third film version of W. Somerset Maugham's classic novel about club-footed medical student Harvey's obsession with unfaithful Cockney waitress Novak lacks the honesty and resonance of the 1934 Bette Davis vehicle. Novak's accomplished performance and grim view of Edwardian London bring some life to the sentimental plot.
Dist.: MGM/UA

OF UNKNOWN ORIGIN 1983 Canadian
★★ **R Horror 1:29**
[✓] Nudity, explicit language, violence
Dir: George Pan Cosmatos *Cast:* Peter Weller, Jennifer Dale, Lawrence Dane, Kenneth Welsh, Shannon Tweed
▶ New York bank executive Weller sends his family to Vermont while he completes a company project, but his privacy is disrupted by a large, extremely aggressive rodent. Shrewd psychological twists perk up an otherwise predictable story line.
Dist.: Warner

O'HARA'S WIFE 1982
★★★★ **PG Drama 1:27**
[✓] Adult situations, explicit language
Dir: William S. Bartman *Cast:* Edward Asner, Mariette Hartley, Jodie Foster, Perry Lang, Tom Bosley, Ray Walston
▶ Hard-working attorney Asner suffers when wife Hartley suddenly dies; then she reappears as a ghost. She offers counsel on his career and travails with daughter Foster and son Lang, but since her ghost is visible only to Asner he's presumed to have gone crazy. Fine performances from quality cast.
Dist.: Vestron

OH DAD, POOR DAD, MAMA'S HUNG YOU IN THE CLOSET AND I'M FEELING SO SAD 1967
☆ **NR Comedy 1:26**
Dir: Richard Quine *Cast:* Rosalind Russell,

Robert Morse, Barbara Harris, Hugh Griffith, Jonathan Winters

▶ An early Arthur Kopit play is turned into an unwatchable mess, with Russell as an ultra-domineering mom who keeps her late husband's corpse in the closet and makes life miserable for unlikeable son Morse. Few laughs in this black comedy, only embarrassment for everyone involved.
Dist.: Paramount

OH, GOD! 1977
★ ★ ★ ★ **PG Comedy 1:44**
☑ Adult humor
Dir: Carl Reiner *Cast:* George Burns, John Denver, Teri Garr, Donald Pleasence, Ralph Bellamy, Dinah Shore
▶ God (Burns) chooses California supermarket manager Denver to spread His good word. This suburban Moses meets some skepticism from the secular world, but soon the media can't get enough of Him. Divine inspiration was casting Burns as a Supreme Being who admits that ostriches and avocados were mistakes and claims the 1969 Mets as His last big miracle. First entry in popular series.
Dist.: Warner

OH, GOD! BOOK II 1980
★ ★ ★ ★ **PG Comedy 1:34**
☑ Adult humor
Dir: Gilbert Cates *Cast:* George Burns, Suzanne Pleshette, David Birney, Louanne, John Louie, Conrad Janis, Howard Duff, Huris Corfield
▶ Less-than-inspired sequel with Burns reprising his role as the Big Guy. This time preteen Louanne gets tapped to persuade a disbelieving world that God is not dead. Havoc ensues at school and at home until Burns intervenes to convince the girl's estranged parents, Pleshette and Birney, and a team of doctors that Louanne isn't loony. Mildly diverting family fare, but the original's edge is gone, especially when Burns is off-screen.
Dist.: Warner

OH, GOD! YOU DEVIL 1984
★ ★ ★ ★ **PG Comedy 1:36**
☑ Explicit language, adult humor
Dir: Paul Bogart *Cast:* George Burns, Ted Wass, Ron Silver, Roxanne Hart, Eugene Roche, Robert Desiderio
▶ New gimmick here: Burns plays both God and the Devil. Struggling musician Wass sells his soul to become a rock superstar, only to find wealth and fame don't compensate for loss of love from his previous life. Ultimately God plays poker with the Devil to save Wass from suicide. Burns, always a rascal, is even better as Satan and supremely carries the picture. **(CC)**
Dist.: Warner

OH HEAVENLY DOG! 1980
★ ★ ★ ★ **PG Comedy/Family 1:43**
☑ Explicit language, mild violence
Dir: Joe Camp *Cast:* Chevy Chase, Jane

Seymour, Omar Sharif, Robert Morley, Alan Sues, Benji
▶ Private eye Chase, murdered during a case, is reincarnated as dog Benji to capture his killers. While pursuing the villains, Chase discovers he's still attracted to girlfriend Seymour, despite his canine `appearance. Third Benji film is racier than expected, with an amazing performance by the adorable pooch. **(CC)**
·*Dist.:* CBS/Fox

OKLAHOMA! 1955
★ ★ ★ ★ ★ **G Musical 2:23**
Dir: Fred Zinnemann *Cast:* Gordon MacRae, Shirley Jones, Charlotte Greenwood, Gloria Grahame, Eddie Albert, Rod Steiger, Eddie Albert, James Whitmore
▶ Rodgers and Hammerstein's landmark musical receives a first-rate, full-bodied film adaptation capturing all the joy and energy of the stage hit. Plot concerns the love affair between Sooner cowboy MacRae and young Laurey (Jones, in her film debut), but supporting cast (particularly Grahame, Greenwood, and Steiger) is most impressive. Oscar-winning score includes "People Will Say We're in Love" and "The Surrey With the Fringe on Top." Choreography by Agnes DeMille. **(CC)**
Dist.: CBS/Fox

OKLAHOMA ANNIE 1952
★ **NR Musical 1:30**
Dir: R. G. Springsteen *Cast:* Judy Canova, John Russell, Grant Withers, Allen Jenkins, Almira Sessions, Frank Ferguson
▶ Sheriff Russell is the heartthrob of rustic shopkeeper Canova, who becomes his deputy after capturing a bank robber. When Russell is kidnapped, it's up to Canova and the other women of the town to take on corrupt politician Ferguson and his illegal gambling house. Corny programmer, but some fun thanks to Canova's rootin' tootin' vocals. Listen to her belt "Have You Ever Been Lonely?" and "Blow the Whistle."
Dist.: Republic

OKLAHOMA KID, THE 1939
★ ★ **NR Western 1:25 B&W**
Dir: Lloyd Bacon *Cast:* James Cagney, Humphrey Bogart, Rosemary Lane, Donald Crisp, Harvey Stephens, Hugh Sothern
▶ Contrived but enjoyable Western ostensibly about the founding of Tulsa. Bogart, a land-grabbing villain, arranges the lynching of a sheriff; Cagney, a noble outlaw nicknamed the Oklahoma Kid who is the sheriff's long-lost son, rides into town for revenge. Stars overcome miscasting by adopting a tongue-in-cheek approach—Cagney even gets to sing "I Don't Want to Play in Your Yard."
Dist.: MGM/UA

OKLAHOMAN, THE 1957
★ ★ **NR Western 1:20**
Dir: Francis D. Lyon *Cast:* Joel McCrea,

Barbara Hale, Douglas Dick, Michael Pate, Anthony Caruso, Esther Dale

▶ Decent-hearted doctor McCrea decides to stay in the Sooner state after his wife dies there on their way West. But evil cattle barons Dexter and Dick vow revenge when he helps an Indian whose land they're trying to steal. Good little Western.
Dist.: MGM/UA

OLD BOYFRIENDS 1979
★ ★ R Drama 1:42
☑ Brief nudity, adult situations, explicit language
Dir: Joan Tewkesbury *Cast:* Talia Shire, Richard Jordan, Keith Carradine, John Belushi, John Houseman, Buck Henry
▶ Los Angeles psychologist Shire conquers depression over her husband's death by contacting past lovers: Jordan, a divorced filmmaker; Belushi, leader of a tacky lounge band; and Carradine, younger brother of a Vietnam fatality. Intriguing premise undone by choppy script (by Paul and Leonard Schrader) and vague point of view. Belushi and Henry offer good comic bits.
Dist.: Nelson

OLD CURIOSITY SHOP, THE 1975 British
★ ★ ★ G Musical 1:58
Dir: Michael Tuchner *Cast:* Anthony Newley, David Hemmings, David Warner, Mona Washbourne, Michael Hordern, Sarah Jane Varley
▶ In nineteenth-century England, Little Nell (Varley) and grandfather Hordern flee from hunchbacked miser Newley, to whom the old man owes money. Adaptation of the Charles Dickens classic is reminiscent of *Oliver*. Plush costumes and sets; Newley also wrote the songs. Entertaining family fare also known as *Mr. Quilp*. **(CC)**
Dist.: Vestron

OLD ENOUGH 1984
★ PG Comedy 1:28
☑ Adult situations, explicit language
Dir: Marisa Silver *Cast:* Sarah Boyd, Rainbow Harvest, Neill Barry, Danny Aiello, Susan Kingsley
▶ Wealthy young New Yorker Boyd strikes up an unlikely friendship with streetwise teenager Harvest, who teaches her about makeup and shoplifting. Modest, low-key coming-of-age comedy features a strong performance by Boyd. First-time director Silver, daughter of Joan Micklin Silver, developed her script at Robert Redford's Sundance Institute.
Dist.: Media

OLD GRINGO 1989
★ ★ ★ ★ R Drama 1:59
☑ Brief nudity, adult situations, violence
Dir: Luis Puenzo *Cast:* Jane Fonda, Gregory Peck, Jimmy Smits, Patricio Contreras, Jenny Gago, Jim Meltzer
▶ In 1914, American spinster Fonda goes to Mexico for governess job and finds herself in the middle of revolution. She is fascinated by cynical old writer Ambrose Bierce (Peck), but it is rebel general Smits who captures her heart. Searching, noble adaptation of the Carlos Fuentes novel trips over its high ambitions in second half but nevertheless conveys an evocative quality. Magnificent performance by Peck as the real-life Bierce, who disappeared in Mexico around that time. Most stirring scene: Peck recalling his youth for Fonda. **(CC)**
Dist.: RCA/Columbia

OLD IRONSIDES 1926
★ NR Action-Adventure 1:51 B&W
Dir: James Cruze *Cast:* Charles Farrell, Esther Ralston, Wallace Beery, George Bancroft, Guy Oliver, George Godfrey
▶ Celebrated activities of the *U.S.S. Constitution* as it routs the pirates on the shores of Tripoli. Hearty seamen Berry, Godfrey, and Oliver are more than a match for Saracens like Boris Karloff (briefly seen as a guard). Silent classic gives a rousing view of history.
Dist.: Paramount

OLD MAID, THE 1939
★ ★ ★ ★ NR Drama 1:35 B&W
Dir: Edmund Goulding *Cast:* Bette Davis, Miriam Hopkins, George Brent, Donald Crisp, Jane Bryan
▶ Davis secretly has an affair with Brent, who is supposed to marry her sister Hopkins. After Brent is killed in the Civil War, Davis gives birth to a girl and then joins Hopkins's household as a spinster aunt. No one knows the secret of daughter Bryan's birth, and Davis fights a losing battle for her love. One of Bette's best performances.
Dist.: MGM/UA

OLD YELLER 1957
★ ★ ★ ★ ★ G Family 1:23
Dir: Robert Stevenson *Cast:* Dorothy McGuire, Fess Parker, Tommy Kirk, Jeff York, Chuck Connors, Kevin Corcoran
▶ Left in charge of the family while father Parker joins a cattle drive, young Texas frontier boy Kirk befriends Old Yeller, a mischievous mongrel with a fearless heart. Their adventures include encounters with bears, wild boars, and a plague of rabies. Heartwarming adaptation of Fred Gipson's novel is an enduring Disney favorite. Followed by *Savage Sam*.
Dist.: Buena Vista

OLIVER! 1968 British
★ ★ ★ ★ G Musical 2:29
Dir: Carol Reed *Cast:* Ron Moody, Oliver Reed, Mark Lester, Shani Wallis, Jack Wild
▶ Romanticized musical version of Dickens's novel *Oliver Twist*. Young orphan Lester is tossed into the London streets, where he falls in with gang of London pickpockets, then is rescued by a wealthy gent who turns out to be his uncle. Fine performances by Moody as head thief, Reed as street thug, and Wild as spunky waif. Film classic won six Oscars includ-

ing Best Picture and Director. Lionel Bart's score (from his play) includes rambunctious "Food, Glorious Food" and plaintive "Where Is Love?" Striking sets vividly re-create London of the 1830s. **(CC)**
Dist.: RCA/Columbia

OLIVER & COMPANY 1988
★ ★ ★ ★ ★ **G Animation 1:12**
Dir: George Scribner *Cast:* Voices of Bette Midler, Billy Joel, Cheech Marin, Richard Mulligan, Dom DeLuise, Robert Loggia
▶ Disney variation on Dickens's *Oliver Twist* tells of orphaned New York kitten befriended by canine Dodger (Joel), human Fagin (DeLuise), and their gang of thieves. Oliver is adopted by a rich girl, then must team with pals to save her from mobster Loggia. Snappy music and fun characterizations (notably Midler's pampered poodle and Marin's streetsmart Chihuahua) make satisfying family fare.
Dist.: Buena Vista

OLIVER'S STORY 1978
★ ★ ★ **PG Romance 1:30**
☑ Adult situations, explicit language
Dir: John Korty *Cast:* Ryan O'Neal, Candice Bergen, Nicola Pagett, Edward Binns, Ray Milland
▶ Sequel to the huge hit *Love Story*. Young attorney O'Neal, still in mourning over wife's death, is all work and no play until he meets fashion heiress Bergen. Both are prisoners of their self-centered, upper-class backgrounds and their romance eventually flounders. Adapted from Erich Segal's novel, well-acted film looks slick but lacks its predecessor's gripping melodrama.
Dist.: Paramount

OLIVER TWIST 1948 British
★ ★ ★ **NR Drama 1:45 B&W**
Dir: David Lean *Cast:* Alec Guinness, John Howard Davies, Robert Newton, Kay Walsh, Anthony Newley, Henry Stephenson
▶ In nineteenth-century England, orphan Oliver Twist (Davies), after daring to ask keepers for more gruel, finds himself out on the street and in the company of thief Fagin (Guinness), the Artful Dodger (Newley), and their gang of teen pickpockets. Magnificently acted and directed adaptation of the Charles Dickens classic; Guinness's performance, although viewed as anti-Semitic upon film's first release, remains especially unforgettable. **(CC)**
Dist.: Paramount

O LUCKY MAN! 1973 British
★ **R Drama 3:01**
☑ Strong sexual content, adult situations, explicit language
Dir: Lindsay Anderson *Cast:* Malcolm McDowell, Ralph Richardson, Rachel Roberts, Arthur Lowe, Helen Mirren
▶ Hustling young salesman McDowell pushes his way to the top in bleak, post-industrial England. Superbly acted by topnotch cast, complex and thought-provoking film was a fa-

vorite of most critics. However, length, surrealism, allegorical intent, and cynicism ("If you've found the reason to live on and not to die—you are a lucky man!") make it rough going for most viewers. Beware of severely edited versions.
Dist.: Warner

OLYMPIA 1936 German
★ **NR Documentary/Sports 3:40 B&W**
Dir: Leni Riefenstahl
▶ Massive documentary on the 1936 Berlin Olympics is one of the most comprehensive and beautiful records of the games. Shot with an eye towards extolling Nazi virtues, film downplays non-Aryans like Jesse Owens, but otherwise presents a fascinating, intimate look at athletes. Several sequences—in particular the majestic diving competition—are edited with breathtaking virtuosity. Various shorter versions are also available.
Dist.: Various

OMEGA MAN, THE 1971
★ ★ ★ **PG Sci-Fi 1:38**
☑ Brief nudity, adult situations, explicit language, violence
Dir: Boris Sagal *Cast:* Charlton Heston, Anthony Zerbe, Rosalind Cash, Paul Koslo, Lincoln Kilpatrick, Eric Laneuville
▶ Most of human life has been killed by germ warfare. Los Angeles scientist Heston immunizes himself and must battle plague-stricken albino mutants known as the Family. Heston discovers a group of disease-free youngsters who may be the key to saving mankind. Visually striking and generally gripping.
Dist.: Warner

OMEGA SYNDROME 1987
★ ★ **R Action-Adventure 1:29**
☑ Adult situations, explicit language, violence
Dir: Joseph Manduke *Cast:* Ken Wahl, Doug McClure, George DiCenzo, Nicole Eggert
▶ Hard-drinking, down-on-his-luck journalist Wahl shakes out of his doldrums when daughter Eggert is kidnapped by neo-Nazi terrorists known as Omega. Teamed with Vietnam buddy DiCenzo, Wahl infiltrates Omega, rescues his daughter, and wastes the fascists in a climactic shoot-out. Formula actioner for diehards only.
Dist.: New World

OMEN, THE 1976
★ ★ ★ ★ **R Horror 1:51**
☑ Explicit language, graphic violence
Dir: Richard Donner *Cast:* Gregory Peck, Lee Remick, David Warner, Billie Whitelaw, Harvey Stephens, Leo McKern
▶ Peck, American ambassador to England, and wife Remick learn that angelic-looking surrogate son Stephens is actually the Antichrist, offspring of Satan. Many gory deaths later, Peck must attempt to kill the boy to avert Armageddon. Lurid and extremely pop-

ular film spawned sequels *Damien—Omen II* and *The Final Conflict.*
Dist.: CBS/Fox

ON A CLEAR DAY YOU CAN SEE FOREVER
1970
★ ★ ★ **G Musical 2:09**
Dir: Vincente Minnelli **Cast:** Barbra Streisand, Yves Montand, Bob Newhart, Larry Blyden, Simon Oakland, Jack Nicholson
▶ Shrink Montand becomes fascinated when patient Streisand recalls past lives under hypnosis. Unaware of the true nature of his experiments (she just wants to beat a smoking habit), she falls in love with him. Tuneful, underrated Streisand vehicle, with spectacular cinematography (especially in the flashbacks), melodic Lerner and Lane score (including title tune and "Come Back to Me"), and fine support from Newhart and Nicholson as Barbra's stepbrother.
Dist.: Paramount

ONCE BITTEN 1985
★ ★ **PG-13 Comedy 1:33**
☑ Brief nudity, adult situations, explicit language, adult humor
Dir: Howard Storm **Cast:** Lauren Hutton, Cleavon Little, Jim Carrey, Karen Kopins, Skip Lackey
▶ Frustrated Los Angeles teenager Carrey has a one-night stand with alluring countess Hutton—unaware that she preys on the blood of virgins. Can Carrey's girlfriend Kopins rescue him from the undead? Despite sultry Hutton, stylish but uninspired comedy quickly grows tedious. **(CC)**
Dist.: Vestron

ONCE IN PARIS 1978
★ ★ **PG Romance 1:39**
☑ Adult situations, explicit language
Dir: Frank D. Gilroy **Cast:** Wayne Rogers, Gayle Hunnicutt, Jack Lenoir, Phillippe March, Clement Harari, Tanya Lopert
▶ American screenwriter Rogers, on assignment in Paris, is shown the town by know-it-all chauffeur Lenoir. Rogers romances beautiful Englishwoman Hunnicutt until Lenoir also beds her. Slight, sedate, and highly personal romance (Lenoir was originally Paris chauffeur to writer/director Gilroy).
Dist.: Media

ONCE IS NOT ENOUGH 1975
★ **R Drama 2:01**
☑ Nudity, adult situations, explicit language
Dir: Guy Green **Cast:** Kirk Douglas, Alexis Smith, David Janssen, George Hamilton, Melina Mercouri, Deborah Raffin
▶ Glossy, superficial adaptation of Jacqueline Susann's best-selling soap opera describes the affairs of various jet-setters, in particular Douglas, an over-the-hill movie producer who marries wealthy lesbian Smith to please his spoiled daughter Raffin. She then seduces playboy Hamilton and writer

Janssen. Also known as *Jacqueline Susann's Once Is Not Enough.*
Dist.: Paramount

ONCE UPON A HONEYMOON 1942
★ **NR Comedy 1:57 B&W**
Dir: Leo McCarey **Cast:** Ginger Rogers, Cary Grant, Walter Slezak, Albert Dekker, Albert Basserman
▶ Romantic triangle set before World War II, with Grant a reporter who lures American stripper-turned-society-woman Rogers from her "businessman" husband Slezak. Slezak, actually a Nazi agent, then chases the couple across Europe. Stars outshine lackluster script.
Dist.: Turner

ONCE UPON A SCOUNDREL 1973
★ ★ **G Family 1:30**
Dir: George Schaefer **Cast:** Zero Mostel, Katy Jurado, Tito Vandis, Priscilla Garcia
▶ Mostel is a tyrannical Mexican land baron who puts a young man in jail to blackmail the fellow's girlfriend into marrying him. Villagers drug Mostel, convince him he is dead, and treat him like a ghost until he undergoes a Scrooge-like transformation and releases the imprisoned man. Cheery, uplifting comedy was Mostel's last film.
Dist.: Prism

ONCE UPON A TIME IN AMERICA 1984
★ ★ ★ ★ **R Crime/Drama 3:48**
☑ Rape, nudity, explicit language, graphic violence
Dir: Sergio Leone **Cast:** Robert De Niro, James Woods, Elizabeth McGovern, Tuesday Weld, William Forsythe, James Hayden
▶ Lengthy, convoluted gangster epic traces the uneasy friendship between Brooklyn thugs De Niro and Woods over a fifty-year span of rape, extortion, and murder. Film's visual sweep achieves an almost operatic intensity, but plot is often incomprehensible. First released here in two drastically shortened and re-edited versions; cassette copies still lack some footage shown in Europe. Leone's final film. **(CC)**
Dist.: Warner

ONCE UPON A TIME IN THE WEST 1969
U.S./Italian
★ ★ ★ **PG Western 2:45**
☑ Rape, explicit language, graphic violence
Dir: Sergio Leone **Cast:** Charles Bronson, Henry Fonda, Claudia Cardinale, Jason Robards, Gabriele Ferzetti, Keenan Wynn
▶ Culmination of director Leone's spaghetti Westerns is an extraordinary look at the settling of the frontier. Cardinale, newly widowed, is drawn into a land war with a railroad magnate. Bronson and Robards are outlaws who defend her against hired killers led by Fonda (outstanding in a rare villainous role). From its brilliant opening credits (featuring Woody Strode and Jack Elam) to its final

shootout, a film of breathtaking scope and detail. Avoid the re-edited shorter version.
Dist.: Paramount

ONCE WE WERE DREAMERS 1987 Israeli
★ NR Drama 1:40
☑ Violence
Dir: Uri Barbash   *Cast:* Kelly McGillis, John Shea, Christine Boisson, Arnon Zadok
▶ Sincere, high-minded drama about the early days of Israel, focusing on a Galilee commune dedicated to equality. A forbidden love affair between McGillis, a beautiful Viennese woman, and violinist Shea threatens to disrupt the delicate balance of the community. Good intentions can't salvage film's plodding style. Also known as *Unsettled Land*.
Dist.: Nelson

ON DANGEROUS GROUND 1951
★ ★ ★ NR Mystery-Suspense 1:22 B&W
Dir: Nicholas Ray   *Cast:* Robert Ryan, Ida Lupino, Ward Bond, Ed Begley, Cleo Moore, Charles Kemper
▶ Burned-out New York cop Ryan is sent to the country to unwind. There he solves the murder of farmer Bond's daughter. Lupino, the blind sister of the murderer, begs Ryan to show mercy to the troubled youth and save him from Bond's implacable revenge. Excellent film noir.
Dist.: Turner

ONE AND ONLY, THE 1978
★ ★ PG Comedy 1:38
☑ Explicit language
Dir: Carl Reiner   *Cast:* Henry Winkler, Kim Darby, Gene Saks, William Daniels, Harold Gould, Herve Villechaize
▶ Brash Midwesterner Winkler moves to New York confident he will become an acting star, but finds success elusive until manager Saks introduces him to the world of professional wrestling. Easygoing comedy presents a warmly nostalgic view of the 1950s.
Dist.: Paramount

ONE AND ONLY, GENUINE, ORIGINAL FAMILY BAND, THE 1968
★ ★ ★ G Family/Musical 1:50
Dir: Michael O'Herlihy   *Cast:* Walter Brennan, Buddy Ebsen, John Davidson, Lesley Ann Warren, Janet Blair, Kurt Russell, Steve Harmon, Richard Deacon, Wally Cox, Goldie Hawn
▶ During the 1888 election, loyal Democrat Brennan stands by his candidate Grover Cleveland. Opposing him is his large brood of Harrison-supporting Republicans. Between political discussions, the family sings the title tune, "The Happiest Girl Alive," and others. Not genuinely original, but certainly genial in the patented Disney manner.
Dist.: Buena Vista

ONE BODY TOO MANY 1944
★ NR Mystery-Suspense/Comedy 1:14 B&W

Dir: Frank McDonald   *Cast:* Jack Haley, Jean Parker, Bela Lugosi, Bernard Nedell, Blanche Yurka, Douglas Fowley
▶ A millionaire's will stipulates the potential beneficiaries must gather in the house with his body. Insurance salesman Haley arrives to ply his wares, but ends up in the middle of mysterious murders. Parker is his love interest, Lugosi the butler who may have done it. Enjoyable genre blend.
Dist.: Cable

ONE CRAZY SUMMER 1986
★ ★ ★ PG Comedy 1:33
☑ Adult situations, explicit language, adult humor
Dir: Savage Steve Holland   *Cast:* John Cusack, Demi Moore, Joel Murray, Bob Goldthwait, Curtis Armstrong, Joe Flaherty
▶ Vacationing on Nantucket, aspiring cartoonist Cusack falls for singer Moore, who's leading a protest against land developer William Hickey. Loose collection of sight gags and brief animated sequences add up to a pleasant but standard teen comedy. **(CC)**
Dist.: Warner

ONE DARK NIGHT 1983
★ ★ PG Horror 1:29
☑ Adult situations, explicit language, violence
Dir: Tom McLoughlin   *Cast:* Meg Tilly, Robin Evans, Leslie Speights, Elizabeth Daily, Adam West, Melissa Newman
▶ Teen Tilly must spend a night in a local mausoleum as part of a sorority initiation. A Russian psychic is buried there and his powers survive the grave to cause trouble for Tilly and her sorority sisters. Some original touches but farfetched plot and mediocre special effects.
Dist.: HBO

ONE DAY IN THE LIFE OF IVAN DENISOVICH 1971 British/Norwegian
★ G Drama 1:40
Dir: Caspar Wrede   *Cast:* Tom Courtenay, Espen Skjonberg, James Maxwell, Alfred Burke, Eric Thompson, Alf Malland
▶ Courtenay is convincingly lean and pallid in this crisp adaptation of Alexander Solzhenitsyn's novel of life in a Soviet concentration camp. Story details a single dawn-to-dusk period, showing the small triumphs and stratagems that keep Courtenay going. Cinematographer Sven Nyqvist's striking images include a fish's head staring up out of a bowl of watery gruel and lines of ragged prisoners crunching off to work against a bracingly white winter landscape.
Dist.: SVS

ONE DEADLY SUMMER 1983 French
★ R Mystery-Suspense 2:10
☑ Rape, nudity, strong sexual content, adult situations, explicit language, violence
Dir: Jean Becker   *Cast:* Isabelle Adjani,

Alain Souchon, Suzanne Flon, Francois Cluzet, Jenny Cleve, Manuel Gelin

▶ Emotionally unstable young Adjani seeks to kill the men who once raped her mother. Only after she has seduced the three en route to her planned revenge does she learn they are not guilty. She is institutionalized while her husband mistakenly slays the innocent men. Adjani sizzles in otherwise pretentious and confused story. **(CC)** S
Dist.: MCA

ONE DOWN, TWO TO GO 1983
☆ **PG Action-Adventure 1:24**
☑ Adult situations, explicit language, violence
Dir: Fred Williamson *Cast:* Jim Brown, Fred Williamson, Richard Roundtree, Jim Kelly, Paula Sills, Laura Loftus

▶ Black-exploitation actors and clichés are dredged up for one last, straight-faced go round, with Roundtree as a karate/boxing promoter who enlists Brown and Williamson to help him take on mobsters. The acting is subamateur; the story is unbelievable; and the budget must have been next to nothing.
Dist.: Media

ONE-EYED JACKS 1961
★ ★ ★ ★ **NR Western 2:21**
Dir: Marlon Brando *Cast:* Marlon Brando, Karl Malden, Pina Pillicer, Katy Jurado, Ben Johnson, Slim Pickens

▶ Bank robber Brando, betrayed by partner Malden, spends five years in a Mexican prison. On release, he confronts Malden, now a sheriff, in Monterey. Brando's only turn at directing is a rambling but often intriguing psychological Western with stunning, Oscar-nominated photography.
Dist.: Paramount

ONE FLEW OVER THE CUCKOO'S NEST 1975
★ ★ ★ ★ ★ **R Comedy/Drama 2:13**
☑ Adult situations, explicit language
Dir: Milos Forman *Cast:* Jack Nicholson, Louise Fletcher, Will Sampson, Brad Dourif, Scatman Crothers, Danny DeVito

▶ Entertaining and moving adaptation of Ken Kesey's antiestablishment novel. Troublemaking convict Nicholson is transferred to a mental hospital. There he tries to rally patients Dourif, DeVito, and Sampson against the iron rule of head nurse Fletcher. Picture swept top five Academy Awards, first to do so in forty years. Nicholson soars.
Dist.: Thorn/EMI

ONE FRIGHTENED NIGHT 1935
★ **NR Mystery-Suspense 1:05 B&W**
Dir: Christy Cabanne *Cast:* Charley Grapewin, Mary Carlisle, Arthur Hohl, Wallace Ford, Lucien Littlefield, Regis Toomey

▶ Anticipation is high among greedy family members when wealthy patriarch Grapewin gathers them together for the reading of his will. When Grapewin's long-lost granddaugh-

ter shows up, she stands to inherit a fortune. Unfortunately, there are two of her, and one's an imposter. Well-crafted mystery.
Dist.: KVC

ONE FROM THE HEART 1982
★ **R Romance/Comedy 1:40**
☑ Brief nudity, adult situations, explicit language
Dir: Francis Coppola *Cast:* Frederic Forrest, Teri Garr, Raul Julia, Nastassia Kinski, Harry Dean Stanton, Lainie Kazan

▶ Longtime Las Vegas lovers Forrest and Garr quarrel on their anniversary. Each cavorts with respective one-night stands Kinski and Julia while wishing they were reunited. Director Coppola hoped to create a homage to old-style Hollywood tinsel, but insubstantial script sabotaged his intent. Picture is lushly gorgeous, with breathtaking sets from Dean Tavoularis and striking cinematography by Vittorio Storaro, but dull result lacks heart.
Dist.: RCA/Columbia

101 DALMATIONS 1961
★ ★ ★ ★ ★ **G Animation 1:19**
Dir: Wolfgang Reitherman, Hamilton Luske, Clyde Geronimi *Cast:* Voices of Rod Taylor, Betty Lou Gerson, J. Pat O'Malley, Martha Wentworth

▶ Male dalmation Pongo arranges for bachelor master to meet pretty woman with female dalmation Perdita. The humans marry, and puppies are soon born. When villainous Cruella De Ville kidnaps the pups to make a fur coat, it's Pongo and Perdita to the rescue. Enthralling family fare has thrills, chills, romance, and comedy.
Dist.: Buena Vista

100 RIFLES 1969
★ ★ ★ **PG Western 1:50**
☑ Adult situations, explicit language, violence
Dir: Tom Gries *Cast:* Jim Brown, Raquel Welch, Burt Reynolds, Fernando Lamas, Dan O'Herlihy

▶ Sheriff Brown pursues renegade halfbreed Reynolds, who has just stolen a shipment of guns for an uprising against sadistic Mexican officer Lamas and railroad tycoon O'Herlihy. Brown's priorities are tested when he falls for Welch, Reynolds's squaw and a Yaqui Indian guerrilla leader. Reynolds's ingratiating performance steals this violent but routine Western.
Dist.: CBS/Fox

ONE MAGIC CHRISTMAS 1985
★ ★ ★ ★ **G Drama/Family 1:40**
Dir: Philip Borsos *Cast:* Mary Steenburgen, Gary Basaraba, Harry Dean Stanton, Arthur Hill, Elisabeth Harnois, Robbie Magwood, Jan Rubes

▶ Impoverished mother Steenburgen sinks into despair as the holidays near, but guardian angel Stanton renews her faith with a series of unexpected miracles. Sincere but sur-

prisingly dark Disney fantasy is an extremely effective Yuletide tearjerker. Climax features Rubes as a touchingly realistic Santa Claus.
Dist.: Buena Vista

ONE MAN FORCE 1988
★ ★ ★ R Action-Adventure 1:45
☑ Adult situations, explicit language, violence
Dir: Dale Trevillion *Cast:* John Matuszak, Ronny Cox, Charles Napier, Sharon Farrell, Sam Jones, Richard Lynch
▶ By-the-book detective Matuszak throws the book away after his partner is killed by drug dealers. Suspended from the force, he goes into private investigation, and discovers that the drug dealers are behind the bizarre kidnapping of a rock star. Ex-football player Matuszak does what is expected of him, and rest of the film delivers its action with solid proficiency.
Dist.: Academy

ONE MAN JURY 1978
★ R Action-Adventure 1:44
☑ Adult situations, explicit language, violence
Dir: Charles Martin *Cast:* Jack Palance, Christopher Mitchum, Pamela Shoop, Angel Tompkins, Joe Spinell, Cara Williams
▶ Palance takes the law into his own hands to deliver a "fair and speedy trial" to thugs, lowlifes, criminals, and others while investigating the slasher killings of pretty young girls. *Death Wish* ripoff looks cheap and dissipates suspense in pointless subplots. Also known as *The Cop Who Played God.*
Dist.: United

ONE MILLION B.C. 1940
★ NR Drama 1:20 B&W
Dir: Hal Roach, Hal Roach, Jr. *Cast:* Victor Mature, Carole Landis, Lon Chaney, Jr., John Hubbard, Mamo Clark, Jean Porter
▶ Wackily serious prehistoric fantasy, with Mature being banished by cave patriarch Chaney and wandering a dinosaur-strewn landscape on the way to a final clinch with refined cave lady Landis. Dinosaurs of the lizard variety typify the cheap special effects. Legendary director D. W. Griffith was briefly involved in making the picture. Remade in 1966 as *One Million Years B.C.*.
Dist.: Fox Hills

ONE MINUTE TO ZERO 1952
★ ★ NR War 1:45 B&W
Dir: Tay Garnett *Cast:* Robert Mitchum, Ann Blyth, William Talman, Richard Egan, Charles McGraw
▶ Combat-hardened Korean War colonel Mitchum finds himself in a moral dilemma as he tries to evacuate U.S. citizens amid flood of refugees and rain of bombs. Mitchum works hard, but despite some real combat footage, overall effort is dour and routine.
Dist.: Turner

ONE MORE SATURDAY NIGHT 1986
★ R Comedy 1:31
☑ Brief nudity, adult situations, explicit language
Dir: Dennis Klein *Cast:* Tom Davis, Al Franken, Moira Harris, Frank Howard, Bess Meyer
▶ Uneventful comedy about mishaps and mixups in the small town of St. Cloud, Minnesota. "Saturday Night Live" veterans Franken and Davis play visiting rock musicians on the prowl for dates; other subplots involve a widower dating for the first time in years and teens wrecking a house during an unplanned party. Bland film was produced by Dan Aykroyd.
Dist.: RCA/Columbia

ONE NIGHT OF LOVE 1934
★ ★ NR Musical 1:20 B&W
Dir: Victor Schertzinger *Cast:* Grace Moore, Tullio Carminati, Lyle Talbot, Mona Barrie, Jessie Ralph, Luis Alberni
▶ After hearing Moore warble in a cafe, vocal teacher Carminati offers to take her on as a protégé. Moore falls in love with him, but imperils her opera debut when she becomes jealous of another student. One of the best movie musicals set in the world of opera. Includes title song and excerpts from *Carmen* and *Lucia de Lammermoor.* Moore was nominated for Best Actress and Louis Silvers won an Oscar for the score.
Dist.: RCA/Columbia

ONE OF OUR AIRCRAFT IS MISSING 1942
British
★ ★ NR War 1:43 B&W
Dir: Michael Powell, Emeric Pressburger
Cast: Godfrey Tearle, Eric Portman, Hugh Williams, Bernard Miles, Hugh Burden, Emrys Jones
▶ During World War II, a British plane is shot down over Nazi-occupied Holland. The crew men hook up with the Dutch Resistance to safely escape the country. Vivid direction creates a hushed, ultrarealistic atmosphere, complementing a suspenseful screenplay that keeps the heroes in constant jeopardy.
Dist.: Republic

ONE OF OUR DINOSAURS IS MISSING 1975
★ ★ ★ G Comedy 1:41
Dir: Robert Stevenson *Cast:* Peter Ustinov, Helen Hayes, Clive Revill, Derek Nimmo, Joan Sims
▶ Chinese spies steal a dinosaur fossil containing top-secret microfilm from a British museum. Scotland Yard is baffled until nanny Hayes and her friends tackle the case. Lower-grade Disney offering filled with weak slapstick chases.
Dist.: Buena Vista

ONE ON ONE 1977
★ ★ ★ ★ PG Drama 1:38
☑ Explicit language

Dir: Lamont Johnson *Cast:* Robby Benson, Annette O'Toole, G. D. Spradlin, Gail Strickland, Melanie Griffith

▶ Benson, a small-town high schooler, wins a basketball scholarship to a large university, but is quickly overwhelmed by coach Spradlin's demanding training regimen. Beautiful tutor O'Toole helps him cope with classes and sports. Inspiring underdog drama was written by Benson and his father, Jerry Segal.

Dist.: Warner

ONE RAINY AFTERNOON 1936
★ NR Comedy 1:18 B&W
Dir: Rowland V. Lee *Cast:* Francis Lederer, Ida Lupino, Hugh Herbert, Roland Young, Erik Rhodes, Mischa Auer

▶ In a Paris movie theater, actor Lederer kisses Lupino, having mistaken her for his lover. The incident causes a public scandal, bringing down the wrath of the law on the thespian. However, Lupino decides she prefers Lederer to her fiancé. A charming confection.

Dist.: Video Yesteryear

ONE SINGS, THE OTHER DOESN'T 1976 French
☆ NR Drama 1:45
☑ Nudity, adult situations
Dir: Agnes Varda *Cast:* Valerie Mairesse, Therese Liotard, Ali Raffi, Robert Dadies

▶ Widely divergent lives of devoted friends Liotard and Mairesse are shown as they work out their liberation through pregnancies, abortions, careers, and marriages. A somewhat preachy polemic, very much an artifact of its era. [S]

Dist.: RCA/Columbia

ONE SUMMER LOVE 1976
★★ PG Drama 1:35
☑ Adult situations, violence
Dir: Gilbert Cates *Cast:* Beau Bridges, Susan Sarandon, Mildred Dunnock, Michael B. Miller, Linda Miller, Ann Wedgeworth

▶ Connecticut mental patient Bridges has trouble adjusting to the real world upon release and seeks comfort from a variety of surrogate mothers. Sarandon, a movie theater concession clerk, falls for his naive view of life and helps him trace his parents. Earnest drama suffers from predictable plotting.

Dist.: HBO

ONE THAT GOT AWAY, THE 1958 British
★★ NR Action-Adventure 1:46 B&W
Dir: Roy (Ward) Baker *Cast:* Hardy Kruger, Colin Gordon, Michael Goodliffe, Terence Alexander, Jack Gwillim, Andrew Faulds

▶ Nazi Luftwaffe pilot Kruger is shot down over Britain and taken prisoner. Kruger brashly boasts to the mild-mannered British that he will escape. With a double-agent in among those who are guarding him, Kruger gets a chance to make good on his boast. Subdued but good-looking suspenser.

Dist.: IUD

1001 ARABIAN NIGHTS 1959
★★★★ NR Animation 1:16
Dir: Jack Kinney *Cast:* Voices of Jim Backus, Kathryn Grant, Dwayne Hickman, Hans Conried, Herschel Bernardi

▶ Baghdad merchant Abdul Azziz Magoo discovers a genie in one of his lamps, leading to magical adventures involving his nephew Aladdin. Charming animated version of the famous Arabian Nights tales was nearsighted Mr. Magoo's feature-film debut. Pleasant musical score by George Duning.

Dist.: RCA/Columbia

ONE TOUCH OF VENUS 1948
★★ NR Musical 1:22 B&W
Dir: William A. Seiter *Cast:* Robert Walker, Ava Gardner, Dick Haymes, Eve Arden, Olga San Juan, Tom Conway

▶ Department store window dresser Walker kisses a statue of Venus, which then comes to life as Gardner. Her romantic spell is so powerful that she not only wins Walker, but brings love to Haymes and San Juan. Cute comic fantasy, based on the Kurt Weill/Ogden Nash/S. J. Perelman stage musical. Songs include "Speak Low" and "Don't Look Now But My Heart Is Showing."

Dist.: Republic

ONE TRICK PONY 1980
★ R Drama 1:40
☑ Nudity, adult situations, explicit language
Dir: Robert M. Young *Cast:* Paul Simon, Blair Brown, Rip Torn, Joan Hackett, Allen Goorwitz, Mare Winningham

▶ Earnest but predictable drama about Simon, a once-popular musician confronting various crises: pressure from record company execs for a new hit, an impending divorce, an affair with a married woman, etc. Simon, who also wrote the script and score (including "Late in the Evening"), gives a creditable performance. Appearances by the B-52's, Sam and Dave, the Lovin' Spoonful, and Lou Reed as an egotistical producer.

Dist.: Warner

ONE, TWO, THREE 1961
★★★ NR Comedy 1:48 B&W
Dir: Billy Wilder *Cast:* James Cagney, Horst Buchholz, Pamela Tiffin, Arlene Francis, Lilo Pulver, Howard St. John, Red Buttons

▶ In West Berlin, Coca-Cola executive Cagney, told to look after the boss's daughter (Tiffin), tries to turn her Communist husband Buchholz into a proper capitalist. Fast-paced and very funny Cold War satire, dominated by Cagney's wonderfully blustering characterization.

Dist.: MGM/UA

ONE WILD MOMENT 1977 French
★ R Drama 1:28
☑ Nudity, adult situations, explicit language
Dir: Claude Berri *Cast:* Jean-Pierre Marielle, Victor Lanoux, Agnes Soral, Christine Dejoux, Martine Sarcey

► On a Riviera vacation, life-long friendship between middle-aged Lanoux and Marielle is spoiled when Marielle has an affair with Lanoux's seventeen-year-old daughter. Well-done, effective film shows poignancy of characters' dilemma. Plot was borrowed for 1984 American film *Blame It on Rio.* [S]
Dist.: RCA/Columbia

ONE WOMAN OR TWO 1985 French
☆ **PG-13 Romance/Comedy 1:37**
☑ Nudity, explicit language
Dir: Daniel Vigne ***Cast:*** Gerard Depardieu, Sigourney Weaver, Michel Aumont, Dr. Ruth Westheimer, Zabou, Jean-Pierre Bisson
► Archaeologist Depardieu discovers remnants of prehistoric woman. Mistaking ad exec Weaver for Westheimer, a philanthropist with cash for future research, Depardieu whisks Weaver off to his dig and falls in love. Harmless romp with fine cast aspires to lunacy of classic screwball comedies but often falls short of the mark.
Dist.: Vestron

ON GOLDEN POND 1981
★★★★★ **PG Drama 1:49**
☑ Explicit language
Dir: Mark Rydell ***Cast:*** Katharine Hepburn, Henry Fonda, Jane Fonda, Dabney Coleman, Doug McKeon, William Lanteau
► Crotchety Yankee retiree Henry Fonda and spunky wife Hepburn find idyllic summer on New England lake disrupted when daughter Jane Fonda and fiancé Coleman leave his unruly son McKeon in their care. He learns to be civil while the old man learns to loosen up and love, so that he and daughter can overcome lifelong hostility. Screenplay by Ernest Thompson from his Broadway hit. Splendid performances from all, but Fonda steals the show in his last film. Oscars went to Fonda (his first in a long and accomplished career), Hepburn, and Thompson.
Dist.: J2 Communications

ON HER MAJESTY'S SECRET SERVICE 1969 British
★★★ **PG Espionage/Action-Adventure 2:20**
☑ Violence
Dir: Peter Hunt ***Cast:*** George Lazenby, Diana Rigg, Telly Savalas, Ilse Steppat, Gabriele Ferzetti, Bernard Lee
► James Bond (Lazenby), while battling archvillain Blofeld's (Savalas) plan to poison international food supply, falls in love with and marries gangster's daughter Rigg. First non-Connery Bond lacks Sean's charisma (although George tries gallantly); otherwise first-class, with terrific chase scenes, more depth and fewer gimmicks than usual. The ill-fated romance with fetching Diana provides some of the most poignant moments in the whole series.
Dist.: MGM/UA

ONION FIELD, THE 1979
★★★★ **R Drama 2:01**
☑ Brief nudity, explicit language, violence
Dir: Harold Becker ***Cast:*** John Savage, James Woods, Franklyn Seales, Ronny Cox, Ted Danson, David Huffman
► In 1963, small-time criminals Woods and Seales kidnap two cops, kill one, and are later apprehended. As surviving policeman Savage struggles with his guilt, the killers manage to frustrate the justice system and avoid the death penalty. Gutsy, realistic, and strongly crafted indictment of the legal system based on the book (a true story) by Joseph Wambaugh. Exceptional performances by Woods and Savage.
Dist.: Nelson

ONLY ANGELS HAVE WINGS 1939
★★★ **NR Drama 2:01 B&W**
Dir: Howard Hawks ***Cast:*** Cary Grant, Jean Arthur, Richard Barthelmess, Rita Hayworth, Thomas Mitchell, Sig Rumann
► Stylized, highly charged adventure about foolhardy aviators under pressure to deliver mail over the Andes Mountains despite constant bad weather. Arrival of showgirl Arthur, who's immediately drawn to top pilot Grant, increases tension among the fliers. Perfect example of golden-era Hollywood storytelling is filled with memorable scenes, particularly a grim dinner after a crash.
Dist.: RCA/Columbia

ONLY THE VALIANT 1951
★ **NR Western 1:45 B&W**
Dir: Gordon Douglas ***Cast:*** Gregory Peck, Barbara Payton, Ward Bond, Gig Young, Lon Chaney, Jr., Neville Brand
► Tough army captain Peck is assigned to defend a mountain pass from Apache attack. Not an easy task: his troops are outnumbered and they hate his disciplinarian ways. Also making Peck's life difficult is his competition with Young for Payton. Average Western with a fine cast.
Dist.: Republic

ONLY TWO CAN PLAY 1962 British
★ **NR Comedy 1:46 B&W**
Dir: Sidney Gilliat ***Cast:*** Peter Sellers, Mai Zetterling, Virginia Maskell, Richard Attenborough, Kenneth Griffiths, Maudie Edwards
► Married librarian Sellers, unhappy with his job, tries to land a promotion through romance with big shot's wife Zetterling. He fails at infidelity while his wife is wooed by poet Attenborough. Amusing adaptation of Kingsley Amis novel *That Uncertain Feeling* features sharp turns by Sellers and Attenborough.
Dist.: RCA/Columbia

ONLY WHEN I LAUGH 1981
★★★★ **R Comedy/Drama 1:55**
☑ Brief nudity, adult situations, explicit language, adult humor
Dir: Glenn Jordan ***Cast:*** Marsha Mason,

Kristy McNichol, James Coco, Joan Hackett, David Dukes

▶ After a stay in a rehab clinic, actress Mason tries to rebuild her relationship with daughter McNichol. Mason, fighting the temptation to drink again when personal and professional problems surface, is wonderful and sympathetic; Coco and Hackett provide able support (all were Oscar-nominated) and McNichol holds her own in this august company. Satisfying Neil Simon screenplay combines one-liners with realistic look at life's disappointments and triumphs.
Dist.: RCA/Columbia

ON THE BEACH 1959
★ ★ ★ NR Drama 2:13 B&W
Dir: Stanley Kramer *Cast:* Gregory Peck, Ava Gardner, Fred Astaire, Anthony Perkins, Donna Anderson

▶ After a nuclear explosion devastates the world, the sole survivors (the crew of a sub captained by Peck and the people of Australia) deal with their impending radioactive doom. Haunting and powerful, superbly performed, and with a strong antiwar statement. From the novel by Nevil Shute.
Dist.: CBS/Fox

ON THE EDGE 1985
★ ★ PG-13 Drama/Sports 1:35
☑ Brief nudity, explicit language
Dir: Rob Nilsson *Cast:* Bruce Dern, John Marley, Bill Bailey, Jim Haynie, Pam Grier

▶ Middle-aged runner Dern, banned from the sport for twenty years, pins his hopes for personal redemption on California's grueling Dipsea Race (renamed Cielo-Sea here), a beautiful but challenging mountain course. Sincere, uplifting film features an inspiring climax.
Dist.: Vestron

ON THE LINE 1985
★ ★ ★ R Action-Adventure 1:45
☑ Nudity, adult situations, explicit language, violence
Dir: Jose Louis Boraw *Cast:* David Carradine, Scott Wilson, Victoria Abril, Sam Jaffe, Jeff Delger, Paul Richardson

▶ Delger and Richardson arrive to become patrolmen on the Texas/Mexico border, where Carradine runs an immigrant smuggling ring. Sadistic patrolman Wilson causes problems when he kills Mexican child in a raid. Delger has married a lovely Mexican prostitute but can't bring her over the border. Lusty but not-very-likable film has hectic pace and lots of action.
Dist.: Nelson

ON THE NICKEL 1980
★ R Drama 1:36
☑ Nudity, adult situations, explicit language, violence
Dir: Ralph Waite *Cast:* Donald Moffat, Ralph Waite, Penelope Allen, Hal Williams, Jack Kehoe

▶ Skid-row melodrama about former bottle hound Moffat who's lifted himself out of the gutter but doesn't know what to do for a second act. His efforts to assist old pal Waite threaten to drag him back down into the world of drunken characters from which he emerged. Very well-photographed, sincere, but maudlin.
Dist.: Vestron

ON THE RIGHT TRACK 1981
★ ★ ★ ★ PG Comedy 1:38
☑ Adult situations, explicit language, mild violence
Dir: Lee Philips *Cast:* Gary Coleman, Maureen Stapleton, Michael Lembeck, Norman Fell, Lisa Eilbacher, Bill Russell

▶ Ten-year-old shoeshine boy Coleman lives in Chicago's Union Station, where his friends include affable bag lady Stapleton. When Coleman uses his psychic powers to pick horses at the racetrack, everyone wants to be his friend. Social worker Lembeck and arcade employee Eilbacher fall in love and rescue Coleman from exploitation.
Dist.: CBS/Fox

ON THE TOWN 1950
★ ★ ★ NR Musical 1:37
Dir: Gene Kelly, Stanley Donen *Cast:* Gene Kelly, Frank Sinatra, Ann Miller, Vera-Ellen, Jules Munshin, Betty Garrett

▶ "Gotta pick up a date, maybe seven or eight" is the mission for sailors Kelly, Sinatra, and Munshin on a one-day leave in "New York, New York, a helluva town." Kelly pursues subway poster girl Vera-Ellen, Sinatra finds romance with cabbie Garrett, and cavemanish Munshin pairs off with Miller, doing a study on prehistoric times. Exuberant musical classic gives you a tour of famous New York City locations to the bounce of a tuneful score by Betty Comden, Adolph Green, Leonard Bernstein, and Roger Edens.
Dist.: MGM/UA

ON THE WATERFRONT 1954
★ ★ ★ ★ NR Drama 1:47 B&W
Dir: Elia Kazan *Cast:* Marlon Brando, Eva Marie Saint, Karl Malden, Lee J. Cobb, Rod Steiger, Leif Erickson

▶ "I coulda been a contender," pleads exboxer-turned-longshoreman Brando to his brother Steiger. Both are involved with corrupt union boss Cobb, responsible for the death of a dock worker, but Brando turns against Cobb under the influence of crusading priest Malden and the dead man's sister, Saint. Hard-hitting and incredibly powerful; deservedly one of the most acclaimed films of all time. Winner of eight Oscars including Picture, Director, Actor (Brando), Supporting Actress (Saint). **(CC)**
Dist.: RCA/Columbia

ON THE YARD 1979
★ ★ ★ R Drama 1:41
☑ Explicit language, violence

Dir: Raphael D. Silver *Cast:* Thomas Waites, John Heard, Mike Kellin, Richard Bright, Joe Grifasi

▶ Conflict escalates between Waites, an inmate who runs the prison black market, and Heard, a convict who cannot pay him back for fifteen packs of cigarettes. Convincing ensemble acting, excellent jazz score, and realistic prison environnment. However, plot lacks focus and tone is generally downbeat.
Dist.: Media

ON VALENTINE'S DAY 1986
★ **PG Drama 1:46**
☑ Adult situations, explicit language
Dir: Ken Harrison *Cast:* William Converse-Roberts, Hallie Foote, Michael Higgins, Steven Hill, Rochelle Oliver, Matthew Broderick
▶ Second in Horton Foote's semiautobiographical cycle of nine plays about a small Texas town is a literate but slow-moving account of various members of the Robedaux family, in particular pregnant Foote, wife of Converse-Roberts. Having eloped on Valentine's Day, 1917, she hopes for a reconciliation with her parents over Christmas. A prequel to *1918*, paired together as *Story of a Marriage* for TV.
Dist.: Warner

OPEN CITY 1945 Italian
★ **NR Drama 1:43 B&W**
Dir: Roberto Rossellini *Cast:* Aldo Fabrizi, Anna Magnani, Marcello Pagliero, Harry Feist, Francesco Grandjacquet, Maria Michi
▶ During World War II, Italian Resistance fighter Pagliero, hunted by the Gestapo, hides with cohort Grandjacquet and his fiancée Magnani. Priest Fabrizi, another underground member, is also endangered as the Nazis close in. Landmark Italian neorealist classic paints a still powerful, stark portrait. Oscar-nominated screenplay co-written by Federico Fellini. Ⓢ
Dist.: Various

OPERATION C.I.A. 1965
★★ **NR Action-Adventure 1:30 B&W**
Dir: Christian Nyby *Cast:* Burt Reynolds, Kieu Chinh, Danielle Aubry, John Hoyt, Cyril Collack
▶ Pretending to be a visiting professor, CIA agent Reynolds snoops around Saigon, hoping to unravel the murder of a fellow agent. In the process he uncovers a plot to gas the U.S. embassy. Reynolds and fellow spies Chinh and Aubry are all attractive, but script is dull and muddled.
Dist.: CBS/Fox

OPERATION PETTICOAT 1959
★★★ **NR Comedy 2:04**
Dir: Blake Edwards *Cast:* Cary Grant, Tony Curtis, Joan O'Brien, Dina Merrill, Arthur O'-Connell
▶ Extremely popular service comedy about a crippled sub captained by Grant but controlled by smooth-talking con man Curtis. As a result of one of Curtis's schemes, Grant finds five beautiful nurses squeezed into the sub's tight confines. Stars make a great comic pair, and they're supported by consistently strong gags. Financially Grant's most successful effort, film inspired a TV movie and brief series.
Dist.: Republic

OPERATION THUNDERBOLT 1978 Israeli
★★★★ **PG Action-Adventure 2:00**
☑ Violence
Dir: Menahem Golan *Cast:* Yehoram Gaon, Klaus Kinski, Assaf Dayan, Sybil Danning, Ori Levy, Arik Lavi
▶ True story of the raid on Entebbe Airport: terrorists hijack Tel Aviv–Paris flight and bring it to Uganda. Israeli soldiers stage a daring mission to rescue them. Straightforward and exciting; enough action to overcome crude direction and unconvincing performances. Some subtitles but most of the dialogue is in English. Nominated for Oscar as Best Foreign Film. Other films about the same event: *Raid on Entebbe* and *Victory at Entebbe*. Ⓢ
Dist.: MGM/UA

OPPORTUNITY KNOCKS 1990
★★★ **PG-13 Comedy 1:45**
☑ Explicit language, violence
Dir: Donald Petrie *Cast:* Dana Carvey, Todd Graff, Julia Campbell, Robert Loggia, Milo O'Shea, Doris Belack
▶ On the run from the mob, con artist Carvey impersonates a business wiz, wooing Campbell to win over her corporate father Loggia. The scam gets complicated when he develops real feelings for her. Lightweight vehicle for the "Saturday Night Live" star. Fans may enjoy his bits of shtick, but neither he nor the writers bother to create a sympathetic characterization. **(CC)**
Dist.: MCA

OPPOSING FORCE 1986
★★★ **R Action-Adventure 1:37**
☑ Rape, nudity, adult situations, explicit language, violence
Dir: Eric Karson *Cast:* Tom Skerritt, Lisa Eichhorn, Anthony Zerbe, Richard Roundtree, Robert Wightman, John Considine
▶ Air Force recruits, including one female, Eichhorn, are dropped on a deserted Philippine island for war games which get murderously out of hand when psychotic commander Zerbe plays for keeps. Well-staged action, good cast, and generally entertaining although short on logic.
Dist.: HBO

OPTIONS 1989
★★ **PG Comedy 1:32**
☑ Mild violence
Dir: Conrad Hool *Cast:* Matt Salinger, Joanna Pacula, John Kani, James Keach
▶ Salinger's an MBA who tracks down real-life stories for the movies. His greedy boss sends him to Africa to look up disinherited princess

Pacula. Despite being a nervous nellie, he saves Pacula when she's kidnapped by her shotgun-toting ex-husband. Pacula is gorgeous, but there's barely a giggle in this bottom-of-the-barrel comedy. Male lead is the son of author J. D. Salinger.
Dist.: Vestron

ORCA 1977
★★★★ **PG Mystery-Suspense 1:32**
☑ Explicit language, violence
Dir: Michael Anderson ***Cast:*** Richard Harris, Charlotte Rampling, Will Sampson, Keenan Wynn, Bo Derek
▶ When fisherman Harris kills pregnant killer whale, he finds himself stalked by her revenge-minded mate. Generates plenty of far-fetched tension and spectacular scares, as when the whale knocks over a house to snack on Bo's leg. Effective Ennio Morricone score; pompous dialogue from Rampling, unbelievably cast as a whale expert.
Dist.: Paramount

ORDEAL BY INNOCENCE 1985
★★ **PG-13 Mystery-Suspense 1:30**
☑ Brief nudity, adult situations, violence
Dir: Desmond Davis ***Cast:*** Donald Sutherland, Sarah Miles, Faye Dunaway, Ian McShane, Christopher Plummer
▶ Dr. Arthur Calgary (Sutherland) returns from a polar expedition to discover that he was the alibi for a man hanged two years earlier for murder. When the police won't reopen the case, Calgary decides to investigate the murder himself. A moderately entertaining mystery marred by a less than riveting plot and rather wooden performances. Still, genre fans will enjoy the usual Agatha Christie mix of suspects and clues.
Dist.: MGM/UA

ORDET 1955 Danish
☆ **NR Drama 2:06 B&W**
Dir: Carl Theodor Dreyer ***Cast:*** Henrik Malberg, Emil Hass Christensen, Preben Lerdorff Rye, Cay Kristiansen, Birgitte Federspiel, Sylvia Eckhausen
▶ Beliefs of devout farming family in Jutland are put to a severe test when mother Federspiel falls ill; brother-in-law Rye, dismissed as simpleminded, claims his divine powers will cure her. Extremely demanding examination of faith has a strong critical reputation; climax is a stunning screen approximation of religious fervor. Deliberate pacing and stylized acting will disappoint casual viewers. Also known as *The Word*. [S]
Dist.: Foothill

ORDINARY PEOPLE 1980
★★★★ **R Drama 2:04**
☑ Adult situations, explicit language
Dir: Robert Redford ***Cast:*** Donald Sutherland, Mary Tyler Moore, Judd Hirsch, Timothy Hutton, Elizabeth McGovern, Dinah Manoff
▶ After a boating accident that kills his older brother and a suicide attempt, Hutton visits shrink Hirsch to deal with his guilt and his emotionally repressed mother Moore. Dad Sutherland and mom gradually grow apart. Oscars for Best Picture, Director, and Supporting Actor (Hutton) went to this immaculately crafted, emotionally wrenching examination of upper-middle-class angst. Superbly performed (especially by Hutton), with wonderful use of suburban Chicago locations.
Dist.: Paramount

ORGANIZATION, THE 1971
★★ **PG Drama 1:47**
☑ Adult situations, explicit language, violence
Dir: Don Medford ***Cast:*** Sidney Poitier, Barbara McNair, Gerald S. O'Loughlin, Sheree North, Fred Beir, Allen Garfield
▶ Poitier reprises his *In the Heat of the Night* role as Virgil Tibbs, a hard-boiled cop trying to break up a drug ring. Antidrug vigilantes are framed for a murder; when Poitier tries to clear them, he's suspended from the force. Above-average cop film with driving action and a strong climax. Look for Ron O'Neal and Raul Julia in small roles. **(CC)**
Dist.: CBS/Fox

ORPHANS 1987
★★ **R Drama 2:00**
☑ Adult situations, explicit language, violence
Dir: Alan J. Pakula ***Cast:*** Albert Finney, Matthew Modine, Kevin Anderson, John Kellogg, Anthony Heald
▶ Orphaned brothers, manipulative Modine and naive Anderson, kidnap alcoholic gangster Finney. A strange family relationship develops as Finney becomes a father figure to his captors. Grandstanding performances by the talented trio get the most out of the juicy dialogue. However, weird characterizations and claustrophobic conflict will limit appeal. From Lyle Kessler's Off-Broadway play. **(CC)**
Dist.: Warner

ORPHEUS 1949 French
☆ **NR Fantasy 1:35 B&W**
Dir: Jean Cocteau ***Cast:*** Jean Marais, François Périer, Maria Casares, Marie Dea, Juliette Greco, Roger Blin
▶ Imagistic fantasy about the love of Casares, the Princess of Death, for poet Marais, and their passage between the worlds of the living and the dead. Set in modern times, the Princess of Death rides in a Rolls Royce, and the characters pass back and forth from one world to the next through the surface of a mirror. Though stylish and beautifully executed, slow, highly symbolic story has limited mainstream appeal. [S]
Dist.: Various

OSA 1985
★ **NR Sci-Fi 1:34**
☑ Explicit language, violence

Dir: Oleg Egorov ***Cast:*** Kelly Lynch, Daniel Grimm, Phillip Vincent, Etienne Chicot, John Forristal

► In another postapocalyptic scenario, conglomerate served by homosexual enforcer Grimm controls all the world's potable water. Lynch has been thirsting for vengeance after Grimm killed her family when she was a child. Now she's grown up, shapely, and going after him with a crossbow. About average for this type of film, with less violence than usual.

Dist.: HBO

OSCAR, THE 1966
★ NR Drama 1:59
Dir: Russell Rouse ***Cast:*** Stephen Boyd, Elke Sommer, Eleanor Parker, Joseph Cotten, Milton Berle, Jill St. John

► Romanticized hokum about actor Boyd nervously waiting through the awards ceremony to see if he's won an Oscar. Best friend Tony Bennett recounts his sordid career from strip joint emcee to over-the-hill matinee idol. Fun on a camp level, and filled with stars: Ernest Borgnine, Walter Brennan, Hedda Hopper, Bob Hope, Merle Oberon, Frank Sinatra, Edie Adams, Peter Lawford, etc.

Dist.: Nelson

OSSESSIONE 1942 Italian
☆ NR Drama 1:52 B&W
Dir: Luchino Visconti ***Cast:*** Massimo Girotti, Clara Calamai, Juan deLanda, Elio Marcuzzo, Dhia Cristani, Vittorio Duse

► Drifter Girotti accepts the hospitality of innkeeper deLanda, and the clandestine favors of his much younger wife Calamai. When Girotti becomes uneasy over the affair, Calamai concocts a scheme to kill her husband, make it look like an accident, and collect the insurance. Visconti's first movie, an unauthorized adaptation of James M. Cain's *The Postman Only Rings Twice*, is not up to the 1946 American film of that book, but has interesting Italian variations. Location shooting heralded a new era of realism in Italian cinema. [S]

Dist.: Film Forum

OSTERMAN WEEKEND, THE 1983
★★★ R Mystery-Suspense 1:42
☑ Nudity, explicit language, violence
Dir: Sam Peckinpah ***Cast:*** Rutger Hauer, John Hurt, Burt Lancaster, Craig T. Nelson, Dennis Hopper, Chris Sarandon

► Television journalist Hauer, told by CIA agent Hurt that his best friends Nelson, Hopper, and Sarandon are Soviet spies, hosts a CIA-monitored gathering. Double crosses and kidnapping are on the weekend agenda. Virile direction by Peckinpah and decent acting, but confused plotting generates little emotional empathy. From the Robert Ludlum novel.

Dist.: HBO

OTELLO 1986 Italian
★★★★ PG Music 2:02
☑ Adult situations
Dir: Franco Zeffirelli ***Cast:*** Placido Domingo, Katia Ricciarelli, Justino Diaz, Petra Malakova

► Pathologically jealous Moorish general Domingo is driven into a murderous frenzy toward his wife Ricciarelli by the machinations of scheming ensign Diaz. Overblown production of Verdi opus may please opera fans. Domingo sings beautifully but looks (thanks to ridiculous dark makeup) awful.

Dist.: HBO

OTHER, THE 1972
★★★ PG Horror 1:40
☑ Adult situations, explicit language, violence
Dir: Robert Mulligan ***Cast:*** Uta Hagen, Diana Muldaur, Chris Udvarnoky, Martin Udvarnoky, Portia Nelson, John Ritter

► In 1930s New England, bizarre murders plague small town. Are the Udvarnoky twins, one good and one evil, involved? Mom Muldaur and grandma Hagen are among those who'd like some answers. Spine-tingling adaptation of the Thomas Tryon best-seller.

Dist.: CBS/Fox

OTHER SIDE OF MIDNIGHT, THE 1977
★★★★★ R Drama 2:49
☑ Nudity, adult situations, explicit language
Dir: Charles Jarrott ***Cast:*** Marie-France Pisier, John Beck, Susan Sarandon, Raf Vallone, Clu Gulager

► During World War II, American pilot Beck seduces, impregnates, and dumps French Pisier. After having an abortion, Pisier uses her wiles to become rich and famous and then plots revenge against Beck and his wife Sarandon. Lavish, swanky, juicy pulp captures author Sidney Sheldon's standard formula for elegant melodrama. Lush Michel Legrand score.

Dist.: CBS/Fox

OTHER SIDE OF THE MOUNTAIN, THE 1975
★★★★ PG Biography 1:41
☑ Adult situations, explicit language
Dir: Larry Peerce ***Cast:*** Marilyn Hassett, Beau Bridges, Belinda Montgomery, Dabney Coleman, Nan Martin, William Bryant

► True story of skier Jill Kinmont (Hassett), whose career ends when a skiing accident leaves her a paraplegic. New beau Bridges gives her hope and romance. She becomes a teacher, but then tragedy strikes Bridges. Inspirational tale will evoke tears; Hassett is excellent. Followed by sequel.

Dist.: MCA

OTHER SIDE OF THE MOUNTAIN PART II, THE 1978
★★★★★ PG Biography 1:39
☑ Adult situations, explicit language
Dir: Larry Peerce ***Cast:*** Marilyn Hassett, Timothy Bottoms, Nan Martin, Belinda Montgomery, Gretchen Corbett

► Continuation of the true story of Olympic

skier Jill Kinmont (Hassett), who suffered paralysis in a skiing accident and the death of her fiancé in a plane crash. Kinmont teaches in L.A. and then vacations in her hometown, where she meets divorced trucker Bottoms who breaks through her resistance to love. Hassett repeats the credible and sympathetic characterization. Bottoms is natural and likable, and the intimate love story delivers a good cry.
Dist.: MCA

OUR DAILY BREAD 1934
★ NR Drama 1:14 B&W
Dir: King Vidor   *Cast:* Karen Morley, Tom Keene, John Qualen, Barbara Pepper, Addison Richards, Harry Holman
▶ Morley and Keene are a struggling farm couple who make a go of it by forming a commune with the homeless. Temptress Pepper diverts Keene temporarily from his mission. Heartfelt Depression-era drama is at times stilted and overly sincere, but packs an undeniably stirring punch during its bravura drought-busting climax. Moving performance by Morley.
Dist.: Nelson

OUR HOSPITALITY 1923
★★ NR Comedy 1:15 B&W
Dir: Buster Keaton, Jack Blystone   *Cast:* Buster Keaton, Natalie Talmadge, Joseph Keaton, Joe Roberts, Leonard Clapham, Craig Ward
▶ Keaton leaves 1830s New York to claim an inheritance in the Deep South. During the journey he befriends Talmadge, unaware that her family has marked him for death because of a long-standing feud. Ingenious, fast-paced, and with a hair-raising finale. Remarkable silent comedy is a perfect introduction to Keaton's work, particularly in this painstakingly restored version by Kevin Brownlow and David Gill.
Dist.: HBO

OUR LITTLE GIRL 1935
★★ NR Family/Drama 1:05 B&W
Dir: John Robertson   *Cast:* Shirley Temple, Rosemary Ames, Joel McCrea, Lyle Talbot, Erin O'Brien-Moore, Poodles Hanneford
▶ Doctor McCrea is more dedicated to his job than to his wife Ames, who turns her attentions to another man. In an effort to bring her parents back together, daughter Temple runs away. Lesser Temple vehicle finds heavy-handed script dampening star's charm. For her die-hard fans only. (CC)
Dist.: Playhouse ©

OUR MAN FLINT 1966
★★★ NR Espionage/Comedy 1:47
Dir: Daniel Mann   *Cast:* James Coburn, Lee J. Cobb, Gila Golan, Edward Mulhare, Benson Fong, Shelby Grant
▶ When an evil organization plots to take over the world by establishing control over global weather, it is up to superspy Derek Flint

(Coburn) to stop them. Perhaps the best of the countless James Bond spoofs of the 1960s, thanks to Coburn's confident tongue-in-cheek flair. Superior to its 1967 sequel *In Like Flint.*
Dist.: CBS/Fox

OUR TOWN 1940
★★★★★ NR Drama 1:30 B&W
Dir: Sam Wood   *Cast:* William Holden, Martha Scott, Frank Craven, Beulah Bondi, Thomas Mitchell, Guy Kibbee
▶ Narrator Craven is our guide to life in pre–World War I Grover's Corners, a small New England town. Holden is a doctor's son who pursues strong-willed Scott over many years; in film's eeriest scene, she encounters reminders of the frailty of human existence during a cemetery hallucination. Adaptation of Thornton Wilder's classic Pulitzer prize–winning play is moving, funny, innocent, and wise.
Dist.: Prism

OUT COLD 1988
★★ R Comedy 1:35
☑ Brief nudity, adult situations, explicit language, violence
Dir: Malcolm Mowbray   *Cast:* John Lithgow, Teri Garr, Randy Quaid, Bruce McGill, Lisa Blount
▶ When crude butcher McGill accidentally freezes to death in his meat closet, his unfaithful wife Garr and hapless partner Lithgow, both involved in the incident, conspire to hide the body. Story owes a nod to *The Postman Always Rings Twice.* Some real belly laughs (most effective running sick joke is McGill's popsicled corpse) but despite a talented cast, humor doesn't go far enough, winding up as watered-down black comedy.
Dist.: HBO

OUTLAND 1981
★★ R Sci-Fi 1:50
☑ Brief nudity, explicit language, graphic violence
Dir: Peter Hyams   *Cast:* Sean Connery, Peter Boyle, Frances Sternhagen, James B. Sikking, Kika Markham, Steven Berkoff
▶ New marshall Connery arrives on moon of Jupiter, just in time to investigate weird mining-camp deaths. When he gets too close to the truth, he's stalked by hired killers. Sturdy story unites Western-style plot with elaborate sci-fi trappings. Violence is more explicit than necessary but sympathetic Connery transcends the flaws. Best scenes: the interplay between Connery and crusty lady doctor Sternhagen.
Dist.: Warner

OUTLAW, THE 1943
★★ G Western 1:43 B&W
Dir: Howard Hughes   *Cast:* Jane Russell, Jack Beutel, Thomas Mitchell, Walter Huston, Joe Sawyer
▶ Wounded by lawman Pat Garrett (Mitchell), famous outlaw Billy the Kid (Beutel) hides out on a desert ranch with his friend Doc Holliday

(Huston). There he falls for the tempestuous Russell (in her film debut). Once-controversial Western seems dull today, although Huston is always interesting. Censored on release for Hughes's preoccupation with Russell's cleavage.
Dist.: Various

OUTLAW BLUES 1977
★ ★ ★ ★ PG Action-Adventure 1:41
☑ Adult situations, explicit language
Dir: Richard T. Heffron *Cast:* Peter Fonda, Susan Saint James, John Crawford, James Callahan, Michael Lerner
► Texas ex-con Fonda has his song stolen by country singer Callahan. Fonda accidentally shoots Callahan trying to retrieve his money, then becomes the center of a statewide manhunt. Singer Saint James helps him escape police while promoting his song into a hit. Lightweight chase film has an appealing country-western score (with Fonda doing his own singing).
Dist.: Warner

OUTLAW JOSEY WALES, THE 1976
★ ★ ★ ★ ★ PG Western 2:16
☑ Rape, brief nudity, explicit language, violence
Dir: Clint Eastwood *Cast:* Clint Eastwood, Chief Dan George, Sondra Locke, Bill McKinney, John Vernon, Sam Bottoms
► When his family is murdered by Union "Redlegs," farmer Eastwood joins Confederate guerrillas. Eastwood escapes from an ambush with a price on his head and flees across the West from his nemesis McKinney. Despite his desire for peace, he encounters violence with marauders and Indians. Strong post–Civil War Western features a large canvas of richly detailed characters and settings.
Dist.: Warner

OUTLAW OF GOR 1989
☆ PG-13 Fantasy 1:29
☑ Violence
Dir: John (Bud) Cardos *Cast:* Urbano Barberini, Rebecca Ferrati, Donna Denton, Jack Palance, Russel Savadier
► Handsome hero Barberini attempts to liberate the planet Gor from slavery under evil high priest Palance. With gladiator-style fights in abundance, but little else besides desert backgrounds to look at, direct-to-video second adaptation of John Normman's fantasy novels lacks any sense of wonder or magic.
Dist.: Warner

OUT OF AFRICA 1985
★ ★ ★ ★ PG Drama 2:44
☑ Adult situations, mild violence
Dir: Sydney Pollack *Cast:* Meryl Streep, Robert Redford, Klaus Maria Brandauer, Michael Kitchen, Malick Bowens
► True story of Danish writer Karen Blixen (Streep), known as Isak Dinesen, who arrives in 1913 Africa to run a coffee plantation. Ignored by husband Brandauer, she develops a spe-

cial relationship with the land, its people, and dashing adventurer Redford. Magnificent cinematography and locations, stunning performances, unusually complex characters, and beautiful John Barry score. Even with its epic trappings, an intimate and beautiful love story. Seven Oscars include Best Picture, Director, Screenplay. **(CC)**
Dist.: MCA

OUT OF BOUNDS 1986
★ ★ ★ R Mystery-Suspense 1:29
☑ Explicit language, violence
Dir: Richard Tuggle *Cast:* Anthony Michael Hall, Jenny Wright, Jeff Kober, Glynn Turman, Raymond J. Barry, Pepe Serna
► Iowa teen Hall visits his brother in L.A., picks up the wrong bag at the airport, and finds himself the target of vicious drug dealers. Farfetched but boasts some tension, action, and surprises. Wright is appealing although Hall suffers from a poorly written part. **(CC)**
Dist.: RCA/Columbia

OUT OF CONTROL 1985
★ R Action-Adventure 1:18
☑ Rape, nudity, adult situations, explicit language, violence
Dir: Allan Holzman *Cast:* Martin Hewitt, Betsy Russell, Claudia Udy, Andrew J. Lederer, Cindi Dietrich, Jim Youngs
► After their senior prom, teens take a plane ride and crash land on a deserted island. Their high jinks (including a rousing game of strip "Spin the Bottle") are rudely disrupted by drug smugglers. Well-shot but rather pointless exercise. Shallow characters, meager plotting.
Dist.: New World

OUT OF SEASON 1975 British
★ R Drama 1:30
☑ Nudity, adult situations, explicit language
Dir: Alan Bridges *Cast:* Cliff Robertson, Vanessa Redgrave, Frank Jarvis, Susan George
► American Robertson wants to rekindle old romance with British hotel-keeper Redgrave, but Redgrave's sexy daughter George keeps getting in the way. Situation seems impossible, and Robertson decides to leave. After sleeping with George, he learns that he is her father. Not much happens here, but script is literate and Redgrave takes it a long way. Also known as *Winter Rates*.
Dist.: United

OUT OF THE BLUE 1980
★ ★ R Drama 1:29
☑ Nudity, strong sexual content, explicit language, violence
Dir: Dennis Hopper *Cast:* Linda Manz, Dennis Hopper, Sharon Farrell, Don Gordon, Raymond Burr, Eric Allen
► Rebellious teen Manz, living with drug-addicted mom Farrell, is reunited with her dad Hopper, who has spent six years in prison for ramming his truck into a school bus. Hopper's drinking and the family's tortured past make

the reunion eventful. Outstanding acting but devastating look at family life is tough to take; not a pretty picture.
Dist.: Media

OUT OF THE DARK 1989
★★ R Horror 1:30
☑ Nudity, strong sexual content, explicit language, violence
Dir: Michael Schroeder *Cast:* Cameron Dye, Karen Black, Bud Cort, Divine, Paul Bartel, Tracey Walter
▶ Ugly, repellent film about a psychotic killer who dons a clown mask to kill women after being titillated by a telephone sex service. Killer may be photographer Dye, or weird accountant Cort. Violence toward women is unsavory and misogynistic. Divine plays a male detective in this, his last movie.
Dist.: RCA/Columbia

OUT OF THE PAST 1947
★★★ NR Mystery-Suspense 1:37 B&W
Dir: Jacques Tourneur *Cast:* Robert Mitchum, Jane Greer, Kirk Douglas, Rhonda Fleming, Richard Webb
▶ Former private eye Mitchum tries to lead a quiet small-town life but ex-lover Greer and her gangster boyfriend Douglas return to both haunt and involve him in murder. Film noir cult classic has it all: an intricate and twisty plot, Tourneur's striking visuals, sizzling Greer, Mitchum at his sardonic best, and fine support from Douglas. Remade in 1984 as *Against All Odds* with Greer playing the mother of her original character.
Dist.: Turner ©

OUT OF TOWNERS, THE 1970
★★★ G Comedy 1:37
Dir: Arthur Hiller *Cast:* Jack Lemmon, Sandy Dennis, Anne Meara, Sandy Baron, Ann Prentiss
▶ Ohio couple Lemmon and Dennis plan a romantic visit to New York before an important job interview, but run into a series of nightmarish disasters: lost luggage, cancelled hotel reservations, muggers, hijackers, etc. Although dismaying to Big Apple's tourist industry, Neil Simon script provides nonstop laughs at a breakneck pace.
Dist.: Paramount

OUTRAGEOUS! 1977 Canadian
★ R Comedy/Drama 1:36
☑ Adult situations, explicit language
Dir: Richard Benner *Cast:* Craig Russell, Hollis McLaren, Richard Easley, Allan Moyle, Helen Shaver, Gerry Salzberg
▶ Released Toronto mental patient McLaren befriends gay hairdresser/female impersonator Russell. McLaren becomes pregnant by another man but miscarries. She then joins Russell when he moves to New York to seek fame and fortune. Cult following found offbeat, low-budget feature hilarious, but not for

mainstream tastes. Followed by *Too Outrageous!* ten years later.
Dist.: RCA/Columbia

OUTRAGEOUS FORTUNE 1987
★★★★ R Comedy 1:32
☑ Adult situations, explicit language
Dir: Arthur Hiller *Cast:* Shelley Long, Bette Midler, Peter Coyote, George Carlin, Robert Prosky, John Schuck
▶ Two would-be actresses, prim and proper Long and rude and earthy Midler, are shocked to discover they share the same lover, Coyote. Although he's apparently killed, the two are convinced he's alive and, pursued by both the KGB and the CIA, they trail him to New Mexico. Antagonistic chemistry between Long and Midler is uproarious while Carlin is a hoot in this briskly entertaining romp.
Dist.: Buena Vista

OUTSIDERS, THE 1983
★★★★ PG Drama 1:27
☑ Explicit language, violence
Dir: Francis Coppola *Cast:* Matt Dillon, Ralph Macchio, C. Thomas Howell, Patrick Swayze, Rob Lowe, Emilio Estevez
▶ In 1966 Oklahoma, troubled teens Dillon, Macchio, and others square off against the preppies. When Macchio accidentally kills a preppie, he and Howell must lay low. Then Macchio dies saving schoolchildren from a fire, causing grief-stricken Dillon to attempt ill-fated robbery. Fine performances from Brat Pack actors and authentic period look. Adapted from the best-selling novel by young adult author S. E. Hinton.
Dist.: Warner

OVERBOARD 1987
★★★★ PG Romance/Comedy 1:52
☑ Explicit language
Dir: Garry Marshall *Cast:* Goldie Hawn, Kurt Russell, Edward Herrmann, Katherine Helmond, Michael Hagerty, Roddy McDowall
▶ Amiable escapist fare about bored heiress Hawn who stiffs redneck carpenter Russell for a $600 fee. When she falls off her yacht and washes ashore with amnesia, widower Russell persuades Hawn she's mother to his bratty children. After initial turmoil in rural pigsty home, Hawn becomes ideal mom to reformed kids. But it isn't long before devious hubby Herrmann shows up to claim her. Hawn, America's favorite airhead, is at her best with real-life beau Russell. (CC)
Dist.: CBS/Fox

OVER THE BROOKLYN BRIDGE 1984
★★ R Romance/Comedy 1:46
☑ Nudity, adult situations, explicit language
Dir: Menahem Golan *Cast:* Elliott Gould, Margaux Hemingway, Sid Caesar, Shelley Winters, Carol Kane, Burt Young
▶ Brooklyn restaurateur Gould seeks to open a more upscale establishment in Manhattan but needs loan from rich uncle Caesar. Cae-

sar and rest of Jewish clan don't approve of Gould's Catholic girlfriend Hemingway and pressure him to wed nice Jewish girl Kane. Melting-pot romantic comedy mixes lifeless direction and stereotypical characters into bland fare.
Dist.: MGM/UA

OVER THE EDGE 1979
★ ★ PG Action-Adventure 1:35
☑ Explicit language, violence
Dir: Jonathan Kaplan *Cast:* Matt Dillon, Vincent Spano, Michael Kramer, Patricia Ludwig, Tom Fergud, Harry Northrup
▶ In model suburb, young tough-guy teens Dillon, Spano, and Kramer kill time with drugs and vandalism. When hardnosed cop Northrup slays Dillon after car theft, kids run amok in fatal binge of violence. Fine young cast in probing look at alienated youth, although story is often familiar. Fine soundtrack; Dillon's screen debut.
Dist.: Warner

OVER THE SUMMER 1984
★ NR Drama 1:40
☑ Rape, nudity, explicit language
Dir: Teresa Sparks *Cast:* Laura Hunt, Willard Millan, Johnson West, Catherine Williams
▶ Atlanta teenager visits her relatives in rural North Carolina. In an eventful stay, she falls in love for the first time, renews her friendship with another seventeen-year-old girl, and fights a rapist. Naturalistic and fresh flavor but thin plot, slow pace, and amateurish acting.
Dist.: Vestron

OVER THE TOP 1987
★ ★ ★ ★ PG Drama/Sports 1:33
☑ Explicit language, violence
Dir: Menahem Golan *Cast:* Sylvester Stallone, Robert Loggia, Susan Blakely, Rick Zumwalt, David Mendenhall
▶ Gentle giant truck driver Stallone battles rich dad-in-law Loggia for custody of son Mendenhall when mom Blakely dies. To earn cash for child support, Stallone enters world arm-wrestling championship. Variation on *The Champ* will delight the legions of Stallone fans. **(CC)**
Dist.: Warner

OWL AND THE PUSSYCAT, THE 1970
★ ★ ★ ★ PG Comedy 1:37
☑ Adult situations, explicit language
Dir: Herbert Ross *Cast:* Barbra Streisand, George Segal, Robert Klein, Allen Garfield, Roz Kelly
▶ Would-be writer Segal informs his landlord of kooky prostitute neighbor Streisand's late-night activities. After she is evicted, she cons her way into becoming his roommate. They fight, argue, and fall in love. Charming if somewhat inconsistent comedy featured Streisand's first nonsinging role. Adapted by Buck Henry from Bill Manhoff's 1964 Broadway hit.
Dist.: RCA/Columbia

OX-BOW INCIDENT, THE 1943
★ ★ ★ ★ NR Western 1:15 B&W
Dir: William Wellman *Cast:* Henry Fonda, Dana Andrews, Harry Morgan, Anthony Quinn, Mary Beth Hughes, William Eythe
▶ Searing indictment of mob rule and vigilante justice is one of the all-time great Westerns and director Wellman's masterpiece. Cowboys Fonda and Morgan ride into a small Nevada town where a local rancher is shot by rustlers. Despite pleas for reason by Fonda and others, a posse forms and apprehends passing farmers Andrews and Quinn. Gritty, compelling drama uses Western setting for morality tale with universal appeal. Based on the novel by Walter Van Tilburg Clark. **(CC)**
Dist.: CBS/Fox

OXFORD BLUES 1984
★ ★ ★ PG-13 Comedy 1:37
☑ Adult situations, explicit language
Dir: Robert Boris *Cast:* Rob Lowe, Ally Sheedy, Amanda Pays, Julian Sands, Julian Firth, Alan Howard
▶ American drop-out Lowe cons his way into Oxford to woo English beauty Pays. He's immediately disliked by the stiff British until he proves his mettle as a rower. Creaky fable of British reserve clashing with American brashness works primarily as vehicle for heartthrob Lowe. **(CC)**
Dist.: CBS/Fox

PACKAGE, THE 1989
★ ★ ★ R Mystery-Suspense 1:47
☑ Explicit language, violence
Dir: Andrew Davis *Cast:* Gene Hackman, Joanna Cassidy, Tommy Lee Jones, John Heard, Pam Grier, Dennis Franz, Kevin Crowley, Ron Dean
▶ Army sergeant Hackman is assigned to take a "package" back to the U.S. from Germany: military prisoner Jones. When Jones escapes after arriving stateside, Hackman, with the help of ex-wife Cassidy, discovers Jones's real identity and a chilling political conspiracy. Cold war thriller successfully uses glasnost as a springboard to revitalize the genre, but overcomplicated script and unsure direction are drawbacks. **(CC)**
Dist.: Orion

PADRE PADRONE 1977 Italian
☆ NR Drama 1:54
☑ Adult situations, violence
Dir: Vittorio Taviani, Paolo Taviani *Cast:* Omero Antonutti, Saverio Marioni, Marcella Michelangeli, Fabrizio Forte
▶ After his abusive father forces him to spend his youth tending sheep, Marioni enters manhood illiterate and unsocialized. Recruited into the army, the language-starved soldier conceives a passion for words, learning Italian, Greek, and Latin, and returns to his childhood home a distinguished writer. Though far from lightweight entertainment, highly origi-

nal direction tells this true story in a unique and arresting fashion. Won both Cannes Golden Palm and International Critics' Prize. [S]
Dist.: RCA/Columbia

PAIN IN THE A—, A 1974 French/Italian
★ PG Comedy 1:30
☑ Adult situations, explicit language
Dir: Edouard Molinaro ***Cast:*** Lino Ventura, Jacques Brel, Caroline Cellier, Nino Castelnuovo, Jean-Pierre Darras
► Brel is a suicidal cuckold who takes a hotel room next door to hitman Ventura. Since a suicide attempt would attract the police, and Ventura is planning a political assassination, the icy killer tries to help the hapless Brel do himself in. Also known as *A Pain in the Neck*, very funny French comedy was basis for less funny American film *Buddy Buddy*. [S]
Dist.: RCA/Columbia

PAINTED DESERT, THE 1938
★ NR Western 1:15 B&W
Dir: Howard Higgin ***Cast:*** William Boyd, Helen Twelvetrees, William Farnum, J. Farrell MacDonald, Clark Gable
► Land prospectors Farnum and MacDonald stumble across an infant in the desert and quarrel over who will raise it. Farnum eventually claims the child, but the feud continues until the grown boy, Boyd, falls in love with Farnum's daughter, Twelvetrees. Gable, her other suitor,is among those opposed to the liaison. Clunky, painfully slow drama with nice views of wide open spaces.
Dist.: Various

PAINT YOUR WAGON 1969
★★ PG Musical 2:46
☑ Adult situations, explicit language
Dir: Joshua Logan ***Cast:*** Lee Marvin, Clint Eastwood, Jean Seberg, Harve Presnell, Ray Walston, The Nitty Gritty Dirt Band
► California prospector Marvin purchases wife Seberg from a Mormon; when she falls for his partner Eastwood, they set up a ménage à trois that shocks their straitlaced neighbors. Lavish production of a Lerner-Loewe stage hit, adapted by Paddy Chayefksy, suffers somewhat from the stars' inability to sing. Songs include "I Talk to the Trees," "They Call the Wind Maria," "Whoop-Ti-Ay."
Dist.: Paramount

PAISAN 1946 Italian
★ NR Drama 1:57 B&W
Dir: Roberto Rossellini ***Cast:*** Carmela Sazio, Dots Johnson, Gar Moore, Bill Tubbs, Harriet White, Maria Michi
► Director Rossellini explores the intimate side of the Allied invasion of Italy in World War II through six short episodes. Alternately touching, violent, romantic, and thought-provoking, the segments include black G.I. Johnson discovering Italian poverty when a street boy steals his shoes, a meeting between U.S. chaplains and Italian monks, and a tragic shoot-out between Nazis and underground partisans. Very strong drama was co-written by Rossellini and future-director Federico Fellini. [S]
Dist.: Various

PAJAMA GAME, THE 1957
★★★ NR Musical 1:41
Dir: George Abbott, Stanley Donen ***Cast:*** Doris Day, John Raitt, Carol Haney, Eddie Foy, Jr., Barbara Nichols
► Highly enjoyable musical about a labor disturbance in a pajama factory: workers seeking a raise appoint Day to negotiate with foreman Raitt, but she lets them down by falling in love with him. Inventive choreography by Bob Fosse complements a bright score, including "Hernando's Hideaway" and Haney's knockout "Steam Heat."
Dist.: Warner

PALEFACE, THE 1948
★★★ NR Western/Comedy 1:31
Dir: Norman Z. McLeod ***Cast:*** Bob Hope, Jane Russell, Robert Armstrong, Iris Adrian, Robert Watson, Iron Eyes Cody
► Sprightly Western farce about dentist Hope with a mail-order degree who marries Calamity Jane (Russell) to keep her out of jail. Hope inadvertently corrals a gang of outlaws, but not before engaging in frequently hysterical parodies of Western clichés. Hope and Russell duet to the Oscar-winning "Buttons and Bows." Followed by *Son of Paleface*.
Dist.: MCA

PALE RIDER 1985
★★★★ R Western 1:56
☑ Explicit language, violence
Dir: Clint Eastwood ***Cast:*** Clint Eastwood, Carrie Snodgress, Michael Moriarty, Christopher Penn, Richard Dysart, Richard Kiel
► Miners in Idaho are harassed by robber baron Dysart and pray for salvation. Into town rides Eastwood, a stranger called the Preacher. When reason doesn't work with Dysart, Eastwood takes off his collar and straps on his six-guns, proving action speaks louder than words. Eastwood has no peer as the silent avenger and his direction brings both reverence and freshness to the Western genre that made him a star. (CC)
Dist.: Warner

PAL JOEY 1957
★★★ NR Musical 1:51
Dir: George Sidney ***Cast:*** Frank Sinatra, Rita Hayworth, Kim Novak, Barbara Nichols, Bobby Sherwood
► Cynical singer Sinatra dreams of opening his own club; wealthy Hayworth will provide financing if he'll abandon his true love Novak. Sparkling Rodgers and Hart score (including "Bewitched, Bothered, and Bewildered," "My Funny Valentine," "The Lady Is a Tramp"), wonderful San Francisco locations, terrific singing and performances (particularly a fetching ca-

nine) in this entertaining adaptation of the John O'Hara story.
Dist.: RCA/Columbia

PALM BEACH STORY, THE 1942
★ ★ ★ NR Comedy 1:28 B&W
Dir: Preston Sturges **Cast:** Claudette Colbert, Joel McCrea, Mary Astor, Rudy Vallee, William Demarest, Sig Arno, Robert Dudley, Jack Norton, Jimmy Conlin
▶ Colbert, the flighty wife of impoverished inventor McCrea, runs off to Palm Beach and attracts mild-mannered millionaire Vallee. When McCrea follows, Vallee's sister Astor sets her sights on him. Witty, cleverly plotted, breathlessly paced love quadrangle from writer/director Sturges. Full of unforgettable comic scenes and characters (Astor's foreign boyfriend "Toto," the Ale & Quail Club, the wealthy "Wienie King").
Dist.: MCA

PALOOKA 1934
★ NR Comedy 1:26 B&W
Dir: Benjamin Stoloff **Cast:** Jimmy Durante, Lupe Velez, Stuart Erwin, Marjorie Rambeau, Robert Armstrong, William Cagney, Thelma Todd
▶ Erwin is comic strip boxer Joe Palooka, who is taken under the wing of veteran manager Durante and turned into a title contender. Cagney (James's brother) is the champion who stands in Joe's way. Frisky romp finds perfectly cast Durante in fine form. Also known as *Joe Palooka*.
Dist.: Cable

PANDEMONIUM 1982
★ PG Comedy 1:21
☑ Explicit language, violence, adult humor
Dir: Alfred Sole **Cast:** Tom Smothers, Carol Kane, Candice Azzara, Miles Chapin, Judge Reinhold
▶ Midwestern cheerleading academy is tormented by a series of brutal murders; Kane, a cheerleader with telekinetic powers, joins stalwart Mountie Smothers in solving the case. Silly takeoff of horror movies features cameos by Tab Hunter, Eve Arden, Pee-wee Herman, etc.
Dist.: MGM/UA

PANDORA'S BOX 1928 German
★ NR Drama 1:50 B&W
Dir: G. W. Pabst **Cast:** Louise Brooks, Fritz Kortner, Franz Lederer, Carl Goetz, Alice Roberts, Daisy d'Ora
▶ Amoral, sexually avaricious Brooks marries Kortner, kills him, romances his son Lederer, then travels from Berlin to London, where she becomes a prostitute. Leaving a trail of destroyed lives in her wake, she meets her match when she picks up a strange man who turns out to be Jack the Ripper. Brooks is devastatingly attractive in this frankly sexual silent masterpiece, making her character's effect on men powerfully believable.
Dist.: Nelson

PAPA'S DELICATE CONDITION 1963
★ ★ ★ ★ NR Comedy 1:38
Dir: George Marshall **Cast:** Jackie Gleason, Glynis Johns, Charles Ruggles, Laurel Goodwin, Linda Bruhl, Ned Glass
▶ In turn-of-the-century Texas, fun-loving railroad supervisor Gleason drinks too much, but daughter Bruhl adores him. However, wife Johns gets fed up, takes the kids, and walks out. A reconciliation eventually occurs. Gleason is quite appealing in this nostalgic charmer. Oscar for Best Song, "Call Me Irresponsible."
Dist.: KVC

PAPERBACK HERO 1975 Canadian
★ R Drama 1:34
☑ Nudity, explicit language
Dir: Peter Pearson **Cast:** Keir Dullea, Elizabeth Ashley, John Beck, Dayle Haddon
▶ Small-town loser Dullea plays hockey, fools around with barmaid Ashley, and dresses up in Western duds to enjoy target practice. Hockey and his Western obsessions lead to a riot, and Dullea faces down local cops in an old fashioned Main Street shoot-out. Fresh characters and backgrounds lend charm to otherwise downbeat and undramatic film.
Dist.: Cinema Group

PAPER CHASE, THE 1973
★ ★ ★ ★ PG Drama 1:51
☑ Adult situations, explicit language
Dir: James Bridges **Cast:** Timothy Bottoms, Lindsay Wagner, John Houseman, Graham Beckel, Edward Herrmann, James Naughton
▶ First-year Harvard law student Bottoms struggles under the stern tutelage of crusty professor Houseman; he also falls in love with Houseman's daughter Wagner. Incisive look at law school features stupendous, Oscar-winning performance by Houseman. Led to television series.
Dist.: CBS/Fox

PAPERHOUSE 1988
★ ★ PG-13 Horror 1:34
☑ Adult situations, explicit language, violence
Dir: Bernard Rose **Cast:** Charlotte Burke, Elliott Spiers, Glenne Headly, Ben Cross, Gemma Jones
▶ Young Burke, confined to home because of an illness, invents an imaginary world through her drawings. Her initially pleasant adventures there with Spiers are menaced by a mysterious nemesis. Rose, a noted rock video director, brings an inventive visual style to underdeveloped plot.
Dist.: Vestron

PAPER LION 1968
★ ★ G Drama/Sports 1:45
Dir: Alex March **Cast:** Alan Alda, Lauren Hutton, Alex Karras, David Doyle, Ann Turkel, Sugar Ray Robinson
▶ To get an inside look at the NFL, writer George Plimpton (Alda) tries out for quarter-

back in the Detroit Lions training camp, despite the doubts of the other players. Generally entertaining with enough humor to keep even non–football fans interested. Several Lions play themselves; based on Plimpton's book.
Dist.: Wood Knapp

PAPER MOON 1973
★ ★ ★ ★ **PG Comedy 1:42 B&W**
☑ Adult situations, explicit language, mild violence
Dir: Peter Bogdanovich *Cast:* Ryan O'Neal, Tatum O'Neal, Madeline Kahn, John Hillerman, P. J. Johnson, Randy Quaid
► In 1936, Bible-selling con artist Ryan O'Neal is forced into driving a foul-mouthed young orphan (played by his real-life daughter Tatum in her film debut) to relatives in Missouri. Along the way they develop a grudging respect for each other, despite the intrusion of flamboyant "showgirl" Trixie Delight (Kahn). Charming, flavorful period piece received a Supporting Actress Oscar for O'Neal (beating out Kahn's nomination). Aided by beautiful B&W photography and a soundtrack of vintage Depression tunes.
Dist.: Paramount

PAPER TIGER 1976 British
★ ★ ★ **PG Action-Adventure 1:41**
☑ Violence
Dir: Ken Annakin *Cast:* David NivenTo, Toshiro Mifune, Hardy Kruger, Ando
► Ando, the young son of Japanese Ambassador Mifune, is regaled by tutor Niven's unlikely tales of heroism during the war. When the two are kidnapped by terrorists, Niven must show his charge how much of a hero he is. Lame screenplay and lackluster direction are further hampered by corny message as a Brit, a German, and a Japanese forget war animosities and band together to save Ando.
Dist.: Nelson

PAPILLON 1973
★ ★ ★ ★ ★ **PG Action-Adventure 2:34**
☑ Adult situations, explicit language, violence
Dir: Franklin J. Schaffner *Cast:* Steve McQueen, Dustin Hoffman, Victor Jory, Anthony Zerbe, Don Gordon, Robert Deman
► True story of unjustly convicted French gangster McQueen and counterfeiter buddy Hoffman who repeatedly attempt to escape from penal colonies in Guiana. After many ordeals in solitary confinement, and a brief, bucolic respite in an Indian village, McQueen's thirst for freedom and desire to break out of the escape-proof Devil's Island grow stronger as he makes a final, desperate bid for liberation. Lengthy film boasts two star turns, exotic locales, and plot extolling human spirit. Screenplay by Dalton Trumbo and Lorenzo Semple, Jr., based on best-seller by the real Papillon, Henri Charrière.
Dist.: CBS/Fox

PARADINE CASE, THE 1948
★ ★ **NR Drama 1:56 B&W**
Dir: Alfred Hitchcock *Cast:* Gregory Peck, Charles Laughton, Ann Todd, Valli, Louis Jourdan, Ethel Barrymore
► Courtroom drama in which married attorney Peck falls in love with client Valli, accused of murdering her wealthy husband. Peck compels Valli's stableman/lover Jourdan to testify and present incriminating evidence. Even the great Hitchcock and a fine cast couldn't overcome a chatty and static script co-written by producer David O. Selznick. **(CC)**
Dist.: CBS/Fox

PARADISE 1982
★ ★ **R Drama 1:35**
☑ Nudity, violence
Dir: Stuart Gillard *Cast:* Phoebe Cates, Willie Aames, Richard Curnock, Tuvia Tavi, Neil Vipond, Aviva Marks
► *Blue Lagoon* without water. In nineteenth-century Turkey, Arabs massacre a Christian caravan; only good-looking teens Cates and Aames survive. Pursued from oasis to oasis by lecherous sheik Tavi, the two unchaperoned youngsters cannot resist each other. Plenty of uncovered skin.
Dist.: Nelson

PARADISE ALLEY 1978
★ ★ ★ **PG Drama 1:49**
☑ Adult situations, explicit language
Dir: Sylvester Stallone *Cast:* Sylvester Stallone, Armand Assante, Anne Archer, Kevin Conway, Joe Spinell, Lee Canalito
► Brothers Stallone, Assante, and Canalito seek to escape the slums of 1940s New York by exploiting Canalito's strength in the wrestling ring. Small-time hood Conway thwarts their plan until hustling con man Stallone shifts into high gear. Sly is everywhere in this picture: star, writer, director (his debut as such), and even crooner of the title song.
Dist.: MCA

PARADISE, HAWAIIAN STYLE 1966
★ ★ **NR Musical 1:31**
Dir: Michael Moore *Cast:* Elvis Presley, Suzanna Leigh, James Shigeta, Donna Butterworth, Marianna Hill
► When he loses his job as an airline pilot, Presley moves to Hawaii to form a charter helicopter service. Although his license is suspended, Presley risks his career to fly a wounded friend to the hospital. Weak plotting fails to capture the lighthearted spirit of the King's earlier *Blue Hawaii*; nondescript songs include "Datin'," "Queenie Wahine's Papaya," and "Bill Bailey, Won't You Please Come Home."
Dist.: CBS/Fox

PARADISE MOTEL 1985
★ **R Comedy 1:30**
☑ Nudity, adult situations, explicit language
Dir: Cary Medoway *Cast:* Gary Hersh-

berger, Jonna Leigh Stack, Robert Krantz, Bob Basso, Rick Gibbs, Jeffrey Jay Hea

► Naive teen Hershberger's father buys resort motel; local Romeo Krantz fakes friendship with him in order to use motel rooms for romantic liaisons with local beauties. Problems ensue when Hershberger falls for Krantz's true girlfriend Stack. Performers bring some spark to routine story.

Dist.: CBS/Fox

PARALLAX VIEW, THE 1974
★★★ R Mystery-Suspense 1:41
☑ Adult situations, explicit language, violence
Dir: Alan J. Pakula ***Cast:*** Warren Beatty, Paula Prentiss, William Daniels, Walter McGinn, Hume Cronyn, Kelly Thordsen

► Investigative reporter Beatty probes the strange deaths of witnesses to the assassination of a Presidential candidate. With help of colleague Prentiss and despite reluctance of editor Cronyn, Beatty soon finds himself neck-deep in an elaborate conspiracy. Taut, intelligent thriller builds suspense with each new piece of evidence.

Dist.: Paramount

PARAMEDICS 1988
★★ PG-13 Comedy 1:31
☑ Brief nudity, adult situations, explicit language
Dir: Stuart Margolin ***Cast:*** George Newbern, Christopher McDonald, Javier Grajeda, Lawrence Hilton-Jacobs, John P. Ryan, Ray Walston

► Fun-loving paramedics Newbern and McDonald enjoy girl-chasing while lifesaving, so their boss assigns them to tough neighborhood as punishment. The guys must deal with terrorists as well as organ snatchers. Rowdy antics include laughs at the expense of ethnic stereotypes and cardiac arrest. Actors seem to be enjoying themselves, although plot is overly familiar.

Dist.: Vestron

PARANOIA 1968 Italian/French
☆ R Horror 1:32
☑ Nudity, strong sexual content, adult situations, explicit language, violence
Dir: Umberto Lenzi ***Cast:*** Carroll Baker, Lou Castel, Collette Descombes, Tino Carraro, Lilla Brignone, Franco Pesce

► In Italy, Americans Castel and Descombes blackmail wealthy widow Baker through seduction and orgies. Lawyer Carraro, apparently her friend, might be involved in the squalid scheme. Not one of Baker's finest hours, although possibly her sleaziest one. Also known as *Orgasmo.*

Dist.: Republic

PARASITE 1982
☆ R Horror 1:25
☑ Nudity, explicit language, graphic violence
Dir: Charles Band ***Cast:*** Robert Glaudini, Demi Moore, Luca Bercovici, James Davidson, Vivian Blaine

► In a postapocalyptic wasteland, scientist Glaudini is infected with a hideous bacteria that multiplies into bloodthirsty parasites. With the help of local lemon grower Moore, he searches for a cure as the parasites eat through his stomach. Repellant horror exploitation filmed in 3-D will lose most of its impact on TV.

Dist.: Embassy

PARDON MON AFFAIR 1977 French
★ PG Comedy 1:45
☑ Brief nudity, explicit language
Dir: Yves Robert ***Cast:*** Jean Rochefort, Claude Brasseur, Guy Bedos, Victor Lanoux, Daniele Delorme, Anny Duperey

► Wacky French comedy of infidelity has businessman Rochefort determined to commit adultery with model Duperey. Also seen are the tangled personal lives of three of Rochefort's friends. Good Gallic fun when it concentrates on Rochefort's efforts to arrange an assignation, but less effective when it turns to dramatic subplots. Inspired 1984's *The Woman in Red.* [S]

Dist.: Nelson

PARDON US 1931
★★ NR Comedy 0:55 B&W
Dir: James Parrott ***Cast:*** Stan Laurel, Oliver Hardy, Wilfred Lucas, Walter Long, James Finlayson, June Marlowe

► During Prohibition, Laurel and Hardy are thrown into jail for brewing their own beer. Once in the Big House, they are forced into an escape attempt with tough prisoner Long, and wind up singing and picking cotton in blackface. Comedy duo's first feature is made up of bits inartistically strung together, but it's still very funny.

Dist.: Nostalgia

PARENTHOOD 1989
★★★★★ PG-13 Comedy/Drama 2:04
☑ Adult situations, explicit language, adult humor
Dir: Ron Howard ***Cast:*** Steve Martin, Mary Steenburgen, Dianne Wiest, Jason Robards, Rick Moranis, Tom Hulce, Martha Plimpton, Keanu Reeves, Harley Kozak, Leaf Phoenix

► Alternately heartbreaking and hilarious look at joys and sorrows of middle-class parenting: Martin tries so hard to be good father that he turns his son into a nervous wreck; his sister-in-law Wiest (Oscar-nominated) contends with teen daughter Plimpton's marriage to Reeves; and yuppie brother-in-law Moranis obsessively tries to turn little daughter into budding genius. Adding to the family troubles is arrival of ne'er-do-well brother Hulce with a gambling problem and an illegitimate son. Excellent ensemble acting highlights screenplay that will strike chord in many homes. (CC)

Dist.: MCA

PARENTS 1988
★ R Horror 1:23
☑ Adult situations, explicit language, violence
Dir: Bob Balaban *Cast:* Randy Quaid, Mary Beth Hurt, Sandy Dennis, Bryan Madorsky, Juno Mills-Cockell, Kathryn Grody
► Young Madorsky, whose father Quaid is engaged in unusual scientific research, is troubled by bloody nightmares and starts to wonder about the strange cuts of meat prepared by his doting mother Hurt. Eccentric blend of 1950s camp and eerie horror doesn't succeed entirely, but offbeat visual style and amusing soundtrack are often delightful.
Dist.: Vestron

PARENT TRAP, THE 1961
★★★★ NR Comedy/Family 2:04
Dir: David Swift *Cast:* Hayley Mills, Maureen O'Hara, Brian Keith, Charles Ruggles, Una Merkel, Leo G. Carroll
► Hayley Mills plays identical twins, the daughters of divorced parents O'Hara and Keith. The girls live apart but finally meet when they attend the same camp and scheme to bring their folks back together. Mills doubles delightfully in delectable Disney antics. Followed by a TV movie sequel in 1986.
Dist.: Buena Vista

PARIS BLUES 1961
★★ NR Drama 1:38 B&W
Dir: Martin Ritt *Cast:* Paul Newman, Joanne Woodward, Sidney Poitier, Diahann Carroll, Louis Armstrong
► Intriguing story about two American musicians, expatriates in post–World War II Paris for the wrong reasons: Poitier fears racism at home, Newman won't give up his stalled classical career. Their lives are changed when they fall in love with tourists Carroll and Woodward. One of the better attempts to capture jazz on film. Duke Ellington received an Oscar nomination for his first-rate score, including "Mood Indigo" and "Sophisticated Lady." (CC)
Dist.: CBS/Fox

PARIS DOES STRANGE THINGS 1957 French
☆ NR Drama 1:38
Dir: Jean Renoir *Cast:* Ingrid Bergman, Jean Marais, Mel Ferrer, Jean Richard, Magali Noel, Juliette Greco
► In nineteenth-century Paris, Polish countess Bergman proves to be a good luck charm with men, her latest beau being ambitious general Marais. However, count Ferrer turns out to be her true love. Overly stylized film should appeal to the director's fans but may leave others shaking their heads. Also known as *Elena and Her Men*.
Dist.: Foothill

PARIS EXPRESS, THE 1953 British
★ NR Mystery-Suspense 1:20
Dir: Harold French *Cast:* Claude Rains,

Marta Toren, Marius Goring, Anouk Aimee, Herbert Lom, Lucie Mannheim
► Formerly dependable clerk Rains begins stealing from his company after uncovering management corruption. Boarding one of the trains that have been passing him by all his life, he heads for Paris—but his idyll ends when he is accused of murder. Adequate adaptation of the Georges Simenon novel, also known as *The Man Who Watched Trains Go By*.
Dist.: MPI

PARIS HOLIDAY 1958
★★ NR Comedy 1:40
Dir: Gerd Oswald *Cast:* Bob Hope, Fernandel, Anita Ekberg, Martha Hyer, Preston Sturges
► American movie star Hope goes to Paris to read a script. When the author is murdered, Hope is blamed. A criminal gang portrayed in the script wants to get its hands on the material, and hit woman Ekberg is dispatched to get Hope out of the way. Some of the bloom was off Hope's rose by the time this slightly plodding comedy came out, but fans won't mind.
Dist.: Unicorn

PARIS, TEXAS 1984 German/French
★ R Drama 2:25
☑ Brief nudity, adult situations, explicit language
Dir: Wim Wenders *Cast:* Harry Dean Stanton, Nastassja Kinski, Dean Stockwell, Hunter Carson, Aurore Clément
► Critically praised drama about drifter Stanton's efforts at reconciling with his son Carson and estranged wife Kinski. Overly long, demanding, but surprisingly positive depiction of loneliness and alienation. Carson (son of Karen Black and writer L. M. Kit Carson) is marvelous in his first film. Screenplay by Sam Shepard, outstanding photography by Robby Mueller, and moody Ry Cooder soundtrack. Many find it slow and pretentious. (CC)
Dist.: CBS/Fox

PARIS WHEN IT SIZZLES 1964
★★ NR Comedy 1:50
Dir: Richard Quine *Cast:* William Holden, Audrey Hepburn, Gregoire Aslan, Raymond Bussieres, Noel Coward, Tony Curtis
► Facing a tight deadline, screenwriter Holden hires secretary Hepburn to help him finish his latest script. Instead of working, they fall in love while acting out fantasy versions of film plots. Despite beautiful locations and numerous cameos (Marlene Dietrich, Mel Ferrer, etc.), a disappointing comedy that fails to establish a consistent tone.
Dist.: Paramount

PARK IS MINE, THE 1985
★★★★ NR Drama/MFTV 1:39
☑ Brief nudity, adult situations, explicit language, violence
Dir: Steven Hilliard Stern *Cast:* Tommy Lee

Jones, Helen Shaver, Yaphet Kotto, Eric Peterson, Lawrence Dane, Peter Devorsky
▶ Emotionally shattered Vietnam vet Jones, using techniques of jungle warfare, captures New York's Central Park to protest government indifference to the plight of his fellow vets. Free-lance TV reporter Shaver risks life to get the scoop while cop Kotto tries to undermine Jones's plan. Thriller with a message. (CC)
Dist.: CBS/Fox

PARLOR, BEDROOM AND BATH 1931
★ **NR Comedy 1:11 B&W**
Dir: Edward Sedgwick *Cast:* Buster Keaton, Charlotte Greenwood, Reginald Denny, Cliff Edwards, Dorothy Christy, Sally Eilers
▶ Suitor Denny is distraught because Eilers won't marry him until her older sister Christy is engaged. After nearly being killed by Denny's car, sign-hanger Keaton is introduced to the sister. Christy falls for Keaton, but becomes insanely jealous when she finds him rehearsing his proposal with another woman. Shot in and around Keaton's posh Beverly Hills mansion, strained talkie has some funny moments, but is not on the level of Keaton's silents.
Dist.: Video Yesteryear

PARTING GLANCES 1986
★ **NR Drama 1:30**
☑ Adult situations, explicit language
Dir: Bill Sherwood *Cast:* Richard Ganoung, John Bolger, Steve Buscemi, Adam Nathan, Kathy Kinney, Patrick Tull
▶ Gay lovers Ganoung and Bolger must separate when Bolger is transferred to Africa. Their last hours together are disrupted by quarrel over care for friend Buscemi, dying of AIDS. Honest, straightforward depiction of contemporary homosexual life mixes laughs and tears while confronting AIDS crisis. (CC)
Dist.: CBS/Fox

PARTNERS 1982
★★★ **R Comedy 1:32**
☑ Adult situations, explicit language, mild violence
Dir: James Burrows *Cast:* Ryan O'Neal, John Hurt, Kenneth McMillan, Robyn Douglass, Jay Robinson, Denise Galik
▶ Macho cop O'Neal must pose as homosexual with genuine gay policeman Hurt to find murderer of male models. Hurt, smitten with his new partner, sulks when O'Neal beds gorgeous photographer Douglass who's linked to killings. Despite his jealousy Hurt comes to the rescue when O'Neal's life is on the line. Shallow parody of homosexual life-styles may please some fans of very broad humor.
Dist.: Paramount

PARTS: THE CLONUS HORROR 1978
★ **R Sci-Fi 1:30**
☑ Nudity, adult situations, explicit language, violence
Dir: Robert Fiveson *Cast:* Tim Donnelly, Dick

Sargent, Peter Graves, Paulette Breen, David Hooks, Keenan Wynn
▶ On an island off southern California, bad Big Brother types are planning to clone entire population of North America. Rebel clone Donnelly loves Breen, but they are being monitored. When Donnelly escapes to nearest city, the guards try to kill him. Naive special effects and little real suspense in this modest, TV movie-style sci-fi effort. Also known as *The Clonus Horror*.
Dist.: Vestron

PARTY ANIMAL 1985
☆ **R Comedy 1:18**
☑ Nudity, adult situations, explicit language
Dir: David Beaird *Cast:* Matthew Causey, Tim Carhart, Robin Harlan, Suzanne Ashley, Jerry Jones, Frank Galati
▶ Inexperienced college student Causey is unable to score with women, unlike his stud roommate Carhart. When former announces he'd sell his soul to change his luck, beautiful Ashley suddenly appears on the scene. Typical low-rent youth comedy has a dumb script and plenty of nudity.
Dist.: Vestron

PARTY CAMP 1986
★ **R Comedy 1:37**
☑ Nudity, adult situations, explicit language
Dir: Gary Graver *Cast:* Andrew Ross, Kerry Brennan, Billy Jacoby, Jewel Shepard, Peter Jason, Kirk Cribb
▶ Party-animal counselor Ross butts heads with disciplinarian camp director Jason. Ross overcomes interference to teach fun-loving to campers and woo sexy lifeguard Brennan. Silly clone of *Meatballs* without laughs or Bill Murray.
Dist.: Vestron

PARTY GIRLS 1929
☆ **NR Drama 1:07 B&W**
Dir: Victor Halperin *Cast:* Douglas Fairbanks, Jr., Jeanette Loff, Judith Barrie, Marie Prevost, John St. Polis, Almeda Fowler
▶ Sharpie Fowler runs a babes-for-hire operation out of Times Square, renting hot-lipped tootsies like Prevost to businessmen for wild parties. Blackmailed into marrying one of the girls, Fairbanks, the son of a company president, is saved from the disgraceful union when she tumbles out a window. Difficult to take seriously.
Dist.: Sinister

PARTY LINE 1988
★ **R Mystery-Suspense 1:31**
☑ Nudity, adult situations, explicit language, violence
Dir: William Webb *Cast:* Richard Hatch, Shawn Weatherly, Leif Garrett, Greta Blackburn, Richard Roundtree, James O'Sullivan
▶ Garrett and Blackburn are a brother and sister psycho kill team who lure their victims through "976" phone numbers. Cop Hatch, D.A. Weatherly, and boss Roundtree are on

their tails. Blackburn is a wonderfully bilious villain in this grubby but fast-paced thriller.
Dist.: SVS

PASCALI'S ISLAND 1988 British
★ PG-13 Drama 1:41
☑ Nudity, adult situations, explicit language, violence
Dir: James Dearden ***Cast:*** Ben Kingsley, Charles Dance, Helen Mirren, George Murcell, Sheila Allen, Stefan Gryff
▶ Political and emotional intrigue on Greek island in 1908. Kingsley, a two-bit spy for the Turks, helps archaeologist Dance dig up ancient artifacts. When Dance romances Austrian expatriate painter Mirren, Kingsley becomes jealous, setting into motion a tragic climax. Low-key drama features fine cast and much local flavor, but may be too cerebral for some.
Dist.: IVE

PASSAGE TO INDIA, A 1984 British
★★★★ PG Drama 2:46
☑ Adult situations, explicit language
Dir: David Lean ***Cast:*** Alec Guinness, Judy Davis, Peggy Ashcroft, James Fox, Victor Banerjee, Nigel Havers
▶ In the 1920s, Havers's mother Ashcroft escorts his bethrothed, young Englishwoman Davis, to India to see him. Alarmed by prevailing British racial prejudice, Davis and Ashcroft seek out locals with help of scholar Fox and soon befriend affable Indian doctor Banerjee. On an ill-fated picnic to rural caves, Davis accuses Banerjee of attempted rape. Intimate story of sexual repression set against sweeping backdrop garnered eleven Oscar nominations, with Ashcroft taking Best Supporting Actress. Based on the novel by E. M. Forster. (CC)
Dist.: RCA/Columbia

PASSAGE TO MARSEILLES 1944
★★ NR Action-Adventure 1:50 B&W
Dir: Michael Curtiz ***Cast:*** Humphrey Bogart, Claude Rains, Michele Morgan, Philip Dorn, Sydney Greenstreet, Peter Lorre
▶ Anti-Nazi French reporter Bogart leads escape of his fellow countrymen from a prison and a ship captained by German sympathizer Greenstreet. Action-packed but far from top-notch Bogie, due to excessive flashbacks in the cluttered plot.
Dist.: Key

PASSENGER, THE 1975 Italian
★ PG Drama 1:59
☑ Violence
Dir: Michelangelo Antonioni ***Cast:*** Jack Nicholson, Maria Schneider, Jenny Runacre, Ian Hendry, Steven Berkoff
▶ In Africa, disaffected journalist Nicholson switches identities with a dead gun runner, gets involved with beautiful young Schneider, and finds himself in danger. Subtle and intelligent performance by Nicholson. Virtuoso camerawork from Antonioni includes one of the most complex final shots in film history. Unusual, provocative, and quite absorbing but strictly for sophisticated tastes.
Dist.: Warner

PASSIONATE THIEF, THE 1960 Italian
☆ NR Comedy 1:45 B&W
Dir: Mario Monicelli ***Cast:*** Anna Magnani, Toto, Ben Gazzara, Fred Clark, Edy Vessel
▶ Little goes right for pickpocket Gazzara, film extra Magnani, and out-of-work actor Toto, whose attempts at petty thievery are sometimes amusingly, sometimes sadly brought to ruin. Based on the stories of Alberto Moravia, tragicomedy works well thanks to sparkling cast. [S]
Dist.: Nelson

PASSION OF JOAN OF ARC, THE 1928 French
★★ NR Drama 1:54 B&W
Dir: Carl Theodor Dreyer ***Cast:*** Maria Falconetti, Eugene Silvain, Maurice Schutz, Michel Simon, Antonin Artaud
▶ Meticulous approach to the inquisition and martyrdom of Joan of Arc in the fifteenth century relies on actual trial transcripts to provide a realistic, often harrowing view of the events. Falconetti, in her only screen role, is unforgettable as the young saint. Silent masterpiece is historically significant for director Dreyer's unprecedented use of close-ups.
Dist.: Foothill

PASSPORT TO PIMLICO 1948 British
★★ NR Comedy 1:25 B&W
Dir: Henry Cornelius ***Cast:*** Stanley Holloway, Hermione Baddeley, Margaret Rutherford, Basil Radford, Naunton Wayne
▶ Post–World War II excavation reveals an ancient French deed granting political autonomy to a London neighborhood. The citizens react by establishing their own country whose new, relaxed laws alarm government officials. Delightful ensemble comedy with an Oscar-nominated screenplay is highly recommended to fans of British humor.
Dist.: Various

PASS THE AMMO 1988
★★★ R Comedy 1:37
☑ Adult situations, explicit language
Dir: David Beaird ***Cast:*** Bill Paxton, Linda Kozlowski, Tim Curry, Annie Potts, Dennis Burkley, Glenn Withrow
▶ Swindled out of $50,000 by phony TV evangelists Curry and Potts, lovers Paxton and Kozlowski try to steal back the cash from the preachers' broadcast studio. Caught in the act, the thieves take Curry and Potts hostage and go public with their plight, leading to raucous climax. Broad and uneven satire of born-again biz has its moments.
Dist.: IVE

PAT AND MIKE 1952
★★★★ NR Comedy 1:35 B&W
Dir: George Cukor ***Cast:*** Spencer Tracy,

Katharine Hepburn, Aldo Ray, William Ching, Sammy White, Charles Buchinski (Bronson)

▶ Sportswoman Hepburn is convinced to turn pro by manager/promoter Tracy. Business relationship turns personal, causing problems with fiancé Ching. Tracy's woes include shady deal with underworld partner Buchinski. Deft comedy with Oscar-nominated script by reknowned duo Garson Kanin and Ruth Gordon was seventh teaming for Tracy and Hepburn. Look for Chuck Connors, on leave from pro baseball career, in film debut, golfer Babe Didrikson, and scene-stealing Ray as oafish boxer.

Dist.: MGM/UA

PATCH OF BLUE, A 1966
★★★★ NR Drama 1:45 B&W
Dir: Guy Green ***Cast:*** Sidney Poitier, Shelley Winters, Elizabeth Hartman, Wallace Ford, Ivan Dixon, John Qualen

▶ Shut-in, blind Hartman, used as housekeeper by prostitute mom Winters, meets young black businessman Poitier on rare trip to park. Shocked by uneducated Hartman's forlorn life, Poitier befriends her despite racist Winters's ire; soon she's in love with him. Sensitive, thoughtful drama avoids sentimentality. Five Oscar nominations with Winters taking Best Supporting Actress.

Dist.: MGM/UA

PATERNITY 1981
★★★★ PG Comedy 1:33
☑ Adult situations, explicit language, adult humor
Dir: David Steinberg ***Cast:*** Burt Reynolds, Beverly D'Angelo, Paul Dooley, Norman Fell, Elizabeth Ashley, Lauren Hutton

▶ Confirmed bachelor Reynolds wants heir but not wife. With help of doctor Fell and attorney Dooley, he contracts with musician/waitress D'Angelo for her to bear his child. Deal sours when she falls in love with him. Lightweight comedy will please Reynolds's fans.

Dist.: Paramount

PAT GARRETT AND BILLY THE KID 1973
★ R Western 1:46
☑ Nudity, adult situations, explicit language, graphic violence
Dir: Sam Peckinpah ***Cast:*** James Coburn, Kris Kristofferson, Bob Dylan, Richard Jaeckel, Jason Robards, Jr., Slim Pickens

▶ Outlaw-turned-sheriff Coburn pursues buddy Kristofferson, a notorious gunslinger, in 1881 New Mexico. Lawman apprehends his old friend, who then escapes for final violent confrontation. Blue-chip director, quality cast, legendary Western story, and soundtrack by Dylan (also his debut as screen actor), but end result is an uneven and unexciting muddle. Recently restored to director Peckinpah's original version.

Dist.: MGM/UA

PATHER PANCHALI 1955 Indian
☆ NR Drama 1:52 B&W
Dir: Satyajit Ray ***Cast:*** Kanu Banerji, Karuna Banerji, Subir Banerji, Runki Banerji, Chunibala Devi

▶ Mother Karuna Banerji is left in charge of aged aunt Devi when husband Kanu Banerji departs their poverty-stricken little town to write. Devi dies, and so does Karuna Banerji's daughter. Son Subir Banerjee carries on. Masterful and moving study of the Indian poor was director Ray's first film. Shot on weekends by an amateur crew on a meager budget, first entry in Ray's Apu trilogy catapulted him to international fame. Ravi Shanker did the music. Followed by *Aparajito* and *The World of Apu.* [S]

Dist.: Foothill

PATHS OF GLORY 1957
★★ NR War/Drama 1:26 B&W
Dir: Stanley Kubrick ***Cast:*** Kirk Douglas, Ralph Meeker, Adolphe Menjou, George Macready, Wayne Morris, Richard Anderson

▶ During World War I, pompous French generals Menjou and Macready order regiment to assault impregnable German position despite protests of commander Douglas. When the attack fails utterly, three soldiers are court-martialed and executed for cowardice in an attempt to cover the high command's ineptitude. Considered by many one of the finest antiwar pics ever, harrowing drama boasts ultrarealistic trench scenes, seamless direction, and stellar performances with Douglas arguably at his best.

Dist.: CBS/Fox

PATRIOT, THE 1986
★ R Action-Adventure 1:25
☑ Nudity, adult situations, explicit language, violence
Dir: Frank Harris ***Cast:*** Gregg Henry, Simone Griffeth, Leslie Nielsen, Michael J. Pollard, Stack Pierce, Jeff Conaway

▶ When lunatics steal a nuclear warhead to sell to the Soviets, scuba expert Henry is called out of retirement. With help of admiral Nellsen and his beautiful daughter Griffeth, Henry saves the day. Clumsy script and technical ineptitude mar underwater action pic.

Dist.: Vestron

PATSY, THE 1964
★★ NR Comedy 1:40
Dir: Jerry Lewis ***Cast:*** Jerry Lewis, Ina Balin, Everett Sloane, Phil Harris, Keenan Wynn, John Carradine

▶ When their meal ticket is killed in a plane crash, show business manager Sloane and his cohorts pluck bellboy Lewis from obscurity to train him for stardom. Lewis fails at first but eventually gets his act together and takes it on "The Ed Sullivan Show." Interesting plot concept deserves more than star's broad clowning.

Dist.: IVE

PATTI ROCKS 1988
★ ★ R Comedy 1:26
☑ Nudity, adult situations, explicit language
Dir: David Burton Morris   *Cast:* Chris Mulkey,
John Jenkins, Karen Landry, David L. Turk
▶ Married Mulkey cons buddy Jenkins into
helping break news of wife and kids to preg-
nant girlfriend Landry. Jenkins beds Landry
and decides to help her raise Mulkey's child.
Chatty comedy skewers male chauvinism
and sexual myths.
Dist.: Virgin

PATTON 1970
★ ★ ★ ★ ★ PG Biography 2:51
☑ Explicit language, violence
Dir: Franklin J. Schaffner   *Cast:* George C.
Scott, Karl Malden, Stephen Young, Michael
Strong, Frank Latimore, James Edwards
▶ Compelling bio of World War II General
George Patton (Scott). A genius of tank war-
fare, Patton's fits of temper and public out-
spokenness put him at odds with his superiors
and eventually cause General Omar Bradley
(Malden) to relieve him of his command in
Sicily. Scott is simply brilliant as a born warrior
doomed to live in an age that no longer glorifies war. Film took eight Academy Awards, including Best Picture, Director, and Actor,
which Scott refused on the premise that actors shouldn't compete with each other.
Dist.: CBS/Fox

PATTY HEARST 1988
★ ★ R Biography 1:48
☑ Nudity, adult situations, explicit language
Dir: Paul Schrader   *Cast:* Natasha Richard-
son, William Forsythe, Ving Rhames, Frances
Fisher, Jodi Long, Olivia Barash
▶ True story of heiress Patty Hearst (Richard-
son), kidnapped, imprisoned, and brain-
washed by the radical Symbionese Liberation
Army. She participates in an SLA bank robbery
before arrest by FBI. Grim rehash of recent his-
tory features innovative direction and superb
Richardson.
Dist.: Media

PAULINE AT THE BEACH 1983 French
☆ R Comedy 1:35
☑ Nudity, explicit language
Dir: Eric Rohmer   *Cast:* Amanda Langlet,
Arielle Dombasle, Pascal Greggory, Feodor
Atkine, Simon de la Brosse, Rosette
▶ Fifteen-year-old Langlet spends summer at
Normandy beach with relatives and learns
about sex, love, and the French passion for
talking about both topics. Relatively plotless
and very chatty, airy comedy is for fans of
director Rohmer only. Striking cinematogra-
phy by the renowned Nestor Almendros.
[S]
Dist.: Media

PAWNBROKER, THE 1965
★ ★ ★ NR Drama 1:56 B&W
Dir: Sidney Lumet   *Cast:* Rod Steiger, Geral-

dine Fitzgerald, Brock Peters, Jaime Sanchez, Thelma Oliver, Marketa Kimbrell
▶ In Harlem, Jewish pawnbroker Steiger, bitter
survivor of the Holocaust, has lost all faith and
doesn't care that shop's black owner Peters is
a pimp and gangster. Social worker Fitzgerald
and employee Sanchez try to shake Steiger
out of his apathy but fail until Sanchez makes
the ultimate sacrifice. Grim social realism,
breakthrough depiction of minorities, and
captivating, Oscar-nominated performance
by Steiger distinguish this important and controversial film.
Dist.: Republic

PAYDAY 1973
★ R Drama 1:43
☑ Nudity, adult situations, explicit language
Dir: Daryl Duke   *Cast:* Rip Torn, Ahna Capri,
Elayne Heilveil, Michael C. Gwynne, Jeff
Morris, Cliff Emmich
▶ Chronicle of last thirty-six hours in life of on-
the-skids country singer Torn. Hard-hitting look
at groupies, bribes, drugs, and hardship of the
road skewers the myth of glamorous performing life. Well-honed script and solid acting, especially bravura Torn, mark this often overlooked but well-regarded film. Discriminating
viewers should take a look.
Dist.: Thorn/EMI

PEANUT BUTTER SOLUTION, THE 1986
Canadian
★ ★ PG Family 1:31
☑ Explicit language
Dir: Michael Rubbo   *Cast:* Mathew
Mackay, Siluck Saysanasy, Alison Podbrey,
Michael Hogan, Michel Maillot, Helen
Hughes
▶ Visiting a haunted house, eleven-year-old
Mackay is so scared that his hair literally falls
out. Ghosts later supply baldness cure, whose
recipe includes peanut butter, but resulting
hair growth is so phenomenal that further
misadventures occur. Offbeat family fare fea-
tures imaginative story line, likable characters,
and fine production values.
Dist.: New World

PEARL OF DEATH, THE 1944
★ ★ NR Mystery-Suspense 1:09 B&W
Dir: Roy William Neill   *Cast:* Basil Rathbone,
Nigel Bruce, Evelyn Ankers, Dennis Hoey,
Miles Mander, Rondo Hatton
▶ Rathbone and Bruce as London's ace de-
tective Sherlock Holmes and his bumbling
sidekick Dr. Watson pursue pearl thief Mander.
Mander employs an evil henchman, the "Ox-
ford Creeper," who kills his victims by snap-
ping their third vertebrae. One of the better
offerings in the Rathbone series climaxes with
battle between Holmes and the Creeper.
Dist.: CBS/Fox

PECK'S BAD BOY 1921
★ NR Comedy 0:51 B&W
Dir: Sam Wood   *Cast:* Jackie Coogan,

Wheeler Oakman, James Corrigan, Doris May, Raymond Hatton, Lillian Leighton
► Coogan, a small boy in a small town, wants very badly to go to the circus. He blackmails his father, frames his sister's beau, and gets into all sorts of comic trouble to achieve his goal. Slight silent film is primarily a vehicle for Coogan's classic child performance.
Dist.: Video Yesteryear

PECK'S BAD BOY WITH THE CIRCUS 1938
★ **NR Comedy 1:06 B&W**
Dir: Edward Cline ***Cast:*** Tommy Kelly, Ann Gillis, Edgar Kennedy, Benita Hume, Billy Gilbert, Spanky McFarland
► Peck's bad boy (Kelly) is back, and he's badder than ever. During an eventful circus trip, he slips the lions sleeping pills, puts on women's clothing, and rides bareback in the center ring. Charmless Kelly is no Jackie Coogan, but Kennedy is very funny as a befuddled lion tamer.
Dist.: Video Yesteryear

PEDESTRIAN, THE 1974 German
★ **PG Drama 1:37**
☑ Adult situations, violence
Dir: Maximilian Schell ***Cast:*** Gustav Rudolf Sellner, Maximilian Schell, Peter Hall, Gila von Weitershausen
► German engineering tycoon Sellner lives the good life until his world begins falling apart. It all culminates when he is charged with annihilating a Greek village during World War II. Gripping drama dealing with the harrowing affects of guilt was Germany's entry for the Best Foreign Film Oscar.
Dist.: Embassy

PEEPING TOM 1960 British
★★★ **NR Mystery-Suspense 1:49**
☑ Brief nudity, adult situations, explicit language
Dir: Michael Powell ***Cast:*** Carl Boehm, Moira Shearer, Anna Massey, Maxine Audley, Esmond Knight, Bartlett Mullins
► Disturbed movie cameraman Boehm tours London murdering women and photographing their death throes. Unique examination of voyeurism is both provocative and distasteful. Savaged by critics on release, cult favorite is now touted by many as a classic psychological study.
Dist.: Admit One Video

PEE-WEE'S BIG ADVENTURE 1985
★★ **PG Comedy 1:27**
☑ Mild violence
Dir: Tim Burton ***Cast:*** Pee-wee Herman, Elizabeth Daily, Mark Holton, Diane Salinger, James Brolin, Morgan Fairchild
► When his beloved bicycle is stolen, Pee-wee travels cross-country to the Alamo to recover it. Along the way, he hooks up with an escaped convict, a waitress who dreams of France, and bikers whom he entertains with a "Tequila" clog dance. Insanely surreal bit of nonsense, full of lunatic gags and bizarrely clever production design. Will appeal to Pee-wee fans of all ages. Fun moment: Pee-wee's encounter with "Large Marge." **(CC)**
Dist.: Warner

PEGGY SUE GOT MARRIED 1986
★★★★ **PG-13 Fantasy 1:43**
☑ Adult situations, explicit language
Dir: Francis Coppola ***Cast:*** Kathleen Turner, Nicolas Cage, Barry Miller, Catherine Hicks, Maureen O'Sullivan, Leon Ames
► Peggy Sue (Turner), the mother of two, is separated from her husband, TV appliance pitchman Cage. She attends her twenty-fifth high school reunion where she's crowned queen, blacks out, and time travels back to 1960. As a teenager with the brain of a grown woman, Peggy Sue has the chance to change her destiny. Will she repeat the same mistakes? Delightful adult fairy tale is provocative, well-acted, and stylishly directed. **(CC)**
Dist.: CBS/Fox

PELLE THE CONQUEROR 1988 Danish
★ **PG-13 Drama 2:30**
☑ Adult situations, violence, nudity
Dir: Billie August ***Cast:*** Max Von Sydow, Pelle Hvenegaard, Erik Paaske, Kristina Tornqvists, Morten Jorgensen
► Impoverished Swede Von Sydow and son Hvenegaard go to Denmark to work on farm. Hvenegaard comes of age as they face many hardships, including a tyrannical overseer. Long, stately epic with affecting moments and insightful political points. Actors (especially the Oscar-nominated Von Sydow) are cast to perfection, but slow pace limits appeal to the discriminating. Won Academy Award as Best Foreign Film. [S]
Dist.: HBO

PENDULUM 1969
★★ **PG Drama 1:46**
☑ Adult situations, explicit language, violence
Dir: George Schaefer ***Cast:*** George Peppard, Jean Seberg, Richard Kiley, Charles McGraw, Madeleine Sherwood, Robert F. Lyons
► After convicted rapist-murderer Lyons wins release on technicality argued by liberal attorney Kiley, irate police captain Peppard takes leave. He's promptly arrested for murder of wife Seberg and her lover and retains Kiley for defense, but breaks out of jail when conviction appears likely. Fascinating premise is given too soft a treatment to be completely satisfying.
Dist.: RCA/Columbia

PENITENT, THE 1988
★ **PG-13 Drama 1:34**
☑ Brief nudity, adult situations
Dir: Cliff Osmond ***Cast:*** Raul Julia, Armand Assante, Rona Freed, Julie Carmen, Lucy Reina
► Struggling farmer Julia learns that his frigid

wife Freed is having an affair with his best friend Assante. Julia retaliates by forcing Assante to play Christ in the local village's yearly reenactment of the Crucifixion. Ponderous melodrama loses focus despite attractive cast.
Dist.: IVE

PENITENTIARY 1979
★ ★ R Action-Adventure 1:39
☑ Nudity, adult situations, explicit language, graphic violence
Dir: Jamaa Fanaka   *Cast:* Leon Isaac Kennedy, Thommy Pollard, Hazel Spears, Badja Djola, Chuck Mitchell, Floyd Chatman
▶ Framed for murder, Kennedy relies on his fists to avoid homosexual advances in prison. His fighting skill leads to a chance for early parole in a boxing championship, but he must first thwart a murder plot by a jealous inmate. Tough, honest prison drama benefits from Kennedy's gritty performance as "Too Sweet." Led to two inferior sequels.
Dist.: Unicorn

PENITENTIARY II 1982
★ R Action-Adventure 1:49
☑ Rape, nudity, adult situations, explicit language, graphic violence
Dir: Jamaa Fanaka   *Cast:* Leon Isaac Kennedy, Ernie Hudson, Glynn Turman, Peggy Blow, Ebony Wright, Mr. T
▶ Sequel to *Penitentiary* finds Too Sweet (Kennedy) ordered to throw his nationally televised boxing match with a prison champ by the villainous Half Dead (Hudson), who's holding Too Sweet's family hostage. Ugly, violent melodrama will disappoint fans of the original.
Dist.: MGM/UA

PENITENTIARY III 1987
★ R Action-Adventure 1:31
☑ Adult situations, explicit language, graphic violence
Dir: Jamaa Fanaka   *Cast:* Leon Isaac Kennedy, Anthony Geary, Steve Antin, Ric Mancini, Kessler Raymond, Magic Schwarz
▶ Boxer Too Sweet (Kennedy), drugged during a match, kills his opponent and winds up in the pen again. Refusing a chance to fight for jailed mobster Geary, he is set upon by Raymond, a vicious midget (and real-life wrestler Haiti Kid). Too Sweet subdues Raymond before facing Geary's monstrous fighter Schwarz. Sequel to *Penitentiary II* continues formula's emphasis on sadism and wooden acting. (CC)
Dist.: Warner

PENN & TELLER GET KILLED 1989
★ R Comedy 1:29
☑ Adult situations, explicit language, violence
Dir: Arthur Penn   *Cast:* Penn Jillete, Teller, Caitlin Clarke, David Patrick Kelly
▶ Real-life magicians Penn & Teller showcase

their mastery of the art and abrasive comic style in this vehicle scripted by the duo. Obnoxious loudmouth Penn brags during a TV appearance that he would enjoy having someone make an attempt on his life. He gets his wish as psycho fan Kelly stalks him. Unfortunately, numerous gags are overplayed to the point of boredom, and director Penn, an odd choice for this project, seems at a loss. (CC)
Dist.: Warner

PENNIES FROM HEAVEN 1981
☆ R Musical 1:48
☑ Nudity, adult situations, explicit language
Dir: Herbert Ross   *Cast:* Steve Martin, Bernadette Peters, Christopher Walken, Jessica Harper, Vernel Bagneris
▶ Stylized, off-beat entertainment, set in 1930s Depression era. Unhappily married sheet-music salesman Martin fantasizes about a more glamourous life with mistress Peters; the two frequently break into song just like Fred and Ginger. Before they can run away together, he's arrested for murder and she becomes a streetwalker. Extraordinary cameo by Walken who strips to "Let's Misbehave." Bold and risky, but not for all tastes. Adapted from the well-received BBC TV series written by Dennis Potter.
Dist.: MGM/UA

PENNY SERENADE 1941
★ ★ ★ ★ NR Drama 2:00 B&W
Dir: George Stevens   *Cast:* Irene Dunne, Cary Grant, Beulah Bondi, Edgar Buchanan, Ann Doran
▶ Journalist Grant weds Dunne and brings her to Japan, where she becomes pregnant but miscarries. Back in the States, the couple adopt a baby but tragedy strikes again. Get out your handkerchiefs for this well-made weeper. Sentimental classic boasts strong performances by Grant (Oscar-nominated), Dunne, and Buchanan.
Dist.: Various   ⓒ

PEOPLE NEXT DOOR, THE 1970
★ R Drama 1:33
☑ Adult situations, explicit language
Dir: David Greene   *Cast:* Deborah Winters, Eli Wallach, Julie Harris, Stephen McHattie, Hal Holbrook, Cloris Leachman
▶ Suburban parents Wallach and Harris discover that their daughter Winters is strung out on LSD. After much hand-wringing, they take action to break her habit and expose the neighborhood drug pusher. Based on a network teleplay, dated cautionary tale has been surpassed by many subsequent and more gut-wrenching efforts.
Dist.: CBS/Fox

PEOPLE THAT TIME FORGOT, THE 1977
British
★ ★ ★ PG Sci-Fi 1:30
☑ Violence
Dir: Kevin Connor   *Cast:* Patrick Wayne,

Doug McClure, Sarah Douglas, Dana Gillespie, Thorley Walters, Shane Rimmer
▶ Sequel to *The Land That Time Forgot*, set in 1918, features Wayne as the leader of search party seeking missing friend McClure. Douglas is a newspaper photographer along for the ride. A dinosaur attack forces the team onto an island containing creatures and cavemen. Not bad, but not as good as the original.
Dist.: Nelson

PEPE LE MOKO 1937 French
★ NR Drama 1:30 B&W
Dir: Julien Duvivier ***Cast:*** Jean Gabin, Mireille Balin, Gabriel Gabrio, Lucas Gridoux
▶ Gangster Gabin avoids arrest as long as he remains in the Casbah section of Algiers. He falls for lovely Balin, and their affair ultimately settles his fate in this elegantly directed melodrama. Gabin is magnetic in the title role, portrayed with equal charisma by Charles Boyer in the slavishly faithful American remake *Algiers*. [S]
Dist.: Various

PERFECT 1985
★★ R Drama 2:00
☑ Brief nudity, adult situations, explicit language
Dir: James Bridges ***Cast:*** John Travolta, Jamie Lee Curtis, Marilu Henner, Laraine Newman, Anne De Salvo, Jann Wenner
▶ *Rolling Stone* magazine reporter Travolta falls for aerobics instructor Curtis while researching a story about the health club/singles scene. They quarrel about his ethics but when the government harasses him to reveal his sources on a computer scandal he uncovers, she stands by her man. Slick, glossy, and superficial but those sweaty bodies, especially Curtis's, are easy to watch. Appearances by Carly Simon and real-life *Rolling Stone* publisher Wenner. **(CC)**
Dist.: RCA/Columbia

PERFECT FURLOUGH, THE 1958
★★★ NR Comedy 1:33
Dir: Blake Edwards ***Cast:*** Tony Curtis, Janet Leigh, Keenan Wynn, Linda Cristal, Elaine Stritch, Troy Donahue
▶ To boost morale, Army psychologist Leigh comes up with a scheme to award a particular G.I. with the furlough of his dreams. Winner turns out to be girl-happy Curtis, who opts for a trip to Paris with a curvaceous starlet. Despite Curtis's plans, Leigh comes along as chaperone. Workmanlike comedy by superior craftsman Blake.
Dist.: KVC

PERFECT MATCH, THE 1987
★★★ PG Comedy 1:32
☑ Explicit language
Dir: Mark Deimel ***Cast:*** Marc McClure, Jennifer Edwards, Diane Stilwell, Rob Paulsen, Wayne Woodsen, Karen Witter
▶ Unlucky-in-love McClure and video store clerk Edwards meet after glamorously misrepresenting themselves through personal ads. On a weekend together in the mountains, they learn the truth about each other, but romance is still possible. Slow to start, but charming, klutzy pair pulls this together.
Dist.: Virgin

PERFECT WITNESS 1989
★★★★ NR Drama/MFTV 1:41
☑ Explicit language, violence
Dir: Robert Mandel ***Cast:*** Aidan Quinn, Brian Dennehy, Stockard Channing, Laura Harrington
▶ Provocative drama about restaurant owner Quinn, an eyewitness to a gangland rubout. He is U.S. attorney Dennehy's perfect witness, but will he be willing to take the stand after his family is threatened? Fine ensemble work highlights this probing crime story which raises important questions about ethical and judicial issues. **(CC)**
Dist.: HBO

PERFORMANCE 1970 British
☆ R Drama 1:46
☑ Adult situations, explicit language, violence
Dir: Donald Cammell, Nicolas Roeg ***Cast:*** James Fox, Mick Jagger, Anita Pallenberg, Michele Breton, Ann Sidney, John Bindon
▶ After killing the wrong man, London gangster Fox hides out in townhouse of decadent rock star Jagger (in his first starring role). Accompanied by groupies Pallenberg and Breton, they embark on an odyssey of drugs, sex, and psychological games. Perverse, sadistic, deliberately bizarre film has some arresting moments (notably Jagger's striptease to his "Memo From Turner") despite an incomprehensible plot.
Dist.: Warner

PERIL 1985 French
☆ R Mystery-Suspense 1:40
☑ Nudity, adult situations, explicit language, violence
Dir: Michel Deville ***Cast:*** Christopher Malavoy, Nichole Garcia, Michel Piccoli, Richard Bohringer, Anemone, Anais Jeanneret
▶ Passions smolder as guitar teacher Malovoy is seduced by the wife of an industrialist, and gets involved with a hitman and a neighbor who photographs his affair. The hitman saves Malovoy, but later tries to kill him as hitman is involved in an intrigue with the industrialist. Not out for traditional suspense, this sexually charged, cerebral thriller makes its mark with a strong mood of paranoid perversity. [S]
Dist.: RCA/Columbia

PERILS OF PAULINE, THE 1947
★★ NR Musical 1:36
Dir: George Marshall ***Cast:*** Betty Hutton, John Lund, Constance Collier, Billy de Wolfe, William Demarest
▶ Stage-smitten Hutton graduates from seamstress to Broadway star, but stomps off

the boards after a fight with love interest Lund. After causing a wild scene on a film set, she wins the title role in *The Perils of Pauline*, a serial. Hutton gives her all in this top-notch musical (very loosely based on the life of silent film star Pearl White), with Frank Loesser songs like "I Wish I Didn't Love You So" and "Poppa Don't Preach to Me."
Dist.: Various

PERMANENT RECORD 1988
★ ★ ★ PG-13 Drama 1:31
☑ Adult situations, explicit language
Dir: Marisa Silver ***Cast:*** Alan Boyce, Keanu Reeves, Michelle Meyrink, Jennifer Rubin, Pamela Gidley
► Subtle, sensitive account of how the lives of various high schoolers are irrevocably changed when their talented classmate Boyce commits suicide. Best friend Reeves suffers the most, but learns to cope with Boyce's decision. Perceptive, low-key drama features music by Joe Strummer, formerly of the Clash. Lou Reed has a brief cameo as himself. (CC)
Dist.: Paramount

PERMISSION TO KILL 1975 British
★ PG Espionage 1:36
☑ Violence, adult situations
Dir: Cyril Frankel ***Cast:*** Dirk Bogarde, Ava Gardner, Bekim Fehmiu, Timothy Dalton, Frederic Forrest
► Exiled Third World Communist Fehmiu is determined to return to his home country and foment trouble. Bogarde heads a mysterious secret security agency that will take whatever actions necessary to keep him from carrying out his intentions. Unrelieved seriousness in a grim, overlong spy story.
Dist.: Nelson

PERSONA 1967 Swedish
☆ NR Drama 1:21 B&W
Dir: Ingmar Bergman ***Cast:*** Liv Ullmann, Bibi Andersson, Gunnar Bjornstrand, Margaretha Krook
► Nurse Andersson takes care of actress Ullmann who has suffered a nervous breakdown and been rendered mute. As the relationship grows closer, a personality transference occurs. Landmark, brilliantly made drama with tremendous performances. Director Bergman's technique is dazzling but demanding; may be too abstract for the casual viewer (especially in the climactic repeated confession sequence). [S]
Dist.: Various

PERSONAL BEST 1982
★ ★ R Drama/Sports 2:01
☑ Nudity, adult situations, explicit language
Dir: Robert Towne ***Cast:*** Mariel Hemingway, Scott Glenn, Patrice Donnelly, Kenny Moore, Jim Moody
► Female track-and-field athletes Hemingway and Donnelly become lovers but their relationship hits the rocks under the pressures of competition. Hemingway eventually finds a new love in male athlete Moore. Compassionate, tasteful handling of the lesbian theme, winning performances (especially Glenn as the coach), intelligent direction, and exciting track footage; plotting is somewhat thin, however.
Dist.: Warner

PERSONALS, THE 1982
★ PG Comedy 1:28
☑ Adult situations, explicit language
Dir: Peter Markle ***Cast:*** Bill Schoppert, Karen Landry, Paul Eiding, Michael Laskin, Vicki Dakil
► "Straight, White, Male, recently divorced, thirty-two, interested in Picasso, Prokofiev, roller skating and Chicken Kiev." With this personals ad, nerdy-but-nice Schoppert meets pretty, literate psychologist Landry. Everything is wonderful until he discovers she's married. Amiable, winsome comedy, set in Minneapolis, features steady performances but no surprises.
Dist.: Nelson

PERSONAL SERVICES 1987 British
★ R Comedy/Drama 1:43
☑ Nudity, strong sexual content, adult situations, explicit language, mild violence
Dir: Terry Jones ***Cast:*** Julie Walters, Alec McCowen, Shirley Stelfox, Danny Schiller, Victoria Hardcastle, Tim Woodward
► Waitress Walters supplements her income by managing apartments rented by prostitutes. When she owes money to her own landlord, she repays him with sexual favors and falls into a new career as call girl and madam. Kinky and witty but overly talky and strictly for adults. Based on the life of English madam Cynthia Payne.
Dist.: Vestron

PETE KELLY'S BLUES 1955
★ ★ ★ NR Drama 1:35
Dir: Jack Webb ***Cast:*** Jack Webb, Janet Leigh, Edmond O'Brien, Peggy Lee, Andy Devine, Lee Marvin
► Interesting, unsentimental gangster drama set in Kansas City during the Roaring Twenties. Webb leads a jazz combo who take on crimelord O'Brien and his extorting henchmen. Lee won an Oscar nomination for her role as O'-Brien's alcoholic mistress. Best for the good score and rare appearances by top jazz musicians Ella Fitzgerald, George Van Eps, Joe Venuti, etc.
Dist.: Warner

PETE 'N' TILLIE 1972
★ ★ ★ PG Drama 1:40
☑ Adult situations, explicit language
Dir: Martin Ritt ***Cast:*** Walter Matthau, Carol Burnett, Geraldine Page, Barry Nelson, René Auberjonois, Lee H. Montgomery
► Ambitious, often charming drama blends comedy and pathos while examining unlikely

marriage between compulsive jokester Matthau and Burnett, an aging woman afraid of spinsterhood. Verges on the mawkish, but redeemed by thoughtful performances. Julius Epstein's adaptation of *Witch's Milk* by Peter DeVries received an Oscar nomination.
Dist.: MCA

PETE'S DRAGON 1977
★ ★ ★ ★ ★ G Musical/Family 2:17
Dir: Don Caffey *Cast:* Helen Reddy, Mickey Rooney, Sean Marshall, Red Buttons, Shelley Winters, Jim Dale
▶ Popular Disney fantasy mixes animation with real characters in this playful romp through Passamaquoddy, Maine, with orphan Pete and his friend Elliot, a bright green dragon with pink wings and the power to make himself invisible. Escaping from awful backwoods Winters, Pete and Elliot share many adventures with friendly lighthouse keeper Rooney and his fair daughter Reddy. Kids will cheer as Elliot's clowning gets Pete into all kinds of trouble. (CC)
Dist.: Buena Vista

PETRIFIED FOREST, THE 1936
★ ★ ★ NR Drama 1:23 B&W
Dir: Archie Mayo *Cast:* Bette Davis, Leslie Howard, Humphrey Bogart, Genevieve Tobin, Dick Foran
▶ Waitress Davis and disillusioned writer Howard are among the captives when criminal Duke Mantee (Bogart) takes hostages at a Southwestern diner. Adaptation of Robert Sherwood play, which both Howard and Bogart starred in on Broadway, is dated and stagy but still engrossing, thanks to Bogart's breakthrough performance and the wistfully romantic Davis.
Dist.: MGM/UA

PET SEMATARY 1989
★ ★ ★ ★ R Horror 1:45
☑ Explicit language, violence
Dir: Mary Lambert *Cast:* Dale Midkiff, Fred Gwynne, Denise Crosby, Brad Greenquist, Michael Lombard, Blaze Berdahl
▶ When the family cat is killed, Midkiff is able to resurrect pet by putting it in Indian burial ground that can revive the dead. When tragedy strikes the family, Midkiff returns to the "Pet Sematary" for help but winds up creating a monster. Chilling, eerie shocker with Lambert's fluid direction overcoming plot flaws. Based on the Stephen King best-seller. (CC)
Dist.: Paramount

PETULIA 1968
★ ★ R Drama 1:45
☑ Adult situations, explicit language
Dir: Richard Lester *Cast:* Julie Christie, George C. Scott, Richard Chamberlain, Arthur Hill, Shirley Knight, Joseph Cotten
▶ Unsettling, beautifully photographed drama about the bittersweet romance between divorced doctor Scott and wealthy

Christie, who may be the victim of abuse from her husband Chamberlain. Penetrating look at San Francisco's hippie movement provides a satirical backdrop to superb cast and absorbing script.
Dist.: Warner

PHANTASM 1979
★ ★ R Horror 1:29
☑ Nudity, explicit language, graphic violence
Dir: Don Coscarelli *Cast:* Michael Baldwin, Bill Thornbury, Reggie Bannister, Angus Scrimm, Ken Jones, Kathy Lester
▶ Oregon orphan Baldwin investigates when friend of older brother Thornbury is killed. Murderous mortician Scrimm is the number-one suspect. Visually imaginative and often quite terrifying, especially when Scrimm and a lethal flying ball are on screen; audiences may find the farfetched plot too silly. Spawned a sequel.
Dist.: Nelson

PHANTASM II 1988
★ ★ R Horror 1:30
☑ Nudity, explicit language, violence
Dir: Don Coscarelli *Cast:* James Le Gros, Reggie Bannister, Angus Scrimm, Paula Irvine, Samantha Phillips, Kenneth Tiger
▶ Le Gros, put in psychiatric clinic after events of *Phantasm*, gets out and finds he wasn't imagining things: murderous mortician Scrimm is back with his flying silver ball to create deadly havoc. Flashy production an improvement over its low-budget predecessor, but farfetched script lacks the first entry's originality. Effective use of special effects and music.
Dist.: MCA

PHANTOM EMPIRE, THE 1989
☆ R Horror 1:30
☑ Explicit language, violence
Dir: Fred Olen Ray *Cast:* Ross Hagen, Jeffrey Combs, Dawn Wildsmith, Sybil Danning, Russ Tamblyn, Susan Stokey
▶ Stokey hires Hagen and Wildsmith to search caves for a lost city. They discover prehistoric bikini-clad women running for their lives from assorted monsters. Moronic adventure with cut-rate production values, godawful acting, and cheesy special effects.
Dist.: Prism

PHANTOM FROM SPACE 1953
☆ NR Sci-Fi 1:12 B&W
Dir: W. Lee Wilder *Cast:* Ted Cooper, Rudolph Anders, Noreen Nash, Harry Landers, Dick Sands, Jack Daley
▶ A strange blip on the nation's radar screens turns out to be a flying saucer whose pilot attacks picnickers. The alien is invisible without his spacesuit, and must be surrounded by his own atmosphere to survive. When scientist Anders gets hold of the alien's tank-like suit, the now-frightened spaceman is doomed.

Not very exciting, but some sympathy for stranded alien.
Dist.: Sinister

PHANTOM OF LIBERTY, THE 1974 French
☆ R Drama 1:44
☑ Adult situations, nudity
Dir: Luis Buñuel *Cast:* Jean-Claude Brialy, Adolfo Celi, Michel Piccoli, Monica Vitti, Paul Frankeur, Helen Perdriere
▶ A compelling nonnarrative with odd jokes and surreal blackouts flowing into one another with dreamlike logic. Main sequence has a well-dressed group seated decorously at toilets set up around a fancy table. One by one they excuse themselves to go devour food in the bathroom. It's a concept that would amuse a five-year-old, or a seventy-five-year-old—director Buñuels's age at the time he made this gleeful experiment in topsy-turveydom. Ⓢ
Dist.: Media

PHANTOM OF THE MALL 1989
☆ R Horror 1:31
☑ Nudity, adult situations, explicit language, violence
Dir: Richard Friedman *Cast:* Derek Rydall, Kari Whitman, Morgan Fairchild, Jonathan Goldsmith, Rob Estes, Pauly Shore
▶ Mayor Fairchild dedicates a shiny new mall that happens to be haunted by disfigured teen Rydall. Rydall stalks air shafts, killing shoppers and rescuing ex-girlfriend Whitman from attacker. Scares are few and far between in this derivative bomb.
Dist.: Fries

PHANTOM OF THE OPERA, THE 1925
★ ★ NR Horror 2:02 B&W
Dir: Rupert Julian *Cast:* Lon Chaney, Mary Philbin, Norman Kerry, Snitz Edwards, Gibson Gowland, Virginia Pearson
▶ Masked phantom Chaney haunts the Paris Opera and guides understudy Philbin to stardom. However, in the justly classic unmasking scene, she encounters the true horror of her mentor's visage. Perhaps because of the subsequent remakes and the Broadway musical, silent film has an overblown reputation, as its story is slow-paced and somber. But no one can deny its visual opulence or the power of Chaney's performance.
Dist.: Video Yesteryear

PHANTOM OF THE OPERA 1943
★ ★ ★ NR Horror 1:32
Dir: Arthur Lubin *Cast:* Nelson Eddy, Susanna Foster, Claude Rains, Edgar Barrier, Leo Carrillo, Jane Farrar
▶ Acid-scarred violinist Rains haunts Paris opera house and promotes the career of protégé Foster. Her beau Eddy finds himself involved when Rains goes on a murderous rampage. Lavish, music-filled production with less emphasis on terror than other versions; nice work by Rains as a sympathetic Phantom.
Dist.: MCA

PHANTOM OF THE OPERA, THE 1989
★ R Horror 1:30
☑ Brief nudity, explicit language, violence
Dir: Dwight H. Little *Cast:* Robert Englund, Jill Schoelen, Alex Hyde-White, Bill Nighy, Stephanie Lawrence
▶ Auditioning for a Broadway show, Schoelen is knocked on the head and transported a hundred years into the past, where she sings at the London Opera House. Englund is the resident phantom, horribly disfigured and driven to serial murder in his obsession for Schoelen. Crass reworking of too-often-told tale substitutes spilled guts for suspense, romance, and genuine terror.
Dist.: RCA/Columbia

PHANTOM OF THE PARADISE 1974
★ ★ PG Musical 1:32
☑ Explicit language, violence
Dir: Brian De Palma *Cast:* Paul Williams, William Finley, Jessica Harper, George Memmoli, Gerrit Graham
▶ Surprisingly sturdy parody of *The Phantom of the Opera* and *Faust*: evil rock promoter Williams steals songs from naive composer Finley who's then horribly scarred in an accident. Finley haunts Williams's rock palace, where he becomes obsessed with young singer Harper. Despite unfocused plot, scores some satirical points, particularly Graham's overdone macho singer. Williams's score received an Oscar nomination.
Dist.: CBS/Fox

PHANTOM TOLLBOOTH, THE 1970
★ ★ ★ G Animation 1:30
Dir: Chuck Jones, David Monahan, Abe Levitow *Cast:* Butch Patrick, voices of Mel Blanc, Daws Butler, Candy CandidoConried, Hans Conried, June Foray
▶ Bored youngster Patrick drives his toy car through a "phantom tollbooth" which appears in his bedroom. He's then transported (and animated) into a wonderful world disrupted by conflict between Letters and Numbers, as each group believes it's more important to society. Charming children's picture offers likable characters, diverting songs, and educational impact.
Dist.: MGM/UA

PHAR LAP 1984 Australian
★ ★ ★ ★ PG Drama/Sports 1:47
☑ Explicit language
Dir: Simon Wincer *Cast:* Tom Burlinson, Ron Leibman, Martin Vaughan, Judy Morris, Celia Deburgh
▶ True story of champion come-from-behind racehorse, Phar Lap, a huge money winner and symbol of hope for Australians in the early 1930s. Owned by American Jewish businessman Leibman, who had to fight anti-Semitism to race the horse, Phar Lap was trained by brutish fanatic Vaughan, but the love of stable boy Burlinson made him the winner of

thirty-seven races in three years. Thoroughbred entertainment. (CC)
Dist.: CBS/Fox

PHASE IV 1974
★ ★ PG Sci-Fi 1:26
☑ Violence
Dir: Saul Bass *Cast:* Nigel Davenport, Mi-
chael Murphy, Lynne Frederick, Alan Gifford,
Robert Henderson, Helen Horton
▶ When humanity is threatened by super-
powered race of ants, scientists Davenport,
Murphy, and Frederick attempt to find a solu-
tion at an Arizona desert lab. Bass, who de-
signed the credits for classic Hitchcock films
like *Vertigo* and *North by Northwest*, makes a
stylish directorial debut.
Dist.: Paramount

PHILADELPHIA EXPERIMENT, THE 1984
★ ★ ★ ★ PG Sci-Fi 1:41
☑ Explicit language, violence
Dir: Stewart Raffill *Cast:* Michael Paré,
Nancy Allen, Bobby DiCicco, Kene Holiday,
Eric Christmas
▶ Sailors Paré and DiCicco time travel from
1940s to 1984 when a clandestine government experiment goes awry. Chased by military men, Paré finds himself confused by a
world in which an actor is President. Allen
helps him elude capture. Lively and inventive
despite illogical plot and uneven performances. An entertaining surprise.
Dist.: HBO

PHILADELPHIA STORY, THE 1940
★ ★ ★ ★ NR Comedy 1:52 B&W
Dir: George Cukor *Cast:* Cary Grant, Katharine Hepburn, James Stewart, Ruth Hussey, John Howard, Roland Young
▶ Priceless romantic comedy about the
chaos before heiress Hepburn's second wedding when her ex-husband Grant and meddling reporter Stewart unexpectedly arrive. Extraordinary acting throughout, with special
kudos to James Stewart's Oscar-winning turn
and Virginia Weidler's sharp-tongued youngster. Glossy adaptation of Philip Barry's Broadway hit betrays its stage origins, but Donald
Ogden Stewart's Oscar-winning screenplay
retains enough sparkling dialogue to make
this consistently delightful.
Dist.: MGM/UA ©

PHOBIA 1980 Canadian
★ R Mystery-Suspense 1:30
☑ Nudity, violence
Dir: John Huston *Cast:* Paul Michael
Glaser, Susan Hogan, John Colicos, David
Bolt, Patricia Collins, David Eisner
▶ Glaser is an experimental psychiatrist who
may or may not be killing off his "guinea pig"
patients. Girlfriend Hogan learns the awful
truth too late to save them. Difficult to believe
Huston directed this unsavory, barely sus-
penseful thriller. (CC)
Dist.: Paramount

PHOENIX THE WARRIOR 1988
☆ NR Action-Adventure 1:26
☑ Nudity, explicit language, violence
Dir: Robert Hayes *Cast:* Persis Khambatta,
Kathleen Kinmont, Peggy Sands, James
Emery, Sheila Howard
▶ A series of wars have destroyed all the
world's males, leaving "The Bitch" (Khambatta) as reigning Queen of the World. A challenge to her dominance comes from female
warrior Phoenix (Kinmont), who arrives on the
scene with—a man! As junky as they come,
with TV-worshipping mutants and nude bathing under a waterfall.
Dist.: SVS

PHONE CALL FROM A STRANGER 1952
★ ★ NR Drama 1:36 B&W
Dir: Jean Negulesco *Cast:* Shelley Winters,
Gary Merrill, Michael Rennie, Keenan Wynn,
Bette Davis, Beatrice Straight
▶ On a plane flight to Los Angeles, lawyer
Merrill befriends three strangers: failed actress
Winters, blustering salesman Wynn, and Ren-
nie, a doctor whose drunken driving has
caused three deaths. Plane crash kills the
three; Merrill decides to break the news to
their survivors, including Wynn's wife Davis. In-
triguing anthology drama features good per-
formances by talented cast. (CC)
Dist.: CBS/Fox

PHYSICAL EVIDENCE 1989
★ ★ ★ R Mystery-Suspense 1:39
☑ Explicit language, violence
Dir: Michael Crichton *Cast:* Burt Reynolds,
Theresa Russell, Ned Beatty, Kay Lenz, Ted
McGinley
▶ Reynolds, a suspended Boston cop who is
the chief suspect in a mobster's murder, is
forced to accept ambitious but inex-
perienced attorney Russell as his lawyer.
Spurning prosecutor Beatty's plea-bargaining
deal, she sets out to prove Reynolds was
framed. Formulaic courtroom drama finds Rus-
sell out of her element, but Reynolds turns in
one of his best performances in years.
Dist.: Vestron

PICASSO TRIGGER 1989
☆ R Action-Adventure 1:39
☑ Nudity, strong sexual content, graphic violence
Dir: Andy Sidaris *Cast:* Steve Bond, Dona
Spier, John Aprea, Hope Marie Carlton, Harold Diamond, Roberta Vasquez
▶ Appearances by six former *Playboy* models
highlight this mixture of martial arts, explosions, and gratuitous nudity. Plot is comic book
spy skullduggery, with Bond heading up
group of fighting experts out to stop bad guy
Aprea from carrying out mass assassination of
federal agents. Lots of heavy action interspersed with soft porn.
Dist.: Warner

PICK A STAR 1937
★ NR Comedy 1:10 B&W

Dir: Edward Sedgwick *Cast:* Jack Haley, Rosina Lawrence, Patsy Kelly, Mischa Auer, Stan Laurel, Oliver Hardy

▶ After being tricked by a contest that promised an entree into pictures, Iowa girl Lawrence navigates Tinseltown byways alongside love interest Haley, with stardom the inevitable outcome. Laurel and Hardy are shoehorned into the plot for a few funny minutes, as are several strained musical numbers, but overall there is not much exciting here, and Haley is particularly drippy. Also known as *Movie Struck.*
Dist.: Cable

PICK-UP ARTIST, THE 1987
★ ★ PG-13 Comedy/Drama 1:21
☑ Adult situations, explicit language
Dir: James Toback *Cast:* Molly Ringwald, Robert Downey, Jr., Dennis Hopper, Danny Aiello, Harvey Keitel

▶ Downey makes a career out of conquering women, until he meets his match in Ringwald who condescends to a one-night stand but won't supply her phone number. Convoluted subplot involves Ringwald's alcoholic gambling father Hopper and gangster Keitel to whom he owes a fortune. Ringwald projects sweetness and sensuality. Lively rock soundtrack with title song by Stevie Wonder. (CC)
Dist.: CBS/Fox

PICKWICK PAPERS 1954 British
★ ★ NR Drama 1:49 B&W
Dir: Noel Langley *Cast:* James Hayter, James Donald, Hermione Baddeley, Hermione Gingold, Joyce Grenfell, Alexander Gauge

▶ Merry, middle-aged Pickwick (Hayter) forms a society devoted to gathering interesting bits of knowledge and taking adventurous field trips. Good-hearted group must get Pickwick out of prison when Baddeley enmeshes him in a breach-of-promise suit. Based on Charles Dickens's first novel, entertaining effort is funny, touching, dramatic, and extremely heartwarming.
Dist.: United

PICNIC 1956
★ ★ ★ ★ NR Drama 1:53
Dir: Joshua Logan *Cast:* William Holden, Rosalind Russell, Kim Novak, Betty Field, Arthur O'Connell, Cliff Robertson

▶ Wanderer Holden hooks up with old pal Robertson in a Kansas town. Robertson's girlfriend Novak falls for Holden, as does teacher Russell. Probing and atmospheric adaptation of the Pulitzer prize–winning William Inge play. Electric Holden/Novak chemistry; tremendous performance from Russell.
Dist.: RCA/Columbia

PICNIC AT HANGING ROCK 1979 Australian
★ ★ PG Drama 1:50
☑ Adult situations, explicit language

Dir: Peter Weir *Cast:* Rachel Roberts, Dominic Guard, Helen Morse, Anne Lambert, Margaret Nelson

▶ On Valentine's Day, 1900, teachers and students from an exclusive Australian girls' boarding school prepare for an excursion to the mysterious Hanging Rock near Mt. Macedon. Three girls and a teacher disappear without explanation. Challenging, inventive adaptation of a John Lindsay novel has an evocative but puzzling atmosphere.
Dist.: Vestron

PICTURE MOMMY DEAD 1966
★ ★ NR Horror 1:28
Dir: Bert I. Gordon *Cast:* Don Ameche, Martha Hyer, Zsa Zsa Gabor, Susan Gordon, Maxwell Reed, Wendell Corey

▶ When Ameche's wife Gabor dies, his daughter Gordon takes it so badly she is institutionalized. Upon her release, her new stepmother Hyer tries to get the family fortune by driving Gordon batty again. Not without a certain sleazy vitality, although Ameche deserves better material.
Dist.: Nelson

PICTURE OF DORIAN GRAY, THE 1945
★ ★ ★ NR Drama 1:50 C/B&W
Dir: Albert Lewin *Cast:* George Sanders, Hurd Hatfield, Donna Reed, Angela Lansbury, Lowell Gilmore, Peter Lawford

▶ Exemplary adaptation of Oscar Wilde's classic novel about nineteenth-century rake Hatfield, who makes a satanic pact to retain his youthful looks while his portrait ages hideously. Strong support from Sanders, as the man who initially corrupts Hatfield, and Oscar-nominated Lansbury as a jilted singer. Harry Stradling's scintillating photography won an Oscar. Original release showed the portrait in Technicolor.
Dist.: MGM/UA

PIECE OF THE ACTION, A 1977
★ ★ ★ ★ PG Comedy 2:15
☑ Explicit language
Dir: Sidney Poitier *Cast:* Sidney Poitier, Bill Cosby, James Earl Jones, Denise Nicholas, Hope Clarke

▶ Follow-up to *Let's Do It Again* is a high-spirited romp about genial con men Poitier and Cosby, forced into supervising tough juvenile delinquents at a community service center. Uplifting social message blends nicely with action and slapstick. Impressive work by Jones as an imposing cop and a good score by Curtis Mayfield add to the fun.
Dist.: Warner

PILLOW TALK 1959
★ ★ ★ ★ NR Romance/Comedy 1:45
Dir: Michael Gordon *Cast:* Rock Hudson, Doris Day, Tony Randall, Thelma Ritter, Nick Adams, Julia Meade

▶ First Hudson-Day teaming is a lighthearted romantic farce about a Manhattan playboy and a no-nonsense interior designer who

grow to hate each other when they're forced to share a party line. Hate turns to love when Hudson finally meets Day at auditions for a Broadway musical. Received five Oscar nominations (including Day and Ritter, her unflappable maid), winning for screenplay by Russell Rouse, Clarence Greene, Stanley Shapiro, and Maurice Richlin.
Dist.: MCA

PIMPERNEL SMITH 1941 British
★ NR Action-Adventure 2:02 B&W
Dir: Leslie Howard   *Cast:* Leslie Howard, Mary Morris, Francis L. Sullivan, Hugh McDermott, Peter Gawthorne, Raymond Huntly
▶ Seemingly mild-mannered archaeologist Howard uses research activities as a cover for anti-Nazi rescue work, sparring with chubby Gestapo nemesis Sullivan, and taking time out to romance Morris. Producer/director/star Howard's update of the *Scarlet Pimpernel* concept to World War II era is good, lively entertainment. Also known as *Mister V.*
Dist.: Video Yesteryear

PING PONG 1987 British
☆ PG Drama
☑ Explicit language
Dir: Po-chih Leong   *Cast:* David Yip, Lucy Sheen, Robert Lee, Lam Fung
▶ London-born Chinese lawyer Sheen is called in to sort out the complex will of an old Chinese restaurant owner. None of his relatives wants to abide by the will, which also requires that his body be returned from London to his home town in Red China. Sheen has an affair with Yip, the old man's son, on his way to reconciling the family. Moderately involving drama gives intriguing glimpse into the London Chinese community.
Dist.: Virgin

PINK CADILLAC 1989
★ ★ ★ PG-13 Comedy 2:02
☑ Explicit language, violence
Dir: Buddy Van Horne   *Cast:* Clint Eastwood, Bernadette Peters, Timothy Carhart, Tiffany Gail Robinson, John Dennis Johnston, Geoffrey Lewis
▶ Bounty hunter Eastwood tracks down bailjumper Peters, who's driven off in a pink Caddie packed with a fortune in criminal currency. When Peters's neo-Nazi ex-husband kidnaps her baby, Eastwood decides to help her before he turns her in. Peters is cute, and Eastwood goes way out of his usual character when he dresses up in funny outfits to con quarry. Beautiful set design, but falls short of Eastwood's other comedies. **(CC)**
Dist.: Warner

PINK FLOYD: THE WALL 1982 British
★ R Music 1:39
☑ Nudity, adult situations, explicit language, violence
Dir: Alan Parker   *Cast:* Bob Geldof, Christine Hargreaves, James Laurenson, Eleanor David, Bob Hoskins
▶ Music from Pink Floyd's best-selling album *The Wall* inspired this relentlessly bleak examination of Pink (Geldof), a tormented rock star who sinks into insanity in his isolated hotel room. Written by former Floyd bassist Roger Waters (although the group itself doesn't appear), and featuring harsh animation by political caricaturist Gerald Scarfe. Good antiwar themes countered by offensively misogynist touches.
Dist.: MGM/UA

PINK NIGHTS 1985
★ ★ PG Comedy 1:24
☑ Adult situations
Dir: Philip Koch   *Cast:* Shaun Allen, Kevin Anderson, Peri Kaczmarek, Larry King, Jonathan Jancovic Michaels, Jessica Vitkus
▶ Teen Anderson has no luck with girls, getting a date with one only after she loses a dare. But a concurrence of events lands three of his ex-dates in his mother's house after she leaves town, and suddenly Anderson's a ladies' man. Refreshingly unslick, good-natured teen comedy is not the usual smutty stuff.
Dist.: New World

PINK PANTHER, THE 1964
★ ★ ★ ★ NR Comedy 1:53
Dir: Blake Edwards   *Cast:* David Niven, Peter Sellers, Capucine, Robert Wagner, Claudia Cardinale
▶ Hilariously incompetent Inspector Clouseau (Sellers) has problems: not only is international jewel thief Niven one step ahead of him but he's also sleeping with Sellers's wife! The film that started all the comic madness (spawning six sequels) introduces the familiar trademarks: Sellers's malapropisms and pratfalls, Edwards's slick slapstick, the animated credits, and Henry Mancini theme music. Still fresh and funny.
Dist.: MGM/UA

PINK PANTHER STRIKES AGAIN, THE 1976 British
★ ★ ★ ★ PG Comedy 1:43
☑ Adult situations
Dir: Blake Edwards   *Cast:* Peter Sellers, Herbert Lom, Lesley-Anne Down, Colin Blakely, Leonard Rossiter
▶ Ex-chief inspector Lom is about to be released from the insane asylum—until an appearance by the bumbling Clouseau (Sellers) causes a relapse. Lom escapes, hires a gang of assassins, and builds a doomsday machine that will destroy an entire city if Sellers is not eliminated. Fourth in the successful free-form comedy series features on-the-mark slapstick antics and the winning Sellers/Lom team.
Dist.: CBS/Fox

PINOCCHIO 1940
★ ★ ★ ★ ★ G Animation 1:28
Dir: Ben Sharpsteen, Hamilton Luske   *Cast:* Voices of Dickie Jones, Christian Rub, Cliff Edwards, Evelyn Venable, Walter Catlett
▶ Magical fantasy about young marionette's

efforts to become a flesh-and-blood boy is among the most accomplished of all Disney features. Rich characterizations (wisecracking Jiminy Cricket, the insidious fox J. Worthington Foulfellow, etc.), astonishing animation, an Oscar-winning score (including Cliff Edwards's version of "When You Wish Upon a Star"), and a plot that alternates between whimsical humor and genuinely frightening sequences has made this a family favorite for five decades. Highly recommended.   (CC)
Dist.: Buena Vista

PIN-UP GIRL 1944
★ ★ ★ **NR Musical 1:23**
Dir: H. Bruce Humberstone   *Cast:* Betty Grable, Martha Raye, John Harvey, Joe E. Brown, Eugene Pallette, Mantan Moreland
▶ Wartime stenographer Grable pretends to be a successful showgirl to get an audition at a top New York nightclub. While developing a romance with war hero Harvey, she becomes famous in her own right through a popular pinup. Grable vehicle is short on energy and interest. Lackluster songs include "Don't Carry Tales Out of School" and "Very Merry Widow." (CC)
Dist.: Key

PIPE DREAMS 1976
★ ★ **PG Drama 1:29**
☑ Adult situations
Dir: Stephen Verona   *Cast:* Gladys Knight, Barry Hankerson, Bruce French, Sherry Bain, Wayne Tippit, Altovise Davis
▶ Knight makes her screen debut in an old-fashioned weeper set in the unlikely locale of Alaska during the pipeline boom. Knight has come to rowdy boom town to find errant (and real-life) husband Hankerson. While trying to woo him from current girlfriend, Knight must resist temptation to join the profession of her prostitute roommate. Poorly directed, badly edited, and clumsily acted, film at least has plenty of songs by Knight and the Pips.
Dist.: Nelson

PIRANHA 1978
★ ★ **R Horror 1:34**
☑ Brief nudity, explicit language, graphic violence
Dir: Joe Dante   *Cast:* Bradford Dillman, Heather Menzies, Kevin McCarthy, Keenan Wynn, Richard Deacon
▶ Killer fish, developed at scientist McCarthy's lab, invade local river, menacing summer camp kids and vacationers. Mountain man Dillman and skip tracer Menzies try to warn the populace. Pretty scary stuff, stylishly directed by Dante and appealingly acted by Dillman and Menzies, although the story (by John Sayles) can't be taken seriously.
Dist.: Warner

PIRANHA II: THE SPAWNING 1983
Italian/U.S.
★ **R Horror 1:30**

☑ Nudity, adult situations, explicit language, violence
Dir: James Cameron   *Cast:* Tricia O'Neil, Lance Henriksen, Steve Marachuk, Ricky G. Paull, Ted Richert
▶ Diving teacher O'Neil and biochemist Marachuk investigate when guests start dropping like flies at a tropical resort. The culprits: deadly piranha. Predictable story but well-done fright scenes, like opening bit of critters attacking a couple making love underwater. Attractive scenery and lead actors.
Dist.: Nelson

PIRATE, THE 1948
★ ★ ★ **NR Musical 1:42**
Dir: Vincente Minnelli   *Cast:* Judy Garland, Gene Kelly, Walter Slezak, Gladys Cooper, Reginald Owen, The Nicholas Brothers
▶ In the nineteenth-century Caribbean, performer Kelly pretends to be a pirate to win Garland away from her older fiancé Slezak. Overly broad MGM musical with a production design almost too loudly colorful. Can be enjoyed for Kelly's acrobatics and the Cole Porter score, which includes "Be a Clown."
Dist.: MGM/UA

PIRATE MOVIE, THE 1982 Australian
★ ★ **PG Musical 1:39**
☑ Explicit language
Dir: Ken Annakin   *Cast:* Kristy McNichol, Christopher Atkins, Ted Hamilton, Bill Kerr, Maggie Kirkpatrick, Garry McDonald
▶ Plain young McNichol, stranded on a beach, dreams of being wooed by handsome pirate's apprentice Atkins. He helps McNichol retrieve her family's stolen treasure from the pirate gang. Modernized version of Gilbert and Sullivan's *The Pirates of Penzance* with clumsily staged dances, bubblegum music, and Atkins's stiff performance. McNichol charmingly emerges unscathed.
Dist.: CBS/Fox

PIRATES 1986 French/Tunisian
★ **PG-13 Action-Adventure/Comedy 2:04**
☑ Explicit language, mild violence, adult humor
Dir: Roman Polanski   *Cast:* Walter Matthau, Cris Campion, Charlotte Lewis, Damien Thomas, Richard Pearson
▶ Peglegged English pirate Matthau and his young mate Campion are imprisoned by Spanish captain Thomas. The pirates attempt mutiny as Matthau seeks treasure and Campion falls for Lewis, Thomas's intended. Burlesque of pirate genre is a gorgeous eyeful of sets and costumes, not to mention attractive Lewis and Campion. The downside: unsympathetic characters, repetitious swashbuckling action, a mush-mouthed Matthau, and a disgusting rat-eating sequence.
Dist.: IVE

PIRATES OF PENZANCE, THE 1983
★ **G Musical 1:52**
Dir: Wilford Leach   *Cast:* Kevin Kline, An-

gela Lansbury, Linda Ronstadt, George Rose, Rex Smith, Tony Azito

▶ Young pirate Smith goes ashore and falls for Ronstadt, daughter of Major General Rose, but is torn between love and duty when Pirate King Kline bounds him to further swashbuckling servitude on a technicality. Leach sweetly re-creates his Broadway staging of the Gilbert and Sullivan operetta; his deliberately artificial-looking production is amusing but somewhat off-putting. Kline does a wonderfully funny and charismatic Errol Flynn parody; Ronstadt sings beautifully, acts less well.

Dist.: MCA

PIT, THE 1984 Canadian
☆ **R Horror 1:36**
☑ Explicit language, violence
Dir: Lew Lehman ***Cast:*** Sammy Snyders, Jeannie Elias, Laura Hollingsworth, Sonja Smits, Laura Press, Andrea Swartz

▶ Spying on his showering babysitter is only one of troubled pre-teen Snyders's antics. He also pushes people into a pit occupied by four, furry, man-eating monsters. A bully, a young neighbor, and a teacher become his victims before authorities step in. Silly horror film fails to find scares, and strives, unsuccessfully, for laughs.

Dist.: Nelson

PIT AND THE PENDULUM, THE 1961
★★ **NR Horror 1:20**
Dir: Roger Corman ***Cast:*** Vincent Price, John Kerr, Barbara Steele, Luana Anders, Anthony Carbone

▶ Price, the son of a Spanish Inquisition torturer, loses his mind after the death of wife Steele. When Steele's brother Kerr investigates, Price hooks him up to the title device. Solid, chilling adaptation of the Edgar Allan Poe short story. One of Corman's and Price's better efforts.

Dist.: Warner

PIXOTE 1981 Brazilian
★ **NR Drama 2:07**
☑ Nudity, strong sexual content, explicit language, violence
Dir: Hector Babenco ***Cast:*** Fernando Ramos da Silva, Marila Pera, Jardel Filho, Rubens de Falco, Elke Maravilha, Tony Tornado

▶ Young da Silva is mistreated in harsh São Paulo reform school and escapes after authorities kill two of his pals. He becomes a drug dealer and then hooks up with prostitute Pera. Brutal atmosphere and nonprofessional cast are impressively realistic; unrelentingly grim, violent tone makes this difficult to watch. Actor da Silva was subsequently shot dead during an armed robbery. [S]

Dist.: RCA/Columbia

P.K. AND THE KID 1982
★★★ **PG-13 Drama 1:29**
☑ Brief nudity, adult situations, explicit language, mild violence
Dir: Lou Lombardo ***Cast:*** Molly Ringwald, Paul LeMat, Alex Rocco, Fionnula Flanagan, Charles Hallahan, Esther Rolle

▶ Ringwald's first starring role has her running away from abusive stepdad Rocco and joining pickup-driver LeMat, an arm wrestler on his way to a championship contest. Rocco pursues the pair, and when he can't stop LeMat from competing, he beats the stuffing out of Ringwald. Hokey film worth seeing for the good vibes between the two leads.

Dist.: Lorimar

PLACE IN THE SUN, A 1951
★★★★ **NR Drama 1:42 B&W**
Dir: George Stevens ***Cast:*** Montgomery Clift, Elizabeth Taylor, Shelley Winters, Raymond Burr, Anne Revere, Herbert Hayes

▶ Weak-willed Clift is romantically linked to factory co-worker Winters until he falls in love with heiress Taylor. Clift plans to wed Taylor, but Winters announces she's pregnant. Confrontation between Clift and Winters, who insists on marriage, ends in tragedy. Remake of *An American Tragedy* (from Theodore Dreiser's novel) won six Academy Awards, including Best Director and Screenplay by Michael Wilson and Harry Brown. Intense close-ups of beautiful-looking lovers Clift and Taylor are one of the film's distinctions, as well as lush score by Franz Waxman.

Dist.: Paramount

PLACES IN THE HEART 1984
★★★★★ **PG Drama 1:51**
☑ Adult situations, explicit language, violence
Dir: Robert Benton ***Cast:*** Sally Field, Danny Glover, Lindsay Crouse, John Malkovich, Ed Harris, Amy Madigan

▶ Heartfelt story of family endurance features Oscar-winning performance by Field as a feisty widow and mother of two who fights tornadoes, falling cotton prices, and the KKK to save her Texas farm from foreclosure in 1935. She hires itinerant Glover and takes in blind tenant Malkovich to help make ends meet. Benton's screenplay, a celebration of traditional American values, also won an Oscar. Nominations included Picture, Director, Supporting Actress (Crouse) and Actor (Malkovich), and Costumes. (CC)

Dist.: CBS/Fox

PLAGUE DOGS, THE 1982
★★★ **NR Animation 1:26**
☑ Explicit language, violence
Dir: Martin Rosen ***Cast:*** Voices of John Hurt, Christopher Benjamin, James Bolam, Nigel Hawthorne, Warren Mitchell

▶ Two dogs escape from the laboratory where scientists have been tormenting them and roam the English countryside. When the scientists reveal they've exposed the dogs to the bubonic plague, the canine hunt intensifies. Striking animation distinguishes this adaptation of Richard Adams's novel, but grim,

often unsettling story is unusual family fare. (CC)
Dist.: Nelson

PLAIN CLOTHES 1988
★ ★ ★ PG Mystery-Suspense 1:38
☑ Explicit language, mild violence
Dir: Martha Coolidge *Cast:* Arliss Howard, Suzy Amis, George Wendt, Diane Ladd, Seymour Cassel, Robert Stack
▶ When a teacher is murdered, young cop Howard, whose brother is the number-one suspect, poses as a high school student in order to investigate. Howard finds romance with English teacher Amis while cracking the case. Mildly amusing humor, promising performances by newcomers Howard and Amis, and sleek production values. (CC)
Dist.: Paramount

PLAINSMAN, THE 1936
★ ★ ★ NR Western 1:53 B&W
Dir: Cecil B. DeMille *Cast:* Gary Cooper, Jean Arthur, James Ellison, Charles Bickford, Porter Hall, Anthony Quinn
▶ Extravagant, fast-paced version of a fictional romance between Wild Bill Hickok (Cooper) and Calamity Jane (Arthur) interrupted by villain Bickford's scheme to sell guns to the Indians. Facts may be inaccurate, but the stars' bickering affair is disarming, and the action (with a proverbial cast of thousands) is furious.
Dist.: MCA

PLANES, TRAINS & AUTOMOBILES 1987
★ ★ ★ R Comedy 1:33
☑ Explicit language, adult humor
Dir: John Hughes *Cast:* Steve Martin, John Candy, Laila Robbins, Michael McKean, William Windom, Kevin Bacon
▶ Uptight Chicago executive Martin, desperate to get home for Thanksgiving despite an indefinitely delayed plane, hooks up with overbearing shower-curtain-ring salesman Candy to make the trip by car and train. Although their trek is a series of comic disasters, Candy slowly melts Martin's reserve. Candy and Martin make a winning team in a contrived (but frequently funny) tale of travel's travails. Highlights: Candy warbling the Flintstones theme and the "Those aren't pillows" bedroom encounter. (CC)
Dist.: Paramount

PLANET OF BLOOD 1966
☆ NR Sci-Fi 1:21
Dir: Curtis Harrington *Cast:* John Saxon, Basil Rathbone, Dennis Hopper, Judi Meredith, Florence Marly
▶ Earth astronauts, responding to strange signals from Mars, rescue alien woman from a wrecked spacecraft. Bad move: she turns out to be a vampire and starts killing off the crew members. Surprisingly effective chiller whose plot may remind you of *Alien*. Also known as *Queen of Blood*.
Dist.: HBO

PLANET OF THE APES 1968
★ ★ ★ ★ G Sci-Fi 1:52
Dir: Franklin J. Schaffner *Cast:* Charlton Heston, Roddy McDowall, Kim Hunter, Maurice Evans, James Whitmore, James Daly
▶ Astronaut Heston crash-lands on planet where evolution has taken an upside-down turn: talking apes rule and humans are mute and enslaved. When Heston is captured by the simian rulers, sympathetic scientist ape couple Hunter and McDowall rally to his side. Terrific sci-fi adventure is witty, thought-provoking, visually exciting, and original, with Heston at his most heroic. Marvelous Oscar-winning monkey makeup. The twist ending still packs a punch. Led to four sequels and a TV series. (CC)
Dist.: CBS/Fox

PLANET OF THE VAMPIRES 1965 Italian
☆ NR Sci-Fi 1:26
Dir: Mario Bava *Cast:* Barry Sullivan, Norma Bengell, Angel Aranda, Evi Mirandi
▶ Spaceship captain Sullivan investigates eerie transmission from the planet Aura. Mysterious killings plague his crew. The culprit: advanced minds seeking bodies to escape Aura. Also known as *The Demon Planet*.
Dist.: HBO

PLAN 9 FROM OUTER SPACE 1959
★ NR Sci-Fi 1:19 B&W
Dir: Edward D. Wood, Jr. *Cast:* Gregory Walcott, Mona McKinnon, Duke Moore, Tom Keene, Bela Lugosi, Vampira
▶ Aliens invade Earth, reviving the dead to take over the planet. First target is Vampira, Lugosi's recently deceased wife. Pilot Walcott and his friends are the only people who can save humanity. Revered by cultists as the worst movie ever made, staggeringly inept horror adventure is actually funnier than many intentional comedies.
Dist.: Media

PLATOON 1986
★ ★ ★ ★ R War 1:59
☑ Explicit language, graphic violence
Dir: Oliver Stone *Cast:* Charlie Sheen, Willem Dafoe, Tom Berenger, Forest Whitaker, Francesco Quinn, John C. McGinley
▶ Harrowing account of life on the front line in Vietnam. Seen through the eyes of young idealist-turned-cynic Sheen, portrait of war as hell pits decent sergeant Dafoe against vicious counterpart Berenger. Blockbuster hit noteworthy for excellent ensemble acting, realistic depiction of jungle warfare, and sympathetic look at individual struggle to cope with the insanity of an unpopular war. Won four Oscars, including Best Picture and Director. (CC)
Dist.: Vestron

PLATOON LEADER 1988
★ ★ R War 1:40
☑ Adult situations, explicit language, graphic violence
Dir: Aaron Norris *Cast:* Michael Dudikoff,

Robart F. Lyons, Rick Hitts, Michael De Lorenzo, Jesse Dabson, William Smith
▶ Rookie first lieutenant Dudikoff must win the respect of battle-scarred veterans in his new platoon while battling hordes of Vietcong on debilitating daily raids. Well-mounted, bloody Vietnam War drama undermined by routine plotting and thin characterizations.
Dist.: Media

PLAYERS 1979
★ ★ PG Drama 2:00
☑ Adult situations, explicit language
Dir: Anthony Harvey *Cast:* Ali MacGraw, Dean Paul Martin, Maximilian Schell, Steve Guttenberg, Melissa Prophet, Pancho Gonzalez
▶ In Mexico, young tennis hustler Martin falls in love with older, kept woman MacGraw, but her wealthy sugar daddy Schell drops in at the most inopportune times. Will MacGraw choose true romance? Will the final score be Money: 40, Love: Love? Great-looking actors, exotic locales, and cameo appearances by tennis stars of the era, including a youthful John McEnroe.
Dist.: Paramount

PLAYING AWAY 1988 British
★ NR Drama 1:40
☑ Adult situations, explicit language
Dir: Horace Ove *Cast:* Norman Beaton, Robert Urquhart, Helen Lindsay, Nicholas Farrell, Trevor Thomas, Elizabeth Anson
▶ Cultures clash on and off the pitch as Beaton leads a team of West Indian cricketeers to an all-white town where they are to play the locals as part of "Third World Week." Encounters between the two ethnic groups range from the romantic to the confrontational. Wise, funny film holds out the possibility of mutual understanding.
Dist.: Nelson

PLAYING FOR KEEPS 1986
★ ★ PG-13 Comedy 1:43
☑ Brief nudity, adult situations, explicit language
Dir: Bob Weinstein, Harvey Weinstein *Cast:* Danny Jordano, Matthew Penn, Leon Grant, Mary B. Ward, Marisa Tomei
▶ Teenager Jordano and his family inherit run-down hotel which he and buddies Penn and Grant decide to rehab into rock 'n' roll resort. Obstacles include back taxes, suspicious townfolk, and politician's plan for chemical waste dump on the site. Lightweight teen comedy sports foot-tapping soundtrack and energetic style.
Dist.: MCA

PLAYING FOR TIME 1980
★ ★ ★ ★ NR Drama/MFTV 2:31
Dir: Daniel Mann *Cast:* Vanessa Redgrave, Jane Alexander, Maud Adams, Shirley Knight, Melanie Mayron
▶ True story of Fania Fenelon (Redgrave), a French cabaret singer who survived Auschwitz

concentration camp by performing in the women's orchestra. Conducted by Alma Rose (Alexander), they were forced to play while inmates were led to the crematoriums. First-rate, uncompromising, and shattering made-for-TV film won four Emmys including Drama Special, Actress (Redgrave), Supporting Actress (Alexander), and Writing (Arthur Miller).
Dist.: Virgin

PLAY IT AGAIN, SAM 1972
★ ★ ★ PG Comedy 1:25
☑ Explicit language
Dir: Herbert Ross *Cast:* Woody Allen, Diane Keaton, Tony Roberts, Jerry Lacy, Susan Anspach, Jennifer Salt
▶ Timid San Francisco film critic Allen, abandoned by bored wife Anspach, is such a mess he can't bring himself to heat up TV dinners—he sucks them frozen. Enter the ghost of Humphrey Bogart (Lacy) to teach Allen about being a man, especially with women ("I never met one who didn't understand a slap in the mouth"). After a series of nightmarish dates, Allen has one-night fling with Keaton, the wife of his best friend Roberts, and gets to live out his *Casablanca* fantasy. From Allen's Broadway play.
Dist.: Paramount

PLAY MISTY FOR ME 1971
★ ★ ★ ★ R Mystery-Suspense 1:42
☑ Adult situations, violence
Dir: Clint Eastwood *Cast:* Clint Eastwood, Jessica Walter, Donna Mills, John Larch, Jack Ging, Irene Hervey
▶ Late-night DJ Eastwood has one-night stand with fan Walter who calls every evening requesting the tune "Misty." When he tries to break off the relationship, she takes increasingly violent steps against him and his girlfriend Mills. Sure-handed directorial debut by Eastwood in a spooky thriller about obsessive love. Song "The First Time Ever I Saw Your Face," sung by Roberta Flack, was a Top Ten hit.
Dist.: MCA

PLAYTIME 1967 French
☆ NR Comedy 1:48
Dir: Jacques Tati *Cast:* Jacques Tati, Barbara Dennek, Jacqueline Lecomte, Valerie Camille, Leon Doyen
▶ Tati's Mr. Hulot stumbles in and out of gently amusing situations while visiting an uncomfortably up-to-date Paris of glass skyscrapers, drugstores, and ultra-modern design. In English dialogue written by Art Buchwald, a busload of American tourists exults that "It's just like home." Screen great Tati's last comedy is dazzlingly unique, but some may become restive owing to the somewhat slow pacing.
Ⓢ
Dist.: Nelson

PLAZA SUITE 1971
★ ★ ★ PG Comedy 1:55
☑ Adult situations

Dir: Arthur Hiller   *Cast:* Walter Matthau, Maureen Stapleton, Barbara Harris, Lee Grant, Louise Sorel, Jenny Sullivan
▶ Matthau assays three different roles in three episodes taking place in one New York Plaza Hotel suite: Stapleton's unfaithful husband; producer attempting to seduce old flame Harris; and father of nervous bride Sullivan, who locks herself in room before wedding. Neil Simon adaptation of his Broadway hit provides good vehicle for Matthau's clowning.
Dist.: Paramount

PLENTY 1985
★ ★ ★ **R Drama 2:04**
☑ Adult situations, explicit language
Dir: Fred Schepisi   *Cast:* Meryl Streep, Charles Dance, Sting, Tracey Ullman, John Gielgud, Ian McKellen
▶ Faithful film version of David Hare's play traces the life of Susan Traherne (Streep). Her happiest moments are as World War II resistance fighter; then her life deteriorates even though she prospers through several careers. Unhappily married to Foreign Service member Dance, she's given to teary pronouncements ("I want to change everything and I don't know how") and, eventually, suffers a nervous breakdown. High-powered supporting cast includes Ullman as Streep's wise-cracking friend and Gielgud as a diplomat.
Dist.: HBO

PLOUGHMAN'S LUNCH, THE 1984 British
☆ **R Drama 1:47**
☑ Adult situations, explicit language
Dir: Richard Eyre   *Cast:* Jonathan Pryce, Tim Curry, Charlie Dore, Rosemary Harris, Frank Finlay, Simon Stokes
▶ Burnt-out journalist Pryce is enamored of young intellectual Dore. He interviews her historian mother Harris and is invited to stay for the weekend. Instead of making his play for Dore, Pryce makes love to Harris. He later regrets his decision when his friend Curry is intimate with Dore. Well-crafted but static study of class differences and cynically detached youth in Thatcher England will appeal only to those with taste for things veddy British.
Dist.: Embassy

PLUMBER, THE 1980 Australian
☆ **NR Drama 1:16**
☑ Adult situations, explicit language
Dir: Peter Weir   *Cast:* Judy Morris, Ivar Kants, Robert Coleby, Candy Raymond
▶ Teasing cat-and-mouse play as work-at-home college professor Morris is suddenly visited by uninvited plumber Kants, who claims he has to fix the pipes. Kants destroys bathroom and drops hints that he's been arrested for rape; Morris's distracted husband Coleby can't be bothered by whole affair. There's one good scare scene in this otherwise one-note demonstration of the incompatibility between intellectuals and the working class. Originally made for Australian TV.
Dist.: Media

PLUNDER ROAD 1957
★ ★ **NR Mystery-Suspense 1:11 B&W**
Dir: Hubert Cornfield   *Cast:* Gene Raymond, Jeanne Cooper, Wayne Morris, Elisha Cook, Jr., Stafford Repp, Michael Fox
▶ After pulling off a daring bullion heist, a gang of crooks divides the take into three trucks and tries to sneak it out of the country. In one truck, Repp thinks his police radio will save him. In the other, Morris and Cook disguise their load as coffee. Gang leader Raymond disguises his gold as bumpers and hubcaps on a Cadillac. Surprisingly good low-budget film noir is gripping throughout.
Dist.: Republic

POCKETFUL OF MIRACLES 1961
★ ★ ★ ★ **NR Comedy 2:16**
Dir: Frank Capra   *Cast:* Glenn Ford, Bette Davis, Hope Lange, Peter Falk, Arthur O'-Connell, Ann-Margret
▶ Soft-hearted gangster Ford sets up alcoholic street vendor Davis in posh Manhattan digs so she can impress European-educated daughter Ann-Margret and her fiancé's wealthy father O'Connell. Chaotic and comic encounters between mobsters, socialites, and street people follow. Capra's last feature is a remake of his earlier and briefer *Lady for a Day*, adapted from a Damon Runyon short story. **(CC)**
Dist.: MGM/UA

POINT, THE 1971
★ ★ ★ ★ **NR Animation/MFTV 1:13**
Dir: Fred Wolf   *Cast:* Narrated by Ringo Starr
▶ In a world where everybody's head is pointed, a little boy whose head is round is persecuted. Whimsical tale takes too long to deliver its simple message. Lightweight songs by Harry Nilsson. Original voice-over by Dustin Hoffman; current version is narrated by Starr.
Dist.: Vestron

POINT BLANK 1967
★ ★ ★ ★ **NR Action-Adventure 1:32**
☑ Violence
Dir: John Boorman   *Cast:* Lee Marvin, Angie Dickinson, Keenan Wynn, Carroll O'Connor, Lloyd Bochner, John Vernon
▶ Marvin, a San Francisco gangster double-crossed by his wife and partner after a gang heist, infiltrates their L.A. mob for revenge. Working with crooked accountant Wynn, he wipes out a series of mobsters while searching for his missing loot. Tense, hard-edged thriller was based on a Donald Westlake novel. **(CC)**
Dist.: MGM/UA

POINTSMAN, THE 1988 Dutch
☆ **R Drama 1:35**
☑ Brief nudity, adult situations

Dir: Joe Dielling *Cast:* Jim van der Woude, Stephane Excoffier, Joose de Puuw

▶ Odd parable about beautiful Frenchwoman Excoffier who misses her train connection. Stranded, she moves into a shack with boorish signal-switcher, or pointsman, van der Woude. As the months pass, they form a rather unusual but powerful bond. With hardly any dialogue and inscrutable message, this one remains accessible only to arthouse audiences. [S]
Dist.: Vestron

POLICE ACADEMY 1984
★ ★ ★ ★ R Comedy 1:36
☑ Nudity, adult situations, explicit language
Dir: Hugh Wilson *Cast:* Steve Guttenberg, Kim Cattrall, George Gaynes, G. W. Bailey, Michael Winslow, Bubba Smith
▶ Assorted misfits, including failed parking lot attendant Guttenberg, bored socialite Cattrall, and hulking florist Smith, enroll in police academy when admissions standards are eliminated. Milquetoast commander Gaynes meekly accepts inept new trainees, but hardnosed chief instructor Bailey is determined to make their lives miserable. Inevitable clashes between Bailey and rookies result until the trainees prove their worth. Raucous and extremely popular comedy pushes limits of taste, usually with outrageous results. **(CC)**
Dist.: Warner

POLICE ACADEMY 2: THEIR FIRST ASSIGNMENT 1985
★ ★ ★ ★ PG-13 Comedy 1:27
☑ Brief nudity, explicit language, adult humor
Dir: Jerry Paris *Cast:* Steve Guttenberg, Bubba Smith, Michael Winslow, Howard Hesseman, George Gaynes, Art Metrano
▶ Sequel to comedy hit. Fresh from their academy training, endearing rookies Guttenberg, Smith, and Winslow are assigned to a crime-ridden precinct run by besieged captain Hesseman. Ambitious lieutenant Metrano, with eye on Hesseman's job, tries to thwart the new cops, but the bumbling misfits fight crime with laughs and soon the neighborhood is safe again. **(CC)**
Dist.: Warner

POLICE ACADEMY 3: BACK IN TRAINING 1986
★ ★ ★ PG Comedy 1:24
☑ Adult situations, adult humor
Dir: Jerry Paris *Cast:* Steve Guttenberg, Bubba Smith, David Graf, Michael Winslow, George Gaynes, Art Metrano
▶ City decides to close one of two police academies, one run by underhanded tough guy Metrano and the other by lovable numbskull Gaynes. All-thumbs alums Guttenberg, Smith, etc., return for decisive drill competition but make poor impression on evaluators. However, when the governor is kidnapped at

a regatta, the misfits prove their true mettle. More boffo laughs in third of series. **(CC)**
Dist.: Warner

POLICE ACADEMY 4: CITIZENS ON PATROL 1987
★ ★ ★ PG Comedy 1:27
☑ Explicit language
Dir: Jim Drake *Cast:* Steve Guttenberg, Bubba Smith, Michael Winslow, David Graf, George Gaynes, G. W. Bailey
▶ More law and little order from the bumbling boys in blue. Academy commander Gaynes initiates civilian crime-fighting program so the Keystone Klones (Guttenberg and rest of the gang) are enlisted to train volunteers. Original nemesis Bailey tries to sabotage their efforts. Prisoners escape and must be apprehended in bang-up finale. Formula losing gas. Gags even more juvenile, but still popular. **(CC)**
Dist.: Warner

POLICE ACADEMY 5: ASSIGNMENT MIAMI BEACH 1988
★ ★ ★ PG Comedy 1:30
☑ Explicit language
Dir: Alan Myerson *Cast:* Bubba Smith, David Graf, Michael Winslow, George Gaynes, G. W. Bailey, Janet Jones
▶ Academy commander Gaynes is to be honored at Miami cop convention, so he, obnoxious rival Bailey, and customary crew of klutzes (Smith, Graf, etc.) fly south. Gaynes accidentally picks up bag of stolen gems at airport and is kidnapped by jewel thieves. In typically inept style, the comic coppers save the day. More silly high jinks from the same boneheaded lawmen, although Steve Guttenberg bowed out of this round. **(CC)**
Dist.: Warner

POLICE ACADEMY 6: CITY UNDER SIEGE 1989
★ ★ PG Comedy 1:27
☑ Mild violence
Dir: Peter Bonerz *Cast:* Bubba Smith, Michael Winslow, David Graf, Marion Ramsey, Leslie Easterbrook, George Gaynes
▶ Commandant Gaynes and his police academy half-wits are assigned by the mayor to thwart a criminal gang and its elusive mastermind. Taken off the investigation when stolen goods are discovered in Gaynes's office, the crew needs a wild chase to solve the case. Zippy cast keeps series rolling along. **(CC)**
Dist.: Warner

POLICE SQUAD! HELP WANTED 1982
★ ★ ★ NR Comedy/MFTV 1:15
Dir: Jim Abrahams, Jerry Zucker, David Zucker, Joe Dante, Reza Badiyi *Cast:* Leslie Nielsen, Alan North, Rex Hamilton, Peter Lupus, Lorne Greene, Florence Henderson
▶ Three episodes of the TV series "Police Squad" featuring Nielsen as the square-jawed cop Frank Drebin. He solves a murder at a check cashing outfit, battles an extortion

ring, and takes on a corrupt boxing promoter. Freewheeling humor, often very funny. Best bits: the visit to Little Italy and "no sax before the fight." Inspired the hugely popular 1988 feature *The Naked Gun.*
Dist.: Paramount

POLLYANNA 1960
★ ★ ★ ★ ★ **NR Family 2:14**
Dir: David Swift ***Cast:*** Hayley Mills, Jane Wyman, Richard Egan, Karl Malden, Nancy Olson, Adolphe Menjou, Donald Crisp, Agnes Moorehead
▶ Orphan Mills, taken in by her New England aunt Wyman, brings sunshine and happiness to previously glum neighbors, including hermit Menjou and hellfire preacher Malden. Wonderful Disney adaptation of Eleanor Porter's novel is sentimental without being sticky. In her American debut, Mills received Oscar statuette for her "outstanding juvenile performance." Menjou's last film. **(CC)**
Dist.: Buena Vista

POLTERGEIST 1982
★ ★ ★ ★ **PG Horror 1:54**
☑ Adult situations, explicit language, graphic violence
Dir: Tobe Hooper ***Cast:*** JoBeth Williams, Craig T. Nelson, Dominique Dunne, Heather O'Rourke, Oliver Robins, Zelda Rubinstein
▶ Suburban couple Williams and Nelson and kids Dunne, O'Rourke, and Robins are harassed by poltergeists (German for "noisy ghosts") in their new home. At first the unseen critters merely rearrange the furniture, but then they turn nasty and abduct O'Rourke. As chaos breaks out, diminutive exorcist Rubinstein, who's pretty spooky herself, must calm the angry spirits and retrieve O'Rourke. Sensational special effects in spine-tingling and gruesome ghost story co-written and co-produced by Steven Spielberg. Not for younger kids.
Dist.: MGM/UA

POLTERGEIST II: THE OTHER SIDE 1986
★ ★ ★ **PG-13 Horror 1:31**
☑ Explicit language, graphic violence
Dir: Brian Gibson ***Cast:*** JoBeth Williams, Craig T. Nelson, Heather O'Rourke, Oliver Robins, Will Sampson, Geraldine Fitzgerald
▶ "They're back!" in sequel to megahit ghost thriller. On the skids after their first bout with poltergeists, downtrodden family Williams, Nelson, etc., move in with Williams's psychic mother Fitzgerald. When Fitzgerald dies, vicious spirits invade the house, wreaking stunning visual havoc. Indian mystic Sampson assists family in warding off evil spirits. Generally satisfying encore, with spellbinding special effects. **(CC)**
Dist.: MGM/UA

POLTERGEIST III 1988
★ ★ **PG-13 Horror 1:37**
☑ Explicit language, violence
Dir: Gary A. Sherman ***Cast:*** Heather

O'Rourke, Zelda Rubinstein, Tom Skerritt, Nancy Allen, Lara Flynn Boyle, Kip Wentz
▶ Reprising her role from prior two films, O'Rourke now lives in care of aunt Allen and uncle Skerritt in their chic Chicago high-rise. But nasty evil spirits just won't leave her alone and soon abduct her and her cousin Boyle to the netherworld. Once again sweet little exorcist Rubinstein comes to the rescue. Story getting awfully familiar; as usual, real stars are special effects. Dedicated to O'Rourke, who passed away during emergency surgery following film's completion.
Dist.: MGM/UA

POLYESTER 1981
★ **R Comedy 1:30**
☑ Explicit language, violence, adult humor
Dir: John Waters ***Cast:*** Divine, Tab Hunter, Stiv Bators, Edith Massey, Mink Stole
▶ Intentionally tacky domestic comedy will probably be appreciated only by cult followers of writer/producer/director John Waters. Transvestite Divine plays the much-beleaguered Baltimore housewife Francine Fishpaw, who fantasizes about dream lover Hunter. Theatrical release gimmick was Odorama card with scratch-and-sniff smells (when Francine smelled something, a number appeared on the screen and audience could sniff the same scent). Definitely not for all tastes or scents.
Dist.: HBO

PONY EXPRESS 1953
★ ★ ★ **NR Western 1:41**
Dir: Jerry Hopper ***Cast:*** Charlton Heston, Rhonda Fleming, Jan Sterling, Forrest Tucker, Michael Moore, Porter Hall
▶ Buffalo Bill Cody (Heston) and Wild Bill Hickok (Tucker) battle would-be California secessionists and warring Sioux to help push mail service through to the Golden State. One of the best of Heston's Westerns fills the air with bullets, tomahawks, and the thud of bad guys biting the dust.
Dist.: KVC

POOR LITTLE RICH GIRL 1936
★ ★ **NR Musical/Family 1:12 B&W**
Dir: Irving Cummings ***Cast:*** Shirley Temple, Alice Faye, Jack Haley, Gloria Stuart, Michael Whalen, Sara Haden
▶ Little rich girl Temple dodges boarding school and, claiming to be an orphan, hooks up with vaudeville duo Faye and Haley. They dance their way to success, ultimately reuniting Temple with her widowed father Whalen and his new love Stuart. One of finer vehicles for puckish moptop, with first-rate production values. Song-and-dance numbers include oft-excerpted "Military Man" (Temple in uniform with rifle) and "You've Got To Eat Your Spinach, Baby." **(CC)**
Dist.: CBS/Fox

POPE OF GREENWICH VILLAGE, THE 1984
★ ★ ★ **R Drama 2:00**

☑ Adult situations, explicit language, violence
Dir: Stuart Rosenberg *Cast:* Eric Roberts, Mickey Rourke, Daryl Hannah, Geraldine Page, Burt Young, Kenneth McMillan
▶ Offbeat slice-of-life tale about punk cousins Roberts and Rourke who rob a Mafia safe and accidentally kill a cop, landing them in deep trouble with both organized crime in Little Italy and the police. Rourke's live-in girl Hannah makes off with the money as the leads struggle desperately to stay alive. Authentic New York City locations. Best performance: Geraldine Page as the slain cop's frumpy mother. Adapted from Vincent Patrick's best-seller.
Dist.: MGM/UA

POPEYE 1980
★ ★ ★ PG Musical 1:54
☑ Explicit language, violence
Dir: Robert Altman *Cast:* Robin Williams, Shelley Duvall, Ray Walston, Paul Dooley, Paul Smith, Richard Libertini
▶ Sailor Popeye (Williams) rows into Sweethaven port searching for his long-lost Pappy (Walston). He falls in love with Olive Oyl (Duvall) though she's engaged to Bluto (Smith); together Popeye and Olive care for foundling Swee'Pea. Eccentric live-action comedy was a critical dud despite inspired casting. Worthy family fare.
Dist.: Paramount

PORK CHOP HILL 1959
★ ★ NR War 1:37 B&W
Dir: Lewis Milestone *Cast:* Gregory Peck, Harry Guardino, Rip Torn, George Peppard, James Edwards, Bob Steele, Woody Strode, Robert Blake, Martin Landau
▶ Peck gives a quietly heroic performance as a Korean War lieutenant ordered to take a strategically worthless hill just as cease-fire talks commence. Despite horrendous fatalities and minimal backup support, Peck and his men battle their way to the top, then learn they must hold the hill against overwhelming enemy onslaughts. Realistic, hard-hitting film features excellent support from Strode and Blake. **(CC)**
Dist.: MGM/UA

PORKY'S 1982 Canadian
★ ★ ★ ★ R Comedy 1:38
☑ Nudity, adult situations, explicit language, adult humor
Dir: Bob Clark *Cast:* Kim Cattrall, Scott Colomby, Kaki Hunter, Nancy Parsons, Alex Karras, Susan Clark, Don Monahan, Mark Herrier, Wyatt Knight, Roger Wilson
▶ Good-natured but extremely raunchy comedy set in 1950s Florida is basically a fast-paced collection of locker room jokes as high school friends—primarily Monahan, Herrier, Knight, and Wilson—try to lose their virginity at a local tavern notorious for its loose women. Megahit comedy inspired a number of sequels; four male stars appeared in the follow-up, *Porky's II: The Next Day.*
Dist.: CBS/Fox

PORKY'S II: THE NEXT DAY 1983 Canadian
★ ★ ★ R Comedy 1:38
☑ Nudity, adult situations, explicit language, mild violence, adult humor
Dir: Bob Clark *Cast:* Dan Monahan, Wyatt Knight, Mark Herrier, Tony Ganios, Kaki Hunter, Scott Colomby, Roger Wilson
▶ The *Porky's* gang production of *Romeo and Juliet* is disrupted by a fundamentalist minister and the Ku Klux Klan who object to the racy language and casting of a Seminole in the lead. Not to worry, the kids manage to outwit their tormentors. Outrageous pranks and sophomoric gags of the original are mixed with a dash of social consciousness.
Dist.: CBS/Fox

PORKY'S REVENGE 1985
★ ★ R Comedy 1:33
☑ Nudity, adult situations, explicit language, graphic violence
Dir: James Komack *Cast:* Dan Monahan, Wyatt Knight, Tony Ganios, Mark Herrier, Kaki Hunter, Chuck Mitchell
▶ Pee Wee (Monahan), Meat (Ganios), and cohorts foil their old nemesis Porky's (Mitchell) plan to fix the high school basketball championship and force Meat to marry his ugly daughter. Tried-and-true horny high jinks superior to the second movie, not as good as the first. Soundtrack, featuring Dave Edmonds, Willie Nelson, and Clarence Clemons, really rocks. **(CC)**
Dist.: CBS/Fox

PORTNOY'S COMPLAINT 1972
★ R Drama 1:42
☑ Nudity, adult situations, explicit language
Dir: Ernest Lehman *Cast:* Richard Benjamin, Karen Black, Lee Grant, Jack Somack, Jeannie Berlin, Jill Clayburgh
▶ Attempt to film Philip Roth's profane novel, a virtual monologue about the miseries of growing up, was universally panned by critics upon its release. Portnoy (Benjamin) recites his sexual hang-ups to his shrink while describing his nagging mother Grant, constipated father Somack, and gentile girlfriend Black. For curiosity seekers only.
Dist.: Warner

PORT OF NEW YORK 1949
★ NR Mystery-Suspense 1:22 B&W
Dir: Laslo Benedek *Cast:* Scott Brady, Richard Rober, K. T. Stevens, Yul Brynner, Arthur Blake
▶ Customs agents Brady and Rober scour New York's waterfront for clues to a drug shipment. Trail leads to a narcotics ring run by Brynner. Modest thriller has good atmosphere but a weak plot. Film debut for Brynner, who sports a full head of hair.
Dist.: Video Yesteryear

PORTRAIT OF A WOMAN NUDE 1983 Italian
☆ **NR Comedy 1:52**
☑ Nudity, explicit language
Dir: Nino Manfredi ***Cast:*** Nino Manfredi, Eleonora Giorgi, Jean-Pierre Cassel, George Wilson, Carlo Bagno
► In Venice, Manfredi/Giorgi marriage breaks up due to boredom. He becomes enamored of a nude woman he sees in a picture and tries to track her down. She turns out to be a hooker who suspiciously resembles his wife. Enchanting performance by Giorgi in a dual role, but overly somber tone is at odds with premise.
Dist.: MCA

PORTRAIT OF JENNIE 1948
★★ **NR Fantasy 1:26 B&W**
Dir: William Dieterle ***Cast:*** Jennifer Jones, Joseph Cotten, Ethel Barrymore, Cecil Kellaway, David Wayne, Lillian Gish
► Painter Cotten is short on money and inspiration until he encounters Jones in Central Park. She is sweet, innocent, and beautiful, but her speech is strangely anachronistic, and she is years older every time they meet. Achingly romantic classic gets lush direction from Dieterle, haunting performance by Jones. Oscar-nominated for cinematography; won for special effects. Based on a novel by Robert Nathan. **(CC)**
Dist.: CBS/Fox

POSED FOR MURDER 1989
★ **R Mystery-Suspense 1:25**
☑ Nudity, adult situations, explicit language, violence
Dir: Brian Thomas Jones ***Cast:*** Charlotte J. Helmkamp, Carl Fury, Rick Gianasi, Michael Merrings, William Beckwith, Roy McArthur
► *Thrill Magazine* gatefold girl Helmkamp (a real-life *Playboy* model) auditions for a horror movie and finds reality even worse: a maniac is killing everyone around her. Her current and former boyfriends are among the suspects. Standard sex and violence combo.
Dist.: Academy

POSEIDON ADVENTURE, THE 1972
★★★★★ **PG Action-Adventure 1:57**
☑ Explicit language, mild violence
Dir: Ronald Neame ***Cast:*** Gene Hackman, Ernest Borgnine, Shelley Winters, Red Buttons, Roddy McDowall, Stella Stevens
► The first and best of the seventies disaster films. Trapped when their luxury liner is capsized by a tidal wave, an all-star cast of survivors must undertake a perilous journey to the bottom—now the top—of the ship. Thrills, chills, and action all the way, with juicy performances from everyone. Our favorite scene: Jewish mama Winters taking her big dive underwater. Oscars for theme song, "The Morning After," and Special Effects; Winters was also nominated. Sequel: *Beyond the Poseidon Adventure.*
Dist.: CBS/Fox

POSITIVE I.D. 1986
★ **R Mystery-Suspense 1:31**
☑ Adult situations, explicit language, violence
Dir: Andy Anderson ***Cast:*** Stephanie Rascoe, John Davies, Steve Fromholz, Laura Lane, Gail Cronauer
► Fort Worth housewife Julie (Rascoe), recovering slowly from a brutal rape-torture and subsequent media-sensation trial, manufactures a new identity as "Bobbie," a blond bombshell who hangs out at a seedy downtown bar. The reason for her double life is revealed when her rapist is released from prison. Compelling low-budget film displays a surprisingly good mix of dark humor and convincing tension.
Dist.: MCA

POSSE 1975
★★★★ **PG Western 1:34**
☑ Adult situations, violence
Dir: Kirk Douglas ***Cast:*** Kirk Douglas, Bruce Dern, Bo Hopkins, James Stacy, Luke Askew, David Canary
► Politically ambitious sheriff Douglas figures that nabbing deadly desperado Dern will help his career. However, the wily criminal resists being captured and used, and a chase follows. Solid Western is consistently entertaining, if not overwhelmingly original. Kirk does a nice job as director and actor; Dern is a worthy adversary.
Dist.: Paramount

POSSESSED 1931
★★ **NR Drama 1:16 B&W**
Dir: Clarence Brown ***Cast:*** Joan Crawford, Clark Gable, Wallace Ford, Skeets Gallagher, John Miljan
► Ambitious factory girl Crawford moves to New York and gets involved with married politician Gable. Their love is threatened when Gable runs for governor and his affair with Crawford becomes an issue in the campaign. Gable and Crawford are near the top of their form in this otherwise ordinary soaper.
Dist.: MGM/UA

POSSESSION 1981 French/German
☆ **R Horror 2:07**
☑ Nudity, adult situations, violence
Dir: Andrzej Zulawski ***Cast:*** Isabelle Adjani, Sam Neill, Heinz Bennent, Margit Carstensen, Michael Hogben, Carl Duering
► Neill comes home from a long absence to discover that wife Adjani has been unfaithful with handsome Bennent, and is also making love to a large, glisteningly tentacled monster. Beast/Adjani union spawns husband look-alike. Impossible to figure out what it all means in clutter of half-baked symbols and disgusting images. [S]
Dist.: Vestron

POSTMAN ALWAYS RINGS TWICE, THE 1946
★★★★ **NR Drama 1:53 B&W**

Dir: Tay Garnett *Cast:* Lana Turner, John Garfield, Cecil Kellaway, Hume Cronyn, Leon Ames, Audrey Totter
▶ Drifter Garfield accepts handyman job at a roadside diner in order to seduce owner Kellaway's wife Turner; she responds with a plot to kill her husband. Classic film noir notable for torrid teaming of Garfield and Turner (who's irresistible in an almost all-white wardrobe) and daring plot. Shrewd adaptation of James M. Cain's novel suggests a great deal despite censorship restrictions. Remade in 1981.
Dist.: MGM/UA

POSTMAN ALWAYS RINGS TWICE, THE 1981
★ ★ ★ R Drama 1:56
☑ Strong sexual content, adult situations, explicit language, violence
Dir: Bob Rafelson *Cast:* Jack Nicholson, Jessica Lange, John Colicos, Michael Lerner, Anjelica Huston
▶ Steamy remake of the 1946 Lana Turner/ John Garfield vehicle, based on James M. Cain's novel. In the Depression thirties, drifter Nicholson begins a torrid affair with Lange, wife of roadhouse owner Colicos. The lovers succeed in murdering Colicos and even manage to escape justice but get their just desserts in the end. Most notorious scene: Nicholson and Lange on the floury kitchen table.
Dist.: CBS/Fox

POT O' GOLD 1941
★ ★ NR Comedy 1:26 B&W
Dir: George Marshall *Cast:* James Stewart, Paulette Goddard, Charles Winninger, Mary Gordon, Frank Melton, Horace Heidt
▶ Inconsequential comedy about the efforts of wealthy harmonica whiz Stewart to promote Heidt's band while pursuing Goddard, the beautiful daughter of a tenement landlady. Stewart succeeds in placing the band on a new radio show financed by his uncle Winninger. Frail story line isn't helped by Stewart's singing or songs like "Hi Cy, What's Cookin'?" Based on a once-popular radio series.
Dist.: Various

POWAQQATSI 1988
☆ G Documentary 1:37
Dir: Godfrey Reggio
▶ Reggio's follow-up to *Koyannisqatsi* contrasts modern urban life with images of nature and Third World cultures. Reggio eschews conventional storytelling and dialogue in favor of an extravagant visual style and bravura editing that make this a treat for the eye and ear if not the mind and heart. Score by Philip Glass.

POWER, THE 1984
★ ★ R Horror 1:26
☑ Explicit language, graphic violence
Dir: Jeffrey Obrow, Stephen Carpenter *Cast:* Susan Stokey, Warren Lincoln, Lisa Erickson, J. Dinan Myrtetus, Chad Christian
▶ Aztec relic that possesses people falls into

the hands of teens who give it to reporter Stokey. Reporter's rejected beau Lincoln falls under statue's influence and goes on a murderous spree. Good special effects and makeup but atrocious acting, clichéd story, and excessive violence.
Dist.: Vestron

POWER 1986
★ ★ R Drama 1:51
☑ Brief nudity, adult situations, explicit language
Dir: Sidney Lumet *Cast:* Richard Gere, Julie Christie, Gene Hackman, Kate Capshaw, Denzel Washington, E. G. Marshall
▶ Media consultant Gere is handsome, ruthless, and for a big enough fee, will transform anyone into a front-running political contender. His ex-mentor Hackman, ex-wife Christie, and senator Marshall, who's involved in a real-estate swindle, ultimately convince Gere to redeem himself by backing an ethical candidate. Well-meaning but witless film with pretty clothes and hip set decorations. (CC)
Dist.: Warner

POWER PLAY 1978 Canadian
★ NR Action-Adventure 1:42
☑ Brief nudity, graphic violence
Dir: Martyn Burke *Cast:* Peter O'Toole, David Hemmings, Donald Pleasence, Barry Morse, Jon Granik, Dick Cavett
▶ In a European country, army officers conspire to overthrow the corrupt government. The coup is a success but O'Toole, one of the conspirators, turns on his erstwhile allies and assumes power himself. Believable performances, acceptable action, but leisurely pacing and overly dry dialogue.
Dist.: Media

P.O.W. THE ESCAPE 1986
★ ★ R War 1:30
☑ Nudity, explicit language, violence
Dir: Gideon Amir *Cast:* David Carradine, Charles R. Floyd, Mako, Steve James, Phil Brock
▶ In North Vietnam, captured American colonel Carradine is slated for execution but offered freedom if he'll help captor Mako escape to the U.S. with his cache of gold. Carradine enters Norris/Stallone territory, delivering the expected macho heroics and nonstop action.
Dist.: Media

POWWOW HIGHWAY 1989
★ ★ ★ R Comedy/Drama 1:31
☑ Brief nudity, adult situations, explicit language, violence
Dir: Jonathan Wacks *Cast:* A Martinez, Gary Farmer, Joanelle Romero, Amanda Wyss, Wayne Waterman
▶ With his sister Romero framed by federal agents because of his opposition to a government deal with his tribe, cynical Cheyenne Indian Martinez flees the reservation with hulk-

ing, childlike Farmer. The latter changes the former's outlook and ends up helping Romero too. Sleeper's initially angry tone shifts into blissful, warm comedy, with wondrous teamwork from Martinez and Farmer.
Dist.: Warner

PRACTICE MAKES PERFECT 1978 French
☆ **NR Comedy 1:44**
☑ Nudity, adult situations
Dir: Philippe de Broca *Cast:* Jean Rochefort, Nicole Garcia, Annie Girardot, Danielle Darrieux, Catherine Alric, Lila Kedrova
▶ Concert pianist Rochefort, although married to gorgeous Garcia and father of three daughters, plays the field as well he plays his instrument, dividing his energy among ex-wives and current lovers until his wife walks out. Insightful romantic comedy features sublime performances by Rochefort and Garcia.
Dist.: RCA/Columbia

PRANCER 1989
★ ★ ★ ★ **G Family 1:43**
Dir: John Hancock *Cast:* Sam Elliott, Rebecca Harrell, Cloris Leachman, Rutanya Alda, John Joseph Duda, Abe Vigoda, Michael Constantine, Boo the Reindeer
▶ In a midwestern town at Christmastime, eight-year-old Harrell finds an injured reindeer which she believes is Santa's very own Prancer. She hides the animal on her widowed dad Elliott's farm and nurses him back to health. Sweet, charming children's fantasy gets gentle yet sure-handed direction by Hancock and a winning performance by Harrell. **(CC)**
Dist.: Nelson

PRAYER FOR THE DYING, A 1987 British
★ ★ **R Drama 1:48**
☑ Brief nudity, adult situations, explicit language, violence
Dir: Mike Hodges *Cast:* Mickey Rourke, Bob Hoskins, Alan Bates, Sammi Davis, Christopher Fulford, Liam Neeson
▶ Rourke, a disillusioned IRA killer, does a hit for mobster Bates. When priest Hoskins witnesses the deed, Rourke uses the confessional to ensure Hoskins's silence, but is still pursued by the police and his employers. Hindered by incomplete characterizations, heavy accents, and overwrought symbolism. Based on the Jack Higgins best-seller. **(CC)**
Dist.: Virgin

PRAY FOR DEATH 1985
★ ★ **R Martial Arts 1:34**
☑ Explicit language, graphic violence
Dir: Gordon Hessler *Cast:* Sho Kosugi, Donna Kei Benz, James Booth, Norman Burton, Michael Constantine
▶ Japanese businessman Kosugi moves to New York and opens a restaurant. When thugs kidnap his son and kill his wife, Kosugi comes out of ninja retirement for revenge. Rousing

fight scenes, acrobatic action, formula plot, and wooden performances.
Dist.: IVE

PREDATOR 1987
★ ★ ★ ★ **R Sci-Fi/Action-Adventure 1:46**
☑ Explicit language, graphic violence
Dir: John McTiernan *Cast:* Arnold Schwarzenegger, Carl Weathers, Elpidia Carrillo, Bill Duke, Jesse Ventura, Sonny Landham, Kevin Peter Hall
▶ Schwarzenegger leads a team of mercenaries into the jungles of Latin America, but they're double-crossed by CIA agent Weathers and forced to battle their way back to a distant rendezvous point. Tension increases as a half-seen enemy (Hall) with amazing powers picks them off one by one. Solid adventure with good special effects is sure to please Schwarzenegger's fans. **(CC)**
Dist.: CBS/Fox

PREHISTORIC WOMEN 1950
☆ **NR Action-Adventure 1:14**
Dir: Gregg Tallas *Cast:* Laurette Luez, Allan Nixon, Joan Shawlee, Judy Landon, Mara Lynn, Jo Carroll Dennison
▶ Camp 1950s skin feature with Nixon and Luez defying predatory female society and a hairy, nine-foot monster to find love. Though it is many million years B.C., primitive women have somehow evolved sophisticated hairdressing techniques as well as lipstick and eyeliner. Really silly.
Dist.: Rhino

PREMATURE BURIAL, THE 1962
★ ★ **NR Horror 1:21**
Dir: Roger Corman *Cast:* Ray Milland, Hazel Court, Richard Ney, Heather Angel, Alan Napier, Dick Miller
▶ Nineteenth-century medical student Milland's one great fear—of being buried alive—becomes reality when a doctor mistakenly declares him dead. Milland escapes to get revenge. Middling entry in Corman's series of Edgar Allan Poe adaptations.
Dist.: Vestron

PREMONITION, THE 1976
★ **PG Horror 1:34**
☑ Violence
Dir: Robert Allan Schnitzer *Cast:* Sharon Farrell, Edward Bell, Jeff Corey, Richard Lynch, Ellen Barber, Danielle Brisebois
▶ Farrell and Bell live in a small town with adoptive daughter Brisebois. Unstable natural mother Barber shows up, wanting her little girl back; Farrell has visions that something awful is about to happen. Parapsychological thriller emphasizes mood over mayhem.
Dist.: Nelson

PRESENTING LILY MARS 1943
★ ★ ★ **NR Musical 1:44 B&W**
Dir: Norman Taurog *Cast:* Judy Garland, Van Heflin, Fay Bainter, Richard Carlson, Spring Byington, Marta Eggerth

▶ Garland enhances this predictable tale of a stagestruck Indiana girl who convinces Broadway producer Heflin to make her a chorus girl in his next show. Despite objections of star Eggerth, Garland becomes a success. Routine songs ("Three O'Clock in the Morning," "Broadway Rhythm") bolster slight plot (based on a novel by Booth Tarkington). With Tommy Dorsey, Bob Crosby, and their orchestras.
Dist.: MGM/UA

PRESIDENT'S ANALYST, THE 1967
★ ★ NR Comedy 1:43
☑ Adult situations, explicit language, violence
Dir: Theodore J. Flicker *Cast:* James Coburn, Godfrey Cambridge, Severn Darden, Joan Delaney, Pat Harrington, William Daniels
▶ Shrink Coburn learns too much in his sessions with the President and tries to escape the pressures of his job, only to become the target of both the U.S. and foreign spies. Wacky satire takes on the CIA, FBI, and international political intrigue. Uneven, but Coburn's cool and some delicious bits (especially the revelation of the identity of "TPC," one of the groups hounding Coburn) make it work.
Dist.: Paramount

PRESIDIO, THE 1988
★ ★ ★ ★ R Mystery-Suspense 1:39
☑ Adult situations, explicit language, violence
Dir: Peter Hyams *Cast:* Sean Connery, Mark Harmon, Meg Ryan, Jack Warden, Dana Gladstone, Mark Blum
▶ When a young female soldier is slain while patrolling the Presidio, the San Francisco Army base, hot-headed police detective Harmon and tough, by-the-book base chief Connery must settle jurisdictional dispute and team to solve the case. Connery's hostility is increased by daughter Ryan's romance with Harmon. Flinty team of Connery and Harmon create sparks in fast-paced, action-packed crime drama.
Dist.: Paramount

PRETTY BABY 1978
★ ★ R Drama 1:50
☑ Nudity, adult situations, explicit language
Dir: Louis Malle *Cast:* Keith Carradine, Susan Sarandon, Brooke Shields, Frances Faye, Antonio Fargas, Genil Graham
▶ In 1917 New Orleans, young Shields follows in the professional footsteps of prostitute mom Sarandon. Photographer Carradine takes pictures of the women and eventually marries Shields. Beautiful period re-creation with a snazzy ragtime score. Some shocking scenes (mostly involving Shields) gave this notoriety, but slow pace and stiff acting hinder story.
Dist.: Paramount

PRETTY IN PINK 1986
★ ★ ★ ★ PG-13 Romance/Comedy 1:36
☑ Adult situations, explicit language
Dir: Howard Deutsch *Cast:* Molly Ringwald, Harry Dean Stanton, Jon Cryer, Andrew McCarthy, Annie Potts, James Spader
▶ Snooty high schoolers look down on poor teen Ringwald with unemployed dad Stanton although her nerdy best pal Cryer loves her. Rich kid McCarthy falls for Ringwald but will peer pressure ruin their prom date? Slight but very sweet: witty dialogue from producer/writer John Hughes, adorable Ringwald, amusing support from Cryer, good rock standards score, and an upbeat finale. (CC)
Dist.: Paramount

PRETTYKILL 1987
★ R Mystery-Suspense 1:35
☑ Nudity, adult situations, explicit language, violence
Dir: George Kaczender *Cast:* David Birney, Season Hubley, Suzanne Snyder, Yaphet Kotto, Susannah York
▶ High-class hooker Hubley takes Snyder under her professional wing. Can Hubley's cop boyfriend Birney save her when Snyder turns out to be a schizoid killer? Unconvincing thriller with cardboard characters, silly screenplay, average production values.
Dist.: Warner

PRETTY SMART 1987
★ R Comedy 1:24
☑ Nudity, strong sexual content, adult situations, explicit language
Dir: Dimitri Logothetis *Cast:* Tricia Leigh Fisher, Lisa Lorient, Dennis Cole, Patricia Arquette, Paris Vaughan
▶ Sisters Fisher and Lorient at posh girls' academy in Greece are divided by their choice of clique. Fisher joins the rebel Subs while Lorient opts for the snooty 'Premes. They are, however, united in their effort to thwart drug-smuggling scheme of principal Cole. Lots of nudity in a silly story.
Dist.: New World

PRETTY WOMAN 1990
★ ★ ★ ★ ★ R Romance/Comedy 1:57
☑ Brief nudity, adult situations, explicit language, violence
Dir: Garry Marshall *Cast:* Richard Gere, Julia Roberts, Ralph Bellamy, Laura San Giacomo, Jason Alexander, Hector Elizondo
▶ After a casual meeting, wealthy corporate raider Gere offers prostitute Roberts $3000 to spend a week with him at a swank Beverly Hills hotel. Real feelings penetrate their business arrangement as he broadens her horizons and she awakens his conscience. Hoary hooker-with-a-heart-of-gold cliché has been cleverly upgraded into an irresistible modern love story. Engaging, marvelously natural performance by Roberts; Elizondo stands out as an understanding hotel manager.
Dist.: Buena Vista

PREY, THE 1983
★ R Horror 1:21
☑ Brief nudity, adult situations, violence
Dir: Edwin Scott Brown *Cast:* Debbie Thureson, Steve Bond, Lori Lethin, Robert Wald, Gayle Gannes
▶ Teens take their van into the mountains to go camping but something tall, gross, and ugly begins to stalk and kill them. A ranger aids the survivors but is soon in danger himself. Routine formula story, blandly cast and dully directed. Fails to deliver requisite thrills.
Dist.: HBO

PRICK UP YOUR EARS 1987 British
☆ R Drama 1:51
☑ Strong sexual content, adult situations, explicit language
Dir: Stephen Frears *Cast:* Gary Oldman, Alfred Molina, Vanessa Redgrave, Wallace Shawn, Lindsay Duncan
▶ True story of the late British playwright Joe Orton (Oldman), who gained renown for his black comedies in the 1960s. His male lover Molina's jealousy of Orton's success led to a tragic conclusion. Literate, candid, superbly performed by Oldman and Molina but very depressing.
Dist.: Virgin

PRIDE AND PREJUDICE 1940
★ ★ ★ ★ NR Comedy 1:58 B&W
Dir: Robert Z. Leonard *Cast:* Greer Garson, Laurence Olivier, Mary Boland, Edna May Oliver, Maureen O'Sullivan, Edmund Gwenn
▶ First-rate adaptation of Jane Austen's classic comedy of manners about the efforts of early nineteenth-century English couple Boland and Gwenn to marry off their five eligible daughters. Garson and Olivier, extremely appealing as antagonistic lovers, make the most of the witty, polished dialogue (by Aldous Huxley and Jane Murfin). Gorgeous set designs by Cedric Gibbons and Paul Groesse received an Oscar.
Dist.: MGM

PRIDE AND THE PASSION, THE 1957
★ ★ NR Action-Adventure 2:12
Dir: Stanley Kramer *Cast:* Cary Grant, Frank Sinatra, Sophia Loren, Theodore Bikel, John Wengraf, Jay Novello
▶ Overblown historical epic about a strategic cannon left behind by retreating Spaniards during 1810 war. Guerrilla leader Sinatra convinces British artillery expert Grant to bring the weapon to Avila, where it will be used against the French. During the perilous journey Grant falls in love with beautiful camp follower Loren. Large-scale spectacle lacks emotion.
Dist.: CBS/Fox

PRIDE OF ST. LOUIS, THE 1952
★ ★ NR Biography/Sports 1:33 B&W
Dir: Harmon Jones *Cast:* Dan Dailey, Joanne Dru, Richard Crenna, Hugh Sanders, James Brown, Leo T. Cleary
▶ True story of baseball star Dizzy Dean (Dai-

ley). While working his way into the big leagues, Dean proposes to Dru and helps his brother Daffy (Crenna) with his own baseball career. Despite a tendency to mangle the language, he becomes a famous announcer once his pitching career is over. Not bad, even for nonbaseball fans.
Dist.: CBS/Fox

PRIDE OF THE YANKEES, THE 1942
★ ★ ★ ★ ★ NR Biography/Sports 2:08 B&W
Dir: Sam Wood *Cast:* Gary Cooper, Teresa Wright, Babe Ruth, Walter Brennan, Dan Duryea, Elsa Janssen
▶ Top-notch story of Lou Gehrig (Cooper), Hall-of-Fame Yankee first baseman, charts his undergrad years at Columbia, choice of pro baseball over postgrad work to pay for operation for mother Janssen, romance with wife-to-be Wright, and spectacular career as part of legendary "Murderer's Row" of the twenties and thirties Yanks. After setting still-unbroken record for 2,130 consecutive games played, "Iron Horse" Gehrig succumbed to the degenerative muscle disease that bears his name, bowing out of baseball in an emotional farewell. First-class production earned ten Oscar nominations; won for Best Editing. **(CC)**
Dist.: CBS/Fox

PRIEST OF LOVE 1981 British
★ ★ R Biography 2:05
☑ Nudity, adult situations, explicit language
Dir: Christopher Miles *Cast:* Ian McKellen, Janet Suzman, Ava Gardner, John Gielgud, Sarah Miles, Penelope Keith
▶ The life and loves of the writer D. H. Lawrence (McKellen), including relationships with wife (Suzman) and patroness of the arts Mabel Dodge Luhan (Gardner). Interesting casting (Gardner looks especially fit) and colorful locations, but rather shapeless narrative fails to give sufficient insight into what made Lawrence tick.
Dist.: HBO

PRIME CUT 1972
★ ★ ★ R Action-Adventure 1:26
☑ Brief nudity, explicit language, violence
Dir: Michael Ritchie *Cast:* Lee Marvin, Gene Hackman, Angel Tompkins, Gregory Walcott, Sissy Spacek
▶ Stylish but brutal thriller about gang warfare between a Chicago mob represented by Marvin and Kansas City upstarts led by Hackman features a memorable opening sequence in which a thug is reduced to sausages. Spacek makes her film debut as a drugged prostitute auctioned off in a cattle warehouse by Hackman's wife Tompkins. **(CC)**
Dist.: Key

PRIME EVIL 1988
☆ R Horror 1:28
☑ Nudity, adult situations, explicit language, graphic violence

Dir: Roberta Findlay *Cast:* William Beckwith, Christine Moore, Tim Gail, Max Jacobs, Mavis Harris, Gary Warner

▶ Satanist Beckwith leads cult of immortals who maintain longevity through sacrifice of blood relatives. This is bad news for virginal Moore, who is set up as a victim by grandfather Jacobs, but nun Harris leaves the convent to stop the dastardly doings. Far from prime evildoings in low-rent production.
Dist.: New World

PRIME OF MISS JEAN BRODIE, THE 1969
British
★ ★ PG Drama 1:56
☑ Nudity, adult situations
Dir: Ronald Neame *Cast:* Maggie Smith, Robert Stephens, Pamela Franklin, Gordon Jackson, Jane Carr, Celia Johnson
▶ In 1932, eccentric Miss Jean Brodie (Smith) teaches at a conservative school for girls in Edinburgh, where she tells her girls to live for beauty, art, and truth. She encourages one girl to become the mistress of Stephens, who is in love with Brodie, and inspires Carr to make a tragic decision. Monumental performance from Smith won her the Oscar for Best Actress. Also nominated for hit song *Jean* by Rod McKuen. Based on the London and Broadway stage hit by Jay Presson Allen, who adapted Muriel Spark's novel.
Dist.: CBS/Fox

PRIME RISK 1985
★ ★ PG-13 Drama 1:38
☑ Brief nudity, explicit language, violence
Dir: Michael Farkas *Cast:* Lee Montgomery, Toni Hudson, Sam Bottoms, Clu Gulager, Keenan Wynn
▶ When computer expert Hudson is turned down for a job by a sexist bank officer, she teams up with aspiring pilot Montgomery, whose bank account has been frozen, in a plot to rob automated teller machines. Unfortunately, they stumble into a deadly conspiracy by foreign spies to undermine the Federal Reserve Bank. Taut, enjoyable thriller with an impressive script by first-time director Farkas.
Dist.: Vestron

PRIME SUSPECT 1988
☆ NR Mystery-Suspense 1:29
☑ Nudity, adult situations, explicit language, graphic violence
Dir: Mark Rutland *Cast:* Susan Strasberg, Frank Stallone, Billy Drago, Doug McClure, Robert F. Lyons, Dana Plato
▶ After witnessing the murder of his girlfriend Plato, suspect Drago is sent to a mental institution. Although psychiatrist Strasberg believes him innocent, he escapes as the killer strikes again. Strasberg's sheriff boyfriend Lyons investigates. Poor production values sink this thriller.
Dist.: SVS

PRIMROSE PATH 1940
★ NR Drama 1:34 B&W

Dir: Gregory La Cava *Cast:* Ginger Rogers, Joel McCrea, Marjorie Rambeau, Henry Travers, Miles Mander, Queenie Vassar
▶ Rogers, whose family lives on the edge of poverty, eagerly accepts a marriage proposal from McCrea, owner of a hamburger stand. He has second thoughts when he learns that her mother Rambeau is a prostitute. Unexpectedly frank and moving story benefits greatly from the leads' sincerity.
Dist.: Turner

PRINCE AND THE PAUPER, THE 1937
★ ★ ★ NR Action-Adventure 2:00 B&W
Dir: William Keighley *Cast:* Errol Flynn, Claude Rains, Henry Stephenson, Barton MacLane, Billy Mauch, Bobby Mauch
▶ Young prince Bobby Mauch, soon to be crowned King Edward VI, trades places with a lookalike beggar (Billy Mauch) for a first-hand look at sixteenth-century London slums. Enemies at court learn of the switch, and proceed with plans to crown the wrong boy. The only one who listens to the prince's pleas is dissolute rake Flynn. Large-scale adaptation of Mark Twain's classic played with high spirits and wit. (CC)
Dist.: Media ⒸC

PRINCE AND THE SHOWGIRL, THE 1957
★ ★ NR Comedy 1:57
Dir: Laurence Olivier *Cast:* Marilyn Monroe, Laurence Olivier, Sybil Thorndike, Richard Wattis, Jeremy Spenser
▶ Charming but low-key comedy set in 1911 London. Carpathian prince Olivier, in town for King George's coronation, invites dizzy showgirl Monroe to dinner in hopes of a quick seduction. Instead, she falls in love and settles a feud between the prince and his son Spenser. Based on a hit play by Terence Rattigan.
Dist.: Warner

PRINCE OF DARKNESS 1987
★ ★ R Horror 1:41
☑ Explicit language, graphic violence
Dir: John Carpenter *Cast:* Donald Pleasence, Jameson Parker, Lisa Blount, Victor Wong, Dennis Dun, Susan Blanchard
▶ Priest Pleasence, scientist Wong, and graduate students, including Parker and Blount, team to fight Satan (imprisoned for centuries in a church basement in the form of a liquid green mass) when the demon threatens to return to life. Carpenter provides genuine jolts, moody atmosphere, intense special effects, and interesting ideas; there may be times, however, when you wish his talky characters would just shut up.
Dist.: MCA

PRINCE OF PENNSYLVANIA, THE 1988
★ ★ ★ R Drama 1:32
☑ Adult situations, explicit language
Dir: Ron Nyswaner *Cast:* Keanu Reeves, Amy Madigan, Bonnie Bedelia, Fred Ward, Joseph De Lisi, Jeff Hayenga
▶ Misunderstood Pennsylvania teenager

Reeves, who prefers working at Madigan's restaurant than with dad Ward in the coal mine, convinces her to aid in plot to kidnap pop and force the sale of his property. Subplot involves wife Bedelia cheating on Ward with Hayenga. Unconventional study of alienation has sharp acting and dialogue even when story veers out of control.
Dist.: RCA/Columbia

PRINCE OF THE CITY 1981
★ ★ ★ R Drama 2:50
☑ Adult situations, explicit language, violence
Dir: Sidney Lumet   *Cast:* Treat Williams, Jerry Orbach, Richard Foronjy, Don Billett, Kenny Marino, Lindsay Crouse
▶ New York narc Williams is torn between moral obligation and loyalty to his partners when he agrees to cooperate in a corruption investigation. Gripping drama manages a complex balancing act, portraying all sides of the characters and issues while evoking sympathy for the tortured Williams. Powerfully directed and co-written by Lumet; strong support by Orbach. Oscar-nominated screenplay was inspired by a true story.
Dist.: Warner

PRINCESS ACADEMY, THE 1987
★ R Comedy 1:30
☑ Adult situations, explicit language, adult humor
Dir: Bruce Block   *Cast:* Eva Gabor, Lu Leonard, Lar Park Lincoln, Richard Paul, Carole Davis
▶ Reform-school teen Lincoln nabs scholarship to posh Swiss academy where pâté eating and shopping are part of the curriculum. Lincoln foils corrupt headmistress Leonard and wins the heart of a titled twit. Crass comedy features lots of jokes about losing virginity and close-ups of manure.
Dist.: Vestron

PRINCESS AND THE PIRATE, THE 1944
★ ★ NR Comedy 1:34
Dir: David Butler   *Cast:* Bob Hope, Virginia Mayo, Walter Brennan, Walter Slezak, Victor McLaglen
▶ Princess Mayo, fleeing arranged marriage, is kidnapped by pirates of the Spanish Main. Actor Hope, longer on shtick than talent, helps her escape. Mindless, glossy period story shows off Hope, Mayo, and Brennan (who provides many of the laughs) to good advantage.
Dist.: Nelson

PRINCESS BRIDE, THE 1987
★ ★ ★ ★ PG Fantasy/Comedy 1:38
☑ Explicit language, mild violence
Dir: Rob Reiner   *Cast:* Cary Elwes, Robin Wright, Mandy Patinkin, Chris Sarandon, Wallace Shawn, Andre the Giant, Billy Crystal
▶ Grandfather Peter Falk's bedtime story features fencing, fighting, torture, giants, mon-

sters, and yes, some kissing. Princess Buttercup (Wright) becomes engaged to Prince Humperdink (Sarandon) after learning her true love Elwes has been killed by pirates. When she's abducted by Shawn, Patinkin, and Andre, a masked stranger appears to rescue her. Enchanting, high-spirited fun is actually an adult fantasy disguised as a children's story. Adapted by William Goldman from his cult novel. **(CC)**
Dist.: Nelson

PRINCESS TAM-TAM 1935 French
☆ NR Drama 1:17 B&W
Dir: Edmond Greville   *Cast:* Josephine Baker, Albert Prejean, Germaine Aussy, Viviane Romance
▶ In a plot reminiscent of *Pygmalion,* French novelist Prejean grooms rough-around-the-edges African Baker, turning her into a lady in the hopes of making his cheating wife jealous. Antique Baker showcase is of interest to film buffs or her fans.
Dist.: Kino

PRINCIPAL, THE 1987
★ ★ ★ ★ R Drama 1:50
☑ Explicit language, violence
Dir: Christopher Cain   *Cast:* James Belushi, Louis Gossett, Jr., Rae Dawn Chong, Michael Wright, J. J. Cohen, Esai Morales
▶ Unruly teacher Belushi is punished with "promotion" to principal of a war-zone high school dominated by drug-dealing ganglord Wright. Teaming with security chief Gossett, baseball bat–wielding Belushi attempts to instill discipline in rowdy students and pride in apathetic teachers. Efforts lead to climactic showdown with Wright. Picture blends comedy and drama, often with unsettling results, but Belushi shines in this ultimately compelling tale.
Dist.: RCA/Columbia

PRISON 1988
★ ★ R Horror 1:42
☑ Adult situations, explicit language, graphic violence
Dir: Renny Harlin   *Cast:* Lane Smith, Viggo Mortensen, Chelsea Field, Andre de Shields, Lincoln Kilpatrick, Ivan Kane
▶ Prison guard Smith stands by as innocent man is electrocuted. Twenty years later, Smith, now warden of the very same prison, is haunted by the vengeful electric ghost of the wrongfully executed man. Low-budget horror pic offers few surprises. **(CC)**
Dist.: New World

PRISONER, THE 1955 British
★ ★ NR Drama 1:31 B&W
Dir: Peter Glenville   *Cast:* Alec Guinness, Jack Hawkins, Raymond Huntley, Wilfrid Lawson, Jeannette Sterke, Ronald Lewis
▶ In an Eastern European, totalitarian country, cardinal Guinness is arrested and accused of treason. Interrogator Hawkins, Guinness's anti-Nazi compatriot during World War II, now finds

himself in opposition as he tries to break his old friend's will. Engrossing drama with excellent performances. Bridget Boland adapted her play.
Dist.: RCA/Columbia

PRISONER OF SECOND AVENUE, THE 1975
★ ★ ★ ★ PG Comedy 1:38
☑ Explicit language, adult humor
Dir: Melvin Frank   *Cast:* Jack Lemmon, Anne Bancroft, Gene Saks, Elizabeth Wilson, Florence Stanley, Maxine Stuart
▶ His nerves already frayed by New York hassles, ad executive Lemmon suffers a nervous breakdown when fired by failing firm. His rock-solid wife Bancroft gets a job and supports Lemmon through hardships with apathetic shrink, obnoxious neighbors, and meddling relatives, but then is also dismissed. Fine comic outing with melancholy edge in another play-into-film by prolific Neil Simon. Look for pre-*Rocky* Stallone in a bit part.
Dist.: Warner

PRISONER OF ZENDA, THE 1937
★ ★ ★ NR Action-Adventure 1:41 B&W
Dir: John Cromwell   *Cast:* Ronald Colman, Madeleine Carroll, Mary Astor, Douglas Fairbanks, Jr., C. Aubrey Smith, Raymond Massey
▶ Visiting Englishman Colman bears a remarkable resemblance to Prince Rudolf, the Ruritanian heir apparent. With evil stepbrother Fairbanks scheming to grab the throne, Colman is persuaded to impersonate the prince, leading to flashy swordfights, narrow escapes, and romance with princess Carroll. Fairbanks and Colman are ideally cast in this first-rate swashbuckling romance.
Dist.: MGM/UA

PRISONER OF ZENDA, THE 1952
★ ★ ★ NR Action-Adventure 1:40
Dir: Richard Thorpe   *Cast:* Stewart Granger, Deborah Kerr, James Mason, Louis Calhern, Jane Greer, Robert Douglas
▶ Third version of Anthony Hope's novel about political intrigue in the mythical kingdom of Ruritania. When crown prince Granger is kidnapped, a lookalike Englishman (also Granger) steps in to replace him and falls in love with beautiful princess Kerr. Thrilling climax features swashbuckling swordplay with oily villain Mason.
Dist.: MGM/UA

PRISONER OF ZENDA, THE 1979
★ ★ ★ PG Comedy 1:48
☑ Adult situations
Dir: Richard Quine   *Cast:* Peter Sellers, Lynne Frederick, Lionel Jeffries, Elke Sommer, Gregory Sierra, Jeremy Kemp
▶ Send-up of many previous incarnations of the film of the same name. In late nineteenth-century London, cabbie is enlisted to impersonate the crown prince of Ruritania (Sellers in both roles) since the prince's evil half-brother Kemp has plans for an assassination. Complications ensue when cabbie Sellers falls in love with prince's fiancée Frederick. Tepid costume comedy worthy for the always entertaining Sellers.
Dist.: MCA

PRISON TRAIN 1938
★ NR Action-Adventure 1:24 B&W
Dir: Gordon Wiles   *Cast:* Fred Keating, Linda Winters, Clarence Muse, Faith Bacon, Alexander Leftwich, Nestor Paiva
▶ After being sentenced by a federal judge to Alcatraz, gangster Keating is put under guard and transported across the country by train. Fellow crooks with unfinished business try to see that Keating doesn't survive the trip. Much expense has been spared, but hard-hitting actioner is fast moving. Also known as *The People's Enemy*.
Dist.: Sinister

PRIVATE BENJAMIN 1980
★ ★ ★ ★ ★ R Comedy 1:50
☑ Brief nudity, explicit language
Dir: Howard Zieff   *Cast:* Goldie Hawn, Eileen Brennan, Armand Assante, Albert Brooks, Sam Wanamaker, Barbara Barrie
▶ Spoiled, rich Hawn, distraught over death of hubby Brooks six hours after wedding, enlists in Army expecting country club life. Imagine Hawn's dismay when she encounters the spartan military, personified by no-nonsense captain Brennan determined to make a soldier out of her. Bouncy and popular comedy is splendid vehicle for Hawn, but Brennan and Brooks are also terrific. Hawn, Brennan, and screenplay were Oscar nominees.
Dist.: Warner

PRIVATE EYES, THE 1980
★ ★ ★ PG Comedy/Family 1:31
☑ Mild violence
Dir: Lang Elliot   *Cast:* Tim Conway, Don Knotts, Trisha Noble, Bernard Fox, Grace Zabriskie, Jogn Fujioka
▶ Klutzy American detectives Conway and Knotts assigned to Scotland Yard must solve the murder of two British aristocrats. Bluebloods' daughter Noble is in danger, since family servants inherit the fortune if she also expires. Lightweight but amiable comedy (co-written by Conway) aims for kids, with plenty of secret passageways, pratfalls, and silly sight gags.
Dist.: Vestron

PRIVATE FILES OF J. EDGAR HOOVER, THE 1977
★ ★ PG Biography 1:22
☑ Explicit language, violence
Dir: Larry Cohen   *Cast:* Broderick Crawford, Jose Ferrer, Rip Torn, Dan Dailey, Michael Parks, Ronee Blakley
▶ Sensationalist biopic of the late FBI chief Hoover (Crawford), whose ironfisted rule over the bureau lasted from 1924 until his death in 1972, is not for admirers of the man. Film paints unflattering portrait of Hoover's professional

tactics and private life, acknowledging his contribution in building the agency into a respected crime-fighting outfit but questioning his disregard for individual rights and pointedly touching on his hypocritical personal standards. Fine portrayal of feud with RFK (Parks).
Dist.: HBO

PRIVATE FUNCTION, A 1985 British
★ **R Comedy 1:33**
☑ Adult situations, explicit language
Dir: Malcolm Mowbray   *Cast:* Michael Palin, Maggie Smith, Denholm Elliott, Liz Smith, Richard Griffiths, Tony Haygarth
▶ Food rationing causes havoc in World War II English town as snobby big-shot Elliott and pals illegally raise a pig for a banquet. Wimpy podiatrist Palin, badgered by his social-climbing wife Smith, pignaps the main course but can't butcher it. Smith, Palin, Elliott, and the pig all deliver outstanding performances, but droll comedy will appeal only to fans of British humor.
Dist.: HBO

PRIVATE HELL 36 1954
★ ★ **NR Mystery-Suspense 1:21 B&W**
Dir: Don Siegel   *Cast:* Ida Lupino, Steve Cochran, Howard Duff, Dean Jagger, Dorothy Malone
▶ Cops Cochran and Duff trace a hot fifty-dollar bill to nightclub singer Lupino, who received it from a fan. Their legwork leads them to an eighty-thousand-dollar stash, the proceeds of a robbery. Cochran wants to keep the money, but Duff thinks they should turn it in. Siegel, directing a screenplay co-written by Lupino, lifts a generic plot up a notch.
Dist.: Republic

PRIVATE INVESTIGATIONS 1987
★ ★ **R Drama 1:31**
☑ Adult situations, explicit language, violence
Dir: Nigel Dick   *Cast:* Clayton Rohner, Ray Sharkey, Paul LeMat, Talia Balsam, Anthony Zerbe, Martin Balsam
▶ Newspaper editor Zerbe investigates drug-dealing cop Sharkey who frames his son Rohner for murder. Rohner seeks sanctuary with new girlfriend Balsam. The young couple, pursued by Sharkey and his murderous cohorts (including LeMat), seek to establish Rohner's innocence and help Zerbe expose police corruption. Serviceable thriller employs brisk action to disguise somewhat familiar tale.
Dist.: CBS/Fox

PRIVATE LESSONS 1981
★ ★ **R Comedy 1:27**
☑ Nudity, adult situations, explicit language
Dir: Alan Myerson   *Cast:* Sylvia Kristel, Howard Hesseman, Eric Brown, Patrick Piccininni, Ed Begley, Jr., Pamela Bryant
▶ Unscrupulous chauffeur Hesseman takes advantage of teen Brown's preoccupation

with sex by having beautiful housekeeper Kristel seduce him. Hesseman then fakes Kristel's death in a blackmail scheme, but true love saves the day. A popular hit on release for its ample nudity, but leering tone grows tedious.
Dist.: MCA

PRIVATE LIFE OF DON JUAN, THE 1934 British
★ **NR Drama 1:20 B&W**
Dir: Alexander Korda   *Cast:* Douglas Fairbanks, Sr., Merle Oberon, Binnie Barnes, Joan Gardner, Benita Hume, Athene Seyler
▶ Fairbanks is the legendary roué who, upon returning to his hometown, discovers a young imposter romancing the local wives in his stead. After the upstart is killed by a jealous husband, Fairbanks tries to convince the townspeople that he is the real Don Juan. Stiff, creaky costumer was Fairbanks's last film.
Dist.: Nelson

PRIVATE LIFE OF HENRY VIII, THE 1933 British
★ ★ **NR Biography 1:37 B&W**
Dir: Alexander Korda   *Cast:* Charles Laughton, Robert Donat, Binnie Barnes, Elsa Lanchester, Merle Oberon, Wendy Barrie
▶ Laughton won an Oscar for his vibrant, full-bodied impersonation of the notorious sixteenth-century English king in this sumptuous historical epic. Story covers Henry's last five marriages, with Laughton's wife Lanchester a standout as the card-cheating Anne of Cleves. Although technically dated, film's blend of spectacle and bawdy humor remains delightful.
Dist.: Various

PRIVATE LIFE OF SHERLOCK HOLMES, THE 1970
★ ★ **PG Mystery-Suspense 2:05**
☑ Adult situations, explicit language
Dir: Billy Wilder   *Cast:* Robert Stephens, Colin Blakely, Genevieve Page, Christopher Lee, Irene Handl, Stanley Holloway
▶ Sherlock Holmes (Stephens) and Doctor Watson (Blakely) investigate a baffling case that involves midgets, the Loch Ness monster, and mystery woman Page. Unusual and absorbing; Wilder takes an adult, revisionist approach to Holmes that brings new complexity to the character.
Dist.: Key

PRIVATE LIVES OF ELIZABETH AND ESSEX, THE 1939
★ ★ ★ **NR Drama 1:46**
Dir: Michael Curtiz   *Cast:* Bette Davis, Errol Flynn, Olivia de Havilland, Donald Crisp, Alan Hale, Vincent Price
▶ Elaborate but historically inaccurate costume epic about the tempestuous relationship between the aging Queen of England and the dashing Earl of Essex is a fine showcase for Davis's marvelous acting. Adapted from Maxwell Anderson's play *Elizabeth the Queen*, with a stirring score by Wolfang Korn-

gold. Davis would repeat her role in 1955's *The Virgin Queen*.
Dist.: MGM/UA

PRIVATE RESORT 1985
★ ★ R Comedy 1:22
☑ Nudity, adult situations, explicit language
Dir: George Bowers   *Cast:* Rob Morrow, Johnny Depp, Emily Longstreth, Karyn O'Bryan, Hector Elizondo, Dody Goodman
► Still another adolescent farce about young boys looking for girls, this time at a Jamaican resort. Jack (teen heartthrob Depp) falls for older woman Longstreth; his friend Morrow chases a waitress. Slapstick plot complications are provided by jewel thief Elizondo.
Dist.: RCA/Columbia

PRIVATE ROAD 1987
★ R Drama 1:37
☑ Nudity, explicit language, mild violence
Dir: Raphael Nussbaum   *Cast:* Greg Evigan, George Kennedy, Mitzi Kapture, Brian Patrick Clarke
► Hotheaded mechanic Evigan is the victim of a hit-and-run accident by unstable heiress Kapture. Afraid of the police, her father Kennedy hides him at home until he recovers. Evigan insinuates himself into the family but faces a setback in a blackmail plot. Twisty plot compensates for a low budget.
Dist.: TWE

PRIVATE SCHOOL 1983
★ ★ R Comedy 1:25
☑ Nudity, explicit language, adult humor
Dir: Noel Black   *Cast:* Phoebe Cates, Betsy Russell, Matthew Modine, Michael Zorek, Ray Walston, Sylvia Kristel
► Leering teen comedy about the efforts of prep school boys to spy on the luscious girls at Cherryvale Academy. Modine's tricks backfire when he's pursued by naughty flirt Russell as well as shy virgin Cates. Plenty of skin on display, but smirking screenplay by humorist Dan Greenburg is a disappointment.
Dist.: MCA

PRIVATES ON PARADE 1984 British
☆ R Comedy 1:38
☑ Nudity, adult situations, explicit language, violence
Dir: Michael Blakemore   *Cast:* John Cleese, Denis Quilley, Patrick Pearson, Michael Elphick, Nicola Pagett, Bruce Payne
► Adaptation of Peter Nichols's stage play concerns a song-and-dance troupe entertaining British soldiers in 1948 Singapore. Farce pits gung-ho, not-too-bright officer Cleese against aging homosexual chorus `director Quilley. Uneven mixture of camp musical comedy and antiwar intrigue doesn't work, although Cleese and especially Quilley are fine.
Dist.: HBO

PRIZE FIGHTER, THE 1979
★ ★ ★ PG Comedy 1:39
☑ Explicit language

Dir: Michael Pierce   *Cast:* Tim Conway, Don Knotts, David Wayne, Robin Clarke, Cisse Cameron, Mary Ellen O'Neill
► In the 1930s, inept boxer Conway and trainer Knotts get involved with fight-fixing gangsters without realizing Conway's sudden winning streak is due to the mob's scams rather than his skills. Third feature teaming of Conway and Knotts is silly, harmless fun with family appeal.
Dist.: Media

PRIZE OF PERIL, THE 1983 French
☆ NR Action-Adventure 1:39
☑ Explicit language, violence
Dir: Yves Boisset   *Cast:* Gerard Lanvin, Michel Piccoli, Marie-France Pisier, Bruno Cremer, Andrea Ferreol
► Piccoli hosts "The Prize of Peril," a television game show in which contestants risk death to win big bucks. Contestant Lanvin lands a pilotless plane and eludes hired killers as the ratings go through the roof. He then tries to expose the corruption behind the contest. Nimble, fast-paced satire from a Robert Sheckley story. Dubbed.
Dist.: Vestron

PRIZZI'S HONOR 1985
★ ★ ★ ★ R Comedy/Drama 2:09
☑ Brief nudity, adult situations, explicit language, violence
Dir: John Huston   *Cast:* Jack Nicholson, Kathleen Turner, William Hickey, Anjelica Huston, Robert Loggia, John Randolph
► Charlie Partana (Nicholson), hit man for the Prizzi family, especially the Don (Hickey), falls for Turner. When he discovers she also kills for a living and, even worse, may have stolen from the Prizzis, Nicholson is confused. "Do I ice her? Do I marry her?" he asks ex-girlfriend Maerose (Oscar winner Angelica Huston), who replies: "Just because she's a thief and a hitter don't mean she ain't a good woman in all other departments." The double crosses turn somersaults in the John Huston/Janet Roach sceenplay, adapted from Richard Condon's witty novel. Copped eight Oscar nominations.
Dist.: Vestron

PRODUCERS, THE 1967
★ ★ ★ ★ NR Musical/Comedy 1:28
Dir: Mel Brooks   *Cast:* Zero Mostel, Gene Wilder, Dick Shawn, Kenneth Mars, Estelle Winwood, Renée Taylor, Christopher Hewitt
► Has-been theatrical producer Mostel and neurotic accountant Wilder conspire to raise money from rich old ladies to produce sure-fire flop, *Springtime for Hitler*. If the show closes on opening night, the swindlers will get rich. To insure failure, they hire terrible writer Mars, transvestite director Hewett, and drugged-out hippie actor Shawn. Top-notch Brooks screenplay won an Oscar. A rare comedy that gets funnier with every viewing.
Dist.: Nelson

PROFESSIONALS, THE 1966
★ ★ ★ ★ PG Western 1:57
☑ Brief nudity, adult situations
Dir: Richard Brooks *Cast:* Burt Lancaster,
Lee Marvin, Robert Ryan, Jack Palance,
Claudia Cardinale, Woody Strode, Ralph
Bellamy
► Cattle baron Bellamy hires four mercenaries to retrieve kidnapped wife Cardinale from
Mexican bandit Palance. The team consists of
specialized experts: explosives wizard Lancaster, sharpshooter Marvin, horse trainer
Ryan, and archer Strode. After a daring raid
on the bandit's hideout, the heroes learn
they've been double-crossed. Thoroughly enjoyable Western with a superb cast features
Oscar-nominated photography by Conrad
Hall.
Dist.: RCA/Columbia

PROJECT X 1987
★ ★ ★ ★ PG Drama 1:47
☑ Explicit language, mild violence
Dir: Jonathan Kaplan *Cast:* Matthew
Broderick, Helen Hunt, Bill Sadler, Johnny
Ray McGhee, Jonathan Stark, Robin Gammell
► Unruly Air Force pilot Broderick is punished
with a new assignment: experimenting on
chimps at a top-secret weapons research
center. With the help of animal psychologist
Hunt, he learns the chimps are being prepared for an unnecessarily fatal test. Sincere
plea for animal rights enhanced by a marvelous performance by Willie as a chimp with the
ability to read sign language. **(CC)**
Dist.: CBS/Fox

PROMISED LAND 1988
★ ★ R Drama 1:35
☑ Adult situations, explicit language, violence
Dir: Michael Hoffman *Cast:* Jason Gedrick,
Kiefer Sutherland, Meg Ryan, Tracy Pollan,
Googy Gress
► Two years after high school, jock-turned-cop Gedrick is visited by old girlfriend Pollan;
his shy friend Sutherland also returns home.
Tragedy is set in motion when Sutherland falls
on the wrong side of the law. Ambitious coming-of-age story covers familiar ground but
does it well. Nicely nuanced performances by
the lead foursome, beautiful cinematography; sometimes too self-consciously arty.
Dist.: Vestron

PROMISES IN THE DARK 1979
★ ★ ★ ★ ★ PG Drama 1:58
☑ Adult situations, explicit language
Dir: Jerome Hellman *Cast:* Marsha Mason,
Ned Beatty, Kathleen Beller, Susan Clark,
Michael Brandon
► Beller, a gallant teenager dying of cancer,
is treated by compassionate but personally
troubled doctor Mason, who must decide
whether or not to keep her on life support.
Modern melodrama featuring first-rate acting
and ultrarealistic production design is an assured tearjerker.
Dist.: Warner

PROM NIGHT 1980 Canadian
★ R Horror 1:31
☑ Brief nudity, adult situations, explicit language, graphic violence
Dir: Paul Lynch *Cast:* Leslie Nielsen, Jamie
Lee Curtis, Casey Stevens, Eddie Benton,
Antoinette Bower
► Four preteens tease a friend until she commits suicide. Six years later they're stalked by
a masked madman on the night of a big
dance. Derivative horror film with a predictably gory plot benefits from a professional turn
by Curtis as the daughter of high school principal Nielsen.
Dist.: Virgin

PROPHECY 1979
★ ★ PG Horror 1:42
☑ Explicit language, graphic violence
Dir: John Frankenheimer *Cast:* Talia Shire,
Robert Foxworth, Armand Assante, Richard
Dysart, Victoria Racimo
► In Maine, government agent Foxworth and
wife Shire investigate when a pollution-caused monster goes on a bloody killing
spree. Some effective scares and nice natural
backgrounds. Unfortunately, the plot is tired,
the monster looks phony, and some may find
the violence distasteful.
Dist.: Paramount

PROTECTOR, THE 1985
★ ★ R Action-Adventure 1:34
☑ Nudity, explicit language, graphic violence
Dir: James Glickenhaus *Cast:* Jackie Chan,
Danny Aiello, Roy Chao, Bill Wallace, Victor
Arnold, Kim Bass
► New York cops Chan and Aiello bust the
rules and plenty of heads pursuing a Hong
Kong drug kingpin who kidnaps an heiress.
Nonstop action includes no-holds-barred barroom brawl, speedboat chase, and a big fight
between Chan and karate champ Wallace.
Gratuitous nudity and violence; Chan has
muscles but little screen presence. **(CC)**
Dist.: Warner

PROTOCOL 1984
★ ★ ★ ★ PG Comedy 1:35
☑ Explicit language, violence
Dir: Herbert Ross *Cast:* Goldie Hawn, Chris
Sarandon, Andre Gregory, Cliff De Young,
Richard Romanus, Ed Begley, Jr.
► Washington cocktail waitress Hawn becomes a national heroine when she accidentally foils an assassination attempt on Arab
sheik Romanus. Hired by the State Protocol
Department, she becomes involved in several
misadventures, including a brawl at a gay-Arab-biker sushi bar. Breezy and lighthearted
romp was tailor-made for Hawn's talents.
(CC)
Dist.: Warner

PROUD REBEL, THE 1958
★ ★ ★ ★ **G Western/Family 1:43**
Dir: Michael Curtiz *Cast:* Alan Ladd, Olivia
de Havilland, Dean Jagger, David Ladd,
Cecil Kellaway, Henry Hull, John Carradine,
Harry Dean Stanton
▶ When son David Ladd becomes mute after
seeing mom killed in the Civil War, father Alan
Ladd takes him north for medical help. Along
the way, the Ladds are helped by spinster de
Havilland as they battle local villains for pos-
session of the boy's beloved dog. Wholesome
and heartwarming family drama with fine fa-
ther-and-son teamwork from the Ladds.
Dist.: Embassy

PROVIDENCE 1977 French
★ **R Drama 1:50**
☑ Adult situations, explicit language
Dir: Alain Resnais *Cast:* Dirk Bogarde, Ellen
Burstyn, John Gielgud, David Warner, Elaine
Stritch
▶ On his deathbed, British novelist Gielgud
spins imaginary stories about son Bogarde,
daughter-in-law Burstyn, and their respective
lovers Stritch and Warner. Baffling adult puzzle
dealing with themes of creativity and death
requires an effort to watch; easier to admire
than enjoy
Dist.: RCA/Columbia

PSYCHIC KILLER 1976
★ ★ ★ **PG Mystery-Suspense 1:30**
☑ Nudity, graphic violence
Dir: Raymond Danton *Cast:* Jim Hutton,
Paul Burke, Della Reese, Rod Cameron,
Aldo Ray, Julie Adams
▶ Hutton, wrongly accused of murder, is com-
mitted to an asylum where he learns the se-
cret of astral projection. Upon his release, he
uses this power to get revenge against his
enemies. Unusual premise given overly grue-
some treatment; above-average B movie
may please genre fans.
Dist.: Nelson

PSYCHO 1960
★ ★ ★ ★ **R Mystery-Suspense 1:49 B&W**
☑ Adult situations, violence
Dir: Alfred Hitchcock *Cast:* Anthony Perkins,
Janet Leigh, Vera Miles, John Gavin, Martin
Balsam, John McIntire
▶ Bank employee Leigh steals money and
takes a room at the spooky Bates Motel. Proprietor Perkins seems like such a nice young
man, but his mom is a tad strange; Leigh then
meets a tragic fate in cinema's most famous
shower scene. Hitchcock's fiendishly clever
tale of madness and murder masterfully creates tension through camera and editing
techniques. Much more unnerving than
today's gory movies. Brilliant Bernard Herrmann score. Two sequels followed more than
twenty years later.
Dist.: MCA

PSYCHO II 1983
★ ★ ★ **R Horror 1:53**

☑ Nudity, adult situations, explicit language, graphic violence
Dir: Richard Franklin *Cast:* Anthony Perkins,
Vera Miles, Meg Tilly, Robert Loggia, Dennis
Franz, Hugh Gillin
▶ Released after twenty-two years in a mental institution, murderer Norman Bates (Perkins,
re-creating his most famous role) moves back
into the old digs, and tries to go straight with
the help of waitress friend Tilly. However, the
cycle of killings begins once more. Surprisingly
effective sequel/homage to the Hitchcock
classic. Twisty, ironic plot and ominous camera angles keep you guessing.
Dist.: MCA

PSYCHO III 1986
★ ★ **R Horror 1:33**
☑ Nudity, explicit language, violence
Dir: Anthony Perkins *Cast:* Anthony Perkins,
Diana Scarwid, Jeff Fahey, Roberta Maxwell,
Hugh Gillin
▶ Norman Bates (Perkins) saves ex-nun Scar-
wid who tries to kill herself at his motel. Other
guests are not so lucky: someone is murdering
them. Norman, is that you? Assured direction
by Perkins, who still can twitch effectively. The
underrated Scarwid offers sturdy support.
However, plot is pretty thin and predictable.
Few scares; not in the league of the original or
Psycho II. (CC)
Dist.: MCA

PSYCHO COP 1989
☆ **R Horror 1:27**
☑ Explicit language, violence
Dir: Wallace Potts *Cast:* Bobby Ray Shafer,
Jeff Qualle, Palmer Lee Todd, Dan Campbell, Cynthia Guyer, Linda West
▶ Three young couples arrive at a deserted
country house and find themselves stalked by
an elusive killer. They're relieved when a policeman shows up, but the man in blue turns
out to be the very maniac who's terrorizing
them. Poorly written, badly acted, and ineptly
directed slasher pic is predictable and
deadly dull.
Dist.: Southgate

PSYCHO GIRLS 1987
☆ **R Horror 1:32**
☑ Adult situations, explicit language,
  graphic violence
Dir: Gerard Ciccoritti *Cast:* John Haslett
Cuff, Darlene Mignacco, Agi Gallus, Rose
Graham, Silvio Oliviero, Pier Giorgio Dicicco
▶ When her parents are poisoned on their an-
niversary, Mignacco is sentenced to an in-
sane asylum. Fifteen years later she escapes
in search of her sister Gallus, the real culprit.
Private eye Cuff is trapped in the middle of
their deadly confrontation in this low-budget
exploitation.
Dist.: MGM/UA

PSYCH-OUT 1968
★ ★ **NR Drama 1:22**

☐ Brief nudity, adult situations, explicit language, violence
Dir: Richard Rush *Cast:* Susan Strasberg, Jack Nicholson, Bruce Dern, Dean Stockwell, Adam Roarke, Max Julien
▶ Deaf teenager Strasberg searches Haight-Ashbury for missing brother Dern. Hippies Nicholson, Roarke, and Julien help her. Meager story line provides vehicle for quaintly dated period atmosphere and dialogue ("Hey, man, I'm hip") and a young Nicholson. A curiosity item.
Dist.: HBO

PT 109 1963
★ ★ NR Biography 2:20
Dir: Leslie H. Martinson *Cast:* Cliff Robertson, Ty Hardin, James Gregory, Robert Culp, Grant Williams
▶ World War II experiences of John F. Kennedy in the South Pacific are the basis for this serviceable naval drama. Robertson turns in a creditable performance as the future President who assumes command of his first vessel and engages in dangerous missions on islands held by the Japanese. Climaxes in a daring escape after the PT boat is rammed by an enemy destroyer.
Dist.: Warner

PUBERTY BLUES 1983 Australian
★ R Comedy 1:27
☐ Nudity, adult situations, explicit language
Dir: Bruce Beresford *Cast:* Neil Schofield, Jad Capelja, Geoff Rhoe, Tony Hughes, Sandy Paul, Leander Brett
▶ Title says it all: the adolescent woes of surfer girls Schofield and Capelja in Sydney. Neither is especially attractive so they must drink, smoke, and swear to get the attention of boys interested only in a little groping. Standard rite-of-passage tale distinguished by candor and Aussie setting.
Dist.: MCA

PUBLIC ENEMY 1931
★ ★ ★ NR Crime 1:23 B&W
Dir: William Wellman *Cast:* James Cagney, Jean Harlow, Eddie Woods, Beryl Mercer, Joan Blondell, Donald Cook, Mae Clark
▶ Gritty cautionary tale about short and violent life of gangster Cagney is still compelling. Cagney and Irish tough buddy Woods embrace lives of crime in south side of Chicago, stealing booze for resale during Prohibition. Soon they're in the thick of gang warfare and its inevitable tragedy, as director Wellman pulls no punches depicting the characters' vicious immorality. Picture made Cagney and his rough-hewn mannerisms an overnight star. Most familiar scene: Cagney smashing grapefruit into face of Clark, who's worn out her welcome.
Dist.: MGM/UA

PULP 1972 British
★ ★ PG Mystery-Suspense 1:35
☐ Adult situations, violence

Dir: Michael Hodges *Cast:* Michael Caine, Mickey Rooney, Lionel Stander, Lizabeth Scott, Nadia Cassini, Al Lettieri
▶ Mystery writer Caine travels to Italy, where he is to interview former movie tough guy Rooney in preparation for ghosting his memoirs. But Rooney is shot before he can finish, and Caine himself is in danger when he discovers that the movie star was involved in a web of shady doings. Spoofish thriller has chucklesome references for film buffs. Rooney is well cast as a combination of George Raft, James Cagney, and Edward G. Robinson.
Dist.: Wood Knapp

PULSE 1988
★ ★ ★ PG-13 Sci-Fi 1:31
☐ Adult situations, explicit language
Dir: Paul Golding *Cast:* Cliff De Young, Roxanne Hart, Joey Lawrence, Matthew Lawrence, Charles Tyner, Dennis Redfield
▶ Young Joey Lawrence, forced to spend the summer with stepmother Hart and father De Young, develops an unnatural fear of household appliances after elderly neighbor Tyner tells him that aliens have sabotaged electric utilities. His phobia proves prophetic in this well-crafted, but bland, shocker. (CC)
Dist.: RCA/Columbia

PUMPING IRON 1977
★ ★ PG Documentary 1:25
☐ Explicit language
Dir: George Butler *Cast:* Arnold Schwarzenegger, Lou Ferrigno, Matty Ferrigno, Victorio Ferrigno, Franco Columbu, Mike Katz
▶ Intriguing look at the Mr. Olympia contest in which Schwarzenegger seeks to defend his title against challenger Ferrigno and others. Ferrigno has the better physique but, even with help of his doting parents and homespun Brooklyn philosophy, he's no match for Schwarzenegger's psych-out ruses. Observant and often witty documentary noteworthy for introducing Schwarzenegger to the American public.
Dist.: RCA/Columbia

PUMPING IRON II: THE WOMEN 1985
★ ★ NR Documentary 1:47
☐ Brief nudity, explicit language
Dir: George Butler *Cast:* Rachel McLish, Bev Francis, Carla Dunlap, Lori Bowen, Kris Alexander, George Plimpton
▶ World's best female body builders gather in Vegas for competition. Judges debate two views of feminine ideal, represented by kittenish McLish and densely muscle-bound Francis. Emceed by "the one and only" Plimpton. (CC)
Dist.: Vestron

PUMPKINHEAD 1989
★ ★ R Horror 1:26
☐ Adult situations, explicit language, graphic violence
Dir: Stan Winston *Cast:* Lance Henriksen,

John Diaquino, Joel Hoffman, Kimberly Ross, Florence Shauffler, Kerry Remsen

▶ When his son is killed in a motorcycle accident, grieving father Henriksen seeks out local witch for revenge against the visitors responsible. She summons Pumpkinhead, a hideous demon whose indiscriminate murders force Henriksen to reconsider his plan. Good intentions and frightening special effects elevate routine plot and characters.
Dist.: MGM/UA

PUNCHLINE 1988
★ ★ ★ ★ **R Comedy/Drama 2:03**
☑ Adult situations, explicit language, adult humor
Dir: David Seltzer   *Cast:* Sally Field, Tom Hanks, John Goodman, Kim Greist, Mark Rydell

▶ Hanks is a failing medical student who does a caustic standup routine at the comedy clubs. Field is a housewife who also wants to be a comedienne, but her family commitments and poor material are a hindrance. The unlikely pair lend each other support and creative guidance on the road to a big audition for a network appearance. The melodramatic script aside, Field shines, and Hanks proves once again he is the most talented and watchable comic actor in film today. **(CC)**
Dist.: RCA/Columbia

PUPPET MASTER 1989
★ **R Horror 1:30**
☑ Nudity, adult situations, explicit language, violence
Dir: David Schmoeller   *Cast:* Paul LeMat, Irene Miracle, Matt Roe, Kathryn O'Reilly, Robin Frates, William Hickey

▶ Psychics LeMat, Roe, and O'Reilly receive telepathic summons to hotel where one of their compatriots has killed himself. Dead man was working on puppets brought to life via ancient Egyptian technique. The murderous little marionettes proceed to menace the psychics. Ingenious special effects highlight well-made flick. **(CC)**
Dist.: Paramount

PURGATORY 1989
☆ **R Action-Adventure 1:32**
☑ Rape, nudity, adult situations, explicit language, violence
Dir: Ami Artzi   *Cast:* Tanya Roberts, Julie Pop, Hal Orlandini, Rufus Swart, Adrienne Pearce, Marie Human

▶ Peace Corps volunteers Roberts and Pop are sentenced to eleven years in African slammer on trumped-up drug charges. There they face rape and abuse before embassy employee Swart helps Roberts escape. Lurid and sleazy South African–shot prison picture features cardboard acting and Roberts in the buff. Best line: "Why don't you take a shower? You'll feel better."
Dist.: New Star

PURPLE HEART, THE 1944
★ ★ ★ **NR War 1:39 B&W**
Dir: Lewis Milestone   *Cast:* Dana Andrews, Farley Granger, Sam Levene, Richard Conte, Tala Birell, Nestor Paiva

▶ After General Dolittle's 1942 raid on Tokyo, eight American flyers led by Andrews are captured by the Japanese and tortured to reveal the origin of their flight. Steadfast flyers reveal nothing, and are tried on trumped up charges. Succeeds in celebrating bravery of U.S. airmen.
Dist.: CBS/Fox

PURPLE HEARTS 1984
★ ★ ★ ★ **R Drama 1:55**
☑ Nudity, explicit language, violence
Dir: Sidney J. Furie   *Cast:* Ken Wahl, Cheryl Ladd, Paul McCrane, Stephen Lee, Annie McEnroe, Cyril O'Reilly

▶ Surgeon Wahl, tending wounded troops in Vietnam, woos nurse Ladd at another Army base. Individual trips to the front and special assignments make their courtship arduous. Then Wahl is shot down behind enemy lines and must fight his way home.
Dist.: Warner

PURPLE PEOPLE EATER 1988
★ **PG Fantasy/Family 1:32**
☑ Explicit language
Dir: Linda Shayne   *Cast:* Ned Beatty, Neil Patrick Harris, Shelley Winters, Peggy Lipton, James Houghton, Thora Birch

▶ While his parents are away in Europe, Harris is befriended by a one-eyed, one-horned Purple People Eater from outer space. Boy and being form a rock band and stage a benefit concert to prevent old folks from eviction. Friendly fare, based on the Sheb Wooley song, should entertain kids. Cameo appearances by Little Richard and Chubby Checker.
Dist.: Media

PURPLE RAIN 1984
★ ★ ★ **R Musical 1:51**
☑ Nudity, adult situations, explicit language, violence
Dir: Albert Magnoli   *Cast:* Prince, Morris Day, Apollonia Kotero, Clarence Williams III, Jerome Benton, Olga Karlatos

▶ Triple-platinum music sensation Prince, in his smashing screen debut as a performer with on- and off-stage problems. He doesn't get along with his troubled parents Karlatos and Williams, quarrels with his band Revolution, and has romance problems with his new girl, stunning Kotero. Jazzy melodrama has color, energy, and lots of rock 'n' roll hits: "Let's Go Crazy," "When Doves Cry," "I Would Die 4 U," "Darling Nikki" and title song. Score won Oscar. **(CC)**
Dist.: Warner

PURPLE ROSE OF CAIRO, THE 1985
★ ★ **PG Comedy 1:22**
☑ Adult situations
Dir: Woody Allen   *Cast:* Mia Farrow, Jeff

Daniels, Danny Aiello, Van Johnson, Alexander Cohen, Milo O'Shea

▶ Frumpy Depression era waitress Farrow, unhappily married to unemployed lout Aiello, finds solace at the movies. On fifth viewing of her favorite flick, *The Purple Rose of Cairo*, handsome actor Daniels steps off the silver screen and into her heart. ("He's fictional, but you can't have everything," muses Farrow.) Meanwhile, pandemonium breaks out on the screen as the stranded actors debate how to end the movie without their leading man. Fresh and inventive, although criticized by some as a one-joke movie. **(CC)**
Dist.: Vestron

PURSUED 1947
★ ★ ★ NR Western 1:41 B&W
Dir: Raoul Walsh *Cast:* Robert Mitchum, Teresa Wright, Judith Anderson, Dean Jagger, Alan Hale, Harry Carey, Jr., John Rodney

▶ Orphan Mitchum, raised by Anderson and Jagger, falls in love with stepsister Wright. She eventually marries him, but only because she seeks revenge for his killing her brother Rodney. Superb Western represents a change of pace for Walsh. His atypically dark, brooding visuals perfectly complement Niven Busch's probing, psychological screenplay. Fine performance by Mitchum as the troubled hero.
Dist.: Republic

PURSUIT OF D.B. COOPER, THE 1981
★ ★ ★ PG Action-Adventure 1:40
☑ Brief nudity, adult situations, explicit language
Dir: Roger Spottiswoode *Cast:* Robert Duvall, Treat Williams, Kathryn Harrold, Paul Gleason, Ed Flanders, R. G. Armstrong

▶ Comedy caper about D. B. Cooper (Williams), real-life antihero who hijacked a plane with a phony bomb and parachuted into legend with $200,000 of extortion money. Speculative film follows attempts of insurance investigator Duvall to track Williams and wife Harrold cross-country to Mexican border. Plenty of chases and amiable characters.
Dist.: Vestron

PURSUIT OF THE GRAF SPEE 1957 British
★ ★ NR War 1:59
Dir: Michael Powell, Emeric Pressberger
Cast: John Gregson, Anthony Quayle, Peter Finch, Ian Hunter, Bernard Lee, Patrick Macnee

▶ The British Navy pursues the deadly German battleship *Graf Spee* (under the command of admiral Finch) to South America. As the Germans try to take refuge in various ports, the British must flush them out. Sea battles are thunderously recreated in this straightforward page out of history.
Dist.: IUD

PURSUIT TO ALGIERS 1945
★ ★ NR Mystery-Suspense 1:05 B&W
Dir: Roy William Neill *Cast:* Basil Rathbone,

Nigel Bruce, Marjorie Riordan, Rosalind Ivan, Martin Kosleck, Leslie Vincent

▶ World's greatest detective Sherlock Holmes (Rathbone) and sidekick Dr. Watson (Bruce) encounter foul play when they escort a Mediterranean prince on sea voyage from England to his home country. Modern take on Arthur Conan Doyle's *The Return of Sherlock Holmes* plays up melodrama while neglecting logic and deduction.
Dist.: CBS/Fox

PUTNEY SWOPE 1969
☆ R Comedy 1:25 C/B&W
☑ Adult situations, explicit language
Dir: Robert Downey *Cast:* Arnold Johnson, Antonio Fargas, Laura Greene, Pepi Hermine, Ruth Hermine, Allen Garfield

▶ Token black ad agency exec Johnson catapulted to helm of firm promptly revamps it into the Truth and Soul agency, firing most whites and refusing to promote booze, cigarettes, or war toys. Madcap, subversive agency is an immediate success but soon falls victim to new internal strife. Influential underground classic, with its anarchic and irreverent sixties style, now seems more artifact than art, although TV commercial spoofs are still hilarious.
Dist.: RCA/Columbia

PYGMALION 1938 British
★ ★ ★ ★ NR Comedy 1:35 B&W
Dir: Anthony Asquith, Leslie Howard *Cast:* Leslie Howard, Wendy Hiller, Wilfrid Lawson, Marie Lohr, David Tree, Scott Sunderland

▶ Top-notch adaptation of the G. B. Shaw play concerns stuffy phonetics professor Howard, who bets friend Lawson he can transform uneducated Cockney flower girl Hiller into an English lady. Howard's rigorous course of diction and etiquette succeeds: Hiller not only passes for a duchess at London society ball, but also wins the love of her tutor. Superior romantic comedy preserved much of the play's barbed dialogue; in fact, Shaw won Oscar for screenplay. Later remade as musical *My Fair Lady*.
Dist.: Nelson

PYX, THE 1973 Canadian
★ ★ R Horror 1:51
☑ Nudity, adult situations, explicit language, violence
Dir: Harvey Hart *Cast:* Karen Black, Christopher Plummer, Donald Pilon, Jean-Louis Roux, Yvette Brind'Amour, Jacques Godin

▶ Detective Plummer investigates the murder of prostitute Black. The trail leads to devil worshippers and a Black Mass as her story unfolds in flashbacks. Hart's direction overcomes plot holes in this above-average shocker. Black sings three of her own songs on the soundtrack.
Dist.: Prism

Q 1982
★ ★ R Horror 1:32

☑ Nudity, explicit language, graphic violence

Dir: Larry Cohen *Cast:* Michael Moriarty, David Carradine, Richard Roundtree, Candy Clark, Malachi McCourt, Ron Cey

▶ Giant winged creature hides out in the top of the Chrysler Building, swooping down on unsuspecting New Yorkers. Detective Carradine investigates while small-time crook Moriarty gets involved. Campy monster flick; more silly than scary. Preposterous plot but Moriarty hams it up, yelling, "Eat him, eat him!" as the beast munches on one of his enemies.

Dist.: MCA

Q&A 1990
★ ★ ★ R Drama 2:14
☑ Brief nudity, adult situations, explicit language, violence

Dir: Sidney Lumet *Cast:* Nick Nolte, Timothy Hutton, Armand Assante, Patrick O'Neal, Lee Richardson, Luis Guzman, Charles Dutton, Jenny Lumet

▶ Inexperienced assistant D.A. Hutton's first case, revered cop Nolte's apparent shooting of a suspect in self-defense, seems open and shut. However, he uncovers not only Nolte's dark side, but a web of corruption involving drug dealers, cops, and officials. Honorable, ambitious drama starts like gangbusters, then falters as focus shifts from the investigation to the bad guys' machinations and Hutton's relationship with ex-girlfriend Lumet. Sharp dialogue captures urban racial tension; Guzman and Assante stand out in an excellent ensemble. **(CC)**

Dist.: HBO

QUACKSER FORTUNE HAS A COUSIN IN THE BRONX 1970 Irish
★ ★ PG Comedy 1:30
☑ Brief nudity, adult situations

Dir: Waris Hussein *Cast:* Gene Wilder, Margot Kidder, Eileen Colgan, Seamus Ford, May Ollis, Liz Davis

▶ Dubliner Wilder makes a living recycling horse manure from streets as fertilizer, enjoying independence, the outdoors, and an affair with customer Colgan. His life takes turn for worse when he falls in love with wealthy American Kidder and Dublin authorities order horses off the streets in favor of cars. Amiable, offbeat comedy features charming Dublin locale and fine, controlled performance by Wilder.

Dist.: VCI

QUADROPHENIA 1979 British
☆ R Drama/Music 1:55
☑ Adult situations, explicit language, violence

Dir: Franc Roddam *Cast:* Phil Daniels, Mark Wingett, Philip Davis, Leslie Ash, Garry Cooper, Sting

▶ Gritty visualization of rock opera written by The Who's Peter Townshend. In 1964 England, young Mod Daniels in dead-end mailroom job joins mates to seek kicks in pills, casual sex, and rumbles with rival Rockers. Solid, involving story of angry young man for fans of The Who's music. Convincing screen debut by rock star Sting as an over-the-hill Mod.

Dist.: RCA/Columbia

QUARTET 1949 British
★ ★ ★ ★ NR Comedy/Drama 2:00 B&W
Dir: Ken Annakin, Arthur Crabtree, Harold French, Ralph Smart *Cast:* Hermione Baddeley, Dirk Bogarde, Mervyn Johns, Cecil Parker, Honor Blackman, Mai Zetterling

▶ Four W. Somerset Maugham tales, introduced by the author: a young man ignores his conservative dad's advice and outwits an adventuress, an aspiring pianist faces a harsh evaluation of his talent, a clerk's obsession with kites upsets his wife and mother, an aging womanizer is angry when his wife writes poems about a younger man (not realizing her subject is the younger him). Crisply produced, swiftly paced, well acted.

Dist.: Warner

QUATERMASS CONCLUSION, THE 1980 British
★ NR Sci-Fi 1:47
Dir: Piers Haggard *Cast:* John Mills, Simon MacCorkindale, Barbara Kellerman, Margaret Tyzack, Brewster Mason

▶ Evil alien employs death ray to suck energy from Earth's children. Scientist Mills and his cohorts feed atom bomb to extraterrestrial to induce terminal indigestion. Intriguing script overcomes mediocre effects and direction. Based on the lead character from popular British TV show and film series.

Dist.: HBO

QUATERMASS EXPERIMENT, THE 1956 British
☆ NR Sci-Fi 1:18 B&W
Dir: Val Guest *Cast:* Brian Donlevy, Margia Dean, Jack Warner, Richard Wordsworth, Thora Hird, Gordon Jackson

▶ Super scientist Quatermass (Donlevy) does battle with an insane creature holed up in Westminister Abbey. Creature was originally an astronaut taken over by an alien fungus. Not much in the way of expensive special effects, but tells its story well, like all the Quatermass series. Also known as *The Creeping Unknown*. Third in series begun with *Five Million Years to Earth*, *Enemy From Space*, and ending with *Quatermass Conclusion*.

Dist.: Discount

QUEEN CHRISTINA 1933
★ ★ NR Drama 1:37 B&W
Dir: Rouben Mamoulian *Cast:* Greta Garbo, John Gilbert, Ian Keith, Lewis Stone, C. Aubrey Smith, Elizabeth Young

▶ Seventeenth-century Swedish queen Garbo flees arranged marriage to pursue Spanish ambassador Gilbert. To learn his real nature she dons men's clothes and pals with

him before revealing her true sex. When her romance with the commoner angers the public, she considers abdicating her throne. Chemistry between off-screen lovers Garbo and Gilbert is electrifying and enhances the heartbreaking ending. A classic; arguably Garbo's best performance.
Dist.: MGM/UA

QUEEN KELLY 1929
☆ **NR Drama 1:16 B&W**
Dir: Erich von Stroheim ***Cast:*** Gloria Swanson, Seena Owen, Walter Byron, Tully Marshall, Wilhelm von Brinken, Madge Hunt
▶ Convent novitiate Swanson falls for prince Byron, despite his betrothal to evil queen Owen. When Byron sneaks Swanson into his palace chambers for a night of love, Owen discovers them and takes sadistic revenge. Though never completed in the way director von Stroheim originally intended, silent romance is strong psychosexual stuff. Lost scenes have been replaced with still photographs in 1985 rerelease.
Dist.: Kino

QUEEN OF HEARTS 1989 British
★★ **NR Drama 1:53**
☑ Adult situations, explicit language, violence
Dir: Jon Amiel ***Cast:*** Anita Zagaria, Joseph Long, Eileen Way, Vittorio Duse, Ian Hawks, Vittorio Amandola
▶ Young Hawks, born in England to Italian Zagaria and Long, tells the passionate, larger-than-life tale of his parents' marriage after they dramatically eloped so his mother would not have to wed Amandola. Years later, when the bitter Amandola shows up to finally stake his claim, it leads to total havoc. Warm, endearingly offbeat comedy has charm enough to spare. **(CC)**
Dist.: Virgin

QUEEN OF SPADES, THE 1949 British
★★ **NR Fantasy 1:39 B&W**
Dir: Thorold Dickinson ***Cast:*** Anton Walbrook, Edith Evans, Yvonne Mitchell, Ronald Howard, Mary Jerrold, Anthony Dawson
▶ Walbrook, an impoverished officer in the nineteenth-century Russian army, learns that elderly countess Evans has a secret for winning at faro. He tries various schemes to pry the information from her but accidentally frightens her to death. Eerie adaptation of classic Alexander Pushkin tale builds smoothly to a sinister climax.
Dist.: HBO

QUERELLE 1983 German
☆ **R Drama 1:46**
☑ Strong sexual content, explicit language, violence
Dir: Rainer Werner Fassbinder ***Cast:*** Brad Davis, Jeanne Moreau, Franco Nero, Laurent Malet, Hanno Poschl, Gunter Kaufmann
▶ Sailor Davis in seedy port deals in opium and murder and has both hetero- and homosexual relations. Confused saga of decadence and decay doesn't work at all despite occasionally intriguing visual experimentation. Difficult-to-watch film was also director Fassbinder's last. [S]
Dist.: RCA

QUEST FOR FIRE 1982 French/Canadian
★★ **R Action-Adventure 1:40**
☑ Nudity, strong sexual content, adult situations, graphic violence, adult humor
Dir: Jean-Jacques Annaud ***Cast:*** Everett McGill, Rae Dawn Chong, Ron Perlman, Nameer El-Kadi, Gary Schwartz
▶ Prehistoric tribe loses its source of fire and sends McGill, Perlman, and El-Kadi in search of flame. Their adventures include encounters with cannibals, marsh-nymph Chong and her more advanced tribe, wooly mammoths, and a saber-toothed tiger. Chong and McGill become mates; she teaches him both tenderness and the art of firemaking. Ambitious saga is generally diverting and often sweetly comic. Remarkably effective languages by novelist Anthony Burgess and body movements by zoologist Desmond Morris. Oscar for costumes.
Dist.: CBS/Fox

QUESTION OF SILENCE, A 1984 Dutch
☆ **R Drama 1:32**
☑ Brief nudity, adult situations, explicit language, violence
Dir: Marleen Gorris ***Cast:*** Cox Habbema, Nelly Fridja, Edda Barends, Henriette Tol, Eddy Brugman, Dolf de Vries
▶ Fridja, Barends, and Tol are arrested for murder of male shopkeeper, whom they beat to a pulp in show of solidarity when he caught one shoplifting. The women, strangers prior to the event, are analyzed by psychiatrist Habbema, who comes to share their hostility to a world run by men. Feminist parable is based on fact. Director Gorris displays originality and attention to character in film with unusual premise. Not for all tastes. [S]
Dist.: Nelson

QUE VIVA MEXICO 1930 U.S./Russian
☆ **NR Drama 1:30 B&W**
Dir: Sergei Eisenstein ***Cast:***
▶ Silent film composed of unedited footage shot by legendary director Eisenstein for a film produced by U.S. author Upton Sinclair about the Mexican revolution. The film was abandoned before completion, and years after the director's death his former assistant edited this together using Eisenstein's notes and script. Episodic story highlights class-struggle between peasants and landowners in a predictable way. Some wonderful images, but on the whole, disappointing.
Dist.: IFE

QUICK AND THE DEAD, THE 1987
★★★★ **NR Western/MFTV 1:30**
☑ Adult situations, violence
Dir: Robert Day ***Cast:*** Sam Elliott, Tom

Conti, Kate Capshaw, Kenny Morrison, Matt Clark
► Devoutly religious frontier family struggles across the harsh Wyoming wilderness to their new homestead. Although attacked by bandits, father Conti refuses to fight and spurns the help of vengeful drifter Elliott. But as the journey progresses, Conti grows so dependent on Elliott that his marriage to Capshaw is threatened. Strong, vigorous adaptation of a Louis L'Amour novel captures the scope and themes of a Western classic. Aided considerably by Dick Bush's stark, beautiful photography.
Dist.: Warner

QUICKER THAN THE EYE 1988
☆ **NR Mystery-Suspense 1:30**
☑ Explicit language, violence
Dir: Nicholas Gessner *Cast:* Ben Gazzara, Mary Crosby, Catherine Jarrett, Robert Liensol, Jean Yanne
► Magician Gazzara, scheduled to appear at a European summit meeting with his assistant Crosby, becomes a political assassination suspect when a terrorist switches places with him and kills an African prime minister. Tired thriller never works up much suspense although Lucerne locations look nice.
Dist.: Academy

QUICKSAND 1950
★ **NR Drama 1:19 B&W**
Dir: Irving Pichel *Cast:* Mickey Rooney, Jeanne Cagney, Barbara Bates, Peter Lorre, Taylor Holmes, Wally Cassell
► Garage mechanic Rooney borrows twenty dollars from the till to pay for a date with Cagney, a local tart. His efforts to replace the small sum progressively enmesh him in greater crimes involving larger sums, until he is part of an attempted murder and a police shoot-out. A good B-movie, with arcade-owner Lorre particularly effective greasing the skids for Rooney's slide.
Dist.: Sinister

QUICKSILVER 1986
★ ★ ★ ★ **PG Drama 1:46**
☑ Explicit language, violence
Dir: Tom Donnelly *Cast:* Kevin Bacon, Jami Gertz, Paul Rodriguez, Rudy Ramos, Andrew Smith, Gerald S. O'Loughlin
► Busted stockbroker Bacon takes job as bicycle messenger. He locks horns with Ramos, drug dealer on wheels, and saves gullible Gertz from Ramos's clutches. Bacon returns to stock market to earn money for messenger buddy Rodriguez, who hopes to open own hot-dog stand. Implausible premise and too many subplots detract from fine performances and slick, MTV filming. Real stars of picture are stuntmen on bicycles and pounding soundtrack. **(CC)**
Dist.: RCA/Columbia

QUIET COOL 1986
★ ★ **R Action-Adventure 1:20**

☑ Explicit language, graphic violence
Dir: Clay Borris *Cast:* James Remar, Adam Howard, Daphne Ashbrook, Jared Martin, Nick Cassavetes, Fran Ryan
► Remar, a New York cop with a low boiling point, travels to northern California to aid old girlfriend Ashbrook, whose brother and sister-in-law have been slain by violent marijuana growers. Ashbrook's vengeful nephew Howard and Remar team up to waste the druggies and their leader Cassavetes. Leads convincing in action pic with often brutal violence.
Dist.: RCA/Columbia

QUIET EARTH, THE 1985 New Zealand
★ **R Drama 1:31**
☑ Nudity, adult situations, explicit language
Dir: Geoff Murphy *Cast:* Bruno Lawrence, Alison Routledge, Peter Smith
► Scientist Lawrence working on malfunctioning top-secret project discovers his efforts have eliminated all human life save for himself, pretty redhead Routledge, and menacing Maori Smith. Lawrence enjoys free material amenities and the company of Routledge until confronted by mystical Smith. Often implausible and inconclusive, antinuke film has fans for Lawrence's performance and technical achievements. **(CC)**
Dist.: CBS/Fox

QUIET MAN, THE 1952
★ ★ ★ ★ **NR Drama/Romance 2:09**
Dir: John Ford *Cast:* John Wayne, Maureen O'Hara, Barry Fitzgerald, Victor McLaglen, Ward Bond, Mildred Natwick
► American boxer Wayne seeks peace in native Ireland after killing man in the ring. Obstacles include tempestuous local beauty O'Hara, who weds Wayne but resents his refusal to demand traditional dowry from her bullying brother McLaglen. When O'Hara tries to run away, Wayne shelves his pacifism for rollicking fight with McLaglen. Spirited and vibrant drama won Best Director Oscar for Ford and Best Cinematography for gorgeous portrayal of Ireland. A classic.
Dist.: Republic

QUILLER MEMORANDUM, THE 1966 British
★ ★ ★ **NR Espionage 1:45**
Dir: Michael Anderson *Cast:* George Segal, Alec Guinness, Max Von Sydow, Senta Berger, George Sanders, Robert Helpmann
► American secret agent Segal is recruited by Brit spy chief Guinness to replace operatives killed during investigation of modern neo-Nazi conspiracy in Berlin. Nazi leader Von Sydow nabs Segal and tortures him to reveal whereabouts of Guinness. Thoughtful spy intrigue, with screenplay by Harold Pinter, forsakes guns and stunts. **(CC)**
Dist.: CBS/Fox

QUINTET 1979
★ **R Drama 1:58**
☑ Adult situations, graphic violence

Dir: Robert Altman *Cast:* Paul Newman, Bibi Andersson, Fernando Rey, Vittorio Gassman, Nina Van Pallandt, Brigitte Fossey
▶ During the future Ice Age, people play a life-or-death game known as Quintet. Into this frozen apocalypse enters life-affirming newcomer Newman, determined to beat the odds of the game. Arty, high-falutin' allegory falls flat on its face. A major disappointment from usually intriguing director Altman.
Dist.: CBS/Fox

QUO VADIS 1951
★ ★ ★ ★ **NR Action-Adventure 2:52**
Dir: Mervyn LeRoy *Cast:* Robert Taylor, Deborah Kerr, Peter Ustinov, Leo Genn, Patricia Laffan, Finlay Currie
▶ Roman commander Taylor falls in love with Christian slave Kerr. When Nero (Ustinov) burns Rome and blames the Christians, Taylor and Kerr are seized for mass executions in the arena. Taylor then leads mob of Christians and disgruntled Romans against the hated Nero. Sweeping costume epic produced with lavish care to detail was box office smash and earned eight Oscar nominations. Somewhere among the thousands of extras are Sophia Loren and Elizabeth Taylor, but attention is better paid to the scene-stealing Ustinov. (CC)
Dist.: MGM/UA

RABID 1977 Canadian
★ **R Horror 1:31**
☑ Nudity, explicit language, graphic violence
Dir: David Cronenberg *Cast:* Marilyn Chambers, Frank Moore, Joe Silver, Howard Ryshpan, Patricia Gage, Susan Roman
▶ An accident and subsequent surgery turn young Chambers into a rabies-infected vampire who terrorizes Montreal and turns her victims into killers like herself. Gruesome and unappealing, although former porn star/Ivory Snow girl Chambers does well enough in her first dramatic role.
Dist.: Warner

RACE FOR YOUR LIFE, CHARLIE BROWN 1977
★ ★ ★ ★ ★ **G Animation 1:15**
Dir: Bill Melendez *Cast:* Voices of Duncan Watson, Greg Felton, Stuart Brotman, Gail Davis, Liam Martin, Kirk Jue
▶ Charlie Brown and company go to summer camp, where they run afoul of bullies who challenge them to a dangerous river-raft race. Heroic efforts by Charlie and Snoopy (riding a motorcycle *Easy Rider*–style) pull the gang through. Solid family fare; bright animation and jazzy musical score.
Dist.: Paramount

RACE WITH THE DEVIL 1975
☆ **PG Drama 1:28**
☑ Adult situations, explicit language, violence
Dir: Jack Starrett *Cast:* Peter Fonda, Warren Oates, Loretta Swit, Lara Parker, R. G. Armstrong, Clay Tanner
▶ Couples Fonda and Parker and Oates and Swit share camper while vacationing in Texas. First night out they see a Satanic cult sacrifice humans and flee in horror. Devil worshippers give chase, pursuing camper across Texas with intent to kill witnesses to their worship. Uneasy blend of horror and chases at least moves quickly.
Dist.: CBS/Fox

RACHEL AND THE STRANGER 1948
★ ★ ★ ★ **NR Romance 1:19 B&W**
Dir: Norman Foster *Cast:* Loretta Young, William Holden, Robert Mitchum, Tom Tully, Sara Haden
▶ In 1820, widowed backwoodsman Holden buys bondswoman Young out of servititude and marries her so that his son will have a mother. Holden's guitar-playing friend Mitchum falls for Young and a love triangle results. Agreeable, appealing performances with Mitchum warbling five songs.
Dist.: Turner

RACHEL PAPERS, THE 1989 British
★ ★ ★ **R Drama 1:32**
☑ Nudity, strong sexual content, explicit language
Dir: Damian Harris *Cast:* Dexter Fletcher, Ione Skye, Jonathan Pryce, James Spader, Bill Patterson, Lesley Sharp
▶ Scheming Fletcher uses a computer to get dating down to a science, but when he meets Skye, all methodology goes out the window. Fletcher pursues her relentlessly until she forgoes boyfriend Spader. Interesting modern romance has well-developed characters, with striking performances by two leads. (CC)
Dist.: CBS/Fox

RACHEL, RACHEL 1968
★ ★ ★ **R Drama 1:41**
☑ Adult situations, explicit language
Dir: Paul Newman *Cast:* Joanne Woodward, James Olson, Kate Harrington, Estelle Parsons, Donald Moffat, Geraldine Fitzgerald
▶ Spinsterish schoolteacher Woodward, upset at the lack of emotional involvement in her life, rejects the lesbian advances of friend Parsons and has her first affair with old classmate Olson. Deeply moving; highlighted by sensitive Oscar-nominated performances by Woodward and Parsons. Also nominated for Best Picture and Director. Newman's first outing behind the camera.
Dist.: Warner

RACING WITH THE MOON 1984
★ ★ ★ **PG Drama 1:49**
☑ Nudity, adult situations, explicit language
Dir: Richard Benjamin *Cast:* Sean Penn, Elizabeth McGovern, Nicolas Cage, John Karlen, Rutanya Alda, Carol Kane
▶ On the eve of their enlistment in the ma-

rines during World War II, best pals Penn and Cage hang out together while Penn woos McGovern, whom he thinks is a wealthy "Gatsby Girl", but who is actually a maid's daughter. Lightweight but likable story has immaculate period details, sweet chemistry between Penn and McGovern, and a warm, nostalgic tone. **(CC)**
Dist.: Paramount

RADIOACTIVE DREAMS 1986
★ R Sci-Fi 1:35
☑ Nudity, explicit language, violence
Dir: Albert Pyun *Cast:* John Stockwell, Michael Dudikoff, Lisa Blount, George Kennedy, Don Murray, Michelle Little
▶ Raised in a fallout shelter after a nuclear war, Stockwell and Dudikoff receive their entire education from pulp mystery novels. They travel through a wasteland filled with mutants, bikers, punks, and beautiful but untrustworthy molls Blount and Little—all searching for the keys to the world's last atomic bomb. Clever but overdone premise wears thin quickly due to confusing plot.
Dist.: Vestron

RADIO DAYS 1987
★ ★ ★ PG Comedy 1:28
☑ Brief nudity, adult situations, explicit language
Dir: Woody Allen *Cast:* Mia Farrow, Seth Green, Julie Kavner, Michael Tucker, Dianne Wiest, Danny Aiello
▶ Depression era lives of young Green and his close-knit if far-from-rich Rockaways family—mom Kavner, dad Tucker, unmarried aunt Wiest—are intercut with more glamorous stories of the radio stars they adore, like rags-to-riches rise of cigarette girl Farrow. Nostalgic, affectionate look back is a series of vignettes, alternately gentle, sweet, and amusing. Best scenes: Green's punishment by a rabbi, Wiest's disastrous date during "War of the Worlds," Farrow's encounter with gangster Aiello.
Dist.: HBO

RAFFERTY AND THE GOLD DUST TWINS 1975
★ ★ ★ R Comedy 1:32
☑ Explicit language
Dir: Dick Richards *Cast:* Alan Arkin, Sally Kellerman, Mackenzie Phillips, Alex Rocco, Harry Dean Stanton, Charles Martin Smith
▶ In Los Angeles, motor vehicles bureau inspector Arkin is kidnapped by aspiring singer Kellerman and teenage runaway Phillips, who demand he take them to New Orleans. Along the way, the threesome draw closer as Kellerman and Arkin become lovers. Good performances with a fresh improvised air although rambling story, not quite comedy or drama, is eccentric and unsatisfying.
Dist.: Warner

RAGE 1972
★ ★ ★ PG Action-Adventure 1:39

☑ Explicit language, violence
Dir: George C. Scott *Cast:* George C. Scott, Richard Basehart, Martin Sheen, Barnard Hughes
▶ Rancher Scott realizes Army's chemical warfare tests are responsible for his son's death. When major Sheen plots a cover-up, Scott is provoked into an explosive vendetta. Scott's directorial debut successfully works up a mood of righteous anger.
Dist.: Warner

RAGE OF HONOR 1987
★ ★ R Martial Arts 1:31
☑ Adult situations, explicit language, violence
Dir: Gordon Hessler *Cast:* Sho Kosugi, Lewis Van Bergen, Robin Evans, Gerry Gibson
▶ Phoenix-based narc Kosugi is determined to get revenge after his partner is tortured and murdered. When his boss (who is in cahoots with the killer) won't cooperate, Kosugi quits his job and tracks the murderer to Buenos Aires. Kosugi delivers the expected action for genre fans but struggles with the English dialogue in the predictable story.
Dist.: Media

RAGE OF PARIS, THE 1938
★ NR Comedy 1:15
Dir: Henry Koster *Cast:* Danielle Darrieux, Douglas Fairbanks, Jr., Mischa Auer, Louis Hayward, Helen Broderick, Charles Coleman
▶ On the way to a modeling assignment, comely Frenchwoman Darrieux accidentally goes to the office of Fairbanks, who thinks she's pulling a blackmail scheme and throws her out. When a pair of real chiselers try to use the innocent Darrieux to soak millionaire Hayward, friend Fairbanks once again gets the wrong impression. Fairly sparkling affair, with Mary Martin making her film debut in a small part.
Dist.: Cable

RAGGEDY MAN 1981
★ ★ ★ ★ PG Drama 1:34
☑ Brief nudity, adult situations, violence
Dir: Jack Fisk *Cast:* Sissy Spacek, Eric Roberts, Sam Shepard, William Sanderson, Tracey Walter, Henry Thomas
▶ During World War II, Texas divorcée Spacek struggles to support her two kids while having an affair with sailor Roberts. Mysterious "raggedy man" Shepard intervenes when angry locals try to rape her. Intimate, sensitive, and low-key with convincing tenderness between Spacek and Roberts. Naturalistic dialogue and fine period atmosphere transcend understated plotting. Favorite scene: Spacek's "Rum & Coca-Cola" dance. Director Fisk is Spacek's husband.
Dist.: MCA

RAGGEDY RAWNEY, THE 1990 British
☆ R Fantasy 1:42
☑ Nudity, adult situations, violence
Dir: Bob Hoskins *Cast:* Dexter Fletcher, Bob

Hoskins, Zoe Nathanson, Jennifer Platt, Dave Hill, Ian Drury

▶ During a war, deserter Fletcher takes refuge in Hoskins's gypsy camp. Pretending to be a mute woman, Fletcher fools Hoskins and others into thinking he is "rawney," or a half-mad, half-magic person, while romancing Hoskins's daughter Nathanson and evading the searches of the army. Weird, incoherent anti-war fantasy.
Dist.: Cannon

RAGING BULL 1980
★ ★ ★ R Biography/Sports 2:09 C/B&W
☑ Adult situations, explicit language, violence
Dir: Martin Scorsese *Cast:* Robert De Niro, Cathy Moriarty, Joe Pesci, Frank Vincent, Nicholas Colasanto, Theresa Saldana

▶ De Niro won an Oscar for his astonishing portrayal of Jake LaMotta, a furious, inarticulate boxer who briefly held the middleweight championship. Told in flashbacks as he prepares for a nightclub performance, unusually intelligent script covers his career, his brush with the mob, and his painful decline. Fights are shown with frightening intensity and brutality, but take second place to uniformly strong acting. Received eight Oscar nominations overall, also winning for Thelma Schoonmaker's dynamic editing.
Dist.: MGM/UA

RAGTIME 1981
★ ★ ★ ★ PG Drama 2:38
☑ Nudity, adult situations, explicit language, violence
Dir: Milos Forman *Cast:* James Cagney, Howard E. Rollins, Jr., Elizabeth McGovern, Mandy Patinkin, Mary Steenburgen, James Olson, Brad Dourif, Kenneth McMillan

▶ In turn-of-the-century New York, white family Olson, Steenburgen, and Dourif take black Rollins's part when he seeks justice from racist fireman McMillan. Police chief Cagney assumes charge as the dispute escalates. Other figures in the period panorama: actress McGovern at apex of violent love triangle and immigrant moviemaker Patinkin. Engrossing, superbly produced adaptation of the E. L. Doctorow best-seller. Cagney, who came out of retirement, and Oscar-nominated Rollins stand out in the great cast. Eight Oscar nominations include Randy Newman's score.
Dist.: Paramount

RAIDERS OF THE LOST ARK 1981
★ ★ ★ ★ ★ PG Action-Adventure 1:55
☑ Explicit language, violence
Dir: Steven Spielberg *Cast:* Harrison Ford, Karen Allen, Wolf Kahler, Paul Freeman, John Rhys-Davies, Denholm Elliott

▶ In 1936, archaeologist/adventurer Indiana Jones (Ford) and his spunky girlfriend Allen battle Nazi-backed rival Freeman in a search for the lost Ark of the Covenant, a biblical relic that contains a powerful supernatural force.

Riproaring, old-fashioned adventure anchored by a wonderfully gritty Ford is perhaps more pure fun than any other recent movie. Rousing John Williams score. Among many exciting scenes: Ford's brief duel with a swordsman, the runaway boulder. Eight Oscar nominations (including Best Picture); won Sound, Visual Effects, Editing, Art Direction. **(CC)**
Dist.: Paramount

RAID ON ENTEBBE 1977
★ ★ ★ NR Drama/MFTV 2:32
Dir: Irvin Kershner *Cast:* Charles Bronson, Peter Finch, Jack Warden, Horst Buchholz, Martin Balsam, Sylvia Sidney

▶ Israeli general Finch leads Bronson, Buchholz, and a team of commandos on a daring rescue of 103 Israeli hostages from a hijacked plane in Uganda. Thoughtful and thrilling made-for-TV drama based on a true 1976 incident. Finch's last screen appearance earned Emmy nomination. Same incident was depicted in *Victory at Entebbe* and *Operation Thunderbolt*.
Dist.: HBO

RAID ON ROMMEL 1971
★ PG War 1:39
☑ Adult situations, explicit language, violence
Dir: Henry Hathaway *Cast:* Richard Burton, John Colicos, Clinton Greyn, Wolfgang Preiss, Danielle De Metz, Karl Otto Alberty

▶ British World War II commando Burton and cohorts penetrate Nazi lines by deliberately allowing capture. Once in POW camp, they escape for sabotage mission. Second-rate actioner recycles desert footage from earlier film *Tobruk*.
Dist.: MCA

RAILWAY CHILDREN, THE 1971 British
★ ★ ★ G Family 1:35
Dir: Lionel Jeffries *Cast:* Dinah Sheridan, Bernard Cribbins, William Mervyn, Iain Cuthbertson, Jenny Agutter, Sally Thomsett

▶ With her husband wrongly imprisoned for treason, Sheridan must move her children to a lower-class home near a railroad on the Yorkshire moors. Wealthy aristocrat Mervyn takes a liking to the youngsters, and helps them clear their father's name. Above-average family-oriented story makes good use of its turn-of-the-century settings.
Dist.: HBO

RAIN 1932
★ ★ NR Drama 1:32
Dir: Lewis Milestone *Cast:* Joan Crawford, Walter Huston, William Gargan, Guy Kibbee, Walter Catlett, Beulah Bondi

▶ Dated adaptation of W. Somerset Maugham's story finds Crawford, a notorious South Seas prostitute, stranded on Pago Pago with dedicated missionary Huston and amorous but naive sergeant Gargan. Huston attempts to reform her but falls prey to her temptations instead. Strong atmosphere and

Huston's superb performance are still interesting. Remade as *Miss Sadie Thompson* in 1953.
Dist.: KVC

RAINBOW, THE 1989 British
★ ★ R Drama 1:44
☑ Nudity, adult situations, explicit language
Dir: Ken Russell *Cast:* Sammi Davis, Paul McGann, Amanda Donohoe, David Hemmings, Glenda Jackson, Christopher Gable
▶ Director Russell returns to the works of D. H. Lawrence twenty years after his acclaimed *Women in Love.* Ursula Brangwen (Davis) falls in love with dashing army officer McGann, but she's learning important lessons about independence from swimming teacher Donohoe. She eventually fights her family to take a teaching position outside their provincial environs. Although Davis is miscast, classy production combined with Lawrence's fascinating characters make this a fine effort. Jackson, who portrayed Ursula's sister in the first film, here plays their mother.
Dist.: Vestron

RAINMAKER, THE 1956
★ ★ ★ ★ NR Comedy/Drama 2:01
Dir: Joseph Anthony *Cast:* Burt Lancaster, Katharine Hepburn, Wendell Corey, Lloyd Bridges, Earl Holliman, Cameron Prud'-homme
▶ Drought-stricken Southwestern town mirrors the arid emotional life of lonely spinster Hepburn (receiving her seventh Oscar nomination) courted half-heartedly by sheriff Corey. Arrival of brash con man Lancaster, who promises rain for one hundred dollars, exposes Hepburn to true romance for the first time. Lancaster's sly performance dominates this pleasant comedy. **(CC)**
Dist.: Paramount

RAIN MAN 1988
★ ★ ★ ★ R Drama 2:13
☑ Adult situations, explicit language
Dir: Barry Levinson *Cast:* Dustin Hoffman, Tom Cruise, Valeria Golino, Jerry Molen, Jack Murdock, Michael D. Roberts
▶ High-pressure Los Angeles salesman Cruise is depending on his estranged father's estate to save his auto franchise but discovers he has an autistic brother Raymond (Hoffman), who has inherited everything except a '49 Buick. Cruise kidnaps Hoffman for a cross-country trip and learns to appreciate his brother's unusual talents. Inspired directing, deeply affecting script, and stellar acting in demanding roles bring unexpected humor and warmth to this unusual road movie. Won four Oscars, including Best Picture, Actor (Hoffman), Director, and Original Screenplay.
Dist.: MGM/UA

RAIN PEOPLE, THE 1969
★ ★ R Drama 1:41
☑ Adult situations, explicit language
Dir: Francis Ford Coppola *Cast:* James Caan, Shirley Knight, Robert Duvall, Marya Zimmet, Tom Aldredge
▶ When she learns she's pregnant, housewife Knight flees Long Island on a cross-country odyssey to find herself. She befriends mildly retarded football player Caan and later has a disturbing encounter with Nebraska cop Duvall. Impressive acting and sympathetic treatment of feminist themes are pluses in this early Coppola film.
Dist.: Warner

RAINTREE COUNTY 1957
★ ★ ★ ★ NR Drama 2:49
Dir: Edward Dmytryk *Cast:* Elizabeth Taylor, Montgomery Clift, Eva Marie Saint, Lee Marvin, Rod Taylor, Agnes Moorehead
▶ Idealist Clift drifts away from high school sweetheart and marries New Orleans belle Taylor. He discovers Taylor's mother died of insanity and it becomes apparent she has inherited family curse. Lavishly mounted Civil War epic with Oscar-nominated Taylor expressing surprising range. Movie has grim history of being shot at time when Clift had his disfiguring car accident, revealing the effects in scenes filmed after his recovery.
Dist.: MGM/UA

RAINY DAY FRIENDS 1985
★ ★ R Drama 1:45
☑ Explicit language, mild violence
Dir: Gary Kent *Cast:* Esai Morales, Chuck Bail, Janice Rule, Carrie Snodgress, Tomi Barrett, John Phillip Law
▶ L.A. street punk Morales learns he has cancer; with the help of fellow patient Bail, he battles a drug habit and authorities who object to his illegal immigrant background. Gutsy little movie packs a surprising punch on a small budget; Morales is sensational.A sleeper.
Dist.: Prism

RAISE THE TITANIC 1980
★ ★ ★ PG Action-Adventure 1:54
☑ Explicit language
Dir: Jerry Jameson *Cast:* Jason Robards, Jr., Richard Jordan, Alec Guinness, Anne Archer, David Selby
▶ When valuable metal is located in the wreck of the *Titanic,* an American team led by Robards and Jordan seek to salvage it before the Russians. Underwater mishaps threaten their effort. Good special effects, especially in the spectacular raising-of-the-*Titanic* sequence, help the unevenly paced story.
Dist.: CBS/Fox

RAISING ARIZONA 1987
★ ★ PG-13 Comedy 1:32
☑ Explicit language, mild violence
Dir: Joel Coen *Cast:* Nicolas Cage, Holly Hunter, Trey Wilson, John Goodman, William Forsythe, Randall (Tex) Cobb
▶ Highly stylized comedy starts brilliantly with a ten-minute prologue describing the marriage between career petty con Cage and

police mug shot photographer Hunter. Childless, they kidnap one of five quints, then confront a series of disasters involving two escaped convicts, deadly biker Cobb, and assorted cops. Intellectual approach to Three Stooges material is alternately grating and hilarious, with good performances undermined by too much silliness. **(CC)**
Dist.: CBS/Fox

RAISIN IN THE SUN, A 1961
★ ★ ★ ★ **NR Drama 2:08 B&W**
Dir: Daniel Petrie *Cast:* Sidney Poitier, Ruby Dee, Claudia McNeil, Diana Sands, Ivan Dixon, Louis Gossett, Jr.
▶ Black family, living in Chicago ghetto, must decide what to do with $10,000 insurance payment. Poitier's dream of starting his own business leads to conflict with mom McNeil, wife Dee, and sister Sands. Towering drama from Lorraine Hansberry's Pulitzer prize–winning play; perfect performances in complex, unstereotyped characterizations evoke laughter and tears.
Dist.: RCA/Columbia

RAMBO: FIRST BLOOD, PART II 1985
★ ★ ★ ★ **R Action-Adventure 1:36**
☑ Explicit language, violence
Dir: George Pan Cosmatos *Cast:* Sylvester Stallone, Richard Crenna, Charles Napier, Steven Berkoff, Julia Nickson, Martin Kove
▶ Rambo (Stallone) is freed from prison by the U.S. Army to locate POWs still being held in Vietnam. He is captured by the Vietnamese and deserted by his own government but that doesn't stop his one-man rescue effort. Literally explosive sequel. Breathless pacing, killings and stunts aplenty, impressive special effects; Stallone perfectly embodies a lean, mean fighting machine. Nickson, as the Vietnamese woman who helps him, adds a touch of humanity. **(CC)**
Dist.: HBO

RAMBO III 1988
★ ★ ★ ★ **R Action-Adventure 1:41**
☑ Lanuguage, violence
Dir: Peter MacDonald *Cast:* Sylvester Stallone, Richard Crenna, Marc de Jonge, Sasson Gabai, Doudi Shoua, Spiros Focus
▶ When his mentor Crenna is captured by the Russians in Afghanistan, Rambo (Stallone) teams up with the Afghan rebels to rescue him and wipe out the Soviets. Third in the series sticks to tried-and-true formula: convincing explosions, narrow escapes, little dialogue, lots of action. Large budget shows on screen: the film looks great. Stallone fans will cheer.
Dist.: IVE

RAMPAGE 1987
★ ★ **R Drama 1:37**
☑ Adult situations, explicit language, graphic violence
Dir: William Friedkin *Cast:* Michael Biehn, Alex McArthur, Nicholas Campbell, Deborah

Van Valkenburgh, John Harkins, Billy Green Bush
▶ Prosecutor Biehn, although personally against capital punishment, is assigned to seek death penalty for serial killer McArthur. McArthur's lawyer Campbell tries to get client off via insanity plea. Becomes a conservative courtroom drama after a lurid opening detailing McArthur's crimes. Interesting presentation of all sides of the issue; convincing performances.
Dist.: HBO

RAMROD 1947
★ ★ **NR Western B&W**
Dir: Andre de Toth *Cast:* Veronica Lake, Joel McCrea, Ian McDonald, Charles Ruggles, Preston Foster, Lloyd Bridges
▶ Ranch-owner Lake defies dad Ruggles and cattle boss Foster when the cow herders band together to keep sheepmen off their range. Ranch foreman McCrea can't go along with Lake's assaults on his honor, or her dishonest approach to battling the cattlers. Coming out from behind her peek-a-boo hair, Lake steals the show from the men in this otherwise standard Western.
Dist.: Republic

RAN 1985 Japanese
★ ★ ★ **R Drama 2:40**
☑ Violence
Dir: Akira Kurosawa *Cast:* Tatsuya Nakadai, Akira Terao, Jinpachi Nezu, Daisuke Ryu, Mieko Harada, Yoshiko Miyazaki
▶ In sixteenth-century Japan, an aging lord gives kingdom to eldest son, not realizing his ambitious daughter-in-law is plotting against him. Youngest son opposes the arrangement and is banished by the foolish old man, who later realizes the truth. Lavish adaptation of Shakespeare's *King Lear* is exciting but long and arduous, with stunning use of color and expert choreography of grueling battle scenes. Will lose some impact on the small screen. Ⓢ
Dist.: CBS/Fox

RANCHO NOTORIOUS 1952
★ ★ ★ **NR Western 1:29**
Dir: Fritz Lang *Cast:* Marlene Dietrich, Arthur Kennedy, Mel Ferrer, Lloyd Gough, Gloria Henry, William Frawley
▶ When his girlfriend is murdered by bandits, innocent cowboy Kennedy embarks on a vendetta that transforms him into a hardened killer. His only clue—"Chuck-a-Luck"—turns out to be an outlaw hideout ruled by glamorous Dietrich. Tensions simmer as Kennedy continues his search by courting Dietrich. Unusually somber Western is an intriguing exploration of hatred and revenge. Gough's name was removed from the credits when he was blacklisted as a Communist.
Dist.: United

RANDOM HARVEST 1942
★ ★ ★ **NR Drama 2:04 B&W**

Dir: Mervyn LeRoy ***Cast:*** Ronald Colman, Greer Garson, Susan Peters, Philip Dorn, Reginald Owen, Edmund Gwenn
► Shell-shocked World War II soldier Colman suffers amnesia and cannot recall his wealthy past. He is nursed to health by dancer Garson and falls in love with her. When new trauma causes him to forget her and return to family and business, she gets job as a secretary to woo him anew. Despite creaky amnesia gimmick, entertaining melodrama moves without being too maudlin, thanks to splendid work by Colman and Garson.
Dist.: MGM/UA

RANSOM 1956
★★★★ NR Drama 1:49
Dir: Alex Segal ***Cast:*** Glenn Ford, Donna Reed, Leslie Nielsen, Juano Hernandez, Robert Keith, Bobby Clark
► Ideal life of successful businessman Ford and wife Reed is shattered when their eight-year-old son Clark is kidnapped. But Ford refuses to give in to the kidnappers' half-million-dollar randsom demand. Taut direction and scripting steadily build tension; first-rate performances add genuine emotion.
Dist.: Vestron

RAPE OF LOVE 1979 French
☆ NR Drama 1:57
☑ Rape, nudity, adult situations, explicit language
Dir: Yannick Bellon ***Cast:*** Nathalie Nell, Alain Foures, Pierre Arditi, Daniel Auteuil, Bernard Granger, Michele Simonnet
► Nurse Nell is brutally raped and humiliated by four young men. As she tries to deal with her experience, her fiancé Foures takes it as a personal affront, while her mother is ashamed. Nell must decide whether to prosecute in light of society's often insensitive treatment of rape victims. Harrowing, involving look at victim's rights raises many issues, but remains decidedly one-sided. Nell turns in a formidable performance. [S]
Dist.: RCA/Columbia

RAPPIN' 1985
★★ PG Drama/Musical 1:32
☑ Adult situations, explicit language, mild violence
Dir: Joel Silberg ***Cast:*** Mario Van Peebles, Tasia Valenza, Charles Flohe, Melvin Plowden, Leo O'Brien, Eriq La Salle
► Van Peebles, a reformed street tough with the gift of gab, returns from prison to Pittsburgh ghetto. There he woos ex-girlfriend Valenza, beats up gang leader Flohe, defeats attempt by greedy landlord to evict tenants prior to gentrification, and cuts a record to earn the dough to save kid brother O'Brien from jail, all in time to rap with homeboys Plowden and La Salle in the musical finale. Sweet and good-natured hokum mainly for urban teens.
Dist.: MGM/UA

RARE BREED, THE 1966
★★★ NR Western 1:37
Dir: Andrew V. McLaglen ***Cast:*** James Stewart, Maureen O'Hara, Brian Keith, Juliet Mills, Don Galloway, David Brian
► British widow O'Hara travels to the States for an experiment with Texas rancher Keith: can English Hereford cows be crossbred with longhorns? Cynical cowboy Stewart must transport O'Hara, daughter Mills, and a bull from St. Louis to Keith's ranch. Wholesome oater sometimes bogged down by sentimentality.
Dist.: MCA

RARE BREED, A 1981
★★ PG Drama 1:34
☑ Explicit language, mild violence
Dir: David Nelson ***Cast:*** George Kennedy, Forrest Tucker, Tracy Vaccaro, Tom Hallick, Don DeFore, William Hicks
► Rich rancher Kennedy buys filly Carnauba for Vaccaro, daughter of best friend Tucker. She raises the horse and stows away when Carnauba is shipped to Italy for further training. Carnauba wins races until filly, Vaccaro, and trainer Hallick are kidnapped for ransom. Wholesome but unsurprising family fare. Based on a true story.
Dist.: IVE

RASHOMON 1950 Japanese
★★ NR Drama 1:27 B&W
Dir: Akira Kurosawa ***Cast:*** Toshiro Mifune, Machiko Kyo, Masayuki Mori, Takashi Shimura
► In twelfth-century Japan, a bandit kills a husband and rapes his wife—or does he? Participants and witnesses give four differing accounts of the tragic incident. Truly timeless work about the nature of truth and justice, magnificently filmed and acted, although American audiences may find stylized performances somewhat remote. Received an honorary Oscar.
Dist.: Nelson

RASPUTIN 1981 Russian
☆ NR Biography B&W/C
Dir: Elem Klimov ***Cast:*** Alexei Petrenko, Anatoly Romashin, Velta Linen, Alice Freindlikh, O. Hine
► Dramatization of the two years before the Russian Revolution, with Czar Nicholas II (Romashin) and the Czarina (Freindlikh) in the thrall of Rasputin (Petrenko), the mad monk whose abuse of influence, wild orgies, and lunatic ways helped erode imperial authority. Wildly overplayed, silly movie was supressed by Brezhnev-era Soviet authorities for being too soft on the Czar. Also known as *Agony*. [S]
Dist.: IFE

RATBOY 1986
★ PG-13 Drama 1:44
☑ Adult situations, explicit language
Dir: Sondra Locke ***Cast:*** Sondra Locke,

Robert Townsend, Christopher Hewett, Larry Hankin, Gerrit Graham, S. L. Baird ·
▶ Directing debut for Locke is a decidedly offbeat parable about half-boy, half-rat outcast Baird, exploited by opportunistic journalist Locke. When the ratboy escapes from his guardian Townsend, Locke must choose between imprisoning him again or granting him freedom. Despite good satirical moments, superficial story fails to generate sympathy.
Dist.: Warner

RAVEN, THE 1935
★ ★ NR Horror 1:01 B&W
Dir: Louis Friedlander (Lew Landers) *Cast:* Boris Karloff, Bela Lugosi, Irene Ware, Lester Matthews, Samuel S. Hinds, Inez Courtney
▶ Teaming of horror greats features Lugosi as a mad doctor who performs plastic surgery on gangster Karloff and makes him look worse. Lugosi then plots vengeance against the family of the woman who jilted him, but Karloff tries to thwart him.
Dist.: MCA

RAVEN, THE 1963
★ ★ G Horror 1:26
Dir: Roger Corman *Cast:* Vincent Price, Peter Lorre, Boris Karloff, Hazel Court, Jack Nicholson, Olive Sturgess
▶ Evil magician Karloff steals good magician Price's wife Court. Price teams up with fellow conjurer Lorre and Lorre's son Nicholson to battle Karloff. Loosely inspired by Edgar Allan Poe's classic poem; Price and Corman mock their more serious Poe films with high spirits and good humor.
Dist.: Warner

RAW DEAL 1986
★ ★ ★ R Action-Adventure 1:37
☑ Explicit language, graphic violence
Dir: John Irvin. *Cast:* Arnold Schwarzenegger, Kathryn Harrold, Sam Wanamaker, Paul Shenar, Robert Davi, Ed Lauter
▶ Disgraced former FBI agent Schwarzenegger busts up the Chicago mobs to redeem himself. Middling action fare doesn't compare well to better Schwarzenegger outings. For those who favor automatic weapons and automatic plot lines. **(CC)**
Dist.: HBO

RAWHEAD REX 1987
★ R Horror 1:29
☑ Adult situations, explicit language, graphic violence
Dir: George Pablou *Cast:* David Dukes, Kelly Piper, Ronan Wilmot, Niall Tobin, Heinrich von Schellendorf, Niall O'Brien
▶ Ugly, red-eyed monster von Schellendorf, a.k.a. Rawhead Rex, Lord of the Dark Times, is unearthed from his tomb in Ireland and goes on a murder spree, assisted by vicar's aide Wilmot. American historian Dukes and wife Piper arrive in town and are soon in the thick of the mayhem. Gory, poorly acted, low-bud-

get horror with formula plot. Nice Irish setting and colorful brogues, though.
Dist.: Vestron

RAWHIDE 1951
★ ★ NR Western 1:26 B&W
Dir: Henry Hathaway *Cast:* Tyrone Power, Susan Hayward, Hugh Marlowe, Dean Jagger, Edgar Buchanan, Jack Elam
▶ Power and Hayward are held prisoner in a stagecoach station by escaped murderer Marlowe and his three companions. While the bad guys prepare to rob the incoming stage, Power and Hayward plot their escape. Middling Western with some good suspense. Also known as *Desperate Siege*.
Dist.: CBS/Fox

RAZORBACK 1984 Australian
★ ★ R Horror 1:35
☑ Rape, explicit language, graphic violence
Dir: Russell Mulcahy *Cast:* Gregory Harrison, Arkie Whitely, Bill Kerr, Chris Haywood, David Argue, Judy Morris
▶ Giant razorback hog in Australian outback devours American newscaster Morris. Hubby Harrison investigates and is ill-treated by suspicious locals. Harrison teams with pretty zoologist Whitely to lead posse that slays marauding pig. Director Mulcahy, weaned on music videos, shoots the Aussie wilderness as a surreal nightmare, but style alone can't overcome plot that's neither scary nor campy.
Dist.: Warner

RAZOR'S EDGE, THE 1946
★ ★ ★ ★ NR Drama 2:26 B&W
Dir: Edmund Goulding *Cast:* Tyrone Power, Gene Tierney, John Payne, Anne Baxter, Clifton Webb, Herbert Marshall
▶ Adaptation of the W. Somerset Maugham novel, with Marshall in the role of the observant author. Idealistic young Power, his life philosophy askew after horror of World War I, struggles with materialistic America and searches abroad for truth. Elegantly shot, well acted, and engrossing. Baxter got Academy Award for Best Supporting Actress.
Dist.: CBS/Fox

RAZOR'S EDGE, THE 1984
★ ★ ★ PG-13 Drama 2:09
☑ Adult situations, explicit language, violence
Dir: John Byrum *Cast:* Bill Murray, Theresa Russell, Catherine Hicks, Denholm Elliott, James Keach, Peter Vaughn
▶ After eye-opening stint as ambulance driver in World War I, young Murray postpones his marriage to Midwestern sweetheart Hicks. He seeks enlightenment in India while she weds his buddy Keach. The three are reunited in Paris, where Hicks and Keach live with her dour rich uncle Elliott, but friendships sour when Hicks ruins Murray's plans to marry local prostitute Russell. Confusing plot and Murray's

discomfort with dramatic material detract; 1946 version holds up better. **(CC)**
Dist.: RCA/Columbia

REACHING FOR THE MOON 1931
★ **NR Comedy 1:12 B&W**
Dir: Edmund Goulding *Cast:* Douglas Fairbanks, Bebe Daniels, Edward Everett Horton, Jack Mulhall, Claude Allister, Bing Crosby
▶ Wall Street financier Fairbanks falls so hard for aviatrix Daniels that he follows her on a transatlantic cruise. Also on board are her English fiancé Allister, his servant Horton, and Crosby, who sings Irving Berlin's "Lower Than Lowdown." Frisky Fairbanks performance highlights luxurious vehicle.
Dist.: Video Yesteryear

REAL GENIUS 1985
★ ★ ★ ★ **PG Comedy 1:46**
☑ Adult situations, explicit language
Dir: Martha Coolidge *Cast:* Val Kilmer, William Atherton, Gabe Jarret, Patti D'Arbanville, Michelle Meyrink, Jonathan Gries
▶ Fifteen-year-old science whiz Jarret enrolls in college and rooms with unorthodox genius senior Kilmer. Each learns from the other amid campus high jinks until they go to work on laser project for unethical prof Atherton. The boys then discover their research will aid development of deadly weapon for the Pentagon. Amiable hybrid comedy combines standard sex jokes and sight gags with more clever lines and sharp satire. **(CC)**
Dist.: RCA/Columbia

REAL LIFE 1979
★ **PG Comedy 1:38**
☑ Explicit language
Dir: Albert Brooks *Cast:* Albert Brooks, Charles Grodin, Frances Lee McCain, Matthew Tobin, J. A. Preston, Lisa Urette
▶ Documentary filmmaker Brooks, backed by think tank and Hollywood studio, moves in with "typical" American family Grodin, McCain, and two kids to chronicle their day-to-day life. Family quickly disintegrates under continual scrutiny of cameras while Brooks grows ever more rabid in pursuit of his vision. Spoof of Hollywood filmmaking and the PBS "American Family" docu-series doesn't hold together, but many individual pieces are terrific.
Dist.: Paramount

REAL MEN 1987
★ ★ ★ **PG-13 Comedy 1:36**
☑ Explicit language, violence
Dir: Dennis Feldman *Cast:* James Belushi, John Ritter, Barbara Barrie, Bill Morey, Iva Anderson, Gail Berle
▶ When Russians kill a CIA agent in touch with aliens about an ecology conspiracy that threatens the world, rogue agent Belushi must convince Milquetoast lookalike Ritter to replace the dead spy. Amid shoot-'em-ups with the Russkies on a wild cross-country trek, Ritter learns to be aggressive and Belushi picks up

some manners. Far-fetched and frantic spy spoof occasionally hits its target. **(CC)**
Dist.: CBS/Fox

RE-ANIMATOR 1985
★ ★ **NR Horror 1:26**
☑ Nudity, explicit language, graphic violence
Dir: Stuart Gordon *Cast:* Jeffrey Combs, Bruce Abbott, Barbara Crampton, David Gale, Robert Sampson, Gerry Block
▶ Based on stories by H. P. Lovecraft, film concerns medical student Combs, who develops serum to bring the dead back to life. Unfortunately, the re-animated return in very bad moods. Combining 1930s-style horror story with 1980s special effects gore, grisly but comically macabre picture has substantial cult following. Original R rating was revoked when producers inserted additional graphic violence on videocassette version.
Dist.: Vestron

REAP THE WILD WIND 1942
★ ★ ★ **NR Action-Adventure 2:04**
Dir: Cecil B. DeMille *Cast:* Ray Milland, John Wayne, Paulette Goddard, Raymond Massey, Robert Preston, Susan Hayward
▶ Ship captain Wayne falls prey to pirates off the coast of Florida; lawyer Milland investigates the case and falls for Wayne's girl Goddard, the feisty owner of a salvage operation. Two-fisted DeMille epic set in the 1840s is immensely entertaining. Climaxed by duel with a giant squid, a stunt that won an Oscar for Special Effects.
Dist.: MCA

REAR WINDOW 1954
★ ★ ★ ★ ★ **PG Mystery-Suspense 1:52**
☑ Adult situations
Dir: Alfred Hitchcock *Cast:* James Stewart, Grace Kelly, Raymond Burr, Thelma Ritter, Wendell Corey, Judith Evelyn
▶ Magazine photographer Stewart, laid up in his Greenwich Village apartment with a broken leg, has nothing to do but spy on his neighbors. He begins to suspect that Burr, the man across the courtyard, has killed his suddenly missing wife. Hitchcock gem has a deceptively simple surface, amazingly sharp psychological insight, and a serious look at voyeurism encased in a gripping thriller plot. Dazzling technique, letter-perfect performances by Stewart and Kelly as his girlfriend. Not to be missed.
Dist.: MCA

REBECCA 1940
★ ★ ★ ★ **NR Drama 2:10 B&W**
Dir: Alfred Hitchcock *Cast:* Laurence Olivier, Joan Fontaine, George Sanders, Judith Anderson, Nigel Bruce, C. Aubrey Smith
▶ After a whirlwind romance, shy Fontaine marries dashing aristocrat Olivier. Moving to his Manderley estate, Fontaine finds herself puzzled and then haunted by his deceased wife Rebecca. Dazzling adaptation of

Daphne du Maurier's novel is a beautifully tense and compelling romance, with an outstanding performance by Anderson as a grim housekeeper. Received an Oscar for George Barnes's cinematography, as well as seven other nominations. Hitchcock's first American work is also his only film to win the Best Picture Oscar. **(CC)**
Dist.: CBS/Fox

REBECCA OF SUNNYBROOK FARM 1938
★ ★ NR Musical/Family 1:20 B&W
Dir: Allan Dwan   *Cast:* Shirley Temple, Randolph Scott, Jack Haley, Gloria Stuart, William Demarest, Bill "Bojangles" Robinson
▶ Aspiring radio star Temple stays at aunt's farm; Scott is the talent scout next door who discovers the little girl's potential. Very loosely based on the classic novel; plot is an excuse for Temple to perform "On the Good Ship Lollipop," "Animal Crackers," and others.
Dist.: CBS/Fox

REBEL 1986 Australian
★ R Drama 1:34
☑ Nudity, adult situations, explicit language, violence
Dir: Michael Jenkins   *Cast:* Matt Dillon, Bryan Brown, Debbie Byrne, Bill Hunter, Ray Barrett, Julie Nihill
▶ In Sydney during World War II, American Marine Dillon goes AWOL and falls in love with married nightclub singer Byrne, whose hubby is off fighting the Axis. Amid shenanigans with waterfront con man Brown, Dillon romances the reluctant Byrne while dodging the local police and American MPs. Low-grade romantic drama with thin plot and confused mix of 1980s tunes sung in wartime setting. For Dillon fans only. **(CC)**
Dist.: Vestron

REBEL LOVE 1985
★ ★ R Drama 1:30
☑ Nudity, adult situations, explicit language
Dir: Milton Bagby, Jr.   *Cast:* Jamie Rose, Terence Knox, Fran Ryan, Carl Spurlock, Rick Waln
▶ The solitary Indiana farm life of Yankee widow Rose is changed by an affair with Confederate spy Knox. Cut-rate Civil War drama is ponderous and unbelievable.
Dist.: Vestron

REBEL ROUSERS 1970
★ ★ R Action-Adventure 1:18
☑ Adult situations, explicit language, violence
Dir: Martin B. Cohen   *Cast:* Cameron Mitchell, Bruce Dern, Jack Nicholson, Diane Ladd, Harry Dean Stanton, Lou Procopio
▶ On a remote stretch of beach, Dern and his motorcycle buddies abduct pregnant girlfriend of architect Mitchell; he turns to local Mexicans armed with pitchforks for help. Violent but predictable low-budget exploitation

highlighted by Nicholson's amusing turn as "Bunny."
Dist.: Media

REBEL WITHOUT A CAUSE 1955
★ ★ ★ ★ NR Drama 1:51
☑ Adult situations, violence
Dir: Nicholas Ray   *Cast:* James Dean, Natalie Wood, Sal Mineo, Jim Backus, Ann Doran, William Hopper
▶ Chronic delinquent teenager Dean tries for fresh start at L.A. school, only to find himself baited into contest of courage by Wood, girlfriend of local tough. Thus begins night of tragedy, as Dean, Wood, and oddball peer Mineo find brief solace with one another from pressures to conform, parents who don't understand, and the longing for adult identity. Bona fide classic still hits all the right notes of teen angst. Splendid performances from Mineo, Wood, and the smoldering Dean; energetic filmmaking from director Ray.
Dist.: Warner

RECKLESS 1984
★ ★ R Drama 1:30
☑ Nudity, adult situations, explicit language, violence
Dir: James Foley   *Cast:* Daryl Hannah, Aidan Quinn, Kenneth McMillan, Adam Baldwin, Cliff De Young, Lois Smith
▶ In small West Virginia town, moody, rebellious teenager Quinn quits football but still manages to romance straitlaced cheerleader Hannah. He battles alcoholic steelworker father McMillan while she copes with dullsville boyfriend Baldwin and mother Smith, whose idea of a tribal rite-of-passage is getting her first credit card. Familiar opposite-side-of-the-tracks teen romance burdened by cumbersome screenplay but boasts great-looking leads, torrid sex scenes, distinctive direction from Foley, and dynamic score.
Dist.: MGM/UA

RECRUITS 1986
☆ R Comedy 1:22
☑ Nudity, adult situations, explicit language
Dir: Rafal Zeilinski   *Cast:* Steve Osmond, Doug Annear, Annie McAuley, Alan Deveau, John Terrell, Lolita David
▶ In the beach town of Clam Cove, sheriff cleans up the streets by deputizing all the thieves, hookers, winos, and bums. Ragtag recruits aren't as inept as expected—they thwart corrupt police chief and run bikers out of town. Cheap carbon copy of *Police Academy* series offers few laughs and technical incompetence.
Dist.: Vestron

RED BADGE OF COURAGE, THE 1951
★ ★ ★ ★ NR War/Drama 1:09 B&W
☑ Adult situations, mild violence
Dir: John Huston   *Cast:* Audie Murphy, Bill Mauldin, Douglas Dick, Royal Dano, John Dierkes, Andy Devine
▶ Adaptation of the well-known Stephen

Crane novel depicts struggle of Union solider Murphy with cowardice during first battle with Confederates. Despite his confidence behind the lines, Murphy freezes at the sight of the enemy, then seeks to hide his panic from his fellow soldiers. Classic film boasts compelling battle sequences and dialogue from writer/director Huston. Murphy was the most-decorated soldier of World War II.
Dist.: MGM/UA

RED BEARD 1965 Japanese
☆ **NR Drama 3:05 B&W**
☑ Violence
Dir: Akira Kurosawa ***Cast:*** Toshiro Mifune, Yuzo Kayama, Yosio Tsuchiya, Reiko Dan, Kyoko Kagawa, Terumi Niki
► Medical soap opera set in nineteenth-century Japan. Mifune is a devoted public clinic doctor trying to convince a younger colleague to dedicate himself to the poor. Episodic structure varies in quality: encounter with a "black widow" psychopath and Mifune disbanding a gang of thugs are thrilling, but other subplots are maudlin. [S]
Dist.: Various

RED DAWN 1984
★★★★ **PG-13 Action-Adventure 1:54**
☑ Adult situations, explicit language, violence
Dir: John Milius ***Cast:*** Patrick Swayze, Charlie Sheen, C. Thomas Howell, Lea Thompson, Powers Boothe, Harry Dean Stanton, Ben Johnson, Jennifer Grey
► Soviet and Cuban troops invade the U.S. after limited nuke attack and occupy Calumet, Colorado, killing many and dispatching remaining adults to "reeducation camps." Cause of freedom is left in hands of teen refugees Swayze, Sheen, Howell, and Thompson, known as the Wolverines. Adopting guerrilla tactics and assisted by downed flyer Boothe, the once-disorganized crew becomes effective nemesis to the Commies. Intriguing premise and fine cast.
Dist.: MGM/UA

RED DESERT 1964 French/Italian
☆ **NR Drama 1:46**
Dir: Michelangelo Antonioni ***Cast:*** Monica Vitti, Richard Harris, Rita Renoir, Carlo Chionetti, Xenia Valderi, Aldo Grotti
► Housewife Vitti grows depressed by the factory-blasted environment of Ravenna. Visiting employment recruiter Harris senses her pain at the barren industrial environment, but husband Chionetti does not understand. Director Antonioni uses a carefully controlled palette to convey the horrors of pollution. Interesting study may not come across for all. [S]
Dist.: Corinth

RED DUST 1932
★★★ **NR Drama 1:23 B&W**
Dir: Victor Fleming ***Cast:*** Clark Gable, Jean Harlow, Mary Astor, Donald Crisp, Gene Raymond, Tully Marshall
► Gable, head of a Far East rubber plantation, has a temporary affair with Harlow, a harlot on the run from the law. When she leaves, Gable takes up with Astor, whose husband lies dying of jungle fever. Harlow's return and the husband's recovery spark a deadly confrontation. Suggestive script and sizzling chemistry between the two stars made this a daring film for its time. It remains a classic, with Gable at his manliest, and Harlow at her most irresistibly seductive. Gable repeated his role in John Ford's 1953 remake *Mogambo*.
Dist.: MGM/UA

RED-HEADED STRANGER 1987
★★ **R Western 1:45**
☑ Explicit language, violence
Dir: William Wittliff ***Cast:*** Willie Nelson, Katharine Ross, Morgan Fairchild, Royal Dano, Sonny Carl Davis
► Eastern parson Nelson travels with unfaithful wife Fairchild to run church in Montana and finds town dominated by bully Dano and his clan. Nelson battles with Dano for the freedom of the townfolk and gets rid of philandering Fairchild for sweet-natured widow Ross. Somber Western, with origin in 1975 album by Nelson, will disappoint fans of the genre, although Nelson is always likable and production values are better than average. **(CC)**
Dist.: Nelson

RED HEAT 1985 U.S./German
★ **NR Drama 1:46**
☑ Nudity, adult situations, explicit language, violence
Dir: Robert Collector ***Cast:*** Linda Blair, Sylvia Kristel, Sue Kiel, William Ostrander, Albert Fortell
► American Blair witnesses the kidnapping of a defector in Berlin and is tossed into an East German prison. Lesbian warden Kristel makes life difficult for Blair and the other prisoners. Linda's soldier boyfriend breaks into the prison to rescue her. Contains all the genre staples: shower scenes, lesbianism, violence, and far-fetched plotting.
Dist.: Vestron

RED HEAT 1988
★★★★ **R Action-Adventure 1:46**
☑ Adult situations, explicit language, graphic violence
Dir: Walter Hill ***Cast:*** Arnold Schwarzenegger, James Belushi, Peter Boyle, Ed O'Ross, Gina Gershon, Larry Fishburne
► Tough, hard-nosed Moscow cop Schwarzenegger is dispatched to Chicago to extradite Soviet narcotics gangster O'Ross. When O'Ross escapes, Schwarzenegger pairs with slovenly, cynical U.S. counterpart Belushi. The two mix like oil and water at first, but soon develop rapport needed to nab the ruthless Russian and his cohorts. Plenty of shoot-outs, chases, and a good measure of humor in this clever take on the buddy-action formula.
Dist.: Vestron

RED HOUSE, THE 1947
★ NR Drama 1:40 B&W
Dir: Delmer Daves **Cast:** Edward G. Robinson, Lon McCallister, Allene Roberts, Judith Anderson, Rory Calhoun, Julie London
▶ Reclusive farmer Robinson warns people not to go into a certain house on his property. Those who ignore his warning are shot by hired man Calhoun. Daughter Roberts and employee McCallister are curious, but Robinson's sister is determined to destroy the house before its secret can be discovered. Robinson makes a furious eccentric in this compelling little drama.
Dist.: Sinister

RED KING, WHITE KNIGHT 1989
★★★ NR Espionage/MFTV 1:45
☑ Adult situations, explicit language, violence
Dir: Geoff Murphy **Cast:** Tom Skerritt, Max Von Sydow, Helen Mirren, Tom Bell
▶ High-level KGB plot to assassinate Gorbachev is leaked to the CIA. They enlist the aid of former agent Skerritt, a bitter, down-and-out ex-alcoholic, to thwart the conspiracy. Fast-paced political thriller features top cast of international stars and an eerie scenario. (CC)
Dist.: HBO

RED PONY, THE 1949
★★★★ NR Family 1:19
Dir: Lewis Milestone **Cast:** Myrna Loy, Robert Mitchum, Louis Calhern, Shepperd Strudwick, Peter Miles, Margaret Hamilton
▶ Young Miles idolizes Mitchum, a hired hand on father Strudwick's ranch. Strudwick's marital problems with Loy upset the youngster; he's comforted when Mitchum helps him train a frail horse. Moving family drama boasts superb photography, beautiful Aaron Copland score, and effectively understated sentiment. Adapted by John Steinbeck from three of his short stories and remade for TV in 1972.
Dist.: Republic

RED RIVER 1948
★★★★ NR Western 2:13 B&W
Dir: Howard Hawks **Cast:** John Wayne, Montgomery Clift, Joanne Dru, Walter Brennan, Coleen Gray, John Ireland
▶ Seminal Western about mammoth cattle drive along the Chisholm Trail to Abilene is one of the true classics of the genre. Wayne is remarkable as cattle baron Tom Dunson; Clift became a star as a foster son who rebels against Dunson's unreasonable discipline. Magnificent photography, rousing score, and hard-as-nails script by Borden Chase and Charles Schnee contribute to film's epic sweep.
Dist.: MGM/UA

REDS 1981
★★★ PG Biography 3:19
☑ Adult situations, explicit language, violence

Dir: Warren Beatty **Cast:** Warren Beatty, Diane Keaton, Jack Nicholson, Maureen Stapleton, Gene Hackman, Edward Herrmann
▶ Radical journalist John Reed (Beatty) has an affair with writer Louise Bryant (Keaton), who leaves behind her middle-class life to marry him. Reed makes his mark when he reports on the tumultuous Russian Revolution. Ambitious, impressive epic successfully mixes passion and politics; interviews with real-life survivors of the period like Henry Miller and Adela Rogers St. John are one of the brilliant strokes. Nominated for Best Picture, Actor, Actress, Supporting Actor (Nicholson, as Bryant's lover, the playwright Eugene O'Neill). Oscars for Best Director, Supporting Actress (Stapleton), Cinematography.
Dist.: Paramount

RED SCORPION 1989
★★★ R Action-Adventure 1:42
☑ Explicit language, graphic violence
Dir: Joseph Zito **Cast:** Dolph Lundgren, M. Emmet Walsh, Al White, T. P. McKenna, Carmen Argenziano, Alex Colon
▶ Soviet agent Lundgren, slated for execution when his mission to Africa fails, escapes to the desert. The natives save him after a scorpion bites him. He then joins the African rebels against his own people. Constant carnage and slam-bang action highlight vehicle for big blond Lundgren.
Dist.: SGE

RED SHOES, THE 1948 British
★★★★ NR Drama/Dance 2:13
Dir: Michael Powell, Emeric Pressburger **Cast:** Moira Shearer, Anton Walbrook, Marius Goring, Robert Helpmann, Albert Basserman, Leonide Massine
▶ Ambitious ballerina Shearer loves composer Goring, but ruthless company director Walbrook disapproves of the relationship. Shearer's conflict between love and career is paralled by the tragic ballet that made her famous, "The Red Shoes." Grandly romantic and beautifully produced; perhaps the best film about ballet. Best Picture nominee; won for Art/Set Decoration and Score.
Dist.: Paramount

RED SONJA 1985
★ PG-13 Action-Adventure 1:29
☑ Adult situations, violence
Dir: Richard Fleischer **Cast:** Arnold Schwarzenegger, Brigitte Nielsen, Sandahl Bergman, Paul Smith, Ernie Reyes, Jr., Ronald Lacey
▶ Female warrior Nielsen acquires special skill at swordplay but must pledge never to make love to a man unless he beats her in a fair fight. Some years later, well-developed Nielsen, aided by even-better-developed mercenary Schwarzenegger, embarks on a mission to retrieve magic talisman from evil queen Bergman and thus save the world from

destruction. Adapted from stories by Robert E. Howard, also creator of *Conan the Barbarian*. Humorless sword-and-sorcery exercise for fans only. **(CC)**
Dist.: CBS/Fox

RED TENT, THE 1971 Italian/Russian
★ ★ ★ **G Action-Adventure 2:01**
Dir: Mikhail K. Kalatozov *Cast:* Sean Connery, Claudia Cardinale, Hardy Kruger, Peter Finch, Massimo Girotti, Luigi Vannucchi
▶ Finch commands an Italian dirigible expedition to North Pole in 1928. When his airship crashes in the North Atlantic, Kruger races team led by Norwegian explorer Roald Amundsen (Connery) to the rescue. Lives of the imperiled men take a back seat to political maneuverings. Impressive location photography adds scope to this exciting drama based on a real-life disaster.
Dist.: Paramount

REEFER MADNESS 1936
☆ **PG Drama 1:12 B&W**
☑ Adult situations
Dir: Louis Gasnier *Cast:* Dorothy Short, Kenneth Craig, Lillian Miles, Dave O'Brien, Thelma White, Carleton Young
▶ Cautionary tale about youngsters who experiment with marijuana and soon become addicted to the evil weed. Depths of debauchery include necking, close dancing, and fast boogie-woogie piano playing; drug use ultimately leads to prison and death. Unintentionally comic, camp classic is favorite of midnight movie audiences.
Dist.: Media

REFLECTION OF FEAR, A 1973
★ ★ ★ **PG Mystery-Suspense 1:29**
☑ Violence
Dir: William A. Fraker *Cast:* Robert Shaw, Mary Ure, Sally Kellerman, Sondra Locke, Signe Hasso
▶ Young Locke, given strange upbringing by mother Ure and grandmother Hasso, makes hazy distinctions between fantasy and reality and believes her doll Aaron is alive. When her dad Shaw shows up to demand divorce so he can marry his girlfriend Kellerman, Locke goes on killing spree. Standard shocker.
Dist.: RCA/Columbia

REFLECTIONS IN A GOLDEN EYE 1967
★ **NR Drama 1:49**
☑ Adult situations, explicit language
Dir: John Huston *Cast:* Elizabeth Taylor, Marlon Brando, Brian Keith, Julie Harris, Zorro David, Robert Forster
▶ Army major Brando hides his homosexuality behind stern discipline and neglects sexpot wife Taylor, leading her to begin affair with colonel Keith, whose psychotic wife Harris enjoys company of gay houseboy David. Add to the equation Peeping Tom underwear fetishist Forster, who stirs Brando's repressed longings, and things really get kinky. Heavy-handed

melodrama of interest for stars only. Based on the Carson McCullers novel.
Dist.: Warner

REFORM SCHOOL GIRLS 1986
★ **R Action-Adventure 1:34**
☑ Nudity, adult situations, explicit language, violence
Dir: Tom DeSimone *Cast:* Sybil Danning, Wendy O. Williams, Pat Ast, Linda Carol, Charlotte McGinnis, Sherri Stoner
▶ Innocent young Carol is convicted and sentenced to nightmarish reform school where she encounters Bible-spouting warden Danning, nasty cell-block matron Ast, and tough lesbian inmate Williams. Campy send-up of women-behind-bars pics has a few yuks but is generally flimsy excuse for hair-pulling brawls and many shower scenes. Williams was former singer for punk group the Plasmatics; Ast appeared in numerous Andy Warhol films.
Dist.: New World

REGGAE SUNSPLASH 1980
★ **NR Documentary/Music 1:47**
☑ Adult situations
Dir: Stefan Paul *Cast:* Bob Marley, Peter Tosh, Third World Band, Burning Spear
▶ Concert footage of 1979's Montego Bay Sunsplash Festival, featuring reggae stars Marley, Tosh, Burning Spear, and Third World. Performances are intercut with backstage interviews. Sloppily shot, with a cloudy political point of view. Worth seeing only if you're a fan of the musicians involved.
Dist.: SVS

REINCARNATION OF PETER PROUD, THE 1975
★ ★ **R Mystery-Suspense 1:45**
☑ Nudity, adult situations, explicit language, violence
Dir: J. Lee Thompson *Cast:* Michael Sarrazin, Jennifer O'Neill, Margot Kidder, Cornelia Sharpe, Paul Hecht, Tony Stephano
▶ Young professor Sarrazin discovers he's inhabited by spirit of cheating husband killed by angry wife Kidder years ago. Kidder realizes Sarrazin is her husband reincarnated and feels some of her original passion return. Matters grow more complex when Kidder's daughter O'Neill falls for Sarrazin. Adaptation of Max Ehrlich's best-selling novel devotes considerable effort to character development, unusual for occult yarns.
Dist.: Vestron

REIVERS, THE 1969
★ ★ ★ ★ **PG Comedy 1:47**
☑ Adult situations, explicit language
Dir: Mark Rydell *Cast:* Steve McQueen, Sharon Farrell, Will Geer, Michael Constantine, Rupert Crosse, Mitch Vogel
▶ At the turn of the century, young rich boy Vogel, chauffeur McQueen, and McQueen's black buddy Crosse drive an expensive auto from Mississippi to Memphis. There Vogel samples the fare at a bordello as McQueen ro-

mances vet hooker Farrell. When Crosse trades car for racehorse, the trio must finagle its return to save Vogel from paying the consequences. Colorful yarn peopled by eccentrics is based on William Faulkner's last novel.
Dist.: CBS/Fox

REJUVENATOR, THE 1988
☆ R Horror 1:30
☑ Explicit language, graphic violence
Dir: Brian Thomas Jones   *Cast:* Vivian Lanko, John MacKay, James Hogue, Katell Pleven, Marcus Powell, Jessica Dublin
▶ Aging actress Dublin pays doctor MacKay to develop a youth serum. The formula works, turning the elderly woman into younger Lanko, but then an unfortunate side effect occurs: Lanko becomes a murderous, brain-eating monster. Frightening, fast-paced, but grisly horror flick.
Dist.: SVS

RELENTLESS 1989
★ ★ ★ R Mystery-Suspense 1:32
☑ Nudity, adult situations, explicit language
Dir: William Lustig   *Cast:* Judd Nelson, Robert Loggia, Leo Rossi, Meg Foster, Patrick O'Bryan
▶ Los Angeles serial killer Nelson randomly picks victims out of the phone book and strikes. Brief flashbacks trace the root of the maniac's psychosis. Meanwhile, bickering cops Rossi and Loggia close in on him. Gripping, tautly directed thriller has complex characters and sharp dialogue, but sometimes goes over the edge into unintentional laughter. Off-center casting of Nelson succeeds. (CC)
Dist.: RCA/Columbia

REMBRANDT 1936 British
★ ★ ★ ★ NR Biography 1:26 B&W
Dir: Alexander Korda   *Cast:* Charles Laughton, Gertrude Lawrence, Elsa Lanchester, Edward Chapman, Walter Hudd, Roger Livesey
▶ Laughton's restrained performance dominates this romanticized version of the final three decades in the master Dutch painter's life. Newly widowed, Rembrandt turns to his housekeeper and sometime-model Lawrence for companionship. Crippling debts and a third marriage to his maid Lanchester leave him on the brink of senility. While not factually accurate, film is an honest, incisive study of the creative process. Magnificent photography illustrates the sources of Rembrandt's inspiration.
Dist.: Nelson

REMOTE CONTROL 1988
☆ R Sci-Fi 1:28
☑ Explicit language, violence
Dir: Jeff Lieberman   *Cast:* Kevin Dillon, Deborah Goodrich, Christopher Wynne, Frank Beddor, Jennifer Tilly, Bert Remsen
▶ Aliens fabricate sci-fi home video that sends viewers on homicidal rampage. Vid

store employee Dillon is fingered by police for subsequent murders and must go on lam with boss Wynne and dream girl Goodrich while attempting to thwart alien plan to take over world by videocassette. Less-than-serious sci-fi mixes suspense and inside jokes. Kids and teens will enjoy it the most.
Dist.: IVE

REMO WILLIAMS: THE ADVENTURE BEGINS 1985
★ ★ ★ ★ PG-13 Action-Adventure 2:01
☑ Explicit language, violence
Dir: Guy Hamilton   *Cast:* Fred Ward, Joel Grey, Wilford Brimley, Kate Mulgrew, J. A. Preston, George Coe
▶ Tough New York City cop Ward is unwillingly enlisted by government higher-up Brimley to assassinate bad guys beyond the reach of justice. After training in martial arts and Zen from oriental mystic Grey, Ward is thrust into conspiracy so elaborate he barely has time for romantic interest Mulgrew. Live-action comic-book movie, based on best-selling pulp novels, boasts impressive stunts and a shrewd turn from Grey, who tells Ward "You move like a pregnant yak."
Dist.: HBO

RENEGADES 1989
★ ★ ★ ★ R Action-Adventure 1:47
☑ Adult situations, explicit language, violence
Dir: Jack Sholder   *Cast:* Kiefer Sutherland, Lou Diamond Phillips, Jami Gertz, Rob Knepper, Bill Smitrovich, Floyd Westerman
▶ Maverick Philadelphia undercover cop Sutherland and Lakota Sioux Phillips band together to snare slimy thief Knepper who has killed Phillips's brother and stolen the sacred Lakota from a Native American museum. Fabulously staged action sequences make up for implausible plot and mystical mumbo jumbo. (CC)
Dist.: MCA

RENT-A-COP 1988
★ ★ ★ R Action-Adventure 1:36
☑ Explicit language, violence
Dir: Jerry London   *Cast:* Burt Reynolds, Liza Minnelli, James Remar, Richard Masur, Dionne Warwick, Robby Benson
▶ Reduced to working as security guard, ex-cop Reynolds is hired as a bodyguard by Minnelli, a high-priced hooker who witnessed a murderous drug bust. Suspects include drug dealer Remar, cop-gone-bad Masur, and high tech madam Warwick, among others. No surprises and few sparks from this poorly plotted shoot-'em-up. (CC)
Dist.: HBO

RENTED LIPS 1988
★ ★ R Comedy 1:22
☑ Nudity, adult situations, explicit language
Dir: Robert Downey   *Cast:* Martin Mull, Dick Shawn, Jennifer Tilly, Robert Downey, Jr., Edy Williams, Kenneth Mars

▶ Mull and Shawn, documentary filmmakers of such epics as *Hello, Mr. Spermwhale*, are lured by promise of funds for pic on Indian farming techniques into taking over helm of porno film stalled in midshoot by director's death. Amid on-set mayhem, including romance between Mull and ditzy singer Tilly and obstruction by fundamentalist preacher Mars, filmmakers attempt to shoot both porno and docu as musicals.
Dist.: IVE

REPO MAN 1984
★ R Action-Adventure/Comedy 1:32
☑ Adult situations, explicit language, violence
Dir: Alex Cox *Cast:* Harry Dean Stanton, Emilio Estevez, Olivia Barash, Tracey Walter, Sy Richardson, Susan Barnes
▶ Middle-class punk Estevez learns how to repossess cars from mentor Stanton, an old-timer who knows all the tricks of the trade. They get involved with pretty Barash and a Chevy Malibu worth $20,000 to someone. Imagine their surprise when they find radioactive aliens in the trunk of the Chevy. Zany and offbeat low-budget film features good performances from the leads, but may be too weird for mainstream audiences.
Dist.: MCA

REPORT TO THE COMMISSIONER 1975
★ ★ PG Action-Adventure 1:52
☑ Adult situations, explicit language, violence
Dir: Milton Katselas *Cast:* Michael Moriarty, Susan Blakely, Yaphet Kotto, Hector Elizondo, Tony King, Michael McGuire
▶ During bust of drug czar King, rookie detective Moriarty kills undercover agent Blakely, not realizing she's also a cop. Other cops, including Moriarty's partner Kotto, derail investigation into Blakely's death. Moriarty and Kotto try to do their jobs but get caught in bureaucratic infighting. Uneven mix of character study and social commentary is not for action fans. Look for Richard Gere in screen debut as a sleazy pimp.
Dist.: MGM/UA

REPULSION 1965 British
★ NR Mystery-Suspense 1:45 B&W
☑ Rape, adult situations, violence
Dir: Roman Polanski *Cast:* Catherine Deneuve, Ian Hendry, Patrick Wymark, John Fraser, Yvonne Furneaux
▶ Extremely repressed Belgian manicurist Deneuve lives in London with her sister Furneaux. She is driven into a mad, murderous rampage when Furneaux brings a lover home and then goes away for two weeks. Scary and controversial thriller builds shocks after a slow opening.
Dist.: Video Dimensions

REQUIEM FOR A HEAVYWEIGHT 1962
★ ★ NR Drama/Sports 1:40 B&W
Dir: Ralph Nelson *Cast:* Anthony Quinn,

Jackie Gleason, Mickey Rooney, Julie Harris, Stanley Adams, Cassius Clay
▶ Over-the-hill boxer Quinn is advised to retire by doctor after beating from younger, faster fighter Clay (before he changed his name to Muhammad Ali). Gleason, Quinn's manager, has lost large bet to mob and fears loss of his meal ticket. Gleason sabotages attempt by social worker Harris to land decent job for Quinn and persuades him to try pro wrestling. Feature version of Rod Serling's Emmy-winning teledrama is still fine, but extra scenes are redundant. Superb Quinn and Gleason, plus cameo by boxing legend Jack Dempsey.
Dist.: MGM/UA

RESCUE, THE 1988
★ ★ ★ PG Action-Adventure 1:38
☑ Explicit language, mild violence
Dir: Ferdinand Fairfax *Cast:* Kevin Dillon, Christina Harnos, Marc Price, Ned Vaughn, Charles Haid, Edward Albert
▶ Four American servicemen are captured by the North Koreans. When the State Department abandons a rescue plan, the captured men's Navy brat offspring (led by punky teen Dillon) stage their own daring mission to liberate their fathers. Flag-waver provides several exciting chase scenes.
Dist.: Buena Vista

RESTLESS 1978 Italian
☆ R Drama 1:15
☑ Adult situations, explicit language, violence
Dir: George Pan Cosmatos *Cast:* Raquel Welch, Richard Johnson, Jack Hawkins, Flora Robson, Renato Romano, Frank Wolff
▶ After his father's death, Johnson leaves England and returns home to Cyprus, where he starts seeing Romano's unhappy wife Welch. When the lovers allow Romano to die in a drowning accident, they face the wrath of local townspeople. Coarse melodrama has little dialogue and even less character development. The sexiest thing Welch does is stomp grapes.
Dist.: Vidmark

RESURRECTION 1980
★ ★ ★ ★ PG Drama 1:43
☑ Adult situations, explicit language
Dir: Daniel Petrie *Cast:* Ellen Burstyn, Sam Shepard, Eva Le Gallienne, Richard Farnsworth, Roberts Blossom
▶ Burstyn, after car accident and near-death experience (represented in a visually eerie sequence), discovers she has a miraculous power to heal others. Her lover Shepard is uneasy about her newfound ability. Simply told yet powerful and fascinating. Graceful, stirring performance by Burstyn (Oscar-nominated, as was Le Gallienne as her grandmother).
Dist.: MCA

RETALIATOR, THE 1987
☆ R Action-Adventure 1:31

☑ Nudity, adult situations, explicit language, violence
Dir: Allan Holzman *Cast:* Robert Ginty, Sandahl Bergman, James Booth, Alex Courtney, Paul W. Walker, Louise Caire Clark
▶ Mercenary Ginty captures Mideast terrorist Bergman; CIA scientists turn her into cyborg programmed to kill her PLO colleagues. But Bergman short-circuits and embarks on rampage against American agents. Can Ginty stop the robot? Standard action exploitation suffers from mechanical acting.
Dist.: Media

RETREAT, HELL! 1952
★ ★ NR War 1:35 B&W
Dir: Joseph H. Lewis *Cast:* Frank Lovejoy, Richard Carlson, Russ Tamblyn, Anita Louise, Ned Young
▶ Early in the Korean War, Marine reservists like Carlson are called to active duty, where they train raw recruits and land at Inchon. They fight their way to within sixty miles of the Chosin reservoir, but must withdraw when the Chinese enter the war. Based on the actual bloody and heroic Marine retreat from Chosin, no-nonsense battle pic is realistically grim.
Dist.: Republic

RETRIBUTION 1987
★ R Horror 1:47
☑ Nudity, adult situations, explicit language, graphic violence
Dir: Guy Magar *Cast:* Dennis Lipscomb, Leslie Wing, Suzanne Snyder, Jeff Pomerantz, Hoyt Axton
▶ Lipscomb fails to commit suicide, then is tortured by recurring nightmares involving murder. Sympathetic shrink Wing can't help. When his gruesome dreams become a reality, Lipscomb becomes number-one suspect of detective Axton. Gut-level psychological thriller has well-executed special effects and tight pacing.
Dist.: Virgin

RETURN, THE 1980
★ ★ NR Sci-Fi 1:31
☑ Explicit language, violence
Dir: Greydon Clark *Cast:* Jan-Michael Vincent, Cybill Shepherd, Martin Landau, Raymond Burr, Neville Brand
▶ Deputy Vincent and scientist Shepherd, having witnessed UFO as children, are reunited in a New Mexico town where they confront an alien visitor. Although story is somewhat implausible, pleasing special effects and likable leads succeed in evoking a sense of wonder.
Dist.: HBO

RETURN FROM THE RIVER KWAI 1988
★ ★ ★ NR War 2:00
☑ Explicit language, violence
Dir: Andrew V. McLaglen *Cast:* Edward Fox, Denholm Elliott, Christopher Penn, Timothy Bottoms, George Takei
▶ In 1945 Thailand, Allied POWs are being shipped to Japan for factory work; Aussie Bottoms plots escape although British officer Fox is doubtful. American pilot Penn eventually comes to their aid. Gets off to a flat start but improves as it goes along. Good performances and a rousing ending, even if the film doesn't live up to the high standards of the original.
Dist.: HBO

RETURN FROM WITCH MOUNTAIN 1978
★ ★ ★ ★ G Action-Adventure/Family 1:33
Dir: John Hough *Cast:* Bette Davis, Christopher Lee, Kim Richards, Ike Eisenmann, Jack Soo, Anthony James
▶ Psychic-powered alien siblings Richards and Eisenmann vacation in Los Angeles. When Eisenmann is kidnapped by mad-scientist Lee and cohort Davis, Richards teams with a street gang to rescue him. First-rate sequel to Disney's 1975 *Escape to Witch Mountain* has appealing performances by Davis, Lee, and the children.
Dist.: Buena Vista

RETURN OF A MAN CALLED HORSE 1976
★ ★ ★ PG Western 2:05
☑ Graphic violence
Dir: Irvin Kershner *Cast:* Richard Harris, Gale Sondergaard, Geoffrey Lewis, William Lucking, Jorge Luke, Enrique Lucero
▶ In 1830, English lord Harris, bored with life among whites, returns to the Yellow Hands, his adopted Indian tribe in America. Tribe is suffering under the attacks of trader Lewis, but Harris reverses the trend after undergoing the breast-piercing Sun Vow ritual once more. As exciting and memorable as the original. Excellent photography but excruciating torture sequences.
Dist.: CBS/Fox

RETURN OF CAPTAIN INVINCIBLE, THE 1983 Australian
★ PG Action-Adventure/Comedy 1:42
☑ Explicit language, mild violence
Dir: Phillipe Mora *Cast:* Alan Arkin, Christopher Lee, Kate Fitzpatrick, Bill Hunter, Graham Kennedy, Michael Pate
▶ American superhero Arkin has become a drunk in Australia after the 1950s McCarthy political climate tarnished his reputation. However, when villainous Lee threatens New York City, the current U.S. President summons the retired Captain Invincible back into action. Offbeat opus features musical numbers by *Rocky Horror Picture Show* team of Richard Hartley and Richard O'Brien.
Dist.: Magnum

RETURN OF FRANK JAMES, THE 1940
★ ★ ★ ★ NR Western 1:33
Dir: Fritz Lang *Cast:* Henry Fonda, Gene Tierney, Jackie Cooper, Henry Hull, John Carradine, Donald Meek, Charles Tannen
▶ Continuation of 1939's *Jesse James* opens with Jesse's murder at the hands of the Ford brothers (Carradine, Tannen). When they're

pardoned, brother Frank (Fonda) vows revenge. Framed for an accidental death during a robbery, he is brought to trial while Carradine gloats in the audience. With the help of intrepid reporter Tierney (in her film debut), justice prevails. Trim, fast-paced Western with a winning performance by Fonda and good photography.
Dist.: CBS/Fox

RETURN OF JOSEY WALES, THE 1986
★★ NR Western 1:30
☑ Rape, explicit language, violence
Dir: Michael Parks ***Cast:*** Michael Parks, Raphael Campos, Charlie McCoy, Bob Magruder, Paco Vela
▶ When marauding Mexican soldiers kidnap his friend and rape and kill his barmaid girlfriend, outlaw Josey Wales (Parks) seeks revenge. The Mexican commander plots several ambushes but Parks survives. Laborious sequel to *The Outlaw Josey Wales* finds uncharismatic Parks failing to effectively follow in Clint Eastwood's footsteps.
Dist.: Magnum

RETURN OF MARTIN GUERRE, THE 1983 French
★ NR Drama 1:51
☑ Adult situations, violence
Dir: Daniel Vigne ***Cast:*** Gerard Depardieu, Nathalie Baye, Roger Planchon, Bernard Pierre Donnadieu, Maurice Barrier
▶ In sixteenth-century France, peasant Martin Guerre leaves wife Baye and child. Nine years later, stranger Depardieu arrives in town and claims to be Guerre; Baye vouches for him but others are not so sure. Absorbing story with fine acting, beautiful photography, and expert period details; slow pacing requires patience. [S]
Dist.: Nelson

RETURN OF SWAMP THING, THE 1989
★ PG-13 Sci-Fi 1:26
☑ Explicit language, violence
Dir: Jim Wynorski ***Cast:*** Louis Jourdan, Heather Locklear, Sarah Douglas, Dick Durock, Joey Sagal, Ace Mask
▶ Continuing adventure of the DC Comics creature, a former scientist turned big and slimy after tangling with researcher Jourdan in the original. Swamp Thing (Durock) again takes on his old enemy, who is trying to use stepdaughter Locklear in a genetic experiment. Beast rescues beauty; can love be far behind? Certainly silly but has appeal to the younger set.
Dist.: RCA/Columbia

RETURN OF THE BADMEN 1948
★★ NR Western 1:31 B&W
Dir: Ray Enright ***Cast:*** Randolph Scott, Robert Ryan, Anne Jeffreys, George "Gabby" Hayes, Steve Brodie, Lex Barker
▶ Retired marshal Scott is forced to don his guns again when the Sundance Kid (Ryan) assembles a who's who of criminals to terrorize the Oklahoma Territory. When not fighting the Youngers, Daltons, and other desperadoes, Scott tries to reform gunslinger Jeffreys. Fast but not very credible; Ryan has the most impact.
Dist.: Turner

RETURN OF THE DRAGON 1974 Hong Kong
★★ R Martial Arts 1:31
☑ Explicit language, violence
Dir: Bruce Lee ***Cast:*** Bruce Lee, Chuck Norris, Nora Miao, Huang Chung Hsun
▶ In Rome, Lee helps family trying to stop evil gang from taking over their restaurant. Among the bad guys: fellow martial arts master Norris. Bad dubbing, ho-hum crime plot, stiff characters and dialogue, but Lee and Norris provide plenty of acrobatic action. Lee, who also wrote the screenplay, died before film's completion.
Dist.: CBS/Fox

RETURN OF THE FLY 1959
★ NR Horror 1:20 B&W
Dir: Edward Bernds ***Cast:*** Vincent Price, Brett Halsey, David Frankham, John Sutton, Dan Seymour
▶ Halsey, son of the ill-fated scientist in 1958's *The Fly*, decides to repeat his dad's work. He too becomes a half-man/half-fly when spy Frankham disrupts the experiment. Halsey's uncle Price helps him. Okay genre effort not in the league of its predecessor.
Dist.: CBS/Fox

RETURN OF THE JEDI 1983
★★★★★ PG Sci-Fi/Action-Adventure 2:12
☑ Adult situations, violence
Dir: Richard Marquand ***Cast:*** Mark Hamill, Harrison Ford, Carrie Fisher, Billy Dee Williams, Anthony Daniels, Alec Guinness
▶ Much-awaited finale to the Star Wars trilogy. Luke (Hamill), Han (Ford), Lando (Williams), Princess Leia (Fisher), and their robot pals are befriended by furry Ewoks in their final battle with Darth Vader and the evil Empire. Along the way, Luke learns the series's most shocking secret: Vader's true identity. Smashing sequel to the elaborate space opera introduces colorful new creatures and features stunning three-way battle climax, adding thrills to the tried-and-true formula. Most exciting scene: the flying chase through the forest. Special effects won an Oscar. **(CC)**
Dist.: CBS/Fox

RETURN OF THE KILLER TOMATOES 1988
★ PG Comedy 1:38
☑ Explicit language
Dir: John DeBello ***Cast:*** Anthony Stark, George Clooney, Karen Mistal, Steve Lundquist, John Astin
▶ Tomatoes have been outlawed in this sequel to *Attack of the Killer Tomatoes*, which means the pizzas delivered by Stark have other ingredients. He falls for lovely Mistal, not knowing that she is the product of mad pro-

fessor Astin's experiment to turn tomatoes into people and take over the world. Innocuous humor has more misses than hits.
Dist.: New World

RETURN OF THE LIVING DEAD, THE 1985
★ ★ R Horror/Comedy 1:31
☑ Nudity, explicit language, graphic violence
Dir: Dan O'Bannon *Cast:* Clu Gulager, James Karen, Don Calfa, Thom Mathews, Beverly Randolph, Jewel Shepard
▶ Medical supply house workers Karen and Mathews accidentally bring zombies back to life by releasing gas from a sealed government drum. Some genuine laughs, clever situations, and pleasing tongue-in-cheek acting, but quite gory; brain-eating zombies will not be to everyone's taste.
Dist.: HBO

RETURN OF THE LIVING DEAD II, THE 1988
★ ★ R Horror/Comedy 1:29
☑ Explicit language, violence
Dir: Ken Wiederhorn *Cast:* James Karen, Thom Mathews, Michael Kenworthy, Marsha Dietlein, Suzanne Snyder, Dana Ashbrook
▶ Can of zombie gas falls off an Army truck and kids break it open. Big mistake: the gas floats into the local graveyard and brings the dead to life to menace the locals. Some laughs and gory effects but few surprises; the original film had a lot more humor. **(CC)**
Dist.: Warner

RETURN OF THE PINK PANTHER, THE 1975
British
★ ★ ★ ★ G Comedy 1:53
Dir: Blake Edwards *Cast:* Peter Sellers, Christopher Plummer, Catherine Schell, Herbert Lom, Peter Arne, Burt Kwouk
▶ Pink Panther diamond is stolen and ex-thief Plummer is blamed. While Plummer seeks real thief to clear his name, chief inspector Lom reluctantly puts blundering detective Sellers on the trail of the crooks. Usual assortment of pratfalls, sight gags, and quotable Clouseauisms results. Fourth Pink Panther picture featured return of inimitable Sellers as Inspector Clouseau after Alan Arkin tried role in third of series.
Dist.: CBS/Fox

RETURN OF THE SECAUCUS 7 1981
★ R Comedy/Drama 1:48
☑ Nudity, adult situations, explicit language
Dir: John Sayles *Cast:* Mark Arnott, Gordon Clapp, Maggie Renzi, Karen Trott, John Sayles
▶ Earnest, intelligent, low budget directorial deubt by Sayles predates similar but more polished *The Big Chill.* Seven political activists from the 1960s, now in their thirties, reunite to spend a weekend in New Hampshire. The group includes a hippie couple, two Washington activists, and several grown-up children who refuse to face the responsibilities of

adulthood. Wall-to-wall talk, but much of it is interesting.
Dist.: RCA/Columbia

RETURN OF THE SEVEN 1966
★ ★ ★ NR Western 1:36
Dir: Burt Kennedy *Cast:* Yul Brynner, Robert Fuller, Warren Oates, Jordan Christopher, Claude Akins, Emilio Fernandez, Rudy Acosta, Elisa Montes, Fernando Rey
▶ Still dressed in black, Winchester-toting Brynner goes to disreputable haunts and recruits a group of gunmen to help him defend a Mexican village being oppressed by local bully Fernandez. No small amount of lead is expended in this rougher sequel to *The Magnificent Seven,* but the result is merely a standard Western of its period, with Brynner the only returning cast member from the original seven.
Dist.: MGM/UA

RETURN OF THE SOLDIER, THE 1985 British
★ NR Drama 1:42
☑ Adult situations, explicit language
Dir: Alan Bridges *Cast:* Alan Bates, Julie Christie, Glenda Jackson, Ann-Margret, Ian Holm
▶ Soldier Bates, shellshocked and amnesiac after World War I, returns home. Snobby wife Christie, old flame Jackson, and Ann-Margret, the cousin who secretly loves him, must deal with his condition. Heavy, ponderous, and depressing despite fine performances and classy production values.
Dist.: HBO

RETURN OF THE VAMPIRE, THE 1943
★ NR Horror 1:09 B&W
Dir: Lew Landers *Cast:* Bela Lugosi, Frieda Inescort, Nina Foch, Roland Varno, Miles Mander, Matt Willis
▶ Lugosi has slept soundly since being despatched in 1931's *Dracula,* but after being awakened by Nazi bombs in World War II London, he goes on a cape-swirling rampage in the company of local werewolf Willis. Neither scary nor atmospheric.
Dist.: RCA/Columbia

RETURN TO HORROR HIGH 1987
★ R Horror 1:35
☑ Nudity, adult situations, explicit language, violence
Dir: Bill Froehlich *Cast:* Lori Lethin, Brendan Hughes, Alex Rocco, Scott Jacoby, Vince Edwards, Maureen McCormick
▶ Movie company shoots at a high school where murders took place a few years back. Someone starts knocking off crew members. A few clever moments elevate this above standard slasher fare, but not many scares and the jokey finale will leave viewers feeling cheated.
Dist.: New World

RETURN TO MACON COUNTY 1975
★ ★ PG Action-Adventure 1:30

☑ Explicit language, violence
Dir: Richard Compton   *Cast:* Nick Nolte, Don Johnson, Robin Mattson, Robert Viharo, Eugene Daniels, Matt Greene
▶ Hot-rodding pals Nolte and Johnson pick up crazy Mattson for drag duel with toughs Daniels and Greene and run-in with cop Viharo. Cheapo exploitation flick used allure of sex and violence to cash in on the success of *Macon County Line*. Young Nolte and Johnson are wasted on inane script.
Dist.: Vestron

RETURN TO OZ 1985
★ ★ **PG Fantasy/Family 1:50**
☑ Violence
Dir: Walter Murch   *Cast:* Fairuza Balk, Nicol Williamson, Jean Marsh, Piper Laurie, Matt Clark
▶ Dorothy (Balk) returns to the Emerald City, now turned into a wasteland by the evil Nome King (Williamson) and Princess Mombi (Marsh). Dorothy sets off to restore order with the help of her talking chicken, a moosehead, a tin man, and a pumpkinhead. Balk is appealing and there are some nice special effects but downbeat tone may alienate those looking for a lighthearted sequel to *The Wizard of Oz*. Dorothy's mechanical companions lack the charm and humanity of their predecessors.
Dist.: Buena Vista

RETURN TO SALEM'S LOT 1987
★ **R Horror 1:40**
☑ Nudity, adult situations, explicit language, violence
Dir: Larry Cohen   *Cast:* Michael Moriarty, Samuel Fuller, Evelyn Keyes, Andrew Duggan, June Havoc
▶ Sequel to TV movie based on the Stephen King novel. Anthropologist Moriarty arrives in Maine for research and soon learns the place is infested with vampires. When Moriarty's son Duggan appears to be on his way to eternal life of bloodsucking, dad teams with Nazi/vampire killer Fuller to rescue son and escape from Salem's Lot. Average vampire effort plays for laughs with scene-stealing turn by legendary director Fuller. History will note this the first film to discuss AIDS risk to vampires.
Dist.: Warner

RETURN TO SNOWY RIVER 1988 Australian
★ ★ ★ **PG Western 1:40**
☑ Explicit language, mild violence
Dir: Geoff Burrowes   *Cast:* Tom Burlinson, Sigrid Thornton, Brian Dennehy, Nicholas Eadie, Mark Hembrow, Bryan Marshall
▶ Adventurer Burlinson returns to reclaim beloved Thornton but faces opposition from dad Dennehy and banker's son Eadie, who covets her for himself. Burlinson pursues when Eadie steals his horses. Sequel to *The Man From Snowy River* sustains hardy formula with

grand, wide-open scenery, handsome horseflesh and humans, and swift pace.
Dist.: Buena Vista

REUBEN, REUBEN 1983
★ ★ **R Comedy/Drama 1:40**
☑ Brief nudity, adult situations, explicit language
Dir: Robert Ellis Miller   *Cast:* Tom Conti, Kelly McGillis, Roberts Blossom, Cynthia Harris, Lois Smith, Kara Wilson
▶ Conti plays a freeloading poet who's lazy, irresponsible, and fascinating to women. A puckish Scotsman, he's transplanted to Connecticut and has roving eyes for farm-bred college girl McGillis. Sophisticated fare, adapted from the Peter DeVries novel, was nominated for two Oscars (Best Actor and Screenplay). **(CC)**
Dist.: CBS/Fox

REUNION IN FRANCE 1942
★ **NR Drama 1:44 B&W**
Dir: Jules Dassin   *Cast:* Joan Crawford, John Wayne, Philip Dorn, Reginald Owen, Albert Basserman, John Carradine
▶ In Nazi-occupied France, Crawford breaks up with her boyfriend Dorn when she discovers he is a collaborator. She comes to the aid of wounded American pilot Wayne and hides him from the Germans. Romance develops but she must contact Dorn to ensure Wayne's safety. Clumsy combination of wartime romance and action. Stars are mismatched but exude charisma.
Dist.: MGM/UA

REVENGE 1990
★ ★ ★ ★ **R Mystery-Suspense 2:04**
☑ Nudity, adult situations, explicit language, violence
Dir: Tony Scott   *Cast:* Kevin Costner, Anthony Quinn, Madeleine Stowe, Sally Kirkland, Joaquin Martinez, James Gammon
▶ After retiring from the Air Force, Costner visits old friend Quinn in Mexico and is drawn to pal's beautiful young wife Stowe. When adulterous affair occurs, Quinn has violent vengeance taken out on the lovers; Costner recuperates and seeks his own revenge. Sexy, steamy suspense, played with passion and punch. Based on the novel by Jim Harrison. **(CC)**
Dist.: RCA/Columbia

REVENGE OF THE CHEERLEADERS 1976
☆ **R Comedy 1:28**
☑ Nudity, adult humor
Dir: Richard Lerner   *Cast:* Jeril Woods, Rainbeaux Smith, Helen Lang, Patrice Rohmer, Susie Elene
▶ Trouble for Aloha High, as Board of Education is planning to close it down and merge it with a vocational school. It's up to Aloha's cheerleaders, including Woods, Smith, and Lang, to stop the merger, using efforts like

drugging the Board and setting off an orgy. Nonamusing teen comedy.
Dist.: Vestron

REVENGE OF THE DEAD 1960
☆ **NR Horror 1:00 B&W**
Dir: Edward D. Wood, Jr.   *Cast:* Criswell, Tor Johnson, Maila "Vampira" Nurmi, Keene Duncan, Valda Hansen, Duke Moore
▶ Duncan is Dr. Acula (get it?), a bogus psychic who teams with henchpeople Johnson and Hansen to stage phony seances. Detective Moore investigates, but the doc's plan backfires when the dead are resurrected to menace him. Typical camp monstrosity from director Wood. Also known as *Night of the Ghouls*.
Dist.: Nostalgia

REVENGE OF THE NERDS 1984
★ ★ ★ ★ **R Comedy 1:30**
☑ Nudity, adult situations, explicit language
Dir: Jeff Kanew   *Cast:* Robert Carradine, Anthony Edwards, Curtis Armstrong, Andrew Cassese, Julie Montgomery, Melanie Meyrink
▶ College freshmen Carradine and Edwards, humiliated by loutish jocks and rejected by cheerleaders, enlist fellow campus outcasts and join previously all-black fraternity. Nerds then gain a measure of vengeance in resulting rivalry with the elitists. Carradine and Edwards excel as the geek leads in this raucous romp. **(CC)**
Dist.: CBS/Fox

REVENGE OF THE NERDS II: NERDS IN PARADISE 1987
★ ★ **PG-13 Comedy 1:29**
☑ Brief nudity, explicit language
Dir: Joe Roth   *Cast:* Robert Carradine, Curtis Armstrong, Timothy Busfield, Andrew Cassese, Larry B. Scott, Courtney Thorne-Smith
▶ The house of geeks, played by Carradine and crew, heads south to Fort Lauderdale for an interfraternity conference. Arch-rival jocks nearly sabotage fun in the sun, but you can't keep a good nerd down, especially when he steals a tank to assure entry into exclusive meetings. Popular sequel features more wacky high jinks, including romance for Carradine with comely hotel clerk Thorne-Smith and nerd pride rap number. **(CC)**
Dist.: CBS/Fox

REVENGE OF THE NINJA 1983
★ ★ ★ **R Martial Arts 1:28**
☑ Nudity, explicit language, graphic violence
Dir: Sam Firstenberg   *Cast:* Sho Kosugi, Keith Vitali, Virgil Frye, Arthur Roberts, Mario Gallo, Grace Oshita
▶ Kosugi, a Japanese immigrant in U.S., conceals ninja heritage until unscrupulous Roberts kidnaps his son. Then it's no-blows-barred action, capped by rooftop free-for-all. Sequel to *Enter the Ninja*, also starring Kosugi (who

choreographed fight scenes). For die-hard kung fu fans.
Dist.: MGM/UA

REVENGE OF THE PINK PANTHER 1978
★ ★ ★ ★ **PG Comedy 1:39**
☑ Explicit language
Dir: Blake Edwards   *Cast:* Peter Sellers, Herbert Lom, Dyan Cannon, Robert Webber, Burt Kwouk, Robert Loggia
▶ Chief Inspector Clouseau (Sellers) is on the loose again in fifth outing (and last for Sellers) of the perennially popular series. In Paris, American heroin dealer Webber plans to kill Clouseau to prove his clout to Mafia. Webber's secretary Cannon spills the beans to Clouseau and the duo team up to thwart heroin ring in Hong Kong climax. Standard Sellers vehicle includes many disguises (look for takeoffs on Toulouse-Lautrec and Don Corleone) and customary brushes with addled former boss Lom and karate-crazy valet Kwouk. Plenty of mileage left.
Dist.: CBS/Fox

REVOLUTION 1985
★ ★ **PG Drama 2:01**
☑ Explicit language, graphic violence
Dir: Hugh Hudson   *Cast:* Al Pacino, Donald Sutherland, Nastassja Kinski, Joan Plowright, Dexter Fletcher, Annie Lennox
▶ Large-scale spectacle of the American Revolution seen from the eyes of Pacino, a New York trapper who becomes an unwilling rebel when his son Fletcher is drafted into the British Army by villainous sergeant Sutherland. He joins a movement that includes wealthy aristocrat Kinski and a loud "Liberty Woman" (rock star Lennox). Stirring battle scenes can't salvage miscasting, incongruous accents, and English locations doubling as American landmarks. **(CC)**
Dist.: Warner

RHINESTONE 1984
★ ★ **PG Musical/Comedy 1:51**
☑ Explicit language
Dir: Bob Clark   *Cast:* Sylvester Stallone, Dolly Parton, Richard Farnsworth, Ron Leibman, Tim Thomerson, Steven Apostle Pec
▶ Country-western singer Parton bets club owner Leibman she can turn anyone into passable country crooner in two weeks. Leibman selects shiftless cabbie Stallone as guinea pig. Parton whisks Stallone off to ol' Tennessee home where she and pappy Farnsworth turn him into Roy Rogers with muscles in time for acid test at Leibman's club. Formulaic but good-natured clash of cultures with superior supporting cast. **(CC)**
Dist.: CBS/Fox

RHINOCEROS 1974
☆ **PG Comedy/Drama 1:44**
☑ Adult situations, explicit language
Dir: Tom O'Horgan   *Cast:* Zero Mostel, Gene Wilder, Karen Black, Robert Weil, Joe Silver

▶ In a city where people are turning into rhinos, meek clerk Wilder tries to hold on to his humanity, even after his girlfriend and best friend both experience the metamorphosis. Eugene Ionesco's anti-conformist, absurdist play translates disappointingly to film because of O'Horgan's unsubtle direction. Talented cast tries too hard. Music by Galt MacDermot.
Dist.: CBS/Fox

RICH AND FAMOUS 1981
★ ★ ★ R Drama 1:57
☑ Nudity, adult situations, explicit language
Dir: George Cukor *Cast:* Jacqueline Bisset, Candice Bergen, David Selby, Hart Bochner, Steven Hill, Meg Ryan
▶ Glossy remake of 1943's *Old Acquaintance* examines a twenty-year friendly rivalry between two Smith College grads: Bisset, a serious novelist who must settle for critical rather than financial success, and Bergen, author of best-selling soap operas. Despite explicit language and preoccupation with sex, doesn't improve on the original. Cukor's last film.
Dist.: MGM/UA

RICH AND STRANGE 1932 British
★ NR Comedy 1:32 B&W
Dir: Alfred Hitchcock *Cast:* Henry Kendall, Joan Barry, Betty Amann, Percy Marmont, Elsie Randolph, Hannah Jones
▶ Lower-middle-class couple Kendall and Barry inherit a fortune and go on a cruise. Once at sea, the newly rich pair ignore each other for new friends, until a swindler cheats Kendall out of his money. On the way home, they are shipwrecked, and learn the lesson that money isn't everything. Cockeyed bit of fun from director Hitchcock.
Dist.: Sinister

RICHARD PRYOR HERE AND NOW 1983
★ ★ ★ R Documentary/Comedy 1:34
☑ Adult situations, explicit language, adult humor
Dir: Richard Pryor *Cast:* Richard Pryor
▶ Filmed in a Bourbon Street theater in New Orleans, fourth Pryor concert film offers the comedian's caustic and obscene comments on such subjects as his acting career, Ronald Reagan, drunks, and racism. Quirkier, funkier, and sometimes more rambling than his earlier performance films. Not for delicate sensibilities. (CC)
Dist.: RCA/Columbia

RICHARD PRYOR—LIVE IN CONCERT 1979
★ ★ ★ ★ NR Documentary/Comedy 1:18
☑ Explicit language, adult humor
Dir: Jeff Margolis *Cast:* Richard Pryor
▶ First of Pryor's concert films (and arguably the best) records the comedian's rib-tickling reactions to being arrested for shooting his car, suffering a heart attack, and being confronted by his grandmother about cocaine use. Also included are diatribes against macho men and rapists. Uncensored and

uncut Pryor talks a blue streak—strictly for adults.
Dist.: Vestron

RICHARD PRYOR LIVE ON THE SUNSET STRIP 1982
★ ★ ★ R Documentary/Comedy 1:21
☑ Explicit language, adult humor
Dir: Joe Layton *Cast:* Richard Pryor
▶ Third Pryor concert film, shot in Los Angeles' Palladium, is another blistering, hilarious monologue on a variety of controversial subjects, particularly sex. Explicit, provocative, and at times oddly moving, especially when Pryor discusses his freebasing accident. Followed by *Richard Pryor Here and Now.*
Dist.: RCA/Columbia

RICHARD'S THINGS 1981 British
☆ R Drama 1:44
☑ Brief nudity, explicit language
Dir: Anthony Harvey *Cast:* Liv Ullmann, Amanda Redman, Tim Piggott-Smith, Elizabeth Springs, David Markham, Mark Eden
▶ After husband Eden dies, Ullmann receives his belongings in a plastic bag and discovers that he was seeing Redman, a younger woman. Liv adjusts to widowhood and has an affair with her spouse's mistress. Intimate, tasteful melodrama with powerhouse performances compensating for molasses pacing.
Dist.: Nelson

RICHARD III 1956 British
★ ★ ★ NR Drama 2:18
Dir: Laurence Olivier *Cast:* Laurence Olivier, John Gielgud, Ralph Richardson, Claire Bloom, Alec Clunes, Cedric Hardwicke
▶ Olivier is riveting as Shakespeare's hunchback king, a volatile combination of cunning and malice who proved to be England's most dangerous ruler. Excellent support from an outstanding cast, beautiful photography, and meticulous production values showcase Olivier's superb Oscar-nominated interpretation.
Dist.: Nelson

RICH KIDS 1979
★ ★ ★ PG Drama 1:36
☑ Adult situations, explicit language
Dir: Robert M. Young *Cast:* Trini Alvarado, Jeremy Levy, Kathryn Walker, John Lithgow, Paul Dooley, Irene Worth
▶ Twelve-year-old Alvarado knows upper-class New Yorker parents Walker and Lithgow are headed for divorce and seeks advice from classmate Levy, who's already been through the mill. Puppy love and parental manipulation ensue. Lightweight drama examines divorce and its innocent victims with intelligence and conviction, but dry, upscale setting and copious talk may be turnoffs.
Dist.: MGM/UA

RIDDLE OF THE SANDS, THE 1984 British
★ ★ NR Action-Adventure 1:42
Ⓥ Brief nudity, mild violence
Dir: Tony Maylam *Cast:* Michael York,
Jenny Agutter, Simon MacCorkindale, Alan
Badel, Jurgen Andersen, Olga Lowe
▶ College chums York and MacCorkindale
go on sailing venture off northern Germany
and make acquaintance of rich German
yachtsman Badel and his daughter Agutter.
As MacCorkindale romances Agutter, he and
York suspect that Badel is helping to plan a
German invasion of England, and attempt to
thwart the attack on their homeland. Pictur-
esque spy drama too slow for savvy audi-
ences, but fine for older kids.
Dist.: VidAmerica

RIDE IN THE WHIRLWIND 1965
★ ★ G Western 1:22
Dir: Monte Hellman *Cast:* Cameron Mitchell, Jack Nicholson, Tom Filer, Millie Perkins,
Katherine Squire, Harry Dean Stanton
▶ Returning from cattle roundup, cowpokes
Mitchell, Nicholson, and Filer share an innocent meal with Stanton, who turns out to be
the leader of a gang of killers. Pursued across
Utah by murderous vigilantes, Nicholson decides to take homesteader's daughter Perkins
hostage. Standard Western of interest for an
early Nicholson performance (he also wrote
the script). Filmed simultaneously with the superior *The Shooting*.
Dist.: VidAmerica

RIDE LONESOME 1959
★ ★ ★ NR Western 1:13
Dir: Budd Boetticher *Cast:* Randolph Scott,
Karen Steele, Pernell Roberts, James Best,
Lee Van Cleef, James Coburn
▶ Bounty hunter Scott stalks outlaw Best
through a harsh landscape. Joining him are
bandits Roberts and Coburn, who could gain
amnesty with Best's corpse, and Steele, whose
husband has disappeared. Following them
are hostile Indians and Van Cleef, Best's
vengeful brother. In addition to meeting every
genre expectation, superb adult Western has
intelligently realized characters, great dialogue, thoughtful plot, and nice ironic
touches. One of director Boetticher's best,
with fine script by Burt Kennedy.
Dist.: Goodtimes

RIDER ON THE RAIN 1970 French/Italian
★ ★ PG Mystery-Suspense 1:54
Ⓥ Rape, violence
Dir: René Clement *Cast:* Charles Bronson,
Marlene Jobert, Annie Cordy, Jill Ireland,
Gabriele Tinti, Jean Gaven
▶ Jobert plays a French housewife who's
raped by a mysterious stranger. She murders
him in self-defense and hides his body from
the authorities, then is menaced by American
agent Bronson, who claims the rapist stole
$60,000. Unnerving thriller with a thoughtful,
unpredictable script and a polished perform-

ance by Bronson. His real-life wife Ireland has
a small role as the owner of a boutique.
Dist.: Monterey

RIDERS ON THE STORM 1988
★ ★ R Comedy 1:32
Ⓥ Adult situations, explicit language, vio-
lence
Dir: Maurice Phillips *Cast:* Dennis Hopper,
Michael J. Pollard, Eugene Lipinski, James
Aubrey, Al Matthews, Nigel Pegram
▶ Madcap Vietnam veterans, led by Hopper,
monitor American TV from a B-29 crammed
with state-of-the-art technology, jamming po-
litical broadcasts with their own propaganda.
Their latest target is right-wing Presidential
candidate Willa Westinghouse (Pegram). In-
ventive but extremely broad satire is sexist,
racist, bizarre, and only infrequently on target.
Dist.: Nelson

RIDE THE HIGH COUNTRY 1962
★ ★ ★ ★ NR Western 1:34
Ⓥ Adult situations, adult humor
Dir: Sam Peckinpah *Cast:* Randolph Scott,
Joel McCrea, Mariette Hartley, Ronald Starr,
R. G. Armstrong, Edgar Buchanan
▶ Two aging former lawmen—McCrea, still
idealistic and dedicated, and Scott, out for his
own interests—escort a shipment of gold from
a mountain mining camp. They also rescue
young bride Hartley from her hideous in-laws,
leading to a gripping chase to safety. Handsome, bittersweet tribute to old Western values is a memorable success due to the stars'
subdued performances. Scott's last film.
Dist.: MGM/UA

RIDE THE MAN DOWN 1952
★ ★ NR Western 1:30
Dir: Joseph Kane *Cast:* Brian Donlevy, Rod
Cameron, Ella Raines, Forrest Tucker, Bar-
bara Britton, J. Carrol Naish
▶ After his boss's death, ranch foreman Cam-
eron tries to protect his spread from greedy
neighbors. Things look bleak as Donlevy and
Tucker are willing to kill to get the Hatchet
Ranch, but Cameron resourcefully finds a way
to even the odds. Average Western, above-
average cast.
Dist.: Republic

RIDING ON AIR 1937
☆ NR Comedy 1:11 B&W
Dir: Edward Sedgwick *Cast:* Joe E. Brown,
Guy Kibbee, Florence Rice, Vinton Haworth,
Anthony Nace, Harlan Briggs
▶ Small-town newspaperman Brown rescues
a flyer from a crash, and is let in on an invention that can control airplanes from afar. Rice
is the girl of his dreams, but her father stands
in the way of their union. After Brown battles
airborne smugglers, the father comes to think
otherwise. Those who are annoyed by Brown's
yowling film persona will not be pleased by
this predictable vehicle.
Dist.: KVC

RIFIFI 1954 French
★ NR Mystery-Suspense 1:55 B&W
Dir: Jules Dassin   *Cast:* Jean Servais, Carl Mohner, Robert Manuel, Jules Dassin, Magali Noel, Marie Sabouret
▶ Four crooks, led by Servais, come up with an ingenious plan to break into an exclusive jewelry store. But while the gang thwarts the store's elaborate security devices, danger threatens in the form of fellow criminals who want in on the action. Gripping suspenser may well have single-handedly founded the caper genre. Still one of the best.   Ⓢ
Dist.: Various

RIGHT HAND MAN, THE 1987 Australian
★ ★ ★ R Drama 1:41
☑ Nudity, adult situations, explicit language, violence
Dir: Di Drew   *Cast:* Rupert Everett, Hugo Weaving, Catherine McClements, Arthur Dignam, Jennifer Claire
▶ Diabetic aristocrat Everett loses his arm in a riding accident. He hires dashing stagecoach driver Weaving to exercise his horses, a move with dire repercussions for Everett's lovely fiancée McClements. Lushly photographed romance set in 1860 Australia undermined by talky, unconvincing plot.
Dist.: New World

RIGHT STUFF, THE 1983
★ ★ ★ ★ PG Action-Adventure 3:16
☑ Adult situations, explicit language
Dir: Philip Kaufman   *Cast:* Sam Shepard, Scott Glenn, Ed Harris, Dennis Quaid, Fred Ward, Barbara Hershey, Kim Stanley, Veronica Cartright, Kathy Baker, Pamela Reed
▶ Rousing, witty adaptation of Tom Wolfe's best-seller, chronicling heroics of test pilot Chuck Yeager (Shepard) and the Mercury astronauts, particularly John Glenn (Harris), Alan Shepard (Glenn), and Gordon Cooper (Quaid). Spectacular flight scenes, genuine depiction of human side of astronauts and their wives, and moving portrayal of Yeager as unsung hero more than compensate for some uneven scenes. Stellar ensemble cast includes Donald Moffat, Levon Helm, Scott Wilson, Jeff Goldblum, and Harry Shearer. Won four technical Oscars.   (CC)
Dist.: Warner

RING OF BRIGHT WATER 1969 British
★ ★ ★ G Family 1:47
Dir: Jack Couffer   *Cast:* Bill Travers, Virginia McKenna, Peter Jeffrey, Jameson Clark
▶ London writer Travers adopts Mij the otter, then leaves the city for Scotland, where man and beast cavort against scenic backgrounds. One heartrending scene toward the end may upset smaller children, but overall this is warm and wonderful family fare.
Dist.: Magnetic

RIO BRAVO 1959
★ ★ ★ ★ NR Western 2:20
Dir: Howard Hawks   *Cast:* John Wayne, Dean Martin, Ricky Nelson, Angie Dickinson, Walter Brennan, Claude Akins
▶ Wayne is John T. (for "Trouble") Chance, a border town sheriff who jails murderer Akins even though his wealthy brother controls the county. Under siege by hired killers, Wayne turns to a motley crew for help: drunken deputy Martin, who's lost his self-respect; crippled oldster Brennan; greenhorn gunslinger Nelson; and the aggressive, leggy showgirl Feathers (Dickinson). Polished, extremely entertaining Western was reworked by director Hawks in the similar *El Dorado* and *Rio Lobo*.
Dist.: Warner

RIO CONCHOS 1964
★ ★ ★ ★ NR Western 1:47
Dir: Gordon Douglas   *Cast:* Richard Boone, Stuart Whitman, Tony Franciosa, Wende Wagner, Jim Brown, Edmond O'Brien
▶ Union captain Whitman orders bigot Boone to discover source of stolen rifles. Joined by Mexican bandit Franciosa and black sergeant Brown, they track the weapons to unrepentant Confederate O'Brien, who is trading them to Apaches to start another Civil War. Hard-edged, action-packed Western features exceptional performance by Boone. Brown's film debut.
Dist.: CBS/Fox

RIO GRANDE 1950
★ ★ ★ ★ NR Western 1:45 B&W
Dir: John Ford   *Cast:* John Wayne, Maureen O'Hara, Ben Johnson, Claude Jarman, Jr., Harry Carey, Jr., Victor McLaglen
▶ Wayne, the commander of a remote Army outpost, repulses Apache attacks while coping with personal problems. His son Jarman, a West Point dropout, has been assigned to the post after enlisting; his estranged wife O'Hara wants Jarman sent home to safety. Leisurely, richly detailed Western, an excellent climax to director Ford's "cavalry trilogy" (*Fort Apache*, *She Wore a Yellow Ribbon*), features stirring Sons of the Pioneers tunes and a fine performance by Johnson as a fugitive horseman.
Dist.: Republic

RIO LOBO 1970
★ ★ ★ ★ G Western 1:54
Dir: Howard Hawks   *Cast:* John Wayne, Jennifer O'Neill, Jorge Rivero, Sherry Lansing, Jack Elam, Chris Mitchum
▶ Howard Hawks's last film features the Duke as a Union soldier who teams with ex-Confederate Rivero to search for a gold-shipment thief and help beleaguered townsfolk against corrupt sheriff. Lively, fun, and action-packed; interesting cast features future producer/studio head Lansing as the woman who gets revenge against the man who scarred her and pairs off with Wayne in the finale. (CC)
Dist.: CBS/Fox

RIOT IN CELL BLOCK 11 1954
★ ★ ★ NR Action-Adventure 1:20 B&W
Dir: Don Siegel *Cast:* Neville Brand, Dabbs Greer, Emile Meyer, Frank Faylen, Leo Gordon, Robert Osterloh
▶ Brand leads fellow inmates in a cell block takeover inspired by inhumane conditions. Warden Meyer is sympathetic, but crazed prisoner Gordon wants bloodshed. Situation gets out of hand when the National Guard is brought in. Hard-hitting action story with an intelligent, even-handed jailer/prisoner dilemma.
Dist.: Republic

RISKY BUSINESS 1983
★ ★ ★ ★ R Comedy 1:39
☑ Nudity, strong sexual content, adult situations, explicit language, adult humor
Dir: Paul Brickman *Cast:* Tom Cruise, Rebecca De Mornay, Curtis Armstrong, Bronson Pinchot, Raphael Sbarge, Joe Pantoliano
▶ Wealthy, sex-starved Chicago teen Cruise uses chance encounter with prostitute De Mornay to establish a one-night bordello in his parents' house while they're out of town. But pimps clean out Cruise's house just as his parents are due back. Although morally vague, disarming comedy is inventive and good-natured. Cruise has a great air-guitar solo to Bob Seeger's "Old Time Rock and Roll."
Dist.: Warner

RITA, SUE AND BOB TOO 1987 British
★ ★ R Comedy 1:35
☑ Brief nudity, strong sexual content, explicit language
Dir: Alan Clarke *Cast:* Michelle Holmes, Siobhan Finneran, George Costigan, Lesley Sharp, Willie Ross, Ghir Kulvindar
▶ Yorkshire teens Holmes and Finneran babysit for married couple Costigan and Sharp. Soon both girls lose their virginity to Costigan. They share him happily until Sharp wises up and packs off with the kids. Further complicating their once-happy triangle is Finneran's pregnancy and Holmes's new Pakistani boyfriend Kulvindar. Deliberately outrageous comedy blends wistful sadness and cheery raunchiness.
Dist.: Warner

RITUALS 1978 Canadian
☆ R Action-Adventure 1:34
☑ Explicit language, graphic violence
Dir: Peter Carter *Cast:* Hal Holbrook, Lawrence Dane, Robin Gammell, Ken James, Gary Reineke
▶ Physician Holbrook goes on an outdoors trip with four doctor pals. Unfortunately, someone with a grudge and a mean temper is stalking the vacationers, using such novel devices as bees and a beaver trap to get his quarry. Ugly thriller churns up some tension, but it's of the most unpleasant kind.
Dist.: Nelson

RITZ, THE 1976
★ ★ R Comedy 1:31
☑ Nudity, strong sexual content, adult situations, explicit language
Dir: Richard Lester *Cast:* Rita Moreno, Jack Weston, Jerry Stiller, Kaye Ballard, F. Murray Abraham, Treat Williams
▶ Small-time businessman Weston, fleeing murderous mobster brother-in-law Stiller, seeks refuge for night in gay bathhouse. Flirtations and much confusion of sexual preference ensue as Weston meets off-key singer Moreno, trench-coated detective Williams, and sharp-tongued gay Abraham. The ante is upped when Stiller and sister Ballard arrive at the bathhouse. Terrence McNally's hit Broadway farce is given a stagy screen adaptation, but much of the wit is still here.
Dist.: Warner

RIVER, THE 1951 Indian
★ NR Drama 1:39
Dir: Jean Renoir *Cast:* Patricia Walters, Nora Swinburne, Arthur Shields, Radha, Adrienne Corri, Thomas E. Breen
▶ Brilliant panorama of life along India's Ganges river, built around a story of the adolescent love of plain Britisher Walters for visiting war-amputee Breen, who finds himself attracted to ravishing Indian girl Radha. Ruled by ancient customs, the lives of the Indians are linked to the image of the river, whose current seems immune to time. Future director Satyajit Ray got his first film experience on this adaptation of a novel by Rumer Godden, with stunning Technicolor cinematography by Claude Renoir.
Dist.: Corinth

RIVER, THE 1984
★ ★ ★ ★ PG-13 Drama 2:02
☑ Adult situations, explicit language, violence
Dir: Mark Rydell *Cast:* Mel Gibson, Sissy Spacek, Scott Glenn, Shane Bailey, Becky Jo Lynch, Don Hood
▶ Hard-headed, debt-ridden farmer Gibson and wife Spacek struggle to keep their riverside farm in business. Gibson must auction belongings and take factory job to make ends meet while Spacek fends off advances of Glenn, an ex-lover who would like to buy the farm. Then rains cause severe flooding and the river becomes foremost threat to survival. Grimly realistic portrait of plight of today's small farmer. Picture nominated for four Oscars, including Spacek as Best Actress. (CC)
Dist.: MCA

RIVERBEND 1989
★ R Drama 1:40
☑ Rape, explicit language, violence
Dir: Sam Firstenberg *Cast:* Steve James, Margaret Avery, Tony Frank, Julius Tennon, Alex Morris, Vanessa Tate
▶ In 1966 Georgia, Avery's husband is gunned

down by bigoted sheriff Frank. Three fugitive Vietnam vets, led by James, arrive in the area. James falls for Avery and the vets train the local blacks to battle their oppressors. Unusual combination of action and social comment suffers from excessive preachiness but has its heart in the right place.
Dist.: Prism

RIVER OF NO RETURN 1954
★ ★ ★ NR Western 1:31
Dir: Otto Preminger   *Cast:* Robert Mitchum, Marilyn Monroe, Rory Calhoun, Tommy Rettig, Murvyn Vye, Douglas Spencer
▶ During the Canadian gold rush, ex-con Mitchum makes arduous raft journey with son Rettig and singer Monroe in pursuit of bad guy Calhoun. Mitchum wins Monroe's love and the respect of his son. River trip provides plenty of physical excitement and star chemistry. CinemaScope film will suffer on TV.
Dist.: CBS/Fox

RIVER RAT, THE 1984
★ ★ ★ PG Drama 1:29
☑ Explicit language, violence
Dir: Tom Rickman   *Cast:* Tommy Lee Jones, Martha Plimpton, Brian Dennehy, Shawn Smith, Nancy Lea Owen
▶ Touching family drama about ex-con Jones trying to win the affection of Plimpton, the thirteen-year-old daughter he's met for the first time. Together they renovate an old boat that once cruised the Mississippi, but Jones's crooked past reappears in the form of corrupt parole officer Dennehy searching for robbery loot. Moving story was developed at Robert Redford's Sundance Institute.   (CC)
Dist.: Paramount

RIVER'S EDGE 1987
★ ★ R Drama 1:39
☑ Adult situations, explicit language, violence
Dir: Tim Hunter   *Cast:* Dennis Hopper, Crispin Glover, Keanu Reeves, Daniel Roebuck, Ione Skye Leitch, Joshua Miller
▶ Young teenager Roebuck murders his girl and friends numbly agree not to inform on him. But one boy, Reeves, feels compelled to speak with the police, setting up conflict with stoned clique leader Glover. Roebuck flees to home of hermit drug-dealer Hopper. Based on fact, critically acclaimed portrait of alienated, small-town youth hits hard. Some may find bleak depiction of violence, drug use, and utter apathy too unsettling.   (CC)
Dist.: Nelson

ROAD GAMES 1981 Australian
★ ★ PG Mystery-Suspense 1:41
☑ Adult situations, explicit language, graphic violence
Dir: Richard Franklin   *Cast:* Stacy Keach, Jamie Lee Curtis, Marion Edward, Grant Page, Bill Stacey, Thaddeus Smith
▶ Truck driver Keach, on long haul from Melbourne to Perth, finds his load getting

heavier—someone has been stashing corpses in the rig. Police suspect Keach is the highway killer, so with help of sympathetic hitchhiker Curtis he tries to apprehend the true murderer and prove his innocence. Offbeat suspenser with plenty of action and Aussie color.
Dist.: Nelson

ROAD HOUSE 1989
★ ★ ★ ★ R Action-Adventure 1:50
☑ Nudity, adult situations, explicit language, violence
Dir: Rowdy Herrington   *Cast:* Patrick Swayze, Kelly Lynch, Sam Elliott, Ben Gazzara, Marshall Teague, Julie Michaels
▶ Swayze, a bouncer with a black belt and a Ph.D. in philosophy, is hired to clean up a small-town saloon controlled by corrupt businessman Gazzara and his kickboxing goons. He does just that, with the help of sultry doctor Lynch and fellow bouncer Elliott. High-powered trash is silly, sexist, violent, and great fun on a moronic level. As Swayze says, "It's my way, or the highway."
Dist.: MGM/UA

ROADHOUSE 66 1984
★ ★ R Action-Adventure 1:34
☑ Nudity, adult situations, explicit language, violence
Dir: John Mark Robinson   *Cast:* Willem Dafoe, Judge Reinhold, Kaaren Lee, Kate Vernon, Stephen Elliot, Alan Autry
▶ Ivy Leaguer Reinhold and hitchhiker Dafoe are stranded overnight in a small Arizona town. After taunts from bullies and a touch of romance with sisters Lee and Vernon, they enter their 1955 T-bird in a drag race. Interesting cast and great soundtrack (including the Pretenders, Dave Edmunds, Los Lobos, etc.) set this a notch above typical action films.
Dist.: CBS/Fox

ROADIE 1980
★ PG Musical 1:45
☑ Adult situations, explicit language
Dir: Alan Rudolph   *Cast:* Meat Loaf, Kaki Hunter, Art Carney, Gailard Sartain, Alice Cooper, Hank Williams, Jr.
▶ Texas trucker Loaf helps musicians with a broken down vehicle and winds up working as a technician on a traveling rock show. He falls for sixteen-year-old groupie Hunter, but she only has eyes for Cooper, whom the two travel to New York to meet. Surprisingly unpretentious, with a great soundtrack featuring Roy Orbison, Cheap Trick, and Jerry Lee Lewis performing some of their best songs in years.
Dist.: Wood Knapp

ROAD TO BALI 1953
★ ★ ★ NR Comedy 1:30
Dir: Hal Walker   *Cast:* Bob Hope, Bing Crosby, Dorothy Lamour, Murvyn Vye, Ralph Moody
▶ Unemployed song-and-dance men Hope and Crosby, hired to dive for buried treasure,

are shipwrecked with princess Lamour. Other mishaps include being caught by cannibals and a volcanic eruption. Mindless fun with stars having an infectious good time. Fetching Edith Head costumes. Only color film of series features cameos by Jane Russell, Dean Martin, and Jerry Lewis.
Dist.: Unicorn

ROAD TO RIO 1947
★ ★ ★ **NR Comedy 1:40 B&W**
Dir: Norman Z. McLeod   *Cast:* Bing Crosby, Bob Hope, Dorothy Lamour, Gale Sondergaard, Frank Faylen, Joseph Vitale
▶ Musician stowaways Crosby and Hope are nonplussed by beautiful passenger Lamour's erratic behavior until they learn she's been hypnotized by Sondergaard into marrying a Brazilian villain. Fifth "Road" entry is one of the best in the series, with the usual array of gags and tunes supported by the zany Wiere Brothers and singing guests the Andrews Sisters.
Dist.: RCA/Columbia

ROAD TO SALINA 1971 French/Italian
★ **R Drama 1:36**
☑ Nudity
Dir: George Lautner   *Cast:* Mimsy Farmer, Robert Walker, Jr., Rita Hayworth, Ed Begley, Bruce Pecheur
▶ Drifter Walker is mistaken by crazy Hayworth for her long-lost son. He assumes that role, becoming involved with his "sister" and in intrigue surrounding the murder of the real son. Over-the-top performances and farfetched screenplay make this enjoyable trash. Considerable nudity, awful rock score.
Dist.: Nelson

ROAD TO UTOPIA 1945
★ ★ ★ **NR Comedy 1:30 B&W**
Dir: Hal Walker   *Cast:* Bing Crosby, Bob Hope, Dorothy Lamour, Hillary Brooke, Douglas Dumbrille, Jack LaRue
▶ Fourth Crosby-Hope teaming could be their best: washed up as vaudevillians, they head for gold-rush Alaska with a stolen mine deed. There they encounter saloon singer Lamour (who croons the pop hit "Personality"), the actual owner of the mine, as well as slimy villain Dumbrille. Full complement of sight gags and one-liners topped off with an amusing voice-over commentary by Robert Benchley.
Dist.: MCA

ROAD WARRIOR, THE 1982 Australian
★ ★ ★ **R Action-Adventure 1:35**
☑ Rape, nudity, explicit language, violence
Dir: George Miller   *Cast:* Mel Gibson, Bruce Spence, Vernon Wells, Emil Minty, Mike Preston, Virginia Hey
▶ Sequel to *Mad Max* continues the story of loner cop Gibson, who battles injustice in a harsh future where fuel is the most precious commodity. Minimalist plot concerns a desert commune besieged by punk villains for their primitive refinery. Influential international hit contains striking sets, startling violence, and

some of the most incredible high-velocity chases every filmed. Followed by *Mad Max Beyond Thunderdome*.
Dist.: Warner

ROARING TWENTIES, THE 1939
★ ★ ★ **NR Crime 1:44 B&W**
Dir: Raoul Walsh   *Cast:* James Cagney, Humphrey Bogart, Priscilla Lane, Gladys George, Jeffrey Lynn
▶ Cagney and Bogart are World War I buddies who make bootlegging fortune. After the stock market crash, Cagney goes straight and turns against Bogart when he menaces Lane, the woman Cagney loves. Riproaring, hugely entertaining gangster classic. Great last line: "He used to be a big shot."
Dist.: MGM/UA   Ⓒ

ROBBERY 1967 British
★ ★ **NR Mystery-Suspense 1:54**
Dir: Peter Yates   *Cast:* Stanley Baker, Joanna Pettet, James Booth, Frank Finlay, Barry Foster, William Marlowe
▶ Baker pulls off a daring jewelry heist to finance his complex scheme to rob a mail train. Breaking money-maven Finlay out of jail to help him, he gathers a group of expert crooks, and proceeds to pull off what appears to be the perfect crime. Unfortunately, there's a woman involved, and they've got inspector Booth on their tail. Inspired by a real-life British train robbery, well-done caper pic hits all the the right notes.
Dist.: Vestron

ROBE, THE 1953
★ ★ ★ ★ **NR Drama 2:15**
Dir: Henry Koster   *Cast:* Richard Burton, Jean Simmons, Victor Mature, Michael Rennie, Jay Robinson, Dean Jagger
▶ Episodic but richly inspirational drama about the impact of Christianity on the Roman tribune (Burton) ordered to crucify Christ. His slave (Mature) obtains Christ's miraculous robe, an object later coveted by mad emperor Caligula. Burton and his lover Simmons must choose between Christian martyrdom and obeying Caligula. Noteworthy as the first feature shot in CinemaScope; won Oscars for Best Costume Design and Art Direction. Mature would repeat his role in the sequel, *Demetrius and the Gladiators*.
Dist.: CBS/Fox

ROBERTA 1935
★ ★ ★ **NR Musical 1:45 B&W**
Dir: William A. Seiter   *Cast:* Irene Dunne, Fred Astaire, Ginger Rogers, Randolph Scott, Helen Westley, Luis Alberni
▶ Wispy plot about romance between football player Scott and Russian emigré clothes designer Dunne in Paris detracts somewhat from the beautiful Jerome Kern/Dorothy Fields/Jimmy McHugh score (including "Smoke Gets in Your Eyes," "Yesterdays," and the Oscar-nominated "Lovely to Look At").

Fred and Ginger play subsidiary roles in this fashion-oriented musical, but they steal the film with their witty duets to "I'll Be Hard to Handle" and "I Won't Dance."
Dist.: MGM/UA

ROBERT ET ROBERT 1979 French
☆ **NR Comedy 1:35**
☑ Adult situations
Dir: Claude Lelouch ***Cast:*** Charles Denner, Jacques Villeret, Jean-Claude Brialy, Macha Meril, Regine
► Cabbie Denner and meek student cop Villeret discover they have much in common: both are lonely guys named Robert who live with their mothers. Friendship forms as they try to meet women. Compasssionate characterizations expertly performed and directed. Bittersweet tone supported by Francis Lai score. [S]
Dist.: RCA/Columbia

ROBIN AND MARIAN 1976
★★★ **PG Romance/Action-Adventure 1:47**
☑ Adult situations, explicit language, violence
Dir: Richard Lester ***Cast:*** Sean Connery, Audrey Hepburn, Robert Shaw, Nicol Williamson, Richard Harris, Ronnie Barker
► Aging Robin Hood (Connery) returns to Sherwood Forest after twenty years of fighting in the Crusades and discovers Maid Marian (Hepburn) has become a nun in his absence. Robin renews their love affair and his battle with the evil Sheriff of Nottingham (Shaw). A supremely moving love story with touches of revisionist satire. Sweet chemistry between Connery and Hepburn (who returned to the screen after a decade in retirement), superb support from Williamson as the loyal Little John, literate screenplay and direction.
Dist.: RCA/Columbia

ROBIN AND THE SEVEN HOODS 1964
★★★ **NR Musical 2:00**
Dir: Gordon Douglas ***Cast:*** Frank Sinatra, Dean Martin, Sammy Davis, Jr., Bing Crosby, Peter Falk, Barbara Rush
► Pleasant musical comedy set in Prohibition-era Chicago. Gangster Sinatra inadvertently donates money to Crosby's orphanage and enjoys the public's acclaim so much he steps up his contributions. Rival mobster Falk doesn't like the competition and sets out to ruin Sinatra's gang. Last Rat Pack film features Oscar-nominated "My Kind of Town" and Falk's amusing rendition of "All for One."
Dist.: Warner

ROBIN HOOD 1973
★★★★ **G Animation 1:23**
Dir: Wolfgang Reitherman ***Cast:*** Voices of Brian Bedford, Phil Harris, Monica Evans, Peter Ustinov, Terry-Thomas, Roger Miller
► Disney variation on the classic legend turns familiar characters into animals (Robin Hood is a fox and Little John is a bear). Otherwise, story is familiar, as Robin battles the evil Sheriff of Nottingham, who bilks the poor, and romances Maid Marian. Up to studio's usual sterling standard. A delight for the eye, and the ear, especially when Miller's rooster/minstrel character sings. **(CC)**
Dist.: Buena Vista

ROBOCOP 1987
★★★★ **R Sci-Fi 1:43**
☑ Explicit language, graphic violence
Dir: Paul Verhoeven ***Cast:*** Peter Weller, Nancy Allen, Daniel O'Herlihy, Ronny Cox, Kurtwood Smith, Miguel Ferrer
► In a grim Detroit future, Weller, a patrolman killed on duty, is reassembled into Robocop, a deadly anticrime machine. Weller's human memories interfere with Robocop's computer programs, leading him on a search for his killers that brings him dangerously close to the leaders of an android company. Eye-opening special effects and nonstop action made this a megahit. **(CC)**
Dist.: Orion

ROBOCOP 2 1990
★★★ **R Sci-Fi/Action-Adventure 1:58**
☑ Adult situations, explicit language, graphic violence
Dir: Irvin Kershner ***Cast:*** Peter Weller, Nancy Allen, Daniel O'Herlihy, Belinda Bauer, Tom Noonan, Gabriel Damon
► Between the municipal takeover schemes of corporate baddie O'Herlihy and the soul-enslaving products of drug mogul Noonan, futuristic Detroit is in the kind of serious trouble from which only man/machine Robocop (Weller) can save it. Having twice the budget of its predecessor, flashy sequel really pumps up the action, with heart-stopping chases, frequent dismemberment, and spectacular puppet animation. As in the original, the script includes a few laughs amid the pounding, relentless violence and noise. **(CC)**
Dist.: Orion

ROBOT MONSTER 1953
☆ **NR Sci-Fi 1:03 B&W**
Dir: Phil Tucker ***Cast:*** George Nader, Claudia Barrett, Selena Royle, Gregory Moffett, John Mylong, George Barrows
► Alien creature, played by Barrows in a gorilla costume and diving helmet, is ordered to destroy life on Earth; Nader and Barrett are two of the humans who try to escape his wrath. Low-budget sci-fi is so ludicrous it has achieved the status of a camp classic. Originally released in 3-D.
Dist.: SVS

ROB ROY, THE HIGHLAND ROGUE 1953
☆ **NR Action-Adventure 1:25 B&W**
Dir: Harold French ***Cast:*** Richard Todd, Glynis Johns, James Robertson Justice, Michael Gough, Finlay Currie, Geoffrey Keen
► In eighteenth-century Scotland, boisterous Todd leads his followers against representatives of German-born King George. Eventually,

a truce is reached, but not before several battles. Johns plays Todd's wife in this uneven, if occasionally rousing, Disney adventure.
Dist.: Buena Vista

ROCCO AND HIS BROTHERS 1960 Italian
☆ **NR Drama 2:14 B&W**
Dir: Luchino Visconti ***Cast:*** Alain Delon, Renato Salvatori, Annie Girardot, Katina Paxinou, Claudia Cardinale, Roger Hanin
► Five brothers and their mother move from the Sicilian countryside to Italy's industrial north. The story of their difficult adjustment is told episodically, concentrating on the tragic triangle among brothers Delon and Salvatori and free-spirited prostitute Giradot. Crude, powerful emotions. [S]
Dist.: Video Dimensions

ROCK AND ROLL HIGH SCHOOL 1979
★ **PG Musical 1:32**
☑ Explicit language
Dir: Allan Arkush ***Cast:*** P. J. Soles, Vincent Van Patten, Clint Howard, Dey Young, Mary Woronov, The Ramones
► At Vince Lombardi High, evil principal Woronov tries to suppress her high-spirited student body, led by the bouncy Soles. Soles succeeds in bringing her favorite group, the Ramones, to the school, setting off a rockin' revolt against authority. Lightweight youth antics set to an energetic beat has inventive humor but little to offer adults.
Dist.: Warner

ROCKET ATTACK, U.S.A. 1959
☆ **NR Sci-Fi 1:11 B&W**
Dir: Barry Mahon ***Cast:*** Monica Davis, John McKay, Daniel Kern, Edward Czerniuk, Philip St. George, Arthur Metrano
► American operative McKay learns from Soviet spy Davis that the Russians are plotting to use the Sputnik satellite to bomb America. McKay races against time to foil the plan before the enemy can take Manhattan. Relic of the pre-Glasnost era may have seemed silly even on initial release.
Dist.: SVS

ROCKET GIBRALTAR 1988
★★★ **PG Drama 1:40**
☑ Adult situations, explicit language
Dir: Daniel Petrie ***Cast:*** Burt Lancaster, Suzy Amis, Patricia Clarkson, Frances Conroy, Sinead Cusack, John Glover
► Grown children and grandchildren gather for dying patriarch Lancaster's birthday party. The adults are too busy to notice when the youngsters decide to grant the old man's wish for a Viking funeral. Lancaster interacts beautifully with the children in this gentle drama; the ending is a tearjerker.
Dist.: RCA/Columbia

ROCKETSHIP X-M 1950
★ **NR Sci-Fi 1:17 B&W**
Dir: Kurt Neumann ***Cast:*** Lloyd Bridges, Osa Massen, Hugh O'Brian, John Emery, Noah Beery, Jr., Morris Ankrum
► Astronauts led by Bridges are en route to the moon when their spaceship is knocked off course to Mars. There they discover the ruins of a civilization that destroyed itself through atomic warfare. Well-made and adequately scripted sci-fi cheapie. New scenes were shot in 1978 and added to that year's videocassette release.
Dist.: Fox Hills

ROCK PRETTY BABY 1956
★ **NR Musical 1:29 B&W**
Dir: Richard Bartlett ***Cast:*** Sal Mineo, John Saxon, Fay Wray, Edward C. Platt, Rod McKuen, Shelley Fabares
► Saxon wants to be a rock 'n' roll singer, but doctor dad Platt doesn't think it's a good idea, though mom Wray is sympathetic. A talent contest offers Saxon and his band (including McKuen) the chance to show the world what they can do. High 1950s camp doesn't amount to much musically or dramatically, but dig that cast.
Dist.: KVC

ROCK, ROCK, ROCK 1956
★★ **NR Musical 1:23 B&W**
Dir: Will Price ***Cast:*** Tuesday Weld, Jacqueline Kerr, Ivy Schulman, Jack Collins, Carol Moss, Alan Freed
► Mean father of teenybopper Weld (in her film debut) closes her charge account before she can buy a strapless gown for her prom. Ridiculous plot is fun on a camp level, but film's real appeal is an amazing collection of rock 'n' roll artists: Chuck Berry ("You Can't Catch Me"), Frankie Lymon and the Teenagers ("I'm Not a Juvenile Delinquent"), the Moonglows, the Flamingos, LaVern Baker, etc.
Dist.: Media

ROCKY 1976
★★★★★ **PG Drama/Sports 1:59**
☑ Explicit language, violence
Dir: John G. Avildsen ***Cast:*** Sylvester Stallone, Talia Shire, Burt Young, Carl Weathers, Burgess Meredith, Thayer David
► Stallone, a club boxer/Mafia thumbbreaker from South Philly, gets unlikely title shot against publicity-hungry heavyweight champ Weathers. Mercilessly conditioned by gruff old trainer Meredith and inspired by shy girlfriend Shire, the Italian Stallion is determined to prove he's no palooka by going the distance with Weathers. Superior Hollywood hokum left crowds cheering and spawned three more films about America's favorite screen pugilist. Oscars for Best Picture, Director, and Editing. Inspirational soundtrack also a hit.
Dist.: MGM/UA

ROCKY II 1979
★★★★★ **PG Drama/Sports 1:58**
☑ Explicit language, violence
Dir: Sylvester Stallone ***Cast:*** Sylvester Stal-

lone, Talia Shire, Burt Young, Carl Weathers, Burgess Meredith, Tony Burton
▶ In the wake of his stunning draw against world champ Weathers, artless club fighter Stallone copes with sudden fame and inability to find work. After marriage to mousy girlfriend Shire, he cannot resist Weathers's taunting challenge for a rematch and resumes training under watchful eye of mentor Meredith, despite objections of Shire. When Shire lapses into coma after childbirth, Stallone may lose will to fight. Generally successful sequel with another spirited finale bout.
Dist.: CBS/Fox

ROCKY III 1982
★ ★ ★ ★ ★ **PG Drama/Sports 1:39**
☑ Explicit language, violence
Dir: Sylvester Stallone *Cast:* Sylvester Stallone, Talia Shire, Carl Weathers, Burt Young, Burgess Meredith, Mr. T
▶ Now a superstar going soft, series hero Stallone loses title to tough and hungry challenger Mr. T in wake of death of longtime trainer Meredith. Determined to regain the heavyweight championship, Stallone learns quickness and moves from previous nemesis Weathers for showdown with Mr. T. Popular myth survives one more installment without losing too much vitality. Look for pre-Hulkmania Hogan in charity exhibition at movie's start.
Dist.: CBS/Fox

ROCKY IV 1985
★ ★ ★ ★ **PG Drama/Sports 1:31**
☑ Explicit language, violence
Dir: Sylvester Stallone *Cast:* Sylvester Stallone, Talia Shire, Burt Young, Carl Weathers, Dolph Lundgren, Brigitte Nielsen
▶ To avenge the death of friend and ex-champ Weathers and to defend the honor of his homeland, beloved boxer Stallone journeys to Russia for grudge match against seemingly superhuman Soviet Lundgren. Lundgren uses science and steroids to prepare for bout, but Rocky preps the old-fashioned way in frigid Siberia while wife Shire reluctantly decides to back him for another head-banger. Critics kvetched about tired boxing formula, but fans stayed in Rocky's corner all the way. **(CC)**
Dist.: CBS/Fox

ROCKY HORROR PICTURE SHOW, THE
1975 British
★ **R Musical/Sci-Fi 1:35**
☑ Brief nudity, adult situations, explicit language
Dir: Jim Sharman *Cast:* Tim Curry, Susan Sarandon, Barry Bostwick, Meat Loaf, Nell Campbell, Richard O'Brien
▶ Riotous, campy, and sexy horror spoof takes innocent couple Sarandon and Bostwick to Gothic home of Transylvanians led by transvestite mad-scientist Curry. Curry and his weirdo minions teach the straitlaced duo a thing or two about loosening up. Picture was originally box-office dud, but word-of-mouth developed unprecedented cult following based on audience interaction with the movie. Actor O'Brien also wrote songs, including "The Time Warp," "Science Fiction Double Feature," and "Sweet Transvestite." For midnight movie types only. Followed by *Shock Treatment.* **(CC)**
Dist.: CBS/Fox

RODAN 1958 Japanese
★ ★ **NR Sci-Fi 1:10 B&W**
Dir: Inoshiro Honda *Cast:* Kenji Sawara, Yumi Shirakawa, Akihiko Hirata, Akio Kobori, Yasuko Nakata
▶ Just when you thought it was safe to go to Tokyo, flying reptile Rodan comes out of hibernation inside a mountain and proceeds to destroy all in its wake. Pretty silly, although those who enjoy *Godzilla* and *Mothra* will be entertained. Dubbed.
Dist.: Vestron

ROE VS. WADE 1989
★ ★ ★ ★ **NR Drama/MFTV 1:40**
Dir: Gregory Hoblit *Cast:* Holly Hunter, Amy Madigan, Terry O'Quinn, Kathy Bates, James Gammon, Annabella Price
▶ Perky Texan Hunter is unmarried, pregnant, and on the wrong side of standing abortion statutes. Teamed with lawyer Madigan, she decides to make a federal case out of it. Result is landmark Supreme Court decision loosening abortion curbs. Hunter's Emmy-winning performance is highlight of this balanced look at an emotionally charged issue.
Dist.: Paramount

ROGER AND ME 1989
★ ★ ★ **R Documentary 1:28**
☑ Violence
Dir: Michael Moore *Cast:* Michael Moore, Bob Eubanks, Pat Boone, Anita Bryant
▶ When General Motors closes plants, causing massive layoffs in his hometown of Flint, Michigan, filmmaker Moore tries to track down elusive GM chairman Roger Smith for an interview. Local workers are more cooperative than GM brass. Moore paints an incisive picture of unemployment, official boosterism, and corporate indifference that is at once sober, ironic, and cuttingly humorous (especially in interviews with celebrities like Eubanks and soon-to-be Miss America Lei Lani Rae Rafko). **(CC)**
Dist.: Warner

ROLLERBALL 1975
★ ★ ★ **R Action-Adventure 2:03**
☑ Adult situations, explicit language, violence
Dir: Norman Jewison *Cast:* James Caan, John Houseman, John Beck, Maud Adams, Moses Gunn, Pamela Hensley
▶ In the future, man's need for violence (now outlawed) is fulfilled by spectator sport rollerball, an amalgam of football, roller derby,

hockey, judo, and motorcycle racing. Caan, the best athlete in the game, is told to retire because he's grown too popular, but he refuses. Corporate/government elite make the game even deadlier to kill Caan. Director Jewison intended to condemn glorification of violence, but gripping rollerball action scenes often have opposite effect.
Dist.: MGM/UA

ROLLER BOOGIE 1979
★ ★ PG Comedy 1:44
☑ Adult situations, explicit language
Dir: Mark L. Lester *Cast:* Linda Blair, Jim Bray, Beverly Garland, Roger Perry, Jimmy Van Patten, Kimberly Beck
▶ Carefree rich girl Blair runs away from Beverly Hills home for roller-skating life in Venice Beach with boyfriend Bray. When mobsters threaten to take over the kids' favorite roller rink, Blair returns home to enlist aid of lawyer father Perry and eventually competes in climactic disco skating contest. Quickie effort to cash in on now defunct roller disco craze looks dated.
Dist.: Media

ROLLERCOASTER 1977
★ ★ ★ ★ PG Action-Adventure 1:58
☑ Explicit language, violence
Dir: James Goldstone *Cast:* George Segal, Richard Widmark, Timothy Bottoms, Henry Fonda, Susan Strasberg, Harry Guardino
▶ Extortionist Bottoms hides bombs in amusement parks and threatens to set them off unless he is paid $1 million. Safety inspector Segal tries to thwart him. Intelligent and involving, with solid performances (especially Bottoms), canny use of everyday settings to increase the tension, sensational rollercoaster sequences. Originally released in Sensurround.
Dist.: MCA

ROLLING THUNDER 1977
★ ★ ★ ★ R Action-Adventure 1:39
☑ Explicit language, graphic violence
Dir: John Flynn *Cast:* William Devane, Tommy Lee Jones, Linda Haynes, James Best, Dabney Coleman, Lisa Richards
▶ After eight years in a Vietcong POW camp, Devane returns to his Texas hometown a hero. But thieves murder his wife and son, and mutilate his hand in a garbage disposal. Aided by fellow ex-POW Jones, Devane sets out to execute the villains. Unusually good action film has an unpredictable script (by Paul Schrader and Heywood Gould) and strong interpretations of intense, complicated characters by Devane and Jones.
Dist.: Vestron

ROLLING VENGEANCE 1987
★ ★ R Action-Adventure 1:31
☑ Rape, adult situations, explicit language, violence
Dir: Steven Hilliard Stern *Cast:* Don Michael Paul, Lawrence Dane, Ned Beatty, Lisa

Howard, Todd Duckworth, Michael J. Reynolds
▶ When he learns that his family has been murdered and his girlfriend raped by redneck thugs who hang out at Beatty's sleazy tavern, young trucker Paul constructs a Monster Truck with seventy-three-inch tires and a 600-horsepower engine to wreak revenge. Fast-paced exploitation features spectacular stunts that demolish over sixty vehicles.
Dist.: Nelson

ROLLOVER 1981
★ ★ ★ R Drama 1:55
☑ Adult situations, explicit language, violence
Dir: Alan J. Pakula *Cast:* Jane Fonda, Kris Kristofferson, Hume Cronyn, Josef Sommer, Bob Gunton
▶ Widow Fonda has affair with wheeler-dealer Kristofferson, who helps her take over late husband's business. High-powered conspiracy involving Arab investment threatens the firm. Complex, disturbing, and topical. Fine Fonda, slick direction, and polished production marred somewhat by excessive talk and miscast Kristofferson.
Dist.: Warner

ROMANCING THE STONE 1984
★ ★ ★ ★ ★ PG Action-Adventure 1:46
☑ Adult situations, explicit language, violence
Dir: Robert Zemeckis *Cast:* Michael Douglas, Kathleen Turner, Danny DeVito, Zack Norman, Alfonso Arau, Manuel Ojeda
▶ Turner, the author of pulp romances, travels with mysterious package to South America to seek kidnapped sister. Norman, DeVito, Ojeda, and other assorted criminals pursue her for the treasure map she unwittingly possesses and soon she's lost in the wilds in her high heels. To her rescue comes adventurer Douglas. They team up to flee the bad guys and seek the treasure. Boisterous, wildly successful adventure with laughs, romance, and real sparks between the leads. Sequel: *The Jewel of the Nile.* (CC)
Dist.: CBS/Fox

ROMAN HOLIDAY 1953
★ ★ ★ ★ ★ NR Romance 1:58 B&W
Dir: William Wyler *Cast:* Gregory Peck, Audrey Hepburn, Eddie Albert, Hartley Power, Tullio Carminati
▶ Sheltered princess Hepburn sneaks away from her official duties to enjoy the sights of Rome. Cynical reporter Peck befriends her, pretending not to know her true identity in hopes of getting a big scoop; but then they fall in love. Rome and Hepburn were never lovelier than in this gloriously romantic tale. The leads and Albert (as Peck's photographer pal) are splendid and the ending movingly bittersweet. Nine Oscar nominations—including Best Picture, Director, and Supporting Actor (Albert)—with Hepburn, scriptwriter Ian

McLellan Hunter, and costumer Edith Head winning.
Dist.: Paramount

ROMAN SCANDALS 1933
★ NR Musical 1:31 B&W
Dir: Frank Tuttle *Cast:* Eddie Cantor, Ruth Etting, Gloria Stuart, David Manners, Edward Arnold, Alan Mowbray
▶ Amusing romp sends Cantor, an Oklahoma delivery boy, to ancient Rome in an extended dream. Food taster for evil emperor Arnold, he's thrown into a wild chariot race parodying *Ben Hur.* Dated but enjoyable comedy highlighted by daring Busby Berkeley numbers, one featuring women (including young Lucille Ball) dressed only in long blond wigs.
Dist.: Nelson

ROMAN SPRING OF MRS. STONE, THE 1961
★ ★ NR Drama 1:44
Dir: Jose Quintero *Cast:* Vivien Leigh, Warren Beatty, Lotte Lenya, Jill St. John. Coral Browne, Jeremy Spenser
▶ Aging actress Leigh finds Rome romance with young Italian gigolo Beatty. Leigh's obsession grows but Beatty eventually jilts her for younger St. John. Poignant but dark love story features solid work from Leigh, Beatty, and Lenya (Oscar-nominated). Based on the Tennessee Williams novel.
Dist.: Warner

ROMANTIC COMEDY 1983
★ ★ ★ PG Romance/Comedy 1:42
☑ Adult situations, explicit language, adult humor
Dir: Arthur Hiller *Cast:* Dudley Moore, Mary Steenburgen, Frances Sternhagen, Janet Eilber, Ron Leibman, Robyn Douglass
▶ As playwrights, the sophisticated Moore and the shy Steenburgen find collaborating on Broadway hits much easier than love; both go through other lovers and spouses before realizing their true feelings for one another. Likable leads but the writing and directing are lackluster. Lush Marvin Hamlisch score, some amusing moments. Based on Bernard Slade's play. **(CC)**
Dist.: CBS/Fox

ROMANTIC ENGLISHWOMAN, THE 1975 British
★ R Drama 1:56
☑ Strong sexual content
Dir: Joseph Losey *Cast:* Glenda Jackson, Michael Caine, Helmut Berger, Kate Nelligan, Beatrice Romand, Michael Lonsdale
▶ Writer Caine works on tale of infidelity and finds life imitating art when wife Jackson has affair with smuggler Berger. Ambitious, sharply acted (by Caine and Jackson) and written (by Tom Stoppard) but overly complex and unsatisfying.
Dist.: Warner

ROMEO AND JULIET 1954 British
★ NR Drama 2:20
Dir: Renato Castellani *Cast:* Laurence Harvey, Susan Shentall, Flora Robson, Mervyn Johns, Bill Travers, Sebastian Cabot
▶ In fifteenth-century Venice, young Romeo (Harvey) and Juliet (Shentall) fall in love despite the fact that their families are engaged in a bloody feud. Photography on pristine fifteenth-century Italian locations results in a painterly masterpiece. Not the liveliest adaptation of a Shakespeare play, but one of the most beautiful to look at. Introduced by John Gielgud.
Dist.: VidAmerica

ROMEO AND JULIET 1966 British
★ NR Dance 2:04
Dir: Paul Czinner *Cast:* Margot Fonteyn, Rudolf Nureyev, David Blair, Desmond Doyle, Michael Sommes, Anthony Dowell
▶ The Royal Ballet's elegant rendering of the classic love story features choreography by Kenneth MacMillan set to the memorable score by Prokofiev. Chance to see Nureyev and Fonteyn, one of the ballet world's greatest partnerships, at the height of their powers makes up for the restrictions the camera imposes on the art form.
Dist.: Corinth

ROMEO AND JULIET 1968 British/Italian
★ ★ ★ ★ PG Romance 2:17
☑ Brief nudity, adult situations, mild violence
Dir: Franco Zeffirelli *Cast:* Olivia Hussey, Leonard Whiting, Milo O'Shea, Michael York, John McEnery, Robert Stephens
▶ In Verona, teenagers Romeo (Whiting) and Juliet (Hussey) fall in love; however, their warring families insure the romance will be starcrossed. Definitive movie version of Shakespeare's play is extremely romantic (particularly in the balcony scene) and gorgeously mounted. Nominated for Best Picture and Director; won for Cinematography and Costume Design. Haunting music by Nino Rota.
Dist.: Paramount

ROMERO 1989
★ ★ PG-13 Biography 1:45
☑ Violence
Dir: John Duigan *Cast:* Raul Julia, Richard Jordan, Ana Alicia, Tony Plana, Harold Gould
▶ True story of El Salvador's Archbishop Romero (Julia). After his friend Jordan is killed, Romero evolves from political passivity to active opposition against the excesses of the right-wing government. Upbeat drama with a thoughtful performance by Julia, although overly obvious direction and dialogue undercuts the inspiration. Produced by the Paulist Brothers, an order of the Catholic Church. **(CC)**
Dist.: Vidmark

ROOFTOPS 1989
★★ R Drama 1:35
☑ Adult situations, explicit language, violence
Dir: Robert Wise   *Cast:* Jason Gedrick, Troy Beyer, Eddie Velez, Tisha Campbell, Alexis Cruz, Allen Payne
▶ Gedrick, an orphaned teen who lives on a Manhattan rooftop, falls for Hispanic Beyer and convinces her to quit working for her drug dealer cousin Velez. The latter takes out his anger on Gedrick's friend Cruz, setting up a rooftop showdown. Director Wise's return to *West Side Story* territory features flashy dance numbers, good-looking cast, and a punchy soundtrack.
Dist.: IVE

ROOM AT THE TOP 1959 British
★★ NR Drama 1:57 B&W
Dir: Jack Clayton   *Cast:* Laurence Harvey, Simone Signoret, Heather Sears, Donald Wolfit, Hermione Baddeley, Ambrosine Philpotts
▶ Incisive story about the rise of ambitious but amoral clerk Harvey in a grimy industrial town. Received six Oscar nominations, winning for Neil Paterson's screenplay and Signoret's haunting performance as an older woman whose life is ruined by Harvey when he leaves her for Sears, the daughter of a prominent businessman. Early example of the new wave of British realistic films was based on a novel by John Braine. Led to a 1965 sequel, *Man at the Top*.
Dist.: Magnetic

ROOM SERVICE 1938
★★ NR Comedy 1:18 B&W
Dir: William A. Seiter   *Cast:* Groucho Marx, Harpo Marx, Chico Marx, Lucille Ball, Ann Miller, Frank Albertson, Donald MacBride
▶ The John Murray–Allen Boretz Broadway comedy, adapted rather uneasily into a Marx Brothers vehicle. Groucho is the struggling producer of a play, trying to get his show off the ground while staying one step ahead of his creditors. Chico is the cheerfully obtuse director and Harpo his sidekick. Only intermittently funny comedy was remade as *Step Lively*.
Dist.: Turner

ROOM WITH A VIEW, A 1986 British
★★★ NR Drama 1:55
☑ Nudity, adult situations
Dir: James Ivory   *Cast:* Maggie Smith, Denholm Elliott, Helena Bonham Carter, Julian Sands, Daniel Day-Lewis, Simon Callow
▶ In 1907 Florence, well-to-do Englishwoman Carter begins to fall in love with socially unsuitable young Sands, son of rough-edged self-made businessman Elliott. Her alarmed chaperone Smith whisks Carter back to England where she's soon engaged to dull, blue-blooded fop Day-Lewis. By coincidence, Elliott and Sands move to the same village so Carter

is caught between passion and propriety. Beautiful production, quality performances, and witty-and-wise screenplay adapted from E. M. Forster novel. Won three Oscars. **(CC)**
Dist.: CBS/Fox

ROOSTER COGBURN 1975
★★★★★ PG Western 1:47
☑ Violence
Dir: Stuart Millar   *Cast:* John Wayne, Katharine Hepburn, Anthony Zerbe, Richard Jordan, Strother Martin, John McIntyre
▶ Hard-drinking one-eyed lawman Wayne, reprising his Oscar-winning role from *True Grit*, pursues outlaws Jordan and Zerbe, who have heisted Army wagon laden with nitroglycerin. On their trail he meets Bible-thumping schoolmarm Hepburn, whose preacher father has been slain by the bad guys. Chauvinist Wayne has his doubts until feisty Hepburn proves a crack shot and ace horsewoman, so the two old coots team up to avenge her father's murder. Sometimes creaky and overly sentimental attempt at Western version of *The African Queen* is saved by presence of two movie legends.
Dist.: MCA

ROOTS 1977
★★★★★ NR Drama/MFTV 9:00
Dir: David Greene   *Cast:* LeVar Burton, John Amos, Ben Vereen, Edward Asner, Louis Gossett, Jr., Sandy Duncan
▶ In 1750, black African Kunte Kinte (played by Burton as a young man, Amos as an older one) is captured by slave traders and taken to America. Kinte attempts to escape several times but freedom is something only his descendents will know. Massive miniseries, part of television history, is unmatched for sheer dramatic impact; from Alex Haley's best-selling account of his own African roots. Available in six ninety-minute tapes.
Dist.: Warner

ROPE 1948
★★★ NR Mystery-Suspense 1:20
Dir: Alfred Hitchcock   *Cast:* James Stewart, Farley Granger, John Dall, Cedric Hardwicke, Joan Chandler, Dick Hogan
▶ Bright but amoral college pals Granger and Dall murder friend Hogan for the intellectual thrill, strangling him with a rope in their apartment. To further their macabre game they hide the corpse on the premises and invite over Hogan's father Hardwicke, fiancée Chandler, and professor Stewart, whose lectures inspired the slaying. As the evening wears on and Hogan's absence becomes alarming, Stewart grows suspicious of his pupils. An experiment for Hitchcock, film was shot in ten-minute takes spliced together to create the illusion of one seamless shot.
Dist.: MCA

ROSALIE 1937
★ NR Musical 2:02 B&W
Dir: W. S. Van Dyke II   *Cast:* Eleanor Powell,

Nelson Eddy, Frank Morgan, Edna May Oliver, Ray Bolger, Ilona Massey
▶ West Point football star Eddy flies to Europe to meet a Vassar girl he'd dated earlier in the year, unaware that she is the princess of a troubled country. Romantic difficulties multiply as revolution breaks out and the royal family must flee to America. Overblown musical has everything but heart. Cole Porter songs include "In the Still of the Night" and "Why Should I Care?"
Dist.: MGM/UA

ROSALIE GOES SHOPPING 1990
☆ **PG Comedy 1:34**
☑ Explicit language
Dir: Percy Adlon *Cast:* Marianne Sägebrecht, Brad Davis, Judge Reinhold, Erika Blumberger, Willy Harlander, Alex Winter
▶ Sägebrecht supports her family of seven in lavish style by juggling twenty-seven credit cards, kiting checks, and taking out loans. Her activities allow her to buy a plane for her nearly blind pilot husband, and eventually save a local mill from takeover by the Japanese. Reinhold is hilarious as Sägebrecht's confessor, but otherwise heavy-handed satire aims tired barbs at already well-punctured target of American consumerism. (CC)
Dist.: Vidmark

ROSARY MURDERS, THE 1987
★ ★ ★ **R Mystery-Suspense 1:41**
☑ Adult situations, explicit language, violence
Dir: Fred Walton *Cast:* Donald Sutherland, Charles Durning, Josef Sommer, Belinda Bauer, James Murtaugh, John Danelle
▶ Serial killer terrorizes Detroit, leaving rosary beads as clues. Unorthodox priest Sutherland tackles the case with beautiful reporter Bauer. Plodding mystery from a script by director Walton and Elmore Leonard. (CC)
Dist.: Virgin

ROSE, THE 1979
★ ★ ★ **R Musical 2:14**
☑ Adult situations, explicit language
Dir: Mark Rydell *Cast:* Bette Midler, Alan Bates, Frederic Forrest, Harry Dean Stanton, David Keith
▶ Oscar-nominated Midler dominates this tragic tale of rock, the road, and redemption. Bette's first screen performance, a composite portrait of several 1960s singers, especially Janis Joplin, is a powerhouse in every way. Enhanced by solid supporting roles from Bates as her overbearing manager and Forrest (nominated for Best Supporting Actor) as her lover. Concert footage features great music: "Stay With Me" and the title tune. (CC)
Dist.: CBS/Fox

ROSEBUD BEACH HOTEL, THE 1984
★ **R Comedy 1:22**
☑ Nudity, adult situations, explicit language
Dir: Harry Hurwitz *Cast:* Colleen Camp,

Peter Scolari, Christopher Lee, Fran Drescher, Eddie Deezen, Monique Gabrielle
▶ Scolari signs on as manager of a second-rate Florida hotel at the suggestion of girlfriend Camp. They deal with the odd staff which includes bellhop/call girl Drescher, while Camp's tycoon father Lee plots to blow up the place for insurance money. Frantic and silly; the supporting cast (especially Drescher) steals it.
Dist.: Vestron

ROSELAND 1977
★ **PG Drama 1:44**
☑ Adult situations
Dir: James Ivory *Cast:* Joan Copeland, Geraldine Chaplin, Lilia Skala, Lou Jacobi, Christopher Walken, Teresa Wright
▶ Three stories set in New York City's Roseland Ballroom: widow Wright is obsessed with her dead husband until she meets the uncouth but sensitive Jacobi; gigolo Walken gets involved with three different women; and an old German woman, Skala, dreams of winning a dance contest. Affecting performances, great dancing, but talky and slow; the stories are rather depressing.
Dist.: Vestron

ROSE MARIE 1936
★ ★ ★ **NR Musical 1:53 B&W**
Dir: W. S. Van Dyke II *Cast:* Jeanette MacDonald, Nelson Eddy, Reginald Owen, Allan Jones, James Stewart, Alan Mowbray
▶ Lavish musical set in Canada: opera star MacDonald enlists Mountie Eddy's help in finding her brother Stewart. Discards most of the Otto Harbach–Oscar Hammerstein II play, but the soaring duets to "Indian Love Call" and others should please fans of light opera. Also known as *Indian Love Call.*
Dist.: MGM/UA

ROSEMARY'S BABY 1968
★ ★ ★ **R Horror 2:17**
☑ Rape, nudity, adult situations, explicit language
Dir: Roman Polanski *Cast:* Mia Farrow, John Cassavetes, Ruth Gordon, Maurice Evans, Ralph Bellamy, Charles Grodin
▶ Stylish classic based on Ira Levin's best-selling novel. When Farrow and Cassavetes move into a beautiful old New York City apartment building, it's to start a new family. Little does Farrow realize that a coven of witches living next door is also eager for her to get pregnant—for a very diabolical reason! Gordon won Best Supporting Actress; Grodin's first film.
Dist.: Paramount

ROUGH CUT 1980
★ ★ ★ ★ **PG Mystery-Suspense 1:51**
☑ Adult situations, explicit language
Dir: Don Siegel *Cast:* Burt Reynolds, Lesley-Anne Down, David Niven, Timothy West, Patrick Magee, Susan Littler
▶ In England, American jewel thief Reynolds plans diamond caper and meets gorgeous

socialite Down, who is working for Scotland Yard inspector Niven. Down falls for Reynolds and becomes his partner in crime. Escapist fare of a high order; slick production, attractive and charming performances, pleasant European locations.
Dist.: Paramount

'ROUND MIDNIGHT 1986 U.S./French
★ ★ ★ R Drama/Music 2:11
☑ Adult situations, explicit language
Dir: Bertrand Tavernier *Cast:* Dexter Gordon, François Cluzet, Gabrielle Haker, Sandra Reaves-Philips, Lonette McKee, Herbie Hancock
▶ Heartfelt tribute to 1950s jazz features a magnetic performance by real-life musician Gordon as Dale Turner, a talented but self-destructive saxophonist whose career is rescued by French fan Cluzet. Loosely based on the friendship between jazz great Bud Powell and Francis Paudras, film is more a series of vignettes than a coherent story. Hancock's score (which includes the title song and "How Long Has This Been Going On?") won an Oscar. Martin Scorsese has a chilling cameo during a brief sequence in New York. **(CC)**
Ⓢ
Dist.: Warner

ROUSTABOUT 1964
★ ★ NR Musical 1:41
Dir: John Rich *Cast:* Elvis Presley, Barbara Stanwyck, Joan Freeman, Leif Erickson, Sue Ane Langdon, Pat Buttram, Jack Albertson, Billy Barty, Richard Kiel
▶ Presley takes a job with Stanwyck's financially troubled carnival, and saves her from bankruptcy with his singing while falling in love with fellow worker Freeman. Enjoyable vehicle for the King, who sings "Little Egypt," "One Track Heart," "Wheels on My Heels," and "Big Love, Big Heartache." Unusual cast includes Raquel Welch in her film debut.
Dist.: CBS/Fox

ROXANNE 1987
★ ★ ★ PG Romance/Comedy 1:47
☑ Adult situations, explicit language
Dir: Fred Schepisi *Cast:* Steve Martin, Daryl Hannah, Shelley Duvall, Rick Rossovich, Fred Willard, Michael J. Pollard
▶ Fire chief Martin has a big nose and a bigger problem: he loves astronomer Hannah, who is hung up on his hunky co-worker Rossovich. Too shy to woo Hannah, Rossovich asks Martin to provide him with love letters and dialogue. Funny, charming update of *Cyrano de Bergerac* is one of the best comedies of recent years. Imaginatively directed by Schepisi, delightfully acted by an acrobatic and poignant Martin. Funniest moment in Martin's screenplay: the barroom list of twenty nasal put-downs. **(CC)**
Dist.: RCA/Columbia

ROYAL WEDDING 1951
★ ★ ★ NR Musical 1:33
Dir: Stanley Donen *Cast:* Fred Astaire, Jane Powell, Peter Lawford, Sarah Churchill, Keenan Wynn
▶ Queen Elizabeth II's wedding to Prince Philip provides the background to a slight romantic comedy about brother-sister team, Astaire and Powell, who find love with dancer Churchill (Sir Winston's daughter) and aristocrat Lawford in London. Despite a smooth score by Alan Jay Lerner and Burton Lane (Oscar-nominated "Too Late Now," "You're All the World to Me," etc.), memorable chiefly for two amazing Astaire routines: one a duet with a hat rack, the other his celebrated dancing-on-the-ceiling sequence.
Dist.: MGM/UA

RUBY 1977
★ ★ R Horror 1:25
☑ Violence
Dir: Curtis Harrington *Cast:* Piper Laurie, Stuart Whitman, Janit Baldwin, Crystin Sinclaire, Paul Kent
▶ Florida drive-in operator Laurie's dead gangster lover rises from his watery grave to get revenge against her and underworld colleagues. Instrument of his ghostly vendetta is the deaf girl he inhabits. Story owes much to superior genre efforts like *Carrie* and *The Exorcist.* Surprisingly good special effects, absurd plotting.
Dist.: United

RUBY GENTRY 1952
★ ★ ★ NR Drama 1:22 B&W
Dir: King Vidor *Cast:* Jennifer Jones, Charlton Heston, Karl Malden, Tom Tully, Bernard Phillips
▶ Jones, sexy girl from the wrong side of the Carolina swamps, loves Heston but is embittered when he marries someone else. She marries his wealthy rival Malden and plots revenge. Lurid, overheated, and quite entertaining melodrama with an intense love/hate relationship between Heston and Jones.
Dist.: CBS/Fox

RUCKUS 1980
★ ★ ★ ★ PG Action-Adventure 1:31
☑ Adult situations, explicit language, violence
Dir: Max Kleven *Cast:* Dirk Benedict, Linda Blair, Ben Johnson, Richard Farnsworth, Matt Clark
▶ Burnt-out Vietnam vet Benedict arrives in small town, runs afoul of local big-shot Johnson and townspeople. Only Johnson's widowed daughter-in-law Blair sides with Benedict as he uses his fighting skills against his tormentors. Well-staged action, good performances, credible middle-American atmosphere.
Dist.: Paragon

RUDE AWAKENING 1989
★ ★ ★ R Comedy 1:40
☑ Brief nudity, explicit language, violence
Dir: Aaron Russo, David Greenwalt *Cast:*

Cheech Marin, Eric Roberts, Julie Hagerty, Robert Carradine, Buck Henry, Louise Lasser, Cindy Williams, Andrea Martin, Cliff De Young
► Hippies Marin and Roberts have spent past twenty years hiding from the feds in a Central American jungle. They learn of a CIA invasion scheme and go to New York to expose it. There they are reunited with old friends like Carradine who have succumbed to the lure of yuppiedom. Good-humored satire's ragged direction doesn't detract from high-spirited scripting and top comic cast. **(CC)**
Dist.: HBO

RUDE BOY 1980 British
★ ★ R Musical 2:13
☑ Explicit language
Dir: Jack Hazan *Cast:* The Clash, Ray Gange, Johnny Green, Barry Baker, Terry McQuade, Caroline Coon
► With little direction in life, cashier Gange gets gig as roadie for his favorite band, the Clash, but manages to mess up and get fired. Good rock music numbers, convincing portrait of alienated punk generation, but unintelligible accents and uneven production values. Strictly for the band's fans.
Dist.: CBS/Fox

RUGGLES OF RED GAP 1935
★ ★ ★ NR Comedy 1:30 B&W
Dir: Leo McCarey *Cast:* Charles Laughton, Mary Boland, Charles Ruggles, ZaSu Pitts, Roland Young
► Very proper English butler Laughton is won by vulgar American millionaire Ruggles in poker game and makes a surprisingly deft transition to the wild, wild West. Charming, sweet, and amusing; Laughton eschews his usual theatrics to deliver a quietly droll and touching performance.
Dist.: MCA

RULES OF THE GAME 1939 French
☆ NR Comedy/Drama 1:46 B&W
Dir: Jean Renoir *Cast:* Marcel Dalio, Nora Gregor, Mila Parely, Jean Renoir, Roland Toutain, Paulette Dubost
► On eve of World War II, French aristocrats, including famous aviator Toutain and his confidante (played by director Renoir), gather at home of dapper toy collector Dalio and his wife Gregor. During a weekend of hunting and partying, various flirtations among both rich and servants merge in chaos ("Stop this farce!" demands Dalio; "Which one?" asks his butler) until one too many cases of mistaken identity brings a tragic end to the high jinks. Satire of morals and manners features splendid performances, especially Dalio and Renoir. [S]
Dist.: Various

RULING CLASS, THE 1972 British
★ ★ PG Comedy/Drama 2:24
☑ Brief nudity, adult situations, explicit language, mild violence, adult humor

Dir: Peter Medak *Cast:* Peter O'Toole, Alastair Sim, Harry Andrews, Arthur Lowe, Coral Browne
► "When I pray to Him, I find I'm talking to myself," explains O'Toole when asked why he fancies himself to be Jesus Christ. O'Toole's family initially indulges his fantasy so they can live off his money, but plots against him as his madness gets out of hand. Brilliant black comedy based on play by Peter Barnes loses some of its impact in screen translation.
Dist.: Nelson

RUMBLE FISH 1983
★ ★ R Drama 1:34 B&W
☑ Nudity, explicit language, violence
Dir: Francis Coppola *Cast:* Matt Dillon, Mickey Rourke, Diane Lane, Dennis Hopper, Diana Scarwid, Vincent Spano
► Troubled Tulsa teenager Dillon, living with alcoholic dad Hopper, gets visit from biker older brother Rourke whom he worships. Rourke's desire to liberate rare fish from pet store leads to conflict with cop. Technically audacious cinematography and sound defeated by arch dialogue and cold characters. From the S. E. Hinton novel.
Dist.: MCA

RUNAWAY 1984
★ ★ ★ PG-13 Sci-Fi 1:40
☑ Brief nudity, explicit language, violence
Dir: Michael Crichton *Cast:* Tom Selleck, Cynthia Rhodes, Kirstie Alley, Gene Simmons, Stan Shaw
► Pretty blond cop Rhodes is assigned to robotics expert Selleck, who suffers from vertigo. They're called in when someone's modifications transform domestic robots into murder machines. Bad guy Simmons (from rock group Kiss) kidnaps Selleck's son and holds him high atop a building under construction. Farfetched formula helped by clever special effects, terrific craftsmanship, and the always easy-to-watch Selleck. **(CC)**
Dist.: RCA

RUNAWAY TRAIN 1985
★ ★ ★ R Action-Adventure 1:47
☑ Explicit language, graphic violence
Dir: Andrei Konchalovsky *Cast:* Jon Voight, Eric Roberts, Rebecca De Mornay, Kyle T. Heffner, John P. Ryan, Kenneth McMillan
► In Alaska, hardened convict Voight breaks out of jail with younger colleague Roberts. They hop a freight but find themselves on a runaway train when the engineer suffers a fatal heart attack. Exciting action and stunts but unsavory characterizations and pretentious dialogue. Intense performances by Voight and Roberts nabbed Oscar nominations. Based on a screenplay by Akira Kurosawa. **(CC)**
Dist.: MGM/UA

RUN FOR THE ROSES 1978
★ ★ PG Family 1:33
☑ Explicit language

Dir: Henry Levin **Cast:** Vera Miles, Stuart Whitman, Sam Groom, Panchito Gomez, Theodore Wilson, Lisa Eilbacher
▶ Horse farm manager Whitman's Puerto Rican stepson Gomez is given a lame colt by the farm's owner. The lad saves up his money for an operation that restores the horse's health, enabling it to race in the Kentucky Derby. Homey heartwarmer is simple but satisfying family fare, save for some mild profanity.
Dist.: Vestron

RUNNING BRAVE 1983 Canadian
★ ★ ★ ★ **PG Biography/Sports 1:46**
☑ Brief nudity, adult situations, mild violence
Dir: D. S. Everett **Cast:** Robby Benson, Pat Hingle, Claudia Cron, Jeff McCracken, August Schellenberg, Graham Greene
▶ True story of Billy Mills (Benson), the American Indian runner who overcame prejudice and personal crises to win a gold medal at the 1964 Olympics. Along the way, he gets support from his WASP wife Cron and tough coach Hingle. Irresistible story with sympathetic hero and thrilling (if predictable) finale; Benson's best screen work to date.
Dist.: Buena Vista

RUNNING MAN, THE 1987
★ ★ ★ **R Sci-Fi/Action-Adventure 1:41**
☑ Explicit language, violence
Dir: Andrew Davis **Cast:** Arnold Schwarzenegger, Maria Conchita Alonso, Yaphet Kotto, Richard Dawson, Jim Brown, Jesse Ventura
▶ In 2017, pilot Schwarzenegger disobeys fascist regime's orders and is forced to become contestant on deadly TV game show. He must run for his life while being hunted down by killers. "I'll be back," Schwarzenegger promises the unctuous host (perfectly cast Dawson) and you know he's not kidding. Fast-moving futuristic fun is noisy but energetic. Based on the novel by Richard Bachman (Stephen King).
Dist.: Vestron

RUNNING ON EMPTY 1988
★ ★ ★ ★ **PG-13 Drama 1:55**
☑ Adult situations, explicit language
Dir: Sidney Lumet **Cast:** Christine Lahti, Judd Hirsch, River Phoenix, Martha Plimpton, L. M. Kit Carson, Steven Hill
▶ Sixties radicals Lahti and Hirsch have been on the lam for fifteen years after blowing up napalm lab, moving from town to town and changing their names to avoid capture by the Feds. When their teenage son Phoenix decides to apply for a Juilliard music scholarship, it precipitates a family crisis. The adults are fine but it is the sensitive Phoenix and the marvelously natural Plimpton as his girlfriend who dominate this provocative and moving story.
Dist.: Warner

RUNNING SCARED 1986
★ ★ ★ ★ **R Action-Adventure 1:47**

☑ Nudity, adult situations, explicit language, violence
Dir: Peter Hyams **Cast:** Gregory Hines, Billy Crystal, Dan Hedaya, Steven Bauer, Jimmy Smits, Darlanne Fluegel
▶ Hectic male-bonding melodrama features top-notch team of Crystal and Hines as two cool Chicago cops looking to retire to Florida after a bloody confrontation with aspiring Spanish godfather Smits. They're forced back onto the streets when Smits kidnaps Crystal's ex-wife Fluegel. Nonstop banter is rowdy, intimate, and often very funny. Fresh action ending staged at Chicago's cavernous Illinois State Building. **(CC)**
Dist.: MGM/UA

RUNNING WILD 1927
★ **NR Comedy 1:08 B&W**
Dir: Gregory La Cava **Cast:** W. C. Fields, Mary Brian, Claude Buchanan, Marie Shotwell, Barney Raskle, Tom Madden
▶ Obsessively superstitious Fields throws a horseshoe over his shoulder, breaks a window, and is chased onto a vaudeville stage where a hypnotism act is in progress. The stage hypnotist convinces Fields he is a "lion," whereupon the formerly Milquetoast husband storms off to put things right in his own home. Delirious silent comedy is a good showcase for Fields's brilliant physical gags and gestural asides.
Dist.: Paramount

RUNNING WILD 1973
★ ★ ★ ★ **G Drama 1:43**
Dir: Robert McCahon **Cast:** Lloyd Bridges, Dina Merrill, Pat Hingle, Morgan Woodward, Gilbert Roland
▶ Merrill, a journalist visiting the high country of Colorado, organizes animal rights campaign when she learns that a herd of wild horses is threatened by a local dog food canning factory. Upbeat, family-oriented drama features a strong cast and beautiful scenery.
Dist.: Paramount

RUNNIN' KIND, THE 1989
★ **R Drama 1:40**
☑ Adult situations, explicit language
Dir: Max Tash **Cast:** David Packer, Pleasant Gehman, Brie Howard, Susan Strasberg, Steven Eckholdt
▶ Slated for a summer job in his dad's law firm, middle-class Ohioan Packer departs for Los Angeles instead when he falls for a female drummer. While his parents hire a private detective to check up on him, Packer throws himself into the club scene and manages an all-girl band. Portrait of L.A. music scene seems authentic, although performances and plotting lack oomph.
Dist.: CBS/Fox

RUN SILENT, RUN DEEP 1958
★ ★ ★ **NR War 1:33 B&W**
Dir: Robert Wise **Cast:** Clark Gable, Burt

Lancaster, Jack Warden, Brad Dexter, Don Rickles, Nick Cravat

▶ World War II sub commander Gable is the only survivor of a Japanese attack. Distrusted by the crew of his new sub (in particular executive officer Lancaster), he embarks on a foolhardy mission to sink an enemy destroyer. Tense, claustrophobic drama adapted from Commander Edward L. Beach's best-seller features a valiant performance by Gable.
Dist.: CBS/Fox

RUSH IT 1984
☆ **NR Comedy 1:30**
☑ Explicit language
Dir: Gary Youngman *Cast:* Judy Kahan, Tom Berenger, John Heard, Christina Pickles
▶ Gung-ho messenger Kahan can't seem to get her love life in gear until she meets artist/fellow-messenger Berenger. After they move in together, Kahan learns that her bed is not the only stop on Berenger's route. Not very funny.
Dist.: Unicorn

RUSSIAN ROULETTE 1975
★ ★ ★ **PG Mystery-Suspense 1:33**
☑ Explicit language, mild violence
Dir: Lou Lombardo *Cast:* George Segal, Cristina Raines, Denholm Elliott, Louise Fletcher, Bo Brundin, Peter Donat
▶ Mountie Segal is assigned to guard Soviet premier Kosygin during Canadian visit. Segal infiltrates local agitators only to discover KGB reactionaries plan to slay the Russian leader and frame the CIA for the hit. Above-average espionage caper gets off to confusing start but soon moves into high gear with Segal effective as rogue detective.
Dist.: CBS/Fox

RUSSIANS ARE COMING, THE RUSSIANS ARE COMING, THE 1966
★ ★ ★ ★ **NR Comedy 2:06**
Dir: Norman Jewison *Cast:* Carl Reiner, Eva Marie Saint, Alan Arkin, Brian Keith, Jonathan Winters, Theodore Bikel
▶ Surprise hit about a Soviet submarine that runs aground off the New England coast. A landing crew led by Arkin takes Reiner hostage and searches for a motorboat to tow the sub off the sandbar. Meanwhile, sheriff Keith and sidekick Winters have their hands full as panic spreads and the town mobilizes to defend itself from an imagined attack. Lighthearted parody of Cold War tension is still effective; Arkin was Oscar-nominated in his screen debut.
Dist.: MGM/UA

RUSSKIES 1987
★ ★ ★ ★ **PG Drama 1:38**
☑ Explicit language
Dir: Rick Rosenthal *Cast:* Whip Hubley, Peter Billingsley, Leaf Phoenix, Stefan DeSalle, Susan Walters, Carole King
▶ On the Fourth of July, Russian radio operator Hubley is shipwrecked on a Key West beach while on a mission. Local kids Billingsley, Phoenix, and DeSalle discover him. Their initial mistrust soon turns to East-West friendship. Amiable civics lesson, especially for younger viewers.
Dist.: Warner

RUSTLERS' RHAPSODY 1985
★ ★ **PG Western/Comedy 1:28**
☑ Explicit language, violence, adult humor
Dir: Hugh Wilson *Cast:* Tom Berenger, G. W. Bailey, Marilu Henner, Andy Griffith, Fernando Rey, Sela Ward, Patrick Wayne
▶ White-suited singing cowboy Berenger aids sheepherders in battle against evil cattlemen and wins the hearts of town "hostess" Henner and colonel's daughter Ward. Cute spoof with amusing supporting cast, especially Henner and Wayne as a good guy hired by the bad guys to confuse Berenger; a bit skimpy on big laughs, however. (CC)
Dist.: Paramount

RUTHLESS PEOPLE 1986
★ ★ ★ ★ **R Comedy 1:38**
☑ Nudity, explicit language, adult humor
Dir: Jerry Zucker *Cast:* Bette Midler, Danny DeVito, Judge Reinhold, Helen Slater, Anita Morris
▶ Spandex miniskirt king DeVito is planning to kill heiress wife Midler when he discovers she's been kidnapped. Abductors Reinhold and Slater demand $500,000 "or else" If Sam calls the cops. He opens champagne, calls his mistress Morris, and promptly alerts the police and media. Cheerfully boisterous comedy about bad manners proves nastiness is its own reward.
Dist.: Buena Vista

RYAN'S DAUGHTER 1970 British
★ ★ ★ ★ **PG Drama 3:18**
☑ Brief nudity, adult situations, explicit language
Dir: David Lean *Cast:* Robert Mitchum, Sarah Miles, John Mills, Christopher Jones, Trevor Howard, Leo McKern
▶ In 1916 Ireland, willful young Miles, married to middle-aged schoolteacher Mitchum, has affair with British major Jones that scandalizes the locals and leads to tragic consequences. Sweeping love story directed on an epic scale. Oscars for Supporting Actor Mills as the village idiot and the lovely cinematography; Miles was nominated for Best Actress.
Dist.: MGM/UA

SABOTAGE 1936 British
★ ★ **NR Mystery-Suspense 1:16 B&W**
Dir: Alfred Hitchcock *Cast:* Sylvia Sidney, Oscar Homolka, John Loder, Desmond Tester, Joyce Barbour, Matthew Boulton
▶ Foreign terrorist Homolka establishes a cover in London as a movie theater manager. His unhappy wife Sidney gradually suspects him, and turns to Scotland Yard undercover agent Loder for help. Chilling thriller based on Joseph Conrad's *The Secret Agent* has a

flawed plot despite impressive work by Sidney. Notable for two of Hitchcock's most famous scenes: a controversial depiction of an explosion and a fascinating murder performed after a screening of Walt Disney's cartoon *Who Killed Cock Robin?*
Dist.: KVC

SABOTEUR 1942
★★★ PG Mystery-Suspense 1:48 B&W
☑ Violence
Dir: Alfred Hitchcock ***Cast:*** Robert Cummings, Priscilla Lane, Otto Kruger, Alan Baxter, Alma Kruger
▶ Cummings, falsely implicated for torching a war factory, embarks on cross-country chase to nab the real culprit, Nazi agent Kruger. Fast-paced thrills from the opening bit with the gas-filled fire extinguisher to the famous cliff-hanging climax at the Statue of Liberty, although callow Cummings is miscast.
Dist.: MCA

SABRINA 1954
★★★★★ NR Romance/Comedy 1:53 B&W
Dir: Billy Wilder ***Cast:*** Humphrey Bogart, Audrey Hepburn, William Holden, Walter Hampden, John Williams, Martha Hyer
▶ After Paris education, chauffeur's daughter Hepburn returns to Long Island estate where dad works and attracts the attention of two scions: swinging swain Holden and his stuffy older brother Bogart. Sparkling romantic triangle, nicely played by the three leads. Oscar for Costume Design.
Dist.: Paramount

SACRED GROUND 1983
★★★ PG Action-Adventure 1:40
☑ Adult situations, violence
Dir: Charles B. Pierce ***Cast:*** Tim McIntire, Jack Elam, Serene Hedin, Mindi Miller, Eloy Phil Casados, L. Q. Jones
▶ Mountain man and Indian wife set up homestead and have child on sacred Indian burial ground. A local tribe discovers them, kidnaps the baby, and kills the wife. Now the father must find a way to get the baby back. The Indian dialogue is wooden, but story is appealing, and Western scenery beautiful. (CC)
Dist.: CBS/Fox

SACRIFICE, THE 1986 Swedish/French
☆ PG Drama 2:25
☑ Brief nudity, adult situations
Dir: Andrei Tarkovsky ***Cast:*** Erland Josephson, Susan Fleetwood, Valerie Mairesse, Allan Edwall, Gudrun Gisladottir, Sven Wollter
▶ On the coast of Sweden, intellectual Josephson is celebrating his birthday with family and friends when it seems that a nuclear blast has occurred. As the night wears on, Josephson makes a mystical and profound sacrifice in the hopes that mankind be spared. Slow-moving, portentous arthouse film is stunningly shot by Sven Nykvist, but ultimately grim and unfathomable. [S]
Dist.: Pacific Arts

SADIE THOMPSON 1928
★ NR Drama 1:37 B&W
Dir: Raoul Walsh ***Cast:*** Gloria Swanson, Lionel Barrymore, Raoul Walsh, Blanche Frederici, Charles Lane, James Marcus
▶ Lusty, freewheeling Sadie Thompson was already famous from W. Somerset Maugham's short story "Rain" and a hit stage adaptation when director Walsh brought her to the screen in the person of Swanson. The story of how Sadie seduces and destroys minister Barrymore smolders with the tense sensuality the silents were so adept at evoking. Since the last reel long ago disintegrated, conclusion has been reconstructed from the original title cards and production stills. Remade as *Rain* and *Miss Sadie Thompson*.
Dist.: Kino

SADIST, THE 1963
☆ NR Mystery-Suspense 1:21 B&W
Dir: James Landis ***Cast:*** Arch Hall, Jr., Helen Hovey, Richard Alden, Marilyn Manning, Don Russell
▶ When their car breaks down on the way to Dodger Stadium, teachers Hovey, Alden, and Manning go to a gas station for help. There they are captured by teacher-hating psycho Hall and his partner Russell, who proceed to torture and murder them. Also known as *Profile of Terror*, crisp thriller was photographed by Vilmos Zsigmond.
Dist.: Rhino

SAD SACK, THE 1957
★★ NR Comedy 1:38 B&W
Dir: George Marshall ***Cast:*** Jerry Lewis, David Wayne, Phyllis Kirk, Peter Lorre, Gene Evans, Liliane Montevecchi
▶ George Baker's popular comic strip about the perennial Army loser gave Lewis his second starring role without Dean Martin. Loosely structured plot sends Lewis to Morocco, where he falls for slinky singer Montevecchi. Spurned, he joins the Foreign Legion, where his photographic memory is exploited by Arab bandit Lorre. Predictable high jinks buoyed by Lorre's amusing performance.
Dist.: RCA

SAFARI 3000 1982
★★ PG Action-Adventure 1:31
☑ Brief nudity, adult situations, explicit language
Dir: Harry Hurwitz ***Cast:*** David Carradine, Stockard Channing, Christopher Lee, Hamilton Camp, Ian Yule
▶ American stunt-driver Carradine teams with live-wire journalist Channing for the African International Rally. Various entanglements over the 2,500-mile course include crumbling bridges, irritable locals, and hostile competitors. Amid such adversity, antagonism between the leads turns to love. Only

mild humor but very attractive visuals of African landscape and fauna.
Dist.: MGM/UA

SAFETY LAST 1923
★ ★ **NR Comedy 1:18 B&W**
Dir: Sam Taylor, Fred Newmeyer   *Cast:* Harold Lloyd, Mildred Davis, Noah Young, Bill Strother, Mickey Daniels
▶ Country boy Lloyd moves to the city, attempts to succeed while winning the girl of his dreams. Upward mobility takes a comic turn when circumstances force him to climb a skyscraper, an amazing sequence that features the immortal image of Lloyd hanging from the face of a clock. Silent classic is filled with nifty sight gags. Lloyd's upbeat persona is a delight.
Dist.: Time-Life

SAHARA 1943
★ ★ ★ ★ **NR War 1:37 B&W**
Dir: Zoltan Korda   *Cast:* Humphrey Bogart, Bruce Bennett, Lloyd Bridges, Rex Ingram, J. Carrol Naish, Dan Duryea
▶ Top-notch World War II adventure about an American tank led by Bogart fleeing the Germans after the fall of Tobruk. Bogart rescues a band of stragglers and finds refuge from the withering heat in the ruins of an Arabian desert village. His men make a heroic stand against a Nazi battalion desperate for water. Canny use of survival themes, racial conflicts, and thrilling battles combine into a superior film with integrity and excitement. Received three Oscar nominations, including Naish's convincing Italian POW.
Dist.: RCA/Columbia

SAHARA 1984
★ **PG Action-Adventure 1:51**
☑ Adult situations, mild violence
Dir: Andrew V. McLaglen   *Cast:* Brooke Shields, Lambert Wilson, John Mills, Horst Buchholz, John Rhys-Davies, Steve Forrest
▶ In 1927, Shields poses as a man to enter Sahara road race. After winning warm-up heat, her identity is revealed and she is kidnapped by tribal leaders; handsome sheik Wilson comes to her rescue. Conventional, nicely mounted filler. Shields is pleasant to watch , but an unconvincing actress.
Dist.: RCA/Columbia

SAIGON COMMANDOS 1988
☆ **R Action-Adventure 1:23**
☑ Nudity, explicit language, violence
Dir: Clark Henderson   *Cast:* Richard Young, P. J. Soles, John Allen Nelson, Jimi B., Jr., Spanky Manikan, Joonee Gamboa
▶ Young is an Army M.P. in Saigon whose superiors are leaning on him to solve a series of killings of drug dealers. Soles is a reporter who goes along with him on the investigation. Cheap, murky crime melodrama never got theatrical release.
Dist.: Media

SAILOR WHO FELL FROM GRACE WITH THE SEA, THE 1976 British
★ ★ ★ ★ **R Drama 1:45**
☑ Nudity, adult situations, explicit language, violence
Dir: Lewis John Carlino   *Cast:* Sarah Miles, Kris Kristofferson, Jonathan Kahn, Margo Cunningham, Earl Rhodes, Paul Tropea
▶ Young Kahn is initially pleased when Kristofferson passionately courts his widowed mother Miles, but friends convince him that the sailor cannot maintain integrity on land. Solemn adaptation of a Yukio Mishima novel gained some notoriety for its graphic eroticism, but story ultimately turns glum and violent.
Dist.: Embassy

SAINT JACK 1979
★ ★ **R Drama 1:50**
☑ Nudity, adult situations, explicit language
Dir: Peter Bogdanovich   *Cast:* Ben Gazzara, Denholm Elliott, James Villiers, Peter Bogdanovich, Lisa Lu
▶ Jack Flowers (Gazzara), a pimp with a heart of gold, runs a bordello in Singapore for U.S. soldiers recovering from the Vietnam war. When local competitors bring down the operation, Flowers works for American mobster Bogdanovich, but draws the line at blackmailing a U.S. senator. Vivid portrayal of the seamier side of Singapore, fine supporting performance from Elliott as a dreamy English accountant who befriends Flowers, and a perfect role for the always interesting Gazzara.
Dist.: Vestron

SAINT JOAN 1957
☆ **NR Drama 1:51 B&W**
Dir: Otto Preminger   *Cast:* Jean Seberg, Richard Widmark, Anton Walbrook, John Gielgud, Harry Andrews
▶ Lackluster historical drama set in 15th-century France about Seberg, a simple country girl who hears voices telling her to lead her people into battle, enabling the Dauphin (Widmark) to be crowned. Undermined by the Earl of Warwick (Gielgud), she is eventually burned at the stake as a witch. Tepid screen version of the G. B. Shaw play. Strong cast overpowers Seberg, who was discovered by Preminger during a huge talent search.
Dist.: Hal Roach   ☐

SAINT STRIKES BACK, THE 1939
★ **NR Mystery-Suspense 1:07 B&W**
Dir: John Farrow   *Cast:* George Sanders, Wendy Barrie, Jonathan Hale, Jerome Cowan, Neil Hamilton, Barry Fitzgerald
▶ Urbane Sanders's first attempt playing Simon Templar finds the English sleuth in San Francisco, helping Barrie solve the murder of her father, who was wrongly implicated in other killings. Second in the series is one of the best, thanks to top cast and direction. Home

video version double billed with Robert Wise's 1946 *Criminal Court.*
Dist.: Turner

SAINT'S VACATION, THE 1941 British
★ NR Mystery-Suspense 1:00
Dir: Leslie Fenton   *Cast:* Hugh Sinclair, Sally Gray, Arthur Macrae, Cecil Parker, Leueen McGrath, Gordon McLeod
▶ During a Swiss vacation, the Saint (Sinclair) gets involved in intrigue surrounding a music box that contains a secret code. A spy ring provides the opposition. Middling entry in the series finds Sinclair not up to George Sanders's standard. Leslie Charteris, creator of *The Saint*, co-wrote the screenplay. Home video version double billed with the 1952 *Narrow Margin.*
Dist.: Turner

SAKHAROV 1984
★ ★ ★ ★ ★ NR Biography/MFTV 1:58
☑ Adult situations
Dir: Jack Gold   *Cast:* Jason Robards, Glenda Jackson, Nicol Williamson, Frank Finlay, Marion Bailey, Michael Bryant
▶ Russian physicist Andrei Sakharov (Robards) speaks out against human rights abuses. He and wife Jackson suffer hardships, persecution, and exile but his actions provoke the conscience of the world; he is eventually awarded the Nobel Peace Prize. Gripping and powerful true story with stirring performances by Robards and Jackson.
Dist.: Prism

SALAAM BOMBAY! 1988 Indian
★ ★ NR Drama 1:53
☑ Adult situations, explicit language
Dir: Mira Nair   *Cast:* Shafiq Syed, Raghubir Yadav, Aneeta Kanwar, Nana Patekar, Chanda Sharma
▶ Indian youngster takes menial jobs after being forced out of home. He befriends drug addict who steals from him and teenage prostitute who seeks to escape pimp. Harrowing and often moving look at the street children of Bombay, wonderfully acted by a nonprofessional cast. Nominated for Best Foreign Film Oscar. Ⓢ
Dist.: Virgin

SALAMANDER 1981 U.S./British/Italian
★ NR Drama 1:41
☑ Brief nudity, adult situations, explicit language, mild violence
Dir: Peter Zinner   *Cast:* Franco Nero, Anthony Quinn, Sybil Danning, Martin Balsam, Claudia Cardinale, Christopher Lee
▶ When an Italian general dies under suspicious circumstances, cop Nero investigates and uncovers a right-wing plot to take over the government. Along the way, Nero has an affair with Polish spy Danning. Serviceable premise, decent acting, breathtaking locations, but tangled plotting and stiff dialogue.
Dist.: Nelson

SALEM'S LOT: THE MOVIE 1979
★ ★ ★ PG Horror 1:51
☑ Mild violence
Dir: Tobe Hooper   *Cast:* David Soul, James Mason, Bonnie Bedelia, Lance Kerwin, Lew Ayres, Elisha Cook, Jr.
▶ Novelist Soul returns to the Maine town of Salem's Lot and discovers his boyhood house has been sold to sinister antique dealer Mason. Supernatural hell breaks loose: vampires materialize and young children disappear. Goose-bumping gimmicks include opening graves, barking doors, creaking fences, and gusting wind. Certain to please fans of Stephen King, who wrote the original novel. Originally shown on television in two parts, videocassette version contains more explicit violence.
Dist.: Warner

SALLY OF THE SAWDUST 1925
☆ NR Comedy 1:31 B&W
Dir: D. W. Griffith   *Cast:* W. C. Fields, Carol Dempster, Alfred Lunt, Erville Alderson, Effie Shannon
▶ Juggler and con man Fields has raised young orphan Dempster in a carnival environment. While attempting to find her real grandparents, Fields and Dempster are arrested and brought before the town judge—who turns out to be the long lost grandfather. Director Griffith's only full-length comedy is beguiling, and considerably aided by Fields's well-timed business. Silent; remade with Fields in 1936 as *Poppy.*
Dist.: Grapevine

SALOME 1953
★ ★ ★ NR Drama 1:43
Dir: William Dieterle   *Cast:* Rita Hayworth, Stewart Granger, Charles Laughton, Judith Anderson, Cedric Hardwicke, Alan Badel
▶ Costly Biblical epic completely distorts story of infamous seductress, presenting her as a secret Christian sympathizer in love with soldier/convert Granger. Still entertaining, with Hayworth especially ravishing during her dance of the seven veils and Laughton chewing the scenery as Herod.
Dist.: RCA/Columbia

SALOME'S LAST DANCE 1988 British
☆ R Drama 1:29
☑ Nudity, adult situations, explicit language
Dir: Ken Russell   *Cast:* Glenda Jackson, Stratford Johns, Nickolas Grace, Douglas Hodge, Imogen Millais-Scott, Denis Ull
▶ In 1892, Oscar Wilde attends secret premiere of his banned play *Salome* in the homosexual brothel that would later figure in his arrest. Amateur cast for the play includes brothel proprietor Johns and his servant Millais-Scott (in her film debut). Overwrought version of an already florid play may strike viewers as camp.
Dist.: Vestron

SALOME, WHERE SHE DANCED 1945
★ NR Drama 1:30
Dir: Charles Lamont *Cast:* Yvonne De
Carlo, Rod Cameron, David Bruce, Walter
Slezak, Albert Dekker, Marjorie Rambeau
▶ Dancer De Carlo wows the crowned heads
of Europe with her Dance of the Seven Veils,
but when she gets tangled with Franco-Prus-
sian intrigue, she hightails it to the American
West with Yank reporter Cameron. There she
does her dance for yahooing gold miners,
and is kidnapped by moony bandit Bruce.
Outrageously bad, and De Carlo's clunky
dancing is a howl.
Dist.: Playhouse

SALSA 1988
★★ PG Drama/Dance 1:36
☑ Adult situations, explicit language
Dir: Boaz Davidson *Cast:* Robby Rosa,
Rodney Harvey, Magali Alvarado, Miranda
Garrison, Moon Orona, Angela Alvarado
▶ Auto mechanic Rosa rehearses feverishly to
win top prize in a Los Angeles salsa contest,
trading in girlfriend Angela Alvarado for older
dancing partner Orona. He also watches over
young sister Magali Alvarado, who's just start-
ing to date. Thin plot doesn't detract from sen-
sational salsa numbers choreographed by
Kenny Ortega (*Dirty Dancing*). Music by Tito
Puente, Celia Cruz, Mongo Santamaria, etc.
Also available in a Spanish language version.
Dist.: Cannon

SALT OF THE EARTH 1953
☆ NR Drama 1:34 B&W
Dir: Herbert Biberman *Cast:* Juan Chacon,
Rosoura Revueltas, Will Geer, Mervin Williams, Frank Talavera, Clinton Jencks
▶ Chacon leads a strike of Mexican-American mine workers, aided by wife Revueltas
and opposed by sheriff Geer. The authorities
start to evict Chacon from his home, but the
miners and their families descend on the proceedings and try to stop them. Producer Paul
Jarrico and director Biberman produced this
politically weighted drama independently
after being blacklisted by Hollywood in the
early fifties.
Dist.: MPI

SALTY 1974
★★★★ G Comedy/Family 1:33
Dir: Ricou Browning *Cast:* Clint Howard,
Mark Slade, Nina Foch, Julius W. Harris,
Linda Scruggs
▶ Orphan Howard and his brother Slade be-
friend an intelligent, fun-loving sea lion fond of
practical jokes. Predictable family-oriented
high jinks aided by pretty Florida locations.
Dist.: Vestron

SALVADOR 1986
★★★★ R Action-Adventure 2:03
☑ Rape, adult situations, explicit language,
graphic violence
Dir: Oliver Stone *Cast:* James Woods,
James Belushi, John Savage, Michael Murphy, Cynthia Gibb, Elpidia Carrillo
▶ Journalist Woods and DJ buddy Belushi go
to El Salvador, where Woods uncovers the corruption and oppression of the U.S.-backed
Salvadoran military while trying to aid girlfriend Carrillo. Vivid, unsettling, hard-hitting,
and real; Stone's direction rivals his *Platoon* for
its sheer intensity. Woods nabbed an Oscar
nomination for his edgy performance as the
real-life Richard Boyle (who was nominated
for co-authoring the script with Stone).
(CC)
Dist.: Vestron

SAME TIME, NEXT YEAR 1978
★★★★★ PG Romance/Comedy 1:59
☑ Adult situations, explicit language, adult
humor
Dir: Robert Mulligan *Cast:* Ellen Burstyn,
Alan Alda, Ivan Bonar, Bernie Kuby
▶ Burstyn and Alda, married but not to each
other, have an annual affair at a California
inn. Over a 26-year period, the one-weekend-
a-year lovers see each other through several
crises. Captivating, warm, witty, and very ro-
mantic, with excellent Burstyn and Alda, well
crafted direction from Mulligan, and sweet
Marvin Hamlisch score. Oscar nominations:
Best Actress (Burstyn), Screenplay Adaptation
(Bernard Slade from his Broadway hit), Song
("The Last Time I Felt Like This"), Cinematography.
Dist.: MCA

SAMMY AND ROSIE GET LAID 1987 British
★★ R Comedy/Drama 1:40
☑ Nudity, adult situations, explicit lan-
guage, violence
Dir: Stephen Frears *Cast:* Shashi Kapoor,
Frances Barber, Ayub Khan Din, Claire
Bloom, Roland Gift, Wendy Gazelle
▶ Pakistani fascist Kapoor visits accountant
son Din and his antiestablishment English wife
Barber in a racially torn London ghetto. Kapoor renews acquaintance with old flame
Bloom but his son's open marriage and countercultural lifestyle shock him. Ambitious,
seething, and rowdy comedy has complex
characters (especially Kapoor) and darkly
funny sexual shenanigans (three couplings in
a montage set to "My Girl"), although political
slant makes it not for all tastes.
Dist.: Warner

SAMMY THE WAY OUT SEAL 1962
★★★ G Family 1:30
Dir: Norman Tokar *Cast:* Robert Culp, Jack
Carson, Billy Mumy, Patricia Barry
▶ Mumy and pal discover an injured seal on
the beach and smuggle it back to their subur-
ban home. The seal is soon healed, but every-
where they stash him, he causes hilarious mis-
haps. Best scene has seal causing havoc in a
supermarket. Originally a two-episode Disney
TV production.
Dist.: Buena Vista

SAMSON AND DELILAH 1950
★ ★ ★ NR Drama 2:07
Dir: Cecil B. DeMille   **Cast:** Victor Mature,
Hedy Lamarr, George Sanders, Angela
Lansbury, Henry Wilcoxon
▶ Extravagant biblical epic about the ill-
fated romance between the legendary muscleman Samson (Mature) and the treacherous Philistine Delilah (Lamarr). Samson first
wins the hand of beautiful princess Lansbury
by killing a lion bare-handed; betrayed, he
lays wastes to the Saran's (Sanders) soldiers
until he is tricked by the wily Delilah. Enormous
cast and intricate special effects helped
make this a popular success. Won Oscars for
costumes and art direction.
Dist.: Paramount

SANDERS OF THE RIVER 1935 British
★ NR Action-Adventure 1:36 B&W
Dir: Zoltan Korda   **Cast:** Leslie Banks, Paul
Robeson, Nina Mae McKinney, Robert
Cochran, Martin Walker, Tony Wane
▶ British officer Banks is about to leave colo-
nial Africa on vacation when trouble breaks
out in the form of tribal king Wane's revolt. The
Englishman is aided by chief Robeson in his
effort to stop Wane. Creaky but still rousing
adventure features powerful Robeson per-
formance. Based on stories by Edgar Wallace.
Also known as *Bosambo.*
Dist.: Nelson

SAND PEBBLES, THE 1966
★ ★ ★ NR Action-Adventure 3:15
Dir: Robert Wise   **Cast:** Steve McQueen,
Richard Attenborough, Richard Crenna,
Candice Bergen, Mako, Marayat Andriane
▶ In China, lone wolf McQueen is assigned to
the engine room of a U.S. Navy gunboat patrolling the Yangtze River. Civil war breaks out,
and ship's captain Crenna must balance di-
plomacy against self-preservation. Meanwhile, McQueen falls in love with missionary
Bergen. Epic adventure about American inter-
vention abroad was nominated for Best Picture, Actor (McQueen), Supporting Actor
(Mako as McQueen's machinist sidekick), and
five technical Oscars.
Dist.: CBS/Fox

SANDPIPER, THE 1965
★ ★ ★ ★ NR Romance 1:57
☑ Adult situations, explicit language
Dir: Vincente Minnelli   **Cast:** Elizabeth Taylor, Richard Burton, Eva Marie Saint, Charles
Bronson, Tom Drake
▶ Classy soap opera set against California's
scenic Big Sur: artist Taylor enrolls her son in
private school run by married clergyman Burton. After initial conflict, a love affair develops
between Taylor and Burton that threatens his
career and marriage to Saint. Slightly dated
but the stars transcend the material. Oscar for
Best Song ("The Shadow of Your Smile").
Dist.: MGM/UA

SANDS OF IWO JIMA, THE 1949
★ ★ ★ ★ NR War 1:50
Dir: Allan Dwan   **Cast:** John Wayne, John
Agar, Adele Mara, Forrest Tucker, James
Brown, Richard Webb
▶ Wayne, winning his first Oscar nomination,
plays a strict sergeant whose expertly trained
men were a major factor in the battle of Iwo
Jima. Realistic plot follows the men through
jungle exercises, harsh fighting on Tarawa,
R&R leaves, and climactic effort to take Mt.
Suribachi. Film is enhanced by use of docu-
mentary war footage and appearances by
three of the soldiers in the famous flag-raising
photograph (Ira Hayes, Rene Gagnon, John
Bradley).
Dist.: Republic

SAN FRANCISCO 1936
★ ★ ★ ★ NR Drama 1:55 B&W
Dir: W. S. Van Dyke II   **Cast:** Clark Gable,
Jeanette MacDonald, Spencer Tracy, Jack
Holt, Ted Healy, Margaret Irving
▶ Barbary Coast gambler Gable and singer
MacDonald fall in love. His rough ways hinder
both the romance and his friendship with
priest Tracy, both of which are further disrupted by the 1906 earthquake. Lusty, brawling saga is a great deal of fun, thanks to the
star power of the leads and the magnificent
earthquake sequence. Many musical numbers include MacDonald's famous warbling of
the title tune.
Dist.: MGM/UA

SANJURO 1962 Japanese
☆ NR Action-Adventure 1:36 B&W
Dir: Akira Kurosawa   **Cast:** Toshiro Mifune,
Tatsuya Nakadai, Takashi Shimura, Yuzo
Kayama, Reiko Dan, Yunosuke Ito
▶ Samurai loner Mifune gets involved in local
politics in nineteenth-century Japan. On the
way to rescue kidnapped chamberlain Ito,
Mifune himself is captured, and must find a
way to float white camelias down the river as
a signal to attack. Slightly tongue-in-cheek
sequel to *Yojimbo* is not one of Kurasawa's
masterpieces, but still enjoyable.   [S]
Dist.: Various

SANSHO THE BAILIFF 1954 Japanese
☆ NR Drama 2:05 B&W
Dir: Kenji Mizoguchi   **Cast:** Kinuyo Tanaka,
Kisho Hanayagi, Kyoko Kagawa, Eitaro
Shindo, Ichiro Sugai, Kikue Mori
▶ In the lawless world of eleventh-century
Japan, a family is assaulted on the road, and
young Hanayagi and his sister Kagawa are
kidnapped and sold as slaves to evil bailiff
Sansho (Shindo). Raised to be cruel himself,
Hanayagi longs for a different life, escapes,
and rises to a position of responsibility. Once
given power, he attempts reforms. Consid-
ered a landmark of world cinema.   [S]
Dist.: SVS

SANTA CLAUS 1985
★ ★ ★ ★ PG Family 1:52

☑ Explicit language
Dir: Jeannot Szwarc *Cast:* Dudley Moore, John Lithgow, David Huddleston, Burgess Meredith, Judy Cornwell
▶ Large-scale fantasy about the origin of Santa Claus (Huddleston), a kindly woodcutter magically transported to a toy-filled workshop at the North Pole. Conflict between bumbling elf Moore and evil toy baron Lithgow provides plot complications. Intricate special effects will enthrall young viewers. Also known as *Santa Claus: The Movie.* (CC)
Dist.: Media

SANTA CLAUS CONQUERS THE MARTIANS 1964
☆ **NR Sci-Fi 1:20**
Dir: Nicholas Webster *Cast:* John Call, Victor Stiles, Donna Conforti, Vincent Beck, Bill McCutheon, Pia Zadora
▶ Santa Claus and two Earthling children are kidnapped by Martians but all ends happily as old St. Nick introduces the joys of Christmas to the angry red planet. Silly screenplay, chintzy sets, and memorably wacky theme song ("Hurray for Santa Claus!") add up to a camp classic.
Dist.: Nelson

SANTA FE TRAIL 1940
★★★★ **NR Western 1:50 B&W**
Dir: Michael Curtiz *Cast:* Errol Flynn, Olivia de Havilland, Raymond Massey, Ronald Reagan, Alan Hale, Van Heflin
▶ Unusual Western set in 1854 Kansas: West Point pals Jeb Stuart (Flynn) and George Custer (Reagan) battle each other over beautiful tomboy de Havilland while infiltrating John Brown's (Massey) dangerous abolitionist movement. Culminates in the famous Harper's Ferry siege. Muddled as history and often uncomfortably pro-slavery, but furious pacing and large-scale action scenes are exciting.
Dist.: Various ⓒ

SAPPHIRE 1959 British
★★ **NR Mystery-Suspense 1:32**
Dir: Basil Dearden *Cast:* Nigel Patrick, Yvonne Mitchell, Michael Craig, Paul Massie, Bernard Miles
▶ In London, a black woman who was passing for white is murdered. Among the many suspects: members of her boyfriend's bigoted family. Absorbing whodunit with a social conscience; fine ensemble acting, tight script, intriguing John Dankworth jazz score. Frank depiction of racial slurs could offend some.
Dist.: IUD

SATAN'S CHEERLEADERS 1977
☆ **PG Horror**
☑ Adult situations, explicit language
Dir: Greydon Clark *Cast:* John Ireland, Yvonne De Carlo, Jack Kruschen, John Carradine, Sydney Chaplin
▶ A devil cult in California goes after a busload of nubile teen cheerleaders. Cheap,

low-budget production features many familiar faces, but is surprisingly mild in the skin/violence department.
Dist.: United

SATISFACTION 1988
★★★ **PG-13 Drama 1:32**
☑ Adult situations, explicit language
Dir: Joan Freeman *Cast:* Justine Bateman, Liam Neeson, Trini Alvarado, Scott Coffey, Britta Phillips, Julia Roberts
▶ Four-girl, one-guy inner-city rock band Mystery wins an audition for a summer-long gig at a posh seaside resort. Lead singer Bateman has a fling with alcoholic, Grammy-winning songwriter Neeson; Phillips overdoses on pills; Roberts finds love in the back of a van. Predictable teen flick isn't helped by nondescript songs. Debbie Harry has a brief cameo. (CC)
Dist.: CBS/Fox

SATURDAY NIGHT FEVER 1977
★★★ **PG Drama/Dance 1:52**
☑ Brief nudity, adult situations
Dir: John Badham *Cast:* John Travolta, Karen Lynn Gorney, Barry Miller, Donna Pescow, Julie Bovasso, Joseph Cali
▶ Blockbuster megahit made Travolta a household name as Tony Manero, a nineteen-year-old paint store salesmen in Brooklyn who lives for Saturday nights at the local disco where he's the star dancer. He enters a dance contest with new partner Gorney, who thinks his life is a "cliché." Not much on plot but great dancing scenes and phenomenally successful, pulse-pounding Bee Gees score. Includes hits "Night Fever," "How Deep Is Your Love," "More Than a Woman," many more. Sequel: *Staying Alive.*
Dist.: Paramount

SATURDAY THE 14TH 1981
★★ **PG Horror/Comedy 1:16**
☑ Explicit language, violence
Dir: Howard R. Cohen *Cast:* Richard Benjamin, Paula Prentiss, Severn Darden, Jeffrey Tambor, Kari Michaelson, Kevin Brando
▶ Benjamin and Prentiss inherit haunted house and try to make the best of it when assorted monsters and spooks make themselves part of the household. Family tires of finding Creature from the Black Lagoon in bath tub, so they throw an exorcism party to rid themselves of the guests that won't leave. Sophomoric horror spoof.
Dist.: Nelson

SATURDAY THE 14TH STRIKES BACK 1988
★ **PG Horror 1:18**
☑ Mild violence
Dir: Howard R. Cohen *Cast:* Ray Walston, Avery Schreiber, Jason Presson, Patty McCormack, Julianne McNamara, Rhonda Aldrich
▶ All the evil in the world is coming up through a crack in the basement of the house that dad Schreiber, mom McCormack, and

grandpa Walston have just moved into. Only teenaged son Presson is aware of the danger. A poor, silly sequel to *Saturday the 14th*.
Dist.: MGM/UA

SATURN 3 1980
★ ★ R Sci-Fi 1:27
☑ Nudity, adult situations, violence
Dir: Stanley Donen *Cast:* Farrah Fawcett, Kirk Douglas, Harvey Keitel, Douglas Lambert, Ed Bishop
▶ Somewhere in deep, dark space, scientists Fawcett and Douglas jog around an enclosed space station. Enter creepy bad guy Keitel, who installs Hector, a lust-crazed humanoid robot who terrorizes the inhabitants of this outer-orbit Garden of Eden. Best scene: Hector's resurrection after he has been dismantled for being randy.
Dist.: CBS/Fox

SAVAGE BEACH 1989
★ R Action-Adventure 1:36
☑ Nudity, explicit language, violence
Dir: Andy Sidaris *Cast:* Dona Speir, Hope Marie Carlton, John Aprea, Michael Shane, Lisa London, Patty Dufek
▶ Undercover agents (and real-life *Playboy* centerfolds) Speir, Carlton, and Dufek are stranded on an island where an elderly Japanese soldier is hoarding gold from World War II. The U.S. military, Japanese agents, and Commie rebels are all out to get the gold, but the girls save the day. Leads drop their tops at the drop of a hat here; frequent shoot-outs should please action fans.
Dist.: RCA/Columbia

SAVAGE DAWN 1985
★ ★ NR Action-Adventure 1:42
☑ Adult situations, explicit language, violence
Dir: Simon Nuchtern *Cast:* George Kennedy, Richard Lynch, Karen Black, Lance Henriksen, Claudia Udy, William Forsythe
▶ Vietnam hero Henriksen visits his vet friend Kennedy, now confined to a wheelchair. They are attacked by a gang of vicious bikers led by Forsythe. Neighbors, including paranoid preacher Lynch and surly bar owner Black, are powerless to stop the villains until Henriksen takes charge. Low-budget exploitation redeemed somewhat by inventive motorcycle stunts.
Dist.: Media

SAVAGE ISLAND 1985 Italian/Spanish
★ R Action-Adventure 1:14
☑ Nudity, explicit language, violence
Dir: Edward Muller *Cast:* Linda Blair, Anthony Steffen, Ajita Wilson, Christina Lai, Leon Askin
▶ Blair, former inmate of women's island prison, seeks revenge on Askin, cohort of the camp's rulers. Rest of the story unfolds in flashback (separate from and mostly irrelevant to Blair's section) as warden and guards

exploit inmates, using them to dig for gems. Idiot plot hook for frequent nude scenes.
Dist.: Vestron

SAVAGE IS LOOSE, THE 1971
★ R Drama
☑ Adult situations, explicit language
Dir: George C. Scott *Cast:* George C. Scott, Trish Van Devere, John David Carson, Lee H. Montgomery
▶ Strange story of incest among a family of three stranded on a desert island. Dad Scott can't handle it when he finds son Carson in the arms of mom Van Devere, and determines to track the boy down. Pet project by director/ producer/distributor/star Scott faced critical disdain and lukewarm box office.
Dist.: VCII

SAVAGE SAM 1963
★ ★ ★ ★ NR Family 1:43
Dir: Norman Tokar *Cast:* Brian Keith, Tommy Kirk, Kevin Corcoran, Dewey Martin, Jeff York, Marta Kristen
▶ When brothers Kirk and Corcoran and their friend Kristen are kidnappped by Indians, their uncle Keith attempts to find them with the help of family dog Savage Sam, the son of Old Yeller. Sturdy sequel to Disney's *Old Yeller* is not nearly as emotionally wrenching as its predecessor.
Dist.: Buena Vista

SAVAGE SEVEN, THE 1968
☆ NR Action-Adventure 1:36
Dir: Richard Rush *Cast:* Robert Walker, Larry Bishop, Adam Roarke, Max Julien, Duane Eddy, Penny Marshall
▶ Roarke and his motorcycle gang cruise into a crumbling American Indian town which is being fleeced by corrupt businessmen. Indians and motorcyclists clash, while Roarke courts an Indian girl. Typical motorcycle gang stuff violently exploits sixties social concerns. Guitarist Eddy and future TV star/director Marshall have little to do.
Dist.: Trylon

SAVAGE STREETS 1984
★ ★ R Action-Adventure 1:33
☑ Rape, nudity, explicit language, graphic violence
Dir: Danny Steinmann *Cast:* Linda Blair, John Vernon, Robert Dryer, Johnny Venocur, Sal Landi
▶ Punks led by Dryer gang rape a deaf-mute and murder a bride on her wedding day. Blair, the deaf-mute's older sister, assembles her girlfriends for revenge. Explicit, often gratuitously violent drama features campy dialogue and a satisfying vigilante theme.
Dist.: Vestron

SAVANNAH SMILES 1982
★ ★ ★ ★ ★ PG Family 1:44
☑ Mild violence
Dir: Pierre DeMoro *Cast:* Mark Miller, Dono-

van Scott, Bridgette Andersen, Peter Graves, Michael Parks, Pat Morita

▶ Poor little six-year-old rich girl Savannah (Andersen) runs away from snooty parents and hooks up with Miller and Scott, a pair of on-the-run criminals with hearts of teddy bears. Holding her for ransom, they set up what turns into a very loving household. Genuine laughs mixed in with moments of true warmth and tenderness. Strong family entertainment; one of the highest-rated movies ever shown on HBO.
Dist.: Nelson

SAVE THE TIGER 1973
★ ★ ★ R Drama 1:42
Dir: John G. Avildsen *Cast:* Jack Lemmon, Jack Gilford, Laurie Heineman, Norman Burton, Thayer David

▶ Oscar-winner Lemmon in a sobering, sensitive portrait of a middle-aged clothing manufacturer whose life and business are failing. In desperation, he decides to burn his factory for the insurance money, despite the objections of partner Gilford. Serious-minded examination of the failure of the American dream feels sluggish at times but packs a powerful punch.
Dist.: Paramount

SAVING GRACE 1986
★ ★ ★ ★ PG Drama 1:52
☑ Explicit language, violence
Dir: Robert M. Young *Cast:* Tom Conti, Giancarlo Giannini, Fernando Rey, Erland Josephson, Edward James Olmos

▶ Sentimental but heartfelt tale about man-of-the-people Pope (Conti) who wanders away from the Vatican one day and ends up in a remote small town without a priest, where everyone pretends to be quarantined in order to receive relief money. Vatican officials Rey and Josephson keep the Pope's absence a secret. Conti succeeds in redeeming the town, including mysterious goatherd Giannini. Pleasant, likable entertainment. **(CC)**
Dist.: Nelson

SAY AMEN, SOMEBODY 1983
★ ★ ★ ★ G Documentary/Music 1:40
Dir: George T. Nierenberg *Cast:* Willie Mae Ford Smith, Thomas A. Dorsey, Sallie Martin, The Barrett Sisters, The O'Neal Brothers, Jackson Price

▶ Jubilant documentary about gospel music, the "sanctified blues." Mixing music scenes with exploration of colorful characters, picture pays special attention to two legends of gospel's roots: "Mother" Smith and Dorsey, the acknowledged "Father of Gospel Music." Uplifting and fascinating.
Dist.: Pacific Arts

SAY ANYTHING 1989
★ ★ ★ ★ PG-13 Romance 1:40
☑ Adult situations, explicit language
Dir: Cameron Crowe *Cast:* John Cusack, Ione Skye, John Mahoney, Lili Taylor, Erik Stoltz, Joan Cusack, Lois Chiles, Jason Gould

▶ Brainy Skye is graduating high school with honors and heading off to college in England. She falls in love with unambitious Cusack, but her father Mahoney objects. Love's course proves rocky as the two try to find some way of working things out. Thoughtful, sensitive romantic comedy is a refreshing change from the usual teen fare. Appealing stars, especially the always winning Cusack, and nicely rounded characters make this one a treat. **(CC)**
Dist.: CBS/Fox

SAYONARA 1957
★ ★ ★ ★ NR Drama 2:31
☑ Adult situations, explicit language
Dir: Joshua Logan *Cast:* Marlon Brando, James Garner, Red Buttons, Miyoshi Umeki, Miiko Taka, Ricardo Montalban

▶ Adapted from the James Michener novel about the love affair between U.S. pilot Brando and Japanese singer Taka during Korean War. Features wonderful performances from quality cast, exotic locale, and convincing story. Winner of four Oscars, including Best Supporting Actor and Actress to Buttons and Umeki.
Dist.: CBS/Fox

SAY YES 1986
★ ★ PG-13 Comedy 1:30
☑ Nudity, adult situations, explicit language
Dir: Larry Yust *Cast:* Lissa Layng, Art Hindle, Logan Ramsey, Jonathan Winters, Maryedith Burrell

▶ Good-natured comedy with a familiar premise: playboy Hindle must marry before his thirty-fifth birthday or lose his immense inheritance. Winters displays his delightful off-the-wall humor as the curmudgeonly grandfather, but story suffers from flat jokes.
Dist.: RCA/Columbia

SCANDAL 1989 British
★ ★ 1:45 Drama R
☑ Nudity, strong sexual content, adult situations, explicit language
Dir: Michael Caton-Jones *Cast:* John Hurt, Joanne Whalley-Kilmer, Bridget Fonda, Ian McKellen, Britt Ekland, Jeroen Krabbe, Roland Gift

▶ True story of the 1963 Profumo scandal, in which the British politician's (McKellen) downfall is brought about by relationship with party girl Christine Keeler (the haunting Whalley-Kilmer), who is also involved with Soviet Krabbe. Beautifully made, extremely evocative of the period, but Caton-Jones's placid direction dampens the subject's sizzling potential. Fonda is amusing, yet the central relationship between Whalley-Kilmer and her apparently asexual mentor Hurt remains teasingly ambiguous. Available in a longer, unrated version.
Dist.: HBO

SCANDALOUS 1984
★ ★ **PG Comedy 1:34**
☑ Adult situations, explicit language
Dir: Rob Cohen   *Cast:* Robert Hays, John
Gielgud, Pamela Stephenson, Jim Dale, M.
Emmet Walsh, Bow Wow Wow
▶ Beautiful con artist Stephenson falls for TV
reporter Hays, much to the dismay of her part-
ner Gielgud. When Hays's wife turns up dead,
Scotland Yard tries to pin the murder on him.
Gielgud and Stephenson are funny when they
impersonate wacky characters as part of the
con, but plot runs out of steam early. Features
an extended and unnecessary concert se-
quence by rock group Bow Wow Wow.
Dist.: Vestron

SCANNERS 1981 Canadian
★ ★ **R Horror 1:42**
☑ Adult situations, graphic violence
Dir: David Cronenberg   *Cast:* Jennifer
O'Neill, Stephen Lack, Patrick McGoohan,
Lawrence Dane, Michael Ironside, Charles
Shamata
▶ Maternity drug with bizarre side effects creates "scanners," humans with telekinetic
powers who can cause others' heads to explode. One such man, Lack, is recruited by
weaponry corporation to infiltrate in-house
conspiracy to take over the world by other
scanners Dane and Ironside. Aided by beautiful scanner comrade O'Neill, Lack battles his
evil counterparts. Literally mind-blowing special effects in the service of average premise
and script.
Dist.: Nelson

SCARECROW 1973
★ **R Drama 1:52**
☑ Adult situations, explicit language, vio-
    lence
Dir: Jerry Schatzberg   *Cast:* Gene Hackman, Al Pacino, Dorothy Tristan, Ann
Wedgeworth, Richard Lynch, Eileen Brennan
▶ Ex-con Hackman, hoping to open a car
wash in Pittsburgh, teams up with merchant
seaman Pacino, who plans reconciliation with
his estranged wife in Detroit, for a journey
across an extremely bleak America. Episodic
road movie features superior performances,
particularly Hackman's unpredictably violent
drifter, but plot often feels aimless.
Dist.: Warner

SCARED STIFF 1987
★ **R Horror 1:23**
☑ Explicit language, graphic violence
Dir: Richard Friedman   *Cast:* Andrew Stevens, Mary Page Keller, Josh Segal, David
Ramsey, William Hindman
▶ Rock singer Keller, her son Segal, and her
psychiatrist boyfriend Stevens move into
Gothic Southern mansion. When Keller suffers
terrifying hallucinations, Stevens at first believes she's having a relapse of a nervous
breakdown. Soon enough the three learn that
their new home is cursed—its original owner

slaughtered innocents in voodoo rituals.
Southern-fried chiller will appeal mainly to
genre fans.
Dist.: Republic

SCARED TO DEATH 1947
☆ **NR Horror 1:09**
Dir: Christy Cabanne   *Cast:* Bela Lugosi,
Douglas Fowley, Joyce Compton, George
Zucco, Nat Pendleton, Angelo Rossitto
▶ A dead woman who was literally frightened
to death looks back on events leading to the
crime. Likely suspects include asylum director
Zucco, evil Lugosi, and his dwarf associate
Rossitto. Although not particularly scary,
Lugosi's only color film is good for a few unin-
tentional chuckles.
Dist.: Video Yesteryear

SCARED TO DEATH 1981
☆ **R Sci-Fi 1:38**
☑ Nudity, explicit language, violence
Dir: William Malone   *Cast:* John Stinson,
Diana Davidson, Jonathon David Moses,
Toni Janotta, Kermit Eller, Walker Edmiston
▶ Police find strange clues as they hunt down
a mad killer who mutilates victims. Investiga-
tion reveals that the killer is a genetic experi-
ment gone horribly wrong. Victims die one by
one before the camera. Production values,
especially the monster, are cheap.
Dist.: Media

SCARFACE 1932
★ ★ **PG Crime/Drama 1:30 B&W**
☑ Adult situations, violence
Dir: Howard Hawks   *Cast:* Paul Muni, Ann
Dvorak, George Raft, Boris Karloff, Karen
Morley, Osgood Perkins
▶ Extraordinary story of Chicago hoodlum
Tony Camonte (Muni), his amoral sister Dvorak, and violent henchman Raft is among the
most violent and shocking gangster movies
ever made. Based on the career of Al Capone, plot is uncompromising in its depiction
of a ruthless, lethal underworld. Plagued by
censors for its suggestions of incest and
twenty-eight on-screen murders, film was
recut by producer Howard Hughes, then withdrawn from circulation for forty years. Muni
and Raft became overnight stars for their brutal performances. Loosely remade in 1983
with Al Pacino.
Dist.: MCA

SCARFACE 1983
★ ★ ★ **R Crime/Drama 2:53**
☑ Nudity, adult situations, explicit lan-
    guage, graphic violence
Dir: Brian De Palma   *Cast:* Al Pacino, Mi-
chelle Pfeiffer, Steven Bauer, Robert Loggia,
Mary Elizabeth Mastrantonio, F. Murray
Abraham
▶ Flashy, big-budget remake of the Howard
Hawks 1932 classic tells the story of Cuban
refugee Tony Montana (Pacino), who rises
from cocaine courier to top kingpin of the
drug world. He takes blond mistress Pfeiffer

from crime boss Loggia, kills Bauer, the lover of his kid sister Mastrantonio, and spirals into a cocaine frenzy that leads to a final shootout in his Miami mansion. Written by Oliver Stone. Very strong violence includes dismemberments, hangings, knifings, etc.
Dist.: MCA

SCARLET CLAW, THE 1944
★ ★ ★ **NR Mystery-Suspense 1:14 B&W**
Dir: Roy William Neill *Cast:* Basil Rathbone, Nigel Bruce, Gerald Hamer, Paul Cavanagh, Arthur Hohl, Kay Harding
▶ In 1944 Canada, Sherlock Holmes (Rathbone) and Dr. Watson (Bruce) attend a conference on the supernatural. The local villagers hold a legendary monster responsible for a rash of murders, but Holmes proves contemporary vengeance is behind the killings. Better-than-average outing for Rathbone and Bruce in modernized version of Arthur Conan Doyle's classics.
Dist.: Various

SCARLET LETTER, THE 1934
★ **NR Drama 1:10 B&W**
Dir: Robert G. Vignola *Cast:* Colleen Moore, Hardie Albright, Henry B. Walthall, Cora Sue Collins, Alan Hale, Virginia Howell
▶ Moore wears a bright-red "A" on her breast as punishment for bearing a child out of wedlock in sixteenth-century Puritan Boston. Daughter Collins capers brightly as the town wonders who her father is. The screenwriters have taken some liberties in this mostly straightforward adaptation of the novel by Nathaniel Hawthorne, but the changes lighten the story agreeably. Remade from 1926 silent, and subsequently done as a 1979 TV movie.
Dist.: Video Yesteryear

SCARLET PIMPERNEL, THE 1934 British
★ ★ **NR Action-Adventure 1:35 B&W**
Dir: Harold Young *Cast:* Leslie Howard, Merle Oberon, Raymond Massey, Nigel Bruce, Bramwell Fletcher, Joan Gardner
▶ As her aristocratic friends are guillotined during the eighteenth-century Reign of Terror, Oberon, a lady in the court of the Prince of Wales, loses faith in her foppish husband Howard—unaware he's secretly the daredevil freeing many of the prisoners. Howard approaches his role with relish in this rousing adaptation of Baroness Orczy's swashbuckling adventure.
Dist.: Various

SCARLET STREET 1945
★ ★ **NR Mystery-Suspense 1:43 B&W**
Dir: Fritz Lang *Cast:* Edward G. Robinson, Joan Bennett, Dan Duryea, Margaret Lindsay, Rosalind Ivan, Jess Barker
▶ Gloomy tale of mild-mannered clerk Robinson's infatuation with Bennett, a mysterious woman he rescues from a mugging. Her secret lover Duryea takes advantage of Robinson's artwork, leading to a murder with an ironic double twist. Remake of 1931's *La Chienne* reteamed three stars from *The Woman in the Window* for a similarly bleak study of revenge.
Dist.: Various

SCARRED 1984
★ **R Drama 1:25**
☑ Nudity, strong sexual content, adult situations, explicit language
Dir: Rose Marie Turko *Cast:* Jennifer Mayo, Jackie Berryman, David Dean, Rico L. Richardson, Debbie Dion, Lili
▶ Single mother Mayo is forced into prostitution to pay the rent, reluctantly allowing Dean to pimp for her. Honest look at unsavory subject suffers from budget restrictions, but realistic view of seedy Los Angeles settings is powerful. Young Mayo is impressive as the resilient heroine.
Dist.: Vestron

SCARS OF DRACULA 1971 British
★ ★ **R Horror 1:33**
☑ Adult situations, explicit language, violence
Dir: Roy Ward Baker *Cast:* Christopher Lee, Dennis Waterman, Jenny Hanley, Christopher Matthews, Patrick Troughton, Michael Gwynn
▶ Lured to Count Dracula's castle by a seductive vampiress, Matthews gets fanged. Young couple Waterman and Hanley battle cobwebs, bats, and worse in search of Matthews. Climactic showdown with Lee, heir to Bela Lugosi as the Dracula of choice.
Dist.: HBO

SCAVENGER HUNT 1979
★ ★ ★ ★ **PG Comedy 1:56**
☑ Explicit language
Dir: Michael Schultz *Cast:* Richard Benjamin, James Coco, Scatman Crothers, Ruth Gordon, Cloris Leachman, Cleavon Little
▶ Broad, frantic comedy with five greedy teams in a mad scramble to fulfill the weird obligations of game manufacturer's will by competing in a treasure hunt. Among their targets to find: obese people, ostriches, toilets, and beehives. All-star cast includes bizarre cameos by Arnold Schwarzenegger, Meat Loaf, Tony Randall, Avery Schreiber, Dirk Benedict, others.
Dist.: CBS/Fox

SCAVENGERS 1988
★ ★ **PG-13 Action-Adventure 1:34**
☑ Explicit language, violence
Dir: Duncan McLachlan *Cast:* Kenneth David Gilman, Brenda Bakke, Crispin De Nys, Cocky Tlhothalemaj
▶ Adventure parody set primarily in Africa, with KGB and CIA agents chasing virile hero Gilman and his girlfriend Bakke for secret information hidden in a Bible. Extended chase featuring vintage planes, tanks, and jeeps is

high-spirited, but generic plot and low production values are big drawbacks.
Dist.: Academy

SCENE OF THE CRIME 1986 French
☆ **NR Drama 1:31**
☑ Nudity, adult situations, explicit language, violence
Dir: Andre Techine *Cast:* Catherine Deneuve, Danielle Darrieux, Wadeck Stanczak, Nicolas Giraudi, Victor Lanoux, Jean Bousquet
▶ Young Giraudi, threatened by deadly drifter Stanczak, draws his repressed mother Deneuve into a mysterious plot involving murder, escaped convicts, and blackmail. Intriguing premise and a polished performance by Deneuve can't overcome murky story line. Best moments involve Deneuve's strained relationship with ex-husband Lanoux. [S]
Dist.: MCA

SCENES FROM A MARRIAGE 1974 Swedish
☆ **PG Drama 2:48**
☑ Adult situations, explicit language
Dir: Ingmar Bergman *Cast:* Liv Ullmann, Erland Josephson, Bibi Andersson, Jan Malmsjo, Anita Wall, Gunnel Lindblom
▶ Challenging, intimately detailed depiction of a troubled marriage focuses on Ullmann's grief at learning her husband Josephson is seeing a younger woman. Edited down from a six-part Swedish TV miniseries, film's incessant close-ups and emotionally traumatic themes are often uncomfortably vivid. [S]
Dist.: RCA/Columbia

SCENES FROM THE CLASS STRUGGLE IN BEVERLY HILLS 1989
★★ **R Comedy 1:42**
☑ Nudity, adult situations, explicit language
Dir: Paul Bartel *Cast:* Jacqueline Bisset, Ray Sharkey, Robert Beltran, Mary Woronov, Arnetia Walker, Ed Begley, Jr., Wallace Shawn, Rebecca Schaeffer, Paul Mazursky, Paul Bartel
▶ Former TV star Bisset is celebrating the death of cheating hubbie Mazursky in the company of assorted over-sexed Beverly Hills residents, including "thinologist" Bartel, playwright Begley, crude Walker, and horny houseboys Beltran and Sharkey. No-holds-barred raunch and lunacy in this hit-or-miss sex comedy. Tragically, the final film of Schaeffer, who was murdered by an obsessed fan soon after film's release. (CC)
Dist.: Virgin

SCENES FROM THE GOLDMINE 1987
★★ **R Drama/Musical 1:45**
☑ Explicit language
Dir: Marc Rocco *Cast:* Catherine Mary Stewart, Steve Railsback, Cameron Dye, Joe Pantoliano, John Ford Coley, Timothy B. Schmit
▶ Keyboard player Stewart joins rock band and becomes involved with lead singer Dye. But when record magnate Pantoliano dangles dollars at Dye, he changes for the worse, stealing Stewart's songs, asking his brother Railsback to quit as band's manager, and developing cocaine addiction. Lots of tunes in credible look at cut-throat music biz.
Dist.: Nelson

SCHIZOID 1980
★★ **R Mystery-Suspense 1:31**
☑ Nudity, adult situations, explicit language, graphic violence
Dir: David Paulsen *Cast:* Klaus Kinski, Marianna Hill, Craig Wasson, Donna Wilkes, Richard Herd, Christopher Lloyd
▶ Newspaper columnist Hill, member of a therapy group run by psychiatrist Kinski, receives evidence about a series of gruesome murders that implicates both Kinski and her estranged husband Wasson. Strong acting adds to the agreeably creepy atmosphere in this crude but effective chiller.
Dist.: MCA

SCHOOL DAZE 1988
★ **R Musical/Comedy 1:54**
☑ Adult situations, explicit language
Dir: Spike Lee *Cast:* Larry Fishburne, Giancarlo Esposito, Tisha Campbell, Kyme, Ossie Davis, Spike Lee
▶ Feisty, often funny, but unstructured and episodic chronicle of life on all-black campus. School is split between conservative Wannabee fraternity and socially conscious, independent Jigaboos. Over homecoming weekend Wannabee head Esposito and Jigaboo leader Fishburne clash over everything except the ineptitude of young frat pledge Lee. Many zippy dance-and-music numbers and spirited lampooning of fraternities in somewhat scattershot satire. (CC)
Dist.: RCA/Columbia

SCHOOL SPIRIT 1985
★ **R Comedy**
☑ Nudity, adult situations, explicit language
Dir: Alan Holleb *Cast:* Tom Nolan, Elizabeth Foxx, Roberta Collins, John Finnegan, Larry Linville, Marta Kober
▶ College student Nolan is killed in a car crash. Heavenly powers that be give him one day back on earth to redeem himself, which he does by exposing corrupt dean Linville and saving the school's traditional "Hog Day" celebrations. Lifeless comedy registers almost nothing on the laugh meter.
Dist.: Media

SCORCHY 1976
★ **R Action-Adventure 1:39**
☑ Nudity, adult situations, explicit language, violence
Dir: Hikmet Avedis *Cast:* Connie Stevens, Cesare Danova, William Smith, Marlene Schmidt, Normann Burton, Joyce Jameson
▶ Seattle drug dealer Danova thinks he's a bad dude—but that's before he meets Stevens, one tough undercover cop who makes

it her mission destroy the sleazeball's vicious heroin empire. Violence and chases by the numbers. Stevens comes out from undercover long enough to do a nude shower scene.
Dist.: Vestron

SCOTT OF THE ANTARCTIC 1948 British
★★ NR Action-Adventure 1:50
Dir: Charles Frend *Cast:* John Mills, Derek Bond, James Robertson Justice, Kenneth More, Christopher Lee, John Gregson
▶ In 1911, Robert Falcon Scott (Mills) plans to become the first man to reach the South Pole. After exhaustive preparation, he sets out with a team that endures incredible hardships, only to discover that a group of Norwegians led by Roald Amundsen have gotten to the Pole first. Now the men must fight their way back through the terrible Antarctic winter. Every detail is authentic in this minutely researched re-creation of Scott's doomed, real-life adventure.
Dist.: Sinister

SCREAM AND SCREAM AGAIN 1970 British
★★ PG Horror 1:35
☑ Adult situations, explicit language, violence
Dir: Gordon Hessler *Cast:* Vincent Price, Christopher Lee, Peter Cushing, Judy Huxtable, Alfred Marks
▶ Gruesome thriller about mad scientist Price conducting amputation experiments for a conspiracy led by vicious sadist Cushing. Lee's murder investigations and subplot about military secrets add unnecessary confusion, but three horror stars are in top form.
Dist.: Vestron

SCREAM, BLACULA, SCREAM 1973
☆ PG Horror 1:35
☑ Adult situations, violence
Dir: Bob Kelljan *Cast:* William Marshall, Don Mitchell, Pam Grier, Michael Conrad, Richard Lawson, Arnita Bell
▶ Grier and Lawson are locked in a power struggle for leadership of a voodoo cult when Lawson revives the bones of Blacula (Marshall), triggering a bloodsucking spree in Los Angeles. Blacula hopes powerful enchantress Grier can cure his problem. Grier is sultry in this adequate sequel to *Blacula*.
Dist.: Orion

SCREAMERS 1981 Italian
☆ R Horror 1:22
☑ Explicit language, graphic violence
Dir: Sergio Martino *Cast:* Barbara Bach, Claudio Cassinelli, Richard Johnson, Joseph Cotten, Beryl Cunningham, Mel Ferrer
▶ Caribbean island ruled by Johnson is home to strange half-fish/half-men created by scientist Cotten and tended by Bach, his daughter. Island also has voodoo graveyards, slinky snakes, smiling skulls, and mushy swamps to spook Cassinelli and other survivors of a

wrecked convict ship. Awful special effects and ludicrous plot.
Dist.: Nelson

SCREAM FOR HELP 1984
★★ R Mystery-Suspense 1:30
☑ Nudity, adult situations, explicit language, violence
Dir: Michael Winner *Cast:* Rachael Kelly, Marie Masters, David Brooks, Lolita Lorre, Rocco Sisto
▶ Young Kelly is convinced that her stepfather Brooks is trying to kill her mother Masters. Police refuse to believe her, even after murderous traps lead to the deaths of a power company worker and her best friend. Effective shocker from the maker of *Death Wish* features some jarringly violent scenes.
Dist.: Warner

SCREAM OF FEAR 1961 British
★★ NR Mystery-Suspense 1:21 B&W
Dir: Seth Holt *Cast:* Susan Strasberg, Ronald Lewis, Ann Todd, Christopher Lee, John Serret, Leonard Sachs
▶ Handicapped Strasberg arrives at a Riviera estate to be reunited with her father, but instead keeps seeing his corpse. Is he dead or is she just imagining this? Chauffeur Lewis romances her while stepmother Todd and doctor Lee are among the suspects. Intriguing if overly contrived mystery.
Dist.: RCA/Columbia

SCREWBALL ACADEMY 1987 Canadian
★ R Comedy 1:27
☑ Nudity, adult situations, explicit language
Dir: John Blanchard *Cast:* Colleen Camp, Kenneth Welsh, Christine Cattell, Charles Dennis, Angus MacInnes, Damian Lee
▶ Thin farce about ad executive Camp making a low-budget feminist film on a resort island where corrupt televangelist Lee is dodging a Federal investigation into his finances. Low-budget attempt at teen-oriented slapstick was filmed in 1983 and never released theatrically.
Dist.: TWE

SCREWBALL HOTEL 1988 British
★ R Comedy 1:41
☑ Nudity, adult situations, explicit language, violence
Dir: Rafal Zielinski *Cast:* Michael C. Bendetti, Jeff Greenman, Kelly Monteith, Corinne Alphen, Charles Ballinger, Laurah Guillen, Andrew Zeller
▶ Fat cadet Greenman and fellow military school discards Bendetti and Zeller try to save Florida hotel from greedy manager Ballinger by organizing illegal gambling casino and turning a Miss Purity contest into an oil wrestling bash. Teasing sex comedy is very tired.
Dist.: MCA

SCREWBALLS 1983
★ R Comedy 1:20
☑ Nudity, explicit language, adult humor

Dir: Rafal Zielinski *Cast:* Peter Keleghan, Linda Shayne, Alan Daveau, Kent Deuters, Jason Warren, Lynda Speciale
▶ Male students at Taft & Adams High School try a variety of tricks to deflower Purity Bush (Speciale), the school's sole remaining virgin. Stunts include a fraudulent medical exam, a strip bowling contest, and visits to the girls' locker room. Raunchy low-brow humor in the *Porky's* mold.
Dist.: Warner

SCROOGE 1970 British
★ ★ **G Musical 1:58**
Dir: Ronald Neame *Cast:* Albert Finney, Alec Guinness, Edith Evans, Kenneth More, Michael Medwin, Laurence Naismith
▶ Glossy, big-budget musical version of classic Christmas tale by Charles Dickens. Old skinflint Finney is transformed overnight by ghosts Guinness, More, and Evans into jolly do-gooder. Distinguished cast, quality production, and music by Leslie Bricusse, author of tunes for *Dr. Doolittle*, make this decent family fare, although critics panned it on release. (CC)
Dist.: CBS/Fox

SCROOGED 1988
★ ★ ★ ★ **PG-13 Comedy 1:41**
☑ Explicit language
Dir: Richard Donner *Cast:* Bill Murray, Karen Allen, John Forsythe, Carol Kane, Bob Goldthwait, David Johansen
▶ Modern-day version of Dickens's *A Christmas Carol* stars Murray as a Scrooge-like network TV mogul who finally learns to put a little love in his heart when visited by ghosts Forsythe, Johansen, and Kane. Hilarious and heartwarming comedy with Murray's trademark brash humor topped off by a surprisingly emotional ending. Among many funny scenes: Murray dictating Christmas gift list ("Towel, towel, VCR. . ."), figuring out how to put antlers on mice, and watching commercial for "Robert Goulet's Cajun Christmas."
Dist.: Paramount

SEA CHASE, THE 1955
★ ★ ★ **NR War 1:57**
Dir: John Farrow *Cast:* John Wayne, Lana Turner, Tab Hunter, David Farrar, Lyle Bettger, James Arness
▶ World War II has broken out, but German freighter captain Wayne wants no part of his country's evil doings. Sailing out of New Zealand, Wayne picks up romantic spy Turner, and tries to outrun both the German and British navies around Cape Horn. Wayne's American drawl is conspicuous amid crew's Katzenjammer accents in this slack, gritless presentation.
Dist.: Warner

SEA DEVILS 1953 British
★ **NR Action-Adventure 1:26**
Dir: Raoul Walsh *Cast:* Rock Hudson, Yvonne De Carlo, Maxwell Reed, Denis O'Dea, Michael Goodliffe, Bryan Forbes
▶ Handsome smuggler Hudson sails beautiful British spy De Carlo to Napoleonic France. He helps her escape when she is captured and they fall in love. Typically virile Walsh adventure is entertaining if far from the director's finest. Borden Chase screenplay loosely based on the Victor Hugo novel *The Toilers of the Sea*.
Dist.: Media

SEA GYPSIES, THE 1978
★ ★ ★ ★ **G Family 1:41**
Dir: Stewart Raffill *Cast:* Robert Logan, Mikki Jamison-Olson, Heather Rattray, Cjon Damitri Patterson, Shannon Saylor
▶ Seattle widower Logan sets sail around world with daughters Saylor and Rattray and two last-minute additions, cute female reporter Jamison-Olson and young black stowaway Patterson. Storm maroons motley crew on Alaskan coast. Agreeable family adventure combines spectacular wildlife and scenery with an engaging Seattle Family Robinson yarn.
Dist.: Warner

SEA HAWK, THE 1940
★ ★ ★ ★ **NR Action-Adventure 2:07 B&W**
Dir: Michael Curtiz *Cast:* Errol Flynn, Brenda Marshall, Claude Rains, Donald Crisp, Flora Robson, Henry Daniell
▶ In the sixteenth century, Queen Elizabeth (Robson) suspects the Spaniards are building an armada to attack England but lacks evidence. Gallant sea captain Flynn combats plot by Spanish ambassador Rains while trying to prove worthy of the love of Rains's beautiful daughter Marshall. Rousing old-fashioned adventure, with action on seas off Spain, England, and Panama, boasts swashbuckling Flynn at his finest.
Dist.: Key

SEANCE ON A WET AFTERNOON 1964 British
★ ★ **NR Mystery-Suspense 1:55 B&W**
Dir: Bryan Forbes *Cast:* Kim Stanley, Richard Attenborough, Mark Eden, Nanette Newman, Judith Donner, Patrick Magee
▶ Inventive, gripping drama about half-crazed psychic Stanley, who forces her weak-willed husband Attenborough to stage the kidnapping of a young girl for publicity purposes. Unpredictable plot twists and cunning direction maintain story's relentless pacing. Stanley received an Oscar nomination for her bravura performance.
Dist.: VidAmerica

SEA OF LOVE 1989
★ ★ ★ ★ ★ **R Mystery-Suspense 1:50**
☑ Nudity, adult situations, explicit language, violence
Dir: Harold Becker *Cast:* Al Pacino, Ellen Barkin, John Goodman, William Hickey, Michael Rooker, Richard Jenkins

▶ Weary alcoholic cop Pacino and good-natured partner Goodman are on the trail of a serial killer who finds her victims through the personals ads. Number-one suspect is sultry divorcée Barkin, who has dated all the dead men, and to whom Pacino finds himself attracted. Routine suspense melodrama given a lift by cynical dialogue and the feverish chemistry between the leads. Pacino gives one of his best performances in years. (CC)
Dist.: MCA

SEARCH AND DESTROY 1981
★ ★ ★ PG Action-Adventure 1:33
☑ Adult situations, explicit language, violence
Dir: William Fruet *Cast:* Perry King, Don Stroud, Tisa Farrow, Park Jong Soo, George Kennedy, Tony Sheer
▶ Special Forces experts King and Stroud abandon Vietnamese officer Soo to care for a wounded buddy. Ten years later, the vindictive Soo stalks the veterans through Niagara Falls, determined to kill them. Kennedy plays a policeman seeking an end to the feud. Good locations add to film's extended chase sequences.
Dist.: Forum

SEARCHERS, THE 1956
★ ★ ★ ★ ★ NR Western 1:59
Dir: John Ford *Cast:* John Wayne, Natalie Wood, Vera Miles, Jeffrey Hunter, Ward Bond, John Qualen
▶ When his brother and sister-in-law are savagely killed by Comanches, Civil War veteran Wayne begins seven-year search for their kidnapped daughter Wood. Wayne delivers arguably the finest performance of his career as a man caught between civilization and savagery in this landmark Western. Director Ford's masterpiece, an important influence on later generations of filmmakers, uses stunning visuals and multiple perspectives to portray a haunting, morally complex story. Wayne's oft-repeated riposte, "That'll be the day," inspired the Buddy Holly tune.
Dist.: Warner

SEA SHALL NOT HAVE THEM, THE 1954 British
★ NR War 1:32 B&W
Dir: Lewis Gilbert *Cast:* Michael Redgrave, Dirk Bogarde, Anthony Steel, Nigel Patrick, Bonar Colleano, Jack Watling
▶ During World War II, airmen Redgrave, Bogarde, Colleano, and Watling are shot down over the North Sea. Possessing important information, they try to survive in a lifeboat. Steel and Patrick are among the would-be rescuers. Suspenseful wartime adventure, not terribly original but strongly acted and directed.
Dist.: Republic

SEASIDE SWINGERS 1965 British
☆ NR Musical 1:34
Dir: James Hill *Cast:* John Leyton, Mike Sarne, Ron Moody, Liz Fraser, Grazina Frame, Susan Baker
▶ Musically inclined teens with summer jobs at a seaside resort prepare to show their stuff on a televised talent show. Grab bag of British entertainment styles gives an interesting glimpse into the cheesy show-biz culture that produced the British pop music explosion of the sixties. Groups include the Mojos, Freddie and the Dreamers, and the Leroys.
Dist.: Nelson

SEASON OF FEAR 1989
★ ★ R Drama
☑ Nudity, adult situations, explicit language, violence
Dir: Doug Campbell *Cast:* Michael Bowen, Ray Wise, Clancy Brown, Clara Wren, Michael J. Pollard
▶ Bowen finds sultry blond Wren in his estranged father Wise's house. After he sleeps with her, he discovers she's his stepmother. Father wants son to join him in a wind-driven energy project, but son gets further involved with stepmother after she stabs loony mechanic Pollard. Sexy, high-class sinning is watchable, but not particularly distinguished.
Dist.: CBS/Fox

SEA WOLVES, THE 1981 British
★ ★ ★ ★ PG Action-Adventure 2:00
☑ Brief nudity, adult situations, explicit language, violence
Dir: Andrew V. McLaglen *Cast:* Gregory Peck, Roger Moore, David Niven, Trevor Howard, Barbara Kellerman, Patrick Macnee
▶ During World War II, aging members of the Calcutta Light Horse, an honorary drinking club in India, undertake a commando raid on Nazi ships anchored in neutral Goa. Led by British intelligence officer Peck, the commandos train for the mission while spy Moore romances double agent Kellerman. Stars bring life to this large-scale adventure based on a true incident.
Dist.: Warner

SECOND CHANCE 1953
★ ★ NR Drama 1:22
Dir: Rudolph Maté *Cast:* Robert Mitchum, Linda Darnell, Jack Palance, Sandro Giglio, Rodolfo Hoyos, Jr., Reginald Sheffield
▶ Mitchum gives a brooding performance as a boxer who flees to Mexico after killing an opponent. He falls for gangster's moll Darnell, a fugitive from a Washington Senate investigation. Arrival of hit man Palance leads the couple to a thrilling climax aboard a damaged mountain cable car. Filmed on location in 3-D.
Dist.: SVS

SECOND CHORUS 1940
★ NR Musical 1:23 B&W
Dir: H. C. Potter *Cast:* Fred Astaire, Paulette Goddard, Burgess Meredith, Charles Butterworth, Artie Shaw, Frank Melton

▶ Rival musicians Astaire and Meredith vie for the affections of their manager Goddard, who lands them gigs with Shaw's band. Below Astaire's high average, although he, Goddard, and Shaw are charming. Meredith's comic relief is leaden. Songs include "Would You Like to Be the Love of My Life?" and "(I Ain't Hep to that Step) But I'll Dig It"; Astaire performs drum and trumpet solos.
Dist.: Cable

SECOND SIGHT 1989
★ ★ **PG Comedy**
☑ Explicit language
Dir: Joel Zwick *Cast:* John Larroquette, Bronson Pinchot, Bess Armstrong, Stuart Pankin, John Shuck, Marisol Masey
▶ Larroquette is running a paranormal detective agency in Boston with psychic Pinchot and Ph.D. Pankin. When nun Armstrong comes to them for help, they get involved in the kidnapping of a Cardinal and his secretary. Smoothie Larroquette comes off best, but cast is called upon to do little here. Weak, inane fluff. **(CC)**
Dist.: Warner

SECOND THOUGHTS 1983
★ ★ ★ **PG Comedy 1:38**
☑ Adult situations, explicit language
Dir: Lawrence Turman *Cast:* Lucie Arnaz, Craig Wasson, Ken Howard, Anne Schedeen, Arthur Rosenberg
▶ San Diego lawyer Arnaz leaves stuffy banking husband Howard for affair with idealistic musician Wasson. Learning she's pregnant, she considers an abortion because Wasson is too immature. Wasson reacts by kidnapping her until she must give birth. Engaging performances compensate for script's labored humor.
Dist.: HBO

SECRET ADMIRER 1985
★ ★ ★ **R Comedy 1:38**
☑ Nudity, adult situations, explicit language
Dir: David Greenwalt *Cast:* C. Thomas Howell, Lori Loughlin, Kelly Preston, Dee Wallace Stone, Cliff De Young, Leigh Taylor-Young, Fred Ward
▶ Bright teen farce about high school student Howell who receives an anonymous love letter. Is the writer his long-suffering pal Loughlin or sexy classmate Preston? Comic complications extend to parents as well when further letters fall into the hands of his mother Stone and Preston's father Ward.
Dist.: HBO

SECRET AGENT 1936 British
★ ★ **NR Mystery-Suspense 1:26 B&W**
Dir: Alfred Hitchcock *Cast:* John Gielgud, Madeleine Carroll, Robert Young, Peter Lorre, Lilli Palmer
▶ British agent Gielgud goes to Switzerland to nab enemy agent and nearly jeopardizes the mission when he and cohort Lorre assassinate the wrong man. First-rate Hitchcock sets up an interesting, morally ambiguous situation and concludes with a terrific train wreck finale.
Dist.: Various

SECRET BEYOND THE DOOR 1948
★ **NR Drama 1:38**
Dir: Fritz Lang *Cast:* Joan Bennett, Michael Redgrave, Anne Revere, Barbara O'Neil, Natalie Schafer, Anabel Shaw
▶ Heiress Bennett meets and marries architectural theorist Redgrave in Mexico, little realizing that he is a screwball with a "thing" about locked doors. Returning with him to his weird household in New York, she discovers that he may have murdered his last wife. Director Lang has a sure hand with the expressionist atmosphere in this fascinating film; just ignore the crude psychologizing.
Dist.: Republic

SECRET CEREMONY 1968 British
★ **R Drama 1:49**
☑ Nudity, adult situations, explicit language, violence
Dir: Joseph Losey *Cast:* Elizabeth Taylor, Mia Farrow, Robert Mitchum, Peggy Ashcroft, Pamela Brown
▶ Aging prostitute Taylor, grieving over the death of her daughter, becomes obsessed with young lookalike Farrow. Entering into a symbolic familial relationship, Taylor follows her home, where stepfather Mitchum reveals Farrow is insane. Glum, murky melodrama is both tedious and confusing. Producers recut scenes and added characters for a TV version that remains equally baffling.
Dist.: KVC

SECRET DIARY OF SIGMUND FREUD, THE 1984
☆ **PG Comedy 1:41**
☑ Adult situations, explicit language
Dir: Danford B. Greene *Cast:* Bud Cort, Carol Kane, Klaus Kinski, Marisa Berenson, Carroll Baker, Dick Shawn
▶ Offbeat comedy about the early life of Dr. Sigmund Freud (Cort), who learns about sex by asking his mother Baker. He experiments with cocaine and hypnotizes his lisping assistant Kane, who falls in love with him and becomes jealous of his first client Berenson. Mostly silly, often dreary, but provides a few laughs. **(CC)**
Dist.: CBS/Fox

SECRET HONOR 1984
★ **NR Drama 1:30**
☑ Explicit language
Dir: Robert Altman *Cast:* Philip Baker Hall
▶ One-man show depicts a frenzied President Nixon pacing around his study while holding forth on the memorable controversies and personalities of his roller-coaster career. Scathing portrait of a paranoid and vindictive politician goes beyond satire to become mean-spirited and malicious; for the curious and Nixon-haters only.
Dist.: Vestron

SECRET LIFE OF AN AMERICAN WIFE, THE 1968
★ R Comedy 1:33
[✓] Brief nudity, adult situations, explicit language
Dir: George Axelrod ***Cast:*** Walter Matthau, Anne Jackson, Patrick O'Neal, Edy Williams, Richard Bull
► When her press agent husband O'Neal neglects her, suburban housewife Jackson poses as a prostitute for macho film star Matthau to regain her self-esteem. Labored and leering farce fails to exploit its immoral premise.
Dist.: CBS/Fox

SECRET LIFE OF WALTER MITTY, THE 1947
★★★ NR Comedy 1:50
Dir: Norman Z. McLeod ***Cast:*** Danny Kaye, Virginia Mayo, Boris Karloff, Fay Bainter, Ann Rutherford, Thurston Hall
► Loose adaptation of James Thurber's short story gave Kaye one of his best roles as a henpecked proofreader tormented by fiancée Rutherford, mother Bainter, boss Hall, and everyday life. His solution is to star in daydreams as a gunslinger, gambler, surgeon, etc., pursuing voluptuous Mayo. Fantasy intrudes into reality when Mayo asks his help against jewel thieves. Highlighted by Kaye's performance of "Anatole of Paris."
Dist.: Nelson

SECRET OF MY SUCCESS, THE 1987
★★★★ PG-13 Comedy 1:50
[✓] Brief nudity, adult situations, explicit language
Dir: Herbert Ross ***Cast:*** Michael J. Fox, Helen Slater, Richard Jordan, Margaret Whitton, John Pankow, Fred Gwynne
► Breezy satire of the business world follows young Kansas college graduate Fox on his improbable climb up the corporate ladder. Combination of luck, wits, and an affair with boss's wife Whitton places him in the position to thwart corporate raider Jordan's sneaky tricks and pursue true love Slater. Stars' charm and cleverly calculating plot made this a popular hit.
Dist.: MCA

SECRET OF NIMH, THE 1982
★★★★★ G Animation 1:22
Dir: Don Bluth ***Cast:*** Voices of Derek Jacobi, Elizabeth Hartman, Dom DeLuise, Hermione Baddeley, John Carradine, Peter Strauss
► Animated adventure of mother field mouse trying to find new home for brood before spring plowing destroys old one. Task is complicated by illness of one child, so buffoon crow, wise owl, and trio of high-IQ rats come to her aid against perils of nature and man. Spectacular animation matches standards of old Disney pics while story will interest kids and adults alike. Superior family fare.
Dist.: MGM/UA

SECRET PLACES 1985 British
★★★ PG Drama 1:38
[✓] Brief nudity, explicit language
Dir: Zelda Barron ***Cast:*** Marie-Theres Relin, Tara MacGowran, Claudine Auger, Jenny Agutter, Cassie Stuart, Klaus Barner
► During World War II, German refugee Relin attends an English girls' school and is ostracized by all students except MacGowran. Her mother Auger is a morphine addict while her physicist father Barner, denounced in Germany by a Nazi son, is interned as enemy alien in nearby camp, so she's intrigued by Relin's colorful presence. Average coming-of-age melodrama. **(CC)**
Dist.: CBS/Fox

SECRETS 1972 British
★★ R Drama 1:26
[✓] Nudity, adult situations
Dir: Philip Saville ***Cast:*** Jacqueline Bisset, Per Oscarsson, Shirley Knight Hopkins, Robert Powell, Tarka Kings, Martin C. Thurley
► Bissett allows herself to be picked up in the park by recent widower Oscarsson. Bisset's husband Powell is having an affair with Hopkins, who is interviewing him as part of a computer training program. Their adolescent daughter is tempting an artist neighbor. Bisset's relatively tame nude scene was heavily promoted when this was first released, but the real appeal here will be to fans of romantic soap.
Dist.: Prism

SECRET WAR OF HARRY FRIGG, THE 1969
★ NR War/Comedy 1:49
Dir: Jack Smight ***Cast:*** Paul Newman, Sylva Koscina, Andrew Duggan, Tom Bosley, John Williams, Charles Gray
► Disappointing World War II comedy about five Allied generals crucial to the war effort but held prisoner in Italy. Brash private Newman, known for his ability to escape jail, is promoted to major general and dropped behind enemy lines to rescue them. Scheme comes to a halt when Newman falls for beautiful warden Koscina. Stars mug broadly in this slow-moving farce.
Dist.: MCA

SEDUCED AND ABANDONED 1964 Italian
☆ NR Comedy 1:58 B&W
Dir: Pietro Germi ***Cast:*** Stefania Sandrelli, Saro Urzi, Lando Buzzanca, Leopoldo Trieste, Paolo Biggio, Aldo Puglisi
► Unprincipled seducer Puglisi impregnates Sandrelli, the fifteen year-old sister of his fiancée, and is trapped between her father and the chief of police. The father wants to kill him; the police chief offers him a choice: marry the girl or go to jail. Puglisi agrees to marry—forgetting that Sandrelli is no passive pussycat. Earthy and very Italian. [S]
Dist.: Foothill

SEDUCTION, THE 1982
★★★ R Mystery-Suspense 1:44

☑ Nudity, explicit language, violence
Dir: David Schmoeller *Cast:* Morgan Fairchild, Michael Sarrazin, Vince Edwards, Andrew Stevens, Colleen Camp
▶ Gorgeous Los Angeles reporter Fairchild is terrorized by psychotic photographer Stevens, who pries into every aspect of her personal life. With her boyfriend Sarrazin and policeman Edwards powerless to help, Fairchild must confront Stevens alone. Uncomfortably voyeuristic plot follows a predictable story line.
Dist.: Media

SEDUCTION OF JOE TYNAN, THE 1979
★ ★ ★ ★ R Drama 1:47
☑ Adult situations, explicit language
Dir: Jerry Schatzberg *Cast:* Alan Alda, Meryl Streep, Barbara Harris, Rip Torn, Melvyn Douglas
▶ Alda, a U.S. Senator from New York, ignores wife Harris for an affair with Streep, a Southern lawyer who's helping with research for a Senate hearing. Ignoring his conscience, he seizes the opportunity for national publicity by selling out elderly colleague Douglas. Not altogether believable script by Alda is enhanced by fine ensemble acting, especially from Streep, Harris, and Torn as an influential, skirt-chasing Southern senator.
Dist.: MCA

SEDUCTION OF MIMI, THE 1974 Italian
★ R Comedy 1:29
☑ Adult situations, explicit language
Dir: Lina Wertmuller *Cast:* Giancarlo Giannini, Mariangela Melato, Agostina Belli, Elena Fiore
▶ Giannini is a slow-witted, vain, and stubborn Communist who gradually compromises his ideals in this satire of sexual and political morals. Various episodes are amusing, but end result is not on a par with director Wertmuller's *Seven Beauties* or *Swept Away*. Hollywood lifted the bare-bones story for the Richard Pryor vehicle *Which Way Is Up?*
Dist.: CBS/Fox

SEEDS OF EVIL 1974
☆ R Mystery-Suspense 1:37
☑ Nudity, adult situations, explicit language
Dir: Jim Kay *Cast:* Joe Dallesandro, Katharine Houghton, Rita Gam, James Congdon
▶ Rich people are being killed by homicidal plants under the care of charismatic hunk gardener Dallesandro. Low-budget horror film has people gaping in horror at innocuous-appearing house plants and Dallesandro tastefully doffing his duds. Provides some camp pleasure. Also known as *The Gardener*.
Dist.: United

SEEMS LIKE OLD TIMES 1980
★ ★ ★ ★ PG Comedy 1:42
☑ Explicit language
Dir: Jay Sandrich *Cast:* Goldie Hawn, Chevy Chase, Charles Grodin, Robert Guillaume, Harold Gould, George Grizzard

▶ Soft-hearted lawyer Hawn is torn between helping her hopeless ex-husband Chase through his bottomless legal problems and keeping up appearances for her current husband Grodin as he runs for California attorney general. Genial Neil Simon script and can't-miss cast are hallmarks of this sweetly zany comedy.
Dist.: RCA/Columbia

SEE NO EVIL 1971 British
★ ★ ★ PG Mystery-Suspense 1:29
☑ Violence
Dir: Richard Fleischer *Cast:* Mia Farrow, Dorothy Alison, Robin Bailey, Diane Grayson, Brian Rawlinson, Norman Eshley
▶ Blinded in an accident, Farrow recuperates at home of her uncle Bailey. A homicidal maniac murders Bailey and his family while she is horseback riding with her fiancé Eshley. Farrow returns to the house alone, discovers the deaths, and must overcome her handicap to defeat the killer. Manipulative but effective thriller offers a fair share of shocks.
Dist.: RCA/Columbia

SEE NO EVIL, HEAR NO EVIL 1989
★ ★ ★ ★ PG-13 Comedy 1:41
☑ Nudity, explicit language, violence, adult humor
Dir: Arthur Hiller *Cast:* Gene Wilder, Richard Pryor, Joan Severance, Kevin Spacey, Anthony Zerbe, Alan North
▶ Deaf newsstand operator Wilder hires blind Pryor as assistant; duo witnesses (as best they can) a murder. When the cops suspect them, they combine to overcome their handicaps to nab gorgeous hitwoman Severance and her partner Spacey. Rude, raucous, vulgar—and undeniably a great deal of fun, thanks to stars' teamwork in their third pairing. Funniest scenes: the bar fight, the boys driving together, and Wilder's "fuzzy wuzzy" lip reading. (CC)
Dist.: RCA/Columbia

SEE YOU IN THE MORNING 1989
★ ★ PG-13 Drama 1:59
☑ Adult situations, explicit language
Dir: Alan J. Pakula *Cast:* Jeff Bridges, Alice Krige, Farrah Fawcett, Drew Barrymore, Lukas Haas, David Dukes, Francis Sternhagen, George Hearn, Theodore Bikel, Linda Lavin
▶ Psychiatrist Bridges, recently divorced from Fawcett, meets photographer Krige, widowed mother of Barrymore and Haas. They marry, but both adults and children find difficulties in creating a new family unit. Openly emotional drama teeters on the edge of excessive sentiment but is ultimately affecting. Gentle Bridges and luminous Krige lead a strong cast. Uneven script combines nice touches (the mutual migraines, Bridges's conversation with the dog) with embarrassing ones (Lavin singing "Auld Lang Syne"). (CC)
Dist.: Warner

SEIZE THE DAY 1986
★ NR Drama/MFTV 1:33
☑ Explicit language
Dir: Fielder Cook *Cast:* Robin Williams, Jerry Stiller, Tony Roberts, Glenne Headly, William Hickey, Joseph Wiseman
► Harassed by his girlfriend and bled dry by his ex-wife, unemployed salesman Williams loses his job and returns home to New York. Old buddies offer smiles but no help while cold-hearted father Wiseman dismisses pleas for aid. Desperate for a big score, Williams gambles his last savings with commodities broker Stiller. Williams shines in a serious role, but bleak portrait of disintegrating life is not for those seeking laughs. Adapted from the Saul Bellow novella.
Dist.: HBO

SEIZURE 1974 Canadian
☆ PG Horror 1:33
☑ Adult situations, explicit language, violence
Dir: Oliver Stone *Cast:* Jonathan Frid, Martine Beswick, Joe Sirola, Christina Pickles, Troy Donahue, Herve Villechaize, Mary Woronov
► Writer Frid's guests are terrorized by three strange characters who come to life from one of his stories. The weekend fun includes a strangling, suicides, an execution, and the hanging of a dog. Stone's slowly paced directorial debut has pretensions to art that dilute story's suspense.
Dist.: Prism

SELL OUT, THE 1976
★★ PG Espionage 1:28
☑ Violence
Dir: Peter Collinson *Cast:* Richard Widmark, Oliver Reed, Gayle Hunnicut, Sam Wanamaker, Ori Levy, Assaf Dayan
► In Israel, CIA agent Widmark comes out of retirement when his friend Reed is placed on both American and Russian hit lists. Also caught in the middle of this intrigue are Israeli officers Levy and Dayan. Standard spy yarn, clumsily directed by Collinson, leaves good cast stranded.
Dist.: Media

SEMI-TOUGH 1977
★★★★ R Comedy/Sports 1:47
☑ Brief nudity, adult situations, explicit language, adult humor
Dir: Michael Ritchie *Cast:* Burt Reynolds, Kris Kristofferson, Jill Clayburgh, Robert Preston, Lotte Lenya, Bert Convy
► Star running back Reynolds and roommate wide receiver Kristofferson pal around with Clayburgh, daughter of team owner Preston. Then Kristofferson joins self-realization cult and convinces Clayburgh to both convert and marry him. Suddenly the odd man out, Reynolds joins the cult to expose its fraudulence and woo Clayburgh for himself. Amiable and often uproarious comedy satirizes both Me

Decade fads and pro football. Based on the best-seller by Dan Jenkins.
Dist.: CBS/Fox

SENATOR WAS INDISCREET, THE 1948
★★★ NR Comedy 1:21 B&W
Dir: George S. Kaufman *Cast:* William Powell, Ella Raines, Peter Lind Hayes, Arleen Whelan, Ray Collins, Allen Jenkins
► Inept senator Powell runs for President, using a diary recording crooked business by party bigwigs to assure nomination. Powell's press agent Hayes gets the blackmail book and must choose between keeping his job or allowing journalist girlfriend Raines to expose the politicians. Only directorial outing for renowned playwright/screenwriter Kaufman has many fine moments.
Dist.: Republic

SENDER, THE 1982 British
★ R Mystery-Suspense 1:32
☑ Explicit language, violence
Dir: Roger Christian *Cast:* Kathryn Harrold, Zeljko Ivanek, Shirley Knight, Paul Freeman, Sean Hewitt, Harry Ditson
► Beautiful psychiatrist Harrold, working with an attempted suicide Ivanek, learns he has the power to telepathically transmit dreams and nightmares. When his mother Knight, who has been raising him as the new Messiah, is murdered, Harrold realizes Ivanek is being framed. Understated psychological thriller was the debut film for director Christian, art designer for *Star Wars* and *Alien*.
Dist.: Paramount

SEND ME NO FLOWERS 1964
★★★ NR Comedy 1:40
Dir: Norman Jewison *Cast:* Rock Hudson, Doris Day, Tony Randall, Paul Lynde, Hal March, Edward Andrews
► Last Hudson-Day teaming takes a slapstick approach to death. Hudson overhears the wrong prognosis at the hospital and assumes he's dying. With his best friend Randall, he searches for a second husband for his soon-to-be-widowed wife Day. She's convinced his strange behavior is a cover-up for an affair. Excellent supporting cast provides plenty of bounce. Day sings the title tune by Hal David and Burt Bacharach.
Dist.: MCA

SENIORS 1978
★ R Comedy 1:28
☑ Nudity, explicit language
Dir: Rod Amateau *Cast:* Jeffrey Byron, Gary Imhoff, Dennis Quaid, Priscilla Barnes, Lou Richards
► Four college buddies con a professor into giving them a $50,000 grant to study "Sex and the College Girl." The boys use the money to rent a lavish house for their "interviews" with buxom coeds. Low-budget sex comedy with a heavy emphasis on nudity and juvenile jokes.
Dist.: Vestron

SENIOR WEEK 1988
★ **NR Comedy 1:28**
🔲 Nudity, adult situations, explicit language
Dir: Stuart Goldman *Cast:* Michael St. Gerard, Garry Kerr, George Klek, Jennifer Gorey, Leesa Bryte, Alan Naggar
▶ Tame student sex comedy about high school threesome St. Gerard, Klek, and Naggar spending seven days before graduation in Daytona Beach. This direct-to-video release may be the last gasp of its genre.
Dist.: Vestron

SENSE OF FREEDOM, A 1981 British
☆ **NR Drama 1:25**
🔲 Nudity, explicit language, graphic violence
Dir: John Mackenzie *Cast:* David Hayman, Alex Norton, Jake D'Arcy, Sean Scanlan, Fulton Mackay
▶ Sleek Scottish hoodlum Hayman is convicted of murder and continues his violent ways in prison. Transferred from big house to big house, Hayman's rage allows him to endure beatings and long stretches in solitary. When his mother dies, he begins to feel remorse and enters a rehab program. Based on a true story, script and imagery are violent, repetitive and depressing.
Dist.: HBO

SENSE OF LOSS, A 1972 U.S./Swiss
☆ **NR Documentary 2:15 C/B&W**
Dir: Marcel Ophuls
▶ Master documentarian Ophuls turns his camera on Northern Ireland, hoping that by throwing light on individuals caught up in that nation's ongoing strife he might illuminate larger issues. While some of the stories captured by his camera are deeply affecting, Ophuls does not help the viewer sort out all the factions, passions, and competing interests. Successful, however, in humanizing some of the death statistics.
Dist.: RCA/Columbia

SENTINEL, THE 1977
★ ★ ★ ★ **R Horror 1:32**
🔲 Nudity, adult situations, explicit language, violence
Dir: Michael Winner *Cast:* Cristina Raines, Chris Sarandon, Martin Balsam, John Carradine, Ava Gardner, Jose Ferrer, Arthur Kennedy, Burgess Meredith
▶ Upset over her father's death, elegant fashion model Raines moves to a Brooklyn Heights apartment, where she is plagued by nightmares, harassed by an evil real-estate agent, and bothered by a blind tenant. When she tells her boyfriend Sarandon she's found the doorway to hell, he wonders if she's losing her mind. All-star cast (including Sylvia Miles, Deborah Raffin, and Eli Wallach) adds gloss to a genuinely creepy plot.
Dist.: MCA

SEPARATE PEACE, A 1972
★ ★ **PG Drama 1:44**

🔲 Adult situations, explicit language
Dir: Larry Peerce *Cast:* Parker Stevenson, John Heyl, Peter Brush, Victor Bevine, William Roerick
▶ In this sensitive adaptation of the John Knowles novel, roommates Stevenson and Heyl have a complex relationship in the insulated world of an affluent New England prep school while World War II rages. Stevenson admires and resents the popular Heyl, an emotional mix that has tragic consequences.
Dist.: Paramount

SEPARATE TABLES 1958
★ ★ ★ **NR Drama 1:38 B&W**
Dir: Delbert Mann *Cast:* Deborah Kerr, Rita Hayworth, David Niven, Wendy Hiller, Burt Lancaster, Gladys Cooper
▶ Moving drama about guests at a modest resort hotel and the tentative relationships they develop in the dining room. Niven brags about his wartime experiences, attracting Kerr, the shy daughter of domineering mother Cooper. Hotel owner Hiller worries about her lover Lancaster, an alcoholic writer whose ex-wife Hayworth arrives unexpectedly. Based on two Terence Rattigan one-act plays, this superbly acted film received seven Oscar nominations, with Niven and Hiller winning for their touching performances.
Dist.: CBS/Fox

SEPARATE VACATIONS 1986
★ **R Comedy 1:31**
🔲 Nudity, adult situations, explicit language, mild violence
Dir: Michael Anderson *Cast:* David Naughton, Jennifer Dale, Mark Keyloun, Laurie Holden, Blanca Guerra
▶ After twelve years of marriage, bored architect Naughton and his wife Dale try a vacation apart: Naughton in Mexico, where he futilely pursues various beauties; Dale at a ski resort, where she catches the eye of a handsome young instructor Keyloun. Uninspired comedy financed by Playboy Enterprises features lackluster premise, weak cast, and predictable jokes.
Dist.: Vestron

SEPARATE WAYS 1981
★ ★ ★ **R Drama 1:32**
🔲 Nudity, adult situations, explicit language
Dir: Howard Avedis *Cast:* Karen Black, Tony Lo Bianco, Arlene Golonka, David Naughton, Jack Carter, Sharon Farrell
▶ Unhappy with husband Lo Bianco, a former race-car driver now bored with his auto dealership, Black tries an affair with young art student Naughton. She moves out and takes a waitressing job at Carter's strip joint when she learns that Lo Bianco is having an affair of his own. Cast tries hard to inject life into a routine melodrama.
Dist.: Vestron

SEPTEMBER 1987
★ **PG Drama 1:22**

☑ Explicit language
Dir: Woody Allen   *Cast:* Mia Farrow, Denholm Elliott, Dianne Wiest, Elaine Stritch, Sam Waterston, Jack Warden
▶ In a Vermont country house, would-be suicide Farrow is visited by mom Stritch, stepdad Warden, best friend Wiest, widowed neighbor Elliott, and tenant Waterston. Elliott loves Farrow, Farrow loves Waterston, Waterston loves Wiest, Wiest may or may not love her husband and kids in Philadelphia. The most burning question: who shot Stritch's lover thirty years ago, mother or daughter? Housebound, talky drama moves as slow as molasses although some of the performances are noteworthy. **(CC)**
Dist.: Orion

SEPTEMBER AFFAIR 1950
★ ★ ★ ★ NR Romance 1:45 B&W
Dir: William Dieterle   *Cast:* Joan Fontaine, Joseph Cotten, Françoise Rosay, Jessica Tandy, Robert Arthur, Jimmy Lydon
▶ Two Americans, unhappily married Cotten and pianist Fontaine, fall in love in Italy. When a plane they were scheduled to be on crashes, they are believed dead and freed to be together. However, responsibilities cast a shadow on their happiness. Effective love story with touching performances by the leads. Score includes Rachmaninoff and Walter Huston singing "September Song".   **(CC)**
Dist.: Paramount

SERGEANT YORK 1941
★ ★ ★ ★ ★ NR Biography 2:14 B&W
Dir: Howard Hawks   *Cast:* Gary Cooper, Walter Brennan, Joan Leslie, George Tobias, Stanley Ridges, Margaret Wycherly
▶ Outstanding biography of Alvin York, the pacifist soldier who single-handedly captured 132 Germans during World War I. Although the battle scenes are shown with superb realism, film's best moments are scenes of York's backwoods upbringing in the hills of Tennessee. Cooper earned an Oscar for capturing the sincerity and nobility behind the hero's shy character. Received eleven nominations overall, also winning for editing.
Dist.: CBS/Fox   ⓒ

SERIAL 1980
★ ★ R Comedy 1:32
☑ Nudity, adult situations, explicit language
Dir: Bill Persky   *Cast:* Martin Mull, Tom Smothers, Sally Kellerman, Tuesday Weld, Bill Macy, Christopher Lee
▶ Satirical look at every seventies fad from hot tubs to religious cults, based on the bestselling novel by Cyra McFadden. In Marin County, California, relationships flounder, the drug culture flourishes, kids are in therapy "to get in touch with their childhood," teenagers run off to join Moonie-type groups, and women gather to raise their consciousness.

Entertaining and right on the money, although much of it is dated now.
Dist.: Paramount

SERPENT AND THE RAINBOW, THE 1988
★ ★ R Mystery-Suspense 1:38
☑ Nudity, adult situations, explicit language, graphic violence
Dir: Wes Craven   *Cast:* Bill Pullman, Cathy Tyson, Zakes Mokae, Paul Winfield, Brent Jennings, Conrad Roberts
▶ Pullman, a Harvard researcher investigating voodoo in Haiti, battles local police while trying to get his hands on a powerful zombie-making powder. Intriguing story, good special effects, picturesque locations, outstanding Mokae; a bit overlong and overcomplicated but consistently interesting.
Dist.: MCA

SERPENT'S EGG, THE 1978 German/U.S.
☆ R Drama 2:00
☑ Adult situations, explicit language, violence
Dir: Ingmar Borgman   *Cast:* Liv Ullmann, David Carradine, Gert Frobe, Heinz Bennent, James Whitmore, Glynn Turman
▶ Against the background of incipient Nazism in 1920s Berlin, Jewish circus performer Carradine hooks up with his brother's widow Ullmann. They encounter old friend Bennent, who may be involved in a sinister scheme. Bergman's first English-language effort is moody and atmospheric but slow-moving, talky, and unevenly acted.
Dist.: Vestron

SERPICO 1974
★ ★ ★ ★ ★ R Biography/Crime 2:10
☑ Adult situations, explicit language, violence
Dir: Sidney Lumet   *Cast:* Al Pacino, Tony Roberts, John Randolph, Jack Kehoe, Biff McGuire, Barbara Eda-Young
▶ Galvanizing, disquieting adaptation of Peter Maas's best-selling book dramatizing the career of real-life undercover cop Frank Serpico (Pacino), whose testimony about police corruption and bribery led to the formation of the Knapp Commission. Riveting, high-energy performance from Pacino as the obsessive "hippie" cop who refuses to compromise.
Dist.: Paramount

SERVANT, THE 1963 British
☆ NR Drama 1:55 B&W
Dir: Joseph Losey   *Cast:* Dirk Bogarde, Sarah Miles, Wendy Craig, James Fox, Catherine Lacey, Richard Vernon
▶ Jaded playboy Fox hires lower-class valet Bogarde to run his London mansion. Bogarde cunningly assumes control of Fox's life in a psychological battle of wits. Challenging examination of power and decadence will reward patient viewers. Screenplay by Harold Pinter, who has a brief cameo as a party-goer.
Dist.: HBO

SESAME STREET PRESENTS: FOLLOW THAT BIRD 1985
★★★★★ G Family 1:28
Dir: Ken Kwapis ***Cast:*** The Sesame Street Gang, Sandra Bernhard, John Candy, Chevy Chase, Joe Flaherty, Dave Thomas
► Big Bird goes to Illinois to live with a family of dodos but misses his pals on Sesame Street. He decides to hit the road back to New York while the Sleaze Brothers (Thomas, Flaherty) try to catch Big Bird for their amusement park. Delightful entertainment for children; all-star Muppet cast includes Cookie Monster, Oscar the Grouch (who does a neat *Patton* parody to open the film). Funny bits from Bernhard and Candy. (CC)
Dist.: Warner

SET-UP, THE 1949
★★★ NR Drama/Sports 1:12 B&W
Dir: Robert Wise ***Cast:*** Robert Ryan, Audrey Totter, George Tobias, Alan Baxter, Wallace Ford, Percy Helton
► Aging fighter Ryan prepares for a meaningless bout, unaware his trainer Helton and local gangster Baxter have fixed the match. Unique boxing drama, played out in real time, is uncompromising in its depiction of the sport as seedy and corrupt. Fight scenes are among the most brutal ever filmed.
Dist.: Blackhawk

SEVEN 1979
★ R Action-Adventure 1:30
☑ Nudity, adult situations, explicit language, violence
Dir: Andy Sidaris ***Cast:*** William Smith, Barbara Leigh, Guich Koock, Art Metrano, Martin Kove, Richard Le Pore, Lenny Montana
► When a series of assassinations hits Hawaii, the government has Smith assemble a crack team of killers to stop the gangsters responsible. The group includes a kung-fu expert, a black drag racer, and two beautiful women prone to baring their breasts. Unflagging action against a lovely Hawaiian background. Acting, dialogue, and story are the weak links.
Dist.: IVE

SEVEN ALONE 1975
★★ G Family 1:36
Dir: Earl Bellamy ***Cast:*** Dewey Martin, Aldo Ray, Anne Collins, Dean Smith, Stewart Peterson, Roger Pancake
► On the way West in the nineteenth century, seven children find themselves orphaned on the Oregon Trail. With two thousand miles yet to go, doughty youngsters press onward. The children are okay, and adult characters like Ray's Dr. Dutch are mildly amusing in this strictly average family adventure.
Dist.: Vestron

SEVEN BEAUTIES 1976 Italian
★★ R Comedy/Drama 1:55
☑ Nudity, explicit language, violence
Dir: Lina Wertmuller ***Cast:*** Giancarlo Giannini, Fernando Rey, Shirley Stoler, Elena Fiore, Enzo Vitale, Mario Conti
► During World War II, Giannini kills his sister Fiore's pim and chooses an insanity plea over a death sentence. The insane asylum becomes intolerable, so Giannini wins release by joining the army. But when he's shipped off to the Russian front he deserts, only to wind up in a Nazi concentration camp, a place so hellish he tries to seduce obese, sadistic warden Stoler to survive. Some will find this portrayal of survivor-without-scruples too disturbing. [S]
Dist.: RCA/Columbia

SEVEN BLOWS OF THE DRAGON 1976 Hong Kong
★ R Martial Arts 1:30
☑ Nudity, violence
Dir: Chang Cheh ***Cast:*** David Chaing, Ti Lung, Wang Chung, Lily Ho, Tetsuro Tamba, Ku Feng
► Ancient China is the setting for a tale of oppression and liberation, with the Sung dynasty sitting heavily on the people, and the "Honorable 108" valorously resisting. Complicated, historically based plot grinds on, with every so often a snappy martial arts sequence soaring and leaping across the screen. Good costumes. Also known as *The Avengers of Death*.
Dist.: Warner

SEVEN BRIDES FOR SEVEN BROTHERS 1954
★★★★ G Musical 1:42
Dir: Stanley Donen ***Cast:*** Howard Keel, Jane Powell, Jeff Richards, Russ Tamblyn, Julie Newmar, Jacques d'Amboise, Marc Platt
► Bachelor brothers live a lonely existence on their Oregon farm until eldest Keel brings home pert wife Powell. She tries to domesticate the rowdy bunch; they proceed to kidnap six pretty girls for wives of their own. One of America's most beloved musicals remains fresh, thanks to strong direction, witty script, tuneful Johnny Mercer–Gene de Paul score, and outstanding choreography by Michael Kidd. Best Picture nominee received an Oscar for musical scoring.
Dist.: MGM/UA

SEVEN BROTHERS MEET DRACULA, THE 1974 British/Hong Kong
★ R Martial Arts 1:12
☑ Nudity, graphic violence
Dir: Roy Ward ***Cast:*** Peter Cushing, David Chiang, Julie Ege, Robin Stewart, Shih Szu, John Forbes-Robertson
► Professor Cushing tries to convince his students that Chinese provinces have their own vampires. The seven fighting brothers go on an expedition to a remote village that was long ago taken over by Count Dracula in the guise of a Chinese warlord. Labored and ab-

surd. Somewhat longer original version called *Legend of the Seven Golden Vampires.*
Dist.: Sinister

SEVEN CITIES OF GOLD 1955
★ ★ NR Action-Adventure 1:43
Dir: Robert D. Webb   ***Cast:*** Richard Egan, Anthony Quinn, Jeffrey Hunter, Rita Moreno, Michael Rennie, Leslie Bradley
▶ In 1769, Spanish captain Quinn leads Father Junipero Serra (Rennie) and a group of soldiers into the American Southwest searching for legendary cities filled with precious metals. Holed up in southern California, the Spaniards fight Indian men, romance Indian woman, and ultimately found the city of San Diego. Entertaining mix of history and fiction, with a good role for Quinn.
Dist.: CBS/Fox

SEVEN DAYS ASHORE 1942
★ NR Comedy 1:14 B&W
Dir: John H. Auer   ***Cast:*** Wally Brown, Alan Carney, Marcy McGuire, Virginia Mayo, Gordon Oliver, Dooley Wilson
▶ Handsome sailor Oliver arrives for San Francisco shore leave with three girlfriends waiting for him. To avoid a confrontation, he recruits hapless cohorts Brown and Carney to even things out. Innocuous showcase for one of Hollywood's least memorable comedy teams. Home video version double billed with 1942's *Hurry, Charlie, Hurry.*
Dist.: Turner

SEVEN DAYS IN MAY 1964
★ ★ ★ NR Mystery-Suspense 2:00 B&W
Dir: John Frankenheimer   ***Cast:*** Kirk Douglas, Burt Lancaster, Fredric March, Ava Gardner, Edmond O'Brien, Martin Balsam
▶ Army colonel Douglas suspects right-wing general Lancaster is plotting to dipose of President March and take over the U.S. government. Douglas alerts March and attempts to thwart the coup. Topical, tense nail-biter with terrific performances. Frankenheimer's superb direction creates the same "it can happen here" feel as his *The Manchurian Candidate.*
Dist.: Paramount

SEVEN DAYS' LEAVE 1942
★ NR Musical 1:27 B&W
Dir: Tim Whalen   ***Cast:*** Victor Mature, Lucille Ball, Harold Peary, Ginny Simms, Peter Lind Hayes, Arnold Stang
▶ Soldier Mature will lose his inheritance unless he marries Ball during his seven-day leave of absence. Only one problem: they've never met. Amusing musical with a likable Lucy. Peary re-creates his radio role of "The Great Gildersleeve." Frank Loesser/Jimmy McHugh score includes "Can't Get Out of This Mood," "Soft Hearted," and "I Get the Neck of a Chicken."
Dist.: Turner

SEVEN DOORS TO DEATH 1944
★ NR Mystery-Suspense 1:04 B&W
Dir: Elmer Clifton   ***Cast:*** Chick Chandler, June Clyde, George Meeker, Michael Raffetto, Gregory Gaye
▶ Chandler, wrongly implicated in a crime he did not commit, attempts to prove his innocence. Cop Raffetto also investigates. The killer could be a neighbor hiding behind any of seven doors, making this the "Let's Make a Deal" of murder mysteries. Mediocre low-budget fare.
Dist.: IVE

7 FACES OF DR. LAO 1964
★ ★ ★ NR Fantasy 1:40
Dir: George Pal   ***Cast:*** Tony Randall, Arthur O'Connell, Barbara Eden, John Ericson, Kevin Tate, Noah Beery, Jr., John Qualen, Lee Patrick
▶ In the Western frontier town of Abalone, crusading newspaper editor O'Connell battles land-grabbing villain Ericson and woos pretty widow Eden. Into town rides oriental magician Randall and a circus troupe of oddities (also played by Randall) to assist O'Connell in his worthy endeavors. Diverting Old West fantasy is distinguished by excellent performance from Randall in multiple roles. Received a special Oscar for makeup (not a regular Academy Award until 1981).
Dist.: MGM/UA

SEVEN HOURS TO JUDGMENT 1988
★ ★ ★ R Mystery-Suspense 1:36
☑ Explicit language, violence
Dir: Beau Bridges   ***Cast:*** Beau Bridges, Ron Leibman, Julianne Phillips, Tiny Ron Taylor, Reggie Johnson
▶ Although he knows they are guilty of murder, judge Bridges is forced to free vicious punks on a technicality. Leibman, the victim's husband, kidnaps Bridges's wife Phillips and gives him seven hours to find the evidence necessary for conviction. Familiar vigilante story given a lift by swift pacing and realistic performances.
Dist.: Media

SEVEN LITTLE FOYS, THE 1955
★ ★ ★ ★ NR Biography/Musical 1:33
Dir: Melville Shavelson   ***Cast:*** Bob Hope, Milly Vitale, George Tobias, Angela Clarke, Herbert Heyes, Richard Shannon, Billy Gray, James Cagney
▶ Charming biography of vaudeville star Eddie Foy (Hope), whose marriage to ballerina Vitale results in seven children. When Vitale dies, Hope molds his brood into a top vaudeville act. Nostalgic songs ("Row, Row, Row," "I'm the Greatest Father of Them All"), surefire gags, a restrained performance by Hope, and a knockout cameo by Cagney (reprising his George M. Cohan role from *Yankee Doodle Dandy*) add up to winning entertainment. Narrated by Eddie Foy, Jr.
Dist.: RCA/Columbia

SEVEN MAGNIFICENT GLADIATORS, THE 1984
★ PG Fantasy 1:26
☑ Violence
Dir: Bruno Mattei ***Cast:*** Lou Ferrigno, Sybil Danning, Brad Harris, Dan Vadis, Carla Ferrigno, Mandy Rice-Davies
▶ Village forced to pay tribute to evil demigod Vadis asks barbarian Ferrigno to free them from slavery. He hires gladiator Harris, fierce but beautiful fighter Danning, and four other unemployed warriors to do battle against the tyrant. Uncredited remake of *The Magnificent Seven* set in mythical times offers plenty of action, but poor dubbing and special effects are obvious.
Dist.: MGM/UA

SEVEN MILES FROM ALCATRAZ 1942
★ NR Action-Adventure 1:02 B&W
Dir: Edward Dmytryk ***Cast:*** James Craig, Bonita Granville, Frank Jenks, Cliff Edwards, George Cleveland, Tala Birell
▶ Title distance is how far convicts Craig and Jenks get when they break out of Alcatraz and take refuge near an isolated lighthouse. The two think they're home free, but then they learn that their hideout is being used by Nazis planning an attack on San Francisco. World War II is raging, and after speeches by lighthouse owner Cleveland and daughter Granville, the two cons weigh the value of their freedom versus the importance of smashing the Nazis. Well-made wartime flag-waver.
Dist.: Turner

SEVEN MINUTES IN HEAVEN 1986
★★★ PG-13 Comedy 1:28
☑ Explicit language
Dir: Linda Feferman ***Cast:*** Jennifer Connelly, Maddie Corman, Byron Thames, Alan Boyce, Polly Draper, Marshall Bell
▶ Appealing coming-of-age comedy set in Ohio. Connelly plays a studious teen competing in an essay contest; she lets mixed-up male friend Thames stay at her house despite rumors about their relationship at school. She also competes with best friend Corman over a handsome classmate. Endearing cast and honest, sympathetic script set this above routine adolescent comedies.
Dist.: Warner

SEVEN-PER-CENT SOLUTION, THE 1976
★★★ PG Action-Adventure 1:53
☑ Adult situations
Dir: Herbert Ross ***Cast:*** Nicol Williamson, Alan Arkin, Robert Duvall, Vanessa Redgrave, Laurence Olivier, Joel Grey, Samantha Eggar
▶ Sherlock Holmes (Williamson) is lured to Vienna by Dr. Watson (Duvall) so that Sigmund Freud (Arkin) can treat the detective for cocaine addiction. The two great minds then team up to solve a mystery. Stylish, original, and an enormous amount of fun. Williamson is brilliant as the high-strung Holmes; he gets outstanding support from Arkin, Duvall, and Olivier (in a delicious cameo as a surprisingly mousy Moriarty). Handsomely mounted, beautifully paced. Literate screenplay by Nicholas Meyer from his best-selling novel.
Dist.: MCA

SEVEN SAMURAI, THE 1954 Japanese
★ NR Action-Adventure 2:21 B&W
Dir: Akira Kurosawa ***Cast:*** Takashi Shimura, Toshiro Mifune, Yoshio Inaba, Seiji Miyaguchi, Minoru Chiaki, Daisuke Kato, Ko Kimura
▶ Seventeenth-century master samurai Shimura agrees to defend villagers from marauders. He assembles a team of six other warriors, trains the villagers in fighting, and leads them against the bandits in an astonishing battle. Sweeping epic is a highly influential classic famed for its thrilling action and sharply realized characters. Remade in the U.S. under its alternate title, *The Magnificent Seven*. Restored, 3:28 minute version is also available. [S]
Dist.: Nelson

SEVEN SINNERS 1940
★★ NR Action-Adventure 1:27 B&W
Dir: Tay Garnett ***Cast:*** John Wayne, Marlene Dietrich, Albert Dekker, Broderick Crawford, Mischa Auer, Billy Gilbert
▶ South Seas nightclub chanteuse Dietrich snags Navy officer Wayne, who has a career to lose by loving the tarnished angel. Other Dietrich admirers include lightfingered magician Auer and bodyguard Crawford. Lots of action and steamy romance, highlighted by a rip-roaring bar fight. Dietrich sings Frank Loesser's excellent "I've Been in Love Before," and looks smashing in Navy whites.
Dist.: KVC

1776 1972
★★★★ G Musical 2:28
Dir: Peter H. Hunt ***Cast:*** William Daniels, Howard da Silva, Ken Howard, Blythe Danner, Ronald Holgate, John Cullum
▶ "I'm obnoxious and disliked," sings acerbic John Adams (Daniels), explaining to Benjamin Franklin (da Silva) why he's a bad choice to write the Declaration of Independence at the first Continental Congress. Young Tom Jefferson (Howard) eventually accepts the job, but will a divided congress approve the document? Occasionally corny but high-spirited tribute to our founding fathers. Stiff staging betrays Broadway origins but the cast is a lot of fun, especially Daniels, da Silva, and Holgate, whose boisterous "Lees of Virginia" number is a comic highlight.
Dist.: RCA/Columbia

SEVENTH SEAL, THE 1956 Swedish
★★ NR Drama 1:45 B&W
Dir: Ingmar Bergman ***Cast:*** Max Von Sydow, Gunnar Bjornstrand, Nils Poppe, Bengt Ekerot, Bibi Andersson, Maud Hansson
▶ Fourteenth-century Swedish knight Von

Sydow returns from the Crusades to his plague-ravaged homeland. He takes on Death in a game of chess and rescues a family from its clutches. Bergman's stunning direction creates a superb medieval tapestry in this haunting foreign classic. Unforgettable performances (especially the moving Von Sydow and the fresh-faced Andersson). $\boxed{S}$
Dist.: Nelson

SEVENTH SIGN, THE 1988
★ ★ ★ R Horror 1:37
☑ Brief nudity, adult situations, explicit language, violence
Dir: Carl Schultz *Cast:* Demi Moore, Michael Biehn, Jurgen Prochnow, Peter Friedman, Manny Jacobs
▶ Pregnant Moore, suffering from horrible nightmares while disasters occur around the world, takes in mysterious boarder Prochnow. Through him, she learns her unborn child's role in saving the world from destruction. Contemporary shocker in the vein of *The Omen*; fast-paced thrills anchored sympathetically by raspy-voiced Moore. (CC)
Dist.: RCA

SEVENTH VEIL, THE 1945 British
★ ★ ★ NR Drama 1:35 B&W
Dir: Compton Bennett *Cast:* James Mason, Ann Todd, Herbert Lom, Hugh McDermott, Albert Lieven, Yvonne Owen
▶ With the aid of psychiatrist Lom, suicidal pianist Todd, an orphan, comes to terms with her feelings toward neurotic Mason, the bachelor cousin who raised her and cultivated her musical talents. Intelligent psycholgical drama won Oscar for Best Screenplay.
Dist.: VidAmerica

SEVENTH VICTIM, THE 1943
★ ★ NR Mystery-Suspense 1:11 B&W
Dir: Mark Robson *Cast:* Kim Hunter, Tom Conway, Jean Brooks, Evelyn Brent, Hugh Beaumont, Isabel Jewell
▶ Hunter, in her film debut, arrives in Greenwich Village to look for her missing sister Brooks. The trail leads to an evil satanic cult. Can Hunter save Brooks before the cult makes her their seventh victim? Intriguing premise given effectively shadowy direction (including a pre-*Psycho* shower scene), but the plot improbabilities pile up.
Dist.: Turnor

7TH VOYAGE OF SINBAD, THE 1958
★ ★ ★ G Fantasy 1:28
Dir: Nathan Juran *Cast:* Kerwin Mathews, Kathryn Grant, Richard Eyer, Torin Thatcher, Alec Mango, Danny Green
▶ Evil magician Thatcher shrinks princess Grant to miniature size; to rescue her, hero Sinbad (Mathews) must battle a fierce Cyclops, an angry mother roc, a fire-breathing dragon, and a living skeleton. Prime example of Arabian Nights entertainment will delight parents as well as children. Lively plot, strong

action, but stars and story are upstaged by Ray Harryhausen's marvelous special effects and a sweeping score by Bernard Herrmann.
Dist.: RCA

SEVEN-UPS, THE 1973
★ ★ PG Action-Adventure 1:43
☑ Explicit language, violence
Dir: Philip D'Antoni *Cast:* Roy Scheider, Tony Lo Bianco, Larry Haines, Victor Arnold, Jerry Leon, Ken Kercheval
▶ Hard-nosed New York cop Scheider runs unorthodox unit employing informants to pursue crooks whose crimes merit prison sentences of seven years or longer. Chief stoolie Lo Bianco uses police info for his own profit until the scam gets one of Scheider's men killed. Director D'Antoni, producer of *Bullit* and *The French Connection*, favors action over character. Best bit: chase sequence in which head car is cut off by a tractor trailer. (CC)
Dist.: CBS/Fox

SEVEN YEAR ITCH, THE 1955
★ ★ ★ NR Comedy 1:45
Dir: Billy Wilder *Cast:* Marilyn Monroe, Tom Ewell, Evelyn Keyes, Sonny Tufts, Robert Strauss, Oscar Homolka
▶ With wife Keyes and son on vacation, high-strung Manhattan publisher Ewell fantasizes an affair with new upstairs neighbor Monroe. Adaptation of a George Axelrod Broadway hit, laden with double entendres, has a disarmingly wistful performance by Monroe. Her stance over a subway grating is one of her most famous poses.
Dist.: CBS/Fox

SEX, LIES AND VIDEOTAPE 1989
★ ★ ★ R Drama 1:40
☑ Adult situations, explicit language
Dir: Steven Soderbergh *Cast:* James Spader, Andie McDowell, Peter Gallagher, Laura San Giacomo, Ron Vawter
▶ Critically acclaimed debut film from Soderbergh is a witty and penetrating look at contemporary relationships. McDowell's husband Gallagher is cheating with her envious sister San Giacomo. Meanwhile, McDowell grows interested in his pal Spader, who can only relate to women by videotaping them talking about sex. Talky and seemingly actionless, but disarmingly original and perceptive look at love and deception. Nominated for Best Original Screenplay Oscar. (CC)
Dist.: RCA/Columbia

SGT. PEPPER'S LONELY HEARTS CLUB BAND 1978
★ PG Musical 1:51
☑ Explicit language
Dir: Michael Schultz *Cast:* Peter Frampton, Barry Gibb, Robin Gibb, Maurice Gibb, Frankie Howerd, Paul Nicholas, Sandy Farina
▶ Misguided effort to provide a story line to the classic Beatles album interprets their songs in weak skits and some funny bits of

camp. Long list of guest performers and cameo appearances (George Burns, Steve Martin, Alice Cooper, Aerosmith, Billy Preston, Peter Allen, Helen Reddy, Connie Stevens, Carol Channing, Leif Garrett, Heart, Seals and Croft, Tina Turner, and Earth, Wind & Fire, among others) can't salvage silly plot.
Dist.: MCA

SHACK OUT ON 101 1955
★ NR Drama 1:20 B&W
Dir: Edward Dein   *Cast:* Terry Moore, Frank Lovejoy, Lee Marvin, Keenan Wynn, Whit Bissell, Frank De Kova
▶ While dealing with several suitors, beautiful waitress Moore also discovers that someone at her roadside diner is a Communist spy. Is it customer Lovejoy, a scientist? Or co-worker Marvin, the short-order cook? Paranoia, 1950s-style, is so overdone that it becomes unintentionally entertaining.
Dist.: Republic

SHADEY 1987 British
★ PG-13 Comedy 1:46
☑ Brief nudity, adult situations, explicit language, violence
Dir: Philip Saville   *Cast:* Antony Sher, Billie Whitelaw, Patrick Macnee, Leslie Ash, Bernard Hepton, Larry Lamb
▶ Auto mechanic Sher, who has the ability to project anyone's thoughts and images onto film, is courted by secret agent Whitelaw in an effort to uncover strategic Russian submarine plans. But pacifist Sher is only interested in earning enough money for a sex-change operation. Offbeat black comedy is short on satisfying laughs. **(CC)**
Dist.: CBS/Fox

SHADOW OF A DOUBT 1943
★★★★ NR Mystery-Suspense 1:48 B&W
Dir: Alfred Hitchcock   *Cast:* Teresa Wright, Joseph Cotten, Macdonald Carey, Henry Travers, Patricia Collinge, Hume Cronyn
▶ Young Wright's placid Santa Rosa life is disrupted by the arrival of her beloved uncle Cotten, a suave, charming intellectual who offers her a glimpse of sophistication. To her dismay, she finds evidence that he could be a notorious mass murderer, and is torn between revealing her fears to detective Carey and protecting her family. Subtle but penetrating thriller is among Hitchcock's most accomplished and unnerving stories. Screenplay by Thornton Wilder, Sally Benson, and Alma Reville.
Dist.: MCA

SHADOW OF THE THIN MAN 1941
★★ NR Mystery-Suspense 1:37 B&W
Dir: W. S. Van Dyke II   *Cast:* William Powell, Myrna Loy, Barry Nelson, Donna Reed, Sam Levene, Stella Adler
▶ Married sleuths Nick (Powell) and Nora (Loy) Charles investigate the deaths of a jockey and a reporter at the racetrack. Fourth entry in the *Thin Man* series provides trademark blend of whodunit plotting and wit.
Dist.: MGM/UA

SHADOW PLAY 1986
★★ R Drama 1:37
☑ Brief nudity, adult situations, explicit language
Dir: Susan Shadburne   *Cast:* Dee Wallace Stone, Cloris Leachman, Ron Kuhlman, Barry Laws, Al Strobel, Delia Salvi
▶ New York playwright Stone, obsessed with her lover's suicide, goes to his hometown and has visions of the dead man. Is this her imagination or is there a more sinister explanation? Stone goes crazy beautifully and Leachman underplays sweetly as the grieving mom. Tense climax, but talkiness drags down earlier sections.
Dist.: New World

SHADOWS RUN BLACK 1984
★ NR Horror 1:29
☑ Nudity, adult situations, explicit language, graphic violence
Dir: Howard Heard   *Cast:* William J. Kulzer, Elizabeth Trosper, Shea Porter, George J. Engelson, Dianne Hinkler, Kevin Costner
▶ Campus killer slices and dices coeds. Cop Kulzer, whose kidnapped daughter may be one of the victims, investigates. Among the suspects: a prestardom Costner (who appears briefly). Shabbily directed, little story momentum, rudimentary acting, gratuitous nudity.
Dist.: Vestron

SHADOWZONE 1989
★★ NR Horror 1:25
☑ Nudity, explicit language, graphic violence
Dir: J. S. Cardone   *Cast:* David Beecroft, James Hong, Shawn Weatherly, Lu Leonard, Louise Fletcher
▶ When a human experimental subject dies in an underground lab, NASA captain Beecroft investigates doctor Hong, who has created a murderous monster with shape-changing powers. Murky visuals and draggy pacing. Outrageous performance by Fletcher as Hong's assistant.
Dist.: Paramount

SHAFT 1971
★★★ R Action-Adventure 1:40
☑ Brief nudity, adult situations, explicit language, violence
Dir: Gordon Parks   *Cast:* Richard Roundtree, Moses Gunn, Charles Cioffi, Gwenn Mitchell, Christopher St. John, Lawrence Pressman
▶ When the Mafia kidnaps Harlem crime boss Gunn's daughter, he hires tough private eye Roundtree to retrieve her. While cop pal Cioffi frets about racially oriented mob war, Roundtree takes care of business with aid of black militant St. John. Gumshoe-with-soul was forerunner of seventies black exploitation pics, but holds up today as urban actioner regard-

less of racial focus. Dynamic score by Isaac Hayes won Oscar for Best Song. Director Parks started as well-known *Life* magazine photographer.
Dist.: MGM/UA

SHAG 1988
★★★ PG Comedy 1:40
☑ Adult situations, explicit language
Dir: Zelda Barron *Cast:* Phoebe Cates, Scott Coffey, Bridget Fonda, Annabeth Gish, Page Hannah, Robert Rusler
▶ Cates, Fonda, Gish, and Hannah are four friends who head to Myrtle Beach, South Carolina, for some fun in the sun in the summer of 1963. Cates, although engaged to someone else, finds true love with handsome Rusler while pudgy Gish falls for Coffey. The girls also find time for plenty of shag dancing. Pleasant beach movie is a throwback to another era.
Dist.: HBO

SHAGGY D.A., THE 1976
★★★ G Comedy/Family 1:31
Dir: Robert Stevenson *Cast:* Dean Jones, Suzanne Pleshette, Tim Conway, Keenan Wynn, Jo Anne Worley, Dick Van Patten
▶ Belated sequel to *The Shaggy Dog* repeats the original's winning blend of slapstick and fantasy. Jones's campaign against comically corrupt district attorney Wynn runs into a snag when an ancient ring turns him into a sheepdog at inopportune moments. Prime Disney fun.
Dist.: Buena Vista

SHAGGY DOG, THE 1959
★★★★ G Comedy/Family 1:44 B&W
Dir: Charles Barton *Cast:* Fred MacMurray, Jean Hagen, Tommy Kirk, Annette Funicello, Tim Considine, Kevin Corcoran
▶ Young Kirk finds a magic ring that turns him into a sheepdog, causing no end of problems for father MacMurray, who's allergic to canines. Kirk later plays a secret part in unmasking a spy ring. Charming Disney fantasy, the studio's first attempt at live-action slapstick, led to *The Shaggy D.A.* almost twenty years later.
Dist.: Buena Vista [C]

SHAKEDOWN 1988
★★★ R Action-Adventure 1:40
☑ Adult situations, explicit language, violence
Dir: James Glickenhaus *Cast:* Peter Weller, Sam Elliott, Patricia Charbonneau, Blanche Baker, Antonio Fargas
▶ Legal Aid lawyer Weller, defending crack dealer accused of killing undercover cop, teams with cop Elliott to investigate police theft of money from drug pushers. Packed with action and impressive stunts; moves along nicely even though farfetched story doesn't always make sense.
Dist.: MCA

SHAKER RUN 1985 New Zealand
★★★ NR Action-Adventure 1:30
☑ Adult situations, explicit language, violence
Dir: Bruce Morrison *Cast:* Cliff Robertson, Leif Garrett, Lisa Harrow, Shane Briant
▶ In New Zealand, American race-car drivers Robertson and Garrett are hired by scientist Harrow to sneak an experiment out of the country and quickly get involved with the army and CIA. Well-crafted with nicely orchestrated chases; however, characterizations and dialogue are rather simplistic.
Dist.: Nelson

SHAKESPEARE WALLAH 1965 Indian
☆ NR Drama 2:00 B&W
Dir: James Ivory *Cast:* Shashi Kapoor, Felicity Kendal, Geoffrey Kendal, Madhur Jaffrey, Laura Liddell
▶ As her family of English Shakesperean actors play to dwindling audiences in India, actress Kendal meets rich Indian Kapoor. A bittersweet, cross-cultural love affair ensues. Director Ivory's meticulous direction captures the end-of-the-empire ennui all too well as his elephantine pacing tries patience. However, Felicity Kendal's passionate performance cuts through the torpor.
Dist.: Nelson

SHAKIEST GUN IN THE WEST, THE 1968
★★★ NR Comedy 1:41
Dir: Alan Rafkin *Cast:* Don Knotts, Barbara Rhoades, Jackie Coogan, Donald Barry, Ruth McDevitt, Frank McGrath
▶ Eastern dentist Knotts travels west, where he is tricked into marrying lady robber Rhoades so she can join a wagon train. When wagoners are attacked by Indians, Rhoades does the sharpshooting, but Knotts takes the credit. The truth revealed, Knotts must rescue his kidnapped bride to reassert his manhood. Unfunny remake of Bob Hope's *Paleface* has the look of sixties TV product.
Dist.: Goodtimes

SHALAKO 1968 British
★ PG Western 1:53
☑ Violence
Dir: Edward Dmytryk *Cast:* Sean Connery, Brigitte Bardot, Stephen Boyd, Jack Hawkins, Peter Van Eyck, Honor Blackman
▶ Turgid Western about stoical guide Connery who rescues British aristocrats from an Indian ambush engineered by untrustworthy range boss Boyd. When the travelers prove ungrateful, Connery shifts his attention to their guest, beautiful countess Bardot, who turns out to be a crack shot. Based on a Louis L'Amour novel.
Dist.: CBS/Fox

SHALL WE DANCE 1937
★★★ NR Musical 1:56 B&W
Dir: Mark Sandrich *Cast:* Fred Astaire, Ginger Rogers, Edward Everett Horton, Eric Blore, Jerome Cowan, Ketti Gallian

▶ Seventh Astaire-Rogers teaming skimps on the dances for thin but elegant comedy about a publicity-inspired romance between an aloof Russian ballet star and a strong-willed American singer. Since the Russian is really Astaire in disguise, true love is inevitable. Remarkable George and Ira Gershwin score includes the Oscar-nominated "They Can't Take That Away from Me," "Let's Call the Whole Thing Off" (performed on roller skates), and "Slap That Bass," but the highlight is an irresistible duet to "They All Laughed."
Dist.: Turner

SHAME 1988 Australian
★ ★ ★ R Drama 1:30
☑ Adult situations, explicit language, violence
Dir: Steve Jodrell   *Cast:* Deborra-Lee Furness, Tony Barry, Simone Buchanan, Gillian Jones, Peter Aanensen, Margaret Ford
▶ Rapists terrorize women in grimy Australian town; female motorcyclist Furness, waiting for repairs to her bike, becomes target of violence when she presses for thugs' arrest. Good acting and unusual approach to vigilante and feminist themes add up to provocative drama.
Dist.: Republic

SHAMPOO 1975
★ ★ ★ R Comedy 1:52
☑ Nudity, adult situations, explicit language
Dir: Hal Ashby   *Cast:* Warren Beatty, Julie Christie, Goldie Hawn, Lee Grant, Jack Warden, Carrie Fisher
▶ Against the background of the 1968 Presidential election, Beverly Hills hairdresser Beatty has affairs with the three women in wealthy Warden's life—wife Grant, mistress Christie, and daughter Fisher—while still seeing his own girlfriend Hawn. However, real happiness eludes him. Saucy, sharply satirical sexual roundelay is at times shocking, notably during Christie's famous under-the-table seduction of Beatty. Ashby's direction and Paul Simon's score expertly capture mood of the times. Oscar for Best Supporting Actress (Grant). **(CC)**
Dist.: RCA/Columbia

SHAMUS 1973
★ ★ PG Action-Adventure 1:31
☑ Adult situations, explicit language, violence
Dir: Buzz Kulik   *Cast:* Burt Reynolds, Dyan Cannon, John P. Ryan, Joe Santos, Georgio Tozzi, Ron Weyand
▶ Brooklyn private eye and part-time pool hustler Reynolds stumbles across a warehouse filled with illegal arms while searching for stolen diamonds. Unlikely help comes in the form of beautiful society heiress Cannon. Swift action and sharp dialogue lift this above standard Reynolds vehicles.
Dist.: RCA/Columbia

SHANE 1953
★ ★ ★ ★ NR Western 1:58
Dir: George Stevens   *Cast:* Alan Ladd, Jean Arthur, Van Heflin, Brandon de Wilde, Jack Palance, Emile Meyer, Ben Johnson, Edgar Buchanan, Elisha Cook, Jr.
▶ Reformed gunfighter Ladd works as hired hand for Wyoming homesteaders Heflin and Arthur, winning admiration of their son de Wilde and love of Arthur. Cattle baron Meyer seeks to drive farmers away and imports hired gun Palance as his intimidator. When Heflin decides to show the other farmers how to face up to Palance and Meyer, Ladd must choose between apathy and return to the gunslinger's wayward life. Classic Western was nominated for five Oscars and won for cinematography.
Dist.: Paramount

SHANGHAI GESTURE, THE 1941
★ NR Drama 1:38
Dir: Josef von Sternberg   *Cast:* Walter Huston, Gene Tierney, Victor Mature, Ona Munson, Maria Ouspenskaya, Phyllis Brooks
▶ Munson is the Asian proprietress of a gambling house threatened with closing by Huston, an old acquaintance and the building's new owner. To save her business, Munson draws Tierney, Huston's daughter, down into her sordid world—only to learn that the three of them are united in a secret shame. Cleaned-up version of the John Colton play originally set in a brothel crawls at a snail's pace despite evocative atmosphere.
Dist.: Mystic Fire

SHANGHAI SURPRISE 1986
★ PG-13 Action-Adventure 1:37
☑ Brief nudity, adult situations, explicit language, mild violence
Dir: Jim Goddard   *Cast:* Sean Penn, Madonna, Paul Freeman, Richard Griffiths, Philip Sayer, Clyde Kusatsu
▶ In 1937, missionary Madonna hires rogue Penn to help her track down valuable opium cargo; they run afoul of various villains who also want the stash. After a good start (credits by Maurice Binder of James Bond fame), escapist fare falls apart due to moldy screenplay, abysmal dialogue, and miscast leads. Freeman outshines the stars; ex-Beatle George Harrison produced and provided the music.
Dist.: Vestron

SHARK 1969 U.S./Mexican
★ PG Action-Adventure 1:32
☑ Adult situations, explicit language, violence
Dir: Samuel Fuller   *Cast:* Burt Reynolds, Arthur Kennedy, Barry Sullivan, Silvia Pinal, Francisco Reyguera, Carlos Barry
▶ When their Sudanese assistant is killed by a shark, boat captain Sullivan and Pinal hire American gunrunner Reynolds to replace him. Sullivan claims to be experimenting to solve

hunger but he's really diving for sunken treasure; Reynolds seeks a piece of the action. Some effective underwater footage, but cheesy production falls apart on land. Burt's character is a boor, although with some moments of cheeky humor.
Dist.: Republic

SHARKS' TREASURE 1975
☆ **PG Action-Adventure 1:35**
☑ Violence
Dir: Cornel Wilde   *Cast:* Cornel Wilde, Yaphet Kotto, John Neilson, Cliff Osmond, David Canary
▶ Aging deep-sea fisher Wilde risks his prized boat in a search for sunken treasure. Caribbean locations, good underwater photography, and frequent shark attacks enliven middling plot and acting. Wilde also wrote and produced.
Dist.: MGM/UA

SHARKY'S MACHINE 1981
★ ★ ★ ★ **R Action-Adventure 1:58**
☑ Brief nudity, adult situations, explicit language, graphic violence
Dir: Burt Reynolds   *Cast:* Burt Roynolds, Rachel Ward, Vittorio Gassman, Bernie Casey, Brian Keith, Charles Durning
▶ Atlanta cop Reynolds, demoted to vice squad after shoot-out, falls for Ward, the high-class call girl he has under surveillance, and uncovers corruption involving her client Gassman, a drug king. Adept performance and direction from Reynolds, sexual chemistry from sultry Ward, realistic and gritty atmosphere. Satisfying although violent.
Dist.: Warner

SHARMA AND BEYOND 1986
★ **NR Drama 1:23**
☑ Brief nudity, explicit language
Dir: Brian Gilbert   *Cast:* Suzanne Burden, Robert Urquhart, Michael Maloney, Antonia Pemberton, Benjamin Whitrow, Tom Wilkinson
▶ Aspiring science fiction writer Maloney falls in love with Burden, the daughter of his hero, author Urquhart. The already neurotic Burden can't figure out whether Maloney really loves her or is just using her to get close to her father. Nice touches, especially the opening sequence of a car racing down the road to the music of Shubert; but the premise is slight and difficult to care about.
Dist.: MGM/UA

SHE 1983 Italian
★ **NR Fantasy 1:46**
☑ Nudity, adult situations, explicit language, graphic violence
Dir: Avi Nesher   *Cast:* Sandahl Bergman, David Goss, Harrison Muller, Quinn Kessler
▶ In a postnuclear-war world, immortal amazon Bergman falls in love with traveler Goss, who is searching for his kidnapped sister. Goss and Bergman battle mutants, vampires, and a mad doctor. Repetitive story and cheap production skimpy on everything but dismembered limbs.
Dist.: Vestron

SHEBA, BABY 1975
★ **PG Action-Adventure 1:30**
☑ Adult situations, violence
Dir: William Girdler   *Cast:* Pam Grier, Austin Stoker, D'Urville Martin, Rudy Challenger, Dick Merrifield, Ernest Cooley
▶ Private eye Grier goes after the seemingly respectable businessman who killed her hard-working father. Packing a .44, the fetchingly attired Grier battles the inevitable minions, then goes gunning for Mr. Big himself. Standard black exploitation, with a sexy Grier.
Dist.: Orion

SHE BEAST, THE 1966 Italian/Yugoslavian
☆ **NR Horror 1:14**
Dir: Michael Reeves   *Cast:* Barbara Steele, John Karlsen, Ian Ogilvy, Mel Welles, Jay Riley, Richard Watson
▶ Ogilvy and Steele make the mistake of honeymooning in Transylvania, which is not only under Communist rule, but is the sleeping place of a hideous eighteenth-century witch. When the couple's car plunges into a lake, the witch rises in Steele's place and starts killing the descendents of her old tormentors. Different, but not good. Director Reeves was only twenty-one when he made this—four years before his suicide.
Dist.: Sinister

SHE DEMONS 1958
☆ **NR Horror 1:20 B&W**
Dir: Richard E. Cunha   *Cast:* Irish McCalla, Tod Griffin, Victor Sen Yung, Rudolph Anders, Gene Roth, Leni Tana
▶ Nazi scientist Anders rules a tropical island, where he robs local beauties of their faces to restore that of his accident-scarred wife. Sexpot McCalla is targeted for fiendish experiments when she and he-man Griffin are stranded on the rumblingly volcanic isle. Femme monsters wear claylike masks and bulky leather bikinis in this awesomely bad horror/adventure item.
Dist.: Sinister

SHE-DEVIL 1989
★ ★ **PG-13 Comedy 1:39**
☑ Adult situations, explicit language
Dir: Susan Seidelman   *Cast:* Meryl Streep, Roseanne Barr, Fd Begley, Jr., Linda Hunt, Sylvia Miles
▶ Dumpy housewife Barr decides to get mad and even when philandering hubbie Begley leaves her for romance novelist Streep. Barr systematically sets about destroying their lives with great relish. Diluted version of Fay Weldon's bitter and darkly funny *Life and Loves of a She-Devil* lacks the nastiness and kick of the book. However, Streep is hilarious as the pretentious, pouty, and perpetually dressed-in-pink novelist. Barr fails to keep up with her. **(CC)**
Dist.: Orion

SHE DONE HIM WRONG 1933
★ ★ ★ NR Comedy 1:06 B&W
Dir: Lowell Sherman   *Cast:* Mae West, Cary
Grant, Gilbert Roland, Owen Moore, Noah
Beery, Sr.
▶ West, a Gay Nineties Bowery bar manager
involved with crime boss Beery and convict
Moore, loses her heart to handsome Salvation
Army captain Grant. One of West's best: she
sings, delivers her patented one-liners, and
makes eyes at Grant in high style against a
lusty period background. Based on West's
play "Diamond Lil."
Dist.: MCA

SHEENA 1984
★ ★ PG Action-Adventure 1:56
☑ Nudity, explicit language, violence
Dir: John Guillermin   *Cast:* Tanya Roberts,
Ted Wass, Donovan Scott, Elizabeth of Toro,
France Zobda
▶ After her parents are killed on an expedi-
tion, blond orphan Roberts grows up to be
Queen of the Jungle. Her ability to communi-
cate with animals helps her fight bad guys
who have framed her mentor for an assassina-
tion. Agreeable updating of a popular comic
strip has a welcome sense of humor, scenic
African backgrounds, cute animals. Roberts is
attractive but lacks charisma. (CC)
Dist.: RCA/Columbia

SHENANDOAH 1965
★ ★ ★ ★ NR Western 1:45
Dir: Andrew V. McLaglen   *Cast:* James
Stewart, Doug McClure, Glenn Corbett, Pa-
trick Wayne, Rosemary Forsyth, Katharine
Ross
▶ Stewart gives a wonderful performance as
a Virginia farmer whose opposition to the Civil
War doesn't prevent tragedy from striking his
family. When his son is arrested by Union sol-
diers, Stewart gathers his clan to rescue him.
Large-scale adventure uses haunting vi-
gnettes to show the personal impact of the
war, with warm humor balancing heartbreaking moments. Inspired a Broadway musical.
Dist.: MCA

**SHERLOCK HOLMES AND THE SECRET
WEAPON** 1943
★ ★ ★ ★ NR Mystery-Suspense 1:08 B&W
Dir: Roy William Neill   *Cast:* Basil Rathbone,
Nigel Bruce, Lionel Atwill, Kaaren Verne
▶ During World War II, Sherlock Holmes (Rath-
bone) dons disguises to ferret a Swiss inventor
away from the Nazis. Holmes's archnemesis
Professor Moriarty (Atwill), working for the Ger-
mans, attempts to foil the great detective.
Rathbone and Bruce are fine (as always) as
the great detective and his bumbling side-
kick. (CC)
Dist.: Various ⓒ

**SHERLOCK HOLMES AND THE SPIDER
WOMAN** 1944
★ ★ ★ NR Mystery-Suspense 1:02 B&W
Dir: Roy William Neill   *Cast:* Basil Rathbone,

Nigel Bruce, Gale Sondergaard, Dennis
Hoey
▶ Sherlock Holmes (Rathbone) almost meets
his match in the fiendishly clever "Spider
Woman" (Sondergaard), who murders men so
she can collect on insurance. She tries to kill
Holmes with a poisonous spider. One of the
better Rathbone-Bruce efforts; Sondergaard
makes a stylish villain.
Dist.: Various

**SHERLOCK HOLMES AND THE VOICE OF
TERROR** 1942
★ ★ NR Mystery-Suspense 1:05 B&W
Dir: John Rawlings   *Cast:* Basil Rathbone,
Nigel Bruce, Evelyn Ankers, Reginald Denny,
Henry Daniell, Lon Chaney, Jr.
▶ Holmes (Rathbone) and Watson (Bruce)
employ some lowlife types to help them infil-
trate a sinister Nazi ring that announces sabo-
tage threats on the radio and then carries
them out. One of the series's better casts; the
"Voice of Terror" broadcasts are quite chilling.
Third Rathbone-Bruce effort was their first in a
modern setting. (CC)
Dist.: Key

SHERLOCK HOLMES FACES DEATH 1943
★ ★ NR Mystery-Suspense 1:08 B&W
Dir: Roy William Neill   *Cast:* Basil Rathbone,
Nigel Bruce, Dennis Hoey, Arthur Margetson,
Hillary Brooke, Halliwell Hobbes
▶ Arthur Conan Doyle's nineteenth-century
story is updated to the World War II era: shell-
shocked officers are treated by Dr. Watson
(Bruce) at mansion belonging to impover-
ished aristocrat Brooke. When Watson's assist-
ant Margetson is stabbed by an unknown as-
sailant, and the manor's clock strikes thirteen
times—a legendary portent of the death—he
calls upon his famous detective friend Holmes
(Rathbone) to solve the mystery. (CC)
Dist.: Key

SHERLOCK HOLMES IN WASHINGTON
1943
★ ★ NR Mystery-Suspense 1:11 B&W
Dir: Roy William Neill   *Cast:* Basil Rathbone,
Nigel Bruce, Marjorie Lord, Henry Daniell,
George Zucco
▶ Matchbook containing important secret in-
formation falls into the hands of a German
agent in America's capital. Holmes and Wat-
son travel to Washington to recover it. Stan-
dard Rathbone-Bruce vehicle. (CC)
Dist.: Key

SHERLOCK, JR. 1924
★ ★ NR Comedy 0:45 B&W
Dir: Buster Keaton   *Cast:* Buster Keaton, Ka-
thryn McGuire, Ward Crane, Joseph Keaton,
Erwin Connolly, Horace Morgan
▶ Framed for a petty crime, film projectionist
Keaton falls asleep and dreams he's entered
Hearts and Pearls, the melodrama he's
screening. The resulting series of wildly inven-
tive sight gags gleefully scramble the rules of
cinematic convention and play havoc with

viewer expectation. Consistently ingenious film may have been the first to break the barrier between viewers and the screen. Keaton broke his neck during one train stunt.
Dist.: Grapevine

SHERMAN'S MARCH 1986
★ NR Documentary 2:35
☑ Adult situations, explicit language
Dir: Ross McElwee
▶ Droll look at the women of the South as seen through the eyes of appreciative fellow Southerner McElwee. When his girlfriend dumps him, he sets out to do a documentary on Gen. Sherman's March during the Civil War. Instead McElwee gets sidetracked and chronicles his near-romances with several unforgettable belles. Unpolished camerawork, but filmmaker's trek is fascinating and very funny.
Dist.: First Run

SHE'S BACK 1989
☆ R Comedy 1:30
☑ Explicit language, violence
Dir: Tim Kincaid *Cast:* Carrie Fisher, Robert Joy, Matthew Cowles, Joel Swetow, Sam Coppola, Donna Drake
▶ When Fisher is killed by robbers who've broken into her house, she comes back as a ghost to urge husband Joy to avenge her. Fisher is worried by Joy's attentions to a ditzy neighbor, but he does her bidding and one by one knocks off the gang of killer-thieves. Feeble comedy is helped by Joy's appealing performance.
Dist.: Vestron

SHE'S GOTTA HAVE IT 1986
★ R Comedy 1:29 B&W
☑ Nudity, strong sexual content, explicit language
Dir: Spike Lee *Cast:* Tracy Camilla Johns, Tommy R. Hicks, John Canada Terrell, Spike Lee, Raye Dowell, Joie Lee
▶ Black Brooklynite Johns juggles three lovers: vain actor Terrell, sensitive romantic Hicks, and jokester Lee. Rough-edged and sexually frank but fresh, vibrant, and very funny; Lee's inventiveness as a writer-director is matched only by his skill as the fast-talking Mars Blackmon. Funniest scenes: the Thanksgiving dinner where Lee boasts of his meeting with Jesse Jackson and the montage of male come-ons. (CC)
Dist.: CBS/Fox

SHE'S HAVING A BABY 1988
★ ★ ★ PG-13 Comedy 1:46
☑ Adult situations, explicit language
Dir: John Hughes *Cast:* Kevin Bacon, Elizabeth McGovern, Alec Baldwin, Isabel Lorca, William Windom, Cathryn Damon
▶ Bacon marries his high school sweetheart McGovern, takes job in advertising, and settles into suburbia. Couple has trouble conceiving while Bacon feels alienated from his new lifestyle. Nice cast and slick production. Upbeat finale will leave viewers in a good mood if mean-spirited earlier sections are overlooked. (CC)
Dist.: Paramount

SHE'S OUT OF CONTROL 1989
★ ★ ★ PG Comedy 1:37
☑ Adult situations, explicit language
Dir: Stan Dragoti *Cast:* Tony Danza, Catherine Hicks, Wallace Shawn, Dick O'Neil, Ami Dolenz, Laura Mooney
▶ Divorced Danza becomes obsessed with daughter Dolenz's dating life after she gets a smashing makeover. Suddenly aware that his little girl has grown up, Danza starts breaking up her dates. Plot is simplistic, and Danza's strangely one-sided view of his daughter's life may strike some as unhealthy. (CC)
Dist.: RCA/Columbia

SHE WORE A YELLOW RIBBON 1949
★ ★ ★ ★ NR Western 1:44
Dir: John Ford *Cast:* John Wayne, Joanne Dru, John Agar, Ben Johnson, Harry Carey, Jr., Victor McLaglen
▶ Second of director Ford's "cavalry trilogy," and the only one in color, stars Wayne as an officer facing retirement whose region is threatened by rampaging Arapahos. Frustrated in his attempts to make peace, and unable to evacuate civilians safely, he decides to confront the Indian chief before he loses his command. Wayne gives a memorable performance in this beautifully detailed Western, with Oscar-winning photography by Winton Hoch. *Fort Apache* and *Rio Grande* are the other entries in the trilogy.
Dist.: Turner

SHINING, THE 1980
★ ★ ★ R Horror 2:24
☑ Nudity, explicit language, graphic violence
Dir: Stanley Kubrick *Cast:* Jack Nicholson, Shelley Duvall, Scatman Crothers, Danny Lloyd, Barry Nelson, Philip Stone
▶ Aspiring writer Nicholson, wife Duvall, and their clairvoyant son Lloyd spend winter a caretaking huge Colorado hotel where, years before, caretaker killed family and self. Lloyd suffers vivid visualizations of the violence; isolation eventually drives Nicholson insane. Longish adaptation of Stephen King novel can be confusing but has plenty of shocks and gore for horror fans. Most frequently mimicked scene: ax-wielding Nicholson hacks door open and grins, "Heeeere's Johnny!"
Dist.: Warner

SHIP OF FOOLS 1965
★ ★ NR Drama 2:30 B&W
Dir: Stanley Kramer *Cast:* Vivien Leigh, Simone Signoret, Jose Ferrer, Lee Marvin, Oskar Werner, George Segal, Michael Dunn, Jose Greco, Elizabeth Ashley
▶ In 1933, events aboard a German-bound ship symbolize the rise of Nazism. Among the passengers: drug addict Signoret and her doctor lover Werner, divorcée Leigh, anti-Se-

mite Ferrer, and dwarf Dunn. Engrossing adaptation of the Katherine Anne Porter best-seller. Outstanding Oscar-nominated performances from Werner, Signoret, and Dunn. A Best Picture nominee; won for Cinematography and Art/Set Direction. (CC)
Dist.: RCA/Columbia

SHIRLEY VALENTINE 1989
★★★ R Comedy 1:48
☑ Brief nudity, adult situations, explicit language
Dir: Lewis Gilbert ***Cast:*** Pauline Collins, Tom Conti, Alison Steadman, Julia McKenzie, Joanna Lumley, Bernard Hill, Sylvia Sims
▶ Successful adaptation of the London and New York stage hit which showcased Collins as the lively but lonely Liverpudlian housewife Shirley Valentine. Married to routine-bound Hill, she rebels and runs off to Greece where she starts an affair with Conti that changes her life. Collins is a pure delight, as is Willy Russell's screenplay based on his hilarious one-woman play. Collins was Oscar-nominated for Best Actress. (CC)
Dist.: Paramount

SHOAH 1985 French
☆ NR Documentary 8:23
☑ Adult situations
Dir: Claude Lanzmann
▶ Monumental examination of the Nazi Final Solution during the years 1943–1944 took twelve years of preparation. Tirelessly and doggedly, filmmaker Lanzmann used extensive interviews and a hidden camera when necessary to illuminate the collective mindset that led to the genocide of millions of Eastern European Jews. Among the most disturbing interviews: the Polish peasants who stood by indifferently as their neighbors were carted off to the camps and the barber who cut the hair of the women about to enter the gas chamber. [S]
Dist.: Paramount

SHOCK 1946
★★ NR Mystery-Suspense 1:10 B&W
Dir: Alfred L. Werker ***Cast:*** Vincent Price, Lynn Bari, Frank Latimore, Anabel Shaw, Michael Dunne, Reed Hadley
▶ Shaw witnesses psychiatrist Price murdering his wife, and tries to alert her former-POW husband Latimore. Price, however, convinces Latimore that Shaw is crazy and seeing things. Conniving with nurse/mistress Bari, Price tries to get Shaw put away—forever. First starring role for Price is a convincing exposé of psychiatric abuse.
Dist.: Cable

SHOCKER 1989
★★ R Horror 1:47
☑ Explicit language, graphic violence
Dir: Wes Craven ***Cast:*** Michael Murphy, Peter Berg, Cami Cooper, Mitch Pileggi, Sam Scarber, Theodore Raimi
▶ The electric chair cannot kill homicidal TV repairman Pileggi, since he is able to transport his spirit into other bodies through TV circuit wiring. Berg is the only surviving member of a family wiped out by Pileggi, and his dreams tell him where Pileggi will strike next. Both end up inside a television for a final confrontation. This repellent effort lacks director Craven's usually interesting special effects.
Dist.: MCA

SHOCK TO THE SYSTEM, A 1990
★★★ R Comedy 1:31
☑ Adult situations, explicit language, mild violence
Dir: Jan Egleson ***Cast:*** Michael Caine, Elizabeth McGovern, Peter Riegert, Swoosie Kurtz, Will Patton, Jenny Wright
▶ New York advertising executive Caine has a huge mortgage, a nagging wife (Kurtz), and a younger office rival (Riegert) who has just been promoted ahead of him. After taking out his frustrations on a panhandler, Caine discovers homicide is his ticket up the corporate ladder. Sly, sophisticated black comedy deserves a new life on video. Charming, skillful Caine performance is one of his best. Cleverly adapted from the Simon Brett novel by Andrew Klavan.
Dist.: HBO

SHOCK TREATMENT 1981
★ PG Musical 1:34
☑ Adult situations, explicit language, adult humor
Dir: Jim Sharman ***Cast:*** Jessica Harper, Cliff De Young, Richard O'Brien, Patricia Quinn, Charles Gray, Ruby Wax
▶ Follow-up to campy cult hit *The Rocky Horror Picture Show* substitutes Harper and De Young for the naive young couple originally played by Susan Sarandon and Barry Bostwick. Duo are guests on "Marriage Maze" TV game show, leading to night of musical debauchery. Despite return of writer/actor/songwriter O'Brien, silly spin-off lacks crude fun of the original. (CC)
Dist.: CBS/Fox

SHOCK WAVES 1977
★ PG Horror 1:24
☑ Violence
Dir: Ken Wiederhorn ***Cast:*** Peter Cushing, Brooke Adams, John Carradine, Fred Buch, Luke Halpin, Jack Davidson
▶ Adams is a passenger on Carradine's yacht, which runs aground on an island inhabited by ex-SS man Cushing and a group of dormant Nazi zombies who never got to show their evil stuff during the war. Making up for lost time, the creatures attack the visitors. Not-so-hot plot generates some shocks. Originally known as *Death Corps.*
Dist.: Prism

SHOESHINE 1946 Italian
★ NR Drama 1:33 B&W
Dir: Vittorio De Sica ***Cast:*** Franco Inter-

lenghi, Annielo Mele, Bruno Ortensi, Pacifico Astrologo
▶ Raw, powerfully emotional story of two homeless shoeshine boys who are thrown into a brutal reform school after their scheme to buy a horse falls afoul of the law. Corrupt guards and filthy conditions prompt an escape—and tragedy. Winner of a special Oscar and a landmark in world cinema; led to reform of Italy's juvenile justice system. [S]
Dist.: Foothill

SHOES OF THE FISHERMAN, THE 1968
★★★★★ G Drama 2:28
Dir: Michael Anderson ***Cast:*** Anthony Quinn, Oskar Werner, John Gielgud, David Janssen, Laurence Olivier, Vittorio De Sica
▶ Archbishop Quinn emerges from twenty-year sentence in Soviet prison camp to become the first non-Italian pope in four hundred years. Quinn must deal with a world facing starvation and nuclear confrontation. Global-sized adaptation of the Morris West best-seller has a superb cast and an epic sweep.
Dist.: MGM/UA

SHOGUN 1981
★★★ NR Action-Adventure/MFTV 2:05
☑ Nudity, adult situations, violence
Dir: Jerry London ***Cast:*** Richard Chamberlain, Toshiro Mifune, Yoko Shimada, Frankie Sakai, Alan Badel, Michael Hordern
▶ Chamberlain, a seventeenth-century Englishman shipwrecked in Japan, becomes a pawn in feudal power struggle as local lord Mifune vies for title of shogun. Star-crossed romance between Chamberlain and concubine Shimada falls victim to politics when couple is captured by one of Mifune's rivals. Highly compressed version of ten-hour TV miniseries.
Dist.: Paramount

SHOGUN ASSASSIN 1980 Japanese/U.S.
★★ R Martial Arts 1:26
☑ Nudity, adult situations, graphic violence
Dir: Robert Houston ***Cast:*** Tomisaburo Wakayama, Masahiro Tomikawa, Kayo Matsuo, Minoru Ohki, Shoji Kobayashi
▶ Curiosity item edited from two episodes in a popular Japanese martial arts series. Adding a new soundtrack and redubbing the characters, American producers fashioned an extremely violent and almost plotless story from *Sword of Vengeance* and *Baby-Cart at the River Styx*, sequels to the stylish *Lightning Swords of Death*. Nonstop action involving an outcast samurai and his young son is dazzlingly bloody, but narration adds unnecessary comic overtones. Providing new voices are Lamont Johnson and Sandra Bernhard.
Dist.: MCA

SHOOTING, THE 1967
★★★ G Western 1:22
☑ Explicit language, violence
Dir: Monte Hellman ***Cast:*** Millie Perkins, Jack Nicholson, Warren Oates, Will Hutchins
▶ Ex-bounty hunter and sidekick hook up with mysterious woman in the desert. A gunslinger follows them, leading to a violent dispute. Offbeat and arty Western filmed simultaneously with *Ride in the Whirlwind* is not for the John Wayne crowd. However, Nicholson is fascinating and cult favorite Hellman provides interesting direction.
Dist.: VidAmerica

SHOOTING PARTY, THE 1985 British
★★ NR Drama 1:48
☑ Brief nudity, explicit language, mild violence
Dir: Alan Bridges ***Cast:*** James Mason, Dorothy Tutin, Edward Fox, Cheryl Campbell, John Gielgud, Gordon Jackson
▶ In pre-World War I England, nobleman Mason plays host to fellow aristocrats for a weekend of hunting at his country estate. Shooting isn't the only thing on the agenda as adultery, romance, and political discussions also occur. The one Mason-Gielgud scene is priceless in this faultlessly acted drama, and the bucolic English countryside provides nice contrast to the violence of the hunt. However, talky story of manners and tradition moves slowly.
Dist.: HBO

SHOOTIST, THE 1976
★★★★★ PG Western 1:39
☑ Adult situations, explicit language, violence
Dir: Don Siegel ***Cast:*** John Wayne, Lauren Bacall, Ron Howard, James Stewart, Richard Boone, Hugh O'Brian
▶ In turn-of-the-century Carson City, famous gunslinger Wayne, dying of cancer, takes room in Bacall's boarding house. Her son Howard worships Wayne but bad guys Boone and O'Brian are determined to shoot him down. Tremendously moving and effective. Director Siegel emphasizes characterization and suspense over the usual genre shoot-outs; Wayne's quietly dignified performance ranks with his finest.
Dist.: Paramount

SHOOT LOUD, LOUDER. . .I DON'T UNDERSTAND 1966 Italian
☆ NR Drama 1:40
Dir: Eduardo De Filippo ***Cast:*** Marcello Mastroianni, Raquel Welch, Guido Alberti, Leopoldo Trieste, Paolo Ricci, Tecla Scarano
▶ Antiques dealer Mastroianni lives with a crazy uncle who communicates only through firecracker explosions. When wealthy neighbor Ricci is murdered, Mastroianni doesn't know if the murder was real or a dream. Boundries between fantasy, reality, dreams, and nightmares are all too permeable in this failed parody of Fellini-style filmmaking. Surreal result is uninvolving. [S]
Dist.: Nelson

SHOOT THE MOON 1982
★ ★ ★ R Drama 2:04
☑ Adult situations, explicit language, violence
Dir: Alan Parker *Cast:* Albert Finney, Diane Keaton, Karen Allen, Peter Weller, Dana Hill
▶ Respected author Finney, the father of four girls, leaves Keaton for younger woman Allen. Keaton battles rejection and despair while considering a divorce and an affair with Weller. Strong acting and incisive writing by Bo Goldman are the highlights of this downbeat melodrama.
Dist.: MGM

SHOOT THE PIANO PLAYER 1960 French
☆ NR Drama 1:25 B&W
Dir: François Truffaut *Cast:* Charles Aznavour, Marie Dubois, Nicole Berger, Michele Mercier
▶ Pianist Aznavour, haunted by his wife's suicide, abandons his career to play in a cheap cafe. Aznavour's quiet existence is disrupted when he gets in a violent dispute with the bartender over the affections of waitress Dubois and his brother gets mixed up with criminals. Masterful mix of different moods from black comedy to tragedy will delight fans of the French New Wave. Soulful performance by Aznavour, catchy score by Georges Delerue. Adapted from a David Goodis novel.
[S]
Dist.: Various

SHOOT TO KILL 1947
★ NR Mystery-Suspense 1:04 B&W
Dir: William Berke *Cast:* Russell Wade, Edmund MacDonald, Vince Barnett, Susan Walters, Douglas Blackley, Nestor Paiva
▶ Film noir told in flashback by Walters, the wife of a gangster who is trying to muscle his way into a crooked municipal power structure. Corrupt district attorney MacDonald and gang-boss Paiva set out to frame the interloper, but Walters and newshound Wade expose their doings. Dark, moody, effective little suspenser.
Dist.: Sinister

SHOOT TO KILL 1988
★ ★ ★ ★ R Action-Adventure 1:46
☑ Adult situations, explicit language, violence
Dir: Roger Spottiswoode *Cast:* Sidney Poitier, Tom Berenger, Kirstie Alley, Clancy Brown, Richard Masur, Andrew Robinson
▶ Savage killer joins a group camping trip led by Alley through Pacific Northwest mountains; San Francisco FBI agent Poitier must depend on Alley's outdoorsman boyfriend Berenger to track the killer down. Familiar manhunt benefits from extraordinary location footage, well-mounted action sequences, and first-rate performance by Poitier, starring in his first film in a decade.
Dist.: Buena Vista

SHOP AROUND THE CORNER, THE 1940
★ ★ ★ NR Romance/Comedy 1:37 B&W
Dir: Ernst Lubitsch *Cast:* James Stewart, Margaret Sullavan, Frank Morgan, Joseph Schildkraut, Sara Haden, Felix Bressart
▶ For feuding Budapest sales clerks Stewart and Sullavan, it is fight at first sight. Both fall for pen pals they've never met, not realizing that the other is actually the object of their written affections. One of the most charming and romantic confections ever to come out of Hollywood features delicately nuanced direction by Lubitsch, marvelous ensemble playing. Remade as the musical *In the Good Old Summertime* and adapted into the Broadway musical *She Loves Me*. **(CC)**
Dist.: MGM/UA

SHOP ON MAIN STREET, THE 1965 Czech
★ ★ NR Drama 2:08 B&W
Dir: Jan Kadar, Elmar Klos *Cast:* Josef Kroner, Ida Kaminska, Hana Slivkova, Frantisek Zvarik, Helena Zvarikov, Martin Holly
▶ In Nazi-occupied Eastern Europe, amiable carpenter Kroner agrees to be "Aryan comptroller" for a Jewish-owned button shop on Main Street to appease nagging wife Slivkova and fascist brother-in-law Zvarik. Kroner learns the store's owner, bankrupt, deaf, and elderly Kaminksa, is not even aware of the war, and he must decide whether or not to abide by an order to deport the town's Jews. Oscar winner for Best Foreign Film. [S]
Dist.: RCA/Columbia

SHORT CIRCUIT 1986
★ ★ ★ ★ ★ PG Sci-Fi/Comedy 1:39
☑ Explicit language, mild violence
Dir: John Badham *Cast:* Steve Guttenberg, Ally Sheedy, Fisher Stevens, Austin Pendleton, G. W. Bailey, Brian McNamara
▶ Lightning strikes robot made for military applications, giving it human qualities. Robot escapes from lab and finds sanctuary with animal-lover Sheedy, who thinks it's an adorable alien. Robot's inventor Guttenberg and Indian colleague Stevens search for their creation while military honcho Bailey orders the errant robot destroyed. Genial box-office smash will delight children of all ages. Followed by sequel. **(CC)**
Dist.: CBS/Fox

SHORT CIRCUIT II 1988
★ ★ ★ ★ PG Sci-Fi/Comedy 1:52
☑ Explicit language
Dir: Kenneth Johnson *Cast:* Fisher Stevens, Michael McKean, Cynthia Gibb, Jack Weston, David Hemblen
▶ Sequel to the popular comedy continues the adventures of Johnny Five, the jerry-rigged robot with superhuman intelligence. This time he helps Stevens, one of his former guardians, foil a jewel robbery while struggling with an idea for a new toy. Lighthearted follow-up should please younger viewers.
Dist.: RCA/Columbia

SHORT EYES 1977
☆ **R Drama 1:44**
☑ Adult situations, explicit language, graphic violence
Dir: Robert M. Young *Cast:* Bruce Davison, Jose Perez, Nathan George, Don Blakely, Shawn Elliot, Tito Goya
▶ Davison, a mild-mannered, middle-class WASP, encounters complex code of rules and dangerous existence when imprisoned in New York City's Tombs jails. The other inmates learn Davison is an accused child molester (a "short eyes" in cellblock slang) and vent their racial and sexual frustrations on him. Powerful and hard-hitting look at underclass of American society is disturbing and unforgettable. Not for those seeking escapist fare.
Dist.: Vestron

SHORT TIME 1990
★★★ **PG-13 Comedy 1:37**
☑ Explicit language, violence
Dir: Gregg Champion *Cast:* Dabney Coleman, Teri Garr, Matt Frewer, Barry Corbin, Joe Pantoliano
▶ Thanks to some mixed-up medical records, policeman Coleman thinks he has only two weeks to live. Ex-wife Garr will receive insurance payments if he dies in the line of duty, so Coleman does everything he can to get himself knocked off. Comedy/action/romance tries to do too much, none of it well. No disgrace for pros Coleman and Garr, and there's an exciting helicopter chase
Dist.: LIVE

SHOT IN THE DARK, A 1964
★★★★ **PG Comedy 1:43**
☑ Adult situations, explicit language
Dir: Blake Edwards *Cast:* Peter Sellers, Elke Sommer, George Sanders, Herbert Lom, Burt Kwouk, Tracy Reed
▶ When Paris maid Sommer is accused of murder, bumbling Inspector Clouseau (Sellers) investigates. Despite all evidence to the contrary and an increasing body count, Clouseau insists on Sommer's innocence and solves the case in his own inimitable fashion. Hilarious follow-up to *The Pink Panther* with classic Sellers-Edwards pratfalls.
Dist.: CBS/Fox

SHOUT, THE 1979 British
☆ **R Drama 1:27**
☑ Nudity, explicit language
Dir: Jerzy Skolimowski *Cast:* Alan Bates, Susannah York, John Hurt, Robert Stephens, Tim Curry
▶ In an English village, Bates, a stranger whose weird powers include the ability to kill by shouting, insinuates himself into the lives of composer Hurt and wife York. She falls under Bates's spell while her husband is exposed to the full power of the shout. Unusual and mysterious but ultimately off-putting. Based on a Robert Graves story.
Dist.: RCA/Columbia

SHOUT AT THE DEVIL 1977
★★★★ **PG Action-Adventure 2:08**
☑ Explicit language, violence
Dir: Peter Hunt *Cast:* Lee Marvin, Roger Moore, Barbara Parkins, Ian Holm, Rene Kolldehoff, Horst Janson
▶ Irish ivory poacher Marvin and English partner Moore run afoul of German commissioner Kolldehoff in 1913 East Africa. Moore and Marvin's daughter Parkins fall in love but when Kolldehoff kills their baby, they seek vengeance by blowing up a German battleship. Rousingly old-fashioned adventure is well mounted and quite pleasing.
Dist.: Vestron

SHOW BOAT 1936
★★ **NR Musical 1:50 B&W**
Dir: James Whale *Cast:* Irene Dunne, Allan Jones, Charles Winninger, Paul Robeson, Helen Morgan, Helen Westley
▶ Aboard a Mississippi River showboat in the 1900s, captain's daughter Dunne falls for gambler Jones while black singer Morgan tries to pass for white. Atmospheric direction from Whale; superb singing and acting by Dunne and Robeson. Magnificent Jerome Kern-Oscar Hammerstein score includes "Ol' Man River," "Can't Help Lovin' Dat Man," and "Bill." Adapted from the Broadway musical based on the Edna Ferber novel.
Dist.: MGM/UA

SHOW BOAT 1951
★★★★ **NR Musical 1:48**
Dir: George Sidney *Cast:* Howard Keel, Kathryn Grayson, Ava Gardner, Joe E. Brown, William Warfield, Agnes Moorehead
▶ MGM remake of the Kern-Hammerstein musical classic is perfectly cast: Grayson as captain Brown's daughter, Keel as her gambler beau, and Gardner as the mulatto star singer forced to flee from the sheriff because the law forbids her marriage to a white. Lovingly produced, beautifully sung, emotional and heartbreaking.
Dist.: MGM/UA

SHOW BUSINESS 1944
★ **NR Musical 1:32 B&W**
Dir: Edwin L. Marin *Cast:* Eddie Cantor, Joan Davis, George Murphy, Nancy Kelly, Constance Moore, Don Douglas
▶ Cantor, Murphy, Davis, and Moore start out in vaudeville, and together make a tuneful rise to Ziegfeld Follies stardom. Though fictional, story mirrors real-life climb of the stars, and Cantor especially has a wonderful time in this rose-colored reminiscence. Uniformly excellent songs include "It Had to Be You" and "While Strolling in the Park One Day."
Dist.: Turner

SHOWDOWN AT BOOT HILL 1958
★ **NR Western 1:12 B&W**
Dir: Gene Fowler, Jr. *Cast:* Charles Bronson, Fintan Meyler, Robert Hutton, John Carradine, Carole Mathews

▶ U.S. marshal Bronson kills a wanted murderer, then heads for the man's hometown to collect the bounty. But townspeople refuse to identify the body. With only barber/undertaker Carradine on his side, Bronson faces agonizing frustration. Young Bronson gets a strong psychological grip on his character in this unusually grown-up Western.
Dist.: Republic

SHOW OF FORCE, A 1990
★ R Drama 1:33
☑ Nudity, adult situations, violence
Dir: Bruno Barreto *Cast:* Amy Irving, Andy Garcia, Lou Diamond Phillips, Kevin Spacey, Priscilla Pointer
▶ TV journalist Irving encounters informer Phillips, FBI agent Spacey, and special prosecutor Garcia as she investigates the killings of two Puerto Rican nationalists. Was the FBI involved in a cover-up of the real motive behind the murders? Irving glows with conviction, but nonsensical, poorly directed attempt at political suspense falls apart around her.
Dist.: Paramount

SHOW PEOPLE 1928
★ NR Comedy 1:22 B&W
Dir: King Vidor *Cast:* Marion Davies, William Haines, Del Henderson, Paul Ralli, Harry Gribbon, Polly Moran
▶ Hollywood celebrates a then recently passed era in its own history, with Davies as a young actress who gets her break making energetic two-reel comedies for a small studio reminiscent of Mack Sennett's. Funny late silent film with a legendary pie fight and a wonderful peek at real-life stars having fun in the studio commissary.
Dist.: MGM/UA

SHRIEK IN THE NIGHT, A 1933
★ NR Mystery-Suspense 1:06 B&W
Dir: Albert Ray *Cast:* Ginger Rogers, Lyle Talbot, Arthur Hoyt, Purnell Pratt, Harvey Clark, Lillian Harmer
▶ Scoop-happy reporters Rogers and Talbot compete against one another for a big story until they come upon some nasty murders in a brand-new apartment complex. Things get hot for Rogers in janitor Clark's furnace, but the newspersons pull together to get the bad guys. Interesting period ephemera in this otherwise throwaway effort.
Dist.: Sinister

SHY PEOPLE 1987
★ ★ R Drama 1:58
☑ Rape, adult situations, explicit language, violence
Dir: Andrei Konchalovsky *Cast:* Jill Clayburgh, Barbara Hershey, Martha Plimpton, Merritt Butrick, John Philbin, Mare Winningham
▶ Manhattan magazine reporter Clayburgh, unruly daughter Plimpton in tow, goes to Louisiana bayou to write an article on her backwoods relative Hershey, a widowed mother of four. A sometimes violent culture clash ensues. Strong performances by Hershey (Best Actress at the Cannes Film Festival) and Clayburgh transcend overbaked script. **(CC)**
Dist.: Warner

SICILIAN, THE 1987
★ R Action-Adventure 1:55
☑ Nudity, explicit language, violence
Dir: Michael Cimino *Cast:* Christopher Lambert, Terence Stamp, Barbara Sukowa, Joss Ackland, John Turturro, Richard Bauer
▶ Sicilian peasant Lambert kills a cop, organizes outlaw band in the mountains, and becomes local folk hero as he battles powerful Mafia chieftain Ackland. Achieves some sweep and color but miscast Lambert fails to convince as a tragic figure. Adapted from the Mario Puzo novel and inspired by a true story.
Dist.: Vestron

SID AND NANCY 1986 British
☆ R Biography/Music 1:53
☑ Nudity, adult situations, explicit language, violence
Dir: Alex Cox *Cast:* Gary Oldman, Chloe Webb, David Hayman, Drew Schofield, Debby Bishop, Tony London
▶ Sordid relationship between Sex Pistols bassist Sid Vicious and junkie groupie Nancy Spungen receives a graphic but sympathetic treatment in this highly stylized punk biography. Oldman and Webb are sensational as the ill-fated pair, but film's unflinching depiction of the drug and punk underworlds is uncomfortably authentic. The music (including a re-creation of Sid's infamous "My Way" rock video) is first-rate. **(CC)**
Dist.: Nelson

SIDEWALKS OF LONDON 1938 British
★ ★ NR Comedy 1:24 B&W
Dir: Tim Whelan *Cast:* Charles Laughton, Vivien Leigh, Rex Harrison, Larry Adler, Tyrone Guthrie, Gus McNaughton
▶ Laughton, a London street entertainer, takes gamin Leigh under his wing when he catches her stealing from a musician. With the help of admirer Harrison, she becomes a famous music hall star, but doesn't forget the man who first helped her. Charming, bittersweet comedy features excellent performances by Laughton and Leigh.
Dist.: KVC

SIDEWINDER 1 1977
★ ★ PG Action-Adventure 1:37
☑ Explicit language
Dir: Earl Bellamy *Cast:* Marjoe Gortner, Michael Parks, Susan Howard, Alex Cord, Charlotte Rae, Barry Livingston
▶ Lots of motorcycles roaring through dirt and mud in this intrigue centering around the sport of motocross racing. Howard takes over a roguish cycle troupe from her late brother and develops a relationship with rider Parks. Gortner is a wild, womanizing racer who joins the group to race for the national championship.

Simpleminded dirt bike jamboree has racing, crashes, and spinouts galore.
Dist.: Nelson

SIEGE OF FIREBASE GLORIA, THE 1989 Australian
★★★ R War 1:40
☑ Explicit language, violence
Dir: Brian Trenchard-Smith *Cast:* Wings Hauser, R. Lee Ermey, Albert Popwell, Robert Arevalo, Mark Neely, Gary Hershberger
► During the Tet offensive, the Vietcong attack Firebase Gloria, an American outpost. Hauser and Ermey lead their outnumbered troops in a valiant defense. Workmanlike effort has some good moments but basically covers the same dramatic territory as other Vietnam movies. Fine performance by Ermey, who contributed to the screenplay.
Dist.: Fries

SIESTA 1987
★★ R Drama 1:37
☑ Rape, nudity, adult situations, explicit language
Dir: Mary Lambert *Cast:* Ellen Barkin, Gabriel Byrne, Julian Sands, Isabella Rossellini, Martin Sheen, Jodie Foster
► Fragmented, experimental drama about daredevil stuntwoman Barkin, whose pursuit of ex-lover Byrne brings her to the brink of madness. Told in flashbacks, story includes Barkin's encounters with jaded aristocrats in Spain and abandoned husband Sheen in Death Valley. Barkin is superb, but debut director Lambert's style is often irritating and pretentious. (CC)
Dist.: Warner

SIGN O' THE TIMES 1987
★★★ PG-13 Documentary/Music 1:30
☑ Adult situations, explicit language
Dir: Prince *Cast:* Prince, Sheila E., Sheena Easton, Dr. Fink, Miko Weaver, Cat
► Concert footage from Prince's European tour shot in Rotterdam and Antwerp. On a stage set resembling a seedy downtown bar district, Prince and his retinue rip through numbers including "Sign o' the Times," "Little Red Corvette," "The Cross," and "U Got the Look." Prince also writhes his way through several dance numbers and sports numerous outrageous costumes. Fans will be in revery while doubters may become converts.
Dist.: MCA

SIGNS OF LIFE 1989
★★★ PG-13 Drama 1:31
☑ Adult situations, explicit language
Dir: John David Coles *Cast:* Beau Bridges, Vincent Phillip D'Onforio, Arthur Kennedy, Kevin J. O'Connor, Will Patton, Kate Reid, Georgia Engel, Kathy Bates, Michael Lewis, Mary Louise Parker
► Closing of crusty Kennedy's Maine shipyard affects the lives of his employees. Foreman Bridges seeks job at his brother-in-law's hardware store but ends up robbing it instead; D'Onoforio will have to institutionalize retarded brother Lewis to leave town with O'-Connor. Gentle, winningly restrained slice of small town life got lost in theaters but should find audience on video. Kennedy stands out in his final film.
Dist.: IVE

SILAS MARNER 1985 British
★ NR Drama/MFTV 1:32
Dir: Giles Foster *Cast:* Ben Kingsley, Jenny Agutter, Patrick Ryecart, Jonathan Coy, Freddie Jones, Frederick Treves
► Falsely accused of theft, weaver Kingsley retires to a hut on the moors, where he lives in bitter isolation until someone abandons an infant on his doorstep. Taking the child in, he risks not only the curiosity of his neighbors, but further emotional loss as well. Consummate artist Kingsley goes straight for the heart in this well-produced adaptation of the George Eliot novel.
Dist.: CBS/Fox

SILENCE, THE 1963 Swedish
☆ R Drama 1:35 B&W
☑ Brief nudity, adult situations
Dir: Ingmar Bergman *Cast:* Ingrid Thulin, Gunnel Lindblom, Jorgen Lindstrom, Hakan Jahnberg
► Two sisters passing through an unnamed country stop at a hotel. Thulin, a frustrated lesbian, is slowly dying of lung disease; her younger sister Lindblom is the mother of the ten-year-old boy who accompanies them. While the boy meets various characters throughout the hotel, Lindblom picks up a waiter, and inflames her sister's desires. Spare, uncomfortable, sometimes obscurely symbolic third part of Bergman's trilogy on faith begun with *Through A Glass Darkly* and *Winter Light.* [S]
Dist.: Various

SILENCE OF THE NORTH 1981 Canadian
★★★★ PG Drama 1:33
☑ Adult situations, explicit language, violence
Dir: Allan King *Cast:* Ellen Burstyn, Tom Skerritt, Gordon Pinsent, Jennifer McKinney, Colin Fox
► True story of Olive Frederickson (Burstyn) who accompanied her trapper husband Skerritt into the northern Canadian wilderness in 1919. Burstyn sees her family through harsh conditions and personal tragedies. Little-known film deserves a bigger reputation; strong story, solid production values, and magnficently sympathetic Burstyn.
Dist.: MCA

SILENT ASSASSINS 1988
★ NR Action-Adventure 1:32
☑ Explicit language, violence
Dir: Lee Doo-yong *Cast:* Sam Jones, Linda Blair, Jun Chong, Philip Rhee, Gustav Vintas, Rebecca Ferrati
► When his partner is killed by ex-CIA agent

Vintas, Los Angeles cop Jones teams up with Chong, whose niece was kidnapped by the villain, and martial arts expert Rhee to get revenge. The stakes are high: Vintas has also nabbed a scientist with a deadly germ warfare formula. Low-rent production has some decent action but indecent acting, dialogue, and music.
Dist.: Virgin

SILENT MADNESS 1984
★ R Horror 1:35
☑ Nudity, adult situations, explicit language, graphic violence
Dir: Simon Nuchtern *Cast:* Belinda Montgomery, Viveca Lindfors, Solly Marx, David Greenan, Sydney Lassick
▶ Brilliant psychiatrist Montgomery learns that homicidal psychopath Marx has been released by mistake from an asylum. She returns to the small-town college where he committed his original murders, and poses as a sorority sister in an effort to capture him. Predictably bloody drama's interesting 3-D effects will lose impact on TV.
Dist.: Media

SILENT MOVIE 1976
★ ★ ★ PG Comedy 1:27
☑ Adult situations
Dir: Mel Brooks *Cast:* Mel Brooks, Marty Feldman, Dom DeLuise, Bernadette Peters, Burt Reynolds, Paul Newman, Sid Caesar, James Caan, Liza Minnelli
▶ Has-been director Brooks and his pals Feldman and DeLuise try to revive their careers by convincing studio chief Caesar to back their silent movie. To win Caesar's support, the guys attempt to sign up big stars like Reynolds, Newman, Caan, and Minnelli. Wild and wacky fun with inventive visual gags. Not strictly a silent: there are music, sound effects, and one line of dialogue spoken by mime Marcel Marceau. Funniest scene: the boys take a shower with Reynolds.
Dist.: CBS/Fox

SILENT NIGHT, BLOODY NIGHT 1973
★ R Horror 1:27
☑ Adult situations, graphic violence
Dir: Theodore Gershuny *Cast:* Patrick O'Neal, James Patterson, Mary Woronov, Astrid Heeren, John Carradine, Walter Abel
▶ Descendent of a madman visits the long-deserted family mansion to investigate some strange goings on there. It seems an ax murderer is on the loose, and many think it's an inmate who's escaped from the local insane asylum. The mayor's daughter, however, may not be so sure. Standard horror fare with disappointing climax.
Dist.: Paragon

SILENT NIGHT, DEADLY NIGHT 1984
★ R Horror 1:19
☑ Nudity, explicit language, graphic violence
Dir: Charles E. Sellier *Cast:* Lilyan Chauvan,

Gilmer McCormick, Toni Nero, Robert Brian Wilson, Britt Leach
▶ Little Billy witnesses parents' murder by man in a Santa Claus suit. He grows up in a Catholic orphanage, where the Mother Superior punishes him for his anti-Christmas feelings. When his toy-store boss makes him don Santa gear, he goes beserk. Lackluster slasher pic whose premise provoked public outcry on original release.
Dist.: IVE

SILENT NIGHT, DEADLY NIGHT PART 2 1987
☆ R Horror 1:28
☑ Rape, nudity, adult situations, explicit language, violence
Dir: Lee Harry *Cast:* Eric Freeman, James P. Newman, Elizabeth Cayton, Jean Miller
▶ While institutionalized, Freeman, younger brother of the killer from *Silent Night, Deadly Night*, recalls emotionally distraught childhood. Upon release, Freeman puts on Saint Nick gear and goes on murderous rampage. Vicious sequel, poorly produced and badly acted.
Dist.: IVE

SILENT PARTNER, THE 1979 Canadian
★ ★ ★ ★ R Mystery-Suspense 1:45
☑ Brief nudity, explicit language, violence
Dir: Daryl Duke *Cast:* Elliott Gould, Susannah York, Christopher Plummer, Celine Lomez, Ken Pogue, John Candy
▶ When crazed robber Plummer attempts hold-up, mild-mannered teller Gould takes advantage of the heist to grab the loot for himself. Plummer menaces Gould for the dough; the two attempt to outwit one another with Lomez, involved with both men, caught in the middle. Exceptional and underrated with clever plotting, fine performances, well-rounded characterizations, and maximum tension.
Dist.: Vestron

SILENT RAGE 1982
★ ★ ★ R Action-Adventure 1:40
☑ Nudity, adult situations, explicit language, graphic violence
Dir: Michael Miller *Cast:* Chuck Norris, Ron Silver, Steven Keats, Toni Kalem, Brian Libby, William Finley
▶ Sheriff Norris figures his job is done when his deputies kill ax murderer Libby. However, a research doctor revives the dead man with a drug, turning him into an indestructible killing machine. It's up to Norris to stop him. Fast-paced, if not quite Norris's best.
Dist.: MCA

SILENT RUNNING 1972
★ ★ ★ G Sci-Fi 1:29
Dir: Douglas Trumbull *Cast:* Bruce Dern, Cliff Potts, Ron Rifkin, Jesse Vint, Steven Brown
▶ Nuclear war has destroyed vegetation on Earth; the only plants left are in a space sta-

tion orbiting Saturn. When the crew's botanist Dern receives orders to destroy them, he rebels and takes over the station. Intriguing but slowly paced drama was the directing debut for Trumbull, who worked on the special effects for *2001: A Space Odyssey*. Music by Peter Schickele, better known as P.D.Q. Bach.
Dist.: MCA

SILENT SCREAM 1980
★ ★ R Horror 1:26
☑ Nudity, adult situations, explicit language, violence
Dir: Denny Harris *Cast:* Rebecca Balding, Cameron Mitchell, Avery Schreiber, Barbara Steele, Steve Doubet, Yvonne De Carlo
▶ College student Balding rents room in spooky boarding house, unaware that landlady De Carlo is hiding her psychotic daughter Steele upstairs. Subsequent brutal murders puzzle detectives Mitchell and Schreiber. Inventive but gory thriller builds up credible chills from a routine formula.
Dist.: IVE

SILK STOCKINGS 1957
★ ★ ★ ★ NR Musical 1:57
Dir: Rouben Mamoulian *Cast:* Fred Astaire, Cyd Charisse, Janis Paige, Peter Lorre, George Tobias, Barrie Chase
▶ In Paris, Hollywood producer Astaire gets involved with Russian agents, in particular pretty comrade Charisse. She's all official business at first, but Astaire manages to overcome the Cold War and warm her up. Remake of *Ninotchka* features some good Cole Porter songs and memorable Astaire dancing. While Garbo was a more convincing Russian, Charisse sure can dance. Score includes "All of You" and "Stereophonic Sound."
Dist.: MGM/UA

SILKWOOD 1983
★ ★ ★ ★ R Biography/Drama 2:11
☑ Brief nudity, adult situations, explicit language, violence
Dir: Mike Nichols *Cast:* Meryl Streep, Kurt Russell, Cher, Craig T. Nelson, Diana Scarwid, Fred Ward
▶ Streep, a scrappy worker at a nuclear plant where employees include her live-in lover Russell and gay roommate Cher, grows disenchanted with lax safety procedures and becomes a union activist. When she discovers boss Nelson is deliberately concealing defects in products that could cause nuclear disasters, she gathers evidence for the press, annoying both management and her colleagues. Based on the true story of Karen Silkwood, topical drama comments on both Middle American blue-collar life and corporate greed and recklessness. Nominated for five Oscars.
Dist.: Embassy

SILVERADO 1985
★ ★ ★ ★ PG-13 Western 2:13
☑ Explicit language, violence

Dir: Lawrence Kasdan *Cast:* Kevin Kline, Scott Glenn, Kevin Costner, Danny Glover, John Cleese, Rosanna Arquette, Brian Dennehy, Linda Hunt
▶ Drifters Kline and Glenn team up with Glenn's hot-blooded younger brother Costner and black cowboy Glover to rid town of corrupt sheriff Dennehy and crooked cattle ranchers. Ripsnorter has it all: epic feel, fascinating characters, Oscar-nominated Bruce Broughton score. Relentless action and unflagging pace combine with touchingly quieter moments, like the gentle friendship between Kline and barmaid Hunt. **(CC)**
Dist.: RCA/Columbia

SILVER BEARS 1978
★ ★ PG Drama 1:53
☑ Adult situations, explicit language
Dir: Ivan Passer *Cast:* Michael Caine, Cybill Shepherd, Louis Jourdan, Tom Smothers, Martin Balsam, David Warner, Jay Leno
▶ Wheeler-dealers Balsam and Caine hire penniless Italian count Jourdan as front for new Swiss bank. With wealthy Persian Warner, they conspire to smuggle silver from Iran. Convoluted plot includes various other bankers, brokers, and silver magnates. Shepherd plays the screwball, unfaithful wife of Smothers; Leno appears as Balsam's car-thief son. Adapted from Paul Erdman's novel.
Dist.: USA

SILVER BULLET 1985
★ ★ ★ R Horror 1:35
☑ Explicit language, graphic violence
Dir: Dan Attias *Cast:* Gary Busey, Corey Haim, Megan Follows, Robin Groves, Terry O'Quinn
▶ Run-of-the-mill werewolf story, written by Stephen King and based on his novella, "Cycle of the Werewolf." Confined to a wheelchair, Haim must convince sister Follows and hard-drinking uncle Busey that a werewolf is responsible for the horrible murders in Tarker's Mills. Eventually, they confront the monster on Halloween eve with the assistance of a silver bullet. **(CC)**
Dist.: Paramount

SILVER CHALICE, THE 1955
★ ★ ★ NR Drama 2:15
Dir: Victor Saville *Cast:* Paul Newman, Virginia Mayo, Pier Angeli, Jack Palance, Natalie Wood, Lorne Greene
▶ Greek sculptor Newman is sold into slavery but wins recognition in Rome. He is commissioned by Christian leaders in Jerusalem to make a religious relic, leading to battles with evil magician Palance and the Roman emperor. Miscast Newman is awkward and self-conscious in his film debut; actor took out an ad asking people not to watch the movie, but it really isn't that bad. Based on the Thomas B. Costain novel.
Dist.: Warner

SILVER DREAM RACER 1983 British
★★ **PG Drama/Sports 1:39**
☑ Adult situations, explicit language
Dir: David Wickes ***Cast:*** Beau Bridges, David Essex, Cristina Raines, Clarke Peters, Harry H. Corbett
▶ Essex is an aspiring world-class biker who has it in for American champ Bridges, responsible for the death of another driver. Forced out of the competition, Essex gets help financing his new motorcycle prototype, the Silver Dream Racer, from Raines, the widow of the dead driver, and enters the big British race. First-rate photography and spectacular track scenes enhance the only slightly above-average plot line.
Dist.: Vestron

SILVER STREAK 1976
★★★★★ **PG Comedy 1:53**
☑ Adult situations, explicit language, mild violence
Dir: Arthur Hiller ***Cast:*** Gene Wilder, Jill Clayburgh, Richard Pryor, Ned Beatty, Patrick McGoohan, Ray Walston
▶ All-star cast of clowns becomes embroiled in a cross-country caper when bookish Wilder, on an L.A. to Chicago train trip, seduces Clayburgh. Everything is blissful until he sees a corpse thrown from the train. With looney, petty thief Pryor, they learn of a murder plot involving missing Rembrandt letters and psychopathic art historian McGoohan. Briskly paced plot culminates in a literally smashing ending.
Dist.: CBS/Fox

SIMON 1980
★ **PG Comedy 1:37**
☑ Explicit language, adult humor
Dir: Marshall Brickman ***Cast:*** Alan Arkin, Austin Pendleton, Judy Graubart, William Finley, Wallace Shawn, Madeline Kahn
▶ Think-tank scientists brainwash professor Arkin into believing he is an alien; experiment gets out of control when Arkin becomes a TV messiah, preaching to the masses. Some funny scenes, like Arkin's pantomine history of evolution, but the humor tends to be uneven. Graubart is quite winning as the girlfriend who tells Arkin he is not from "out of space." "That's 'outer space'!" protests Arkin.
Dist.: Warner

SIMON OF THE DESERT 1965 Mexican
☆ **NR Drama 0:47 B&W**
☑ Nudity
Dir: Luis Buñuel ***Cast:*** Claudio Brook, Silvia Pinal, Hortensia Santovena, Enrique Alverez Felix
▶ A holy man lives on a platform on top of a pillar, performing miracles for the crowd and undergoing lascivious temptations from Satan (Pinal). One of director Buñuel's funniest and most concise statements on the irredeemability of mankind. [S]
Dist.: Various

SIMPLE STORY, A 1979 French
★ **NR Drama 1:47**
☑ Brief nudity, adult situations
Dir: Claude Sautet ***Cast:*** Romy Schneider, Bruno Cremer, Claude Brasseur, Arlette Bonnard
▶ Schneider is a thirty-nine-year-old woman undergoing a personal crisis when husband Cremer leaves her and their teenage son and she becomes pregnant by lover Brasseur. Understated, penetrating look at mid-life crisis is buoyed by radiant Schneider's performance. A Best Foreign Film Oscar nominee. [S]
Dist.: RCA/Columbia

SINBAD AND THE EYE OF THE TIGER 1977 British
★★★ **G Fantasy/Family 1:53**
Dir: Sam Wanamaker ***Cast:*** Patrick Wayne, Taryn Power, Margaret Whiting, Jane Seymour
▶ Sinbad (Wayne) comes to the aid of his princess-fiancée Seymour when her brother is transformed into a baboon by his evil stepmother Whiting. Along the way, the brave sailor fights numerous monsters (courtesy of special effects whiz Ray Harryhausen). Good fun for youngsters although bland acting may not hold adult viewers.
Dist.: RCA/Columbia

SINBAD THE SAILOR 1947
★★★★ **NR Action-Adventure 1:57**
Dir: Richard Wallace ***Cast:*** Douglas Fairbanks, Jr., Maureen O'Hara, Anthony Quinn, Walter Slezak, Jane Greer, Mike Mazurki
▶ On a mysterious island, Sinbad (Fairbanks) races against evil emir Quinn in pursuit of the legendary treasure of Alexander the Great and wins the love of the beautiful O'Hara. Saturday matinee–style escapism: alabaster palaces and slender minarets sparkle in Technicolor with Fairbanks adding a dash of panache to the many escapes.
Dist.: Turner

SINCERELY CHARLOTTE 1986 French
★ **NR Drama 1:32**
☑ Nudity, adult situations, explicit language, mild violence
Dir: Caroline Huppert ***Cast:*** Isabelle Huppert, Niels Arestrup, Christine Pascal, Nicolas Wostrikoff, Jean-Michel Ribes, Philippe Delevingne
▶ Red-headed nightclub singer Huppert goes on the lam after she's suspected in her boyfriend's murder. Unable to prove her innocence, Huppert runs to the suburbs, where she steals previous boyfriend Arestrup from his level-headed wife. Although Huppert is captivating, this film winks at low moral doings, and ends with crime having paid. Director is Huppert's sister. [S]
Dist.: RCA/Columbia

SINCERELY YOURS 1955
★★ **NR Drama 1:55**
Dir: Gordon Douglas ***Cast:*** Liberace,

Joanne Dru, Dorothy Malone, Alex Nicol, William Demarest, Lori Nelson

▶ Pianist Liberace goes deaf and becomes a recluse. He watches others through a telescope and acquires lip-reading ability. His enthusiasm for life renewed, he helps those less fortunate. Liberace fans might enjoy his patented outrageous outfits and musical numbers (including "Chopsticks"), but the script is unintentionally funny.74
Dist.: Warner

SINCE YOU WENT AWAY 1944
★ ★ ★ ★ NR Drama 2:52 B&W
Dir: John Cromwell *Cast:* Claudette Colbert, Jennifer Jones, Shirley Temple, Joseph Cotten, Monty Woolley, Robert Walker, Lionel Barrymore, Agnes Moorehead, Hattie McDaniel, Keenan Wynn

▶ Sentimental masterpiece examines the impact of World War II on the home front, in particular housewife Colbert and daughters Jones and Temple as they wait for news from their enlisted husband and father. Cotten offers solid support as a long-term friend of the family. Filled with heartbreaking moments and warmly nostalgic views of small-town life, film received nine Oscar nominations, winning for Max Steiner's lush score.
Dist.: CBS/Fox

SINFUL LIFE, A 1989
☆ R Comedy 1:30
☑ Adult situations, explicit language
Dir: William Schreiner *Cast:* Anita Morris, Rick Overton, Dennis Christopher, Blair Tefkin, Mark Rolston, Cynthia Szigeti

▶ Negligent single mother Morris tries to clean up her act before the school authorities take overgrown, baby-talking daughter Tefkin away from her. Bidding for respectability, Morris tries to trap janitor Overton and credit manager Christopher into matrimony. The characters do not transcend their piggishness here, and vulgar attempt at black comedy fails to amuse.
Dist.: RCA/Columbia

SING 1989
★ ★ ★ PG-13 Musical 1:37
☑ Explicit language
Dir: Richard Baskin *Cast:* Lorraine Bracco, Peter Dobson, Jessica Steen, Louise Lasser, George DiCenzo, Patti LaBelle, Rachel Sweet

▶ Central Brooklyn High School is about to be closed, threatening the continuation of its yearly, teen-affirming musical show. Fiesty teacher Bracco enlists tough kid Dobson and demure Steen to put on this year's extravaganza. With the help of hip cheerleader Sweet, the performance is a blockbuster. An old-fashioned screen musical in modern dress, film is bursting with energy, pluck, and new talent.
Dist.: RCA/Columbia

SINGING THE BLUES IN RED 1986 Germany
☆ NR Drama 1:50
☑ Adult situations
Dir: Kenneth Loach *Cast:* Gerulf Pannach, Fabienne Babe, Cristine Rose, Sigfrit Steiner, Krutina

▶ Protest balladeer Pannach switches loyalties from East to West Germany. He is appalled by crass Western attempts to exploit his decision, and with the help of French journalist Babe, he sets off in search of his father who had crossed over to the West many years before. Heavy drama makes its now-dated political points without subtlety or humor.
Ⓢ
Dist.: JCI

SINGIN' IN THE RAIN 1952
★ ★ ★ ★ ★ NR Musical 1;43
Dir: Gene Kelly, Stanley Donen *Cast:* Gene Kelly, Debbie Reynolds, Donald O'Connor, Jean Hagen, Cyd Charisse, Rita Moreno

▶ In the late 1920s, Hollywood silent-movie star Kelly adjusts to the coming of sound and romances young actress Reynolds. Kelly's co-star Hagen wants him for herself and schemes against Reynolds. Perhaps the greatest musical of them all is consistently witty, tuneful, and exuberant. Many unforgettable numbers: O'Connor's pratfalls to "Make 'Em Laugh," the justly famous title tune, the lyrical Kelly-Reynolds "You Were Meant for Me" duet in an empty studio. **(CC)**
Dist.: MGM/UA

SIN OF HAROLD DIDDLEBOCK, THE 1947
★ ★ NR Comedy 1:30 B&W
Dir: Preston Sturges *Cast:* Harold Lloyd, Frances Ramsden, Rudy Vallee, Jimmy Conlin, Edgar Kennedy, Raymond Walburn

▶ Inventive comedy opens with Lloyd's football heroics from 1925's *The Freshman*, then jumps twenty years to show that he never rose above bookkeeper. After being fired, Lloyd gets first drink from barkeep Kennedy. "Sir, you arouse the artist in me," says Kennedy as he mixes concoction that sends straightlaced Lloyd on a mad spree that includes purchasing a circus. Underrated Sturges work is just a few shades below his best; sweet Lloyd/Ramsden relationship adds poignance to the humor. Producer Howard Hughes reedited and released the film in 1950 as *Mad Wednesday*, with ten minutes cut from original.
Dist.: Various

SIROCCO 1951
★ ★ ★ NR Mystery-Suspense 1:38 B&W
Dir: Curtis Bernhardt *Cast:* Humphrey Bogart, Marta Toren, Lee J. Cobb, Everett Sloane, Gerald Mohr, Zero Mostel

▶ Downbeat love triangle set in 1920s Syria. Bogart is a black-market gunrunner supplying arms to rebel Arabs; when threatened by Cobb, a French officer, he retaliates by stealing Cobb's girlfriend Toren. But his better instincts take hold when Cobb is kidnapped by

the rebels. Effort to recapture the magic of *Casablanca* suffers from gloomy plot and lack of romance.
Dist.: RCA/Columbia

SISTERHOOD, THE 1988
☆ **R Action-Adventure 1:16**
☑ Violence
Dir: Cirio H. Santiago *Cast:* Rebecca Holden, Chuck Wagner, Lynn-Holly Johnson, Barbara Hooper, Henry Strzalkowski, Robert Dryer
▶ In a male-dominated, postapocalyptic world, Johnson lives with her little brother and communicates psychically with a wild hawk. When her brother is murdered by marauders, she joins up with the Sisterhood, a band of female warriors led by Holden. Together they set out for the forbidden zone to rescue imprisoned sisters. May be among the most laughably bad of the *Mad Max* clones.
Dist.: Media

SISTER KENNY 1946
★ ★ ★ **NR Biography 1:56 B&W**
Dir: Dudley Nichols *Cast:* Rosalind Russell, Alexander Knox, Dean Jagger, Philip Merivale, Beulah Bondi, Charles Dingle
▶ Moving, thoughtful tribute to Elizabeth Kenny, an Australian nurse who fought for decades to have her polio rehabilitation therapy accepted by the medical establishment. Russell received an Oscar nomination for her loving portrayal of Kenny; Knox, who also worked on the screenplay with director Nichols and Mary McCarthy, plays a Scottish doctor who was one of her few allies.
Dist.: Turner

SISTERS 1973
★ **R Horror 1:33**
☑ Adult situations, explicit language, violence
Dir: Brian De Palma *Cast:* Margot Kidder, Jennifer Salt, Charles Durning, Bill Finley, Lisle Wilson, Barnard Hughes
▶ Staten Island reporter Salt thinks she's witnessed a murder, but police refuse to believe her. She hires detective Durning to tail suspect Kidder while conducting her own dangerous investigation. Film borrows liberally from *Rear Window*, but director De Palma adds unnerving touches. Added benefits are inventive split-screen techniques and an eerie Bernard Herrmann score.
Dist.: Warner

SISTER SISTER 1988
★ ★ **R Mystery-Suspense 1:30**
☑ Nudity, adult situations, explicit language, violence
Dir: Bill Condon *Cast:* Eric Stoltz, Jennifer Jason Leigh, Judith Ivey, Dennis Lipscomb, Anne Pitoniak
▶ Dank Southern gothic mystery/horror about sisters Ivey and Leigh, who turn their Louisiana bayou mansion into a bed and breakfast guest house. Ivey resents the attention her younger sister receives from handsome guest Stoltz. Things turn for the worse when their dog is decapitated, the handyman is sliced up in the swamp, and little sister begins hearing voices from the past. Steamy atmosphere and capable performances aid sluggish plot.
Dist.: New World

SITTING DUCKS 1979
☆ **R Comedy 1:30**
☑ Adult situations, explicit language
Dir: Henry Jaglom *Cast:* Michael Emil, Zack Norman, Patrice Townsend, Irene Forrest, Richard Romanus, Henry Jaglom
▶ Goofs Emil and Norman swipe the receipts from a mob numbers game and drive south towards Costa Rica. On the way, they pick up waitress Forrest and abandoned date Townsend. Unknown to the heroes, the two women are actually mob killers hired to get them. As in most of Jaglom's films, much of the dialogue here was improvised, and much of it concerns sex. The result is mostly annoying.
Dist.: Media

SIX PACK 1982
★ ★ ★ ★ **PG Comedy 1:48**
☑ Adult situations, explicit language, mild violence
Dir: Daniel Petrie *Cast:* Kenny Rogers, Diane Lane, Erin Gray, Barry Corbin, Terry Kiser, Anthony Michael Hall
▶ Racer Rogers, attempting to make a comeback after an accident, catches six orphans stripping his car. After this rocky start, the kids wear down Rogers's resistance to them and a warm relationship develops. Down-home tale has easy-going charm; Rogers makes a pleasant feature film debut and the kids are cute as a bug. Songs by Rogers, Crystal Gayle, and Merle Haggard.
Dist.: CBS/Fox

SIXTEEN CANDLES 1984
★ ★ ★ ★ **PG Comedy 1:33**
☑ Brief nudity, adult situations, explicit language
Dir: John Hughes *Cast:* Molly Ringwald, Anthony Michael Hall, Paul Dooley, Carlin Glynn, Blanche Baker, Michael Schoeffling
▶ Sweet sixteen turns sour for student Ringwald: parents Dooley and Glynn are so crazed by sister Baker's wedding they forget Molly's birthday; crush on high school hunk Schoeffling appears unrequited; and attention only comes from not-so-meek geek Hall. Good-natured, lowbrow comedy mixes rowdy laughs with sweetly accurate portrayal of puberty blues. Directorial debut for Hughes and launching pad for careers of Ringwald and Hall.
Dist.: MCA

16 DAYS OF GLORY 1986
★ ★ ★ **G Documentary/Sports 2:25**
Dir: Bud Greenspan *Cast:* Narrated by: David Perry
▶ Documentary about the 1984 Summer

Olympics in Los Angeles. Among the featured stories: hurdler Edwin Moses's attempt to extend his seven-year winning streak, swimmer Rowdy Gaines winning the gold medal denied him by the 1980 boycott, and the thrilling decathalon duel between Germany's Jurgen Hingsen and England's Daley Thompson. Incredible camerawork puts you right in the middle of the action; unfortunately, the austere narration distances you from it. **(CC)**
Dist.: Paramount

16 DAYS OF GLORY PART II 1986
★ ★ ★ **G Documentary/Sports 2:27**
Dir: Bud Greenspan *Cast:* Narrated by: David Perry
▶ More footage from the 1984 Summer Olympics covering Carl Lewis's attempt to duplicate Jesse Owens's feat of winning four gold medals, diver Greg Louganis's victory, and the heroics of cyclist Connie Carpenter-Phinney and the United States Men's Gymnastics Team. Follow-up to *16 Days of Glory* repeats the same virtues and flaws of the original. (CC)
Dist.: Paramount

'68 1988
☆ **R Drama 1:37**
☑ Nudity, adult situations, explicit language
Dir: Steven Kovacks *Cast:* Eric Larson, Robert Locke, Neil Young, Sandor Tecsi, Anna Dukasz, Mirlan Kwun
▶ While the sixties cultural revolution explodes around him, Hungarian immigrant Tecsi opens a restaurant in San Francisco. Among the strains in his life are sons Larson and Locke: one is kicked out of Berkeley and goes to work for motorcycle shop owner Young; and the other realizes he is gay at his Army induction. Not so much about the title year as it is a family melodrama, with familiar conflicts.
Dist.: New World

SIX WEEKS 1982
★ ★ ★ ★ **PG Drama 1:47**
☑ Adult situations, explicit language
Dir: Tony Bill *Cast:* Dudley Moore, Mary Tyler Moore, Katherine Healy, Shannon Wilcox, Joe Regalbuto, John Harkins
▶ Married politician Dudley Moore gets involved with cosmetics mogul Mary Tyler Moore and her dying daughter Healy. Romantic feelings grow between Dudley and Mary as they help make Healy's last weeks meaningful. High-grade tearjerker doesn't insult your intelligence; the leads play off one another with humor and sensitivity, and Healy is very appealing.
Dist.: RCA/Columbia

SKELETON COAST 1988
★ **R Action-Adventure 1:38**
☑ Explicit language, violence
Dir: John (Bud) Cardos *Cast:* Ernest Borgnine, Robert Vaughn, Oliver Reed, Herbert Lom, Daniel Greene, Leon Isaac Kennedy
▶ Borgnine recruits a motley commando unit

to go into Angola and rescue his son, who's fallen into the hands of Communists and is being tortured by East German Vaughn. A run-in with evil South African diamond boss Reed adds to the stakes, putting the commandos in the way of a fortune in diamonds. Stereotyped characters and a too-complex plot sink this poorly shot actioner.
Dist.: Nelson

SKIN DEEP 1989
★ ★ ★ **R Comedy 1:41**
☑ Nudity, adult situations, explicit language
Dir: Blake Edwards *Cast:* John Ritter, Vincent Gardenia, Alyson Reed, Joel Brooks, Julianne Phillips, Chelsea Field, Raye Hollit
▶ Ritter, ostensibly a successful author, tries to cure writer's block with alcohol and obsessive womanizing. His slapstick journey includes encounter with bodybuilding champion Hollit and startling incident with a new brand of condoms. Episodic comedy has overtones of director Edwards's more successful *10*.
Dist.: Media

SKIN GAME, THE 1931 British
★ **NR Drama 1:26 B&W**
Dir: Alfred Hitchcock *Cast:* Edmund Gwenn, Jill Esmond, John Longdon, C. V. France, Helen Haye, Phyllis Konstam
▶ Gwenn and France are the patriarchs of two rival families, one aristocratic and the other nouveau, who are competing for land rights. Director Hitchcock later disowned this suspenseless, dated story, based on a play by John Galsworthy. Lifeless and talky.
Dist.: Sinister

SKIN GAME 1971
★ ★ ★ ★ **PG Western/Comedy 1:42**
☑ Explicit language, mild violence
Dir: Paul Bogart *Cast:* James Garner, Louis Gossett, Jr., Susan Clark, Brenda Sykes, Edward Asner, Andrew Duggan
▶ Two pre–Civil War con men run imaginative scam: "slaveowner" Garner sells "slave" Gossett to dupes and then helps him escape for next sucker. Comfortable ruse runs afoul of con woman Clark, who steals their money and Garner's heart, slave girl Sykes, who wins Gossett's love, suspicious slave trader Asner, and abolitionists who insist on "freeing" Gossett. Amiable comedy with heart makes case for human dignity.
Dist.: Warner

SKI PATROL 1990
★ ★ **PG Comedy 1:31**
☑ Explicit language, adult humor
Dir: Richard Correll *Cast:* Roger Rose, Yvette Nipar, T. K. Carter, Martin Mull, Leslie Jordan, Ray Walston
▶ Pops Walston runs a ski resort that is threatened by yuppie developer Mull, who is not above using dirty tricks to sabotage the slopes. Fun-loving ski-patrollers like Rose do zany stunts, get in romantic tangles, and make life miserable for their martinet leader

Jordan. Ski scenes add some movement, but *Police Academy* formula is very tired.
Dist.: RCA/Columbia

SKIP TRACER 1979 Canadian
★ ★ NR Mystery-Suspense 1:30
☑ Brief nudity, explicit language
Dir: Zale R. Dalen *Cast:* David Petersen, John Lazarus, Rudy Szabo, Mike Grigg
▶ Driven to win loan agency's "Man of the Year" for fourth time, debt collector Petersen takes his job seriously, callously repossessing the merchandise of those who skip payments. But when his efforts have unforeseen tragic consequences, obsessed Petersen must reassess his life. Low-budget character study can be slow-paced, but is well written and credible.
Dist.: HBO

SKI TROOP ATTACK 1959
☆ NR War 1:03 B&W
Dir: Roger Corman *Cast:* Michael Forest, Frank Wolff, Wally Campo, Richard Sinatro, Sheila Carol, Roger Corman
▶ During World War II, tough sergeant Wolff and lieutenant Forest lead their Allied ski troop on a mission to destroy a bridge in German territory. Lovely Carol initially helps them, but her motives turn out to be purely Aryan. Minor but still zippy Corman effort features the director in a brief bit as a Nazi skier.
Dist.: Sinister

SKY HIGH 1985
★ ★ NR Comedy 1:40
☑ Nudity, explicit language, violence, adult humor
Dir: Nico Mastorakis *Cast:* Daniel Hirsch, Clayton Norcross, Frank Schultz, Lauren Taylor, Janet Taylor, Karen Verlaine
▶ While vacationing in Greece, three teenagers looking for dates find themselves dealing with the KGB when they come into possession of an audio tape that can cause hallucinations and even kill. Not to worry, they also find girlfriends. Beautiful scenery, bonehead screenplay.
Dist.: Vestron

SKY PIRATES 1986 Australian
★ ★ PG-13 Action-Adventure 1:28
☑ Violence
Dir: Colin Eggleston *Cast:* John Hargreaves, Meredith Phillips, Max Phipps, Bill Hunter, Simon Chilvers, Alex Scott
▶ In 1945, pilot Hargreaves, accompanied by reverend Chilvers, crashes near Easter Island due to a tablet planted by aliens. Hargreaves is then court-martialed, but escapes with Chilvers's daughter Phillips to battle Phipps for the magical object. Confusing and farfetched. (CC)
Dist.: CBS/Fox

SKY RIDERS 1976
★ ★ ★ ★ PG Action-Adventure 1:33
☑ Adult situations, violence

Dir: Douglas Hickox *Cast:* James Coburn, Susannah York, Robert Culp, Charles Aznavour, Werner Pochath, Zouzou
▶ When wife York is kidnapped by terrorists, wealthy industrialist Culp turns to her ex-husband Coburn for help. He assembles a team of mercenaries and leads a daring attack by hang-glider on the mountain fortress where York is being held. Shot on location in Greece, film offers marvelous scenery and thrilling aerial sequences.
Dist.: CBS/Fox

SKY'S THE LIMIT, THE 1943
★ ★ NR Musical 1:29 B&W
Dir: Edward H. Griffith *Cast:* Fred Astaire, Joan Leslie, Robert Benchley, Robert Ryan, Elizabeth Patterson
▶ Minor musical about a wartime romance between Astaire, an aviation hero disguised as an ordinary citizen, and Leslie, a journalist dedicated to the war effort. Undistinguished except for Astaire's brilliant "One for My Baby" and the Oscar-nominated "My Shining Hour."
Dist.: Turner

SLAM DANCE 1987
★ R Mystery-Suspense 1:40
☑ Nudity, adult situations, explicit language, violence
Dir: Wayne Wang *Cast:* Tom Hulce, Virginia Madsen, Mary Elizabeth Mastrantonio, Adam Ant, Harry Dean Stanton, Millie Perkins
▶ Down-on-his-luck Los Angeles cartoonist Hulce, deserted by wife Mastrantonio, is accused of murdering romantic fling Madsen. Pursued by cop Stanton, Hulce finds himself neck-deep in conspiracy as he attempts to exonerate himself. Stylish thriller can be too self-consciously hip, but likable Hulce and subculture setting compensate for many flaws. (CC)
Dist.: CBS/Fox

SLAP SHOT 1977
★ ★ ★ ★ R Comedy/Sports 2:03
☑ Brief nudity, adult situations, explicit language, violence
Dir: George Roy Hill *Cast:* Paul Newman, Michael Ontkean, Lindsay Crouse, Jennifer Warren, Melinda Dillon, Strother Martin
▶ Player-coach Newman revives minor-league hockey team's flagging fortunes by turning the players from skaters into fighters. Sensitive Ivy League teammate Ontkean resists the brawling while, off the ice, womanizer Newman pursues Ontkean's wife Crouse and others. Rowdy, unruly, and uproarious; Newman is perfect. The raw language is hilarious but keep the kiddies out of earshot.
Dist.: MCA

SLATE, WYN & ME 1987 Australian
★ R Drama 1:30
☑ Explicit language
Dir: Don McLennan *Cast:* Sigrid Thornton,

Simon Burke, Martin Sacks, Tommy Lewis, Lesley Baker, Harold Bigent

▶ Vietnam vet Burke and his brother Sacks kill a cop during a bank robbery and are forced to kidnap Thornton, the only witness, when they flee into Australia's remote Outback. At first fearful for her life, Thornton learns to exploit the brothers for her own ends. Despite beautiful locations, unfocused chase lacks excitement.
Dist.: Nelson

SLAUGHTER 1972
★ R Action-Adventure 1:32
☑ Nudity, explicit language, violence
Dir: Jack Starrett *Cast:* Jim Brown, Stella Stevens, Rip Torn, Don Gordon, Cameron Mitchell, Marlene Clark
▶ Hoodlums make the mistake of killing ex-Green Beret Brown's parents. Once he dispatches the killers, Brown takes on criminal boss Torn in Mexico. Black exploitation fans will get what they expect as Brown goes through gun-blazing, chest-baring paces.
Dist.: CBS/Fox

SLAUGHTER HIGH 1987
★ R Horror 1:30
☑ Nudity, explicit language, violence
Dir: George Dugdale, Mark Ezra, Peter Litten *Cast:* Caroline Munro, Simon Scuddamore, Carmine Iannoccone, Donna Yeager, Sally Cross, Kelly Baker
▶ Cruel high school students tormenting classmate Scuddamore with practical jokes accidentally scar him for life. Years later he returns disguised as a court jester to kill them. Routine horror film filled with gratuitously bloody violence. Also known as *April Fool's Day*. Available in an unrated version.
Dist.: Vestron

SLAUGHTERHOUSE 1988
★ R Horror 1:25
☑ Explicit language, graphic violence
Dir: Rick Roessler *Cast:* Sherry Bendorf, Don Barrett, William Houch, Joe Barton, Jane Higginson
▶ California radio station sponsoring a "Pig Out" weekend sends a group of teens on a tour of the local pig slaughterhouse. Owner Barrett and his retarded son Barton, angry at losing the slaughterhouse in a tax dispute, respond by murdering the visitors. Uninspired horror exploitation attempts touches of black humor.
Dist.: Nelson

SLAUGHTERHOUSE FIVE 1972
★★ R Sci-Fi 1:44
☑ Nudity, adult situations, explicit language, violence
Dir: George Roy Hill *Cast:* Michael Sacks, Ron Leibman, Valerie Perrine, Sharon Gans, Roberts Blossom, Kevin Conway
▶ Sacks plays an ordinary guy who finds himself traveling in time and space between three situations: as a World War II POW during

the brutal bombing of Dresden, a middle-class husband and father, a and caged prisoner kept in captivity with sexy lover Perrine by alien beings. Complex, ambitious adaptation perfectly captures the spirit of Kurt Vonnegut's acclaimed novel.
Dist.: MCA

SLAUGHTERHOUSE ROCK 1988
☆ R Horror 1:30
☑ Nudity, explicit language, violence
Dir: Dimitri Logothetis *Cast:* Nicholas Celozzi, Tom Reilly, Donna Denton, Toni Basil, Hope Marie Carlton, Steven Brian Smith
▶ Celozzi, haunted by nightmares involving crimes committed on Alcatraz Island, is told by teacher Denton to confront the dreams at the source. Accompanied by his friends, he does and encounters a really nasty spirit. Nonsensical story favors eerie effects over coherent plotting. Music by Devo.
Dist.: SVS

SLAUGHTER IN SAN FRANCISCO 1981
Hong Kong
☆ R Martial Arts 1:27
☑ Adult situations, explicit language, violence
Dir: William Lowe *Cast:* Don Wong, Chuck Norris, Sylvia Channing, Robert Jones, Dan Ivan
▶ When his former partner is murdered, ex-cop Wong relies on his martial arts prowess to track down the killers. Bland kung-fu filler of interest only for an early villainous role by Norris. Set in Daly City (outside San Francisco), shot in 1973, and released here in 1981 to capitalize on Norris's star power.
Dist.: Nelson

SLAUGHTER'S BIG RIP-OFF 1973
★ R Action-Adventure 1:33
☑ Nudity, explicit language, violence
Dir: Gordon Douglas *Cast:* Jim Brown, Ed McMahon, Brock Peters, Don Stroud, Gloria Hendry, Dick Anthony Williams
▶ Sequel to 1972's *Slaughter* finds Brown targeted for revenge by the crime syndicate he attacked in the first outing. Syndicate head McMahon orders Brown's girlfriend Hendry blown up. Brown is once again an excellent action hero in this violent pic.
Dist.: CBS/Fox

SLAVE GIRLS FROM BEYOND INFINITY 1987
☆ R Sci-Fi 1:12
☑ Nudity, adult situations, explicit language, violence
Dir: Ken Dixon *Cast:* Elizabeth Cayton, Cindy Beal, Brike Stevens, Don Scribner, Carl Horner, Kirk Graves
▶ Three beautiful escaped convicts crashland on a jungle planet ruled by the evil Zed. He forces them into a deadly hunt in which they are the prey. Campy, low-budget adventure is primarily an excuse to see the statu-

esque leads running through woods in lingerie.
Dist.: Urban Classics

SLAVE OF LOVE, A 1978 Russian
☆ **NR Drama 1:34**
Dir: Nikita Mikhalkov *Cast:* Elena Solovey, Rodion Nakhapetov, Alexander Kaliagin, Oleg Basilashvili, Konstantin Grigoryev
► A troupe of actors and filmmakers work on a celluloid potboiler in the Crimea during the 1917 Revolution. While they are engrossed in their small intrigues and romances, history overtakes them in the form of civil war. A propagandistic view of Russian history, but enjoyable and beautifully photographed, especially a striking image of heroine Solovey being borne into the future on a sunshine yellow trolley. [S]
Dist.: RCA/Columbia

SLAVES OF NEW YORK 1989
☆ **R Drama 2:05**
☑ Brief nudity, adult situations, explicit language
Dir: James Ivory *Cast:* Bernadette Peters, Chris Sarandon, Mary Beth Hurt, Madeline Potter, Adam Coleman Howard, Mercedes Ruehl, Betty Comden, Steve Buscemi, Tama Janowitz, Tammy Grimes
► Totally pretentious, uninvolving journey through New York's "Downtown," populated by struggling artists and their hangers-on. Peters is painter Coleman Howard's much-maligned hat-maker girlfriend, "slave" to his abominable behavior and infidelity because he holds the lease to their loft. Flat screenplay by Tama Janowitz, based on her novel. Ivory flounders in what is uncharted territory for him. (CC)
Dist.: RCA/Columbia

SLAYGROUND 1984 British
★ **R Action-Adventure 1:29**
☑ Explicit language, violence
Dir: Terry Bedford *Cast:* Peter Coyote, Mel Smith, Billie Whitelaw, Philip Sayer, Bill Luhrs
► Professional thief Coyote accidentally kills a young girl in upstate New York. Her father hires vicious hit man Sayer for revenge. Coyote flees to England, where amusement park owner Whitelaw involves him in another robbery. Stylish but shallow thriller has a good climax in the amusement park.
Dist.: HBO

SLEEPAWAY CAMP 1983
★★ **R Horror 1:25**
☑ Explicit language, graphic violence
Dir: Robert Hiltzik *Cast:* Mike Kellin, Felissa Rose, Jonathan Tierston, Karen Fields, Christopher Collet
► A young girl witnesses the death of her family in a boating accident near Camp Arawak. Years later teen Rose returns to the camp, which is subsequently plagued by violent murders. Some effective shocks in this low-budget production.
Dist.: Media

SLEEPAWAY CAMP 2: UNHAPPY CAMPERS 1988
★ **R Horror/Comedy 1:20**
☑ Nudity, adult situations, explicit language, graphic violence
Dir: Michael A. Simpson *Cast:* Pamela Springsteen, Brian Patrick Clarke, Renée Estevez, Walter Gotell, Susan Marie Snyder, Heather Binion
► Prim camp counselor Springsteen (sister of Bruce) is actually an inventive psychopathic killer, flushing one victim down the toilet and barbecuing others. Virginal Estevez (sister of Emilio Estevez and Charlie Sheen) tries to stop her. Dark doings evince surprising sense of blackly comic humor.
Dist.: Nelson

SLEEPAWAY CAMP 3: TEENAGE WASTELAND 1989
★ **R Horror/Comedy 1:19**
☑ Nudity, adult situations, explicit language, graphic violence
Dir: Michael A. Simpson *Cast:* Pamela Springsteen, Tracy Griffith, Michael J. Pollard, Mark Oliver, Kim Wall
► Rich and poor kids are joined at an experimental camp built on the site where Springsteen previously rampaged. Guess what? She's back, disguised as a camper and ready to murder at the sight of a promiscuous teen. Continues series' tradition of campy comic carnage. Springsteen is the cutest killer you'd ever care to see.
Dist.: Nelson

SLEEPER 1973
★★★ **PG Comedy 1:28**
☑ Adult situations, explicit language
Dir: Woody Allen *Cast:* Woody Allen, Diane Keaton, John Beck, Mary Gregory, Don Keefer
► Health food store owner Allen wakes up after minor ulcer surgery to discover he's been frozen for 200 years. U.S. is now a dictatorship; reluctant milquetoast Allen is recruited by rebellious underground scientists who defrosted him. To evade capture by police, he pretends to be a robot servant to flaky poet Keaton, eventually drawing her into web of politics and romance. Superb early Allen mixes one-liners with stylish slapstick—don't miss his wrestling match with future's answer to instant pudding. Bouncy jazz and ragtime score performed by Allen and the Preservation Hall Jazz Band.
Dist.: MGM/UA

SLEEPING BEAUTY 1959
★★★★★ **G Animation 1:15**
Dir: Clyde Geronimi *Cast:* Voices of Eleanor Audley, Verna Felton, Barbara Jo Allen, Barbara Luddy, Mary Costa, Bill Shirley
► Animated version of the Charles Perrault

fairy tale, with music from the Tchaikovsky ballet. Evil fairy casts spell on Princess causing eternal sleep. Good fairies must assist Prince's attempt to undo the black magic. Disney spared no expense to make film the pinnacle of animation technology, so movement and detail are remarkable, culminating in Prince's fight with evil dragon. A classic for young and old alike.
Dist.: Buena Vista

SLEEPING DOGS 1977 New Zealand
★ ★ NR Mystery-Suspense 1:47
☑ Nudity, explicit language, violence
Dir: Roger Donaldson *Cast:* Sam Neill, Melissa Donaldson, Bernard Kearns, Ian Mune, Clyde Scott, Warren Oates
▶ In the future, New Zealand has become a police state. Seeking solitude on an off-shore island, Neill is framed by Maori revolutionaries and imprisoned by authorities. Escaping jail, he is pursued by American mercenary Oates. Politicized by encounter with corrupt government, Neill tries to join insurgents, only to learn they are led by wife's lover Mune (also screenplay author). Plenty of action and intrigue in this paranoid thriller.
Dist.: VidAmerica

SLEEPING TIGER, THE 1954 British
★ NR Drama 1:29 B&W
Dir: Victor Hanbury (Joseph Losey) *Cast:* Dirk Bogarde, Alexis Smith, Alexander Knox, Hugh Griffith, Patricia McCarron, Maxine Audley
▶ Bogarde is caught when he attempts to burglarize psychiatrist Knox's home. Instead of turning him over to the police, Knox attempts to rehabilitate Bogarde as a psychological experiment. Complicating his task is his wife Smith, who is attracted to the criminal. Unlikely plot uplifted by cast and director, who used pseudonym due to blacklist.
Dist.: Corinth

SLEEPWALK 1987
☆ NR Mystery-Suspense 1:18
☑ Explicit language
Dir: Sara Driver *Cast:* Suzanne Fletcher, Ann Magnuson, Dexter Lee, Stephen Chen, Tony Todd
▶ Computer programmer Fletcher, who shares apartment with young son Lee and sexy Magnuson, is hired to translate stolen ancient Chinese manuscript. Events that ensue reflect stories in the document: Magnuson goes bald and Lee is kidnapped. Outlandish oddity from Driver, producer of *Stranger Than Paradise*, will alienate all but the most adventurous viewer.
Dist.: Orion

SLEUTH 1972
★ ★ ★ ★ PG Mystery-Suspense 2:18
☑ Adult situations, explicit language, violence
Dir: Joseph L. Mankiewicz *Cast:* Laurence Olivier, Michael Caine, Alec Cawthorne,

Margo Channing, John Matthews, Teddy Martin
▶ Anthony Shaffer's hit play is a dazzling showcase for Olivier and Caine, both Oscar-nominated as ingenious antagonists playing a deadly cat-and-mouse game. Olivier, a detective novelist, tricks Caine (his wife's lover) into committing a crime, but Caine turns the tables on him. Stars are supported by smooth direction and absorbing writing. Red herrings extend to credits as well (including a "performance" by *All About Eve*'s Margo Channing).
Dist.: Media

SLIGHTLY HONORABLE 1940
★ NR Mystery-Suspense 1:23 B&W
Dir: Tay Garnett *Cast:* Pat O'Brien, Edward Arnold, Broderick Crawford, Ruth Terry, Alan Dinehart, Eve Arden
▶ Law partners O'Brien and Crawford profit from government deals, but wind up in trouble when shady politician Arnold frames O'Brien for a series of killings. While fending off the advances of nightclub singer Terry, O'Brien tries to unravel the mystery, never guessing that Crawford knows more than he lets on. Okay mystery has a few laughs.
Dist.: Foothill

SLIGHTLY SCARLET 1955
★ ★ NR Mystery-Suspense 1:30 B&W
Dir: Allan Dwan *Cast:* John Payne, Arlene Dahl, Rhonda Fleming, Kent Taylor, Ted de Corsia, Lance Fuller
▶ Gangster de Corsia enlists henchman Payne to discredit a mayoral candidate. Payne finds dirt on the man's sister Dahl and secretary Fleming, but then risks de Corsia's wrath when he alters the scheme after falling for Fleming. Compelling adaptation of the James M. Cain novel, *Love's Lovely Counterfeit*.
Dist.: Buena Vista

SLIME PEOPLE, THE 1962
★ NR Sci-Fi 1:16 B&W
Dir: Robert Hutton *Cast:* Robert Hutton, Robert Burton, Susan Hart, William Boyce, Les Tremayne
▶ Prehistoric creatures known as slime people menace outer Los Angeles after an atomic test stirs their underground sleep. A scientist, his daughter, an adventurer, and a soldier seek shelter inside a meat locker, a move which undoubtedly saved on the budget but subtracted from the thrills. Shots of monsters in the fog would have had a certain spooky poetry if they had been exposed properly. Mostly pretty silly.
Dist.: Various

SLIPPING INTO DARKNESS 1989
★ R Drama 1:27
☑ Nudity, adult situations, explicit language, violence
Dir: Eleanor Gaver *Cast:* Michelle Johnson,

John DiAquino, Neill Barry, Anastasia Fielding, Cristen Kaufman, Vyto Ruginis
► When retarded Barry is run over by a train while drunk, ex-biker DiAquino suspects local rich girls Johnson, Fielding, and Kaufman gave him the fatal booze. He and his pals kidnap the trio to learn the truth. Honest attempt at wrestling with small town psychosis is heavy sledding due to sketchy screenplay and nasty chararacterizations. Also known as *Born to Lose*.
Dist.: Virgin

SLIPSTREAM 1989
★ ★ ★ PG-13 Sci-Fi 1:32
☑ Adult situations, explicit language, violence
Dir: Steven Lisberger   *Cast:* Mark Hamill, Bob Peck, Bill Paxton, Kitty Aldridge, Ben Kingsley, F. Murray Abraham
► Reunion of *Star Wars* lead Hamill and producer Gary Kurtz features former as a futuristic bounty hunter whose android prisoner Peck is stolen by rival Paxton. Hamill pursues the duo; they flee through a wind tunnel called "Slipstream." Imposing visuals and rousing action overcome thin characterizations and pretentious dialogue.
Dist.: Virgin

SLOANE 1986
★ ★ NR Action-Adventure 1:35
☑ Nudity, adult situations, explicit language, violence
Dir: Daniel Rosenthal   *Cast:* Robert Resnik, Debra Blee, Raul Aragon, Victor Ordonez, Carissa Carlos, Ann Milhench
► Private investigator Resnik is sent to Manila to locate kidnapped Milhench. There he teams with Milhench's sister Blee, his Filipino pal Aragon, and Aragon's pretty sister Carlos. When not bedding down with Carlos, Resnik busies himself with chases, brawls, and shootouts. B-grade actioner with no surprises.
Dist.: Vestron

SLOW BURN 1989
☆ R Action-Adventure 1:34
☑ Rape, explicit language, violence
Dir: George Jay Blood III   *Cast:* Todd Allen, Charles Grant, Jack Starrett, Dedee Pfeiffer, Mitch Pileggi
► While camping, hunting guide Grant and banker brother Allen run afoul of backwoods types who have crucified their friend and kidnapped Pfeiffer. They free her but the lowlifes don't give up easily. Rockies scenery and Pfeiffer are easy to take; sadistic story is not. Also known as *Brothers in Arms*.
Dist.: Republic

SLUGGER'S WIFE, THE 1985
★ ★ ★ PG-13 Comedy 1:44
☑ Adult situations, explicit language
Dir: Hal Ashby   *Cast:* Michael O'Keefe, Rebecca De Mornay, Randy Quaid, Martin Ritt, Cleavant Derricks, Lisa Langlois
► Slumping baseball player O'Keefe goes on

hitting tear when De Mornay, the rock singer he starts dating, attends games. His batting average soars, so they marry. Then her career takes off and she stops watching him play. Both marriage and O'Keefe's hitting skills fall apart. Somewhat sluggish comedy written by Neil Simon. **(CC)**
Dist.: RCA/Columbia

SLUMBER PARTY MASSACRE 1982
★ R Horror 1:18
☑ Nudity, explicit language, graphic violence
Dir: Amy Jones   *Cast:* Michele Michaels, Robin Stille, Michael Villela, Andre Honore, Debra Deliso, Gina Mari
► Killer Villela escapes from jail and employs power drill to methodically kill valley girls during a slumber party. Attempt at tongue-in-cheek spoof misses mark and instead works as average horror with a few gags. Screenplay by feminist novelist Rita Mae Brown provides many opportunities for actresses to disrobe. Popular enough at drive-ins to spawn a sequel.
Dist.: Nelson

SLUMBER PARTY MASSACRE II 1987
☆ R Horror 1:15
☑ Nudity, adult situations, explicit language, graphic violence
Dir: Deborah Brock   *Cast:* Crystal Bernard, Kimberly McArthur, Juliette Cummins, Patrick Lowe, Heidi Kozak, Atanas Ilitch
► On teen getaway weekend, Bernard, young sister of victim from original film, suffers nightmare about marauding rocker Ilitch wielding drill-bit guitar. Ilitch suddenly materializes on premises and starts killing Bernard's pals in gory fashion. Sequel abandons humor for straight B-grade horror.
Dist.: Nelson

SLUMBER PARTY '57 1977
☆ R Comedy 1:29
☑ Nudity, strong sexual content, adult situations, explicit language, adult humor
Dir: William A. Levey   *Cast:* Noelle North, Bridget Hollman, Debra Winger, Mary Ann Appleseth, Rainbeaux Smith, Janet Wood
► Teen girlfriends at a party describe their first sexual encounters. Winger takes on a gang of bikers; another girl is seduced by an older man; a third visits a hayloft with her riding instructor; etc. Flashbacks provide plenty of nudity and raunchy language in this soft-core exploitation. Soundtrack includes Patti Page, Dinah Washington, and Jerry Lee Lewis.
Dist.: Vestron

SMALL CHANGE 1976 French
★ ★ PG Comedy 1:45
☑ Brief nudity, explicit language
Dir: François Truffaut   *Cast:* Geory Desmouceaux, Philippe Goldman, Claudio Deluca, Frank Deluca, Richard Golfier
► Truffaut's loving, lyrical, and often surprisingly funny tribute to the spirit of childhood

and the gift for survival. Film relates a series of vignettes about the lives of a group of children from the French town of Thiers. Not much on plot, but still vintage Truffaut. Original and insightful, with superb acting by the children. [S]
Dist.: Warner

SMALL CIRCLE OF FRIENDS, A 1980
★★★ R Drama 1:52
☑ Adult situations, explicit language, violence
Dir: Rob Cohen ***Cast:*** Karen Allen, Brad Davis, Jameson Parker, Shelley Long, John Friedrich
► In the late 1960s, Harvard journalism major Davis moves in with art student Allne. When they have problems, she leaves for med student Parker. Eventually Allen decides to bed both men at once. Attractive leads give competent performances but seldom rise above the clichéd—and now dated—plot.
Dist.: Key

SMALL TOWN GIRL 1953
★★★ NR Musical 1:30
Dir: Leslie Kardos ***Cast:*** Jane Powell, Farley Granger, Ann Miller, S. Z. Sakall, Bobby Van, Billie Burke, Robert Keith, Fay Wray, Nat King Cole
► Small town judge Keith tosses wealthy womanizer Granger into jail for speeding. His sentence turns out to be life with Keith's daughter Powell, who becomes his true love. Wholesome, bouncy musical. Numbers include Cole singing the Oscar-nominated "My Flaming Heart" and Miller performing "I've Got to Hear That Beat," but the best scene is Van exuberantly jumping his way through town.
Dist.: MGM/UA

SMALL TOWN IN TEXAS, A 1976
★★★★ PG Action-Adventure 1:36
☑ Explicit language, violence
Dir: Jack Starrett ***Cast:*** Timothy Bottoms, Susan George, Bo Hopkins, Art Hindle, John Karlen, Buck Fowler
► Texas ex-con Bottoms returns home for revenge on corrupt sheriff Hopkins, who framed him. He and girlfriend George find evidence that Hopkins is plotting a political assassination, but the knowledge proves deadly as they're involved in a nonstop chase. Highlighted by scores of stunts involving cars, trains, and motorcycles.
Dist.: Vestron

SMARTEST GIRL IN TOWN 1936
☆ NR Comedy 0:58
Dir: Joseph Santley ***Cast:*** Gene Raymond, Ann Sothern, Helen Broderick, Eric Blore, Erik Rhodes, Harry Jans
► Broderick suffers marriage to a penniless good-for-nothing, so she advises sister Sothern to find a rich husband and forget about Raymond. What neither sister realizes is that Raymond is really a millionaire only pretending to be poor so as to be loved for himself. Mix-up is all straightened out by the end of this cheery little romp.
Dist.: Turner

SMASHING THE RACKETS 1937
★ NR Crime 1:05 B&W
Dir: Lew Landers ***Cast:*** Chester Morris, Frances Mercer, Bruce Cabot, Rita Johnson, Donald Douglas, Ben Welden
► Morris, playing a thinly disguised Thomas Dewey, stars as a crusading district attorney who attempts to disinfect a crime-infested city. The underworld unites to stop him but he persists in his battle. Less-than-smashing, although efficient, B-movie. Home video version double billed with 1950's *Hunt the Man Down.*
Dist.: Turner

SMASH PALACE 1982 New Zealand
★ NR Drama 1:47
☑ Nudity, adult situations, explicit language, violence
Dir: Roger Donaldson ***Cast:*** Bruno Lawrence, Anna Jemison, Greer Robson, Keith Aberdein, Les Kelly
► Mechanic Lawrence enjoys quiet life running auto junkyard; his wife Jemison grows bored, has an affair, and leaves him. When she gets a court order to keep him away from their daughter Robson, a frustrated Lawrence kidnaps the child. Good acting and production values, but predictable story and slow pacing make interest wander.
Dist.: Vestron

SMASH-UP, THE STORY OF A WOMAN 1947
★★★ NR Drama 1:43 B&W
Dir: Stuart Heisler ***Cast:*** Susan Hayward, Lee Bowman, Marsha Hunt, Eddie Albert, Carl Esmond, Carleton Young
► Nightclub chanteuse Hayward helps boost husband Bowman to radio stardom, then takes a back seat as wife and mother. During Bowman's long absences, Hayward becomes a lonely, jealous drunk, and begins behaving irrationally. Hayward was nominated for an Oscar for her work in this emotion-wringing tale of a woman brought low by her generous impulses. Scripted by John Lawson from a story by Dorothy Parker and Frank Cavett; also known as *A Woman Destroyed.*
Dist.: Turner

SMILE 1975
★ PG Comedy 1:53
☑ Adult situations, explicit language
Dir: Michael Ritchie ***Cast:*** Bruce Dern, Barbara Feldon, Michael Kidd, Geoffrey Lewis, Annette O'Toole, Melanie Griffith
► Amusing look at beauty contests takes place during the final days of an intense pageant in Santa Rosa, California. Plot switches dizzyingly among contestants, judges, organizers, and bystanders in a series of sight gags that satirize middle-class America with often uncomfortable accuracy. Dern, the head judge and a mobile home salesman, and

Kidd, a burnt-out choreographer, stand out in the good cast. Later adapted into a Broadway musical.
Dist.: MGM/UA

SMILES OF A SUMMER NIGHT 1957 Swedish
★ ★ NR Comedy 1:48 B&W
Dir: Ingmar Bergman *Cast:* Ulla Jacobsson, Eva Dahlbeck, Margit Carlquist, Harriet Andersson, Gunnar Bjornstrand, Jarl Kulle
▶ In turn-of-the-century Sweden, a lawyer, his virginal bride, his son, and his old flame gather for a country weekend in which lovers break up and unite in new pairs. Bergman's most enchanting film is wise, amusing, and beautifully mounted without avoiding his usual serious concerns. The basis for the Broadway musical, "A Little Night Music." Ⓢ
Dist.: Nelson

SMILIN' THROUGH 1941
★ NR Musical 1:40 B&W
Dir: Frank Borzage *Cast:* Jeanette MacDonald, Gene Raymond, Brian Aherne, Ian Hunter, Francis Robinson, Patrick O'Moore
▶ Crusty old Aherne won't let niece MacDonald see beau Raymond, alluding to a long ago incident when Raymond's father accidentally killed Aherne's wife in a fit of jealousy. Listless musical remake of the 1932 classic boasts then husband-and-wife team of MacDonald and Raymond. Songs include "Drink to Me Only With Thine Eyes" and Georges Bizet's "Ouvre Ton Coeur."
Dist.: MGM/UA

SMITHEREENS 1982
★ R Drama 1:30
☑ Adult situations, explicit language
Dir: Susan Seidelman *Cast:* Susan Berman, Brad Rinn, Richard Hell, Nada Despotovich
▶ Oddly realistic punk/teen flick marks the directorial debut of Seidelman. Very low-budget tale of Jersey woman Berman who has little talent but lots of spunk, struggling to make it in the rock world while working in a copy shop. She loves surly rocker Hell who treats her badly; she abuses the decent Montana boy Rinn who wants to marry her. Credible performances and colorful junkheap locations shot in New York City. Independent film will not appeal to all.
Dist.: Media

SMOKEY AND THE BANDIT 1977
★ ★ ★ ★ ★ PG Action-Adventure/Comedy 1:36
☑ Explicit language
Dir: Hal Needham *Cast:* Burt Reynolds, Sally Field, Jackie Gleason, Paul Williams, Jerry Reed, Pat McCormick
▶ Truckers Reynolds and Reed transport bootleg beer across state lines, pursued by redneck sheriff Gleason. Along the way, Reynolds romances hitchhiking bride-to-be Field. Fast-moving fun, with thrilling car chases and stunts, relaxed electricity generated by Reynolds and Field (a real-life couple at the time),

broadly amusing support from Reed and Gleason.
Dist.: MCA

SMOKEY AND THE BANDIT II 1980
★ ★ ★ ★ PG Action-Adventure/Comedy 1:41
☑ Explicit language, adult humor
Dir: Hal Needham *Cast:* Burt Reynolds, Sally Field, Jerry Reed, Jackie Gleason, Dom DeLuise, Paul Williams
▶ The cargo this time for truckers Reynolds and Reed is a pregnant elephant to be delivered to the Republican convention. Reynolds also attempts to win Field back from the sheriff's son and Gleason gives chase in three roles (the sheriff, a patrolman, and a mountie). Knockabout sequel with wild and wooley stunts and racy humor; DeLuise steals the show as a gynecologist who treats the elephant.
Dist.: MCA

SMOKEY AND THE BANDIT—PART 3 1983
★ ★ PG Action-Adventure/Comedy 1:25
☑ Nudity, explicit language, adult humor
Dir: Dick Lowry *Cast:* Jackie Gleason, Jerry Reed, Paul Williams, Pat McCormick, Colleen Camp, Mike Henry
▶ The wealthy Enoses (Williams, McCormick) bet retiring sheriff Buford T. Justice (Gleason) that he can't make a Miami-Austin trip in twenty-four hours and hire Reed to make Gleason's task difficult. Smutty sex jokes abound as third entry fails to compare to its predecessors. Burt Reynolds makes a cameo; the film misses his starring presence.
Dist.: MCA

SMOKEY BITES THE DUST 1981
★ ★ PG Action-Adventure/Comedy 1:29
☑ Brief nudity, adult situations, explicit language, mild violence, adult humor
Dir: Charles B. Griffith *Cast:* Jimmy McNichol, Janet Julian, Walter Barnes, Patrick Campbell, Kari Lizer, William Forsythe
▶ High school hotshot McNichol kidnaps homecoming queen Julian; her sheriff father Barnes leads the pursuit. Literally one long chase with little in the way of character development or plot. No relation to the *Smokey and the Bandit* series.
Dist.: Nelson

SMOOTH TALK 1985
★ PG-13 Drama 1:32
☑ Adult situations, explicit language
Dir: Joyce Chopra *Cast:* Treat Williams, Laura Dern, Mary Kay Place, Levon Helm, Sara Inglis, Margaret Welch
▶ Provocative drama about suburban California teen Dern's initiation into adulthood opens with a realistic look at problems with parents Place and Helm, then veers into an unnerving encounter with edgy drifter Williams. Adaptation of the short story "Where Are You Going? Where Have You Been?" by

Joyce Carol Oates features knowing performances by Dern and Williams.
Dist.: Vestron

SNAKE EATER 1989
☆ R Action-Adventure 1:35
☑ Nudity, adult situations, explicit lan-
guage, violence
Dir: George Erschbamer *Cast:* Lorenzo
Lamas, Josie Bell, Robert Scott, Ronnie
Hawkins, Cheryl Jeans, Larry Csonka
▶ When his parents are killed and his sister
kidnapped during their houseboat vacation,
tough cop Lamas, formerly a member of the
Marine squad known as "Snake Eaters," sets
out to even the score. Low-rent *Rambo* knock-
off provides routine action and abysmal act-
ing.
Dist.: Media

SNAKE PEOPLE 1968 U.S./Mexican
☆ NR Horror 1:30
Dir: Jhon Ibanez *Cast:* Boris Karloff, Julissa,
Charles East, Ralph Bertrand, Tongolele,
Quintin Bulnes
▶ On the South Pacific island of Korbai, plan-
tation owner Karloff warns French officer Ber-
trand about the native voodoo/zombie cult.
Karloff's temperence-worker niece Julissa
then becomes a target of the cultists. One of
Karloff's last films is a cheaply made, sad affair
in which star is mostly off-screen. Draggy pac-
ing, chintzy music, and bad dubbing add up
to no scares. Also known as *Isle of the Snake
People.*
Dist.: Various

SNOOPY COME HOME 1972
★ ★ ★ ★ ★ G Animation 1:21
Dir: Bill Melendez *Cast:* Voices of Chad
Webber, Robin Kohn, Stephen Shea, David
Carey, Johanna Baer
▶ Second feature based on Charles Schulz's
comic-strip characters is a delightful family
film concentrating on the headstrong Snoopy.
Pooch learns he was originally owned by Lila,
and leaves home with Woodstock to visit her
in the hospital. Charlie Brown and his friends
search frantically for him. Good animation
and songs by Richard and Robert Sherman
add to the fun. Sequel to *A Boy Named
Charlie Brown.* (CC)
Dist.: CBS/Fox

SNOWBALL EXPRESS, THE 1972
★ ★ ★ ★ G Comedy/Family 2:00
Dir: Norman Tokar *Cast:* Dean Jones,
Nancy Olson, Harry Morgan, Keenan Wynn,
Johnnie Whitaker
▶ New York accountant Jones inherits a ski
resort in the Colorado Rockies. Expecting a
glamorous chalet, he heads west with his
family to discover a wreck on the verge of ruin.
Despite hard work, they encounter disaster
after disaster, culminating in an extended
chase on snowmobiles. Typical Disney slap-
stick delivered with polish and flair.
Dist.: Buena Vista

SNOWS OF KILIMANJARO, THE 1952
★ ★ ★ NR Drama 1:57
Dir: Henry King *Cast:* Gregory Peck, Susan
Hayward, Ava Gardner, Hildegarde Neff,
Leo G. Carroll, Torin Thatcher
▶ Successful author Peck, stricken with fever on
an African safari, reviews his past loves with
dark beauty Gardner, European countess
Neff, and American heiress Hayward. In his de-
lirium he doubts his accomplishments until
Hayward courageously defends him. Loosely
adapted from a series of Ernest Hemingway
stories, although more closely based on the
author's own life.
Dist.: Various

SNOW WHITE AND THE SEVEN DWARFS
1937
★ ★ ★ ★ ★ G Animation 1:23
Dir: David Hand *Cast:* Voices of Adriana
Caselotti, Harry Stockwell, Lucille Laverne,
Moroni Olsen, Billy Gilbert
▶ Once upon a time an evil queen, jealous of
fair Snow White, ordered her huntsman to slay
the girl. Instead, he hid her deep in the forest
where she moved in with seven eccentric but
adorable dwarfs. Enduring classic, a landmark
in animation, still delights young and old, although the smallest children may be frightened by some scary moments. Songs include
perennial favorites "Whistle While You Work"
and "Heigh-Ho." Received a special Oscar for
"significant screen innovation."
Dist.: Buena Vista

SNOW WHITE AND THE THREE STOOGES
1961
★ ★ NR Family 1:47
Dir: Walter Lang *Cast:* Moe Howard, Larry
Fine, "Curly" Joe DeRita, Carol Heiss, Patricia Medina, Edson Stroll
▶ Real-life 1960 Olympic figure-skating star
Heiss flees evil stepmother Medina and hides
out with Howard, Fine, and DeRita in the forest. When Heiss falls into an enchanted sleep,
handsome prince Stroll meanders in to wake
her. Heiss skates in this colorful production, but
nonviolent Stooges are not funny, and everyone else is lifeless. (CC)
Dist.: CBS/Fox

S.O.B. 1981
★ ★ R Comedy 2:01
☑ Brief nudity, adult situations, explicit lan-
guage, violence
Dir: Blake Edwards *Cast:* Julie Andrews,
William Holden, William Mulligan, Robert
Preston, Robert Vaughn, Larry Hagman,
Loretta Swit, Larry Hagman, Marisa Beren-
son, Shelley Winters, Rosanna Arquette,
Robert Loggia
▶ Crazed Hollywood producer Mulligan has a
nervous breakdown after his big-budget musi-
cal starring wife Andrews flops at the box of-
fice. He becomes obsessed with recutting the
film, adding his wife's nudity, to garner an X
rating. Among the vipers in his life: director-in-

residence Holden, boozy "Dr. Feelgood" Preston, pushy gossip-monger Swit, and ruthless studio head Vaughn. Wickedly right-on performances from stellar cast in this offbeat take on Hollywood hustlers.
Dist.: CBS/Fox

SO DEAR TO MY HEART 1949
★★★★ NR Family 1:22
Dir: Harold Schuster, Hamilton Luske ***Cast:*** Burl Ives, Beulah Bondi, Bobby Driscoll, Harry Carey, Luana Patten, Raymond Bond
▶ Indiana farmboy Driscoll dreams of winning blue ribbon for his black sheep at the county fair, but must find a way to earn the entry fee first. Superb Disney blend of nostalgia, adventure, charming animated sequences, and lively songs will delight children and parents alike.
Dist.: Buena Vista

SODOM AND GOMORRAH 1963 U.S./Italian
★★★ NR Drama 2:28
Dir: Robert Aldrich ***Cast:*** Stewart Granger, Pier Angeli, Stanley Baker, Rossana Podesta, Anouk Aimee, Claudia Mori
▶ Lot (Granger) and the Jews visit those sin-filled cities of Sodom and Gomorrah, which are ruled by sexy queen Aimee. Resisting temptation, and heeding God's advice, Lot leads his people away from the soon-to-be-destroyed burgs. Angeli plays Lot's wife in this lusty, large-scaled epic. **(CC)**
Dist.: CBS/Fox

SO FINE 1981
★★ R Comedy 1:29
☑ Adult situations, explicit language
Dir: Andrew Bergman ***Cast:*** Ryan O'Neal, Jack Warden, Mariangela Melato, Richard Kiel, Fred Gwynne
▶ Fussy English professor O'Neal is kidnapped by the Mafia to help father Warden revive the family garment business—and pay back a major mob loan. Caught romancing gangster Kiel's wife Melato, Ryan escapes in her jeans, which split to reveal his backside and instantly create a new fashion sensation. Somewhat shapeless but altogether harmless little comedy with a fine O'Neal. Directorial debut for Bergman, author of the much funnier film, *The In-Laws.*
Dist.: Warner

SOFT SKIN, THE 1964 French
☆ NR Drama 1:58 B&W
Dir: François Truffaut ***Cast:*** Jean Desailly, Françoise Dorléac, Nelly Benedetti, Daniel Ceccaldi, Laurence Badie, Jean Lanier
▶ Famous writer Desailly gets involved with stewardess Dorléac while his relationship with wife Benedetti deteriorates. Eventually, Benedetti learns of the infidelity, leading to a stunning conclusion. Truffaut's gracefully understated direction and subtle performances add nuance to the slim, mechanical story. [S]
Dist.: Key

SOLARBABIES 1986
★★ PG-13 Sci-Fi 1:34
☑ Violence
Dir: Alan Johnson ***Cast:*** Richard Jordan, Jami Gertz, Jason Patric, Lukas Haas, Sarah Douglas, Charles Durning
▶ Orphans in a futuristic wasteland devoid of water find the Bodhi, a magical sphere that leads them out of their harsh prison. Pursued by Jordan, the chief of the state police, they search for an answer to the planet's crisis. When evil scientist Douglas steals the Bodhi, the children must attack her stronghold. Elaborate fantasy from producer Mel Brooks is dry and stale. **(CC)**
Dist.: MGM/UA

SOLDIER, THE 1982
★★★ R Action-Adventure 1:30
☑ Explicit language, graphic violence
Dir: James Glickenhaus ***Cast:*** Ken Wahl, Klaus Kinski, William Prince, Alberta Watson, Jeremiah Sullivan
▶ Russian terrorists steal enough plutonium to destroy Saudi Arabia's oil fields, then order Israel to pull back from the West Front. America's only resort is the Soldier (Wahl), a secret agent who battles his way around the world for a solution to the Russian plot. Top-notch stunts (including a breathtaking ski chase) and rapid pace compensate for confusing plot and thin characters. **(CC)**
Dist.: Nelson

SOLDIER BLUE 1974
★★★★ PG Western 1:49
☑ Nudity, adult situations, explicit language, graphic violence
Dir: Ralph Nelson ***Cast:*** Candice Bergen, Peter Strauss, Donald Pleasence, Bob Carraway, Jorge Rivero, Dana Elcar
▶ Bergen, a white woman kidnapped by the Cheyennes, and cavalry private Strauss are the only survivors of a brutal massacre by the U.S. Army. They encounter further horrifying violence as they struggle to the safety of an Army outpost. Attempt to describe the plight of the Indians in terms of a Vietnam allegory has dated this Western badly.
Dist.: Nelson

SOLDIER IN THE RAIN 1963
★★★ NR Drama 1:28 B&W
Dir: Ralph Nelson ***Cast:*** Jackie Gleason, Steve McQueen, Tuesday Weld, Tony Bill, Tom Poston, Lew Gallo, Adam West
▶ Supply officer McQueen and career sergeant Gleason share an uneasy relationship on a Southern Army base, especially after McQueen introduces him to a beautiful young Weld. Uneven mixture of slapstick comedy and maudlin sentimentality features an accomplished performance by Gleason and an amusing role by West as a captain. Based on a William Goldman novel. **(CC)**
Dist.: CBS/Fox

SOLDIER OF FORTUNE 1955
★★★ NR Action-Adventure 1:36
Dir: Edward Dmytryk ***Cast:*** Clark Gable, Susan Hayward, Michael Rennie, Gene Barry, Tom Tully, Alex D'Arcy
► American housewife Hayward searches Hong Kong for kidnapped husband Barry; hard-bitten smuggler Gable learns he's held captive in Communist China, and organizes rescue mission with local chief of police Rennie. Improbable but smoothly entertaining drama benefits from beautiful Hong Kong locations. Adapted by Ernest K. Gann from his novel.
Dist.: CBS/Fox

SOLDIER OF ORANGE 1979 Dutch
★★★ R Drama 2:45
☑ Nudity, violence
Dir: Paul Verhoeven ***Cast:*** Rutger Hauer, Jeroen Krabbe, Peter Faber, Edward Fox, Susan Penhaligon
► In World War II Holland, a group of college pals band together to battle German invaders. One Jewish member is captured and tortured while another must join the Germans to save his fiancée; a third pursues a traitor. Epic story rouses utmost sympathy for the heroes and antipathy for the Nazi villains. Solid performances and careful period re-creation, although story is a bit disjointed. [S]
Dist.: Media

SOLDIER'S STORY, A 1984
★★★★ PG Mystery/Suspense 1:41
☑ Explicit language, violence
Dir: Norman Jewison ***Cast:*** Howard E. Rollins, Jr., Adolph Caesar, Dennis Lipscomb, Art Evans, Denzel Washington, Larry Riley, Robert Townsend, Patti LaBelle
► In 1944, Rollins, a black military attorney from Washington, arrives at segregated Fort Neal, Louisianna, to investigate the murder of Caesar, master sergeant to an all-black unit. Series of flashbacks reveals a number of suspects with plenty of motive to kill the hard-nosed sarge. Arresting performances and tightly woven psychological plot adapted from Charles Fuller's Pulitzer prize–winning drama, *A Soldier's Play*. **(CC)**
Dist.: MGM/UA

SOLDIER'S TALE, A 1988 New Zealand
★★ R Romance 1:37
☑ Adult situations, explicit language, violence
Dir: Larry Parr ***Cast:*** Gabriel Byrne, Marianne Basler, Paul Wyett, Judge Reinhold
► At the end of World War II, British soldier Byrne meets French farm girl Basler, who has run afoul of the Resistance because of her previous involvement with a German soldier. They fall in love and Byrne tries to keep her safe. Reinhold has a small role as Byrne's American rival for Basler.
Dist.: MGM/UA

SOLE SURVIVOR 1984
★ R Horror 1:30
☑ Brief nudity, adult situations, explicit language
Dir: Thom Eberhardt ***Cast:*** Anita Skinner, Kurt Johnson, Caren Larkey
► Advertising producer Skinner, the only survivor of an airplane wreck, recuperates and has romance with doctor Johnson. She returns to work and is menaced by murderous incarnations of corpses from the crash. Gets off to an interesting start but plot bogs down in loose ends and red herrings.
Dist.: Vestron

SOLO 1978 Australian/New Zealand
☆ NR Drama 1:37
☑ Nudity, adult situations
Dir: Tony Williams ***Cast:*** Vincent Gil, Lisa Peers, Martyn Sanderson, Jock Spence, Perry Armstrong, Davina Whitehouse
► Hitchhiker Peers is picked up by widowed pilot Gil. They become romantically involved, but it takes a solo flight and plane crash by Gil's young son for the taciturn flyer to open up emotionally. Stylish filmmaking and professional performances. However, meandering plot and pointless romance leave you wanting more.
Dist.: Vestron

SOLOMON AND SHEBA 1959
★★ NR Drama 2:19
Dir: King Vidor ***Cast:*** Yul Brynner, Gina Lollobrigida, George Sanders, David Farrar, Marisa Pavan, Alejandro Rey
► Lavish biblical epic about the famed Israeli king Solomon (Brynner) and his fateful affair with the beautiful Queen of Sheba (Lollobrigida) includes most of the familiar Solomon stories: building the Great Temple, settling a dispute over an infant, challenging the Egyptians and his power-hungry brother Sanders. Sheer spectacle helps overcome historical inaccuracies. Original star Tyrone Power died during filming and can be glimpsed in some shots.
Dist.: Key

SOMEBODY UP THERE LIKES ME 1956
★★★★ NR Biography/Sports 1:53 B&W
Dir: Robert Wise ***Cast:*** Paul Newman, Pier Angeli, Sal Mineo, Eileen Heckart, Everett Sloane, Harold J. Stone
► True story of boxer Rocky Graziano (Newman) who goes through poverty, prison, and troubled army stint. With the support of his devoted wife Angeli, he rises to the middleweight championship. Inspiring and hard-hitting, both in and out of the ring (with the big fight climax especially exciting). Newman is terrific as the tough but vulnerable Graziano. Oscars for Cinematography and Art Direction. **(CC)**
Dist.: MGM/UA

SOME CAME RUNNING 1958
★★★★ NR Drama 2:16

Dir: Vincente Minnelli *Cast:* Frank Sinatra, Shirley MacLaine, Dean Martin, Martha Hyer, Arthur Kennedy, Nancy Gates
► Failed writer Sinatra returns to his home town after World War II with loose and goofy MacLaine in tow. While romancing the local women and hanging out with gambler Martin, Sinatra fails to amuse his older brother Kennedy, who is hiding his own peccadilloes. MacLaine and Martin shine in this brilliant dissection of postwar malaise. Adapted well from James Jones's sprawling novel.
Dist.: MGM/UA

SOME GIRLS 1988
★ ★ R Romance/Comedy 1:34
☑ Nudity, adult situations, explicit language
Dir: Michael Hoffman *Cast:* Patrick Dempsey, Jennifer Connelly, Andre Gregory, Sheila Kelly, Florinda Bolkan, Lila Kedrova
► American college student Dempsey visits girlfriend Connelly in Quebec City for Christmas. When she dumps him, he turns his romantic attentions to her two sisters. Scenic vehicle for the appealing Dempsey, nicely supported by fetching Connelly and Gregory as her offbeat father.
Dist.: MGM/UA

SOME KIND OF HERO 1982
★ ★ R Comedy 1:37
☑ Adult situations, explicit language, violence
Dir: Michael Pressman *Cast:* Richard Pryor, Margot Kidder, Ray Sharkey, Ronny Cox
► After six years in a POW camp, Vietnam veteran Pryor returns home a national hero, only to discover his wife's in love with another man, his bookstore is bankrupt, and his mother is in a $1200-a-month nursing home. He meets sympathetic hooker Kidder and turns to a life of crime. Mediocre movie (adapted from James Kirkwood's novel) is redeemed by the ever-entertaining, multitalented Pryor.
Dist.: Paramount

SOME KIND OF WONDERFUL 1987
★ ★ ★ ★ PG-13 Comedy/Drama 1:33
☑ Adult situations, explicit language
Dir: Howard Deutsch *Cast:* Eric Stoltz, Mary Stuart Masterson, Lea Thompson, Craig Sheffer, John Ashton, Elias Koteas
► Stoltz, a sensitive high schooler from wrong side of tracks, pursues gorgeous Thompson, the girlfriend of wealthy brat Sheffer. Tomboyish best pal Masterson helps Stoltz even though she secretly loves him. Warm, funny, and affecting as producer-writer John Hughes expertly explores the universal dilemmas of teens. Masterson's performance is truly some kind of wonderful. **(CC)**
Dist.: Paramount

SOME LIKE IT HOT 1959
★ ★ ★ ★ NR Comedy 2:00 B&W
Dir: Billy Wilder *Cast:* Marilyn Monroe, Tony Curtis, Jack Lemmon, Joe E. Brown, Pat O'Brien, George Raft

► Musicians Curtis and Lemmon are wanted men when they witness a gangland rubout in 1920s Chicago, so they don drag and join an all-girl band bound for Florida. Complications arise when Curtis falls for ukelele player Monroe and millionaire Brown pursues Lemmon. Hilarious classic, one of the funniest films ever, is as fresh today as when it was made. Lemmon and Curtis are incredible in drag and Monroe has never been more disarming. Best scenes: Lemmon's burst of happiness after Brown proposes to him, Curtis's Cary Grant impression.
Dist.: MGM/UA

SOMEONE BEHIND THE DOOR 1971 French
★ PG Drama 1:37
☑ Adult situations, violence
Dir: Nicholas Gessner *Cast:* Charles Bronson, Anthony Perkins, Jill Ireland, Henri Garcin, Adriano Magestretti
► Found wandering on a beach, amnesia victim Bronson is brought to neuropsychologist Perkins, who realizes that Bronson has just killed a woman. Perkins manipulates Bronson to take murderous revenge on unfaithful wife Ireland. Banal script doesn't really explore the characters.
Dist.: Unicorn

SOMEONE TO LOVE 1987
★ NR Romance 1:49
☑ Adult situations, explicit language
Dir: Henry Jaglom *Cast:* Orson Welles, Henry Jaglom, Andrea Marcovicci, Michael Emil, Sally Kellerman, Oja Kodar, Stephen Bishop, Kathryn Harold
► Autobiographical mock-documentary stars Jaglom as filmmaker fighting with girlfriend Marcovicci and throwing a singles-only Valentine's Day party where he questions guests about love. Self-lacerating humor saves this from preciousness. Highlight is last section, in which Welles pontificates delightfully. **(CC)**
Dist.: Paramount

SOMEONE TO WATCH OVER ME 1987
★ ★ ★ ★ R Mystery-Suspense 1:46
☑ Adult situations, explicit language, violence
Dir: Ridley Scott *Cast:* Tom Berenger, Mimi Rogers, Jerry Orbach, Lorraine Bracco, John Rubinstein, Andreas Katsulas
► When society beauty Rogers witnesses a mob killing, happily married, working-class cop Berenger is assigned to protect her. As two fall in love, much to dismay of Berenger's wife Bracco and boss Orbach, hit man Katsulas stalks Rogers. Unable to get near enough to Rogers to kill her, Katsulas abducts Bracco and her kids. Glossy suspense from master image-maker Scott looks terrific, with fine performances from romantic leads and supporting cast.
Dist.: RCA/Columbia

SOMETHING FOR EVERYONE 1970
★ ★ R Comedy 1:50

☑ Adult situations
Dir: Harold Prince   *Cast:* Angela Lansbury, Michael York, Anthony Corlan, Heidelinde Weis, Eva-Maria Meineke, Jane Carr
▶ Down-on-her-luck European countess Lansbury hires stranger York as footman. York proceeds to have an affair with Lansbury's son Corlan while also wedding a wealthy young girl, an arrangement that helps restore Lansbury's fortune. Picturesque production, stylishly directed and well-played. However, weird story and perverse characterizations will leave audiences shaking their heads.
Dist.: CBS/Fox

SOMETHING OF VALUE 1957
★ ★ ★ ★ NR Drama 1:53 B&W
Dir: Richard Brooks   *Cast:* Rock Hudson, Sidney Poitier, Dana Wynter, Wendy Hiller, Frederick O'Neal
▶ Hudson and Poitier, childhood pals, work together on Hudson's father's plantation in Kenya. When Poitier is driven away by an act of racial discrimination and joins the radical Mau Mau terrorists, Hudson finds himself at odds with his friend. Exciting story steadily increases tension after slow start. Based on the novel by Robert C. Ruark.
Dist.: MGM/UA

SOMETHING SHORT OF PARADISE 1979
★ ★ ★ PG Romance/Comedy 1:27
☑ Brief nudity, adult situations, explicit language
Dir: David Helpern, Jr.   *Cast:* Susan Sarandon, David Steinberg, Jean-Pierre Aumont, Marilyn Sokol, Joe Grifasi, David Rasche
▶ Magazine writer Sarandon and movie publicist Steinberg become lovers. However, their inability to make a commitment and a misunderstanding involving French actor Aumont jeopardize the relationship. Lightweight fare has thin story but appealing central couple.
Dist.: Vestron

SOMETHING SPECIAL 1986
★ ★ PG-13 Comedy 1:26
☑ Adult situations, explicit language
Dir: Paul Schneider   *Cast:* Pamela Segall, Eric Gurry, Patty Duke, John Glover, Seth Green, Mary Tanner
▶ Teenage girl Milly (Segall) wishes she could be a boy and wakes up to find wishes do come true. "Willy" must then learn how to fight, talk dirty, and other important skills in a man's world. Farfetched comedy covers familiar territory; pleasant cast does evoke a few smiles.
Dist.: Magnum

SOMETHING TO SING ABOUT 1937
★ NR Musical 1:33 B&W
Dir: Victor Schertzinger   *Cast:* James Cagney, Evelyn Daw, William Frawley, Mona Barrie, Gene Lockhart, Richard Tucker
▶ Thinking his Hollywood career has gone bust, band leader Cagney goes back to New York and marries long-time love Daws. When

he comes home from the honeymoon, however, he's offered a big studio contract with a catch—he's got to pretend to be single. Singing, dancing satire of the studio system lets an exuberant Cagney strap on his taps and hoof a bit. Rest of production, including songs, is less memorable.
Dist.: Video Yesteryear

SOMETHING WICKED THIS WAY COMES 1983
★ ★ PG Sci-Fi 1:34
☑ Adult situations, explicit language
Dir: Jack Clayton   *Cast:* Jason Robards, Jonathan Pryce, Diane Ladd, Pam Grier, Vidal Peterson, Shawn Carson
▶ In turn-of-the-century Illinois, teen Peterson has uneasy relationship with elderly dad Robards. When Pryce brings a mysterious carnival to town, Peterson and his pal Carson turn to Robards for help after they uncover dark secrets. Well-wrought drama has eerie atmosphere and refreshing human scale despite a few awkward moments. Most chilling scene: Pryce tearing out pages in fiery bursts from a book representing different stages of Robards's life. Adapted by Ray Bradbury from his novel.
Dist.: Buena Vista

SOMETHING WILD 1986
★ ★ R Comedy/Drama 1:53
☑ Nudity, adult situations, explicit language, violence
Dir: Jonathan Demme   *Cast:* Jeff Daniels, Melanie Griffith, Ray Liotta, Margaret Colin, Dana Preu
▶ Conservative New York accountant Daniels falls in with unpredictable flirt Griffith, who drives him to her Pennsylvania high school reunion. Offbeat comedy takes an unexpected twist to drama when Griffith introduces Daniels to husband Liotta, a frenzied ex-con. Compelling, beautifully nuanced story ultimately seems too disjointed, but contains many fine vignettes and a knockout soundtrack. Great supporting cast and amusing cameos by directors John Sayles and John Waters.
Dist.: HBO

SOMETIMES A GREAT NOTION 1971
★ ★ ★ PG Drama 1:55
☑ Adult situations, explicit language, violence
Dir: Paul Newman   *Cast:* Paul Newman, Henry Fonda, Lee Remick, Michael Sarrazin, Richard Jaeckel, Linda Lawson
▶ Oregon lumbering family is pressured by neighbors to join a strike; crusty patriarch Fonda and his son Newman decide to honor their contract despite escalating violence. Sincere adaptation of Ken Kesey's sprawling novel is noteworthy for Jaeckel's Oscar-nominated performance as Newman's brother. Charlie Pride's rendition of "All His Children"

also received an Oscar nomination. Also known as *Never Give an Inch.*
Dist.: MCA

SOMEWHERE IN TIME 1980
★ ★ ★ ★ **PG Fantasy/Romance 1:43**
☑ Adult situations, explicit language
Dir: Jeannot Szwarc *Cast:* Christopher Reeve, Jane Seymour, Christopher Plummer, Teresa Wright, Bill Erwin, George Voskovec
▶ Playwright Reeve sees picture of 1912 actress Seymour and falls in love. Through self-hypnosis, he travels back in time to be with her, but Seymour's jealous manager Plummer tries to sabotage their romance. Entrancing love story with a basic sincerity that touches the heart. Melodic John Barry score, gorgeous cinematography, Oscar-nominated costumes, and beautiful Mackinac Island, Michigan, locations; adapted by Richard Matheson from his novel, *Bid Time Return.*
Dist.: MCA

SOMEWHERE, TOMORROW 1984
★ ★ ★ ★ **PG Fantasy 1:31**
☑ Explicit language
Dir: Robert Wiemer *Cast:* Sarah Jessica Parker, Nancy Addison, Tom Shea, Rick Weber, Paul Bates, John Evans
▶ Young Parker will lose her beloved horse farm if her mother remarries, and hopes teenaged Shea will help by boarding his horse in her stables. When she discovers Shea is actually a ghost, she enlists him in a different scheme with unexpected results. Overlooked comic fantasy is an understated, charming examination of adolescent love.
Dist.: Media

SONG OF BERNADETTE, THE 1943
★ ★ ★ ★ ★ **NR Biography 2:40 B&W**
Dir: Henry King *Cast:* Jennifer Jones, Charles Bickford, Vincent Price, Lee J. Cobb, William Eythe, Gladys Cooper
▶ Nineteenth-century French peasant girl Bernadette Soubirous (Jones) sees a vision of Virgin Mary. Despite skepticism of many, Bernadette persists in her story; soon religious pilgrims flock to her home in Lourdes, seeking the healing waters of a spring miraculously appearing at site of apparition. On advice of a priest, she backs out of marriage and joins nunnery where jealous nun Cooper and cold-hearted official Price punish her for perceived blasphemy. Long but well-crafted inspirational film won four Oscars, including Best Actress for Jones.
Dist.: CBS/Fox

SONG OF FREEDOM 1936 British
★ **NR Drama 1:20 B&W**
Dir: J. Elder Wills *Cast:* Paul Robeson, Elizabeth Welch, George Mozart, Esme Percy, Arthur Williams, Robert Adams
▶ Once a British stevedore, now a respected concert singer, Robeson possesses a medallion that he thinks holds the clue to his true ancestry in Africa. Traveling to the Dark Continent, he discovers that he is heir to an island throne. Determined to be an enlightened monarch, he devotes himself to eradicating superstition and battling the witch doctors. Singing and acting, Robeson is electrifying, as always. But the rest of the movie is forgettable.
Dist.: Cable

SONG OF NORWAY 1970
★ **G Biography/Music 2:22**
Dir: Andrew L. Stone *Cast:* Toralv Maurstad, Florence Henderson, Christina Schollin, Frank Porretta, Robert Morley, Edward G. Robinson
▶ Bloated, inaccurate biography of Norwegian classical composer Edvard Grieg (Maurstad) unwisely adds English lyrics to his music and suggests a romantic rivalry between his patron Therese Berg (Schollin) and his first cousin (Henderson, who also sings). Even the beautiful scenery (filmed in Super Panavision) will lose its impact on TV.
Dist.: CBS/Fox

SONG OF THE ISLANDS 1942
★ **NR Musical 1:15**
Dir: Walter Lang *Cast:* Betty Grable, Victor Mature, Jack Oakie, Thomas Mitchell, George Barbier, Billy Gilbert
▶ Youngsters Grable and Mature fall in love despite objections from fathers Mitchell and Barbier. The oldsters are feuding over a stretch of Hawaiian beach and try everything to keep the young lovers apart. Tropical garb allows Grable to show plenty of leg in this sunny, dance-filled musical. Tunes include "Sing Me a Song of the Islands" and "What's Buzzin' Cousin." **(CC)**
Dist.: Key

SONG OF THE SOUTH 1946
★ ★ ★ ★ **G Musical/Family 1:34**
Dir: Harve Foster, Wilfred Jackson *Cast:* James Baskett, Bobby Driscoll, Ruth Warrick, Hattie McDaniel, Luana Patten, Lucile Watson
▶ Driscoll goes to live on grandmother's plantation during the Civil War. Elderly black slave Uncle Remus (Baskett) befriends the lad and entertains him with stories of Brer Rabbit. Vibrant, tender tale of brotherhood from Disney will appeal to young and old alike. Lively mixture of animation (used to illustrate Uncle Remus's stories) and live action. Oscars for Best Song ("Zip-a-dee Doo-Dah") and Baskett (honorary).
Dist.: Buena Vista

SONG OF THE THIN MAN 1947
★ ★ **NR Mystery-Suspense 1:26 B&W**
Dir: Edward Buzzell *Cast:* William Powell, Myrna Loy, Keenan Wynn, Dean Stockwell, Gloria Grahame, Jayne Meadows
▶ Musicians, gamblers, and singer Grahame are among the possible suspects when Nick (Powell) and Nora (Loy) Charles investigate the shipboard murder of a bandleader. Final

entry in the series is far from peak form although Powell and Loy are still charming.
Dist.: MGM/UA

SONG TO REMEMBER, A 1945
★ ★ ★ NR Biography/Music 1:52
Dir: Charles Vidor *Cast:* Cornel Wilde, Merle Oberon, Paul Muni, Stephen Bekassy, Nina Foch, George Coulouris
▶ Nineteenth-century Polish composer Frederic Chopin (Wilde) is taken to Paris by his mentor Joseph Elsner (Muni). There Chopin rises to stardom and has a torrid romance with writer George Sand (Oberon); under her influence, he turns against Elsner. Lavish story of great personal peaks and heartbreaking lows; Wilde and the grand music earned two of six Oscar nominations.
Dist.: RCA/Columbia

SONGWRITER 1984
★ ★ R Musical/Comedy 1:34
☑ Nudity, adult situations, explicit language
Dir: Alan Rudolph *Cast:* Willie Nelson, Kris Kristofferson, Melinda Dillon, Rip Torn, Lesley Ann Warren, Richard C. Sarafian
▶ Country-western duo Nelson and Krisofferson part company so that Nelson can become a songwriter. Singer Warren gets a big hit with one of Nelson's songs and tries to seduce him, but he's only interested in getting back ex-wife Dillon. Satire of the country music biz is best when the two leads are singing. (CC)
Dist.: RCA/Columbia

SON OF CAPTAIN BLOOD, THE 1964
U.S./Italian/Spanish
☆ NR Action-Adventure 1:28
Dir: Tulio Demicheli *Cast:* Sean Flynn, Ann Todd, Alessandra Panaro, Jose Nieto, John Kitzmiller, Raffaele Baldassarre
▶ The son of Errol Flynn plays the son of Flynn's character in 1935's *Captain Blood,* going to sea against mother Todd's wishes and running into his father's old pirate nemesis Nieto. Colorful settings, but the pirate clichés are thirty years older and that much more tired here.
Dist.: Prism

SON OF DRACULA 1943
★ ★ NR Horror 1:20 B&W
Dir: Robert Siodmak *Cast:* Lon Chaney, Jr., Robert Paige, Louise Allbritton, Evelyn Ankers, Frank Craven, Samuel S. Hinds
▶ Hungarian Count Alucard (Chaney) journeys to Louisiana, where he steals lovely Allbritton away from boyfriend Paige. She thinks she's entering high society, but Paige unearths disturbing secrets about Alucard's past. Inaccurate title (capitalizing on Universal Studio's string of successful horror films) disguises surprisingly effective vampire tale.
Dist.: MCA

SON OF FLUBBER 1963
★ ★ ★ ★ G Comedy 1:40 B&W
Dir: Robert Stevenson *Cast:* Fred MacMurray, Nancy Olson, Keenan Wynn, Tommy Kirk, Elliott Reid, Joanna Moore, Leon Ames, Ed Wynn, Charlie Ruggles, William Demarest
▶ Professor MacMurray has a new invention called "dry rain," but unfortunately hasn't worked out all the bugs. Meanwhile, the school football team uses his "flubbergas" to win the big game. On the domestic front, his wife Olson becomes jealous of his old girlfriend Moore. Frolicsome Disney sequel to *The Absent Minded Professor.*
Dist.: Buena Vista

SON OF FRANKENSTEIN 1939
★ ★ ★ NR Horror 1:39 B&W
Dir: Rowland V. Lee *Cast:* Basil Rathbone, Boris Karloff, Bela Lugosi, Lionel Atwill, Josephine Hutchinson, Donnie Dunagan
▶ Rathbone, Dr. Frankenstein's son, returns from America to dad's castle. He meets Ygor (Lugosi), the broken-necked survivor of a hanging, who helps Rathbone revive monster Karloff, only to use the monster for his own sinister purposes. Terrific third entry in the series, best remembered as the movie that introduced Lugosi's unforgettably creepy Ygor characterization.
Dist.: MCA

SON OF KONG 1933
★ ★ NR Sci-Fi 1:10 B&W
Dir: Ernest B. Schoedsack *Cast:* Robert Armstrong, Helen Mack, Frank Reicher, John Marston, Victor Wong, Lee Kohlmar
▶ Promoter Armstrong and his crew return to Skull Island and discover King Kong's son, a cuddly, thirty-foot albino. After Armstrong rescues "Baby Kong" from quicksand, the ape returns the favor by saving the explorers from various creatures. Sequel emphasizes humor and pathos over original's terrifying power. Touching ending.
Dist.: Media

SON OF MONTE CRISTO, THE 1940
★ NR Action-Adventure 1:42 B&W
Dir: Rowland V. Lee *Cast:* Louis Hayward, Joan Bennett, George Sanders, Ralph Byrd, Clayton Moore
▶ The Count of Monte Cristo (Hayward) pretends to be a foolish fop, but is really the heroic leader of the resistance to ruthless villain Sanders, who is trying to take over a Balkan nation. Bennett plays the duchess whom Hayward aids. Exciting swordplay, lavish sets and costumes adorn Alexandre Dumas–inspired adventure.
Dist.: Video Yesteryear

SON OF PALEFACE 1952
★ ★ ★ NR Comedy 1:35
Dir: Frank Tashlin *Cast:* Bob Hope, Jane Russell, Roy Rogers, Douglass Dumbrille, Bill Williams
▶ Harvard grad Hope comes west to claim gold hidden by his legendary Indian-fighter dad. Curvy cafe singer–outlaw Russell and government agent Rogers help him. Sequel to

the 1948 *Paleface*; Hope's nifty timing keeps it perking with nice support from Russell, Rogers, and Trigger.
Dist.: RCA/Columbia

SON OF THE SHEIK, THE 1926
☆ NR Action-Adventure 1:12 B&W
Dir: George Fitzmaurice   *Cast:* Rudolph Valentino, Vilma Banky, Agnes Ayres, Karl Dane, Bull Montana
▶ Valentino plays both father and son in this sly, swashbuckling silent. As the son, Valentino falls for dancer Banky, whose father has him kidnapped by thieves. When Valentino is freed, he must teach the bad guys manners at the end of a saber. Valentino's last is a real audience pleaser, strong in every department. Sequel to *The Sheik*.
Dist.: Cable

SONS OF KATIE ELDER, THE 1965
★ ★ ★ NR Western 2:02
Dir: Henry Hathaway   *Cast:* John Wayne, Dean Martin, Martha Hyer, Michael Anderson, Jr., Earl Holliman, George Kennedy
▶ Four brothers reunited by their mother's death learn their father was murdered and put aside their differences to search for the killers. Gunman Wayne, gambler Martin, silent killer Holliman, and college graduate Anderson are imprisoned and threatened by a lynching party before they uncover the truth. Sprawling Western with an especially physical performance by Wayne.
Dist.: Paramount

SONS OF THE DESERT 1933
★ ★ ★ ★ NR Comedy 1:09 B&W
Dir: William A. Seiter · *Cast:* Stan Laurel, Oliver Hardy, Charley Chase, Mae Busch, Dorothy Christy, Lucien Littlefield
▶ The boys are afraid to tell their wives about the Chicago convention of their fraternal order Sons of the Desert, so Ollie fakes a cold and claims he's leaving with Stan for a Hawaiian cure. Their plan naturally backfires with hilarious results in this short, sweet, near-perfect comedy. Fans consider this the best of Laurel and Hardy's feature films.
Dist.: Nostalgia

SOPHIE'S CHOICE 1982
★ ★ ★ ★ R Drama 2:31
☑ Adult situations, explicit language, mild violence
Dir: Alan J. Pakula   *Cast:* Meryl Streep, Kevin Kline, Peter MacNicol, Rita Karin, Stephen D. Newman
▶ Streep's Oscar-winning performance as Sophie dominates this powerful film version of William Styron's best-selling novel. In a Brooklyn boarding house after World War II, southern writer MacNicol meets Sophie, a beautiful Polish Holocaust survivor, and her lover Kline, a Jewish biologist. While the multifaceted plot spirals towards its ultimately tragic conclusion, the characters reveal their long-hidden se-

crets. Also nominated for Best Screenplay, Cinematography, Score, and Costumes.
Dist.: CBS/Fox

SORORITY BABES IN THE SLIMEBALL BOWL-A-RAMA 1988
★ R Horror/Comedy 1:18
☑ Nudity, explicit language, graphic violence
Dir: David DeCoteau   *Cast:* Linnea Quigley, Michelle Bauer, Andras Jones, Robin Rochelle, Brinke Stevens, Kathi Obrecht
▶ Sorority pledges Bauer and Stevens, assigned to steal a bowling trophy for initiation, break into the same bowling alley that Quigley is robbing. The girls drop the trophy, unleashing a little creature who grants them each a wish but then turns them into monsters. Gleeful, mean-spirited humor lives up to the title.
Dist.: Urban Classics

SORORITY HOUSE MASSACRE 1986
★ R Horror 1:14
☑ Nudity, adult situations, explicit language, graphic violence
Dir: Carol Frank   *Cast:* Angela O'Neill, Wendy Martel, Pamela Ross, Nicole Rio, John C. Russell
▶ Vacation weekend empties out Theta Omega sorority house except for psychology major Martel, shy pledge O'Neill, and two friends who fall victim to escaped mental patient Russell. O'Neill learns she is Russell's sister, the only survivor of a mass murder years earlier, before confronting her brother in a bloody climax. Inventive photography helps routine slasher plot.
Dist.: Warner

SORROW AND THE PITY, THE 1970 Swiss
★ PG Documentary 4:20 B&W
☑ Explicit language
Dir: Marcel Ophuls
▶ Compelling documentary interweaves current-day interviews and extraordinary period footage to create masterful portrait of French collaboration with Nazis during World War II. Chilling revelations as former SS men portray themselves as benevolent conquerors while Frenchmen try to rationalize their behavior. Subtlety and length limit appeal. Dubbed and subtitled versions available. Nominated for Best Documentary.   S
Dist.: RCA/Columbia

SORROWFUL JONES 1949
★ ★ ★ NR Comedy 1:28 B&W
Dir: Sidney Lanfield   *Cast:* Bob Hope, Lucille Ball, William Demarest, Bruce Cabot, Thomas Gomez, Tom Pedi, Mary Jane Saunders
▶ Uncredited remake of *Little Miss Marker* with Hope surprisingly restrained as a bookie forced to care for young Saunders when her father skips town. Broadway singer Ball and a collection of typical Damon Runyon eccentrics aid Hope with his new paternal duties.

sentimental rather than snappy. Introduced by Walter Winchell. [S]
Dist.: MCA

SORRY, WRONG NUMBER 1948
★ ★ ★ ★ NR Mystery-Suspense 1:29 B&W
Dir: Anatole Litvak *Cast:* Barbara Stanwyck, Burt Lancaster, Ann Richards, Wendell Corey, Ed Begley, William Conrad
▶ Bed-ridden, neurotic, and rich Stanwyck overhears phone conversation in which a murder is planned. She soon suspects she is the intended victim, but the police won't believe her paranoid tale. Her only hope is to get through to her hard-to-reach businessman husband Lancaster. Classic suspense earned Oscar nomination for Stanwyck. Adapted from renowned twenty-two-minute radio play written by Lucille Fletcher and starring Agnes Moorehead.
Dist.: Paramount

SOTTO. . .SOTTO 1985 Italian
☆ R Comedy 1:45
☑ Adult situations, explicit language, adult humor
Dir: Lina Wertmuller *Cast:* Enrico Montesano, Veronica Lario, Luisa de Santis, Massimo Wertmuller
▶ Super-macho carpenter Montesano is thrown for a loop when wife Lario tells him she loves someone else. He turns to de Santis for comfort, not realizing that she is the object of Lario's affections. Spirited but overly frenetic sexual satire. Funniest scene: Montesano and the priest during confession. [S]
Dist.: RCA/Columbia

SOUL MAN 1986
★ ★ ★ PG-13 Comedy 1:45
☑ Adult situations, explicit language
Dir: Steve Miner *Cast:* C. Thomas Howell, Rae Dawn Chong, James Earl Jones, Arye Gross, James B. Sikking
▶ Along with best friend Gross, rich southern Californian Howell is accepted into Harvard Law School, but father Sikking refuses to pay tuition and he isn't eligible for financial aid. With tanning pills and afro wig, he wins a minority scholarship—but can he pass as a soul brother? In his "black-like-me" identity, Howell discovers many truths about racial stereotyping and falls for lovely co-ed Chong. Amusing story line, solid performances, and zippy pacing. Jones excels as Howell's intimidating law professor. Howell and Chong later married. (CC)
Dist.: New World

SOUNDER 1972
★ ★ ★ ★ G Family 1:45
Dir: Martin Ritt *Cast:* Cicely Tyson, Paul Winfield, Kevin Hooks, Carmen Mathews, Taj Mahal, James Best
▶ Adaptation of a William Armstrong novel in which Depression-era black sharecropper Winfield steals food to feed family and must serve year sentence at work camp. Wife Tyson is left to run farm and tend younger kids with help of eldest son Hooks. Superior drama distinguished by story of universal appeal and first-rate performances, especially Hooks as youth on verge of manhood. Top-notch score by Mahal (also in screen debut). Moving family fare nominated for Best Picture, Actor, Actress, and Adaptation. (CC)
Dist.: Paramount

SOUND OF MUSIC, THE 1965
★ ★ ★ ★ ★ G Musical 2:54
Dir: Robert Wise *Cast:* Julie Andrews, Christopher Plummer, Eleanor Parker, Peggy Wood, Angela Cartwright, Richard Haydn
▶ Vibrant musical based on true story of singing Von Trapp family's flight from Austria to Switzerland during World War II. Nun-turned-governess Andrews helps stern widower Plummer guide his flock of kids through good times and bad and eventually softens Plummer for marriage. Memorable songs from Rodgers and Hammerstein's Broadway hit include "My Favorite Things," "Do-Re-Mi," "Climb Every Mountain," and title tune. Alpine scenery and Andrews's singing made film one of most popular of all time. Winner of five Oscars, including Best Picture. (CC)
Dist.: CBS/Fox

SOUP FOR ONE 1982
★ R Comedy 1:24
☑ Brief nudity, adult situations, explicit language, adult humor
Dir: Jonathan Kaufer *Cast:* Saul Rubinek, Marcia Strassman, Gerrit Graham, Teddy Pendergrass, Richard Libertini, Andrea Martin
▶ Nice Jewish boy Rubinek, tired of Manhattan singles scene, seeks dream mate for wedded bliss. When various dates disappoint him, womanizer friend Graham takes him to a singles weekend at Catskills hotel. There he meets Strassman, but she rejects him until he bullies his way into her heart. As the altar looms near, however, Rubinek gets cold feet. Erratic satire with likable cast but tired observations.
Dist.: Warner

SOUTHERN COMFORT 1981
★ ★ ★ R Action-Adventure 1:46
☑ Explicit language, graphic violence
Dir: Walter Hill *Cast:* Keith Carradine, Powers Boothe, Fred Ward, Franklyn Seales, T. K. Carter, Peter Coyote
▶ Nine National Guardsmen on weekend manuevers in a Louisiana swamp harass Cajun locals and steal some canoes. The Cajuns respond by tracking the interlopers and killing them one by one, often in grisly fashion. Soon only Guardsmen Carradine and Boothe are left, hoping to escape the cat-and-mouse game alive. Well-crafted although somewhat pointless drama with lots of action and fine performances.
Dist.: Embassy

SOUTHERNER, THE 1945
★ ★ NR Drama 1:31 B&W
Dir: Jean Renoir   *Cast:* Zachary Scott, Betty Field, Beulah Bondi, Jean Vanderwilt, Jay Gilpin, J. Carrol Naish
▶ .Haunting account of a Texas family's dogged attempts to establish a farm on poor land. Scott, the father, gives up a factory job to work an arid stretch while repairing a run-down shack for his wife Field and children Vanderwilt and Gilpin. Vindictive neighbor Naish refuses to help even when Gilpin falls ill. Director Renoir received an Oscar nomination for his sensitive, uplifting depiction of a heroic battle against poverty.
Dist.: Various

SOUTH OF RENO 1988
☆ R Drama 1:38
☑ Adult situations, explicit language, violence
Dir: Mark Rezyka   *Cast:* Jeffrey Osterhage, Lisa Blount, Joe Phelan, Lewis Van Bergen, Julia Montgomery, Bert Remsen
▶ In the Nevada desert, Osterhage is so lonely that he throws nails on the road to stop cars. His wife Blount cheats on him with mechanic Van Bergen but he is unable to stop their relationship. Osterhage also dreams of escaping to Reno. Effectively spare dialogue and artful cinematography, but characters are too quiet to be interesting.
Dist.: Republic

SOUTH OF ST. LOUIS 1949
★ NR Western 1:28
Dir: Ray Enright   *Cast:* Joel McCrea, Alexis Smith, Zachary Scott, Dorothy Malone, Douglas Kennedy, Victor Jory
▶ During the Civil War, Unionist Jory wrecks the ranch owned by Texans McCrea, Scott, and Kennedy, driving Kennedy into the Rebel army, and the two others into a gunrunning plot. Jory has ideas along similar lines, and conflict occurs. On the way to putting the bad guys in their place, McCrea and Kennedy trade girlfriends Smith and Malone. Well-staged action, but a simpler plot would have helped.
Dist.: Republic

SOUTH PACIFIC 1958
★ ★ ★ ★ NR Musical 2:29
Dir: Joshua Logan   *Cast:* Mitzi Gaynor, Rossano Brazzi, Ray Walston, John Kerr, Juanita Hall, France Nuyen
▶ Screen version of the smash Broadway musical, based on the James Michener book, takes place on remote South Pacific island during World War II. Midwestern nurse Gaynor falls in love with widowed plantation owner Brazzi while young Marine Kerr woos native girl Nuyen. Story may be merely serviceable, but with sensational Rodgers and Hammerstein score, who cares? Tunes include "I'm Gonna Wash That Man Right Out of My Hair," "There

Is Nothing Like Dame," "My Girl Back Home," and "Some Enchanted Evening." (CC)
Dist.: CBS/Fox

SOYLENT GREEN 1973
★ ★ ★ PG Sci-Fi 1:37
☑ Adult situations, explicit language
Dir: Richard Fleischer   *Cast:* Charlton Heston, Leigh Taylor-Young, Chuck Connors, Joseph Cotten, Brock Peters, Edward G. Robinson
▶ In 2022, overpopulated world is so depleted of resources that most people subsist on a waferlike food known as soylent. Detective Heston investigates assassination of industrialist Cotten who discovered a terrifying secret about the foodstuff. Passable sci-fi noteworthy as legendary Robinson's final movie. Dying of cancer during shoot, he delivered a dignified and poignant performance.
Dist.: MGM/UA

SPACEBALLS 1987
★ ★ PG Comedy 1:36
☑ Explicit language
Dir: Mel Brooks   *Cast:* Mel Brooks, John Candy, Rick Moranis, Bill Pullman, Daphne Zuniga, Dick Van Patten
▶ Evil planet Spaceball has run out of air so leader Brooks and underling Dark Helmet (Moranis) conspire to steal atmosphere of neighboring Druidia, ruled by kind king Van Patten. Moranis kidnaps Van Patten's daughter Zuniga as hostage. To the rescue come space maverick Pullman and man-dog sidekick Candy, fresh from training by mini-guru Yogurt (also Brooks). Broad and often erratic parody of *Star Wars* and other sci-fi epics. Best moments come from Moranis's wimpy Napoleonic parody of Darth Vader.
Dist.: MGM/UA

SPACECAMP 1986
★ ★ ★ ★ PG Action-Adventure 1:47
☑ Explicit language
Dir: Harry Winer   *Cast:* Kate Capshaw, Lea Thompson, Kelly Preston, Larry B. Scott, Leaf Phoenix, Tate Donovan
▶ Teens attend a summer program at the NASA Space Center, where astronaut Capshaw teaches them about the shuttle. Jinx, a friendly but imperfect robot, arranges for them to be launched on an actual mission. When Capshaw is injured, the youngsters must rely on their knowledge and grit to return to Earth safely. Optimistic view of space travel was released just after the *Challenger* disaster.
Dist.: Vestron

SPACEHUNTER: ADVENTURES IN THE FORBIDDEN ZONE 1983
★ ★ PG Sci-Fi 1:29
☑ Explicit language, violence
Dir: Lamont Johnson   *Cast:* Peter Strauss, Molly Ringwald, Ernie Hudson, Michael Ironside, Beeson Carroll, Andrea Marcovicci
▶ Wars and plagues reduce the planet Terra Eleven to a wasteland. Mercenary loner

Strauss rockets there to rescue three kidnapped travelers, teaming up with orphaned "Earther" girl Ringwald to battle Bat People, cyborg gladiators, and the evil Overdog. Routine space epic, shot in 3-D, will lose most of its impact on TV. **(CC)**
Dist.: RCA/Columbia

SPACE MOVIE, THE 1978
★ ★ ★ **NR Documentary 1:18**
Dir: Tony Palmer
▶ Examination of American space exploration focuses on the flight of Apollo 11, which first placed men on the moon; also includes other missions (like a glimpse at Skylab). Intelligently made documentary highlighted by breathtaking, previously unreleased NASA footage. Powerful score by Mike Oldfield.
Dist.: Warner

SPACE RAGE 1987
★ **R Sci-Fi 1:18**
☑ Explicit language, violence
Dir: Conrad E. Palmisano   *Cast:* Richard Farnsworth, Michael Paré, John Laughlin, Lee Purcell, William Windom
▶ Futuristic planet Proxima Centauri 3 provides the backdrop for a sustained battle between bounty hunters and vicious escaped con Paré who's kidnapped warden Windom and his wife Purcell. Farnsworth, leader of the bounty hunters, adds some dignity to this cut-rate sci-fi Western. Subtitle: *Breakout on Prison Planet.*
Dist.: Vestron

SPACE RAIDERS 1983
★ ★ **PG Sci-Fi 1:23**
☑ Explicit language, violence
Dir: Howard R. Cohen   *Cast:* Vince Edwards, David Mendenhall, Patsy Pease, Thom Christopher, Luca Bercovici, Drew Synder
▶ In an authoritarian future, ten-year-old Mendenhall stows away on spaceship stolen by rebels. Mendenhall idolizes outlaws' leader Edwards, who tries unsuccessfully to return kid to home. When evil alien Snyder snatches him for ransom, Edwards and gang come to his rescue. Special effects and score were lifted from producer Roger Corman's previous hit, *Battle Beyond the Stars.* Low-budget entry in the space genre.
Dist.: Warner

SPARTACUS 1960
★ ★ ★ ★ **NR Drama 3:05**
Dir: Stanley Kubrick   *Cast:* Kirk Douglas, Laurence Olivier, Tony Curtis, Jean Simmons, Charles Laughton, Peter Ustinov
▶ In 73 B.C., gladiator-slave Douglas leads revolt of fellow slaves against tyrannical Roman senator Olivier. Aiding Douglas in his fight: his lover Simmons and his friend Curtis. Exciting, old-fashioned epic with terrific battles and passionate performance by Douglas leading

the great cast; more conventional and more accessible than Kubrick's later films.
Dist.: MCA

SPASMS 1983 Canadian
★ **R Horror 1:27**
☑ Nudity, explicit language, graphic violence
Dir: William Fruet   *Cast:* Peter Fonda, Oliver Reed, Kerrie Keane, Al Waxman, Miguel Fernandes, Marilyn Lightstone
▶ Scholar Reed is bitten by a huge snake that kills his brother. When the reptile is captured in New Guinea, Reed realizes he can communicate with it telepathically. Working with ESP expert Fonda, he searches desperately for the snake, aware it is one of the guardians to the gates of hell. Illogical low-budget horror has compelling special effects and a larger-than-life performance by Reed.
Dist.: HBO

SPECIAL DAY, A 1977 Italian/Canadian
★ ★ **NR Drama 1:46**
☑ Adult situations, explicit language
Dir: Ettore Scola   *Cast:* Sophia Loren, Marcello Mastroianni, John Vernon, Francoise Berd, Nicole Magny, Patrizia Basso
▶ When most of Rome turns out for Hitler and Mussolini's 1938 meeting, harried housewife Loren and tormented homosexual Mastroianni are among few who stay away. Loren seduces Mastroianni before each returns to dreary existence. Fine turns by Italy's two biggest stars, with Oscar nominations for Best Actor and Foreign Film.   Ⓢ
Dist.: RCA/Columbia

SPECIAL DELIVERY 1976
★ ★ **PG Comedy 1:39**
☑ Adult situations, explicit language
Dir: Paul Wendkos   *Cast:* Bo Svenson, Cybill Shepherd, Michael Gwynne, Tom Atkins, Sorrell Booke
▶ Jobless Vietnam vet Svenson robs a bank, loses his gang, and caches the loot in a mailbox. Artist Shepherd witnesses the stashing, falls for Svenson, and tries to thwart the efforts of druggie Gwynn, who also has eyes on the swag. Not many laughs here, and there's little to sympathize with in bank-robbing Svenson.
Dist.: Vestron

SPECTER OF THE ROSE 1946
☆ **NR Drama 1:30 B&W**
Dir: Ben Hecht   *Cast:* Judith Anderson, Michael Chekhov, Ivan Kirov, Viola Essen, Lionel Stander
▶ Ballet dancer Kirov suffers hallucinations in which he slits a woman's throat. Fellow dancer Essen loves him, and marries him in the belief that she can cure him. A movie that stands way out from the pack, comedy/mystery/melodrama was penned, produced, and directed by Hecht. Crisp, unusual dialogue spills generously from vividly realized characters

like impressario Chekhov and ballet doyenne Anderson. A must for the adventurous.
Dist.: Republic

SPEEDTRAP 1977
★ ★ **PG Action-Adventure 1:38**
☑ Explicit language
Dir: Earl Bellamy *Cast:* Joe Don Baker, Tyne Daly, Richard Jaeckel, Robert Loggia, Morgan Woodward, Lana Wood
▶ A mysterious car thief who calls himself the Roadrunner has been stealing expensive cars; private detective Baker and policewoman Daly try to catch him. For fans of car chases, a feast of metal-crunching, tire-squealing mayhem, with great crashes and amazing stunts.
Dist.: Media

SPEEDWAY 1968
★ ★ **G Musical 1:30**
Dir: Norman Taurog *Cast:* Elvis Presley, Nancy Sinatra, Bill Bixby, Gale Gordon, William Schallert
▶ Top race-car driver Presley learns his manager Bixby has mishandled his money. IRS agent Sinatra falls for Presley, and helps pay off his debts. Formula wears thin in the King's twenty-seventh film. Sinatra warbles "Your Groovy Self"; other songs include "Who Are You? (Who Am I?)" and "He's Your Uncle, Not Your Dad."
Dist.: MGM/UA

SPEED ZONE 1989
★ ★ **PG Comedy 1:35**
☑ Explicit language
Dir: Jim Drake *Cast:* John Candy, Donna Dixon, Matt Frewer, Joe Flaherty, Tim Matheson, Mimi Kuzyk, Melody Anderson, Shari Belafonte, Peter Boyle, Eugene Levy
▶ When fun-hating cop Boyle busts all the Cannonball Run racers on the eve of the coast-to-coast dash, the driving devolves upon a mixed bag of latecomers and hangers-on. Leadfoot derbyists include parking lot attendant Candy piloting for car dealer Levy; gambler and hitman Frewer and Flaherty; and brainy-but-beautiful MIT grads Belafonte and Anderson. Despite presence of many former "SCTV" stars, this entry stalls at the starting line. Lack of continuity is especially bad.
Dist.: Media

SPELLBINDER 1988
★ **R Horror 1:39**
☑ Adult situations, explicit language, violence
Dir: Janet Greek *Cast:* Timothy Daly, Kelly Preston, Rick Rossovich, Audra Lindley, Anthony Crivello, Diana Bellamy
▶ Lawyer Daly rescues beautiful Preston from brutal boyfriend Crivello. Daly and Preston become lovers, but she then reveals her past association with Satanic cult, which now aims to make her a human sacrifice. Daly battles

the evil gang on her behalf. Two good plot twists help this modest but unconvincing tale.
Dist.: CBS/Fox

SPELLBOUND 1945
★ ★ ★ ★ **NR Mystery-Suspense 1:52 B&W**
Dir: Alfred Hitchcock *Cast:* Ingrid Bergman, Gregory Peck, Michael Chekhov, Leo G. Carroll, John Emery, Wallace Ford, Rhonda Fleming
▶ Peck, the new psychiatrist at an asylum, is discovered to be a fraud by staff doctor Bergman; she helps uncover a secret he has been blocking about a murder. Intriguing romance with a psychoanalytic background features a number of good Hitchcock twists and a bizarre dream sequence by Salvador Dali. Received six Oscar nominations, winning for Miklos Rozsa's lush score.
Dist.: CBS/Fox

SPETTERS 1980 Dutch
★ **R Drama 1:49**
☑ Nudity, strong sexual content, explicit language
Dir: Paul Verhoeven *Cast:* Toon Agterberg, Hans Van Tongeren, Rutger Hauer, Maarten Spanjer, Renee Soutendijk, Marianne Boyer
▶ Aimless youths Agterberg, Van Tongeren, and Spanjer have little to do in Rotterdam but work and ride motorcycles, aspiring to mimic champ racer Hauer. Enter vampy temptress Soutendijk, hoping to attach herself to the one with best shot for fame and fortune and initiating rivalry between the pals. Sexy study of wayward youth, although heedless hedonism and alienated leads will leave some cold.
Ⓢ
Dist.: Embassy

SPHINX 1981
★ ★ ★ **PG Mystery-Suspense 1:57**
☑ Adult situations, explicit language, violence
Dir: Franklin J. Schaffner *Cast:* Frank Langella, Lesley-Anne Down, John Gielgud, Maurice Ronet, Martin Benson, Vic Tablian
▶ On a research trip to Cairo, Egyptologist Down witnesses murder of crooked antiquities dealer Gielgud. Villains mark her for death while French journalist Ronet and local artifacts authority Langella are curious about her role in the murder. Despite these distractions, Down finds a secret tomb in which she becomes trapped. Striking scenery and exotic Egyptian lore occasionally marred by confusing story line.
Dist.: Warner

SPIDER BABY, THE MADDEST STORY EVER TOLD 1964
☆ **NR Horror 1:20 B&W**
Dir: Jack Hill *Cast:* Lon Chaney, Jr., Sid Haig, Jill Banner, Mantan Moreland, Beverly Washburn, Carol Ohmart
▶ Chaney caretakes a trio of cretinous siblings suffering from something called "Merrye's Syndrome," which renders them cannibals.

Some unscrupulous cousins are plotting to cheat the three out of the mansion in which they live, but Chaney is determined to prevent that from happening. Unique film was almost forgotten, but received wild praise upon video release. Also known as *The Liver Eaters*, grotesque item is a must for fans of the truly weird.
Dist.: Sinister

SPIES 1928 German
★ **NR Espionage 2:10 B&W**
Dir: Fritz Lang   *Cast:* Rudolph Klein-Rogge, Gerda Marcus, Willy Fritsch, Lupu Pick, Fritz Rasp, Hertha von Walther
▶ In London, agent Fritsch battles Klein-Rogge, whose front as a banker covers a devious criminal mind and a foreign espionage ring encompassing colonel Rasp, opium addict von Walther, and lovely spy Marcus. Paranoid, intricate thriller, masterfully directed by Lang, includes several exciting sequences. German title: *Spione*.
Dist.: Video Yesteryear

SPIES LIKE US 1985
★ ★ ★ ★ **PG Comedy 1:43**
☑ Explicit language, mild violence, adult humor
Dir: John Landis   *Cast:* Dan Aykroyd, Chevy Chase, Steve Forrest, Donna Dixon, Bruce Davison, William Prince
▶ Inept government employees Aykroyd and Chase are recruited and trained as spies for dangerous mission in Afghanistan and USSR. After blundering their way through various crises, they realize they're disposable decoys intended to distract the Soviets. Aykroyd and Chase then team up with Dixon, one of the real agents, to avert end of civilization. Uneven comedy doesn't always fulfill its fine premise, but Aykroyd and Chase fans won't be disappointed. **(CC)**
Dist.: Warner

SPIKE OF BENSONHURST 1988
★ ★ **R Comedy 1:41**
☑ Explicit language, violence
Dir: Paul Morrissey   *Cast:* Ernest Borgnine, Sasha Mitchell, Anne De Salvo, Maria Pitillo, Sylvia Miles, Geraldine Smith, Ta'isa Soto
▶ Middling Brooklyn prizefighter Mitchell seeks help with career from local Mafia don Borgnine and lands gig as low-level hood. But when Mitchell seduces Borgnine's daughter Pitillo, the don banishes him to a Puerto Rican neighborhood where he is idolized for his mob connections. Mitchell takes on the local drug dealers while trying to get back in Borgnine's good graces. Campy, off-the-wall comedy from Morrissey, director of Andy Warhol films.
Dist.: Virgin

SPIKER 1985
★ ★ **R Drama/Sports 1:44**
☑ Nudity, adult situations, explicit language
Dir: Roger Tilton   *Cast:* Patrick Houser, Kristi

Ferrell, Jo McDonnel, Stephen Burns, Christopher Allport, Michael Parks
▶ Pals Houser and Burns try out for Olympic volleyball and discover coach Parks has demeanor of a drill sergeant. Houser romances old flame Ferrell, who's writing thesis on the sport, while Burns quits after row with Parks during Japan tour. Meanwhile other player Allport suffers from marital woes due to constant travel. Fine depiction of matches undermined by melodramatic antics.
Dist.: Vestron

SPINOUT 1966
★ ★ ★ **NR Musical 1:30**
Dir: Norman Taurog   *Cast:* Elvis Presley, Shelley Fabares, Diane McBain, Deborah Walley, Cecil Kellaway, Una Merkel
▶ Race car driver Presley has more girls than he can handle, including spoiled millionairess Fabares and the drummer in his band. Other band members envy their leader, but some end up with girls of their own as plot races to its speedway conclusion. Many bad songs here, but "Smorgasbord" may be among the King's all-time worst. Rest of film is average Presley fare.
Dist.: MGM/UA

SPIRAL STAIRCASE, THE 1946
★ ★ ★ **NR Mystery-Suspense 1:23 B&W**
Dir: Robert Siodmak   *Cast:* Dorothy McGuire, George Brent, Ethel Barrymore, Kent Smith, Gordon Oliver, Elsa Lanchester
▶ Madman kills deformed women in turn-of-the-century New England village; McGuire, a mute servant in invalid Barrymore's gothic mansion, realizes she may be the next victim. Marvelous thriller exploits every nook and cranny in the spooky setting to provoke terror. Remade with Jacqueline Bisset in 1975.
Dist.: Magnetic

SPIRAL STAIRCASE, THE 1975 British
★ ★ ★ **NR Mystery-Suspense 1:29**
☑ Explicit language, violence
Dir: Peter Collinson   *Cast:* Jacqueline Bisset, Christopher Plummer, Sam Wanamaker, Mildred Dunnock, Gayle Hunnicutt, Elaine Stritch
▶ Attractive young Bisset loses voice as result of severe emotional trauma and moves into old New England house with frail grandmother Dunnock, stern nurse Stritch, psychologist uncle Plummer, and his secretary Hunnicutt. Local cop Wanamaker searches for psychopath killer who victimizes the handicapped. Remake of 1946 classic suspenser uses gimmick of pursued woman whose screams can't be heard.
Dist.: Warner

SPIRIT OF ST. LOUIS, THE 1957
★ ★ ★ ★ **NR Biography 2:17**
Dir: Billy Wilder   *Cast:* James Stewart, Patricia Smith, Murray Hamilton, Bartlett Robinson, Robert Cornthwaite, Marc Connelly
▶ Stirring version of Charles Lindbergh's fa-

mous 1927 solo flight across the Atlantic, with Stewart delivering a bravura performance as the heroic pilot. Flashbacks during the journey reveal Lindbergh's struggling years as a stunt flier and air-mail pilot. Inspirational, uplifting story was based on the best-selling autobiography.
Dist.: Warner

SPITFIRE 1942 British
★ **NR Biography 1:29 B&W**
Dir: Leslie Howard *Cast:* Leslie Howard, David Niven, Rosamund John, Roland Culver, Anne Firth, David Horne
▶ True story of R. J. Mitchell (Howard), the Englishman who developed the Spitfire fighter plane. The visionary Mitchell faced opposition from a skeptical airline industry until the plane proved its worth during World War II. Niven plays his test pilot pal in this first-rate biography.
Dist.: Video Yesteryear

SPLASH 1984
★ ★ ★ ★ **PG Comedy 1:50**
☑ Brief nudity, adult situations, explicit language, mild violence, adult humor
Dir: Ron Howard *Cast:* Tom Hanks, Daryl Hannah, John Candy, Eugene Levy, Dody Goodman, Shecky Greene
▶ Lonely New York bachelor Hanks is saved from drowning off Cape Cod by mermaid Hannah. Sprouting legs, she finds him in the city where, once his shock has worn off, they fall in love. Romance is complicated by Hannah's inability to live out of water more than six days and attempts by zoologist Levy to apprehend and study her. Enormously popular comedy mixes old-fashioned love story with fish-out-of-water jokes. Candy is hilarious as Hanks's lecherous older brother while Goodman steals scenes as a dim-witted secretary.
Dist.: Buena Vista

SPLATTER UNIVERSITY 1984
☆ **R Horror 1:20**
☑ Adult situations, explicit language, graphic violence
Dir: Richard W. Haines *Cast:* Francine Forbes, Dick Biel, Cathy Lacommare, Ric Randig, Joanna Mihalakis, Denise Texeira
▶ Forbes, a new instructor at a Catholic university, learns her predecessor was stabbed to death in a murder that remains unsolved. Despite assurances of creepy school head Biel, the killer returns to slay others and stalk Forbes. Low-budget horror offers nothing new to genre. Available in an unrated version.
Dist.: Vestron

SPLENDOR IN THE GRASS 1961
★ ★ ★ **NR Drama/Romance 2:04**
Dir: Elia Kazan *Cast:* Natalie Wood, Warren Beatty, Pat Hingle, Audrey Christie, Barbara Loden, Zohra Lampert, Sandy Dennis
▶ Contrived but effective soap opera set in 1920s Kansas with Wood and Beatty as teenagers indulging in a forbidden love affair de-

spite the objections of their parents. Oscar-winning screenplay by William Inge (who has a cameo as a minister) verges on the maudlin, but breathlessly romantic story is a good showcase for the stars. Film debuts for Beatty and Dennis.
Dist.: Warner

SPLIT DECISIONS 1988
★ ★ ★ ★ **R Drama/Sports 1:35**
☑ Adult situations, explicit language, violence
Dir: David Drury *Cast:* Gene Hackman, Jeff Fahey, Jennifer Beals, Craig Sheffer, John McLiam
▶ When boxer Fahey refuses to throw a fight, mobsters beat him up and his opponent-to-be throws him out a window to his death. Fahey's brother Sheffer forsakes college to train for grudge match with killer. Father Hackman and grandfather McLiam, both boxing vets, had higher hopes for Sheffer but soon they're in his corner, training him mercilessly. Sheffer romances Fahey's girl Beals before climactic fight for revenge.
Dist.: Warner

SPLIT IMAGE 1982
★ ★ ★ **R Drama 1:51**
☑ Adult situations, explicit language, mild violence
Dir: Ted Kotcheff *Cast:* Michael O'Keefe, Karen Allen, Peter Fonda, Elizabeth Ashley, James Woods, Brian Dennehy
▶ Bright college jock O'Keefe is lured by dewey-eyed siren Allen to join bizarre cult run by ascetic guru Fonda and soon renounces his family and former life. O'Keefe's well-to-do parents Dennehy and Ashley hire deprogrammer Woods to kidnap son and break him of cult's hold. O'Keefe weakens, however, when Fonda and Allen come looking for him. Thought-provoking topical drama boasts superior cast.
Dist.: Embassy

SPLIT SECOND 1953
★ **NR Mystery-Suspense 1:26 B&W**
Dir: Dick Powell *Cast:* Stephen McNally, Alexis Smith, Jan Sterling, Keith Andes, Arthur Hunnicutt, Paul Kelly
▶ Smith, Sterling, Hunnicutt, and others are taken hostage in a deserted Nevada town by escaped con McNally's gang. Turns out there's a good reason why the town's empty: it's about to be nuked in a government atomic test. Good performances in this compelling directorial debut for Powell.
Dist.: Turner

SPLITZ 1984
☆ **PG-13 Comedy 1:29**
☑ Brief nudity, adult situations, explicit language
Dir: Domonic Paris *Cast:* Robin Johnson, Patti Lee, Barbara M. Bingham, Shirley Stoler, Chuck McQuary
▶ At Hooter College, female rock band helps

nerd sorority win strip basketball and lingerie wrestling contests, much to the dismay of dictator dean Stoler who wants to replace their house with a sewage plant. *Porky's* clone features surprisingly little nudity and insulting ethnic stereotypes.
Dist.: Vestron

SPOILERS, THE 1942
★★ NR Western 1:27 B&W
Dir: Ray Enright ***Cast:*** Marlene Dietrich, Randolph Scott, John Wayne, Margaret Lindsay, Harry Carey, Richard Barthelmess
▶ During the Alaskan gold rush, prospector Wayne is cheated out of his claim by crooked official Scott. Bad blood between Wayne and Scott continues in rivalry over saloon-owner Dietrich, whom they both admire. Lively, earthy saga culminates in one of the most elaborate and imitated barroom brawls in cinema.
Dist.: MCA

SPONTANEOUS COMBUSTION 1989
★ R Horror 1:40
☑ Explicit language, graphic violence
Dir: Tobe Hooper ***Cast:*** Brad Dourif, Cynthia Bain, Jon Cypher, William Prince, Dey Young, Melinda Dillon
▶ Dourif has the power to reduce people to piles of flaming ashes. He discovers that he and his parents were victims of a radiation experiment conducted by mogul Prince. Doomed to melt down himself, Dourif seeks fiery revenge. Director Hooper is usually a reliable source of scares, but this is too tongue-in-cheek to generate concern for the main character's fate. **(CC)**
Dist.: Media

SPOOKS RUN WILD 1941
★ NR Comedy 1:05 B&W
Dir: Phil Rosen ***Cast:*** Bela Lugosi, Leo Gorcey, Huntz Hall, Bobby Jordan, David Gorcey, Sammy Morrison
▶ The East Side Kids leave the city for sleepaway camp but decide to sneak out for dates. When one kid is injured, they find refuge in the house of Lugosi, a magician with a mute dwarf assistant named Luigi. Is Lugosi the maniac who's been stalking the countryside? It helps if you like low comedy. Sample dialogue: "I don't like that guy's altitude."
Dist.: Goodtimes

SPORTING CLUB, THE 1971
☆ R Drama 1:44
☑ Brief nudity, explicit language, violence
Dir: Larry Peerce ***Cast:*** Robert Fields, Maggie Blye, Nicolas Coster, Jack Warden, Richard Dysart
▶ An upper-class group spends a weekend at an exclusive Michigan club where memberships are handed down from father to son. The drinking and partying soon escalate into violent war games, climaxing in a fatal duel. Irritating adaptation of the Thomas McGuane novel with hateful characters and self-conscious direction.
Dist.: Nelson

SPRING BREAK 1983
★★ R Comedy 1:41
☑ Nudity, adult situations, explicit language, adult humor
Dir: Sean S. Cunningham ***Cast:*** David Knell, Perry Lang, Steve Bassett, Paul Land, Corinne Alphen, Donald Symington
▶ Virginal college boys Knell and Lang, on spring vacation in Fort Lauderdale, meet experienced party vets Land and Bassett, who introduce them to beer, wet T-shirt contests, and willing women. Knell's politician stepfather Symington, leery of bad press, sends henchman to end boys' escapades and close motel housing them, but timely blackmail scheme assures the fun won't stop. Harmless teen comedy is reminiscent of beach-blanket pics of early sixties.
Dist.: RCA/Columbia

SPRING FEVER 1983 Canadian
★★★ PG Comedy/Sports 1:40
☑ Adult situations, explicit language
Dir: Joseph Scanlan ***Cast:*** Susan Anton, Frank Converse, Jessica Walter, Stephen Young, Carling Bassett, Shawn Foltz
▶ Las Vegas showgirl Anton escorts daughter Bassett to Junior National Tennis Championships in Florida. Reigning champ Foltz and snobby rich mom Walter lead others to ostracize Anton and Bassett. Anton romances reporter Converse while Bassett casually hustles older males on tennis court. Sports real-life tennis stars Bassett and Foltz.
Dist.: Vestron

SPRING SYMPHONY 1986 German
☆ PG-13 Biography/Music 1:46
☑ Adult situations
Dir: Peter Schamoni ***Cast:*** Nastassia Kinski, Herbert Gronemeyer, Rolf Hoppe, Anja-Christine Preussler, Edda Seippel, Andre Heller
▶ Life story of composer Robert Schumann (Gronemeyer) centers on his romance with Kinski, the musically gifted daughter of renowned music teacher Hoppe. Schumann studies under Hoppe and blossoms into major pianist-composer. Teacher and pupil have falling out when Hoppe tries to end Schumann's romance with Kinski. [S]
Dist.: Vestron

SPRINGTIME IN THE ROCKIES 1942
★★★★ NR Musical 1:31
Dir: Irving Cummings ***Cast:*** Betty Grable, John Payne, Carmen Miranda, Cesar Romero, Harry James, Jackie Gleason
▶ Bickering Broadway stars Grable and Payne separate and accidentally wind up at the same resort on the banks of Lake Louise. While Harry James and his Music Makers swing up a storm on the bandstand, Grable pretends to romance leering Romero, and Payne

appears to be headed for the arms of bizarre Brazilian Miranda. Romero is at his big-shouldered best here. In fact, no one fails to excel in this near-perfect forties musical. Songs include "Chattanooga Choo Choo" and "I Had the Craziest Dream." **(CC)**
Dist.: Key

SPY IN BLACK, THE 1939 British
★ ★ **NR Espionage 1:22 B&W**
Dir: Michael Powell *Cast:* Conrad Veidt, Valerie Hobson, Sebastian Shaw, Marius Goring, June Duprez, Helen Haye
▶ During World War I, German U-Boat captain Veidt's mission takes him to the Scottish isles, where he encounters teacher Hobson, who's working for his side. Or is she? Hobson's ultimate loyalty is one of the many intriguing issues in this well-plotted, skillfully directed thriller. Also known as *U-Boat 29.*
Dist.: Nelson

SPY WHO CAME IN FROM THE COLD, THE 1965
★ ★ ★ ★ **NR Espionage 1:52 B&W**
Dir: Martin Ritt *Cast:* Richard Burton, Claire Bloom, Oskar Werner, Peter Van Eyck, Sam Wanamaker, George Voskovec
▶ Burned-out British spy Burton is recalled from Berlin for mission to eliminate Van Eyck, head of East German counter-espionage. Elaborate ruse in London, during which he romances Bloom, a librarian with Communist sympathies, discredits Burton as drunken foul-up ready to defect. Burton painfully learns he is merely a pawn in larger scheme. Grimly realistic depiction of espionage was adapted from the John le Carré best-seller. **(CC)**
Dist.: Paramount

SPY WHO LOVED ME, THE 1977 British
★ ★ ★ ★ **PG Espionage/Action-Adventure 2:05**
☑ Adult situations, violence
Dir: Lewis Gilbert *Cast:* Roger Moore, Barbara Bach, Curt Jurgens, Richard Kiel, Caroline Munro, Walter Gotell
▶ Shipping magnate Jurgens steals both American and Soviet subs, hoping to start World War III and build new underseas civilization in aftermath of destruction. Agent 007 must team with beautiful Russian agent Bach to thwart Jurgens's plan. Tenth Bond epic introduced the toothy Jaws (Kiel). Don't miss the opening ski sequence with breathtaking stunt at climax. Carly Simon's theme song was a pop hit.
Dist.: MGM/UA

SQUARE DANCE 1987
★ ★ ★ **PG-13 Drama 1:52**
☑ Adult situations, explicit language
Dir: Daniel Petrie *Cast:* Jane Alexander, Jason Robards, Winona Ryder, Rob Lowe, Deborah Richter, Guich Koock
▶ Texas teenager Ryder, who lives with farmer grandfather Robards, goes to the city to start relationship with trashy mother Alexander,

whom she never really knew. Ryder comes of age and gets involved with retarded Lowe. Sensitive and well-crafted. Ryder is winning; Lowe and Alexander are effective in departures from their usual screen personas.
Dist.: Pacific Arts

SQUEEZE, THE 1977 British
☆ **NR Drama 1:46**
☑ Nudity, violence
Dir: Michael Apted *Cast:* Stacy Keach, Freddie Starr, Edward Fox, Stephen Boyd, David Hemmings, Carol White
▶ Keach is private investigator who comes out of an alcoholic treatment program and into a kidnapping case involving his now-remarried ex-wife White, held by a gang of thugs led by Irish-accented Boyd. Plodding drama makes up for lack of style and originality by nasty, sadistic doings.
Dist.: Warner

SQUEEZE, THE 1987
★ ★ **PG-13 Comedy 1:42**
☑ Adult situations, explicit language
Dir: Roger Young *Cast:* Michael Keaton, Rae Dawn Chong, John Davidson, Meat Loaf, Joe Pantoliano, Danny Aiello
▶ Down-on-his-luck artist Keaton finds a dead body and a mysterious package in his ex-wife's apartment. Thugs pursue him while collection agent Chong helps him uncover a lottery scam. Outlandish but entertaining mixture of laughs and action never takes itself too seriously; appealing performances by Keaton and Chong.
Dist.: HBO

SQUEEZE PLAY 1980
★ **R Comedy 1:32**
☑ Nudity, adult situations, explicit language
Dir: Samuel Weil *Cast:* Jim Harris, Jenni Hetrick, Rick Getlin, Al Corley
▶ In a New Jersey town, the men are so obsessed with softball that they ignore women. When one woman is denied a place on the team, the ladies retaliate by forming their own squad to take on the guys. Maintains the noisy atmosphere of a wild party, including a wet T-shirt contest.
Dist.: HBO

SQUIRM 1976
★ **PG Horror 1:33**
☑ Explicit language, violence
Dir: Jeff Lieberman *Cast:* Don Scardino, Patricia Pearcy, R. A. Dow, Jean Sullivan, Peter MacLean, Fran Higgins
▶ Georgia storm downs power lines over a nest of sandworms, turning them into vicious man-eaters. Nearby town succumbs to panic as voracious worms go on an eating spree. Low-budget thriller is scary as well as preposterous; opening credits claim plot is based on a true story.
Dist.: Vestron

STACKING 1987
★ ★ ★ **PG Drama 1:49**
☑ Adult situations, explicit language
Dir: Martin Rosen **Cast:** Christine Lahti,
Frederic Forrest, Megan Follows, Jason Ge-
drick, Raymond Baker, Peter Coyote
▶ When her husband is injured, wife Lahti and
daughter Follows run the family farm them-
selves. Hard-drinking hired hand Forrest,
Lahti's old flame, helps out and develops feel-
ings for Follows. Homespun and honest, with
natural performances and lovely Montana
scenery. Slow pace poses a problem.
Dist.: Nelson

STACY'S KNIGHTS 1983
★ ★ ★ **PG Drama 1:34**
☑ Adult situations, explicit language, mild
violence
Dir: Jim Wilson **Cast:** Andra Millian, Kevin
Costner, Eve Lilith, Mike Reynolds, Garth
Howard, Ed Semenza
▶ Shy Millian is a born cardsharp. Her lover
Costner helps her win big but the casinos re-
sort to cheating and murder to stop the duo.
Millian decides to get even. A sleeper; attrac-
tive cast does well in this underdog tale.
Dist.: Vestron

STAGECOACH 1939
★ ★ ★ ★ **NR Western 1:39 B&W**
Dir: John Ford **Cast:** Claire Trevor, John
Wayne, Andy Devine, John Carradine,
Thomas Mitchell, Louise Platt, George Bancroft, Donald Meek
▶ Eight people ride a stagecoach through
Apache territory to the town of Lordsburg,
where they are joined by escaped convict
Wayne. Lawman Bancroft arrests Wayne, who
has plans to avenge his brother's and father's
murders. Prostitute Trevor falls in love with the
rangy outlaw as Indians attack. Classic film
was director Ford's first Western since silent era
and marked beginning of unparalleled work
in the genre. Mitchell won Supporting Oscar;
Wayne became a star. Oscar for Best Score;
remade twice.
Dist.: Warner

STAGE DOOR 1937
★ ★ ★ ★ **NR Drama 1:31 B&W**
Dir: Gregory La Cava **Cast:** Katharine Hep-
burn, Ginger Rogers, Adolphe Menjou, Gail
Patrick, Andrea Leeds, Constance Collier,
Eve Arden, Franklin Pangborn, Jack Carson,
Lucille Ball, Ann Miller
▶ Marvelous adaptation of an Edna Ferber–
George S. Kaufman play about struggling ac-
tresses rooming at the Footlights Club blends
drama, comedy, and unbeatable dialogue
into a bittersweet tribute to ambition and en-
durance. Hepburn (with her memorable line
"The calla lilies are in bloom again") is a
wealthy dilettante whose motives are ques-
tioned by earthy Rogers; Leeds won an Oscar
nomination as a despairing artist.
Dist.: Turner

STAGE DOOR CANTEEN 1943
★ ★ ★ **NR Musical 2:12 B&W**
Dir: Frank Borzage **Cast:** Cheryl Walker, William Terry, Marjorie Riordan, Lon McCallister,
Margaret Early, Michael Harrison
▶ New York's famous World War II club for enlisted men is the setting for flimsy romance
among soldiers on leave and three hostesses,
but picture's real asset is its incredible array of
over seventy guest stars, ranging from Katharine Hepburn to Harpo Marx to Tallulah Bankhead to Johnny Weissmuller. Katherine Cornell, in her only film appearance, performs
from *Romeo and Juliet*; Peggy Lee, Gracie
Fields, Count Basie, Benny Goodman, Yehudi
Menuhin, and Ray Bolger offer "Why Don't You
Do Right," "We Mustn't Say Goodbye," and
other songs.
Dist.: Various

STAGE FRIGHT 1950
★ ★ ★ **NR Mystery-Suspense 1:50 B&W**
Dir: Alfred Hitchcock **Cast:** Jane Wyman,
Marlene Dietrich, Michael Wilding, Richard
Todd, Alastair Sim, Kay Walsh
▶ Acting student Wyman hides ex-boyfriend
Todd, who claims his mistress Dietrich framed
him for murder. Playing detective, Wyman
takes a job as Dietrich's maid to learn the
truth. Arrival of suave but suspicious policeman Wilding complicates the plot. Tricky, underrated mystery falls short of Hitchcock's best
work, but offers more than enough humor and
suspense. Dietrich is superb singing Cole Porter's "The Laziest Gal in Town."
Dist.: Warner

STAGE STRUCK 1957
★ **NR Drama 1:35**
Dir: Sidney Lumet **Cast:** Henry Fonda,
Susan Strasberg, Joan Greenwood, Christopher Plummer, Herbert Marshall
▶ Young New Englander Strasberg comes to
New York to be an actress, and snags the
hearts of producer Fonda, playwright Plummer, and actor Marshall. Fonda won't help her
career for ethical reasons until temperamental star Greenwood walks out his production,
and Strasberg triumphs in her place. Familiar
story based on the play *Morning Glory* by Zoe
Atkins; filmed before 1933.
Dist.: VCI

STAKEOUT 1987
★ ★ ★ ★ **R Comedy/Drama 1:55**
☑ Nudity, adult situations, explicit language, violence
Dir: John Badham **Cast:** Richard Dreyfuss,
Emilio Estevez, Madeleine Stowe, Aidan
Quinn, Dan Lauria, Forest Whitaker
▶ When dangerous killer Quinn escapes
prison, detectives Dreyfuss and Estevez stake
out home of Quinn's girlfriend Stowe. Surveillance grows complicated when Dreyfuss falls
in love with Stowe. Meanwhile, Quinn draws
closer to her home, where he stashed loot
years before. Popular cops-and-robbers com-

edy rehashes buddy-cop formula with great success due to fine performances and plenty of laughs. **(CC)**
Dist.: Buena Vista

STALAG 17 1953
★ ★ ★ ★ ★ **NR Comedy/Drama 2:00 B&W**
Dir: Billy Wilder   *Cast:* William Holden, Don Taylor, Otto Preminger, Robert Strauss, Peter Graves, Harvey Lembeck
▶ In a World War II POW camp, loner-hustler Holden rejects patriotism and escape plans of cohorts to pursue life of comfort. Camp commandant Preminger repeatedly thwarts escape efforts, so other Americans suspect Holden of spying. But when captured pilot Taylor faces execution for sabotage of German train, Holden turns from heel to hero. Classic war drama mixes laughs with intrigue. Holden won an Oscar in this adaptation of the Broadway play. Real-life producer-director Preminger shines as vicious Nazi.
Dist.: Paramount

STALKING MOON, THE 1969
★ ★ ★ **G Western 1:49**
Dir: Robert Mulligan   *Cast:* Gregory Peck, Eva Marie Saint, Robert Forster, Noland Clay, Russell Thorson, Frank Silvera
▶ On the eve of his retirement, long-time Army scout Peck helps rescue Saint from an extended captivity with the Apaches. Her brutal Indian husband will not let her get away so easily however, and as Peck leads the woman and her child to safety, he begins to stalk them. Takes a long time getting to final confrontation.
Dist.: Warner

STAND ALONE 1985
★ ★ ★ ★ **R Drama 1:34**
☑ Explicit language, violence
Dir: Alan Beattie   *Cast:* Charles Durning, Pam Grier, James Keach, Bert Remsen, Barbara Sammeth, Lu Leonard
▶ Decorated World War II veteran Durning witnesses murder by drug dealers and assists police detective Keach. Lawyer Grier advises Durning not to testify against "cocaine cowboys," but Durning, fed up with society's tolerance of crime, fingers the guilty parties and then arms himself with war souvenirs for showdown. Good chance to see Durning in a leading role.
Dist.: New World

STAND AND DELIVER 1988
★ ★ ★ ★ **PG Biography 1:43**
☑ Explicit language
Dir: Ramon Menendez   *Cast:* Edward James Olmos, Lou Diamond Phillips, Rosana de Soto, Andy Garcia, Will Gotay, Virginia Paris
▶ True story of Los Angeles math teacher Jaime Escalante (Olmos) whose charismatic tutelage guided students from poor Hispanic background to record success on advanced math placement exams. Despite authorities

who suspect they cheated, Escalante and the kids overcome the odds. An inspirational tale to cherish; powerhouse performance by Oscar-nominated Olmos mixes wry humor, toughness, and tenderness. **(CC)**
Dist.: Warner

STAND BY ME 1986
★ ★ ★ ★ **R Drama 1:29**
☑ Explicit language
Dir: Rob Reiner   *Cast:* Wil Wheaton, River Phoenix, Corey Feldman, Jerry O'Connell, Kiefer Sutherland, John Cusack
▶ Twelve-year-old writer-to-be Wheaton joins misunderstood tough Phoenix, daredevil Feldman, and overweight wimp O'Connell in adventurous search for the body of a boy killed by train. Camping trip provides laughs, thrills, and tears, leading to climactic standoff with town bully Sutherland. Sweetly comic rite-of-passage drama is based on a short story by Stephen King. Narrated by Richard Dreyfuss, who plays the grownup Wheaton. **(CC)**
Dist.: RCA/Columbia

STAND UP AND CHEER 1934
★ **NR Musical 1:09 B&W**
Dir: Hamilton MacFadden   *Cast:* Warner Baxter, Madge Evans, Theresa Gardella, Skins Miller, Stepin Fetchit, Shirley Temple
▶ In the midst of the Great Depression, newly named "Secretary of Entertainment" Baxter puts together an entertainment-packed variety show to shake the country out of the blues. Fascinating glimpse at second-string thirties entertainers includes Fetchit discoursing with a penguin, Miller as a comic hillbilly, and Gardella as Aunt Jemima. Temple went into this film an unknown toddler and came out a star after her performance of "Baby Take a Bow."
Dist.: CBS/Fox

STANLEY 1972
★ **PG Horror 1:46**
☑ Explicit language, violence
Dir: William Grefe   *Cast:* Chris Robinson, Alex Rocco, Susan Carroll, Steve Alaimo, Mark Harris, Paul Avery
▶ Crazed Vietnam vet Robinson keeps a shackful of snakes. His enemy is Rocco, a man who makes snakeskin wallets. By the end of the film, Robinson has sicced his snakes on everybody he doesn't like. Produced during the wave of swarming animal horror films sparked by *Willard*, story sounds like it might be worth a few yucks, but isn't.
Dist.: VidAmerica

STANLEY & IRIS 1990
★ ★ ★ ★ **PG-13 Drama 1:44**
☑ Adult situations, explicit language
Dir: Martin Ritt   *Cast:* Jane Fonda, Robert De Niro, Swoosie Kurtz, Martha Plimpton, Harley Cross, Jamey Sheridan
▶ Recently widowed factory worker Fonda meets co-worker De Niro and learns the secret he tries so desperately to hide: he's illiterate. Fonda finally coaxes De Niro into letting her

teach him to read, and romance blossoms despite troubling personal problems. Over-earnest romance often comes across as too syrupy, and it's hard to believe Fonda as a working-class woman, even though she gives a secure performance. Older viewers, however, should find its old-fashioned sensibility appealing. **(CC)**
Dist.: MGM/UA

STAR CHAMBER, THE 1983
★ ★ ★ ★ R Drama 1:49
☑ Adult situations, explicit language, graphic violence
Dir: Peter Hyams *Cast:* Michael Douglas, Hal Holbrook, Sharon Gless, Yaphet Kotto, James B. Sikking, Joe Regalbuto
▶ Young judge Douglas, disgusted with crooks getting off on technicalities, is recruited by colleague Holbrook for vigilante group of justices. However, Douglas turns against the group when they slate innocent men for death. Exciting and provocative story deals intelligently with serious issues while not stinting on thrilling chases, crisp dialogue, and sharp plot twists.
Dist.: CBS/Fox

STARCHASER: THE LEGEND OF ORIN 1985
★ ★ PG Animation 1:38
☑ Explicit language, violence
Dir: Steven Hahn *Cast:* Voices of Joe Colligan, Carmen Argenziano, Noelle North, Anthony Delongia, Les Tremayne
▶ Orin, enslaved with his people by robot rulers of underground Mineworld, escapes with the help of a jeweled sword hilt. He hooks up with an adventurer and a beautiful princess. Together they battle the robots. Originally released in 3-D; loses some impact on video. Good animation compensates for script flaws.
Dist.: KVC

STARCRASH 1979 Italian
★ PG Sci-Fi 1:36
☑ Mild violence
Dir: Lewis Coates (Luigi Cozzi) *Cast:* Marjoe Gortner, Caroline Munro, Christopher Plummer, David Hasselhoff, Robert Tessier, Joe Spinell
▶ Evil inventor of doom machine sets out to destroy the universe; outer-space pilots Gortner and Munro try to stop him. Moves fast but not convincingly; flat dialogue and acting (save for the dependable Plummer), laughable costumes lead to unintentional comedy.
Dist.: Nelson

STAR CRYSTAL 1986
☆ R Sci-Fi 1:34
☑ Explicit language, violence
Dir: Lance Lindsay *Cast:* C. Jutson Campbell, John W. Smith, Faye Bolt, Taylor Kingsley, Marcia Linn
▶ In 2032, scientific expedition to Mars picks up alien who kills most humans on space station. Survivors seek to flee on shuttle to earth, but alien tags along for more mayhem and

murder. Low-budget sci-fi entry suffers from uneven script.
Dist.: New World

STARDUST MEMORIES 1980
★ PG Comedy 1:31 B&W
☑ Adult situations, explicit language, adult humor
Dir: Woody Allen *Cast:* Woody Allen, Charlotte Rampling, Jessica Harper, Marie-Christine Barrault, Tony Roberts, Daniel Stern, Amy Wright
▶ Troubled film director Allen escapes for seminar at resort hotel where he relives old romances in his head while carrying on new ones in the flesh. Meanwhile fans and critics alike complain his recent self-indulgent films aren't as good as earlier comedies. Pseudo-autobiographical effort comically skewers both Allen and his devotees. Many find the laughs are buried under the surrealistic style and somewhat mean-spirited tone.
Dist.: CBS/Fox

STAR 80 1983
★ ★ R Biography 1:43
☑ Nudity, adult situations, explicit language, graphic violence
Dir: Bob Fosse *Cast:* Mariel Hemingway, Eric Roberts, Cliff Robertson, Carroll Baker, Roger Rees, David Clennon
▶ Sleazy hustler Paul Snider (Roberts) discovers beautiful teen Dorothy Stratten (Hemingway) hawking ice cream in Vancouver and soon persuades her to pose nude. Photos lead to spread in *Playboy* and marriage of Stratten to Snider despite warnings from publisher Hugh Hefner (Robertson). When Stratten's acting career takes off, she leaves Snider who seeks revenge in gory fashion. Quality filmmaking from director Fosse and excellent work by two leads, but story is depressing and Roberts's character disturbing to watch.
Dist.: Warner

STAR IS BORN, A 1937
★ ★ ★ ★ NR Drama 1:51
Dir: William Wellman *Cast:* Fredric March, Janet Gaynor, Adolphe Menjou, Lionel Stander, Andy Devine, May Robson
▶ Unknown actress Gaynor marries alcoholic movie star March. She tries to help him as she becomes a star and he goes personally and professionally downhill. Despite two subsequent remakes, this may be the finest of the three; Gaynor's innocence and March's poignance are extremely moving. One of the all-time great emotional closing lines: "This is Mrs. Norman Maine."
Dist.: Various

STAR IS BORN, A 1954
★ ★ ★ ★ ★ PG Musical 2:34
☑ Adult situations
Dir: George Cukor *Cast:* Judy Garland, James Mason, Charles Bickford, Jack Carson, Tom Noonan
▶ Hard-drinking actor Mason on his way

down the Hollywood ladder marries ingenue Garland on her way up. Mason deteriorates as Garland watches helplessly. Tearjerker with tunes pulls out all the stops dramatically (Mason's harrowing "I need a job!" speech at the Oscar ceremonies) and musically (Garland's memorable torch song, "The Man Who Got Away"). Reissued version has extra numbers and cut footage reinserted.
Dist.: Warner

STAR IS BORN, A 1976
★★★★★ R Musical 2:20
⊙ Brief nudity, adult situations, explicit language
Dir: Frank Pierson *Cast:* Barbra Streisand, Kris Kristofferson, Paul Mazursky, Gary Busey, Oliver Clark, Sally Kirkland
▶ Remake of 1937 and 1954 films changes venue from movies to music. Over-the-hill rock star Kristofferson falls in love with unheralded singer Streisand. As her career skyrockets and his declines, their marriage heads towards a tragic end. Familiar story mishandled in new version, but Streisand's big production numbers will wow fans. Song "Evergreen," by Streisand and Paul Williams, won Oscar.
Dist.: Warner

STARLIGHT HOTEL 1988 New Zealand
★★★ PG Drama 1:30
⊙ Explicit language
Dir: Sam Pillsbury *Cast:* Peter Phelps, Greer Robson, Marshall Napier, Alice Fraser, Patrick Smyth, Bruce Phillips
▶ In Depression-era New Zealand, thirteen-year-old Robson, deserted by her father, runs away from her aunt and uncle. She meets sympathetic fugitive Phelps and a close relationship forms as they go on the lam. Commonplace plot, acted and directed with sensitivity against stunning scenery.
Dist.: Republic

STARMAN 1984
★★★★ PG Fantasy/Romance 1:55
⊙ Adult situations, explicit language, violence
Dir: John Carpenter *Cast:* Jeff Bridges, Karen Allen, Charles Martin Smith, Richard Jaeckel, Robert Phalen, Tony Edwards
▶ Shipwrecked extraterrestrial Bridges abducts widow Allen for help getting to rendezvous with mother ship. Government agents pursue them. During cross-country chase Allen loses fear of the alien and falls for him. Charming and uplifting love story in sci fi wrapping carried by strong turns from fetching Allen and impressively convincing Bridges. **(CC)**
Dist.: RCA/Columbia

STAR OF MIDNIGHT 1935
★ NR Mystery-Suspense/Comedy 1:30 B&W
Dir: Stephen Roberts *Cast:* William Powell, Ginger Rogers, Paul Kelly, Gene Lockhart, Ralph Morgan, Leslie Fenton
▶ When he becomes a suspect in an actress's

disappearance and a columnist's murder, lawyer Powell must find the culprit to prove his innocence. While solving the mystery, the attorney finds time for drinking and romance with Rogers. Nifty mystery-comedy provides plenty of opportunities for Powell's wit.
Dist.: Turner

STARS AND BARS 1988
★ R Comedy 1:38
⊙ Brief nudity, adult situations, explicit language
Dir: Pat O'Connor *Cast:* Daniel Day-Lewis, Harry Dean Stanton, Spalding Gray, Joan Cusack, Martha Plimpton, Steven Wright, Matthew Cowles, Maury Chaykin, Dierdre O'Connell, Will Patton, Glenne Headly, Laurie Metcalf
▶ Proper English art dealer Day-Lewis takes job in New York gallery and must fend off advances of owner's fifteen-year-old daughter Plimpton and amorous New Yorker Cusack. First major project is trip to Georgia to purchase rare painting from backwoods Southerner Stanton and his inbred clan. Brit-out-of-water comedy boasts terrific cast but tends to be broad and uneven. **(CC)**
Dist.: RCA/Columbia

STARS LOOK DOWN, THE 1940 British
★★★ NR Drama 1:50 B&W
Dir: Carol Reed *Cast:* Michael Redgrave, Margaret Lockwood, Emlyn Williams, Nancy Price, Edward Rigby, Cecil Parker
▶ College-educated Redgrave, son of miner Rigby, returns to his hometown and tries to help the miners. A strike and underground disaster make life hard for the men; Redgrave must also deal with unfaithful wife Lockwood. Outstanding adaptation of the A. J. Cronin novel.
Dist.: KVC

STARSTRUCK 1982 Australian
★ PG Musical/Comedy 1:35
⊙ Brief nudity, adult situations, explicit language
Dir: Gillian Armstrong *Cast:* Jo Kennedy, Ross O'Donovan, Pat Evison, Margo Lee, Max Cullen, Ned Lander
▶ Fourteen-year-old hustler O'Donovan schemes to make singing star of cousin Kennedy. New punk look and publicity stunt turn Kennedy into a media hit, but to succeed she must compromise her art and abandon O'Donovan. When family business teeters on edge of bankruptcy, O'Donovan and Kennedy reunite to seek grand prize in talent contest. Updated take on old-style "let's put on a show" yarns mixes mild spoof with serious musical numbers.
Dist.: Nelson

STARTING OVER 1979
★★★★ R Romance/Comedy 1:45
⊡ Adult situations, explicit language
Dir: Alan J. Pakula *Cast:* Burt Reynolds, Jill

Clayburgh, Candice Bergen, Mary Kay Place, Frances Sternhagen, Charles Durning
▶ Poignant and clever look at life after marriage from writer James L. Brooks: divorced writer Reynolds, dumped by wife Bergen, tries to start over with teacher Clayburgh. Bergen's reappearance threatens the new relationship. Reynolds's understated performance is one of his best; Clayburgh and Bergen (both Oscar-nominated) are disarming. Funniest scene: Reynolds's nervous breakdown at Bloomingdale's.
Dist.: Paramount

STAR TREK—THE MOTION PICTURE 1979
★ ★ ★ ★ G Sci-Fi 2:12
Dir: Robert Wise *Cast:* William Shatner, Leonard Nimoy, DeForest Kelley, James Doohan, Persis Khambatta, Stephen Collins, George Takei, Walter Koenig
▶ Mysterious, gigantic cloud heads from outer space towards Earth; starship *Enterprise* investigates. Captain Kirk (Shatner), Spock (Nimoy), and crew learn their nemesis is a living machine, superintelligent but without emotions. It takes over body of ship's navigator Khambatta and will wipe out the human race unless quick thinking by crew can save the day. First big-screen outing for characters of cult TV series can be ponderous. Next three sequels are livelier.
Dist.: Paramount

STAR TREK II: THE WRATH OF KHAN 1982
★ ★ ★ ★ PG Sci-Fi 1:53
☑ Explicit language, violence
Dir: Nicholas Meyer *Cast:* William Shatner, Leonard Nimoy, DeForest Kelley, Ricardo Montalban, James Doohan, Kirstie Alley, Walter Koenig, George Takei
▶ Evil outlaw Montalban, exiled years before by Kirk (Shatner), escapes in stolen starship and lays trap for nemesis, stealing Genesis technology that can destroy or re-create whole planets. Kirk leaves desk-jockey admiral's job to lead ragtag crew and veteran officers in battle of wits with malevolent Montalban. Sequel has much more life than original. Top-notch effects, hammy turn by Montalban, warm repartee among Kirk and Co., climactic phaser-'em-up, and tearjerker ending add up to engaging trek.
Dist.: Paramount

STAR TREK III: THE SEARCH FOR SPOCK 1984
★ ★ ★ ★ PG Sci-Fi 1:45
☑ Violence
Dir: Leonard Nimoy *Cast:* William Shatner, Leonard Nimoy, DeForest Kelley, James Doohan, George Takei, Walter Koenig, Christopher Lloyd, Judith Anderson
▶ Having given his life to save his friends in *Star Trek II*, Spock (Nimoy) is buried on experimental planet Genesis. When it appears the planet may have brought Spock back to life, Captain Kirk (Shatner) and his loyal officers

steal their mothballed ship to rescue him. There they find a youth who may be Spock regenerated and an ambitious Klingon (Lloyd) who hopes to steal the power of Genesis. Third offering to Trekkies combines wit and action and shrewdly emphasizes winning characters instead of special effects. (CC)
Dist.: Paramount

STAR TREK IV: THE VOYAGE HOME 1986
★ ★ ★ ★ PG Sci-Fi 1:59
☑ Explicit language
Dir: Leonard Nimoy *Cast:* William Shatner, Leonard Nimoy, DeForest Kelley, James Doohan, George Takei, Walter Koenig, Cahterine Hicks, Jane Wyatt
▶ Returning home in Klingon vessel to face punishment for theft and destruction of *Enterprise* and other infractions, Kirk (Shatner), Spock (Nimoy), and crew discover unidentified probe is laying waste to Earth. Probe will quit destruction only when answered by call of now-extinct humpback whale, so heroes time-travel to twentieth-century San Francisco to whalenap specimens from biologist Hicks. Generally series lose gas with each outing, but plentiful humor and nifty ecology story make fourth entry arguably the best of the TV spin-offs. (CC)
Dist.: Paramount

STAR TREK V: THE FINAL FRONTIER 1989
★ ★ ★ ★ PG Sci-Fi 1:45
☑ Explicit language, violence
Dir: William Shatner *Cast:* William Shatner, Leonard Nimoy, DeForest Kelley, Laurence Luckinbill, David Warner, James Doohan, Walter Koenig, Nichelle Nichols, George Takei
▶ Cult leader Luckinbill takes over remote planetary outpost to lure starship to the scene, then hijacks *Enterprise* for journey through universe's Barrier and a meeting with God; Kirk is skeptical ("Why does God need a starship?" he wonders) but Spock has a strange reluctance to stop Luckinbill. Fifth outing undeservedly got worst reviews of series. Thunderously paced, ultimately heartfelt, and provocative. Intense, charismatic performance by Luckinbill makes him one of series' best guest stars. (CC)
Dist.: Paramount

START THE REVOLUTION WITHOUT ME 1970
★ ★ ★ PG Comedy 1:30
☑ Brief nudity, adult situations, explicit language, violence
Dir: Bud Yorkin *Cast:* Gene Wilder, Donald Sutherland, Hugh Griffith, Billie Whitelaw, Victor Spinetti, Orson Welles
▶ Peasant twins and their aristocrat counterparts are mixed up at birth; years later, the now-grown mismatched sets (each played by Wilder and Sutherland) find themselves on opposite sides of the French Revolution. Generally amusing if uneven slapstick fun has gar-

nered a cult following since its initial release.
Dist.: Warner

STAR WARS 1977
★★★★★ PG Sci-Fi/Action-Adventure 2:01
[✓] Adult situations, mild violence
Dir: George Lucas ***Cast:*** Harrison Ford, Mark Hamill, Carrie Fisher, Alec Guinness, Peter Cushing, David Prowse, Anthony Daniels, Kenny Baker
▶ High-tech, action-packed reworking of old Saturday matinee serials portrays efforts of adventurer Hamill and his mystic mentor Guinness to rescue princess Fisher from clutches of evil despot Cushing and his sinister minion Darth Vader (with voice of James Earl Jones). They are assisted by mercenary maverick Ford and trio of nonhumans, who reluctantly join rebel forces in attempt to defeat Cushing and his menacing Death Star. Fun and funny, box office legend changed Hollywood's approach to filmmaking. Winner of six technical Oscars and Best Score by John Williams. *The Empire Strikes Back* and *Return of the Jedi* completed trilogy. **(CC)**
Dist.: CBS/Fox

STATE FAIR 1945
★★★★ NR Musical 1:40
Dir: Walter Lang ***Cast:*** Jeanne Crain, Dana Andrews, Dick Haymes, Vivian Blaine, Charles Winninger, Fay Bainter
▶ Midwestern family finds adventure and romance at the Iowa State Fair. Dad Winninger and mom Bainter vie for hog and mincemeat honors. Son Haymes falls for married singer Blaine while daughter Crain meets reporter Andrews. Brimming with color and charm; grand Rodgers and Hammerstein score includes the Oscar-winning "It Might as Well Be Spring." Remake of 1933 film, remade again in 1962. **(CC)**
Dist.: CBS/Fox

STATE FAIR 1962
★★★ NR Musical 1:58
Dir: Jose Ferrer ***Cast:*** Pat Boone, Bobby Darin, Pamela Tiffin, Ann-Margret, Alice Faye, Tom Ewell
▶ Third and worst remake of the Rodgers and Hammerstein musical switches the setting from Iowa to Texas. Farmer Ewell, son Boone, and daughter Tiffin go to Dallas with mom Faye, her brandied mincemeat, and a prize hog. Ann-Margret and Darin are the farm kids' sophisticated love interests. New songs written by Rodgers especially for this version include "More Than Just a Friend" and "This Isn't Heaven."
Dist.: CBS/Fox

STATE OF SIEGE 1973 French
★ NR Drama 2:00
[✓] Graphic violence
Dir: Costa-Gavras ***Cast:*** Yves Montand, Renato Salvatori, O. E. Hasse, Jacques Weber
▶ U.S. official Montand is kidnapped and interrogated by rebel guerrillas in Uruguay. The incident nearly brings down the government. Challenging but difficult to watch: political slant is controversial (some would say anti-American), the rebels are largely faceless, and Montand's character is clearly unsavory. The acting is excellent. [S]
Dist.: RCA/Columbia

STATE OF THE UNION 1948
★★★★ NR Drama 1:50 B&W
Dir: Frank Capra ***Cast:*** Spencer Tracy, Katharine Hepburn, Van Johnson, Angela Lansbury, Adolphe Menjou, Lewis Stone
▶ Idealistic millionaire Tracy, separated from wife Hepburn, is persuaded by lover and newspaper publisher Lansbury to run for Republican Presidential nomination. Hepburn agrees to pose as loving spouse for campaign but cannot tolerate changes in Tracy's values as he succumbs to fevered ambitions of Lansbury, party boss Menjou, and publicity flack Johnson. Nonetheless, Hepburn finds herself falling back in love. Some topical commentary is dated, but collision of morals and expediency in politics still remain pertinent subjects. All-star cast shines.
Dist.: MCA

STATIC 1985
☆ NR Comedy 1:33
[✓] Explicit language
Dir: Mark Romanek ***Cast:*** Keith Gordon, Amanda Plummer, Bob Gunton, Barton Heyman, Lily Knight, Jane Hoffman
▶ After a car crash claims his parents, Arizonian Gordon tries to create television set that can contact heaven; all he gets is static. Depressed, he hijacks a bus to call attention to his invention. Introverted performance by Gordon, who co-wrote script with Romanek, sets the tone for muted satire.
Dist.: Forum

STATION WEST 1948
★★ NR Western 1:20 B&W
Dir: Sidney Lanfield ***Cast:*** Dick Powell, Jane Greer, Agnes Moorehead, Burl Ives, Tom Powers, Gordon Oliver
▶ When two guards are murdered shipping gold, military man Powell goes undercover in a western town to investigate. The local crime boss turns out to be sexy Greer; Ives is a singing innkeeper who warbles "The Sun Is Shining Warm." Intriguing, intelligently plotted Western.
Dist.: Turner

STAY AS YOU ARE 1978 Italian
★★ NR Romance 1:45
[✓] Nudity, adult situations, explicit language
Dir: Alberto Lattuada ***Cast:*** Marcello Mastroianni, Nastassia Kinski, Francisco Rabal, Monica Randal
▶ In Florence, middle-aged Mastroianni is pursued by gorgeous young student Kinski. He is reluctant to consummate the relationship

because it turns out she might be his daughter by a former lover. Luscious Italian scenery and both Mastroianni and the frequently nude Kinski are perfectly cast; however, slow-moving story never catches fire. [S]
Dist.: Warner

STAY AWAY, JOE 1968
★ ★ PG Musical 1:42
☑ Adult situations
Dir: Peter Tewksbury *Cast:* Elvis Presley, Burgess Meredith, Joan Blondell, Quentin Dean, Katy Jurado, Thomas Gomez
▶ Presley, the half-breed son of Indian Meredith, gets a congressman to work out a deal involving cattle raising and government aid to the reservation. At the same time, he romances Dean behind the back of Blondell, her restrictive mom. All-around bad entertainment, with songs including "U.S. Male."
Dist.: MGM/UA

STAY HUNGRY 1976
★ ★ R Comedy/Drama 1:42
☑ Nudity, adult situations
Dir: Bob Rafelson *Cast:* Jeff Bridges, Sally Field, Arnold Schwarzenegger, Fannie Flagg, Scatman Crothers
▶ Wealthy Southern scion Bridges invests in local gym, is befriended by bodybuilder Schwarzenegger and blue collar worker Field, and battles corrupt business types who covet the property Quirky, ambitious plot is a bit too self-consciously eccentric, but leads give natural and unassuming performances.
Dist.: CBS/Fox

STAYING ALIVE 1983
★ ★ ★ PG Drama/Dance 1:36
☑ Adult situations, explicit language
Dir: Sylvester Stallone *Cast:* John Travolta, Cynthia Rhodes, Finola Hughes, Steve Inwood, Julie Bovasso, Frank Stallone
▶ *Saturday Night Fever* sequel takes place five years later as Travolta, now a dancer living in Manhattan, auditions for every musical in town and romances dancers Rhodes and Hughes. Cheerless wisecracks, run-of-the-mill dancing, and a few pleasant new Bee Gees songs (although most of the music is by Frank Stallone, Sly's brother). **(CC)**
Dist.: Paramount

STAYING TOGETHER 1989
★ ★ ★ R Drama 1:31
☑ Nudity, adult situations, explicit language
Dir: Lee Grant *Cast:* Sean Astin, Stockard Channing, Melinda Dillon, Jim Haynie, Levon Helm, Dermot Mulroney, Tim Quill, Daphne Zuniga, Dinah Manoff
▶ Brothers Quill, Mulroney, and Astin work in dad Haynie's chicken restaurant and deal with personal crises, such as sale of family business, Quill's affair with politician Channing, and Mulroney's pursuit of Zuniga, who is engaged to another. Solid direction and writing effectively evoke emotions of everyday ex-

istence. Vivid ensemble led by charming young starring trio. **(CC)**
Dist.: HBO

STEALING HEAVEN 1989 British
★ R Romance 1:50
☑ Nudity, adult situations
Dir: Clive Donner *Cast:* Derek de Lint, Kim Thomson, Denholm Elliott, Bernard Hepton, Kenneth Cranham, Patsy Byrne
▶ In twelfth-century France, philosopher de Lint and pretty scholar Thomson fall in love. He tries to remain true to his vow of chastity but they become lovers, bringing the wrath of the church upon them. Literate screenplay and accomplished acting but very dry story based on the lives of Abelard and Heloise. Available in an unrated version.
Dist.: Virgin

STEALING HOME 1988
★ ★ ★ ★ PG-13 Drama 1:38
☑ Adult situations, explicit language
Dir: Steven Kampmann, Will Aldis *Cast:* Mark Harmon, Jodie Foster, Blair Brown, Jonathan Silverman, Harold Ramis, John Shea
▶ His career on the skids, baseball player Harmon returns home upon learning of childhood friend Foster's suicide. Memories of the unforgettable Foster help Harmon come to terms with his own life. Sentimental story pulls out all the stops; Foster is superb.
Dist.: Warner

STEAL THE SKY 1988
★ ★ ★ NR Action-Adventure/MFTV 1:48
☑ Adult situations, explicit language
Dir: John Hancock *Cast:* Mariel Hemingway, Ben Cross, Sasson Gabai, Mark Rolston, Nicolas Surovy, Ronald Guttman
▶ Iraqi pilot Cross romances American Hemingway, not realizing that she is an agent of the Israeli secret service. Her cover is blown when she asks him to defect with one of his nation's new MIG fighters, but she proves her sincerity by helping his wife and children escape in a heart-pounding chase through the desert. Good air action, but Cross is wooden and Hemingway doesn't look her best.
Dist.: Image

STEAMBOAT BILL, JR. 1928
★ ★ ★ NR Comedy 1:11 B&W
Dir: Charles Riesner *Cast:* Buster Keaton, Ernest Torrence, Tom Lewis, Tom McGuire, Marion Byron, Joe Keaton
▶ Steamboat Bill (Torrence), a Mississippi riverboat pilot, is counting on his college-educated son to help stave off bankruptcy, but Junior (Keaton) turns out to be a fop in love with his father's rival. Dazzling silent comedy traces Keaton's progress from wastrel to hero in a series of breathtaking sight gags. Climactic typhoon sequence contains one of the most dangerous stunts ever filmed: entire wall of an actual house collapses on Keaton,

who's saved by standing where an upstairs window lands.
Dist.: Video Yesteryear

STEAMING 1986 British
☆ R Drama 1:35
☑ Nudity, explicit language
Dir: Joseph Losey *Cast:* Vanessa Redgrave, Sarah Miles, Diana Dors, Patti Love, Brenda Bruce, Felicity Dean
▶ Group of women share confidences and form close relationships in a London steambath. When the bath is slated for demolition, they band together to protest. Strong cast with Love and Dors especially shining. However, talkiness, thick accents, and dated feminist slant severely limit appeal. Based on the Nell Dunn play.
Dist.: New World

STEEL DAWN 1987
★ ★ R Action-Adventure 1:40
☑ Brief nudity, violence
Dir: Lance Hool *Cast:* Patrick Swayze, Lisa Niemi, Christopher Neame, Brion James, Brett Hool, Anthony Zerbe
▶ In a postnuclear future, wandering swordsman Swayze befriends widow Niemi (Swayze's real-life wife) and her son Hool. Greedy land baron Zerbe wants Niemi's land for its precious water supply and dispatches assassin Neame to kill Swayze. Story derivative of *Mad Max* has impressive swordplay and charismatic Swayze.
Dist.: Vestron

STEELE JUSTICE 1987
★ ★ ★ R Action-Adventure 1:35
☑ Brief nudity, adult situations, explicit language, violence
Dir: Robert Boris *Cast:* Martin Kove, Sela Ward, Ronny Cox, Bernie Casey, Joseph Campanella, Soon-Teck Oh
▶ Vietnam vet Kove, having trouble adjusting to civilian life, battles old war enemy Oh, who has come to California to run the Black Tiger, an organization that deals drugs and harasses Vietnamese immigrants. Nonstop action with perfectly cast Kove a sympathetic underdog hero. **(CC)**
Dist.: Paramount

STEEL MAGNOLIAS 1989
★ ★ ★ ★ ★ PG Comedy/Drama 1:58
☑ Brief nudity, adult situations, explicit language
Dir: Herbert Ross *Cast:* Sally Field, Dolly Parton, Shirley MacLaine, Daryl Hannah, Olympia Dukakis, Julia Roberts, Sam Shepard, Tom Skerritt, Dylan McDermott, Kevin J. O'Connor
▶ Heartfelt, hilarious homage to five endearing and wacky Southern belles, who prove each other's most comforting source of strength. Field is a concerned mother whose beautiful diabetic daughter Roberts insists on having a child, even though her doctor forbids it. Lending support and laughs are Par-

ton, the owner of a hair salon who's just hired myopic beauty school valedictorian Hannah; nasty MacLaine who's been in a bad mood for forty years; and stalwart Dukakis. Adapted by Robert Harling from his hit Off-Broadway play. From among a resplendent cast, Roberts was singled out with an Oscar nomination as Best Supporting Actress. **(CC)**
Dist.: RCA/Columbia

STEELYARD BLUES 1973
★ ★ ★ PG Comedy 1:32
☑ Explicit language
Dir: Alan Myerson *Cast:* Jane Fonda, Donald Sutherland, Peter Boyle, Garry Goodrow, Howard Hesseman, John Savage
▶ Dated, offbeat comedy about hippies who reconstruct a World War II plane to fly them away from conventional society. Sutherland is an ex-con obsessed with demolition derbies; his brother Hesseman, also his parole officer, takes a dim view of the airplane scheme. Zany characters include master of transvestite disguises Boyle, frizzy-haired prostitute Fonda, and mental institution escapee Savage.
Dist.: Warner

STELLA 1990
★ ★ ★ ★ PG-13 Drama 1:46
☑ Brief nudity, adult situations, explicit language
Dir: John Erman *Cast:* Bette Midler, John Goodman, Trini Alvarado, Stephen Collins, Marsha Mason, Eileen Brennan, Linda Hart, Ben Stiller
▶ Barmaid Midler, impregnated by medical student Collins, turns down his marriage proposal and raises daughter Alvarado herself. Midler, later realizing her daughter would be better off with her wealthy father, makes a noble sacrifice to ensure Alvarado's future. *Stella Dallas*, cannily updated by screenwriter Robert Getchell, still packs a tearjerking emotional punch. Magnetic star turn by Midler.
Dist.: Buena Vista

STELLA DALLAS 1937
★ ★ ★ NR Drama 1:46 B&W
Dir: King Vidor *Cast:* Barbara Stanwyck, John Boles, Alan Hale, Anne Shirley, Marjorie Main, Barbara O'Neil
▶ In a small New England town, social climber Stanwyck uses improvement course to woo upper-class husband Boles. Once married, however, Stanwyck reverts to her loud, vulgar self, driving Boles to arms of former sweetheart O'Neil and dismaying their daughter Shirley. Stanwyck was nominated as Best Actress for performance as misfit mother in this peerless tearjerker. Remade in 1990 as *Stella*.
Dist.: Nelson

ST. ELMO'S FIRE 1985
★ ★ ★ ★ R Comedy/Drama 1:48
☑ Adult situations, explicit language
Dir: Joel Schumacher *Cast:* Emilio Estevez, Rob Lowe, Andrew McCarthy, Judd Nelson,

Ally Sheedy, Mare Winningham, Andie Mac-Dowall, Demi Moore

▶ Georgetown University grads face a difficult transition to the real world: virginal social worker Winningham yearns for charming but irresponsible Lowe, struggling writer McCarthy battles lawyer Nelson for Sheedy's affections, Estevez madly pursues older MacDowell, Moore deals with drug addiction and office romance. Slick story of emerging yuppies has energetic cast (with winsome Winningham faring best) but shallow characterizations. Funniest line: "When I grow up I want to be a bag lady. . .of course, I'd have alligator bags." John Parr title song was a big hit.   **(CC)**
Dist.: RCA/Columbia

STEPFATHER, THE 1987
★ ★ ★ R Mystery-Suspense 1:29
☑ Nudity, adult situations, explicit language, violence
Dir: Joseph Ruben   *Cast:* Terry O'Quinn, Jill Schoelen, Shelley Hack, Charles Lanyer, Stephen Shellen
▶ Sensitive teen Schoelen, inexplicably troubled about her new stepfather O'Quinn, checks into his background. Could he be the same man who recently massacred another family? Taut, convincing thriller by Donald Westlake builds to a graphically violent climax. O'Quinn, impressive in a measured, incisive performance, and assured direction place this well above routine slasher films.
Dist.: Nelson

STEPFATHER 2: MAKE ROOM FOR DADDY 1989
★ R Mystery-Suspense 1:26
☑ Adult situations, explicit language, graphic violence
Dir: Jeff Burr   *Cast:* Terry O'Quinn, Meg Foster, Caroline Williams, Mitchell Laurence, Jonathan Brandis
▶ Family-killer O'Quinn escapes from a mental hospital, masquerades as a therapist, and wins single mom Foster, a patient in his group session. On the way to the altar with the unsuspecting Foster, O'Quinn chillingly alternates between warm fatherliness with her son Brandis and murderous rage at those who stand in the way of his schemes. Another well-modulated performance by O'Quinn, but this sequel quickly sinks to the level of a mediocre slasher pic.
Dist.: HBO

STEP LIVELY 1944
★ ★ NR Musical 1:28 B&W
Dir: Tim Whelan   *Cast:* Frank Sinatra, George Murphy, Adolphe Menjou, Gloria De Haven, Eugene Pallette, Walter Slezak
▶ Musical version of the play *Room Service* stars Sinatra as a playwright whose producer Murphy is big on talk but short on funds. Sinatra falls for De Haven as Murphy scrambles to put on his show and avoid paying the hotel bill. Sammy Cahn/Jule Styne score includes

"As Long as There's Music" and "Where Does Love Begin?"
Dist.: Turner

STEPPENWOLF 1974
☆ R Drama 1:45
☑ Nudity, adult situations
Dir: Fred Haines   *Cast:* Max Von Sydow, Dominique Sanda, Pierre Clementi, Carla Romanelli, Roy Bosier
▶ Von Sydow, determined to commit suicide when he turns fifty, decides to live a little first. Drugs, dancing, and Sanda's charms are just some of the things he encounters in his quest for self-knowledge. Brave attempt at adapting Herman Hesse's novel, mixing live action and animation, is better visually than dramatically due to unfocused narrative and stiff philosophical dialogue. Von Sydow is superb.
Dist.: Vidmark

STERILE CUCKOO, THE 1969
★ ★ ★ PG Comedy/Drama 1:47
☑ Adult situations, explicit language
Dir: Alan J. Pakula   *Cast:* Liza Minnelli, Wendell Burton, Tim McIntire, Elizabeth Harrower
▶ Minnelli earned her first Oscar nomination in this sensitive story of young love between college students. As the outspoken Pookie Adams, Minnelli pursues the shy Burton. Their romance hits a snag when she announces she's pregnant. Directorial debut for Pakula, who shows a sure hand with the material. Theme song, "Come Saturday Morning," was also Oscar-nominated.
Dist.: Paramount

STEVIE 1978 British
★ PG Biography 1:42
☑ Explicit language
Dir: Robert Enders   *Cast:* Glenda Jackson, Mona Washbourne, Alec McCowen, Trevor Howard
▶ Adaptation of Hugh Whitemore's play about the profoundly witty English poet, Stevie Smith. In a tour-de-force performance, Jackson portrays Stevie in all her glory: funny, fragile, demanding, suicidal, and brave. Washbourne is the dotty aunt with whom Stevie lived; McCowen, her one-time fiancé. Sepia-toned flashbacks and readings of Stevie's poetry (including her most famous and prophetic poem, "Not Waving But Drowning") slow the pace.
Dist.: Nelson

ST. HELENS 1981
★ ★ ★ PG Action-Adventure 1:37
☑ Explicit language, violence
Dir: Ernest Pintoff   *Cast:* Art Carney, David Huffman, Cassie Yates, Albert Salmi
▶ Drama about the May 18, 1980, eruption of Mount St. Helen's in southeastern Washington. More entertaining than factual, film details the interaction of various residents during the weeks preceding the event. Among the characters: stubborn old coot Carney, who refuses

to leave his mountaintop home, hell-bent geologist Huffman, his pushy girl Yates, and greedy local entrepreneur Salmi. Interesting weaving of special effects and real footage.
Dist.: Vestron

STICK 1985
★ ★ ★ R Action-Adventure 1:49
☑ Adult situations, explicit language, violence
Dir: Burt Reynolds *Cast:* Burt Reynolds, Candice Bergen, George Segal, Charles Durning
► Ex-con Stick (Reynolds) tries to pick up the pieces of his life after seven years in prison but becomes involved in seeking revenge when his pal is murdered by drug king Durning. He takes chauffeur job with Palm Beach millionaire Segal, who does business with Durning. Segal's financial advisor Bergen plays Reynolds's love interest. Competent adaptation of Elmore Leonard novel never sizzles, despite star cast and sun-bleached Miami locations. (CC)
Dist.: MCA

STICKY FINGERS 1988
★ ★ PG-13 Comedy 1:37
☑ Adult situations, explicit language, violence
Dir: Catlin Adams *Cast:* Helen Slater, Melanie Mayron, Carol Kane, Christopher Guest, Danitra Vance, Eileen Brennan
► Flaky East Village musicians Slater and Mayron go on spending spree and land in hot water with cops and assorted thugs when drug-dealer pal leaves them $900,000 in cash. Two stars are likable in this visually inventive film; however, frenetic sitcom plot has too many shrill scenes of Slater and Mayron screaming at each other. (CC)
Dist.: Media

STILETTO 1969
★ R Action-Adventure 1:38
☑ Adult situations, explicit language, violence
Dir: Bernard Kowalski *Cast:* Alex Cord, Britt Ekland, Patrick O'Neal, Joseph Wiseman, Barbara McNair, Roy Scheider
► Hired gun Cord lives the high life working for mob don Wiseman. Cord decides to turn over a new leaf but learns that breaking off is hard to do. Decent cast fails to breathe life into undistinguished adaptation of the Harold Robbins novel.
Dist.: Nelson

STILL OF THE NIGHT 1982
★ ★ ★ PG Mystery-Suspense 1:27
☑ Brief nudity, adult situations, explicit language, violence
Dir: Robert Benton *Cast:* Meryl Streep, Roy Scheider, Jessica Tandy, Sandra Botsford, Josef Sommer
► Psychologist Scheider is visited by Streep, the neurotic mistress of his recently murdered patient Sommer. She's the key suspect in the murder but, despite warnings from his psychiatrist mother Tandy, Scheider falls for Streep anyway. Will his attraction prove fatal? Visual tribute to the stylized films of Hitchcock features an attractive, pedigree cast and several suspenseful moments.
Dist.: MGM/UA

STILL SMOKIN' 1983
★ ★ R Comedy 1:31
☑ Nudity, explicit language, violence
Dir: Thomas Chong *Cast:* Cheech Marin, Thomas Chong, Carol Van Herwijnen, Shirleen Stoker
► Cheech & Chong go to Amsterdam in this random assortment of unrelated skits aimlessly strung together. The word "man" is used, at last count, 4,587 times. Entertaining for diehard fans only, man.
Dist.: Paramount

STING, THE 1973
★ ★ ★ ★ ★ PG Comedy 2:09
☑ Adult situations, explicit language
Dir: George Roy Hill *Cast:* Paul Newman, Robert Redford, Robert Shaw, Charles Durning, Eileen Brennan, Ray Walston
► In 1930's Chicago, Redford teams with con man Newman to stage elaborate "sting" and bilk gangster Shaw. One of the most intricate plots in movie history will have you continually guessing and smiling in this tremendously entertaining comedy. Gorgeously mounted period settings enhanced by tinkling Scott Joplin piano rag score, oodles of charm and pizzazz from Newman and Redford (Oscar-nominated). Seven Oscars include Best Picture, Director, Screenplay, and Music Adaptation (Marvin Hamlisch).
Dist.: MCA

STING II, THE 1983
★ ★ ★ PG Comedy 1:42
☑ Adult situations, explicit language, violence, adult humor
Dir: Jeremy Paul Kagan *Cast:* Jackie Gleason, Mac Davis, Teri Garr, Karl Malden, Oliver Reed
► In 1940, New York con man Gleason and boxer Davis stage ring hustle to "sting" mobster Reed and racketeer Malden out of big bucks. Garr plays a co-conspirator whose ultimate loyalty is uncertain. Good cast and some nice plot surprises but sophomoric humor lacks the cleverness of the Oscar-winning original.
Dist.: MCA

STINGRAY 1978
★ PG Action-Adventure 1:39
☑ Explicit language, violence
Dir: Richard Taylor *Cast:* Christopher Mitchum, Sherry Jackson, Les Lannom, Bill Watson, Sondra Theodore, Bert Hinchman
► In St. Louis, pals Mitchum and Lannom purchase a little red Corvette, not realizing that bad guys (led by bad gal Jackson) have stashed cash and drugs inside. The crooks

want their cache back, leading to chases and car crashes. Speedy vehicle motors along efficiently.
Dist.: Nelson

STIR CRAZY 1980
★ ★ ★ ★ ★ **R Comedy 1:51**
☑ Adult situations, explicit language
Dir: Sidney Poitier *Cast:* Richard Pryor, Gene Wilder, JoBeth Williams, George Stanford Brown, Craig T. Nelson, Barry Corbin
▶ Blockbuster hit about lunatic friends Wilder and Pryor, who leave New York for an easier life out west but are arrested for a robbery they didn't commit. Sentenced to 120 years in an Arizona prison, they attempt to outwit sadistic wardens, scheming guards, and fellow prisoners. Explosively funny moments. Chemistry between leads overcomes somewhat predictable plot.
Dist.: RCA/Columbia

STITCHES 1985
★ **R Comedy 1:27**
☑ Nudity, explicit language, adult humor
Dir: Alan Smithee *Cast:* Parker Stevenson, Geoffrey Lewis, Eddie Albert, Brian Tochi, Robin Dearden
▶ Medical school is short on money; after partying students wreck the dean's house, fundraising seems increasingly unlikely. Other antics for the rowdy crew include dressing up as cadavers and watching naked women through a one-way mirror. Extremely broad humor is strictly for the undiscriminating.
Dist.: Media

ST. IVES 1976
★ ★ ★ ★ **PG Action-Adventure 1:34**
☑ Violence
Dir: J. Lee Thompson *Cast:* Charles Bronson, John Houseman, Jacqueline Bisset, Maximilian Schell, Harry Guardino, Elisha Cook, Jr., Daniel J. Travanti, Jeff Goldblum
▶ Novelist Bronson, a former crime reporter, is enticed by attorney Houseman into recovering account books that figure in a mob trial. He becomes the target of both sides of a gang war as he deals with crooked psychiatrist Schell and beautiful femme fatale Bisset. Above-average Bronson vehicle is restrained and genuinely perplexing.
Dist.: Warner

STOLEN LIFE, A 1946
★ ★ **NR Drama 1:47 B&W**
Dir: Curtis Bernhardt *Cast:* Bette Davis, Glenn Ford, Dane Clark, Walter Brennan, Charlie Ruggles, Bruce Bennett
▶ Davis plays twins competing for the affections of lighthouse inspector Ford. One of the twins is good, the other evil—and Ford marries the evil one. But when the married twin is killed in a boating accident, the good twin keeps it a secret and takes her sister's place in the marriage. Two Bettes are even better than

one in this fine hankie-wringer remade from a 1939 British film.
Dist.: MGM/UA

STONE BOY, THE 1984
★ ★ ★ ★ **PG Drama 1:28**
Dir: Christopher Cain *Cast:* Robert Duvall, Glenn Close, Frederic Forrest, Wilford Brimley, Jason Presson, Gail Youngs, Cindy Fisher
▶ Young farm boy Presson kills his brother in a hunting accident and is thrown into a nearly catatonic state. Unable to communicate with parents Close and Duvall, he moves in with his grandfather Brimley, but eventually runs away to his aunt in Reno. Compelling drama of a family's adjustment to a tragic death is moving and provocative, although slow at times. (CC)
Dist.: CBS/Fox

STONE COLD DEAD 1980 Canadian
★ ★ **R Mystery-Suspense 1:40**
☑ Nudity, explicit language, violence
Dir: George Mendeluk *Cast:* Richard Crenna, Paul Williams, Linda Sorensen, Belinda J. Montgomery, Alberta Watson, George Chuvalo
▶ A sniper preys on prostitutes with a high-powered, long-range rifle; homicide inspector Crenna investigates and undercover cop Montgomery poses as a call girl to help him. Workmanlike tale hits all the tried-and-true notes. Casting is a mixed bag: Crenna suits his role to a tee, but Williams is bizarrely cast as a sleazy pimp.
Dist.: Media

STONE KILLER, THE 1973
★ ★ ★ **R Action-Adventure 1:35**
☑ Adult situations, explicit language, violence
Dir: Michael Winner *Cast:* Charles Bronson, Martin Balsam, David Sheiner, Norman Fell, Ralph Waite, Eddie Firestone
▶ Rapid, hard-edged, extremely violent thriller about ex–New York cop Bronson battling Mafia don Balsam's mass-murder plot. His efforts to combat the scheme are hampered by Balsam's use of Vietnam vets without prison records. Good Bronson vehicle based on John Gardner's *A Complete State of Death*.
Dist.: RCA/Columbia

STONES OF DEATH 1988 Australian
★ **R Horror 1:30**
☑ Adult situations, violence
Dir: James Bogle *Cast:* Kerry McKay, Tom Jennings, Zoe Carides, Eric Oldfield
▶ Teenagers suffer nightmares and wake up with a stone that aborigines believe marks possessor for death. Sure enough, the teens are murdered. Could this be related to a haunted cave where a massacre took place years before? Australian setting is novel backdrop for plot reminiscent of recent American horror films.
Dist.: SVS

STOP MAKING SENSE 1984
★★ NR Documentary/Music 1:28
Dir: Jonathan Demme ***Cast:*** David Byrne, Tina Weymouth, Chris Frantz, Jerry Harrison, Steve Scales, Alex Weir
▶ Concert film from the Talking Heads 1983 tour combines iconoclastic lighting and stage design, elements of Japanese kabuki theater, rear projection of thought-poems, riveting presence of lead singer Byrne, and seamless direction by Demme. Byrne and top-notch band perform sixteen songs (three extra on home video version) including "Psycho Killer," "Life During Wartime," and "Burning Down the House." Considered by some the best concert film ever. Byrne's Big Suit shouldn't be missed.
Dist.: RCA/Columbia

STOPOVER TOKYO 1957
★★★ NR Espionage 1:40
Dir: Richard L. Breen ***Cast:*** Robert Wagner, Joan Collins, Edmond O'Brien, Ken Scott, Reiko Oyama, Larry Keating
▶ Well-crafted espionage thriller concerns American spy Wagner ordered to protect dignitary Keating in Tokyo from a Communist assassination plot. Keating refuses to believe anyone intends to kill him while Collins, Wagner's romantic interest, grows unhappy with his excessive dedication to his job. Scenic tour of Japan and intelligent drama are the strengths of this adaptation of John P. Marquand's novel.
Dist.: CBS/Fox

STORM 1985 Canadian
☆ NR Action-Adventure 1:21
☑ Adult situations
Dir: David Winning ***Cast:*** David Palfy, Stan Kane, Tom Schioler, Harry Freedman, Lawrence Elion
▶ Students Palfy and Schioler journey deep into the Alberta woods to play a survival game. There they stumble across three elderly crooks searching for buried loot from a 1946 robbery, leading to an extended chase through forest. Ambitious first effort by director Winning suffers from minuscule budget and weak plotting.
Dist.: Warner

STORM IN A TEACUP 1937 British
★★ NR Comedy 1:27 B&W
Dir: Victor Saville, Ian Dalrymple ***Cast:*** Vivien Leigh, Rex Harrison, Cecil Parker, Sara Allgood, Arthur Wontner, Ivor Barnard
▶ Young newspaperman Harrison arrives for work in a small town, where he falls in love with Leigh, daughter of the town's wealthiest and most powerful man. Harrison crosses Leigh's father when he defends an elderly lady whose dog is about to be executed for a license violation. With the love of Leigh at stake, Harrison winds up in court against the old man. Fine wit in this Capraesque British comedy.
Dist.: KVC

STORMY MONDAY 1988 British
★ R Drama 1:33
☑ Nudity, adult situations, explicit language, violence
Dir: Mike Figgis ***Cast:*** Melanie Griffith, Tommy Lee Jones, Sting, Sean Bean
▶ Young Bean goes to work for Newcastle, England, club owner Sting, whose place is coveted by ruthless American businessman Jones. As Jones uses violence to get what he wants, Bean gets involved with his girlfriend Griffith. Talented cast and Figgis create effective melancholy mood and sense of impending danger; suffers from sketchy plotting and characterizations. **(CC)**
Dist.: Paramount

STORMY WEATHER 1943
★★ NR Musical 1:18 B&W
Dir: Andrew L. Stone ***Cast:*** Lena Horne, Bill "Bojangles" Robinson, Cab Calloway, Katherine Dunham, Fats Waller, Nicholas Brothers
▶ All-star black musical uses song-and-dance numbers to describe turning points in vaudeville dancer Robinson's life from 1911 to 1936, including his troubled relationship with wife Horne. Waller performs "Ain't Misbehavin'," Bojangles Robinson shows off his famous soft shoe routines, and Horne does a stellar version of the title song. Coleman Hawkins and many other jazz stars add specialty numbers. **(CC)**
Dist.: CBS/Fox

STORY OF ADELE H., THE 1975 French
★ PG Drama 1:38
☑ Adult situations, explicit language
Dir: François Truffaut ***Cast:*** Isabelle Adjani, Bruce Robinson, Sylvia Marriott, Reubin Dorey, Joseph Blatchley
▶ Beautiful but often baffling study of Adele H. (Adjani), daughter of the nineteenth-century writer Victor Hugo, and her unrequited passion for callous British officer Robinson. Adele's obsession leads her to the brink of insanity as she follows her lover from Nova Scotia to Barbados. Complex film received an Oscar nomination for Adjani's controlled acting. [S]
Dist.: Warner

STORY OF LOUIS PASTEUR, THE 1936
★★★ NR Biography 1:25 B&W
Dir: William Dieterle ***Cast:*** Paul Muni, Josephine Hutchinson, Anita Louise, Donald Woods, Porter Hall, Akim Tamiroff
▶ Nineteenth-century French scientist Louis Pasteur (Muni) defies the scorn of the medical establishment to develop vaccines for anthrax and rabies. Conventional but engrossing; Muni won a well-deserved Best Actor Oscar. Best Picture nominee.
Dist.: MGM/UA

STORY OF ROBIN HOOD, THE 1952
★★★ NR Action-Adventure 1:23
Dir: Ken Annakin ***Cast:*** Richard Todd, Joan

Rice, Peter Finch, James Hayter, James Robertson, Martita Hunt

▶ Exemplary Disney version of the classic adventure casts Todd as the bandit of Sherwood Forest, with Finch suitably villainous as the nefarious Sheriff of Nottingham. Elaborate production with fast pacing and high spirits will entertain parents and children alike.
Dist.: Buena Vista

STORY OF RUTH, THE 1960
★ ★ ★ **NR Drama 2:12**
Dir: Henry Koster *Cast:* Elana Eden, Stuart Whitman, Tom Tryon, Peggy Wood, Viveca Lindfors, Jeff Morrow

▶ Moabite Ruth (Eden) renounces her pagan background and embraces the Jewish religion, but the Israelites don't intially embrace her back. She marries Boaz (Whitman), who champions her cause. Directed with a heavy hand, and not in the league of other biblical epics. Good score by Franz Waxman.
Dist.: CBS/Fox

STORY OF VERNON AND IRENE CASTLE, THE 1939
★ ★ ★ **NR Biography/Musical 1:33 B&W**
Dir: H. C. Potter *Cast:* Fred Astaire, Ginger Rogers, Edna May Oliver, Walter Brennan, Lew Fields, Etienne Girardot

▶ Enjoyable biography of the Castles, the most popular dancing team of the early twentieth century, with Astaire and Rogers lovingly re-creating their best routines in over thirty musical numbers ("Row, Row, Row," "The Yama Yama Man," "Rose Room," etc.). Plot describes their marriage, rigorous training, rise to fame in Europe and America, and Vernon's tragic early death. Last film together for Astaire and Rogers until 1949's *The Barkleys of Broadway*.
Dist.: Turner

STOWAWAY 1936
★ ★ **NR Musical/Family 1:26 B&W**
Dir: William A. Seiter *Cast:* Shirley Temple, Robert Young, Alice Faye, Eugene Pallette, Helen Westley, Arthur Treacher

▶ Orphaned in China when her missionary parents are murdered, Temple falls asleep in Young's car and ends up on a luxury liner. At sea, Young and Faye decide to marry so they can adopt the child, who is instrumental in keeping them together when their relationship falters. One of Temple's best features star doing impressions and speaking Chinese. (CC)
Dist.: CBS/Fox

STRAIGHT TIME 1978
★ ★ ★ **R Crime/Drama 1:54**
☑ Nudity, explicit language, violence
Dir: Ulu Grosbard *Cast:* Dustin Hoffman, Theresa Russell, Harry Dean Stanton, Gary Busey, M. Emmet Walsh

▶ Armed robber Hoffman is paroled after six years in prison. He has an affair with employment agency worker Russell but is unable to stay straight, getting involved with other ex-cons on a robbery spree. Gritty and refreshingly real evocation of the underworld; exceptional performances by Hoffman and first-rate supporting cast.
Dist.: Warner

STRAIGHT TO HELL 1987
☆ **R Comedy 1:26**
☑ Explicit language, violence
Dir: Alex Cox *Cast:* Sy Richardson, Joe Strummer, Dick Rude, Grace Jones, Elvis Costello, Dennis Hopper

▶ In Spain, bank robbers bury their money in the desert after their car breaks down. They go into town and battle various types who also want the loot. Strange spoof of spaghetti Westerns misfires: self-indulgent humor, repulsive characters, overdone acting. (CC)
Dist.: CBS/Fox

STRAIT-JACKET 1964
★ ★ **NR Horror 1:29 B&W**
Dir: William Castle *Cast:* Joan Crawford, Diane Baker, Leif Frickson, Howard St. John, John Anthony Hayes, George Kennedy

▶ After murdering her husband and his lover with an axe, Crawford spends twenty years in an insane asylum. Upon release she seeks out daughter Baker, a sculptor, but is horrified when axe murders resume. Mild shocker written by Robert Bloch has a few effective chills.
Dist.: RCA/Columbia

STRANGE BEHAVIOR 1981 Australian/New Zealand
★ **R Horror 1:39**
☑ Explicit language, violence
Dir: Michael Laughlin *Cast:* Michael Murphy, Louise Fletcher, Dan Shor, Fiona Lewis, Dey Young, Marc McClure

▶ In a midwestern college town, sheriff Murphy battles scientists whose experiments turn students into killers. Standard scare tactics, farfetched plotting. Fletcher and Murphy are fine but deserve better material. Australian locations pass convincingly for America.
Dist.: RCA/Columbia

STRANGE BREW 1983
★ ★ **PG Comedy 1:30**
☑ Explicit language, mild violence, adult humor
Dir: Dave Thomas, Rick Moranis *Cast:* Dave Thomas, Rick Moranis, Max Von Sydow, Paul Dooley, Lynne Griffin

▶ SCTV's Moranis and Thomas reprise their beer-guzzling McKenzie Brothers characterizations. The likable "hosers" get the job of their dreams when they are hired to work in a brewery. They uncover evil brewmeister Von Sydow's scheme to conquer the world. Gentle and sweet spirited, even when the gags are less than sophisticated.
Dist.: MGM/UA

STRANGE CARGO 1940
★ ★ **NR Action-Adventure 1:45 B&W**

Dir: Frank Borzage *Cast:* Clark Gable, Joan Crawford, Ian Hunter, Peter Lorre, Albert Dekker, Paul Lukas
▶ Gable leads a group of prisoners out of Devil's Island, picking up tough dance hall dame Crawford on the way. Jammed together with the Christlike Hunter in a small, open boat, hardened convicts undergo individual religious conversions. Gable and Crawford do their jobs competently in this not entirely successful attempt at an inspirational adventure.
Dist.: MGM/UA

STRANGE INVADERS 1983
★ ★ PG Sci-Fi 1:34
☑ Explicit language, violence
Dir: Michael Laughlin *Cast:* Paul LeMat, Nancy Allen, Diana Scarwid, Michael Lerner, Louise Fletcher, Wallace Shawn
▶ Columbia University professor LeMat searches for his missing wife Scarwid in midwestern town taken over by alien beings. Reporter Allen aids LeMat as the aliens also nab his daughter. Stylish direction and acting evoke the classic 1950s sci-fi films; modest special effects, several clever touches.
Dist.: Vestron

STRANGE LOVE OF MARTHA IVERS, THE 1946
★ ★ ★ NR Drama 1:57 B&W
Dir: Lewis Milestone *Cast:* Barbara Stanwyck, Kirk Douglas, Lizabeth Scott, Van Heflin, Judith Anderson, Darryl Hickman
▶ Douglas uses his knowledge about Stanwyck's past to force her to marry him. A visit from childhood friend Heflin threatens to uncover her long-hidden secret, throwing Douglas and Stanwyck into a panic. Stanwyck attacks her evil role with gusto in this strong melodrama. Douglas's film debut.
Dist.: KVC

STRANGER, THE 1946
★ ★ ★ ★ NR Mystery-Suspense 1:31 B&W
Dir: Orson Welles *Cast:* Orson Welles, Loretta Young, Edward G. Robinson, Philip Merivale, Richard Long, Byron Keith
▶ Federal agent Robinson, searching for an escaped Nazi criminal, centers in on a small Connecticut town where gentle professor Welles is marrying judge's daughter Young. Robinson doggedly uncovers evidence which places Young's life in jeopardy. Beautifully executed thriller features a strong script, memorable climax, and a chilling performance by Welles. **(CC)**
Dist.: Various Ⓒ

STRANGER AND THE GUNFIGHTER, THE 1976 Italian/Hong Kong
★ ★ PG Western/Martial Arts 1:47
☑ Brief nudity, violence
Dir: Anthony M. Dawson (Antonio Margheriti) *Cast:* Lee Van Cleef, Lo Lieh, Patty Shepard, Femi Benussi
▶ Gunslinger Van Cleef and Chinese martial arts expert Lieh team up to find Lieh's family fortune in the Old West. Stiff acting, silly musical score, but fast-paced action combines flying-through-the-air kung-fu with old-fashioned Western shoot-outs. Good cinematography.
Dist.: RCA/Columbia

STRANGER IS WATCHING, A 1982
★ ★ ★ R Mystery-Suspense 1:32
☑ Adult situations, explicit language, graphic violence
Dir: Sean S. Cunningham *Cast:* Kate Mulgrew, Rip Torn, James Naughton, Shawn Von Schreiber, Barbara Baxley, Frank Hamilton
▶ Mad killer Torn kidnaps young Von Schreiber, who witnessed his crime, and newscaster Mulgrew, who covered the story. Torn keeps them prisoner under Grand Central Station and demands ransom from Von Schreiber's father Naughton. Effective direction and Lalo Schifran music generate tension throughout. Based on the Mary Higgins Clark best-seller.
Dist.: MGM/UA

STRANGER ON THE THIRD FLOOR, THE 1940
★ ★ NR Mystery-Suspense 1:04 B&W
Dir: Boris Ingster *Cast:* Peter Lorre, John McGuire, Margaret Tallichet, Charles Waldron, Elisha Cook, Jr., Charles Halton
▶ Reporter McGuire fingers taxi driver Cook for murder after seeing him fleeing the scene of a crime. But real killer Lorre is still loose, and when McGuire himself is arrested on circumstantial evidence, it's up to girlfriend Tallichet to pursue the culprit. A close, menacing atmosphere pervades this small masterpiece. The dream sequence is a classic.
Dist.: Nostalgia

STRANGERS KISS 1984
★ R Drama 1:33 C/B&W
☑ Explicit language
Dir: Matthew Chapman *Cast:* Peter Coyote, Victoria Tennant, Blaine Novak, Dan Shor, Richard Romanus, Linda Kerridge
▶ On a 1955 Hollywood movie set, actor Novak gets involved with co-star Tennant. As the plot of their movie increasingly reflects real life, the lovers must deal with manipulative director Coyote and Tennant's gangster boyfriend Romanus. Polished production, haunting jazz score, solid acting. However, repetitive scenes of moviemaking slow down the pace, and the characters and romance fail to hold interest.
Dist.: HBO

STRANGERS ON A TRAIN 1951
★ ★ ★ ★ NR Mystery-Suspense 1:41 B&W
Dir: Alfred Hitchcock *Cast:* Farley Granger, Ruth Roman, Robert Walker, Leo G. Carroll, Patricia Hitchcock, Marion Lorne
▶ Walker is mesmerizing as a devious psychopath who lures tennis star Granger into a bizarre plan to exchange murders. If Granger

refuses to kill Walker's father, he'll be arrested for strangling his wife. Classic thriller improves with each viewing. Dazzling plot and dialogue (adapted by Raymond Chandler from Patricia Highsmith's novel), startling performance by Lorne as Walker's mother, and justly famed sequences in an amusement park and tennis stadium place this at the top of Hitchcock's work. Inspiration for *Throw Mama From the Train*.
Dist.: Warner

STRANGERS WHEN WE MEET 1960
★ ★ ★ NR Drama 1:57
Dir: Richard Quine *Cast:* Kirk Douglas, Ernie Kovacs, Kim Novak, Barbara Rush, Walter Matthau, Kent Smith
▶ Architect Douglas designs a house for eccentric writer Kovacs while carrying on affair with married Novak. As the house goes up, Douglas agonizes about whether he should leave his family for Novak, and neighbor Matthau makes eyes at Douglas's neglected wife. Lots of effort went into this adultery-in-the-suburbs soap opera, but the actors seem uninvolved and the plot never catches fire. The house is beautiful, though.
Dist.: RCA/Columbia

STRANGER THAN PARADISE 1984
★ R Comedy 1:29 B&W
☑ Adult situations, explicit language
Dir: Jim Jarmusch *Cast:* John Lurie, Eszter Balint, Richard Edson, Cecillia Stark, Danny Rosen, Rammellzee
▶ Two-bit Newark gambler Lurie plays reluctant host to Hungarian cousin Balint until she moves to Cleveland. A year later, Lurie and pal Edson decide to visit Balint, then take her to Florida. The Sunshine State turns out to be less than paradise, until Balint accidentally receives a stash of drug profits. Hip road movie using extremely dry humor and static long takes was a critical darling, but many find it simply strange.
Dist.: CBS/Fox

STRANGE SHADOWS IN AN EMPTY ROOM 1977
☆ R Mystery-Suspense 1:39
☑ Adult situations, violence
Dir: Alberto DeMartino *Cast:* Stuart Whitman, John Saxon, Martin Landau, Tisa Farrow, Gayle Hunnicutt, Carole Laure
▶ Information is hard to come by as detective Whitman slugs and shoots his way through the city trying to find who killed his sister. Sleazy, poorly scripted tale.
Dist.: Vestron

STRANGLER, THE 1964
★ ★ ★ NR Mystery-Suspense 1:29 B&W
Dir: Burt Topper *Cast:* Victor Buono, David McLean, Diane Sayer, Davey Davison, Ellen Corby, Michael M. Ryan
▶ Warped relationship with his mother Corby has forged serial killer Buono's murderous personality. He slays several Boston women as

cop McLean closes in on him. Inspired by the real-life Boston Strangler, effective thriller features one of Buono's creepiest performances.
Dist.: CBS/Fox

STRANGLER OF THE SWAMP 1945
☆ NR Horror 1:00 B&W
Dir: Frank Wisbar *Cast:* Rosemary La Planche, Robert Barrat, Blake Edwards, Charles Middleton, Effie Parnell, Nolan Leary
▶ The inhabitants of a village are frightened by the ghost of an innocent man lynched many years earlier who periodically returns to kill in revenge. La Planche takes over her grandfather's ferry boat when he is murdered, and offers her life to the ghost when it threatens her boyfriend Edwards. Cheap, but tense, with good direction and imaginative sets.
Dist.: SVS

STRATEGIC AIR COMMAND 1955
★ ★ ★ NR Drama 1:54
Dir: Anthony Mann *Cast:* James Stewart, June Allyson, Frank Lovejoy, Barry Sullivan, Alex Nicol, Bruce Bennett
▶ Due to a critical shortage of pilots, baseball player Stewart is ordered back into the service to fly new jets for the SAC. At first antagonistic over his fate, Stewart learns to appreciate the importance of the unit. Shot with the cooperation of the armed forces, film features outstanding aviation footage but a less-than-inspired earthbound plot.
Dist.: Paramount

STRAWBERRY BLONDE, THE 1941
★ ★ ★ NR Comedy 1:37 B&W
Dir: Raoul Walsh *Cast:* James Cagney, Olivia de Havilland, Rita Hayworth, Jack Carson, Alan Hale, George Tobias
▶ Dentist Cagney loses strawberry blond Hayworth to dishonest pal Carson, marries wholesome de Havilland instead, and takes prison rap for one of Carson's scams. Years later, Cagney has a chance for revenge but realizes his life turned out for the best after all. Warm and wonderful Americana, with marvelous turn-of-the-century period re-creation, robust Cagney, and winning de Havilland.
Dist.: MGM/UA

STRAWBERRY STATEMENT, THE 1970
★ R Drama 1:43
☑ Brief nudity, adult situations, explicit language, violence
Dir: Stuart Hagmann *Cast:* Bruce Davison, Kim Darby, Bud Cort, Murray MacLeod, Danny Goldmann, Bob Balaban
▶ Dated "message" film about the 1968 Columbia University riots shows how uninvolved student Davison becomes a rebel leader when he falls for hippie classmate Darby. Muddled adaptation of a novel by James Simon Kunen sacrifices realism for sensationalized portrayals of police brutality. Screenplay by Israel Horovitz; soundtrack includes songs

by Crosby, Stills, Nash, and Young; Joni Mitchell; and Thunderclap Newman.
Dist.: MGM/UA

STRAW DOGS 1972
★★ R Drama 1:54
☑ Rape, adult situations, explicit language, graphic violence
Dir: Sam Peckinpah ***Cast:*** Dustin Hoffman, Susan George, Peter Vaughn, T. P. McKenna, Del Henney, Ken Hutchison
► American mathematician Hoffman moves to a remote Cornish village with his wife George to escape violence. When George is raped by local thugs, Hoffman resorts to brutality for revenge. Raw, distasteful film provoked controversy on release for its endorsement of violence, but weak characters and plot lessen its effectiveness.
Dist.: CBS/Fox

STRAY DOG 1949 Japanese
☆ NR Drama 2:02 B&W
Dir: Akira Kurosawa ***Cast:*** Toshiro Mifune, Takashi Shimura, Keiko Awaji, Ko Kimura
► Detective Mifune has his gun stolen on a crowded bus and makes it his mission to get it back. Feeling personally responsible for the crimes committed with the weapon, he searches through the underworld, all the while seemingly chasing his own criminal tendencies. A fascinating look at Japanese life just after the war, stylistically problematic Kurasowa offering succeeds best as a character study of a troubled cop. [S]
Dist.: Various

STREAMERS 1983
★ R Drama 1:58
☑ Brief nudity, adult situations, explicit language, graphic violence, adult humor
Dir: Robert Altman ***Cast:*** Matthew Modine, Michael Wright, Mitchell Lichtenstein, David Alan Grier, Albert Macklin, Guy Boyd, George Dzundza
► Wright, a fiery recruit from the black ghetto, serves as catalyst for simmering tensions in a barracks filled with paratroopers awaiting assignment in Vietnam. Adaptation of David Rabe's hard-hitting play suffers from overacting and unconvincing cinematic tricks. Dzundza delivers the best performance as a boozy sergeant.
Dist.: Media

STREET ASYLUM 1990
★ NR Action-Adventure 1:34
☑ Nudity, strong sexual content, Adult situations, explicit language, graphic violence
Dir: Gregory Brown ***Cast:*** Wings Hauser, G. Gordon Liddy, Alex Cord, Roberta Vasquez, Sy Richardson, Brion James
► After being shot by an unknown assailant, Los Angeles cop Hauser is assigned to the Scum Quelling Urban Assault Division (S.Q.U.A.D.). Discovering that the unit's officers have been turned into suicidal killing machines via mind control devices, he attempts to expose the conspiracy. Relentlessly sleazy thriller features Liddy's tightly pitched performance as a politician with something to hide.
Dist.: Magnum

STREETCAR NAMED DESIRE, A 1951
★★★★ PG Drama 2:02 B&W
☑ Adult situations
Dir: Elia Kazan ***Cast:*** Vivien Leigh, Marlon Brando, Kim Hunter, Karl Malden, Rudy Bond
► "I've always depended on the kindness of strangers," says fragile Southern belle Blanche DuBois (Leigh), visiting sister Stella (Hunter); but Blanche can't depend on the kindness of Stella's brutal husband, Stanley Kowalski (Brando). His resentment of her presence leads to conflict and a powerful climax. Superb adaptation of the Tennessee Williams play with a towering Oscar-nominated performance by Brando; Oscar-winning ones by Leigh, Hunter, and Malden. Best Picture nominee. (CC)
Dist.: Warner

STREET HERO 1984 Australian
★ NR Drama 1:40
☑ Adult situations, explicit language, violence
Dir: Michael Pattinson ***Cast:*** Vincent Colosimo, Sigrid Thornton, Sandy Gore, Bill Hunter, Ray Marshall
► Teenage mob courier Colosimo finds refuge from dreary life when girlfriend Thornton and music teacher Gore convince him to join school band as drummer. Colosimo also must deal with mom's abuse by her drunken husband. Teen flick is slickly produced and directed but suffers from cloudy plotting.
Dist.: Vestron

STREET JUSTICE 1989
★ R Action-Adventure 1:34
☑ Adult situations, explicit language
Dir: Richard C. Sarafian ***Cast:*** Michael Ontkean, Joanna Kerns, Catherine Bach, J. D. Cannon, Jeanette Nolan, Richard Cox
► Rogue CIA agent Ontkean escapes from a decade behind the Iron Curtain to find his remarried wife committed to defeating a corrupt mayor. Ontkean secretly aids his wife and teenage daughter by battling bad cops while eluding evil CIA pursuers. Functional but slow genre piece hampered by stodgy star, who plays most of the movie in a Rambo headband.
Dist.: Warner

STREET LAW 1978 Italian
☆ NR Action-Adventure 1:21
☑ Explicit language, violence
Dir: Enzo Castellari ***Cast:*** Franco Nero, Giancarlo Prete, Barbara Bach
► Bank robbers take Nero hostage and beat him. After his release, his wife wants him to let the police investigate. When the cops provide little help, Nero takes the law into his own

hands to get revenge. Even the gun shots sound phony in this poorly dubbed and badly done crime drama.
Dist.: VidAmerica

STREET MUSIC 1983
★ R Comedy/Drama 1:30
☑ Nudity, adult situations, explicit language
Dir: Jenny Bowen *Cast:* Elizabeth Daily, Larry Breeding, Ned Glass, Marjorie Eaton, W. F. Walker, Miriam Phillips
▶ Elderly inhabitants of a San Francisco residential hotel fight in vain to save it from demolition. Street singer Daily and her tour bus driver boyfriend Breeding are younger tenants whose romance fades as the battle unfolds. Humanistic independent film helped by sexy Daily, hurt by flaccid narrative.
Dist.: Vestron

STREET PEOPLE 1976 U.S./Italian
☆ R Action-Adventure 1:32
☑ Nudity, explicit language, violence
Dir: Maurizio Lucidi *Cast:* Roger Moore, Stacy Keach, Ivo Garrani, Fausto Tozzi, Ettore Manni, Ennio Balbo
▶ An Italian mafioso smuggles crosses filled with heroin into San Francisco, earning the ire of Moore, himself the nephew of a Cosa Nostra member. With his pal Keach, a racing car driver, Moore zooms around Italy and San Francisco, expending ammunition and burning rubber. Needs a better story to hang all the violence on.
Dist.: Vestron

STREET SCENE 1931
★ NR Drama 1:20 B&W
Dir: King Vidor *Cast:* Sylvia Sidney, William Collier, Jr., David Landau, Estelle Taylor, Walter Miller
▶ Thirties period piece, adapted by Elmer Rice from his long-running Pulitzer prize–winning play, set on a single Manhattan street in the West Sixties. Major plot episode is Landau's murderous revenge on his wife, who is having an affair with the milkman. Nice street ambiance; Alfred Newman's theme music will be immediately familiar, having been used in numerous contexts since.
Dist.: Video Yesteryear

STREET SMART 1987
★★★ R Drama 1:36
☑ Brief nudity, adult situations, explicit language, violence
Dir: Jerry Schatzberg *Cast:* Christopher Reeve, Kathy Baker, Morgan Freeman, Mimi Rogers, Andre Gregory, Jay Patterson
▶ Journalist Reeve makes a big career move by passing off a story about a fictitious pimp as truth. He gets more trouble than he bargained for when actual pimp Freeman, accused of murder, attempts to use him as an alibi. Baker is haunting as a prostitute, Oscar-nominated Freeman is mesmerizing, and Reeve is solid as

the unsympathetic protagonist in this savvy drama. (CC)
Dist.: Media

STREETS OF FIRE 1984
★★★ PG Action-Adventure 1:34
☑ Adult situations, explicit language, violence
Dir: Walter Hill *Cast:* Michael Paré, Diane Lane, Rick Moranis, Amy Madigan, Willem Dafoe, Deborah Van Valkenburgh
▶ Bikers in a vaguely futuristic ghetto kidnap rock singer Lane; tough loner Paré, aided by an even tougher Madigan, scours the underworld to rescue her. Subtitled "A Rock 'n' Roll Fable," highly stylized drama plays like a feature-length music video. Dafoe is appropriately menacing as the villain. Strong score by Ry Cooder features his band and the Blasters. (CC)
Dist.: MCA

STREETS OF GOLD 1986
★★★★ R Drama/Sports 1:35
☑ Explicit language, violence
Dir: Joe Roth *Cast:* Klaus Maria Brandauer, Adrian Pasdar, Wesley Snipes, Angela Molina, Elya Baksin, Rainbow Harvest
▶ Predictable boxing drama with a commanding performance by Brandauer as a Russian banned from fighting for his Jewish religion. Emigrating to Coney Island, he trains promising youths Pasdar and Snipes for spots on the U.S. team and a chance for revenge against his former coach. Fights are staged realistically, and clash-of-cultures theme works due to Brandauer's conviction.
Dist.: Vestron

STREETWALKIN' 1985
★ R Drama 1:23
☑ Nudity, strong sexual content, adult situations, explicit language, graphic violence
Dir: Joan Freeman *Cast:* Melissa Leo, Julie Newmar, Dale Midkiff, Antonio Fargas, Leon Robinson, Annie Golden
▶ Leo supports her little brother by working as a hooker. She flees when pimp Midkiff goes on a murderous rampage but eventually she must take the law into her own hands. Effectively captures the seamier side of New York City and Leo is sympathetic; however, appeal limited by endless brutality towards women and miscast Midkiff, who is too clean-cut for his role.
Dist.: Vestron

STREETWISE 1985
★★ NR Documentary 1:32
☑ Brief nudity, adult situations, explicit language
Dir: Martin Bell
▶ Oscar-nominated no-holds-barred look at Seattle street kids. They beg, turn tricks, eat from dumpsters, drink, live in deserted buildings, and form close friendships amidst the hardships and depravity. Strong stuff cap-

tured with insight and compassion is depressing but compelling. Produced by Willie Nelson.
Dist.: New World

STRIKE 1924 Russian
★ **NR Drama 1:21 B&W**
Dir: Sergei Eisenstein *Cast:* Gregori Alexandrov, Maxim Strauch, Mikhail Gomarov, Alexander Antonov, Judith Glizer
▶ In 1912 Russia, factory workers unite to strike against their oppressive bosses. The powers that be sic the fire and police departments on the workers, leading to a climactic brutal attack. If Eisenstein's politics seem simplistic, his stirring, kinetic technique is anything but.
Dist.: Video Yesteryear

STRIKE IT RICH 1989 British
★ **PG Comedy 1:278**
☑ Adult situations, explicit language
Dir: James Scott *Cast:* Molly Ringwald, Robert Lindsay, John Gielgud, Max Wall, Simon de la Brosse
▶ Lackluster romantic comedy harkens back to the films of the thirties and forties, but without the class. Lovers Ringwald and Lindsay arrive in Monte Carlo, where they will wed and honeymoon at the expense of his millionaire boss Gielgud. When Gielgud proves a no-show, Lindsay hits the roulette table with amazing results. Lindsay tries valiantly, but his pairing with Ringwald lacks the necessary chemistry and sparkle. Loosely based on Graham Greene's *Loser Takes All*. **(CC)**
Dist.: HBO

STRIKE UP THE BAND 1940
★★★ **NR Musical 2:00 B&W**
Dir: Busby Berkeley *Cast:* Mickey Rooney, Judy Garland, Paul Whiteman, June Preisser, William Tracy, Ann Shoemaker
▶ Rooney's the whole show in this high-spirited musical. As an aspiring drummer desperate to win a new band contest sponsored by Paul Whiteman and His Orchestra, he drums, sings, dances, and plays the xylophone while assembling crackerjack young musicians. Rooney wisely chooses Garland over rich girl Preisser for vocalist. Songs include Oscar-nominated "Our Love Affair" and "Heaven Will Protect the Working Girl."
Dist.: MGM/UA

STRIPES 1981
★★★★ **R Comedy 1:46**
☑ Nudity, adult situations, explicit language, mild violence
Dir: Ivan Reitman *Cast:* Bill Murray, Harold Ramis, John Candy, Warren Oates, P. J. Soles, Sean Young, John Larroquette, Judge Reinhold
▶ After losing his job and girlfriend, down-on-his-luck degenerate Murray enlists in the Army with best friend Ramis. They clash with stern Sgt. Oates and "borrow" a top-secret mobile weapons center, but prove their mettle by saving the world from nuclear war. Top-rank,

low-down tomfoolery; Murray's brand of sarcasm has never been funnier, whether urging his fellow soldiers into action with "We're the U.S. Army. . .we're ten and one!" or exhorting overweight recruit Candy to become a "lean, mean fighting machine." **(CC)**
Dist.: RCA/Columbia

STRIPPED TO KILL 1987
★★ **R Action-Adventure 1:26**
☑ Nudity, adult situations, explicit language, violence
Dir: Katt Shea Ruben *Cast:* Kay Lenz, Greg Evigan, Norman Fell, Tracy Crowder, Athena Worthey
▶ Serial killer terrorizes dancers at Los Angeles topless bars; posing as a stripper, undercover cop Lenz offers herself as bait to catch the murderer. Above-average exploitation offers good performances, convincingly tawdry settings, and a puzzling plot.
Dist.: MGM/UA

STRIPPED TO KILL II 1989
★ **R Mystery-Suspense 1:22**
☑ Nudity, adult situations, explicit language, violence
Dir: Katt Shea Ruben *Cast:* Maria Ford, Eb Lottimer, Karen Mayo Chandler, Birke Tan, Marjean Holden, Debra Lamb
▶ Los Angeles stripper Ford is haunted by nightmares in which she kills her co-workers. When her colleagues start getting murdered, she becomes a suspect, although cop Lottimer finds himself attracted to her. Tawdry, distasteful, but far from unwatchable. Way-out plot doesn't stint on kinkiness.
Dist.: MGM/UA

STRIPPER, THE 1963
★★ **NR Drama 1:35 B&W**
Dir: Franklin J. Schaffner *Cast:* Joanne Woodward, Richard Beymer, Carol Lynley, Claire Trevor, Robert Webber, Gypsy Rose Lee
▶ Stripper Woodward returns to her hometown and has an affair with Beymer, the young son of old friend Trevor. However, her tawdry past and brutal manager-boyfriend Webber threaten her happiness. Standout performances by Woodward and Trevor enliven a flat screenplay.
Dist.: Key

STROKER ACE 1983
★★★ **PG Action-Adventure/Comedy 1:34**
☑ Adult situations, explicit language, violence
Dir: Hal Needham *Cast:* Burt Reynolds, Loni Anderson, Jim Nabors, Ned Beatty, Parker Stevenson, Bubba Smith
▶ Race car driver Reynolds signs promotion deal with fast-food chicken mogul Beatty. Soon Reynolds wants out of the contract and into the arms of Beatty's virginal assistant Anderson. Combination of Reynolds's quips, Anderson's looks, and Needham's elaborate car

stunts is good-natured and amiable if not terribly sophisticated.
Dist.: Warner

STROMBOLI 1950 Italian
☆ **NR Drama 1:21 B&W**
Dir: Roberto Rossellini   *Cast:* Ingrid Bergman, Mario Vitale, Renzo Cesana, Mario Sponza
▶ Refugee Bergman marries Italian fisherman Vitale to get out of a displaced persons camp, only to find herself imprisoned in a life of hardship and toil among the poor residents of a rocky volcanic isle. In her efforts to escape, she attempts to seduce a priest and makes a play for the lighthouse keeper. Dreary and depressing in the extreme, movie's interest comes from the then-scandalous affair between Bergman and director Rossellini.
Dist.: United

STRYKER 1983 Filipino
☆ **R Action-Adventure 1:20**
☑ Rape, nudity, explicit language, graphic violence
Dir: Cirio H. Santiago   *Cast:* Steve Sandor, Andria Savio, William Ostrander, Michael Lane, Julie Gray, Monique St. Pierre
▶ In a postnuclear wasteland, colonies compete for scarce water. Savio learns of a spring but is intercepted by nasty chieftain; heroic Sandor rescues her. Strike *Stryker* from your must-see list if excessive violence and sadism, such as villain urinating on thirsty prisoner, offend you.
Dist.: Nelson

STUCK ON YOU 1983
★ **R Comedy 1:30**
☑ Nudity, strong sexual content, adult situations, explicit language
Dir: Michael Herz   *Cast:* Prof. Irwin Corey, Virginia Penta, Mark Mikulski, Albert Pia, Norma Pratt
▶ Live-in couple Penta and Mikulski break up and go before judge Corey to divide their property. Corey discusses their problems in the context of history (going back to Adam and Eve); the lovers recall happier times and eventually reconcile. Vulgar bathroom humor includes spitting, vomiting, burping, and flatulence. Lovely Penta deserves better.
Dist.: Nelson

STUD, THE 1978 British
★ **R Drama 1:30**
☑ Nudity, adult situations, explicit language
Dir: Quentin Masters   *Cast:* Joan Collins, Oliver Tobias, Sue Lloyd, Mark Burns, Walter Gotell, Emma Jacobs
▶ Tobias, a waiter in a London disco, earns promotion to manager when he he satisfies insatiable sexual appetite of Collins, wife of club owner Gotell. Tobias has ambitions to open own club, but entry into the upper class seems unlikely since he can't keep hands off Gotell's daughter Jacobs. Screenplay by pulp novelist Jackie Collins (sister of Joan) from her book.
Dist.: HBO

STUDENT NURSES 1970
★ **R Drama 1:25**
☑ Nudity, adult situations, explicit language, violence
Dir: Stephanie Rothman   *Cast:* Elaine Giftos, Karen Carlson, Brioni Farrell, Barbara Leigh, Reni Santoni, Richard Rust
▶ Enjoyably trashy exploitation about four beautiful nurses in their last year of school. Giftos falls in love with a dying patient; Carlson breaks off an affair with an abortionist; Leigh is raped by a drug addict; Farrell joins a revolutionary terrorist movement. Low-budget Roger Corman production led to four lesser sequels. Followed by *Private Duty Nurses.*
Dist.: Nelson

STUDENT TEACHERS, THE 1973
☆ **R Drama 1:19**
☑ Nudity, adult situations, explicit language, violence
Dir: Jonathan Kaplan   *Cast:* Susan Damante, Brooke Mills, Brenda Sutton, Nora Heflin, Dick Miller, John Kramer
▶ Offshoot of Roger Corman's *Student Nurses* series provides a titillating look at an "alternative learning" high school threatened with closing by a series of rapes. Lively debut for director Kaplan, who would later helm *Project X.* Look quickly for Chuck Norris in a tiny role. Followed by *Summer School Teachers.*
Dist.: Nelson

STUDY IN SCARLET, A 1933
★ ★ **NR Mystery-Suspense 1:12 B&W**
Dir: Edwin L. Marin   *Cast:* Reginald Owen, Anna May Wong, June Clyde, Alan Dinehart, Warburton Gamble, Alan Mowbray
▶ Sherlock Holmes (Owen) and Dr. Watson (Gamble) investigate when members of the mysterious "Scarlet Ring" organization are murdered. The clues include nursery rhymes sent to the victims before their deaths. Intriguing mystery is one of the better pre–Basil Rathbone efforts.
Dist.: Video Yesteryear

STUDY IN TERROR, A 1965 British
★ ★ **NR Mystery-Suspense 1:35**
Dir: James Hill   *Cast:* John Neville, Donald Houston, John Fraser, Anthony Quayle, Robert Morley, Barbara Windsor, Cecil Parker, Kay Walsh, Frank Finlay
▶ Overlooked Sherlock Holmes mystery has Neville assaying a younger, more forceful version of the famous detective. Plot pits him against real-life criminal Jack the Ripper, the notorious murderer of prostitutes. Compact, action-filled film features good support by veteran character actors Parker and Walsh, with Finlay an amusing Inspector Lestrade.
Dist.: RCA/Columbia

STUFF, THE 1985
☆ **R Horror/Comedy 1:33**
☑ Explicit language, violence
Dir: Larry Cohen ***Cast:*** Michael Moriarty, Andrea Marcovicci, Garrett Morris, Paul Sorvino, Scott Bloom, Danny Aiello
▶ New dessert sensation, promoted with slick advertising, threatens ice cream sales. Ice cream industry hires private eye Moriarty and publicist Marcovicci to learn production secret of "the Stuff." Meanwhile, as consumers become addicted to the menacing, mind-controlling Stuff, now-bankrupt cookie king Morris and anti-Communist militia leader Sorvino join fight against the Stuffies. Some laughs but little real horror. **(CC)**
Dist.: New World

STUNT MAN, THE 1979
★★★ **R Drama 2:11**
☑ Brief nudity, adult situations, explicit language, violence
Dir: Richard Rush ***Cast:*** Peter O'Toole, Steve Railsback, Barbara Hershey, Sharon Farrell, Allen Goorwitz, Alex Rocco
▶ Fugitive Railsback, a Vietnam vet, wanders onto a movie set and accidentally causes death of a stuntman; director O'Toole decrees Railsback must replace the dead man. Railsback romances film's leading lady Hershey when not learning movie trickery from mentor O'Toole. Soon Railsback suspects O'Toole plans to kill him in a stunt while police draw closer. Delightful movie-about-movies constantly flimflams viewers. O'Toole steals every scene as an egomaniacal director.
Dist.: CBS/Fox

STUNTS 1977
★★ **PG Mystery-Suspense 1:30**
☑ Adult situations, explicit language, violence
Dir: Mark L. Lester ***Cast:*** Robert Forster, Fiona Lewis, Joanna Cassidy, Darrell Fetty, Bruce Glover, Jim Luisi
▶ Someone is killing stuntmen on a movie set. When his brother becomes one of the victims, daredevil Forster joins the production to uncover the murderer. Well-crafted sleeper with solid direction and performances. Whodunit aspect is fairly predictable but still worth a look.
Dist.: HBO

ST. VALENTINE'S DAY MASSACRE, THE 1967
★★★ **NR Crime 1:40**
Dir: Roger Corman ***Cast:*** Jason Robards, Jr., George Segal, Ralph Meeker, Jean Hale, Clint Ritchie, Joseph Campanella
▶ Vivid, unexpectedly accurate version of Chicago gang war between Al Capone (Robards) and Bugs Moran (Meeker) shows their growing hostility in violent flashbacks before meticulously reconstructing the famous 1929 garage killing spree. Cameos include Bruce Dern as a mechanic and Jack Nicholson as a thug who poisons his bullets.
Dist.: CBS/Fox

SUBURBIA 1984
☆ **R Drama 1:39**
☑ Nudity, adult situations, explicit language, graphic violence
Dir: Penelope Spheeris ***Cast:*** Chris Pederson, Bill Coyne, Jennifer Clay, Tim O'Brien, Michael Bayer
▶ Punk teens rebel against their bad upbringings (alcoholic mothers, homosexual and abusive fathers) and crumbling neighborhood by forming a group called "The Rejected." They run afoul of local rednecks who blame them for the area's condition. Grim and unconvincing.
Dist.: Vestron

SUBWAY 1985 French
☆ **R Drama 1:44**
☑ Adult situations, explicit language
Dir: Luc Bresson ***Cast:*** Christopher Lambert, Isabelle Adjani, Richard Bohringer, Michel Galabru, Jean-Hugues Anglade
▶ Thief Lambert steals documents from wealthy man's wife Adjani and then escapes into band of bums, bohemians, and crooks who live in the Paris subway. Adjani follows him underground, where love blooms although Lambert must still avoid subway security and her husband's hired gun. Stylized filmmaking can't save stupid story. **(CC)**
Dist.: Key

SUBWAY TO THE STARS 1988 Brazilian
☆ **R Drama 1:43**
☑ Nudity, adult situations, explicit language
Dir: Carlos Diegues ***Cast:*** Guilherme Fontes, Milton Gonçalves, Taumaturgo Ferreira, Ana Beatriz Wiltgen, Zé Trindade, Miriam Pires
▶ Struggling saxophone player Fontes celebrates new job with girlfriend Wiltgen, who subsequently disappears. He searches through seamier side of Rio de Janeiro for her and is involved in an aborted robbery plan. Downbeat drama lacks the joy and passion of same director's *Bye, Bye, Brazil.* [S]
Dist.: New World

SUCCESS IS THE BEST REVENGE 1984 British
☆ **NR Drama 1:30**
☑ Nudity, adult situations, explicit language
Dir: Jerzy Skolimowski ***Cast:*** Michael York, Anouk Aimee, John Hurt, Janna Szerzerbic, Michael Lyndon, Jane Asher
▶ In London, Polish dissident York, hard pressed to raise cash for a stage production, is too precoccupied to realize his teenage son Lyndon is unhappy and plotting a return to Poland. Central situation fails to work up much drama despite Skowlimowski's economical direction and some fine acting.
Dist.: Magnum

SUDDEN DEATH 1985
★ ★ R Action-Adventure 1:30
☑ Rape, nudity, adult situations, explicit
   language, graphic violence
Dir: Sig Shore   *Cast:* Denise Coward, Frank
Runyeon, Jamie Tirelli, Robert Trumbull, Rebecca Holden, J. Kenneth Campbell
▶ New York businesswoman Coward is raped
and beaten. When the cops are unable to
catch her attackers, Coward buys a gun, uses
herself as bait, and lures rapists to their
deaths. Female *Death Wish* pulls few punches
in the action department; slickly done but exploitative.
Dist.: Vestron

SUDDEN IMPACT 1983
★ ★ ★ ★ R Action-Adventure 1:57
☑ Rape, brief nudity, explicit language,
   graphic violence
Dir: Clint Eastwood   *Cast:* Clint Eastwood,
Sondra Locke, Pat Hingle, Bradford Dillman,
Paul Drake
▶ "Go ahead, make my day," says San Francisco's toughest cop Dirty Harry (Eastwood) to
hold-up thugs. After dispatching them in his
usual fashion, Harry investigates brutal murders of men who were involved in a rape ten
years back and is attracted to artist Locke
who may hold a clue. Hard-hitting and pulse-
pounding; Eastwood invests the familiar formula with new vitality. **(CC)**
Dist.: Warner

SUDDENLY 1954
★ ★ ★ NR Drama 1:15 B&W
Dir: Lewis Allen   *Cast:* Frank Sinatra, Sterling
Hayden, James Gleason, Nancy Gates, Kim
Charney, Paul Frees
▶ Secret Service agents check security for
Presidential visit to the small town of Suddenly.
Disguised as FBI agents, psychopath Sinatra
and two henchmen take hostages in house
overlooking the railroad station where the
President will stop. Sinatra is riveting as an am-
oral assassin in this tense and chillingly pre-
scient drama. The computer-colorized version
unfortunately gives Sinatra brown eyes.
Dist.: Various   C

SUDDENLY, LAST SUMMER 1959
★ ★ ★ NR Drama 1:54 B&W
Dir: Joseph L. Mankiewicz   *Cast:* Elizabeth
Taylor, Katharine Hepburn, Montgomery
Clift, Albert Dekker, Mercedes McCambridge
▶ Wealthy Hepburn offers brain surgeon Clift
a big donation to his hospital if he will loboto-
mize her niece Taylor. Clift spends time with
Taylor and, as family skeletons pour out of the
closet, he realizes she isn't insane. Outrageous, lurid, and fascinating drama whose
florid performances perfectly fit writer Tennessee Williams's near-camp style. Both Taylor
and Hepburn nabbed Oscar nominations.
Dist.: RCA/Columbia

SUGARBABY 1985 German
★ NR Comedy/Drama 1:27
☑ Nudity, adult situations
Dir: Percy Adlon   *Cast:* Marianne Sägebrecht, Eisi Gulp, Toni Berger, Manuela
Denz, Will Spindler
▶ Overweight fraulein Sägebrecht works by
day in a mortuary and spends lonely nights
eating herself silly. Her life changes when she
spies handsome subway conductor Gulp,
who becomes the object of her pent-up
desires. Sägebrecht trails him until finally they
meet and enjoy a passionate affair based on
shared affection for sweets. Definitely different,
offbeat, and stylized comedy was remade as
an American TV movie. S
Dist.: Warner

SUGAR CANE ALLEY 1983
French/Martinique
★ PG Drama 1:43
☑ Adult situations
Dir: Euzhan Palcy   *Cast:* Garry Cadenat,
Darling Legitimus, Douta Seck, Laurent
Saint-Cyr, Joby Bernabe, Marie-Jo Descas
▶ In 1930s Martinique, blacks have little
choice but to work the cane fields; impoverished orphan Cadenat is encouraged by
grandmother Legitimus to escape that fate
through education. He learns lessons at
school well enough to win a scholarship but is
also exposed to racism. Richly rendered if
overlong. Infectious performance by Cadenat. S
Dist.: Media

SUGARLAND EXPRESS, THE 1974
★ ★ ★ PG Drama 1:49
☑ Explicit language, violence
Dir: Steven Spielberg   *Cast:* Goldie Hawn,
Ben Johnson, Michael Sacks, William Atherton, Gregory Walcott, Louise Latham
▶ When Texas authorities threaten to take
away her baby, determined mother Hawn
springs husband Atherton from jail and leads
police and reporters on a fast-paced chase
along rural highways and back roads. Consistently engrossing drama, based on a true story,
has strong characters as well as technically
accomplished action sequences. Spielberg's
theatrical directing debut.
Dist.: MCA

SUICIDE CLUB, THE 1988
☆ R Drama 1:30
☑ Explicit language
Dir: James Bruce   *Cast:* Mariel Hemingway,
Robert Joy, Lenny Henry, Madeleine Potter,
Michael O'Donoghue, Alice Drummond
▶ Heiress Hemingway, guilty over her brother's
suicide, attends Long Island masquerade
party featuring a card game in which the win-
ner is murdered. Intrigued, she returns for an-
other party, despite objections of boyfriend
Joy. Dull, preposterous drama was "sug-
gested" by a Robert Louis Stevenson story.
Dist.: Academy

SULLIVAN'S TRAVELS 1941
★ ★ ★ ★ **NR Comedy 1:31 B&W**
Dir: Preston Sturges *Cast:* Joel McCrea, Veronica Lake, Robert Warwick, William Demarest, Porter Hall, Robert Greig, Jimmy Conlin, Al Bridge, Franklin Pangborn
▶ Tired of making comedies like *Ants in Your Pants of 1939*, Hollywood director McCrea disguises himself as a hobo for a solo journey to discover the real America as research for his planned epic, *Oh Brother, Where Art Thou?* At first his over-zealous staff exploits the trip as a publicity stunt; giving them the slip with failed actress Lake, McCrea discovers a heartland of unanticipated danger. Unique combination of slapstick, pathos, and devastating satire is among the most perceptive movies ever made about Hollywood. Supporting cast shines in another masterpiece by writer-producer-director Sturges.
Dist.: MCA

SUMMER 1986
☆ **R Comedy 1:30**
☑ Nudity, adult situations, explicit language
Dir: Eric Rohmer *Cast:* Marie Rivière, Lisa Heredia, Beatrice Romand, Rosette, Eric Hamm
▶ Paris secretary Rivière's summer vacation plans are thrown into tizzy when a friend cancels on her. Restless and unhappy, she bounces between the city and various holiday spots until an encounter with a young man in a station. Individual reactions will vary, depending on how one responds to the willful, obstinate, but ultimately moving heroine. Ends with one of the most transcendent moments in Rohmer's career. ⓢ
Dist.: Media

SUMMER CAMP NIGHTMARE 1987
★ ★ **PG-13 Drama 1:25**
☑ Rape, adult situations, explicit language, violence
Dir: Bert L. Dragin *Cast:* Chuck Connors, Charles Stratton, Adam Carl, Harold Pruett, Melissa Brennan
▶ Cautionary drama about a boys' camp ruled by strict disciplinarian Connors. Idealistic counselor Stratton organizes a revolt, locking up the adults and taking command of a nearby girls' camp as well. Muddled script based on *The Butterfly Revolution* by William Butler suffers from obvious plotting and overacting. **(CC)**
Dist.: Nelson

SUMMER HEAT 1987
★ ★ **R Drama 1:30**
☑ Adult situations, explicit language, violence
Dir: Michie Gleason *Cast:* Lori Singer, Anthony Edwards, Bruce Abbott, Kathy Bates, Clu Gulager, Jessie Kent
▶ Tobacco country of North Carolina, 1937, provides backdrop for torpid love triangle among farmer Edwards, young wife Singer,

and hired hand Abbott. Subtle adaptation of Louise Shivers's *Here to Get My Baby Out of Jail* features beautiful production values but suffers from extremely slow pacing.
Dist.: Paramount

SUMMER LOVERS 1982
★ ★ **R Romance 1:38**
☑ Nudity, strong sexual content, adult situations, explicit language
Dir: Randal Kleiser *Cast:* Peter Gallagher, Daryl Hannah, Valerie Quennessen, Barbara Rush, Carole Cook
▶ Young American couple Gallagher and Hannah vacation in the Aegean. Gallagher starts seeing French girl Quennessen; Hannah responds by finding another guy, but then opts for a ménage à trois with Gallagher and Quennessen. Not much of a story, but the stars and the Greek scenery are simply gorgeous.
Dist.: Nelson

SUMMER OF '42 1971
★ ★ ★ **PG Drama 1:44**
☑ Adult situations, explicit language
Dir: Robert Mulligan *Cast:* Jennifer O'Neill, Gary Grimes, Jerry Houser, Oliver Conant, Katherine Allentuck, Christopher Norris
▶ Teenager Grimes summers on New England island and shares growing pains with constantly horny pal Houser and younger, introspective sidekick Conant. Grimes develops crush on beautiful war bride O'Neill, but she thinks he's just a sweet kid. Anxious to lose virginity, Grimes and Houser pore over marriage manual and muster courage to buy condoms. For Grimes, however, sexual initiation must await a tragedy of World War II. Familiar teen territory given sweet and tender presentation. Nominated for four Oscars; winner for Michel Legrand's popular score.
Dist.: Warner

SUMMER PLACE, A 1959
★ ★ ★ **NR Drama 2:10**
Dir: Delmer Daves *Cast:* Robert Egan, Dorothy McGuire, Sandra Dee, Arthur Kennedy, Troy Donahue, Constance Ford
▶ Successful businessman Egan returns to Maine resort where ex-girlfriend McGuire is trapped in an unhappy marriage with alcoholic loser Kennedy. While Egan rekindles his romance with McGuire, daughter Dee falls for McGuire's son Donahue. Plush but superficial adaptation of Sloan Wilson's best-seller was a box office hit, helped immeasurably by Max Steiner's unforgettable theme song.
Dist.: Warner

SUMMER RENTAL 1985
★ ★ ★ **PG Comedy 1:28**
☑ Adult situations, explicit language
Dir: Carl Reiner *Cast:* John Candy, Richard Crenna, Rip Torn, Karen Austin, Kerri Green
▶ Burnt-out air traffic controller Candy takes his family for a Florida vacation. A series of comic disasters gives Candy little rest and he runs afoul of snobby Crenna. Candy gets a

chance for revenge in a boat race against Crenna. Slight but lazily enjoyable. Candy is a pleasing everyman hero and Austin gives sturdy support as his understanding wife. (CC)
Dist.: Paramount

SUMMER SCHOOL 1987
★ ★ ★ ★ **PG-13 Comedy 1:38**
☑ Explicit language, violence
Dir: Carl Reiner *Cast:* Mark Harmon, Kirstie Alley, Robin Thomas, Patrick Labyorteaux, Courtney Thorne Smith, Dean Cameron
▶ Summer-school teacher Harmon has to whip remedial students into shape to pass the big test or face losing his job. Harmon pursues fellow teacher Alley, who initially resists but then helps him. Jolly, low-brow humor with enough vulgar jokes to give teens a good time. Harmon displays an ingratiating personality. (CC)
Dist.: Paramount

SUMMER SCHOOL TEACHERS 1977
☆ **R Comedy 1:25**
☑ Nudity, strong sexual content, explicit language
Dir: Barbara Peters *Cast:* Candice Rialson, Pat Anderson, Rhonda Leigh Hopkins, Will Carney, Grainger Hines, Dick Miller
▶ Midwesterners Rialson, Anderson, and Hopkins become teachers in Los Angeles. Rialson tries to form a girls' football team and has an affair with another teacher, Anderson teaches chemistry and takes up with one of her students, and Hopkins has two affairs of her own between photography classes. Attractive cast gives performances above genre average although story is predictable.
Dist.: Nelson

SUMMER STOCK 1950
★ ★ ★ ★ **NR Musical 1:49**
Dir: Charles Walters *Cast:* Judy Garland, Gene Kelly, Eddie Bracken, Gloria De Haven, Marjorie Main, Phil Silvers
▶ New England farm girl Garland plays reluctant host to Kelly's theatrical troupe when her sister De Haven invites them to use the family barn for a summer production. Despite her initial misgivings, Garland eventually contracts the stage bug herself. High-spirited MGM fun with great stepping and singing from Kelly and Garland. Best number: "Get Happy."
Dist.: MGM/UA

SUMMER STORY, A 1988 British
★ ★ ★ **PG-13 Drama 1:35**
☑ Nudity, adult situations
Dir: Piers Haggard *Cast:* Imogen Stubbs, James Wilby, Susannah York, Jerome Flynn, Sophie Ward, Ken Colley
▶ Old-fashioned, tragic romance is set in turn-of-the-century England, where beautiful farm girl Stubbs meets lawyer Wilby when he injures his leg hiking in the moors. Suitor Flynn and her guardian York are against the romance, but Stubbs runs away to meet her lover in a sea-side town. Lovely performances by Stubbs and Wilby, insightful look at class differences, and emotional ending make this a real tearjerker.
Dist.: Media

SUMMERTIME 1955
★ ★ ★ ★ **NR Romance 1:39**
Dir: David Lean *Cast:* Katharine Hepburn, Rossano Brazzi, Darren McGavin, Isa Miranda, Mari Aldon, Gaitano Audiero
▶ American spinster Hepburn vacations in Venice, befriends street youth Audiero, and has ill-fated affair with antique-store proprietor Brazzi. Lovely, bittersweet, and scenic adaptation of the Arthur Laurents play *The Time of the Cuckoo*. Hepburn and Lean were Oscar-nominated.
Dist.: Nelson

SUMMER WISHES, WINTER DREAMS 1973
★ ★ ★ **PG Drama 1:35**
☑ Adult situations, explicit language
Dir: Gilbert Cates *Cast:* Joanne Woodward, Martin Balsam, Sylvia Sidney, Dori Brenner, Win Forman, Tresa Hughes
▶ When mother Sidney dies, housewife Woodward realizes she can no longer hide her dissatisfaction with her marriage. European vacation with husband Balsam, reviving his memories of service in World War II, leads to an attempt to confront their problems. Strong performances and earnest tone undermined by frequently tedious plot. Both Woodward and Sidney (returning to film after a sixteen-year hiatus) received Oscar nominations.
Dist.: RCA/Columbia

SUNBURN 1979
★ **PG Mystery-Suspense/Comedy 1:40**
☑ Adult situations, explicit language, mild violence
Dir: Richard C. Sarafian *Cast:* Farrah Fawcett-Majors, Charles Grodin, Art Carney, Joan Collins, William Daniels, John Hillerman
▶ In Acapulco, insurance investigator Grodin examines a possible murder which involves $5 million. Grodin enlists Fawcett-Majors to pose as his wife to help him enter city society; he's also assisted by retired detective Carney. Fawcett-Majors and Acapulco are easy on the eyes, but plot and characterizations are tired.
Dist.: Paramount

SUNDAY, BLOODY SUNDAY 1971 British
★ ★ **R Drama 1:50**
☑ Nudity, adult situations, explicit language
Dir: John Schlesinger *Cast:* Glenda Jackson, Peter Finch, Murray Head, Peggy Ashcroft, Tony Britton, Maurice Denham
▶ In London, divorced personnel worker Jackson and prominent physician Finch are both in love with young pop sculptor Head. At first all agree Head will divide attentions between Jackson and Finch, but arrangement falls victim to normal pitfalls of romantic triangles. Shrewd, sophisticated study of hetero- and

homosexual relationships and identities written by film critic–novelist Penelope Gilliat. Jackson, Finch, and director Schlesinger were all Oscar-nominated.
Dist.: Key

SUNDAY IN THE COUNTRY, A 1984 French
☆ **NR Drama 1:34**
☑ Adult situations
Dir: Bertrand Tavernier *Cast:* Lous Decreux, Sabine Azema, Michel Aumont, Genevieve Mnich, Monique Chaumette
▶ In turn-of-the-century France, elderly impressionist painter Decreux awaits the Sunday visit of his children: stuffy son Aumont accompanied by his pious wife Mnich, and beautiful free-spirit Azema, who always inspires her father. Small, delicately crafted film is expertly built on nuance and mood; enchanting and rewarding. [S]
Dist.: MGM/UA

SUNDAYS AND CYBELE 1962 French
★★ **NR Drama 1:50 B&W**
Dir: Serge Bourguignon *Cast:* Hardy Kruger, Patricia Gozzi, Nicole Courcel, Daniel Ivernel, Michel de Re
▶ War vet Kruger returns home from battle and befriends orphan Gozzi. A warm relationship develops, but the locals misunderstand its innocent nature, leading to a tragic conclusion. Moving and original study of a provocative subject won Best Foreign Film Oscar. [S]
Dist.: Foothill

SUNDAY TOO FAR AWAY 1975 Australian
★ **NR Drama 1:38**
☑ Explicit language
Dir: Ken Hannam *Cast:* Jack Thompson, Max Cullen, John Ewart, Reg Lyle
▶ Slice of Australian outback life focuses on sheep shearer Thompson and his co-workers, who work with intensity because they get paid per animal and then blow off steam at the local bar. Shearers go on strike when their bonus is withdrawn but must contend with replacement scabs. Sense of workers' isolation is well-rendered but subject is remote for American audiences.
Dist.: Embassy

SUNDOWN 1941
★ **NR Drama 1:30 B&W**
Dir: Henry Hathaway *Cast:* Gene Tierney, Bruce Cabot, George Sanders, Harry Carey, Carl Esmond, Dorothy Dandridge
▶ The Nazis are running guns to North African natives during World War II, and Army officer Sanders and local commissioner Cabot are out to stop it. Tierney, adopted daughter of an Arab trader, helps them by feigning to join Nazi chief Esmond. Sun, sand, and tedium.
Dist.: Cable [C]

SUNDOWNERS, THE 1960
★★★ **NR Drama 2:13**
Dir: Fred Zinnemann *Cast:* Deborah Kerr, Robert Mitchum, Peter Ustinov, Glynis Johns, Dina Merrill, Chips Rafferty
▶ Excellent family drama, filmed on location in Australia, follows the adventures of headstrong father Mitchum who prefers odd jobs on the open road to the security of a home, despite the pleas of wife Kerr to settle down. Sheep drive, forest fire, and adventures with a race horse provide a strong counterpoint to Kerr's warmly emotional performance. Received five Oscar nominations, including Johns's role as a spirited hotel owner.
Dist.: Warner

SUNRISE AT CAMPOBELLO 1960
★★★ **NR Biography 2:23**
Dir: Dore Schary *Cast:* Ralph Bellamy, Greer Garson, Hume Cronyn, Jean Hagen, Ann Shoemaker
▶ In the 1920s, Franklin Delano Roosevelt (Bellamy) is stricken with polio and paralyzed. His wife Eleanor (Garson) and his friend Cronyn give him the courage to attempt to walk again. Inspirational true story features Bellamy's outstanding impersonation of FDR, which is matched by Garson's Oscar-nominated turn. Adapted by Schary from his Broadway hit.
Dist.: Warner

SUNSET 1988
★★★ **R Mystery-Suspense 1:47**
☑ Adult situations, explicit language, mild violence
Dir: Blake Edwards *Cast:* Bruce Willis, James Garner, Malcolm McDowell, Mariel Hemingway, Kathleen Quinlan, Jennifer Edwards
▶ Real-life lawman Wyatt Earp (Garner) serves as technical advisor on movie starring 1920s screen hero Tom Mix (Willis). The pair team up to solve the murder of a local madam involved with movieland elite. Garner's gallantry, Willis (surprisingly effective playing it straight), and snazzy Roaring Twenties wrapping overcome plot flaws. (CC)
Dist.: RCA/Columbia

SUNSET BOULEVARD 1950
★★★ **NR Drama 1:50 B&W**
Dir: Billy Wilder *Cast:* William Holden, Gloria Swanson, Erich von Stroheim, Nancy Olson, Jack Webb, Buster Keaton, Fred Clark, Cecil B. DeMille
▶ "I am big—it's the pictures that got small!" claims faded silent screen queen Norma Desmond (Swanson). She hires disillusioned screenwriter Holden to aid her film comeback. He becomes her lover and is entrapped in her demented lifestyle. Immortal screen classic, one of Hollywood's sharpest looks at itself, is haunting and poignant all at once (especially in the bridge-game scene). Tremendous performances by Swanson and Holden (both Oscar-nominated, as was the picture, von Stroheim as Swanson's faithful butler, and

Olson). Three Oscars, including Best Screenplay.
Dist.: Paramount

SUNSET STRIP 1986
★ ★ NR Action-Adventure 1:24
☑ Adult situations, explicit language, violence
Dir: William Webb ***Cast:*** Tom Eplin, Cheri Cameron Newell, Danny Williams, John Mayall
▶ Photographer gets unwittingly involved in mob plot to take over Sunset Strip club. When the photographer's best pal is murdered, he finds both the police and the mob (who think he has evidence against them) on his trail. Mediocre story and acting.
Dist.: Vestron

SUNSHINE BOYS, THE 1975
★ ★ ★ ★ PG Comedy 1:51
☑ Adult situations, explicit language
Dir: Herbert Ross ***Cast:*** George Burns, Walter Matthau, Richard Benjamin, Lee Meredith, Carol Arthur, Howard Hesseman
▶ Scheming agent Benjamin plans to reunite his irritable comedian uncle Matthau with former partner Burns for TV special. Except the problem is the two vaudeville vets hate each other, so rehearsals are a running feud. Adaptation of Neil Simon Broadway hit is amusing and heartwarming. Comeback role for Burns (first film since 1939) won Oscar for Best Supporting Actor.
Dist.: MGM/UA

SUPERDAD 1974
★ G Family 1:36
Dir: Vincent McEveety ***Cast:*** Bob Crane, Barbara Rush, Kurt Russell, Joe Flynn, Kathleen Cody, Dick Van Patten
▶ Crane, disapproving of daughter Cody's choice of companions (especially boyfriend Russell), decides to spend more time with her. Cody isn't too pleased with the arrangement; mom Rush attempts to tone down the "superdad." Lighthearted Disney comedy provides painless entertainment. Crane is perfectly cast.
Dist.: Buena Vista

SUPER FLY 1972
★ ★ R Action-Adventure 1:31
☑ Nudity, adult situations, explicit language, violence
Dir: Gordon Parks, Jr. ***Cast:*** Ron O'Neal, Sheila Frazier, Carl Lee, Julius W. Harris, Charles McGregor, Sig Shore
▶ Cocaine dealer O'Neal dreams of one big score before retirement with girlfriend Frazier. With partner Lee, O'Neal seeks help from mentor Harris, who directs the two to big drug source: corrupt police inspector Shore. Things heat up for O'Neal when both Lee and Shore double-cross him. Most successful of '70s black exploitation pics boasts hard-hitting depiction of seedy underworld and hit soundtrack from Curtis Mayfield. Story with coke dealing hero seems dated today.
Dist.: Warner

SUPER FUZZ 1981
★ ★ ★ PG Comedy 1:37
☑ Explicit language, violence
Dir: Sergio Corbucci ***Cast:*** Terence Hill, Ernest Borgnine, Joanne Dru, Marc Lawrence
▶ Exposed to radiation due to Everglades nuke test, rookie cop Hill finds himself with extraordinary powers. Hill and partner Borgnine proceed to bust up mob counterfeiting ring. Modest escapism has interesting premise.
Dist.: Nelson

SUPERGIRL 1984
★ ★ PG Fantasy/Action-Adventure 1:45
☑ Mild violence
Dir: Jeannot Szwarc ***Cast:*** Faye Dunaway, Helen Slater, Peter O'Toole, Mia Farrow, Peter Cook, Brenda Vaccaro, Simon Ward
▶ Superman's teenage cousin Supergirl (Slater) comes to small midwestern town to recover her planet's life-sustaining device. She must battle evil priestess Dunaway, who gets hold of it first. Kids should enjoy this although it's not up to the level of the *Superman* series. Slater is perfectly cast, but Dunaway camps it up mercilessly and steals the show.
Dist.: IVE

SUPERMAN 1978
★ ★ ★ ★ PG Fantasy/Action-Adventure 2:23
☑ Explicit language, mild violence
Dir: Richard Donner ***Cast:*** Christopher Reeve, Marlon Brando, Gene Hackman, Margot Kidder, Glenn Ford, Valerie Perrine, Ned Beatty, Glenn Ford, Jackie Cooper
▶ When planet Krypton explodes, scientist Brando sends his only son in a rocket to Earth. After the superpowered being is raised by Pa Kent (Ford) in Kansas, he goes to the city, adopts the identity of mild-mannered reporter Clark Kent, falls for Lois Lane (Kidder), and battles villainous Lex Luthor (Hackman). Extravaganza impressively combines special effects, comic book heroics, and tongue-in-cheek comedy. Reeve plays Superman/Clark Kent with infectious humor and his aerial romance with Kidder is surprisingly lyrical. Funniest moment: Reeve's phone booth reaction. Led to three sequels.
Dist.: Warner

SUPERMAN II 1981
★ ★ ★ ★ ★ PG Fantasy/Action-Adventure 2:07
☑ Adult situations, violence
Dir: Richard Lester ***Cast:*** Christopher Reeve, Margot Kidder, Gene Hackman, Terence Stamp, Sarah Douglas, Jackie Cooper, Ned Beatty, Valerie Perrine
▶ Brash, irreverent sequel to *Superman* pits the Man of Steel (Reeve) against three supercriminals from Krypton determined to rule Earth. Love affair with reporter Lois Lane (Kid-

der) and the wily schemes of arch-criminal Lex Luthor (Hackman) provide unexpected obstacles to Superman's efforts. Strong direction concentrates on the humor and humanity behind the inspired special effects. Hackman, Stamp, and Douglas are memorable villains in the series's wildest, funniest episode. Followed by *Superman III*.
Dist.: Warner

SUPERMAN III 1983
★ ★ ★ **PG Fantasy/Action-Adventure 2:05**
☑ Adult situations, mild violence
Dir: Richard Lester   *Cast:* Christopher Reeve, Richard Pryor, Robert Vaughn, Annette O'Toole, Pamela Stephenson, Jackie Cooper, Annie Ross
▶ Man of Steel (Reeve) returns to Smallville for high school reunion. When Superman thwarts plan to control weather satellite, villain Vaughn has computer whiz Pryor make artificial Kryptonite to stop him. Third installment in the series is lots of fun with more emphasis on comedy than action. Reeve shines in the sequence where Superman goes bad, drinking, womanizing, and straightening up the Leaning Tower of Pisa. The underrated O'Toole (as Lana Lang) is Clark Kent's old sweetheart.
Dist.: Warner

SUPERMAN IV: THE QUEST FOR PEACE 1987
★ ★ **PG Fantasy/Action-Adventure 1:30**
☑ Explicit language, violence
Dir: Sidney J. Furie   *Cast:* Christopher Reeve, Gene Hackman, Jackie Cooper, Margot Kidder, Mariel Hemingway, Marc McClure, Jon Cryer
▶ Superman (Reeve) rids the world of nuclear weapons in response to a child's letter; Lex Luthor (Hackman) takes advantage of the situation to create a nuclear-powered villain to fight the Man of Steel. Fourth in the series is still enjoyable; special effects seem a bit skimpy but Reeve and Hemingway (as the daughter of the Daily Planet's new owner, who tries to turn paper into a sensationalist tabloid) are charming. Cleverest scene: Reeve trying to be in two places at once for dates with Hemingway and Lois Lane (Kidder). **(CC)**
Dist.: Warner

SUPERMAN AND THE MOLE MEN 1951
★ **NR Fantasy 0:58 B&W**
Dir: Lee Sholem   *Cast:* George Reeves, Phyllis Coates, Jeff Corey, Walter Reed, J. Farrell MacDonald, Stanley Andrews
▶ Pilot episode of the long-running TV series finds *Daily Planet* reporters Clark Kent (Reeves) and Lois Lane (Coates) investigating strange disturbance near an oil-mining town. Talky story skimps on special effects, but Reeves provides an interesting contrast to latter-day Superman Christopher Reeve.
Dist.: Warner

SUPERNATURALS, THE 1986
★ **R Drama 1:20**

☑ Explicit language, violence
Dir: Armand Mastroianni   *Cast:* Maxwell Caulfield, Nichelle Nichols, Talia Balsam, Bradford Bancroft, LeVar Burton, Bobby DiCicco
▶ During the Civil War, a group of Confederate soldiers are killed when Union counterparts force them across a minefield. In the present, sergeant Nichols commands a unit of soldiers in the area. The Confederate zombies come back to life to menace them. Straight-to-video release doesn't aim high. **(CC)**
Dist.: Nelson

SUPERSTITION 1985
★ ★ **NR Horror 1:24**
☑ Explicit language, graphic violence
Dir: James W. Roberson   *Cast:* James Houghton, Albert Salmi, Lynn Carlin, Larry Pennell, Heidi Bohay
▶ In 1692, a demonically possessed woman is drowned for being a witch. The woman's spirit returns in the present to menace residents of an old house. Good production values, decent acting, but routine screenplay lacks suspense and surprises.
Dist.: Vestron

SUPPORT YOUR LOCAL SHERIFF! 1969
★ ★ ★ ★ **G Western/Comedy 1:32**
Dir: Burt Kennedy   *Cast:* James Garner, Joan Hackett, Walter Brennan, Harry Morgan, Jack Elam, Bruce Dern
▶ Amiable spoof of Westerns, with Garner giving an adroit performance as a peace-loving drifter who becomes the unwilling sheriff of a gold-mining boomtown. Aided by town drunk Elam as his deputy, he arrests immature killer Dern and faces down Dern's father Brennan (lampooning his *My Darling Clementine* role) in a smart parody of shoot-outs. **(CC)**
Dist.: CBS/Fox

SURE THING, THE 1985
★ ★ ★ ★ **PG-13 Comedy 1:34**
☑ Adult situations, explicit language
Dir: Rob Reiner   *Cast:* John Cusack, Daphne Zuniga, Viveca Lindfors, Tim Robbins, Boyd Gaines, Nicollette Sheridan
▶ College party animal Cusack strikes out with women, including prim and proper coed Zuniga. Over Christmas break, mismatched duo share ride to California, where Zuniga will visit equally uptight beau Gaines while Cusack has high hopes for gorgeous surfer girl Sheridan, billed as a "sure thing." The two bicker but love blossoms. Romantic road comedy with overtones of 1934's *It Happened One Night* was surprise hit. **(CC)**
Dist.: Nelson

SURF NAZIS MUST DIE 1987
☆ **R Comedy 1:20**
☑ Nudity, adult situations, explicit language, violence
Dir: Peter George   *Cast:* Barry Brenner, Gail Neely, Michael Sonye, Dawn Wildsmith, Tom Shell

▶ Killing and surfing are two of the Surf Nazi gang's favorite activities on California beaches. Victim's mother Neely buys gun, grenades, and motorcycle to get revenge. Overdrawn, cartoonish humor provides some laughs although many will find this racist and repulsive. Neely, however, is wonderful.
Dist.: Media

SURF II 1984
☆ **R Comedy 1:26**
☑ Nudity, adult situations, explicit language, mild violence, adult humor
Dir: Randall Badat *Cast:* Eddie Deezen, Linda Kerridge, Lyle Waggoner, Ron Paillo, Ruth Buzzi, Eric Stoltz
▶ Wimpy chemist Deezen plots to rid Southern California beaches of surfers by making them drink Buzz Cola, soft drink that literally rots the brain. Healthy bodies, silly humor (including an eating contest and autopsy), and one-note performance by Jerry Lewis clone Deezen in this *Beach Blanket Bingo* satire.
Dist.: Media

SURRENDER 1987
★ ★ ★ **PG Romance/Comedy 1:36**
☑ Adult situations, explicit language
Dir: Jerry Belson *Cast:* Sally Field, Michael Caine, Steve Guttenberg, Peter Boyle, Jackie Cooper, Iman
▶ Wealthy writer Caine, tired of being taken to the cleaners in divorce proceedings, pretends to be poor. Struggling artist Field falls for him, but money worries and Field's lawyer beau Guttenberg provide obstacles to the affair. Sparkling chemistry between Field and Caine, funny support from Guttenberg, and the most bizarre chance meeting in recent films (Field and Caine are stripped and tied up together when terrorists invade a party). (CC)
Dist.: Warner

SURVIVAL GAME 1987
★ **R Action-Adventure 1:32**
☑ Adult situations, explicit language, violence
Dir: Herb Freed *Cast:* Mike Norris, Deborah Goodrich, Seymour Cassel, Arlene Golonka, Ed Bernard
▶ Survival-camp trainee Norris (son of Chuck) meets Goodrich in car crash and falls for her. When Goodrich and her ex-1960s drug guru dad Cassel are kidnapped, Norris battles the abductors. Martial arts master Norris proves himself to be chip-off-the-old-chopping-block and Cassel is hilarious.
Dist.: Media

SURVIVAL QUEST 1989
★ ★ **R Action-Adventure 1:30**
☑ Explicit language, violence
Dir: Don Coscarelli *Cast:* Lance Henriksen, Dermot Mulroney, Mark Rolston, Steve Antin, Paul Provenza, Traci Lin
▶ Instructor Henriksen takes six people out to the Rockies for a wilderness course. When an insane member of a rival school shoots their teacher, the students' new skills are tested as they attempt to reach civilization before being hunted down. Simplistic plot rendered with skill. Bland characters, good stunts, pretty scenery. (CC)
Dist.: CBS/Fox

SURVIVAL RUN 1980
★ ★ **R Action-Adventure 1:30**
☑ Rape, explicit language, violence
Dir: Larry Spiegel *Cast:* Peter Graves, Ray Milland, Vincent Van Patten, Pedro Armendariz, Jr., Alan Conrad
▶ Five teens led by Van Patten are stranded in the desert when their van breaks down during a carefree outing. Accidentally stumbling upon Graves, Milland, and their drug-running gang, the young people are forced to flee, then fight for their lives. Standard teens-in-danger plot establishes bad guys with pointless rape and murder.
Dist.: Media

SURVIVOR, THE 1980 Australian
★ ★ **NR Mystery-Suspense 1:24**
☑ Adult situations, explicit language, graphic violence
Dir: David Hemmings *Cast:* Robert Powell, Jenny Agutter, Joseph Cotten, Angela Punch-McGregor, Ralph Cotterill, Peter Sumner
▶ When a 747 explodes shortly after takeoff, only pilot Powell survives. He investigates the tragedy and is caught in a web of occult terror and corporate conspiracy. Strong opening will hook viewers, but pacing falls off after rapid start. Intriguing supernatural elements, restrained performances.
Dist.: Warner

SURVIVORS, THE 1983
★ ★ ★ **R Comedy 1:43**
☑ Explicit language, violence, adult humor
Dir: Michael Ritchie *Cast:* Robin Williams, Walter Matthau, Jerry Reed, James Wainwright, Kristen Vigard, Annie McEnroe
▶ Executive Williams is fired on the same day Matthau loses his gas station. The luckless pair then witness Reed committing hold-up; they hide in a survivalist camp as Reed pursues them. Mixture of black humor and blunt slapstick is uneven, but the two stars generate laughs. (CC)
Dist.: RCA/Columbia

SUSANA 1951 Mexican
☆ **NR Drama 1:12 B&W**
Dir: Luis Buñuel *Cast:* Rosita Quintana, Fernando Soler, Victor Manuel Mendoza, Matilde Palou
▶ Beautiful young reprobate Quintana escapes from a detention home and hides out on an isolated plantation estate. After being taken in by the family, she repays their kindness with seduction, trickery, and disruptive

immorality. Overheated tale of a minor vixen is best appreciated by Buñuel's fans. [S]
Dist.: Media

SUSANNAH OF THE MOUNTIES 1939
★ ★ **NR Drama 1:18 B&W**
Dir: William A. Seiter *Cast:* Shirley Temple, Randolph Scott, Margaret Lockwood, J. Farrell MacDonald, Moroni Olsen
▶ Blackfoot Indians kill Temple's parents, leaving her in the charge of Mountie Scott and his girlfriend Lockwood. Further friction between whites and Indians is fomented by an evil medicine man, and Temple must save Scott from being burned at the stake. Minor Temple vehicle gives star only one musical number.
Dist.: CBS/Fox

SUSAN SLEPT HERE 1954
★ ★ **NR Comedy 1:38**
Dir: Frank Tashlin *Cast:* Dick Powell, Debbie Reynolds, Anne Francis, Horace McMahon, Glenda Farrell, Alvy Moore
▶ Screenwriter Powell needs first-hand research on young social miscreants, so two friendly cops hand him Reynolds, a certifiable juvenile delinquent who proves to be more than a handful. Powell's girlfriend Francis suspects hanky panky between the two. Winking, leering sex humor from a more repressed era.
Dist.: VCI

SUSPECT 1987
★ ★ ★ ★ ★ **R Mystery-Suspense 2:01**
☑ Explicit language, violence
Dir: Peter Yates *Cast:* Cher, Dennis Quaid, Liam Neeson, John Mahoney, Joe Mantegna, Philip Bosco
▶ Cher is a public defender who puts her career in jeopardy when she becomes involved with juror Quaid during the murder trial of homeless Neeson, who is also a deaf-mute. Her case is hindered by tough-as-nails judge Mahoney, macho prosecutor Mantegna, and sleazy, corrupt senator Bosco. Well-done courtroom whodunit features excellent cast and creditable script.
Dist.: RCA/Columbia

SUSPICION 1941
★ ★ ★ ★ **NR Mystery-Suspense 1:40 B&W**
Dir: Alfred Hitchcock *Cast:* Cary Grant, Joan Fontaine, Cedric Hardwicke, Nigel Bruce, Dame May Whitty, Isabel Jeans
▶ Fontaine, a spinsterish wallflower from a wealthy family, weds flamboyant playboy Grant, disregarding rumors about his past. Soon spendthrift Grant is in financial hot water and Fontaine fears he'll kill her for insurance money. When Grant's best pal Bruce dies, Fontaine's suspicions peak. Fine Hitchcock suspenser will please fans and newcomers alike. Fontaine is memorable in an Oscar-winning turn.
Dist.: Turner [C]

SUSPIRIA 1977 Italian
★ **R Horror 1:32**

☑ Graphic violence
Dir: Dario Argento *Cast:* Jessica Harper, Stefania Casini, Alida Valli, Joan Bennett, Udo Kier
▶ American Harper enrolls in German dancing school where evil doings pile up: two girls are murdered on her first night, worms and bats plague the dorm, and her best friend disappears. Argento's overripe technique and use of wall-to-wall electronic music borders on the ridiculous but nevertheless creates a genuinely horrific mood. A cult favorite.
Dist.: Magnum

SUZANNE 1981 Canadian
☆ **R Romance 1:54**
☑ Nudity, adult situations, explicit language
Dir: Robin Spry *Cast:* Jennifer Dale, Winston Rekert, Gabriel Arcand, Ken Pogue, Helen Hughes, Michael Ironside
▶ Middle-class Montrealite Dale grows up torn between two lovers: handsome rake Rekert and quiet but solid Arcand. The former impregnates her but then is imprisoned; the latter eventually marries her and brings up the child. Overly maudlin love story carried by the lovely Dale.
Dist.: Vestron

SVENGALI 1931
★ **NR Drama 1:21 B&W**
Dir: Archie Mayo *Cast:* John Barrymore, Marian Marsh, Donald Crisp, Carmel Myers, Bramwell Fletcher, Luis Alberni
▶ Former model Marsh takes up singing under the tutelage of Barrymore, who sidelines as a hypnotist. Eventually he uses his hypnotic powers to guide her to stardom. Wild sets and imaginative photography are the stars of this poorly scripted remake of silent *Trilby*. Written by J. Grubb Alexander from a novel by George du Maurier.
Dist.: Cable

SWAMP THING 1982
★ ★ **PG Sci-Fi 1:30**
☑ Brief nudity, explicit language, violence
Dir: Wes Craven *Cast:* Louis Jourdan, Adrienne Barbeau, Ray Wise, David Hess, Nicholas Worth, Dick Durack
▶ Scientist Wise tries to combine plant and animal characteristics but formula turns him into monster when villain Jourdan interferes. Jourdan hunts the Swamp Thing; government agent Barbeau battles the bad guy and wins the heart of the creature. Tongue-in-cheek entertainment inspired by the DC Comics character. Sequel: *Return of the Swamp Thing*.
Dist.: Nelson

SWAMP WOMEN 1955
★ **NR Action-Adventure 1:13**
Dir: Roger Corman *Cast:* Michael Connors, Marie Windsor, Beverly Garland, Carole Matthews, Susan Cummings
▶ Geologist Connors is boating through the Louisiana swamps when he is set upon by three love-starved women's prison escapees

searching for a cache of hidden diamonds. Among the femmes is Matthews, an undercover policewoman who is far from indifferent to Connors's manly charms. Super-schlock for Corman-cultists. Also known as *Swamp Diamonds* and *Cruel Swamp*.
Dist.: Sinister

SWANN IN LOVE 1984 French
☆ **R Drama 1:50**
☑ Nudity, strong sexual content, adult situations, explicit language
Dir: Volker Schlondorff ***Cast:*** Jeremy Irons, Ornella Muti, Alain Delon, Fanny Ardant, Marie-Christine Barrault
▶ In the 1880s, aristocrat Irons falls for Muti, an enigmatic Parisian of scandalous reputation. He jeopardizes his social standing to marry her but the relationship slowly deteriorates. Flawless visuals, technically superb production, and knockout performances from Irons, Delon, and Ardant, but film suffers from stately pace, cryptic resolution, and lack of genuine passion, in spite of some graphic sex scenes. Adapted from Marcel Proust's *Remembrance of Things Past*. [S]
Dist.: Media

SWAP, THE 1980
★ **R Drama 2:00**
☑ Nudity, adult situations, explicit language
Dir: Jordan Leondopoulos, John C. Broderick ***Cast:*** Robert De Niro, Jarred Mickey, Jennifer Warren, Terrayne Crawford, Martin Kelley, Viva
▶ New York film editor De Niro, hoping to raise money for a documentary about Richard Nixon, spends a weekend with a crowd of wealthy characters on Long Island. Originally released in 1971 as *Sam's Song*; director Broderick shot new footage for 1980 rerelease in theaters and on video. Flawed and pretentious result is of note only for early performance by De Niro.
Dist.: Vestron

SWARM, THE 1978
★★ **PG Horror 1:56**
☑ Adult situations, mild violence
Dir: Irwin Allen ***Cast:*** Michael Caine, Henry Fonda, Katharine Ross, Richard Widmark, Olivia de Havilland, Fred MacMurray
▶ Scientist Caine and general Widmark lead the effort to stop a swarm of African killer bees who terrorize the Southwest. A military base, a small town flower festival, and the city of Houston are among the bees' targets. Plenty of action and creepy moments; marred by talkiness and stereotyped characters.
Dist.: Warner

SWEENEY TODD, THE DEMON BARBER OF FLEET STREET 1936 British
☆ **NR Horror 1:08 B&W**
Dir: George King ***Cast:*** Tod Slaughter, Bruce Seton, Stello Rho, Eve Lister, Ben Soutten, D. J. Williams
▶ Barber Slaughter has a trap door under his chair that propels wealthy customers into his basement. Once there, they are robbed and cooked into pies for sale in the shop next door. Based on the play that inspired the Stephen Sondheim musical *Sweeney Todd*, overly histrionic British horror offering doesn't scare or otherwise compel interest. Also known as *The Demon Barber of Fleet Street*.
Dist.: Video Yesteryear

SWEET BIRD OF YOUTH 1962
★★★ **NR Drama 2:00**
Dir: Richard Brooks ***Cast:*** Paul Newman, Geraldine Page, Shirley Knight, Ed Begley, Rip Torn, Mildred Dunnock
▶ Seedy Hollywood has-been Page accompanies boyfriend Newman on a visit to his home town, where the would-be actor confronts his past. Knight is the girl Newman once got pregnant, Begley is her politician father, and Torn is the wronged brother bent on violent retribution. Newman, Page, and Torn recreate their Broadway roles in this cleaned-up, but still fascinating, version of Tennessee Williams's stage hit.
Dist.: MGM/UA

SWEET CHARITY 1969
★★★★ **G Musical 2:15**
Dir: Bob Fosse ***Cast:*** Shirley MacLaine, Sammy Davis, Jr., John McMartin, Ricardo Montalban, Chita Rivera, Paula Kelly, Stubby Kaye
▶ After being literally dumped by boyfriend, dance-hall hostess MacLaine has brief fling with movie star Montalban and tries for relationship with the more stable McMartin. Tuneful good time features energetic direction by Fosse and loads of waifish charm from MacLaine. Exuberant Cy Coleman–Dorothy Fields score includes "If My Friends Could See Me Now" and "Hey, Big Spender." Based on the Broadway musical, in turn adapted from Federico Fellini's *Nights of Cabiria*.
Dist.: MCA

SWEET COUNTRY 1987
★★ **R Drama 2:30**
☑ Nudity, adult situations, explicit language, violence
Dir: Michael Cacoyannis ***Cast:*** Jane Alexander, John Cullum, Carole Laure, Franco Nero, Joanna Pettet, Randy Quaid
▶ In 1973, American activist Alexander, her teacher-husband Cullum, and their daughters Laure and Pettet get involved in political intrigue when Chilean Marxist leader Allende is overthrown. Weighty subject matter elicits sympathy, but flat dialogue, miscast actors, and dull pacing fail to engage the audience.
Dist.: Magnum

SWEET DREAMS 1985
★★★★ **PG-13 Biography/Music 1:55**
☑ Adult situations, explicit language, violence
Dir: Karel Reisz ***Cast:*** Jessica Lange, Ed

Harris, Ann Wedgeworth, David Clennon, James Staley

▶ True story of country singer Patsy Cline (Lange) traces her romance with abusive redneck husband Harris, her rise to stardom, and her tragic plane-crash death. Solid and affecting with meticulous direction by Reisz, tangy down-home dialogue, marvelous soundtrack of Cline's hits (including "Walking After Midnight," "Blue Moon of Kentucky," the title tune), Oscar-nominated performance by Lange, and superb support from Harris and Wedgeworth as Lange's salt-of-the-earth mom.
Dist.: HBO

SWEETHEARTS 1938
★ NR Musical 2:00
Dir: W. S. Van Dyke II *Cast:* Jeanette MacDonald, Nelson Eddy, Frank Morgan, Ray Bolger, Florence Rice, Mischa Auer
▶ Married Broadway stars MacDonald and Eddy want a hiatus from their show after a six-year run. They consider going Hollywood, but producer Morgan and other assorted hangers-on scheme to keep them in New York. Witty Dorothy Parker/Alan Campbell screenplay makes this one of the team's best vehicles. Songs include title tune and "Pretty as a Picture." MGM's first three-strip Technicolor movie won an Oscar for cinematography.
Dist.: MGM/UA

SWEET HEARTS DANCE 1988
★ ★ ★ R Drama 1:42
☑ Brief nudity, adult situations, explicit language
Dir: Robert Greenwald *Cast:* Don Johnson, Susan Sarandon, Jeff Daniels, Elizabeth Perkins, Kate Reid, Justin Henry
▶ Vermont carpenter Johnson suffers thirtysomethingish crisis and walks out on wife Sarandon and three kids; his best pal Daniels, a principal, falls in love with teacher Perkins, but she is iffy about marriage. Ernest Thompson screenplay has message as comfy as its New England atmosphere. Neat change-of-pace performance by Johnson, who leads a strong cast, but sluggish script and lack of strong focus detract.
Dist.: RCA/Columbia

SWEETIE 1989 Australian
☆ NR Drama 1:30
☑ Nudity, strong sexual content, adult situations, explicit language
Dir: Jane Campion *Cast:* Genvieve Lemmon, Karen Colston, Tom Lycos, Michael Lake, Jon Darling, Dorothy Barry, Michael Lake
▶ Colston and her live-in boyfriend Lycos have houseguests: her overweight, spoiled-rotten, aspiring-singer/sister Lemmon and her manager/lover Lake. Colston can't bear having sis around, and matters get worse when their father, who has always doted on Lem-

mon, arrives to do more of the same. Unlikable characters, unfocused screenplay, and generally distasteful tone make this one hard to take.
Dist.: IVE

SWEET LIBERTY 1986
★ ★ ★ PG Comedy 1:47
☑ Brief nudity, adult situations, explicit language
Dir: Alan Alda *Cast:* Alan Alda, Michael Caine, Michelle Pfeiffer, Bob Hoskins, Lillian Gish, Saul Rubinek
▶ Hollywood filmmakers descend on small Long Island town to shoot adaptation of Revolutionary War saga written by college professor Alda. Hack screenwriter Hoskins has rewritten Alda's tale with eye on box office; youthful director Rubinek refuses to accommodate Alda's desire for changes. However, Alda quickly learns vain stars Caine and Pfeiffer have real clout and ingratiates himself into their good graces. Amiable comedy tweaks both moviemaking and bed-hopping on campus and film locations. **(CC)**
Dist.: MCA

SWEET LIES 1988
★ ★ ★ R Romance/Comedy 1:26
☑ Brief nudity, adult situations, explicit language
Dir: Nathalie Delon *Cast:* Treat Williams, Joanna Pacula, Julianne Phillips, Laura Manszky, Norbert Weisser
▶ American detective Williams, in Paris to investigate insurance fraud, becomes object of bet between Pacula and Phillips as to who will bed him first. Complications arise when both gals fall for him. Slipshod but ingratiating farce with appealing performers and picture-postcard views of Paris. **(CC)**
Dist.: CBS/Fox

SWEET LORRAINE 1987
★ ★ PG-13 Drama 1:31
☑ Adult situations, explicit language
Dir: Steve Gomer *Cast:* Maureen Stapleton, Trini Alvarado, Lee Richardson, John Bedford Lloyd, Freddie Roman, Giancarlo Esposito
▶ Modest, wistful account of a summer season at a run-down Catskills resort facing bankruptcy. Young Alvarado pitches in to help her grandmother, resort owner Stapleton, and finds herself growing increasingly attached to the staff and guests. Charmingly sentimental and nostalgic despite unfocused plot and subdued style.
Dist.: Paramount

SWEET REVENGE 1987
★ R Action-Adventure 1:19
☑ Nudity, adult situations, explicit language, violence
Dir: Mark Sobel *Cast:* Nancy Allen, Ted Shackelford, Martin Landau, Sal Landi, Michelle Little
▶ Reporter Allen investigates Far East white

slavery ring, is kidnapped, and brought before ringleader Landau. American smuggler Shackelford helps Allen escape. Low-budget heroics in the vein of *Romancing the Stone*.
Dist.: Media

SWEET 16 1983
★★ R Horror 1:25
☑ Adult situations, explicit language, graphic violence
Dir: Jim Sotos ***Cast:*** Bo Hopkins, Susan Strasberg, Don Stroud, Dana Kimball, Patrick Macnee
▶ Typical teens-in-peril suspenser takes place in small-town Texas. Old Indian is accused of two teen murders and hanged by townsfolk. Plot also involves violating sacred Indian burial ground and a suspect with a bad case of split personality. Climaxes in a gory and bloody sweet sixteen party.
Dist.: Vestron

SWEET SMELL OF SUCCESS 1957
★★★★ NR Drama 1:36 B&W
Dir: Alexander Mackendrick ***Cast:*** Burt Lancaster, Tony Curtis, Susan Harrison, Martin Milner, Barbara Nichols, Sam Levene
▶ Publicist Curtis's unscrupulous existence depends on getting clients' names into Lancaster's newspaper column. Thus he is compelled to obey when Lancaster asks him to break up his sister Harrison's relationship with Milner. Blistering, cynical look at Broadway. Memorably nasty dialogue highlights hard-edged Ernest Lehman/Clifford Odets screenplay. Lancaster's tightly constricted characterization is perfectly complemented by Curtis's energetic one.
Dist.: MGM/UA

SWEET SWEETBACK'S BAADASSSSS SONG 1971
☆ R Drama 1:37
☑ Nudity, strong sexual content, adult situations, explicit language
Dir: Melvin Van Peebles ***Cast:*** Melvin Van Peebles, Rhetta Hughes, Simon Chuckster, John Amos
▶ Nicknamed "Sweetback" by prostitute who seduced him as young boy, sex performer Van Peebles beats two cops who arrest him. Police pursue him as he visits a variety of women. Chase ends in climactic showdown at Mexican border. Sexy and stylish low-budget classic caused great controversy when released. A one-man show from Van Peebles as director, writer, producer, composer, and star. Not for the faint of heart, but daredevils will be amply rewarded.
Dist.: Magnum

SWEET WILLIAM 1979 British
★ R Drama 1:32
☑ Brief nudity, adult situations, explicit language
Dir: Claude Whatham ***Cast:*** Sam Waterston, Jenny Agutter, Anna Massey, Geraldine James, Daphne Oxenford, Rachel Bell
▶ With her boyfriend away in America, Londoner Agutter has affair with Waterston, a lying womanizer who can't keep his hands off his former wives or any other lady for that matter. She then becomes pregnant. Small-scaled story just never gets going due to tiresome characters and miscast Waterston.
Dist.: Prism

SWEPT AWAY. . . 1975 Italian
★★★ R Comedy 1:56
☑ Nudity, strong sexual content, adult situations, explicit language, adult humor
Dir: Lina Wertmuller ***Cast:*** Giancarlo Giannini, Mariangela Melato
▶ Shrewish capitalist Melato is rich, haughty, liberated, and miserable. Peasant sailor Giannini is a macho Communist continually humiliated by employer. When quirk of fate maroons them on deserted isle, their roles reverse as master becomes slave en route to love. Moral fable with surprise twist at end employs gorgeous cinematography, passionate performances from leads, and laughs rooted in truth. Resulting mix of sex and politics can both outrage and delight. [S]
Dist.: RCA/Columbia

SWIMMER, THE 1968
★ PG Drama 1:34
☑ Adult situations
Dir: Frank Perry ***Cast:*** Burt Lancaster, Janice Rule, Janet Landgard, Tony Bickley, Marge Champion, Nancy Cushman
▶ Based on a short story by John Cheever, episodic drama concerns efforts of middle-aged adman Lancaster to traverse Connecticut suburb by swimming from pool to pool of friends and neighbors. At each stop he encounters someone whose life he's touched, setting off memories and fantasies which gradually reveal the disorder of his life. Intriguing look at upper-class manners and hypocrisy marred by vague and inconclusive ending. Debut score by Marvin Hamlisch.
Dist.: RCA/Columbia

SWIMMING TO CAMBODIA 1987
★ NR Documentary 1:27
☑ Explicit language
Dir: Jonathan Demme ***Cast:*** Spalding Gray
▶ Performance artist Gray recounts his experiences in Thailand while playing a small part in *The Killing Fields*. Cleverly understated direction by Demme effectively transfers Gray's stage monologue to the screen, but only the adventurous will warm to his rambling, seriocomic anecdotes.
Dist.: Warner

SWIM TEAM 1979
★ PG Comedy 1:32
☑ Brief nudity, explicit language
Dir: James Polakoff ***Cast:*** James Daughton, Stephen Furst, Richard Young, Jenny Neumann, Buster Crabbe
▶ Coach Daughton attempts to reverse swim team's losing ways through hard work and

practice. However, his infidelity to star swimmer/girlfriend Neumann jeopardizes that goal. Cast looks great, acts not so great. Furst provides a few funny moments in a screenplay that gives him little to do.
Dist.: Prism

SWING HIGH, SWING LOW 1937
★ NR Drama 1:35 B&W
Dir: Mitchell Leison   *Cast:* Carole Lombard, Fred MacMurray, Charles Butterworth, Jean Dixon, Dorothy Lamour, Anthony Quinn
▶ Soon after meeting on shipboard, trumpeter MacMurray and singer Lombard are stranded in Panama. After they marry, MacMurray returns to New York, where he becomes a star and begins squiring sultry Lamour. Lombard wants out of the marriage, until MacMurray begins a downward spiral only she can halt. Engrossing remake of *Dance of Life* was later done as *When My Baby Smiles at Me.*
Dist.: Cable

SWING SHIFT 1984
★ ★ ★ PG Drama 1:40
☑ Adult situations, explicit language
Dir: Jonathan Demme   *Cast:* Goldie Hawn, Kurt Russell, Christine Lahti, Ed Harris, Fred Ward, Holly Hunter
▶ When husband Harris enlists in World War II Navy, Hawn takes riveter job at a Santa Monica factory. Soon she's romanced by coworker Russell, who plays trumpet at dance hall owned by Ward, the former boyfriend of her best pal Lahti. Cozy Hawn-Russell affair pops a seam when Harris gets wind of adultery and Lahti entertains Russell for night. An admirable attempt to portray contributions of working women in preliberation era, but wartime romance doesn't pass muster. Terrific supporting work from underrated Lahti earned Oscar nomination.
Dist.: Warner

SWING TIME 1936
★ ★ ★ ★ NR Musical 1:44 B&W
Dir: George Stevens   *Cast:* Fred Astaire, Ginger Rogers, Victor Moore, Helen Broderick, Eric Blore, Betty Furness
▶ Gambling dancer Astaire goes to New York to earn money for a wedding, but falls in love with dance instructor Rogers instead. One of the best Astaire-Rogers teamings features wonderful comic support from Moore and Broderick, an unforgettable Jerome Kern-Dorothy Fields score (including the Oscar-winning "The Way You Look Tonight"), and unparalleled dancing—particularly Astaire's Oscar-nominated "Bojangles of Harlem" and a dazzling tap duet to "Pick Yourself Up."
Dist.: Turner

SWISS CONSPIRACY, THE 1975 U.S./German
★ PG Action-Adventure 1:31
☑ Brief nudity, violence
Dir: Jack Arnold   *Cast:* David Janssen,

Senta Berger, John Ireland, John Saxon, Elke Sommer, Ray Milland
▶ Swiss bank customers are confronted by an extortionist who demands big bucks to keep their numbered accounts secret. Private detective Janssen is hired to uncover the blackmailer. Perplexing plot does nicely in keeping viewers off-balance. Glamorous cast and Swiss locations provide added attractions.
Dist.: United

SWISS FAMILY ROBINSON 1960
★ ★ ★ ★ G Family 2:06
Dir: Ken Annakin   *Cast:* John Mills, Dorothy McGuire, James MacArthur, Janet Munro, Sessue Hayakawa, Tommy Kirk
▶ Delightful adaptation of Johann Wyss's novel about a nineteenth-century family fleeing Napoleon who are shipwrecked on the tropical paradise of Tobago. Inventive father Mills and sons MacArthur and Kirk construct an ingenious island fortress to repel attacks by pirate Hayakawa. Above-average Disney adventure features lush settings, boisterous humor, and nonstop action.
Dist.: Buena Vista

SWITCHBLADE SISTERS 1975
☆ R Drama 1:31
☑ Rape, adult situations, explicit language
Dir: Jack Hill   *Cast:* Robbie Lee, Joanne Nail, Monica Gayle, Kitty Bruce, Marlene Clark, Michael Miller
▶ A punk deb gang led by Lee is sent off to a girls' detention home after they knife a man in an elevator. A decent girl is accidentally rounded up with these bad types, and she finds herself involved in rape and violence. Shoddy entry in the girls' reformatory genre is good for a few camp laughs, but there are much better examples out there. Also known as *The Jezebels* and *The Playgirl Gang.*
Dist.: Monterey

SWITCHING CHANNELS 1988
★ ★ ★ PG Comedy 1:45
☑ Adult situations, explicit language
Dir: Ted Kotcheff   *Cast:* Burt Reynolds, Kathleen Turner, Christopher Reeve, Ned Beatty, Henry Gibson
▶ Fourth (and least successful) remake of the Hecht-MacArthur play *The Front Page,* updated from newspaper room to TV studio. Director Reynolds still loves ex-wife/news anchor Turner, who is engaged to business tycoon Reeve. Reynolds tries to delay the wedding by assigning Turner to the story of a convicted murderer (Gibson) about to be executed. Some funny bits but no sizzle or chemistry between the leads; lackluster direction. Stick to the Roz Russell-Cary Grant 1940 sparkler, *His Gal Friday.*
Dist.: RCA/Columbia

SWORD AND THE ROSE, THE 1953
★ ★ ★ NR Drama 1:31
Dir: Ken Annakin   *Cast:* Richard Todd, Gly-

nis Johns, James Robertson Justice, Michael Gough, Jane Barrett, Peter Copley
► Mary Tudor (Johns), sister of Henry VIII (Justice), loses her heart to commoner Todd but agrees to marry an aged French king to maintain peace. When he dies, Duke of Buckingham (Gough) attempts to usurp Todd's place. Elaborate but historically inaccurate Disney epic is filled with sweeping spectacle and high spirits. Based on Charles Major's *When Knighthood Was in Flower.*
Dist.: Buena Vista

SWORD AND THE SORCERER, THE 1982
★★ R Fantasy 1:40
☑ Brief nudity, adult situations, explicit language, violence
Dir: Albert Pyun ***Cast:*** Lee Horsley, Kathleen Beller, George Maharis, Simon MacCorkindale, Richard Lynch, Richard Moll
► Evil spirits bring about downfall of a good king. King's son Horsley is aided by a mysterious sword as he fights for the oppressed, wins the heart of Beller, and restores the kingdom to deserving hands. Good pacing and production values in this overplotted fantasy. Horsley exhibits grace and verve.
Dist.: MCA

SWORD IN THE STONE, THE 1963
★★★★ G Animation 1:15
Dir: Wolfgang Reitherman ***Cast:*** Voices of Rickie Sorenson, Sebastian Cabot, Karl Swenson, Junius Matthews, Alan Napier
► Simplified adaptation of T. H. White's Camelot stories concerns training of Wart, the young lad destined to become King Arthur. Guided by Merlin the Magician, Wart is transformed into various animals to learn how to rely on his intellect rather than his brawn. Blustering Merlin provides most of the fun in this overlooked Disney cartoon. **(CC)**
Dist.: Buena Vista

SWORD OF DOOM, THE 1967 Japanese
☆ NR Martial Arts 2:02 B&W
Dir: Kihachi Okamoto ***Cast:*** Tatsuya Nakadai, Toshiro Mifune, Yuzo Kayama, Michiyo Aratma, Ichiro Nakaya, Yoko Naito
► In Medieval Japan, brutal samurai Nakadai kills an innocent old man, then proceeds to challenge other samurai. Kayama is the brother of one of Nakadai's victims, who now stalks him in search of vengeance. Standard sword-flailing samurai pic, with Mifune in a minor role. [S]
Dist.: Nelson

SWORD OF GIDEON 1986
★★★★ NR Action-Adventure/MFTV 2:28
☑ Violence
Dir: Michael Anderson ***Cast:*** Steven Bauer, Rod Steiger, Colleen Dewhurst, Michael York, Robert Joy, Peter Dvorsky
► After the 1972 Munich Olympics massacre, Israeli officer Steiger enlists the aid of captain Bauer in putting together a special team of commandos who will kill terrorists responsible for the deaths of innocent Israelis. Other members include English explosives expert York and veteran soldier of fortune Dvorsky. Thrill-packed mission moves from sands of Jordan desert to the piazzas of Rome and the streets of New York.
Dist.: HBO

SWORD OF LANCELOT 1963 British
★★ NR Action-Adventure 1:55
Dir: Cornel Wilde ***Cast:*** Cornel Wilde, Jean Wallace, Brian Aherne, George Baker, Archie Duncan, Michael Meacham
► Sir Lancelot (Wilde) and Queen Guinevere (Wallace) fall in love, although she is married to King Arthur (Aherne). The affair leads to exile for the knight and a convent for the Queen, until circumstances later reunite the lovers. Colorful pageant of romance and action.
Dist.: MCA

SWORD OF THE VALIANT 1984 British
★★ PG Action-Adventure 1:42
☑ Violence
Dir: Stephen Weeks ***Cast:*** Miles O'Keeffe, Sean Connery, Cyrielle Claire, Leigh Lawson, Trevor Howard, Peter Cushing
► Knight O'Keeffe decapitates magician Connery, a challenger to King Arthur's (Howard) court. Connery resurrects self and gives O'Keeffe one year to solve a riddle or face death. Decent script and showy production; Connery is strong as always but direction is lackluster.
Dist.: MGM/UA

SYBIL 1976
★★★★ NR Biography/MFTV 3:18
Dir: Daniel Petrie ***Cast:*** Joanne Woodward, Sally Field, Brad Davis, Martine Bartlett, Jane Hoffman, William Prince
► Psychiatrist Woodward probes the mind of disturbed Field who, as consequence of childhood trauma, developed seventeen personalities. Emmy-winning miniseries proved extremely popular with viewers and critics. Field's memorable performance in a challenging role revitalized her dormant career. Based on a true story from the book by Flora Rheta Scheiber.
Dist.: CBS/Fox

SYLVESTER 1985
★★★★ PG Family 1:43
☑ Explicit language, mild violence
Dir: Tim Hunter ***Cast:*** Melissa Gilbert, Richard Farnsworth, Michael Schoeffling, Constance Towers
► Orphaned tomboy Gilbert trains wild jumping horse Sylvester while protecting her younger brothers from state social workers. Crusty trainer Farnsworth helps Gilbert and Sylvester prepare for big meet. Old-fashioned entertainment with a satisfying story. Gilbert is sweet, Farnsworth real and likable. **(CC)**
Dist.: RCA/Columbia

SYLVIA 1985 New Zealand
★ ★ **PG Biography 1:38**
☑ Adult situations, explicit language
Dir: Michael Firth **Cast:** Eleanor David,
Nigel Terry, Tom Wilkinson, Mary Regan,
Martyn Sanderson
▶ True story based on the best-sellers *Teacher*
and *I Passed This Way* by educator Sylvia Ash-
ton-Warner. Teacher David and headmaster
husband Wilkinson come to impoverished
New Zealand village. David finds traditional
curriculum fails with Maori kids; she reaches
them with her own brand of instruction, but
runs afoul of bureaucrat Terry. Underdog-
against-the-system tale has broad appeal.
(CC)
Dist.: CBS/Fox

SYLVIA SCARLETT 1935
★ ★ **NR Drama 1:37**
Dir: George Cukor **Cast:** Katharine Hepburn, Cary Grant, Brian Aherne, Edmund
Gwenn, Natalie Paley, Dennie Moore
▶ Disguising daughter Hepburn as a man,
Gwenn, her ne'er-do-well father wanted by
police, sneaks into England. There they are
tricked by Cockney charmer Grant who later
joins them in a series of money-making
schemes culminating in a seaside theater engagement. Odd blend of drama and comedy lacks a consistent tone, but Hepburn (in
the first of four films with Grant) is impressive in
a daring cross-dressing role.
Dist.: Nostalgia

TABLE FOR FIVE 1983
★ ★ ★ ★ **PG Drama 1:57**
☑ Adult situations, explicit language
Dir: Robert Lieberman **Cast:** Jon Voight,
Marie-Christine Barrault, Richard Crenna,
Millie Perkins, Roxana Zal
▶ Divorced dad Voight picks up his three kids
from ex-wife Perkins on an ocean cruise to
Egypt. On board, he meets pretty blond Bar-
rault. Dad and estranged kids are having trou-
ble adjusting to each other when news comes
that mom has been killed in a car accident.
Crenna plays the stepfather who fights Voight
for custody of the children. Slick tearjerker fea-
tures exotic locales.
Dist.: CBS/Fox

TABU 1931
☆ **NR Drama 1:22 B&W**
Dir: F. W. Murnau **Cast:** Anna Chevalier,
Matahi, Hitu, Jean, Jules, Kong Ah
▶ Native Tahitian girl Chevalier is conse-
crated to the gods and off limits to mortal men
like Matahi, the pearl diver she loves. To keep
the young lovers apart, the high priest steals
her away on his boat, with Matahi swimming
in pursuit. When documentary director Robert
Flaherty dropped out of this project halfway
through, Murnau was left to create a sumptuously poetic tale of South Seas romance—
capturing that part of the world perhaps more
beautifully than any film since. Cinematogra-

pher Floyd Crosby won an Oscar for his work.
Murnau died in an auto accident before the
premiere.
Dist.: Facets

TAFFIN 1988 British/U.S
★ **R Drama 1:32**
☑ Nudity, adult situations, explicit lan-
guage, violence
Dir: Francis Megahy **Cast:** Pierce Brosnan,
Ray McAnally, Alison Doody, Jeremy Child,
Dearbhia Molloy
▶ Debt collector Brosnan rethinks his priorities
when he learns athletic field in his Irish home
town is the planned site of dangerous chemi-
cal plant. He mounts campaign against
plant's owners and resorts to violence when
hired thugs attack local conservationists.
Dreary attempt at socially redeeming drama
isn't helped by weak acting.
Dist.: MGM/UA

T.A.G.: THE ASSASSINATION GAME 1982
★ ★ **PG Mystery-Suspense/Comedy 1:31**
☑ Adult situations, explicit language, violence
Dir: Nick Castle **Cast:** Robert Carradine,
Linda Hamilton, Perry Lang, Bruce Abbott,
Kristine DeBell, Frazer Smith
▶ College students unwind with hunter-prey
game using harmless dart guns. School paper
editor Carradine spies lovely co-ed Hamilton
playing game and follows her under ruse of
writing article. Meanwhile Abbott gets shot by
player and decides to up the ante: he stalks
quarry with lethal ammo. Promising comic
start abandoned when picture shifts into standard thriller gear.
Dist.: Nelson

TAI-PAN 1986
★ ★ ★ **R Action-Adventure 2:07**
☑ Nudity, adult situations, violence
Dir: Daryl Duke **Cast:** Bryan Brown, Joan
Chen, John Stanton, Tom Guinee, Bill Lead-
bitter, Kyra Sedgwick
▶ Based on James Clavell's best-seller, histori-
cal epic depicts life of "Tai-Pan" (Brown),
trade leader for European community in nine-
teenth-century Hong Kong. Principal player in
China-Britain opium war, Scotsman Tai-Pan
has other woes as well: son Guinee won't for-
give father for mistress Chen, while nasty rival
Stanton and his vicious son Leadbitter seek to
bankrupt him. Filmed on location, multiplot-
ted potboiler has something for everyone.
(CC)
Dist.: Vestron

TAKE A HARD RIDE 1975
★ ★ **PG Western 1:43**
☑ Violence
Dir: Anthony M. Dawson (Antonio Marg-
heriti) **Cast:** Jim Brown, Lee Van Cleef,
Fred Williamson, Catherine Spaak, Jim Kelly,
Dana Andrews
▶ Honest cowboy Brown treks across Western
wilderness to deliver $86,000 from dying

rancher boss Andrews to his family. He is pursued by happy-go-lucky gambler Williamson, who decides to team up with the cowboy when vicious bounty hunter Van Cleef trails them both. Standard spaghetti Western with one new twist: good guys are black while bad dudes are white.
Dist.: CBS/Fox

TAKE DOWN 1979
★ ★ ★ ★ PG Drama/Sports 1:47
☑ Explicit language
Dir: Kieth Merrill   *Cast:* Edward Herrmann, Kathleen Lloyd, Lorenzo Lamas, Maureen McCormick, Nick Beauvy, Kevin Hooks
▶ Perennial football losers, tiny Utah high school starts wrestling team in hopes of gaining revenge. Shakespeare scholar Herrmann, with no knowledge of sport, is assigned to coach squad. He learns to enjoy the boys and the job when wife Lloyd urges him to stop being such a stiff. His primary challenge: to convince star athlete Lamas to learn to be a winner and not drop out of school. Uplifting and light-hearted.
Dist.: Unicorn

TAKE ME OUT TO THE BALL GAME 1949
★ ★ ★ NR Musical 1:33
Dir: Busby Berkeley   *Cast:* Frank Sinatra, Esther Williams, Gene Kelly, Betty Garrett, Edward Arnold, Jules Munshin
▶ Pleasant turn-of-the-century musical combines baseball, gambling, and vaudeville into an undemanding trifle. Singers Sinatra and Kelly, teammates on the semipro summer circuit, are pleasantly surprised when their club is purchased by beautiful new manager Williams. Evil gambler Arnold almost leads Kelly astray, but Williams sets him straight. Classic title tune and Kelly's "The Hat My Father Wore on St. Patrick's Day" are highlights; Betty Comden and Adolph Green worked on the rest of the score.
Dist.: MGM/UA

TAKE THE MONEY AND RUN 1969
★ ★ PG Comedy 1:25
☑ Adult situations, explicit language
Dir: Woody Allen   *Cast:* Woody Allen, Janet Margolin, Marcel Hillaire, Jacquelyn Hyde, Lonny Chapman
▶ Inept crook Allen tries to support wife Margolin through life of crime, is caught and imprisoned, but later escapes. Very amusing documentary-style satire is Allen's directorial debut. Funniest scenes: Allen attempting to rob bank with illegible stick-up note ("Does this say gun or gub?" the teller wonders) and interracial chain gang posing as "really close family" after escaping.
Dist.: CBS/Fox

TAKE THIS JOB AND SHOVE IT 1981
★ ★ ★ PG Comedy 1:40
☑ Brief nudity, adult situations, explicit language, adult humor
Dir: Gus Trikonis   *Cast:* Robert Hays, Art Carney, Barbara Hershey, David Keith, Tim Thomerson, Martin Mull
▶ Johnny Paycheck's hit country-western song provides the inspiration for an appealing comedy about overachiever Hays, who's sent to his hometown of Dubuque to revamp the local brewery. Encounters with old friends and former lover Hershey convince him to reorder his priorities. Good score and cameos by country-western stars Paycheck, Charlie Rich, David Allan Coe, etc., boost predictable plot. (CC)
Dist.: Nelson

TAKING OF PELHAM ONE TWO THREE, THE 1974
★ ★ ★ ★ R Action-Adventure 1:44
☑ Adult situations, explicit language, violence
Dir: Joseph Sargent   *Cast:* Walter Matthau, Robert Shaw, Martin Balsam, Hector Elizondo, Jerry Stiller, Kenneth McMillan
▶ Four criminals led by Shaw hijack a Bronx subway and demand one million dollars ransom from transit cop negotiator Matthau. Taut, fast-paced thriller with welcome comic touches features convincing settings, strong action, and first-rate performances by Matthau and Shaw. Based on John Godey's novel.
Dist.: MGM/UA

TAKIN' IT ALL OFF 1988
☆ NR Comedy 1:31
☑ Nudity, adult situations, explicit language
Dir: Ed Hansen   *Cast:* Kitten Natividad, Fred Hampton, Farley Maynard
▶ When a stripping school faces eviction, the gals decide to raise money by putting on a show. Alas, one shy young lady can't bring herself to take it all off, so Betty Bigones (Natividad) is enlisted to help out. The acting here won't win any Oscars.
Dist.: Vestron

TALE OF TWO CITIES, A 1935
★ ★ ★ ★ NR Drama 2:01 B&W
Dir: Jack Conway   *Cast:* Ronald Colman, Elizabeth Allan, Edna May Oliver, Blanche Yurka, Basil Rathbone, Reginald Owen
▶ A far, far better film than any other adaptation of the Charles Dickens French Revolution classic. Solid storytelling given handsome production by David O. Selznick. Yurka is memorable as literature's most evil knitter, Madame DeFarge; Colman's Sydney Carton is heroic and moving, especially in his climactic martyrdom.
Dist.: MGM/UA

TALE OF TWO CITIES, A 1958 British
★ ★ NR Drama 1:57 B&W
Dir: Ralph Thomas   *Cast:* Dirk Bogarde, Dorothy Tutin, Cecil Parker, Christopher Lee, Ian Bannen, Donald Pleasence
▶ In Paris and London during the French Revolution, English lawyer Bogarde finds purpose in life helping those threatened by French reb-

els. His resemblance to the husband of the woman he loves leads to a noble act of courage. Adaptation of Charles Dickens classic is well done but the Ronald Colman version still stands apart.
Dist.: VidAmerica

TALES FROM THE CRYPT 1972 British
★ ★ **PG Horror 1:32**
☑ Violence
Dir: Freddie Francis *Cast:* Ralph Richardson, Joan Collins, Ian Hendry, Nigel Patrick, Peter Cushing, Richard Greene
▶ Anthology horror film, adapted from E.C. comics, features five characters confronted by crypt keeper Richardson as their stories unfold. Creepiest episodes: Collins being menaced by a psychotic Santa at Christmas, an adaptation of "The Monkey's Paw" in which three wishes on a magical object go disastrously wrong, and Price's run-in with a wall of razor blades. Superior fare of its kind. Sequel: *Vault of Horror.*
Dist.: Prism

TALES FROM THE DARKSIDE 1990
★ ★ ★ **R Horror 1:35**
☑ Adult situations, explicit language, violence
Dir: John Harrison *Cast:* Deborah Harry, Christian Slater, David Johansen, William Hickey, James Remar, Rae Dawn Chong
▶ Glossy dramatizations of three short stories narrated by a young boy trying to stave off an assault by cannibal housewife Harry. Based on works by Stephen King, Arthur Conan Doyle, and *Beetlejuice*-scripter Michael McDowell, segments include a cat avenging the deaths of laboratory animals, a crazed mummy terrorizing frat kids, and a gargoyle stalking New York's SoHo. Good production values can't distinguish this from TV's multitude of horror anthology shows.
Dist.: Paramount

TALES OF ORDINARY MADNESS 1983 Italian/French
☆ **NR Drama 1:47**
☑ Nudity, strong sexual content, adult situations, explicit language, violence
Dir: Marco Ferreri *Cast:* Ben Gazzara, Ornella Muti, Susan Tyrrell, Tanya Lopert, Roy Brocksmith, Katia Berger
▶ Los Angeles skid-row writer Gazzara has unusual sexual encounters with several women: he trails home blond bombshell Tyrrell and rapes her, spars with nymphomaniac ex-wife Lopert, and romances self-destructive prostitute Muti with tragic results. Unblinking look at dregs of society is based on works of poet Charles Bukowski, later used for *Barfly.*
Dist.: Vestron

TALES OF TERROR 1962
★ ★ **NR Horror 1:30**
Dir: Roger Corman *Cast:* Vincent Price, Peter Lorre, Basil Rathbone, Maggie Pierce, Joyce Jameson, Debra Paget

▶ Three-part horror omnibus adapted from Edgar Allan Poe stories: in "Morella," grieving widower Price forces a gruesome encounter between daughter Pierce and his mummified wife; in "The Black Cat," Lorre, an alcoholic cuckold, entombs his wife Jameson and lover Price behind a basement wall; "The Case of Mr. Valdemar" concerns evil doctor Rathbone's plot to keep Price comatose while stealing his wife Paget. Uneven anthology features a marvelous comic turn by Lorre and unusual color design.
Dist.: Warner

TALK OF THE TOWN, THE 1942
★ ★ ★ **NR Comedy 1:58 B&W**
Dir: George Stevens *Cast:* Cary Grant, Jean Arthur, Ronald Colman, Edgar Buchanan, Glenda Farrell, Rex Ingram
▶ Escaped fugitive Grant hides in schoolteacher Arthur's home, which has just been rented to Supreme Court nominee Colman. Posing as a gardener, Grant engages Colman in a debate over tolerance in the law while wooing Arthur. Stars are extremely appealing in this witty comedy, winner of seven Oscar nominations.
Dist.: RCA/Columbia

TALK RADIO 1988
★ ★ ★ **R Drama 1:50**
☑ Adult situations, explicit language, violence
Dir: Oliver Stone *Cast:* Eric Bogosian, Ellen Greene, Leslie Hope, Alec Baldwin, John C. McGinley, John Pankow
▶ Dallas talk show host Bogosian rises to nationwide syndication with abrasive style. His insistence on abusing callers provokes crazies in audience and leads to violent conclusion. Bogosian, re-creating his stage role, is dynamic. Stone's moving camera keeps talky but sharp-edged script running; however, some may find obnoxiousness of lead character and downbeat ending off-putting. Based on the Bogosian play and the real-life killing of DJ Alan Berg.
Dist.: MCA

TALK TO ME 1984
★ ★ ★ **NR Drama 1:35**
☑ Adult situations, explicit language
Dir: Julius Potocsny *Cast:* Austin Pendleton, Michael Murphy, Barbara Eda Young, Louise Fletcher, Dan Shor, Michael Tolan
▶ Lifelong stutterer Pendleton avoids his problem, preferring to immerse himself in work. Tiring of his dilemma, Pendleton enrolls in speech therapy institute and meets others who share his disability. With help of tough-but-fair instructor Murphy and new friend Young, he conquers impediment. All profits from inspirational film go to Hollins Communication Research Institute in Virginia, site of Pendleton's cure. **(CC)**
Dist.: CBS/Fox

TALL BLOND MAN WITH ONE BLACK SHOE, THE 1972 French
★ **PG Mystery-Suspense/Comedy 1:29**
☑ Adult humor
Dir: Yves Robert ***Cast:*** Pierre Richard, Bernard Blier, Jean Rochefort, Mireille Darc, Jean Carmet
► Innocent musician Richard becomes pawn of French intelligence director Rochefort in plan to trip up his overly ambitious assistant Blier. Richard also gets involved with gorgeous spy Darc. Understated humor is frequently charming. Spawned a French sequel and American remake (*The Man With One Red Shoe*). [S]
Dist.: RCA/Columbia

TALL IN THE SADDLE 1944
★★★★ **NR Western 1:19 B&W**
Dir: Edwin L. Marin ***Cast:*** John Wayne, Ella Raines, Ward Bond, George "Gabby" Hayes, Don Douglas
► Cowhand Wayne takes ranch job and discovers his cousin has been killed. The Duke learns that corrupt judge Bond covets the ranch and was responsible for the murder. Wayne falls for owner's niece Raines while battling Bond. Rip-roaring, unpretentious fun with shoot-outs, fistfights, chases galore.
Dist.: Turner [C]

TALL MEN, THE 1955
★★ **NR Western 2:01**
Dir: Raoul Walsh ***Cast:*** Clark Gable, Jane Russell, Robert Ryan, Cameron Mitchell, Juan Garcia, Harry Shannon
► Gable and Mitchell play cowpoke brothers and former Confederate raiders who sign up for a Texas-to-Montana cattle drive. Their obstacles include fraud scheme by wealthy businessman Ryan; romantic problems with Russell, the only survivor of an Indian massacre; fierce blizzard; and ambush in a narrow canyon. Elaborate Western fails to deliver enough action.
Dist.: CBS/Fox

TAMARIND SEED, THE 1974
★★★★ **PG Romance/Espionage 2:03**
☑ Mild violence
Dir: Blake Edwards ***Cast:*** Julie Andrews, Omar Sharif, Anthony Quayle, Dan O'Herlihy, Sylvia Sims, Oscar Homolka
► While vacationing in Barbados, English civil servant Andrews and Soviet diplomat Sharif fall in love. Respective governments spy on each when Andrews returns to London and Sharif resumes embassy job in Paris. Lovers can't bear to be apart, so Sharif trades political asylum for info on British politician O'Herlihy, a spy for Russians. Fine romantic drama with star cast is more cloak than dagger as love conquers all, even the Cold War.
Dist.: CBS/Fox

TAMING OF THE SHREW, THE 1967 U.S./Italian
★★★★ **NR Comedy 2:04**
Dir: Franco Zeffirelli ***Cast:*** Elizabeth Taylor, Richard Burton, Michael York, Cyril Cusack, Michael Hordern, Natasha Pyne
► In the sixteenth-century, rich Italian merchant Hordern despairs of ever marrying off his tempestuous daughter Taylor, until Burton shows up seeking a wealthy wife. Taylor vows to resist but romantic sparks fly as Burton woos her. Lusty, lavish, and energetic; then-married Taylor and Burton bring charisma and chemistry to this very entertaining Shakespeare adaptation.
Dist.: RCA

TAMMY AND THE BACHELOR 1957
★★★ **NR Comedy 1:29**
Dir: Joseph Pevney ***Cast:*** Debbie Reynolds, Leslie Nielsen, Walter Brennan, Mala Powers, Fay Wray, Mildred Natwick
► Plane crash brings rich Nielsen and rural Reynolds together. Nielsen takes Reynolds home to meet the family and, despite culture clash, all ends happily. Sweet and likable comedy was first in the series and probably the best. Charming Reynolds sings the theme song with the Ames Brothers.
Dist.: MCA

TAMMY AND THE DOCTOR 1963
★★ **NR Comedy 1:28**
Dir: Harry Keller ***Cast:*** Sandra Dee, Peter Fonda, Macdonald Carey, Beulah Bondi, Margaret Lindsay, Adam West
► Innocent country girl Dee gets hospital job. Nurse Lindsay befriends Dee and doctor Fonda (in his film debut) falls in love with her. Fonda's boss Carey disapproves of the romance. However, love finds a way in this corny but entertaining third entry in the series.
Dist.: MCA

TAMPOPO 1987 Japanese
★★ **NR Comedy 1:54**
☑ Nudity, adult situations, adult humor
Dir: Juzo Itami ***Cast:*** Tsutomu Yamazaki, Nobuko Miyamoto, Koji Yakusho, Ken Watanabe, Rikiya Yasuoka, Kinzo Sakura
► Mysterious stranger Yamazaki drives into town and helps sweet widow Miyamoto (director Itami's wife) develop ace recipe for her noodle shop. Delectable concoction combines movie references (if Clint Eastwood were a Japanese chef, he might be the delightfully taciturn Yamazaki), food, and eroticism (especially in the startling sequence of an egg being passed between mouths). [S]
Dist.: Republic

TANGO & CASH 1989
★★★★ **R Action-Adventure 1:38**
☑ Brief nudity, adult situations, explicit language, graphic violence
Dir: Andrei Konchalovsky ***Cast:*** Sylvester Stallone, Kurt Russell, Teri Hatcher, Jack Palance, Brion James, James Hong
► Stallone and Russell are two Los Angeles cops who are too different from one another

to get along. But when drug lord Palance sends them to prison on a frame-up, they have to work together to bust out and clear their names. Slam-bang action the way the pros do it, with a big budget and foolproof script.
Dist.: Warner

TANGO BAR 1989 Argentinian/Puerto Rican
☆ **NR Dance 1:30**
☑ Brief nudity, mild violence
Dir: Marcos Zurinaga   *Cast:* Raul Julia, Valeria Lynch, Ruben Juarez
▶ A nightclub act featuring Julia, Lynch, and Juarez is the framing device for what is essentially a history of dance in Argentina. The stars sing a few tunes, and the Tango Argentino dancers perform in period dress. Best parts, however, are film clips of the tango Hollywood-style, featuring the dance as performed by everyone from Rudolph Valentino to the Flintstones. Julia is a genial host, but leadfooted nondance material drags this movie down. ⒮
Dist.: Warner

TANK 1984
★ ★ ★ ★ **PG Action-Adventure/Comedy 1:53**
☑ Nudity, adult situations, explicit language, violence
Dir: Marvin J. Chomsky   *Cast:* James Garner, Shirley Jones, C. Thomas Howell, G. D. Spradlin, Jenilee Harrison
▶ Army major Garner rescues Howell, his falsely arrested son, by driving a Sherman tank into town, grabbing the boy, and high-tailing it for the state border. Improbable loners-versus-corrupt-system story with Spradlin as a bad sheriff and Jones as Garner's understanding wife. **(CC)**
Dist.: MCA

TAP 1988
★ ★ ★ ★ **PG-13 Drama/Dance 1:50**
☑ Explicit language
Dir: Nick Castle   *Cast:* Gregory Hines, Sammy Davis, Jr., Suzzanne Douglas, Savion Glover, Joe Morton, Harold Nicholas
▶ Talented tap dancer Hines gets out of jail after serving robbery hitch. He rejoins girlfriend Douglas and retired dancer Davis and fights the lure of crime to develop his art. Occasionally contrived plotting is vehicle for superlative dancing by Hines, who holds his own even when dancing with old-time greats, like Nicholas. Davis's last role is one of his best screen performances.
Dist.: RCA/Columbia

TAPEHEADS 1988
★ ★ **R Comedy 1:37**
☑ Brief nudity, adult situations, explicit language
Dir: Bill Fishman   *Cast:* John Cusack, Tim Robbins, Mary Crosby, Connie Stevens, Don Cornelius, Clu Gulager
▶ After getting fired, young security guards

Cusack and Robbins try their hands at the video business, accidentally coming into possession of a tape damaging to politician Gulager. Thugs search for the tape as the buddies rise to the top. Brash spoof of the music biz has some clever send-ups of rock videos but little to entertain older viewers.
Dist.: Pacific Arts

TAPS 1981
★ ★ ★ ★ **PG Drama 2:01**
☑ Brief nudity, explicit language, violence
Dir: Harold Becker   *Cast:* Timothy Hutton, George C. Scott, Ronny Cox, Sean Penn, Tom Cruise
▶ General Scott and cadet major Hutton deal with mounting pressures at a military school beset by financial problems. When the trustees announce plans to close the academy to build condos on the property, frustrated students seize the campus. Hutton tries to quell the heat, with tragic consequences. Solid cast and well-crafted production, although the ending may seem predictable. Good chance to spot early work by Penn and Cruise.
Dist.: CBS/Fox

TARAS BULBA 1962
★ ★ **NR Drama 2:02**
Dir: J. Lee Thompson   *Cast:* Tony Curtis, Yul Brynner, Christine Kaufmann, Sam Wanamaker, Brad Dexter, Guy Rolfe
▶ Muddled tale of sixteenth-century Cossack leader Brynner forced into exile; his son Curtis incurs his wrath by romancing beautiful heathen Kaufmann. Large-scale battle sequences add some excitement to this extremely loose adapation of a Nikolai Gogol story, but Curtis's Bronx accent and clichéd plotting are major drawbacks.
Dist.: MGM/UA

TARGET 1985
★ ★ ★ ★ **R Action-Adventure 1:57**
☑ Brief nudity, adult situations, explicit language, violence
Dir: Arthur Penn   *Cast:* Gene Hackman, Matt Dillon, Gayle Hunnicutt, Victoria Fyodorova, Josef Sommer, Guy Boyd
▶ When wife Hunnicutt is kidnapped in Paris, Dallas lumberyard owner Hackman and son Dillon fly there to investigate. When assassins try to kill Hackman, he reveals former life as CIA agent to stunned Dillon. Action scenes are both hair-raising and funny. Hackman turns in usual solid performance while Dillon convincingly portrays slack-jawed kid who can't believe lethargic pop is really ace spy. **(CC)**
Dist.: CBS/Fox

TARGET EAGLE 1984 Spanish/Mexican
★ ★ ★ **NR Action-Adventure 1:30**
☑ Explicit language, violence
Dir: J. Anthony Loma   *Cast:* George Rivero, Maud Adams, George Peppard, Max Von Sydow, Chuck Connors

▶ Soldier of fortune Rivero, recruited to spy on heroin ring, impresses them enough to join the gang. Asked to hang glide onto an Arab yacht and pick up the drugs, he soon uncovers bigger stuff—namely stolen plutonium intended for a Libyan bomb factory. Spurts of action but fine actors wasted. Badly dubbed and edited.
Dist.: Media

TARGETS 1968
★ **PG Mystery-Suspense 1:30**
☑ explicit violence
Dir: Peter Bogdanovich   *Cast:* Boris Karloff, Tim O'Kelly, Nancy Hsueh, James Brown, Sandy Baron, Peter Bogdanovich
▶ Horror-movie star Karloff plans to retire while real-life monster Kelly goes on shooting spree that starts with Kelly's family, includes innocent bystanders, and eventually targets Karloff in a chilling drive-in climax. Bogdanovich's directorial debut is timely and ambitious.
Dist.: Paramount

TARKA THE OTTER 1979 British
★★★★ **G Family 1:31**
Dir: David Cobham   *Cast:* Narrated by Peter Ustinov
▶ Tarka (ancient name meaning Little Wanderer) the otter loses his parents to hunters and their hounds, led by the fearsome Deadlock. Orphaned otter journeys downriver to estuary where he learns to fend for himself. He meets young female White Tip and two return to his river home. There he must fight to death against Deadlock to defend mate and their cubs. Top-notch wildlife footage; superior family fare.
Dist.: TWE

TARZAN, THE APE MAN 1932
★★★ **NR Action-Adventure 1:39 B&W**
Dir: W. S. Van Dyke II   *Cast:* Johnny Weissmuller, Maureen O'Sullivan, C. Aubrey Smith, Neil Hamilton, Doris Lloyd, Cheetah the Chimp
▶ First of a long series of jungle adventures starring Olympic swimming star Weissmuller as Edgar Rice Burroughs's hero packs plenty of action and excitement into an enjoyably dated plot about members of an English safari in search of an ivory-filled elephants' graveyard. O'Sullivan, daughter of expedition leader Smith, is a fetching partner to the ape man, who delivers the immortal line "Me Tarzan, you Jane." Amusing, racy classic was remade in 1959 and 1981. Sequel: *Tarzan and His Mate.*
Dist.: MGM/UA

TARZAN, THE APE MAN 1981
★ **R Action-Adventure 1:52**
☑ Nudity, adult situations, explicit language
Dir: John Derek   *Cast:* Bo Derek, Richard Harris, Miles O'Keeffe, John Phillip Law, Akushula Selayah
▶ Victorian explorer Harris, his virginal daughter Derek, and handsome photographer Law

fall prey to heathen savages in darkest Africa. O'Keeffe, a mute muscleman raised by apes, saves Derek from a horrible fate. Plot of Edgar Rice Burroughs's classic adventure is largely discarded, as are Derek's clothes, in this campy, inept remake of the 1932 film. Closing credits were the subject of a court battle with the Burroughs estate.
Dist.: MGM/UA

TASTE OF HONEY, A 1962 British
★ **NR Drama 1:40 B&W**
Dir: Tony Richardson   *Cast:* Rita Tushingham, Dora Bryan, Robert Stephens, Murray Melvin, Paul Danquah
▶ Fatherless British teen Tushingham has affair with black sailor Danquah. When her mother Bryan remarries and her lover goes back to sea, Tushingham moves in with gay pal Melvin, who takes care of her. Slow beginning, talkiness, and heavy accents may make some restless; however, perfect performances (especially Tushingham) elicit touching moments.
Dist.: American Video

TATTOO 1981
★ **R Mystery-Suspense 1:43**
☑ Nudity, explicit language, violence
Dir: Bob Brooks   *Cast:* Bruce Dern, Maud Adams, Leonard Frey, Rikki Borge, John Getz, Peter Iacangelo
▶ Tattoo artist Dern, hired by fashion magazine to paint temporary tattoos for bathing suit promotion, becomes infatuated with striking model Adams. She at first returns his interest but soon finds his notions of women and dating too old-fashioned for her liberated lifestyle. His passion then becomes dangerously obsessive as he decides to use her body as a canvas for his artwork. Fine premise fizzles after promising start.
Dist.: CBS/Fox

TAXI DRIVER 1976
★★★★ **R Drama 1:53**
☑ Explicit language, graphic violence
Dir: Martin Scorsese   *Cast:* Robert De Niro, Jodie Foster, Cybill Shepherd, Harvey Keitel, Peter Boyle, Albert Brooks
▶ Introverted ex-Marine De Niro takes job as night shift cab driver in New York that proves a relentless tour of dark side of humanity. De Niro's anxieties become unbearable: rejected by All-American beauty Shepherd and taunted by pimp Keitel over teen prostitute Foster, he vents his tensions in a spree of violence. Frightening look at urban underbelly features superb performances and striking images. Haunting score was the last work by longtime Hitchcock collaborator Bernard Herrmann. Nominated for four Oscars.
Dist.: RCA/Columbia

TAXING WOMAN, A 1987 Japanese
☆ **NR Comedy 2:07**
☑ Nudity, adult situations, explicit language, violence

Dir: Juzo Itami *Cast:* Nobuko Miyamoto, Tsutomu Yamazaki, Masahiko Tsugawa, Hideo Murota, Shuji Otaki, Daisuke Yamashita

▸ Dauntless Japanese tax investigator Miyamoto graduates from small-time operations to the most lucrative: nailing wealthy tax cheat Yamakazi. Sharp satire can be appreciated by anyone who's ever had a run-in with the IRS. Director Itami reunites his two favorite stars: real-life wife Miyamoto and Yamakazi, who also starred in *Tampopo* and *The Funeral* together. [S]

Dist.: Fox/Lorber

TAXING WOMAN'S RETURN, A 1989
Japanese
☆ **NR Comedy 2:07**
☑ Nudity, adult situations, explicit language v, violence
Dir: Juzo Itami *Cast:* Nobuko Miyamoto, Rentaro Mikuni, Toru Masuoka, Masahiko Tsugawa, Mihoko Shibata, Haruko Kato

▸ Miyamoto reprises her role in *A Taxing Woman* as the intrepid tax investigator. This time she's hot on the trail of dirty old man Mikuni, leader of a bogus church that is using its tax-exempt status to build high-rise office space in land-starved Japan. Fans of Itami's brand of scathing social satire will savor this follow-up. [S]

Dist.: New Yorker

TEACHERS 1984
★★★★ **R Comedy/Drama 1:46**
☑ Nudity, adult situations, explicit language, violence
Dir: Arthur Hiller *Cast:* Nick Nolte, Judd Hirsch, JoBeth Williams, Ralph Macchio, Lee Grant, Richard Mulligan

▸ Williams, a lawyer and former student of burnt-out but beloved teacher Nolte, is suing J.F.K. High School because her client graduated but can't read. Fighting the case are conservative vice principal Hirsch and caustic school board advisor Grant. Romancing Williams and caught in-between the battle lines, Nolte also deals with rebellious student Macchio. First-rate cast and some fine comic moments in this critique of public education. (CC)

Dist.: CBS/Fox

TEACHER'S PET 1958
★★ **NR Comedy 2:00**
Dir: George Seaton *Cast:* Clark Gable, Doris Day, Gig Young, Mamie Van Doren, Nick Adams, Marion Ross

▸ Journalism teacher Day criticizes newspaper editor Gable. He poses as student, becomes her star pupil, then falls for Day and tries to win her away from shrink Young (Oscar nominated). Winning leads in this bright and breezy newspaper comedy.

Dist.: KVC

TEENAGE DEVIL DOLLS 1962
☆ **NR Drama 1:28 B&W**
Dir: B. Lawrence Price, Jr. *Cast:* Barbara Marks, Robert A. Sherry, Robert Norman, Elaine Lindenbaum, Joel Climenhaga

▸ Deadpan rendering of young Marks's spiral into degradation, beginning with her fall into the wrong company and addiction to marijuana. A serious car crash fails to set her straight, and before long she's selling the stuff as well as using it. Told entirely through voice-over narration, sensational exploitation picture is watched today for laughs. Also known as *One Way Ticket to Hell.*

Dist.: Rhino

TEENAGE MUTANT NINJA TURTLES 1990
★★★★ **PG Action-Adventure 1:33**
☑ Explicit language, violence
Dir: Steve Barron *Cast:* Judith Hoag, Elias Koteas, Michael Turney, Jay Patterson, Louis Cantarini, Josh Pais

▸ Sewer-dwelling, humanoid turtles Raphael, Donatello, Leonardo, and Michaelangelo fight crime in New York City, especially a Japanese gang called the Foot. When the Foot kidnaps the Turtles' rat mentor Splinter, the foursome, along with human pals Koteas and Hoag, go after the Shredder, the Foot's evil genius. Smash-hit film and national kiddie phenomonena; parents who allow their children to see this may find themselves obliged to purchase expensive tie-in paraphernalia.

Dist.: IVE

TEENAGERS FROM OUTER SPACE 1959
☆ **NR Sci-Fi 1:26 B&W**
Dir: Tom Graeff *Cast:* Tom Graeff, Dawn Anderson, Harvey B. Dunn, Bryant Grant, Tom Lockyear

▸ Aliens wielding flesh-searing ray guns are prepared to use Earth as pasturage for their "gargons," giant-sized lobsters who graze on humans. Sensitive alien Graeff falls for Earth girl Anderson and attempts to thwart the plans of his fellow invaders. Really bad, but considering the ultra-low budget, one-man show from producer/writer/director/editor/actor Graeff is something of an achievement for not being much worse.

Dist.: Sinister

TEENAGE ZOMBIES 1958
☆ **NR Horror 1:73 B&W**
Dir: Jerry Warren *Cast:* Don Sullivan, Steve Conte, Katherine Victor, Paul Pepper, Bri Murphy, Mitzi Albertson

▸ On a desolate island, scientist Victor plans a Communist takeover of the world via a special nerve gas that turns its victims into mindless slaves. When a group of water-skiing teenagers stumbles onto the plot, they are endangered by a man in a gorilla suit. Really bad.

Dist.: Sinister

TEEN WITCH 1989
★★ **PG-13 Comedy 1:36**
☑ Adult situations, explicit language
Dir: Dorian Walker *Cast:* Robyn Lively, Dan

Gauthier, Joshua Miller, Caren Kaye, Dick Sargent, Zelda Rubenstein
▶ As predicted by palm reader Rubenstein, bookish teen Lively gains occult ability on her sixteenth birthday. Powers provide her with popularity, spots in the school play and cheerleading squad, and jock of her dreams Gauthier. Cheerfully mindless fare pleasantly performed, dully directed. Some teen appeal but little to offer their elders.
Dist.: Media

TEEN WOLF 1985
★ ★ ★ ★ **PG Comedy 1:32**
☑ Adult situations, explicit language
Dir: Rod Daniel   *Cast:* Michael J. Fox, James Hampton, Susan Ursitti, Jerry Levine, Matt Adler, Lorie Griffin
▶ Typical teen Fox suffers usual woes: school basketball team is so bad he's on verge of quitting, love for popular beauty Griffin goes unrequited, and perky Ursitti won't leave him alone. Then Fox discovers he's a werewolf. Being mean and hairy does wonders for his basketball game and love life, but sudden success goes to Fox's head until Ursitti tames his ego. Always likable Fox is a howl in good-natured but predictable comedy. Followed by sequel. (CC)
Dist.: Paramount

TEEN WOLF TOO 1987
★ **PG Comedy 1:35**
☑ Adult situations, explicit language
Dir: Chris Leitch   *Cast:* Jason Bateman, Kim Darby, John Astin, Paul Sand, James Hampton, Estee Chandler
▶ Bateman, cousin of Michael J. Fox character from *Teen Wolf*, enrolls in college on boxing scholarship despite real interest in veterinary medicine. To satisfy crusty dean Astin and boxing coach Sand and impress girlfriend Chandler, Bateman plays human punching bag to more-talented opponents until genetics bring out his inhuman side and he becomes scourge of the ring and campus hero. Fox-less sequel lacks punch.
Dist.: Paramount

TELEFON 1977
★ ★ ★ ★ **PG Espionage/Action-Adventure 1:43**
☑ Adult situations, explicit language, violence
Dir: Don Siegel   *Cast:* Charles Bronson, Lee Remick, Donald Pleasence, Tyne Daly, Patrick Magee, Sheree North
▶ KGB renegade Pleasence, upset with softening of superpower hostilities, treks to U.S. to activate Soviet saboteurs planted during Cold War. When they wreak havoc on American military bases to start World War III, crack Russian agent Bronson is dispatched to thwart the runaway Red with help of local liaison Remick, who's actually a CIA double agent. First-rate espionage yarn with a timely premise.
Dist.: MGM/UA

TELEPHONE, THE 1988
☆ **R Drama 1:22**
☑ Adult situations, explicit language
Dir: Rip Torn   *Cast:* Whoopi Goldberg, Elliott Gould, John Heard, Severn Darden, Amy Wright, Ronald J. Stallings
▶ Goldberg, an out-of-work actress with a botched love life, unpaid bills, and dumpy apartment, vents frustrations on phone, employing various accents and persona. Her agent Gould offers no hope for future. When macho phone repairman Heard arrives to disconnect line for nonpayment, Goldberg cracks up. Disappointing and claustrophobic one-woman show. Goldberg unsuccessfully sued to prevent film's release. (CC)
Dist.: New World

TELL ME A RIDDLE 1980
★ ★ **PG Drama 1:33**
☑ Explicit language
Dir: Lee Grant   *Cast:* Melvyn Douglas, Lila Kedrova, Brooke Adams, Dolores Dorn, Bob Elross, Jon Harris
▶ Elderly couple Douglas and Kedrova, immigrants from Russia in 1920s, quarrel over his desire to sell home to move into retirement community and her need to lose herself in novels and scrapbooks of past. When they learn Kedrova suffers from terminal cancer, the couple visits peppy granddaughter Adams in San Francisco. Sincere and restrained look at pitfalls of old age can be slow and downbeat, but Douglas and Kedrova bring depth and credibility to lead roles.
Dist.: Media

TELL ME THAT YOU LOVE ME 1985
★ ★ **NR Drama 1:31**
☑ Adult situations, explicit language
Dir: Tzipi Trope   *Cast:* Nick Mancuso, Belinda Montgomery, Ken Walsh, Andre Pelletier, Barbara Williams
▶ Reporter Montgomery, investigating battered wives, suffers marital woes of her own when lawyer husband Mancuso announces plan to work for a year in another city. He moves out and she invites abused spouse Williams to move in. Montgomery then copes with amorous advances of Walsh, her best friend's husband, and efforts of Mancuso to woo her to new home. Soap opera examination of contemporary adult situations and emotional traumas.
Dist.: Vestron

TELL-TALE HEART, THE 1963 British
★ **NR Horror 1:21 B&W**
Dir: Ernest Morris   *Cast:* Laurence Payne, Adrienne Corri, Dermot Walsh, Selma Van Dias, John Scott, John Martin
▶ Handicapped Payne loves pretty neighbor Corri, but she prefers his best friend Walsh. Payne murders Walsh and hides his corpse. Thump, thump, thump. . .is that the sound of the dead man's heart the killer hears? Above-

average horror was adapted from the classic Edgar Allan Poe short story.
Dist.: Loonic

TELL THEM WILLIE BOY IS HERE 1969
★ ★ ★ **PG Drama 1:37**
☑ Adult situations, explicit language, violence
Dir: Abraham Polonsky *Cast:* Robert Redford, Katharine Ross, Robert Blake, Susan Clark, Barry Sullivan, Mikel Angel
▶ In 1909 California, strong-willed Indian Blake woos fellow tribe member Ross against objections of her father Angel; Blake kills Angel in self-defense during quarrel. Lawman Redford, urged on by romantic interest Clark and racist rancher Sullivan, must reluctantly pursue Blake and Ross into the wilderness. Polonksy's first directing assignment after being blacklisted tries too hard to capture history of whites versus Indians in a nutshell, but Redford's struggle of conscience and the rugged scenery are compelling.
Dist.: MCA

TEMPEST 1982
★ ★ **PG Comedy 2:22**
☑ Adult situations, explicit language
Dir: Paul Mazursky *Cast:* John Cassavetes, Gena Rowlands, Susan Sarandon, Molly Ringwald, Raul Julia, Vittorio Gassman
▶ Prosperous New York architect Cassavetes, in mid-life crisis, leaves wife Rowlands and whisks daughter Ringwald away to barren Greek island. With aid of new girlfriend Sarandon and lecherous goatherd Julia, Cassavetes sets up rural housekeeping and seeks peace with uneven results, until Rowlands and casino magnate beau Gassman interrupt the isolation. Offbeat comedy with meditations on mortality and human frailty is loosely based on Shakespeare's *The Tempest.*
Dist.: RCA/Columbia

TEMPTER, THE 1974 Italian
☆ **R Horror 1:36**
☑ Nudity, explicit language, violence
Dir: Alberto de Martino *Cast:* Carla Gravina, Mel Ferrer, Arthur Kennedy, George Coulouris, Alida Valli, Anita Strindberg
▶ *The Exorcist,* Italian style, as paralyzed and possessed Gravina begins gyrating and spewing to beat the Devil. Father Ferrer interrupts his dalliance with Strindberg to call in clerics to wrestle the malevolent incubus. Repulsive and badly made. Scenes of animal violence are offensive.
Dist.: Embassy

10 1979
★ ★ ★ **R Comedy 2:03**
☑ Nudity, strong sexual content, adult situations, explicit language
Dir: Blake Edwards *Cast:* Dudley Moore, Bo Derek, Julie Andrews, Robert Webber, Dee Wallace
▶ Hollywood songwriter Moore, in throes of male menopause, deserts singer girlfriend Andrews to pursue stunning newlywed Derek, with whom he's become obsessed even though he's never spoken to her. Overcoming all sorts of pitfalls and pratfalls, Moore finally catches up with Derek on honeymoon in Acapulco, only to discover he's not as sexually liberated as he believed. Plenty of physical comedy, skillfully handled by director Edwards. Hugely popular film exposed newcomer Derek to moviegoers.
Dist.: Warner

TENANT, THE 1976 French/U.S.
☆ **R Mystery-Suspense 2:05**
☑ Explicit language, graphic violence
Dir: Roman Polanski *Cast:* Roman Polanski, Isabelle Adjani, Shelley Winters, Melvyn Douglas, Jo Van Fleet, Bernard Fresson
▶ Oddball Parisian loner Polanski moves into seedy apartment previously occupied by woman who committed suicide. He gradually becomes convinced that landlord Douglas, concierge Winters, and previous tenant's friend Adjani are part of conspiracy to drive him to suicide. Eccentric, darkly comic study of burgeoning madness will disappoint fans of conventional horror.
Dist.: Paramount

TEN COMMANDMENTS, THE 1923
★ ★ **NR Drama 2:26 B&W**
Dir: Cecil B. DeMille *Cast:* Theodore Roberts, Charles de Roche, Estelle Taylor, Richard Dix, Rod La Rocque, Leatrice Joy
▶ The Book of Exodus, complete with parting of the Red Sea, destruction of the golden calf, Moses (Roberts), Ramses (de Roche), and a cast of many thousands. First part is legendary for the huge, lavishly detailed sets and literal army (a U.S. Cavalry division) of extras. Less well-known second part shows modern-day consequences of breaking commandments, with Dix and La Rocque playing brothers on opposite sides of the sin question. Spectacular, but not as impressive as DeMille's 1956 remake.
Dist.: Paramount

TEN COMMANDMENTS, THE 1957
★ ★ ★ ★ ★ **G Drama 3:39**
Dir: Cecil B. DeMille *Cast:* Charlton Heston, Anne Baxter, Yul Brynner, Yvonne De Carlo, Cedric Hardwicke, Edward G. Robinson, Debra Paget, John Derek
▶ Massive biblical epic, DeMille style, retells the Old Testament story of Moses (Heston) from his humble birth to his role as the man who leads the Jewish people out of Egypt and to the Promised Land. Strong cast (especially Brynner as rival King Ramses), magnificent production values (Oscar-winning special effects), and fine dramatic tension. Everyone's favorite scene: the parting of the Red Sea. Grand-scale religious entertainment for the whole family.
Dist.: Paramount

TENDER MERCIES 1983
★ ★ ★ ★ **PG Drama 1:29**
☑ Adult situations, explicit language
Dir: Bruce Beresford   *Cast:* Robert Duvall, Tess Harper, Allan Hubbard, Betty Buckley, Ellen Barkin, Wilford Brimley
▶ Stark, compelling drama about alcoholic ex-country star Mac Sledge (Duvall) and his struggle for personal redemption with Harper, the widowed owner of a ramshackle Texas motel. Duvall (who wrote and sang his tunes) won an Oscar for his incisive performance, as did Horton Foote for his moving, subdued screenplay. Equally fine are Barkin as Sledge's troubled daughter, and Buckley as his ex-wife and a popular singer.
Dist.: HBO

TENDER YEARS, THE 1948
★ **NR Drama 1:21**
Dir: Harold Schuster   *Cast:* Joe E. Brown, Richard Lyon, Noreen Nash, Charles Drake, Josephine Hutchinson, James Millican
▶ Change-of-pace dramatic role for Brown, effectively playing a reverend who battles dog fights in his town. The clergyman steals a pooch to protect it from this "sport." A court decides his fate. Animal rights activists will certainly agree with film's sincere conclusion.
Dist.: IVE

TEN FROM YOUR SHOW OF SHOWS 1973
★ ★ ★ ★ **G Comedy/MFTV 1:31 B&W**
Dir: Max Liebman   *Cast:* Sid Caesar, Imogene Coca, Carl Reiner, Howard Morris, Louis Nye, Swen Swanson
▶ Ten excerpts from "Your Show of Shows," landmark 1950s TV comedy starring Caesar and Coca in various skits written by then-fledgling talents such as Mel Brooks, Woody Allen, and Larry Gelbart. Best bits are two spoofs: "From Here to Obscurity" with seaside lovers Caesar and Coca doused with buckets of water, and "This Is Your Story" in which emcee Reiner is wickedly impervious to humiliation brought upon guest Caesar by review of his life. Only drawback to anthology of classic live comedy: kinescopes from which film is assembled give it crude, grainy look.
Dist.: Media

TEN LITTLE INDIANS 1975 British
★ ★ ★ **PG Mystery-Suspense 1:38**
☑ Violence
Dir: Peter Collinson   *Cast:* Oliver Reed, Elke Sommer, Richard Attenborough, Gert Frobe, Herbert Lom, Charles Aznavour
▶ Bland version of the often-filmed Agatha Christie classic. Ten guests are invited to an isolated hotel in Iran where a mysterious murderer bumps them off one by one. Christie's plot defeated by Collinson's flat direction.
Dist.: Nelson

TENNESSEE'S PARTNER 1955
★ ★ ★ **NR Western 1:27**
Dir: Allan Dwan   *Cast:* John Payne, Ronald

Reagan, Rhonda Fleming, Coleen Gray, Anthony Caruso, Morris Ankrum
▶ When ranchhand Reagan saves gambler Payne's life during a barroom brawl, Payne proceeds to take over Reagan's life. Offering unwanted advice about women, gambling, and gunfights, he becomes a serious obstacle to Reagan's happiness with girlfriend Gray. Quirky Western loosely based on a Bret Harte short story has a subtle moral. Look closely for Angie Dickinson as one of madam Fleming's girls.
Dist.: Buena Vista

10 RILLINGTON PLACE 1971 British
★ ★ ★ **PG Drama 1:51**
☑ Adult situations, explicit language, violence
Dir: Richard Fleischer   *Cast:* Richard Attenborough, John Hurt, Judy Geeson, Pat Heywood, Isobel Black, Phyllis McMahon
▶ Attenborough is John Reginald Christie, serial rapist/murderer who tells neighbor Hurt he can abort wife Geeson's unwanted baby. Attenborough slays Geeson and couple's other child. Hurt is hanged for the crime because of Attenborough's perjury, leaving the killer free to commit more crimes. Somber and frightening depiction is based on a true story of innocent man's execution, which led to abolition of capital punishment in Britain.
Dist.: RCA/Columbia

TENTH VICTIM, THE 1965 Italian
★ ★ **NR Sci-Fi 1:32**
Dir: Elio Petri   *Cast:* Marcello Mastroianni, Ursula Andress, Elsa Martinelli, Salvo Randone, Massimo Serato
▶ In legalized murder game set in the future, hunter Andress seeks her much coveted "tenth victim"; her chosen quarry, Mastroianni, would also like to kill Andress, but things get complicated when the would-be killers fall in love. Charismatic leads and stylish direction grace provocative but thin screenplay. Dubbed.
Dist.: Nelson

10 TO MIDNIGHT 1983
★ ★ ★ ★ **R Action-Adventure 1:42**
☑ Nudity, adult situations, explicit language, violence
Dir: J. Lee Thompson   *Cast:* Charles Bronson, Lisa Eilbacher, Andrew Stevens, Gene Davis, Wilford Brimley, Geoffrey Lewis
▶ Hard-boiled L.A. cop Bronson trails slasher Davis, whose next victim might be Bronson's daughter Eilbacher. Convinced of Davis's guilt but lacking evidence to convict him, Bronson tries unsuccessfully to frame the killer and is dismissed from the police force. Davis, once again free, stalks Eilbacher, prompting Bronson to take matters into own hands. Vigilante Bronson at his best.
Dist.: MGM/UA

TEN WANTED MEN 1955
★ ★ **NR Western 1:20**

Dir: H. Bruce Humberstone *Cast:* Randolph Scott, Jocelyn Brando, Richard Boone, Alfonso Bedoya, Donna Martell, Skip Homeier
▶ Greedy landowner Boone brings in hired guns to taunt law-abiding neighbor Scott, whose nephew has won the affections of local belle Martell. Feud degenerates into a gun-blazing seige and deadly duel between the two prinicpals. Brando is good as the widow who hopes to snag Scott once the smoke has cleared.
Dist.: RCA/Columbia

TEQUILA SUNRISE 1988
★★★ R Drama 1:56
☑ Adult situations, explicit language, violence
Dir: Robert Towne *Cast:* Mel Gibson, Michelle Pfeiffer, Kurt Russell, Raul Julia, J. T. Walsh, Arliss Howard
▶ High school friends Gibson, a retired cocaine dealer, and Russell, a Los Angeles narcotics cop, fall for beautiful Pfeiffer, owner of a trendy restaurant. Or is Russell using Pfeiffer to implicate Gibson in a major drug deal? Attractive stars make the most of director Towne's often confusing screenplay, infusing remarkable romantic chemistry into weak action sequences.
Dist.: Warner

TERMINAL CHOICE 1985 Canadian
★★ R Mystery-Suspense 1:39
☑ Brief nudity, adult situations, explicit language, violence
Dir: Sheldon Larry *Cast:* Joe Spano, Diane Venora, David McCallum, Robert Joy, Don Francks, Ellen Barkin
▶ Computer-automated hospital is plagued by a series of fatal mechanical malfunctions. Suspects include alcoholic surgeon Spano, his ex-girlfriend Venora, and sneaky lawyer Francks. Superior cast outweighs farfetched plot in this moderately suspenseful medical drama.
Dist.: Vestron

TERMINAL ENTRY 1987
★ R Action-Adventure 1:37
☑ Nudity, adult situations, explicit language, violence
Dir: John Kincaide *Cast:* Eddie Albert, Yaphet Kotto, Paul Smith, Heidi Helmer, Patrick Labyorteaux, Tracy Brooks Swope
▶ Teen computer hackers break into the Terminal Entry program and mistake it for an interactive antiterrorist game. Unfortunately, the program is actually an information source for Middle Eastern killers intent on assassinating the President. Federal security agents Albert and Kotto must find the hackers and the terrorists before an important peace conference begins. Despite good twists, clever premise isn't exploited effectively.
Dist.: Celebrity

TERMINAL ISLAND 1973
☆ R Action-Adventure 1:28

☑ Nudity, adult situations, explicit language, violence
Dir: Stephanie Rothman *Cast:* Phyllis Elizabeth Davis, Don Marshall, Barbara Leigh, Sean Kenny, Roger Mosley, Tom Selleck
▶ Inmates at an anything-goes maximum security penitentiary off the coast of California include mercy-killing doctor Selleck and tough hood Davis. Although Selleck's role in this sleazy exploitation is minuscule, he's used it on TV talk shows to make fun of his early hunk image. Not worth staying up for.
Dist.: United

TERMINAL MAN, THE 1974
★★★ PG Sci-Fi 1:44
☑ Violence
Dir: Mike Hodges *Cast:* George Segal, Joan Hackett, Richard Dysart, Michael C. Gwynne, Donald Moffat, Jill Clayburgh
▶ Computer expert Segal develops murderous impulses after an accident; surgeon Dysart implants a microchip into his brain to control his violent tendencies. But a malfunction turns Segal into a killing machine. Grim adaptation of Michael Crichton's best-seller is often unpleasantly violent.
Dist.: Warner

TERMINATOR, THE 1984
★★★★ R Sci-Fi/Action-Adventure 1:47
☑ Nudity, adult situations, explicit language, graphic violence
Dir: James Cameron *Cast:* Arnold Schwarzenegger, Michael Biehn, Linda Hamilton, Paul Winfield, Lance Henriksen
▶ Twenty-first-century killer cyborg Schwarzenegger travels in time to the present to assassinate Hamilton, the future mother of human race's savior; futuristic resistance fighter Biehn follows to save her. Biehn and Hamilton fall in love as they are pursued by Schwarzenegger. Blistering saga has it all: relentless pacing, incredible action, humor, and surprisingly affecting characterizations. A genre movie with guts and brains.
Dist.: HBO

TERMS OF ENDEARMENT 1983
★★★★★ PG Comedy/Drama 2:12
☑ Adult situations, explicit language
Dir: James L. Brooks *Cast:* Shirley MacLaine, Debra Winger, Jack Nicholson, Jeff Daniels, John Lithgow, Danny DeVito
▶ Multi-Oscar winner—Best Picture, Director, Screenplay (Brooks), Actress (MacLaine), Supporting Actor (Nicholson)—explores the relationship between neurotic MacLaine and her determined daughter Winger, who marries philandering teacher Daniels against her mother's wishes. Endearing, full-bodied characterizations from extraordinary cast, especially Nicholson as the womanizing, over-the-hill astronaut MacLaine loves. Based on the novel by Larry McMurtry. (CC)
Dist.: Paramount

TERROR, THE 1963
★ ★ NR Horror 1:21
Dir: Roger Corman *Cast:* Boris Karloff, Jack Nicholson, Sandra Knight, Dick Miller, Dorothy Neuman, Jonathan Haze
▶ Napoleonic officer Nicholson keeps encountering—but losing—the beautiful Knight. Arriving at baron Karloff's castle, he sees a portrait of the girl, whom the older man claims is his late wife. Corman evokes a neatly gloomy atmosphere that makes the many plot holes easier to take; Nicholson contributes an early, overdone performance. Shot in three days on *The Raven* sets.
Dist.: Various

TERROR BY NIGHT 1946
★ ★ ★ NR Mystery-Suspense 1:00 B&W
Dir: Roy William Neill *Cast:* Basil Rathbone, Nigel Bruce, Alan Mowbray, Dennis Hoey, Renee Godfrey
▶ On a London-Edinburgh train, a diamond is stolen and its owner murdered. Sherlock Holmes (Rathbone) and Watson (Bruce) examine the various suspects and unmask the guilty party. Taut and tense mystery is one of the better Rathbone-Bruce efforts. **(CC)**
Dist.: Various ☐C

TERROR IN THE WAX MUSEUM 1973
☆ PG Horror 1:29
☑ Violence
Dir: Georg Fenady *Cast:* Ray Milland, Broderick Crawford, Elsa Lanchester, Maurice Evans, Shani Wallis, John Carradine, Louis Hayward, Patric Knowles
▶ Carradine is murdered just as he's about to sell his wax museum to Crawford. Lanchester takes over the place, but the killings, apparently by wax figures come to life, continue. Could sculptor Milland be behind this? Terrific cast in a mediocre plot that you've seen many times before.
Dist.: Vestron

TERROR IS A MAN 1959 Filipino
★ NR Horror 1:29 B&W
Dir: Gerry DeLeon *Cast:* Francis Lederer, Greta Thyssen, Richard Derr, Oscar Keesee
▶ Shipwrecked sailor Derr finds himself on Blood Island, where mad scientist Lederer has transformed a leopard into a hybrid half-man, half-beast. The monster kidnaps Lederer's wife Thyssen, and both men set out in pursuit. First in a flood of Filipino horror pics is a respectable variation on the *Island of Lost Souls* theme. Also known as *Blood Creature*.
Dist.: Sinister

TERRORISTS, THE 1975 British
★ PG Action-Adventure 1:29
☑ Explicit language, violence
Dir: Casper Wrede *Cast:* Sean Connery, Ian McShane, Norman Bristow, John Cording, Isabel Dean, William Fox
▶ In Norway, terrorists hijack a plane and hold British diplomats hostage. Security chief Connery, after attempting a negotiated solution,

takes action against the hijackers. Topical thriller has a couple of suspenseful sequences. However, not even Connery's dependably strong presence can overcome the flaccid direction and screenplay. Also known as *Ransom*. **(CC)**
Dist.: CBS/Fox

TERRORNAUTS, THE 1967 British
☆ NR Sci-Fi 1:15
Dir: Montgomery Tully *Cast:* Simon Oates, Zena Marshall, Charles Hawtrey, Patricia Hayes, Stanley Meadows, Max Adrian
▶ Scientist Oates, his co-workers, and their building are transported to a planet where evil aliens are plotting against Earth. Oates and company must figure out how to save the world. Moody adaptation of the Murray Leinster novel *The Wailing Asteroid*.
Dist.: Nelson

TERROR OF TINY TOWN, THE 1938
☆ NR Western 1:06 B&W
Dir: Sam Newfield *Cast:* Billy Curtis, Little Billy, Yvonne Moray, Billy Platt
▶ The first (and probably last) all-midget Western in movie history. Bad guy Billy attempts to get his greedy little hands on Tiny Town land by creating feuds between ranchers. Equally diminutive good guy Curtis thwarts him. Literally small in scope and pretty silly.
Dist.: Video Yesteryear

TERROR TRAIN 1980 Canadian
★ ★ R Horror 1:37
☑ Nudity, adult situations, explicit language, graphic violence
Dir: Roger Spottiswoode *Cast:* Ben Johnson, Jamie Lee Curtis, Hart Bochner, David Copperfield, Derek MacKinnon, Sandee Currie
▶ Practical joke by medical students backfires when their victim goes insane. Three years later he sneaks aboard a chartered train to kill his tormentors during their masquerade party. Presence of veteran actors Curtis and Johnson (playing a friendly conductor) elevate this slightly above other slasher films. Directing debut for Spottiswoode.
Dist.: CBS/Fox

TERRORVISION 1986
☆ R Horror 1:23
☑ Nudity, adult situations, explicit language, graphic violence
Dir: Ted Nicolaou *Cast:* Jennifer Richards, Diane Franklin, Gerrit Graham, Mary Woronov, Chad Allen, Alejandro Rey
▶ Typical suburban family receives a strange signal from outer space on their new satellite dish. Curiosity turns to horror when a revolting monster suddenly pops out of their TV set. Weak attempt at satire relies heavily on disgusting slime special effects.
Dist.: Vestron

TERROR WITHIN, THE 1989
★ R Horror 1:26

☐ Rape, adult situations, explicit language, graphic violence
Dir: Thierry Notz   *Cast:* George Kennedy, Andrew Stevens, Starr Andreeff, Terri Treas, John LaFayette, Yvonne Saa
▶ After a plague kills most of humanity, Kennedy and other scientists are trapped by gargoyles in an underground bunker. Saa gives birth to a mutating monster that stalks the scientists down dark corridors. Inferior imitation of *Alien* delivers a few scares with mechanical competence.
Dist.: MGM/UA

TERRY FOX STORY, THE 1983
★ ★ ★ ★ NR Biography/MFTV 1:37
☑ Adult situations, explicit language
Dir: Ralph L. Thomas   *Cast:* Eric Fryer, Robert Duvall, Michael Zelniker, Chris Makepeace, Rosalind Chao
▶ True story of courage and heroism dramatizes the life of Terry Fox (Fryer), the Canadian who, despite his leg amputation, ran three thousand miles across Canada. His effort raised more than $20 million for cancer research. Duvall plays Bill Vigers, the public relations man who befriends Fox; Makepeace appears as Terry's brother and Chao, his girlfriend. HBO's first original film.
Dist.: Vestron

TESS 1980 French/British
★ ★ ★ PG Drama 2:55
☑ Adult situations
Dir: Roman Polanski   *Cast:* Nastassia Kinski, Peter Firth, Leigh Dawson, John Collin, Tony Church
▶ Thomas Hardy's classic 1891 tale about the enchanting Tess (Kinski), a free spirit who is seduced, impregnated, and abandoned by her cousin Dawson. She finds love with Angel Clair (Firth) but he, too, abandons her when he discovers the secret of her past affair. Old-fashioned, gloriously detailed film won Oscars for Cinematography, Art Direction, and Costume Design.
Dist.: RCA/Columbia

TESTAMENT 1983
★ ★ ★ PG Drama 1:30
☑ Adult situations, explicit language
Dir: Lynne Littman   *Cast:* Jane Alexander, William Devane, Ross Harris, Lukas Haas, Roxana Zal, Philip Anglim
▶ Typical suburban mom Alexander sends commuter hubbie Devane off to work in San Francisco and copes with errands and kids Harris, Haas, and Zal on seemingly average day, only to witness drastic changes in wake of nuclear holocaust. Contamination by radioactive fallout, isolation from rest of world, breakdown of law, and shortages of basic supplies become the new norm as death and despair sweep through once-placid community. Restrained, sure-handed look at morbid topic carried by Oscar-nominated Alexander.

Rebecca De Mornay and Kevin Costner appear in bit roles.   (CC)
Dist.: Paramount

TESTAMENT OF DR. MABUSE, THE 1933 German
☆ NR Action-Adventure 2:00 B&W
Dir: Fritz Lang   *Cast:* Rudolf Klein-Rogge, Oskar Beregi, Gustav Diesl, Karl Meixner, Klaus Pohl, Camilla Spira
▶ Sequel to the silent *Dr. Mabuse, The Gambler* has the fiendish Klein-Rogge locked in an insane asylum, where his spirit takes over the mind of Beregi, the asylum's director. Using his respectable position as a front, Beregi forms a group devoted to bringing down society by acts of terrorism and chaos. Unsettling thriller creates an effective air of menace.   Ⓢ
Dist.: Nelson

TEST OF LOVE, A 1985 Australian
★ ★ ★ PG Drama 1:33
☑ Adult situations
Dir: Gil Brealey   *Cast:* Angela Punch-McGregor, Drew Forsythe, Tina Arhondis, Charles Tingwell, Monica Maughan, Mark Butler
▶ Young Arhondis, brain-damaged at birth, has lived for years in home for spastics. New doctor McGregor believes Arhondis, although physically incapacitated, is mentally alert and perhaps of above-average intelligence. She teaches Arhondis to communicate by signs and symbols. Ultimately, McGregor initiates court contest to free girl from institution. Moving drama is based on a true story.
Dist.: MCA

TEX 1982
★ ★ ★ PG Drama 1:43
☑ Adult situations, explicit language, mild violence
Dir: Tim Hunter . *Cast:* Matt Dillon, Jim Metzler, Meg Tilly, Bill McKinney, Ben Johnson, Emilio Estevez
▶ Left alone for long stints by widower father McKinney, high school senior Metzler struggles to raise younger brother Dillon. Dillon's unsupervised life results in tentative experiences with drugs, alcohol, girls, class differences, crime, and death. Best pal Estevez pushes drugs while his tomboy sister Tilly catches Dillon's eye; their rich father Johnson doesn't approve of either hanging out with poor boy Dillon. Adapted from the novel by S. E. Hinton.
Dist.: Buena Vista

TEXAS 1941
★ ★ ★ ★ NR Western 1:33 B&W
Dir: George Marshall   *Cast:* William Holden, Glenn Ford, Claire Trevor, George Bancroft, Edgar Buchanan
▶ Friends and Confederate veterans Holden and Ford split up to escape a posse who mistakenly think they have robbed a stage. When they next meet, it is on opposite sides of some shady cattle business, and as rivals for

the hand of Trevor. Nonstop plot is a strong showcase for the talents of the young stars.
Dist.: RCA/Columbia

TEXAS CHAINSAW MASSACRE, THE 1974
★ R Horror 1:23
☑ Graphic violence
Dir: Tobe Hooper **Cast:** Marilyn Burns, Gunnar Hansen, Allen Danzinger, Paul A. Partain, William Vail, Edwin Neal
▶ Five friends travel through Texas and discover a seemingly deserted house that turns out to be not so empty: residents include a crazy father and his two sons who proceed to menace the hapless group with hammers, meat hooks, and chainsaws. Horrifying and suspenseful but also quite violent and repellent. **(CC)**
Dist.: Media

TEXAS CHAINSAW MASSACRE PART 2 1986
☆ NR Horror 1:35
☑ Explicit language, graphic violence
Dir: Tobe Hooper **Cast:** Dennis Hopper, Caroline Williams, Bill Johnson, Jim Siedow, Bill Moseley, Lou Perry
▶ Sequel to cult horror classic brings back chili chef Siedow and his clan of cannibalistic corpse-robbers. Bible-thumping Texas Ranger Hopper seeks to avenge murder of kin in earlier pic while local DJ Williams, hoping to expose slash-happy family, winds up a screaming captive in an underground chamber of horrors. Tongue-in-cheek script offers some laughs, but slice-and-dice exploitation is for diehards only.
Dist.: Media

TEXAS DETOUR 1978
★ R Action-Adventure 1:32
☑ Rape, brief nudity, explicit language
Dir: Hikmet Avedis **Cast:** Patrick Wayne, Priscilla Barnes, Cameron Mitchell, Lindsay Bloom, R. G. Armstrong, Mitch Vogel
▶ The cops are no help when stuntman Wayne, brother James, and sister Bloom have their souped-up van swiped by thugs halfway between California and Nashville. The stranded threesome get a job on a ranch, acquire local lovers, and go after the bad guys themselves. Rousing B-movie action, but shallow characters. Music performed by Flo and Eddie.
Dist.: Prism

TEXAS LADY 1955
★ ★ NR Western 1:26
Dir: Tim Whelan **Cast:** Claudette Colbert, Barry Sullivan, Greg Walcott, Walter Sande, John Litel, Ray Collins
▶ Idealistic newspaper editor Colbert battles corrupt cattlemen Sande and Collins. Gambler Sullivan shows up, seeking revenge against Colbert for a past wrong, but then falls under her spell and joins the fight against her

enemies. Colbert's personality transcends a bland vehicle.
Dist.: Republic

THANK GOD IT'S FRIDAY 1978
★ ★ PG Musical/Comedy 1:29
☑ Explicit language
Dir: Robert Klane **Cast:** Donna Summer, Valerie Landsburg, Terri Nunn, Chick Vennera, Ray Vitte, Mark Lonow
▶ One night in the lives of a crowd at a Los Angeles disco. Ensemble turns include unknown singer Summer in first break en route to stardom, dance-crazy Mexican-American Vennera who wins big boogie contest, underage girls Landsburg and Nunn who get first taste of nightclub life, and disco's manic DJ Vitte. In smaller parts are Jeff Goldblum and Debra Winger; the Commodores appear in finale as themselves. Summer's hit "Last Dance" won an Oscar.
Dist.: RCA/Columbia

THANK YOUR LUCKY STARS 1943
★ ★ NR Musical 2:07 B&W
Dir: David Butler **Cast:** Eddie Cantor, Joan Leslie, Dennis Morgan, Dinah Shore, S. Z. Sakall, Edward Everett Horton, Bette Davis, Errol Flynn, Humphrey Bogart, John Garfield, Olivia de Havilland, Ida Lupino, Ann Sheridan
▶ Dated but enjoyable concoction about Cantor producing a show with Sakall and Horton was Warner Brothers' contribution to the World War II effort. Their top stars and contract players appear in a variety of song-and-dance numbers to benefit the Hollywood Canteen. Highlights include Davis belting out the Oscar-nominated "They're Either Too Young or Too Old" and Flynn performing the sly "That's What You Jolly Well Get." Shore's film debut.
Dist.: MGM/UA

THAT CHAMPIONSHIP SEASON 1982
★ ★ R Drama 1:49
☑ Adult situations, explicit language, violence
Dir: Jason Miller **Cast:** Bruce Dern, Robert Mitchum, Stacy Keach, Martin Sheen, Paul Sorvino
▶ Four teammates join their ex-coach Mitchum for the twenty-fourth annual reunion of their high school basketball team, the champs of 1957. The booze flows freely and the talk turns personal. In various ways, each of the men reveals himself as a washout; the only real "winner" is the team member who failed to show up. Excellent cast, especially Mitchum, but the upbeat ending denies everything that has gone on beforehand. Director Miller adapted his own Pulitzer prize–winning play.
Dist.: MGM/UA

THAT COLD DAY IN THE PARK 1969
☆ R Drama 1:46

☑ Brief nudity, adult situations, explicit language, violence
Dir: Robert Altman **Cast:** Sandy Dennis, Michael Burns, Susanne Benton, Luana Anders, John Garfield, Jr., Michael Murphy
▶ During a dreary day in the park, lonely spinster Dennis finds Burns and brings him home. Although he doesn't care for her, she becomes increasingly obsessive and imprisons him in her apartment. Early effort from Altman is dank and depressing. Director fails to rein in Dennis's occasionally touching but overly mannered performance.
Dist.: Republic

THAT DARN CAT 1965
★ ★ ★ ★ **G Family 1:56**
Dir: Robert Stevenson **Cast:** Hayley Mills, Dean Jones, Dorothy Provine, Roddy McDowall, Neville Brand, Elsa Lanchester, William Demarest, Frank Gorshin, Ed Wynn
▶ Amusing Disney romp about a kidnapped banker who hides clue to his whereabouts on the collar of Mills's Siamese cat; FBI agent Jones is dragged through entertaining slapstick situations keeping an eye on the feline. Bright cast helped by comic pros Demarest, Gorshin, and Wynn.
Dist.: Buena Vista

THAT GIRL FROM PARIS 1936
★ **NR Musical 1:45 B&W**
Dir: Leigh Jason **Cast:** Lily Pons, Jack Oakie, Gene Raymond, Herman Bing, Mischa Auer, Lucille Ball
▶ Real-life diva Pons plays a French opera star trying to hide from U.S. immigration agents. Going incognito, she takes a job warbling with a swing orchestra. Band leader Raymond falls for her, and gets a big surprise when he finds out who she is. Bubbly, tuneful mix of highbrow and low, with songs like "Moon Face" and Strauss's "The Blue Danube" done swing style. Remade as *Four Jacks and a Jill*.
Dist.: Turner

THAT HAMILTON WOMAN 1941
★ ★ ★ ★ **NR Biography/Drama 2:05 B&W**
Dir: Alexander Korda **Cast:** Vivien Leigh, Laurence Olivier, Alan Mowbray, Gladys Cooper, Henry Wilcoxon, Sara Allgood
▶ During the Napoleonic era, beautiful Leigh weds ambassador Mowbray, becomes Lady Hamilton, then falls for Lord Nelson (Olivier), the famous naval commander. Their scandalous romance shocks the world and ends in tragedy. The glamour and magic of then reallife spouses Leigh and Olivier make this lovingly produced true story one of the most achingly romantic movies of all time. Heart-tugging curtain line: "There was no then, there was no after."
Dist.: Nelson

THAT'LL BE THE DAY 1974 British
★ **PG Drama 1:26**
☑ Explicit language

Dir: Claude Whatham **Cast:** David Essex, Ringo Starr, Rosemary Leach, James Booth, Billy Fury, Keith Moon
▶ Real-life musician Essex brings depth and insight to his role as an alienated youth in late 1950s England who dreams of becoming a rock star. Loosely inspired by the life of John Lennon, film provides accurate look at early music scene in working-class Britain. Sequel: *Stardust*.
Dist.: HBO

THAT OBSCURE OBJECT OF DESIRE 1977
French/Spanish
☆ **R Comedy 1:40**
☑ Nudity, adult situations, explicit language
Dir: Luis Buñuel **Cast:** Fernando Rey, Angela Molina, Carole Bouquet, Julian Bertheau, Andre Weber, Milena Vukotic
▶ Against a background of terrorist attacks, rich widower Rey falls for a younger woman and pursues her obsessively. The object of Rey's desire has a personality so complex that the part is played by two different actresses (the volcanic Molina and the willowy Bouquet). Oscar nominations for Best Foreign Film and Screenplay Adaptation went to Buñuel's last movie. Ⓢ
Dist.: Nelson

THAT'S ADEQUATE 1988
☆ **R Comedy 1:20**
☑ Nudity, explicit language
Dir: Harry Hurwitz **Cast:** Tony Randall, James Coco, Jerry Stiller, Anne Meara, Ina Balin, Ann Bloom, Robert Townsend, Irwin Cory, Susan Dey, Robert Downey, Jr., Richard Lewis, Chuck McCann, Peter Reigert, Brother Theodore, Robert Vaughn, Bruce Willis
▶ Mock documentary about a fictional movie studio, beginning with its origins in the 1930s making films like *Sluts of the South* and *Young Adolf*, taking it to later TV offerings like *Father Knows Beaver*. Surprisingly unfunny, considering the potential of the premise.
Dist.: Southgate

THAT'S DANCING! 1985
★ ★ ★ ★ **G Dance 1:44**
Dir: Jack Haley, Jr. **Cast:** Gene Kelly, Sammy Davis, Jr., Mikhail Baryshnikov, Liza Minnelli, Ray Bolger
▶ Clips trace the history of dance on film, including Depression-era Busby Berkeley, teaming of young Shirley Temple and tap master Bill Robinson, Fred Astaire and Gingor Rogers, and contemporary ballet and rock dancing. Other noteworthy appearances include Jimmy Cagney, Ruby Keeler, Ann Miller, Cyd Charisse, and, in pitch to younger viewers, John Travolta and Michael Jackson. Dance jamboree has some slow spots, but highlights can't be beat.
Dist.: MGM/UA

THAT'S ENTERTAINMENT! 1974
★ ★ ★ ★ ★ **G Musical 2:12**

Dir: Jack Haley, Jr. *Cast:* Fred Astaire, Liza Minnelli, Frank Sinatra, Bing Crosby, Gene Kelly, Elizabeth Taylor

▶ Compilation of the best numbers from classic MGM musicals may be even more fun than its sources because you don't have to sit through dialogue scenes (writer-director Haley's narration is intelligent and unobtrusive). Among many highlights: young Judy Garland singing "Dear Mr. Gable" to a photo of Clark Gable, Esther Williams's lavish water ballets, and Astaire dancing on the ceiling in *Royal Wedding.*
Dist.: MGM/UA

THAT'S ENTERTAINMENT, PART 2 1976
★ ★ ★ ★ G Musical 2:13
Dir: Gene Kelly *Cast:* Fred Astaire, Gene Kelly

▶ Sequel to *That's Entertainment* provides more clips from MGM musical greats as well as material from the studio's non-musical classics (like the Marx Brothers' hilarious stateroom scene from *A Night at the Opera* and William Powell, Myrna Loy, and Asta in *The Thin Man*). In between, Kelly and Astaire narrate and show they can still hoof effectively in new numbers made especially for this film.
Dist.: MGM/UA

THAT SINKING FEELING 1983 Scottish
☆ PG Comedy 1:22
☑ Adult situations
Dir: Bill Forsyth *Cast:* Robert Buchanan, John Hughes, Billy Greenlees, Douglas Sannachan, Alan Love, Danny Benson

▶ Gang of unemployed Glasgow youths rob stainless steel sinks from factory, then must find a way to fence their booty. Laconic caper captures Forsyth's distinctive comic sensibility and visual style in its earliest form. Director's debut was shot in 16mm and released in this country after the success of his later *Gregory's Girl* and *Local Hero.*
Dist.: Nelson

THAT'S LIFE! 1986
★ ★ ★ PG-13 Comedy/Drama 1:42
☑ Explicit language
Dir: Blake Edwards *Cast:* Julie Andrews, Jack Lemmon, Sally Kellerman, Robert Loggia, Rob Knepper

▶ It's Lemmon's sixtieth birthday and he's suffering a bad case of male menopause in this seriously funny Edwards comedy. Lemmon has everything a man could want, but he's throwing tantrums like a childish brat, he's also making everyone miserable, including his wife Andrews (a.k.a. Mrs. Edwards), a show biz singer with very real problems of her own. **(CC)**
Dist.: Vestron

THAT TOUCH OF MINK 1962
★ ★ ★ NR Comedy 1:39
Dir: Delbert Mann *Cast:* Cary Grant, Doris Day, Gig Young, Audrey Meadows, John Astin, Dick Sargent

▶ Out-of-work Day meets rich Grant when his

limo goes through a puddle and splashes her. Grant tries to woo the virginal Day with wealth and charm. Will she succumb to his advances? Familiar story works nicely, thanks to amusing Oscar-nominated screenplay and pleasant performances. Cameos by Mickey Mantle, Roger Maris, and Yogi Berra.
Dist.: Republic

THAT UNCERTAIN FEELING 1941
★ ★ NR Comedy 1:23 B&W
Dir: Ernst Lubitsch *Cast:* Merle Oberon, Melvyn Douglas, Burgess Meredith, Alan Mowbray, Eve Arden, Harry Davenport

▶ Park Avenue wife Oberon, ignored by insurance executive husband Douglas, meets grumpy pianist Meredith at her psychiatrist's office. When their fling threatens the marriage, Douglas schemes to get Oberon back. Lesser Lubitsch effort is still sparkling fun, thanks to acerbic script and Meredith's performance as the musician fond of saying, "Phooey."
Dist.: Video Yesteryear ☐

THAT WAS ROCK (THE T.A.M.I./T.N.T. SHOW) 1984
★ ★ ★ NR Music/MFTV 1:32 B&W
Dir: Steve Binder, Larry Peerce *Cast:* Chuck Berry, James Brown, Ray Charles, Marvin Gaye, The Rolling Stones, The Supremes, Bo Diddley, Smokey Robinson and the Miracles, Ike and Tina Turner

▶ *The T.A.M.I. Show* (1964) and *The Big T.N.T. Show* (1966) were two of the greatest rock 'n' roll extravaganzas; this compilation features the best of both with a remastered soundtrack. Since both were shot on videotape and transferred to film, picture quality is poor. However, unbeatable stars are captured in incredible performances. Also known as *Born to Rock: The T.A.M.I. Show/The T.N.T. Show.*
Dist.: Media

THAT WAS THEN. . .THIS IS NOW 1985
★ ★ ★ R Drama 1:43
☑ Adult situations, explicit language, mild violence
Dir: Christopher Cain *Cast:* Emilio Estevez, Craig Sheffer, Kim Delaney, Jill Schoelen, Barbara Babcock, Morgan Freeman

▶ Disillusioned orphan Estevez has been raised by widow Babcock and her son Sheffer. They take different paths towards adulthood: Sheffer romances cute waitress Delaney and takes on responsibilities, while Estevez deals drugs and steals cars. Estevez's deviant behavior puts strain on once-close friendship. Adaptation of S. E. Hinton novel, with screenplay by Estevez, has fine cast, but is unrelentingly glum. **(CC)**
Dist.: Paramount

THEATRE OF BLOOD 1973 British
★ ★ R Horror/Comedy 1:44
☑ Explicit language, graphic violence
Dir: Douglas Hickox *Cast:* Vincent Price, Diana Rigg, Ian Hendry, Robert Morley, Coral Browne, Jack Hawkins

▶ Mad ham Price lives out an actor's ultimate revenge fantasy: with the aid of his daughter Rigg, he literally knocks the critics dead in the styles of his favorite Shakespearean scenes. Ghoulishly funny stuff, deliciously acted by Price and Rigg, has earned cult movie status.
Dist.: MGM/UA

THELONIOUS MONK: STRAIGHT, NO CHASER 1989
☆ **NR Documentary/Music 1:30 C/B&W**
☑ Adult situations
Dir: Charlotte Zwerin *Cast:* Thelonius Monk, Thelonious Monk, Jr., Charlie Rouse, Harry Colomby, Nica de Koenigswarter, Bob Jones
▶ Portrait of Thelonius Monk, one of the most influential jazz musicians of his time, employs excerpts from a West German television documentary filmed in 1967–68, recent interviews with colleagues and family, and rare archival photographs. Emphasis is on Monk's idiosyncratic piano style; very little about the man is revealed. Best appreciated by his fans. Produced by Clint Eastwood. **(CC)**
Dist.: Warner

THEM! 1954
★★★ **NR Sci-Fi 1:34 B&W**
Dir: Gordon Douglas *Cast:* James Whitmore, Edmund Gwenn, Joan Weldon, James Arness, Onslow Stevens, Chris Drake
▶ New Mexico State Troopers Whitmore and Drake find a terrified girl inside the remains of a trailer home; scientist Gwenn and his daughter Weldon discover that nearby radiation tests have spawned a nest of vicious, giant ants. Working with FBI agent Arness, they trace the ants to the storm sewers of Los Angeles. Influential, often terrifying adventure boasts marvelous special effects and a thoughtful script. Look for Fess Parker and Leonard Nimoy in small roles.
Dist.: Warner

THERE'S A GIRL IN MY SOUP 1970 British
★★ **R Comedy 1:35**
☑ Adult situations, explicit language
Dir: Roy Boulting *Cast:* Peter Sellers, Goldie Hawn, Diana Dors, Nicky Henson, Tony Britton
▶ In London, womanizing English TV host Sellers falls for free-spirited American Hawn, but her unfaithful fiancé Henson creates problems for the relationship. Sellers and Hawn bring chemistry and comic skill to an amusing but thin screenplay.
Dist.: RCA/Columbia

THERESE 1986 French
☆ **NR Drama 1:30**
☑ Adult situations
Dir: Alain Cavalier *Cast:* Catherine Mouchet, Aurore Prieto, Sylvie Habault, Chislaine Mona, Helene Alexandridis, Clemence Massart
▶ Teenaged Mouchet overcomes the objections of the church to take the veil and become a "bride of Christ." Her religious passion is revealed through a series of stark, visually powerful tableaux, culminating in her untimely death from tuberculosis. Very slow pacing, but Mouchet is radiant with a rapturous faith. Based on the famous diaries of Saint Therese. ☒
Dist.: Circle

THERE'S NO BUSINESS LIKE SHOW BUSINESS 1954
★★★★★ **NR Musical 1:57**
Dir: Walter Lang *Cast:* Ethel Merman, Donald O'Connor, Marilyn Monroe, Dan Dailey, Mitzi Gaynor, Johnny Ray
▶ Vaudeville couple Merman and Dailey and their kids Gaynor, O'Connor, and Ray form a successful act. Ray leaves to become a priest and O'Connor suffers through rocky romance with opening act Monroe but, in the end, all realize there's no business like show business. Marvelous Irving Berlin score includes "Alexander's Ragtime Band," Monroe singing "Heat Wave," and Merman belting title tune. **(CC)**
Dist.: CBS/Fox

THERE WAS A CROOKED MAN. . . 1970
★★★ **R Western/Comedy 2:03**
☑ Nudity, adult situations, explicit language, mild violence
Dir: Joseph L. Mankiewicz *Cast:* Kirk Douglas, Henry Fonda, Hume Cronyn, Warren Oates, Burgess Meredith, Lee Grant
▶ Outlaw Douglas pulls off big heist but is then arrested. Sheriff Fonda, who nabbed Douglas, becomes prison warden and tries to reform conditions. Douglas cooperates with Fonda but secretly plans to escape and reclaim his loot. Fascinating and outrageous Western is a bit overlong, but the cast (especially Douglas and Fonda) is outstanding.
Dist.: Warner

THESE THREE 1936
★★★ **NR Drama 1:33 B&W**
Dir: William Wyler *Cast:* Miriam Hopkins, Merle Oberon, Joel McCrea, Bonita Granville, Margaret Hamilton, Walter Brennan
▶ Boarding-school brat Granville (Oscar nominated) spreads lies about officials Hopkins, Oberon, and McCrea, the man they both love, leading to personal and professional trouble for the threesome. Excellent acting and masterful direction highlight Lillian Hellman's adaptation of her play *The Children's Hour.* Dated but worthwhile.
Dist.: Nelson

THEY ALL LAUGHED 1981
★★ **PG Romance/Comedy 1:55**
☑ Adult situations, explicit language
Dir: Peter Bogdanovich *Cast:* Audrey Hepburn, Ben Gazzara, John Ritter, Colleen Camp, Dorothy Stratten, Patti Hansen
▶ Private eyes Gazzara and Ritter are assigned to tail beautiful wives Hepburn and Stratten and fall in love with their respective quarries. Meanwhile country-western singer

Camp and sultry cabbie Hansen provide additional romantic entanglements, while others at agency have love complications of their own. Terrific-looking cast and authentic Manhattan setting, but romantic comedy never really takes off. Director Bogdanovich dedicated film to Stratten, killed by her husband after film's completion; her story was filmed as *Star 80*.
Dist.: Vestron

THEY CALL ME BRUCE 1982
★ ★ PG Action-Adventure/Comedy 1:27
☑ Brief nudity, explicit language, violence
Dir: Elliot Hong   *Cast:* Johnny Yune, Margaux Hemingway, Ralph Mauro, Pam Huntington
▶ Totally inept Mafia cook Yune was named for famed karate champ Bruce Lee. He drops out of karate school but accidentally becomes a hero when he foils a robbery. Chopsocky spoof also known as a *A Fistful of Chopsticks*. Sequel: *They Still Call Me Bruce*.
Dist.: Vestron

THEY CALL ME MISTER TIBBS! 1970
★ ★ ★ PG Mystery-Suspense 1:48
☑ Adult situations, explicit language, violence
Dir: Gordon Douglas   *Cast:* Sidney Poitier, Martin Landau, Barbara McNair, Anthony Zerbe, Jeff Corey, David Sheiner
▶ Tough cop Poitier investigates prostitute's murder; his close friend, activist priest Landau, is chief suspect. Poitier's aggressive pursuit of all likely killers leads to several threats on his life. Poitier re-created his enormously popular *In the Heat of the Night* character Virgil Tibbs and made his uncredited directorial debut by helming a number of scenes. Third (and last) in series of Tibbs films was *The Organization*.
Dist.: Key

THEY CALL ME TRINITY 1971 Italian
★ ★ G Western 1:49
Dir: E. B. Clucher (Enzo Barboni)   *Cast:* Terence Hill, Bud Spencer, Farley Granger, Steffen Zacharias, Dan Sturkie, Gisela Hahn
▶ Lighthearted spoof of spaghetti Westerns about amoral sheriff Hill and his dopey half-brother Spencer, who are unexpectedly forced to defend a Mormon family from Mexican bandits. Surprise international success led to sequel *They Still Call Me Trinity*.
Dist.: Nelson

THEY CAME FROM BEYOND SPACE 1967 British
☆ NR Sci-Fi 1:25
Dir: Freddie Francis   *Cast:* Robert Hutton, Jennifer Jayne, Zia Mohyeddin, Bernard Kay, Michael Gough, Geoffrey Wallace
▶ Aliens crash their rocketship on the moon. They travel to Earth, where they use their astral power to possess humans for labor. A steel plate in scientist Hutton's head enables him to resist the extraterrestrial takeover. Dependable Gough is the lead invader, but this sci-fi flick is strictly routine.
Dist.: Nelson

THEY CAME FROM WITHIN 1975 Canadian
☆ R Horror 1:27
☑ Nudity, adult situations, explicit language, graphic violence
Dir: David Cronenberg   *Cast:* Paul Hampton, Joe Silver, Lynn Lowry, Allen Magicovsky, Susan Petrie, Barbara Steele
▶ Scientist specializing in parasites infects his mistress with a mutant bug that turns her into a sexually voracious maniac. She subsequently spreads the parasite to most of the occupants of a Canadian high rise. Intriguing allegory on venereal disease features incredibly disgusting special effects. Also known as *Shivers* and *The Parasite Murders*.
Dist.: Vestron

THEY CAME TO CORDURA 1959
★ ★ NR Western 2:03
Dir: Robert Rossen   *Cast:* Gary Cooper, Rita Hayworth, Van Heflin, Tab Hunter, Richard Conte, Dick York
▶ In 1916, accused coward Cooper and alleged traitor Hayworth accompany five American army heroes on a forced march through the Mexican desert. During the arduous journey, Cooper proves his actual worth and the others demonstrate their darker natures. Gritty and tough; Cooper and Hayworth are quite affecting.
Dist.: RCA/Columbia

THEY DIED WITH THEIR BOOTS ON 1941
★ ★ ★ NR Western 2:18 B&W
Dir: Raoul Walsh   *Cast:* Errol Flynn, Olivia de Havilland, Arthur Kennedy, Charley Grapewin, Anthony Quinn
▶ True story of General George Custer (Flynn) traces his early days at West Point, his courtship and marriage to de Havilland, his military triumphs, and the Little Big Horn massacre. As a history lesson, the movie is distorted; as large-scale entertainment, amazingly exciting. Flynn is outstanding.
Dist.: Key   ©

THEY DRIVE BY NIGHT 1940
★ ★ NR Drama 1:33 B&W
Dir: Raoul Walsh   *Cast:* George Raft, Ann Sheridan, Ida Lupino, Humphrey Bogart, Alan Hale, Roscoe Karns
▶ Trucker brothers Raft and Bogart encounter dangers in life on the road: Bogart is crippled after a crash while Raft gets involved with Lupino, the scheming wife of boss Hale. Gripping and realistic, with hard-nosed acting and direction.
Dist.: CBS/Fox   ©

THEY GOT ME COVERED 1943
★ ★ NR Comedy 1:34 B&W
Dir: David Butler   *Cast:* Bob Hope, Dorothy Lamour, Otto Preminger, Lenore Aubert, Donald Meek

▶ Reporter Hope, canned for making wrong prediction about World War II, gets redemption by uncovering Nazi bigwig Preminger's plot to destroy Washington. Fast-paced and enormously funny comedy with Hope at his peak, wisecracking his way out of tight spots with clever one-liners, ably supported by lovely Lamour and a hairy Preminger.
Dist.: Nelson

THEY KNEW WHAT THEY WANTED 1940
★ NR Drama 1:30 B&W
Dir: Garson Kanin   *Cast:* Carole Lombard, Charles Laughton, William Gargan, Harry Carey, Frank Fay, Karl Malden
▶ California grape grower Laughton woos waitress Lombard by mail. She accepts his marriage proposal, but then learns that he used handsome Gargan's picture as his own. A love triangle ensues. Gargan was Oscar-nominated, but Lombard shines in this adaptation of Sidney Howard's Pulitzer Prize–winning play, which was later the basis of the Broadway musical *Most Happy Fella*.
Dist.: Turner

THEY LIVE 1988
★★ R Sci-Fi 1:37
☑ Nudity, explicit language, violence
Dir: John Carpenter   *Cast:* Roddy Piper, Keith David, Meg Foster, George "Buck" Flower, Peter Jason, Raymond St. Jacques
▶ Construction worker Piper acquires special pair of sunglasses that reveal seemingly normal folk as aliens. Piper becomes a hunted man as he teams with co-worker David to stop the invaders. Intriguing paranoid premise provides vehicle for breathlessly paced stunts and escapes.
Dist.: MCA

THEY LIVE BY NIGHT 1949
★★ NR Drama 1:35 B&W
Dir: Nicholas Ray   *Cast:* Farley Granger, Cathy O'Donnell, Howard da Silva, Jay C. Flippen, Helen Craig, Will Wright
▶ Naive convict Granger joins hardened criminals da Silva and Flippen in an escape attempt. Wounded in an accident, he's nursed to health by equally naive teen O'Donnell, who quickly falls in love. The two are hounded by police until they meet a tragic fate. A classic example of film noir. Ray's directing debut is a moody, tense study of implacable destiny. Based on Edward Anderson's novel *Thieves Like Us*, and remade under that title in 1974.
Dist.: Hollywood Home Theatre

THEY MADE ME A CRIMINAL 1939
★★ NR Drama 1:32 B&W
Dir: Busby Berkeley   *Cast:* John Garfield, Gloria Dickson, Claude Rains, Ann Sheridan, May Robson, Billy Halop, Leo Gorcey, Bobby Jordan, Huntz Hall, Gabriel Dell
▶ Boxing champ Garfield, told he has murdered a reporter, flees to Arizona under an assumed name. Pursued by detective Rains,

he finds a measure of self-respect on a farm for juvenile delinquents. Will he sacrifice his freedom to help the boys in a prize fight? The Dead End Kids (Halop, Gorcey, Jordan, Hall, Dell) provide some humor in this dated but sincere drama.
Dist.: Various

THEY MIGHT BE GIANTS 1971
★★ G Comedy/Drama 1:38
Dir: Anthony Harvey   *Cast:* George C. Scott, Joanne Woodward, Jack Gilford, Rue McClanahan, Lester Rawlins, Kitty Winn
▶ New York psychiatrist Dr. Watson (Woodward) examines patient Scott, who believes he is Sherlock Holmes. This unusual Holmes-Watson team stumbles into a mystery as Scott's relative Rawlins schemes to get his hands on the family fortune. Scott has a grand time in this unusual, interesting item; Woodward plays off him skillfully. Adapted by James Goldman from his play.
Dist.: MCA

THEY'RE PLAYING WITH FIRE 1984
★★ R Mystery-Suspense 1:36
☑ Strong sexual content, violence
Dir: Howard Avedis   *Cast:* Sybil Danning, Eric Brown, Andrew Prine, Paul Clemens, Gene Bicknell, K. T. Stevens
▶ College student Brown is seduced by sexy professor Danning. She and her husband Prine then blackmail Brown into scaring his grandmother to death. Tasteless and pedestrian, with stomach-turning violence and explicit sex scenes.
Dist.: HBO

THEY SAVED HITLER'S BRAIN 1964
☆ NR Sci-Fi 1:14
Dir: David Bradley   *Cast:* Walter Stocker, Audrey Caire, Carlos Rivas, John Holland
▶ Caire and husband Stocker, looking for missing relatives, encounter group of unrepentant Nazis instead. The boys have indeed saved the Fuëhrer's cranium and plot to take over the world. Campy and so inept that it provides unintentional laughs.
Dist.: United

THEY SHALL HAVE MUSIC 1939
★ NR Musical 1:41 B&W
Dir: Archie Mayo   *Cast:* Jascha Heifetz, Joel McCrea, Walter Brennan, Andrea Leeds, Gene Reynolds, Terry Kilburn
▶ Violin virtuoso Heifetz inspires impoverished youth Reynolds to take up music. When his instructor Brennan's school is threatened with foreclosure, Reynolds convinces Heifetz to give a benefit concert. Obvious, sentimental screenplay, but classical music fans will enjoy Heifetz's renditions of Tchaikovsky, Saint Saëns, and Mendelssohn pieces.
Dist.: Nelson

THEY SHOOT HORSES, DON'T THEY? 1969
★★ PG-13 Drama 2:01

☑ Adult situations, explicit language, violence
Dir: Sydney Pollack *Cast:* Jane Fonda, Michael Sarrazin, Susannah York, Gig Young, Red Buttons, Bonnie Bedelia
▶ Chicago dance marathon of 1930s serves as microcosm of life. Disagreeable loner Fonda, pregnant farm girl Bedelia, sultry aspiring actress York, and sailor Buttons are among the marathoners goaded toward self-destruction by sadistic emcee Young over period of weeks for $1500 prize. Fonda established herself as a serious actress, standing out among many splendid performances. Nominated for nine Oscars; Young won Supporting Actor.
Dist.: CBS/Fox

THEY STILL CALL ME BRUCE 1987
★ PG Comedy 1:35
☑ Adult situations, explicit language, mild violence
Dir: Johnny Yune, James Orr *Cast:* Johnny Yune, David Mendenhall, Pat Paulsen, Joey Travolta, Robert Guillaume, Carl Benson
▶ Sequel to *They Call Me Bruce* offers more of the same childish humor, with producer/director/writer Yune still frisky as a martial artist with two left fists. This time out, he's finagled by bad guy Benson into fighting a five-time karate champ called "The Executioner" on national TV. Jokes fall flat, and racial stereotypes may offend.
Dist.: New World

THEY WENT THAT-A-WAY AND THAT-A-WAY 1978
★ ★ ★ PG Comedy 1:35
☑ Adult situations
Dir: Edward Montagne, Stuart E. McGowan
Cast: Tim Conway, Chuck McCann, Richard Kiel, Dub Taylor, Reni Santoni, Lenny Montana
▶ Pint-sized Conway and king-sized McCann are small town cops pretending to be prisoners to uncover whereabouts of stolen loot. No one knows they're really cops but the governor, and when he dies, hapless pair must scheme their way out of trouble. Sight gags may amuse children, but parents will find nothing fresh here.
Dist.: Nelson

THEY WERE EXPENDABLE 1945
★ ★ ★ ★ NR War 2:15 B&W
Dir: John Ford *Cast:* Robert Montgomery, John Wayne, Donna Reed, Jack Holt, Ward Bond, Leon Ames
▶ Classic World War II adventure about the doomed battle for the Philippines concentrates on Montgomery, the leader of a squad of PT boats, and his second-in-command Wayne, an officer impatient with the company's minor duties until his men fall victim to overpowering Japanese. Despite story's tragic outcome, director Ford emphasizes the heroic in inspiring vignettes of fighting. Montgomery's role was based on PT captain John

Bulkeley, who won the Congressional Medal of Honor.
Dist.: MGM/UA ⓒ

THEY WON'T BELIEVE ME 1947
★ ★ NR Drama 1:35 B&W
Dir: Irving Pichel *Cast:* Robert Young, Susan Hayward, Jane Greer, Rita Johnson, Tom Powers, George Tyne
▶ Grim tale of amoral rake Young's affairs with writer Greer and secretary Hayward as he tries to hold onto wealthy wife Johnson. A timely accident seems to solve his problems, but in an unexpected twist he is arrested in a suicide case. Strong drama features a great trick ending. Young is impressive in a rare villainous role.
Dist.: Nostalgia

THIEF 1981
★ ★ ★ ★ R Crime 1:58
☑ Adult situations, explicit language, violence
Dir: Michael Mann *Cast:* James Caan, Tuesday Weld, Willie Nelson, James Belushi, Robert Prosky
▶ Character portrait examines diamond thief Caan's struggle to remain independent of mob influence. Caught between the middle class values of wife Weld and criminal ambitions of vicious mob boss Prosky, Caan decides to pull one last diamond heist to get enough money to live straight. Nelson plays Caan's jailhouse mentor. Gripping and meticulously crafted drama was first theatrical film for Mann.
Dist.: MGM/UA

THIEF OF BAGDAD, THE 1924
★ NR Fantasy 2:35 B&W
Dir: Raoul Walsh *Cast:* Douglas Fairbanks, Julanne Johnston, Anna May Wong, Sojin, Snitz Edwards, Charles Belcher
▶ Disguised as a nobleman, thief Fairbanks wins the love of princess Johnston. To marry her, he must compete with other suitors for an exotic prize, and with that object in mind embarks on a delightful fantasy quest. Upon his return, he uses magic to battle an evil Mongol who threatens the Princess's city. Full of still-amazing visual effects, cheerfully fast-moving silent classic is not to be missed.
Dist.: Various

THIEF OF BAGDAD, THE 1940 British
★ ★ ★ ★ NR Fantasy/Action-Adventure 1:46
Dir: Michael Powell, Ludwig Berger, Tim Whelan *Cast:* Sabu, Conrad Veidt, John Justin, June Duprez, Rex Ingram
▶ Thief Sabu is aided by genie Ingram and a magic carpet in his quest to help prince Justin regain his kingdom from evil magician Veidt. The ultimate Arabian Nights movie is a treat for the eye and ear, with wondrous special effects (including a giant spider and a flying toy horse), perfect casting, exceptional music score, and larger-than-life storytelling. Three

Oscars (Special Effects, Color Cinematography, Art Direction).
Dist.: Various

THIEF OF HEARTS 1984
★ ★ ★ R Drama 1:40
☑ Nudity, strong sexual content, explicit language, violence
Dir: Douglas Day Stewart *Cast:* Steven Bauer, Barbara Williams, John Getz, David Caruso, Christine Ebersole, George Wendt
▶ San Francisco thief Bauer robs house with help from buddy Caruso, taking private journals belonging to the beautiful Williams. Obsessed with the fantasies Williams has written in her journal, Bauer spies on her; eventually, they fall in love. Beautifully shot, well acted and edited; weak dialogue hurts intriguing story. Video features more explicit sex than the theatrically released version. (CC)
Dist.: Paramount

THIEF WHO CAME TO DINNER, THE 1973
★ ★ ★ PG Comedy 1:45
☑ Adult situations, explicit language
Dir: Bud Yorkin *Cast:* Ryan O'Neal, Jacqueline Bisset, Warren Oates, Jill Clayburgh, Ned Beatty
▶ Bored computer programmer O'Neal chucks the straight life to become Houston's most successful jewel thief. He falls for society girl Bisset, befriends insurance investigator Oates, and is seduced by his ex-wife Clayburgh. Caper comedy is harmless enough but short on laughs.
Dist.: Warner

THIN BLUE LINE, THE 1988
★ ★ ★ ★ NR Documentary 1:46
☑ Explicit language, violence
Dir: Errol Morris *Cast:* Randall Adams, David Harris, Edith James, Dennis White, Sam Kittrell
▶ Unnerving study of the chance encounter in 1976 between hitchhiker Randall Adams and runaway David Harris that led to the murder of a Texas policeman. Although proclaiming his innocence, Adams was sentenced to death on Harris's testimony. But through adroit recreations and interviews, director Morris reveals the possibility of a horrible miscarriage of justice. Ominous Philip Glass score adds to the tension in this first-rate documentary, which helped convince Texas Court of Criminal Appeals to overturn Adams's conviction.
Dist.: HBO

THING, THE 1951
★ ★ ★ ★ NR Sci-Fi 1:20 B&W
Dir: Christian Nyby *Cast:* Kenneth Tobey, Margaret Sheridan, Robert Cornthwaite, Douglas Spencer, James Young, James Arness
▶ Arctic scientists uncover a frozen alien that, when thawed, runs amok through their isolated outpost. Influential, thrilling study of a peer group's grace under pressure is among the best of all sci-fi films. Rich characters, rapid

dialogue, exotic Dimitri Tiomkin score, and streamlined direction (often credited to producer Howard Hawks) add up to immensely exciting entertainment. Full title: *The Thing From Another Planet.* Remade in 1982.
Dist.: Turner ⓒ

THING, THE 1982
★ ★ ★ R Sci-Fi 1:49
☑ Explicit language, graphic violence
Dir: John Carpenter *Cast:* Kurt Russell, A. Wilford Brimley, T. K. Carter, David Clennon, Keith David, Richard Dysart
▶ American scientists at remote Antarctic research center stumble across a buried spaceship and unleash a fierce alien capable of transforming into any shape. Technically accomplished remake of the 1951 film remains truer to John W. Campbell, Jr.'s novella *Who Goes There?,* but tension and characterizations take a back seat to gruesome special effects.
Dist.: MCA

THINGS ARE TOUGH ALL OVER 1982
★ ★ R Comedy 1:30
☑ Nudity, adult situations, explicit language, adult humor
Dir: Thomas K. Avildsen *Cast:* Cheech Marin, Thomas Chong, Shelby Fiddis, Rikki Marin, Evelyn Guerrero, Rip Taylor
▶ Comics Cheech and Chong in dual roles: their usual buffoonish selves and the rich Arabs who hire them in Chicago to drive a limo carrying secret stash of $5 million. High jinks revolve around loss of the money and attempts to recover the loot before meeting employers in Las Vegas. Fans will be delighted by comics' customary clowning.
Dist.: RCA/Columbia

THINGS CHANGE 1988
★ ★ PG Comedy 1:40
☑ Brief nudity, adult situations, explicit language
Dir: David Mamet *Cast:* Don Ameche, Joe Mantegna, Robert Prosky, J. J. Johnston, Ricky Jay, Mike Nussbaum
▶ Italian shoeshine man Ameche, bearing uncanny resemblance to mobster facing jail term, agrees to take the rap and enter prison; guard Mantegna decides to give him a final whirl at Lake Tahoe. Bittersweet fable written by director Mamet and Shel Silverstein has glowing performance by Ameche and intermittently sharp dialogue, but leaden pacing and trick ending are drawbacks.
Dist.: RCA/Columbia

THINGS TO COME 1936 British
★ ★ NR Sci-Fi 1:32 B&W
Dir: William Cameron Menzies *Cast:* Raymond Massey, Ralph Richardson, Edward Chapman, Margaret Scott, Cedric Hardwicke, Maurice Bradell
▶ In a war-ravaged, plague-ridden future, despot Richardson rules over the remains of Everytown until Massey and a team of scien-

tists bring peace and build a new world. Years later, artist Hardwicke leads a rebellion against the soulless, high-tech society. Visually stunning science fiction epic, with screenplay by H. G. Wells from his essay *The Shape of Things to Come,* suffers somewhat from stilted dialogue and lack of drama.
Dist.: Various

THIN MAN, THE 1934
★★★★ NR Mystery-Suspense 1:33 B&W
Dir: W. S. Van Dyke II *Cast:* William Powell, Myrna Loy, Maureen O'Sullivan, Nat Pendleton, Cesar Romero, Edward Ellis, Porter Hall, Edward Brophy
▶ Wealthy heiress O'Sullivan contacts retired detective Nick Charles (Powell) to find her missing father Ellis. Nick's wife Nora (Loy) and dog Asta provide invaluable assistance in cracking the case. Sparkling adaptation of Dashiell Hammett's novel introduced one of film's best-loved duos. The tipsy, wisecracking, and happily married Charleses inspired five lesser sequels, a TV series, and countless imitators—although the "Thin Man" sobriquet actually refers to Ellis, not Powell.
Dist.: MGM/UA

THIN MAN GOES HOME, THE 1944
★★ NR Mystery-Suspense 1:40 B&W
Dir: Richard Thorpe *Cast:* William Powell, Myrna Loy, Gloria De Haven, Anne Revere, Lucile Watson, Harry Davenport
▶ Nick and Nora Charles (Powell, Loy) return to his hometown to see parents Davenport and Watson, but their vacation is cut short when they investigate the murder of a local painter. Fifth installment in the series plays up laughs over suspense; still smoothly entertaining.
Dist.: MGM/UA

THIRD DEGREE BURN 1989
★★★ NR Drama/MFTV 1:37
☑ Nudity, adult situations, explicit language, violence
Dir: Roger Spottiswoode *Cast:* Treat Williams, Virginia Madsen, Richard Masur, CCH Pounder
▶ Williams is a down-on-his-luck private eye paid to follow the luscious Madsen by her filthy rich husband. Williams and Madsen fall for each other, but when the husband turns up dead, Williams finds himself trapped in a tightly woven web of deceit. Madsen shines as mood shifts between sunny Taos and rainy, sinister Seattle. **(CC)**
Dist.: Paramount

THIRD MAN, THE 1949 British
★★★ NR Mystery-Suspense 1:45 B&W
Dir: Carol Reed *Cast:* Orson Welles, Joseph Cotten, Valli, Trevor Howard, Paul Hoerbiger, Ernst Deutsch
▶ Haunting, superbly directed classic improves with each viewing. Cotten is marvelous as a writer of pulp Westerns searching the ruins of post-WWII Vienna for his friend Harry

Lime (Welles), and he's matched by Howard's effortless performance as a British major. Justifiably famed for its intriguing Graham Greene script, Oscar-winning photography (by Robert Krasker), and unforgettable Anton Karas zither score. Also available in an edition containing film's original trailer.
Dist.: Various

THIRD MAN ON THE MOUNTAIN 1959
★★★★ NR Action-Adventure/Family
1:47
Dir: Ken Annakin *Cast:* James MacArthur, Michael Rennie, Janet Munro, James Donald, Herbert Lom, Laurence Naismith
▶ When his father is killed trying to climb the Matterhorn, young MacArthur vows to complete the ascent. First he must learn the fundamentals of mountain climbing from Rennie. Excellent Disney drama has excitement, breathtaking scenery, and worthwhile themes for younger viewers. Based on *Banner in the Sky* by James Ramsey Ullmann (who appears in a cameo with MacArthur's real-life mother Helen Hayes).
Dist.: Buena Vista

13 GHOSTS 1960
★ NR Horror 1:28 B&W
Dir: William Castle *Cast:* Charles Herbert, Jo Morrow, Martin Milner, Rosemary DeCamp, Margaret Hamilton, Donald Woods
▶ Struggling paleontologist Woods and his family inherit an old house from their late uncle. The good news is there's a fortune hidden inside; the bad news is the place is haunted by thirteen ghosts who terrorize the clan. Tacky chiller with slipshod production values; does have a few laughs. Hamilton is a treat as the housekeeper.
Dist.: RCA/Columbia

13 RUE MADELEINE 1947
★★★ NR Mystery-Suspense 1:35 B&W
Dir: Henry Hathaway *Cast:* James Cagney, Annabella, Richard Conte, Frank Latimore, Walter Abel, Sam Jaffe
▶ Adventurer Cagney trains crack unit of agents to discover German rocket site in France before the Allied invasion. The mission is threatened by the presence of a German agent within Cagney's group. Documentary-style classic, based on a true story, delivers maximum tension; Cagney is first-rate.
Dist.: CBS/Fox

THIRTEENTH GUEST, THE 1932
★ NR Mystery-Suspense 1:09 B&W
Dir: Albert Ray *Cast:* Ginger Rogers, Lyle Talbot, J. Farrell MacDonald, Paul Hurst, James C. Eagles
▶ On the thirteenth anniversary of a fatal dinner party, the thirteen guests have reconvened. This time, however, a hooded killer is determined that none of the guests will live to see the fourteenth anniversary. Rogers is knee

deep in corpses and peril in this old-fashioned whodunit.
Dist.: Turner

30 FOOT BRIDE OF CANDY ROCK, THE
1959
★ ★ ★ NR Comedy 1:13
Dir: Sidney Miller   *Cast:* Lou Costello, Dorothy Provine, Gale Gordon, Jimmy Conlin, Charles Lane
▶ When his girlfriend Provine mysteriously grows into a thirty-foot giant, garbage man-amateur scientist Costello marries her and tries to correct the condition with one of his inventions. Amusing spoof is pleasantly tacky; Costello's last film.
Dist.: RCA/Columbia

30 IS A DANGEROUS AGE, CYNTHIA 1968
British
★ NR Comedy 1:24
Dir: Joseph McGrath   *Cast:* Dudley Moore, Eddie Foy, Jr., Suzy Kendall, Patricia Routledge, Duncan MacRae, Michael MacLiammoir
▶ Shy pianist Moore, feeling pressured by his impending thirtieth birthday, vows to write a hit musical and get married within six weeks. Boyish charm and dry wit from Moore (who cowrote the screenplay), but uneven plotting goes off on too many tangents.
Dist.: RCA/Columbia

39 STEPS, THE 1935 British
★ ★ ★ ★ NR Mystery-Suspense 1:26 B&W
Dir: Alfred Hitchcock   *Cast:* Robert Donat, Madeleine Carroll, Lucie Mannheim, Godfrey Tearle, Peggy Ashcroft, John Laurie
▶ Donat, a Canadian vacationing in London, learns of a foreign spy ring from British agent Mannheim. When dying Mannheim turns up in Donat's room and delivers a map of Scotland, police pursue Donat for murder as villains chase him for the map. Flight to Scotland involves reluctant ally Carroll and encounter with master spy Tearle. Breakthrough film for Hitchcock, loosely based on the John Buchan novel, established him as master of suspense.
Dist.: Various

THIRTY-NINE STEPS, THE 1980 British
★ ★ ★ ★ PG Mystery-Suspense 1:42
☑ Adult situations, explicit language, mild violence
Dir: Don Sharp   *Cast:* Robert Powell, David Warner, John Mills, Eric Porter, Karen Dotrice, George Baker
▶ In 1914, British colonel Mills, with info on Prussian plot to start World War I, seeks refuge in home of stranger Powell. Villain Warner and his assassins slay Mills and pursue Powell, believing he has conspiracy plan, while police suspect Powell is Mills's killer. Fleeing for his life, Powell finds ally Dotrice, who believes him innocent. Chase through trains and Scottish moors leads to climax atop Big Ben. Contemporary version sticks closer to John Buchan's

novel than Hitchcock's renowned 1935 adaptation.
Dist.: Media

THIRTY SECONDS OVER TOKYO 1944
★ ★ ★ NR War 2:18 B&W
Dir: Mervyn LeRoy   *Cast:* Van Johnson, Spencer Tracy, Robert Walker, Phyllis Thaxter, Robert Mitchum, Don DeFore
▶ World War II American pilot Johnson participates in General Doolittle's (Tracy) inaugural bombing raid on Japan. When his plane crashes near China, Johnson faces hardship and injury. Fact-based and first rate, with strong performances from Johnson, Tracy, and Thaxter (as Johnson's understanding wife). Oscar-winning special effects.
Dist.: MGM/UA

THIS GUN FOR HIRE 1942
★ ★ ★ NR Mystery-Suspense 1:21 B&W
Dir: Frank Tuttle   *Cast:* Alan Ladd, Veronica Lake, Robert Preston, Laird Cregar, Tully Marshall, Marc Lawrence
▶ Taut but bleak melodrama about hired killer Ladd, double-crossed by Nazi double agent Cregar and pursued through a hostile urban landscape by police. Nightclub singer Lake becomes an unwilling accomplice as he seeks revenge. Adaptation of a Graham Greene novel made Ladd a star, and led to three further teamings with Lake.
Dist.: MCA

THIS HAPPY FEELING 1958
★ ★ ★ NR Comedy 1:32
Dir: Blake Edwards   *Cast:* Debbie Reynolds, Curt Jurgens, John Saxon, Alexis Smith, Mary Astor, Estelle Winwood
▶ Retired from the stage, leading man Jurgens raises horses in Connecticut, dining on the creations of his eccentric cook Winwood, and attempting to cool the ardor of former leading lady Smith. When fresh young Reynolds makes an appearance, the aging thespian begins to feel coltish, and the girl is torn between his elegant attentions and those of coeval Saxon. An old story, but writer/director Edwards makes it bright and lively.
Dist.: KVC

THIS IS ELVIS 1981
★ ★ ★ ★ PG Documentary/Biography 1:41 C/B&W
☑ Adult situations, explicit language
Dir: Malcolm Leo, Andrew Solt   *Cast:* Elvis Presley, David Scott, Paul Boensch III, Johnny Harra, Rhonda Lyn, Dana MacKay
▶ Controversial biography of Elvis Presley combines documentary footage, home movies, film and concert clips, and staged reconstructions for a definitive look at the King's career. Opening with his death at age forty-two, film uses flashbacks to trace his rise from truck driver to international star. Cooperation of Col. Tom Parker (Presley's manager) and inclusion of thirty-eight songs add to authenticity,

although his late decline receives glossy treatment.
Dist.: Warner

THIS ISLAND EARTH 1955
★ NR Sci-Fi 1:27
Dir: Joseph Newman   *Cast:* Jeff Morrow, Faith Domergue, Rex Reason, Lance Fuller, Russell Johnson
▶ When his planet faces destruction in an outer-space war, alien Morrow recruits Earth scientists Reason and Domergue for help. Will they reach Morrow's world in time to save it? Imaginative special effects and story, but laughable dialogue. Although dated, has cult following among genre fans.
Dist.: MCA

THIS IS SPINAL TAP 1984
★ R Comedy 1:22
☑ Adult situations, explicit language
Dir: Rob Reiner   *Cast:* Michael McKean, Christopher Guest, Harry Shearer, Rob Reiner, Tony Hendra, June Chadwick
▶ Underrated cult gem is a scathing satire about the rock music business where "there's such a fine line between clever and stupid." Reiner appears as a documentary filmmaker covering the fictional rock group Spinal Tap, in the U.S. to promote their newest album, "Smell the Glove." Good-natured spoof recounts the group's rise from obscurity to "one of England's loudest bands." Original Spinal Tap songs include "Listen to the Flower People" and their current hit, "Big Bottom," extolling the virtues of a lover's rear end.
Dist.: Nelson

THIS IS THE ARMY 1943
★★ NR Musical 2:01
Dir: Michael Curtiz   *Cast:* George Murphy, Ronald Reagan, Joan Leslie, Alan Hale, Dolores Costello, Kate Smith
▶ During World War II, lieutenant Reagan, son of producer Murphy, gets the assignment of putting together a morale-boosting revue for the troops. Irving Berlin wrote the score (and appears in the "Oh, How I Hate to Get Up in the Morning" number) for this patriotic tribute. Sentimental and endearing songs include "God Bless America" and "This Is the Army, Mr. Jones."
Dist.: Video Treasures

THIS LAND IS MINE 1943
★★ NR Drama 1:43 B&W
Dir: Jean Renoir   *Cast:* Charles Laughton, Maureen O'Hara, George Sanders, Walter Slezak, Kent Smith, Una O'Connor
▶ Timid Laughton teaches school and tries to stay out of trouble in Nazi-occupied Europe. When the Germans pick him up as a hostage, his mother buys his freedom by informing on a partisan. Shamed by her actions, Laughton is given the opportunity to redeem himself in a dramatic courtroom confrontation. As World War II propaganda, director Renoir's work-in-exile seems remarkably fair in acknowledging

the human frailty of both his heroes and villains.
Dist.: Turner

THIS MAN MUST DIE 1970 French
★ PG Mystery-Suspense 1:58
☑ Adult situations, violence
Dir: Claude Chabrol   *Cast:* Michel Duchaussoy, Jean Yanne, Caroline Cellier, Marc DiNapoli, Maurice Pialat, Lorraine Rainer
▶ When his son is killed by hit-and-run driver Yanne, widower Duchaussoy swears revenge. He seduces the driver's sister-in-law Cellier to get close to his quarry, only to learn that others have targeted Yanne for murder. Tense, twisty, and superbly crafted. Dubbed.
Dist.: CBS/Fox

THIS PROPERTY IS CONDEMNED 1966
★★★★ NR Drama/Romance 1:50
☑ Adult situations, mild violence
Dir: Sydney Pollack   *Cast:* Natalie Wood, Robert Redford, Charles Bronson, Mary Badham, Kate Reid, Robert Blake
▶ Adaptation of a Tennessee Williams one-act play concerns beautiful Wood, stifled by life in mother Reid's boarding house for railway workers. She falls madly in love with newcomer Redford, who arrives to lay off railroad men. When he's driven out of town, Wood plans to flee with him, but circumstances and her own pride lead to a tragic conclusion. Fine performances from all, with Wood especially affecting. Francis Ford Coppola cowrote screenplay.
Dist.: Paramount

THIS SPORTING LIFE 1963 British
★★ NR Drama/Sports 2:14 B&W
Dir: Lindsay Anderson   *Cast:* Richard Harris, Rachel Roberts, Alan Badel, William Hartnell, Colin Blakely, Vanda Godsell
▶ "You see something you want and you go out and get it. It's as simple as that." Armed with this credo, Harris leaves life as miner to win fame and fortune as aggressive rugby player. All that eludes him is Roberts, the widow with whom he lodges. She eventually yields to his persistent efforts, but their affair fails due to his insensitivity. Scathing portrayal of man-as-beast also boasts powerful rugby footage. Harris and Roberts were both Oscar nominees.
Dist.: Paramount

THOMAS CROWN AFFAIR, THE 1968
★★★ R Mystery-Suspense 1:42
☑ Brief nudity, adult situations, explicit language, violence
Dir: Norman Jewison   *Cast:* Steve McQueen, Faye Dunaway, Paul Burke, Jack Weston, Biff McGuire, Yaphet Kotto
▶ Insurance investigator Dunaway matches wits with McQueen, a wealthy Boston crook who has pulled off daring bank heist. They fall in love while playing cat and mouse. Exciting caper features jazzy Jewison direction and

sizzling McQueen/Dunaway chemistry (especially in the sexiest chess game scene in film history). Oscar for Best Song, "The Windmills of Your Mind."
Dist.: CBS/Fox

THOROUGHLY MODERN MILLIE 1967
★ ★ NR Musical 2:18
Dir: George Roy Hill *Cast:* Julie Andrews, Mary Tyler Moore, Carol Channing; John Gavin, James Fox, Beatrice Lillie
▶ Flapper Andrews arrives in Roaring Twenties New York with the modern notion of marrying her boss Gavin. However, love rears its head in the form of Fox and adventure follows when a white slavery ring kidnaps Andrews's roommate Moore. Crammed with music, fun, and nifty performances (Channing was Oscar nominated but don't overlook the delightful Fox). Received seven Oscar nominations, winning for Best Original Score.
Dist.: MCA

THOSE CALLOWAYS 1965
★ ★ ★ ★ NR Family 2:11
Dir: Norman Tokar *Cast:* Brian Keith, Vera Miles, Brandon de Wilde, Walter Brennan, Ed Wynn, Linda Evans
▶ New Englander Keith and son de Wilde go fur trapping to support a bird sanctuary, but outside interests have less bucolic intentions for the town. Miles is Keith's understanding wife; Evans the girl who wins de Wilde's heart. Warmhearted Disney effort, a bit overlong and sentimental, but overall quite enjoyable.
Dist.: Buena Vista

THOSE LIPS, THOSE EYES 1980
★ ★ R Drama 1:46
☐ Nudity, adult situations, explicit language
Dir: Michael Pressman *Cast:* Frank Langella, Tom Hulce, Glynnis O'Connor, Kevin McCarthy, Jerry Stiller
▶ In 1950s Cleveland, stagestruck premed student Hulce gets a job with summer theater, finds romance with chorus girl O'Connor, and is taken under wing of leading man Langella, who gives him lessons in life. Sweet and simple, but a bit tepid and slow. Langella is terrific.
Dist.: MGM/UA

THOSE MAGNIFICENT MEN IN THEIR FLYING MACHINES 1965
★ ★ ★ G Comedy 2:13
Dir: Ken Annakin *Cast:* Stuart Whitman, Sarah Miles, James Fox, Alberto Sordi, Robert Morley, Benny Hill
▶ Morley, a 1910 British press baron, offers prize for air race from London to Paris, hoping to prove Commonwealth reigns over skies as well as seas. Competitors include Royal Navy airman Fox with stiff upper lip, Italian count Sordi, and barnstorming American Whitman. Fox and Whitman also vie for attentions of Morley's lovely daughter Miles. Well-meaning

and lighthearted comedy makes fine family fare, despite occasionally sluggish lapses.
Dist.: CBS/Fox

THOUSAND CLOWNS, A 1965
★ ★ NR Comedy 1:58 B&W
Dir: Fred Coe *Cast:* Jason Robards, Barbara Harris, Martin Balsam, Barry Gordon, Gene Saks, William Daniels
▶ Delightful, funny adaptation by Herb Gardner of his Broadway play about Robards, an unemployed TV writer living with twelve-year-old nephew Gordon. They share a nonconformist philosophy, as one morning uncle advises boy: "You're about to see the scariest thing on earth—people on their way to work." But social worker Daniels insists Robards get a job or lose custody of boy. Title song by saxophonist Gerry Mulligan and wife, actress Judy Holliday.
Dist.: CBS/Fox

THOUSANDS CHEER 1944
★ ★ ★ NR Musical 2:06
Dir: George Sidney *Cast:* Gene Kelly, Kathryn Grayson, Mary Astor, Jose Iturbi, John Boles
▶ During World War II, circus performer Kelly finds army life intolerable; he woos colonel's daughter Grayson in hopes of winning a transfer but then actually falls in love. Wartime rouser crammed to the brim with tunes climaxes with a big show featuring zillions of MGM stars (Mickey Rooney, Judy Garland, Lucille Ball, Eleanor Powell, Red Skelton, Donna Reed, Lena Horne, Frank Morgan, June Allyson, Gloria De Haven, and others).
Dist.: MGM/UA

THREADS 1984 British
★ ★ ★ NR Drama/MFTV 1:50
☐ Adult situations, explicit language, violence
Dir: Mick Jackson *Cast:* Karen Meagher, Reece Dinsdale, Rita May, Nicholas Lane, Victoria O'Keefe
▶ Meagher, Dinsdale, and other citizens of a British industrial city go about their lives until war breaks out and their town takes a direct nuclear hit. Survivors riot for food, storm the hospitals, starve, and descend into savagery. Bleak, disturbing, and scientifically realistic look at nuclear aftermath packs more wallop than other presentations of this subject.
Dist.: New World

THREAT, THE 1949
★ NR Mystery-Suspense 1:05 B&W
Dir: Felix E. Feist *Cast:* Charles McGraw, Virginia Grey, Michael O'Shea, Julie Bishop, Frank Conroy, Robert Shayne
▶ After escaping from prison, psychopath McGraw kidnaps those who contributed to his conviction, including district attorney Conroy, cop O'Shea, and Grey. Detective Shayne gets on the killer's trail. Superior thriller, extremely suspenseful, deserves greater renown. Home

video version double billed with 1941's *Lady Scarface*.
Dist.: Turner

THREE AGES, THE 1923
★★ NR Comedy 1:25 B&W
Dir: Buster Keaton, Eddie Cline ***Cast:*** Buster Keaton, Wallace Beery, Margaret Leahy, Joe Roberts, Lilian Lawrence, Oliver Hardy
▶ Keaton battles Beery for the love of Leahy in different historical epochs in a takeoff on D. W. Griffith's *Intolerance*. In prehistoric times, Keaton rides to his lady love on a stop-animated dinosaur; in Roman times, he defeats Beery in a wintertime chariot race; and in the modern era, he competes with his rival in a zany football game. Early Keaton feature takes some time building to the chase. Worth waiting for: the star's precipitous tumble down the side of a building, breaking through several awnings, and landing on the back of a fire truck.
Dist.: Video Yesteryear

THREE AMIGOS! 1986
★★ PG Comedy 1:43
☑ Explicit language, mild violence
Dir: John Landis ***Cast:*** Steve Martin, Chevy Chase, Martin Short, Patrice Martinez, Joe Mantegna, Alfonso Arau
▶ Silent-screen heroes Martin, Chase, and Short, mistaken for the real article by Martinez, are summoned to Mexican village to fight bandito Arau. The bumbling trio are in for a rude awakening as they think they've been signed for a personal appearance. Nutty and amiable if not sidesplitting. Best laughs: Randy Newman's songs (including one with singing horses), Martin's rousing "Everyone has an El Guapo in his life" speech.
Dist.: HBO

THREE BROTHERS 1982 Italian
☆ PG Drama 1:53
☑ Adult situations
Dir: Francesco Rosi ***Cast:*** Charles Vanel, Philippe Noiret, Michele Placido, Vittorio Mezzogiorno, Andrea Ferreol, Sara Tafuri
▶ Three estranged brothers are summoned home to attend their mother's funeral. With contrasting beliefs and temperaments, the brothers argue, console their father, and confront their past. Graceful, poetical, impeccably painted; a movingly sympathetic evocation of family life. Splendid music by Piero Piccioni. [S]
Dist.: Nelson

THREE CABALLEROS, THE 1945
★ G Animation 1:10
Dir: Norman Ferguson ***Cast:*** Aurora Miranda, Carmen Molina, Dora Luz; voices of Sterling Holloway, Clarence Nash, Jose Oliveira
▶ Generally delightful mix of short sequences loosely based around the friendship between Donald Duck, Mexican rooster Panchito, and Brazilian parrot Jose Cariocoa. Created to boost America's wartime "Good Neighbor Policy," feature has some of Disney's most spectacular animation along with trivial, travelogue filler. Mix of live action and animation was the best of its kind until *Who Framed Roger Rabbit*. Special treats include a chorus line of giant, throbbing cacti, and rambunctious title-song sequence.
Dist.: Buena Vista

THREE COINS IN THE FOUNTAIN 1954
★★★★ NR Drama 1:41
Dir: Jean Negulesco ***Cast:*** Clifton Webb, Dorothy McGuire, Jean Peters, Louis Jourdan, Maggie McNamara, Rossano Brazzi
▶ Three single Americans—secretary McNamara, executive Peters, and writer's assistant McGuire—pin their hopes for romance on Rome's Fountain of Trevi. McNamara snares Italian prince Jourdan, Peters reforms gigolo Brazzi, and McGuire finds true love with her boss Webb. Slight, predictable drama given a tremendous boost by Milton Krasner's Oscar-winning location photography and Frank Sinatra's beautiful version of the title song (also an Oscar winner for Jule Styne and Sammy Cahn).
Dist.: CBS/Fox

THREE DAYS OF THE CONDOR 1975
★★★★★ R Mystery-Suspense 1:57
☑ Adult situations, explicit language, violence
Dir: Sydney Pollack ***Cast:*** Robert Redford, Faye Dunaway, Cliff Robertson, Max Von Sydow, John Houseman
▶ In New York, CIA researcher Redford has seemingly innocuous job of reading novels until his entire office is wiped out and he's targeted for death by his superiors. He kidnaps innocent bystander Dunaway to help him and a wary love affair ensues. Riveting story enhanced by evocative direction by Pollack, top-notch performances (Von Sydow shines as a gentlemanly hit man), and intelligent plotting. Haunting climax.
Dist.: Paramount

THREE FACES WEST 1940
★★ NR Drama 1:19 B&W
Dir: Bernard Vorhaus ***Cast:*** John Wayne, Sigrid Gurie, Charles Coburn, Spencer Charters, Roland Varno, Russell Simpson
▶ Coburn and daughter Gurie, refugees from Nazi Austria, settle in America's Midwest, where local boy Wayne falls for Gurie. While thinking that he's lost Gurie to Varno, a young Austrian officer, Wayne leads the community on a harrowing treck to Oregon to escape ravaging dust storms. Interesting Wayne outing is an unusual combination of European politics and Westward Ho adventure. Also known as *The Refugee*.
Dist.: Republic

3:15—MOMENT OF TRUTH 1986
★ R Drama 1:35
☑ Nudity, adult situations, explicit language

Dir: Larry Gross   *Cast:* Adam Baldwin, Deborah Foreman, René Auberjonois, Ed Lauter, Joseph Brutsman, Scott McGinnis
► Gang-rumble film stars Baldwin as a former member of East L.A. leather and chain gang, the Cobras. After a drug bust, he is branded a traitor and must contend with gang leader De La Paz, wicked principal Auberjonois, frightened girlfriend Foreman, and nerdy friend Brutsman. Final confrontation is after school.
Dist.: Media

THREE FOR BEDROOM C 1952
★ NR Comedy 1:14
Dir: Milton H. Bren   *Cast:* Gloria Swanson, James Warren, Fred Clark, Hans Conried, Steve Brodie, Janine Perreau
► Aboard a New York-to-Hollywood train, film star Swanson and her young daughter find themselves accidentally sharing scientist Warren's compartment. Predictably, this chance meeting leads to romance. Even Swanson's style can't save this sub-par screenplay. Margaret Dumont has a small role.
Dist.: IVE

THREE FOR THE ROAD 1987
★ ★ ★ PG Comedy 1:30
☑ Adult situations
Dir: B.W.L. Norton   *Cast:* Charlie Sheen, Kerri Green, Alan Ruck, Sally Kellerman, Blair Tefkin
► Sheen, an ambitious senator's aide, agrees to escort boss's troubled daughter Green to a reform school and brings his obnoxious roommate Ruck along for the ride. Sheen handcuffs himself to Green to prevent her from escaping to visit divorced mom Kellerman, which she manages to do anyway. Plot offers few surprises.
Dist.: IVE

THREE FUGITIVES 1989
★ ★ ★ ★ PG-13 Comedy 1:36
☑ Explicit language, violence
Dir: Francis Veber   *Cast:* Nick Nolte, Martin Short, Sarah Rowland Doroff, James Earl Jones, Kenneth McMillan, Alan Ruck
► Criminal Nolte gets out of jail, enters bank to open account, and is taken hostage by novice bank robber Short. The cops figure Nolte is involved, and he is forced on the lam with Short and his little daughter Doroff. Frisky formula filmmaking longer on energy than inspiration. Nolte and Short work well together, and the Nolte/Doroff relationship is very sweet. Funniest scene: Short in drag. Director Veber's remake of his own French film, *Les Fugitifs.*
Dist.: Buena Vista

THREE GODFATHERS 1948
★ ★ ★ ★ NR Western 1:45
Dir: John Ford   *Cast:* John Wayne, Pedro Armendariz, Harry Carey, Jr., Ward Bond, Mildred Natwick, Jane Darwell
► Sentimental version of an oft-filmed story

about Wayne, Armendariz, and Carey, outlaws chased into the desert by a posse. They find pregnant Natwick who dies giving birth, and vow to bring the child to New Jerusalem, Arizona. Oddly touching and not without moments of humor. Director Ford's first color film was dedicated to Carey's father, Harry Carey, Sr., a Western veteran who appeared in a 1916 version of the story.
Dist.: MGM/UA

THREE HUSBANDS 1950
★ NR Comedy 1:18 B&W
Dir: Irving Reis   *Cast:* Eve Arden, Ruth Warrick, Howard da Silva, Shepperd Strudwick, Emlyn Williams, Robert Karnes
► Wealthy lady-killer Williams dies and leaves letters to Strudwick, da Silva, and Karnes—men with whose wives he'd had affairs. The letters tell how he was able to do it, and as the husbands reflect in flashback, they must confront their own deficiencies as spouses. Brisk, pleasing farce inspired by the similarly themed *Letter to Three Wives.*
Dist.: Video Dimensions

THREE IN THE ATTIC 1968
★ ★ R Comedy 1:30
☑ Nudity, strong sexual content, adult situations, explicit language
Dir: Richard Wilson   *Cast:* Christopher Jones, Yvette Mimieux, Judy Pace, Maggie Thrett, Nan Martin, John Beck
► College womanizer Jones seduces Mimieux but can't settle down with one girl; Pace becomes yet another conquest. Mimieux, Pace, and Thrett, Jones's third lover, get revenge by trapping him in an attic and wearing him out sexually. Strong on sex but lacking in subtlety.
Dist.: Nelson

THREE IN THE CELLAR 1970
★ ★ R Comedy 1:34
☑ Nudity, adult situations
Dir: Theodore J. Flicker   *Cast:* Wes Stern, Joan Collins, Larry Hagman, Judy Pace, David Arkin, Nira Barab
► Stern is a poetry student determined to get back at college prez Hagman by seducing wife Collins, daughter Barab, and secretary Pace. Campus is crawling with student revolutionaries, black militants, and national guardsmen. Offers crudely humorous peek at period attitudes. Also known as *Up in the Cellar.*
Dist.: HBO

THREE KINDS OF HEAT 1987
★ ★ R Action-Adventure 1:27
☑ Adult situations, explicit language, violence
Dir: Leslie Stevens   *Cast:* Robert Ginty, Victoria Barrett, Shakti, Sylvester McCoy, Barry Foster, Jeannie Brown
► Secret agent Ginty tracks down nefarious Chinese mobster McCoy with the help of beautiful New York police officer Barrett and

exotic Hong Kong cop Shakti. Trail leads from Big Apple to London warehouse filled with explosives. Routine mayhem presented with little flair. **(CC)**
Dist.: Warner

THREE LITTLE WORDS 1950
★ ★ ★ ★ **NR Musical 1:42**
Dir: Richard Thorpe *Cast:* Fred Astaire, Red Skelton, Vera-Ellen, Arlene Dahl, Keenan Wynn, Gale Robbins, Debbie Reynolds
▶ Biography of 1920s songwriting team Bert Kalmar and Harry Ruby features fourteen of their best songs: "Who's Sorry Now," "Hooray for Captain Spaulding," "She's Mine, All Mine," more. Plot sticks to the facts, following the unlikely friendship of vaudeville dancer Kalmar (Astaire) and aspiring baseball player Ruby (Skelton) through their split-up and reconciliation. Reynolds sparked her career with "I Wanna Be Loved by You," but highlight is Astaire's surrealistic duet with Vera-Ellen to "Mr. and Mrs. Hoofer at Home."
Dist.: MGM/UA

THREE LIVES OF THOMASINA, THE 1963
★ ★ ★ ★ **NR Fantasy/Family 1:35**
Dir: Don Chaffey *Cast:* Patrick McGoohan, Susan Hampshire, Karen Dotrice, Laurence Naismith, Jean Anderson, Finlay Currie
▶ Scottish veterinarian McGoohan decides his daughter Dotrice's sick cat Thomasina must be put to sleep, but the pet escapes and hides with Hampshire, a recluse with mysterious powers. She later uses the feline to mend rift between McGoohan and Dotrice. Heartwarming Disney adaptation of a Paul Gallico story will thrill children.
Dist.: Buena Vista

THREE MEN AND A BABY 1987
★ ★ ★ ★ ★ **PG Comedy 1:39**
☑ Explicit language
Dir: Leonard Nimoy *Cast:* Tom Selleck, Steve Guttenberg, Ted Danson, Nancy Travis, Margaret Colin, Philip Bosco
▶ New York bachelors Selleck, Guttenberg, and Danson fall into fatherhood when an infant girl is left on their doorstep. The guys make hilarious transition from party boys to proud papas. Frothy, foolproof entertainment was major box office smash. Selleck demonstrates deft comic touch, and the baby is adorable. Confident direction by Nimoy leaves no diaper joke unturned. Based on the French *Three Men and a Cradle*.
Dist.: Buena Vista

THREE MEN AND A CRADLE 1985 French
★ ★ ★ **PG-13 Comedy 1:46**
☑ Brief nudity, adult situations, explicit language
Dir: Coline Serreau *Cast:* Roland Giraud, Michel Boujenah, André Dussolier, Philippine Leroy Beaulieu
▶ Warm and winning comedy about three Parisian bachelors who suddenly find themselves in charge of the infant girl one of them

has unknowingly fathered. Grappling with diapers, formulas, and all-night crying jags, the men eventually fall hopelessly in love with the tiny baby. One of France's all-time top grossing films was nominated for a foreign language Oscar and remade in the U.S. as *Three Men and a Baby*. ⒮
Dist.: Vestron

THREE MUSKETEERS, THE 1935
★ ★ **NR Action-Adventure 1:37 B&W**
Dir: Rowland V. Lee *Cast:* Walter Abel, Paul Lukas, Ian Keith, Onslow Stevens, Margot Graham, Heather Angel
▶ Alexandre Dumas's familiar tale of D'Artagnan (Abel) joining the musketeers and defending the French throne against all schemers and plotters gets a surprisingly flat adaptation from Lee and co-screenwriter Dudley Nichols. Abel lacks the proper panache; Lukas outshines him as Athos.
Dist.: Turner

THREE MUSKETEERS, THE 1948
★ ★ ★ **NR Action-Adventure 2:05**
Dir: George Sidney *Cast:* Lana Turner, Gene Kelly, Van Heflin, Angela Lansbury, June Allyson, Vincent Price
▶ Country youth D'Artagnan (Kelly) arrives in seventeenth-century Paris and joins the fabled musketeers led by Heflin. The swordsmen thwart a plot against the throne by evil prime minister Price and countess co-conspirator Turner. Adaptation of the Alexandre Dumas classic is frisky fun, thanks to Kelly's fast footwork and stylish production.
Dist.: MGM/UA

THREE MUSKETEERS, THE 1974 British
★ ★ ★ ★ **PG Action-Adventure 1:45**
☑ Adult situations, violence
Dir: Richard Lester *Cast:* Oliver Reed, Michael York, Richard Chamberlain, Raquel Welch, Frank Finlay, Geraldine Chaplin, Charlton Heston, Faye Dunaway
▶ In seventeenth-century France, bumpkin York befriends more worldly Reed, Chamberlain, and Finlay, leaders of the king's guard known as the Musketeers. His new pals are only interested in brawling, boozing, and wenching until York romances queen Chaplin's lady-in-waiting Welch. She reveals a plan to besmirch milady's honor and wrest power from the weak-willed king, sending the quartet into action. Rollicking, often slapstick version of the oft-filmed Dumas tale. Sequel: *The Four Musketeers*.
Dist.: USA

THREE O'CLOCK HIGH 1987
★ ★ **PG-13 Comedy 1:41**
☑ Explicit language, violence
Dir: Phil Joanou *Cast:* Casey Siemaszko, Anne Ryan, Richard Tyson, Jeffrey Tambor, Philip Baker Hall, John P. Ryan
▶ Nerdy teen Siemaszko upsets the new school bully Tyson, a hulking transfer student who challenges him to a fight after class. Sie-

maszko spends the rest of the day dreading the confrontation. Capable cast and amusing directorial flourishes rank this slightly above similar adolescent comedies.
Dist.: MCA

THREEPENNY OPERA, THE 1931 German
★ **NR Musical 1:52 B&W**
Dir: G. W. Pabst *Cast:* Rudolf Forster, Carola Neher, Reinhold Schunzel, Lotte Lenya, Fritz Rasp, Valeska Gert
▶ Infamous outlaw Mackie Messer (Forster) announces his engagement to Neher, daughter of the king of the beggars (Rasp). Rasp threatens to disrupt upcoming coronation ceremonies if the wedding goes through. Prostitute Lenya, who sings a dazzling "Pirate Jenny," betrays Mack the Knife to the police. Technically dated version of the Bertolt Brecht/Kurt Weill play, itself based on John Gay's eighteenth-century classic *The Beggar's Opera*, effectively captures atmosphere of pre-Nazi Germany. Remade with Sammy Davis, Jr., in 1963. [S]
Dist.: Nelson

THREE PENNY OPERA 1963 German
★ **NR Musical 2:04**
Dir: Wolfgang Staudte *Cast:* Sammy Davis, Jr., Curt Jurgens, June Ritchie, Hildegard Neff, Marlene Warrlich, Lino Ventura, Gert Frobe
▶ Stylized but plodding adaptation of the classic Weill/Brecht musical features uncharismatic Jurgens miscast as Mack the Knife, the ruthless ladies man/killer who walks the streets of nineteenth-century London. Ritchie is Polly Peachum, the bad man's young paramour; Davis is the Ballad Singer, whose rendition of "Mack the Knife" is a highlight.
Dist.: Nelson

THREE SECRETS 1950
★ **NR Drama 1:38 B&W**
Dir: Robert Wise *Cast:* Eleanor Parker, Patricia Neal, Ruth Roman, Frank Lovejoy, Ted de Corsia, Larry Keating
▶ When a five-year-old boy is trapped in the wreckage of a plane, Neal, Parker, and Roman—all of whom gave up a child for adoption five years previous—arrive at the site. Flashbacks tell their separate stories as a rescue effort unfolds. Openly emotional drama, acted and directed with conviction.
Dist.: Republic

THREE STOOGES MEET HERCULES, THE 1962
★ ★ ★ **NR Comedy 1:20 B&W**
Dir: Edward Bernds *Cast:* Moe Howard, Larry Fine, "Curly" Joe De Rita, Vicki Trickett, George N. Neise, Samson Burke
▶ Predictable family-oriented slapstick as the latter-day edition of the Stooges travel in a time machine to ancient Greece. Dressed in togas and sandals, the boys form a conga line on a slave galley, encounter a Siamese twin cyclops, and add pie-fighting to a chariot race.
Dist.: Goodtimes

3:10 TO YUMA 1957
★ **NR Western 1:32 B&W**
Dir: Delmer Daves *Cast:* Van Heflin, Glenn Ford, Felicia Farr, Richard Jaeckel, Leora Dana, Henry Jones
▶ Family man Heflin takes job escorting killer Ford on a train to the Yuma prison. Ford's gang shows up to help him escape as respect grows between between outlaw and guard. Suspenseful Western with impressive performances and unusual psychological insight; based on a story by Elmore Leonard.
Dist.: RCA/Columbia

THREE THE HARD WAY 1974
★ ★ **R Action-Adventure 1:33**
☑ Nudity, explicit language, violence
Dir: Gordon Parks, Jr. *Cast:* Jim Brown, Fred Williamson, Jim Kelly, Sheila Frazier, Jay Robinson, Alex Rocco
▶ Record producer Brown, PR man Williamson, and karate whiz Kelly uncover a plot by white fascists to poison blacks by tainting municipal water supplies. When the bad guys abduct Brown's girlfriend Frazier, the threesome seek deadly revenge. Cynical, humorless black exploitation movie has good stunts by Hal Needham's Stunts Unlimited group.
Dist.: Xenon

THREE WARRIORS 1977
★ ★ ★ ★ **G Family 1:49**
Dir: Kieth Merrill *Cast:* McKee (Kiko) Red-Wing, Charles White Eagle, Randy Quaid, Lois Red Elk
▶ American Indian boy RedWing returns to the reservation to visit his dying grandfather and uncovers a plot by white ranchers to steal protected wild horses. With help of federal wildlife officer Quaid, he uses traditional Indian strategies to thwart the rustlers. Good performances from untrained actors in this sincere, appealing tale.
Dist.: HBO

THREE WORLDS OF GULLIVER, THE 1960
★ ★ **NR Fantasy/Family 1:39**
Dir: Jack Sher *Cast:* Kerwin Mathews, June Thorburn, Jo Morrow, Lee Patterson
▶ Eighteenth-century English doctor Mathews joins ship's crew and is swept overboard for adventures among the tiny inhabitants of Lilliput and the giants of Brobdingnag. Ray Harryhausen special effects and Bernard Herrmann score highlight this worthwhile adaptation of Jonathan Swift's *Gulliver's Travels*. Ideal for the younger set.
Dist.: RCA/Columbia

THRESHOLD 1983
★ ★ ★ **PG Drama 1:37**
☑ Nudity, explicit language
Dir: Richard Pearce *Cast:* Donald Suther-

land, Mare Winningham, Jeff Goldblum, John Marley, Sharon Acker
▶ Renowned surgeon Sutherland and biologist Goldblum team up to develop artificial heart. When patient Winningham suffers irreparable damage, Sutherland implants the experimental device in her. Low-key and credible, with noteworthy Sutherland and Goldblum, winning Winningham. One caveat: surgery scenes are quite graphic.
Dist.: CBS/Fox

THRILLKILL 1984 Canadian
★ NR Mystery-Suspense 1:38
☑ Adult situations, violence
Dir: Anthony Kramreither, Anthony D'Andrea ***Cast:*** Robin Ward, Gina Massey, Laura Robinson, Diana Reis, Colleen Embree, Kurt Reis
▶ A toy company is a front for a gang of embezzlers who use computers to skim corporate funds. Before being killed, embezzler Reis leaves clues to the whereabouts of a hidden fortune to kid sister Massey. Zippy camerawork and editing can't help murky plot.
Dist.: CBS/Fox

THRILL OF IT ALL, THE 1963
★★★ NR Comedy 1:47
Dir: Norman Jewison ***Cast:*** Doris Day, James Garner, Arlene Francis, Edward Andrews, ZaSu Pitts, Reginald Owen
▶ Ordinary housewife Day forsakes home and hearth to become a big hit as TV commercial spokeswoman. Her neglected hubby Garner has trouble dealing with her success and schemes to restore things to normal. Bright and clever vehicle for the stars.
Dist.: MCA

THRONE OF BLOOD 1957 Japanese
★ NR Drama 1:38 B&W
Dir: Akira Kurosawa ***Cast:*** Toshiro Mifune, Isuzu Yamada, Takashi Shimura, Minoru Chiaki
▶ Violent, breathtakingly beautiful adaptation of Shakespeare's *Macbeth* set in feudal Japan, with Mifune as the paranoid king, and Yamada as his goading wife. Director Kurasawa tells the bloody tale of murderous usurpation through vivid, silken imagery and stylized, Noh-like acting. Stunning finale is piercingly graphic. [S]
Dist.: Various

THROUGH A GLASS DARKLY 1960 Swedish
★ NR Drama 1:31 B&W
Dir: Ingmar Bergman ***Cast:*** Harriet Andersson, Gunnar Bjornstrand, Max Von Sydow, Lars Passgard
▶ Mentally unstable Andersson leaves institution and spends summer with family on island. Her father Bjornstrand, husband Von Sydow, and brother Passgard are unable to help as she descends into madness once more. Dark but involving psychodrama won Best Foreign Film Oscar. [S]
Dist.: Nelson

THROW MOMMA FROM THE TRAIN 1987
★★★★ PG-13 Comedy 1:28
☑ Adult situations, explicit language, mild violence
Dir: Danny DeVito ***Cast:*** Billy Crystal, Danny DeVito, Anne Ramsey, Kim Greist, Rob Reiner, Kate Mulgrew
▶ Teacher Crystal suffers writer's block because ex-wife Mulgrew stole his manuscript and turned it into a best-seller. One of Crystal's students, DeVito, endures bullying, grotesque mother Ramsey. When Crystal advises DeVito to see Hitchcock's *Strangers on a Train*, student thinks teacher means to suggest they kill each other's nemesis, just as in the movie. Trouble breaks loose when DeVito keeps his end of bargain. Best are hilarious writer's block gags and diabolical but childlike DeVito. (CC)
Dist.: Orion

THUNDER ALLEY 1985
★★★ R Drama 1:41
☑ Nudity, adult situations, explicit language
Dir: J. S. Cardone ***Cast:*** Roger Wilson, Jill Schoolen, Scott McGinnis, Cynthia Eilbacher, Leif Garrett, Clancy Brown
▶ Tucson keyboardist McGinnis forms rock 'n' roll band, but hostility of lead singer Garrett deters ace guitarist Wilson from joining. Wilson eventually signs on and group's success seems assured; he and McGinnis romance Schoelen and Eilbacher, who work at ice cream parlor. When McGinnis gets involved with drugs, band's fortunes predictably take a turn for worse.
Dist.: MGM/UA

THUNDERBALL 1965 British
★★★★ PG Espionage/Action-Adventure 2:12
☑ Adult situations, violence
Dir: Terence Young ***Cast:*** Sean Connery, Claudine Auger, Adolfo Celi, Luciana Paluzzi, Rick Van Nutter
▶ Fourth outing for 007 (Connery) has him battling evil SPECTRE, led by eye-patched villain Celi and his seductive sidekick Paluzzi. Celi has hijacked two NATO atom bombs and demands multimillion-dollar ransom. Search for bombs leads Bond to Bahamas for encounters with bikini-clad women (including skindiving dish Auger) and underwater shoot-'em-up finale. Droll Connery, eye-catching scenery, and spectacular underwater footage are highlights.
Dist.: MGM/UA

THUNDER BAY 1953
★★★ NR Action-Adventure 1:42
Dir: Anthony Mann ***Cast:*** James Stewart, Joanne Dru, Gilbert Roland, Dan Duryea, Harry Morgan, Marcia Henderson
▶ Stewart and Duryea team up to drill for "black gold" in Gulf of Mexico, constructing stormproof oil-rig platform. Local shrimp fisherman, already suffering tough times, aren't

keen about newcomers. Tensions peak when Stewart and Duryea romance local Louisiana girls Dru and Henderson. Wildcatters must then battle elements, financial crisis, and angry mob. Plenty of action and fine cast make for entertaining yarn.
Dist.: MCA

THUNDERBOLT AND LIGHTFOOT 1974
★ ★ ★ R Action-Adventure 1:54
☑ Adult situations, explicit language, violence
Dir: Michael Cimino *Cast:* Clint Eastwood, Jeff Bridges, George Kennedy, Geoffrey Lewis, Catherine Bach, Gary Busey
▶ Amiable drifter Bridges hooks up with ex-thief Eastwood on the lam from cohorts Kennedy and Lewis, who believe Eastwood set them up and took loot in robbery of years past. When Kennedy and Lewis apprehend the duo, a truce is struck: they'll rob the same bank the same way. Engrossing caper features fully realized characters and commendable acting, especially from Bridges. First feature outing for writer/director Cimino.
Dist.: MGM/UA

THUNDER IN THE CITY 1937 British
★ NR Comedy 1:26 B&W
Dir: Marion Gering *Cast:* Edward G. Robinson, Luli Deste, Constance Collier, Ralph Richardson, Nigel Bruce, Arthur Wontner
▶ Wisecracking American promoter Robinson goes to London, where he jousts with somber, conservative British business types like Bruce and Richardson. Satisfactory comedy of cultural contrasts, with a perfectly cast Robinson, and Bruce at his befuddled best.
Dist.: KVC

THUNDER ROAD 1958
★ ★ NR Action-Adventure 1:32 B&W
Dir: Arthur Ripley *Cast:* Robert Mitchum, Gene Barry, Jacques Aubuchon, Keely Smith, Trevor Bardette, Jim Mitchum
▶ Korean vet Robert Mitchum reestablishes his Tennessee moonshine business, fighting off Aubuchon's mob hit men and antibootlegging Fed Barry while dissuading his brother (his real-life son Jim Mitchum) from a life of crime. Mitchum produced, wrote the story and theme song "Whippoorwill" (which he later made a hit song), and gave one of his most enjoyable performances in this influential cult film. Good car chases and pop star Smith's offbeat role add to the fun.
Dist.: MGM/UA

THUNDER RUN 1986
★ ★ PG-13 Action-Adventure 1:31
☑ Explicit language, violence
Dir: Gary Hudson *Cast:* Forrest Tucker, John Ireland, John Shepherd, Jill Whitlow, Wally Ward, Cheryl M. Lynn
▶ Retired trucker Tucker agrees to transport shipment of plutonium across Nevada despite presence of heavily armed terrorists who need the ore to build nuclear weapons.

Tucker's last film is half dull chase, half teenage high jinks from Sheperd and his adolescent friends.
Dist.: Media

THX 1138 1971
★ ★ PG Sci-Fi 1:28
☑ Brief nudity, adult situations, violence
Dir: George Lucas *Cast:* Robert Duvall, Donald Pleasence, Don Pedro Colley, Maggie McOmie, Ian Wolfe, Sid Haig
▶ Computers run a futuristic subterranean society where love and sex are outlawed while daily drug dose represses free will. Young rebels Duvall and McOmie cease taking drug and discover romance. Imprisoned for insubordination, they team with fellow convict Pleasence and attempt escape to aboveground world. Arresting but grim feature debut for director Lucas.
Dist.: Warner

TICKET TO HEAVEN 1981 Canadian
★ ★ ★ PG Drama 1:48
☑ Explicit language
Dir: Ralph L. Thomas *Cast:* Nick Mancuso, Meg Foster, Saul Rubinek, Kim Cattrall, R. H. Thomson, Jennifer Dale
▶ In wake of break-up with girlfriend, young Canadian Mancuso vacations in San Francisco and is seduced into joining religious cult by group's spooky cheerleaders Foster and Cattrall. Soon thoroughly brainwashed by propaganda and spartan regimen, Mancuso rejects family and past. Best friend Rubinek and pro deprogrammer Thomson set out to liberate Mancuso from cult's clutches. Chilling and realistic look at exploitation of vulnerable minds by fraudulent, profit-hungry religions.
Dist.: MGM/UA

TICKLE ME 1965
★ ★ NR Musical 1:30
Dir: Norman Taurog *Cast:* Elvis Presley, Julie Adams, Jocelyn Lane, Jack Mullaney, Merry Anders, Bill Williams
▶ Singing rodeo star Presley forsakes hard riding for a handyman's job at Adams's all-girl dude ranch and beauty spa. He romances beautiful Lane and rescues her from kidnappers determined to steal her gold mine, while singing "Dirty, Dirty Feeling," "Night Rider," "It Feels So Right," and other tunes. More gags than usual in this middling Presley vehicle.
Dist.: CBS/Fox

TIE ME UP! TIE ME DOWN! 1990 Spanish
☆ NC-17 Comedy 1:41
☑ Nudity, adult situations, explicit language, violence
Dir: Pedro Almodóvar *Cast:* Victoria Abril, Antonio Banderas, Loles Leon, Francisco Rabal, Julieta Serrano
▶ Recently released mental patient Banderas kidnaps porno star Abril. When she refuses to marry him, he ties her up. Eventually, Abril falls in love with her captor. Typically strong art direction and plotting compensate

for film's deliberately controversial story line.
Ⓢ
Dist.: RCA/Columbia

TIGER AND THE PUSSYCAT, THE 1967 Italian
★ NR Comedy/Drama 1:45
Dir: Dino Risi *Cast:* Vittorio Gassman, Ann-
Margret, Eleanor Parker, Caterina Boratto,
Eleonora Brown, Fiorenzo Fiorentini
► In Rome, married Italian Gassman becomes enamored with a younger woman,
sexy American art student Ann-Margret, despite her previous affair with his son. Gassman
runs off to Paris with his lover and considers
ending his marriage. Energetic direction and
acting enliven trite story.
Dist.: Nelson

TIGER BAY 1959 British
★ ★ NR Drama 1:45 B&W
Dir: J. Lee Thompson *Cast:* John Mills, Horst
Buchholz, Hayley Mills, Yvonne Mitchell,
Megs Jenkins, Anthony Dawson
► Smashing film debut for Hayley Mills, who
plays a young girl of the Cardiff slums who
witnesses sailor Buchholz killing his girlfriend.
Stealing the murder weapon, she is pursued
by Buchholz, who gradually develops a
grudging respect for her. John Mills (Hayley's
real-life father) is a police detective who
forces her to choose between her new friend
and justice. Unusual material receives a fresh,
absorbing treatment.
Dist.: Paramount

TIGER'S TALE, A 1988
★ ★ R Comedy 1:37
☑ Nudity, adult situations, explicit language
Dir: Peter Douglas *Cast:* Ann-Margret, C.
Thomas Howell, Charles Durning, Kelly Preston, Ann Wedgeworth, William Zabka
► Texas teen Howell falls for ex-girlfriend Preston's divorced mother Ann-Margret. Unexpected pregnancy (courtesy of Preston
punching hole in mom's diaphragm) complicates the relationship. Adolescent wish-ful-
fillment plot has tangy small-town atmosphere and luscious Ann-Margret investing
her role with shading and wit.
Dist.: Paramount

TIGER WARSAW 1988
★ ★ ★ R Drama 1:32
☑ Adult situations, explicit language
Dir: Amin Chandrini *Cast:* Patrick Swayze,
Piper Laurie, Barbara Williams, Bobby
DiCicco, Lee Richardson, Mary McDonnell
► When McDonnell plans marriage, black
sheep brother Swayze returns home after fifteen years. Mother Laurie is glad to see him,
but father Richardson doesn't want him
around due to rift from years ago. While coping with family woes, Swayze chums with old
pal DiCicco and rediscovers magic with former girlfriend Williams. Competently crafted
working-class melodrama.
Dist.: SVS

TIGHTROPE 1984
★ ★ ★ ★ R Mystery-Suspense 1:54
☑ Nudity, adult situations, explicit language, violence
Dir: Richard Tuggle *Cast:* Clint Eastwood,
Genevieve Bujold, Dan Hedaya, Alison Eastwood, Jennifer Beck, Marco St. John
► Eastwood adds new depth to his macho
persona in this twisty, satisfying thriller. A New
Orleans vice cop separated from his wife and
caring for two daughters, he searches for a
serial killer whose victims are the same prostitutes he frequently visits. Intelligent script and
direction effectively exploit French Quarter
settings without sensationalizing story's
seedier aspects. That's Eastwood's real-life
daughter Alison playing his older girl. **(CC)**
Dist.: Warner

TILL DEATH DO US PART 1972
☆ PG Mystery-Suspense 1:26
☑ Adult situations, explicit language, adult
humor
Dir: Timothy Bond *Cast:* James Keach,
Claude Jutra, Helen Hughes, Jack Creley,
Mott Craven, Candace O'Connor
► Reporter Keach attends weekend therapy
session at mansion of unorthodox marriage
counselor Jutra. When someone starts murder-
ing the patients, Keach investigates. B-movie
attempt at black comedy has skimpy plot
and overly broad performances.
Dist.: Vestron

TILLIE'S PUNCTURED ROMANCE 1914
★ ★ NR Comedy 1:17 B&W
Dir: Mack Sennett *Cast:* Charlie Chaplin,
Marie Dressler, Mabel Normand, Edgar
Kennedy, Charlie Chase, The Keystone Kops
► City slicker Chaplin steals farm girl Dressler's
money, then drops her for Normand. He
changes his mind when Dressler inherits three
million dollars. Flimsy, incoherent oddity was
the first feature-length comedy; fans will want
to see Chaplin in a non–"Little Tramp" role.
Good moment: Charlie takes Normand to see
the movie *Double Crossed.*
Dist.: Various

TILL MARRIAGE DO US PART 1974 Italian
★ ★ R Comedy 1:37
☑ Nudity, adult situations, explicit language
Dir: Luigi Comencini *Cast:* Laura Antonelli,
Alberto Lionello, Michele Placido, Jean Rochefort, Karin Schubert
► On her wedding night, virginal Antonelli
learns groom Lionello is actually her stepbrother. He runs off to war, forcing her to ease
her frustrations with ardent Rochefort and
chauffeur Placido. Glossy showcase for voluptuous Antonelli has beautiful turn-of-the-century settings.
Dist.: Vestron

TILL THE CLOUDS ROLL BY 1946
★ ★ ★ NR Biography/Musical 2:17
Dir: Richard Whorf *Cast:* Robert Walker,
Van Heflin, Lucille Bremer, Dorothy Patrick

▶ Composer Jerome Kern (Walker) rises to the top of Broadway and London stages. Along the way, he gets married, suffers the death of his mentor, and deals with other backstage problems. Thin story line bolstered by MGM stars (Frank Sinatra, Judy Garland, Lena Horne, Dinah Shore, and others) performing Kern's classic music (like "I Won't Dance," "Yesterdays," and selections from *Show Boat*).
Dist.: Various

TILL THE END OF TIME 1946
★★ NR Drama 1:45 B&W
Dir: Edward Dmytryk *Cast:* Dorothy McGuire, Guy Madison, Robert Mitchum, Bill Williams, Tom Tully, William Gargan
▶ After World War II, marines Madison, Mitchum, and Williams return to the home front to face civilian life. Madison has a romance with war widow McGuire, Mitchum drinks to ease his head injury, and handicapped Williams tries to adjust to his disability. Moving drama with Mitchum leading a superb ensemble. Perry Como sings the Chopin-inspired hit title song.
Dist.: Turner

TIM 1979 Australian
★★★★ NR Drama 1:30
☑ Adult situations
Dir: Michael Pate *Cast:* Mel Gibson, Piper Laurie, Alwyn Kurts, Pat Evison, Peter Gwynne, Deborah Kennedy
▶ Fortyish Laurie falls for mentally retarded gardener Gibson and helps him through personal crises. Gibson's sister Kennedy objects to the relationship. Tender and compassionate, with lovely low-key performances by Gibson and Laurie. Based on the novel by Colleen McCullough.
Dist.: Media

TIME AFTER TIME 1979
★★★★ PG Sci-Fi 1:52
☑ Adult situations, explicit language, violence
Dir: Nicholas Meyer *Cast:* Malcolm McDowell, Mary Steenburgen, David Warner, Charles Cioffi, Joseph Maher, Patti D'Arbanville
▶ Victorian English writer H. G. Wells (McDowell) thinks he's unleashed a madman on Utopia when Jack the Ripper (Warner) steals his time machine and goes to present-day San Francisco. McDowell pursues Warner and finds romance with bank employee Steenburgen. Imaginative and literate adventure features engaging performances by McDowell and Steenburgen (husband and wife in real life), clever plotting, and amusing touches intelligently mixed with a thought-provoking message.
Dist.: Warner

TIME BANDITS 1981 British
★★ PG Fantasy/Comedy 1:55
☑ Explicit language, violence, adult humor
Dir: Terry Gilliam *Cast:* Craig Warnock,

David Rappaport, Kenny Baker, Sean Connery, David Warner, Ralph Richardson, John Cleese
▶ Bored English schoolboy Warnock is whisked away by ragtag group of midget bandits, former employees of the Supreme Being (Richardson), who have stolen map of creation to travel through time and space in search of riches. Many adventures lead to battle with Evil (Warner), who wants map for own nefarious purposes. Antics of boy and "little people" include cameos by Connery as Agamemnon and Cleese as Robin Hood. Inventive, witty fun for young and old alike. Baker was R2D2 in *Star Wars*.
Dist.: Paramount

TIME FOR REVENGE 1983 Argentinian
☆ NR Drama 1:53
☑ Brief nudity, adult situations, explicit language, graphic violence
Dir: Adolfo Aristarain *Cast:* Frederico Luppi, Haydee Padilla, Julio De Grazia, Rodolfo Ranni, Ulises Dumont, Aldo Barbero
▶ Explosive thriller about dynamite expert Luppi's devious efforts to defraud a crooked mining company by faking an accident. When bogus mishap actually turns fatal, Luppi, must carry on the deception to expose the company's corrupt practices. Brutal, somewhat irrational, but technically well done.
S
Dist.: Nelson

TIME GUARDIAN 1987 Australian
★ PG Sci-Fi 1:39
☑ Brief nudity, violence, explicit language
Dir: Brian Hannant *Cast:* Tom Burlinson, Carrie Fisher, Dean Stockwell
▶ A battle in a another dimension sends futuristic good guys (including Fisher) into present-day Australia, but bad guys from their century also show up in pursuit. Silly script and cheesy special effects; kids may enjoy the hectic action scenes.
Dist.: Nelson

TIME MACHINE, THE 1960
★★★ G Sci-Fi 1:43
Dir: George Pal *Cast:* Rod Taylor, Yvette Mimieux, Alan Young, Sebastian Cabot, Tom Helmore, Whit Bissell
▶ Victorian inventor Taylor develops time machine and travels ahead into the twentieth-century. After encountering world wars, he goes to the year 802,701 and helps a peaceful blond race battle apelike predators. Terrific adaptation of the H. G. Wells novel features marvelous Oscar-winning special effects, solid Taylor, and an intelligent screenplay.
Dist.: MGM/UA

TIME OF DESTINY, A 1988
★★ PG-13 Drama 1:58
☑ Explicit language, violence
Dir: Gregory Nava *Cast:* William Hurt, Timothy Hutton, Melissa Leo, Francisco Rabal, Stockard Channing, Megan Follows

▸ Basque-American Hurt vows revenge when his dad dies the night Hutton elopes with his sister Leo. In World War II, Hurt gets sent to Hutton's unit and tries to kill him. Old-fashioned soap opera has excellent acting despite sappy melodramatics. Hurt does nicely in an unsympathetic role.
Dist.: Nelson

TIME OF TEARS 1988
★ **NR Drama 1:35**
☑ Adult situations, explicit language
Dir: Costa Mantis ***Cast:*** Frank Urso, Angelo Madrigale, Sharon Westley, Lou Liotta
▸ After the death of his grandfather, young Madrigale is befriended by elderly long-lost relative Urso who helps him cope with the loss. Sincere and unassuming drama has its heart in the right place, but low budget and slow pacing lead to lack of real punch.
Dist.: New World

TIME OF THE GYPSIES 1990 Yugoslavian
☆ **R Drama 2:22**
☑ Nudity, adult situations
Dir: Emir Kusturica ***Cast:*** Davor Dujmovic, Bora Todorovic, Ljubica Adzovic, Husnija Hasimovic, Sinolicka Trpkova, Zabit Memedov
▸ A rambling, poetic tale of contemporary gypsy life, built around the practice of smuggling gypsy children to foreign cities where they are forced to steal and beg. Dujmovic is a teenager who rises through the ranks of petty crime only to discover that he has been played for a fool by the chief crook. Story partakes of gypsy magic, fantasy, and tragic fatalism. [S]
Dist.: RCA/Columbia

TIMERIDER 1983
★★★ **PG Fantasy/Action-Adventure 1:33**
☑ Adult situations, explicit language, violence
Dir: William Dear ***Cast:*** Fred Ward, Belinda Bauer, Peter Coyote, Richard Masur, Ed Lauter
▸ Motorcyclist Ward gets lost during desert race and finds himself in the midst of time-travel experiment. Transported back to 1877 California, he gets involved with outlaws and beautiful gunslinger Bauer. Easygoing entertainment with intriguing premise and surprising sense of humor.
Dist.: Pacific Arts

TIMES OF HARVEY MILK, THE 1984
★★★★ **NR Documentary 1:28**
☑ Adult situations, explicit language
Dir: Robert Epstein ***Cast:*** Harvey Milk, Dan White, George Moscone
▸ Oscar-winning documentary follows career of Harvey Milk, the first openly gay person elected to San Francisco's City Council. The homosexual community is outraged when Council member Dan White murders Milk and Mayor George Moscone. Compelling film examines White's trial (based on the infamous Twinkies defense) and release as well as Milk's influence on San Francisco politics. Narrated by Harvey Fierstein.
Dist.: Pacific Arts

TIMES SQUARE 1980
★ **R Drama 1:51**
☑ Brief nudity, explicit language
Dir: Alan Moyle ***Cast:*** Tim Curry, Trini Alvarado, Robin Johnson, Peter Coffield, Herbert Berghof
▸ Wealthy teenager Alvarado, neglected by her politician father, runs away with rebellious mental patient Johnson to New York's Times Square. Alvarado becomes a stripper and Johnson a punk-rock star; sinister radio DJ Curry turns them into media celebrities. Ambitious soundtrack can't salvage this highly contrived and sanitized look at runaways.
Dist.: HBO

TIME STANDS STILL 1982 Hungarian
★ **NR Drama 1:39**
☑ Nudity, adult situations, explicit language, mild violence
Dir: Peter Gothar ***Cast:*** Istvan Znamenak, Henrik Pauer, Sandor Soth, Peter Galfy, Aniko Ivan, Agi Kakassy
▸ In 1963 Hungary, Znamenek and Pauer, teenage sons of an exiled dissident, have problems with school, politics, and romance. They befriend the school punk and discuss escaping to the West. Director Gothar uses inventive visuals and American rock music to evoke the period and reflect the characters' restlessness, but critically praised film seems to lose something on video. [S]
Dist.: RCA/Columbia

TIME TO DIE, A 1983
★ **R Drama 1:31**
☑ Nudity, adult situations, explicit language, violence
Dir: Matt Cimber ***Cast:*** Edward Albert, Jr., Rod Taylor, Rex Harrison, Linn Stokke, Raf Vallone, Cor Van Rijn
▸ American Albert tracks down the Nazis who tortured him and killed his wife during the war. Chief villain Harrison is now a respected politician, and his henchmen are determined to stop Albert and make Harrison the next leader of Germany. An effective international thriller based on a short story by Mario Puzo. Also known as *Seven Graves for Rogan.*
Dist.: Media

TIME TO LOVE AND A TIME TO DIE, A 1958
★★ **NR Drama 2:12**
Dir: Douglas Sirk ***Cast:*** John Gavin, Lilo Pulver, Jock Mahoney, Don DeFore, Keenan Wynn, Klaus Kinski
▸ A look at the closing days of World War II from the point of view of an ordinary German. Soldier Gavin returns home from the Russian front to a hometown corrupted and demoralized by aerial bombardment and political hypocrisy. After a hasty romance and marriage to Pulver, Gavin returns to the front. Based on

Erich Maria Remarque's novel, poignant offering features the author in a small role.
Dist.: KVC

TIME TRACKERS 1989
★ **PG Sci-Fi 1:27**
☑ Explicit language
Dir: Howard R. Cohen *Cast:* Will Shriner, Ned Beatty, Kathleen Beller, Lee Bergere, Alex Hyde-White, Bridget Hoffman
► When villainous Bergere steals her father's time machine, Beller, accompanied by scientists Shriner and Hoffman, journeys back from 2033 to 1991 to stop him from changing history. Los Angeles cop Beatty joins the crew when the chase ends up in twelfth-century England. Brisk direction and ingratiating cast overcome below-par special effects to create a pleasant time trip.
Dist.: MGM/UA

TIME TRAVELERS, THE 1964
★ ★ **NR Sci-Fi 1:22**
Dir: Ib Melchior *Cast:* Preston Foster, Phil Carey, Merry Anders, John Hoyt, Steve Franken
► Scientists develop a time machine and travel to 2071. They find the world devastated by a nuclear war; the few remaining humans are fighting a race of mutants while using androids to build a spaceship for escape to another planet. A neglected genre treat makes up for moderate budget with clever story and brisk pace.
Dist.: HBO

TIME WALKER 1982
★ ★ **PG Horror 1:23**
☑ Explicit language, violence
Dir: Tom Kennedy *Cast:* Ben Murphy, Nina Axelrod, Kevin Brophy, James Karen, Austin Stoker, Shari Belafonte-Harper
► American archaeologist Murphy transports Egyptian mummy to California campus. When valuable jewels are stolen from the mummy's sarcophagus, it comes to rampaging life. Some spookiness and genuine jolts although plot gets increasingly farfetched as it goes along.
Dist.: Nelson

TIN DRUM, THE 1980 German
★ **R Drama 2:22**
☑ Rape, nudity, strong sexual content, adult situations, explicit language, violence
Dir: Volker Schlondorff *Cast:* David Bennent, Angela Winkler, Mario Adorf, Daniel Olbrychski, Katharina Thalbach, Heinz Bennent
► Adaptation of world-renowned novel by Günter Grass tells of young Bennent, who rebels against bleak world of Nazi Germany in unusual ways: he becomes obsessed with banging on toy tin drum, develops glass-shattering scream, and refuses to grow bigger. With these bizarre talents, tiny Bennent survives World War II as entertainer for Nazis even

as he staunchly opposes them; rest of family suffers horrors of dictatorship and war. Haunting performance by Bennent in unusual, surreal winner of Oscar for Best Foreign film.
Ⓢ
Dist.: Warner

TIN MAN 1987
★ ★ ★ **NR Drama 1:35**
☑ Nudity, adult situations, explicit language
Dir: John G. Thomas *Cast:* Timothy Bottoms, Deana Jurgens, John Phillip Law, Troy Donahue, Gerry Black
► Genius deaf boy Bottoms develops computer through which he can hear and speak. Jurgens, a teacher for deaf, finds work for Bottoms with a computer outfit. Operation restores Bottoms's hearing and love blooms between him and Jurgens. Their subsequent love affair suffers when Bottoms falls under the spell of evil corporate executive Donahue. Often melodramatic treatment of original premise.
Dist.: Media

TIN MEN 1987
★ ★ ★ **R Comedy 1:52**
☑ Adult situations, explicit language
Dir: Barry Levinson *Cast:* Richard Dreyfuss, Danny DeVito, Barbara Hershey, John Mahoney, Jackie Gayle, J. T. Walsh
► Baltimore aluminum siding salesmen Dreyfuss and DeVito feud when their Cadillacs collide. Battle between "tin men" escalates until Dreyfuss seduces DeVito's wife Hershey. Meanwhile, a state commission investigates scams used by Dreyfuss, DeVito, and cohorts to sucker prospective customers. Leads are fine as macho, pig-headed foes, but real stars are · ensemble of supporting tin men and comic dialogue by writer-director Levinson. (CC)
Dist.: Buena Vista

TIN STAR, THE 1957
★ ★ ★ ★ **NR Western 1:33 B&W**
Dir: Anthony Mann *Cast:* Henry Fonda, Anthony Perkins, Betsy Palmer, Michael Ray, Neville Brand, John McIntire
► Former sheriff/bounty hunter Fonda rides into town and teaches rookie lawman Perkins the tricks of the trade. Together the tough guy and the tenderfoot battle vigilante gunman Brand. Fine Western concentrates on characters rather than action.
Dist.: KVC

TINTORERA 1978 British/Mexican
☆ **R Action-Adventure 1:31**
☑ Nudity, violence
Dir: Rene Cardona, Jr. *Cast:* Susan George, Fiona Lewis, Hugo Stiglitz, Andres Garcia, Jennifer Ashley, Robert Guzman
► South of the border, yacht-owner Stiglitz and hustler Garcia hunt sharks and pretty blonds like Lewis and George. After a shark makes a meal out of his friends, Stiglitz vows revenge on the sea-going killer. Much shedding of garments and gnashing of teeth in this

low-budget *Jaws* exploiter. The underwater footage is good, however, and the real sharks are scary.
Dist.: Media

T-MEN 1947
★ **NR Crime 1:31 B&W**
Dir: Anthony Mann   *Cast:* Dennis O'Keefe, Alfred Ryder, June Lockhart, Wallace Ford, Charles McGraw, Mary Meade
▶ Treasury agents O'Keefe and Ryder undercover to crack a counterfeiting ring. The mission is jeopardized when heinous hit man McGraw, not above murdering a colleague via steam bath, discovers their identity. Smashing direction by Mann pushes this thriller to intense, memorable heights.
Dist.: IVE

T.N.T. JACKSON 1975
☆ **R Martial Arts 1:13**
☑ Nudity, adult situations, explicit language, violence
Dir: Cirio Santiago   *Cast:* Jeanne Bell, Stan Shaw, Pat Anderson, Ken Metcalf, Leo Martin, Chris Cruz
▶ Former real-life centerfold Bell's brother has disappeared in Hong Kong. When she goes looking for him, she finds herself mixed up with heroin dealer Shaw, whose criminal boss suspects Bell of being a police informer. She lives up to her nickname by blasting them all to kingdom come in an explosion of martial arts fury. Bell is stiff in this third-rate clobberfest.
Dist.: Nelson

TOAST OF NEW ORLEANS, THE 1950
★ **NR Musical 1:37**
Dir: Norman Taurog   *Cast:* Kathryn Grayson, Mario Lanza, David Niven, J. Carrol Naish, James Mitchell, Rita Moreno
▶ Fisherman Lanza, enchanted by diva Grayson, coincidentally sings well enough for her manager Niven to turn him into an opera star. However, the road to Grayson's heart is not as easy. Cornball plot best ignored in favor of the music and 1900s New Orleans settings. Opera excerpts from Bizet and Puccini interspersed with Sammy Cahn/Nicholas Brodszky score that includes the Oscar-nominated "Be My Love" and "I'll Never Love You."
Dist.: MGM/UA

TOAST OF NEW YORK, THE 1937
★ ★ ★ **NR Biography 1:49 B&W**
Dir: Rowland V. Lee   *Cast:* Edward Arnold, Cary Grant, Frances Farmer, Jack Oakie, Donald Meek, Clarence Kolb
▶ Lively, entertaining biography of robber baron Jim Fisk, who amassed post-Civil War fortune by defrauding Cornelius Vanderbilt, only to lose everything in a scheme to corner the gold market. Arnold approaches his role as "Jubilee Jim" with relish, while Grant brings touch of elegance to character based on Jay Gould. Farmer is charming as Josie Mansfield, center of a tragic love triangle.
Dist.: Turner

TO BE OR NOT TO BE 1942
★ ★ ★ ★ **NR Comedy 1:42 B&W**
Dir: Ernst Lubitsch   *Cast:* Carole Lombard, Jack Benny, Robert Stack, Felix Bressart, Lionel Atwill, Sig Rumann
▶ In this black comedy classic, droll Benny is a Polish actor trying to outwit the Nazis and, in her last film, Lombard exudes glamour as his flirtatious wife. Lubitsch's direction subtly interweaves comedy and more serious themes as writer Edwin Justis Mayer provides some darkly funny lines: "So they call me Concentration Camp Erhardt!" and "What he did to Shakespeare, we're doing to Poland." Inspired the Mel Brooks 1983 remake.
Dist.: Vestron

TO BE OR NOT TO BE 1983
★ ★ **PG Comedy 1:47**
☑ Explicit language, mild violence
Dir: Alan Johnson   *Cast:* Mel Brooks, Anne Bancroft, Tim Matheson, Charles Durning, Jose Ferrer, Christopher Lloyd
▶ In 1939 Warsaw, hammy theatre troupe leader Brooks, being cuckolded by co-star wife Bancroft with soldier Matheson, must impersonate top ranking Nazi to get his company out of German-occupied Poland. Remake of 1942 classic is broad but good-natured. Bancroft shines. Funniest scene: Bancroft and Brooks dueting "Sweet Georgia Brown" in Polish. **(CC)**
Dist.: CBS/Fox

TOBOR THE GREAT 1954
☆ **NR Sci-Fi 1:17 B&W**
Dir: Lee Sholem   *Cast:* Charles Drake, Karin Booth, Billy Chapin, Taylor Holmes, William Schallert
▶ Young Chapin's grandfather invents a robot. The kid becomes attached to the mechanical man, who attempts a rescue when bad guys kidnap Chapin and the old man. Strange sci-fi effort, cheaply produced and blandly acted, emphasizes emotion over action.
Dist.: Republic

TOBRUK 1967
★ ★ ★ **NR War 1:50**
Dir: Arthur Hill   *Cast:* Rock Hudson, George Peppard, Nigel Green, Guy Stockwell, Jack Watson, Norman Rossington
▶ Competent World War II drama about a daring mission across the African desert to destroy Nazi supplies at Tobruk. German Jews posing as Axis troops and commandos disguised as POWs undertake the trek. Hudson and Green, the respective American and British leaders, suspect a traitor when they are unexpectedly ambushed. Large-scale action scenes boost familiar plot.
Dist.: MCA

TOBY MCTEAGUE 1986 Canadian
★ ★ ★ ★ **PG Family 1:35**
☑ Explicit language
Dir: Jean-Claude Lord   *Cast:* Yannick Bis-

son, Winston Rekert, Timothy Webber, Stephanie Morgenstern, Andrew Bednarski, Liliane Clune
► Far in the frozen north, widowed dad Rekert may lose his business if he doesn't win the big dog sledding race. Son Bisson runs away to the mountains, where he's caught in a terrible storm and learns some important lessons from an old Indian trapper. When Rekert breaks his leg, a chastened Bisson takes his dad's place in the crucial competition. Nice-looking dogs, fresh faces, and old-fashioned family values.
Dist.: Nelson

TOBY TYLER, OR TEN WEEKS WITH A CIRCUS 1960
★★★ NR Family 1:36
Dir: Charles Barton *Cast:* Kevin Corcoran, Henry Calvin, Gene Sheldon, Bob Sweeney, Mr. Stubbs, James Drury
► At the turn of the century, young Corcoran runs away from his family and joins the circus, where he is befriended by concessioner Sweeney and chimp Mr. Stubbs. The boy gets to perform and learn about life, but he eventually discovers there's no place like home. Entertaining Disney adaptation of the James Otis Kaler novel.
Dist.: Buena Vista

TO CATCH A KING 1983
★★★ NR Action-Adventure/MFTV 1:53
☑ Adult situations, mild violence
Dir: Clive Donner *Cast:* Robert Wagner, Teri Garr, Barbara Parkins, Horst Janson, Marcel Bozzuffi
► In World War II Lisbon, American nightclub owner Wagner teams with beautiful cabaret singer Garr to thwart Nazi plan to kidnap the Duke and Duchess of Windsor. Race-against-time tension blends with foreign intrigue and romance in this adaptation of the Jack Higgins best-seller.
Dist.: Prism

TO CATCH A THIEF 1955
★★★★ NR Drama 1:46
Dir: Alfred Hitchcock *Cast:* Cary Grant, Grace Kelly, Jessie Royce Landis, John Williams, Charles Vanel, Brigitte Auber
► Lightweight but elegant drama about dashing, retired cat burglar Grant, the chief suspect when daring jewel thefts plague hotels along the French Riviera. Grant must catch the culprit to exonerate himself; alluring heiress Kelly offers herself as bait. Suspense is downplayed for frequently audacious double entendres, gorgeous Edith Head costumes, and scenic, Oscar-winning photography by Robert Burks.
Dist.: Paramount

TO DIE FOR 1989
★ R Horror 1:32
☑ Adult situations, explicit language, graphic violence
Dir: Deren Sarafian *Cast:* Brendan Hughes,

Sydney Walsh, Amanda Wyss, Scott Jacoby, Steve Bond, Duane Jones
► Dracula (Hughes) buys a Los Angeles house from real estate agent Walsh and falls head over fangs for her. The feeling may be mutual but won't be consummated if her boyfriend Jacoby and rival vampire Bond have their way. Average bloodsucking antics could have used a more charismatic count than the wan Hughes.
Dist.: Academy

TOGETHER? 1979 Italian
☆ R Drama 1:42
☑ Nudity, adult situations, explicit language, violence
Dir: Armenia Balducci *Cast:* Jacqueline Bisset, Maximilian Schell, Terence Stamp, Monica Guerritore
► A memorable weekend at a beach house with lawyer Schell and his wife, fashion designer Bisset. Macho Schell cannot handle his wife's successful career, and his obstinacy leads to tragedy. Bisset is strong in this psychologically intense battle of the sexes. Lush score by Burt Bacharach and Paul Anka. Also known as *I Love You, I Love You Not.*
Dist.: Embassy

TO HAVE AND HAVE NOT 1944
★★★★ NR Drama 1:40 B&W
Dir: Howard Hawks *Cast:* Humphrey Bogart, Walter Brennan, Lauren Bacall, Dolores Moran, Hoagy Carmichael, Marcel Dalio
► Fishing charter captain Bogart agrees to run guns for Free French forces to help sultry saloon singer Bacall escape the Nazis. Intensely romantic World War II drama is famous as the film that brought Bogey and Bacall together, but other aspects of this loose adaptation of Ernest Hemingway's best-seller hold up equally well. Bacall's film debut includes her unforgettable "whistling" sequence as well as two charming songs with Carmichael; Brennan offers solid comic support as an addle-brained rummy. Screenplay by Jules Furthman and William Faulkner.
Dist.: MGM/UA [C]

TO HELL AND BACK 1955
★★★ NR Biography 1:46
Dir: Jesse Hibbs *Cast:* Audie Murphy, Marshall Thompson, Jack Kelly, Susan Kohner, Charles Drake, David Janssen
► Murphy gives a disarming performance as himself in this drama based on his best-selling autobiography. His childhood as son of Texas sharecroppers and rejection by Marines and Navy in World War II are tastefully depicted, but film's highlights are strong battle scenes as the Army private rises through the ranks to win the Congressional Medal of Honor.
Dist.: MCA

TO KILL A MOCKINGBIRD 1962
★★★★ NR Drama 2:09 B&W
Dir: Robert Mulligan *Cast:* Gregory Peck,

Mary Badham, Phillip Alford, John Megna, Brock Peters, Robert Duvall

▶ In a prejudice-filled 1930s Alabama town, widowed lawyer Peck tries to raise children Badham and Alford while defending Peters, a black unjustly accused of rape. A masterpiece in which director Mulligan creates a portrait of time and place that is at once haunting, nostalgic, and clear-eyed. Magnificent performance by Peck nabbed one of film's three Oscars (Screenplay Adaptation, Art Direction/Set Decoration); also nominated for Best Picture and Supporting Actress for Badham, who gave one of the most natural child performances ever. Based on Harper Lee's Pulitzer prize-winning novel.
Dist.: MCA

TO KILL A PRIEST 1988 U.S./French
★ R Drama 1:57
☑ Adult situations, explicit language, violence
Dir: Agniezska Holland   *Cast:* Christopher Lambert, Ed Harris, Joanne Whalley, Joss Ackland, David Suchet, Tim Roth
▶ True story, based on the 1984 murder of a Polish clergyman by Communist security police, features Harris as the Polish officer obsessed with silencing pro-Solidarity priest Lambert. Although Harris begins to see the merits of Lambert's views, the Father's martyrdom is a fait accompli. Well-intentioned and atmospheric but never quite catches fire. (CC)
Dist.: RCA/Columbia

TOKYO JOE 1949
★★★ NR Drama 1:22 B&W
Dir: Stuart Heisler   *Cast:* Humphrey Bogart, Florence Marly, Alexander Knox, Sessue Hayakawa, Lora Lee Michel, Jerome Courtland
▶ Returning to Japan after the war, former nightclub owner Bogart discovers that the wife he deserted has married another man. But the baby she bore is Bogart's, and when Japanese war criminals kidnap the child, he must battle for both their lives. Middle-of-the-road action drama buoyed by Bogey charisma.
Dist.: RCA/Columbia

TOKYO OLYMPIAD 1966 Japanese
★★ NR Documentary/Sports 2:34
Dir: Kon Ichikawa
▶ Dazzling documentary on the 1964 Tokyo Olympics is one of the greatest testimonials to athletics ever filmed. Working with hundreds of technicians, director Ichikawa fashioned a breathtaking mosaic of gymnasts, swimmers, racers, and onlookers. Among the highlights are future heavyweight champ Joe Frazier's gold-winning performance and his roommate Bob Hayes's hundred-yard dash. An hour cut from the original U.S. release has recently been restored.
Dist.: Various

TOKYO POP 1988
★★ R Drama 1:37
☑ Adult situations, explicit language
Dir: Fran Rubel Kazui   *Cast:* Carrie Hamilton, Yutaka Tadokoro, Taiji Tonoyoma, Tetsura Tanba, Masumi Harukawa, Toki Shiozawa
▶ Young American rock singer Hamilton travels to Tokyo on a whim. She soon attracts the attentions of Tadokoro, who feels a tall blond vocalist will give his struggling rock band an edge over the competition. East-meets-West romance combined with rising star saga is an extended music video primarily for teens. Hamilton is comedienne Carol Burnett's daughter.
Dist.: Warner

TOKYO STORY 1953 Japanese
☆ NR Drama 2:14 B&W
Dir: Yasujiro Ozu   *Cast:* Chishu Ryu, Chieko Higashiyama, So Yamamura, Haruko Sugimura, Setsuko Hara
▶ Elderly couple Ryu and Higashiyama visit their grown children in Tokyo. The children are too busy with their own lives to deal with the oldsters, and pack them off to a noisy resort. Unhappy, the parents are on their way home when tragedy cuts short the journey. Deeply rooted in Japanese culture, moving, critically acclaimed study of family dynamics may be too static for some. Ⓢ
Dist.: Corinth

TO LIVE AND DIE IN L.A. 1985
★★★ R Mystery-Suspense 1:56
☑ Nudity, explicit language, graphic violence
Dir: William Friedkin   *Cast:* William L. Petersen, Willem Dafoe, John Pankow, John Turturro, Darlanne Fluegel, Dean Stockwell
▶ When counterfeiter Dafoe causes the death of a Secret Service agent, Petersen, the dead man's partner, relentlessly seeks revenge. Petersen's new cohort Pankow intially objects to his methods but becomes caught up in his obsession. Cynical but riveting thriller features complex (although unsympathetic) characters, twisty story, and a great chase scene as Petersen drives against L.A. freeway traffic. Hit theme song by Wang Chung. (CC)
Dist.: Vestron

TOMB OF LIGEIA, THE 1965 British
☆ NR Horror 1:20
Dir: Roger Corman   *Cast:* Vincent Price, Elizabeth Shephard, John Westbrook, Oliver Johnston
▶ Final entry in Corman's series of Edgar Allan Poe adaptations stars Price as a widower obsessed with the memory of his wife. He marries Shephard, who resembles the late Ligeia, whose menacing spirit causes trouble for the newlyweds. Screenplay by Robert Towne.
Dist.: HBO

TOMBOY 1985
★★ R Romance/Comedy 1:30
☑ Nudity, adult situations, explicit language, mild violence
Dir: Herb Freed *Cast:* Betsy Russell, Jerry Dinome, Kristi Somers, Richard Erdman, Phillip Sterling, Eric Douglas
▶ Female mechanic Russell shows little interest in men until she meets handsome racer Dinome. When their romance hits the rocks, she makes a bet that climaxes in a car race between them. Delivers nudity and soft-core sex but avoids offending; Russell and Somers are pleasant company.
Dist.: Vestron

TOM BROWN'S SCHOOL DAYS 1940
★ NR Drama 1:21
Dir: Robert Stevenson *Cast:* Cedric Hardwicke, Freddie Bartholomew, Jimmy Lydon, Billy Halop, Polly Moran, Gale Storm
▶ Young Tom Brown (Lydon) enters a nineteenth-century English boarding school and is bullied by roughnecks. As Brown matures and deals with the tough guys, harsh headmaster Hardwicke imposes his iron will to clean up the school. Solid, if somewhat dated, adaptation of the Thomas Hughes classic.
Dist.: Video Yesteryear

TOM BROWN'S SCHOOLDAYS 1951 British
★★ NR Drama/Family 1:33 B&W
Dir: Gordon Parry *Cast:* John Howard Davies, Robert Newton, Diana Wynyard, Hermione Baddeley, Kathleen Byron, John Forrest
▶ Well-mounted version of Thomas Hughes's 1857 novel about the adventures of young Brown (Davies) at Rugby, an exclusive English boys' school dominated by bullies. Forrest portrays Brown's nemesis Flashman (later the hero of a series of comic novels by George MacDonald Fraser); Newton is the novice headmaster who treats his students with unprecedented respect.
Dist.: Prism

TOM HORN 1980
★★★★ R Western 1:37
☑ Adult situations, explicit language, violence
Dir: William Wiard *Cast:* Steve McQueen, Linda Evans, Richard Farnsworth, Slim Pickens, Billy Green Bush, Elisha Cook, Jr.
▶ In 1901, legendary bounty-hunter Tom Horn (McQueen) is hired by Wyoming cattlemen to kill rustlers. The hunter does his job but, when he no longer fits into his employers' schemes, is framed for murder. Cynical and timely; McQueen, in one of his last performances, is sympathetic as the real-life martyr. Nice support from Farnsworth.
Dist.: Warner

TOM JONES 1963 British
★★★ NR Comedy 2:08
Dir: Tony Richardson *Cast:* Albert Finney, Susannah York, Hugh Griffith, Edith Evans, Joyce Redman, Diane Cilento

▶ In nineteenth-century England, rakish young orphan Finney makes time with the ladies while making his way in the world; a rival plots against him for the affections of virginal heiress York. Stunning adaptation of Henry Fielding's classic novel works like a charm, thanks to Richardson's wonderfully playful direction. Among many standout scenes: the eating orgy between Finney and Redman. Oscars for Best Picture, Director, Score, and Screenplay Adaptation. Acting nominations went to Finney, Redman, Evans, Cilento, and Griffith.
Dist.: CBS/Fox

TOMMY 1975 British
★ PG Musical 1:51
☑ Adult situations
Dir: Ken Russell *Cast:* Ann-Margret, Oliver Reed, Roger Daltrey, Elton John, Eric Clapton, Keith Moon
▶ Abused by his parents Reed and Ann-Margret, Tommy (Daltrey) grows up a deaf, dumb, and blind pinball wizard and the leader of a bizarre religious cult. Flamboyant adaptation of Pete Townshend's famous rock opera contains some startling cameos (notably Tina Turner as the Acid Queen and Jack Nicholson as a doctor), but some viewers may not swallow the sight of Ann-Margret dancing in baked beans. The Who (Townshend and Daltrey's rock group) appear briefly.
Dist.: RCA/Columbia

TOMORROW 1972
★★★★ NR Drama 1:42 B&W
Dir: Joseph Anthony *Cast:* Robert Duvall, Olga Bellin, Sudie Bond, Richard McConnell, Peter Masterson, William Hawley
▶ Meticulous, slowly paced adaptation of a William Faulkner short story about poor Mississippi farmer Duvall, who cares for pregnant Bellin after she's abandoned by her husband and family. When she dies giving birth, he raises her son as his own—only to lose him in a cruel twist. Duvall is magnificent in a stark, unpolished drama that captures the atmosphere of Faulkner's work. Screenplay by Horton Foote.
Dist.: Media

TOMORROW NEVER COMES 1978
British/Canadian
★ PG Drama 1:46
☑ Adult situations, explicit language, violence
Dir: Peter Collinson *Cast:* Oliver Reed, Susan George, Stephen McHattie, Donald Pleasence, John Ireland, Raymond Burr
▶ When McHattie discovers his girlfriend George at a resort hotel with another man, he goes off his rocker, shoots the man, and takes her hostage. Reed and Burr are cops with conflicting notions of how to solve the siege. Simplistic story gets nastily efficient direction from Collinson.
Dist.: Unicorn

TOM SAWYER 1973
★ ★ ★ ★ **G Musical/Family 1:21**
Dir: Don Taylor *Cast:* Johnnie Whitaker, Celeste Holm, Jeff East, Warren Oates, Jodie Foster, Lucille Benson
▶ Musical adaptation of Mark Twain's classic story of boy's adventures in 1830s Midwest features Whitaker as Tom Sawyer, Holm as warm but impatient Aunt Polly, East as dropout Huck Finn, Oates as town drunk Muff Potter, and young, scene-stealing Foster as Becky Thatcher. First-rate family entertainment with screenplay and music by Richard and Robert Sherman, composers of *Mary Poppins*. Picture earned Oscar nominations for Set Decoration, Costume Design, and Score. Best tunes: "Freebootin'," sung by Whitaker and Oates, and "A Man's Gotta Be What He's Born to Be," from Oates and East. **(CC)**
Dist.: MGM/UA

TOM THUMB 1958
★ ★ **G Fantasy 1:32**
Dir: George Pal *Cast:* Russ Tamblyn, Alan Young, Peter Sellers, Terry-Thomas, Jessie Matthews, June Thorburn
▶ Thumb-sized lad Tamblyn is beloved by townsfolk for his high spirits; evil Sellers and Terry-Thomas want to use Tamblyn for no good but are foiled. Oscar-winning special effects from technical master George Pal highlight adaptation of the Charles Perrault fairy tale; kids of all ages should have a good time.
Dist.: MGM/UA

TONIGHT AND EVERY NIGHT 1945
★ ★ ★ **NR Musical 1:32**
Dir: Victor Saville *Cast:* Rita Hayworth, Janet Blair, Lee Bowman, Marc Platt, Leslie Brooks, Stephen Crane
▶ "The show must go on" for entertainers Hayworth, Blair, and others who perform despite the Nazi blitz outside their London theater. Wartime romance is tough too, as Hayworth discovers in a hit-and-miss affair with charming R.A.F. pilot Bowman. Prime musical product from Hollywood's golden era features songs "You Excite Me," "The Boy I Left Behind," and Oscar-nominated "Anywhere."
Dist.: RCA/Columbia

TONY ROME 1967
★ ★ **NR Mystery-Suspense 1:51**
Dir: Gordon Douglas *Cast:* Frank Sinatra, Jill St. John, Richard Conte, Sue Lyon, Gena Rowlands, Simon Oakland
▶ Miami private eye Sinatra gets involved with blackmailers, junkies, and killers when he rescues alcoholic heiress Lyon from a seedy motel. Sinatra's comfortable performance and frequent action boost extremely confusing plot. Followed by *Lady in Cement*.
Dist.: CBS/Fox

TOO BEAUTIFUL FOR YOU 1990 French
☆ **NR Comedy/Drama 1:31**
☑ Adult situations, explicit language
Dir: Bertrand Blier *Cast:* Gerard Depardieu,

Josiane Balasko, Carole Bouquet, Rolande Blanche
▶ Prosperous French businessman Depardieu finds himself in an ironic situation: he is married to the stunningly beautiful Bouquet, but becomes smitten with plain Jane office temp Balasko. Scintillating romantic ménage à trois exploits the hilarious plot twist for all it's worth, with a bewildered Depardieu asking himself "How can it be?" **S**

TOO LATE THE HERO 1970
★ ★ ★ **PG War 2:13**
☑ Explicit language, violence
Dir: Robert Aldrich *Cast:* Michael Caine, Cliff Robertson, Henry Fonda, Ian Bannen, Harry Andrews, Denholm Elliott
▶ During World War II, American Robertson and Brit Caine are chosen for dangerous mission to destroy Japanese encampment on Pacific island. Although they don't get along, they prove their heroism. Macho derring-do is familiar but fast-paced in the patented Aldrich fashion. Also known as *Suicide Run*.
Dist.: CBS/Fox

TOOLBOX MURDERS, THE 1977
☆ **R Horror 1:33**
☑ Nudity, adult situations, explicit language, graphic violence
Dir: Dennis Donnelly *Cast:* Cameron Mitchell, Pamelyn Ferdin, Wesley Eure, Nicholas Beauvy, Aneta Corseaut, Kelly Nichols
▶ Los Angeles building superintendent Mitchell sure takes his daughter's death hard. Using the tools of his trade, he goes on a murderous rampage against women, killing Nichols with a nail gun and tying Ferdin to a bed. A victim's brother investigates. Reportedly a favorite of horror author Stephen King, but most will find this ugly and excessively violent.
Dist.: VCI

TOO MANY GIRLS 1940
★ ★ **NR Musical 1:25 B&W**
Dir: George Abbott *Cast:* Lucille Ball, Richard Carlson, Ann Miller, Eddie Bracken, Francis Langford, Desi Arnaz
▶ When heiress Ball goes to college, her father hires four young men to look after her. The foursome turn the school's failing football team into a winner. Innocuous but upbeat musical, adapted from the Rodgers and Hart Broadway show. Songs include "I Didn't Know What Time It Was" and "Love Never Went to College." First teaming of Lucy and Desi led to their marriage.
Dist.: Turner

TOO SCARED TO SCREAM 1985
★ ★ **R Drama 1:39**
☑ Nudity, adult situations, explicit language, violence
Dir: Tony Lo Bianco *Cast:* Mike Connors, Anne Archer, Leon Isaac Kennedy, Ian McShane, Ruth Ford, John Heard, Maureen O'Sullivan
▶ When a woman is stabbed to death in a

posh Manhattan high rise, tough cop Connors convinces his partner Archer to pose as a tenant to lure the killer out of hiding. Chief suspect is Shakespeare-quoting doorman McShane, who lives in a luxurious brownstone with his invalid mother, O'Sullivan. Although graphic at times, unpretentious drama follows a comfortable formula.
Dist.: Vestron

TOOTSIE 1982
★★★★★ **PG Comedy 1:56**
☑ Adult situations, explicit language
Dir: Sydney Pollack   *Cast:* Dustin Hoffman, Jessica Lange, Teri Garr, Dabney Coleman, Bill Murray, Charles Durning
▶ Bona fide blockbuster features Hoffman as a New York actor who has become, in his agent's (director Pollack) words, "a cult failure." He can't earn enough money to mount roommate Murray's play, *Return to Love Canal,* so he dresses as a woman and lands a role on a popular soap opera. Complications arise when he falls for co-star Lange and then almost becomes engaged to her father Durning. Remarkably funny comedy offers many astute observations about sexual roles. Nominated for ten Oscars; Lange won for Best Supporting Actress. **(CC)**
Dist.: RCA/Columbia

TO PARIS WITH LOVE 1955 British
★★ **NR Comedy 1:18 B&W**
Dir: Robert Hamer   *Cast:* Alec Guinness, Odile Versois, Vernon Gray, Jacques Francois, Elina Labourdette, Austin Trevor
▶ Guinness, a wealthy, retired English colonel, takes his son Gray to Paris. Both father and son plot to fix the other up with a woman, which is when Versois and Labourdette enter the picture. A romantic quadrangle is the result. Lightly amusing fare features a neat turn by Guinness.
Dist.: VidAmerica

TOPAZ 1969
★★ **PG Mystery-Suspense 2:07**
☑ Violence
Dir: Alfred Hitchcock   *Cast:* John Forsythe, Frederick Stafford, Dany Robin, Karin Dor, John Vernon, Michel Piccoli
▶ CIA agent Forsythe and French counterpart Stafford find themselves up to their necks in intrigue involving the 1962 Cuban Missile Crisis. The trail leads Stafford to corruption and double crosses within his own organization. Adaptation of the Leon Uris best-seller evokes some tension, but overall one of Hitchcock's lesser efforts.
Dist.: MCA

TOP GUN 1986
★★★★★ **PG Action-Adventure 1:50**
☑ Adult situations, explicit language
Dir: Tony Scott   *Cast:* Tom Cruise, Kelly McGillis, Anthony Edwards, Tom Skerritt, Val Kilmer, John Stockwell
▶ Hotshot, rule-breaking Navy fighter pilot

Cruise and his partner Edwards are sent to Top Gun school where one percent of fighter pilots learn the 1980s high-tech style of dogfighting. Cruise's attitude problem gets him in trouble with leader Skerritt, rival pilot Kilmer, and instructor-love interest McGillis. He triumphs to save the day, shoot down a few Commie MIGs and get the girl. Eye-popping flying footage, smugly macho Cruise, relentless rock music soundtrack (including the Oscar-winning "Take My Breath Away" by Berlin), and superslick production values turned this into a major blockbuster hit.
Dist.: Paramount

TOP HAT 1935
★★★★ **NR Musical 1:39 B&W**
Dir: Mark Sandrich   *Cast:* Fred Astaire, Ginger Rogers, Edward Everett Horton, Helen Broderick, Erik Rhodes, Eric Blore
▶ In London, song-and-dance man Astaire falls for his downstairs neighbor Rogers, but true love runs a rocky course when she mistakenly assumes he is married to her friend Broderick. Absolutely divine, with Astaire and Rogers at their peaks. Many romantic moments: Astaire spreading sand on the floor so as not to disturb Rogers during a tap routine, the duo getting caught in the rain to the strains of "Isn't This a Lovely Day," and their "Cheek to Cheek" duet. Best Picture nominee also features able comic support from Horton, Rhodes, and Blore.
Dist.: Turner

TOPKAPI 1964
★★★ **NR Comedy 2:00**
Dir: Jules Dassin   *Cast:* Melina Mercouri, Peter Ustinov, Maximilian Schell, Robert Morley, Akim Tamiroff, Gilles Segal
▶ Dazzling caper movie about an attempt by a disparate band of inventors, con artists, and acrobats to steal a priceless dagger from a heavily guarded Turkish museum. Mercouri (director Dassin's real-life wife) assembles the team, unaware that the paunchy final member (Ustinov) is a police informer. Funny, unpredictable, and highlighted by a bravura sequence detailing the break-in. Ustinov won a Supporting Actor Oscar for his perfect comic timing. Based on an Eric Ambler novel.
Dist.: CBS/Fox

TOPPER 1937
★★★★ **NR Fantasy/Comedy 1:36 B&W**
Dir: Norman Z. McLeod   *Cast:* Cary Grant, Constance Bennett, Roland Young, Billie Burke, Eugene Pallette, Arthur Lake
▶ Freewheeling couple Grant and Bennett are killed in a drunk-driving accident and become ghosts. Needing to accomplish a good deed to reach heaven, they teach stuffy banker Young the lighter side of life. Whimsical fun with three top performances and terrific effects. Led to two sequels, a TV series, and made-for-TV remake.
Dist.: Hal Roach Studios ⒸＣ

TOPPER RETURNS 1941
★ ★ ★ ★ NR Fantasy/Comedy 1:22
Dir: Roy Del Ruth *Cast:* Joan Blondell, Roland Young, Carole Landis, Billie Burke, Dennis O'Keefe, Eddie "Rochester" Anderson
▶ Bubbly Blondell is murdered by a mysterious man in black, and her ghost summons the reluctant Topper (Young) to help her find the culprit. Amusing mishaps in spooky old house as invisible spectre keeps getting Topper into undignified positions. Last of series features more slapstick than its predecessors, including a nice bit with Anderson and a trained seal.
Dist.: Various Ⓒ

TOPPER TAKES A TRIP 1938
★ ★ ★ NR Fantasy/Comedy 1:25
Dir: Norman Z. McLeod *Cast:* Constance Bennett, Roland Young, Billie Burke, Alan Mowbray, Franklin Pangborn, Verree Teasdale
▶ First sequel to *Topper* finds Young involved in marital woe. Wife Burke suspects him of hanky-panky after catching him chatting with toothsome ghost Bennett. Needing a good deed to get into heaven, Bennett follows Young and divorce-bent Burke to Paris to patch things up. Almost as good as the original.
Dist.: Various Ⓒ

TOP SECRET 1984
★ ★ PG Comedy 1:30
☑ Mild violence, adult humor
Dir: Jim Abrahams, David Zucker, Jerry Zucker *Cast:* Val Kilmer, Lucy Gutteridge, Omar Sharif, Jeremy Kemp, Peter Cushing, Michael Gough
▶ American rock star Kilmer performs in East Germany and gets involved in intrigue involving beautiful Gutteridge, whose father has been kidnapped by Nazi organization. Painless lunacy mixes scattered hits with many misses. Funniest moments: the musical numbers, Sharif's bout with a trash compactor, and Kilmer's introduction to French spy "Deja Vu" ("Haven't we met somewhere before, monsieur?"). **(CC)**
Dist.: Paramount

TORA! TORA! TORA! 1970 U.S./Japanese
★ ★ ★ G War 2:23
Dir: Richard Fleischer, Toshio Masuda, Kinji Fukasaku *Cast:* Martin Balsam, Soh Yamamura, Jason Robards, Joseph Cotten, Tatsuya Mihashi, E. G. Marshall
▶ Lavish and accurate re-creation of events leading up to Japanese sneak attack on Pearl Harbor in 1941. Japanese plan to further expansionist goals despite reservations of admiral Yamamura assigned to lead assault. Meanwhile, American military men go about peacetime business, ignoring warnings of suspicious intelligence officer Marshall. Talky first half redeemed by impressive action sequences in climax. Two versions of film were

shot, each showing one nation's side: U.S. version bombed, but Japanese was huge hit.
Dist.: CBS/Fox

TORCHLIGHT 1985
★ R Drama 1:32
☑ Adult situations, explicit language
Dir: Tom Wright *Cast:* Pamela Sue Martin, Steve Railsback, Ian McShane, Al Corley
▶ Lackluster cautionary tale about cocaine addiction was co-written and associate produced by Martin. She stars as a successful artist who falls in love with architect Railsback. They marry and are happy but by their first anniversary, he has begun free-basing cocaine with evil drug dealer McShane. Some pulp vitality but, overall, a predictable soap opera as subtle as a sledgehammer.
Dist.: Nelson

TORCH SONG 1953
★ ★ ★ NR Drama 1:30
Dir: Charles Walters *Cast:* Joan Crawford, Michael Wilding, Gig Young, Marjorie Rambeau, Harry Morgan, Dorothy Patrick
▶ Crawford, a temperamental musical stage star who has alienated everyone around her, hires blind pianist Wilding as an arranger. He stands up to her nonsense and she finds herself falling in love with him. Hokey but highly effective love story. As Crawford's mother, Rambeau was nominated for Best Supporting Actress Oscar. Songs include "Tenderly" and "Blue Moon."
Dist.: MGM/UA

TORCH SONG TRILOGY 1988
★ ★ ★ R Comedy/Drama 2:06
☑ Adult situations, explicit language
Dir: Paul Bogart *Cast:* Harvey Fierstein, Anne Bancroft, Matthew Broderick, Brian Kerwin, Karen Young, Eddie Castrodad
▶ Gay female impersonator finds search for Mr. Right rocky, until he meets and falls in love with bisexual teacher Kerwin. Fierstein's fiery mom Bancroft still won't accept her son's homosexuality and keeps trying to find him a nice Jewish girl. He finds greater purpose in life when he adopts troubled gay teen Castrodad as his son. Frank adaptation of Fierstein's Tony-winning play will merit kudos from the discerning although humorous moments work better than the dramatic ones.
Dist.: RCA/Columbia

TORMENT 1986
★ ★ R Mystery-Suspense 1:23
☑ Explicit language, violence
Dir: Samson Aslanian, John Hopkins *Cast:* Taylor Gilbert, William Witt, Eve Brenner, Warren Lincoln, Najean Cherry, Stan Weston
▶ Moody thriller about psychotic killer Witt preying on single women in San Francisco. He singles out detective's fiancée Gilbert as his next victim, and traps her in the remote house of her crippled future mother-in-law, Brenner.

Despite budget constraints, inventive directing provides some effective shocks.
Dist.: Nelson

TORN CURTAIN 1966
★ ★ ★ PG Espionage 2:05
☑ Violence
Dir: Alfred Hitchcock **Cast:** Paul Newman, Julie Andrews, Lila Kedrova, Hansjorg Felmy, Tamara Toumanova, Ludwig Donath
► Nuclear physicist Newman defects from West to East, taking puzzled girlfriend/assistant Andrews with him. Soon she understands his plan: he dupes East German scientist Donath into revelations about Soviet missile program. Can they escape to the free world with the info? Not one of Hitchcock's better outings.
Dist.: MCA

TORRENTS OF SPRING 1990 French/Italian
☆ PG-13 Drama 1:33
☑ Adult situations
Dir: Jerzy Skolimowski **Cast:** Timothy Hutton, Nastassja Kinski, Valeria Golino, William Forsythe, Urbano Barberini, Francesco De Sapio
► Dashing nineteenth-century nobleman Hutton falls for Golino, the daughter of Italian pastry makers. He's ready to sell his serfs and fight a duel for her—until he meets Kinski, wife of a childhood friend. Torn between two lovers, he throws his destiny up for grabs. Lush score and gorgeous costumes, but acting is poor and characters' motives confusing. Based on a short story by Ivan Turgenev.
Dist.: HBO

TORSO 1974 Italian
☆ R Horror 1:30
☑ Nudity, strong sexual content, explicit language, graphic violence
Dir: Sergio Martino **Cast:** Suzy Kendall, Tina Aumont, Luc Meranda, John Richardson, Robert Bisacco, Angela Covello
► As several of her classmates are killed and mutilated by a madman, American exchange student Kendall is befriended by professor Richardson. Although her pal Aumont discovers a key clue, it is Kendall who ends up alone in a deserted house with the killer. Lurid trash, directed with flash. Dull performances.
Dist.: Prism

TORTURE CHAMBER OF DR. SADISM, THE 1967 German
☆ NR Horror 1:30
Dir: Harald Reinl **Cast:** Christopher Lee, Lex Barker, Karin Dor, Carl Lange, Vladimir Medar
► Evil count Lee needs the blood of thirteen virgins for eternal life, but is executed after getting to only twelve. Brought back to life by servant Lange, he gathers a group including Dor and Barker to his castle as part of a plot to kill number thirteen. Barker winds up spread-eagled under a Edgar Allan Poe–style pendulum in this imaginatively visualized horror cheapie. Also known as *The Blood Demon* and *Castle of the Walking Dead.*
Dist.: Magnum

TO SIR, WITH LOVE 1967 British
★ ★ ★ ★ NR Drama 1:45
Dir: James Clavell **Cast:** Sidney Poitier, Judy Geeson, Lulu, Suzy Kendall, Christian Roberts, Faith Brook
► Black teacher Poitier takes job in London's toughest slum. The kids resist him at first but he wins their respect through unorthodox lessons and treating them as equals. Heartfelt and moving drama with an uplifting message. Poitier is terrific, interacting beautifully with his young charges. Lulu sings the hit title song.
Dist.: RCA/Columbia

TOTAL RECALL 1990
★ ★ ★ ★ ★ R Sci-Fi 1:49
☑ Nudity, adult situations, explicit language, graphic violence
Dir: Paul Verhoeven **Cast:** Arnold Schwarzenegger, Rachel Ticotin, Sharon Stone, Ronny Cox, Michael Ironside, Marshall Bell
► Construction worker Schwarzenegger buys a memory implant that gives him the experience of a vacation on Mars. To his surprise, the implant triggers memories of his forgotten life as a secret agent, and thrusts him into a deadly battle with Martian dictator Cox and his henchman Ironside. One of the most original and surprising sci-fi plots of recent years gets splashy treatment from Verhoeven. Expensive production shows every penny on screen. Inspired by the Philip K. Dick story, "We Can Remember It for You Wholesale."
Dist.: IVE

TO THE SHORES OF TRIPOLI 1942
★ NR War 1:25
Dir: H. Bruce Humberstone **Cast:** John Payne, Maureen O'Hara, Randolph Scott, Nancy Kelly, William Tracy, Maxie Rosenbloom
► Wealthy, insolent Payne enlists in the Marines and conflicts with hard-nosed drill sergeant Scott. Eventually, basic training changes Payne, and he falls in love with Navy nurse O'Hara. Patriotic rouser is manipulative but told with verve. Scott stands out.
Dist.: CBS/Fox

TOUCH AND GO 1980 Australian
★ NR Comedy 1:32
☑ Adult situations
Dir: Peter Maxwell **Cast:** Wendy Hughes, Chantal Contouri, Carmen Duncan, Jeanie Drynan, Liddy Clark
► Three seemingly normal, well-to-do women become masked thieves, pulling off heists to support a school for the underprivileged. The ladies attempt their biggest caper to date at a resort on the Great Barrier Reef. Sit-commish screenplay fails to explore the characters or create a compelling plot.
Dist.: VidAmerica

TOUCH AND GO 1986
★ ★ ★ ★ **R Drama 1:41**
☑ Brief nudity, adult situations, explicit language, violence
Dir: Robert Mandel *Cast:* Michael Keaton, Maria Conchita Alonso, Ajay Naidu, Maria Tucci, Max Wright
▶ Hotshot hockey jock Keaton is attacked by gang and captures Naidu, one of the punks. Tough-talking kid charms Keaton and takes him home where he meets and falls for the youth's mom, Alonso. Their budding relationship hits many snags, but this stand-up-and-cheer sleeper delivers in the end. Both Keaton and Alonso are charming.
Dist.: HBO

TOUCHED 1982
★ ★ ★ **R Drama 1:29**
☑ Adult situations, explicit language
Dir: John Flynn *Cast:* Robert Hays, Kathleen Beller, Ned Beatty, Gilbert Lewis, Lyle Kessler
▶ Mental patient Hays escapes from an institution and finds a job at boardwalk amusement park. He returns to the asylum to free his schizophrenic girlfriend, Beller, hoping to establish an independent life. Sincere, uplifting drama is a bit too predictable, despite fine performances by Hays and Beller.
Dist.: Media

TOUCHED BY LOVE 1980
★ ★ ★ ★ **PG Drama 1:34**
☑ Explicit language
Dir: Gus Trikonis *Cast:* Deborah Raffin, Diane Lane, Michael Learned, John Amos, Cristina Raines, Mary Wickes
▶ Nursing trainee Lena Canada (Raffin) develops friendship with a young cerebral palsy victim (Lane) and encourages her to write to her idol, Elvis Presley. Responsive to the girl's plight, Presley becomes a supportive pen pal. Earnest, sentimental drama, based on a true story by Canada, features effectively restrained performances and an uplifting theme.
Dist.: RCA/Columbia

TOUCH OF CLASS, A 1973
★ ★ ★ **PG Romance/Comedy 1:45**
☑ Adult situations, explicit language
Dir: Melvin Frank *Cast:* Glenda Jackson, George Segal, Paul Sorvino, Hildegard Neil, Cec Linder, K. Callan
▶ In London, married American insurance agent Segal meets divorced Englishwoman Jackson during Hyde Park baseball game. They embark on initially casual affair, but true love rears its difficult head. Brightly funny and breezily whimsical, with bubbling chemistry between Segal and Oscar-winning Jackson.
Dist.: Media

TOUCH OF EVIL 1958
★ ★ ★ **NR Mystery-Suspense 1:35 B&W**
Dir: Orson Welles *Cast:* Charlton Heston, Janet Leigh, Orson Welles, Joseph Calleia, Akim Tamiroff, Valentin de Vargas
▶ In a U.S.-Mexican border town, Mexican cop Heston and corrupt gringo detective Welles lock horns while investigating murder of local bigwig. When Welles frames an innocent man for the crime, Heston tries unsuccessfully to blow the whistle. Welles and drug dealer Tamiroff retaliate by framing Heston's wife Leigh for sordid crimes. Compelling portrayal of decadence and deception opens with spectacular three-minute shot that ranks among best in film history. Look for unbilled cameos by Marlene Dietrich, Mercedes McCambridge, Zsa Zsa Gabor, and Joseph Cotten.
Dist.: MCA

TOUGH ENOUGH 1983
★ ★ ★ **PG Drama 1:46**
☑ Nudity, adult situations, explicit language, violence
Dir: Richard Fleischer *Cast:* Dennis Quaid, Carlene Watkins, Stan Shaw, Pam Grier, Warren Oates, Wilford Brimley
▶ Aspiring country-western singer Quaid enters a local "Toughman" boxing competition, and catches the eye of shady promoter Oates, who promises him a chance to sing on national TV if he will throw a prizefight. Oates gives a delicately shaded performance in his last film role; Quaid is appealing both in the ring and with a guitar.
Dist.: CBS/Fox

TOUGHER THAN LEATHER 1988
☆ **R Musical 1:32**
☑ Nudity, adult situations, explicit language, graphic violence
Dir: Rick Rubin *Cast:* Joseph Simmons, Darryl McDaniels, Jason Mizell, Richard Edson, Jenny Lumet, Rick Rubin, Russell Simmons, Larry Kase, Tim Summer
▶ Rappers Run-DMC (Simmons, McDaniels, Mizell) reunite after Simmons is released from prison. Group is signed by shady mogul Rubin, who becomes object of trio's revenge when he kills one of their friends. Crude effort mistakenly emphasizes parody plot over music, disappointing all but the most hardcore rap fans; others will be offended at the sexist and racist humor. Some amusement from co-screenwriter Ric Menello's performance.
Dist.: RCA/Columbia

TOUGH GUYS 1986
★ ★ ★ ★ **PG Comedy 1:42**
☑ Adult situations, explicit language
Dir: Jeff Kanew *Cast:* Burt Lancaster, Kirk Douglas, Charles Durning, Alexis Smith, Dana Carvey, Darlanne Fluegel
▶ In their seventh film teaming, Lancaster and Douglas play two elderly convicts, the last successful train robbers in America, who find it hard to cope with a strange new Los Angeles after thirty years in jail. Lancaster, suffering in a nursing home, and Douglas, offered a series of demeaning jobs, join up for one last rob-

bery. Wonderful stars provide all the luster in this slight comedy.
Dist.: Buena Vista

TOUGH GUYS DON'T DANCE 1987
★ ★ R Mystery-Suspense 1:48
☑ Nudity, adult situations, explicit language
Dir: Norman Mailer *Cast:* Ryan O'Neal, Isabella Rossellini, Debra Sandlund, Wings Hauser, Lawrence Tierney, John Bedford Lloyd
▶ Adaptation by Norman Mailer of his novel about booze, drugs, murder, and sex in Provincetown, Cape Cod. Writer O'Neal wakes up after drunken binge caused by departure of unfaithful wife Sandlund to find blood in his car and severed head buried under dope stash. Local police chief Hauser fingers O'Neal for crimes, leading O'Neal to uncover wholesale cocaine deal and sexual intrigue in attempt to prove innocence. Convoluted plot plagued by frequent flashbacks and heavy-handed narration.
Dist.: Media

TOWERING INFERNO, THE 1974
★ ★ ★ ★ PG Action-Adventure 2:45
☑ Explicit language, violence
Dir: John Guillermin, Irwin Allen *Cast:* Paul Newman, Steve McQueen, William Holden, Faye Dunaway, Fred Astaire, Susan Blakely, Richard Chamberlain, O. J. Simpson
▶ During dedication party, San Francisco skyscraper goes up in flames, trapping celebrants on top floors. Newman is the stunned architect, Holden the greedy developer who cost-cut architect's safety features, and McQueen the heroic fire chief who seeks to minimize loss of life and douse the flames. First-rate visual spectacle overcomes sometimes silly personal drama. Grand disaster epic earned seven Oscar nominations, including Best Picture and Supporting Actor (for Astaire); winner for Cinematography and Editing. (CC)
Dist.: CBS/Fox

TOWN CALLED HELL, A 1971 British/Italian
☆ R Western 1:35
☑ Brief nudity, adult situations, violence
Dir: Robert Parrish *Cast:* Robert Shaw, Stella Stevens, Martin Landau, Fernando Rey, Telly Savalas
▶ In 1905 Mexico, widow Stevens comes to a small town searching for her husband's killer. Suspects include bandit leader Savalas, rebel-turned-soldier Landau, and Shaw, a revolutionary hiding in priest's robes. Boring, frequently incomprehensible mess riddled with bizarre flashbacks. Enlivened somewhat by three large-scale shoot-outs.
Dist.: Goodtimes

TOWN THAT DREADED SUNDOWN, THE 1976
★ ★ ★ R Mystery-Suspense 1:30
☑ Violence
Dir: Charles B. Pierce *Cast:* Ben Johnson,

Andrew Prine, Dawn Wells, Jimmy Clem, Charles B. Pierce, Cindy Butler
▶ Unsolved murder spree in Texarkana during the summer of 1946 is the basis of an effective, low-budget thriller. Documentary approach shows town's growing panic and the inability of local law officers to pinpoint the killer, identified only by his hooded mask. Texas Ranger Johnson, brought in to help, is also stymied by lack of evidence.
Dist.: Warner

TOXIC AVENGER, THE 1985
★ R Comedy 1:25
☑ Explicit language, graphic violence
Dir: Michael Herz, Samuel Weil *Cast:* Andree Maranda, Mitchell Cohen, Jennifer Baptist, Cindy Manion, Robert Prichard
▶ Skinny nerd falls into a vat of toxic waste and emerges as the Toxic Avenger (Cohen), a liberal monster determined to clean up his corrupt hometown. While dispatching his enemies, he falls for a beautiful blind girl (Maranda) who fixes him Drano sandwiches. Tongue-in-cheek tone and pro-environment stance don't atone for film's tawdry style. Followed by *Toxic Avenger Part II.*
Dist.: Vestron

TOXIC AVENGER PART II, THE 1989
★ ★ R Comedy 1:35
☑ Nudity, adult situations, explicit language, violence
Dir: Lloyd Kaufman, Michael Herz *Cast:* Ron Fazio, John Altamura, Phoebe Legere, Rikiya Yasouka, Tsutomu Sekine, Mayako Katsuragi
▶ After the evil Apocalypse Corp. blows up the Tromaville Home for the Blind (where his girlfriend Legere lives), the Toxic Avenger is tricked into going to Japan. There he is reunited with his father Yasuoka but eventually returns home to take on the bad guys. Sequel repeats original's goofy, sleazeball humor, occasionally getting laughs. (CC)
Dist.: Warner

TOY, THE 1982
★ ★ ★ ★ PG Comedy 1:42
☑ Explicit language
Dir: Richard Donner *Cast:* Richard Pryor, Jackie Gleason, Ned Beatty, Scott Schwartz, Teresa Ganzel
▶ Business tycoon Gleason tells bratty son Schwartz he can have anything in the store for Christmas. The boy selects janitor Pryor, an out-of-work writer. Eventually, Pryor teaches Schwartz about love, hope, politics, racial tolerance, and nuclear physics—but not before they share many very funny adventures. Excellent cast will delight kids. Remake of a French comedy by Francis Veber.
Dist.: RCA/Columbia

TOY SOLDIERS 1984
★ R Action-Adventure 1:31
☑ Nudity, adult situations, explicit language, violence

Dir: David Fisher *Cast:* Jason Miller, Cleavon Little, Terri Garber, Rodolfo De Anda, Douglas Warhit
▶ When her friends are taken hostage by Central American guerrillas, feisty coed Garber forms a rescue mission with grizzled captain Miller and neighborhood tough Little. Mindless adventure is often unintentionally funny.
Dist.: New World

TRACKER, THE 1987
★ ★ ★ ★ NR Western/MFTV 1:55
☑ Nudity, adult situations, explicit language, violence
Dir: John Guillermin *Cast:* Kris Kristofferson, Scott Wilson, David Huddleston, Mark Moses, Karen Kopins, John Quade
▶ Kristofferson was the greatest Indian fighter and scout of his day. When erudite son Moses returns from law school in the East, Kristofferson hopes he'll take over the family ranch, but Moses wants to pursue a career. Their divergent views of life and justice are put to the test as they band together to track a murderous religious fanatic who has kidnapped two women. One of the best Westerns of recent years; exciting action sequences and striking scenery complement a moving father and son relationship.
Dist.: HBO

TRACK OF THE MOONBEAST 1976
☆ NR Horror 1:30
☑ Violence
Dir: Dick Ashe *Cast:* Chase Cordell, Donna Leigh Drake, Gregorio Sala, Francine Kessler, Joe Blasco
▶ When a meteor lands in New Mexico, a fragment beans mineralogist Cordell in the noggin. Later, he wishes he had ducked, because he mutates into a monstrous lizard. Rick Baker contributed make-up effects to an otherwise limp genre effort. Acting, direction, and screenplay are inept.
Dist.: Prism

TRACK 29 1988
☆ R Drama 1:30
☑ Rape, adult situations, explicit language
Dir: Nicolas Roeg *Cast:* Theresa Russell, Gary Oldman, Christopher Lloyd, Sandra Bernhard, Colleen Camp, Seymour Cassel
▶ Bored Texas housewife Russell, whose doctor husband Lloyd is more interested in model trains and nurse Bernhard than in her, meets mysterious Englishman Oldman. Is he the son she abandoned years ago or a figment of her imagination? Oddball story given dash by Roeg's direction and performances by Russell and Oldman, but many viewers will be left scratching heads in bewilderment. Written by Dennis Potter.
Dist.: Warner

TRADING HEARTS 1988
★ ★ ★ PG Drama 1:30
☑ Adult situations, explicit language

Dir: Neil Leifer *Cast:* Raul Julia, Beverly D'Angelo, Jenny Lewis, Parris Buckner, Robert Gwaltney, Mark Harris
▶ Cut by his team, Red Sox pitcher Julia is pounced on by Lewis, a cute tomboy desperate for a new dad. But her lounge-singing mom D'Angelo can't stand Julia, a problem that doesn't deter young Lewis. Nostalgic drama by sportswriter Frank Deford captures 1957 Miami effectively, but low-key plot offers few surprises.
Dist.: IVE

TRADING PLACES 1983
★ ★ ★ ★ ★ R Comedy 1:56
☑ Nudity, adult situations, explicit language, adult humor
Dir: John Landis *Cast:* Dan Aykroyd, Eddie Murphy, Ralph Bellamy, Don Ameche, Denholm Elliott, Jamie Lee Curtis
▶ Powerhouse casting sparks this hit comedy about role reversals. How will black con artist Murphy and stuffy Main Line financier Aykroyd react to switching professions? Millionaire brothers Bellamy and Ameche engineer the plot on a whim. Feisty hooker Curtis teaches Aykroyd how to survive on the streets while Murphy adjusts to a new world of wealth and privilege. Excellent script and brilliant performance by Murphy highlight an enjoyably shrewd film. **(CC)**
Dist.: Paramount

TRAIL OF THE PINK PANTHER 1982
★ ★ ★ PG Comedy 1:37
☑ Brief nudity, explicit language, adult humor
Dir: Blake Edwards *Cast:* Peter Sellers, David Niven, Herbert Lom, Richard Mulligan, Joanna Lumley, Robert Loggia
▶ Once again the Pink Panther diamond is stolen from mythical city of Lugash and Inspector Clouseau (Sellers) is sent to investigate the theft. Sellers's plane disappears so he's presumed dead. French TV reporter Lumley then interviews detective's colleagues and family, setting up flashbacks to previous movies. Attempt to continue popular series despite death of star is strange brew of new footage and old outtakes, but worthy for previously unreleased Sellers gags. Followed by *The Curse of the Pink Panther.*
Dist.: CBS/Fox

TRAIN ROBBERS, THE 1973
★ ★ ★ ★ PG Western 1:28
☑ Explicit language
Dir: Burt Kennedy *Cast:* John Wayne, Ann-Margret, Rod Taylor, Ben Johnson, Christopher George, Ricardo Montalban
▶ Outlaw's widow Ann-Margret proposes deal to aging Civil War vet Wayne: for a reward, help her return $500,000 in stolen bank funds hidden by hubby so family honor is restored. Widow, war vet, and hired hands set off for Mexican badlands, site of buried loot; in pursuit are enigmatic loner Montalban and

gunmen hired by outlaw's former partners. Fine, old-style horse opera, Wayne's 149th screen appearance, features surprise ending. *Dist.:* Warner

TRAMPLERS, THE 1966 Italian
★ NR Western 1:45
Dir: Albert Band *Cast:* Joseph Cotten, Gordon Scott, James Mitchum, Franco Nero, Ilaria Occhini, Emma Vannoni
▶ Family feud, Texas-style: after the Civil War, Scott and Mitchum argue with despotic father Cotten over slavery and other issues. The boys leave home with a herd of cattle, but the family tensions erupt in violence. Way below-average Western, a definite low point in Cotten's career.
Dist.: Nelson

TRANCERS 1985
★★ PG-13 Sci-Fi 1:17
☑ Explicit language, violence
Dir: Charles Band *Cast:* Tim Thomerson, Helen Hunt, Michael Stefani, Art La Fleur, Biff Manard
▶ Stefani, the sinister ruler of future Los Angeles, returns to the present-day city to kill the ancestors of his enemies. He's followed by Trooper Jack Deth (Thomerson), who teams up with beautiful guide Hunt to stop Stefani's scheme. Low-budget variation on *The Terminator* offers enough clever touches to remain intriguing. Also known as *Future Cop*.
Dist.: Vestron

TRANSATLANTIC MERRY-GO-ROUND 1934
★ NR Musical 1:28
Dir: Benjamin Stoloff *Cast:* Gene Raymond, Jack Benny, Nancy Carroll, Sydney Howard, Mitzi Green, Sid Silvers, William Boyd, The Boswell Sisters, Sam Hardy, Shirley Grey, Sidney Blackmer, Ralph Morgan
▶ Benny is the master of ceremonies for a shipboard show that dominates the ostensible story, an assembly of subplots involving Morgan's unfaithful wife Grey, gambler Hardy, alcoholic Howard, and others. Highlighted by Benny's clowning and the Boswell Sisters singing "Rock and Roll" and "If I Had a Million Dollars."
Dist.: IVE

TRANSFORMERS—THE MOVIE 1986
★★ PG Animation 1:26
☑ Explicit language
Dir: Nelson Shin *Cast:* Voices of: Eric Idle, Judd Nelson, Leonard Nimoy, Robert Stack, Lionel Stander, Orson Welles
▶ Autobots, good robots who can transform themselves into cars and dinosaurs, among other things, battle the villainous Decepticons for control of their world. Aiding the bad guys is a villainous planet (voice of Welles); leading the good guys is Autobot Hot Rod (voice of Nelson). Kids who enjoy the original toys might like this, but their parents may be offended by the film's commercial implications.
Dist.: Fries

TRANSMUTATIONS 1987 British
☆ R Horror 1:43
☑ Adult situations, violence
Dir: George Pavlou *Cast:* Denholm Elliott, Steven Berkoff, Larry Lamb, Miranda Richardson, Art Malik, Nicola Cowper
▶ Drug experiments by mad doctor Elliott turn people into underground mutants. When prostitute Cowper is kidnapped by these beings, gangster Berkoff hires detective Lamb to rescue her. Mesmerizing visuals but muddled storytelling and torpid pacing. Also known as *Underworld*.
Dist.: Vestron

TRANSYLVANIA 6-5000 1985
★★ PG Horror/Comedy 1:30
☑ Mild violence
Dir: Rudy DeLuca *Cast:* Jeff Goldblum, Joseph Bologna, Ed Begley, Jr., Carol Kane, Geena Davis, Jeffrey Jones, John Byner
▶ Tabloid paper sends reporters Goldblum and Begley to investigate rumors of modern-day ghouls. Begley loses his heart to village vampire Davis, while Goldblum grapples with servile mayor Jones, mad doctor Bologna, and Kane, the sex-starved wife of incompetent butler Byner. Frantic horror spoof with talented cast but few real laughs. **(CC)**
Dist.: New World

TRANSYLVANIA TWIST 1989
★★ PG Comedy 1:22
☑ Explicit language, mild violence
Dir: Jim Wynorski *Cast:* Robert Vaughn, Teri Copley, Steve Altman, Jay Robinson, Steve Franken, Howard Morris
▶ Altman accompanies pop star Copley to her ancestral home in Transylvania to retrieve an invaluable occult book from the estate of her recently deceased father. Copley's uncle, vampire Vaughn, won't give up the tome, as it contains an incantation for summoning Satan. Witty writing and broad slapstick combine for primo high jinks in the manner of Mel Brooks; abundant laughs put this a cut above most recent horror spoofs.
Dist.: MGM/UA

TRAPEZE 1956
★★★ NR Drama 1:45
Dir: Carol Reed *Cast:* Burt Lancaster, Tony Curtis, Gina Lollobrigida, Katy Jurado, Thomas Gomez, Johnny Puleo
▶ Lancaster, a former trapeze acrobat famous for performing triple somersault prior to an injury, works as rigger for Parisian circus. Newcomer Curtis persuades him to return to trapeze as "catcher" to help younger man perfect famed triple. Two aerialists become close until scheming tumbler Lollobrigida, hoping to move up to more prestigious trapeze act, turns her feminine charms on both men. Spectacular trapeze footage and colorful three-ring atmosphere.
Dist.: CBS/Fox

TRASH 1970
☆ NR Drama 1:43
☑ Nudity, strong sexual content, adult situations, explicit language, violence
Dir: Paul Morrissey *Cast:* Joe Dallesandro, Holly Woodlawn, Jane Forth, Michael Sklar, Geri Miller, Andrea Feldman
▶ Junkie hustler Dallesandro is made impotent by frequent drug abuse, causing problems with girlfriend Woodlawn and customers. Semblance of plot and Morrissey's controlled direction make this one of the more accessible of Andy Warhol's Factory films, but trademark assault on decorum will still prove rough going for most.
Dist.: Paramount

TRAVELING MAN 1989
★ ★ ★ ★ NR Drama/MFTV 1:45
☑ Adult situations, explicit language
Dir: Irvin Kershner *Cast:* John Lithgow, Jonathan Silverman, Margaret Colin, John Glover, Chynna Phillips
▶ Traveling salesman Lithgow is upset when boss Glover puts unscrupulous newcomer Silverman on his route. Lithgow teaches the kid the tricks of the trade but is horrified by Silverman's corruption. Meanwhile, romance with Colin could provide a new life for the roadweary veteran. Neat mixture of comedy and drama features vivid performances in a naturalistic David Taylor screenplay.
Dist.: HBO

TRAVELLING NORTH 1988 Australian
★ PG-13 Drama 1:35
☑ Explicit language
Dir: Carl Schultz *Cast:* Leo McKern, Julia Blake, Graham Kennedy, Henri Szeps, Michele Fawdon, Diane Craig
▶ Cantankerous Melbourne civil engineer McKern retires at age seventy and coaxes widow Blake to start new life in subtropical northern Australia. Spectacular scenery, new friends Kennedy and Szeps, and sexual reawakening make their domestic arrangement a success until McKern's health deteriorates. Crotchety but endearing McKern and luminous Blake excel in often humorous and always touching down-under drama.
Dist.: Virgin

TRAXX 1988
★ R Comedy 1:25
☑ Brief nudity, adult situations, explicit language, violence
Dir: Jerome Gary *Cast:* Shadoe Stevens, Priscilla Barnes, Willard E. Pugh, Robert Davi, John Hancock
▶ Ex-cop-turned-mercenary Stevens returns to Texas town to start cookie business. Hoping for reward money from sexy mayor Barnes, he teams with black sidekick Pugh to clean up crime-ridden neighborhood and take on local mafia. Impish crime comedy aided and abetted by Stevens's droll spirit.
Dist.: HBO

TREASURE ISLAND 1934
★ ★ ★ NR Action-Adventure 1:45 B&W
Dir: Victor Fleming *Cast:* Wallace Beery, Jackie Cooper, Lionel Barrymore, Otto Kruger, Lewis Stone, Nigel Bruce, Douglass Dumbrille
▶ Dying sailor passes a treasure map to young English lad Cooper, who takes a job as cabin boy on a ship bound for the secret island. Long John Silver (Beery), a treacherous pirate, leads a rebellion that endangers Cooper and captain Stone. Large-scale adaptation of Robert Louis Stevenson's classic adventure is first-rate on all levels, with Beery particularly boisterous in one of his best roles. Remade in 1950 and 1972.
Dist.: MGM/UA

TREASURE ISLAND 1950
★ ★ ★ ★ G Family 1:36
Dir: Byron Haskin *Cast:* Bobby Driscoll, Robert Newton, Basil Sydney, Walter Fitzgerald, Denis O'Dea, Ralph Truman
▶ Young Driscoll inherits treasure map from aged captain; accompanied by lawyer Fitzgerald and doctor O'Dea, he sets out for the remote island, unaware that his ship's crew is made up of bloodthirsty pirates. Superb Disney adventure is the best version of Robert Louis Stevenson's classic, with an especially strong performance by Newton (who repeated his role in 1954's *Long John Silver*). Bloodier moments were trimmed from the original to gain a G rating.
Dist.: Buena Vista

TREASURE ISLAND 1989
★ ★ ★ ★ ★ NR Action-Adventure/MFTV 2:12
Dir: Fraser Heston *Cast:* Christian Bale, Oliver Reed, Christopher Lee, Richard Johnson, Julian Glover
▶ From the dark tables of the Admiral Benbow Inn to the bright beaches of the Carribean, grizzled Long John Silver (Heston) leads young Jim Hawkins (Bale) on a merry, swordflashing adventure in search of buried dubloons. Nice ensemble acting in this rougher, somewhat un-romanticized version of the Robert Louis Stevenson classic. Writer/director/producer is star Heston's son.
Dist.: Turner

TREASURE OF MATECUMBE 1976
★ ★ G Family 1:57
Dir: Vincent McEveety *Cast:* Robert Foxworth, Joan Hackett, Johnny Doran, Vic Morrow, Jane Wyatt, Billy Attmore
▶ In the Reconstruction-era South, young Doran teams with former slave Attmore to evade bad guy Morrow and revive a plantation by recovering the treasure lying in a sunken ship lying off the coast. Kids won't sit still through the first hour of this slow-paced family adventure, though things do pick up

toward the end, and a roaring hurricane brings the action to a rousing conclusion. *Dist.:* Buena Vista

TREASURE OF THE AMAZONS, THE 1985
Mexican
☆ **NR Action-Adventure 1:44**
☑ Nudity, adult situations, explicit language, graphic violence
Dir: Rene Cardona, Jr. *Cast:* Stuart Whitman, Emilio Fernandez, Donald Pleasence, Bradford Dillman, John Ireland
▶ Low-rent hokum set in South America about an Amazonian expedition searching for lost gold. Whitman plays an irascible guide; Pleasence is an ex-Nazi whose native wife helps him through the jungle. Inept plot features plenty of violence.
Dist.: Vestron

TREASURE OF THE SIERRA MADRE, THE 1948
★ ★ ★ ★ **NR Action-Adventure 2:06 B&W**
Dir: John Huston *Cast:* Humphrey Bogart, Walter Huston, Tim Holt, Bruce Bennett, Barton MacLane, Alfonso Bedoya
▶ Down-and-out Americans Bogart and Holt seek to change their luck by teaming with veteran prospector Huston to mine for gold in Mexican mountains. Trio strikes paydirt and accumulates riches, causing Bogart and Holt to grow paranoid about being robbed by comrades. Timeless masterpiece employs action and intrigue to examine corruption of human spirit. Film won Oscars for father-son team John Huston (Director and Screenplay) and Walter Huston (Supporting Actor), an Academy first.
Dist.: MGM/UA

TREASURE OF THE YANKEE ZEPHYR 1983
Australian/New Zealand
★ ★ ★ **PG Action-Adventure 1:38**
☑ Adult situations, explicit language, violence
Dir: David Hemmings *Cast:* Ken Wahl, George Peppard, Lesley Ann Warren, Donald Pleasence
▶ Elderly Pleasence discovers wreck of World War II plane filled with gold bars and is kidnapped by wealthy villain Peppard. Pleasence's daughter Warren and partner Wahl team up to rescue him and beat Peppard to the treasure. Above-average genre effort with plenty of action.
Dist.: Vestron

TREE GROWS IN BROOKLYN, A 1945
★ ★ ★ ★ **NR Drama 2:08 B&W**
Dir: Elia Kazan *Cast:* Dorothy McGuire, Joan Blondell, James Dunn, Peggy Ann Garner, Lloyd Nolan, Ted Donaldson
▶ Classic, endearing tale of bright young Garner's coming of age in a Brooklyn tenement. She's a dreamer who idolizes her alcoholic, ne'er-do-well father, Dunn, and resents her down-to-earth mother, McGuire. Blondell plays a beloved aunt. Oscars for Dunn and

Garner. Kazan's directorial debut. Based on the popular novel by Betty Smith. **(CC)**
Dist.: CBS/Fox

TREMORS 1990
★ ★ ★ ★ **PG-13 Horror 1:38**
☑ Explicit language, violence
Dir: Ron Underwood *Cast:* Kevin Bacon, Fred Ward, Finn Carter, Michael Gross, Reba McEntire, Bobby Jacoby
▶ Strange seismic activity under an isolated Nevada town turns out to be four giant worms who burst from the ground to devour human prey. Geologist Carter and handyman Bacon investigate, while survivalist Gross and wife McEntire wind up battling the ferocious creatures in their basement rec room. Uncertain tone mars otherwise entertaining monster pic. Country music megastar McEntire deserves some points for choosing this unusual vehicle for her film debut. **(CC)**
Dist.: MCA

TRENCHCOAT 1983
★ ★ **PG Comedy 1:31**
☑ Explicit language, violence
Dir: Michael Tuchner *Cast:* Margot Kidder, Robert Hays, David Suchet, Gila von Weitershausen, Daniel Faraldo, Ronald Lacey
▶ Court stenographer Kidder travels to Malta to write a mystery novel, then finds herself in the middle of an international plot to steal plutonium. Hays, a handsome stranger with uncertain motives, offers help when Kidder is kidnapped by Arabs. Attempt by Disney Studio to broaden its image offers engaging performances and beautiful scenery along with a farfetched plot.
Dist.: Buena Vista

TRESPASSES 1987
★ **R Drama 1:40**
☑ Rape, nudity, adult situations, explicit language, violence
Dir: Loren Bivens, Adam Roarke *Cast:* Robert Kuhn, Van Brooks, Mary Pillot, Adam Roarke, Lou Diamond Phillips, Ben Johnson
▶ Rancher Kuhn and married Pillot fall in love after he saves her from a rape attack. Her husband hires the men who attacked her to get revenge on Kuhn. Turgid Texas melodrama is slow-moving and suspenseless. Phillips co-wrote the script.
Dist.: Academy

TRIAL, THE 1963
☆ **NR Drama 1:58 B&W**
Dir: Orson Welles *Cast:* Anthony Perkins, Jeanne Moreau, Romy Schneider, Elsa Martinelli, Suzanne Flon, Orson Welles
▶ Kafka's classic story of anxiety and paranoia gets the Welles treatment. Perkins is Joseph K., who wakes one morning to find himself arrested, accused, and ostracized for a crime no one sees fit to mention. A bedridden Welles is his attorney, and Welles's servant Schneider becomes his mistress. Individual scenes are knockouts, but this is arty and self-

conscious to the point of appearing to parody its genre.
Dist.: Various

TRIBUTE 1981 Canadian
★ ★ ★ ★ **PG Comedy/Drama 1:59**
☑ Nudity, adult situations, explicit language
Dir: Bob Clark *Cast:* Jack Lemmon, Robby Benson, Lee Remick, Kim Cattrall, Colleen Dewhurst, John Marley
▶ Intellectual Benson is estranged from Lemmon, his frenetic, extroverted dad, a New York press agent who has just been diagnosed with terminal cancer. Aided by ex-wife/mom Remick, the two are reconciled and Benson arranges a testimonial for Lemmon in a Broadway theater. Moving family drama, powered by Lemmon's bravura performance. Based on the Broadway play by Bernard Slade, which starred the Tony-winning Lemmon.
Dist.: Vestron

TRICK OR TREAT 1986
★ **R Horror 1:37**
☑ Brief nudity, explicit language, violence
Dir: Charles Martin Smith *Cast:* Marc Price, Tony Fields, Lisa Orgolini, Doug Savant, Ozzy Osbourne, Gene Simmons
▶ Funny premise has dead heavy-metal star Fields returning to life when his record is played backward by high-school geek Price. Reborn rocker takes revenge on Price's jock enemies, then goes evilly wild on his own nemeses, including anti-rock preacher Osborne. Silly but well-made teen revenge movie has loud music and inside jokes for metalheads.
Dist.: Lorimar

TRICK OR TREATS 1982
★ **R Horror/Comedy 1:31**
☑ Explicit language, violence
Dir: Gary Graver *Cast:* Jackelyn Giroux, Peter Jason, Carrie Snodgress, David Carradine, Chris Graver
▶ Terrified babysitter horror spoof. Parents Snodgress and Carradine leave practical-joker son Graver with pretty blond sitter Giroux on Halloween eve. They are unknowingly stalked by Snodgress's first husband Jason, who has just escaped from the local insane asylum. Amiable tone, a few chuckles, and minor gore.
Dist.: Vestron

TRIO 1950 British
★ ★ **NR Drama 1:22 B&W**
Dir: Ken Annakin, Harold French *Cast:* James Hayter, Kathleen Harrison, Anne Crawford, Nigel Patrick, Jean Simmons, Michael Rennie
▶ Superbly entertaining follow-up to 1949's *Quartet* has W. Somerset Maugham introducing dramatizations of three more of his stories: "The Verger," "Mr. Know-All," and "Sanitorium." Each short piece is a classic of its kind,

skillfully blending wit, charm, and the author's flair for dramatic turnaround.
Dist.: Axon

TRIP, THE 1967
★ ★ **NR Drama 1:25**
☑ Nudity, adult situations, explicit language, violence
Dir: Roger Corman *Cast:* Peter Fonda, Susan Strasberg, Bruce Dern, Dennis Hopper, Dick Miller, Peter Bogdanovich
▶ Dated psychedelia from the era when folks didn't "just say no." Troubled TV director Fonda hooks up with guru Dern and decides to take LSD. The drug inspires a series of fantasies and unusual situations. Screenplay by Jack Nicholson.
Dist.: Vestron

TRIPLE ECHO 1973 British
★ **R Drama 1:30**
☑ Adult situations, explicit language
Dir: Michael Apted *Cast:* Glenda Jackson, Oliver Reed, Brian Deacon, Jenny Lee Wright
▶ Young soldier Deacon goes AWOL to live with lover Jackson. To fool the authorities, Deacon grows his hair long, dons a dress, and pretends to be Jackson's sister. Trouble comes in the form of tank-driving sergeant Reed, who takes a fancy to the ersatz lass. Intriguing situation is not fully explored; heavy and obscure. Also known as *Soldier in Skirts*.
Dist.: Paragon

TRIP TO BOUNTIFUL, THE 1985
★ ★ ★ ★ **PG Drama 1:46**
☑ Adult situations
Dir: Peter Masterson *Cast:* Geraldine Page, John Heard, Carlin Glynn, Richard Bradford, Rebecca De Mornay, Kevin Cooney
▶ In 1947, elderly widow Page lives in Houston with son Heard and daughter-in-law Glynn, but longs for one last visit to her hometown, Bountiful. One day she runs away, boarding a bus where she meets De Mornay, the young wife of a soldier. Seeing her old, tumbled-down home brings back a flood of memories. Richly detailed but slow moving drama won Page Best Actress Oscar. Horton Foote's screenplay was nominated. **(CC)**
Dist.: Nelson

TRIUMPH OF SHERLOCK HOLMES, THE 1935 British
★ **NR Mystery-Suspense 1:23 B&W**
Dir: Leslie S. Hiscott *Cast:* Arthur Wontner, Lyn Harding, Leslie Perrins, Jane Carr, Ian Fleming, Charles Mortimer
▶ Sherlock Holmes (Wontner) retires, but an intriguing murder case brings him back into action. Despite the skepticism of Dr. Watson (Fleming) and Inspector Lestrade (Mortimer), Holmes senses the involvement of Professor Moriarty (Harding). The answer to the mystery may not be elementary, but unfortunately the stage-bound filmmaking and acting are. Wontner looks right but lacks spark as Holmes;

Harding is a hammy villain. Based on Sir Arthur Conan Doyle's *The Valley of Fear.*
Dist.: Goodtimes

TRIUMPH OF THE SPIRIT 1989
★ ★ ★ R Biography 2:00
☑ Adult situations, graphic violence
Dir: Robert M. Young   *Cast:* Willem Dafoe, Edward James Olmos, Robert Loggia, Wendy Gazelle, Kelly Wolf, Costas Mandylor
▶ True story of Greek-Jewish boxer Salamo Arouch (Dafoe), who is sent with his family to Auschwitz by the Nazis. When the Germans stage boxing matches among inmates, Arouch must literally fight to survive: losers are sent to the gas chambers. Young's direction and the screenplay are overly blunt, but this Holocaust story's basic power is undeniable. (CC)
Dist.: RCA/Columbia

TRIUMPH OF THE WILL 1935 German
★ NR Documentary 1:50 B&W
Dir: Leni Riefenstahl
▶ Chilling documentary of Nazi rallies in Nuremberg, 1934, is among the most influential pieces of propaganda ever filmed. Shot with cooperation of armed forces, this powerful record remains fascinating despite distasteful subject matter. Opening sequence depicting Hitler's descent from majestic clouds is often cited as a perfect montage.
Dist.: Various

TRIUMPHS OF A MAN CALLED HORSE 1983 U.S./Mexican
★ ★ ★ ★ PG Western 1:26
☑ Explicit language, violence
Dir: John Hough   *Cast:* Richard Harris, Michael Beck, Ana De Sade, Anne Seymour, Vaughn Armstrong, Buck Taylor
▶ In 1875, English nobleman Harris, captured by Sioux and inducted into tribe thirty years previous, is now an aged warrior determined to halt invasion of Indian territory by gold prospectors. Gunmen, hoping to rile Sioux onto warpath, kill Harris. His son Beck, aided by feisty Crow girl De Sade, must fill father's moccasins in battle against outsiders. Preceded by *A Man Called Horse* and *Return of a Man Called Horse.*
Dist.: HBO

TROJAN WOMEN, THE 1972 Greek/U.S.
☆ PG Drama 1:25
☑ Adult situations
Dir: Michael Cacoyannis   *Cast:* Katharine Hepburn, Irene Papas, Genevieve Bujold, Vanessa Redgrave, Patrick Magee, Brian Blessed
▶ Powerhouse cast headlines adaptation of the classic Euripides tragedy. When Helen (Papas) is abducted by Hecuba's (Hepburn) son Paris, the Greeks attack Troy, killing all the men and sending the women, including Redgrave and Bujold, off to slavery. Filmed translations of classic tragedies are inherently problematic and the stagnant mounting here doesn't do justice to the four marvelous actresses.
Dist.: IVE

TROLL 1986
★ ★ PG-13 Horror 1:23
☑ Explicit language, violence
Dir: John Buechler   *Cast:* Michael Moriarty, Shelley Hack, Nan Hathaway, Jennifer Beck, June Lockhart, Phil Fondacaro
▶ Book reviewer Moriarty, wife Hack, and kids Hathaway and Beck move into new San Francisco apartment. Soon evil troll possesses Beck, causing havoc at home and trouble in other apartments. Good witch Lockhart enlists aid of Hathaway to defeat troll. Undemanding genre exercise.
Dist.: Vestron

TROMA'S WAR 1988
☆ R Action-Adventure 1:39
☑ Nudity, explicit language, violence
Dir: Michael Herz   *Cast:* Carolyn Beauchamp, Sean Bowen, Michael Ryder, Patrick Weathers, Jessica Dublin, Steven Crossley
▶ Surviving a plane crash on a jungle island, an assortment of citizens from Tromaville, N.J., discover that the island is being used by terrorists to launch an invasion against the U.S. Patriotic Tromavillians thwart the terrorists and save America. Though deliberately tasteless, witless, and cheap-looking, this fails to amuse even on a camp level.
Dist.: Media

TRON 1982
★ ★ ★ PG Animation/Sci-Fi 1:36
☑ Mild violence
Dir: Steven Lisberger   *Cast:* Jeff Bridges, David Warner, Cindy Morgan, Bruce Boxleitner, Barnard Hughes, Dan Shor
▶ In the future, most lives are controlled by the Master Computer. Evil executive Warner secretly plots to control the computer. Freethinking computer whiz Bridges, seeking to prove Warner stole programs he created, is transformed into miniaturized prisoner of Master Computer's microcircuits. There Bridges and friends must engage Warner and Master Computer in video game warfare. Disney adventure combines live-action with animation. Breathtaking video game action compensates for confusing plot.
Dist.: Buena Vista

TROOP BEVERLY HILLS 1989
★ ★ ★ ★ PG Comedy 1:40
☑ Explicit language
Dir: Jeff Kanew   *Cast:* Shelley Long, Craig T. Nelson, Betty Thomas, Mary Gross, Jenny Lewis, Stephanie Beacham
▶ Long is a shopaholic Beverly Hills housewife who becomes den mother to a troop of "Wilderness Girls." Nasty scout leader Thomas goes berserk when pampered Long moves a camp-out to a hotel bungalow, and teaches her girls decidedly nonwilderness crafts like

jewelry appraisal and sushi appreciation. In the end, heroine and troop have to prove their mettle in grueling Jamboree hike. Formula comedy works, thanks to sparkling star. (CC)
Dist.: RCA/Columbia

TROUBLE IN MIND 1985
★ ★ R Drama 1:52
☑ Nudity, adult situations, explicit language, violence
Dir: Alan Rudolph *Cast:* Kris Kristofferson, Genevieve Bujold, Lori Singer, Keith Carradine, Joe Morton, Divine
▶ After serving a prison sentence, ex-detective Kristofferson moves into apartment over a diner run by former lover Bujold. He is drawn into the lives of small-time hood Carradine and girlfriend Singer. When crime kingpin Divine orders hit on Carradine, Kristofferson intervenes for Singer's sake. Moody, atmospheric, and often meandering yarn spells trouble for many fans of director Rudolph and adventurous may find rewards. (CC)
Dist.: Nelson

TROUBLE IN PARADISE 1932
★ ★ NR Comedy 1:23 B&W
Dir: Ernst Lubitsch *Cast:* Herbert Marshall, Miriam Hopkins, Kay Francis, Charles Ruggles, Edward Everett Horton, C. Aubrey Smith
▶ Suave jewel thief Marshall worms his way into the household of rich Parisian widow Francis, only to find that his rival and ex-lover Hopkins also has designs on the widow's fortune. Sly, elegant trifle may be the most sophisticated and enjoyable of director Lubitsch's comedies. Horton is hilarious as one of the thieves' former victims.
Dist.: MCA

TROUBLE IN THE GLEN 1953 British
☆ NR Comedy 1:31
Dir: Herbert Wilcox *Cast:* Margaret Lockwood, Orson Welles, Forrest Tucker, Victor McLaglen, John McCallum, Janet Barrow
▶ Domineering South American mogul Welles moves to the Scottish highlands and quickly gets into a battle with residents over the use of a local highway. American Tucker tries to mediate the dispute and ends up winning Welles's daughter Lockwood. Welles's performance provides most of the fun here. Screenwriter Frank S. Nugent adapted a Maurice Walsh story, as he did in *The Quiet Man*.
Dist.: Republic

TROUBLE WITH ANGELS, THE 1966
★ ★ ★ NR Comedy/Family 1:52
Dir: Ida Lupino *Cast:* Rosalind Russell, Hayley Mills, June Harding, Binnie Barnes, Camilla Sparv, Gypsy Rose Lee
▶ Mother Superior Russell has heavenly hands full with mischievous convent students Mills and Harding, whose pranks scandalize the nuns. Russell manages to tame Mills and bring out her more serious instincts. Genial comedy

spawned sequel *Where Angels Go—Trouble Follows.*
Dist.: RCA/Columbia

TROUBLE WITH GIRLS, THE 1969
★ ★ ★ G Musical 1:44
Dir: Peter Tewksbury *Cast:* Elvis Presley, Marlyn Mason, Nicole Jaffe, Sheree North, Vincent Price, John Carradine
▶ Presley leads an old-time variety entertainment troupe through the 1920s Midwest. Carradine is a visiting Shakespearean, Price a pompous moral reformer, and their stories intersect with numerous backstage romances and intrigues all broadly nostalgic in tone. Uncharacteristic Elvis vehicle has the King singing only one complete song, the minor hit "Clean Up Your Own Backyard."
Dist.: MGM/UA

TROUBLE WITH HARRY, THE 1955
★ ★ ★ PG Comedy 1:39
Dir: Alfred Hitchcock *Cast:* Shirley MacLaine, John Forsythe, Edmund Gwenn, Mildred Natwick, Mildred Dunnock, Jerry Mathers
▶ Vermont hunter Gwenn stumbles across corpse and, believing he's the accidental killer, buries the body. But dead man "Harry" refuses to stay buried: repeated discovery of corpse sets about romance between Gwenn and middle-aged spinster Natwick and between local artist Forsythe and Harry's widow MacLaine. Offbeat black comedy sports fine cast, saucy dialogue, and striking shots of New England in autumn. Screen debut for MacLaine; catchy score by Bernard Herrmann was first in famed collaboration with director Hitchcock.
Dist.: MCA

TROUBLE WITH SPIES, THE 1987
★ PG Comedy 1:29
☑ Brief nudity, explicit language, mild violence
Dir: Burt Kennedy *Cast:* Donald Sutherland, Ruth Gordon, Ned Beatty, Robert Morley, Lucy Gutteridge, Michael Hordern
▶ Bumbling British agent Sutherland is sent by superior Morley to Mediterranean isle of Ibiza to ferret out Soviet spies who perfected truth serum. Sutherland takes room at hotel and romances proprietor Gutteridge. When unknown assailants attempt but fail to kill Sutherland, he suspects other guests Beatty, Gordon, and Hordern. Inspector Clouseau-style shenanigans don't quite work in this unfunny, unsatisfying spy concoction.
Dist.: HBO

TRUCK STOP WOMEN 1974
★ R Action-Adventure 1:28
☑ Nudity, adult situations, explicit language, violence
Dir: Mark L. Lester *Cast:* Claudia Jennings, Lieux Dressler, John Martino, Dennis Fimple, Dolores Dorn
▶ Restaurant fronting for prostitution ring is so

successful that the Mafia muscles in for a cut. Good-natured but badly dated sleaze features plenty of truck chases and nudity. Dressler stands out as a cynical madam. *Dist.:* Vestron

TRUE BELIEVER 1989
★ ★ ★ ★ **R Mystery-Suspense 1:44**
☑ Explicit language, violence
Dir: Joseph Ruben *Cast:* James Woods, Robert Downey, Jr., Margaret Colin, Yuji Okumoto, Kurtwood Smith, Tom Bower
► Lawyer Woods, an activist in the sixties, has settled into a lucrative but morally despicable practice of defending drug dealers. His long-dormant idealism is reawakened when he sets out to prove that convict Okumoto is innocent of an eight-year-old Chinatown murder. Riveting, both in and out of the courtroom, with gut-grabbing direction by Ruben. Commanding performance by Woods is ably supported by Downey as his young associate. (CC)
Dist.: RCA/Columbia

TRUE BLOOD 1988
★ ★ ★ **R Action-Adventure 1:37**
☑ Adult situations, explicit language, violence
Dir: Frank Kerr *Cast:* Jeff Fahey, Chad Lowe, Sherilyn Fenn, James Tolkan, Billy Drago, Ken Foree
► Brothers Fahey and Lowe are separated during a crime in which a cop is killed. Ten years later, they meet again, with Lowe now a law-abiding ex-Marine, and Fahey working for criminal gang-boss Drago. Can Lowe bring his brother back from a life of crime? Solid action and well-drawn characters.
Dist.: RCA/Columbia

TRUE CONFESSIONS 1981
★ ★ ★ **R Drama 1:48**
☑ Nudity, adult situations, explicit language, violence
Dir: Ulu Grosbard *Cast:* Robert De Niro, Robert Duvall, Charles Durning, Ed Flanders, Burgess Meredith, Rose Gregorio
► In 1930s Los Angeles, shabby police detective Duvall, investigating brutal slaying of girl, follows the trail to building contractor Durning, a major contributor to the wealthy parish run by ambitious priest De Niro, Duvall's brother. Brothers clash as Duvall, formerly corrupt and now in pursuit of justice no matter the cost, exhorts worldly De Niro to assist in arrest of Durning. Slow but sure-handed character study mixes the disparate views of a sleazy crime underworld and the church. Adapted by John Gregory Dunne and wife Joan Didion from his novel.
Dist.: MGM/UA

TRUE GRIT 1969
★ ★ ★ ★ ★ **G Western 2:08**
Dir: Henry Hathaway *Cast:* John Wayne, Glen Campbell, Kim Darby, Jeff Corey, Robert Duvall, Dennis Hopper, Jeremy Slate, Strother Martin
► Feisty young Darby hires hard-drinking, over-the-hill U.S. Marshall Wayne to pursue Corey, her father's killer, into Indian territory. Straight-arrow Texas Ranger Campbell joins them in chase leading to shootouts with outlaws Duvall and Hopper and brushes with Indians. Immensely popular adaptation of the Charles Portis best-seller offers much to admire: sure-handed direction from veteran Hathaway (seventy-one years old at time), romantic cinematography, and charming interaction of Wayne and Darby. Wayne won first Oscar in forty years on screen, and reprised his role in 1975's *Rooster Cogburn*.
Dist.: Paramount

TRUE LOVE 1989
★ **R Comedy 1:24**
☑ Adult situations, explicit language
Dir: Nancy Savoca *Cast:* Annabella Sciorra, Ron Eldard, Star Jasper, Aida Turturro, Roger Rignack, Michael J. Wolfe
► Spirited comedy about the impending marriage of Bronx working-class couple Sciorra and Eldard. Surrounded by beer-guzzling buddies, Eldard proves irresponsible and uncommitted, but Sciorra's determined to get him to the altar regardless of what it takes. Rooted in ethnic New York humor, sly look at contemporary love rituals proves a solid directing debut for Savoca.
Dist.: MGM/UA

TRUE STORIES 1986
★ **PG Musical/Comedy 1:51**
☑ Adult situations
Dir: David Byrne *Cast:* David Byrne, John Goodman, Swoosie Kurtz, Spalding Gray, Annie McEnroe, Joe Harvey Allen
► Narrator Byrne leads tour of small town Virgil, Texas, on state's 150th anniversary. Musical encounters with eccentric citizens include lovable bachelor Goodman advertising for wife; Kurtz, who hasn't left bed in years; and lying Allen who claims to have written "Billie Jean" and be pals with Rambo. Directing debut for Byrne, lead singer of rock group Talking Heads, has charming bits and lively tunes by Byrne and band, but patronizing tone and frequent flat spots sabotage effort. (CC)
Dist.: Warner

TUCKER: THE MAN AND HIS DREAM 1988
★ ★ ★ ★ **PG Biography 1:51**
☑ Explicit language
Dir: Francis Ford Coppola *Cast:* Jeff Bridges, Joan Allen, Martin Landau, Frederic Forrest, Mako, Dean Stockwell, Elias Koteas, Christian Slater, Don Novello
► True story of 1940s inventor Preston Tucker (Bridges). Although his plan to make a luxurious, safe, and affordable automobile was destroyed by big-business conspiracy, his essential optimism remained unvanquished. Coppola directs with a technical exuberance

and Bridges performs with an upbeat energy perfectly reflecting their visionary subject in this irresistible biography. Dazzling production design, bouncy Joe Jackson score, and an Oscar-nominated supporting performance by Landau as Bridges's business partner.
Dist.: Paramount

TUCK EVERLASTING 1980
★ ★ ★ NR Family 1:40
Dir: Frederick King Keller *Cast:* Margaret Chamberlain, James McGuire, Paul Flessa, Fred A. Keller, Sonia Raimi, Bruce D'Auria
► Young girl is introduced to the Tuck family, wealthy New Yorkers whose estate contains a mysterious spring. The Tucks reveal the secret of their drinking water, only to fall victim to an unscrupulous stranger who greedily attempts to steal their land. Despite budget restrictions, an intelligent, rewarding family film adapted from Natalie Babbitt's absorbing novel.
Dist.: Vestron

TUFF TURF 1985
★ ★ ★ R Drama 1:52
☑ Nudity, adult situations, explicit language, graphic violence
Dir: Fritz Kiersch *Cast:* James Spader, Kim Richards, Robert Downey, Jr., Paul Mones, Matt Clark, Claudette Nevins
► Spader, a Connecticut youth transferred to tough Los Angeles high school, becomes the target of a gang of thugs when he pursues beautiful moll Richards. Visually stylish drama features a strong soundtrack (including Marianne Faithfull and Jim Carroll) and a good performance by Downey as Spader's only friend. (CC)
Dist.: New World

TULIPS 1981 Canadian
★ PG Comedy 1:32
☑ Adult situations, explicit language
Dir: Stan Ferris *Cast:* Gabe Kaplan, Bernadette Peters, Henry Gibson, Al Waxman, David Boxer
► Suicidal tuba player Kaplan hires hit man Gibson to knock him off. Gibson is determined to complete the assignment, even after Kaplan falls in love with fellow suicidal-type Peters, and decides life is worth living after all. Peters is appealingly kooky, but film is a hodgepodge, having been directed by Waxman, Mark Warren, and Rex Bromfield, and ultimately credited to the fictitious Ferris.
Dist.: Nelson

TULSA 1949
★ ★ NR Drama 1:30
Dir: Stuart Heisler *Cast:* Susan Hayward, Robert Preston, Pedro Armendariz, Lloyd Gough, Chill Wills, Ed Begley
► Hayward enters the oil business to avenge the death of her father at the hands of petroleum magnate Gough. But she finds herself joining Gough in a massive drilling project that disgusts environmentally minded boyfriend Preston. Preston's worst fears come true

when a fiery disaster erupts, and all their lives are imperiled. With lots to look at, big melodrama sweeps the viewer along.
Dist.: Cable

TUMBLEWEEDS 1925
★ NR Western 1:21 B&W
Dir: King Baggot *Cast:* William S. Hart, Barbara Bedford, Lucien Littlefield, J. Gordon Russell, Richard R. Neill
► Cowboy hero Hart wants to settle down with Bedford in western Oklahoma. But the government is restricting access, and would-be settlers are forced to line up on the border waiting for the cannon shot that will set off a mad dash for territory. Hart gets to the border late, but once he's off, his race through the horse and wagon pack is thrilling. Accurate restaging of the great Oklahoma Land Race is the highlight of this silent Western.
Dist.: Video Yesteryear

TUNES OF GLORY 1960 British
★ ★ ★ NR Drama 1:47
Dir: Ronald Neame *Cast:* Alec Guinness, John Mills, Dennis Price, Susannah York, John Fraser
► Scottish colonel Guinness drinks too much and maintains loose discipline; his men adore him. When by-the-book Mills arrives to replace Guinness, intraregiment conflict is created. Masterful drama, with towering performances by Guinness and Mills. Oscar-nominated screenplay by James Kennaway, adapted from his novel.
Dist.: Nelson

TUNNEL 1988 Spanish
☆ R Drama
☑ Nudity, adult situations, explicit language
Dir: Antonio Drove *Cast:* Jane Seymour, Peter Weller, Fernando Rey, Victoria Zinni, Marga Herrera, Oscar San Juan
► In 1940s Argentina, painter Weller becomes obsessed with Seymour, whom he spots engrossed in his work at an art show. When she suddenly disappears from the gallery, he finds out where she lives, and his efforts to become part of her life turn desperate and deadly. Lush romantic melodrama looks classy, but takes itself too seriously.
Dist.: Vestron

TUNNELVISION 1976
★ R Comedy 1:08
☑ Nudity, explicit language, adult humor
Dir: Brad Swirnoff, Neil Israel *Cast:* Phil Proctor, Rich Hurst, Laraine Newman, Howard Hesseman, Roger Bower, Ernie Anderson
► Collection of irreverent skits purporting to show how TV had advanced by 1985 is a tasteless and uneven hodgepodge of parodies and one-liners that are often extremely dated. Frequent cameos by future stars (Chevy Chase, Ron Silver, Tom Davis, Al Franken, etc.) can't salvage the endless Richard Nixon jokes.
Dist.: MPI

TURK 182! 1985
★ ★ ★ ★ PG-13 Drama 1:36
☑ Adult situations, explicit language
Dir: Bob Clark *Cast:* Timothy Hutton, Robert Urich, Kim Cattrall, Robert Culp, Darren McGavin, Peter Boyle
▶ Renegade graffiti artist Hutton avenges the injustices done to his firefighter brother Urich, disabled in the line of duty. His acts of rebellion catch the attention of the entire city, culminating in a climatic scheme to disrupt the lighting of the Queensboro Bridge during a celebration. Cattrall plays a social worker romantically involved with Hutton. Street-smart script will have viewers rooting for the underdog. **(CC)**
Dist.: CBS/Fox

TURNAROUND 1987
★ ★ R Action-Adventure 1:37
☑ Adult situations, explicit language, violence
Dir: Ola Solum *Cast:* Eddie Albert, Doug McKeon, Gayle Hunnicutt, Tim Maier, Jonna Lee
▶ A biker gang terrorizes Albert and grandson McKeon, both of whom are practicing magicians. When the police prove to be no help, prestidigitatory pair trick the bikers into coming after them again—only this time, twosome have magical surprises up their sleeves. Obvious revenge scenario, but less violent than most of this type.
Dist.: Palisades

TURNER & HOOCH 1989
★ ★ ★ ★ ★ PG Comedy 1:40
☑ Explicit language, violence
Dir: Roger Spottiswoode *Cast:* Tom Hanks, Mare Winningham, Craig T. Nelson, Reginald VelJohnson, Scott Paulin, Beasley the Dog
▶ When a friend is murdered, fussy police detective Hanks takes in the only witness, a mangy junkyard dog named Hooch. The sloppy canine proceeds to drool over and destroy much of the cop's belongings, but ultimately proves to be man's best friend. Surefire crowd pleaser with nifty comic chemistry between the accomplished Hanks and his adorably ugly canine co-star. Jokes, including lots of dog slobber, may aim low, but score frequently. Winningham is sweet as the veterinarian/love interest. **(CC)**
Dist.: Buena Vista

TURNING POINT, THE 1977
★ ★ ★ ★ PG Drama/Dance 1:59
☑ Adult situations, explicit language
Dir: Herbert Ross *Cast:* Shirley MacLaine, Anne Bancroft, Mikhail Baryshnikov, Tom Skerritt, Leslie Browne, Martha Scott
▶ Longterm friendship between Bancroft, a famous ballerina, and MacLaine, a former dancer who gave up her career to be a wife and mother in Oklahoma, is threatened when MacLaine's daughter Browne, a promising ballerina, has a shot at the kind of career her mother gave up. Baryshnikov, in his film debut, co-stars as Browne's partner on stage and in the bedroom; Skerritt plays MacLaine's husband. High-quality soap opera enlivened by extraordinary dancing. Eleven Oscar nominations.
Dist.: CBS/Fox

TURTLE DIARY 1986 British
★ ★ ★ PG Drama 1:36
☑ Adult situations, explicit language
Dir: John Irvin *Cast:* Glenda Jackson, Ben Kingsley, Michael Gambon, Richard Johnson, Harriet Walter, Jeroen Krabbe
▶ Lonely Londoners Kingsley and Jackson share a passion for sea turtles. With the help of sympathetic zookeeper Gambon, they devise a plan to free turtles from the zoo and bring them to sea. Slyly intelligent and touchingly humane. Harold Pinter's screenplay refreshingly avoids clichés. Subtle performances by the leads, but slow pace and film's narrow scope may not appeal to mainstream audiences.
Dist.: Vestron

TWELVE ANGRY MEN 1957
★ ★ ★ NR Drama 1:35 B&W
Dir: Sidney Lumet *Cast:* Henry Fonda, Lee J. Cobb, Martin Balsam, Jack Klugman, Ed Begley, Jack Warden, E. G. Marshall, John Fiedler
▶ Jurors convene to decide on a seemingly cut-and-dried murder case. Eleven vote guilty but holdout Fonda gradually convinces others of his views, although Cobb (the angriest of the angry men) fights him all the way. One-set movie is incredibly engrossing; co-producer Fonda leads an outstanding ensemble. Oscar nominations for Picture, Director, Screenplay (Reginald Rose, who adapted his television play). **(CC)**
Dist.: CBS/Fox

TWELVE CHAIRS, THE 1970
★ ★ G Comedy 1:33
Dir: Mel Brooks *Cast:* Ron Moody, Frank Langella, Dom DeLuise, Mel Brooks, Bridget Brice
▶ In 1927 Russia, fallen aristocrat Moody is informed by dying mama that ten years ago she hid a cache of jewels in one of twelve matching chairs. His search for the chairs takes him across Russia and into Siberia, aided by beggar Langella and priest DeLuise, who heard mama's dying confession. Don't miss Brooks's tune, "Hope for the Best (Expect the Worst)."
Dist.: Media

TWELVE O'CLOCK HIGH 1949
★ ★ ★ ★ ★ NR War 2:12 B&W
Dir: Henry King *Cast:* Gregory Peck, Hugh Marlowe, Gary Merrill, Dean Jagger, Millard Mitchell, Paul Stewart
▶ Compelling World War II drama examines how the burdens of leadership affect Peck,

commander of a B-17 bomber squadron stationed in England. At first a strict disciplinarian, he loses objectivity when he starts to identify with his men. Influential film highlighted by adroit use of combat footage and Oscar-winning support by Jagger. Loosely based on the experiences of Maj. Gen. Frank Armstrong.
Dist.: CBS/Fox

TWENTIETH CENTURY 1934
★ ★ ★ ★ NR Comedy 1:31 B&W
Dir: Howard Hawks *Cast:* John Barrymore, Carole Lombard, Roscoe Karns, Walter Connolly, Ralph Forbes, Etienne Girardot
▶ Delightful screwball farce about egomaniacal director Barrymore who pins his fading fortunes on former protégé Lombard, now a Hollywood goddess engaged to lunkhead football player Forbes. Barrymore's zany schemes to win back Lombard during a train journey from Chicago to New York range from dazzling insults to camel imitations. Brilliant script by Ben Hecht and Charles MacArthur inspired the Broadway musical *On the Twentieth Century*.
Dist.: RCA/Columbia

20,000 LEAGUES UNDER THE SEA 1954
★ ★ ★ ★ G Sci-Fi 2:07
Dir: Richard Fleischer *Cast:* Kirk Douglas, James Mason, Paul Lukas, Peter Lorre, Robert J. Wilke, Carleton Young
▶ Walt Disney classic based on the novel by Jules Verne. In 1868, professor Lukas, his aide Lorre, and harpoonist Douglas are taken prisoner by visionary scientist Captain Nemo (Mason) on his advanced submarine, the *Nautilus*. Nemo plans to use his craft to enforce world peace; Douglas tries to stop him. Beautifully crafted and acted, particularly Mason and Lorre. Oscars for Special Effects and Art/Set Decoration.
Dist.: Buena Vista

TWICE DEAD 1988
★ R Horror 1:30
☑ Nudity, adult situations, explicit language, graphic violence
Dir: Bert Dragin *Cast:* Tom Breznahan, Jill Whitlow, Jonathan Chapin, Christopher Burgard
▶ Chapin, a long-dead actor, comes to the aid of teenagers Breznahan and Whitlow when they move into his old house and are terrorized by a gang of punks. Ghostly presence gruesomely picks off punks one by one, saving the leader (also played by Chapin) for an especially horrible demise. Predictable story has very bloody ending.
Dist.: Nelson

TWICE IN A LIFETIME 1985
★ ★ ★ R Drama 1:45
☑ Adult situations, explicit language
Dir: Bud Yorkin *Cast:* Gene Hackman, Ellen Burstyn, Ann-Margret, Ally Sheedy, Amy Madigan, Brian Dennehy
▶ Powerhouse cast enhances familiar story of

middle-aged Hackman, who leaves wife Burstyn for barmaid Ann-Margret. The breakup causes havoc for the couple's daughters Madigan and Sheedy. Madigan cannot forgive her father but, despite her objections, Sheedy invites him to her wedding. Emotionally charged domestic drama will strike a responsive chord in many viewers. (CC)
Dist.: Vestron

TWICE TOLD TALES 1963
★ ★ NR Horror 2:00
Dir: Sidney Salkow *Cast:* Vincent Price, Sebastian Cabot, Mari Blanchard, Brett Halsey, Richard Denning, Beverly Garland
▶ Price has three roles in a solid adaptation of Nathaniel Hawthorne stories: "Dr. Heidegger's Experiment" tells of Cabot's revival of dead wife Blanchard, who reveals a secret about Price; "Rappaccini's Daughter" has been raised on deadly herbs for Price's sadistic experiment; star visits *The House of the Seven Gables* and encounters a ghost.
Dist.: MGM/UA

TWILIGHT'S LAST GLEAMING 1977
U.S./German
★ ★ ★ ★ R Drama 2:24
☑ Adult situations, explicit language, violence
Dir: Robert Aldrich *Cast:* Burt Lancaster, Richard Widmark, Charles Durning, Melvyn Douglas, Paul Winfield, Burt Young
▶ Vietnam vet Lancaster takes over Strategic Air Command base and attempts to blackmail President Durning into revealing the true reasons for our country's involvement in the war. Despite predictable plotting, ambitious, high-powered thriller offers a convincing indictment of military arrogance.
Dist.: CBS/Fox

TWILIGHT ZONE—THE MOVIE 1983
★ ★ ★ PG Sci-Fi 1:41
☑ Explicit language, graphic violence
Dir: John Landis, Steven Spielberg, Joe Dante, George Miller *Cast:* Vic Morrow, Scatman Crothers, Kathleen Quinlan, Kevin McCarthy, Jeremy Licht, William Schallert, John Lithgow, Dan Aykroyd, Albert Brooks
▶ Anthology of four supernatural tales, three based on old "Twilight Zone" episodes, gained considerable notoriety for the death of Morrow during a Vietnam battle sequence. Other stories include a saccharine fantasy about an old age home, a chilling version of "It's a Good Life" in which a child's magical powers turn his home into a terrifying cartoon, and a breathtaking "Nightmare at 20,000 Feet," with Lithgow as a paranoid airplane passenger who sees a monster lurking on the wing. Narrated by Burgess Meredith.
Dist.: Warner

TWINS 1988
★ ★ ★ ★ PG Comedy 1:43
☑ Adult situations, explicit language, violence

Dir: Ivan Reitman *Cast:* Danny DeVito, Arnold Schwarzenegger, Kelly Preston, Chloe Webb, Bonnie Bartlett, Marshall Bell
▶ Schwarzenegger and DeVito are fraternal twins, spawned by a scientific experiment and separated at birth. Schwarzenegger, raised by a scientist on a remote island, is now an intellectual straight-shooter. DeVito, kicked out of convent school for corrupting a nun, is a womanizing, thieving hustler. Reunited twins search for their long-lost mom while evading hit man who's after DeVito's hide. Broad, outlandish comic fare, with DeVito carrying most of the comic muscle.
Dist.: MCA

TWINS OF EVIL 1972 British
★ R Horror 1:27
☑ Nudity, adult situations, violence
Dir: John Hough *Cast:* Madeleine Collinson, Mary Collinson, Peter Cushing, Kathleen Bryon, Dennis Price, Damien Thomas
▶ The Collinson twins are orphans taken in by their uncle Cushing, an ace witch hunter. The bad twin gets involved with vampire Thomas, who turns her into a bloodsucker. Cushing is tricked into thinking the good twin is the vampire. Former *Playboy* playmates Madeleine and Mary are an eyeful in an above-par fright movie.
Dist.: VidAmerica

TWIST, THE 1976 French
☆ NR Comedy 1:45
☑ Nudity, adult situations, explicit language
Dir: Claude Chabrol *Cast:* Bruce Dern, Stephane Audran, Ann-Margret, Charles Aznavour, Curt Jergens, Maria Schell
▶ Comedy of manners with American writer Dern married to fiery Frenchwoman Audran, who fantasizes that Dern is having an affair with translator Ann-Margret. Dern, in turn, begins to suspect that his wife is having her own affair. Hard to tell what the story is getting at, and romantic intrigues are not very interesting.
Dist.: IVE

TWIST AND SHOUT 1986 Danish
★ R Drama 1:47
☑ Nudity, strong sexual content, adult situations
Dir: Billie August *Cast:* Adam Tonsberg, Lars Simonsen, Camilla Soeberg, Ulrikke Juul Bondo, Thomas Nielsen, Lone Lindorff
▶ Round-robin of teen love in Denmark: straitlaced blond Bondo dotes on handsome drummer Tonsberg; Tonsberg and voluptuous beauty Soeberg are madly in love; Tonsberg's best pal Simonsen has unrequited crush on Bondo. When Soeberg gets pregnant and rejects Tonsberg after abortion, he reevaluates Bondo's romantic overtures. Sequel to director August's *Zappa.* [S]
Dist.: HBO

TWISTER 1989
☆ PG-13 Drama 1:33
☑ Adult situations, explicit language
Dir: Michael Almereyda *Cast:* Harry Dean Stanton, Suzy Amis, Crispin Glover, Dylan McDermott, Jenny Wright, Charlaine Woodard
▶ Strange Kansas family led by Stanton includes layabout daughter Amis and would-be artist son Glover. Siblings are determined to find the mother who abandoned them years before, but only Stanton knows the real secret of her disappearance. Truly weird melodrama is quirky in the extreme, and may have been intended to be a comedy.
Dist.: Vestron

TWO DAUGHTERS 1961 Indian
☆ NR Drama 1:54 B&W
Dir: Satyajit Ray *Cast:* Anil Chatterjee, Chandana Bannerjee, Soumitra Chatterjee, Aparna des Gupta, Sita Mukherji, Gita Dey
▶ Two sensitively directed short stories from India's greatest filmmaker: "The Postmaster" stars Bannerjee as a young orphan girl who develops a close relationship with postmaster Anil Chatterjee. "Samapti" tells of law student Soumitra Chatterjee, who eschews his mother's choices for his bride to marry des Gupta. Also known as *Teen Katya.* [S]
Dist.: Nelson

TWO ENGLISH GIRLS 1971 French
★ NR Drama 1:48
☑ Strong sexual content, adult situations
Dir: François Truffaut *Cast:* Jean-Pierre Leaud, Kika Markham, Stacey Tendeter, Sylvia Marriott, Marie Mansart, Philippe Leotard
▶ At the turn of the century, Frenchman Leaud romances two proper Welsh sisters, Markham and Tendeter. Markham is fragile, but desperately passionate; Tendeter is virginal and realistic about love; and both are profoundly attached to their free-loving Frenchman. Critically acclaimed romance is based on a novel by Henri-Pierre Roch. Twenty-four minutes were added to a later version, released in 1984. [S]
Dist.: Key

TWO-FACED WOMAN 1941
★ NR Comedy 1:34 B&W
Dir: George Cukor *Cast:* Greta Garbo, Melvyn Douglas, Constance Bennett, Roland Young, Robert Sterling, Ruth Gordon
▶ Garbo is worried that new husband Douglas will fall for his old girlfriend, playwright Bennett, so she pretends to be her own twin in an effort to distract his wandering tendencies. But Douglas is onto her scheme, and has fun pretending to be seduced by the ersatz sister. Garbo's last film is mildly entertaining, but she may have been miscast in this uncharacteristic comedy.
Dist.: MGM/UA

TWO FOR THE ROAD 1967 British
★★ NR Drama 1:53
Dir: Stanley Donen *Cast:* Audrey Hepburn,

Albert Finney, Eleanor Bron, William Daniels, Claude Dauphin, Jacqueline Bisset
▶ Trip to France by an unhappily married couple—architect Finney and disillusioned wife Hepburn—prompts a series of flashbacks showing their earlier relationship. Despite irritatingly trendy direction, a generally satisfying romance highlighted by Bron's amusing turn as an American tourist and Henry Mancini's lush score. Oscar-nominated screenplay by Frederic Raphael.
Dist.: CBS/Fox

TWO GIRLS AND A SAILOR 1944
★ ★ NR Musical 2:04 B&W
Dir: Richard Thorpe *Cast:* Van Johnson, June Allyson, Gloria De Haven, Jimmy Durante, Tom Drake, Lena Horne, Gracie Allen, Jose Iturbi, Buster Keaton
▶ In New York, sailor Johnson and soldier Drake meet singing sisters Allyson and De Haven. A love quadrangle ensues, complicated by the secret of Johnson's wealth, but all ends happily. Sprightly fun, with lots of terrific music, including Durante's "Inka Dinka Doo" and Horne's "Paper Doll."
Dist.: MGM/UA

TWO HUNDRED MOTELS 1971
☆ R Musical 1:38
☑ Nudity, explicit language, adult humor
Dir: Frank Zappa, Tony Palmer *Cast:* Ringo Starr, Theodore Bikel, Keith Moon, Jimmy Carl Black, The Mothers of Invention, Frank Zappa
▶ Ostensibly about exploits of rock band on tour, with the Mothers of Invention as themselves and bewigged, goateed Starr as bandleader Zappa, film is more a hodgepodge of visual effects and music laced with Zappa's trademark subversive wit. Predecessor to music videos was first color feature to be shot on tape and transferred to film. Result is uneven and often unsettling, but some moments are truly inspired.
Dist.: MGM/UA

TWO LOST WORLDS 1950
★ NR Action-Adventure 1:03 B&W
Dir: Norman Dawn *Cast:* James Arness, Laura Elliot, Bill Kennedy, Gloria Petroff, Tom Hubbard, Jane Harlan
▶ After suffering an injury, American boat captain Arness recuperates in Australia. He falls in love with local lady Elliot, who is then abducted by pirates. Rescuing her is only half the battle: a volcano and a shipwreck are also part of the adventure. Crudely made, not very thrilling.
Dist.: SVS

TWO MOON JUNCTION 1988
★ ★ R Drama 1:44
☑ Nudity, strong sexual content, explicit language, mild violence
Dir: Zalman King *Cast:* Sherilyn Fenn, Richard Tyson, Louise Fletcher, Kristy McNichol, Martin Hewitt, Burl Ives

▶ Southern deb Fenn bypasses square fiancé Hewitt to find sexual fulfillment with carny lug Tyson. McNichol is a loose midway girl, and Fletcher is a family matriarch in this torrid, lust-laden trip to the class-anxious precincts of plantationland.
Dist.: RCA/Columbia

TWO MULES FOR SISTER SARA 1970
★ ★ ★ ★ PG Western 1:45
☑ Adult situations, explicit language, violence
Dir: Don Siegel *Cast:* Clint Eastwood, Shirley MacLaine, Monolo Fabregas, Alberto Morin, Armando Silvestre, John Kelly
▶ During the Mexican Revolution, taciturn drifter Eastwood rescues nun MacLaine from rapists, then reluctantly agrees to help her attack a French fortress. Eastwood is troubled by his unnatural attraction to MacLaine, who eventually reveals a surprising background. Apart from the bloody climax, a lighthearted Western showcasing the stars' natural charm.
Dist.: MCA

TWO OF A KIND 1983
★ ★ ★ PG Fantasy 1:27
☑ Adult situations, explicit language, violence
Dir: John Herzfeld *Cast:* Olivia Newton-John, John Travolta, Charles Durning, Beatrice Straight, Scatman Crothers, Oliver Reed
▶ Angels Durning, Straight, and Crothers convince God (voice of Gene Hackman) to put the Apocalypse on hold, claiming they can prove the existence of selflessness on earth by following the lives of two star-crossed lovers: New York inventor Travolta, in debt to the Mob, and aspiring actress Newton-John, working as a bank teller. He tries to rob her bank, she steals his loot. Satan (Reed) himself appears to thwart them but love—and salvation—triumphs. (CC)
Dist.: CBS/Fox

TWO RODE TOGETHER 1961
★ ★ ★ NR Western 1:49
Dir: John Ford *Cast:* James Stewart, Richard Widmark, Shirley Jones, Linda Cristal, Andy Devine, John McIntire
▶ Cavalry lieutenant Widmark agrees to pay corrupt sheriff Stewart five hundred dollars for each hostage taken from the Comanche tribe who kidnapped them years earlier, but their mission leads to bloodshed and tragedy. Somber, thoughtful Western features a convincing performance by Stewart in an atypical role.
Dist.: RCA/Columbia

2001: A SPACE ODYSSEY 1968 U.S./British
★ ★ ★ G Sci-Fi 2:18
Dir: Stanley Kubrick *Cast:* Keir Dullea, Gary Lockwood, William Sylvester, Daniel Richter, Leonard Rossiter
▶ In 2001, the discovery of a mysterious monolith beneath moon's surface initiates voyage

to Jupiter. In deep space, computer HAL (voice of Douglas Rain) goes berserk; astronauts Dullea and Lockwood seek to turn off the machine that runs the ship. Landmark special effects movie with ape-to-astronaut theme evokes widespread opinions; with minimal dialogue and ambiguous ending leaving many unmoved. Virtuoso visuals (Oscar winner for special effects), filmed in widescreen Cinerama, lose impact on video.
Dist.: MGM/UA

2010 1984
★ ★ ★ ★ **PG Sci-Fi 1:56**
☑ Explicit language, mild violence
Dir: Peter Hyams *Cast:* Roy Scheider, John Lithgow, Helen Mirren, Bob Balaban, Keir Dullea
► Sequel to *2001: A Space Odyssey* finds U.S. and Russia on brink of war, but scientists unite to locate missing spaceship from *2001*. American leader Scheider, guilt-ridden by role in original mission, brings along colleagues Lithgow and Balaban for journey to Jupiter on Soviet craft skippered by Mirren. Scientists reactivate computer HAL (voice of Douglas Rain), encounter lone survivor of *2001* launch (Dullea), and discover truth of mystic monolith. High-tech sequel has more drama and humanity than original.
Dist.: MGM/UA

TWO TICKETS TO BROADWAY 1951
★ **NR Musical 1:46**
Dir: James V. Kern *Cast:* Tony Martin, Janet Leigh, Gloria De Haven, Eddie Bracken, Ann Miller, Barbara Lawrence
► Leigh leaves her Vermont hometown to make it in New York show biz. She joins De Haven's all-girl act and finds romance with singer Martin. However, incompetent agent Bracken's machinations almost sink her love life and career. Lighthearted and lively. Songs include "The Closer You Are," "Let the Worry Bird Worry for You," and "Big Chief Hole-in-the-Ground."
Dist.: Turner

TWO WAY STRETCH 1960 British
★ **NR Comedy 1:20 B&W**
Dir: Robert Day *Cast:* Peter Sellers, Wilfrid Hyde-White, Lionel Jeffries, Liz Fraser, Maurice Denham
► Sellers is a prisoner enjoying all the comforts of home when former partner Hyde-White comes to him proposing the perfect heist. There's only one catch: they have to break out of prison to pull it off. Very funny, with an involving plot; Sellers is wonderful.
Dist.: HBO

TWO WOMEN 1961 Italian
★ **NR Drama 1:39 B&W**
Dir: Vittorio De Sica *Cast:* Sophia Loren, Jean-Paul Belmondo, Eleonora Brown, Raf Vallone, Renato Salvatori
► During World War II, Italian mother Loren and adolescent daughter Brown attempt to survive as the Allies invade and the Germans retreat. Both fall for farmer's son Belmondo but hardships ensue after the women are raped by Allied soldiers. Their efforts to deal with the attack and Brown's burgeoning womanhood make for an emotion-packed, immensely moving film. Staggering performance by Loren nabbed Best Actress Oscar. **(CC)** Ⓢ
Dist.: Nelson

TYCOON 1947
★ ★ ★ **NR Drama 2:08**
Dir: Richard Wallace *Cast:* John Wayne, Laraine Day, Cedric Hardwicke, Judith Anderson, James Gleason, Anthony Quinn
► Mining magnate Hardwicke hires engineer Wayne to build a railroad over the Andes but balks at Wayne's plan for an expensive bridge instead of a hazardous tunnel. Wayne further complicates matters by falling for Hardwicke's daughter Day. Lengthy but engrossing drama with the Duke performing smartly in an atypical role.
Dist.: Turner

UFORIA 1980
☆ **PG Sci-Fi 1:34**
☑ Adult situations, explicit language, mild violence
Dir: John Binder *Cast:* Cindy Williams, Harry Dean Stanton, Fred Ward, Beverly Hope Atkinson, Harry Carey, Jr., Diane Deifendorf
► Drifter Ward falls for Williams, a born-again supermarket checkout clerk who believes she's been chosen as a Noah for an imminent UFO expedition. Bogus faith healer Stanton publicizes her mission in an effort to earn money. Eccentric but good-natured blend of comedy, romance, and science fiction may please fans of the offbeat.
Dist.: MCA

UGETSU 1953 Japanese
☆ **NR Drama 1:36 B&W**
Dir: Kenji Mizoguchi *Cast:* Machiko Kyo, Massayuki Mori, Kinuyo Tanaka, Sakae Ozawa, Mitsuko Mito, Sugisaku Aoyama
► In sixteenth-century Japan, brothers Ozawa and Mori make pots and dream of being important men. While war rages around them, Mori leaves his wife and is made a pampered prisoner by a beautiful female ghost. Ozawa leaves his family and becomes a swaggering samurai. Both men are almost destroyed by their fantasies, and their families are shattered. There is pure artistry at work in the carefully controlled imagery, but the mix of reality and supernatural in this critically hailed film requires considerable concentration. Also known as *Ugetsu Monogatari.* Ⓢ
Dist.: Video Yesteryear

UGLY AMERICAN, THE 1963
★ ★ **NR Drama 2:00**
Dir: George Englund *Cast:* Marlon Brando, Eiji Okada, Sandra Church, Pat Hingle, Arthur Hill, Jocelyn Brando

▶ Former journalist Brando is appointed ambassador to Vietnam-like country. Although he is friendly with rebel leader Okada, Brando finds himself caught between government and Communist factions. Cautionary tale of political intrigue highlighted by Brando's change-of-pace performance.
Dist.: MCA

UGLY DACHSHUND, THE 1966
★★★★ NR Comedy/Family 1:33
Dir: Norman Tokar ***Cast:*** Dean Jones, Suzanne Pleshette, Charles Ruggles, Kelly Thordsen, Mako
▶ The ugly dachshund is actually a Great Dane who grows up with the smaller breed and adopts their mannerisms. Husband Jones enters the big beast against one of his wife Pleshette's dachshunds in a dog show. Friendly Disney antics stolen by the four-legged thespians.
Dist.: Buena Vista

UHF 1989
★ PG-13 Comedy 1:37
☑ Explicit language, adult humor
Dir: Jay Levey ***Cast:*** Weird Al Yankovic, Victoria Jackson, Kevin McCarthy, Michael Richards, David Bowe, Billy Barty
▶ Yankovic inherits a floundering TV station and rehabs it with crazy shows of his own devising. Result is a few mildly amusing parodies, but Yankovic does not have enough comedic presence to carry the picture, and childish, undisciplined humor is tired and overfamiliar. (CC)
Dist.: Orion

ULTIMATE THRILL, THE 1974
★ PG Mystery-Suspense 1:50
☑ Adult situations, violence
Dir: Robert Butler ***Cast:*** Barry Brown, Britt Ekland, Eric Braeden, Michael Blodgett, John Davis Chandler, Paul Felix
▶ Ekland, married to executive Brown, carries on with other men. He learns of her infidelity and goes crazy, tailing his wife and murdering her lovers. Some nice mountain backdrops but ultimately nothing thrilling. Also known as *The Ultimate Chase*.
Dist.: Congress

ULTIMATE WARRIOR, THE 1975
★★ R Sci-Fi 1:34
☑ Adult situations, explicit language, violence
Dir: Robert Clouse ***Cast:*** Yul Brynner, Max Von Sydow, Joanna Miles, William Smith, Richard Kelton
▶ Twenty-first century New York City, decimated by plagues, provides the battleground for fight to the finish between commune headed by Von Sydow and deadly rivals led by Smith. Brynner, a hero known as Knife Fighter, arrives to lead Von Sydow's sister Miles to safety in New Jersey. Routine adventure marred by cheap special effects.
Dist.: Warner

ULYSSES 1955 Italian
★★ NR Action-Adventure 1:44
Dir: Mario Camerini ***Cast:*** Kirk Douglas, Anthony Quinn, Silvana Mangano, Rossana Podesta
▶ Adventurer Douglas suffers amnesia after fighting in the Trojan War. As he recovers on an island in the care of princess Podesta, his wife Mangano is pursued by his rival Quinn. Douglas's brawny heroics highlight this exciting adapation of Homer's *The Odyssey*. Dubbed.
Dist.: Warner

ULYSSES 1967
★★ NR Drama 2:20 B&W
Dir: Joseph Strick ***Cast:*** Barbara Jefford, Milo O'Shea, Maurice Roeves, T. P. McKenna, Martin Dempsey, Sheila O'Sullivan
▶ Ambitious adaptation of one of this century's greatest works of literature. O'Shea is impotent Irish Jew Leopold Bloom, walking the streets of Dublin, hooking up with poet Roeves, and reflecting on wife Jefford's infidelity and on tragedies in his past. Uneven, but captures some of author James Joyce's spirit.
Dist.: Mystic Fire

ULZANA'S RAID 1972
★★ R Western 1:43
☑ Brief nudity, adult situations, explicit language, graphic violence
Dir: Robert Aldrich ***Cast:*** Burt Lancaster, Bruce Davison, Jorge Luke, Richard Jaeckel, Joaquin Martinez, Lloyd Bochner
▶ Liberal lieutenant Davison, on the trail of renegade Apaches, comes into conflict with scout Lancaster, a hardened veteran who shows no mercy for the savages. Tough, extremely violent Western can be viewed as a provocative allegory on the Vietnam War. Third teaming of Lancaster and director Aldrich (after *Apache* and *Vera Cruz*).
Dist.: MCA

UMBERTO D 1955 Italian
★ NR Drama 1:29 B&W
Dir: Vittorio De Sica ***Cast:*** Carlo Battisti, Maria Pia Casilio, Lina Gennari
▶ Old-age pensioner Battisti struggles desperately to keep himself from being thrown out of his apartment. He tries to raise money by selling his belongings and borrowing from his friends, but only his faithful dog Flick stands by him to the end. Poignant, critically acclaimed, and quite depressing. [S]
Dist.: Nelson

UMBRELLAS OF CHERBOURG, THE 1964 French
★ NR Musical 1:31
Dir: Jacques Demy ***Cast:*** Catherine Deneuve, Nino Castelnuovo, Anne Vernon, Marc Michel, Ellen Farner, Mireille Perrey
▶ Young lovers Deneuve and Castelnuovo are separated when he's drafted into the army for two years; her pregnancy forces a hard decision steeped in sorrow. Cinematic

operetta, in which all dialogue is sung, features haunting music by Michel Legrand and a stunning young Deneuve. However, mainstream audiences will be put off by this stylized experiment. Oscar-nominated for Best Foreign Film, Story and Screenplay, Song ("I Will Wait For You"), and Score. Available dubbed. [S]
Dist.: USA

UNAPPROACHABLE, THE 1984 German
☆ **NR Comedy/Drama 1:32**
☑ Adult situations
Dir: Krzysztof Zanussi ***Cast:*** Leslie Caron, Daniel Webb, Leslie Malton
▶ Reclusive retired actress Caron lives near Berlin in a mansion with her maid Malton. The household is invaded by Webb, a young man who claims to be a crime victim but may have more sinister intentions. Interminable gabfest never rises above its pretensions, despite a game cast.
Dist.: MGM/UA

UNBEARABLE LIGHTNESS OF BEING, THE 1988
★★★ **R Drama/Romance 2:52**
☑ Nudity, strong sexual content, adult situations, explicit language
Dir: Philip Kaufman ***Cast:*** Daniel Day-Lewis, Juliette Binoche, Erland Josephson, Lina Olin, Derek de Lint, Pavel Landowsky
▶ In Prague, 1966, just before Russian invasion of Czechoslovakia, promiscuous young surgeon Day-Lewis, dedicated to privacy and loneliness, enjoys unfettered life—a "lightness of being." Then he meets romantic waitress Binoche; she and the arrival of Russian tanks prompt Day-Lewis to reconsider philosophy of life. Day-Lewis, Binoche, and his on-again, off-again lover, Olin, all flee to safety of Geneva for further explorations of fidelity, eroticism, and politics. Fine young cast in a sensuous and provocative adaptation of the novel by Czech author Milan Kundera. (CC)
Dist.: Orion

UNCLE BUCK 1989
★★★★ **PG Comedy 1:40**
☑ Adult situations, explicit language
Dir: John Hughes ***Cast:*** John Candy, Amy Madigan, Jean Louisa Kelly, Gaby Hoffman, Macaulay Culkin, Elaine Bromka
▶ Parents put teenaged daughter Kelly and small son Hoffman under charge of slovenly uncle Candy. Kelly is hostile when Candy tries to interfere with her love life, though she comes to see that he's actually a cool guy after he helps her get back at a two-timing boyfriend. Many of the characters' motives are obscure, but Candy is jovially agreeable, and Kelly is super as the embittered teen. (CC)
Dist.: MCA

UNCOMMON VALOR 1983
★★★★ **R Action-Adventure 1:45**
☑ Explicit language, violence
Dir: Ted Kotcheff ***Cast:*** Gene Hackman, Patrick Swayze, Robert Stack, Randall "Tex" Cobb, Fred Ward, Reb Brown
▶ Grieving Hackman, convinced son is still alive ten years after he was reported missing in action in Vietnam, traces him to a prison camp in Laos. Financed by oil tycoon Stack, whose boy is also missing, Hackman assembles former members of son's Marine outfit for rescue mission. After an attempt by CIA to derail raid, Hackman and crew sneak into Laos. Plenty of gut-busting action, rough-and-ready heroes, and impressive stunts in upbeat film. (CC)
Dist.: Paramount

UNDEFEATED, THE 1969
★★★ **G Western 1:59**
Dir: Andrew V. McLaglen ***Cast:*** John Wayne, Rock Hudson, Roman Gabriel, Tony Aguilar, Lee Meriwether, Merlin Olsen
▶ In post-Civil War Mexico, Union officer Wayne, on mission to deliver horse herd, meets up with Southern counterpart Hudson. The two former foes team up when they run afoul of Mexican general Aguilar. The Duke, Hudson, and football stars Gabriel and Olsen add up to lots of beefy macho in an otherwise middling vehicle. (CC)
Dist.: CBS/Fox

UNDERACHIEVERS, THE 1987
★ **R Comedy 1:27**
☑ Nudity, adult situations, explicit language
Dir: Jackie Kong ***Cast:*** Edward Albert, Barbara Carrera, Michael Pataki, Susan Tyrrell, Mark Blankfield, Vic Tayback
▶ Failed shortstop Albert becomes narc at a combination reformatory-high school specializing in remedial education. Albert's arrest rate plummets when he falls for beautiful counselor Carrera, an unwilling accomplice in her colleague Tyrrell's dope ring. Low-budget, lowbrow high jinks climax in an extended catfight between Carrera and Tyrrell.
Dist.: Vestron

UNDER CAPRICORN 1949
★★★★ **NR Drama 1:57**
Dir: Alfred Hitchcock ***Cast:*** Ingrid Bergman, Joseph Cotten, Michael Wilding, Margaret Leighton, Cecil Parker
▶ Bergman, a seemingly frail alcoholic, is tormented by husband Cotten in nineteenth-century Australia. Wilding, a visitor from Ireland, upsets the household when he tries to free Bergman from her bondage. Leighton plays an evil housekeeper in love with Cotten. Obscure, unusual, slowly paced, and with little suspense; may disappoint Hitchcock fans.
Dist.: Prism

UNDER COVER 1987
★★★ **R Action-Adventure 1:34**
☑ Adult situations, explicit language, violence
Dir: John Stockwell ***Cast:*** David Neidorf,

Jennifer Jason Leigh, Barry Corbin, David Harris, Kathleen Wilhoite, John Philbin
▶ When his fellow cop is killed, Baltimore plainclothes expert Neidorf infiltrates South Carolina high school to break up drug ring. Helped by his beautiful new partner Leigh, Neidorf gathers evidence which is inexplicably ignored by his boss, Corbin. Overaged stars are too implausible for this routine tale. Stockwell's directing debut. **(CC)**
Dist.: Warner

UNDER FIRE 1983
★ ★ ★ ★ R Drama 2:08
☑ Brief nudity, adult situations, explicit language, graphic violence
Dir: Roger Spottiswoode **Cast:** Nick Nolte, Gene Hackman, Joanna Cassidy, Ed Harris, Jean-Louis Trintignant, Richard Masur
▶ Explosive tale of journalists covering Nicaraguan conflict combines complex politics, gritty action, and a convincing love triangle into engrossing entertainment. Hardened photo-journalist Nolte tests his objectivity when asked to stage a pro-terrorist picture that could contribute to the fall of Somoza's regime. Superb performances by Hackman, as a cynical editor, and Harris, as a gung-ho mercenary, add to picture's depth.
Dist.: Vestron

UNDER MILK WOOD 1973 British
☆ PG Drama 1:30
☑ Adult situations, explicit language
Dir: Andrew Sinclair **Cast:** Richard Burton, Elizabeth Taylor, Peter O'Toole, Glynis Johns, Vivien Merchant, Sian Phillips
▶ Episodic look at the people of Llaregubb, a Welsh fishing village, cuts among a variety of characters: blind sea captain O'Toole, shrewish butcher Merchant, local prostitute Taylor, etc. Based on a Dylan Thomas radio play, film offers engaging dialogue and settings but very little drama. Burton provides voice-over and appears briefly in transitions.
Dist.: CBS/Fox

UNDERSTUDY: GRAVEYARD SHIFT II, THE 1988
★ ★ R Horror 1:28
☑ Nudity, adult situations, explicit language, violence
Dir: Gerard Ciccoritti **Cast:** Wendy Gazelle, Mark Soper, Silvio Oliviero, Ilse Von Glatz, Tim Kelleher, Leslie Kelly
▶ Vampire Oliviero causes havoc on a horror movie set when he takes over for the leading man and begins a campaign of surreptitious blood sucking. Crewmember Soper must shoot pool with Oliviero for soul of starlet Gazelle. Erotic and scary, with good cast of unknowns. Sequel to *Graveyard Shift*.
Dist.: Virgin

UNDER THE BOARDWALK 1988
★ ★ R Drama 1:40
☑ Adult situations, explicit language, violence

Dir: Fritz Kiersch **Cast:** Keith Coogan, Danielle von Zerneck, Corky Carroll, Sonny Bono, Roxana Zal, Richard Joseph Paul
▶ Wealthy Californian von Zerneck falls for Valley guy Paul, her brother's rival in upcoming surfing competition, while Paul's nerdy cousin Coogan romances wave whiz Zal. In climactic meet Paul must either win the title for the honor of the Valley or give up the $5,000 prize for von Zerneck's love. Stale surfer saga with plenty of pecs and bikinis.
Dist.: New World

UNDER THE CHERRY MOON 1986
★ PG-13 Drama 1:40 B&W
☑ Adult situations, explicit language, violence
Dir: Prince **Cast:** Prince, Jerome Benton, Kristin Scott-Thomas, Steven Berkoff, Francesca Annis, Emmanuelle Sallet
▶ Bronx expatriate Prince searches for love on the French Riviera, settling on Scott-Thomas, an heiress to a shipping fortune. Romance hits a snag when Prince's best friend Benton questions his motives. Extravagant throwback to 1940s glamour musicals suffers from terminally silly plot. Although "Kiss" and other tunes from Prince's platinum album *Parade* are featured on soundtrack, film lacks musical scenes. **(CC)**
Dist.: Warner

UNDER THE GUN 1989
★ ★ R Action-Adventure 1:29
☑ Brief nudity, explicit language, violence
Dir: James Sbardellati **Cast:** Sam Jones, Vanessa Williams, John Russell, Michael Halsey, Sharon Williams, Bill McKinney
▶ St. Louis cop Jones goes to Los Angeles to get Russell, the plutonium-dealing crook who killed his brother. He links up with Williams, Russell's lawyer, who must be rescued when she's kidnapped by the bad guys. Dull, dismal thriller is Williams's film debut.
Dist.: Magnum

UNDER THE RAINBOW 1981
★ ★ PG Comedy 1:38
☑ Brief nudity, adult situations, explicit language, violence
Dir: Steve Rash **Cast:** Chevy Chase, Carrie Fisher, Eve Arden, Joseph Maher, Robert Donner, Billy Barty
▶ Scores of little people gather at a Hollywood hotel hoping for parts as Munchkins in *The Wizard of Oz;* talent scout Fisher, babysitting them, faces additional chaos from Secret Service agent Chase, a Japanese spy, visiting royalty, and midget assassins. Bright premise wears out quickly in this labored comedy.
Dist.: Warner

UNDER THE RED ROBE 1937 British
★ NR Action-Adventure 1:22 B&W
Dir: Victor Seastrom **Cast:** Conrad Veidt, Raymond Massey, Annabella, Romney Brent, Sophie Stewart, F. Wyndham Goldie
▶ In musketeer-era France, evil Cardinal Rich-

elieu snatches inveterate duellist Veidt from the gallows and sends him on a secret mission to capture a Protestant nobleman suspected of fomenting discontent. Veidt and comic servant Brent insinuate themselves into the nobleman's castle, where Veidt falls in love with his host's sister, Annabella. Pouchy, middle-aged Veidt is not the usual swashbuckling hero, and Annabella's acting is dreadful, but there's good, corny fun here.
Dist.: United

UNDER THE ROOFS OF PARIS 1930 French
★ NR Drama 1:32 B&W
Dir: René Clair ***Cast:*** Albert Prejean, Pola Illery, Gaston Modot, Edmond Greville, Paul Olivier, Bill Bocket
▸ When street singer Prejean is arrested for a crime he didn't commit, girlfriend Illery and best pal Greville wind up in each other's arms. At first he's upset, but when he sees that the two really are in love, he rejoins the couple as their friend. Simple tale, beautifully told on striking sets. [S]
Dist.: Video Yesteryear

UNDER THE VOLCANO 1984
★★ R Drama 1:52
☑ Nudity, adult situations, explicit language
Dir: John Huston ***Cast:*** Albert Finney, Jacqueline Bisset, Anthony Andrews, Ignacio Lopez Tarso, Katy Jurado, James Villiers
▸ In 1938, crises overwhelm alcoholic ex-British consul Finney on the Day of the Dead (November 1) in Mexico, despite the efforts of his estranged wife Bisset and half-brother Andrews to help. Ambitious attempt to adapt Malcolm Lowry's novel fails to capture book's dense symbolism, but offers strong performances, beautiful Gabriel Figueroa photography, and assured direction. Finney and soundtrack composer Alex North received Oscar nominations.
Dist.: MCA

UNDERWATER! 1955
★ NR Action-Adventure 1:39
Dir: John Sturges ***Cast:*** Jane Russell, Gilbert Roland, Richard Egan, Lori Nelson, Robert Keith, Jayne Mansfield
▸ Adventurer Roland joins Egan and wife Russell as they dive for Spanish gold in the Caribbean. While priest/advisor Keith looks on, they gingerly attempt to recover treasure from a sunken galleon perched on an underwater cliff. Not much excitement in this Howard Hughes-produced adventure, which pinned its hopes on Russell's figure and then-novel scuba diving.
Dist.: Turner

UNDERWORLD U.S.A. 1961
★★ NR Crime 1:38 B&W
Dir: Samuel Fuller ***Cast:*** Cliff Robertson, Dolores Dorn, Beatrice Coll, Larry Gates, Paul Dubov
▸ A child witnesses his dad's murder by four syndicate leaders. Growing up to become hoodlum Robertson, he joins the gang to get revenge against the killers. Explosive pace, moody direction, and intense performances deliver excitement.
Dist.: RCA/Columbia

UNEARTHLY, THE 1957
☆ NR Horror 1:13 B&W
Dir: Brooke L. Peters ***Cast:*** John Carradine, Allison Hayes, Myron Healey, Sally Todd, Tor Johnson
▸ Mad scientist Carradine lures victims to his secret lair, where he is conducting glandular experiments supposed to lead to eternal life. Among his would-be victims are escaped con Healey and attractive Hayes. Carradine's mutant helper Johnson helps turn the trick in Healey's favor when the hero makes his move. Camp laughs include *Plan 9 From Outer Space* vet Johnson given the unusual opportunity to speak.
Dist.: Rhino

UNFAITHFULLY YOURS 1948
★★★ NR Comedy 1:45 B&W
Dir: Preston Sturges ***Cast:*** Rex Harrison, Linda Darnell, Barbara Lawrence, Rudy Vallee, Kurt Kreuger, Lionel Stander
▸ Famed British conductor Harrison suspects hanky-panky between sexy young wife Darnell and his handsome personal secretary Kreuger. That night Harrison leads orchestra in three symphonies; mood of each causes him to imagine trio of different resolutions to romantic dilemma, including murder. Splendid Harrison carries fanciful farce by writer-director Sturges. Some flat moments in music-inspired fantasies; brilliant comic bits are compensation.
Dist.: CBS/Fox

UNFAITHFULLY YOURS 1984
★★★ PG Comedy 1:36
☑ Brief nudity, adult situations, explicit language, mild violence, adult humor
Dir: Howard Zieff ***Cast:*** Dudley Moore, Nastassja Kinski, Albert Brooks, Armand Assante, Richard Libertini, Cassie Yates
▸ Stylish remake of the 1948 Preston Sturges film about famous conductor Moore, who learns agent Brooks has assigned private eye to tail Moore's gorgeous young wife Kinski. Circumstantial evidence suggests Kinski has been having affair with violinist Assante, leading Moore to imagine murdering Kinksi and framing Assante for crime. When Moore tries to turn fantasy into fact, scheme goes comically awry. (CC)
Dist.: CBS/Fox

UNFORGIVEN, THE 1960
★★★ NR Western 2:05
Dir: John Huston ***Cast:*** Burt Lancaster, Audrey Hepburn, Audie Murphy, John Saxon, Charles Bickford, Lillian Gish
▸ Sprawling Western about a Texas cattle family battling Kiowa Indians over Hepburn,

an Indian orphan adopted by matriarch Gish. Uneven plot forsakes genuinely interesting racial themes and suggestions of incest (between Hepburn and Lancaster, playing Gish's blood son) for rousing attacks and fights.
Dist.: MGM/UA

UNHOLY, THE 1988
★ ★ R Horror 1:40
☑ Nudity, adult situations, explicit language, violence
Dir: Camilo Vila *Cast:* Ben Cross, Hal Holbrook, Jill Carroll, Trevor Howard, Ned Beatty, Nicole Fortier
▶ Archbishop Holbrook assigns previously invincible priest Cross to rid a New Orleans parish of the devil. Satanic cult prepares to sacrifice virgin waitress Carroll, while Cross battles Fortier, an incredibly erotic demon. Powerful stars lift this above similar horror vehicles.
Dist.: Vestron

UNHOLY ROLLERS, THE 1972
★ ★ R Action-Adventure 1:28
☑ Nudity, adult situations, explicit language, violence
Dir: Vernon Zimmerman *Cast:* Claudia Jennings, Louis Quinn, Betty Anne Rees, Roberta Collins, Alan Vint, Candice Roman
▶ Factory worker Jennings enters the roller derby circuit determined to become a star. Her teammates are dismayed when she rejects staged brawls and phony fights for real violence. Low-budget Roger Corman production may be the best film ever about roller derbies.
Dist.: HBO

UNIDENTIFIED FLYING ODDBALL, THE 1979
★ ★ ★ G Fantasy/Comedy 1:33
Dir: Russ Mayberry *Cast:* Dennis Dugan, Ron Moody, Jim Dale, Kenneth More, John Le Mesurier
▶ American scientist Dugan and his robot duplicate are transported into England during the reign of King Arthur (More). There Dugan runs afoul of the sorcerer Merlin (Moody). Disney high jinks adapted from Mark Twain's *A Connecticut Yankee in King Arthur's Court.*
Dist.: Buena Vista

UNION CITY 1980
☆ PG Drama 1:25
☑ Explicit language, violence
Dir: Mark Reichert *Cast:* Dennis Lipscomb, Deborah Harry, Irina Maleeva, Everett McGill, Sam McMurray, Pat Benatar
▶ Insecure husband Lipscomb, suspicious of slatternly wife Harry, murders an innocent drifter before succumbing to madness. Gloomy film noir set in 1953 was based on Cornell Woolrich's "The Corpse Next Door." Acting debut for Harry, former singer for rock group Blondie.
Dist.: RCA/Columbia

UNION PACIFIC 1939
★ ★ ★ NR Western 2:15 B&W

Dir: Cecil B. DeMille *Cast:* Barbara Stanwyck, Joel McCrea, Robert Preston, Akim Tamiroff, Brian Donlevy, Anthony Quinn
▶ Railroad executive McCrea builds the Union Pacific across the post–Civil War West, although bad guys, including his old war buddy Preston, try to stop him. Stanwyck, the woman involved with both men, reforms Preston. History-based tale provides larger-than-life excitement.
Dist.: MCA

UNMARRIED WOMAN, AN 1978
★ ★ ★ R Drama 2:04
☑ Nudity, adult situations, explicit language
Dir: Paul Mazursky *Cast:* Jill Clayburgh, Alan Bates, Michael Murphy, Cliff Gorman, Lisa Lucas, Kelly Bishop
▶ New Yorker Clayburgh faces difficult adjustment to single life when husband Murphy walks out for younger woman. After one-night stand with heel Gorman, she finds new love with passionate artist Bates, but maintains her hard-won independence. A winning drama whose sensitive script and direction convey contemporary humor, razor-sharp insight, and bright New York City atmosphere. Oscar-nominated Clayburgh is fabulous. A Best Picture nominee.
Dist.: CBS/Fox

UNREMARKABLE LIFE, AN 1989
★ PG Drama 1:38
☑ Adult situations
Dir: Amin Q. Chaudhri *Cast:* Patricia Neal, Shelley Winters, Mako, Rochelle Oliver, Charles Dutton, Lily Knight
▶ After living together for many years, middle-aged sisters Neal and Winters are jolted out of complacency when good-humored Asian mechanic Mako takes a romantic interest in Neal. Bitter and domineering Winters tries to keep Neal from reciprocating, but Neal struggles for independence. Despite clumsy direction, clichéd drama has its moments thanks to piece-of-cake performances from the three veteran leads.
Dist.: SVS

UNSEEN, THE 1980
★ R Horror 1:31
☑ Rape, nudity, explicit language, graphic violence
Dir: Peter Foleg *Cast:* Barbara Bach, Sydney Lassick, Stephen Furst, Lelia Goldoni, Karen Lamm, Doug Barr
▶ TV reporter Bach and two colleagues covering a Danish heritage festival in California are forced to stay in a remote mansion where Lassick and his sister Goldoni are hiding a dark family secret in the basement. Unimaginative horror film fails to exploit its incest premise with conviction.
Dist.: VidAmerica

UNSINKABLE MOLLY BROWN, THE 1964
★ ★ NR Biography/Musical 2:08
Dir: Charles Walters *Cast:* Debbie Rey-

nolds, Harve Presnell, Ed Begley, Jack Kruschen, Hermione Baddeley, Harvey Lembeck
▶ True story of Brown (Reynolds), who rises from poverty when her husband Presnell becomes rich. Acceptance in posh society eludes her until she achieves fame surviving the wreck of the *Titanic*. Oscar-nominated Reynolds is the prime attraction here. Based on the Broadway hit; hummable score by Meredith Wilson (*The Music Man*).
Dist.: MGM/UA

UNTIL SEPTEMBER 1984
★ ★ ★ **R Romance 1:35**
☑ Nudity, adult situations, explicit language
Dir: Richard Marquand *Cast:* Karen Allen, Thierry Lhermitte, Christopher Cazenove, Marie-Catherine Conti, Nitzi Saul
▶ Star-crossed romance between Allen, an American stranded in Paris, and Lhermitte, a well-to-do banker whose wife and children are in the country until September. The couple spend three idyllic weeks exploring Paris and the surrounding countryside. Will their summer love end? City of Lights never looked better; neither have the attractive leads. **(CC)**
Dist.: MGM/UA

UNTOUCHABLES, THE 1987
★ ★ ★ ★ ★ **R Action-Adventure 2:00**
☑ Explicit language, violence
Dir: Brian De Palma *Cast:* Kevin Costner, Sean Connery, Charles Martin Smith, Andy Garcia, Robert De Niro, Billy Drago, Richard Bradford, Jack Kehoe, Patricia Clarkson
▶ Smashing account of Federal agent Elliot Ness's (Costner) efforts to nab crimelord Al Capone (De Niro) is nonstop entertainment in the best Hollywood manner. Loosely inspired by the famous TV series, David Mamet's script offers excellent roles for Garcia (an Italian sharpshooter) and Drago (Capone's psychotic hitman Frank Nitti), but Connery steals the film in his Oscar-winning turn as an honest street cop who lends a guiding hand to Ness. Bravura shootout in Chicago's Union Station is only one of many highlights.
Dist.: Paramount

UP FROM THE DEPTHS 1979
★ **R Horror 1:25**
☑ Brief nudity, adult situations, explicit language, graphic violence
Dir: Charles B. Griffith *Cast:* Sam Bottoms, Suzanne Reed, Virgil Frye, Kedric Wolf, Charles Howerton
▶ Monstrous fish attacks visitors to a Hawaiian tourist resort, prompting locals to stage contest to capture it. Many lives are lost as the fish proves smarter than anticipated. Low-rent *Jaws* rip-off filmed in the Philippines makes a few stabs at humor, but its satire is as weak as the bloody action.
Dist.: Vestron

UP IN ARMS 1944
★ **NR Musical 1:46**
Dir: Elliott Nugent *Cast:* Danny Kaye, Dana

Andrews, Constance Dowling, Dinah Shore, Louis Calhern, Margaret Dumont
▶ The Army is sorry when it drafts Kaye: he's the world's most nervous hypochondriac. Admirer Shore has just what will cure him, but first she has to tear his eyes away from attractive nurse Dowling. Clever songs like "Melody in 4-F" and "The Lobby Number" are among Kaye's best, but frenetic star will get on some viewers' nerves.
Dist.: Nelson

UP IN SMOKE 1978
★ ★ ★ **R Comedy 1:27**
☑ Nudity, adult situations, explicit language
Dir: Lou Adler *Cast:* Cheech Marin, Thomas Chong, Stacy Keach, Edie Adams, Tom Skerritt, Zane Buzby
▶ Genial, irreverent comedy about barrio hustler and rich hippie searching for dynamite pot introduced comedy team Cheech and Chong to feature films. Bawdy, drug-oriented humor is broad and juvenile, but duo's good spirits are infectious. Keach mugs shamelessly as a redneck cop in pursuit of the pair; Buzby as a crazed hitchhiker has the most bizarre gags. Sequel: *Cheech & Chong's Next Movie*.
Dist.: Paramount

UP THE ACADEMY 1980
★ ★ **R Comedy 1:27**
☑ Explicit language, adult humor
Dir: Robert Downey *Cast:* Ron Leibman, Wendell Brown, Tom Citera, J. Hutchinson, Ralph Macchio, Tom Poston, Barbara Bach
▶ Raunchy teen comedy set in a military academy ruled by a sadistic major (Leibman, who had his name removed from film's publicity) is alternately tasteless, crude, and surprisingly funny. Poston is amusing as a swishy dance instructor; Bach has a cameo as a weapons instructor. Presented by *Mad* magazine.
Dist.: Warner

UP THE CREEK 1984
★ ★ **R Comedy 1:35**
☑ Nudity, adult situations, explicit language, violence
Dir: Robert Butler *Cast:* Tim Matheson, Jennifer Runyon, Stephen Furst, Dan Monahan, Jeff East, Blaine Novak
▶ Four college misfits led by Matheson must win white-water raft race to graduate; they're opposed by East's cruel preppies and Novak's vicious military academy rejects. Fitfully inspired comedy stretches thin; Chuck the Wonder Dog steals film in a hilarious charades sequence.
Dist.: Vestron

UP THE SANDBOX 1972
★ ★ **R Comedy/Drama 1:38**
☑ Adult situations, explicit language, violence
Dir: Irvin Kershner *Cast:* Barbra Streisand, David Selby, Barbara Rhodes, Jane Hoffman, Jacobo Morales, Ariane Heller

▶ New York housewife Streisand, mother of two with a third on the way, is unappreciated by professor husband Selby. She finds solace in fantasies about Africa, Fidel Castro, abortion, and other subjects. Uneven but challenging change-of-pace for Streisand. Based on the novel by Anne Richardson Roiphe.
Dist.: Warner

UPTOWN SATURDAY NIGHT 1974
★ ★ ★ PG Comedy 1:44
☑ Adult situations, explicit language, violence
Dir: Sidney Poitier *Cast:* Sidney Poitier, Bill Cosby, Harry Belafonte, Flip Wilson, Richard Pryor, Rosalind Cash
▶ Pals Poitier and Cosby sneak away from their wives and go to a gambling house. When the joint is robbed, the guys lose a wallet containing a winning lottery ticket. In their attempt to recover the item, they encounter gangster Belafonte, preacher Wilson, and others. Uproarious comedy led to sequel *Let's Do It Again*. Poitier holds his own among the all-star comic cast
Dist.: Warner

UP YOUR ALLEY 1989
★ ★ R Comedy 1:28
☑ Explicit language, violence
Dir: Bob Logan *Cast:* Linda Blair, Murray Langston, Bob Zany, Ruth Buzzi, Johnny Dark, Jack Hanrahan
▶ When someone murders Los Angeles homeless people, reporter Blair goes undercover to investigate. She gets romantically involved with beggar Langston (who co-wrote script), who is later unjustly accused of the crimes. Homelessness played for laughs is surprisingly amusing, although Buzzi's overstated performance as a sex-crazed bag lady is hard to take. Yakov Smirnov and Tom Dreesen are among the comics in brief parts.
Dist.: IVE

URBAN COWBOY 1980
★ ★ ★ ★ PG Romance 2:15
☑ Adult situations, explicit language, violence
Dir: James Bridges *Cast:* John Travolta, Debra Winger, Scott Glenn, Madolyn Smith, Barry Corbin
▶ Tough-talking but soft-hearted honky-tonk romance between refinery worker Travolta and Winger, a girl he picks up at the world-famous Gilley's bar. They marry but face troubles: while Travolta wrestles both Gilley's mechanical bull and debutante Smith, bad guy Glenn catches Winger on the rebound. Familiar boy-meets-girl tale enlivened by down-home Texas flavor, sassy soundtrack, and electrifying chemistry between leads. Sexiest scene: Winger rides the bull.
Dist.: Paramount

URGH! A MUSIC WAR 1982
☆ R Documentary/Music 2:04
☑ Adult situations, explicit language

Dir: Derek Burbidge *Cast:* Devo, The Go-Gos, Dead Kennedys, The Police, Joan Jett, UB40
▶ Concert film shot in New York, California, France, and England eschews interviews to concentrate on the music, mostly New Wave and punk. Thirty-seven different acts perform. If you like these groups, you'll enjoy this well-produced rockumentary. Otherwise, stay away. Our favorites: the Police and UB40.
Dist.: CBS/Fox

USED CARS 1980
★ ★ ★ R Comedy 1:52
☑ Brief nudity, explicit language, adult humor
Dir: Robert Zemeckis *Cast:* Kurt Russell, Jack Warden, Gerrit Graham, Frank McRae, Deborah Harmon, Joe Flaherty
▶ The Fuchs brothers (Warden, in a dual role) compete viciously with rival car dealerships. When the kindly Fuchs dies, aspiring politician and master salesman Russell disregards ethics in an epic battle of wits with the nasty Fuchs brother. Breathless, tasteless, insulting, genuinely inventive comedy is remarkably funny until the forced climax. Kudos to Peanuts, a brilliant pooch. Produced by Steven Spielberg and John Milius.
Dist.: RCA/Columbia

UTOPIA 1950 French
★ NR Comedy 1:20 B&W
Dir: Leo Joannon *Cast:* Stan Laurel, Oliver Hardy, Suzy Delair, Max Elloy
▶ Laurel and Hardy are shipwrecked on a uranium-laden island, where they set up Hardy as the head of an "ideal state." Last film of the legendary comedy duo is depressingly unfunny, with a terminally ill Laurel seemingly unaware of where he is, and Hardy randomly inflecting his lines. If you love the team, avoid this. Also known as *Atoll K* and *Robinson Crusoeland*.
Dist.: Video Yesteryear

UTU 1983 New Zealand
☆ R Action-Adventure 1:44
☑ Brief nudity, adult situations, violence
Dir: Geoff Murphy *Cast:* Anzac Wallace, Bruno Lawrence, Wi Kuki Kaa, Tim Elliot, Ilona Rodgers, Tania Bristowe
▶ When nineteenth-century Maori native Wallace discovers his tribe has been slaughtered by European troops, he gathers followers and declares war on whites. The cycle of "utu" is continued when Lawrence seeks revenge against Wallace for his wife's death. Soldiers also pursue the Maori in this exotic, beautifully photographed epic. **(CC)**
Dist.: CBS/Fox

U2: RATTLE AND HUM 1988
★ ★ ★ PG-13 Documentary/Music 1:39 C/B&W
☑ Explicit language
Dir: Phil Joanou *Cast:* Bono Vox, The Edge, Larry Mullen, Jr., Adam Clayton, B. B. King

▶ American odyssey of U2 rock group alternates concert footage with scenes of four band members discovering their stateside musical roots. Quartet re-records hit "I Still Haven't Found What I'm Looking For" with Harlem gospel singers and cuts "Love Comes to Town" with bluesmaster King. Concert tunes include cover versions of Beatles' "Helter Skelter" and Bob Dylan's "All Along the Watchtower."
Dist.: Paramount

VAGABOND 1986 French
☆ **NR Drama 1:45**
☑ Nudity, adult situations, explicit language
Dir: Agnes Varda ***Cast:*** Sandrine Bonnaire, Macha Meril, Stephane Freiss, Laurence Cortadellas, Marthe Jarnias, Yolande Moreau
▶ In the south of France, eighteen-year-old Bonnaire hitchhikes, does odd jobs, lives in a tent through the winter, forms fleeting relationships with those she encounters, and meets a tragic fate. Bonnaire's performance is haunting in this finely detailed portrait, although the vivid depiction of her lifestyle is extremely depressing. [S]
Dist.: Pacific Arts

VALENTINO RETURNS 1989
★★ **R Drama 1:30**
☑ Nudity, explicit language
Dir: Peter Hoffman ***Cast:*** Barry Tubb, Frederic Forrest, Veronica Cartwright, Jenny Wright, Miguel Ferrer, Leonard Gardner
▶ During the 1950s, small-town teen Tubb gets into scrapes with the law and bikers and has romance with trashy Wright. Meanwhile, his mom Cartwright walks out on alcoholic, philandering dad Forrest. Good cast, but coming-of-age tale lacks fire due to aimless plotting. Gardner, who adapted his short story "Christ Has Returned to Earth and Preaches Here Nightly," plays Forrest's pal.
Dist.: Vidmark

VALET GIRLS 1987
★ **R Comedy 1:23**
☑ Nudity, adult situations, explicit language
Dir: Rafal Zielinski ***Cast:*** Meri D. Marshall, April Stewart, Mary Kohnert, Christopher Weeks, Patricia Scott Michel
▶ Aspiring singer Marshall, psychology major Stewart, and Southern belle Kohnert displace three jealous male carhops at a slimy agent's endless parties. The boys respond with a series of practical jokes, hoping to get the girls fired. Brainless comedy fails to deliver enough gags.
Dist.: Vestron

VALLEY GIRL 1983
★★ **R Romance/Comedy 1:39**
☑ Nudity, explicit language
Dir: Martha Coolidge ***Cast:*** Nicolas Cage, Deborah Foreman, Colleen Camp, Frederic Forrest, Michael Bowen
▶ Foreman is like totally a valley girl and must choose between surfer boyfriend Bowen and Cage, the punkish Hollywood dude she meets at a party. Meanwhile, she has to work in the totally gross health food store run by Forrest and Camp, her hippie parents. Slightly better-than-average teen flick was inspired by the pop song.
Dist.: Vestron

VALLEY OF THE DOLLS 1967
★★ **PG Drama 2:03**
☑ Adult situations, explicit language
Dir: Mark Robson ***Cast:*** Barbara Parkins, Patty Duke, Susan Hayward, Sharon Tate, Martin Milner, Lee Grant
▶ Parkins, Duke, and Tate seek show business fame and fortune but soon run into professional problems, drugs, bad affairs, and disease. Trashy and vulgar with little redeeming social value; nevertheless, kind of fun. Based on Jacqueline Susann's best-seller.
Dist.: CBS/Fox

VALLEY OF THE SUN 1942
★ **NR Western 1:24 B&W**
Dir: George Marshall ***Cast:*** Lucille Ball, James Craig, Cedric Hardwicke, Dean Jagger, Peter Whitney, Billy Gilbert
▶ Government investigator Craig pretends to be a renegade scout to expose the criminal doings of Jagger, a corrupt Indian agent. Cross-purposes are intensified as both men court local restaurateur Ball. Fairly interesting duel of personalities in old Arizona.
Dist.: Turner

VALMONT 1989
★★ **R Drama 2:14**
☑ Brief nudity, adult situations
Dir: Milos Forman ***Cast:*** Colin Firth, Annette Bening, Meg Tilly, Fairuza Balk, Sian Phillips, Fabia Drake, Jeffrey Jones, Henry Thomas, T. P. McKenna
▶ Close on the heels of Stephen Frears's *Dangerous Liaisons*, Forman's interpretation of Choderlos de Laclos's shocking tale of sexual manipulation and debauchery in late eighteenth-century France fails to come to life. Adjustments to the story dilute its impact, but the higher budget shows in production design and costumes. Handsome Firth suffers from an underwritten character, while Bening does a one-note Cheshire cat impersonation. If you want your story with bite and tension, go with the Frears version.
Dist.: Orion

VAMP 1986
★ **R Horror 1:34**
☑ Nudity, adult situations, explicit language, violence
Dir: Richard Wenk ***Cast:*** Chris Makepeace, Grace Jones, Robert Rusler, Gedde Watanabe, Sandy Baron, Dedee Pfeiffer
▶ Fraternity pledges Makepeace and Rusler agree to provide stripper for upcoming party. With Watanabe, they journey to nightclub that's actually den of vampires. Dazzling stripper Jones sinks her teeth into Rusler while

Makepeace, Watanabe, and cute waitress Pfeiffer try to flee from monsters. Uneven genre hybrid emphasizes dark terrors lurking beneath swinging nightlife. **(CC)**
Dist.: New World

VAMPING 1984
★★ R Drama 1:30
☑ Brief nudity, adult situations, explicit language, violence
Dir: Frederick King Keller *Cast:* Patrick Duffy, Catherine Hyland, Rod Arrants, Fred A. Keller, David Booze
▶ Down-on-his-luck saxophonist Duffy robs widow Hyland's mansion, making off with valuable ring and love letters from her late husband. Letters inspire both Duffy's sax playing and heart: he winds up in bed with Hyland, only to be tailed by mysterious man who may or may not be a cop. Wildly convoluted plot, passive role for Duffy, and downbeat ending derail promising start.
Dist.: CBS/Fox

VAMPIRE AT MIDNIGHT 1988
★★ R Horror 1:33
☑ Nudity, explicit language, violence
Dir: Gregory McClatchy *Cast:* Jason Williams, Gustav Vintas, Lesley Milne, Esther Alise, Jeanie Moore, Robert Random
▶ L.A. police detective Williams pursues vampire Vintas, who's leaving a trail of bodies. Vintas is a hypnotherapist whose gaze mesmerizes women; they become either victims or servant drones. Williams's pianist girlfriend Milne falls under Vintas's spell; he must battle to save her life and end threat to city. Bloodsucking thrills and bevy of undraped beauties should please fans of genre. **(CC)**
Dist.: Key

VAMPIRE BAT, THE 1933
★ NR Horror 1:11 B&W
Dir: Frank Strayer *Cast:* Lionel Atwill, Fay Wray, Dwight Frye, Maude Eburne, George E. Stone, Lionel Belmore
▶ When a sudden spate of mysterious murders occurs, superstitious villagers suspect that local bats are draining the blood of the victims. But it is actually mad-scientist Atwill, who is feeding an artificial life form, as assistant Wray learns to her peril. Respectable horror offering from the golden age satisfies with familiar faces and good atmosphere.
Dist.: Cable

VAMPIRE'S KISS 1988
★ R Horror 1:43
☑ Nudity, adult situations, explicit language, violence
Dir: Robert Bierman *Cast:* Nicolas Cage, Maria Conchita Alonso, Jennifer Beals, Elizabeth Ashley, Kasi Lemmons, Bob Lujan
▶ Swinging Manhattan yuppie Cage picks up beautiful Beals in singles bar. One catch: Cage thinks she's made him a vampire. He grows increasingly manic at work, then completely cracks up, going on psychotic killing

spree while begging for someone to end his misery. Fine cast wasted as seriocomic start degenerates into unanticipated mayhem made worse by Cage's frantic overacting.
Dist.: HBO

VAMPYR 1932 French/German
★ NR Horror 1:10 B&W
Dir: Carl Theodor Dreyer *Cast:* Julian West, Henriette Gerard, Jan Hieronimko, Maurice Schutz, Rena Mandel, Sybylle Schmitz
▶ While exploring a remote village, naturalist West learns that a vampire is slowly destroying the inhabitants. Demanding, slowly paced adaptation of Sheridan le Fanu's *In a Glass Darkly* is historically significant for its subtly eerie tone and Rudolph Maté's extraordinary photography. Evocative score by Wolfgang Zeller and almost complete absence of dialogue add to unnerving atmosphere. [S]
Dist.: Various

VAN, THE 1977
☆ R Comedy 1:30
☑ Nudity, explicit language
Dir: Sam Grossman *Cast:* Stuart Getz, Deborah White, Harry Moses, Marcie Barkin, Bill Adler, Danny DeVito
▶ High schooler Getz buys a flashy van to improve his chances with women. The move works fine with everyone except White, the girl he really wants. He must also challenge the local bully to a drag race to meet the van payments. Easygoing, but totally juvenile, drive-in fare.
Dist.: United

VANISHING POINT 1971
★★★ PG Drama 1:38
☑ Explicit language, violence
Dir: Richard C. Sarafian *Cast:* Barry Newman, Cleavon Little, Dean Jagger, Victoria Medlin, Robert Donner, Severn Darden
▶ Driver Newman makes impossible bet that he can zip from Colorado to California in fifteen hours. Blind disc jockey Little learns of his quest and advises him over the air how to avoid the pursuing cops. Bizarre but compelling chase movie. Busy musical score includes numbers by Kim Carnes, Jerry Reed, and Delaney and Bonnie.
Dist.: CBS/Fox

VANISHING WILDERNESS 1974
★★★★★ G Documentary 1:26
Dir: Arthur Dubs, Heinz Seilmann
▶ Scenic documentary travels 32,000 miles from Alaska to Florida, examining plight of wildlife from polar bears to pelicans. Outstanding family fare with a message features breathtaking photography and narration by cowboy actor Rex Allen.
Dist.: Media

VAN NUYS BLVD. 1979
★ R Action-Adventure 1:33
☑ Nudity, adult situations, explicit language, violence

Dir: William Sachs   *Cast:* Bill Adler, Cynthia Wood, Dennis Bowen, Melissa Prophet, David Hayward, Tara Strohmeier
▶ Restless Adler leaves his rural home in search of the California good life. In Los Angeles, he is exposed to the joys of cruising, hot rodding, disco, and pinball before falling in love with his gorgeous drag race rival Wood. Typical teen movie combo of cars and couplings. Wood is a former *Playboy* Playmate.
Dist.: United

VARIETY 1926 German
☆ **NR Drama 1:34 B&W**
Dir: E. A. Dupont   *Cast:* Emil Jannings, Maly Delschaft, Lya DePutti, Warwick Ward
▶ Trapeze artist Jannings leaves his wife to form an act with seductress DePutti. Ward, a more successful trapezist, invites them to join his act, but his real motive is to get DePutti. The huge, muscular Jannings discovers what is going on, and goes into a murderous rage. Powerful picture making, revealing Weimar Germany from surprising camera angles and inventive points of view.
Dist.: Video Dimensions

VARIETY LIGHTS 1950 Italian
☆ **NR Drama 1:33 B&W**
Dir: Federico Fellini, Alberto Lattuada   *Cast:* Peppino De Filippo, Carla Del Poggio, Guilietta Masina, John Kitzmiller, Dante Maggio, Checco Durante
▶ Young village girl Del Poggio runs away to join a group of traveling performers, pestering manager De Filippo and the rest of the troupe to take her on as a dancer. Once accepted, she becomes the troupe's star attraction, and soon leaves the tattered little band behind for the big time. Don't look for director Fellini's famous flamboyance in his first film; co-director Lattuada helped keep the lid on for this enjoyable, bittersweet tale.   [S]
Dist.: Corinth

VELVET TOUCH, THE 1948
★ **NR Mystery-Suspense 1:37 B&W**
Dir: John Gage   *Cast:* Rosalind Russell, Leo Genn, Claire Trevor, Sydney Greenstreet, Leon Ames, Frank McHugh
▶ Russell thinks she's gotten away with murder when she clubs theatrical producer Ames to death with a statuette. Detective Greenstreet pins the crime on Trevor, Ames's innocent former lover; Russell then must face the agonies of her conscience. Clever mystery ties resolution to Ibsen's *Hedda Gabler*, a role Russell is playing on the stage.
Dist.: Turner

VELVET VAMPIRE, THE 1971
☆ **R Horror 1:21**
☑ Nudity, adult situations, explicit language, graphic violence
Dir: Stephanie Rothman   *Cast:* Michael Blodgett, Sherry Miles, Celeste Yarnall, Jerry Daniels, Gene Shane
▶ Newlyweds Blodgett and Miles fall under

the spell of sexy art patron Yarnall, who reveals an unhealthy thirst for blood at her desert hideaway. Stylish but ultimately farfetched horror marred by weak acting.
Dist.: Nelson

VENDETTA 1986
★ ★ **R Action-Adventure 1:29**
☑ Rape, nudity, adult situations, explicit language, graphic violence
Dir: Bruce Logan   *Cast:* Karen Chase, Lisa Clarson, Lisa Hullana, Linda Lightfoot, Sandy Martin, Michelle Newkirk
▶ Innocent Newkirk, serving prison sentence for slaying would-be rapist, is killed by gang of lesbian toughs. Newkirk's sister Chase, a professional stunt woman and kung fu expert, intentionally gets herself incarcerated to seek revenge. Series of vendetta murders leads to showdown with gang leader Martin. Violent and sensationalist women-behind-bars pic lacks usual tongue-in-cheek humor of genre.
Dist.: Vestron

VENGEANCE VALLEY 1951
★ ★ **NR Western 1:23**
Dir: Richard Thorpe   *Cast:* Burt Lancaster, Robert Walker, Joanne Dru, Sally Forrest, John Ireland, Hugh O'Brian
▶ Slow-paced Western about feuding foster brothers: Walker, a cad trying to gain control of a large ranch, Lancaster, a do-gooder unaware of Walker's true intentions. Subplot about an illegitimate baby made this an eyebrow-raiser in the fifties; cattle roundup sequences and a fiery Lancaster still hold interest.
Dist.: Goodtimes

VENOM 1982 British
★ ★ **R Mystery-Suspense 1:32**
☑ Explicit language, violence
Dir: Piers Haggard   *Cast:* Klaus Kinski, Oliver Reed, Nicol Williamson, Sarah Miles, Sterling Hayden, Lance Holcomb
▶ German criminal Kinski, aided by butler Reed, attempts to kidnap rich boy Holcomb from London townhouse. Unbeknownst to hoodlums, Holcomb has inadvertently acquired deadly black mamba snake. Reptile escapes, threatening all in home, including boy's protective grandfather Hayden. Superior cast in average suspense thriller.
Dist.: Vestron

VENUS IN FURS 1970 British/German/Italian
☆ **R Mystery-Suspense 1:26**
☑ Nudity, adult situations, explicit language, violence
Dir: Jess Franco   *Cast:* James Darren, Barbara McNair, Maria Rohm, Klaus Kinski, Dennis Price, Margaret Lee
▶ Musician Darren sees sickos Kinski, Lee, and Price murder a woman and dispose of her body. Much to his surprise, the woman pops up alive in a nightclub, and later takes revenge on her "killers" while making love to

them. Moody tale of sexual confusion is more than a little confused itself.
Dist.: Republic

VERA CRUZ 1954
★★★ **NR Western 1:34**
Dir: Robert Aldrich ***Cast:*** Gary Cooper, Burt Lancaster, Denise Darcel, Cesar Romero, Sarita Montiel, Ernest Borgnine
▸ American mercenaries Cooper and Lancaster form a wary alliance while guiding a gold shipment to Emperor Maximilian's Vera Cruz fortress. Beautiful aristocrat Darcel convinces Cooper to hand the loot over to Juarez's rebels, but Lancaster has his own plans for the gold. Solid, action-packed Western has a small role by Charles Bronson under his Buchinski surname.
Dist.: Key

VERDICT, THE 1982
★★★★★ **R Drama 2:09**
☑ Adult situations, explicit language, mild violence
Dir: Sidney Lumet ***Cast:*** Paul Newman, Charlotte Rampling, Jack Warden, James Mason, Milo O'Shea, Lindsay Crouse
▸ Alcoholic Boston lawyer Newman gets one last stab at redemption when he takes on the medical establishment and the church in a malpractice suit against a Catholic hospital. Complicating his task: big-time opposing attorney Mason, unsympathetic judge O'Shea, and mystery woman Rampling. Superlative courtroom drama works up maximum empathy for the underdog. Concise direction by Lumet, daring and subtle performance by Newman, and incisive David Mamet script. Oscar nominations: Best Picture, Director, Screenplay, Actor, Supporting Actor (Mason).
Dist.: CBS/Fox

VERNE MILLER 1987
★ **NR Crime 1:35**
☑ Explicit language, violence
Dir: Rod Hewitt ***Cast:*** Scott Glenn, Barbara Stock, Thomas G. Waites, Lucinda Jenney, Andrew Robinson, Diane Salinger
▸ True story of Verne Miller (Glenn), former South Dakota sheriff who served time for embezzlement before going to Chicago, where he worked as hit man for Al Capone (Waites). Eventually Miller found himself targeted for death by Capone. Limp directing and scripting fail to do justice to interesting subject. Good production values.
Dist.: Nelson

VERTIGO 1958
★★★★★ **PG Mystery-Suspense 2:00**
☑ Adult situations
Dir: Alfred Hitchcock ***Cast:*** James Stewart, Kim Novak, Barbara Bel Geddes, Tom Helmore, Henry Jones, Ellen Corby
▸ Retired detective Stewart is hired by old friend Helmore to tail his unstable wife Novak. Stewart becomes obsessed with his quarry, but his fear of heights leads to tragedy. A masterpiece whose hypnotic direction conveys emotion and meaning with every shot, leading to a climax of almost unbearable intensity. Stewart's complex performance and Bernard Herrmann's score add to the haunting mood.
Dist.: MCA

VERY PRIVATE AFFAIR, A 1962
French/Italian
★★ **NR Drama 1:35**
Dir: Louis Malle ***Cast:*** Brigitte Bardot, Marcello Mastroianni, Gregor von Ressori, Eleonore Hirt, Ursula Kubler, Dirk Sanders
▸ Unconvincing depiction of the rise to fame of Swiss model (Bardot) and her subsequent withdrawal from public life when the pressures of stardom grow too strong. Theatrical director Mastroianni tries to protect her privacy in this moody drama based on several incidents in Bardot's life. [S]
Dist.: MGM/UA

VIBES 1988
★★ **PG Comedy 1:39**
☑ Explicit language, violence
Dir: Ken Kwapis ***Cast:*** Cyndi Lauper, Jeff Goldblum, Peter Falk, Julian Sands, Googy Gress, Michael Lerner
▸ Psychics Lauper and Goldblum meet at seminar conducted by ESP expert Sands and are soon recruited by Falk to find his missing son in the mountains of Ecuador. Once in the Andes, they learn Falk has a more nefarious purpose. Singer Lauper's screen debut is fluffy, unconvincing fare.
Dist.: RCA/Columbia

VICE SQUAD 1982
★★★ **R Action-Adventure 1:37**
☑ Nudity, strong sexual content, adult situations, explicit language, graphic violence
Dir: Gary A. Sherman ***Cast:*** Season Hubley, Gary Swanson, Wings Hauser, Pepe Serna, Beverly Todd, Joseph DiGiroloma
▸ Young mother Hubley reluctantly works as prostitute to support child. When vicious pimp Hauser slays another hooker, vice squad cop Swanson persuades Hubley to work undercover to capture the killer. Average sleazy crime drama offers few surprises.
Dist.: Nelson

VICE VERSA 1988
★★★ **PG Comedy 1:37**
☑ Adult situations, explicit language
Dir: Brian Gilbert ***Cast:*** Judge Reinhold, Fred Savage, Corinne Bohrer, Swoosie Kurtz, Jane Kaczmarek, David Proval
▸ Father-son role reversal comedy boasts memorable performances from both Reinhold and Savage. Reinhold brings vigor and freshness to his role as an eleven-year-old interested in heavy metal and his pet frog. Savage also excels as kid with the brain of a yuppie executive. Cleverer and a lot more fun

than similarly plotted *Like Father, Like Son*.
(CC)
Dist.: RCA/Columbia

VICIOUS 1988 Australian
☆ **NR Drama 1:30**
☑ Nudity, adult situations, explicit language, graphic violence
Dir: Karl Zwicky *Cast:* Tamblyn Lord, Craig Pearce, Tiffiny Dowe, John Godden, Kelly Dingwall, Leather
▶ Upper-class teenager Lord hooks up with young low-lifes who lure him into a life of crime. The gang picks up Dowe on a joyride; attraction builds between her and Lord, but further violence occurs. Repellent behavior by the main characters, especially toward women, limit the appeal of this nasty story.
Dist.: SVS

VICTIM 1961 British
★★★★ **NR Drama 1:40 B&W**
Dir: Basil Dearden *Cast:* Dirk Bogarde, Sylvia Sims, Dennis Price, Anthony Nichols, Nigel Stock, Peter McEnery
▶ Homosexual lawyer Bogarde finds his marriage and career endangered when his young lover McEnery kills himself. Bogarde pursues the blackmailers responsible for McEnery's death. Powerful statement approaches subject matter with tact and dignity. Crisply directed and well played by all.
Dist.: Nelson

VICTOR/VICTORIA 1982
★★★★ **PG Musical/Comedy 2:14**
☑ Adult situations, explicit language
Dir: Blake Edwards *Cast:* Julie Andrews, Robert Preston, James Garner, Lesley Ann Warren, Alex Karras
▶ Down-on-her-luck actress Andrews is starving in 1930s Paris when she meets Preston, a similarly unemployed entertainer. Together, they create a nightclub act by passing Andrews off as a guy who impersonates women. She/he is an overnight sensation but complications arise when American tycoon Garner falls in love and sets out to prove Andrews is all woman. Meanwhile, Garner's obnoxious girlfriend Warren spreads the rumor that he's in love with a man. Screamingly funny comedy of errors.
Dist.: MGM/UA

VICTORY 1981
★★★★ **PG War/Drama 1:56**
☑ Explicit language, violence
Dir: John Huston *Cast:* Michael Caine, Sylvester Stallone, Max Von Sydow, Pele, Werner Roth, Carole Laure
▶ Nazi propaganda officer Von Sydow organizes soccer match in Paris between Allied POW all-stars and German national squad. Caine, head of POW squad, plans escape for team during game, so tough American Stallone breaks out of camp to notify French Resistance and then returns to play goalie. During game Allies must choose between escape and victory. Rousing drama from veteran director Huston boasts unusual premise and world-famous soccer stars, including legendary Pele and former New York Cosmos player Roth.
Dist.: Warner

VIDEO DEAD, THE 1987
★★ **R Horror 1:30**
☑ Explicit language, violence
Dir: Robert Scott *Cast:* Roxanna Augesen, Rocky Duvall, Vickie Bastel, Sam David McClelland, Michael St. Michaels, Jennifer Miro
▶ TV set is accidentally delivered to writer St. Michaels. Even when unplugged, it plays same black-and-white zombie movie. Zombies walk out of set and kill him. Months later siblings Augesen and Duvall move into house; they and neighbors are threatened by zombies. Low-budget nonsense.
Dist.: Nelson

VIDEODROME 1983 Canadian
★ **R Horror 1:27**
☑ Nudity, strong sexual content, adult situations, explicit language, graphic violence
Dir: David Cronenberg *Cast:* James Woods, Deborah Harry, Sonja Smits, Peter Dvorsky, Les Carlson, Jack Creley
▶ In the near future, Woods, unsavory head of sleazy Toronto cable TV station, becomes obsessed with torture-mutilation program called "Videodrome." Woods learns images have irreversible effect on viewers; he and kinky girlfriend Harry succumb to dire effects of Videodrome. Intriguing premise of TV displacing reality is overwhelmed by confusing technospeak and grandiose plot.
Dist.: MCA

VIEW TO A KILL, A 1985 British
★★★★ **PG Espionage/Action-Adventure 2:11**
☑ Adult situations, explicit language, violence
Dir: John Glen *Cast:* Roger Moore, Christopher Walken, Tanya Roberts, Grace Jones, Patrick Macnee, Patrick Bauchau
▶ Investigating murder of fellow British agent in Alps, James Bond (Moore) narrowly escapes on one ski from Soviet assassins. Trail leads to Russian spy Walken with a plan to destroy Silicon Valley, home of U.S. computer industry, by inducing an earthquake. Jones is Walken's evil assistant; Roberts is at first his unwitting dupe, then Moore's ally and romantic interest. Moore's efforts to thwart Walken lead to two climaxes: one below ground, the other on top of Golden Gate Bridge. **(CC)**
Dist.: CBS/Fox

VIGILANTE 1982
★★ **R Action-Adventure 1:30**
☑ Rape, nudity, adult situations, explicit language, graphic violence
Dir: William Lustig *Cast:* Robert Forster, Fred

Williamson, Richard Bright, Rutanya Alda, Don Blakely, Joseph Carberry

▶ When thugs attack his wife and murder their young son, New York blue-collar worker Forster seeks justice in court, but simpleton judge and crooked lawyer spring hoods. Forster then joins neighborhood vigilantes, led by co-worker Williamson, for spree of retribution killings. Hard-hitting action yarn, in tradition of *Death Wish* pictures, is only for those with stomach for extreme violence.
Dist.: Vestron

VIKINGS, THE 1958
★ ★ ★ **NR Action-Adventure 1:54**
Dir: Richard Fleischer *Cast:* Kirk Douglas, Tony Curtis, Ernest Borgnine, Janet Leigh, James Donald, Alexander Knox

▶ Viking prince Douglas and slave Curtis, half-brothers (although they don't know it) and rivals for the love of princess Leigh, fight each other but later team up when their father Borgnine is killed. Brawny and muscular. Curtis and Douglas provide plenty of heroics; Leigh contributes sex appeal.
Dist.: MGM/UA

VILLAGE OF THE DAMNED 1960 British
★ ★ **NR Sci-Fi 1:18 B&W**
Dir: Wolf Rilla *Cast:* George Sanders, Barbara Shelley, Michael Gwynn, Laurence Naismith, Martin Stephens

▶ In an English village, women become mysteriously pregnant and give birth to a race of superpowered kids. When the children evince evil intent, scientist father Sanders tries to stop them. Spooky and unusual, with moody direction and chilling child actors. Based on the novel *The Midwich Cuckoos* by John Wyndham; led to sequel *Children of the Damned.*
Dist.: MGM/UA

VILLAGE OF THE GIANTS 1965
★ ★ **NR Sci-Fi 1:22**
Dir: Bert I. Gordon *Cast:* Tommy Kirk, Beau Bridges, Ron Howard, Johnny Crawford, Joy Harmon, Toni Basil

▶ Teens go on a rampage after being turned into giants by young scientist Howard's new type of food. Low-rent shenanigans with an inane screenplay supposedly inspired by the H. G. Wells novel *The Food of the Gods.*
Dist.: Nelson

VILLAIN STILL PURSUED HER, THE 1940
★ **NR Comedy 1:08 B&W**
Dir: Edward Cline *Cast:* Anita Louise, Richard Cromwell, Hugh Herbert, Alan Mowbray, Buster Keaton, Joyce Compton, Margaret Hamilton, Billy Gilbert

▶ A blackguard plots to foreclose a farm mortgage, leaving sweet Louise and her widowed mother out in the cold. Louise's beau is too busy getting drunk to be of much help until Keaton, who gives the best performance, comes to his aid. Extremely broad satire of old-fashioned melodrama seems as dated as its target.
Dist.: Video Yesteryear

VINDICATOR, THE 1986 Canadian
★ ★ **R Horror 1:2**
☑ Brief nudity, explicit language, violence
Dir: Jean-Claude Lord *Cast:* Terri Austin, Richard Cox, Pam Grier, Maury Chaykin, David McIlwraith

▶ Brilliant scientist Cox develops indestructible cyborg killer and is slain by jealous colleague McIlwraith. He then installs Cox's brain in cyborg prototype, but creature escapes before installation of control mechanism and goes on rampage. Also released as *Frankenstein '88*, low-budget updating of Mary Shelley classic works best as camp. **(CC)**
Dist.: CBS/Fox

VIOLATED 1984
★ **R Action-Adventure 1:28**
☑ Nudity, adult situations, violence
Dir: Richard Cannistraro *Cast:* J. C. Quinn, April Daisy White, John Heard, Lisanne Falk, Samantha Fox, Jonathan Ward

▶ Actress White, raped by gangsters at a party, gets involved with policeman Quinn. In a twist of fate, the same thugs run afoul of the mob, and killer Heard hires Quinn, who is also a hired gun, to rub out one of White's tormentors. Exploitation item is short on logic and talent save for the dependable Heard.
Dist.: Vestron

VIOLENT ONES, THE 1967
☆ **NR Drama 1:36**
Dir: Fernando Lamas *Cast:* Fernando Lamas, Aldo Ray, Tommy Sands, David Carradine, Melinda Marx, Lisa Gaye

▶ When Marx (Groucho's daughter) is beaten and raped in a small Mexican town, sheriff Lamas takes three suspects into custody. The townspeople form a lynch mob. The sheriff must keep his captives safe while trying to nab the real culprit. Overheated, but effective, drama.
Dist.: Republic

VIOLENT YEARS, THE 1956
☆ **NR Drama 0:57 B&W**
Dir: William M. Morgan (Franz Eichorn)
Cast: Jean Moorehead, Barbara Weeks, Arthur Millan, Theresa Hancock, Joanne Cangi, J. Stanford Jolley

▶ Newly discovered trash written by schlock king Edward D. Wood, Jr., (*Plan 9 From Outer Space*) has the seemingly demure daughter of a journalist going on a robbing, killing, and petting spree with a gang of teen-girl hellions. Judge Jolley gives them a stern scolding in court. Also known as *Female.*
Dist.: Rhino

VIOLENT ZONE 1989
☆ **NR Action-Adventure 1:30**
☑ Brief nudity, adult situations, explicit language, violence

Dir: John Garwood   *Cast:* John Jay Douglas, Christopher Weeks, Chard Hayward, Cynthia Killion
▶ An eccentric Beverly Hills millionaire asks a retired Chicago cop, whose life he saved in World War II, to find his son, a POW last seen on a Pacific island in 1974. The lawman joins a scruffy band of misfits for the mission. Does not live up to its title: too much talk, too little action.
Dist.: Southgate

VIOLETS ARE BLUE 1986
★ ★ ★ **PG-13 Romance 1:26**
☑ Brief nudity, adult situations
Dir: Jack Fisk   *Cast:* Sissy Spacek, Kevin Kline, Bonnie Bedelia, John Kellogg, Jim Standiford, Augusta Dabney
▶ Spacek, a successful photojournalist, and Kline, a married newspaper editor, are former high school sweethearts reunited fifteen years after they were romantically involved. They try to fight their feelings for each other but their old passion is rekindled. They collaborate on a local story and then have the opportunity to work together on a Paris assignment. Will Kline give up wife Bedelia and his teenage son? Tender and touching love story directed by Spacek's husband.   **(CC)**
Dist.: RCA/Columbia

VIPER 1988
★ ★ ★ **R Action-Adventure 1:34**
☑ Explicit language, graphic violence
Dir: Peter Maris   *Cast:* Linda Purl, James Tolkan, Jeff Kober, Ken Foree, Chris Robinson, David M. Sterling
▶ Washington housewife Purl discovers that her workaday husband was actually a secret agent after he is killed by Tolkan, the head of his security command. With the help of reporter Kober, Purl stocks up on ammo and flees to a country cabin for a dawn shoot-out with the secret commandos. Good action, with a strong, sympathetic heroine.
Dist.: Fries

VIRGINIAN, THE 1929
★ **NR Western 1:30 B&W**
Dir: Victor Fleming   *Cast:* Gary Cooper, Richard Arlen, Walter Huston, Mary Brian, Chester Conklin, Eugene Pallette
▶ Cattleman Cooper is forced to hang three rustlers, including an old friend, alienating girlfriend Brian. After a reconciliation, Cooper and Brian are set to wed—but first, Cooper and head rustler Huston must have a showdown in the street. Best version of oft-filmed Owen Wister novel contains the line: "If you want to call me that, smile." Cooper is rugged in his classic role.
Dist.: KVC

VIRGIN QUEEN, THE 1955
★ ★ **NR Biography 1:32**
Dir: Henry Koster   *Cast:* Bette Davis, Richard Todd, Joan Collins, Herbert Marshall, Dan O'Herlihy, Rod Taylor

▶ In sixteenth-century England, explorer Walter Raleigh (Todd) wins the heart of elderly Queen Elizabeth (Davis, who played the same role in 1939's *The Private Lives of Elizabeth and Essex*). She is willing to finance his expeditions but becomes jealous when he rebuffs her in favor of lady-in-waiting Collins. Well made and well cast; Davis is first-rate. **(CC)**
Dist.: CBS/Fox

VIRGIN QUEEN OF ST. FRANCIS HIGH, THE 1987 Canadian
☆ **PG Comedy 1:34**
☑ Adult situations
Dir: Francesco Lucente   *Cast:* Joseph R. Straface, Stacy Christensen, J. T. Wotton, Anna-Lisa Iapaolo, Lee Barringer, Bev Wotton
▶ Socially inept high schooler Straface bets tough guy Barringer he can lure stuck-up virgin Christensen to no-tell motel for hanky panky by summer's end. Christensen accepts Straface's invite to bungalow but insists he act like a gentleman. He does just that and two develop chaste friendship. Low-budget teen comedy resists usual descent into sexploitation. Beware bottom-of-the barrel production values.
Dist.: Media

VIRGIN SOLDIERS, THE 1969 British
★ ★ **R Drama 1:36**
☑ Nudity, adult situations, explicit language, mild violence
Dir: John Dexter   *Cast:* Hywel Bennett, Nigel Patrick, Lynn Redgrave, Nigel Davenport, Rachel Kempson, Tsai Chin
▶ Inexperienced young troops fret about arms and love in rebel-plagued Malaya of the 1950s. Romantically naive Bennett longs for schoolteacher Redgrave, but realizes manhood in bed with a local hooker and in battle with attacking guerrillas. Youthful follies are amusingly portrayed, but violence seems to come out of nowhere.
Dist.: RCA/Columbia

VIRGIN SPRING, THE 1960 Swedish
★ **NR Drama 1:28 B&W**
Dir: Ingmar Bergman   *Cast:* Max Von Sydow, Brigitta Valberg, Gunnel Lindblom, Brigitta Pettersson, Axel Duberg
▶ When his young daughter Pettersson is raped and killed in medieval Sweden, Von Sydow takes violent revenge on the perpetrators. His faith in God is shaken until a miracle occurs. Grim but gripping tale nabbed Foreign Film Oscar. Available dubbed. Ⓢ
Dist.: Nelson

VIRIDIANA 1961 Spanish
★ **NR Drama 1:30 B&W**
Dir: Luis Buñuel   *Cast:* Silvia Pinal, Francisco Rabal, Fernando Rey, Margarita Lozano, Victoria Zinny, Teresa Rabal
▶ Pinal, raised in a sheltered convent, is ordered to visit her wealthy uncle Rey before

taking vows. When he commits suicide, she turns his estate into a refuge for beggars. Director Buñuel's first film in his native Spain after a twenty-five-year exile was immediately banned by authorities for its political implications. Haunting mixture of blasphemy and surrealism will reward discriminating viewers. [S]
Dist.: Hollywood Home Theatre

VIRUS 1982 Japanese
★★ PG Sci-Fi 1:42
☑ Explicit language, violence
Dir: Kinji Fukasaku *Cast:* Sonny Chiba, Chuck Connors, Stephanie Faulkner, Glenn Ford, Olivia Hussey, Robert Vaughn
▸ Virus released in plane crash kills most of humanity; nuclear explosions wipe out the rest, except for a few hardy survivors in the Antarctic. Large-scale disaster epic with an international cast of stars contains beautiful South Pole sequences.
Dist.: Media

VISION QUEST 1985
★★★★ R Drama/Sports 1:47
☑ Adult situations, explicit language, violence
Dir: Harold Becker *Cast:* Matthew Modine, Linda Fiorentino, Michael Schoeffling, Ronny Cox, Harold Sylvester, Charles Hallahan
▸ Coming-of-age story set in Spokane focuses on high school wrestler Modine, who embarks on a personal mission to lose weight for an important match. Beautiful older Fiorentino, boarding in his house, becomes a tempting distraction. Predictable plot enhanced by convincing, attractive stars. Madonna appears briefly in a nightclub performance. (CC)
Dist.: Warner

VISIONS OF EIGHT 1973
★★ G Documentary/Sports 1:45
Dir: Milos Forman, Kon Ichikawa, Claude Lelouch, Juri Ozerov, Arthur Penn, Michael Pfleghar, John Schlesinger, Mai Zetterling
▸ The 1972 Munich Olympics as viewed by eight world-class directors. Highlights include Lelouch's look at the losers, *Amadeus* director Forman's intercutting of decathalon entrants with Beethoven's Ninth Symphony, and Schlesinger's marathon episode, which also shows the tragic murder of eleven Israeli athletes. Uneven but compelling.
Dist.: RCA/Columbia

VISITING HOURS 1982 Canadian
★★ R Horror 1:45
☑ Brief nudity, adult situations, explicit language, graphic violence
Dir: Jean-Claude Lord *Cast:* Michael Ironside, Lee Grant, Linda Purl, William Shatner, Harvey Atkin
▸ Psychotic killer Ironside, who likes to photograph his victims, fails in his first attempt to murder TV reporter Grant. He stalks her through a hospital in this crude but undeniably effective shocker. Purl is appealing as Grant's nurse.
Dist.: CBS/Fox

VISITOR, THE 1979 U.S./Italian
★★ R Horror 1:30
☑ Adult situations, explicit language, graphic violence
Dir: Michael J. Paradise (Giulio Paradisi)
Cast: Mel Ferrer, Glenn Ford, Lance Henriksen, John Huston, Joanne Nail, Shelley Winters
▸ Atlanta millionaire Ferrer wants his wife to deliver another demonic child like their daughter; when she refuses, his satanic cult tortures her. Detective Ford, investigating the group, meets a gruesome end. Visually stylish but predictable effort features Hitchcockian bird attacks and a cameo by director Sam Peckinpah as an abortionist.
Dist.: Vidmark

VISITORS, THE 1989 Swedish
☆ R Horror 1:42
☑ Adult situations, explicit language, violence
Dir: Joakim Ersgard *Cast:* Keith Berkeley, Lena Endre, John Force, John Olson, Joanna Berg, Brent Landiss
▸ After moving to Sweden, an American advertising executive settles into a spooky house with his wife and two children. Dad has marital and professional problems, but his worries are just starting: the attic is possessed by an evil demon. Some chills, but the first half hour is awfully slow going. Awkwardly dubbed.
Dist.: Vidmark

VITAL SIGNS 1990
★★★ R Drama 1:43
☑ Nudity, adult situations, explicit language, violence
Dir: Marisa Silver *Cast:* Adrian Pasdar, Diane Lane, Jimmy Smits, Laura San Giacomo, Norma Aleandro, Jack Gwaltney
▸ Young doctors confront life, death, careers, and love in a modern hospital. Pasdar romances aspiring pediatrician Lane while trying to live up to the reputation of his surgeon dad. Financially strapped Gwaltney competes for surgery berth while his marriage to waitress wife San Giacomo hits the rocks. Overloaded script delivers expected hospital suds, but gory operation scenes will turn a few stomachs. (CC)
Dist.: CBS/Fox

VIVACIOUS LADY 1938
★★★ NR Comedy 1:30 B&W
Dir: George Stevens *Cast:* Ginger Rogers, James Stewart, Charles Coburn, James Ellison, Beulah Bondi, Frances Mercer
▸ Small-town professor Stewart falls in love with New York nightclub singer Rogers. After they marry, Stewart takes Rogers to his hometown, but worries about how his disapproving parents Coburn and Bondi will react. Sparkling fun with a nifty cast, but contrived plot

keeps Stewart and Rogers apart for too long.
Dist.: Media

VIVA KNIEVEL! 1977
★ ★ **PG Drama 1:44**
☑ Explicit language, violence
Dir: Gordon Douglas   *Cast:* Evel Knievel, Gene Kelly, Lauren Hutton, Red Buttons, Leslie Nielsen, Frank Gifford
▶ Showcase for formerly notorious daredevil Knievel finds him visiting orphanages, performing motorcycle stunts, falling for glamorous reporter Hutton, rescuing alcoholic mechanic Kelly from despair, and stopping evil druglord Nielsen from smuggling a fortune in cocaine into the country. Scary stunts add some bite.
Dist.: Warner

VIVA LAS VEGAS 1964
★ ★ ★ **NR Musical 1:26**
Dir: George Sidney   *Cast:* Elvis Presley, Ann-Margret, Cesare Danova, William Demarest, Nicky Blair, Jack Carter
▶ Desperate to beat wealthy rival Danova in the Las Vegas Grand Prix, singing race-car driver Presley becomes a hotel waiter to buy a new engine. The King romances the hotel's beautiful swimming instructor Ann-Margret with "What'd I Say," "The Yellow Rose of Texas," and other tunes before competing in the big race. Silly but satisfying fluff enhanced by Ann-Margret's considerable skills.
Dist.: MGM/UA

VIVA MAX! 1969
★ ★ ★ **G Comedy 1:33**
Dir: Jerry Paris   *Cast:* Peter Ustinov, Pamela Tiffin, Jonathan Winters, John Astin, Harry Morgan, Keenan Wynn
▶ Mexican general Ustinov leads his troops on a quixotic mission: a modern-day retaking of the Alamo. National Guard general Winters, police chief Morgan, and assorted other ineffectuals are involved in the American counterattack. Nifty comic premise gets only mild execution from the director, but a large cast of clowns keeps the movie afloat. Winters turns in the best performance.
Dist.: Republic

VIVA ZAPATA! 1952
★ ★ ★ **NR Biography 1:53 B&W**
Dir: Elia Kazan   *Cast:* Marlon Brando, Jean Peters, Anthony Quinn, Joseph Wiseman, Arnold Moss, Alan Reed
▶ Meticulous biography of Emiliano Zapata (Brando), an illiterate Mexican peasant who helped unseat the corrupt President Diaz in 1911 and then briefly led the country. Downbeat John Steinbeck screenplay describes Zapata's courtship of merchant's daughter Peters and troubles with his alcoholic brother Eufemio (Quinn, who won Supporting Oscar), as well as the labyrinthine politics that thwarted the popular revolution. Impressive production is brooding and slowly paced.
Dist.: CBS/Fox

VOGUES 1937
★ **NR Musical 1:48**
Dir: Irving Cummings   *Cast:* Warner Baxter, Joan Bennett, Helen Vinson, Mischa Auer, Alan Mowbray, Jerome Cowan
▶ Fashion salon owner Baxter endures the demands of socialite Bennett, wife Vinson, and the depredations of rival couturier Vinson. Plot is mainly an excuse for a parade of high-fashion clothing on the backs of comely models, all in glorious Technicolor. Delicious piece of popular history, with singing, dancing, and some acrobatic roller skaters.
Dist.: Axon

VOLUNTEERS 1985
★ ★ ★ **R Comedy 1:47**
☑ Adult situations, explicit language, adult humor
Dir: Nicholas Meyer   *Cast:* Tom Hanks, John Candy, Rita Wilson, Tim Thomerson, Gedde Watanabe, George Plimpton
▶ Insolent preppie playboy Hanks, on the run from mob loansharks, finds himself shanghaied into a Peace Corps project to build a bridge for poor Thai peasants. His partners include beautiful Long Island idealist Wilson and inept American patriot Candy, who's later brainwashed by Communists. Broad, genial satire takes a scattershot approach to its 1962 targets.
Dist.: HBO

VON RYAN'S EXPRESS 1965
★ ★ ★ **NR War 1:57**
Dir: Mark Robson   *Cast:* Frank Sinatra, Trevor Howard, Raffaela Carra, Brad Dexter, Sergio Fantoni, James Brolin
▶ American flier Sinatra, newly imprisoned in Italy, is scorned by his fellow POWs until he proves his courage in a daring jailbreak. Italians aid the escape attempt, but the Nazis mount an all-out assault on the prisoners as they flee to Switzerland. Straightforward, no-frills adventure boasts strong cast and impressive action sequences.
Dist.: CBS/Fox

VOYAGE OF THE DAMNED 1976
British/Spanish
★ ★ ★ **PG Drama 2:14**
☑ Adult situations, explicit language
Dir: Stuart Rosenberg   *Cast:* Faye Dunaway, Max Von Sydow, Oskar Werner, Malcolm McDowell, Orson Welles, James Mason, Lee Grant, Ben Gazzara, Julie Harris, Wendy Hiller, Denholm Elliott
▶ True story of ill-fated 1939 voyage of German liner *St. Louis* is the basis for an often heartbreaking drama. Nazi propagandists filled the ship with Jewish passengers who hoped to emigrate to Cuba but were subsequently denied entry permits. Von Sydow makes a strong impression as the boat's captain. Grant was Oscar-nominated.
Dist.: CBS/Fox

VOYAGE TO THE BOTTOM OF THE SEA 1961
★★★ **NR Sci-Fi 1:45**
Dir: Irwin Allen ***Cast:*** Walter Pidgeon, Joan Fontaine, Barbara Eden, Peter Lorre, Robert Sterling, Michael Ansara
► Admiral Pidgeon commands crew of ultra-advanced nuclear submarine. He attempts to save the world from radiation-induced destruction by shooting missiles into space. Oddly mixed cast, decent effects, middling screenplay; spawned the television series of the same name. (CC)
Dist.: CBS/Fox

WACKIEST SHIP IN THE ARMY, THE 1961
★★ **NR Comedy 1:39**
Dir: Richard Murphy ***Cast:*** Jack Lemmon, Ricky Nelson, John Lund, Chips Rafferty, Tom Tully, Warren Berlinger
► During World War II, lieutenant Lemmon must lead a motley crew on a run-down vessel for a mission inside Japanese territory. Lemmon clowns, Nelson sings, and the antics are appropriately wacky. Pleasant but far from memorable service comedy inspired the television series of the same name.
Dist.: RCA/Columbia

WACKO 1983
★ **R Comedy 1:24**
☑ Explicit language, violence
Dir: Greydon Clark ***Cast:*** Joe Don Baker, Stella Stevens, George Kennedy, Julia Duffy, Scott McGinnis, Jeff Altman
► Limp spoof of horror movies parodies everything from *Psycho* to *Halloween*, but fails to connect with solid gags. Baker plays a sheriff on the trail of a "lawnmower killer" tormenting the teenagers at Hitchcock High during their annual Pumpkin Dance; subsequent mayhem includes mad scientists, a football game, and an elephant.
Dist.: Vestron

WAGES OF FEAR, THE 1955 French/Italian
★ **NR Action-Adventure 2:20**
Dir: Henri-Georges Clouzot ***Cast:*** Yves Montand, Charles Vanel, Vera Clouzot, Folco Lulli, Peter Van Eyck, William Tubbs
► When an oil fire breaks out in a South American country, Montand, Vanel, Lulli, and Van Eyck are hired to drive trucks containing nitroglycerine through dangerous mountains. One wrong move means instant death. One of the most hair-raising cinematic journeys ever; blistering direction and incredible physical production combine for suspense with an existential edge. Remade in America as 1977's *Sorcerer*. [S]
Dist.: Various

WAGNER 1983 Austrian/British/Hungarian
☆ **NR Biography 5:00**
☑ Adult situations, explicit language, violence
Dir: Tony Palmer ***Cast:*** Richard Burton, Vanessa Redgrave, Gemma Craven, Laszlo Galffi, John Gielgud, Ralph Richardson
► Burton plays the great composer whose grandiose operas and mystical theories of art, politics, and German culture have remained controversial and influential to this day. Craven is his put-upon first wife; Redgrave, his fanatically devoted second. Burton's Wagner is cool, egomaniacal and unsympathetic. Period details are terrific; and overall result is a vivid panorama of late nineteenth-century Europe.
Dist.: Nelson

WAGONMASTER 1950
★★★ **NR Western 1:26 B&W**
Dir: John Ford ***Cast:*** Ward Bond, Ben Johnson, Harry Carey, Jr., Joanne Dru, Jane Darwell, Alan Mowbray
► Bond leads a Mormon wagon train to Utah in search of religious freedom. Outlaws and Indians are encountered along the way but cowboys Johnson and Carey help them make the perilous journey. One of John Ford's more overlooked efforts is marvelously crafted and very involving.
Dist.: Turner [C]

WAITING FOR THE MOON 1987
☆ **PG Drama 1:28**
☑ Adult situations, explicit language
Dir: Jill Godmilow ***Cast:*** Linda Hunt, Linda Bassett, Bernadette Lafont, Bruce McGill, Andrew McCarthy, Jacques Boudet
► Fictionalized version of the relationship between Alice B. Toklas (Hunt) and Gertrude Stein (Bassett) presents hypothetical episodes from their lives in 1936. Slow, muddled, and pretentious drama offers some pretty images but almost no insight into their characters. Produced for PBS's "American Playhouse." (CC)
Dist.: CBS/Fox

WAIT UNTIL DARK 1967
★★★★ **NR Mystery-Suspense 1:48**
Dir: Terence Young ***Cast:*** Audrey Hepburn, Alan Arkin, Richard Crenna, Efrem Zimbalist, Jr., Jack Weston, Samantha Jones
► New York commercial artist Zimbalist unwittingly brings doll stuffed with heroin home to blind wife Hepburn. Psychotic criminal Arkin and henchmen Crenna and Weston lure Zimbalist away from apartment and try to retrieve drugs. Hepburn must find a way to even the odds with the crazed Arkin in a climactic showdown. Edge-of-your-seat thriller, based on Broadway play, is carried by Hepburn, who spent weeks wearing eye shades to prepare for role.
Dist.: Warner

WAKE ISLAND 1942
★★ **NR War 1:27 B&W**
Dir: John Farrow ***Cast:*** Brian Donlevy, Robert Preston, Macdonald Carey, Albert Dekker, Walter Abel, Barbara Britton
► Donlevy and Dekker lead the handful of

Marines and construction workers left to defend tiny Wake Island in the opening days of World War II. With incredible valor, the Americans hold out against waves of Japanese invaders, but with U.S. forces stretched thin throughout the world, there is no help forthcoming. Nominated for four Oscars, warrouser hits home like a sledgehammer.
Dist.: MCA

WAKE OF THE RED WITCH 1948
★ ★ NR Action-Adventure 1:46 B&W
Dir: Edward Ludwig *Cast:* John Wayne, Gail Russell, Gig Young, Adele Mara, Luther Adler, Eduard Franz
▶ Sea captain Wayne and powerful trader Adler have a bitter rivalry, competing for both the love of Russell and the riches of a South Sea Island. The seaman's adventures include battling an octopus and a climactic attempt to salvage a treasure-filled sunken ship. Vigorous, picturesque adventure.
Dist.: Republic

WALK, DON'T RUN 1966
★ ★ ★ ★ NR Comedy 1:56
Dir: Charles Walters *Cast:* Cary Grant, Samantha Eggar, Jim Hutton, John Standing, Miiko Taka, Ted Hartley
▶ Pleasant remake of *The More the Merrier* updates the story to 1964 Tokyo, where hotel rooms are at a premium due to the Olympics. Industrialist Grant (playing the old Charles Coburn role) rents room from embassy secretary Eggar, then gives half his share to Hutton, a member of the U.S. walking team. Subsequent romance is predictable but amusing. Grant's last film.
Dist.: RCA/Columbia

WALKER 1987
★ R Biography/Action-Adventure 1:35
☑ Nudity, explicit language, violence
Dir: Alex Cox *Cast:* Ed Harris, Richard Masur, René Auberjonois, Keith Szarabajka, Sy Richardson, Peter Boyle, Marlee Matlin
▶ Based on the true story of American soldier of fortune William Walker (Harris), who proclaimed himself president of Nicaragua in 1855. Hired by robber baron Cornelius Vanderbilt (Boyle), mercenary Harris leads invasion force into Central America and displaces existing government. Director Cox intended to satirize modern American interference in Nicaragua, using moments such as Harris reading about himself in *Newsweek* to drive home his point, but result misfires.
Dist.: MCA

WALKING TALL 1973
★ ★ ★ R Action-Adventure 2:05
☑ Adult situations, explicit language, violence
Dir: Phil Karlson *Cast:* Joe Don Baker, Elizabeth Hartman, Gene Evans, Noah Beery, Jr., Brenda Benet, John Brascia
▶ Tennessee sheriff Baker, fed up with gambling, moonshining, and prostitution in his county, wields baseball bat to clean out hoods. Criminal kingpins retaliate, severely beating Baker and killing his wife Hartman. Now really mad, sheriff goes on rampage to end problem once and for all. Based on true-life story of legendary sheriff Buford Pusser, runaway hit inspired two sequels, *Walking Tall, Part 2* and *Final Chapter—Walking Tall*, a TV movie, *A Real American Hero*, and a short-lived network series.
Dist.: Vestron

WALKING TALL, PART 2 1975
★ ★ ★ PG Action-Adventure 2:09
☑ Adult situations, explicit language, violence
Dir: Earl Bellamy *Cast:* Bo Svenson, Luke Askew, Noah Beery, Jr., Robert DoQui, John Chandler, Bruce Glover
▶ In sequel to *Walking Tall*, Svenson plays Tennessee sheriff Buford Pusser. Angered by events related in first film, local crime conglomerate tries repeatedly to slay Svenson. Patched-up sheriff then uses favorite baseball bat to bash a few heads. Pusser was supposed to play himself, but legendary hero died in a mysterious car crash just prior to film's shooting.
Dist.: Vestron

WALKING THE EDGE 1985
★ ★ R Action-Adventure 1:33
☑ Nudity, explicit language, graphic violence
Dir: Norbert Meisel *Cast:* Robert Forster, Nancy Kwan, Joe Spinell, A. Martinez, Aarika Wells, Wayne Woodson
▶ Cab driver/part-time numbers runner Forster gets involved with vigilante Kwan seeking to avenge murder of husband and son by nasty hoodlum Spinell and his thugs. Kwan slays some of her kin's murderers and hides out at Forster's home. When Spinell's men kill Forster's buddy Martinez, Forster catches revenge bug himself. Average actioner will appeal to genre fans.
Dist.: Vestron

WALK IN THE SPRING RAIN, A 1970
★ ★ PG Romance 1:38
☑ Adult situations
Dir: Guy Green *Cast:* Ingrid Bergman, Anthony Quinn, Fritz Weaver, Katherine Crawford, Tom Fielding
▶ On a trip to the South, Bergman, wife of urban academic Weaver, finds romance with rural married man Quinn. Obstacles to their happiness include his son Fielding and her daughter Crawford. Love story features good performances from the dependable Bergman and Quinn.
Dist.: RCA/Columbia

WALK IN THE SUN, A 1945
★ ★ ★ NR War 1:57 B&W
Dir: Lewis Milestone *Cast:* Dana Andrews, Richard Conte, John Ireland, George Tyne, Lloyd Bridges, Sterling Holloway

▶ The story of an infantry platoon's attack on a Nazi hideout in Italy, from their beach landing in Salerno to their final objective, a farmhouse six miles inland. Early fatalities put sergeant Andrews in command of a mixed bag of personalities. Adaptation of Robert Rossen's novel concentrates as much on depicting men under stress as on action.
Dist.: Various

WALK INTO HELL 1957 Australian
☆ **NR Action-Adventure 1:33**
Dir: Lee Robinson *Cast:* Chips Rafferty, Françoise Christophe, Reginald Lye, Pierre Cressoy
▶ Adventurer Rafferty leads doctor Christophe and wheeler-dealer Lye into the New Guinea jungle to look for oil. They find the black gold, but restless ·natives may prevent them from getting out alive, much less rich. New Guinea scenery is more vivid than the ordinary story. Produced by Rafferty.
Dist.: Nelson

WALK LIKE A MAN 1987
★ ★ ★ **PG Comedy 1:26**
☑ Explicit language
Dir: Melvin Frank *Cast:* Howie Mandel, Christopher Lloyd, Cloris Leachman, Colleen Camp, Amy Steel
▶ Lost in wilderness as child and raised by wolves for twenty-nine years, Mandel is discovered by biologist Steel and returned to civilization. Scurrying around on all fours, Mandel is reunited with debt-ridden brother Lloyd, his alcoholic wife Camp, and eccentric rich mother Leachman. Steel teaches Mandel human behavior and falls in love with him, while Lloyd tries to swindle his brother out of inheritance.
Dist.: MGM/UA

WALK ON THE WILD SIDE 1962
★ ★ ★ ★ **NR Drama 1:54 B&W**
Dir: Edward Dmytryk *Cast:* Laurence Harvey, Jane Fonda, Capucine, Anne Baxter, Barbara Stanwyck
▶ Texan Harvey searches for his long-lost love Capucine and finds her in a New Orleans whorehouse. Unfortunately, tough madam Stanwyck won't give her up without a fight. Spicy soap opera has wisecracking Fonda and terrific credit sequence (featuring a black cat and Elmer Bernstein's distinctive title tune). Drawbacks are an uneven story and draggy pacing.
Dist.: RCA/Columbia

WALL STREET 1987
★ ★ ★ ★ **R Drama 2:08**
☑ Nudity, adult situations, explicit language
Dir: Oliver Stone *Cast:* Michael Douglas, Charlie Sheen, Daryl Hannah, Martin Sheen, Terence Stamp, Hal Holbrook
▶ Ambitious stock broker Charlie Sheen is lured into insider trading scheme by unscrupulous bigwig financier Douglas. Soon Sheen is living the good life, buying a luxury apartment and squiring around beautiful decorator Hannah. But when Douglas schemes to buy and dismantle the airline employing Sheen's dad Martin Sheen, the corrupt broker has a crisis of conscience. Director Stone's morality tale is slick and entertaining. Douglas won Best Actor Oscar with lines like: "Lunch is for wimps, pal." **(CC)**
Dist.: CBS/Fox

WALTZ ACROSS TEXAS 1983
★ ★ ★ **PG Romance 1:39**
☑ Brief nudity, adult situations, explicit language
Dir: Ernest Day *Cast:* Anne Archer, Terry Jastrow, Noah Beery, Jr., Mary Kay Place, Richard Farnsworth, Josh Taylor
▶ Ivy League geologist Archer clashes with down-home Texas wildcatter Jastrow until they team up to drill for oil. Workers dislike having a woman boss and the well turns up dry, but Jastrow and Archer fall in love. They decide to give oil biz one more shot. Romance of opposites carried by fine supporting cast.
Dist.: Vestron

WALTZ OF THE TOREADORS 1962 British
★ **NR Comedy 1:45**
Dir: John Guillermin *Cast:* Peter Sellers, Dany Robin, Margaret Leighton, John Fraser, Cyril Cusack, Prunella Scales
▶ Retired army officer Sellers, unhappily married to Leighton, seeks to resume relationship with old flame Robin, but is beaten to the punch by his young assistant, Fraser. Okay adaptation of the play by Jean Anouilh features good work from Sellers and the supporting cast.
Dist.: Various

WANDERERS, THE 1979
★ ★ ★ **R Drama 1:53**
☑ Adult situations, explicit language, violence
Dir: Philip Kaufman *Cast:* Ken Wahl, John Friedrich, Karen Allen, Toni Kalem, Alan Rosenberg, Jim Youngs
▶ High schoolers Wahl and Friedrich in an Italian gang called the Wanderers have run-ins with rival gangs. Encounters with ethnic counterparts end mostly in harmless bluster, but brushes with shaved-headed Baldies and vicious Duck Boys result in violence. Meanwhile boys pursue Allen and Kalem, using ploys like strip poker. Despite unevenness of plot and tone, adaptation of Richard Price's novel set in the Bronx, 1963, is a cult favorite due to spirited cast and director Kaufman's fresh approach to familiar material.
Dist.: Warner

WANNSEE CONFERENCE, THE 1984 Austrian/German
☆ **NR Drama 1:27**
Dir: Heinz Schirk *Cast:* Dietrich Mattausch, Gerg Bockmann, Friedrich Beckhaus, Gunter Spoerrie, Martin Luttge, Peter Fritz
▶ Gripping, real-time re-creation of an actual

event: the 1942 conference at which Nazi leaders discussed how to put the Final Solution into effect. Most of the dialogue is delivered verbatim from the meeting's minutes, and the Nazis discuss with chilling matter-of-factness programs that will exterminate millions. Lays bare the banality of evil. [S]
Dist.: Prism

WANTED: DEAD OR ALIVE 1987
★ ★ ★ ★ R Action-Adventure 1:44
☑ Explicit language, graphic violence
Dir: Gary A. Sherman *Cast:* Rutger Hauer, Robert Guillaume, Gene Simmons, Mel Harris, William Russ, Susan McDonald
▶ Bounty hunter Hauer, an ex–CIA agent, is hired by former boss Guillaume to capture terrorist Simmons. Hauer will get a bonus if he brings in Simmons alive. When Simmons slays Hauer's buddy Russ and girlfriend McDonald, bonus incentive becomes incidental. Action fans will be enthralled, but squeamish should stay away. Loosely based on 1950s TV series of same name starring Steve McQueen; tight-lipped Hauer plays McQueen's grandson. **(CC)**
Dist.: New World

WAR AND LOVE 1985
★ ★ PG-13 War/Drama 1:52
☑ Adult situations, violence
Dir: Moshe Mizrahi *Cast:* Sebastian Keneas, Kyra Sedgwick, David Spielberg, Cheryl Gianini, Eda Reiss-Merin, Brita Youngblood
▶ In 1939, young Jew Keneas flees the Warsaw ghetto by posing as Christian after the Nazi invasion. He falls in love with Sedgwick, a Jew using the same ruse to survive; together they dodge Nazis to smuggle food to friends and family. Separated when captured by Germans, the two vow to be reunited some day. True story of Jack Eisner, film's producer, is given uninspired treatment by director Mizrahi.
Dist.: MGM/UA

WAR AND PEACE 1956 U.S./Italian
★ ★ NR Action-Adventure 3:28
Dir: King Vidor *Cast:* Audrey Hepburn, Henry Fonda, Mel Ferrer, Vittorio Gassman, John Mills, Anita Ekberg
▶ Sprawling melodrama centered on a romantic triangle between prince Ferrer, his good friend Fonda, and young beauty Hepburn prior to and during Napoleon's invasion of Russia. Old-fashioned Hollywood spectacle, based on Tolstoy's epic novel, has first-rate cast, sweeping story, and terrific battle scenes. However, length and erratic script are drawbacks.
Dist.: Paramount

WAR AND PEACE 1968 Russian
★ PG Action-Adventure 6:10
☑ Adult situations, explicit language, violence
Dir: Sergei Bondarchuk *Cast:* Lyudmila Savelyeva, Sergei Bondarchuk, Vyacheslav

Tikhonov, Viktor Stanitsyn, Kira Golovko, Oleg Tabakov
▶ Elaborate, extremely long production of Tolstoy's epic novel may be the most expensive movie ever made, as the Soviets claim it cost $100 million. Authentic battle scenes and sequences featuring Russian aristocracy in genuine settings are impressive, but the drama and emotion get lost in the fuss. Dubbed into English; original uncut version ran 8:27.
Dist.: Paramount

WARGAMES 1983
★ ★ ★ ★ PG Drama 1:52
☑ Explicit language, mild violence
Dir: John Badham *Cast:* Matthew Broderick, Ally Sheedy, Dabney Coleman, John Wood, Barry Corbin, Juanin Clay
▶ Brilliant but bored teen Broderick spends most of his time fooling with his home computer. He and girlfriend Sheedy accidentally tap into a Pentagon computer and, thinking they're playing a game, put U.S. defense network on full alert against presumed Soviet attack. Government bigwig Coleman and his men search for Broderick; he seeks out Wood, the computer's programmer, before nuclear war breaks out. Blockbuster hit entertains with thrilling end-of-the-world scenario and engaging Broderick. **(CC)**
Dist.: MGM/UA

WARLOCK 1959
★ ★ ★ NR Western 2:01
Dir: Edward Dmytryk *Cast:* Richard Widmark, Henry Fonda, Anthony Quinn, Dorothy Malone, Dolores Michaels, Wallace Ford
▶ Unusually complex Western about a frontier town terrorized by bandits that hires gunslinger Fonda as sheriff. With the help of club-footed sidekick Quinn, he imposes a measure of security, but at a stiff price. Widmark is the deputy who must stand up to Fonda. Dark psychological twists enhance frequent gunfights. **(CC)**
Dist.: CBS/Fox

WARLOCK 1989
★ ★ ★ R Horror 1:30
☑ Adult situations, explicit language, violence
Dir: Steve Miner *Cast:* Lori Singer, Julian Sands, Richard E. Grant
▶ Evil entity Sands escapes the gallows in seventeenth-century Boston and surfaces in present-day Los Angeles searching for the divided sections of a "Devil's Bible." Witchfinder Grant pursues him across time, and across the country. Sands is smooth and slimy as he leads Grant and helper Singer on a lively, violent, and effects-filled chase.
Dist.: New World

WARLORDS 1988
☆ R Action-Adventure 1:27
☑ Nudity, explicit language, violence
Dir: Fred Olen Ray *Cast:* David Carradine,

Sid Haig, Ross Hagen, Fox Harris, Robert Quarry, Dawn Wildsmith

▶ In a post-holocaust future, crazed mutants have kidnapped soldier-of-fortune Carradine's wife and a scientist. Tough-but-sexy redhead Wildsmith joins the Carradine rescue mission. Dime store production has repellent characterizations, bad dialogue, and a plot reminiscent of better movies.
Dist.: Vidmark

WARLORDS FROM HELL 1988
☆ **NR Action-Adventure 1:40**
☑ Explicit language, violence
Dir: Clark Henderson *Cast:* Jeffrey D. Rice, Brad Henson, Mark Merry
▶ Two Americans are motorcycling through Mexico when they are captured by a vicious gang of drug-dealing bikers. The bikers also kidnap a local woman, force her to sleep with the leader, and make the prisoners harvest their marijuana crop. Lurid doings awkwardly filmed and acted.
Dist.: Warner

WARLORDS OF THE 21ST CENTURY 1982
☆ **PG Action-Adventure 1:31**
☑ Adult situations, explicit language, violence
Dir: Harley Corkliss *Cast:* Michael Beck, Annie McEnroe, James Wainwright, John Ratzenberger, Randolph Powell, Bruno Lawrence
▶ In the future, "oil wars" have depleted most of world's fuel, leaving vehicles useless and civilization in ruins. Marauding pirate Wainwright, with secret gasoline supply and a band of thugs, loots and kills all in his path. His daughter McEnroe, appalled by dad, runs away to peace-loving commune, aided by motorcycle-riding loner Beck. When Wainwright seeks daughter, Beck must fight for her independence. Cheap rip-off of *The Road Warrior* will disappoint all but die-hard genre fans.
Dist.: Nelson

WAR LOVER, THE 1962 British
★ ★ **NR War 1:45 B&W**
Dir: Phillip Leacock *Cast:* Steve McQueen, Robert Wagner, Shirley Anne Field, Gary Cockrell, Michael Crawford
▶ In World War II England, daredevil bomber pilot McQueen and his more cautious colleague Wagner fall in love with Englishwoman Field. The fliers' lives are endangered during a large-scale mission. Adaptation of the John Hersey novel features fine flying sequences but spends too much time on the ground.
Dist.: RCA/Columbia

WARM NIGHTS ON A SLOW MOVING TRAIN 1987 Australian
★ **NR Drama 1:31**
☑ Brief nudity, adult situations, explicit language
Dir: Bob Ellis *Cast:* Wendy Hughes, Colin

Friels, Norman Kaye, John Clayton, Rod Zuanic, Peter Whitford
▶ Catholic school art teacher Hughes takes care of her morphine-addicted, handicapped brother and makes ends meets by working as a prositute on the Melbourne-Sydney train. She avoids emotional involvement with men until she meets smooth-talking Friels. Gloomy drama long on talk and short on real erotic charge, despite Hughes's allure.
Dist.: Prism

WARM SUMMER RAIN 1989
★ **R Drama 1:22**
☑ Nudity, strong sexual content, explicit language
Dir: Joe Gayton *Cast:* Kelly Lynch, Barry Tubb, Ron Sloan
▶ After attempting suicide, troubled Lynch leaves the hospital and wakes up next to tuxedo-clad fugitive Tubb. They have sex and talk about their pasts. He claims to have killed his fiancée; she discusses her suicide attempt. Dramatically inert screenplay fails to make characters sympathetic, but does give Lynch some meaty monologues.
Dist.: RCA/Columbia

WARNING SIGN 1985
★ ★ ★ **R Sci-Fi 1:39**
☑ Explicit language, violence
Dir: Hal Barwood *Cast:* Sam Waterston, Kathleen Quinlan, Yaphet Kotto, Jeffrey DeMunn, Richard Dysart, G. W. Bailey
▶ At a secret germ warfare laboratory in Utah run by fanatical scientist Dysart, gene-splicing experiment goes awry and turns all workers into homicidal zombies. Local sheriff Waterston seeks to control zombies and rescue researcher wife Quinlan before she succumbs. Army major Kotto arrives with troops to assist Waterston while microbiologist DeMunn seeks cure. Intriguing premise and competent action. **(CC)**
Dist.: CBS/Fox

WAR OF THE ROSES, THE 1989
★ ★ ★ **R Comedy 1:56**
☑ Adult situations, explicit language, violence
Dir: Danny DeVito *Cast:* Michael Douglas, Kathleen Turner, Danny DeVito, Marianne Sägebrecht, Sean Astin, Heather Fairfield
▶ Vitriolic comedy about the horrors of divorce starts with the storybook romance of Turner and Douglas, who meet on Nantucket during a school break. Two kids, a law practice, and one beautiful antiques-filled home later, they decide to split, but each wants the house. Turner calls in lawyer DeVito, and one of the vulgarest, most vicious, and hilarious divorces ever begins. Stinging direction from DeVito stays true to its black comedy dictates, copping out only when it comes to the fate of the family pooch. **(CC)**
Dist.: CBS/Fox

WAR OF THE WILDCATS 1943
★ ★ NR Western 1:42 B&W
Dir: Albert S. Rogell   *Cast:* John Wayne, Martha Scott, Albert Dekker, Gabby Hayes, Marjorie Rambeau, Dale Evans
▶ Driven out of town after she writes a scandalous book, schoolmarm Scott winds up on a train in the company of cowboy Wayne and oilman Dekker, who later compete for the right to drill oil on Indian land. Wayne sides with the Indians to get the lease, and, while romancing Scott, races against time to deliver the oil. The Duke is two-fisted and effective in this solid Western, as are Roy Rogers stalwarts Hayes and Evans. Also known as *In Old Oklahoma.*
Dist.: Republic

WAR OF THE WORLDS, THE 1953
★ ★ ★ G Sci-Fi 1:25
Dir: Byron Haskin   *Cast:* Gene Barry, Ann Robinson, Les Tremayne, Robert Cornthwaite, Lewis Martin, Cedric Hardwicke
▶ Martians invade the Earth, sending ordinary Americans fleeing in terror from their heat rays. Caught in the crossfire: Pacific Tech scientist Barry and his girlfriend Robinson. The excitement and thrills are virtually nonstop, thanks to amazing Oscar-winning special effects and breathless pacing. Scariest moments: the Martians zapping preacher who tries to reason with them and Robinson's encounter with an alien.
Dist.: Paramount

WAR PARTY 1989
★ ★ ★ R Action-Adventure 1:39
☑ Explicit language, graphic violence
Dir: Franc Roddam   *Cast:* Billy Wirth, Kevin Dillon, Tim Sampson, Jimmie Ray Weeks, M. Emmet Walsh, Dennis Banks
▶ Modern-day Montana re-creation of an old Indian battle goes disastrously wrong when a bigoted white uses real bullets, killing one of the Indians. Dillon and Wirth retaliate, then escape to the hills. The police and a redneck posse pursue. Gripping combination of social comment and action betrays a heavy hand only at its climax. Best performance: Walsh as the bounty hunter.
Dist.: HBO

WARRIOR AND THE SORCERESS, THE 1984
★ R Action-Adventure 1:21
☑ Nudity, violence
Dir: John Broderick   *Cast:* David Carradine, Luke Askew, Maria Socas, Anthony DeLongis, Harry Townes
▶ Holy warrior Carradine arrives in village where rival clans vie for control of water well while oppressing peasants. Mercenary Carradine plays each side against the other. Then, with gift of magic sword from bare-chested sorceress Socas, he fights to free hapless villagers. Low-budget remake of plots from

Yojimbo and *A Fistful of Dollars* has sufficient swordplay and kung fu to satisfy action fans.
Dist.: Vestron

WARRIOR OF THE LOST WORLD 1985 Italian
☆ R Sci-Fi 1:30
☑ Violence
Dir: David Worth   *Cast:* Robert Ginty, Donald Pleasence, Fred Williamson, Persis Khambatta, Harrison Muller, Janna Ryan
▶ In the future, nuclear war has destroyed civilzation and left remnants of humanity under sway of ruthless dictator Pleasence and his terrorizing troops. Nameless warrior Ginty on supersonic motorcycle helps rebel leader Muller and feisty daughter Khambatta attempt overthrow of despot. Second-rate spaghetti sci-fi strikes out.
Dist.: HBO

WARRIOR QUEEN 1986
★ R Drama 1:20
☑ Rape, nudity, adult situations, explicit language, violence
Dir: Chuck Vincent   *Cast:* Sybil Danning, Donald Pleasence, Richard Hill, J. J. Jones, Tally Chanel, Samantha Fox
▶ Cheesy exploitation filmed in Italy purports to offer an inside look at decadent aristocrats cavorting under the shadow of Vesuvius. Danning, the well-endowed queen, bids on a few slaves, but her role is almost as brief as Pleasence's (playing Pompei's Mayor Clodius). Climactic eruption was lifted from other films. Cassette version, unrated by MPAA, contains additional sex scenes.
Dist.: Vestron

WARRIORS, THE 1955
★ NR Action-Adventure 1:25
Dir: Henry Levin   *Cast:* Errol Flynn, Joanne Dru, Peter Finch, Yvonne Furneaux, Michael Hordern
▶ After the British defeat the French during the Hundred Years War, French count Finch kidnaps English lady Dru to entrap British prince Flynn. Flynn infiltrates Finch's troops incognito. Outstanding production values and dependable Flynn combine for above-average genre fare.
Dist.: CBS/Fox

WARRIORS, THE 1979
★ ★ ★ R Action-Adventure 1:29
☑ Explicit language, violence
Dir: Walter Hill   *Cast:* Michael Beck, James Remar, Thomas Waites, Dorsey Wright, Brian Tyler, David Harris
▶ During delegate rally of two-hundred street gangs in the Bronx, one gang leader is assassinated by a lunatic. Angry delegates wrongfully accuse the Warriors and seek violent retribution. Flight back to Warriors' Coney Island turf is filled with fights against vicious rivals and encounters with bizarre denizens of the night. Nonstop pace, stark but hypnotic images,

and unusual gang motifs distinguish actioner tinted with fantasy.
Dist.: Paramount

WARRIORS OF THE WASTELAND 1984 Italian
☆ R Sci-Fi 1:27
☑ Rape, nudity, adult situations, explicit language, graphic violence
Dir: Enzo Castellari *Cast:* Timothy Brent, Fred Williamson, Anna Kanakis, Vennatino Venantini, George Eastman, Andrea Coppola
▶ In the wake of nuclear holocaust, lone heroes Brent and Williamson protect religious leader Venantini and flock from violent marauders in souped-up cars. Thugs abduct and rape Brent, causing crisis of confidence, but pep talk from Williamson restores fighting spirit. Venantini's murder leads to final confrontation. Low-budget schlock with some truly distasteful scenes is yet another retread of *The Road Warrior*.
Dist.: HBO

WAR WAGON, THE 1967
★ ★ ★ NR Western 1:41
Dir: Burt Kennedy *Cast:* John Wayne, Kirk Douglas, Howard Keel, Robert Walker, Jr., Keenan Wynn, Bruce Dern
▶ Framed by a greedy mine owner, Wayne sets out for revenge upon release from jail. The target: an armor-plated wagon holding a fortune in gold dust. Douglas, originally hired to kill the Duke, joins forces with Wayne's men in the daring heist. Sharp-tongued Indian Keel and irascible codger Wynn offer strong comic support in this fast-paced, funny Western.
Dist.: MCA

WASH, THE 1988
★ NR Drama 1:34
☑ Adult situations
Dir: Michael Toshiyuki Uno *Cast:* Mako, Nobu McCarthy, Patti Yasutake, Marian Yue, Sab Shimono, Shizuko Hoshi
▶ In San Jose's Japantown, McCarthy leaves Mako, her husband of forty years, although she continues to do his laundry. Widower Shimono woos McCarthy while Mako must deal with his anger over the separation and other issues. Sensitive drama conveys insight, although filmmaking lacks punch. Produced by "American Playhouse."
Dist.: Academy

WASP WOMAN, THE 1959
★ NR Horror 1:06 B&W
Dir: Roger Corman *Cast:* Susan Cabot, Fred (Anthony) Eisley, Barboura Morris, Michael Marks, William Roerick, Frank Gerstle
▶ Essence of wasp is the prime ingredient of scientist Marks's formula for rejuvenation, and it's just the thing for youth-obsessed cosmetics queen Cabot. Unfortunately, scientist's concoction turns Cabot into a buzzing killer after nightfall. Lovers of ridiculous horror movies will find this irresistible.
Dist.: Sinister

WATCHED! 1972
☆ R Drama 1:35
☑ Explicit language
Dir: John Parsons *Cast:* Stacy Keach, Harris Yulin, Brigid Polk, Denver John Collins
▶ Former lawyer and narcotics officer Keach slowly comes unravelled as he agonizes over past loves and busts via tapes made by chief narc Yulin. Slow-paced, technically weak film aspires to statement about privacy, surveillance, and sixties politics, but lacks a compelling story or interesting lead character.
Dist.: Vestron

WATCHER IN THE WOODS, THE 1981
★ ★ ★ PG Family 1:24
☑ Mild violence
Dir: John Hough *Cast:* Bette Davis, Carroll Baker, David McCallum, Lynn-Holly Johnson, Kyle Richards, Ian Bannen
▶ Youngsters Johnson and Richard, in England for the summer, move into eccentric recluse Davis's secluded mansion with their parents. Ghost of blindfolded girl and other specters haunt the family. Johnson learns Davis's daughter disappeared during seance thirty years prior—could the phantom be the long-lost girl? Familly tare from Disney offers creepy supernatural story, teen sleuth for kids, and immortal Davis for older crowd.
Dist.: Buena Vista

WATCHERS 1988
★ ★ R Sci-Fi 1:32
☑ Adult situations, explicit language, graphic violence
Dir: Jon Hess *Cast:* Corey Haim, Barbara Williams, Michael Ironside, Lala, Duncan Fraser, Blu Mankuma
▶ Secret government project develops a brainy dog that can type and play Scrabble and an unearthly monster called Oxcom that hates the brilliant canine. The dog escapes to hide in a small town with Haim and his mom Williams. Oxcom pursues its nemesis, killing those in its way, while ruthless government agent Ironside tracks both runaways. Adapted from the Dean R. Koontz novel.
Dist.: IVE

WATCH ON THE RHINE 1943
★ ★ ★ NR Drama 1:54 B&W
Dir: Herman Shumlin *Cast:* Bette Davis, Paul Lukas, Geraldine Fitzgerald, Lucile Watson, Beulah Bondi, George Coulouris
▶ Respectful adaptation of Lillian Hellman's ground-breaking antifascist play concerns European family visiting relatives in Washington on the eve of World War II. Father Lukas (in an Oscar-winning performance) is threatened with blackmail by a German informer, but doesn't lose faith in his ideals. Screenplay by Dashiell Hammett.
Dist.: Key

WATER 1986 British
★ PG-13 Comedy 1:35
☑ Adult situations, explicit language

Dir: Dick Clement *Cast:* Michael Caine, Valerie Perrine, Brenda Vaccaro, Billy Connolly, Leonard Rossiter, Jimmie C. Walker
► Economically depressed British island in Caribbean, run by pot-smoking governor Caine and his bird-brained wife Vaccaro, is ignored by the world. Then an abandoned oil rig spews forth Perrier water, causing Cuba, England, and France to compete for control of the valuable well. Meanwhile wealthy environmentalist Perrine makes pitch of her own to Caine. Uneven comedy has few effervescent moments.
Dist.: Paramount

WATER BABIES, THE 1979 British
★ ★ ★ ★ **NR Animation 1:33**
Dir: Lionel Jeffries *Cast:* James Mason, Billie Whitelaw, Bernard Cribbins, Tommy Pender, Joan Greenwood, David Tomlinson
► In combination of live-action and animation, young chimney sweep Pender in 1850 England is wrongfully accused of theft by bosses Mason and Cribbins. To escape from pursuers, Pender dives into a pond. Trapped underwater, he encounters animated world populated by pond dwellers with human traits. With aid of fairy godmother, Pender helps "water babies" in battle against bad fish. Appealing diversion for youngsters, but adults may get restless. Based on Charles Kingsley's classic children's tale.
Dist.: Nelson

WATERHOLE #3 1967
★ ★ ★ **NR Western 1:35**
Dir: William Graham *Cast:* James Coburn, Carroll O'Connor, Margaret Blye, Claude Akins, Timothy Carey, Bruce Dern, Joan Blondell, James Whitmore
► Broad, racy spoof of Westerns finds crooked cavalry sergeant Akins, apoplectic sheriff O'-Connor, his nubile daughter Blye, and charming con man Coburn all racing for a fortune in gold hidden in the desert. Good bits by Blondell and Whitmore, bawdy situations (notably Coburn's "assault with a friendly weapon"), and smart dialogue add up to amusing entertainment.
Dist.: Paramount

WATERLOO BRIDGE 1940
★ ★ ★ **NR Romance 1:43 B&W**
Dir: Mervyn Leroy *Cast:* Vivien Leigh, Robert Taylor, Lucile Watson, C. Aubrey Smith, Maria Ouspenskaya, Virginia Field
► During World War I air raid, dancer Leigh and army officer Taylor meet on London's Waterloo Bridge. They fall in love but, when he is presumed dead, she sinks into prostitution to support herself. When he returns alive, her past haunts their renewed chance at happiness. Highly emotional heartbreaker with lovely Leigh-Taylor chemistry and a tearjerker ending. Based on the Robert Sherwood play. (CC)
Dist.: MGM/UA Ⓒ

WATERMELON MAN 1970
★ ★ **R Comedy 1:40**
☑ Adult situations, explicit language
Dir: Melvin Van Peebles *Cast:* Godfrey Cambridge, Estelle Parsons, Howard Caine, Mantan Moreland, Erin Moran, D'Urville Martin
► White conservative Cambridge must eat his own bigoted words when he wakes up one morning to find himself a black man. His wife Parsons and business associates have a tough time adjusting to his new state. Racy satire of racism scores salient social points although some of it is a bit obvious.
Dist.: RCA/Columbia

WATERSHIP DOWN 1978 British
★ ★ ★ ★ **PG Animation 1:32**
☑ Violence
Dir: Martin Rosen *Cast:* Voices of John Hurt, Ralph Richardson, Denholm Elliott, Zero Mostel, Richard Briers, Harry Andrews
► In a rabbit warren, prophet Hazel warns of impending destruction of home and leads group of male believers on a perilous search for a new place to live. Surviving dogs, owls, foxes, and men, they reach a hill called Watership Down. There they must lure women away from neighboring clan of hostile rabbits. Well-handled adaptation of Richard Adams's allegorical novel offers thoughtful entertainment for all ages.
Dist.: Warner

WAVELENGTH 1983
★ ★ ★ **PG Sci-Fi 1:27**
☑ Nudity, explicit language, violence
Dir: Mike Gray *Cast:* Robert Carradine, Cherie Currie, Keenan Wynn, Cal Bowman, James Hess, Terry Burns
► In an underground Hollywood Hills facility, the Air Force conducts medical experiments on three extraterrestrials. Rock musician Carradine and girlfriend Currie discover apparently abandoned site and investigate with help of grizzled prospector Wynn. Soon trio is also held captive by military and must befriend somewhat intimidating aliens. Reasonably diverting sci-fi fare boasts inventive soundtrack by rock group Tangerine Dream.
Dist.: Nelson

WAXWORK 1988
★ **R Horror 1:37**
☑ Adult situations, explicit language, graphic violence
Dir: Anthony Hickox *Cast:* Zach Galligan, Deborah Foreman, Michelle Johnson, David Warner, Patrick Macnee, John Rhys-Davies
► Galligan and Foreman are among six college kids invited to wax museum owner Warner's midnight opening. The kids should have stayed in bed—the relics come to murderous life. Polished surface but lackluster direction; young cast plays it strictly tongue-in-cheek. Goriest scene: the vampire done in by

the wine rack. Also available in an unrated version.
Dist.: Vestron

WAY AHEAD, THE 1944 British
★★ NR War 1:31 B&W
Dir: Carol Reed   *Cast:* David Niven, Stanley Holloway, James Donald, John Laurie, Leslie Dwyer, Trevor Howard, Peter Ustinov, Leo Genn, Raymond Lovell
▶ England is in trouble at the start of World War II, and Niven is ordered to whip a handful of raw recruits from various ranks of civilian life into soldiers. Group grumbles, but coheres in time to fight Nazis in North Africa. Superior male bonding saga, co-written by Ustinov and introducing Howard to the screen. Also known as *The Immortal Batallion*.
Dist.: Video Yesteryear

WAY DOWN EAST 1920
★ NR Drama 3:12 B&W
Dir: D. W. Griffith   *Cast:* Lillian Gish, Richard Barthelmess, Lowell Sherman, Burr McItosh, Kate Bruce, Mary Hay
▶ Innocent country girl Gish is seduced by sophisticated city fellow Sherman and must flee her town in the dead of winter when she gives birth to a child. Trapped on an ice flow heading toward a waterfall, she appears doomed. Will hero Barthelmess be able to save her? This silent melodrama's story seemed old-fashioned even in 1920, but director Griffith and star Gish masterfully wring from it every last gasp and tear.
Dist.: Video Yesteryear

WAY OUT WEST 1937
★★★★★ G Comedy 1:05 B&W
Dir: James W. Horne   *Cast:* Stan Laurel, Oliver Hardy, James Finlayson, Sharon Lynne, Stanley Fields, Rosina Lawrence
▶ Laurel and Hardy head for the frontier town of Brushwood Gulch to hand over a gold mine deed to their friend's daughter; bartender Mickey Finn (Finlayson) learns of the deed and sets out to steal it from the boys. Genial Western spoof may be the duo's best feature: marvelous gags, perfect timing, and charming soft-shoe versions of "Trail of the Lonesome Pine" and "Commence Dancing" add up to sheer delight.
Dist.: Various   C

WAY WEST, THE 1967
★★★ NR Western 2:02
Dir: Andrew V. McLaglen   *Cast:* Kirk Douglas, Robert Mitchum, Richard Widmark, Lola Albright, Michael Witney, Stubby Kaye, Sally Field
▶ Limp adaptation of A. B. Guthrie's Pulitzer prize-winning novel concerns wagon train led by widowed senator Douglas and aging scout Mitchum across the Oregon Trail. Newlywed Witney leaves wife for Field (in her film debut), then provokes war with the Sioux.

Mitchum's brooding performance can't salvage meandering plot.
Dist.: Wood Knapp

WAY WE WERE, THE 1973
★★★★★ PG Romance 1:58
☑ Adult situations, explicit language
Dir: Sydney Pollack   *Cast:* Barbra Streisand, Robert Redford, Bradford Dillman, Murray Hamilton, Viveca Lindfors, Lois Chiles
▶ Hugely popular romance about the unlikely courtship and marriage of political activist Streisand and WASPy Ivy League writer Redford. After World War II they move to California, where she reads scripts and turns his novel into a movie. Hollywood blacklisting makes their political differences even harder to live with. One of the great screen romances, with true chemistry between the leads, was adapted by Arthur Laurents from his novel. Nominated for five Oscars, including Streisand as Best Actress; won for score and for hit title song.
Dist.: RCA/Columbia

W.C. FIELDS STRAIGHT UP 1986
★★★ NR Documentary 1:30
Dir: Joe Adamson   *Cast:* Narrated by Dudley Moore, W. C. Fields, Leonard Maltin, Joseph L. Mankiewicz, Ronald J. Fields
▶ Emmy-winning documentary about the great comedian destroys many myths about Fields's personal life (for example, his tombstone does not read "I'd rather be in Philadelphia"). Interweaves brief but insightful interviews with W. C.'s grandson/biographer Ronald J. Fields and others with clips from his funniest movies. Suitable for fans and the uninitiated.
Dist.: Vestron

WE ALL LOVED EACH OTHER SO MUCH 1977 Italian
★ NR Comedy 2:04
☑ Nudity, adult situations, explicit language
Dir: Ettore Scola   *Cast:* Nino Manfredi, Vittorio Gassman, Aldo Fabrizi, Stefania Sandrelli, Giovanna Ralli, Stefano Satta Flores
▶ Wry, nostalgic comedy follows the lives of buddies Gassman, Manfredi, and Flores from their days as anti-Nazi partisans to bitter, successful, or disillusioned middle age. All three are involved with Sandrelli, an aspiring actress whose career apex is as an extra in *La Dolce Vita*. Delightful sequences pay homage to film buffs and directors with cameos by Vittorio de Sica, Federico Fellini, and Marcello Mastroianni.   S
Dist.: RCA/Columbia

WEAVERS: WASN'T THAT A TIME!, THE 1982
★★ PG Documentary/Music 1:18
☑ Explicit language
Dir: Jim Brown   *Cast:* Lee Hays, Pete Seeger, Ronnie Gilbert, Fred Hellerman, Arlo Guthrie, Don McLean
▶ Happy, tuneful document of the 1980 reunion of The Weavers, an early fifties singing

group who sparked a popular revival of folk and traditional music with songs like "Goodnight Irene" and "This Land Is Your Land." Includes concert footage and sentimental account of group's blacklisting for Stalinist politics. Group member Hays died six months after recording narration.
Dist.: MGM/UA

WEDDING, A 1978
★ **PG Comedy 2:00**
☑ Brief nudity, adult situations, explicit language
Dir: Robert Altman ***Cast:*** Carol Burnett, Mia Farrow, Lillian Gish, Geraldine Chaplin, Howard Duff, Lauren Hutton, Vittorio Gassman, Desi Arnaz, Jr., Amy Stryker, John Cromwell
► Forty-eight-character extravaganza explores traumas of disastrous wedding between offspring of nouveau riche Southerners and old Midwestern money. Director Altman's satire of the wealthy suffers from meanness of spirit; his use of multiple plots and ensemble cast works much better in *Nashville*.
Dist.: CBS/Fox

WEDDING IN BLOOD 1973 French/Italian
☆ **PG Mystery-Suspense 1:38**
☑ Adult situations, violence
Dir: Claude Chabrol ***Cast:*** Stephane Audran, Michel Piccoli, Claude Pieplu, Clothilde Joano, Eliana de Santis
► Sexy Audran grows tired of marriage to Pieplu, and has an affair with the far more fascinating Piccoli. To get rid of his own wife, Piccoli slips her some poison. Then he and Audran plot to kill Pieplu. Marital stew has a suspenseful savor, thanks to director Chabrol. [S]
Dist.: RCA/Columbia

WEDDING MARCH, THE 1928
☆ **NR Drama 1:52 B&W/C**
Dir: Erich von Stroheim ***Cast:*** Erich von Stroheim, Fay Wray, ZaSu Pitts, George Fawcett, Maude George, George Nicholls
► In imperial Austria, wastrel prince von Stroheim falls madly in love with working-class Wray. The prince seduces the girl amid falling apple blossoms alongside the Danube, but the appearance of "The Iron Man," a legendary spectre, seems to presage doom. Aside from gross scenes with Wray's butcher suitor, this silent masterpiece seems too short—and is, since latter half has been lost. What is left (including several minutes in Technicolor) is top-drawer filmmaking and pure, tragic romance.
Dist.: Paramount

WEEDS 1987
★★★ **R Drama 1:59**
☑ Nudity, adult situations, explicit language, violence
Dir: John Hancock ***Cast:*** Nick Nolte, Lane Smith, Rita Taggart, John Toles-Bey, Joe Mantegna, William Forsythe
► Sentenced for life, prisoner Nolte forms a theater company to perform his play about life behind bars. Drama critic Taggart writes a favorable review and works to get him released. On the outside, he continues his theatrical work and romances Taggart. When the troupe has financial problems, Nolte considers committing another robbery to pay expenses. Nolte showcase is talky but the characters are well drawn. Based on a true story.
Dist.: HBO

WEEKEND AT BERNIE'S 1989
★★★ **PG-13 Comedy 1:41**
☑ Adult situations, explicit language, violence
Dir: Ted Kotcheff ***Cast:*** Andrew McCarthy, Jonathan Silverman, Terry Kiser, Catherine Mary Stewart, Don Calfa, Catherine Parks
► Co-workers McCarthy and Silverman are thrilled when boss Kiser invites them to his beach house, but they arrive to find him dead. Not wanting their weekend spoiled, they prop him up and pretend he's alive. Lunatic farce milks many laughs out of its wild premise. Snappy direction by Kotcheff (who appears briefly as Silverman's father) and sly scene stealing by Kiser as the corpse with the permanent smirk. Funniest sight gag: Kiser waterskiing.
Dist.: IVE

WEEKEND PASS 1984
★ **R Comedy 1:29**
☑ Nudity, adult situations, explicit language, violence
Dir: Lawrence Bassoff ***Cast:*** D. W. Brown, Peter Ellenstein, Patrick Hauser, Chip McAllister, Pamela G. Kay, Hilary Shapiro
► Four sailors finish basic training in San Diego and celebrate with a weekend pass to L.A. Among their adventures: a strip joint, an aerobics class, a visit to Watts, and a comeuppance for one sailor who looks up his old (and now snobby) girlfriend. Standard fare doesn't pay off.
Dist.: Vestron

WEEKEND WARRIORS 1986
★★ **R Comedy 1:29**
☑ Nudity, adult situations, explicit language, adult humor
Dir: Bert Convy ***Cast:*** Chris Lemmon, Vic Tayback, Lloyd Bridges, Graham Jarvis, Daniel Greene, Marty Cohen
► In 1961, show biz types spend weekends in the Air Force Reserve, but prefer high jinks to soldiering. When the men are slated for inspection, they must get their act together or be sent off to fight. More profanity and flatulence than real wil; however, the young cast is appealing and some of the tasteless humor hits home. Also known as *Hollywood Air Force Base*.
Dist.: Vestron

WEE WILLIE WINKIE 1937
★★ **NR Family 1:15 B&W**
Dir: John Ford ***Cast:*** Shirley Temple, Victor

McLaglen, C. Aubrey Smith, June Lang, Michael Whalen, Cesar Romero
▶ Rudyard Kipling story becomes a charming vehicle for Temple, who stops a rebel uprising in colonial India by bringing irascible British colonel Smith and insurgent leader Romero to the negotiating table. Unlikely pairing of Temple and McLaglen is surprisingly successful.
Dist.: Playhouse

WEIRD SCIENCE 1985
★ ★ ★ ★ PG-13 Fantasy/Comedy 1:33
☑ Brief nudity, explicit language, adult humor
Dir: John Hughes *Cast:* Anthony Michael Hall, Kelly LeBrock, Ilan Mitchell-Smith, Bill Paxton, Suzanne Snyder, Robert Downey, Jr.
▶ Nerdy teens Hall and Mitchell-Smith create fantasy woman LeBrock with a computer. LeBrock teaches them to fight bullies, solve family problems, and win girls their own age. Frisky, wild, and woolly, with Hall showing nice comic timing. Best scene: LeBrock meets the parents. (CC)
Dist.: MCA

WELCOME HOME 1989
★ ★ ★ ★ R Drama 1:36
☑ Adult situations, explicit language
Dir: Franklin J. Schaffner *Cast:* Kris Kristofferson, JoBeth Williams, Sam Waterston, Brian Keith, Thomas Wilson Brown, Trey Wilson
▶ It's quite a surprise when Williams comes face-to-face with husband Kristofferson seventeen years after he was supposed to have been killed in Cambodia. Williams has remarried, and Kristofferson's reappearance triggers anguish and ambivalence in, among others, Dad Keith and son Brown. Good tear-jerking drama has heartfelt ending. Includes music by Willie Nelson and Henry Mancini.
Dist.: RCA/Columbia

WELCOME TO 18 1986
★ ★ PG-13 Comedy/Drama 1:31
☑ Brief nudity, adult situations, explicit language
Dir: Terry Carr *Cast:* Courtney Thorne-Smith, Mariska Hargitay, Jo Ann Willette, Cristen Kauffman, John Putch, Erich Anderson
▶ After high school graduation, California girls Thorne-Smith, Hargitay, and Willette take jobs at a Nevada resort. There they help new friend Kauffman escape the clutches of gangster Anderson. Teen flick has thoughtful aspirations above the run-of-the-mill; nicely cast and shot, although transvestite comic relief is pretty weak.
Dist.: IVE

WELCOME TO L.A. 1976
★ R Drama 1:46
☑ Nudity, adult situations, explicit language
Dir: Alan Rudolph *Cast:* Keith Carradine, Geraldine Chaplin, Sally Kellerman, Lauren Hutton, Harvey Keitel, Sissy Spacek
▶ Songwriter Carradine arrives in Los Angeles and gets involved with a variety of women,

including his dad's girlfriend Hutton, married Chaplin, realtor Kellerman, and maid Spacek. Director Rudolph shows talent but an excess of self-consciousness; moody movie lacks the humor he brought to his later (and superior) *Choose Me.*
Dist.: CBS/Fox

WE OF THE NEVER NEVER 1983 Australian
★ G Drama 2:12
☑ Adult situations, explicit language, violence
Dir: Igor Auzins *Cast:* Angela Punch-McGregor, Arthur Dignam, Tony Barry, Tommy Lewis, Lewis Fitz-Gerald
▶ True story of Jeannie Gunn (Punch-McGregor), who followed husband Dignam to a remote cattle station in the Australian outback, and proved that she could get along in the rough-and-tumble society of wranglers and aborigines. Lead characters are noble and civilized, but best part of the film is its incorporation of aboriginal world view, and delightful tribal extras. Spectacular camerawork amid sweeping landscapes.
Dist.: RCA/Columbia

WE'RE NO ANGELS 1955
★ ★ ★ NR Comedy 1:46
Dir: Michael Curtiz *Cast:* Humphrey Bogart, Aldo Ray, Peter Ustinov, Joan Bennett, Basil Rathbone, Leo G. Carroll
▶ Criminals Bogart, Ray, and Ustinov escape from Devil's Island. They intend to rob struggling couple Bennett and Carroll, but instead decide to help them fight their evil relative Rathbone. Amusing trifle with nifty comic performances by Bogart and company. Remade in 1989.
Dist.: Paramount

WE'RE NO ANGELS 1989
★ ★ PG-13 Comedy 1:41
☑ Brief nudity, adult situations, explicit language, violence
Dir: Neil Jordan *Cast:* Robert De Niro, Sean Penn, Demi Moore, Hoyt Axton, Bruno Kirby, Ray McAnally, James Russo, Wallace Shawn
▶ Dim-witted cons De Niro and Penn inadvertently escape prison when killer Russo drags them along during a bust-out. Coming to a small Northern border town, they are mistaken for lost priests. They take part in the charade, hoping to eventually get to Canada. Film's humor depends too much on De Niro's incessant mugging and the duo's mutiliation of the English language and religious dogma. Labored mistaken-identity script by David Mamet was very loosely based on the Humphrey Bogart film of the same name.
Dist.: Paramount

WESTERNER, THE 1940
★ ★ ★ ★ NR Western 1:40 B&W
Dir: William Wyler *Cast:* Gary Cooper, Walter Brennan, Doris Davenport, Fred Stone, Chill Wills, Forrest Tucker, Dana Andrews
▶ Drifter Cooper, sentenced to hang by the

infamous Judge Roy Bean (Brennan), postpones his execution by promising to introduce Bean to his idol, Lily Langtry. Sly, unpredictable Western is a consistent delight. Brennan won his third Oscar (the first actor to do so) for his wily performance. Film debuts for Tucker and Andrews.
Dist.: Embassy

WESTERN UNION 1941
★★★★ NR Western 1:31
Dir: Fritz Lang ***Cast:*** Randolph Scott, Robert Young, Dean Jagger, Virginia Gilmore, John Carradine, Barton MacLane
► Spirited account of the building of the first telegraph across the Wild West, with an appealing Scott as a reformed outlaw and scout. Obstacles include storms, Indians, and Scott's former gang of bandits. Gilmore provides the love interest as a telegraph operator torn between the outlaw and Eastern dandy Young.
Dist.: CBS/Fox

WEST SIDE STORY 1961
★★★★ NR Musical 2:35
Dir: Robert Wise, Jerome Robbins ***Cast:*** Natalie Wood, Richard Beymer, Russ Tamblyn, Rita Moreno, George Chakiris, John Astin
► Shakespeare's *Romeo and Juliet* updated to a New York ghetto: Puerto Rican Wood falls in love with white Beymer, but their respective warring gangs make the romance ill-fated. Smashing adaptation of the Broadway hit with magnetic Jerome Robbins choreography, glorious Sondheim-Bernstein score ("Tonight," "Maria," "I Feel Pretty"), outstanding performances, and authentic New York City locations. Ten Oscars include Best Picture, Director, Supporting Actor (Chakiris), Supporting Actress (Moreno), and a special award for Robbins. **(CC)**
Dist.: MGM/UA

WESTWARD HO, THE WAGONS 1956
★★ NR Family/Western 1:30
Dir: William Beaudine ***Cast:*** Fess Parker, Kathleen Crowley, Jeff York, David Stollery, Sebastian Cabot, Doreen Tracey
► Frontier scout Parker leads an Oregon-bound wagon train through Indian country. Episodes on the trek involve a desperate Indian attack, an Indian bid to buy a little blond girl, and Parker's growing interest in pretty pioneer Crowley. Though second unit direction is handled by stunt veteran Yakima Canutt, Disney adventure never gets interesting. Features four of the original Mouseketeers.
Dist.: Buena Vista

WESTWORLD 1973
★★★ PG Sci-Fi 1:29
☑ Adult situations, graphic violence
Dir: Michael Crichton ***Cast:*** Yul Brynner, Richard Benjamin, James Brolin, Alan Oppenheimer, Victoria Shaw, Dick Van Patten
► Vacationers Benjamin and Brolin take time off at ultra-futuristic resort where amazingly lifelike robots simulate Old West characters. Fun and games come to a rude end when gunslinger Brynner malfunctions and starts stalking guests. Inventive and stylish action spiced with ironic humor. Brynner is perfectly cast as the implacable menace.
Dist.: MGM/UA

WE THE LIVING 1942 Italian
☆ NR Drama 2:52
☑ Adult situations
Dir: Goffredo Alessandrini ***Cast:*** Alida Valli, Rossano Brazzi, Fosco Giachetti, Giovanni Grasso
► Love triangle in 1920s Leningrad between engineering student Valli, fugitive Brazzi, and party-man Giachetti. Adapted from autobiographical first novel by libertarian theorist Ayn Rand, film faded into obscurity after it was banned by Mussolini. Rand and her followers rediscovered it in the sixties and cut it from four hours to its present length, finally releasing it after her death in 1984. Not worth the wait; politically schematic presentation is slow, stodgy, and stylistically old-fashioned. [S]
Dist.: JCI

WETHERBY 1985 British
☆ R Drama 1:37
☑ Brief nudity, adult situations, explicit language, violence
Dir: David Hare ***Cast:*** Vanessa Redgrave, Ian Holm, Judi Dench, Marjorie Yates, Tom Wilkinson, Joely Richardson
► In a small English village, a stranger kills himself at the house of schoolteacher Redgrave. Secrets in Redgrave's past emerge as the police investigate. Interesting performances (with Redgrave's real-life daughter Richardson playing her in flashbacks), but many will find slack pacing and bewildering plot off-putting. **(CC)**
Dist.: MGM/UA

WE THINK THE WORLD OF YOU 1988 British
★★ PG Drama 1:34
☑ Adult situations, explicit language
Dir: Colin Gregg ***Cast:*** Alan Bates, Gary Oldman, Frances Barber, Liz Smith, Max Wall, Kerry Wise
► Nineteen-fifties London provides the setting for offbeat struggle over German shepherd Evie by wealthy Bates and his jailed lover, Oldman. Bates, concerned about dog's welfare, must also contend with Oldman's wife Barber and parents' desire for the pet. Low-key, emotionally detached adaptation of Joseph R. Ackerley's novel may please pet fanciers. Amusing cameo by Ryan Batt, perhaps the world's ugliest infant.
Dist.: Nelson

WHALES OF AUGUST, THE 1987
★★ NR Drama 1:30
☑ Explicit language
Dir: Lindsay Anderson ***Cast:*** Bette Davis, Lil-

lian Gish, Ann Sothern, Vincent Price, Harry Carey, Jr.
▶ Davis and Gish are elderly sisters living on the coast of Maine. Davis is going blind and, possibly, senile. Sothern is a family friend who tries to convince them to sell the house. Neighbor Price is forced to look for a place to live after his landlady dies. Not much plot but old-timer cast works hard to generate emotion. First-rate production and gorgeous views of Maine. Sothern was Oscar nominated.
Dist.: Nelson

WHAT COMES AROUND 1985
★★ PG Comedy 1:28
☑ Explicit language, mild violence
Dir: Jerry Reed ***Cast:*** Jerry Reed, Bo Hopkins, Barry Corbin, Arte Johnson
▶ Band leader Corbin manages Reed, a country-western singer with a drinking problem. Reed is kidnapped by his brother Hopkins and delivered to a rehab to dry out. While there, the guys discover Corbin has been stealing millions from Reed, and plot a revenge involving several diesel trucks. Harmless shaggy-dog mixture of comedy, car chases, and country music doesn't really cook. (CC)
Dist.: Nelson

WHAT EVER HAPPENED TO AUNT ALICE? 1969
★★ PG Mystery-Suspense 1:41
☑ Violence
Dir: Lee H. Katzin ***Cast:*** Geraldine Page, Ruth Gordon, Rosemary Forsyth, Robert Fuller, Mildred Dunnock, Peter Bonerz
▶ Mad Page hires maids, then kills and robs them. Aunt Alice (Gordon) goes undercover as Page's next employee when her pal becomes a victim; Gordon's nephew Fuller provides support. More chills from producer Robert Aldrich in the vein of his *What Ever Happened to Baby Jane?* and *Hush Hush . . .Sweet Charlotte.*
Dist.: CBS/Fox

WHAT EVER HAPPENED TO BABY JANE? 1962
★★★ NR Horror 2:12 B&W
Dir: Robert Aldrich ***Cast:*** Bette Davis, Joan Crawford, Victor Buono, Anna Lee, Marjorie Bennett
▶ In a rotting Los Angeles mansion, former child star Davis terrorizes her wheelchair-bound sister Crawford in revenge for Crawford's greater success in movies. First teaming of the screen superstars inspired a rash of grisly horror films featuring older actresses. Powerful and unsettling story received Oscar nominations for Davis and Buono, her unbalanced piano accompanist; won for Norma Koch's costume design.
Dist.: Warner

WHAT HAVE I DONE TO DESERVE THIS? 1985 Spanish
☆ R Comedy 1:40
☑ Nudity, adult situations, explicit language, violence
Dir: Pedro Almodóvar ***Cast:*** Carmen Maura, Luis Hostalot, Angel De Andrés-López, Gonzalo Suarez, Veronica Forque, Juan Martinez
▶ Cleaning lady Maura scrubs floors to support her family, but they hardly seem worth the trouble. She has an abusive husband in love with someone else, one son who sells drugs, and another who sleeps with older men. She sells the latter to a dentist and eventually gets rid of her spouse in this stinging black comedy. [S]
Dist.: CineVista

WHAT PRICE GLORY? 1952
★★★★ NR Comedy 1:50
Dir: John Ford ***Cast:*** James Cagney, Dan Dailey, Robert Wagner, Corinne Calvet, William Demarest, James Gleason
▶ Soldiers Cagney and Dailey have a love/hate relationship in France during World War I. When they are not fighting the enemy, they fight each other and vie for the affections of Frenchwoman Calvet. Genial remake of the 1926 silent classic works best as a vehicle for Cagney's comic carousing and sparring with Dailey.
Dist.: CBS/Fox

WHAT'S NEW, PUSSYCAT? 1965
★★ NR Comedy 1:48
Dir: Clive Donner ***Cast:*** Peter O'Toole, Peter Sellers, Woody Allen, Romy Schneider, Paula Prentiss, Ursula Andress
▶ Womanizer O'Toole visits neurotic shrink Sellers for help but is unable to thwart gorgeous gals (including Schneider and Andress) from pursuing him. Allen wrote the screenplay and co-stars, stealing scenes as an extremely frustrated strippers' assistant. Freewheeling, uneven, but often very funny. Tom Jones sings the Bacharach-David title tune.
Dist.: CBS/Fox

WHAT'S UP, DOC? 1972
★★★★ G Comedy 1:30
Dir: Peter Bogdanovich ***Cast:*** Barbra Streisand, Ryan O'Neal, Kenneth Mars, Madeline Kahn, Austin Pendleton
▶ Zany Streisand and eccentric professor O'Neal become involved in a wild chase to recover four identical flight bags containing top-secret information, a wealth of jewels, Ryan's musical rocks, and Streisand's clothes. Great cast of clowns led a marvelous Kahn as O'Neal's uptight fiancée.
Dist.: Warner

WHAT'S UP, TIGER LILY? 1966
★ PG Comedy 1:19
☑ Explicit language, violence
Dir: Woody Allen ***Cast:*** Tatsuya Mihashi, Miya Hana, Eiko Wakabayashi, Tadao Nakamura, Woody Allen
▶ Japanese imitation James Bond movie about a devious plot to steal the world's best

egg-salad recipe. Allen took a third-rate Japanese spy movie and redubbed it using the voices of his friends, including then-wife Louise Lasser. Cute idea, goofy dialogue, and outlandish plot deliver a fair amount of laughs but eventually wear thin.
Dist.: Vestron

WHAT WAITS BELOW 1984
★ PG Horror 1:22
☑ Violence
Dir: Don Sharp ***Cast:*** Robert Powell, Lisa Blount, Timothy Bottoms, Richard Johnson, Anne Heywood, Liam Sullivan
► Powell is a mercenary helping Army officer Bottoms set up a signal station in an ancient Central American cavern. Mysterious killings there are soon traced to a lost tribe of mummy-like mutants who occupy underground world. Some suspense in this standard genre item, filmed in interesting caves in Alabama and Tennessee. Also known as *Secret of the Phantom Caverns.*
Dist.: Vestron

WHEEL OF FORTUNE 1941
★ NR Action-Adventure 1:23 B&W
Dir: John H. Auer ***Cast:*** John Wayne, Frances Dee, Edward Ellis, Wallace Ford, Ward Bond, Harold Huber
► When his best friend is murdered, small-town attorney Wayne goes to the big city to investigate. The trail leads him to corrupt politician Ellis, although romance develops between Wayne and Ellis's daughter Dee. Painless if unmemorable thriller is also known as *A Man Betrayed.*
Dist.: Republic

WHEN A STRANGER CALLS 1979
★★★★ R Mystery-Suspense 1:40
☑ Explicit language, violence
Dir: Fred Walton ***Cast:*** Carol Kane, Charles Durning, Rachel Roberts, Ron O'Neal, Colleen Dewhurst, Tony Beckley
► Babysitter Kane is tormented by threatening phone calls. Tracing the calls, police officer Durning discovers caller Beckley is in her house. Beckley murders the children and is sent to an asylum where, seven years later, he escapes to find Kane, who now has young children of her own. Durning, now a private investigator, returns to track him down. Genuinely scary and suspenseful woman-in-jeopardy thriller.
Dist.: RCA/Columbia

WHEN FATHER WAS AWAY ON BUSINESS
1985 Yugoslavian
★ R Comedy 2:22
☑ Nudity, adult situations, explicit language
Dir: Emir Kusturica ***Cast:*** Moreno D'E Bartolli, Miki Manojlovic, Mirjana Karanovic, Mustafa Nadarevic, Mira Furian
► Dad isn't really away on business, but in a Communist reeducation camp, as young D'E Bartolli narrates in this charmingly bittersweet reminiscence of family life in Yugoslavia during the politically twisted fifties. While living outside the camp, D'E Bartolli falls in love with the TB-striken girl next door and gets himself in trouble during his sleepwalking episodes. [S]
Dist.: Media

WHEN GANGLAND STRIKES 1956
☆ NR Drama 1:10 B&W
Dir: R. G. Springsteen ***Cast:*** Raymond Greenleaf, Marjie Millar, John Hudson, Anthony Caruso, Slim Pickens, Morris Ankrum
► Prosecutor Greenleaf goes against his professional principles to protect his daughter from blackmailing gangsters. But when they frame her for murder, Greenleaf defends her when she goes to trial. Pickens is good in this not very believable tale.
Dist.: Republic

WHEN HARRY MET SALLY. . . 1989
★★★★★ R Romance/Comedy 1:36
☑ Adult situations, explicit language
Dir: Rob Reiner ***Cast:*** Billy Crystal, Meg Ryan, Carrie Fisher, Bruno Kirby, Lisa Jane Persky
► Crystal and Ryan meet as college students sharing a ride to New York and years later form friendship, despite his insistence that sex will always prevent a man and a woman from ever really being friends. She disagrees but his theory is put to the test when they fall in love. Hugely popular crowd pleaser, snappily directed and acted. Highlights of Nora Ephron's clever, Oscar-nominated screenplay: Ryan's celebrated fake orgasm demonstration, Crystal's explanation of a "low maintenance woman." **(CC)**
Dist.: Nelson

WHEN THE LEGENDS DIE 1972
★★ PG Drama 1:45
☑ Adult situations, explicit language
Dir: Stuart Millar ***Cast:*** Richard Widmark, Frederic Forrest, Luana Anders, Vito Scotti, Herbert Nelson, John War Eagle
► Indian Forrest leaves the reservation, joins the rodeo, and becomes star rider under hard-drinking old pro Widmark's guidance. A close relationship develops between the two although Widmark tries to exploit his protégé. Widmark and Forrest give fine performances.
Dist.: CBS/Fox

WHEN THE WHALES CAME 1989 British
★ PG Drama 1:40
☑ Adult situations
Dir: Clive Rees ***Cast:*** Paul Scofield, Helen Mirren, Helen Pearce, Max Rennie, David Suchet, Barbara Jefford
► Life is hard on a windswept island off the coast of England, most of whose population relocated there after a strange curse dried up the wells on another island. Children Pearce and Rennie befriend Scofield, an old woodcarver who alone knows the secret of the tusked whales threatening to hurl themselves

onto the beach. Haunting, lyrical fantasy features good performances by the kids. **(CC)**
Dist.: CBS/Fox

WHEN THE WIND BLOWS 1988 British
☆ **NR Animation/Adult 1:25**
☑ Adult situations
Dir: Jimmy T. Murakami **Cast:** Voices of Peggy Ashcroft, John Mills
▶ Ordinary couple reminisce about the past and worry about the future when nuclear war breaks out. Their fallout shelter ultimately offers little protection as the effects of radiation become apparent. Cartoon overstates commendable message; dry British humor and one-dimensional animation quickly grow tiresome. Raymond Briggs adapted from his bestseller; title song by David Bowie.
Dist.: IVE

WHEN TIME RAN OUT 1980
★ ★ ★ **PG Drama 2:01**
☑ Adult situations, explicit language
Dir: James Goldstone **Cast:** Paul Newman, Jacqueline Bisset, William Holden, Red Buttons, Ernest Borgnine, James Franciscus
▶ Hawaiian hotel and oil field owned by Holden are endangered when nearby volcano erupts. Wildcatter Newman attempts to lead girlfriend Bisset and others to safety on high ground. Tremendous cast, workmanlike dialogue, lots of lava in standard disaster genre brew from the master, Irwin Allen.
Dist.: Warner

WHEN WORLDS COLLIDE 1951
☆ **G Sci-Fi 1:22**
Dir: Rudolph Maté **Cast:** Barbara Rush, Richard Derr, John Hoyt, Larry Keating, Peter Hanson, Frank Cady
▶ Scientists predict the impending destruction of Earth as runaway planet and star head our way. Wealthy businessmen finance spaceship to start human race again on another planet but must face the wrath of those left behind. Classic genre movie combines emphasis on human aspect with Oscar-winning special effects.
Dist.: Paramount

WHERE ARE THE CHILDREN? 1986
★ ★ ★ ★ **R Mystery-Suspense 1:37**
☑ Adult situations, explicit language, violence
Dir: Bruce Malmuth **Cast:** Jill Clayburgh, Max Gail, Harley Cross, Elisabeth Harnois, Barnard Hughes, Frederic Forrest
▶ When her two children are kidnapped, Clayburgh is forced to confront a similar tragedy in her past. Contrived but effective thriller about a sensitive issue builds to a shocking climax. Beautiful Cape Cod locations and strong performances by Hughes and Forrest are bonuses. **(CC)**
Dist.: RCA/Columbia

WHERE EAGLES DARE 1968
★ ★ ★ ★ **PG War 2:38**
☑ Adult situations, explicit language, mild violence
Dir: Brian G. Hutton **Cast:** Richard Burton, Clint Eastwood, Mary Ure, Patrick Wymark, Michael Hordern, Donald Houston
▶ Crack commandos led by Burton and Eastwood attack a Nazi fortress in the Alps to free an Allied general, but their mission is endangered by a double agent. Thrilling World War II drama has relentless pacing and extraordinary stunts. Alistair MacLean later turned his screenplay into a novel.
Dist.: MGM/UA

WHERE'S POPPA? 1970
★ ★ ★ **R Comedy 1:23**
☑ Adult humor
Dir: Carl Reiner **Cast:** George Segal, Ruth Gordon, Ron Leibman, Trish Van Devere, Barnard Hughes, Vincent Gardenia
▶ Because his senile mother Gordon makes relationships with women impossible, New York City attorney Segal, who's vowed never to put her in a nursing home, considers scaring mom to death. Irreverent and outrageous black comedy features inspired teamwork by Segal and Gordon, ably supported by Van Devere as the nurse who falls for Segal and Leibman as his gorilla suit-wearing brother. **(CC)**
Dist.: CBS/Fox

WHERE THE BOYS ARE 1960
★ ★ ★ **NR Comedy 1:39**
Dir: Henry Levin **Cast:** Dolores Hart, George Hamilton, Yvette Mimieux, Jim Hutton, Paula Prentiss, Connie Francis
▶ College girls Hart, Mimieux, Prentiss, and Francis head for Fort Lauderdale during spring break. Hart loses her heart to Ivy Leaguer Hamilton; Mimieux gets involved with a womanizer; awkward Prentiss has clumsy romance with Hutton; and Francis gets to sing title song on her way to love. Entertaining smash period hit is now a nostalgic cult item.
Dist.: MGM/UA

WHERE THE BOYS ARE '84 1984
★ ★ **R Comedy 1:35**
☑ Nudity, adult situations, explicit language
Dir: Hy Averback **Cast:** Lisa Hartman, Russell Todd, Lorna Luft, Wendy Schall, Howard McGillin, Lynn-Holly Johnson
▶ Hartman, Luft, Schall, and Johnson are a college foursome who find love on the Fort Lauderdale beach. Among their adventures: a drunk-driving charge, a Hot Bod contest, and Hartman's romance with a musician. Deep it's not, but has toe-tapping music and acres of bared tanned skin from a good-looking cast. Luft, although a bit long in the tooth for her role, steals her scenes. Remake of the 1960 film. **(CC)**
Dist.: CBS/Fox

WHERE THE BUFFALO ROAM 1980
★ **R Comedy 1:36**

☑ Adult situations, explicit language, adult humor
Dir: Art Linson　*Cast:* Bill Murray, Peter Boyle, Bruno Kirby, René Auberjonois, R. G. Armstrong, Danny Goldman
▶ Uneven comedy loosely based on "gonzo" journalist Dr. Hunter S. Thompson (Murray) takes a scattershot, often confusing approach to the writer's coverage of marijuana trials, political campaigns, and Las Vegas. Episodic structure undermines the gags, although Boyle is excellent as Thompson's attorney friend. Music by Neil Young.
Dist.: MCA

WHERE THE GREEN ANTS DREAM 1984
German
☆ **R Drama 1:40**
☑ Nudity, explicit language
Dir: Werner Herzog　*Cast:* Bruce Spence, Wandjuk Marika, Roy Marika, Ray Barrett, Norman Kaye, Colleen Clifford
▶ Australian aborigines protest a mining company's blasting tests on sacred land. Court decides against them, with tragic results. Memorable scene has a tribal group performing a ritual in the aisle of a supermarket built over another sacred site. Although more accessible than director Herzog's other projects, the primitive world view seems more hare-brained than profound.
Dist.: Media

WHERE THE HEART IS 1990
★ **R Comedy 1:34**
☑ Nudity, adult situations, explicit language
Dir: John Boorman　*Cast:* Dabney Coleman, Uma Thurman, Joanna Cassidy, Crispin Glover, Suzy Amis, Christopher Plummer, David Hewlett
▶ Wealthy construction mogul Coleman thinks his children are spoiled, so he sends them to live in an abandoned Brooklyn building. Friendships with bum Plummer and designer Glover help them adjust; Amis's body painting on Thurman leads to success. Ambitious parable aims for magic, doesn't quite get there. Boorman's direction is more confident than his screenplay (co-written with daughter Telsche); cast and production are eye-catching but dramatically uncertain. (CC)
Dist.: Buena Vista

WHERE THE RED FERN GROWS 1974
★ ★ ★ **G Family 1:37**
Dir: Norman Tokar　*Cast:* James Whitmore, Beverly Garland, Jack Ging, Lonny Chapman, Stewart Petersen, Jill Clark
▶ In 1930s Oklahoma, young Petersen lives on a struggling farm with his family, including grandpa Whitmore. The lad buys two dogs and has some happy times with them before tragedy occurs. Well-intentioned. The cute pooches will entertain small fry, but draggy pacing and soggy story limit adult appeal.
Dist.: Vestron

WHERE THE RIVER RUNS BLACK 1986
★ ★ ★ **PG Action-Adventure 1:36**
☑ Brief nudity, mild violence
Dir: Christopher Cain　*Cast:* Charles Durning, Alessandro Rabelo, Ajay Naidu, Peter Horton, Conchata Ferrell, Dana Delany
▶ Rabelo is raised by dolphins after his parents are killed. After being placed in an orphanage and looked after by priest Durning, the boy must adjust to civilization and get revenge against his mom's killer. Authentic Brazilian locations, stunning camerawork and music create an unusual fable that will appeal to families. (CC)
Dist.: CBS/Fox

WHERE TIME BEGAN 1978 Spanish
★ ★ ★ **G Sci-Fi 1:26**
Dir: Piquer Simon　*Cast:* Kenneth More, Pep Munne, Jack Taylor, Yvonne Sennis, Frank Branna
▶ Professor More leads an intrepid group of adventurers down into the crater of an extinct volcano where they discover a hidden world of prehistoric monsters and other astounding anachronisms. Retelling of Jules Verne's *Journey to the Center of the Earth* has better special effects than previous adaptations. Good childrens' matinee feature.
Dist.: Nelson

WHICH WAY IS UP? 1977
★ ★ ★ **R Comedy 1:34**
☑ Explicit language, adult humor
Dir: Michael Schultz　*Cast:* Richard Pryor, Morgan Woodward, Lonette McKee, Margaret Avery, Marilyn Coleman, Bebe Drake-Hooks
▶ Through a quirk of fate, California citrus picker Pryor becomes union hero. New notoriety leads to career opportunities, so Pryor leaves wife Avery and moves to Los Angeles for fast-lane lifestyle, including urban beauty McKee and sell-out to corporate cash. Based on Italian director Lina Wertmuller's *The Seduction of Mimi*, tale of man's corruption and self-redemption never quite works, but Pryor's antics provide continual laughs.
Dist.: MCA

WHICH WAY TO THE FRONT? 1970
★ ★ **G Comedy 1:36**
Dir: Jerry Lewis　*Cast:* Jerry Lewis, John Wood, Jan Murray, Steve Franken, Willie Davis, Dack Rambo
▶ During World War II, wealthy Lewis, rejected for the military, raises his own private army and stages European invasion. Subsequent high jinks include an encounter with Hitler. Low-brow humor hits occasional targets.
Dist.: Warner

WHILE THE CITY SLEEPS 1956
★ ★ ★ **NR Mystery-Suspense 1:40 B&W**
Dir: Fritz Lang　*Cast:* Dana Andrews, Ida Lupino, Rhonda Fleming, George Sanders, Thomas Mitchell, John Drew Barrymore, Vin-

cent Price, Howard Duff, James Craig, Sally Forrest

▶ Inheriting a New York tabloid, playboy Price offers its top job to whomever tracks down "The Lipstick Killer." Mitchell, Sanders, and Craig enlist the aid of various female acquaintances to entrap the elusive fiend, but it is smart reporter Andrews who finally confronts him in a dramatic standoff on subway tracks. Tight little thriller benefits from a good script and an experienced cast.
Dist.: VCI

WHISKY GALORE! 1949 British
★ ★ NR Comedy 1:23 B&W
Dir: Alexander Mackendrick *Cast:* Basil Radford, Catherine Lacey, Bruce Seton, Joan Greenwood, Gordon Jackson, Wylie Watson

▶ Wartime shortages cut off remote Scottish island's whisky supply; the islanders are overjoyed when a ship filled with liquor sinks just offshore. However, strict Home Guard officer Radford wants to turn the cargo over to authorities, prompting ingenious schemes to liberate it. Delightful comedy based on a true incident is a genuine treat for fans of British humor. American title: *Tight Little Island.*
Dist.: HBO

WHISTLE BLOWER, THE 1987 British
★ PG Mystery-Suspense 1:50
☑ Explicit language, violence
Dir: Simon Langton *Cast:* Michael Caine, James Fox, Nigel Havers, Felicity Dean, John Gielgud, Kenneth Colley

▶ When a colleague is arrested for spying, British intelligence agent Havers complains to his father, salesman Caine. As the unfolding spy scandal results in a number of suspicious deaths, Caine finds his faith in social values undermined. Suspenseful intrigue eschews action for cogent critique of English class system. (CC)
Dist.: Nelson

WHISTLE DOWN THE WIND 1961 British
★ ★ NR Family 1:39 B&W
Dir: Bryan Forbes *Cast:* Hayley Mills, Alan Bates, Bernard Lee, Diane Holgate, Alan Barnes, Norman Bird

▶ English children Mills, Holgate, and Barnes find fugitive Bates in family barn and believe he is Jesus returned to earth. As events increasingly parallel Christ's life, they care for Bates and hide him from their elders. Fascinating tale of childhood innocence moves swiftly to a memorable conclusion. Poignant performances by the kids; Bates is equally excellent.
Dist.: Nelson

WHISTLE STOP 1946
★ NR Drama 1:25 B&W
Dir: Leonide Moguy *Cast:* George Raft, Ava Gardner, Victor McLaglen, Tom Conway, Jorja Curtright, Florence Bates

▶ Gardner returns to her little home town to renew her romance with the shiftless Raft, but saloon owner Conway makes a play for her. Raft's efforts to pull himself together and go to work are thwarted when Conway tries to frame him for murder. Unimpressive drama notable mainly for the prominence and attractiveness of young Gardner.
Dist.: Various

WHITE CHRISTMAS 1954
★ ★ ★ ★ NR Musical 2:00
Dir: Michael Curtiz *Cast:* Bing Crosby, Danny Kaye, Rosemary Clooney, Vera-Ellen, Dean Jagger

▶ Army pals Crosby and Kaye learn that their old general Jagger's ski resort is facing bankruptcy; they stage a musical benefit that climaxes with Crosby's rendition of the classic title tune. Irving Berlin score includes "Blue Skies," "Snow," and the Oscar-nominated "Count Your Blessings Instead of Sheep." Borrows heavily from the superior *Holiday Inn.* (CC)
Dist.: Paramount

WHITE DAWN, THE 1974
★ ★ PG Action-Adventure 1:50
☑ Adult situations, violence
Dir: Philip Kaufman *Cast:* Warren Oates, Timothy Bottoms, Louis Gossett, Jr., Simonie Kopapik, Joanasie Salamonie, Pilitak

▶ In 1896, whalers Oates, Bottoms, and Gossett are rescued in the Arctic by Eskimo tribe. Their Western values soon conflict with the ethics of their hosts. Beautiful cinematography and startlingly authentic production values enliven this offbeat adventure.
Dist.: Paramount

WHITE GHOST 1988
☆ R Action-Adventure 1:33
☑ Adult situations, explicit language, violence
Dir: B. J. Davis *Cast:* William Katt, Rosalind Chao, Martin Hewitt, Wayne Crawford, Reb Brown, Raymond Ma

▶ Vietnamese peasants believe that a pale spirit is going through the jungle collecting the souls of dead American soldiers. In fact, it's Katt, an ex-POW wearing white makeup and conducting a one-man war. Army brass send Katt's old Green Beret rival Crawford into the bush to get him out. Stilted, direct-to-video action film never works up excitement.
Dist.: TWE

WHITE HEAT 1949
★ ★ ★ ★ NR Crime/Drama 1:54 B&W
Dir: Raoul Walsh *Cast:* James Cagney, Edmond O'Brien, Virginia Mayo, Margaret Wycherly, Steve Cochran

▶ Criminal Cagney has an obsessive soft spot for his ma (Wycherly), but a hard edge and quick gun for everyone else. Lawman O'Brien goes undercover and befriends Cagney in an effort to get the goods on him. One of Cagney's most riveting performances reaches its peak in the literally explosive ending. Memo-

rable scene: jailed Cagney learning ma's fate. **(CC)**
Dist.: MGM/UA ⓒ

WHITE HELL OF PITZ PALU, THE 1929 German
★ **NR Drama 1:33 B&W**
Dir: G. W. Pabst, Arnold Fanck *Cast:* Leni Reifenstahl, Gustav Diessl, Ernst Peterson
▶ Aged mountaineer Diessl joins young Peterson and Reifenstahl as they climb Pitz Palu, a mountain that has claimed many lives. When they are trapped in an ice cave, one must make the supreme sacrifice to save the others. Beautiful, documentary-style silent. Reifenstahl later became a controversial but much-admired director/photographer.
Dist.: Grapevine

WHITE LIGHTNING 1973
★★★★ **PG Action-Adventure 1:41**
☑ Adult situations, explicit language
Dir: Joseph Sargent *Cast:* Burt Reynolds, Jennifer Billingsley, Ned Beatty, Bo Hopkins, Matt Clark, Louise Latham
▶ Framed bootlegger Reynolds is offered freedom if he informs on his moonshine cohorts. Reynolds agrees for ulterior motives: he wants to find his brother's killers. Top-notch car chases and hard-edged action lift this above typical redneck melodramas. Reynolds repeated his role in 1976's *Gator.*
Dist.: MGM/UA

WHITE LINE FEVER 1975
★★★★ **PG Action-Adventure 1:30**
☑ Adult situations, explicit language, violence
Dir: Jonathan Kaplan *Cast:* Jan-Michael Vincent, Kay Lenz, Slim Pickens, L. Q. Jones, Don Porter, Sam Laws
▶ Sturdy B movie about Air Force vet Vincent who discovers first-hand that the produce trucking industry is corrupt. Despite bribes, beatings, and blackmail, he maintains his integrity and exposes the villains with the help of supportive wife Lenz. Assured direction and knockout truck stunts have made this a cult favorite.
Dist.: RCA/Columbia

WHITE MISCHIEF 1988 British
☆ **R Drama 1:40**
☑ Nudity, adult situations, explicit language, violence
Dir: Michael Radford *Cast:* Sarah Miles, Joss Ackland, John Hurt, Greta Scacchi, Charles Dance, Geraldine Chaplin, Ray McAnally, Murray Head, Trevor Howard
▶ During World War II, knockout Scacchi marries elderly Ackland and follows him and his money to Kenya's Happy Valley, a bastion for decadent, bored Brits who spend their days and nights drinking, doing drugs, and sleeping around. When superstud Dance gets shot, jealous Ackland becomes the prime suspect. Deliciously naughty and voyeuristic drama was based on the book by James Fox, in turn

based on a true incident. Superior acting and production values. Howard's final film role.
Dist.: Nelson

WHITE NIGHTS 1985
★★★★ **PG-13 Drama 2:15**
☑ Explicit language, violence
Dir: Taylor Hackford *Cast:* Mikhail Baryshnikov, Gregory Hines, Isabella Rossellini, Helen Mirren, Jerzy Skolimowski, Geraldine Page
▶ Former Soviet ballet star Baryshnikov, a defector to West, survives plane crash in Russia but is captured by the government he fled years before. Soviets put Baryshnikov in care of American tap dancer Hines and Russian wife Rossellini. Hostility erupts as Hines must convince Baryshnikov to dance with Kirov Ballet again, but shared interest in dance and freedom soon leads to friendship and plans for escape. Gripping drama mixes thrills and sensational dancing. **(CC)**
Dist.: RCA/Columbia

WHITE OF THE EYE 1988
★★ **R Mystery-Suspense 1:50**
☑ Adult situations, explicit language, violence
Dir: Donald Cammell *Cast:* David Keith, Cathy Moriarty, Alan Rosenberg, Art Evans, Michael Greene, Danielle Smith
▶ Arizona audio expert Keith, unfaithful to wife Moriarty, becomes cop Evans's number one suspect in series of local housewife murders. Moriarty and daughter Smith are menaced by the killer. Glitzy-looking production with style to burn gives new life to old formula. Good performances, especially the earthy Moriarty, and interesting script twists; however, fractured narrative and weird ending will leave some with bad taste. **(CC)**
Dist.: Paramount

WHITE ROSE, THE 1983 German
★ **NR Drama 1:48**
☑ Brief nudity, explicit language, violence
Dir: Michael Verhoeven *Cast:* Lena Stolze, Martin Benrath, Wulf Kessler, Werner Stocker, Oliver Siebert, Ulrich Tucker
▶ In Munich, 1942, student underground group the White Rose rebels against Nazis. True story of suppressed uprising centers on Benrath and Stolze, the siblings who are tried and executed as leaders of insurrection. Historically interesting subject gets flat, uninspired treatment. Ⓢ
Dist.: MGM/UA

WHITE SHEIK, THE 1951 Italian
☆ **NR Comedy 1:28 B&W**
Dir: Federico Fellini *Cast:* Alberto Sordi, Brunella Bova, Leopoldo Trieste, Giulietta Masina
▶ Dreamy Bova slips away from stern husband Trieste to meet Sordi, the romantic lead in her favorite magazine photo story. While Bova is quickly disillusioned when she meets her ideal, Trieste makes excuses for her ab-

sence, and worries that they will miss a scheduled meeting with the Pope. Not one of director Fellini's masterpieces, but still a cheerful satire of celebrity. [S]
Dist.: Video Dimensions

WHITE TOWER, THE 1950
★ NR Drama 1:38
Dir: Ted Tetzlaff   *Cast:* Glenn Ford, Claude Rains, Lloyd Bridges, Valli, Cedric Hardwicke
▶ Occasional mountaineer Ford reluctantly joins arrogant German climber Bridges as he leads a party on the first assault of a particulalry deadly Swiss Alp. Valli, Rains, and Hardwicke are among the climbers, each of whom will work through a private agenda on the hazardous journey. Not much of an adventure, but the well-written script really gets into the characters. Vivid Technicolor.
Dist.: Turner

WHITE WATER SUMMER 1987
★ ★ ★ PG Action-Adventure 1:30
☑ Explicit language, mild violence
Dir: Jeff Bleckner   *Cast:* Kevin Bacon, Sean Astin, Jonathan Ward, K. C. Martel, Matt Adler, Caroline McWilliams
▶ Wealthy youngster Astin joins three other boys at summer camp. Counselor Bacon proves demanding and unyielding during a tough wilderness expedition up a fast-moving river and a frightening rock climb. Beautiful nature photography and realistic coming-of-age theme should please teen viewers.
Dist.: RCA/Columbia

WHITE ZOMBIE 1932
★ ★ NR Horror 1:13 B&W
Dir: Victor Halperin   *Cast:* Bela Lugosi, Madge Bellamy, Robert Frazer, Brandon Hurst, Joseph Cawthorn, John Harron
▶ Voodoo master Lugosi, who turns Haitians into zombies, does the same for soon-to-be-married visitors Bellamy and Harron at the behest of bad guy Frazer. While among the living dead, Bellamy is ordered by Lugosi to kill her new husband. Unfairly forgotten gem from classic era of Hollywood horror is strongly atmospheric. Filmed hot on the heels of *Dracula* with Lugosi in his prime.
Dist.: Video Yesteryear

WHO DONE IT? 1942
★ NR Comedy 1:15 B&W
Dir: Erle C. Kenton, Basil Dearden   *Cast:* Bud Abbott, Lou Costello, Patric Knowles, Louise Allbritton, William Gargan, William Bendix
▶ Abbott and Costello work as soda jerks on the busy ground floor of a building housing the studios of a big radio network. Longing to break into broadcasting, they pose as detectives when a network president is murdered during a show. Good period comedy with glossy photography.
Dist.: MCA

WHO FRAMED ROGER RABBIT 1988
★ ★ ★ ★ ★ PG Animation/Comedy 1:36
☑ Explicit language, violence
Dir: Robert Zemeckis   *Cast:* Bob Hoskins, Christopher Lloyd, Joanna Cassidy, Stubby Kaye, Alan Tilvern, Richard Le Parmentier
▶ Top-grossing film of 1988, an amazing blend of live action and animation, takes place in a 1947 Hollywood where cartoon characters are second-class citizens relegated to the Toon Town ghetto. Private eye Hoskins reluctantly agrees to help slapstick star Rabbit, prime suspect in producer's murder. Hilarious, fast-paced, technically breathtaking, and filled with many cartoon cameos. Stolen by Rabbit's sultry wife Jessica and her booby trap (Kathleen Turner does her speaking voice, Amy Irving her song).
Dist.: Buena Vista

WHO IS KILLING THE GREAT CHEFS OF EUROPE? 1978
★ ★ ★ PG Mystery-Suspense 1:52
☑ Adult situations, explicit language
Dir: Ted Kotcheff   *Cast:* George Segal, Jacqueline Bisset, Robert Morley, Jean-Pierre Cassel, Philippe Noiret, Jean Rochefort
▶ International gourmet magazine runs articles on world's greatest meal, featuring six courses by six world-class chefs. One by one the chefs are murdered in the manner of their featured dish. (Pity the poor cook who prepared the pressed duck!) Dessert chef Bisset fears for her life as police investigate. Suspects include magazine's publisher Morley and Bisset's jealous ex-husband Segal, a fast-food franchiser. Laughs and intrigue abound in diverting romp with fine cast and scenes in the world's finest restaurants.
Dist.: CBS/Fox

WHO KILLED MARY WHATS'ERNAME? 1971
★ PG Mystery-Suspense 1:30
☑ Adult situations, explicit language
Dir: Ernie Pintoff   *Cast:* Red Buttons, Alice Playton, Sam Waterston, Sylvia Miles, Conrad Bain, Norman Rose
▶ Nobody cares about the murder of a prostitute except diabetic ex-prizefighter Buttons, who moves into her old apartment and sets out to find her killer. Along the way, he meets young filmmaker Waterston and good-natured hooker Miles. Standard mystery with depressingly authentic slum settings has good acting from Buttons and Miles.
Dist.: Prism

WHO'LL STOP THE RAIN? 1978
★ ★ ★ ★ R Drama 2:06
☑ Brief nudity, adult situations, explicit language, violence
Dir: Karel Reisz   *Cast:* Nick Nolte, Tuesday Weld, Michael Moriarty, Anthony Zerbe, Richard Masur, Ray Sharkey
▶ Vietnam vet Nolte agrees to smuggle two pounds of heroin to California for his best

friend Moriarty, then is forced on the run by double-crossing narcotics agent Zerbe. Somewhat sanitized adaptation of Robert Stone's *Dog Soldiers* is still a gripping, powerful study of corruption and heroism.
Dist.: MGM/UA

WHOLLY MOSES! 1980
★ ★ **PG Comedy 1:43**
⊘ Adult situations, explicit language, adult humor
Dir: Gary Weis   *Cast:* Dudley Moore, Laraine Newman, James Coco, Paul Sand, Jack Gilford, Dom DeLuise
▶ Moore, a slave in ancient Egypt, overhears God's instructions to Moses and, thinking the words are for him, sets out to lead the Jews from Pharaoh's tyranny to the promised land. Naturally, Moses beats him to the punch at every turn. Fine cast and cameos by Richard Pryor, John Houseman, Madeline Kahn, and John Ritter wasted in second-rate comedy.
Dist.: RCA/Columbia

WHOOPEE! 1930
★ **NR Musical 1:33**
Dir: Thornton Freeland   *Cast:* Eddie Cantor, Eleanor Hunt, Paul Gregory, John Rutherford, Ethel Shutta, Spencer Charters
▶ Early sound and color joy has hypochondriac Cantor getting into love scrapes in the Arizona ranch country. Adapted from a Flo Ziegfeld stage extravaganza, plot mixes silly (and racially offensive) cowboy and Indian business with unusually fresh and vital Busby Berkeley dance sequences. Nurse Shutta stops the show with a raw, sexy Charleston; songs include "Making Whoopee" and "My Baby Just Cares for Me." Look for a young Betty Grable in the opening number.
Dist.: Nelson

WHOOPEE BOYS, THE 1986
★ ★ **R Comedy 1:28**
⊘ Brief nudity, adult situations, explicit language, adult humor
Dir: John Byrum   *Cast:* Michael O'Keefe, Paul Rodriguez, Denholm Elliott, Carole Shelley, Andy Bumatai, Eddie Deezen
▶ Con artist O'Keefe enters Elliott's etiquette school to win Shelley away from her snob fiancé. His friend Rodriguez indulges in frequent practical jokes while O'Keefe learns the secrets of becoming a perfect gentleman. Tasteless comedy feels unfocused due to improvisational style.
Dist.: Paramount

WHOOPS APOCALYPSE 1986 British
★ **R Comedy 1:29**
⊘ Nudity, explicit language, adult humor
Dir: Tom Bussman   *Cast:* Loretta Swit, Peter Cook, Michael Richards, Rik Mayall, Ian Richardson, Herbert Lom
▶ When Caribbean general Lom invades a British Central American colony, Prime Minister Cook responds by sending troops. The English win the war but their princess is kidnapped by

mercenary Richards. Good cast works overtime to inject some hilarity into the skimpy story, but laughs run out of steam quickly. Swit co-stars as the President of the United States.
Dist.: MGM/UA

WHO'S AFRAID OF VIRGINIA WOOLF? 1966
★ ★ ★ **NR Drama 2:09 B&W**
Dir: Mike Nichols   *Cast:* Elizabeth Taylor, Richard Burton, George Segal, Sandy Dennis
▶ New England English professor Burton and wife Taylor invite younger faculty couple Segal and Dennis to their home for drinks. Drunken arguments and mind games between Burton and Taylor reveal their suppressed frustrations and disappointments. Searing drama features Burton and Taylor at pinnacle of their marriage and acting talents. Nominated for thirteen Academy Awards, film won five Oscars for Best Actress (Taylor), Supporting Actress (Dennis), Cinematography, Art Direction, and Costume Design. Adaptation of Edward Albee's Broadway hit was feature debut for director Nichols.
Dist.: Warner

WHOSE LIFE IS IT, ANYWAY? 1981
★ ★ ★ ★ **R Drama 1:58**
⊘ Nudity, adult situations, explicit language
Dir: John Badham   *Cast:* Richard Dreyfuss, John Cassavetes, Christine Lahti, Bob Balaban, Kenneth McMillan, Kaki Hunter
▶ Dreyfuss's rising career as a sculptor is terminated when auto crash leaves him paralyzed. His depression grows so profound he hires attorney Balaban to argue for his right to die. Hospital head Cassavetes and sympathetic doctor Lahti seek to convince Dreyfuss to live. Sure-handed direction by Badham and convincing performance from Dreyfuss elevate potentially sentimental subject into effective drama. Based on the hit Broadway play by Brian Clark.
Dist.: MGM/UA

WHO'S HARRY CRUMB? 1989
★ ★ ★ **PG-13 Comedy 1:27**
⊘ Adult situations, explicit language, adult humor
Dir: Paul Flaherty   *Cast:* John Candy, Jeffrey Jones, Annie Potts, Barry Corbin, Tim Thomerson, Shawnee Smith
▶ Candy is Harry Crumb, a detective so inept that kidnapper Jones enlists him to solve his crime, figuring the case won't be cracked. The joke's on Jones, as Candy, with help from the victim's sister Smith, stumbles his way to a solution. Broad slapstick fun with ingenious sight gags anchored by surprisingly affecting Candy/Smith relationship. Comic highlights: Candy's impersonation of an Indian and bout with a ceiling fan.
Dist.: RCA/Columbia

WHO SLEW AUNTIE ROO? 1971
★ ★ **PG Horror 1:29**

☑ Adult situations, violence
Dir: Curtis Harrington   *Cast:* Shelley Winters, Ralph Richardson, Mark Lester, Lionel Jeffries, Hugh Griffith, Chloe Franks
▶ In England, American widow Winters remains obsessed with the memory of her late daughter. She takes in orphan Franks, who reminds her of the child, but Franks's brother Lester becomes suspicious of Winters's ultimate intent. Bizarre and not quite satisfying, although the cast is strong.
Dist.: Vestron

WHO'S MINDING THE MINT? 1967
★ ★ ★ ★ NR Comedy 1:38
Dir: Howard Morris   *Cast:* Jim Hutton, Dorothy Provine, Milton Berle, Joey Bishop, Bob Denver, Walter Brennan
▶ Hapless Hutton, a worker at the U.S. Mint, accidentally destroys $50,000. To keep his job, he enlists a motley crew—ice cream man Denver, pawnbroker Berle, retiree Brennan, and sewer man Bishop—in a scheme to replace the loot. Hilarious gem evokes freshly minted laughs.
Dist.: Goodtimes

WHO'S THAT GIRL 1987
★ PG Comedy 1:34
☑ Explicit language
Dir: James Foley   *Cast:* Madonna, Griffin Dunne, John Mills, Haviland Morris, John McMartin, Bibi Besch
▶ On the day before his wedding to an heiress, lawyer Dunne is asked to escort feisty ex-con Madonna from New York to Philadelphia. Supposedly easy trip turns to chaos with the introduction of a cheetah, gun-runners, cops, and romance. Throwback to 1930s screwball comedies borrows heavily from *Bringing Up Baby*. Madonna's version of the title tune became a pop hit.   (CC)
Dist.: Warner

WHY ME? 1984
★ ★ ★ ★ NR Drama/MFTV 1:40
Dir: Fielder Cook   *Cast:* Glynis O'Connor, Armand Assante, Craig Wasson, Annie Potts, Michael Sacks, William Windom
▶ True story of Leola Mae Harmon, an Air Force nurse whose face was destroyed in a head-on car collision. Unable to deal with the repercussions of the accident, her husband Wasson walks out on her, but dedicated plastic surgeon Assante gives her the courage to continue despite the odds of her ever living a normal life. Poignant, inspiring drama features fine performance from O'Connor. Michael Westmore was awarded an Emmy for makeup.
Dist.: TWE

WHY SHOOT THE TEACHER? 1982
Canadian
★ ★ NR Drama 1:40
☑ Adult situations, explicit language
Dir: Silvio Narizzano   *Cast:* Bud Cort,
Samantha Eggar, Chris Wiggins, Gary Reineke, John Friesen, Michael J. Reynolds
▶ In 1930s Saskatchewan, immature Cort travels to prairies to teach in one-room school. Hardships such as the severe winter and social isolation are balanced by occasional joys of hard-working farm life and delights of innocent young minds introduced to knowledge. Wryly humorous, wistful, small-scale drama delivers on all counts.
Dist.: Embassy

WICKED LADY, THE 1945 British
★ NR Drama 1:44 B&W
Dir: Leslie Arliss   *Cast:* Margaret Lockwood, James Mason, Patricia Roc, Michael Rennie, Griffith Jones, Felix Aylmer
▶ In Restoration England, high-born lady Lockwood leads a secret life as a criminal. Though betrothed to the respectable Jones, she secretly romances bandit Mason. Mason fans won't want to miss him at his dashing young best. Rest of the film not is not very good. Remade in 1983.
Dist.: Axon

WICKED LADY, THE 1983 British
★ R Action-Adventure 1:39
☑ Nudity, adult situations, explicit language, violence
Dir: Michael Winner   *Cast:* Faye Dunaway, Alan Bates, John Gielgud, Denholm Elliott, Prunella Scales, Oliver Tobias
▶ Dunaway, a fetching seventeenth-century aristocrat, turns to highway robbery to relieve her boredom, helped in more ways than one by randy bandit Bates. Lively remake of a 1945 film spoofs costume dramas by concentrating on nudity and sex. Dunaway cracks a mean bullwhip in the funniest scene.
Dist.: MGM/UA

WICKED STEPMOTHER 1989
★ PG-13 Horror/Comedy 1:32
☑ Explicit language, violence, adult humor
Dir: Larry Cohen   *Cast:* Bette Davis, Barbara Carrera, Colleen Camp, David Rasche, Lionel Stander, Tom Bosley
▶ Rasche and wife Camp return home after a vacation and discover her widowed dad Stander has married Davis, a horrible woman who turns out to be a witch. Later, Davis's equally evil daughter Carrera makes trouble for the family. Promising premise gets lost in the ineffective telling. Davis left the set after dispute with writer/director Cohen; her character was written out of the movie's second half.
Dist.: MGM/UA

WICKER MAN, THE 1975 British
★ R Horror 1:43
☑ Nudity, adult situations, explicit language, violence
Dir: Robin Hardy   *Cast:* Edward Woodward, Christopher Lee, Diane Cilento, Britt Ekland, Ingrid Pitt, Lindsay Kemp
▶ Woodward, a policeman searching for lost

young girl, travels to Summerisle, a remote Scottish island whose inhabitants have an unusual fondness for heathen rituals. Obscure, slowly paced drama has a small cult reputation for its Anthony Shaffer script and tongue-in-cheek performance by Lee.
Dist.: Magnum

WIFEMISTRESS 1979 Italian
★ ★ R Drama 1:38
☑ Nudity, adult situations
Dir: Marco Vicario *Cast:* Laura Antonelli, Marcello Mastroianni, Leonard Mann, Olga Karlatos, Anne Belle, Gastone Moschin
▶ In turn-of-the-century Italy, Mastroianni disappears after getting involved in murder. His sickly wife Antonelli investigates his affairs, discovers his infidelities, and develops new vitality as she takes a lover of her own. Secretly spying on his wife, Mastroianni falls in love all over again. Lusty and sumptously filmed.
☒
Dist.: RCA/Columbia

WILBY CONSPIRACY, THE 1975
★ ★ ★ PG Action-Adventure 1:41
☑ Adult situations, explicit language, violence
Dir: Ralph Nelson *Cast:* Sidney Poitier, Michael Caine, Nicol Williamson, Prunella Gee, Persis Khambatta, Saeed Jaffrey
▶ In South Africa, black antiapartheid leader Poitier goes on the lam with white fugitive Caine while racist policeman Williamson chases them both. Fast-paced and slick mayhem with a message and a terrific cast. (CC)
Dist.: MGM/UA

WILD ANGELS, THE 1966
★ PG Action-Adventure 1:33
☑ Adult situations, explicit language, violence
Dir: Roger Corman *Cast:* Peter Fonda, Nancy Sinatra, Bruce Dern, Lou Procopio, Michael J. Pollard, Diane Ladd
▶ Fonda, leader of leather-clad biker gang, kidnaps injured buddy Dern from hospital while cohorts wreak mayhem on staff and patients. When Dern dies, gang takes over church for drunken, orgiastic funeral ceremony, causing retaliation by local townspeople. First in wave of biker movies released in late sixties was panned by critics but earned $25 million on budget of $350,000. Actual Hell's Angels play bit parts.
Dist.: Embassy

WILD BUNCH, THE 1969
★ ★ ★ R Western 2:23
☑ Brief nudity, adult situations, explicit language, graphic violence
Dir: Sam Peckinpah *Cast:* William Holden, Ernest Borgnine, Robert Ryan, Edmond O'-Brien, Warren Oates, Ben Johnson, Strother Martin, Bo Hopkins
▶ Unable to adapt to 1913's automobiles and machine guns, bank robbers flee to Mexico,

where they become unwilling accomplices in a revolutionary movement. Magisterial Western, once controversial for its unprecedented violence, now has all the earmarks of a genuine classic. Editing, photography, directing, and performances are all extraordinary. Cassette version contains additional sequences cut from original release.
Dist.: Warner

WILDCATS 1986
★ ★ ★ ★ R Comedy 1:46
☑ Brief nudity, adult situations, explicit language
Dir: Michael Ritchie *Cast:* Goldie Hawn, Swoosie Kurtz, Robyn Lively, Brandy Gold, James Keach, Nipsey Russell
▶ Divorcée Hawn, determined to coach high school football, takes tough assignment at an inner-city ghetto school. She wins over her athletes through perseverance and wit, then battles her ex-husband for custody of her daughters. Winning comedy makes expert use of Hawn's charm. (CC)
Dist.: Warner

WILD COUNTRY, THE 1971
★ ★ ★ G Family 1:32
Dir: Robert Totten *Cast:* Steve Forrest, Vera Miles, Jack Elam, Ron Howard, Frank De Kova, Morgan Woodward
▶ In the 1880s, aspiring rancher Forrest moves wife Miles and family from Pittsburgh to Wyoming, only to discover the land he's purchased is inhabited by mountain man Elam and his Indian sidekick De Kova. Others woes include fire, tornado, and refusal of nasty neighbor Woodward to share water rights. Superior Disney fare centers on rite-of-passage for teen son Howard.
Dist.: Buena Vista

WILD DUCK, THE 1983 Australian
★ ★ PG Drama 1:36
☑ Explicit language
Dir: Henri Safran *Cast:* Liv Ullmann, Jeremy Irons, Lucinda Jones, John Meillon, Arthur Dignam, Michael Pate
▶ In the course of two days and nights, the lives of married couple Irons and Ullmann and their teen daughter Jones are destroyed by the reappearance of Irons's boyhood friend Dignam, a stern moralist who corrects the lies which previously allowed the family to peacefully coexist. Well-cast adaptation of classic Ibsen play moves slowly.
Dist.: Vestron

WILDERNESS FAMILY, PART 2, THE 1978
★ ★ ★ ★ G Family 1:45
Dir: Frank Zuniga *Cast:* Robert Logan, Susan Damante Shaw, Heather Rattray, Ham Larsen, George "Buck" Flower, Brian Cutler
▶ Sequel to popular *Adventures of the Wilderness Family* portrays further Rocky Mountain exploits of former city-dwellers living in remote log cabin. Parents Logan and Shaw savor life

away from the rat race while kids Rattray and Larsen enjoy company of animals, both tamed and wild. Sole human visitors are crusty old trapper Flower and mail pilot Cutler. The real stars in this wholesome adventure are the animals and stunning mountain landscapes.
Dist.: Media

WILD GEESE, THE 1978 British
★ ★ ★ ★ R Action-Adventure 2:14
☑ Explicit language, violence
Dir: Andrew V. McLaglen *Cast:* Richard Burton, Roger Moore, Richard Harris, Stewart Granger, Hardy Kruger, Jack Watson
▶ British industrialist Granger hires veteran warrior Burton to organize rescue of democratic African leader deposed by dictator. With help of old fighting chums Moore and Harris, Burton leads successful mission. Granger then strikes a deal with the new dictator to resume his old business, so he cancels the air evacuation and leaves the gaggle of mercenaries to their fate. First-rate action boasts sturdy cast and well-staged derring-do. A sequel followed in 1985.
Dist.: CBS/Fox

WILD GEESE II 1985 British
★ ★ ★ R Action-Adventure 2:05
☑ Adult situations, explicit language, violence
Dir: Peter Hunt *Cast:* Scott Glenn, Laurence Olivier, Barbara Carrera, Edward Fox, Robert Webber, Robert Freitag
▶ American TV network commissions mercenary Glenn and debonair sidekick Fox to bust Nazi war criminal Rudolf Hess (Olivier) out of impregnable Spandau prison. Ambushes, double-crosses, and kidnapping of journalist Carrera ensue as soldiers of fortune encounter hostile Germans, Soviets, and Palestinians. Premise is far-fetched, but action fans will not be disappointed. Dedicated to Richard Burton, who died before reprising role from hit original.
Dist.: Warner

WILD GUITAR 1962
☆ NR Drama 1:27 B&W
Dir: Ray Dennis Steckler *Cast:* Arch Hall, Jr., Arch Hall, Sr., Nancy Czar, Ray Dennis Steckler, Marie Denn, Al Scott
▶ Hall, Jr., is a cycle-riding rock singer who goes to California and enters a talent contest. Signed by corrupt promoter Hall, Sr., he is fleeced mercilessly, with kidnapping and worse indignities in store. So bad it's awesome. Hall, Sr., produced under a pseudonym. Most of the actors are amateurs.
Dist.: Rhino

WILD HORSE HANK 1979 Canadian
★ ★ ★ NR Action-Adventure 1:34
☑ Explicit language, mild violence
Dir: Eric Till *Cast:* Linda Blair, Michael Wincott, Al Waxman, Pace Bradford, Richard Crenna
▶ Feisty college student Blair discovers unsa-

vory rustlers led by Waxman rounding up a herd of wild horses to be slaughtered and sold for dog food. With the rustlers in hot pursuit, Blair frees the horses and begins a desperate race to drive them to safety on a government preserve. Young horse-lovers will enjoy.
Dist.: Vestron

WILD IN THE COUNTRY 1961
★ ★ NR Drama/Musical 1:54
Dir: Philip Dunne *Cast:* Elvis Presley, Hope Lange, Tuesday Weld, Millie Perkins, Rafer Johnson, John Ireland
▶ Presley is a backwoods delinquent groomed for a widowed psychiatrist Lange for a literary career. The King also must decide between over-confident Weld and her shy rival Perkins. Unexpectedly sincere drama was written by Clifford Odets. Songs include "I Slipped, I Stumbled, I Fell," and "In My Way."
Dist.: CBS/Fox

WILD IN THE STREETS 1968
★ PG Drama 1:37
☑ Adult situations, explicit language, violence
Dir: Barry Shear *Cast:* Shelley Winters, Christopher Jones, Diane Varsi, Ed Begley, Hal Holbrook, Richard Pryor
▶ Rebellious teen Jones runs away from home and within years becomes world's most-idolized entertainer, living millionaire's life in Beverly Hills with flower child mistress Varsi and fawning entourage (including Pryor). Next challenge for Jones: by doping Congress with LSD, he persuades the legislators to lower the minimum age for voting and holding office to fourteen. Jones is soon elected President and sends anyone over thirty-five-years old to compulsory "retirement camps." Sixties satire, critics' favorite when released, may seem dated.
Dist.: HBO

WILD LIFE, THE 1984
★ R Comedy 1:36
☑ Nudity, adult situations, explicit language, adult humor
Dir: Art Linson *Cast:* Christopher Penn, Eric Stoltz, Rick Moranis, Lea Thompson, Jenny Wright, Hart Bochner
▶ Responsible teen Stoltz graduates from high school, moves into own apartment, and takes in bowling alley co-worker Penn as roommate to make ends meet. Swinging singles they're not: Penn's girl Wright leaves while Stolz's former steady Thompson has fling with older policeman Bochner. Their answer is to party hearty. Uneven and episodic teen comedy mostly misfires. **(CC)**
Dist.: MCA

WILD MAN 1989
☆ NR Action-Adventure 1:57
☑ Nudity, explicit language, violence
Dir: Fred J. Lincoln *Cast:* Don Scribner, Michelle Bauer, Kathleen Middleton, Travis Silver, Ginger Lynn Allen, James L. Newman

▶ Las Vegas casino manager Scribner battles drug czar Newman with the help of a mystical Indian ring that brings him back from the dead after being killed. Between resurrections, Scribner finds time for love with newscaster Bauer although his own ex-wife Middleton is involved with the villain. Wild plot derailed by dull filmmaking.
Dist.: Celebrity

WILD ONE, THE 1954
★ ★ ★ NR Drama 1:19 B&W
Dir: Laslo Benedek *Cast:* Marlon Brando, Mary Murphy, Robert Keith, Lee Marvin, Jay C. Flippen, Peggy Maley
▶ Biker Brando and his gang, the Black Rebels, disrupt life in a small town while he romances Murphy, daughter of the sheriff. Second gang of bikers, headed by Brando's former riding buddy Marvin, rides into town, causing angry townsfolk to take matters into their own hands. Original biker movie was also one of the first films to deal with alienated youth. Somewhat dated by its successors, but worthy for Brando's performance, one of his best. **(CC)**
Dist.: RCA/Columbia

WILD ORCHID 1990
☆ R Drama 1:43
☑ Nudity, strong sexual content, Adult situations, explicit language
Dir: Zalman King *Cast:* Mickey Rourke, Jacqueline Bisset, Carré Otis, Assumpta Serna, Bruce Greenwood, Oleg Vidov
▶ Innocent American Otis sent to work on a real estate deal in Rio De Janeiro, where boss Bisset bustles with business, and mogul Rourke makes eyes at her. After a few voyeuristic and participatory sexual experiences, Otis sees the world in a new light, and prepares to cure Rourke's impotence. Little more than soft-core sex.
Dist.: RCA/Columbia

WILD ORCHIDS 1929
★ NR Drama 1:42 B&W
Dir: Sidney Franklin *Cast:* Greta Garbo, Lewis Stone, Nils Asther
▶ While visiting Java with distracted husband Stone, Garbo and Javanese prince Asther become attracted to one another. Jealous Stone feels the pair's heat, and prepares to shoot Asther while they are out hunting. Garbo's radiant presence raises this draggy silent above the ordinary.
Dist.: MGM/UA

WILD PAIR, THE 1987
★ ★ R Action-Adventure 1:28
☑ Nudity, adult situations, explicit language, violence
Dir: Beau Bridges *Cast:* Beau Bridges, Bubba Smith, Lloyd Bridges, Gary Lockwood, Raymond St. Jacques, Danny De La Paz
▶ Black L.A. cop Smith and white FBI agent Beau Bridges form grudging friendship, investigating ghetto drug ring run by bar owner St. Jacques. Trail leads to group of white supremacists led by ex-colonel Lloyd Bridges, aided by corrupt police captain Lockwood. When racists kidnap and torture Smith, Beau Bridges turns into a one-man army. Uninspired *Lethal Weapon* clone is for hard-core action fans.
Dist.: Media

WILD PARTY, THE 1975
★ R Drama 1:35
☑ Nudity, adult situations, explicit language, violence
Dir: James Ivory *Cast:* James Coco, Raquel Welch, Perry King, Tiffany Boiling, David Dukes, Royal Dano
▶ In the 1920s, fading silent movie comic Coco throws huge bash. He gets drunk as his girlfriend Welch falls for younger man King, a triangle that leads to tragedy. Ivory lays on the gloomy atmosphere and wall-to-wall music way too thick in this ambitious failure. Welch and Coco struggle dutifully with ludicrous dialogue. Story loosely resembles the Fatty Arbuckle scandal.
Dist.: Nelson

WILDROSE 1984
★ NR Drama/Romance 1:35
☑ Brief nudity, adult situations, explicit language, violence
Dir: John Hanson *Cast:* Lisa Eichhorn, Tom Bower, James Cada, Cinda Jackson, Dan Nemanick, Lydia Olson
▶ Divorced Eichhorn, a truck driver in a Minnesota strip mine, is demoted to all-male pit crew due to recession. At first she resists advances of co-worker Bower but soon succumbs to his charms. When both are laid off, she must consider his offer to move to Lake Superior shore to operate fishing business. Modest romantic drama best for small moments of blue-collar life.
Dist.: Vestron

WILD ROVERS 1971
★ ★ ★ ★ PG Western 1:49
☑ Explicit language, violence
Dir: Blake Edwards *Cast:* William Holden, Ryan O'Neal, Karl Malden, Tom Skerritt, Lynn Carlin, Joe Don Baker
▶ Older ranch worker Holden and his young sidekick O'Neal embark on bank holdup, but soon find themselves on the lam from the law and heading for Mexico. Rare foray into Western territory for writer/director/producer Edwards, who elicits outstanding performances from the two stars.
Dist.: MGM/UA

WILD STRAWBERRIES 1959 Swedish
★ ★ NR Drama 1:30
Dir: Ingmar Bergman *Cast:* Victor Sjostrom, Bibi Andersson, Ingrid Thulin, Gunnar Bjornstrand, Jullan Kindahl, Folke Sundquist
▶ En route to receive honorary degree, elderly medical professor Sjostrom reviews his life

while coping with difficult car passengers, including disenchanted daughter-in-law Thulin and Andersson, who resembles the sweetheart of his youth. Flashbacks and dream sequences provide the film's most memorable moments. Generally considered director Bergman's finest work, touching drama is a must for film buffs; others will find it too symbolic and intellectual. $\boxed{S}$
Dist.: Various

WILD THING 1987
★ PG-13 Action-Adventure 1:32
☑ Adult situations, explicit language, violence
Dir: Max Reid *Cast:* Rob Knepper, Kathleen Quinlan, Robert Davi, Betty Buckley, Maury Chaykin
▶ Knepper, orphaned at age three in Montreal, learns to survive on his own into adulthood, becoming legend as "the wild thing" in the inner-city jungle known as the Zone. Leaping from rooftops and materializing out of alleys, he protects the ghetto's street people from villains. Intriguing premise gets confused and uninteresting treatment; best part of film is title song, the sixties hit by Chip Baker and the Troggs.
Dist.: Paramount

WILLARD 1971
★ ★ PG Horror 1:35
☑ Explicit language, violence
Dir: Daniel Mann *Cast:* Bruce Davison, Ernest Borgnine, Elsa Lanchester, Sondra Locke, Michael Dante
▶ Mild-mannered young Davison, mistreated by cruel boss Borgnine and others, discovers he can communicate with rats and train them to follow his orders. Davison gets revenge but eventually finds drawbacks to rats as man's best friends. Diabolically clever genre flick is alternately creepy and poignant. Best line: "Tear him up." Spawned sequel *Ben.*
Dist.: Prism

WILLOW 1988
★ ★ ★ ★ PG Fantasy 2:04
☑ Violence
Dir: Ron Howard *Cast:* Val Kilmer, Jean Marsh, Joanne Whalley, Warwick Davis, Patricia Hayes, Ruth and Kate Greenfield
▶ Evil queen Marsh casts infant into river lest the child fulfill prophecy of unseating the villainous ruler. Amiable dwarf Davis rescues child and, with help of valiant mercenary Kilmer, sets out to defeat Marsh. Sprawling fantasy created by George Lucas with plenty of action and derring-do, featuring dragons, fairies, sorcerers, wicked witches, heroes, and damsels in distress. A feast for eyes and imagination, though some effects will lose impact on video. **(CC)**
Dist.: RCA/Columbia

WILL PENNY 1968
★ ★ ★ NR Western 1:49
Dir: Tom Gries *Cast:* Charlton Heston, Joan

Hackett, Donald Pleasence, Bruce Dern, Lee Majors, Ben Johnson
▶ After running afoul of evil preacher Pleasence, grizzled cowboy Heston befriends widow Hackett and her son. Heston falls for Hackett and protects her from Pleasence's wrath. Overlooked on first release but reputation has deservedly grown over the years; features one of Heston's subtlest performances and gritty Gries direction.
Dist.: Paramount

WILLY WONKA AND THE CHOCOLATE FACTORY 1971
★ ★ ★ ★ G Musical/Family 1:38
Dir: Mel Stuart *Cast:* Gene Wilder, Jack Albertson, Peter Ostrum, Michael Bollner, Ursula Reit, Denise Nickerson
▶ Wilder, the mysterious owner of a fantastical chocolate factory, holds a contest in which five winners are awarded tour of plant and lifetime supply of sweets. His real motive: to find an honest child to be his heir. Young lad Ostrum wins coveted tour and takes along bed-ridden grandfather Albertson, but Wilder's tests may prove too tempting for any child. Musical adaptation of Roald Dahl's popular children's book will please the young.
Dist.: Warner

WIMPS 1987
★ R Comedy 1:34
☑ Nudity, adult situations, explicit language
Dir: Chuck Vincent *Cast:* Louie Bonanno, Deborah Blaisdell, Jim Abele, Jane Hamilton, Eddie Prevot, Derrick Roberts
▶ Brainy nerd freshman Bonanno helps college jocks with homework. Soon he's persuaded to help star quarterback Abele woo fetching librarian Blaisdell, who has been turned off by Abele's rah-rah demeanor. Bonanno writes love letters to Blaisdell in Abele's name while falling for her himself. Updating of classic tale *Cyrano de Bergerac* lacks muscle.
Dist.: Vestron

WINCHESTER '73 1950
★ ★ ★ NR Western 1:32 B&W
Dir: Anthony Mann *Cast:* James Stewart, Shelley Winters, Dan Duryea, Stephen McNally, Millard Mitchell, Charles Drake, Will Geer, Rock Hudson, Tony Curtis
▶ Stewart delivers a brooding, magnetic performance as a drifter obsessed with recovering a rifle stolen from him during a sharpshooting contest. After encounters in grim trading posts, Indian ambushes, and attacks on homesteaders, his odyssey forces him to confront a dark secret in his past. Disturbing psychological themes were a major influence on subsequent Westerns. First teaming of Stewart and director Mann.
Dist.: MCA

WIND, THE 1928
☆ NR Drama 1:28 B&W
Dir: Victor Seastrom *Cast:* Lillian Gish, Lars

Hanson, Montagu Love, Dorothy Cumming, Edward Earle, William Orlamond
▶ Innocent country girl Gish marries a rough cowboy. Left alone when he's off on a roundup, she is visited in her home by Love during a violent windstorm. When Love tries to assault her, she kills him, burying the body outside. The wind uncovers the grave, and seems to drive Gish insane with its relentless fury. Full of dreamlike imagery, silent melodrama has great pictorial appeal.
Dist.: MGM/UA

WIND, THE 1987
☆ **NR Mystery-Suspense 1:32**
☑ Explicit language, violence
Dir: Nico Mastorakis ***Cast:*** Meg Foster, Wings Hauser, Robert Morley, Steve Railsback, David McCallum, John Michaels
▶ Mystery writer Foster rents house on Greek island from eccentric owner Morley, despite his warnings of dangerous wind in region and presence of creepy caretaker Hauser. Foster begins to write mystery based on Morley and Hauser, which is soon mimicked by real life. Predictable suspenser has few scares.
Dist.: Vestron

WIND AND THE LION, THE 1975
★★★★ **PG Action-Adventure 1:59**
☑ Adult situations, explicit language, violence
Dir: John Milius ***Cast:*** Sean Connery, Candice Bergen, Brian Keith, John Huston, Geoffrey Lewis, Steve Kanaly
▶ When rebellious Arab chieftain Connery kidnaps beautiful American Bergen in 1904, President Teddy Roosevelt (Keith) threatens to send Marines to rescue her. Meanwhile, Germany sends troops to northern Africa, hoping to turn delicate situation to its advantage. Splendid performance by Connery as strong-willed, full-of-life rogue carries this colorful adventure. Keith as Connery's respected adversary is also fine. Nominated for two technical Oscars.
Dist.: MGM/UA

WINDOM'S WAY 1957 British
★★ **NR Drama 1:48**
Dir: Ronald Neame ***Cast:*** Peter Finch, Mary Ure, Natasha Parry, Robert Flemyng, Michael Hordern, John Cairney
▶ Idealistic doctor Finch is caught between striking rubber workers and the government in politically turbulent Malaya. Putting his pacifistic principles to work, Finch tries to negotiate a settlement between the violently inclined antagonists. Star is earnest and effective in this well-done drama, loosely based on a true story.
Dist.: VidAmerica

WINDWALKER 1981
★★★★ **PG Drama 1:47**
☑ Violence
Dir: Kieth Merrill ***Cast:*** Trevor Howard, Nick Ramus, James Remar, Serene Hedin, Dusty Iron Wing McCrea, Silvana Gallardo
▶ In the late eighteenth-century, dying Cheyenne warrior Howard tells two grandsons of murder of his wife Hedin and abduction of his son Ramus by rival Crows years before. Howard dies but is brought back to life to complete his mission of finding his lost son and punishing the Crow. Unusual, extremely effective drama uses Indian languages and English subtitles for authentic treatment of Native American culture. Set against striking backdrop of Utah's Wasatch Mountains. [S]
Dist.: CBS/Fox

WINDY CITY 1984
★ **R Drama 1:42**
☑ Adult situations, explicit language
Dir: Armyan Bernstein ***Cast:*** John Shea, Kate Capshaw, Josh Mostel, Jim Borelli, Jeffrey DeMunn, Eric Pierpoint
▶ Lifelong Chicago friends, now in their thirties, struggle with fast-fading dreams. Mailman Shea still hopes to be a writer while Capshaw, the woman he loves, plans to wed another. Shea's comedian pal Mostel has tasted success, but he's dying of leukemia. Shea assembles the old gang for final cruise with Mostel. Well-intentioned drama is maudlin and melodramatic. (CC)
Dist.: CBS/Fox

WINGS 1927
★★ **NR War 2:19 B&W**
Dir: William Wellman ***Cast:*** Clara Bow, Gary Cooper, Richard Arlen, Buddy Rogers, El Brendel, Jobyna Ralston
▶ Silent classic soars in the air with amazing footage from former pilot Wellman, and on the ground with stirring story of World War I flyers Arlen and Rogers, pals but rivals for the same gal, who discover the excitement, romance, and horrors of battle. Winner of the first Best Picture Oscar.
Dist.: Paramount

WINGS OF DESIRE 1988 German/French
☆ **PG-13 Drama 2:10 C/B&W**
☑ Explicit language
Dir: Wim Wenders ***Cast:*** Bruno Ganz, Solveig Dommartin, Otto Sander, Curt Bois, Peter Falk
▶ Intensely lyrical fantasy about guardian angels watching over the citizens of West Berlin became an art-house favorite for its exquisite Henri Alékan photography and romantic screenplay (by director Wenders and Peter Handke). Ganz is unexpectedly moving as an angel who yearns to become human; Falk adds an amusing cameo as an American movie star with a surprising secret. [S]
Dist.: Orion

WINNERS TAKE ALL 1987
★★ **PG-13 Drama/Sports 1:42**
☑ Brief nudity, adult situations, explicit language
Dir: Fritz Kiersch ***Cast:*** Don Michael Paul,

Kathleen York, Robert Krantz, Deborah Richter, Courtney Gains, Paul Hampton
▶ Dirt-track motorcycle superstar Krantz returns home for race and romances Richter, girlfriend of talented also-ran Paul. Paul challenges Krantz on dirt track and loses badly. Spunky trainer York helps Paul regain confidence for big showdown in Dallas. Plenty of romance and even more motorcycle action in amiable *Rocky* on wheels. **(CC)**
Dist.: Nelson

WINNING 1969
★★★ PG Drama/Sports 2:03
☑ Adult situations, explicit language, mild violence
Dir: James Goldstone *Cast:* Paul Newman, Joanne Woodward, Robert Wagner, Richard Thomas, David Sheiner, Clu Gulager
▶ Car racer Newman marries divorcée Woodward and adopts her teen son Thomas. Couple are apart during racing season but reunite for Indianapolis 500. There Newman spends so much time with his car that Woodward succumbs to the amorous advances of rival driver Wagner. Above-average drama about man obsessed with winning has spectacular racing footage and strong turns from Newman and Woodward.
Dist.: MCA

WIN, PLACE OR STEAL 1975
★ PG Comedy 1:21
☑ Adult situations
Dir: Richard Bailey *Cast:* Dean Stockwell, Russ Tamblyn, Alex Karras, McLean Stevenson, Alan Oppenheimer, Kristina Holland
▶ Tamblyn and Karras are a mismatched pair of losers who team up with Stockwell on a get-rich-quick-scheme that involves trickery with a pari-mutuel betting machine. Mildly amusing, TV-style racetrack comedy, with good performances by Karras and hardworking minor characters. Also known as *Three for the Money* and *Another Day at the Races*.
Dist.: Vestron

WINSLOW BOY, THE 1950 British
★ NR Drama 1:57 B&W
Dir: Anthony Asquith *Cast:* Robert Donat, Margaret Leighton, Cedric Hardwicke, Francis L. Sullivan, Frank Lawton, Neil North, Basil Radford, Wilfrid Hyde-White, Ernest Thesiger
▶ Retired bank official Hardwicke hires Donat, a prominent lawyer, to defend fourteen-year-old son North, a young naval cadet accused of stealing a postal order. Though the ensuing notoriety causes difficulties for family members, Hardwicke and Donat go to the wall against the tough British naval and legal establishment. Brilliant drama from a play by Terrence Rattigan based on an actual trial.
Dist.: HBO

WINTER FLIGHT 1986 British
★★ NR Drama/Romance 1:43
☑ Adult situations, explicit language
Dir: Roy Battersby *Cast:* Reece Dinsdale,

Nicola Cowper, Gary Olsen, Sean Benn, Beverly Hewitt, Shelagh Stephenson
▶ Bittersweet romance portrays sometimes rocky development of relationship between innocent airman Dinsdale, in charge of keeping birds off runway at RAF base, and more worldly barmaid Cowper. When Cowper reveals she's pregnant by Dinsdale's predecessor, he nonetheless offers to marry her and can't understand her hesitancy. Simple drama with message ending convinces, but strong English accents could cause some problems.
Dist.: MGM/UA

WINTER KILLS 1979
★★★★ R Comedy/Drama 1:37
☑ Nudity, adult situations, explicit language, violence
Dir: William Richert *Cast:* Jeff Bridges, John Huston, Anthony Perkins, Richard Boone, Anthony Perkins, Sterling Hayden, Eli Wallach, Toshiro Mifune, Dorothy Malone, Elizabeth Taylor
▶ Seriocomic adaptation of the Richard Condon novel loosely based on the Kennedy family. Nineteen years after the assassination of a President, his half-brother Bridges pursues new conspiracy evidence which may implicate their father Huston, the country's richest man. Farfetched cult favorite has many loose screws but always outrages and delights. Stunningly shot by Vilmos Zsigmond.
Dist.: Nelson

WINTER LIGHT 1963 Swedish
☆ NR Drama 1:20 B&W
Dir: Ingmar Bergman *Cast:* Ingrid Thulin, Gunnar Bjornstrand, Max Von Sydow, Gunnel Lindblom
▶ Stark story of a preacher who has lost his faith, is losing his congregation, and can offer no consolation to a fisherman despairing over the possibility of nuclear war. After the fisherman kills himself, the preacher must confront an empty universe. Powerful, step-by-step dissection of disillusionment stands between *Through a Glass Darkly* and *The Silence* in Bergman's trilogy on faith.
Dist.: Various

WINTER OF OUR DREAMS 1982 Australian
★ NR Drama 1:29
☑ Adult situations, explicit language
Dir: John Duigan *Cast:* Judy Davis, Bryan Brown, Cathy Downes, Baz Luhrman, Peter Mochrie, Mervyn Drake
▶ Upscale Sydney bookseller Brown ventures into red light district to learn how ex-girlfriend committed suicide. There he meets waifish prostitute/junkie Davis. Despite sexual attraction, two remain just friends as he helps her kick heroin while she reveals life's underbelly to him. Well-acted drama gets mired in relentless earnestness and gloom.
Dist.: USA

WINTER PEOPLE 1988
★ PG-13 Drama 1:50
☑ Adult situations, explicit language, violence
Dir: Ted Kotcheff *Cast:* Kurt Russell, Kelly McGillis, Lloyd Bridges, Mitchell Ryan, Amelia Burnette, Jeffrey Meek
▶ Backwoods melodrama about Depression-era clockmaker Russell and his daughter who get stranded in a North Carolina mountain town. They take refuge from the cold with McGillis, mother of an illegitimate baby and object of a bloody feud between two families. Lovely camerawork can't make up for the slow-as-molasses pacing and creaky plot.
Dist.: Nelson

WINTERSET 1936
☆ NR Drama 1:18 B&W
Dir: Alfred Santell *Cast:* Burgess Meredith, Margo, Eduardo Ciannelli, Paul Guilfoyle, John Carradine, Edward Ellis
▶ Impulsive young Meredith is determined to prove that father Carradine was innocent of the murder he was convicted of twenty years earlier. Flashback shows how radical Carradine was prosecuted more for his political beliefs than for the actual murder. Adapted from Maxwell Anderson's play, which took its inspiration from the real-life Sacco and Vanzetti case, stiff, stagey effort never convinces.
Dist.: Cable

WIRED 1989
★ R Biography 1:52
☑ Nudity, adult situations, explicit language
Dir: Larry Peerce *Cast:* Michael Chiklis, Ray Sharkey, J. T. Walsh, Patti D'Arbanville, Lucinda Jenney, Alex Rocco
▶ Adaptation of Bob Woodward's best-seller about comedian/actor John Belushi features Sharkey as a Puerto Rican cabbie/guardian angel who takes Belushi (Chiklis) on a tour of his fast-lane life, including his rise to fame on "Saturday Night Live," his movie success, and the drug problem that would kill him. Done in by fractured screenplay and frenetic direction. Chiklis captures comic's surface, but not his spirit.
Dist.: IVE

WIRED TO KILL 1986
★ ★ R Sci-Fi 1:36
☑ Explicit language, graphic violence
Dir: Franky Schaeffer *Cast:* Emily Longstreth, Matt Hoelscher, Merritt Butrick, Frank Collison, Garth Gardner, Kristina David
▶ After massive plague in 1998 Los Angeles, normal humans in quarantine zone are on defensive from marauding renegades. One such gang slays Hoelscher's family and beats him so badly he loses use of his legs. With help of girlfriend Longstreth, techno-wizard seeks revenge from his wheelchair. B-grade action with explicit violence is for hard-core thrill-seekers.
Dist.: Vestron

WISDOM 1986
★ ★ R Drama 1:49
☑ Brief nudity, adult situations, explicit language, violence
Dir: Emilio Estevez *Cast:* Emilio Estevez, Demi Moore, Tom Skerritt, Veronica Cartwright, William Allen Young, Richard Minchenberg
▶ Pegged for life as a criminal because of teen car theft, Estevez can't find a steady job. He decides to become a latter-day Robin Hood, torching bank mortgages of those threatened with foreclosure. After initial reluctance, girlfriend Moore joins him for traveling crime spree. Directing and writing debut for twenty-three-year-old star Estevez. (CC)
Dist.: Warner

WISE BLOOD 1979
★ PG Drama 1:48
☑ Adult situations, explicit language
Dir: John Huston *Cast:* Brad Dourif, Ned Beatty, Harry Dean Stanton, Dan Shor, Amy Wright, Mary Nell Santacroce
▶ Obsessed with religion, Army veteran Dourif forms the Church of Christ Without Christ in rural Georgia, but finds unexpected competition from fraudulent managers and preachers. One-of-a-kind film adapted from Flannery O'Connor's novel is bleak, haunting, and funny. Quirky drama's light-hearted blasphemy and astonishing violence will reward discriminating viewers. Huston, directing his thirty-third feature, has an amusing cameo as a preacher.
Dist.: MCA

WISE GUYS 1986
★ ★ ★ R Comedy 1:32
☑ Explicit language, violence, adult humor
Dir: Brian De Palma *Cast:* Danny DeVito, Joe Piscopo, Harvey Keitel, Ray Sharkey, Dan Hedaya, Captain Lou Albano
▶ Mafia gofers DeVito and Piscopo lose $10,-000 belonging to boss Hedaya at race track; Hedaya tells each separately to kill the other. The two flee to Atlantic City, hoping to win back missing money, with hitman Albano in pursuit. Slight, padded excursion into humor by director De Palma doesn't click. (CC)
Dist.: CBS/Fox

WISH YOU WERE HERE 1987 British
★ ★ R Drama 1:30
☑ Adult situations, explicit language
Dir: David Leland *Cast:* Emily Lloyd, Tom Bell, Clare Clifford, Barbara Durkin, Geoffrey Hutchings, Charlotte Barker
▶ Spunky but troubled teen Lloyd suffers growing pains in British seaside resort during the 1950s. Still aching from death of her mom years before, Lloyd rebels against her father, Bell; ill-fated sexual encounters ensue, including one with her father's sleazy friend Hutchings. Familiar drama delivers taunting performance by Lloyd as a precocious free spirit.
Dist.: Fries

WITCHBOARD 1987
★★ R Horror 1:38
☑ Nudity, explicit language, violence
Dir: Kevin S. Tenney *Cast:* Todd Allen, Tawny Kitaen, Stephen Nichols, Kathleen Wilhoite, Burke Byrnes
▶ Evil spirit of drowned boy uses ouija board with mysterious qualities as a bridge to the real world, endangering Kitaen, who's unaware of the board's powers. Low-budget horror works up some good chills when the spirit reveals its true identity. Extremely brief cameo by comedienne Rose Marie.
Dist.: Magnum

WITCHCRAFT THROUGH THE AGES 1922
Swedish
★ NR Drama 2:11 B&W
☑ Nudity, violence
Dir: Benjamin Christensen *Cast:* Maren Pedersen, Clara Pontoppidan, Elith Pio, Oscar Stribolt, Tora Teje, Johs Andersen
▶ Spooky exploitation from Sweden purportedly tells the story of witchcraft and satanism from the earliest days through the then-present. Film shows ancient books and drawings, and reenacts satanic rituals. Graphic images of witches undergoing torture at the hands of the Church and other occasions for violence and nudity are what have kept this film in print. Also known as *The Witches* and *Haxan.*
Dist.: Various

WITCHERY 1989 Italian
★ NR Horror 1:36
☑ Rape, nudity, adult situations, explicit language, violence
Dir: Fabrizio Laurenti *Cast:* David Hasselhoff, Linda Blair, Catherine Hickland, Annie Ross, Hildegard Knef, Leslie Cumming
▶ A group including writer Cumming, photographer Hasselhoff, and pregnant Blair are stranded on a deserted New England island haunted by Knef, a former silent film star turned murderous witch. Blair is possessed, and the rest are killed off one by one in brutal fashion. Mean, poorly scripted direct-to-video release is for die-hard horror fans only.
Dist.: Vidmark

WITCHES OF EASTWICK, THE 1987
★★★ R Fantasy/Comedy 1:58
☑ Adult situations, explicit language
Dir: George Miller *Cast:* Jack Nicholson, Michelle Pfeiffer, Susan Sarandon, Cher, Veronica Cartwright, Richard Jenkins
▶ Pfeiffer, Sarandon, and Cher, independent women stifled by small-town New England life and frustrated by lack of eligible men, dream of a "tall dark prince traveling under a curse." Soon the "witches" see their wish fulfilled: lecherous millionaire Nicholson moves into town and quickly seduces all three. But when the witches realize Nicholson is a woman-hating devil, they cast a spell to get rid of him. Hamming Nicholson carries uneven but fun

romp, loosely based on the John Updike novel. (CC)
Dist.: Warner

WITCHFIRE 1986
★ R Mystery-Suspense 1:32
☑ Nudity, adult situations, explicit language, violence
Dir: Vincent J. Primitera *Cast:* Shelley Winters, Frances De Sapio, Corrine Chateau, Gary Swanson
▶ Mental patient Winters, distraught over death of beloved psychiatrist, leads fellow inmates De Sapio and Chateau in an escape from the hospital. Convinced they're witches, trio tries to raise the dead doctor in an abandoned mansion. When Swanson stumbles onto property, the madwomen believe he's the resurrected shrink and abduct him. Little real suspense, although Winters gets some laughs. Best line: "I may be insane, but I'm not stupid."
Dist.: Lightning

WITHNAIL AND I 1987 British
☆ R Comedy 1:48
☑ Adult situations, explicit language
Dir: Bruce Robinson *Cast:* Richard E. Grant, Paul McGann, Richard Griffiths, Ralph Brown, Michael Elphick, Daragh O'Mallery
▶ In London, 1969, roommates Grant and McGann, fed up with the hedonistic excesses of the decade, trek to country for soul-cleansing weekend in a cottage owned by Griffiths, Grant's homosexual uncle. Restorative holiday doesn't turn out as expected, especially when Griffiths makes a play for McGann. Writer-director Robinson offers some funny dialogue, but excessive talk make this offbeat comedy rough going for many American viewers.
Dist.: Media

WITHOUT A CLUE 1988
★★★★ PG Mystery-Suspense 1:47
☑ Mild violence
Dir: Thom Eberhardt *Cast:* Michael Caine, Ben Kingsley, Jeffrey Jones, Lysette Anthony, Paul Freeman, Nigel Davenport
▶ New take on the Sherlock Holmes/Dr. Watson sleuthing team makes Watson (Kingsley) the brilliant detective. Wishing to remain anonymous, he hires drunken actor Caine to play the role of Holmes, master deducer. When they investigate sudden influx of counterfeit five-pound notes, Caine's degeneracy offsets his public relations value. Kingsley meanwhile begins to long for the praise he deserves. Plenty of bawdy wit.
Dist.: Orion

WITHOUT A TRACE 1983
★★★★★ PG Drama 1:59
☑ Adult situations, explicit language
Dir: Stanley Jaffe *Cast:* Kate Nelligan, Judd Hirsch, David Dukes, Stockard Channing, Jacqueline Brookes, Daniel Corkill
▶ New York professor Nelligan and ex-hus-

band Dukes learn their six-year-old son Corkill has disappeared on way to school. Police detective Hirsch doggedly pursues case as initial press furor fades over course of months. Nelligan bears up admirably under stress of child loss and continuing marital strife, but Hirsch suspects she's losing her grip on reality when she consults a psychic for help finding Corkill. Nelligan shines in a drama taken in part from a true story.
Dist.: CBS/Fox

WITHOUT RESERVATIONS 1946
★ ★ **NR Comedy 1:47 B&W**
Dir: Mervyn LeRoy *Cast:* Claudette Colbert, John Wayne, Don DeFore, Anne Triola, Frank Puglia, Phil Brown
▶ Writer Colbert, journeying to Hollywood for her book's film adaptation, meets soldier Wayne, who criticizes her novel without knowing who she is. She thinks him well cast as both the movie's and her own leading man, but keeps her identity secret from him. Breezy, likable trifle with nice chemistry between Colbert and Wayne. Look for cameos by Cary Grant, Jack Benny, Louella Parsons, and LeRoy.
Dist.: Turner

WITHOUT WARNING 1980
★ **R Sci-Fi 1:29**
☑ Adult situations, explicit language, violence
Dir: Greydon Clark *Cast:* Jack Palance, Martin Landau, Cameron Mitchell, Ralph Meeker, Sue Ane Langdon, Larry Storch
▶ Four teens are warned by gas station owner Palance not to go near the lake. The kids do so anyway and encounter killer alien on the loose. Complicating their slim chances for survival: trigger-happy veteran Landau, who mistakes the teens for extraterrestrials. As ridiculous as it sounds.
Dist.: HBO

WITHOUT YOU I'M NOTHING 1990
☆ **R Comedy 1:34**
☑ Nudity, adult situations, explicit language
Dir: John Boskovich *Cast:* Sandra Bernhard, John Doe, Steve Antin, Lu Leonard, Ken Foree
▶ Movie adaptation of comedienne Bernhardt's off-Broadway show in which she pokes fun at racism, homophobia, and relations between the sexes. Making the most of the big screen, Bernhard expands her stage routine to encompass bits of visual business that sometimes accentuate and sometimes contradict the points she appears to be trying to make. More anger than laughs.
Dist.: HBO

WITH SIX YOU GET EGGROLL 1968
★ ★ ★ **G Comedy 1:35**
Dir: Howard Morris *Cast:* Doris Day, Brian Keith, Barbara Hershey, Pat Carroll, George Carlin, Alice Ghostley
▶ Day, widowed mom with three sons, falls for Hershey's widowed dad Keith. They marry, then must deal with their feuding offspring. After some comic shenanigans, the kids see the family light. Friendly and pleasant. Most heartwarming scene: Day gives Hershey tomorrow's chores.
Dist.: CBS/Fox

WITNESS 1985
★ ★ ★ ★ ★ **R Drama 1:52**
☑ Nudity, adult situations, explicit language, violence
Dir: Peter Weir *Cast:* Harrison Ford, Kelly McGillis, Alexander Godunov, Josef Sommer, Lukas Haas, Jan Rubes
▶ Amish boy Haas, on trip to Philadelphia with widowed mother McGillis, witnesses murder. Streetwise cop Ford learns killer was narcotics cop and reports finding to superior Sommer. When a cop tries to kill Ford, he flees with Haas and McGillis to Amish farm run by Rubes, her father-in-law. Cross-cultural romance blooms between Ford and McGillis, to chagrin of her Amish suitor Godunov. Top-notch yarn combines star-crossed love story and suspenseful action. Film received eight Oscar nominations, including Ford as Best Actor; won two, including Original Screenplay.
Dist.: Paramount

WITNESS FOR THE PROSECUTION 1957
★ ★ ★ ★ **NR Mystery-Suspense 1:54 B&W**
Dir: Billy Wilder *Cast:* Marlene Dietrich, Tyrone Power, Charles Laughton, Elsa Lanchester, John Williams, Henry Daniell
▶ Movie version of the hit play by Agatha Christie returns retired attorney Laughton to court to defend drifter Power, accused of murdering rich widow for money. Power's wife Dietrich could offer his only alibi, but she isn't allowed to testify in his behalf. Classy drama with surprise ending was nominated for six Oscars, including Best Picture, Director, Actor (Laughton), and Supporting Actress (Lanchester).
Dist.: CBS/Fox

WIZ, THE 1978
★ ★ ★ **G Musical 2:14**
Dir: Sidney Lumet *Cast:* Diana Ross, Michael Jackson, Richard Pryor, Lena Horne, Nipsey Russell, Ted Ross
▶ Movie version of all-black Broadway musical, based on L. Frank Baum's novel and the 1939 Judy Garland movie, casts Ross as Harlem-dwelling twenty-four-year-old Dorothy. From the ghetto she's transported to Oz, where scarecrow Jackson, tin man Russell, and lion Ted Ross escort her to wizard Pryor, who may help her return to New York. Expensive song-and-dance extravaganza has terrific cast and creative sets, but musical numbers fall flat.
Dist.: MCA

WIZARD, THE 1989
★ ★ ★ **PG Action-Adventure 1:37**
☑ Explicit language

Dir: Todd Holland   *Cast:* Fred Savage, Luke Edwards, Jenny Lewis, Christian Slater, Beau Bridges

▶ Thirteen-year-old Savage sneaks Edwards, his disturbed younger brother, out of a hospital. The boys run away from home and head for California, where video whiz Edwards can enter a big Nintendo tournament. Bridges is their concerned dad, Lewis the girl who joins them on the road. Slickly contrived vehicle for Savage should please his young fans, but plugs for Nintendo and Universal Studios (where film climaxes) will leave adults cold. *Dist.:* MCA

WIZARD OF LONELINESS, THE 1988
★★★ PG-13 Drama 1:50
☑ Adult situations, explicit language, violence
Dir: Jenny Bowen   *Cast:* Lukas Haas, Lea Thompson, Lance Guest, John Randolph, Dylan Baker

▶ Small-scale family melodrama set in Vermont during World War II. Haas, a spoiled L.A. brat, is sent to small town to live with his grandparents after his mother dies and his father is shipped off to fight. His life is greatly affected by his disabled uncle (Guest) and aunt (Thompson), who gives birth to an illegitimate child. Good cast and excellent production values compensate for rather disparate story.
Dist.: Virgin

WIZARD OF MARS 1964
☆ NR Sci-Fi 1:21
Dir: David L. Hewitt   *Cast:* John Carradine, Roger Gentry, Vic McGee, Jerry Rannow, Eve Bernhardt

▶ Astronaut Gentry and his crew crash-land on Mars and find traces of a vanished civilization. With oxygen running perilously low, their only hope of return is to find "Wizard" Carradine. Some may think this is bad enough to be entertaining, others will be bored. Also known as *Horrors of the Red Planet.*
Dist.: Republic

WIZARD OF OZ, THE 1939
★★★★★ G Fantasy 1:42 C/B&W
Dir: Victor Fleming   *Cast:* Judy Garland, Ray Bolger, Bert Lahr, Jack Haley, Margaret Hamilton, Frank Morgan, Billie Burke, Charley Grapewin

▶ Hollywood's most enduring fantasy has delighted generations of viewers with its Harold Arlen–E. Y. Harburg songs, remarkable cast, and marvelous plot. Free adaptation of L. Frank Baum's classic about a Kansas girl's adventures in a magical kingdom has become a rite of passage for children, who are unfailingly moved by the special effects and music. Won Oscars for "Over the Rainbow," Herbert Stothart's score, and a special award for Garland. Remade in 1978 as *The Wiz;* sequels include the animated *Journey Back to Oz* and Disney's *Return to Oz.* Fiftieth anniversary

videocassette offers restored Technicolor version.
Dist.: MGM/UA

WIZARD OF SPEED AND TIME, THE 1989
★★★★ PG Comedy 1:35
☑ Explicit language
Dir: Mike Jittlov   *Cast:* Mike Jittlov, Richard Kaye, Lucky Straeker, Paige Moor, Brian Lucas, Philip Michael Thomas

▶ Unique comedy about free-lance special-effects master Jittlov's efforts to prove his skills while working on a big TV special. Kaye, one of the show's producers, tries to thwart Jittlov, and a presidential speech threatens to preempt the debut, but the young effects man produces a three-minute sequence that provides the film with a daffy climax. A hyperactive, live cartoon, and one-man show for producer/director/writer/star Jittlov.
Dist.: SGE

WIZARDS 1977
★★ PG Animation/Adult 1:20
☑ Explicit language, violence
Dir: Ralph Bakshi   *Cast:* Voices of Bob Holt, Jesse Wells, Richard Romanus, David Proval, James Connell, Steve Gravers

▶ In a post-atomic holocaust civilization set in the far-off future, mutants and an evil wizard wage war against a good wizard and peaceful elves. Fantasy fable finds talented Bakshi in a lighter mood than in his urban cartoons, although ponderous allegorical touches leave this somewhere between child and adult audiences. Excellent animation. [CC]
Dist.: Playhouse

WIZARDS OF THE LOST KINGDOM 1985
★★ PG Fantasy/Action-Adventure 1:16
☑ Mild violence
Dir: Hector Olivera   *Cast:* Bo Svenson, Vidal Peterson, Thom Christopher, Barbara Stock, Maria Socas, Dolores Michaels

▶ Wandering warrior Svenson decides to help young prince Peterson, whose father has been murdered and his kingdom overrun by evil magician Christopher. Tacky, low-budget sword-and-sorcery may appeal to kids.
Dist.: Media

WOLF AT THE DOOR 1987 French/Danish
☆ R Biography 1:32
☑ Nudity, adult situations, explicit language
Dir: Henning Carlsen   *Cast:* Donald Sutherland, Max Von Sydow, Valerie Morea, Merete Voldstedlund, Fanny Bastien

▶ In 1843 Paris, forty-five-year-old Paul Gauguin (Sutherland) is living a bohemian life after Polynesian sojourn. His post-Impressionist work is laughed at and he's debt-ridden. Private life is muddled by wife Voldstedlund and four kids he has deserted, former mistress Bastien, and Javanese slave girl Morea. He discusses art with playwright and art critic August Strindberg (Von Sydow). Tame retelling of artist's life,

although Sutherland delivers a compelling performance. (CC)
Dist.: CBS/Fox

WOLFEN 1981
★★ R Horror 1:55
☑ Nudity, adult situations, explicit language, graphic violence
Dir: Michael Wadleigh ***Cast:*** Albert Finney, Diane Venora, Gregory Hines, Edward James Olmos, Tom Noonan, Dick O'Neill
▶ New York City detective Finney and psychologist Venora team up to solve a series of murders. The trail leads to a group of American Indians and a race of supernaturally powered wolves. Astonishing camerawork and special effects, droll black humor from Finney and Hines (as the coroner), and appealing Venora compensate for ambitious but uneven screenplay. Some real scares although violence is a bit excessive.
Dist.: Warner

WOLF LAKE 1979
★ R Drama 1:27
☑ Rape, adult situations, explicit language, violence
Dir: Burt Kennedy ***Cast:*** Rod Steiger, David Huffman, Robin Mattson, Jerry Hardin, Richard Herd, Paul Mantee
▶ Vietnam deserter Huffman and girlfriend Mattson are living at a Canadian lodge when Steiger's hunting party shows up. Having lost a son in the war, Steiger is plenty mad when he discovers Huffman's status and aims to make him his quarry. Grim story of post-Vietnam angst.
Dist.: Prism

WOLF MAN, THE 1941
★★★ NR Horror 1:10 B&W
Dir: George Waggner ***Cast:*** Claude Rains, Lon Chaney, Jr., Evelyn Ankers, Ralph Bellamy, Maria Ouspenskaya, Bela Lugosi
▶ While out on the English moors, Chaney is bitten by a werewolf. When a full moon rises, the helpless Chaney is transformed into a murderous wolf man. Bone-chilling genre classic delivers deliciously ominous atmosphere. Ouspenskaya as a gypsy seer and Rains as Chaney's concerned dad stand out in the top-drawer cast. Spawned sequel (*Frankenstein Meets the Wolf Man*) and many variations.
Dist.: MCA

WOMAN IN GREEN, THE 1945
★★ NR Mystery-Suspense 1:08 B&W
Dir: Roy William Neill ***Cast:*** Basil Rathbone, Nigel Bruce, Hillary Brooke, Henry Daniell, Paul Cavanagh, Matthew Boulton
▶ Famed Baker Street sleuth Sherlock Holmes (Rathbone) investigates a series of mutilation murders that leaves Scotland Yard puzzled. Holmes follows the trail to a confrontation with Moriarty (Daniell), his arch-enemy, long presumed dead. Fatigue of long-running series reveals itself in lackluster performances (save for villainous Daniell) and uninspired script.
Dist.: Various

WOMAN IN RED, THE 1984
★★★ PG-13 Comedy 1:26
☑ Brief nudity, adult situations, explicit language
Dir: Gene Wilder ***Cast:*** Gene Wilder, Charles Grodin, Joseph Bologna, Judith Ivey, Kelly LeBrock, Gilda Radner
▶ Wilder, an advertising executive married to Ivey, suffers a mid-life crisis when he falls for leggy model LeBrock. His friends Bologna and Grodin have their own romantic problems. Best running gag: spurned co-worker Radner takes her revenge on Wilder's car. Remake of French farce *Pardon Mon Affaire* is paper-thin but sweetly amusing. Won Best Original Song Oscar for Stevie Wonder's "I Just Called to Say I Love You."
Dist.: Vestron

WOMAN IN THE DUNES 1964 Japanese
☆ NR Drama 2:03 B&W
Dir: Hiroshi Teshigahara ***Cast:*** Eiji Okada, Kyoko Kishida, Koji Mitsui, Hiroko Ito, Sen Yano
▶ Entomologist Okada is trapped in a sand pit with a beautiful woman. Unable to escape, and forced to labor for a group of villagers, he forms a relationship with the woman, and comes to terms with his existence. Dreamlike parable was nominated for Best Foreign Film Oscar, and director Teshigahara was first Japanese ever nominated for Best Director. Not an easy film to watch. [S]
Dist.: Video Dimensions

WOMAN IN THE MOON 1929 German
☆ NR Sci-Fi 2:36 B&W
Dir: Fritz Lang ***Cast:*** Klaus Pohl, Willy Fritsch, Gustav von Wangenheim, Gerda Maurus, Fritz Rasp
▶ Believing there is gold on the moon, bankers sponsor a trip there by a special rocketship launched from a pool of water. The space travelers experience the rigors of blast-off, then are able to chuck their precautionary diving suits and walk around the moon in street clothes, thanks to an Earth-like atmosphere. Much historical interest and unintentional humor in this silent sci-fi adventure from the director of *Metropolis*, including the fact that it originated the 5–4–3–2–1. . . countdown adapted by real-life rocketeers. German title: *Frau im Mond*.
Dist.: Video Yesteryear

WOMAN NEXT DOOR, THE 1981 French
★ R Drama 1:46
☑ Brief nudity, adult situations, explicit language, violence
Dir: François Truffaut ***Cast:*** Gerard Depardieu, Fanny Ardant, Henri Garcin, Michele Baumgartner, Veronique Silver, Phillipe Morier-Genoud

▶ Depardieu and Ardant play former lovers, now married to others, who are coincidentally reunited when they become neighbors. Their feelings reignited, they resume their relationship, but tragedy looms. Considering the cast and director, this should have been better. Truffaut's accomplished but too-cool direction drains the passion out of the material. S

Dist.: Key

WOMAN OBSESSED, A 1959
★★★ NR Drama 1:42
Dir: Henry Hathaway *Cast:* Susan Hayward, Stephen Boyd, Barbara Nichols, Dennis Holmes, Theodore Bikel, Ken Scott
▶ In the nineteenth century, widow Hayward marries Boyd after hiring him as a farmhand. Holmes, her son from a previous marriage, rebels against rough-hewn but well-meaning new dad. While struggling with family conflicts, threesome must also battle nature amid spectacular Canadian forest settings. Theme of improvised family life is very contemporary and comfortably integrated with elements of outdoor adventure.
Dist.: Academy

WOMAN OF DISTINCTION, A 1950
★★ NR Comedy 1:25 B&W
Dir: Edward Buzzell *Cast:* Rosalind Russell, Ray Milland, Edmund Gwenn, Janis Carter, Mary Jane Saunders, Francis Lederer
▶ Russell, a stuffy women's college dean, knows nothing of relaxation or romance. Then gossip columnist Carter spreads scandalous rumors about her and visiting professor Milland. Russell holds the famed Milland responsible, but soon succumbs to his charms. Romantic comedy boasts slapstick energy and top-notch Russell. Lucille Ball makes cameo appearance as herself in opening sequence.
Dist.: RCA/Columbia

WOMAN OF PARIS, A 1923
★ NR Drama 1:23 B&W
Dir: Charles Chaplin *Cast:* Edna Purviance, Adolphe Menjou, Carl Miller, Lydia Knott, Charles French, Clarence Geldert
▶ Country girl Purviance leaves behind fiancé Miller and goes to Paris, where she becomes a courtesan to wealthy Menjou. Miller comes back to her, but his mother interferes with their potential happiness. Elegantly directed, ironic melodrama, unseen for over fifty years, shows a different side to Chaplin's great talent. Director's first dramatic feature and first nonstarring vehicle. Home video version includes Chaplin short *Sunnyside.*
Dist.: Playhouse

WOMAN OF THE YEAR 1942
★★★★ NR Comedy 1:52 B&W
Dir: George Stevens *Cast:* Spencer Tracy, Katharine Hepburn, Fay Bainter, Reginald Owen, William Bendix, Minor Watson
▶ Down-to-earth sportswriter Tracy and sophisticated columnist Hepburn wed in an attraction of opposites. Marriage hits the rocks as Hepburn fails to balance love and work. Delightful Tracy-Hepburn vehicle (their first together) with the stars in top form. Feminists may blanche at the notorious scene in which Hepburn struggles in the kitchen. Witty screenplay nabbed Oscar.
Dist.: MGM/UA

WOMAN'S FACE, A 1941
★★ NR Drama 1:45 B&W
Dir: George Cukor *Cast:* Joan Crawford, Melvyn Douglas, Conrad Veidt, Reginald Owen, Albert Basserman, Marjorie Main
▶ Remake of a 1937 Ingrid Bergman Swedish film depicts Crawford as woman disfigured during her youth and bitterly seeking revenge on the world. Penniless aristocrat Veidt uses his wiles to enlist her in a murder plot, but when physician Douglas performs successful plastic surgery on her face, Crawford changes her outlook on life. Well-crafted drama with Crawford at the peak of her powers.
Dist.: MGM/UA

WOMAN TIMES SEVEN 1967
★★ NR Comedy 1:39
Dir: Vittorio De Sica *Cast:* Shirley MacLaine, Peter Sellers, Rossano Brazzi, Alan Arkin, Vittorio Gassman, Michael Caine, Lex Barker, Philippe Noiret, Robert Morley, Elsa Martinelli
▶ MacLaine fans will enjoy seeing her play seven different parts in this episodic movie. Among the roles: a widow wooed by suitor Sellers at her husband's funeral, a wife upset with her writer husband's obsession with fictional creations, and an adulterous lover whose suicide pact with beau Arkin goes awry.
Dist.: Nelson

WOMAN WHO CAME BACK, THE 1945
★ NR Horror 1:09 B&W
Dir: Walter Colmes *Cast:* John Loder, Nancy Kelly, Otto Kruger, Ruth Ford, Harry Tyler, Jeanne Gail
▶ Kelly arrives in a New England village where her ancestor once framed an innocent victim for witchcraft. She believes herself cursed and, when bizarre events happen, the locals agree to the point of mob violence. Loder is Kelly's boyfriend, the handsome doctor who believes her innocent. Unusual tale is worth a look.
Dist.: SVS

WOMEN, THE 1939
★★★★ NR Comedy 2:13 B&W/C
Dir: George Cukor *Cast:* Norma Shearer, Joan Crawford, Rosalind Russell, Mary Boland, Paulette Goddard, Joan Fontaine
▶ Unique behind-the-scenes look at society women gossiping, catfighting, and stealing husbands is superb entertainment thanks to its all-female cast, superior dialogue (adapted by Anita Loos and Jane Murfin from Claire Boothe Luce's Broadway hit), and

smooth direction. Amoral sales clerk Crawford and Russell, who has an amazing nervous breakdown, are standouts among the many stars. Brief Adrian fashion show was filmed in Technicolor.
Dist.: MGM/UA

WOMEN IN LOVE 1970 British
★ R Drama 2:10
☑ Nudity, strong sexual content, adult situations, adult humor
Dir: Ken Russell   *Cast:* Alan Bates, Oliver Reed, Glenda Jackson, Jennie Linden, Eleanor Bron, Alan Webb
▶ Lushly sensual adaptation of D. H. Lawrence novel explores romantic-sexual interplay between sisters Jackson and Linden and Bates and Reed, the close friends the women love. Visually stunning battle-of-the-sexes was nominated for four Academy Awards, with Jackson getting nod for Best Actress. Challenging and provocative film will not suit all tastes.
Dist.: MGM/UA

WOMEN ON THE VERGE OF A NERVOUS BREAKDOWN 1988 Spanish
★★ R Comedy 1:28
☑ Adult situations, explicit language
Dir: Pedro Almodóvar   *Cast:* Carmen Maura, Antonio Banderas, Julieta Serrano, Maria Barranco, Rossy De Palma, Fernando Guillen
▶ Actress Maura is on the edge after break-up with womanizing lover Guillen. While attempting to reach him, she is thrown into a wild plot involving Guillen's wife, his new lover, his son, his son's girlfriend, an eccentric taxi driver, cops, terrorists, and a bowl of spiked gazpacho. Stylishly vibrant direction by Almodóvar and marvelous cast (led by magnificent Maura and the striking De Palma) combine to create outrageous lunacy. Nominated for Best Foreign Film Oscar.   [S]
Dist.: Orion

WOMEN'S CLUB, THE 1987
★ R Comedy 1:26
☑ Strong sexual content, explicit language, adult humor
Dir: Sandra Weintraub   *Cast:* Michael Paré, Maud Adams, Eddie Velez, Dotty Coloroso
▶ Struggling L.A. scriptwriter Paré loses both his waitering job and girlfriend Coloroso. Adams offers him work in a posh women's health club where he's supposed to have sex with wealthy L.A. ladies. Shoddy production generates no real excitement.
Dist.: Vestron

WOMEN'S PRISON MASSACRE 1985 Italian/French
★ NR Action-Adventure 1:29
☑ Rape, nudity, adult situations, explicit language, graphic violence
Dir: Gilbert Roussel   *Cast:* Laura Gemser, Gabriele Tinti, Lorraine de Selle, Ursula Flores, Maria Romano

▶ Sentenced to depraved prison, framed sexpot Gemser becomes a pawn in her lesbian cellmates' war against the warden. Relentlessly lurid exploitation was filmed under the title *Emanuelle's Escape From Hell* as a companion piece to *Caged Women*. Unintentionally funny drama features grotesque overacting, poor dubbing, and a budget so small the producers could only afford a dozen prisoners.
Dist.: Vestron

WONDERFUL WORLD OF THE BROTHERS GRIMM, THE 1962
★★★ G Musical 2:09
Dir: Henry Levin   *Cast:* Laurence Harvey, Carl Boehm, Claire Bloom, Walter Slezak, Barbara Eden, Oscar Homolka, Yvette Mimieux, Russ Tamblyn, Buddy Hackett, Terry-Thomas
▶ Fictionalized account of the lives of the Grimm brothers (Harvey, Boehm) frames three of their fairy tales: in "The Dancing Princess," a woodsman wins the king's daughter; "The Cobbler and the Elves" finds an overworked shoemaker saved by friendly sprites; "The Singing Bone" is an amusing struggle between a servant and his master over credit for killing a dragon. Disappointing whimsy despite George Pal special effects and star-filled cast.
Dist.: MGM/UA

WONDERLAND 1989 British
☆ R Drama 1:43
☑ Nudity, adult situations, explicit language, violence
Dir: Philip Saville   *Cast:* Emile Charles, Tony Forsyth, Robert Stephens, Clare Higgins, Bruce Payne, Robbie Coltrane
▶ Artistically ambitious tale of homosexual teenage friends Charles and Forsyth who witness a murder at a drag club. When the pair abscond to a seaside resort with opera singer Stephens, they are stalked by the drag club's silent, sword-wielding killer. Lurid fantasy plot goes off in too many directions.
Dist.: Vestron

WONDER MAN 1945
★★★★ NR Musical 1:38
Dir: H. Bruce Humberstone   *Cast:* Danny Kaye, Virginia Mayo, Vera-Ellen, Donald Woods, S. Z. Sakall, Allen Jenkins
▶ When flashy nightclub performer Kaye is murdered by gangsters, his spirit enters the body of his shy, bookish, identical-twin brother (also played by Kaye). Fiancée Mayo is confused, and the gangsters are furious, as the surviving brother outwits them to give evidence to the D.A. Kaye, as usual, knocks himself out to entertain.
Dist.: Nelson

WOODEN HORSE, THE 1950 British
★★ NR War 1:41 B&W
Dir: Jack Lee   *Cast:* Leo Genn, David Tomlinson, Anthony Steel, David Greene, Peter Burton, Patrick Waddington

▶ POW drama has British prisoners using a vaulting horse in the camp's exercise yard to cover their tunneling operations. Genn, Tomlinson, and Steel then escape and attempt to reach friendly territory. Suspenseful drama based on an actual World War II escape by Brits from Stalag Luft III.
Dist.: HBO

WOODSTOCK 1970
★ ★ R Documentary/Music 3:00
☑ Nudity, explicit language
Dir: Michael Wadleigh   *Cast:* Jefferson Airplane, Joe Cocker, Crosby, Stills, and Nash, Jimi Hendrix, Santana, The Who, Richie Havens, Ten Years After, Sly and the Family Stone
▶ Oscar-winning documentary records communal, three-day 1969 outdoor rock concert in the Summer of Love. Behind-the-scenes footage is mixed with classic performances by era's rock greats. Highlights: Cocker's "With a Little Help from My Friends," The Who's "Summertime Blues," Airplane's "Volunteers," and Jimi Hendrix's acid-rock "The Star-Spangled Banner." Future director Martin Scorsese apprenticed as an editor on project. Rock and nostalgia buffs will be delighted, but video lessens impact.
Dist.: Warner

WORDS AND MUSIC 1948
★ ★ ★ NR Biography/Musical 1:59
Dir: Norman Taurog   *Cast:* Mickey Rooney, Tom Drake, Ann Sothern, Perry Como, Janet Leigh, Betty Garrett, Judy Garland, Gene Kelly, Lena Horne, June Allyson
▶ Life story of the composers Richard Rodgers (Drake) and Lorenz Hart (Rooney). Rodgers finds true love with Leigh; Hart suffers romantic setbacks. Far from factual but still fun, thanks to MGM stars belting out team's classic tunes. Horne's "The Lady Is a Tramp" and Allyson's "Thou Swell" stand out among over thirty songs.
Dist.: MGM/UA

WORKING GIRL 1988
★ ★ ★ ★ R Romance/Comedy 1:55
☑ Nudity, adult situations, explicit language
Dir: Mike Nichols   *Cast:* Harrison Ford, Sigourney Weaver, Melanie Griffith, Alec Baldwin, Joan Cusack, Philip Bosco
▶ Wall Street secretary Griffith is long on brains but short on luck. When scheming boss Weaver tries to steal her idea, Griffith finds success is best revenge: she impersonates a bigwig and puts together big money deal with broker Ford. Fabulous corporate fairy tale for the eighties. Star-making performance by Griffith mixes tenderness and grit; Cusack shines as her best friend from Staten Island. Good line: "I sing and dance in my underwear sometimes but that doesn't make me Madonna." Nominated for six Oscars, including Best Picture, Director, Actress (Griffith), Sup-

porting Actress (Weaver and Cusack); won for Carly Simon's song "Let the River Run."
Dist.: CBS/Fox

WORKING GIRLS 1987
★ NR Drama 1:33
☑ Nudity, strong sexual content, explicit language
Dir: Lizzie Borden   *Cast:* Louise Smith, Ellen McElduff, Amanda Goodwin, Marusia Zach, Janne Peters, Helen Nicholas
▶ Unvarnished study of typical day at a Manhattan brothel shows the mechanics of prostitution without condemning or praising the "work." Intellectually intriguing subject marred by stiff acting and tiny budget; feminist director Borden's antierotic approach is worthwhile but predictable.
Dist.: Nelson

WORLD ACCORDING TO GARP, THE 1982
★ ★ ★ R Comedy/Drama 2:16
☑ Nudity, adult situations, explicit language, violence
Dir: George Roy Hill   *Cast:* Robin Williams, Mary Beth Hurt, Glenn Close, John Lithgow, Jessica Tandy, Swoosie Kurtz, Hume Cronyn, Amanda Plummer
▶ Williams gives a gentle screen performance as T. S. Garp, writer, family man, husband to winsome Hurt, and bastard son of feminist Close. Life's absurdities, tragedies, and joys provide fuel for Garp's art. Screenwriter Steve Tesich's adaptation transforms John Irving's sprawling best-seller into a concise script. Alternately lyrical (Williams writing "Magic Gloves") and funny (Lithgow's reaction to an accident involving Hurt's lover). Oscar-nominated performances by Close and Lithgow as a transsexual ex–football star.
Dist.: Warner

WORLD APART, A 1988 British
★ ★ ★ ★ PG Drama 1:53
☑ Adult situations, explicit language, violence
Dir: Chris Menges   *Cast:* Barbara Hershey, Jodhi May, Jeroen Krabbe, Carolyn Clayton-Cragg, Merav Gruer, Yvonne Bryceland
▶ In 1963, a crackdown on antiapartheid protests causes dissident Krabbe to flee South Africa, leaving behind wife Hershey and daughters May, Clayton-Cragg, and Gruer. Eldest, thirteen-year-old May, seeks affection from mother, but dedicated Hershey is too wrapped up in politics. May's resentment grows as Hershey takes greater risks on behalf of oppressed blacks. Sensitive tale of motherhood and apartheid as seen through teen's eyes is based on screenwriter Shawn Slovo's own life.
Dist.: Media

WORLD GONE MAD 1933
☆ NR Mystery-Suspense 1:13 B&W
Dir: Christy Cabanne   *Cast:* Pat O'Brien, Evelyn Brent, Richard Tucker, Mary Brian, Louis Calhern, J. Carrol Naish, Neil Hamilton

▶ Wisecracking reporter O'Brien discovers that gangster Tucker was responsible for killing an uncooperative district attorney, and is plotting to kill current office holder Hamilton. He looks for help from gangster girlfriend Brent, but winds up in trouble when the mob appears ready to take him for a ride. Snappy dialogue, but the plot is full of holes.
Dist.: Cable

WORLD GONE WILD 1988
★ R Sci-Fi 1:34
☑ Rape, nudity, adult situations, explicit language, graphic violence
Dir: Lee H. Katzin *Cast:* Bruce Dern, Michael Paré, Catherine Mary Stewart, Adam Ant, Anthony James, Rick Podell
▶ Postapocalyptic survivors jealously guarding their precious water are attacked by vicious thugs led by the androgynous Ant, who quotes the writings of Charles Manson as inspiration. Elder statesman Dern hires mercenary Paré to help in the battle. Low-budget *Mad Max* clone has appealing tongue-in-cheek humor. (CC)
Dist.: Media

WORLD IS FULL OF MARRIED MEN, THE 1979 British
★ R Drama 1:47
☑ Nudity, strong sexual content, explicit language
Dir: Robert Young *Cast:* Anthony Franciosa, Carroll Baker, Sherrie Cronn, Gareth Hunt, Georgina Hale, Paul Nicholas
▶ Married womanizer Franciosa thinks he can have his cake and eat it too, until he finds himself falling in love with Cronn, a cool model with ideas of her own. His downfall is completed when wife Baker has an affair with young rock star Nicholas in the back of a limousine. Glitzy, lurid trash adapted by Jackie Collins from her own novel. Also known as *The Good Time Girls.*
Dist.: Key

WORLD OF APU, THE 1959 Indian
☆ NR Drama 1:43 B&W
Dir: Satyajit Ray *Cast:* Soumitra Chatterjee, Sharmila Tagore, Alok Chakravarty, Swapan Mukherji
▶ By Indian custom, bride Tagore must remain a perpetual spinster after her wedding is cancelled when the bridegroom proves to be insane. But wedding guest and aspiring novelist Chatterjee defies tradition and marries her himself, only to be devastated when she dies soon after, leaving a son. Final entry in director Ray's Apu trilogy, begun with *Pather Panchali* and *Aparajito,* is piercingly observed. A critically hailed masterpiece for the discerning.
Ⓢ
Dist.: Video Yesteryear

WORLD OF HENRY ORIENT, THE 1964
★ ★ ★ NR Comedy 1:55
Dir: George Roy Hill *Cast:* Peter Sellers, Angela Lansbury, Paula Prentiss, Tippy Walker, Merrie Spaeth, Phyllis Thaxter
▶ Henry Orient (Sellers) specializes in piano concerts (in which he's fair to middling) and womanizing (at which he's a pro). Teenagers Walker and Spaeth worship Orient and obsessively follow him around New York; he makes Walker's mom Lansbury his next conquest. Exceptional performances by the youngsters and adults highlight bewitching comedy. (CC)
Dist.: CBS/Fox

WORLD OF SUZIE WONG, THE 1960
★ ★ NR Drama 2:09
Dir: Richard Quine *Cast:* William Holden, Nancy Kwan, Sylvia Syms, Michael Wilding, Laurence Naismith, Jacqueline Chan
▶ Against the colorful backdrop of a neon-lit Hong Kong, artist Holden grapples with his feelings for prostitute Kwan. While Holden runs through the money supply that was to sustain him for a year, Kwan cares for a child she has borne in secret. Slit-skirted Kwan looks great in her film debut, but Holden and rest of drama never get out of low gear.
Dist.: Paramount

WORLD'S GREATEST ATHLETE, THE 1973
★ ★ ★ ★ G Comedy/Family 1:29
Dir: Robert Scheerer *Cast:* Jan-Michael Vincent, John Amos, Roscoe Lee Browne, Tim Conway, Dayle Haddon, Nancy Walker
▶ After Tarzan-like upbringing in Africa, Vincent comes to America. There his athletic prowess helps beleaguered college coach Amos revive his long-suffering team. Never less than playful and amusing Disney fare. Howard Cosell appears in a cameo.
Dist.: Buena Vista

WORLD'S GREATEST LOVER, THE 1977
★ ★ PG Comedy 1:29
☑ Explicit language
Dir: Gene Wilder *Cast:* Gene Wilder, Carol Kane, Dom DeLuise, Fritz Feld, Cousin Buddy, Matt Collins
▶ In the 1920s, Milwaukee baker Wilder answers the call when a Hollywood studio holds nationwide talent hunt to find the next Valentino. Wilder's wife Kane has a crush on the real Valentino (Collins) which threatens their marriage. He helps Wilder win her back. Handsomely produced, although the fun wears thin.
Dist.: CBS/Fox

WORTH WINNING 1989
★ ★ ★ PG-13 Comedy 1:43
☑ Adult situations, explicit language
Dir: Will MacKenzie *Cast:* Mark Harmon, Madeleine Stowe, Lesley Ann Warren, Maria Holvoe, Mark Blum, Andrea Martin
▶ Friends bet ladies' man Harmon that he can't become engaged to three women within three months. Designated fiancées are bimbo Holvoe, housewife Warren, and pianist Stowe, all of whom eventually discover the

wager and put the smug lothario through some character-building paces. Easygoing sex comedy has some laughs, but Harmon never seems to get the full measure of what he deserves for his deceptions.
Dist.: CBS/Fox

WRAITH, THE 1986
★ ★ PG-13 Horror 1:32
☑ Adult situations, explicit language, violence
Dir: Mike Marvin **Cast:** Charlie Sheen, Nick Cassavetes, Sherilyn Fenn, Randy Quaid, Griffin O'Neal, Clint Howard
▶ In an Arizona town, mysterious driver Sheen appears to battle gang leader Cassavetes and his cohorts in a series of deadly drag races. Is Sheen one of Cassavetes's victims, back from the beyond? Ideal drive-in fare: far-out story, original touches, and sense of humor compensate for unbelievable villains. Quaid steals the show as the sheriff.
Dist.: Vestron

WRITTEN ON THE WIND 1957
★ ★ ★ NR Drama 1:39
Dir: Douglas Sirk **Cast:** Rock Hudson, Lauren Bacall, Robert Stack, Dorothy Malone, Robert Keith, Grant Williams
▶ Hard-drinking Texas oil scion Stack marries Bacall; Stack's best pal Hudson also falls for her, although Stack's trampy sister Malone adores Hudson. Combustible combination leads to impotence, suspicions of infidelity, a miscarriage, and a shooting. Lurid, overwrought, yet enthralling and emotion-packed. Oscar for Best Supporting Actress (Malone).
Dist.: MCA

WRONG BOX, THE 1966 British
★ ★ NR Comedy 1:47
☑ Adult situations, mild violence
Dir: Bryan Forbes **Cast:** John Mills, Ralph Richardson, Michael Caine, Peter Cook, Dudley Moore, Nanette Newman
▶ Irreverent adaptation of the Robert Louis Stevenson-Lloyd Osbourne novel concerns Victorian-era brothers Mills and Richardson, who must outlive each other to inherit trust fund. Neither codger seems likely to die, so offsprings Moore and Cook conspire to speed the process. Antics include unscrupulous doctor Sellers and hot-blooded lovers Caine and Newman, constrained by morals of era. Plot and gags sometimes stumble, but madcap yarn of sex, greed, body-snatching, and homicide offers more than enough laughs.
Dist.: RCA/Columbia

WRONG GUYS, THE 1988
★ ★ PG Comedy 1:26
☑ Adult situations, mild violence
Dir: Danny Bilson **Cast:** Louie Anderson, Richard Lewis, Richard Belzer, Franklyn Ajaye, Tim Thomerson, John Goodman
▶ Former Cub Scout Anderson calls together his old troup, including neurotic Lewis, earnest DJ Ajaye, horny dress designer Belzer, and dumb surfer Thomerson, for adult reunion. Escaped killer Goodman stalks the overgrown campers. Silly but almost sweet; oversized Anderson in Scout uniform is hard to resist. Funniest moment: Goodman humming "Tammy" while loading his machine gun. (CC)
Dist.: New World

WRONG IS RIGHT 1982
★ ★ R Action-Adventure/Comedy 1:57
☑ Adult situations, explicit language, violence
Dir: Richard Brooks **Cast:** Sean Connery, Katharine Ross, Robert Conrad, George Grizzard, Leslie Nielsen, Ron Moody
▶ Network anchorman Connery finds himself up to his neck in intrigue when U.S. politicians, the CIA, an Arab king, and a Khaddafi-like madman vie for possession of a pair of A-bombs. Ambitious, fast-paced combination of satire and action is too jumbled for its own good, but Connery and company do well.
Dist.: RCA/Columbia

WRONG MAN, THE 1957
★ ★ ★ NR Biography/Mystery-Suspense 1:45 B&W
Dir: Alfred Hitchcock **Cast:** Henry Fonda, Vera Miles, Anthony Quayle, Harold J. Stone, Nehemiah Persoff, Esther Minciotti
▶ New York jazz musician Fonda, wrongly accused of robbery, is arrested and tried. When the case against Fonda looks convincing, his wife Miles cracks up and is institutionalized. Based on a true story, documentary-style drama depicts case of musician Manny Balestrero through actual events and sites. Result is Hitchcock's bleakest and, to many, most tedious film, forgoing even the usual cameo by the director.
Dist.: Warner

WUTHERING HEIGHTS 1939
★ ★ ★ ★ ★ NR Drama/Romance 1:44 B&W
Dir: William Wyler **Cast:** Laurence Olivier, Merle Oberon, David Niven, Geraldine Fitzgerald, Flora Robson, Donald Crisp
▶ In nineteenth-century England, orphan stable-boy Olivier is taken in by Yorkshire family and falls in love with daughter Oberon. Oberon marries wealthy Niven but her ill-fated involvement with Olivier continues. Grandly passionate adapation of the Emily Brontë classic boasts superlative direction and performances. One of the most romantic movies of all time. Seven Oscar nominations include Best Picture, Actor (Olivier), Supporting Actress (Fitzgerald); won for Cinematography.
Dist.: Embassy

WUTHERING HEIGHTS 1954 Mexican
☆ NR Drama 1:30 B&W
Dir: Luis Buñuel **Cast:** Iraseme Dilian, Jorge Mistral, Lilia Prado, Ernesto Alonso, Luis Aceves Castaneda
▶ Buñuel's version of the Charlotte Brontë

classic moves the action from England to Mexico, where his Heathcliff (Mistral) and Cathy (Dilian) play out the tragic love that transcends her marriage to another, and even death. With a Spanish title that translates as *The Abyss of Passion*, film has a dark emphasis, and is perhaps more faithful to the original for that reason. Bold, brilliant, and disturbing imagery—the ending especially. [S]
Dist.: Nelson

WUTHERING HEIGHTS 1971 British
★★★ G Drama/Romance 1:45
Dir: Robert Fuest ***Cast:*** Anna Calder-Marshall, Timothy Dalton, Harry Andrews, Pamela Brown, Ian Ogilvy
► Remake of the 1939 classic is actually more faithful to the Emily Brontë novel than its predecessor. Calder-Marshall and Dalton are spirited as the doomed lovers; Ogilvy assays the David Niven role as the wealthy husband. The authentic locations help, but the end result lacks the power and chemistry of the original. Michel Legrand contributes a syrupy score.
Dist.: HBO

XANADU 1980
★★ PG Musical 1:36
☑ Explicit language
Dir: Robert Greenwald ***Cast:*** Olivia Newton-John, Gene Kelly, Michael Beck, James Sloyan, Dimitra Arliss, Katie Hanley
► Mythological muse Newton-John comes to life and inspires artist Beck to build roller disco. Man and muse fall in love but can the mixed relationship work? Agreeably silly story embellished with top-ten soundtrack. Highlights: Newton-John singing "Magic" and dueting with Kelly on old-fashioned "Whenever You're Away From Me."
Dist.: MCA

X—THE MAN WITH X-RAY EYES 1963
★ NR Sci-Fi 1:20
Dir: Roger Corman ***Cast:*** Ray Milland, Diana Van Der Vlis, Harold J. Stone, Don Rickles, John Hoyt
► Doctor Milland discovers the ability to see through things. The power proves a double-edged gift: he loses his job, is reduced to carnival attraction managed by Rickles, and descends into physical pain and madness. Minor visionary classic builds to a shattering conclusion; striking Floyd Crosby cinematography and top Milland performance.
Dist.: Warner

XTRO 1983 British
★ R Sci-Fi 1:22
☑ Nudity, adult situations, explicit language, graphic violence
Dir: Harry Bromley Davenport ***Cast:*** Philip Sayer, Bernice Stegers, Danny Brainin, Simon Nash, Maryam d'Abo
► Sayer returns to family after three-year absence due to alien kidnapping. In interim, he has become killer monster, and soon turns his son Nash into a similar aberration. Low-budget hodgepodge of familiar genre elements. Acting and special effects leave a lot to be desired.
Dist.: HBO

X, Y AND ZEE 1972 British
☆ PG Drama 1:50
☑ Brief nudity, adult situations, explicit language
Dir: Brian G. Hutton ***Cast:*** Elizabeth Taylor, Michael Caine, Susannah York, Margaret Leighton, John Standing
► Widow York wins heart of married architect Caine. Caine's rejected wife Taylor wages war to break up lovers; at one point she even resorts to seduction of the bisexual York. Charismatic star trio deserves better material.
Dist.: RCA/Columbia

YAKUZA, THE 1975
★★★ R Action-Adventure 1:52
☑ Adult situations, explicit language, violence
Dir: Sydney Pollack ***Cast:*** Robert Mitchum, Takakura Ken, Brian Keith, Herb Edelman, Richard Jordan, Kishi Keiko
► Daughter of U.S. shipping magnate Keith is kidnapped by the Yakuza, Japan's answer to the Mafia, to force him to deliver a cache of arms. Keith dispatches old Army buddy Mitchum to retrieve her, despite Mitchum's painful memories of star-crossed love affair with Keiko, sister of Yakuza gangster Ken. Clash-of-cultures yarn mixes action, romance, intrigue, and an ancient code of honor. Screenplay by Paul Schrader and Robert Towne.
Dist.: Warner

YANKEE DOODLE DANDY 1942
★★★★★ NR Biography/Musical 2:06
B&W
Dir: Michael Curtiz ***Cast:*** James Cagney, Joan Leslie, Walter Huston, Irene Manning, Rosemary DeCamp, Richard Whorf
► Classic portrait of show biz legend George M. Cohan (Cagney), the playwright, songwriter, singer, dancer, and actor. Born on the Fourth of July, Cohan started off in vaudeville and rose to become one of Broadway's brightest stars. Patriotic numbers include "You're a Grand Old Flag," "Over There," and the sing-along title tune. Nominated for seven Academy Awards and winner of three, including Best Actor for Cagney.
Dist.: MGM/UA [C]

YEARLING, THE 1946
★★★★ G Family 2:14
Dir: Clarence Brown ***Cast:*** Gregory Peck, Jane Wyman, Claude Jarman, Jr., Chill Wills, Clem Bevans, Margaret Wycherly
► Moving adaptation of Marjorie Kinnan Rawlings's classic novel about a poor Florida boy whose attachment to an orphaned fawn endangers his father Peck's small farm. Oscar-

winning photography, set designs, and beautifully nuanced performances contribute to the story's superb moral. Jarman received a special Oscar for his role as Peck's son.
Dist.: MGM/UA

YEAR MY VOICE BROKE, THE 1988
Australian
★ ★ PG-13 Drama 1:43
☑ Adult situations
Dir: John Duigan *Cast:* Noah Taylor, Leone Carmen, Ben Mendelsohn, Graeme Blundell, Lynette Curran, Malcolm Robertson
▶ Fourteen-year-old Taylor watches in dismay as childhood friend/sweetheart Carmen, a year older and maturing faster, falls for jock Mendelsohn. Taylor tries in vain to help Carmen when first encounters with adulthood lead to tragedy. Sensitive, well-handled coming-of-age drama won Australian Oscar-equivalent for Best Picture.
Dist.: IVE

YEAR OF LIVING DANGEROUSLY, THE 1983
Australian
★ ★ ★ PG Drama 1:55
☑ Adult situations, explicit language, violence
Dir: Peter Weir *Cast:* Mel Gibson, Sigourney Weaver, Linda Hunt, Michael Murphy, Bill Kerr, Noel Ferrer
▶ In 1965, Indonesia stands on brink of civil war. Novice Australian journalist Gibson befriends savvy, mystical photographer Hunt (playing the role of a man). Hunt shows him the ropes and introduces him to beautiful British embassy employee Weaver. When Weaver tips Gibson to secret report of Communist arms delivery, he must choose between betraying sources and breaking exclusive scoop. Ambitious drama made Gibson's reputation as a serious actor; Hunt won Supporting Oscar.
Dist.: MGM/UA

YEAR OF THE DRAGON 1985
★ ★ ★ R Action-Adventure 2:16
☑ Nudity, adult situations, explicit language, graphic violence
Dir: Michael Cimino *Cast:* Mickey Rourke, John Lone, Ariane, Leonard Termo, Raymond J. Barry, Caroline Kava
▶ Ambitious police captain Rourke seeks to clean up gangland violence in New York's Chinatown, putting him at odds with violent new crime boss Lone. Rourke enlists aid of Ariane, a pretty Chinese TV reporter, to publicize his crusade and soon romances her, much to the dismay of his estranged wife Kava. Self-important script, but fast-paced yarn should delight action fans.
Dist.: MGM/UA

YELLOWBEARD 1983
★ ★ PG Comedy 1:37
☑ Nudity, explicit language, violence, adult humor
Dir: Mel Damski *Cast:* Graham Chapman, Peter Boyle, Cheech Marin, Thomas Chong, Peter Cook, Madeline Kahn, Martin Hewitt
▶ Pirate Chapman busts out of jail and tries to recover fortune in buried treasure. Also looking for the loot: Chapman's son Hewitt, the pirate's old flame Kahn, and evil navy man Boyle. All-star cast of comic cut-ups generates laughs out of sheer energy and talent, although the script has too many uninspired stretches.
Dist.: Vestron

YELLOW SUBMARINE 1968 British
★ ★ ★ ★ G Animation 1:25
Dir: George Dunning *Cast:* Voices of John Clive, Geoffrey Hughes, Peter Batten, Dick Emery, Paul Angelus
▶ The Beatles travel by yellow submarine to a fantasy land where their music and love triumph over the evil Blue Meanies. Richly imaginative and clever, with eye-popping pop art animation. Actors provide the speaking voices of the Beatle characters, but the group itself supplies the wonderful soundtrack ("Lucy in the Sky With Diamonds," "Nowhere Man," "Eleanor Rigby," "All You Need Is Love," "Only a Northern Song", more).
Dist.: MGM/UA

YENTL 1983
★ ★ ★ ★ PG Musical 2:13
☑ Adult situations, mild violence, adult humor
Dir: Barbra Streisand *Cast:* Barbra Streisand, Mandy Patinkin, Amy Irving, Nehemiah Persoff, Steven Hill, Ruth Goring
▶ After the death of her father Persoff, headstrong Yentl (Streisand) disguises herself as a boy to study at an all-male yeshiva in turn-of-the-century Eastern Europe. Befriended by fellow student Patinkin and his fiancée Irving, Yentl finds her disguise has serio-comic results. Sterling performances and good production values highlight this adaptation of Isaac Bashevis Singer's short story; a joy for Streisand fans, but may seem long to others. Five nominations, including Oscar-winning score.
Dist.: MGM/UA

YES, GIORGIO 1982
★ ★ PG Comedy 1:50
☑ Adult situations, explicit language
Dir: Franklin J. Schaffner *Cast:* Luciano Pavarotti, Kathryn Harrold, Eddie Albert, Paola Borboni, James Hong, Beulah Quo
▶ On a concert tour of the U.S. with manager Albert, superstar tenor Fini (Pavarotti) loses his voice, then his heart to Harrold, a throat specialist called in to cure him. The singing here is exceptional (no surprise), but script never makes passion between the lead characters even remotely believable, especially when Pavarotti's on-lines include: "You are thirsty plant. Fini can water you."
Dist.: MGM/UA

YOJIMBO 1962 Japanese
★ ★ NR Action-Adventure 1:50 B&W

Dir: Akira Kurosawa *Cast:* Toshiro Mifune, Eijiro Tono, Seizaburo Kawazu, Isuzu Yamada, Hiroshi Tachikawa, Kyu Sazanka
► Engrossing, action-packed "samurai Western" about nineteenth-century professional killer Mifune, who gains control of a warring village by playing both sides against each other. Unexpectedly tough and funny, with a commanding performance by Mifune and first-rate direction. Prime inspiration for *A Fistful of Dollars.* [S]
Dist.: Nelson

YOL 1982 Turkish
☆ **PG Drama 1:54**
☑ Adult situations, violence
Dir: Serif Goren *Cast:* Tarik Akan, Serif Sezer, Halil Ergun, Meral Orhonsoy, Necmettin Cobanoglu, Semra Ucar
► Five Turkish prisoners, given temporary leaves of absence, find unhappy family situations and death waiting for them on the outside. Exotic glimpse into a harsh world where fear and hardship are a way of life is emotionally sincere but technically crude. Screenwriter-editor Yilmaz Guney supervised production while still in prison himself. Shared Cannes Film Festival award with *Missing.* [S]
Dist.: RCA/Columbia

YOLANDA AND THE THIEF 1945
★★ **NR Musical 1:48**
Dir: Vincente Minnelli *Cast:* Fred Astaire, Lucille Bremer, Frank Morgan, Mildred Natwick, Mary Nash, Leon Ames
► Astaire pretends to be an angel to bilk innocent convent-educated Bremer out of her fortune. However, he falls in love with his quarry. Offbeat but rewarding: Astaire and Bremer work together charmingly and Minnelli provides his usual skillful use of color and production design.
Dist.: MGM/UA

YONGARI: MONSTER FROM THE DEEP
1967 Korean
☆ **NR Horror 1:40**
Dir: Kiduck Kim *Cast:* Yungil Oh, Chungim Nam, Soonjai Lee, Moon Kang, Kwang Ho Lee
► Giant lizard, awakened by an earthquake, heads for Korea, where he steps on buildings, guzzles gasoline, and shows a strange fondness for Seoul music. Koreans eventually wipe him out with ammonia. Not much different from similar happenings across the Yellow Sea. Also known as *Yongkari: Monster from the Deep* and *Monster Yongkari.*
Dist.: Orion

YOR, THE HUNTER FROM THE FUTURE 1983
Italian
★ **PG Sci-Fi 1:29**
☑ Violence
Dir: Anthony M. Dawson (Antonio Margheriti) *Cast:* Reb Brown, Corinne Clery, John Steiner, Carole Andre, Alan Collins, Syshe Gul
► In a post-holocaust future, caveman Brown battles dinosaurs and other prehistoric monsters. Next he takes on evil overlord Steiner and destructive robots to save Clery's tribe. Brown's discovery of his secret past evens the odds against Steiner. B-grade sci-fi, shot in Italy and Turkey, is mainly for genre fans.
Dist.: RCA/Columbia

YOU CAN'T CHEAT AN HONEST MAN 1939
★★ **NR Comedy 1:16 B&W**
Dir: George Marshall *Cast:* W. C. Fields, Edgar Bergen, Constance Moore, Mary Forbes, Thurston Hall, Eddie "Rochester" Anderson
► Struggling circus owner Fields feuds with featured act Bergen; Bergen falls in love with Fields's daughter Moore, but she considers marrying a rich guy to aid dad. The combination of Fields and ventriloquist Bergen (along with dummies Charlie McCarthy and Mortimer Snerd) adds up to a consistently frisky and funny vehicle.
Dist.: KVC

YOU CAN'T FOOL YOUR WIFE 1940
★ **NR Comedy 1:08 B&W**
Dir: Ray McCarey *Cast:* Lucille Ball, James Ellison, Robert Coote, Virginia Hale, Emma Dunn, Elaine Shepard
► Mother-in-law Dunn butts into the happily humdrum marriage of daughter Ball so often that hubby Ellison calls it quits. But Ball won't be bounced that easily, and tries to get him back by masquerading as the glamorous Mercedes Vasquez. Middle-of-the-road comedy has its moments, thanks to Lucy.
Dist.: Turner

YOU CAN'T HURRY LOVE 1988
★ **R Comedy 1:32**
☑ Nudity, adult situations, explicit language
Dir: Richard Martini *Cast:* David Packer, David Leisure, Scott McGinnis, Bridget Fonda, Anthony Geary, Frank Bonner, Charles Grodin, Kristy McNichol, Sally Kellerman
► Dumped by his fiancée, young Ohioan Packer moves to L.A. to pursue swinging lifestyle with hipster cousin McGinnis, who's housesitting Beverly Hills mansion for ad exec Leisure. Packer has nothing but trouble with the opposite sex—until he meets dream date Fonda. Lightweight but likable comedy. Leisure is recognizable as Joe Izuzu, lying pitchman of TV fame.
Dist.: Vestron

YOU CAN'T TAKE IT WITH YOU 1938
★★★★★ **NR Comedy 2:06 B&W**
Dir: Frank Capra *Cast:* James Stewart, Jean Arthur, Edward Arnold, Lionel Barrymore, Mischa Auer, Spring Byington, Ann Miller
► Screen version of the Moss Hart–George S. Kaufman Broadway hit chronicles the adventures of an eccentric family. When eligible daughter Arthur falls in love with charming

Stewart, son of stuffed-shirt conservatives, comic conflict results. Stewart and Arthur share a delightful scene in a posh restaurant. Nominated for seven Oscars, winning for Best Picture and Director.
Dist.: RCA/Columbia

YOU LIGHT UP MY LIFE 1977
★★★ PG Drama 1:31
☑ Adult situations
Dir: Joseph Brooks *Cast:* Didi Conn, Joe Silver, Michael Zaslow, Stephen Nathan, Melanie Mayron, Jerry Keller
▶ Young woman aspires to be pop singer-songwriter, but her father, a second-rate Borscht Belt comic, insists she follow in his footsteps. To further her ambitions, she breaks engagement to sweet tennis instructor Nathan for casting-couch affair with movie director Zaslow. Written, produced, and directed by Brooks, meandering drama examines difficulty of romance in show biz. Brooks-composed title track won Oscar and Grammy.
Dist.: RCA/Columbia

YOU'LL NEVER GET RICH 1941
★★★★ NR Musical 1:29 B&W
Dir: Sidney Lanfield *Cast:* Fred Astaire, Rita Hayworth, Robert Benchley, John Hubbard, Osa Massen, Frieda Inescort
▶ Choreographer Astaire loves dancer Hayworth but hurts her by participating in producer Benchley's scheme to fool his wife. Drafted into the Army, Astaire gets a second chance when Hayworth visits soldier-beau Hubbard. One of Astaire's best non-Rogers films has surprising chemistry between him and sexy Hayworth (a swell dancer). Benchley provides snappy comic support. Oscar-nominated Cole Porter score and song, "Since I Kissed My Baby Goodbye."
Dist.: RCA/Columbia

YOUNG AND INNOCENT 1937 British
★★ NR Mystery-Suspense 1:23 B&W
Dir: Alfred Hitchcock *Cast:* Nova Pilbeam, Derrick de Marney, Percy Marmont, Edward Rigby, Mary Clare, John Longden
▶ Policeman's daughter Pilbeam befriends de Marney, a suspect in a murder case, and embarks on a mad dash for the real killer while a manhunt closes in. Buoyant, light-hearted thriller, one of Hitchcock's most-overlooked films, contains some of his best sequences, including a dazzling game of blind man's bluff and frightening coal mine accident.
Dist.: Various

YOUNG AT HEART 1954
★★★★ NR Musical 1:57
Dir: Gordon Douglas *Cast:* Doris Day, Frank Sinatra, Gig Young, Ethel Barrymore, Dorothy Malone, Alan Hale, Jr.
▶ Day falls for composer Young, unaware that her sister Malone also loves him. Sinatra, Young's cynical partner, then tries to win Day's heart. Glossy musical remake of the 1938

soap opera *Four Daughters* includes "Just One of Those Things," "One for My Baby," and "Someone to Watch Over Me."
Dist.: Republic

YOUNGBLOOD 1986
★★★★ R Drama/Sports 1:50
☑ Nudity, adult situations, explicit language, violence
Dir: Peter Markle *Cast:* Rob Lowe, Patrick Swayze, Cynthia Gibb, Ed Lauter, Jim Youngs, George Finn
▶ Canadian farm boy Lowe leaves home to pursue hockey career with semi-pro team; coach Lauter tries to mold talented Lowe into a star. Romance with Lauter's daughter Gibb leads to benching while rivalry erupts with Finn, a goon from another squad. When Finn cracks a teammate's skull, Lowe wants to quit the violent sport. Swayze plays his best friend on team.
Dist.: MGM/UA

YOUNG DOCTORS IN LOVE 1982
★★ R Comedy 1:31
☑ Brief nudity, adult situations, explicit language, adult humor
Dir: Garry Marshall *Cast:* Michael McKean, Sean Young, Harry Dean Stanton, Patrick Macnee, Hector Elizondo, Pamela Reed, Dabney Coleman
▶ Soapy send up of the medical profession features doctor McKean, who hates blood, sexy intern Young with a strange disorder, Mafia lieutenant Elizondo who dresses in drag, deranged surgeon Coleman, prune-faced head nurse Reed, lab worker Stanton who confuses urine specimens—and lots of jokes about bodily fluids and functions. Silly but occasionally savvy.
Dist.: Vestron

YOUNG EINSTEIN 1989 Australian
☆ PG Comedy 1:32
☑ Adult situations, explicit language
Dir: Yahoo Serious *Cast:* Yahoo Serious, Odile Le Clezio, John Howard, Pee Wee Wilson, Su Cruickshank
▶ Revisionist look at the life of scientist Albert Einstein (Serious) plunks character down in 1906 Australia, where he not only comes up with the theory of relativity but discovers rock 'n' roll and surfing to boot. Daffy comic antics are often funny, but offbeat humor may not please everyone; Serious is definitely not for the serious.
Dist.: Warner

YOUNG FRANKENSTEIN 1974
★★★★ PG Comedy 1:46 B&W
☑ Adult humor
Dir: Mel Brooks *Cast:* Gene Wilder, Peter Boyle, Madeline Kahn, Teri Garr, Marty Feldman, Cloris Leachman
▶ Mad takeoff on the monster genre with Wilder as Frankenstein's grandson who returns to Transylvania, reworks his ancestor's experiment, and, this time, gets it right. As the man-

made monster, Boyle is hysterical and touching, especially in top hat and tails singing "Puttin' on the Ritz." Memorable performances from Feldman as Wilder's hunchback assistant, lab assistant Garr, and Kahn as the monster's girl. Marvelous, moody, and fun.
Dist.: CBS/Fox

YOUNG GUNS 1988
★ ★ ★ R Western 1:37
☑ Adult situations, explicit language, violence
Dir: Christopher Cain **Cast:** Emilio Estevez, Kiefer Sutherland, Lou Diamond Phillips, Charlie Sheen, Dermot Mulroney, Casey Siemaszko, Terence Stamp, Jack Palance
▶ Ensemble piece recasts Billy the Kid myth with Hollywood's hot male stars to little effect. Estevez essays the famous killer who finds himself and five followers on the wrong side of the law during 1878 New Mexico range wars. Stamp (his foster father) and villain Palance bring some dignity to loud, violent, but routine plot; hard rock soundtrack proves major drawback. Sequel in 1990.
Dist.: Vestron

YOUNG LIONS, THE 1958
★ ★ ★ ★ NR Drama 2:51 B&W
Dir: Edward Dmytryk **Cast:** Marlon Brando, Montgomery Clift, Dean Martin, Hope Lange, Maximilian Schell, Barbara Rush
▶ Adaptation of the Irwin Shaw novel depicts the effects of World War II upon three very different men. Brando, an idealistic young German officer, embraces Hitler as cure for nation's ills, but war turns him against the Nazis. American soldiers Clift and Martin becomes pals as they struggle with personal problems: Jewish Clift fights anti-Semitism in American ranks as entertainer Martin struggles with cowardice. Nominated for three technical Oscars.
Dist.: CBS/Fox

YOUNG MAN WITH A HORN 1950
★ ★ ★ ★ NR Drama/Musical 1:52 B&W
Dir: Michael Curtiz **Cast:** Kirk Douglas, Lauren Bacall, Doris Day, Hoagy Carmichael, Juano Hernandez, Mary Beth Hughes
▶ Douglas, inspired by jazz trumpeter Hernandez, takes up horn playing to escape ghetto. His talent leads to New York gigs, friendship with vocalist Day, and marriage to socialite Bacall, but marital discord and an untimely death result in alcoholism. Classic drama with top-notch cast and terrific music (jazz great Harry James dubs for Douglas) was inspired by life of trumpeter Bix Beiderbecke.
Dist.: Warner

YOUNG MR. LINCOLN 1939
★ ★ ★ ★ ★ NR Biography 1:40 B&W
Dir: John Ford **Cast:** Henry Fonda, Alice Brady, Marjorie Weaver, Arleen Whelan, Eddie Collins, Pauline Moore
▶ Early years in the life of Abraham Lincoln are shown with insight and humor. Fonda gives an uncanny impression of the President, haunted by his lost love Ann Rutledge (Moore) and struggling as a backwoods lawyer in the early 1800s. Second half is devoted to an engrossing trial, which displays Lincoln's subtle wit. Lamar Trotti's story received an Oscar nomination.
Dist.: CBS/Fox

YOUNG NURSES, THE 1973
★ R Drama 1:15
☑ Nudity, strong sexual content, explicit language, mild violence
Dir: Clinton Kimbro **Cast:** Jean Manson, Ashley Porter, Angela Gibbs, Zack Taylor, Richard Miller
▶ Adventures of three beautiful nurses prove moderately entertaining in this low-budget exploitation. Manson falls in love with a sailor; Porter must choose between rich boyfriend and work at a medical clinic; Gibbs uncovers a hospital drug ring run by an unethical doctor (director Sam Fuller in a brief cameo). Fourth entry in Roger Corman's "Nurses" series has a heavy emphasis on sex; followed by *Candy Stripe Nurses.*
Dist.: Nelson

YOUNG PHILADELPHIANS, THE 1959
★ ★ ★ NR Drama 2:16 B&W
Dir: Vincent Sherman **Cast:** Paul Newman, Barbara Rush, Alexis Smith, Brian Keith, Robert Vaughn, Diane Brewster
▶ Newman plays a Philadelphia lawyer of dubious heritage who passes up marriage to society girl Rush in order to further his ambitions. Later, Newman defends army buddy Vaughn on a murder charge; in the process, he gets in touch with his more idealistic side and wins back Rush. Newman and a solid supporting cast make this engrossing drama work.
Dist.: Warner

YOUNG SHERLOCK HOLMES 1985
★ ★ ★ ★ PG-13 Action-Adventure 1:50
☑ Violence
Dir: Barry Levinson **Cast:** Nicholas Rowe, Alan Cox, Sophie Ward, Anthony Higgins, Susan Fleetwood, Freddie Jones
▶ Entertaining romp from producer Steven Spielberg asks what might have happened if Sherlock Holmes and Dr. John Watson first met as teenage students. The answer is elementary: adventures on a par with the later exploits of the Arthur Conan Doyle hero. Young detective Rowe and sidekick Cox, along with romantic interest Ward, investigate a series of murders. Best bits: roots of Holmes's trademark pipe, deerstalker cap, violin playing, and bachelorhood.
Dist.: Paramount

YOUNG WARRIORS 1983
★ R Action-Adventure 1:45
☑ Rape, nudity, strong sexual content, explicit language, graphic violence
Dir: Lawrence D. Foldes **Cast:** Richard Roundtree, James Van Patten, Ernest Borg-

nine, Anne Lockhart, Linda Day Shawn, Dick Shawn

▶ When violent thugs gang rape and murder a young woman, her cop father Borgnine follows normal procedures with partner Roundtree in pursuit of goons. Van Patten, anguished brother of the victim, grows impatient; he and fraternity mates assemble arsenal for vigilante action. Revenge drama lacks subtlety.
Dist.: MGM/UA

YOUNG WINSTON 1972 British
★ ★ **PG Biography 2:25**
☑ Explicit language, violence
Dir: Richard Attenborough *Cast:* Simon Ward, Anne Bancroft, Robert Shaw, John Mills, Jack Hawkins, Edward Woodward
▶ True story of Winston Churchill (Ward) traces his early years, including adventures as war correspondent in India and South Africa, the death of his father (Shaw), first political defeat, and first election to Parliament. Largescale and exciting. Ward is fine; Bancroft holds her own in the great English cast.
Dist.: RCA/Columbia

YOU ONLY LIVE ONCE 1937
★ ★ ★ ★ **NR Drama 1:26 B&W**
Dir: Fritz Lang *Cast:* Henry Fonda, Sylvia Sidney, Barton MacLane, Jean Dixon, William Gargan
▶ Ex-con Fonda tries to reform with wife Sidney, but is sentenced to prison for a crime he didn't commit. After killing a man during a jailbreak, he and Sidney go on the lam, but find the law closing in on them. Haunting variation on the Bonnie and Clyde story with superlative performances and direction.
Dist.: Media

YOU ONLY LIVE TWICE 1967 British
★ ★ ★ ★ **PG Espionage/Action-Adventure 1:55**
☑ Adult situations, violence
Dir: Lewis Gilbert *Cast:* Sean Connery, Donald Pleasence, Akiko Wakabayashi, Mie Hama, Teru Shimada, Karin Dor
▶ From his Japanese volcano headquarters, archvillain Blofeld (Pleasence) nabs Russian and American space capsules in hopes of starting a world conflict; agent James Bond (Connery) must stop him. One of the best of the series features totally in-stride Connery, exotic Japanese locations, zippy pacing, great gadgets (especially a miniature flying machine) and chases. Nancy Sinatra sings the title tune.
Dist.: MGM/UA

YOU'RE A BIG BOY NOW 1967
★ **NR Comedy 1:36**
Dir: Francis Ford Coppola *Cast:* Elizabeth Hartman, Geraldine Page, Julie Harris, Peter Kastner, Rip Torn, Karen Black
▶ Lighthearted coming-of-age comedy describes Kastner's introduction to sex, drugs, and love after fleeing his doting Long Island

parents for a position as Manhattan librarian. His futile obsession with dancer Hartman eventually leads to romance with shy Black. Strong performances and bouncy Lovin' Spoonful soundtrack help episodic, occasionally arch plot.
Dist.: Warner

YOURS, MINE AND OURS 1968
★ ★ ★ ★ **NR Comedy 1:51**
Dir: Melville Shavelson *Cast:* Lucille Ball, Henry Fonda, Van Johnson, Tom Bosley, Ben Murphy, Tracy Nelson
▶ Fonda is a widower with ten kids who meets Ball, a widow with eight of her own. The two fall in love and marry, learning that patience is indeed a virtue with a brood of eighteen children. Charming family comedy based on a true story is winningly play by pros Ball and Fonda.
Dist.: MGM/UA

YOU TALKIN' TO ME? 1987
★ **R Drama 1:37**
☑ Explicit language, violence
Dir: Charles Winkler *Cast:* Jim Youngs, James Noble, Faith Ford, Mykel T. Williamson, Bess Motta, Rex Ryon
▶ Aspiring actor Youngs fancies himself another Robert De Niro and moves to Los Angeles, only to discover his dark, brooding type is no longer in fashion. Dying his hair blond and adopting a laid-back surfer manner, he quickly lands dishy girlfriend Ford. She gets him work on dad Noble's racist TV show, much to the dismay of black pal Williamson. Uneven effort switches midway from comedy to social drama.
Dist.: MGM/UA

YOU WERE NEVER LOVELIER 1942
★ ★ **NR Musical 1:37 B&W**
Dir: William A. Seiter *Cast:* Fred Astaire, Rita Hayworth, Adolphe Menjou, Xavier Cugat, Leslie Brooks, Adele Mara
▶ South American hotel magnate Menjou, concerned about daughter Hayworth's lack of interest in romance, tries to stir her up with flowers and letters from a phantom lover he's created. Hayworth mistakes down-on-his-luck entertainer Astaire for the phony suitor. Classic escapist fare uses first-class score by Johnny Mercer–Jerome Kern for delightful song-and-dance numbers like "Dearly Beloved," "I'm Old-Fashioned," and the title tune. Nominated for three Oscars.
Dist.: RCA/Columbia

YURI NOSENKO, KGB 1986
★ ★ **NR Espionage/MFTV 1:29**
☑ Explicit language
Dir: Mick Jackson *Cast:* Tommy Lee Jones, Oleg Rudnick, Josef Sommer, Ed Lauter, Stephen Newman, Alexandra O'Karma
▶ True story of KGB defector Yuri Nosenko (Rudnick), who agreed to provide information about Lee Harvey Oswald in the 1960s. CIA agent Jones is assigned the task of learning

whether Nosenko is a true defector or a KGB plant. Gripping drama re-creates grueling interrogations and baffling clues; acclaimed performances by Jones and Rudnick.
Dist.: HBO

Z 1969 French
★ ★ ★ **PG Drama 2:07**
☑ Violence
Dir: Costa-Gavras *Cast:* Yves Montand, Jean-Louis Trintignant, Irene Papas, Jacques Perrin, Charles Denner, François Périer
▶ Powerful drama turns 1963 assassination of Greek liberal Gregorios Lambrakis into a hard-hitting, often dazzling thriller. Montand plays the murdered leader; Trintignant is appointed investigating magistrate in what the government hopes will be a whitewash of the facts. But he uncovers corruption that ultimately leads to a coup. Oscar winner for Best Foreign Film and Editing.
Dist.: RCA/Columbia

ZABRISKIE POINT 1970
☆ **R Drama 1:52**
☑ Nudity, adult situations, explicit language, violence
Dir: Michelangelo Antonioni *Cast:* Mark Frechette, Daria Halprin, Rod Taylor, Paul Fix, G. D. Spradlin, Bill Garaway
▶ Frechette, a student radical framed for murder, steals an airplane and flies to Death Valley, where secretary Halprin introduces him to drugs and orgies. Dated counterculture epic seemed confusing and self-indulgent when released, but now provides a visually interesting time capsule of the hippie movement. Soundtrack includes songs by Pink Floyd, Grateful Dead, and Rolling Stones; Sam Shepard and Clare Peploe worked on the screenplay.
Dist.: MGM/UA

ZACHARIAH 1970
★ ★ **PG Western/Musical 1:33**
☑ Explicit language
Dir: George Englund *Cast:* John Rubinstein, Don Johnson, Pat Quinn, Elvin Jones, Country Joe and the Fish, Doug Kershaw
▶ In the 1870s, restless youth Rubinstein embarks on gunslinger career with best pal Johnson. Encounters with gang of outlaws (played by Country Joe and the Fish), fast-drawing Jones, and legendary tomboy Quinn lead duo to divergent lives. Hailed as first rock Western, uneven yarn mixes performances by rock bands in cowboy garb, spoofs of genre, and hip pacifist ending. Comedy troupe The Firesign Theater cowrote script but asked to be removed from credits.
Dist.: CBS/Fox

ZAPPED! 1982
★ ★ ★ **R Comedy 1:38**
☑ Nudity, adult situations, explicit language
Dir: Robert J. Rosenthal *Cast:* Scott Baio, Willie Aames, Heather Thomas, Scatman Crothers, Felice Schacter
▶ Shy teen genius Baio dabbles in botany experiment and accidentally gives himself telekinetic powers. Outgoing buddy Aames wants him to use psychic prowess to beat the odds in Las Vegas, but Baio's more interested in employing mind-over-matter to disrobe high school girls. Sex comedy climaxes in parody of *Carrie,* as Baio's libido and powers run amok at senior prom.
Dist.: Nelson

ZARDOZ 1974 British
☆ **R Sci-Fi 1:44**
☑ Nudity, adult situations, explicit language, violence
Dir: John Boorman *Cast:* Sean Connery, Charlotte Rampling, Sara Kestelman, John Alderton, Niall Buggy
▶ In the twenty-third century, society is divided into barbarians and an elite group of intelligent but sterile immortals. Brainy barbarian Connery invades the enclave of the latter, gets involved with Rampling and Kestelman, and turns the society upside down. Visually extravagant (watch out for that flying head) and wildly ambitious but not always in control. Best moments: Connery being tested for potency, the revelation of what the title means.
Dist.: CBS/Fox

ZED AND TWO NOUGHTS, A 1985 British/Dutch
☆ **NR Drama 1:55**
☑ Nudity, adult situations, explicit language, violence
Dir: Peter Greenaway *Cast:* Andrea Ferreol, Brian Deacon, Eric Deacon, Frances Barber, Joss Ackland
▶ Obscure, pretentious examination of the relationship between amputee Ferreol and twin zookeepers (Brian and Eric Deacon) who become obsessed with animal liberation. Nonlinear plot also includes meditations on Vermeer, mythology, and mirrors. Shot and scored with great care, although touches like time-lapse photography of decaying flesh will obviously not appeal to all. Title spells out "zoo."
Dist.: Pacific Arts

ZELIG 1983
★ ★ **PG Comedy 1:19 B&W/C**
☑ Adult situations, explicit language, adult humor
Dir: Woody Allen *Cast:* Woody Allen, Mia Farrow, Garrett Brown, Stephanie Farrow, Will Holt, Sol Lomita
▶ Documentary-style comedy follows the fictional life of Leonard Zelig (Allen), who has the chameleonlike power to transform himself into almost anyone: Indian, rabbi, Chinaman. Dedicated shrink Farrow works to give Zelig a single personality. Clever editing of actual newsreel footage from the thirties and forties places Zelig next to Pope Pius XI, Fanny Brice, Herbert Hoover, even Hitler. Technical masterpiece with some truly inspired sight gags and

poignant moments unfortunately wears thin and may be best appreciated by sophisticated viewers.
Dist.: Warner

ZELLY AND ME 1988
★★★ PG Drama 1:27
☑ Adult situations
Dir: Tina Rathborne *Cast:* Isabella Rossellini, Glynis Johns, Alexandra Johnes, Kaiulani Lee, David Lynch, Joe Morton
▶ In 1958, young orphan Johnes lives in a Virginia mansion with cold, overbearing grandmother Johns; her only loving relationship is with governess Rossellini. When Johnes's fixation on Joan of Arc leads the girl to self-mutilation, Rossellini looks to her suitor Lynch for help in moving the child to a healthier environment. Psychological drama stars real-life couple Rossellini and noted film director Lynch. (CC)
Dist.: RCA/Columbia

ZERO BOYS, THE 1986
★★ NR Action-Adventure 1:29
☑ Adult situations, explicit language, graphic violence
Dir: Nico Mastorakis *Cast:* Dan Hirsch, Kelli Maroney, Tom Sholl, Jarod Moses, Crystal Carson, John Michaels
▶ Four buddies take part in weekend survivalist games. The fun takes a deadly turn when they encounter a deserted house and a brutal killer. Professionally crafted but somewhat unsavory; Moses is excellent. Best line: "Freud, he's the dude who changed it all."
Dist.: Vestron

ZERO FOR CONDUCT 1933 French
☆ NR Drama 0:48 B&W
Dir: Jean Vigo *Cast:* Jean Dasté, Louis Lefébvre, Gilbert Pruchon, Constantin Kelber, Gerard de Bedarieux
▶ At a French boarding school, the stern staff, including a dwarf headmaster, try to suppress their charges. The children will have none of it and stage a rebellion. Landmark movie, short in length but not in influence. Director Vigo and cinematographer Boris Kaufman produce images that are at once lyrical and surreal. French title: *Zéro de Conduite.* [S]
Dist.: Video Yesteryear

ZERO TO SIXTY 1978
★ PG Comedy 1:40
☑ Adult situations, explicit language, adult humor
Dir: Don Weis *Cast:* Darren McGavin, Sylvia Miles, Joan Collins, Denise Nickerson, The Hudson Brothers, Lorraine Gary
▶ Alimony-saddled McGavin joins zany car repossession team as partner to teen dynamo Nickerson, but gets in dutch with the mob for taking an auto with a body in the trunk. Problems multiply as McGavin falls for curvaceous Collins and a jealous Nickerson zeroes in on her delinquent TransAm. Moves quickly and effortlessly, with lots of action and crazy humor. Also known as *Snatch.*
Dist.: Nelson

ZIEGFELD FOLLIES 1946
★★★ NR Musical 1:50
Dir: Vincente Minnelli *Cast:* William Powell, Fred Astaire, Gene Kelly, Judy Garland, Lena Horne, Fanny Brice, Red Skelton, Lucille Bremer
▶ Powell, reprising his *Great Ziegfeld* role, imagines a star-studded review from his new home in heaven. Following routines include first Astaire/Kelly teaming in "The Babbit and the Bromide," amusing Garland sketch about an audition, Skelton's idea of a TV liquor commercial, elaborate "Limehouse Blues" with Astaire and Bremer. Extravagant fun in the MGM style.
Dist.: MGM/UA

ZIEGFELD GIRL 1941
★★ NR Musical 2:11 B&W
Dir: Robert Z. Leonard *Cast:* James Stewart, Judy Garland, Hedy Lamarr, Lana Turner, Jackie Cooper, Philip Dorn, Tony Martin, Edward Everett Horton, Eve Arden, Al Shean
▶ Lavish but ploddingly told story of Turner, Garland, and Lamarr rising from obscurity to become stars of the Ziegfeld Follies. Stewart, Cooper, and Dorn are the men loved, lost, or left behind in the ladies' glittering ascent. Uneven song mix includes "I'm Always Chasing Rainbows," "You Stepped Out of a Dream" and "Mr. Gallagher and Mr. Shean." Busby Berkeley choreographed the endless parade of elaborate showgirl finery.
Dist.: MGM/UA

ZOMBIE 1979 Italian
☆ NR Horror 1:31
☑ Nudity, explicit language, graphic violence
Dir: Lucio Fulci *Cast:* Tisa Farrow, Ian McCulloch, Richard Johnson, Al Cliver
▶ An abandoned yacht drifts into New York harbor bearing a zombie who eats an investigator who comes on board. Reporter McCulloch and Farrow, daughter of the yacht's owner, trace the boat's route back to the Caribbean, where they discover an island being overrun by flesh-gobbling corpses. Grisly and excruciating, but not frightening or enjoyable on any level.
Dist.: Magnum

ZOMBIE HIGH 1987
★ R Horror 1:31
☑ Explicit language, violence
Dir: Ron Link *Cast:* Virginia Madsen, Richard Cox, Kay Kuter, James Wilder, Paul Williams
▶ Madsen is mystified that all the guys at her new school are dull grinds who read the *Wall Street Journal.* Then she discovers that Cox and other professors are gaining immortality by availing themselves of student brain tissue.

A glowing Madsen breathes life into fanciful, but not very exciting proceedings.
Dist.: Palisades

ZOMBIE ISLAND MASSACRE 1984
☆ **R Horror 1:35**
☑ Nudity, adult situations, explicit language, violence
Dir: John N. Carter   *Cast:* David Broadnax, Rita Jenrette, Tom Cantrell, Diane Clayre Holub
▶ American tourists in Caribbean sign up for special trip to remote island to witness voodoo rites. There they get more than they bargained for, as cannibal zombies knock them off, one by one. Drive-in fare stars Jenrette, ex-wife of the Congressman indicted in the Abscam sting and later subject of a *Playboy* spread.
Dist.: Media

ZOMBIE NIGHTMARE 1986
☆ **R Horror 1:23**
☑ Nudity, violence
Dir: Jack Bravman   *Cast:* Adam West, Jon-Mikl Thor, Francesca Boncorsa, Manuska Rigaud, Frank Dietz, Linda Singer
▶ When husband Thor is killed by a gang of teens in a hit-and-run accident, Boncorsa has him revived voodoo style by witch doctor Rigaud, who uses him to carry out her own agenda of revenge against police chief West. Real-life heavy-metal rock muscieman Thor is more interesting on stage than in this moronic, direct-to-video release.
Dist.: New World

ZOMBIES OF MORA TAU 1957
☆ **NR Horror 1:10 B&W**
Dir: Edward L. Cahn   *Cast:* Gregg Palmer, Allison Hayes, Autumn Russell, Joel Ashley, Morris Ankrum, Marjorie Eaton
▶ On an island off the coast of Africa, zombies are doomed to guard a cache of diamonds left undersea. When Palmer and Ashley come upon the scene, zombies try to kill them as they have other treasure hunters, but this time the undead sentinals may have met their match. Clumsy, second-rate horror filler.
Dist.: RCA/Columbia

ZONE TROOPERS 1985
★ ★ **PG Sci-Fi 1:28**
☑ Explicit language, violence
Dir: Danny Bilson   *Cast:* Timothy Van Patten, Tim Thomerson, Biff Manard, Art La Fleur, William Paulson
▶ During World War II, a platoon of American soldiers, including tough sarge Thomerson, greenhorn private Van Patten, dumb-but-lovable corporal La Fleur, and obnoxious journalist Manard, gets caught behind enemy lines. While trying to escape, they encounter a wrecked spacecraft and rescue the surviving alien from Nazis. Unusual sci-fi premise renders competent war saga.
Dist.: Vestron

ZOO GANG, THE 1986
★ ★ **PG-13 Comedy/Drama 1:37**
☑ Explicit language, violence
Dir: Pen Densham, John Watson   *Cast:* Jackie Earle Haley, Eric Gurry, Tiffany Helm, Jason Gedrick, Ben Vereen
▶ Scruffy teens Haley, Gurry, Helm, and Gedrick turn an abandoned building into a nightclub. Neighborhood toughs prey on the club, so, with help of alcoholic ex-wrestler Vereen, the kids must fight for their right to party. Teen turf war should appeal to peer group.
Dist.: New World

ZORBA THE GREEK 1964
★ ★ ★ **NR Drama 2:26 B&W**
Dir: Michael Cacoyannis   *Cast:* Anthony Quinn, Alan Bates, Irene Papas, Lila Kedrova, George Foundas, Eleni Anousaki
▶ Life-embracing Greek peasant Quinn befriends uptight Englishman Bates. Although their involvements with widow Papas and elderly prostitute Kedrova are ultimately tragic, Bates loosens up under Quinn's tutelage. Highly emotional and strongly recommended experience; Quinn's Oscar-nominated turn is magnificent. Best Picture nominee won Best Supporting Actress (Kedrova), Cinematography, and Art Direction.
Dist.: CBS/Fox

ZORRO, THE GAY BLADE 1981
★ ★ **PG Comedy 1:34**
☑ Explicit language, adult humor
Dir: Peter Medak   *Cast:* George Hamilton, Lauren Hutton, Brenda Vaccaro, Ron Leibman, Donovan Scott, James Booth
▶ Hamilton, the son of legendary masked rider Zorro, must continue family tradition of aiding the oppressed. When a busy social life takes up too much of his time, he enlists the aid of his homosexual brother (also Hamilton). Their cause: pretty newcomer Hutton, who seeks to organize peasant revolt against local tyrant Leibman. Broad spoof is inconsistent.
Dist.: CBS/Fox

ZOTZ! 1962
★ **NR Family 1:27 B&W**
Dir: William Castle   *Cast:* Tom Poston, Julia Meade, Jim Backus, Fred Clark, Cecil Kellaway, Margaret Dumont
▶ Mild-mannered professor Poston comes into possession of an ancient coin that causes people to move in slow motion. He can't interest the Pentagon in his discovery, but Khrushchev has his agents kidnap Poston's comely colleague Meade to get their hands on it. Poston is appealingly fuddled, and children will enjoy this comedy/fantasy.
Dist.: RCA/Columbia

ZULU 1964 British
★ ★ ★ **NR Action-Adventure 2:15**
Dir: Cy Endfield   *Cast:* Stanley Baker, Jack Hawkins, Michael Caine, Ulla Jacobsson, James Booth, Nigel Green
▶ True story of 1879 Zulu attack on the British.

Co-producer Baker plays the brave commander who rallied the outnumbered English forces to an inspiring victory. Caine, in his first major role, is outstanding as an upper-crust officer. Well-crafted storytelling with enthralling battle scenes.
Dist.: Nelson

ZULU DAWN 1980 U.S./Dutch
★ ★ ★ **PG Action-Adventure 1:57**
☑ Violence

Dir: Douglas Hickox *Cast:* Burt Lancaster, Peter O'Toole, Simon Ward, John Mills, Denholm Elliott
▶ True story of the 1879 Battle of Islandhlwana in which the British Army's inferior numbers and inappropriate fighting methods led to defeat by the Zulu nation. Old-fashioned epic has impressive location shooting and vividly staged battle scenes, but the human drama suffers from stereotyped characters and uninspired script.
Dist.: TWE